CONSOLIDATED INDEXES TO BRITISH
GOVERNMENT PUBLICATIONS 1936-1970

D0233138

Consolidated indexes to British government publications 1936-1970

Vol. 1 of *Catalogues and indexes of British government publications 1920-1970*

CHADWYCK-HEALEY LTD, BISHOPS STORTFORD
SOMERSET HOUSE INC, TEANECK

1974

© 1974 Chadwyck-Healey Ltd

*Catalogues and indexes of British
government publications 1920-1970*
are jointly republished in 5 volumes by:

Chadwyck-Healey Ltd
45 South Street, Bishops Stortford, Hertfordshire, UK
ISBN 0 85964 006 X

Somerset House Inc.
417 Maitland Avenue,Teaneck, New Jersey 07666, USA
ISBN 0 914146 04 1

Printed in England

CONSOLIDATED INDEX TO GOVERNMENT PUBLICATIONS
1936-1940

INDEX

References are to pages of the Annual Catalogues. See opposite page.
Abbreviations.—In addition to the abbreviations in general use, the following are used · Cmd.=Command Paper ; (N.P.)=Non-Parliamentary.
Cross References are to entries consisting of, or beginning with, the word or words indicated.

FOREWORD

When changes were made in the annual catalogue of Government Publications in 1936 it was intended to produce every five years a consolidated index, and for this purpose the annual catalogues from that date have been paginated consecutively in periods of five years.

The war delayed the preparation of these indexes, of which this is the first. The second, for 1941–45, is in course of printing. If these five-yearly indexes are found to be of service to librarians and others who need to make frequent references to official publications an index for 1946–50 will be put in hand.

It is suggested that the annual catalogues for 1936–40 should be bound with this consolidated index, the annual index pages (which are excluded from the pagination) being discarded.

This consolidated index volume covers the titles of new publications issued in the period, revised editions and reprints at amended prices. References to Statutory Rules and Orders have, however, been omitted as it was felt that their inclusion would be of little value, particularly as full indexes to this class of publication are provided in the Guide to Government Orders.

The page numbering of the annual catalogues indexed in this consolidation is as follows :

1936	...	...	1 to 234
1937	...	...	235 to 460
1938	...	...	461 to 695
1939	...	...	696 to 943
1940	...	...	944 to 1,072

Abandoned Mines, Plans of, Catalogues, 411, 647, 897
Abbeys, Guides to, 157, 691, 928
A.B.C. Calculator for Average Quality Unlined Canvas Delivery Hose, 1036
Aberdeen :
 Arrangements for increasing demand for Milk, 432, 670
Asylum for the Blind Scheme, 200, 425
Corporation :
 (Administration, Finance, etc.) Order Confirmation Act, 972
 —Bill, 734, 945
 (General Powers) Order Confirmation Act, 756—Bill, 475, 499
 Order Confirmation Act, 70— Bill, 17
 (Streets, Buildings, Sewers, etc.) Order Confirmation Act, 70— Bill, 17, 41
 (Water, Gas, Electricity and Transport) Order Confirmation Act, 301—Bill, 246, 270
Dee Tidal Nets, Sea Trout from, 201
Milk Marketing Scheme, 204
Port Labour in, Report, 404
Aberdeenshire Educational Trust Scheme, 199, 425
Aberystwyth Rural District Council Act, 302
Abortion :
 Bovine, Contagious, 594
 Interdepartmental Committee on, Report, 870
Abram Colliery, Boiler Explosion, 435
Abrasive Wheels .
 Installation and Working of, Factory Form, 879
 Safety Precautions, etc., 167, 170
 Use of, 882
Abyssinia. See Ethiopia ; Haile Selassie.
Access to Mountains :
 Act, 753
 Bill, 246, 270, 493, 498, 700, 703, 718, 725, 727, 731
Accessions, etc. (Treaties), Lists of :
 Cmd. 5088, 49
 Cmd. 5376, 275
 Cmd. 5654, 502
 Cmd. 5930, 736
 Cmd. 6148, 964
Accident· Proneness among Motor Drivers, 1055

Accidents :
 Colliery, Funds. Cmd. 5167, 50
 Factory and Workshop, Notice of Accident, 167
 Mines :
 Accidents from falls of ground 186, 900
 and Quarries :
 Form, 640
 Deaths caused by, 184, 411, 648, 898, 1053
 Non-fatal, Annual Return Form, 412
 Road :
 Fatal, during 1935, 218
 Involving Personal Injury and Fatal :
 Annual Return, 1935, 27
 Annual Return Forms, 170
 School Laboratories, 430, 668
 Shipping, Casualties to, and Deaths on Vessels registered in U.K., 209
 Rehabilitation of Persons Injured by, Interim Report, 392
 See also Aircraft Accident ; Cyclists ; Electrical Accidents ; Employers' Liability ; Eye Accidents ; Factories ; Factory and Industrial Explosions ; Industrial Accidents ; Railway Accidents ; Rehabilitation ; Road Accidents ; Shipping Casualties ; Workmen's Compensation ; Wrecks.
Accountancy, Careers, 174, 887
Accountant :
 Branch of R.A.F., 136, 596
 In Edinburgh (Scottish Education Dept.), 203, 430, 668, 913
Accountants. Edinburgh Chartered Accountants Annuity, etc. Fund (Consolidation and Amendment) Order Confirmation :
 Act, 298
 Bill, 18, 42
Accounts :
 Public, Committee of, Reports, 24, 31
 See also Finance Accounts ; Public Accounts.
Accumulator Cut-outs or Reverse Current Relays, Specification, 853
Accumulators :
 Electric, Factory Form, 631
 Electrical, Specification, 854
 Sulphuric Acid for, Specification, 854
Acetic Acid Bacteria, 192

1

ACE-AIR | 1936-40

Acetylene Gas, etc., Safety Measures, 167, 395
Actinomyces, 1056
Active Carbon, Production of, from Bituminous Coal, 660
Acts:
  of Parliament. *See* Parliament.
  of Privy Council of England, 655
  See also Emergency Acts; titles of Acts.
Adam, Bell, Gibson and Stewart Bursaries Trust Scheme, 199, 425
Adaptation of Shelter in Houses, 1038
Adder s.t., explosion, 672
Addington, Lord, Chairman, Local Government and Public Health Consolidation Committee, *which see.*
Additional Pay, War Office Publications (N.P.), 1066
Adelphi Estate Act, 525
Aden:
  Colonial Annual Reports, 377, 860, 1031
  Draft Instructions to Governor and Commander-in-Chief. *Cmd. 5222*, 55
  Flag Badge, 611
  See also Gulf of Aden.
Adjutants, Army, Additional Pay of, 1066
Administration:
  of Justice:
    (Miscellaneous Provisions) Act, 523—Bill, 462, 465, 473, 487, 489, 494, 497
    (Wales)—Bill, 265
    See also Justice
  Scottish, Committee on, Report. *Cmd. 5563*, 289
Administrative:
  Memo., Board of Education, 865
  Service Lists, Colonial, 152, 279, 610, 1031
Admiral Graf Spee:
  Account of Events up to the Self-destruction of, 1018
  Distinguished Service Awards in recognition of the gallant and successful Action with, 1048
Admiralty:
  Civil Service Arbitration Tribunal Awards, 639, 888
  Examinations, 146–7, 374, 604–5, 857
  Instructions, 1018
  Publications (N.P.), 125, 353, 586, 841, 1018
Adoption:
  of Children:
    Act, 295
    (Regulation) Bill, 498
  Societies and Agencies. *Cmd. 5499*, 284
Adult Education:
  Amending Regs. No. 1, 865
  in Wales, Report, 386
  Scotland:
    Classes, etc., 669
    Residential Institutions, List of, 669
  See also Education.
Advertisements:
  Air, Bill, 498
  Control of Employment, Draft Order, Report on, 957
  Restriction of Advertisement (War Risks Insurance):
    Act, 756
    Bill, 709, 734
  See also Licensing of Advertisements.
Advisory Leaflets, *see* Agricultural.
Aerated:
  Water:
    Regs., 395
    Syphons. *See* Import Duties Advisory Committee.
  Waters Trade, Wages, 642, 889, 1046
Aerial:
  Navigation in the Antarctic, Exchange of Notes, France, Australia, New Zealand. *Cmd. 5900*, 520
  Wire, Specifications, 368, 600
    See also Steel Aerial Wire.
Aerodromes. *See* Land Aerodromes.
Aerodynamics: Reports of Aeronautical Research Committee, 146, 370, 602
Aero-Engines:
  Aeronautical Research Committee Publications (N.P.), 143, 370, 602, 856
  Air Ministry Publications (N.P.), 696, 851
  Cheetah IX, 1028
  Gas Starter Systems for, 365
  Handbooks, etc., 136
  Production of, Note on Policy of H.M. Government. *Cmd. 5295*, 61
Aerological Work, Height-Computer for use in, 646
Aeronautical:
  Radio Service. *See* Civil Aeronautical Radio Service.
  Research Committee Publications (N.P.), 143, 370, 602, 856, 1027
Aeronautics, History and Development of, 414
Aeroplane:
  Tutor, 1027
  Wings, etc., De-icing of, 598
Aeroplanes:
  Design Requirements for, 138, 365, 598, 852, 1028
  Doping Schemes, Specification, 141
  Handbooks, etc., 136, 363, 597, 851
  See also Civil Aeroplanes; Landplanes.

Afforestation in the Lake District, 159
Africa:
  British East, Economic Condition., 211
  Customs Tariffs, 153, 380
  Fauna and Flora of, International Conference for the protection of, 683
  Importation of Spirituous Beverages:
    Cmd. 5205, 54
    Cmd. 5486, 28.
    Cmd. 5814, 514
    Cmd. 6082, 747
  Locust Outbreaks in, 447, 927
  See also British East Africa; French West Africa; Portuguese West Africa; South Africa; West Africa; East Africa; Empire Air Mail Scheme; Portuguese East Africa; South West Africa; Tropical Africa; Civil Air Transport Service.
African Pencil Cedar, Properties of, 659
Aged Persons, Rehousing of:
  Circular, 666
  Report. *Cmd. 7598*, 512
Aggregates and Workability of Concrete, 662
Agricultural:
  Bulletins, 132, 360, 593, 848, 1023
  Colleges (Scotland) Additional Grants, 1060
  Development Act, 753—Bill, 706, 721, 725, 730, 732
    Assistance to Barley Growers. *Cmd. 6077*, 746
  Dwelling-houses, Valuation of, Bill, 36
  Education, Vocational, in Colonial Empire, 381
  Holdings Act, 295
  Leaflets, 134, 362, 595, 849, 1023
    Scotland, 196, 424, 664, 909
  Machinery Testing Committee, Certificates and Reports, 132, 359, 592, 848
  Market Reports, 132, 359, 592, 848
  Marketing:
    Act (1933) Amendment Bill, 271
    Development Schemes. *Cmd. 5285*, 60
    Schemes, Annual Reports:
      Cmd. 5284, 60
      Cmd. 5734, 508
      Cmd. 6030, 743
    See also Milk Marketing Scheme.
  Population, Scotland. *See* Housing (Agricultural Population).
  Prices, Index Number of, 592
  Produce:
    Output and Prices, 359, 593, 848
    Prices and Supplies, 132, 359
      Scotland, 196
Agricultural (*continued*):
  Research:
    Council:
      Publications: (N.P.), 418, 656, 904
      Reports and Accounts:
        Cmd. 5293, 60
        Cmd. 5662, 503
        Cmd. 5379, 275
        Cmd. 5768, 510
        Cmd. 5965, 739
        Cmd. 6146, 964
    Institutes Reports on, 132, 359,
    Workers, Lists of, 171, 633, 882
  Service Lists, Colonial, 380, 610
  Societies, Annual Return Forms, 387, 617, 870, 1034
  Statistics, 132, 359, 593, 848
    Scotland, 196, 663, 909, 1059
  Wages (Regulation):
    Act, 1924, Report of Proceedings under, 132, 359, 593
    Amendment Act, 971
      Bill, 946, 962
        Scotland, Act, 971
          Bill, 947, 962
    (Scotland) Act, 297
      Bill, 236, 238, 245, 259, 262, 267, 269
  Workers:
    Bothies and Chaumers for the accommodation of, 666
    Number of, 359, 593, 848
Agriculture:
  Act, 297
    Bill, 245, 246, 269, 270
    Memo. *Cmd. 5493*, 284
    Part IV, Date to come into operation, Circular and Memo., 619, 620
  and Fisheries, Ministry of, Publications (N.P.), 132, 359, 592, 848, 1023
  and Forestry Research Workers, List of, 1038
  and Horticulture, List of Books in Ministry of Agriculture and Fisheries Library, 849
Careers, 174
Colonial Directors of, Conference, 616
Damage by Rabbits, Reports, 235, 237
Department of, for Scotland:
  Annual Reports:
    Cmd. 5126, 48
    Cmd. 5410, 278
    Cmd. 5736, 508
    Cmd. 5968, 739
  Civil Service Abritration Tribunal Award, 402
  Publications (N.P.), 196, 424, 663, 909, 1059

Agriculture (*continued*):
  Development:
    Commissioners' Reports, 20, 248
    Fund Accounts, 20, 35
      Colonial, 23
  Imperial Agricultural Bureaux Publications (N.P.), 171
  Journal, 134, 362, 595, 849, 1023
    Scotland, 196, 424, 664, 909, 1059
  Land Division, Annual Report, 134
  (Miscellaneous War Provisions) Act, 971
    Bill, 946, 962
    No. 2 Act, 972
      Bill, 948, 963
  See also Crops; Dairy; Farming; Live Stock; Modern Agriculture; Tithe; Unemployment Insurance.
Agriculture, Horticulture, and Forestry, Careers, 887
Air:
  Advertisements Bill, 498
  Almanac, 363, 597, 851, 853, 855, 1024
  Attack:
    Protection of Fire Brigade Premises against, 880
      Scotland, 915
    Shelter from, 878
    Vulnerability of Capital Ships. *Cmd. 5301*, 61
  Carriage by. *See* Carriage by Air.
  Council Instructions for the R.A.F., 139, 365, 599, 853, 1024
  Ensign Order, Civil, 364
  Estimates, 25, 252, 480, 714, 953
    Supplementary, 24, 31, 254, 481, 487, 714, 719, 721, 953
    Memos., 47, 276, 504, 738
  Facilities. *See* Naval and Air Facilities.
  Force:
    Act, 67, 298, 524, 756, 972
    Appropriation Accounts, 24, 251, 478, 712
    Army and Air Force (Annual) Act, 65
      Bill, 8, 37
    British:
      Forces in Egypt, Immunities and Privileges. *Cmd. 5270*, 59
      Official Photographs, 1039
    Examinations, 139, 147, 150, 151, 374, 376, 377, 598, 605, 607, 857, 859, 860
    Gross and Net Cost, 22, 251, 479, 712
    Honours, 1050
    Law, Manual of, 137, 363, 851, 1024
    List (Air Force List), 137, 364, 596, 851
    Medical Examination for fitness for flying, 1025
Air (*continued*):
  Force (*continued*):
    Nursing and Auxiliary Services, Retired Pay, Pensions, Allowances, Gratuities, etc., for Members of, 723, 960
    Officers and Men mentioned for Distinguished Services, 1050
    Reserve:
      and Auxiliary Forces, Regs., 140, 852
      National Health Insurance, Contributory Pensions, etc., 139
      See also Reserve Forces.
    Retired Pay, Pensions, Allowances, Gratuities, etc., Members of, 723
    See also Army and Air Force; H.M. Forces; Military and Air Forces; Navy, Army and Air Force; New Zealand.
  Forces, Employment of, with the Army in the Field, 450
  Mail Scheme. *See* Empire Air Mail.
  Ministry:
    Assistant Surveyor, examination, 147
    Civil Service Arbitration Tribunal Award, 639
    Civilian Employees, 138, 365, 598, 852, 1024
    (Heston and Kenley Aerodromes Extension) Act, 754
      Bill, 706, 707, 720, 721, 729, 731
    Meteorological Radio Stations:
      Map showing stations, 410
      Weather Reports from, forms 408, 645, 647
    Permanent Secretary to:
      Report on discussions. *Cmd 5254*, 57
      Minute by Prime Minister. *Cmd. 5255*, 57
    Publications (N.P.), 136, 363, 596, 851, 1024
  Navigation:
    Act, 66
      Bill, 15, 17, 36, 40, 41
    Canada and U.S.A. *Cmd. 6067*, 745
    Customs Forms, 155
    Directions, 137, 597, 1024
    (Financial Provisions) Act, 523
      Bill, 469, 494
    Hungary and U.K.:
      Cmd. 5535, 287
      Cmd. 5765, 510
    Irish Free State and U.S.A. *Cmd. 5711*, 506
    Manual of, 137, 597, 1024

Air (*continued*):
  Navigation (*continued*):
    Meteorology in relation to, 409, 646
    Regulation of. *Cmd. 5332*, 63
    Regs., 851, 1024
    Signal Book, 1025
  Navigator's, Civil, Licence, Examination Papers, 364
  Photographs, Surveying from, 684
  Photography, Organisation and Training, 137, 851, 1024
  Pilot, 138, 364, 597, 851
  Raid:
    Damage, 878
    Precautions:
      Act, 522
        Bill, 247, 271, 272
        Circular, 624
        Classification of Local Authorities for purposes of calculating Exchequer Grant. *Cmd. 5596*, 291
      Approval of Expenditure Scotland, Circular, 670
      Civil Estimates, 480, 715
      Department of Health for Scotland Publications (N.P.), 911
      England and Wales, 165, 393
      for Government Contractors, 851
      Home Office Publications (N.P.), 624, 876
      in Museums, Picture Galleries and Libraries, 941
      in Schools, 614, 866, 1032
        Scotland, 668, 913
        Wales, 616, 868
      Ministry of Health Publications (N.P.), 876
      Ministry of Home Security Publications (N.P.), 882, 1037
      (Postponement of Financial Investigations) Bill, 963
      Provision of Hospital Accommodation, 619
      School, 624
      Scotland, 204, 431
      Scottish Office Publications (N.P.), 669
    Risks in Hospitals, Precautions against, 873
    Shelters:
      Home Office Publications (N.P.), 876
      Ministry of Home Security Publications (N.P.), 1037
      Report of Lord Privy Seal's Conference. *Cmd. 6006*, 742
      Report to Lord Privy Seal on Policy. *Cmd. 5932*, 736
      See also Steel Shelters.
Air (*continued*):
  Raid (*continued*):
    Wardens, Home Office Publications (N.P.), 878
    Works. *See* Rating and Valuation (Air Raid Works).
  Raids:
    Protection against, 930
    What you must know and do, 1037
  Receiver:
    Factory Forms, 629, 1036
    Mines and Quarries Forms, 650
  Services:
    Appropriation Accounts, 24, 951
    between London and Lisbon, Exchange of Notes, Portugal and U.K. *Cmd. 5995*, 741
    between South Africa and Portuguese East Africa, Agreement, Portugal and South Africa. *Cmd. 5707*, 506
    between South West China and British Ports, Exchange of Notes, China and U.K. *Cmd. 6122*, 749
    over China, Exchange of Notes, China and U.K. *Cmd. 5712*, 506
    over Siam, India, and Burma, Exchange of Notes, Siam, India and U.K. *Cmd. 5651*, 502
    See also Civil Air Transport Services; Empire Air Mail.
  Speed Indicators. *See* Speed Indicators.
  Survey Committee:
    Professional Paper, 684
    Report, 448
  Traffic, Liquid Fuel and Lubricants used in, Exemption from Taxation, International Conference. *Cmd. 6001*, 741
  Transport:
    Establishment of Air Transport Lines, Italy and U.K. *Cmd. 5652*, 503
    Exchange of Notes, U.S.A. and Canada. *Cmd. 6210*, 968
    Greece and U.K., Convention:
      Cmd. 6097, 748
      Cmd. 6207, 968
    Relief from Double Income Tax on Air Transport Profits, France and U.K. *Cmd. 6126*, 750
    Services. *See* Civil Air Transport; Civil Aviation; Empire Air Mail.
    Taxation of Profits:
      Germany, Agreement. *Cmd. 5652*, 502
      Netherlands. *Cmd. 5279*, 59
  Votes, 20, 26, 249, 256, 264, 484, 711, 717, 951

Aircraft :
Accident :
City of Khartoum. Cmd. 5220, 55
Loss of aircraft G-ADUU *Cavalier. Cmd. 5975*, 739
and Aircraft Motors, Efficiency Certificates for, Agreement, Germany and South Africa. *Cmd. 5705*, 506
Bomb, High Explosive, Diagram, 878
Bombing by Italian Military Aircraft of British Red Cross Ambulance in Ethiopia. *Cmd. 5160*, 50
Bonding and Screening and Earth Systems for all W/T Purposes, Specifications, 369, 855
Damage caused by, to third parties. *Cmd. 5056*, 43
Exemption of, from Duties on Fuel and Lubricants, Netherlands. *Cmd. 5074*, 45
Ice :
Accretion on, 410
Formation on, 599
See also De-Icing.
Owners and Ground Engineers, Notices to, 364, 598, 851
Personnel, Identity Documents for :
Australia, New Zealand, India, U.K., and Netherlands. *Cmd. 6130*, 750
Belgium, Australia, New Zealand, India, and U.K. *Cmd. 5764*, 516
Denmark and U.K., Australia, New Zealand, and India. *Cmd. 5586*, 291
France and U.K. *Cmd. 6125*, 750
France, India and U.K. *Cmd. 5922*, 736
Norway, Australia, New Zealand, India, and U.K. *Cmd. 5653*, 502
Portugal and South Africa. *Cmd. 5565*, 289
Portugal, Australia, New Zealand, India, and U.K. *Cmd. 6209*, 968
Sweden, Australia, New Zealand, India, and U.K. *Cmd. 5842*, 516
Switzerland and U.K. *Cmd. 5857*, 517
Piratical Acts in the Mediterranean by. *Cmd. 5569*, 290
Plywood for Lightly Stressed Parts, Specification, 1029
Production, Ministry of, Publications (N.P.), 1028
Propulsion of, 187
Reciprocal Exemption of Aircraft from Duties on Fuel and Lubricants, Exchange of Notes, Switzerland and U.K. *Cmd. 5846*, 516
Specifications, 140
Airdrie Burgh Extension, etc., Order Confirmation Act, 298
Bill, 18, 41
Airmen of Medical and Dental Branches, R.A.F., Training of, 369, 599, 853
Airscrew :
De-icing Fluid, Specification, 855
Forgings, Specification, 141
Mahogany Substitutes for, Specification, 142
Airship Linen Fabric, Specification, 141
Airspeed Indicators, Pressure Heads, Specification, 599
Airways :
of a Mine, Mines and Quarries Form, 651
See also British Overseas Airways.
Airworthiness :
Certificates for Exported Aircraft, Exchange of Notes, U.S.A. and Canada. *Cmd. 5928*, 736
Handbook for Civil Aircraft, 138, 364, 598, 852, 1024
Alcazar s.t., Wreck Report, 920
Alcohol :
and Alcoholometers, 694
its Action on the Human Organism, 904
See also Isopropyl Alcohol.
Aldridge Urban District Council Act, 525
Alexander, Sir H., Scottish Housing Advisory Committee, Reports :
Cmd. 5462, 281
Cmd. 5798, 512
Alexandra Mills, Batley, Explosion of Economiser, 434
Alfa-Laval Combine Recorder Milking Machine, 592
Algae. *See* Tertiary Siphoneous Algae.
Algeria, Economic Conditions, 439
Aliens :
Certificates of Naturalisation, Annual Returns, 261, 488, 722
Refugees from Germany, Status of, *Cmd. 5338*, 64
Restriction (Blasphemy) (No. 2), Bill, 497
Returns :
Annual :
Cmd. 5430, 279
Cmd. 5727, 507
Cmd. 6036, 743
Quarterly :
Cmd. 5892, 43
Cmd. 5176, etc., 51
Cmd. 5176—III, 272
Cmd. 5455, etc., 281
Cmd. 5455—III, 500
Cmd. 5749, etc., 509
Cmd. 5749—III, 735
Cmd. 6025, etc., 743

Aliens (*continued*)
Who entered and left U.K. in 1935, Statistics. *Cmd. 5195*, 53
See also British Nationality ; Naturalization.
Alimentary Infections, Precautions against the spread of, 1034
Alkali, etc., Works, Reports on, 160, 388, 618, 870
Allan-Fraser, Patrick, Trust Scheme, 198
Allegory of Abundance, Botticelli, 694
Allen, W., Sound Transmission in Buildings, 1058
All Hallows Lombard Street Act, 757
Allied Forces Act, 972
Bill, 948, 963
Allotment Societies, Annual Return Forms, 387, 616, 870, 1034
Allotments :
Acquisition and Cultivation, 133
Allotment Cultivation, 362
Allowance Regulations, Army, 221, 684
Allowances :
Army, 221, 448, 455, 928, 1066, 1070
Civil Service Arbitration Tribunal Awards, 401, 638, 887, 1042
Industrial Court Awards, 403, 640, 888, 1042
National Arbitration Tribunal Awards, 1043
Subsistence, Report of Civil Service National Whitley Council, 220
Alloys of Metal. *See* Metal Alloys.
Alma Road Hospital, Rotherham, Dangerous Drugs, 626
Almonds. *See* Import Duties Advisory Committee.
Alness, Lord, Chairman :
Committee on application of the University Courts of the Universities of Scotland for a Grant, Report. *Cmd. 5735*, 508
Night Baking Committee, Report. *Cmd. 5525*, 286
Scottish Departmental Committee on Nursing, Report. *Cmd. 5866*, 518
Alphabets, Roman, 943
Altimeters, Specifications, 140, 853
Aluminising, Specification, 369
Aluminium Welding Flux, Specification, 366
Aluminium-Alloy Bars, Castings, Sheets, Strips, Tubes, etc., Specifications, 141, 366, 600, 854, 1025, 1029
Aluminium-Bronze Sand or Die Castings, Specifications, 1028
Aluminium-Nickel-Iron Bronze Bars, Forgings, and Stampings, Specification, 1028
Amani, East African Agricultural Research Station, Reports, 151, 377 609, 860, 1031
Amble, Geology, 194
Ambulance :
Factories and Workshops, 170
for Factories, Welfare Pamphlet, 1037
Ambulances :
Conversion of Commercial Vehicles for use as, 625
Department of Health for Scotland Publications (N.P.), 911
Ministry of Health Publications (N.P.), 871, 876
Statement. *Cmd. 6061*, 745
See also Small Ambulances.
America : Calendar of State Papers, 416
See also British North America ; South America ; United States of America.
America and West Indies, Calendar of State Papers, 655, 903
American :
Gooseberry Mildew, 135
Mail Contract, 28
Ammeters, Specifications, 127, 354, 843, 930
Ammonia, Users of, Air Raid Precautions to be taken by, 1038
Amos, A. : Ensilage, 593
Ampere, Absolute Determination of, 661
Amphibians, Instructions for Collectors, 460
Amulree, Lord, Chairman, Holidays with Pay Committee :
Minutes of Evidence, 402, 640
Report. *Cmd. 5724*, 507
Anaerobic Organisms, 1056
Anaesthesia in Casualty Service, 1060
Anaesthetic Explosions. *See* Explosions.
Analysts. *See* Public Analysts.
Ancient Monuments and Historic Buildings :
Office of Works Guides, 231, 457, 691, 938
Royal Commission :
Publications (N.P.), 423, 663, 908
Reports :
Anglesey. *Cmd. 5483*, 283
Middlesex. *Cmd. 5530*, 286
Westmorland, Interim Report. *Cmd. 5179*, 52
Westmorland, Inventory, 195
Anderson, D., Air Raid Shelter Policy, Report. *Cmd. 5932*, 736
Anderson, Sir J., Chairman, Committee on Evacuation, Report. *Cmd. 5837*, 515
Anderson, J.G.C., The Granites of Scotland, 907
Andrew, J. H., Metallurgical Examination of Colliery Haulage Drawgear, 413
Andrewes, C. H., Epidemic Influenza, 657

Androgenic and Ostrogenic Activity, Estimation of, 904
Anemograph, behaviour of, at Lizard, 181
Anemometers at Southport, Comparison of Records, 181
Angles. *See* Tidal Angles.
Anglesey : Ancient Monuments of :
Interim Report. *Cmd. 5483*, 283
Inventory, 423
See also East Anglesey.
Anglo Australian s.s., Wreck Report, 673
Anglo-Egyptian Sudan. *See* Sudan.
Anglo-Scottish Railways Assessment Authority, Reports, 160, 388, 618, 870
Anglo-Turkish (Armaments Credit) Agreement Act, 523
Bill, 472, 496
Angola :
Air Services with South Africa. *Cmd. 6231*, 970
Economic Conditions, 439
Shirt, Specification, 452
Angora Wool Production, Modern, 850
Angus Educational Trust :
(Additional Endowment) (No. 1) Scheme, 427, 664
Scheme, 425
Angus s.t., Wreck Report, 675
Anhydrite, 661
Aniline Vapour, Detection of, 908
Animal :
Management, Army, 684
Tissues, Microbiology in the Preservation of, 420
Transport, Army, 688
Animals :
Air Raid Precautions for, 877
Breeding of, 360
Keeping of, 391
Protection of :
Bill, 1937, 267
Bills, 1939, 728
(Prevention of Deer Hunting) Bill, 729
See also Cattle ; Live Stock ; Vivisection ; Cinematograph Films (Animals) ; Diseases of Animals ; Living Animals ; Performing Animals ; Destructive Animals ; Protection of Animals ; Royal Society.
Ankle Boots Specifications :
Army, 932
Navy, 452
Annagher s.s., Wreck Report, 920
Annealing, Factory Form, 630
Annual Holiday Bill, 41, 255, 262, 271
Annuities :
Edinburgh Chartered Accountants' Annuity, etc. (Consolidation and Amendment) Order Confirmation Bill, 18, 42
Annuities (*continued*) :
See also Government Insurance ; National Debt ; Tithes.
Anodic Oxidation of Aluminium, etc., Specifications, 369, 601
Antarctic, Aerial Navigation in, Exchange of Notes, France, Australia, New Zealand, and U.K. *Cmd, 5900*, 520
Anthrax, Leaflet, 595
Anti-Aircraft :
Artillery, Instruments, Army, Directions, 221
Defence, Army Units, 222, 458
Gunnery, Notes on, 684
Searchlight Drills, 448, 684
Small Arms Training, 456
Anti-Dilution Cylinder-Head Gasket, 592
Anti-Freezing :
Grease, Specifications, 367, 1025
Oil, Specifications, 366, 854
Anti-Gas :
Clothing :
Decontamination of, from Blister Gases, 877
Specifications, 933, 1069
Instructional Diagrams, 624
Protection :
of Babies and Young Children, 877
of Houses, 624
Scotland, 670
Schools, Civilian, 624
Training, 165, 166, 223, 393, 625
Scotland, 431
Revised Syllabus, 877
Antigens and Antibodies, Chemistry of, 657
Anti-Misting Compound, Specification, 1026
Antiquity, Classical, in Renaissance Painting, 694
Anti-Tank Rifle, Small Arms Training, 456
Anti-Tuberculosis Service in Wales and Monmouthshire, Committee of Inquiry Report, 870
Anti-Venereal Measures in certain Scandinavian Countries, 622
Anvils, Specification, 686
Aphis. *See* Woolly Aphis.
Apitong, Forest Products Research Records, 420
Appeal, Court of. *See* Supreme Court.
Appendicitis, 904
Appendix Certificates of Tonnage, Exchange of Notes, U.S.A. and Canada. *Cmd. 6131*, 750
Apple Trees. *See* Winter Pruning.
Apples :
and Pears, Production and Trade, 633

Apples (*continued*) :
Canker, 134
Cider Apple Production, 301
Commercial Apple Production, 394
Home Storage of, 362
Intensive Systems of Apple Production, 593
Production :
and Trade, 171, 398, 633
Systems of, 133
Applications of Reinforced Concrete to Wartime Building, 1056
Applied :
Geophysics, 187
Mechanics, Examples in, 586
Work and Patchwork, 695
Appointment :
Army, 229, 687, 936, 1071
Pay, Appointment, etc., Army, 454
with British Military Missions, 448
Appropriation Acts, 66, 297, 523, 753, 754, 972
Approved :
Homes for Mental Defectives, 381, 863
Schools, List of, 669
See also Schools.
Societies. *See* National Health Insurance.
Aprons, Anti-Gas, Specifications, 933, 1069
See also Rubber Aprons.
Aquamarine s.t., Wreck Report, 920
Arabia. *See* Saudi Arabia.
Arabian Sea, Marine Deposits of, 942
Arabic :
Examination Papers, R.A.F., 147
Interpretership, Examinations, 605
Arable :
Crops of the Farm, 1023
Land :
Thistles on, 36[illegible]
Weeds of, 594
Arandora Star Inquiry. *Cmd. 6238*, 970
Arbitration :
Bills, 19, 266
Board of, Awards, 638, 1041
Convention of Oct. 25, 1905, Iceland, and various countries, Renewal of. *Cmd. 5448*, 280
See also Civil Service ; National.
Arch Construction without Centering, Building Bulletin, 1056
Archaeology, Field, 188
Architects Registration :
Act, 523
Bill, 236, 266, 271, 467, 482, 489, 494
Architecture, Careers, 401
Ardrossan-Brodick Contract, Post Office, 30
Areas, Population and Valuation of Counties, Burghs, and Parishes in Scotland, 428
Argentine :
Anglo-Argentine Meat Trade, Joint Committee of Inquiry into, Report. *Cmd. 5839*, 516
Economic Conditions, 211, 439, 676, 920
Imported Food Certificates, 618
Scotland, 666
Regulation of Beef Imports into U.K., Exchange of Notes with U.K. *Cmd. 5941*, 737
Trade and Commerce Agreement with U.K. *Cmd. 5324*, 63
Supplement to Board of Trade Journal, 208
Argyll :
Duchess of, Death, 895, 1071
National Forest Park, Guide to, 617
Arkwright, Sir J., Chairman, Foot and Mouth Disease Research Committee, Report, 361
Armaments :
Credit for Turkey, Agreements with U.K. :
Cmd. 5755, 509
Cmd. 6119, 749
Defence Expenditure, Statement. *Cmd. 5374*, 275
London Naval Conference :
Documents, 158
Memo. *Cmd. 5137*, 49
London Naval Treaty Bill, 42
Naval, Limitation of, Treaty. *Cmd.* 5136, 48
Profits Duty, Charge of, *Cmd. 6046*, 744
See also Arms ; Munitions ; Naval Armament ; Small Arms.
Armed Forces (Conditions of Service) Act, 754
See also National Service (Armed Forces).
Armoured :
Cars, 449
Fighting Vehicles, Machine Gun Mountings and Appurtenances for use in, 456
Armourers, Army, Instructions for 222
Arms :
Export Prohibition, List of Goods, 1063
Flags, Badges of British Dominions, 153, 380, 611, 862, 1031
Royal Commission on Private Manufacture of and Trading in :
Minutes of Evidence, 195
Report. *Cmd. 5292*, 60
Statement relating to Report. *Cmd. 5451*, 281
Small, care of, etc., 230
See also Armaments ; Firearms ; Small Arms.

ARM-BAR | 1936-40

ARM— INDEX 1936–40

Armstrong, A., Science in the Army, 653
Armstrong, F. H., Kiln-Seasoning Treatments of Teak, etc., 659
Army :
Acts, 67, 298, 524, 756, 972
and Air Force (Annual) Acts, 65, 296, 522, 753, 971
Bills, 8, 37, 238, 267, 465, 494, 700, 728, 946, 962
Annual Reports :
Cmd. 5104, 47
Cmd. 5398, 277
Cmd. 5686, 504
Cmd. 5950, 738
Appropriation Accounts, 24, 250, 478, 712, 951
Billeting in Emergency, Prices to be paid, 685, 929
British Forces in Egypt, Immunities and Privileges. *Cmd. 5270*, 59
British Official Photographs, 1039
Estimates, 24, 252, 480, 714, 953
Memos. :
Cmd. 5109, 47
Cmd. 5381, 276
Cmd. 5681, 504
Cmd. 5948, 737
Supplementary, 24, 31, 254, 481, 492, 714, 719, 721, 954
Examinations, 150, 225, 376, 451, 605, 607, 685, 857, 859
Subjects, 151
Gross and Net Cost, 22, 251, 479, 712, 953
List (Army List), 222, 448, 684, 929, 1066
Military Manœuvres Commission. *Cmd. 5103*, 47
New Army Divisions, History of the Great War, 883
Officers and Men mentioned for Distinguished Services, 1050
Orders (Army Orders), 222, 448, 684, 929, 1066
For Special Army Orders, see subject.
Pay, Allowances, etc. *Cmd. 5696*, 505
Prize Money and Legacy Funds, etc., Royal Hospital, Chelsea, Accounts, 32, 261, 488, 722
Reserve, War Office Publications (N.P.), 228, 230, 453, 688, 690, 934, 1070
and Auxiliary Forces, Insurance, 934
Schools, War Office Publications (N.P.), 936
Science in the, 653
Tradesmen. *See* Tradesmen.
Votes, 21, 26, 249, 256, 477, 484, 712, 717, 952
Army (*continued*) :
War Office Publications (N.P.), 221, 448, 684, 928, 1066
See also Territorial Army ; H.M. Forces ; Royal Ordnance Factories ; Militia ; Navy, Army ; Reserve Forces.
Aromatic Hydrocarbons, Production of, from Phenols, 660
Arran. *See* Island of Arran.
Arseniuretted Hydrogen Poisoning, 1067
Arsine, Detection of, 907
Art :
Advanced Art Education in London, 155
and Industry, Council for, Reports, 917, 434
Eumorfopoulos Collection of Chinese Art, 234
Examinations, 156, 384, 614, 866, 1032
Royal College of :
Annual Report of Council, 867
Prospectuses, 157, 385, 615
Royal Fine Art Commission Report. *Cmd. 5610*, 293
Scottish Everyday Art, Exhibition, 203
Schools, Burnham Committee Report on Scales of Salaries for Teachers, 866
Subjects, 615
Teacher's Diploma, 155, 614, 865
Technical and Art Education, List of Institutions, 158
Works of. *See* Import Duties Advisory Committee.
See also Museums ; National Museums.
Artificial :
Flower Trade, Wages, 891
Horizons, Specification, 599
Lighting, effect on performance of Worsted Weavers, 657
Limbs, Handbook, 902
Pneumothorax, 192
Silk Fabrics for Parachutes, Specification, 855
Artillery :
Electricity and Service Electrical Apparatus as applied to, 930
Royal Regiment of :
Seniority Lists, 690
Standing Orders, 937
See also Coast Artillery ; Royal Mortar Artillery.
Artists' Brushes, etc., Specification, 686
Asama Maru, Removal of German Citizens from, Correspondence between Japan and U.K. *Cmd. 6166*, 965
Asbestos Fibre Jointing, Specifications, 1026
Asbestosis. *See* Silicosis.

INDEX 1936–40 —AUS

Ascothoracica, 942
Ashby, s.s., Wreck Report, 438
Ashdown Forest Act, 300
Ashes, Nuisance from, Model Byelaws, 391
Ashington, Geology, 194
Ashley Road, Parkstone, Dorset, Explosion in Baking Oven, Report, 435
Ashpits, Cleaning of, Model Byelaws, 391
Asia. *See* Western Asia.
Asilidae, 943
Asphalt, Mastic for Roofing, 419
Assistance. *See* Mutual Assistance ; Public Assistance ; Unemployment Assistance.
Assistant Instructors in Signalling, Army, War Appointments and Additional Pay, 1067
Assize, Commissioners of, Returns :
Cmd. 5592, 291
Cmd. 5874, 518
Assurance :
Companies :
(Amendment) Bill, 272
Returns, 206, 434, 672, 917
of Victory, 884
See also Industrial Assurance ; Insurance.
Assyrian Sculptures, 693
Astronomer Royal for Scotland, Annual Reports, 203, 430
Astronomical :
Ephemeris, 126, 354, 587, 842, 1018
Results from Observations, 188, 653, 901, 1054
Astronomy, Magnetism and Meteorology, Observations in, 188, 653, 901, 1054
Athenian Black-Figure Vases, 941
Athlone, Earl of, Chairman, Interdepartmental Committee on Nursing Services, Report, 874
Atkey, Sir A., Chairman, Joint Advisory Committee on River Pollution, Report, 392
Atlantic. *See* South Atlantic.
Atlas Mixing House, Explosion in, 626
Atmosphere :
Lowest Hundred Metres of, Temperature, 896
Upper, Soundings of, 646, 896
Atmospheric :
Pollution, Investigation of, 192, 419, 657, 904, 1056
Pressure Gauges, Specification, 853
Temperatures, Egypt, 409
Attorney. *See* Powers of Attorney.
Auctioneering, Careers, 401
Auctioneers and House Agents (Protection of Public against Abuses) Bill, 38, 266
Audit :
Service List, Colonial, 862
Stamp Duty, Circular, 619
See also District Audit.
Austen, E. E., The House-Fly as a Danger to Health, 942
Austenitic Cast Iron Pots, Specification, 369
Australia :
Aerial Navigation in Antarctic, Exchange of Notes with France and U.K. *Cmd. 5900*, 520
and New Zealand, Disposal of Property, U.S.A., Convention. *Cmd. 5269*, 59
Arbitration, Convention of Oct. 25, 1905, with various countries, Renewal of. *Cmd. 5448*, 280
British War Memorial Cemeteries and Graves in Egypt, Agreement with Egypt. *Cmd. 5618*, 293
Commercial :
Agreements with Switzerland. *Cmd. 5960*, 738
Relations, Exchange of Notes with :
Brazil. *Cmd. 6214*, 968
Greece. *Cmd. 6243*, 970
Treaty with Czechoslovakia. *Cmd. 5649*, 502
Economic Conditions, 439, 676, 920
Empire Air Mail Scheme. *Cmd. 5414*, 278
Supplementary Arrangements. *Cmd. 5497*, 284
Extradition :
Convention with Luxemburg. *Cmd. 5416*, 378
Supplementary Convention with Ecuador. *Cmd. 5614*, 293
Identity Documents for Aircraft Personnel, Exchange of Notes :
Cmd. 5586, 291
Cmd. 6130, 750
Imported Food Certificates, 162, 618, 620
Scotland, 666
Limitation of Naval Armament, International Treaty. *Cmd. 5561*, 289
Merchant Shipping, Service to and from Western Canada, 208
Regulation of Beef Imports into U.K., Correspondence. *Cmd. 5943*, 737
Trade :
Agreements :
France, Belgium, Czechoslovakia, 208
Japan. *Cmd. 5860*, 517
Discussions with U.K. *Cmd. 5805*, 513

AUS— INDEX 1936–40

Australia (*continued*) :
War :
Cemeteries in Iraq, Agreement. *Cmd. 5196*, 53
Graves Agreement. *Cmd. 5068*, 44
See also British War Memorials ; Extradition ; Identity Documents.
Australian Wool, Establishment of a Reserve in U.S.A. *Cmd. 6242*, 970
Austria :
Application of Treaties between U.K., Germany and Austria, Exchange of Notes, Germany and U.K. *Cmd. 5888*, 519
Commercial Relations with Canada. *Cmd. 5233*, 56
Economic Conditions, 676
Austria-Hungary, Suez Maritime Canal, Free Navigation of, International Convention. *Cmd. 5623*, 500
Austrian :
Civilian Internees, Categories of Persons Eligible for Release. *Cmd. 6217*, 968
Loan Guarantee Act, 1933, Statement of Guarantee and Account, 958
Autoclaves and Vulcanisers, Factory Form, 1042
Automatic :
Controls, Rubber Tubing for, Specification, 855
Telephone Circuit Elements, 653
Telephony, Post Office Publications (N.P.), 902
Auxiliary :
Air Force. *See* Air Force Reserve.
Climatological Stations, Instructions to Observers at, 1052
Fire Service :
Home Office Publications (N.P.), 631, 1036
List and Index of Circulars, 880
Scottish Office Publications (N.P.), 670
Volunteers, Enrolment of, 880
Forces. *See* Reserve and Auxiliary Forces.
Military Pioneer Corps :
Formation of, 929
Palestinian Companies, Allowances issuable to Married Officers, 1067
Reserve Forces, Unemployment Insurance, 1070
Territorial Service :
Formation of, 690
War Office Publications (N.P.), 1070, 1072
Aviation. *See* Civil Aviation.
Aviators, Meteorology for, 896, 1052
Avoidance of Corruption. *See* Corruption.
Avon. *See* Bristol Avon.
Avon, River, s.t., Wreck Report, 438
Awards to Inventors, Royal Commission on, Final Report. *Cmd. 5594*, 291
Axbridge Rural District Council Act, 72
Axe Handles. *See* Import Duties Advisory Committee.
Axeman, Army Trade of, 929
Axminster, Sunday Entertainments, 953
Aylesbury, Sunday Entertainments, 485
Ayr :
Burgh Order Confirmation Bill, 963
Register of Sasines, 417
Ayrshire Educational Trust :
(Additional Endowments) (No. 1) Scheme, 664
(Additional Endowments and Amendment) (No. 1) Scheme, 910
Scheme, 200, 425

B

Babies and Young Children, Anti-gas Protection of, 877
Bacillary White Diarrhoea of Chicks, 363
Bacillus Salmonicida Bacteriophage, 665
Backstays for Use in Mines, 1054
Backward Children, Education of, 384
Bacon :
and Hams, Bacteria in the curing of, 1057
Curing on the Farm, 1023
Industry :
Act, 524
Bill, 471, 472, 486, 490, 494, 496, 497
(Amendment) Act, 752
Bill, 499, 698, 728
Marketing Scheme, 848
Production and Trade, 171, 398, 634
Bacteria :
Acetic Acid, 192
in the Curing of Bacon and Hams, 1057
Sulphur, 192
Bacterial Nutrition, 191
Bacteriological :
Examination of Water Supplies, 871
Tests for Milk, 164
Bacteriologist. *See* Dairy Bacteriologist.
Bacup Provisional Order Confirmation Act, 759
Bill, 701, 731
Badges :
Auxiliary Fire Service, 631, 1036
Scotland, 670
for Volunteers, A.R.P., 393, 624
Scotland, 431
of British Dominions, 153, 380, 611
862, 1031
Baffin Bay, Earthquake, Seismic Wave from, 408

INDEX 1936–40 —BAR

Bag Trades Wages, 642, 891
See also Paper Bag Trade ; Sack and Bag Trade.
Bagasse. *See* Import Duties Advisory Committee.
Baggage, Army, Conveyance of, 229, 449, 685, 929, 1066
Bahamas, Colonial Reports, 378, 860
Bahrein, Transit Dues. *Cmd. 5168*, 51
Bailiffs. *See* County Court Bailiffs.
Baillie, Sir J., Chairman, Road Motor Transport Industry (Goods), Committee on Regulation of Wages, etc. :
Minute of Evidence, 404
Report. *Cmd. 5440*, 280
Baird Trust Order Confirmation Act, 760
Bill, 708, 734
Baking :
Industry (Hours of Work) Act, 523
Bill (formerly Bakehouses Bill), 468, 485, 490, 492, 495, 497
Oven, Explosion in, Report, 435
Trade, Wages, 889, 1045
See also Night Baking.
Ballistic Consequences of assuming a Rate of Burning for a Propellant proportional to the Gas Density, 230
Balloons, Kite :
Silk Fabric for, Specification, 855
Soft Cotton Cord for, Specification, 601
Baltic Redwood, Data on, 420
Balvenie Castle, Banffshire, guide, 231
Bananas, Production and Trade, 171, 398, 633
Banbury Waterworks Act, 301
Bandar Shahpour, s.s., Wreck Report, 438
Banffshire :
Bursary Trust Scheme, 199, 425
Educational Trust Scheme, 200, 425
Bangkok–Hong Kong, Civil Air Transport Service. *Cmd. 5871*, 518
Bangor Corporation Act, 525
Bankers' Returns, 180, 407, 644, 893, 1048
Bank :
Holiday, 4 September 1939, Proclamation, 893
Notes. *See* Currency and Bank Notes.
Banking :
Accounts. *See* Czechoslovakia.
and the Money Market, Careers, 174, 887
Industry. *See* Unemployment Insurance.
Societies, Annual Return Forms, 387, 617, 869, 1034
Bankruptcy :
and Companies (Winding Up) Proceedings, Accounts, 19, 248, 256, 484, 718, 957
Bankruptcy (*continued*) :
Annual Reports, 206, 434, 672, 1063
(Scotland) Act, 295
Statistics, Scotland :
Cmd. 5210, 54
Cmd. 5547, 288
Cmd. 5779, 511
Cmd. 6078, 746
Banks. *See* Post Office Savings Banks ; Trustee Savings Banks ; International Savings Banks ; Savings Banks.
Baptista Boazio, Map of Iceland, 694
Barbados, Colonial Reports, 151, 378, 609, 860
Barber, D. R., The Efficiency of Baths used for the Hot-Water Treatment of Narcissus Bulbs, 361
Barclay, A., Chemistry, 414
Barford Invicta Boiler and Sterilising Chest, 132
Barkas, W. W., Moisture in Wood in Relation to Strength and Shrinkage, 659
Barker, T. P., Cider Apple Production, 361
Barley :
Growers, Assistance to. *Cmd. 6077*, 746
Growing of, 850
Production and Trade, 171, 398, 634, 883
Barlow, Sir M., Chairman, Royal Commission on Geographical Distribution of the Industrial Population :
Minutes of Evidence, 423, 663, 908
Report. *Cmd. 6153*, 964
Barnet District Gas and Water Act, 300
Barnsley :
Corporation Act, 299
Provisional Order Confirmation Act, 71
Bill, 12, 40
Barnsley—Warren House Seam, Survey of Coal Resources, 906
Baroda. *See* Bombay.
Baron Polwarth, s.s., Wreck Report, 438
Baronesa, s.s., Boiler Explosion, Report, 1061
Barony of Vaux of Harrowden, Proceedings and Evidence taken before the Committee of Privileges, 466
Barr, J., Chairman, Committee on Scottish Building Costs, Report. *Cmd. 5977*, 739
Barrack Services, Army, 230, 456, 690, 937, 1071
Barrell, H. :
Determination of the Fundamental Standards of Length, etc., 661
Relations between Wave-Lengths of Light and Fundamental Standards of Length, 661

1936-40 | BAR-BRA

BAR— *INDEX 1936–40*

Bars, Specifications, 141, 366–8, 600–1, 854–5, 1025–9
Basements, Air Raid Shelters in, 878
Basic :
  Slag, 363
  Training in Air Raid Precautions, 1038
Basketware. *See* Merchandise Marks.
Bass and Fibre Trade, Wages, 890, 1046
Bastardy (Blood Tests) Bill, 474, 707
Basutoland :
  Colonial Reports, 151, 378, 609, 860
  Commercial Relations with Swaziland, Bechuanaland, Mozambique. *Cmd. 5807*, 513
  Flags and Badges, 380
Bateson, R. G. :
  Kiln-Drying Schedules, 659
  Methods of Kiln Operation, 420
  Timber Seasoning, 659
Bath Corporation Act, 302
Bathing Pools, Model Byelaws, 391
Baths :
  for Hot Water Treatment of Narcissus Bulbs, 361
  Swimming, Model Byelaws, 391
Battersea Power Station, Chimney Gases, Treatment. *Cmd. 5572*, 290
Battle :
  of the Marne, Administrative Tour of the Battlefield, 449
  of the River Plate, Account of Events, 1018
Bayflower, s.t., Wreck Report, 438
Bayonet Training, Small Arms Training, 456
Beans, 133
  Culture of, 134
  Production and Trade, Soya Beans, 634
  Production, Trade, and Consumption, Soya Beans, 883
  See also Import Duties Advisory Committee.
Beatsa, s.s., Wreck Report, 675
Beaumont Seam, Survey of National Coal Resources, 421
Bechuanaland :
  Colonial Reports, 151, 378, 609, 860
  Commercial Relations with Swaziland, Basutoland, and Mozambique. *Cmd. 5807*, 513
  Flags and Badges, 380
  Imported Food Certificate, 389
    Scotland, 428
Bed-bug, 460
Bedford :
  Joint Hospital Provisional Order Confirmation Act, 67
    Bill, 6, 36
  Provisional Order Confirmation Act, 298
    Bill, 236, 265
  Sunday Entertainments, 955
Bedwellty Urban District Council Act, 69
Beef :
  and Veal Customs Duties :
    Act, 295
    Bill, 43, 236
  Production and Trade, 171, 398, 634
  Regulation of Imports into U.K. :
    Correspondence, Australia, New Zealand, Eire, and U.K. *Cmd. 5943*, 737
    Exchange of Notes, Argentine, Brazil, Uruguay and U.K. *Cmd. 5941*, 737
  See also Import Duties Advisory Committee.
Beekeepers, Intending, Advice to, 363
Beeswax, Marketing of, 361
Beet. *See* Sugar Beet.
Beetles :
  Flea, 362, 849
  injurious to Timber and Furniture, 1057
Beggars, Census of, Scotland, Form, 431
Beibl Cymraeg, Suggestions to Teachers for Celebrations of St. David's Day, 616
Belgian Congo :
  Economic Conditions, 676
  Uganda and Ruanda-Urundi, Sanitary Convention with U.K. *Cmd. 6064*, 745
Belgium :
  Boundary between Tanganyika and Ruanda - Urundi; *Cmds. 5075, 5076*, 45
    Treaty with U.K. *Cmd. 5777*, 511
  Commercial :
    Agreement with South Africa. *Cmd. 5708*, 506
    Relations with Irish Free State. *Cmd. 5562*, 289
  Economic Conditions, 211, 439
  Identity Documents for Aircraft Personnel, Exchange of Notes with various countries. *Cmd. 5764*, 510
  Imported Food Certificates, 161, 618
    Scotland, 666
  International Position of. *Cmd. 5437*, 279
  Parcel Post between U.K. and Belgium, Agreement with U.K. *Cmd. 5858*, 517
  Proposals drawn up by Belgium, France, U.K. and Italy. *Cmd. 5134*, 48
    Correspondence with Belgian and French Ambassadors. *Cmd. 5149*, 49

INDEX 1936–40 —BIR

Belgium (*continued*) :
  Trade :
    Agreement with Australia, 208
    Arrangement with New Zealand. *Cmc. 5359*, 274
  Uganda and the Belgian Congo and Ruanda-Urundi, Sanitary Convention with U.K. *Cmd. 6064*, 745
  Water Rights on Boundary between Tanganyika and Ruanda-Urundi, Agreement with U.K. *Cmd. 5778*, 511
Bell, R. D., Chairman, Commission of Inquiry into Financial Position, etc., of Nyasaland, Report, 611
Bell, T. D., Turkeys, 360
Belligerent Rights at Sea, Correspondence between Italy and U.K. *Cmd. 6191*, 967
Bells, Cycle. *See* Import Duties Advisory Committee.
Belts and Harness, Safety, Specifications, 140, 366
Bending Wood :
  by Hand, Methods of, 420
  Machinery and Equipment used for, 659
Bendix Ltd., Tyseley, Birmingham, Boiler Explosion, 206
Benefice Buildings (Postponement of Inspections and Repayment of Loans) Measure, 947, 948, 973
Benefices. *See* Union of Benefices.
Beneficial Insects, 848
Benevolent Societies, Annual Return Forms, 387, 617, 869, 1034
Bengali Books in the Library of the British Museum, 941
Bensham Seam, Survey of Coal Resources, 906
Benzene Vapour, Detection of, 907
Bergius Process, Action of Hydrogen upon Coal, 193
Berkham(p)ste(a)d :
  Castle, Guide, 231
  Sunday Entertainments, 491
Berkshire County Council Act, 299
Berlin. *See* Civil Air Transport Services.
Bermuda :
  Civil Air Transport Service, Bermuda–New York
    Cmd. 5237, 56
    Cmd. 5870, 518
  Colonial Reports, 151, 378, 609, 860
  Economic Conditions, 439
  Militia Artillery, etc., Peace Establishments, 454
Besano, Lombardy, Triassic Fishes of, 943
Bespoke Tailoring Trade, Wages, 1046
Best, A. C., Abnormal Visibility at Malta, 897
Bethesda Provisional Order Confirmation Act, 760
  Bill, 701, 731
Bethnal Green Museum, Guide, 695
Betting :
  and Bookmakers Bill, 495
  (No. 1) Bill, 36
  Racecourse. *See* Racecourse Betting.
Beverages, Spirituous, Importation into Africa :
  Cmd. 5205, 54
  Cmd. 5814, 514
Beveridge, J. B., Studies in Nutrition, 1056
Bexhill, Sunday Entertainments, 955
Bichloride, Mercury. *See* Import Duties Advisory Committee.
Bicycles, Army, care, inspection and repair of, 230
Bideford Electricity Order, 213
Bigg, W. H., Ice Formation in Clouds in Great Britain, 646
Bihar, Resignation of Ministry. *Cmd 5674*, 504
Bilham, E. G. :
  Effects of Obstacles on Sunshine Records, 409
  Height-Computer for Use in Aerological Work, 646
Billericay, Sunday Entertainments, 487
Billeting. *See* Army.
Bills :
  of Health. *See* Health.
  Private :
    Common Form Clauses in, Report of Committee, 32
    Opposed Private Bills Committee, 18
Biochemical Activities of Acetic Acid Bacteria, 192
Biological :
  Action of X and Gamma Rays, 419
  Remains in Marine Deposits, 942
  Standards, Reports on, 904
Biology :
  Careers, 401
  Examination Papers, Science Scholarships, 384, 866
  of Marine Deposits of the Arabian Sea, 942
  Short History of, 901
Bird, G., Studies in Road Friction, 422
Bird Sanctuaries in Royal Parks, Reports :
  England, 232, 457, 691, 938
  Scotland 205, 433, 671, 916
Birds :
  and their Eggs, 694
  See also Importation of Plumage; Wild Birds.

BIR— *INDEX 1936–40*

Birkett, W. N., Interdepartmental Committee on Abortion, Report, 870
Birmingham Corporation Acts, 72, 973
Birmingham, Tame and Rea Main Sewerage District Provisional Order Confirmation Act, 302
  Bill, 243, 268
Birthday Honours, King's, 407, 644, 893
Births, etc. *See* Registrar-General.
Birtley, s.s., Wreck Report, 211
Biscuits, Provision of, at Courses of Instruction for Unemployed Boys and Girls, 643
Bitumens and Bitumen-Filler Mixtures, Rigidity Modulus of, 907
Bituminous :
  Coal, Production of Active Carbon from, 660
  Road Materials, Mechanical Testing of, 907
Black :
  Currants, " Reversion " in, 135
  Dot Disease of Potato, 850
  Leather Shoes, Specification, 933
  Scurf of Potato, 595
Blackboards, Specification, 452
Blackburn :
  Corporation Act, 526
  Provisional Order Confirmation :
    Acts, 757, 973
    Bills, 698, 727, 946, 962
Black-out :
  Factory Ventilation in the, 1036
  Ventilation in the, 1038
Blackpool Improvement Act, 535
Blackpool, Lytham St. Annes, and Fleetwood, Electricity Breakdown, Report, 926
Blades, Hacksaw, Specification, 226, 686
Blanesburgh, Lord, Chairman, Advisory Committee on the Welfare of the Blind, Report, 393
Blank Cinematograph Film. *See* Import Duties Advisory Committee.
Blankets, Specifications, 226, 452, 687, 932
Blasphemy. *See* Aliens Restriction.
Bledisloe, Viscount, Chairman, Rhodesia-Nyasaland Royal Commission, Report. *Cmd. 5949*, 737
Blind :
  Aberdeen Asylum for the Blind Scheme, 200
  Certification of Blindness, 161
  Persons :
    Act, 522
    Bill, 271, 462, 493
      Circulars :
        England, 618
        Scotland, 667
        Wales, 623
Blind (*continued*) :
  Persons (*continued*) :
    Welfare of :
      Circular, 388
      Reports of Advisory Committee, 393
  Students, Training of, Lists of Institutions, 155, 614, 866
  Welfare of, Handbook, 876
Blindness :
  due to Cataract :
    England, 618
    Wales, 623
  Prevention of, 388
    Wales, 393
  See also Prevention and Treatment of Blindness.
Blister Gases, Decontamination of Clothing from, 877
Blocks, Wooden. *See* Import Duties Advisory Committee.
Blood :
  Groups, International Nomenclature of, 1067
  Tests. *See* Bastardy.
  Transfusion. *See* Traumatic Shock.
Blood-sucking Flies, British, 941
Blow Lamps, Factory Form, 630
Blue Angola Shirt, Specification, 452
Blueness of the Sky, Polarity of the Air and Gradient Wind, Relation between, 646
Blyth Scholarship Trust Scheme, 198, 199, 426
Board for Suitcases, etc. *See* Import Duties Advisory Committee.
Boats :
  Fishing, Exhibition, 187
  Folding Boat Equipment, Army, 223
  See also Fishing Boats; Shipping; Ships.
Boazio, Baptista, Map of Iceland, 694
Bodkin, Sir A. H., Chairman, Departmental Committee on Sharepushing, Report. *Cmd. 5539*, 287
Bodkins. *See* Import Duties Advisory Committee.
Bognor and District Gas and Electricity Act, 758
Bognor Regis Urban District Council Act, 72
Boiler :
  Barford Invicta, and Sterilising Chest, 132
  Explosion Acts, Working of, Annual Reports, 206, 434, 672, 917
  Explosion Reports, 206, 434, 672, 1061
  Halliday Oil-fired, 592

INDEX 1936–40 —BRA

Boilers :
  Factory Forms, 879
  See also Fire Engine Steam Boilers Steam Boilers.
Bolts. *See* Door Bolts; Steel Bolts.
Bomb. *See* Aircraft Bomb; High Explosive Bombs; Incendiary Bombs.
Bombay, Baroda and Central India Railway Act, 525
Bombing by Italian Military Aircraft of the British Red Cross Ambulance in Ethiopia. *Cmd. 5160*, 50
Bomb-resisting Shelters, 877
Bombsight Brackets, Rubber Pads for, Specification, 1026
Bombyliidae, 943
Bon Voisinage Agreement and Exchanges of Notes, Egypt, Italy and U.K. *Cmd. 5726*, 507
Bonded Warehouses, 154, 382, 612, 863, 1032
Bonding and Screening, etc., for all W/T Purposes on Aircraft, Specifications, 369, 855
Bonds. *See* Drawn Bonds; National War Bonds; Victory Bonds.
Bones, Absorption of, in Skull of Salmon, 665
Bonny Water, Rivers Pollution Prevention, Report, 429
Bookbinding, History of, 941
Bookcases, 943
Bookmakers. *See* Betting and Bookmakers.
Books. *See* Bengali Books.
Boot :
  and Floor Polish Trade, Wages, 642, 889, 1046
  and Shoe Repairing Trade, Wages, 404, 642, 890, 1046
  Pullovers. *See* Pullovers, Boot or Shoe.
Booth, N., Action of Hydrogen upon Coal, 660
Bootle Corporation Act, 759
Boots, Specifications, 452, 687, 932
Boredom in Repetitive Work, 418
Borneo. *See* North Borneo.
Borough Councils. *See* Metropolitan Borough Councils.
Borstal :
  Experiments in Vocational Guidance, 418
  Institutions :
    Board of Arbitration Award, 1041
    Directory, 169, 306, 634, 881
Boscawen, Sir A. G., Chairman, Transport Advisory Council, Reports, 447, 682
Botanic Gardens. *See* Edinburgh; Kew.
Bothies, Model Byelaws, 666
Botticelli, Allegory of Abundance, 694
Bottles, Hot-water, Import Duties. *Cmd. 6072*, 60
Bottling of Fruit, 1059
Boundaries. *See* Glasgow Boundaries.
Boundary Rights. *See* Mozambique Ruanda-Urundi.
Bournemouth :
  Corporation (Trolley Vehicles) Order Confirmation Act, 525
    Bill, 270, 466, 493
  Enteric Fever in, Report, 392
  Gas and Water Acts, 525, 973
Bovine Contagious Abortion, 594
Box Trade, Wages, 642, 891
  See also Paper Box; Tin Box.
Boys :
  and Girls in Greater London, Employment for, 641
  employed in Coal Mines, Safety Principles for, 384
  Holidays for, etc., Factory Forms, 627
  Night Work, Factory Forms, 167
  Secondary School, Careers for, 174
  See also Coal Mines (Employment of Boys); Unemployed Boys.
Braces, Specification, 687
Bracken, 595
Bradford :
  Electricity Breakdown Report, 212
  Provisional Order Confirmation Act, 760
    Bill, 701, 731
Brady, F. L., External Rendered Finishes, 657
Brass, J., Report on Explosion at Gresford Colliery. *Cmd. 5358*, 274
Brass Pins. *See* Merchandise Marks.
Brass Tubes, Wire, Rivets, etc., Specifications, 368, 600
Braxy, Louping-Ill, and Tick-Borne Fever, 909
Brazell, J. H., Relation between Blueness of the Sky, Polarity of the Air, and Gradient Wind, 646
Brazil :
  Commercial :
    Agreement with South Africa. *Cmd. 6132*, 750
    Relations :
      Exchange of Notes with Australia. *Cmd. 6214*, 968
      with Canada. *Cmd. 5821*, 514
      with Newfoundland. *Cmd. 5268*, 58
      with U.K. *Cmd. 5267*, 58
  Economic Conditions, 211, 439, 676, 920
  Imported Food Certificates, 388, 619
    Scotland, 428
  Regulation of Beef Imports into U.K., Exchanges of Notes. *Cmd. 5941*, 737

BRA-BYS | 1936-40

BRA— INDEX 1936–40

Brazil Nuts. *See* Import Duties Advisory Committee.
Breathing Apparatus. *See* Oxygen Breathing Apparatus.
"Breathing Machines" and their Use in Treatment, Report, 1055
Breeding :
Animal, 360
Oysters in Tanks, 361
Plankton Organisms of South-west North Sea, 361
Breeds, British, of Live Stock, 593
Breeze and Clinker Aggregates, Properties, etc., 192
Brentford and Chiswick :
Corporation Act, 69
Sunday Entertainments, 485
Brentwood, Sunday Entertainments, 952
Bressey, Sir C., Highway Development Survey, 1937, Greater London, Report, 677
Bricklaying in Cold Weather, Precautions for, 1057
Bricks. *See* Clay Bricks ; Merchandise Marks.
Bridge :
Charing Cross, Report, 214
Works, Standard Forms, Conditions of Tender and Contract, 218, 680
Bridge of Allan Gas Order Confirmation Act, 67
Bridgwater Extension Provisional Order Confirmation Act, 525
Bill, 272, 464
Bridlington Provisional Order Confirmation Act, 301
Bill, 240, 269
Bridport Joint Hospital District Provisional Order Confirmation Act, 68
Bill, 8, 37
Brighton :
Corporation :
Act, 70
(Transport) Act, 527
Generating Station Extension Electricity Orders, 213
Marine Palace and Pier Acts, 67, 973
Brighton, Hove and Worthing Gas Act, 299
Bristol :
Avon, Milk Wastes on the, 594
Coal Mines Scheme Amendment, 192
Corporation Act, 527
Ministry of Health Provisional Order Confirmation Act, 68
Bill, 9, 38
Transport Act, 302
Waterworks Act, 759
Britannia Steam Ship Insurance Association Ltd., War Risks Insurance, 724
British :
Airways :
Experimental flights for development of certain Air Services, Agreement. *Cmd. 5524*, 286
Regular services to Holland, North Germany and Scandinavia, Agreement. *Cmd. 5203*, 53
See also Civil Air Transport Services.
and Foreign :
Medals, 414, 900
State Papers, 158, 386, 616, 1033
Blood-sucking Flies, 941
Breeds of Live Stock, 593
Broadcasting Corporation :
Annual Reports :
Cmd. 5088, 46
Cmd. 5406, 278
Cmd. 5668, 503
Cmd. 5951, 738
Drafts of Royal Charter, Licence, etc. *Cmd. 5329*, 63
Lambert *v* Levita Case :
Cmd. 5337, 64
Minute by Prime Minister. *Cmd. 5405*, 277
Postmaster-General and Minister of Information, Agreement with. *Cmd. 6177*, 966
Colonial Empire, Story of, 860
Columbia. *See* Trail.
Commonwealth Scientific Conference, Report. *Cmd. 5341*, 273
Death Duties Acts, Supplement, 399
Dependencies in West Africa, Economic Conditions, 439
Documents on the Origin of the War, 158, 616
East Africa :
Economic Conditions, 211, 439, 920
Flags and Badges, 380
Higher Education in, Report of Commission, 380
East African Coffee, Importation of, Exchange of Notes, France and U.K. *Cmd. 5558*, 289
Empire :
Constitution of, 616
Shipping, Geographical Distribution of, 586
Statistical Abstracts :
Cmd. 5582, 290
Cmd. 5872, 518
Cmd. 6140, 751
Expeditionary Force, Powers of the Commander-in-Chief, 929
Fishing :
and Coastal Craft, 414
Vessels Mutual War Risks Association, 723

INDEX 1936–40 —BRO

British (*continued*) :
Forces, Photographs of, 1039
Guiana :
Colonial Reports, 151, 609, 860, 1031
Economic Conditions, 439
Local Legislature, 710
Refugee Commission :
Report. *Cmd. 6014*, 742
Appendices. *Cmd. 6029*, 743
Honduras :
Colonial Reports, 151, 378, 609, 860
Economic Conditions, 439, 676
Local Legislature, 710
Pitch Pine, Properties of, 420
Imperial Calendar and Civil Service List, 205, 433, 671, 916, 1062
India. *See* India.
Iron and Steel Industry, Memo. on Clause 6 of Finance Bill, 1936. *Cmd. 5201*, 53
Marine Mutual Insurance Association, 724
Meteorological Stations used in preparation of Synoptic Reports, Gazetteer of, 645
Military Missions, Appointments with, 448
Museum :
Act, 523
Bill, 471, 497
Annual Reports, 186, 413, 652, 900
Civil Service Arbitration Tribunal Award, 640
Publications, 459, 693, 941
Museum (Natural History) :
Annual Reports, 186, 413, 652, 900
Publications, 460, 694, 941
Nationality and Status of Aliens :
Bill, 470
Amendment Bill, 267
North America Act, 971
Bill, 948, 963
Official Postcards, Photographs of the British Forces, 1039
Overseas Airways Act, 754
Bill, 707, 722, 730, 732, 733
Statement of Guarantee, 957
Purbeck Charophyta, 941
Rainfall, 180, 408, 645, 896
Red Cross Society :
Air Raid Precautions, 165
Scottish Branch, 204
Bombing of Ambulance by Italian Military Aircraft in Ethiopia. *Cmd. 5160*, 50
Shipowners, Memo. on Wartime Financial Arrangements with H.M. Government. *Cmd. 6218*, 969
British (*continued*) :
Shipping :
Assistance to, Memo. on proposals. *Cmd. 6060*, 745
(Assistance) Act, 1935, Accounts of advances under, 35, 263, 487, 723, 961
(Assistance) Bill, 1938, 732
(Continuance of Subsidy) Acts, 65, 296
Bills, 8, 37, 237, 266
See also Tramp Shipping Subsidy.
in the Orient, Report, 918
Ships :
Registry of, 209, 437, 674, 919
Reinsurance Agreements, 959
Signal Letters of, 209, 437, 674, 919, 1061
See also Ships.
Solomon Islands, Colonial Report, 378
Somaliland, Grazing Rights and Transit Traffic. *Cmd. 5775*, 511
Sugar :
Corporation Ltd., Incentive Agreement with Ministry of Agriculture and Fisheries, 596
Subsidy, Balance Sheets of Companies. *See* Sugar.
Transatlantic Territories, Naval and Air Facilities for the United States in, and United States Destroyers, Exchange of Notes. *Cmd. 6224*, 969
War :
Debt. *See* United States of America.
Memorial Cemeteries and Graves in Egypt, Agreement between Egypt and various countries. *Cmd. 5618*, 293
Memorials, Transfer to French State of Property in the Sites of, Convention, Canada, Australia, France and U.K. *Cmd. 6003*, 741
West Indies :
Calendar of State Papers, 416
Customs Tariffs, 380
Economic Conditions, 439
Britton, C. E., Meteorological Chronology to A.D. 1450, 408
Brixham Gas and Electricity Act, 525
Broadcasting :
Civil Estimates, 252, 480, 481, 715, 954
Committee Report. *Cmd. 5091*, 46
Memo. by Postmaster-General. *Cmd. 5207*, 54
Services in the Colonies, Committee on, Interim Report, 379
Supplement, 862

BRO— INDEX 1936–40

Broadcasting (*continued*) :
School 203
Use of, in the cause of Peace, International Convention :
Cmd. 5505, 285
Cmd. 5714, 506
See also British Broadcasting.
Broadcasts of Weather Reports from Air Ministry Meteorological Stations, 408, 645
Broadstairs :
and District Electricity Act, 299
and St. Peters, Sunday Entertainments, 482
Brodick. *See* Ardrossan.
Bromsgrove, Sunday Entertainments, 952
Brontes, s.t., Boiler Explosion, 435
Bronze. *See* Lead Bronze.
Bronzing, Regs. for, Factory Forms, 1036
Brooks, J., Curing of Bacon, 1057
Broom :
Handles, Specification, 1063
Trade, Wages, 890, 1046
Brooms and Brushes, Specifications, 686, 931
Brough, J., Triassic Fishes of Besano, Lombardy, 943
Broussonetia Papyrifera (Paper Mulberry). *See* Import Duties Advisory Committee.
Brown, H. G., Chairman, Committee on the Production of Civil Aeroplanes, Report. *Cmd. 6038*, 743
Browne, G. St. J. Orde, Labour Conditions in West Indies, Report. *Cmd. 6070*, 746
Brunei, Colonial Reports, 151, 378, 609, 1031
Brush :
and Broom Trade, Wages, 890, 1046
Handles, Specification, 1063
Brushes, Specifications, 686, 931
Brussels. *See* Civil Air Transport Services.
Bryn Navigation Colliery, Explosion, 672
Buchan, S., Water Supply of London from Underground Sources, 907
Buckhaven and Methil Burgh Order Confirmation Act, 68
Bill, 12, 39
Buckingham's Charity (Dunstable) Act, 70
Bill, 9, 38
Buckles, Merchandise Marks. *Cmd. 6080*, 746
Bucks Water :
Act, 301
Board Provisional Order Confirmation Act, 527
Bill, 471, 496
Buckton Vale Works, Stalybridge, Explosion, 672
Budapest. *See* Civil Air Transport Services.
Budget :
Disclosure Enquiry :
Minutes of Evidence, 166
Report of Tribunal. *Cmd. 5184*, 52
Financial Statements by Chancellor of the Exchequer, 27, 257, 484, 718, 723, 957, 959
Income Tax Statements, Tables. *Cmd. 6107*, 748
Bug, Bed, 460
Bugle Sounds, Army, 937
Builders, Institute of, National Certificates and Diplomas, 204
Building :
Byelaws :
Department of Health for Scotland Publications (N.P.), 429
Ministry of Health Publications (N.P.), 389
Costs, Scottish, Committee on, Report. *Cmd. 5977*, 739
Estates, Practice Leaflet for Solicitors, 179
Factory Forms, 627
Industry :
Choice of Occupation Leaflet, 174
Workmen's Compensation Forms, 170, 397, 633
Materials :
(Charging and Supply) Bill, 36
Freezing of, 658
Trades, Import Duties, Reports, 208, 436
Programmes, Local Authority, Planning and Priority, Scotland, 432
Research Board Publications (N.P.), 192, 419, 657, 904, 1056
Science Abstracts, 519, 658, 905, 1057
Societies :
Act, 753
Bill, 728
No. 2 Bill, 707, 721, 725, 728, 731
Registry of Friendly Societies, Publications (N.P.), 159, 387, 617, 869, 1034
See also Modern Building.
Buildings :
Fumigation of. *See* Hydrogen Cyanide.
in course of Construction, Cranes, etc., at, 395
in which Marriages may be solemnised, 417, 903, 1055
Model Byelaws, 621
Noise in, Reduction, 904
Planning of, for Public Elementary Schools, 156

INDEX 1936–40 —BYS

Buildings (*continued*) :
Sound Transmission in, 1058
See also Ancient Monuments ; Aberdeen Corporation (Streets) ; Glasgow Streets ; Public Buildings ; School Buildings ; Commercial Buildings ; Commercial and Industrial Buildings ; Essential Buildings ; Light Construction Buildings ; Benefice Buildings ; Hut Type Buildings ; War Department ; Works and Buildings.
Buildwas Abbey, Shropshire, Guide, 457
Bulbs :
Commercial Bulb Production, 848
Diseases of, 849
Pickers of, Model Byelaws, 621
Supplies, 171, 398, 634, 883
See also Narcissus Bulbs.
Bulgaria :
Economic Conditions, 439, 920
Imported Food Certificate, 389
Scotland, 428
Military, Naval, and Air Clauses of the Treaty of Neuilly, etc., Exchange of Notes with U.K. *Cmd. 5954*, 738
Bullet Proof Safety Glass for Windscreen Panels, Specification, 933
Bullion, Imports and Exports, 155, 383, 614, 865
Bulverhythe Stream. *See* Old Haven.
Bunching or Stranding, Electrical Specifications, 452
Bunting, Specifications, 933, 1069
Buoyage. *See* Maritime Buoyage.
Burgess Hill Water Act, 299
Burghs, Scotland, Model Byelaws for Regulating Building in, 429
Burial Ground. *See* Stanmore.
Burma :
Air Services over Siam, India and Burma, Exchange of Notes, Siam, India and U.K. *Cmd. 5651*, 502
Civil Service Examinations, 374, 605, 1030
Criminal Law Amendment (Amendment) Act, 30
Customs Tariff, 674
Frontier Forces at, 259
Nationality of Persons affected by the Re-delimitation of the boundary between Burma (Tenasserim) and Siam. *Cmd. 5475*, 282
Office List, 1038
Police Service, Examinations, 376, 607
Standing Orders, House of Lords, 5, 17
Trade and Commerce with Japan :
Cmd. 5504, 285
Cmd. 5636, 501
See also Government of Burma ; India and Burma ; Rangoon.
Burnet, F. M., The Use of the Development Egg in Virus Research, 418
Burnett, A., Mintlaw, Industrial Court Award, 888
Burnham :
and District Water Provisional Order Confirmation Act, 758
Bill, 704, 729
Committee Reports on Scales of Salaries for Teachers, 866
Burnley, Electricity, 440
Burns, Dangers from, 167
Bursary Schemes, Education (Scotland) Act 1918, Circular, 913
Burton-on-Trent, Electricity, 921
Bury and District Joint Hospital District Provisional Order Confirmation Act, 67
Bill, 6
Bury Hill, s.s., Wreck Report, 438
Bus Strikes. *See* London Central Omnibus Services.
Bush Fruits, 848
Business :
Appointments, Acceptance by Officers of the Crown Services. *Cmd. 5517*, 285
of Courts Committee, Report. *Cmd. 5506*, 44
Premises, Air Raid Precautions, 166, 393
Scotland, 431
Businesses, Miscellaneous, Societies carrying on, Annual Return Form, 387
Busmen. *See* London Central Busmen.
Busty Seam, Survey of Coal Resources, 660
Butcher, R. W. :
Effects of Milk Wastes on the Bristol Avon, 594
Survey of River Tees, 422
Butler, G. G., Cultivation of Vaccinia on the Chorid-Allantoic Membranes of Chick Embryos, 874
Butter, Production and Trade, 171, 398, 883
Butterfly Migrations in the Tropics, 460
Buttermaking, Faults and Difficulties in, 850
Button Manufacturing Trade, Wages, 642, 1045
Buttons, Merchandise Marks. *Cmd. 6080*, 746
Buxton, J. B., Tuberculin Tests in Cattle, 904
Buzzard, The, 134
Byelaws : *See* Building Byelaws ; Model Byelaws.
Byssinosis : Workmen's Compensation and Benefit (Byssinosis) Act, 972
Bill, 948

1936-40 | CAB-CEY

CAB— INDEX 1936–40

C

Cabbage Aphis, 135, 1024
Cabbages and Related Green Crops, 1023
Cabinets :
  and Bookcases, 943
  Vertical Filing, Specification, 931
Cable. *See* Electrical Cable ; Telegraph Cable ; Flexible Cable ; Kite Balloon Cable.
Cable and Wireless, Ltd., changes in arrangements with H.M. Government and reduction in Empire Cable and Wireless Rates. *Cmd. 5716*, 507
Cabs and Private Hire Vehicles, Inter-departmental Committee on, Report. *Cmd. 5938*, 737
Cadet Training, Army, 685, 929
Cadetships. *See* Naval Cadetships.
Cadman, Lord, Chairman, Civil Aviation Committee of Inquiry, Report. *Cmd. 5685*, 504
Cadmium Plating, Specification, 369, 1027
Cadogan, Hon. E., Chairman, Departmental Committee on Corporal Punishment, Report. *Cmd. 5684*, 504
Caicos Islands, Colonial Reports, 152, 610, 1031
Caisse de la Dette Publique Egyptienne, Convention relative to Abolition of, *Cmd. 6244*, 970
Caisteil na Stroine, Guide to, 691
Caithness :
  Educational Trust Scheme, 200, 426
  Index to Particular Register of Sasines, 903
Cakes, Oil, Use of, 360
Calanus finmarchicus :
  and other Copepods in Scottish Waters, 427
  Distribution, Breeding, etc., 361
Calcium Sulphate Plasters, 657
Calculator for Average Quality Unlined Canvas Delivery Hose, 1036
Caldew s.t. and *Ospray II* s.t., Collision, 210
Caledonian Omnibus Co. Ltd., Dumfries, Industrial Court Award, 641
Calendars. *See* British Imperial Calendar ; Public Record Office.
Calenders and Extruders, Guarding of, Committee on :
  Interim Report, 632
  Final Report, 1036
Calf Rearing, 360
Calico :
  and Cambric for Oil-dressed Fabrics, Specification, 1069
  Shirt, Specification, 686
Calman, W. T., Crustacea : Caridae, 942
Calne Water Provisional Order Confirmation Act, 526
  Bill, 470, 495
Camberley Staff College :
  Examinations, 225, 451
  Regs., 456, 690, 937
Cambria, s.s., Wreck Report, 920
Cambridgeshire :
  Census, 190
  Soils of, 361
Camera Shutters. *See* Focal-Plane Camera Shutters.
Cameras. *See* High-speed Cameras.
Cameroons :
  under British Mandate, Colonial Reports, 152, 379, 610, 862
  under French Mandate, Economic Conditions, 439
Camouflage of Large Installations, 877
Camp Kit Allowance, Army, 929, 1067
Campbeltown Harbour Water and Gas Order Confirmation Act, 67
Camps Act, 753
  Bill, 701, 728, 730
Camps, Annual, Officers Training Corps, Army, 229
Canada :
  Air :
    Navigation, Exchange of Notes with U.S.A. *Cmd. 6067*, 745
    Transport Services, Exchange of Notes with U.S.A. *Cmd. 6210*, 968
  Airworthiness Certificates for Exported Aircraft, Exchange of Notes with U.S.A. *Cmd. 5928*, 736
  Appendix Certificates of Tonnage, Exchange of Notes with U.S.A. *Cmd. 6131*, 750
  Arbitration Convention of Oct. 25, 1905, with various countries, renewal of. *Cmd. 5448*, 280
  British War Memorial Cemeteries and Graves in Egypt, agreement with Egypt. *Cmd. 5618*, 293
  Commerce and Navigation, Convention with France. *Cmd. 5581*, 290
  Commercial Relations with :
    Austria. *Cmd. 5233*, 56
    Germany. *Cmds. 5231, 5232*, 56
    Hayti. *Cmd. 5445*, 280
    Poland. *Cmd. 5598*, 292
    United States of America. *Cmd. 5597*, 292
    Uruguay. *Cmd. 5578*, 280
  Competency Certificates or Licences for Piloting Civil Aircraft, Exchange of Notes with U.S.A. *Cmd. 6066*, 745
  Consular Fees on Certificates of Origin, Exchange of Notes with Roumania. *Cmd. 5447*, 280

INDEX 1936–40 —CAR

Canada (*continued*) :
  Customs Treatment of Imports, Exchange of Notes with Japan. *Cmd. 5577*, 290
  Economic Conditions, 211, 676, 920
  Imported Food Certificates, 618, 619
    Scotland, 666
  Income Tax on Non-Resident Individuals and Corporations, Convention with U.S.A. *Cmd. 5852*, 517
  Limitation of Naval Armament, International Treaty. *Cmd. 5561*, 289
  Load Line Convention, U.S.A. *Cmd. 5234*, 56
  Military Forces raised in, Mutual Powers of Command, 1070
  Naval Armaments Treaty. *Cmd. 5136*, 48
  Operation of the Smelter at Trail, British Columbia, Convention with U.S.A. *Cmd. 5444*, 280
  Payments for the Exchange of Goods, Agreement with Germany. *Cmd. 5580*, 290
  Preservation of Halibut Fishing Industry of North Pacific Ocean and Bering Sea, Convention with U.S.A. *Cmd. 5850*, 516
  Prevention of Double Taxation of Income, Arrangement with Netherlands East Indies. *Cmd. 5940*, 737
  Shipping Service, Western Canada—Australia—New Zealand, 208
  Sockeye Salmon Fisheries in Fraser River System, Convention with U.S.A. *Cmd. 5851*, 517
  Trade Agreement with :
    Guatemala. *Cmd. 6240*, 970
    Hayti. *Cmd. 6095*, 748
    United Kingdom. *Cmd. 5382*, 276
  War Cemeteries in Iraq, Agreement. *Cmd. 5196*, 53
  War Graves Agreement. *Cmd. 5068*, 44
  See also Eastern Canadian ; Commercial ; Agreements ; Trade Agreements ; British War Memorials.
Canal. *See* Railway and Canal.
Cancer :
  Act, 752
    Bill, 409, 699, 727, 728
    Circulars, 879
      Scotland, 911
      Wales, 876
  Extent to which patients can receive treatment, 875
  Provision of Radio-therapeutic Departments in General Hospitals, 392
Candidates (Local Government) Election Deposit Bill, 269
Canes, Import Duties. *Cmd. 5216*, 55
Canker, Apple, 134
  See also Stem Canker.
Canned :
  and Dried Fruit Supplies, 171, 633
  Food, Trade in, 883
  Fruit, Production and Trade, 398, 633
  Ham and Bacon. *See* Import Duties Advisory Committee.
  Meat, Production and Trade, 171, 634
Cannock :
  Chase, Coal Mines Scheme, 182, 411, 648
  Electricity Orders, 213
Canteen Meals for School Children, 867
Canteens at Small Factories, 1037
Canterbury :
  Gas and Water Act, 527
  Provisional Order Confirmation Act, 972
    Bill, 734, 946
Canton and Enderbury Islands, Exchange of Notes, U.S.A. and U.K. *Cmd. 5989*, 740
Canvas. *See* Cotton Canvas
Canvas Shoes, Specification, 452, 933
Canvey Island :
  Sunday Entertainments, 952
  Urban District Council Act, 302
Cap :
  Comforter, Specifications, 933, 1069
  F.S., Cover, Anti-Gas No. 1, Specification, 1069
  Trade, Wages, 890, 1047
Cape :
  Anti-gas, Specifications, 933, 1069
  Observatory, Publications, 653, 901
  Oilskin, Specification, 687
Cape Matapan, s.t., Wreck Report, 438
Capital Expenditure, Survey of Prospective Works, 619
Capitulations, Abolition of :
  in Egypt :
    Cmd. 5491, 283
    Cmd. 5630, 294
  in Morocco and Zanzibar :
    Cmd. 5538, 287
    Cmd. 5646, 501
Caps, Specification, 932
Capsids, Fruit Tree, 362, 595
Capsules, Lead, Import Duties. *Cmd. 5170*, 51
Carbon :
  Bisulphide Vapour, Detection of, 908
  Monoxide, Detection of, 1058
  Steel Bars, etc., Specifications, 140, 366
Carbonaceous Materials, Freenian Assay for, 660
Carbonisation, Low Temperature, 906

CAR— INDEX 1936–40

Carbonising Plant of Coal and Allied Industries, Ltd., Report of Test, 101
Carburettors, De-icing Spirit for, Specification, 855
Card Room Workers, Compensation for, Report of Committee, 878
Cardiac Enlargement in Disease of the Heart, Development of, 419
Cardiazol Treatment, 611
Cardiff :
  and Forest of Dean Division, Mines Reports, 184, 412, 648, 898
  Corporation (Trolley Vehicles) Order Confirmation Act, 973
    Bill, 962
  Extension Act, 302
Cardiganshire, Strata Florida Abbey, Guide to, 232
Care and Custody of A.R.P. Equipment, 1038
Careers, 174, 401, 638, 887
Caricature, Exhibition of, 941
Caridea, 942
Caries in Children's Teeth, Influence of Diet, 191
Carlisle Castle, Cumberland, Guide, 457
Carnations, 850
Carnegie Park and Scott Orphanage Trust Scheme, 197, 199
Carnock, Lord, Chairman, Joint Committee on Breaking up of Streets by Statutory Undertakers, Report, 698
Carpet, Cork, Specification, 452
Carpet-Knotting and Weaving, 943
Carpets. *See* Import Duties Advisory Committee.
Carpets, Rugs and Mats, Specifications, 1068
Carriage. *See* Invalid Carriage.
Carrick, Register of Sasines, 417
Carriers' Licences, Period of Validity, Report, 682
Carron, River :
  Rivers Pollution Prevention, Report, 429
  Sea Trout of, 665
Carrot Fly, 1023
Carrots. *See* Import Duties Advisory Committee.
Carrying Vessels (Ships), Nationality of, 437, 674
Cars, Armoured, 449
Carshalton, Sunday Entertainments, 478
Cart Navigation. *See* Paisley Corporation.
Cartridge Cases. *See* Merchandise Marks.
Cartwright, K. St. G., Dry Rot in Wood, 659
Cased Tubes, Merchandise Marks. *Cmd. 6094*, 747
Casein, Production and Trade, 398, 883
Cases :
  Mattress, Specification, 932
  Packing, Specifications, 225, 686, 931
  Pillow, Specification, 687
  Sporting Cartridge. *See* Merchandise Marks.
Cash Accounts, Army, 225, 491, 685, 930
Cassell, Sir F., Compulsory Insurance Committee, Report. *Cmd. 5528*, 286
Cast Iron Piston Ring Pots, Specification, 1057
Castings, Specifications, 366, 368, 600, 854, 1027
Castle Acre Priory, Norfolk, Guide, 231
Castlecary, Railway Accident, 667
Castles, Guides to. *See* Ancient Monuments.
Castor :
  Oil, Specification, 1025
  Seed. *See* Import Duties Advisory Committee.
Casual :
  Poor. *See* Public Assistance.
  Wards, Costing Returns, 162, 389, 620, 873
Casuals, Medical Attention and Treatment of, 163
Casualties :
  Air Raid, 873, 1034
  on Ships registered in the U.K., 1064
Casualty Service :
  Anaesthesia in, 1060
  Stretcher Support, A.R.P., 624
Catalogues, Trade. *See* Import Duties Advisory Committee.
Cataract. *See* Blindness.
Catchment Boards. *See* Land Drainage.
Caterham and Woldingham, Electricity, 921
Caterpillars, Surface, 525
Catgut, Sterilised, Surgical, 161, 165
Cathcart, E. P. :
  A Dietary Survey in Terms of Actual Foodstuffs consumed, 418
  (Chairman) Scottish Health Services Committee, Summary of Report, 429
  Studies in Nutrition, 1036
Cathedral Canonries. *See* Ely.
Cathedrals (Houses of Residence) Measure, 10, 72
  Report by Ecclesiastical Committee, 11
Cattle :
  Dairy, Register of, 133, 361
  Industry (Emergency Provisions) Act 1936, 66
    Acts, Particulars of Additional Arrangements, 133
    Bill, 17, 41
    Extension of Period. *Cmd. 5199*, 53
    Memo. on Financial Resolution. *Cmd. 5223*, 55

INDEX 1936–40 —CEY

Cattle (*continued*) :
  Insurance Society, Annual Return Form, 1031
  Mastitis in, 850
  Production and Trade, 171, 398, 634
  Subsidy Proposals. *Cmd. 5362*, 274
  Tuberculin Tests in, 904
Causes of Death. *See* Death.
Cauvin's Trust Scheme, 197, 198
  See also Dean's Orphanage.
Cavalier, Aircraft G–ADUU, Report on loss of. *Cmd. 5975*, 739
Cavalry Training, 449
Cawley, C. M., Hydrogenation-Cracking of Tars, 421, 906
Cayman Islands, Colonial Reports, 151, 378, 609, 860
Cedar, African, Pencil, Properties of, 659
Celery, Leaf Spot of, 1073
Celestine and Strontianite, 661
Cellular Underclothing, Specification, 452
Celluloid :
  Dolls and Rattles. *See* Import Duties Advisory Committee.
  Use of, in Manufacture of Toys, Fancy Goods, etc., Departmental Committee Report. *Cmd. 5790*, 512
Cellulose :
  Acetate Sheets, Specification, 368
  Enamels and Primer, Specifications, 366, 854, 1025, 1028
  Ethyl, Specification, 1027
  Matt, Finishes and Primer, Specifications, 143, 1026
  Sheet, Specification, 601
  Solutions :
    Regs., 1934, Factory Forms, 631, 880
    Repair of Drums or Tanks, 395
    Use and Storage of, 167
Cement :
  Conservation of, 1036
  Unhydrated Portland, Carbonation of, 192
Cements, Solubility of, 905
Cemeteries :
  British War, in Iraq. *Cmd. 5196*, 53
    See also Graves.
  British War Memorial, in Egypt, Agreement between Egypt and various Countries. *Cmd. 5618*, 293
Cemetery. *See* Torquay Cemetery.
Cemetery, General, Act, 299
Censorship of Mails. *See* Mails.
Census :
  Mechanically-propelled Vehicles, 445, 681
  of Production Act, 752
    Bill, 475, 499, 714
  Population, 189, 417, 1055
  Production, 673, 917, 1063
Census (*continued*) :
  Road Traffic, 218, 445, 924
  Seamen, 208, 433, 673, 750
  Vagrants, Beggars, Migratory Poor, Scotland, Form, 431
Centipedes, 595
Central :
  Advisory Water Committee :
    Draft of a Water Undertakings Bill. *Cmd. 5987*, 740
    First Report, 618
    Second Report. *Cmd. 6986*, 740
  Coal Mines Scheme Amendments, 182
  Coalfield, Scotland, Economic Geology of, 660
  Electricity Board Publications, 212, 677, 926, 1064
  England :
    Electricity (Alteration and Extension) Scheme, 936, 937
    Geological Survey, 194
  Government and Finance, Civil Estimates, 25, 480, 715, 954
  Housing Advisory Committee Publications, 160, 618, 870
  India Railway. *See* Bombay.
  Midwives Board Reports, 160, 388, 618, 870
    Scotland, 201, 666, 911
  Valuation Committee Annual Reports, 165, 623, 875
Ceratopogonidae, 943
Cereals, Feeding Stuffs for use with, in Pig Feeding, 362
Cerebro-spinal Fever, Memo., 1034, 1060
Cerement-making Trade, Wages, 404, 890, 1046
Ceremonial :
  Air Force, 138
  Army, 223, 449, 685
  Coronation, 407
Certification Mark for :
  Filtration Plant, Poison Gases, 393, 877
  Respirators, 624
Certified :
  Institutions for Mental Defectives, 381, 611, 863
  Special Schools, Lists of, 383, 614, 866
Certifying Hospitals. *See* Maternity Nurses ; Midwives.
Cesspools, Cleansing of, Model Byelaws, 391
Ceylon :
  Civil Service Examinations, 605, 1030
  Colonial Reports, 151, 378, 609, 860
  Constitution of. *Cmd. 5910*, 521
  Post and Telegraph Department, Examination, 150

Chain Trade, Wages, 890
Chains and other Lifting Gear, Use of, 1037
Chains, Ropes, Lifting Tackle, etc., Factory Forms, 630, 879
Chairmen of Traffic Commissioners, etc. (Tenure of Office) Act, 297
Bill, 243, 266
Chairs, Typist, Specification, 686
Challenge of Youth, Circular, 1032
Chalmers, D. K. M., Epidemic Influenza, 657
Chambers, E. G., Accident Proneness among Motor Drivers, 1055
Chamomile Flowers, Import Duties. Cmd. 5247, 57
Chancel Repairs. See Ecclesiastical Dilapidations.
Chancery Proceedings, Early, List of, 189
Chandler v. Webster, Report of Law Revision Committee. Cmd. 6009, 742
Channel Islands :
Civil Air Transport Services to and from U.K. Cmd. 5894, 520
National Service (Channel Islands) Act, 971
Bill, 947, 963
Chapels, Licensing. See Marriage (Licensing of Chapels).
Chaplains of Territorial Army, Outfit Allowances, 935
Chaplin, C. J. :
Development of a Minimum Structural Grade for Redwood, 906
Strength Tests of Structural Timbers, 420
Charcoal, Manufacture of, in Portable Kilns, 906
Charges : Railway Control, Consultative Committee Reports, 1064
Charing Cross Bridge, Report, 214
Charitable :
and Reformatory Institutions, Annual Return Forms, 394
Collections (Regulation) Bill, 498
See also House to House Collections.
Charities :
(Fuel Allotments) Act, 753
Bill, 482, 498, 499, 701, 712
See also Collecting Charities.
Charity Commissioners' Annual Reports :
Cmd. 5150, 49
Cmd. 5421, 279
Cmd. 5719, 507
Cmd. 5992, 740
Charles II, Calendar of State Papers, 655
Charlestown Bleach Works, Glossop, Boiler Explosion, 206
Charophyta, British Purbeck, 941

Chartered and other Bodies (Temporary Provisions) Act, 756
Bill, 709, 754
Charteris, Sir E., Standing Commission on Museums and Galleries, Report, 652
Charts, Admiralty, Catalogue of, 127, 354, 587, 843
Chatham, Rochester and District, Electricity, 440, 677
Chatwin, C. P., East Anglia and adjoining areas, Geological Survey, 421
Chaumers, Model Byelaws, 666
Checker, Army Trade of, 1066
Cheese, Production and Trade, 171, 398, 883
Cheese-making, 593
Cheetah IX Aero-Engine, 1028
Chelmsford, Electricity, 921
Chelsea, Royal Hospital, Army Prize Money and Legacy Funds, etc., Accounts, 32, 261, 488, 722
Cheltenham and Gloucester Joint Water Board Act, 72
Chemical :
and Allied Trades, Census of Production, 1063
Composition of Foods, 1055
Survey. See Physical and Chemical Survey.
Trades, Import Duties Act Inquiry Report, 208
Warfare, Medical Manual of, 929, 1036
Works Regs., Factory Form, 1036
Chemist. See Government Chemist.
Chemistry :
Careers, 401
Examinations, Science Scholarships, 384, 614, 866
National Certificates in, 383
of Antigens and Antibodies, 657
Pure, History and Development, 414
Research, 192, 658
Short History of, 901
Chepping Wycombe, Sunday Entertainments, 713
Cheriton, s.t., Wreck Report, 920
Cherries, Preserved. See Import Duties Advisory Committee.
Cherry Sawfly, 134
Cheshire :
Census, 417
Coal Mines Scheme, 411
See also Lancashire and Cheshire.
Cheshunt, Sunday Entertainments, 486
Chest, Dressing, Specification, 686
Chester and Derby Provisional Order Confirmation Act, 68
Bill, 6
Chewing Gum Base. See Import Duties Advisory Committee.

Chichester :
Corporation Act, 527
Sunday Entertainments, 486
Chick Embryos, Cultivation of Vaccinia on the Chorio-Allantoic Membranes of, 874
Chickens, Rearing of, 360
Chicks, Bacillary White Diarrhoea of, 360
Chief Royal Engineer, Army, Honorary Appointment of, 1067
Child Welfare. See Maternity and Child Welfare.
Children :
Adoption of :
Act, 295
(Regulation), Act 753
Bill, 498, 701, 702, 716, 725, 728, 730
and Young Persons :
Act, 523
Bill, 468, 483, 494, 497 (as Children and Young Persons Act (1933) Amendment Bill), 271
(Scotland) Act, 296
Bill, 235, 237, 239, 268
Table of Comparison, 430
Custody of, (Scotland) Act, 752
Bill, 475, 492, 498, 499, 712
Employment of, Byelaws, Scotland, 430
under School Age, Circular, 161
with Defective Hearing, Committee of Inquiry into Problems relating to, Report, 614
See also Boys ; Deaf Children ; Girls ; Juvenile ; School Children ; Backward Children ; Defective Children ; Education (Deaf Children) ; Lunacy ; Babies ; Young Children ; Evacuated School Children ; Reception of Children.
Children's :
Branch, Work of, Report, 626
Homes (Poor Law), Costing Returns, 162, 389, 620, 873
Chile :
Commercial Agreements with U.K. : Cmd. 5650, 502
Cmd. 5972, 739
Economic Conditions, 211, 439
Imported Food Certificate, 618
Scotland, 666
Chilled Beef. See Import Duties Advisory Committee.
Chimney :
Gases, Treatment of, at new Battersea Power Station, Report. Cmd. 5572, 290
Sweepers Acts (Repeal) Act, 523
Bill, 471, 495

Chimneys, Building, 658, 904
China :
Air Services :
between South West China and British Ports, Exchange of Notes with U.K. Cmd. 6122, 749
over China, Exchange of Notes with U.K. Cmd. 5712, 506
(Currency Stabilisation) Act, 752
Bill, 699, 728
Economic Conditions, 439
Local Issues at Tientsin, Arrangement between Japan and U.K. Cmd. 6212, 968
Chinese :
Art. See Art.
Currency Stabilisation Fund Arrangements. Cmd. 5963, 738
Interpretership Examinations, 605
Woven Fabrics, 695
Chiswick. See Brentford.
Chlorine, Detection of, 908
See also Liquid Chlorine.
Choice :
and Adaptation of Shelter in Houses, 1038
of Careers Series, 401, 638, 889
of Occupation Leaflets, 401
Cholderton and District Water Provisional Order Confirmation Act, 526
Bill, 470, 495
Cholera, Fowl, 595
Chopra, B., Stomatopoda, 942
Chorio-Allantoic Membranes of Chick Embryos, Cultivation of Vaccinia on, 874
Christchurch :
Corporation Act, 973
Enteric Fever in, Report, 392
Christison, M. H., Bacillus Salmonicida, Bacteriophage, 665
Chrome :
Effects of, on the Skin, 395
Zinc, Specification, 601
Chrome-Molybdenum Steel Tubes, Specifications, 1026
Chromium-Alloy Bars, Tubes, etc., Specifications, 600
Chromium - Aluminium - Molybdenum Steel, Specification, 1028
Chromium-Molybdenum Steel, Specifications, 1025, 1026, 1029
Chromium-Nickel Non-corrodible Steel, Specifications, 141
Chromium-Steel, Specifications, 366
Sheets and Strips, 1025
Sheets, Wire, Rods, 366
Tubes, 825, 1028
Chromium-Steel, Specifications, 366
Chronological Table and Index of the Statutes, 205, 433, 671, 917

Chrysanthemum Midge, 363, 595, 850
Chrysanthemums, 133
Church :
Estates Commissioners, Annual Reports :
Cmd. 5148, 49
Cmd. 5434, 279
Cmd. 5691, 505
Cmd. 6035, 743
Temporalities in Wales :
Accounts, 20, 35, 264, 711, 725
Annual Reports :
Cmd. 5148, 57
Cmd. 5534, 287
Cmd. 5822, 514
Cmd. 6083, 747
See also Liverpool City Churches ; Methodist Church ; St. Nicholas, Millbrook ; Welsh Church.
Church Stretton Provisional Order Confirmation Act, 527
Bill, 471, 496
Cider Apple Production, 361
Cinematograph :
Act, 1909, Commission on Administration of, Report, 878
Films :
Act, 522
Bill, 265, 271, 462, 463, 464, 465, 480, 490, 493, 494 (Animals) Act, 297
Bill, 243, 245, 259, 266, 269, 270
Council, Annual Report, 722
Factory Form, 880
Legislation on, Proposals. Cmd. 5529, 286
See also Films ; Import Duties Advisory Committee.
Fund Accounts, 20, 254, 264, 491, 950
News Films (Prevention of Abuses) Bill, 733
Circular Saws, 659
Cirencester :
Gas Act, 69
Provisional Order Confirmation Act, 527
Bill, 472, 496
Sunday Entertainments, 955
Citex Oil Wharves Ltd., Explosion, 626
Citrus Fruit, Production and Trade, 171, 398, 633
City :
Hospital, Nottingham, Dangerous Drugs, 878
of London (Various Powers) Acts, 299, 757
City of Khartoum, Aircraft Accident. Cmd. 5220, 55

Civil :
Aeronautical Radio Service, Q Code, 365, 599, 853
Aeroplanes, Committee on the Production of, Report. Cmd. 6038, 743
Air :
Ensign Order, 364
Guard Bulletin, 852
Navigator's Licence, Examination Papers, 364
Transport Services :
Agreements with British Airways Ltd. :
England – South America and England–Germany and Scandinavia, experimental flights and surveys. Cmd. 5524, 286
London – Brussels ; London–Berlin and Warsaw ; London–Frankfurt and Budapest. Cmd. 6005, 741
London–Lisbon. Cmd. 5898, 520
Agreements with Imperial Airways Ltd. :
Bangkok–Hong Kong. Cmd. 5871, 518
Bermuda–New York. Cmd. 5870, 518
connecting Hong Kong and West Africa with the main Empire Air Routes. Cmd. 5688, 504
England–South Africa ; Egypt–South Africa. Cmd. 5404, 277
European Services. Cmd. 6004, 741
Khartoum–West Africa : Cmd. 5403, 277
Cmd. 5723, 507
Cmd. 6052, 744
and Kisumu–Lusaka. Cmd. 5770, 510
Penang–Hong Kong. Cmd. 5396, 277
Agreement with various companies, Channel Islands–Isle of Man–U.K. Cmd. 5894, 520
See also Air Services ; Air Transport ; Empire Air Mail Scheme.
Aircraft :
Airworthiness Handbook for, 138, 364, 598, 852, 1024
Navigator's Licence, Examination Papers, 598, 852, 1024
See also Civil Air Navigator's Licence

Civil (continued) :
Aircraft (continued) :
Piloting Certificates of Competency or Licences for, Exchange of Notes, Canada and U.S.A. Cmd. 6066, 745
Airworthiness Committee Report, De-Icing of Aeroplane Wings, etc., 598
Appropriation Accounts, 20, 248, 476, 711, 949
Aviation :
Air Transport Services :
Bermuda–New York. Cmd. 5237, 56
England–Scandinavia. Cmd. 5203, 53
England–South Africa. Cmd. 5325, 63
See also Agreements (under Civil Air Transport Services above).
Committee of Inquiry into, Report. Cmd. 5685, 504
Communications Handbook, 852
Development of, Report. Cmd. 5351, 273
Medical examination for fitness for flying, 139
Progress of, Annual Reports, 138, 364, 598, 852
Statistical and Technical Review, 598
See also Air ; Civil Air Transport Services above ; Empire Air Mail Scheme.
Aviation Department :
Committee of Inquiry into Working of, Report. Cmd. 5864, 518
Publications (N.P.), 598, 852, 1024
Contingencies Fund Accounts, 251, 264, 717, 957
Defence Act, 753
Bill, 703, 706, 728, 730, 731
Provisional List of Areas to which Part III of the Bill is proposed to be applied, 877
Circular, 877
Employment for Regular Soldiers, 449, 685
Estimates :
25, 252, 253, 480, 481, 715, 716, 951, 953, 954, 955
Supplementary, 21, 24, 25, 29, 31, 35, 251, 260, 480, 488, 713, 715, 721, 722, 959
Revised :
Education, Scotland, 258
Eire Services and Irish Land Purchase, 488
Statements of Excess, 25, 254, 481
Votes on Account, 25, 481

Civil (continued) :
Estimates (continued) :
Memoranda :
1936, Education. Cmd. 5106, 47
1937, Education. Cmd. 5387, 276
Judicial Statistics :
England and Wales :
Cmd. 5277, 59
Cmd. 5560, 289
Cmd. 5859, 517
Cmd. 6135, 751
Scotland :
Cmd. 5210, 54
Cmd. 5547, 288
Cmd. 5779, 511
Cmd. 6078, 746
List Acts :
1936, 65
Bill, 11, 38
1937, 296
Bill, 241, 268
Report, 258
List Pensions, List of, 31, 259, 484, 718, 957, 960
Report from Select Committee, 27
Service :
Admission of Women to the Diplomatic and Consular Services. Cmd. 5166, 50
Arbitration Tribunal Awards, 401, 638, 887, 1042
British Imperial Calendar and Civil Service List, 205, 433, 671, 916, 1062
Commission Publications, 146, 274, 604, 857, 1030
Examinations, 146, 274, 604, 857, 1030
Ex-Servicemen employed in Government Departments. Cmd. 5257, 58
His Majesty's Ministers and Heads of Public Departments, 205, 433, 671, 916, 1062
Industrial Court Awards, 174
National Whitley Council Reports, 220, 683
Regs. of, 647
Sick Leave Regs., 928
Subsistence Allowances, 220
See also Appropriation Accounts ; Estimates ; Public Departments ; Government Departments ; Crown Services ; India ; Burma.
Staffs Employed in Government Departments :
Cmd. 5256, 58
Cmd. 5333, 63
Cmd. 5543, 287
Cmd. 5815, 514

Civilian :
Anti-Gas Schools, 624
Duty Respirators :
Record Card, 1037
with Microphone Attachments, 882
Employees at Air Ministry Establishments, 138, 365, 598, 852, 1024
Internees, Categories of Persons eligible for Release, etc. :
Enemy Nationality :
Cmd. 6223, 969
Cmd. 6233, 970
German and Austrian. Cmd. 6217, 968
Respirators :
held by the public, Inspection of, 1037
Local Storage and Distribution of, 625
Requirements of, 877
Staff, War Office, Regs., 929, 1067
Clacton-on-Sea Pier and Harbour Order Confirmation Act, 526
Bill, 470, 495
Clacton Urban District Council Act, 526
Claims Commission, Army, 1067
Clamps, Specifications, 226, 1068
Clan Malcolm, s.s., Wreck Report, 210
Clark, H. L., Ophiuroidea, 942
Clarke, S. H :
Growth, Structure and Properties of Wood, 906
Gurjun, Apitong, Keruing, Kapur, and Allied Timbers, 420
Clarke 1880 Figure, Geodetic Tables for, 225
Clasps, Merchandise Marks. Cmd. 6080, 746
Classes :
Continuation, Scotland, 203, 204
Public Elementary Schools, 157
Classical Antiquity in Renaissance Painting, 694
Classics, Suggestions for Teaching, 866
Clauses, Common Form, in Private Bills, Report, 32
Clay :
Bricks, Conservation of, 1056
Trade, Import Duties Acts, Reports, 208, 436
Cleansing :
of Earth Closets, Privies, Ashpits, and Cesspools, Model Byelaws, 391
Public, Street, Costing Returns, 389, 620
See also Public Cleansing.
Clear Varnish for Internal Protection of Drinking Water Tanks, Specification, 1028
Clearing Offices. See Debts Clearing Offices.

30

Cleethorpes :
Corporation (Trolley Vehicles) Provisional Order Confirmation Act, 300
Bill, 241, 267
Sunday Entertainments, 955
See also Grimsby Corporation.
Clergy :
(National Emergency Precautions) Measure, 706, 760
Pensions :
(Amendment) Measure, 10, 72
Report by Ecclesiastical Committee, 10
(Widows and Dependants) Measure, 10, 72
Report by Ecclesiastical Committee, 10
Clerical :
and Secretarial Work, Choice of Careers, 174
Classes, Civil Service Arbitration Tribunal Awards, 639
Staffs, Temporary, employed in Government Departments :
Cmd. 5626, 294
Cmd. 5909, 521
Work :
Daylight Illumination necessary, 422
for Women, Careers, 638
Clerks of Stationery, Notes for, 433
Clevedon Water Provisional Order Confirmation Act, 302
Bill, 244, 468
Clifford's Tower, York Castle, Guide, 231
Clifton Electrically Heated Steam Boiler, 359
Climatological Observations, Pocket Register for, 408
Clinic. See Model Health Clinic.
Clinker Aggregates, Properties, etc., 192
Cloakrooms, Factories and Workshops, 170
Clogs, Specification, 452
Close Rolls, Calendars of, 189, 417, 655
Closets. See Earth Closets.
Cloth, Lasting, Specification, 932
Clothes Horse, Specification, 686
Clothing :
and Necessaries, Army, Vocabulary, 223
and Shoes for Physical Training, 156, 158
Army, War Office Publications (N.P.), 449, 452, 685, 686, 929, 931, 1067
Decontamination of, from Blister Gases, 877
Fabrics, Water-proofing, Specification, 932
Materials, Specification, 931
of the Army, 223

Clothing (continued) :
Trade, Census of Production, 673
Trade(s), Wages, 404, 1046
Trades, Import Duties Act, Report, 208
See also Oilskin Clothing ; Protective Clothing ; Women's Light Clothing.
Cloths, Specifications, 452, 686, 931, 1069
Cloud Forms, Definitions and Photographs, 896
Clouds, Ice Formation in, 646
Clover Rot, 135
Clovers, Weed Seeds in, 363
Clowes, G. S. Laird, British Fishing and Coastal Craft, 414
Club Root, 135
Clubs :
Annual Returns Forms, 387, 617, 870, 1034
Bill, 1939, 698
Registration Bill, 727
(Scotland) Bill, 37
Clyde :
Lighthouses Consolidation Order Confirmation Bill, 948, 963
Valley Electrical Power Order Confirmation Act, 301
Bill, 245, 270
Clydebank :
Burgh Order Confirmation Act, 524
Bill, 247, 272
Launching Ceremony, Air Navigation Regs., 597
Coal :
Act, 1938, 523
Bill, 271, 465, 466, 469, 471, 472, 493, 494, 497
Assurances in connection with Schemes for organised selling in the Coal Industry. Cmd. 5693, 505
Memo. Cmd. 5593, 291
Central Valuation Board, Valuation Regions and Regional Allocations. Cmd. 5904, 520
Statements of Guarantees and Accounts, 718, 957
Action of Hydrogen upon, 193, 660
and Allied Industries, Ltd., Carbonising Plant, Report of Test, 421
Commercial, Analysis of, 421, 906
Commission :
Accounts, 952
Report, 958
Drying and Pulverising Plants, Safety Precautions, 395
Dust, Precautions against :
Circular, 899
Mines and Quarries Forms, 1035
Freeman Assay for, 660
Increased Use of, for Bunkering, Report of Committee, 647

Coal (continued) :
Industry, Return showing action taken on Recommendations in Report of Royal Commission, 697
Measure Rocks, Classification, Nomenclature, and Relative Strengths, 413
Methods of Analysis, 1057
Mine Refuse :
Coal Mine Refuse (Public Health) Act, 754
Bill, 271, 492, 498, 499, 700, 701, 702, 717, 733
Public Health (Coal Mine Refuse) (Scotland) Act, 753
Bill, 700, 728, 730
Mines :
Abstract and General Regs., 1054
Bill, 38
District Schemes : 411, 648, 898
Reports on Working of :
Cmd. 5062, 44
Cmd. 5474, 282
Cmd. 5773, 511
Cmd. 6170, 965
(Employment of Boys) Act, 297
Bill, 42, 238, 240, 252, 262, 266, 269
Explosions, Comparison between Britain and France. Cmd. 5566, 289
Explosives in, Safe Use of, 651
General Regs., 1938, Part II, Circular, 899
Mines Department Publications (N.P.), 411, 647, 897
Precautions against Coal Dust, Circular, 899
Regs., Coal Mines Act 1911, 182
Reorganisation Commission Report. Cmd. 5069, 44
Royal Commission on Safety in : Minutes of Evidence, etc., 195, 196, 424, 663
Report. Cmd. 5890, 519
War Levy Scheme, Explanatory Memo. Cmd. 6236, 970
Mining Industry :
Boys employed in, Safety Principles, West Riding of Yorkshire, 984
Statistical Summaries :
Annual :
Cmd. 5142, 49
Cmd. 5427, 279
Cmd. 5709, 505
Cmd. 5983, 740
Quarterly :
Cmd. 5057, 43
Cmd. 5138, 49
Cmd. 5198, 53
Cmd. 5278, 59

Coal (continued) :
Mining Industry (continued) :
Statistical Summaries (continued) :
Quarterly (continued) :
Cmd. 5340, 273
Cmd. 5419, 278
Cmd. 5508, 285
Cmd. 5559, 289
Cmd. 5635, 500
Cmd. 5698, 505
Cmd. 5785, 511
Cmd. 5862, 517
Cmd. 5918, 735
Cmd. 5978, 739
Cmd. 6049, 744
Cmd. 6104, 748
Oil from, Sub-committee of Committee for Imperial Defence, Report. Cmd. 5665, 503
(Registration of Ownership) Act, 297
Bill, 242, 243, 244, 270
Research Syndicate, Ltd., Retort of, Report of Test, 193
Resources, National, Survey of, 421, 660, 906, 1057
Sale of, Weights and Measures (Scotland) Act, 66
Seams of North Staffordshire, 421
Coal, Coke, and Manufactured Fuel, Departmental Committee on the Distribution of, Minutes of Evidence, 648, 898
Coast :
Artillery Rangefinders, Drill for, 449, 685
Premature or Unsightly Development on Sea Coast, 620
Protection Act, 753
Bill, 497, 498, 702, 704, 715, 726, 727, 731
Coastal Craft, British, Historical Review and Descriptive Catalogue, 414
Coasting Vessels Mutual War Risks Association Ltd., War Risks Insurance, 723
Coastwise Shipping, Service and Rates, 682
Coatbridge Burgh Extension, etc., Order Confirmation Act, 300
Bill, 245, 270
Coating of Metal Sheets, Factory Form, 1036
Coats, Specifications, 226, 687, 932, 1069
Coccidiosis in Poultry, 955
Cockburn, A. W., Chairman, Hops Reorganisation Commission Report, 594
Cockroach, Life History, etc., 694
Cocoa, Production and Trade, 172, 398, 634
See also West African Cocoa.
Code, Q. See Civil Aeronautical Radio Service.

32

Codex Sinaiticus :
and Codex Alexandrinus, 941
Scribes and Correctors of, 693
Codling Moth, 134, 849
Coffee, Production and Trade, 172, 398, 634
See also British East African Coffee.
Coffin Furniture, etc., Trade, Wages, 404, 890, 1046
Coffins. See Egyptian Mummies.
Coils, Aluminium Coated Aluminium Alloy, Specification, 855
Coin, Imports and Exports, 155, 383, 614, 865
See also India.
Coinage Offences Act, 65
Bill, 6, 7, 38
Coir, Production, Trade and Consumption, 883
Coke :
Methods of Analysis, 1057
Use of, in Open Domestic Grates, 421
See also Coal, Coke.
Colchester Provisional Order Confirmation Act, 757
Bill, 699, 727
Cole, H. A., Experiments in the Breeding of Oysters in Tanks, 361, 849
Cole, W. T., Occurrence of H. Influenzae in the Trachea, 875
Coles, F. E., Dust-Storms in Iraq, 646
Collars, Specification, 687
Collecting Charities (Regulation) Bill, 246, 462, 467, 473
Collecting Societies, Annual Return Form, 387, 617, 869, 1034
Collections. See House to House Collections ; National Collections.
Collectors, Instructions for, 694
Colleges :
R.A.F., Cranwell, Regs. 140
See also Agricultural Colleges ; French and German Schools ; Training Colleges ; Universities and Colleges.
Collieries. See Coal Mines.
Colliery :
Accident Funds. Cmd. 5167, 50
Haulage Drawgear, Metallurgical Examination of, 413
Ropes in Service, Examination of, 651
Winding Ropes :
Corrosion of, 413
Fibre Cores for, 901
Collins, A R , Aggregates and Workability of Concrete, 661
Colne Valley :
and Northwood Electricity Act, 69
Water Act, 759
See also Hertfordshire County Council.

Colombia :
Economic Conditions, 910
Treaty of Friendship, Commerce, and Navigation, Exchange of Notes with U.K. Cmd. 5945, 738
Colonial :
Administrative Service List, 379, 610, 1034
Agricultural Service List, 380, 610
Allowance, Army, 930
Audit Service List, 862
Broadcasting, Choice of Suitable Wave Lengths for, 862
Dependencia, British Empire, Legislation relating to the Introduction of Plants into, 381
Development :
Advisory Committee :
Cmd. 5202, 53
Cmd. 5537, 287
Cmd. 5789, 512
Cmd. 6062, 745
and Welfare :
Act, 927
Bill, 947, 948, 962, 963
Statement of Policy on. Cmd. 6175, 966
Fund Accounts, 23, 251, 478, 712, 951
Directors of Agriculture, Conference, 610
Divorce. See Indian and Colonial Divorce.
Empire :
Conditions and Cost of Living in, 380
Economic Survey of, 611, 1031
in 1937–38, Statement. Cmd. 5760, 510
in 1938–39, Statement. Cmd. 6023, 742
Marketing Board, 860
Nutrition in, Report. Cmd. 6050–1, 744
Nutrition Policy, 153
Story of, 860
Vocational Technical Education in, 1032
Forest Service List, 152, 862
Legal Service List, 153, 380, 610, 862
Medical Service List, 153, 380, 610, 1032
Office Publications (N.P.), 151, 377, 609, 860, 1031
Police Service List, 862
Provident Funds, Report of Committee. Cmd. 5219, 55
Regs., 610, 862, 1031
Service, Officers in, Pensions to Widows and Orphans. Cmd. 5219, 55
Stocks, Treasury List of, 32, 261, 488, 723

Empire (continued) :
Students Committee, Report, 862
Veterinary Service List, 380, 862
Colonies :
Broadcasting Services in, Committee on, Interim Report, Supplement, 862
Trade with Netherlands. Cmd. 5061, 44
See also Air Navigation ; Colonial.
Coloured :
Cotton Waste, Specification, 1069
Light for Motor Car Headlights, use of, 422
Colouring, Fish. See Sea Fish.
Columns :
for Factory Buildings, 1056
See also Reinforced Concrete Columns.
Colwyn Bay :
Provisional Order Confirmation Act, 298
Bill, 237, 265
See also Llandudno.
Combatant Officers, Army, New Conditions of Service for, 685
Combination Suits, Specifications, 932, 1068
Combing Machines in the Cotton Spinning Trade, Prevention of Accidents on, 1035
Combs, Hair, Import Duties. Cmd. 5159, 50
Command :
Mutual Powers of, Military Forces, 1070
Papers. See Parliament.
Commander-in-Chief, British Expeditionary Force, Powers of, 929
Commerce :
Award of National Certificates to Students in Colleges or Schools, 866
Board of Education Endorsed Certificate, award of, 615
Commercial :
Agreements, Conventions, etc. :
Argentine and U.K. Cmd. 5324, 63
Austria and Canada. Cmd. 5233, 56
Belgium :
and Irish Free State. Cmd. 5562, 289
and South Africa. Cmd. 5708, 506
Brazil :
and Australia. Cmd. 6214, 968
and Canada. Cmd. 5821, 514
and Newfoundland. Cmd. 5268, 58
and South Africa. Cmd. 6132, 963
and U.K. Cmd. 5267, 58
Burma and Japan. Cmd. 5636, 501

Commercial (continued):
Agreements, Conventions, etc. (continued):
Chile and U.K.:
Cmd. 5650, 502
Cmd. 5972, 739
Colombia and U.K. Cmd. 5958, 738
Cuba and U.K.:
Cmd. 5383, 276
Cmd. 5867, 518
Cmd. 6152, 964
Czechoslovakia:
and Australia. Cmd. 5649, 502
and South Africa. Cmd. 5704, 506
Denmark and U.K.:
Cmd. 5942, 737
Cmd. 6112, 749
Dominican Republic and Newfoundland. Cmd. 6208, 968
Egypt:
and Palestine. Cmd. 5361, 274
and South Africa. Cmd. 6134, 750
France:
and Canada. Cmd. 5581, 290
and South Africa:
Cmd. 5843, 516
Cmd. 5844, 516
and U.K. with Tunis. Cmd. 5622, 294
(on behalf of Morocco) and U.K. Cmd. 5823, 514
Germany and Canada. Cmd. 5231–2, 56
Greece and Australia. Cmd. 6243, 970
Guatemala and Canada. Cmd. 5280, 514
Hayti and Canada. Cmd. 5445, 280
Iraq and Palestine. Cmd. 5372, 275
Italy:
and South Africa. Cmd. 5702, 505
and U.K.:
Cmd. 5306–7, 61
Cmd. 5345–6, 273
Cmd. 5669, 503
Cmd. 5694–5, 505
Japan and India. Cmd. 5600, 292
Muscat and U.K. Cmd. 6037, 743
Netherlands:
and Irish Free State. Cmd. 5447, 280
and New Zealand. Cmd. 5812, 513
and South Africa. Cmd. 5818, 514
Peru and U.K. Cmd. 5288, 60

Commercial (continued):
Agreements, Conventions, etc. (continued):
Poland:
and Canada. Cmd. 5598, 292
and U.K.:
Cmd. 5599, 292
Cmd. 5997, 741
Portugal and South Africa. Cmd. 5085, 45
Roumania and U.K.:
Cmd. 6018, 742
Cmd. 6111, 749
Salvador and Canada. Cmd. 5824, 514
Siam and U.K.:
Cmd. 5608, 292
Cmd. 5731, 508
Swaziland, Basutoland, Bechuanaland and Mozambique. Cmd. 5807, 513
Switzerland:
and Australia. Cmd. 5960, 738
and New Zealand. Cmd. 5838, 515
Turkey and U.K. Cmd. 6151, 964
United States of America and Canada. Cmd. 5697, 292
Uruguay and Canada. Cmd. 5576, 290
See also Payments Agreements; Trade Agreements; Trade and Commerce; Trade and Payments.
and Industrial Buildings, Windows in, Protection of, 1037
Apple Production, 594
Buildings, Air Raid Shelters for Persons working in, 876
Bulb Production, 848
Flower Production, 594, 849
Fruit Tree Spraying, 848
Gas Act, 973
Grades of Coal, Analysis of, 906
Horticulture, 850
Mahoganies and Allied Timbers, 659
Premises, Wartime Lighting Restrictions for, 878
Quality Steel Tubes, Specifications, 1029
Services conducted by Government Departments. See Government Departments.
Treaties:
Hertzlets, 158, 386, 616
with Foreign Powers, Lists, 158, 386, 616, 869, 1033
Commissioners of Assize, Returns: Cmd. 5592, 291
Commissions, R.A.F., Regs., 136, 138, 139
Commodity Insurance. See War Risks.

Common:
Form Clauses:
Committee on, Standard Clauses, 170, 397
in Private Bills, Report, 32
Lodging Houses, Model Byelaws, 621
Commons, House of. See Parliament.
Communal Feeding in Wartime, 1035
Community Life in New Housing Schemes, Scotland, 201
Companies:
Act, 1929, Table, 917
Act (1929) Amendment Bill, 499
Annual Reports, 207, 435, 673, 917
See also Bankruptcy and Companies.
Compasses:
Gyro, Sperry, Manual, 127
Magnetic, Specification, 140
Compensation:
(Defence) Act, 754
for Industrial Diseases, 166
National Health Insurance, Form,391
See also Card Room Workers; Loss of Employment; Workmen's Compensation.
Composite Goods, Import Duties. Cmd. 5241, 57
Composts, 363
Compressed Asbestos Fibre Jointing, Specifications, 1026
Compulsory Insurance, Departmental Committee on:
Minutes of Evidence, 207
Index, 435
Report. Cmd. 5528, 286
Concrete:
Aggregates, 192
and Workability of, 662
Control of Moisture Content, 422
Piles, Stresses in, 658
Road Construction:
Machinery used in, 907
on the Reichsautobahnen, 926
Structures exposed to Sea Water, 193, 420, 658
under Load, Creep or Flow of, 1056
See also Reinforced Concrete.
Concreting and Bricklaying in Cold Weather, Precautions for, 1057
Confectionery. See Sugar Confectionery.
Confirmation of Executors. See Executors.
Congleton Provisional Order Confirmation Act, 958
Bill, 701, 730
Congo. See Belgian Congo.
Coniferae and other Gymnosperms, 638
Connaught, H.R.H. Prince Arthur of, Death, 644
Conon, River, Trout of, 665
Conscription of Wealth. See Wealth.
Conservancy Authorities, River, Income and Expenditure, Forms, 390

Consolidated Fund:
Abstract Accounts, 22, 250, 477, 712, 951
Acts, 65, 295, 296, 522, 752, 971, 972
Bills, 7, 8, 37, 38, 265, 267, 465, 494, 728, 962, 963
Appropriation Bills: 41, 270, 498, 733, 963
Constabulary, Inspectors of, Reports:
England and Wales, 24, 255, 480, 717, 958
Scotland:
Cmd. 5128, 48
Cmd. 5412, 278
Cmd. 5687, 505
Cmd. 5988, 740
Cmd. 6193, 967
Constance, s.s., Boiler explosion, 206
Constants, Physical, of Pure Metals, 194
Constitution of Marriage. See Marriage.
Constitutions of all Countries, 616
Construction of Flats for the Working Classes, Committee on, Report, 389
Constructional Work, Workmen's Compensation Forms, 170, 397, 632
Consular:
and Diplomatic Services, Admission of Women to. Cmd. 5166, 50
Fees on Certificates of Origin, Roumania and Canada. Cmd. 5447, 280
Service, Examinations, 147, 374, 605, 1030
Visas on Bills of Health, Abolition of, Exchange of Notes:
France and U.K. Cmd. 6187, 966
India and French Indochina.
Consumers' Council Bill, 498
Container, tinplate, Corrosion by Food Products, 193
Continuation Classes, Scotland, 669
See also Schools.
Contraband, Articles to be treated as, in the War with Italy, 1049
Contraceptives (Regulation) Bill, 494, 498
Contractors. See Government Contractors.
Contracts:
in connection with Defence Programme, Report, 256
See also Prime Cost Contracts; War Damage.
Contributory:
Negligence, Report of Law Revision Committee. Cmd. 6032, 743
Pensions. See National Health Insurance and Contributory Pensions; Widows', Orphans', etc.
Control:
Board of:
Annual Reports, 489, 722
Publications (N.P.), 153, 381, 611, 863

Control (continued):
Board of (continued):
Scotland, Annual Reports:
Cmd. 5124, 48
Cmd. 5408, 278
Cmd. 5715, 506
Cmd. 5970, 739
of Employment. See Employment.
Controls,Lubricating Oil,Specification,367
Conversion Loans:
under Finance Act 1934, Accounts, 258, 264, 718, 722
4½ per cent., 1940–44, 1048
Conveyancing Amendment (Scotland) Act, 522
Bill, 247, 466, 484, 490, 493, 494
Convict Prisons, Director of, Annual Reports:
Cmd. 5430, 279
Cmd. 5675, 504
Cmd. 5868, 518
Cmd. 6137, 751
Conway Gas Act, 973
Conybeare, E. T., Outbreak of Food Poisoning due to Salmonella, Type "Dublin", 622
Cook, F. C., Chairman, Street Lighting Committee, Final Report, 446
Cookery, Naval, Manual of, 354
Cooking:
Military, Manual of, 453
Utensils, Specifications, 226, 452
Cooks, Army, Pay, etc., 1066
Cookson Floating Zenith Telescope, Observ..tions with, 901
Coolers, Oil, Specification, 599
Co-operative Societies, Statistical Summaries, 160, 387, 618, 870
Copper Tubes for Honeycomb Type Radiators, Specification, 1029
Copra, Production and Trade,172,634,883
Corals. See Solitary Corals.
Corbridge Roman Station (Corstopitum), Guide to, 691
Cord. See Soft Cotton Cord.
Cord Rings. See Shock Absorber Cord Rings.
Cordage. See Plaited Flax Cordage; Silk Cordage.
Cords. See Electric Cords.
Cores. See Fibre Cores.
Cork:
Carpet, Specification, 452
Jointing Material, Specification, 367
Corn:
Production Acts (Repeal) Act, 64
Sweet, 850
Cornwall Electric Power Acts, 69, 973
Coronation:
Edward VIII, Proclamation, 180
George VI:
Air Navigation Directions, 364

Control (continued):
George VI (continued):
Ceremonial, 407
Coronation Day to be Public Holiday, 407
Souvenirs. See Import Duties.
Coroners, Report of the Departmental Committee. Cmd. 5070, 44
Coroners' Investigations, Statistics:
Cmd. 5185, 52
Cmd. 5520, 286
Cmd. 5690, 505
Cmd. 5878, 519
Cmd. 6167, 965
Corporal Punishment, Departmental Committee Report. Cmd. 5684, 504
Corrosion:
Inhibitor, Specification, 1029
of Colliery Winding Ropes, 413
of Tar Stills, 658
of Tinplate Container by Food Products, 193
Protection against, Specifications,369
Corruption, Avoidance of, Bill, 732
Corset Trade, Wages, 404, 890, 1046
Corsham Water Provisional Order Confirmation Act, 758
Bill, 703, 729
Cost of Living in the Colonial Empire,380
Costa Rica, Economic Conditions, 211,676
Costing:
Return Forms:
Certified Institutions, Mental Hospitals, etc., 154
General Hospitals, Maternity Homes, etc., 162
Returns:
Board of Control Publications (N.P.), 154, 381, 611, 863
Ministry of Health Publications (N.P.), 162, 389, 620, 873
Costs, Taxation of, House of Lords Standing Orders, 17
Costume Trade, Wages, 405, 891, 1048
Cotswold. See North Cotswold.
Cottages. See Housing (Rural Cottages); Rural Cottage.
Cotton:
and Rubber, Exchange of Agreement, U.S.A. and U.K. Cmd. 6043, 744
Canvas, Specification, 1029
Cord for Kite Balloons, Specification, 601
Drawers, Specification, 686
Fabric:
Mercerised, Specification, 369
Scoured, Specification, 855
Fabrics:
Import Duties. Cmd. 5243,5251,57
Specifications, 226, 452, 600, 1029, 1068

Cotton (continued):
Handkerchief Trade, Wages, 405, 890, 1047
Industry:
Acts:
1938, 522
Bill, 271, 462, 477
1940, 971
Bill, 945, 962
Operatives in, Respiratory Dust Disease, 191
(Reorganisation) Act, 573
Bill, 705, 706, 707, 720, 726, 728, 730, 732
Reorganisation of, Legislation. Cmd. 5935, 736
(Reorganisation) (Postponement) Act, 755
Bill, 709, 734
Manufacturing Industry:
Prices for Weaving, 175
Wages for Weavers. See Weavers.
Production, Trade and Consumption, 171, 398, 634, 883
Sheets and Sheeting, Specifications 687, 932
Shirt, Specification, 452
Spinning:
Industry:
Act, 65
Bill, 8, 26, 34, 37, 40
Trade, Prevention of Accidents on Combing Machines, 1035
Tapes, Specification, 855
Waste:
Reclamation Trade, Wages, 642, 1046
Specifications, 1069
Webbing (Anti-Gas Clothing), Specification, 933
Cottonseed, Production, Trade and Consumption, 172, 634, 883
Coulsdon and Purley:
Sunday Entertainments, 257
Urban District Council Act, 301
Councils. See County Councils; Metropolitan Borough Councils.
Councillors, Parish and Rural District, election of, 394
Counterfeiting. See Coinage Offences.
Country:
Control of Premature and Unsightly Development in the, 620
Planning. See Town and Country Planning.
Countryside, Preservation of, Report, 623
County:
Councils Association Expenses (Amendment) Act, 296
Bill, 238, 266

County (continued):
Court:
Auditors, Civil Service Arbitration Tribunal Award, 639
Bailiffs, Scales of Pay, Allowances, Award, 402
Courts:
Accounts, 255, 483, 713, 952
Bill, 36
Districts, Parishes, etc., in, Index, 643
Judges, Salaries. Cmd. 5309, 61
London, Directory, 407
See also Judicial Statistics.
Egg-laying Trials, Certificates, 361, 594, 849
of London Electric Supply Company, Electricity, 921
Courses of Instruction:
Army, 223, 449, 685, 929
in First Aid, A.R.P., 877
See also Holiday Courses; Unemployed Boys and Girls; Vacation Courses; Modern Languages Courses; Refresher Courses.
Court-Martial:
Naval, Procedure, 354
Trials by; 231
See also Courts-Martial.
Courts. See County Courts; Crime; Judicial; Law; Legal; Police; Scottish Land Court; Solicitors; Supreme Court; Juvenile Courts; Lancaster (Court of Chancery); London County Courts; Session, Court of; Sheriff Court; Summary Jurisdiction; University Courts; Industrial Court; International Justice; Thailand.
Courts (Emergency Powers):
Act, 754
Amendment Act, 971
Bill, 947, 948, 963
(Scotland) Act, 755
Bill, 708, 734
Courts-Martial Committee, Army and Air Force, Report. Cmd. 6200, 967
Covenant of the League of Nations. See League of Nations.
Coventry Corporation Acts, 71,759
Coventry Corporation Specifications, 932, 933, 1069
Cowell, F. R., Brief Guide to Government Publications, 671
Cowen, E. H., Epidemic Influenza,657
Cowes:
Pier and Harbour Provisional Order Confirmation Act, 70
Bill, 13, 39
Urban District Council Act, 526
Crafts, School, Exhibitions of, 971
Craig-an-Eran, s.t., Wreck Report, 675
Cramps, Specifications, 226, 1068

Cranes :
at Buildings in course of Construction, Register, 395
Derrick, Use of, 882
Register of Examinations, Factory Forms, 630
Crang, B. A., Preserves from the Garden, 1023
Crankcase Forgings, Specification, 854
Cranwell, R.A.F. College :
Admission to, 140, 365, 853
Examinations, 150, 376, 607, 859, 1031
Crates or Skeleton Cases, Specification, 1063
Crawford and Balcarres, Earl of, Chairman, Royal Fine Art Commission, Report. *Cmd. 5610*, 293
Crawford, O. G. S., Strip-map of Litlington, 653
Crawhall, T. C., Very Low Temperatures, 415
Cream Cheeses, 1023
Credit, Vote of, 723, 955
Supplementary, 1940, 959, 960
Statement. *Cmd. 6198*, 967
Creeping Thistles, 664
Crematorium, Mortlake, Act, 72
Crete. *See* " Imperia " M/Y.
Crew Spaces, Instructions, 437
Crewe Corporation Act, 525
Criccieth Castle, Guide to, 938
Cricket Bat Willow, Cultivation, 159
Crime :
Psychological Treatment of, 881
Scientific Investigation of, Report of Advisory Committee, 170
Criminal :
Appeal Act, 522
Investigation, Scientific Aids to, 170
Justice Bill, 498, 718, 726, 729
Procedure (Scotland) Act, 523
Bill, 272, 470, 485, 490, 495
Statistics :
England and Wales :
Cmd. 5185, 52
Cmd. 5520, 286
Cmd. 5690, 505
Cmd. 6167, 965
Scotland :
Cmd. 5299, 61
Cmd. 5580, 291
Cmd. 5878, 519
Cmd. 6150, 964
Crinkle of Potatoes, 595
Crookall, R., Kidston Collection of Fossil Plants, 660
Crop Plants, Cultivated, of British Empire and Anglo-Egyptian Sudan, 173
Crops :
Acreage and Production, 132, 359, 593, 848
Scotland, 196
Crops (*continued*) :
for Pickling, 593
Insect Pests of, 849
(Prevention of Damage) Bill. *See* Prevention of Damage by Rabbits Bill.
Production in Frames, 360
Rotation of, 133
Crown :
Gall, 1023
Lands :
Accounts, 27, 250, 476, 711, 951
Act, 66
Bill, 16, 30, 36
Commissioners, Annual Reports, 154, 381, 612, 863
Ministers of the Crown (Emergency Appointments) Act, 754
Office Fees, Honours and Dignities, Reports of Committee :
Interim. *Cmd. 5450*, 280
Final. *Cmd. 5767*, 510
Services, Acceptance of Business Appointments by Officers. *Cmd. 5517*, 285
Crown's Nominee Accounts, 220, 447, 683, 927
Croydon :
Airport Regs., 364
Corporation Act, 759
Typhoid Fever, Report. *Cmd. 5664*, 503
Crude Sewage, Discharge of, into River Mersey, 662
Cruelty to Animals. *See* Royal Society.
Cruikshank and Ross, Newburgh, Industrial Court Award, 888
Crustacea, 942
Crystal Symmetry, 941
Cuba :
Commercial Agreements with U.K. :
Cmd. 5383, 276
Cmd. 5867, 518
Cmd. 6152, 964
Economic Conditions, 439
Culag (Lochinver) Pier and Harbour Provisional Order Confirmation Act, 300
Bill, 242, 268
Cultivation, Allotment, 362
Cultures. *See* Type Cultures.
Cumberland :
Coal Mines Scheme, 183, 411
Coalfield, Survey of, 660, 1057
Cunard Insurance Fund Accounts, 35, 260, 488, 720
Cunard-White Star :
Agreement :
re R.M.S. *Queen Mary* and New Ship No. 552. *Cmd. 5397*, 277
with Treasury. *Cmd. 5725*, 507
American Mail Contract, 28

Cunningham :
Register of Sasines, 417
Susan, Paisley, Industrial Court Award, 888
Cupboards : Specifications, 931
See also English Cupboards.
Cupro-nickel and Gilding-metal Coated Steel Cups. *See* Import Duties Advisory Committee.
Curia Regis Rolls, 655
Curing. *See* Bacon Curing.
Curled Hair, Specification, 687
Currants :
Black, " Reversion " in, 135
Production and Trade, 171, 398, 633
Currency :
and Bank Notes Act, 1928, Fiduciary Note Issues, 712, 955
Treasury Minute, 959
and Bank Notes Act, 1939, 752
Bill, 697, 727
(Defence) Act, 754
See also China (Currency Stabilisation) ; Chinese Currency.
Current :
Official Statistics, Guide to, 447, 683, 927
Periodicals in the Science Museum Library, 652, 901
Currents. *See* Indian Ocean ; South Pacific Ocean.
Curtain, Anti-Gas, for Steel Helmet, Specifications, 933, 1069
Custody of Children. *See* Children.
Customs :
and Excise :
Annual Reports of Commissioners :
Cmd. 5296, 61
Cmd. 5573, 500
Cmd. 5876, 518
Cmd. 6098, 748
Examinations, 148, 375, 606, 858
Publications (N.P.), 154, 382, 612, 863, 1032
Tariffs of the U.K., 154, 382, 612, 864, 1032
Beef and Veal Customs Duties Bill, 43
British Indian, Passengers' Baggage Regs., 172, 399
Classification of certain Pneumatic Tyres, Poland and U.K. *Cmd. 6044*, 301
Forms, 154, 382, 612, 864, 1032
Isle of Man, Accounts, 221, 447, 683, 927
Tariff and Valuations, British India, 436
Tariffs :
Burma, 674
of the Colonial Empire, 153, 380, 611
Customs (*continued*) :
Treatment of Imports, Japan and Canada. *Cmd. 5577*, 290
See also Import Duties ; Tariffs ; Isle of Man ; Beef and Veal ; Excise Duty ; Import, Export and Customs.
Cutlery :
Specifications, 686, 931
Trade, Wages, 176, 404, 1045
Cut-Outs. *See* Accumulator Cut-Outs.
Cutworms or Surface Caterpillars, 595
Cyanide :
Poisons, Precautions to be taken in use of Cyanide Compounds, 395
Vapours, Hydrogen, Detection of, 666
Cycle Bells. *See* Import Duties Advisory Committee.
Cyclists, Accidents to, Report, 682
Cylindrical Multi-Tubular Steam Boilers, Factory Form, 1036
Cyprus : Colonial Reports, 151, 378, 609, 860
See also Nicosia.
Czech Refugee Trust Fund. *Cmd. 6076*, 746
Czechoslovakia :
Correspondence respecting. *Cmd. 5847*, 516
Economic Conditions, 439
Financial Assistance to, Agreement with France and U.K. *Cmd. 5933*, 736
(Financial Assistance) Act, 752
Bill, 697, 727
(Financial Claims and Refugees) Act, 971
Bill, 945, 962
Scheme for disposal of Financial Claims Funds. *Cmd. 6154*, 964
Frontiers between Czechoslovakia and Germany. *Cmd. 5908*, 521
Further Documents, including the Munich Agreement. *Cmd. 5848*, 516
Imported Food Certificate, 619
(Restriction on Banking Accounts, etc.), Act, 752
Bill, 699, 728
Trade Agreement with Australia, 208
See also Commercial Agreements.

D

Dairies. *See* Milk and Dairies.
Dairy :
Bacteriologists, Work of, 656
Cattle, Register of, 133, 361, 633, 849
Farm, Godford Park, Awliscombe, Devon, Boiler Explosion, 206

Dairy (*continued*) :
Farms, Report Card for Inspection of, 201
Produce :
Cost of Production, Scotland, 424
Production and Trade, 171, 398, 883
Supplies, 171, 398, 633, 883
Research, 656
Dalton-in-Furness Urban District Council Act, 71
Damage :
by Rabbits, Report, 235, 237
caused by Aircraft to Third Parties. International Convention. *Cmd. 5056*, 43
Prevention of Damage by Rabbits Act, 753
Bill, formerly Crops (Prevention of Damage), 474, 475, 697, 698, 707, 721, 726, 728, 732
See also War Damage.
Dampier, Sir W. C., Chairman, Committee of Inquiry into Land Settlement, Report, 889
Damsons and Plums, 135
Dandini, s.t., Boiler Explosion, 434
Dangerous Drugs, Home Office Publications (N.P.), 394, 626, 878
Daniel, A., Whitecairns, Industrial Court Award, 888
Daniel Owen, Celebration of St. David's Day, 158
Danish, Interpretership, Examinations, 607
Danube. *See* European Commission.
Danzig, Imported Food Certificates, 161, 618
Scotland, 666
Darby Thatching Needle, 359
Dardanelles, Regime of the Straits, Conventions :
Cmd. 5249, 57
Cmd. 5551, 288
Darlington Corporation Trolley Vehicles (Additional Routes) Provisional Order Confirmation Act, 69
Bill, 12, 39
Dartford :
Sunday Entertainments, 714
Tunnel Act, 302
Davidson, D. du B., Chairman, Committee on Expenditure in respect of Evacuated School Children, Report, 1032
Davidson, Viscount, Chairman, Departmental Committee on Ordnance Survey, Final Report, 596
Davies, C., Chairman, Anti-Tuberculosis Service in Wales and Monmouthshire, Committee of Inquiry, Report, 870
Davies, F. M., An Account of the Fishing Gear of England and Wales, 361
Davies, W. W., Stresses in Reinforced Concrete Piles during Driving, 658
Davis, A. H., Reduction of Noise in Buildings, 904
Davy, M. J. B., Interpretive History of Flight, 414
Day, W. R., Spring Frosts, 386
Day School :
Certificates, Examinations, Scotland, 203, 431, 668, 911
Code, 1939, Memos., 668, 914
Grant Earning, Statistical List, 889
System, Position of Technical Education in, 431
Daylight Illumination :
necessary for Clerical Work, 422
Seasonal Variation of, 194
de Clifford, Lord, Trial of, 5
See also Trial of Peers.
de L'Isle and Dudley, Lord, Manuscripts, 189
De la Warr, Earl, Chairman, Committee on Nutrition in the Colonial Empire, Report. *Cmds. 6050, 6051*, 744
Deaf :
Children :
Hearing and Speech, 419
(School Attendance) Bill, 42
See also Education (Deaf Children).
Dundee and Angus Trust for the Education of the Deaf Scheme, 198
Northern Counties Trust for Education of Deaf, 199
Deal, Sunday Entertainments, 257
Dean, A. R., Kiln-Seasoning Treatments of Teak, etc., 659
Dean, Forest of :
Coal Mines Scheme, 898, 1053
National Forest Park Committee Report, 617
Dean Orphanage and Cauvin's Trust :
Scheme, 197, 198
(Amendment) Scheme, 426, 427
Death, Causes of, Manual of International List of, 1055
Deaths :
on Ships registered in the U.K., 437, 674, 1064
Prince Arthur of Connaught, 644
Princess Louise of Argyll, 895
Queen of Norway, 644
See also Accidents ; Registrar-General.
Debates. *See* Parliamentary Publications ; Publications and Debates.
Debris, Clearance of, A.R.P., 878
Debt. *See* United States of America ; National Debt ; Regimental Debts.
Debt Collectors (Registration and Licensing) Bill, 731

Debts Clearing Offices :
Accounts, 477, 711, 950
Anglo-Spanish Account, 250
Annual Report, 207
Decay :
in Imported Timber, Causes of, 420
of Timber and its Prevention, 659
Decays, Principal, of Softwoods, 906
Decennial Supplements, Registrar-General :
England and Wales, 190, 656
Scotland, 202
Deck :
Manning of Foreign Going Ships. *See* Ships.
Sheathing for Ships, 435
Decode for use with International Code for Wireless Weather Messages from Ships, 647
Decontamination :
Services, Organisation, A.R.P., 625
See also Clothing.
Decorticated ground-nuts. *See* Import Duties Advisory Committee.
Dee, Tidal Nets, Aberdeen, Notes on Sea Trout from, 201
Deeds :
Register of, 903
See also Middlesex Deeds.
Deer and Ground Game (Scotland) Bill, 699, 700, 729
Defective :
Children, Educational Care of, 430
Hearing, Children with, Report of Committee, 614
Students, Training of, Institutions, 155, 614, 866
Defence :
against Gas, Army, 450
Contracts in connection with Defence Programme, Report, 256
Emergency, Road Transport for, 925
Expenditure on. *Cmd. 5114*, 47
Loans :
Act, 1937, 296
Bill, 237, 266
Act, 1939, 752
Bill, 728
Memos. :
Cmd. 5368, 275
Cmd. 5945, 737
Ministry of Defence (Creation) Bill, 36
Regulations, 1939 :
Action taken under Reg. 18B, Reports, 727, 930, 933, 936, 961
as amended to Sept. 21, 1939, 927
as amended to Dec. 11, 1939, and including Orders to Feb. 6, 1940, 1065
as amended to various dates in 1940, 1065
Defence (*continued*) :
Regulations, 1939 (*continued*) :
(Finance) Regs., as amended to Sept. 3, 1940, 1065
Instructions with regard to the detention in prison establishments of persons detained in pursuance of Regulation 18B. *Cmd. 6162*, 965
Statements :
Cmd. 5107, 47
Cmd. 5374, 275
Cmd. 5682, 501
Cmd. 5944, 737
See also Air Raid Precautions ; Arms ; Armaments ; Anti-Aircraft Defence ; National Defence ; Civil Defence ; Imperial Defence Committee ; Structural Defence.
Defences, Military Engineering, 454
Definitions, Statutory, Index to, 188
de Gaulle, General, French Volunteer Force, Exchange of Letters with Prime Minister. *Cmd. 6220*, 969
De-Icing :
Fluid, Specifications, 855, 1029
of Aeroplane Wings, etc., 598
Spirit for Carburettors, Specification, 855
Delevigne, Sir M., Chairman, Interdepartmental Committee on Rehabilitation of Persons injured by Accidents, Report, 875
Delta Iron and Steel Works, Derwenthaugh, Co. Durham, Boiler Explosion, 206
Demolition of Individual Unfit Houses. *See* Unfit Houses.
Demotic Papyri in the British Museum, 941
Denaro, L. F., External Rendered Finishes, 657
Denbighshire, East. *See* Wrexham.
Denmark :
Commercial Agreement with U.K. :
Cmd. 5942, 737
Cmd. 6112, 749
Economic Conditions, 211, 676
Extradition Treaty of March 31, 1873, Convention with U.K. *Cmd. 5919*, 735
Identity Documents for Aircraft Personnel, Exchange of Notes with various countries. *Cmd. 5586*, 291
Imported Food Certificate, 389
Scotland, 428
Load Line Certificates. *Cmd. 5441*, 280
Naval Armament, International Agreement. *Cmd. 5999*, 741
Trade and Commerce Agreements with U.K. :
Cmd. 5206, 54
Cmd. 5400, 277
See also Extradition.

DEN-EBO | 1936-40

DEN— *INDEX 1936–40*

Dental :
Branches of R.A.F., Training of Airmen, 369, 599, 853
Corps, Army, 223, 455, 689, 936, 1071
Disease in the Island of Lewis, 1055
Officers, Manual (R.A.F.), 599, 853, 1025
Dentistry, Careers, 401, 887
Dentists, Duties of, under Dangerous Drugs Acts, 626
Dependant's Allowance, Army, 1066
Introduction of, 929
Men serving in H.M. Forces during the present War. *Cmd. 6186*, 966
" Depressed Areas ". *See* " Special Areas ".
Depressions :
as Vortices, 896
Kinematical Features of, 408
Deputies and Shotfirers (Safety Lamps) Order, 1938, 899
Derby :
Corporation (Trolley Vehicles) Provisional Order Confirmation Act, 69
Bill, 12, 38
Electricity, 677
See also Chester and Derby.
Derbyshire :
and Nottinghamshire, Electricity, 921
Census, 190
Coalfield, Survey of, 421, 906
Electricity Order, 213
Traction Act, 68
Derrick Cranes :
Factory Form, 630
Use of, 882
Derwent Valley Water Act, 526
Design :
In Education, Industry, etc., Board of Trade Publications (N.P.), 434
Recommendations for, Steel Structures Research Committee, 194
Requirements for Aeroplanes, 138, 365, 598, 1028
Design, Patents, Trade Marks, Annual Reports, 27, 257, 485, 719, 958
Desks, Specifications, 452, 686
Despatch of Business at Common Law, Report of Royal Commission. *Cmd. 5065*, 44
Destroyers. *See* United States Destroyers.
Destructive Animals Bill, 473
Detective Work and Procedure, Departmental Committee Report, 626
Detectors. *See* Firedamp Detectors.
Deterioration of Structures of Timber, Metal, and Concrete exposed to the action of Sea Water, 193, 420, 658
Detonation in Solid Explosives, High-Speed Cameras for Measuring the Rate of, 413
Developing Egg in Virus Research, Use of, 418
Development :
Commissioners, Annual Reports, 20, 248, 475, 710, 952
Fund Accounts, 22, 35, 478, 712, 951
of Cardiac Enlargement in Disease of the Heart, 419
Schemes, Annual Reports :
Cmd. 5742, 508
Cmd. 6008, 742
See also Colonial Development; Industrial Development; Highway Development; Restriction of Ribbon Development; Agricultural Development.
Devils, Sand, 181
Diamond-Back Moth, 134
Diarrhoea. *See* Bacillary White Diarrhoea.
Diatomaceous Earth. *See* Import Duties Advisory Committee.
Dibutyl Phthalate, Specification, 141
Diet :
Influence of, on Caries in Children's Teeth, 191
of Families in the Highlands and Islands of Scotland, Inquiry into, 1056
Dietary :
Military, Manual of, 453
Survey in terms of Actual Foodstuffs consumed, 418
Digestive Disturbances of London Transport Workers, Investigation, 418
Dignities. *See* Crown Office Fees; Honours and Dignities.
Dilapidations. *See* Ecclesiastical Dilapidations.
Dines, L. H. G., Comparison between Geostrophic Wind, Surface Wind and Upper Winds, etc., 646
Diphtheria, Artificial Immunity against, 1034
Diplomas :
Art Teachers, 155
Electrical Engineering, 156
National Institute of Builders, 204
See also Certificates.
Diplomatic :
Privileges (Extension) Bill, 949
Service, Examinations, 374, 605
See also Consular and Diplomatic Service.
Directional Gyro, Specification, 140
Directory, Board of Education (Welsh Department), 868
Disability Pensions. *See* Soldiers' Allowances, etc.

INDEX 1936–40 —DOU

Disablement Allowances to Local Defence Volunteers, 1067
Discipline. *See* Naval Discipline.
Diseases :
Industrial, Compensation for, Third Report of Departmental Committee, 166
in Gardens and Small Orchards, Control of, 595
Notification of, Factory Form, 629
of Animals Acts and Orders, Ministry of Agriculture and Fisheries Publications (N.P.), 133, 361, 594
of Fish Act, 296
Bill, 18, 43, 240, 257, 267
of Poultry, 360, 593
Respiratory Dust, in Operatives in Cotton Industry, 191
Disinfection. *See* Poultry Market, etc.
Dispensing, Army, 685
Disputes, International. *See* International Disputes.
Distemper, Matt Finish, Specification, 1029
Distinguished Service Awards, etc., 894, 1048
Distressed Areas. *See* Special Areas.
Distribution of the Industrial Population. *See* Industrial Population.
District Probate Registries :
Draft Order, 1938, 487
Salary Scales, Award, 402
Disused Burial Grounds Act (1884) Amendment Bill, 727
Dividends. *See* Limitation of Dividends.
Divorce :
and Nullity of Marriage (Scotland) Bill, 247
(Scotland) Act, 523
Bill, 18, 267, 461, 468, 490, 494, 495
See also Matrimonial Causes; Indian and Colonial Divorce.
Dixon, A. L., Chairman, Departmental Committee on Detective Work and Procedure, Report, 626
Dixon, F. E., Fog on the Mainland and Coasts of Scotland, 897
Docking and Nicking of Horses (Prohibition) Bills, 247, 461, 462, 493, 732
Docks :
Demand for Timber in, 617
Factory Forms, 627
Regs., 395
Sunderland. *See* Wear Navigation.
Workmen's Compensation Forms, 170, 397, 632
See also Mersey Docks.
Dockyard Accounts, 26, 255, 483, 716, 956
Doctors. *See* General Practitioners; Medical Officers; Medical Practitioners.
Doctors and Dentists, Duties of, under Dangerous Drugs Acts, 626
Doctrine of Consideration, Report of Law Revision Committee. *Cmd. 5449*, 280
Documents. *See* Identity Documents; Official Documents.
Documents, British, on the Origin of the War, 158, 616
Dogs :
Amendment Act, 522
Bill (formerly Dogs Act (1871) Amendment Bill), 271, 462, 464, 494
Experiments on, Bill, 731
Prohibition of Vivisection on, (Scotland) Bill, 42, 498
Protection of Bill, 39
Dolls, Celluloid. *See* Import Duties Advisory Committee.
Dolomite, 943
Domestic :
Embroidery, English, 695
Grates, Open, Use of Coke in, 421
Preservation of Fruit and Vegetables, 132, 360
Proceedings. *See* Summary Procedure (Domestic Proceedings).
Science, Careers, 401
Surface Shelters, 1038
Erection of, 877
Utensils, Galvanised, Specifications, 226, 686, 931, 1068
Dominica Act, 522
Bill, 247, 272
Dominican Republic :
Commercial Relations with Newfoundland. *Cmd. 6208*, 968
Economic Conditions, 211, 676
Dominions :
Governors of, Pensions Act, 65
Bill, 13
Income Tax in, 635, 884, 1039
See also Arms, Flags and Badges.
Donald, G. H., Manufacture of Charcoal in Portable Kilns, 906
Donaldson Trust Scheme, 200, 426
Doncaster :
Area Drainage Act, 524
Corporation (Trolley Vehicles) Provisional Order Confirmation Act, 69
Bill, 12, 38
Door Bolts of Iron or Steel, Report. *Cmd. 5619*, 294
Doping Schemes, Aeroplane, Specification, 141
Dormant Funds in Court, 644
Dorward House (Montrose) Scheme, 197
Dotted Manner, Prints in the, 459
Double Nationality, Military Obligations. *Cmd. 5460*, 281
Doule, Loch, Sea Trout of, 665

DOV— *INDEX 1936–40*

Dover :
Corporation Act, 72
Electricity, 440
Dowlas, Undyed and Tan, Specification, 226
Downshire, Marquess of, Manuscripts, 189, 655
Drainage. *See* Land Drainage; Public Health (Drainage of Trade Premises).
Draining, Mole, 849
Drawers, Specifications, 226, 452, 686, 931
Drawgear. *See* Colliery Haulage.
Drawings :
and Etchings by Rembrandt in British Museum, List, 693
and Water Colours in British Museum, Handbook, 941
Facsimiles of, 694
Gallery, British Museum, Guide to exhibits in, 459
See also Import Duties Advisory Committee.
Drawn Bonds, Treasury Notice of Numbers of, 1049
Dress Regs. :
Army, 450, 685, 1067
for Officers of the R.A.F., 138, 1024
Dressed Leather. *See* Import Duties Advisory Committee.
Dressing Chest, Specification, 686
Dressing Table, Specification, 686
Dressmaking and Women's Light Clothing Trade, Wages, 404, 642, 890, 1046
Dried Fruit Supplies, 398, 633
Drift. *See* Surface Water Drift.
Drill :
and Ceremonial, R.A.F., 138
Elementary, Army, 685, 930
Drink Trade, Census of Production, 1063
Drinking Water Tanks :
Clear Varnish for internal protection of, specification, 1028
Protection against Corrosion, Specification, 369
Drive. *See* Flexible Drive.
Driver (Excavator), Army Trade of, 1066
Drivers. *See* Motor Drivers.
Driving and Maintenance for Mechanical Vehicles (Wheeled), Army, 685, 929
Droitwich Canals (Abandonment) Act, 759
Drug Traffic, National Health Insurance, 873
Drugs :
Hospital Exemption and Approved Institution Orders, 166, 167
Sale of, 162, 390
See also Dangerous Drugs; Food and Drugs.
Drum Trade, Wages, 405, 890, 1047
Drums :
or Tanks, Explosions during Inspection and Repair of, Factory Form, 880
which have contained Cellulose Solutions or Inflammable Solvents, Repair of, 395
Dry Rot :
in Wood, 659
Investigations in an Experimental House, 420
of Potatoes, 1023
Drying. *See* Kiln Drying.
Drying Cylinder Explosion, Report, 365
Duck :
and Geese, Wild Birds Protection Act, 753
Bill, 474, 499, 700
Cotton, Specification, 1068
Ducks :
and Ducklings, Salmonella Infections of, 850
and Geese, 360
Dukinfield. *See* Stalybridge.
Dumbarton Burgh :
Order Confirmation Act, 972
Bill, 710, 734, 945
Water Order Confirmation Act, 526
Bill, 470, 496
Dumbartonshire. *See* Dunbartonshire.
Dumbreck Colliery, Fire, Reports. *Cmd. 5863*, 517
Dumfriesshire :
Educational Trust :
Scheme, 200, 426
(Additional Endowment and Amendment) (No. 1) Scheme, 664, 910
Electricity, 440
Dunbartonshire :
County Council (Kirkintilloch Street Improvement Order, Confirmation Act, 760
Bill, 708, 732
Educational Trust Scheme, 199, 426
Electricity, 921
Duncan Macleod of Skeabost Scholarship Fund Scheme, 1059
Dundee :
and Angus Trust for the Education of the Deaf Scheme, 198
Corporation Order Confirmation :
Act, 1936, 67
Act, 1939, 757
Bill, 704, 731
Harbour and Tay Ferries (Superannuation) Order Confirmation Act, 758
Bill, 704, 731
High School (Amendment) Scheme, 198, 199

INDEX 1936–40 —EBO

Dundee (*continued*) :
Institute of Art and Technology :
Scheme, 1059
(Amendment) (No. 1) Scheme, 664, 910
Dunstable Gas and Water Act, 300
Dunstanburgh Castle, Northumberland, Official Guide, 231
Dunster. *See* Minehead.
Durham :
and Northumberland Coalfield, Survey, 421
Census, 417
Coal Mines Scheme, 183, 411, 648
Coalfield, Survey, 660, 906
Public Service Vehicle Operators, Industrial Court Award, 888
Durward, J., Upper Winds Measured at :
M/Y " Imperia ", Mirabella Bay, Crete, 410
Nicosia (Cyprus), 897
Dust :
Coats, Specification, 932
Nuisances from, Model Byelaws, 391
Respirator, Fitting and Maintenance of, Factory Form, 879
See also Coal Dust; Mine Dust.
Dusters, Specification, 687
Dusts, Mine, Analysis of, 651
Dust-Storms in Iraq, 646
Dutch, Interpretership, Examination, 857
Dwellings. *See* Movable Dwellings.
Dyed and Printed Textiles, Guide to, 695
Dyeing, Fish. *See* Sea Fish.
Dynamo Lighting Equipment for Cycles. *See* Import Duties Advisory Committee.
Dysentery, Lamb, 362

E

Ealing :
and Shepherds Bush Railway Extension. *See* Great Western Railway.
Extension Provisional Order Confirmation Act, 298
Bill, 237, 265
Earsdon Joint Hospital District Provisional Order Confirmation Act, 299
Bill, 42, 237
Earth :
Closets, Cleansing, Model Byelaws, 391
Diatomaceous. *See* Import Duties Advisory Committee.
Electric Field of, Point Discharge in, 180
Systems for W/T Purposes on Aircraft, Specifications, 369, 855
Earthquake. *See* Baffin Bay.
Easby Abbey, Yorkshire, Guide to, 231
Easels, Specification, 452
East Africa. *See* Africa; British East Africa; Portuguese East Africa.
East African Agricultural Research Station. *See* Amani.
East Anglesey Gas Act, 299
East Anglia :
and Midlands, Guide to Ancient Monuments, 231
Geological Survey, 421
Eastbourne Extension Act, 300
East Craigs, Potato Trials and Collections at, 425, 664, 909
East Denbighshire. *See* Wrexham.
Eastern Canadian Spruce, Data on, 420
Eastern Valleys (Monmouthshire) Joint Sewerage District Provisional Order Confirmation Act, 759
Bill, 704, 729
East Hertfordshire Joint Hospital District Provisional Order Confirmation Act, 298
Bill, 237, 265
East India :
Budget, 261, 488, 722
Constitutional Reforms :
Elections. *Cmd. 5589*, 291
Resignation of Ministries in Bihar and the United Provinces. *Cmd. 5674*, 504
India Office Publications (N.P.), 399, 634
Loans raised in England, 399, 884, 1038
Progress and Condition, 256
Statistical Abstracts :
Cmd. 5424, 279
Cmd. 5804, 513
Cmd. 6079, 746
Tribal Disturbances in Waziristan. *Cmd. 5495*, 284
See also India.
East India Loans Act, 296
Bill, 236, 265
Memo. *Cmd. 5352*, 273
East Indies. *See* Netherlands East Indies.
East Lothian :
County Council :
Act, 69
Order Confirmation Act, 68
Bill, 9
Water Order Confirmation Act, 525
Bill, 468, 495
East Midlands Forensic Science Laboratory, Nottingham, Dangerous Drugs, 394
East Riding. *See* Yorkshire.
Eastry, Sunday Entertainments, 29
East, W. N., Psychological Treatment of Crime, 881
Eastwood, T., Gosforth District, Geological Survey, Memoir, 421
Ebonite, Loaded, Specifications, 587, 1019

Ecclesiastical :
Commissioners :
Annual Reports :
Cmd. 5151, 49
Cmd. 5433, 279
Cmd. 5759, 510
Cmd. 6022, 742
(Powers) Measures, 11, 72, 470, 528
Committee Reports on various Measures. See titles of Measures.
Dilapidations (Chancel Repairs) Measure, 947, 948, 973
Officers' Remuneration Measure, 700, 760
Echinoidea, 942
Echo Sounding Gear, 586
Economic :
Advisory Council, Locust Control, 447, 927
Collaboration, Agreement, Italy and U.K. Cmd. 6128, 750
Series :
Agriculture, 133, 361, 594
British Museum (Natural History), 460, 694, 941
Survey of Colonial Empire, 380, 611, 1031
Economiser :
Examination of :
Factory Forms, 629
Mines and Quarries Form, 650
Explosions, Reports, 434
Ecuador :
Economic Conditions, 439, 920
Extradition, Supplementary Convention with U.K., etc. Cmd. 6614, 293
Edible :
and Poisonous Fungi, 1023
Fats, Rancidity in, 659
Edinburgh :
Accountant (Scottish Educational Dept.) in, Report of, 203, 430, 668
Border Counties Association Educational Trust Schemes, 910, 1059
Castle, Guide, 231
Corporation Order Confirmation :
Act, 1936, 67
Bill, 8
Act, 1937, 301
Bill, 245, 270
Educational Endowments Scheme, 200, 427, 665, 910
Gazette, 197, 425, 664, 909, 1059
Royal Botanic Gardens Publications, (N.P.), 203, 430, 668, 913, 1060
Royal Maternity and Simpson Memorial Hospital Order Confirmation Act, 298
Bill, 238, 267

Edinburgh (continued) :
Trust for the University Education of Women Scheme, 198
University :
Additional Bursaries (No. 2) Scheme, 198, 199, 426
Fellowships, Scholarships and Bursaries (Amendment) Scheme, 198, 199, 426
See also Royal Observatory.
Education :
Act, 1936, 66
Bill, 12, 15, 17, 28, 34, 36, 39, 41
Areas, Scotland, Statistics, 203, 431, 660, 914
Authorities : Scotland, List of, 203, 669
See also Local Education Authorities.
Board of :
Annual Reports :
Cmd. 5290, 60
Cmd. 5564, 289
Cmd. 5776, 511
Cmd. 6013, 742
Grant Regs., 865, 868, 1033
Publications (N.P.), 155, 383, 614, 865, 1032
Civil Estimates : 25, 252, 480, 715, 954
Memos. :
Cmd. 5106, 47
Cmd. 5837, 276
Cmd. 5678, 504
Cmd. 5959, 738
Cmd. 6179, 966
Committee of Council (Scotland). Cmd. 5140, 49
(Deaf Children) Act, 296
Bill (formerly Deaf Children, School Attendance), 237, 238, 267
Design in, 434
(Emergency) Act, 755
Bill, 708, 734
(Emergency) (Scotland), Act, 755
Bill, 708, 734
in Scotland :
Annual Reports :
Cmd. 5140, 49
Cmd. 5428, 279
Cmd. 5709, 506
Cmd. 6007, 742
Scottish Education Department, Publications (N.P.), 203, 430, 668, 913, 1060
Civil Estimates, Revised, 1937, 258
in the Colonies, Advisory Committee on, Report, 1031

Education (continued) :
in Wales :
Annual Reports :
Cmd. 5178, 52
Cmd. 5478, 283
Cmd. 5799, 513
Cmd. 6042, 744
Welsh Department, Publications (N.P.), 158, 386, 616, 868, 1033
in Windward and Leeward Islands, 863
Payment of Travelling Expenses, Appointed Day, Scotland, 203
Schemes for Provision of (Scotland), 203
(Scotland) Act, 66
Bill, 16, 29, 34, 36, 40
Explanatory Circular, 203
Technical and Art Education, List of Institutions, 158
Technical Education :
in Continuation Classes (Scotland), 203
in North Wales, 158
See also Art ; Examinations ; Physical Education ; Scholarships ; Schools ; Teachers ; Training Colleges ; Agricultural Education ; Elementary Education ; Higher Education ; Technical Education ; Adult Education ; Further Education ; Public Education ; Secondary Education ; Veterinary Education ; Health Education ; Vocational Technical Education.
Educational :
Administration in England and Wales, Selection of Charts, 156
Appointments Overseas, 131, 669
Development, Administrative Programme, 156, 158
Endowments (Scotland) Commission, Publications (N.P.), 197, 425, 664, 910, 1059
Exhibition, Oxford, Charts, 156
Films :
Convention. Cmd. 5155, 50
Proces-Verbal facilitating the International Circulation of. Cmd 6221, 969
Pamphlets :
Board of Education, 156, 384, 614, 866
Post Office, 514, 683, 902
Scottish Education Department, 669, 914
Services, Scottish, 669
System :
in England and Wales, 384
Structure of, 866
Training, Army, 223, 450, 685, 930, 1067
Edward III, Calendar of Inquisitions, 189
Post Mortem, 189

Edward VII Welsh National Memorial Association Act, 757
Edward VIII :
Appointments to Royal Household, 180
Birthday Honours, 180
Declaration of Abdication Act, 67
Bill, 19, 43
List of Names of Corporations and Bodies presenting Addresses of Sympathy and Congratulations, 180, 197
Proclamation on Accession, 180, 188, 197
Facsimile, 205
Speech to Parliament, 18
Edwards, F. W., British Blood-Sucking Flies, 941
Eelworm, Potato Root. 363
Egg-Laying Trials, County, Certificates, 133, 361, 594, 849
Egg Products, Production and Trade, 171, 398, 883
Eggs :
Birds, Instructions for Collectors, 694
Maintenance of Egg Size, 362
Packing of, 362
Production and Trade, 171, 398, 883
Egypt :
Atmospheric Temperature, 408
Bon Voisinage Agreement with Italy and U.K. Cmd. 5726, 507
British Forces in, Immunities and Privileges :
Cmd. 5270, 59
Cmd. 5360, 274
British War Memorial Cemeteries and Graves in. Agreement with U.K., etc. Cmd. 5618, 293
Capitulations in, Abolition. Cmd. 5491, 283
Civil Air Transport Service, Egypt-South Africa :
Cmd. 5325, 63
Cmd. 5404, 277
Commercial Relations with Palestine. Cmd. 5361, 274
South Africa. Cmd. 6134, 750
Convention relative to the Abolition of the Caisse de la Dette Publique Egyptienne. Cmd. 5544, 970
Economic Conditions, 439, 920
Financial Questions affecting the Anglo-Egyptian Sudan, Agreement. Cmd. 5319, 62
Lake Tsana and Suez Canal, Exchange of Notes with Italy and U.K. Cmd. 5923, 736
Map to illustrate Treaty of Alliance. Cmd. 5308, 61
Order in Council, 1937, Index to, 616

Egypt (continued) :
Taxation, etc., of Pensions of Retired Foreign Officials, Djibouti and U.K. Cmd. 5630, 501
Telecommunications, Egypt and U.K. Cmd. 5640, 501
Tonnage Measurement, Agreement with U.K. Cmd. 5994, 740
Treaty of Alliance with U.K. Cmd. 5861, 517
Egyptian :
Mummies and Coffins, 693
Religious Papyri, Catalogue of, 694
Stelae, Hieroglyphic Texts from, 941
Eire :
Agreements with U.K. Cmd. 5728, 507
Air Navigation, Exchange of Notes with U.S.A. Cmd. 5711, 506
Civil Estimates, Revised, 488
(Confirmation of Agreements) Act, 522
Bill, 467, 494
Post Offices in, 902
Regulation of Beef Imports into U.K., Correspondence. Cmd. 5943, 737
Transfer of Harbour Defence Equipment to. Cmd. 5809, 513
See also Trade Agreements.
Elastic Lace. See Import Duties Advisory Committee.
Election Deposit. See Candidates (Local Government).
Elections :
General Election, 1935, expenses, etc., 32
(Motor Cars) Bill, 271
Parish, etc., circulars, 394
See also East India ; Parliamentary Elections ; Local Elections ; Local Government Elections.
Electors, Register of. See Local Elections
Electric :
Accumulator Regs., Factory Form, 631
Arc Welding Memo., 395
Cables, Specifications, 686, 930, 931, 1062, 1068
Cords, Specifications, 931, 1068
See also Flexible Electric Cords.
Field of the Earth, Point Discharge in, 181
Illumination, Principles, etc., 187
Power Acts, 68, 69
Electrical :
Accidents, 167, 395, 630, 880
Accumulators, Specification, 254
and Radio Notes for Wireless Operators 1024

Electrical (continued) :
Apparatus :
as applied to Artillery, 390
Examination of, 651
Flameproof, Test and Certification of, 651
Minimum Requirements, 140
Specifications, 366
Engineering, National Certificates and Diplomas in, 156, 384
Equipment of Excavating Machinery, 411
Generators, Specification, 366
Inspector of Mines, Reports, 411, 648, 898
Machinery and Apparatus, Survey of Trade in, 171
Power, Trolley Vehicles. See Trolley Vehicles.
Specifications, 452, 930, 1062, 1068
Telecommunication Apparatus, Specification, 1019
Electricians, Coal Mines, Regs. to be supplied to, 899
Electricity :
and Service Electrical Apparatus as applied to Artillery, 930
Commission Publications (N.P.), 212, 440, 682, 926, 1065
Meters, Testing and Certification of, 683
on Rain, 645
Supply :
(Meter Charges) Bill, 731
(Meters) Act, 65
Bill, 7, 9, 37, 39
Regs., 212
Undertakings, Returns relating to, 926
See also, Gas, Electricity.
See also Central Electricity Board Publications ; Ministry of Transport Publications ; Mines and Quarries Forms.
Elementary :
Drill, Army, 223, 930
Education, Cost per Child, 156, 384, 614, 866
Meteorology, Short Course in, 645
Schools. See Public Elementary Schools ; Senior Public Elementary Schools.
Elgin and Lossiemouth Harbour Order Confirmation Act, 301
Bill, 246, 270
Elizabeth :
Calendar of State Papers, 189
Patent Rolls, 903
Ellice Islands. See Gilbert and Ellice Islands.
Elm, Rock, as Rough Timber, Specification, 140
El Salvador, Economic Conditions, 211, 920

Ely :
Cathedral Canonries Act, 972
Paper Works, Cardiff, Explosion, 671
Embrey, G., Ltd., Bakery of, Explosion, 672
Embroideries, English, 943
Embroidery, English, Domestic, 695
Embryos. See Chick Embryos.
Emergency :
Acts and Statutory Rules and Orders, Lists of, 916, 1062
Commissions, Army, 1067, 1070
Fire Brigade Organisation :
England and Wales, 595, 631, 880
Scotland, 432, 670, 915
Hospital Organisation :
England and Wales, 872
First Aid Posts and Ambulances, Statement. Cmd. 6081, 745
Scotland, 911
Medical Services Memoranda :
England and Wales, 873, 1034
Scotland, 911, 1060
Powers (Defence) Act, 1939, 754
Bill, 733
Instructions with regard to the detention in prison establishments of persons detained in pursuance of Reg. 18B. Cmd. 6162, 965
Powers (Defence) Act, 1940, 971
Bill, 962
Powers (Defence) (No. 2) Act, 1940, 972
Bill, 948, 963
Relief Organisation for persons rendered homeless by enemy attack, 1060
Statutory Rules and Orders, Lists of, 916, 1062
Water Supplies for Fire Fighting, 880
Work, Prime Cost Contracts for, 882, 1038
Emmens, C. W., Variables affecting the Estimation of Androgenic and Oestrogenic Activity, 904
Empire :
Air Mail Schemes (Agreements, etc., with Imperial Airways Ltd.) :
Carriage of Empire first class mail. Cmd. 5414, 278
Christmas Mails and extension to Sydney. Cmd. 5497, 284
Kisumu-Lusaka Auxiliary Service :
Cmd. 5523, 286
Extension. Cmd. 5616, 293
Malaya-U.K. Cmd. 5676, 504
Singapore-Sydney. Cmd. 5813, 514
Operation on route between U.K. and South Africa. Cmd. 5501, 284

Empire (continued) :
Air Mail Schemes (Agreements, etc., with Imperial Airways Ltd.) (continued) :
South Africa (Empire) Agreement, Extensions :
Cmd. 5616, 293
Cmd. 5769, 510
Colonial. See Colonial Empire.
Exhibition :
(Glasgow), Exhibit, 620
(Scotland) Order Confirmation Act. 525
Bill, 247, 272
Settlement :
Empire Settlement Act, 296
Bill, 236, 265
Home and Empire Settlement Bill, 42
Memo. Cmd. 5326, 63
Survey Officers, Conference, 153
Timbers, 905
Employees. See Civil Staffs ; Civilian Employees ; Staffs.
Employers' Liability :
Act, 1880, Statistics of Compensation and Proceedings under :
Cmd. 5557, 288
Cmd. 5722, 507
Cmd. 5955, 738
Cmd. 6203, 967
Bill, 1936, 36, 42
Insurance :
Certificate of Auditors of Accident Officers' Association :
Cmd. 5309, 54
Cmd. 5522, 286
Cmd. 5800, 513
Cmd. 6075, 746
Limitation of Charges. Cmd. 6223, 969
Employment :
Control of :
Act, 756
Bill, 708, 733
Draft Order, Report on, 957
Hours of. See Hours of Employment.
of Air Forces with Army, 450
of Boys. See Coal Mines (Employment of Boys).
of Children, Scotland, Byelaws, 430
of Women and Young Persons Act, 65
Bill, 16, 26, 34. 37
Shift System in Factories and Workshops (Consultation of Workpeople) Ballot Paper, 168
See also Unemployment ; Hours of Employment ; Juvenile Employment ; Loss of Employment ; Young Persons.

ENA-FAU | 1936-40

ENA— INDEX 1936–40

Enactments :
  Postponement of, (Special Provisions) Act, 756
  Bill, 734
  See also Special Enactments.
Enamelling. *See* Vitreous Enamelling.
Enamels, Specifications, 366, 854, 1025
Enderbury Island. *See* Canton.
Endowments. *See* Educational Endowments.
Enemy :
  Attack, Emergency Relief Organisation for persons rendered homeless by, 1060
Enemy :
  Attack, Emergency Relief Organisation for persons rendered homeless by, 1060
  Nationality, Civilian Internees of, Categories of Persons eligible for release :
    Cmd. 6223, 969
    Cmd. 6233, 970
  Trading with the Enemy Act, 755
    Bill, 708, 733
Enfield, Sunday Entertainments, 482
Engine Speed Indicator, Flexible Drive for, Specifications, 140, 369, 855, 1027
Engineer :
  Army, Chief Royal, Honorary Appointment, 1067
  Services, Army, 223, 450, 685, 930, 1067
  Training, Army, 450
Engineering :
  Careers, 174
  Construction, Works of, Factory Forms, 627
  Industry, Occupations in, 401
  Inspectors, Post Office, Civil Service Arbitration Tribunal Award, 1042
  Military, 223
  Royal Scholarships Examination Papers, 364, 614, 866
  Trade :
    Census of Production, 917
    Import Duties Reports, 208, 436
  See also Electrical Engineering; Field Engineering; Military Engineering.
Engineers :
  Ground, Notices to, 138, 364, 598, 851
  in Mercantile Marine, Examinations, 673, 918, 1061
  Royal, Pocket Book, 455
  See also Mechanical Engineers.
Engines. *See* Aero Engines; Marine Engines.
England :
  Central, Geological Survey, 194
  Mid-East and South-East, Electricity Schemes, 212
England–Scandinavia, Air Transport Services. *Cmd. 5203*, 53
England–South Africa, Air Transport Services. *Cmd. 5325*, 63
English :
  Channel, Salinity and Temperature of, 133
  Costume, 460
  Cupboards, Cabinets and Bookcases, 943
  Domestic Embroidery, 695
  Embroideries, 943
  Embroidery, Flowers in, 943
  Plaice-Marking Experiments, 595
  Pottery, 234
Ensign, Civil Air, Order, 364
Ensilage, 593
Enteric Fever in Bournemouth, Poole and Christchurch, 392
Entertainments. *See* Sunday Entertainments.
Ephemeroptera, 943
Epidemic Influenza, 657
Epidemics in Schools, 657
Epidemiology, Experimental, 191
Epsom :
  and Ewell, Sunday Entertainments, 486
  and Walton Downs Regulation Act, 71
Equalisation. *See* Exchange Equalisation.
Equipment :
  Branch, R.A.F., Conditions of entry, etc., 138, 598
  of the Army, 450, 685
  of the Working Class Home, 434
  Regs., Army, 224, 225
Equitation, Army, 688
Erikson, Dagny, Pathogenic Anaerobic Organisms, 1056
Ernst, E. G., Chairman, British Guiana Refugee Commission, Report and Appendices. *Cmd. 6014, 6029*, 742, 743
Errand Boys, Holidays for, Factory Forms, 627
Esher, Sunday Entertainments, 250
Essential Buildings and Plant (Repair of War Damage) Act, 754
  Circular, 872
    Scotland, 914
Essential Commodities Reserves Act, 523
  Bill, 472, 490
Essex :
  Census, 190
  Provisional Order Confirmation Act, 71
    Bill, 14, 39
  South East :
    Joint Hospital District Provisional Order Confirmation Act, 301
      Bill, 240, 269
    Waterworks Act, 68

INDEX 1936–40 —EXC

Estate Agency, Careers, 401
Estates :
  and Treasure Trove in Scotland, Account of Receipts and Payments, 205
  Ultimus Haeres, 208, 433, 671, 915, 1061
  See also Church Estates; Municipal Housing Estates.
Estimated Populations, Scotland, 432
Estimates :
  East India, 399
  Select Committee Reports, 30, 256, 260, 487, 721
  See also Civil Estimates; Air Estimates; Army Estimates; Navy Estimates; Revenue Department Estimates.
Estonia :
  Economic Conditions, 211, 920
  Extradition, Exchange of Notes with South Africa. *Cmd. 6027*, 743
  Imported Food Certificate, 389
    Scotland, 428
Etchings by Rembrandt in British Museum, List, 693
Ether. *See* Ethylene Glycol.
Ethiopia :
  and Italy, Dispute between :
    Bombing by Italian Military Aircraft of British Red Cross Ambulance. *Cmd. 5160*, 50
    Correspondence, Papers, etc. *Cmd. 5071, 5072*, 44
    Petroleum, etc., Report. *Cmd. 5094*, 46
    Rescue and Relief of British and Foreign Nationals at Addis Ababa. *Cmd. 5213*, 54
  Discovering of Abyssinia, 693
  Order in Council, 1934, 158
  See also Haile Selassie.
Ethyl Cellulose, Specification, 1027
Ethylene Glycol, Specifications, 601, 855, 1026, 1029
Eumorfopoulos Collection of Chinese Art, 234
Euphausiacea and Mysidacea, 942
Europe. *See* North West Europe.
European :
  Commission of the Danube :
    Entry of Germany into, etc. *Cmd. 6068*, 746
    Exercise of Powers and Privileges and Immunities of Personnel, etc. :
      Cmd. 5946, 737
      Cmd. 6069, 746
  Settlement :
    Diplomatic Discussions. *Cmd. 5143*, 49
    German Proposals. *Cmd. 5175*, 51
Euthanasia, Voluntary (Legislation), Bill, 18
Evacuated School Children :
  Education of, 866
    Wales, 868
  Expenditure in respect of, Committee on, Report, 1032
Evacuation Scheme. *See* Government Evacuation Scheme.
Evergreen, s.t., stranding, 210
Evesham and Pershore Joint Hospital District Provisional Order Confirmation Act, 298
  Bill, 42, 236
Evidence :
  Act, 1938, 523
    Bill, 461, 463, 495
  and Powers of Attorney Act, 971
    Bill, 946, 947, 963
Evocation, Right of, from Siamese Courts, Exchanges of Notes between Siam and U.K. :
  Cmd. 5611, 293
  Cmd. 5921, 735
Ewell. *See* Epsom.
Ewing, A. W. G., and I. R., The Use of Hearing Aids, 418
Examinations :
  Air Ministry, 138, 139, 147
  Army, 150, 225, 376, 451, 685, 930
  Art, 156, 384, 614, 866, 1032
  Civil Aircraft Navigator's Licence, 364, 598, 852, 1024
  Civil Service Commission, 146, 374, 604, 857, 1030
  Higher School Certificate, Report, 867
  Leaving Certificate, Day School, etc., Scotland, 203, 431, 668, 914
  Mercantile Marine, 209, 673, 918, 1061
  Mines, 184, 411, 648, 898, 1053
  Police, Scotland, 670
  Scholarships, various, 156
  Science Scholarships, 384, 614, 866
  Senior Leaving Certificate, 913
  Skippers and Second Hands of Fishing Boats, 436
  Whitworth Scholarships, Regs. for, 866
  See also Medical Examination; Physical Examination; Metallurgical Examination; Bacteriological Examination; Special Army Examination.
Examiners : Mines Department Publications (N.P.), 899
Examples in Navigation, 1018
Excavating Machinery at Quarries, Electrical Equipment, 411
Excess Profits Duty, Lists of Orders, 399

EXC— INDEX 1936–40

Exchange Equalisation Account Act, 296
  Bill, 244, 269
  Memo. *Cmd. 5498*, 284
Exchequer :
  and Audit Departments (Temporary Provisions) Act, 755
    Bill, 733
  Contributions to Local Revenues, 481, 795, 954
Excise. *See* Customs and Excise.
Execution of Trusts. *See* Trust.
Executors, Confirmation of (War Service) (Scotland), Act, 972
  Bill, 947, 963
Exercises :
  A.R.P., Notes on, 878
  R.A.F., 597, 851
Exeter Extension Act, 757
Exhibition :
  Galleries, British Museum, Guide, 459
  of Atom Tracks, Catalogue, 414
  See also Empire Exhibition.
Exmouth, s.t., Wreck Report, 675
Expenditure :
  in respect of Evacuated School Children, Committee on, Report, 1032
  Public, Accounts, 257, 485, 719
  See also Income and Expenditure; National Expenditure; Public Income.
Experimental Work on Highways Technical Committee Publications (N.P.), 926
Experiments :
  Drift Bottle, 428
  English Plaice Marking, 595
  in Anti-Gas Protection of Homes, 624
    Scotland, 670
  in Breeding of Oysters, 361
  on Dogs Bill, 731
  on Living Animals, Licences granted, etc., 32, 259, 487, 721
Expiring Laws Continuance :
  Acts, 65, 67, 297, 752, 756
  Bills, 19, 41, 43, 247, 271, 475, 499, 734, 963
Explosions :
  Anaesthetic, in Operating Theatres, 160
  at Mossfield Colliery. *Cmd. 6227*, 969
  at North Gawber (Lidgett) Colliery, Yorkshire. *Cmd. 5214*, 54
  at Valleyfield Colliery. *Cmd. 6226*, 969
  Boiler, 206, 434, 672, 1061
  during inspection of Drums, etc., Factory Form, 880
  Home Office Publications (N.P.), 169, 626
Explosions (*continued*) :
  See also Coal Mines; Boiler Explosions Acts.
Explosives :
  Authorised, List of, 167, 394, 626, 879, 1035
  Conveyance of, on roads, 879
  H.M. Inspectors of, Annual Reports :
    Cmd. 5263, 58
    Cmd. 5541, 287
    Cmd. 5838, 516
    Cmd. 6103, 748
  Mines and Quarries Forms, 650, 1053
  See also Mines; Solid Explosive; High Explosive.
Export :
  Control, Tests of Goods, 1063
  Council, Work of. *Cmd. 6183*, 966
  Credits Guarantee Department :
    Agreement with Soviet Trade Representative. *Cmd. 5253*, 57
    Examinations, 1030
  Guarantees :
    Acts, 297, 752
    Bills, 245, 269, 499, 697
    Memo. *Cmd. 5467*, 282
  List, 154, 382, 612
  See also Goods; Import, Export.
Exportation of Horses Bill, 37
Exported Aircraft, Certificates of Airworthiness, Exchange of Notes, U.S.A. and Canada. *Cmd. 5928*, 736
Expulsion Orders. *See* Violence.
Ex-Service Men :
  Condition of, Reports made to Prime Minister. *Cmd. 5738*, 508
  Employed in Government Departments :
    Cmd. 5257, 58
    Cmd. 5536, 287
    Cmd. 5816, 514
  and Women, Voluntary Organisations etc. for assisting, Guide, 415
External Rendered Finishes, Survey of Continental Practice, 657
Externally Fired Egg-ended Steam Boilers, Factory Form, 879
Extracted Meals, Use of, 360
Extradition :
  Australia, New Zealand, Luxembourg, and U.K., Conventions :
    Cmd. 5416, 278
    Cmd. 5811, 513
  Denmark and U.K. *Cmd. 5172*, 51
  Ecuador and U.K., Supplementary Convention. *Cmd. 5614*, 293
  Estonia and South Africa. *Cmd. 6027*, 743
  Hungary and U.K. :
    Cmd. 5311, 62
    Cmd. 5550, 288

INDEX 1936–40 —FAU

Extradition (*continued*) :
  Iceland and U.K. :
    Cmd. 5919, 735
    Cmd. 6083, 747
  Luxembourg and U.K. *Cmd. 6087*, 747
Extruders, Guarding of, Committee on, Reports, 632, 1037
Eye Accidents, Protection against, Factory Form, 880
Eyeglass Frames, etc., Merchandise Marks, Report. *Cmd. 6147*, 751
Eyestrain, Industrial, Special Measures needed where fine work is done, 395

F

Fabric Mouldings for Magneto Gear Wheels, Specification, 1028
Fabrics. *See* Chinese Woven Fabrics; Light Cotton Fabric; Oil-dressed Fabric.
Facsimiles of Drawings (British Museum), 694
Factories :
  Accidents in, 396, 631, 881
  Act, 297
    Bill, 243, 244, 246, 259, 262, 265, 268, 269, 270
    Duties of Local Authorities, 646
    Guide to, 626
    Memo. *Cmd. 5366*, 275
  Air Raid Precautions, 166
  Chief Inspector of, Annual Reports :
    Cmd. 5230, 55
    Cmd. 5514, 285
    Cmd. 5802, 513
    Cmd. 6081, 747
  Economical Type Designs—Single Storey Factories, 1056
  Emergency Protection in, 1038
  First Aid and Ambulance for, 1037
  Home Office Publications (N.P.), 166, 393
  Hours of Employment of Women and Young Persons. *Cmd. 6182*, 966
  Lighting in, 397, 632, 1043
  Means of Escape in case of Fire, 626
  Medical Supervision in, Memo., 1042
  Opened, extended, and closed, 209, 674, 919
  Protective Clothing for persons employed in, 1037
  Seats for Workers in, 1048
  Shift System. *See* Women and Young Persons.
  Ventilation in, 395, 397, 1038
  See also Alkali; Royal Ordnance Factories; Small Factories.
Factors. *See* Tidal Angles.
Factory :
  and Industrial Accidents, Descriptions, 396
  and Workshops Acts, Abstract, 167
  Buildings, 1056
  Forms, 167, 394, 627, 879, 1035, 1042
  Ventilation in the Black-Out, 1036
Faculty Jurisdiction Measure, 470, 528
Faint Stars, Catalogue of, 901
Falkland Islands :
  Badge, 380
  Colonial Reports, 151, 378, 860, 1031
Falmouth :
  Docks Act, 759
  Lord, Chairman :
    Departmental Committee on Imposition of Penalties by Marketing Boards, etc., Report. *Cmd. 5980*, 740
    Sub-Committee of Imperial Defence Committee, Coal from Oil, Report. *Cmd. 5665*, 503
  Pier and Harbour Provisional Order Confirmation Act, 300
    Bill, 242, 267
  Provisional Order Confirmation Acts, 68, 759
    Bills, 9, 38, 704, 730
False Indications of Origin on Goods, International Agreement. *Cmd. 5832*, 515
Family :
  Allowances, Army, 685, 930, 1067
  and Dependants Allowances, Army, 1068
  Provision. *See* Inheritance.
Fancy Feather Trade, Wages, 891
Farm :
  and Factory Cheese-making, 593
  Animals, some diseases of, 132
  Poisonous Plants on the, 593
  Workers in Scotland. *Cmd. 5217*, 55
Farmer, E., Accident Proneness among Motor Drivers, 1055
Farming in Scotland, Economic Reports, 197, 425, 664, 1059
Farms. *See* Dairy Farms.
Farmyard Manure, 849
Farnham Gas and Electricity Act, 973
Farnworth. *See* Radcliffe.
Faroe-Shetland Channel, Surface Water Drift, 428
Farquharson, J. S., Blueness of the Sky, 646
Fast Brown V Base. *See* Import Duties Advisory Committee.
Fat lambs, production of, 850
Fatigue and Boredom in Repetitive Work, 418
Fats. *See* Edible Fats.
Faulkner, Sir A., Chairman, Committee on Possibility of Increased Use of Coal for Bunkering Purposes, Report, 647

Fauna and Flora, Protection of :
  Africa, International Conference, 683
  International Convention. *Cmd. 5280*, 60
Faversham, Sunday Entertainments, 491
Favorita, s.t., Wreck Report, 438
Feather Pillows and Slips, Specifications, 687, 932
Feathers, Specification, 687
Federated Malay States, Colonial Reports, 151, 378, 609, 860, 1031
Feeding :
  Habits of the Haddock in Scottish Waters, 428
  Poultry, Essential Points in, 362
  Stuffs :
    for use with Cereals in Pig Feeding, 362
    Home Grown, 848
    Residual Values of, 425, 1059
    See also Fertilisers and Feeding Stuffs.
  See also Communal Feeding.
Fees :
  House of Lords, Standing Orders, 17
  Medical Practitioners called in by Midwives, Circular, 162
  See also County Courts ; Crown Office ; Survey.
Fellowships. *See* Edinburgh University.
Felt. *See* Import Duties Advisory Committee.
Felt Hoods. *See* Import Duties Advisory Committee.
Feltham, Sunday Entertainments, 952
Felton, J. R., Report on Explosion at Markham Colliery. *Cmd. 5456*, 281
Fencing :
  and other Safety Precautions for Transmission Machinery, 167
  of Machinery :
    in Tinplate Factories, 632
    Woodworking, 632
Ferguson and Muirhead, Renfrew, Industrial Court Award, 888
Ferguson Bequest Fund Order Confirmation Act, 301
  Bill, 245, 270
Ferguson, T., Anti-Venereal Measures, etc., 622
Ferries. *See* Harbours, Piers and Ferries.
Ferrocyanide, Potassium. *See* Import Duties Advisory Committee.
Ferro-Silicon. *See* Import Duties Advisory Committee.
Fertility :
  and Animal Breeding, 360
  See also Land Fertility.
Fertiliser Salts, Import Duties. *Cmd. 5294*, 60
Fertilisers :
  and Feeding Stuffs Act (1926) Amendment Bill, 728
  in Modern Agriculture, 849
  Potash, 134
  Residual Values, 425, 1059
Fettes Endowment (Amendment) :
  Scheme, 427, 664
  (No. 2) Scheme, 910
Fever. *See* Cerebro-spinal Fever ; Tickborne Fever.
Fibre :
  Cores for Colliery Winding Ropes, 413, 900
  Jointing, Compressed Asbestos, Specification, 1026
  Trade, Wages, 890, 1046
Fibres. *See* Industrial Fibres.
Fiduciary Note Issues, Treasury Minutes, 712, 713, 955
Field :
  Allowance, Army, 1068
  Allowance and Colonial Allowance, 930
  Archaeology, 188
  Engineering, Army, 451
  Peas, Growing of, for Stock Feeding Purposes, 1024
  Service Regs., Army, 225, 451, 930
  Sketching, Army, 229, 453, 688, 934, 1070
  Training, Navy, 353
Fife :
  County Council Order Confirmation Bill, 963
  Educational Trust Scheme, 198, 427
Fighting Vehicles, Armoured, Machine Gun Mountings in, 456
Fiji, Colonial Reports, 151, 609, 861
Files, Specification, 226
Filey, Sunday Entertainments, 953
Filing Cabinets and Cupboards, Specifications, 931
Film Base, Photographic, Import Duties. *Cmd. 5264*, 58
Films :
  Departmental Committee on :
    Minutes of Evidence, 207
    Report. *Cmd. 5320*, 62
  Educational :
    Convention. *Cmd. 5155*, 50
    Procès-Verbal facilitating the International Circulation of. *Cmd. 6221*, 969
  See also Cinematograph Films ; Slow-burning Films.
Filters. *See* Oil Filters ; Petrol Filters.
Filth, Nuisances from, Model Byelaws, 391
Filtration, Poison Gases, Certification Mark, 393, 977

Finance :
  Accounts of U.K., 29, 259, 486, 720, 959
  Act :
    1926 (S.10), Report of a Committee appointed by the Board of Trade. *Cmd. 5157*, 50
    1934, Statements of Conversion Loans, etc., 29, 258, 264, 484, 718, 722, 958
    1936, 66
      Bill, 16, 38, 40
        Memo. on Clause 6. British Iron and Steel Industry. *Cmd. 5201*, 53
    1937, 297
      Bill, 245, 267, 270
    1938, 523
      Bill, 495, 497
    1939, 753
      Bill, 706, 729, 731
    1939 (No. 2), 755
      Bill, 708, 734
    1940, 971
      Bill, 947, 963
    1940 (No. 2), 972
      Bill, 948, 962, 963
  Acts, Supplements, 173, 400
Financial :
  Instructions, Army, 225, 451, 685, 930, 1068
  Statement. *See* Budget.
  Statistics, Local Government, 621, 874, 1035
Finch, J. C. W., Chairman, National Forest Park Committee (Snowdonia), Report, 386
Finchley, Sunday Entertainments, 482
Findlay, W. P. K. :
  Decay of Timber and its Prevention, 659
  Dry Rot in Wood, 659
  Dry Rot Investigation in an Experimental House, 420
  Principal Decays of Softwoods used in Great Britain, 906
Fine Rolls, Calendars, 189, 416, 903, 1054
Finger Prints, Classification and Uses, 631
Finishes, External Rendered, Survey of Continental Practice, 657
Finland :
  Economic Conditions, 611, 909
  Importation of Wheaten Flour, Exchange of Notes with U.K. *Cmd. 5515*, 285
  Imported Food Certificate, 389
    Scotland, 428
  See also Naval Armament.
Fir, Douglas, British Columbia, 193
Fire :
  Appliances, Emergency, Care of, 880
Fire (*continued*) :
  Application of, Small Arms Training, 456, 937
  at Dumbreck Colliery. *Cmd. 5863*, 517
  Brigade :
    Services Report. *Cmd. 5224*, 55
    Premises, Protection of, against Air Attack, 880
      Scotland, 915
    Pumps, Care and Maintenance of, 880
  Brigades :
    Act, 524
      Bill, 472, 473, 486, 490, 495, 496, 498
      Circulars, 620, 631, 881
        Scotland, 670, 915
    Division Publications (N.P.), 631, 880, 1036
    Home Office Publications (N.P.), 395, 631
    Scottish Office Publications (N.P.), 432, 670
  Engine Steam Boilers, Factory Form, 880
  Extinguishers, Specifications, 140
  Factories, Means of Escape, 626
  Fighting, Emergency Water Supplies, 880
  Insurance Bill, 37
  Precautions, etc. :
    Home Office Publications (N.P.), 625
    Incendiary Bombs, 877
    Scottish Office Publications (N.P.), 669
  Protection, Hints to Householders, 168
  Risks at Generating Stations, etc., 683
  Service :
    Commission, 880
      Scotland, 915
    Volunteers, Auxiliary, Enrolment of, 880
  Services : Army, 928, 1066
    See also Local Fire Services.
  Tender, General Purpose, 881
Firearms :
  Act, 296
    Bill, 19, 235, 236
  (Amendment) Act, 66
    Bill, 3, 16, 18, 31, 34, 37, 40
  Certificates, Forms, 396
Fireboat, 941
Firedamp :
  Detectors, Report, 648
  Mines Department Publications (N.P.), 186
Firemen :
  Home Office Publications (N.P.), 880
  Mines Department Publications (N.P.), 899, 1054
  See also Police and Firemen.

Fire-Resistance Tests, Specification, 140
First Aid :
  and Ambulance for Factories, 1037
  and Nursing for Gas Casualties, 625
  Courses of Instruction, A.R.P., 877
  Factory Form, 631
  for detached personnel in the tropics and sub-tropics, R.A.F., 365, 833, 1025
  in the Navy, 352, 1018
  Mines and Quarries Form, 649
  Parties, Training and Work of, 877
  Posts, 393, 432, 624
    and Ambulance Services :
      Circular, 871
        Scotland, 911
        Wales, 876
      Statement. *Cmd. 6061*, 745
    and Points, 871
      Scotland, 911
      Wales, 876
    Collective Training for, 872
      Scotland, 911
      Wales, 876
    Memo for Guidance of Personnel, 873
      Scotland, 911
Fish :
  Culture in ponds, 132
  Frying, Model Byelaws, 391
  Gallery, British Museum, Illustrated Guide to, 460
  Import Duties. *Cmd. 5098*, 46
  Instructions for Collectors, 460
  John Murray Expedition, 942
  Lemon Soles, Marking Experiments in Scottish Waters, 201
  Meal. *See* White-Fish Meal.
  Oils. *See* Import Duties Advisory Committee.
  Size Limits, International Convention. *Cmd. 5494*, 284
  Wet, Salted, Spilt. *See* Import Duties Advisory Committee.
  White Fish Industry. *Cmd. 5130*, 48
  See also Sea Fish ; Diseases of Fish ; Silver Fish ; Fisheries ; Triassic Fishes.
Fishenden, M., Heat Transmissions, Calculation of, 1058
Fisher, Sir W., Chairman, Departmental Committee on Pensions for Members of the House of Commons, Report. *Cmd., 5624*, 294
Fisheries. *See* Agriculture and Fisheries ; Sea Fisheries ; Herring ; Salmon ; Whaling ; Fishery Board ; Sea Fishing ; Sockeye Salmon ; Halibut ; Scottish Fisheries.
Fishermen, Share, Unemployment Insurance, 178
Fishery :
  Board for Scotland :
    Annual Reports :
      Cmd. 5127, 48
      Cmd. 5411, 278
      Cmd. 5721, 507
      Cmd. 5971, 739
    Publications (N.P.), 201, 427, 665, 910, 1060
  Investigations, 133, 361, 591, 819, 1023
Fishguard and Goodwick Urban District Council Act, 69
Fishing :
  Boats :
    British, Exhibition, 187
    Skippers and Second Hands of, Examination Regs., 436
  Craft, British, Historical Review, 414
  Gear of England and Wales, 361
  Nets, Size of Meshes, International Convention. *Cmd. 5494*, 284
  Vessels Co-operative Insurance Society Ltd., War Risks Insurance, 723
  See also Sea Fishing.
Fitness. *See* National Fitness ; Physical Fitness.
Fitness Wins, 615
Fitzmaurice, R. :
  Principles of Modern Building, 658, 904
  Sound Transmission in Buildings, 1058
Fixed Trusts, Report of Departmental Committee. *Cmd. 4249*, 58
Flags :
  of all Nations, 125, 353
  of British Dominions, 153, 380, 611, 862
Flame :
  Gas and, Mines, 900
  Safety Lamps, 186
    Care of, 899
    Detection of Firedamp with, 897
Flameproof Electrical Apparatus, Test and Certification, 651
Flannel :
  Drawers, Specification, 931
  Shirts, Specification, 932
Flannelette, Specification, 1069
Flats :
  for the Working Classes, Construction of, Final Report, 389
  owned by Local Authorities, Rents. *Cmd. 5527*, 286
Flax :
  and Hemp :
    Cordage, Plaited, Specifications, 854, 1026
    Trade Wages, 176, 404, 890, 1045

Flax (*continued*) :
  Production, Trade, and Consumption, 171, 398, 634, 883
  Spinning and Weaving, Factory Form, 630
Flea Beetles, 362, 849
Fleas, 460
  as a Menace to Man and Domestic Animals, 694
Fleet :
  Coronation Review, Air Navigation, 364
  Officers of, Uniform Regs., 587, 842
  Orders, 125, 353, 586, 841
  Small Arm Courses for, Royal Naval Handbook, 842
  See also Navy.
Fleets of various Countries, Particulars of :
  Cmd. 5371, 275
  Cmd. 5666, 303
  Cmd. 5936, 737
Fleetwood. *See* Blackpool.
Flesh, Rabbits for, 595, 850, 1023
Flett, Sir J. S., the First Hundred Years of the Geological Survey of Great Britain, 422
Flexible :
  Cables, Electricity, 1053
  Drive for Engine Speed Indicator, Specification, 143, 369, 855, 1027
  Electric :
    Cables, Specification, 930
    Cords, Specification, 931, 1068
  Steel Wire Rope for Kite Balloon Cables, Specification, 1029
  Wire Rope, Specification, 367
Flies. *See* British Blood-sucking Flies.
Flight, Interpretive History of, 414
Flights in the Tropics and Sub-Tropics, Medical Notes, etc., 139
Flints, Sturge Collection of, 694
Floodlighting Playgrounds and Playing Fields, 867
Floor Polish Trade Wages, 642, 889, 1046
Flora. *See* Fauna ; Nasopharyngeal Bacterial Flora.
Floral Display at Kew Gardens, 173
Flour. *See* Wheat Flour.
Flower, Commercial Production, 133, 594, 849
  See also Artificial Flower.
Flower, W. D. :
  An Investigation into the Variation of the Lapse Rate of Temperature in the Atmosphere near the Ground at Ismailia, Egypt, 408
  Temperature and Relative Humidity in the Atmosphere over Lower Egypt, 409
Flowering Plants in Pots, 849
Flowers :
  In English Embroidery, 913
  Pickers of, Model Byelaws, 621
  Spring, and grown under Glass, 133, 849
  Summer, 594
  Supplies, 171, 398, 634, 883
Fluids, various, Specifications, 1026, 1029
Flume. *See* Venturi Flume.
Flutter, Aeronautical Research Committee Publications (N.P.), 373
Flux, Aluminium Welding, Specification, 366
Fly, Sheep Maggot, 664
  See also Carrot Fly ; House Fly ; Onion Fly.
Flying :
  Control of :
    Report of Committee. *Cmd. 5961*, 738
    Memo. *Cmd. 6045*, 744
  Medical Examination for Fitness for, 139, 365, 599, 853, 1025
  Training Manual, 365, 598
Focal-Plane Camera Shutters, Proofed Fabric for, Specification, 1029
Fodder :
  Conservation, 904
  Crops, Preservation of, 418
Fog :
  on the Mainland and Coasts of Scotland, 897
  Signals, List of, 354, 598, 843
Fogg, A., Friction of an Oscillating Bearing, 661
Folding :
  Boat Equipment, 223
  Desks, Specification, 686
Foliage and Foliage Plants, 594
Folkestone :
  Pier and Lift Act, 299
  Water Act, 760
Food :
  and Drugs :
    Act, 523
      Bill, 464, 467, 469, 470, 497
        Draft by Local Government and Public Health Consolidation Committee. *Cmd. 5629*, 500
      Circulars, 620, 623
      Procedure under, 873
      Tables of Comparison, etc., with earlier Acts, 873
    Circular, 872
      Wales, 876
    Sale of, 162, 620, 873
  and Feeding Habits of the Haddock in Scottish Waters, 428
  and Health, 620
  Certificates. *See* Public Health (Imported Food).
  Chemical Composition of, 1055

Food (*continued*) :
Circulars, 666, 911
Council Reports, 436, 673, 918
Defence Bill, 732
(Defence Plans) Department, Report, 673
Education Memoranda, 1032
for Live Stock, White Fish Meal, 360
from the Garden, 849
Investigation Board Publications (N.P.), 193, 420, 659, 905, 1057
Lead in, 623
Memoranda, 390, 620
Ministry of, Publications (N.P.), 1033
of North Sea Herring, 361
Poisoning due to Salmonella, Type "Dublin" and conveyed by Raw Milk, 622
Preservatives in, Circular, 1034
Preserving Trade :
Board. *See* Sugar Confectionery.
Wages, 405
Products, Corrosion by Tinplate Container, 193
Protection against Poison Gas, 1033
Saleof, (WeightsandMeasures) Act, 64
Schools in Wartime, 1033
Trades :
Census of Production, 1063
Import Duties Act Inquiry Report, 208
See also Canned Food ; Home-produced Foods ; Public Health (Imported Food).
Foodstuffs, Protection of, against Poison Gas, 394
Foot, I., Chairman, Committee on Fire-damp Detector Regs., Report, 648
Foot-and-Mouth Disease Research Committee Report, 361
Foot Rot of Sheep, 695
Forces : *See* House of Commons (Service in H.M. Forces) ; Military and Air Forces ; Military Forces ; Allied Forces ; French Volunteer Force ; National Service ; Naval and Marine Forces.
Foreign :
Judgments. *See* Judgments.
Medals, 414, 900
Officials. *See* Retired Foreign Officials.
Office :
Examinations, 374, 605, 1030
Publications (N.P.), 158, 386, 616, 869, 1033
Plate, Hall-marking of, Act, 753
Bill, 499, 702, 715
Services, Civil Estimates, 25, 253, 480, 715, 954
State Papers, 158, 386, 616, 1033
Foreign (*continued*) :
Stone Implements, Selection of, 694
Telegrams and Radiotelegrams, 415, 654, 902
Trade and Commerce Accounts, 209, 436, 673, 918
Volunteers, Withdrawal of, from Spain, Correspondence with Italian Government. *Cmd. 5570*, 290
Foreigners, Marriage with, Act, 64
Forest :
Ashdown, Act, 300
Nurseries and Plantations, Methods of Establishing, 386, 869
of Dean :
Coal Mines Scheme, 183, 1053
National Forest Park Committee Report, 617
See also Cardiff.
Park Committee, National, Report (Snowdonia), 386
Products :
Minor, of the British Empire, Index, 171
Research Board Publications (N.P.), 193, 420, 659, 906, 1057
Service List, Colonial, 152, 862
Forestry :
Afforestation in the Lake District, 159
Careers, 174, 888
Commission :
Annual Reports, 27, 258, 485, 720
Publications (N.P.), 159, 386, 617, 869
Practice, 386, 869
Research Workers, List of, 882
See also Agriculture and Forestry.
Forfar Corporation Water Order Confirmation Act, 525
Bill, 466, 494
Forgings, Specifications, 368, 1025
Formosa, Economic Conditions, 211
Forster, Sir J., Chairman :
Commission on Trinidad and Tobago Disturbances, 1937, Report. *Cmd. 5641*, 501
Committee on Effects of Working Conditions upon the Health of Central London Busmen, Report, 889
Court of Inquiry on stoppage of London Central Omnibus Services :
Interim Report. *Cmd. 5454*, 281
Report. *Cmd. 5464*, 282
Fort William, Electricity, 677
Fossil :
Orthoptera Ensifera, 942
Plants, Kidston Collection, 660
Foundling Hospital Act, 69
Fourah Bay College, Freetown, Report, 862

Fowey Pier and Harbour Provisional Order Confirmation Act, 300
Bill, 242, 268
Fowl :
Cholera, 595
Paralysis, 135
Pest, 362
Pox, 362, 1023
Fowler "Three-Thirty" Diesel Crawler Tractor, 132
Fox, Sir C., Illustrated Regional Guide, South Wales, 691
Fox, E. N., Stresses in Reinforced Concrete Piles, 658
Foxon, G. E. H., Stomatopod Larvae, 942
Frames, Crop Production in, 360
Framlingham Castle, Guide to, 691
France :
Abolition :
of Capitulation in Morocco and Zanzibar, Convention with U.K. :
Cmd. 5538, 287
Cmd. 5646, 501
of Consular Visas on Bills of Health, Exchange of Notes with U.K. *Cmd. 6187*, 966
See also Reciprocal Abolition *below*.
Aerial Navigation in Antarctic, Exchange of Notes with Australia, New Zealand, U.K. *Cmd. 5900*, 520
Commerce and Navigation Convention with Canada. *Cmd. 5581*, 290
Commercial Relations with Tunis, France and U.K. *Cmd. 5622*, 294
Despatch from H.M. Ambassador in Paris. *Cmd. 6159*, 965
Exemption of Military Aircraft from Duties on Fuel and Lubricants, Exchange of Notes with U.K. *Cmd. 5998*, 741
Financial Assistance to Czechoslovakia, Agreement with Czechoslovakia and U.K. *Cmd. 5933*, 736
Fleet, particulars of :
Cmd. 5371, 275
Cmd. 5666, 503
Cmd. 5936, 737
French :
Telegraph Cable between Mauritius and Reunion :
Cmd. 6127, 750
Cmd. 6194, 967
Volunteer Force, Exchange of letters between the Prime Minister and General de Gaulle. *Cmd. 6220*, 969
France (*continued*) :
Identity Documents for Aircraft Personnel, Exchange of Notes :
with India and U.K. *Cmd. 5922*, 736
with U.K. *Cmd. 6125*, 750
Importation of Raffia, Coffee and Gum, Exchange of Notes with U.K. *Cmd. 5558*, 289
Imported Food Certificate, 161, 619
International :
Position of Belgium. *Cmd. 5437*, 279
Trade, Report by M. van Zeeland. *Cmd. 5648*, 502
Legal Proceedings, Conventions :
Cmd. 5182, 52
Cmd. 6206, 968
Legalisation of certain Official Documents, Agreement with U.K. *Cmd. 5476*, 282
Limitation of Naval Armament, International Treaty. *Cmd. 5564*, 289
Loan to Poland, Agreement with Poland and U.K. *Cmd. 6110*, 749
Mutual Assistance Treaty with Turkey and U.K. :
Cmd. 6123, 750
Cmd. 6165, 965
Naval Armaments Treaty. *Cmd. 5136*, 48
New Hebrides Protocol, Exchanges of Notes with U.K. *Cmd. 6184*, 966
Opium Smoking Agreement. *Cmd. 5401*, 277
Proposals drawn up by Belgium, France, U.K., and Italy. *Cmd. 5734*, 48
Correspondence with Belgian and French Ambassadors. *Cmd. 5149*, 49
Reciprocal :
Abolition of Consular Visas on Bills of Health, Exchange of Notes, India and French Indo-China. *Cmd. 5920*, 735
Enforcement of Judgments. *Cmd. 5235*, 56
Exemption from Income Tax of Air Transport Profits, Agreement with U.K. *Cmd. 6126*, 750
Rubber, Regulation of Production and Export :
Cmd. 5236, 56
Cmd. 5384, 276
Suez Maritime Canal, Free Navigation of, International Convention. *Cmd. 5623*, 500
Trade Agreement with Australia, 208

France (*continued*) :
Transfer to French State of Property in the Sites of British War Memorials, Convention with Canada, Australia, New Zealand, and U.K. *Cmd. 6003*, 741
War Graves Agreement. *Cmd. 5068*, 44
See also Commercial Agreements.
Franco-Soviet Treaty, the Treaty of Locarno and the Demilitarised Zone in the Rhineland, Memo. by German Government. *Cmd. 5118*, 47
Frankfurt. *See* Civil Air Transport.
Fraser River System. *See* Sockeye Salmon Fisheries.
Fraud, Prevention of (Investments) Act, 752
Bill, 492, 498, 499, 698, 699, 711, 729
See also Statute of Frauds.
Free :
Navigation of Suez Canal, International Convention. *Cmd. 5623*, 500
Postage. *See* Local Government Elections.
Freeman Assay for Coal and Carbonaceous Materials, 660
Freezing of certain Building Materials, 658
Freight Ships :
Instructions for Masters, 437, 918
Specification for fitting, 919, 1061
French :
and German :
Assistants in Scottish Schools and Training Colleges, 668, 913
Schools and Colleges, Scottish Assistants in, 913
Assistants in Scottish Schools, 430
Examinations, 606, 607
Indo-China, Reciprocal Abolition of Consular Visas on Bills of Health, Exchange of Notes with India. *Cmd. 5920*, 735
Interpretership, Examinations, 150, 859
Schools and Colleges, Scottish Assistants in, 203, 668
Telegraph Cable between Mauritius and Reunion, Convention between France and U.K. *Cmd. 6194*, 967
Volunteer Force, Exchange of letters between the Prime Minister and General de Gaulle. *Cmd. 6220*, 969
West Africa, Economic Conditions, 439
See also Africa.
Frequency and Power-Factor Meters, Specification, 930
Freshwater Fisheries. *See* Salmon and Freshwater Fisheries.
Friction of an Oscillating Bearing, 661
Friendly Societies :
Accounts, 221, 447, 684, 928, 1065
Act, 295
Annual Reports, 28, 159, 255, 487, 950
Publications (N.P.), 159, 387, 617, 869, 1033
Friendship, Treaty of, Colombia and U.K. *Cmd. 5958*, 738
Frome, Sunday Entertainments, 953
Frontier Questions, Agreement, Palestine, Syria and the Lebanon. *Cmd. 6065*, 745
Frontiers between Germany and Czechoslovakia. *Cmd. 5908*, 521
Frosts, Spring, 386
Fruit :
Bottling of, 195, 1059
Crops, Manuring of, 361
Domestic Preservation of, 132, 360
Nutritive Value of, 191
Pectins, 905
Pests and Diseases in Gardens and Small Orchards, Control of, 595
Pickers, Model Byelaws, 621
Production, 360, 848
and Trade, 171, 398, 633
Supplies, 171, 398, 634, 883
Tree :
Capsids, 362, 595
Red Spiders, 595
Spraying, Commercial, 848
See also Canned Fruit ; Bush Fruits ; Tree Fruits.
Frying, Fish, Model Byelaws, 391
Fuel :
Allotments. *See* Charities.
Exemption of Aircraft from Duties :
Netherlands. *Cmd. 5074*, 45
Switzerland. *Cmd. 5846*, 516
Research Board Publications (N.P.), 193, 421, 659, 906, 1057
Scales of, Army, 456, 686
See also Coal, Coke and Manufactured Fuel ; Liquid Fuel ; Manufactured Fuel ; Motor Fuel.
Fugitive Criminal. *See* Extradition.
Fumes. *See* Nitrous Fumes.
Fumigation :
of Insect Pests in Stored Produce, 1057
with Hydrocyanic Acid Gas, 595
See also Hydrogen Cyanide.
Fundamental :
Standards of Length, etc., 661
Stars, Apparent Places of, 1018
Funeral Directors (Registration) Bill, 468
Fungi, Edible and Poisonous, 1023
Fur :
Rabbits for, 595, 850, 1023
Trade Wages, 642, 890, 1046
Furnishing of Working Class Home, 434

Furniture :
Beetles injurious to, 1057
Manufacturing Trade Wages, 1045
See also School Furniture ; Coffin Furniture.
Further Education, England and Wales, award of Board of Education Endorsed Certificate in Commerce, 615
Fustian Cutting Trade, Wages, 176, 1045

G

Gaboon Mahogany :
Okoume. *See* Import Duties Advisory Committee.
Plywood. *See* Import Duties Advisory Committee.
Gall. *See* Crown Gall.
Galleries. *See* National Museums ; Picture Galleries.
Galvanised Domestic Utensils, Specifications, 686, 931, 1068
Gambia :
Colonial Reports, 151, 378, 609, 861
Economic Conditions, 439
Game. *See* Deer and Ground Game.
Gamma Rays, Biological Action, 419
Gangrene. *See* Gas Gangrene.
Ganzoni, Sir J., Chairman, Select Committee on Medicine Stamp Duties, Report etc., 252
Gapes in Poultry, 134
Garden :
Food from the, 849
Plants. *See* Ornamental Garden Plants.
Preserves from the, 1023
Trenches, 625
Gardeners, Private. *See* Unemployment Insurance.
Gardens :
Control of Fruit Pests and Diseases in, 595
Scotland's War, 909
See also Edinburgh ; Kew.
Gardiner, J. S. :
Ecology of Solitary Corals, 942
Madreporaria, 942
Gareloch, s.s., Wreck Report, 210
Garments, Rubber-proofed, Specification, 688
Garner, H. V., Manures and Manuring, 360
Garrett, A. W., Chairman, Committee on Fencing of Heavy Power Presses, Report, 889
Garrison and Regimental Institutes, Army, 451, 930, 1068
Garscube Lands, Electricity, 677
Gas :
Air Raid Precautions :
England and Wales, 165, 166
Scotland, 204
and Air Raids, Protection against, 930
and Flame, Mines, 900
and Steam Vehicles (Excise Duties) Act, 971
Bill, 734, 945
Casualties :
First Aid and Nursing for, 625
Medical Treatment of, 394
Defence against, 223, 450
Detection and Identification Service, 882
Examiner's Ordinary Reports (Recording Apparatus), Forms, 207
Fund Accounts, 207, 436, 673, 918
Gangrene, Notes on the Diagnosis and Treatment of, 1056
Mains and Services, Cutting and **Welding Operations**, Factory Forms, 879, 880, 1036
Measurement of, 15, 16
Personal Protection against, 625
Poisoning, Atlas of, 394, 625
Prices :
Report, 239
Report and Evidence, etc., 235
Producer. *See* Government Emergency.
Sheffield No. 2 Order (1936), Modifications by Select Committee, 238
Starter Systems for Aero Engines, 365
Supplies in West of Scotland, 207
Undertakings, Returns, 208, 436, 674, 918, 1063
Vans and Gas Chambers, 165
See also Chimney Gases ; Poison Gas ; Toxic Gases ; Hydrocyanic Acid Gas ; Anti-Gas ; Blister Gases ; War Gases ; Commercial Gas ; Producer Gas.
Gas, Electricity and Water Undertakings, Select Committee on, Minutes of Evidence, etc., 702
Gas, Light and Coke Company :
No. 1 Act, 71
No. 2 Act, 72
Gasholders. *See* Water Sealed Gasholders.
Gasket. *See* Headen Keil.
Gassing, Dangers from, 167
Gateshead :
and District Tramways and Trolley Vehicles Act, 527
Corporation Act, 526
See also Newcastle.

1936-40 | GAU-GRA

GAU— INDEX 1936–40

Gauges :
Pressure, Specification, 140, 853
Screw, 661
Testing, 143, 1030
Geese :
Rearing and Marketing of, 362
See also Duck and Geese.
General :
Board of Control for Scotland. *See* Control, Board of.
Cemetery Act, 299
Duties Branch of R.A.F. :
Commissions in, 598, 852
Regs., 139, 365
Hospitals :
Acute, Cost of, 390
Costing Returns Forms etc., 389, 620, 873
Provision of Radiotherapeutic Departments for Cancer, 392
Instrument Equipment for Aircraft, 139
Lighthouse Fund Accounts, 22, 249, 478, 713, 953
Post Office. *See* Post Office.
Practitioners, Remuneration of, Maternity Services, Scotland, 429
Principles of Wartime Building, 1056
Purpose Fire Tender, 881
Register Office and its Origins, 417
Service Medal with Clasp, " Palestine ", 930
Stores, Specifications, 452
Waste Materials Reclamation Trade, Wages, 405, 890, 1046
Generating Stations, etc., Fire Risks at, 683
Generation of Electricity, 212, 440, 683, 927
Generators, Electrical, Specification, 366
See also Motor Generators.
Geneva Convention Act, 296
Bill, 18, 43, 252, 262
Geodetic Tables for the Clarke 1880 Figure, 225
Geographical :
Distribution :
of British Empire Shipping, 126, 586
of the Industrial Population, Royal Commission, Minutes of Evidence, 422, 663, 908
Globes, Merchandise Marks. *Cmd. 6086*, 747
Geological :
Column, Guide to, 660
Survey and Museum Publications (N.P.), 194, 421, 660, 906, 1058
Geology, Examinations, Science Scholarships, 384, 614, 866
Geophysical Memoirs, 181, 408, 645, 896
Geophysics, Applied, 187
George V :
Death of, etc., 180, 197
Memorial Fund, Contribution to. *Cmd. 6041*, 744
George VI :
Appointment of Commission delegated to act in the absence of, 893
Birthday Honours, 407, 644, 893
Message to the Army, 934
Proclamation of Accession, 180, 188, 197
Proclamation, Facsimile, 205
Speech to Parliament, 246, 474, 709
See also Coronation ; Regency.
George, T. N., South Wales, Geological Survey, 421
Georgette, s.t., s.t. and *Pretoria*, collision, 210
Geostrophic Wind, Surface Wind, and Upper Winds, Comparison, 646
German :
Aggression on Norway, English Translation of White Paper issued by Norwegian Government, 1039
and Austrian Civilian Internees, Categories of Persons eligible for Release. *Cmd. 6217*, 968
Assistants in Scottish Schools and Training Centres, 430, 668, 913
Citizens, Removal of, from the Japanese ship *Asama Maru*, Correspondence between Japan and U.K. *Cmd. 6166*, 965
Interpretership, Examinations, 376
Military Terms and Abbreviations, Vocabulary of, 930
Schools and Colleges, Scottish Assistants in, 203, 668, 913
Germany :
Air Transport Services to. *Cmd. 5524*, 286
Application of Treaties between Germany, Austria and U.K., Exchange of Notes. *Cmd. 5888*, 519
Commercial Relations with Canada. *Cmds. 5231, 5232*, 56
Concrete Road Construction on the Reichsautobahnen, 926
Correspondence with U.K. *Cmd. 6102*, 748
Documents concerning German Polish Relations and Outbreak of Hostilities between Great Britain and Germany. *Cmd. 6106*, 748
Economic Conditions, 211
Efficiency Certificates for Aircraft and Aircraft Motors, Agreement with South Africa. *Cmd. 5705*, 506
Entry into European Commission of the Danube, and Accession of Germany and Italy to Sinaia Arrangement of Aug. 18, 1938. *Cmd. 6068*, 746

INDEX 1936–40 —GLA

Germany (*continued*) :
European Settlement Proposals. *Cmd. 5175*, 51
Extension to Sudetenland of the Anglo-German Transfer Agreement of July 1, 1938, and Supplementary Agreement of Aug. 13, 1938. *Cmd. 6047*, 744
Final Report on the circumstances leading to the termination of Sir N. Henderson's Mission to Berlin. *Cmd. 6115*, 749
Fleet, particulars of :
Cmd. 5371, 275
Cmd. 5666, 503
Cmd. 5936, 737
Frontiers between Czechoslovakia and. *Cmd. 5908*, 521
German Nationals in, Treatment of. *Cmd. 6210*, 749
Imported Food Certificates, 620
Limitation of Naval Armament, etc., Agreement with U.K. *Cmd. 5519*, 286
Memo. by German Government respecting Franco-Soviet Treaty, Treaty of Locarno, and Demilitarised Zone in the Rhineland. *Cmd. 5118*, 47
North, Agreement for Air Services to. *Cmd. 5338*, 64
Notification that state of War exists between His Majesty and Germany, 893
Payments for the Exchange of Goods, Agreement with Canada. *Cmd. 5580*, 290
Physical Education in, 384
Proposals drawn up by Representatives of Belgium, France, U.K., and Italy. *Cmd. 5134*, 48
Correspondence with Belgian and French Ambassadors. *Cmd. 5149*, 49
Refugees from, Status of :
Cmd. 5338, 64
Cmd. 5780, 511
Cmd. 5929, 736
Cmd. 6222, 969
Suez Maritime Canal, Free Navigation of, International Convention. *Cmd. 5623*, 500
Taxation of certain Profits arising from Air Transport, Agreement with U.K. *Cmd. 5652*, 502
War Graves Agreement. *Cmd. 5068*, 44
See also Naval Armament ; Payments Agreements ; Trade Agreements ; Transfer Agreement.
Gibb, M. S., Chairman, Departmental Committee on Examination of Engineers in Mercantile Marine, Report, 673
Gibbons, S. G., Calanus finmarchicus and Copepods in Scottish Waters in 1933, 427
Gibraltar :
Colonial Reports, 151, 378, 609, 861
Meteorological Reports, 410, 647
Gilbert and Ellice Islands :
Colonial Reports, 378, 609, 861
Flag Badge, 611
Gilding-metal coated steel cups. *See* Import Duties Advisory Committee.
Gillingham, Sunday Entertainments, 257
Gilmour, H., Production of Active Carbon from Bituminous Coal, 660
Gilmour, Sir J., Chairman :
Committee on Scottish Administration, Report. *Cmd. 5563*, 289
Select Committee on Official Secrets Acts, Report, 488
Girls :
in Greater London, Employment for, 641
Secondary School, Careers, 404
Unemployed, Instruction for, 177
See also Unemployed Boys and Girls.
Gjers, Mills and Co., Ltd., Explosion, 672
Glanrhyd, s.s., Wreck Report, 675
Glanville, S. R. K., Demotic Papyri in the British Museum, 941
Glanville, W. H. :
Aggregates and Workability of Concrete, 661
Creep or Flow of Concrete under Load, 1056
Moment Redistribution in Reinforced Concrete, 904
Stresses in Reinforced Concrete Piles during Driving, 658
Glasgow :
Boundaries Order Confirmation Act, 525
Bill, 247, 272
City of, Royal Technical College Scheme, 198
Corporation Order Confirmation Acts, 68, 299, 756
Bills, 9, 240, 268, 475, 499
Educational Trust Scheme, 199, 426
Port Labour in, Board of Inquiry Report, 404
Street, Sewers and Buildings Consolidation Order Confirmation Act, 299
Bill, 242, 268
Supply of Milk at reduced rates for Children, 204
Water and Tramways Order Confirmation Act, 972
Bill, 945
See also Royal Samaritan Hospital.

GLA— INDEX 1936–40

Glass :
Protection, Factories, Circular, 1042
Stained, 234
Vitreous Enamelling of, Factory Form, 630
See also Safety Glass ; Bullet Proof Safety Glass.
Globes. *See* Geographical Globes ; Hurricane Lamps.
Gloucester :
Cheltenham and, Joint Water Board Act, 72
Pier and Harbour Order Confirmation Act, 69
Bill, 13, 39
Gloucestershire : Census, 190
See also West Gloucestershire.
Glover, J. A., Committee of Inquiry into Problems relating to Children with Defective Hearing, Report, 614
Glover, R. E., Tuberculin Tests in Cattle, 904
Gloves, Specifications, 931, 933
Anti-Gas, Specifications, 1069
Glues, Synthetic Resin, Specification, 600
Glycol. *See* Ethylene Glycol.
Godalming, Sunday Entertainments, 952
Godbert, A. L., Analysis of Mine Dusts, 651
Goggle Glass, Specification, 1028
Goitre, Endemic, Relation of Iodine Contents of Water, Milk, and Pasture, 192
Gold Alloys. *See* Metal Alloys.
Gold Coast :
Colonial Reports, 151, 378, 609, 861
Economic Conditions, 439
Goldie, A. H. R. :
Depressions as Vortices, 896
Kinematical Features of Depressions, 408
Gombe, Course for Training of Visiting Teachers, Report, 1031
Gooch, G. P., British Documents on the Origin of the War, 158, 616
Good Conduct Pay, Army, Grant of, 1070
Goods :
Export :
Guarantee Agreements :
Greece. *Cmd. 6072*, 746
Poland. *Cmd. 6093*, 747
Prohibition, List of, 918
Prices of, Act, 755
Bill, 709, 734
Vehicles :
Licensing Statistics, 213
Road Transport :
for a Defence Emergency, 925
Industry, Committee on Regulation of Wages, 176
Goods (*continued*) :
See also Manufactured Goods, Merchandise Marks ; Household Goods ; Made-up Goods ; Piece Goods ; Supplies, Limitation of.
Goodwick. *See* Fishguard.
Gooseberries, 1023
Gooseberry :
Mildew, American, 135
Sawfly, 134
Gorell, Lord, Chairman, Committee on Control of Flying, Report. *Cmd. 5961*, 738
Gosforth District, Geological Survey, 421
Gosport :
Corporation Act, 757
Water Act, 300
Gothic, m.v., Wreck Report, 675
Gothic Star, s.s., Explosion, 672
Gough, C. M., The Use of Asphalt Mastic for Roofing, 419
Government :
and Other Stocks (Emergency Provisions) Act, 755
Bill, 733
Chemist, Annual Reports, 160, 388, 870, 618
Contractors, Air Raid Precautions for, 851
Control of Railways :
Estimates of Net Revenue. *Cmd. 6216*, 968
Financial Arrangements. *Cmd. 6168*, 965
Department Specifications. *See* Specifications.
Departments :
Civil Staffs employed :
Cmd. 5543, 287
Cmd. 5815, 514
Ex-Service Men employed :
Cmd. 5536, 287
Cmd. 5816, 514
Temporary Clerical and Typing Staffs employed :
Cmd. 5626, 294
Cmd. 5909, 521
Trading and Commercial Services, Accounts, 22, 250, 478, 713, 949
See also Civil Service ; Crown Service ; Public Departments.
Emergency Type Gas Producer, Notes on, 1053
Evacuation Scheme :
Department of Health for Scotland Publications (N.P.), 911, 1060
Educational Provision, 913
Ministry of Health Publications (N.P.), 872, 1034

INDEX 1936–40 —GRA

Government (*continued*) :
Insurance and Annuities, Accounts, 26, 256, 483, 717, 957
Laboratory, Annual Reports, 160, 388, 618, 870
of Burma :
Act, 1935, 65
as amended, 972
Amendments to be made by the India and Burma (Miscellaneous Amendments) Bill. *Cmd. 5990*, 740
Commencement and Transitory Provisions, Memo. *Cmd. 5181*, 52
Delimitation of Constituencies. *Cmd. 5101*, 46
House of Representatives, Explanatory Memo. *Cmd. 5133*, 48
Instrument of Instructions, Draft, 35
Senate Elections, Explanatory Memo. *Cmd. 5133*, 48
See also Burma.
of India :
Act, 1935, 65
as amended, 972
Amendments to be made by the India and Burma (Miscellaneous Amendments) Bill. *Cmd. 5990*, 740
Index to, 1038
Proclamation of Emergency under, 951
Act (Amendment) Act, 754
Commencement and Transitory Provisions, Memo. *Cmd. 5181*, 52
Delimitation of Constituencies, etc. :
Vol. I : Report. *Cmd. 5099*, 46
Vol. II : Proposals. *Cmd. 5100*, 46
Vol. III. Evidence, 172
Distribution of Revenue, Memo. *Cmd. 5181*, 52
Excluded and partially excluded areas, Recommendations of Provincial Governments. *Cmd. 5064*, 44
Financial Enquiry, Report by Sir Otto Niemeyer. *Cmd. 5163*, 50
Views of Provincial Governments, etc. *Cmd. 5064*, 44
Instrument of Instructions, Draft, 35
Provincial Legislative Assemblies and Provincial Legislative Councils, Memo. *Cmd. 5133*, 48
(Reprinting) Act, 65
Scheduled Castes, Explanatory Memo. *Cmd. 5133*, 48
Publications, 433, 671, 916, 1062
Government (*continued*) :
Governors of Dominions. *See* Dominions.
Gowers, E. A., Chairman, Coal Commission, Reports, 958
Gradient Wind and Blueness of the Sky, Relation between, 646
Grading of Aggregates and Workability of Concrete, 662
Graf Spee. *See Admiral Graf Spee.*
Graham, J. & W., Linwood Toll, Elderslie, Industrial Court Awards, 888
Graham, M., Phytoplankton and the Herring, 595
Grain :
Cargoes, Memo., 208
Crops, Production and Trade, 171, 398, 634, 883
Infestation :
by Insects, 1048
Survey Committee, 907
Prices of, Scotland, 196
Grammar Schools, Report, 615
Grampian Electricity Supply Order Confirmation Act, 68
Bill, 11, 38
Grangemouth Burgh Extension Order Confirmation Act, 299
Bill, 241, 268
Granite, Import Duties. *Cmd. 5276*, 59
Granites of Scotland, 907
Grant Trust Scheme, 199, 426
Grant-Earning Day Schools and Institutions, Statistical List of, 669
Grants :
Calculations in third fixed grant period, Local Government (Scotland), 204
Midwifery Training, 1035
to Research Workers and Students, 194, 422, 661, 907, 1058
See also Mess Grants ; University Grants.
Grapes :
Merchandise Marks Report. *Cmd. 5147*, 49
Production and Trade, 171, 398, 633
Graphited Grease, Specification, 855
Grass :
Drying, 418, 904
Land :
Improvement of, 593
Poor, Ploughing and Re-seeding, 909
Thistles in, 362
Weeds of, 593
Grasses, Weed Seeds in, 363
Grates. *See* Domestic Grates.
Gratuities :
Hotels and Restaurants, Bill, 42
See also Air Force ; Air Force Reserve ; Naval Reserves.

GRA— INDEX 1936-40

Graves:
Agreement, War Graves. Cmd. 5068, 44
British War Memorial, in Egypt, Agreement between Egypt and Canada, Australia, New Zealand, South Africa, India, and U.K. Cmd. 5618, 293
See also Cemeteries; Imperial War Graves.
Gravesend and Milton Waterworks Act, 69
Grazing Rights and Transit Traffic in British Somaliland. Cmd. 5775, 511
Grazings. See Hill Grazings.
Grease. See Anti-Freezing Grease; Graphited Grease; High Melting Point Grease.
Great:
Barrier Reef Expedition, Scientific Reports, 942
Orme Tramways Act, 68
War: History of, 398, 633, 883
See also War; British Documents.
Western Railway:
Act, 299
(Additional Powers) Act, 71
(Ealing and Shepherds Bush Railway Extension) Act, 70
Industrial Court Awards, 640
Yarmouth, Sunday Entertainments, 956
Great Admiral, s.t., Explosion, 672
Greater London. See London.
Greece:
Air Transport Services, Conventions with U.K.:
Cmd. 6097, 748
Cmd. 6207, 968
Commercial Relations, Exchange of Notes with Australia. Cmd. 6243, 970
Economic Conditions, 439, 676
Guarantee Agreement with U.K. Cmd. 6072, 746
Legal Proceedings Conventions:
Cmd. 5146, 49
Cmd. 5643, 501
Payments due to British Subjects in respect of Expropriation of Landed Properties. Cmd. 5260, 58
Reciprocal Exemption from Income Tax on certain profits or gains from an agency. Cmd. 5318, 62
Greek Loan Accounts, 21, 27, 249, 256, 478, 484, 712, 718, 958, 965
Green Belt (London and Home Counties) Act, 527
Green, T. A., Radium Beam Therapy Research, 657

Greenock Burgh Extension, etc., Order Confirmation Act, 298
Bill, 236
Greenwich:
Hospital and Travers Foundation; Accounts, 26, 256, 483, 717, 957
Estimated Income and Expenditure, 28, 258, 485, 719, 958
Observatory, Publications (N.P.), 653, 901, 1054
Grenada, Colonial Reports, 378, 609, 1031
Grenade, Small Arms Training, 456
Gresford Colliery, Explosion. Cmd. 5358, 274
Grey Squirrels, 362, 848
Grime, G., Stresses in Reinforced Concrete Piles during Driving, 658
Grimes Graves, Weeting, Norfolk, Guide, 231
Grimethorpe. See Hemsworth.
Grimmett, L. G., Radium Beam Therapy Research, 657
Grimsby Corporation:
(Grimsby, Cleethorpes and District Water, etc.) Act, 299
(Trolley Vehicles). See Trolley Vehicles.
Grinding of Metals, Factory Forms, 1042
Grindley, J.:
Chemical Methods for the Study of River Pollution, 1023
Effects of Milk Wastes on the Bristol Avon, 594
Ground:
Engineers. See Engineers, Ground.
Game. See Deer and Ground Game.
Nuts, Production and Trade, 172, 634, 883
See also Import Duties Advisory Committee.
Growmore Bulletins, 849, 1023
Growth and Structure of Wood, 420
Guarantees. See Export Guarantees;
Coal Act; Overseas Trade Guarantees;
Trade Facilities Acts.
Guatemala:
Commercial Relations with Canada. Cmd. 5820, 514
Economic Conditions, 439
Trade Agreement with Canada. Cmd. 6240, 970
Guernsey:
Gift of 3½ per cent. War Stock. Cmd. 6084, 747
Securities, Restrictions, and Returns, 893
Guiana. See British Guiana.
Guildford:
Cathedral Measure, 464, 528

INDEX 1936-40

Guildford (continued):
Corporation Act, 527
Provisional Order Confirmation Act, 301
Bill, 240, 269
Gulf of Aden and Red Sea, Exchange of Water between, 942
Gum:
Chewing, Base. See Import Duties Advisory Committee.
Kauri. See New Zealand.
Gun:
Drills, Handbooks, etc., Army, 227, 453, 688
Mountings, Shock Absorber Cord Rings for, Specification, 1025
Gunnery, Anti-Aircraft, 448, 689
Guns, Machine, care of, etc., 230
Gurjun, Forest Products Research Records, 420
Gymnasia, Schools and Educational Institutions, Planning, 157, 867
Gymnasium:
Trousers, Specification, 932
Vest, Specification, 931, 1068
Gymnosperms. See Coniferae.
Gypsum and Anhydrite, 661
Gyro, Directional, Specification, 140

H

Hacksaw Blades, Specifications, 226, 686
Haddock:
in Scottish Waters, Food and Feeding Habits, 428
Stocks of, North-East Atlantic, 427
Hague, The, Colonial Report, 377
Haile Selassie, Emperor of Ethiopia (Property) Bill, 496
Hailey, Lord, Chairman, Lord Privy Seal's Conference on Air Raid Shelters, Report. Cmd. 6006, 742
Hailsham Water Provisional Order Confirmation Act, 758
Bill, 703, 729
Haines, B. B.:
Curing of Bacon, 1057
Microbiology in the Preservation of the Hen's Egg, 905
Hair:
Combs. See Combs.
Curled, Specifications, 226, 687
Mattresses, Specifications, 932, 1069
Nets. See Nets.
Hair, Bass and Fibre Trade, Wages, 890, 1046
Haircutting, Army, Allowance, 1067
Hairdressers (Registration) Bill, 41, 244, 463, 728
Haldane's Trust Scheme, 198

—HAR

Hales, J. S., Use of Coke in Open Domestic Grates, 421
Half-Standard Apple Trees, 1023
Halibut Fishery of Northern Pacific Ocean and Bering Sea, Preservation of, Convention, U.S.A. and Canada. Cmd. 5850, 516
Halifax Provisional Order Confirmation Acts, 301, 525
Bills, 243, 268, 271, 463
Hall, J. A., International Temperature Scale, etc., 661
Halliday Oil-Fired Boiler and Sterilising Chest, 592
Hall-Marking. See Foreign Plate.
Halnan, E. T., The Scientific Principles of Poultry Feeding, 360
Ham and Bacon preserved in Airtight Containers. See Import Duties Advisory Committee.
Hamilton Burgh Order Confirmation Acts, 524, 760
Bills, 247, 272, 708, 732
Hammers, Specifications, 226, 686, 931
Hammond, J., Fertility and Animal Breeding, 360
Hamond, J. B., Nuts, 361
Hampshire Basin, Geological Survey, 194
Hampton Court Palace, Photographs of, 663
Hams, Production and Trade, 171, 398, 634
Hand and Machine Milking, 595
Handkerchief Trade, Wages, 405, 890, 1047
Handkerchiefs. See Import Duties Advisory Committee.
Handles for Brooms, Brushes, Mops, etc., Specifications, 1063
Handwriting:
for various Examinations held by Civil Service Commissioners, 377
of Adequate Proficiency, Civil Service, 150
Hanley, F., The Soils of Cambridge-shire, 361
Hanley, J. A., Improvement of Grass Land, 593
Hansard. See Parliamentary Publications (Debates).
Hanwell. See Poor's Allotment.
Hanwood Coalfield, 661
Harbour:
Defence Equipment, transfer to Eire. Cmd. 5809, 513
Dues, Isle of Man, Accounts, 221, 447, 683, 927, 1065
Harbours:
Demand for Timber in, 617
Development Commissioners' Report, 248

HAR— INDEX 1936-40

Harbours (continued):
Workmen's Compensation Forms, 170, 397, 632
Harbours, Piers and Ferries (Scotland) Act, 296
Bill, 239, 255, 262, 265, 266
Circular, 432
Harness:
Makers, Army, Handbook, 1071
Safety, Specification, 140, 366
Harris, P., Circular Saws, 659
Harris, T. M., British Purbeck Charophyta, 941
Harrison, L. W., Anti-Venereal Measures, 622
Harrison, Sir E. R., Digest and Index of Official Reports of Tax Cases, 400
Harrogate, Sunday Entertainments, 953
Harrowden. See Barony of Vaux.
Hartlepool. See West Hartlepool.
Hartley, G. W., Salmon caught in the Sea:
Island of Soay and Ardnamurchan, 910
North-West Sutherland, 1936, 427
West Sutherland, 665
Hartley, Sir H., Chairman, Emergency Conversion of Motor Vehicles to Producer Gas, Committee on, Report, 1053
Harwich Harbour Act, 526
Haslemere, Sunday Entertainments, 250
Hastings:
Corporation (General Powers) Act, 300
Extension Act, 300
Pier Act, 300
Provisional Order Confirmation Act, 757
Bill, 698, 727
Sunday Entertainments, 955
Hat, Cap, and Millinery Trade Wages, 405, 890, 1047
Hats. See Import Duties Advisory Committee.
Haughton, J. L., Magnesium and its Alloys, 422
Haulage. See Road Haulage.
Haulage, Drawgear, Colliery, Metallurgical Examination of, 413
Hayti:
Commercial Agreement with Canada. Cmd. 5445, 280
Economic Conditions, 211, 676
Trade Agreement with Canada. Cmd. 6095, 748
Headen Keil Anti-Dilution Cylinder-Head Gasket, 592
Headlights. See Motor Car Headlights.
Heads of Public Departments. See Public Departments.

Health:
Bills of, Reciprocal Abolition of Consular Visas on, Exchange of Notes:
France and U.K. Cmd. 6187, 966
India and French Indo-China. Cmd. 5920, 735
Board of (Welsh) Publications (N.P.), 876, 1035
Civil Estimates, 25, 253, 481, 715, 954
Conditions in Air Raid Shelters, Lord Horder's Committee Recommendations. Cmd. 6234, 970
Department of Health for Scotland:
Annual Reports:
Cmd. 5123, 48
Cmd. 5407, 278
Cmd. 5713, 506
Cmd. 5969, 739
Publications (N.P.), 201, 428, 666, 911, 1060
Education, Suggestions on, 1033
Food and, 620
Ministry of:
Annual Reports:
Cmd. 5287, 60
Cmd. 5516, 285
Cmd. 5801, 513
Cmd. 6089, 747
Publications (N.P.), 160, 388, 618, 870, 1034
of London Central Busmen, Report, 889
of the Army, 228, 453, 688, 933
of the Navy, 126, 353, 841
of the Royal Air Force, 139, 699, 852
of the School Child, 156, 385, 615, 1033
Resorts and Watering Places Act, 66
Bill, 16, 17, 40, 41
Services:
in Receiving Areas, Government Evacuation Scheme, 911
London, extract from Annual Report of Ministry of Health, 164
Bill:
Cmd. 5204, 54
Committee on, Summary of Report, 429
Visitors:
Refresher Courses for, 429, 666, 912
Training, 619
See also Industrial Health; National Health; Public Health; School Health.
Hearing:
and Speech in Deaf Children, 419
Physiology of, 191, 418
See also Defective Hearing.
Heart:
and Great Vessels, Disease of, Course of the Oesophagus, 191
Disease, Cardiac Enlargement, 419

INDEX 1936-40

Heat Transmission, Calculation of, 1058
Heathfield and District Water Provisional Order Confirmation Act, 71
Bill, 39
Heating:
and Ventilation, Warmth Factor in Comfort at Work, 191
for Wartime Factories, 1056
Heavy:
Cotton Tapes, Specification, 855
Power Presses, Fencing of, Report of Committee, 880
Hedge and Tree Stump Clearings, 133
Height:
and Range Finder, Anti-Aircraft, 221
Computer for use in Aerological Work, 646
Heliographic, Photo, Results, 188
Helston and Porthleven Water Provisional Order Confirmation Act, 71
Bill, 16, 39
Hemel Hempstead:
Provisional Order Confirmation Act, 759
Bill, 704, 730
Sunday Entertainments, 956
Hemp:
Production, Trade and Consumption, 171, 398, 634, 883
Spinning and Weaving, Factory Form, 630
Trade, Wages, 176, 404, 890, 1045
Henderson, Sir N., Final Report on the circumstances leading to termination of his Mission to Berlin. Cmd. 6115, 749
Henderson, Sir V., Chairman, Committee on use of Celluloid in the manufacture of Toys, Fancy Goods, etc., Report. Cmd. 5790, 512
Hendre Hall Farm, St. Mellons, Boiler Explosion, 206
Henry III:
Close Rolls, etc., 189, 416, 655
Curia Regis Rolls, 655
Liberate Rolls, 416
Henry IV, Close Rolls, 655
Henry V:
Close Rolls, 655
Fine Rolls, 189, 416, 903, 1054
Henry, Sir E. R., Classification and uses of Finger Prints, 631
Hen's Egg, Microbiology in Preservation, 905
Herbs, 133
Hereford Corporation Act, 71
Herefordshire, Census, 190
Herring:
Food of, North Sea, 361
Fund Advances Account, 250, 476, 492, 950

—HIG

Herring (continued):
Industry:
Act, 523
Bill, 470, 495, 496
Board, 264, 432, 510
Provision for electing Members of, by persons engaged in the Herring Industry, Report, 670
Hertfordshire:
County Council (Colne Valley Sewerage, etc.) Act, 301
North, Joint Hospital District Provisional Order Confirmation Act, 71
Bill, 14, 40
Hertslet's Commercial Treaties, 158, 386, 616, 1033
Heston:
and Isleworth, Sunday Entertainments, 259
and Kenley Aerodromes Extension, Air Ministry, 254
Bill, 706, 707, 720, 721, 729
Hetherington, Sir H., Chairman, Royal Commission on Workmen's Compensation, Minutes of Evidence, 909, 1058, 1059
Heysham. See Morecambe.
Heywood and Middleton Water Board Provisional Order Confirmation Act, 758
Bill, 704, 730
Heywood, G. S. P., Lapse Rate of Temperature in the Lowest Hundred Metres of the Atmosphere, 896
Hickling, C. F., English Plaice-Marking Experiments, 594
Hides:
and Leather, Specifications, 686, 931
and Skins, Factory Form, 631
Hieroglyphic Texts from Egyptian Stelae, 941
High:
Chromium Non-corrodible Steel:
Streamline Wires, Specifications, 600
The Road, Specification, 600
Court: Appeals, National Defence Contribution, 1039
See also Supreme Court.
Explosive:
Bombs, Protection against, Training, 877
Instructional Diagrams, 878
Melting Point Grease, Specification, 1027
Tensile Cold Headed Steel Bolts, Specification, 1027
Velocity Stream, an Orifice Method of Producing, 1027

Higher:
Education:
in East Africa, Report of Commission, 380
in Malaya, Report of Commission, 863
School Certificate Examination, Report, 867
Highland Orphanage Trust Scheme, 199, 426
Highlands:
and Islands Educational Trust Scheme, 199, 426
Northern, Scotland, Geology, 194
See also Western Islands.
High-speed Cameras for measuring Rate of Detonation in Solid Explosives, 413
Highway:
Authorities, Road and Bridge Works, Standard Forms, Conditions of Tender and Contract, 218
Development Survey, Greater London, Report, 677
Highways:
Experimental Work on. See Experimental Work.
Protection Bill, 721, 726, 727, 732
Hill, A. B.:
Investigation into the Sickness Experience of London Transport Workers, 418
Nasopharyngeal Bacterial Flora of Different Groups of Persons, 875
Hill Grazings in Scotland, Stock Carrying Capacity of, 909
Hindley, Sir C., Chairman, Interdepartmental Committee on Cabs and Private Hire Vehicles, Interim Report. Cmd. 5938, 737
Hinton, C. L., Fruit Pectins, 905
Hire-Purchase Act, 523
Bill, 271, 467, 472, 482, 490, 493, 497
H. M. Forces:
Personnel in Egypt, Immunities and Privileges. Cmd. 5360, 274
Voluntary Organisations and Funds for assisting Ex-Service Men and Women, Guide to, 415
See also reference from Forces.
Historic Buildings. See Ancient Monuments.
Historical Manuscripts, Royal Commission on, Publications (N.P.), 189, 416, 654, 903
History of Parliament, Committee on, Publications (N.P.), 165, 624
Hitler: How Hitler made the War, 884
Hoare, A. H.:
Manuring of Vegetable Crops, 593
Nuts, 361
Hodder, s.t., Wreck Report, 920

Hodge, R. E., Kiln-drying Schedules, 659
Hodson, W. E. H., Narcissus Pests, 848
Hoisting Machines, Factory Form, 630
Hoists, Factory Forms, 629
Holditch Colliery, Explosion. Cmd. 5720, 507
Holiday Courses on the Continent for instruction in Modern Languages, etc., 157, 385, 615, 867
See also Vacation Courses.
Holidays:
and Suspensions in relation to Unemployment Insurance, Report, 643
Factory Forms, 627
Royal Proclamation declaring Coronation Day, May 12, 1937, to be a Bank Holiday and a Public Holiday, 407
with Pay:
Act, 524
Bill, 473, 497
Collective Agreements between Organisations of Employers and Workpeople, 888
Committee on:
Minutes of Evidence, 402, 640
Report. Cmd. 5724, 507
Trade Board Orders, 889, 1046
Holland:
Agreement for Air Services to. Cmd. 5203, 53
Anti-Venereal Measures in, 622
Hollingworth, S. E.:
Gosforth District, Memoir, Geological Survey, 421
Mineral Resources of Great Britain, 661
Hollow-ware Trade, Wages, 405, 890, 1045
Home:
and Empire Settlement Bill, 42
as an Air Raid Shelter, 1038
Department, Civil Estimates, 25, 253, 481, 715, 954
Office:
Examinations, 149, 606, 858
Publications (N.P.), 165, 393, 624, 876, 1035
Schools, Directory of, 396, 532, 881
Protection of your, against Air Raids, 626
Security, Ministry of, Publications (N.P.), 882, 1037
Storage of Apples and Pears, 362
Teaching, Sub-Committee on (Welfare of the Blind), Report, 393
Trade, Limitation of:
Consumer Goods:
Explanatory Memo., 1063
Persons entered in the Home Trade Register, 1064

Home (continued):
Trade, Limitation of (continued):
Textiles:
Explanatory Memo., 1063
List of Wholesale Dealers and Producersof Made-upGoods for Export, 1063
Home-grown:
Feeding Stuffs, 848
Timbers, 420, 906
Home-produced Foods, Cooking of, 813
Homes. See Children's Homes; Maternity Homes; Remand Homes; Working Class Homes; Nursing Homes; Probation Homes; Approved Homes.
Homework, 384
Honduras. See British Honduras.
Honey, Marketing of, 361
Honeycomb Type Radiators, Copper or Copper Alloy Tubes for, Specification, 1029
Hong Kong:
Civil Air Transport Service to and from Penang. Cmd. 5396, 277
Colonial Reports, 151, 609, 861
Imported Food Certificates, 389
Scotland, 428
Mui Tsai in, 48, 381
Honours:
and Dignities, Committee on:
Interim Report. Cmd. 5450, 280
Report. Cmd. 5767, 510
Lists, 180, 407, 644, 893, 1050
See also Crown Office Fees.
Hood, Anti-Gas, Specification, 933
Hood, s.t., Wreck Report, 675
Hoods, Wool, Felt. See Import Duties Advisory Committee.
Hook and Eye and Snap Fastener Trades Wages, 405, 891, 1047
Hooks, Factory Form, 630
Hop Pickers, Model Byelaws, 621
Hope Mortification Scheme, 198
Hops:
Marketing Scheme as amended, 849
Reorganisation Commission for England, Report, 594
Horder, Lord, Conditions in Air Raid Shelters, Recommendations. Cmd. 6234, Cmd. 6245, 970
Horizons, Artificial, Specification, 970
Horizontal Milling Machines, Regs., 395
Hornchurch Urban District Council Act, 72
Hornsea Provisional Order Confirmation Act, 301
Horse, Clothes, Specification, 686
Horsemanship, Equitation, and Animal Transport, 688

Horses:
Docking and Nicking of (Prohibition), Bill, 247, 461, 462, 494
Exportation of, Act, 296
Bill, 37, 241, 258, 265, 268
Management of Young, 595
Horsforth Provisional Order Confirmation Act, 527
Bill, 471, 496
Horticulture:
Careers, 174, 887
Commercial, 850
Hospital:
Boards. See Joint Hospital Boards.
Committees. See Isolation Hospital Committees.
Nursing, Conditions of Service, 872
Wales, 876
Hospitals:
Board of Control Publications (N.P.), 153, 381, 611, 863
Circulars, 666
Department of Health for Scotland Publications (N.P.), 911
Departmental Committee on Cost of, Final Report, 620
Circular, 619
included in the Emergency Scheme, Records to be kept by, 1060
Ministry of Health Publications (N.P.), 160, 388, 619, 872
See also Voluntary Hospitals; Local Authorities (Hours of Employment); Midwives; Military Hospitals.
Hostels. See Probation Homes.
Hostilities, Premises damaged by, Committee on the Responsibility for the Repair of, Report. Cmd. 5934, 736
Hotels and Restaurants (Gratuities) Bill, 42
Hotplates, SteamTube, FactoryForm, 879
Hot-water:
Bottles. See Bottles.
Treatment of Narcissus Bulbs, Efficiency of Baths, 361
Hours of:
Employment:
(Conventions) Act, 65
Bill, 37
Factory Forms, 627
of Young Persons, Report. Cmd. 5394, 276
Poll. See Local Government (Hours of Poll).
Work, International Labour Conference, League of Nations. Cmd. 5113, 47
House:
Agents. See Auctioneers.
Closing Order, Scotland, 201
Construction, 1056

House (continued):
Experimental, Dry Rot Investigations in, 420
Fly as a Danger to Health, 942
of Commons:
Members Fund Act, 753
Bill, 707, 731, 732
(Service in His Majesty's Forces) Act, 754
Bill, 733
See also Parliament; Parliamentary Publications.
of Laity:
(Co-opted Members) Measure, 238, 302
Report of Ecclesiastical Committee, 239
(Postponement of Election) Measure, 709, 760
of Lords. See Parliament; Parliamentary Publications.
Production, Position, 163, 390, 621, 873
Refuse, Removal of, Model Byelaws, 391
to House Collections Act, 753
Bill (formerly Charitable Collections (Regulation)), 701, 702, 705, 706, 717, 726, 728, 732
Household Goods, etc., Trade, Wages, 405, 890, 1047
Houses:
Cathedrals (Houses of Residence). See Cathedrals.
CommonLodging, ModelByelaws, 621
Experiments in Anti-Gas Protection of, 624
Scotland, 670
Mental Defectives, 153
owned by Local Authorities, Rents of:
Cmd. 5527, 286
Cmd. 5913, 735
Shelter in, Choice and Adaptation of, 1038
Valuation of Agricultural Dwelling-Houses Bill, 36
We Live in, 873
See also Unfit Houses.
Housing:
About Housing, 873
Act:
1914, Accounts and Expenditure under, 260, 487, 721
1935, Circulars, 161
Scotland, 201
1936, 66
Bill, 7, 8, 16, 41
Comparison with earlier Acts, 163
Acts:
Interest on Loans, 1034
Postponement of Work, 872

Housing (continued):
(Agricultural Population) (Scotland) Act, 523
Bill, 264, 265, 271, 272, 465, 496
Circular, 666
Associations: Ministry of Health Publications (N.P.), 870, 872
Central Housing Advisory Committee, Rural Housing Sub-Committee Report, 160
Community Life in New Housing Schemes, Scotland, 201
(Emergency Powers) Act, 754
Estates. See Municipal Housing Estates.
Extracts from Annual Reports of Ministry of Health, 390
Finance and Letting (Scotland), 201
(Financial Provisions):
Act, 522
Bill, 464, 493
Circulars and Memoranda, 619, 621
(Scotland) Act, 752
Bill, 475, 492, 498, 499, 711
Circular, 912
Memo., 912
Loans, Rate of Interest, Circulars, 388, 871
Measurement of Rooms (Scotland), 201
of Young Married Couples, 912
Organisation of Schemes, 666
Overcrowding:
Operation of Provisions of 1935 Act, Circular, 388
Reports, Scotland, Circular, 428
Scotland. Cmd. 5171, 51
Planning and Priority in Local Authority Building Programmes, Scotland, 432
Rent Rebates, Scotland, Circular, 428
Repair of War Damage, Circular, 872
(Rural Cottages Protection) Bill
(Rural Workers):
Act, 1937, 295
Acts, Circulars, 162
Amendment Act, 523
Bill, 468, 494, 495, 496
Circular, 619
Scotland, 666
Societies, Annual Return Forms, 387, 617, 870, 1034
See also Flats; Rural Housing; Town and Country Planning; Rehousing; Scottish Housing; Central Housing Advisory Committee.
Housing, House Property, Slum Clearance, Position, 163, 390, 621, 873
Hove. See Brighton.
Howden Trust Scheme, 198, 200

Howes, H., Ducks and Geese, 360
Hubert, W. H. de B., Psychological Treatment of Crime, 881
Huddersfield:
Corporation:
Act, 300
Trolley Vehicles:
Act, 69
Order Confirmation Act, 973
Bill 962
Ministry of Health Provisional Order Bill, 962
Hudson Bay Marine Insurance Rates, 208, 369, 918
Hudspeth, H. M.:
Coal Measure Rocks, Part I, Classification, Nomenclature, and Relative Strengths, 413
Explosions in Coal Mines, a Comparison between Great Britain and France, Report. Cmd. 5566, 289
Hughes, D. L., Epidemic Influenza, 657
Hull. See Kingston-upon-Hull.
Humidity:
Average for British Isles, 645
Factory Forms, 629
in Atmosphere over Lower Egypt, 409
Humphreys, G. W., Chairman, Construction of Flats for the Working Classes Committee, Final Report, 389
Hungary:
Air Navigation Conventions with U.K.:
Cmd. 5535, 287
Cmd. 5765, 510
Economic Conditions, 211, 676, 921
Extradition Treaties:
Cmd. 5311, 62
Cmd. 5550, 288
Imported Food Certificate, 389
Scotland, 428
Legal Proceedings, Convention. Cmd. 5190, 53
Payments Agreement with U.K., 206
Huntingdonshire, Census, 190
Hurricane Lamps and Globes, Specifications, 931
Hurst, B. L., Air Raid Shelter Policy. Cmd. 5932, 736
Hut Type Buildings, Design of, 1056
Hutchenson's Educational Trust Scheme, 200, 426
Huts. See Small Huts.
Hyde. See Stalybridge.
Hydraulic Mechanisms, Fluid for, Specifications, 1026
Hydrocarbons. See Aromatic Hydrocarbons.
Hydrocyanic Gas, Fumigation with, 595
Hydrogen:
Action of, upon Coal, 193, 660

Hydrogen (continued):
Cyanide:
Fumigation:
of Buildings, Forms, 881
of Ships with, 390
(Fumigation) Act, 296
Bill, 16, 238, 268
Vapour, Detection of, 662
Sulphide, Detection of, 422
Hydrogenation-cracking of Tars, 421, 660, 906
Hydrographic:
Publications (N.P.), 127, 534, 587, 643, 1019
Surveying, Manual of, 843
Hydrography of the Red Sea, 942
Hydrometric Tables, 181, 1052
Hypoglycaemic Shock Treatment in Schizophrenia, 153, 611
Hypothetical Town, Sketch of Emergency Fire Brigade Organisation for, 395

I

Ice:
Accretion on Aircraft, 410
Formation:
in Clouds, 646
on Aircraft, 899
Iceland:
Arbitration Convention of October 25, 1905, with various countries, Renewal of. Cmd. 5448, 280
Economic Conditions, 439
Imported Food Certificate, 162, 389
Scotland, 428
Icing. See De-icing.
Iddesleigh, s.s., stranding, 210
Ilford Corporation Act, 300
IlfracombeUrbanDistrictCouncilAct, 72
Ilkley Provisional Order Confirmation Act, 972
Bill, 734, 946
Illumination:
Electric, Principles etc., 187
Research Board Publications (N.P.), 194, 422
Standard, of Test Types, Certification of Blindness, 161
See also Lighting; Lights.
Imperia, M/Y, Mirabella Bay, Crete, Upper Winds at, 410
Imperial:
Agricultural Bureaux Publications (N.P.), 171, 693, 882, 1038
Airways Ltd. See Civil Air Transport; Empire Air Mail.
Calendar and Civil Service List, 433, 671, 916, 1062
College of Science and Technology, Reports, 157, 385, 615, 867, 1033
Conference, Summary of Proceedings. Cmd. 5482, 283

Imperial (continued):
Continental Gas Association Act, 68
Defence Committee Publications (N.P.), 171, 398, 633, 883
Economic Committee Publications (N.P.), 171, 398, 633, 883, 1038
Institute Publications (N.P.), 172, 399, 634, 694, 883, 943
Services, Civil Estimates, 25, 252, 480, 715, 954
Shipping Committee Publications (N.P.), 208, 436, 918
Standards, Comparisons, 218
Telegraphs Act, 523
Bill, 473, 495
Trade Agreements. See Trade Agreements.
War Graves Commission Publications (N.P.), 172, 399, 634, 883, 1038
War Museum Publications (N.P.), 413, 652, 900
Import:
and Export List, 154, 382, 612
Certificates of Origin and Interest, 820
Duties:
Act, Inquiry Reports, 208, 436, 673, 917
Advisory Committee, Reports etc.:
1936:
Ham and Bacon preserved in Airtight Containers. Cmd. 5633, 500
Additional:
No. 1. Wooden Blocks. Cmd. 5067, 44
No. 2. Stuffing Material. Cmd. 5083, 45
No. 3. Dressed Leather. Cmd. 5108, 47
No. 4. Felt hats and hat shapes. Cmd. 5110, 47
No. 5. Soya Bean cake, meal, oil, sunflower seed oil, and safflower seed oil. Cmd. 5115, 47
No. 6. Locks and padlocks. Cmd. 5116, 47
No. 7. Potatoes. Cmd. 5135, 48
No. 8. Hair combs. Cmd. 5159, 50
No. 9. Sodium bichromate and potassium bichromate. Cmd. 5164, 50
No. 10. Capsules, lead. Cmd. 5170, 51
No. 11. Casseine. Cmd. 5183, 52
No. 12. Starches, various. Cmd. 5211, 54
No. 13. Potatoes. Cmd. 5212, 54

Import Duties Advisory Committee Reports etc. (continued):
1936 (continued):
Additional (continued):
No. 14. Paper yarn fabrics. Cmd. 5215, 54
No. 15. Track-laying tractors. Cmd. 5227, 55
No. 16. Composite Goods. Cmd. 5241, 57
No. 17. Weft pile fabrics. Cmd. 5243, 57
No. 18. Battery-operated portable electric lamps. Cmd. 5246, 57
No. 19. Dried Chamomile flowers. Cmd. 5247, 57
No. 20. Weft pile fabrics. Cmd. 5251, 57
No. 21. Glazed tiles. Cmd. 5258, 58
No. 22. Hair nets made from human hair. Cmd. 5261, 58
No. 23. Felt hats and hat shapes. Cmd. 5265, 58
No. 24. Endless band Knives. Cmd. 5266, 59
No. 25. Typewriters and parts thereof. Cmd. 5272, 59
No. 26. Hot water bottles, rubber. Cmd. 5273, 59
No. 27. Granite, manufactured. Cmd. 5276, 59
Nos. 28 and 29. Iron and steel products. Cmd. 5289, 60
No. 30. Art Silk Duties
No. 2. Coronation Souvenirs, including articles made of silk. Cmd. 5313, 62
No. 31. Rubber aprons.
No. 32. Knives. Cmd. 5339, 64
Drawback:
No. 1. Wheat in grain. Cmd. 5063, 44
No. 2. Fish. Cmd. 5098, 46
No. 3. Soya beans. Cmd. 5152, 49
No. 4. Castor seed. Cmd. 5156, 50
No. 5. Manufactures of linen and tissue made from paper yarn. Cmd. 5169, 51
No. 6. Linseed Oil. Cmd. 5192, 53
No. 7. Canes. Cmd. 5216, 55

Import Duties Advisory Committee Reports, etc. (continued):
1936 (continued):
Additional (continued):
No. 8. Photographic film base. Cmd. 5264, 58
No. 9. Soya bean oil. Cmd. 5327, 63
Exemptions:
No. 1. Oxalic acid. Cmd. 5073, 44
No. 2. Potatoes. Cmd. 5135, 48
No. 3. Alloys of metal, containing silver or gold. Cmd. 5208, 54
No. 4. Potatoes. Cmd. 5212, 54
No. 5. Rags, various. Cmd. 5226, 55
No. 6. Naphthol. Cmd. 5244, 57
No. 7. Fertiliser Salts. Cmd. 5294, 60
No. 8. Oxalic acid. Cmd. 5331, 63
No. 9. Boot or Shoe Pullovers. Cmd. 5335, 64
Silk Duties:
No. 1. Artificial silk yarn or straw. Cmd. 5312, 62
No. 2. Coronation Souvenirs. Cmd. 5313, 62
1937:
Additional:
No. 1. Tomatoes. Cmd. 5367, 275
No. 2. Needles and bodkins. Cmd. 5389, 276
No. 3. Iron and steel products. Cmd. 5389, 276
No. 4. Parts of Umbrellas, Sunshades, and walkingsticks. Cmd. 5391, 276
No. 5. Iron or Steel screws. Cmd. 5436, 279
No. 6. Iron and Steel goods. Cmd. 5463, 281
No. 7. Iron and Steel goods. Cmd. 5510, 285
No. 8. Wool Felt Hoods. Cmd. 5545, 287
No. 9. Broussonetia Papyrifera (Paper Mulberry). Cmd. 5567, 289
No. 10. Carrots. Cmd. 5623, 294
No. 11. Celluloid Dolls and Rattles. Cmd. 5361, 294
No. 12. Weft Pile Velvets. Cmd. 5632, 294

Import Duties Advisory Committee Reports, etc. (continued):
1937 (continued):
Beef and Veal Duties, Drawback:
No. 1. Beef and Veal. Cmd. 5481, 283
No. 2. Chilled Beef. Cmd. 5578, 290
Drawback:
No. 1. Dressed Leather. Cmd. 5390, 276
No. 2. Unrefined Fish Oils. Cmd. 5418, 278
No. 3. Castor Seed. Cmd. 5438, 279
No. 4. Soya Beans. Cmd. 5458, 281
No. 5. Decorticated ground-nuts. Cmd. 5469, 282
No. 6. Cupro-nickel and gilding metal coated steelcups. Cmd. 5500, 284
No. 7. Rough turned wooden blocks. Cmd. 5502, 284
No. 8. Axe handles of wood. Cmd. 5511, 285
No. 9. Linseed and linseed oil. Cmd. 5512, 285
No. 10. Board for suitcases, etc. Cmd. 5531, 287
No. 11. Square-sawn wood and veneers for Sewing-machine woodwork. Cmd. 5532, 287
No. 12. Iron or Steel wheels. Cmd. 5602, 292
Exemptions:
No. 1. Trade Catalogues. Cmd. 5355, 274
No. 2. Drawings. Cmd. 5356, 274
No. 3. Used Railway Rails. Cmd. 5373, 275
No. 4. Pig-iron. Cmd. 5389, 276
No. 5. Fast Brown V Base. Cmd. 5413, 278
No. 6. Iron and steel products. Cmd. 5417, 278
No. 7. Gaboon Mahogany. (Okoume). Cmd. 5465, 282
No. 8. Mother of Pearl, etc. Cmd. 5484, 283
No. 9. Ferro-Silicon. Cmd. 5492, 284
No. 11. Diatomaceous Earth. Cmd. 5546, 288

Import Duties Advisory Committee Reports, etc. (continued):
1937 (continued):
Exemptions (continued):
No. 12. Ground Sumach Leaves. Cmd. 5601, 292
No. 13. Insoluble Quebracho Extract. Cmd. 5605, 292
No. 14. Bagasse. Cmd. 5606, 292
No. 15. Works of Art. Cmd. 5615, 293
General Ad Valorem Duty Reduction No. 1. Iron and Steel Goods. Cmd. 5510, 285
Milk Products. Cmd. 5591, 291
Substitution No. 1. Peppercorns. Cmd. 5620, 294
1938:
Additional:
No. 1. Lithopone. Cmd. 5655, 502
No. 2. Carpets. Cmd. 5656, 502
No. 3. Handkerchiefs. Cmd. 5687, 504
No. 4. Pot Scourers. Cmd. 5740, 508
No. 5. Pig Iron. Cmd. 5743, 508
No. 6. Cycle Bells and Dynamo Lighting Equipment for cycles. Cmd. 5771, 510
No. 7. Felt made of animal hair. Cmd. 5808, 513
No. 10. Insulated Iron or Steel Staples. Cmd. 5912, 521
No. 11. Weft Pile Velvets. Cmd. 5914, 521
Beef and Veal Duties, Drawback No. 1. Chilled Beef. Cmd. 5737, 508
Drawback:
No. 1. Unperforated Zinc Sheets. Cmd. 5642, 501
No. 2. Leg frames for Sewing-machine tables. Cmd. 5659, 502
No. 3. Metal-bodied aerated water syphons. Cmd. 5660, 503
No. 4. Soya beans for Soya bean flour. Cmd. 5683, 504
No. 5. Solid Insoluble Quebracho Extract. Cmd. 5700, 505
No. 6. Brazil nuts in shell. Cmd. 5751, 509

Import Duties Advisory Committee Reports, etc. (continued):
1938 (continued):
Drawback (continued):
No. 7. Soya beans. Cmd. 5782, 511
No. 8. Eggs in shell. Cmd. 5783, 511
No. 9. Linseed and linseed oil. Cmd. 5786, 511
No. 10. Chewing gum base. Cmd. 5791, 512
No. 11. Cupro-nickel and gilding-metal coated steelcups. Cmd. 5825, 515
No. 12. Board for Suit cases. Cmd. 5826, 515
No. 14. Blank Cinematograph Film. Cmd. 5830, 515
No. 15. Unblanched shelled almonds. Cmd. 5841, 515
No. 16. Square-sawn Wood and Veneers for Sewing-machine woodwork. Cmd. 5856, 517
No. 17. Certain square-cut Wood. Cmd. 5915, 521
Exemptions:
No. 1. Certain Alloys or mixtures of metal. Cmd. 5689, 505
No. 2. Pig iron. Cmd. 5743, 508
No. 3. Raw Oiticica Oil. Cmd. 5810, 513
No. 4. Scientific films and sound track negatives. Cmd. 5831, 515
No. 5. Certain Organic Intermediate Products. Cmd. 5887, 519
No. 6. Pig iron. Cmd. 5891, 520
No. 7. Silicon alloys. Cmd. 5911, 521
1939:
Additional:
No. 1. Works of Art. Cmd. 5985, 740
No. 2. Potassium Ferrocyanide. Cmd. 6000, 741
No. 3. Carrots. Cmd. 6011, 742
No. 4. Rolling Mill Machinery. Cmd. 6024, 743
No. 5. Preserved Cherries. Cmd. 6057, 745
Nos. 6 and 7. Iron and steel goods. Cmd. 6071, 746

Import Duties Advisory Committee Reports, etc. (continued):
1939 (continued):
Additional (continued):
Key Industry No. 1. Mercury Bichloride. Cmd. 6053, 745
Drawback:
No. 1. Castor Seed. Cmd. 5976, 739
No. 2. Unrefined fish oils. Cmd. 6040, 744
No. 4. Linseed and linseed oil. Cmd. 6085, 747
No. 5. Soya beans. Cmd. 6090, 747
No. 6. Chewing gum base. Cmd. 6091, 747
Elastic Lace and Lace Net. Cmd. 6124, 750
Exemptions:
No. 1. Unwrought alloys of metal. Cmd. 5937, 737
No. 2. Ouricury wax. Cmd. 5966, 738
No. 3. Matrices. Cmd. 5984, 740
No. 4. Works of Art. Cmd. 5985, 740
No. 5. Rapidogen Navy Blue R. Cmd. 6033, 743
Gaboon Mahogany Plywood. Cmd. 6113, 749
Substitution:
No. 1. Eggs not in shell. Cmd. 5925, 736
No. 2. Zinc or spelter. Cmd. 6023, 743
(Emergency Provisions) Act, 755
Bill, 733
Exemption of Aircraft from, on Fuel and Lubricants, Netherlands. Cmd. 5074, 45
Spirituous Beverages into Africa:
Cmd. 5205, 54
Cmd. 5814, 514
Cmd. 6082, 747
Licensing Department Publications (N.P.), 1063
Import, Export, and Customs Powers (Defence) Act, 754
Importation:
of Plumage (Prohibition) Act (1921) Amendment Bills, 38, 42, 497, 499
of Spirituous Beverages into Africa. See Import Duties.
Imported:
Bullion, Statement, 383
Cattle Marking. See Cattle Subsidy.
Coin, Statement, 383
Food. See Public Health (Imported Food).

Imported (continued):
Food Certificates, 161, 388, 618, 871
Scotland, 428, 666
Goods, Merchandise Marks. See Merchandise Marks.
Timber, Causes of Stain and Decay in, 420
Imports:
Control of, Notice to Importers, 1063
Customs Treatment of, Exchange of Notes, Canada and Japan. Cmd. 5577, 290
into Italy, Quotas for, Exchange of Notes, Italy and U.K. Cmd. 6020, 742
into United Kingdom, Tabular Statement, 126
of Poultry. See Poultry and Poultry Products.
Imprisonment in Default of Payment, 168
Improvement of Grass Land, 593
Incapacitating Sickness in the Insured Population of Scotland, 201, 428, 912
Incendiary Bombs, Home Office Publications (N.P.), 877
Incentives, Some Experimental Studies, 191
Inchcolm Abbey, Fife, Guide, 457
Inchmaholme, Priory, Guide, 232
Income:
and Expenditure, Public, Accounts, 257, 485, 719, 957
Tax:
Act, 1918, and Finance Acts, Supplements, 173, 400, 635, 1039
Bill, Draft. Cmd. 5132, 48
Codification Committee, Report etc. Cmds. 5131, 5132, 48
Dominions, 884
Inland Revenue Publications (N.P.), 635
on Air Transport Profits, France and U.K. Cmd. 6126, 750
on Non-Resident Individuals and Corporations, Convention Canada and U.S.A. Cmd. 5852, 517
Prevention of Double Taxation, Arrangement, Netherlands East Indies and Canada. Cmd. 5940, 737
Procedure (Emergency Provisions) Act, 755
Bill, 733
Reciprocal Exemption from, on certain profits or gains arising from an agency, Greece. Cmd. 5318, 62
Tables, 173, 399, 748, 1039
Dominions, 884

1936-40 | INC-ISM

INC— INDEX 1936–40

Increase of Rent and Mortgage Interest:
(Restrictions) Act, 522
Bill, 466, 467, 484, 490, 493, 494, 495
Circular, 619
Scotland, 670
(War Restrictions) Act, 64
India:
Air Services over Siam, India, Burma, Exchange of Notes, Siam and U.K. *Cmd. 5651*, 502
and Burma:
(Emergency Provisions) Act, 971
Bill, 945
(Existing Laws) Act, 295
Bill, 19, 43
(Miscellaneous Amendments) Act, 971
Bill, 700, 710, 729, 734, 945
Amendments made by the Bill to certain Acts. *Cmd. 5990*, 740
Office List, 1038
Orders, House of Lords, 5, 17
and the War:
Announcements and Correspondence, *Cmd. 6129*, 750
Communique. *Cmd. 6196*, 967
Statements:
Cmd. 6121, 749
Cmd. 6219, 969
Cmd. 6235, 970
British:
Customs Regs. relating to Passengers' Baggage, 172, 399, 883, 1038
Tariff, etc., 208
Board of Trade Journal Supplements, 436
War Memorial Cemeteries and Graves in Egypt, Agreement with Egypt. *Cmd. 5618*, 293
Civil Service, Examinations, 147, 149, 151, 375, 377, 605, 606, 860, 1030
Commercial Relations with Japan. *Cmd. 5600*, 292
Conditions and Prospects of U.K. Trade in, 921
East. *See* East India.
Economic Conditions, 211
Empire Air Mail Scheme. *Cmd. 5414*, 278
Supplemental Arrangement. *Cmd. 5481*, 281
Identity Documents for Aircraft Personnel, Exchange of Notes:
with Australia, New Zealand, U.K. and Netherlands. *Cmd. 6130*, 750
with France and U.K. *Cmd. 5922*, 736
with Various Countries. *Cmd. 5586*, 291
India (*continued*):
Limitation of Naval Armament, International Treaty. *Cmd. 5561*, 289
Nationality of Persons affected by the Re-Delimitation of the Boundary between Burma (Tenasserim) and Siam, Agreement. *Cmd. 5475*, 282
Naval Armaments Treaty. *Cmd. 5136*, 48
Navy, Examinations, 376, 607, 859, 1030
North-west Frontier, Despatch, 407
Office Publications (N.P.), 172, 399, 634, 883, 1038
Opium Smoking Agreement. *Cmd. 5401*, 277
Police, Examinations, 150, 376, 607
Reciprocal Abolition of Consular Visas on Bills of Health, Exchange of Notes with French Indo-China. *Cmd. 5920*, 735
Rubber, Regulation of Production and Export of, Agreements:
Cmd. 5236, 56
Cmd. 5384, 276
Sanitary Control over Mecca Pilgrims at Kamaran Island, Exchange of Notes, Netherlands. *Cmd. 6096*, 748
Social Service in, 884
Tonnage Measurement Agreement, Application to India. *Cmd. 5994*, 740
Trade Agreement with U.K. *Cmd. 5966*, 739
War:
Cemeteries in Iraq, Agreement. *Cmd. 5196*, 53
Graves Agreement. *Cmd. 5068*, 44
West. *See* West India.
See also Government of India.
Indian:
and Colonial Divorce Jurisdiction Act, 971
Bill, 947, 963
Coins in British Museum, Catalogue of, 459
Families, Family Allowance, 1067
Finance Acts, 30, 259, 486, 719
Naval Reserve Forces (Discipline) Act, 719
Navy. *See* Royal Indian Navy.
Ocean:
Currents, 181, 1032
John Murray Expedition, 942
Tariff (Third Amendment) Act, 719
Indicating Ammeters, Voltmeters, Wattmeters, etc., Specification, 930
Indications. *See* False Indications.
Indicators. *See* Speed Indicators; Turn Indicators; Engine Speed Indicators; Longitudinal Incline Indicators; Airspeed Indicators.

INDEX 1936–40 —INS

Indies. *See* Netherlands East Indies; West Indies.
Individual Unfit Houses, Demolition of, 870
Indo-China. *See* French Indo-China.
Industrial:
Accidents, 168, 395, 631, 881
and Commercial Premises, Wartime Lighting Restrictions for, 878
and Provident Societies:
(Amendment) Act, 64
Annual Reports, 387, 617, 869
Return Forms, 1034
Assurance:
and Friendly Societies (Emergency Protection from Forfeiture) Act, 971
Bill, 945, 946, 962
Commissioner, Annual Reports, 28, 255, 488, 950
Statistical Summaries, 160, 387, 618, 870
Buildings. *See* Commercial and Industrial Buildings.
Court:
Awards, 174, 403, 640, 888, 1042
Disputes between Plasterers and Joiners in Scotland, Report. *Cmd. 5554*, 288
Development, Survey of, 209, 437, 673, 717
Diseases, Compensation. *See* Workmen's Compensation.
Eyestrain, Special Measures needed where Fine Work is done, 395
Fibres, Production, Trade and Consumption, 171, 398, 634, 883
Health:
in War, 1055
Research Board Publications (N.P.), 191, 418, 657, 904, 1055
Lead Poisoning, Factory Form, 1036
Museum, Exhibits, 165, 631
Organic Solvents, Toxicity of, 418
Population, Geographical Distribution of, Royal Commission on:
Evidence, etc., 423, 663, 908
Report. *Cmd. 6153*, 964
Premises, Air Raid Precautions, 393
Scotland, 431
Property, Protection of, International Convention. *Cmd. 5833*, 515
Research. *See* Scientific and Industrial Research.
Undertakings, Air Raid Precautions in, 876
Workers, Weight Lifting by, 396
Industries, Safeguarding. *See* Safeguarding of Industries.
Industry:
Civil Estimates, 25, 253, 481, 715, 954
Industry (*continued*):
Council for Art and Industry Publications (N.P.), 434, 917
Toxic Gases in, 422, 662, 907, 1058
See also Cotton Industry.
Infanticide Act, 523
Bill, 42, 247, 461, 466, 496
Infantry:
Range Finder, 688
Section Leading, 934
Training, 688
Infirmary. *See* Royal Sheffield Infirmary.
Infections. *See* Alimentary Infections; Salmonella Infections.
Inflammable Solvents, Repair of Drums or Tanks, 395
Influenza:
Epidemic, 657
Memo., 874
Occurrence of H. Influenza in the Trachea, 875
Information, Ministry of, Publications (N.P.), 884, 1039
Ingots, Metal, Specifications, 367, 369, 1026, 1027
Inheritance (Family Provision) Act, 523
Bills, 42, 37, 256, 262, 264, 267, 271, 272, 466, 471, 476, 497
Injuries. *See* Personal Injuries.
Ink. *See* Marking Ink.
Inland:
Revenue:
Board of, Publications (N.P.), 173, 399, 635, 884, 1039
Civil Service Arbitration Tribunal Awards, 401, 639, 887, 1042
Commissioners of, Annual Reports:
Cmd. 5015, 43
Cmd. 5297, 272
Cmd. 5574, 500
Cmd. 5865, 735
Cmd. 6099, 964
Examination Papers. *See* Civil Service Commission.
Water Survey Committee Publications (N.P.), 163, 390, 621, 874
Innerpeffray Mortification Scheme, 198, 200, 426
Innes, Sir C., Chairman, Ships Replacement Committee, Report. *Cmd. 5494*, 281
Ino, s.s., Wreck Report, 675
Inquisitions, Calendars of, 189, 416, 655
Insect Pests:
Fumigation of, in Stored Produce, 1057
of Crops, 133, 849
Insects:
Beneficial, 848
Infestation of Grain by, 1058
Insoluble Quebracho Extract. *See* Import Duties Advisory Committee.

INS— INDEX 1936–40

Institutional Poor Relief, Costing Return Forms, 389, 620, 873
Institutions:
Board of Control Publications (N.P.), 153, 381
Ministry of Health Publications (N.P.), 389, 392
Training of the Blind, 155
See also Local Authorities (Hours of Employment).
Instruction. *See* Courses of Instruction.
Instructions for Collectors, British Museum (Natural History), 694
Instrument:
Equipment, General, for Aircraft, 139
Manual (Air), 599, 852, 1021
Panels, Rubber Tubing for, 855
Instruments, Testing of, 143, 1030
Insulated Iron or Steel Staples. *See* Import Duties Advisory Committee.
Insurance:
Careers, 638
Civil Estimates, 25, 252, 480, 715, 954
Fire, Bill, 37
Industry. *See* Unemployment Insurance.
Rates. *See* Marine Insurance Rates.
Ships, Committee on, Report. *Cmd. 5439*, 273
See also Compulsory Insurance; National Health Insurance; Unemployment Insurance; Cunard Insurance; Employer's Liability; Government Insurances; Assurance Companies; National Insurance; Marine Insurance; Health and Unemployment Insurance; War Risks Insurance.
Insured Population of Scotland. *See* Incapacitating Sickness.
Intelligence Corps, Army, Formation of, 1070
Intending Bee-keepers, Advice to, 363
Interest. *See* Housing Loans; Rent and Mortgage.
Internal Rust Spot of the Potato Tuber, 595
International:
Disputes, Pacific Settlement of, *Cmd. 5947*, 737
Institute of Refrigeration, Establishment of:
Cmd. 5747, 509
Cmd. 5889, 519
Justice, Permanent Court of, Optional Clause of Statute:
Cmd. 6108, 748
Cmd. 6185, 966
International (*continued*):
Labour Conference:
Conventions, Draft Conventions, Recommendations, etc. adopted at:
20th Session. *Cmd. 5305*, 61
21st Session. *Cmd. 5392*, 276
22nd Session. *Cmd. 5393*, 276
23rd Session. *Cmd. 5584*, 291
24th Session. *Cmd. 5874*, 318
25th Session. *Cmd. 6141*, 751
Hours of work, etc., replies of H.M. Government *Cmd. 5113*, 47
Proposed Action regarding Conventions and Draft Conventions:
Cmd. 5078, 45
Cmd. 5141, 49
Cmd. 5745, 508
Cmd. 5924, 736
Recruiting Workers, etc., Convention concerning. *Cmd. 5886*, 519
Nomenclature of Blood Groups, 1067
Penal and Penitentiary Commission, Prisoners, Treatment of, Standard Minimum Rules, 169
Position of Belgium. *Cmd. 5437*, 279
Radiocommunication Regs., 654
Settlements, Bank for, Immunities of:
Cmd. 5344, 273
Cmd. 5489, 283
Status of Refugees. *Cmd. 5347*, 273
Telegraph Regs., 654
Telephone Regs., 654
Temperature Scale, 661
Tin Control Scheme, Papers. *Cmd. 5879*, 519
Trade, Report presented by M. Van Zeeland to U.K. and France. *Cmd. 5648*, 502
Internees, Persons eligible for release:
Enemy Nationality:
Cmd. 6223, 969
Cmd. 6233, 970
German and Austrian. *Cmd. 6217*, 968
Interpolation and Allied Tables, 126
Interpretership Examinations, 150, 605, 607, 857, 859
Intoxicating Liquors:
Annual Return Forms, 396, 631, 632, 881
Licensing Statistics:
Cmd. 5304, 61
Cmd. 5585, 291
Cmd. 5869, 518
Cmd. 6145, 751
Scotland:
Cmd. 5547, 287
Cmd. 5779, 511
Cmd. 6078, 746
See also Spirituous Beverages.

INDEX 1936–10 —ISM

Invalid Carriage and Perambulator Trade Wages 176, 642, 891, 1047
Inventions. *See* Patents.
Inventors, Awards to, Royal Commission on, Report. *Cmd. 5594*, 291
Investment Societies, Annual Return Forms, 387, 617, 869, 1034
Investments. *See* Fraud.
Iodine Contents of Water, Milk and Pasture, Relationship to Occurrence of Endemic Goitre. 192
Iran: Economic Conditions, 676
See also Persia.
Iraq:
British War Cemeteries, etc. *Cmd. 5196*, 53
Commercial Relations with Palestine. *Cmd. 5372*, 275
Dust Storms in, 646
Economic Conditions, 211, 676
Legal Proceedings in Civil and Commercial Matters, Convention with U.K. *Cmd. 5369*, 275
Meteorological Reports, 410, 694
Railway System, Agreements with U.K.:
Cmd. 5173, 51
Cmd. 5282, 60
Winds over, 410
Ireland: Map of, 694
See also Eire; Irish Free State; Northern Ireland.
Irish:
Free State:
Commercial Relations with:
Belgium. *Cmd. 5562*, 289
Netherlands. *Cmd. 5442*, 28
Trade and Payments Agreement with Turkey. *Cmd. 5443*, 280
See also Eire.
Land:
Boundary Customs Form, 154
Purchase:
Fund Accounts, 23, 251, 480, 711, 950
Services, Civil Estimates, Revised, 488
Sailors' and Soldiers' Land Trust, 220, 683, 927, 1065
Iron:
and Steel:
Goods. *See* Import Duties Advisory Committee.
Industry:
Memo. on Clause 6 of Finance Bill, 1936. *Cmd. 5201*, 53
Position and Future Development, Report. *Cmd. 5507*, 285
Products, Import Duties. *Cmd. 5289*, 60
Iron (*continued*):
and Steel (*continued*):
Trades:
Census of Production, 917
Import Duties Inquiry Reports, 208, 436
Door Bolts, Report. *Cmd. 5619*, 294
Gas Mains. *See* Wrought Iron Gas Mains.
Oreworking, Restoration of Land affected by, Report of Committee, 875
Pig. *See* Import Duties Advisory Committee.
Pins. *See* Merchandise Marks.
Pots, Austenitic, Specification, 369
Products. *See* Import Duties Advisory Committee.
Screws for Wood. *See* Import Duties Advisory Committee.
Sheets and Strips, Specifications, 600
Specifications, 368
Staples. *See* Import Duties Advisory Committee.
Wheels. *See* Import Duties Advisory Committee.
Irvine and District Water Board Order Confirmation Act, 525
Bill, 473, 498
Irvine, J. M., Chairman, Board of Inquiry on Port Labour in Aberdeen and Glasgow, Report, 404
Irwell Valley Water Board Act, 526
Island:
of Arran Piers Order Confirmation Act, 526
Bill, 473, 498
of Lewis, Dental Disease in, 1025
of Soay and Ardnamurchan, Salmon caught in the Sea, 910
Islands, Highlands and, Educational Trust Scheme, 199, 426
Isle:
of Arran, Ardrossan—Brodick Contract, 30
of Ely, Census, 190
of Man:
Accounts of Customs Duties, etc., 221, 447, 683, 927, 1065
(Customs) Acts, 66, 297, 524, 753, 972
Bills, 17, 41, 245, 270, 473, 497, 708, 732, 948, 963
Mines in, List of, 899
Quarries in, List of, 900
Securities, Restrictions and Returns, 893
(War Legislation) Act, 754
Bill, 733
Isleworth. *See* Heston.
Ismailia, Egypt, Variation of Lapse Rate of Temperature in Atmosphere, 408

ISO-LAN | 1936-40

ISO— INDEX 1936–40

Isolation Hospital Committees, Provisions of Public Health Act, 1936, 388
  Wales, 393
Ison, H. C. K., Corrosion of Tar Stills, 658
Iso-propyl Alcohol, Specification, 1026
Italian :
  Aircraft, bombing of British Red Cross Ambulance in Ethiopia. *Cmd. 5160*, 60
  Interpretership Examinations, 605, 607
Italian Prince, s.s., Wreck Report, 920
Italy :
  Agreement with U.K. *Cmd. 5726*, 507
  Anglo-Italian Clearing Office Accounts, 711, 950
  Belligerent Rights at Sea, Correspondence with U.K. *Cmd. 6191*, 967
  Bon Voisinage Agreement, etc., with Egypt and U.K. *Cmd. 5726*, 507
  Commercial :
    Agreement with U.K. *Cmd. 5345*, 273
    and Payments Agreements with U.K. :
      Cmd. 5306, 61
      Cmd. 5307, 61
    Exchanges and Payments Agreement with U.K. *Cmd. 5346*, 273
  Declaration by Italy and U.K. bringing into force Protocol of April 16, 1938, etc., with Exchange of Notes with the Egyptian Government regarding Lake Tsana and the Suez Canal. *Cmd. 5923*, 736
  Economic Collaboration Agreement with U.K. *Cmd. 6128*, 750
  Entry of Germany into the European Commission of the Danube, Accession of Germany and Italy to the Sinaia Arrangement. *Cmd. 6068*, 746
  Establishment of Air Transport Lines, Exchange of Notes with U.K. *Cmd. 5670*, 503
  Fleet, particulars of :
    Cmd. 5371, 275
    Cmd. 5666, 503
    Cmd. 5936, 737
  Imported Food Certificates, 619
  Mediterranean Declarations :
    Cmd. 5348, 273
    Cmd. 5429, 279
  Proclamation specifying articles to be treated as Contraband in the war with Italy, 1049
  Proposals drawn up by Belgium, France, U.K., and Italy. *Cmd. 5134*, 48
    Correspondence with Belgian and French Ambassadors. *Cmd. 5149*, 49
  Quotas for Imports into, Exchange of Notes with U.K. *Cmd. 6020*, 742
Italy (*continued*) :
  Regulation of Trade in Medicinal Products, Agreement. *Cmd. 6199*, 967
  Suez Maritime Canal, Free Navigation of, International Convention. *Cmd. 5623*, 500
  Withdrawal of Foreign Volunteers from Spain. *Cmd. 5570*, 290
  See also Commercial Agreements ; Payments Agreements ; Ethiopia.

J

Jackets, Specifications, 687, 932
  Anti-Gas, Specification, 1069
  Oilskin, Specification, 227
Jakeman, C., Friction of an Oscillating Bearing, 661
Jamaica :
  Colonial Reports, 378, 609, 861
  Dependency, Cayman Islands, Colonial Report, 151
  See also Kingston.
James Laing's Bursary Trust Scheme, 200, 426
Japan :
  and Japanese Mandated Territory, Economic Conditions, 211
  Commercial Relations with India. *Cmd. 5600*, 292
  Customs Treatment of Imports, Exchange of Notes with Canada. *Cmd. 5577*, 290
  Fleet, Particulars of :
    Cmd. 5371, 275
    Cmd. 5666, 503
    Cmd. 5936, 737
  Local Issues at Tientsin, Arrangement with U.K. *Cmd. 6212*, 968
  Opium Smoking Agreement. *Cmd. 5401*, 277
  Removal of German Citizens from the Japanese Ship *Asama Maru*, Correspondence with U.K. *Cmd. 6166*, 965
  Termination of Perpetual Leases in. *Cmd. 5548*, 288
  Trade and Commerce with Burma. *Cmd. 5504*, 285
  See also Trade Agreements.
Japanese, Interpretership Examinations, 857
Japp, Sir H., Air Raid Policy, Report. *Cmd. 5932*, 736
Jarrow Corporation Act, 759
Jay, B. Alwyn, Structure, Properties and Utilisation of Timber, 415
Jedda, Treaty of, Modification. *Cmd. 5380*, 276

INDEX 1936–40 **—KEI**

Jeffrey, Sir J., Chairman, Local Government and Public Health Consolidation (Scotland) Committee, Memo. *Cmd. 5962*, 738
Jeffrey, R., Metallurgical Examination of Colliery Haulage Drawgear, 413
Jersey, Securities, Restrictions and Returns, 893
Jerseys, Specifications, 687, 932
Jewellery Trade, Design in, 434
Johnson, E., Nature and Characteristic Features of Post-Normal Occlusion, 419
Johnson, N. K., Lapse Rate of Temperature in the Lowest Hundred Metres of the Atmosphere, 896
Johnson, W. A. :
  Back-stays for use in Mines, 1054
  Metallurgical Examination of Colliery Haulage Drawgear, 413
Johnston, Logan and, School Scheme, 198, 200
Johnstone Burgh Order Confirmation Act, 299
  Bill, 241, 268
Johnstone, K. H. :
  Commercial Flower Production, 594, 849
  Flowering Plants in Pots, 849
Johore, Colonial Reports, 151, 378, 609, 861
Joiners and Plasterers in Scotland, Disputes between, Report. *Cmd. 5554*, 288
Joint Hospital Boards, Provisions of Public Health Act, 1936, 388
  Wales, 393
Jointing :
  Compressed Asbestos Fibre, Specification, 1026
  Compound, Specification, 601
  Material, Cork, Specification, 367
Jones, J., Report on explosion at Gresford Colliery. *Cmd. 5358*, 274
Jones, R. C. B., Geological Survey, Wigan District, 661
Joseph Medill, m.v., Wreck Report, 211
Journalism, Careers, 401
Journalists (Registration) Bill, 41, 42, 271
Judges, County Court. *See* Salaries.
Judgments, Foreign, Reciprocal Enforcement :
  Belgium. *Cmd. 5321*, 62
  France. *Cmd. 5235*, 56
Judicature. *See* Supreme Court.
Judicial Statistics : Police Return Forms, 168
  See also Civil Judicial Statistics ; Criminal Statistics.
Judiciary (Safeguarding) Bill, 18, 41, 247
Junior :
  Leaving Certificates, 668, 913
  Technical Schools :
    Review of, 384
    Teaching in, 384
Jurisdiction. *See* Foreign Jurisdiction ; Summary Jurisdiction.
Justice :
  Administration of :
    (Emergency Provisions) :
      Act, 754
        Bill, 701, 702, 730
      (Northern Ireland) Act, 755
        Bill, 708, 733
      (Scotland) Act, 754
        Bill, 732
    See also Administration.
  See also Criminal Justice ; International Justice.
Justices of the Peace (Scotland) Bill, 498
Jute :
  Fabrics, Specification, 686
  Factory Form, 630
  Production, Trade and Consumption, 171, 398, 634, 883
  Trade Wages, 405, 890, 1045
  Webbing, Specification, 140
Juvenile :
  Contributors. *See* National Health Insurance.
  Courts, Constitution of, 671
  Employment, Ministry of Labour Publications (N.P.), 176, 403, 641, 889
Juveniles. *See* Boys ; Children ; Girls ; Young Persons.

K

Kales, 135
Kamaran Island, Sanitary Control over Mecca Pilgrims at, Netherlands, India and U.K. *Cmd. 6096*, 748
Kantorowicz, O., Very Low Temperatures, 415
Kaolin, Specification, 601
Kapur, Forest Products Research Records, 420
Kathiawar, m.v., Wreck Report, 675
Kavak, s.s., Explosion, 672
Kedah, Colonial Reports, 151, 378, 609, 861
Keg and Drum Trade Wages, 405, 890, 1047
Keighley Provisional Order Confirmation Act, 526
  Bill, 468, 494
Keith, J., Chairman, Departmental Committee on Poor Law in Scotland, Report. *Cmd. 5803*, 513

KEL— INDEX 1936–40

Kelantan, Colonial Reports, 151, 378, 609, 861
Kenley. *See* Heston and Kenley.
Kennett, Lord, Chairman, Committee on the Restoration of Land affected by Iron Ore Working, Report, 875
Kensington Palace, Guide to, 231
Kent :
  Coal Mines Scheme, Amendment, 183
  Duchess of, Birth of a Daughter, 180
  Electric Power Act, 300
  North West, Joint Water Act, 70
  See also South Kent.
Kentbrook, s.s., Wreck Report, 211
Kenya :
  Colonial Reports, 151, 153, 378, 380, 609, 861
  Economic Conditions, 211, 439, 920
  Imported Food Certificates, 619, 871
  Native Affairs, Reports on, 611, 862, 1032
  Railways and Harbours Administration, Flag Badge, 380
Kerosene Tank Explosion, 626
Kerr, J. (late), Trustees of, Methlick, Industrial Court Award, 888
Kerridge, P. M. T., Hearing and Speech in Deaf Children, 419
Kersey Waistcoat, Specification, 932
Keruing, Forest Products Research, Records, 420
Kettering, Sunday Entertainments, 488
Kew :
  Observatory, Seismology at, 896
  Royal Botanic Gardens Publications (N.P.), 173, 400, 638, 887, 1041
Keyhaven, Pier and Harbour Provisional Order Confirmation Act, 70
  Bill, 13, 39
Khaki Drill Dust Coats, Specification, 932
Khartoum. *See* Civil Air Transport.
Kidston Collection of Fossil Plants, 660
Kiers, Factory Form, 630
Kilburn Seam, National Coal Resources, 1057
Kiln Operation, Methods of, 420
Kiln-drying Schedules, 659
Kiln-seasoning Treatments of Teak, etc., 659
Kilns : Timber, Types of, 193
  See also Portable Kilns.
Kilsyth and Kirkintilloch, Economic Geology of Coalfield, 660
Kincardineshire Educational Trust Scheme, 198
Kinematical Features of Depressions, 408
King Edward the Seventh Welsh National Memorial Association Act, 972
King, J. D., Dental Diseases in the Island of Lewis, 1055
King, J. G. :
  Action of Hydrogen upon Coal, 660
  Hydrogenation-cracking of Tars, 421, 906
  Production of Active Carbon from Bituminous Coal, 660
King's :
  and Lord Treasurer's Remembrancer, Administration of Estates and Treasure Trove in Scotland, Accounts, 205
  Enemy Risks. *See* War Risks Insurance.
  Library, British Museum, Guide to Exhibition in, 941
  Own Malta Regiment, Peace Establishments, 454
  Regulations :
    and Admiralty Instructions, 126, 353, 586, 842, 1018
    and Air Council Instructions for the R.A.F., 139, 365, 599, 853, 1024
    for the Army and Army Reserve, 228, 453, 688, 934, 1070
Kings and Queens of England (V. and A. Museum), 460
Kingsbridge and Salcombe Water Board Act, 300
Kingston :
  Jamaica, Upper Winds at, 410
  upon Hull :
    Corporation Act, 69
    Provisional Order Confirmation Act, 299
      Bill, 238, 265
  upon Thames Generating Station, Electricity Breakdown, Report, 926
Kingston Cornelian, s.t., Boiler Explosion, 435
Kinross. *See* Perth.
Kirby Hall, Northamptonshire, Guide, 457
Kirkcaldy Corporation Order Confirmation Act, 757
  Bill, 699, 728
Kirkcudbright. *See* Stewartry of Kirkcudbright.
Kirkintilloch. *See* Dunbartonshire ; Kilsyth.
Kisumu–Lusaka. *See* Civil Air Transport ; Empire Air Mail.
Kit, Camp, Allowance, Army, 929
Kitchen and Refreshment Rooms, House of Commons, Reports, 27, 259, 486, 717, 957
Kite Balloon :
  Cable, Flexible Steel Wire Rope for, Specification, 1029

INDEX 1936–40 **—LAN**

Kite Balloon (*continued*) :
  Soft Cotton Cord for, Specification, 601
Knight, R. A. G. :
  Kiln-seasoning Treatments of Teak, etc., 659
  Moisture Content Determination, 906
Knitted Cotton Drawers, Specification, 686
Knives, Import Duties :
  Cmd. 5339, 64
  Endless Band. *Cmd. 5266*, 58
Kohl-Rabi, 850
Korea, Economic Conditions, 211
Kyle, Register of Sasines, 417

L

Labelling. *See* Surgical Ligatures.
Laboratories. *See* Government Laboratories ; School Laboratories ; National Physical Laboratory.
Laboratory Diagnosis of Psittacosis, 392
Labour :
  and National Service, Ministry of, Publications (N.P.), 1041
  Civil Estimates, 25, 253, 481, 715, 954
  Conference. *See* International Labour Conference.
  Gazette, 176, 404, 641, 889, 1043
  Ministry of :
    Annual Reports :
      Cmd. 5145, 49
      Cmd. 5431, 271
      Cmd. 5717, 507
      Cmd. 6016, 742
    Publications (N.P.), 174, 401, 638, 887
  Port. *See* Port Labour.
  Statistics of U.K. *Cmd. 5556*, 288
  Wastage, 191
  See also Native Labour.
Lace :
  Elastic. *See* Import Duties Advisory Committee.
  Finishing Trade, Wages, 642, 1046
Lady Jeannette, s.t., Wreck Report, 920
Laganbank, m.v., Wreck Report, 675
Laing, James. *See* James Laing.
Laing, F., The Cockroach : Its Life History and how to deal with it, 694
Laity. *See* House of Laity.
Lake District, Afforestation in, 159
Lamb :
  Dysentery, 362
  Production and Trade, 171, 398, 634
Lambert *v* Levita. *See* Broadcasting.
Lambs. *See* Fat Lambs.
Laminated :
  Compressed Wood, Specification, 1026
Laminated (*continued*) :
  Synthetic Resin Bonded Mouldings, Specification, 1030
Lamps :
  Electric, Import Duties. *Cmd. 5246*, 57
  See also Blow Lamps ; Safety Lamps.
Lanarkshire :
  County Council Order Confirmation Act, 760
    Bill, 708, 732
  Educational Trust Scheme, 200, 426
  Electricity, 677
Lancashire :
  and Cheshire Coal Mines Scheme, 411, 648
  Cheese, 1023
  Coal Mines Scheme Amendments, 183
  Coalfields, Survey of, 660
  County Council (Rivers Board and General Powers) Act, 527
  Electric Power Act, 300
Lancaster :
  Electricity Orders, 213
  Provisional Order Confirmation Act, 70
    Bill, 12, 39
Land :
  Acquisition of, Restriction of River Development, 218
  Aerodromes, Planning and Zoning of, 598, 852
  and Estate Agency, Careers, 401
  and Housing Societies, Annual Return Forms, 387, 617, 870, 1034
  Change of Ownership, Tithe Act, 1936, 206
  Court. *See* Scottish Land Court.
  Division, Annual Report, 134, 362, 595
  Drainage :
    Act, 1930 :
      Handbook, 134
      Operations and Proceedings under, Report, 362
    Catchment Boards, Receipts and Expenditure, Forms, 163, 390, 621
    Drainage Authorities, Receipts and Expenditure, Forms, 163, 390, 621, 874, 1035
    Lee Conservancy Catchment Board Act, 70
    Provisional Order :
      Bill No. 1, 16, 39
      Bill No. 2, 16, 39
      (Louth Drainage District) Confirmation Act, 527
        Bill, 472, 496
    River Conservancy Authorities, Income and Expenditure, 163
    Stour, River (Kent), Provisional Order Confirmation Act, 70

Land (continued):
Drainage (continued):
Witham and Steeping Rivers Provisional Order Confirmation Act, 70
Fertility:
Committee Report, 595
Research Fund Accounts, 713, 950
Palestine Land Transfers Regulations, Letter to the Secretary-General of the League of Nations. Cmd. 6180, 966
Purchase. See Irish Land Purchase; Northern Ireland.
Registration:
Act, 66
Bill, 14, 30, 36
Forms, 179, 406, 644
Registry:
Examinations, 858
Mapping Assistants, 149, 150
Publications (N.P.), 179, 406, 644, 892
Restoration of. See Iron Ore Working.
Settlement on, Report of Committee. 889
Societies. See Land and Housing Societies.
Tax Commissioners Act, 522
Bill, 271, 464
Transport, Handbook, 187
Trust. See Irish Sailors' and Soldiers' Land Trust.
Uses of Lime on, 362
Values (Rating) Bill, 271
See also Arable Land; Grass Land; Crown Land; Mortgaged Land; War Damage to Land.
Landholders. See Small Landholders.
Landing Approach Installations, V.H.F., Radiobeacon, 852
Landlord and Tenant (War Damage) Act, 754
Landplanes, Flying Training Manual, 598
Lands:
Crown. See Crown Lands.
Valuation (Scotland) Amendment Act, 321
Bill, 493
Landward Areas of Counties, Scotland. Emergency Fire Brigade Measures in, 570
Model Byelaws for regulating Building in, 429
Langdon, J. N.:
Fatigue and Boredom in Repetitive Work, 418
Machine and the Worker, 657
Languages:
Examinations, 374, 376, 605

Languages (continued):
Modern, Instruction in:
HolidayCourses, 157, 385, 615, 867
Three-Year Courses, 914
Lanolin, Specifications, 1026, 1027, 1029
Lanolin - Resin Solution, Pigmented, Specification, 600
Lap Straps, Specification, 366
Lapse Rate of Temperature in the Lowest Hundred Metres of the Atmosphere, 896
Large Installations, Camouflage of, 877
Larvae, Stomatopod, 942
Latitude, Variation of, 901
Latvia:
Economic Conditions, 676
Imported Food Certificate, 389
Scotland, 428
Legal Proceedings in Civil and Commercial Matters, Conventions with U.K.:
Cmd. 6109, 748
Cmd. 6181, 966
Lauan, Forest Products Research Record, 193
Launching. See Tyneside Launching Ceremony.
Laundries:
Abstract of Factory and Workshops Acts, 167
Factory Form, 394
Laundry:
Machinery:
Factory Form, 631
Safety Precautions in the Installation and Use of, 395
Trade:
Occupations in, 401
Wages, 176, 405, 890, 1047
Lavatories in the Palace of Westminster, 17
Lavender, Cultivation etc. of, 135
Law:
Careers, 174
Civil Estimates, 25, 253, 481, 715, 954
of Libel:
(Amendment) Bill, 498
(Damages) Amendment Bill, 42
of Property Act:
1925 (Amendment) Bill, 243
1939, 752
Reform (Miscellaneous Provisions) (Scotland) Act, 972
Bill, 707, 947, 963
Reporting Committee, Report, 1052
Revision Committee Reports:
Cmd. 5334 (Statutes of Limitation), 64
Cmd. 5449 (Statute of Fraud and the Doctrine of Consideration), 280
Cmd. 6009, 742
Cmd. 6032, 743

Law (continued):
Royal Commission on the Despatch of Business at Common Law, Report. Cmd. 5065, 44
See also Courts of Law; Legal; Legislation; Air Force Law; Expiring Laws; Military Law; Nationality Laws; Pension Law; Poor Law; Temporary Laws; Private Legislation.
Lawson, W. & F., Premises of, Explosion, 672
Laxford System, Sea Trout of, 201
Le Quesne, C. T., Chairman, Committee on Pensions for Unmarried Women:
Minutes of Evidence, 683, 927
Report. Cmd. 5991, 740
Lea, C. H., Rancidity in Edible Fats, 659
Lea, F. M.:
Pozzolanas and Lime-Pozzolana Mixes, 1056
Solubility of Cements, 905
Lead:
Bronze Ingots and Bars, Specifications, 1026, 1027
Capsules. See Capsules.
Compounds, Women and Young Persons employed in processes involving the use of, Factory Form, 630.
in Food, 623
Poisoning, Factory Form, 1036
Leadership, Elements of, 689
Leaf:
Mould, Tomato, 595
Spot of Celery, 1023
Leaf-drop Streak of Potatoes, 595
Leaf-warblers, 941
League of Nations:
Assembly Reports:
16th. Cmd. 5053, 43
17th. Cmd. 5365, 274
18th. Cmd. 5625, 294
19th. Cmd. 5899, 520
20th. Cmd. 6160, 965
Covenant, 158
Protocol for Amendment. Cmd. 5884, 519
Dispute between Ethiopa and Italy:
Cmd. 5071, 5072, 44
Cmd. 5094. Petroleum, etc., 46
Mandated Territories, Reports on, 152, 379, 610, 862
Prisoners, Treatment of. Standard Minimum Rules, 169
See also International Labour Conference.
Leak, Radiator, Compound, Specification, 601
Leasehold Property (Repairs) Act, 523
Bill, 271, 468, 484, 490, 494
Leases. See Perpetual Leases.

Leather:
Dressed, Import Duties. Cmd. 5108, 47
Shoes, Specification, 933
Slipper, Specification, 452
Specification, 686, 931
Trade:
Census of Production, 673
Import Duties Act Inquiry Report, 208
See also Import Duties Advisory Committee.
Leather-soled brown canvas shoes, Specification, 452
Leaves, Ground Sumach. See Import Duties Advisory Committee.
Leaving Certificate Examinations, etc., 203, 430, 668, 913, 1060
Lebanon:
Economic Conditions, 212, 676
Frontier Questions, Agreement with Palestine and Syria. Cmd. 6065, 745
Imported Food Certificate, 871
Lee, A. W.:
Seismology at Kew Observatory, 896
Travel Times of Seismic Waves:
from the Baffin Bay Earthquake of Nov. 20, 1933, 408
P. & S., 645
Lee Conservancy:
Act, 526
Catchment Board Acts, 70
Leeds Provisional Order Confirmation Act, 71
Bill, 13, 39
Leek, Smut, 135
Leeward Islands:
Colonial Reports, 609, 861, 1031
Education in, 863
Leg Frames for Sewing Machine Tables. See Import Duties Advisory Committee.
Legal:
Aid in the High Court, 407
Proceedings, Conventions, etc.:
France:
Cmd. 5182, 52
Cmd. 6206, 968
Greece:
Cmd. 5144, 49
Cmd. 6643, 501
Hungary. Cmd. 5190, 53
Iraq. Cmd. 5503, 173
Latvia:
Cmd. 6109, 748
Cmd. 6181, 966
Lithuania. Cmd. 5197, 53
Netherlands. Cmd. 5490, 283
Switzerland:
Cmd. 5658, 502
Cmd. 5973, 739
Turkey. Cmd. 5996, 741

Legal (continued):
Proceedings, Conventions, etc. (continued):
Yugoslavia:
Cmd. 5101, 50
Cmd. 5542, 287
Service List, Colonial, 153, 380, 610, 862
Legalisation of certain official documents, Agreement between France and U.K. Cmd. 5446, 282
Legation to Lithuania, 167, 927
Anti-gas, 1069
Oilskin, 227
Legislation:
relating to introduction of Plants into Colonial Dependencies of the British Empire, 381
Tables showing the effect of, etc., 205
See also Private Legislation; Isle of Man.
Legislatures, Colonies, 933
Legitimacy Act, 522
Leicestershire:
and South Derbyshire Coalfield, 660, 1057
Census, 417
Electricity Orders, 213
Lemon Soles:
Age and Growth of, 910
Factors in the growth of, 1060
Marking Experiments in Scottish Waters, 201
Length. See Fundamental Standards.
Letterpress Printing, Regs. for Bronzing, Factory Form, 1036
Letters: Patent. See Malta.
See also Signal Letters.
Levita, Lambert v. See Broadcasting.
Lewis. See Island of Lewis.
Lewis-Faning, E.:
Mortality Rates in Urban Communities, 623
Seasonal Incidence of Mortality in England and Wales and in the U.S.A., 1055
Leyton Provisional Order Confirmation Act, 757
Bill, 598, 727
Liability for War Damage. See War Damage.
Libel. See Law of Libel.
Liberate Rolls, Calendar of, 416
Librarianship, Careers, 638
Libraries, A.R.P. in, 941
Library, National, of Scotland Publications (N.P.), 202, 429, 667, 1060
Licences. See Broadcasting: Goods Vehicles; Road Traffic (Driving Licences); Petroleum; Vivisection; Civil Aircraft; Road Vehicles; Road Traffic (Licensing of Vehicles); Debt Collectors; Methylated Spirits; Intoxicating Liquors; Marriage (Licensing of Chapels).

Licensing:
Act, 293
(Amendment) Bill, 36
Authorities, Road and Rail Traffic, Reports, 218, 435, 680, 924
(Declaration of Justices) Bill, 730
Intoxicating Liquors:
Annual Return Forms; Annual Statistics. See Intoxicating Liquors.
of Administrators (Ireland) Bill, 246, 247
State Management Districts, Annual Reports, 32, 260, 488, 722
Vehicles, Goods, Statistics, 213
Life:
Saving Appliances (Shipping), 208, 674
Tables, Registrar-General's Decennial Supplement, 190
Lifting Appliances, etc.:
at Buildings in course of Construction, Register, 394
Factory Form, 630, 879
Mines and Quarries Form, 650
Lifts: Factory Forms, 629, 630
See also Folkestone.
Ligatures. See Surgical Ligatures.
Light:
Alloy Airscrew Forgings, Specifications, 141, 1028
Clothing. See Women's Light Clothing.
Construction Buildings, 866
Cotton Fabric, Specification, 600
Machine Gun, Small Arms Training, 456
Nickel-Copper Alloy Rods, Wire, Tubes, and Rivets, Specifications, 1028
Railways:
Acts, etc., Reports of Proceedings, etc., 214, 441, 677, 921
Returns of Capital, Receipts, etc., 214
through Window Glasses, Transmission of, 194
Wave Lengths of, 661
See also Coloured Light; Illumination.
Lighthouse. See Clyde Lighthouse; General Lighthouse.
Lighthouses and other Aids to Navigation, International Technical Conference, Report, 221, 928
Lighting:
Air Raid Precautions, 624
during Blackout Hours in Ship-building and Ship-repairing Yards, 1037
Electric, principles, etc., 187
Equipment for Cycles. See Import Duties Advisory Committee.

Lighting (continued):
in Factories:
and Workshops, Welfare Pamphlet, 397
Departmental Committee Reports, 632, 1043
Road Vehicles, Memo., 446
Street, Departmental Committee on, Final Report, 446
See also Illumination; Artificial Lighting; Time Lighting.
Lightning. See Fog Signals.
Lightweight Concrete Aggregates, 192
Limbs. See Artificial Limbs.
Lime:
and its uses on the Land, 362
Use of, in Agriculture, 593
Lime-Pozzolana Mixes, 1056
Liming of Soils, 909
Limitation:
Act, 753
Bill, 468, 472, 474, 475, 497, 499, 701, 716, 726
Lincolnshire, Census, 190
Lindsey:
North, Water Board Provisional Order Confirmation Act, 759
Bill, 301, 751
North East, Joint Hospital District Provisional Order Confirmation Act, 68
Bill, 68
Linen:
and Cotton Handkerchief etc. Trade, Wages, 405, 890, 1047
and Jute Fabrics, Specification, 931
Fabric, Airship, Specifications, 141
Fabrics, Specification, 686
Manufactures of, Import Duties. Cmd. 5169, 51
Piece Goods Trade, Wages, 1047
Towels, Specification, 452
Lines, Natural and Tarred, Specification, 226
Linfield Factory, Belfast, Boiler Explosion, 206
Lining of Trenches, Specifications, 626, 878
Linnaeus, C., Systema Naturae, 943
Linoleum, Specification, 452
Linseed: Production, Trade and Consumption, 172, 634, 883
See also Import Duties Advisory Committee.
Linseed Oil. See Import Duties Advisory Committee.
Lipscomb, J. K., Ducks and Geese, 360
Liquid:
Chlorine, Handling, Storage and Use, 395, 880
Fuel and Lubricants used in Air Traffic, Exemption from Taxation, International Conference. Cmd. 6001, 741

Liquid-phase Continuous Plant, Development of, 660
Liquors. See Intoxicating Liquors.
Lisbon. See Civil Air Transport Services.
Lister Institute of Preventive Medicine. See Type Cultures.
Lithographic Printing, Regs. for Bronzing, Factory Form, 1036
Lithophone. See Import Duties Advisory Committee.
Lithuania:
Economic Conditions, 211
Imported Food Certificate, 389
Scotland, 428
Legal Proceedings Convention. Cmd. 5197, 53
Litlington, Strip Map of, 653
Little:
Main Steam, Survey of Coal Resources, 660
Owl, 362, 595
Littler, T. S., The Use of Hearing Aids, 418
Littlestone on Sea and District Water Provisional Order Confirmation Act, 973
Bill, 701, 962
Liver Boiling Installations, Explosions from, Reports, 435
Liverpool:
and London War Risks Insurance Association Ltd., 724
City Churches Act, 1897 (Amendment) Measure, 469, 528
Corporation Act, 72
Electricity Orders, 213
Exchange Act, 298
Royal Children's Hospital, Dangerous Drugs Orders, 166, 167
United Hospital Act, 302
See also Senior Public Elementary Schools.
Livestock:
Commission Report, 596
Cost of Production, Scotland, 424
Industry Act, 297
Bill, 42, 240, 242, 244, 257, 262, 267, 270
Number of, 132, 359, 848
Rations for, 133, 848
White-fish Meal as a Food for, 360
See also Cattle.
Living Animals, Experiments on, 259, 487
Lizard, Behaviour of the Anemograph at, 181
Llandrindod Wells Provisional Order Confirmation Act, 527
Bill, 471, 496
Llanelly District Traction Act, 69
Llwchwr Electricity Orders, 213

Load Line :
Certificates :
Denmark. *Cmd. 5441*, 280
Norway. *Cmd. 5336*, 64
Sweden. *Cmd. 5180*, 52
Convention, Canada and U.S.A.
Cmd. 5234, 35
Loaded Ebonite, Specification, 587
Loan :
Agreement, Spain and U.K. :
Cmd. 6189, 967
Cmd. 6230, 970
Societies, Annual Return Forms,
387, 617, 869, 1034
Loans : Facilities Bill, 732
See also East India ; Local Loans ;
Greek Loans ; Public Works
Loans ; Conversion Loans ;
Defence Loans ; Housing Loans ;
Poland ; National Loans ;
Austrian Loan.
Local :
Authorities :
Air Raid Precautions, 393
Scotland, 431, 432
and Local Government Officers
(Joint Councils) Bills, 495, 729
Building Programmes, Planning,
etc., Scotland, 432
Duties of :
Factories Act 1937, 626
Milk and Dairies Orders, 594
(Enabling) Bills, 37, 42, 493, 727
(Hours of Employment in con-
nection with Hospitals and
Institutions) Bill, 267, 271
Members of, Disabilities arising
out of Interest in Contracts,
etc. *Cmd. 5962*, 738
Powers under Physical Training
and Recreation Act, 1937,
385
Communications and Reporting of
Air Raid Damage, 625, 878
Defence Volunteers, Disablement
Allowances, 1067
Education Authorities, Lists of, 157,
385, 867
Wales and Monmouthshire, 386,
868
Elections :
and Register of Electors (Tempor-
ary Provisions) Act, 1939,
755
Bill, 708, 734
Bill, 1940, 949, 963, 964
(Proportional Representation) Bill
492, 498
Fire Services :
in Rural Districts, 881
in Small Burghs and Landward
Areas, 915

Local *(continued)* :
Government :
Act, 1929, Investigation under
S.110, Report, 251
Amendment (Scotland) Act, 753
Bill, 703, 719, 726, 728, 729
and other Officers, Superannua-
tion, Model Form of Agree-
ment, 390
and Public Health Consolidation :
Committee :
Draft Bills :
Food and Drugs. *Cmd.
5629*, 500
Public Health. *Cmd.
5060*, 44
Reports :
Cmd. 5059, 43
Cmd. 5628, 500
(Scotland) Committee, Memo.
Cmd. 5962, 738
Calculations of Grants for Third
Fixed Grant Period (Scotland),
204
Careers, 401
Elections (Free Postage) Bill,
729
Financial Statistics, 390, 621,
874, 1035
(Financial Provisions) :
Act, 296
Bill, 237, 266
(Scotland) Act, 296
Bill, 239, 266
(Hours of Poll) Act, 523
Bill, 472, 487, 494, 497
in the Tyneside Area, Report of
the Royal Commission. *Cmd.
5402*, 277
(Members' Travelling Expenses)
Act, 296
Bill, 239, 267
Officers, Departmental Commit-
tee on, Circular, 161
(Scotland) Act, 1929 :
Investigation under S.72,
Report, 254
Third Fixed Grant Period,
Estimated Populations, 432
Staffs (War Service) Act, 755
Bill, 733
Circular, 913
Standard Clauses, 170
Superannuation :
Act, 1937, 297
Bill, 244, 245, 259, 262,
268, 270
Circulars, 389, 618, 871,
874
Memo. *Cmd. 5452*, 281
Act, 1939, 753
Bill, 700, 728

Local *(continued)* :
Government *(continued)* :
Superannuation *(continued)* :
Actuarial Valuation, Circular,
872
Additional Contributory Pay-
ment, Circular, 620
Administration Circulars, 619,
871
Allocation of Part of Bene-
fits to Wife or Husband,
621
Scotland, 671
England and Scotland, Circu-
lar, 871
Mental Hospital, etc., Em-
ployment, Circular, 620
Model Combination Scheme,
621
Reckoning of Service on Trans-
fer, Circular, 620
(Scotland) Act, 297
Bill, 245, 260, 262, 268,
270
Circulars, 433, 916
Memo. *Cmd. 5453*, 281
Service of Registration Offi-
cers, Circular, 619
Surrender of Allowance, Cir-
cular, 871
Scotland, 916
Teachers, Circular, 871
Transfer Value, Circulars, 620,
871
Legislation : Clauses, Private Bill
Procedure, Reports, 257
Legislatures, Colonies, Protectorates,
etc., 710
Loans :
Fund Accounts, 23, 231, 477, 491,
950
Housing. *See* Housing Loans.
Revenues, Exchequer Contributions
to Civil Estimates, 25, 252, 481,
715, 954
Storage and Distribution of Civilian
Respirators, 625
Taxation Returns :
England and Wales. *See* Local
Government Financial Statis-
tics.
Scotland, 201, 433, 1061
Unemployment Index, 176, 404, 641,
889
Locarno, Treaty of, Memo. by German
Government respecting Franco-Soviet
Treaty, Treaty of Locarno, and
Demilitarised Zone in Rhineland.
Cmd. 5118, 47
Loch Buie, s.t., Wreck Report, 438
Loch Doule (Dhughaill), Western Ross-
shire, Sea Trout of, 665

Lochaber Water Power Order Confirma-
tion Acts :
1938, 526
Bill, 472, 497
1940, 973
Bill, 947, 963
Lochinver. *See* Culag.
Locks and Padlocks, Import Duties.
Cmd. 5216, 47
Locust Outbreak in Africa and Western
Asia, Reports, 447, 927
Lodging Houses, Model Byelaws, 621
Loftman, Army Trade of, 1066
Logan and Johnston School Scheme,
198, 200
London :
and Home Counties Traffic Advisory
Committee Publications (N.P.),
214, 441, 677, 922
and Middlesex (Improvements, etc.)
Act, 71
and North Eastern Railway :
Act, 1938, 526
Collision at Castle Cary, 677
General Powers Act, 72
Industrial Court Awards, 403,
641, 888, 1042
London Transport Act, 72
Order Confirmation Act, 69
Bill, 9
(Superannuation Fund) Act, 757
Building Acts (Amendment) Act,
760
Census, 417
Central :
Busmen, Effects of Working Con-
ditions upon Health of, Report,
889
Omnibus Services, Stoppage of,
Court Inquiry, Reports :
Cmd. 5454 (Interim), 281
Cmd. 5464, 282
See also London Transport
Workers.
City of (Various Powers) Act, 757
County :
Council :
(General Powers) Acts, 69,
301, 526, 760, 973
Bill, 1937, Memo. *Cmd.
5426*, 279
(Improvements) Act, 760
(Money) Acts, 71, 299, 526,
759, 973
(Tunnel and Improvements)
Act, 527
Courts Directory, 407
of :
Electric Supply Co. (Surrey)
Electricity Order, 921
Water Supply of, from Under-
ground Sources, 907

London *(continued)* :
Employment for Boys and Girls,
Greater London, 641
Gas Undertakings (Regulation) Act,
760
Gazette, 180, 407, 544, 893, 1048
Government Act, 793
Bill, 697, 702, 703, 706, 731
Health Services, Extract from Annual
Report of Ministry of Health, 164
Highway Development Survey,
Greater London, Report, 677
Midland and Scottish Railway :
Acts, 69, 300, 525, 757
Ardrossan-Brodick Contract, 30
Industrial Court Awards, 403,
641, 889, 1043
Order Confirmation Act, 259
Bill, 240, 268
National Museums and Galleries of :
Brief Guide to, 916
Lectures, etc., 186, 901
Naval :
Conference :
Documents, 158
Memo. *Cmd. 5137*, 49
Treaty Act, 297
Bill, 42, 246
Passenger Transport :
Acts, 72, 301, 527, 760
Board :
Increases of Fares, Reports,
1064
Railways, Staff employed,
217, 444, 680
Post Office Guide, 415, 654, 902
Post Offices and Streets, 416,654,1054
Public Health (London) Act, 66
Bill, 6, 7, 14, 15, 41
Regional Advisory Council for
Juvenile Employment Publica-
tions (N.P.), 403, 641, 889
Remission of Rates (London) Act, 971
Bill, 947, 963
Steam Ship Owners' Mutual Insu-
rance Association, Ltd., War Risks
Insurance, 724
Tower of, Guide, 457
Transport Workers, Investigation
into Sickness Experience, 418
Long, H. C. :
Poisonous Plants on the Farm, 593
Weeds :
of Arable Land, 594
of Grass Land, 593
Long Service Pay, Army, Grant of, 1070
Longitudinal Incline Indicators, Speci-
fication, 599
Longwell, J., Survey of River Tees, 422
Lonsdale, T. :
Mechanical Testing of Bituminous
Road Materials, 907

Lonsdale, T. *(continued)* :
Rigidity Modulus of Bitumens and
Bitumen-Filler Mixtures, 907
Lord :
Advocate's Department, Civil Ser-
vice Arbitration Tribunal Awards,
638, 888
Chancellor's Department Publica-
tions (N.P.), 407, 645, 1052
Lord Beaconsfield, s.t., Explosion, 672
Lord Runciman, s.t., Wreck Report, 438
Lords :
House of. *See* Parliamentary Publi-
cations.
Spiritual and Temporal, List and
Roll of, 18, 238, 474, 709
Loss of Employment (Compensation)
Bill, 269, 271
Lossiemouth. *See* Elgin.
Lothian :
Homes Trust Scheme, 198
late Marquess of, H.M. Ambassador
at Washington, Speech. *Cmd.
6239*, 970
See also East Lothian.
Lotteries. *See* Betting and Lotteries.
Loughborough College, Dangerous Drugs
Order, 166
Louping-Ill, 909
Louse, The, Memo., 1035
Loveday, T., Chairman, Committee on
Veterinary Education in Great Britain,
Report, 596
Lovell, R., Nasopharyngeal Bacterial
Flora of Different Groups of Persons,
875
Low :
Temperature :
Carbonisation, 906
Stoving Enamel, Specification,
1058
Temperatures, 415
Tensile Cold Headed Steel Bolts,
Specification, 1027
Lower Egypt, Temperature and Relative
Humidity in the Atmosphere, 409
Lowestoft, Sunday Entertainments, 955
L. T. Varnished Insulating Tubing,
Specification, 369
Lubricants :
Exemption of Aircraft from Duties on :
France. *Cmd. 5998*, 741
Netherlands. *Cmd. 5074*, 45
Switzerland. *Cmd. 5846*, 516
used in Air Traffic, Exemption from
Taxation, International Con-
ference. *Cmd. 6001*, 741
Lubricating Oil, Controls, Specification,
367
Lubrication Research Publications
(N.P.), 194, 661
Lucerne, Agriculture Leaflet, 134

Luke, Lord, Chairman, Advisory Com-
mittee on Nutrition, Report, 391
Lunacy :
and Mental Deficiency :
Education of Mentally Defective
Children, 430
See also Control, Board of.
Board (Scotland) Salaries and Clerks
Act, 521
Lusaka. *See* Civil Air Transport.
Luton :
Extension Provisional Order Confir-
mation Act, 757
Bill, 698, 727, 729
Provisional Order Confirmation Act,
68
Bill, 8, 37
Water Provisional Order Confirma-
tion Act, 758
Bill, 703
Lutyens, Sir E., Highway Develop-
ment Survey, 1937, Greater London,
Report, 677
Luxembourg :
Economic Conditions, 211, 439
Extradition Conventions :
Australia, New Zealand, U.K. :
Cmd. 5416, 278
Cmd. 5811, 513
U.K. *Cmd. 6087*, 747
Lymantriidae, 943
Lympne Air Port, Regs., 364
Lysioquilla Maculata, 942
Lyte, Sir H. C. Maxwell, Catalogue of
Manuscripts and other Objects in the
Museum of the Public Record Office,
656
Lytham St. Annes. *See* Blackpool.

M

(Note : *The prefixes " Mac " and " Mc "
are both treated for the purpose of alphabetical order as if they were written
" Mac ".*)

MacBrayne, Messrs. David, Ltd., Con-
tract for maintenance of transport
services in Western Highlands and
Islands of Scotland, 492
McCance, R. A., Chemical Composition
of Foods, 1055
Macclesfield Corporation Act, 759
McDermott, L. H., Daylight Illumina-
tion necessary for Clerical Work, 421
Macdonald, A. J., Turkeys, 360
MacDougall, D., Production of Active
Mineral Bromine from Bituminous Coal, 660
Macfarlane, P. R. C. :
Salmon of the River Carron, 665
Salmon of the Upper Solway District,
665

McGill, J. M., Barrhead, Glasgow,
Industrial Court Award, 888
MacGregor, M., Synopsis of the Mineral
Resources of Scotland, 1058
Machine :
and the Worker, 657
Guns :
Care, Inspection and Repair of, 230
Light, Small Arms Training, 456
Range Table for, 455
Milking, 595
Machine-feeding Processes, Study of, 657
Machinery :
and its uses in Concrete Road Con-
struction, 907
Attendants, Factory Form, 630
Electrical, Survey of Trade in, 171
Fencing of :
Tinplate Factories, 632
Woollen and Worsted Factories,
170
Rating of, Panel of Referees, 389
Rolling Mill. *See* Import Duties
Advisory Committee.
See also Agricultural Machinery ;
Woodworking Machinery.
Machines. *See* " Breathing Machines "
Mackenzie Bequest Scheme, 664, 910
Mackenzie, I., Bacillus Salmonicida
Bacteriophage, 665
Mackenzie, S., Cancer, Extent to which
Patients receive Treatment, 875
Mackie, T. J., Bacillus Salmonicida
Bacteriophage, 665
Mackinnon-Macneill Trust Scheme, 199,
200, 426
McLean, Sir W. H., Chairman, Commis-
sion on Higher Education in Malaya,
Report, 863
McMahon, Sir H. *See* Palestine.
Madagascar, Imported Food Certificate,
161, 389
Scotland, 428
Made-up :
Goods, Cotton, Rayon and Linen :
Explanatory Memo., 1063
List of Manufacturers of Con-
trolled Goods, 1063
for Export, List of Wholesale
Dealers and Producers, 1063
Textiles Trade Wages, 405, 890, 1047
Madreporaria, 942
Magazine Clothing, Specifications, 452, 932
Magazines for Powder, Specification for
building, 919
Magdalen Hospital :
Bill, 239, 267
Charity Scheme Confirmation Act, 300
Magistrates, Metropolitan Police Courts.
See Salaries.
Magna Carta, 1054
Magnesite, 943

Magnesium :
and its Alloys, 422
Specifications (Magnesium Alloy), 141, 142, 143, 366, 367, 369, 600, 601, 1054
Magnesium, Magnesite and Dolomite, 943
Magnesium-Aluminium Alloy Tubes, etc., Specifications, 954, 955
Magnetic :
and Meteorological Observations, 188, 653, 901
Compasses, Specification, 140
Magnetism :
Observations in, 653, 901, 1054
Wireless Telegraphy, 587
Magnetism, Astronomy, and Meteorology, Observations in 1934, 188
Magneto Parts, Steel Strips for, Specifications, 141, 142
Magneto-Theodolite, 415
Mahoganies, Commercial, 659
Mahogany :
as Rough Timber, Specification, 366
African, Properties of, 193
Gaboon. *See* Import Duties Advisory Committee.
Gaboon, Plywood. *See* Import Duties Advisory Committee.
Substitutes, Specification, 142
Maidenhead Water Provisional Order Confirmation Act, 300
Bill, 242, 268
Mails :
Censorship of, Correspondence between U.K. and U.S.A. *Cmd. 6156*, 964
See also Empire Air Mail ; Post.
Main :
Line Railway Companies, Conveyance of Merchandise by Rail, 926
Seam, Survey or Coal Resources, 660
Maitland, A., Chairman, Departmental Committee on the cost of Hospitals and other Public Buildings, Report 620
Maize, Production and Trade, 171, 398, 634, 883
Major Planets, Observations of, 653
Malaria, Public Health and Medical Subjects Reports, 622, 623
Malay States, Colonial Reports, 151, 152, 378, 379, 609, 610, 860, 861, 1031
Malaya :
Economic Conditions, 439, 921
Higher Education in, Report of Commission, 863
Mui Tsai in, 381
Maldon, Essex, Periwinkle Fishery, 134
Male Young Persons, Factory Forms, 627, 628
Malling, Sunday Entertainments, 952
Malta :
Abnormal Visibility at, 897
H.M. Dockyard, Civil Service Arbitration Tribunal Awards, 402, 888
King's Own Malta Regiment, Peace Establishments, 454
(Letters Patent) Act, 66
Bill, 9, 40
Meteorological Reports, 410, 647
Religious Questions in. *Cmd. 5975*, 500
Winds over, 410
See also Royal Malta Artillery.
Malvern, Sunday Entertainments, 956
Man, Isle of. *See* Isle of Man.
Manchester :
Corporation Acts, 72, 526
Ship Canal Act, 72
Mandated Territories :
Trade with Netherlands. *Cmd. 5061*, 44
See also League of Nations ; Air Navigation ; Colonies.
Manganese, 694
Steel Castings, Specification, 600
Manganese-Molybdenum Steel Tubes, Specifications, 1026, 1027
Mansfield District Traction Act, 259
Manson Bequest :
(Keiss) Caithness Scheme, 199, 200
(Moray and Nairn) Scheme, 199, 200
Mansonia, Properties of, 193
Mantle, etc., Trades Wages, 405, 891, 1048
Manufactured :
Fuel. *See* Coal, Coke, etc.
Goods, Marking of, Bill, 727
Manure, Farmyard, 849
Manures, 360
and Manuring, 1023
Artificial, Valuation of, 134
Manuring of Fruit Crops, 361
Manuscripts. *See* Historical Manuscripts.
Map :
Reading, Army, 229, 453, 688, 934, 1070
Reading, Photo Reading and Field Sketching, Army, 453, 688, 934, 1070
Weather, 647, 897
See also Litlington.
Maps :
for use in connection with R.A.F. Schemes, 625
Ireland, 694
Notes on the Making of, 689
Margaret Stephen, s.t., Wreck Report, 210
Margarine. *See* Merchandise Marks.
Margate Provisional Order Confirmation Act, 758
Bill, 701, 730

Margate, Broadstairs and District Electricity Act, 299
Maria de Larrinaga, s.s., Wreck Report, 916
Marine :
Boiler in s.s. *Baronesa*, Explosion, Report, 1061
Deposits :
of the Arabian Sea, 942
Stratification of Biological Remains in, 942
Engines, Handbook of Collections, 652
Forces. *See* Naval and Marine Forces.
Insurance :
Market, Re-Insurance of, Provisional Scheme. *Cmd. 6002*, 741
Rates, Hudson Bay, Report, 918
Mercantile. *See* Mercantile Marine ; Polish Mercantile Marine ; Merchant Shipping.
Observer, 181, 408, 646, 896
Observer's Handbook, 409
Mariners, Notices to, 128, 355, 588, 844, 1019
Marines :
Examinations, 150, 376, 607, 918, 1031
Extension of Term of Service, Proclamation, 894
Marriage Allowance for Officers. *Cmd. 5746*, 509
Royal Marines Act, 754
Bill, 708, 733
See also Navy and Marines.
Maritime :
Buoyage, Uniform System of, International Agreement. *Cmd. 5590*, 291
Directory. *See* Mercantile Navy List.
Museum. *See* National Maritime Museum.
Marketing Boards, Departmental Committee on Imposition of Penalties by, Report. *Cmd. 5980*, 740
Markets. *See* Livestock Markets.
Markham Colliery, Derbyshire, Explosion, Report. *Cmd. 5456*, 281
Marking. *See* English Plate Marking ; Hall Marking ; Foreign Plate ; Manufactured Goods.
Marking Ink, Specification, 1068
Marks. *See* Certification Mark ; Merchandise Marks ; Trade Marks ; Patents, Designs and Trade Marks.
Marne, Battle of the, 223, 449
Marrack, J. R., Chemistry of Antigens and Antibodies, 657
Marriage :
Act, 1898, Rules and Regs., 190
Act, 1939, 753
Bill, 493, 498, 702, 704, 719, 732
Allowance. *See* Marines ; Navy.
Bill, 1936, 36, 37, 41
Constitution of, Law of Scotland, Report. *Cmd. 5354*, 274
(Licensing of Chapels) Measure, 463, 464, 528
(Scotland) Act, 753
Bill, 474, 494, 499, 705, 720, 726, 730
(Scotland) (Emergency Provisions) Act, 971
Bill, 947, 963
See also Matrimonial Causes ; Divorce.
Marriages :
Buildings :
in which Marriages may be solemnised under the provisions of the Marriage (Navy, Army, and Air Force Chapels) Act, 1932, List, 417
registered or disused for Marriages, List of, 417
Provisional Orders Confirmation Acts :
1936, 70
Bill, 12, 38
1937, 300
Bill, 241, 267
1938, 526
Bill, 468, 495
Registration of. *See* Registrar-General.
Validity Act, 753
Bill, 702, 731
Married :
Couples, Young, Housing of, 912
Officers, Allowances, Army, 928, 1066, 1070
Marshall, F. H. A., Fertility and Animal Breeding, 360
Marshall Trust Scheme, 199, 200, 426
Marske-by-the-Sea. *See* Saltburn.
Marwick, A. H. D., The Shape of Road Agregate and its Measurement, 422
Mary, Queen of Scots, State Papers, 189, 417
See also Philip and Mary.
Maryport :
Harbour Act, 757
Pier and Harbour Provisional Order Confirmation Act, 70
Bill, 13, 39
Mason, M., Preserves from the Garden, 1023
Master's and Crew Spaces (Ships), Instructions, 437

Masters of Freight Ships and Transports, Instructions for, 437, 918, 1064
Mastic, Asphalt, for Roofing, 419
Mastitis in Cattle, 850
Material, Testing of, at A.I.D. Test Houses, 1030
Maternal :
Mortality :
Medical Practitioners called in by Midwives, 619
Wales, 623
Reports, etc. *Cmd. 5422*, 279
Circular, 388
Wales. *Cmd. 5423*, 279
Circular, 393
Welfare Circular, 201
Maternity :
and Child Welfare :
Department of Health for Scotland Publications (N.P.), 429, 666
Ministry of Health Publications (N.P.), 160, 621, 912
Homes and Hospitals, Costing Returns, 162, 389, 620, 873
Nurses, Scotland, Circulars, 429, 1060
Services (Scotland) Act, 296
Bill, 41, 42, 239, 252, 263, 266
Mathematics :
Alternative Scheme of, for Technical and Rural (Boys) Courses, 914
Note as to, 204
Short History of, 901
Mathews, D. D., Aggregates and Workability of Concrete, 661
Mathews, D. J., Velocity of Sound in Pure Water and Sea Water, 847
Matlock Provisional Order Confirmation Acts :
1936, 68
Bill, 8, 37
1939, 758
Bill, 701, 730
Matrices. *See* Import Duties Advisory Committee.
Matrimonial :
and other matters, Summary Procedure. *See* Summary Procedure (Domestic Proceedings).
Causes (formerly Marriage) Act, 297
Bill, 241, 244, 245, 251, 262, 266, 270
(as "Marriage Bill"), 36, 37, 41
Mats, Specification, 1068
Matt Pigmented :
Lanolin-Resin Finishes, Specifications, 1027, 1029
Oil Varnishes and Primer, Specification, 1026
Mattick, A. T. R., Handling of Milk and Milk Products, 360
Mattress Cases, Specification, 1069
Mattresses, Hair, Specifications, 932, 1069
Maude, Sir J., Chairman, Town and Country Planning Advisory Committee, Report on Preservation of the Countryside, 623
Maudslay Collection of Maya Sculptures in British Museum, Guide to, 694
Mauritius : Colonial Reports, 152, 378, 861
See also French Telegraph.
Maxwell, Sir A., Chairman, Departmental Committee on Courts of Summary Jurisdiction in the Metropolitan Area, Report, 394
Maya Sculptures. *See* Maudslay Collection.
Maybury, Sir H. P., Chairman, Committee to consider the Development of Civil Aviation in the U.K., Report. *Cmd. 5351*, 273
Mayne, J. E. O., The Effect of Fibre Cores on Internal Corrosion in Colliery Winding Ropes, 413
Meadow Saffron, 363
Meals :
at Courses of Instruction, 643
extracted, Use of, 360
See also Canteen Meals.
Measurement :
of Gas, 15, 16
of Rooms (Scotland), 201
Time, Handbook of Collections, 189, 415
Tonnage, of Ships, 437, 919
Measures :
Church Assembly, 72, 302, 528, 760, 973
See also Weights and Measures.
Meat :
Inspection of, 360
Production and Trade, 171, 398, 634
Trade, Anglo-Argentine, Joint Committee of Inquiry into, Report. *Cmd. 5839*, 516
See also Retail Meat Dealers.
Mecca Pilgrims, Sanitary Control over, at Kamaran Island, Netherlands, India and U.K. *Cmd. 6096*, 748
Mechanical :
Engineers :
Coal Mines, Regs., to be supplied to, 899
National Certificates, etc., of the Institution of Mechanical Engineers, Award of, 914
Road Vehicles, Collection at Science Museum, 187
Testing of Bituminous Road Materials, 907
Vehicles, Wheeled, Driving and Maintenance, Army, 685, 929

Mechanically-propelled Vehicles :
Noise in the operation of, 214, 441
Number registered, 219, 443, 681, 925
Mechanics, Applied, Examples in, 586
Medals :
British and Foreign, 414, 900
General Service, Palestine, 930
Medical :
and Dental :
Branches, R.A.F., Training, 599, 853
Officers, R.A.F., Manual, 599, 853, 1025
Assistance, Society registered for, Annual Return Form, 1034
Attention and Treatment of Casuals, 161
Branches, R.A.F., Training of Airmen, 369
Corps, Army, War Office Publications (N.P.), 229, 455, 689, 936, 1071
Examination :
for Fitness for Flying, 139, 365, 599, 853, 1025
of Recruits, Army, 454
Guide, Ship Captain's, 919
Inspection and Treatment, Unemployed Boys and Girls, 177
Manual of Chemical Warfare, 1067
Notes and First-Aid Treatment, Tropics and Sub-Tropics, R.A.F., 139, 365, 853, 1025
Officers :
at First Aid Posts, Memo for guidance of, 873
Scotland, 911
of R.A.F. :
Guidance in Selection of Recruits, 653
Manual for, 139, 365
Practitioners :
called in by Midwives, Fees, 162, 619, 1034
Communications (Privilege) Bill, 235
Women :
Employment of, Army, 937
Uniform for, 1072
Research Council :
Annual Reports :
Cmd. 5079, 45
Cmd. 5378, 275
Cmd. 5671, 503
Cmd. 5939, 737
Cmd. 6163, 965
Publications (N.P.), 191, 418, 657, 904, 1055
Scales, Merchant Shipping, 209
Service List, Colonial, 153, 380, 610, 1031
Medical (*continued*) :
Services, Army, 229, 453, 688, 934, 1070
See also Emergency Medical Services.
Subjects, Public Health and, Reports, 392, 622, 874
Supervision in Factories, Memo., 1042
Treatment :
at Courses of Instruction, 643
of Gas Casualties, 394
Uses of Radium, 192, 419, 657, 1055
Medicinal Products, Trade in, Agreement between Italy and U.K. *Cmd. 6199*, 967
Medicine :
Careers, 401
Stamp Duties, Reports, 32, 252
See also War Medicine.
Medicines and Surgical Appliances (Advertisement) Bill, 36
Mediterranean :
Declarations by Italy and U.K. :
Cmd. 5348, 273
Cmd. 5429, 279
Piracy in. *Cmds. 5568, 5569*, 289
Medway Conservancy Act, 759
Meeting. *See* Public Meeting.
Melrose Abbey, Guide and Plan, 691
Membranes. *See* Chorio-Allantoic Membranes.
Memorials. *See* British War Memorials.
Men Teachers and National Service, 913
Mental :
Defect, Clinical and Genetic Study of, 657
Deficiency :
Act, 523
Bill, 470, 495
(Scotland) Act, 971
Bill, 945, 962
See also Control, Board of ; Lunacy.
Menzies, W. J. M., The Movement of Salmon marked in the Sea, 427, 665
Meranti, Forest Products Research Record, 493
Mercantile :
Marine :
Board of Trade Publications (N.P.), 207, 435, 673, 917
Ministry of Shipping Publications (N.P.), 1061
See also Navy, Army, Air Force and Mercantile Marine ; Polish Mercantile Marine.
Navy List, 209, 438, 674, 919, 1061
Mercerised Cotton Fabric, Specification, 369

Merchandise :
Conveyance by Rail, Proposals, 926
Marks :
(Amendment) Bill, 1938, 493
Bill, 1939, 731
(Imported Goods), Reports :
Buckles, Slides, Clasps and
Buttons. Cmd. 6080, 746
Cased Tubes. Cmd. 6094, 747
Door Bolts. Cmd. 5619, 294
Geographical Globes. Cmd.
6086, 747
Grapes. Cmd. 5147, 49
Margarine. Cmd. 4907, 521
Sanitary Ware of Pottery.
Cmd. 5753, 509
Spectacle Frames, Fronts, etc.
Cmd. 6147, 751
1937 :
No. 1. Picture or Greeting
Postcards. Cmd. 5472,
282
Exemption Direction No.
1. Bricks and Tiles.
Cmd. 5473, 283
1938 :
No. 2. Textile Smallwares.
Cmd. 5638, 501
No. 3. Sporting Cartridge
Cases. Cmd. 5729, 507
No. 4. Basketware. Cmd.
5796, 512
No. 5. Various articles
worn with watches.Cmd.
5819, 514
No. 6. Solid-headed pins
of brass, iron or steel.
Cmd. 5835, 515
Merchant :
Navy :
Careers, 401
Meritorious Service Awards and
Commendations, 1049
Shipping :
Act, 1906, Reports of cases, 255,
483, 717
Act, 1937, 296
Bill, 237, 252, 263, 265
Acts, 1894 to 1932 (Dispensing
Powers), Report by Board of
Trade, 25
Air Raid Precautions, 166
(Carriage of Munitions to Spain)
Act, 67
Bill, 18, 42
Instructions to Surveyors, 435
Medical Scales, 209
Principal Acts of Parliament,
Regs., etc., Lists of, 209, 437,
674, 919, 1061
(Salvage) Act, 972
Bill, 948, 963

Merchant (continued) :
Shipping (continued) :
(Spanish Frontiers Observation)
Act, 296
Bill, 237, 238, 266
(Superannuation Contributions)
Act, 297
Bill, 247, 272
See also Load Line Certificates.
Mercury Bichloride. See Import Duties
Advisory Committee.
Meritorious Service Awards and Com-
mendations, 1049
Mersey :
Docks and Harbour Board Act, 58
Railway Power and Pumping
Stations, Labourer, Industrial
Court Award, 175
River, Discharge of Crude Sewage
into, 662
Merthyr Tydfil Corporation Act, 759
Merton and Morden Urban District
Council Act, 72
Meshes of Fishing Nets, International
Convention. Cmd. 5494, 284
Mess Grants,Initial,Territorial Army,934
Messages, Wireless, Weather, 182
Messengers, Fire Brigades, Uniform, 880
Messrooms and Canteens at Small
Factories, 1037
Metal :
Alloys containing silver or gold,
Import Duties. Cmd. 5208, 54
Deterioration of structure of, exposed
to Sea Water, 193, 420, 658
Parts, Protection against Corrosion,
Processes for Cleaning, etc., Speci-
fications, 369, 1027
Plating, Specifications, 369
Sheets,Coatingof,FactoryForm,1036
Unwrought Alloys of. See Import
Duties Advisory Committee.
Vitreous Enamelling of, Factory
Form, 630
Wares. See Stamped or Pressed
Metal Wares.
See also Non-ferrous Metals.
Metal-bodied Aerated Water Syphons.
See Import Duties Advisory Com-
mittee.
Metalliferous Mines, 185, 412, 651, 900,
1053
See also Mines and Quarries Forms.
Metallising, Specification, 369
Metallurgical Examination of Colliery
Haulage Drawgear, 413
Metallurgy Research Board Publica-
tions (N.P.), 422
Metals :
Grinding of, Factory Forms, 1042
Pure, Physical Constants, 194
See also Non-Ferrous Metals.

Meteorological :
Glossary, 896
Magazine, 181, 408, 646, 896, 1052
Observations, 188, 653, 901
Observer's Handbook, 409, 1052
Office Publications (N.P.), 180, 408,
645, 896, 1052
Telegraphy, Instructions for, 1052
Meteorology, 645
Elementary, Short Course in for
Aviators, 896, 1052
in relation to Air Navigation, 646
Modern, Introduction to, 897
Observations in, 653, 901, 1054
Meters, Testing of, 440
See also Electricity Meters ; Elec-
tricity Supply (Meters).
Methil. See Buckhaven.
Methodist Church Act, 757
Methylated Spirits :
(Sale by Retail) (Scotland) Act, 297
Bill, 239,243,256,263,266,267,269
See also Licensing.
Metropolitan :
Area, Courts of Summary Jurisdic-
tion in, Report, 394
Borough Councils (Proportional Rep-
resentation) Bill, 268
Police :
Commissioners' Annual Reports :
Cmd. 5165, 50
Cmd. 5457, 281
Cmd. 5761, 510
Cmd. 6073, 746
Cmd. 6201, 967
Courts, Accounts. See Fund
below.
Duties in Air Raid Precaution
Schemes, 393
Examinations, 150, 376, 606, 858
Fund Accounts, 28, 258, 485, 719,
958
Guide, 943
Laboratory,Dangerous Drugs,394
Office Publications (N.P.), 943
Water Board Act, 760
Mexico :
Economic Conditions, 213
Expropriation of Oil Properties in.
Cmd. 5758, 510
Mice, Destruction of, 849
See also Rats and Mice.
Microbiology in the Preservation of :
Animal Tissues, 404
the Hen's Egg, 905
Middlesex :
County Council :
(General Powers) Act, 528
(Sewerage) Act; 527
Deeds Act, 971
Bill, 947, 963
Hospital Act, 525

Middlesex (continued) :
Land Registry, Deeds, Form, 179
London and, (Improvements) Act, 71
Mid-East England :
and South-East England, Electricity
Schemes, 212
Electricity (Alteration and Exten-
sion) Scheme, 926
Midge, Chrysanthemum, 363, 595, 850
Midland :
(Amalgamated) District Coal Mines
Scheme, 183, 648
and North Midland Division, Report
of H.M. Inspector of Mines, 184
and Southern Division, Mines,
Report, 898
Division, Mines, Reports, 411, 648
Valley of Scotland, Geology, 194
Midlands :
East Anglia and, Guide to Monu-
ments, 231
See also North Midlands ; North-
West Midlands ; West Midlands.
Midlothian Educational Trust (Amend-
ment and Additional Endowments)
(No. 1) Scheme, 664, 910
Mid-Southern Electricity Orders, 213
Mid-Staffordshire Joint Hospital District
Provisional Order Confirmation Act,
757
Bill, 474, 496, 498
Mid-Sussex Joint Hospital District Pro-
visional Order Confirmation Act, 68
Bill, 6, 36
Midwifery Training, 619, 1035
Midwives :
Act, 66
Bill, 16, 30, 34, 37, 40
Circulars, 161, 618, 871, 876
Qualifications of Supervisors, 388
See also Central Midwives Board ;
Medical Practitioners.
Migrations. See Butterfly Migrations.
Migratory Poor, Census of, Form, 431
Mildew, American Gooseberry, 135
Milford Haven and Tenby Water Act,
759
Military :
Aircraft, Exemption from Duty on
Fuel and Lubricants, France and
U.K. Cmd. 5998, 741
and Air Forces (Prolongation of
Service) Act, 755
Bill, 708, 733
Cooking and Dietary, Manual of, 453
Engineering, 454
Forces :
Allowances for Dependents of
Men Serving in. Cmd. 6138,
751
Disabled, etc., Pay, Pensions,
etc. Cmd. 6205, 968

Military (continued) :
Forces (continued) :
Mutual Powers of Command
raised in Canada and U.K.,1070
Retired Pay, Pensions, etc., for
Members of. Cmd. 6105, 748
Honours, 1050
Hospitals, Pharmacopoeia for use in,
689, 1071
Law, Manual of, 454, 688, 934, 1070
Manoeuvres Commission, Report.
Cmd. 5103, 47
Missions. See British Military Mis-
sions.
Obligations in cases of Double
Nationality. Cmd. 5460, 281
Pioneer Corps, Auxiliary, Forma-
tion, 929
Police Manual, 230, 934
Promotions, 644
Railways Rule Book, 934
Staff Changes, 893, 1048
Terms and Abbreviations, German,
Vocabulary, 930
Training :
Act, 753
Bill, 702, 729, 730
Act, 1939, and Reserve and
Auxiliary Forces Act, 1939,
Monetary Assistance to per-
sons liable to Training or Ser-
vice, in respect of Dependants,
etc. Cmd. 6043, 744
Consequential Provisions Circu-
lar, 913
Militia :
Mobilisation, 934
Regs. for, 934
Milk :
Acts, amendments proposed to be
made by the Milk (Extension and
Amendment) Bill. Cmd. 5772, 511
(Amendment) Act, 297
Bill, 246, 270
Memo. Cmd. 5506, 285
and Dairies :
Acts and Orders, 594
Circular, 619
Guide to Powers and Duties
of Local Authorities, 594
Arrangement for increasing demand :
England and Wales, 135, 363,
596, 850
Scotland, 204, 432, 670, 915
Bacteriological :
Grading of, 191
Tests for, 164
Container,"Perga"SingleService,848
Distribution, Costs and Profits, 436,
1033
Distributive Trade, Wages, 176, 642,
891, 1047

Milk (continued) :
(Extension and Amendment) Act, 523
Bill, 497
(Extension of Temporary Provi-
sions) Act, 65
Bill, 7, 37
Memo. Cmd. 5092, 46
Handling of, 360
Industry Act, 753
Bill, 499
(No. 2) Bill, 706, 731
Iodine Content of, Relationship to
Occurrence of Endemic Goitre, 192
Marketing Scheme :
amended to August 3, 1937, 596
Reports of Committee of Investi-
gation on Complaints, 135
Scotland, 205
Modern Milk Production, 593
Nutritive Value of, 164
Policy. Cmd. 5533, 287
Preserved, Production and Trade,
171, 398, 883
Products :
Handling of, 360
See also Import Duties Advisory
Committee.
Provision of :
at a reduced price for Mothers
and Children, 911, 915
at Courses of Instruction, 643
for School Children, 203
Quality of, Circumstances affecting,
849
Reorganisation Commission Report,
133
Special Designations :
Circulars, 161, 162, 164, 620
Scotland, 201, 666
Report Card for Dairy Forms, 201
Supply of Cheap Milk to Welfare
Authorities, 672
Wales, 876
Wastes on the Bristol Avon, Effect
of, 594
Ways of using Nature's best food,
1032
Milking :
Hand and Machine, 595
Machine, Alfa-Laval, 592
Milk-sampling Plunger, " Spanate ", 848
Miller, A. T., Chairman of Committee
on Insurance of Ships, Report. Cmd.
5349, 273
Miller, R. A., Studies in Road Friction,
422
Millinery Trade, Wages, 405, 890, 1047
Milling Machines, Horizontal, Regs., 395
Millipedes and Centipedes, 595
Mills : Restoration of, in Rural Areas
Bill, 497
See also Paper Mills.

Milne, Lord, Chairman, Central Advi-
sory Water Committee :
Draft of a Water Undertakings Bill.
Cmd. 5987, 740
Report, 618
Second Report. Cmd. 5986, 740
Milne's Institution Trust Scheme, 199,
426
Milton. See Gravesend ; Sittingbourne.
Mine Dust, Analysis of, 651
Mines and Quarries Form, 1054
Minehead and Dunster, Electricity, 440
Mineral :
Deposits, Location of, 187
Gallery, British Museum, Guide to,
460
Industry of the British Empire and
Foreign Countries, 172, 399, 634,
694, 883, 943
Resources :
of Great Britain, Special Reports,
661
of Scotland, Synopsis, 1058
See also Nationalisation of Mines.
Miner's :
Nystagmus, Workmen's Compensa-
tion Questions, Report of Com-
mittee. Cmd. 5657, 502
Welfare, Annual Reports, 185, 412,
649, 899
Mines :
Abandoned, Plans of, 182
Air Raid Shelters for Persons working
in, Memo. on Revised Code, 876
and Quarries Forms, 185, 412, 649,
899, 1053
Back-stays for use in, 1054
Deaths caused by accidents at,
1053
Department Publications (N.P.), 182,
411, 647, 897, 1053
Examinations, 373
Workmen's Compensation Forms,
397, 632
See also Coal ; Metalliferous Mines ;
Nationalisation of Mines ; Mining.
Minimum Structural Grade for Red-
wood, 906
Mining :
Industry :
Act, 1926, Reports by Board of
Trade :
Cmd. 5162, 50
Cmd. 5370, 275
Cmd. 5701, 505
Cmd. 5982, 740
(Amendment) Act, 753
Bill, 721, 726, 729
(Welfare Fund) Act, 752
Bill, 698, 706, 714, 726, 727
Subsidence Bill, 705, 720, 726, 731

Ministers :
and Heads of Public Departments,
List of, 205, 433, 671, 916, 1062
of the Crown Act, 296
Bill, 241, 267, 268
See also Crown.
Minley Manor. See Camberley.
Minster Lovell Hall, Guide to, 938
Mint, Royal, Annual Reports, 413, 652,
900
Mirabella Bay. See " Imperia ", M/Y.
Miscellaneous :
Clothing Materials, Army, Specifica-
tion, 1068
Series :
1890 :
No. 1. Religious Questions in
Malta. C. 5975, 500
1935 :
No. 5. League of Nations,
16th Assembly, Report.
Cmd. 5053, 43
No. 6. Damage caused by
Aircraft to Third Parties on
the Surface, International
Convention. Cmd. 5056,
43
1936 :
No. 1. Limitation of Naval
Armament, U.K., Canada,
Australia, New Zealand,
India, U.S.A., and France.
Cmd. 5136, 48
No. 2. London Naval Con-
ference, Memo. Cmd. 5137,
49
No. 3. Diplomatic Discus-
sions towards European
Settlement. Cmd. 5143, 49
No. 4. Correspondence with
Belgian and French Ambas-
sadors on Cmd. 5134. Cmd.
5149, 49
No. 5. Admission of Women
to the Diplomatic and Con-
sular Services. Cmd. 5166,
50
No. 6. German Proposals for
a European Settlement.
Cmd. 5175, 51
No. 7. Regulation of Air
Navigation. Protocols
regarding amendment of
Brussels Convention. Cmd.
5332, 63
1937 :
No. 1. Bank of International
Settlements, Immunities of.
No. 2. League of Nations,
17th Assembly, Report.
Cmd. 5365, 274

Miscellaneous Series (*continued*) :
- 1937 (*continued*) :
  - No. 3. Regulations of Sugar Production and Marketing, International Agreement. *Cmd. 5461*, 281
  - No. 4. Regulation of Whaling, International Agreement. *Cmd. 5487*, 283
  - No. 5. Regulation of sizes of Meshes of Fishing Nets and the Size Limits of Fish, International Agreement. *Cmd. 5494*, 284
  - No. 6. Use of Broadcasting in the cause of Peace, International Convention. *Cmd. 5505*, 285
  - No. 7. Abolition of Capitulations in Morocco and Zanzibar, Convention, France and U.K. *Cmd. 5538*, 287
  - No. 8. Uniform System of Maritime Buoyage, International Agreement. *Cmd. 5590*, 291
- 1938 :
  - No. 1. International Trade, Report by M. van Zeeland. *Cmd. 5648*, 502
  - No. 2. Immunity of State-owned Ships. *Cmd. 5672*, 503
  - No. 3. Immunity of State-owned Ships, Supplementary Protocol. *Cmd. 5673*, 503
  - No. 4. International Institute of Refrigeration, establishment of. *Cmd. 5747*, 509
  - No. 5. Status of Refugees from Germany. *Cmd. 5780*, 511
  - No. 6. Regulation of Whaling. *Cmd. 5827*, 515
  - No. 7. Correspondence respecting Czechoslovakia. *Cmd. 5847*, 516
  - No. 8. Czechoslovakia, further documents including the Munich Agreement. *Cmd. 5848*, 516
  - No. 9. Covenant of the League of Nations, Protocol for Amendment. *Cmd. 5884*, 519
  - No. 10. League of Nations, 19th Assembly, Report. *Cmd. 5899*, 520
  - No. 11. Frontier between Germany and Czechoslovakia. *Cmd. 5908*, 521

Miscellaneous Series (*continued*) :
- 1939 :
  - No. 1. European Commission of the Danube, Exercise of Powers and Privileges and Immunities of Personnel. *Cmd. 5946*, 737
  - No. 2. International Disputes, General Act for the pacific settlement of. *Cmd. 5947*, 737
  - No. 3. Palestine, Correspondence between Sir Henry McMahon and the Sharif Hussein of Mecca. *Cmd. 5957*, 738
  - No. 4. Ottoman Empire, Future Status of certain parts of. *Cmd. 5964*, 739
  - No. 5. Sanitary Conference at Paris. *Cmd. 5979*, 739
  - No. 6. Limitation of Naval Armament, Denmark, Finland, Norway, Sweden, and U.K. *Cmd. 5999*, 741
  - No. 7. Liquid Fuel and Lubricants used in Air Traffic, Exemption from Taxation, International Conference. *Cmd. 6001*, 741
  - No. 8. Germany and U.K., Correspondence. *Cmd. 6102*, 748
  - No. 9. Germany, Documents concerning German-Polish relations and outbreak of hostilities between Great Britain and Germany. *Cmd. 6106*, 748
  - No. 10. International Justice, Optional Clause of Statute of Permanent Court of. *Cmd. 6108*, 748
- 1940 :
  - No. 1. League of Nations, 20th Assembly, Report. *Cmd. 6160*, 965
  - No. 2. Palestine Land Transfers Regs. *Cmd. 6180*, 966
  - No. 3. International Justice, Optional Clause of Statute of Permanent Court of. *Cmd. 6185*, 966

Missions. *See* British Military Missions.
Mites, Poultry, 849
Model :
- Byelaws, 164, 391, 621
  - Scotland, 429, 666
- Health Clinic, 622
- Rules for Approved Societies, National Health Insurance, 622

Modern :
- Agriculture, Fertilizers in, 828
- Building, Principles of, 658, 904
- Languages, Instruction in, Holiday Courses on the Continent, 385, 615
- Meteorology, Introduction to, 897
- Milk Production, 593
- Rabbit Keeping, 1023

Mohair, Production, Trade and Consumption, 634, 883
Moisture :
- Content Determination of Timber, 906
- in Wood in relation to Strength and Shrinkage, 659

Mold Electricity Order, 213
Mole Draining, 849
Monckton, Sir W., Chairman, Departmental Committee on Distribution of Coal, Coke, and Manufactured Fuel, Minutes of Evidence, 648, 898
Money :
- Market, Banking, Careers, 174
- Resolutions, Procedure, Report, 260

Monier-Williams, G. W., Lead in Food, 623
Monmouthshire :
- and South Wales Employers' Mutual Indemnity Society Limited Act, 973
- Anti-Tuberculosis Service, Committee of Inquiry, Report, 870
- Census, 190
- *See also* Secretary of State.

Monoxide. *See* Carbon Monoxide.
Monuments. *See* Ancient Monuments.
Moonrise and Moonset, 354, 587, 842, 1018
Moore, W. C., Diseases of Bulbs, 849
Mop Handles, Specification, 1063
Mops, Specification, 686
Moran, T., Curing of Bacon, 1057
Moray and Nairn Educational Trust :
- Scheme, 426
- (Additional Endowment) (No. 1), 427, 664

Morden. *See* Merton.
Morecambe and Heysham Provisional Order Confirmation Act, 302
- Bill, 240, 270

Morellet, L. & J., Tertiary Siphoneous Algae in the W. K. Parker Collection, 943
Morgan Rotary Retort, Report of Test, 660
Morocco :
- Abolition of Capitulations.
  - *Cmd. 5538*, 287
  - *Cmd. 5646*, 501
- Commercial Relations between the U.K. and the French and Tangier Zones of the Shereefian Empire, Treaty, France and U.K. *Cmd. 5823*, 514
- Economic Conditions, 439, 921
- Imported Food Certificate, 871

Morreau, C. J., Reduction of Noise in Buildings, 904
Morrison, R. P., Explosion at Valleyfield Colliery, Report. *Cmd. 6226*, 969
Morrison's Academy Trust Scheme, 199, 200, 426
Mortality :
- Maternal. *See* Maternal Mortality.
- Rates in Urban Communities, 623
- Seasonal Incidence of, England, Wales and U.S.A., 1055

Mortar Training, Army, 230
Mortensen, Th., Echinoidea of the Murray Expedition, 942
Mortgage :
- Certificate, Customs, 155
- Interest. *See* Increase of Rent.

Mortgaged Land, Possession of (Emergency Provisions) Act, 755
- Bill, 708, 734

Mortgagees, Proceedings by, 407
Mortlake Crematorium Act, 72
Morton, G., Chairman, Poor Persons' Representation (Scotland) Committee, Report. *Cmd. 5435*, 279
Mortuaries and Post-Mortem Rooms, Model Byelaws, 621
Mosaic of Potatoes, 595
Mosquito :
- Boots, Specification, 452
- Nuisances, 1035

Mosquitoes, 943
- Longevity of, 623

Mossfield Colliery, Explosion at. *Cmd. 6227*, 969
Mossley. *See* Stalybridge.
Mother of Pearl. *See* Import Duties Advisory Committee.
Motherwell and Wishaw :
- Burgh Order Confirmation Act, 300
  - Bill, 245, 270
- Electricity, etc., Order Confirmation Act, 760
  - Bill, 708, 732

Moth, Pine Shoot, 159
Moths, Leaflets, 134, 849, 1023
Motor :
- Bus Drivers and Conductors, Northampton, Industrial Court Award, 175
- Car Headlights, Coloured Light for, 422
- Cars, Elections. *See* Elections (Motor Cars).
- Drivers :
  - Accident Proneness among, 1055
  - (Signals) Bill, 493
- Generators, Specification, 854
- Transport Industry Wages. *See* Road Motor Transport.
- Vehicles :
  - Emergency Conversion of, to Producer Gas, Committee on, Report, 1053

Motor (*continued*) :
- Vehicles (*continued*) :
  - (Forfeiture) Bill, 246
  - Index Marks, List and Directory of Registration and Licensing Authorities, 682
  - Offences relating to :
    - Forms, 169, 396, 632, 881
    - Returns, 29, 258, 485, 720
  - Survey of Trade in, 398
  - *See also* Goods Vehicles ; Mechanically-propelled Vehicles.
- Vessels. *See* Ships.

Mould, Tomato Leaf, 595
Mouldings, Specifications, 367, 855, 1030
Mountains. *See* Access to Mountains.
Movable Dwellings, 388
Movement :
- Control (Overseas in War), Instructions for, Army, 688
- (War), Manual of, 454

Moyne, Lord, Chairman, West India Royal Commission, Recommendations. *Cmd. 6174*, 966
Mozambique :
- Boundary between Tanganyika and, Exchange of Notes, Portugal and U.K. *Cmd. 5661*, 503
- Commercial Relations with Swaziland, Basutoland, Bechuanaland. *Cmd. 5807*, 513
- Native Labour, etc. :
  - *Cmd. 5085*, 45
  - *Cmd. 5703*, 506
  - *Cmd. 5817*, 514

Mucocutaneous Tertiary Syphilis, Treatment, 419
Mui-Tsai :
- in Hong Kong. *Cmd. 5121*, 48
- in Hong Kong and Malaya, 381

Mulberry, Paper. *See* Import Duties Advisory Committee.
Mumbles Pier Act, 757
Mummies. *See* Egyptian Mummies.
Municipal Housing Estates, Management of, Report, 618
- Circular, 620

Munitions, Carriage of, to Spain. *See* Merchant Shipping.
Munro, J. W., Infestation of Grain by Insects, 1058
Murchison of Taradale Memorial Trust Scheme, 200, 426
Murray, A. M. T. :
- Dietary Survey in terms of the Actual Foodstuffs Consumed, 418
- Studies in Nutrition, 1056

Murray, John, Expedition, Scientific Reports, 942
Murray's Bequest Scheme, 199, 200
Muscat, Treaty of Commerce and Navigation with U.K. *Cmd. 6037*, 743
Muscidae, 943
Muscinae, 943
Museums :
- Industrial, exhibits, 167
- Practical Geology, 194
- *See also* National Museums and Galleries ; Science Museum ; Victoria and Albert Museum ; British Museum.

Museums, Picture Galleries, and Libraries, Air Raid Precautions in, 941
Mushroom-growing, 593
Music :
- Printing, History of, 941
- Teaching of, Suggestions, 386

Mustering and Pay of Army Tradesmen in War, 1070
Mutton, Production and Trade, 171, 398, 634
Mutual Assistance Agreements :
- Poland and U.K. :
  - *Cmd. 6101*, 748
  - *Cmd. 6144*, 751
- Turkey, France, and U.K. *Cmd. 6123*, 750

Mycology Series, 420, 659
Mysidacea, 942

N

In order that compounds can be listed in proper alphabetical sequence, the practice of using a single heading has not been followed in the case of the words New *and* North.

Nairn. *See* Moray and Nairn.
Nall, G. H. :
- Sea Trout of River Carron and Loch Doule, 665
- Sea Trout of River Conon, 665

Napthol, Import Duties. *Cmd. 5244*, 57
Narcissus Bulbs, efficiency of Baths used for the Hot-water Treatment of, 361
Narrow Brick Retorts, Low Temperature Carbonisation, 906
Nasopharyngeal Bacterial Flora of Different Groups of Persons, 875
National :
- Advisory Councils for Juvenile Employment, Reports, 403
- Arbitration Tribunal Awards, 1043
- Certificates, Board of Education Publications (N.P.), 866, 868
- Coal Resources, Physical and Chemical Survey of, 660, 906, 1057
- Coke and Oil Co., Ltd., Erith, Report of Test on Plant, 421
- Collections, Illustrated Catalogue of Publications, 615
- Committee for the Training of Teachers (Scotland), 203, 669

National (*continued*) :
- Debt :
  - Annuities Accounts, 91, 951, 190, 715, 955
  - Funds left in Trust. *Cmd. 5186*, 52
  - Position of Certain Funds :
    - *Cmd. 5466*, 282
    - *Cmd. 5744*, 508
    - *Cmd. 6017*, 742
    - *Cmd. 6202*, 967
  - Returns showing liabilities of the State, etc. :
    - *Cmd. 5271*, 39
    - *Cmd. 5549*, 288
    - *Cmd. 5836*, 515
    - *Cmd. 6092*, 747
    - *Cmd. 6228*, 969
  - Sinking Funds, Accounts, 29
- Defence :
  - Companies, Outfit Allowance, 935
  - Contribution :
    - Appeals to High Court, etc., 1059
    - Charge of. *Cmd. 5485*, 283
- Emergency Precautions, Clergy, Measure, 706, 760
- Expenditure, Select Committee on, Reports, 950, 957, 960
- Fitness :
  - Council Publications (N.P.), 615, 867
  - The First Steps, 385
- Forest Park Committee (Snowdonia) Report, 386
- Galleries Publications (N.P.), 186, 187
  - Scotland, 202
  - *See also* National Museums.
- Gallery :
  - and Tate Gallery, Annual Reports, 414, 652
  - Publications (N.P.), 694
  - Scotland, Annual Reports, 429, 667, 912
- Health, Widows', Orphans', and Old Age Pensions and Unemployment Insurance :
  - Army, 934
  - Reserve and Auxiliary Forces and Auxiliary Territorial Service, 1070
- Health Insurance :
  - Act, 66
    - Bill, 6, 7, 12, 13, 46
  - Act (Amendment) Act, 296
    - Bill, 237, 266
  - Acts, Summary of, 164, 622
  - Advances of Benefit in Compensation Cases, etc., 391
  - (Amendment) Act, 522
    - Bill, 272, 463

National (*continued*) :
- Health Insurance (*continued*) :
  - and Contributory Pensions :
    - (Emergency Provisions) Act, 754
      - Bill, 733
    - Outline of Schemes in U.K., 874
  - Approved Societies :
    - Assets and Liabilities, Report. *Cmd. 5496*, 284
    - List of, 391
    - Model Rules for, 622
  - Army, 934
  - Decisions as to Liability, 164, 391, 622, 874, 1035
  - Drug Tariff, 873
  - Forms, 391, 622
  - Fund :
    - Accounts, 23, 27, 252, 479, 714, 951
    - Accounts showing the Nature and Amount of the Securities held, 254, 479, 714, 954
  - (Juvenile Contributors and Young Persons) Act, 297
    - Bill, 247, 269, 271, 272
  - Model Rules for Approved Societies, 622
  - Personnel of R.A.F., 139, 599
  - Transfer, Forms, 164, 391
- Insurance :
  - Act, 522
  - Audit Department, Annual Reports, 186, 413, 652, 900, 1054
  - Scottish Union and, Company's Act, 757
- Library of Scotland, 202, 429, 667, 912, 1060
- Loans :
  - Act, 1939, 755
    - Bill, 734
  - Act, 1940, 971
    - Bill, 945, 962
      - Memo. *Cmd. 6155*, 964
  - No. 2 Act, 1940, 971
    - Bill, 963
- Maritime Museum, Greenwich, Publications (N.P.), 414, 652, 900
- Museums and Galleries :
  - of London :
    - Brief Guide to, 414, 916
    - Lectures, Special Exhibitions, etc., 652, 901
  - Publications (N.P.), 652, 900
  - Standing Commission on, Report, 652
  - *See also* Museums.
- Physical Laboratory, 194, 422, 661, 907, 1058
- Portrait Gallery, 187, 414, 652, 907

NAT— INDEX 1936-40

National (continued) :
Radium Trust and Radium Commission Reports :
Cmd. 5112, 47
Cmd. 5342, 273
Cmd. 5612, 293
Cmd. 5883, 519
Cmd. 6161, 965
Rat Week Posters, 850
Registration :
Act, 755
Bill, 733
Army, 934
Form, 882
Savings Committee Reports, 221, 447, 683, 927
Service :
(Armed Forces) Act, 1939, 754
Bill, 733
British Subjects liable for Service, Proclamation, 894
Decisions by Umpire in respect of Application of Postponement of Liability to be called up for Service, 1045
Pay of Soldiers enlisted under, 935
(Armed Forces) Act, 1940, 971
Bill, 962
Campaign : Enrolment of Volunteers :
A.R.P., 674
Auxiliary Fire Services, 880
(Channel Islands) Act, 971
Bill, 947, 963
Teachers and, 913
See also Labour.
Trust :
Acts, 300, 759
for Scotland Order Confirmation Acts, 67, 757
Bill, 1938, 475, 499
War Bonds, 1945-47, Notice, 1052
Whitley Council Reports :
Promotion Procedure, 683
Subsistence Allowances, 220
Nationalisation of Mines and Minerals Bill, 265, 492
Nationality :
Laws, Conflict of. Cmd. 5553, 288
of Carrying Vessels, Overseas Trade of U.K., 437, 674
of Persons affected by the Re-Delimitation of the Boundary between Burma (Tenasserim) and Siam. Cmd. 5475, 282
of Seamen, 435, 673
See also British Nationality.
Native Labour. See Mozambique.
Natural History Museum :
Annual Reports, 186, 413, 652, 900
Publications (N.P.), 460, 694, 941

Natural Sciences, Careers, 401
Naturalisation :
Forms, 881
Returns, 32, 261, 722
See also Aliens.
Nautical Almanac, 126,354,587,842,1018
Naval :
and Air Facilities for the United States in British Transatlantic Territories and United States Destroyers, Exchange of Notes. Cmd. 6224, 969
and Marine Forces (Temporary Release from Service) Bill, 963
Armament : Limitation, etc. :
Denmark, Finland, Norway, Sweden, and U.K. Cmd. 5999,741
France, U.S.A., Canada, Australia, India, New Zealand, and U.K. :
Cmd. 5136, 48
Cmd. 5561, 289
Germany and U.K. :
Cmd. 5519, 286
Cmd. 5637, 504
Cmd. 5795, 512
Cmd. 5834, 515
Poland and U.K. :
Cmd. 5739, 508
Cmds. 5916, 5917, 735
Protocol modifying Treaty of March 25, 1936. Cmd. 5781, 510
Soviet Union and U.K. :
Cmd. 5518, 285
Cmd. 5679, 504
Cmd. 5794, 512
Cmd. 6074, 746
Cadetships, Special Entry, Entrance Examination, 1030
Conference. See London Naval Conference.
Cookery, Manual of, 354
Court Martial Procedure, 354
Discipline :
Act, 524
(Amendment) Act, 523
Bill, 496, 497
Establishments, Examinations, 146
Reserve :
Officers, Regs., 842
Regs., 587
See also Indian Naval Reserve.
Treaty. See London Naval Treaty.
Naval, Military, and Air Force Honours, 1050
Navigable Waters, Oil in, Act, 64
Navigating Officers, Merchant Navy, Careers, 401
Navigation :
Admiralty Publications (N.P.), 125, 254, 586
Aids, 1022

Navigation (continued) :
and Shipping of the U.K., Annual Statements, 209, 437, 674, 1064
Colombia and U.K., Treaty. Cmd. 5958, 738
Cuba and U.K., Exchange of Notes. Cmd. 5867, 518
Examples in, 1018
France and Canada, Convention. Cmd. 5581, 290
Lighthouses and Other Aids to, 221, 928
Manual, 842, 1018
Muscat and U.K., Treaty. Cmd. 6037, 743
Netherlands and South Africa, Exchange of Notes. Cmd. 5818, 516
Peru and U.K., Agreement. Cmd. 5288, 60
Siam and U.K., Treaty. Cmd. 5731, 508
See also Air Navigation ; Aerial Navigation ; Free Navigation ; Paisley Corporation ; Trade and Navigation ; Transatlantic Steam Navigation ; Wear Navigation.
Navigators. See Civil Air(craft) Navigators.
Navy :
Admiralty Publications (N.P.), 125, 353, 586, 841, 1018
Ankle Boots, Specification, 452
and Marines (Wills) Act, 754
Appropriation Accounts, 24, 250, 478, 712, 951
Dockyard Accounts, 26, 255, 483, 716, 956
Estimates. See Estimates.
Examinations, 150,374,604,859,1030
First-Aid in, 353, 1018
Fleet Orders, 125
Gross and Net Cost, 22, 251, 479, 712, 953
Health of, 353, 126, 841
King's Regs. and Admiralty Instructions, 126, 353, 586, 842
List, 126, 354, 587, 842
Appendix, 1018
Marriage Allowances for Officers. Cmd. 5746, 509
Proclamations, 894
Royal Naval Sick Berth Staff, Manual of Instruction, 126
Statement of Excess, 254
Submarine Warfare, Rules. Cmd. 5302, 61
Votes, 21, 27, 256, 477, 483, 712, 717, 955
Vulnerability of Capital Ships to Air Attack. Cmd. 5301, 61
See also Estimates ; Fleet ; Marine ; Merchant Navy.

NET— INDEX 1936-40

Navy, Army, Air Force and Mercantile Marine Pensions Act, 754
Bill, 733
Navy, Army and Air :
Estimates, 1940. Cmd. 6176, 966
Force :
Examination Papers, 1031
Proclamations, 893
Necrosis, Net, of the Potato Tuber 595
Needle Trades, Occupation in, 174, 401
Negatives, Sound Track. See Import Duties Advisory Committee.
Negligence. See Contributory Negligence.
Nelson Electricity Orders, 213
Net :
Necrosis. See Necrosis.
Trade, Wages, 177, 642, 891, 1047
Netherlands :
Commercial Relations with Irish Free State. Cmd. 5442, 280
Duties on Fuel and Lubricants, Aircraft, Exemption. Cmd. 5074, 45
East Indies :
Economic Conditions, 211, 676
Prevention of Double Taxation of Income, Arrangement with Canada. Cmd. 5940, 737
Economic Conditions, 211, 676
Identity Documents for Aircraft Personnel, Exchange of Notes with Australia, New Zealand, India, and U.K. Cmd. 6130, 750
Imported Food Certificate, 618
Scotland, 666
Legal Proceedings Convention with U.K. Cmd. 5490, 283
Opium Smoking Agreement. Cmd. 5401, 277
Rubber, Regulation of Production and Export, Agreements :
Cmd. 5236, 56
Cmd. 5384, 276
Sanitary Control over Mecca Pilgrims at Kamaran Island, Exchange of Notes with India and U.K. Cmd. 6096, 748
Suez Maritime Canal, Free Navigation of, International Convention. Cmd. 5623, 500
Taxation :
of Air Transport Profits. Cmd. 5279, 59
of Profits or Gains arising through an Agency. Cmd. 5191, 53
Trade with British Colonies, etc. Cmd. 5061, 44
Netley Abbey, Hampshire, Guide, 457

106

107

NET— INDEX 1936-40

Nets :
Fishing, Size of Meshes, International Convention. Cmd. 5494, 284
Hair, Import Duties. Cmd. 5261, 58
Neuilly, Treaty of, Military, Naval and Air Clauses of, Exchange of Notes, Bulgaria and U.K. Cmd. 5954, 738
Neuroptera, 943
Neurosis in Wartime, Memo., 1054
Nevard, E. H. :
Development of a Minimum Structural Grade for Redwood, 906
Strength Tests of Structural Timbers, 420
Nevinson, J. L., Catalogue of English Domestic Embroidery, 695
Newall, H. E., Hydrogenation-cracking of Tars, 660
Newark-on-Trent, Sunday Entertainments, 956
Newbury :
Provisional Order Confirmation Act, 757
Bill, 699, 727
Sunday Entertainments, 953
Newcastle :
and District Electricity, 677
and Gateshead Waterworks Acts, 527, 972
War Risks Indemnity Association Ltd., 724
Newcastle-under-Lyme Corporation Act, 300
Newcastle-upon-Tyne :
Corporation :
Act, 301
(Trolley Vehicles) Order Confirmation :
Act, 1937, 298
Bill, 237, 265
Act, 1938, 527
Bill, 471, 495
Electricity, 677
Saint Mary Magdalene Hospital Act, 973
Trolley Vehicles Order Confirmation Act, 1940, 973
Bill, 962
New Forest, Protection of, 869
Newfoundland :
Commercial Relations :
with Brazil. Cmd. 5268, 58
with the Dominican Republic. Cmd. 6208, 968
Commission of Government, Report :
Cmd. 5117, 47
Cmd. 5425, 279
Cmd. 5741, 508
Cmd. 6010, 742
Payments to be made to the Sinking Fund, 21

Newfoundland (continued) :
Trade with Netherlands. Cmd. 5061, 44
Newhaven and Seaford Water Provisional Order Confirmation Act, 758
Bill, 703, 729
New Hebrides :
Colonial Reports, 152, 378, 609, 861, 1031
Condominium, Treasury Minute. Cmd. 5286, 60
Modification of Protocol, France and U.K. Cmd. 6184, 966
Newquay and District Water Acts, 300, 759
News Films. See Cinematograph News Films.
New Sarum, Electricity, 440
New Streets, Model Byelaws, 391, 621
Newton Elm, s.s., Explosion, 672
New Year's Honours. See London Gazette.
New York-Bermuda, Civil Air Transport Services :
Cmd. 5237, 56
Cmd. 5870, 518
New Zealand :
Aerial Navigation in the Antarctic, Exchange of Notes with France and U.K. Cmd. 5900, 520
Arbitration Convention with various countries, renewal of. Cmd. 5448, 280
Beef Imports into U.K., Regulation of, Correspondence. Cmd. 5943, 737
Economic Conditions, 211, 439
Extradition :
Australia, Luxembourg and U.K., Convention. Cmd. 5416, 278
Ecuador, Supplementary Convention. Cmd. 5614, 293
Identity Documents for Aircraft Personnel, Exchange of Notes with various countries. Cmd. 5586, 291
Imported Food Certificate, 618
Scotland, 666
Kauri Gum, Importation of, Exchange of Notes, France and U.K. Cmd. 5558, 289
Limitation of Naval Armament, International Treaty. Cmd. 5561, 289
Naval Armaments Treaty. Cmd. 5136, 48
Payments Agreement with Germany. Cmd. 5732, 508
Shipping Service to Western Canada, 208

New Zealand (continued) :
Trade :
Agreement with Germany. Cmd. 5733, 508
Arrangement with Belgium. Cmd. 5359, 274
Discussions with U.K. Cmd. 6059, 745
War Cemeteries in Iraq. Cmd. 5196,53
War Graves Agreement. Cmd. 5063, 44
See also British War Memorial ; Australia and New Zealand ; Commercial Agreements ; Extradition ; Identity Documents.
Nicholson, H. H., The Soils of Cambridgeshire, 361
Nickel :
Plating, Specification, 369
Wire and Rivets, Specification, 601
Nickel-Chromium Steel :
Specification, 600
Tools, Specification, 1068
Nickel-Chromium-Iron Alloy Sheets and Strips, Specifications, 369, 1026
Nickel - Chromium - Molybdenum Steel, Specification, 368, 1025
Nickel-Copper Alloy :
Bars and Strips, Specification, 854
Tubes, Specification, 1029
Nickel-Steel Tools, Specifications, 1068
Nicking of Horses. See Horses.
Nicosia, Upper Winds at, 897
Niemeyer, Sir Otto, Report on Indian Financial Enquiry. Cmd. 5163, 50
Views of Provincial Governments, etc. Cmd. 5181, 52
Nigeria :
Colonial Reports, 152, 609, 861
Economic Conditions, 439
(Remission of Payments) Act, 297
Bill, 245, 269
Memo. Cmd. 5488, 283
Night :
Baking, Report. Cmd. 5525, 286
Work, Factory Forms, 167
Nippon, Imported Food Certificates, 871
Nith, River, Salmon Fisheries, 201
Nitrate, Nitrite, and Bacteria in Curing of Bacon and Hams, 1057
Nitrous Fumes, Detection of, 907
Noise :
in Buildings, Reduction of, 904
in the Operation of Mechanically-propelled Vehicles, 214, 441
Nollington Court, s.s., Wreck Report, 675
Nominee Account, Crown's, 220, 447, 683, 927
Non-aggression Treaty between Thailand and U.K. :
Cmd. 6211, 968
Cmd. 6241, 970

INDEX 1936-40 —NOR

Non-Combatant Corps, War Office Publications (N.P.), 1070
Non-corrosive Steel Strip, Specification, 1078
Non-ferrous Metals Trade :
Census of Production, 917
Import Duties Act Enquiry Reports, 208, 436
Non-Immigrant Passport Visa Fees, Agreement, U.S.A. and South Africa. Cmd. 5706, 505
Non-provided Schools. See Schools.
Norfolk :
Castle Acre Priory, Guide, 225
Census, 190
Grimes Graves, Weeting, Guide, 231
Norham Castle, Northumberland, Guide, 231
Norman, J. R., Fishes, 942
Northallerton Urban District Council Act, 973
North America. See British North America.
Northampton, Motor Bus Drivers and Conductors, Industrial Court Award, 175
North Borneo, Arms, 153
North Cotswold Rural District Council Act, 302
North East England (Alteration and Extension) Scheme, Electricity, 926
North East Lindsey. See Lindsey.
Northern :
Counties Trust for the Education of the Deaf Scheme, 199
Division, Mines, Reports, 184, 412, 648, 898
Highlands, Scotland, Geology, 194
Ireland :
Air Navigation, Royal Procession, 364
Civil Service Examinations, 147, 374, 605, 1030
Land Purchase Accounts, 252, 480, 723, 961
Rhodesia :
Colonial Reports, 152, 379, 609, 1031
Economic Conditions, 921
Financial Position, 611
Northern Duke, s.t., Wreck Report, 438
North Gawber (Lidgett) Colliery, Yorkshire, Explosion. Cmd. 5214, 54
North Herts. See Hertfordshire.
North Lindside Naval Base, Barrow-in-Furness, Dangerous Drugs, 394
Northwest Power Act, 757
North Metropolitan Electric Power Supply Acts, 69, 299
North Midland Division, Mines, Reports, 412, 648, 898
North Northumberland, Electricity Orders, 213

108

109

1936-40 | NOR-PAL

NOR— INDEX 1936–40

North of England Protecting and Indemnity Association, War Risks Insurance, 724
North Sea :
Herring :
Food of, 361
Movements of, 428
Surface Water Drift, Upper Water Circulation, 428
North Staffordshire Coal Mines Scheme, 183, 411, 648, 898, 1053
Northumberland :
and Durham Coalfield Survey, 421, 660, 906
Coal Mines Scheme, 183, 411, 898
North, Electricity Orders, 213
Tynemouth Priory and Castle, Guide, 232
Warkworth Castle, Hermitage, Guides, 232
North Wales :
Coal Mines Scheme, 184, 411
Coalfield, Survey of, 660
See also North West England.
North West England and North Wales (Alteration and Extension) Scheme, Electricity, 926
North Western :
Division, Mines, Reports, 184, 412, 648, 898
Forensic Science Laboratory, Preston, Dangerous Drugs, 878
North West Europe, Weather in, 647
North West Frontier, India, Despatch, 407
North West Kent. *See* Kent.
North West Midlands Joint Electricity Authority Order Confirmation :
Act, 1938, 525
Bill, 464, 493
Act, 1939, 758
Bill, 704, 730
Northwood. *See* Colne Valley.
Norway :
Death of H.M. the Queen of, 644
Economic Conditions, 211, 676
Exemption from Taxation of Profits or Gains :
Cmd. 6039, 744
Cmd. 6195, 967
German Aggression of, English Translation of White Paper issued by Norwegian Government, 1039
Identity Documents for Aircraft Personnel, Exchange of Notes with various countries. *Cmd. 5653*, 502
Imported Food Certificates, 619
Load Line Certificates. *Cmd. 5336*, 64
Sale Prices in, of Whisky produced in the U.K., Exchange of Notes with U.K. *Cmd. 6178*, 966
Norwegian, Interpretership Examinations, 859
Norwich Provisional Order Confirmation Act, 973
Bill, 947, 962
Notices to Mariners. *See* Mariners.
Nottingham Corporation Act, 528
Nottinghamshire :
and Derbyshire :
Electricity Order, 213
Traction Act, 68
Census, 190
Coalfield, Survey of, 906
Coal Mines Scheme, 411
Electricity, 921
Nowell, W., Chairman, Commission on the Marketing of West African Cocoa, Report. *Cmd. 5845*, 516
Noxious Matter or Liquid, Removal through Streets, Model Byelaws, 391
Nuffield, Lord, Production of Aero-Engines, Note on Policy of H.M. Government. *Cmd. 5295*, 61
Nuisances :
from Snow, Filth, etc., Model Byelaws, 391
See also Mosquito Nuisances.
Nullity of Marriage. *See* Divorce.
Nuneaton Extension Provisional Order Confirmation Act, 525
Bill, 463, 493
Nurseries. *See* Forest Nurseries.
Nursery Schools, Lists, 155, 156, 383, 614, 866
Nurses :
Royal National Pension Fund for Nurses Act, 68
Training of, Report of Scottish Departmental Committee. *Cmd. 5093*, 46
See also Maternity Nurses.
Nursing :
and Kindred Services, Careers, 174, 638
for Gas Casualties, 625
Homes :
Mental Defectives, 153
Model Byelaws, 621
Registration :
Circulars, 162, 618
(Scotland) Act, 524
Bill, 470, 486, 490, 494, 496, 490
Circular, 618
in the Army, 688
Profession, Scottish Central Emergency Committee for, Circular, 911
Scottish Departmental Committee Report on. *Cmd. 5866*, 518
Service, Territorial Army, Standing Orders, 457

INDEX 1936–40 —OFF

Nursing (*continued*) :
Services, Interdepartmental Committee on, Report, 874
See also Air Force ; Air Force Reserve ; Hospital Nursing ; Princess Mary's.
Nutation, Constant of, 901
Nutrition :
Advisory Committee on, Report, 391
Bacterial, 191
Circular, 388
in the Colonial Empire :
Policy, 153
Report of Committee. *Cmds. 6050, 6051*, 744
Nutritive Value of Fruits, Vegetables, and Nuts, 191
Nuts :
Brazil. *See* Import Duties Advisory Committee.
Decorticated Ground. *See* Import Duties Advisory Committee.
Ground, Production, Trade and Consumption, 172, 634, 883
Nutritive Value of, 191
Nyasaland :
Colonial Reports, 152, 379, 861
Economic Conditions, 212, 921
Financial Position, 611
Rhodesia–Nyasaland Royal Commission, Report. *Cmd. 5949*, 737
Nystagmus. *See* Miner's Nystagmus.

O

Oak, Forest Products Research Board Publications (N.P.), 193
Oats :
Leaflet, 850
Production and Trade, 171, 398, 634, 883
Observatories :
Publications (N.P.), 187, 188, 203, 430, 653, 668, 901, 913, 1054
Year Book, 181, 409, 646, 896
Observer's Primer, 1053
Observers at Auxiliary Climatological Stations, Instructions to, 1052
Obstacles, Effects on Sunshine Records, 409
Occlusion, Post-normal, Nature and Characteristic Features, 419
Occultations, Prediction and Reduction of, 354
Occupation, Choice of, Leaflets, 174, 401
Occupational Mortality, 656
Occupations. *See* Reserved Occupations.
Ocean :
Currents :
Indian, 1052
South Pacific, 897
Island, Meteorological Observations at, 408
Passages for the World, 844
Ocean Duke, s.t., Wreck Report, 438
Oesophagus in Health and in Disease of the Heart and Great Vessels, 191
Offences relating to Motor Vehicles. *See* Motor Vehicles.
Offenders, Probation of. *See* Probation.
Offensive :
or Noxious Matter or Liquid, Removal of through Streets, Model Byelaws, 391
Trades, Model Byelaws, 391
Officers :
and Men mentioned for Distinguished Services, 1050
and Sergeants Messes 935, 1070
Army, War Office Publications (N.P.), 934, 1066, 1070
Fire Brigade, Ranks and Uniforms, 880
Scotland, 915
Local Government. *See* Local Authorities.
of the Fleet, Uniform Regs., 842
R.A.F. Dress Regs. for, 1024
Responsible for A.R.P. Training, Manual for, 1038
Training Corps :
Examinations, 451, 685, 930
Regs., 229, 454, 689, 935, 1070
See also Married Officers ; Medical Officers.
Offices :
Regulation Bill, 36, 41
Reorganisation of, (Scotland) Act, 753
Bill, 498, 700, 715, 726, 728
Official :
Documents, Legalisation of, Agreement between France and U.K. *Cmd. 5476*, 282
List, Registrar-General's, 189, 417, 656, 903, 1055
Publications. *See* Government Publications.
Secrets :
Act, 756
Bill, 498, 706, 697, 728
Acts, Select Committee on, Report, Proceedings, etc., 488, 718
(Amendment) Bill, 495
Shorthand Writers in the Supreme Court, Report of Committee. *Cmd. 5395*, 277
Statistics, Current, Guide to, 220, 447, 683, 927

OHM— INDEX 1936–40

Ohm, Determination of, 661
Oil :
Cakes and Extracted Meals, Use of, 360
Coolers, Specification, 599
Filters, Specification, 854
Fish. *See* Import Duties Advisory Committee.
from Coal, Sub-Committee of Committee of Imperial Defence, Report. *Cmd. 5665*, 503
in Navigable Waters Act, 64
Linseed. *See* Import Duties Advisory Committee.
Palm Products, Production, Trade and Consumption, 883
Properties in Mexico, Expropriation of. *Cmd. 5758*, 510
Report of Experts of League of Nations. *Cmd. 5094*, 46
Storage Tanks, Factory Form, 879
Tanks of Ships, Welding Operations on, Factory Form, 1036
Temperature Thermometers, Specification, 140
Varnishes and Primer, Specifications, 143, 854, 1026
See also Castor Oil.
Oil-dressed Fabrics, Specifications, 687, 933, 1069
Oilseeds, Production, Trade and Consumption, 172, 634, 883
Oilskin :
Anti-gas Clothing and Equipment, Decontamination of, from Blister Gas, 877
Clothing, Specifications, 226, 687, 933, 1069
Oiticica Oil. *See* Import Duties Advisory Committee.
Old Age :
and Widows' Pensions Act, 1940, 971
Bill, 946, 962
Explanatory Memo. *Cmd. 6204*, 967
Report of the Financial Provisions of the Bill relating to Contributory Pensions and Health Insurance. *Cmd. 6169*, 965
Pensions :
Act, 1936, 66
Bill, 6, 7, 13, 40
See also Widows', Orphans'.
Oldbury. *See* Smethwick.
Oldham, C. H., Strawberries, 360
Old Mill, Congleton, Cheshire, Boiler Explosion, 206
Oldroyd, H., British Bloodsucking Flies, 941
Oleo Shock Absorber Struts, Fluid for, Specification, 1026
Olive Oil, Production, Trade and Consumption, 172, 634, 883
Oliver, Roland, Chairman, Army and Air Force Courts-Martial Committee, Report. *Cmd. 6200*, 967
Omnibus Strike. *See* London Central Omnibus Services.
One-teacher Schools, Physical Training in, 669
Onion :
and Leek Smut, 135
Fly, 850
Open Domestic Grates, Use of Coke in, 421
Operating Theatres, Anaesthetic Explosions in, 160, 161
Ophiuroidea, 942
Ophthalmia Neonatorum, Circular, 387
Opium Smoking, International Agreement. *Cmd. 5401*, 277
Opposed Private Bill Committees, Reports, 18, 47, 461, 697
Optical :
Aids, 614
and Other Instruments, Repair of, 229, 454
Orchards, Control of Fruit Pests and Diseases in, 595
Ordnance :
Corps, Army, 455
Factories. *See* Royal Ordnance Factories.
Services, Army, 229, 448, 684
Survey :
Annual Reports, 188, 901
Departmental Committee on, Reports, 136, 596
Publications (N.P.), 83, 415, 653
Organic :
Halogen Compounds, Detection of, 1058
Intermediate Products. *See* Import Duties Advisory Committee.
Solvents, Industrial Toxicity of, 418
Orient, British Shipping in, Report, 918
Orifice Method of Producing a High Velocity Stream, 1027
Origin :
Certificates, Consular Fees on, Exchange of Notes, Roumania and Canada. *Cmd. 5447*, 280
of Goods. *See* False Indications.
Ornamental Garden Plants, Pests of, 360
Orphans' Pensions. *See* Widows.
Orsett, Sunday Entertainments, 26
Oscillating Bearing Friction of 661
Oscillators. *See* Quartz Oscillators.
Ospray II, s.t., and *Caldew*, s.t., collision, 210
Osseine, Import Duties. *Cmd. 5183*, 52
Ossett Corporation Act, 526

INDEX 1936–40 —PAL

Ostrich and Fancy Feather and Artificial Flower Trade, Wages, 891
Oswestry Corporation Act, 750
Ottoman Empire, Future Status of certain parts of. *Cmd. 5964*, 739
Ouricury Wax. *See* Import Duties Advisory Committee.
Outdoor Relief, Administration of, 389
Wales, 393
Outfit Allowance, Army, 935, 1070
Out-patient Treatment, Provision of, 873, 1034
Outworkers, Factory Form, 629
Oven, Baking, Explosion in, Report, 435
Ovens, Steam Tube, Factory Form, 879
Overall Trousers, Specification, 932
Overalls, Specifications, 932, 1068
Overboots, Anti-gas, Specifications, 933, 1069
Overcrowding. *See* Housing.
Overmittens, Anti-gas, Specifications, 933, 1069
Oversea :
Settlement Board, Reports :
Cmd. 5314, 62
Cmd. 5766, 510
Trade of U.K., Nationality of Carrying Vessels, 437, 674
Overseas :
Reception of Children, Interdepartmental Committee Report. *Cmd. 6213*, 968
Settlement Committee, Report. *Cmd. 5200*, 53
Territories Bill, 473
Trade :
Department of :
Examinations, 374, 605, 1030
Publications (N.P.), 211, 439, 676, 920
Guarantees Act, 753
Bill, 706, 731
Overshirts, Serge, Specification, 932
Overshoes, Magazine, Specification, 452
Overtime, Inland Revenue, Civil Service Arbitration Tribunal Awards, 639, 888
Owen, Daniel, Celebration, St. David's Day, 159
Owls, 134, 362, 595
Oxalic Acid. *See* Import Duties Advisory Committee.
Oxford :
Ancient Monuments :
Inventory, 908
Report. *Cmd. 6142*, 751
Educational Exhibition, Charts, 156
Provisional Order Confirmation Act, 758
Bill, 704, 730
Variations of Temperature at, 409
Oxidation. *See* Anodic Oxidation.
Oxy-acetylene Processes, Safety Measures, 167, 395
Oxygen :
Administration, 1034
Breathing Apparatus, Rubber Tubing for, Specification, 142, 368, 1026
Oyster Beds in South Wales, 134
Oysters, Breeding of, in Tanks, 361, 849

P

Pace, J., Curing of Bacon, 1057
Pacific Ocean. *See* South Pacific Ocean.
Packing :
Cases, Specification, 225, 686, 1062
of Eggs, 362
Padlocks. *See* Locks.
Pads. *See* Rubber Pads.
Paignton Pier and Harbour Provisional Order Confirmation Act, 70
Bill, 14, 39
Paint, Petrol Resisting, Specification, 1027
Painted Textiles, Guide to, 695
Painting, Factory Forms, 628, 630
See also Renaissance Painting.
Paisley Corporation :
(Cart Navigation) Order Confirmation Act, 756
Bill, 475, 499
(General Powers) Order Confirmation Act, 525
Bill, 463, 494
Order Confirmation Act, 1937, 301
Bill, 246, 260
Palestine :
and Trans-Jordan, Colonial Reports, 152, 379
Colonial Reports, 610, 862
Commercial Relations :
with Egypt. *Cmd. 5361*, 274
with Iraq. *Cmd. 5372*, 275
Correspondence :
between Sir Henry McMahon and the Sharif Hussein of Mecca in 1915 and 1916. *Cmd. 5957*, 738
Report of Committee. *Cmd. 5974*, 739
with the Palestine Arab Delegation and the Zionist Organisation. *Cmd. 1700*, 500
Frontier Questions, Agreement with Syria and the Lebanon. *Cmd. 6065*, 745
General Service Medal, 930
High Commissioner, Badge, 153
Land Transfer Regulations. *Cmd. 6180*, 966

Palestine (continued):
Partition Commission Report. Cmd. 5854, 517
Policy in, Statements:
Cmd. 5513, 285
Cmd. 5634, 500
Cmd. 6019, 742
Proposed New Constitution for. Cmd. 5119, 47
Royal Commission:
Colonial Office Publications (N.P.), 381
Report. Cmd. 5479, 283
Statement by H.M. Government. Cmd. 5883, 520
U.S.A., Rights in. Cmd. 5544, 283
Winds over, 410
Palestinian Companies, Auxiliary Military Pioneer Corps, Allowances issuable to Married Officers, 1067
Palm:
Kernels, Production and Trade, 172, 634
Oil, Production and Trade, 172, 634
Palmer, J. H., Development of Cardiac Enlargement in Disease of the Heart, 419
Panama:
and Panama Canal Zone, Economic Conditions, 676
Canal, Measurement of Vessels, 919
Economic Conditions, 211
Paper:
Bag Trade, Wages, 642, 891, 1047
Box Trade, Wages, 642, 891, 1046
Control of, Lists of Merchants authorised to deal in Waste Paper-making Materials, 917, 1063
Insulated Cables, Specification, 686
Mills, Accidents in, Committee to consider the prevention of, Report, 624
Mulberry. See Import Duties Advisory Committee.
Trade, Import Duties Reports, 208, 436
Yarn:
Fabrics, Import Duties. Cmd. 5215, 54
Tissues made from, Import Duties. Cmd. 5169, 51
Papyri. See Demotic Papyri; Egyptian Papyri.
Papyrifera Broussonetia (Paper Mulberry). See Import Duties Advisory Committee.
Parachute:
and Personnel Safety Equipment Manual, 140, 365, 599
Harness Webbing, Specification, 1027
Shroud Lines, Silk Cordage for, Specification, 140

Parachutes:
Artificial Silk Fabric for, Specification, 855
Silk Fabric for, Specification, 600, 854, 1026
Paraguay:
Economic Conditions, 439
Imported Food Certificate, 619
Paralysis, Fowl, 135
Parcel Post between U.K. and Belgium, Agreement. Cmd. 5858, 517
Parish Elections, Circulars, 394
Park Hospital, London, Dangerous Drugs, 167
Parker, W. K., Collection, Tertiary Siphoneous Algae in, 943
Parking Places, Model Byelaws, 164
Parks. See National Forest Park; Royal Parks.
Parliament:
Act (1911) Amendment Bill, 42
Common Form Clauses in Private Bills, 32
History of, 165
Committee on, Publications (N.P.), 624
House of Commons:
Biographies of Members, 165
Election, 1933, expenses, 32
Kitchen and Refreshment Rooms, 27, 259, 486
Pensions for Members of, Departmental Committee on, Report. Cmd. 6624, 294
Sessional Printed Papers, Titles and Contents:
Session 1935-36, 248
Session 1936-37, 476
Standing Orders, 33, 261, 476, 488
House of Lords:
Lords Spiritual and Temporal, Roll of, 18, 246, 474, 709
Offices, Select Committee on, Reports, 11, 18, 237, 242, 246, 473, 475, 702, 708, 710, 946
Scottish Appeals, Statistics. Cmd. 5210, 54
Scottish Representative Peers to sit and vote in Parliament, 5
Standing Orders, 5, 17
Trial:
of Lord de Clifford, 5
of Peers (Abolition of Privilege) Bill, 5, 6, 40
King's Speech, 18, 246, 474, 709, 948
Ministers and Heads of Public Departments, 205, 433, 671, 916, 1062
Procedure relating to Money Resolutions, Select Committee on, Report, 260

Parliament (continued):
Prolongation of, Act, 972 Bill,948,963
Refreshment Rooms and Lavatories in the Palace of Westminster, 17
Temporary Laws, Register, 29
Parliamentary:
Counsel Office Publications (N.P.), 188
Elections:
(Compulsory Voting) Bills, 271, 730
Mr. Speaker's Seat, Select Committee on, Report, 718
Papers, List of, 20, 248
Publications:
Acts:
Local and Private, 67, 298, 524, 756, 972
Public General, 64, 294, 521, 751, 971
Command Papers, 43, 272, 500, 735, 964
House of Commons:
Bills, 36, 265, 492, 727, 962
Debates, 20, 33, 265, 492, 727, 961
Papers, 20, 248, 475, 710, 949
House of Lords Papers, Bills and Debates, 5, 235, 461, 697, 945
Measures, Church Assembly, 72, 302, 528, 760, 973
Parsnips, Cultivation of, 362
Parsonages Measure and Report, 469, 528
Partitions (Building), 658, 904
Pass of Ballater, s.t., Wreck Report, 920
Passenger Tax, Isle of Man, Accounts, 221, 447, 683, 927, 1065
Passenger Transport. See London Passenger Transport Board.
Passport. See Non-Immigrant Passport.
Passports. See Seamen's Discharge Books.
Pasture:
Iodine Contents, relationship to occurrence of Endemic Goitre, 192
Poor Upland, Improvement of, 362
Patchwork, 695
Patent:
Medicines. See Medicine Stamp Duties; Medicines and Surgical Appliances.
Office, Civil Service Arbitration Tribunal Award, 401
Rolls, Calendars of, 189, 655, 903
Patents and Designs:
Act, 1907, as amended, 756
Act, 1938, 524
(Limits of Time) Act, 753
Bill, 698, 699, 705, 720, 726, 728, 730

Patents, Designs, and Trade Marks. See Design.
Patents, Designs, Copyright, and Trade Marks (Emergency) Act, 755
Bill, 708, 734
Patents, etc. (International Conventions) Act, 523
Bill, 247, 461, 462, 468, 485, 490, 493, 495
Pathogenic Anaerobic Organisms, 1056
Paton Brothers and Bannatyne, Renfrew, Industrial Court Award, 888
Patrick Allan-Fraser Trust Scheme, 198
Pay:
Army, 454, 689, 934, 1066, 1070
Improvements. Cmd. 5695, 505
Duties Manual, 229
See also Board of Arbitration Awards; Civil Service Arbitration Tribunal Awards; Industrial Court Awards; Fees; Wages; General Practitioners; Holidays with Pay; Marines; Naval Reserves; Navy; Salaries; Road Haulage; Air Force; Air Force Reserve; Ecclesiastical Officers; Military Forces; Teachers' Salaries; Retired Pay.
Pay, Appointment, Promotion, and Non-effective Pay of the Army, 229
Payman, W., High-Speed Cameras for measuring rate of detonation in solid explosives, 413
Paymaster Cadetships in the Royal Navy, Entrance Examinations, 1030
Payments:
Agreements:
Germany:
and Canada. Cmd. 5580, 290
and New Zealand. Cmd. 5732, 508
and U.K.:
Cmd. 5787, 512
Cmd. 5881, 519
Hungary and U.K., 206
Italy and U.K.:
Cmd. 5307, 61
Cmd. 5346, 273
Cmd. 5669, 503
Cmd. 5695, 505
Roumania and U.K.:
Cmd. 5174, 51
Cmd. 5187, 52
Cmd. 5470, 282
Cmd. 5471, 282
Cmd. 5587, 291
Cmd. 5588, 291
Cmd. 5613, 293
Cmd. 5718, 507
Cmd. 5797, 512
Cmd. 5840, 516
Cmd. 6063, 745
Cmd. 6215, 968

Payments (continued):
Agreements (continued):
Spain and U.K.:
Cmd. 5058, 43
Cmd. 5097, 46
Cmd. 5250, 57
Cmd. 6188, 966
Cmd. 6229, 969
Turkey and U.K. Cmd. 6171, 965
Yugoslavia and U.K. Cmd. 5323, 63
See also Trade Agreements; Trade and Payments Agreements; Commercial Agreements.
due to British Subjects in respect of Expropriation of Landed Properties in Greece. Cmd. 5260, 58
Remission of. See Nigeria.
Peace:
Bill, 37, 42, 271
Broadcasting in the cause of, International Convention:
Cmd. 5505, 285
Cmd. 5714, 506
Establishments, Army, 229, 454
Peace, T. R., Spring Frosts, 386
Pear and Cherry Sawfly, 134
Pears:
Home Storage of, 362
Production and Trade, 171, 398, 633
Peas, Green, and Beans, Culture of, 134
Pectins, Fruit, 905
Peel, Earl, Chairman, Palestine Royal Commission:
Colonial Office Publications(N.P.),381
Report. Cmd. 5479, 283
Peerage Law Declaration Bill, 238
Penang–Hong Kong, Civil Air Transport Service. Cmd. 5396, 277
Penalties, Imposition of, by Marketing Boards and other similar bodies, Departmental Committee on, Report. Cmd. 5980, 740
Pencil Cedar, African, Properties of, 659
Pendennis, s.s., Wreck Report, 211
Pendlebury. See Swinton.
Pennines and Adjacent Areas, Geology, 194
Penrose, L. S., Clinical and Genetic Study of Mental Defect, 657
Pensions:
Acts (Amendment) Bill, 498, 499
Civil Estimates, Supplementary, 496
for Members of House of Commons, Departmental Committee on, Report. Cmd. 5624, 294
(Governors of Dominions), etc., Act, 65
Bill, 13
Law and Regs. of the Civil Service, 447

Pensions (continued):
Minister of, Annual Reports, 25, 248, 476, 710, 721
Ministry of, Publications (N.P.), 902, 1054
Royal National Pensions Fund for Nurses Act, 68
Widows and Orphans of Officers in Colonial Service. Cmd. 5219, 55
See also Civil List; Clergy Pensions; Old Age Pensions; Superannuation; Widows, Orphans, and Old Age.
Pentelow, F. T. K.:
Effects of Milk Waste on the Bristol Avon, 594
Survey of River Tees, 422
Penzance Corporation Act, 528
People. See Representation of the People.
Peppercorns. See Import Duties Advisory Committee.
Peppermint, Cultivation and Distillation, 134
Perambulator Trade. See Invalid Carriage.
Performing Animals (Regulation):
Bill, 272
Amendment Bill, 475
No. 2 Bill, 475
" Perga " Single Service Milk Container, 848
Periodicals. See Current Periodicals.
Periwinkle Fishery, Maldon, Essex, 134
Perlis, Colonial Reports, 152, 379, 610, 861
Permanent Lining of Trenches, Specifications, 626, 878
Perpetual Leases in Japan, Termination of. Cmd. 5448, 288
Pershore. See Evesham.
Persia, Tariff Autonomy of. Cmd. 5054,43
See also Iran.
Persian Gulf, Economic Conditions, 439
Personal:
Injuries (Emergency Provisions) Act, 754
Bill, 733
Protection against Gas, 625
Satires, Catalogue of, 694
Personnel:
Army, Conveyance of, 229, 449, 685, 929, 1066
Safety Equipment for. See Parachute.
Perth:
and Kinross Educational Trust Scheme, 199, 427
Corporation Order Confirmation Act, 67
Bill, 7
Homes Trust Scheme, 200, 426

Peru:
Commerce and Navigation Agreement with U.K. Cmd. 5288, 60
Economic Conditions, 676
Pests:
and Diseases in the Vegetable Garden, 1023
of Grain and other Stored Produce, 907
of Ornamental Garden Plants, 360
See also Fruit Pests; Insect Pests; Narcissus Pests.
Peters, R. J., Analysis of Results of Treatment of Syphilis, 419
Peters, S. P., Sea Breezes at Worthy Down, Winchester, 897
Petrol:
Filters, Specification, 854
Resisting Paint, Specification, 1027
Petroleum:
Dispute between Ethiopia and Italy, Report by Committee of Experts on Co-ordination of Measures. Cmd. 5094, 46
Spirit Tank, Explosion, 169
Transfer of Licences Act, 66
Bill, 14
Pharmacopoeia for use in Military Hospitals, 689, 1071
Pharmacopoeial Formulas for Potent Drugs, Unification of, International Agreement. Cmd. 6117, 749
Pharmacy:
and Poisons Act, 1933, Memoranda on the Provisions of, 169
Careers, 174, 887
Phenols, Production of Aromatic Hydrocarbons from, 660
Philip and Mary, Calendars of Patent Rolls, 189, 655, 903
Philippine Islands, Economic Conditions, 676
Phillips, D. W., Coal Measure Rocks, 413
Phlyctaenachlamys Lysiosquillina Gen. and Sp. Nov., a Lemellibranch Commensal in the Burrows of Lysiosquilla Maculata, 942
Phosgene, Detection of, 908
Phosphate, Distribution of, Fisheries, 595
Phosphor Bronze Bars and Tubes, Specification, 854
Photo Reading, Army, 229, 453, 688, 934, 1070
Photographic Film Base, Import Duties. Cmd. 5264, 58
Photographs: of the British Forces, 1039
See also Air Photographs.
Photography, Air, Organisation and Training, 137
Photo-heliographic Results, 188, 653, 901

Phylloscopus, Systematic Review of, 941
Physical:
and Chemical Survey of National Coal Resources, 421, 660, 906, 1057
and Recreational Training:
Army, 1071
Navy, 1018
Constants of Pure Metals, 194
Education:
England and Wales, Circulars, 156, 158
in Germany, 384
Scotland, Circulars, 203
Examination of Recruits, Army, 454, 689
Fitness for Youths and Men, Girls and Women, 385
Recreation and Service, Youth, 1032
Training:
and Recreation Act, 297
Bill, 242, 258, 263, 266, 268
Memo. Cmd. 5364, 274
Powers of Local Authorities, 385
Scotland, 432
Army, 229, 454, 689, 936
See also Social and Physical Training; Physical and Recreational Training.
Board of Education Publications (N.P.), 385
Clothing and Shoes for, 156
Wales, 158
Corps, Army, 1066
Equipment, Specifications, 225, 226
for Children, Wales, 616
for Schools, Syllabus, 1033
See also Social and Physical Training.
in One-Teacher and other Small Schools, 669
Instructors, Army, Pay, 1066
Planning, Construction and Equipment of Gymnasia in Schools, etc., 1047
Tables, Auxiliary Territorial Service, 1071
Physically Defective Children, Education and Care of, Scotland, 430
Physics:
Careers, 401
Examinations, Science Scholarships, 384, 614, 866
Short History of, 901
Physiology of Hearing, Committee on, Reports, 418
Phytoplankton and the Herring, 134, 595
Picador, s.t., Wreck Report, 438

1936-40 | PIC-PRE

PIC— INDEX 1936–40

Pick, F., Chairman, Design and the Designer in Industry, 434
Pick, W. H., Short Course in Elementary Meteorology, 645
Pickers, etc., of Fruit, Flowers, Bulbs, Roots, and Vegetables, Model Byelaws, 621
Pickling, Crops for, 593
Picture :
Galleries, A.R.P. in, 941
Postcards. *See* Merchandise Marks
Piece Goods and Made-up Goods (Cotton, Rayon, and Linen) :
Explanatory Memo., 1063
List of Manufacturers of Controlled Goods, 1063
Piers. *See* Island of Arran ; Harbours, Piers and Ferries.
Piezo-Electric Quartz, Notation for, 661
Pig :
Feeding, 134, 424
Feeding Stuffs for use with Cereals in, 362
Products, 171, 398, 633, 883
Pig-iron. *See* Import Duties Advisory Committee.
Pig-keeping, 593
Pigmented :
Cellulose Acetate Sheets, Specification, 368
Lanolin-Resin Solution, Specifications, 600, 1026, 1028, 1029
Oil Varnishes and Primer, Specifications, 854, 1026, 1028
Varnish Jointing Compound, Specifications, 601, 1026
Pigs, Production and Trade, 171, 398, 634
Piles. *See* Reinforced Concrete Piles.
Pillow Cases and Slips, Specifications, 687, 932
Pillows, Feather, Specifications, 226, 687, 932
Pilot Books :
Air, 138, 364, 597, 851
Hydrographic, 128, 355, 589, 944, 1020
Pilotage :
Authorities, Limitation of Liability Act, 66
Bill, 11, 29, 34, 36
in U.K., Returns, 33, 261, 489, 723
Pim, Sir A., Chairman, Northern Rhodesia Commission, Report, 611
Pin, Hook and Eye, and Snap Fastener Trade, Wages, 405, 891, 1047
Pine :
Pitch. *See* British Honduras.
Shoot Moth, Studies on, 159
Pink Rot of Potatoes, 595
Pins. *See* Merchandise Marks.
Pioneer Corps, British Official Photographs, 1039
Pippard, W. R., Calcium Sulphate Plasters, 657
Piracy in the Mediterranean. *See* Mediterranean.
Pistol, Small Arms Training, 586
Pistols, Revolver, Instructions for Armourers, Army, 222
Piston Ring Pots, Specification, 1027
Pitcairn Island, Colonial Report, 611
Pitch Pine. *See* British Honduras.
Plaice-Marking Experiments, 595
Plaited Flax and Hemp Cordage, Specifications, 854, 1026
Planes, Specifications :
Iron, 226
Wood, 931
Planetary Co-ordinates, 842
Planets. *See* Major Planets.
Plankton Organisms, Distribution, etc., 361
Planning. *See* Town and Country Planning ; Underground Water Planning.
Plans and Maps, Making of, 689
Plant :
of the National Coke and Oil Co., Ltd., Erith, Kent, Report of Test, 321
See also Essential Buildings and Plant.
Plantation Crops, Production and Trade, 172, 398, 634
Plantations :
Journals of the Commissioners for Trade and, 189, 655
See also Forest Nurseries.
Plants :
Crop, cultivated, of British Empire and Anglo-Egyptian Sudan, 173
Introduction into the Colonial Dependencies of the British Empire, Legislation, 381
See also Ornamental Garden Plants ; Seeds ; Fossil Plants ; Poisonous Plants ; Flowering Plants.
Plasterers and Joiners in Scotland, disputes between, Report. *Cmd. 5554*, 288
Plasters, Calcium Sulphate, 657
Plate. *See* Hallmarking.
Plating. *See* Metal Plating ; Cadmium Plating ; Zinc Plating.
Playgrounds. *See* Street Playgrounds.
Playing-field Facilities, Preservation of, 615
Playing-fields, Floodlighting, 867
Pledge, H. T., Science since 1500, 901
Ploughing and Re-seeding Poor Grass Land, 909
Ploughley, Sunday Entertainments, 952
Plumage. *See* Importation of Plumage.
Plums and Damsons, 135

INDEX 1936–40 —POO

Plymouth :
Earl of : Chairman, Committee on Broadcasting Services in the Colonies, Interim Report, 379
Supplement, 862
Extension Act, 526
Pier and Harbour Order Confirmation Act, 527
Bill, 471, 495
Plympton St. Mary :
Electricity, 921
Provisional Order Confirmation Act, 71
Bill, 12, 40
Plywood :
for lightly-stressed parts of Aircraft, Specification, 1029
Packing Cases, Specification, 1063
See also Import Duties Advisory Committee.
Pneumatic Tyres, Customs Classification of, Poland and U.K. *Cmd. 5644*, 501
Pneumothorax, Artificial, 192
Pocock, R. W., Geological Survey, Shrewsbury District, 661
Point Discharge in the Electric Field of the Earth, 181
Poison Gas :
Air Raid Precautions, 393, 624
Scotland, 431
Atlas, 394
Certification Mark for Filtration Plants, 877
Food and its Protection against, 1033
Poisoning :
Factory Form, 629
See also Food Poisoning ; Gas Poisoning.
Poisons :
Form of application to sell, 169
Memoranda, 169
See also Pharmacy and Poisons ; Cyanide Poisons.
Poland :
Customs Classification of Pneumatic Tyres, Exchange of Notes with U.K. *Cmd. 5644*, 501
Commercial :
Agreements with U.K. :
Cmd. 5599, 292
Cmd. 5997, 741
Relations with Canada. *Cmd.* [illegible], [illegible]
Documents concerning German-Polish Relations and Outbreak of Hostilities between Great Britain and Germany. *Cmd. 6106*, 748
Economic Conditions, 211, 439, 676
Guarantees in connection with Export of Goods from U.K. to Poland, Agreement. *Cmd. 6093*, 747
Poland (*continued*) :
Imported Food Certificate, 389
Scotland, 428
Limitation of Naval Armament, etc., Agreements with U.K. :
Cmd. 5739, 508
Cmd. 5916, 735
Cmd. 5917, 735
Loan to, Agreement with France and U.K. *Cmd. 6110*, 749
Mutual Assistance, Agreements with U.K. :
Cmd. 6101, 748
Cmd. 6144, 751
Utilisation of Units of the Polish Mercantile Marine in the prosecution of the War against Germany, Exchange of Notes with U.K. *Cmd. 6172*, 965
Polarity of the Air and Blueness of the Sky, Relation between, 646
Police :
Air Raids Precautions, 625
and Firemen (War Service) Act, 755
Bill, 708, 733
Duties in A.R.P. Schemes, 393
Scotland, 431
Examinations, Scotland, 670
Return Forms, Judicial Statistics, 178
Scientific Aids to Criminal Investigation, 170
See also India ; Metropolitan Police ; Military Police ; Constabulary ; Burma ; Colonial Police.
Poliomyelitis, Acute, Memo., 388
Polish Mercantile Marine. *See* Poland.
Polish Trade. *See* Boot and Floor Polish.
Political :
and Personal Satires, Catalogue of, 694
Fund of an Unregistered Trade Union, Return Forms, 617, 870, 1034
Poll, Hours of. *See* Local Government.
Pollution. *See* Atmospheric Polution ; River Polution ; Water Pollution.
Pontypool Gas and Water Act, 300
Poole :
Corporation Act, 302
Enteric Fever in, Report, 392
Pools, Bathing, Model Byelaws, 391
Poor :
Casual. *See* Public Assistance.
Grass Land, Ploughing and Re-seeding, 909
Law :
(Amendment) Act, 1938, 522
Bill, 1939, 731
(No 2) Bill, 1937, 247, 272, 461, 463, 494

POO— INDEX 1936–40

Poor (*continued*) :
Law (*continued*) :
Hospitals, Institutions, etc., Costing Returns, 162, 389, 620, 873
in Scotland, Departmental Committee on, Report. *Cmd. 5803*, 513
Persons, Committees, List of, 407
Persons' Representation (Scotland) Committee, Report. *Cmd. 5435*, 279
Relief :
Annual Statements, 29, 261, 488, 720
Ministry of Health Publications (N.P.), 162, 389, 620, 873, 1035
Upland Pasture, Improvement of, 362
See also Migratory Poor.
Poor's Allotment :
in Hanwell Charity Scheme Confirmation Act, 525
Bill, 466, 494
in Hornsey Charity Scheme Confirmation Act, 973
Bill, 947, 963
in Walton-upon-Thames Confirmation Act, 299
Bill, 239, 267
Popham, M. L., Phlyctaenachlamys Lysiosquillina, etc., 942
Population :
Estimated, Scotland, 916
of Counties, Burghs and Parishes in Scotland, Return, 428
(Statistics) Act, 522
Bill, 271, 462, 493
See also Registrar-General ; Census ; Industrial Population ; Insured Population ; Estimated Populations ; Housing (Agricultural Population) ; School Population.
Porcelain of the Far East, Handbook, 459
Pork, Production and Trade, 171, 398, 634
Port :
Labour in Aberdeen and Glasgow, Board of Enquiry Report, 404
of Manchester Provisional Order Confirmation Act, 298
Bill, 236
Sanitary Authorities, Provisions of Public Health Act, 1936, 388
Wales, 393
Port Glasgow Burgh and Harbour Order Confirmation Act, 759
Bill, 706, 731
Portable Kilns, Manufacture of Charcoal in, 906
Porthleven. *See* Helston.
Portobello Land, Electricity Orders, 213
Portugal :
Air Services :
between London and Lisbon, Exchange of Notes with U.K. *Cmd. 5995*, 741
between South Africa and Portuguese East Africa. *Cmd. 5707*, 506
between South Africa and Portuguese West Africa. *Cmd. 6081*, 970
Boundary between Tanganyika and Mozambique, Exchange of Notes with U.K. *Cmd. 5661*, 503
Commercial Relations between Swaziland, Basutoland, Bechuanaland, and Mozambique, Agreement with U.K. *Cmd. 5807*, 513
Economic Conditions, 211, 676
Identity Documents for Aircraft Personnel, Exchange of Notes :
with Australia, New Zealand, India, and U.K. *Cmd. 6209*, 968
with Union of South Africa. *Cmd. 5565*, 289
Native Labour from Mozambique, Railway Matters and Commercial Intercourse. *Cmd. 5085*, 45
Opium Smoking Agreement. *Cmd. 5401*, 277
Portuguese :
East Africa, Economic Conditions, 676
See also Portugal.
Interpretership Examinations, 605
West Africa, Economic Conditions, 439
See also Portugal.
Possession of Mortgaged Land. *See* Mortgaged Land.
Post :
and Telegraph Department, Ceylon, Examination, 150
Office :
American Mail Contract, 28
and Telegraph :
Act, 971
Bill, 947, 963
(Money) Acts :
1937, 297
Bill, 243, 269
Memo. *Cmd. 5468*, 282
1939, 753
Bill, 704, 730
Ardrossan-Brodick Contract, 30
Civil Service Arbitration Tribunal Awards, 401, 638, 887, 1042
Commercial Accounts, 20, 248, 476, 710, 949
Examinations, 148, 376, 607, 859, 1031

INDEX 1936–40 —PRE

Post (*continued*) :
Office (*continued*) :
Fund :
Accounts, 20, 248, 477, 711, 950
Statements showing Surplus 35, 263, 489, 724, 961
Guide, 188, 416, 654, 902, 1054
London, 415
Publications (N.P.), 188, 415, 653, 902, 1054
Savings Bank Accounts, 221, 447, 684, 928, 1065
Sites Acts :
1936, 69
Bill, 5, 31, 39
1938, 526
Bill, 467, 485, 493, 495
See also Empire Air Mail Schemes.
Postage. *See* Local Government Elections.
Postal Services, Army, War, Manual of, 449
Postcards. *See* British Official Postcards ; Merchandise Marks.
Post-Mortem :
Inquisitions, Calendar, 655
Rooms, Model Byelaws, 621
Post-Normal Occlusion, Nature and Characteristic Features, 419
Postponement of Enactments. *See* Enactments.
Pot Scourers. *See* Import Duties Advisory Committee.
Potash Fertilisers, 134
Potassium :
Bichromate. *See* Sodium Bichromate.
Ferrocyanide. *See* Import Duties Advisory Committee.
Potato :
Leaf Roll, 850
Root Eelworm, 363
Potatoes :
Department of Agriculture for Scotland Publications (N.P.), 197, 424, 664, 909, 1059
Dry Rot of, 1023
Ministry of Agriculture and Fisheries Publications (N.P.), 135, 593, 595
Skin Spot and Silver Scurf of, 362
Wart Disease of, 1024
See also Import Duties Advisory Committee.
Potent Drugs, Unification of Pharmacopoeial Formulas for, International Agreement. *Cmd. 6117*, 749
Pots, Cast Iron, Specification, 369
Potteries. *See* Staffordshire Potteries.
Pottery :
and Porcelain of the Far East, Handbook, 459
English, 234
Industry, Design in, 434
Pottery (*continued*) :
Worker's Register, 882
See also Merchandise Marks.
Poultry :
and Poultry Products (Regulation of Imports) Bill, 269
Coccidiosis in, 595
Feeding :
Essential Points in, 362
Scientific Principles of, 360
Gapes in, 134
Industry Bill, 704, 706, 729, 732
Mites, 849
Products, Supplies, 390, 633, 883
Some Diseases of, 360, 593
Supplies, 171
Technical Committee of Great Britain, Report, 596
Power Presses :
Safety Precautions, 167
See also Heavy Power Presses
Power-Factor Meters, Specification, 930
Powers of Attorney Act, 971
Bill, 946, 947, 963
Pox, Fowl, 362
Pozzolanas and Lime-Pozzolana Mixes, 1056
Practice Leaflet for Solicitors, 407, 893
Practitioners. *See* Medical Practitioners ; General Practitioners.
Pratt, D. D., Corrosion of Tar Stills, 658
Precipitation, atmospheric, summaries of, 181, 410, 647, 1053
Predictor, Anti-Aircraft, 221
Premature or unsightly development in the country or on the sea coast, 620
Premises damaged by Hostilities, Committee on the Responsibility for the Repair of, Report. *Cmd. 5934*, 736
Preparatory Schools, Lists of, 157, 385, 616, 868
Preservation :
Domestic, of Fruit and Vegetables, 360
of Animal Tissues, Microbiology in, 420
of the Countryside, 623
See also Ancient Monuments.
Preservatives, Wood, 420
Methods of applying, 193
Preserved Cherries. *See* Import Duties Advisory Committee.
Preserves from the Garden, 1023
Preserving. *See* Food Preserving ; Fruit and Vegetable.
Pressed Metal Wares Trade, Wages, 405, 891, 1048
Presses. *See* Power Presses ; Heavy Power Presses.
Pressure :
Atmospheric, Summaries of, 181, 410, 647, 1053
Gauges. *See* Gauges.

Pressure (continued) :
Heads for Air Speed Indicators, Specification, 599
Pretoria, s.s., and s.t. Georgette, collision, 210
Prevention :
and Treatment of Blindness (Scotland) Act, 523
Bill, 272, 467, 480, 490
of Damage by Rabbits :
Bill (formerly Crops (Prevention of Damage) Bill), 474, 475
of Fraud. See Investments.
Prime Cost Contracts, Ministry of Home Security Publications (N.P.), 882, 1038
Primers, specifications, 143, 854, 1025
Princess Louise, Duchess of Argyll, Death, 895
Princess Mary's Royal Air Force Nursing Service, 853, 1025
Pringle, J., South Wales, Geological Survey, 421
Printed Textiles, Guide to, 695
Printing :
and Allied Trades in Scotland, 434
Method of Recording Road Service Texture, 907
Notes on preparing Copy, 433
Printing, Music Printing, and Bookbinding, History of, 941
Prints :
and Drawings Gallery, British Museum, Guide to Exhibitions in, 459
in the Dotted Manner, 459
Priory of Inchmaholm, Guide, 232
Prison Service, Hours of Duty, Board of Arbitration Award, 1041
Prisoners :
of War, 1071
Treatment of, Standard Minimum Rules, 169
Prisons :
and Borstal Institutions, Board of Arbitration Award, 1041
Annual Reports :
England and Wales :
Cmd. 5153, 50
Cmd. 5430, 279
Cmd. 5675, 504
Cmd. 5868, 518
Cmd. 6137, 751
Scotland :
Cmd. 5125, 48
Cmd. 5409, 278
Cmd. 5710, 506
Cmd. 5967, 739
Private :
Bills. See Parliament.
Hire Vehicles. See Cabs.
Legislation :
Procedure (Scotland) Act, 66
Bill, 7, 13, 16, 41

Private (continued) :
Legislation (continued) :
(Scotland) Procedure Publications (N.P.), 202, 429, 667, 912, 1060
Manufacture of Arms. See Arms.
Privies, Cleansing of, Model Byelaws, 391
Privileges, Committee of, Reports, 487, 960
Privy :
Council :
Acts of, 655
Publications (N.P.), 188
Seal of Scotland, Register, 417
Prize :
Act, 754
Money. See Army Prize Money.
Probate. See Non-contentious Probate ; District Probate Registries.
Probation :
Homes and Hostels, Directory of, 169, 396, 632, 881
of Offenders :
Act, 295
Circular, 671
Home Office Publications (N.P.), 632
Officers, Directory of, 169, 396, 632, 881
Proceedings by Mortgagees, 407
Produce. See Stored Produce.
Producer Gas, Emergency Conversion of Vehicles to, Report, 1053
Production. See Census of Production.
Productive Societies, Annual Return Forms, 617, 869, 1034
Professional :
Notes (Meteorological), 181, 409, 646, 897
Papers (Ordnance Survey), 653
Proficiency Pay, Army, 935
Profitableness of Farming in Scotland, 197, 425, 664, 1059
Profits :
Excess Duty, Lists of Orders, 899
or Gains arising through an Agency, Agreement, Norway and U.K. Cmd. 6039, 744
Prognostic Value of some Psychological Tests, 191
Prohibition of Vivisection on Dogs (Scotland) Bill, 42, 498
Prolongation of Parliament Act, 972
Bill, 948, 963
Promotion, Army, 229, 454, 689, 936, 1066
Proofed Fabric for Focal-plane Camera, Specification, 1029
Property :
Disposal of, Convention between Australia, New Zealand, and U.S.A. Cmd. 5269, 59
Landed Properties in Greece, Expropriation of. Cmd. 5260, 58

Property (continued) :
War Damage to, Committee on Principles of Assessment, Final Report. Cmd. 6197, 967
See also Law of Property ; Leasehold ; Haile Selassie ; Industrial Property ; War Dept.
Proportional Representation. See Local Elections ; Metropolitan Borough.
Propulsion of Aircraft, 187
Prosecutions, Religious, (Abolition) Bill, 37, 267
Prospective Works, Survey of, Capital Expenditure, 619
Protection :
of Animals Bill, 267, 493
No. 2, 495
No. 3, 497
of Dogs Bill, 39
of your Home against Air Raids, 626
Protective Clothing for Persons employed in Factories, 1037
Protectorates :
Trade with Netherlands. Cmd. 5061, 44
See also Air Navigation ; Colonies.
Proud, S., Upper Winds at Kingston, Jamaica, 410
Provident Societies :
Annual Reports, 387, 617, 869
See also Industrial and Provident.
Provincial Offices of the Post Office, 416
Provisional Orders. See Marriages.
Prytherch, W. E., Magnesium and its Alloys, 422
Psittacosis, Laboratory Diagnosis of, 392
Psychodidae, 943
Psychological :
Tests, Prognostic Value of, 191
Treatment of Crime, 881
Public :
Accounts, Committee Reports, 28, 252, 260, 480, 487, 714, 721, 955, 959
Analysts, Circular, 872
Wales, 876
Assistance, Circular, 871
Buildings :
Departmental Committee on cost of:
First Report, 390
Circular, 388
Final Report, 620
Overseas, Civil Estimates, 25
Business, Colonial Regs., 380, 610, 862, 1031
Cleansing and Refuse Disposal, Costing Returns, etc., 162, 389, 620, 873
Departments :
Gross and Net Cost, 22, 251, 479, 712, 953
Heads of, Lists, 205, 433, 671, 916, 1062
See also Civil Service ; Government Departments.

Public (continued) :
Education in Scotland, Administration of, 889
Civil Estimates, 954
Elementary Schools :
Burnham Committee Report, Scales of Salaries for Teachers, 866
List of, and Certified Efficient Schools, 867
Statistics, 157, 385, 615, 867
Wales, List of, 868
See also Senior Public Elementary Schools.
Health :
Act, 66
Bill, 8, 12, 14, 17, 19, 41
Draft. Cmd. 5060, 44
Memo. Cmd. 5238, 56
Ministry of Health Publications (N.P.), 388, 392
Acts Amendment Act, 751
and Medical Subjects, Reports, 392, 622, 874
(Coal Mine Refuse) :
Act, 754
Bill, 37, 211, 492, 498, 499, 700, 702, 717, 733
(Scotland) Act, 753
Bill, 700, 702, 730
Consolidation Committee :
Draft of a Food and Drugs Bill. Cmd. 5629, 500
Report. Cmd. 5628, 500
(Drainage of Trade Premises) Act, 296
Bill, 11, 13, 15, 40, 237, 243, 259, 263, 267, 269
(London) Act, 66
Bill, 6, 7, 14, 15, 41
Imported Food Certificates, 161, 388, 618, 871, 1034
Scotland, 428, 666
Preservatives, etc., in Food, Circular, 1034
State of, Annual Reports, 164, 392, 622, 874
Income and Expenditure Accounts, 28, 257, 485, 719, 957
Meeting Act (1908) Amendment Bill, 37, 271, 489, 490
Officers, Colonial, 380, 1031
Order Act, 67
Bill, 42
Places (Order and Decency) Bill, 497, 499
Record Office Publications (N.P.), 189, 416, 655, 903, 1054
Records (Scotland) Act, 296
Bill, 236, 242, 258, 263, 266, 268
Refreshment Bill, 37, 42, 43

Public (continued) :
Right of Way. See Housing.
Sanitary Conveniences, Model Byelaws, 621
Service Vehicles, Road Transport for a Defence Emergency, 925
Sewers :
Contribution by Frontagers, 11, 13
Discharge of Trade Effluent into, 621
See also Aberdeen Corporation.
Social Services, expenditure, etc. :
Cmd. 5310, 62
Cmd. 5609, 293
Cmd. 5906, 521
Trustee :
Act, 295
Annual Reports, 189, 416, 654, 902
(General Deposit Fund) Act, 753
Bill, 499, 703, 719
Water Supply, Consolidation and Amendment of the Law relating to. Cmd. 5986, 740
Works :
Loan :
Board, Annual Reports, 221, 447, 684, 928
Commissioner, Land Settlement Accounts, 223
Loans :
Act, 1936, 65
Bill, 43
Act, 1937, 296
Bill, 236, 247, 272
Act, 1939, 752
Bill, 475, 499
No. 2 Act, 1938, 522
Publications :
and Debates, Reports, 255, 487, 954
See also Government Publications.
Publishing, Careers, 401
Puerperal :
Pyrexia, Circular, 871
Sepsis, Control of, 875
Pullovers, Boot or Shoe, Import Duties. Cmd. 5335, 64
Pulverising Plants, Precautions, 395
Pumps. See Fire Brigade Pumps.
Punishment. See Corporal Punishment.
Pupil Teachers in Army Schools, 936
Pupils' :
Progress (Schools), 914
Record Cards (Schools), 913
Purchase Tax Bill, 962
Pure Chemistry, History and Development, 414
Purley. See Coulsdon and Purley.
Pwllbach Colliery, Ystalyfera, Explosion from an Accumulator, Report, 435
Pyefinch, K. A., Acanthoracica, 942
Pyjamas, Specification, 452
Pyrexia. See Puerperal Pyrexia.

Q

" Q " Code. See Civil Aeronautical Radio Service.
Qantas Empire Airways Ltd., Empire Air Mail Scheme, Singapore–Sydney. Cmd. 5813, 514
Quail Protection Act, 522
Bill, 247, 272
Quarries :
Inspector of, Examination, 375
Mines Department Publications (N.P.), 184, 411, 648, 899, 1053
Workmen's Compensation Forms, 170, 397, 632
Quarrington Court, s.s., Wreck Report, 675
Quarter Sessions Committee Report. Cmd. 5252, 57
Quartz :
Oscillators, 1058
Piezo-Electric, Notation for, 661
Quays :
Workmen's Compensation Forms, 170, 397, 632
Quebracho Extract. See Import Duties Advisory Committee.
Queen Anne's Bounty :
Annual Reports, Accounts, 189, 416, 654, 902, 1054
(Powers) Measures, 235, 302, 699, 760
Report on, 235
Queen Elizabeth, Patent Rolls, 903
Queen Elizabeth, R.M.S., Launching Ceremony, Air Navigation Regs., 597
Queen Mary, Appointments to Royal Households, 180
Queen Mary, R.M.S., Agreement. Cmd. 5397, 271
Queen's Army Schoolmistresses, etc., 230, 454, 936
Queens of England, 460
Quetta, Staff College, examination for admission, 225
Quotas for Imports into Italy, Exchange of Notes, Italy and U.K. Cmd. 6020, 742

R

Rabbit Keeping, 1023
Rabbits :
Damage by, Report, 235, 237
See also Prevention of Damage by Rabbits.
for Fun and Flesh, 595, 850, 1023
Race Investigation of the Herring Population of Scottish Waters, 427
Racecourse Betting Control Board Reports, 29, 259, 486, 720, 958

Radcliffe, Farnworth and District Gas Act, 525
Radiator :
Leak Compound, Specification, 601
Temperature Thermometers, Specification, 140
Radiators. See Honeycomb Type Radiators.
Radio :
Notes for Wireless Operators, 1024
Service. See Civil Aeronautical Radio Service.
Signals, Admiralty List of, 1022
Station. See Air Ministry Meteorological Radio Station.
Radiobeacon. See V. H. F. Radiobeacon.
Radiocommunication, International Regs., 654
Radio-Meteorological Stations, Map, 647
Radiotelegrams, 188, 415, 654, 902
Radio - Therapeutic Departments for Cancer in General Hospitals, Memo., 392
Radium :
Beam Therapy Research, 657
Medical Uses of, 192, 419, 657, 1055
See also National Radium Trusts.
Rae, B. B. :
Age and Growth of Lemon Soles in Scottish Waters, 910
Factors in the Growth of Lemon Sole, 1060
Rae, Sir J., Chairman, Committee of Inquiry into working of Directorate of Operational Services and Intelligence of the Civil Aviation Department, Report. Cmd. 5864, 518
Raffia, Importation of, Exchange of Notes, France and U.K. Cmd. 5558, 289
Ragwort, 362
Rags, Import Duties. Cmd. 5226, 55
Railway :
and Canal Commission, Annual Reports :
Cmd. 5439, 280
Cmd. 5855, 517
Cmd. 6012, 742
Assessment Authorities, Annual Reports, 160, 392, 623, 875
Anglo-Scottish, 164, 388, 618, 870
Companies :
Charges Report, 1064
Industrial Court Award, 1043
See also Main Line Railway Companies.
Control. See Charges.
Freight Rebates Act, 67
Bill, 18, 42
Rails. See Import Duties Advisory Committee.

Railway (continued) :
Rates Tribunal Publications (N.P.), 214, 441, 678, 922
Shopmen, Industrial Court Awards, 174, 404, 640, 888, 1043
Statistics, 443, 679, 924
Railways :
Accidents :
Annual Reports :
Cmd. 5221, 55
Cmd. 5477, 283
Cmd. 5806, 513
Cmd. 6054, 745
Quarterly Reports, 214, 441, 677, 922
Report on Collision at Castle Cary, 677
Act, 1921 (reprinted), 752
Proceedings under, 214, 677, 921
(Agreement) Act, 65
Agreement (Powers) Bill, 963
Capital, Traffic, Receipts, and Working Expenditure Returns, 216
Government Control of. Cmd. 6168, 965
Estimates of, Net Revenue. Cmd. 6216, 968
Iraq :
Cmd. 5173, 51
Cmd. 5282, 60
Ministry of Transport Publications (N.P.), 444, 677, 921
of Great Britain, Return, 217
Staff employed, etc., Returns, 217
Traffic carried, etc., Returns, 217
Workmen's Compensation Forms, 170, 397, 632
See also Light Railways ; Military Railways.
Rain, Electricity on, 645
Rainfall, Meteorological Office Publications (N.P.), 180, 408, 645, 896
Rains, Production and Trade, 171, 398, 633
Raitt, D. S., The Haddock Stocks of the North-East Atlantic, 427
Ramsey and St. Ives Joint Water District Provisional Order Confirmation Act, 70
Bill, 13, 39
Ramsgate, Sunday Entertainments, 260
Rancidity in Edible Fats, 659
Range Table for Vickers Machine Gun, 455
Rangefinders :
Anti-Aircraft, 221
Coast Artillery, 685
Infantry, 688
Rangoon (Emergency) Security Act, 491
Rapeseed, Production and Trade, 172, 634
Raphael, Virgin and Child, 694

1936-40 | RAP-ROA

RAP— INDEX 1936–40

Rapidogen Navy Blue R. *See* Import Duties Advisory Committee.
Raspberries, Cultivation, 131
Rat Week Posters, 850
Rates :
and Rateable Values, 164, 392, 623, 875
Scotland, 916
Remission of, (London) Act, 971
Bill, 947, 963
Ratifications, Accessions, Withdrawals, etc., Supplementary Lists :
Cmd. 5086, 45
Cmd. 5376, 389
Cmd. 5654, 502
Cmd. 5930, 736
Cmd. 6148, 964
Rating :
and Valuation :
Act, 297
Bill, 244, 269
Product of Rates and Receipts, Circular, 618
(Air Raid Works) :
Act, 524
Bill, 497
(Scotland) Act, 524
Bill, 497
Assessment Committees Report Forms, 165, 392, 623, 875, 1035
Central Valuation Committee, Annual Reports, 165, 392, 623, 875
(Postponement of Valuations) :
Act, 1938, 522
Bill, 464, 494
Act, 1940, 971
Bill, 947, 963
Third Valuation Lists, Circular, 619
of Machinery, Panel of Referees, 389
See also Land Values ; Railway Rates Tribunal ; Voluntary Hospitals.
Rations :
and Allowances in lieu, Army, 455
for Livestock, 133, 848
Rats :
and how to exterminate them, 360, 848
and Mice :
(Destruction) Act, 732
Destruction of, 849
Rattles, Celluloid. *See* Import Duties Advisory Committee.
Raw :
Milk, Outbreak of Food Poisoning due to Salmonella, Type " Dublin " 622
Oiticica Oil. *See* Import Duties Advisory Committee.
Rawmarsh Provisional Order Confirmation Act, 527
Bill, 471, 496
Rayon, Production, Trade and Consumption, 171, 398, 634, 883
See also Piece-Goods.
Reading :
Corporation Trolley Vehicles Provisional Order Confirmation Act, 69
Bill, 13, 38
Sunday Entertainments, 956
Ready-Made and Wholesale Bespoke Tailoring Trade, Wages, 405, 891, 1047
Rearing :
of Calves, 360
of Chickens, 360
of Geese, 362
Receivers, Steam, Factory Form, 879
Reception of Children Overseas, Departmental Committee, Report. *Cmd. 6213*, 968
Record :
Cards, Pupils, 914
Publications. *See* Public Record Office.
Recreation and Physical Fitness for Youths and Men, Girls and Women, 388
See also Physical Training.
Recruiting :
Army :
Annual Reports :
Cmd. 5104, 47
Cmd. 5398, 277
Cmd. 5686, 504
Cmd. 5950, 738
Regs., 230, 455, 689, 936
of Workers. *See* League of Nations.
Recruits :
Air Force Instructions for guidance of Medical Officers in the selection of, 853
Army, Physical Examination of, etc., 454, 689, 936
Red :
Sea :
and Gulf of Aden, Exchange of Water between, 942
General Hydrography of, 942
Spider, 850
Fruit Tree, 595
Redcar Corporation Act, 526
Re-Delimitation of the Boundary between Burma (Tenasserim) and Siam, Nationality of persons affected. *Cmd. 5475*, 282
Redemption Annuities. *See* Tithes.
Redwood :
Baltic, Data on, 420
Minimum Structural Grade for, 906
Reeds Holme Works, Rawtenstall, Explosion, 672

INDEX 1936–40 —REQ

Reefflower, s.t., Wreck Report, 920
Reform. *See* Law Reform.
Reformatory Institutions, Annual Return Forms, 394
Refresher Courses for Health Visitors, 429, 666, 912
Refreshment :
Rooms :
and Kitchens, House of Commons, Select Committee Reports, 27, 259, 486, 717, 957
and Lavatories in the Palace of Westminster, 17
Public, Bill, 37
Refrigeration :
International Institute. *See* International.
Very Low Temperature, Survey, 187
Refugees :
from Germany, Status of :
Cmd. 5538, 64
Cmd. 5780, 511
Cmd. 5929, 736
Cmd. 6222, 969
International Status of. *Cmd. 5347*, 273
See also British Guiana Refugee Commission ; Czech Refugee Trust Fund.
Refuse Collection and Disposal, 162, 389, 620, 873
See also Public Health (Coal Mine Refuse).
Regal, s.t., Wreck Report, 675
Regency Act, 296
Bill, 236, 265, 266
Regimental :
Debts Act Regs., 455
Institutes, Conduct of, 451, 930, 1068
Regional Commissioners Act, 754
Register of Electors. *See* Local Elections.
Registered Friendly Societies, Annual Return Forms, 617, 869, 1033
Registers and Records :
of Scotland, Publications, 189, 417, 656, 903
School, 865
Registrar-General of Birth, Deaths and Marriages Publications (N.P.) :
England and Wales, 190, 417, 656, 903, 1033
Scotland, 202, 430, 667, 912, 1060
Registrars, Treasury Instructions to, 1049
Registration Officers, List of, 190, 417, 656
Registries. *See* District Registries ; District Probate Registries.
Registry of Ships, 209, 437, 674, 919
Regnum Animale, 943
Rehabilitation of Persons injured by Accidents, Reports, 392, 875
Rehousing of Aged Persons :
Report. *Cmd. 5798*, 512
Circular, 666
Reichsautobahnen, Germany, Concrete Road Construction on, 926
Reigate, Sunday Entertainments, 491
Reinforced Concrete :
Columns, Strength and Deformation of, 658
Piles, Stresses in, during Driving, 658
Studies in, 658, 904, 1056
Wartime Building Bulletins, 1056
Reinsurance of British Ships. *See* War Risks Insurance.
Relief. *See* Emergency Relief ; Poor Relief.
Religious :
Papyri, Egyptian, Catalogue of, 694
Prosecutions (Abolition) Bill, 37, 267
Remand Homes, Directory, 397
Rembrandt, Drawings and Etchings in British Museum, List, 693
Remission of Rates. *See* Rates.
Remount :
Manual, Army, 455
Regs., 455, 689, 936, 1071
Remuneration. *See* General Practitioners ; Ecclesiastical Officers ; Pay.
Renaissance Painting, Classical Antiquity in, 694
Rendered Finishes, External, 657
Rendle, B. J., Growth and Structure of Wood, 420
Rendle, J., Commercial Mahoganies and Allied Timbers, 659
Renfrewshire Educational Trust Scheme, 199, 200, 426
Rent :
and Mortgage Interest Restrictions Act, 754
Circular, 872
Restriction :
Acts, Interdepartmental Committee Report. *Cmd. 5621*, 294
Government Policy. *Cmd. 5667*, 503
See also Increase of Rent.
Rents of Houses and Flats owned by Local Authorities :
Cmd. 5527, 286
Cmd. 5910, 736
Repair of Drums, etc., Factory Forms, 395
Repairs. *See* Works and Repairs.
Representation of the People :
Acts (Amendment) Bills, 37, 498
(Publication of Register) Bill, 698
Reptiles, Instructions for Collectors, 460
Requisitioned Buildings. *See* War Department.

RES— INDEX 1936–40

Rescue Parties and Clearance of Debris, Air Raid Precautions, 166, 868
Research :
Aeronautical, 143, 370, 602, 856, 1072
Agricultural. *See* Agricultural Research.
Department, Woolwich, 230
Development Commissioners, Annual Report, 20
Government Laboratory, Annual Report, 160
Industrial Health, 191, 418, 657, 1055
Medical, 191, 418, 657, 904, 1055
Scientific and Industrial, 192, 419, 657, 904, 1056
Workers and Students :
Agriculture and Forestry, List of, 882, 1038
Grants to, 194, 422, 661, 907, 1058
See also National Physical Laboratory.
Reseau Mondial, 181, 410, 647, 1053
Re-seeding Poor Grass Land, 909
Reserve :
and Auxiliary Forces :
Act, 753
Bill, 702, 729, 730
Circular, Consequential Provisions, 913
Forces Act, 296
Bill, 236, 266
See also Army Reserve ; Naval Reserve ; Naval Volunteer Reserve ; Supplementary Reserve.
Reserved Occupations :
Cmd. 5926, 736
Cmd. 6015, 742
(N.P.), 889, 1045
Residential Institutions for Treatment of Tuberculosis, List, 392
Residual Values of Feeding Stuffs and Fertilisers, 425, 1059
Resin :
Sheets and Mouldings, Specification, 855
Specification, 601, 1026
See also Synthetic Resin Glues.
Respirators :
Army, 930
Care and Repair of, 930
Inspection and Repair of, 1037
Lost or Damaged by Members of the Public, Charges for, 1037
Mark, Certification, 165, 624
See also Civilian Respirator ; Civilian Duty Respirator.
Respiratory Dust Disease in Operatives in the Cotton Industry, Investigation, 191
Restaurants. *See* Hotels and Restaurants.
Restoration of Mills in Rural Areas Bill, 497
Restriction of Ribbon Development :
Acquisition of Land, 218
Act, 1935 :
Circular, 875
Decisions by Minister of Transport on Appeals, 680, 924
Directions, 218
Standard widths for roads, 218
Retail :
Bespoke Tailoring Trade, Wages, 177, 405, 1046
Distribution, Careers, 638
Distributive :
Societies, Annual Return Forms, 387, 617, 869, 1034
Trades, Wages, etc., Report, 889
Meat Dealers' Shops (Sunday Closing) Act, 66
Bill, 9, 13, 27, 36, 38, 41
Memos., 397, 632
Milk Distribution in Great Britain, Costs and Profits of, Report, 436
Trading Safeguards. *See* Shops.
Retired :
Foreign Officials, Taxation of Pensions of, Egypt and U.K. *Cmd. 5639*, 501
Pay :
Members of the Air Force and of the Nursing and Auxiliary Services thereof disabled, and for Widows, Children and Dependents of such members deceased in consequence of the present War, 960
Members of the Military Forces disabled, and of the Widows, Children, and Dependents of such members deceased in consequence of the present War, 968
Retort :
of the Coal Research Syndicate Ltd., Report of test, 193
See also Morgan Rotary Retort.
Retorts. *See* Narrow Brick Retorts.
Reunion, French Telegraph Cable between Mauritius and, Conventions, France and U.K. :
Cmd. 6127, 750
Cmd. 6194, 967
Revenue :
Act, 294
and Expenditure, Statements by the Chancellor of the Exchequer. *See* Budget.
Departments :
Appropriation Accounts, 21, 248, 476, 711, 949
Estimates, 25, 251, 253, 480, 716, 721, 954

INDEX 1936–40 ROA

Revenue (*continued*) :
Departments (*continued*) :
Estimates (*continued*) :
Memos, 253, 480, 716
Vote on Account, 253
Gross and Net Cost, 22, 251, 479, 712, 953
See also Inland Revenue.
Reverse Current Relays, Specification, 753
" Reversion " in Blackcurrants, 135
Revetments, Sandbag, Construction, Maintenance, and Replacement of, 1038
Revolver, Instructions for Armourers, 222
Rhagionidae, 943
Rhineland, Demilitarised Zone, Memo. by German Government. *Cmd. 5118*, 47
Rhodesia :
Economic Conditions, 212
See also Northern Rhodesia ; Southern Rhodesia.
Rhodesia–Nyasaland Royal Commission, Report. *Cmd. 5949*, 737
Rhopalocera, 943
Rhymney Valley Sewerage :
Board Act, 68
District and Western Valleys (Monmouthshire) Sewerage District Provisional Order Confirmation Act, 301
Bill, 240, 269
Ribble Sea Fisheries Order Confirmation Act, 70
Ribbon Development. *See* Restriction of Ribbon Development.
Rice, Production and Trade, 171, 398, 634, 883
Richards, T. G., Typewriters, History and Development, 653
Richardson, N. A., Wood Preservatives, 420
Richborough Castle, Kent, Guide, 232
Richmond (Surrey) Corporation Act, 300
Rickmansworth :
and Uxbridge Valley Water Acts, 69, 299, 526
Sunday Entertainments, 483
Riding Establishments :
Act, 754
Bill, 705, 721, 727, 731
(Registration and Inspection) Bill, 497
Ridley, Viscount, Chairman, Interdepartmental Committee on Rent Restrictions Acts, Report. *Cmd. 5621*, 294
Rifles, Small Arms Training, 456
Rigging for Aircraft, 150
Right or Wrong?, 689
Rigidity Modulus of Bitumens and Bitumen-Filler Mixtures, 907
Rings :
Factory Forms, 630
See also Shock Absorber Rings.
Ripon Provisional Order Confirmation Act, 71
Bill, 12, 41
Ritchie, A., Food and Feeding Habits of the Haddock in Scottish Waters, 428
River :
Conservancy Authorities, Income and Expenditure, Forms, 163, 390, 621, 874
Plate, Battle of, Account of Events, 1018
Pollution :
Chemical Methods for the Study of, 1023
Joint Advisory Committee on, Report, 392
River Avon, s.t., Wreck Report, 438
Rivers Pollution Prevention :
Act, 521
Scotland, Suggested Amendments of the Law, 202
Scottish Advisory Committee on, Report, 392
River-System, Water Survey of, 163
Rivets, Specifications, 141, 143, 367, 369, 600, 601, 855, 1028
Road :
Accidents :
Fatal, during 1935, 218
involving personal injury :
Annual Returns, 27, 256, 484, 680, 718
Forms, 170, 444, 680, 924
Prevention of, Reports, 462, 473, 697, 699
and Bridge Works, Standard Forms, etc., 218, 680
and Rail Traffic Act, 1933, Reports of Licensing Authorities, 218, 435, 680, 924
Aggregate, Shape and Measurements, 422
Construction. *See* Concrete Road Construction.
Friction, Studies in, 194, 422
Fund :
Accounts, 22, 250, 477, 712, 951
Annual Reports, 218, 445, 924, 1064
Haulage Wages :
Act, 523
Bill, 494
No. 2, 468, 469, 471, 495, 497
Order, 1045
Proposals and Directions in force, 1045
See also Trade Boards.
Materials. *See* Bituminous Road Materials.

ROA-SAN | 1936-40

ROA— INDEX 1936–40

Road (*continued*) :
Motor Transport Industry (Goods), Committee on Regulation of Wages and Conditions of Service :
Minutes of Evidence, 176, 404
Report. *Cmd. 5440*, 280
Passenger Transport Industry, Industrial Court Award, 1043
Research Publications, 194, 422, 662, 907, 1058
Safety among School Children, 218, 914
Surface Texture, a Printing Method of Recording, 907
Surfaces, 194
Traffic :
Act, 296
Bill, 42, 239, 255, 263, 266
Aids to the movement of, in absence of street lighting, 876
(Amendment) Bill, 37, 247
Authorisation of Signs, 218
Census, 218, 445, 924
Commissioners' Reports, 220
(Driving Licences) Act, 65
Bill, 9, 28, 34, 36, 38
(Licensing of Vehicles) Bill, 266
Signs, 445
Transport for a Defence Emergency, Organisation of, 925
Vehicles :
Lighting of, 446
Lights carried by, 882
Registration and Licensing :
List of Authorities, 682
Returns, 219, 445, 681, 925
Trades, Import Duties Inquiry Report, 208
Roads :
Acquisition of Land, 218
Building of, etc. (Military Engineering), 223
Civil Estimates, 252, 480, 715, 954
Construction. *See* Concrete Road Construction.
Conveyance of Explosives on, 879
Department Publications (N.P.), 926
Experimental Work on, 220, 446, 682, 926
Lay-out and Construction, 446
Standard Widths, 218
Trunk, Bill, 19, 41, 42, 43
Roberts, C. H., Chemical Methods for the Study of River Pollution, 1023
Roberts, E. J. :
Grass Drying, 418
Fodder Conservation, 904
Robertson, J. A., The Sprat and the Sprat Fishery of England, 595
Robertson, T., Geological Survey, Shrewsbury District, 661
Robertson, William, Bursary Trust Scheme, 198
Rochdale Corporation Act, 300
Roche Abbey, Yorkshire, Guide, 232
Rochester :
Corporation Act, 70
See also Chatham.
Rock Elm as Rough Timber, Specification, 140
Rockley, Lord, Chairman, Royal Commission on Safety in Coal Mines :
Minutes of Evidence, etc., 424, 663
Report. *Cmd. 5890*, 519
Rocks. *See* Coal Measure Rocks.
Rodger, A., A Borstal Experiment in Vocational Guidance, 418
Rods, Metal, Specifications, 367, 600, 1028
Rolling Mill Machinery. *See* Import Duties Advisory Committee.
Rolls, Calendars, etc. *See* Public Record Office.
Roman Alphabets, 943
Romford Gas Act, 525
Roofing, Use of Asphalt Mastic for, 419
Rooms, Measurement of, Housing, Scotland, 201
Root Vegetables, 849
Roots, Pickers of, Model Byelaws, 621
Rope :
Colliery Winding, 185
Corrosion of, 413
Fibre Cores for, 901
Hemp, Specification, 226
Steel Wire, Specification, 367
See also Sisal Rope ; Flexible Steel Wire Rope ; Wire Rope.
Rope, Twine and Net Trade, Wages, 177, 642, 891, 1047
Ropes :
Examination of, Mines and Quarries Form, 650
Register of, Factory Form, 879
Rorke, M., Anti-Venereal Measures, etc., 622
Rose, W. C. C., Gosforth District, Memoir, Geological Survey, 421
Rosher, A. B., H. Influenza in the Trachea, 875
Roslin, s.t., Wreck Report, 675
Ross, W. D., Chairman, Departmental Committee on Compensation for Card Room Workers, Report, 878
Rot. *See* Dry Rot ; Foot Rot ; Pink Rot ; Watery Wound Rot.
Rotary Transformers and Motor Generators, Specification, 854
Rotation of Crops, 133
Rothbury, Geology, 194
Rotherham Corporation Act, 300
Rothesay :
Corporation Gas Order Confirmation Act, 67

INDEX 1936–40 —ROY

Rothesay (*continued*) :
Harbour Order Confirmation Act, 525
Bill, 247, 272
Water Order Confirmation Act, 298
Bill, 238, 267
Rots, Principal, of English Oak, 193
Roumania :
Acceptance of Seamen's Discharge Books in lieu of Passports, Exchange of Notes with U.K. *Cmd. 5645*, 51
Anglo-Roumanian Clearing Offices, 950
Commercial, etc., Relations with U.K. :
Cmd. 6018, 742
Cmd. 6111, 749
Consular Fees on Certificates of Origin, Exchange of Notes with Canada. *Cmd. 5447*, 280
Economic Conditions, 211, 439
Imported Food Certificates, 162, 389
Scotland, 428
Payments Agreements with U.K. :
Cmd. 5174, 51
Cmd. 5187, 52
Cmd. 5470, 282
Cmd. 5471, 282
Cmd. 5587, 291
Cmd. 5588, 291
Cmd. 5613, 293
Cmd. 5718, 507
Cmd. 5797, 512
Cmd. 5840, 516
Rowley Regis. *See* Smethwick.
Royal :
Air Force. *See* Air Force.
Appointments, 1051
Army :
Medical Corps, Standing Orders, etc., 455, 689, 936, 1071
Ordnance Corps, Standing Orders, 455
Service Corps, Standing Orders, etc., 455, 689, 936, 1071
Artillery, Standing Orders, 455, 690
Botanic Gardens. *See* Edinburgh ; Kew.
College :
of Art :
Council, Annual Report, 869
Prospectus, 157, 385, 615
of Surgeons, Dangerous Drugs, 626
Commissions :
Publications (N.P.), 195, 423, 663, 908, 1058
Reports :
Despatch of Business at Common Law. *Cmd. 5065*, 44
Private Manufacture of and Trading in Arms. *Cmd. 5292*, 60
Royal (*continued*) :
Engineers :
Field Engineering, Manual, 451
Pocket Book, 455
Fine Art Commission, 6th Report. *Cmd. 5610*, 293
Gwent Hospital (Newport and Monmouth Hospital), Dangerous Drugs, 394
High School Endowment Scheme, 196
Horse Artillery, Seniority Lists, 455, 690
Hospital, Chelsea, Army Prize Money and Legacy Funds, etc., Accounts, 32, 261, 488, 722
Households, Appointments by H.M. the King and H.M. the Queen, 180
Indian Navy, Entrance Examination, 1030
Liverpool Children's Hospital, Dangerous Drugs, 166
Malta Artillery, New Conditions of Service for Officers, 936
Marines. *See* Marines.
Military :
Academy, Woolwich, Examination, 150
College, Sandhurst, Examinations, 150, 376, 607, 859, 1031
Mint, Annual Reports, 413, 652, 900
National Pension Fund for Nurses Act, 68
Naval Reserve. *See* Naval Reserve.
Navy. *See* Navy.
Observatory, Edinburgh, Publications (N.P.), 261, 668, 913
Ordnance Factories :
Accounts, 26, 255, 483, 716, 956
Civil Service Arbitration Tribunal Award, 402
Estimates, 24, 25, 31, 254, 481, 714, 716
Parks, Bird Sanctuaries in, 457, 691
Scotland, 433, 671, 916
Regiment of Artillery, Seniority Lists, Standing Orders, etc., 455, 690, 937
Samaritan Hospital for Women, Glasgow, Order Confirmation Act, 301
Bill, 245, 270
Scholarships, 156, 384, 614, 866
Scottish Museum :
Catalogue of Fossils in, 194
Reports, 431, 669, 914
Sheffield Infirmary and Hospital Act, 525
Society for the Prevention of Cruelty to Animals Act, 972
Technical College, Scheme, City of Glasgow, 198
Wanstead School Act, 757

ROY— INDEX 1936–40

Royal (*continued*) :
Warrants, Tradesmen holding, List of, 644
Ruanda-Urundi and Tanganyika, Boundary between :
Cmd. 5075, 45
Cmd. 5076, 45
Cmd. 5777, 511
Cmd. 5778, Water Rights, 511
Ruanda-Urundi, Uganda, and the Belgian Congo, Sanitary Convention, Belgium and U.K. *Cmd. 6064*, 745
Rubber :
and Cotton, Exchange of, Agreement, U.S.A. and U.K. *Cmd. 6048*, 744
Aprons, Import Duties. *Cmd. 5316*, 62
Boots, Specification, 688
Gloves, Anti-Gas, Specifications, 1069
Manufacturing Trade, Wages, 891, 1047
Pads for Bomb Sight Brackets, Specification, 369
Production and Trade, 172, 398, 634
Proofed :
Fabric for Riveted Tanks, Specification, 142
Garments, Specification, 688
Leggings, Specification, 933
Reclamation Trade, Wages, 1046
Regulation of the Production and Export of :
Cmd. 5236, 56
Cmd. 5384, 276
Cmd. 5901, 520
Cmd. 5901 (corrected reprint), 735
Soled Canvas Shoes, Specification, 752
Trade Conference :
Interim Report, 632
Final Report, 1037
Tubing, Specifications, 142, 366, 855, 1026
Vulcanised Expanded, Specification, 1027
Rubbish, Nuisances from, Model Byelaws, 391
Rugs, Specification, 1068
Ruislip-Northwood, Sunday Entertainments, 260
Rumore, s.s., Wreck Report, 920
Rural :
Areas :
A.R.P. in, 877
Demolition of Unfit Houses. *See* Unfit Houses.
Restoration of Mills, Bill, 497
Cottage Competition, Plans and Designs, 667
Cottages Protection. *See* Housing (Rural Cottages Protection).
District Councillors, Election of, 394
Rural (*continued*) :
Districts, Emergency Fire Brigade Measures in, 631
Housing :
in Scotland :
Report. *Cmd. 5462*, 281
Circular, 428
Manual (Housing (Financial Provisions) Act, 1938), 623
Sub-Committee Reports, 160, 392
Workers. *See* Housing (Rural Workers).
Russell, Sir E. J., Fertilisers in Modern Agriculture, 848
Russell, W. T., Appendicitis, 904
Russia. *See* Union of Soviet Socialist Republics.
Russian, Interpretership Examination, 857
Rust, Preventive, Temporary, Specification, 1025
Rust-Spot, Internal, of the Potato Tuber, 595
Rutherglen Burgh Order Confirmation Act, 524
Bill, 247, 272
Rutland, Census, 190
Ruwenzori Expedition, 1934–1935, 943
Rye, Production and Trade, 634, 883

S

Sack and Bag Trade Wages, 642, 891, 1047
Saddle and Harness Makers and Textile Refitters, Handbook, 1071
Safeguarding of Industries :
Articles Chargeable with Duty, 437, 674
Report of Committee. *Cmd. 5157*, 50
Safety :
Belts and Harness, Specifications, 140, 366
Conventions. *See* Merchant Shipping.
Equipment. *See* Parachute.
Glass :
for Plane Goggle and Spectacle Glass, Specification, 1028
See also Bullet-proof Safety Glass.
in Coal Mines. *See* Royal Commission.
in Mines Research Board Publications (N.P.), 185, 413, 651, 900, 1054
Lamps, 186, 899
See also Flame Safety Lamps.
Pamphlets, 396, 532, 882, 1037
Precautions :
Anaesthetic Explosions in Operating Theatres, 160, 161

INDEX 1936–40 —SAN

Safety (*continued*) :
Precautions (*continued*) :
Electricity Supply Regs., 167, 168, 170
For Woodworking Machinery, 630, 631
Factory Forms, 395
in the installation and use of laundry machinery and plant, 631
Principles for Boys employed in Coal Mining, 384
Safflower Seed Oil, Import Duties. *Cmd. 5115*, 47
Sagitta setosa, Sagitta elegans, Distribution, Breeding, etc., 631
Sailing :
Ships, History and Development, 187
Vessels, Workmen's Compensation Forms, 170, 397, 633
Sailors and Soldiers, Irish. *See* Irish Sailors and Soldiers.
St. Albans Joint Hospital District Provisional Order Confirmation Act, 68
Bill, 6, 36
St. Andrew's Ambulance Association, Air Raid Precautions, 204
St. Benedict's Hospital, London, Dangerous Drugs, 167
Saint Conan, s.s., Wreck Report, 1061
St. David's Day, Celebration of, 159, 616
St. Delphine, s.t., Wreck Report, 920
St. Helena, Colonial Reports, 152, 379, 610, 861
St. Helens :
Corporation (Trolley Vehicles) Provisional Order Confirmation Act, 758
Bill, 703, 729
Electricity Orders, 152
Provisional Order Confirmation Act, 71
Bill, 12, 17, 40
St. Ives. *See* Ramsey and St. Ives.
St. John Ambulance Brigade, Air Raid Precautions, 165
St. Lucia :
Arms, 1031
Flag Badge, 862
Colonial Reports, 152, 379, 610, 1031
Saint Mary Magdalene Hospital (Newcastle-upon-Tyne) Act, 973
St. Nicholas Millbrook (Southampton) Church (Sale) Act, 757
St. Olave's Hospital, London, Dangerous Drugs Order, 167
Saint Paul's and Saint James' Churches (Sheffield) Act, 302
St. Peter's :
Chapel (Stockport) Act, 759
Hospital, London, Dangerous Drugs, 167
See also Broadstairs.
St. Sebastian, s.t., Wreck Report, 920
St. Vincent, Colonial Reports, 152, 379, 610, 1031
Sal-d Crops, 133
Salads and Vegetables, Food Memo., 1032
Salaries. *See* Statutory Salaries ; Pay ; Civil Service Arbitration Tribunal Awards ; Remuneration ; Teachers' Salaries.
Salcombe. *See* Kingsbridge.
Sale :
Certificate (Customs), 155
of Food (Weights and Measures) Act, 64
Salford Corporation Act, 528
Salinity and Temperature of the English Channel, 133
Salisbury :
Marquess of, Manuscripts, 654
Sunday Entertainments, 952
Salmon :
and Freshwater Fisheries, Annual Reports, 363, 596
Fisheries (Scotland) Bill, 496
See also Fishery Board for Scotland ; Sockeye Salmon Fisheries.
Salmonella :
Infections of Ducks and Ducklings, 850
Type " Dublin ", Outbreak of Food Poisoning due to, 622
Saltburn and Marske-by-the-Sea Urban District Council Act, 525
Salvador, Commercial Relations with Canada. *Cmd. 5824*, 514
Sanatoria :
Costing Returns, 162, 389, 620, 873
List of, 392
Sanctuaries, Bird. *See* Royal Parks.
Sand Devils, 181
Sandbag Revetments, Construction, Maintenance and Replacement of, 1038
Sandgate Castle, s.s., Wreck Report, 675
Sandhurst. *See* Royal Military College.
Sandwich, Sunday Entertainments, 956
Sanitary :
Accommodation, Factories and Workshops, 170
Authorities. *See* Port Sanitary Authorities.
Control. *See* Mecca Pilgrims.
Conveniences, Public, Model Byelaws, 621
Convention :
International :
Cmd. 5979, 739
Cmd. 6114, 749
See also Belgium.
Ware of Pottery. *See* Merchandise Marks.
Sanquhar Coalfield, Geology, 194

1936-40 | SAN-SHI

SAN— INDEX 1936–40

San Salvador, s.s., Wreck Report, 438
San Sebastian, s.s., Wreck Report, 438
Sasines, Register of, 417
Index, 903
Satires, Political and Personal, Catalogue, 694
Saudi Arabia :
Modification of the Treaty of Jedda. *Cmd. 5380*, 276
Transit Dues at Bahrein. *Cmd. 5168*, 31
Saunders, O. A., Heat Transmission, Calculation of, 1058
Savage, R. E., Food of North Sea Herring, 361
Savings :
Banks :
and Friendly Societies, Accounts, 221, 447, 684, 928, 1068
See also Post Office Savings Banks ; Trustee Savings Banks.
See also National Savings ; War Savings.
Sawfly, Pear and Cherry, 132
Saws :
Circular, 659
Specifications, 452, 686
Scabies, 1036
Scaffolding :
at Buildings in course of construction, Register 395
Factory Form, 630
Tubular, 223
" Scaldwell " Steriliser, 132
Scale Absorption in Salmon, 427
Scandinavia, Air Services to :
Cmd. 5203, 53
Cmd. 5524, 286
Scandinavian Countries, Anti-Venereal Measures in, 622
Scarborough Provisional Order Confirmation Act, 525
Bill, 464, 493
Schizophrenia, Hypoglycaemic Shock Treatment in, 153, 611
School :
Age, Children under, 161
Attendance :
Deaf Children, Bill, 42
Scotland, 430, 668
Suggestions for Procedure, 384, 386
Boys, Secondary, Careers for, 887
Broadcasting (Scotland), 403
Buildings and their Equipment, 669
Certificates, Examinations, Scotland, 430
See also Day School Certificates ; High School Certificates.
Child, Health of the, 157, 385, 615, 1033
School (*continued*) :
Children :
Canteen Meals for, 867
Provision of Milk for (Scotland), 203
Road Safety among, 218, 914
Supply of Milk at reduced rates, 135
Scotland, 204
Crafts, Exhibition of, 917
Furniture, Army, Specifications, 452, 686
Girls, Secondary, Careers for, 401, 887
Health Records and Annual Reports, Revision of, 666
Laboratories, Accidents in. *See* Accidents.
Population in Scotland, 430
Registers and Records, Time-tables, etc., 865
Teachers (Superannuation) Act, 522
Schooling in an Emergency, 866
Schoolmistresses. *See* Queen's Army Schoolmistresses.
Schools :
A.R.P. Schools, 624
A.R.P. in, 614, 867, 1032
Scotland, 668, 913
Wales, 616, 868
Certified Efficient Schools, List of, 157
Day School System of Scotland, Technical Education in, 431
Epidemics in, 657
French and German, Scottish Assistants in, 203, 430, 913
Grant-Earning, 204, 669
Gymnasia in, 157, 867
Home Office, Directory, 169, 396, 632, 881
in War-Time, Memo., 867, 1033
Non-provided, grants, 156, 158
Physical Training for, Syllabus, 1033
Voluntary Schools, Scotland, List of, 203, 669
See also Borstal Institutions ; Public Elementary Schools ; Secondary Schools ; Anti-Gas Schools ; Approved Schools ; Certified Special Schools ; Day Schools ; French Schools ; Grammar Schools ; Nursery Schools ; One-Teacher Schools ; Scottish Schools ; Small Schools ; Technical High Schools ; Army Schools.
Schuster, Sir C., Chairman, Committee on Fees and Duties payable to Public Funds on the Grant of Honours and Dignities, Reports :
Cmd. 5450, 280
Cmd. 5767, 510

INDEX 1936–40 —SEA

Schuster, Sir G., Chairman, Joint Committee of Inquiry into Anglo-Argentine Meat Trade, Report. *Cmd. 5839*, 516
Science :
and Technology. *See* Imperial College.
Domestic, Careers, 401
in the Army, 653
Museum Publications (N.P.), 187, 414, 652, 901
Pure and Applied, Classification for Works on, 187
Scholarships, Exams., 156, 384, 614, 866
since 1500, 901
Scientific :
Aids to Criminal Investigation, 170
and Industrial Research, Department of :
Annual Reports :
Cmd. 5350, 273
Cmd. 5647, 501
Cmd. 5927, 736
Publications (N.P.), 192, 419, 657, 904, 1056
Conference, British Commonwealth, Report. *Cmd. 5341*, 273
Films. *See* Import Duties Advisory Committee.
Investigations, Fisheries, Scotland, 427, 910, 1060
Sclerotinia Disease of Potatoes and other Plants, 135
Scotland :
Geology of, 194
West, Gas Supplies in, 207
Scott, Alexander, Hospital Order Confirmation Act, 68
Bill, 11
Scott, C. M., Biological Action of X and Gamma Rays, 419
Scott Orphanage, Carnegie Park and, Trust Scheme, 197, 199
Scottish :
Administration Committee, Report. *Cmd. 5563*, 289
Assistants in French and German Schools and Colleges, 203, 668, 913
Building Costs, Committee on, Report. *Cmd. 5977*, 739
Central Emergency Committee for the Nursing Profession, Circular, 911
Departments, Publications (N.P.) (*Scottish Office, Scottish Home Department, Scottish Education Department ; Department of Health for Scotland, etc.*), 196, 424, 663, 909, 1059
District Coal Mines Scheme, 183, 411, 648, 1053
Scottish (*continued*) :
Ecclesiastical Commissioners' Report. *Cmd. 5692*, 505
Educational Services, 669
Everyday Art Exhibition, 203
Fisheries Advisory Council Bill, 948
Health Services :
Report of Committee. *Cmd. 5204*, 54
Summary of Report, 429
Highlands :
Dornoch and District, Electricity, 677
See also Western Highlands.
Housing Advisory Committee Reports :
Rehousing of Aged Persons. *Cmd. 5798*, 512
Circular, 666
Rural Housing in Scotland. *Cmd. 5462*, 281
Land Court :
Act, 523
Bill, 466, 484, 490, 493
Annual Reports :
Cmd. 5188, 52
Cmd. 5509, 285
Cmd. 5792, 512
Cmd. 6044, 744
Publications (N.P.) 431, 669, 914
Milk Marketing Scheme, 1933 area, Arrangements for increasing demand for milk, 204
Representative Peers to sit and vote in Parliament, 5
Schools and Training Centres, French and German Assistants in, 430, 668, 913
Union and National Insurance Company's Act, 757
Woollen Industry, Design in, 434
Scoured Cotton Fabric, Specification, 855
Scourers. *See* Import Duties Advisory Committee.
Scrase, F. J., Electricity of Rain, 645
Screening and Earth Systems for W/T purposes on Aircraft, Specifications, 369, 855
Screens, Thermometer, of the Stevenson Type, 410
Screw Gauges, 661
Screws. *See* Import Duties Advisory Committee.
Sculptures :
Assyrian, 693
Maya, 694
Scurf. *See* Black Scurf.
Sea :
Belligerent Rights at, Correspondence between Italy and U.K. *Cmd. 6191*, 967

SEA— INDEX 1936–40

Sea (*continued*) :
Breezes at Worthy Down, Winchester, 897
Coast. *See* Coast.
Fish :
(Dyeing and Colouring Prohibition) Bill, 270
Industry Act, 523
Bill, 265, 271, 466, 468, 482, 490, 493, 495
Fisheries :
Annual Reports, 136, 363, 596
Provisional Order Bills : 14, 39
Ribble Order Confirmation Act, 70
Scotland, Order confirming Byelaw No. 43, amending Byelaw No. 17, 114
Statistical Tables, 136, 363, 596, 850
Scotland, 201, 428, 665, 910
(Tollesbury and West Mersea) Order Confirmation Act, 758
Bill, 700, 728
Truro Order Confirmation Act, 70
Fishing Service, Examinations, etc., 209, 435, 673, 918
Transport Service Regs., 437, 919, 1061
Trout :
of Laxford System (Loch Stack and Loch More), 200
of River Carron and Loch Doule, 665
of River Conon, 665
Sea Valour, s.s., Wreck Report, 920
Seaford. *See* Newhaven.
Seals, Catalogue of, 900
Seamanship Manual, 587
Seamen :
Census, 208, 435, 673, 917
Centres for treatment of venereal disease, 165
Seamen's Discharge Books, Acceptance of, in lieu of passports, Roumania and U.K. *Cmd. 5645*, 501
Seaplanes, Reports of Aeronautical Research Committee, 146, 373
Searchlight Drills, Anti-Aircraft, 448, 684
Searchlights, 222
Manual of Anti-Aircraft Defence, 448
Sears, J. E. :
Delimitations of the Fundamental Standards of Length, etc., 661
Relationship between Wavelengths of Light and Fundamental Standards of Length, 661
Seasonal Workers, Scotland, Accommodation for, Model Byelaws, 666
Seasoning :
Series, Forest Products Research, 659
Timber, 659
Seats for Workers in Factories, 1048
Second Hands of Fishing Boats, Examination Regs., 136
Secondary :
Education :
Consultative Committee on, Report, 615
Cost per Pupil, 868
Scotland, Leaving Certificate Examinations, 431, 669, 914
Schools :
and Preparatory Schools recognised as efficient, Lists of :
England, 157, 385, 616, 868
Wales, 386, 868
on the Grant List, Statistics, 868, 616
Organisation and Curriculum of Sixth Forms, 614
Scotland, List of, 203, 669
Technical Subjects in, 669
Secretarial and Clerical Work, Careers, 174, 638
Secretary :
of State for Wales and Monmouthshire Bill, 271
Permanent, to Air Ministry, Report on discussions. *Cmd. 5254*, 57
Minute by Prime Minister. *Cmd. 5255*, 57
Secrets. *See* Official Secrets.
Sectional Steel Shelters, Protection Afforded, Report. *Cmd. 6055*, 745
Securities :
Treasury Directions, 1049
(Validation) Act, 972
Bill, 948
Sedgefield, Sunday Entertainments, 482
Seeds :
Lists of, Royal Botanic Gardens :
Edinburgh, 203, 430, 913
Kew, 173, 400, 887
See also Flower Seeds ; Weed Seeds.
Seismic Waves :
from the Baffin Bay Earthquake, Travel of, 408
Travel-Times of, 645
Seismology at Kew Observatory, 896
Selby Provisional Order Confirmation Act, 301
Bill, 240, 269
Self-Acting Mules, Factory Form, 630
Selkirkshire Educational Trust (Amendment and Additional Endowments) (No. 1) Scheme, 427, 665, 910
Semi-Technical-Scale Plant, Operation of, 906
Senior Leaving Certificate, Scotland, 913, 1060
Senior Public Elementary Schools (Liverpool Act, 754
Bill, 707, 722, 731

INDEX 1936–40 SHI—

Seniority Lists. *See* Royal Artillery ; Royal Horse Artillery.
Sepsis. *See* Puerperal Sepsis.
Seraya, Meranti and Lauan, 193
Serge Overshirts, Specification, 932
Sergeants' Messes, Grants, 935, 1070
Serges, Specifications, 452, 686, 1068
Service :
and Rates, Coastwise Shipping, Report, 602
Corps. *See* Royal Army Service Corps.
Electrical Apparatus as applied to Artillery, 930
Sesame Seed, Production and Trade, 172, 634
Settlement. *See* Empire Settlement ; Oversea Settlement ; Home and Empire.
Seven-Figure Trigonometrical Tables, 842
Sevenoaks :
Sunday Entertainments, 491
Water Provisional Order Confirmation Act, 300
Bill, 242, 268
Sewage :
Disposal Works, Costing Returns, 162, 389, 620, 873
See also Crude Sewage.
Sewerage. *See* Middlesex ; Rhymney Valley.
Sewers. *See* Glasgow Streets ; Public Sewers ; Aberdeen Corporation.
Sewing Machine :
Oil, Specification, 366
Tables, Leg Frames for. *See* Import Duties Advisory Committee.
Woodwork. *See* Import Duties Advisory Committee.
Sewings-Cotton, Linen, Silk, Specification, 932
Seychelles, Colonial Reports, 152, 610, 861
Shackles, Factory Form, 630
Shafts, Mines and Quarries Form, 650
Shakespeare, G., Chairman, Interdepartmental Committee on Reception of Children Overseas, Report. *Cmd. 6213*, 968
Shanghai, Imported Food Certificates, 388, 618
Scotland, 666
Share-pushing, Report. *Cmd. 5539*, 287
Shaw, J. F., Low Temperature Carbonisation, etc., 906
Shaw, W. V., Report on outbreak of Enteric Fever in the County Borough of Bournemouth and in the Boroughs of Poole and Christchurch, 392
Sheaf Brook, s.s., Wreck Report, 210
Sheathings, Deck, for Ships, 435
Sheds, Model Byelaws, 164, 621
Sheep :
Foot Rot of, 393
Maggot Fly, 664
Production and Trade, 171, 398, 634
Stocks Valuation (Scotland) Act, 296
Bill, 42, 238, 249, 263, 265
Stomach Worms in, 135
Sheeting, Cotton, Specification, 687, 932
Sheeting Cotton, Grey, Specification, 1068
Sheets :
and Sheeting, Specification, 226
Cotton, Specification, 687, 932
Metal, Specification, 141, 366, 600, 854
Pigmented Cellulose Acetate, Specification, 368
Synthetic Resin, Specification, 369, 855
Various, Specification, 1025
Sheffield :
and District Gas Act, 526
Corporation Acts, 299, 760
Gas :
(Consolidation) Act, 756
No. 2 Order, 1936, modifications proposed by Select Committee, 238
Infirmary. *See* Royal Sheffield Infirmary.
Shelled Almonds. *See* Import Duties Advisory Committee.
Shelter from Air Attack, 878
Shelters. *See* Air Raid Shelters ; Bomb Resisting Shelters ; Domestic Surface Shelters ; Steel Shelters ; Surface Shelters.
Shepherd, W. C. F., High-Speed Cameras for measuring Rate of Detonation in Solid Explosives, 413
Shepherd's Bush Railway Extension. *See* Great Western Railway.
Sheppey Water Act, 299
Sherardising, Specification, 369
Sheriff Courts (Scotland) Act, 755
Bill, 733
Sherlock, R. L. :
Guide to Geological Column, 660
Mineral Resources of Great Britain, 661
Shift :
System. *See* Employment of Women and Young Persons.
Workers, Young Persons, Factory Forms, 628
Ship Captain's Medical Guide, 919
Shipbuilding :
and Ship-repairing Yards, Lighting during Blackout Hours, 1037
Demand for Timber in, 617
Dockyard Accounts, 26, 255, 483, 716, 956

SHI-SOU | 1936-40

SHI— INDEX 1936–40

Shipbuilding (*continued*) :
  Trade, Census of Production, 917
Shipley Provisional Order Bill, 963
Shipowners. *See* British Shipowners.
Shipping :
  Casualties and Deaths, 209, 437, 674, 1064
  Geographical Distribution of British Empire Shipping, 126
  Ministry of, Publications (N.P.), 916, 1061
  Navigation and. *See* Navigation and Shipping.
  Service between Western Canada and Australia–New Zealand, 208
  Suez Canal, Annual Returns, 158, 386, 616, 869, 1033
  See also Admiralty Publications; Board of Trade Publications; Imperial Shipping Committee Publications; British Shipping; Tramp Shipping; Merchant Shipping.
Ship-repairing, Dockyard Accounts. *See* Shipbuilding.
Ships :
  and Aircraft (Transfer Restriction) Act, 754
  Casualties. *See* Shipping.
  Foreign-going, Deck manning of :
    Correspondence with Merchant Shipping Advisory Committees. *Cmd. 5242*, 57
    Instructions, 207
    Report. *Cmd. 5096*, 46
  Fumigation of, with Hydrogen Cyanide, 390
  Insurance of, Report. *Cmd. 5349*, 273
  Mercantile Marine Surveyors. *See* Ship's Provisions.
  Piracy in Mediterranean. *Cmd. 5568–9*, 290
  Registry of. *See* Registry of Ships.
  Re-insurance Agreements, 959
  Replacement Committee, Report. *Cmd. 5459*, 281
  Sailing. *See* Sailing Ships.
  Signal Letters of. *See* Signal Letters.
  Vulnerability of Capital Ships to Air Attack. *Cmd. 5301*, 61
  Wireless Weather Messages from, Decode, 182, 647
  Wreck Reports, 210, 438, 675, 916, 1061
  See also Load Line Convention; Navigation; Pilot; Pilotage; Boats; British Fishing and Coastal Craft; British Ships; Cunard White Star; Fishing Boats; Fleets; Freight Ships; Sailing Vessels; Steamships; Coastwise Shipping; State-owned Ships; Merchant Ships.
Ships' Provisions, Inspectors of, 207, 673, 917
Shipwreck :
  Societies registered for assistance, Annual Return Forms, 387, 617, 869, 1034
  Wreck Reports. *See* Ships.
Shirtings, Specification, 452, 931, 1068
Shirtmaking Trade, Wages, 405, 891, 1047
Shirts, Specifications, 226, 452, 686, 932, 1068
Shock. *See* Wound Shock.
Shock-Absorber :
  Cord Rings for Gun Mountings, Specification, 1025
  Struts, Fluid for, Specification, 1026
Shoe :
  Pullovers. *See* Pullovers.
  Repairing Trade. *See* Boot and Shoe.
Shoes :
  for Physical Training, 156, 158
  Specifications, 452, 932
Shopkeepers, Poisons Memo., 169
Shops :
  Act, 1934 :
    Forms, 1037
      Scotland, 1061
    Memo., 1037
      Scotland, 1061
  Act, 1936, 66
    Bill, 5, 6, 16, 29, 34, 37, 39
  Bill, 1937, 266
  Bill, 1939, 727
  (Hours of Closing) Act, 752
  (Retail Trading Safeguards) Bill, 42
  Sunday Closing of, 632
  (Sunday Trading Restriction) Act, 66
    Bill, 9, 10, 15, 16, 17, 27, 34, 36, 38, 41, 42
    (Amendment) Bills, 42, 255, 263, 266, 496, 731
    Memos., 397, 632
  Window Displays and Illuminated Signs, 882
Shoreham Harbour Act, 302
Shorthand Writers in Supreme Court, Report. *Cmd. 5395*, 277
Shot-firers, Mines Department Publications (N.P.), 899
Shovels, Specification, 226
Shrewsbury District, Geological Survey, 661
Shropshire :
  Census, 190
  Coal Mines Scheme, 183, 411, 898
Shropshire, Worcestershire and Staffordshire Electric Power (Consolidation) Act, 526
  Bill, 467

INDEX 1936–40 —SIP

Shute, P. G., Longevity of Mosquitoes, etc., 623
Siam :
  Air Services over Siam, India and Burma, Exchange of Notes with India and U.K. *Cmd. 5651*, 502
  Economic Conditions, 439
  Nationality of Persons affected by the Re-Delimitation of the Boundary between Burma (Tenasserim) and Siam. *Cmd. 5475*, 282
  Opium Smoking Agreement. *Cmd. 5401*, 277
  Rubber, Regulation of Production and Export, Agreements :
    Cmd. 5236, 56
    Cmd. 5384, 276
  Siamese Courts, Right of Evocation from, Exchange of Notes with U.K. *Cmd. 5611*, 293
  Treaties of July 14, 1925, with U.K., continuance of rights under :
    Cmd. 5607, 292
    Cmd. 5730, 507
  Treaties of Commerce and Navigation with U.K. :
    Cmd. 5608, 292
    Cmd. 5731, 508
  See also Thailand.
Siberite, s.t., Wreck Report, 210
Sick Leave Regs., Civil Service, 928
Sickness :
  Absence and Labour Wastage, 191
  Experience of London Transport Workers, Investigation, 418
  Incapacitating, in the Insured Population of Scotland, 201, 428, 912
Sierra Leone :
  Colonial Reports, 152, 379, 610, 861
  Economic Conditions, 439
Signal :
  Book for use in Air Navigation, 1025
  Card, Admiralty, 587
  Letters of British Ships, 209, 437, 674, 919, 1061
  Training, Army, 230, 456, 690
Signaller's Pocket Book, Army, 222
Signals :
  Air Raid Warning, 625
  Fog and Visual Time, 127, 354, 587, 843, 1019
  Radio, 1022
  Wireless, Admiralty List of, 132, 359, 592, 847
  See also Motor Drivers (Signals).
Signs, Traffic, 218, 445, 926, 1064
Silage, Making, without Expensive Buildings, 850
Silhouettes of Aircraft, 140
Silico-Manganese Steel Bars, Specification, 366
Silicon :
  Alloys. *See* Import Duties Advisory Committee.
  Wire and Rivets, Specification, 601
Silicon-Aluminium Alloy Forgings, Specification, 369, 1029
Silicon-Brass :
  Sheets, Specification, 1028
  Tubes, Specification, 369
Silicon-Chromium Valve Steel Forgings or Stampings, Specification, 143
Silicon-Iron Bronze Castings, Specification, 601
Silicosis :
  Pottery Worker's Register, 882
  Workmen's Compensation Forms, 170
Silk :
  Cordage for Parachute Shroud Lines, Specification, 140, 1028
  Fabric :
    for Kite Balloons, Specification, 855
    for Parachutes, Specification, 600, 854, 855, 1026
    See also Artificial Silk Fabric
  Production and Trade, 171, 398, 634, 883
  See also Import Duties Advisory Committee.
Silver :
  Fish and Firebrat, 941
  Scurf of Potatoes, 362
  See also Metal Alloys.
Silversmithing, Design in, 434
Simmons, Sir L., Special Mission to the Vatican, Religious Questions in Malta. *C. 5975*, 500
Simonds, Mr. Justice, Law Reporting Committee, Report, 1052
" Simplex " Oilskin Clothing, Specifications, 933
Simpson, G. C., Ice Accretion on Aircraft, 410
Simpson, J. S., Rosehearty, Industrial Court Award, 888
Simpson Memorial Hospital. *See* Edinburgh.
Simuliidae, 943
Singapore Strait and Approaches, Tidal Stream, Tables, 1022
Singapore–Sydney, Empire Air Mail Scheme. *Cmd. 5813*, 514
Sinking Funds. Accounts, 29, 259, 485, 720, 958
Sinton, J. A. :
  Infective Material for the Practice of Malaria-Therapy, 622
  Longevity of Mosquitoes in relation to Transmission of Malaria in Nature, 623
Siphonaptera, 943

SIS— INDEX 1936–40

Sisal Ropes, Specification, 1068
Sitka Spruce, Specifications, 1025
Sittingbourne and Milton, Sunday Entertainments, 264
Six-Quarters Seam, Survey of Coal Resources, 1057
Sixth Forms. *See* Secondary Schools.
Size Limits of Fish, International Convention. *Cmd. 5494*, 284
Skeleton Cases, Specification, 1063
Sketching, Field, Army, 688, 934
Skidding, Road Research Board Publications (N.P.), 194
Skill, Acquisition of, 191
Skin :
  Effects of Chrome on, 395
  Spot of Potatoes, 362
Skins. *See* Hides.
Skippers and Second Hands of Fishing Boats, Examination Regs., 436
Sky. *See* Blueness of the Sky.
Slag, Basic, 363
Sleeve-Control Trunk and Auto-Manual System, Telephones, 902
Slides, Merchandise Marks. *Cmd. 6080*, 746
Slippers, Specification, 452
Slough :
  Provisional Order Confirmation Act, 758
    Bill, 704, 730
  Sunday Entertainments, 32
Slow-Burning Films, Position of, under the Cinematograph Act, Report and Circular, 878
Slugs, 362
Slum Clearance, position, 163, 390, 621, 873
Small :
  Ambulances, Stretcher Carrying Fitments for, 871
    Scotland, 911
    Wales, 876
  Arms :
    Care, inspection and repair of, 230
    Courses for H.M. Fleet, Royal Naval Handbook, 842
    Training, Army, 230, 456, 690, 937
  Factories, Messrooms and Canteens at, 1037
  Holding or Allotment Societies, Annual Return Forms, 387, 617, 870, 1034
  Huts, Type Designs for, 1056
  Landholders (Scotland) :
    Act (1911) Amendment Bill, 272
    Acts, Proceedings under :
      Reports :
        Cmd. 5792, 512
        Cmd. 6044, 744
      Appendices, 204, 431, 669, 914
  Schools, Physical Training in, 669
Smallman, A. B., Cancer, Memo. on Provision of Radio-Therapeutic Departments in General Hospitals, 392
Smallpox, Memo., 623
Small-scale Liquid Phase Continuous Plant, Development of, 660
Smallwares, Textile. *See* Merchandise Marks.
Smart, J., British Blood-sucking Flies, 941
Smelter, Operation of, at Trail, British Columbia, Convention between U.S.A. and Canada. *Cmd. 5444*, 280
Smethwick, Oldbury, Rowley Regis, and Tipton Transport Act, 757
Smith, B., Gypsum and Anhydrite, 661
Smith, W., Epidemic Influenza, 657
Smocks, Lasting, Specification, 932
Smoke Abatement, Model Byelaws, 391
  See also Atmospheric Pollution.
Smyth, C., Nature and Characteristic Features of Post-Normal Occlusion, 419
Snails, 362
Snap Fastener Trade, Wages, 405, 891, 1047
Snell, Lord, Arandora Star Inquiry. *Cmd. 6238*, 970
Snodgrass, W. R., Analysis of Results of Treatment of Syphilis, 419
Snow, Nuisances from, Model Byelaws, 391
Snowdonia, National Forest Park Committee Report, 386
Snowfall in British Isles, 647
Soaps, Specification, 226
Soay. *See* Island of Soay.
Social :
  and Physical Training Grant Regs., 868
    Amending Regs. No. 1, 1033
  Service :
    in India, 884
    Public, Expenditure, :
      Cmd. 5609, 293
      Cmd. 5906, 521
  Services in Courts of Summary Jurisdiction, Report. *Cmd. 5122*, 48
  Work, Women, Careers, 887
Societies :
  Friendly. *See* Registry of Friendly Societies.
  (Miscellaneous Provisions) Act, 971
    Bill, 946, 962
Sockeye Salmon Fisheries in the Fraser River System, Convention, U.S.A. and Canada. *Cmd. 5851*, 517
Socks, Specification, 687
Sodbury, Sunday Entertainments, 956

INDEX 1936–40 —SOU

Sodium bichromate and potassium bichromate, Import Duties. *Cmd. 5164*, 50
Soft :
  Aluminium Alloy Tubes, Specification, 1029
  Cotton Cord for Kite Balloons, Specification, 601
  Fruits, production, 360
Softwoods, Principal Decays of, 906
Soil Analysis, 135, 850, 1024
Soils :
  Liming of, 909
  of Cambridgeshire, 261
Soldiers :
  Civil Employment for, 449, 685
  See also Irish Soldiers and Sailors; War Office Publications.
Soles. *See* Lemon Soles.
Solicitors :
  Act (1936), 66
    Bill, 7, 15, 30, 34, 38, 40
  Amendment (Scotland) Bill, 464, 466, 474, 495, 499
  Bill, 700, 704, 707, 947, 948
  (Disciplinary Committee) Act, 755
    Bill, 708, 732
  (Emergency Provisions) Act, 971
    Bill, 945, 946, 962
  Practice Leaflets, 179, 407
Solid :
  Explosives, High-Speed Camera for measuring Rate of Detonation, 413
  Insoluble Quebracho Extract. *See* Import Duties Advisory Committee.
Solid-headed Pins of Brass, Iron or Steel. *See* Merchandise Marks.
Solihull Urban District Council Act, 71
Solitary Corals, Ecology of, 942
Solomon Islands. *See* British Solomon Islands.
Solubility of Cements, 905
Solvents. *See* Organic Solvents.
Somaliland :
  Economic Conditions, 439
  Meteorological Observations in, 408
  See also British Somaliland.
Somerset :
  and Wilts Provisional Order Confirmation Act, 298
    Bill, 237, 265
  Coal Mines Scheme, 183, 411
Sound :
  Localisation of, 191
  Transmission in Buildings, 1058
  Velocity of, in Pure Water and Sea Water, 847
Sound-Track Negatives. *See* Import Duties Advisory Committee.
South :
  Africa :
    Air Services :
      Portuguese East Africa. *Cmd. 5707*, 506
      Portuguese West Africa. *Cmd. 6231*, 970
    British War Memorial Cemeteries and Graves in Egypt. *Cmd. 5618*, 293
    Civil Air Transport Service. *Cmd. 5325*, 63
      To and from Egypt. *Cmd. 5404*, 277
    Commercial Relations with Egypt. *Cmd. 6134*, 750
    Economic Conditions, 211
    Efficiency Certificates for Aircraft and Aircraft Motors, Agreement with Germany. *Cmd. 5705*, 506
    Extradition :
      Exchange of Notes with Estonia. *Cmd. 6027*, 743
      Supplementary Agreement with Ecuador. *Cmd. 5614*, 293
    Flags and Badges, 380
    Identity Documents for Aircraft Personnel, Exchange of Notes with Portugal. *Cmd. 5565*, 289
    Imported Food Certificates, 162, 389, 871
      Scotland, 428
    Native Labour from Mozambique. *Cmd. 5085*, 45
    Non-Immigrant Passport Visa Fees, Agreement with U.S.A. *Cmd. 5706*, 506
    War Cemeteries in Iraq, Agreement. *Cmd. 5196*, 53
    War Graves Agreement. *Cmd. 5068*, 44
    See also Empire Air Mail; Commercial Agreements.
  America, Air Transport Services to. *Cmd. 5524*, 286
  Atlantic, Meteorological Observations in, 408
  Derbyshire Coalfield, 660, 1057
  Essex. *See* Essex.
  Kent Water Provisional Order Confirmation Act, 758
    Bill, 703, 729
  Metropolitan Gas Act, 71
  Nottinghamshire Joint Hospital District Provisional Order Confirmation Act, 299
    Bill, 238, 266
  Pacific Ocean Currents, 897
  Shields Corporation (Trolley Vehicles) Order Confirmation Act, 587
    Bill, 701, 728

South (*continued*) :
Staffordshire :
Coal Mines Scheme Amendments, 184
Joint Hospital District Provisional Order Confirmation Act, 757
Bill, 499, 698
Joint Smallpox Hospital District Provisional Order Confirmation Act, 68
Bill, 6
Waterworks Acts, 69, 759
Suburban Gas Acts, 71, 973
Wales :
Coal Mines Scheme, 184, 411, 648, 1053
Geological Survey, 421
Illustrated Regional Guide, 691
See also Monmouthshire ; South-West England.
South-East :
Cornwall. *See* Cornwall.
England Electricity (Alteration and Extension Scheme), 926, 927, 1065
Essex. *See* Essex.
South-Eastern Gas Corporation Limited, Associated Companies, Bill, Report on, 947
Southall, Sunday Entertainments, 716, 953
Southampton :
Corporation Act, 302
Harbour Act, 759
Southend-on-Sea Corporation (Trolley Vehicles) Order Confirmation Act, 758
Bill, 703, 729
Southern :
Division, Mines, Reports, 412, 648, 898
Railway :
Acts, 79, 299, 759, 526
Industrial Court Awards, 403, 640
Rhodesia :
Constitution, Proposed Amendment. *Cmd. 5218*, 55
Economic Conditions, 921
Imported Food Certificate, 389
Scotland, 428
Southport, Anemometers at, comparison of records, 181
Southwark Cathedral Measure, 239, 302
South-West :
Africa, Imported Food Certificate, 619
China–British Ports, Air Service. *Cmd. 6122*, 749
England and South Wales Electricity (Alteration and Extension) Scheme, 1065
Midlands Electricity Special Order, 1064
Sou'wester, Oilskin, Specification, 687, 933
Soviet Union. *See* Union of Soviet Socialist Republics.
Soya Bean Cake, Meal, Oil ; Import Duties :
Cmd. 5115, 47
Cmd. 5327, 63
Soya Beans :
Production, Trade and Consumption, 172, 634, 883
See also Import Duties Advisory Committee.
Spain :
Carriage of Munitions to, Merchant Shipping, Act, 67
Bill, 18, 42
Debts Clearing Office Accounts, 250, 477, 711, 950
Extension of Non-Intervention Agreement and withdrawal of foreign volunteers, etc. *Cmd. 5793*, 512
International Committee for Application of Agreement for Non-Intervention :
Cmd. 5300, 61
Cmd. 5521, 286
Loan Agreement with U.K. :
Cmd. 6189, 967
Cmd. 6230, 970
Observation of Frontiers, Resolution relating to Scheme. *Cmd. 5399*, 277
Payments Agreements with U.K. :
Cmd. 5058, 43
Cmd. 5097, 46
Cmd. 5250, 57
Suez Maritime Canal, Free Navigation of, International Convention. *Cmd. 5623*, 500
Trade and Payments Agreements with U.K. :
Cmd. 6188, 966
Cmd. 6229, 969
Withdrawal of Foreign Volunteers from, Correspondence with the Italian Govt. *Cmd. 5570*, 290
See also Merchant Shipping (Spanish Frontiers Observation).
Spanish, Interpretership, Examinations, 374, 607
Sparkes, F. N. :
Control of the Moisture Content of Aggregates for Concrete, introducing a new Vibration Method, 422
Machinery and its uses in Concrete Road Construction, 907
Sparking Plugs, Graphited Grease for Threads of, Specification, 855
Spear and Creeping Thistles, 664

Special :
Areas :
Agreement between Treasury and Special Areas Reconstruction Association Ltd., 32
(Amendment) Act, 296
Bill, 239, 267
Statement. *Cmd. 5386*, 276
Commissioners' Reports :
England and Wales :
Cmd. 5090, 46
Cmd. 5303, 61
Cmd. 5595, 291
Cmd. 5896, 520
Scotland :
Cmd. 5089, 46
Cmd. 5245, 57
Cmd. 5604, 292
Cmd. 5905, 521
Committee of Inquiry into Land Settlement, Report, 889
Mortality Rates in " Depressed Areas ", 623
Reconstruction (Agreement) Act, 65
Bill, 11, 38
Army Examination, 1071
Enactments (Extension of Time) Act, 971
Bill, 945, 946, 962
Schools, List of, 383, 615, 866
Specifications :
Air Ministry, 140, 366, 599, 853, 1025
A.R.P. Department, 626, 878
Auxiliary Fire Service, 631, 1036
Board of Trade, 919
Ministry of Aircraft Production, 1028
Ministry of Shipping, 1061
Ministry of Supply, 1062
War Office, 225, 452, 686, 930, 1068
Wireless, 127, 354, 587, 843, 1019
Spectacle :
Frames, etc., Merchandise Marks Report. *Cmd. 6147*, 751
Glass, Specification, 1028
Speech in Deaf Children, 419
Speed Indicators, Specifications :
Air, 140
Engine, 140
Flexible drive for, 143, 369
Spelter. *See* Import Duties Advisory Committee.
Spen Valley Dairy Co., Ltd., Explosion from Sterilising Tank, 435
Spence Bursary Trust Scheme, 199, 200, 426
Spens, W., Chairman, Consultative Committee on Secondary Education, Report, 615
Sperry Gyro Compass Manual, 127, 842
Spices, Production and Trade, 172, 398, 634
Spiders. *See* Red Spider ; Fruit Tree Red Spiders.
Spier's Trust Scheme, 199, 200, 426
Spindles Board :
Accounts, 264, 492, 949
Reports :
Cmd. 5579, 290
Cmd. 5873, 513
Cmd. 6157, 964
Spinning :
and Weaving Flax and Tow, Factory Form, 530
See also Cotton Spinning.
Spirits, Bonded Warehouse Procedure, 154
Spirituous Beverages, Importation into Africa, Reports :
Cmd. 5205, 54
Cmd. 5486, 283
Cmd. 5814, 514
Cmd. 6082, 747
Split Pins, Specifications, 367, 600
Sponge, Cloths, Specification, 1069
Sporting Cartridge Cases. *See* Merchandise Marks.
Spraing of the Potato Tuber, 595
Sprat and the Sprat Fishery of England, 595
Spratt, H. P. :
Marine Engines, Handbook of Collections, 652
One Hundred Years of Transatlantic Steam Navigation, 652
Spraying, Fruit Tree, 848
Spring Frosts, 386
Springs :
Steel, Specification, 600
Valve. *See* Valve Springs.
Spruce, Eastern Canadian, data on, 420
Spurrey, 134
Square-cut Wood. *See* Import Duties Advisory Committee.
Square-sawn Wood and Veneers for Sewing Machine Woodwork. *See* Import Duties Advisory Committee.
Squirrels, Grey, 848
Staff College, Camberley, Regs., 690
Staffordshire :
and Worcestershire Canal Act, 973
County Council Act, 299
Potteries Water Board Act, 302
Technical College, Dangerous Drugs, 166
See also North Staffordshire ; South Staffordshire.
Staffs. *See* Civilian Employees ; Railways ; Government Departments.
Stain in Imported Timber, Causes of, 420
Stained Glass, 234
Stalybridge Hyde Mossley and Dukinfield Transport and Electricity Board Acts, 70, 759
Stamp Duty. *See* Audit Stamp Duty ; Medicine Stamp Duties.
Stamped or Pressed Metal Wares Trade, Wages, 405, 891, 1048

Stampings, Specification, 1028
Stancrest s.s. Wreck Report, 675
Standard :
Clauses, Recommendations of Committee on Common Form Clauses, 170, 397
Owners' Mutual War Risks Association, Ltd., 724
Standards :
Imperial, Comparison of, 210
of Length. *See* Fundamental Standards.
Staniland, L. N., The Efficiency of Baths used for the Hot-Water Treatment of Narcissus Bulbs, 361
Stanmore Unused Burial Ground Act, 527
Staples, *See* Import Duties Advisory Committee.
Starches, Import Duties. *Cmd. 5211*, 54
Stars :
Catalogue of, 901
Fundamental. *See* Fundamental Stars.
Proper Motions of, 187
State :
Institutions, Mental Defectives, List, 381
Management Districts Annual Reports, 32, 260, 488, 722
Papers :
British and Foreign, 158, 386, 616, 1033
Calendars of, 189, 416, 655, 903
Scholarships, 157, 385, 616, 866
Statelessness, Certain case of. *Cmd. 5552*, 288
State-owned Ships, Immunity of :
Unification of certain rules. *Cmd. 5672*, 503
Supplementary Protocol. *Cmd. 5673*, 503
Stationery :
Clerks of, Notes for, 433
Office Publications (N.P.), 205, 433, 671, 916, 1062
Services, Civil Estimates 25, 253, 481, 715, 954
Statistical :
Abstract :
for British Empire :
Cmd. 5298, 61
Cmd. 5582, 290
Cmd. 5872, 518
Cmd. 6140, 751
for the U.K. :
Cmd. 5144, 49
Cmd. 5353, 273
Cmd. 5627, 500
Cmd. 5903, 735
Cmd. 6232, 970
Review of England and Wales, 191, 418, 656, 903, 1055
Statistics, Current Official, Guides to, 220, 447, 683, 927
Status :
of Aliens. *See* British Nationality.
of Refugees. *See* Refugees.
Statute :
Law Committee Publications (N.P.), 205, 433, 671, 917, 1062
of Frauds, Report of Law Revision Committee. *Cmd. 5449*, 280
Statutes :
Chronological Table and Index, 433, 671, 917, 1062
of Limitation, Report of Law Revision Committee. *Cmd. 5334*, 64
Errata, 273
Statutory :
Definitions, Index, 188
Rules and Orders, 74, 304, 530, 762, 974
Emergency, List of, 916, 1062
Volumes, 434, 671, 917, 1062
Salaries Act, 296
Bill, 241, 266
Memo. on Financial Resolution. *Cmd. 5309*, 61
Steam :
Boilers :
Factory Forms, 629, 879, 1036, 1042
Mines and Quarries Forms, 650
See also Boiler Explosions.
Mill, Fazeley, Boiler Explosion, 435
Navigation, Transatlantic, 652
Receiver, Factory Forms, 629, 879, 1036, 1042
Tube Ovens and Hotplate, Factory Form, 879
Vehicles. *See* Gas and Steam Vehicles.
Steamboat Service. *See* Thames River.
Steam-heated Baking Oven, Explosion in, Report, 435
Steamships, Workmen's Compensation Forms, 170, 397, 633
Steel :
British Iron and Steel Industry, Memo. on Clause 6 of Finance Bill, 1936. *Cmd. 5201*, 53
Cups. *See* Import Duties Advisory Committee.
Door Bolts. *Cmd. 5619*, 294
Goods. *See* Import Duties Advisory Committee.
Industry. *See* Iron and Steel Industry.
or Wrought Iron Gas Mains, Cutting and Welding Operations, Factory Forms, 879, 1036
Pins. *See* Merchandise Marks.

Steel (*continued*) :
Products :
Import Duties. *See* Iron and Steel Products.
Specifications, 366, 600, 854, 1026
Cupboards, 951
Helmets, Anti-Gas Curtain for, 933, 1069
Screws for Wood. *See* Import Duties Advisory Committee.
Shelters :
Cases of Flooding, 877
Sectional, Standard of Protection afforded, Report. *Cmd. 6055*, 745
Specifications, 366, 1025
Staples. *See* Import Duties Advisory Committee.
Structures Research Committee Publications (N.P.), 194, 662
Trade, Import Duties Report, 436
Wheels. *See* Import Duties Advisory Committee.
Steelwork. *See* Structural Steelwork.
Steering Gear Committee Reports :
Cmd. 5120, 48
Cmd. 5225, 55
Stelae. *See* Egyptian Stelae.
Stellar Parallaxes, 653
Stem Canker of Potato, 595
Sterilising :
Chest :
Barford Invicta, 132
Halliday Oil-fired Boiler and, 592
Tank explosion at premises of Spen Valley Dairy Co. Ltd., Report, 435
Steriliser, " Scaldwell ", 132
Stevens, W. C. :
Machinery and Equipment used for bending Wood, 659
Methods of bending Wood by Hand, 420
Stevenson, W. D. H., Cultivation of Vaccinia on the Chorio-Allantoic Membranes of Chick Embryos, 874
Stewart, W., Chairman, Departmental Committee on questions under Workmen's Compensation Acts, Report. *Cmd. 5657*, 502
Stewartry of Kirkcudbright Educational Trust (Additional Endowments and Amendment) (No. 1) Scheme, 664, 910
Still, M., Nature and Characteristic Features of Post-Normal Occlusion, 419
Still-births, Registration of, (Scotland) Act, 523
Bill, 468, 483, 490, 493, 494
Circular, 666
Stills. *See* Tar Stills.
Stinging Nettles, 134
Stirling :
Burgh Order Confirmation Act, 759
Bill, 706, 731
Castle, Guide to, 232, 691
Stirlingshire Educational Trust Scheme, 199, 200, 426
Stock-carrying Capacity of Hill Grazings in Scotland, 909
Stockings, Specification, 226, 687, 932, 1068
Stockings Seam, Survey of Coal Resources, 660
Stocks :
Colonial, Treasury List of, 32, 261, 488, 723
See also Government and other Stocks ; War Stock.
Stockton-on-Tees :
Corporation Act, 528
Provisional Order Confirmation Act, 69
Bill, 10, 38
Stomach Worms in Sheep, 135
Stomatopod Larvae, 942
Stomatopoda, 942
Stomoxydinae, 943
Stone Implements, Foreign, Selection of, 694
Stonehaven, Rt. Hon., Viscount, Chairman, Committee on Administration of the Cinematograph Act, 1909, Report, 878
Stonehenge :
Guide, 232
To-day and Yesterday, 691
Storage. *See* Home Storage.
Stored Produce, Fumigation of Insect Pests in, 1057
Stores Branch R.A.F. (Non-Equipment Branch), 138
Storms, Dust, in Iraq, 646
Stoving Enamel, Specifications, 854, 1025, 1028
Straits :
Dardanelles, Regime of, Convention :
Cmd. 5249, 57
Cmd. 5551, 288
Settlements, Colonial Reports, 379, 610, 1031
Straker, Edith, Nasopharyngeal Bacterial Flora of Different Groups of Persons, 875
Stranding, Electrical, Specification, 452
Straps, Lap, Specifications, 366
Strata Florida Abbey, Guide, 232, 938
Stratiomyiidae, 943
Strawberries, 360
Strawberry, 595
Culture, 909

STR-TEC | 1936-40

STR— *INDEX 1936-40*

Street :
Cleansing, 162
Playgrounds Act, 523
Bill, 274,463,469,482,490,493,497
Trading (Regulation) Bill, 493
Streets :
Breaking up, by Statutory Undertakings, Joint Committee of House of Lords and House of Commons, Report, 698
Cleansing of, Costing Returns, 389, 620, 873
Lighting of, Departmental Committee, Final Report, 446
London PostOfficesand,416,654,1054
New, Model Byelaws, 391, 621
See also Aberdeen Corporation ; Glasgow Streets.
Strength Tests of Structural Timbers, 420, 906
Stresses in Reinforced Concrete Piles during Driving, 658
Stretcher Cover, Anti-Gas, Specification, 1069
Stretcher-carrying Fitments. *See* Small Ambulances.
Stretchers, A.R.P., 624, 625
Strip-map of Litlington, 653
Strips, Metal, Specifications, 141, 142, 366, 854, 1025
Strontianite, 661
Stroud District Water Board, etc., Act, 759
Structural :
Defence, A.R.P., 877
Grade, Minimum Development, for Redwood, 906
Steelwork for Single-storey Factories, 1056
Timbers, Strength Tests of, 420, 906
Structure of Wood, 420
Structures of Timber, Metal, and Concrete exposed to the action of Sea Water, Deterioration of, 193
Stuart-Harris, C. H., Epidemic Influenza, 657
Stubbings, H. G. :
Marine Deposits of the Arabian Sea, 942
Stratification of Biological Remains in Marine Deposits, 942
Students. *See* Blind Students ; Colonial Students.
Stuffing Material, Import Duties. *Cmd. 5083*, 45
Sturge Collection of Flints, 694
Submarine Warfare, Rules of. *Cmd. 5302*, 61
Submarines, Piratical Attacks in the Mediterranean by. *Cmd. 5568*, 289
Subscription Rates, 233, 458, 692, 939
Subsidence. *See* Mining Subsidence.
Subsistance Allowances, Civil Service, 220
Subterranean Structural Conditions, Investigation, 187
Sub-Tropics, Medical Notes and First Aid for detached personnel in, 365, 853, 1025
Sudan :
Administration, etc., Reports :
Cmd. 5281, 60
Cmd. 5575, 290
Cmd. 5895, 735
Cmd. 6139, 964
Almanac, 456, 696, 937
Cultivated Crop Plants of, 173
Financial Questions. *Cmd. 5319*, 62
Wadi Halfa, Upper Winds at, 181
Sudetenland, Extension to, of the Anglo-German Transfer Agreement of July 1, 1938 and the Supplementary Agreement of Aug. 13, 1938. *Cmd. 6047*, 744
Suez Canal :
Exchange of Notes, Italy, Egypt, and U.K. *Cmd. 5923*, 736
Free Navigation of, International Convention. *C. 5623*, 500
Shipping and Tonnage, 158, 386, 616, 869, 1033
Suffolk, Census, 190
Sugar :
Balance Sheets of Companies, 33, 249
Beet :
Growing, 134, 850
on the Continent, 133
Commission, Reports, 363, 596
Confectionery Trade, Wages, 405, 891, 1048
Industry :
Incentive Agreement between the Minister of Agriculture and Fisheries and The British Sugar Corporation Ltd., 596
(Reorganisation) Act, 65
Bill, 9, 11, 27, 34, 36, 38, 39
Amalgamation of Beet Sugar Manufacturing Companies. *Cmd. 5139*, 49
Memo. *Cmd. 5080*, 45
Production and Trade, 172, 398, 634
Regulation of Production and Marketing, International Agreement. *Cmd. 5461*, 281
Suit, Combination, Specification, 227, 687, 932
Suit-cases, Board for. *See* Import Duties Advisory Committee.
Sulphate. *See* Calcium Sulphate.
Sulphide, Hydrogen, Detection of, 422
Sulphonamide Derivatives, 1071
Sulphur :
Bacteria, 192
Dioxide, Detection of, 907

INDEX 1936-40 —SUR

Sulphuric Acid for Accumulators, Specification, 854
Sumach Leaves. *See* Import Duties Advisory Committee.
Summary :
Jurisdiction, Courts of, in the Metropolitan Area, Report, 394
Procedure (Domestic Proceedings) (formerly Matrimonial and other matters) Act, 297
Bill, 239, 245, 258, 263, 265, 269, 270
Summer :
Flowers, 594
Vest, Specification, 932
" Summit " Folding Milk-Sampling Plunger, 848
Sun, Photographs of, 188
Sunday :
Closing :
of Shops, 397, 632
See also Retail Meat Dealers.
Trading. *See* Shops (Sunday Trading).
Sunderland :
Corporation Acts, 67, 759
Dock. *See* Wear Navigation.
Steamships Mutual War Risks Association, 724
Sunflower Seed Oil, Import Duties. *Cmd. 5115*, 47
Sunrise and Sunset, 354, 587, 842, 1018
Sunshades. *See* Import Duties Advisory Committee.
Sunshine :
Effects of Obstacles on Records, 410
Particulars of, 182, 409, 647, 897
Superannuation :
Contributions, Officers appointed from Local Authorities, Unemployment Assistance Board, 639
Schemes (War Service) Act, 971
Bill, 947, 963
Teachers in Contributory Service in Schools not Grant-aided, 21
(Various Services) Act, 522
Bill, 271, 463, 481, 490, 493
See also Local Government ; Merchant Shipping ; Teachers' Superannuation ; Pensions.
Superheater :
Factory Form, 629
Mines and Quarries Form, 650
Supervision of Midwives. *See* Midwives.
Supplementary Reserve, Army, 230, 454, 690, 935, 1070
Regs., 456
Supplies, Limitation of :
Miscellaneous :
Explanatory Memos., 1063, 1064
List of Persons entered in the Home Trade Register, 1064
Supplies, Limitations of (*continued*) :
Woven Textiles :
Explanatory Memo., 1063
List of Persons entered on the Limitation of Supplies (Woven Textiles) Register, 1064
See also Wartime Building Supplies.
Supply, Ministry of :
Act, 753
Bill, 704, 705, 730, 732
Estimates 1940. *Cmd. 6176*, 966
Publications (N.P.), 917, 1062
Transfer of Powers, Proposals. *Cmd. 6034*, 743
Supply, Transport and Barrack Services, Army, 230, 456, 690, 937, 1071
Supreme Court of Judicature :
Accounts, 21, 253, 477, 713, 950
(Amendment) :
Act, 1937, 297
Bill, 247, 271
Act, 1938, 524
No. 2 Bill, 1938, 496
High Court and Court of Appeal, Accounts, 220, 447, 683, 927, 1065
Legal Aid in the High Court, 407
Northern Ireland. *See* Land Purchase.
Official Shorthand Writers in, Report. *Cmd. 5395*, 277
See also Judicial Statistics.
Surface :
and Upper Winds, Monthly Percentage Frequencies, 897
Caterpillars, 595
Shelters, Domestic, 1038
Water :
Drift, North Sea and Faroe–Shetland Channel, 428
YearBookofGreatBritain,621,874
Winds, Monthly Normals, etc., 410
See also Geostrophic Wind.
Surgeons, Royal College of, Dangerous Drugs, 626
Surgery, Veterinary, Careers, 638
Surgical :
Appliances, Medicines and (Advertisement) Bill, 36
Catgut, 161, 165
Ligatures and Sutures, Labelling, Circular, 389
Surrey :
County Council Acts, 72, 526
See also West Surrey.
Sur-Tax Tables, 400, 1039
Survey :
Artillery, 449
Fees and Expenses payable in connection with Board of Trade Surveys, Mercantile Marine, 673
of Industrial Development, 209, 437, 674

SUR— *INDEX 1936-40*

Survey (*continued*) :
of Life Saving Appliances, Shipping, 674
of Master's and Crew's Spaces, Instructions, 437
of National Coal Resources, 421
of Prospective Works, 619
of River Tees, 423
of Ships, Instructions to Surveyors, 435
Officers, Empire, Conference, 153
See also Economic Survey ; Geological Survey ; Inland Water Survey ; Air Survey ; Highway Development Survey ; Ordnance Survey ; Physical and Chemical Survey.
Surveying :
Careers, 401
See also Hydrographic Surveying.
Surveyors :
Instructions for, 179
Mercantile Marine Department Staff of, 673, 917
Nautical, examination, 150
Ships', Instructionsto, List of, etc., 435
Surveyors' Certificates, Mines, 184, 411, 648, 898, 1053
Sutcliffe, R. C., Meteorology for Aviators, 896, 1052
Sutherland :
Educational Trust Scheme, 198
Kyle of, district, Sea Trout, 201
See also West Sutherland.
Sutherland, J. (Peterhead) Ltd., Industrial Court Award, 888
Sutton and Cheam, Sunday Entertainments, 258
Sutures, Labelling. *See* Surgical Ligatures.
Swaffham Water Provisional Order Confirmation Act, 758
Bill, 704, 729
Swahili, Interpretership Examinations, 857
Swansea :
and District Transport Act, 69
Division, Mines Reports, 184, 412, 648, 898
" Swayback " in Lambs, 1024
Swaziland :
Colonial Reports, 152, 379, 861
Commercial Relations with Basutoland, Bechuanaland, Mozambique. *Cmd. 5807*, 513
Flags and Badges, 380
Sweater, White, Specification, 686
Sweden :
Economic Conditions, 439, 921
Identity Documents for Aircraft Personnel, Exchange of Notes. *Cmd. 5842*, 516
Sweden (*continued*) :
Imported Food Certificates, 618
Scotland, 666
Load Line Certificates Agreement. *Cmd. 5180*, 51
See also Naval Armament.
Swedes, 850
Sweet Corn, 850
Swimming Baths, Model Byelaws, 391
Swindon, Sunday Entertainments, 956
Swinton and Pendlebury Corporation Act, 526
Switzerland :
Commercial :
Agreement with Australia. *Cmd. 5960*, 738
Relations with New Zealand. *Cmd. 5828*, 515
Economic Conditions, 212, 676
Exemption of Aircraft from Duties on Fuel and Lubricants, Exchange of Notes with U.K. *Cmd. 5846*, 516
Identity Documents for Aircraft Personnel. Exchange of Notes with U.K. *Cmd. 5857*, 517
Imported Food Certificates, 389
Scotland, 428
Legal Proceedings, Conventions with U.K. :
Cmd. 5658, 502
Cmd. 5973, 739
Swivels, Factory Form, 630
Sydney–Singapore Empire Air Mail Scheme. *Cmd. 5813*, 514
Synoptic Reports, Gazeteer of British Meteorological Stations, 182
Synthetic Resin :
Bonded Fabric Mouldings, 367, 1028
Glues, Specification, 600
Sheets and Mouldings, Specifications, 369, 855
Syphilis, Treatment, 419
Syphons. *See* Import Duties Advisory Committee.
Syria :
and the Lebanon, Economic Conditions, 212, 676
Frontier Questions, Agreement with Palestine and the Lebanon. *Cmd. 6065*, 745
Imported Food Certificate, 871
Systema Naturae, 943

T

Tabanidae, 943
Table Poultry Production, 850
Tables, Specifications, 686
Taf Fechan Water Supply Act, 300
Taigel, P. G., Back-Stays for use in Mines, 1054

INDEX 1936-40 —TEC

Tailoring Trade, Wages, 177, 405, 1046
See also Ready-made Tailoring.
Tait, J. B., Surface Water Drift in the Northern and Middle Areas of the North Sea and in the Faroe-Shetland Channel, 428
Talley Abbey, Guide to, 691
Tanganyika :
Boundaries. *See* Mozambique ; Ruanda-Urundi.
Colonial Reports, 152, 439, 610, 862
Economic Conditions, 211, 439, 920
Tangier Zone. *See* Morocco.
Tank :
Training, Army, 230, 456
See also Kerosene Tank.
Tanks :
Explosions during Inspection and Repair of, Factory Form, 880
Oysters, Breeding of, 361
Rubber-proofed Fabric for, 142
See also Drinking-Water Tanks ; Oil Storage Tanks ; Sterilising Tanks.
Tape. *See* Cotton Fabrics.
Tapes, Cotton, Specification, 855
Tar Stills, Corrosion of, 658
Taradale. *See* Murchison of Taradale.
Tariff :
Autonomy of Persia. *Cmd. 5054*, 43
See also British India ; Customs ; Import Duties ; Drug Tariff.
Tars, Hydrogenation-Cracking of, 421, 660, 906
Tartans, Specification, 452, 686, 931
Tate Gallery, Annual Reports, 186, 414, 652
Tate, G. F., Leeds, Industrial Court Award, 888
Tattersall, C. E. C., Carpet-knotting and Weaving, 943
Tattersall, W. M., Euphausiacea and Mysidacea, etc., 942
Tatton Estate Act, 525
Taunton Corporation Act, 302
Tawny Owl, 362, 595
Tax :
Cases, Reports and Leaflets, 173, 365, 884, 1039
Inland Revenue Publications (N.P.), 173, 399, 635, 884, 1039
See also Income Tax ; Land Tax ; Passenger Tax ; Purchase Tax ; Sur-Tax.
Taxation :
Netherlands :
Air Transport Profits. *Cmd. 5279*, 59
Profits or Gains arising through an Agency. *Cmd. 5191*, 53
of Pensions of Retired Foreign Officials, Egypt and U.K. *Cmd. 5639*, 501
Taxation (*continued*) :
of Profits arising from Air Transport, Agreement, Germany and U.K. *Cmd. 5652*, 502
See also Customs ; Import Duties ; Local Taxation ; Tariffs.
Taxes, Inspector of, Examination, 149
Tay River :
Ferries. *See* Dundee Harbour.
Salmon of, 201
Taylor, s.s., Wreck Report, 675
Taylor, H. V. :
Commercial Flower Production, 594
Flowering Plants in Plots, 849
Fruit Production, 360
Spring Flowers and Flowers grown under Glass, 849
Tchernavin, V. : Absorption of Bones in Skull of Salmon during their Migration to Rivers, 665
Tea, Production and Trade, 172, 398, 634
Teachers :
and National Service, 913
Art, Diploma, 155, 614, 865
Handbook of Suggestions for, 385
National Committee for Training of, Scotland, 203, 669
Number employed, etc., 157, 615
Pupil, in Army Schools 230
St. David's Day Celebration, 158, 616
Salaries, Burnham Committee Reports, 866
Superannuation :
Act, 1937, 297
Bill, 243, 269
Explanatory Memo., 385
Allocation of Pensions Rules :
included in Teachers (Superannuation) Act, Explanatory Memo., 385
(Scotland), 1937, Tables, 914
(War Service) Act, 755
Bill, 733
See also Superannuation ; School Teachers.
Training of, 1033
Teaching :
in Junior Technical Schools, 384
of Classics, Suggestions for, 866
Profession in Scotland, 914
See also Home Teaching.
Teak, Kiln-seasoning Treatments of, 659
Technical :
Education :
Co-operation in, 384
in the Colonial Empire, Survey of, 1032
Position in the Day School System of Scotland, Report, 431
See also Education.
High Schools, Report, 615

TEC—   *INDEX 1936–40*

Technical (continued):
Pamphlets for Workmen (Post Office), 188
Pay, Grant of, Army, 1072
Schools:
and Art Schools, Teachers' Reports, 866
Junior. See Junior Technical Schools.
Subjects in Secondary Schools, 669
Technology. See Imperial College.
Tees:
River, Survey of, 423
Valley Water Board Provisional Order Confirmation Act, 70
Bill, 13, 39
Teeth:
Children's, Caries in, Influence of Diet, 191
Structure of, as shown by X-Ray Examination, 1055
Telecommunication Apparatus, Electrical, Specification, 1019
Telecommunications, Egypt and U.K. Cmd. 5640, 501
Telegrams:
and Radiotelegrams, Table of Charges, 188
See also Foreign Telegrams.
Telegraph:
International, Regs., 654
Services Accounts, 248, 476, 710, 949
Wireless, Operators' Handbook, 416
See also Post Office Publications (N.P.); Post Office and Telegraph; Imperial Telegraphs; Wireless Telegraph.
Telegraphy. See Meteorological Telegraphy; Wireless Telegraphy; Telephony.
Telephone:
International, Regs., 654
Post Office Educational Pamphlets, 902
Relay, General Principles and Practical Applications, 653
Services Accounts, 248, 476, 710, 949
Telephony:
and Telegraphy, Line, Army, 230
See also Automatic Telephony.
Telescope. See Cookson Floating Zenith Telescope.
Television, Development and General Principles, 414
Temperance (Scotland) Act, 1913, Return of Voting Areas, 916
Temperature:
Atmospheric, Summaries of, 1053
Equivalent, of a Room and its Measurement, 192
Monthly and Annual Summaries, 181
Salinity and, of English Channel, 133

Temperature (continued):
Scale, International, 661
Weekly particulars, 182
Woollen and Worsted Factories, 170
See also Meteorological Office Publications (N.P.).
Temperatures:
Low, Survey 187
Very Low, 415
Temperley, H., British Documents on the Origin of the War, 150, 616
Temporary:
Clerical and Typing Staffs employed in Government Departments: Cmd. 5626, 294
Laws, Register of, 29, 260, 491, 724, 961
Queen's Army Schoolmistresses, Information for Guidance of Candidates, 454
Rust Preventive, Specification, 1025
Tenant. See Landlord and Tenant.
Tenby. See Milford Haven.
Tents, Model Byelaws, 164, 621
Territorial:
Army:
Finances, etc.:
Cmd. 5275, 59
Cmd. 5571, 290
History of the Great War, 397
Mounted Divisions, etc., in the Great War, 171
Nursing Service, 457
Peace Establishments, 454
Regs., 231, 456
See also War Office Publications (N.P.).
Service. See National Health.
Territories. See Overseas Territories.
Tertiary Siphonous Algae in the W. K. Parker Collection, 943
Testing:
Memorandum (Mines), 651
Of Materials, etc., at the A.I.D. Test House, 143, 601, 855, 1030
Textile:
Refitters Handbook, 1071
Smallwares. See Merchandise Marks.
Trade:
Census of Production, 673
Import Duties Act Inquiry Report, 208
Textiles:
Award of National Certificates to Students in Technical Colleges and Schools, 868
Home Trade in, Limitation of: Explanatory Memo., 1063
List of Manufacturers of Controlled Goods, 1063

150

INDEX 1936–40   —TIP

Textiles (continued):
Home Trade in, Limitation of (continued):
List of Wholesale Dealers and Producers of Made-up Goods for Export, 1063
Specifications, 142, 452, 686, 931, 1068
See also Made-up Textiles; Woven Textiles.
Thailand:
Economic Conditions, 971
Right of Evocation from Siamese Courts, Exchange of Notes with U.K. Cmd. 5921, 735
Treaty of Non-Aggression with U.K.: Cmd. 6211, 968
Cmd. 6241, 970
See also Siam.
Thames River Steamboat Service Bill, 728
Thatching Needle, Darby, 359
Theodolite, Magneto, 415
Thermometer Screens of the Stevenson Type, 410
Thermometers:
Factory Form, 629
Specifications, 140
Thetis, H.M.S., Tribunal of Enquiry into the Loss of, Report. Cmd. 6190, 967
Thewlis, J., Structure of Teeth as shown by X-Ray examination, 1055
Thirsk District Water Provisional Order Confirmation Act, 973
Bill, 947, 962
Thistles:
in Grass Land, 362
on Arable Land, 362
Spear and Creeping, 664
Thomas, F. G.:
Creep or Flow of Concrete under load, 1056
Studies in Reinforced Concrete, 658, 904
Thomas Hardy, s.t., Wreck Report, 438
Thomas Thresher, s.t., Wreck Report, 438
Thomas, W. N., Experiments on Freezing of certain Building Materials, 658
Thomas, W. R., Cardiazol Treatment and present application of Hypoglycaemic Shock Treatment in Schizophrenia, 611
Thompson, E. F.:
Exchange of Water between the Red Sea and the Gulf of Aden, 942
General Hydrography of the Red Sea, 942
Thompson, W. R., Some Beneficial Insects, 848
Thornhill, Basin of, Geology, 194
Thornton Cleveleys Improvement Act, 71
Thornton, L. H. D., Outbreak of Food Poisoning due to Salmonella, Type " Dublin ", 622

Thurrock. See West Thurrock.
Thurso, Electricity, 213, 440
Tkehurst, C. B., Systematic Review of Genus Phylloscopus, 941
Tick-borne Fever, 909
Tidal:
Angles and Factors, Tables of, 1022
Prediction by Admiralty Methods, Forms, 131, 1022
Tide Tables, 131, 358, 592, 847, 1023
Tides. See Torres Strait.
Tientsin, Local Issues at, Arrangement between Japan and U.K. Cmd. 6212, 968
Ties, Specification, 687
Tiles:
Glazed, Import Duties. Cmd. 5258, 58
in Victoria and Albert Museum, Guide 843
See also Merchandise Marks.
Timber:
Beetles injurious to, 1057
Decay of, 659
Demand for:
in Shipbuilding and in Docks and Harbours, 617
in Wood Turning, 139
Home-grown, Handbook, 420
Kilns, Types of, 193
Mahogany Substitutes, Specification, 142
Moisture Content Determination, 906
Rock Elm as Rough Timber, 140
Seasoning, 659
Series, 193
Structural, Strength Tests, 193, 420
Structure, Properties, and Utilisation of, 415
Structures exposed to Sea Water, 193, 420, 658
Trades, Import Duties Act Inquiry Reports, 208, 436
Walnut as Rough Timber, 140
See also Dry Rot; Imported Timber; Wood.
Time:
Measurement, Handbook, 187, 415
Signals. See Signals.
Tin:
Box Trade, Wages, 642, 891, 1048
Control Scheme, International, Papers. Cmd. 5879, 519
Mines, special rules, 185
Tin-Iron Brass Tubes, Specifications, 368, 600
Tinplate:
Container, Corrosion by Food Products, 193
Factories, Safety Precautions, 632
Tintagel Castle, Guide to, 938
Tipton. See Smethwick.

151

TIT   *INDEX 1936–40*

Tithe:
Act, 66
Bill, 14, 16, 17, 30, 34, 38, 40, 41
Accounts, 479, 716, 953
Circulars, 161, 162, 619
Redemption:
Annuities, Forms, 205, 206, 434
Commission Publications (N.P.), 205, 434
Rentcharge, Royal Commission:
Appendices to Minutes of Evidence, 176
Report. Cmd. 5095, 46
Statement by H.M. Govt. Cmd. 5102, 46
Tiverton Corporation Act, 759
Tobacco:
Bonded Warehouse Procedure, 154
Production and Trade, 172, 398, 634
Trade:
Census of Production, 1063
Wages, 891, 1048
Tobago. See Trinidad.
Togoland, Colonial Reports, 152, 379, 610, 862
Tollesbury and West Mersea Sea Fisheries Order Confirmation Act, 758
Bill, 700, 728
Toluol, Specification, 141
Tomato Leaf Mould, 135, 595
Tomatoes. See Import Duties Advisory Committee.
Tomlin, Lord, Chairman, Royal Commission on Awards to Inventors, Final Report. Cmd. 5594, 291
Tomlinson, G. J. F., Chairman, Colonial Students' Committee, Report, 862
Tonbridge Water Provisional Order Confirmation Act, 301
Bill, 242, 268
Tongan Islands, Colonial Reports, 379, 610, 861
Tonks, L. H., Geological Survey, Wigan District, 661
Tonnage:
and Shipping. See Suez Canal.
Measurement of Ships:
Agreement, Egypt and U.K. Cmd. 5994, 740
Instructions, 437, 999
(Ships), Appendix Certificates of, Exchange of Notes, U.S.A. and Canada. Cmd. 6131, 750
Tools, Specifications, 226, 1068
See also Woodworkers' Tools.
Toro, Course for Training of Visiting Teachers held at, Report, 1031
Torpedoes, Salvage of. Cmd. 5774, 511
Torquay:
Cemetery Act, 973
Corporation Act, 301
Electricity Orders, 213

152

Torquay (continued):
Provisional Order Confirmation Act, 526
Bill, 470, 495
Torres Strait, Tides, Currents and Tidal Streams, 132
Tow, etc., Spinning and Weaving, Factory Form, 630
Towels, Specification, 226, 452
Terry, Cotton, 932
Tower of London, Guide, 457
Town and Country Planning:
Act:
Circulars, 620, 872
Summary of Provisions, 875
Extracts from Annual Reports of Ministry of Health, 390, 623
in Scotland, 429
Memo., 875
Model Clauses, 202, 392, 623, 875
Toxic Gases in Industry, 422, 662, 907, 1058
Toxicity of Industrial Organic Solvents, 418
Toy Manufacturing Trade, Wages, 405, 891, 1048
Tractors:
Fowler " Three-Thirty " Diesel Crawler, 132
Track-laying, Import Duties. Cmd. 5227, 55
Trade:
Agreements:
Argentine and U.K. Cmd. 5324, 63
Australia:
and France, Belgium, Czechoslovakia, 208
and U.K. Cmd. 5805, 513
Belgium and New Zealand. Cmd. 5359, 274
Burma and Japan. Cmd. 5636, 501
Canada and U.K. Cmd. 5382, 276
Denmark and U.K. Cmd. 5206, 54
Eire and U.K. Cmd. 5748, 509
Germany:
and New Zealand. Cmd. 5733, 508
and U.K. Cmd. 5881, 519
Hayti and Canada. Cmd. 6095, 748
India and U.K. Cmd. 5966, 739
Japan and Australia. Cmd. 5860, 517
Netherlands and U.K. Cmd. 5061, 44
New Zealand and U.K. Cmd. 6059, 745
Roumania and U.K. Cmd. 6063, 745
Turkey and U.K. Cmd. 5274, 59

153

Trade (continued):
Agreements (continued):
U.S.A.:
and Canada. Cmd. 5892, 520
and U.K. Cmd. 5882, 519
Exchange of Letters, Canada and U.K. Cmd. 5897, 520
Yugoslavia and U.K. Cmd. 5323, 63
See also Commercial Agreements; Payments Agreements.
and Clearing Agreements, Turkey and U.K.:
Cmd. 5756, 509
Cmd. 5981, 740
Cmd. 6118, 749
Cmd. 6133, 750
and Commerce:
Agreements:
Burma and Japan. Cmd. 5504, 284
Denmark and U.K. Cmd. 5400, 277
See also Commercial Agreements.
Foreign Accounts, 209, 436, 673, 918, 1032
and Industry, Civil Estimates, 25, 248, 481, 715, 954
and Navigation of the U.K., Accounts, 20, 21, 22, 248, 249, 475, 479, 710, 713, 949
and Payments Agreements:
Guatemala and Canada. Cmd. 6240, 970
Roumania and U.K. Cmd. 6225, 968
Spain and U.K.:
Cmd. 6188, 966
Cmd. 6229, 969
Turkey:
and Irish Free State. Cmd. 5443, 280
and U.K. Cmd. 6171, 965
Uruguay and U.K. Cmd. 5343, 273
U.S.A. and U.K. Cmd. 6158, 964
Yugoslavia and U.K. Cmd. 5540, 287
See also Commercial Agreements; Payments Agreements.
and Plantations, Commissioners, Journal, 189, 655
Board of:
Examinations, 150, 377
Civil Service Arbitration Tribunal Award, 887
Publications (N.P.), 206, 434, 1029
Boards:
and Road Haulage Wages (Emergency Provisions) Act, 971
Bill, 945, 962

Trade (continued):
Boards (continued):
Orders, Wages, 176, 404, 642, 889, 1043
Catalogues. See Import Duties Advisory Committee.
Effluents from Trade Premises, 621
Facilities Acts, Statement of Guarantees, etc., 29, 258, 484, 718, 958
in Medicinal Products, Agreement between Irish and U.K. Cmd. 6199, 967
Marks:
Act, 1938, 522
Bill, 461, 462, 463, 494
(Amendment) Act, 1937, 297
Bill, 18, 235, 236, 244, 259, 263, 266, 269
Paper showing how Trade Marks Acts are affected. Cmd. 5328, 68
Reports, 27, 257
See also Patents.
Negotiations with U.S.A., 674
of the U.K. with British Countries and Foreign Countries, 155, 383, 611, 865, 1032
Premises, Drainage. See Public Health (Drainage of Trade Premises).
Statistics, U.K., new classification, 436
Union Act, 522
Unions, Friendly Societies Forms, 159, 387, 617, 870, 1034
Trade; International Trade.
Tradesmen:
Army, Mustering and Pay, 934, 1070
holding Royal Warrants, List of, 644
Trading:
Accounts. See Government Departments.
with the Enemy. See Enemy.
Traffic:
carried by Trains, etc., 443, 679, 924
Commissioners:
Annual Reports, 220, 446, 926
See also Chairman of Commissioners.
London and Home Counties, Advisory Committee Annual Reports, 667, 922
Signs. See Signs.
See also Transit Traffic.
Trail, British Columbia, Operation of Smelter at, Convention between U.S.A. and Canada. Cmd. 5444, 281
Training:
and Exercises, A.R.P., Notes on, 878
and Leadership, Elements of, 689
Centres. See Scottish Societies.
Colleges, Lists of, 158, 616, 868
Scotland, 203, 669

TRA-TRE | 1936-40

Training (*continued*):
- Regs., Army, 231, 691, 937
  - Vocational, 929
- *See also* Military Training; Physical Training; Physical and Recreational Training; Midwifery Training; Teachers.

Tramcars and Light Railways (Street and Road) and Trolley Vehicles Undertakings, Returns, 220, 447, 682

Tramp Shipping:
- Administrative Committee Reports:
  - *Cmd. 5084*, 45
  - *Cmd. 5291*, 60
  - *Cmd. 5363*, 274
  - *Cmd. 5555*, 288
  - *Cmd. 5750*, 509
- Subsidy:
  - Continuance of. *Cmd. 5357*, 274
  - Distribution of:
    - *Cmd. 5129*, 48
    - *Cmd. 5420*, 278
  - Memo. *Cmd. 5082*, 45
- *See also* British Shipping (Continuance of Subsidy).

Tramways. *See* Tramcars.

Transatlantic Steam Navigation, 1838–1938, 652

Transfer Agreement, Germany and U.K. *Cmd. 5788*, 512
- Supplementary Agreements:
  - *Cmd. 5829*, 515
  - *Cmd. 5880*, 519
  - *Cmd. 5885*, 519

Transformers. *See* Rotary Transformers.

Transit Traffic in British Somaliland. *Cmd. 5775*, 511

Transjordan:
- Colonial Reports, 152, 379, 610, 862
- Winds over, 410

Transparent Synthetic Resin Sheets and Mouldings, Specification, 855

Transport:
- Advisory Council Reports, 447, 682, 926
- Careers, 401
- Ministry of:
  - Civil Service Arbitration Tribunal Award, 402
  - Publications (N.P.), 212, 440, 667, 921, 1064
- Services, Army, 230, 456, 690, 937, 1071
- *See also* Air Transport; Animal Transport; Civil Air Transport; London Transport; Road Transport; Sea Transport; London Passenger Transport.

Transportation on the Western Front, 397, 633

Transports. *See* Masters of Freight Ships and Transports.

Traumatic Shock and Blood Transfusion, Treatment of, Wound Shock, 1056

Travelling Expenses, 203, 296

Travers Foundation. *See* Greenwich Hospital.

Treachery Act, 971
- Bill, 962

Treasury:
- Books, Calendars of, 417, 903
- Chest Fund Accounts, 33, 476, 489, 949
- Instructions to Registrars, 1049
- Notice of Numbers of Drawn Bonds, 1049
- Publications (N.P.), 220, 683, 927, 1065

Treated Ethylene Glycol, Specification, 601, 855

Treaty Series:
- 1935:
  - No. 43. Persia, Tariff Autonomy. *Cmd. 5054*, 43
  - No. 44. Ratifications, Accessions, Withdrawals, etc., Supplementary List of. *Cmd. 5086*, 45
  - No. 45. Index. *Cmd. 5087*, 46
- 1936:
  - No. 1. Netherlands, Trade with British Colonies, etc. *Cmd. 5061*, 44
  - No. 2. War Graves, Agreement. *Cmd. 5068*, 44
  - No. 3. Netherlands, Reciprocal Exemption of Aircraft from Duties on Fuel and Lubricants. *Cmd. 5074*, 45
  - No. 4. Portugal and Union of South Africa, Native Labour, etc. *Cmd. 5085*, 45
  - No. 5. Spain, Payments Agreement. *Cmd. 5097*, 46
  - No. 6. Educational Films. *Cmd. 5155*, 50
  - No. 7. Saudi Arabia, Transit Dues at Bahrein. *Cmd. 5168*, 51
  - No. 8. Denmark, Extradition. *Cmd. 5172*, 51
  - No. 9. Sweden, Load Line Certificate. *Cmd. 5180*, 52
  - No. 10. Netherlands, Taxation of Profits or Gains arising through an Agency. *Cmd. 5191*, 53
  - No. 11. Hungary, Legal Proceedings. *Cmd. 5190*, 53
  - No. 12. General Index, 1933–1935. *Cmd. 5193*, 53
  - No. 13. Iraq, British War Cemeteries. *Cmd. 5196*, 53
  - No. 14. Lithuania, Legal Proceedings. *Cmd. 5197*, 53

Treaty Series (*continued*):
- 1936 (*continued*):
  - No. 15. Canada and Germany, Commercial Relations. *Cmd. 5232*, 56
  - No. 16. Canada and Austria, Commercial Relations. *Cmd. 5233*, 56
  - No. 17. Canada and U.S.A., Load Lines. *Cmd. 5234*, 56
  - No. 18. France, Reciprocal Enforcement of Judgments. *Cmd. 5235*, 56
  - No. 19. Canada and Germany, Commercial Relations. *Cmd. 5231*, 56
  - No. 20. Rubber, Regulation of Production and Export. *Cmd. 5236*, 56
  - No. 21. Spain, Payments Agreement. *Cmd. 5250*, 57
  - No. 22. Greece, Payments due to British Subjects in respect of Expropriation of Landed Properties. *Cmd. 5260*, 58
  - No. 23. Brazil, Commercial Relations. *Cmd. 5267*, 58
  - No. 24. Newfoundland and Brazil, Commercial Relations. *Cmd. 5268*, 58
  - No. 25. Turkey, Trade and Clearing. *Cmd. 5274*, 59
  - No. 26. Netherlands, Taxation of Air Transport Profits. *Cmd. 5279*, 59
  - No. 27. Fauna and Flora, Protection. *Cmd. 5280*, 60
  - No. 28. Iraq, Transfer of Railways. *Cmd. 5282*, 60
  - No. 29. Submarine Warfare, Rules of. *Cmd. 5302*, 61
  - No. 30. Greece, Income Tax. *Cmd. 5318*, 62
  - No. 31. Belgium, Judgments. *Cmd. 5321*, 62
  - No. 32. Norway, Load Line Certificates. *Cmd. 5336*, 64
  - No. 33. Refugees from Germany, Status of. *Cmd. 5338*, 64
  - No. 34. Supplementary List of Ratifications, Withdrawals, etc. *Cmd. 5376*, 275
  - No. 35. Index. *Cmd. 5377*, 275
- 1937:
  - No. 1. Uruguay, Trade and Payments. *Cmd. 5343*, 273
  - No. 2. Italy, Commercial Agreement. *Cmd. 5345*, 273
  - No. 3. Italy, Commercial Exchanges and Payments. *Cmd. 5346*, 273

Treaty Series (*continued*):
- 1937 (*continued*):
  - No. 4. International Status of Refugees. *Cmd. 5347*, 273
  - No. 5. Belgium and New Zealand, Trade Arrangement. *Cmd. 5359*, 274
  - No. 6. Egypt, Immunities and Privileges of British Forces. *Cmd. 5360*, 274
  - No. 7. Egypt and Palestine, Commercial Relations. *Cmd. 5361*, 274
  - No. 8. Iraq, Legal Proceedings. *Cmd. 5369*, 275
  - No. 9. Iraq and Palestine, Commercial Relations. *Cmd. 5372*, 275
  - No. 10. Saudi Arabia, Modification of Treaty of Jedda. *Cmd. 5380*, 276
  - No. 11. Rubber, Regulation of Production and Export. *Cmd. 5384*, 276
  - No. 12. Denmark, Trade and Commerce. *Cmd. 5400*, 277
  - No. 13. Control of Opium Smoking. *Cmd. 5401*, 277
  - No. 14. Italy, Mediterranean. *Cmd. 5429*, 279
  - No. 15. Denmark, Load Line Certificates. *Cmd. 5441*, 280
  - No. 16. Netherlands and Irish Free State, Commercial Relations. *Cmd. 5442*, 280
  - No. 17. Turkey and Irish Free State, Trade and Payments. *Cmd. 5443*, 280
  - No. 18. United States and Canada, Claims arising from the operation of the Smelter at Trail, British Columbia. *Cmd. 5444*, 280
  - No. 19. Hayti and Canada, Commercial Relations. *Cmd. 5445*, 280
  - No. 20. Roumania and Canada, Consular Fees on Certificates of Origin. *Cmd. 5447*, 280
  - No. 21. Canada, Australia and New Zealand and Iceland, Arbitration Convention of Oct. 25, 1905, Renewal. *Cmd. 5448*, 280
  - No. 22. Double Nationality, Military Obligations. *Cmd. 5460*, 281
  - No. 23. Siam and India, Nationality of persons affected by the redelimitation of the boundary between Burma (Tenasserim) and Siam. *Cmd. 5475*, 282

Treaty Series (*continued*):
- 1937 (*continued*):
  - No. 24. France, Legalisation of certain Official Documents. *Cmd. 5476*, 282
  - No. 25. Bank for International Settlements, Immunities of. *Cmd. 5489*, 283
  - No. 26. Finland, Importation of Wheaten Flour. *Cmd. 5515*, 285
  - No. 27. Yugoslavia, Trade and Payments. *Cmd. 5540*, 287
  - No. 28. Yugoslavia, Legal Proceedings. *Cmd. 5542*, 287
  - No. 29, Japan, Termination of Perpetual Leases. *Cmd. 5548*, 28 8
  - No. 30. Regime of the Straits (Dardanelles) Convention. *Cmd. 5551*, 288
  - No. 31. Certain Cases of Statelessness. *Cmd. 5552*, 288
  - No. 32. Hungary, Extradition. *Cmd. 5550*, 288
  - No. 33. Conflict of Nationality Laws, International Convention. *Cmd. 5553*, 288
  - No. 34. France, Importation of certain Raffia, Coffee, and Gum. *Cmd. 5558*, 289
  - No. 35. Belgium and Irish Free State, Commercial Relations. *Cmd. 5562*, 289
  - No. 36. Limitation of Naval Armament. *Cmd. 5561*, 289
  - No. 37. Portugal and South Africa, Identity Documents for Aircraft Personnel. *Cmd. 5565*, 289
  - No. 38. Piratical Attacks in the Mediterranean by Submarines. *Cmd. 5568*, 289
  - No. 39. Piratical Attacks in the Mediterranean by Surface Vessels and Aircraft. *Cmd. 5569*, 290
  - No. 40. Uruguay and Canada, Commercial Relations. *Cmd. 5576*, 290
  - No. 41. Japan and Canada, Customs Treatment of Imports. *Cmd. 5577*, 290
  - No. 42. Germany and Canada, Payments for the Exchange of Goods. *Cmd. 5580*, 290
  - No. 43. France and Canada, Commerce and Navigation. *Cmd. 5581*, 290
  - No. 44. Denmark and U.K., Australia, New Zealand, and India. Identity Documents for Aircraft Personnel. *Cmd. 5586*, 291
  - No. 45. Roumania, Commercial Payments. *Cmd. 5587*, 291

Treaty Series (*continued*):
- 1937 (*continued*):
  - No. 46. Roumania, Payments Agreement, Supplementary. *Cmd. 5588*, 291
  - No. 47. U.S.A. and Canada, Commercial Relations. *Cmd. 5597*, 292
  - No. 48. Poland and Canada, Commercial Relations. *Cmd. 5598*, 292
  - No. 49. Poland, Commercial Agreement, Amendment. *Cmd. 5599*, 292
  - No. 50. Japan and India, Commercial Relations. *Cmd. 5600*, 292
  - No. 51. Roumania, Payments (Amendment) Agreement of May 27, 1937, modification. of. *Cmd. 5613*, 293
  - No. 52. Ecuador, Extradition. *Cmd. 5614*, 293
  - No. 53. Egypt and Canada, Australia, India and U.K., British War Memorial Cemeteries and Graves in Egypt. *Cmd. 5618*, 293
  - No. 54. France, Commercial Relations with Tunis. *Cmd. 5622*, 294
  - No. 55. Egypt, Abolition of Capitulations in, Final Act, Convention, etc. *Cmd. 5630*, 294
  - No. 56. Ratifications, Accessions, Withdrawals, etc., Supplementary List. *Cmd. 5654*, 502
  - No. 57. Index. *Cmd. 5663*, 503
- 1938:
  - No. 1. Japan, Trade and Commerce with Burma. *Cmd. 5636*, 501
  - No. 2. Germany, Limitation of Naval Armament, etc. *Cmd. 5637*, 501
  - No. 3. Egypt, Taxation, etc., of Pensions of Retired Foreign Officials. *Cmd. 5639*, 501
  - No. 4. Egypt, Telecommunications. *Cmd. 5640*, 501
  - No. 5. Greece, Legal Proceedings in Civil and Commercial Matters. *Cmd. 5643*, 501
  - No. 6. Poland, Customs Classification of certain Pneumatic Tyres. *Cmd. 5644*, 501
  - No. 7. Roumania, Acceptance of Seamen's Discharge Books in lieu of Passports. *Cmd. 5645*, 501
  - No. 8. France, Abolition of Capitulations in Morocco and Zanzibar. *Cmd. 5646*, 501

Treaty Series (*continued*):
- 1938 (*continued*):
  - No. 9. Czechoslovakia and Australia, Commercial Treaty. *Cmd. 5649*, 502
  - No. 10. Chile, Temporary Commercial Agreement. *Cmd. 5649*, 502
  - No. 11. Siam, India and U.K., Air Services over Siam, India and Burma. *Cmd. 5651*, 502
  - No. 12. Germany, Exemption from Taxation of certain Profits arising from Air Transport. *Cmd. 5652*, 502
  - No. 13. Norway and U.K., Australia, New Zealand and India, Identity Documents for Aircraft Personnel. *Cmd. 5653*, 502
  - No. 14. Portugal, Boundary between Tanganyika Territory and Mozambique. *Cmd. 5661*, 503
  - No. 15. Italy, Establishment of Air Transport Lines. *Cmd. 5670*, 503
  - No. 16. Italy, Commercial Exchanges and Payments. *Cmd. 5669*, 503
  - No. 17. U.S.S.R., Limitation of Naval Armament. *Cmd. 5679*, 504
  - No. 18. Italy, Commercial Agreement. *Cmd. 5694*, 505
  - No. 19. Italy, Commercial Exchanges and Payments Agreement. *Cmd. 5695*, 505
  - No. 20. Italy and South Africa, Commercial Agreement. *Cmd. 5702*, 505
  - No. 21. Portugal and South Africa, Native Labour from Mozambique. *Cmd. 5703*, 506
  - No. 22. Czechoslovakia and South Africa, Commercial Agreement. *Cmd. 5704*, 506
  - No. 23. Germany and South Africa, Efficiency Certificates for Aircraft and Aircraft Motors. *Cmd. 5705*, 506
  - No. 24. U.S.A. and South Africa, Non-Immigrant Passport Visa Fees. *Cmd. 5706*, 506
  - No. 25. Portugal and South Africa, Air Services between South Africa and Portuguese East Africa. *Cmd. 5707*, 506
  - No. 26. Belgium and South Africa, Commercial Agreement. *Cmd. 5708*, 506
  - No. 27. U.S.A. and Irish Free State, Air Navigation. *Cmd. 5711*, 506

Treaty Series (*continued*):
- 1938 (*continued*):
  - No. 28. China, Air Services over. *Cmd. 5712*, 506
  - No. 29. Broadcasting in the cause of Peace. *Cmd. 5714*, 506
  - No. 30. Roumania, Payments (Amendment) Agreement of May 27, 1937, Supplementary Agreement. *Cmd. 5718*, 507
  - No. 31. Italy, Egypt and U.K., Bon Voisinage Agreement and Exchanges of Notes. *Cmd. 5726*, 507
  - No. 32. Siam, Treaties of July 14, 1925, temporary continuance of rights under. *Cmd. 5730*, 507
  - No. 33. Siam, Treaty of Commerce and Navigation. *Cmd. 5731*, 508
  - No. 34. Germany and New Zealand, Payments Agreement. *Cmd. 5732*, 508
  - No. 35. Germany and New Zealand, Trade Agreement. *Cmd. 5733*, 508
  - No. 36. Turkey, Trade and Clearing. *Cmd. 5756*, 509
  - No. 37. Regulation of Whaling, International Agreement. *Cmd. 5767*, 509
  - No. 38. Belgium and U.K., Australia, New Zealand, and India, Identity Documents for Aircraft Personnel. *Cmd. 5764*, 510
  - No. 39. Hungary, Air Navigation. *Cmd. 5765*, 510
  - No. 40. Salvage of Torpedoes. *Cmd. 5774*, 511
  - No. 41. Belgium, Boundary between Tanganyika and Ruanda-Urundi. *Cmd. 5777*, 511
  - No. 42. Belgium, Water Rights on the Boundary Between Tanganyika and Ruanda-Urundi. *Cmd. 5778*, 511
  - No. 43. Limitation of Naval Armament. *Cmd. 5781*, 511
  - No. 44. Roumania, Payments Technical (Amendment) Agreements. *Cmd. 5797*, 512
  - No. 45. Portugal, Commercial Relations between Swaziland, Basutoland, Bechuanaland, and Mozambique. *Cmd. 5807*, 513
  - No. 46. Luxembourg, Australia, New Zealand and U.K., Extradition. *Cmd. 5811*, 513
  - No. 47. Netherlands and New Zealand, Commercial Relations. *Cmd. 5812*, 513

Treaty Series (*continued*) :
1938 (*continued*) :
No. 48. Portugal and South Africa, Native Labour from Mozambique. *Cmd. 5817*, 514
No. 49. Netherlands and South Africa, Commerce and Navigation. *Cmd. 5818*, 514
No. 50. Guatemala and Canada, Commercial Relations. *Cmd. 5820*, 514
No. 51. Brazil and Canada, Commercial Relations. *Cmd. 5821*, 514
No. 52. Salvador and Canada, Commercial Relations. *Cmd. 5824*, 514
No. 53. Switzerland and New Zealand, Commercial Relations. *Cmd. 5828*, 515
No. 54. False Indications of Origin on Goods, International Agreement. *Cmd. 5832*, 515
No. 55. Protection of Industrial Property, International Convention. *Cmd. 5833*, 515
No. 56. Germany, Limitation of Naval Armament. *Cmd. 5834*, 515
No. 57. Roumania, Commercial Payments. *Cmd. 5840*, 516
No. 58. Sweden, Australia, New Zealand, India, and U.K., Identity Documents for Aircraft Personnel. *Cmd. 5842*, 516
No. 59. France and South Africa, Commercial Agreement. *Cmd. 5843*, 516
No. 60. France and South Africa, Commercial Agreement. *Cmd. 5844*, 516
No. 61. Switzerland, Exemption of Aircraft from Duties on Fuel and Lubricants. *Cmd. 5846*, 516
No. 62. U.S.A. and Canada, Preservation of the Halibut Fishery of Northern Pacific Ocean and Bering Sea. *Cmd. 5850*, 516
No. 63. U.S.A. and Canada, Sockeye Salmon Fisheries in the Fraser River System. *Cmd. 5851*, 517
No. 64. U.S.A. and Canada, Income Tax on Non-resident Individuals and Corporations. *Cmd. 5852*, 517
No. 65. Switzerland, Identity Documents for Aircraft Personnel. *Cmd. 5857*, 517
No. 66. Japan and Australia, Trade Agreement. *Cmd. 5860*, 517
No. 67. Cuba, Commercial Agreement. *Cmd. 5867*, 518
No. 68. Germany, Transfer Agreement. *Cmd. 5880*, 519
No. 69. Germany, Payments (Amendment) Agreement. *Cmd. 5881*, 519
No. 70. Germany, Transfer Agreement. *Cmd. 5885*, 519
No. 71. Germany, Application of Treaties between Germany, Austria and U.K. *Cmd. 5888*, 519
No. 72. Establishment of International Institute of Refrigeration. *Cmd. 5889*, 519
No. 73. France, Australia, New Zealand, and U.K., Aerial Navigation in Antarctic. *Cmd. 5900*, 520
No. 74. Rubber, Regulation of Production and Export. *Cmd. 5901*, 520, 735
No. 75. Ratifications, Accessions, Withdrawals, etc. *Cmd. 5930*, 736
No. 76. Index. *Cmd. 5931*, 736
1939 :
No. 1. Poland, Limitation of Naval Armament. *Cmd. 5916*, 735
No. 2. Poland, Limitation of Naval Armament. *Cmd. 5917*, 735
No. 3. France, Reciprocal Abolition of Consular Visas on Bills of Health, Exchange of Notes, India and French Indo-China. *Cmd. 5920*, 735
No. 4. Siam, Right of Evocation from Siamese Courts. *Cmd. 5921*, 735
No. 5. France, India and U.K., Identity Documents for Aircraft Personnel. *Cmd. 5922*, 736
No. 6. Italy, Declaration bringing into force the Protocol of April 16, 1938, with Exchanges of Notes with the Egyptian Government regarding Lake Tsana and the Suez Canal. *Cmd. 5923*, 736
No. 7. U.S.A. and Canada, Certificates of Airworthiness for Exported Aircraft. *Cmd. 5928*, 736
No. 8. Status of Refugees coming from Germany. *Cmd. 5929*, 736
No. 9. Czechoslovakia, France and U.K., Financial Assistance to Czechoslovakia. *Cmd. 5933*, 736

Treaty Series (*continued*) :
1939 (*continued*) :
No. 10. Netherlands East Indies and Canada, Prevention of Double Taxation of Income. *Cmd. 5940*, 737
No. 11. Argentine, Brazil, Uruguay and U.K., Regulation of Beef Imports into U.K. *Cmd. 5941*, 737
No. 12. Bulgaria, Military, Naval and Air Clauses of the Treaty of Neuilly, etc. *Cmd. 5954*, 738
No. 13. Colombia, Prolongation of Treaty of Friendship, Commerce and Navigation of Feb. 16, 1866. *Cmd. 5958*, 738
No. 14. Switzerland and Australia, Commercial Agreement. *Cmd. 5960*, 738
No. 15. Chile, Commercial Agreement. *Cmd. 5972*, 739
No. 16. Switzerland, Legal Proceedings. *Cmd. 5973*, 739
No. 17. Turkey, Trade and Clearing Agreement. *Cmd. 5981*, 740
No. 18. Regulation of Whaling, International Agreement. *Cmd. 5993*, 740
No. 19. Egypt, Tonnage Measurement. *Cmd. 5994*, 740
No. 20. Portugal, Air Service between London and Lisbon. *Cmd. 5995*, 741
No. 21. U.S.A., Administration of the Islands of Canton and Enderbury. *Cmd. 5989*, 740
No. 22. Poland, Commercial Agreement. *Cmd. 5997*, 741
No. 23. France, Exemption of Military Aircraft from Duties on Fuel and Lubricants. *Cmd. 5998*, 741
No. 24. France, Transfer to French State of Property in the Sites of British War Memorials. *Cmd. 6003*, 741
No. 25. Roumania, Commercial and Economic Relations. *Cmd. 6018*, 742
No. 26. Italy, Quotas for Imports into. *Cmd. 6020*, 742
No. 27. Estonia and South Africa. Extradition. *Cmd. 6027*, 743
No. 28. General Index, 1936–38. *Cmd. 6031*, 743
No. 29. Muscat, Treaty of Commerce and Navigation. *Cmd. 6037*, 743
No. 30. Germany, Extension to Sudetenland of the Anglo-German Transfer Agreement of July 1, 1938 and the Supplementary Agreement of Aug. 13, 1938. *Cmd. 6047*, 744
No. 31. U.S.A., Exchange of Cotton and Rubber. *Cmd. 6048*, 744
No. 32. Roumania, Trade and Payments. *Cmd. 6063*, 745
No. 33. Belgium, Sanitary Convention, Uganda and the Belgian Congo and Ruanda-Urundi. *Cmd. 6064*, 745
No. 34. Palestine and Syria and the Lebanon, Frontier Questions. *Cmd. 6065*, 745
No. 35. U.S.A. and Canada, Certificates of Competency or Licences for piloting Civil Aircraft. *Cmd. 6066*, 745
No. 36. U.S.A. and Canada, Air Navigation. *Cmd. 6067*, 745
No. 37. Danube. Entry of Germany into the European Commission of the Danube, the Accession of Germany and Italy to the Sinaia Arrangement of Aug. 18, 1938, etc. *Cmd. 6068*, 746
No. 38 Exercise of the Powers of the European Commission of the Danube. *Cmd. 6069*, 746
No. 39. Soviet Union, Limitation of Naval Armament. *Cmd. 6074*, 746
No. 40. Iceland, Extradition Treaty of March 31, 1873, Supplementary Convention. *Cmd. 6083*, 747
No. 41. Hayti and Canada, Trade Agreement. *Cmd. 6095*, 748
No. 42. Netherlands, India and U.K., Sanitary Control over Mecca Pilgrims at Kamaran Island. *Cmd. 6096*, 748
No. 43. France, Loan to Poland. *Cmd. 6110*, 749
No. 44. Roumania, Commercial Payments. *Cmd. 6111*, 749
No. 45. Denmark, Commercial Agreement, April 11, 1933, Modification of. *Cmd. 6112*, 749
No. 46. International Sanitary Convention modifying Convention of June 21, 1926. *Cmd. 6114*, 749
No. 47. Potent Drugs, Unification of Pharmacopoeial Formulas for, International Agreement. *Cmd. 6117*, 749

Treaty Series (*continued*) :
1939 (*continued*) :
No. 48. Turkey, Trade and Clearing. *Cmd. 6118*, 749
No. 49. Turkey, Armaments Credit for. *Cmd. 6119*, 749
No. 50. France, Identity Documents for Aircraft Personnel. *Cmd. 6125*, 750
No. 51. France, Reciprocal Exemption from Income Tax of Air Transport Profits. *Cmd. 6120*, 750
No. 52. China, Air Service between South West China and British Ports. *Cmd. 6122*, 749
No. 53. Netherlands, Identity Documents for Aircraft Personnel. *Cmd. 6130*, 750
No. 54. U.S.A. and Canada, Appendix Certificates of Tonnage. *Cmd. 6131*, 750
No. 55. Brazil and South Africa, Commercial Agreement. *Cmd. 6132*, 750
No. 56. Turkey, Trade and Clearing. *Cmd. 6133*. 750
No. 57. Egypt and South Africa, Commercial Relations. *Cmd. 6134*, 750
No. 58. Poland, Mutual Assistance. *Cmd. 6144*, 751
No. 59. Ratifications, Accessions, Withdrawals, etc. *Cmd. 6148*, 964
No. 60. Index. *Cmd. 6149*, 964
1940 :
No. 1. Turkey, Commercial Relations. *Cmd. 6151*, 964
No. 2. Cuba, Commercial Agreement of February 19, 1937, Modification of. *Cmd. 6152*, 964
No. 3. U.S.A., Trade Agreement. *Cmd. 6158*, 964
No. 4. Turkey, France and U.K., Treaty of Mutual Assistance. *Cmd. 6165*, 965
No. 5. Poland, Utilisation of Units of Polish Mercantile Marine in the Prosecution of the War against Germany. *Cmd. 6172*, 965
No. 6. Norway, Sale Prices in Norway of Whisky produced in the U.K. *Cmd. 6178*, 966
No. 7. Latvia, Legal Proceedings in Civil and Commercial Matters. *Cmd. 6181*, 966
No. 8. France, Exchanges of Notes. *Cmd. 6184*, 966
No. 9. France, Abolition of Consular Visas on Bills of Health. *Cmd. 6187*, 966
No. 10. France, French Telegraph Cable between Mauritius and Reunion. *Cmd. 6194*, 967
No. 11. Norway, Exemption from Taxation of Profits or Gains. *Cmd. 6195*, 967
No. 12. France, Legal Proceedings. *Cmd. 6200*, 968
No. 13. Greece, Air Transport Services. *Cmd. 6207*, 968
No. 14. Dominican Republic and Newfoundland, Commercial Relations. *Cmd. 6208*, 968
No. 15. Portugal, Identity Documents for Aircraft Personnel. *Cmd. 6209*, 968
No. 16. U.S.A. and Canada, Air Transport Services. *Cmd. 6210*, 968
No. 17. Brazil and Australia, Commercial Relations. *Cmd. 6214*, 968
No. 18. Roumania, Trade and Payments. *Cmd. 6215*, 968
No. 19. Educational Films, International Circulation of. *Cmd. 6221*, 969
No. 20. Status of Refugees coming from Germany. *Cmd. 6222*, 969
No. 21. U.S. Destroyers and Naval and Air Facilities for U.S.A. in British Transatlantic Territories. *Cmd. 6224*, 969
No. 22. Spain, Trade and Payments. *Cmd. 6229*, 969
No. 23. Spain, Loan Agreement. *Cmd. 6230*, 970
No. 24. Angola and Union of South Africa, Air Services. *Cmd. 6231*, 970
No. 25. Guatemala and Canada, Trade Agreement. *Cmd. 6240*, 970
No. 26. Thailand, Treaty of Non-Aggression. *Cmd. 6241*, 970
No. 27. Establishment of a reserve of Australian Wool in U.S.A. *Cmd. 6242*, 970
No. 28. Greece and Australia, Commercial Relations. *Cmd. 6243*, 970
No. 29. Egypt, Abolition of the "Caisse de la Dette Publique Egyptienne", Convention. *Cmd. 6244*, 970
Tree. *See* Fruit Tree.
Tree Fruits, 848
Tree-Stump Clearing, 133
Trencherbone Seam, Survey of Coal Resources, 660

Trenches, Home Office Publications (N.P.), 625, 878
Trengganu :
Colonial Reports, 152, 379, 610, 861
Flags, 153, 611
Tretower Court, Guide, 691
Trial :
of Lord de Clifford, 5
of Peers (Abolition of Privilege) Bill, 5, 6, 40
Trials by Court Martial, 231
Triassic Fishes of Besano, Lombardy, 943
Tribal Disturbances in Waziristan. *Cmd. 5495*, 284
Trichoptera, 943
Trigonometrical Tables, Seven-figure, 842
Tring Gas Act, 70
Trinidad and Tobago :
Colonial Reports, 152, 379, 862
Disturbances, Commission on, Report. *Cmd. 5641*, 501
Trinity House Publications (N.P.), 221, 928
Trolley Vehicles. *See* Tramcar.
Tropical :
Africa, Welfare of Women. *Cmd. 5784*, 511
Helmet, Anti-Gas Cover, Specification, 933, 1069
Tropics and Sub-Tropics, R.A.F. Personnel in, Medical Notes and First Aid Treatment, 139, 365, 853, 1025
Trotter, F. M., Gosforth District Memoir, Geological Survey, 421
Trousers, Specifications, 932
Anti-Gas, 1069
Oilskin, 687
Trout. *See* Sea Trout.
Truck Act, 971
Bill, 948, 963
Trumbull, William, the Elder, Papers of, 189, 655
Trumpet :
and Bugle Sounds, Army, 231, 937
Calls, R.A.F., 601, 855
Trunk :
Acts, Memo., 297
Demand Service, Telephones, 902
Roads Act, 295
Bill, 19, 41, 43
Truro Sea Fisheries Order Confirmation Act, 70
Trusses and Purlins for Factory Buildings, 1056
Trust. *See* National Trust.
Trustee :
Public. *See* Public Trustee.
Savings Banks :
and Friendly Societies, Accounts, 221, 448, 684, 928, 1065
Inspection Committee Reports, 221, 448, 684, 928, 1066
Trusts :
Execution of, (Emergency Provisions) Act, 755
Bill, 734, 908
Fixed, Report of Departmental Committee. *Cmd. 5259*, 58
Tsana, Lake, and Suez Canal, Exchange of Notes, Egypt, Italy, and U.K. *Cmd. 6923*, 736
Tuberculin Tests in Cattle, 901
Tuberculosis :
Circular, 619
Residential Treatment of, Costing Return Forms, 162, 389, 620, 873
See also Anti-Tuberculosis ; Sanatoria.
Tubes, Specifications, 140, 366, 600, 854, 1026
See also Cased Tubes.
Tubing :
L. T. Varnished Insulating, Specification, 369
See also Rubber Tubing.
Tuckwell, H. & Sons, Ltd., Oxford, Drivers and Statutory Attendants, Wages, etc., 175
Tunbridge Wells, Sunday Entertainments, 956
Tunis, Commercial Relations with France and U.K. *Cmd. 5622*, 294
Tunisia, Economic Conditions, 676
Tunnel. *See* London County Council.
Turkey :
Anglo-Turkish Clearing Office, Accounts, 711
Armaments Credit for, Agreement with U.K. :
Cmd. 5755, 509
Cmd. 6119, 749
Commercial Relations, Exchange of Notes. *Cmd. 6151*, 964
Debts Clearing Offices Accounts, 950
Economic Conditions, 439, 921
Guarantees in connection with Export to Turkey of Goods manufactured in U.K., Agreements :
Cmd. 5754, 509
Cmd. 6173, 966
Legal Proceedings Convention. *Cmd. 5996*, 741
Mutual Assistance Treaty with France and U.K. :
Cmd. 6123, 750
Cmd. 6165, 965
Regime of the Straits, Convention. *Cmd. 5249*, 57
Suez Maritime Convention, Free Navigation, International Convention. *C. 5623*, 500

Turkey (*continued*) :
Trade :
and Clearing Agreements, etc., with U.K. :
Cmd. 5274, 59
Cmd. 5756, 509
Cmd. 5981, 740
Cmd. 6118, 749
Cmd. 6133, 750
and Payments Agreements :
with Irish Free State. *Cmd. 5443*, 280
with U.K. *Cmd. 6171*, 965
See also Anglo-Turkish Armaments.
Turkeys, 360
Turkish, Interpretership Examination, 859
Turks and Caicos Islands, Colonial Reports, 152, 610, 1031
Turn Indicators, Specifications, 140, 366
Turnbull, J. :
Commercial Apple Production, 594
Commercial Fruit-Tree Spraying, 848
Turner, F. G., Concrete Road Construction on the Reichsautobahnen, 926
Turner, N., Methods of Bending Wood by Hand, 420
Turnips, Swedes, and Kohl-Rabi, 850
Tutor Aeroplane, 1027
Tweeds, Specifications, 452, 686, 931
Twill, Waterproofed and Dyed Cotton, Specification, 1030
Twine Trade, Wages, 177, 642, 891, 1047
Twines, Specification, 226, 1068
Tynemouth :
Corporation Act, 758
Priory and Castle, Guide, 232
Provisional Order Confirmation Act, 302
Bill, 240, 269
Tyneside :
Launching Ceremony, Air Navigation Regs., 851
Local Government, Report of Royal Commission. *Cmd. 5402*, 277
Type :
Cultures maintained at Lister Institute of Preventive Medicine, Catalogue, 191
Designs for Small Huts, 1056
Typewriters :
History and Development, 653
Import Duties. *Cmd. 5272*, 59
Typhoid Fever, 875
at Croydon, Report. *Cmd. 5664*, 503
Typing :
Staffs. *See* Temporary.
Tables, Specification, 686
Typist Chairs, Specification, 686
Tyres. *See* Pneumatic Tyres.

U

Uckfield :
Electricity, 440
Water Act, 69
Uganda :
and the Belgian Congo and Ruanda-Urundi, Sanitary Convention. *Cmd. 6064*, 745
Colonial Reports, 152, 379, 610, 862
Economic Conditions, 211, 439, 920
Ullswater Report. *See* Broadcasting.
Ultimus Haeres. *See* Estates.
Umbrellas. *See* Import Duties Advisory Committee.
Unblanched Shelled Almonds. *See* Import Duties Advisory Committee.
Unclassified Services, Estimates, 954
Underclothing, Cellular, Specification, 452
Underground Water Planning of Water Resources and Supplies, 618
Unemployed :
Boys and Girls, Instruction for, 177 403, 643
Persons in receipt of Poor Relief, 391
Unemployment :
Absorption of Unemployed into Industry, Discussions between Minister of Labour and Representatives of certain Industries. *Cmd. 5317*, 62
Assistance :
Allowances, Return of. *Cmd. 5240*, 56
See also Civil Estimates
Board :
Annual Reports :
Cmd. 5177, 52
Cmd. 5526, 286
Cmd. 5752, 509
Cmd. 6021, 742
Civil Service Arbitration Tribunal Awards, 639, 1042
See also Civil Estimates.
Determination of Need and Assessment of Needs :
Draft Regs., 31, 727
Memos. :
Cmd. 5228, 5229, 55
Cmd. 6143, 751
House of Commons Paper, 960
(Emergency Powers) Act, 755
Bill, 733
(Temporary Provisions) :
Act, 1935 (Termination). *Cmd. 5239*, 56
Amendment Act, 295
Bill, 42, 236
Memo. *Cmd. 5322*, 63
(Extension) Act, 65
Bill, 5, 37
Winter Adjustments, Draft Regs., 486

Unemployment (*continued*) :
Fund :
Accounts, 23, 27, 251, 480, 711, 951
Financial Condition, 25, 252, 482, 716
General Account, Letter from Unemployment Insurance Statutory Committee. *Cmd. 5603*, 292
Investment Accounts, 257, 484, 718, 959
Insurance :
Acts :
Summary of (1937), 406
1938, 522
Bill, 247, 272, 461, 462, 493
1939, 753
Bill, 703, 719, 726, 728, 730
1940, 972
Bill, 948, 963
Additional :
Benefits, Draft Order, 482
Days and Waiting Period, Draft Order (H.C. Paper), 253
Agriculture :
Act, 65
Bill, 8, 26, 34, 37, 38
Additional Benefits and Reduction in Contributions, Draft Order, 482
Contributions, Agriculture Miscellaneous Provisions, Draft Regs., Report, 178
Crediting of Contributions, Draft Regs., Report, 178
Insurable Employments, Draft Regs., Report, 643
Long Hirings in, Draft Regs., Report, 178
Persons employed in, and otherwise :
Benefit, Draft Regs., Report, 178
Miscellaneous, Draft Regs., Report, 178
Private Gardeners Draft Order, 35
Air Force Personnel, 139
(Amendment) Bill, 267
Anomalies, Seasonal Workers, Amendment, Draft Orders, 30, 31
Army, 934
Benefit :
Amendment, Draft Regs., Report, 178
Claims for, Decisions by Umpire on, 177, 405, 643, 892, 1048
Unemployment (*continued*) :
Insurance (*continued*) :
Benefit (*continued*) :
Increase of :
and Reduction in Contributions, Draft Order, 716
in respect of Dependent Children, Draft Order, 956
Miscellaneous Provisions, Draft Regs., Report, 643
Payments made. *Cmd. 5240*, 56
Contributions :
Amendment, Draft Regs., Report, 178
Draft Regs., Report, 1939, 891
Weekly Rates, Reduction, Draft Order, 26
Courts of Referees, Draft Regs., Report, 178
Crediting of Contributions, Amendment, Draft Regs., Report, 643
Determination of Questions, Draft Regs., Report, 178
Education Authorities Administrative and Choice of Employment Expenses, Draft Regs., Report, 178
(Emergency Powers) Act, 755
Bill, 733
Employment, Draft Regs., Reports :
outside the U.K., 178
under Public or Local Authorities and Temporary Police Employment (Exclusion), 178
Extension to Outdoor Private Domestic Servants, Report, 406
Holidays and Suspensions, Report, 643
Inconsiderable Employments, Amendment, Draft Regs., Report, 178
Inspectors, Draft Regs., Report, 178
Insurable Employments, Draft Regs., Reports, 178, 406, 643
Mercantile Marine Exclusion, Draft Regs., Report, 178
Mixed Employment, Report, 406
Non-manual Workers, Remuneration Limit, Report, 178
of Soldiers of Army Reserve, Supplementary Reserve, Territorial Army, Auxiliary Territorial Service, etc., 1072
Payment of Travelling Expenses, Draft Regs., Report, 178
Personnel of R.A.F., 599

Unemployment (*continued*) :
Insurance (*continued*) :
Post Office Claimants, Draft Regs., Report, 178
Private Gardeners :
Draft Order, 35
Report, 32
Share Fishermen, Report, 178
Special :
Arrangements, Draft Regs., Report, 178
Amendment, 406
Schemes, Draft Regs., Report, 892
Statutory Committee Reports (N.P.), 406, 643, 892, 955
See also Civil Estimates.
Local, Index, 176, 404, 641, 889
(Northern Ireland Agreement) :
Act, 65
Bill, 7, 37
Memo. *Cmd. 5081*, 45
Unfederated Malay States, Colonial Reports, 378, 609, 861
Unfit Houses in Rural Areas, Demolition of, 870, 871
Uniforms :
Auxiliary Fire Service, 631, 1036
Mercantile Marine, 918
Officers :
and Messengers, Fire Brigades, 880, 915
of the Fleet, Regs., 587, 842
(Restriction). *See* Public Order.
Union :
of Benefices (Amendment) Measure, 10, 72
Report by Ecclesiastical Committee, 10
of South Africa. *See* South Africa.
of Soviet Socialist Republics :
Agreement with Export Credits Guarantee Department. *Cmd. 5253*, 57
Fleet, particulars of :
Cmd. 5371, 275
Cmd. 5666, 503
Franco-Soviet Treaty, Memo. by German Government. *Cmd. 5118*, 47
Limitation of Naval Armament, etc., Agreement. *Cmd. 5518*, 285
Protocol modifying. *Cmd. 6074*, 746
Suez Maritime Canal, Free Navigation of, International Convention. *Cmd. 5623*, 500
United :
Kingdom Mutual War Risks Assurance Ltd., 724
United (*continued*) :
States of America :
Administration of the Islands of Canton and Enderbury, Exchange of Notes. *Cmd. 5989*, 740
Air :
Navigation, Exchanges of Notes :
with Canada. *Cmd. 6067*, 745
with Irish Free State. *Cmd. 5711*, 506
Transport Services, Exchange of Notes with Canada. *Cmd. 6210*, 968
Airworthiness Certificates for Exported Aircraft, Exchange of Notes with Canada. *Cmd. 5928*, 736
and Australia and New Zealand, Disposal of Real and Personal Property, Convention. *Cmd. 5269*, 59
and Canada, Load Lines Convention. *Cmd. 5234*, 56
Appendix Certificates of Tonnage. Exchange of Notes with Canada. *Cmd. 6131*, 750
British War Debt Papers :
Cmd. 5189, 52
Cmd. 5330, 63
Cmd. 5480, 283
Cmd. 5617, 293
Cmd. 5763, 510
Cmd. 5902, 520
Cmd. 6026, 743
Censorship of Mails, Correspondence with U.K. *Cmd. 6156*, 964
Certificates of Competency or Licences for piloting Civil Aircraft, Exchange of Notes with Canada. *Cmd. 6066*, 745
Claims arising from the Operation of the Smelter at Trail, British Columbia, Convention with Canada. *Cmd. 5444*, 280
Commercial Relations with Canada. *Cmd. 5597*, 292
Conveyance of Mails to, 28
Destroyers and Naval and Air Facilities for the United States in British Transatlantic Territories, Exchange of Notes. *Cmd. 6224*, 969
Economic Conditions, 439
Establishment of a reserve of Australian Wool in U.S.A. *Cmd. 6242*, 970
Exchange of Cotton and Rubber, Agreement. *Cmd. 6048*, 744

United States of America (*continued*) :
Fleet, particulars of :
Cmd. 5371, 275
Cmd. 5666, 503
Cmd. 5936, 737
Imported Food Certificate, 389
Scotland, 428
Income Tax on Non-resident Individuals and Corporations, Convention with Canada. *Cmd. 5852*, 517
Limitation of Naval Armament, International Treaty. *Cmd. 5561*, 289
Naval Armament Treaty. *Cmd. 5136*, 48
Non-Immigrant Passport Visa Fees, Agreement with South Africa. *Cmd. 5706*, 506
Preservation of the Halibut Fishery of Northern Pacific Ocean and Bering Sea, Convention with Canada. *Cmd. 5850*, 516
Rights in Palestine. *Cmd. 5544*, 287
Seasonal Incidence of Mortality in, 1055
Sockeye Salmon Fisheries in the Fraser River System, Convention with Canada. *Cmd. 5851*, 517
Speech by the late Marquis of Lothian. *Cmd. 6239*, 970
Trade :
Agreement with U.K. *Cmd. 6158*, 964
Negotiations with U.K., 674
Universities :
and Colleges (Emergency Provisions) Act, 755
Bill, 708, 733
State Scholarships tenable at, Candidates, 157, 385, 616
University :
Candidates, Conditions of Appointment to Commissions in R.A.F., 365, 598, 852
Courts, Scotland, Report of the Special Committee on Application for a Grant. *Cmd. 5735*, 508
Grants Committee Reports, 221, 448, 684, 928, 1066
Unmarried Women, Committee on Pensions for :
Minutes of Evidence, 683, 927
Report. *Cmd. 5991*, 740
Unperforated Zinc Sheets. *See* Import Duties Advisory Committee.
Unrefined Fish Oils. *See* Import Duties Advisory Committee.
Unsightly Development in the Country and on the Sea Coast, 620
Unused Burial Ground, Stanmore, Act, 527
Unwrought Alloys of Metal. *See* Import Duties Advisory Committee.
Uphall Works, Ilford, Explosion, 672
Upland Pasture, Poor, Improvement of, 362
Upper :
Atmosphere, Soundings of, 646, 896
Solway District, Salmon of, 665
Water Circulation, North Sea, 428
Winds :
at Kingston, Jamaica, 410
at Nicosia, Cyprus, 897
measured at M/Y Imperia, Mirabella Bay, Crete, 410
Measurement of, by means of Pilot Balloons, 410
Monthly Percentage Frequencies, 410, 897
See also Geostrophic Wind.
Urban Communities, Mortality Rates in, 623
Urquhart Castle, Guide to, 691
Uruguay :
Beef Imports into U.K., Regulation of. *Cmd. 5941*, 737
Commercial Relations with Canada. *Cmd. 5576*, 290
Economic Conditions, 212
Imported Food Certificate, 618
Scotland, 666
Trade and Payments Agreement. *Cmd. 5343*, 273
Users of Ammonia, Air-Raid Precautions to be taken by, 1038
Uthwatt, A. A., Chairman :
Committee on the Liability for War Damage to the Subject-matter of Contracts, Report. *Cmd. 6100*, 748
Committee on the Principles of Assessment of War Damage, Reports :
Cmd. 6136, 751
Cmd. 6197, 967
Committee on the Responsibility for the Repair of Premises damaged by Hostilities, Report. *Cmd. 5934*, 736
Utilisation Series, 617
Uxbridge. *See* Rickmansworth.

V

Vacation Courses, 158, 386, 616, 868
See also Holiday Courses.
Vaccinia, Cultivation of, on the Chorio-Allantoic Membranes of Chick Embryos, 874
Vagrancy in Scotland, Report. *Cmd. 5194*, 53
Vagrants, Census of, Scotland, Form, 431
Valleyfield Colliery, Explosion at, Report. *Cmd. 6226*, 969

1936-40 | VAL-WAU

VAL— INDEX 1936–40

Valuation :
  of Agricultural Dwelling-houses Bill, 36
  See also Rating and Valuation; Customs; Sheep Stocks; Central Valuation Committee.
Valve :
  Seats, Forgings for, etc., Specification, 141
  Springs, Steel for, Specification, 140
Van Boys, Factory Form, 627
van Sommeren, V. D., A Preliminary Investigation into the Courses of Scale Absorption in Salmon, 427
van Zeeland, Report on International Trade. *Cmd. 5648*, 502
Vans, Model Byelaws, 164, 621
Vapour. *See* Hydrogen Cyanide Vapour.
Vardulia, s.s., Wreck Report, 210
Variables in the Selected Areas at 75 deg. and 60 deg. North Declination, 913
Varnish Jointing Compound, Pigmented, Specification, 601
Varnishes, Specifications, 143, 854, 1026, 1028
Vases. *See* Athenian Black Figure Vases.
Vaux. *See* Barony of Vaux.
Veal. *See* Beef and Veal; Import Duties Advisory Committee.
Vegetable :
  Crops, Manuring of, 593
  Garden, Pests and Diseases in, 1023
  Oils and Oilseed, Production, Trade and Consumption, 172, 634, 883
Vegetables :
  and Home-produced Foods, Cooking of, 913
  Domestic Preservation of, 132, 360
  Nutritive Value of, 191
  Pickers of, Model Byelaws, 621
  Root, 849
  Supplies, 171, 398, 634, 883
  See also Salads and Vegetables.
Vehicle Trade :
  Census of Production, 917
  Import Duties Reports, 208, 436
Velocity of Sound. *See* Sound.
Velvets, Weft Pile. *See* Import Duties Advisory Committee.
Veneers for Sewing-machine Woodwork. *See* Import Duties Advisory Committee.
Venereal Disease :
  Anti-Venereal Measures in certain Scandinavian Countries, 622
  Centres for Seamen, 165, 1035
  Memo., 231
Venice, State Papers and Manuscripts relating to English Affairs, 416, 903
Ventilation :
  in the Blackout, 1038
  of Factories and Workshops, 395, 397, 1037
    in the Blackout, 1036
  Physiological Study, 191
Venturi Flume, Uniformity of the Stream issuing from, 1027
Verbal Methods, Assessment of Psychological Qualities by, 657
Vernon, P. E., Assessment of Psychological Qualities by Verbal Methods, 657
Versailles. *See* Peace Treaty.
Vertical Filing Cabinets, Cupboards, Specifications, 931
Verticillium Wilt and the Black Dot Disease of the Potato, 850
Very Low Temperatures, 415
Vests, Specifications, 226, 686, 931
  Gymnasium, 1068
Veterinary :
  Corps, Services, etc., Army, 231, 449, 1067
  Education in Great Britain, Committee on, Report, 596
  Reduction of Charges, 360
  Service List, Colonial, 380, 862
  Surgeon, Careers, 638
V. H. F. Radiobeacon Landing-approach Installations, 852
Vices, Clamps, etc., Specifications, 226, 1068
Vickers Machine-Gun :
  Range Table for, 455
  Tank Training, Army, 456
Victoria and Albert Museum Publications (N.P.), 234, 460, 695, 943
Victory :
  Assurance of, 884
  Bonds, 180, 407, 644, 893
Vigoureux, P. :
  Absolute Determination of the Ampere, 661
  Determination of the Ohm, etc., 661
  Quartz Oscillators, 1058
Virgin and Child, Raphael, 694
Virus :
  Diseases of Potatoes, 595
  Research, Use of developing egg, 418
Violence, Prevention of (Temporary Provisions) Act, 753
  Bill, 707, 732
  Report on Orders, etc., made under the Act, 723, 950, 958, 959
Visa Fees. *See* Non-immigrant Visa Fees.
Visas. *See* Consular Visas.
Visibility, Abnormal, at Malta, 897
Visiting Teachers, Course for the training of, held at Toro and Gombe, Northern Provinces, Nigeria, Report, 1031
Visitors. *See* Health Visitors.

INDEX 1936–40 —WAL

Visual Time Signals. *See* Signals.
Vitreous Enamelling of Metal or Glass, Factory Form, 630
Vivisection. *See* Experiments on Living Animals; Prohibition of Vivisection.
Vocational :
  Agricultural Education in the Colonial Empire, 381
  Guidance, a Borstal Experiment in, 418
  Technical Education in the Colonial Empire, 1032
  Training, Army, 685, 929
Voltage Regulators, Specification, 854
Voltmeters, Specifications, 127, 354, 843, 930
Voluntary :
  Euthanasia (Legislation) Bill, 18
  Hospitals :
    (Paying Patients) Act, 65
      Bill, 5, 28, 37
    (Relief from Rating) Bill, 498
  Organisations and Funds assisting Officers, Men and Women who served in H.M. Forces, 415
  Schools. *See* Schools.
Volunteers :
  (Air Raid Precautions), Badges for, 393
    Scotland, 431
  See also Foreign Volunteers; French Volunteer Force; Local Defence Volunteers.
Vortices, Depressions as, 896
Vote of Credit, 723, 955
  Statement. *Cmd. 6198*, 967
  Supplementary, 1940, 959, 960
Votes. *See* Air Votes; Army Votes; Navy Votes.
Voting :
  Areas, Temperance (Scotland) Act, 1913, 916.
  See also Parliamentary Elections.
Voyage Regs., Army, 231, 457, 691, 937
Vulcanised Expanded Rubber, Specification, 1027
Vulcanisers, Factory Form, 1042
Vulnerability of Capital Ships to Air Attack. *Cmd. 5301*, 61

W

Wadebridge Rural District Council Act, 301
Wadi Halfa, Sudan, Upper Winds, 181
Wages :
  Agricultural Wages (Regulation) Act, 1924, Report of Proceedings under, 132
  Approved Schools, 166
  Civil Service Arbitration Tribunal Awards, 401, 638, 1042
Wages (*continued*) :
  Industrial Court Awards, 174, 403, 640, 888, 1042
  Railways, Staff, 444, 680
  Retail Distributive Trades, Report, 889
  Trade Boards Orders 176, 404, 642, 889, 1045
  Wool Textile Industry in Yorkshire, 179
  See also Salaries; Agricultural Wages; Road Motor Transport Industry; Road Haulage.
Waistcoat, Kersey, Specification, 932
Wakefield Corporation Act, 526
Wales :
  Anti-Tuberculosis Service in, Committee of Inquiry, Report, 870
  Census, 190
  Church Temporalities in :
    Accounts, 20, 35, 264, 711, 725
    Annual Reports :
      Cmd. 5248, 57
      Cmd. 5534, 287
      Cmd. 5822, 574
      Cmd. 6088, 747
  Education in :
    Cmd. 5178, 52
    Cmd. 5475, 283
    Cmd. 5799, 573
    Cmd. 6042, 744
  Maternal Mortality in, Report. *Cmd. 5423*, 279
  North Wales Electric Power Act, 69
  Technical Education in, 158
  See also Board of Education (Welsh Department) Publications (N.P.); Welsh Board of Health Publications (N.P.); North Wales; South Wales; Secretary of State; Administration of Justice; Monmouthshire.
Walker, A., New Aberdour, Industrial Court Award, 888
Walker, Sir H., Reports on Explosions :
  Gresford Colliery. *Cmd. 5358*, 274
  Wharncliffe Woodmoor Colliery. *Cmd. 5503*, 284
Walking Sticks. *See* Import Duties Advisory Committee.
Wallace, J. C., Potatoes, 593
Wallace, T., Manuring of Fruit Crops, 361
Wallet, Anti Gas, Specification, 1069
Walls :
  Building, 658, 904
  for Factory Buildings, 1056
Walnut as Rough Timber, 140
Walsall Corporation :
  Act, 759
  (Trolley Vehicles) Provisional Order Confirmation Act, 300
    Bill, 242, 268

WAL INDEX 1936–40

Waltham :
  Holy Cross Urban District Council Act, 299
  Joint Hospital District Provisional Order Confirmation Act, 298
    Bill, 237, 265
Walton :
  and Weybridge, Sunday Entertainments, 478
  Downs. *See* Epsom.
Walton-upon-Thames. *See* Poor's Allotment.
Wandsworth and District Gas Act, 299
War :
  Bonds, National, 1945–7, Notice, 1052
  Cemeteries in Iraq. *Cmd. 5196*, 53
  Charities Act, 971
    Bill, 947, 963
    Forms, 1030
  Damage :
    Bill, 963
    Liability for :
      (Miscellaneous Provisions) Act, 755
        Bill, 708, 733
      to the Subject Matter of Contracts, Committee on, Report. *Cmd. 6100*, 748
    Repair of, 914
    to Land (Scotland) Act, 754
    to Property :
      Committee on Principles of Assessment of, Reports :
        Cmd. 6136, 751
        Cmd. 6197, 967
      Report and Statement of Government Policy. *Cmd. 6116*, 749
  Debt. *See* United States of America.
  Department :
    Buildings, etc., Schedule of Prices, 937, 1072
    Clerks, Industrial Court Award, 174
    Property Act, 523
      Bill, 469, 497
  Gardens, Scottish, 909
  Gases, Detection and Identification of, 882
  Graves :
    Agreement. *Cmd. 5068*, 44
    Imperial War Graves Commission Publications (N.P.), 172, 399, 634, 883, 1038
  Great. *See* Great War.
  How Hitler made the War, 884
  India and the War :
    Announcement and Correspondence. *Cmd. 6129*, 750
    Communique. *Cmd. 6196*, 967
War (*continued*) :
  India and the War (*continued*) :
    Statements :
      Cmd. 6121, 749
      Cmd. 6219, 969
      Cmd. 6235, 970
  Industrial Health in, 1055
  Legislation. *See* Isle of Man.
  Levy. *See* Coal Mines.
  Medicine, Bulletins of, 1056
  Memoranda, 1056
  Memorial Cemeteries and Graves in Egypt, Agreement. *Cmd. 5018*, 293
  Memorials. *See* British War Memorials.
  Museum, Imperial, Publications (N.P.), 652, 900
  Notification that state of War exists between His Majesty and Germany, 893
  Office :
    Civil Service Arbitration Tribunal Awards, 639, 1042
    Examinations, 147, 377, 605, 608, 860
    Publications (N.P.), 221, 448, 684, 928, 1066
  Pay to Soldiers, 1072
  Risks Insurance :
    Act, 1939, 754
      Bill, 707, 732
      Part II :
        Memo. *Cmd. 6056*, 735
        Paper showing Amendments proposed to be made by the War Damage Bill. *Cmd. 6237*, 970
    Bill, 1940, 962
    Commodity Insurance, Explanatory Note. *Cmd. 6192*, 967
    Insurance of Goods against King's Enemy Risks, Memo. *Cmd. 6056*, 745
    Re-insurance of British Ships, Agreements between Board of Trade and various organisations, 723, 724, 959, 960
      Draft Agreement. *Cmd. 6058*, 745
  Savings (Determination of Needs) Bill, 963
  Service. *See* Education (Scotland); Local Government Staffs; Executors; Superannuation.
  Stock, Gift by Guernsey. *Cmd. 6084*, 747
  Wounds, Scheme for the Bacteriological Investigation of, 1056
Ward, D. C. L., Anti-Venereal Methods in certain Scandinavian Countries, 622
Ward, F. A. B., Handbook of Collections illustrating Time Measurement, 415

INDEX 1936 40 —WAU

Wardens, Air Raid, Home Office Publications (N.P.), 394, 625, 878
Ware, W. M., Mushroom Growing, 592
Warehouses, Bonded, 151, 382, 612, 863, 1032
  Factory Forms, 627
Warfare. *See* Chemical Warfare; Submarine Warfare.
Warkworth :
  Castle, Guide, 232, 457
  Harbour Act, 68
  Hermitage, Guide, 232
Warmth Factor in Comfort at Work, 191
Warning Signals, Air Raid, 625
Warrants. *See* Royal Warrants.
Warrington Corporation :
  Act, 300
  Water Act, 528
Wart Diseases of Potatoes, 135, 1024
  Varieties immune from, 197, 425, 661, 909, 1059
Wartime :
  Building :
    Bulletins, 1056
    Supplies, Schedule of, 1072
  Communal Feeding in, 1035
  Financial Agreements between H.M. Government and British shipowners. *Cmd. 6218*, 969
  Food in Schools, Memo., 1033
  Lighting Restrictions, 878, 882
  Schools in, Memo., 867
Warwickshire :
  Coal Mines Scheme, 184, 411, 648, 1053
  Electricity Orders, 213
Washing :
  and Haircutting, Army, 1067
  Facilities, Factories and Workshops, 170
  of Factories, Factory Form, 628
Washstand, Specification, 686
Wasps, 136
Waste :
  Cotton. *See* Cotton Waste.
  Materials Trades, Wages, 405, 890, 1046
  Paper Making Materials, List of Merchants authorised to deal in, 917, 1063
Watches, various articles worn with. *See* Merchandise Marks.
Water :
  Bacteriological Examination of Water Supplies, 874
  Circulation and Drift, etc., North Sea, 428
  Drinking, Factories and Workshops, 170
  Exchange of, between Red Sea and Gulf of Aden, 942
  Iodine Content, Relationship to occurrence of Endemic Goitre, 192
  Pollution Research Board Publications (N.P.), 195, 423, 662, 908, 1058
  Power. *See* Lochaber.
  Prevention of Waste, etc., Model Byelaws, 164
  Resources and Supplies, Reports from Joint Committee, 9, 17
  Rights on boundary between Tanganyika and Ruanda-Urundi :
    Cmd. 5076, 45
    Cmd. 5778, 511
  Supply :
    Bill, 1939, 720, 726, 727, 730, 732
    Biology of, 694
    Military Engineering, 454
    of London from Underground Sources, 907
  Survey of a River-System, 163
  Undertakings :
    Bill, 1939, 703, 705, 707, 733
      Draft prepared by Central Advisory Water Committee. *Cmd. 5987*, 740
    Report by Joint Committee, 706
    Safeguards to be adopted in day-to-day administration of, 876
    See also Gas, Electricity and Water Undertakings.
  See also Aerated Water; Inland Water; Surface Water; Underground Water; Central Advisory Water Committee; Emergency Water Supplies; Public Water Supply.
Water-colours in British Museum, Handbook, 941
Watering Places. *See* Health Resorts and Watering Places.
Waterproof Cover, Specification, 932, 1069
Waterproofed and Dyed Cotton :
  Fabric, Specification, 1029
  Twill, Specification, 1030
Waterproofing of Clothing Fabrics, Specification, 932
Water-sealed Gasholders, Factory Forms, 879, 1036
Watery Wound Rot of Potatoes, 595
Watford :
  Corporation Act, 302
  Sunday Entertainments, 485
Wath-upon-Dearne Provisional Order Confirmation Act, 527
  Bill, 472, 496
Watkins, C. M., The use of Asphalt Mastic for Roofing, 419
Watson, Sir Duncan, Chairman, Poultry Technical Committee of Great Britain, Report, 596
Wattmeters, Specification, 930
Waugh, P., Madreporaria, 942

WAV-WOR | 1936-40

Wave-lengths :
for Colonial Broadcasting, Choice of, 862
of Light, National Physical Laboratory Publications (N.P.), 661
Waves. *See* Seismic Waves.
Wax, Ouricury. *See* Import Duties Advisory Committee.
Waziristan :
Operations in, 644, 893
Tribal Disturbances in. *Cmd. 5495*, 284
Wealth, Conscription of (Preparatory Provisions) Bill, 729
Weapon Training, 690, 893
Wear Navigation and Sunderland Dock Acts, 527, 757
Weather :
Manual, 847
Maps, 1053
Messages. *See* Wireless.
See also Meteorological Office Publications (N.P.).
Weavers :
Industrial Court Award, 175
Rates of Wages, Application for Order to be made, Report, 402
See also Worsted Weavers.
Weaving :
Flax and Tow, etc., Factory Form, 630
See also Carpet-Knotting.
Webbing :
Cotton, Anti-Gas Clothing, Specification, 933
Jute, Specification, 140
See also Parachute Harness Webbing.
Webster. *See* Chandler *v* Webster.
Wedd, G. B., Geological Survey, Shrewsbury District, 661
Weed Seeds in Grasses and Clovers, 363
Weeds :
of Arable Land, 594
of Grass Land, 593
Suppression of, 849
Weevils, Wingless, 134
Weft Pile Velvets. *See* Import Duties Advisory Committee.
Weight Lifting by Industrial Workers, 396
Weights and Measures :
Acts, 66, 294
Bill (1936), 12, 15, 29, 34, 39, 41
Acts, Reports by Board of Trade on Proceedings under, 210, 435, 675, 919
Comparisons of Standards, 210
Notices of Examinations of Patterns, 210, 438, 675, 919, 1064
Sale :
of Coal (Scotland) Act, 66
of Food (Weights and Measures) Act, 64
(Scotland) Bill, 15, 31, 38, 40
Weir, Viscount, Chairman, Conference on War Damage to Property Report. Statement on Government Policy, *Cmd. 6116*, 749
Welding :
Electric Arc, Memo., 395
Flux, Aluminium, Specification, 366
of Steel Structures, 662
Operations, Factory Forms, 879, 1036
Rod, Specification, 366
Welfare :
Fund. *See* Mining Industry (Welfare) Fund.
of Blind, Circular, 667
See also Blind Persons.
of Women in Tropical Africa, *Cmd. 5784*, 511
of Youth, 1060
Pamphlets (Factories etc.), 170, 397, 1037, 1048
See also Colonial Development and Welfare ; Maternity and Child Welfare ; Miners' Welfare.
Wellshill Girls' School, etc., Trust Scheme, 199
Welsh Church (Amendment) Act, 523
Bill, 462, 487, 494
Wembley Provisional Order Confirmation Act, 759
Bill, 701, 731
Wessex Electricity :
Acts, 300, 973
Orders, 921, 1064
West :
Africa :
British Dependencies in, Economic Conditions, 439
See also Civil Air Transport Services ; Africa ; South-West Africa ; French West Africa ; Portuguese West Africa.
African Cocoa, Commission on the Marketing of, Report. *Cmd. 5845*, 516
Gloucestershire Water Act, 760
Ham Corporation Act, 299
Hartlepool :
Corporation (Trolley Vehicles) Order Confirmation Act, 526
Bill, 471, 496
Provisional Order Confirmation Act, 71
Bill, 11, 40
India Royal Commission, Recommendations. *Cmd. 6174*, 966
Indies :
Calendars of State Papers, 655, 903
Customs Tariffs, 153
Labour Conditions in. *Cmd. 6070*, 746
Local Legislatures, 710
See also British West Indies.

West (*continued*) :
Midland Forensic Science Laboratory, Dangerous Drugs, 626
Midlands Joint Electricity Authority Order Confirmation Act, 527
Bill, 471, 495
of England Mutual War Risks Association Ltd., 724
Riding of Yorkshire :
Census, 1055
Safety Principles for Boys employed in Coal Mining, 384
Surrey Water Acts, 525, 759
Sutherland, Salmon Caught in Sea, 665
Thurrock Estate Act, 526
Yorkshire Gas Distribution Act, 528
Western :
Asia, Locust Outbreak, 447, 927
Front, Transportation on, 398, 633
Highlands and Islands of Scotland, Contract with Messrs. David MacBrayne, Ltd., for Maintenance of Transport Services, 492
Painted, Dyed and Printed Textiles, 695
Valleys (Monmouthshire) Sewerage District. *See* Rhymney.
Westminster, Palace of, Refreshment Rooms and Lavatories, 17
Westmorland, Ancient and Historical Monuments :
Inventory, 195
Report. *Cmd. 5179*, 52
Weston, H. C., Effects of Conditions of Artificial Lighting on Performance of Worsted Weavers, 657
Wey Valley Water Act, 973
Weybridge. *See* Walton.
Whaling, Regulation of, International Agreements :
Cmd. 5487, 283
Cmd. 5757, 509
Cmd. 5827, 515
Cmd. 5993, 740
Wharncliffe Woodmoor Colliery Explosion. *Cmd. 5503*, 284
Wharves :
Factory Forms, 627
Workmen's Compensation Forms, 170, 397, 632
What Every Mining Man should Know series, 651, 900
Wheat :
(Amendment) Act, 753
Bill, 703, 705, 719, 726, 728, 729, 732
Commission, Report on Administration of Wheat Act, 1932, 594
Fund Accounts, 28, 254, 480, 715, 953
Growing, 1024
Import Duties. *Cmd. 5063*, 44
Production and Trade, 171, 398, 634, 883
Wheaten Flour, Importation into Finland. *Cmd. 5515*, 285
Wheat-Flour, Production and Trade, 171, 398, 634, 883
Wheatley Lime Seam, 421
Wheels :
Abrasive. *See* Abrasive Wheels.
Iron or Steel. *See* Import Duties Advisory Committee.
Whisky produced in U.K., Sale Prices in Norway of, Exchange of Notes. *Cmd. 6178*, 966
Whitby, Sunday Entertainments, 953
White :
Canvas Shoes, Specification, 933
Cotton Waste, Specification, 1069
Fish Meal as Food for Live Stock, 360
Herrings. *See* Cured White Herrings.
Metal Ingots, Specification, 142, 367
" White Papers ". A colloquial term for House of Commons Papers and Command Papers. *See* Parliamentary Publications.
Whitehaven Harbour Act, 301
Whitehead, T. H., Shrewsbury District, Geological Survey, 661
Whitewashing, Factory Form, 628
Whitley Bay Pier and Harbour Provisional Order Confirmation Act, 70
Bill, 14, 39
Whitley Council. *See* Civil Service.
Whitworth Scholarships, 156, 384, 614, 866
Wholesale :
and Productive Societies, Annual Return Forms, 387, 617, 869, 1034
Bespoke Tailoring Trade, Wages, 405, 891, 1047
Mantle and Costume Trade, Wages, 405, 891, 1048
Whyte, Sir W. E., Chairman, Scottish Advisory Committee on Rivers Pollution Prevention, Report, 429
Widdowson, E. M., Chemical Composition of Foods, 1055
Widows and Orphans of Officers in Colonial Service, Pensions, Report. *Cmd. 5219*, 55
Widows', Orphans', and Old Age Contributory Pensions :
Accounts, 23, 250, 478, 714, 952
Act, 66
Bill, 6, 7, 12, 13, 40
Army, 934
Outline of Schemes in U.K., 874
Personnel of the R.A.F., 139, 599
(Voluntary Contributors) Act, 296
Bill, 240, 241, 257, 263, 267
Report by Government Actuary. *Cmd. 5415*, 278
Wigan District, Geological Survey, 661

Wild Birds :
(Duck and Geese) Protection Act, 753
Bill, 487, 499, 700
Protection :
Act, 751
(Scotland) Bill, 42
Willenhall Urban District Council Act, 757
William III, Calendar of State Papers, 416, 655
Williams, E. H., Chemical Methods for the Study of River Pollution, 1023
Williams, F. A., Action of Hydrogen upon Coal, 660
Willow, Cricket Bat, Cultivation, 159
Willow-Warblers, 941
Wills. *See* Navy and Marines (Wills).
Wilson Airways Ltd., Kisumu–Lusaka Auxiliary Service. *Cmd. 5523*, 286
Wilson, C. T. R., Expansion Chamber Method, Atom Tracks, 414
Wilson, Sir D. H., Chairman, Departmental Committee on Lighting in Factories, Report, 632
Wilson, G., Pests of Ornamental Garden Plants, 360
Wilson, I. G. H., Cardiazol Treatment, and Present Application of Hypoglycaemic Shock Treatment, 611
Wilson, J. S. :
Printing Method of recording Road Surface Textures, 907
Rigidity Modulus of Bitumens and Bitumen-Filler Mixtures, 907
Wilson, W. K., Modern Rabbit Keeping, 1023
Wilt. *See* Verticillium Wilt.
Wiltshire. *See* Somerset and Wilts.
Wimpenny, E. S., The Distribution, Breeding and Feeding of some important Plankton Organisms of the South-West North Sea in 1934, 361
Winchester :
Corporation Act, 69
See also Worthy Down.
Winchester Castle, m.v., Wreck Report, 211
Winding Machinery, Mines and Quarries Form, 650
Window Glasses, Transmission of Light through, 194
Windows in Commercial and Industrial Buildings, Protection of, 1037
Winds :
Relation between Blueness of the Sky and Gradient Wind, 646
See also Meteorological Office Publications (N.P.) ; Geostrophic Wind ; Upper Winds.
Windscreen Panels, Bullet Proof Safety Glass for, Specification, 855
Windscreens, Safety Glass for, Specification, 600
Windward and Leeward Islands, Education in, 863
Wine, Production and Trade, 171, 398, 633
Wines and Spirits, Bonded Warehouse Procedure, 154
Winter :
Moths, 849
Pruning Bush and Half-Standard Apple Trees, 1023
Vest, Specification, 932
Wire, Specifications, 143, 367, 600, 855, 1026, 1028
Wire Rope, Specifications, 367, 854, 1029
Wireless :
Operators :
Electrical and Radio Notes for 1024
Handbook for, 654
Signal Training, 456, 690
Signals, Admiralty List of, 132, 359, 592, 847
Telegraph :
Installations, Survey of, 919
Operators, Handbook for, 416
Telegraphy :
Admiralty Handbook of, 587
Bonding and Screening and Earth Systems, Aircraft, Specifications, 369, 855
Specifications, Wireless Telegraphy Board, 354, 587, 843, 1019
Telephone on Aircraft, Specification, 143
Weather Messages, 182, 410, 647, 897
Wireworms, 850
Wisbech :
Joint Isolation Hospital District Provisional Order Confirmation Act, 298
Bill, 237, 268
Water Provisional Order Confirmation Act, 302
Bill, 243, 268
Wishaw. *See* Motherwell.
Withdrawals, Accessions, Ratifications, etc., Supplementary Lists of (Treaty Series) :
Cmd. 5086, 45
Cmd. 5376, 275
Cmd. 5654, 502
Cmd. 5930, 736
Cmd. 6148, 964
Woldingham, Electricity, 921
Wolverhampton Corporation Act, 71
Women :
and Young Persons, Employment of :
Factory Forms, etc., 394, 627, 879

Women (*continued*) :
and Young Persons, Employment of (*continued*) :
in Factories, Hours of Employment, Report. *Cmd. 6182*, 966
See also Employment of Women and Young Persons Act.
Admission to Diplomatic and Consular Services. *Cmd. 5166*, 50
Conductors, Industrial Court Awards, 1043
Medical Practitioners, Army :
Employment of, 937
Uniform for, 1072
Secretarial and Clerical Work, Careers, 638
Welfare of, in Tropical Africa. *Cmd. 5784*, 511
See also Unmarried Women.
Women's Light Clothing Trade, Wages, 404, 890, 1046
Scotland, 642
Wood :
Bending :
by Hand, Methods, 420
Machinery, 659
Practice of, 193
Bursary Trust Scheme, 199, 200
Dry Rot in, 659
for Sewing Machine Woodwork. *See* Import Duties Advisory Committee.
Growth, Structure, Properties, 420, 906
Moisture in, in relation to Strength and Shrinkage, 659
Planes, Specification, 931
Preservatives, 420
Methods of applying, 193
See also Laminated Compressed Wood ; Timber.
Wood, C. A. P., Radium Beam Therapy Research, 657
Wood Green, Sunday Entertainments, 260
Wood, H. :
Movements of Herring in the Northern North Sea, 428
Race Investigation of the Herring Population of Scottish Waters, 427
Wood, R. G., Corrosion of Tar Stills, 658
Wood, T. B., Rations for Livestock, 848
Woodbridge, Electricity Orders, 213
Wooden :
Axe Handles. *See* Import Duties Advisory Committee.
Blocks. *See* Import Duties Advisory Committee.
Parts (Aeroplanes, etc.), Protection of, Specification, 369
Woodhall Spa Urban District Council Act, 301
Woodhead, D. W., High-speed Cameras for Measuring Rate of Detonation in Solid Explosives, 413
Woodhead, Sir J., Chairman, Palestine Partition Commission, Report. *Cmd. 5854*, 517
Woodman, H. E. :
Ensilage, 593
Home Grown Feeding Stuffs, 848
Use of Oil Cakes and Extracted Meals, 360
White Fish Meal as a Food for Live Stock, 360
Woodruffe, D., The Story of the British Colonial Empire, 860
Wood-turning, Demand for Timber, 159
Woodworkers' Tools, Specifications, 226, 931
Woodworking Machinery :
Fencing and other Safety Precautions, 632
Safety Hints, Precautions, etc., Factory Forms, 167, 630, 879
Woodworking Services, 659
Wool :
Felt Hoods. *See* Import Duties Advisory Committee.
Production, Trade and Consumption, 172, 398, 634, 883
Textile Industry in Yorkshire, Wages, etc., 179
See also Angora Wool.
Woollen :
and Worsted Factories, Conference Report, 170
Industry. *See* Scottish Woollen Industry.
Vest, Specification, 932
Woolly Aphis, 362
Woolwich :
Research Department, 230
Royal Military Academy, Entrance Examinations, 150, 376, 607, 859, 1031
Worcestershire :
Coal Mines Scheme, Amendments, 184
See also Staffordshire and Worcestershire.
Workers in Factories, Seats for, 1048
Working :
Class Home, Furnishing and Equipment, 434
Classes, Construction of Flats, Committee on, Final Report, 389
Men's Clubs, Annual Return Form, 159, 387, 617, 869, 1034
Workington Corporation Act, 527
Workmen's Compensation :
Act, 1925, Summary, 899
Acts (1925–1934) Amendment Bill, 498
Acts (1925–1940), Memo. on, 1037
(Amendment) Act, 523
Bill, 271, 463, 482, 493

Workmen's Compensation (*continued*) :
and Benefit (Byssinosis) Act, 972
Bill, 948
Annual Return Forms, 170, 397, 632, 882
Bills, 36, 41, 271, 498
Compensation for Industrial Diseases, 3rd Report of Departmental Committee, 166
Departmental Committee on, Report. *Cmd. 5657*, 502
Factory Form, 629
Royal Commission, Minutes of Evidence, 909, 1058
Statistics :
   Cmd. 5077, 45
   Cmd. 5557, 288
   Cmd. 5722, 507
   Cmd. 5955, 738
   Cmd. 6203, 967
(Supplementary Allowances) Act, 972
Bill, 962
   No. 2, 948, 963
Forms, 1037
Workroom, Number of Persons who may be employed in a, Factory Form, 629
Works :
and Buildings, Ministry of, Publications (N.P.), 1072
and Repairs, War Department Schedule of Prices, 231, 937, 1072
Councils Bill, 272
of Art. *See* Import Duties Advisory Committee.
Office of :
   Civil Service Arbitration Tribunal Award, 639
   Publications (N.P.), 231, 457, 691, 938
   Scotland, 433, 671, 916
Services. *See* Civil Estimates.
See also Public Works ; Prospective Works ; Rating and Valuation (Air Raid Works) ; Road and Bridge Works.
Workshops :
Employment of Young Persons in, 913
See also Factories and Workshops.
World Consumption of Wool, 399, 634, 883
Worms, Stomach, in Sheep, 135
Worsted Weavers, Effects of Conditions of Artificial Lighting on Performance, 657
Worsteds, Specifications, 452, 686, 1068
Worthing. *See* Brighton, Hove and Worthing.
Worthy Down, Winchester, Sea Breezes at, 897
Wound Shock, Treatment of, 1056
Wounds. *See* War Wounds.

Woven :
Fabrics, Chinese, 695
Textiles. Limitation of Supplies : Explanatory Memo., 1063
List of persons entered on the Limitation of Supplies (Woven Textiles) Register, 1064
Wreck Reports, 210, 438, 675, 916, 1061
Wrexham and East Denbighshire Water Act, 71
Wright, Lord, Chairman, Law Revision Committee, Reports :
   Cmd. 5449, 280
   Cmd. 6009, 742
   Cmd. 6032, 743
Wright, W. B., Wigan District, Geological Survey, 661
Wringers, Fomentation, Specification, 226
Wrought :
Iron Gas Mains, Cutting and Welding Operations on, Factory Forms, 879, 1036
Light Aluminium Alloy Sheets and Strips, Specification, 1026
Wyatt, S. :
Fatigue and Boredom in Repetitive Work, 418
Machine and the Worker, 657

X

X and Y Rays, Biological Action of, 419
X-Ray Examination, Structure of Teeth as shown by, 1055

Y

Yachts. *See* Ships.
Yatton. *See* Clevedon.
Yeadon Water Provisional Order Confirmation Act, 302
Bill, 243, 268
Yeovil, Sunday Entertainments, 955
Ymarferion Corff, Tablau, 616
York :
Castle, Clifford's Tower, Guide, 231
Gas Act, 71
Water Provisional Order Confirmation Act, 758
Bill, 703, 729
Yorkshire :
East and North Ridings, Census, 190
Electric Power Act, 68
Mines, Reports, 184, 412, 648, 898
Roche Abbey, Guide, 232
Survey of Coalfield, 421

Yorkshire (*continued*) :
Wool Textile Industry, Wages, etc., 179
See also West Yorkshire ; West Riding.
Yorkshire, Nottinghamshire and Derbyshire Coalfield, Survey of, 906
Young :
Children, Anti-gas Protection of, 877
Horses, Rearing and Management of, 595
Married Couples, Housing of, 913
Persons :
   Employment of :
     in Factories, Workshops, etc., 913
     in Shops, Forms, 1037
     Scotland, 1061
   (Employment) Act, 524
     Bill, 468, 470, 471, 473, 497
     Forms, 633, 882, 915
     Memos., 633, 915
   Factory Forms, 627, 628
   Hours of Employment, Report. *Cmd. 5394*, 276
   See also Boys ; Children ; Employment of Women ; Girls ; Juvenile ; Women and Young Persons ; National Health Insurance (Juvenile Contributors).
Workers, Safety of, Factory Form, 879
Young, M. :
Appendicitis, 904
Nature and Characteristic Features of Post-normal Occlusion, 419
Younger, H. W., Chairman, Accidents in Paper Mills, Committee to consider prevention of, Report, 624
Your Home as an Air Raid Shelter, 1038

Youth :
Challenge of, Circular, 1032
Physical Recreation and Service, 1032
Welfare of, 913, 1060
Ystradgynlais, Electricity Orders, 213
Yugoslavia :
Economic Conditions, 212, 676
Imported Food Certificate, 161, 389
Scotland, 428
Legal Proceedings, Conventions with U.K. :
   Cmd. 5161, 50
   Cmd. 5542, 287
Trade and Payments Agreements with U.K. :
   Cmd. 5323, 63
   Cmd. 5540, 287

Z

Zanzibar :
Abolition of Capitulations in :
   Cmd. 5538, 287
   Cmd. 5646, 501
Colonial Reports, 152, 379, 610, 862
Zeuner, F. E., Fossil Orthoptera Ensifera, 942
Zinc :
Chrome, Specification, 601
Plating, Specification, 369, 1027
Sheets. *See* Import Duties Advisory Committee.
Zinc or Spelter. *See* Import Duties Advisory Committee.
Zionist Organisation and Palestine Arab Delegation, Correspondence. *Cmd. 1700*, 500

CONSOLIDATED INDEX
TO GOVERNMENT
PUBLICATIONS
1941-1945

INDEX

Abbreviations : In addition to the abbreviations in general use, the following are used :—*Cmd.*=Command Paper ; (N.P.)=Non-Parliamentary.

Cross References are to entries consisting of, or beginning with, the word or words indicated.

FOREWORD

The first five-yearly consolidated index to Government Publications covering the years 1936–40 was published in November 1952 (price 6s. 0d.).

This second index for the years 1941–45 is compiled on the same lines and includes the titles of new publications issued in the period, revised editions and reprints at amended prices. Commencing with the year 1941 Statutory Rules and Orders were omitted from the Annual Catalogues. For those issued during the period covered by this Index reference should be made to the separate Annual Lists and, for those still in force, to the Guide to Government Orders.

It is suggested that the annual catalogues for 1941–45 should be bound with this consolidated index, the annual index pages (which are excluded from the pagination) being discarded.

The page numbering of the annual catalogues indexed in this consolidation is as follows :

1941	... ...	1 to 68
1942	... ...	69 to 125
1943	... ...	126 to 189
1944	... ...	190 to 254
1945	... ...	255 to 336

A

Abercrombie, Sir P., Greater London Plan 1944, 325
Aberdeen :
   Corporation (Fish Market Rates) Order Confirmation Act, 87
   Bill, 80
   Oakbank School Trust (Amendment) No. 1 Scheme :
      1944, 244
      1945, 322, 323
Abrasive Wheels, Installation and Working of, Factory Form, 164
Absence :
   from Work, 242
   Record Cards, 103
   Sickness, 242, 318
Absenteeism among Women, 178
Abyssinian Campaigns, 100, 302
Accessions, etc., Supplementary Lists :
   Cmd. 6253, 16
   Cmd. 6329, 81
   Cmd. 6431, 141
Accidents :
   at Mines and Quarries :
      Death by, 55, 98, 156, 220, 299
      Form, 157
   from Falls of Roof, etc., at Coal Faces, 220
   Notice of, Factory Form, 42, 164
   Personal Factor in, 113
   Railway, 333
   Register of (Factories etc.), 307
   See also Factory Accidents ; Road Accidents.
Accommodation :
   in the Palace of Westminster, Report, 192
   See also Temporary Accommodation.
Accountancy, Careers, 305
Accounts. *See* Public Accounts.
Accumulator. *See* Electric Accumulator.
Acetylene Gas, etc., Safety Measures in the use of, Factory Form, 228

Acid. *See* Fatty Acid.
Acoustics. *See* Sound Insulation.
Acquisition of Land. *See* Land.
Actions, Limitation of, and Bills of Exchange, Report. *Cmd. 6591*, 274
Acts of Parliament, 22, 86, 144, 207, 281
Actuarial Work, Careers, 305
Administration, Officers in Charge, Army, Power in Relation to Losses—Writing off, 67
Admiralty :
   Examinations, 32, 95, 153, 216
   Instructions, 25
   Publications (N.P.), 25, 88, 147, 210, 285
Adult Education :
   Amending Regs., 34, 96, 154, 217
   Grants, Report. *Cmd. 6574*, 207
Advertising, Careers, 305
Aerated :
   Water, Factory Form, 228
   Waters Trade, Wages, 50, 109, 175, 238
Aerial :
   Navigation, International Sanitary Convention. *Cmd. 6638*, 276
   Wire. *See* Steel Aerial Wire.
Aerodrome Construction, 78
Aerodromes, Sites and Construction, 10
Aeronautical :
   Radio Service. *See* Civil Aeronautical Radio Service.
   Research Committee Publications (N.P.), 32, 94, 153, 215, 292
Aeronautics, A College of, Report, 212
Africa :
   British Military Administration of Occupied Territories in. *Cmd. 6589*, 273
   See also East Africa ; French Equatorial Africa ; Portuguese East Africa ; South Africa ; West Africa ; Italian East Africa ; North Africa ; British East Africa.
African :
   Auxiliary Pioneer Corps, Formation of, 120

1

AFR—   *INDEX 1941-45*

African (continued) :
Society, Mass Education in, Report, 217
See also South African.
Agricultural :
Bureaux. See Imperial Agricultural Bureaux.
Colleges (Scotland) Additional Grants, 180
Credit Society, Annual Return Form, 98
Drainage, 244
Education :
in England and Wales, Postwar, Report of Committee on. Cmd. 6433, 141
in Scotland, Report. Cmd. 6704, 280
Employment, provision in Secondary Schools of courses preparatory to, Report, 295
Engineering Record, 317
Improvement Council for England and Wales, Report, 148
Machinery Testing Committee Certificates and Reports, 25, 88
Policy, Long Term, Principles and Objectives of, Report, 149
Population. See Housing.
Research :
Council :
Accounts :
Cmd. 6257, 17
Cmd. 6344, 82
Cmd. 6434, 141
Publications (N.P.), 178, 318
Organisation and Development of, Report. Cmd. 6421, 141
Station, Amani, Annual Reports, 33, 95
Society, Annual Return Forms, 36, 98, 156
Statistics, 25
Workers, Weekly Expenditure, 52
Agriculture :
Advisory Leaflets, 26, 89, 148, 211, 280
and Fisheries, Ministry of, Publications (N.P.), 25, 88, 148, 211, 285
(Artificial Insemination) Bill, 270, 271
Bulletins, 25, 88, 148, 211, 285
Careers, 305
Department of, for Scotland, Publications (N.P.), 58, 115, 179, 244, 321

Agriculture (continued) :
in the West Indies, 95
Journal, 26, 89, 141, 211, 286
Scotland, 58, 115, 179, 244, 321
(Miscellaneous Provisions) Acts : 1941, 23
Bill, 3, 16
1943, 145
Bill, 81, 126, 127, 139
1944, 208
Bill, 191, 202
Report of Select Committee on National Expenditure, 9
Unemployment Insurance (Contributions) (Agriculture) Order 1942
Draft, 76
Aid, Mutual, Reports on :
Cmd. 6483, 144
Cmd. 6570, 207
Air :
Almanac, 28, 90, 149, 211, 286
Battle of Malta, 223
Council Instructions for the R.A.F., 28, 91, 148, 212, 287
Estimates, 8, 74, 133, 196, 261
Force :
Act, 1939, Amendments, 23, 87, 146, 283
Awards, 53, 111, 240, 316, 176
Examination, Special Provisional Regs., 28
Law, Manual of, 90, 149, 211, 286
Members of, Pay, Pensions, etc., 133, 136, 193, 199
New Broadcasts by, 160
Nursing Service Regs., 212
Pensions, etc., 265, 266
R.A.F. Middle East, 303
See also Air Ministry Publications (N.P.) below.
Ministry :
Establishments, Civilian Employees at, Regs., 28, 91, 149, 287
Publications (N.P.), 28, 90, 149, 211, 286
Navigation, £11
Act (1920), 281
Directions, 212
Regs., 28, 149
Signal Book for use in, 28
of Glory, 100
Raid Precautions :
Act, 1937. Report on working of the financial provisions. Cmd. 6356, 82

INDEX 1941-45   **—ALU**

Air (continued) :
Raid Precautions (continued)
in Schools, 59
Ministry of Home Security Publications (N.P.), 38, 99, 158, 222, 302
(Postponement of Financial Investigation) Act, 22
Raids :
Compensation for Civilians injured or killed in, 55
What you must know and do, 38
Receivers, Factory Form, 104
Services :
Appropriation Accounts, 7, 73, 76, 131, 194, 260
Vote of Credit, 134
Australia and Portuguese Timor. Cmd. 6266, 17
British. Cmd. 6712, 281
to Battle, By, 302
Training Corps, Rules and Regs., 212, 287
Transport :
British. Cmd. 6605, 274
International. Cmd. 6561, 206
Services,Exchange of Notes,U.S.A and Canada. Cmd. 6230, 21
See also Great Western Railway ; London and North Eastern Railway ; London Midland and Scottish Railway ; Southern Railway.
Votes, 9, 76, 134, 197, 262
We speak from the, 101
Airborne Divisions, British, Account of, 302
Aircraft :
Engines,Testing of,Factory Form, 228
Industry, Labour in the, 11
is Missing, One of our, 112
Log Book, 212
Production :
Ministry of :
Publications (N.P.), 28, 91, 149, 212, 287
Work of (Housing), 78
Report on, 136
See also Civil Aircraft ; Lightning and Aircraft.
Air-Sea Rescue, 100
Airworthiness :
Certificates for Export. Exchange of Notes, U.S.A. and New Zealand. Cmd. 6272, 18
Handbook for Civil Aircraft, 28

Alcohol, Excise Restrictions on Distillation, etc. Cmd. 6622, 275
Aliens :
Certificates of Naturalisation, Annual Returns, 10, 75, 132, 136, 259
See also British Nationality.
Allied :
Ministers of Education, Conference of. See Education.
Plan for Education, 329
Powers :
(Maritime Courts) Act, 22
Bill, 15
(War Service) Act, 86
Bill, 69, 70, 80
War Effort, Co-ordination of, Agreement. Cmd. 6332, 81
Allotment Society, Annual Return Form, 36, 98, 156
Allotments from Pay, Army, 66
Allowances :
Army (War Office Publications), 62, 120, 184, 250, 330
See also Dependant's Allowances ; Family Allowances; Pay and Allowances ; Forces ; Rent Allowances.
Alness, Lord (Chairman), Committee on Agricultural Education in Scotland, Report. Cmd. 6704, 280
Aluminium :
Alloy :
Bars, Extruded Sections, and Forgings, Specifications, 29, 92, 93
Castings, Specifications, 92, 93
Notched Bars and Ingots for remelting, Specifications, 31
Sand Castings, etc., Specifications, 29
Sheets and Coils, Specifications, 92
Tubes, etc., Specifications, 30, 31, 92
and Aluminium Alloy :
Plating, Process for cleaning prior to painting, Specification, 32
Rivets, Identification Colouring, Specification, 32
Notched Bars and Ingots for remelting, Specification, 30
Pistons, the Turning of, with Diamond Tools, 246
Aluminium–Copper–Nickel Alloy Cold Headed Bolts, Specification, 31

2

3

ALU—   *INDEX 1941-45*

Aluminium–Magnesium Alloy :
Castings, Specifications, 29
Sand or Die Castings, Specifications, 92
Aluminium–Manganese Alloy Sheets and Coils, Specification, 91
Aluminium–Nickel–Iron Bronze Bars, Forgings and Stampings Specifications, 91
Aluminium–Nickel–Silicon Brass :
Bars, Specification, 92
Tubes, Specification, 92
Amani, East African Agricultural Research Station, Annual Reports, 33, 95
America. See British North America ;
United States of America.
American Gooseberry Mildew, 90
Ammeters, Specification, 121
Ammon, Lord (Chairman), Committee of Enquiry into the London Dock Dispute, Report, 307
Ammonia, Wearing of War Respirators in the presence of, 38
Amos, A., Ensilage, 36, 211
Amputations. See Emergency Amputations.
Ancient Monuments and Historic Buildings, Official Guides, 188
Anderson, Dr. David (Chairman), Steel Structures Committee, Report, 254
Anglesey County Council (Water, etc.) Act, 209
Animal :
Breeding, 148, 286
Feeding Stuffs (Ministry of Food Publications), 97
Animals. See Aquatic Animals.
Annuities. See National Debt Annuities ; Redemption Annuities.
Anthrax, 286
Symptoms and Precautions, Factory Form, 43
Anti-Aircraft Defences, Story of, 160
Anti-Freezing Oil, Specification, 28, 93
Anti-Gas :
Clothing, Specifications, 65, 122
Precautions for Merchant Shipping, 28, 222
Wallet, No. 1, Specification, 65
Anti-Personnel Bomb, German, Instructional Diagram, 223
Aphides. See Apple Aphides ; Currant and Gooseberry Aphides ; Plum Aphides.
Aphis. See Cabbage Aphis ; Woolly Aphis.

Apparel :
and Textiles Orders, Registers, etc., 117, 182, 246, 325
Utility and Non-Utility, Traders' Guide to Price Control, 119
See also Cloth and Apparel ; Utility Apparel ; Fur Apparel.
Appeal, Court of. See Supreme Court.
Apple :
and Pear :
Canker, 27
Scab, 90, 211
Aphides, 27
Blossom Weevil, 89
Mildew, 27
Sawfly, 89
Sucker, 89
Apples :
and Pears Home Storage of, 90
Blossom Wilt of, 89
Brown Rot, 89
Applied Physics, Award of National Certificates, 297
Appointment, Army, War Office Publications (N.P.), 67, 123, 187, 252, 332
Appointments, Higher, Report. Cmd. 6576, 273
Apprentice Tradesmen, Army, Pay, 66
Apprenticeship. See Building Apprenticeship.
Appropriation :
Accounts. See names of Departments, etc.
Acts :
1941, 23
1941, No. 2, 23
1942, 86
Bill. See Consolidated Fund.
1942, No. 2, 86
Bill. See Consolidated Fund.
1942, No. 3, 86
Bill. See Consolidated Fund.
1943, 145
Bill. See Consolidated Fund.
1943, No. 2, 145
Bill. See Consolidated Fund.
1944, 208
Bill. See Consolidated Fund.
1944, No. 2, 208
Bill. See Consolidated Fund.
1945, 282
Bill. See Consolidated Fund.
Approved :
Schools (Scotland) List of, 180
Societies. See National Health Insurance.

Aprons, Specification, 65
Aquatic Animals, Composition of Depot Fats of, 115
Arabia. See Saudi Arabia.
Arc Welding. See Electric Arc Welding.
Arch Designs. See Centreless Arch Designs.
Architect, Training of the, 155
Architecture, Careers, 305
Arctic War, 321
Argentina :
Commercial Conditions in, 317
Wheat Discussions at Washington. Cmd. 6371, 83
Ark Royal, 100, 159
Armed Forces, Pay and Allowances. Cmd. 6385, 84
Armistice, Conditions of. See Bulgaria ; Finland ; Italy ; Roumania.
Armoured Corps, Royal, 332
Arms :
of H.M. Dominions, 216
See also Flags, Badges and Arms.
Army :
Act, 1940, Amendments, 87, 146, 208
Air Corps, Formation of, 120
and Air Force (Annual) Acts :
1941, 23
Bill, 15
1942, 86
Bill, 80
1943, 145
Bill, 139
1944, 208
Bill, 202
1945, 282
Bill, 270
Appropriation Accounts, 7, 9, 72, 76, 131, 194, 259
Vote of Credit, 1943, 134
at War, 39, 68, 100, 159, 224
Cadets, Pre-Service Physical Training and Recreation for, 252
Council, Message to Army, 332
Dental Corps, War Office Publications (N.P.), 187, 252
Destruction of an, 101
Estimates, 8, 73, 132, 196, 262
Examinations, 32
Fire Services in War, 230, 350
Increase of certain Pensions. Cmd. 6572, 207
List, 63, 120
Man-Power in the, 12
Orders, 63, 120, 185, 250, 330

Army (continued) :
Pay, Pensions and other Grants for Officers, Soldiers and Nurses disabled, etc. Cmd. 6653, 277
Prize Money and Legacy Funds, etc., Royal Hospital, Chelsea, Accounts, 9, 14, 136
Reserve, War Office Publications (N.P.), 63, 63, 123, 186, 252, 330
Retired Pay, Pensions, etc., for Officers, Soldiers and Nurses disabled, etc. Cmd. 6649, 105
Votes, 8, 75, 131, 196, 361
Arsine, Detection of, 115
Art :
and Industry, Council for, Report, 302
Careers, 305
Examinations in, 34, 96, 155, 218
See also Works of Art.
Arterial Injuries, Early Diagnosis and Treatment, 242
Arthur Jenkins Indemnity Act, 23
Bill, 3, 16
Artificial :
Flower Trade, Wages, 50
Insemination. See Agriculture.
Limbs, Report, 317
Silk Fabric, Specification, 94
Artists' Brushes, Specification, 64
Asbestos :
Fibre Jointing, Specification, 30, 94
Industry Regs., Factory Form, 164
Ascot District Gas and Electricity Act, 209
Asia. See South East Asia.
Asphalt Carpets, Recommendations for, 57
Asquith, Mr. Justice (Chairman), Royal Commission on Equal Pay, Minutes of Evidence, 321
Assheton, Rt. Hon. Ralph (Chairman), Committee on the Training of Civil Servants, Report. Cmd. 6525, 205
Assistance :
Board, Report for 1944. Cmd. 6700, 280
See also Public Assistance ; Unemployment Assistance.
Assurance :
Companies Bill, 272
See also Industrial Assurance.
Astronomical Ephemeris, 25, 88, 147
Atkinson, Mrs. Creswick, A.R.P. at Home, 99
Atlantic :
Bridge, 302

4

5

ATL-BUI | 1941-45

Atlantic (continued) :
 Charter. Cmd. 6511, 204
 Joint Declaration by President of U.S.A. and Mr. Winston Churchill. Cmd. 6321, 21
Atmospheric Pollution in Leicester, 319
Atomic :
 Bomb, Statements relating to the, 328
 Energy, 298
Atrocities. See German Attrocities.
Attorney. See Evidence.
Auctioneering, Careers, 305
Australia :
 Commercial Conditions in, 317
 Co-operation regarding Armistice, Civil Aviation, etc., Agreement with New Zealand. Cmd. 6513, 204
 Disposal of Real and Personal Property, Convention with U.S.A., New Zealand and U.K. Cmd. 6268, 18
 Establishment of an Air Service between Australia and Portuguese Timor. Exchange of Notes with Portugal. Cmd. 6266, 17
 Extradition. Supplementary Convention to Treaty with Paraguay, New Zealand, South Africa and U.K. Cmd. 6410, 85
 Wheat Discussions at Washington. Exchanges of Notes with Argentina, Canada, U.S.A. and U.K. Cmd. 6371, 83
Australian :
 Army at War, 216
 Surpluses, Statement of Policy. Cmd. 6287, 19
Authorised Explosives, Lists of, 222, 301
Auxiliary Territorial Service :
 Medical Services, 76
 War Office Publications (N.P.), 121, 185, 250, 330
Aviation. See Civil Aviation ; International Civil Aviation.
Aviators, Meteorology for, 54, 112
Axis :
 Oppression of Education, 101, 159, 160
 Rule :
  Rationing under, 101
  Women under, 160, 224
  System of Hostages, 101, 159
Ayr Burgh Order Confirmation Act, 23
Ayre, A. L. (Chairman), Committee on Hydrocarbon Oil Duties, Report. Cmd. 6615, 275

B

Baby is coming, When your, 160
Bacon :
 and Hams, Home Curing of, 27, 286
 Home Curing of, 211
Bactericides, Economy in the use of, 242
Badges :
 of H.M. Dominions, 216
 See also Flags.
Bag Trade :
 Wages, 50, 51, 239
 See also Paper Bag Trade.
Baker, S. J. (Chairman), Sub-Committee of the Police Council, Report on Income Tax on Rent Allowances, 302
Baking Trade, Wages, 50, 110, 111, 175, 176, 239, 315
Balfour, G. (Chairman), Committee on Cement Production, Report. Cmd. 6282, 19
Balfour, Lord (Chairman), Committee on Hill Sheep Farming in Scotland, Report. Cmd. 6494, 203
Balloon Sites, 5
Balls, Punching, etc., Specification, 64
Banbury Water Provisional Order Confirmation Act, 146
Bank :
 Notes. See Currency and Bank Notes.
 of England Bill, 258, 268, 271, 272
Bankers' Returns, 53, 112, 176, 240
Banking :
 and Insurance, Careers, 305
 Man-power in, Committee on, Report. Cmd. 6402, 85
 Society, Annual Return Forms, 36, 98, 156
Banks. See Post Office Savings Banks ; Savings Banks ; Trustee Savings Banks.
Barbados, West Indian Conference held in, Report, 217
Barkas, W. W., Swelling Stresses in Gels, 320
Barley :
 Eyespot of, 286
 Take-all or Whiteheads of, 27
Barnard, G. P., Circular Dividing Apparatus for Angular and Linear Measurement, 320
Barnborough Main Colliery, Upheaval of Floor, Report. Cmd. 6414, 140

Barnsley :
 Main Colliery, Explosions at, Report. Cmd. 6387, 84
 See also Beckett Hospital.
Barrack Services Regs., Army, 67, 124, 187, 252
Barracks. See Detention Barracks.
Barristers, Careers, 306
Bars, Specifications, 29, 30, 91, 92, 93
Basic English, Prime Minister's Statement. Cmd. 6511, 204
Baths. See Nitrate Salt Baths.
Battle :
 of Britain, 39, 101
 of Egypt, 159
 of Flanders, 68
Beale, Sir S. (Chairman), Scheme for ensuring fair shares of supplies to small retailers of clothing, 119
Bean :
 Beetles, 89
 Thrips, 90
 Weevils, 89
Beard, J. R. (Chairman), Electrical Installations Committee, Report, 254
Beaton, C., Air of Glory, 100
Beaumaris Castle, Guide to, 188
Beckett Hospital and Dispensary, Barnsley, Act, 209
Bed-Bug Infestation, Committee on, Report, 113
Bedding :
 Lists of Manufacturers and Wholesalers, 117, 182
 Utility and Non-Utility, Traders' Guide to Price Control, 119
Bee-Keepers, Advice to, 27, 286
Bee-Keeping, 25, 285
Bees, Diseases of, 286
Beet Eelworm, 149
Beetle. See Colorado Beetle ; Flea-Beetle ; Raspberry Beetle ; Chafer Beetles ; Pea and Bean Beetles.
Before We Go Back, 243
Belgian Congo :
 Finance and the Purchase of Commodities. Agreement between Belgium and U.K. Cmd. 6248, 16
 Regulation of Purchases of Commodities from, Agreement between Belgium and U.K. Cmd. 6365, 83
Belgium :
 Monetary Agreement with U.K. Cmd. 6557, 206

Belgium (continued) :
 Production and Export of Tin. Agreement with Bolivia, Netherlands and U.K. Cmd. 6396, 85
 Property in U.K. belonging to persons resident in, Agreement with U.K. Cmd. 6665, 278
 Protocol between U.K. and, regarding Mutual Aid. Cmd. 6620, 275
 See also Belgian Congo.
Bending Brakes, Report, 305
Benefit, Increase of. See Unemployment Insurance.
Benevolent Society, Annual Return Forms, 36, 97, 156
Benwick Internal Drainage District, Land Drainage Provisional Order Confirmation Act, 24
Berkshire, Hospital Services of, 300
Berlin Conference. See Foreign Ministers.
Best, R. D. (Chairman), Council for Art and Industry, Report, 326
Bethnal Green Tube Station Shelter Accident, Report. Cmd. 6583, 273
Betterment. See Compensation.
Beveridge, Sir W. H. (Chairman) :
 Fuel Rationing Report. Cmd. 6352, 82
 Skilled Men in the Services, Committee on, Reports :
  Cmd. 6307, 20
  Cmd. 6339, 81
 Social Insurance and Allied Services :
  Report. Cmd. 6404, 85
  Appendix G. Cmd. 6405, 85
  Report in Brief, 120
Bewley, W. F., Tomatoes, 26
Billeting, Army, 185
Bills of Exchange, Report. Cmd. 6591, 274
Bilston Corporation Act, 87
Birthday Honours. See London Gazette.
Births. See Registrar-General.
Bisulphide. See Carbon Bisulphide.
Black :
 Currant Gall Mite, 89
 Currants, Reversion in, 90
 Dot of Potato, 90
 Leg of Potatoes, 89
 Scurf of Potato, 90
Blackout :
 of Windows, Timber Economy, 189
 Ventilation in, 38
Blades. See Hacksaw Blades.

Blind :
 Public Assistance and Welfare of the, 157, 158, 180
 Welfare of, War Savings, 37
Blister Gas, Instructions for Handling, etc., 222
Blood :
 Groups, Determination of, 178
 Transfusion Services, Account of, 303
Blossom Wilt of Apples, 89
Blue Drill Hospital Clothing, Specifications, 65
Boarding Schools, Wartime Diet in, 96
Boilers. See Steam Boilers.
Bolivia. Production and Export of Tin, Agreement with Belgium, Netherlands and U.K. Cmd. 6396, 85
Bolts, Specifications, 31, 92, 93
Bomb. See Incendiary Bomb ; Atomic Bomb.
Bombay Baroda and Central Indian Railway Act, 87
Bomb - damaged Houses, Repair of, 114
Bomber Command, 39
" Bomber Command Continues ", 100, 159, 223
Bonded Warehouses, List of, 33, 95, 154, 217, 295
Bonds, etc. (London Gazette), 240
 See also Victory Bonds.
Book-keeping :
 for the Small Farmer, 179
 See also Farm Book-keeping.
Boot :
 and Floor Polish Trade, Wages, 50, 110, 175, 238, 315
 and Shoe Repairing Trade, Wages, 50, 110, 175, 238, 315
Boots, Specification, 65
Borstal Institutions, Directory of, 99
Borstals, Prisons and, 302
Boundary Commission :
 for England, 1944, Report on abnormally large constituencies. Cmd. 6634, 276
 See also Local Government (Boundary Commission).
Box Trade. See Paper Box Trade ; Tin Box Trade.
Boxes, Nest, 211
Boxing Gloves, Specification, 64
Boys' Clothing, Prices, etc., 183, 248, 326, 328
Brakes. See Bending Brakes.

Brassieres :
 List of Manufacturers, 61
 Prices, etc., 183
Brazil, Commercial Conditions in, 317
Breast Feeding of Infants, 221
Breeding. See Animal Breeding.
Bretton Woods :
 Agreements Bill, 272
 Conference, Final Act. Cmd. 6546, 206
 Monetary and Financial Conference. See United Nations.
Brewing, Careers, 305
Brick Industry, Committee on, Reports, etc., 125, 189
Bricks. See Common Bricks ; Sand-lime Bricks.
Bridge Design and Construction, 333
Bridgwater Gas Act, 146
Brigade Commanders, Army, Powers in relation to Losses—Writing off, 67
Briggs Motor Bodies, Ltd., Trade Dispute, Report of Court of Inquiry. Cmd. 6284, 19
Briggs, M.S., Training of the Architect, 195
Brightness Contrast, Effect of, 318
Britain, Battle of. See Battle of Britain.
British :
 Air :
  Services. Cmd. 6712, 281
  Transport. Cmd. 6605, 274
  Airborne Divisions, Account of, 302
  and Indian Troops in North Africa, 223
  Broadcasting Corporation Accounts. Cmd. 6705, 280
  Commonwealth, Migration within. Cmd. 6658, 277
  East Africa, Commercial Conditions in, 317
  Farming, 1939–44, Story of, 303
  India, Statistical Abstracts :
   Cmd. 6333, 81
   Cmd. 6441, 142
  Nationality and Status of Aliens Act, 145
  Bill, 71, 126, 139
  North America Act, 145
  Bill, 128
  Overseas Airways Corporation and R.A.F. Transport Command, Relationship between, Correspondence, etc., 140
  Further correspondence. Cmd. 6442, 142
  Rainfall, 54

British (continued) :
 Settlements Bill, 258, 271
 Shipowners, Wartime Financial Arrangements with, Report, 265
 Shipping (Assistance) Act, 1935, Accounts, 14, 78, 193, 200, 267
 Ships :
  Re-insurance Agreements, 76, 137, 198, 260
  Signal Letters of, 59, 125
  Tanks, 100
 Broadcasting, Civil Estimates, 7, 8, 74, 132, 133, 195, 261
 Broadcasts by R.A.F., 160
 Broccoli (Winter) and Summer Cauliflower, 286
 Brood, Foul, 211
 Broom Trade, Wages, 315
 Brown :
  Rot :
   of Apples, 89
   of Plum, 27
  Scale, 148
 Brown, D. Clifton (Chairman), Boundary Commission for England, Report on abnormally large constituencies. Cmd. 6634, 276
 Brown, Miss E. O., Natural Lighting of Houses and Flats, 243
 Brown, W. B., Control of Insects infesting Dried Fruits, 114
 Browne, G. J. St. O., Labour Conditions : in Ceylon, Mauritius and Malaya. Cmd. 6423, 141
  in West Africa. Cmd. 6277, 18
 Brush and Broom Trade. See Broom.
 Brushes. See Artists' Brushes ; Painters' Brushes.
 Brussels Sprouts, 149
 Buchenwald Camp, Report of Parliamentary Delegation. Cmd. 6626, 276
 Buckinghamshire, Hospital Services of, 300
 Bucks Water Board Provisional Order Confirmation Act, 146
 Bill, 139
 Budget. See Financial Statement ; India.
 Bug. See Bed-Bug ; Fruit Tree Capsid Bugs.
 Building :
  and Civil Engineering :
   Industries in Wartime, 334
   Production in, 334
  and Engineering Construction, Record of Working Hours, Factory Form, 104

Building (continued) :
 Apprenticeship and Training Council, Reports, 253, 334
 Codes of Practice, Committee for, Reports, 189
 Contracts, the Placing and Management of, Report, 253
 Crafts, 297
 Draft Regs., (School Premises), Memo. and Circulars, 217, 218
 Factories Regs., Draft of New Code, 305
 Industry :
  Careers, 305
  Training. Cmd. 6428, 141
  Report, 189
  in the U.S.A., Methods of, 253
  Materials and Housing Bill, 258, 272
 Operations :
  Abstract of Provisions of the Factories Act, 1937, Factory Form, 228
  and Works of Engineering Construction (Welfare and Safety Provisions) Order, 1941, Memo., 43
  Payment by Results, 125, 189, 253
  Research Board Publications, 56, 114, 242
  Restrictions (Wartime Contraventions) Bill, 258, 268, 269, 271
  Sale of Land for Building Purposes, 324
  Schools Regs., Memo., 295
  Science Abstracts, 56, 114, 178, 242, 319
  Sites, Welfare Amenities for, Factory Form, 104
  Standard Schedule of Prices, 125
 Supplies. See Wartime Building Supplies.
 Studies. See Post-War Building Studies.
 the use of Standards in, 254
 See also Wartime Building.
Buildings :
 Fumigation of. See Hydrogen Cyanide.
 Lighting of, Report, 334
 of the War Department, Schedule of Prices for Works and Repairs, 125, 188, 252
 Painting of, Report, 254
 registered for marriages, 55, 113, 177, 241, 318
 Requisitioned, Release of, 263

Buildings (continued) :
War Damage to, 250
See also Lands and Buildings ;
Requisitioned Buildings ; Works
and Buildings ; Ancient Buildings ;
Single Storey Buildings ; Business
Buildings ; Farm Buildings ;
Requisitioned Land and Build-
ings ; School Buildings.
Bulb Eelworm, 90
Bulbs. See Onion Bulbs.
Bulgaria :
Conditions of Armistice. Cmd. 6587,
273
Notification of State of War with, 54
Bullet Proof Safety Glass for Wind-
screen Panels, Specification, 30
Bullfinch, 149
Bullion, Imports and Exports, 34
Burial Grounds. See Welsh Church.
Burma :
and Thailand, Boundary between.
Exchange of Notes, Thailand and
U.K. Cmd. 6262, 17
Front, Account of, 303
Office List, 302
Statement of Policy by H.M.
Government. Cmd. 6635, 276
See also Government and Burma ;
India and Burma.
Burnham Committee on Scales of
Salaries for Teachers, Reports,
297
Burns :
and Scalds, Studies of, 319
First Aid Treatment of, 58
Hospital Treatment of, 116, 244
Burrows, Roland (Chairman). New-
castle-upon-Tyne Inquiry, Report,
Cmd. 6522, 205
Bursaries. See Education Authority.
Burt, Sir George (Chairman), Inter-
Departmental Committee on House
Construction, Report, 253
Bush Fruits. 66
Business :
Administration, Training for, Report,
Cmd. 6673, 278
Buildings, Report, 334
Premises. See Fire Prevention ;
Retail Business Premises.
Scheme (War Damage), Statement of
Receipts and Payments, 201
Businesses. See Retail Businesses.
Butler, C. G., Bee-keeping, 285
Butter. See Whey Butter.

Button Manufacturing Trade, Wages,
51, 111, 175, 238
By Air to Battle, 302

C

Cabbage :
Aphis, 149
Caterpillars, 26
Root Fly, 26
Cables. See Electric Cables ; Electrical
Cables ; Flexible Electric Cables.
Cadets. See Army Cadets ; Service
Cadets.
Cadetships. See Naval Cadetships.
Caernarvon :
Castle, Guide to, 188
Provisional Order Confirmation Act,
87
Bill, 70, 80
Calais, Defence of, 39, 101
Calcium Sulphate Plasters, 56
Calendars. See Record Publications.
Calling Up :
of the 1922 and Younger Age
Classes, 59
See also Civil Servants.
Calves :
" Husk " or " Hoose " in, 211
White Scour in, 148
Camborne Water Act, 24
Camel Hair, Processes, Factory Form, 164
Cameroons under French Mandate,
Commercial and Economic Relations
with U.K. :
Cmd. 6249, 16
Cmd. 6345, 82
Campaign Stars, Clasps and Defence
Medal :
Approved Recommendations. Cmd.
6633. 276
Special Army Order, 330
Camps :
Act, 282
Bill, 256
See also Militia Camps.
Canada :
Air Transport Services, Exchange of
Notes with U.S.A. Cmd. 6320, 21
Avoidance of Double Taxation, etc.,
Convention with U.S.A. Cmd.
6383, 84

Canada (continued) :
Commercial :
Conditions in, 317
Modus Vivendi, Exchange of Notes
with Ecuador. Cmd. 6409, 85
Relations, Exchange of Notes
with Paraguay. Cmd. 6274, 18
Emergency Regulation of the Level
of Rainy Lake, etc., Convention
with U.S.A. Cmd. 6276, 18
Establishment of a Board of Enquiry
for the Great Lake Fisheries.
Exchange of Notes with U.S.A.
Cmd. 6273, 18
Exemptions from Exchange Control
Measures, Exchange of Notes with
U.S.A. Cmd. 6319, 21
Food Consumption Levels in, 219
Great Lakes–St. Lawrence Basin,
Exchange of Notes with U.S.A.
Cmd. 6303, 20
Load Line Regs. for Vessels engaged
in International Voyages on the
Great Lakes, Exchange of Notes
with U.S.A. Cmd. 6302, 20
Military Forces raised in Canada and
in U.K., Mutual Powers of Com-
mand, 122
Trade Agreements :
with Uruguay. Cmd. 6275, 18
with U.S.A. Cmd. 6246, 16
What do they Eat in U.S.A.,
Canada and Britain, 219
Wheat Discussions at Washington,
Exchanges of Notes with Argen-
tina, Australia, U.S.A. and U.K.
Cmd. 6371, 83
Canadian Honours. See London Gazette.
Canals. See London Midland and Scot-
tish Railway.
Cancer, Mule Spinners in, 306
Canker. See Apple and Pear Canker ;
Stem Canker.
Cannock Urban District Council Act, 24
Canteens :
in Youth Clubs, 295
See also School Canteens ; Service
Canteens.
Canvas, Rope and Cordage, Rot-proof-
ing of, Specification, 94
Cap Trade, Wages, 51, 110
Cape, Anti-Gas, Specification, 65
Capital :
Issues Control. Cmd. 6645, 277
See also German Capital.

Carbon :
Bisulphide, Precautions against
dangers of poisoning, etc., Factory
Form, 164
Monoxide :
Detection of, 115
Poisoning, 42, 307
Steel :
for Valve Springs, Specification,
28
Strips, Specification, 93
Carburettors, Testing of, Factory Form,
228
Cardiff Corporation Acts, 24, 146
Careers, Ministry of Labour and
National Service Publications (N.P.),
305
Cargoes :
Salvage of, Report, 137
See also Grain Cargoes.
Carmichael, A. D. (Chairman), Scheme
for ensuring fair shares of supplies
to Small Retailers of Hollow-ware,
119
Carpets. See Tar Carpets.
Carr, Sir Cecil (Chairman), Committee
on Electoral Law Reform, Interim
Report. Cmd. 6606, 274
Carriageway Designs for Roads other
than Public Highways, 115
Carrot Fly, 26, 211
Cartwright, K. St. G., Dry Rot in Wood,
320
Cash issued to Soldiers in Debt, Restric-
tions on, 252
Cast Iron Piston Ring Pots, Specifica-
tions, 92, 93
Castings, Specifications, 91, 92, 93
Catchment Boards, Receipts and Expen-
diture of, 37
Catering :
Corps, Army, Formation of, 63
Wages :
Act, 145
Bill, 127, 138, 139
Commission Reports :
Annual, 199, 267
Rehabilitation of the Catering
Industry, 306
Remuneration and Conditions
of Employment, 227
Staggering of Holidays, 306
Wages Board :
for Industrial Catering.
Cmd. 6509, 204

Catering (continued) :
for Licensed Non-Residen-
tial Establishments.
Cmd. 6612, 275
for Licensed Restaurants.
Cmd. 6601, 274
for Unlicensed Non-Resi-
dential Establishments.
Cmd. 6569, 207
for Unlicensed Resident
Establishments.
Cmd. 6706, 280
Caterpillars. See Cabbage Caterpillars ;
Surface Caterpillars.
Cattle :
Insurance Society, Annual Return
Form, 156
Liver Rot, 90
Cauvins Trust. See Dean Orphanage.
Cauliflower, Summer, 286
Celery :
Leaf Spot, 90
Fly, 89
Cellular Rubber Sheet. Specification
93
Celluloid, Regs. for the Manufacture of,
etc., Factory Form, 43
Cellulose Solutions. Regs. Factory Form,
43
Cement Production, Committee on,
Report. Cmd. 6282, 19
Census :
East India, Abstract of Tables. Cmd.
6435, 141
of Production, Committee Report.
Cmd. 6686, 279
Centipedes, 89
Central :
Advisory Water Committee, Report.
Cmd. 6465, 143
Coal Mines Scheme, 54, 98
Electricity Board :
Increase of Borrowing Powers,
Draft Special Order, 60
Publications (N.P.), 95, 216
Government and Finance, Civil Esti-
mates, 7, 74, 132, 195, 261
India Railway. See Bombay.
Ordnance Depots and Production of
Obsolete Stores, Report, 136
Centreless Arch Destgus, 36
Cereal Diseases, 286
Cereals, Wheat Control in, 149, 286
Cerebro-Spinal Fever among Troops,
Memo. on, 121
Cerement-making Trade, Wages, 51, 110

Ceylon :
Constitutional Reform, Report. Cmd.
6677, 279
Statement of Policy. Cmd. 6690,
279
Defence Force, Colonial Officers,
Powers of Command. 250, 330
Labour Conditions in, Report. Cmd.
6423, 141
Ceylonese Soldiers, Issues of Pay and
Proficiency Pay to, 66
Chief Needles, 93
Chalk. See French Chalk.
Chalmers, R. (Chairman), Mechanical
Installations Committee, Report, 254
Chancellor, Lt.-Col. Sir J. R. (Chairman),
Committee on Veterinary Practice by
Unregistered Persons, Report. Cmd.
6611, 275
Charlock, Destruction of, 89
Chartered and Other Bodies :
(Resumption of Elections) Bill, 257,
271
(Temporary Provisions) Act, 22
Bill, 2
Chasteney, H. E. (Chairman), Dust in
Steel Foundries Committee, Report,
238
Chattels. See Private Chattels.
Cheddar Cheese, 89
Cheese. See Cheshire Cheese ; Cheddar
Cheese ; Lancashire Cheese.
Cheesemaking :
Starters for, 27, 287
See also Farm and Creamery Cheese-
making.
Chelsea. See Royal Hospital.
Chemical :
Controls, Report, 200
Engineering, Careers, 306
Survey. See Physical and Chemical
Survey.
Warfare, Medical Manual of, 63, 185
Works, Factory Forms, 43
Chemistry and Physics, Careers, 306
Cheshire Cheese, 27
Chesterfield and Bolsover Water Act,
209
Chevrons for War Service, Grant of.
Cmd. 6463, 143
Children :
and Young Persons :
Act, 1933. Order Revoking
Licence, 37
in need of Care and Protection,
Scotland, Circular, 245

Children (continued) :
Employment in Entertainments, 75,
296
Feeding of, from one to five years, 99
Hostels for, 116
in Occupied Lands, Story of, 329
Over Two in Wartime Nurseries, 99
Temporary Migration of, (Guardian-
ship) Act, 22
Bill, 2, 15
See also Evacuated School Children ;
Growing Children ; Pre-School
Children ; Refugee Children ;
" Difficult " Children ; Guardian-
ship ; Mothers and Young Child-
ren ; Handicapped Children.
Chile :
Commercial Conditions in, 317
Temporary Commercial Agreement
with U.K. Cmd. 6322, 21
Chiltern Hills Spring Water Provisional
Order Confirmation Act, 146
Bill, 139
China, Relinquishment of Extra-Terri-
torial Rights in. Treaty with U.K.
and India. Cmds. 6417, 6456, 140,
142
Chippings, Naturally Coloured, Sources
of, in Great Britain, 57
Christmas Greetings, Exchange between
the President of the U.S.A. and the
Prime Minister, 185
Chrome. See Zinc Chrome.
Chromium :
Steel, Specification, 30
See also Nickel Chromium.
Chromium-Molybdenum Steel, Specifi-
cation, 30
Chromium–Nickel :
Heat Resisting Steel :
Rods and Wire, Specifications, 31
Sheets and Coils, Specifications.
31
Tubes, Specification, 31
Non-Corrodible Steel :
Sheets and Coils, Specifications,
91
Welding Rods and Wire, Speci-
fications, 94
Chronic :
Pulmonary Disease in South Wales
Coalminers, 113, 319
Rheumatic Diseases, Report, 321
Chronological Table and Index of the
Statutes, 181
Chrysanthemum Midge, 211, 286

Church :
Councils. See Parochial Church
Councils.
Temporalities in Wales, Accounts,
5, 14, 78, 197, 200, 268
Work, Careers, 305
See also Welsh Church.
Churchill, Winston :
Atlantic Charter. Cmd. 6321, 21
Correspondence with H.M. the King
on the Conquest of Sicily, 187
Exchange of Christmas Greetings
with the President of U.S.A., 185
Cinematograph :
Film :
Industry, 247
Manufacture of, Regs., Factory
Form, 43
Fund Account, 5, 13, 78, 136, 201,
268
Cipher Operations, Royal Corps of Sig-
nals, Pay, 121
Circular Dividing Apparatus, Notes on
the use of, 333
Citizenship, Training for, 117, 323
Report, Cmd. 6495, 203
Citrine, Sir W. (Chairman), Committee
on Regional Boards, Report. Cmd.
6360, 82
City of London (Various Powers) Act, 209
Civil :
Aeronautical Radio Service, " Q "
Code, 28
Aircraft :
Airworthiness Handbook for, 28
Navigator's Licence, Examina-
tion Papers, 90
Appropriation Accounts, 5, 72, 131,
134, 194, 197, 259, 263
Aviation :
Communications Handbook, 212,
31
Department Publications (N.P.),
90
Ministry of :
Act, 282
Bill, 256, 270
Publications (N.P.), 294
See also International Civil Avia-
tion
Awards and Commendations, 53, 111,
176, 240
Contingencies Fund, Accounts, 10,
75, 132, 198, 264
Defence, 11

CIV— INDEX 1941–45 —COA

Civil (continued) :
Defence (continued) :
Ministry of Home Security Publications (N.P.), 222
(Suspension of Powers) Bill, 258, 271
Training Pamphlet, 158
War Pensions for Members of Civil Defence Services, Explanatory Notes, 241
Employment, Reinstatement in :
Act, 208
Bill, 190, 202
Decisions by Umpire, 238, 314
Engineering :
Award of Higher National Certificates, 155, 245
Careers, 306
Codes of Practice Committee for, Reports, 189
Payment by Results, 253
Estimates :
1940, Supplementary, 7
1941, 7, 8
Statement of Excess, 135
Supplementary, 12, 72, 73, 74
1942, 74
Revised (Treasury and Subordinate Departments), 77
Statement of Excess, 199
Supplementary, 77, 78, 131, 132
1943, 132, 133
Supplementary, 135, 194, 195
1944, 195, 196
Supplementary, 199, 202, 259
Vote on Account, 196
1945, 261, 262
Supplementary, 265, 267
Servants :
Calling Up of, Committee on, Interim Report. Cmd. 6301, 20
Training of, Committee on, Report. Cmd. 6525, 205
Service :
Administrative Class. Cmd. 6680, 279
Arbitration Tribunal Awards, 42, 103, 163, 227, 306
Careers, 305
Commission Publications (N.P.), 32, 95, 153, 216, 294
Examinations, 294
Organisation and Control, 78
Pensions : Forms, etc., for Pensioners claiming Increase, 249

14

Civil (continued) :
Service (continued) :
Recruitment to Established Posts in, during the Reconstruction Period. Cmd. 6567, 207
Scientific. Cmd. 6679, 279
Civilian :
Clothing (Restrictions) Order, Specifications, 247
Consumption, Impact of the War on, 328
Employees at Air Ministry Establishments. See Air Ministry.
Non-Industrial Staffs (War Office), Subsistance Allowance, 124
Staff Regs., War Office, 63, 121, 185, 250, 330
Technical Corps (Air Ministry), 28
Civilians :
employed at Air Ministry Establishments. See Air Ministry.
in Japanese or Japanese-Occupied Territory, Handbook for Relatives, etc., 252
injured or killed in Air Raids, Compensation for, 55
Mass Miniature Radiography of, 319
Travelling Regs. (War Office), 124
War Pensions for, Explanatory Notes, 241
Clackmannan Educational Trust :
(Additional Endowment and Amendment) (No. 1) Scheme, 180
(Amendment) (No. 1) Scheme, 244
Clark, Kathleen C., Mass Radiography of Civilians, 319
Classes, Compulsory Day Continuation, Report, 180
Clearing Offices. See Debts Clearing Offices.
Clegg, H. A., How to keep well in War-time, 160
Clerks. See Justices' Clerks.
Clifford'sTower, York Castle, Guide to, 188
Cloakrooms and Washing Facilities, etc., in Factories, 315
Cloth :
and Clothing :
Board of Trade Publications (N.P.), 325
Education Circulars, 296
and Apparel :
Explanatory Notes for Traders, 61
Registers, 61, 119
Rationing, 154, 155, 217, 218
Answers to Questions on, 60, 118

B

Cloth, Clothing, Footwear, and Knitting Wool, Rationing, 34, 35, 36, 96, 97
Clothes Rationing Manual for Manufacturers, 118
Clothing :
Army, War Office Publications (N.P.), 63
Board of Trade Publications (N.P.), 246
Coupon Quiz, 60
Decontamination of, from Persistent Gases, 100
Education Circulars, 217, 218
Factories, List of Firms entered on the Designation List, 117
Prices, Related Schedules, 183
Quiz, 118, 182, 247
Rationing. See Cloth ; Cloth, Clothing.
Scheme for ensuring Fair Shares of Supplies to Small Retailers, 119
Specifications, 122, 186, 251
See also Oilskin Clothing ; Women's Light Clothing ; Salvaged Clothing ; Second-hand and Salvaged Clothing.
Cloud Forms, 54
Clover Rot, 90
Club Root, 27, 211
Clubs :
Annual Return Form, 37, 97, 98, 156
See also Youth Clubs.
Clyde, J. L., Report on Government Contracts in Scotland. Cmd. 6393, 84
Clyde Lighthouses Consolidation Order Confirmation Act, 23
Clydebank and District Water Order Confirmation Act, 146
Bill, 139
Coal. Cmd. 6364, 82
Coal :
Act :
1933, Statement of Guarantees and Account, 134, 198
1943, 145
Bill, 128, 139
Charges Account. Cmd. 6617, 275
Commission Accounts, 7, 72, 131, 198, 264
Report, 264
(Concurrent Leases) Act, 86
Bill, 69
Dust Explosions. Report. Cmd. 6450, 142
Faces, Accidents from Falls of Roof, 220

15.

Coal (continued) :
Industry Nationalisation :
Cmd. 6716, 281
Bill, 272
Mines :
Acts, 1887 to 1937, Abstract, Mines and Quarries Form, 157
Central (Coal Mines) Scheme, 98
Explosives in Coal Mines Order, 1943, Circular, 157
General Regs., Mines and Quarries Form, 55
Guaranteed Wage Levy, Explanatory Memo. Cmd. 6278, 18
Ministry of Fuel and Power Publications (N.P.), 220, 299
Parts of Abstract and General Regs. to be supplied to Underground Workmen in " Naked Light " mines, 98
Regulations and Orders relating to Safety and Health, 54
Mining :
Industry :
Board of Investigation into Wages, Reports, 104, 163
Committee on Recruitment of Juveniles, Reports, 98, 156
Financial Position. Cmd. 6617, 275
Report. Cmd. 6610, 275
Production, 75
See also Opencast Coal Production.
Resources, National, Survey of, 115, 243
Supply, 9, 13
See also Opencast Coal.
Coal-carrying Vessels, Instructions to Surveyors, 125
Coalfields :
Ministry of Fuel and Power Publications (N.P.), 299
See also Scottish Coalfields ; South Wales Coalfield.
Coalminers. See South Wales Coalminers.
Coals of South Wales, 115
Coastal Command, 159
Coasting and Short Sea Trades in Europe, 334
Coat, Oilskin, Simplex, Specification, 122
Coatbridge and Springburn Elections (Validation) Act, 283
Bill, 257, 271
Coats, Specifications, 65

COC— INDEX 1941–45 —COO

Cocoa Control in West Africa, Report. Cmd. 6554, 206
Code, " Q ". See Civil Aeronautical Radio Service.
Codes of Practice. See Civil Engineering.
Codling Moth, 89
Coffin Furniture and Cerement Making Trade, Wages, 51, 110
Cohen, Sir B. (Chairman), Committee on Artificial Limbs, Report, 317
Cohen, Mr. Justice (Chairman), Company Law Amendment Committee :
Minutes of Evidence, 182, 247, 325
Report. Cmd. 6659, 277
Coils, Specifications, 31, 91, 92
Coin, Imports and Exports, 34
Cold-Headed Bolts, Specifications, 92, 93
Collars, Specification, 64
Collecting Society, Annual Return Forms, 36, 98, 156
Colleges. See Training Colleges ; County Colleges ; Agricultural Colleges ; Universities and Colleges.
Colliery Management, Careers, 305
Colombia, Commercial Conditions in, 317
Colonial :
and Field Allowances, Army, 250
Corps, etc., Awards for disability or death, 63
Development :
Advisory Committee, Final Report. Cmd. 6298, 20
and Welfare :
Act :
1940 :
Report. Cmd. 6422, 141
Returns of Schemes made under :
Cmd. 6457, 142
Cmd. 6532, 205
House of Commons Paper, 265
1945, 282
Bill, 270
Despatch. Cmd. 6713, 281
Fund Accounts, 7, 72
Empire, Labour Supervision in, 154
Office Publications (N.P.), 33, 95, 154, 216, 295
Policy in Wartime, Certain Aspects of. Cmd. 6299, 20
Products Research Council, Annual Report. Cmd. 6535, 205

16

Colonial (continued) :
Regs., 33, 295
Research Reports :
Cmd. 6486, 144
Cmd. 6535, 205
Cmd. 6663, 278
War Risks Insurance (Guarantees) Act, 23
Bill, 2, 15
Colonies :
Higher Education in. Cmd. 6647, 277
Training of Nurses for. Cmd. 6672, 278
Colonisation. See Jewish Colonisation.
Colorado Beetle, 26
Colwyn Bay. See Conway and Colwyn Bay.
Combined :
Colonial and Field Allowances, Army, 250
Food Board, Report of Special Joint Committee, 219
Operations, 159, 223, 302
Raw Materials Board, Annual Reports, 241, 348
Command Papers, 16, 81, 140, 203, 273
Commercial :
Agreement (Temporary), Chile and U.K. Cmd. 6332, 21
Conditions, Reviews of, 317
Crops for Pickling, 88
Gas Act, 283
Modus Vivendi, Exchange of Notes, Ecuador and Canada. Cmd. 6409, 85
Relations :
Cameroons under French·Mandate and U.K. :
Cmd. 6249, 16
Cmd. 6345, 82
French Equatorial Africa and U.K. :
Cmd. 6281, 19
Cmd. 6346, 82
Paraguay and Canada. Cmd. 6274, 18
Vegetable Crops, Manuring, 89, 148, 211
Commission Combing and Recombing Schedule, 327
Commissions. See Emergency Commissions.
Common :
Bricks, Firing of, 189
Scab of the Potato, 26
Worms of the Pig, 90

Communications Handbook. See Civil Aviation.
Community :
Centres, 218
Feeding in Wartime, 37
Company Law Amendment Committee :
Minutes of Evidence, 182, 247, 325
Report. Cmd. 6659, 277
Compass. See Gyro-Compass.
Compensation :
and Betterment, Expert Committee on :
Interim Report. Cmd. 6291, 19
Final Report. Cmd. 6386, 84
for Civilians injured or killed in Air Raids, 55
of Displaced Officers (War Service) Act, 282
Bill, 255, 270
See also National Health Insurance ; Land and Buildings ; Workmen's Compensation ; Equal Compensation.
Competency Certificates, Mines, Examinations, 220, 299
Compressed Asbestos Fibre Jointing, Specifications, 30, 92
Compulsory :
Day Continuation Classes, Report, 180
Retirement of Women Officers, Army, 67
Concentration of Production. See Production.
Concrete. See Reinforced Concrete ; Lightweight Concrete Aggregates.
Condensed Milk, 157
Confectionery. See Sugar Confectionery.
Congenital Deaf-Mutism in Scotland, Report, 321
Congo. See Belgian Congo.
Connah's Quay Gas Act, 209
Connaught, Duke of, Death, 111, 121
Conscientious Objectors. See National Service.
Consolidated Fund :
Accounts, 6, 72, 130, 194, 260
Acts :
1941, 22, 23
Bills, 15, 16
Appropriation Bills, 15, 16
1942, 86
Bills, 80
Appropriation Acts, 86
Bills, 80, 81

Consolidated Fund (continued) :
Acts (continued) :
1943, 145
Bills, 138
Appropriation Acts, 145
Bills, 140
1944, 207, 208
Bills, 202, 203
Appropriation Acts, 208
Bills, 203
1944–5, 282
Bills, 270
Appropriation Act, 282
Bill, 271
1945–6, 283
Bill, 271
Constabulary. See Police.
Constituencies. See Parliamentary Constituencies.
Constructional Work. See Civil Engineering.
Consumer Rationing :
Order, 1941, Explanatory Notes for Traders, 61
(Consolidation) Order, Registers, 182, 246, 325
Containers and Straps, Lists of Manufacturers, 183, 247, 326
Contract. See Prime Cost Contract.
Contracts, 7
See also Building Contracts ; Law Reform ; Government Contracts ; International Labour Conference ; Public Accounts.
Contributory :
Negligence. See Law Reform.
Pensions. See National Health Insurance ; Widows', Orphans', etc.
Control, Board of, Publications (N.P.), 33
Controlled Prices. See Retail Controlled Prices.
Conway and Colwyn Bay Joint Water Supply Board Provisional Order Confirmation Act, 283
Bill, 270
Cook, T., Limited Guarantee. See Railway Companies.
Cookery, the A.B.C. of, 298
Cooking :
Appliances, Schedules, etc., 68, 125, 334
Utensils, Specification, 64
Cooper, Rt. Hon. Lord (Chairman), Committee on Hydro-Electric Development in Scotland, Report. Cmd. 6406, 85

17

Copper Tubes, Specification, 92
Corbet, A. S., Insect Pests of Food, 219
Cord Rings. *See* Shock Absorber Cord Rings.
Cordage :
  Rot-proofing of, Specification, 94
  See also Nylon Cordage ; Plaited Cordage.
Cords. *See* Flexible Electric Cords.
Corn, Sweet, 149
Corps :
  Divisional and Brigade Commanders, Army Powers in relation to Losses —Writing off, 67
  Warrant, Army, 63
Corrosion, Protection of Magnesium-Rich Alloy Parts against, Specification, 32
Corset Trade, Wages, 51, 110, 315
Corsets, Corset Belts and Brassieres :
  Lists of Manufacturers, 61, 117, 182, 246
  Prices, 183
Cost :
  Accountancy, Careers, 305
  of Living Index Number, Method of Compilation, 228
Costume Trade, Wages, 52, 110, 315
Cotranwar Charter Party, Form, 253
Cotton :
  Drawers, Specification, 64
  Duck. *See* Waterproofed and Dyed Cotton Duck.
  Fabric, Specifications, 29, 31, 93, 94
  Handkerchief Trade, Wages, 50, 110, 239
  Hospital Clothing, Specifications, 65, 122
  Industry, Interim Report, 306
  Sheets and Sheeting, Specification, 65
  Spinning Industry, Report, 306
  Textiles Mission to the U.S.A., Report, 241
  Waste Reclamation Trade, Wages, 51, 110, 175, 238
  Webbing, Specification, 93
Country Planning. *See* Town and Country Planning.
County :
  Colleges, Further Education in, 296
  Courts Accounts, 7, 73, 132, 195, 261
Court. *See* County Courts ; Industrial Court ; Maritime Courts ; Supreme Court ; Welsh Courts ; Juvenile Court ; High Court ; International Justice.
Court-Martial, Notes on Procedure, etc., 331
Courts (Emergency Powers) :
  Act, 145
    Bill, 126
      Report by Joint Committee, 127
        Proceedings and Minutes of Evidence, 127
  Amendment Act, 86
    Bill, 70
  (Scotland) Act, 207
    Bill, 129
Coventry Corporation Act, 87
Covers, Waterproof, Specification, 65
Cox, C. W. M. (Chairman), Adult and Mass Education Sub-Committee of the Advisory Committee on Education in the Colonies, Report, 217
Crane Flies, 27
Crang, B. A., Preserves from the Garden, 148
Creamery Cheesemaking, 26
Credit, Vote of :
  1940, Supplementary, 7
  1941, 7
    Statement. *Cmd. 6279*, 18
    Supplementary, 12, 14, 75
  1942, 75
    Statement. *Cmd. 6363*, 82
    Supplementary, 77, 78, 131
  1943, 131
    Statement. *Cmd. 6445*, 142
    Supplementary, 133, 137, 193
  1944, 193
    Statement. *Cmd. 6524*, 205
    Supplementary, 198, 199, 200, 259
  1945, 259, 267
    Statement. *Cmd. 6630*, 276
    Supplementary, 265
  See also Appropriation Account.
Crete. *See* Greece and Crete.
Criccieth Castle, Guide to, 188
Crigglestone Colliery, Explosion at, Report. *Cmd. 6327*, 81
Crimea Conference, Report of. *Cmd. 6598*, 274
Crimes. *See* War Crimes.
Criminals. *See* War Criminals.
Crop Production in Frames and Cloches, 88, 148
Crops :
  Diseases of, 148
  for Pickling, 26
  See also Fruit Crops ; Salad Crops ; Commercial Crops.

Cross Infection in Hospitals, Control of, 242
Crown :
  Gall, 90
  Lands :
    Act, 145
      Bill, 81
    Commissioners of, Accounts, 9, 73, 130, 194, 260
  Ministers of the, and House of Commons Disqualification Act, 86
    Bill, 80
Culinary Herbs, 89
Culture. *See* Learning.
Cunard Insurance Fund Accounts, 5, 71, 130, 194, 263
Curing. *See* Home Curing.
Currant and Gooseberry Aphides, 148
Currants. *See* Black Currants.
Currency and Bank Notes Act, 1928, Fiduciary Notes Issue, 6, 11, 12, 14, 76, 78, 80, 134, 136, 138, 196, 199, 202, 264, 266, 269
Curtain, Anti-Gas, for Steel Helmets, Specification, 65
Customs :
  and Excise :
    Annual Reports of the Commissioners. *Cmd. 6703*, 280
    Publications (N.P.) (including Customs Forms), 33, 95, 154, 217, 295
  See also Isle of Man.
Cutlery :
  Grinding of, Factory Form, 43
  Trade Wages, 49, 51, 111, 176, 239
Cutters of Horizontal Milling Machines, Safety Precautions, Factory Form, 228
Cutworms or Surface Caterpillars, 27
Cyanide. *See* Hydrogen Cyanide.
Cycles. *See* Road Transport Lighting.
Cylinders for Liquefiable Gases, 320
Cyprus and Egypt, Trade between, Exchange of Notes between Egypt and U.K. *Cmd. 6305*, 20
Czechoslovak :
  Financial Claims Fund Accounts, 135, 197, 264
  Refugee Fund Accounts, 9, 77, 135, 197, 264
Czechoslovakia :
  Monetary Agreement with U.K. *Cmd. 6694*, 280
  Money and Property Agreement with U.K. *Cmd. 6695*, 280
Czechoslovakia (*continued*) :
  Policy of H. M. Government in the U.K. in regard to, Exchange of Notes with U.K. *Cmd. 6379*, 84

D

Daddy Longlegs, 27
Dainty Dishes for the Queen, 245
Dairies :
  Treatment and Disposal of Waste Waters from, 115
  See also Food and Drugs.
Dairy Equipment, Cleansing of, 157
Damage. *See* War Damage.
Damsons, 211
Dancing, Careers, 306
Danger Buildings of Explosive Works, Factory Form, 43
Dangerous Goods, Stowage of, in Ships, 188, 253
Danish Council in London Publications (N.P.), 295
Dashpot Hydraulic Fluid, Specification, 94
Davidson, D. du B. (Chairman), Committee on Expenditure in respect of Evacuated School Children, Report, 35
Dawson of Penn, Rt. Hon. the Viscount (Chairman), Committee on Tuberculosis in Wartime, Report, 113
Dawson, W. M., A Study of Variations in Output, 242
Day Continuation Classes, Compulsory, Report, 180
Deaf-Mutism, Congenital, Report, 321
Dean Orphanage and Cauvin's Trust (Amendment) (No. 2) Scheme, 58
Death, Manual of the International List of Causes of, 241
Deaths :
  by accidents at Mines and Quarries, 55, 98, 156, 220, 299
  Registration. *See* Registrar-General.
Debates. *See* House of Commons Papers ; House of Lords Papers ; Publications and Debates.
Debt :
  Restrictions on Cash Issued to Soldiers etc. in Debt, 252
  See also National Debt.
Debts Clearing Offices Accounts, 7, 72, 130, 195, 260

Decontamination :
  of Clothing, 100
  of Materials, 100, 222
  Services, Organisation of, 100
Decorations and Medals :
  Grant of, in Time of War. *Cmd. 6463*, 143
  War Office Publications (N.P.), 185
Defence :
  (Finance) Regulations, 1939, Treasury Notice, 240
  Medal. *See* Campaign Stars.
  of Calais, 39, 101
  Regs., 1939 :
    Action taken under 18B, Reports, 6, 8, 9, 11–14, 72, 74–79, 131, 133, 135, 136, 137, 138, 194, 196, 197, 198, 199, 200, 201, 259, 260, 262, 263, 264, 265
    As amended up to various dates, 62
    Volumes, 119, 120, 184, 249, 328
  See also National Defence ; Civil Defence ; Ceylon Defence ; Emergency Powers.
De-Icing Fluid, Specification, 92
de la Warr, Earl (Chairman), Committee on Hill Sheep Farming in England and Wales, Report. *Cmd. 6498*, 203
Delevingne, Sir M., Coal Dust Explosions, Report. *Cmd. 6450*, 142
de Lisle and Dudley, Lord, MSS., 113
Demobilisation. *See* Manpower, Reallocation.
Demonstration Houses, 253
Denbigh Castle, Guide to, 188
Denmark :
  Monetary Agreement with U.K. *Cmd. 6671*, 278
  Money and Property in, Agreement with U.K. *Cmd. 6717*, 281
Denmark's Fight against Germany, 295
Dental Corps, Army, 67, 124, 187, 252, 332
Dentistry :
  Careers, 305
  Interdepartmental Committee on, Interim Report. *Cmd. 6565*, 207
Dependants, Payments to, after Death of Soldier, 123
Dependants' :
  Allowances :
    Army, War Office Publications (N.P.), 62, 63, 120, 121, 250
    Members of H.M. Forces. *Cmd.* [illegible], 81
Dependants (*continued*) :
  Allowances (*continued*) :
    Men serving in H.M. Forces during the present War. *Cmd. 6260*, 17
  Pensions, Soldiers', 252
Deportation. *See* Slave Labour.
Depot Fats of Aquatic Animals, Composition of, 114
Derbyshire :
  Coalfield, National Coal Resources, 115, 243
  See also South Derbyshire.
Dermatitis, Factory Forms, 42, 104, 164
Derwent Valley Water Act, 209
Design and the Designer :
  in the Dress Trade, 302
  in the Light Metal Trades, 326
Designated Clothing Factories, List of Clothing Factories entered on the Designation List, 117
Designs. *See* Centreless Arch Designs ; Patents and Designs.
Despatches Emblem, 251
  Grant of. *Cmd. 6463*, 143
Destruction of an Army, 101
Detector Tippets :
  Fabric for, Specification, 65
  Specification, 65
Detention Barracks, Prime Minister's Committee of Inquiry into, Report. *Cmd. 6484*, 144
Determination of Needs. *See* Needs.
Development :
  Fund Accounts, 6, 72, 130, 194, 260
  See also Colonial Development ; Ribbon Development ; Scientific Research ; Research and Development.
Diamond Tools, the Turning of Aluminium Pistons with, 246
Diamond-Back Moth, 148
Die-Back Disease of Gooseberries, 90
Diet. *See* Wartime Diet.
Dietics, Careers, 304
" Difficult " Children, Hostels for, 221
Diocesan :
  Education Committees Measure, 129, 146
  Reorganisation Committees Measure, 2, 24
Diphtheria, Epidemiology of, during the last Forty Years, 178

Diplomatic Privileges (Extension) Acts :
  1941, 22
  1944, 208
    Bill, 191, 192, 203
Direct Grant Grammar Schools, Circular, 296
Disability. *See* Incumbents' Disability ; Soldiers' Disability.
Disablement Allowances to Members of Home Guard, 121
Disabled Persons :
  (Employment) Act, 208
    Bill, 140, 190, 202
  Rehabilitation and Resettlement of, Interdepartmental Committee on, Report. *Cmd. 6415*, 140
Discipline. *See* Naval Discipline.
Diseases :
  and Injuries, Provisional Classification of, 242
  See also Pests and Diseases.
Dispensers' Clothing, Specifications, 65
Displaced Officers. *See* Compensation.
Dispossession, Acts of, in Enemy Occupied Territory, Inter-Allied Declaration. *Cmd. 6418*, 140
Disqualification. *See* House of Commons.
Distinguished Conduct Medal, Efficiency Classification of Soldiers, 185
Distribution of Industry Act, 282
  Bill, 257, 265, 266, 270, 271
Divisional Commanders, Army, Powers in relation to losses—Writing off, 67
Divorce. *See* Indian Divorce.
Dock :
  Disputes, etc. *See* London Dock ; Port Transport Industry.
  Labour :
    in Merseyside, Manchester and Preston Areas, Explanatory Memo., 68
    in the Port of Glasgow, Explanatory Memo., 68
    in the Port of Greenock, Explanatory Memo., 68
    Schemes, Explanatory Memo., 42
  Workers (Regulation of Employment) Bill, 258, 268, 269, 271, 272
Docks, Factory Forms, 42, 104, 228
Documents :
  Select Committee on Disposal and Custody of, Reports, 75, 78, 135
  See also Secret German Documents.
Dollar Academy Trust (Amendment) (No. 1) Scheme, 58, 116
Domestic :
  and Industrial Quarrels, Prices, etc., 248
  Employment, Postwar Organisation of, Report. *Cmd. 6650*, 277
  Help, Committee on Minimum Rates of Wages, etc., Report. *Cmd. 6481*, 144
  Preservation of Fruit and Vegetables, 148
  Science, Careers, 305
  Utensils, Galvanised, Specification, 122
Dominions :
  Income Tax, 39
  Office Publications (N.P.), 154
Doncaster Provisional Order Confirmation Bill, 256, 271
Donkin, S. B., Report on Severn Barrage Scheme, 300
Double Taxation, Avoidance of, Convention between U.S.A. and Canada. *Cmd. 6383*, 84
Douching. *See* Eye Douching.
Doughty, Sir C. (Chairman), Court of Inquiry concerning Disputes :
  at Briggs Motor Bodies Ltd. *Cmd. 6284*, 18
  between the Clerical and Administrative Workers' Union and certain Colliery Companies in South Wales and Monmouthshire. *Cmd. 6493*, 144
Douglas Fir, Specification, 30, 93
Douglas, J. B. (Chairman), Scottish Land Settlement Committee, Report. *Cmd. 6577*, 273
Dower, J., Report on National Parks in England and Wales. *Cmd. 6628*, 276
Downshire, Marquess of, MSS., 113
Downy Mildew of the Onion, 26
Drainage :
  Agricultural, 244
  Authorities, Receipts and Expenditure Forms, 37, 99
  See also Land Drainage.
Dramatic Art, Careers, 306
Drawers, various, Specifications, 64
Dress, Army, Distinctions in, 251
Dressmaking and Women's Light Clothing Trade, Wages, 51, 110, 238, 315
Dried :
  and Condensed Milk, 157
  Fruits, Control of Insects infesting, 114
  Separated Milk, Allocation to School Canteens, etc., 34, 36, 154, 155

Drift Nets Mending Trade, Wages, 49
Drilling Machine Spindles, Fencing of, Factory Form, 164, 228
Drive. *See* Flexible Drive.
Drop Hammers, Safety of, Factory Form, 228
Drugs :
Economy in the Use of, in Wartime, 56, 242
See also Food and Drugs.
Drum Trade, Wages, 51, 110, 111, 175, 239, 315
Dry Rot :
in Wood, 320
of Potatoes, 27
of Turnips and Swedes, 58
Duck. *See* Flax Duck ; Waterproofed and Dyed Cotton Duck.
Ducks and Geese, 26
Duckworth, J., Substitute Feeding Stuffs, 148
Dudley, Earl of (Chairman), Design of Dwellings Committee, Report, 221
Dumbarton Oaks :
Commentary on Proposals. *Cmd. 6571*, 207
Conversations on World Organisation. *Cmd. 6560*, 206
Dumfries Electricity (Extension) Special Order, 118
Draft, 60
Dumfriesshire Educational Trust (Amendment) (No. 2) Scheme, 116, 180
Duncan Macleod of Skeabost Scholarship Fund Scheme, 58
Dunne, L. R., Report on Accident at Bethnal Green Tube Station Shelter. *Cmd. 6583*, 273
Durham :
Coalfield, Report, 299
District Coal Mines Scheme, 54
Dust :
in Steel Foundries, Report, 238
Suppression, Co-ordination of, 220, 300
See also Coal Dust ; Silica.
Dwellings, Design of, Report, 221
Dysentery. *See* Lamb Dysentery.

E

Earning, High, Instances of, Report, 263

East :
Africa :
Commercial Conditions in, 317
Inter-Territorial Organisation in, 295
Military Operations, 1914–16, 39
See also British East Africa ; Portuguese East Africa.
African Agricultural Research Station, Amani, Annual Reports, 33, 95
India :
Census, Abstract of Tables. *Cmd. 6435*, 141
(Finance Act, 1944), 199
(Finance Act, 1945), 265
Indian Wool Regs. for Factories in which East Indian Wool is used, Factory Form, 104
Indies. *See* Netherlands East Indies.
Midlands :
Area, Hospital Services, 300
Electricity District (Amendment) Special Order, 118
of Malta, West of Suez, 160
Surrey Gas Act, 24
Worcestershire Water Act, 24
Eastern Area, Hospital Services, 300
Ebbw Vale Urban District Council Act, 24
Ebonite. *See* Loaded Ebonite.
Ecclesiastical :
Commissioners (Powers) Measure, 69, 87
Committee Reports, 190, 193, 256
Economic :
Advisory Council Publications (N.P.), 328
Relations :
Cameroons under French Mandate and U.K. *Cmd. 6345*, 82
French Equatorial Africa and U.K. :
Cmd. 6281, 19
Cmd. 6346, 82
Ecuador, Commercial Modus Vivendi. Exchange of Notes with Canada. *Cmd. 6409*, 85
Eden, Rt. Hon. Anthony, Speech delivered at the Mansion House. *Cmd. 6289*, 19
Edge Tools, Grinding of, Regs., Factory Form, 43
Edinburgh :
Castle, Guide to, 188
Gazette, 58, 116, 180, 244, 321

Edinburgh (*continued*) :
Merchant Company Endowments (Amendment) Order Confirmation Acts :
1943, 146
Bill, 81
1944, 209
Bill, 202
University of, Munro Lectureship Schemes, 244, 323
Education :
Act, 208
Bill, 140, 190, 191, 192, 202, 203
Explanatory Memo. *Cmd. 6492*, 144
Allied Ministers of, Conference, 295
Story of the Conference, 329
Army Education Scheme, 330
Authority Bursaries, Report. *Cmd. 6573*, 207
Axis Oppression of, 101, 159, 160
Board of :
Civil Estimates :
1941, 7, 8
Memo. *Cmd. 6526*, 17
1942, 74
Memo. *Cmd. 6343*, 82
1943, 132, 133
Memo. *Cmd. 6429*, 141
Grant Regs., 34, 35, 96, 97, 154, 155
Publications (N.P.), 34, 96, 154
in African Society, 217
in Scotland :
Scottish Education Department Publications (N.P.), 59, 116, 180, 245, 322
Summary Reports :
Cmd. 6317, 21
Cmd. 6370, 83
Cmd. 6452, 142
Cmd. 6540, 205
Cmd. 6667, 278
Ministry of :
Civil Estimates :
1944, 195
Memo. *Cmd. 6508*, 204
1945, 261
Memo. *Cmd. 6629*, 276
Grant Regs., 217, 218
Publications (N.P.), 217, 295
(Scotland) Acts :
1918, Circulars, 59, 180, 245
1942, 86
Bill, 16
Circular, 116

Education (*continued*) :
(Scotland) Acts (*continued*) :
1945, 282
Bill, 203, 265, 266, 270, 271
Explanatory Memo. *Cmd. 6602*, 274
Circulars, 322
Welsh Department, Publications (N.P.), 35, 97, 155, 218, 297
See also Adult Education ; Diocesan Education ; Health Education ; Oversea Education ; Post-War Agricultural Education ; Sex Education ; Veterinary Education ; Higher Education ; Technical Education.
Educational :
Endowments (Scotland), 58, 116, 180, 244, 322
Pamphlets, 96, 155
Property, War Damage to, 34, 36
Reconstruction. *Cmd. 6458*, 142
System in England and Wales, 96, 296
Training, Army, 185, 331
Edwards, W., Geology of the Country around Wakefield, 57
Eelworm. *See* Beet Eelworm ; Potato Root Eelworm ; Root-Knot Eelworm ; Stem and Bulb Eelworm.
Efficiency :
Medal and Efficiency Decoration, 121, 185
See also Physical Efficiency ; Visual Efficiency.
Egypt :
Battle of, 159
Commercial Conditions in, 317
Correspondence with U.K. concerning Egyptian Foreign Exchange Requirements. *Cmd. 6582*, 273
Trade between Cyprus and, Exchange of Notes with U.K. *Cmd. 6305*, 20
Eighth Army, 224
Eire, Post Offices in, 55
Elections :
and Jurors Bill, 258, 272
Report of Select Committee, 267
See also Local Elections ; Parliament ; Chartered and other Bodies ; Coatbridge ; Parliamentary Elections.

Electoral :
Law Reform, Interim Report. *Cmd. 6606*, 274
Machinery, Committee on, Report. *Cmd. 6408*, 85
Reform and Redistribution of Seats, Conference on, Letters from Mr. Speaker to the Prime Minister :
Cmd. 6534, 205
Cmd. 6543, 206
Registration Regs. *Cmd. 6466*, 143
Electors. *See* Local Elections ; Parliamentary Constituencies ; Parliamentary Electors.
Electric :
Accumulator Regs., Factory Form, 43
Arc Welding :
Factory Forms, 104, 307
in Ship Construction, 285
Cables, Specifications, 64, 122
Cords, Specifications, 64
Undertakings. *See* Hydro-electric Undertakings.
Welding in Shipbuilding, 210
Electrical :
Energy in Premises, Regs. for the Generation of, Factory Form, 42
Engineering, Careers, 306
Installations, Report, 254
Research and Testing, etc., Mines, 220
Specifications, 64, 121, 181, 185, 324
Electricity :
Board of Trade Publications (N.P.), 60, 118
Commission Publications (N.P.), 36, 97, 218
Form of Accounts for a Local Authority, 36
in Mines, 55
Committee on Amendment of General Regs. governing the use of, Report, 55
Installation and Use of, Mines and Quarries Form, 220
Regs., Factory Form, 228
Electro-Plating Shops, Air Raid Precautions, 38
Elementary Flying Training, 149
Elliot, Rt. Hon. W. (Chairman) :
Committee on Voluntary Aid Detachments, Report. *Cmd. 6448*, 142
Herring Industry Committee, Report. *Cmd. 6503*, 204
Higher Education in West Africa, Commission on, Report. *Cmd. 6655*, 277

Emblem for Mention in Despatches, 251
Emergency :
Amputations, 56
Commissions, Army Officers promoted to, 66
Hospitals, List of, 117
Laws (Transitional Provisions) Bill, 269, 272
Legislation Measures, 193, 284
Medical Services :
Instructions, 37
Memoranda, 58, 116, 157, 221, 244
Pipe Repairs, 56
Powers (Isle of Man Defence) Act, 145
Bill, 139
Relief Organisation, 116
Statutory Rules and Orders, Lists of, 60
Empire :
Timbers, Handbook of, 179, 320
See also Colonial Empire.
Employers' Liability :
Act, 1880, 281
Insurance, Limitation of Charges :
Cmd. 6297, 20
Cmd. 6377, 83
Cmd. 6478, 143
Cmd. 6541, 205
Cmd. 6676, 279
Employment :
Conditions of, Domestic Help. *Cmd. 6481*, 144
Policy. *Cmd. 6527*, 205
Problems of Post-war entry of Juveniles into, 109
See also Children ; Civil Employment ; Disabled Persons ; Juvenile Employment ; Agricultural Employment ; Dock Workers ; Private Domestic Employment ; Trade and Employment.
Enamel. *See* Stoving Enamel.
Endowments. *See* Educational Endowments ; Episcopal Endowments ; Edinburgh Merchant Company Endowments.
Enemies. *See* Limitation (Enemies and War Prisoners).
Enemy :
Occupied Territory, Acts of Dispossession in, Inter-Allied Declaration. *Cmd. 6418*, 140
Territories, Dates on which certain Territories became or ceased to be, 316

Enemy (*continued*) :
Trading with the, Legislation in force, 119, 248, 328
Engine Log Book, 212
Engineer Services, Army, 63, 121, 185, 251, 331
Engineering :
Agricultural Engineering Record, 317
Careers, 306
Construction :
Provisions of the Factories Act, 1937, Factory Form, 228
Record of Working Hours, Factory Form, 104
(Welfare and Safety Provisions) Order, 1941, Memo., 43
Work of, Draft Regs., 307
Science Scholarship Examination, 296
Undertaking in Scotland, Dispute at, Report. *Cmd. 6474*, 143
See also Civil Engineering ; Mechanical Engineering ; Production Engineering ; Building and Civil Engineering.
Engineers :
Mercantile Marine, Examinations, 125
Quality Control for, 324
See also Royal Electrical and Mechanical Engineers.
Enginemen. *See* Winding Enginemen.
Engines. *See* Aircraft Engines.
Engledow, F. L. :
Chairman), Committee on Farm Buildings, Report, 286
Report on Agriculture, Fisheries, Forestry and Veterinary Matters, West Indies. *Cmd. 6608*, 274
English, Teaching of, in England, 35
Enlisted Boys, War Pay, 187
Ensilage, 26, 211
Enterprise. *See* Private Enterprise.
Entertainment. *See* Public Entertainment.
Entertainments, Employment of Children in, 35, 296
Episcopal :
Endowments and Stipends Measures, 71, 146
Pensions Measure, 256, 284
Equal :
Compensation, Select Committee on, Report, Proceedings, etc., 133
Pay, Royal Commission on, Minutes of Evidence, 321

Equipment (A.R.P.), Care and Custody of, 38, 100, 223
Eritrea and Somalia, British Military Administration in, 224
Ermine Moths, 211
Erysipelas. *See* Swine Erysipelas.
Essential Work (Building and Civil Engineering) Order, Memo. on (Payment by Results), 125, 189, 253
Essex. *See* Herts and Essex.
Estate :
Agency, Careers, 305
Duty. *See* India.
Estimates. *See* Air Estimates ; Army Estimates ; Civil Estimates ; Navy Estimates ; Revenue Departments ; National Income.
Ethiopia, Agreements with U.K. :
Cmd. 6334 (and Military Convention), 81
Cmd. 6584, 273
Ethylene Glycol, Specification, 89
European (Central) Inland Transport, Agreements :
Cmd. 6640, 276
Cmd. 6685, 279
Evacuated School Children, Committee Report, 85
Evacuation. *See* Government Evacuation Scheme.
Eve, Sir Malcolm Trustram (Chairman), Building Apprenticeship and Training Council, Reports, 253, 334
Evershed, Mr. Justice (Chairman) :
Cotton Spinning Industry Commission, Report, 306
Port Transport Industry Committee, Report, 314
Evidence and Powers of Attorney Act, 145
Bill, 139
Ewes, Twin Disease, 27
Examinations :
Civil Aviation Department, 90
Civil Service Commission, 32, 95, 153, 216, 294
Competency and Surveyors' Certificates, Mines, 220, 299
in Art, 34, 96, 155, 218
Inspector of Weights and Measures, 328
Mercantile Marine, 125
Police (Scotland) Examinations Board, 245
Science Scholarships, 96, 218, 296

Examinations (continued) :
Special Air Force, Provisional Regs., 28
Surveyors' Certificates, Mines, 55, 156
See also Secondary Schools.
Excess Profits Tax Leaflets, 101, 160, 224, 303
Exchange :
Bills of, Report. Cmd. 6591, 274
Control Measures, Exemption from, Exchange of Notes between U.S.A. and Canada. Cmd. 6319, 21
Exchequer Contributions to Local Revenues, Civil Estimates, 7, 8, 74, 132, 133, 195, 196, 261
Excise. See Customs and Excise.
Expanded Rubber Sheet, Specification, 30
Expenditure. See National Expenditure ; Public Income and Expenditure ; Weekly Expenditure.
Expiring Laws Continuance Acts :
1940, 22
1941, 23
Bill, 16
1942, 86
Bill, 81
1943, 145
Bill, 140
1944 Bill, 203
1945, 282
Bill, 258, 271
Explosion and Gassing Risks in the Cleaning, Examination and Repair of Stills, Tanks, etc., Factory Form, 228
Explosions. See Coal Dust Explosions.
Explosives :
Acts, 1875 and 1893, Guide to, 37
Authorised, Lists of, 99, 158, 222, 301
Conditions of Stowage on board ship, 125, 188, 253, 333
Conveyance of, on Roads, 215
Home Office Publications (N.P.), 37
in Coal Mines Order, 1943, Circular, 187
Sale of, 301
Special Rules for Use of, 55, 220
Works, Danger Buildings of, Factory Form, 43
See also Government Explosives ; High Explosive.
Export :
Control of, Lists of Goods, 61, 118, 183, 247, 326

Export (continued) :
Guarantees Act, 282
Bill, 270
List, 96
of Goods. See Goods.
Trade of the U.K., Accounts, 248, 326
Exporters. See Registered Exporters.
Extradition :
of Offenders. Agreement between Saudi Arabia and U.K. Cmd. 6382, 84
Supplementary Convention to Treaty of Sept., 1908 between Paraguay, Australia, New Zealand, South Africa and U.K. Cmd. 6410, 85
Extra-Statutory Wartime Concessions in the Administration of Inland Revenue Duties. Cmd. 6559, 206
Extra-Territorial Rights in China, Relinquishment of, Treaty between China, U.K. and India :
Cmd. 6417, 140
Cmd. 6456, 142
Eye-douching, Instructions for, 37
Eyespot of Wheat and Barley, 286

F

Faber, Dr. Oscar (Chairman), Reinforced Concrete Structures Committee, Report, 254
Factories :
Act, 1937, Guide to, 158
Chief Inspectors of, Annual Reports :
Cmd. 6251, 16
Cmd. 6316, 21
Cmd. 6397, 85
Cmd. 6471, 143
Cmd. 6563, 207
Cmd. 6698, 280
Cloakrooms, etc., in, 315
First-Aid Services, 315
Luminising (Health and Safety Provisions), Factory Forms, 104, 228
Medical Supervision in, Memo., 228
Reports of Select Committee on National Expenditure, 9
Seats for Workers in, 315
Testing of Aircraft Engines, Carburettors, etc., Factory Form, 228
See also Royal Ordnance Factories ;
Single Storey Factories ; Clothing Factories ; Milk Products Factories.

Factory :
Accidents, How they Happen, 104
Construction and Equipment of a, 12
Forms, 42, 104, 163, 228, 307
near Glasgow, Investigation into certain Complaints, Report, 137
Orders, 228
Welfare Work outside the. Cmd. 6310, 20
Fair Wages Resolution. Cmd. 6399, 85
Falls of Roof and Sides at Coal Faces, Accidents from, 220
Family :
Allowances :
Act, 283
Bill, 257, 270, 271
Army, War Office Publications (N.P.), 63, 121, 184, 250, 330
Memo. Cmd. 6354, 82
and Dependants' Allowances, Army, 121
Fancy Leather Trade, Wages, 50
Far East, Additional Pay for H.M. Forces. Cmd. 6553, 206
Farm :
and Creamery Cheese Making, 26
Book-keeping, 148
Buildings, Report, 286
Mechanisation, Developments in, 317
Farmers' Income Tax, 148
Farming. See British Farming ; Hill Sheep Farming.
Fatigue, Prevention of, 242
Fats. See Depot Fats.
Fatty Acid Derivatives, Mode of Occurrence, in Living Tissues, 114
Feather Trade. See Ostrich and Fancy Feather.
Feathers, Specification, 65
Fedden, Sir A. H. R., (Chairman, Committee on the Establishment of a School of Aeronautical Science, Report, 212
Feeding. See Breast Feeding ; Community Feeding ; Poultry Feeding.
Feeding-Stuffs :
Composition and Nutritive Value, 89, 211
Residual Values, 58, 244
Substitute, 148, 286
See also Animal Feeding Stuffs.
Fees. See Tuition Fees.
Fencing :
Equipment, Specifications, 64
of Power Presses, 307

Fergusson, D. (Chairman), Agricultural Improvement Council for England and Wales, Report, 148
Fertilisers, Residual Values of, 58, 244
Fertility :
and Animal Breeding, 148, 286
See also Land Fertility.
Fever. See Cerebro-Spinal Fever.
Fibre Jointing, Compressed Asbestos, Specifications, 92
Fiduciary Note Issue, Treasury Minutes, 6, 11, 12, 14, 76, 78, 80, 134, 136, 138, 196, 199, 264, 266, 269
Field :
Allowances, Army, 250
Mice, Notes on, 285
Peas for Stock Feeding, 27
Fife County Council Order Confirmation Act, 23
Fiji, Sugar Industry of, Report, 295
File-Cutting by Hand, Factory Form, 42
Film :
Strips, 218
See also Cinematograph.
Finance :
Accounts of the U.K., 11, 77, 135, 199, 265
Acts :
1934, Accounts, etc., 11, 13, 76, 79, 135, 199, 264
1941, 23
Bill, 2, 15
Memo. on the Clauses relating to Tax-Free Income. Cmd. 6283, 19
1942, 86
Bill, 69, 80
1943, 145
Bill, 128, 139
1944, 208
Bill, 191, 202
1944-5, 282
Bill, 270
Bill No. 2, 271
1945-6, Bill, 258, 272
See also Indian Finance Act.
Defence Regs. 1939 :
Acquisition of Securities, Treasury Directions, 111
as amended up to various dates, 62, 120
See also Civil Estimates ; War Finance.
Financial :
Conference. See United Nations.

Financial (continued) :
Institutions, Army, 63
Powers :
of Commands, Subordinate Formations, and Units, Statement of, 121
(U.S.A. Securities) Act, 21
Bill, 15
Draft Regs. Cmd. 6296, 19
Pensions. See Local Government
Statement by the Chancellor of the Exchequer, 10, 76, 134, 198, 264
Supplementary (1945), 267
Finchale Priory, Guide to, 188
Findlay, W. P. K., Dry Rot in Wood, 320
Finland :
Conditions of Armistice. Cmd. 6586, 273
Indebtedness between U.K. and Finland. Cmd. 6664, 278
Notification of State of War with, 54
Fir. See Douglas Fir.
Fire :
Appliances, 222
Brigade Pensions, Instructions to Pensioners claiming Increase, 222
Fighting, Water Problems, explained, 99
Guard :
(Business and Government Premises) Order, 1943, Form of Application for approval of arrangements, 223
Regs., 1943, etc., Explanatory Memo., 158
Guards :
Handbook, 100
Payment of, Report, 134
Precautions, 100
in Schools, 301
Prevention (Business Premises) No. 2 Order, 1941, Explanatory Memo., 38
Supplement, 100
Protection, 100
of Structural Steelwork, 56
Service Department Publications (N.P.), 99, 158, 222
Services :
Army, 301
in War, 120, 250
(Emergency Provisions) Act, 22
Bill, 15
See also National Fire Services.
Stops for Timber Roots, 56

Firearms Form, 158
Firebars and Ship Fires, ???
Firemanship, Manual of, 158, 222
Firemen. See Police and Firemen.
Fires, Ship, 222
First to be Freed, 224, 302
First-Aid :
and Nursing for Gas Casualties, 158
for Civil Defence Purposes, Training, 100
in the Royal Navy, 147
Service in Factories, 315
Treatment of Burns, 58
Firth of Forth Area, Classes of Persons permitted to enter, 252
Fisheries. See Agriculture and Fisheries ; Great Lakes Fisheries ; Scottish Fisheries ; International Fisheries ; West India Royal Commission.
Fishing :
Industry. See Inshore Fishing Industry.
Vessels, Reinsurance Agreements, 80, 137, 199
Fitments, Timber Economy, 125, 189
Fitzgerald, M. (Chairman), Departmental Committee on Valuation for Rates, Report, 222
Five-Figure Logarithm Tables, 246
Flags :
Flying of, on Motor Cars, Army, 121
of All Nations, Admiralty Book of, 25
Flags, Badges and Arms of the Dominions, 33, 216
Flanders, Battle of, 68
Lord Gort's Despatches, 54
Flats, Natural Lighting of, 243
Flax :
and Hemp Trade, Wages, 50, 110, 175, 238, 315
and Tow, Spinning and Weaving, Factory Forms, 104, 164
Duck, Specification, 64
See also Home Flax Production.
Flea Beetles, 27
Fleet :
Air Arm, 160, 302
Mediterranean, 224
The Silver Fleet, 177
See also Officers of the Fleet.
Fleming, Lord (Chairman), Committee on Public Schools :
Report, 218
Special Report (Abolition of Tuition Fees in Grant-Aided Secondary Schools), 154

Flesh, Rabbits for, 27
Flexible :
Drive for Engine-Speed Indicator, Specification, 32
Electric :
Cables, Specifications, 64, 122
Cords, Specifications, 64
Paint, Specification, 94
Flies. See Narcissus Flies ; Cabbage Root Fly ; Carrot Fly ; Crane Flies ; Onion Fly ; Greenhouse White Fly ; Bulb Fly ; Wheat Bulb Fly ; Celery Fly ; Mangold Fly.
Flooding, Cases of, in Steel Shelter, 38
Floor Polish Trade, Wages, 50, 110, 175, 238, 315
Floors, Report, 334
Flower. See Artificial Flower.
Fluid for Hydraulic Mechanisms, Specifications, 30, 92
Fly. See references from Flies.
Fly-Catcher, Spotted, 211
Food :
and Agriculture :
Conference :
Final Act. Cmd. 6451, 142
Section Reports. Cmd. 6461, 143
Organisation. See United Nations.
and Drugs (Milk and Dairies) Act, 208
Bill, 191, 202
and its protection against Poison Gas, 36
Consumption Levels in the U.S.A., Canada and U.K., 219
Education Memos., 33, 96
from Overseas, 35
from the Garden, 26
Insect Pests of, 298
Investigation Board Publications (N.P.), 57, 114, 179, 243, 320
Labelling and Advertising of. Cmd. 6482, 144
Ministry of, Publications (N.P.), 36, 97, 155, 219, 298
Preserving Trade, Wages, 52, 111, 175, 239, 315
Prices, Retail List of, 97
Production. See Wireworms.
Situation. 1943. India. Cmd. 6479, 143
Yeast, Nutritive Value, 319
Your Baby's, in Wartime, 101
See also Wartime Food ; Imported Food.

Foods included in " Points " Rationing Scheme, List of, 97
Foot Rot in Sheep, 27
Footwear :
Lists of Manufacturers, 61, 118, 182, 246, 325
Rationing, 34, 35, 36, 59, 96, 97, 154, 155, 217, 218, 296
Answers to Questions on, 60, 118
See also Utility Footwear.
Forces :
Additional Financial Benefits in respect of Service in the Far East. Cmd. 6553, 206
below Officer Rank, Allowances, Pensions, Gratuities, etc. Cmd. 6715, 281
Increased Financial Provision for Members of. Cmd. 6581, 204
Postal Voting for, Report. Cmd. 6581, 273
Retired Pay, Pensions and other Grants Cmd. 6558, 206
War Pensions, Improvement in. Cmd. 6514, 181
See also Military Forces ; Naval Forces ; Troops.
Foreign :
Currencies, Treasury Notice, 240
Ministers, Establishment of a Council of (Berlin Conference). Cmd. 6689, 279
Office Publications (N.P.), 156, 219, 298
Service :
Act, 145
Bill, 128, 139
Reform of the. Cmd. 6420, 141
Services, Civil Estimates, 7, 74, 132, 195, 261
Forest :
of Dean Coal and Iron-Ore Field, Geology of, 145
Policy, Post-War, Reports :
Cmd. 6447, 142
Cmd. 6500, 203
Products Research Publications (N.P.), 57, 179, 320
Forestry :
Act, 282
Bill, 256, 265, 266, 270, 271
Careers, 306
Commission Publications (N.P.), 299
See also West India Royal Commission.
Forgings, Specifications, 29, 91, 92, 93

Formulary :
  for use in Military Hospitals, 121
  National War, 37, 157, 301
Forster, Sir J. (Chairman), Committee on the Recruitment of Juveniles into the Coal Mining Industry :
  Report, 98
  Supplemental Report, 156
Fougasse, The Little Less, 39
Foul Brood, 27, 90, 211
Foundries. *See* Steel Foundries.
Four-Figure Tables and Constants for the use of Students, 35
France :
  Agreements with U.K. :
    Financial. *Cmd. 6613*, 275
    Industrial, Literary and Artistic Property. *Cmd. 6674*, 278
    Money and Property. *Cmd. 6675*, 278
  Relief from Double Taxation. *Cmd. 6692*, 280
  Despatch to H.M. Ambassador in Paris. *Cmd. 6662*, 278
Franchise. *See* Indian Franchise.
Fraser, Sir John (Chairman), Medical Advisory Committee (Scotland), Report on Venereal Diseases. *Cmd. 6518*, 204
Fraud, Prevention of (Investments), 327
Freedom in the Air, There's, 224
Freight Ships :
  Conveyance of Explosives in, 125, 188, 253
  Sea Transport Service Regs., 125
French :
  Chalk, etc., Specifications, 94
  Equatorial Africa, Commercial and Economic Relations with U.K. :
    Cmd. 6281, 19
    Cmd. 6346, 82
French, Sir H. (Chairman), Conference on Post-War Loaf, Report. *Cmd. 6701*, 280
Frequency and Power-Factor Meters, Specification, 121
Friendly Societies :
  Accounts, 62, 120, 184, 249, 299
  Registry of, Publications (N.P.), 36, 97, 156, 219, 299
  Savings Banks and Friendly Societies Accounts, 329
Frit Fly, 148
Front Line, 101, 224, 302
Fruit :
  Crops, Manuring, in Wartime, 26

Fruit (*continued*) :
  Domestic Preservation of, 148
  from the Garden, 89
Tree :
  Capsid Bugs, 89
  Red Spider, 26
Trees :
  Silver Leaf Disease, 90
  See also Stone Fruit Trees.
Fruits :
  Tree, 211
  See also Bush Fruits ; Dried Fruits.
Fuel :
  Allowances, Army, 184
  and Light Allowances, Army, 250
  and Power :
    Ministry of :
      Act, 282
      Bill, 256, 270
      Publications (N.P.), 98, 156, 220, 299
      Report on, 135
      Statistical Digest : *Cmd. 6538*, 205
        Cmd. 6639, 276
  Efficient Use of, 220
  Installations. *See* Solid Fuel Installations.
  Rationing Report. *Cmd. 6352*, 82
  Research Board Publications (N.P.), 115, 243
  See also Patent Fuel.
Fumigation :
  of Buildings. *See* Hydrogen Cyanide.
  with Hydrocyanic Acid Gas, 27
Fundamental Stars, Apparent Places of, 25, 88, 147, 210, 285
Funeral Expenses of Officers, Army, whose deaths result from Enemy Action, 64
Fur :
  Apparel, List of Manufacturers, 61, 118, 182, 246, 325
  Rabbits for, 27
  Trade, Wages, 51, 239
Furness Abbey, Guide to, 188
Furnished Houses :
  (Rent Control) Bill, 269, 272
  Rent of Furnished Houses Control (Scotland) Act, 145
    Bill, 129, 140
Furnishings. *See* Household Furnishings.
Furniture :
  Manufacturing Trade, Wages, 50, 51, 110
  See also Coffin Furniture ; Utility Furniture.

Further Education in County Colleges, 296
Fustian Cutting Trade, Wages, 50
Fyfe, W. Hamilton (Chairman), Advisory Council on Education, Reports :
  Compulsory Day Continuation Classes, 180
  Special Committee. *Cmd. 6593*, 274

G
Gall. *See* Crown Gall.
Galvanised Domestic Utensils, Specification, 122
Games, Shoes for, 245
Gangrene, Gas, Notes on, 178
Garden :
  Food from the, 26
  Preserves from the, 26
  See also Vegetable Garden.
Gardening. *See* Kitchen Gardening.
Garments. *See* Knitted Cloths, etc.
Garrett, A. W. (Chairman), Committee appointed to consider methods of suppression and removal of dust containing silica in the Pottery Industry, Report, 175
Garrison and Regimental Institutes, Conduct of, Army, 64, 121
Gas :
  and Chemical Engineering, Careers, 306
  Casualties, First Aid and Nursing, 158
  Detection and Identification Service, 38, 223
  Fund Accounts, 61, 119, 183, 220, 299
  Gangrene, Notes on, 178
  Industry, Report. *Cmd. 6699*, 280
  Installations, Report, 254
  Producer, Government Utility, Instruction Book, 188
  See also Hydrocyanic Acid Gas ; Poison Gas ; War Gases ; Toxic Gases ; Acetylene Gas ; Anti-Gas ; Blister Gas ; Commercial Gas ; Liquefiable Gases ; South Suburban Gas.
Gas-contaminated Persons, Treatment of, 37
" Gascoigne " Auto-Releaser Milking Plant, 88
Gassing Risks in the Cleaning, etc., of Stills, Tanks, etc., Factory Form, 228

Gastritis, Parasitic, in Sheep, 211
Gateshead. *See* Newcastle and Gateshead ; Newcastle-upon-Tyne.
Gauge Making and Measuring, Notes on, 115
Gauges, Screw, Notes on, 243
Geese, 26
  Rearing of, 148
Gels, Swelling Stresses in, 320
General :
  Merchandise Quotas, 119
  Service Corps, Army, Formation of, 121
  Waste Materials Reclamation Trade, Wages, 51, 175, 238
Geological Survey and Museum Publications (N.P.), 57, 115, 320
Geophysical Memoirs, 240
George VI :
  Birthday Honours. *See* London Gazette.
  Correspondence with Prime Minister on Conquest of Sicily, 187
  Message :
    to the Forces, 332
    to the Home Guard, 186, 251
  Speech to Parliament, 3, 70, 129, 193, 257
German :
  Anti-Personnel Bomb, Instructional Diagram, 223
  Atrocities, Molotov Notes on, 101
  Capital, Penetration of, into Europe, 101, 160
  Documents seized during raid on Lofoten Islands. *Cmd. 6270*, 18
  Military Terms and Abbreviations, Vocabulary of, 185
Germany :
  Denmark's Fight against, 295
  Joint action in the War against ; Agreement between Soviet Union and U.K. *Cmd. 6304*, 20
  Target, Germany, 219
  Treaty for an Alliance in the War against Hitlerite Germany, etc., between U.S.S.R. and U.K. :
    Cmd. 6368, 83
    Cmd. 6376, 83
  Unconditional Surrender of. *Cmd. 6648*, 277
Gill, C. L. (Chairman), Committee convened by the R.I.B.A., Report (Walls, Floors and Roofs), 334
Gillingham Corporation Act, 209

Girls :
  Registration of, 96, 97
  Training and Service for, 97
Girls' Apparel, Clothing, Utility Clothing, etc., Prices, etc., 183, 247, 248, 326, 328
Glasgow :
  Dock Labour in, Explanatory Memo., 68
  See also Port Glasgow.
Glass. *See* Safety Glass ; Bullet-Proof Safety Glass ; Plane Safety Glass.
Glentrool, National Forest Park Committee Report, 299
Glider Pilot Regiment and Parachute Regiment, Formation of, 121
Glossary, Meteorological, 177
Gloucester, Duchess of, Birth of a Son, 54
Gloves :
  Board of Trade Publications (N.P.), 61, 118, 182, 246, 325
  Schedules, 249, 328
  Specifications, 65
  Rubber, Anti-Gas, 122
  See also Knitted Goods.
Glycol. *See* Ethylene Glycol.
Goat Hair, Processes, Factory Form, 164
Goddard, Lord Justice :
  Hereford Juvenile Court Inquiry, Report of Tribunal. *Cmd. 6485*, 144
  Procedure at a Case heard at Longton, Report, 301
Good :
  Conduct Pay, Army, 66, 123, 124
  Fare in Wartime, 35, 96
Goodenough, Sir William (Chairman), Medical Schools Committee, Report, 221
Goodrich Castle, Guide to, 188
Goods :
  and Services (Price Control) Act, 23
    Bill, 2, 15
  Control of Export, List of Goods, 61
    Traffic. *See* Road Goods Traffic.
Gooseberries, 27
  Die-back Disease of, 90
Gooseberry :
  Aphides, 148
  Cluster-Cup Rust, 90
  Mildew, American, 90
  Red Spider, 27
  Sawfly, 89
Gort, Lord, Despatches, 54
Gosport Water Act, 23
Government :
  Chemist, Publications (N.P.), 157

Government (*continued*) :
  Contracts in Scotland, Report. *Cmd. 6393*, 84
  Control of Railways :
    Estimates of pooled revenue, etc., *Cmd. 6252*, 16
    Financial Arrangements. *Cmd. 6314*, 21
  Department Specifications. *See* Specifications.
  Departments :
    Staffs employed in. *Cmd. 6718*, 281
    Trading or Commercial Services, Accounts, 5, 72, 130
  Evacuation Scheme, Hostels for Children, 116
  Explosives, Conveyance of, Ministry of War Transport Publications (N.P.), 125, 188, 253
  of Burma :
    Act, 1935, as amended, 283
    (Temporary Provisions) Act, 282
      Bill, 271
  of India Act, 1935, as amended, 146
  Publications, Consolidated List, 60, 117, 181, 245, 323
  Surplus Stores, Disposal of. *Cmd. 6539*, 205
  Utility Gas Producer, Instruction Book, 188
  See also Local Government.
Graham, Robert, of Fintry, MSS., 113
Grain :
  Cargoes, 59
  Weevils, 90
Grammar Schools, 296, 298
Grampian Electricity :
  (Argyll) Special Order, 60
  Supply Order Confirmation Bill, 15
Grand Union Canal Act, 146
Grant-Aided Secondary Schools, Abolition of Tuition Fees in, Special Report, 154
Grants. *See* Adult Education Grants.
Graphited Wax, Specification, 93
Grass, Root and Vegetable Seed Crops, Threshing of, 286
Gratuities. *See* Forces.
Graves. *See* Imperial War Graves.
Great :
  Lakes Fisheries, Establishment of a Board of Enquiry for, U.S.A. and Canada. *Cmd. 6273*, 18
  Lakes—St. Lawrence Basin, Exchange of Notes between U.S.A. and Canada. *Cmd. 6303*, 20

Great (*continued*) :
  War, History of, 39
  Western Railway :
    (Air Transport) Act (1928–9), 283
    (Superannuation) Fund Act, 24
    (Variation of Directors Qualification) Act, 24
Greater London Plan, 325
Greece :
  and Crete, Campaign in, 101, 159
  Relations of Learning and Culture, Convention with U.K. *Cmd. 6250*, 16
  Situation in. *Cmd. 6592*, 274
Green Manuring, 90
Greene, Rt. Hon. Lord (Chairman), Board of Investigation into Coal Mining Industry, Wages Issue, 104
  Supplemental Report, 104
Greenhouse White Fly, 27
Greenock :
  Dock Labour in, Explanatory Memo., 68
  Port and Harbours Order Confirmation Acts :
    1941, 24
      Bill, 2, 15
    1943, 146
      Bill, 139
Greenwich Hospital and Travers Foundation :
  Accounts, 11, 77, 135, 198, 265
  Estimated Income and Expenditure, 13, 77, 135, 199, 267
Grey Squirrels, 26, 89, 148
Grinding of Cutlery and Edge Tools Regs., Factory Form, 43
Groceries and Provisions, Retail Controlled Prices, 219, 286
Growing Children, Wartime Food for, 16
Growmore Bulletins, 26, 89, 148, 211, 286
Guardianship (Refugee Children) Act, 207
  Bill, 129
Guaranteed Wage Levy, Coal Mines, Explanatory Memo. *Cmd. 6278*, 18
Guarantees. *See* Export Guarantees.
Guillotines and Shears, 307
Guppy, E. M., Rock Wool, 320
Gyro-Compass, Admiralty (Sperry Type), Manual of, 88

H
Hacksaw Blades, Specification, 64
Haemoglobin Levels in Great Britain, 319

Hailey, Lord (Chairman), Colonial Research Committee, Progress Report. *Cmd. 6496*, 144
Hair. *See* Camel Hair ; Goat Hair.
Halcrow, Sir W., Report on Severn Barrage Scheme, 300
Halifax, Viscount, H.M. Ambassador to Washington, Speech. *Cmd. 6264*, 17
Halnan, E. T. :
  Scientific Principles of Poultry Breeding, 211
  Wartime Poultry Feeding, 89
Hammers, Specification, 64
  See also Drop Hammers.
Hammond, J., Fertility and Animal Breeding, 148
Hamp, S. (Chairman), Business Buildings Committee, Report, 334
Hampton Court Palace, Guide to, 188
Hams, Home Curing of, 27, 211, 286
Hancock, Miss Florence, Report on Post-war Organisation of Private Domestic Employment. *Cmd. 6650*, 277
Hand-Knitting Yarn, List of Manufacturers, 61, 182, 247, 325
Handicapped :
  Children (Form of Certificate) Order, 322
  Pupils and Medical Services Regs., 296
Handkerchief Trade, Wages, 50, 110, 239
Hankey, Lord (Chairman) :
  Committee on Imperial Agricultural Bureaux, Report, 159
  Higher Appointments Committee, Report. *Cmd. 6576*, 273
  Television Committee, Report, 318
" Hanovia " Ultra-Violet Water Steriliser, 25
" Hansard " *See* Parliamentary Debates.
Harbour Dues, Isle of Man, Accounts, 62
Hardknott, National Forest Park Committee, Report, 299
Harlech Castle, Guide, 334
Harrogate Provisional Order Confirmation Act, 146
  Bill, 139
Hart, P. D'Arcy, Mass Miniature Radiography of Civilians, etc., 319
Hat, Cap and Millinery Trade Wages, 51, 110
Hatching, 26
Haulage. *See* Road Haulage.
Hawfinch and Bullfinch, 149
Hay, Ian, Battle of Flanders, 68

HEA—   INDEX 1941-45

Head :
  Injury, Cases of, Glossary of Psycho-
    logical Terms used in, 56
  Lice, Control of, 157
Heads of Public Departments, List of, 60
Headwear, Lists of Manufacturers, etc.,
  118, 182, 246, 325
Health :
  and Industrial Efficiency, Scottish
    Experiments, 180
  and Welfare of Women in War
    Factories, Report, 130
  Civil Estimates, 8, 74, 132, 195, 261
  Department, for Scotland :
    Publications (N.P.), 58, 116, 180,
      244, 321
    Summary Reports :
      Cmd. 6308, 20
      Cmd. 6372, 83
      Cmd. 6462, 143
      Cmd. 6545, 206
      Cmd. 6661, 277
  Education, Suggestions on, 155
  Hints, Simple, 96
  Insurance. See National Health
    Insurance.
  Ministry of :
    Publications (N.P.), 37, 99, 157,
      221, 300
    Summary Reports :
      Cmd. 6340, 81
      Cmd. 6394, 84
      Cmd. 6468, 143
      Cmd. 6562, 207
      Cmd. 6710, 281
  Register, Factory Form, 228
  Research in Industry, 318
  Welsh Department of, Publications
    (N.P.), 158, 222, 301
  See also Industrial Health ; National
    Health Service ; Public Health ;
    Local Government and Public
    Health.
Heat-Treated Milk :
  Phosphatased Test for, 157
  (Prescribed Tests) Order, 221
Heating, 179
Hedge and Tree-Stump Clearing, 88
Helmets, Fencing, Specification, 64
Helmsley Castle, Guide to, 188
Hemp. See Flax and Hemp.
Henderson, W. C. (Chairman), Retail
  Trade Committee, Reports, 62, 119
Herbs. See Culinary Herbs ; Medicinal
  Herbs.

Hereford Juvenile Court Enquiry,
  Report. Cmd. 6485, 144
Herring :
  Fund Advances Accounts, 6, 73, 130,
    137, 259
  Industry :
    Act, 208
    Bill, 202
    Committee on, Report. Cmd.
      6503, 204
    Scheme, 1935, Amending Scheme,
      323
Herts and Essex Water Act, 209
Hetherington, Sir H. (Chairman) :
  Committee on Minimum Wages,
    etc., in connection with Special
    Arrangements for Domestic Help,
    Report. Cmd. 6481, 144
  Committee on Post-War Hospitals
    in Scotland, Report. Cmd. 6472,
    143
  Royal Commission on Workmen's
    Compensation, Report. Cmd. 6588,
    273
Heyworth, G. (Chairman), Gas Industry
  Committee, Report. Cmd. 6699, 280
Hides :
  and Leather, Specification, 64
  and Skins, Regs., Factory Form, 43
Higgins, A. E. H., Control of Insects
  infesting Dried Fruits, 114
High :
  Altitude Controls Lubricant, Speci-
    fication, 94
  Court. See Supreme Court.
  Earnings, Instances of, Report, 263
  Explosive Instructional Diagrams,
    223
  Tensile Cold Headed Bolts, Specifi-
    tion, 92
Higher :
  Appointments, Report. Cmd. 6576,
    273
  Education :
    in the Colonies. Cmd. 6647, 277
    in West Africa. Cmd. 6655, 277
    in West Indies. Cmd. 6654, 277
    Technological, Report, 096
  National Certificates, Board of Edu-
    cation Publications (N.P.), 35
Highland :
  Division, 101, 160
  Regiment, Formation of, 123
Hill Sheep Farming :
  in England and Wales. Cmd. 6498, 203
  in Scotland. Cmd. 6494, 203

Hindley, Sir C. (Chairman), Codes of
  Practice Committee for Civil Engineer-
  ing, etc., Reports, 189
Hinton, H. E., Insect Pests of Food, 219,
  298
His Majesty's :
  Forces. See Forces.
  Minesweepers, 160, 224, 303
  Submarines, 303
Historic Buildings. See Ancient Monu-
  ments.
Historical Manuscripts Commission Pub-
  lications (N.P.), 112
Hogs Mill River. See Land Drainage.
Hoists, Precautions in the Installation
  and Working of, Factory Forms, 164,
  228
Holidays :
  Staggering of, Report, 306
  with Pay, Trade Board Orders, 50,
    111, 176, 239
Hollow-Ware :
  Scheme for ensuring Fair Shares of
    Supplies to Small Retailers, 119
  Trade, Wages, 50, 110, 175, 238
Home :
  Department, Civil Estimates, 7, 74,
    132, 195, 261
  Flax Production, Report, 134
  Guard :
    Administration and Cost of, 200
    Disabled, etc., Pensions. Cmd.
      6326, 22
    Measures to be provided for by
      Defence Regs. Cmd. 6325, 23
    Pensions and other Grants for
      Members :
        Cmd. 6449, 142
        Cmd. 6536, 204
        Cmd. 6558, 206
    War Office Publications (N.P.),
      65, 121, 186, 251, 331
    See also Ulster Home Guard.
  Office Publications (N.P.), 37, 99,
    158, 222, 301
  Security, Ministry of, Publications
    (N.P.), 38, 99, 158, 222, 302
  Trade :
    Limitation of, Textiles Memo., 61
    Register, Lists of Persons, 61,
      119, 183, 248, 327
Home-Curing of Bacon and Hams, 27
Home-Grown Timbers, Handbook, 57
Homeless, Care of the, 99, 116, 221
Homes, Planning our New, 244

Honours, Birthday and New Year. See
  London Gazette.
Hook and Eye Trade, Wages. 51, 111,
  176, 239
" Hoose " in Calves, 211
Horizontal Milling Machines Regs.,
  Factory Form, 43
Horticulture, Careers, 305
" Hortvet " Test of Milk, Report, 321
Hose. See Rubber Hose.
Hospital :
  Administration, Careers, 306
  Clothing, Specifications, 65, 122
  Infection of Wounds, Prevention of,
    56
  Problems. See Post-War Hospital
    Problems.
  Rehabilitation Department, Organi-
    sation of, Memo., 157
  Treatment of Burns, 116
Hospitals :
  Control of Cross Infection in, 242
  Staffing the, 301
  Surveys of Services, 300
  See also Mental Hospitals ; Emerg-
    ency Hospitals ; Military Hospitals.
Hostages, Axis System of, 101, 159
Hostels :
  for Children, 116
  Allocation of dried separated
    milk, 34
  for " Difficult " Children, 221
Hours of Work, Lost Time, and Labour
  Wastage, 113
House :
  Construction, Report, 253
  Mice, Notes on, 285
  of Commons :
    Bills, 11, 80, 138, 202, 270
    Bills, Reports, Estimates, etc.,
      Lists of, 4, 71, 129, 193
    Conduct of a Member, Select
      Committee on, Report, 11
    Disqualification (Temporary Pro-
      visions) Acts :
        1941, 22
        Bill, 15
        1942, 145
        Bill, 139
      1944, 208
        Bill, 190, 202
    Return of Certificates, 262
    Kitchen and Refreshment Rooms,
      Reports, 11, 75, 134, 197, 264
    Library, Select Committee
      Reports, 265, 268

House (continued) :
  of Commons (continued) :
    Members :
      Fund Accounts, 12, 73, 131,
        194, 261
      General Financial Position,
        199
    Offices or places of profit under
      the Crown, Select Commit-
      tee on, Minutes of Evidence,
      13
    Ministers of the Crown and House
      of Commons Disqualification
      Act, 86
      Bill, 80
    Papers and Debates, 4, 71, 129,
      193, 239
    Privileges, Committee of,
      Reports, 12
    Procedure, Select Committee
      Reports, 267
    Public Business, 79
    Rebuilding, Minutes of Evidence
      and Report, 200
    (Redistribution of Seats) Act, 208
      Bill, 192, 203
      See also Electoral Reform.
    Sessional Printed Papers, 4, 71,
      130, 193, 259
    Standing Orders, 78, 263
  of Lords :
    Journals, 1, 69, 126, 190, 255
    List and Roll of the Lords Spiritual
      and Temporal, 2, 3, 126, 190,
      255, 257
    Offices, Select Committee on,
      Reports, 2, 69, 71, 127, 128,
      129, 191, 192, 193, 255, 256,
      257, 258
    Papers, Bills, Debates, 1, 69, 129,
      190, 255
    Private Bills, etc., Select Com-
      mittee appointed to consider
      cost of, Report, 128
    Procedure, Select Committee on,
      Reports, 69, 127, 128
Household :
  Furnishings, Traders' Leaflet, 248
  Goods :
    Trade, Wages, 50, 239
    See also Linen and Cotton Hand-
      kerchief.
  Textiles, Board of Trade Publica-
    tions (N.P.), 119, 326
Houses :
  Natural Lighting of, 243

Houses (continued) :
  of Parliament :
    Members serving in H.M. Forces.
      Cmd. 6366, 17
    See also House of Commons ;
      House of Lords ; Palace of
      Westminster ; Parliament.
  Selling Price of, Report. Cmd. 6670,
    279
  See also Bomb-damaged Houses ;
    Furnished Houses ; Demonstra-
    tion Houses ; New Houses.
Housing. Cmd. 6609, 275
  Act, 1914, Account, 5, 120, 184, 249,
    329
  Acts, etc., Interest on Loans, 37
  (Agricultural Population) (Scotland)
    Act, 145
    Bill, 139
  Contracts, Progress Charts for, 334
  Estates, Municipal, Management of,
    300
  Management, Careers, 306
  Manual, 253
  Private (Rural Workers) :
    Act, 1942, 86
    (Amendment) Bill, 1945, 271
    (Scotland) Act, 208
      Bill, 192
  Sites, Advance Preparation of, 246
  Society, Annual Return Forms, 36,
    98, 156
  (Temporary Accommodation) Act,
    208
    Bill, 192, 202, 203
  Temporary Programme. Cmd. 6686.
    Bill, 202
  (Temporary Provisions) Act, 208
    Bill, 202
  Work of the Ministry of Aircraft
    Production, 78
  See also Rural Housing ; Building
    Materials.
How to keep well in Wartime, 160
Howes, H., Ducks and Geese, 26
Hughes, D. E. R., A Study of Variations
  in Output, 264
Hungary, Notification of State of War
  54
" Husk " or " Hoose " in Calves, 211
Hydraulic Mechanisms, Fluid for, Speci-
  fication, 30
Hydrocarbon Oil Duties, Report. Cmd.
  6616, 275

Hydrocyanic Acid Gas, Fumigation
  with 27
Hydro-Electric (Scotland) :
  Development (Scotland) :
    Act, 145,
    Bill, 128, 138, 139, 140
    Committee Report. Cmd. 6406,
      85
  Constructional Schemes :
    No. 1, Explanatory Memo.
      Cmd. 6606, 274
    No. 2, Confirmation Order, 279
      Explanatory Memo. Cmd.
        6660, 277
    No. 3, Confirmation Order,
      323
      Explanatory Memo. Cmd.
        6691, 279
  Undertakings :
    in Scotland, Report. Cmd. 6526,
      205
    (Valuation for Rating) (Scotland)
      Act, 282
      Bill, 203, 256, 263, 266, 270
Hydrogen :
  Cyanide :
    Fumigation of Buildings Regs.,
      Forms, 99
    Vapour, Detection of, 115
  Sulphide, Detection of, 179
Hygiene and Sanitation, Army Manual
  of, 65
Hygrometric Tables, 177

I

Icy Roads, Salt Treatment for, 57
Illumination and Visual Efficiency, Rela-
  tion between, 318
Imperial :
  Agricultural Bureaux Publications
    (N.P.), 38, 100, 159, 223, 302
  Defence Committee Publications
    (N.P.), 39
  Economic Committee, Annual
    Report, 39
  Services, Civil Estimates, 7, 74, 132,
    195, 261
  War Graves Commission Publica-
    tions (N.P.), 39, 100, 223, 302
Import :
  and Export List, 96
  Restrictions, Debts Clearing Offices,
    Accounts, 195, 260
  Trade of the U.K., Accounts, 327

Imported Food Certificate, 221
Ince, Sir G. H (Chairman), Committee
  on Juvenile Employment Service,
  Report, 307
Incendiary Bombs and Fire Precautions,
  100
Incident Control (A.R.P.), 223
Income Tax :
  Act, 282
    Bill, 257, 270, 271
  Dominions, 39
  (Employments) Act, 145
    Bill, 129
  Extra-Statutory Wartime Conces-
    sions. Cmd. 6659, 206
  Inland Revenue Publications (N.P.),
    39, 101, 160, 224, 303
  (Offices and Employments) Act, 208
    Bill, 190, 202
  on Rent Allowances, Police Report,
    302
  Quiz for Wage Earners, 101
Incumbents (Disability) Measure. 256
Indemnity. See National Fire Services.
India :
  and Burma :
    (Postponement of Elections) Act,
      23
      Bill, 3
    (Temporary and Miscellaneous
      Provisions) Act, 86
      Bill, 81
    and the War. Text of Announce-
      ment. Cmd. 6293, 19
    (Attachment of States) Act, 208
      Bill, 190
    British Expenditure in, Report, 264
    Budget Speech, 223
    Central. See Bombay.
    (Estate Duty) Act, 282
      Bill, 255
    (Federal Court Judges) Act, 86
      Bill, 3, 4, 16
    Food Situation. 1943. Cmd. 6472,
      143
    Lord Privy Seal's Mission, Statement
      and Draft Declaration. Cmd. 6350,
      82
    (Miscellaneous Provisions) Act, 208
      Bill, 191, 202
    Navy, Examinations, 32, 33, 95
    Office Publications (N.P.), 223, 302
    (Proclamations of Emergency) Bill,
      258, 272

IND—   *INDEX 1941-45*   *INDEX 1941-45*   **—JAM**

India (continued):
Relinquishment of Extra-Territorial Rights in China, Treaty with U.K. and China:
Cmd. 6417, 140
Cmd. 6456, 142
Statement:
of Policy of H.M. Government. Cmd. 6652, 277
on the Congress Party's Responsibility for the Disturbances in India, 1942-43. Cmd. 6430, 141
Welfare of Troops in India Command, etc., Report. Cmd. 6578, 207
See also British India; East India; Government of India.
Indian:
Divorce Act, 283
Bill, 257, 271
Finance Acts, 199, 265
Franchise Act, 283
Bill, 257, 271
Navy. See Royal Indian Navy.
Troops in North Africa, Story of, 223
Indiarubber Regs., Factory Form, 104
Indicating Ammeters, Voltmeters, etc., Specification, 121
Indies. See Netherlands East Indies; West Indies.
Industrial:
Assurance, Manpower in, Committee on, Report. Cmd. 6402, 85
Court Awards, 43, 104, 228, 307
Courts, Reports of Courts of Inquiry:
Cmd. 6474, 143
Cmd. 6493, 144
Cmd. 6499, 203
Dermatitis, Factory Forms, 164
Design, Council of, Publications (N.P.), 302
Disease, Factory Form, 164
Efficiency. See Health and Industrial Efficiency.
Health:
and Efficiency Pamphlets, 178, 242
Conference, Report of Proceedings, 165
Research Board Publications (N.P.), 113, 178, 242, 318
Injuries. See National Insurance.
Injury Insurance Schemes. Cmd. 6551, 206
Overalls, Prices, etc., 248, 326
Policy, Statement. Cmd. 6294, 19

Industrial (continued):
Relations Handbook, 229
Research. See Scientific and Industrial Research.
Workers:
Weekly Expenditure, 52
Weight Lifting by, 238
Industry:
and Commerce, Careers, 306
Civil Estimates, 7, 74, 132, 195, 261
Health Research in, 318
Recording of Sickness Absence in, 242
Toxic Gases in, 115, 179
Women in, Sickness among, 318
See also Art and Industry; Distribution of Industry.
Infant Mortality in Scotland, Report, 180
Infants:
and Pre-School Children, Feeding of, 116
Breast Feeding of, 221
Infants' Apparel, Utility Clothing, etc., Board of Trade Publications (N.P.), 183, 248, 326
Infection. See Cross Infection; Hospital Infection.
Infectious Disease, Notification of, Forms, 99, 157
Infestation by Lice, 37
Information, Ministry of:
Publications (N.P.), 39, 100, 223, 302, 159
Wartime Social Survey, 74
See also Polish Ministry of Information.
Ingots, Specifications, 30, 31
Injuries. See Personal Injuries; Arterial Injuries; National Insurance (Industrial Injuries); Diseases and Injuries.
Injury Insurance. See Industrial Injury Insurance.
Inland:
Revenue:
Board of, Publications (N.P.), 39, 101, 160, 227, 303
Duties, Extra-Statutory Wartime Concessions. Cmd. 6559, 206
Transport. See European (Central) Inland Transport.
Insect Pests of Food, 219, 298
Insects infesting Dried Fruit, Control of, 114

Insemination. See Agriculture (Artificial Insemination).
Inshore Fishing Industry Bill, 258, 267, 269, 271
Installations. See Electrical Installations; Gas Installations; Mechanical Installations; Solid Fuel Installations.
Instructors. See Local Instructors.
Instrumental Manual (Air), 28
Instruments. See Service Instruments; Optical Instruments.
Insulating Material, Specifications, 31
Insulation. See Sound Insulation.
Insurance:
Careers, 305
Civil Estimates, 7, 8, 74, 132, 195, 261
Manpower in, Committee on, Report. Cmd. 6402, 85
See also Cunard Insurance; Employers' Liability Insurance; Health and Unemployment Insurance; National Health Insurance; Unemployment Insurance; War Damage Insurance; War Risks Insurance; Social Insurance.
Inter-Allied Meetings held in London, Reports of Proceedings:
Cmd. 6285, 19
Cmd. 6315, 21
International:
Air Transport. Cmd. 6561, 206
Civil Aviation Conference Final Act, etc. Cmd. 6614, 275
Clearing Union, Proposals for. Cmd. 6437, 141
Code of Signals, 188
Exchange Union, Tentative Draft Proposals of Canadian Experts, 154
Fisheries Conference, Final Act. Cmd. 6496, 144
Justice, Report on the future of the Permanent Court of. Cmd. 6531, 205
Labour Conference:
Proposed action:
Cmd. 6407, 85
Cmd. 6475, 143
Cmd. 6702, 280
Reports:
Cmd. 6331, 81
Cmd. 6547, 206
List of Causes of Death, Manual, 241

International (continued):
Monetary Fund, Joint Statement by Experts. Cmd. 6519, 204
Sanitary Convention:
Cmd. 6637, 276
for Aerial Navigation. Cmd. 6638, 276
Invalid Carriage Trade, Wages, 111, 175, 239
Investment Society, Annual Return Form, 36, 98, 156
Investments. See Fraud.
Iran. See Persia.
Iraq:
Commercial Conditions in, 317
Foreign Exchange Requirements, Agreement with U.K. Cmd.6646,277
Ireland. See Northern Ireland.
Irish:
Land Purchase Fund Accounts, 6, 73, 156, 196, 262
Sailors and Soldiers Land Trust Account, 62
Irvine, Sir J. (Chairman), Commission on Higher Education in the Colonies, Report. Cmd. 6654, 277
Irwell Valley Water Board Act, 284
Bill, 270
Isle of Man:
Account of Revenue and Expenditure, 62
(Customs) Acts:
1941, 23
Bill, 15
1942, 86 .
Bill, 80
1943, 145
Bill, 139
1944, 208
Bill, 202
1945 Bill, 258, 272
Defence. See Emergency Powers.
(Detention) Act, 22
Bill, 15
Italian East Africa, Conquest of, 101
Italy:
Armistice with. Cmd. 6693, 280
Debts Clearing Offices Accounts, 7, 72, 130
Works of Art in, Losses and Survivals, 293

J
Jackets, Specifications, 65, 122
Jamaica Constitution, Despatch to the Governor. Cmd. 6427, 141

JAP—   *INDEX 1941-45*   *INDEX 1941-45*   **—LAN**

Japan, Notification of State of War with, 54
Japanese:
Territory, Prisoners of War and Civilians in, Handbook for Relatives, etc., 252
Underground Activities in the Netherlands East Indies, 112
Jeffery, Sir J. (Chairman), Local Government and Public Health Consolidation (Scotland) Committee:
Draft of a Local Government (Scotland) Bill. Cmd. 6477, 143
Report. Cmd. 6476, 143
Jelly, Orange Juice, 296
Jenkins, Arthur, Indemnity Act, 23
Bill, 3, 16
Jerseys, Specification, 122
Jesse, F. Tennyson, Saga of San Demetrio, 101
Jewish Colonisation Association Act, 209
Jews, Persecution of, 160
Joint Planning (War), Organisation for, 82
Joint-Ill in Young Lambs, 89
Jointing:
Mortars for Brickwork, 56
See also Compressed Asbestos Fibre Jointing.
Jones, W. (Chairman), Advisory Committee on the Treatment and Rehabilitation of Coal Miners in the South Wales Region, suffering from Pneumokoniosis, Report, 220
Journalism and Publishing, Careers, 306-
Judicature. See Supreme Court.
Jurors. See Elections and Jurors.
Justice. See International Justice; Law and Justice.
Justices (Supplemental List) Act, 22
Bill, 2, 15
Justices' Clerks, Departmental Committee on, Report. Cmd. 6507, 204
Jute:
Spinning and Weaving, Factory Form, 164
Trade, Wages, 50, 110, 175, 239
Webbing, Specification, 94
Juvenile:
Court Inquiry, Hereford, Report. Cmd. 6485, 144
Employment Service:
Pamphlet, 229
Report, 307
Offenders (Scotland) Circular, 245
Offences, 37, 59

Juveniles:
Problems of Post-War Entry into Employment, 109
Recruitment into Coal Mining Industry, Committee on, Reports, 98, 156

K
Keddie, J. A. G., Congenital Deaf Mutism in Scotland, 321
Keg and Drum Trade, Wages, 51, 110, 111, 175, 239, 315
Kennet, Lord (Chairman):
Calling-up of Civil Servants, Committee on, Interim Report. Cmd. 6301, 20
Man Power in Banking and Allied Businesses and in Ordinary Insurance and in the Industrial Insurance, Committee on, Report. Cmd. 6402, 85
Kent Coalfield, Report, 299
Kerley, P.:
Mass Miniature Radiography of Civilians, etc., 319
Radiological Appearances of Early Pulmonary Tuberculosis, 157
Kestrel, 148
Kiers Regs., Factory Form, 43
Killey, R., Water Problems in Fire Fighting explained, 99
King, Admiral E. J., Commander-in-Chief, U.S. Fleet, Report to Secretary of U.S. Navy, 219
King George VI. See George VI.
King's:
Birthday Honours. See London Gazette.
Regs.:
and Admiralty Instructions, 25, 88, 147, 210, 285
and Air Council Instructions for the R.A.F., 28, 91, 149, 212, 287
for the Army and the Army Reserve, 65, 123, 186, 251, 331
Speech to Parliament. See His Majesty's Speech.
Kitchen:
and Refreshment Rooms. See House of Commons.
Gardening in Scotland, Guide to, 321
Machinery, 125

Knitted:
Apparel, prices, etc., 183, 248
Cloth and Knitwear, List of Manufacturers, 61
Cloths, Garments, etc., Schedules 119, 184
Cotton Drawers, Specification, 64
Goods, Lists of Manufacturers, etc., 118, 182, 246, 325
See also Utility Knitted Goods.
Knitting:
for the Army, 326
Wool, Rationing, 34, 35, 36, 59, 96, 97, 154, 155, 217, 218
Yarn, Board of Trade Publications (N.P.), 60, 325
See also Hand Knitting Yarn.
Knitwear, List of Manufacturers, 61
Kohlrabi, 148
Kultur, Nazi, in Poland, 318

L
Labour:
and National Service, Ministry of, Publications (N.P.), 42, 103, 163, 227, 305
Civil Estimates, 8, 74, 132, 195, 261
Conditions in Ceylon, Mauritius and Malaya, Reports. Cmd. 6423, 141
Conference. See International Labour Conference.
Gazette, 44, 105, 165, 229, 307
in Filling Factories, 12
in the Aircraft Industry, 11
Output of, 12
Problems, 5
Supervision in the Colonial Empire, Report of, 76
Supply of, 76
Wastage, 113
See also Dock Labour; Slave Labour.
Lace, Lists of Manufacturers and Wholesalers, 118, 182
Lackey Moth, 211
Lamb Dysentery, 27
Lambs, "Swayback" in, 27, 286
See also Young Lambs.
Lancashire Cheese, 27
Land:
Acquisition of, (Authorisation Procedure) Bill, 272
Agency, Careers, 306

Land (continued):
and Buildings:
Requisitioning and Compensation, Report. Cmd. 6313, 21
War Damage to, 62, 120, 250
and Housing Society, Annual Return Forms, 36, 98, 156
at War, 303
Change of Ownership, Form, 181
Compulsory Purchase of, Scotland, 322
Drainage:
(Benwick Internal Drainage District) Provisional Order Confirmation Act, 24
Provisional Order Bill, 14, 80 (Scotland) Act, 15, 22
Bill, 1, 15
(Surrey County Council) (Hogs Mill River Improvements) Provisional Order Confirmation Act, 87
Fertility (Research) Fund Accounts, 5, 14, 130, 197, 260
Purchase. See Irish Land Purchase; Supreme Court of Judicature, Northern Ireland.
Registration Forms, 52, 53, 111
Registry Publications (N.P.), 52, 176, 240, 315
Requisitioning. See Land and Buildings above; Landlord and Tenant.
Sale of, for Building Purposes, 324
Settlement in Scotland, Report. Cmd. 6577, 273
Transfer Committee Report. Cmd. 6467, 143
Trust. See Irish Soldiers and Sailors.
Use, Control of. Cmd. 6537, 205
Utilisation of, in the Rural Areas of Scotland, Report. Cmd. 6440, 140
War Damage to, (Scotland) Act, 23
Bill, 3, 15
See also Crown Lands; Requisitioned Land; Settled Land.
Landlord and Tenant:
(Requisitioned Land) Act:
1942, 86
Bill, 16, 69, 80
1944, 207
Bill, 129, 190
(War Damage) (Amendment) Act, 23
Bill, 2, 15
Landrail, 149
Language Teaching in Primary Schools (Wales), 298

Lanolin-Resin :
Finishes, Specifications, 30, 93
Solution, Specifications, 29, 92
Lapwing, 149
Laundry Trade, Wages, 51, 110, 175, 239, 315
Law :
and Justice, Civil Estimates, 7, 74, 132, 195, 261
Careers, 306
Conditions in Occupied Territories, 329
Officers Act, 208
Bill, 202
Reform :
(Contributory Negligence) Act, 282
Bill, 255, 257, 265, 266, 270, 271
(Frustrated Contracts) Act, 145
Bill, 128, 139
See also Electoral Law Reform.
Laws. See Expiring Laws ; Military Law ; Temporary Laws ; Air Force Law ; Company Law ; Acts.
Lea, F. M., Lightweight Concrete Aggregates, 242
Lead Bronze Seal Ring Pots, Specification, 30
Leadership, Youth, Careers, 306
Leaf Spot of Celery, 90
Learning and Culture, Convention, Great Britain and Greece. Cmd. 6250, 16
Leases. See Wartime Leases.
Leather :
or Textile Containers or Straps, Lists of Manufacturers, 183, 247, 326
Specification, 64
Lebanon, Statements of Policy by H.M. Government. Cmd. 6600, 274
Ledingham, Sir J. (Chairman), Committee on Bed - Bug Infestation, Report, 113
Leek Smut, 27
Legal :
Aid and Legal Advice in England and Wales, Report. Cmd. 6641, 276
Proceedings, Convention, Turkey and U.K. Cmd. 6292, 19
Process, Service of, on Forces, 240
Leggings, Specifications, 122
Legislation. See Emergency Legislation ; Private Legislation ; Trading with the Enemy.
Leicester, Atmospheric Pollution in, 319

Leicestershire and South Derbyshire Coalfield, National Coal Resources, 115
Lemon-peeling, Effects on the Skin, Factory Form, 164
Lend-Lease :
Act, Government Policy in connection with the use of materials received under the. Cmd. 6311, 21
Operations. 17th. Report to Congress, 219
Leopard Moth, 149
Liabilities (Wartime Adjustment) :
Act :
1941, 22
Bill, 1, 2, 15
1944, 208
Bill, 191, 192, 203
(Scotland) Act, 282
Bill, 255, 257, 270
Liability Insurance. See Employers' Liability Insurance.
Librarianship, Careers, 306
Libya, First Campaign in, 101
Libyan Campaign, Diary of, 101
Lice :
Head, Control of, 157
Infestation by, 37
Licensed Premises. See War Damaged Licensed Premises.
Licensing :
Act, 1921, State Management Districts, Annual Reports, 4, 71, 130
Planning (Temporary Provisions) Act, 282
Bill, 203, 255, 256, 270
Statistics, Annual Return Forms, 37, 158, 222
Life Blood, 303
Light :
Allowances, Army, 185
See also Fuel and Light Allowances.
Alloy Airscrew Forgings, Specification, 29
Clothing Trade. See Women's Light Clothing.
Metal Trades, Design and the Designer in, 164
Lighthouses. See Clyde Lighthouses.
Lifts, Precautions in the Installation and Working of, Factory Forms, 164, 228
Lighting, 178
See also Buildings ; Road Transport Lighting ; Natural Lighting.
Lightning and Aircraft, 112

Lights :
and Sound Signals, Survey of, 333
Survey, Instructions, 59
Lightweight :
Concrete Aggregates, 242
Silk Fabric, Specifications, 31, 93
Limbs, Artificial, Report, 317
Limitation. See Actions ; Supplies.
Lindsey, Twelfth Earl of, MSS., 113
Linen :
and Cotton Handkerchief Trade, Wages, 50, 110, 239
Fabric and Tape, Specifications, 94
Piece Goods Trade, Wages, 50, 110, 239
Lines, Natural and Tarred, Specification, 122
Linklater, E. :
Defence of Calais, 39, 101
Northern Garrisons, 39
Lipscombe, J. K., Ducks and Geese, 26
Liquefiable Gases, Cylinders for, 320
Liquid :
Manure Tanks, 27
Milk, Supplies for Schools and School Canteens, 34, 36
Little Less, The, 39
Liver Rot in Sheep and Cattle, 90
Liverpool Hydraulic Power Act, 146
Living. See Cost of Living.
Llantrisant Colliery, Explosion at, Report. Cmd. 6328, 81
Load Line :
Certificate Form, 68
Regulations for Vessels engaged in International Voyages on the Great Lakes, U.S.A. and Canada. Cmd. 6302, 20
Loaded Ebonite, Specification, 25
Loading. See Power Loading.
Loaf, Post-War, Report. Cmd. 6701, 280
Loan :
Society, Annual Return Forms, 36, 98, 156
Supplementary Agreement, between Spain and U.K. Cmd. 6267, 18
Loans :
(Postponement of Repayment) Measure, 70, 87
See also Housing, etc., Loans ; Local Loans ; National Loans ; Public Works Loans ; Local Authorities Loans.

Local :
and Private Acts, 23, 87, 146, 208, 283
Authorities Loans Act, 282
Bill, 203, 255, 270
Authority Pensions, Instructions to Pensioners claiming increase, 221
Education Authorities, etc., Clerks of Councils and Authorised Officers, Addresses and Telephone Numbers, 296
Elections :
and Register of Electors (Temporary Provisions) Acts :
1940, 22
1941, 23
Bill, 3, 16
1942, 86
Bill, 81
1943, 145
Bill, 140
Bill (1944), 203
(Service Abroad) Act, 283
Bill, 257, 271
Government :
and Public Health Consolidation (Scotland) Committee :
Draft of a Local Government (Scotland) Bill. Cmd. 6477, 143
Report. Cmd. 6476, 143
(Boundary Commission) Act, 282
Bill, 257, 270
(Financial Provisions) :
Act, 1941, 23
Bill, 15
Bill, 1945, 272
(Scotland) :
Act, 1941, 23
Bill, 15
Bill, 1945, 272
Instructors, Training of, L.A.R.P., 158
Loans Fund Accounts, 6, 73, 131, 195, 261
Revenues, Exchequer Contributions to, Civil Estimates, 7, 8, 74, 132, 133, 195, 261
Location of Retail Businesses Orders, 1941, Explanatory Memo., 61
Locomotives, etc., Regs., Factory Form, 42
Lodging Allowance, Army, 250
Lofoten Islands, Secret German Documents seized during raid on. Cmd. 6270, 18

Log Books, 212
Loganberry, 149
Logarithm Tables, 246
London :
and North Eastern Railway :
Act, 1944, 209
(Air Transport) Act, 1928–29, 283
City of :
Report on Post-War Reconstruction, Observations by Royal Fine Arts Commission, 321
(Various Powers) Act, 283
County Council :
(Money) Acts, 24, 87, 146, 209, 284
Gazette, 53, 111, 176, 240, 316
Greater London Plan, 1944, 325
Hospitals Services of, 300
Passenger Transport Act, 87
Post Office Guide, 55, 112, 177
London, Midland and Scottish Railway :
Act, 1941, 24
Act, 1945, 283
Air Transport Act, 283
Canals Act, 283
Order Confirmation Act, 87
Bill, 81
Long :
Distance Road Goods Traffic. Cmd. 6506, 204
Service Pay, Army, 66, 123, 124
Long-eared Owl and Short-eared Owl, 149
Long-term Agricultural Policy, Principles and Objectives of, Report, 149
Longton, Stoke-on-Trent, Report of Inquiry, 301
Longwall Faces, Power Loading and Roof Control, 229
Lord Chancellor's Department Publications (N.P.), 177, 240, 316
Lords. See House of Lords.
Losses, etc., and Extra-Regulation Expenditure, Army, Powers in relation to, 123
Lost Time and Labour Wastage, 113
Lothian Home Trust (Amendment) (No. 1) Scheme, 1945, 322
Loughborough Corporation Act, 209
Loveday, T. (Chairman) :
Advisory Committee on Agricultural Education, Report, 295
Committee on Veterinary Education in Great Britain, Report. Cmd. 6517, 204

Lovern, J. A. :
Composition of the Depot Fats of Aquatic Animals, 115
Mode of Occurrence of Fatty Acid Derivatives in Living Tissues, 115
Low Temperature Stoving Enamel, Specification, 91
Lowland Regiment, Formation of, 123
Lubricant. See High Altitude Control Lubricant.
Lucerne, 89, 148
Lubrication, Factories (Health and Safety Provisions), Factory Form, 104
Lunacy Act, 1922, 281
Luxmoore, Rt. Hon. Lord Justice (Chairman), Committee on Post-War Agricultural Education in England and Wales, Report. Cmd. 6433, 141
Lythgoe, J. (Chairman), Superannuation Sub-Committee of Nurses and Midwives Salaries Committee, Report. Cmd. 6603, 274

M

MacGregor, Sir A. (Chairman), Sub-Committee of the Scientific Advisory Committee, Report, Freezing Point (Hortvet) Test of Milk, 321
Machine :
Milking, 27
Tools, etc., Safety of, Factory Forms, 164, 228, 307
Machinery. See Agricultural Machinery ; Electrical Machinery.
McIntyre, J. G. (Chairman), Hydro-Electric Undertakings in Scotland, Report. Cmd. 6526, 205
McNair, Sir Arnold (Chairman), Committee on Supply, Recruitment and Training of Teachers and Youth Leaders, Report, 218
McNair, W. L. (Chairman), Committee on Limitation of Actions and Bills of Exchange, Report. Cmd. 6491, 144
MacNeice, L., Meet the U.S. Army, 160
Made-up Textiles Trade, Wages, 111
Maggot. See Sheep Maggot.
Magnesium :
Alloy Bars, Specifications, 29, 92
and Magnesia, Production of, Report, 195
(Grinding of Castings and other Articles) Order, 1943, Factory Form, 164

Magnesium–Aluminium Alloy Sheets and Strips Specifications, 91
Magnesium–Rich Alloy Parts, Protection of, against Corrosion, Specification, 92
Magpie Moth, 89
Maids' Clothing, Prices, etc., 183, 248, 326
Maintained Secondary Schools, Principles of Government in. Cmd. 6523, 205
Major War Criminals. See War Criminals.
Make do and Mend, 160
Malaria nursing in India thank return from Service in Malarious Areas, 68, 187, 251
Malaya, Labour Conditions in, Report. Cmd. 6423, 141
Male Nursing, Careers, 306
Malkin, Sir William (Chairman), International Committee on the Future of the Permanent Court of International Justice, Report. Cmd. 6531, 205
Malta :
Air Battle of, 223
Arms and Flag Badge, 216
East of Malta, West of Suez, 160
Maltese :
Colonial Officers, Powers of Command, 187
Personnel serving with the Malta Signal Company, Pay of, 66
Man, Isle of. See Isle of Man.
Manchester, Dock Labour in. Explanatory Memo., 68
Manganese–Molybdenum Steel, Specification, 29
Manganese–Nickel–Molybdenum Steel, Specification, 31
Mangolds, 149
and Turnips, Storing, 27
Manpower :
Britain's Mobilisation for War, 224
in Banking and Allied Businesses and in Ordinary Insurance and in Industrial Assurance, Committee on, Report. Cmd. 6402, 85
in the Army, 12
Policy, Memo. Cmd. 6324, 21
Re-allocation of :
between Armed Forces and Civilian Employment. Cmd. 6548, 206
between Civilian Employments. Cmd. 6568, 207
Release of R.A.F. Personnel, 287

Manton, S. M., Insect Pests of Food, 298
Manufacture and Supply. Control of, and Limitation of Supplies (Miscellaneous) Quotas, Explanatory Memo., 118
Manure :
Poultry, 211
Seaweed as, 149
Tanks. See Liquid Manure.
Manuring :
Commercial Vegetable Crops in Wartime, 89, 148, 211
Dual Crops in Wartime, 89
See also Green Manuring.
Manuscripts. See Historical Manuscripts.
Manvers Main Colliery, Explosion at, Report. Cmd. 6088, 279
Maps. See Weather Maps.
Marine Transportation and Litigation Agreement between U.S.A. and U.K. Cmd. 6416, 140
Marines :
Examinations, 32, 33, 95, 153
The Royal Marines (Spanish edn.), 303
their Achievements, 1939–43, 224
See also Forces.
Maritime Courts. See Allied Powers.
Markham, Miss V. :
(Chairman), Committee on Amenities and Welfare Conditions in the three Women's Services, Report. Cmd. 6384, 84
Report on Post-War Organisation of Private Domestic Employment. Cmd. 6650, 277
Marquis, Sir F. (now Lord Woolton) (Chairman), Dress Committee of Council for Art and Industry, Report, 302
Marriage :
(Members of His Majesty's Forces) Act, 23
Bill, 3, 16
(Scotland) Act, 86
Bill, 69
Marriages :
Buildings registered for, 55, 113, 177, 241, 318
Provisional :
Order Confirmation Act, 146
Bill, 139
Orders Act, 24
Bill, 2, 15
See also Provisional Orders (Marriages).
Registration. See Registrar-General.
See also Matrimonial Causes.

Married Officers, etc., Army Allowances, 62, 123, 185, 250
Marriott, R. :
  Absenteeism among Women, 178
  A Study of Variations in Output, 242
Marshall, F. H. A., Fertility and Animal Breeding, 148, 286
Mason, M., Preserves from the Garden, 148
Mass :
  Education in African Society, Report, 217
  Miniature Radiography of Civilians for the detection of Pulmonary Tuberculosis, 319
Masters of Transports, Instructions for, 68
Materials :
  Decontamination of, 100, 222
  See also Raw Materials ; Waste Materials.
Maternity Nurses, 58
Matrimonial Causes :
  (Trial in the Provinces) Committee, Report. *Cmd. 6480,* 144
  (War Marriages) Act, 208
  Bill, 192, 203
Matt Pigmented :
  Lanolin-Resin Finishes, Specifications, 30, 93
  Synthetic Resin Primer, Specification, 93
Mauritius, Labour Conditions in, Report. *Cmd. 6423,* 141
Meadow Saffron, 90
Meals. *See* School Meals ; Milk and Meals.
Measurement, Angular and Linear, Circular Dividing Apparatus for, 320
Measures :
  passed by the National Assembly of the Church of England, 24, 87, 146, 209, 284
  See also Weights and Measures.
Mechanical :
  Engineering, Awards of National Certificates and Diplomas to Students at Colleges or Schools for Further Education, 35
  Engineers, Careers, 306
  Installations, Report, 254
Mechanisms. *See* Hydraulic Mechanisms.
Medal, Defence. *See* Campaign Stars.
Medals :
  Grant of, in time of War. *Cmd. 6463,* 143
  War Office Publications, (N.P.), 185

Medical :
  Assistance, Society registered for, Annual Return Forms, 36, 97, 156
  Auxiliary Services, Careers, 306
  Corps, Army, 67, 124, 187, 252, 332
  Diseases in Tropical and Subtropical Areas, 66, 123, 187
  Memoranda, 157
  Personnel (Priority) Committee, Interim Reports, 99
  Practitioners, Women, Army, Pay, etc., 124
  Research Council Publications (N.P.), 56, 113, 178, 242, 318
  Scales, Merchant Vessels, 333
  Schools, Report, 221
  Services :
    Army, Regs., etc., 66, 123, 187, 251, 331
    of the W.R.N.S., A.T.S., and W.A.A.F., 76
    See also Handicapped Pupils ; Emergency Medical Services.
  Subjects, Public Health and, Reports, 221
  Supervision in Factories, Memo., 228
  Treatment and Special Centres, 37
  Use of Sulphonamides, 319
Medicinal :
  Herbs, 26
  Plants, Cultivation of, 88
Medicine :
  and Surgery, Careers, 306
  See also Social Medicine ; War Medicine.
Medicines. *See* Pharmacy and Medicines.
Mediterranean Fleet, 224
Meningococcal Meningitis, Sulphonamides in the treatment of, 244
Men's Clothing, etc., Board of Trade Publications (N.P.), 183, 248, 326
Mental :
  Hospitals, Arrangement, Planning and Construction, 33
  Nurses :
    Reports :
      Cmd. 6488, 144
      Cmd. 6542, 206
      Cmd. 6684, 279
    S.C. Notes, 301
  Nursing, Report, 301
Mercantile Marine :
  Examination of Engineers, 125
  Personnel Scheme, Extension of, 112
  See also Pensions (Mercantile Marine).

Merchant :
  Navy Clothing, Prices, etc., 248
  Shipbuilding and Repairs, 12, 78
Shipping :
  Anti-Gas Precautions, 38, 222
  International Agreement on Co-ordinated Control. *Cmd. 6556,* 206
  Ministry of Shipping and Ministry of War Transport Publications (N.P.), 68, 188, 253, 333
  Vessels, Purchase by Allied Governments from H.M. Government, Memo. *Cmd. 6373,* 83
Merchantmen at War, 303
Mersey Docks and Harbour Board Act, 283
Merseyside, Dock Labour in, Explanatory Memo., 68
Mess Hire Allowances, Army, 250
Metal (Wares) Trade. *See* Light Metal Trades ; Stamped or Pressed Metal Wares.
Metalliferous Mines, Mines and Quarries Form, 157
Metallurgy, Award of National Certificates, 297
Metals. *See* Non-ferrous Metals.
Meteorological Office Publications (N.P.), 54, 112, 177, 240, 316
Meteorology for Aviators, 54, 112
Metropolitan Police :
  Examination, 95
  Reports (Annual) of Commissioner :
    Cmd. 6536, 205
    Cmd. 6627, 276
Mexico, Commercial Conditions in, 317
Mice, Note on, 285
Middle East :
  Air Operations in, 303
  Civil and Military Expenditure in, 265
Middleham Castle, Guide to, 188
Middlesex County Council Act, 283
Midge :
  Chrysanthemum, 211, 286
  Pear, 286
Midland :
  (Amalgamated) Coal Mines Scheme, 54
  Region, Coalfields of, Report, 299
Midlands. *See* East Midlands ; North-West Midlands.
Mid-Wessex Water Acts, 23, 87
Midwifery, Careers, 306

Midwives :
  Salaries :
    Recommendations, 301
    Report of Committee. *Cmd. 6406,* 142
  S.C. Notes, 301
  Superannuation of, Report. *Cmd. 6603,* 274
Migration within the British Commonwealth. *Cmd. 6658,* 277
Mildew. *See* Apple Mildew ; American Gooseberry Mildew ; Downy Mildew.
Military :
  Appointments, 54, 111, 176, 240
  Convention, Ethiopia and U.K. *Cmd. 6334,* 81
  Forces, Disabled etc. Members of, Pay and Pensions, etc. :
    Cmd. 6419, 141
    Cmd. 6473, 143
    Cmd. 6489, 144
  Hospitals, Formulary for use in, 121
  Law, Manual of, 66, 123, 187, 251, 332
  Medal, Efficiency Classification of Soldiers, 185
  Operations, East Africa, 1914–16, 39
  Police, Corps of, Pay, 66
  Railways Rule Book, 123
  Terms and Abbreviations, German, Vocabulary of, 185
Militia Camps, charges made in connection with the Construction of :
  Report by Mr. Justice Simonds. *Cmd. 6271,* 18
  Report of Select Committee on National Expenditure, 9
Milk :
  and Meals, Circulars, 296, 298
  Distributive Trade, Wages, 50, 51, 110, 175, 239
  Freezing Point (Hortvet) Test of, Report, 321
  Heat Treatment of, Circular, 244
  Herds, Veterinary Examination, 157
  in Schools Scheme : Children receiving Milk under, etc. :
    Cmd. 6361, 82
    Cmd. 6366 (Scotland), 83
    Cmd. 6443, 142
    Cmd. 6444, 142
  Keeping Quality of, 99
  Measures to improve the Quality of the Nation's Milk Supply. *Cmd. 6454,* 142
Ministry of Health Circulars, 157

Milk (*continued*) :
  Pasteurisation, 37
  Policy, Memo. *Cmd. 6362,* 82
  Products Factories, Treatment and Disposal of Waste Waters from, 115
  (Special Designations) Regs., 1936–42, 99
  See also Dried Separated Milk ; Liquid Milk ; Ropy Milk ; Heat-treated Milk ; Food and Drugs ; Raw Milk ; School Meals.
Milking :
  Plant, " Gascoigne " Auto-Releaser, 88
  See also Hand and Machine Milking.
Millinery Trade, Wages, 51, 110
Milling Machines :
  Horizontal, Regs., Factory Form, 43
  Safety Precautions, Factory Form, 228
Millipedes and Centipedes, 89
Milne, Lord (Chairman), Central Advisory Water Committee, Report. *Cmd. 6465,* 143
Mineral Deficiencies in Plants, Diagnosis of, 178, 318
Miners. *See* South Wales Coalminers.
Miners' Welfare Commission Publications (N.P.), 317
Mines :
  and Quarries Forms, 55, 98, 157, 220, 300
  Department Publications (N.P.) 54
  Civil Estimates, 8
  Electricity in :
    Circular, 55
    Committee on the Amendment of the General Regs. governing the use of, Report, 55
  Ministry of Fuel and Power Publications (N.P.), 98, 156, 220, 299
  See also Coal Mines ; Metalliferous Mines.
Minesweepers, H.M., 160, 224, 303
Mining :
  Industry (Welfare Fund) Act, 145
  Bill, 129
  People, 317
  See also Coal Mining.
Mining, Gas and Chemical Engineering, Careers, 306
Ministers :
  and Heads of Public Departments, 60
  of the Crown (Transfer of Functions) Bill, 272

Miscellaneous Series :
  1941 :
    No. 1. Inter-Allied Meeting held in London, Report of Proceedings. *Cmd. 6285,* 19
    No. 2. Speech by Rt. Hon. Anthony Eden. *Cmd. 6289,* 19
    No. 3. Inter-Allied Meeting held in London, Report of Proceedings. *Cmd. 6315,* 21
  1942 :
    No. 1. Regulation of Production and Marketing of Sugar. *Cmd. 6395,* 84
  1943 :
    No. 1. Inter-Allied Declaration against Acts of Dispossession in Enemy Occupied Territory. *Cmd. 6418,* 140
    No. 2. Foreign Service, Proposals for Reform of the. *Cmd. 6420,* 141
    No. 3. Food and Agriculture, United Nations Conference, Final Act. *Cmd. 6451,* 142
    No. 4. Food and Agriculture, United Nations Conference, Section Reports. *Cmd. 6461,* 143
    No. 5. International Fisheries Conference, Final Act. *Cmd. 6496,* 144
    No. 6. United Nations Relief and Rehabilitation Administration, Resolutions and Reports. *Cmd. 6497,* 203
  1944 :
    No. 1. Whaling, Protocol on the International Regulation of. *Cmd. 6510,* 204
    No. 2. Report on the future of the Permanent Court of International Justice. *Cmd. 6531,* 205
    No. 3. International Agreement on Principles having reference to the Continuance of Co-ordinated Control of Merchant Shipping. *Cmd. 6556,* 206
    No. 4. Dumbarton Oaks Conversations on World Organisation. *Cmd. 6560,* 206
    No. 5. United Nations Relief and Rehabilitation Administration, Resolutions adopted at Second Session. *Cmd. 6566,* 207

Miscellaneous Series (*continued*) :
  1945 :
    No. 1. Conditions of Armistice with Roumania. *Cmd. 6585,* 273
    No. 2. Conditions of Armistice with Finland. *Cmd. 6586,* 273
    No. 3. Conditions of Armistice with Bulgaria. *Cmd. 6587,* 273
    No. 4. Food and Agriculture Organisation of the United Nations, Documents. *Cmd. 6590,* 274
    No. 5. Crimea Conference, Report. *Cmd. 6598,* 274
    No. 6. International Civil Aviation Conference, Part I, Final Act and Appendices I–IV. *Cmd. 6614,* 275
    No. 7. International Sanitary Convention, 1944. *Cmd. 6637,* 276
    No. 8. International Sanitary Convention for Aerial Navigation. 1944. *Cmd. 6638,* 276
    No. 9. Commentary on the Charter of the United Nations. *Cmd. 6666,* 278
    No. 10. Prosecution and Punishment of War Criminals. *Cmd. 6668,* 278
    No. 11. Agreement establishing the Preparatory Commission of the United Nations. *Cmd. 6669,* 278
    No. 12. United Nations Relief and Rehabilitation Administration, Resolutions adopted by the Council at its Third Session. *Cmd. 6682,* 279
    No. 13. European Central Inland Transport Organisation. *Cmd. 6685,* 279
    No. 14. Establishment of a Council of Foreign Ministers. *Cmd. 6689,* 279
    No. 15. Trade and Employment, Proposals for an International Conference. *Cmd. 6709,* 281
    No. 16. Final Act of United Nations Conference for establishment of an Educational, Scientific and Cultural Organisation. *Cmd. 6911,* 281
Mitchell, G. H., Geology of the country around Wakefield, 57

Mite. *See* Blackcurrant Gall Mite ; Pear leaf Blister Mite ; Tyroglyphid Mites.
Mobilisation and Reconversion (U.S.A.), Problems of, Report, 298
Modern Rabbit Keeping, 26
Mold Gas and Water Provisional Order Confirmation Act, 87
Bill, 70, 80
Mole, The, 211, 286
Molotov Notes on German Atrocities, 101
Monckton, Sir W. :
  (Chairman), Committee on Alternative Remedies (Workmen's Compensation), etc., Reports :
    Cmd. 6580, 273
    Cmd. 6642, 276
  Report on the Boarding Out of Dennis and Terence O'Neill. *Cmd. 6636,* 276
Monetary :
  and Financial Conference. *See* United Nations.
  Belgium and U.K., Agreement. *Cmd. 6557,* 206
  Fund. *See* International Monetary Fund.
Money and the Post-War World, 329
Monmouthshire, Hospital Services of, 301
Monoxide. *See* Carbon Monoxide.
Monuments. *See* Ancient Monuments.
Moore, W. C. :
  Cereal Diseases, 286
  Fungus, Bacterial and other Diseases of Crops, 148
Moore-Brabazon, Lieut.-Col. J. T. C. (Chairman), Severn Barrage Committee, Report, 328
Morbidity Statistics, Provisional Classification of Diseases and Injuries, 242
Morocco, Final Act of Conference concerning the re-establishment of the International Regime in Tangier. *Cmd. 6678,* 279
Morris, Sir Harold (Chairman), Court of Inquiry into Wages and Hours of Work in the Wool-combing Section of the Wool Textile Industry in Yorkshire. Report. *Cmd. 6499,* 203
Morris, J. W. :
  (Chairman) :
    Committee on Selling Price of Houses, Report. *Cmd. 6670,* 278

Morris, J. W. (continued) :
(Chairman) (continued) :
Committee on War-damaged
Licensed Premises and Recon-
struction, Report. Cmd. 6504,
204
Requisitioning of Land and Build-
ings and Compensation, Report.
Cmd. 6313, 21
Mortality. See Infant Mortality.
Mortars. See Jointing Mortars.
Mosaic Disease and Streak of Tomato, 89
Mosquito Nuisances in Great Britain,
Control of, Memo., 157
Moth. See Codling Moth ; Magpie Moth ;
Winter Moths ; Diamond-backed
Moth ; Leopard Moth ; Vapourer
Moth ; Ermine Moths ; Raspberry
Moth ; Lackey Moth.
Mothers and Young Children, Advisory
Committee on, Report, 221
Motion Study, Theory and Application
of, 287
Motor Transport, Civil Defence, 223
Mould. See Tomato Leaf Mould.
Mouldings, Specifications, 30, 93
Moyne, Lord (Chairman), West India
Royal Commission :
Reports : Cmd. 6607, 274 Cmd. 6608,
274
Statement of Action taken on Recom-
mendations. Cmd. 6656, 277
Mozambique Convention of Sept. 11,
1928, as amended, Exchange of
Notes between Portugal and South
Africa. Cmd. 6306, 20
Mule Spinners' Cancer, 306
Municipal Housing Estates, Manage-
ment of, Report, 300
Munro Lectureship Schemes, 244, 323
Munster, Earl of, Report on Welfare of
Troops in India and South East Asia
Commands. Cmd. 6578, 207
Murray, Sir D. King (Chairman), Scot-
tish Coalfields Committee, Report.
Cmd. 6575, 207
Murton Colliery Explosion, Report.
Cmd. 6418, 140
Music, Careers, 306
Mussel Scale, 148
Mustard Beetles, 89
Mutual Aid :
Agreement between U.S.A. and U.K. :
Cmd. 6341, 82 Cmd. 6391, 84
Reports on :
Cmd. 6483, 144 Cmd. 6570, 207

50

N

N.A.A.F.I., 75
Narcissus Flies, 148
National :
Arbitration Tribunal Awards, 44,
105, 165, 229, 308
Certificates :
in Applied Physics, 297
in Metallurgy, 297
Coal Resources, Physical and Chemi-
cal Survey of, 115
Debt :
Annuities Account, 11
Position of certain Funds :
Cmd. 6286, 19
Cmd. 6369, 83
Cmd. 6453, 142
Cmd. 6544, 206
Cmd. 6649, 277
Returns :
Cmd. 6309, 20
Cmd. 6390, 84
Cmd. 6549, 206
Cmd. 6470, 144
Cmd. 6657, 277
Defence Contribution Leaflets, 39,
102, 160, 303
Expenditure, Select Committee on :
Minutes of Proceedings, 4, 13,
129, 193, 259, 265
Reports :
1939-40 :
Departments' replies to
Recommendations, 10
1940-41 :
Departments' Replies to
Recommendations, 12
Work of the Committee, 13
Appointment of a Co-
ordinating Sub-Commit-
tee, 72
Departments' replies to
Recommendations, 72,
77, 78, 80
Membership of Co-ordina-
ting and Investigating
Sub-Committee, 75
Organisation of the Com-
mittee, 80
Work of the Committee,
78
1942-43 :
Departments' Replies to
Recommendations, 134,
135, 137

National (continued) :
Expenditure, Select Committee on
(continued) :
Reports (continued) :
1942-43 (continued) :
Organisation of the Com-
mittee, 138
Work of the Committee,
137
1943-44 :
Departments' Replies to
Recommendations, 197,
199, 201
Examination of National
Expenditure, 200
Work of the Committee,
201
1944-45 :
1st. Organisation of the
Committee, 262
2nd. Release of Requi-
sitioned Land, etc., 263
3rd. Instances of High
Earnings, 263
4th. British Expenditure
in India, 264
5th. Wartime Financial
Arrangements with
British Shipowners, 265
6th. Civil and Military
Expenditure in the
Middle East, 265
7th. Research and
Development, Warlike
Stores, 265
8th. Work of the Com-
mittee, 265
Fire :
Service, 78
Drill Book, 99
Services Regulations (Indemnity)
Act, 208
Bill, 203
Forest Park Committee Reports, 299
Health :
Insurance :
Approved Societies, List of, 99
Civil Estimates, 261
Decisions as to Liability, 99,
221
Fifth Valuation of the Assets
and Liabilities of Approved
Societies, Summary Report.
Cmd. 6455, 142
Funds, Accounts, 8, 9, 72, 73,
131, 133, 195, 196, 262

National (continued) :
Health (continued) :
Service. Cmd. 6502, 204
The Proposals in Brief, 221
Health Insurance Contributory Pen-
sions, and Workmen's Compensa-
tion Act, 23
Bill, 3, 15
Report on Financial Provisions
of Part I of the Bill. Cmd.
6290, 19
Health, Widows', Orphans', and Old
Age Contributory Pensions and
Unemployment Insurance of Per-
sonnel of the R.A.F., 91
Income and Expenditure, Analyses
and Estimates :
Cmd. 6261, 17
Cmd. 6347, 82
Cmd. 6438, 141
Institute of Agricultural Engineering
Publication (N.P.), 317
Insurance :
(Industrial Injuries) Bill, 269,
271, 272
Explanatory Memo. Cmd.
6651, 277
Ministry of, Act, 208
Bill. See Social Insurance.
Loans Acts :
1941, 22
Bill, 15
1942, 86
Bill, 80
1943, 145
Bill, 139
1944, 208
Bill, 202
1945, 282
Bill, 270
Milk Testing and Advisory Scheme,
157
Parks :
in England and Wales, Report.
Cmd. 6628, 276
Scottish, Report. Cmd. 6631, 276
Physical Laboratory Publications
(N.P.), 115, 243, 320
Register, U.K. and Isle of Man,
Statistics of Population, 241
Service :
Acts :
1941, 22
Bill, 2, 15
1941 (No. 2), 23
Bill, 4, 16

51

National (continued) :
Service (continued) ;
Acts (continued) :
1942, 86
Bill, 81
Decisions by the Umpire, 49, 109,
175, 238, 314
(Foreign Countries) Act, 86
Bill, 70, 80
Proclamation, 54
(Release of Conscientious Objec-
tors) Bill, 203, 271
See also Labour and National
Service.
Union of General and Municipal
Workers, Report into a dispute
with Trent Guns and Cartridges
Ltd. Cmd. 6300, 20
War Formulary, 37, 99, 157, 221, 301
Water Policy. Cmd. 6507, 204
Whitley Council Committee Report.
Cmd. 6567, 207
Nationality. See British Nationality.
Nation's Schools, The, 296
Natural Lighting of Houses and Flats,
243
Naturalisation Certificates, Annual
Returns, 10, 75, 132, 136, 259
Nautical Almanac, 35, 88, 147, 210, 285
Naval :
and Marine Forces (Temporary
Release from Service) Act, 22
Architecture, Careers, 306
Auxiliary Personnel Scheme, Exten-
sion of, 112
Awards, 53, 111, 176, 240
Cadetships, Special Entry, Entrance
Examinations, 33, 95
Discipline :
Act, 23
(Amendment) Act, 23
Bill, 2
Forces (Extension of Service) Act, 208
Bill, 129
Service, Release from, 285
Sick Berth Staff, Handbook, 210, 285
Navigation :
Manual, 88
See also Air Navigation.
Navigators. See Civil Aircraft Navi-
gators.
Navy :
Admiralty Publications, 25, 88, 147,
210, 283
and the Y Scheme, 210

Navy (continued) :
Appropriation Account, 6, 73, 131,
194, 260
Estimates, 8, 74, 133, 196, 262
Examinations, 32, 95, 153, 216, 294
List and Appendix, 25, 88, 147, 210,
285
Royal Naval Volunteer Reserve Act,
86
Bill, 69
Votes, 9, 75, 133, 196, 262
See also Fleet ; Forces ; Armed
Co-operation ; Collaboration ; etc.
Forces ; United States Navy ;
Queen Wilhelmina's Navy.
Navy, Army and Air :
Force Institutes, Committee on,
Report, 67
Services, Appropriation Accounts,
10, 76, 134
Nazi Kultur in Poland, 318
Needs, Determination of, Act, 22
Bill, 14
Memo. Cmd. 6247, 16
Report on Administration. Cmd.
6338, 81
See also Pensions and Determination
of Needs ; Supplementary Pen-
sions ; Unemployment Assistance.
Negligence, Contributory. See Law
Reform.
Nelson, Sir G. H. (Chairman), Census of
Production Committee, Report. Cmd.
6687, 279
Nerve Injuries. See Peripheral Nerve
Injuries.
Nest Boxes, 211
Net Trade, Wages, 51, 111, 176, 239, 315
Netherland :
East Indies, A Decade of Japanese
Underground Activities, 112
Government Information Bureau
Publications (N.P.). 112, 177,
241
Netherlands :
Monetary Agreement with U.K.
Cmd. 6681, 279
Production and Export of Tin,
Agreement with Belgium, Bolivia
and U.K. Cmd. 6396, 85
Netley Abbey, Guide to, 188
Nets. See Drift Nets.
Nettles. See Stinging Nettles.
New :
Houses in Scotland, Distribution of,
Report. Cmd. 6552, 206
Parishes Measure, 71, 146

52

New (continued) :
Vessels Built on Government
Account, Purchase by British
Shipowners, Memo. Cmd. 6357,
82
Year's Honours. See London Gazette.
Zealand :
Certificates of Airworthiness for
Export, Exchange of Notes
with U.S.A. Cmd. 6272, 18
Commercial Conditions in, 317
Co-operation Collaboration ; etc.
Agreement with Australia.
Cmd. 6513, 204
Disposal of Real and Personal
Property, Convention with
Australia, U.S.A. and U.K.
Cmd. 6268, 18
Extradition, Supplementary Con-
vention with Paraguay, Austra-
lia, South Africa, and U.K.
Cmd. 6410, 85
Imported Food Certificate, 221
Surpluses, Statement of Policy.
Cmd. 6288, 19
Newcastle and Gateshead Waterworks
Act, 87
Newcastle-upon-Tyne :
and Gateshead Gas Act, 23
Corporation (Trolley Vehicles) Order
Confirmation Act, 284
Bill, 271
Inquiry, Report. Cmd. 6522, 205
Newson-Smith, Sir Frank (Chairman),
Committee on Training for Business
and Administration, Report. Cmd.
6673, 278
Nickel-Chromium Case-Hardening Steel,
Specification, 93
Nickel-Chromium-Iron Alloy Sheets and
Strips, Specification, 92
Nickel-Chromium-Molybdenum Steel.
Specifications, 31, 93
Nigeria, Proposals for Revision of Con-
stitution. Cmd. 6599, 274
Nightjar, 148
1939-43 Star and Clasp, Grant of. Cmd.
6463, 143
Nitrate Salt Baths, Factory Forms,
228
Noel Baker, P. (Chairman), Committee
on Road Safety, Interim Report, 333
Non-Corrodible Steel :
Specifications, 93, 94
Tubes, Specification, 93
Wire, Aerial, Specification, 29

Non-Ferrous Metals, Report, 254
Non-Wool Cloth, Lists of Manufacturers,
118, 182, 247
Normand, Lord (Chairman), Committee
on Utilisation of Land in Rural
Areas of Scotland, Report. Cmd. 6440,
141
North :
Africa, Victory in, Thanks of Houses
of Parliament to H.M. Forces,
187
Junction Bee British North America
Basingstoke. See Wessex.
Lindsey Water Board Provisional
Order Confirmation Act, 209
Bill, 202
Midland Coalfield, Report, 299
Staffordshire District Coal Mines
Scheme, 54
Wales. See North-West England.
Northampton Corporation Act, 146,
208
North-Eastern Coalfield, Report, 299
Northern :
Ireland :
(Miscellaneous Provisions) Act,
282
Bill, 270
See also Supreme Court.
Northumberland :
and Cumberland Coalfields, Report,
299
District Coal Mines Scheme, 54
North-West :
England and North Wales Elec-
tricity :
(Alteration and Extension)
Scheme, 95, 97
(Alteration) Scheme, 216, 218
Midlands :
Electricity District (Meaford
Generating Station) Special
Order, 118
Draft, 60
Joint Electricity Authority Order
Confirmation Act, 209
Bill, 202
North-Western :
Area, Hospital Services of, 300
Coalfields, Report, 299
Norway, Monetary Agreement with U.K.
Cmd. 6697, 280
Norway's :
Fight since April 1940, 243
Role on the Northern Front, 321

53

    INDEX 1941–45

Norwood, Sir C. (Chairman), Committee of the Secondary School Examinations Council, Report (Curriculum and Examinations in Secondary Schools), 155
Not Yet Five, 96
Nottinghamshire Coalfield, National Coal Resources, 115, 243
Nurses :
  Acts :
    1943, 145
    Bill, 139
    1945, 282
    Bill, 255
  Circulars, 300
  and Midwives, Superannuation of, Report. *Cmd. 6603*, 274
  (Scotland) Act, 145
    Bill, 127, 128, 139, 140
  Training of, for the Colonies, Report. *Cmd. 6672*, 278
  See also Maternity Nurses ; Mental Nurses ; Staff Nurse.
Nurses' :
  Salaries :
    Committee Reports :
      1st. *Cmd. 6424*, 141
        Supplement, 157
      2nd. *Cmd. 6439*, 141
      Scottish Committee Reports :
        Interim. *Cmd. 6425*, 141
          Notes on Report, 180
        2nd. *Cmd. 6439*, 141
        3rd. *Cmd. 6505*, 204
      Mental Nurses Sub-Committee, Report. *Cmd. 6488*, 144
      S.C. Notes, 221, 301
  Uniforms, Prices etc., 327
Nursing :
  and Midwifery Services, Careers, 306
  for Gas Casualties, 158
  Services, Pensions, etc. :
    Air Forces, 133, 136
    Military Forces. *Cmd. 6489*, 144
  See also Princess Mary's R.A.F. Nursing Service ; Queen Alexandra's Imperial Nursing Service ; Queen Alexandra's Imperial Military Nursing Service.
Nutrition, Manual of, 298
Nutritive Values of Wartime Foods, 319
Nylon Yarn, Specification, 93

O

Oakbank School Trust (Amendment) Schemes :
  (No. 1), 1944, 244
  (No. 1), 1945, 322, 323
Oats, 89
O.B.E., Additional Statute, etc., 53
Obsolete Stores, Production of, Report, 136
Ocean Front, 303
Occupations. *See* Reserved Occupations.
Occupied Territories, Conditions in, 101, 159, 160, 224, 249
Officers :
  of the Fleet, 25
  See also War Office Publications ; Married Officers ; Women Officers ; Displaced Officers.
Official :
  List, Registrar-General's, 55, 113
  Visitors, Entertainment within Great Britain, 251
Ogilvie, L., Diseases of Vegetables, 26, 286
Oil :
  Dermatitis, Factory Forms, 104, 164
  Duties. *See* Hydrocarbon Oil Duties.
  Varnish, Pigmented, Specifications, 29, 91
  See also Anti-Freezing Oil ; High Altitude Controls Lubricant.
Oilskin Clothing, etc. :
  Inspection and Repair, 38, 158, 223
  Specifications, 65, 122
Oilskins :
  Prices, etc., 327
  Utility, Schedule, 249
Old Age Pensions. *See* Widows', Orphans', etc.
Oldham, C. H., Strawberries, 211
Oliver, Mr. Justice (Chairman), Prime Minister's Committee of Inquiry into Detention Barracks, Report. *Cmd. 6484*, 144
O'Neill Inquiry, Report. *Cmd. 6636*, 276
Onion :
  and Leek Smut, 27
  Bulbs, White Rot Disease, 26
  Crops, Weed Control by Sulphuric Acid Sprays, 90, 149
  Downy Mildew of, 26
  Fly, 27
  See also Wild Onion.
Onions and Related Crops, 148

   —PAR

O

Opencast Coal :
  Mission to the U.S.A., Report, 334
  Production, Report, 199
Open-textured Asphalt Carpets, Recommendations, 57
Operating Aprons, Specification, 65
Operations, Combined, 223
Optical Instruments, Elements of, Report, 179
Optics :
  and Orthoptics, Careers, 306
  and their Application to Service Instruments, Elementary Notes, 66, 187
Orange Juice Jelly, 296
Orange-peeling, Effects on the Skin, 164
Orchard Spraying for Commercial Growers, 148
Orderly-Room Serjeants, Promotion of, 66
Ordnance :
  Corps, Royal Army, Conditions of Service on transfer to, from R.A.S.C., 121
  Factories. *See* Royal Ordnance Factories.
Organisation. *See* Static Organisation.
Orkney Educational Trust (Amendment) (No. 1) Scheme, 1945, 322, 323
Orphans. *See* War Orphans.
Orphans' Pensions. *See* Widows', Orphans', etc.
Orr, Sir J. B. (Chairman), Sub-Committee of the Scientific Advisory Committee, Report (Infant Mortality in Scotland), 160
Ostrich and Fancy Feather and Artificial Flower Trade, Wages, 50
Outfit Allowance, War Office Publications (N.P.), 65, 66, 123, 185
Output, A Study of Variation in, 242
Over to You, 160
Overalls :
  Prices, etc., 183, 248, 326
  Specifications, 247
Overboots, Specifications, 65, 122
Oversea Education, 154, 217, 295
Overseas Trade, Department of, Publications (N.P.), 317
Overtime Register, 307
Owl. *See* Long-eared Owl.
Oxfordshire, Hospital Services of, 300
Oxy-Acetylene Processes, Safety Measures in the Use of, Factory Form, 228
Oxygen Administration, 221

P

Pacific, Story of the War in, 303
Pads. *See* Rubber Pads.
Paint. *See* Flexible Paint ; Silicate Paint.
Painters' Brushes, Specification, 64
Painting :
  Factory Forms, 163, 164
  of Buildings, Report, 254
  See also Wartime Painting.
Palace of Westminster, Accommodation in, Reports, 192, 255, 256
Palache, A. (Chairman), Cinematograph Films Council Committee, Report on Tendency to Monopoly in the Cinematograph Film Industry, 247
Palestine, Commercial Conditions in, 317
Paper :
  Bag Trade, Wages, 50, 111, 175, 239
  Box Trade, Wages, 50, 111, 239
  Control, List of Merchants authorised to deal in Waste Paper-making materials, 324
  Sheet, Synthetic Resin Bonded, Specification, 88
  See also Waste Paper.
Parachute Regiment, Formation of, 121
Paraguay :
  Commercial Relations, Exchange of Notes with Canada. *Cmd. 6274*, 18
  Extradition, Supplementary Convention to Treaty of Sept. 12, 1908 with Australia, New Zealand, South Africa and U.K. *Cmd. 6410*, 85
Parasitic Gastritis in Sheep, 211
Paria, Gulf of, Submarine Areas. Treaty between Venezuela and U.K. : *Cmd. 6359*, 82
  Cmd. 6400, 85
Parishes. *See* New Parishes.
Park. *See* National Parks ; National Forest Park.
Parliament :
  (Elections and Meeting) Act, 145
    Bill, 129, 140
  King's Speech to, 3, 70, 129, 193, 257
  Prolongation of, Acts :
    1941, 23
      Bill, 16
    1942, 86
      Bill, 80
    1943, 145
      Bill, 140

    INDEX 1941–45

Parliament (*continued*) :
  Prolongation of, Acts (*continued*) :
    1944, 208
      Bill, 203
    Thanks of, to Forces, 187, 333
  See also House of Commons ; House of Lords ; Ministers.
Parliamentary :
  Constituencies, Returns showing number of Electors, 194, 266
  Elections (Proxy and Postal Votes), Details of Service Applications for Postal Voting, Number of Votes cast, etc., at General Election of July, 1945, 268
  Electors (Wartime Registration) Act, 208
    Bill, 202
  Publications :
    Acts :
      Local and Private, 23, 87, 146, 208, 283
      Public General, 22, 86, 144, 207, 281
      Reprinted under Specific Authority, 23, 87, 146, 208, 283
    Command Papers, 16, 81, 140, 203, 273
    Lists of, 4, 71, 129, 193, 259
    House of Commons Papers, Debates, Bills, 4, 71, 129, 193, 259
    House of Lords Papers, Debates, Bills, 1, 69, 126, 190, 255
    Measures, Church Assembly, 24, 87, 146, 209, 284
Parochial Church Councils (Powers) Measure, 284
Parsnips, 286
Passenger :
  Steamships, Survey of, 125, 188
  Tax, Isle of Man, Account, 62
  Transport Facilities, 78
Pasteurisation. *See* Milk.
Patent :
  Fuel Manufacture (Health and Welfare) Order, Factory Form, 228
  Rights and Information, Interchange of, Agreement between U.S.A. and U.K. *Cmd. 6392*, 84
Patents and Designs Acts :
  Report. *Cmd. 6618*, 275
  1907, as amended, 208
  1942, 86
    Bill, 3, 16

Paterson, C. C. (Chairman), Lighting Committee of the D.S.I.R., Report, 333
Patos, Island of :
  Anglo-Venezuelan Treaty (Island of Patos) Act, 86
    Bill, 69
  Status of, Treaty between Venezuela and U.K. *Cmd. 6401*, 85
Pay :
  and Allowances of the Armed Forces. *Cmd. 6385*, 84
  Army, War Office Publications (N.P.), 62, 121, 251, 187, 330
  as you Earn, Guide, 225
  Military Forces, Disabled etc. Members of : *Cmd. 6419*, 141
    Cmd. 6473, 143   *Cmd. 6489*, 144
  R.A.F., Disabled etc. Members of, 133, 136
  See also Civil Service Arbitration Tribunal Awards ; Industrial Arbitration Awards ; Industrial Court Awards ; Forces ; Holidays with Pay ; Wages ; Salaries ; Equal Pay.
Paymaster Cadetships in the Royal Navy, Entrance Examination, 33
  Payment by Results, 125, 189, 253
Payments :
  Agreement, Turkey and U.K. *Cmd. 6269*, 18
  to Dependants after Death of Soldier, 123
Pea and Bean :
  Beetles, 89
  Thrips, 90
  Weevils, 89
Peace and War, 156
Pear :
  Canker, 27
  Leaf Blister Mite, 148
  Midge, 286
  Scab, 90, 211
Pears. *See* Apples and Pears.
Peas. *See* Field Peas.
Peers. *See* House of Lords ; Scottish Representative Peers.
Pembrokeshire County Council Act, 87
Penicillin, Use of, in treating War Wounds, 242
Penny Rate, Product of, 221
Pensions :
  and Determination of Needs Act, 145
    Bill, 128, 129
  Public Assistance and Welfare of the Blind, 157, 158, 180

Pensions (*continued*) :
  Appeal Tribunals :
    Act, 145
      Bill, 128, 139
    Notes for the Guidance of Appellants, 240
  Army, 123
  Civil Estimates, 7, 8, 74, 132, 133, 195, 261
  Declaration by Pensioner claiming an Increase, 38
  for Families of H.M. Forces. *Cmd. 6318*, 21
  Home Guard, Disabled etc. Members of. *Cmd. 6449*, 142
  Improved Rates for Members of H.M. Forces. *Cmd. 6342*, 82
    (Increase) Act, 208
      Bill, 190, 202
    Circulars, 221, 300
  (Mercantile Marine) Act, 86
    Bill, 69, 80
  Military Forces, Disabled etc. Members of : *Cmd. 6419*, 141
    Cmd. 6473, 143
    Cmd. 6489, 144
  Ministry of, Publications (N.P.), 55, 112, 241, 317
  R.A.F., Disabled etc. Members of, 133, 136
  See also National Health Insurance and Contributory Pensions ; Police Pensions ; Police Widows' Pensions ; Supplementary Pensions ; Widows', Orphans' and Old Age Contributory Pensions ; War Pensions ; Army ; Air Force ; Home Guard ; Forces ; War Pensions ; Civil Service Pensions ; Fire Brigade Pensions ; Local Authority Petitions.
People, Helping the, to Help Themselves, 249
Perambulator and Invalid Carriage Trade, Wages, 111, 175, 239
Percy, Lord Eustace (Chairman), Committee on Higher Technological Education, Report, 333
Perfumery and Toilet Preparations, Manufacturers and Traders Guide, 119
Peripheral Nerve Injuries, Aids to Investigation of, 178
Persia :
  Commercial Conditions in, 317
  Treaty of Alliance with U.S.S.R. and U.K. *Cmd. 6335*, 81

   —PIC

P

Personal :
  Injuries (Civilians) Schemes, Explanatory Notes, 55, 241
  Property. *See* Real and Personal Property.
Personnel :
  Management, Careers, 306
  who are Prisoners of War or are reported Missing, Pay and Allowances, 67
Perth Homes Trust (Amendment) (No. 1) Scheme, 1945, 322, 323
Peru, Commercial Conditions in, 317
Pests :
  and Diseases in the Vegetable Garden, 26
  See also Insect Pests.
Petitions. *See* Public Petitions.
Petrol and Tyres, Economy in the Use of, 100
Petroleum Agreement, U.S.A. and U.K. *Cmd. 6555*, 206
Pharmacy :
  and Medicines Act, 23
    Bill, 3, 15, 16
  Careers, 306
Phemister, J., Rock Wool, 320
Phosgene, Detection of, 115
Phosphatase Test for Heat Treated Milk, 157
Physical :
  and Chemical Survey of the National Coal Resources, 115
  and Recreational Training, Army, 67
  Efficiency Preparation for Service Cadets, 332
  Training :
    Equipment, Specification, 64
    Facilities for, 296
    for Schools, Syllabus of, 155
    Grant Regs. (Scotland), 322
    Pre-Service, for Army Cadets, 252
    Shoes for, 245
    Tables and Recreational Handbook, W.A.A.F., 28
    See also Social and Physical Training.
Physics :
  Award of National Certificates, 297
  Careers, 306
Pickling :
  Commercial Crops for, 88
  Crops for, 26

Piece Goods :
  Board of Trade Publications (N.P.), 325
  See also Linen Piece Goods ; Woven Piece Goods.
Pig, Common Worms of, 90
Pigmented :
  Lanolin-Resin :
    Finishes, Specification, 29, 93
    Solution, Specification, 30, 92
  Oil Varnish, Specification, 29, 91
  Synthetic Resin Primer and Finish, Specification, 93
Pin, Hook and Eye, and Snap Fastener Trades, Wages, 51, 111, 176, 239
Pink Rot of Potatoes, 90
Pioneer Corps :
  Combatant Status, 123
  See also African Auxiliary Pioneer Corps.
Pipe Repairs. *See* Emergency Pipe Repairs.
Pippard, W. R., Calcium Sulphate Plasters, 56
Piston Ring Pots, Specifications, 92, 93
Pistons. *See* Aluminium Pistons.
Plaited Cordage, Specification, 29
Plane Safety Glass, Specification, 91
Planning :
  our New Homes, 244
  See also Joint Planning ; Works and Planning ; Town and Country Planning ; Licensing Planning.
Plants :
  Mineral Deficiencies in, 178, 318
  See also Medical Plants.
Plasters. *See* Calcium Sulphate Plasters.
Plastics, Report, 254
Plate. *See* Tin Plate.
Platinum Thermocouples for use in Liquid Steel, 115
Plum :
  Aphides, 89
  Brown Rot, 29
Plumbing, Report, 254
Plums and Damsons, 211
Plywood for Lightly Stressed Parts of Aircraft, Specification, 30
Pneumoconiosis :
  Treatment and Rehabilitation of Coal Miners suffering from, Report, 220
  See also Workmen's Compensation (Pneumoconiosis).
Pocket Book, Seaman's, 210
"Points" Rationing Scheme, List of Foods included in, 97

Poison Gas, Food and its Protection against, 36
Poisoning. *See* Carbon Monoxide.
Poisons, Form of Application to sell, 99
Poland :
  Mutual Assistance, Agreement with U.K. *Cmd. 6616*, 275
  Nazi Kultur in, 318
Polarographic and Spectrographic Analy- sis of High Purity Zinc etc., 324
Pole, Sir Felix J. C. (Chairman), Private Enterprise Housing Committee, Report, 221
Police :
  and Firemen (War Service) Act, 208
    Bill, 190, 202
  (Appeals) Act, 145
    Bill, 81
    Bill, 1945, 271, 272
  Careers, 306
  Declaration by a Pensioner claiming Increase, 158
  (H.M. Inspectors of Constabulary) Act, 282
    Bill, 270
  Income Tax on Rent Allowances, Report, 302
  Instructions to Pensioners claiming Increase, 222
  (Overseas Service) Bill, 258
  Pension, Reassessment of Increase, 38
  Regs. :
    England and Wales, 302
    Scotland, 323
  (Scotland) Examinations Board, Question Papers, 245
  Warnings, Report, 323
  Widows' Pensions, Departmental Committee on, Report. *Cmd. 6312*, 21
  (Women) Regs. :
    England and Wales, 302
    Scotland, 323
  See also Military Police ; Metropolitan Police.
Polish Ministry of Information Publica- tions (N.P.), 318
Polish Trade. *See* Boot and Floor Polish.
Political Fund of an Unregistered Trade Union, Annual Return Form, 36, 98, 156
Polling Day, Postponement of, Act, 282
  Bill, 271
Pollution. *See* Water Pollution ; Atmospheric Pollution.
Polwarth, Lord, MSS., 113
Pontypool Gas and Water Act, 283

Poole Provisional Order Confirmation Act, 87
  Bill, 70, 80
Population :
  Current Trend in Great Britain. *Cmd. 6358*, 82
  Statistics of, 241
Port Transport Industry, Report, 314
Portable Equipment (Cooking Appliances), 125
Portchester Castle, Guide to, 188
Port-Glasgow Gas and Burgh Order Con- firmation Act, 284
  Bill, 257
Ports, Seamen's Welfare in, 314
Portsmouth Water Act, 24
Portugal :
  Commercial Conditions in, 317
  Delimitation of the Southern Rhodesia–Portuguese East Africa Frontier, Exchange of Notes with U.K. *Cmd. 6280*, 19
  Establishment of an Air Service between Australia and Portuguese Timor, Exchange of Notes with Australia. *Cmd. 6266*, 17
  Mozambique Convention of Sept. 11, 1928, as amended, Exchange of Notes with South Africa. *Cmd. 6306*, 20
Portuguese East Africa–Southern Rhodesian Frontier, Delimitation of, Exchange of Notes, Portugal and U.K. *Cmd. 6280*, 19
Post :
  Office :
    and Telegraph (Money) Act, 86
      Bill, 80
    Commercial Accounts, 4
      Examinations, 95, 153, 216, 294
    Fund Account, 5
    Guide, 55, 112, 177, 318
    Savings Banks Accounts. 62, 120, 184, 249, 320
    Offices in the U.K. and Eire, 55
  Postal :
    Services. *See* Post Office Guide.
    Voting :
      for the Forces, Seamen, and Workers abroad, Report. *Cmd. 6581*, 273
    See also Parliamentary Elections.
  Postponement of Polling Day Act, 282
    Bill, 271

Post-War :
  Agricultural Education in England and Wales, Committee on, Report. *Cmd. 6433*, 141
  Building Studies, 253, 334
  Credits :
    and Dependants' Allowances, Members of H.M. Forces. *Cmd. 6336*, 81
    for Soldiers, Auxiliaries of the A.T.S., etc., 123
  Employment Policy. *Cmd. 6527*, 205
  Forest Policy :
    Cmd. 6447, 142
    Cmd. 6500, 203
  Hospital Problems in Scotland, Committee on, Report. *Cmd. 6472*, 143
  Loaf, Report. *Cmd. 6701*, 280
  Reconstruction. *See* London.
  Youth Service in Wales, Report, 298
Potato :
  Department of Agriculture for Scotland Publications (N.P.), 58, 116, 244
  Fund Account, 135
  Ministry of Agriculture and Fisheries Publications (N.P.), 26, 58, 149, 211
Potter, H. V. (Chairman), Plastics Committee, Report, 254
Potter, J. M. S., Fruit from the Garden, 89
Potteries. *See* Staffordshire Potteries.
Pottery :
  Industry, Dust containing Silica, Report, 175
  Regs., Factory Form, 164, 307
  Scheme for ensuring fair shares of supplies to small retailers, 119
Poultry :
  Feeding :
    Scientific Principles of, 211
    Wartime, 89, 148
  Keeping :
    Folding System of, 90
    on the General Farm, 25
  Worms in, 149
Powdery :
  Mildew of Vines, 286
  Scab of Potatoes, 89
Power :
  Loading, Ministry of Fuel and Power Publications (N.P.), 220

Power (*continued*) :
  Presses :
    Fencing and other Safety Precautions for, Factory Form, 164, 307
    Safety in use of, Reports, 314
Power-Factor Meters, Specification, 121
Practice Leaflet for Solicitors, 53
Pram Rugs. *See* Knitted Cloths.
Pre-Natal Allowances, 148
Pre-School Children, Feeding of, 116
Preserves from the Garden, 26, 89, 148
Preserving. *See* Food Preserving.
Pressed Metal Wares Trade, Wages, 50, 51, 110, 176, 239
Presses. *See* Power Presses.
Preston, Dock Labour in, Explanatory Memo., 68
Pre-War Trade Practices, Restoration of, Act, 86
    Bill, 16, 69
Price :
  Control :
    (Regulation of Disposal of Stocks) Act, 145
      Bill, 129
    Related Schedules, 326, 327
  Stabilisation and Industrial Policy, Statement. *Cmd. 6294*, 19
Prices :
  and Margins, 119
  Standard Schedule of (Building), 125
  See also Retail Food Prices.
Primary and Secondary Schools, Ministry of Education Publications (N.P.), 296
Prime :
  Cost Contract for Repair of War Damage to Dwellings, 334
  Minister :
    Letters from Mr. Speaker to the, on Electoral Reform and Redistribution of Seats :
      Cmd. 6534, 205
      Cmd. 6543, 206
    Statement on Basic English. *Cmd. 6511*, 204
    See also Churchill, Winston.
Primer, Matt Pigmented Synthetic Resin, Specification, 93
Princess Mary's Royal Air Force Nursing Service, Regs., 212, 287
Prisoners :
  of War, War Office Publications (N.P.), 67, 123, 187, 252, 332
  See also Limitation (Enemies and War Prisoners).

Prisons and Borstals, 302
Private :
  Acts. *See* Parliamentary Publications.
  Bills :
    Rules for the Practice and Procedure of the Court of Referees, 263
    Select Committee appointed to consider the Cost of, Report, 128
    Standing Orders, Reports, 230, 261
  Chattels Scheme (War Damage), Receipts and Payments, 79, 138, 201
  Domestic Employment, Post-war Organisation of, Report. *Cmd 6650*, 277
  Enterprise Housing, Report, 221
  Legislation (Scotland) Committee, Publications (N.P.), 58, 116, 180, 245, 321
  Privileges :
    Committee of :
      Minutes of Evidence, 136
      Reports, 12, 77, 135, 199, 263, 268
    See also Diplomatic Privileges.
Privy Council Office Publication (N.P.), 318
Prize :
  Deposit Account, 197, 200
  Money. *See* Army Prize Money.
  Salvage Act, 207
    Bill, 190
Probate Engrossment Follower, 177
Probation :
  Homes and Hostels, Directory of, 99
  Officers, Directory of, 99
  Records, 38
Procedure in the Public Business. *See* Public Business.
Production :
  Authorities Guide, 177, 241
  Concentration of, Explanatory Memo. *Cmd. 6258*, 17
  Engineering, Award of Higher National Certificates, 35, 117
  Government Statement, 13
  Ministry of :
    Publications (N.P.), 177, 241, 318
    Regional Organisation of, Report, 199

Production (*continued*) :
  Office of the Minister of. *Cmd. 6337*, 81
  Opencast Coal, Report, 199
  Organisation of, 76
  War Materials, 78
Productive Society, Annual Return Forms, 36, 98, 156
Professional Notes, Meteorological, 111
Profit, Offices or Places of, under the Crown, Select Committee on, Report and Minutes of Evidence, 13
Profits. *See* Excess Profits.
Programme and Progress, 254
Prolongation of Parliament Acts :
  1941, 23
    Bill, 16
  1942, 86
    Bill, 80
  1943, 145
    Bill, 140
  1944, 208
    Bill, 203
Promotion, Army, 66, 67, 123, 124, 187, 252, 332
Proofed Fabrics, Specifications, 93, 94 for Focal-Plane Camera Shutters, 30
Property. *See* Educational Property ; Real and Personal Property.
Protected :
  Areas, Classes of Person permitted to enter, 252
  Work, Schedule of, 49
Provisional Orders (Marriages) Confirmation Acts :
  1941, 24
    Bill, 2, 15
  1945, 283
    Bill, 270
Provisions, Retail Controlled Prices, 298
Proxy and Postal Votes. *See* Postal Voting ; Parliamentary Elections.
Pruning Stone Fruit Trees, 27
Psychological Terms, Glossary, 56
Public :
  Accounts, Committee of, Reports, Proceedings, Minutes of Evidence, Action etc., 12, 77, 78, 85, 129, 136, 196, 200, 265, 269
  and Other Schools (War Conditions) Act, 208
    Bill, 1, 2, 15
  Assistance and Welfare of the Blind, 157, 158, 180

Public (*continued*) :
  Business :
    Colonial Regs., 33
    House of Commons, 79
    Procedure in, Report and Evidence, 267
  Departments :
    Heads of, 60
    See also Government Departments.
  Entertainment, Safety in places of, ???
  Health :
    and Medical Subjects, Reports, 221 (Imported Food) Regs., 221 (Scotland) Bill, 257, 268, 269, 272
    See also Local Government and Public Health.
  Income and Expenditure, Accounts, 11, 76, 134, 198, 264
  Officers, Colonial Regs., 33
  Petitions, Committee on, Special Report, 198
  Relations Branches of Service Departments, Report on, 134
  Schools, Report, 254
  Utility Undertakings, War Damage to. *Cmd. 6403*, 85
  Works Loans Act, 208
    Bill, 202
  Publications :
    and Debates, Reports, 5, 74, 200
    See also Government Publications.
Publishing, Careers, 306
Pulmonary :
  Disease :
    in South Wales Coalminers, 113, 178
    See also Chronic Pulmonary Disease.
  Tuberculosis :
    among recruits for H.M. Forces, Report on use of mass miniature radiography in the detection of. *Cmd. 6353*, 82
    Civilians, Mass miniature radiography for the detection of, 319
    Early, Radiological Appearances of, 157
Punching Balls, Specification, 64
Punishment for War Crimes, 101, 160, 224
Pupils. *See* Handicapped Pupils.
Pupils' Record Cards, 245

Q

" Q " Code, Civil Aeronautical Radio Service, 28
Qu'aiti State, National Flag, 33
Quality Control :
Film Strips, 218
for Engineers, 324
Quarries. See Mines and Quarries.
Quays, Factory Forms, 104, 228
Queen :
Alexandra's Imperial Nursing Sèrvices :
Pay and Allowances, 123
Uniform Allowances, 250
War Service Increments, 332
Women Officers in, 188
Elizabeth Hospital for Children Act, 87
Victoria School, 124
Scholarship Fund Scheme, 180, 244
Wilhelmina's Navy, 241
Queen's Army Schoolmistresses, Acting Schoolmistresses and Pupil Teachers, Revised Rates of Pay, 67

R

Rabbit Keeping, 26
Rabbits :
Diseases of, 149
for Flesh and Fur, 27, 148
Radar, 298
Radio :
Aids to Landing Approach, Notes on, 294
for Civil Aviation, Third Commonwealth and Empire Conference, 294
Service. See Civil Aeronautical Radio Service.
Radiography. See Pulmonary Tuberculosis.
Radiological Appearances of Early Pulmonary Tuberculosis, 157
Rail and Road Transport, Report, 197
Railway :
Companies (Thos. Cook Ltd., Guarantee) Act, 87
Freight Rebates Act, 145
Bill, 127, 128, 150

Railways :
Accidents on, 333
Agreement (Powers) Act, 22
Government Control of :
Estimates of Pooled Revenue, etc.:
Cmd. 6252, 16
Cmd. 6349, 82
Cmd. 6436, 141
Cmd. 6512, 204
Cmd. 6619, 275
Financial Arrangements. Cmd. 6314, 21
See also Military Railways.
Rainfall. See British Rainfall.
Rainy Lake, etc., Emergency Regulation of the Level of, U.S.A. and Canada. Cmd. 6276, 18
Ramsey, Sir J. D. (Chairman), Scottish National Parks Survey Committee, Report. Cmd. 6631, 276
Raspberries, Cultivation of, 148
Raspberry :
Beetle, 27, 148
Diseases in Scotland, 179, 321
Moth, 148
Rates :
and Rateable Values in England and Wales, 301
in Scotland, Return of, 323
Valuation for, Departmental Committee on, Report, 222
Ratifications, etc., Supplementary Lists :
Cmd. 6253, 17
Cmd. 6329, 81
Cmd. 6431, 141
Rating :
and Valuation :
Assessment Committee, Report Forms, 37, 99, 157, 222, 301
Product of a Penny Rate, 221
(War Damage) (Scotland) Act, 22
Bill, 15
See also Hydro-Electric Undertakings ; Scottish Rating.
Rationing :
under Axis Rule, 101
See also Consumer Rationing ; Fuel Rationing.
Rations and Allowances in lieu, Army, 187
Rats :
and how to destroy them, 285
and how to exterminate them, 26
Raw :
Materials :
Board, Combined, Reports, 177, 241, 318

Raw (continued) :
Materials (continued) :
contaminated by Blister Gas, Handling and Treatment of, 222
Guide, 181
Supplements, 246, 324
Milk, Restriction on the supply, 221
Ready-made and Wholesale Bespoke Tailoring Trade, Wages, 51, 110, 239, 315
Real and Personal Property, Disposal of, Convention, U.S.A., Australia, New Zealand and U.K. Cmd. 6268, 18
Reception Areas, Conditions in, Report, 37
Reciprocal Aid in the prosecution of the War against Aggression, U.S.A. and U.K. Cmd. 6389, 84
Reconnaissance Corps, Amalgamation with the Royal Armoured Corps, 250
Reconstruction :
Finance Corporation, Agreement with U.K. Cmd. 6295, 19
Office of the Minister of, Publications (N.P.), 241
See also War-damaged Licensed Premises.
Reconversion (U.S.A.), Problems of, Report, 298
Record :
Card, Pupil's, 245
Publications (N.P.), 112
Records. See Probation Records.
Recreation :
and Social and Physical Training, Facilities for, 296
Pre-Service, for Army Cadets, 252
Red :
Oxide of Iron Mixture, Specification, 90
Spider, 90, 149
See also Fruit Tree Red Spider ; Gooseberry Red Spider.
Redemption Annuities Notice, 27, 181
Reed, Guy, The Little Less, 39
Rees-Thomas, W. (Chairman), Committee on Mental Nursing, Report, 301
Reform. See Electoral Reform ; Electoral Law Reform ; Law Reform.
Refractory Materials Regulations, 1931, Factory Form, 164
Refreshment Rooms. See House of Commons.
Refugee Children. See Guardianship.

Refugees. See Czechoslovak Refugee Fund
Refuse. See Town Refuse.
Regency Act, 145
Bill, 129
Regimental Institutes, Army, Rules for Conduct of, 64, 121
Regional Boards, Committee on, Report. Cmd. 6360, 82
Register of Electors. See Local Elections.
Registered :
Exporters, Lists of, 118, 182
Friendly Society, Annual Return Form, 36, 97
Registers :
in Primary and Secondary Schools, 296
See also Parliamentary Constituencies.
Registrar-General of Births, Deaths and Marriages Publications (N.P.) :
England and Wales, 55, 113, 177, 241, 318
Scotland, 58, 116, 180, 245, 322
Registrars, Instructions to, 177
Registration :
Officers, Lists of, 177, 241, 318
of Youth, 34, 36
Rehabilitation. See Disabled Persons ; Hospital ; United Nations.
Reid, C. C. (Chairman), Technical Advisory Committee on Coal Mining, Report. Cmd. 6610, 275
Reinforced Concrete Structures :
Report, 254
Resistance to Air Attack, 56
Release :
and Resettlement, 314
from the Army, War Office Publications (N.P.), 332
Relief :
Organisation, Emergency, 116
See also United Nations.
Religious :
Instruction in Schools in Scotland, Memo. Cmd. 6426, 141
Persecution, 101, 159
Remand Homes, Report. Cmd. 6594, 274
Remount Service, Amalgamation with Army Veterinary Service, 67
Rent :
Allowances (Police), Income Tax on, Report, 302
Control, Report. Cmd. 6621, 275
of Furnished Houses Control (Scotland) Act, 145
Bill, 129, 140

62

63

Reorganisation Areas Measure, 190, 209
Repair of War Damage Act, 22
Bill, 15
Representation of the People Acts :
1922, 281
1945, 282
Bill, 203, 255, 270
Requisitioned :
Buildings of the War Department, Abridged Schedule of Prices for Works and Repairs, 125
Land :
and Buildings, Release of, Report, 263
and War Works Act, 283
Bill, 256, 270, 271
See also Landlord and Tenant.
Requisitioning. See Land and Buildings.
Rescue :
Incidents, Notes for the Guidance of Wardens, 158
Service :
Basic Training, 223
Manual, 100
Research :
and Development, Warlike Stores, Report, 265
Workers, Grants to, 320
Reserve. See Army Reserve ; Supplementary Reserve.
Reserved Occupations and Protected Works, Schedule of, 49
Resettlement, Release and, 314
Residential Schools, Allocation of dried separated milk to, 34, 36
Resignation of Women Officers, Army, 67
Resin :
Specification, 92
See also Synthetic Resin.
Respirators :
Inspection and Repair of, 38, 158, 223
See also War Respirators.
Restoration of Pre-War Trade Practices Bill, 16
Restriction of Ribbon Development. See Ribbon Development.
Resuscitation, Equipment, Organisation, etc., Army, 67, 124, 332
Retail :
Bespoke Tailoring Trade, Wages, 50, 110, 239
Business Premises, Reinstatement in, Bill, 191

Retail (continued) :
Businesses, Location of, Orders, 1941, Explanatory Memo., 61
Controlled Prices (Food), Lists of, 155, 219, 298
Distributive Society, Annual Return Form, 36, 98, 156
Food Prices, List of, 97
Non-Food Trades, Concentration in, Report, 119
Trade Committee, Reports, 62, 119
Retailers. See Small Retailers.
Retirement. See Compulsory Retirement.
Revenue Departments :
Appropriation Accounts, 5, 72, 130, 194, 260
Estimates, 8, 74, 132, 133, 196, 261
Rheumatic Diseases, Chronic, Report, 321
Rhodesia. See Southern Rhodesia.
Rhubarb, 211, 286
Ribbon Development, Restriction of :
Memo., 253
(Temporary Development) Act, 145
Bill, 128, 149
Richmond Castle, Guide to, 188
Rickets, Incidence of, in Wartime, 221
Ridley, Lord (Chairman), Interdepartmental Committee on Rent Control, Report. Cmd. 6621, 275
Rings. See Shock Absorber Cord Rings.
River :
Boards, Central Advisory Water Committee, Third Report. Cmd. 6465, 143
Conservancy Authorities, Receipt and Expenditure Forms, 37, 99
Road :
Accidents, Return, 3
Fund :
Accounts, 6, 71, 130, 194, 259
Annual Reports, 68, 125, 188, 253, 333
Goods Traffic, Long Distance. Cmd. 6506, 204
Haulage :
Organisation, Lists of Offices, 253, 333
Markings. See White Line Road Markings.
Research Laboratory Publications (N.P.), 57, 115, 179, 243
Safety, Interim Report, 333
to Tokyo and Beyond, 298

Road (continued) :
Transport :
Lighting (Cycles) Act, 282
Bill, 193
See also Rail and Road Transport.
Work Contract, 11
Roadhead Supports, Mines, Safety Pamphlets, 220
Roads :
Civil Estimates, 7, 8, 74, 132, 133, 261
Conveyance of Explosives on, 222
Layout and Construction, 188
Tar-Surface Dressings for, 243
See also Snow ; Trunk Roads.
Robinson, Sir R. L. (Chairman), Post-War Forest Policy, Report. Cmd. 6447, 142
Roche Abbey, Guide to, 188
Roche, Lord (Chairman), Departmental Committee on Justices' Clerks, Report. Cmd. 6507, 204
Rock Wool, 320
Rods, Specifications :
Chromium - Nickel Non - Corrodible Steel Welding, 94
Steel, 31
Rogers, H. R. (Chairman) :
Safety in the Use of Power Presses, Committee on, Report, 314
Safety of Heavy Power Presses, Committee on, Report, 305
Rogers, R. J. (Chairman), Gas Installations Committee, Report, 254
Roman Amphitheatre, Caerleon, Guide to, 188
Rommel, They sought out, 101
Roof :
Control at Longwall Faces, 220
over Britain, 160, 224
Roofs :
Report, 334
See also Timber Roofs.
Roosevelt, Franklin D. :
Addresses and Messages of, 156
Exchange of Christmas Greetings with Prime Minister, 185
Lease-Lend Operations, 17th Report to Congress, 219
Root :
and Vegetable Seed Crops, Threshing of, 286
Vegetables, 88
Root-knot Eelworm in Glasshouses, 27
Rope :
Rot-proofing of, Specification, 94
Walks, Factory Form, 43

Rope, Twine and Net Trade, Wages, 51, 111, 176, 239, 315
Ropes. See Sisal Ropes.
Ropy Milk, 27
Rot, Dry, in Wood, 320
Rotations, 211
Rot-proofing of Canvas, Rope and Cordage, Specification, 94
Roumania :
Conditions of Armistice. Cmd. 6585, 273
Debts Clearing Offices, Accounts, 7, 72, 130
Notification of State of War with, 54
Royal :
Air Force. See Air Force.
Armoured Corps, 332
Amalgamation with Reconnaissance Corps, 250
Army :
Medical Corps, War Office Publications (N.P.), 67, 124, 187, 252, 330
Ordnance Corps, Conditions of Service on transfer from R.A.S.C., 121
Reserve, War Office Publications (N.P.), 330
Commissions Publications (N.P.), 321
Electrical and Mechanical Engineers, War Office Publications (N.P.), 124
Hospital, Chelsea, Accounts, 9, 14, 79, 136, 201, 268
Household Appointments, 53
Indian Navy, Examinations, 32, 33, 95, 153, 216, 294
Marines, 303
See also Marines.
Naval :
Sick Berth Staff, Handbook, 210, 285
Volunteer Reserve Act, 86
Bill, 69
Navy. See Navy.
Norwegian Government Information Office Publications (N.P.), 243, 321
Ordnance Factories :
Accounts, 9
Investigation into complaints, 87
Ruanda-Urundi, Regulation of Purchases of Commodities, Agreement, Belgium and U.K. Cmd. 6365, 83
Rubber :
Gaskets for Magneto Terminals, Specification, 91
Gloves, Anti-Gas, Specification, 122

64

65

Rubber (continued):
Hose, Specifications, 30, 92
Manufacturing Trade, Wages, 51, 111, 176, 315
Overboot, Anti-Gas, Specifications, 65, 122
Pads for Bomb Sight Brackets, Specification, 29
Proofed:
Fabrics, Specifications, 31, 94
Leggings, Specification, 122
Reclamation Trade, Wages, 51, 110, 176, 315
Sheet, Specifications, 30, 93
Solvent, Specification, 29
Tubing, Specifications, 91, 92
Watch Holders, Specification, 91
See also Indiarubber.
Rural:
Areas:
Households in, Weekly Expenditure, 52
Land Utilisation in, Committee on, Report. Cmd. 6378, 84
Scotland. Cmd. 6440, 141
Housing:
Circulars, 221, 222
Report, 222
Water Supplies and Sewerage Act, 208
Bill, 191, 202
Circular, 300
Workers. See Housing (Rural Workers).
Rushcliffe, Lord (Chairman):
Land Transference Committee, Report. Cmd. 6467, 143
Legal Aid and Legal Advice in England and Wales, Committee on, Report. Cmd. 6641, 276
Midwives Salaries Committee, Report. Cmd. 6460, 142
Nurses' Salaries Committee, Reports: Cmd. 6424, 141
Supplement, 157
Cmd. 6487, 144
Mental Nurses Sub-Committee, Report. Cmd. 6542, 206
Training of Nurses for the Colonies, Committee on, Report. Cmd. 6672, 278
Russell, W. T., Epidemiology of Diphtheria during the last forty years, 178
Russia. See Union of Soviet Socialist Republics.

S

Sack and Bag Trade Wages, 51, 239
Sackville, Major-General Lord, MSS., 113
Safety:
and Health, Mines, Regs., 54
Circular, Mines, 300
Glass, Specifications, 29, 91
in Mines Research Board, Annual Reports, 55, 98, 157, 220, 300
in Places of Public Entertainment, 222
Measures in Use of Acetylene Gas, etc., Factory Form, 228
of Machine Tools and other plant, Factory Forms, 228
Pamphlets:
Factories, etc., 238
Mines, 220, 300
Sailors. See Irish Sailors.
Saint Lawrence Basin–Great Lakes, Exchange of Notes, U.S.A. and Canada. Cmd. 6303, 20
Salad Crops, 26
Salads and Vegetables, 35
Salaries. See Civil Service Arbitration Tribunal ; National Arbitration Tribunal ; Midwives' Salaries ; Nurses' Salaries ; Teachers' Salaries.
Salisbury, Marquess of, MSS., 112
Salt:
Baths, Nitrate, Factory Forms, 228
Treatment for Icy Roads, 57
Salvage. See Prize Salvage.
Salvaged Clothing, Lists of Wholesalers, 118, 184
San Demetrio, Saga of, 101
Sanders, H. G., Rotations, 211
Sand-lime Bricks, 114
San Francisco Conference. See United Nations.
Sanitary Convention. See International Sanitary Convention.
Sanitation. See Hygiene and Sanitation.
Saudi Arabia:
Extradition of Offenders, Agreement with U.K. Cmd. 6382, 84
Friendship and Neighbourly Relations, Agreement with U.K. Cmd. 6380, 84
Trade Agreement with U.K. Cmd. 6381, 84

Savings:
Banks:
and Friendly Societies, Accounts, 62, 120, 184, 249, 329
See also Post Office Savings Banks ; Trustee Savings Banks.
See also War Savings.
Sawfly. See Apple Sawfly ; Gooseberry Sawfly.
Saws, Specification, 64
Scab. See Apple and Pear Scab ; Common Scab.
Scabies, 37
and how to deal with it, 99, 158
Prevalence and Control of. Cmd. 6355, 82
Scalds, Studies of, 319
Scale. See Brown Scale ; Mussel Scale.
Scholarships. See State Scholarships ; Science Scholarships ; Whitworth Scholarships.
School:
Attendance (Scotland), 322
Buildings (Scotland), Report, 334
Canteens:
Allocation of dried separated milk, 34, 36
Supplies of Liquid Milk, 34, 36
Children. See Evacuated School Children.
Meals and Milk, Children receiving:
England and Wales:
Cmd. 6361, 82
Cmd. 6443, 142
Cmd. 6530, 205
Cmd. 6644, 277
Scotland:
Cmd. 6366, 83
Cmd. 6444, 142
Cmd. 6553, 205
Cmd. 6643, 276
Medical Service, Scotland, 321
Premises, Building Standards for, 217, 218, 295
Registers and Records in Primary and Secondary Schools, 296
Schoolmistresses. See Queen's Army Schoolmistresses.
Schools:
Air Raid Precautions in, 59
Closure of and Exclusion from, 96
Fire Precautions in, 301
in Wartime, 39, 96
Public and other, (War Conditions) Act, 22
Bill, 1, 2, 15

Schools (continued):
Standard Construction for, Report, 253
See also Residential Schools ; Boarding School ; Home Office Schools ; Milk in Schools ; Approved Schools ; Grant-aided Secondary Schools ; Secondary Schools ; Medical Schools ; Public Schools ; Ministry of Education Publications ; Scottish Education Department Publications.
Science:
Awards Amending Regs., 96
Careers, 306
Scholarships Examinations, 96, 296
Scientific:
and Industrial Research, Department of, Publications (N.P.), 56, 114, 178, 242, 319
Research and Development. Cmd. 6514, 204
Sclerotinia Disease of Potatoes, 149
Scott, Rt. Hon. Lord Justice (Chairman), Committee on Land Utilisation in Rural Areas, Report. Cmd. 6378, 84
Scottish:
Coalfields, Report on. Cmd. 6575, 207, 273
Departments, Publications (N.P.) (Department of Agriculture for Scotland ; Edinburgh Gazette ; Educational Endowments (Scotland) Commission ; Department of Health for Scotland ; Private Legislation (Scotland) Procedure ; Registrar-General of Births, Deaths and Marriages for Scotland ; Scottish Education Department ; Scottish Home Department ; Scottish Office). 58, 115, 179, 244, 321
District Coal Mines Scheme, 54
Fisheries Advisory Council Act, 22
Nurses. See Nurses.
Rating System, Committee on, Report. Cmd. 6595, 274
Representative Peers, Election of Representatives to sit and vote in Parliament, 257
Scour. See White Scour.
Scoured Cotton Fabric, Specification, 31, 93
Screw Gauges, Notes on, 243

Scurf. See Black Scurf.
Sea Transport Regs., 125, 188, 253, 333
S.E.A.C. Souvenir, 303
Seaman's Pocket Book, 210
Seamen, Postal Voting for, Report. Cmd. 6581, 273
Seamen's Welfare in Port, Reports: Cmd. 6411, 85
N.P.P., 314
Seats for Workers in Factories, 315
Seaweed as Manure, 149
Secondary:
Aluminium and Aluminium Alloy Notched Bars and Ingots for Remelting, Specifications, 30, 31
Schools:
Circulars, 296
Curriculum and Examinations in, Report, 155
Maintained, Principles of Government in. Cmd. 6523, 205
See also Grant-aided Secondary Schools.
Second-hand and Salvaged Clothing, Lists of Wholesalers, 118, 184
Second-in-Command, Appointment of, Army, 124
Secret German Documents seized during the raid on the Lofoten Islands. Cmd. 6270, 18
Secretarial Work, Careers, 306
Securities:
Acquisition of, Treasury Directions, 111
Instructions to Registrars of, 112, 177
(Validation) Act, 86
Bill, 80
Seed Testing, 90
Seeing, 178
Seligman, R. (Chairman), Non-ferrous Metals Committee, Report, 254
Senior Leaving Certificate, 59, 116, 180, 245
Serge Hospital Clothing, Specification, 65
Serjeants. See Orderly-Room Serjeants.
Serjeants' Messes, Army Office Publications (N.P.), 66
Service:
Book, Teacher's Copy of, 35
Cadets, Physical Efficiency Preparation for, 352
Canteens, Organisation of, Report. 67
Corps, Royal Army, Conditions of Service on transfer to R.A.O.C., 121
Instruments, Optics and their Application, Elementary Notes, 66

Services Clothing Rationing, 248
Settled Land and Trustee Acts (Court's General Powers) Act, 145
Bill, 126, 127, 159
Settlements. See British Settlements.
Severn Barrage:
Committee Report (1933), 238
Scheme, Report on, 300
Sewerage. See Rural Water Supplies.
Sex Education in Schools and Youth Organisations, 155
Shakespeare, Sir G. (Chairman):
Conditions in Reception Areas, Committee on, Report, 37
Medical Personnel (Priority) Committee, Interim Reports, 99
Sharples, G. R. (Chairman), Acoustics Committee of the Building Research Board, Report, 254
Shaw, A. G., An Introduction to the Theory and Application of Motion Study, 287
Shawcross, W. Hartley (Chairman), Catering Wages Commission, Report. Cmd. 6509, 204
Shears, 307
Sheep:
Farming. See Hill Sheep Farming.
Foot Rot in, 27
Liver Rot, 90
Maggot, 26
Stomach Worms in, 90, 211
Sheet. See Rubber Sheet.
Sheeting, Cotton, Specification, 65
Sheets:
Metal, Specifications, 91, 92
See also Cotton Sheets ; Steel Sheets.
Sheffield and East Midlands Area, Hospital Services of, 300
Shelter:
at Home, 38
Design and Strengthening, 100
Shelters. See Steel Shelters.
Shepherd, C. Y., Sugar Industry of Fiji, 295
Shift System in Factories, 307
Ship:
Construction, Application of Electric Arc Welding to, 285
Fires, 222
Shipbuilding:
Electric Welding in, 210
Regs., Factory Form, 43
See also Merchant Shipbuilding.

Shipley Provisional Order Confirmation Act, 74
Shipowners. See British Shipowners.
Shipowners, Shipmasters and Shippers, Notice to, Conditions of Stowage of explosives on board ship, 125
Shipping:
Forms, 59
Ministry of, Publications (N.P.), 59
Select Committee on National Expenditure, Report of, 10, 12
See also British Shipping ; Merchant Shipping.
Shiprepairing. See Merchant Shipbuilding.
Ships:
and Cargoes, Salvage of, Report, 137
Stowage of Explosives in, 188, 253
See also British Ships ; Freight Ships ; Vessels ; Passenger Steamships.
Ships' Stores Dealers, Lists of, 118, 182
Shipwreck:
Preservation of Life at Sea after, Guide to, 178
Society registered for assistance in, Annual Return Form, 36, 97, 156
See also Wreck Reports.
Shirtmaking Trade, Wages, 54, 110, 239
Shock. See Wound Shock.
Shock-Absorber Cord Rings for Gun Mountings, 29
Shoe Repairing Trade, Wages, 49, 50, 110, 175, 238, 315
Shoes:
for Physical Training and Games, 245
Specification, 65
Shops, New, Opening of, and Restriction on Categories of Goods sold in single Shops, Report, 62
Short-eared Owl, 149
Shot Firing in relation to Power Loading (Mines), 220
Shute, P. G., Control of Mosquito Nuisances in Great Britain, 157
Sicily, Conquest of, Letters exchanged between H.M. the King and the Prime Minister, 187
Sick Berth Staff, Royal Naval, Handbook, 210, 285
Sick-leave Regs. applicable to Temporary and Unestablished Employees, Memo., 120
Sickness:
Absence in Industry, Recording of, 242
among Women in Industry, 318

Signal:
Book for use in Air Navigation, 78
Card, 210
Letters of British Ships, 59, 125, 333
Signals:
International Code of, 188
See also Sound Signals.
Signs. See Traffic Signs.
Silica:
Dust containing, in the Tile Making and Pottery Industry, Report, 175
Gel, Specification, 30
Silicate Paint for Timber, Specification, 30
Silicon–Aluminium Alloy:
Castings, Specification, 91
Forgings, Specifications, 29, 92
Silicon–Nickel–Copper Alloy Bars, Specifications, 93
Silicosis, Pottery, Regs., 307
Silk:
Fabrics, Specifications, 30, 91, 93, 94
Tape for Parachutes, Specification, 29
See also Artificial Silk.
Silver:
Fleet, 177
Leaf Disease of Fruit Trees, 90
Scurf of Potatoes, 90
Simmonds, O. (Chairman), Committee on the Brick Industry, Reports, 125, 188
Simon, Lord (Chairman), Royal Commission on Population, Statement, 321
Simonds, Mr. Justice, Militia Camps, Charges made in connection with the construction of, Report. Cmd. 6271, 18
Simple Health Hints, 96, 155
Simplex Oilskin Clothing, Specifications, 65, 122
Simpson, G. C., Lightning and Aircraft, 112
Single-Storey:
Buildings, Construction of, Factory Form, 164
Factories for War Industries, Standard Designs, 56
Sinking Fund, Accounts, 12, 77, 135, 198, 265
Sinton, J. A., Control of Mosquito Nuisances in Great Britain, 157
Sisal Ropes, Specification, 122
Sites. See Building Sites.
Sitka Spruce or Approved Substitutes, Specification, 91

SKI— INDEX 1941-45

Skilled Men in the Services, Committee
on, Reports :
Cmd. 6307, 20
Cmd. 6339, 81
Skillman, E. E., Rhubarb, 211, 286
Skin Spot and Silver Scurf of Potatoes,
90
Skins. See Hides and Skins.
Slave Labour and Deportation, 249
" Sleepy " Disease, 26
Sleeves, Dispensers, Specification, 65
Slugs and Snails, 27, 286
Small :
Ermine Moths, 211
Retailers, Schemes for ensuring fair
shares of supplies, 119
Smallholding Society, Annual Return
Forms, 36, 98, 156
Smith, T., The Natural Lighting of
Houses and Flats, 243
Smut. See Onion and Leek Smut.
Snails. See Slugs and Snails.
Snap Fastener Trade. See Pin, Hook
and Eye, etc.
Snell, Lord (Chairman), Departmental
Committee on Police Widows' Pen-
sions, Report. Cmd. 6312, 21
Sneyd Colliery, Explosion at, Report.
Cmd. 6412, 140
Social :
and Physical Training :
Facilities for, 296
Grant Regs., 35
Amending, 218
Provisional (Scotland), 322
Insurance :
and Allied Services :
Report. Cmd. 6404, 85
Appendix G. Cmd. 6405, 85
in Brief, 120
Brief Guide, 241
Ministry of, Bill, 192, 203
Act. See National Insurance.
Part. I. Cmd. 6550, 206
Part II. Workmen's Compensa-
tion. Cmd. 6551, 206
Medicine, Scottish Experiment in,
180
Work, Careers, 306
Soft :
Aluminium Alloy Sheets and Coils,
Specification, 92
Rubber Sheet, Specification, 30
Soil :
Analysis, 90
Sterilisation, 211, 286

Soldiers :
in Debt, Restriction on Cash issued
to, 252
War Office Publications (N.P.), 62,
120
Soldiers' :
Disability and Dependants' Pensions,
252
Welfare, 68
Solicitors :
Act, 23
Bill, 1, 3, 15
Careers, 306
Practice Leaflet for, 53
Solid Fuel Installations, Report, 254
Solomon, M. E., Tyroglyphid Mites in
Stored Products, 179
Solvent. See Rubber Solvent.
Somalia, British Military Administra-
tion in, 224
Sorn, Lord (Chairman), Committee on
Scottish Rating System, Report. Cmd.
6595, 274
Soulbury, Lord (Chairman), Commission
on Ceylon Constitutional Reform,
Report. Cmd. 6677, 279
Sound :
Insulation and Acoustics, Report,
254
Signals, Survey, Instructions, 59, 333
South :
Africa :
Extradition, Supplementary Con-
vention to Treaty of Sept. 12,
1908 with Paraguay, Australia,
New Zealand and U.K. Cmd.
6410, 85
Mozambique Convention of Sept.
11, 1928, as amended, Exchange
of Notes with Portugal. Cmd.
6306, 20
African Honours, 240
Derbyshire Coalfield, National Coal
Resources, 115
Shields Corporation Act, 284
Suburban Gas Act, 283
Wales :
and Monmouthshire, Hospital Ser-
vices of, 304
Coalfield, Isovol Map, 243
Coalminers, Chronic Pulmonary
Disease in, 113, 178, 319
Coals of, 115
Electric Power :
Act, 87
Special Order, 60

South-East Asia Command, Welfare of
Troops in, Report. Cmd. 6578, 207
South-Eastern Gas Corporation Limited
(Associated Companies) Act, 23
Southern :
Railway :
(Air Transport) Act, 283
(Superannuation Fund) Act, 24
Rhodesia–Portuguese East Africa
Frontier, Delimitation of, Ex-
change of Notes, Portugal and
U.K. Cmd. 6280, 19
Sou'-wester, Oilskin, Specification, 65
Soviet Union. See Union of Soviet
Socialist Republics.
Spain :
Debts Clearing Office, Accounts, 7,
72, 130
Supplementary Loan Agreement with
U.K. Cmd. 6267, 18
Speaker, Letters from the, to the Prime
Minister, on Electoral Reform and
Redistribution of Seats :
Cmd. 6534, 205
Cmd. 6543, 206
Special :
Producers, Lists of, 118, 182, 247
Schools, Qualifications of Teachers,
296
Specifications :
Civilian Clothing, 247
Electrical, 324
Ministry of Aircraft Production, 28,
91, 149, 212, 287
Ministry of Supply, 181
Utility Footwear, 183, 248, 328
War Office, 64, 121, 185, 251, 331
Wireless Telegraphy Board, 25, 88,
147, 285
Spehe, s.s., Wreck Report, 253
Spider. See Red Spider ; Fruit Tree Red
Spider ; Gooseberry Red Spider.
Spindles :
Board Accounts, 4, 71, 131
See also Drilling Machine Spindles.
Spirit Tables, 157
Spotted :
Fly Catcher, 211
Wilt of Tomato, 27
Spraying. See Orchard Spraying.
Springburn. See Coatbridge.
Spruce. See Sitka Spruce.
Spurrey, 90
Squirrels. See Grey Squirrels.
Stabilisation Fund. See United and
Associated Nations.

Staff :
Nurse, Abolition of Rank of, 67
See also Civilian Staff.
Staffordshire :
Potteries Stipendiary Justice Act,
283
See also North Staffordshire.
Stamped and Pressed Metal Wares
Trade, Wages, 50, 51, 110, 176, 239
Standard Tanker Bill of Lading, etc., 334
Standards :
for School Premises, Memo., 217
in Building, the Use of, 254
Standing Orders. See House of Com-
mons ; Private Bill.
Stanley Electricity Special Order, 60
Stars :
Campaign. See Campaign Stars.
Fundamental, Apparent Places of
the, 25, 88, 147, 210, 285
Starters for Cheese Making, 27, 286
State :
Management Districts, Annual
Reports, 4, 71, 130, 194, 259, 267
Scholarships Regs., 35, 96, 296
State-owned Assets, Report, 137
Static Organisation at Home, 252
Stationery :
Office Publications (N.P.), 60, 117,
181, 245, 323
Services, Civil Estimates, 8, 74, 132,
195, 261
Statistical Quality Control, Film Strips,
218
Statute Law Committee Publications
(N.P.), 60, 117, 181, 246, 323
Statutes, Chronological Table and Index,
181
Statutory Rules and Orders :
Lists of, 60, 117, 181, 246, 323
Select Committee on :
Minutes of Evidence, 269
Minutes of Proceedings, 200, 265
Reports, 200, 264, 267, 269
Volumes, 60, 117, 181, 246, 323
Steam Boilers, Factory Forms, 42, 104
Steamships. See Passenger Steamships.
Steel :
Aerial Wire, Specifications, 29
Foundries, Dust in, Report, 238
Rods and Wire, Specification, 31
Sheets and Coils, Specifications, 31
Shelters, Cases of Flooding, 38
Specifications, 28, 93
Structures, Report, 254
Tubes, Specifications, 21, 93

70

71

STE— INDEX 1941-45

Steelwork. See Structural Steelwork.
Stem :
and Bulb Eelworm, 90
Canker of Potato, 90
Sterilisation. See Soil Sterilisation.
Stills, Explosion and Gassing Risks in
Cleaning, etc., Factory Form, 228
Stinging Nettles, 89
Stipends. See Episcopal Endowments
and Stipends.
Stock, F. G. L., A Study of Variations in
Output, 242
Stockdale, Sir F., Development and
Welfare in the West Indies, Report,
154, 295
Stockings, Specifications, 64, 122
Stoker's Manual, 300
Stomach Worms in Sheep, 90, 211
Stone Fruit Trees, Pruning, 27
Stonehenge, Guide to, 188
Stored Products, Tyroglyphid Mites in,
320
Stores :
Government Surplus, Disposal of.
Cmd. 6539, 205
See also Warlike Stores.
Stoving Enamel, Specification, 91
Strait Waistcoats, Specification, 65
Straps. See Containers and Straps ;
Leather or Textile Containers.
Strawberries, 211
Stripe Cotton Hospital Clothing, Speci-
fication, 65
Strips, Metal, Specifications, 91, 93
Structural Steelwork, Fire Protection of,
56
Submarine Areas of the Gulf of Paria,
Treaty between Venezuela and U.K. :
Cmd. 6359, 82 Cmd. 6400, 85
Submarines. See H.M. Submarines.
Subsistence Allowance, Civilian Non-
Industrial Staffs, War Office, 124
Substitute Feeding Stuffs, 148, 286
Sub-tropical Areas, Medical Diseases in,
66, 123, 187
Sugar :
Confectionery and Food Preserving
Trade, Wages, 52, 111, 176, 239
Industry :
Act, 86
Bill, 16
Select Committee on,
Report, 75
of Fiji, Report, 295
(Research and Education) Fund
Accounts, 9, 73, 133, 195, 260

Sugar (continued) :
Production and Marketing of, Proto-
col to International Agreement.
Cmd. 6395, 84
Sulphide. See Hydrogen Sulphide.
Sulphonamides :
Medical Use of, 178, 319
in the Treatment of Meningococcal
Meningitis, Report, 244
Sulphur Dioxide, Detection of, 115
Sunderland Corporation Act, 146
Sunflowers, 90
Cultivation, etc., 149
Superannuation. See Pensions ; Rail-
way Clearing System ; Southern Rail-
way ; Teachers' Superannuation ;
Nurses and Midwives.
Supplementary :
Pensions :
(Determination of Need and
Assessment of Needs) (Amend-
ment) Draft Regs., Memos. :
Cmd. 6265, 17
Cmd. 6375, 83
Cmd. 6464, 143
Cmd. 6490, 144
Report on the Administration of
the Determination of Needs
Act, 1941. Cmd. 6338, 81
Reserve, Army, War Office Publica-
tions (N.P.), 67, 252
Supplies :
and Services (Transitional Powers)
Bill, 257, 258, 271, 272
Limitation of, Board of Trade Publi-
cations (N.P.), 61, 119, 183, 248,
327
Supply :
Ministry of :
Appropriation Account, 7
Publications (N.P.), 117, 181, 246,
324
Services, 10
Transport and Barrack Services,
Regs., Army, 67, 124, 187, 252,
333
Supports at Faces, Defects in, Mines
Safety Pamphlet, 220
Supreme Court :
(Northern Ireland) Act, 86
Bill, 71
of Judicature :
Accounts, 6, 71, 130, 137, 202,
267
(Amendment) Act, 207
Bill, 190, 202

Supreme Court (continued) :
of Judicature (continued) :
High Court and Court of Appeal,
Accounts, 62, 120, 184, 249, 329
Northern Ireland Land Purchase
Accounts, 13, 79, 136, 200, 267
Prize and Deposit Accounts, 133,
197, 200, 267
Surface :
Caterpillars, 27
Dressings (Road), Recommendations
for, 57
Surgery, Careers, 306
Surplus Stores, Government, Disposal
of. Cmd. 6539, 205
Survey :
Computations, 68
of Lights and Sound Signals, Instruc-
tions, 59, 333
of Passenger Steamships, Instruc-
tions, 59, 125
See also Geological Survey.
Surveying, Careers, 306
Surveyors :
Instructions to, Ministry of Trans-
port Publications (N.P.), 59, 125,
333
of Works, Army, 66
Surveyors' Certificates, Mines, Examina-
tions, 55, 156, 220, 299
Sutcliffe, R. C., Meteorology for Avia-
tors, 54, 112
Sutherland, J. (Chairman), National
Forest Park Committee (Glentrool),
Report, 298
Swan, J. R. (Chairman), Departmental
Committee on Patents and Designs
Acts, Report. Cmd. 6618, 275
Swarbrick, T., Hedge and Tree Stump
Clearing, 88
" Swayback " in Lambs, 27, 286
Sweden :
Commercial Conditions in, 317
Monetary Agreement with U.K.
Cmd. 6604, 264
Swedes, 148
See also Turnips and Swedes.
Sweet Corn, 149
Swine Erysipelas, 26
Synthetic Resin :
Bonded Paper Sheet, Specification,
88
(Phenolic) Moulding Materials and
Mouldings, Specifications, 30, 93
Primer and Finish, Specification,
93

Syria and Lebanon, Statements of
Policy by H.M. Government. Cmd.
6600, 274
Syringes, Sterilisation, Use and Care of,
319

T

Tables and Constants for use of Students,
296
Tailoring Trade, Wages, 50, 51, 110, 239,
315
Take-all or Whiteheads of Wheat and
Barley, 27
Tams, W. H. T., Insect Pests of Food,
219
Tangier. See Morocco.
Tanker. See Standard Tanker.
Tanks :
Explosion and Gassing Risks in
Cleaning, etc., Factory Form, 228
See also British Tanks ; Liquid
Manure Tanks.
Tape. See Linen Tape ; Silk Tape.
Tar :
Carpets and Surface Dressings,
Roads, Recommendations, 57, 179,
243
Oil Winter Washes, Specifications
and Methods of Analysis, 26
Target Germany, 219
Tariff. See Customs.
Tatchell, S. (Chairman) :
Plumbing Committee of Building
Research Board, Report, 254
Standards Committee, Report (The
Use of Standards in Building), 254
Taunton Corporation Act, 23
Tax :
Cases, Leaflets and Reports, 39, 102,
160, 265
See also Income Tax ; Passenger
Tax ; Excess Profits Tax ;
Farmers' Income Tax.
Taxation. See Double Taxation.
Taylor, H. V., Rhubarb, 211, 286
Taylor, Professor T. M. (Chairman),
Scottish Nurses' Salaries Committee,
Reports :
Cmd. 6425, 141
Notes on the Report, 180
Cmd. 6439, 141
Cmd. 6488 (Mental Nurses Sub-
Committee Report), 144
Cmd. 6505, 204

72

73

TAY—   *INDEX 1941–45*

Taylor, W. (Chairman), Inquiry Committee on the Standardisation of the Elements of Optical Instruments, Report, 179
Tea Cloths, Rationing, 154, 155, 217, 218
Teachers :
  and Youth Leaders, Supply, Recruitment and Training of, Report, 218
  Emergency Recruitment and Training, Circulars. 217, 218
  in Special Schools, Qualifications, 298
  Scales of Salaries, 297
    Scotland, 322
    Suggestions for, 97
  (Superannuation) Act, 282
    Bill, 255, 270
    Circulars, 296, 298
    Directions, 218
  Supply, Recruitment and Training in the period immediately following the war, Report. *Cmd. 6501*, 203
  Training :
    Scotland, 322
    Supplementary Regs., 35, 97, 155, 218, 297
    Technical, 296
Teacher's Copy of Service Book, 35
Teaching as a Career, 297
Tea-making Appliances, 125
Technical :
  Corps, Civilian (Air Ministry), 28
  Education, Report. *Cmd. 6593*, 274
  Pay, Army, 66, 68, 124, 187
  Teachers, Training of, 296
Technological Education, Higher, Report, 296
Telegraph :
  Act, 145
  Bill, 139
  Services :
    Accounts, 4
    See also London Post Office Guide.
  See also Post Office and Telegraph.
Telegraphy. *See* Meteorological Telegraphy ; Wireless Telegraphy.
Telephone Services :
  Accounts, 4
  See also London Post Office Guide.
Television Committee Report, 318
Temporary :
  Accommodation :
    Memo., 222
    Scotland, 244
    See also Housing.

Housing Programme. *Cmd. 6686, 279*
Laws, Registers of, 13, 79, 137, 201, 268
Migration of Children (Guardianship), Act, 22
  Bill, 2, 15
Tenant. *See* Landlord and Tenant.
Tenders for Treasury Bills, 240
Territorial :
  Army :
    Nursing Service, Women Officers, 188
    See also War Office Publications (N.P.).
  Service. *See* Auxiliary Territorial Service.
Territories. *See* Occupied Territories.
Teviot, Lord (Chairman), Interdepartmental Committee on Dentistry, Interim Report. *Cmd. 6565*, 207
Textile Containers. *See* Leather or Textile Containers.
Textiles :
  and Clothing, Specifications, 64, 122, 186, 251
  See also Woven Textiles ; Apparel and Textiles ; Household Textiles ; Made-up Textiles ; Cotton Textiles.
Thailand :
  Boundary between Burma and, Exchange of Notes with U.K. *Cmd. 6262*, 17
  Notification of State of War with, 112
There's Freedom in the Air, 224
Thermocouples. *See* Platinum Thermocouples.
Thomas, Sir C. J. H. (Chairman), Tithe Redemption Commission, Report, 137
Thomas, W. R. (Chairman), Interdepartmental Committee on Mental Nursing, Report, 301
Thompson, B. C., Mass Miniature Radiography of Civilians, etc., 319
Thompson, F. L., Merseyside Plan 1944, 325
Thornley, S. K. (Chairman), Painting of Buildings Committee, Report, 254
Thornton, W. M. (Chairman), Committee on the Amendment of the General Regs. governing the Use of Electricity in Mines, Report, 55
Thrips. *See* Pea and Bean Thrips.
Tiger Kills, 223
Tile Making, Dust containing Silica, Report, 175

INDEX 1941–45   **—TRA**

Timber :
  Economy, 125, 189
  in Building, 114
  Wartime, 254
  Production, 13
  Roofs, Fire Stops for, 56
Timbers :
  for Aircraft, Decay and Insect Damage in, 175
  See also Empire Timbers.
Tin :
  Box Trade, Wages, 52, 110, 239
  Plate Cooking Utensils, Specification, 64
  Production and Export of, Agreement, Belgium, Bolivia, U.K. and the Netherlands. *Cmd. 6396*, 85
Tintern Abbey, Guide to, 188
Tippets. *See* Detector Tippets.
Tithe :
  Act, 1936, Accounts, 10, 74, 132, 195, 260
  Redemption Commission :
    Publications (N.P.), 181
    Reports, 137, 267
Titmice, 211
Tobacco Trade, Wages, 111, 176
Today's Children—Tomorrow's Hope, 329
Toilet Preparations :
  Manufacturer's and Trader's Guide, 119
  Register, List of Persons, 61, 119, 183, 248, 327
Tomato :
  Leaf Mould, 27
  Mosaic Disease and Streak of, 89
  Wilt or " Sleepy " Disease, 26
Tomatoes, 26
  Spotted Wilt, 27
Tomlinson, G. (Chairman), Interdepartmental Committee on Rehabilitation and Resettlement of Disabled Persons, Report. *Cmd. 6415*, 140
Tools. *See* Edge Tools ; Woodworkers' Tools ; Diamond Tools ; Machine Tools.
Tow, Spinning and Weaving, Factory Forms, 104, 164
Towards a World of Plenty, 329
Towels, Rationing, 154, 155, 217, 218, 296

Town :
  and Country Planning :
    Act, 208
    Bill, 192, 202, 203
    (Interim Development) :
      Act, 145
      Bill, 126, 127, 128, 139
    (Scotland) Act, 145
      Bill, 129, 139
    Minister of, Act, 145
      Bill, 126, 138
    Ministry of, Publications (N.P.), 181, 246, 324
    (Scotland) Act, 282
      Bill, 256, 263, 266, 270
      Explanatory Memo., 321
  Planning, Careers, 306
  Refuse and Soil Improver, 27
Toxic Gases in Industry, 115, 179
Toy Manufacturing Trade, Wages, 50, 52, 176, 315
Trade :
  Agreements :
    Saudi Arabia and U.K. *Cmd. 6381*, 84
    Turkey and U.K. *Cmd. 6269*, 18
    Uruguay and Canada. *Cmd. 6275*, 18
    U.S.A. and Canada. *Cmd. 6246*, 16
  and Employment, Proposals for Consideration by an International Conference. *Cmd. 6709*, 281
  between Cyprus and Egypt, Exchange of Notes between Egypt and U.K. *Cmd. 6305*, 20
  Board of, Publications (N.P.) (including Board of Trade Journal), 60, 117, 182, 246, 325
  Boards Orders, Wages, 49, 109, 175, 238, 315
  Civil Estimates, 8, 74, 132, 195, 261
  Dispute at Briggs Motor Bodies Ltd., Report of Court of Enquiry. *Cmd. 6284*, 19
  Facilities Acts, Accounts etc , 11, 76, 135, 198, 264
  of the U.K. :
    Accounts, 4
    with British Countries and Foreign Countries, 34, 96
  Operations for which Bonus Rate are fixed, 188
  Practices. *See* Pre-war Trade Practices.
  Union, Annual Return Form, 36, 98, 156

TRA—   *INDEX 1941–45*

Tradesmen. *See* Apprentice Tradesmen.
Tradesmen's Rates of Pay, Army, Regs. governing issue, 124
Trading :
  Accounts and Balance Sheets, Government Departments, 5, 72, 130, 194, 260
  with the Enemy, Legislation in Force, 119, 248, 328
Traffic :
  Signs :
    Authorisation of, 253
    Directions, 253
  See also Road Goods Traffic.
Trail, R. R., Radiological Appearances of Early Pulmonary Tuberculosis, 157
Training :
  Manual (A.R.P.), 100
  See also Physical and Recreational Training ; Social and Physical Training ; Physical Training ; Teachers ; Girls ; Citizenship ; Building Industry ; Educational Training.
  Colleges recognised by the Board of Education, 155
Transfusion Services, Official Account of, 303
Trans-Jordan, Agreement with Great Britain. *Cmd. 6323*, 21
Transport :
  Civil Estimates, 8, 74, 132, 195, 261
  goes to War, 101
  Select Committee on National Expenditure, Report, 12
  Services Regs., Army, 67, 124, 187, 252
  See also Air Transport ; Sea Transport ; Passenger Transport ; War Transport ; International Air Transport ; Motor Transport ; Road Transport ; European Inland Transport.
Transportation. *See* Marine Transportation.
Transports. *See* Masters of Transports.
Travelling Regs. for Civilians (War Office), 124
Travers' Foundation. *See* Greenwich Hospital.
Treason Act, 283
  Bill, 256
Treasury :
  Bills, Tenders for, 240
  Chest Fund, Accounts, 5, 75, 133, 196, 263

Treasury—*continued*
  Publications (N.P.), 62, 119, 181, 249, 328
Treated Ethylene Glycol, Specification, 29
Treaty Series :
  1940 :
    No. 30. Trade Agreement, U.S.A. and Canada. *Cmd. 6246*, 16
    No. 31. Notifications, Accessions Withdrawals etc *Cmd 6253*, 17
    No. 32. Index. *Cmd. 6254*, 17
  1941 :
    No. 1. Finance and the Purchase of Commodities, Belgium and U.K. *Cmd. 6248*, 16
    No. 2. Bases leased to U.S.A. *Cmd. 6259*, 17
    No. 3. Burma and Thailand, Boundary between. *Cmd. 6262*, 17
    No. 4. Air Service between Australia and Portuguese Timor. *Cmd. 6266*, 17
    No. 5. Supplementary Loan Agreement, Spain and U.K. *Cmd. 6267*, 18
    No. 6. Disposal of Real and Personal Property, U.S.A., Australia, New Zealand and U.K. *Cmd. 6268*, 18
    No. 7. Trade and Payments Agreement, Turkey and U.K. *Cmd. 6269*, 18
    No. 8. Certificates of Airworthiness for Export, U.S.A. and New Zealand. *Cmd. 6272*, 18
    No. 9. Establishment of a Board of Enquiry for the Great Lakes Fisheries, U.S.A. and Canada. *Cmd. 6273*, 18
    No. 10. Commercial Relations, Paraguay and Canada. *Cmd. 6274*, 18
    No. 11. Trade Agreement, Uruguay and Canada. *Cmd. 6275*, 18
    No. 12. Emergency Regulation of the Level of Rainy Lake and of the Level of other Boundary Waters in the Rainy Lake Watershed. *Cmd. 6276*, 18

INDEX 1941–45   **—TRE**

Treaty Series (*continued*) :
  1941 (*continued*) :
    No. 13. Delimitation of the Southern Rhodesia–Portuguese East Africa Frontier. *Cmd. 6280*, 19
    No. 14. Legal Proceedings in Civil and Commercial Matters, Turkey and U.K. *Cmd. 6292*, 19
    No. 15. Joint Action in the War against Germany, Soviet Union and U.K. *Cmd. 6304*, 20
    No. 16. Trade between Cyprus and Egypt. *Cmd. 6305*, 20
    No. 17. Reciprocal Recognition of Load Line Regulations for Vessels engaged in International Voyages on the Great Lakes. *Cmd. 6302*, 20
    No. 18. Great Lakes–St. Lawrence Basin, U.S.A. and Canada. *Cmd. 6303*, 20
    No. 19. Mozambique Convention of Sept. 11, 1928, as amended. Portugal and South Africa. *Cmd. 6319*, 21
    No. 20. Exemptions from Exchange Control Measures, U.S.A. and Canada. *Cmd. 6319*, 21
    No. 21. Air Transport Services, U.S.A. and Canada. *Cmd. 6320*, 21
    No. 22. Temporary Commercial Agreement, Chile and U.K. *Cmd. 6322*, 21
    No. 23. Ratifications, Accessions, Withdrawals, etc. *Cmd. 6329*, 81
    No. 24. Index. *Cmd. 6330*, 81
  1942 :
    No. 1. Regulation of Purchases of Commodities from the Belgian Congo and Ruanda-Urundi, Belgium and U.K. *Cmd. 6365*, 83
    No. 2. Alliance against Hitlerite Germany and her Associates in Europe, etc., U.S.S.R. and U.K. *Cmd. 6376*, 83
    No. 3. Policy of H.M. Government in regard to Czechoslovakia. *Cmd. 6379*, 83
    No. 4. Avoidance of Double Taxation, etc., U.S.A. and Canada. *Cmd. 6383*, 84

Treaty Series (*continued*) :
  1942 (*continued*) :
    No. 5. Declaration by United Nations. *Cmd. 6388*, 84
    No. 6. Reciprocal Aid in the Prosecution of the War against Aggression. U.S.A. and U.K. *Cmd. 6389*, 84
    No. 7. Mutual Aid in the Prosecution of the War against Aggression. U.S.A. and U.K. *Cmd. 6391*, 84
    No. 8. Interchange of Patent Rights and Information, U.S.A. and U.K. *Cmd. 6392*, 84
    No. 9. Tin, Production and Export, Belgium, Bolivia, Netherlands and U.K. *Cmd. 6396*, 85
    No. 10. Submarine Areas of the Gulf of Paria, Venezuela and U.K. *Cmd. 6400*, 85
    No. 11. Status of Island of Patos, Venezuela and U.K. *Cmd. 6401*, 85
    No. 12. Commercial Modus Vivendi, Ecuador and Canada. *Cmd. 6409*, 85
    No. 13. Extradition, Paraguay, Australia, New Zealand, South Africa and U.K. *Cmd. 6410*, 85
    No. 14. Ratifications, Accessions, Withdrawals, etc. *Cmd. 6431*, 141
    No. 15. Index. *Cmd. 6432*, 141
  1943 :
    No. 1. Marine Transport and Litigation, U.S.A. and U.K. *Cmd. 6416*, 140
    No. 2. Relinquishment of Extra-Territorial Rights in China, China, India and U.K. *Cmd. 6456*, 142
    No. 3. United Nations Relief and Rehabilitation Administration. *Cmd. 6491*, 144
  1944. No documents *in this series were issued in 1944.*
  1945 :
    No. 1. Mutual Aid, Belgium and U.K. *Cmd. 6620*, 275
    No. 2. European Inland Transport. *Cmd. 6660*, 276

TRE—   *INDEX 1941–45*   *INDEX 1941–45*   **—UNI**

Treaty Series (*continued*):
1945 (*continued*):
No. 3. Property in U.K. belonging to persons resident in Belgium. *Cmd. 6665*, 278
No. 4. Monetary Agreement, Denmark and U.K. *Cmd. 6671*, 278
No. 5. Rights of Industrial, Literary and Artistic Property. *Cmd. 6674*, 278
No. 6. Money and Property which have been subjected to Special Measures, France and U.K. *Cmd. 6675*, 278
No. 7. Monetary Agreement, Netherlands and U.K. *Cmd. 6681*, 279
No. 8. Monetary Agreement, Czechoslovakia and U.K. *Cmd. 6694*, 280
No. 9. Property, etc., Czechoslovakia and U.K. *Cmd. 6695*, 280
No. 10. Monetary Agreement, Norway and U.K. *Cmd. 6697*, 280
No. 11. Money and Property, Denmark and U.K. *Cmd. 6717*, 281

Tree Fruits, 211
Trees. *See* Fruit Trees; Stone Fruit Trees.
Tree-Stump Clearing, 88
Trent Guns and Cartridges Ltd., Report into Dispute with National Union of General and Municipal Workers. *Cmd. 6300*, 20
Trevelyan, G. M. (Chairman), National Forest Park Committee (Hardknott), Report, 299
Trichomonas Disease, 149
Triumph in Disaster, 295
Troops in India and South East Asia Commands, Welfare of, Report. *Cmd. 6578*, 207
Tropical:
and Sub-Tropical Areas, Medical Diseases in, Memos., 66, 123, 187
Dress, Outfit Allowance, Army, 123
Trotter, F. M., Geology of Forest of Dean Coal and Iron-Ore Field, 115
Trousers, Specifications, 65, 122
Trunk Roads Bill, 269, 271, 272

Trustee:
Savings Banks and Friendly Societies, Accounts, 62, 120, 184, 249, 299
(War Damage Insurance) Act, 23 Bill, 2
Tuberculosis:
in Wartime, Committee on, Report, 113
See also Pulmonary Tuberculosis.
Tubing. *See* Rubber Tubing.
Tuition Fees in Grant-aided Secondary Schools, Abolition of, Report, 154
Tunisia, 224
Turkey:
Commercial Conditions in, 317
Debts Clearing Office Accounts, 7, 72, 130
Legal Proceedings in Civil and Commercial Matters, Supplementary Convention with U.K. *Cmd. 6292*, 19
Trade and Payments Agreements with U.K.:
Cmd. 6269, 18
Cmd. 6632, 276
Turner, J. S. (Chairman), Solid Fuel Installations Committee, Report, 254
Turnip Gall Weevil, 90
Turnips and Swedes, Dry Rot of, 58
Turnips, Swedes and Kohlrabi, 148
Twin Disease in Ewes, 27
Twine Trade, Wages, 51, 111, 176, 239
Tyres, Economy in Use of, 100
Tyroglyphid Mites in Stored Products, 179, 320

U

Ulster Home Guard, Honours, 240
Ultimus Haeres, Scotland, Account and List of Estates, 59
"Umavoil" Standard Tanker Voyage Charter Party, 334
Unemployment:
Assistance:
and Supplementary Pensions, Report on the Administration of the Determination of Needs Act, 1941. *Cmd. 6338*, 81
Civil Estimates, 7, 8, 74, 132, 133, 195, 196, 261

Unemployment (*continued*):
Assistance (*continued*):
Determination of Need and Assessment of Needs (Amendment) Draft Regs., Explanatory Memos.:
Cmd. 6263, 17
Cmd. 6374, 83
Draft Regs., 1943, Explanatory Memo. *Cmd. 6490*, 144
Fund:
Accounts, 6, 73, 131, 197, 260
Financial Condition, Reports on, 9, 134, 197, 263
Investment Accounts, 10, 77, 136, 198, 264
Insurance:
Civil Estimates, 7, 8, 74, 132, 133, 195, 196, 261
(Contributions) (Agriculture) Order, 1942, Draft, 76
Decisions by the Umpire, 52, 111, 176, 239, 315
(Increase of Benefit) Act, 208 Bill, 192, 203
Personnel of the R.A.F., 91
Statutory Committee Reports, 9, 76
Uniform:
Allowance, Nursing Services, Army, 250
Regs. for Officers of the Fleet, 25
Uniforms:
Civil Defence, 223
Nurses', Prices, etc., 327
Union of Soviet Socialist Republics:
Alliance:
in the War against Hitlerite Germany, etc., Treaty with U.K.:
Cmd. 6368, 83
Cmd. 6376, 83
Treaty of, with Persia and U.K. *Cmd. 6335*, 81
Joint Action in the War against Germany, Agreement with U.K. *Cmd. 6304*, 20
United:
and Associated Nations Stabilisation Fund, U.S. Proposal, 156
Kingdom:
Food Consumption Levels in, 219
War Effort, Statistics. *Cmd. 6564*, 207
Maritime Authority:
Planning Committee, Report, 253
Publications (N.P.), 334

United (*continued*):
Nations:
Charter, etc., San Francisco Conference, 329
Commentary on. *Cmd. 6666*, 278
Declaration by. *Cmd. 6388*, 84
Educational and Cultural Organisation:
Draft Proposals, 295
Final Act. *Cmd. 6711*, 281
Food and Agriculture Organisation:
Documents relating to, 274
Story of, 329
Information Organisation Publications (N.P.), 249, 329
Introduction to, 329
Monetary and Financial Conference:
Final Act. *Cmd. 6546*, 206
Story of, 329
Supplementary Documents. *Cmd. 6597*, 274
Preparatory Commission:
Agreement establishing the Commission. *Cmd. 6669*, 278
Publications (N.P.), 329
Relief and Rehabilitation Administration:
Agreement. *Cmd. 6491*, 144
Publications (N.P.), 250, 329
Reports and Papers (2nd Session), 329
Resolutions, on:
adopted at 1st Session. *Cmd. 6497*, 203
adopted at 2nd Session. *Cmd. 6566*, 207
adopted at 3rd Session. *Cmd. 6682*, 279
Story of, 249
Today and Tomorrow, 329
States of America:
Air Transport Services, Exchange of Notes with Canada. *Cmd. 6320*, 21
Atlantic Charter, Joint Declaration by President of U.S.A. and Mr. Winston Churchill. *Cmd. 6321*, 21
Avoidance of Double Taxation, Conventions:
with Canada. *Cmd. 6383*, 84
with U.K.: *Cmd. 6624*, 275
Cmd. 6625, 275

UNI—   *INDEX 1941–45*   *INDEX 1941–45*   **—VOT**

United (*continued*):
States of America (*continued*):
Bases leased to, Agreement. *Cmd. 6259*, 17
Certificates of Airworthiness for Export, Exchange of Notes with New Zealand. *Cmd. 6272*, 18
Commercial Conditions in, 317
Co-ordination of the Allied War Effort, Agreement with U.K. *Cmd. 6332*, 81
Cotton Textiles Mission to, Report, 241
Disposal of Real and Personal Property, Convention with U.K., Australia, and New Zealand. *Cmd. 6268*, 18
Emergency Regulation of the Level of Rainy Lake and of the Level of other Boundary Waters in the Rainy Lake Watershed, Convention with Canada. *Cmd. 6276*, 18
Establishment of a Board of Enquiry for the Great Lakes Fisheries, Exchange of Notes with Canada. *Cmd. 6273*, 18
Exemption from Exchange Control Measures, Exchange of Notes with Canada. *Cmd. 6319*, 21
Financial:
Agreement with U.K. (Washington Negotiations). *Cmd. 6708*, 281
Statistical Material presented during the Negotiations. *Cmd. 6707*, 281
Powers (U.S.A. Securities) Act, 23
Bill, 15
Draft Regs. *Cmd. 6296*, 19
Food Consumption Levels in, 219
Great Lakes–St. Lawrence Basin, Exchange of Notes with Canada. *Cmd. 6303*, 20
Interchange of Patent Rights and Information, Agreement with U.K. *Cmd. 6392*, 84
Marine Transport and Litigation, Agreement with U.K. *Cmd. 6416*, 140
Materials received under the Lease-Lend Act, Policy of H.M. Government in connection with. *Cmd. 6311*, 21

United (*continued*):
States of America (*continued*):
Meet the U.S. Army, 160
Methods of Building in, 253
Mutual Aid in the Prosecution of the War against Aggression, Agreement with U.K.:
Cmd. 6341, 82
Cmd. 6391, 84
Official Documents reprinted by H.M.S.O., 156, 219, 298
Petroleum Agreements with U.K.:
Cmd. 6555, 206
Cmd. 6683, 279
President of. *See* Roosevelt.
Reciprocal:
Aid in the Prosecution of the War against Aggression, Exchange of Notes with U.K. *Cmd. 6389*, 84
Recognition of Load Line Regs. for Vessels engaged in International Voyages on the Great Lakes, Exchange of Notes with Canada. *Cmd. 6302*, 20
Speech by Viscount Halifax, H.M. Ambassador at Washington. *Cmd. 6264*, 17
Trade Agreement with Canada. *Cmd. 6246*, 16
(Visiting Forces) Act, 86 Bill, 70
What do they Eat in U.S.A., Canada and Britain? 219
Wheat Discussions at Washington, Exchanges of Notes with Argentine, Australia, Canada and U.K. *Cmd. 6371*, 83
Universities and Colleges (Trust) Act, 145 Bill, 138
Upper Winds, Measurement of, 317
Uruguay:
Commercial Conditions in, 317
Trade Agreement with Canada. *Cmd. 6275*, 18
Uthwatt, Hon. Mr. Justice (Chairman), Expert Committee on Compensation and Betterment, Reports:
Cmd. 6291, 19
Cmd. 6386, 84
Utility:
and Non-Utility Cloth, Apparel, Bedding, Household Textiles, Traders' Guide to Price Control, 119

Utility—*continued*
Apparel, etc., Schedules, 183, 248, 326
Footwear, Specifications, 183, 248
Furniture, Board of Trade Publications (N.P.), 183, 248
Gas Producer, Instruction Book, 188
Knitted Goods, Schedules, 119, 249, 184
Oilskins, Schedule, 249

V

Validation of Wartime Leases Act, 208 Bill, 203
Valuation:
for Rates, Departmental Committee on, Report, 222
See also Rating and Valuation; Hydro-Electric Undertakings; War Damage (Valuation Appeals).
Vapourer Moth, 148
Varnish. *See* Pigmented Oil Varnish.
Vaughan-Lee, A. C., Report on Severn Barrage Scheme, 300
Vegetable:
Crops, Manuring, 89, 148, 211
Garden, Pests and Diseases in, 26
Seed Crops, Threshing of, 286
Vegetables:
Diseases of, 26, 286
Domestic Preservation of, 148
Victory with, 321
See also Root Vegetables; Salads and Vegetables.
Venereal Diseases, Report. *Cmd. 6518*, 204
Venezuela:
Anglo-Venezuelan Treaty (Island of Patos) Act, 86 Bill, 69
Island of Patos, Status of, Treaty with U.K. *Cmd. 6401*, 85
Submarine Areas of the Gulf of Paria, Treaty with U.K.:
Cmd. 6359, 82
Cmd. 6400, 85
Ventilation:
and Heating, Lighting and Seeing, 178
Factory Form, 42
in the Blackout, 38
Verticillium Wilt and Black Dot of Potato, 90

Vessels. *See* Coal-carrying Vessels; Fishing Vessels; Merchant Vessels; New Vessels; Ships.
Veterinary:
Education in Great Britain, Committee on, Report. *Cmd. 6517*, 204
Matters. *See* West India Royal Commission.
Practice by Unregistered Persons, Report. *Cmd. 6611*, 275
Surgery, Careers, 306
Vick, G. R. (Chairman), Committee of Enquiry on I.C.C. Remand Homes, Report. *Cmd. 6594*, 274
Victoria Cross, Efficiency Classification of Soldiers, 185
Victory:
Bonds, 53, 112, 177
with Vegetables, 321
Vines, Powdery Mildew of, 286
Virus Disease of Potatoes, 27, 211
Visiting Forces:
(British Commonwealth) Act, 1933, Order and Regulation made under, 124
See also United States of America.
Visitors. *See* Official Visitors.
Visual Efficiency and Illumination, Relation between, 318
Vivian, Sir S. P. (Chairman), Committee on Electoral Machinery, Report. *Cmd. 6408*, 85
Voles, Notes on, 285
Voltmeters, Specification, 121
Voluntary Aid Detachments:
War Office Publications (N.P.), 68, 123, 124, 187, 252, 333
Vote of Credit:
1940 Supplementary, 7
1941, 7
Statement. *Cmd. 6279*, 18
Supplementary, 12, 14, 75
1942, 75
Statement. *Cmd. 6363*, 82
Supplementary, 77, 78, 131
1943, 131
Statement. *Cmd. 6445*, 142
Supplementary, 135, 137, 193
1944, 193
Statement. *Cmd. 6524*, 205
Supplementary, 198, 199, 200, 259
1945, 259, 267
Statement. *Cmd. 6630*, 276
Supplementary, 265
See also Appropriation Accounts.

Votes:
  Number of, cast at General Election, 1945, 268
  See also Air Votes; Army Votes; Navy Votes.
Voting. See Postal Voting.
Voyage, Regs., Army, 68, 124, 187, 252, 333
Vulcanised Rubber Sheet, Specification, 30

W

Wage Levy. See Guaranteed Wage Levy.
Wage-earners. See Weekly Wage-Earners.
Wage-Earners' Income Tax Bill, 140
Wage-Earners' (Income Tax (Employments) Act), 145
Wages:
  Councils Act, 282
  Bill, 203, 255, 270
  Port Transport Industry, Report, 314
  See also Civil Service Arbitration Tribunal Awards; Industrial Court Awards; National Arbitration Tribunal Awards; Trade Boards Orders; Road Haulage Wages; Fair Wages; Coal Mining Industry; Catering Wages; Domestic Help; Pay.
Waistcoats, Specifications, 65
Wakefield, Geology of the Country around, 67
Wales. See Church Temporalities; South Wales; North West England; Post-War Youth Service.
Wallace, J. C., Potatoes, 88
Wallace, T.:
  Diagnosis by Visual Symptoms of Mineral Deficiencies in Plants, 178
  Manuring Fruit Crops in Wartime, 26
Wallet, Anti-Gas, Specification, 65, 122
Walls, Floors and Roofs, Report, 334
War:
  against Aggression:
    Principles applying to Mutual Aid in the Promotion of, Agreement between U.S.A. and U.K.:
      Cmd. 6341, 82
      Cmd. 6391, 83
    Reciprocal Aid in the Prosecution of, Exchange of Notes, U.S.A. and U.K. Cmd. 6389, 84

War (continued):
  against Germany, Joint Action in, Agreement between Soviet Union and U.K. Cmd. 6304, 20
  Army at, 39, 68, 100, 101, 159, 224
  Crimes, Punishment for, 101, 160, 224
  Criminals:
    Prosecution and Punishment of: Agreement. Cmd. 6668, 278
    Indictment. Cmd. 6696, 280
    Trial of, Regs., 333
  Damage:
    Acts:
      1941, 22
      Bill, 1, 15
      Practice Notes, 120
      1943, 145
      Bill, 127, 139
      Report by Joint Committee, 127
      Proceedings and Minutes of Evidence, 127
    (Amendment) Acts:
      1942, 86
      Bill, 69, 70, 80
      1943, 145
      Bill, 126, 138
    Business Scheme, Statement of Receipts and Payments, 201, 268
    Commission Publications (N.P.), 62, 120, 250, 330
    (Extension of Risk Period) Act, 23
      Bill, 15
    Insurance:
      Trustee (War Damage Insurance) Act, 23
        Bill, 2
      Landlord and Tenant (War Damage) (Amendment) Act, 23
        Bill, 2, 15
      Practice Notes, 330
      Private Chattels Scheme, Statements of Receipts and Payments, 79, 138, 201, 268
      Rating (War Damage) (Scotland) Act, 22
        Bill, 15
      Repair of, Act, 23
        Bill, 15
      Statement of Payments and Contributions, 79, 137, 201, 268
      to Educational Property, 34, 36

War (continued):
  Damage (continued):
    to Land (Scotland) Act, 23
      Bill, 3, 15
    to Land and Buildings:
      Explanatory Pamphlet, 62
      Form, 120
    to Public Utility Undertakings. Cmd. 6403, 85
      (Valuation Appeals) Bill, 257, 272
  Department:
    Works and Repairs:
      to Buildings, etc., Schedule of Prices for, 125, 188
      to Requisitioned Buildings, etc., Abridged Schedule of Prices, 125
      Wartime Painting Services to Buildings, Schedule of Prices, 252
  Effort:
    of the U.K., Statistics. Cmd. 6564, 207
    See also Allied War Effort.
  Finance, Sources of:
    Cmd. 6261, 17
    Cmd. 6347, 82
    Cmd. 6438, 141
    Cmd. 6520, 204
    Cmd. 6623, 275
  Formulary. See National War Formulary.
  Gases, Nature, Effects, etc., 38, 100
  Graves. See Imperial War Graves Commission.
  India and the, Text of Announcement. Cmd. 6293, 19
  Marriages. See Matrimonial Causes.
  Materials, Production, 78
  Medicine, Bulletins of, 56, 114, 178, 242, 319
  Memoranda (Medical Research Council), 56, 178, 242, 319
  Notifications of a State of War with various Countries, 54
  Office:
    Claims Commission, Report, 136
    Examination Papers, 33
    Publications (N.P.), 62, 120, 184, 250, 330
  Orphans Act, 86
    Bill, 16, 69
  Peace and, 156
  Pensions:
    Changes in. Cmd. 6459, 142

War (continued):
  Pensions (continued):
    for Civilians and Members of the Civil Defence Services, Explanatory Notes, 241
    Improvement in. Cmd. 6714, 281
  Planning, Organisation of. Cmd. 6351, 82
  Prisoners:
    War Office Publications (N.P.), 272
    See also Limitation (Enemies and War Prisoners).
  Production, Methods of Settling Prices for War Stores, Report, 137
  Respirators, Wearing of, in the presence of Ammonia, 38
  Risks:
    Colonial War Risks Insurance (Guarantees) Act, 23
      Bill, 2, 15
    (Commodities) Insurance Fund Accounts, 262
  Insurance:
    Act, 1939, printed as amended, 62
    Re-insurance Agreements, 76, 80, 137, 198, 199, 200, 260, 268
  Savings, Welfare of the Blind, 37
  Service:
    Allied Powers (War Service) Act, 86
      Bill, 69, 70, 80
  Services:
    Appropriation Accounts, 197, 263
    Civil Estimates, 74, 132, 195, 261
    Transport, Ministry of, Publications (N.P.), 68, 125, 180, 253, 333
    Work, Women on, 318
    Workers, Postal Voting for, Report. Cmd. 6581, 273
  Works. See Requisitioned Land.
  Wounds, Use of Penicillin in treating, 242
    See also Great War.
  War-damaged Licensed Premises and Reconstruction, Committee on, Report. Cmd. 6504, 204
  Wardens, Notes for the Guidance of, at Rescue Incidents, 158
  Warehouses:
    Bonded, Lists of, 33, 95, 154, 217, 295
    Factory Form, 228
  Warfare. See Chemical Warfare.

82

83

Wark, Lord (Chairman), Court of Inquiry concerning a Dispute at an Engineering Undertaking in Scotland, Report. Cmd. 6474, 143
Warkworth Castle, Guide to, 188
Warlike Stores, Research and Development, Report, 265
Warning, Police, Report, 323
Warrington:
  Corporation Act, 284
  Provisional Order Confirmation Act, 209
    Bill, 202
Wart Disease of Potatoes, 27, 90
Wartime:
  Building:
    Bulletins, 56, 114
    Standard of, 189
    Supplies, Schedule of, 68, 189, 254
  Colonial Policy, in Certain Aspects of. Cmd. 6299, 20
  Community Feeding in, 37
  Concessions in Administration of Inland Revenue Duties, List of. Cmd. 6559, 206
  Diet in Boarding Schools, 96
  Food for Growing Children, 101
  Foods, Nutritive Values of, 319
  Good Fare in, 35, 96
  Leases, Validation of, Act, 206
    Bill, 191, 192, 203
  Painting Services. See War Department.
  Poultry Feeding, 89, 148
  Registration. See Parliamentary Electors.
  Road Notes, 57, 115, 179, 243
  Schools in, 39
  Timber Economy, 254
  Tuberculosis in, Committee on, Report, 113
Washing of Factories, Factory Form, 163
Washington Negotiations. See United States of America.
Waste:
  Materials Reclamation Trade, Wages, 57, 175, 238
  Paper and Waste Paper-making Materials, Lists of Merchants, 117, 324
  Waters from Dairies and Milk Products Factories, Treatment and Disposal of, 115
  See also Cotton Waste.

Watch Holders, Specifications, 91
Water:
  Act, 282
  Bill, 256, 264, 266, 270
  Circular, 300
  Table of Comparison, 301
  Central Advisory Water Committee, 3rd Report. Cmd. 6465, 143
  Policy, National. Cmd. 6515, 204
  Pollution Research Board Publications (N.P.), 57, 115, 170, 243, 330
  Problems in Fire Fighting explained, 99
  (Scotland) Bill, 269, 271
  Steriliser, "Hanovia", 25
  Supplies. See War Water Supplies.
  Undertakings Bill, 127, 128, 139
  See also Aerated Waters; Waste Waters.
Waterproof Covers, Specification, 65
Waterproofed and Dyed Cotton:
  Duck, Specification, 30
  Fabrics, Specifications, 30
Waterproofs, Prices etc., 327
Watery Wound Rot of Potatoes, 90
Wattmeters, Specification, 121
Wax. See Graphited Wax.
Weather:
  Maps, Preparation of, 112, 177, 241, 316
  Reports, 317
Webbing. See Cotton Webbing; Jute Webbing.
Wedgwood, Sir R. (Chairman), Matrimonial Causes (Trial in the Provinces) Committee, Report. Cmd. 6480, 144
Weed Control:
  by Sulphuric Acid Sprays, 90, 149
  in Cereals, 286
Weeds, Suppression of, 89
Weekly:
  Expenditure of Working-Class Households in the U.K., 52
  Wage-Earners, Taxation of:
    Cmd. 6348, 82
    Cmd. 6469, 143
    Popular Edition, 184
Weevils. See Apple Blossom Weevil; Grain Weevils; Pea and Bean Weevils; Turnip Gall Weevil; Wingless Weevils.
Weight-lifting by Industrial Workers, 238
Weights and Measures, Examination of Patterns, 62, 119, 184, 249, 328
Weir, Sir C., Scheme for ensuring fair shares of supplies to small retailers of pottery, 119

Welding. See Electric Welding; Electric Arc Welding.
Welfare:
  Amenities for Building Sites, Factory Form, 104
  Conditions in the three Women's Services, Committee on, Report. Cmd. 6384, 84
    outside the Factory and Seamen's Welfare in Port. Cmd. 6411, 85
  Pamphlets (Factories etc.), 215
    Work outside the Factory. Cmd. 6310, 20
    See also Blind; Soldiers' Welfare; Colonial Development; Miners' Welfare; Seamen's Welfare; West Indies.
Welsh:
  Church (Burial Grounds) Act, 282
    Bill, 270
  Courts Act, 86
    Bill, 81
  Reconstruction Advisory Council, Report, 241
Wessex (North Basingstoke) Electricity Special Order, 60
West:
  Africa:
    Cocoa Control in, Report. Cmd. 6554, 206
    Higher Education in, Report. Cmd. 6655, 277
    Labour Conditions in. Cmd. 6277, 18
  India Royal Commission:
    Report. Cmd. 6607, 274
    Report on Agriculture, Fisheries, Forestry and Veterinary Matters. Cmd. 6608, 274
    Statement of Action taken on Recommendations. Cmd. 6656, 277
  Indian Conference, Report, 217
  Indies:
    Agriculture in, 95
    Development and Welfare, Reports, 154, 295
    Higher Education in, Report. Cmd. 6654, 277
  Midlands Area, Hospital Services of, 300
  Riding. See Yorkshire.
Westminster. See Palace of Westminster.
Weston, H. C., The Relation between Illumination and Visual Efficiency, 318

Weston, W. G. (Chairman), United Maritime Authority Planning Committee, Report, 255
Weston-super-Mare Provisional Order Confirmation Bill, 256, 271
Wetherby District Water Provisional Order Confirmation Act, 146
  Bill, 139
Whaling, International Regulation of. Cmd. 6510, 204
Wharves, Factory Forms, 104, 228
Wheat:
  and Barley, Eyespot of, 286
  Bulb Fly, 148
  Discussions at Washington, Exchange of Notes between Argentina, Australia, Canada, U.K. and U.S.A. Cmd. 6371, 83
  Fund Accounts, 10, 75, 133, 196, 260
  Growing, 90
  Take-all or Whiteheads of, 27
Wheels. See Abrasive Wheels.
Whelan, C. B., Report by Lord Goddard on Procedure at a Case heard before two Justices at Longton, Stoke-on-Trent, 301
Whey Butter, 27
White:
  Fly, Greenhouse, 27
  Line Road Markings, 179
  Rot Disease of Onion Bulbs, 26
  Scour in Calves, 148
White, G. H. G. (Chairman), Committee on Seamen's Welfare in Ports, Report, 314
Whiteheads of Wheat and Barley, 27
Whitewashing of Factories, Factory Form, 130
Whitworth Scholarships, 96, 218, 296
Wholesale:
  Bespoke Tailoring Trade, Wages, 51, 110, 239, 315
  Mantle and Costume Trade, Wages, 52, 110, 315
  Annual Return Form, 36, 98, 156
Why is She Away, 318
Widows' Pensions. See Police Widows.
Widows', Orphans' and Old Age Contributory Pensions:
  Accounts, 10, 75, 134, 197, 263
  Care of the R.A.F., 91
Wild Onion, 90
William Pit, Explosion at, Report. Cmd. 6367, 83

84

85

Wills (Probate Engrossment Form), 177
Wilson,W.K.,Modern Rabbit Keeping,26
Wimpey, Messrs. Geo. & Co. Ltd., Allocation of Government Contracts in Scotland. *Cmd. 6393*, 84
Winding Enginemen, Mines and Quarries Forms, 55
Winds. *See* Upper Winds.
Windows, etc., and their Blackout, 189
Wingless Weevils, 148
Winter :
    Moths, 89
    Washes. *See* Tar Oil Winter Washes.
Winterton, Earl (Chairman), Select Committee on House of Commons (Rebuilding), Report, 200
Wire, Specifications, 29, 31, 94
Wireless Telegraphy Board Specifications, 25, 88, 147, 285
Wireworms, 27, 148
    and Food Production, 211
Wisbech Corporation Act, 209
Wise Eating in Wartime, 160
Withdrawals, etc., Supplementary Lists :
    Cmd. 6253, 17
    Cmd. 6329, 81
    Cmd. 6431, 141
Women :
    Absenteeism among, Emergency Report, 178
    and Young Persons :
        Overtime Register, 307
        Shift System, 307
    in Industry, Sickness among, 318
    in War Factories, Health and Welfare, Report, 130
    Medical Practitioners, Army, Pay etc., 124
    Officers, War Office Publications (N.P.), 67, 123, 124, 188
    on War Work, Study of, 318
    under Axis Rule, 160, 224
Women's :
    Auxiliary Air Force :
        Medical Services, 76
        Physical Training Tables and Recreational Handbook, 28
    Clothing :
        Prices etc., 183, 248, 326
        Specifications, 247
    Light Clothing Trade, Wages, 51, 110, 238, 315
    Royal Naval Service, Medical Services, 76
    Services, Amenities and Welfare Conditions in, Report. *Cmd.6384*, 84

Wood, Dry Rot in, 320
Wood, Sir Robert (Chairman), Standard Construction for Schools Committee, Report, 253
Woodman, H. E. :
    Composition and Nutritive Value of Feeding Stuffs, 88, 211
    Ensilage, 26, 211
Woodworkers' Tools, Specification, 64
Woodworking Machinery, Regs., 307
Wool :
    Cloth, etc., Board of Trade Publications (N.P.), 118, 182, 247, 325
    Processes, Factory Form, 164
    Yarn and Wool Cloth, Prices, etc., 248
    See also Knitted Wool ; East Indian Wool.
Woolcombing, Wages, 203
Woolly Aphis, 27
Worcestershire. *See* East Worcestershire.
Work, Absence from, 242
Worker, Young, 229
    in Factories, Seats for, 315
    See also Housing (Rural Workers).
Working :
    Men's Club, Annual Return Form, 36, 97, 156
    Pay,Army,Suspension of Grants of,68
    Working-Class Households in the U.K., Weekly Expenditure, 52
Workington Provisional Order Confirmation Act, 209
    Bill, 191
Workmen's Compensation :
    Act, 1925 :
        Notice of Accidents, Factory Form, 164
        Summary, Mines and Quarries Form, 98
    Act, 1943, 145
        Bill, 81, 126
    Acts, Memos., 222
    (Contributory Negligence), Reports :
        Cmd. 6580, 273   *Cmd. 6642*, 276
    (Pneumoconiosis) Bill, 258, 272
    Royal Commission on, Report. *Cmd. 6588*, 273
    Social Insurance, Part II. *Cmd. 6551*, 206
    Supplementary Allowances and Temporary Increases, Forms, 158
    (Temporary Increases) Act, 145
        Bill, 129, 140
    See also National Health Insurance.

Works :
    and Buildings, Ministry of :
        Publications (N.P.), 68
        Two Appointments in, 77
    and Planning :
        Minister of, Act, 86
        Bill, 69, 80
        Circular, 125
        Ministryof,Publications(N.P.),125
        and Repairs. *See* War Department.
    Cost of (War Damage), 250
    Ministry of, Publications (N.P.), 188, 253, 334
    of Art in Italy, Losses and Survivals in the War, 293
    of Engineering Construction. *See* Engineering.
    Services, Civil Estimates, 7, 74, 132, 195, 261
    See also Public Works ; War Works.
Workshop Calculations, 52, 111
World :
    Economy, the United States in the, 219
    Organisation. *See* Dumbarton Oaks.
Worms :
    in Poultry, 149
    See also Common ; Stomach Worms.
Wound :
    Shock, Treatment of, 242, 319
    Stripes, Grant of. *Cmd. 6463*, 143
Wounds :
    Prevention of "HospitalInfection", 56
    See also War Wounds.
Woven Cloth, Piece Goods, etc., Board of Trade Publications (N.P.), 61, 118, 182, 247, 325
Wray, D. A., Geology of the country around Wakefield, 57
Wreck Report, 253
Wyatt, S. :
    Absenteeism among Women, Report, 178
    Certified Sickness Absence among Women in Industry, A Study of, 318
    Variations in Output, A Study of, 252
    Women on War Work in four Factories, A Study of, 318

Y

Y Scheme. *See* Navy.
Yarn. *See* Hand Knitting Yarn ; Knitting Yarn ; Nylon Yarn ; Worsted Yarn.

Yeast. *See* Food Yeast.
York Castle, Clifford's Tower, Guide to, 188
Yorkshire :
    Area, Hospital Services of, 300
    Registries (West Riding) Amendment Act, 209
    Wages and Hours of Work in the Woolcombing Section of the Wool Textiles Industry in, Report. *Cmd. 6499*, 203
Yorkshire, Nottinghamshire and Derbyshire Coalfield, National Coal Resources, 115, 243
Young :
    Lambs, Joint-Ill in, 89
    Persons :
        aged16,Registration96,97,154,155
        Building and Engineering Construction, Record of Working Hours, 104
        Factory Forms, 104, 163
        in need of Care and Protection (Scotland) Circular, 245
        See also Children and Young Persons.
    Worker, The, 229
Youth :
    Clubs, Canteens in, 295
    in a City, 155
    Leaders. *See* Teachers.
    Leadership, Careers, 306
    Needs of, in these Times, 323
    Registration, 34, 36, 116
        Cmd. 6446, 142
    Service :
        after the War, Report, 158
        Corps, 34, 35
        Emergency Courses of Training, 96
        Post-War, in Wales, 298
        Purpose and Content of, 297
    Scheme :
        in Scotland, 245
        Revision of Machinery, 116
    Youth's Opportunity, Further Education in County Colleges, 296
    Youths' Clothing, etc., Prices, 183, 248, 326

Z

Zinc :
    and Zinc Alloys, Polarographic and Spectrographic Analysis of, for Die Casting, 324
    Chrome, Specifications, 30, 92

H.M. STATIONERY OFFICE
CATALOGUE SERVICE

The catalogue service provided by H.M. Stationery Office includes, in addition to the annual Consolidated List of Government Publications, facilities enabling interested persons to keep themselves informed about official publications at daily, weekly, or monthly intervals.

The series of Sectional Lists, each of which catalogues the publications sponsored by a particular Government Department, cater for those whose interests are more specialised.

A leaflet giving full particulars of the catalogue service may be obtained from any of the addresses on cover p. iv.

CONSOLIDATED INDEX TO GOVERNMENT PUBLICATIONS

1946-1950

FOREWORD

Two previous Consolidated Indexes to Government Publications have already been issued covering the years 1936 to 1940 and 1941 to 1945 (prices 6s. 0d. and 5s. 0d. respectively). This Index is compiled on the same lines and includes the titles of new publications, revised editions and reprints at amended prices.

As in the second index Statutory Rules and Orders and Statutory Instruments are omitted and the Annual Lists of these items which are issued separately should be consulted for those issued during the period. Information concerning those still in force is provided by the Guide to Government Orders.

It is suggested that the annual catalogues for 1946–50 should be bound with this consolidated index, the annual index pages (which are excluded from the pagination) being discarded.

The page numbering of the annual catalogues indexed in this consolidation is as follows :

1946	....	1 to 120
1947	....	121 to 266
1948	....	267 to 444
1949	....	445 to 667
1950	....	669 to 886

INDEX

Abbreviations : In addition to the abbreviations in general use, the following are used :—*Cmd.* = Command Paper ; (N.P.) = Non-Parliamentary.

Cross References are to entries consisting of, or beginning with, the word or words indicated.

A

Aaria, Wreck Report, 636
Aaron, R. I. (Chairman), Central Advisory Council for Education, Wales, Report : Future of Secondary Education in Wales, 543
A.B.C. of :
  Fish Cookery, 760
  Preserving, 544
ABDA. Despatch by Supreme Commander, 436
Aberayron Division, Justices, 55
Abercrombie, Sir Patrick : Clyde Valley Regional Plan, 612
Aberdeen Harbour Confirmation Acts :
  1946, 52
    Bill, 11, 29
  1949, 514
    Bill, 459, 487
  1950, 725
    Bill, 672, 698
Aberdeenshire Educational Trust Scheme, 92, 231
Abergavenny. *See* Marquess of Abergavenny.
Abnormal Visibility at Malta, 84
Abrasives, Their Manufacture and Use in Germany, 624
Absence Record Cards, 207
Acarine Disease :
  Examination of Bees for, 737
  of Bees, Leaflet, 333
Access :
  to Mountains, S.R. & O.s and S.I.s Revised, 835
  to the Countryside. *See* Footpaths.
Accessions. *See* Ratifications.
Accident Reports :
  Aircraft, 180, 337, 489, 523, 744
  Boiler Explosion, 417
  Railway, 107, 247, 418, 634, 850
Accidents :
  How they happen and how to prevent them, 576, 793
  Injuries to Army Motor Cyclists, 607
Accommodation and Water Supply, Field Engineering, 437

Accountancy and Cost Accountancy, Careers, 75
Accounts. *See* Public Accounts ; also names of special accounts, Departments, services, etc.
Achimota, Film strip, 534
Acorns and Beechmast as Feeding Stuffs, 737
Acquisition of Land :
  Assessment of Compensation Act, 170
  Authorisation Procedure :
    Act, 49
    Bill, 6, 7, 18, 27, 28
    Circular, 101
    (Scotland) Act, 172
    Bill, 124, 129
Activities of UNESCO, 259, 653
Acts :
  of Parliament, 47, 170, 324, 506, 718
  of the Privy Council, Charles I, 882
Actuarial Work, Careers, 75, 207
Addu Atoll, Agalega Islands, and Tristan da Cunha, Climates of, 815
Adelges :
  attacking spruce and other conifers, 65
  Cooleyi, 354
Aden :
  Colonial Reports, 343, 531, 749
  Disturbances in, Report, 344
  S.R. & O.s and S.I.s Revised, 835
Adhesives :
  for Wood, Requirements and Properties of, 87, 828
  Selected Government Research Reports, 846
Adjustment of Fares, London Passenger Transport Board, 106
Administration :
  of Estates :
    Act, 722
    S.R. & O.s and S.I.s Revised, 835
  of Justice :
    Act, 326
    (Pensions) Act, 720
    Bill, 676, 699, 700
    (Scotland) Act, 329
    Bill, 299, 303

ADM—   *INDEX 1946–50*

Administrative :
Personnel and Budgetary Questions, 110
Tribunal Statute and Rules, 859
Admiralty Publications (N.P.), 53, 176, 332, 515, 728
Adoption :
Act, 719
Bill, 483, 671, 672, 674, 675, 681, 698
of Children :
Acts :
1948, 327
1949, 512
Bill, 455, 457, 461, 470, 481, 485, 487
1950, 722
Memorandum, 671, 690, 787
(Regulation) Act, 723
(Scotland) Act, 722
Adult Education :
Activities for Public Libraries, 870
Current Trends and Practices, 872
Adur II, Wreck Report, 421
Advertisements, Control of, Circulars, 409, 622
Advertising :
Careers, 75
Stations (Rating) Act, 324
Advertising, Labelling, and Composition of Food, 544
Advice to Intending Beekeepers, 178
Advisory Leaflets. *See under subject or Department.*
Ae, Forest of, 354
Aegean, Naval Operations, 386
Aerial Navigation, International Sanitary Convention. *Cmd. 6944*, 44
Aerodrome :
Approach Lights, 366
Obstruction Charts, 791
Aerodromes :
Directory of International, 574
Air Routes and Ground Aids Division Report, 790
United Kingdom, 524
See also Air Pilot.
Aerological Observations, T-ϕ Gram of, 221
Aeronautical :
Agreement and Contract, Tables, 572
Agreements and Arrangements, Tables, 790
Charts, 572
Production Progress Report, 790

Aeronautical *(continued)*:
Fixed Telecommunication, European —Mediterranean, 790
Research :
Committee Publications (N.P.), 93, 729
Council Reports and Memoranda, 233, 401, 617, 730
Aeronautics :
Heavier-than-air Aircraft, History and Development, 542, 826
Lighter-than-air Aircraft, Brief Outline of History and Development of the Balloon and Airship, 826
Aeroplanes, Design Requirements for, 406, 619, 837
Africa :
British :
Military Administration of Occupied Territories, 437
Territories in East and Central. *Cmd. 7987*, 709
West, Economic Survey, 632
Central and East, Report on Tobacco, 533
Customs Tariffs, 60
East :
and Central, Grain Storage in, 750
Flag Badges, 751
High Commission Reports, 534, 751
Labour Conditions in, 61
Education for Citizenship, 344
International Status of South-West, Advisory opinion, 792
Introducing :
East and Central, 534
West, Film strip, 534
Picture Sets, 364, 533
Portuguese East, Economic Survey, 632
Posters, 364
South :
Agreement with U.K. in connection with establishment of Civil Air Services. *Cmd. 7858*, 700, 744
Commercial Conditions in Union of, 102
Royal Voyage to, 176
Territories under U.K. Mandate. *Cmd. 6840, 6935*, 37, 43
Trypanosomiasis in, 345
Tropical, Weather on West Coast, 596
Tsetse Flies in, 345

Africa *(continued)* :
Wall Maps, 535, 346, 364
West, Customs Tariff, 533
See also Vegetable Oil.
African :
Administration, Journal, 531, 748
Aid to Britain Fund, 249
Campaign from El Alamein to Tunis, 384
Doctors in Training, Film Strip, 534
Labour Efficiency Survey, 531
Land Tenure, Bibliography, 748
Oilseeds Mission Report, 345
Pioneer Corps, Change of Designation, 114
Studies, 194
Africa–Indian Ocean :
and Middle East :
Frequency Assignments Planning Meeting, Report, 791
Special Meeting on Fixed Services, final report, 790
Region Supplementary Procedures, 572
Agalega Islands. *See* Addu Atoll.
Agar, British Seaweeds and their Utilisation in Preparation, 559
Aggrey in Africa, 363
Agreements with U.K. : *See* names of countries concerned.
Agricultural :
Advisory Services in European Countries, Working Party Report, 759
and Horticultural Institutes Report, 177
Aspects in Germany, 410
Credits Acts, 327, 508
Development :
of the Middle East, 106
(Ploughing up of Land) Act, 48
Bill, 5, 27
Engineering Record, 55, 178, 265, 336, 519, 740
Extension and Advisory Work with special reference to the Colonies, 531
Holdings, 89
Act, 329, 333, 724
Bill, 270, 274, ?75, 302
Explanatory Memo. and Tables of Comparison, 333
(Scotland) Act, 510, 724, 736
Bill, 445, 446, 447, 484

Agricultural *(continued)* :
Land :
Commission :
Accounts, 684, 738
Reports, 463, 677, 696, 738
Rights and Obligations of Landlords, Tenants, and Occupiers, 333
Safeguarding of, 840
Marketing :
Act, 511
Bill, 303, 451, 453, 467, 481, 484, 486
Bill, 1950, 681
Mission to South America, 334
Population, Development Charge on Houses, 409
Produce (Grading and Marking) Act, 722
Reconstruction. *See* European Programmes.
Requisites in Latin America, Report, 865
Research Council Publications (N.P.), 390, 603, 736
Services, Select Committee on Estimates Report, 476, 480
Statistics, 177, 333, 396, 516, 736
See also Food and Agriculture.
Studies, 433, 656, 873
Survey of Scotland, 39
Valuation Reports, 333, 738
Wages :
Act, 328
Bill, 270, 272, 273, 302
(Regulation) Acts :
1946, 172
Bill, 29, 30, 148
Standing Committee Minutes, 140
1949, 507
Bill, 280
(Scotland) Act, 510
Bill, 278, 445, 446, 447, 484
Agriculturalists. *See* Biologists.
Agriculture :
Acts, 173, 333
Accounts, 738
and Agricultural Holdings Acts, Rights and Obligations, 517
Advisory Leaflets, 55, 178, 333, 516, 736
(Scotland) :
Act, 170
Scotland, 610
and Fisheries, Ministry of :
Act, 170

AGR—   *INDEX 1946–50*

Agriculture *(continued)* :
and Fisheries, Ministry of *(continued)* :
Publications (N.P.), 53, 177, 333, 516, 737
S.R. & O.s and S.I.s Revised, 835
Annual Report, 55
(Artificial Insemination) Act, 48
Bill, 5, 14
Bills, 30, 127, 130, 131, 148, 149, 280
Explanatory Memo. *Cmd.6996*, 47
Standing Committee Minutes, 134
Bulletins, 54, 177, 334, 517, 738
Careers, 75
Circular, 54
Colonial Research Recommendations Report, 344
Contribution to saving of Foreign Exchange. *Cmd. 7072*, 155
Department of, for Scotland, Publications (N.P.), 89, 228, 396, 609, 736
Economic Series, 518
Emergency Payments Act, 172
Bill, 123, 148
in Scotland, Reports :
Cmd. 7717, 496
Cmd. 7950, 707, 736
in Tropical African Colonies, Native, 751
International Institute Dissolution. *Cmd. 7413*, 312
Journal, 55, 178, 265, 328, 518, 739
Scottish, 89, 228, 266, 335, 609, 736
Miscellaneous Provisions Acts :
1949, 511
Bill, 455, 469, 481, 483, 484
1950, 719, 724
Bill, 673, 681, 698
Overseas Reports, 54, 177, 334, 517
(Miscellaneous War Provisions) Act, 724
Programme for 1950 World Census, 617
(Scotland) :
Act, 1948, 328
Bill, 150, 272, 274, 276, 286, 294, 300, 301
Explanatory Memo. *Cmd. 7175*, 162
Bill, 1949, 463
Specialist Conference in, 741
Technical Bulletin, 518
Agriculturists, Horticulturists, and Domestic Producer, Report on Provision of Part-Time Instruction, 517

Aid to Britain Fund, South African, 249
Air :
Almanac, 56, 179, 336, 519, 740
and Traffic Control Rules, 367, 574
Bases in the Caribbean Area and Bermuda, Agreement with U.S.A. *Cmd. 7389*, 310
Corporations Act, 719
Bill, 447, 460, 488
Statement of Guarantee, 682, 685, 854
Council :
Instructions. *See* King's Regulations.
S.R. & O.s and S.I.s Revised, 835
Estimates, 17, 18, 137, 283, 466, 681, 740
Memoranda :
Cmd. 7053, 154
Cmd. 7329, 306
Cmd. 7634, 491
Cmd. 7898, 703
Force :
Act, Amendments, 50,173,519,740
Awards, etc. *See* London Gazette.
Bill. *See* Army.
Chapels. *See* Naval.
Design Requirements for Aeroplanes, 406
Examinations, 183
Law, Manual of, 56, 179, 336, 519
Lists, 444, 519, 740
Pay, Pensions, etc., for Members Disabled, 21, 26, 141
Psychological Disorders in Flying Personnel, 179
Reserve :
Act, 719
Bill, 672, 674, 675, 698
and Auxiliary Air Force, S.R. & O.s and S.I.s Revised, 835
S.R. & O.s and S.I.s Revised, 835
See also Army and Air Force.
Hygiene, Studies in, 603
Mail Study, 572
Ministry :
Establishments, Civilians employed at, Regs., 56
Publications (N.P.), 56, 179, 336, 519, 740
Navigation :
Act, 172
Bill, 13, 122, 123, 147
Aids to Safety, Agreement with U.S.A. *Cmd. 7622*, 490

Air *(continued)* :
Navigation *(continued)* :
Communications and Radio Aids, 573
Directions, 57, 181, 338, 524
Meeting, 790
Order, 744
Regional Meeting Reports, 572
Regs., 57, 181, 338
Services, Procedures for, 364, 574
S.R. & O.s and S.I.s Revised, 835
(Victory Celebrations) Regs., 57
See also International Civil Aviation Organisation
Operations :
by Air Defence of Great Britain and Fighter Command, 386
by Allied Expeditionary Air Force in North West Europe, 219
in Greece, 219
Pilot, 524
Binder, 743
Services :
Agreements, etc. :
Argentina. *Cmd. 6856*, 38
Canada. *Cmd. 7857*, 700
Ceylon. *Cmd. 7859*, 700
Chile. *Cmd. 7234*, 166
Colombia. *Cmd. 7272*, 169
Cuba. *Cmd. 7393*, 310
Eire. *Cmd. 6793*, 34
Greece :
Cmd. 6722, 30
Cmd. 7348–9, 307
Netherlands :
Cmd. 6893, 40
Cmd. 7144, 160
Norway. *Cmd. 6913*, 42
Pakistan. *Cmd. 7922*, 705
Philippine Republic. *Cmd. 7341*, 307
Portuguese Territories :
Cmd. 6739, 31
Spain. *Cmd. 8112*, 718
Sweden. *Cmd. 7008*, 152
Switzerland (between and beyond). *Cmd. 7953*, 707
Turkey :
Cmd. 6755, 32
Cmd. 6928, 43
U.S.A. *Cmd. 6747*, 32

Air *(continued)* :
Services *(continued)* :
Appropriation Accounts, 14, 134, 281, 464, 683, 740
Expenditure and Receipts, 1939–43. *Cmd. 6856*, 38
in Europe, Exchange of Notes with Greece. *Cmd. 7678*, 494
Statement, 285
Supplementary Estimates, 466, 695, 740
Traversing British and Portuguese Territories :
Cmd. 6740, 31
Cmd. 6920, 43
Survey Research Papers, 346
Transport :
Advisory Council Reports, 472, 685, 744
Agreements :
Brazil :
Cmd. 6962, 45
Cmd. 6977, 46
China, *Cmd. 7211*, 165
France. *Cmd. 6787*, 34
Iceland. *Cmd. 7996*, 710
Statistical Summary, 573
Votes, 17, 136, 139, 683, 740
Treasury Minutes, 287, 466, 470, 685, 854
Aircraft :
Accident :
Investigation :
Manual of, 790
Procedure. *Cmd. 7564*, 322
Reports, 180, 337, 489, 523, 744
Airworthiness of, 791
and Equipment, Agreements :
Belgium. *Cmd. 7039*, 153
Czechoslovakia. *Cmd. 7187*, 163
Denmark. *Cmd. 7660*, 493
France. *Cmd. 7131*, 159
Netherlands. *Cmd. 7011*, 152
Norway. *Cmd. 7095*, 157
Builders, 203
Certification of Civil Aircraft and Approval of Equipment. *Cmd. 7705*, 496
Condensation trails from, 84
Convention on International Recognition of Rights. *Cmd. 7510*, 318
Establishment, Farnborough, Account of, 406
Airfield Construction, Scientific and Industrial Research Publications (N.P.), 88

1946-50 | AIR-ASP

AIR— INDEX 1946–50

Airfields :
Meteorology of, 595
(Provisional) Military Engineering, 438
Airline Abbreviations, 366
Airmen. *See* Merchant Airmen.
Airmet Broadcasts, 221
Airways Corporations Act, 511
Bill, 457, 475, 481, 485, 486
Standing Committee Debate, 681
Airworthiness Division Final Report, 574
Albania. *See* Corfu Channel Case.
Alderney. Report of Committee of Privy Council. *Cmd. 7805*, 503
Alexander of Tunis, Viscount :
African Campaign, 384
Conquest of Sicily, 384
Alexander Scott's Hospital Order Confirmation Act, 513
Bill, 455, 486
Alien, S.R. & O.s and S.I.s Revised, 835
Aliens :
Naturalisation Returns, 13, 22, 142, 298, 677, 782
Registration Form, 201
Restriction :
Act, 721
Amendment Act, 507
Alirmay, Wreck Report, 854
Alkali, etc., Works :
Chief Inspector's Reports, 199, 358, 558, 779
Regulation Act, 325
(Scotland) Bill, 699
S.R. & O.s and S.I.s Revised, 835
Allen, H. B., Rural Education and Welfare in the Middle East, 109
Allen, P. (Chairman), Police Council, Report, 362
Alliance :
and Mutual Assistance, Treaty with French Republic :
Cmd. 7058, 154
Cmd. 7217, 165
Treaty with Transjordan. *Cmd. 7368*, 308
Allied :
Armies in Italy, Sept. 1943–Dec. 1944, Despatch, 812
Commission for Austria Publications (N.P.), 179
Expeditionary Force, Report, 114
Kommandatura of Berlin publication, 536
Allied (*continued*) :
Ministers of Education, Conference, 52
Allotments :
Act, 719
Bill, 694, 698, 784
Advisory Committee Report, 738
(Scotland) Act, 719
Bill, 670, 672, 673, 674, 689, 692, 694, 698, 699, 784
Allowances :
War Office Publications (N.P.), 114, 260, 437, 660, 879
See also Family Allowances ; Unemployment.
Alloys. *See* Aluminium.
Allsop, G. :
Exploders for simultaneous firing of shots, 775
Intrinsic safety of electrical apparatus, 67, 357
Alternative Remedies, Departmental Committee on, Final Report. *Cmd. 6860*, 39
Altmark, Correspondence between U.K. and Norway. *Cmd. 8012*, 711
Aluminium :
Alloys for Naval Use, Report, 53
and Aluminium Alloys in the Food Industry, 392
Goods, Export Licence, 845
Amani, East African Agricultural Research Institution Reports, 60, 185, 531
Ambulance Services, Estimates, Select Committee Report, 689, 785
Amendments made by Acts, etc., Directions for noting, 249, 421, 637
America :
Farm Machinery Mission, 54
Plumbing in, 394
See also North America.
American :
Aid and European Payments :
Accounts, 473, 692, 854
(Financial Provisions) Act, 510
Bill, 303, 448
Among those present, 71
Analgesia in Childbirth Bill, 474, 481, 483, 486, 681
Analysis of Concretes, 829
Anatomy :
and Physiology, Principles of, 56, 741
S.R. & O.s and S.I.s Revised, 835
Anchau Rural Development and Settlement Scheme, 343

INDEX 1946–50 —ARA

Anchor and Chain Cable, S.R. & O.s and S.I.s Revised, 835
Anchors and Chain Cables Act, 506
Ancient Monuments, etc. :
Consolidation and Amendment Act, 507
Guides, 117, 263, 440, 663, 882
Scotland, Royal Commission :
Publications (N.P.), 89
Report. *Cmd. 7967*, 708
S.R. & O.s and S.I.s Revised, 835
Sites, Excavation of, 664
Anderson College of Medicine Trust Scheme, 614, 831
Anderson, J. G. C. : Limestones of Scotland, 606
Anemometers, Exposure of, 221
Anemone, Commercial Growing, 737
Anglo-Egyptian Treaty, 1936, Negotiations for Revision. *Cmd. 7179*, 163
Anglo-Norwegian Fisheries Case, 575,792
Angwin, Sir S. (Chairman), Telecommunications Research Committee, Report, 395
Anhydrite. *See* Plasters.
Animal :
Diseases in Europe, Some Important, 873
Feedstuffs, Commodity series, 873
Health :
Colonial Research Recommendations, 344
Leaflets, 334, 517, 738
Services Report, 738
Animals :
Act, 1948, 328
Bill, 272, 285, 294, 299, 300
Baiting of, Bill, 474, 481, 483
Bill, 1949, 463
S.R. & O.s and S.I.s Revised, 835
Ankara. *See* Turkey.
Annecy Protocol of Terms of Accession and Schedules of Tariff Concessions. *Cmd. 7792*, 501, 652
Ant Pest, Biology and Control, 736
Anthrax, 76, 517
S.R. & O.s and S.I.s Revised, 835
Anti-Aircraft Defence of the U.K., 220
Antibiotics, Expert Committee Report, 877
Antibodies in Foot-and-Mouth Disease, 603
Ants in the House, 737
Aphides, Currant and Gooseberry, 178
Apparatus and Materials for Teaching Science, Inventories of, 870
Apparel :
and Textiles Orders, Board of Trade Publications (N.P.), 101, 241, 409, 623, 841
Cloth, Utility Schedule Amendments, 628, 847
Utility, Maximum Prices and Charges Order, 843
Appeal, Court of. *See* High Court.
Appeals Decisions, Town and Country Planning, 409
Appearance of Housing Estates, 358
Appellate Jurisdiction Act, 172
Bill, 123, 147
Apple :
and Pear Tree, Winter Pruning, 516
Blossom Weevil, 178
Mildew, 178
Apples :
and Pears, 54, 335, 738
Commercial Varieties, 516
Home Storage of, 178
Rootstocks, 333
Spraying Programme, 333
Factors in the marketing of home-produced apples in England and Wales, 518
Marketing Leaflet, 335
Refrigerated Gas Storage of, 828
Storage of, 604
See also Tree Fruits.
Appleton, Sir Edward (Chairman) : British Commonwealth Scientific Official Conference, Report. *Cmd. 6970*, 45
Appliances. *See* Machines.
Applied Work and Patchwork, Notes on, 877
Appointments, Services. *See* London Gazette.
Apprenticeship, Building, 263
Appropriation :
Accounts. *See* Credit ; *also* names of Departments, etc.
Acts, 49, 173, 329, 511, 719
Approved :
Homes for Mental Defectives, 187
Schools :
and Remand Homes, 69
See also Making Citizens.
Estimates, Select Committee Report, 678, 785
Scottish Advisory Council Report, 230
Societies, Absorption of Staffs, 221
Arab States in the Middle East, U.N. Social Welfare Seminar for, 869

ARB— INDEX 1946–50

Arbitration :
Acts :
1946, 170
1949, 508
1950, 719
Bill, 672, 674, 675, 698
Clauses (Protocol) Act, 171
S.R. & O.s and S.I.s Revised, 835
Arbroath Gas :
Order Confirmation Act, 173
Provisional Order Bill, 13, 30
[illegible]
Welding. *See* Electric Arc Welding.
Welds. *See* Examination of Arc Welds.
Archibald, Dr. E. S., Imperial Agricultural Bureaux Conference Report. *Cmd. 6971*, 46
Architects, Northern Ireland, S.R. & O.s and S.I.s Revised, 835
Architecture :
Careers, 75, 793
Technical Register, 593
Archives. *See* Italian Archives.
Arctic Seas, Monthly Ice Charts, 815
Ardler Junction Railway Accident Report, 634
Ardrossan Gas :
Order Confirmation Act, 52
Provisional Order Bill, 11, 29
Area Gas Boards, Loans proposed to be raised, 472
Argentina :
Air Services Agreement. *Cmd. 6848*, 38
Avoidance of Double Taxation on income derived from sea and air transport. *Cmd. 7721*, 497
Commercial Agreement. *Cmd. 7123*, 159
Economic Agreement. *Cmd. 6953*, 44
Overseas Economic Survey, 416
Sale of British-owned Railways in, Exchange of Notes with U.K. *Cmd. 7405*, 311
Trade and Payments Agreements :
Cmd. 7346, 307
Cmd. 7735, 498
Cmd. 8079, 716
Argyll Forest Park Guide, 195
Arkell, W. J. : Geology of the Country around Weymouth, Swanage, Corfe, and Lulworth, 226
Armed Forces :
and Auxiliary Services, Strength and Casualties. *Cmd. 6832*, 37
Armed Forces (*continued*) :
(Housing Loans) Act, 512
Bill, 461, 487
Memorandum. *Cmd. 7828*, 504
Mutual Forbearance concerning claims against Members and Civilian Employees, Exchange of Notes with U.S.A. *Cmd. 7501*, 318
Needs for Land for Training and other purposes. *Cmd. 7278*, 169
Western Union, Agreement relative [illegible]
Brussels Treaty Powers :
Cmd. 7868, 701
Cmd. 8057, 715
Armistice Agreement, Hungary. *Cmd. 7280*, 169
Arms :
and Ammunition, S.R. & O.s and S.I.s revised, 835
and the Men, 742
of H.M. Dominions, 186
See also Flags.
Arms, Ensigns, Flags, and Royal Styles and Titles, S.R. & O.s and S.I.s Revised, 835
Armstrong, F. H. : Flooring Hardwoods, 392
Army :
Accidents resulting in injury to Army motor cyclists, 607
Acts and Amendments, 50, 173, 437, 879
Additional Pay, 878
Allowances, 260, 437, 660, 879
and Air Force :
(Annual) Acts :
1946, 49
Bill, 6, 27
1947, 172
Bill, 124, 148
1948, 328
Bill, 271, 300
1949, 510
Bill, 451, 484
Courts-Martial Report. *Cmd. 7608*, 489
1950, 719
Bill, 669, 697
Pensioners, Recall of, Bill, 278, 279
(Women's Service) Act, 328
Bill, 268, 299
Appropriation Accounts, 14, 134, 281, 464, 684
Auxiliary Territorial Service Regulation Amendments, 879

INDEX 1946–50 —ASP

Army (*continued*) :
Awards. *See* London Gazette.
Cadet Force Regs., 114, 261, 660, 879
Classification and Pay, 661
Dental Corps, Women Officers' Pay, 115
Dependent's Allowances, 114, 663
Detailed Statement of Expenditure and Receipts for the years 1939–43. *Cmd. 6857*, 38
Estimates, 17, 18, 136, 137, 284, 285, [illegible]
Memoranda :
Cmd. 7332, 306
Cmd. 7896, 703
Cmd. 7052, 154
Examinations, 183
Fire Services :
in War, 261
Regs., 437, 879
General Education Handbook Amendment, 661
Health, Statistical Report, 661
Lists, 444, 660, 879
National Service Men Regs., 880
Officers Pay, 880
Orders, 114, 261, 437, 660, 879
Ordnance Services Regs., 114, 261, 437
Pay, Appointment, Promotion, etc., 262, 439, 662, 881
Pay, Pensions, etc. :
Cmd. 6799, 35
Cmd. 6947, 44
Cmd. 6995, 47
Cmd. 7096, 157
Post-War Code of Pay, etc., for Commissioned Officers. *Cmd. 6750*, 32
Regular Officers holding Permanent Commissions, Retirement, etc., 662
Release Regs., 440
Reserve Act, 719
Bill, 672, 674, 675, 698
Report (and on Air Force Reserve Bill), 674
Retired Pay, Pensions, etc. *Cmd. 7699*, 495
S.R. & O.s and S.I.s Revised, 835
Statement of sums required to make good an excess on grants, 20
Territorial Regs., 663, 881
Votes, 135, 139, 283, 287, 467, 470, 683, 685, 854, 879
Arnold, A. H. M. : Alternating Currents Resistance of Non-Magnetic Conductors, 88
Aronson, V. R. :
(Chairman), Wages Council Commission, Report on applications for establishment of a Wages Council for the rubber proofed garment making industry, 811
Draft Blasting Special Regs. Report, 578
Art :
and History, Protection of Treasures in War Areas, 440
Book Jacket, [illegible]
Careers, 75
Commission. *See* Royal Fine Art.
Early :
Christian and Byzantine, 659
Mediaeval, in the North, 659
Education, 63
Examinations, 191, 541, 757
Report, 349
Rules and Syllabuses, 350
Museums in need, 653
Royal College of, Prospectus, 191
Rules governing the award of the Ministry's Diplomas and Certificates in, 758
See also Works of Art.
Articled Clerks. *See* Public Notaries.
Artificial :
Incubation, 516
Insemination. *See* Agriculture.
Limbs, Reports, 222, 389, 820
Artillery, Royal Regiment of, Standing Order Amendments, 663
Artistes. *See* Variety.
Arts Council of Great Britain, Select Committee on Estimates Report, 678, 785
Ascot Race Course Act, 330
Ashbury, Wreck Report, 249
Ashdown Forest Act, 514
Ashes, Combustible Material in, 722
Asia :
and the Far East :
Economic :
Commission, 653
Bulletin, 861
Survey, 645, 862
Working Group Report, 425
South and South-East, Colombo Plan for Economic Development. *Cmd. 8080*, 716
South-East, Wall Map, 535
Askwith Memorandum, 69
Asparagus, 738
Aspen, Raising from Seed, 553

Asquith, Sir Cyril (Chairman): Royal Commission on Equal Pay, Report. *Cmd. 6937*, 43
Assessment of Disablement due to Specific Injuries. *Cmd. 7076*, 156
Assistance:
Board Reports:
Cmd. 6883, 40
Cmd. 7184, 163
Cmd. 7502, 318
See also National Assistance.
Assuan, Wreck Report, 109
Assurance Companies:
Act, 1946, 48
Bill, 4, 15, 26
Act, 1949, 509
Acts, Summary of Business, 841
Astley Ainslie Hospital Confirmation Act, 51
Bill, 8, 28
Aston, G. H., Sound Insulations of Partitions, 394
Astronomical Navigation Tables, 336
Asylums Officers' Superannuation Act, 325
Atkinson, E. H. T. (Chairman), Central Price Regulation Committee, Report, Prices of Radio Valves, 105
Atlantic:
Battle of the, 71
Ocean:
Monthly Meteorological Charts, 386
Surface Current Charts, 84
Temperatures, Monthly Sea Surface, 815
Atmospheric Pollution, Investigation of, Report, 604
Atomic:
Bombs at Hiroshima and Nagasaki, 69
Energy:
Act, 50
Bill, 11, 28, 29
Control of:
International, 864
Scientific and Technical Commission Report, 110
Commission, Official Records, 110, 250, 422, 642, 859
International Bibliography on, 642
Reports, 64, 258, 406
S.R. & O.s and S.I.s Revised, 835
Warfare, 783
Attempted Rape Act, 328
Bill, 150, 268

Auchinleck, Gen. Sir C. J. L.:
Operations in:
Indo-Burma Theatre based on India, 385
Middle East, 383
Auctioneering and Estate Agency, Careers, 75
Auctions (Bidding Agreements) Act, 507
Audit. See Exchequer.
Audley End:
Guide, 882
Topographical Index of State Room Pictures, 883
Aurora and associated magnetic storm, 386
Australia:
Commonwealth of, S.R. & O.s and S.I.s Revised, 835
Film Strip and Lecture Notes, 751
Introducing, Picture Set, 751
Overseas Economic Survey, 845
Specialist Conference in Agriculture, Report, 741
Wall Map, 346
Australian and New Zealand Waters, Monthly Sea Surface Temperatures, 595
Austria:
British:
Expenditure in, Select Committee Report, 23
Forces of Occupation in Germany and, Treaty with Belgium. *Cmd. 6790*, 34
Control:
Commission Publications (N.P.), 179
Machinery and Zones of Occupation, Agreements concerning. *Cmd. 6958*, 44
Deferment of certain claims. *Cmd. 7186*, 163
Payments Agreement. *Cmd. 6891*, 40
Restitution of Monetary Gold, Protocol with U.S.A. and France. *Cmd. 7265*, 168
Sterling Payments Agreement. *Cmd. 7909*, 704
Works of Art in, Losses and survivals, 56
Autosexing poultry breeds, 737
Auxiliary:
and Reserve Forces:
Act, 719
Bill, 459, 462, 485, 488
Disablement Allowances and Pensions, 437

Auxiliary (continued):
Services, Strength and Casualties. *Cmd. 6832*, 37
Territorial Service, War office Publications (N.P.), 114, 261, 437, 660, 879
Averages of:
Bright Sunshine for the British Isles, 386
Humidity for the British Isles, 595
Aviation:
Meteorology:
Azores, 595
of the routes:
Castel Benito–Cairo, 815
Marseilles–Castel Benito, 815
South America, 595
Weather Forecasts Code, 84
See also Civil Aviation.
Aviators, Meteorology for, 84, 387
Awards to Inventors, Royal Commission on, Reports:
Cmd. 7586, 323
Cmd. 7832, 504
Awbery, S. S.: Malaya and Singapore Labour and Trade Union Organisation Report, 584
Aycliffe Development Corporation Reports, 469, 476, 694
Ayrshire, Geology of Central, 829
Azores:
Aviation Meteorology, 595
Transit facilities to British Military Aircraft. *Cmd. 7499*, 317
See also Portugal.

B

Bacon Industry, S.R. & O.s and S.I.s Revised, 835
Bacteriology of Spray-dried Egg, 224
Badges. See Flags.
Baffin Bay, Monthly Meteorological Charts, 814
Bagenal, N. B.: Fruit growing areas of the Hastings Beds in Kent, 517
Baghdad. See Haifa–Baghdad; Iraq.
Bahama Islands and Belgium, Agreement for Reciprocal Protection of Trade Marks. *Cmd. 8089*, 717
Bahamas:
Colonial Reports, 343, 532
S.R. & O.s and S.I.s Revised, 835
Bahrein, Aircraft Accident Report, 338

Bailey Bridge, 115, 662
Military Engineering, 438
Normal Uses, 880
Bainbridge, Sir Clive (Chairman), Committee to formulate proposals for a Central Institute of Management, 102
Bainton Public Level Crossing, Railway Accident Report, 634
Baiting of Animals Bill, 474, 481, 483, 681
Baker, A. R.: Intrinsic Safety of Electrical Apparatus, 357
Baker, Rt. Hon. H. T. (Chairman), New Forest Committee, Report. *Cmd. 7245*, 167
Baker, S. J.: Police Council Report, 202
Bakery Diplomas, Arrangements and Conditions for the Award of, 758
Balance of Payments:
Cmd. 7324, 306
Cmd. 7520, 319
Cmd. 7928, 705
Cmd. 8065, 715
United Nations, 423, 432
Balerno Junction, Railway Accident, Report, 850
Balfour of Burleigh, Lord (Chairman), Housing Management Sub-Committee: Management of Municipal Housing Estates, 559
Balkans, Special Committee Reports, 428, 649, 865
Ball-clay Industry Inquiry, 102
Balmuccley Level Crossing, Railway Accident Report, 107
Bamangwato Tribe, Succession to Chieftainship. *Cmd. 7913*, 704
Bamford, Sir E. St. J. (Chairman), Taxation and Overseas Minerals Departmental Committee, Report. *Cmd. 7728*, 497
Banbury Corporation Act, 173
Bank:
Holiday, Special Proclamation, 594
Notes. See Currency.
of England:
Act, 48
Bill, 3, 4, 27
Charter. *Cmd. 6752*, 32
Reports:
Cmd. 7115, 158
Cmd. 7411, 311
Cmd. 7759, 499
Cmd. 8002, 710
S.R. & O.s and S.I.s Revised, 835
of Ireland, S.R. & O.s and S.I.s Revised, 835

Bankers' Returns, 219, 594, 812
Banking, Careers, 75, 368
Bankruptcy:
Act, 1950, 721
(Amendment) Act, 507
(Scotland) Act, 507
S.R. & O.s and S.I.s Revised, 835
Banks. See Trustee Saving Banks.
Barbados:
Colonial Reports, 343, 749
S.R. & O.s and S.I.s Revised, 835
Barclay, A.: Pure Chemistry, 192
Barkas, W. W.: Swelling of wood under Stress, 605
Barker, J.: Preservation of fruit and vegetables by freezing, 392
Barley. See Grain Crops; Wheat
Barlow, Sir Alan (Chairman), Committee on Scientific Manpower. *Cmd. 6824*, 36
Barnett, G. R. (Chairman):
Cotton Industry Committee, Reports, 208
Safeguarding of Milling Machines, 210
Barnsley:
Corporation Act, 514
Geology of the country around, 393
Main Colliery, Explosion Report. *Cmd. 7300*, 305
Barrack Services. See Supply.
Barrett, D.: Islamic Metalwork in the British Museum, 741
Barrington-Wood, V. M. (Chairman), London Plan Working Party, Report, 633
Barristers, Careers, 75
Barrs Bay, Northern Ireland, Aircraft Accident Report, 180
Barry, Rear-Admiral, Attack on *Tirpitz* by Midget Submarines, 384
Basic:
Facts about the United Nations, 250, 423, 859
Rescue (Civil Defence), 783
Training, Manual of, Pamphlets, 783
Basildon Development Corporation Report, 694
Basingwerk Abbey, Guide, 117
Bastardy, England. S.R. & O.s and S.I.s Revised, 835
Basutoland:
Colonial Reports, 343, 536, 753
S.R.O.s and S.I.s Revised, 835
Batavia:
Consular Commission Report, 867

Batavia (continued):
Security Council Consular Commission, 866
Bateson, D. L. (Chairman), Employment of Children as Film Actors, etc., Report. *Cmd. 8005*, 711
Bath Extension Act, 725
Battersea North and South, Boundary Commission Report. *Cmd. 7745*, 498
Battle:
against Disease:
Film Strip, 534
Picture Set, 532
against Ignorance:
Film Strip, 534
Picture Set, 532
against Poverty:
Film Strip, 534
Picture Set, 532
for Output, 223
of the Atlantic, 71
of the River Plate, 219
Bean Weevils, 178
Beardmore, Wm. & Co. Ltd., Boiler Explosion Report, 417
Beaton, N. S. (Chairman), Committee on Ferries in Great Britain, Report, 417
Bechuanaland Protectorate:
Colonial Reports, 343, 536, 753
Succession to Chieftainship of the Bamangwato Tribe. *Cmd. 7913*, 704
Water Resources Report, 533
Bed Bug, 612
Bee:
Diseases, England. S.R. & O.s and S.I.s Revised, 835
Hives, 738
Beech:
in Great Britain, General Volume Table for, 769
Mast. See Acorns.
Beekeepers, Advice to intending, 516
Beekeeping, Migratory, 516
S.R. & O.s and S.I.s Revised, 835
Bees:
Acarine Disease in, 333
Examination of, for Acarine Disease, 737
in Orchards, Importance of, 333
Beeswax, Preparation of, 516
Beet, Sugar:
Singling to Delivery, 516
Sowing to Singling, 516
Beetles. See under names of beetles.

Beetroot, Recommended grades for, 335
Beira, Port of, and connected Railways, Convention between U.K., Southern Rhodesia and Portugal:
Cmd. 7983, 709
Cmd. 8061, 715
Beirut, General Conference Records, 654
Belfast Aircraft Accident Report, 337
Belgian Congo, Review of Commercial Conditions, 841
Belgium:
Civil Administration and Jurisdiction, Exchange of Notes. *Cmd. 6875*, 39
Disposal of property of Belgian and British Merchant Seamen, Exchange of Notes. *Cmd. 6908*, 42
Incidents involving H.M. Forces, Claims Agreement. *Cmd. 6802*, 35
International Authority for Ruhr, Agreement. *Cmd. 7685*, 494
Loan Agreement. *Cmd. 7811*, 503
Military Operations in, 1918, 362
Monetary Agreements:
Cmd. 7057, 154
Cmd. 7264, 168
Cmd. 7823, 504
Cmd. 7856, 506
Cmd. 7930, 705
Cmd. 8029, 712
Mutual:
Aid to Merchant Shipping, Expenditure. *Cmd. 7283*, 169
Understanding of Intellectual, Artistic and Scientific Activities, Convention for the Promotion of:
Cmd. 6841, 37
Cmd. 7002, 47
Overseas Economic Survey, 416, 845
Privileges and Facilities for British Forces in Belgium, Treaties:
Cmd. 6790, 34
Cmd. 7624, 490
Reciprocal:
Abolition of Visas, Exchange of Notes. *Cmd. 7038*, 153
Compensation in respect of War Damage, Exchange of Notes. *Cmd. 7495*, 317
Protection of Trade Marks, Belgium and the Bahama Islands, Agreement. *Cmd. 8089*, 717
Social Security Convention with U.K. *Cmd. 7911*, 704

Belgium (continued):
Supply of Aircraft and Equipment, Agreement. *Cmd. 7039*, 153
Bell, H. E., Italian Archives during the War and at the close, 179
Belsen Trial Reports, 259
Bending Brakes Report, 577
Benefices:
(Exercise of Rights of Presentation) Measure, 727
(Suspension of Presentation) Measure, 6, 7, 52
Amendment Measures, 457, 727
Ecclesiastical Committee Report, 457
Benefits, Death. See National Insurance (Industrial Injuries).
Benzole:
and Toluene from Coal Gas, Report, 771
Technical Committee Report, 355
Berkhamsted Castle, Guide, 263
Berlin:
Air Lift, 519
Aircraft Accident Report. *Cmd. 7384*, 309
Conference, Protocol of the Proceedings. *Cmd. 7087*, 156
Kommandatura Order, 536
Question referred to United Nations. *Cmd. 7534*, 320
Bermuda:
Colonial Reports, 343, 531, 749
Conference on Civil Aviation. *Cmd. 6747*, 32
Free Importation of Goods into the Leased Bases. *Cmd. 7000*, 47
Petition for Appointment of a Royal Commission. *Cmd. 7093*, 157
S.R. & O.s and S.I.s Revised, 835
Telecommunications Conference:
Cmd. 6818, 36
Cmd. 6837, 37
Bernadotte, F.: Progress Report on Palestine. *Cmd. 7530*, 320
Bespoke Tailoring, Choice of Careers, 793
Best, A. C.: Abnormal Visibility at Malta, 84
Betrothal of Princess Elizabeth, King's Consent, 220
Betterment:
and Lotteries Act, 1442
See also Dog Racecourse: Street Betting.
Betting, Lotteries and Gaming, Royal Commission on, Minutes of Evidence, 608, 822

Bevan, W. F.: Report on Boiler Explosion in Glasgow, 417
Beveridge, W. I. D.: Cultivation of Viruses and Rickettsiae in Chick Embryo, 86
Beverley Corporation Act, 331
Beware Firedamp, 355
Bibliographical Series, 642
Bibliography, Selected, 872
Bickley, F.: Hastings Manuscript Report, 223
Bilharziasis in Africa, 877
Bilingualism in the Secondary School in Wales, 543
Bin Ventilation, 177
Biological:
and Medical Committee, Report, 826
Standardisation, Expert Committee on, 876
Standards, Reports, 603, 813
Biologists and Agriculturists, Demand for persons with professional qualifications, 811
Birch in Great Britain, General Volume Table for, 769
Birds:
in London, Reports, 441, 663, 883
See also Wild Birds.
Birmingham:
Boundary Commission Report. *Cmd. 7787*, 501
Corporation Acts, 52, 331
University Act, 330
Birth:
of a Daughter to their Royal Highnesses the Princess Elizabeth and the Duke of Edinburgh, 812
of a Son to their Royal Highnesses the Princess Elizabeth and the Duke of Edinburgh, 386
Births. *See* Registrar-General's Returns; Notification of Births.
Biscuits. *See* Cakes.
Bishop Auckland, Local Study, 350
Bishops (Retirement) Measure, 676
Ecclesiastical Committee Report, 676
Bishop's Palace, Guides:
Lamphey, 440
St. Davids, 117
Bismarck, Sinking of, 220
Bituminous:
Coatings for the protection of iron and steel against corrosion, 225
Materials. *See* Soils.
Bizonal Fusion Agreement with U.S.A.:
Cmd. 7287, 170
Bizonal Fusion Agreement with U.S.A. (*continued*):
Cmd. 7623, 490
Cmd. 7742, 498
Cmd. 7757, 499
Exchanges of Notes regarding Financial Issues:
Cmd. 7990, 710
Cmd. 8001, 710
Black Currants and Red Currants, 736
Blackhead in Turkeys, 334
Blackquarter, Quarter Ill, or Blackleg, 333, 738
Blenkinsop, A. (Chairman), Publicity for Local Government Consultative Committee, Report, 782
Bletchley Railway Accident Report, 418
Blind:
Persons Act, 723
Welfare of. *See* Disabled Persons (Employment).
Blindness:
in British African and Middle East Territories, Report, 343
in England and Wales, Causes of, 813
See also Monocular Blindness.
Blocklaying, Work Study in, 394
Blood Groups (Rh) and their Clinical Effects, 391
Blow-down, 773
Boarding:
and Hospital Special Schools, 541
Education, 63, 64
Special Schools, 62
Boarding-out of Children and Young Persons, 69
Boarer's Manor Way Occupation Level Crossing, Railway Accident Report, 850
Boiler:
Corrosion and Water Treatment, 332
Explosion Reports, 246, 417, 632, 848
Boilers:
Effect of certain factors on the efficiency of a hand-fired natural-draught Lancashire Boiler, 606
Fuel Efficiency Bulletins, 773
Bolton:
Corporation Act, 513
Wanderers Football Ground Disaster, Inquiry. *Cmd. 6846*, 38
Bomb and Mine Clearance Clasp, 261
Bonded Warehouses, Lists of, 61, 187, 265, 346, 537, 754
Bonding new concrete to old, 604
Bonus Schemes for Fuel Economy in Industry, 772

Book:
Jacket, Art of the, 659
of Needs, 206, 653
Bookmakers, S.R. & Os. and S.I.s Revised, 835
Boot and Shoe Manufacture, Careers, 577
Bootle:
Boundary Commission Report. *Cmd. 8100*, 718
Extension Act, 725
Boots and Shoes, Working Party Report, 106
Borneo, Cultivation of Cocoa, 344
Borough, Municipal, England, S.R. & O.s and S.I.s Revised, 835
Borrowing (Control and Guarantees):
Act, 49
Bill, 7, 8, 9, 18, 19, 27, 28, 29
Statement of Guarantees, 296
S.R. & O.s and S.I.s Revised, 835
Borstal Institutions:
Directory, 70
S.R. & O.s and S.I.s Revised, 835
Borstals. *See* Prisons.
Boschma, Dr. Hilbrand: Lernaediscus pusillus n.sp., 742
Botanic Garden:
Edinburgh, Notes, 613, 822
Kew, Bulletin, 576
Bothwell Castle, Guide, 263
Boundary Commission Reports:
England:
Cmd. 7260, 168
Cmd. 7745, 498
Cmd. 7787, 501
Cmd. 8100, 718
New Constituencies. *Cmd. 7400*, 311
Northern Ireland. *Cmd. 7231*, 166
Scotland. *Cmd. 7270*, 169
Wales. *Cmd. 7274*, 169
See also Local Government; Representation of the People.
Bourne End Railway Accident Report, 107
Bovine Contagious Abortion, 55, 517
Boxing and Wrestling, 879
Brabazon I, Cost of Construction. Select Committee on Estimates, Report, 286, 293
Bracken Eradication, 516
Bradford Corporation Act, 513
Provisional Order Bill, 300
Bradlaw, R. V. (Chairman), U.K. Dental Mission, Report on New Zealand School Dental Nurses, 781
Brassieres, Board of Trade Publications (N.P.), 104
Braxy, 334
Bray, F. (Chairman), Committee on Art Examinations, Report, 349
Brazil:
Air Transport Agreement:
Cmd. 6962, 45
Cmd. 6977, 46
Boundary with British Guiana, Exchange of Notes. *Cmd. 6965*, 151
Commercial Transactions, Exchange of Notes. *Cmd. 8068*, 715
Cultural Conventions:
Cmd. 7134, 159
Cmd. 7606, 489
Effect on the entry and residence of foreigners, Exchange of Notes. *Cmd. 8032*, 713
Economic and Commercial Interest, Exchange of Notes. *Cmd. 6952*, 44
Overseas Economic Survey, 416
Trade:
Agreement. *Cmd. 7768*, 500
with Canada. *Cmd. 6966*, 45
and Payments Agreement. *Cmd. 7438*, 313
Prolongation of, Exchange of Notes. *Cmd. 7730*, 497
Brazing, 100
Breconshire:
County Council Act, 51
Police Forces Enquiry Report, 362
Breeding Livestock adapted to unfavourable environments, 433
Bretton Woods Agreement:
Act, 48
S.R. & O.s and S.I.s Revised, 835
Brewing, Careers, 75, 207, 577
Brick:
Industry:
Amenities in, 263
Labour Requirements in, 263
See also National Brick.
Bricklaying in Cold Weather, 882
Brickmaking, 263
See also Clay.
Bricks:
Clay Building, 394
Sand-lime, Special Report, 394
Brickwork, Some common defects in, 829
Bridge Works. *See* Road and Bridge.
Bridges:
S.R. & O.s and S.I.s Revised, 835
See also Bailey Bridge.

Bridging, Pocket Books (Royal Engineers), 438, 439
Bridgnorth. *See* Dudley.
Brierley, Prof. J. L. (Chairman), Double Day-shift Working, Committee Report. *Cmd. 7147*, 160
Brierly, Prof. J. N. (Chairman), Court of Inquiry regarding dispute between London Master Printers Association and London Society of Compositors. *Cmd. 8074*, 716
Brighstone Down Aircraft Accident Report, 337
Brighton Corporation:
Act, 331
(Trolley Vehicles) Order Confirmation Act, 174
Bill, 128, 148
Bristol:
and Gloucester District, Regional Geology, 393
and Somerset Coalfield Survey, 66
Corporation Act, 725
Election (Validation) Act, 49
Bill, 6, 27
Provisional Order Confirmation Act, 330
Bill, 274, 300
Britain:
Aids:
Colonial Progress, Film Strip, 751
the Colonies, Picture Set, 750
and the Colonies, 343
and the United Nations, 353
Fights:
Locusts, Film Strip, 534
Sleeping Sickness, Film Strip, 534
"Britain Can Make It" Exhibition, related publications, 71
Britain's Forests, 354, 553, 769
British:
Achievement, Something Done, 363
African and Middle East Territories, Blindness in, 343
Agricultural Machinery Mission to Canada, 623
and American Zones of Occupation, Germany, Memorandum of Agreement:
Cmd. 6986, 46
Cmd. 7001, 47
and Foreign State Papers, 353, 547, 761
Armed Forces pending withdrawal from French Territory, Facilities, Agreement with France. *Cmd. 7523*, 319
British (*continued*):
Bark-beetles, 65
Broadcasting Corporation:
Accounts. *Cmd. 6758*, 32
Annual Reports and Accounts:
Cmd. 6985, 46
Cmd. 7319, 306
Cmd. 7506, 318
Cmd. 7770, 500
Cmd. 8044, 741
and Musicians' Union, Report of the Independent Committee, 577
Licence and Agreement with Postmaster-General. *Cmd. 6975*, 46
Royal Charter for Continuance of. *Cmd. 6974*, 46
Select Committee Report, 21
Caribbean:
Area, Unification of Public Services, 749
Colonies:
Photo-poster, 788
Wall map, 535
Standing Closer Association Committee Report, 749
Coaster, Official Story, 246
Committee on the Preservation and Restitution of Works of Art, Archives and other Material, Publications (N.P.), 56
Commonwealth:
and Empire, Handbook, 71
Leaflets, 363
Scientific Conference Reports, 45, 225, 741
Statistical Abstract, 714
Council, Select Committee on Estimates, Report, 286, 293
Dependencies in the Far East, 1945–9. *Cmd. 7709*, 496
East Africa, Economic Survey, 416
Electricity Authority:
Loans proposed to be raised, 682, 684, 688
Reports and Accounts, 691
Statements of Guarantee on Stock issued, 288, 471, 686
Empire Forestry Conference:
Proceedings, 553
Statistics, 354
European Airways Corporation:
Annual Reports and Accounts, 146, 297, 477, 691

British (*continued*):
European Airways Corporation (*continued*):
Statements of Guarantee on loans proposed to be raised and stock issued, 468, 472, 686
Expenditure in Germany, 144
Export Trade Research Organisation Report on Packaging Consumer Goods for the Canadian Market, 846
Film Institute:
Act, 510
Bill, 453, 485
Report. *Cmd. 7361*, 308
Fishing Boats and Coastal craft, 826
Foreign Policy, Documents on, 194, 353, 547, 761
Goodwill Trade Mission to Egypt, Report, 102
Guiana:
and British Honduras, Report of the Settlement Commission. *Cmd. 7533*, 320
Boundary line with Brazil, Exchange of Notes. *Cmd. 6965*, 151
Colonial Reports, 343, 531, 532
Free Importation of Goods into Leased Bases. *Cmd. 7000*, 47
S.R. & O.s and S.I.s Revised, 835
Sugar Industry Report, 535
Honduras:
Boundaries. *Cmd. 6934*, 43
Colonial Reports, 343, 531, 532, 749
S.R. & O.s and S.I.s Revised, 835
Imperial Calendar and Civil Service List, 93, 231, 400, 616, 834
Industries Fair, Supplement to Board of Trade Journal, 844
Intelligence Objectives Sub-Committee Reports, 103, 410, 623, 841
Isles Weather Chart, 596
Military:
Administration of Occupied Territories in Africa, 437
Fixed Assets in Italy, Exchange of Notes. *Cmd. 7377*, 309
Museum:
Act, 49
Bill, 7, 28
(Natural History) Publications (N.P.), 719, 520, 741
Publications (N.P.), 520, 741
S.R. & O.s and S.I.s Revised, 835
National Hive, 737
British (*continued*):
Nationality:
Act, 329
Bill, 268, 275, 277, 301, 302
and Status of Aliens Act, 329
S.R. & O.s and S.I.s Revised, 835
Naval Vessels, Transfer Agreement with China. *Cmd. 7457*, 315
North America Acts:
1946, 49
Bill, 7, 28
1949, 310
Bill, 450, 484
1949 (No. 2), 512
Bill, 460, 487
Overseas Airways:
Act, 1939, Statement, 136
Corporation:
Annual Reports and Accounts, 280, 297, 476, 691
Statements of Guarantee on loans proposed to be raised and stock issued, 21, 466, 469, 477, 682
Pacific Fleet, Assault on Okinawa, 385
Parliamentary Delegation to Greece, Report, 194
Rainfall, 595, 814
Regional Geology, 226, 393
Seaweeds and their Utilisation in the Preparation of Agar, 559
Settlements Act, 48
Shipping (Assistance) Act Accounts, 25, 146, 297
South American Airways Corporation:
Loans proposed to be raised, 298
Reports and Accounts, 280, 297, 477
Stock issued, 468
Territories in East and Central Africa, 1945–50. *Cmd. 7987*, 709
Tourist and Holidays Board, Select Committee on Estimates, 677
Transport Commission:
Act, 513
Bill, 673, 725
Order Confirmation Act, 330
Bill, 277, 302
Reports and Accounts, 477, 691
Statements of Guarantee, 281, 285, 286, 288, 289, 290, 292, 296, 470, 472, 474, 479, 683, 684, 688, 689, 690, 692, 694, 696

British (*continued*) :
War :
Economy, 639
Relief Story : Friends in Need, 194
Way and Purpose, 437
West :
Africa, Civil Services, 186
Indian Colonies :
Conference. *Cmd. 7291*, 304
Conference on Closer Associa-
tion, 344
Indies :
Development and Welfare, 186
Nutrition in, 61
Review of Commercial Con-
ditions, 102
Wines, Sweet, S.R. & O.s and S.I.s
Revised, 835
Zone Review, 61, 187, 266, 346, 536
Broadcasting :
Civil Estimates, 137, 284, 285, 466,
467, 681
European Convention. *Cmd. 7946*,
707
from Ceylon, Copy of Agreement.
Cmd. 7974, 709
in the Far East, Copy of Agreement.
Cmd. 7584, 323
Policy. *Cmd. 6852*, 38
See also British Broadcasting Cor-
poration.
Broadstairs. *See* Margate.
Broch, Hjalmar : John Murray Expedi-
tion Scientific Report, 179
Broccoli and Cauliflower, Recommended
Grades for, 335
Bromborough Dock Act, 52
Bromehead, C. E. N. : Geology of the
Country around Barnsley, 393
Brook, Sir F. (Chairman), Police Council
Committee, Report on Police Uni-
form, 362
Brooke, 709
Brooke-Popham, Sir Robert : Opera-
tions in the Far East, 384
Brough Castle Guide, 663
Brown, C. A. (Chairman) :
Committee on Organisation of Domes-
tic Food Producers, Report, 738
Interdepartmental Committee on
Survey Staffs, Report, 820
Brown, Rt. Hon. D. Clifton (Chairman),
Boundary Commission, Reports :
Cmd. 7231, 166
Cmd. 7260, 168
Cmd. 7270, 168
Cmd. 7274, 169

Brown, E. D. : Natural Lighting of
Houses and Flats, 227, 394
Brown, G. (Chairman) :
Allotments Advisory Committee, Re-
port, 738
Smallholdings Advisory Council, Re-
port, 518
Brown, V. : Aircraft Accident Reports,
180, 337, 523, 744
Browne, Major G. St. J. Orde, Labour
Conditions in East Africa, Report, 61
Browney Railway Accident Report, 107
Brownlee, K. A. : Industrial Experi-
mentation, 238, 620
Brunei, Colonial Reports, 343, 531, 532,
749
Brussels :
Copyright Convention, 624
Sprouts, 54, 55
See also Belgium.
Bryan, A. M. :
(Chairman), Committee of Inquiry
into Precautions necessary to
secure Safety in the use of Explo-
sives in Coal Mines, Report, 775
Explosion Reports :
Burngrange Mine. *Cmd.7221*, 165
Ingham Colliery. *Cmd. 7434*, 313
Whitehaven, Williams Colliery :
Cmd. 7236, 166
Cmd. 7410, 311
Bryan, J. :
Experiments on Preservation of Mine
Timber, 605
Methods of applying Wood Preser-
vatives, 87
Bucks Water Board Act, 51
Budget :
and your Pocket, 541
Disclosure, Select Committee Report,
146
Estimates for UNESCO, 653, 870
See also Financial Statement.
Build the Ships, 71
Builder :
and the State, 263
Machines for the Modern, 883
Building :
(Amendment) Regulations, Factory
Form, 370, 371, 372
and Civil Engineering :
during the War, Payment by
Results, Report, 264
Production in, 117
Works, General Conditions for
Government Contracts, 441,664

Building (*continued*) :
and Quantity Surveying, Supply and
Demand for Persons with Profes-
sional Qualifications, 811
Apprenticeship :
and Training Council Reports,
264, 664
Recruiting and Training, Special
Report, 664
Award of National Diplomas and
Certificates to Students, 350
Bricks of the U.K., Clay, 883
Bulletins (Education), 541, 746
Career, Choice of, 577
Codes of Practice Committee Report,
441
Contracts. *See* Programme and Pro-
gress.
for Health, 435
for Peace, 643
in Britain Today, 664
Industry, Careers, 75
Licences, Food and Drugs Act, 352
Materials :
and Components :
Distribution of, 441
Price Control, 118
and Housing :
Accounts, 134, 470, 679
Acts, 48, 724
Architectural Use of, 117
on Made-up Ground or Filling, 827
Operations, Working Party Report,883
Pattern Staining, 606
Regulations :
Amendment, 541
Revision, Report, 369
Research :
and Development Council Advi-
sory Council Report, 664
Department of Scientific and
Industrial Research Publica-
tions (N.P.), 86, 225, 391, 604,
826
Restrictions (Wartime Contraven-
tion) Act, 49
(Safety, Health and Welfare) Regs.,
370, 371, 372
Science Abstracts, 86, 225, 391, 604,
827
Societies Statistical Summary, 554
Society, S.R. & O.s and S.I.s Re-
vised, 835
Studies. *See* National Building
Studies ; Post War Building
Studies.

Building (*continued*) :
Trades Exhibition, 263
Use of Timber in, 664
Buildings :
Condensation Problems, 827
Historic. *See* Ancient Monuments.
registered for Marriage, etc., 224, 390,
776
Buildwas Abbey, guide, 117
Built-up Areas, Design and Layout of
Roads, 108
Bulbs, Diseases of, 517
Bulgaria :
Draft Peace Treaty. *Cmd. 6895*, 41
Revival of Pre-war Treaties and
Agreements. *Cmd. 7395*, 310
Peace Treaty :
Cmd. 7022, 152
Cmd. 7026, 153
Cmd. 7483, 316
Treaty of Peace Act, 172
Bill, 148
Bulgaria, Hungary, and Roumania,
Interpretation of Peace Treaties,
Advisory Opinion, 792
Bull, J. W., Boiler Explosion Reports,
746
Bullard, Sir Reader (Chairman) :
Treasury Committee Notes on Awards
made to Post-Graduate Students, 421
Burfield, S. T. : Great Barrier Reef
Expedition Scientific Report, 742
Burgess, R. E. : Survey of Existing
Information and Data on Radio Noise
over the frequency range 1–30 Mcs.,
227
Burgh :
Castle, Suffolk, guide, 440
Police (Scotland) Act, 506
Code of Modified Provisions, 612
Scotland, S.R. & O.s and S.I.s
Revised, 835
Burma :
and Bay of Bengal, Air Operations,
384
Avoidance of Double Taxation and
the Prevention of Fiscal Evasion
with respect to Taxes on Income.
Cmd. 7935, 706
Campaign in, 71
Commercial Relations, Exchange of
Notes. *Cmd. 7902*, 703
Compensation for premature termi-
nation of Service. *Cmd. 7189*, 163
Conversation with Delegation from.
Cmd. 7029, 153

18   19

Burma (*continued*) :
Forces, Definition of Corps, 261
Frontier Areas, Committee of In-
quiry Report. *Cmd. 7138*, 160
Hard Currency Areas, Agreement to
control Burma's Expenditure in.
Cmd. 7560, 322
Independence Act, 173
Bill, 132, 150
Jurisdictional and Fiscal Immunities
to be accorded to personnel of the
U.K. Forces in. *Cmd. 7355*, 308
Legislature Act, 49
Bill, 7, 9, 28
Loan Agreement. *Cmd. 8007*, 711
Office List, 71, 186
Official Story of Air War, 520
Operations in, 384
Recognition of Burmese Indepen-
dence and related matters, Treaty.
Cmd. 7360, 308
S.R. & O.s and S.I.s Revised, 835
Treaty. *Cmd. 7240*, 167
See also China.
Burnet, F. M. : Inoculation of Viruses
and Rickettsiae in Chick Embryo, 86
Burngrange Mine Explosion and Fire
Report. *Cmd. 7221*, 165
Burnham Committee Reports, Scales of
Salaries for Teachers, 190, 351, 758
Burrell, D. H. (Chairman), Police Coun-
cil Committee : Police Rent and
Supplementary Allowances, 362
Burrough, Admiral Sir H. M. : Naval
War in North-West Europe, 383
Burrows, F. J. (Chairman), Agricultural
Land Commission, Romney Marsh
Investigation Report, 518
Burrows, Roland (Deputy Chairman),
Boundary Commission, Report. *Cmd.
8100*, 718
Burrs Mount, Aircraft Accident Report,
180
Bursaries :
Education Authority Regs., Scot-
land, 91
for persons over school age, 91
Burt, Sir G. M. (Chairman) :
Building Research Board, Reports,
391
House Construction, Reports, 118,
664
Burton Agnes, Railway Accident Re-
port, 247
Business :
Management. *See* Professions.

Business (*continued*) :
Names :
Registration of, Act, 48
S.R. & O.s and S.I.s Revised, 836
Premises, Tenure and Rents, Report.
Cmd. 7706, 496
Training Scheme, Tutors, 95
Butler, C. G. : Bee Hives, 738
Butler, Rohan : Documents on British
Foreign Policy, 194, 353, 547, 761
Buying for our home, 71
Byelaws, Model, 290, 362
Byfleet, Railway Accident, Report, 247
Byland Abbey, guide, 117
Byng, E. S. (Chairman), London Regional
Advisory Council, Report : Youth
Employment, 593
Byrne, Hon. Mr. Justice (Chairman),
Departmental Committee on Depo-
sitions, Report. *Cmd. 7639*, 491

C

Cabbages, 54, 516
Cabbages, Brussels Sprouts, and Miscel-
laneous Green Crops, 335
Cabinet :
Mission. *See* India.
Office Publications, 743
Cable :
and Wireless :
Act, 50
Bill, 10, 11, 28, 29
Special Report, 21
Ltd. :
Accounts :
Cmd. 7181, 163
Cmd. 7467, 315
Cmd. 7743, 498
Cmd. 8019, 712
Proposed transfer to public
ownership. *Cmd. 6805*, 35
S.R. & O.s and S.I.s Revised, 836
Drum Specification, 406
Cables, Trailing, Committee Reports,
198
Cacao in the Gold Coast, Swollen Shoot
Disease, 535
Cadet Forces Medal :
Committee on the grant of Honours,
Decorations and Medals. *Cmd.
7879*, 702
Cadets. *See* Army Cadet Force.

Caernarvon Pier and Harbour Confirma-
tion Act, 726
Bill, 672, 698
Caerleon Roman Amphitheatre, guide,882
Caesar, Triumph of, 883
Caicos Islands. *See* Turks and Caicos.
Cake and Pudding Mixtures, Labelling,
760
Cakes, Puddings, Biscuits, and Scones,
760
Calabria, Action with Italian Fleet, 384
Caledonian Insurance Company Act, 51
Calendars. *See* Public Record Office
Publications.
Callaghan, James, M.P. (Chairman),
Road Safety Committee, Report, 635
Calorie Requirements Committee Re-
port, 874
Calves :
Husk or Hoose in, 334
White Scour in, 334
Camberwell, Bristol, and Nottingham
Election (Validation) Act, 51
Bill, 6, 27
Cambial Injuries in a Pruned Stand of
Norway Spruce, 769
Cambrai, Battle of, 568
Cambrakenneth Abbey, Guide, 882
Cameron, J., Port Transport Industry
Inquiry Report, 217
Cameron, John (Chairman), Legal Aid
and Legal Advice in Scotland Com-
mittee Report. *Cmd. 6925*, 43
Cameron, John B., Knoydart Estate
Report, 610
Cameroons :
under French Administration, Trus-
teeship Agreement. *Cmd. 7198*, 156
under U.N. Trusteeship :
Trusteeship Agreement, 432
Cmd. 7082, 164
Reports on Administration, 344,
532, 750
See also Togoland.
Camp Structures, Handbook, 437, 880
Campaign in Burma, 71
Campbeltown Water, etc., Order Confir-
mation Act, 51
Bill, 10, 29
Camping, Organised, 350
Camps, Organising International Volun-
tary Work, 655
Canada :
Air Services, Agreement and Ex-
change of Notes with U.K. *Cmd.
7857*, 700

Canada (*continued*) :
and Newfoundland :
Agreement entered into between.
Cmd. 7605, 489
Wall Map, 346
British Agricultural Machinery
Mission to, Report, 623
Defence Installation Agreement with
Newfoundland and U.K. *Cmd.
8323*, 36
Dominion of. S.R. & O.s and S.I.s
Revised, 836
Economic and Commercial Condi-
tions, 416
Exports to, Report, 624
Financial Agreement and Agreement
on the Settlement of War Claims
with U.K. *Cmd. 6904*, 41
Prospects for U.K. Exports in, 415
Tariff and Trade Agreement at
Geneva, Report on. *Cmd. 7258*,
168
Trade Agreement with Brazil. *Cmd.
6966*, 45
United Kingdom Engineering Mission
Report, 631
Canadian :
Army :
at War, 57, 180
Historical Summary, 1939–45,
337
Campaign in Italy and Sicily, 57
Market, Packaging Consumer Goods
for, 846
Treaty Series :
Cmd. 6900, 41
Cmd. 6948, 44
Cmd. 6966, 45
Canal :
and Navigable River, S.R. & O.s and
S.I.s Revised, 836
Boat, England, S.R. & O.s and S.I.s
Revised, 836
See also Forth and Clyde Ship Canal.
Cancer :
Act, 723
Registration in England and Wales,
776
Researches on the Radiotherapy of
Oral Cancer, 813
See also Medical and Population
Subjects.
Cape :
Observatory, Annals, 777
Spartivento, Action between British
and Government Forces, 385

20   21

CAP—   *INDEX 1946-50*

Capital :
Expenditure, Programme of, 200
Investment :
in 1948. *Cmd. 7268*, 169
in 1950, Educational Building,
757, 758
Issues Control. *Cmd. 7281*, 169
Punishment :
Cmd. 7419, 312
Royal Commission, Minutes of
Evidence, 608, 824
Captain Cook's Kangaroo, Identity of,
742
Car Loading, Automatic, Report on, 557
Carbon Monoxide, Methods for Detec-
tion, 607, 830
Garcroft Railway Accident Report, 107
Cardiff :
Cake Coffee Boiler Explosion Report,
417
Corporation :
Act, 52
(Extension of Time) Act, 330
Extension Act, 725
Care :
and Maintenance of Fittings and
Equipment in the Modern Home,
780
of Children Committee. *Cmd. 6922*,
43
of Farm-stored Grain, 730
of the Trawler's Fish, 604
Career, Forestry as a, 553
Careers, Ministry of Labour Publica-
tions (N.P.), 75, 207, 368, 577, 793
Cargo Handling Gear, 439
Caribbean :
Area, Agreement for the Establish-
ment of the Caribbean Commis-
sion. *Cmd. 7679*, 494
British Standing Closer Association
Committee Report, 749
Colonies :
Film Strip, 534
Picture Sets, 533
Commission, Agreement for the
Establishment of. *Cmd. 7000*, 47
Free Importation of Goods Into
Leased Bases. *Cmd. 7000*, 47
Regional Air Navigation Meeting
Final Report, 790
Unification of Public Services, 749
Carisbrooke Castle Guide, 440
Carlgren, Oskar : Great Barrier Reef
Expedition 1928–9, Scientific Report,
742

Carlisle :
Boundary Commission Report. *Cmd.
8100*, 718
Extension Act, 725
Carpet-knotting and weaving, Notes on,
877
Carpets, Working Party Report, 416
Carr, Sir C. (Chairman) : Electoral Law
Reform Committee Final Report.
Cmd. 7286, 304
Carriage :
by Air Act, 723
of Goods by Sea Act, 507
Carrier-borne Aircraft Attack on
Kirkenes and Petsamo, 385
Carrot Fly, 178
Carr-Saunders, Sir A. (Chairman) :
Commission on University Educa-
tion in Malaya, Report, 344
Royal Commission on Population.
Reports and Papers of Statistics
Committee, 825
Special Committee on Education for
Commerce, Report, 541
Carter, Sir Archibald (Chairman) : Mono-
polies and Restrictive Practices Com-
mission, Report on Supply of Dental
Goods, 695
Cartography, Murdoch, 866
Cartwright, K. St. G., Decay of Timber,
226
Casagrande, Dr. L., Application of
Electro-osmosis to practical problems
in foundations and earthworks, 225
Castel Benito, Civil Aircraft Accident
Report, 744
Castle Acre Priory Guide, 117
Casualties. *See* Strength and Casualties ;
U-Boat Casualties.
Catering :
Careers, 75
Industry Training, 63, 64
Report, 75
Wages :
Act, 509
Report, 298
Commission Reports :
Annual, 22, 103, 280, 298,
480, 710
Development of Catering,
Holiday, and Tourist Ser-
vices, 76
Operation of Catering Wages
Boards. *Cmd. 6776*, 33
S.R. & O.s and S.I.s Revised, 836
Catford, Railway Accident Report, 247

   INDEX 1946-50   —CHA

Catherine McCraig's Trust (Amendment)
Schemes, 92, 231
Cattewater Pier and Harbour :
Order Confirmation Act, 726
Provisional Order Bill, 672, 698
Cattle :
Grids :
for Private Farm and Estate
Roads, 739
See also Highways.
Infertility of, 334
Mastitis in, 334
Stomach Worms in, 738
Tuberculosis of, 178
Cauliflower Mosaic, 737
Cauliflowers, Recommended Grades for,
335
Cavity Party Wall Construction for
Sound Insulation, 827, 882
Cayman Islands, Colonial Reports, 343,
749
Celluloid :
and Cinematograph Film Act, 326
Storage Report. *Cmd. 7929*, 705
Cement Costs Report, 264
Censorship of Plays (Repeal) Bill, 479,
482, 483, 488, 681
Census :
England and Wales, 1931, General
Report, 776
of Distribution, Report. *Cmd. 6764*,
33
of Production Act, 170
S.R. & O.s and S.I.s Revised, 836
Central :
Africa, Groundnuts Production. *Cmd.
7030*, 153
Electricity Board :
(Increase of Borrowing Powers)
Special Order, 66
(Keadby Generating Station
Lands) Special Order, 355
Publications (N.P.), 57, 180
England, Geology of, 226
Government, etc., Civil Estimates,
137, 284, 466, 681
Health Services Council Reports, 779
Heating Plants, Control of Excess
Air on, 772
Institute of Management, Report,
102
Land Board :
Practice Notes, 522, 610
Publications, 743
Reports, 475, 691

Central *(continued)* :
Office of Information :
Publications, 788
Reports :
Cmd. 7567, 322
Cmd. 7830, 504
Statistical Office Publications, 109,
250, 266, 422, 641, 743
Transport Consultative Committee
for Great Britain, Annual Report,
684
Ceramics Industry in Germany, 1939–45,
842
Cereal Diseases, Recognition and Con-
trol, 335
Cerebro-Spinal Fever Report, 229
Ceremonial :
Manual of, Amendments, 261, 437
1950 (Provisional), 880
Certified :
Institutions for Mental Defectives, 187
Places of Worship, 558
Ceylon :
Air Services, Agreement with U.K.
Cmd. 7589. 700
Broadcasting from, Copy of Agree-
ment. *Cmd. 7974*, 709
Independence Act, 173
Bill, 132, 150
Proposals for conferring fully respon-
sible status within the British
Commonwealth of Nations. *Cmd.
7257*, 168
S.R. & O.s and S.I.s Revised, 836
Sterling Assets and Monetary Co-
operation, Exchanges of Letters
with U.K. :
Cmd. 7422, 312
Cmd. 7766, 500
Chafer Beetles, 354, 737
Chaffinch. *See* Goldfinch.
Chains and other lifting gear, Use of.
Cmd. 7830, 504
Challenge and Response (Emergency
Scheme for the Training of Teachers),
757
Chancery, Scotland. S.R. & O.s and
S.I.s Revised, 836
Changing Schools, Our, 757
Channel Islands :
Excluded from provisions of General
Agreement on Social Security,
Exchange of Notes with France.
Cmd. 8096, 718
Proposed Reform Report. *Cmd.
7074*, 156

22   23

CHA—   *INDEX 1946-50*

Channel Islands *(continued)* :
(Representation) Measure, 514
Chaplains, Pay of Officiating, 663
Charges Consultative Committee Re-
ports, 106, 246
Charity :
Commissioners, Report, 743
England, S.R. & O.s and S.I.s
Revised, 836
of Walter Stanley in West Bromwich,
Bill, 401, 487
Scotland, S.R. & O.s and S.I.s
Revised, 836
Charles I, Acts of the Privy Council, 882
Charles II Domestic Silver, 659
Charlock. *See* Yellow Charlock
Chart :
depicting Ribands and Emblems of
Orders, Decorations, and Medals,
437
Regional, South East Africa, 574
Charter of the United Nations and
Statute of the International Court of
Justice, 207, 423
Cmd. 7015, 152
Index, 251
Chartered :
and other Bodies :
(Resumption of Elections) Act, 48
(Temporary Provisions), S.R. &
O.s and S.I.s Revised, 836
Associations, S.R. & O.s and S.I.s
Revised, 836
Tonnage, Government owned, Dis-
posal of, Invitation to tender, 107
Charterhouse. *See* Sutton.
Charting the Seas in Peace and War, 176
Charts of the Western North Pacific
Ocean, Quarterly Surface Current, 596
Chasteney, H. E. (Chairman) : Report
on Conditions in Ironfoundries, 210
Chatwin, C. P. : British Regional
Geology, East Anglia, 393
Checkweighing, S.R. & O.s and S.I.s
Revised, 836
Cheese. *See* Milk and Cheese.
Cheesemaking, Starters for, 178
Cheeseman, E. E. : Report on Cultiva-
tion of Cocoa, 344
Chelsea Royal Hospital Account, 138
Chemical :
Engineering, Technical Register, 211
Laboratories, Safety Measures in, 607
Methods for determination of
Uranium in minerals and ores, 830
Products Committee, Reports, 544, 759

Chemical *(continued)* :
Progress, Handbook, 225
Treatment for icy roads, 227
Warfare. *See* Civil Defence.
Chemistry :
Manual of, for Dispensers, 114
Pure, Historical Review, 192
Research Reports, 225, 391, 604, 828
Technical Register, 593
Chemotherapeutic and other studies of
Typhus, 224
Cherries. *See* Plums.
Cheshire :
and Chester Police Forces, proposed
compulsory amalgamation, 564
and Lancashire County Councils
(Runcorn–Widnes Bridge, etc.)
Act, 174
Mid and South East, Water Board
Act, 51
Representation of the People Bill,
proposed new constituencies :
Cmd. 7397, 310
Cmd. 7425, 312
Chester Station Railway Accident Re-
port, 634
Chewton Common Aircraft Accident
Report, 180
Chichester Provisional Order Confir-
mation Act, 513
Bill, 457
Chicago Air Transit Agreement, Ex-
change of Notes with France. *Cmd.
7194*, 164
Chick Embryo. *See* Cultivation.
Child :
and Youth Welfare, 643, 860
Care :
Scottish Advisory Council, Com-
mittee Reports, 832
Training. *Cmd. 6760*, 32
named Marika, 870
Nutrition, Expert advice on, 436
Welfare Films, International Index,
870
Childbirth, Analgesia, Bill, 474, 481, 483,
486
Child-minders. *See* Nurseries.
Children :
Acts :
1948, 328
Bill, 267, 269, 270, 271, 275,
291, 294, 300, 301
Summary. *Cmd. 7306*, 305
1949, 506
Bill, 463

   INDEX 1946-50   —CIN

Children *(continued)* :
Acts *(continued)* :
(Appeal Tribunal) Rules, 561
and the Cinema. *Cmd. 7945*, 706
and Young Persons :
Act, 723
Licence, 783
(Scotland), 723
Forms, 614
Records, 614
Boarding out, 69
S.R. & O.s and S.I.s Revised,
836
Care of, Committee Report. *Cmd.
6922*, 43
Education of Handicapped Children
and Young Persons in Independent
Schools and otherwise than at
School, 757, 758
Educationally sub-normal or mal-
adjusted, provision for boarding
school, 63, 64
employed as film actors, etc. *Cmd.
8005*, 711
of Europe, 870
To the Children from the United
Nations, 652
under 13 years of age, In the class-
room with, 655
War-handicapped, Report on Euro-
pean situation, 873
War's Victims, 653
with defective hearing, Inquiry, 756
See also Homeless Children.
Children's :
Communities, 870
Diets, Study of, 224
Emergency Fund, International Re-
port, 644
Gallery. *See* Science Museum.
Chile :
Agreements with U.K. :
Air Services. *Cmd. 7234*, 166
Commercial :
Cmd. 7013, 152
Cmd. 7178, 162
Military Service. *Cmd. 7580*, 323
Payments. *Cmd. 7497*, 317
Review of Commercial Conditions,
632
Chimneys, Smoky, 827
China :
Air Transport Agreement with U.K.
Cmd. 7211, 165
Burma–Yunnan boundary, Exchange
of Notes. *Cmd. 7246*, 167

China *(continued)* :
Prevention of Smuggling between
Hong Kong and Chinese Ports
and the Exchange of Notes with U.K.
Cmd. 7615, 490
Relinquishment of Extra-Territorial
Rights, Treaty with Canada. *Cmd.
6948*, 44
Seas and North Pacific Ocean,
Weather in, 815
Trade Mission Report, 416
Transfer of British Naval Vessels,
etc., Agreement with U.K. *Cmd.
7457*, 315
China-Clay :
Working Committee Report. *Cmd.
6748*, 32
Working Party Report, 416
Chinese Porcelain, Handbook to the
W. G. Gulland Bequest, 877
Chlorine. *See* Toxic Gases.
Choosing Council Tenants, Report, 778
Chopin, Frederic, 871
Chorley, Lord (Chairman) : Higher Civil
Service Remuneration, Report. *Cmd.
7635*, 491
Christmas Picture Book, 351
Chronological Table and Index of the
Statutes, 93, 232, 616
Chrysanthemum Eelworm, 516
Chrysanthemums, 517
Church :
Assembly Measures. *See* Public
General Acts.
Commissioners Measures, 12, 175
Report, 12
Dignitaries (Retirement) Measure,
450
Report, 450
of Scotland :
Act, 722
Lord High Commissioner, Bill,
299
S.R. & O.s and S.I.s Revised,
836
Trust (Amendment) Order Con-
firmation Act, 330
Bill, 274, 301
Temporalities in Wales, Accounts,
22, 143, 292
Work. Careers, 368
Cinema :
Children and the. *Cmd. 7945*, 706
Use of Mobile Cinema and Radio
Vans in Fundamental Education,
872

24   25

Cinematograph :
Act, 325, 507
and Cinematograph Films, S.R. & O.s and S.I.s Revised, 836
Film Production (Special Loans) :
Account, 695
Acts, 510, 719
Bills, 303, 446, 448, 484, 673, 698
Films :
Act, 328
Bill, 150, 268, 269, 299, 300
Council :
Recommendations, 245
Reports, 23, 686
Distribution and Exhibition, 842
Inquiry Report. Cmd. 7837, 505
Fund Accounts and Reports, 53, 146, 466, 690
Circulars and Administrative Memoranda, Ministry of Education, 541
Citizens growing up, 541
Citizenship in Africa, Education for, 344
City of London :
(Tithes) Act, 174
(Various Powers) Acts, 51, 513, 725
City of Madras Boiler Explosion Report, 633
Civic Restaurants :
Act, 172
Bill, 30, 123, 136, 147, 148
Standing Committee Debates, 280
List of, 545
Civil :
Aircraft :
Accident Reports, 337, 523, 744
Navigator's Licence, Examinations, 57, 181
Report. Cmd. 7705, 496
Appropriation Accounts, 14, 18, 134, 138, 281, 464, 678, 682
Aviation :
Acts :
1946, 49
Bill, 9, 10, 27, 28, 29
Standing Committee
Minutes, 21
Forms, 200
Statement of Guarantee, 298
1949, 511
Bill, 446, 455, 456, 486
Statements of Guarantee, 468, 472
1950, 724
Accident Investigation Procedure Report. Cmd. 7564, 322

Civil (continued) :
Aviation (continued) :
Communications Handbook, 57, 524
Conference, Bermuda. Cmd. 6747, 32
Convention on International Recognition of Rights in Aircraft. Cmd. 7510, 318
Estimates, 137
Examination Papers, 57, 218, 525
Ministry of, Publications (N.P.), 57, 180, 337, 523, 743
Order, 744
Radio :
Aids for Demonstrations, 57
Systems for, 57
Reports, 338, 744
Recruitment, Training, and Licensing, Committee on, Report. Cmd. 7746, 498
See also Merchant Airmen.
Awards. See London Gazette.
Contingencies Fund Accounts, 20, 140, 287, 469, 478, 693
Defence :
Act, 329
Bill, 279, 303
Evacuation Memoranda, 778, 780
Corps, Training Memoranda, 562, 783
Manual of Basic Training, 562, 683
(Suspension of Powers) Act, 48
Employment, Reinstatement in :
Bill, 699
Decisions by the Umpire, 81, 218, 382, 592, 810
Engineering :
Careers, 75
Codes of Practice Committee Report, 441
Technical Register, 811
See also Building and Civil Engineering.
Estimates, 14, 16, 17, 21, 22, 135, 136, 137, 138, 142, 143, 283, 284, 285, 291, 466, 467, 469, 474, 681, 684, 688
Judicial Statistics, Scotland. Cmd. 7821, 504
List, Select Committee Report, 146
Servants, Political Activities. Cmd. 7718, 496

Civil (continued) :
Service :
Arbitration Tribunal Awards, 76, 208, 369, 577, 793
Careers, 75, 368, 793
Commission :
Estimates, Select Committee Report, 293, 468
Publications (N.P.), 58, 182, 339, 526, 745
(Fees), S.R. & O.s and S.I.s Revised, 836
Commissioners Report, 748
List. See British Imperial Calendar.
Methods used in British Zone of Germany. Cmd. 7804, 502
National Whitley Council Report, 421
Staff Relations, 641
Working Conditions, 422
Services Reports :
British West Africa, 186
Kenya, Tanganyika, Uganda, and Zanzibar, 344
Northern Rhodesia and Nyasaland, 344
Civilian Staff Regulations, 114, 261, 437
Civilians employed at Air Ministry Establishments, Regs., 56, 179, 336, 519, 740
Clam Wreck Report, 854
Clapham, Sir John (Chairman), Committee on Social and Economic Research. Cmd. 6868, 39
Clark, N. O. : Study of Mechanically produced foam for combating petrol fires, 225
Clark, W. E. le Gros : History of Primates, 742
Clarke, Sir F. :
(Chairman) Central Advisory Council for Education, Out of School, 350
School and Life, 192
Clarke, S. H. : Gurjun, Apitong, Keruing, Kapur, and Allied Timbers, 605
Classification :
and Pay of Soldiers, 661
of Diseases and Injuries, 391
Clatworthy, Arthur Alfred, Inquiry into the case of. Report. Cmd. 6736, 31
Clay :
and floor tiles, lifting of, 827
Brickmaking in Great Britain, 883
Building Bricks, 394

Clay (continued) :
The getting of, 263
See also China Clay.
Cleary, Sir W. (Chairman) :
Committee on School Sites and Building Procedure, 63
Technical Working Party on School Construction, 351
Clergy Pensions :
Measure, 331
Report by Ecclesiastical Commissioners, 267
(Older Incumbents) Measure, 331
(Supplementary Pensions) Measure, 7, 52
Clergymen of the Church of England. See Election of a Member.
Clerk of the Crown in Chancery, S.R. & O.s and S.I.s Revised, 836
Click Mill, Dounby, Orkney, guide, 663
Close Rolls. See Public Record Office Publications.
Cloth :
and Clothing :
Board of Trade Publications (N.P.), 102
Education Circulars, 62, 63
and Household Textiles, Board of Trade Publications (N.P.), 242, 628, 843
Clothing :
Factory, Career, 793
Industry Development Council Order, 629
Mission to Canada Report, 624
Quiz, 102, 242
Working Party Reports, 246
Cloud :
Atlas for Aviators, 84, 814
Card for Observers, 814
Forms, 595
Amendment List, 814
Clow, Sir A. (Chairman), Electricity Peak Load Problem Committee Report. Cmd. 7464, 315
Clowes, G. S. Laird : Sailing Ships, their History and Development, 192, 351
Clute, S.R. & O.s and S.I.s Revised, 836
Clyde :
Estuary Committee Report, 106
Navigation :
Order Confirmation Act, 725
(Superannuation) Order Confirmation Act, 512
Bill, 484

Clyde (continued) :
Valley Regional Plan, 612
See also Forth and Clyde.
Clyde, J. L. (Chairman), Committee on Homeless Children (Scotland) Report. Cmd. 6911, 42
Clydebank Burgh Order Confirmation Act, 512
Bill, 449, 484
Coal, 355
Agreement with U.S.A. and France regulating export from Western Zones of Germany. Cmd. 7165, 162
Ash and Coke Ash, Improved methods for the quantitative analysis of, 829
Commission :
Accounts, 19, 139, 289
Report, 22
Committee Report, 544
Dust :
Explosions, Prevention of, 198
Precautions against (Mines and Quarries Form), 66
FaceWorkers, Apprenticeship for, 196
Handling and Storage of, 773
Industry :
Act, 511
Bill, 299, 303, 451, 452, 453, 457, 458, 467, 482, 484, 486, 487
(No. 2) Act, 512
Bill, 460, 487
Bill (1950), 681
Nationalisation Act, 49
Bill, 7, 8, 9, 19, 27, 28, 29
Accounts, 286, 471, 679
S.R. & O.s and S.I.s Revised, 836
to Copyright, S.R. & O.s and S.I.s Revised, 836
Miner, The future of the, 66
Mines :
Act (1950), 721
Acts, Regulations and Orders, 196
(Protection of Animals) Bill, 483
Mining :
Industry, Statistical Statements :
Cmd. 6777, 33
Cmd. 6814, 36
Cmd. 6830, 37
Cmd. 6851, 39
Cmd. 6914, 42
Cmd. 6969, 45
Cmd. 7045, 154
Cmd. 7219, 165
Cmd. 7220, 165

Coal (continued) :
Mining (continued) :
(Subsidence) Act, 719
Bill, 671, 672, 673, 697, 698
Organisation. See European Coal Organisation.
Production and Marketing of Opencast Coal, Select Committee on Estimates, 471, 475
Reserves and Production, First Appraisal of Results, 87
Tar. See German Coal Tar.
Coal, Iron and Steel Industries of Western Europe, Schuman Plan. Cmd. 7970, 708
Coalfields :
Regional Survey Reports, 66
See also Ruhr Coalfields.
Coast Protection Acts :
1949, 511
Bill, 278, 445, 447, 448, 459, 475, 482, 484, 486
1950, 724
Bill, 681
Coastal :
Craft. See British Fishing Boats.
Forces Actions, 386
Coastguard, S.R. & O.s and S.I.s Revised, 836
Coatbridge Burgh Extension, etc., Order Confirmation Act, 330
Bill, 133, 150
Coccidiosis in Poultry, 334
Cockfighting Bill, 455, 486
Cocoa :
Commodity Report, 873
Cultivation of, Report, 344
Future Marketing of West African. Cmd. 6950, 44
Research Conference Report, 60
Cod. See Salted Cod.
Codes :
Binder, 573
of Practice :
Committee Report, 441
Guides to good building, 441
Codnor Park and Langley Mill Railway Accident Report, 634
Coed-y-Brenin, Britain's Forests, 769
Coffee Boiler Explosion Report, 417
Cohen, Sir H. (Chairman) :
Joint Committee on Prescribing, Report, 779

Cohen, Sir H. (Chairman) (continued) :
Joint Sub-Committee of the Standing Medical Pharmaceutical and General Practitioner Advisory Committees, Report on Definition of Drugs, 779
Cohen, J. : Recruitment and Training of Nurses, Working Party Report, 360
Cohen, Sir L. L. (Chairman), Royal Commission on Awards to Inventors, Reports :
Cmd. 7586, 323
Cmd. 7832, 504
Coin, S.R. & O.s and S.I.s Revised, 836
British Possessions and Protectorates, 836
Coinage :
Act, 59
Bill, 11, 29
Offences Act, 508
Coity Castle, guide, 117
Coking Practice, Experiments, 87
Colds or Contagious Catarrh in Poultry, 178, 334
Cole, H. A. : Setting behaviour of larvae of the European flat oyster, 518
Collective Self-defence, Treaty of Economic, Social, and Cultural Collaboration. Cmd. 7367, 308
Colleges. See Training Colleges.
Colliery :
Accident Funds (Great Britain) Return. Cmd. 8101, 718
Explosion Report. Cmd. 7410, 311
Management, Careers, 75
Ropes in Service, Examination of, 196
Collins, A. R. : Grading of Aggregates and Workability of Concrete, 227
Collins, Commodore J. A. : Battle of Java Sea, 385
Colne Valley Water Act, 50
Colombia :
Air Services, Agreement. Cmd. 7272, 169
Commercial Conditions, 410
Overseas Economic Survey, 845
Colombian-Peruvian Asylum Case, Report of Judgments, Advisory Opinions and Orders, 575, 792
Colombo Plan for the Co-operative Economic Development of South and South-East Asia, Report. Cmd. 8080, 716
Colonial :
and other Territories (Divorce Jurisdiction) Act, 719
Bill, 669, 697

Colonial (continued) :
Annual Reports, 343
Court- of Admiralty and Vice-Admiralty Court, S.R. & O.s and S.I.s Revised, 836
Development :
and Welfare :
Acts :
1949, 511
Bill, 457, 485
1950, 720
Bill, 675, 699
Returns of Schemes, 21, 142, 291, 475, 689
S.R. & O.s and S.I.s Revised, 836
Corporation, Reports and Accounts, 474, 689
Estimate, 292
Economic Development :
Film Strip, 534
Picture Set, 533
Empire :
Picture Sets, 364, 532, 750
Production of fish in, 535
Reports :
1939–47. Cmd. 7167, 162
1947–8. Cmd. 7433, 313
Forces and Military Missions, Officers and Other Ranks serving with, Special Army Order, 662
Geology and Mineral Resources, 750
Loans Act, 511
Bill, 303, 457, 486
Mining Policy, Memorandum, 60
Naval Defence Act, 510
Bill, 279, 446, 484
Office :
Lists, 186, 344, 533, 750
Map Supplement, 344
Publications (N.P.), 60, 185, 343, 531, 748
Plant and Animal Products, 750
Primary Products Committee Reports, 344, 533
Prisoner, S.R. & O.s and S.I.s Revised, 836
Quiz, 752
Regulations, 60
Reports, 343, 531, 749
Research :
in Agriculture, Animal Health, and Forestry, Recommendations for Organisation of, Report, 344
Publications, 345, 533, 750

Colonial (continued) :
Research (continued) :
Reports :
1945-6, 186
1946-7. Cmd. 7151, 161
1947-8. Cmd. 7433, 313
Cmd. 7739, 498
Cmd. 8063, 715
Studies, 752
Road Problems, Nigeria, 750
Service :
Appointments in, 749
as a Career, 750
Organisation, 60
Post-war Training Report, 60
Stock :
Act, 329
Bill, 278, 302
S.R. & O.s and S.I.s Revised, 836
Territories Reports :
1948-9. Cmd. 7715, 496
1949-50. Cmd. 7958, 707
Colonies :
Agricultural Extension, 531
fight Leprosy, Film Strip, 534
Higher Education in. Cmd. 7331, 305
in Pictures, 533
Introducing the, 534
Colour reproductions of paintings, Catalogues of :
Prior to 1860, 870
1860 to 1949, 653
Colourwashes on External Walls, 827
Combined :
Intelligence Objectives Sub-Committee, Reports on German Industry, 103
Power and Heating, 773
Combustible Material in Ashes, 772
Combustion, Control of Air for, 773
Command Papers, 30, 151, 304, 488, 700
Commerce :
Award of National Certificates in, 350
See also Industry.
Commercial :
Agreements. See Names of countries.
Air Service Agreement with Luxembourg. Cmd. 7445, 314
Anemone growing, 737
Art, Career, 75
Conditions, Reviews of, 102, 846
Flower Production, 54
Horticulture, 55
Advice to Beginners, 178, 516
Mahoganies and Allied Timbers, 392

Commercial (continued) :
Pilot's Licence (Flying Machines), 575, 744
Relations and Export Department Publications, 632
Transactions, U.K. and Brazil. Cmd. 8068, 715
Varieties of Apples and Pears, 516
Violet growing, 737
Commissioners of Prisons and Directors of Convict Prisons, Reports :
Cmd. 7010, 152
Cmd. 7146, 160
Cmd. 7271, 169
Cmd. 7475, 316
Cmd. 7777, 500
Commissions :
Army, 263
Short Service :
Royal Army Medical Corps, 116
Royal Army Veterinary Corps, 661
Committee of Privileges Report, 14
Commodity :
Reports, 873
Series Bulletins, 656, 873
Common :
England, S.R. & O.s and S.I.s Revised, 836
Insect Pests of Stored Food Products, 742
Prayer Book, Catalogue of Exhibition, 520
Services. See Estimates.
Worms of the Pig, 738
Commonwealth :
Agricultural Bureaux Publications (N.P.), 345, 535, 752
Economic Committee Publications (N.P.), 345, 535, 752
of Nations :
Handbook, 535
Material available to Schools and Public, 753
Wall Map, Principle Products, 708
Posters, 364
Relations Office Publications (N.P.), 186, 346, 536, 753
Shipping Committee Publications (N.P.), 346
Telegraphs :
Bill, 452, 483
Agreement. Cmd. 7582, 488
Trade, 535, 752

Communal Laundry Facilities, Inquiry, 883
Communication and Radio Aids, 573
Community Centres :
Village Halls, and Playing Fields, Planning for, 230
See also Youth Leader.
Compaction of Soil, Performance of Plant, 830
Companies :
Act :
1947, 173
Bill, 13, 121, 122, 123, 124, 131, 148
Standing Committee Minutes, 143
1948, 328
Articles of Association, 410
Bill, 269, 270, 273, 280, 301
Table of Comparison, 410
Report of Inspection of A. Reyrolle & Co. Ltd., 629
Annual Reports, 410, 624, 842
General Report for 1939-45, 242
S.R. & O.s and S.I.s Revised, 836
Compensation :
and Superannuation of Staffs of Approved Societies, 388
for British Property affected by Czechoslovak Measures of Nationalisation, etc. Cmd. 7797, 502
by Yugoslav Measures of Nationalisation, etc. Cmd. 7600, 488
for Disablement or Death due to War Injury suffered by Civilians, Agreement between U.K. and France. Cmd. 8000, 710
for premature termination of Services :
Burma. Cmd. 7189, 163
India. Cmd. 7116, 158
Motor Insurers' Bureau, 107
of Victims of Uninsured Drivers, 247
S.R. & O.s and S.I.s Revised (Defence), 836
See also War Damage ; Workmen's Compensation.
Competency Certificates, Examinations, 66, 196
Compressed Air, Industrial Use of, 773
Conciliation Act, 506
Concrete :
Design of Mixers, 394, 830
Effect of Batching Errors on Uniformity, 394

Concrete (continued) :
Kerbs. See Kerbs.
Plant for Prestressing, 883
Practical Work, 439
Workability of, 227
See also Soils, Concrete, and Bituminous Materials.
Concretes, Analysis of, 829
Concreting :
and bricklaying in cold weather, 394
in cold weather, 882
Condensation :
in domestic chimneys, 827
problems in building, 827
Trails :
from Aircraft, 84
Notes for use of pilots, 84
Confederation of Shipbuilding and Engineering Unions, Claim for a 40-hour week. Cmd. 7036, 153
Conference :
and General Services, Department of (United Nations), Glossary of Technical Terms, 423
Manual, UNESCO, 870
Conifer Heart Rot, 354
Coniferous Woodland, Replanting of, 770
Conifers, Phomopsis Diseases of, 553
Conington North Railway Accident Report, 634
Conscientious Objectors. See National Service.
Conservation :
and Utilisation of Resources, Scientific Conference on, 867
of Nature :
in England and Wales :
Circular, 840
Report. Cmd. 7122, 159
in Scotland. See National Parks.
Consol. Radio Aid to Navigation, 338, 744
Consolidated :
Bills, First Report, 7
Fund :
Abstract Accounts, 16, 136, 281, 464, 677
Acts :
1946, 49
Bill, 27
1947, 172
Bill, 148
1948 No. 1, 328
Bill, 300
1949 No. 1, 510
Bill, 484

30   31

Consolidated (continued) :
Fund (continued) :
Acts (continued) :
1950, 719
Bill, 697
(Appropriation) Bills, 29, 150, 302, 487, 699
Consolidation :
Bills, 127, 446, 447, 456, 670, 674
of Enactments, 812
(Procedure) Act, 510
Bill, 451, 485
Excise Duties in Mechanically Propelled Vehicles, 455
Marriage, 454
Memoranda, 671, 690, 787
Solemnisation and Registration of Marriages in England, 594
Constable, Small Picture Book, 877
Constables. See Special Constables.
Constabulary, Inspectors' Reports :
England and Wales, 22, 143, 289, 688, 784
Scotland :
Cmd. 6936, 43
Cmd. 7247, 167
Cmd. 7529, 320
Cmd. 7741, 472
Cmd. 7965, 708
Constants, Formulae, and Methods used for computing in the Transverse Mercator Projection, 820
Constitution of UNESCO, 653
Construction :
and Heating of Commercial Glasshouses, 517
of a Factory Heat Balance, 773
of London Airport and Civil Service Commission, Select Committee on Estimates Report, 468
Constructional Work, Codes of Practice Committee Report, 441
Consul, British, S.R. & O.s and S.I.s Revised, 836
Consular :
Convention with U.S.A. Cmd. 7642, 491
Conventions Act, 510
Bill, 450, 484
Consultant Services, Development of, 781
Consultants. See Remuneration of Consultants.

Consumer Rationing (Consolidation) Order, Registers, etc., 101, 242, 410, 623
Contact Men. See Intermediaries.
Containers and Straps Order, Registers, 102
Contingent Allowance, 660
Contracts for Building and Civil Engineering Works, 441
Contributions to Local Revenues. See Civil Estimates.
Contributory Pensions, Increase of :
Regs., 221
Selected Decisions by Umpire, 388
Control :
Board of, Publications (N.P.), 187, 777
Scotland, 610, 753
Commission for Germany Publications (N.P.), 61, 187, 346, 537, 753
Machinery and Zones of Occupation in Austria, Agreement. Cmd. 6958, 45
of Air for Combustion, 773
of Atomic Energy, 110
of Excess Air on Steam Raising and Central Heating Plants, 772
of Midges, 397
of Sicilian Straits during final stages of the North African Campaign, 386
Controlled :
Grazing with Electric Fencing, 737
Prices, Retail, 194
Convention on Genocide, 653
Conventions, Agreements, etc., Relating to Transport and Communications questions, 424
Conversion :
of Existing Houses, Report, 67
Tables, 754
Conveyance of Explosives on Roads, 361
Conveyancing :
and Law of Property, Scotland, S.R. & O.s and S.I.s Revised, 836
Amendment (Scotland) Act, 509
Convict Prisons. See Commissioners of Convict Prisons.
Convoys to North Russia, Despatches, 812
Cook, E. R. (Chairman), United Kingdom Clothing Mission to Canada, Report, 624
Cook, Sir F. (Chairman) :
Design and Layout of Roads in Built-up Areas, Report, 109
Traffic Signs, Report, 109, 420

Cookery :
Fish, 353
See also ABC of Cookery.
Cooking Appliances Schedule, 664
Cool Storage of Fruit and Vegetables, 392
Cooling :
Firebars in Industrial Furnaces and Boilers, 773
of Air by Rain as a factor in Convection, 596
Coombe, G. A. (Chairman), Surveyor's Panel, Valuation and Estate Management, of the Building and Civil Engineers' Committee, Technical Register, 811
Cooper, Lord (Chairman) :
Clyde Estuary Committee, Report, 106
Special Committee regarding increased grant for Universities of Scotland, Report. Cmd. 6853, 38
Co-operative :
Movement in the Colonies, 60
Societies, Statistical Summary, 354, 554, 771
Copper :
and Galvanised Steel in the same hot water system, Use of, 827
Goods, Open General Export Licence, 845
Coppock, R. (Chairman), Central Housing Advisory Committee, Care and Maintenance of Fittings and Equipment in the Modern House, 780
Copyright :
Act, 507
Bulletins, 654, 871
International Convention for the protection of literary and artistic works. Cmd. 7816, 503
Laws, Exchange of Notes with U.S.A. Cmd. 6991, 46
Corbet, A. S. : Common Insect Pests of Stored Food Products, 742
Corfe, Geology of the country around, 226
Corfu Channel Case, Reports of Judgments, Advisory Opinion, and Orders, 367, 575, 792
Cork and Orrery, Earl of. Norway Campaign Despatch, 219
Corn Sales Act, 170
Cornish Pilchard Fishery in 1947-8, Experiments on, 739
Cornwall, Saxton's Map, 741, 750

Corona, 533, 750
Coroner, England :
S.R. & O.s and S.I.s Revised, 836
to District Auditor, England, S.R. & O.s and S.I.s Revised, 836
Coroners Act, 606
Corps :
Definition of, 114, 261
Warrant Amendment, 261
Corsets, Board of Trade Publications (N.P.), 101, 104
Coryza, "Cold", and Sinusitis in Poultry, 517
Cost :
Accountancy. See Accountancy.
of Home Information Services, Committee Report. Cmd. 7836, 505
of House Building, Reports, 358, 780
of Living Advisory Committee Report. Cmd. 7077, 156
Costing Statistics, England and Wales, 757
Costs :
and Prices, Statement. Cmd. 7321, 306
in Criminal Cases Act, 170
Costume, Nineteenth Century, 260
Cotton :
(Centralised Buying) Act, 172
Bill, 30, 123, 147
Accounts, 469, 677
Standing Committee Minutes, 138
Centralised Buying Bill, 280
Industry :
Development Council Order, Proposals for, 415
Interim Report, 76
Joint Advisory Committee Reports, 208
S.R. & O.s and S.I.s Revised, 836
War Memorial Trust Act, 173
Manufacturing Commission Reports, 369, 578
(Raw Material) Schedule, 415
Spinning :
Industry, Report, 76
(Re-equipment Subsidy) Act, 328
Bill, 272, 287, 294, 300, 463
Textiles Machinery Industry Report, 238
Weaving Factories, Agreement concerning fencing of machinery, etc., 578
Working Party Report, 106
See also Utility Apparel Cloth.
Cotton, Rayon, and Linen Schedules, 631, 847

32   33

COT—   INDEX 1946–50

Cotton, Rayon, and Silk Industries in Germany, Developments, 623
Council :
of Europe :
Consultative Assembly : papers, 754
Establishment of a Preparatory Commission. *Cmd. 7687*, 494
Explanatory Note. *Cmd. 7686*, 494
General Agreement on Privileges and Immunities. *Cmd. 7780*, 500
Reports :
Cmd. 7807, 503
Cmd. 7838, 505
Cmd. 7954, 707
Cmd. 8082, 716
Cmd. 8083, 717
Statute. *Cmd. 7720*, 497
Tenants, Choosing, 778
Councillors. *See* Elections ; Parish Councillors.
County :
Council, S.R. & O.s and S.I.s Revised, 836
Councils Association :
Expenses (Amendment) Act, 172
Bill, 123, 147
(Scotland) Act, 50
Bill, 11, 29
Court :
England, S.R. & O.s and S.I.s Revised, 836
Manual, 83
Procedure, Committee Reports :
Cmd. 7468, 315
Cmd. 7668, 493
Courts Accounts, 15, 137, 283, 464, 679
Police Forces, Amalgamation, Inquiry Report, 362
Courier, UNESCO, 433
Court :
of Appeal. *See* High Court.
of Session, Edinburgh, Publications, 90
Courtney, Sir C. L. (Chairman) :
Tudor Aircraft Committee of Inquiry Reports :
Cmd. 7307, 305
Cmd. 7478, 316
Courts (Emergency Powers), S.R. & O.s and S.I.s Revised, 836
Courts-Martial :
(Appeals) Bill, 700

Courts Martial (*continued*) :
Army and Air Force, Report. *Cmd. 7608*, 489
Rules of Procedure, 263, 437
Coussey, His Honour Mr. Justice J. H. (Chairman) : Committee on Constitutional Reform, Gold Coast. Report, 534
Coventry Corporation Act, 331
Cowden and Hever Railway Accident Report, 634
Cowes Aerodrome Civil Aircraft Accident Report, 744
Cow-houses in Modern Practice, 739
Cowley, C. M. : Extraction of Ester Waxes from British Lignite and Peat, 87
Cowmanship, Essentials of good, 737
Cracking in Masonry Construction of Concrete or Sand-lime Bricks, Avoidance of, 827
Cracoe, Hebden, and District Electricity Special Order, 355
Crare Pier and Harbour Order Confirmation Act, 513
Bill, 456
Cranes, Steam. *See* Boilers.
Crawley Development Corporation Reports, 469, 694
Credit, Vote of. *See* Appropriation Accounts.
Cremation :
Committee Report. *Cmd. 8009*, 711
S.R. & O.s and S.I.s Revised, 836
Crematorium. *See* Middlesex Crematorium.
Creosote-Pitch Mixture, 773
Crete, Battle of, 385
Crew, Professor F. A. E. (Chairman) : Scientific Advisory Committee, Report on Control of Midges, 90
Crew Spaces. *See* Master's and Crew Spaces.
Crewe Corporation Act, 513
Crick, W. F. (Chairman) : Committee on the form of Government Accounts. Final Report. *Cmd. 7969*, 708
Cricket Bat Willow, Cultivation of, 65
Crime :
Action taken by Local Authorities, 674
Large number accompanied by violence, 671
See also Prevention of Crime.
Crimea Conference, Protocol of the Proceedings at Yalta. *Cmd. 7088*, 156

Criminal :
Appeal Act, 506
Evidence Act, 325
Jurisdiction, International Historical Survey, 648
Justice :
Acts :
1948, 329
Bill, 150, 271, 272, 274, 275, 276, 277, 278, 286, 295, 300, 302
1950, 722
(Scotland) Act, 719
Bill, 278, 445, 479, 482, 484, 487
Explanatory Memorandum, 832
Recommitted Bill, 479, 482, 681
Law Amendment Bill, 700
Procedure, S.R. & O.s & S.I.s Revised, 836
Statistics :
Cmd. 7227, 166
Cmd. 7428, 312
Cmd. 7528, 320
Cmd. 7733, 497
Cmd. 7993, 710
Scotland :
Cmd. 7505, 318
Cmd. 7554, 321
Cmd. 7595, 488
Cmd. 7708, 496
Cmd. 7980, 709
Criminals. *See* War Criminals.
Cromer Urban District Council Act, 330
Croney, D. : Damage to Roads caused by Drought of 1947, 607
Crookall, R. : British Regional Geology, 393
Crop :
Plants, Diseases of, 335
Production in Frames and Cloches, 177, 334
Crops, Fertiliser Placement of Arable, 610
Crown :
Jewels, 664
Lands :
Accounts, Commissioners', 16, 136, 283, 464, 679
Act, 327
S.R. & O.s and S.I.s Revised, 836
Proceedings :
Acts :
1947, 172
Bill, 122, 123, 124, 130, 148
1950, 724

Crown (*continued*) :
Proceedings (*continued*) :
List of Authorised Government Departments, 249
S.R. & O.s and S.I.s Revised, 836
Remedy against the Crown as Occupier Bill, 122
Crown's Nominee Accounts, 109, 249, 421, 638, 855
Croxden Abbey, Guide, 117
Croydon :
Aircraft Accident Reports, 180, 181, 523
Borough of (Rating) Act, 174
Cruelty to Animals Act :
Application for Licence, Experiments on living animals, 361
Certificates, 361, 562
Cuba :
Air Services Agreement. *Cmd. 7393*, 310
Overseas Economic Survey, 845
Reciprocal Notification of the Imprisonment or Death in Prison of British and Cuban Nationals, Exchange of Notes. *Cmd. 7143*, 160
Cuckoo, 333
Cucumber :
Marketing Scheme. *See* Tomato.
Mosaic, 516
Culbin, Britain's Forests, 553
Culinary Herbs and their Cultivation, 335
Cultivation :
of Cocoa, Report, 344
of Viruses and Rickettsiae in the Chick Embryo, 86
Cultural Conventions with :
Brazil :
Cmd. 7134, 159
Cmd. 7606, 489
Cmd. 8032, 713
Czechoslovakia :
Cmd. 7155, 161
Cmd. 7263, 168
France :
Cmd. 7386, 310
Cmd. 7450, 314
Luxembourg. *Cmd. 8013*, 711
Netherlands :
Cmd. 7509, 318
Cmd. 7984, 709
Norway :
Cmd. 7338, 306
Cmd. 7748, 498
Cumberland County Council Act, 331

34

INDEX 1946–50   —CUM

35

CUN—   INDEX 1946–50

Cunard Insurance Fund Accounts, 20, 134, 281, 469, 677
Cunningham, Sir A. B. :
Action against an Italian convoy, 385
Action with Italian Fleet off Calabria, 384
Battle of Crete, 385
Coastal Forces Actions, 386
Control of Sicilian Straits, 386
Invasion of Sicily, 812
Fleet Air Arm operations against Taranto, 220
Matapan, Battle of, 220
Mediterranean Convoy Operations, 385
North African Landings, 594
Operations in connection with landings in the Gulf of Salerno, 812
Transportation of Army to Greece and Evacuation from Greece, 385
Currant and Gooseberry Aphides, 178
Currants, Black and Red, 736
Currency :
and Bank Notes Act, Treasury Minutes, 21, 26, 142, 146, 281, 283, 285, 295, 464, 475, 477, 481, 682, 688, 696, 855
(Defence), S.R. & O.s and S.I.s Revised, 836
Rehabilitation in the Netherlands, 389
Curtain Net, Board of Trade Publications (N.P.), 103
Curteis, Sir A. T. B. : Mediterranean Convoy Operations, 385
Curtis, Miss Myra (Chairman) : Care of Children Committee, Reports :
Cmd. 6760, 32
Cmd. 6922, 42
Customs :
and Excise :
Commissioners' Reports :
Cmd. 6951, 101
Cmd. 7252, 167
Cmd. 7547, 321
Cmd. 7834, 505
Publications (N.P.) and Customs Forms, 61, 137, 346, 537, 754
S.R. & O.s and S.I.s Revised, 836
Tariff in the United Kingdom, 347
Tariffs :
of the Colonial Empire, 60, 533
Protocol. *Cmd. 8050*, 714
Unions, 4, 24
See also Isle of Man.
Cuthbertson, D. P. : Report on Nutrition in Newfoundland, 186

Cutlery :
Wages Council Report, 76
Working Party Report, 246
Cutter, Wholesale Clothing Manufacture, Career, 793
Cwm Mountains, Civil Aircraft Accident Report, 338
Cyanide Compounds, Precautions in the use of, 76
Cyprus :
Colonial Reports, 343, 531, 532, 749
Constitution, Despatch, 344
Goodwill Trade Commission, Report, 245
S.R. & O.s and S.I.s Revised, 837
Czechoslovak Claims Fund and Refugee Fund Accounts, 18, 289, 471, 679, 690
Czechoslovakia :
Compensation for British Property affected by Nationalisation. *Cmd. 7797*, 502
Cultural Convention :
Cmd. 7155, 161
Cmd. 7263, 168
Monetary Agreement. *Cmd. 7174*, 162
Exchanges of Notes prolonging :
Cmd. 7585, 323
Cmd. 7625, 490
Cmd. 7667, 493
Cmd. 7719, 496
Cmd. 7772, 500
Mutual Upkeep of War Graves. *Cmd. 7691*, 495
Plan for Allocation of a Reparation Share to Non-repatriable Victims of German Action. *Cmd. 7255*, 168
Purchase of Surplus Stores. *Cmd. 7085*, 156
Settlement of certain Intergovernmental Debts. *Cmd. 7798*, 502
S.R. & O.s and S.I.s Revised, 837
Sterling Payments Agreement. *Cmd. 7781*, 501
Supply of Aircraft and Equipment, Agreement. *Cmd. 7187*, 163
Trade and Financial Agreement. *Cmd. 7799*, 502

D

Dairies, Farm, 739
Dairy :
Produce, Production Trade and Consumption, 345, 752
Products, Commodity Series, 434, 656

Dakar-Yoff, French West Africa, Aircraft Accident Report, 338
Dale, Judge E. T. (Chairman) : Departmental Committee on Industrial Diseases, Report. *Cmd. 7557*, 321
Dalley, F. W. : Trade Union Organisations and Industrial Relations in Trinidad, Report, 186
Damage :
to Roads caused by the Drought of 1947, 607
See also War Damage.
Damp-proof courses in parapet walls, 827
Damsons, 55
See also Plums.
Dancing, Career, 75
Dangerous Drugs :
Acts, 178, 327, 722, 723
(Amendment) Act, 720
Bill, 676, 699
Doctors and Dentists, Memorandum as to Duties, 361
Estimated World Requirements, 251
S.R. & O.s and S.I.s Revised, 837
United Nations Conference, 251
Daniel Kamau becomes a Bus Conductor, film strip, 534
Darkness into Daylight, 351
Darlington Corporation Trolley Vehicles (Additional Routes) Order Confirmation Acts :
1948, 330
Bill, 275, 301
1950, 725
Bill, 698
Dartford Tunnel (Extension of Time) Act, 514
Dartmouth Castle guide, 440
Darwen Corporation Act, 331
Darwin, Sir C. (Chairman) : Advisory Committee on Artificial Limbs, Reports, 222, 389, 820
Data on Urban and Rural Population in recent Censuses, 867
Davey, N. : Bonding New Concrete to Old, 604
Davidson, Viscount (Chairman) :
Departmental Committee on Ordnance Survey, Report, 55
Goodwill Trade Mission to Iraq, Report, 245
Davies, C. (Chairman) : London Regional Planning :
Administration Committee, Report, 622
Advisory Committee, Report, 101

Davies, W. Tudor : Report on Nigeria, 61
Davis, A. G. : Geology Bulletin, 521
Davis Strait, monthly meteorological charts, 814
Davy, M. J. B. :
Aeronautics, History and Development :
Heavier-than-air Aircraft, 542, 826
Lighter-than-air Aircraft, 826
Interpretive History of Flight, 542
Daylight Factors, Protractors for the computation of, 86
Dazzle on roads, Measures for the prevention of, 607
DDT, Some properties and applications of, 97
Dean, Forest of, Guide, 195
Death :
Benefits. *See* National Insurance (Industrial Injuries).
Causes of. *See* International Statistical Classification.
Duties, S.R. & O.s and S.I.s Revised, 837
Deaths :
by accident at Mines and Quarries, Number of, 66, 196, 355, 554, 771
Registration. *See* General Register Office Publications (N.P.).
Debates. *See* House of Commons ; House of Lords ; Publications and Debates.
Debenham, F. : Water Resources of Bechuanaland Protectorate, Northern Rhodesia, Nyasaland Protectorate, Tanganyika Territory, Uganda, and Kenya ; Report, 833
Debt. *See* National Debt.
Debts :
Clearing Offices :
Accounts, 15, 136, 280, 468, 679
Act, 329
Bill, 278, 303
Regimental, Regs., 263
Decennial Supplement, Registrar-General's, 224
Decorations :
and Medals, Chart depicting, 437
See also Insignia ; Orders.
Dedication of Woodlands, 354, 769
Deeds of Arrangement, England. S.R. & O.s and S.I.s Revised, 837

36

INDEX 1946–50   —DEE

37

Defamation, Law of, Report. *Cmd. 7536*, 320

Defective hearing, Children with, Inquiry Committee Report, 756

Defence :
Appropriation Account, 678
Assistance, Mutual, Agreement with U.S.A. *Cmd. 7894*, 703
Central Organisation for. *Cmd. 6923*, 43
Collective, under the Brussels and North Atlantic Treaties. *Cmd. 7883*, 702
Estimates, 284, 285, 466, 475, 681, 682, 689
  Select Committee Reports, 486, 676, 677
Ministry of, Act, 171
  Bill, 12, 29
  Regulations, 109, 421
Services :
  Select Committee Reports, 676, 677
  Storage and Maintenance, Report, 689
Statement relating to :
  Cmd. 6743, 31
  Cmd. 7042, 154
  Cmd. 7327, 306
  Cmd. 7631, 491
  Cmd. 7895, 703
See also Civil Defence.

Definitions of items and units in Statistical Digest, 422

Degaussing. *See* Naval Mining and Degaussing.

Delegations to the United Nations, 112, 251, 423, 643

Demographic Yearbook, 643

Demolitions, Pocket Books, Royal Engineers, 439

Denmark :
British Forces in, Settlement of Claims, Agreement. *Cmd. 7460*, 915
Closer Economic Co-operation. *Cmd. 7884* 702
Convention for Avoidance of Double Taxation and Prevention of Fiscal Evasion, with respect to Taxes on Income :
  Cmd. 7926, 705
  Cmd. 8023, 712
Extension of Anglo-Danish Monetary Agreement to Faroe Islands. Exchange of Notes. *Cmd. 7592*, 324

Denmark *(continued)* :
Further provision for supply of certain Aircraft and Equipment, Agreement. *Cmd. 7660*, 493
Green Crop Drying, Report, 334
Industrial Property Agreement. *Cmd. 7208*, 164
Monetary Agreements :
  1945, Exchange of Notes prolonging validity of. *Cmd. 8055, 714*
  1950. *Cmd. 8104*, 718
Overseas Economic Survey, 632
Participation in the Occupation of Germany, Agreement. *Cmd. 7164*, 162
Supply of Aircraft and Equipment, Agreement. *Cmd. 7141*, 160
Trade and Commerce Agreements :
  Cmd. 7786, 501
  Cmd. 7986, 709
Visas, Reciprocal Abolition of :
  Exchange of Notes. *Cmd. 7101*, 157
  Extension. *Cmd. 7577*, 323
  Singapore and Malaya, Deletion from List of Territories covered. *Cmd. 8036*, 713

Denning, Mr. Justice (Chairman) :
Matrimonial Causes Committee, Reports :
  Cmd. 6881, 40
  Cmd. 6945, 44
  Cmd. 7024, 152

Dental :
Goods. *See* Monopolies and Restrictive Practices.
Nurses. *See* New Zealand.
Practitioners :
  Chairside Times, Working Party Report, 559
  Remuneration of, Committee Report. *Cmd. 7402*, 311

Dentist. S.R. & O.s and S.I.s Revised, 837

Dentistry
Careers, 208
Interdepartmental Committee Final Report. *Cmd. 6727*, 31

Dentists Act, 507

Dependants' Allowances, Army, 114

Depositions, Report of Departmental Committee. *Cmd. 7639*, 491

Derailments :
Bill : Select Committee, House of Lords, Report, 671

Derby Corporation *(continued)* :
(Trolley Vehicles) Order Confirmation Act, 51
  Bill, 9, 28

Derbyshire and Nottinghamshire Electric Power Special Order, 66

Dermatitis among French polishers, 76

Derrick Cranes, Use of, 593

Derricks, Erection of, Railway Bridging, 439

Design : 568, 788
  at Work, 568
  of Buildings for grass drying plants, 739
  of Forms, 639
  Quiz, wall cards, 363
  Requirements for Aeroplanes, 619, 837

Design '46, 71

Designs :
S.R. & O.s and S.I.s Revised, 837
See also Patents and Designs.

Destruction :
of Enemy Raider by H.M.S. *Devonshire*, 385
of Yellow Charlock, 55, 737

Destructive Insect and Pest, S.R. & O.s and S.I.s Revised, 837

Detention in Approved Schools, Period of, 399

Deterioration of Cast Iron and Spun Iron Pipes, 780

Devastated :
Areas, Reconstruction in, Report, 427
Countries, Financial Needs of, 251

Development :
and Road Improvement Funds Act, 507
and Welfare in the West Indies, 186, 750
Areas :
  Administration of, Select Committee on Estimates Report, 140
  Industrial Opportunities, 104
Charges in respect of Minerals, 743
Fund :
  Accounts, 57, 135, 283, 464, 677
  S.R. & O.s and S.I.s Revised, 837
  of Inventions Act, 329
  Bill, 271, 277, 291, 294, 301, 302
  Standing Committee Debates, 463
  Account, 695

Deviation Curve, 57

Devon :
Saxton's Map, 741
See also North Devon.

Devonshire, Duke of (Chairman) : Cocoa Research Committee Report, 60

Dewey, H.: British Regional Geology, 393

Diakanoff, A. : Type specimens of certain oriental Eucosmidae and Carposinidae (Microlepidoptera), 741

Diamond Tools :
Fine boring with, 97
Manufacture and Use in Germany, 410

Dickinson, H. W. : Garret Workshop of James Watt, 542

Diego Suaroz, Capture of, 384

Dieppe Raid, 220

Dietary Surveys, Technique and Interpretation, 874

Dietetics, Careers, 75

Diets for Individual Children, 224

Differences in dispensing practice between England and Wales and Scotland, Report, 359

Digest of Statistics. *See* Statistics.

Dimensional Analysis of Engineering Designs, 406

Dines, H. G. : Geology of the country around Witney, 226

Diocesan Education :
Committee Measure, 727
Committees Measure, 1943 (Amendment) Measure, 676
Ecclesiastical Committee Report, 676

Diphtheria :
Immunisation Records Cards, 397
in two areas of Great Britain, Study of, 813
Report, 397

Diplomatic :
Correspondence, Transmission by Post, Exchange of Notes with Norway. *Cmd. 7146, 160*
Privileges :
  Extension Acts :
    1946, 49
      Bill, 7, 10, 28
    1950, 719
      Bill, 669, 670, 697, 698
    S.R. & O.s and S.I.s Revised, 837

Dirleton Castle guide, 882

Disabled Persons :
(Employment). S.R. & O.s and S.I.s Revised, 837

Disabled Persons *(continued)* :
in Government Employment, Statements :
  Cmd. 7303, 305
  Cmd. 7591, 488
  Cmd. 7848, 505
  Cmd. 8099, 718
Rehabilitation and Resettlement Reports, 81, 592
Welfare of the Blind, 67

Disablement due to specified injuries. *Cmd. 7076*, 156

Discipline :
Courts-Martial Procedure, 263
See also Naval Discipline.

Discrimination, Main types and causes, 860

Disease, Nomenclature of, 360

Diseases :
of Animals Act, 325
  Report of Proceedings, 517
  Act, 1950, 719
  Bill, 671, 674, 675, 698
of Children, Common Communicable, Active Immunisation against, Report, 876
of Crop Plants, 335
of Fish Act, 327
of the Rabbit, 333, 738
of Vegetables, 738
See also Medical Diseases ; International Statistical Classification.

Dishorning, Substitute for, 517, 738

Disorders in Eastern Provinces of Nigeria, Proceedings of Commission, 751

Dispensing, Manual of, 114

Displaced Persons :
Agreement with Yugoslavia. *Cmd. 7232*, 166
and Poles, Cost of, Select Committee on Estimates Report, 293
and Refugees, United Nations Committee Report, 424
  Select Committee on Estimates Report, 284
See also Refugees.

Disposal :
of Government Ships, 107
of Stores in Middle East, Agreement with U.S.A. *Cmd. 7471*, 315
of Surplus Stores, 104
  and fixed assets, Select Committee on Estimates Report, 479

Disposal *(continued)* :
of Unused Drawing Rights :
  France. *Cmd. 7900*, 703
  Germany. *Cmd. 7901*, 703

Dispute between the National Coal Board and the National Union of Colliery Winding Enginemen, Report, 283

Dissolution of Parliament, Proclamation, 812

Distempers on Walls and Ceilings, 827

Distinguished Conduct Medal, Special Army Order, 437

Distress, England, S.R. & O.s and S.I.s Revised, 837

Distribution :
of German Enemy Property Act, 512
  Bill, 461, 487, 488
of Industry. *Cmd. 7540*, 320
  Act, 719
  Bill, 670, 697
  S.R. & O.s and S.I.s Revised, 837

District :
Auditor. England. S.R. & O.s and S.I.s Revised, 837
Commissioner, Film Strip, 534
Council, England :
  to Exchange Control. S.R. & O.s and S.I.s Revised, 837
Council, Scotland. S.R. & O.s and S.I.s Revised, 837

Heating :
in American Housing, Report, 557
Interim Memorandum on, 87

Disturbances :
in Aden, Report, 344
in the Gold Coast, Report, 344

Dittybox, the Navy's Own Magazine, 53, 176, 332, 515

Divorce, S.R. & O.s and S.I.s Revised, 837

Dobson, A. T. A. (Chairman) : International Overfishing Conference Standing Advisory Committee Report. *Cmd. 7387*, 310

Dock Workers :
Inquiry Report, 81
(Regulation of Employment) :
  Act, 48
  S.R. & O.s and S.I.s Revised, 837

Docking and Nicking of Horses Act, 511
  Bill, 456, 475, 482, 483, 486
  Standing Committee Debates, 681

Docks :
Regulations, Factory Form, 76
Strikes, Review of. *Cmd. 7851*, 505

Doctor appointed to Hospitals, Exchange of Notes with Portugal. *Cmd. 7383*, 309

Doctors :
and Dentists, Memorandum on Duties under Dangerous Drugs Acts, 381
See also General Practitioners.

Documents :
on British Foreign Policy, 333
United Nations :
  Check List, 643
  Index, 860

Dodecanese Islands, Transfer of responsibility for administration, Exchange of Notes with Greece. *Cmd. 7142*, 160

Dog Racecourse Betting :
S.R. & O.s and S.I.s Revised, 837
(Temporary Provisions) Act, 172
  Bill, 123, 124, 148

Dogs :
Act, 170
S.R. & O.s and S.I.s Revised, 837

Dolbadarn Castle, guide, 440

Dollar Outpayments, Control of. *Cmd. 7210*, 164

Dolls and Dolls' Houses, 878

Dolphins. *See* Whales.

Domestic :
Coal Consumers' Council Reports, 292, 475, 689
Drainage Report, 264
Food Production Report, 738
Fuel Policy, Report. *Cmd. 6762*, 33
Heating :
  by Solid Fuel, 827
  in America, 66
Hot Water Supply in Great Britain, Inquiry into, 883
Preservation of Fruit and Vegetables, 517
Producers. *See* Agriculturists.
Pottery, Related Schedule, 240
Science, Careers, 75, 793

Dominica, Colonial Reports, 531, 532

Dominican Republic, Review of Commercial Conditions, 842

Dominion Wool Disposals Ltd. Accounts :
  Cmd. 6855, 38
  Cmd. 7714, 496
  Cmd. 7867, 701
  Cmd. 7962, 708

Dominions :
Office Publications (N.P.), 62
Pensions of Governors Act, 328

Don Valley Boundary Commission Report. *Cmd. 8100*, 718

Donatello's Relief of the Ascension with Christ giving the keys to St. Peter, 659

Doncaster :
Boundary Commission Report. *Cmd. 8100*, 718
Corporation Act, 725
Provisional Order Confirmation Act, 50
Railway Accident Report, 418

Donkin, W. C. : Northumberland and Tyneside, 241

Double :
Day-shift Working, Report. *Cmd. 7147*, 160
Income Tax, Agreement with Eire. *Cmd. 7182*, 163
Taxation, Avoidance of :
  France. *Cmd. 6987*, 46
  U.S.A. :
    Cmd. 6589, 38
    Cmd. 6890, 40
    Cmd. 6902, 41

Doughty, C. (Chairman) : Industrial Court Inquiry Report, Wire and Wire Rope Industry. *Cmd. 7097*, 157

Douglas, Air Chief Marshal Sir Sholto :
Air Operations by Fighter Command, 386
Liberation of Europe, 220

Douglas Park Railway Accident Report, 418

Dover :
Castle guide, 117
Corporation Act, 725
Harbour Acts, 513, 725

Draft Blasting Special Regs., 578

Drainage. *See* Domestic Drainage.

Dramatic Art, Careers, 75

Drawing Rights, Agreement with Turkey. *Cmd. 7905*, 704

Dress :
Army, 261
Designing, Careers, 793

Dressmaking, Careers, 793

Drill. *See* Elementary Drill.

Drinking Glasses, Picture Book, 260

Driving Licences. *See* Road Traffic.

Drogheda, Earl of (Chairman) : Cinematograph Films Council, Report, 842

Drug Supervisory Body: Estimated World Requirements of :
Dangerous Drugs, 423
Narcotic Drugs, 423, 860
Drugs :
Commission on Narcotic Drugs, Publications, 861
Definitions of, Report, 779
Expert Committee on Drugs liable to produce Addiction, Report, 877
Protocol amending Agreements, Conventions, and Protocols on Narcotic Drugs. Cmd. 7135, 159
See also Dangerous Drugs ; Food and Drugs ; Narcotic Drugs.
Dry Rot, 882
In Potatoes, 737
Dryburgh Abbey, guide, 440
Drying in the Heavy Clay Industries, 883
DSIR, 604
DTD Specifications. See Specifications.
Dudley :
and Bridgnorth, Geological Survey Memoirs, 226
Corporation Act, 174
Dufton, A. F. : Protractors for the Computation of Daylight Factors, 86
Duke of Edinburgh. See Princess Elizabeth.
Duncan, J. (Chairman) : Land Drainage (Scotland) Committee Report. Cmd. 7948, 707
Dundee :
Corporation :
(Administration and General Powers) Order Confirmation Act, 725
Bill, 697
Order Confirmation Acts :
1946, 51
Bill, 8, 28
1947, 174
Bill, 130, 149
1949, 512
Bill, 279, 303
Harbour and Tay Ferries Order Confirmation :
Act, 1949, 512
Bill, 279, 303
Bill, 1950, 699
Dunham, K. C. : Geology of the Northern Pennine Orefield, 606
Dunkeld Cathedral guide, 882
Dunkirk, Evacuation of, 219
Duties, List of. See Organisation Charts.

E

Earl's Palace, Kirkwall, guide, 440
Early :
Christian and Byzantine Art, 659
Mediaeval Art in the North, 659
Stuart Silver, 878
Easby Abbey, guide, 440
East :
Africa :
Groundnuts Production Scheme : Cmd. 7030, 153
Cmd. 7314, 305
Inter-territorial Organisation, Revised Proposals, 386
Labour Conditions in, 61
African Agricultural Research Institute Reports, 60, 185, 531
Anglia and adjoining areas, British Regional Geology, 393
European Studies. See Oriental.
Grinstead Gas and Water Act, 50
Kilbride New Towns Act, 229
Shalford Public Level Crossing Railway Accident Report, 850
Yorkshire and Lincolnshire, Geology, 393
East, SirN.: Society and the Criminal, 564
Eastern :
and Pacific Customs Tariffs, 533
Dependencies, Introducing the, 534
Pacific Ocean, Monthly Meteorological Charts, 814
Region, Scottish Hospitals Survey, Report, 90
Eastham, T. : Case of Arthur Alfred Clatworthy, Report, 31
Eastwood, C. G. (Chairman) : Colonial Primary Products Committee, Report, 344
Eastwood, T. : British Regional Geology, 88
Eastwood, W. S. : Radioactive Tracers in Metallurgical Research, 838
Ecclesiastical :
Commissioners :
(Curate Grants) Measure, 7, 52
(Loans for Church Training Colleges) Measure, 514
(Provision for Unbeneficed Clergy) Measure, 514
Amendment Measure, 514
Committee Reports, 12, 125, 267, 450, 451, 457, 461, 673, 676
Dilapidations :
(Amendment) Measure, 175

Ecclesiastical (continued) :
Dilapidations (continued) :
(Chancel Repairs) Measure, 514
Measure, 1950, 727
Law, England, S.R. & O.s and S.I.s Revised, 837
ECE in Action, 643
Echo-sounding and the Pelagic Fisheries, 739
Economic :
Affairs, Department of (United Nations) Publications, 251,424,643
and Employment Commission Reports, 425, 426
and Social :
Council (United Nations) Publications, 111, 251, 424, 644, 861
Projects, Catalogues of, 645, 862
Bulletin for Europe, 643, 861
Changes in 1948, Supplement, 643
Commission for Europe, 433
Transport Statistics, 861
Co-operation :
Administration, Report on Programme, 544
Agreement with U.S.A. :
Cmd. 7446, 314
Cmd. 7469, 315
Cmd. 7961, 700
Declaration approving recommendations for closer economic co-operation with Denmark, Norway, and Sweden. Cmd. 7884, 702
Reports :
Cmd. 7570, 322
Cmd. 7654, 492
Cmd. 7702, 495
Cmd. 7776, 500
Cmd. 7844, 505
Cmd. 7890, 703
Cmd. 7960, 708
Cmd. 8028, 712
Cmd. 7862 (Memorandum), 701
Development :
in Selected Countries, Plans, Programmes, and Agencies, 861
Technical Assistance for, 652
Discussions. See Tripartite Economic Discussions.
Information Unit Publications, 541
Reconstruction in Devastated Areas, 427
Report, World Economic Situation, 424

Economic (continued) :
Research Report. Cmd. 6868, 39
Review of Food and Agriculture, 434
Series :
Agriculture and Fisheries, 178, 335, 518, 738
British Museum, 521, 742
Situation and Prospects of Europe, Survey of, 424
Statistics, International Conference relating to, 862
Survey :
1947. Cmd. 7046, 154
1948. Cmd. 7344, 307
Popular Edition, 389
1949. Cmd. 7647, 492
1950. Cmd. 7915, 704
Asia and the Far East, 645, 862
Europe, 645, 862
Latin America, 865
Mission for Middle East, Report, 860
See also Overseas Economic Surveys.
Economic, Social, and Cultural Collaboration and Collective Self-Defence :
Cmd. 7367, 308
Cmd. 7599, 488
Economisers, Unorthodox use of, 773
Economy Memoranda :
Lead, 441
Timber, 264, 664
Ecuador, Overseas Economic Survey, 845
Ede, Rt. Hon. H. Chuter (Chairman) : Committee of Privy Council, Island of Alderney, Report. Cmd. 7805, 503
Edgware Railway Accident Report, 108
Edinburgh :
and Midlothian Water Order Confirmation Act, 513
Bill, 456, 486
Castle, guide, 440
Corporation Order Confirmation Act, 725
Bill, 698
Gazette, 90, 229, 397, 611, 756
Merchant Company Widows' Fund (Amendment) Order Confirmation Act, 330
Bill, 132, 150
Monuments and Constructions, Royal Commission Report. Cmd. 7967, 708
University (Additional Bursaries) Scheme, 831

Edmonds, Brig.-Gen. Sir J. E., History of the Great War, 202, 568
Edmunds, F. H. : British Regional Geology, Central England District, 226
Education :
Acts :
1946, 49
Bill, 6, 17, 26, 27, 28
1949, 509
1950, 724
Administration in Wales, 350
Adult, Summary Report of International Conference, 653
Authorities (Scotland) Grant Regs., 614
by Radio, 872
Circulars, etc., 62, 350, 541, 543, 757
England, S.R. & O.s and S.I.s Revised, 837
Estimates, 16, 187, 284, 285, 466, 681
Memoranda on :
Cmd. 6781, 34
Cmd. 7060, 155
Cmd. 7356, 308
Expenditure of Local Education Authorities, 541, 543
for Commerce, Special Committee Report, 541
for Industry and Commerce, 191
for Librarianship, 771
for Management, 191
Fundamental, 654, 871, 872
General, Handbook, 661
Handicapped Children, etc., 757, 873
Higher :
in the Colonies. Cmd. 7331, 306
Technological Education, Future Development for, 757
in Malaya, Commission Report, 344
in Rural Wales, 543
in Wales, 352
Future of Secondary Education, 543
in West Africa, 534
International :
Conference on Public Education, 433, 654, 871
Yearbook, 654, 871
Local Authorities List, 350
Minister of, UNESCO General Conference Report :
Cmd. 7863, 701
Cmd. 8066, 758
Ministry of, Publications (N.P.), 62, 190, 349, 541, 756

Education (continued) :
Miscellaneous Provisions Act, 328
Bill, 272, 273, 288, 295, 299, 300, 301
Standing Committee Debates, 463
of Backward Children, 541
Problems in, 872
Reports :
Cmd. 7426, 312
Cmd. 7724, 497
Cmd. 7967, 707
Rules, 542, 758
Scotland :
Acts :
1946, 49
Bill, 5, 11, 28
1949, 507, 510
Bill, 297, 299, 302, 303, 448
1950, Bill, 681
Index, 831
Acts :
Edinburgh University (Additional Bursaries) Scheme, 831
Endowment Scheme, 831
Advisory Council Report. Cmd. 7005, 151
Catherine McCaig's Trust (Amendment) Scheme, 399
Circulars, 91, 831
Draft University of Glasgow, Anderson College of Medicine, Trust Scheme, 614
(Exemptions) Act, 172
Bill, 124, 125, 148
Meals Service (Scotland) Regs., 91
Reports :
Cmd. 6887, 40
Cmd. 7089, 156
Cmd. 7319, 319
Cmd. 7656, 492
Cmd. 7914, 704
Scottish Education Department Publications (N.P.), 91, 230, 399, 614, 831
S.R. & O.s and S.I.s Revised, 837
Statistics relating to, 351, 398
University, Report, 614
Welsh Department, Publications (N.P.), 63, 192, 352, 543, 758
See also Fundamental Education ; Further Education ; Primary Education ; Secondary Education ; Oversea Education ; Higher Education.

Education, Science, and Culture of War-devastated countries, Book of Needs in, 653
Educational :
Building, 541, 543
Capital Investment, 757, 758
Commission :
Agreement for Establishment, with U.S.A. Cmd. 7527, 319
Establishment in U.K. Cmd. 7666, 493
Endowments (Scotland) Acts, Schemes approved, 92, 231
Foundations in the County of Hertford, Scheme, 757
Reconstruction, Temporary International Council for, 655
Training, 114, 437
Educationally Sub-normal and maladjusted children, Boarding School provision for, 63, 64
Edwards, Sir L. (Chairman) : Working Party on Ship Repairing Facilities, 729
Edwards, L. J. (Chairman) : Publicity for Local Government, Consultative Committee, 201
Eel, the Common, and its Capture, 399
Eelworm, Stem and Bulb, 178
Effect :
of Soil Foundation on the Road Surface, 395
of Variations in Output on Heat Consumption, 772
Efficiency :
Decoration, 114, 661
Medal, 114
Efficient :
Operation of Steam Engines, 773
Use :
of Fertilisers, 874
of Fuel, 196
of Steam, 355
Egerton, Sir A. R. (Chairman) : Committee of the Building Research Board, Reports on Heating and Ventilation :
of Dwellings, 117
of Schools, 264
Egham Urban District Council Act, 331
Egg :
Bacteriology of Spray-dried, 224
Production, Rearing of fowls for, 516
Eggs :
Home preservation, 516
Testing for Quality, 546
See also Poultry.

Egypt :
British Goodwill Trade Mission to, Report, 102
Equality of Treatment in regard to War Damage Compensation, Exchange of Notes with U.K. Cmd. 7710, 496
Financial Agreements :
Cmd. 7163, 162
Cmd. 7305, 305
Cmd. 7675, 494
Foreign Exchange Requirements, Correspondence with U.K. :
Cmd. 6720, 30
Cmd. 6792, 34
Cmd. 7100, 157
International Sanitary Convention for Aerial Navigation with Declaration :
Cmd. 6989, 46
Cmd. 6999, 47
Negotiations for Revision of the Anglo-Egyptian Treaty of 1936. Cmd. 7179, 163
Overseas Economic Survey, 416
Eire :
Air Services Agreement. Cmd. 6793, 34
Double Income Tax Agreement. Cmd. 7182, 163
Review of Commercial Conditions, 102
Trade Agreement. Cmd. 7504, 318
Volunteers. See Unemployment Insurance Act (Eire Volunteers).
Eisenhower. See Supreme Commander.
Elasticity of Wood and Plywood, 391
Election :
Commissioners Act, 719
Bill, 447, 460, 488
Expenses, 20, 691, 783, 833
of a Member (Clergymen of the Church of Ireland), Select Committee Report, 687
Elections :
and Jurors Act, 48
County, Borough, and District Councils, 562
Parish Councillors, 562
Select Committee Reports, 16, 17
See also Chartered and other Bodies.
Electoral :
Law Reform, Committee Report. Cmd. 7286, 304
Registers Act, 512
Bill, 461, 487, 488

Electoral (continued) :
Registration (Scottish Home Department) Report. Cmd. 7004, 151
Electors in Parliamentary Constituencies :
England and Wales. Cmd. 7840, 505
Scotland. Cmd. 7841, 505
Electric :
Arc Welding, 176
Fencing, Controlled Grazing, 737
Illumination, 192
Lighting :
Act, 507, 721
(Clauses) Act, 325, 721
Power Engineering in Germany during 1939–45, 623
Electrical :
Apparatus Intrinsic Safety Report, 357
Engineering :
Standard Extra High Tension Overhead Lines, 439
Technical Register, 593
Specifications, 238
Electricity :
Act, 173
Bill, 129, 130, 131, 147, 149, 150
Standing Committee Minutes, 141
Commission Publications (N.P.), 64, 193, 352, 543
Commissioners' Final Report, 772
Committee (European Recovery Programme) Reports, 544
Fire Risks at Generating Stations, 774
Fuel Economy by saving, 772
Peak Load Problem, Committee Report. Cmd. 7464, 315
Reports and Accounts. 679. 680. 691, 692, 771, 772
S.R. & O.s and S.I.s Revised, 837
Statements of Guarantee :
Loans proposed to be raised, 288, 290, 295, 296, 477, 682, 684, 688, 856
Stock issued. 288. 290. 295. 296, 471, 686, 856
Sub-Committee Reports, 208, 369, 578, 794
(Supply) Acts :
Engineering and Financial Statistics, 64, 193, 352, 554, 772
Generation of Electricity in Great Britain, 193, 543
Overhead Line Regs., 193
Regulations, 554
Special Orders, 355

Electricity (continued) :
Supply Areas. Cmd. 7007, 152
Electro-Osmosis, Application of, 225
Elementary Drill (All Arms) Manual, 261
Elgin Cathedral guide, 882
Elizabeth, Calendar of Patent Rolls, 390
Elliott, J., Inquiry into the Case of. Report. Cmd. 6933, 43
Elliott, Lt. Col. Rt. Hon. W. E. (Chairman) : Wool Marketing Committee, Report, 55
Ellice Islands. See Gilbert and Ellice Islands.
Ellis, A. W. M. (Chairman) : Royal Commission on Population, Report of Biological and Medical Committee, 826
Elm Disease, 195
El Salvador, Review of Commercial Conditions, 632
Emblems for Mentions in Dispatches and for King's Commendations, 261
Embroideries, Persian, 878
Embroidery, Flowers in English, 260
Emergency :
Economic Committee for Europe, 64
Food Committee Reports, International, 435
Laws :
(Miscellaneous Provisions) Act, 328
Bill, 132, 150
(Transitional Provisions) :
Act, 1946, 48
Bill, 4
Bill, 1947, 150
Legislation, Continuance of. Cmd. 8069, 716
Poultry Feeding, 55
Powers (Defence) Act, 723
Emigrant Ships, Instructions relating to, 417
Emmerson, Sir H. (Chairman) : Building Research and Advisory Council, Report, 664
Empire :
Forests and the War, Statistics, 354
Information Services Publications (N.P.), 363
See also British Commonwealth.
Empire Clansman, Wreck Report, 249
Empire Waveney, Wreck Report, 421
Employer and Worker. Cmd. 7018, 152
Employers' :
Associations, etc., Directory, 208, 369

Employers' (continued) :
Liability Insurance (Limitation of Charges) :
Cmd. 6872, 39
Cmd. 7169, 162
Employment :
and Training :
Act, 328
Bill, 273, 289, 295, 300, 301
Standing Committee Debates, 463
S.R. & O.s and S.I.s Revised, 837
and Unemployment Tables, 208, 369, 578
Full Employment :
Implementation of Policies, Report, 865
Maintenance of, 648
National and International Measures for, 866
of Children, Report. Cmd. 8005, 711
of Women and Young Persons Acts, 722, 723
See also Industry ; Civil Employment ; Trade.
Endowed Schools Acts, Scheme, 687, 757
Endowments. See Educational Endowments.
Energy Yielding Components of Food and Computation of Calorie Values, 434
Enfield Explosion Report, 417
Engine Log Book, 338
Engineer :
and Ship Surveyor, Examination, 59
Services (Peace) Regs., 114
Engineering :
and Allied Employers National Federation and Confederation of Shipbuilding and Engineering Unions, Dispute Report. Cmd. 7511, 318
and Financial Statistics. See Electricity (Supply) Acts.
Apprentice, Examination Papers, 238
Careers, 207
Mission. See United Kingdom.
Products, Standardisation of, 621
Record, Agricultural, 55
Standards : Pocket Books, Royal Engineers, 439
See also Civil Engineering ; Production Engineering ; Programme and Progress ; Chemical Engineering ; Mechanical Engineering ; Military Engineering.

Engines :
Heavy Oil, 773
Shunting. See Boilers.
English :
Domestic Embroidery of the 16th and 17th Centuries, Catalogue of, 878
Embroidery, Flowers in, 878
Wrought Iron Work, 878
Enterprise Scotland Exhibition Publications (N.P.), 203
Entertainment :
Army, 660
Departmental and Official, Select Committee on Estimates Report, 476
Official Visitors, Special Army Order, 661
Entertainments Duty, S.R. & O.s and S.I.s Revised, 837
Entomology Bulletin, 741
Entrepot Cool Storage of Fruit and Vegetables, 392
Environmental Sanitation, Expert Committee Report, 876
Epidemics in Schools, Analysis of Data collected, 813
Epidemiological and Vital Statistics, 436, 659, 875
Epine Wreck Report, 421
Epsom Station Railway Accident Report, 850
Equal Pay, Royal Commission on :
Appendices to Minutes of Evidence, 89
Report. Cmd. 6937, 43
Equipment :
of the Farm, Leaflets, 739
Wire Specifications, 406
See also Machinery ; School Furniture.
Equivalent :
Headwinds :
Application of Upper-Wind Statistics to Air Route Planning, 815
on some of the principal Air Routes of the World, 815
Metric Values in Scientific Papers, Inclusion of, 394
Eritrea, United Nations Commission Report, 864
Essential Commodities Reserves, S.R. & O.s and S.I.s Revised, 837
Essentials of Good Cowmanship, 737

Essex, Representation of the People Bill, proposed new Constituencies :
Cmd. 7397, 310
Cmd. 7425, 312
Esso Saranac, Explosion on Board, Report, 417
Estate :
Agency and Auctioneering, Careers, 75
Development and Management in War-Damaged Areas, Report, 241
Expenditure. See Scottish Farm Rents.
Management. See Valuation.
Estates, Administration of. S.R. & O.s and S.I.s Revised, 837
Estate Wages, Extraction from British Lignite and Peat, 87
Estimates. See Civil Estimates ; Defence Estimates ; Air Estimates ; Army Estimates ; Navy Estimates.
Select Committee Reports, 21, 22, 23, 134, 140, 143, 144, 280, 284, 286, 292, 293, 298, 468, 471, 473, 475, 476, 479, 480, 676, 677, 678, 685, 689, 690, 692, 695
Index to Reports, 678, 785
Minutes of Proceedings, 462
Ethiopia :
Description of the Kenya/Ethiopia Boundary, Agreement amending. Cmd. 7374, 309
Regulation of Mutual Relations, Agreement. Cmd. 7722, 497
Eton Rural District Council Act, 725
Europe :
Council of :
General Privileges and Immunities. Cmd. 7780, 500
Publications, 754
Reports :
Cmd. 7807, 503
Cmd. 7808, 505
Cmd. 8082, 716
Cmd. 8083, 717
Despatch on Naval War in North West, 383
Economic :
Bulletin, 643, 861
Commission for, 433
Survey, 1948, 645
Interim Report of Economic Commission, 861
Recovery in, 858
Weather Chart of North-West, 596

European :
and Mediterranean Region :
Air Navigation Meeting Report, 572
Frequency Assignment Planning, Meeting Report, 791
Manual Binder, 367
Broadcasting Convention :
Cmd. 7774, 500
Cmd. 7946, 707
Central Inland Transport Organisation Agreement. Cmd. 6919, 42
Coal Organisation, Agreements :
Cmd. 6732, 31
Cmd. 7041, 154
Co-operation, Memoranda :
covering revised United Kingdom programme. Cmd. 7545, 321
relating to Economic Affairs. Cmd. 7862, 701
submitted to the Organisation (4-year plan). Cmd. 7572, 320
Economic Co-operation :
Convention for. Cmd. 7388, 310
Final Act, 2nd Session. Cmd. 7796, 502
Organisation, Publications, 194, 353, 544, 759
Health Conference, 658
Jewry and Palestine :
Report of Inquiry. Cmd. 6808, 35
Maps relating to the Report, 65
Languages, Examination Papers, 342
Payments :
Agreements, drawing rights in favour of :
Greece. Cmd. 7802, 502
Turkey. Cmd. 7652, 492
Union (Financial Provisions) Act, 720
Bill, 676, 699
Printed Textiles, 878
Programmes of Agricultural Reconstruction and Development, 434
Recovery Programme :
Popular Account, 541
Reports, 544, 759
Social Welfare Seminar, United Nations, 869
Steel Trends in the setting of the World Market, 862
Union, Council of Europe :
Agreement for the Establishment of a Preparatory Commission. Cmd. 7687, 494

European (continued) :
Union, Council of Europe (continued) :
Statute of the Council .
Cmd. 7686, 494
Cmd. 7778, 500
Explanatory Note. Cmd. 7720, 497
Euston Station Railway Accident Report, 850
Evacuation Memorandum on Short Term Plan for, 778
Evagoras Expansion Report, 859
Evans, Sir G. (Chairman) : Settlement Commission on British Guiana and British Honduras, Report. Cmd. 7533, 320
Evasions of Petrol Rationing Control, Report. Cmd. 7372, 309
Eve, Sir M. T. (Chairman) :
Building Apprenticeship and Training Council, Report, 264
Local Government Boundary Commission, Report, 285
War Damage Commission, Report, 250
Evershed, Hon. Mr. Justice (Chairman) :
Cotton Spinning Industry Report, 76
Cotton Textiles Machinery Industry Committee of Investigation, Report, 238
Evershed, Rt. Hon. Sir R. : Supreme Court Practice and Procedure Committee, Report. Cmd. 7764, 499
Everyman's United Nations, 426
Evesham, Vale of, Survey of Soils and Fruit, 517
Evidence. S.R. & O.s and S.I.s Revised, 837
Ewes, Twin Diseases in, 738
Examination :
of Arc Welds in the Shipyard, 53
of Bees for Acarine Disease, 737
of Masters and Mates, Regs., 417, 849
Examinations :
Admiralty, 332, 515, 728
Art, 191, 350, 541, 757
Committee Report, 349
Civil Aviation, 57, 181, 338, 525, 744
Commercial Subjects, 58, 182, 339, 526, 745
Competency and Surveyor's Certificates, Mines, 66
Education, Ministry of, 191
Fuel and Power, Ministry of, 196, 355, 555, 772
in Secondary Schools, 63, 64, 191, 541, 543

Examinations (continued) :
Police (Scotland), 700
Scottish Education Department, 231, 399, 614, 851
Senior Leaving Certificate, 92, 231
Supply, Ministry of, 238
Transport, Ministry of, 247, 417, 633, 849
War Office Staff College Entrance, 440
Excavation of Ancient Sites, 664
Excess Profits Tax Leaflets, 91, 201, 361, 569, 788
S.R. & O.s and S.I.s Revised, 837
Exchange Control :
Acts :
1947, 172
Bill, 29, 30, 122, 147
Memorandum. Cmd. 6954, 44
1950, 724
S.R. & O.s and S.I.s Revised, 837
Exchequer and Audit Department Acts :
1947, 141
1948, 326
1950, 720
Bill, 675, 699
Excise Duties on Mechanically Propelled Vehicles, 455
Exeter Provisional Order Confirmation Act, 330
Bill, 274, 300
Exhibition of 1851, Commemorative Album, 878
Exhibitions :
and Fairs, Report. Cmd. 6782, 34
Protocol modifying the International Conventions. Cmd. 7736, 498
Expeditionary Force :
Camp Structure Amendments, 880
Camps, 438
General Hospitals, 438
Expenditure :
Estimated (1949). Cmd. 7697, 495
Preliminary Estimates, United Nations, 112
See also National Income and Expenditure.
Expenses :
of Members of Local Authorities, Report. Cmd. 7126, 159
See also Members' Expenses ; Election Expenses.
Experiments :
on Living Animals :
Application for Licence, 361

Experiments (continued) :
on Living Animals (continued) :
Returns, 475, 695, 783
on the Preservation of Mine Timber, 605
Expiring Laws Continuance Acts :
1946, 48
Bill, 12, 29
1947, 171, 173
Bill, 132, 150
1948, 329
Bill, 278, 302
1949, 511
No. 2 Bill, 460, 487
1950, 720
Bill, 675, 699
Exploders for Simultaneous Firing of Shots, 775
Explosions :
Barnsley Main Colliery. Cmd. 7300, 305
Boiler, 417
Burngrange Mine. Cmd. 7221, 165
Harrington Colliery. Cmd. 7222, 165
Ingham Colliery. Cmd. 7434, 313
Whitehaven " William " Colliery :
Cmd. 7336, 166
Cmd. 7410, 311
Explosive and Filling Factory, Fire Fighting in, 837
Explosives :
Acts :
Forms, 201, 361, 562
Small Firework Factories, 69, 783
Summary, 361
Authorised List of, 69, 201, 361, 562, 783
in Coal Mines, Safety in the use of, Report on necessary precautions, 775
on Roads, Conveyance of, 361
Order in Council, 562
Reports :
Cmd. 6976-6983, 151
Cmd. 7214, 165
Cmd. 7543, 320
Cmd. 7869, 701
Revised Classified List, 949
Export :
and Slaughter of Horses, Report. Cmd. 7888, 703
Guarantee Acts :
1948, 329
Bill, 276, 301
1949, 510
Bill, 448, 483
1950, 718

Export (continued) :
Licences, 845
List, 62, 188
Promotion Department Publications (N.P.), 246, 416, 632
Trade, Promotion of. See Exhibitions and Fairs.
Exportation of Horses :
Act, 326
(Amendment) Bill, 483
Exporters, Registers of, 241, 242
Exports :
in Canada and the U.S.A., Prospects, 415
to Canada, Report, 624
We live by, 246
Expropriation of German Enemy Property in Spain and Liquidation of Balances and Payments between Spain and Germany. Cmd. 7558, 322
Extradition Agreement with Saudi-Arabia. Cmd. 7066, 155
Eyespot of Wheat and Barley, 55
Eyles, V. A.: Geology of Central Ayrshire, 829

F

Fabrics. See Furnishing Fabrics.
Factories :
Acts :
1948, 329
Bill, 270, 276, 301
Regs., 369
1950, 723
Short Guide, 578
Chief Inspector's Reports :
Cmd. 6992, 46
Cmd. 7299, 304
Cmd. 7621, 490
Cmd. 7839, 505
Factors :
Act, 506
in marketing of home-produced apples in England and Wales, 518
Factory :
Forms, 76, 209, 369, 578, 794
Heat Balance, Construction of, 773
Orders, 373
Faculty of Homoeopathy Act, 725
Fair Wages Poster, 76
Fairs. See Exhibitions and Fairs.
Fairweather, H. M. (Chairman) : Codes of Practice Committee, Report, 441

50

Falkland Islands :
Arms, 751
Colonial Reports, 531, 749
Flag Badge, 751
Falmouth Docks Act, 513
False Oaths (Scotland) Act, 327
Famagusta, Wreck Report, 636
Families and Genera of Living Rodents, 521
Family :
Allowance Regs., 115
Allowances :
Acts :
1945 Memorandum, 84
1950, 724
See also Unemployment.
Fantee, Wreck Report, 854
Far East :
British Dependencies in. Cmd. 7709, 496
Broadcasting in. Cmd. 7584, 323
Operations in, 384
See also Asia.
Fares :
London Passenger Transport Board, Adjustment, 106
Railway, Report, 246
Faringdon, Lord (Chairman) : Sub-Committee of Central Housing Advisory Committee : Appearance of Housing Estates, 358
Farleigh Hungerford Castle, guide, 117
Farm :
Advisory Methods for Grassland Improvement, 759
Book-keeping, 397, 518
Buildings :
in North America, 54
in Scotland, 118
Case Studies, 55, 336
Dairies, 739
Fences, 739
Machinery :
in North America, Report, 54
Use of, 336
Mechanisation :
Development in, Quarterly Review, 55
Inquiry Cases, 179
National Institute of Agricultural Engineering Publications (N.P.), 55
Progress and Economic Problems, 874

51

Fertiliser (continued) :
Placement for Arable Crops, 610
Fertilisers :
and Feeding Stuffs :
Act, 722
Residual Values of :
Calculation of, 610
Report, 736
Commodity Series, 656, 873
Efficient Use of, 874
Survey of Trade in, 753
Fertility :
Data in Population Censuses, 867
See also Land Fertility.
Festival of Britain :
Education Circulars, 757, 758
(Sunday Opening) Bill, 676, 699
(Supplementary Provisions) Act, 512
Bill, 461, 487, 488
See also Public Works.
Fforde, Sir A. (Chairman) : Cement Costs Report, 264
Fiber, World Supply, 435
Fibers, Commodity Series, 656, 873
Fiduciary Note Issue, 281, 283, 285, 295, 464, 475, 477, 481, 682, 688, 696, 855
Field :
Archaeology, 222
Astronomy, 880
Engineering Manual, 437
Information Agency, Technical, Reports on German Industry, 108
Sketching. See Map Reading.
Fife County Council Order Confirmation Act, 725
Bill, 487
Fifty Facts about UNRRA, 113
Fighter Command, Air Operations, 386
Figure Drawings, 660
Fiji :
Colonial Reports, 531, 749
Learning to be Doctors in, 364
Film :
Production Costs, Working Party Report, 624
Strips and Lecture Notes, 534, 751
Studio Committee, Report, 411
Technical Needs, Report, 260
See also British Film Institute ; Press.
Films :
on Art, 871
See also Cinematograph ; Motion Picture.
Finance :
Accounts, 21, 141, 292, 474, 687

Finance (continued) :
Acts :
1946, 48, 49
No. 2, 48
Bill, 10, 28, 29
1947, 172
Bill, 130, 133, 148, 149, 150
1948, 329
No. 2, 328
Bill, 275, 300, 301
1949, 511
Bill, 457, 485, 486
1950, 719
Bill, 673, 697, 698
Reprinted :
1909-10, 325
1943, 724
Accounts, 20, 140, 288, 472, 685, 687
(New Duties) Act, 326
Financial :
Agreements with :
Canada. Cmd. 6904, 41
Egypt :
Cmd. 7163, 162
Cmd. 7305, 305
Cmd. 7675, 494
France :
Cmd. 6988, 46
Cmd. 7430, 313
India :
Cmd. 7195, 164
Cmd. 7342, 307
Cmd. 7472, 316
Cmd. 7760, 499
Iraq :
Cmd. 7201, 164
Cmd. 7269, 169
Cmd. 7490, 317
Italy. Cmd. 7118, 158
Pakistan :
Cmd. 7343, 307
Cmd. 7479, 316
Cmd. 7765, 499
Cmd. 8008, 711
South Africa. Cmd. 7210, 164
United States. Cmd. 7210, 164
Matters outstanding as a result of termination of Mandate of Palestine, Settlement of, Agreement with Israel. Cmd. 7941, 706
Needs of the devastated countries, 251
Questions, Settlement of Agreement with Poland. Cmd. 7148, 160

52

Financial (continued) :
Statement (Budget), 19, 139, 287, 470, 685
Supplementary, 1947–8, 146
Statistics. See Local Government.
Financing :
Economic Development in under-developed countries, Methods of, 862
Improvements to land and buildings, 739
Finchale Priory, guide, 882
Findlay, W. P. K.: Decay of Timber and its Prevention, 226
Fine :
Boring with Diamond Tools, 97
Ceramics Industry in Germany, 1939–45, 842
Rolls, Calendars of. See Public Record Office Publications.
Finland :
Draft Peace Treaty. Cmd. 6897, 41
Insurance and Re-insurance Contracts, Agreement relating to. Cmd. 7886, 702
Overseas Economic Survey, 632
Payments Agreements :
Cmd. 7166, 162
Cmd. 8006, 701
Revival of Prewar Treaties and Agreements. Cmd. 7395, 310
Treaties of Peace :
Cmd. 7022, 152
Cmd. 7026, 153
Cmd. 7484, 316
Treaty of Peace Act, 172
Bill, 148
Finniston, H. M. : Radioactive Tracers in Metallurgical Research, 838
Finsbury, Boiler Explosion Report, 632
Fir, Douglas, Two Leaf-cast Diseases, 553
Fire :
and Explosion in Underground Car Parks, Precautions against, Report, 883
at Merthyr House, James Street, Cardiff, Report. Cmd. 6877, 40
at the premises of Alfred Harris & Co. Ltd., Richmond. Cmd. 7440, 313
Brigades Advisory Council Committee, Report, 201
Drill Book, National Fire Service, 563
Fighting :
Equipment, 623
in Explosive and Filling Factories, etc., 619, 837
See also Civil Defence.

Fire (continued) :
Grading of Buildings, 117
Precautions in the Home, 783
Prevention and Fire Fighting :
at Harbours where Explosives are involved, Instructions on, 837
in Ships in Port, Working Party Report, 849
Proofing of Fabrics, 226
Research Board, Reports, 604, 828
Service :
Department Publications (N.P.), 565
Drill Book, 783
Services :
Act, 172
Bill, 127, 128, 129, 147, 149
Standing Committee Minutes, 141
Reprint, 724
Reports :
Cmd. 7763, 499
Cmd. 8049, 714
Scotland, Report. Cmd. 8034, 713
See also Army Fire Services.
Firearms Forms, 202, 361, 562
Firedamp, Beware (How it can be detected by means of the Flame Safety Lamp), 355
Firemanship, Manual of, 69, 562
Firemen's Pension Scheme, 563
Fires, Building :
Investigation of, 829
Radiation from, 829
First :
Aid. See Civil Defence.
Fruit and Tenth Measure, 331
Fiscal :
Commission Report, 425
Evasion, Prevention of :
Cmd. 6859, 38
Cmd. 6890, 40
Cmd. 6902, 40
Fish :
Care of the Trawlers, 604
Cookery, 353
ABC of, 760
Diseases of, Act, 327
Freezing and Cold Storage of, 828
Frying and Offensive Trades, 68, 751
Production in the Colonial Empire, 535
See also White Fish.
Fisheries :
Bulletin, 434, 656, 874

53

FIS—   *INDEX 1946-50*

Fisheries (*continued*) :
General Fisheries Council for the Mediterranean, Agreement for the Establishment of. *Cmd. 8011*, 711
in Wartime, Report, 54
Indo-Pacific Fisheries Council, Agreement for the establishment of :
  Cmd. 7590, 324
  Cmd. 7845, 505
International North-West Atlantic Fisheries :
  Conference. *Cmd. 7658*, 492
  Convention. *Cmd. 8071*, 716
Scotland, Reports :
  Cmd. 7726, 497, 700
  Cmd. 7979, 709
Sea, Statistics, 335
Statistics, Yearbook, 434
Fishery :
Harbours Act, 326
Investigations, 54, 518, 739
Fishing :
Boats. *See* Sea Fishing Boats.
Industry. *See* Trawler Fishing Industry ; Inshore Fishing Industry.
Fitness. *See* Standards of Fitness.
Fittings and Equipment in the Modern Home, Care and Maintenance of, 780
Fitzgerald, T. : Civil Service of Northern Rhodesia and Nyasaland, 344
Fitzgerald, W. J. (Chairman) : Commission of Inquiry into Disorders in the Eastern Provinces of Nigeria, Report, 751
Fixed Equipment of the Farm :
Leaflets, 739
Papers read at Winchester Conference, 739
Flags of all Nations, Amendment, 515
Flags, Badges and Arms of Dominions, 186, 751
Flameproof :
Enclosure of Electrical Apparatus, 198
Testing, 355
Flash Steam and Vapour Recovery, 779
Thermal Effects, Design of, 827
Flat Concrete Roofs in relation to Thermal Effects, Design of, 827
Flax Retting with Aeration, 395
Flea Beetles, 737
Fleas as a menace to Man and Domestic Animals, 521
Fleming, Sir A. P. M. (Chairman) : Electrical Engineering Sub-Committee, Technical Register, 593
Flett, Sir J. S. : Geology of the Lizard and Meneage, 226

Flight, Interpretive History of, 542
Flint Implements, 741
Flocks on Range, Housing System for, 516
Floods. *See* Harvest Home.
Floor :
and Wall Tiler, 793
Finishes for Houses and other non-industrial buildings, 829
Flooring :
Hardwoods, 392
Softwoods, Wear and Anatomical Structure, 605
Floors, Granolithic Concrete, 827
Flour Mills, Control of Insect Pests in, 193
Flower Production. *See* Commercial Flower Production.
Flowering Plants in Pots, 54
Flowers :
and Shrubs, Pests of, 738
in English Embroidery, 260, 878
Flowers, J. : Report on fire at Merthyr House, James Street, Cardiff. *Cmd. 6877*, 40
Flue Gases, Recovery of waste heat from, 773
Fluke or Liver Rot in Sheep, 334
Fly. *See* Carrot Fly.
Flying :
Accidents due to Weather, How to avoid, 84
Bombs and Rocket Offensives, 386
Flying-Boat Base Committee Report, 181
Foliage and Foliage Plants, 54
Food :
Advertising, Labelling, and Composition of, 544
and Agricultural :
  Conference, United Nations. *Cmd. 7631*, 31
  Statistics, Monthly Bulletin, 434, 657, 874
  Yearbooks, 874
and Agriculture :
Organisation :
  Constitution, Rules and Regs., 873
  Publications, 433, 656, 873
  Rice, International Commission. *Cmd. 7611*, 489
  United Nations Agreement. *Cmd. 6955*, 44
  World Food Proposals. *Cmd. 7031-2*, 153

54

—FOR

Food (*continued*) :
and Agriculture (*continued*) :
  Report on Committee, 544
  State of, 657, 874
and Coal, Post-war Shortages of, 424
and Drugs :
  Act, 1950, 723
  Acts, Circulars, 67, 352, 353
  (Milk and Dairies) Act, 509
  (Milk, Dairies, and Artificial Cream), 760
  Act, 719
  Bill, 671, 674, 675, 698
  (Whalemeat) Regs., 545, 612, 760
and Nutrition, 193, 353, 545, 761
Bulletin, 760
Circulars, 760
Composition Tables for International Use, 874
Consumption Levels in U.K. :
  Cmd. 7203, 164
  Cmd. 7842, 505
Control 1939 to 1945, 64
Handling, Wrapping, and Delivery, 546
Investigation :
  Board Reports, 392, 604, 828
  Index to Literature, 87, 392, 604
  Leaflets, 392, 604, 828
  Reports, 392
  Technical Paper, 604
Labelling Order, 353
Manufacturing Industry in Germany during 1939-45, 623
Ministry of :
  Financial Powers Bill, 303
  Publications (N.P.), 64, 193, 352, 544, 760
  Select Committee on Estimates, Report, 677
Poisoning, 559, 561
Science Abstracts, 604, 828
World Shortage, Reviews :
  Cmd. 6785, 34
  Cmd. 6879, 40
Foods :
Chemical Composition, 86
commonly used in Tropical Countries, Tables of Representative Values, 86
Foot :
Rot :
  and similar diseases of Tomato and other plants, 736
  in Sheep, 334
Foot-and-Mouth Disease, 517
Antibodies in, 603

Foot-and-Mouth Disease (*continued*) :
Leaflet, 517
Virus, Quantitative Study of, 603
Footpaths and Access to the Countryside. *Cmd. 7207*, 164
Footwear : Board of Trade Publications (N.P.), 101, 246, 416, 631, 847
Forbes, Sir C. M. : Attack on Saint Nazaire, 220
Forces :
Call-up. *Cmd. 6831*, 37
Careers, 368, 793
Pay, Pensions, etc. *Cmd. 7124*, 159
Foreign :
Compensation Act, 719
  Bill, 671, 697
Memorandum and Draft of Orders in Council. *Cmd. 7942*, 706
Decorations, 219
Exchange :
  Control Regs., 220
  Position of the Devastated Countries, 424
Postwar Contribution of British Agriculture to the Saving of. *Cmd. 7072*, 155
Requirements, Prolongation of Existing Arrangements :
  Egypt. *Cmd. 7100*, 157
  Iraq. *Cmd. 7110*, 158
Marriage Act, 172
  Bill, 124, 125, 129, 148
Ministers, Council of. Report. *Cmd. 7729*, 497
Office :
  (German Section) Staff, Select Committee on Estimates Report, 293
  Publications (N.P.), 64, 194, 353, 546, 761
Policy, Documents on, 194, 353, 764
Trade, Statistical Bulletin, 759
Forest :
Inventory, Planning National, 874
Nurseries and Plantations, 65
Officer, Careers, 75, 207, 793
Operations, 65
Park Guides, 195
Products :
  Research Publications, 87, 226, 392, 605, 828
  Statistics, Yearbook of, 435, 657, 874
Records, 553, 769
Research Report, 769

55

FOR—   *INDEX 1946-50*

Forestry :
Act, 172
  Bill, 12, 13, 122, 147
  Reprint of 1909 Act, 326
and Forest Products :
  Studies, 874
  World Situation, 435
as a Career, 65, 195, 333
Colonial Research Recommendations Report, 344
Commission Publications (N.P.), 65, 194, 354, 553, 769
Select Committee on Estimates Report, 677
Commissioners' Reports, 134, 146, 291, 473, 694
Conference, British Empire, 194
Leaflets, 65, 195, 354, 553, 770
(Transfer of Woods) Act, 48
Forests, Britain's, 769
Forgery Act, 326
Forms, Design of, 639
Formulary. *See* National War Formulary.
Forster, Sir John (Chairman) :
Catering Wages Commission Report. *Cmd. 8004*, 710
Difference between the two sides of the National Council for the Omnibus Industry on the Trade Union application for a National Wages and Conditions Agreement. *Cmd. 6796*, 35
Industrial Court of Inquiry Report. *Cmd. 7511*, 318
Mining Dispute, Court of Inquiry Report, 283
Port Transport Industry Inquiry Report, 81
Savoy Hotel Ltd., Court of Inquiry Report. *Cmd. 7266*, 168
Shipbuilding Employers' Federation and the Confederation of Shipbuilding and Engineering Unions on the Trade Union claim for a 40-hour week of 5 days, Court of Inquiry Report. *Cmd. 7036*, 153
Smithfield Market. *Cmd. 6932*, 43
Trawler Fishing Industry. *Cmd. 6882*, 40
Fort William, Industrial Fluorosis, 603
Forth :
and Clyde Ship Canal Group, Report, 106

Forth (*continued*) :
Road Bridge Order Confirmation Acts :
  1947, 173
  Bill, 124, 148
  1950, 725
  Bill, 698
Forward, F. A. :
Land Transport Handbook, 192
Mechanical Road Vehicles, Descriptive Catalogue, 542
Railway Locomotives and Rolling Stock, 542
Foster, John (Chairman) :
British Broadcasting Corporation and Musicians' Union, Report of Independent Committee, 577
Railway Shopmen Board of Conciliation Report, 592
Railways Conciliation and Salaried Grades Report, 592
Foster, W. (Chairman) : Apprenticeship for Coal Face Workers, Report, 196
Four Figure Tables and Constants for Use of Students, 541
Fowl :
Paralysis, 517
Pest, 178, 334
Pox, 334
Typhoid, 334
Fox Hunting, Prohibition of, Bill, 483
Fracture of Mild Steel Plate, 332
Frames and Cloches, Crop Production in, 177, 334
Framlingham Castle, guide, 117
France :
Air Services Agreement. *Cmd. 6787*, 34
Allocation of a Reparation Scheme to Non-Repatriable Victims of German Action, Plan for. *Cmd. 7255*, 168
and Belgium, Military Operations, 202
Application of French Nationality to British Subjects in Tunisia. *Cmd. 7117*, 158
Compensation for Disablement or Death due to War Injury suffered by Civilians, Agreement. *Cmd. 8000*, 710
Cultural Convention :
  Cmd. 7888, 34
  Cmd. 7450, 314
Defence of Madagascar and Reunion. *Cmd. 0980*, 46

56

—FRE

France (*continued*) :
Disposal of Unused Drawing Rights, Memorandum. *Cmd. 7900*, 703
Double Taxation Relief. *Cmd. 6987*, 46
Exchanges of Notes :
  extending time limit of the Anglo-French Agreement of August 1945. *Cmd. 6977*, 42
  modifying the provision of the Supplementary Financial Agreement of April 1946. *Cmd. 7112*, 158
Exclusion from Franc Area of :
  French Somali Coast. *Cmd. 7731*, 497
  Lebanon. *Cmd. 8070*, 716
  Syria. *Cmd. 7408*, 311
Expropriation of German Enemy Property in Spain and Liquidation of Balances and Payments between Spain and Germany. *Cmd. 7558*, 322
Facilities, etc., for British Armed Forces pending withdrawal from French Territory. *Cmd. 7523*, 319
Financial Agreements :
  Cmd. 6809, 35
  Cmd. 6988, 46
  Cmd. 7430, 313
International :
  Administration of Tangier, Agreement for re-establishment. *Cmd. 6899*, 41
  Authority for the Ruhr, Agreement. *Cmd. 7685*, 494
Sanitary Convention :
  Cmd. 6899, 46
  for Aerial Navigation. *Cmd. 6999*, 47
Military Operations in, 1918, 362
Mutual :
  Abolition of Visas. *Cmd. 7003*, 151
  Application of the Chicago Air Transit Agreement. *Cmd. 7194*, 164
Proposed cession of territory in the Zeila area to Ethiopia. *Cmd. 7768*, 499
Reciprocal Military Air Transit Facilities. *Cmd. 7524*, 319
Settlement of Inter-custodial Conflicts relating to German Enemy Assets. *Cmd. 7551*, 321

France (*continued*) :
Social Security Agreements, etc. :
  Cmd. 7455, 314
  Cmd. 7651, 492
  Cmd. 7816, 503
  Cmd. 7906, 704
  Cmd. 7911, 704
Supply of Aircraft and Equipment, Exchange of Notes. *Cmd. 7787*, 159
Treaty of Alliance and Mutual Assistance with U.K. :
  Cmd. 7058, 154
  Cmd. 7217, 165
War Damage Compensation, Exchange of Notes. *Cmd. 7012*, 152
See also European Union.
Franco-Egyptian Case concerning the protection of French Nationals and Protected Persons in Egypt, Order, 792
Franz Haniel Mine Technical Report, 357
Fraser, Sir Bruce A. :
Contribution of British Pacific Fleet to the Assault on Okinawa, 385
Sinking of the *Scharnhorst*, 220
Fraser, F. C. : Stranded Whales and Turtles, 522
Fraser, Sir John (Chairman) : Laboratory Services Medical Advisory Committee, Report, 229
Fraser, J. H. : Distribution of Thalicacea in Scottish Waters, 616
Fraser, R. : Incidence of Neurosis among Factory Workers, 224
Fraud. *See* Prevention of Fraud.
Fraudulent Mediums Bill, 696, 699, 700
Freedom of Information :
  and of the Press, Commission on Human Rights, Report, 425
  Comments of Governments, 425
  Conference on, 645
Freezing and Cold Storage of Fish, 828
Freezing-point Test of Milk, Report, 398
French :
Egyptian and Protected Persons in Egypt. *See* Franco-Egyptian Case.
Paintings, 660
Polishers, Dermatitis among, 76
French, Sir Henry L. (Chairman) : Cost of Home Information Services, Report. *Cmd. 7836*, 505
Frequency Assignment Planning Meetings Reports, 791
Freshwater and Salmon Fisheries Research Reports, 832

57

Friendly Societies :
 Accounts, 110, 250, 422
 Acts, 325, 506
 Registry of, Publications (N.P.) (including Annual Return Forms and Statistical Summaries), 65, 195, 354, 553, 770
Friends in Need, 194
From Pachino to Ortona : The Canadian Campaign in Sicily and Italy, 57
Frontier Workers, Western Union Convention. Cmd. 7971, 708
Frost Damage to Roads, Some Cases of, 607
Frosts. See Spring Frosts.
Fruit :
 and Vegetables :
  Cool Storage of, 392
  Physics of Drying in Heated Air, 392
 Preservation by Freezing, 392
 Bud Development, 177
 Domestic Preservation, 517
 Production and Trade, 536
Fruit-growing Areas of the Hastings Beds in Kent, 517
Fruit-tree :
 Capsid Bugs, 333
 Raising, 54
 Rootstocks and Propagation, 517
 Red Spider, 516
Fruit-trees, Pruning Stone, 178
Fruits, Tree, 610
Fuel :
 Abstracts, 266, 392, 605, 828
 and Power :
  Ministry of, Publications (N.P.), 66, 196, 355, 554, 771
  Statistical Digests :
   Cmd. 6920, 42
   Cmd. 7548, 321
 and the Future, Conference Proceedings, 355
 Economy :
  at Collieries, 773
  by saving :
   Electricity, 772
   Water, 773
  in Industry, Bonus Scheme for, 772
 Efficiency :
  Bulletins, 772
  News, 774
 Efficient Use of, 196
 Research :
  Board Report, 829

Fuel (continued) :
 Research (continued) :
  Experiments in Coking Practice, 87
  Survey Papers, 87, 829
  Technical Papers, 87, 226, 606
 Saving in Factories and Commercial Premises, 773
 See also Domestic Fuel Policy.
Fuel, Power, and Heat Costing, 773
Fumes from Oil Bonded Cores, 796
Fumigation with Methyl Bromide, 202
Fundamental :
 Education, 260, 654, 871
 Human Rights, 645
 Stars, Apparent Places of, 53, 176, 332, 515, 728
Fungi :
 Edible and Poisonous, 54, 177
 pathogenic to Man and Animals, Nomenclature of, 831
Fungicides. See Insecticides.
Fur Apparel, Board of Trade Publications (N.P.), 101, 104, 623, 847
Furnaceman's Manual, 773
Furnaces :
 Cooling Firebars in Industrial Furnaces and Boilers, 773
 Insulation of, 772
Furneaux, B. S. : Fruit-growing Areas of the Hastings Beds in Kent, 517
Furnished Houses (Rent Control) Act, 49, 509
 Bill, 3, 5, 13, 27
Furnishing :
 Fabrics, 71
 to fit the Family, 203
Furniture :
 Georgian, 244
 How to buy, 363
 Industry, Proposals for a Development Council, 415
 Making, Cards for Wall Display, 363
 Price Control, 244, 414, 628, 842
 Utility, Catalogue, 246
 Working Party Report, 106
 See also School Furniture.
Further Education, 191
 Homecraft, 63, 64
 Nursery Students, 63
Future :
 Development of Higher Technological Education, Report, 757
 of the Coal Miner, 66

Fyfe, Sir W. H. (Chairman) :
 Primary Education, Advisory Council on Education in Scotland. Cmd. 6973, 151
 Special Committee on Scottish Technical Education, Report. Cmd. 6786, 34

G

Gaberdine Raincoats, Related Schedule, 843
Gaddum, J. H. : Methods of Biological Assay depending on a Quantal Response, 603
Gallant Action by H.M.I.S. Bengal and M.V. Ondina with two Japanese Raiders, 385
Galleries. See Museums and Galleries.
Galley Hill Skeleton, Reconsideration of, 521
Gambia, Colonial Reports, 343, 531, 532
Game, P. M. : Rocks collected in Oman, Arabia, 742
Gaming. See Betting.
Gander Airport to be used by United States Airlines, Exchange of Notes with U.S.A. Cmd. 7157, 161
Gane, R. : Preservation of Fruit and Vegetables by Freezing, 392
Gardens, 360
Garland, C. E. : Harrison's Digest and Index to Tax Cases, 790
Garratt, G. R. M. : 100 Years of Submarine Cables, 826
Garret Workshop of James Watt, 542
Garrett, Sir D. T. : Report on Inspection of A. Reyrolle & Co. Ltd., 629
Garrett, Sir W. (Chairman) :
 Brick Industry Report, 263
 Industrial Injuries Advisory Council, Report on Tuberculosis, etc. Cmd. 8093, 717
Garston Channel, Liverpool, Aircraft Accident Report, 523
Garton Railway Accident Report, 634
Gas :
 Act, 329
 Bill, 274, 275, 277, 289, 295, 299, 301, 302
 Standing Committee Debates, 463
 Arbitration Tribunal Rules, 555
 Burners, Operation and Maintenance, 772

Gas (continued) :
 Council, Statements of Guarantee :
  Loans proposed, 466, 690, 694
  Stock issued, 473, 474, 475, 477, 686, 694
 Examiner's Working Notebook, 411
 Fund Accounts, 66, 196, 355
 Producers, Operation of, 773
 Regulation Act, 170
 Supply Areas. Cmd. 7313, 305
  Revised. Cmd. 7424, 312
 Undertakings :
  Forms, 411
  General Notification of Gas Referees, 243
  Returns, 66, 355, 555
 Users, Practical Economy Points, 772
Gas, Light, and Coke Company Act, 51
Gater, G. H. (afterwards Sir G. Gater), (Chairman) :
 Building Apprenticeship and Training Council Reports, 664
 Film :
  Production Costs Working Party, Report, 624
  Studio Committee, Report, 411
Gateshead and District Tramways Act, 725
Gathering Grounds Report, 359
Gauge Making and Measuring, 88
General :
 Assembly :
  Publications, 111, 253, 426, 645, 862
  Report. Cmd. 7320, 306
 Conference Records, Mexico, Report, 654
 Lighthouse Fund Accounts, 145, 293, 475, 690
 Practitioners, Remuneration of. Cmd. 6810, 35
 Register Office Publications (N.P.), 85, 224, 390, 558, 776
 Registry Office (Scotland) Publications (N.P.), 91, 230, 398, 611, 777
 Service Medal, Grant of, 261, 437
Generating Stations, Fire Risks, etc., 774
Generic Revision of Achilidae, 741
Geneva :
 Conference on Tariffs and Trade. Cmd. 7276, 169
 Convention :
  Act, 508
  See also Tariffs.
Genocide :
 Committee Report, 426

Genocide (continued) :
 Convention of : What the United Nations is doing, 653
Geodetic and Topographical Surveys, 61
Geography, Some Suggestions on teaching, 872
Geological :
 and Mineralogical Investigations, Scientific Reports, Title Page and Index, 742
 Survey, Publications (N.P.), 88, 226, 392, 606, 777
Geology :
 Bulletin, 521, 741
 and Mineral Resources, British Commonwealth Specialist Conference on, Report, 606
 Technical Register, 593
Geophysical Memoirs, 386, 595, 814
George VI, Speeches to Parliament, 12, 131, 278, 669, 675
George, T. N. : British Regional Geology, 393
Georgian Furniture, 260
German :
 and Japanese Industry Reports, 411, 624
 Classified Index, 400
 Technical Index, 413
 Assets :
  in Italy. Cmd. 7223, 165
  in Spain. Cmd. 7535, 320
  in Sweden. Cmd. 7241, 167
 Settlement Agreements :
  with France. Cmd. 7551, 321
  with Netherlands. Cmd. 7803, 502
 Battleships, Report on the circumstances in which they proceeded from Brest to Germany. Cmd. 6775, 33
 Coal Tar and Benzole Industries, 1939–45, 841
 Enemy Property, Distribution of, Act, 512
  Bill, 461, 487, 488
 Foreign Policy, Documents on, 549, 764
 Gas Turbine Developments, 623
 Industry Reports, 103, 243, 842
 Law, Manual of, 764
 Major War Criminals Trials. See War Criminals.
 Medical War Crimes, Scientific Results, 549
 Motor Roads, Report, 395
 Potash Syndicate Loan Act, 725

German (continued) :
 Wool Industry, 623
German-owned Patents. Cmd. 7359, 308
Germany :
 Abrasives, Manufacture and Use, 624
 Accord of Events leading up to a reference of the Berlin Question to the United Nations. Cmd. 7534, 320
 Accounts of the Joint Export-Import Agency, Report of Price Waterhouse & Co. Cmd. 7978, 709
 Agricultural Aspects, 410
 British :
  Expenditure in. Select Committee on Estimates Reports, 144, 280
  Forces of Occupation, Treaty with Belgium. Cmd. 6790, 34
 Charter of the Allied High Commission. Cmd. 7727, 497
 Coal Exports from the three Western Zones, Agreement to enable. Cmd. 7165, 162
 Collision between a Viking Air Liner and a Soviet Service Aircraft, Court of Inquiry Report. Cmd. 7384, 309
 Control Commission Publications, 61, 187, 346, 537, 753
 Cotton, Rayon, and Silk Industries, Developments in the, 623
 Electric Power Engineering during 1939–45, 623
 Food Manufacturing Industry during 1939–45, 623
 Fine Ceramics Industry, 842
 Ferrous Metal Industry, 1939–45, 623
 Green Crop Conservation, 517
 Industrial Relations, 1945–9. Cmd. 7923, 705
 Inter-governmental group on the safeguarding of Foreign Interests in Germany. Cmd. 7850, 505
 International Authority for the Ruhr, Agreement. Cmd. 7685, 494
 Leather Industry, 841
 Losses and Survivals of Works of Art in the War, 56
 Methods used to assist Local Government and Civil Service in the British Zone, Report on. Cmd. 7804, 502
 Most - favoured - nation Treatment, Agreement. Cmd. 7876, 702
 Motor Car Industry 1939–45, 624

Germany (continued) :
 Occupation of, Agreement regarding participation of a Danish contingent :
  Cmd. 7164, 162
  Cmd. 7785, 501
 Packaging during 1939–45, 842
 Paint Industry during 1939–45, 841
 Programme for, Memorandum on measures agreed. Cmd. 7677, 494
 Purchase and Collection of Scrap in, Select Committee on Estimates Report, 293
 Railways during 1939–45, 623
 Regulation of Payments, Agreement with Military Governors. Cmd. 7824, 504
 Reparations and Restitution of Monetary Gold, Additional Protocol. Cmd. 7476, 316
 Tariff of the Western Zones, Statement regarding. Cmd. 7790, 501
 Three-Power Meeting in Paris. Cmd. 7849, 505
 Textile Industry, 410
 Tuberculosis in the British Zone, 353
 University Reform, 552
 Unused Drawing Rights, Memorandum regarding Disposal. Cmd. 7901, 703
 Western : Most-favoured-nation Treatment :
  Exchange of Notes with U.S.A. : Cmd. 7447, 314
  Cmd. 7470, 314
  under Military Occupation. Cmd. 7539, 320
Getting on Together, 541
Giant Squid, 742
Gibbs-Smith, C. H. : Man Takes Wings, 336
Gibraltar, Colonial Reports, 343, 532, 749
Gibson, C. W. (Chairman) : Housing Management Sub-Committee Report : Selection of Tenants and Transfers and Exchanges, 561
Gidea Park, Railway Accident Report, 247
Gilbert and Ellice Islands, Colonial Reports, 532, 749
Gilliatt, Sir W. (Chairman) : Council of Royal College of Obstetricians and Gynaecologists, Report, 825
Gilling East Division, Report. Cmd. 6783, 34

Girdwood, J. G. (Chairman) : Cost of House Building Committee Reports, 358, 780
Girls' Apparel, Utility, Board of Trade Publications (N.P.), 104
Gisborough Priory, guide, 117
Glanders and Farcy, 334
Glanville, W. H. :
 Impressions of Roads and Road Research in North America, 227
 Grading of Aggregates and Workability of Concrete, 227
Glasgow :
 Corporation :
  Act, 52
  Order Confirmation Acts :
   1946, 51
    Bill, 8, 28
   1948, 330
    Bill, 270, 299
   1949, 513
    Bill, 455, 486
 Sewage Order Confirmation Bill, 699
 Cross Railway Accident Report, 634
 University of :
  Anderson College of Medicine Trust Scheme, 831
  St. Mungo's College Endowment Scheme, 831
Glass :
 Industry of Germany, 410
 Victoria and Albert Museum Collection, 113
 See also Pottery.
Glasshouses, Construction and Heating of Commercial, 517
Glassware, Hand-blown Domestic, 246
Glen :
 More, National Forest Park Guide, 553
 Trool, National Forest Park Guide, 770
Gloag, J. : Good Design, Good Business, 203
Gloucester :
 Boundary Commission Report. Cmd. 8100, 718
 Corporation Act, 50
 District, British Regional Geology, 393
 Extension Act, 725
 Order Confirmation Acts :
  1947, 174
   Bill, 128, 148
  1948, 330
   Bill, 274, 301

Gloucestershire, West, Boundary Commission Report. Cmd. 8100, 718
Glover, J. A. (Chairman): Committee of Inquiry Report, Children with Defective Hearing, 756
Gloves, Board of Trade Publications (N.P.), 101, 104, 242, 244, 246, 413, 631, 847
Gneisenau. See German Battleships.
Goethe:
  Anniversary, 871
  UNESCO's Homage, 654
Gold:
  captured by Allied Forces, Protocol. Cmd. 7244, 167
  Coast:
    Colonial Reports, 343, 531, 749
    Constitutional Reform, 534
    Disturbances, 344
    Studies in Mental Illness, 750
  looted by Germany, Agreement for the return of. Cmd. 7456, 314
Goldfinch, Chaffinch, and Greenfinch, 737
Good:
  Conduct Medal, 262
  Design, Good Business, 203
Goodrich Castle, guide, 440
Goods and Services (Price Control), Board of Trade Publications (N.P.), 102, 243, 413, 628, 842
Goodwill Trade Mission Report, Iraq, Syria, Lebanon, and Cyprus, 245
Gooseberries, 610
Gooseberry:
  Aphides, 178
  Red Spider Mite, 516
  Sawfly, 333
Gordon, I.: John Murray Expedition, Scientific Report, 742
Gordon, Major K.: Petroleum and Synthetic Oil Industry of Germany, Report, 197
Gorell, Rt. Hon. Lord, Regents Park Terrace, Report. Cmd. 7094, 157
Gorman, William (Chairman): Court of Inquiry into Printing Trades Dispute, Report. Cmd. 6912, 42
Goswick, Railway Accident Report, 418
Goth, Wreck Report, 854
Gould, R. M. (afterwards Sir R.) (Chairman):
  Cost of Living Advisory Committee, Report. Cmd. 7077, 156
  Electricity, Committee Reports, 208, 369, 578

Government:
  Accounts, Committee on the Form of. Report. Cmd. 7969, 708
  and Industry, 421
  Chemist, Report, 777
  Contracts, Fair Wages Poster, 76
  Control of Railways, Estimates:
    Cmd. 7106, 157
    Cmd. 7399, 311
  Department Specifications, 97, 115, 261, 406, 438, 620, 661, 837, 880
  Departments:
    Development by, 840
    Staffs employed in:
      Cmd. 6763, 33
      Cmd. 6842, 37
      Cmd. 6936, 43
      Cmd. 7027, 153
      Cmd. 7086, 156
      Cmd. 7139, 160
      Cmd. 7213, 165
      Cmd. 7277, 169
      Cmd. 7370, 309
      Cmd. 7461, 315
      Cmd. 7522, 319
      Cmd. 7571, 322
      Cmd. 7646, 492
      Cmd. 7716, 496
      Cmd. 7770, 500
      Cmd. 7829, 504
      Cmd. 7887, 702
      Cmd. 7968, 708
      Cmd. 6780, 33
      Cmd. 8090, 717
    Suggestion Schemes, 641
  Employment. See Disabled Persons.
  Hospitality, 476
    Departmental Entertainment and Official Entertainment in the Armed Forces, Select Committee on Estimates Report, 678
  Information Services:
    Estimated Expenditure. Cmd. 7949, 707
    Select Committee on Estimates Report, 690
  of Northern Ireland (Loan Guarantee) Act, 326
  Pattern of, 364
  Printing Office, Ottawa, Royal Commission Report, 199
  Publications, Consolidated Lists, 93, 231, 400, 616, 834
  Ships, Disposal of, 107
  Surplus Stores, 104, 238, 245

Government (continued):
  See also Central Government; Local Government.
Government-owned Tonnage, Disposal of, 107
Governors of Dominions, etc., Pensions Act, 328
Gowers, Sir E. A. (Chairman):
  Health, Welfare, and Safety in Non-Industrial Employment, Committee of Inquiry, Report. Cmd. 7664, 493
  Houses of Outstanding Historic or Architectural Interest, Committee on, Report, 857
  Royal Commission on Capital Punishment, Minutes of Evidence, 608, 824
  Scottish Home Department Committee, Report on Closing Hours of Shops. Cmd. 7105, 157
Gowing, M. M.: British War Economy, 639
Grade Assessment and Certification Service as an Assistance to the Horticultural Industry, Scheme, 739
Grading of Aggregates and Workability of Concrete, 227
Graduates, University, Careers, 75
Grafting Fruit Trees, 227
Grain:
  Bulletin, 656, 737
  Care of farm-stored, 737
  Cargoes, Memorandum, 247
    Supplement, 849
  Commodity Report, 873
  Crops, Production and Trade, 752
  Infestation by Insects, 227
  Preservation in Storage, 433
  Storage in East and Central Africa, Report, 750
  Thieves of Stored Grain, How to fight them, 435
  Weevils, 516
  See also World Grain Position.
Grampian Highlands, British Regional Geology, 393
Granolithic Concrete Floors, 827
Grant of General Service Medal, 261
Granton Harbour Order Confirmation Act, 725
  Bill, 699
Grants:
  to Educational Authorities, 399
  to Research Workers and Students, 393

Grants (continued):
  Training, in Agricultural Science, Notes on, 591
  See also Pensions.
Granulated Blast Furnace Slags for the Manufacture of Portland Blast Furnace Cement, Investigations on, 829
Grass drying plants, Design of buildings, 739
Grassland Improvement, Farm Advisory Methods for, 759
Gratuities. See War Gratuities; Pay; Retired Pay; etc.
Gravel:
  Problems, Committee on, 101
  See also Sand and Gravel.
Graves. See Imperial War Graves.
Gravity Warm Air System, 196
Graysigg and Oxenholme Railway Accident Report, 247
Grazing, Controlled, with Electric Fencing, 737
Great:
  Anniversaries, 871
  Barrier Reef Expedition, Reports. 521, 742
  War, History of, 70, 202, 568
  Western Railway Act, 51
Yarmouth:
  Pier and Harbour Order Confirmation Act, 726
  Bill, 672, 698
Greater London:
  Plan, 241
  Water Supplies, Report, 359
Greaves, R. I. N.: Preservation of Proteins by drying, with special reference to the production of dried human serum and plasma for transfusion, 86
Greece:
  Additional Drawing Rights for the purpose of European Payments Agreement, Agreement establishing. Cmd. 7802, 502
  Air Services in Europe:
    Cmd. 6722, 30
    Cmd. 7348, 307
    Cmd. 7678, 494
    Cmd. 8022, 712
  Allied Mission to observe the Greek Elections, Report. Cmd. 6812, 35
  British:
    Legal Mission to, Report. Cmd. 6838, 37

Greece (continued):
  British (continued):
    Parliamentary Delegation, Report, 194
  Commercial Conditions, 632
  FAO Mission Reports, 435
  Financial and Economic Agreement. Cmd. 6733, 31
  Losses and Survivals of Works of Art in the War, 56
  Maintenance of a Royal Air Force Communications Flight in, Exchange of Notes. Cmd. 7193, 163
  Money and Property subjected to special measures during Enemy Occupation. Cmd. 7094, 157
  Report by Supreme Allied Commander, Mediterranean, 661
  Transfer of responsibility for the administration of the Dodecanese Islands. Cmd. 7142, 160
  Transportation of Army to and Evacuation from, 385
Greek:
  Elections. See Greece.
  Frontier Incidents, UN Committee of Investigation, 866
Green Crop:
  Conservation in Germany, 517
  Drying in Holland, Sweden, Denmark, 334
Greenfinch. See Goldfinch.
Greenland and Barents Sea, Monthly Meteorological Charts and Ocean Current Chart, 814
Greenock Port and Harbours Order Confirmation Act, 725
  Bill, 699
Greenwich:
  Hospital:
    Act, 172
    Bill, 12, 30
    and Travers Foundation:
      Accounts, 19, 139, 286, 472, 686
      Estimated Income and Expenditure, Statements, 21, 142, 289, 475, 687
  Observatory Publications, 777
Gregory, R. C. L.: County Court Manual, 83
Grenada, Colonial Report, 749
Grey Squirrels, 333
Grimes Graves, Weeting, guide, 882
Grimsby Corporation Act, 513
Grimsby Town, Wreck Report, 249

Griseburn Railway Accident Report, 634
Groceries and Provisions, Retail Price Lists, 194, 352, 546
Groundnuts:
  in East Africa, Scheme. Cmd. 7314, 305
  in East and Central Africa. Cmd. 7030, 153
Growing:
  Field Peas for Stock Feeding, 737
  Food for Health and Profit, 178
Growmore Bulletins, 33, 333
Guardians' Allowances Regs., 388
Guardianship (Refugee Children) Act, 509
Guatemala, Commercial Conditions, 632
Guenault, E. M.:
  Explosives for Simultaneous Firing of Shots, 775
  Intrinsic Safety of Electrical Apparatus, 357
  See also Allsop, G.
Guernsey. See Jersey.
Guiana. See British Guiana.
Guidance, Manual of, 757, 758
Guide for Lecturers and Teachers, 428
Guides to Official Sources, 777
Guillebaud, C. W. (Chairman): Railway Companies Court of Inquiry, Report. Cmd. 7161, 161
Guindey, M. (Chairman): European Economic Co-operation Committee on Payments Agreement, Report, 353
Gulland Bequest, Handbook to, 877
Gun Barrel Proof Act, 726
Gunn, W. C.: Bed Bug, 612
Guppy, E. M.:
  Roadstone, 88
  Special Report on the Mineral Resources of Great Britain: Rock Wool, 606
Gurjun, Apitong, Keruing, Kapur, and Allied Timbers, 605
Gurkhas, Pay of Gratuities to, 34
Guthrie, H. W. (afterwards the Hon. Lord Guthrie) (Chairman): Committee on Tenure of Shops and Business Premises in Scotland, Reports:
  Cmd. 7603, 489
  Cmd. 7903, 703
Guttman, E.: Readjustment in Civil Life of Soldiers discharged from the Army on account of Neurosis, 68
Gymnastic Training for Boys, 191
Gypsum and Anhydrite Plasters, 606, 881

H

Haberler, G.: Prosperity and Depression, 256
Habitation, Standards of Fitness for, 201
Hackney Carriages (London) Bill, 699
Haddington Aircraft Accident Report,181
Haifa–Baghdad Road, Agreement with Transjordan. Cmd. 7062, 153
Hairdressers (Registration) Bill, 469, 482, 483, 484, 661
Halil, Miton, Report, 648
Halifax Corporation Act, 514
Hallen Marsh Railway Accident Report, 247
Hallifax, Rear-Admiral H. R. C.: Battle of Narvik, 219
Halnan, E. T.: Scientific Principles of Poultry Feeding, 334
Ham House Guide, 878
Hamilton, Sir H. (Chairman): Commonwealth Economic Committee, Report, 535
Hampshire Basin, Geology of, 393
Hampton Court Palace, 883
  Guide, 263
  Plan, 440
Hanbury-Williams, J. C. (Chairman): British Goodwill Trade Mission to Egypt, Report, 102
Hancock, Judge E. (Chairman): Interdepartmental Committee, Assessment of Disablement due to specified injuries, Report. Cmd. 7076, 156
Hancock, W. K.: British War Economy, 639
Hand Knitting Yarn, List of Manufacturers, 102
Handbook:
  for Wireless Operators, 389
  General Assembly of United Nations, 111
  United Nations, 111
Handicapped Pupils, Boarding Schools and Special Homes for, 62
Handling and Storage of Coal, 773
Handling, Wrapping, and Delivery of Food, 546
Hand-operated Turntable Ladder, Instruction Book, 565
Handwriting, Teaching of, 433
Hankey, Rt. Hon. Lord (Chairman), Chemists, Physics, Technical Registers, 593
Hansard. See House of Commons Debates; House of Lords Debates.

Hard:
  Currency Areas, Agreement with Burma to control Burma's Expenditure in. Cmd. 7560, 322
Fibers, Commodity Report, 873
Hardie, S. J. L. (Chairman): Jute, Working Party Report, 416
Harding, J. P.: On some species of Lernaea, 742
Hardknott National Forest Park Guide, 553
Hardman, D. R. (Chairman): National Advisory Council, Education for Industry and Commerce, Report, 191
Hardwicke Railway Accident Report,634
Hardwoods:
  Flooring, 392
  Sowing or Planting, 194
Harlow Development Corporation Report, 469, 476, 694
Harragin, Sir W.: Civil Services of British West Africa, 186
Harrington Colliery Explosion Report. Cmd. 7222, 165
Harris & Co. Ltd., Richmond, Report on Fire at premises of. Cmd. 7440, 313
Harris Lebus Ltd., Boiler Explosion Report, 632
Harris, P.: Handbook of Woodcutting, 87, 828
Harris, Sir S. (Chairman): Marriage Guidance, Grants for Development. Cmd. 7566, 322
Harrison's Digest and Index of Tax Cases, 790
Harrow Boundary Commission Report. Cmd. 7745, 498
Hartlepool Pier and Harbour Order Confirmation Act, 726
  Bill, 672, 698
Hartwell, F. J.: Intrinsic Safety of Electrical Apparatus, 357
Harvest Home, 335
Harwich Harbour Act, 513
Harwood, Admiral Sir H. H.:
  Battle of River Plate, 219
  Battle of Sirte, 220
  Coastal Forces Actions, 386
Hastings:
  Beds in Kent, Fruit Growing Areas of, 517
  Manuscripts, Reports, 223
Hatfield:
  Development Corporation Reports, 476, 694
  Railway Accident Report, 108

HAU—   INDEX 1946–50

Haulage. See Road Haulage.
Havana. See Tariffs and Trade ; Trade and Employment.
Havant and Waterloo Urban District Council Act, 173
Hawkers Act, 721
Hay, Ian :
  Arms and the Men, 743
  Post Office Went to War, 85
  Royal Ordnance Factories, 1939–48, 620
Hayman, R. W. : Families and Genera of Living Rodents, 521
Headquarters of the United Nations, Permanent, Report, 255, 256
Headwear, Board of Trade Publications (N.P.), 101
Health :
  Central Health Services Council : Report, 779
  Scottish Health Services Council Joint Committee on Prescribing, Report, 779
  Conference. See International Health Conference.
  Department of, for Scotland :
    Publications (N.P.), 90, 239, 397, 612, 777
    Reports :
      Cmd. 7188, 163
      Cmd. 7453, 314
      Cmd. 7659, 492
      Cmd. 7921, 705
  Legislation, International Digest of, 659, 876
  Ministry of :
    Publications (N.P.), 67, 199, 358, 558, 779
    Reports :
      Cmd. 7119, 158
      Cmd. 7441, 313
      Cmd. 7734, 497
      Cmd. 7910, 704
  National. See National Health.
  of the Army, Statistical Report, 661
  of the School Child, Reports, 350, 541
  Service, Scotland, 398
  Statistics, Expert Committee on, Report, 876, 877
  Welsh Board of, Publications (N.P.), 69, 201, 361, 561, 782
  See also National Health ; Public Health.

Health, Welfare, and Safety in Non-Industrial Employment, Hours of Employment of Juveniles, Committee of Inquiry Report. Cmd. 7664, 493
Hearing :
  Aids and Audiometers, Report, 225
  Pupils who are defective in, Report. Cmd. 7866, 832
Hearmon, R. F. S. : Elasticity of Wood and Plywood, 391
Heat :
  and Power Linkage, 773
  Consumption, Effect of Variations in Output on, 772
  Costing. See Fuel.
  for Agriculture and Horticulture, 355
  Stroke Centre, Expeditionary Force General Hospitals, 438
Heating :
  and Ventilation, 117
  of Schools, Report, 264
  Domestic :
    by Solid Fuel, 827
    in America, Report, 66
    in Small Dwelling Houses, Gravity Warm Air System, 196
Heavy :
  Clothing, Working Party Report, 246
  Rain on Aircraft, Possible Effects of, 815
Heavy-oil Engines, 773
Hebden. See Cracoe.
Heighington Railway Accident Report, 850
Helmore, Air Commodore W. (Chairman) : Committee on Certification of Civil Aircraft and Approval of Equipment, Report. Cmd. 7705, 496
Helston and Porthleven Water Act, 174
Hemel Hempstead Development Corporation Report, 469, 476, 694
Hemsworth. See Pontefract.
Henderson, Sir H. D. (Chairman) : Royal Commission on Population : Economic Committee Report, 826 Memoranda, 826
Report. Cmd. 7695, 495
Heneage, Lt.-Col. Sir A. (Chairman) : Gathering Grounds Sub-Committee, Report, 359
Henry VI, Close Rolls, 223
Hensall Station Railway Accident Report, 634

INDEX 1946–50

Hepburn, H. A. (Chairman) :
  Conditions in Iron Foundries, Report by Joint Standing Committee on Practical Methods of reducing fumes from Oil Bonded Cores, 796
  Safety in the Use of Power Presses, Joint Standing Committee Report, 810
Herbert, Sir E. (Chairman) : Committee on Intermediaries. Cmd. 7904, 704
Herne Hill, Railway Accident Report, 418
Herring :
  Industry :
    Accounts, 15, 135, 281, 465, 679
    Board, Reports :
      Cmd. 6957, 45
      Cmd. 7284, 304
      Cmd. 7561, 322
      Cmd. 7762, 499
      Cmd. 7975, 709
  See also White Fish.
Hetherington, Sir H. J. W. (Chairman) : Port Transport Industry, Committee of Inquiry Report, 217
Hetherington, Sir R. (Chairman) : Civil Engineer's Panel of Engineering Committee, Technical Register, 811
Hey, M. H., Mineral Species and Varieties Index, 742
Hickling, C. F. : Recovery of a Deep Sea Fishery, 54
High :
  Court :
    and County Court Judges Act, 719
    Bill, 670, 697
    and Court of Appeal Accounts, 109, 249, 421, 639, 856
  Wycombe Corporation Act, 52
Higher :
  Agricultural Education, England and Wales. Cmd. 6728, 31
  Civil Service Remuneration, Report. Cmd. 7635, 491
  Education in the Colonies, Reports :
    Cmd. 7331, 306
    Cmd. 7801, 502
  National Certificates in Production Engineering, Award of, 350
  Training for the Police Service in England and Wales, Report. Cmd. 7070, 155
Highland Development, Programme of. Cmd. 7976, 709
Highway Code, 247

—HOF

Highways (Provision of Cattle Grids) Act, 179
  Bill, 671, 673, 697, 698, 699
Hill Farming :
  Act, 1946, 49
    Reprinted, 509
  Bill, 11, 27, 29
  Standing Committee Minutes, 22
  Bill, 1950, 699
Hill, Lt.-Col. F. G. : Departmental Committee on Deterioration of Cast Iron and Spun Iron Pipes, Interim Report, 780
Hill, J. B. : Geology of the Lizard and Meneage, 226
Hill, Sir R. : Air Operations by Air Defence of Great Britain and Fighter Command, 386
Hilliard, Nicholas, Exhibition, 260
Hinton, H. E. : Common Insect Pests of Stored Food Products, 742
Hire Purchase Act, 509
Historic Buildings. See Ancient Monuments.
Historical :
  Development of Private Bill Procedure and Standing Orders of the House of Commons, 514
  Manuscripts, Royal Commission on, 223
  Monuments, Royal Commission on, 609
  Museum of Register House, Edinburgh, guide, 603
History :
  of the Great War, 362, 568
  of the United Nations War Crimes Commission, 422
Hive, British National, 737
H.M. Ministers and Heads of Public Departments, 93, 232, 400, 616, 834
H.M. Submarines, Polish edition, 203
Hobday, S. R. (Chairman) : Rivers Pollution Prevention Sub-Committee Report, 561
Hobhouse, Sir A. :
  National Parks Committee, Report. Cmd. 7121, 158
  Special Report on Footpaths and Access to the Countryside. Cmd. 7207, 164
Hodgson, W. C. : Experiments on Cornish Pilchard Fishery in 1947–8, 739
Hodson, W. E. H. : Narcissus Pests, 54
Hoffert, W. H. (Chairman) : Benzole Technical Committee, Report, 355

HOG—   INDEX 1946–50

Hogging and Sacking Tests, Reports, 53, 332, 729
Hogsmill River. See Land Drainage.
Hokusai, 520
Holdings. See Agricultural Holdings.
Holidays with Pay Act, 509
Holland, Green Crop Drying, Report, 334
Holland, Sir Eardley (Chairman) : Council of Royal College of Obstetricians and Gynaecologists, Report on Family Limitation, 825
Holmes, Sir M. (Chairman) :
  British Caribbean Area Commission, Unification of Services Report, 749
  Civil Services of Kenya, Tanganyika, Uganda, and Zanzibar, Report, 344
  Secondary Schools Examinations Council Report, 191
Holmfirth Road Accident Report, 419
Holt, G. W. C. : Families and Genera of Living Rodents, 521
Holyroodhouse Abbey and Palace, 663
Home :
  Department, Scottish, Publications (N.P.), 92, 231, 399, 614, 832
  Guard, Pay, Pensions, etc. :
    Cmd. 6898, 41
    Cmd. 7696, 157
    Cmd. 7711, 496
    Information Services, Cost of, Report. Cmd. 7836, 505
  Office :
    Evidence submitted to Royal Commission on Justices of the Peace, 396
    Publications (N.P.), 69, 201, 361, 561, 782
    Schools, Directory of, 70
    Preservation of Eggs, 516
    Trade Register, Board of Trade Publications (N.P.), 102, 105
    Waters and North Eastern Atlantic, Weather in, 815
Homecraft, Further Education, 63, 64
Homeless Children, Report, 871
  Scotland. Cmd. 6911, 42
Homes :
  Modernising our, 229
  See also Approved Homes.
Honduras :
  British. See British Guiana ; British Honduras.
  Republic of, Commercial Conditions, 632
Honey Fungus, 354

Honey, W. B. : Glass Museum Collection, 113
Honeyman, G. G. :
  Building Regs., Revision Report, 369
  (Chairman), Wages Councils Acts Commission of Inquiry, Reports, 218, 382
Hong Kong :
  and Chinese Ports, Prevention of Smuggling, Exchange of Notes with China. Cmd. 7615, 490
  Colonial Reports, 343, 532, 749
  Despatches on Operations in, 384
  Film Strip, 751
  Picture Sets, 533
Honours, Decorations and Medals :
  Committee on Grant of, Reports :
    Cmd. 6833, 37
    Cmd. 7035, 153
    Cmd. 7254, 168
    Cmd. 7725, 497
    Cmd. 7878, 702
    Cmd. 7879, 702
    Cmd. 7907, 704
  River Yangtze Service. Cmd. 7813, 503
Hood, S. W. (Chairman) : Manufactured Meat Products Working Party Report, 761
Hopestar Wreck Report, 854
Hopkins, Sir Richard (Chairman) : Census of Distribution Committee, Report. Cmd. 6764, 33
Hops :
  Marketing Scheme, 739
  Red Spiders on, 333
  Reorganisation Commission for England, Report, 178
Horne, F. R. (Chairman) : Committee on Qualitative Control of Seeds, Report, 739
Horses :
  Docking and Nicking, Act, 511
    Bill, 456, 465, 482, 483
  Live, Export Licence, 845
Horticultural :
  Institutes, Report, 177
  Produce (Saleson Commission) Act, 722
Horticulture :
  Careers, 75
  See also Commercial Horticulture ; Agriculturists.
Hosiery :
  and Knitwear Trade, Proposals for Development, 415
  Working Party Report, 106

INDEX 1946–50

Hospital :
  Administration, Careers, 75
  Endowments Fund Account, 689
  Surveys, 67
  See also Scottish Hospitals.
Hospitals Directory, England and Wales, 599
Hostels, Select Committee on Estimates Reports, 476, 678
Hotel Industry, Catering Wages Commission Report. Cmd. 8004, 710
Hours :
  Closing of Shops, Report. Cmd. 7105, 157
  of Labour. See Time.
  of Work in the Principal Mining and Manufacturing Industries, Proposed Action by H.M. Government. Cmd. 7037, 156
House :
  Construction, 664
    New Methods of, 441, 883
  Design, 779
  Foundations on Shrinkable Clays, 827
  Letting and Rating (Scotland) Act, 325
  of Commons :
    Bills, 26, 147, 299, 483, 697
    Debates, 12, 23, 24, 26, 134, 144, 145, 147, 280, 294, 296, 298, 299, 462, 481, 681, 693, 694, 696, 697
    Historical Development of Private Bill Procedure and Standing Orders, 514
    (Indemnification of Certain Members) Act, 511
    Bill, 457, 486
    Journals, 13, 134, 280, 463
    Kitchen and Refreshment Rooms, Reports, 19, 140, 466, 686
    Library, Select Committee Reports, 13, 18
    Members' Fund. Cmd. 7282, 169
      Accounts, 15, 136, 284, 468, 683
      Act, 328
      Bill, 273, 300
    Select Committee Report, 142
    Statement on Financial Position, 21
    Model Clauses, 514, 727
    Papers, 13, 133, 279, 462, 676
    Procedure, Select Committee Reports, 13, 14

—HOU

House (continued) :
  of Commons (continued) :
    (Redistribution of Seats) Acts :
      1947, 172
      Bill, 13, 30, 122, 147
      1949, 511
      Bill, 446, 451, 486
    Sessional Printed Paper, 279, 280, 463, 680
    Standing :
      Committee Debates, 13, 14, 24, 25, 26, 134, 280, 293, 294, 295, 299, 463, 481, 482, 493, 681, 694, 696
      Orders, 131, 292, 294, 463
    Votes and Proceedings, 265
  of Laity (Co-opted Members) Measure, 727
  of Lords :
    Debates, 12, 13, 121, 131, 133, 267, 277, 278, 279, 462, 669, 675, 676
    Journal, 121, 277
    Manuscripts, 445
    Minutes of Proceedings, 278
    Model Clauses, 514, 727
    Offices, Select Committee Reports, 5, 7, 10, 11, 13, 124, 125, 130, 132, 270, 273, 277, 279, 451, 456, 460, 669, 674, 676
    Papers and Bills, 3, 121, 267, 445, 669
    Procedure, Select Committee Report, 126
    Standing Orders, 131, 276, 277, 280, 459
    Refuse, Removal of, 781
    Sparrow, 178
  House-building, Cost of, 358, 780
  Houseflies, Advisory Leaflet, 737
  Housefly, Economic Series, 742
  Household Textiles, Board of Trade Publications (N.P.), 103, 104, 243, 246, 416, 629, 631, 844
  Houses :
    for Owner-Occupation in Scotland, Report. Cmd. 6741, 31
    of outstanding historic or architectural importance, 857
    owned by local authorities in Scotland, Rents of. Cmd. 8046, 714
    Siting of, Notes, 841
    Structural Requirements for, 394
Housing :
  Accounts, 19, 138

Housing (continued) :
Act :
Accounts, 110, 421, 640, 857
See also Building Materials.
1914, 507
1949, 511
Bill, 454, 456, 473, 482, 484,
485, 487
Reprinted Act, 7, 24
Standing Committee Debates,
681
(Additional Powers) Act, 721
and Town and Country Planning
Bulletins, 648, 865
District Heating in American, 557
Estates, Appearance of, 358
Expenditure, Select Committee on
Estimates, Reports, 23, 134
(Financial)
and Miscellaneous Provisions)
Act, 49
Bill, 6, 26, 27, 28
Reports under the Act, 142,
291, 474, 685
Summary of the Act with
Explanatory Notes, 67, 69
Provisions) :
Act, 723
(Scotland) Act, 49
Bill, 7, 20, 26, 28
Reports under the Act,
142, 291, 474, 688
Handbook, Scottish, 779
in West Africa, Film Strip, 534
Index to Circulars, 200
Ireland Act, 326
Management :
Careers, 75, 207
in Scotland, Report. Cmd. 6901,
41
of Housing Estates, Report, 559
Manual, 559
Programme. Cmd. 7021, 152
Returns :
(England and Wales) ·
Cmd. 6744, 32
Cmd. 6766, 33
Cmd. 6807, 35
Cmd. 6825, 36
Cmd. 6845, 37
Cmd. 6870, 39
Cmd. 6889, 40
Cmd. 6910, 42
Cmd. 6940, 43
Cmd. 6960, 45
Cmd. 6997, 47

70

Housing (continued) :
Returns (continued) :
(England and Wales) (continued) :
Cmd. 7019, 152
Cmd. 7055, 154
Cmd. 7079, 156
Cmd. 7113, 158
Cmd. 7129, 159
Cmd. 7152, 161
Cmd. 7176, 162
Cmd. 7204, 164
Cmd. 7215, 165
Cmd. 7242, 167
Cmd. 7261, 168
Cmd. 7288, 170
Cmd. 7310, 305
Cmd. 7333, 306
Cmd. 7365, 308
Cmd. 7390, 310
Cmd. 7417, 312
Cmd. 7442, 313
Cmd. 7488, 317
Cmd. 7553, 321
Cmd. 7619, 490
Cmd. 7681, 494
Cmd. 7753, 499
Cmd. 7808, 503
Cmd. 7871, 701
Cmd. 7938, 706
Cmd. 7998, 710
Cmd. 8072, 716
Appendix B, 68, 200, 359, 560,
780
(Scotland). These Returns bear
the next Command Number to
the Return for England and
Wales in each case and are to be
found on the same pages.
(Rural Workers) Act, 171
(Scotland) Acts :
1949, 511
Bill, 457, 474, 482, 484, 486
1950, 719
Bill, 672, 674, 675, 681, 699
Table of Comparison. 778
Summary :
Cmd. 7507, 318
Cmd. 7526, 319
Cmd. 7569, 322
Cmd. 7594, 488
Cmd. 7640, 491
Cmd. 7663, 493
Cmd. 7701, 495
Cmd. 7723, 497
Cmd. 7769, 500
Cmd. 7782, 501

Housing (continued) :
Summary (continued) :
Cmd. 7833, 505
Cmd. 7855, 700
Cmd. 7889, 703
Cmd. 7919, 705
Cmd. 7963, 708
Cmd. 7981, 709
Cmd. 8025, 712
Cmd. 8056, 715
Cmd. 8092, 717
Systems for Flocks on Range, 516
Temporary, Programme. Cmd. 7304,
305
(Temporary Accommodation) Act,
173
Bill, 133, 150
Accounts, 286, 470, 679
Town Planning, Act, 47, 48
Housing Progress, 359, 559
Howe Corporation Act, 174
How :
Britain was fed in Wartime, 64
Glasshouse Growers can save fuel, 773
the United Nations began, 869
to buy :
Furniture, 363
Things for the kitchen, 363
to find out about the United Nations,
865
to look after a boiler plant, 773
Howitt, Sir Harold : Rhodesia Rail-
ways Ltd., Report, 62
H.R.H. Princess Elizabeth ·
Birth of a Princess, 812, 879
Birthday Anniversary, 261
Huddersfield :
Corporation Act, 513
Order Confirmation Act, 330
Bill, 274, 300
Hughes, G. : Papers and Discussions of
the Fifth International Conference of
Ship Tank Superintendents, 606
Hughes, R. Moelwyn :
Bolton Wanderers Football Ground
Disaster Report. Cmd. 6846, 38
(Chairman) :
Catering Wages Commission, Re-
port. Cmd. 7191, 163
Cotton Manufacturing Commis-
sion, Report, 578
Greater London Water Supplies,
Departmental Committee, Re-
port, 359
Hughes-Hallett, Capt. J. : Dieppe Raid,
220

71

Human :
Beings, Our Rights as, 867
Milk, Wartime Studies, 813
Performance, Research on the
Measurement of, Report, 813
Rights :
Commission on, Reports, 425,
426, 861, 862
International Bill of, 194
Universal Declaration. Cmd.
7662, 493
Yearbooks, 428, 653, 865
See also UNESCO.
Humidity, Averages of, for British
Isles, 595
Humphrys, Major H. J. (Chairman) :
Committee on Shotfiring in York-
shire, Report, 357
Explosion at Barnsley Main Colliery,
Report. Cmd. 7300, 305
Hungary :
Armistice Agreement. Cmd. 7280,
169
Draft Peace Treaty. Cmd. 6894,
40
Exchange of Notes amending the
Anglo-Hungarian Payments Agree-
ment. Cmd. 7892, 703
Interpretation of Peace Treaty, Advi-
sory Opinion, 792
Payments Agreement. Cmd. 6915, 42
Revival of Pre-war Treaties and
Agreements. Cmd. 7395, 310
Treaties of Peace :
Cmd. 7022, 152
Cmd. 7026, 153
Cmd. 7485, 316
Treaty of Peace Act, 172
Bill, 148
Hunt, F. W. (Chairman) : Jute Industry
Report, 76
Huntingtower Castle guide, 882
Hurcomb, Sir Cyril (Chairman) : Com-
mittee on Bird Sanctuaries in the
Royal Parks, Reports, 441, 663, 883
Hurst Castle, guide, 663
Husk or Hoose in Calves, 334
Hutcheson, Joseph (Chairman) : Euro-
pean Jewry and Palestine, Report.
Cmd. 6808, 35
Hutchinson, A. S. (Chairman) : Central
Fire Advisory Council Technical Com-
mittee, Report, 201
Hutson, L. W. (Chairman) : National
Brick Advisory Council Technical
Committee, Report, 263

HUX— INDEX 1946-50

Huxley, Dr. J. F. (Chairman) : Wild
Life Conservation Committee, Report.
Cmd. 7122, 159
Hybrid :
Bills (Procedure in Committee),
Select Committee on, Report, 292
Maize (Corn) in European Countries,
Report, 758
Hydro-Electric Development (Scotland) :
Accounts, 470, 688
Constructional Schemes Confirma-
tion Orders, 92, 231
Explanatory Memoranda :
Cmd. 6967, 45
Cmd. 7040, 154
Cmd. 7180, 163
Cmd. 7250-1, 167
Cmd. 7378, 309
Cmd. 7491, 317
Cmd. 7521, 319
Cmd. 7612, 489
Cmd. 7617-8, 490
Cmd. 7641, 491
Cmd. 7653, 492
Cmd. 7683, 494
Cmd. 7916, 704
Cmd. 7920, 705
Cmd. 7932, 706
Cmd. 8084, 717
Statements of Guarantee, 20, 140,
288, 685, 857

I

ICAO Circulars, 573, 791
Ice :
Charts :
Monthly, Arctic Seas, 815
Western North Atlantic, 84
Cream Sampling, 515
Iceland :
Air Services Agreement, Cmd. 7996,
710
Reciprocal Abolition of Visas :
Agreement. Cmd. 7159, 161
Extension of. Cmd. 7574, 323
Deletion of Singapore and Malaya
from list of territories covered.
Cmd. 8037, 713
Reykjavik Airfield :
Reversion to Icelandic Govern-
ment. Cmd. 6993, 47
Transfer to Icelandic Govern-
ment. Cmd. 6994, 47

72

Icy Roads, Chemical Treatment for, 227
Ideal Home Exhibition. See Housing
Progress.
Ideas for your Home, 788
Ilford Corporation (Drainage) Act, 726
Illicit Traffic in Narcotic Drugs, 424
Illumination :
Electric, 192
Research Technical Paper, 595
Imperial :
Agricultural Bureaux :
Annual Reports, 70, 202, 362
Conference Report. Cmd. 6971,
46
Calendar. See British Imperial Calen-
dar.
Defence Committee Publications
(N.P.), 70, 202, 362, 568
Economic Committee Publications
(N.P.), 363
Institute Publications (N.P.), 363,
568
Order of the Crown of India Awards,
219
Service Medal Awards, 219, 383, 384
Standards, Report on Comparisons,
844
War Graves Commission Publica-
tions (N.P.), 71, 203, 363, 568, 787
Import :
Control, More Consumer Goods, etc.,
freed, 844
Duties, Relaxation of, 630
Licensing Relaxations, 630
List, 62, 187
Restrictions, Accounts. See Debts
Clearing Offices.
Import, Export, and Customs Powers
(Defence) Act, 509
Importation of Animals Act, 507
Imported Food Regulations, 545
Impressions of Roads and Road Research
in North America, 227
Improved Methods for the Quantitative
Analysis of Coal Ash and Coke Ash,
629
Improving Marginal Land, 610
Inchcolm Abbey, guide, 882
Income :
and Expenditure of the U.K. Cmd.
7371, 309
Tax :
Act, 309, 724
and Finance Acts, Supple-
ments, 204, 364, 569, 788
Forms, 364

Income (continued) :
Tax (continued) :
and Death Duties on Woodlands,
65
Tables, 73, 204, 364
Wear and Tear Allowances for
Machinery or Plant, 788
See also Personal Incomes.
Increase :
in the length of full-time National
Service with the Armed Forces.
Cmd. 8050, 712
of Contributory Pensions Regs.,
Selected Decisions by the Umpire,
388
of Rent and Mortgage Interest Res-
trictions Act, 509
Increased Mechanisation in the United
Kingdom Ports, Working Party Re-
port, 849
Incubation, Artificial, 516
Incumbents (Discipline) Measure, 11,
175
(Amendment) Measure, 673, 743
Report, 673, 743
India :
Cabinet Mission :
Conference with Viceroy and
Representatives of the Con-
gress Party and Muslim League,
Correspondence and Docu-
ments. Cmd. 6829, 37
Congress Party and Muslim
League, Correspondence. Cmd.
6861, 39
Sikhs, Indian States, and Euro-
pean Community, Papers
relating to. Cmd. 6862, 39
Statement by Cabinet Mission
and the Viceroy. Cmd. 6821, 36
Statements replying to Pro-
nouncements by the Indian
Parties and Memorandum on
the States' Treaties and Para-
mountcy. Cmd. 6835, 37
(Central Government and Legisla-
ture) Act, 49
Bill, 4, 5, 27
Command Operations, 384
Commercial Conditions, 102
Compensation for Premature Termi-
nation of Services. Cmd. 7116,
158
(Consequential Provision) Act, 512
Bill, 462, 487
Economic Survey, 632

INDEX 1946-50 —IND

India (continued) :
Financial Agreement. Cmd. 7195,
164
Extensions :
Cmd. 7342, 307
Cmd. 7472, 316
Cmd. 7760, 499
Imperial Order of the Crown, Awards,
219
Office :
and Burma Office List, 71, 188,
303
Publications (N.P.), 71, 203
(Proclamation of Emergency) Act, 48
Bill, 4
Recapitulation of Terms and Assur-
ances given to Officers of the Civil
Services. Cmd. 7192, 163
Social Service, 71
Indian :
Independence Act, 172
Bill, 130, 149
Ocean :
Monthly Meteorological Charts,
814
Weather, 816
Policy :
Cmd. 7047, 154
Cmd. 7136, 159
Indictments Act, 326
Indies. See West Indies.
Indo-Burma Theatre Operations, 385
Indo-Pacific Fisheries Council, Estab-
lishment of :
Cmd. 7590, 324
Cmd. 7848, 505
Industrial :
Assurance :
and Friendly Societies Acts :
1948, 328
Bill, 150, 271, 273, 285,
295, 300, 301
1950, 722
Bill, 463
Statistical Summaries, 354, 554,
771
Reports of Selected Disputes, 770
Classification, Standard, 422
Coal Consumers Council Reports,
292, 475, 689
Court Awards, 210, 373, 580, 796
Courts, Reports of Courts of Inquiry :
Cmd 7025, 152
Cmd. 7036, 153
Cmd. 7097, 157
Cmd. 7511, 318

73

Industrial (continued) :
Design, Council of, Publications (N.P.), 71, 203, 363, 568, 787
Diseases, Report. *Cmd. 7557*, 321
Experimentation, 98, 238, 406, 620
Fibres, 345
Fluorosis, 603
Health Research Board Publications, 86, 234, 391, 603
Injuries :
Advisory Council Report on Tuberculosis in relation to Nurses and other Health Workers. *Cmd. 8093*, 820
Fund Accounts, 473, 687
See also National Insurance.
Lung Diseases of Iron and Steel Foundry Workers, 798
Organisation :
and Development Act, 173
Account, 696
Proposals, 415, 629
Bill, 127, 129, 147, 148, 149, 280
Opportunities in the Development Areas, 104
Production, Interim Index, 641
Productivity Reports :
Cmd. 7665, 493
Cmd. 7991, 710
Property Rights, Agreements for Preservation or Restoration :
Cmd. 7111, 158
Cmd. 7784, 501
Relations :
Handbook, 210, 373, 798
in Germany, 1945–9. *Cmd. 7923*, 705
Salvage and Recovery, 844
Use :
of Compressed Air, 773
of Liquid Fuel, 773
Waste Waters, Treatment and Disposal, 394
Wounds of the Hands, Infection and Sepsis in, 813
Industrialists' Reports. See German Industry ; German and Japanese Industry.
Industry :
and Commerce :
Careers, 208
Education for, 757
and Employment in Scotland :
Cmd. 7125, 159
Cmd. 7459, 315
Cmd. 7676, 494

Industry (continued) :
and Employment in Scotland (continued) :
Cmd. 7937, 706
See also Scots at Work.
Distribution of. *Cmd. 7540*, 320
Research in, 394
Infants' Utility Clothing, Board of Trade Publications (N.P.), 104, 105, 245, 415, 629, 844
Infection :
and Sepsis of Industrial Wounds of the Hands, 813
See also Salmonella.
Infectious Disease, Notification of, 200
Infertility in Cattle, 334
Infestation :
Control, Rats and Mice, 64
of Grain by Insects, 227
Inflationary and Deflationary Tendencies, 424, 648
Influence of Home and Community on Children under 13 Years of Age, 655
Information :
Central Office of :
Publications (N.P.), 71, 203, 363, 569, 788
Reports :
Cmd. 7567, 322
Cmd. 7830, 504
Cmd. 8081, 716
on Non-Self-Governing Territories, 344
Ingham Colliery, Thornhill, Explosion Report. *Cmd. 7434*, 313
Inglis, Professor Sir C. (Chairman) :
Railway (London Plan) Committee Reports, 108, 419
Inheritance (Family Provision) Act, 723
Initial Training of Volunteers, Civil Defence Corps, 783
Injuries. See Diseases ; Industrial Injuries ; National Insurance.
Inland :
Revenue :
Publications (N.P.), 71, 204, 364, 569, 788
Reports :
Cmd. 6769–74 inclusive, 33
Cmd. 7067, 155
Cmd. 7738, 498
Cmd. 7362, 308
Cmd. 8052, 714
Transport Committee, Agreement, 861
Insect Pests of Food, 193
See also Infestation of Grain.

Insecticides :
and Fungicides, Specifications and Methods of Analysis, 518
Expert Committee Report, 876
Insecticides, Fungicides, and Weedkillers, Precautions in use of, 737
Insects, Instructions for Collectors, 521
Inshore Fishing Industry Act, 48
Insignia of Orders, Decorations, and Medals and Medal Ribbons, Instructions regarding wearing, 661
Installation and Maintenance of Boiler House Instruments, 773
Institute of Journalists, Memorandum to Royal Commission on the Press, 228
Insulation of Furnaces, 772
Insurance :
Careers, 75, 368
Fund, Motor Vehicles, Agreement concerning Compulsory Insurances, 107
See also National Insurance ; Unemployment Insurance ; National Health Insurance.
Interconnected Power Systems in the U.S.A. and Western Europe, Report, 759
Interdepartmental Committee on Social and Economic Research Publications, 777
Intergovernmental Claims, Exchange of Notes with U.S.A. *Cmd. 7132*, 159
Intermediaries, Report of Committee.
Cmd. 7904, 704
Internal Financial Stability, 544, 759
International :
Advisory Social Welfare Services, 869
Arbitral Awards, Reports, 648, 865
Artistic and Scientific Activities, Convention with Belgium :
Cmd. 6841, 37
Cmd. 7002, 47
Bibliography of Translations, 872
Bill of Human Rights, 194
Bureau of Education Publications, 654, 871
Capital Movements during the Inter-War Period, 865
Cartels, League of Nations Memorandum, 424
Civil Aviation :
Protocol relating to Amendment to the Convention. *Cmd. 7202*, 164
Organisation, Publications, 366, 571, 790

International (continued) :
Code of Signals, Supplement, 850
Commodity :
Arrangements, Review, 428
Problems, Reviews, 649, 865
Conference on Safety of Life at Sea.
Cmd. 7492, 317
Conventions for the suppression of Traffic in Women and Children, 429
Co-operation at Work, 865
Court of Justice :
Publications, 207, 367, 575, 792
Statute. *Cmd. 7015*, 152
Criminal Jurisdiction, Historical Survey of the Question, 648
Digest of Health Legislation, 876
Economic Organisations (Transition from War to Peace), 194
Emergency Food Committee, Report, 435
Fellowships, 865
Health Conference, 111, 424, 436
Institute of Agriculture, Dissolution and Transfer. *Cmd. 7413*, 312
Investment Report, 759
Journal of Law and Legislation, 435
Labour :
Conference :
Proposals regarding Constitution of the International Labour Organisation. *Cmd. 6746*, 32
Proposed Action :
Cmd. 7626, 490
Cmd. 7703, 495
Cmd. 7704, 496
Cmd. 7865, 701
Cmd. 7956, 707
Cmd. 8070, 716
Reports :
Cmd. 6828, 36
Cmd. 7037, 153
Cmd. 7071, 155
Cmd. 7109, 158
Cmd. 7133, 159
Cmd. 7185, 163
Cmd. 7273, 169
Cmd. 7296, 304
Cmd. 7437, 313
Cmd. 7452, 314
Cmd. 7568, 322
Cmd. 7638, 491
Cmd. 7852, 700
Organisation :
Final Articles Revision Convention. *Cmd. 7516*, 319

International (continued) :
Labour (continued) :
Organisation (continued) :
Instruments for amending the Constitution :
Cmd. 6880, 40
Cmd. 7452, 314
Law Commission :
Publications, 647, 865
Ways and means of making evidence of customary International Law more readily available, 492
Meteorological Code, 387, 814
Military Tribunal Publications, 207, 367, 575
Monetary Fund and International Bank for Reconstruction and Development :
Articles of Agreement. *Cmd. 6885*, 40
Inaugural Meetings. *Cmd. 6800*, 35
Northwest Atlantic Fisheries Conference, Final Acts and Convention. *Cmd. 7658*, 492
Organisations (Immunities and Privileges) Act, 720
Bill, 671, 674, 698
Overfishing Conference :
Cmd. 6791, 34
Cmd. 7387 (Final Report), 310
Radio Regulations, 389
Refugee Organisation, Constitution of. *Cmd. 7934*, 706
Rice Commission :
Constitution :
Cmd. 7611, 489
Cmd. 8118, 718
Report, 873
Sanitary Convention :
for Aerial Navigation :
Modifications, Declarations by Egypt and France. *Cmd. 6999*, 47
Prolongation and Modification. *Cmd. 6944*, 44
Modifications, Declarations by Egypt and France. *Cmd. 6989*, 46
Prolongation and Modification. *Cmd. 6943*, 44
Social Science Bulletin, 654, 871
Statistical Classification of Diseases, Injuries, and Causes of Death, Manual of, 558, 776

International (continued) :
Status of South West Africa, Report, 792
Tax Agreements, 643
Telecommunication Convention and related documents. *Cmd. 7466*, 315
Temperature Scale of 1948, 829
Timber Conference, Report, 435
Whaling :
Conference. *Cmd. 7043*, 154
Convention :
Cmd. 7604, 489
Cmd. 6853, 506
Further Amendment to Schedule. *Cmd. 7918*, 705
Wheat Agreement :
Cmd. 7382, 309
Cmd. 7680, 494
Cmd. 7819, 514
Yearbook of Education, 654, 871
Interpolation and Allied Tables, 176
Interpretation Act, 324
Interpretership Examinations, 183, 185
Inter-Territorial Organisations in East Africa, Revised Proposals, 186
Intra-European Payments :
and Compensations, Agreements :
Cmd. 7546, 321
Cmd. 7812, 503
Supplementary Protocols :
Cmd. 7693, 495
Cmd. 8010, 711
Intrinsic Safety of Electrical Apparatus, Report, 357
Introducing the Colonies, 534
Invasion of Sicily, 812
Inventions. See Development.
Inventors, Awards to, 89
Royal Commission Reports :
Cmd. 7586, 323
Cmd. 7832, 504
Inverness :
Burgh Order Confirmation Acts :
1947, 174
Bill, 130, 149
1948, 330
Bill, 277, 302
County Council (Armadale Pier and Harbour, etc.) Order Confirmation Bill, 700
Water Order Confirmation Act, 51
Bill, 6, 27
Investigation into the Economics of Milk Production in Scotland, 396
Investigations on Building Fires, 829

Investment (Control and Guarantees) :
Bill, 26
Memorandum. *Cmd. 6726*, 31
See also Borrowing (Control and Guarantees).
Investments, Prevention of Fraud, 105
Ipswich :
Corporation :
Act, 331
(Trolley Vehicles) Order Confirmation Act, 51
Bill, 9, 28
Dock Act, 726
Iran, Economic Survey, 416
Iraq :
Economic Survey, 632
Financial Agreements :
Cmd. 7201, 164
Cmd. 7269, 169
Cmd. 7490, 317
Foreign Exchange Requirements :
Cmd. 6742, 31
Cmd. 6803, 35
Cmd. 7110, 158
Government Commission Inquiry into cause of Aircraft Accident near Az-Zubair, 338
Status of Diplomatic Mission in London. *Cmd. 6918*, 42
Treaty of Alliance. *Cmd. 7309*, 305
Iraq, Syria, the Lebanon, and Cyprus, Goodwill Trade Mission Report, 245
Ireland :
Act, 511
Bill, 453, 485, 486
See also Northern Ireland ; European Union.
Irish :
Free State :
(Agreement) Act, 326
(Consequential Provisions) Act, 171
Land :
Act, 170
Purchase Fund Accounts, 16, 138, 283, 465
Sailors' and Soldiers' Land Trust Accounts, 249, 421, 640, 857
Iron :
and Steel :
Act, 511
Bill, 299, 302, 452, 456, 457, 459, 460, 469, 482, 484, 485, 486, 487
Standing Committee Debates, 681
Statement of Guarantee, 692

Iron (continued) :
and Steel (continued) :
Committee, European Recovery Programme Interim Report, 544
Distribution, Notes for Consumers, 406
Goods, Open General Export Licence, 845
Industry, Reports. *Cmd. 6811*, 35
Ore, Resources and Utilisation, 870
Ironfoundries, Conditions in, 210
Ironstone Industry, Report. *Cmd. 6906*, 41
Irrigation, with notes on crops to which it is applicable, 178
Irvine, Sir J. C. (Chairman) : Inter-University Council, Report on Higher Education in the Colonies. *Cmd. 7801*, 502
Islamic Metalwork in the British Museum, 741
Isle of Man :
Aircraft Accident Report, 523
(Customs) Acts :
1946, 48, 49
No. 2 Bill, 10, 29
1947, 173
Bill, 131, 149
1948, 329
Bill, 277, 302
1949, 511
Bill, 458, 486
1950, 720
Bill, 673, 698
Harbours Act, 172
Bill, 13, 147
Israel :
Continuance in force of 1947 Arrangement for Avoidance of Double Taxation and Prevention of Fiscal Evasion with respect to Taxes on Income. *Cmd. 7912*, 704
Settlement of Financial Matters outstanding as a result of termination of the Mandate for Palestine. *Cmd. 7941*, 706
Italian :
Archives during the War and at its close, 179
Campaign, Reports, 115, 438
Convoy attacked, 385
Fleet :
Disposal of Excess Units :
Cmd. 7078, 156
Cmd. 7323, 306
Cmd. 7353, 307

Italian (continued) :
Fleet (continued) :
off Calabria, 384
Italy :
AirServicesAgreement.Cmd.7899,703
British Military Fixed Assets. Cmd.
7377, 309
Draft Peace Treaty. Cmd. 6892, 40
Financial Agreement. Cmd. 7118, 158
German Assets in, Memorandum.
Cmd. 7223, 165
Losses and Survivals of Works of Art
in the War, 56
Military Operations, 568
Mutual Abolition of Visas :
Cmd. 7295, 304
Extension. Cmd. 7578, 323
Singapore and Federation of
Malaya deleted from list of
Territories covered. Cmd. 8083,
713
Protocol relating to the Restitution
of Monetary Gold. Cmd. 7298, 304
Recruitment of Italian :
Skilled Workers for Employment
in Kenya, Agreement. Cmd.
7525, 319
Workers for Employment in
Foundries in U.K., Agreement.
Cmd. 7168, 162
Return of Gold Captured by the
Allied Forces. Cmd. 7244, 167
Revival of Pre-War Treaties and
Agreements :
Cmd. 7395, 310
Cmd. 7943, 706
Settlement of Debts due to Italy
under Anglo-Italian Clearing
Agreement. Cmd. 7518, 319
Sterling Payments Agreement. Ex-
changes of Notes :
Cmd. 7587, 324
Cmd. 7775, 500
Cmd. 7877, 702
Cmd. 8014, 711
Cmd. 8024, 712
Cmd. 3333, 717
Treaties of Peace :
Cmd. 7022, 152
Cmd. 7026, 153
Treaty of Peace Act, 172
Bill, 148
Withdrawal of British Forces and
Transfer of Responsibility, Agree-
ment. Cmd. 7158, 161
See also European Union.

Items and Units, Definitions of, 422
Itshide Rubber Company, Explosion
Report. 632
Izard, C. G. (Chairman) : Staffing Advi-
sory Committee, Report, 388

J

Jackson, E. J. W. : (Chairman) : Youth
Leaders and Community Centre War-
dens Committee, Report, 543
Jackson, H. : South Wales Outline
Plan, 622
Jacob, G. H. Lloyd (Chairman) : Retail
Price Maintenance Committee, Re-
port. Cmd. 7696, 495
Jamaica :
Colonial Reports, 343, 531, 749
See also British West Indies.
James Clunies Wreck Report, 854
Jameson, Sir W. (Chairman) : Expert
Committee on Psychologists and Psy-
chiatrists in the Services, Report, 223
Japan :
Sea and Adjacent Waters, Sea Sur-
face Temperatures and Surface
Currents, 815
Textile Mission to, Report, 105
See also Soviet Union.
Japanese :
Economy, 415
Industry, Reports. See German and
Japanese Industry.
Larch in Great Britain, Revised
Yield Tables, 553
Jarrow Boundary Commission Report.
Cmd. 8100, 718
Java Sea, Battle of, 385
Jenkins, Rt. Hon. Lord Justice (Chair-
man) : Leasehold Committee Report.
Cmd. 7982, 709
Jenkinson, H. : Italian Archives during
the War and at its close, 179
Jersey and Guernsey (Financial Provi-
sions) Act, 173
Bill, 132, 150
Jerusalem City Plan, 389
Jewellery and Silverware :
Industry, Proposals for Development
Council, 415
Working Party Report, 198
Jewish Community in Palestine, System
of Education, Report, 61

Jobson, M. (Chairman) : Homes Com-
mittee of Scottish Advisory Council on
Child Care, Report, 832
John, D. D. : Notes on Asteroids in the
British Museum (Natural History),
742
John Murray Expedition, Scientific Re-
ports, 742
Johnson, F. C. (Chairman) : Witnesses
Allowances Order, Report, 202
Johnson, N. K. : Professional Notes,
387
Johnstone, Katherine H. : Commercial
Flower Production, 54
Joint :
Consultation, Training within Indus-
try, Works Information and Per-
sonnel Management Conference,
Report, 373
Objective Intelligence Agency, Re-
ports on German Industry, 103
Joint-ill in Young Lambs, 738
Jolly, J. C. : Inquiry Reports :
John Elliott. Cmd. 6933, 43
Proposed Compulsory Amalgama-
tion of Police Forces of Cheshire
and Chester, 564
Ware Case. Cmd. 7049, 154
Jones, Mr. Justice A. (Chairman) :
County Courts Committee, Reports :
Cmd. 7468, 315
Cmd. 7668, 493
Jones, Sir C. (Chairman) : Geologists
Sub-Committee, Technical Register,
593
Jones, C. Bryner (Chairman) : Welsh
Agricultural Land Sub-Commission,
Report on Malltraeth Marsh, 739
Jones, Sir C. W. (Chairman) : West
Indian Shipping Services, Report, 346
Jones, E. W. K. : Setting Behaviour of
Larvae of the European Flat Oyster,
etc., 518
Jones, F. E. : Weathering Tests on
Asbestos Cement Roofing Materials,
225
Jones, J. H. : Report on Road Acci-
dents, 108
Jones, Dr. J. W. : Studies of the scales
of young salmon in relation to growth,
migration, and spawning, 518
Jones, N. H. (Chairman) : Wool Textile
Industry, Committee Reports, 218,
593
Jones, R. C. B. : Geology of Southport
and Formby, 393

Jones, Professor W. R. (Chairman) :
Ball-clay Industry, Inquiry Report,
102
China Clay, Working Committee Re-
port. Cmd. 6748, 32
Journalism and Publishing, Careers, 75,
208, 793
Journalists :
National Union of (Royal Commis-
sion on the Press), 228
Professional Training of, 872
See also Institute of Journalists.
Judges Pensions (India and Burma) Act,
329
Bill, 279, 303
Judgments, Advisory Opinions, and
Orders (International Court of Jus-
tice), 367, 575, 792
Judicature. See Supreme Court.
Juries Act, 510
Bill, 303, 448, 449, 450, 484
Jurors. See Elections and Jurors.
Justice. See Criminal Justice ; Law and
Justice.
Justices :
of the Aberayron Division, Report of
Inquiry. Cmd. 7061, 155
of the Peace :
Act, 719
Royal Commission on :
Evidence, 89, 227, 396
Report. Cmd. 7463, 315
Jute :
Commodity Report, 873
Industry :
Factory Advisory Committee Re-
port, 76
in Germany, 1939-45, 623
Working Party, Report, 416
Juvenile :
Delinquency, Memorandum on, 563
Employment Executive Memoran-
dum, 208

K

Kapiti Phonolites and Kenytes in
Kenya Colony, 742
Kathiri State Arms, 186
Kauffman, Henrik (Chairman) : Econo-
mic and Social Council, Special Tech-
nical Committee Report on Relief
NeedsafterterminationofUNRRA, 252

Keen, Dr. B. A. :
Agricultural Development in the
Middle East, 106
(Chairman) : Vegetable Oil and Oil
seed produced in the West African
Colonies, Report, 186
Kellaway, B. A. : British Regional
Geology, 393
Kenilworth Castle, guide, 440
Kent, Proposed new Constituencies :
Cmd. 7397, 310
Cmd. 7425, 312
Kent, Surrey, Sussex, and Middlesex,
Saxton's Maps, 741
Kenya :
added to Lists of Territories covered
by Visa Abolition Agreements :
Cmd. 7847, 505
Cmd. 7964, 706
Bus Driver, Film Strip, 534
Colonial Reports, 343, 531, 749
Colony and Protectorate, Report on
Native Affairs, 344
Economic Survey, 416
Recruitment of Italian Skilled
Workers for employment in. Cmd.
7525, 319
Report on Civil Service, 344
Water Resources, Report, 533
Kenya–Ethiopia Boundary Agreement.
Cmd. 7374, 309
Kerbs, Concrete, Causes and Preven-
tions of Failures, 830
Kew Bulletin, 75, 207, 368, 576, 822
Key Industry Duty, Notes, 344
Kidwelly Castle, guide, 117
Kielder, Britain's Forests, 769
Kilbride. See East Kilbride.
Killick, Brigadier A. H. (Chairman) :
Building and Quantity Surveyors'
Panel, Building and Civil Engineers
Committee Technical Register, 811
King and Queen, Their Majesties' Silver
Wedding Anniversary, 440
King George III Collection of Scientific
Instruments, Handbook, 542
King, J. G. : Extraction of Ester Waxes
from British Lignite and Peat, 87
King's Regulations, etc. :
Admiralty Instructions, 53, 176, 332,
515, 728
Air Council Instructions, 56, 179,
336, 520, 740
Army and Army Reserve, 115, 262,
438, 661, 880
Women's Royal Air Force, 740

Kingsley, Mary, 363
Kingston-upon-Hull Order Confirmation
Act, 174
Bill, 128, 148
Kinnear, S. A. (Chairman) : Committee
of Scottish Police Council, Report on
Police Uniform, 615
Kirby Hall, guide, 263
Kirkby Aircraft Accident Report, 180
Kirkcaldy Burgh Extension, etc., Order
Confirmation Bill, 675, 699
Kirkenes and Petsamo, Carrier-Borne
Aircraft Attack, 385
Kirkham Priory, guide, 117
Kirkwall, Earl's Palace, guide, 440
Kitchen and Refreshment Rooms Re-
ports. See House of Commons.
Knackers' Yard Order, 545
Knight, R. A. G. : Requirements and
Properties of Adhesives for Wood, 87,
828
Knitted Apparel and Knitted Goods,
Board of Trade Publications (N.P.),
101, 105, 415, 630, 631, 845
Knitwear. See Hosiery.
Knoydart Estate, Report, 610
Korea :
and the United Nations, 865
Summary of events relating to, 1950.
Cmd. 8078, 716
United Nations Commissions, Re-
ports, 428, 646, 647, 865, 866

L

Labelling of Food Order, 760
Laboratories, Chemical, Safety Measures
in, 607
Laboratory :
Methods for work with plant and soil
nematodes, 518
of the Air, 406
Services, Report, 229
Labour :
and National Service, Ministry of :
Publications (N.P.), 75, 207, 368,
576, 793
Reports :
Cmd. 7225, 165
Cmd. 7559, 322
Cmd. 7825, 304
Cmd. 8017, 712
Conference. See International Labour
Conference.

Labour (continued) :
Gazette, 76, 216, 373, 569, 790
Party, Evidence to Royal Commis-
sion on Justices of the Peace, 396
Statistics, 390, 777
See also East Africa.
Lace, Working Party Report, 246
Lace, Lace Net, and Woven Curtain Net,
Board of Trade Publications (N.P.),
101, 242, 409, 410, 623, 841
Lace, etc. : East African Rice Mission
Report, 534
Ladder, Hand-operated Turntable,
Instruction Book, 565
Lagging hot and cold water systems in
houses, 881
Laidlaw, C. P. (Chairman) : Scottish
Building Costs Committee, Report, 398
Lambert, M. : Documents on British
Foreign Policy, 761
Lambs :
Swayback in, 334
Young, Joint-ill in, 738
Lamington Railway Accident Report,
418
Lamps. See Safety Lamps.
Lancashire :
Electric Power Special Order, 66
See also Cheshire and Lancashire.
Lancaster, Duchy of, Evidence sub-
mitted to Royal Commission on
Justices of the Peace, 396
Lancum, F. H. : Wild Birds and the
Land, 335
Land :
Campaign in North Africa, 203
Charges Forms, 359
Drainage :
(Scotland) :
Act, 171
Committee Report. Cmd.
7948, 707
(Surrey County Council) (Hogs-
mill River Improvement)
(Amendment) Order Confirma-
tion Act, 726
Bill, 670, 697
Fertility (Research) Fund Accounts
Report, 14, 135, 281, 297, 479,
690, 739
Fund, National, Account, 286
Purchase Account, Northern Ireland,
182, 284, 476, 667
See also Irish Land Purchase.
Registration in Scotland, Report.
Cmd. 7451, 354

Land (continued) :
Registry Publications (N.P.), 82, 218,
383, 593, 811
Settlement (Facilities) Act, 326
Transport, Handbook, 192, 542
See also Acquisition of Land.
Landlord and Tenant (Rent Control)
Act, 511
Bill, 303, 119, 150, 152, 152, 494, 495
Landlords, Tenants, and Occupiers of
Agricultural Land, Rights and Obliga-
tions, 333, 517
Lands :
Tribunal Act, 511
Bill, 450, 454, 484, 485
See also Crown Lands.
Langleecrag Wreck Report, 636
Langley, Brigadier C. A. : Railway
Accident Reports, 247, 418, 419, 634,
635, 850, 851
Larch :
Canker, 354
European, General Volume Tables, 769
Japanese, Revised Yield Tables, 553
Lass o' Doune, Wreck Report, 249
Latent Heat, Sensible Use of, 772
Lateral Deviation of Radio Waves
reflected at the Ionosphere, 606
Latin America :
Agricultural Requisites, Report, 865
Economic :
Commission for, 653
Development, 865
Survey, 1948, 865
Laundry Facilities. See Communal
Laundry Facilities.
Law :
Air Force, Manual of, 336
and Legislation, International Jour-
nal, 435
Careers, 75
German, Manual of, 764
Military, Manual of, 439
ofDefamation, Report. Cmd.7536,320
ofProperty(Amendment)Acts,171,327
Officers' Department Publications
(N.P.), 82, 219, 383, 593, 811
Reform :
(Frustrated Contracts) Act, 509
(Miscellaneous Provisions) Acts :
1934, 508
1949, 512
Bill 456, 459, 460, 461,
471, 482, 483, 487
Standing Committee
Debates, 681

Law (continued) :
Reform (continued) :
(Personal Injuries Act), 328
Bill, 132, 133, 151, 274, 289, 295, 301
Standing Committee Debates, 463, 485
See also Military Law.
Laws. See Expiring Laws ; Temporary Laws.
Laying :
of Documents before Parliament (Interpretation) Act, 329
Bill, 276, 302
of Linoleum upon Concrete Floors, 394
Screeds as an underlay for floor coverings, 882
Layton, Vice-Admiral Sir G. : Loss of H.M.S. Prince of Wales and Repulse, 384
Lead :
Economy Memorandum, 441
Paint (Protection against Poisoning) Act, 722
League of Nations Mandates, Terms of, 112
Leake, J. P. : Boiler Explosion Report, 417
Leasehold :
Committee Report. Cmd. 7982, 709
Property :
(Repairs) Act, 723
(Temporary Provisions) Bill, 699
Lease-lend, etc. Settlements :
Cmd. 6778, 33
Cmd. 6813, 36
Leather :
Bookbindings, Preservation of, 741
Manufacturing and related industries in Germany, 1939-45, 841
Substitutes for, A study of, 98
Lebanon :
Deletion from French Franc Area Territories. Cmd. 8075, 716
Goodwill Trade Mission Report, 215
Settlement of Pending Cases before the Lebanese Mixed Courts. Cmd. 7154, 161
Lecturers and Teachers, guide, 428
Lee, A. G. (Chairman) : Staffing Advisory Committee, Absorption of Staffs of Approved Societies, 221
Lee, A. R. : Types of Road Surfacing and Maintenance using Tar or Asphaltic Bitumen, 394

Lee Conservancy :
Board, Statement of Guarantee, 281
Catchment Board Act, 726
Leeds :
City of, Boundary Commission Report. Cmd. 8100, 718
Order Confirmation Act, 174
Bill, 128, 148
Leeks, 737
Leeward Islands, Colonial Reports, 534, 741
Legal :
Aid :
and Advice Act, 511
Bill, 303, 454, 470,482,484,485
Standing Committee Debates, 681
Summary of the proposed new service. Cmd. 7563, 322
and Legal Advice in Scotland, Report. Cmd. 6925, 43
and Solicitors (Scotland) Act, 511
Bill, 303, 454, 470, 482, 487
Standing Committee Debates, 681
Explanatory Memorandum. Cmd. 7562, 322
Scheme (Scotland), 832
under the Legal Aid and Advice Act, 813
Commission, ICAO, Minutes and Documents, 791
Committee, ICAO, Minutes and Documents, 366, 574, 791
Legitimacy Acts, 327, 722
Leicester, Report of Abandonment, 637
Leicestershire and Rutland County Police Proposed Compulsory Amalgamation, Report, 783
Leith Harbour and Docks Order Confirmation Act, 726
Bill, 673, 698
Lemon, Sir E. (Chairman) : Standardisation of Engineering Products, Report, 621
Leprosy, 363
Letchworth and District Electricity Special Orders, 196, 355
Letters, Despatches, and State Papers relating to negotiations between England and Spain, Calendar of, 822
Lettuces, Recommended grade for, 518
Leucotomy. See Pre-frontal Leucotomy.
Lewis, Mr. Justice (Chairman) : Army and Air Force Court-Martial Committee, Report. Cmd. 7608, 489

Lewis, W. A. : Damage to roads caused by drought, 1947, 607
Lewis-Faning, E. : Family Limitation and its influence on human fertility,825
Leyton Corporation Act, 726
Liberal Party, Evidence to Royal Commission on Justices of the Peace, 396
Liberating World Trade, 865
Liberation of Europe, 220
Liberties of the Subject Bill, 671
Librarianship :
Careers, 75, 208, 577
Education for, 871
Libraries, UNESCO Publications, 260, 433, 654, 872
Library :
United Nations Publications, 429, 648, 865
See also Public Library.
Libya, Report of the United Nations Commissioner in, 865
Licences, 845
Licensing :
Acts :
1921, 171
1949, 511
Bill, 303, 453, 456, 457, 459, 469, 482, 484, 485, 486
Standing Committee Debates, 861
(Amendment) (Tied Houses) Bill, 483
Authorities :
for Goods Vehicles, Report, 851
for Public Service Vehicles, Reports, 633
Planning (Temporary Provisions) Act, 49
Bill, 6, 28
Circular, 101
Statistics Annual Return Forms, 69, 202, 361, 563
Lichfield Railway Accident Report, 108
Life Saving Appliances, Instructions as to Survey, 418
Lifeboat Portable Radio Equipment Performance Specification, 821
Lighting of Houses and Flats, 227
Lilienthal, D. E. (Chairman) : Committee on Atomic Energy, Report, 64
Lime in Agriculture, Use of, 334
Limes for Mortar, 882
Limestones of Scotland, 606
Limitation :
of Actions, Report. Cmd. 7740, 498
of Supplies, Board of Trade Publications (N.P.), 105, 245, 415

Lincolnshire and East Yorkshire, Geology of, 393
Lindisfarne Priory, guide, 663
Lindsay of Birke, Lord (Chairman) : Interdepartmental Committee Report, Expenses of Members of Local Authorities. Cmd. 7126, 159
Line Communication, Royal Signals, Handbook, 440, 881
Linen. See Cotton ; Utility Apparel Cloth.
Linlithgow Palace, guide, 440
Linoleum, Working Party Report, 246
Linseed and Flax, Weed Control in, 556
Liquid Fuel, Industrial Use of, 773
Lisbon. See Portugal.
Littlehampton Railway Accident Report, 850
Liver Rot in Sheep, 334
Liverpool :
Langton Dock Boiler Explosion Report, 633
Lime Street Station, Railway Accident Report, 850
(Speke) Airport, Accident Report, 180
(Walton) Boundary Commission Report. Cmd. 8100, 718
Livestock :
and Meat, 434, 656
Rations for, 334
Livingstone, David, 363
Lizard and Meneage, Geology of, 226
Llawhaden Castle, guide, 263
Lloyd, T. A. : South Wales Outline Plan, 622
Loadsheet, M.C.A. Form, 525
Loan :
Agreements :
Belgium. Cmd. 7811, 503
Export-Import Bank of Washington :
Cmd.:7550, 321
Cmd. 7636, 491
Cmd. 7881, 702
Cmd. 8053, 714
to Burma. Cmd. 8007, 711
Loans :
Sanctioning of, 780
See also Local Loans.
Local :
and Personal Acts, 512, 725
and Private Acts, 50, 173, 329
Authorities, Expenses of Members. Cmd. 7126, 159

Local (continued) :
Education Authorities, List, 350
Government :
Acts :
1894, 47
1948, 328
Bill, 150, 268, 269, 280, 283, 295, 299, 300
Part I. Cmd. 7253, 167
Part II. Cmd. 7256, 168
1949, 508
Bill, 463
Boundary Commission :
(Dissolution) Act, 512
Bill, 460, 486
Practice Notes, 48, 219
Reports, 139, 285, 472
Careers, 368
Financial :
Provisions :
Act, 48
Bill, 3
(Scotland) Act, 48
Bill, 4, 14
Statistics, 68, 200, 359, 560, 781
(Ireland) Act, 326
Manpower Committee Report. Cmd. 7870, 701
Methods used in British Zone of Germany. Cmd. 7804, 502
Publicity for, Report, 782
(Scotland) Act, 172
Bill, 12, 123, 128, 131, 149
Explanatory Memorandum. Cmd. 7068, 155
Memorandum on Procedure, 613
(Scotland) Bill, 1950, 695, 696, 699, 786
Service, Careers, 208
Land Charges Forms, 68, 200, 359, 560
Loans Fund Accounts, 16, 137, 285, 467, 678
Revenues, Exchequer Contributions, Estimates, 137, 284, 466, 682
Locust, 363
See also Red Locust.
Locusts, International Convention for Permanent Control of Outbreak Areas. Cmd. 7783, 501
Lofoten Islands, Raid on Military and Economic Objectives, 385
Log Book, Variable Pitch Propellor, 525

London :
Airport, 181, 339
Aircraft Accident Report, 337, 338
Construction of, Estimates, Select Committee Reports, 293, 468
Ground Traffic Movement, 745
and North Eastern Railway :
Act, 175
Order Confirmation Act, 173
Bill, 12
and Thames Valley, British Regional Geology, 256
Area Passenger Charges Scheme, 853
Bridge Station, Railway Accident Reports, 418, 850
Building (Amendment) Act, 727
Clay at Lower Swanwick, 521
Conference Tripartite Talks. Cmd. 7977, 709
County Council :
(General Powers) Acts, 175, 331, 725
Improvements Act, 330
(Money) Acts, 51, 174, 331, 531, 726
Woolwich Subsidences Act, 726
Gazette, 82, 219, 383, 593, 812
Government Act, 720
Bill, 673, 698
Master Printers Association and the London Society of Compositors, Report of Court of Inquiry. Cmd. 8074, 716
Necropolis Act, 51
Passenger Transport Act, 175
Plan, Working Party Report, 633
Planning Administration Committee Report, 622
Post Offices and Streets, 223, 389, 821
Regional Planning, Advisory Committee Report, 101
Traffic (Annual Reports),418, 633, 850
Transport Stock, Statement of Guarantee, 281
London, Midland, and Scottish Railway :
Acts :
1946, 51
1947, 174
Order Confirmation Act, 51
Bill, 8, 28
Long :
Leases (Temporary Provisions) (Scotland) Bill, 700
Service Medal, 262

Long, A. J. (Chairman) : Report of Inquiry into fire at premises of A. Harris & Co. Ltd., Richmond. Cmd. 7440, 313
Long Eaton Urban District Council Act, 51
Long-eared Owl and Short-eared Owl, 737
Longthorpe Tower, Peterborough, guide, 663
Loop Aerial Correction Curve, 67
Lord :
Chancellor's Department, Publications (N.P.), 83, 220, 386, 594, 813
High Commissioner (Church of Scotland), Act, 328
Bill, 272, 299
Lords Spiritual and Temporal, Roll of, 12, 131, 278, 669, 675
Loss of Employment (Compensation) Bill, 483
Lothian Homes Trust, 92
Lotteries. See Betting.
Loughborough Railway Accident Report, 634
Louisa Colliery Explosion Report. Cmd. 7347, 307
Louping Ill in Sheep, 334
Loveday, Dr. T. (Chairman) : Advisory Committee on Agricultural Education, Reports :
Agricultural and Horticultural Institutes, 177
Agriculturists and Domestic Producers, Part-time Instruction, 517
Higher Agricultural Education in England and Wales. Cmd. 6728, 31
Lovell, R. A. : Road Accident Report, 419
Low Temperature Carbonisation, 606
Lucas, Lord : Working of the Agricultural Marketing Acts, Report, 178
Lucerne, 178
Lugard, Frederick, 363
Lulworth, Geology of the country around, 226
Lunacy :
Acts, 324, 506
and Mental :
Deficiency, Reports, 22, 142
Treatment, Reports, 296, 476
Lunson, E. A. : Sand Storms on the Northern Coasts of Libya and Egypt, 815
Luton Corporation Act, 174

Luxembourg :
Commercial Air Service, Reciprocal Facilities for the operation of, Agreement. Cmd. 7445, 314
Cultural Convention with U.K. Cmd. 8013, 711
Economic Survey, 416
International Authority for Ruhr, Agreement. Cmd. 7685, 494
Money and Property subjected to Special Measures, Agreement. Cmd. 7023, 152
Reciprocal Abolition of Visas :
Agreement. Cmd. 7059, 155
Extension. Cmd. 7579, 323
Singapore and Federation of Malaya deleted from list of Territories covered. Cmd. 8039, 713
Social Security Convention with U.K. Cmd. 7911, 704
See also Belgium ; •European Union.
Lydford Castle, guide, 233
Lyle, O. : Efficient Use of Steam, 355
Lynn, C. W. : Agricultural Extension and Advisory Work, with special reference to the Colonies, 531
Lynskey, Sir G. J. (Chairman) : Tribunal to inquire into allegations reflecting on the official conduct of Ministers of the Crown and other Public Servants :
Evidence, 564
Report. Cmd. 7616, 490

M

(Note.—For alphabetical purposes, all forms and contractions of the prefix " Mac " are treated as if they were in fact spelled " Mac ".)

MacBrayne, David, Ltd. : Agreement for maintenance of certain transport services in Western Highlands and Islands of Scotland, 141
McCaig's, Catherine, Trust Amendment Scheme, 231
McCance, R. A. : Medical Research Council Publications, 86
McClelland, W. (Chairman) : Advisory Council on Education in Scotland, Reports on Children who are defective in :
Hearing. Cmd. 7866, 701
Vision. Cmd. 7885, 702

Macclesfield Order Confirmation Acts :
  1948, 330
    Bill, 274, 301
  1950, 513
    Bill, 457
McDonald, T. P. : Aircraft Accident
  Report, 523
Macgregor, A. G. :
  and Macgregor, M. : British Regional
    Geology, 393
  Geology of Central Ayrshire, 829
MacGregor, A. S. M. (Chairman) : Scien-
  tific Advisory Committee, Reports :
  Control of Midges, 397
  Neo-Natal deaths due to Infection,
    229
  Tuberculous Meningitis treated with
    Streptomycin, 613
Machine Tools, 759
  Export Licence, 845
Machinery :
  and Equipment, Export Availabili-
    ties and Delivery Periods, 759
  or Plant, Income Tax Wear and Tear
    Allowances, 788
Machines :
  and Appliances in Government
    Offices, 249
  for the Modern Builder, 833
Mackworth, N. H. : Researches on the
  measurement of Human Performance,
  813
McManaway, Rev. J. G., Order in
  Council. Cmd. 8067, 715
MacMichael, Sir H. : Reports on :
  Malaya, 61
  Malta, 186
Macmillan, Rt. Hon. H. P. B. (Chair-
  man) : Court of Investigation into
  Tudor IV Aircraft Accident, Report.
  Cmd. 7517, 319
Macmillan, Lord (Chairman) : Land
  Registration in Scotland, Report.
  Cmd. 7451, 314
McMullen, Col. D. : Railway Accident
  Reports, 634, 635, 850
McNair, Sir Arnold (Chairman) : Com-
  mission of Inquiry on System of Edu-
  cation of Jewish Community in
  Palestine, Report, 61
McNair, W. : Civil Aircraft Accident
  Report, 744
McNee, Professor J. W. (Chairman) :
  Scientific Advisory Committee :
  Cerebro-Spinal Fever, Report, 229
  Diphtheria, Report, 397

Maconochie, R. H. (Chairman) : Com-
  mittee on Poaching and Illegal Fishing
  of Salmon and Trout in Scotland.
  Cmd. 7917, 704
Madagascar, Defence of, Agreement
  with France. Cmd. 6986, 46
Maes Howe, Orkney, guide, 440
Magdalena, Wreck Report, 637
Maggot, Sheep, 178
Mahoganies and Allied Timbers, 392
Maids' Underwear, Utility, Board of
  Trade Publications (N.P.), 104
Maidstone Corporation (Trolley Vehicles)
  Order Confirmation Act, 51
  Bill, 9, 28
Maintenance :
  of Full Employment, and Analysis,
    648
  on Industrial Boiler Plant, 773
  Orders Act, 720
    Bill, 483, 669, 670, 673, 688, 694,
      697, 698, 699, 786
Maize. See Grain Crops.
Major :
  Economic Changes in 1948, 48
  War Criminals. See War Criminals.
Making Citizens, 69
Malaria :
  British Commonwealth Leaflet, 363
  Control, WHO Bulletin, 658
  Expert Committee Report, 876
  Film Strip, 534
Malaya :
  Air Operations during Campaigns in
    Malaya and Netherlands East
    Indies, 384
  and Borneo :
    Film Strip, 534
    Picture Set, 533
  and Singapore, Labour and Trade
    Union Organisation in, Report, 534
  Awards, 812
  Colonial Report, 749
  Cultivation of Cocoa, Report, 344
  Federation of :
    Constitutional Proposals. Cmd.
      7171, 162
    Deletion from list of Territories
      covered by Visa Abolition
      Agreement. Cmd. 8036–43,
      713, 714
    Honours, Decorations and Medals for
      Service in. Cmd. 7907, 704
    Mission to, Report, 61
    Operations in Malaya Command, 384
    Rubber-growing Smallholdings, 345

Malaya (continued) :
  Trade and Payments with Singapore
    and Netherlands Indies. Cmd.
    7487, 317
  University Education Commission
    Report, 344
Malayan :
  Rubber, Picture Sets, 750
  Union :
    and Singapore :
      Statement of Policy on Future
        Constitution. Cmd. 6724, 30
      Summary of proposed Con-
        stitutional Arrangements.
        Cmd. 6749, 32
    Colonial Report, 532
Male Nursing, Careers, 208
Malltraeth Marsh Investigation Report,
  739
Malta :
  Constitutional Reform, Statement of
    Policy. Cmd. 7014, 152
  Finances of the Government of, Re-
    port, 61
  Financial and Economic Assistance,
    Recent Requests for, 534
  Reconstruction Act, 172
    Bill, 30, 122
  Report on, 186
  Works of Art in, Losses and Sur-
    vivals in the War, 56
Maltby, Air Vice-Marshal Sir P. : Air
  Operations during campaigns in
  Malaya and Netherlands Indies, 384
Maltby, Maj.-Gen. C. M. : Operations in
  Hong Kong, 384
Maltese :
  Islands, Interim Report on Financial
    and Economic Structure, 751
  Units, Service Retired Pay, Pen-
    sions, etc., 662
Man :
  takes Wings, 336
  the Tool-Maker, 520, 742
Management :
  in Farming, 518
  Notes on Servicemen's Resettlement,
    81
  See also Institute of Management.
Managing and Manuring Orchard Soils, 737
Manchester :
  Corporation Acts, 51, 726
  Parish of :
    Division Act, 1850, Amendment
      Measure, 331
    Revenues Measure, 514

Manchester (continued) :
  Ship Canal Acts, 50, 513, 726
  (Victoria) Railway Accident Report,
    418
Mandate. See Trusteeship Territories.
Mandated and Trust Territories Act, 327
  Bill, 132, 150
Mangotsfield Railway Accident Report,
  850
Manpower :
  Committee Report, 544
  Conference, Committee of European
    Economic Co-operation, Reports,
    353
  See also Scientific Manpower ; Local
    Government ; Scottish Local
    Government.
Mantegna, Andrea, Paintings by, 883
Manufactured Meat Products, Working
  Party Report, 761
Manufacturers, Registers of. See Board
  of Trade Publications.
Manufacturing Industries, Proposed
  action by H.M. Government concern-
  ing Wages and Hours of Work. Cmd.
  7037, 153
Manuring of Commercial Vegetable
  Crops, 335
Manuscripts. See Public Record Office
  Publications.
Map Reading, Photo Reading, and Field
  Sketching, Manual of, 662
Mapping. See Air Survey.
Maps :
  Saxton's, 741
  Wall, 346, 535
  See also Weather Maps.
Margam Museum, guide, 663
Margate, Broadstairs, and District Elec-
  tricity Special Order, 66
Marginal Farms, Scotland's, 228
Marine :
  Navigation, Radio Aids to, 107, 247
  Observer, 221, 387, 595, 814
  Observer's Handbook, 815
  Radar, Performance Standards, 418
  Surveys, etc., Fees and Expenses
    payable, 849
  Transportation and the Litigation
    Agreement of 1942, Modified Ex-
    change of Notes with U.S.A. Cmd.
    7218, 165
Marines. See Royal Marines.
Maritime :
  Conference, Act and Documents, 648
  Conventions Act, 325

Maritime (continued) :
  Directory. See Mercantile Navy List
  Radio Service, European Conven-
    tion. Cmd. 7773, 500
  Transport Committee Report, Euro-
    pean Recovery Programme, 544
Marketing :
  Leaflets, 335, 518, 739
  of Horticultural Produce in England
    and Wales, 335
Markwick, A. H. D. : Road Research
  Publications, 88
Marley, W. G. : Radioactive Tracers in
  Metallurgical Research, 838
Marquess of Abergavenny's Estate Act,
  52
Marriage :
  Acts :
    1898, 325
    1949, 511
      Bill, 446, 454, 458, 487
      Reprinted Act, 724
  Bar in the Civil Service, Report.
    Cmd. 6886, 40
  (Enabling) Bill, 447
  Guidance, Report. Cmd. 7566, 322
  (Licensing of Chapels) Measure,
    514
  with Foreigners Act, 325
Marriages Provisional Orders Bills, 128,
  148, 457, 485
Married Women :
  (Maintenance) Act, 512
    Bill, 455, 461, 473, 482, 483, 485,
      487
  Standing Committee Debates, 681
  (Restraint upon Anticipation) Act,
    512
    Bill, 455, 456, 457, 487
Marshall :
  Aid. See Recovery in Europe.
  Plan, Reports on, 194
Marshall, S. M. : British Seaweeds and
  their utilisation in the preparation of
  Agar, 559
Marshmoor Railway Accident Report,
  247
Martin, W. J. : Physique of Young
  Adult Males, 603
Masonry, Weathering, Preservation and
  Maintenance, 827
Masons, Recruitment of, Special Report,
  664
Massey, Rt. Hon. V. (Chairman) : Com-
  mittee on Museums and Galleries,
  Report. Cmd. 6827, 36

Masterman, J. C. (Chairman) : Political
  Activities of Civil Servants, Report.
  Cmd. 7718, 496
Master's and Crew Spaces, 107
Mastitis in Cattle, 334
Matapan, Battle of, 220
Mathematics :
  Primary Schools, Introduction to,
    671
  Secondary Schools, 831
Matrimonial Causes :
  Acts :
    1937, 508
    1950, 720
      Bill, 671, 672, 674, 698
  Committee on Procedure, Reports :
    Cmd. 6881, 40
    Cmd. 6945, 44
    Cmd. 7024, 152
  in the High Court of England and
    Declarations of the Legitimacy and
    Validity of Marriage and of British
    Nationality, Memorandum, 671,
    690, 787
Matters of Life and Death, 390
Mattersey Priory, guide, 882
Matthew, R. H. : Clyde Valley Regional
  Plan, 612
Matthews, D. D. : Grading of Aggre-
  gates and Workability of Concrete, 227
Maude, J. C. (Chairman) : Committee of
  Inquiry into murder of a Master at
  Sandon Farm Approved School, Re-
  port. Cmd. 7150, 161
Mauritius :
  Colonial Reports, 343, 532
  Revision of the Constitution. Cmd.
    7228, 166
Meals Service. See Education in Scotland.
Measures passed by the National Assem-
  bly of the Church of England, 52, 175,
  331, 727
  See also Public General Acts.
Meat :
  Manufacturing Premises, 545
  Production, Trade and Consumption,
    Summary Figures, 435, 752
  Products. See Manufactured Meat
    Products.
Mechanical :
  Engineering, Technical Register, 811
  Road Vehicles, Descriptive Cata-
    logue, 542
Mechanically :
  Produced Foam for combating Petrol
    Fires, 225

Mechanically (continued) :
  Propelled Vehicles Returns, 248,
    420, 635, 851
Mechanics, Examples in Applied, 728
Mechanisation :
  of Milk Production, 55
  of Sugar Beet Crop, North America,
    177
Medals :
  Committee on the Grant of. Cmd.
    7035, 153
  General Service, 261
  Long Service and Good Conduct, 262
  Special Army Orders, 880
  See also Honours.
Medical :
  Act, 720
    Bill, 669, 670, 671, 674, 698
  and Population Subjects, Studies on,
    224, 558, 776
  Auxiliary Service, Careers, 208
  Certificates, Interdepartmental Com-
    mittee Report, 560
  Diseases in Tropical and Sub-Tropi-
    cal Areas, Memoranda, 262, 662
  Guide, Ship's Captain's, 109
  Officers, Public Health, Salaries, 358
  Partnerships, Legal Committee Re-
    port. Cmd. 7565, 322
  Practitioners and Pharmacists Act,
    328
    Bill, 132, 133, 150
  Record Cards, 784
  Research :
    Council Publications (N.P.), 86,
      224, 391, 603, 813
    in War. Cmd. 7335, 306
  Scales, Merchant Shipping, 107, 418,
    633
  Services of the Army, Regs., 115
Medicinal Plants, Cultivation of, 177
Medicine :
  Careers, 75
  See also Preventive Medicine.
Mediterranean :
  Colonies :
    Film Strips, 534
    Picture Set, 533
  Convoy Operations, 385
  Customs Tariffs, 60, 533
  General Fisheries Council, Agree-
    ment for establishment. Cmd.
    8011, 711
  Weather, 816
Melrose Abbey, guide, 663

Members' :
  Expenses, Select Committee Report,
    18
  Fund, Select Committee Report,
    142
Meneage. See Lizard.
Men's Clothing, etc., Board of Trade
  Publications (N.P.), 104, 244
Mental :
  Defectives, List of State Institutions,
    187
  Deficiency :
    Acts, 509, 722
    See also Lunacy ; Scottish
      Lunacy.
  Health, 436
    Expert Committee Report, 876
    Services, Provisions relating to,
      360
  Illness on the Gold Coast, Studies,
    750
Nurses :
  Salaries S.C. Notes, 68, 200
  Scottish :
    Circulars, 397
    Salaries Committee Report.
      Cmd. 7239, 304
Patients' Affairs Order (Northern
  Ireland), 563
Treatment Report. See Lunacy.
Meningitis, Tuberculous, treated with
  Streptomycin, 613
Menzies, W. J. M. : Common Eel and its
  capture, 399
Mercantile :
  Marine Engineers Examinations, 247
  Navy List and Maritime Directory,
    418, 850
  Supplements, 419
Merchandise Marks Act, 720
Merchant :
  Airmen, Account of British Civil
    Aviation, 71
  Shipping :
    Acts :
      1948, 328
        Bill, 268, 269, 276, 291,
          295, 300
      1950, 720
        Bill, 463, 670, 697
        Earlier Acts reprinted, 722,
          723
    Lists of Acts, etc., relating to, 107,
      418, 633
    Safety and Load Line Conven-
      tions Act, 327

Merchant (continued):
  Shipping (continued):
    (Safety Convention) Act, 511
    Bill, 454, 473, 482, 484, 485
    Standing Committee Debates, 681
    Wireless Telegraphy Act, 507
    See also Medical Scales.
  Ships:
    Radar for, 107, 223
    Radio for, 223, 600
    Steamers and Motorships, Handbook of Collections illustrating, 542
    Vessels lost or damaged by enemy acting during Second World War, 176
Merchants House of Glasgow (Crematorium) Order Confirmation Act, 726
    Bill, 673, 699
Mersey:
    Docks and Harbour Board Act, 726
    Tunnel Act, 513
Merstham Quarry Tunnel Railway Accident Report, 635
Merthyr, Lord (Chairman): Interdepartmental Committee on Rag Flock Acts, Report. Cmd. 6866, 39
Merthyr Tydfil Corporation Act, 331
Mesozoic Ironstones of England, 606
Metal Windows, Fixing, Pointing, and Glazing, 882
Metalliferous Mines:
    Act, 720
    Regulation Act, 720
Metallurgy. See Aluminium Alloys.
Metals:
    and Minerals Panel, Report, 534
    Non-ferrous, Committee Report, 544
Meteorological:
    Division, ICAO, Report, 791
    Office Publications (N.P.), 84, 221, 386, 595, 814
    Telecommunications Meeting, Report, 574
Meteorological, Chemical, and Physical Investigations, 742
Meteorology:
    Convention of the World Meteorological Organisation. Cmd. 7989, 709
    for Aviators, 387, 595
    See also Air Pilot.
Method of determining the Polar Diagrams of Long Wire and Horizontal Rhombic Aerials, 394
Methyl Bromide Fumigation, 202

Metropolitan:
  Police:
    Annual Reports:
      Cmd. 6871, 39
      Cmd. 7156, 161
      Cmd. 7406, 311
      Cmd. 7737, 498
      Cmd. 7985, 709
    at War, 221
    Courts, Examinations, 184
    Water Board Act, 51
  Mexborough and Swinton (Trolley Vehicles) Order Confirmation Act, 174
    Bill, 128, 148
  Mexican Cultural Mission Programme, 812
Mexico:
  City UNESCO Conference, Documents, 351
  Compensation in respect of Expropriated Petroleum Industrial Properties, Agreements:
    with Mexican Eagle Oil Company. Cmd. 7275, 169
    Economic Survey, 632
Mice. See Infestation Control.
Micro-organisms, Culture Collections, 225
Mid and South East Cheshire Water Board Act, 51
Middle East:
  Agricultural Development of, 106
  Blindness in British African and Middle East Territories, 343
  Operations in, 383
  Rural Education and Welfare, 109
  Science, 107
  Settlement of:
    Interests in Joint Installations, Agreement with U.S.A. Cmd. 7514, 319
    Lend-Lease Interest in future sales of Surplus Stores, Agreement with U.S.A. Cmd. 7613, 318
Middlesex:
  County Council Act, 726
  Proposed New Constituencies:
    Cmd. 7397, 310
    Cmd. 7426, 312
  South West Crematorium, 174
    Order Confirmation Act, 726
    Bill, 671, 697
Mid-East England Electricity (Alteration and Extension) Scheme:
  Adopted, 180
  Prepared, 193

Midges, Control of, 90, 397
Mid-Northamptonshire Water Board Order Confirmation (Special Procedure) Act, 512
  Bill, 452, 484, 486
Mid-Southern Utility Acts, 50, 726
Midwifery, Career. See Nursing.
Midwives:
  (Amendments) Act, 720
    Bill, 669, 672, 697, 698
    Salaries, 68, 360
    Working Party Report, 560
Migration Statistics, Problems of, 867
Migratory Beekeeping, 516
Milbourn, P. E. (Chairman), Working Party on Increased Mechanisation in United Kingdom Ports, Report, 849
Mildenhall Wreck Report, 637
Mildew, Apple, 178
Miles, A. A.: Infection and Sepsis in Industrial Wounds of the Hand, 813
Military:
  Air Transit Facilities, Agreement with France. Cmd. 7524, 319
  Awards, 219
  Chapels. See Naval.
  Engineering, 115, 262, 438, 662, 880
  Government Gazette, 61, 187, 346, 536
  Law, Manual of, 115, 262, 439, 880
  Nursing Services (India), 115
  Operations:
    France and Belgium, 202, 362
    Italy, 568
  Service, Agreement with Chile. Cmd. 7580, 323
  Tribunal. See War Criminals.
Milk:
  and Cheese Factories, Hours of Work for Women and Young Persons, 210
  and Dairies Regs., 545, 561, 760
  Better Utilisation of, 656
  Distribution Report. Cmd. 7414, 312
  Economics of Production in Scotland, Investigation Reports, 396, 609
  Freezing Point Test Report, 397
  in North America. See Agriculture Overseas.
  Pasteurised, Prescribed Tests for, 67
  Production:
    in North America, 177
    Mechanisation, 55
  Scottish Testing Scheme, 90
  Services, Scotland, Report, 610

Milk (continued):
  (Special Designations) Act, 510
    Bill, 278, 445, 448, 452, 469, 482, 484
    Standing Committee Debates, 681
  Milking Parlour, Summary of Modern Practice, 739
  Milling Machines, Safeguarding of, Interim Report, 210
Milne, Sir D. (Chairman): Scottish Local Government Manpower Committee, Report. Cmd. 7951, 707
Milngavie, Aircraft Accident Report, 180
Mineral:
  Development Report. Cmd. 7732, 497
Industry:
  British Empire and Foreign Countries, Statistics, 363
  of the British Commonwealth, 568
  Oil in Food Order, 545
    Amendment, 760
  Resources of Great Britain, Reports, 606
  Species and Varieties, Index, 742
Mineralogy Bulletin, 742
Mines and Quarries, Ministry of Fuel and Power Publications (N.P.), 66, 196, 355, 555, 774
Mining:
  and Manufacturing Industries, Proposed Action by H.M. Government concerning Wages and Hours of Work. Cmd. 7037, 153
  Examinations (Certificates of Competency) Rules, 775
  in the Ruhr, Technique of, 197
Industry:
  Entrants Pamphlets, 191
  Provision of Employment in South Wales for persons suspended from the mining industry on account of silicosis and Pneumoconiosis. Cmd. 6719, 30
  Visual Training Aids, 67
  Subsidence, Report of Committee. Cmd. 7637, 491
Minister of Food (Financial Powers) Act, 510
  Bill, 448
Ministerial Salaries Act, 49
  Bill, 8, 28
Ministers:
  and Heads of Public Departments, Lists of, 93, 232, 400, 616, 834

Ministers (continued):
  of the Crown:
    (Transfer of Functions) Act, 48
      Bill, 5, 27
    (Treasury Secretaries) Act, 173
      Bill, 133, 150
Ministry of Defence Act, 171
Minorities, Definition and Classification of, 866
Minster Lovell Hall, guide, 263
Mint. See Royal Mint.
Miscellaneous Financial Provisions Acts:
  1946, 49
    Bill, 5, 27
  1950, 720
    Bill, 698
Misconduct Form, 202
Missing Persons, Conference on Declaration of Death of, Final Act and Convention, 860
Mitchell, G. H.: Geology of the country around Barnsley, 393
Mitchell, Sir M. E. (Chairman): Sub-Committee of Central Housing Advisory Committee, Report on Standards of Fitness for Habitation, 201
Mites associated with Stored Food Products, 335
Moberley, Sir W. (Chairman): University Grants Committee, Report, 513
Model:
  Byelaws, 68, 200, 360, 362, 546, 778, 781
  Clauses, Parliament, 514, 727
  Standing Orders, Contracts, 560
Modern Cartography, 866
Modernising our Homes, 229
Mollison, P. L.: Rh Blood Groups and their Clinical Effects, 391
Monaco, Agreement for Reciprocal Abolition of Visas. Cmd. 7589, 324
Monckton, Sir W. T. (Chairman): Departmental Committee on Alternative Remedies. Cmd. 6860, 39
Monetary Agreements:
  Belgium:
    Cmd. 7057, 154
    Cmd. 7864, 168
    Cmd. 7823, 504
    Cmd. 7856, 504
    Cmd. 7930, 705
    Cmd. 8029, 712
  Czechoslovakia:
    Cmd. 7174, 156
    Cmd. 7585, 323
    Cmd. 7625, 490

Monetary Agreements (continued):
  Czechoslovakia (continued):
    Cmd. 7667, 493
    Cmd. 7719, 496
    Cmd. 7772, 500
  Denmark:
    Cmd. 7592, 324
    Cmd. 8055, 714
    Cmd. 8104, 718
  Netherlands:
    Cmd. 7051, 154
    Cmd. 7381, 309
    Cmd. 7531, 320
    Cmd. 7806, 503
    Cmd. 7854, 506
  Norway:
    Cmd. 7162, 161
    Cmd. 7474, 316
    Cmd. 7672, 493
    Cmd. 8095, 717
  Portugal:
    Cmd. 6798, 35
    Cmd. 7050, 154
    Cmd. 7302, 305
    Cmd. 7401, 311
    Cmd. 7713, 496
    Cmd. 7959, 707
  Spain:
    Cmd. 7090, 158
    Cmd. 7160, 161
  Sweden:
    Cmd. 7170, 162
    Cmd. 7259, 168
    Cmd. 7964, 495
    Cmd. 7861, 701
    Cmd. 8105, 717
  Switzerland:
    Cmd. 6756, 32
    Cmd. 7669, 493
    Cmd. 7952, 707
  Money:
    and Property subjected to special measures in consequence of enemy occupation, Agreements:
      Luxembourg. Cmd. 7023, 152
      Yugoslavia. Cmd. 7601, 489
Monmouthshire. See South Wales.
Monocular Blindness, 779
Monopolies and Restrictive Practices:
  Commission, Report on Supply of Dental Goods, 695
  (Inquiry and Control) Act, 329
    Bill, 276, 277
    Report under, 683
Monopoly (Inquiry and Control) Bill, 275, 276, 277, 291, 295, 300, 301, 302, 463

Montagu, M. F. A.: Galley Hill Skeleton, Reconsideration of, 521
Montgomeryshire:
  Circuit Order in Council, 594
  Police Forces Enquiry, 362
Monthly:
  Bulletin of Statistics, 258, 432, 652, 869
  Digest of Statistics, 250, 422, 641, 743
  Report, Control Commission for Germany, 187, 346
  Weather Report, 221, 387, 596, 817
Monuments. See Ancient Monuments.
Moonlight, Wreck Report, 636
Moore, J. L. M.: Railway Accident Reports, 418, 634, 850
Moore, W. C.:
  Cereal Diseases, Recognition and Control, 335
  Diseases:
    of Bulbs, 517
    of Crop Plants, 335
Moorfields Westminster and Central Eye Hospital Act, 51
Mops, Specification, 438
Moran, Lord: Scientific Results of German Medical War Crimes, 549
Morbidity Statistics, Classification of Diseases for, 391
Morley Order Confirmation Act, 513
  Bill, 457
Morris, T. N.: Preservation of Fruit and Vegetables by Freezing, 391
Morrison Old Colliery Explosion, Report. Cmd. 7347, 307
Morrison's Academy Trust (Amendment) (No. 1) Scheme, 92
Morrison-Scott, T. C. S.: Identity of Captain Cook's Kangaroo, 742
Mortar for Brickwork, Block Construction, and Masonry, 829
Mortlake Crematorium Board Order Confirmation Act, 51
  Bill, 5, 26
Mortuaries and Post Mortem Rooms, Model Byelaws, 781
Mosquito Nuisances in Great Britain, Memorandum on Measures for the Control of, 560
Mosquitos, 742
Mosses, Woodland, 194
Most-favoured-nation Treatment:
  Free Territory of Trieste. Cmd. 7470, 315
  Western Germany:
    Cmd. 7447, 314

Most-favoured-nation Treatment (continued):
  Western Germany (continued):
    Cmd. 7539, 320
    Cmd. 7643, 491
    Cmd. 7876, 702
Moth, Magpie, 178
Motion Picture Industry, Agreement with U.S.A. Cmd. 7421, 312
Motor:
  Car Industry in Germany, 1939–45, 624
  Fuel, Use of, by Government Departments, 292
  Insurers' Bureau (Compensation of Victims of Uninsured Drivers), 107, 247
  Manufacturing Industry, National Advisory Council Report, 238
  Spirit (Regulation) Act, 328
    Bill, 272, 273, 300, 301
  Transport. See Road
  Vehicle Insurance Fund, Agreement concerning Compulsory Insurance, 107
Vehicles:
  Index Marks, 109
  Returns of Offences, 145, 296, 474, 784
Motspur Park Junction Railway Accident Report, 418
Mottingham Railway Accident Report, 108
Mount, Lt.-Col. A. H. L.: Railway Accident Reports, 418, 419
Mountbatten Estate, Report from Personal Bills Committee, 452
Mourant, A. E.: Rh Blood Groups and their Clinical Effects, 391
Muir-Wood, H. M.: Succession of Life through Geological Time, 522
Municipal Housing Estates, Management of, Report, 559
Munro, Professor J. W.:
  British Bark Beetles, 65
  Infestation of Grain by Insects, 227
Murray Expedition Scientific Reports and Publications, 179, 522
Murray, M.A.: Thyroid Enlargement, 391
Murray, S. S.: Report on Tobacco, 533
Museum, 433, 655, 872
  Monographs, 660
Museums and Galleries, Report. Cmd. 6827, 36
Mushroom Growing, 54, 738

Music, Careers, 75
Mutual Aid. Cmd. 6931, 43
See also Alliance and Mutual Assistance.

N

N.A.A.S. Quarterly Review, 518, 739
Nabuco (Great Anniversaries series), 871
Nairobi, 345
Narcissus :
Flies, 737
Pests, 54
Narcotic Drugs :
International Control :
Cmd. 7671, 493
Cmd. 7874, 701
United Nations Publications, 256, 423, 424, 425, 643, 644, 648, 860, 861
Narcotics Bulletin, 648, 866
Narvik, Battle of, 219
Nash, T. A. M. : Tsetse flies in British West Africa, 345
National :
Agricultural Advisory Service Journal, 518, 739
and International Measures for Full Employment, 866
Arbitration Tribunal Awards, 77, 210, 373, 583, 799
Assistance :
Act, 328, 724
Bill, 150, 269, 272, 284, 295, 300
Standing Committee Debates, 463
Explanatory Memorandum. Cmd. 7423, 312
Summary of the Provisions. Cmd. 7248, 167
Draft Amendment Regs., Explanatory Memorandum. Cmd. 7936, 706
Registration and Inspection of Disabled and Old Persons' Homes, 559, 561
Board Reports :
Cmd. 7767, 500
Cmd. 8030, 713
Brick Advisory Council Publications, 263, 883
Building Studies, 394, 441, 557, 606, 829, 883

National (continued) :
Certificates, Award of :
in Commerce, 350
in Naval Architecture, 191
in Production Engineering, 350
Coal Board :
Dispute with Workers' Union, Report, 283
Reports and Accounts, 286, 291, 474, 688
Commissions, Handbook of, 872
Debt :
Commissioners' Accounts, 137, 138, 148, 149
Position of certain Funds :
Cmd. 6839, 37
Cmd. 7190, 166
Reduction :
Cmd. 7454, 314
Cmd. 7751, 499
Cmd. 8054, 714
Returns :
Cmd. 6924, 43
Cmd. 7229, 166
Cmd. 7477, 316
Cmd. 7771, 500
Cmd. 8053, 715
Defence :
Canadian Ministry of, Publications, 180, 337
Contribution Leaflets, 73, 204, 570
Farm Survey of England and Wales, 55
Film Finance Corporation, Report and Accounts. Cmd. 7927, 705
Fire Service Drill Book, 69, 563
Forest Park Guides, 195, 354, 553, 770
Gallery. See Museums and Galleries.
Grid and Reference System, 85, 600
Health :
Insurance :
Forms, 84, 222, 360
Fund Accounts, 17, 19, 136, 139, 282, 287, 465, 471
Service :
Act, 50
Bill, 10, 11, 12, 29
Standing Committee Minutes, 22
Summary of Proposed New Service. Cmd. 6761, 32
Administration of, 473
Allocation of Pension, 360
Scotland, 397

National (continued) :
Health (continued) :
Service (continued) :
(Amendment) Act, 512
Bill, 459, 460, 475, 482, 485, 486, 488
Standing Committee Debates, 681
Circulars, 358, 361
Development of Consultant Services, 781
Mental Health Services, 360
Scotland :
Act, 172
Bill, 29, 30, 124, 138, 148, 149
Standing Committee Debates, 280
Summary of Proposed New Service. Cmd. 6496, 44
Superannuation Scheme, 360
Explanatory Memorandum, 779
Scotland, 379
Explanatory Memorandum, 779
Services Administration, Select Committee on Estimates Report, 678
Income :
and Expenditure of the U.K. :
Cmd. 6784, 34
Cmd. 7099, 157
Cmd. 7371, 309
Cmd. 7649, 492
Cmd. 7933, 706
Statistics, 648, 866
Institute of Agricultural Engineering Publications (N.P.), 55, 178, 336, 519, 740
Insurance :
Acts :
1911, 325
1946, 49
Bill, 8, 20, 26, 27, 29
Summary of the main provisions of the National Insurance Scheme. Cmd. 6729, 31
Report on financial provisions of the Bill. Cmd. 6730, 31
1949, 511
Bill, 458, 486

National (continued) :
Insurance (continued) :
Acts (continued) :
Amendment Regs., Reports, 463, 465, 468, 472, 474, 476, 477, 478, 480
Decisions by the Commissioner on Claims, 818, 388, 599
Preliminary Draft Amendment Regs., 463, 598, 599, 688, 818, 819
Audit Department Annual Reports, 85, 221
(Existing Pensioners) Fund Accounts, 477, 687
Funds Account, 473, 687
(Industrial Injuries) Acts :
1946, 49
Bill, 5, 14, 27, 29
Proposed changes in Death Benefits, Explanatory Memorandum. Cmd. 6738, 31
1948, 328
Bill, 273, 300
Forms, 388
Ministry of, Publications (N.P.), 84, 221, 388, 597, 817
Modification of Local Government Superannuation Schemes (Scotland) Regs., Explanatory Note, 231
Regulations, 222, 388
Reports, 289, 290, 291, 292, 298, 683, 684, 686, 687, 691, 695, 696
Cmd. 7955, 707
Scheme, Family Guide, 389
(Seasonal Workers) Regs., Preliminary Draft, 818
Land Fund Accounts, 286, 471, 477, 690, 857
Museums and Galleries :
Publications, 85
Standing Committee Report, 496
Nursery Examination Board Certificate, 63
Parks :
and Access to the Countryside, 840
Act,.719, 724
Bill, 458, 460, 461, 462, 473, 482, 484, 486, 487, 681
Circular, 840

National (continued) :
Parks (continued) :
and the Conservation of Nature in Scotland, Report. Cmd. 7235, 166
Commission Report. Cmd. 7121, 158
Physical Laboratory Publications (N.P.), 88, 227, 394, 606, 829
Plans, Professional Paper, 820
Progress in Food and Agriculture Programmes, 657
Radium Trust and Radium Commission, Reports :
Cmd. 6817, 36
Cmd. 7127, 159
Cmd. 8087, 717
Service :
Acts :
1947, 172
Bill, 126, 128, 148, 149
1948, 329
Bill, 370, 276, 302
1950, 720, 724
Bill, 674, 699
(Amendment) Acts, 510, 724
Bill, 279, 303
Decisions of the Umpire, 81, 217, 382, 592
Draft of Bill to substitute 24 months for 18 months as term of wholetime service. Cmd. 8031, 713
Increase in the length of full-time service. Cmd. 8026, 712
Pay of soldiers deemed enlisted under, 662
(Release of Conscientious Objectors) Act, 49
Bill, 3, 4, 1, 27
Theatre Act, 510
Bill, 303, 488
Trust for Scotland Order Confirmation Act, 174
Bill, 130, 150
Union of Colliery Winding Enginemen, Dispute with National Coal Board, Report, 283
War Formulary, 200, 360, 561
Nationalisation. See Coal Industry.
Nationality : Application of French Nationality to British Subjects in Tunisia, Exchange of Notes with France. Cmd. 7117, 158
Nations of the Commonwealth, Picture Set, 751

Native Agriculture in Tropical African Colonies, Report on a Survey of Problems in Mechanisation, 751
Natural :
Durability of Timber, 605
Lighting of Homes and Flats, 394, 227
Science in Primary Schools, Introduction to, 654
Naturalisation Forms, 70, 362, 563, 784
See also Aliens.
Nature Reserves in Scotland, Report. Cmd. 7814, 503
See also Conservation of Nature.
Nauru :
Proposed Trusteeship Agreement for Mandated Territory, 428, 432
Trusteeship Agreement. Cmd. 7290, 304
Nautical Almanac, 53, 176, 332, 515, 728
Naval :
Architecture :
Careers, 75
Certificates in, 191
College, Dartmouth, Entrance Examination, 332
Commission, Establishment of :
Cmd. 7078, 156
Cmd. 7323, 306
Cmd. 7353, 307
Discipline Act :
As amended, 727
Report of Committee appointed to consider administration of justice. Cmd. 8094, 717
Establishments, Use of, for Production and Export Drive, 293, 471
Forces (Enforcement of Maintenance Liabilities) Act, 172
Bill, 124, 147
General Service Medal. Cmd. 7813, 503
Mining and Degaussing, 85
Records, Catalogue of, 822
War in North West Europe, 383
Naval, Military, and Air Force Chapels, List of, 558
Navigation :
Examples in, 728
Log, 525
Manual, 515
See also Air Navigation ; Trade and Navigation ; Aerial Navigation ; Marine Navigation ; Weaver Navigation.
Navigational Warnings, 221

Navigator. See Civil Aircraft.
Navy :
Appropriation Accounts, 14, 134, 281, 463, 682
Dockyard and Production Accounts, 469, 682
Estimates, 17, 18, 136, 137, 283, 285, 466, 681
Statements :
Cmd. 7054, 154
Cmd. 7337, 306
Cmd. 7629, 491
Cmd. 7897, 703
Examinations, 58, 183, 184, 185
Expenditure :
and Receipts, 1939–43, Detailed Statement. Cmd. 6858, 38
Statement, 1948, 285
List and Appendices, 53, 176, 332, 444, 516, 729
Votes, 18, 138, 287, 466, 470, 683, 685
See also Admiralty.
Nazeing Wood or Park Act, 124
Neal, L. (Chairman) : Central Advisory Committee : Estate Development and Management in War Damaged Areas, 241
Needs of War-devastated countries in Education, Science, and Culture, 251
Neonatal :
Deaths due to Infection, 229
Mortality and Morbidity Report, 561
Nepal, Treaty with U.K. Cmd. 8077, 716
Netherlands :
Air Services Agreements :
Cmd. 6893, 40
Cmd. 7114, 160
Avoidance of Double Taxation :
and Prevention of Fiscal Evasion with respect to taxes on income :
Cmd. 7555, 321
Cmd. 8015, 711
with respect to Duties on Estates of deceased persons :
Cmd. 7556, 321
Cmd. 8016, 712
Cultural Conventions with U.K. :
Cmd. 7509, 318
East Indies. See Malaya.
Economic Survey, 845
Government, White Paper regarding measures for Currency Rehabilitation, 389
International Authority for the Ruhr, Agreement. Cmd. 7685, 494

Netherlands (continued) :
Monetary Conventions :
Cmd. 6921, 42
Cmd. 7051, 154
Cmd. 7381, 309
Cmd. 7531, 320
Cmd. 7806, 503
Cmd. 7854, 506
Reciprocal Abolition of Visas :
Cmd. 7123, 157
Cmd. 7860, 700
Cmd. 8040, 713
Release of Netherlands Money and Property held by the U.K. Custodian of Enemy Property. Cmd. 7644, 492
Settlement :
for U.K. Purchases under Long Term Contracts. Cmd. 7843, 505
of conflicting claims to German Enemy Assets. Cmd. 7803, 502
of Wartime Debts. Cmd. 7833, 308
Social Security Convention. Cmd. 7911, 704
Supply of Aircraft and Equipment, Agreement. Cmd. 7011, 152
Trade and Payments between Singapore and Federation of Malaya and Netherlands Indies. Cmd. 7487, 317
Neurosis :
among factory workers, 224
See also Soldiers discharged from the Army.
Neveria, Hogging and Sagging Tests, 53, 729
New :
Forest :
Act, 511
Bill, 278, 445, 449, 450, 451, 485
Committee Report. Cmd. 7245, 167
Guinea Trusteeship Agreement, 164, 433
Hebrides, Colonial Report, 532
Home, 71, 363
Horizons in the East, 858
Secondary Schools, Building Bulletin, 756
Southgate Railway Accident Report, 419
Streets, Model Byelaws, 68

New (*continued*) :
Towns :
Act 49,
Bill, 9, 10, 28, 29
Standing Committee
Minutes, 21
Memoranda :
Cmd. 6801, 6804, 35
Cmd. 6850, 38
Cmd. 6867, 6874, 39
Accounts, 471, 679
Designation Orders :
East Kilbride, 229
Glenrothes, 397
Reports :
Development Corpora-
tions, 469, 476, 477, 694
New Towns Committee :
Interim. *Cmd. 6759*,
32
Second Interim. *Cmd.
6794*, 34
Final. *Cmd. 6876*, 39
Zealand :
Constitution (Amendment) Act,
173
Bill, 133, 150
Economic Survey, 845
School Dental Nurses, Report of
U.K. Mission, 781
Wall Map, 346
See also Australian.
Newcastle, Bridgend, guide, 882
Newcastle-upon-Tyne Corporation Act,
51
Newcombia, Hogging and Sagging Tests,
332
Newfoundland :
(Consequential Provisions) Act, 720
Bill, 669, 697
Defence Installations in, Agreement
with Canada. *Cmd. 6823*, 36
deletion from list of Territories
covered by Visa Abolition Agree-
ment. *Cmd. 7750*, 509
Financial and Economic Position,
Report. *Cmd. 6849*, 38
(Liberation) Bill, 448
Nutrition in, 186
Terms of Union with Canada. *Cmd.
7605*, 489
Newhaven and Seaford Sea Defences
Act, 175
Newnham, E. V. : Climates of Addu
Atoll, Agalaga Islands, and Tristan
da Cunha, 815

Newport (Isle of Wight) Corporation
Act, 51
Newsam, Sir F. (Chairman) :
Higher Training for Police Service,
Report. *Cmd. 7070*, 155
Police Post War Committee, Report,
564
Newton, C. M. (Chairman) : Civil Avia-
tion Accident Investigation Pro-
cedure. Report. *Cmd. 7564*, 322
Newton, L. : British Seaweeds and their
utilisation in the preparation of Agar,
559
Nicol, A. D. I. : Intrinsic Safety of
Electrical Apparatus, 67
Nigeria :
Colonial Reports, 343, 532, 749
Cost of Living, etc., Inquiry, 61
Disorders, Eastern Provinces, 751
Road Problems, 750
Nigerians train at Yaba Higher College,
Film Strip, 534
Nineteenth Century Costume, 260
Nitrous Fumes in Industry, Methods for
detection of, 830
Noise in British Homes, 394
Noltland Castle, guide, 882
Nomenclature of Disease, 360
Non-European Officers, Pay of, 881
Non-ferrous metal Industry in Germany
during 1939–45, 624
Non-repatriable Victims of German
Action, Agreement on Plan for alloca-
tion of Reparation Share. *Cmd. 7255*,
168
Non-self-governing Territories :
and Trust Territories, Memorandum.
Cmd. 8035, 713
United Nations Publications, 112,
356, 344, 649, 866
What the United Nations is doing,
653
Norfolk Central, Boundary Commission
Report. *Cmd. 8100*, 718
Norham Castle, guide, 117
Normandy Landings, Assault Phase,
220
Normanton and Wakefield, Boundary
Commission Report. *Cmd. 7745*, 498
North :
African Landings Despatch, 594
America, Development of Poultry
Industry, 177
Atlantic :
Council, Fourth Session. *Cmd.
7977*, 709

North (*continued*) :
Atlantic (*continued*) :
Regional :
Air Navigation Meeting, Re-
port, 573
Manual, 574
Treaty. *Cmd. 7789*, 501
Events leading up to. *Cmd.
7692*, 495
Text. *Cmd. 7657*, 492
Borneo :
Arms, 751
Colonial Reports, 532, 749
Flag Badge, 751
Sovereign Rights and Assets,
Transfer to the Crown, Agree-
ment, 61
Cumberland Water Board Act, 175
Devon Water Board Act, 50
Eastern :
Area, Hospital Service, 67
Regional, Scottish Hospitals Sur-
vey, 90
of Scotland Hydro-electric Board,
Report and Accounts, 833
Pacific Regional Air Navigation
Meeting, Report, 572
Wales :
Ancient Monuments Guide, 441
British Regional Geology, 393
West :
England and North Wales
Electricity (Alteration and
Extension) Scheme, 64, 180
Midlands Joint Electricity Order
Confirmation Act, 51
Bill, 6, 27
North, G. (Chairman), Interdepartmen-
tal Committee on Social and Econo-
mic Research, Reports :
Cmd. 7537, 320
Cmd. 8091, 717
Northampton Order Confirmation Act,
330
Bill, 274, 301
Northern :
Highlands, British Regional Geology,
393
Ireland :
Act, 172
Bill, 128, 148
Boundary Commission Report.
Cmd. 7231, 166
History, Resources and People,
199
Supreme Court Rules, 564

Northern (*continued*) :
Ireland (*continued*) :
See also Supreme Court of Judi-
cature.
Region, Scottish Hospitals Survey
90
Rhodesia :
Colonial Reports, 532, 749
Water Resources, Report, 533
Northmet Power Act, 52
Northolt Airport, 339
Northumberland and Tyneside, Biblio-
graphy, 241
Northwood Railway Accident Report,
108
Norway :
Abolition of Visas :
Cmd. 7073, 156
Cmd. 7575, 323
Cmd. 7610, 489
Cmd. 8041, 714
Air Communications Agreement.
Cmd. 6913, 42
Campaign, 1940, Despatch, 219
Closer Economic Co-operation. *Cmd.
7884*, 702
Correspondence respecting the Ger-
man steamer *Altmark*. *Cmd. 8012*
711
Cultural Conventions :
Cmd. 7338, 306
Cmd. 7748, 498
Economic Survey, 845
Monetary Conventions :
Cmd. 7162, 161
Cmd. 7474, 316
Cmd. 8095, 717
Cmd. 7672, 493
Ocean Weather Station Agreement
Cmd. 7688, 495
Participation of a Norwegian Brigade
Group in the Occupation of Ger-
many. *Cmd. 7226*, 166
Supply of certain Aircraft and Equip-
ment, Agreement. *Cmd. 7095, 157*
Transmission of Diplomatic Corres-
pondence :
by Air Mail. *Cmd. 7315*, 305
by Post. *Cmd. 7145*, 160
Norwich :
Extension Act, 726
North, Boundary Commission Re-
port. *Cmd. 8100*, 718
Order Confirmation Act, 52
Bill, 9, 28
Railway Accident Report, 635

Not yet five, 63
Notation for Survey Maps, 241
Notice of Accidents Act, 325
Notification of Births Act, 325
Nottingham :
Corporation Act, 174
Election (Validation) Bill, 6, 27
University of, Act, 512
Nottinghamshire and Derbyshire Trac-
tion Act, 174
Nuremberg Trials. *See* War Criminals.
Nurseries :
and Child Minders Regulation Act,
329
Bill, 274, 275, 300, 302
See also Forest Nurseries.
Nurseries, Nursery Schools, etc., Salaries
of non-domestic Staff, 358
Nurses :
Act, 511
Bill, 451, 453, 455, 460, 486, 487
Recruitment and Training, Working
Party Reports, 201, 360
Registration :
Act, 721
(Ireland) Act, 721
(Scotland) Act, 512
Bill, 455, 461, 479, 482, 487
Standing Committee Debates, 681
Nurses' Salaries :
Circulars, Scotland, 397
Committee Report, Scotland. *Cmd.
7238*, 304
Notes and Recommendations, 68, 200
See also Mental Nurses.
Nursing :
and Midwifery Services, Careers, 793
Male, Careers, 208
Services :
Pay and Pensions. *Cmd. 7124*,
159
See also Military Nursing Services
(India).
Sister and Aide-de-Camp to the King,
Honorary, Appointment, 662
Nutrition :
Expert Committee Report, 877
in the British West Indies, 61
Manual of, 193
Problems of Rice-eating Countries in
Asia, 435
See also Food and Nutrition.
Nutritional :
Anaemia of Young Pigs, 334
Deficiencies in Livestock, 433
Studies, 874

Nyasaland :
Civil Services Report, 344
Colonial Reports, 343, 532, 749
Water Resources Report, 533

O

Oak in Great Britain, General Volume
Table for, 769
Oakley, K. P. :
British Regional Geology, Central
England District, 226
Galley Hill Skeleton, Reconsidera-
tion of, 521
Man the Tool-maker, 520, 742
Succession of Life through Geological
Time, 522
Oakley Station Railway Accident Re-
port, 850
Oaksey, Rt. Hon. Lord (Chairman) :
Police Conditions of Service, Reports :
Cmd. 7674, 494
Cmd. 7831, 504
Oat Varieties, 396
Oats, 333
Obscene Publications :
Agreement for Supression, 866
International Convention, 644, 649
See also Traffic in Obscene Publica-
tions.
Occupation of Germany :
and Austria, Privileges and Facili-
ties for British Troops in Belgium,
Treaty. *Cmd. 7624*, 490.
British Zone, Agreement with Nor-
way. *Cmd. 7226*, 166
Participation of :
Danish Contingent. *Cmd. 7593*,
324
Norwegian Brigade.*Cmd.7614*,489
Occupational Diseases, Notes on Diag-
nosis of, 200
Ocean :
Station Vessel Manual, 791
Weather Stations :
Agreement with Norway and
Sweden. *Cmd. 7688*, 495
International Agreement. *Cmd.
7818*, 504
O'Dea, W. T. :
Darkness into Daylight, 351
Electric Illumination, 192
Handbook of collections illustrating
Radio Communication, 542

Offences relating to Motor Vehicles. *See
Motor Vehicles.*
Offenders :
Probation of, Regs., 784
Treatment and Rehabilitation of, 616
Officers :
Mess Contributions and Subscrip-
tions, 439
Pay, Special Army Order, 662
See also War Office Publications.
Official :
Conduct of Ministers of the Crown,
etc., Inquiry Report (" Lynskey
Tribunal "). *Cmd. 7616*, 490
Lists, Registrar-General's, 224, 390,
776
Oil :
Committee Report, 544
in Navigable Waters, 722
Refinery Expansion Report, 544
See also Vegetable Oil.
Oil-mining Law, Agreement with Trans-
jordan. *Cmd. 7063*, 155
Oilseed Mission for Venezuela, Report,
656
Oilseeds Mission Report, 345
Oilskins, Board of Trade Publications, 104
Okinawa Assault, Contribution of British
Pacific Fleet, 385
Old :
Age :
and Widows' Pension Act, 1940,
Explanatory Memorandum.
Cmd. 6959, 45
Pensions Act, 1936, Financial
Instructions, Committees.
Cmd. 7091, 157
People, Welfare of, 612
Sarum, guide, 882
Soar, Plaxtol, guide, 882
Oldbury Corporation Act, 513
Oldham Extension Act, 726
Oliver, G. H., M.P., Electoral Registra-
tion Report. *Cmd. 7004*, 151
Oliver, Isaac, and Nicholas Hilliard
Exhibition, 260
Omnibus Industry, Report.*Cmd.6796*,35
One Hundred Years of Submarine
Cables, 826
O'Neill, D. E. (Chairman) : Working
Party on Fire Prevention and Fire
Fighting in Ships in Port, Report, 849
Onions, 737
and Related Crops, 517
Weed Control in, 55
White Rot, 516

Opencast Coal, Production and Market-
ing, Select Committee on Estimates,
Report, 471, 475
Operation :
and Maintenance of Gas Burners, 772
of Gas Producers, 773
T.I.C.E.R., 655
Ophthalmic :
Medical Practitioners, Working
Party Report, 781
Opticians, Working Party Report,
781, 782
Opium Board Reports, 256, 429, 649, 867
Opium-smoking, United Nations Con-
ference, 256
Optics and Orthoptics, Careers, 75, 208
Oral Cancer, Researches on the Radio-
therapy of, 813
Orchard :
Renovation, 333
Soils, Managing and Manuring, 178,
737
Orchards, Importance of Bees in, 333
Order of Thistle, Appointments, 219
Orders, Decorations, and Medals :
Insignia of, 661
Lists of, and order in which to be
worn, 219, 594
Ordnance :
Factories, Use in connection with
production and export drive, 293,
471
Survey :
Departmental Committee Final
Report, 55
Publications, 85, 222, 600, 820
Organisation :
and Methods Division, Publications,
858
and Procedure of United Nations
Commissions, 649, 866
Charts and Lists of Duties, 640
Organised Camping, 350
Organising International Voluntary
Work Camps, 654
Oriental Painted, Dyed, and Printed
Textiles, Brief Guide, 878
Oriental, Slavonic, East European and
African Studies, Report, 194
Origins and Purpose, 71, 535
Orkney and Shetland, Monuments and
Constructions in, Report. *Cmd. 6788*,
34
See also Ancient Monuments.
Ormskirk, Boundary Commission Re-
port. *Cmd. 8100*, 718

Orr, A. P., British Seaweeds and their utilisation in the preparation of Agar, 559
Orthoptics. See Optics.
Osborne, guide, 117
Our :
Changing Schools, 757
Gardens, 360
Money, 363
Rights as Human Beings, 867
Ouse. See River Great Ouse.
Out of School, 350
Outdoor :
Salad Crops, 334
Tomato, 737
Overfishing. See International Overfishing Conference.
Oversea Education, 61, 186, 345, 535, 751
Overseas :
Economic Surveys, 416, 632, 845
Food Corporation Reports and Accounts, 477, 691
Resources Development :
Acts :
1948, 328
Bill, 150, 268
Standing Committee Minutes, 146
1949, 511
Bill, 459, 463, 486
Accounts, 468, 479, 690, 751, 761
Territories Committee Report, 544
Trade :
of the U.K., Statistics, 630, 846
Report, 845
See also British Overseas Airways.
Owl, Long-eared and Short-eared, 737
Oxenholme. See Grayrigg.
Oxford :
and District Gas Order, 451
City of, Inventory of Historical Monuments, 609
Oxley, T. A. : Grain Storage in East and Central Africa, 750
Oyster, European Flat, Setting Behaviour of Larvae, 518

P

Pacific :
Area, Customs Tariffs, 60
Islands :
at War, 71

Pacific (continued) :
Islands (continued) :
Film Strip, 534
Picture Set, 533
Trusteeship Agreement. Cmd. 7233, 166
Ocean :
North, Weather in, 815
Western, Meteorological Chart, 387
Operations in South West, 436
Region, Supplementary Procedures, 575
Western, Wall Map, 535
Packaging :
Consumer Goods for the Canadian Market, 846
in Germany during 1939–45, 842
Page, L. : Evidence to Royal Commission on Justices of the Peace, 396
Paiforce, 662
Paint Industry in Germany, 1939–45, 841
Painting :
New Plaster and Cement, 394, 881
Preparation of Metal Surfaces for, 882
Paintings, Catalogues of Colour Reproductions, 653, 870
Paints, 630
Paisley Corporation Order Confirmation Act, 174
Bill, 130, 150
Pakenham, Rt. Hon. Lord (Chairman) :
Flying Boat Base Committee, Report, 181
Pakistan :
Air Services Agreement. Cmd. 7922, 705
Extension of Financial Agreement :
Cmd. 7343, 307
Cmd. 7765, 499
Cmd. 8008, 711
Financial Agreement and certain Financial Provisions, Exchange of Letters. Cmd. 7479, 516
Industrial Mission Report, 846
Palace of Linlithgow, guide, 440
Palestine :
Act, 328
Bill, 270, 300
Acts of Violence, Statement of Information. Cmd. 6873, 39
Commission Reports, 435, 866
Conciliation Commission Report, 860
Customs Tariffs, 60

Palestine (continued) :
Government of, Publication (N.P.), 389
Progress Reports of United Nations Mediator, 320, 646, 647
Proposals for the future of. Cmd. 7044, 154
Security Council Truce Commission, 649
System of Education in the Jewish Community, 61
Termination of Mandate, Statement, 353
United Nations Publications, 194, 255, 428, 645, 646, 647, 866, 867
See also European Jewry.
Palestinian Question, Ad Hoc Committee on, Records, 862
Pamela, Wreck Report, 249
Paper, Problem of Newsprint and other printing, 872
Parachute, Constitution of Regiment, 661
Parade and Rifle Drill, Royal Naval Handbook of, 729
Paraguay, Trade and Payments Agreement :
Cmd. 7940, 706
Cmd. 8021, 712
Parasite Service Reports, 345
Parcq, Rt. Hon. Lord du (Chairman) :
Royal Commission on Justices of the Peace :
Evidence, 89, 227
Report. Cmd. 7463, 315
Paris Conference on Reparation. Cmd. 6721, 30
Parish :
Councillors, Election of, 70
of Manchester :
Division Act, 1850 (Amendment) Measure, 331
Revenues Measure, 514
Park, Mungo, 363
Parker, H. W. : Stranded Whales and Turtles, 522
Parking :
of Motor Cars in Lighted Streets Bill, 700
Places :
Memorandum, 107
Model Byelaws, 362
Parks. See National Parks.
Parliament :
Act, 507, 512
Bill, 133, 150, 278, 302, 460, 487
Statement. Cmd. 7380, 309

Parliament (continued) :
Proclamation on Dissolution, 812
Prorogued, 812
Square (Improvements) Bill, 462, 479, 487, 488
Parliamentary :
Constituencies, Returns, 17, 141
Election Orders, 362, 832
Elections, Scotland :
Forms, 833
Returning Officers, 615
Papers :
General Alphabetical Index, 25, 279, 280
Lists of, 463, 680
Parochial Church Councils (Powers) :
Measure, 777
(Amendment) Measure, 450, 514
Ecclesiastical Committee Report, 450
Parsnips, Recommended Grades for, 335
Parsonages :
Measure, 331
Amendment Measure, 125
Part, G. M. : Volcanic Rock from the Cape Verde Islands, 742
Particular Lion : Children's Guide to the Enterprise Scotland Exhibition, 203
Partnership Act, 324, 721
Party Walls between Houses, Fire Resistance and Sound Insulation, 606
Passenger :
and Emigrant Ships, Abstract of Law relating to, 418
Ships engaged in Special Trades in the Far East, Instructions as to Survey, 633
Steamships, Instructions as to Survey, 634
Passports and Frontier Formalities, Preparation of World Conference on, 252
Pasteurised Milks, Prescribed Tests, 67
Pastoral Reorganisation Measure, 451, 514
Ecclesiastical Committee Report, 451
Patent :
Rights and Information, Agreement with U.S.A. Cmd. 6795, 34
Rolls, Calendars, 390
Patents :
Act, 719
Bill, 487
and Designs :
Act, 509, 511
Bill, 447, 449, 453, 454, 458, 459, 475, 482, 486

Patents (continued) :
and Designs (continued) :
Act (continued) :
Draft Bill. Cmd. 6745, 492
Standing Committee Minutes, 475
Act as amended, 50
Bill, 4, 5, 19, 27
Acts, Departmental Committee Reports :
Cmd. 6782, 34
Cmd. 7206, 164
Patents, Designs and Trade Marks, Reports, 473, 687
Paterson, T. (Chairman) : Scottish Housing Advisory Committee on Local Authorities' Methods of allocating Tenancies : Choosing Council Tenants, 778
Pathology of Hydrocephalus, 603
Pattern Staining in Buildings, 606, 827
Patterson, E. F. : Northumberland and Tyneside, 241
Pay :
and Marriage Allowances of Members of the Forces. Cmd. 7588, 324
See also publications of the various Service Departments ; Salaries ; National Arbitration Tribunal Awards, etc.
Pay, Pensions, etc. :
Army. Cmd. 6947, 44
Military Forces :
Cmd. 6799, 35
Cmd. 6995, 47
Pay, Retired Pay, Service Pensions and Gratuities for Members of the Women's Services. Cmd. 7607, 489
Payment by Results in Building and Civil Engineering during the War, 264
Payments :
Agreements :
Chile. Cmd. 7497, 317
Committee Report, 452
Finland. Cmd. 7166, 162
Hungary. Cmd. 7892, 703
Peru. Cmd. 7498, 317
Soviet Union. Cmd. 7431, 313
Uruguay. Cmd. 7340, 306
U.S.A. and French Military Governors of Germany. Cmd. 7824, 504
Balance of :
Cmd. 7324, 306
Cmd. 7520, 319
Cmd. 7648, 492

Payments (continued) :
Balance of (continued) :
Cmd. 7793, 501
Cmd. 7928, 705
Cmd. 8066, 715
Pea :
and Bean Weevils, 178
Moth, 333
Peabody Donation Fund Act, 331
Peace :
Building for, 643
Treaties :
Act, 172
Bill, 148
Bulgaria :
Cmd. 6895, 41
Cmd. 7022, 152
Cmd. 7483, 316
Finland :
Cmd. 6897, 41
Cmd. 7022, 152
Cmd. 7484, 316
Hungary :
Cmd. 6894, 40
Cmd. 7022, 152
Cmd. 7026, 153
Cmd. 7485, 316
Interpretation of :
Certain procedural questions, 575
Order, 792
Italy :
Cmd. 6892, 40
Cmd. 7022, 152
Cmd. 7026, 153
Cmd. 7481, 316
Roumania :
Cmd. 6896, 41
Cmd. 7022, 152
Cmd. 7026, 153
Cmd. 7486, 317
Peach Leaf Curl, 333
Peak Steam Demands, Cause Effect and Cure, 773
Pears :
Recommended Grades, 518
Refrigerated Gas Storage, 664
See also Apples ; Tree Fruits.
Peas :
for drying, 737
for market, canning, and drying, 738
for stock feeding, 737
Peat, Winning, Harvesting, and Utilisation, 395

Peers. See Scottish Representative Peers
Pembrokeshire. See South Wales Coal field.
Penal Servitude Act, 324
Pendennis Castle, guide, 263
Penicillin :
Act, 172
Bill, 133, 130, 110
(Merchant Ships) Bill, 675, 700
Synthesis of, Principles applying to Exchange of Information, Agreement with U.S.A. Cmd. 6737, 32
Penman, W. (afterwards Sir W.) (Chairman) :
Dental Practitioners Working Party, Report, 559
Differences in Dispensing Practice between England and Wales and Scotland, Report, 359
Ophthalmic :
Medical Practitioners Working Party Report, 781
Opticians, Report on average time taken to test sight, etc., 781, 782
Penmanshiel Tunnel Railway Accident Report, 850
Pennines and adjacent areas, Geology, 393
Penrith and the Border, Boundary Commission Report. Cmd. 8100, 718
Pensions :
Allocation of, Memoranda, 110, 421, 563, 858
Appeal Tribunals :
Act, 510
Bill, 279, 303, 446
Assessment Appeals, 386
Notes, 813
(Northern Ireland) Amendment Rules, 813
Notes for the guidance of appellants, 220
Army, Increase of, 261
(Governors of Dominions, etc.) Act, 328
Bill, 133, 150
Home Guard, etc. :
Cmd. 7183, 163
Cmd. 7711, 496
(Increase) Act. 172, 724
Bill, 30, 122
Circular, 67
Declaration Forms, 249
Military Forces or Home Guard. Cmd. 7096, 157

Pensions (continued) :
Ministry of :
Publications (N.P.), 222, 389, 600, 820
Reports, 296, 478, 691
Officers, Soldiers and Nurses. Cmd. 7108, 158
Old Age, Widows', and Blind Persons', Increase. Cmd. 6818, 40
Tribunal Notes and Digests, 220
See also Air Force ; Army ; Home Guard ; Contributory Pensions, Old Age Pensions ; Pay ; War Pensions ; Clergy Pensions ; Police Pensions; National Health Service ; U.S.A. Veterans ; Retired Pay.
Pensionability of Unestablished Civil Service. Cmd. 6942, 44
Pensioners' Questions Answered, 249
People's Dispensary for Sick Animals Act, 513
Percentage Frequencies of various Visibility Ranges, 596
Percival, Lt. Gen. A. E. : Operations in Malaya Command, 384
Performing Animals (Regulation) Act Application Forms, 202
Periodicals, Hand List of Short Titles, 826
Perjury Act, 170
Permanent Central Opium Board, Reports, 429, 649, 867
Perry, W. L. M. : Design of Toxicity Tests, 813
Persia and Iraq Command Official Story, 662
Persian ·
Embroideries, 878
Woven Fabrics, Brief Guide to, 878
Personal :
Bills, Committee Report on Mountbatten Estate, 452
Flying Log Book, 57, 181
Incomes, Costs and Prices. Cmd. 7321, 306
Personnel Management :
Careers, 75, 208, 577
Conference Report, 373
Perth, County of, Morrison's Academy Trust (Amendment) (No. 1) Scheme, 92
Peru :
Air Services Agreement. Cmd. 7394, 310

Peru (continued) :
  Commercial :
    Agreement. Cmd. 7931, 705
    Conditions, Review of, 416
  Economic Survey, 632
  Payments Agreement. Cmd. 7498, 317
Pest Infestation Reports, 606, 829
Pests :
  of Flowers and Shrubs, 738
  See also Insect Pests ; Prevention of Damage by Pests.
Pet Animals Bill, 475, 482, 483, 486, 681
Peterlee Development Corporation Reports, 476, 694
Petrol :
  Rationing :
    Evasions of Control. Cmd. 7372, 309
    for Private Cars and Motor Cycles, 357
    Stations, Technical Committee Report, 634
  See also Motor Spirit.
Petroleum :
  and Synthetic Oil Industry of Germany, Report, 197
  (Production) Act, 723
  (Transfer of Licences) Act, 508
Petrology of the Northampton Sand Ironstone Formation, 606
Petsamo. See Kirkenes.
Pevensey Castle, guide, 117
Peveril Castle, guide, 882
Pharmaceutical Industry in Germany, 1939–45, 841
Pharmacists. See Medical Practitioners.
Pharmacopeias, Unification of, Expert Committee Report, 876, 877
Pharmacy :
  and Medicine Act, 724
  and Poisons Act :
    Form of Application, 563
    Memoranda, 70
    Provisions affecting shops other than Chemists' Shops, 362
  Careers, 208, 793
Phemister, J. :
  British Regional Geology, Scotland, 393
  Rock Wool, 608
Philip, J. R. (Chairman) : Milk Services, Scotland, Report, 610
Philippine Republic :
  Air Services Agreement. Cmd. 7341, 307

Philippine Republic (continued) :
  Commercial Conditions, Review of, 846
  Reciprocal Exemption from Stamp Duty, etc., Property occupied for Diplomatic Purposes. Cmd. 7744, 498
Phillips, E. W. S. : Identification of Softwoods, 605
Phillips, Sir T. W. (Chairman) : Working Party on Building Operations, Report, 883
Phomopsis Disease of Conifers, 553
Photo Reading. See Map Reading.
Photographic Industry in Germany, 1939–45, 623
Physical Training :
  and Recreation Act, Circular, 92
  Act, reprinted, 723
  Basic and Battle, 661, 879
  Facilities for, 91
  for Schools, Syllabus for, 542
  Grants. See Social.
  Reference Book, 194
Physics :
  of drying in heated air, with particular reference to fruit and vegetables, 392
  Technical Register, 593
Physiology and Anatomy, Principles of, 56
Physique of Young Adult Males, 603
Pianos, Open General Licence, 845
Piercy, Rt. Hon. Lord (Chairman) :
  National Youth Employment Council, Report on Youth Employment Service, 811
  Second Reorganisation Commission for England, Hops. Report, 178
Pig, Common Worms of, 738
Piggott, W. R. : Method of determining the Polar Diagrams of Long Wire and Horizontal Rhombic Aerials, 394
Pigs, Nutritional Anaemia in, 334
Pike, Major D. F. B. : Accidents resulting in Injuries to Army Motor Cyclists, 607
Pilchard Fishery. See Cornish Pilchard Fishery.
Pilcher, Sir G. St. C. (Chairman), Naval Discipline Committee on Administration of Justice, Report. Cmd. 8094, 717
Pile, Sir F. A. : Anti-Aircraft Defences of the U.K., Despatches, 220
Pilot Error, 336

Pilotage :
  Act, 721
  Authorities (Limitation of Liability) Act, 508
Pilots :
  and Navigators, Meteorological Handbook for, 595
  of Aeroplanes, Instrument Rating for, 525
Pilots' :
  Licences, 525, 744
  Pilotage, 525
Pine :
  Scots, General Volume Tables, 769
  Shoot Beetles, 354
Pintail, Wreck Report, 637
Pioneers who served, 363
Pipes, Cast Iron and Spun Iron, Interim Report on Deterioration of, 780
Pit Silage, 610
Pit-props, 65, 770
Place Names, Abbreviations of, 790
Places of Worship (Enfranchisement) Act, 326
Plague :
  Control, 436
  Expert Committee Report, 876
Plain Words, 422
Planetary Co-ordinates, 177
Planktonic Copepoda, Free-swimming, 179
Planned Seeing, 741
Planners, Qualifications of, Committee Report. Cmd. 8059, 715
Planning :
  a National Forest Inventory, 874
  Acts, Schemes in Force, 409
  Enterprise, 229
  See also Town and Country Planning.
Plant :
  and Animal Nutrition in relation to Soil and Climate Factors, Report, 741
  Breeders in Canada and U.S.A., List of, 874
  for Prestressing Concrete, New Appliances developed, 883
  Performance of, 830
Plant, Professor Sir A. (Chairman) :
  Distribution and Exhibition of Cinematograph Films, Report. Cmd. 7837, 505
Plantation Crops, Production, Trade and Consumption, 345, 752
Plantations. See Forest.
Plasma. See Proteins.

Plaster Mixes for Inside Work, 882
Pla: 'ering, 827
Plasterers, 793
Plasters, Gypsum and Anhydrite, 606, 881
Plasters, Mortars and External Renderings, Sands for, 829
Platt, B. S. :
  Nutrition in the British West Indies, 61
  Representative Values for Foods, Tropical Countries, 86
Pledge, H. T. : Science since 1500, 85
Plenderleith, H. J. : Preservation of Leather Bookbindings, 741
Plumbing in America, 394
Plums :
  and Cherries, 334
  and Damsons, 55, 737
  See also Tree Fruits.
Plymouth Extension Act, 726
Plympton St. Mary Rural District Council Act, 51
Plywood. See Timber.
Pneumoconiosis. See Silicosis ; Workmen's Compensation.
Poaching and Illegal Fishing of Salmon and Trout in Scotland. Cmd. 7197, 704
Pocket Books, Royal Engineers, 439
Pocock, R. W. : Dudley and Bridgnorth, Geology, 226
Points Values, Rations, Availability of Coupons, etc., 64
Poisons. See Pharmacy.
Poland :
  Compensation for British Interests affected by Polish Nationalisation Law. Cmd. 7403, 311
  FAO Mission Report, 435
  Money and Property subjected to Special Measures, Agreement. Cmd. 7627, 490
  Restitution of Monetary Gold looted by Germany. Cmd. 7749, 498
  Settlement of Financial Questions : Cmd. 6864, 39 Cmd. 7148, 160
  Sterling Payments Agreement. Cmd. 7352, 307
  Trade and Finance Agreement. Cmd. 7628, 491
Polesworth Railway Accident Report, 419
Police :
  Act, 49, 170

Police (continued) :
  Act (continued) :
    Bill, 6, 16, 27
    Enquiry, 362
  (Appeals) Act, 722
  Careers, 208, 368
  Conditions of Service :
    Memorandum of Evidence, 564, 615
    Reports : Cmd. 7674, 494 Cmd. 7831, 504
  Council :
    Committee Report, 202
    Report, 362
  Forces, Inquiries into proposed compulsory amalgamation :
    Cheshire and Chester, 564
    Leicestershire and Rutland, 783
  (Overseas Service) Act, 48
  Pay and Conditions of Service. Cmd. 7707, 496
  Pensions :
    Act, 328, 722
    Bill, 269, 299
    Summary. Cmd. 7312, 305
    Regulations, 563
  Post-War Committee Report, 564
  Rent and Supplementary Allowances, Report, 362
  (Scotland) :
    Act, 49
    Bill, 6, 7, 11, 28
    Regulations, 231, 399
  Service Training. Report. Cmd. 7070, 155
  Uniform, Reports, 362, 615
  (Women) (Scotland) Regulations, 231, 399
  See also Metropolitan Police ; Burgh Police ; Constabulary.
Poliomyelitis, Survey of Outbreak in Scotland, 779
Polish :
  Nationalisation Law. Cmd. 7403, 311
  Resettlement :
    Act, 172, 510
    Bill, 123, 147, 148
    Corps, Formation of, 116
    Select Committee on Estimates, Reports, 468, 678
  Political :
    Activities of Civil Servants. Cmd. 7718, 496
    Rights of Women, 649

Pollitt, H. W. W. : Colonial Road Problems, 750
Pollution. See Water Pollution.
Pontefract :
  and Hemsworth Rural Deaneries (Transfer) Measure, 331
  Electricity Special Order, 196, 355
Poor Relief, Returns, 140, 146, 296
Pope-Hennessy, J. : Donatello's Relief of the Ascension, 658
Poplar Planting, 354
Population :
  Commission Report, 425
  Estimates. See General Register Office Publications.
  Census, Methods, 867
  of Trust Territories, Reports on, 649
  of Western Samoa, Report, 431
  Royal Commission on :
    Papers, 700, 825, 826
    Report. Cmd. 7695, 495
  Studies, 867
  World Trends, 870
Porpoises. See Whales.
Port :
  Construction. See Military Engineering.
  of London Act, 726
  Transport Industry, Reports, 81, 217
Porter, Lord (Chairman) : Committee on Law of Defamation. Cmd. 7536, 320
Porthleven. See Helston.
Ports, U.K., Increased Mechanisation in, Report, 849
Portsmouth Corporation :
  Act, 51
  (Trolley Vehicles) Order Confirmation Act, 330
  Bill 275, 301
Portugal :
  Air Services Agreements :
    Cmd. 6739 and 6740, 31
    Cmd. 6927 and 6929, 43
  Appointment of Doctors to Hospitals. Cmd. 7383, 309
  Azores, Facilities in, Agreement. Cmd. 6854, 38
  Economic Survey, 632
  Monetary Agreements :
    Cmd. 6798, 35
    Cmd. 7050, 154
    Cmd. 7302, 305
    Cmd. 7401, 311
    Cmd. 7713, 496
    Cmd. 7959, 707

Portugal (continued) :
  Port of Beira and Connected Railways, Convention :
    Cmd. 7983, 709
    Cmd. 8061, 766
  Transit Facilities in Azores. Cmd. 7499, 317
Portuguese Africa, Economic Surveys, 632
Possible Effects of Heavy Rain on Aircraft, 596
Post :
  Office :
    Act, 326, 506
    and Telegraph (Money) Acts :
      1946, 49
      Bill, 7, 27
      1948, 326, 328
      Bill, 151, 268
      1950, 720
      Bill, 669, 697
    Commercial Accounts, 463, 677, 695
    Examinations, 58, 182, 185
    Guide, 223, 389, 602, 821
    Publications (N.P.), 85, 223, 389, 602, 821
    Review of Year's Activities, 821
    Savings Banks Accounts, 110, 249, 422, 641, 858
    Select Committee on Estimates, Report, 690
    went to War, 85
  Offices :
    and Streets, London, 223, 389, 821
    in the U.K., 85, 389, 602
  Postal :
    Addresses, 602
    Agreement concerning Insured Letters and Boxes. Cmd. 7795, 502
  Post-graduate Students, Notes on Awards made to, 421
  Post-War :
    Building Studies, 117, 264, 883
    Child. See Teacher.
    Code of Pay, etc., Commissioned Officers of the Armed Forces. Cmd. 6760, 32
  Potato :
    and Tomato Blight, 516
    Crops :
      Register of Certified, 90, 228, 397, 610, 736
      Spread of Virus Diseases in, 390

Potato (continued) :
  Storage Mission to U.S. and Canada, Report, 390
  Trials and Collections, 397, 610, 736
  Tuber Eelworm, 737
  Virus Diseases, 737
Potatoes :
  Dry Rot in, 737
  New varieties since 1939, 397
  Ware, 736
Potters Bar Railway Accident Report, 108
Pottery :
  and Glass, 878
  Careers, 793
  (Health and Welfare) Special Regs., 217
  Draft, Public Inquiry Report, 810
  Regulations, 210
  Working Party Report, 106
  See also Domestic Pottery.
Poultry :
  and Eggs, 434, 873
  Autosexing Breeds, 737
  Coccidiosis, 334
  Colds or Contagious Catarrh, 178, 334
  Coryza Colds and Sinusitis in, 517
  Feeding :
    Emergency, 55
    Scientific Principles of, 334
  Fold System of Keeping, 737
  Industry, Development in North America, 177
  Manure, 737
  Nutrition, Theory and Practice, 737
  Salmonella Infection, 55, 334
  Tuberculosis in, 738
  Worms in, 517
Power :
  Combined Power and Heating, 773
  Costing. See Fuel.
  Presses, Safety in the Use of, 810
  Stowing in the Ruhr and Saar Districts of Germany and the Limburg District of Holland, Report, 557
Power, Sir A. J. : Naval Operations, Ramree Island Area, 384
Practical Economy Points for Industrial Gas Users, 772
Practice :
  Leaflet for Solicitors, 811

Practice (continued) :
Notes :
Local Government Boundary Commission, 82, 219
Scotland, 522
Supplement, 743
Practitioners. See General Practitioners.
Prediction Diagrams for Radiation Fog, 596
Pre-frontal Leucotomy in 1,000 cases, 187
Prematurity, Expert Group on, Report, 877
Preparatory Commission, United Nations, 112, 256
Preparing Metal Surfaces for Painting, 882
Preocolly Water Act, 726
Preservation :
of certain Unfit Houses, Model Forms, 780
of the Rights of the Subject Bill, 125
of Trees and Woodlands, 622
Preserving, A.B.C. of, 544
Presiding Officers and Clerks, Instructions to, 833
Press, Royal Commission on :
Memoranda of Evidence, 228, 396
Minutes of Evidence :
Various Command Papers, pages 305 to 318 inclusive
Index. Cmd. 6973, 151
Report. Cmd. 7700, 495
Press, Film and Radio : UNESCO Publications, 260, 433, 655, 872, 873
Preston Corporation Act, 175
Preston, R. St. J. : Bituminous Coatings for the Protection of Iron and Steel against Corrosion, 225
Prestwick Airport, 525
Prevention :
of Crime Act, 170
of Damage by Pests Act, 511
Bill, 278, 279, 303, 457, 472, 483, 485
Standing Committee Debates, 681
of Fraud (Investments), 105, 245, 415, 846
of Waste of Water, 200
Preventive Medicine Handbook, 179
Price :
Control :
Building Materials and Components, 118
Related Schedules, 103, 243, 413, 628, 842
Lists, Retail, 193

Price, Sir K. W. (Chairman) : Committee on Requirements and Supply of Timber and Plywood, Report, 630
Price, Waterhouse & Co., Report on Accounts of Joint Import-Export Agency, Germany. Cmd. 7978, 709
Prices :
Standard Schedule of, 264
War Department Schedule of, 663
Pridham-Whippell, Vice-Admiral Sir H. D., Coastal Forces Actions Despatch, 386
Primary :
and Secondary Schools in England and Wales, recognised as efficient, 757
Education, Report of Advisory Council on Education in Scotland. Cmd. 6973, 151
School in Scotland, Memorandum on Curriculum, 831
Primates, History of, 522, 742
Prime Minister's Visit to the United States, Communique, etc. Cmd. 8110, 718
Prince of Wales, Loss of, 384
Princess Elizabeth :
Birth of a Prince, 386, 437
Letter of Appreciation for Wedding Present, 262
Princess Elizabeth's and Duke of Edinburgh's Annuities Act, 328
Pringle, J. : British Regional Geology, South Wales, 393
Printed Textiles, European, 878
Printing Trades Dispute, Report. Cmd. 6912, 42
Prinz Eugen. See German Battleships.
Prison :
Act, 506
Commission Examinations, 59
Services, Careers, 368
Prisoners of War, Pages, 116
Prisons :
and Borstals, Statement of Policy and Practice in Administration, 784
in Scotland, Reports :
Cmd. 7747, 498
Cmd. 7966, 708
See also Commissioners of Prisons.
Private :
Bill Procedure and Standing Orders in the House of Commons, Historical Development, 331

Private (continued) :
Development on Agricultural Land, Permission for, 101
Flying, Preliminary Report, 181
Legislation (Scotland) Procedure Publications (N.P.), 90, 229, 398, 613, 821
Pilot's Licence, Extracts from Air Pilot, 525
Street Works Act, 721
Privileges, Committee of, Reports, 14, 23, 136, 142, 143, 287, 478
Privy Council Office Publications, 223, 389, 603, 822
Prize :
Act, 329
Bill, 278, 303
Deposit Account, 283
Money granted to the Navy, Marines, and Air Force. Cmd. 7549, 321
Probation :
and Supervision Particulars, 362, 564
of Offenders :
England, 784
Grant (Deduction) Regulations, 564
Officers :
Directory of, 70, 202, 564
(Superannuation) Act, 172
Bill, 128, 149
Records Cover, 202, 362
Service, 202
Amendments, 784
Scotland, 231
with a Condition of Residence (as it affects Children and Young Persons), Report, 92
Problems of Social Policy, 743
Procedure :
of the House, Select Committee Reports, 13, 23, 126
Records, 858
Rules of, Amendments, 263
Proctor, P. D. (Chairman) : Local Government Manpower Committee Report. Cmd. 7870, 701
Production Engineering, Award of Higher National Certificates, 350
Professional :
Bodies, Requirements in terms of General Certificate of Education, 757
Notes, Meteorological Office, 84, 387, 596, 815
Papers, Ordnance Survey, 820
Qualifications, Technical Register, 593, 811

Professions and Business Management, Opportunities in, Careers Guide, 793
Profits Tax :
Act, 511
Bill, 460, 487
See also Excess Profits Tax.
Programme and Progress, Charts for Civil Engineering and Building Contracts, Preparation of, 664
Prohibition of Fox Hunting Bill, 483
Projection Tables for the Transverse Mercator Projection of Great Britain, 820
Promotion, Army, 262
Properties of Road Tars and Asphaltic Bitumens in relation to Road Construction, 395
Property. See Law of Property ; Money and Property.
Prorogation of Parliament, Proclamation on, 812
Prospect for the Land, 822
Prospects for U.K. Exports in Canada and U.S.A., 415
Prosperity and Depression, 256
Protection :
of Animals :
(Hunting and Coursing Prohibition) Bill, 283
(Scotland) Act, 326
of Treasures of Art and History in War Areas, 440
Proteins, Preservation of, by drying ; with special reference to the production of dried human serum and plasma for transfusion, 86
Provisional :
Classification of Diseases and Injuries, 391
Orders (Marriages) Confirmation Acts, 174, 513
Pruning Stone Fruit Trees, 178
Psychological Disorders in Flying Personnel of the R.A.F., 179
Psychologists and Psychiatrists in the Services, 223
Psycho-therapeutic Treatment of certain Offenders, 399
Public :
Accounts, Committee of, Reports, 13, 18, 21, 22, 138, 142, 143, 285, 293, 469, 474, 476, 684, 687, 691, 786
Administration, Bibliography for Organisation and Methods, 858
Bills, Returns, 293, 480, 693

Public (continued) :
Boards, List of Members. Cmd. 8106, 718
Bodies (Admission of Press) Bill, 483
Debt, 1914-46, 424
Education, International Conference, 654
General Acts and Church Assembly Measures, 47, 170, 327, 510, 719
Health :
Act, 722
and Medical Subjects, Reports, 68, 561
(Coal Mine Refuse) (Scotland) Act, 509
(Drainage of Trade Premises) Act, 508
(Imported Food) Regs., 199, 352, 545, 760
(London) Act, 723
Medical Officers, Salaries, 69, 358
(Scotland) Act, 48, 506
State of, Annual Report, 48
Income and Expenditure, Accounts, 20, 140, 288, 472, 686
Libraries Act, 170
Library Extension, 872
Notaries :
(War Service of Articled Clerks) Act, 50
Bill, 11, 29
See also Solicitors.
Offices (Site) Act, 173
Bill, 128, 147, 149
Select Committee Minutes, 141
Order Act, 723
Record Office Publications (N.P.), 223, 390, 603, 822
Records :
Guide to, 603
(Scotland) Act, 508
Registers and Records (Scotland) Acts :
1948, 329
Bill, 133, 267, 276, 302
1950, 720
Bill, 669, 697
Rights of Way, 840
Safety, 622
Street Works Act, 325
Trustee Office Report, 822
Utilities Street Works Act, 720
Bill, 670, 671, 672, 674, 698, 699
Works :
Building, Codes of Practice, 441

Public (continued) :
Works (continued) :
(Festival of Britain) Act, 510
Bill, 449, 450, 483, 484
Loan Board Reports, 110, 249, 422, 641, 858
Loans Acts :
1946, 49
Bill, 6, 27
1946 (No. 2), 50
Bill, 11, 29
1948, 328
Bill, 133, 150
1949, 512
Bill, 464, 481
1950, 720
Bill, 676, 699
Publications and Debates, Select Committee Reports, 23, 143, 293, 475, 693
Publicity for Local Government, Reports, 201, 782
Publishing :
Careers, 75
See also Journalism.
Puddings. See Cakes.
Pulpy Kidney Disease, 55, 517
Pulverised Coal, Characteristics of, 226
Pupils who are defective :
in Hearing. Cmd. 7866, 701
in Vision. Cmd. 7885, 702
Purchase and Collection of Scrap in Germany, Select Committee on Estimates, Report, 293
Pushkin, 1799-1837, 871
Pyx Chamber, Westminster Abbey, guide, 663

Q

" Q " Code, 57, 181, 339
Qu'aiti, Arms, 186
Qualification Pay, 116
Qualifications of Planners, Committee Report. Cmd. 8059, 715
Qualitative Control of Seeds, Committee Report, 739
Quantitative Study of Foot and Mouth Disease Virus, 603
Quantity :
Surveyors, Royal Engineers, Warrant, 440
Surveying. See Building.

Quarries :
Act, 721
and Gravel Pits, List of, 395
General Regulations Abstract, 357
See also Mines and Quarries.
Quarter III. See Blackquarter.
Queen Alexandra's Imperial Military Nursing Service, 262, 263, 662
Quilting, Notes on, 878

R

Rabbit :
Diseases of, 333, 738
Keeping, 334
Rabbits for Flesh and Fur, 55
Rabies, Expert Committee Report, 877
Race, R. R. : Rh Blood Groups and their Clinical Effects, 391
Racecourse. See Dog Racecourse Betting.
Racking for Ordnance Services, 114
Radar for Merchant Ships, 107
Radcliffe, Sir C. J. (Chairman) : British Film Institute, Committee Report. Cmd. 7361, 308
Radiation from Building Fires, 829
Radio :
Aids :
to Civil Navigation, 57
to Marine Navigation, 107, 247
and Radar for Merchant Ships, 223, 389
Communication, History and Development, Handbook, 542
Education by, 872
Facilities, 574
for Merchant Ships, 223, 602, 821
Noise, Survey of Existing Information, 227
Research Publications, 227, 394, 606, 829
Systems for use in Civil Aviation, 57, 339
Technical Needs, 260
Training for, 872
Valves, Prices, Report, 105
See also Consol ; International Radio ; Maritime Radio Service ; Press.
Radioactive :
Mineral Deposits, Prospector's Hand book to, 606
Substances Act, 328
Bill, 125, 270, 271, 300

Radioactive (continued) :
Traces in Metallurgical Research, 838
Radiocommunications, European Regional Convention for Maritime Mobile Radio Service. Cmd. 7947, 707
Radiography, Field Service Handbook, 116
Radiotelephone Service, Agreement with Soviet Union. Cmd. 7028, 153
Radiotelephony Procedure, 339, 525
Radium :
in Industry, Use of, 209
See also National Radium Trust.
Radley, W. G. (Chairman) : Radio Aids and Audiometers, Report, 225
Radnorshire Police Forces Enquiry, 362
Raffles, Thomas Stamford, 363
Rag Flock Acts, Interdepartmental Committee Report. Cmd. 6866, 39
Raglan Castle, Monmouthshire, guide, 882
Raids on Military and Economic Objectives, Lofoten Islands and Vaagso Islands, 385
Railway :
Accident Reports, 107, 247, 418, 634, 850
and Canal Commission (Abolition) Act, 510
Bill, 278, 303, 446
Bridging, Military Engineering, 439
Clearing System Superannuation Fund Act, 330
Companies :
(Accounts and Returns) Act, 325
Adjustment of Rates, Fares and Charges, 246
Charges Consultative Committee Proceedings, 106
Report of Court of Inquiry. Cmd. 7161, 161
Construction and Operation Requirements, 108, 851
Delegation, Payments Agreement with Uruguay. Cmd. 7106, 157
Development, London Plan, Working Party Report, 633
Locomotive and Rolling Stock, Descriptive Catalogue, 542
(London Plan) Committee Reports, 108, 419
Rates and Charges for Merchandise. See Transport Tribunal.
Shopmen, Report, 592

Railways:
Conciliation and Salaried Grades, Report, 592
Government Control of:
Cmd. 6797, 35
Cmd. 7106, 157
Cmd. 7399, 311
of Germany during 1939–45, 623
Sale of British-owned Railways in Argentina. Cmd. 7405, 311
Staff Returns, 108, 248, 419
Statistical Returns, 108, 247, 419
(Valuation for Rating) Act, 49
Bill, 9, 28
Select Committee Minutes, 21
Raincoats, Gaberdine, Related Schedule, 843
Rainfall:
British, Reports, 595, 814
in East Scotland in relation to the Synoptic Situation, 596
Register of, 84
Raising of Aspen from Seed, 553
Ramree Island Area, Naval Operations, 384
Ramsay, Admiral Sir B. N.:
Assault Phase of the Normandy Landings, 220
Evacuation of Dunkirk, 219
Ramsay, Sir J. D. (Chairman): Scottish National Parks Committee:
National Parks and the Conservation of Nature in Scotland. Cmd. 7235, 166
Nature Reserves in Scotland. Cmd. 7814, 503
Ramsay, Sir M. G. (Chairman): Civil Service National Whitley Council Reports, 641
Ramsbottom, J. E.: Fire Proofing of Fabrics, 226
Ramsden, Lord (Chairman): Committee on Exhibitions and Fairs for Promotion of Export Trade, Report. Cmd. 6782, 34
Rance, Major-Gen. Sir H. (Chairman): British Caribbean Standing Closer Association Committee Report, 749
Rape. See Attempted Rape.
Raphael Cartoons, 878
Raspberry:
Beetle, 55
Cultivation, 178, 736
Diseases in Scotland, 228, 610
Rates:
and Fares, Railway, Report, 246

Rates (continued):
and Rateable Values, England and Wales, 201, 360, 561, 782
in Scotland, etc., Returns, 399, 615, 833
of Wages. See Time.
Ratifications, Accessions, Withdrawals, etc. (Treaties and Agreements):
Cmd. 7016, 152
Cmd. 7292, 304
Cmd. 7597, 488
Cmd. 7873, 701
Rating and Valuation:
Act, 508
Acts:
Circulars, 67
Forms and Reports, 69, 201, 360, 561
Rationing:
A Study of, 86
of Cloth, Clothing, etc., Supplementary Coupons, 63, 190
Rations for Livestock, 334
Rats and Mice, Infestation Control, 64
Raw:
Cotton Commission, Reports and Accounts, 472, 685
Materials Guide, 105, 630
Rayon. See Cotton; Linen; Utility Cloth.
Reaction of Oxygen with Tar Oils, 607
Read, H. H.: British Regional Geology, Grampian Highlands, 393
Reading Corporation (Trolley Vehicles) Order Confirmation Act, 51
Bill, 9, 28
Ready Reckoners, 641
Rearing Fowls for Egg Production, 516
Recall of Army and Air Force Pensioners Act, 329
Recapitulation of Terms and Assurances given to Officers of the Civil Services of India in connection with the Constitutional Changes. Cmd. 7192, 163
Recognition of Schools, etc., as efficient, 542
Reconditioning in Rural Areas, 201
Reconnaissance Pocket Book, Royal Engineers, 439
Reconstruction:
in Devasted Areas, 427
Programme, UNESCO Report on Effectiveness, 872
Record Office. See Public Record Office.

Recovery:
in Europe, First two years of Marshall Aid, 858
of a Deep Sea Fishery, 54
of Waste Heat from Flue Gases, 773
Recreation and Social and Physical Training, Facilities for, 91
Recruitment:
and Training:
of Nurses, 201, 360
of Youth Leaders and Organisers, 92
of Masons, Special Report, 664
Reculver, guide, 263
Red:
Cross Conventions, Final Act of Conference for revision of Geneva Convention. Cmd. 8033, 713
Locust, Permanent Control of Outbreak Areas, International Convention. Cmd. 7560, 492
Spider Mite on Glasshouse Crops, 516
Red Gauntlet, Wreck Report, 421
Redcar Pier and Harbour Order Confirmation Act, 330
Bill, 275, 301
Redevelopment of Central Areas, 409
Redistribution of Seats in House of Commons Bill, 13, 30
Reduction of Sound Transmission through Concrete Floors, 827
Rees, Sir F.: Welsh Slate Industry, Report, 264
Rees, His Honour Judge Tudor: Report on Inquiry into proposed compulsory amalgamation of Police Forces of Leicestershire and Rutland, 783
Rees, W. J.: On a giant squid, 742
Rees-Williams, D. R. (Chairman): Burma Frontier Areas Committee of Inquiry, Report. Cmd. 7138, 160
Reference Pamphlets, United Nations, 867
Refrigerated Gas Storage:
of Apples, 828
of Pears, 604
Refugee Children, Greek, Fate of, 870
Refugees:
and Displaced Persons, United Nations Publications, 424, 653
Travel Documents for, Agreement. Cmd. 7033, 153
Refuse, House, Duties in connection with removal of, 781
Regent's Park Terraces, Report. Cmd. 7094, 157

Regimental:
Debts Regulations, 263
Honours, 116
Regional Air Navigation Meetings, Reports, 572
Registered:
Designs Act, 719
Bill, 447, 459, 487
Provident Societies, General Statistical Summary, 554
Trade Unions, Statistical Summary, 354, 554, 771
Registers. See Public Registers.
Registrar-General. See General Register Office.
Registration:
of Births, Deaths and Marriages (Scotland) (Amendment) Act, 508
of Business Names Act, 47, 721
Officers, Lists of, 224, 390, 558, 776
Registry. See Friendly Societies; Ships.
Regulation of Railways Act, 170
Rehabilitation:
and Resettlement of Disabled Persons, Reports, 81, 592
Medical Advisory Committee (Scotland) Report, 90
Reigate Corporation Act, 50
Reina del Pacifica, Wreck Report, 421
Reinstatement in Civil Employment:
Act, 720
Bill, 676, 699, 700
Decisions, 218
Reith, Lord (Chairman): New Towns Committee, Reports, 32, 34, 39
Related Schedules. See Price Control.
Release:
Leave, Pay and Allowances, 115
from the Army, 116, 440
of R.A.F. Personnel, 56
Relief Needs after termination of UNRRA, 252, 425
Remand Homes:
Directory of, 70
Remuneration and Conditions of Service, Report, 69
Treatment and Rehabilitation of Offenders, Report, 92
Remedy against the Crown as Occupier Bill, 122
Remuneration:
of Consultants and Specialists. Cmd. 7420, 312
of General Dental Practitioners. Cmd. 7402, 311
Renfrew, Airport for Glasgow, 525

Rennell of Rodd, Lord, British Military Administration of Occupied Territories in Africa, 437
Rent:
and Mortgage Interest Restrictions (Amendment) Act, 508
Control:
in England and Wales, Summary of Main Provisions, 842
See also Landlord and Tenant.
of Houses owned by Local Authorities in Scotland. Cmd. 8046, 714
Restrictions (Notices of Increase) Act, 722
Reorganisation Areas Measure, 1944, Amendment Measure, 461, 727
Ecclesiastical Committee Report, 461
Reparation:
Germany:
Agreement. Cmd. 7173, 162
and Restitution of Monetary Gold, Additional Protocol. Cmd. 7476, 316
Paris Conference, Final Act. Cmd. 6721, 30
Reparations for Injuries suffered in the Service of the United Nations, 575
Replanting of Felled Coniferous Woodland in relation to Insect Pests, 770
Representation:
of the Laity (Amendment) Measure, 727
of the People:
Acts:
1948, 329
Bill, 275, 276, 277, 299, 300, 301, 302
Boundary Commission Reports:
Cmd. 7400, 311
Cmd. 7425, 312
Proposed new Constituencies:
Cmd. 7363, 308
Cmd. 7397, 310
1949, 511
Bill, 446, 451, 456, 460, 486
Notes for Candidates on Changes in the Law, 516
1918, 721
(Amendment) (No. 2) Bill, 699
Repulse, Loss of, 384
Requirements:
and Properties for Adhesives in Wood, 828
for Passenger Lines and Recommendations for Goods Lines, 108, 851

Requisitioned:
Land and War Works Acts:
1945, Order, 248
1948, 328
Bill, 150, 268, 299
Property, Release of, Select Committee on Estimates, Report, 140
Resale Price Maintenance, Report. Cmd. 7696, 495
Research:
and Development, Select Committee on Estimates, Report, 143
in Industry, 394
Laboratories, United Nations, Question of establishing, 649
on the Radiotherapy of Oral Cancer, 813
Publications of Research Departments (N.P.), 86, 89, 224, 390, 603, 826
Reports, Selected Government, 630, 846
Workers and Students, Notes on Grants awarded, 393, 607, 830
Researches on the Measurement of Human Performance, 813
Reservoirs, Record relating to, 70
Resettlement. See Servicemen's Resettlement; Rehabilitation.
Residual Values of Fertilisers and Feeding Stuffs, 736
Restaurants. See Civic Restaurants.
Restitution:
of Forfeited Service, 813
of Identifiable Property to Victims of Nazi Oppression, 537
of Monetary Gold looted by Germany:
Cmd. 7265, 168
Cmd. 7749, 498
Restoration of Pre-War Trade Practices Act, 720
Bill, 676, 699, 700
Restormel Castle, guide, 263
Restrictive Practices. See Monopolies.
Retail:
Price Lists, 64, 194, 353, 761
Prices, Interim Index, 218
Method of Construction and Calculation, 810
Retired:
Officers, Navy List of, 516
Pay, Pensions and Gratuities, 881
Orders in Council, 447, 478, 601, 821

Retired (continued):
Pay, Pensions and Gratuities (continued):
Royal Warrants:
Cmd. 7699, 495
Cmd. 7712, 496
Cmd. 7286 and 7287, 540
Retiring Officers, Allocation of Pension, Explanatory Memorandum, 421
Returning Officer, Abstract of Duties, 833
Revenue Departments:
Appropriation Accounts, 14, 17, 135, 281, 464, 678, 695, 755, 788
Estimates, 137, 284, 467, 681, 682
Review of Areas, Local Government Boundary Commission, 82
Reykjavik Airfield:
Reversion to Iceland. Cmd. 6993, 47
Transfer to Iceland. Cmd. 6994, 47
Reynolds, B. J. (Chairman): Approved Schools and Remand Homes, Report, 69
Reyrolle & Co. Ltd., Inspection of, Report, 629
Rheola, Britain's Forests, 769
Rhodes Trust Act, 52
Rhodesia:
Northern. See Northern Rhodesia.
Railways Ltd.:
(Pension Schemes and Contracts) Act, 513
Report, 62
Southern:
and Portugal, Convention with U.K., Port of Beira and Connected Railway:
Cmd. 7983, 709
Cmd. 8061, 715
Wall Map, 752
Rhubarb, 517
Rhuddlan Castle, guide, 663
Ribands and Emblems of Orders, etc., Chart depicting, 437
Rice:
Bulletin, 434
Commodity Report, 873
Diets, 656
East African Mission Report, 534
International Commission:
Constitution:
Cmd. 7611, 489
Cmd. 8118, 718
Report, 874
Meeting, Report, 435
Study Group, Report, 657
See also Grain Crops.

Rice-eating Countries in Asia, Nutrition Problems, 435
Richards, T.: Handbook of Collection illustrating Typewriters, 351
Richardson, L.: Geology of the Country around Witney, 226
Richardson, L. D.: Experiments on Cornish Pilchard Fishery, 739
Richardson, N. A.: Experiments on Preservation of Mine Timber, 605
Richborough Castle, guide, 117
Richey, J. E.: British Regional Geology, Scotland, 393
Riding Establishments Act, 509
Rievaulx Abbey, guide, 117
Rifle Drill. See Parade.
Rights:
and Duties of States, Preparatory Study, 647
and Obligations of Landlords, Tenants and Owner-Occupiers of Agricultural Land, 333
as Human Beings, 867
of the Subject, Preservation of, Bill, 125
of Way Act, 508
Righted Vaccines, their Production and Use in the Field, 657
Ritchie, Professor J. (Chairman):
Scottish Wild · Life Conservation Committee:
National Parks and Conservation of Nature in Scotland. Cmd. 7235, 166
Nature Reserves in Scotland. Cmd. 7814, 503
River:
Boards:
Acts:
1948, 328
Bill, 132, 133, 151, 273, 287, 295, 300
1950, 724
Bill, 463
Guide to Powers and Functions, 739
Great Ouse (Flood Protection) Act, 725
Plate, Battle of, Despatch, 210
Pollution, Prevention of, Report, 561
(Prevention of Pollution) Bill, 699
Rivers Pollution Prevention Act, 506
Road:
Abstracts, 830
Accidents, 108, 419
and Bridge Works, 248

ROA— INDEX 1946-50

Road (continued) :
and Motor Transport :
Draft Provisions, 635
United Nations Conference. Cmd.
7997, 710
and Rail Traffic Act, 723
Report of Licensing Authorities
for Goods Vehicles, 851
Back to Health, 201
Fund :
Accounts, 14, 134, 282, 464,
478
Administration of, Reports, 419,
635, 851
Haulage :
Cases, Tribunal Decisions, 852
Industry, Court of Inquiry Re-
port. Cmd. 7025, 152
Organisation, List of Offices, 108
Research :
in North America, 227
Publications (N.P.), 88, 227, 394,
607, 830
Safety, Reports, 248, 635
Surfacing and Maintenance using Tar
or Asphaltic Bitumen, 394, 830
Traffic :
Act, 508, 722
Acts. See Motor Vehicles.
(Amendment) Act, 723
(Driving Licences), 280
Act, 172
Standing Committee
Minutes, 26
Transport Lighting Act, 507
Vehicles, Mechanically-propelled,
Returns, 109, 248, 420, 635, 851
Roads :
Act, 722
Design and Layout in Built-up Areas,
109
Filling and Sealing Materials for
Joints in Concrete Roads, 607
Improvement Act, 327
Military Engineering, 438
Special Roads Bill, 298, 299, 303,
110, 119, 151
See also Trunk Roads.
Roadstone :
Geological Aspects and Physical
Tests, 88
Tests, Significance of, 395
Roberts, Mrs. J. (Chairman) : Boarding-
out Committee of Scottish Advisory
Council on Child Care, 832

Robertson, T. : Limestones of Scotland,
606
Rochdale :
Canal Act, 513
Corporation Act, 331
Rock Wool, 606
Rocks :
Collected by W. Thesiger in Oman,
742
Guide to Collection, British Museum
(Natural History), 522
Rodents, Families and Genera of living,
521, 522
ROF : Story of the Royal Ordnance
Factories, 620
Rogers, H. R. (Chairman) : Joint Stand-
ing Committee on Safety of Heavy
Power Presses : Report on Bending
Brakes, 577
Roman Amphitheatre, Caerleon, guide,
882
Romanesque Art, 878
Romney Marsh Investigation Report,
518
Ronaldsway, Isle of Man, Aircraft Acci-
dent Report, 337
Rook, 333
Roosevelt Memorial Act, 50
Bill, 11, 12, 29
Root Vegetables, 54
Root-knot Eelworm in Glasshouses, 333
Rootstocks for Apples and Pears 333
Ropes. See Colliery Ropes.
Rosebery, Earl of (Chairman) : Export
and Slaughter of Horses, Departmen-
tal Committee Report. Cmd. 7888,
703
Rosetta Stone, 741
Roseveare, Sir M. P. (Chairman) :
Working Party on Supply of Women
Teachers, Report, 543
Ross and Cromarty County Council
(Kyle of Lochalsh Fishery Pier) Order
Confirmation Bill, 700
Ross, W. : Lateral Deviation of Radio
Waves reflected at the Ionosphere, 666
Ross, Sir W. D. (Chairman) : Royal
Commission on the Press, Report.
Cmd. 7700, 495
Rotating Wing Activities in Germany,
1939-45, 623
Rotations, 334
Rotherham Corporation Act, 52
Roumania :
Revival of Prewar Treaties and
Agreements. Cmd. 7395, 310

INDEX 1946-50

Roumania (continued) :
Treaty of Peace :
Cmd. 7480, 317
Act, 172
Bill, 148
Commentary :
Cmd. 7022, 152
Cmd. 7026, 153
Draft. Cmd. 6896, 41
Interpretation of, Advisory
Opinion, 792
Round Oak Steel Works (Level Crossing)
Act, 330
Rowland Case, Inquiry Report. Cmd.
7049, 154
Roxburgh Educational Trust (Addi-
tional Endowment and Amendment)
Schemes, 614, 831
Royal :
Air Force Communications, Flight
Maintenance, Exchange of Notes
with Greece. Cmd. 7193, 163
Alexandra and Albert School Act, 513
Army Medical Corps, War Office
Publications, 115, 263
Bank of Scotland Officers' Widows'
Fund Order Confirmation Act, 513
Bill, 455, 486
Botanic Gardens :
Edinburgh, 91, 398, 822
Kew, 368, 575, 822
College of Art, Prospectus, 63, 191
Commissions :
Non-Parliamentary Publications,
89, 227, 396, 608, 822
Parliamentary Publications :
Ancient and Historical Monu-
ments and Constructions of
Scotland : Report on City
of Edinburgh. Cmd. 7967,
708
Awards to Inventors, Re-
ports :
Cmd. 7586, 323
Cmd. 7832, 504
Fine Art, Reports :
Cmd. 6819, 36
Cmd. 1613, 489
Cmd. 7988, 709
Population, Report. Cmd.
7695, 495
Press :
Index to Minutes of Oral
Evidence. Cmd. 7690,
495
Report. Cmd. 7700, 495

—RUR

Royal (continued) :
Commissions (continued) :
Holloway College Act, 513
Hospital, Chelsea, Accounts, 138,
287, 470, 685
Marines Acts :
1947, 171
Bill, 13, 30, 151
1948, 328
Bill, 268
Mint, Annual Reports, 396, 609, 826
Navy :
Design Requirements for Aero-
planes, 406
See also Navy.
Observatory Publications, 613, 777
Observer Corps Medal, Committee on
the Grant of Honours Decorations
and Medals. Cmd. 7878, 702
Patriotic Fund Corporation Act, 720
Bill, 671, 697
Review of the Territorial Army, 440
Scottish Museum Publication (N.P.),
398
Signals Handbook of Line Communi-
cation, 440, 881
Warrant Holders List, 219, 440, 594,
812
Ruanda-Urundi Trusteeship Agreement,
433
Cmd. 7196, 164
Rubber :
in Engineering, 98
Industry in Germany, 410
Rubber-growing Smallholdings of
Malaya, 345
Rubber-proofed :
Clothing, 246
Garment-making Industry, Appli-
cation for Establishment of Wages
Council, Report, 811
Ruhr :
Coalfield, Technical Reports, 67, 197,
357, 557
International Authority for, Agree-
ment. Cmd. 7880, 494
Ruislip Aircraft Accident Report, 180, 338
Rules of Procedure :
for Courts-Martial, 263
for General Conference, UNESCO, 260
Runcorn. See Cheshire and Lancashire
County Councils.
Runcorn-Widnes Bridge Act, 726
Rural :
Deaneries of Pontefract and Hems-
worth (Transfer) Measure, 331

118

119

RUR— INDEX 1946-50

Rural (continued) :
District Councillors. See Parish
Councillors.
Education and Welfare in the Middle
East, Report, 109
Housing Sub-Committee Report, 201
Water Supplies and Sewerage Act,
Circular, 69
Welfare, Essentials of, 657
Rushden District Gas Act, 51
Russia :
Convoys to North Russia, Despatch,
812
See also Soviet Union.
Russian Studies, 63, 64
Rutland. See Leicestershire.
Rye. See Grain Crops.
Ryle, J. A. : Thyroid Enlargement, 391

S

Sachs, E. : Report on Public Inquiry
into Draft Pottery (Health and Welfare) Special Regulations, 810
Safeguarding of Industries. See Key
Industry Duty.
Safety :
and Health, Regulations and Orders,
557
Circulars, 67, 198, 357, 557, 775
in Mines Research Publications, 67,
198, 357, 557, 775
in Use :
of Explosives in Coal Mines, Report, 775
of Power Presses, Report, 810
Lamps :
in Coal Mines, Report, 67
Test and Approval of, 776
Measures in Chemical Laboratories,
607
of Employment (Employers' Liability) Bill, 483
of Heavy Power Presses, Report, 577
of Life at Sea, Final Act of International Conference. Cmd. 7492,
317
Pamphlets, 198, 357, 382, 593, 775,
810
Precautions in Schools, 350
Requirements in Theatres and other
Places of Entertainment, Manual
of, 564
See also Road Safety.

Safety, Health and Welfare Museum,
Outline Guide, 81
Safford, A. (Chairman) : Interdepart-
mental Committee on Medical Certi-
ficates, Report, 560
Sailing Ships, History and Development,
192, 351
St. Agnes, Wreck Report, 367
St. Amandus, Wreck Report, 421
St. Andrews :
Cathedral, guide, 882
Links Order Confirmation Act, 173
Bill, 13, 30
St. Boniface Down Aircraft Accident
Report, 337
St. Helena, Colonial Reports, 532, 749
St. Helens Corporation (Electricity and
General Powers) Act, 331
St. John's Chapel, Beverley, Act, 726
St. Lucia, Colonial Reports, 343, 532, 749
St. Mawes Castle, guide, 440
St. Mungo's College, University of
Glasgow, Endowments Scheme, 831
St. Nazaire, Attack on, Despatch, 220
St. Olave's Priory, Herringfleet, guide,
663
St. Vincent, Colonial Reports, 343, 532,
749
Salad Crops, 334
under Glass, 738
Salaries. See National Arbitration Tri-
bunal Awards ; Nurses' Salaries ;
Midwives' Salaries ; Teachers'
Salaries ; Civil Service Arbitration ;
Industrial Court Awards ; Mental
Nurses ; Nurseries ; Public Health
Medical Officers ; Pay.
Sale :
of British-owned Railways in
Uruguay, Agreement. Cmd. 7629,
491
of Food (Weights and Measures) Act,
327
Salerno, Gulf of, Operations in connec-
tion with Landings, 812
Salford Corporation Acts, 331, 514
Salisbury, Sir E. (Chairman) : Biologists
and Agriculturists Sub-Committee,
Technical Register, 811
Salmon :
and Freshwater Fisheries :
Act, 508
(Protection) (Scotland) Bill, 699
and Trout in Scotland, Poaching and
Illegal Fishing of, Report. Cmd.
7917, 704

INDEX 1946-50

Salmon (continued) :
Fisheries, 399
See also Freshwater.
Studies of the scales of young
salmon in relation to growth,
migration, and spawning, 518
Salmonella Infection of Poultry, 55, 334
Salted Cod and related Species, 657
Vivendi. Cmd. 6816, 36
Rumkey, Wreck Report, 421
Samoa, Western :
Population Report, 431
Trusteeship Agreement. 433
Cmd. 7197, 164
United Nations Mission Report, 653
Samplers, Picture Book, 260
Sampampa, Wreck Report, 249
Samwater, Wreck Report, 249
Sand :
and Gravel, Reports, 409, 841
Storms on the Northern Coasts of
Libya and Egypt, 815
Sand-lime (and Concrete) Bricks, 394
Sandringham Aircraft, Accident to, 338
Sands for Plasters, Mortars and External
Renderings, 829
Sanitary Convention. See International
Sanitary Convention.
San Marino, Mutual Abolition of Visas.
Cmd. 7825, 504
Addition of Keyna. Cmd. 7964, 708
Sansom, C. H. : Cultivation of Water-
cress, 172
Sarawak :
Arms and Flag Badge, 186
Colonial Reports, 532, 749
Cultivation of Cocoa, Report, 344
Social Science Research in, Report, 752
Sargon, Wreck Report, 637
Saudi Arabia :
Extradition of Offenders. Cmd.
7066, 155
Friendship and Neighbourly Rela-
tions, Agreement. Cmd. 7084, 156
Trade Agreement. Cmd. 7065, 155
Treaty of Jedda, Prolongation of.
Cmd. 7064, 155
Savings :
Bank Acts :
1948, 327
Bill, 297, 299, 302, 303
1949, 510
Bill, 446
Standing Committee Debate,
681

—SCH

Savings (continued) :
Banks and Friendly Societies Ac-
counts, 110, 249, 422, 611, 858
See also Post Office Savings
Banks ; Trustee Savings
Banks.
Savoy Hotel Ltd., Report on Dispute.
Cmd. 7266, 168
Savoys, 316
Sawyer, F. C. : Identity of Captain
Cook's Kangaroo, 742
Sawyer, J. S. : Possible Effects of Heavy
Rain on Aircraft, 596, 815
Saxton's Maps, 741
Scalloway Castle, guide, 882
Scarborough Castle and Headland, guide,
117
Scarborough, Earl of (Chairman) : Inter
departmental Commission of Inquiry
on Oriental, Slavonic, East European
and African Studies, 194
Scharnhorst, Sinking of, 220
See also German Battleships.
Schedule of Prices. See Prices.
Scholarship, State, 190
School :
and Life, 192
Broadcasting, 872
Child, Health of, 350
Construction, Technical Working
Party Report, 351
Furniture and Equipment, 118
Leaving Age, Raising of, 230
Psychologists, 433
Registers and Records in Primary
and Secondary Schools, 349
Sites and Building Procedure, 63
Teachers (Superannuation) Act, 170,
171
Young Citizens at, 832
Schoolbell in the Wilderness, 872
Schools :
Approved, Salaries and Conditions of
Service in, 230
Boarding, Special and Homes for
Handicapped Pupils, 62
Choice of, 757, 758
Independent, 541, 543
Mathematics in Secondary, 831
New Primary, 541, 757, 758
New Secondary, 706, 757, 758
Recognition as efficient, 63, 757
Story of, 541
See also Remand Homes ; Making
Citizens.

120

121

Schuman Plan : French Proposals for Western European Coal, Iron and Steel Industries. *Cmd. 7970*, 708
Schuster, Sir G. E. :
  Financial and Economic Structure of Maltese Islands, 751
  Qualifications of Planners, Report. *Cmd. 8059*, 715
Science :
  at War, 395
  Careers, 75, 368
  Inventories of Apparatus and Materials for Teaching, 871
  Laboratories in Need, 655
  Liaison, 655
  Museum Publications (N.P.), 63, 191, 351, 542, 826
  Museums in Need, 655
  of Weather, Handbook, 826
  Scholarship Examination, 191
  since 1500, 85
  Teachers in devastated countries, Suggestions for, 655
Scientific :
  and Industrial Research ; Department of :
    Publications (N.P.), 86, 225, 391, 604, 826
    Reports :
      Cmd. 7761, 499
      Cmd. 8045, 714
  Conference on the Conservation and Utilisation of Resources, Proceedings, 867
  Instruments, King George III Collection, 542
  Investigations, 616
  Man-power, Report. *Cmd. 6824*, 36
  Official Conference, British Commonwealth, Report. *Cmd. 6970*, 45
  Policy, Reports :
    Cmd. 7465, 315
    Cmd. 7755, 499
    Cmd. 7992, 710
  Principles of Poultry Feeding, 334
  Studies undertaken by Members of the Colonial Medical Service, Notes on, 751
Scilly, Isles of, guide, 882
Scones. *See* Cakes.
Scotland :
  Agricultural Survey of, 89
  British Regional Geology, 393
  Church of, Lord High Commissioner, Bill, 299
  County Councils Association Act, 50

Scotland (*continued*) :
  House Letting and Rating Act, 325
  Industry and Employment in :
    Cmd. 7676, 494
    Cmd. 7937, 706
  North of, Hydro-electric Board Construction Schemes, Explanatory Memorandum. *Cmd. 7617*, 490
  Western Highlands and Islands, Agreement for Maintenance of Transport Services, 141, 467
Scotland's Marginal Farms, 228
Scots :
  at Work, 231
  Pine and other Conifers, Yield Tables, 65
Scott, T. E. (Chairman) : Architects Sub-Committee, Technical Register, 593
Scottish :
  Administration, Handbook of, 833
  Advisory Council After-Care Committee Report, 832
  Affairs. *Cmd. 7308*, 305
  Agricultural Economics, 736
  Agriculture (Quarterly Journal), 89, 238, 396, 609, 736
  Borstal System, Report, 231
  Building Costs Report, 398
  Departments, Publications (N.P.), 89, 228, 396, 609, 736, 831, 832, 833
  Education Report. *Cmd. 7519*, 319
  Farm Rents and Estate Expenditure, 397
  Farming, 90, 228, 736
  Home Department Electoral Registration Report. *Cmd. 7004*, 151
  Hospitals Survey Reports, 90
  Leaving Certificate, 614
  Local Government Manpower Committee Report. *Cmd. 7951*, 707
  Lunacy and Mental Deficiency Laws, Report. *Cmd. 6834*, 37
  Milk Testing Scheme, 778
  Moorlands, Studies of Tree Growth, 354
  Nurses' Salaries Committee Report. *Cmd. 7238*, 304
  Prison System Report, 616
  Representative Peers, Minutes of Meetings, 130, 669
  Silver, Exhibition Catalogue, 398
  Technical Education, Report. *Cmd. 6786*, 34
  United Services Museum, guide, 664, 883

Sea :
  Fish Industry Bill, 474, 483, 485, 681
  Fishing Boats, Tonnage Measurement, 106
Fisheries :
  Statistical Tables, 335, 518, 739
  See also Fisheries in Wartime.
  Surface Temperatures, Monthly, 815
Seafarers, Hygiene of, 877
Seaford. *See* Newhaven.
Sealing Mechanism of Flexible Packings, 406
Search, Official Certificate of, 200
Seasonal :
  Variation of Daylight Illumination, 393
  Workers, Report of National Insurance Advisory Committee, 478
  Seats for Workers in Factories, 593
  Second Drove Level Crossing Railway Accident Report, 850
Secondary :
  Departments, Schemes of Work for, 831
  Education :
    in Wales, Future of, 543
    New, 191
    Report, 192
    Scotland. *Cmd. 7005*, 151
  Schools Examination Council, Reports, 191, 350, 352
  Secret and Confidential Information communicated to Agents of a Foreign Power, Royal Commission Report, 199
  Secretarial Work, Careers, 75, 368
  Secretary of State for Wales and Monmouthshire Bill, 483
  Security Council, United Nations, Publications, 112, 256, 429, 649, 867
  Security, Wreck Report, 636
  Seed Potatoes, Export Licence, 845
  Seeds Act, 170
Selected :
  Disputes referred to Registrar of Friendly Societies, Reports, 770
  Government Research Report, 630, 846
  Selection of Tenants and Transfers and Exchanges, 561
  Selling through Display, 363
Senior :
  Commercial and Airline Transport Pilots' Licences, 744
  Leaving Certificate (Scotland) :
    Examination Papers, 92
    Proposed Changes, 399

Sensible Use of Latent Heat, 772
Seretse Khama. *See* Bechuanaland.
Serum : *See* Proteins.
Service :
  Book, Teacher's Copy, 758
  Emoluments. *Cmd. 8027*, 712
  of certain Senior Officers. *Cmd. 8047*, 714
  See also National Service.
Serviceman's Resettlement, 81
Services. *See* Engineers Services.
Sessional Printed Papers, Titles and Contents, 463, 680
Setting Behaviour of Larvae of European Flat Oyster, 518
Settlement of Claims under specific Agreements between U.K. and U.S.A. *Cmd. 7615*, 319
Settled Land Act, 722
Seven to Eleven, Your Children at School, 541
Sewage and Sullage Disposal Works, etc., 438
Sewell, R. B. S. : John Murray Expedition, Report, 179
Sewerage. *See* Rural Water Supplies.
Sex and Age Distribution of the Civilian Population, Estimates, 558
Seychelles, Colonial Reports, 343, 532
Shaldon Bridge. *See* Teignmouth.
Shanklin Beach Aircraft Accident Report, 337
Shaw, J. F. : Low Temperature Carbonisation, 606
Shaw, W. A. : Calendar of Treasury Books, 224
Shearman, H. : Northern Ireland, History, Resources and People, 199
Sheep :
  Dipping Bath, 55
  Fluke or Liver Rot, 334
  Foot Rot in, 334
  Louping Ill, 334
  Maggot, 178, 517
  Nostril Fly, 334
  Stomach Worms, 517
Sheffield :
  Order Confirmation Act, 330
  Bill, 274, 300
  University (Lands) Act, 330
Shere Aircraft Accident Report, 180
Sherlock, R. L. :
  Geological Column exhibited in Museum of Practical Geology, 88

Sherlock, R. L. (*continued*) :
  Geology of London and Thames Valley, 226
Shetland. *See* Orkney.
Ship :
  Canal. *See* Forth and Clyde.
  Captain's Medical Guide, 109, 420
  Repairing Facilities on Merseyside, Working Party Report, 729
  Surveyor, Examinations, 59, 183, 185
  Tank Superintendents, International Conference, 606
  Welding Committee Reports, 332, 516, 729
Shipbuilding :
  and Marine Engineering in Germany, 410
  and Ship Repairing Regulations, Revision of, 810
  Employers' Federation, Trade Union Claim for a forty-hour week. *Cmd. 7036*, 153
Shipping :
  Arrangements, United Maritime Authority. *Cmd. 6754*, 32
  Casualties and Deaths, Return 852
  in the United Kingdom Ports, Turn-round, Report, 420
  Maritime Consultative Organisation Conference. *Cmd. 7412*, 312
  Movements at U.K. Ports, 1939–45, 105
  Provisional Maritime Consultative Council, Agreement for Establishment of. *Cmd. 7137*, 160
  See also British Shipping ; Merchant Shipping ; West Indian.
Ships :
  Government, Disposal of, 107
  of the Royal Navy, Statement of Losses, 177, 729
  Registry of, Supplements, 419, 635, 729
Shop Premises in Scotland, Tenure, Report. *Cmd. 7285*, 170
Shops :
  Act, 507, 508, 720
  Bill, 671, 672, 674, 675, 698
  and Business Premises in Scotland, Tenure of, Reports :
    Cmd. 7603, 489
    Cmd. 7903, 703
  Hours of Closing :
    Act, 722
    Cmd. 7105, 157
  (Sunday Trading Restriction) Act, 508

Shoreham Harbour Acts, 330, 725
Short Service Engagements, Commissions, etc., Army, 114, 116, 263
Shrewsbury Order Confirmation Act, 331
  Bill, 274, 301
Siam, F.A.O. Mission Report, 656
Sicilian Straits, Control of, North African Campaign, 386
Sicily :
  Conquest of, 384
  Invasion of, 812
Sickness :
  Absence in Industry, Recording of, 391
  Benefit, Decisions on Claims, 388
  in Population of England and Wales, 558
Sierra Leone, Colonial Reports, 343, 532, 749
Signal :
  Card, 516
  Letters of British Ships, 109, 248, 420, 636, 852
Signatures, etc., concerning Multilateral Conventions and Agreements, 868
Signs. *See* Traffic Signs.
Silage from Sugar Beet Tops, 737
Silicosis and Pneumoconiosis, Provision of Employment in South Wales for persons suspended from the Mining Industry on account of. *Cmd. 6719*, 30
Silk Industry. *See* Cotton.
Silver :
  Early Stuart, 878
  Wedding Anniversaries of Their Majesties, 338, 340
Silverware. *See* Jewellery.
Simon of Wythenshawe, Lord (Chairman) : Distribution of Building Materials and Components, Committee Report, 441
Simpson, B. E. : Thyroid Enlargement, 391
Simpson, J. B. :
  Geology of Central Ayrshire, 606
  Limestones of Scotland, 606
Sinclair, J. A. : Railway Accident Report, 850
Singapore :
  Arms, 751
  Colonial Reports, 343, 532, 749
  Deletion from List of Territories covered by Visa Abolition Agreement. *Cmd. 8036–43* inclusive, 713, 714

Singapore (*continued*) :
  Flag Badge, 751
  Labour Organisation. *See* Malaya.
  Trade and Payments with Malaya and Netherlands Indies, Regulation of. *Cmd. 7487*, 317
  See also Malayan Union.
Singleton, J. E. (Joint Chairman) : European Jewry and Palestine, Report. *Cmd. 6808*, 35
Sinking :
  Funds Accounts, 21, 141, 289, 473, 687
  of the German Supply Ship *Python*, 385
Sirte, Battle of, 220
Site Costing for Builders, 441
Sites and Monuments of History and Art and Archaeological Excavations, Problems of Today, 872
Siting of Houses, Notes on, 841
Skara Brae, Orkney, guide, 882
Skegness Pier :
  and Harbour Order Confirmation Act, 51
  Provisional Order Bill, 9, 28
Skenfrith Castle, guide, 663
Skillman, E. : Irrigation, with notes on crops to which it is applicable, 178
Skylark 6, Wreck Report, 109
Slade, Hon. Sir G. (Chairman) : Legal Committee on Medical Partnerships, Report. *Cmd. 7565*, 322
Slate. *See* Welsh Slate Industry.
Slaughter of Animals :
  Act, 508
  (Amendment) Bill, 699
  (Scotland) Act, 511
    Bill, 455, 469, 483
    Standing Committee Debates, 681
Slavonic Studies. *See* Oriental.
Slough Corporation Act, 513
Sludging and Corrosion in Benzole Absorption Plants, 355
Small :
  Dwellings Acquisition Act, 721
  Landholders and Agricultural Holdings (Scotland) Act, 508
  Vertical Boilers, Steam Cranes, and Shunting Engines, 773
Smallholdings :
  Advisory Council Report, 518
  Centralised Services, Report and Accounts, 739
Smallpox, Vaccination against, Memorandum, 360

Smart, J. : Instructions for Collectors' Insects, 521
Smetswick Corporation Act, 331
Smith, B. : British Regional Geology, North Wales, 393
Smith, D. N. : Natural Durability of Timber, 605
Smith, Sir F. (Chairman) : Road Research Board Report, 607
Smith, H. W. (Chairman) : Pensionability of Unestablished Civil Servants. *Cmd. 6942*, 44
Smith, T. : Natural Lighting of Houses and Flats, 227, 394
Smith, W. C. : Mineralogy, Notes on Kapiti Phonolites and Kenytes in Kenya Colony, 742
Smithfield Market, Report. *Cmd. 6932*, 44
Smoke :
  and its Measurement, 88
  from Merchant Ships, Reduction of, 226
Smoky Chimneys, 827
Snow Fences, 830
Snowdonia National Forest Park Guide, 354
Social :
  Affairs, United Nations Department of, Population Division Reports, 431
  and Economic Research :
    Interdepartmental Committee on, Publications (N.P.), 777
  Labour Statistics, 390
  Reports :
    Cmd. 6868, 39
    Cmd. 7537, 320
    Cmd. 8091, 717
  and Medical Assistance, Convention between the Brussels Treaty Powers. *Cmd. 7973*, 709
  and Physical Training Grant Regs., 543
  Policy, Problems of, 743
  Progress, Technical Assistance for, 869
  Science Research in Sarawak, 752
  Security :
    Agreements with France :
      Cmd. 7455, 314
      Cmd. 7651, 492
      Cmd. 7906, 704
      Cmd. 7911, 704
    Convention with Belgium, France, Luxembourg, and Netherlands. *Cmd. 7911*, 704

Social (continued):
Service in India, 71
Services (Northern Ireland Agreement) Act, 510
Bill, 449, 484
Work, Careers, 205, 793
Society and the Criminal, 564
Softwoods, Identification of, 605
Soil:
Conservation, International Study, 433
Sterilisation, with special reference to Glasshouse Crops, 177
Survey:
Procedure, 830
and its application to Road Construction, 88
Research Board Report, 736
Soils, Concrete, and Bituminous Materials, 88, 607
Solar Radiation at Kew Observatory, 814
Soldier, Improvements in the Way of Life, 115
Soldiers discharged from the Army on account of Neurosis, Re-adjustment in Civil Life, 68
Soldiers' Gratuities. See War Gratuities.
Solicitors:
Act, 720
Bill, 669, 676, 699
Amendment (Scotland) Bill, 132
Careers, 195
Practice Leaflets, 82, 811
Public Notaries Act, 510
Bill, 303, 448
Solid and Laminated Wood Bending, 395
Solomon Islands Protectorate:
Colonial Report, 532
Flag Badge and Arms, 186
Somali Coast, exclusion from Franc Area. Cmd. 7731, 497
Somaliland:
Colonial Reports, 532, 749
Draft Trusteeship Agreement for territory under Italian administration, Special Report, 865
Provisions in respect of territory under Italian administration. Cmd. 8085, 717
Some:
Correlation Coefficients between certain Upper Air data, 596
Studies of current economic conditions in Scottish Farming, 736
Suggestions on the teaching of Geography, 872

Somerset Coalfield. See Bristol.
Somerville, Admiral Sir J.:
Action between British and Italian Forces off Cape Spartivento, 385
Gallant Action by H.M.I.S. Bengal and M.V. Ondina with two Japanese Raiders, 385
Mediterranean Convoy Operations, 385
Something Done, 363
Sorsby, A.: Causes of Blindness in England and Wales, 813
Soulbury, Lord (Chairman): Scales of Salaries for Teaching Staffs:
Farm Institutes, 191, 351
Training Colleges, 351
Sound:
Insulation:
in Traditional Construction, 827
of Partitions, 394
Transmission through Concrete Floors, Reduction of, 827
South:
Africa:
Royal Voyage to, 176
Union of:
Commercial Conditions, 102
Financial Agreement. Cmd. 7230, 166
African Aid to Britain Fund, 249
America, British Agricultural Mission, Report, 334
Croydon:
Aircraft Accident Report, 337
Railway Accident Report, 419
Eastern Region, Scottish Hospital Survey Report, 90
Lancashire Transport Act, 330
Metropolitan Gas Act, 174
Molton Order Confirmation Act, 513
Bill, 457
Pacific Commission, Agreement. Cmd. 7104, 157
Rock, Northern Ireland, Aircraft Accident Report, 181
Shields:
Boundary Commission Report. Cmd. 8100, 718
Extension Act, 726
Staffordshire Waterworks Act, 726
Suburban Gas Act, 330
Wales:
and Monmouthshire, Illustrated Regional Guide, 663, 882
Coalfield, Regional Survey Report, 66

South (continued):
Wales (continued):
Outline Plan, 622
Explanatory Memorandum, 622
Provision of Employment for persons suspended from the Mining Industry on account of silicosis and pneumoconiosis. Cmd. 6719, 30
West:
England and South Wales Electricity (Alteration and Extension) Prepared Scheme, 64
Middlesex Crematorium Act, 174
Western Area, Hospital Services, 67
Southampton Harbour Act. 513
Southend-on-Sea Corporation Act, 174
Southern:
Railway Act, 174
Rhodesia, Commercial Conditions, 102
Southern Opal, Boiler Explosion Report, 633
Southport and Formby, Special Order, 393
Southwold Pier and Harbour Order Confirmation Act, 513
Bill, 456
Soviet Union:
Direct Radiotelephone Service, Agreement. Cmd. 7028, 153
Entry into war against Japan, Agreement. Cmd. 6735, 31
Payments Agreement. Cmd.7431,313
Return of Warships:
Cmd. 7323, 306
Cmd. 7353, 307
Trade:
and Finance Agreement. Cmd. 7439, 313
and Payments Agreement. Cmd. 7297, 304
See also Russia.
Spain:
Air Services Agreement. Cmd. 8112, 718
Assumption by Allied Control Council of Powers of Disposal in regard to German Enemy Assets in Spain. Cmd. 7535, 320
Commercial Conditions, 102
Economic Survey, 632
Expropriation of German Enemy Property in Spain and the Liquidation of Balances and Payments between Spain and Germany. Cmd. 7558, 322

Spain (continued):
Monetary Agreement:
Cmd. 7090, 156
Cmd. 7160, 161
Sterling Payments Agreement. Cmd. 7596, 488
Trade and Payments Agreement:
Cmd. 7449, 314
Cmd. 7689, 495
Cmd. 8003, 710
Sparkes, F. N.: Impressions of Roads and Road Research in North America, 227
Sparrow, House, 178
Spath, L. F.: A new Tithonian Ammonoid Fauna from Kudistan, Northern Iraq, 741
Special:
Army Orders. See War Office Publications.
Constables Act, 171
Educational Treatment, 63
Producers, Board of Trade Publications, 243
Report Series. See Medical Research Council.
Roads Act, 510
Bill, 298, 299, 303, 448, 449, 451, 485
Standing Committee Debates, 681
Species maintained in the National Collection of Type Cultures, List of, 813
Specifications:
Army, 114, 438
D.T.D., 98, 239, 406, 620, 838
Electrical, 97, 238, 406, 620, 837
General Stores, 261, 880
Telephone Cables, 619
Textiles and Clothing, 261, 661
Specimen Forms, Civil Aviation Exams, 181
Speke, Aircraft Accident Report, 180
Spelling Reform Bill, 483
Spens, Sir W. (Chairman): Interdepartmental Committee on Remuneration of:
Consultants and Specialists. Cmd. 7420, 312
General Practitioners. Cmd. 6810, 35
General Dental Practitioners. Cmd. 7402, 311
Spiders, Red, on Hops and other crops in the open, 333
Spirit Tables, 540

Spratt, H. P.:
Merchant Steamers and Motor Ships Handbook of Collections illustrating, 542
Outline History of Transatlantic Steam Navigation, 826
Spray-dried Egg. See Egg.
Spraying Programme for Apples and Pears, 333
Spread of Virus Diseases in the Potato Crop, 390
Spruce:
and other conifers, Adelges attacking, 65
Bark Beetle, 354
Squirrels, Grey, 333
Staff:
Civilian Regulations, 261
College, War Office:
Entrance Examination, 440
List, 440, 881
Relations in the Civil Service, 641
Stafford, Railway Accident Report, 247
Staffordshire Potteries Water Board Act, 513
Staffs of Approved Schools, Absorption of, 221
Stamp Act, 324, 721
Stamps in Current Use, British Colonial, 749
Standard:
Industrial Classification, 422
Schedule of Prices, 264
Standardisation of Engineering Products, Report, 6, 21
Standards:
and Recommended Practices, Civil Aviation, 575, 791
in Building, Further Uses of, 118
of Fitness for Habitation, Report, 201
Standing:
Committee Debates, 145, 147, 294, 299, 463, 481, 694
Committees Return, 146, 293, 480, 693
Orders:
House of Commons, 133, 292, 294, 459
House of Lords, 3, 131, 276, 277, 280
Proposed under the Laying of Documents before Parliament (Interpretation) Bill, 276
Revision, Select Committee Report, 292

Standon Farm Approved School, Report of Committee of Inquiry. Cmd. 7150, 161
Stanhope, Earl (Chairman): National Museums and Galleries Commission, Report, 396
Stanier, Sir W. A. (Chairman): Mechanical Engineers' Panel of the Engineering Committee, Technical Register, 811
Stanley's Charity (West Bromwich) Scheme Confirmation Act, 725
Star Almanac for Land Surveyors, 729
Stars:
Second Cape Catalogue, 777
See also Fundamental Stars.
Starters for Cheese-making, 178
State:
Institutions for Mental Defectives, List of, 187
Management Districts Reports, 26, 146, 297, 677, 696, 784, 833
Papers. See Calendar.
Statelessness, A Study of, 869
Statement relating to Defence. Cmd. 7327, 306
Stationery Office Publications (N.P.), 93, 231, 400, 616, 834
Statistical:
Abstract for the British Commonwealth:
Cmd. 7224, 165
Cmd. 8051, 714
Bulletins, 64, 346, 537, 759
Classification of Diseases, International, 558
Digests, 198, 775
Methods, Studies and Reports, 432
Review of England and Wales, 85, 224, 390, 558, 776
Sampling, Statement, 425, 432
Summaries:
Civil Aviation, 575, 792
Friendly Societies, 354, 554, 771
Tables, Sea Fisheries, 739
Yearbook, United Nations, 869
Statistics:
Agricultural, 396
Scotland, 736
Annual Abstract, 422, 641, 743
Civil Judicial. Cmd. 7821, 504
Criminal:
England and Wales:
Cmd. 7428, 312
Cmd. 7733, 497
Cmd. 7993, 710

Statistics (continued):
Criminal (continued):
Scotland:
Cmd. 7505, 318
Cmd. 7695, 488
Cmd. 7708, 496
Cmd. 7980, 709
Economic, International Conference, 060
Education:
Cmd. 7426, 312
Costing, 787
Engineering and Financial, 352, 554
Epidemiological and Vital, 436, 659, 875
Food and Agricultural, 434, 657, 874
Foreign Trade, Bulletin, 759
Monthly:
Bulletin, United Nations, 258, 432, 652, 869
Digest, 110, 250, 422, 641, 743
Morbidity, 391
Narcotics, 649
National Income, 648
of Various Countries, 866
of Trade Act, 172
Bill, 30, 127, 128, 148, 149
Standing Committee Debates, 280
Minutes, 139
Overseas Trade of the U.K., 630
Studies in Official, 641
Timber, 657, 874
Trade with 50 overseas countries, 846
See also Power Products; Fuel and Power; Licensing; Local Government; Railways; Sea Fisheries.
Status of Women, 425, 644
Statute:
of the International Law Commission, 647
Law:
Committee Publications (N.P.), 93, 232, 400
Revision Acts:
1948, 329
Bill, 270, 273, 275, 302
1950, 720
Bill, 462, 669, 670, 674, 697
Statutes:
Chronological Table and Index, 93, 616
in Force, Index, 834
Revised, Directions for noting, 249
Statutory:
Instruments:
Act, 49
Bill, 3, 4, 5, 27

Statutory (continued):
Instruments (continued):
Lists of, 332, 616, 728
(Parliamentary Control) Bill, 483
Select Committee:
Minutes, 285 to 293, 295, 297, 465-6, 468 to 470, 472 to 475, 478-9, 684-5, 687-8, 692, 696
Reports, 282, 285, 289, 292, 293, 297, 468, 479, 679, 686, 689, 690, 693, 694, 695
Orders (Special Procedure):
Act, 48
(Substitution) Order, Draft. Cmd. 7756, 499
Publications Office Publications (N.P.), 616, 834
Rules and Orders:
Lists, Indexes, Volumes, etc.; see under Statute Law Committee Publications and Statutory Publications Office Publications in the catalogues.
Select Committee:
Memoranda, 16
Reports, 17, 18, 19, 21, 22, 23, 26, 140, 141, 143, 146
Statutory Instruments Revised, 834
Steam:
Control of 'Excess' Air on Steam Raising and Central Heating Plant, 772
Efficient Use of, 355
Engines, Efficient Operation of, 773
Flash Steam and Vapour Recovery, 773
Peak Demands, 773
Power, 773
Process and Heating, 773
Superheated, 772
Thermostatic Control for hot water and steam, 772
Utilisation of, 773
Steel. See European Steel; Iron and Steel.
Stephens, J. V.: Geology of the country around Barnsley, 393
Sterling:
Assets and Monetary Co-operation, U.K. and Ceylon:
Cmd. 7422, 312
Cmd. 7766, 500
Payments Agreements:
Austria. Cmd. 7909, 704

Sterling (continued) :
Payments Agreements (continued) :
Czechoslovakia. Cmd. 7781. 501
Finland. Cmd. 8006, 711
Italy :
Cmd. 7587, 324
Cmd. 7775, 500
Cmd. 7877, 702
Cmd. 8014, 711
Cmd. 8024, 712
Cmd. 8085, 717
Poland. Cmd. 7352, 307
Spain. Cmd. 7596, 488
Stevenage Development Corporation Reports, 469, 694
Stevens, W. C. : Solid and Laminated Wood Bending, 395
Stevenson, Air Vice Marshal D. F. : Air Operations in Burma and Bay of Bengal, 384
Stinging Nettles, 737
Stirling Castle, guide, 440
Stock Issues under the Transport Act, Statements of Guarantee, 281, 285, 286, 288, 289, 290, 292, 296
Stockport Railway Accident Report, 635
Stocks, Mr. M. D. (Chairman) : Midwives Working Party Report, 560
Stocks, P. :
Regional and Local Differences in Cancer Death Rates, 224
Sickness in the Population of England and Wales, 558
Stockton-on-Tees Order Confirmation Act, 330
Bill, 274, 301
Stomach Worms :
in Cattle, 738
in Sheep (Parasitic Gastritis), 517
Stonemasonry, Careers, 793
Storage :
and Maintenance in the Defence Services, 689
Potato, Report of Mission to U.S. and Canada, 390
Storing and Drying Grain, 656
Stornoway Harbour Order Confirmation Acts, 330, 512
Bill, 132, 150, 279, 303
Stowting, Aircraft Accident Report, 180
Straight, W. (Chairman) : Special Advisory Committee, Private Flying, Report, 181
Straits Settlements (Repeal) Act, 49
Bill, 3, 27

Stranded Whales and Turtles, Guide for Identification, 522
Straps. See Containers and Straps.
Strata Florida Abbey, guide, 663
Stratford :
Boiler Explosion Report, 417
Railway Accident Report, 247
Strathmiglo Railway Accident Report, 851
Strauss, G. R. (Chairman) : Road Safety Committee, Report, 248
Strawberries, 177, 517
Strawberry :
Cultivation, 610
Diseases, 396, 610
Street :
Betting Act, 325
Playgrounds Act, 723
Streptomycin, 436
Stroud and Thornbury, Boundary Commission Report. Cmd. 8100, 718
Structure of the United Nations, 258
Struggle for lasting Peace, 869
Strutt, H. A. (Chairman) : Cremation Committee, Report. Cmd. 8009, 711
Student Employees, Western Union Convention. Cmd. 7972, 708
Studies of certain Scottish Moorlands in relation to Tree Growth, 354
Study :
Abroad, International Handbook, 655, 872
Introduction to United Nations, 652
Sturdee Rose, Wreck Report, 249
Stylasteridae (Hydrocorals), 179
Subjects, Preservation of the Rights of, Bill, 125
Submarine Cables, One Hundred Years of, 826
Submarines, H.M. (Polish Edition), 203
See also Battle of the Atlantic.
Succession Duty Act, 324
Sudan :
Reports on Administration, etc. :
Cmd. 7316, 305
Cmd. 7346, 307
Cmd. 7581, 323
Cmd. 7835, 505
Review of Commercial Conditions, 246
Suez Canal, Return of Shipping and Tonnage for 1945, 65
Suffolk, Saxton's Map, 741
Sugar :
Beet :
Feeding Tops Green, 516

Sugar (continued) :
Beet (continued) :
Mission, Report, 177
Pulp for Feeding, 737
Recognition and Control of Diseases, 517
Singling to Delivery, 516
Sowing to Singling, 516
Tops, Silage from, 737
Yellows, 737
Commodity Report, 873
Industry :
of British Guiana, Report, 535
(Research and Education) Fund Accounts, 14, 135, 282, 468, 679, 691
Prolongation of International Agreement :
Cmd. 6949, 44
Cmd. 7237, 166
Cmd. 7542, 320
Cmd. 8086, 717
Suggestion Schemes in Government Departments, 641
Suggestions for Teachers, Handbook, 192, 543
Sullivan, A. P. L. : Report of Inquiry into Fire at Ferring Grange Hotel. Cmd. 7048, 154
Summary Jurisdiction (Scotland) Act, 721
Summer Flowers, 54
Summertime Act, 172
Bill, 123, 147
Sun, Mercury and Venus, Results of Meridian Observations, 777
Sunderland :
Corporation Act, 174
Extension Act, 726
See also Wear
Sunflowers as a Seed Crop, 516
Sunshine, Bright, Averages for the British Isles, 386
Superannuation :
Acts :
1946, 49
Bill, 9, 28
1948, 326
1949, 511
Bill, 454, 473, 483, 484, 485, 486
1950, 720, 724
Bill, 676, 681, 699
Appeal Determinations, 780
Draft Rules for Teachers, Scotland, 831

Superannuation (continued) :
Acts (continued) :
Scheme for National Health Service, 782
Asylum Officers, Act, 325
(Miscellaneous Provisions) Act, 328
Bill, 272, 285, 295, 299, 300
Standing Committee Debates, 463
Scheme for Teachers (Scotland), 399, 614
See also Teachers' Superannuation ;
National Health Service.
Superheated Steam, 772
Supplies :
and Services :
(Extended Purposes) Act, 173
Bill, 131
(Transitional Powers) Act, 48
Bill, 150
See also Limitation of Supplies.
Supply, Ministry of, Publications (N.P.), 93, 233, 401, 617, 837
Supply, Transport and Barrack Services Regulations, 116, 263, 663, 881
Support at Roadheads, 775
Suppression :
of Traffic in Women and Children, United· Nations Publications, 429
of Weeds, 333
Supreme :
Allied Commander, Mediterranean, Report on Operations in Southern France, 115
Commander, Report on Operations in Europe, 114
Court :
of Judicature :
Accounts, 23, 282, 297, 479 (Amendment) Act, 50
Bill, 133, 267, 268, 299
(Circuit Officers) Act, 50
Bill, 10, 12, 29
(Consolidation) Act, 722
Northern Ireland Land Purchase Accounts, 22, 282, 296, 476, 690
Order in Council, 594
Northern Ireland Winter Assize Orders, 362, 564, 784
Practice and Procedure, Report. Cmd. 7764, 499
Prize and Deposit Accounts, 25, 282, 297, 480
Rules, Northern Ireland, Order in Council, 362, 564

Surgery, Careers, 75
Surplus Stores, 104, 238, 245
Purchase by Czechoslovakia. Cmd. 7085, 156
Surrey, Proposed new Constituencies :
Cmd. 7397, 310
Cmd. 7425, 312
Surtax Tables, 204
Survey :
Maps, Notation for, 241
of current Inflationary and Deflationary Tendencies, 424
of Noise in British Homes, 394
of the Soils and Fruit in the Vale of Evesham, 517
of the Trade in Fertilisers, 753
Survey '49, 603
Survey '50, 822
Surveying, Careers, 208
Surveyors of Customs and Excise, Arbitration Tribunal Award, 76
Surveyors, Shipowners, Shipmasters and Shippers, Instructions and Notices to, 849
Surveyors' Certificates, Examinations, 66, 196
Sussex, East, Proposed new Constituencies :
Cmd. 7397, 310
Cmd. 7425, 312
Sutcliffe, R. C. : Meteorology for Aviators, 84, 595
Sutton's Hospital in Charterhouse :
Bill, 150, 268
Charity Scheme Order Confirmation Act, 330
Swan, K. R. (Chairman) : Patents and Designs Acts Departmental Committee, Reports :
Cmd. 6789, 34
Cmd. 7206, 164
Swanage :
Geology of the country around, 226
Pier and Harbour Order Confirmation Act, 330
Bill, 275, 301
Swayback in Lambs, 334
Swaziland, Colonial Reports, 343, 536
Sweden :
Air Services Agreement. Cmd. 7008, 152
Avoidance of Double Taxation and Prevention of Fiscal Evasion with respect to Taxes on Income :
Cmd. 7670, 493
Cmd. 7800, 502

Sweden (continued) :
Closer Economic Co-operation. Cmd. 7884, 702
Economic Survey, 845
German Assets, Agreement regarding Liquidation. Cmd. 7241, 167
Green Crop Drying, 334
Monetary Agreements :
Cmd. 7269, 168
Cmd. 7170, 162
Cmd. 7694, 495
Cmd. 7861, 701
Cmd. 8105, 718
Ocean Weather Station Agreement. Cmd. 7688, 495
Reciprocal Abolition of Visas :
Cmd. 7103, 157
Cmd. 7576, 323
Cmd. 8042, 714
Swedes, Recommended Grades for, 335
Swedish Aircraft Accident Report. Cmd. 7609, 489
Sweet Corn, 516
Swelling of Wood under Stress, 605, 830
Swinbank, W. C. : Prediction Diagrams for Radiation Fog, 596
Swindon Corporation Acts, 124, 514
Swine :
Erysipelas, 517
Fever, 333, 517
Swinton. See Mexborough.
Switzerland :
Air Services Agreement. Cmd. 7953, 707
Economic Survey, 416
German Property in, Agreement concerning Liquidation. Cmd. 6884, 40
Monetary Agreements :
Cmd. 6756, 32
Cmd. 7669, 493
Cmd. 7952, 707
Reciprocal Abolition of Visas :
Cmd. 7149, 160
Cmd. 7573, 322
Cmd. 8043, 714
Swollen Shoot Disease of Cacao in the Gold Coast, 535
Syfret, E. N. :
Capture of Diego Suarez, 384
Mediterranean Convoy Operations, 385
Synthetic Fats, Potential contribution towards world food requirements, 657
Syria :
Exclusion from French Franc Area. Cmd. 7408, 311

Syria (continued) :
Goodwill Trade Mission Report, 245
Settlement of Pending Cases before the Syrian Mixed Courts. Cmd. 7140, 160
Sywell Aerodrome, Aircraft Accident Report, 337

T

Tailoring, Bespoke, Careers, 793
Taints in Milk, 55
Take-all or Whiteheads of Wheat and Barley, 178
Tanganyika :
Civil Service, 344
Colonial Report, 345
Economic Survey, 416
Population of, 649
Reports on Administration, 535, 752
Trusteeship Agreement, 433
as approved by United Nations. Cmd. 7081, 156
Water Resources Report, 533
Tangier, Re-establishment of the International Administration. Cmd. 6899, 41
Tank Production. See Wartime Tank Production.
Tantallon Castle, guide, 882
Tar :
Oils, Reaction of Oxygen with, 607
Surface Dressings, Recommendations, 227
Taranto, Fleet Air Arm Operation, 220
Tariffs :
and Trade :
Annecy Negotiations Report. Cmd. 7792, 501
General Agreement, 258, 432, 652 :
Cmd. 7791, 501
Documents relating to :
Cmd. 7376, 309
Cmd. 7544, 320
Provisional Consolidated Text and Text of Related Documents. Cmd. 8048, 714
Report on Discriminatory Application of Import Restrictions, 869
Geneva Negotiations Report. Cmd. 7288, 168
of the Western Zones of Germany, Statement. Cmd. 7790, 501
See also Customs and Excise.

Tatchell, S. (Chairman) : Plumbing Committee, Building Research Board, Domestic Drainage Report, 264
Tate Gallery. See Museums.
Tax Cases :
Harrison's Digest and Index, 790
Leaflets, 73, 204, 364, 570, 788
Reports, 75, 206, 365, 571, 790
Taxation :
Agreements :
Argentina. Cmd. 7721, 497
Burma. Cmd. 7935, 706
Denmark :
Cmd. 7926, 705
Cmd. 8023, 712
Eire. Cmd. 7182, 163
Israel. Cmd. 7912, 704
Netherlands :
Cmd. 8015, 711
Cmd. 8016, 712
Sweden :
Cmd. 7670, 493
Cmd. 7800, 502
and Overseas Minerals. Cmd. 7728, 497
on Foreign Trade and Investment, Effects of, 869
Taylor, Very Rev. C. W. G. (Chairman) :
Scottish Advisory Council, Reports on :
Psycho-therapeutic Treatment of certain Offenders, 399
Treatment and Rehabilitation of Offenders, 230
Taylor, H. V. : Commercial Flower Production, 54
Taylor, J. H. : Petrology of the Northampton Sand Ironstone Formation, 606
Taylor, T. M. (Chairman) : Committee of Inquiry into Tenure of Shop Premises in Scotland, Report. Cmd. 7258, 168
Teacher :
and the Post-war Child in Devastated Countries, 260
Training :
Primary, 872
Technical, 757, 758
Teacher's Copy of Service Book, 63, 758
Teachers :
Draft Superannuation Rules, Scotland, 831
Education and Training of, 655
Guide for Lecturers and, 428
Programme of Short Courses for, 63

Teachers (continued) :
(Scotland) Superannuation Scheme, 399
Suggestions for, 192, 543
Superannuation Acts :
Allocation of Pensions, Rules, 192
Full Time Service, 757, 758
trained in Emergency Colleges, Two-Year Part Time Study, 541, 543
Training of :
Report. Cmd. 6723, 30
Scotland, 92
Teachers' :
Salaries, 92, 192, 230, 351, 542, 758
Superannuation, Scotland, 91, 92, 614
Teaching :
about the United Nations and Specialised Agencies, 655, 869
as a Career, 351
of Handicrafts in Secondary Schools, 871
of Reading, 654
Staffs of Farm Institutes, Salaries, 191
Teasel, Wreck Report, 421
Technical :
Assistance for Social Progress, 652, 869
and Scientific Register, 593, 811
Bulletin, 518
Colleges, Research in 63, 64
Report Series, 876
Technology in Universities, 877
Tees Conservancy Acts, 52, 726
Teesside Railless Traction Board (Additional Routes) Order Confirmation Act, 513
Bill, 456, 485
Tehran Conference, Military Conclusions. Cmd. 7092, 157
Teignmouth and Shaldon Bridge Act, 513
Telecommunications :
Agreements :
between represented at Bermuda Conference :
Cmd. 6810, 27
Cmd. 7994, 710
between U.S.A. and British Commonwealth Governments :
Cmd. 6818, 36
Cmd. 7810, 503
and Equipment in Germany, 1939–45, 842
Arrangements, Protocol between U.S.A. and U.K. Cmd. 6836, 37

Telecommunications (continued) :
Fundamental Research Problems, 395
United Nations Committee Report, 428
Telegraph :
Act, 512
Bill, 460, 486
(Construction) Act, 325
See also Post Office.
Telephone :
Cables, Specification, 619
Kiosks, Colour of, 622
Temperance (Scotland) Act, Return of Voting Areas, 833
Temperature Averages for British Isles, 386
Temporary :
Housing Programme. Cmd. 7304, 305
Laws, Register of, 23, 146, 297, 684
Tenancy of Shops (Scotland) :
Act, 510
Bill, 449, 466, 483, 484
Standing Committee Debates, 681
Consideration of Principles, 466
Tenant. See Landlord.
Tenants, Selection of, and Transfers and Exchanges, Report, 561
Tendring Hundred Water and Gas Act, 174
Bill, Special Committee Report, 125
Tents, Vans, Sheds, etc., Model Byelaws, 560
Tenure :
and Rents of Business Premises :
Cmd. 7603, 489
Cmd. 7706, 496
of Shops and Business Premises in Scotland :
Cmd. 7255, 170
Cmd. 7903, 703
Terrington, Lord (Chairman) : Industrial Court Inquiry, Road Haulage Industry, Report. Cmd 7025, 152
Territorial :
Army, Regs. 116, 263, 440, 663, 881
Royal Review, Exchange of Messages, 440
See also Corps Warrant.
Auxiliary Service, War Office Publications (N.P.), 114, 261, 440, 660
Testing Memoranda, 67, 198, 776
Teviot, Lord (Chairman) : Interdepartmental Committee on Dentistry, Final Report. Cmd. 6727, 31

Textbooks and Teaching Materials Handbook, 872
Textile Mission to Japan, Report, 105
Textiles :
and their Testing, 630
Committee Report, 544
See also Specifications ; Apparel and Textiles ; Board of Trade Publications.
Thailand :
Commercial Conditions, 846
Educational Mission Report, 872
Thaliacea in Scottish Waters, Distribution of, 616
Thames :
Conservancy Act, 726
Bill, 673
Valley, London and, Geology, 226
Theatres, Safety Requirements in, 564
Theatrical Employees Registration Act, 171
Theiler of Onderstepoort, 363
Theoretical Aspects of Pressure-pattern Flying, 595
Therapeutic Substances Act, 722
Thermal Insulation of Buildings, 664, 772
Thermostatic Control for hot water and steam, 772
These Rights and Freedoms, 869
Thetford Priory, guide, 117
Thieves of Stored Grain, How to fight them, 435
Things we see, 363
This is our Power, 655
This or That, 203
Thistle, Order of, Appointment, 219
Thomas, Sir B. (Chairman) : Transport Tribunal Consultative Committee :
Proceedings, 852
Report, 853
Thomas, E. L. : Readjustment in Civil Life of Soldiers discharged from the Army on account of Neurosis, 68
Thomas, H. A. : Survey of Existing Information and Data on Radio Noise over the frequency range 1·30 m /cs, 227
Thomas, H. D., Geology Bulletin, 521
Thomas Altoft, Wreck Report, 421
Thompson, F. L. (Chairman) : London Regional Planning Technical Sub-Committee, Report, 101
Thornton, Dr. H. G. : Culture Collections of Micro-organisms, 225
Threave Castle, guide, 440

Thyroid Enlargement, 391
Tiger Triumphs, 71
Tiler, Floor and Wall, Careers, 793
Timber :
Balsa, Export Licence, 848
and Plywood, Report, 630
Committee Report, 544
Control, Select Committee on Estimates Report, 692
Decay of, and its prevention, 226
Floors to prevent Dry Rot, Design of 827
for Building Work in Scotland, Use of, 264, 883
in all Building Work, Use of, 264, 664
Industry in Germany, 410
Licence, Softwood and Mining, 845
Mine, Experiments on Preservation, 605
Natural Durability of, 605
Statistics, 657, 874
See also International Timber.
Time :
and Labour on the Farm, 519
Measurement, 192, 826
Rates of Wages and Hours of Labour, 81, 218, 593, 811
Tinkinswood and St. Lythams Long Cairns, guide, 882
Tintagel Castle, guide, 882
Tintern Abbey, guide, 882
Tirpitz attacked by Midget Submarines, 384
Tithe :
Act :
Accounts, 15, 136, 282, 467, 677
(Amendment) Bill, 676
Redemption Commission Publications, 146, 183, 682, 840, 846
Tithes. See City of London (Tithes).
Titmuss, R. H. : Problems of Social Policy, 743
Tizard, Sir H. (Chairman) :
Advisory Council on Scientific Policy, Report. Cmd. 7465, 315
Committee on Industrial Productivity, Report. Cmd. 7665, 493
To the Children from the United Nations, 652
Tobacco :
Prospects of Increased Production in Central and East Africa, 533
(Unmanufactured) Open General Licence, 845
Tobago. See Trinidad

Togoland :
Administration Reports, 345, 535, 752
and the Cameroons, Trusteeship under the U.K. Mandate. Cmd. 6863, 39
Trusteeship Agreement, 433
as approved by United Nations :
Cmd. 7083, 156
Cmd. 7199, 164
Joint Preparations Register, 105, 245, 416
Tomato :
and Cucumber Marketing Draft Scheme, 740
and other plants, Foot Rot and similar diseases, 736
Tomatoes :
Cultivation, Diseases and Pests, 334, 738
Home-produced, Factors affecting marketing in Great Britain, 738
Outdoor, 737
Recommended Grades for, 518
Tonga, Colonial Reports, 343, 532, 749
Tonks, L. H. : Geology of Southport and Formby, 393
Tonnage Measurements, Instructions, 248, 633
Tools :
Machine, 759
See also Diamond Tools.
Tooth, G. : Studies in Mental Illness in the Gold Coast, 750
Topographical Surveys. See Geodetic.
Torquay Order Confirmation Act, 174
Bill, 128, 148
Torrington, Boundary Commission Report. Cmd. 8190, 718
Torry Research Station Controlled Fish Smoking Kiln, 828
Tourist Services. See Catering Wages.
Tovey, Admiral Sir J. C. :
Carrier-borne Aircraft Attack on Kirkenes and Petsamo, 385
Coastal Forces Actions, 386
Convoys to North Russia, 812
Raids on Military and Economic Objectives :
in the Lofoten Islands, 385
in the Vaagso Islands, 385
Sinking of the Bismarck, 220
Towards World Understanding, 655, 872

Tower of London, guide, 117, 440
Town :
and Country Planning :
Act, 173
Bill, 126, 129, 130, 131, 147, 148, 149
Explanatory Memorandum.
Cmd 7006, 151
Standing Committee :
Debates, 280
Minutes, 139
Bill, 1950, 700
Careers, 75, 208, 577
(Control of Advertisement) Regs.,
Explanatory Memorandum,
612, 623
Development Charges, Notes on, 522
General Development Order, Explanatory Memorandum, 409
Scotland, 398
(General Interim Development) Order (Scotland), 1946, Explanatory Memorandum, 90
(Grants) (Scotland) Regs., Memo, 779
Ministry of, Publications (N.P.),
including Appeals Decisions
Bulletins, Circulars, etc., 101,
241, 408, 621, 840
(Scotland) Act, 173
Bill, 129, 130, 131, 147, 149, 150
Explanatory Memorandum.
Cmd. 7034, 153
Memorandum. Cmd. 7075, 156
Standing Committee :
Minutes, 142
Planning. See Housing.
Tenants (Ireland) Act, 325
Towyn Trewan Common Act, 726
Toxic Gases in Industry, Methods of Detection, 88, 395, 607, 830
Toxicity Tests, Design of, 813
Toys and Indoor Games, Board of Trade Publications (N.P.), 245, 415
Track Standards, 557
Tractor Ploughing, 519
Trade :
Agreements :
Eire. Cmd. 7504, 318
Saudi Arabia. Cmd. 7065, 155
Yugoslavia. Cmd. 7602, 489

Trade (continued) :
and Commerce Agreements with Denmark :
Cmd. 7786, 501
Cmd. 7986, 709
and Employment :
Conference, 432
Report. Cmd. 7212, 165
Havana Charter for an International Trade Organisation.
Cmd. 7375, 309
United Nations Reports, 259
and Finance Agreement with U.S.S.R. Cmd. 7439, 313
and Financial Agreements :
Czechoslovakia. Cmd. 7799, 502
Poland. Cmd. 7628, 491
and Investment, Foreign, Effects of Taxation on, 869
and Navigation Accounts, 15, 133, 135, 136, 280, 282, 462, 465, 683, 684
and Payments Agreements :
Argentina :
Cmd. 7346, 307
Cmd. 7735, 498
Cmd. 8079, 716
Brazil :
Cmd. 7438, 313
Cmd. 7730, 497
Netherlands. Cmd. 7487, 317
Paraguay :
Cmd. 7940, 706
Cmd. 8021, 712
Soviet Union. Cmd. 7297, 304
Spain :
Cmd. 7449, 314
Cmd. 7689, 495
Cmd. 8003, 710
Barriers, Attack on, 852
Board of, Publications (N.P.), including Board of Trade Journal, 101, 241, 409, 623, 841
Committee Report, European Recovery Programme, 544
Disputes :
Act, 721
and Trade Unions Act, 49
Bill, 6, 26
Facilities Act, 121
Accounts, 20, 140, 288, 472, 685
in Fertilisers, Survey of, 753
Mission to China, Report, 416
of the United Kingdom, 62, 105, 190, 349, 540, 755

Trade (continued) :
Unions :
Congress, Evidence to Royal Commission on Justices of the Peace, 396
Organisations and Industrial Relations in Trinidad, Report, 186
Unions :
Directory, 879
See also Employers' Associations ; Trade Disputes.
See also Tariffs and Trade ; Statistical Abstract ; Statistics of Trade ;
Meat Trade ; Foreign Trade ;
Commonwealth Trade ; Overseas Trade.
Trading :
Accounts and Balance Sheets, 14, 135, 281, 464, 682
with the Enemy :
Act, 723
Legislation in force, 105, 631
Trafalgar Estates Act, 172
Bill, 30, 124
Select Committee Minutes, 136, 146
Traffic :
in Obscene Publications, 426, 644, 862
in Women and Children, 426, 429, 644, 862
London, Report, 418
Signs :
Authorisation of, 248, 852
Departmental Committee Reports, 109, 42
Direction, 248
See also Road Traffic.
Trailing Cables Committee Reports, 198
Training :
Colleges in England and Wales, 192, 543, 758
Grants, etc., Notes on, 391, 603
of Technical Teachers, 757
Rural Leaders, 874
within Industry, 218, 373
Transatlantic Steam Navigation, Outline History, 826
Transfusion, Serum and Plasma for. See Proteins.
Transit Facilities in the Azores, Agreement with Portugal. Cmd. 7499, 317
Transjordan :
Agreements :
Haifa-Baghdad Road. Cmd. 7062, 155

Transjordan (continued) :
Agreements (continued) :
Transjordan Oil Mining. Law.
Cmd. 7063, 155
Customs Tariffs, 60
Treaty of Alliance :
Cmd. 6779, 33
Cmd. 6916, 42
Cmd. 7368, 308
Cmd. 7404, 311
Translations :
Books and Periodicals, Commission
Report, 62
International Bibliography of, 872
Transmissions of Land and Charges on
Death, 811
Transport :
Act, 173, 724
Bill, 30, 125, 128, 129, 130, 131,
148, 149
Standing Committee Minutes, 139
Statements of Guarantee, 281,
285, 286, 288, 289, 290, 292,
296, 297, 470, 472, 474, 479,
683, 684, 685, 688, 690, 691,
692, 694, 695, 696, 859
(Amendment) Bill, 675, 676, 699
and Communications :
Conventions, 424
Reports, 425, 426, 861
Review, 424, 643, 869
Arbitration Tribunal :
Practice Directions, 636
Scottish Division, 852
Road Haulage Cases Decisions, 852
Commission. See British Transport
Commission.
Ministry of, Publications (N.P.), 106,
246, 417, 632, 848
Statistics, Economic Commission for
Europe, 861
Tribunal, Publications, 852, 853
See also European Central Inland
Transport ; Land Transport ;
Supply, Transport and Barrack
Services.
Transportation, Railway Bridging, 439
Transverse Mercator Projection of Great
Britain, Projection Tables for, 820
Travel Document for Refugees, Adop-
tion of, Agreement of Intergovern-
mental Conference. Cmd. 7033, 153
Travers Foundation. See Greenwich
Hospital.
Trawler Fishing Industry, Report. Cmd.
6882, 40

Treasury :
Books, Calendars of, 224, 822
Chest Fund Accounts, 18, 139, 285,
468
Publications (N.P.), 109, 249, 421,
637, 854
Secretaries. See Ministers of the
Crown.
Treaties :
and International Agreements regis-
tered with United Nations, 432,
652, 869
Catalogue of Exhibition, 390
of Peace Act, 172
Bill, 124, 148
Systematic Survey, 652
with ex-enemy countries. Cmd.
7395, 310
Treatment and Rehabilitation of
offenders, 616
Treaty :
between Burma and U.K. Cmd.
7240, 167
of Economic, Social and Cultural
Collaboration and Collective Self-
Defence between the United Kingdom, Belgium, France, Luxembourg and the Netherlands. Cmd.
7367, 308
Series :
Command Papers. See next entry.
United Nations. See Treaties and
International Agreements.

TREATY SERIES

1946 :
1. European Coal Organisation.
Cmd. 6732, 31
2. Greece, Financial and Economic
Agreement. Cmd. 6733, 31
3. U.S.A., Civil Aviation Conference,
Bermuda. Cmd. 6747, 32
4. U.S.A., Exchange of Information
relating to synthesis of Penicillin.
Cmd. 6757, 32
5. Mexico, Compensation for Expropriated Petroleum Industry
Properties. Cmd. 6768, 33
6. Switzerland, Monetary Agreement. Cmd. 6756, 32
7. France, Air Transport Agreement.
Cmd. 6787, 34
8. Greece, Money and Property subjected to special measures. Cmd.
6780, 33

138

Treaty Series, 1946 (continued) :
9. Portugal, Monetary Agreement.
Cmd. 6798, 35
10. U.S.A., Interchange of Patent
Rights and Information. Cmd.
6795, 34
11. Belgium, Claims for Incidents
involving H.M. Forces. Cmd.
6802, 35
12. France, Supplementary Financial Agreement. Cmd. 6809, 35
13. U.S.A., Settlement Lend-lease,
etc. Cmd. 6813, 36
14. Salvador, Renewal of Commercial Modus Vivendi. Cmd. 6816, 36
15. U.S.A., European Jewry and
Palestine. Cmd. 6822, 36
16. U.S.A., Telecommunications.
Cmd. 6836, 37
17. Bermuda Telecommunications
Conference Agreement. Cmd.
6837, 37
18. U.S.A., Marine Transport and
Litigation. Cmd. 6847, 38
19. Belgium, Civil Administration
and Jurisdiction in liberated
Belgian Territory. Cmd. 6875, 39
20. International Labour Organisation. Cmd. 6880, 40
21. United Nations, International
Monetary Fund and International
Bank for Reconstruction and
Development, Articles of Agreement. Cmd. 6885, 40
22. U.S.A., Avoidance of Double
Taxation. Cmd. 6890, 40
23. Netherlands, Air Services. Cmd.
6893, 40
24. France, Re-establishment of
International Administration of
Tangier. Cmd. 6899, 41
25. U.S.A. and Canada. Unemployment Insurance. Cmd. 6900, 41
26. U.S.A., Double Taxation on
Income. Cmd. 6902, 41
27. Prosecution and Punishment of
War Criminals. Cmd. 6903, 41
28. U.S.A., Use and disposal of captured enemy vessels. Cmd. 6905, 41
29. Turkey, Trade and Payments
Agreement. Cmd. 6907, 42
30. Belgium, Disposal of Property of
Belgian and British Merchant
Seamen who die while serving in
British and Belgian ships. Cmd.
6908, 42

Treaty Series, 1946 (continued) :
31. Norway, Air Communication
Cmd. 6913, 42
32. Transjordan, Treaty of Alliance
Cmd. 6916, 42
33. France, extending time limit o
Anglo-French Agreement o
August 1945. Cmd. 6917, 42
34. European Central Inland Tran
port Organisation. Cmd. 6919, 4
35. Portugal, Air Services. Cm
6927, 43
36. Portugal, Air Services. Cm
6929, 43
37. Netherlands, Monetary Agree
ment. Cmd. 6921, 42
38. Turkey, Air Services. Cm
6928, 43
39. Iceland, Reversion of Reykjavi
Airfield. Cmd. 6993, 47
40. Iceland, Transfer of Reykjavi
Airfield. Cmd. 6994, 47
41. International Sanitary Conver
tion, Protocol. Cmd. 6943, 44
42. International Sanitary Conver
tion for Aerial Navigation, Prot
col. Cmd. 6944, 44
43. Canada and China, Relinquis!
ment of Extra-territorial Right
Cmd. 6948, 44
44. Regulation of Whaling, Inter
national Agreement. Cmd. 694.
44
45. Sugar, Protocols prolongin
International Agreement. Cm
6949, 44
46. Argentina, Economic Agreemen
Cmd. 6953, 44
47. United Nations Food and Agr
culture Organisation. Cmd. 695.
44
48. Turkey, Liquidation of Un
executed Judgment of Anglc
Turkish Mixed Arbitral Tribuna
Cmd. 6956, 45
49. U.S.A., U.S.S.R. and France
Control Machinery and Zones c
Occupation in Austria. Cmd. 695!
45
50. United Nations Educationa
Scientific and Cultural Organisa
tion. Cmd. 6963, 45
51. Brazil, Boundary Line wit!
British Guiana. Cmd. 6965, 151
52. Brazil and Canada, Trade Agree
ment. Cmd. 6966, 45

139

Treaty Series, 1946 (continued) :
53. U.S.A., Financial Agreement.
Cmd. 6968, 45
54. Brazil, Air Transport. Cmd.
6977, 46
55. France, Defence of Madagascar
and Reunion. Cmd. 6986, 46
56. France, Relief from Double
Taxation. Cmd. 6987, 46
57. France, Financial Agreement.
Cmd. 6988, 46
58. International Sanitary Convent
tion, with declarations by Egypt
and France. Cmd. 6989, 46
59. Netherlands, Supply of Aircraft
and Equipment. Cmd. 7011, 152
60. France, Supply of Aircraft and
Equipment. Cmd. 7012, 152
61. International Regulation of
Whaling. Cmd. 6990, 46
62. U.S.A., Copyright Laws. Cmd.
6991, 46
63. U.S.A., Free Importation of
Goods into Leased Bases, Bermuda, Caribbean and British
Guiana. Cmd. 7000, 47
64. International Sanitary Convention for Aerial Navigation, Declarations by Egypt and France. Cmd.
6999, 47
65. America, Zones of Occupation in
Germany. Cmd. 7001, 47
66. Belgium, Intellectual, Artistic
and Scientific Activities. Cmd.
7002, 47
67. United Nations Charter and
International Court of Justice
Charter. Cmd. 7015, 152
68. Sweden, Air Services. Cmd.
7008, 152
69. Chile, Temporary Commercial
Agreement. Cmd. 7013, 152
70. International Agreement for the
Regulation of Whaling. Cmd.
7009, 152
71. France, Mutual Abolition of
Visas. Cmd. 7003, 151
72. Ratifications, Accessions, Withdrawals, etc., Supplementary List
for 1943–6. Cmd. 7016, 152
73. Index, 1943–6. Cmd. 7017, 152
1947 :
1. Luxembourg, Money and Property
subjected to special measures in
consequence of enemy occupation.
Cmd. 7023, 152

Treaty Series, 1947 (continued) :
2. U.S.S.R., Direct Radiotelephone
Agreement. Cmd. 7028, 153
3. Travel Document for Refugees,
Adoption of, Intergovernmental
Conference. Cmd. 7033, 153
4. Belgium, Reciprocal Abolition of
Visas. Cmd. 7038, 153
5. Belgium, Supply of Aircraft and
Equipment. Cmd. 7039, 153
6. European Coal Organisation
Agreement, Protocol for prolongation of. Cmd. 7041, 154
7. Luxembourg, Reciprocal Abolition of Visas. Cmd. 7059, 155
8. Belgium, Supplementary
Monetary Agreement. Cmd. 7057,
155
9. Portugal, Supplementary
Monetary Agreement. Cmd. 7050,
155
10. Netherlands, Supplementary
Monetary Agreement. Cmd. 7051,
155
11. Transjordan, Agreement respecting Haifa-Baghdad Road. Cmd.
7062, 155
12. Transjordan, Agreement respecting the Transjordan Oil Mining
Law. Cmd. 7063, 155
13. Saudi-Arabia, Exchange of Notes
prolonging the Treaty of Jedda.
Cmd. 7064, 155
14. Saudi-Arabia and Koweit, Trade
Agreement. Cmd. 7065, 155
15. Saudi-Arabia and Koweit, Agreement for Extradition of Offenders.
Cmd. 7066, 155
16. Norway, Mutual Abolition of
Visas. Cmd. 7073, 156
17. Saudi-Arabia, Agreement for
Friendship and Neighbourly Relations. Cmd. 7084, 156
18. Czechoslovakia, Purchase of
Surplus Stocks. Cmd. 7085, 156
19. Tanganyika, Trusteeship Agreement as approved by United
Nations. Cmd. 7081, 156
20. Cameroons, Trusteeship Agreement as approved by United
Nations. Cmd. 7082, 156
21. Togoland, Trusteeship Agreement as approved by United
Nations. Cmd. 7083, 156
22. General Index 1939–46. Cmd.
7098, 157

140

Treaty Series, 1947 (continued) :
23. Spain, Monetary Agreement.
Cmd. 7090, 156
24. Norway, Supply of Aircraft and
Equipment. Cmd. 7095, 157
25. Denmark, Reciprocal Abolition
of Visas. Cmd. 7101, 157
26. Netherlands, Reciprocal Abolition of Visas. Cmd. 7102, 157
27. Sweden, Reciprocal Abolition of
Visas. Cmd. 7103, 157
28. Whaling, Supplementary Protocol. Cmd. 7107, 158
29. France, Exchange of Notes
modifying Supplementary Agreement of April 1946. Cmd. 7112,
158
30. France, Application of French
Nationality to British Subjects in
Tunisia. Cmd. 7117, 158
31. Italy, Financial Agreement.
Cmd. 7118, 158
32. Argentina, Prolongation of Commercial Agreement. Cmd. 7123, 159
33. France, Supply of Aircraft and
Equipment. Cmd. 7131, 159
34. U.S.A., Interpretation of para. 6
of Agreement on Settlement of
Intergovernmental Claims. Cmd.
7132, 159
35. Protocol amending Agreements,
Conventions and Protocols on
Narcotic Drugs. Cmd. 7135, 159
36. United Maritime Consultative
Council, Agreement for establishment of a Provisional Maritime
Consultative Council. Cmd. 7137,
160
37. Syria, Settlement of Pending
Cases before Syrian Mixed Courts
Cmd. 7140, 160
38. Denmark, Supply of Aircraft and
Equipment. Cmd. 7141, 160
39. Greece, Transfer of Responsibility of Administration of
Dodecanese Islands. Cmd. 7142,
160
40. Cuba, Reciprocal Notification of
Imprisonment or Death in Prison
of British and Cuban Nationals.
Cmd. 7143, 160
41. Netherlands, Air Services Agreement. Cmd. 7144, 160
42. Norway, Transmission by Post
of Diplomatic Correspondence.
Cmd. 7145, 160

Treaty Series, 1947 (continued) :
43. Switzerland, Reciprocal Aboli
tion of Visas. Cmd. 7149, 160
44. Poland, Settlement of outstand
ing Financial Questions. Cm
7148, 160
45. Lebanon, Settlement of Pendin
Cases before Lebanese Mixe
Courts. Cmd. 7154, 161
46. U.S.A., Use of Gander Airport b
United States Airlines. Cmd. 7157
161
47. Italy, Agreement for withdrawa
of British Forces and Transfer o
Responsibility. Cmd. 7158, 161
48. Spain, Supplementary Monetar
Agreement. Cmd. 7160, 161
49. Iceland, Reciprocal Abolition o
Visas. Cmd. 7159, 161
50. Norway, Supplementar
Monetary Agreement. Cmd 716!
161
51. Egypt, Financial Agreemen
Cmd. 7163, 162
52. Denmark, Participation of
Danish Contingent in occupatio
of Germany. Cmd. 7164, 162
53. U.S.A. and France, Regulatio
of Coal Exports from the thre
Western Zones of Germany. Cm
7165, 162
54. Italy, Agreement for Recruit
ment of Italian Workers i
foundries in the U.K. Cmd. 7168, 16:
55. Sweden, Supplementary
Monetary Agreement. Cmd. 7170
162
56. Agreement on Reparations from
Germany. Cmd. 7173, 162
57. Czechoslovakia, Monetary Agree
ment. Cmd. 7174, 162
58. Chile, Commercial Agreemen
Renewal. Cmd. 7178, 162
59. Austria, Deferment of Claims
Cmd. 7186, 163
60. Czechoslovakia, Supply of Air
craft and Equipment. Cmd. 7187, 164
61. Greece, Maintenance of R.A.F
Communications Flight. Cmd.
7193, 163
62. France, Mutual Application of
Chicago Air Transit Agreement.
Cmd. 7194, 164
63. Not published.
64. Ruanda-Urundi, Trusteeship
Agreement. Cmd. 7196, 164

141

Treaty Series, 1947 (*continued*) :
65. Western Samoa Trusteeship Agreement. *Cmd. 7197*, 164
66. Cameroons, Trusteeship Agreement. *Cmd. 7198*, 164
67. Togoland, Trusteeship Agreement. *Cmd. 7199*, 164
68. New Guinea, Trusteeship Agreement. *Cmd. 7200*, 164
69. Denmark, Industrial Property Agreement. *Cmd. 7208*, 164
70. U.S.A., Air Services. *Cmd. 7209*, 164
71. China, Air Transport. *Cmd. 7211*, 165
72. Norway, Participation in occupation of British Zone of Germany. *Cmd. 7226*, 166
73. France, Treaty of Alliance and Mutual Assistance. *Cmd. 7217*, 165
74. U.S.A., Treaty modifying Marine Transportation and Litigation Agreement of December, 1942. *Cmd. 7218*, 165
75. Italy, U.S.A. and France, German Assets in Italy. *Cmd. 7223*, 165
76. Pacific Islands, Trusteeship Agreement. *Cmd. 7233*, 166
77. Yugoslavia, Displaced Persons. *Cmd. 7232*, 166
78. Sugar, Protocol prolonging International Agreement. *Cmd. 7237*, 166
79. Italy, Return of Gold captured at Fortezza. *Cmd. 7244*, 167
80. China and Burma, Burma–Yunnan Boundary. *Cmd. 7246*, 167
81. U.S.A., France, Czechoslovakia and Yugoslavia, Agreement for non-repatriable victims of German action. *Cmd. 7255*, 168
82. Czechoslovakia, Cultural Convention. *Cmd. 7263*, 168
83. Belgium, Monetary Agreement. *Cmd. 7264*, 168
84. Sweden, Monetary Agreement. *Cmd. 7259*, 168
85. U.S.A., France and Austria, Restitution of Monetary Gold looted by Germany. *Cmd. 7265*, 168
86. Iraq, Financial Agreement. *Cmd. 7269*, 169

Treaty Series, 1947 (*continued*) :
87. U.S.A., Agreement on Tariffs and Trade. *Cmd. 7276*, 169
88. Belgium, Mutual Aid Agreement, Merchant Shipping Expenditure. *Cmd. 7283*, 169
89. Nauru, Trusteeship Agreement. *Cmd. 7290*, 304
90. Ratifications, Accessions, Withdrawals, etc. *Cmd. 7292*, 304
91. Index, 1946–7. *Cmd. 7293*, 304
1948 :
1. U.S.A., Leased Base at Argentina, Newfoundland. *Cmd. 7294*, 304
2. Italy, Mutual Abolition of Visas. *Cmd. 7295*, 304
3. U.S.A., France and Italy, Protocol relating to restitution of monetary gold. *Cmd. 7298*, 304
4. U.S.A., Bizonal Fusion Agreement. *Cmd. 7301*, 305
5. Portugal, Abrogation of Supplementary Monetary Agreement. *Cmd. 7302*, 305
6. Egypt, Financial Agreement. *Cmd. 7305*, 305
7. Norway, Transmission of Diplomatic Correspondence by Air Mail. *Cmd. 7315*, 305
8. Uruguay, Payments Agreement. *Cmd. 7340*, 306
9. Philippine Republic, Air Services. *Cmd. 7341*, 307
10. Greece, Air Services in Europe. *Cmd. 7348*, 307
11. Greece, Air Services between Athens and Cairo. *Cmd. 7349*, 307
12. Poland, Sterling Payments Agreement. *Cmd. 7352*, 307
13. Four Power Naval Commission, Disposal of Excess Units of Italian Fleet, Return to Soviet Union of Warships on Loan. *Cmd. 7353*, 307
14. Whaling, Protocol for 1947–8 Season. *Cmd. 7351*, 307
15. German-owned Patents, Final Act of Conference. *Cmd. 7350*, 308
16. Burma, Recognition of Burmese Independence and related matters. *Cmd. 7360*, 308
17. Netherlands, Settlement of Wartime Debts. *Cmd. 7358*, 308
18. Ethiopia, Agreement amending description of Kenya–Ethiopia Boundary. *Cmd. 7374*, 308

Treaty Series, 1948 (*continued*) :
19. Italy, British Military Fixed Assets. *Cmd. 7377*, 309
20. Netherlands, Supplementary Monetary Agreement. *Cmd. 7381*, 309
21. Portugal, Appointment of Doctors to Hospitals. *Cmd. 7383*, 309
22. U.S.A. Air Bases in the Caribbean Area and Bermuda. *Cmd. 7389*, 310
23. Poland, Compensation for British Interests affected by Polish Nationalisation Law. *Cmd. 7403*, 310
24. Peru, Air Services. *Cmd. 7394*, 310
25. Portugal, Monetary Agreement. *Cmd. 7401*, 311
26. Transjordan, Treaty of Alliance. *Cmd. 7404*, 311
27. Argentina, Sale of British-owned Railways. *Cmd. 7405*, 311
28. France, Exclusion of Syria from French Franc Area. *Cmd. 7408*, 311
29. United Nations, Dissolution of International Institute of Agriculture and transfer of its functions and assets. *Cmd. 7413*, 312
30. Turkey, Air Services. *Cmd. 7429*, 312
31. France, Financial Agreement. *Cmd. 7430*, 313
32. Soviet Union, Payments Agreement. *Cmd. 7431*, 313
33. Brazil, Trade and Payments Agreement. *Cmd. 7438*, 313
34. Soviet Union, Trade and Finance Agreement. *Cmd. 7439*, 313
35. Luxembourg, Reciprocal Facilities for Commercial Air. Service. *Cmd. 7445*, 314
36. France, Cultural Convention. *Cmd. 7450*, 314
37. Spain, Trade and Payments Agreement. *Cmd. 7449*, 314
38. U.S.A., France and International Settlement Bank, Return of gold looted by Germany. *Cmd. 7456*, 314
39. China, Transfer of British Naval Vessels, and waiver of claims for loss of other vessels. *Cmd. 7457*, 314

Treaty Series, 1948 (*continued*) :
40. Denmark, British Forces in, Settlement of Claims. *Cmd. 7460*, 315
41. U.S.A., Economic Co-operation. *Cmd. 7469*, 315
42. U.S.A., Application of Most-favoured-nation Treatment to Western Germany and the Free Territory of Trieste. *Cmd. 7470*, 315
43. World Health Organisation Final Act. *Cmd. 7458*, 315
44. France, Facilities for British Armed Forces pending withdrawal. *Cmd. 7523*, 319
45. France, Reciprocal Military Air Transport Facilities. *Cmd. 7524*, 319
46. Norway Monetary Agreement. *Cmd. 7474*, 316
47. International Labour Organisation. Instrument for amendment of Constitution. *Cmd. 7452*, 314
48. Netherlands, Regulation of Trade and Payments between Singapore and Federation of Malaya and Netherlands East Indies. *Cmd. 7487*, 316
49. Iraq, Prolongation of Supplementary Financial Agreement. *Cmd. 7490*, 316
50. Italy, Peace Treaty. *Cmd. 7481*, 316
51. Italy, Peace Treaty, Maps. *Cmd. 7482*, 316
52. Bulgaria, Peace Treaty. *Cmd. 7483*, 316
53. Finland, Peace Treaty. *Cmd. 7484*, 316
54. Hungary, Peace Treaty. *Cmd. 7485*, 316
55. Roumania, Peace Treaty. *Cmd. 7486*, 317
56. Belgium, Reciprocal Compensation in respect of War Damage. *Cmd. 7495*, 317
57. Chile, Payments Agreement. *Cmd. 7497*, 317
58. Peru, Payments Agreement. *Cmd. 7498*, 317
59. Portugal, Transit Facilities in the Azores to British Military Aircraft. *Cmd. 7499*, 317
60. U.S.A., Mutual Forbearance concerning claims against members and civilian employees of their respective Armed Forces. *Cmd. 7501*, 318

Treaty Series, 1948 (*continued*) :
61. U.S.A., Settlement of Lend-Lease Interest in future sales of surplus stores in the Middle East. *Cmd. 7513*, 318
62. U.S.A., Settlement on interests in joint installations in the Middle East. *Cmd. 7514*, 319
63. U.S.A., Settlement of claims under specific argeements. *Cmd. 7515*, 319
64. International Labour Conference, Final Articles Revision Convention. *Cmd. 7516*, 319
65. Additional Protocol on reparation from Germany and restitution of monetary gold. *Cmd. 7476*, 316
66. U.S.A., Settlement of debts due to Italy under the Anglo-Italian Clearing Agreement. *Cmd. 7518*, 319
67. Italy, Agreement for recruitment of Italian skilled workers for employment in Kenya. *Cmd. 7525*, 319
68. Netherlands, Monetary Agreement. *Cmd. 7531*, 320
69. U.S.A., Establishment of U.S. Educational Commission in U.K. *Cmd. 7527*, 319
70. Spain, Disposal of German Enemy Assets. *Cmd. 7535*, 320
71. France, U.S.A. and Spain, Expropriation of German Enemy Property in Spain and Liquidation of balances and payments between Spain and Germany. *Cmd. 7558*, 322
72. U.S.A., Ferrous Scrap Export. *Cmd. 7538*, 320
73. Sugar, Prolongation of International Agreement for regulating production and marketing. *Cmd. 7542*, 320
74. France, Settlement of Intercustodial Conflicts relating to German Enemy Assets. *Cmd. 7551*, 321
75. Burma, Agreement to control Burma's expenditure in hard currency areas. *Cmd. 7560*, 322
76. Switzerland, extension of Visa Abolition Agreement. *Cmd. 7573*, 322
77. Iceland, extension of Visa Abolition Agreement. *Cmd. 7574*, 323

Treaty Series, 1948 (*continued*) :
78. Norway, extension of Visa Abolition Agreement. *Cmd. 7575*, 323
79. Sweden, extension of Visa Abolition Agreement. *Cmd. 7576*, 323
80. Denmark, extension of Visa Abolition Agreement. *Cmd. 7577*, 323
81. Italy, extension of Visa Abolition Agreement. *Cmd. 7578*, 323
82. Luxembourg, extension of Visa Abolition Agreement. *Cmd. 7579*, 323
83. Chile, Military Service. *Cmd. 7580*, 323
84. Czechoslovakia, Prolongation of Monetary Agreement of November 1945. *Cmd. 7585*, 323
85. U.S.A., Duty Free Treatment of American Relief Goods. *Cmd. 7583*, 323
86. Monaco, Reciprocal Abolition of Visas. *Cmd. 7589*, 324
87. Italy, Sterling Payments Agreement. *Cmd. 7587*, 324
88. Denmark, Monetary Agreement. *Cmd. 7592*, 324
89. Denmark, Participation of Danish contingent in occupation of Germany. *Cmd. 7593*, 324
90. Spain, Sterling Payments Agreement. *Cmd. 7596*, 488
91. Ratifications, Accessions, Withdrawals, etc. *Cmd. 7597*, 488
92. Index, 1948. *Cmd. 7598*, 488
1949 :
1. Belgium, France, Luxembourg and Netherlands, Economic, Social and Cultural Collaboration and Collective Self-Defence. *Cmd. 7599*, 488
2. Yugoslavia, Compensation for British Property, etc., affected by Yugoslav Measures of Nationalisation, etc. *Cmd. 7600*, 488
3. Yugoslavia, Money and property subjected to special measures in consequence of enemy occupation. *Cmd. 7601*, 489
4. Yugoslavia, Trade Agreement. *Cmd. 7602*, 489
5. Whaling, International Convention for Regulation. *Cmd. 7604*, 489

Treaty Series, 1949 (*continued*) :
6. Brazil, Cultural Convention. *Cmd. 7606*, 489
7. Norway, extension of Visa Abolition Agreement to Norwegian Overseas Territories. *Cmd. 7610*, 489
8. Norway, prolongation of Agreement for participation of Norwegian Brigade Group in occupation of Germany. *Cmd. 7614*, 489
9. China, Prevention of smuggling between Hong Kong and Chinese ports. *Cmd. 7615*, 490
10. Poland, Money and property subjected to special measures. *Cmd. 7627*, 490
11. U.S.A., Aids to the Safety of Air Navigation. *Cmd. 7622*, 490
12. U.S.A., prolongation of Bizonal Fusion Agreement. *Cmd. 7623*, 490
13. Belgium, Privileges and facilities for British Forces in Belgium in connection with occupation of Germany and Austria. *Cmd. 7624*, 490
14. Czechoslovakia, prolongation of Monetary Agreement. *Cmd. 7625*, 490
15. Poland, Trade and Finance Agreement. *Cmd. 7628*, 491
16. Uruguay, Sale of British-owned Railways. *Cmd. 7629*, 491
17. Agreement on Most-favoured-nation Treatment for Western Germany. *Cmd. 7643*, 491
18. Netherlands, Release of Netherlands money and property held by the U.K. Custodian of Enemy Property. *Cmd. 7644*, 492
19. France, Social Security Agreement. *Cmd. 7651*, 492
20. Denmark, Supply of Aircraft and Equipment. *Cmd. 7660*, 493
21. U.S.A., Establishment of U.S. Educational Commission in U.K. *Cmd. 7666*, 493
22. Czechoslovakia, Monetary Agreement. *Cmd. 7667*, 493
23. Switzerland, prolongation of Monetary Agreement. *Cmd. 7669*, 493
24. Norway, Monetary Agreement. *Cmd. 7672*, 493
25. Egypt, Financial Agreement. *Cmd. 7675*, 494

Treaty Series, 1949 (*continued*) :
26. Greece, Air Services in Europe. *Cmd. 7678*, 494
27. France, Netherlands and U.S.A., Establishment of Caribbean Commission. *Cmd. 7679*, 494
28. Belgium, France, Luxembourg, Netherlands, U.S.A. and Germany, Establishment of an International Authority for the Ruhr. *Cmd. 7685*, 494
29. Norway and Sweden, Weather Stations Agreement. *Cmd. 7688*, 495
30. Spain, Trade and Payments Agreement. *Cmd. 7689*, 495
31. Czechoslovakia. Mutual Upkeep of War Graves. *Cmd. 7691*, 495
32. Establishment of Preparatory Commission of the Council of Europe. *Cmd. 7687*, 494
33. Sweden, Monetary Agreement. *Cmd. 7694*, 495
34. Portugal, prolongation of Monetary Agreement of April 1946. *Cmd. 7713*, 496
35. Egypt, Equality of treatment in regard to war damage compensation. *Cmd. 7710*, 496
36. Czechoslovakia, prolongation of Monetary Agreement. *Cmd. 7719*, 496
37. Argentina, Avoidance of Double Taxation on income derived from sea and air transport. *Cmd. 7721*, 497
38. Ethiopia, Regulation of Mutual Relations. *Cmd. 7722*, 497
39. Brazil, prolongation of Trade and Payments Agreement. *Cmd. 7730*, 497
40. France, exclusion of French Somali Coast from Franc Area. *Cmd. 7731*, 497
41. U.S.A., Bizonal Fusion Agreement. *Cmd. 7742*, 498
42. Philippine Republic, Reciprocal exemption from Stamp Duty of leases, etc., in respect of property occupied for diplomatic purposes. *Cmd. 7744*, 498
43. Norway, Cultural Convention. *Cmd. 7748*, 498
44. U.S.A., France and Poland. Restitution of monetary gold looted by Germany. *Cmd. 7749* 498

Treaty Series, 1949 (continued) :
45. Denmark, Iceland, Italy, Luxembourg, Norway, Sweden and Switzerland, deletion of Newfoundland from list of territories covered by Visa Abolition Agreement. Cmd. 7759, 499
46. U.S.A., Bizonal Fusion Agreement. Cmd. 7757, 499
47. France, Proposed cession of territory in the Zeila Area to Ethiopia. Cmd. 7758, 499
48. Brazil, Trade Agreement. Cmd. 7768, 500
49. Czechoslovakia, Monetary Agreement. Cmd. 7772, 500
50. Italy, Sterling Payments Agreement. Cmd. 7775, 500
51. European Union, Statute of the Council of Europe. Cmd. 7778, 500
52. Czechoslovakia, Sterling Payments Agreement. Cmd. 7781, 501
53. International Convention for permanent control of outbreak areas of red locust. Cmd. 7783, 501
54. Agreement for preservation or restoration of industrial property rights affected by Second World War. Cmd. 7784, 501
55. Denmark, prolongation of Agreement for participation of Danish contingent in occupation of Germany. Cmd. 7785, 501
56. North Atlantic Treaty. Cmd. 7789, 501
57. Universal Postal Convention. Cmd. 7794, 501
58. Postal Agreement concerning insured letters and boxes. Cmd. 7795, 502
59. European Economic Co-operation, Final Act, Second Session. Cmd. 7796, 502
60. Czechoslovakia, Compensation for British property, etc., affected by Nationalisation, etc. Cmd. 7797, 502
61. Czechoslovakia, Settlement of Intergovernmental Debts. Cmd. 7798, 502
62. Czechoslovakia, Trade and Financial Agreement. Cmd. 7799, 502

Treaty Series, 1949 (continued) :
63. Sweden, Convention for Avoidance of Double Taxation and prevention of fiscal evasion with respect to taxes on income. Cmd. 7800, 502
64. Greece, additional drawing rights for purpose of European Payments Agreement. Cmd. 7802, 502
65. International Wheat Agreement. Cmd. 7819, 504
66. Netherlands, extension of Monetary Agreement. Cmd. 7806, 503
67. France, Social Security. Cmd. 7816, 503
68. International Agreement regarding production and marketing of sugar. Cmd. 7817, 503
69. Belgium, prolongation of Monetary Agreement. Cmd. 7823 504
70. San Marino, Mutual 'Abolition of Visas. Cmd. 7825, 504
71. U.K., U.S.A. and French Military Governors of Germany, Agreement regulating Payments. Cmd. 7824, 504
72. Netherlands, Settlement for U.K. purchases under long term contracts. Cmd. 7843, 505
73. Establishment of Indo-Pacific Fisheries Council. Cmd. 7845, 505
74. Denmark, Iceland, Italy, Luxembourg, Norway, Sweden and Switzerland, addition of Kenya to list of territories covered by Visa Abolition Agreement. Cmd. 7847, 505
75. International Whaling Convention, amendments to schedule. Cmd. 7853, 505
76. Anglo-Netherlands Monetary Agreement. Cmd. 7854, 506
77. Belgium, prolongation of Monetary Agreement. Cmd. 7856, 506
78. Ratifications, Accessions, Withdrawals, etc. Cmd. 7873, 701
79. Index. Cmd. 7882, 702
1950 :
1. Netherlands, Visa Abolition Agreement. Cmd. 7860, 700
2. Sweden, Monetary Agreement. Cmd. 7861, 701
3. U.S.A., Establishment of U.S. Air Base in Trinidad. Cmd. 7864, 701

Treaty Series, 1950 (continued) :
4. International Control for Narcotic Drugs outside scope of Convention of July 1931. Cmd. 7874, 701
5. Yugoslavia, Payment of Balance of compensation for British property, etc., affected by Yugoslav measures of Nationalisation. Cmd. 7875, 702
6. Yugoslavia, Trade Agreement. Cmd. 7880, 702
7. Most-favoured-nation Treatment for areas of Western Germany under Military Occupation. Cmd. 7876, 702
8. Italy, Sterling Payments Agreement. Cmd. 7877, 702
9. Finland, Insurance and Reinsurance Contracts. Cmd. 7886, 702
10. United Nations, General Convention on Privileges and Immunities. Cmd. 7891, 703
11. Hungary, amendment of Anglo-Hungarian Payments Agreement of August 1946. Cmd. 7892, 703
12. U.S.A., Visas. Cmd. 7893, 703
13. U.S.A., Mutual Defence Assistance Agreement. Cmd. 7894, 703
14. France, Disposal of unused drawing rights. Cmd. 7900, 703
15. Germany, Disposal of unused drawing rights. Cmd. 7901, 703
16. Burma, Commercial Relations pending conclusion of a new Treaty of Commerce and Navigation. Cmd. 7902, 703
17. Turkey, establishment of drawing rights for purposes of European Payments Agreement. Cmd. 7905, 703
18. Austria, Sterling Payments Agreement. Cmd. 7909, 704
19. Israel, continuance in force of 1947 arrangement for avoidance of double taxation, etc. Cmd. 7912, 704
20. International Whaling Convention, further agreement to schedule. Cmd. 7918, 705
21. U.S.A., amendment to Agreement relating to ferrous scrap metal. Cmd. 7925, 705
22. Portugal, modification and prolongation of Monetary Agreement of April 1946. Cmd. 7959, 707

Treaty Series, 1950 (continued) :
23. Belgium, prolongation of Monetary Agreement. Cmd. 792 705
24. Peru, continuance in force of Commercial Agreement. Cm 7931, 705
25. Constitution of Internation Refugee Organisation. Cmd. 793 706
26. Israel, Settlement of financ matters outstanding as a result termination of Mandate of Pale tine. Cmd. 7941, 706
27. Italy, Revival of certain pre-w treaties. Cmd. 7943, 706
28. U.S.A., Additional funds f continued operation of U.S. Ed cational Commission in U.K. Cm 7944, 706
29. European Regional Conventic for Maritime Mobile Radio Servic Cmd. 7947, 707
30. European Broadcasting Cor vention. Cmd. 7946, 707
31. Switzerland, Monetary Agre ment. Cmd. 7952, 707
32. U.S.A., amendment of Econom Co-operation Agreement. Cm 7961, 708
33. San Marino, addition of Kenya list of territories covered by Vi Abolition Agreement. Cmd. 796 708
34. Netherlands, Cultural Conve tion. Cmd. 7984, 709
35. Denmark, Trade and Commerc Cmd. 7986, 709
36. Convention of the Worl Meteorological Organisation. Cm 7989, 709
37. Telecommunications, Final A and Agreement. Cmd. 7994, 71
38. U.S.A., Final issues arising out Bizonal Fusion Agreement. Cm 8001, 710
39. Spain, Trade and Paymen Agreement, prolongation. Cm 8003, 710
40. Finland, Sterling Paymen Agreement. Cmd. 8006, 711
41. Australia, India, Ceylon and Ceylon, Loan to Burma. Cm 8007, 711
42. Italy, extension of Sterling Pa ments Agreement. Cmd. 8014, 71

Treaty Series, 1950 (continued) :
43. Netherlands, Avoidance of Double Taxation, etc. Cmd. 8015, 711
44. Netherlands, Avoidance of Double Taxation with respect to duties on estates of deceased persons. Cmd. 8016, 712
45. Paraguay, Trade and Payments Agreement. Cmd. 8021, 712
46. Greece, Exchange of Notes regarding Air Services in Europe. Cmd. 8022, 712
47. Denmark, Avoidance of Double Taxation, etc. Cmd. 8023, 712
48. Italy, extension of Sterling Payments Agreement. Cmd. 8024, 712
49. Belgium, prolongation of Monetary Agreement. Cmd. 8029, 712
50. Brazil, Cultural Convention. Cmd. 8032, 713
51. Denmark, deletion of Singapore and Federation of Malaya from list of territories covered by Visa Abolition Agreement. Cmd. 8036, 713
52. Iceland, deletion of Singapore and Federation of Malaya from list of territories covered by Visa Abolition Agreement. Cmd. 8037, 713
53. Italy, deletion of Singapore and Federation of Malaya from list of territories covered by Visa Abolition Agreement. Cmd. 8038, 713
54. Luxembourg, deletion of Singapore and Federation of Malaya from list of territories covered by Visa Abolition Agreement. Cmd. 8039, 713
55. Netherlands, deletion of Singapore and Federation of Malaya from List of territories covered by Visa Abolition Agreement. Cmd. 8040, 713
56. Norway, deletion of Singapore and Federation of Malaya from list of territories covered by Visa Abolition Agreement. Cmd. 8041, 714
57. Sweden, deletion of Singapore and Federation of Malaya from list of territories covered by Visa Abolition Agreement. Cmd. 8042, 714

Treaty Series, 1950 (continued) :
58. Switzerland, deletion of Singapore and Federation of Malaya from list of territories covered by Visa Abolition Agreement. Cmd. 8043, 714
59. Customs Tariff Protocol. Cmd. 8050, 714
60. Denmark, prolongation of Monetary Agreement. Cmd. 8055, 714
61. Southern Rhodesia and Portugal, Port of Beira and connected railways. Cmd. 8061, 715
62. International Fisheries Convention for North-west Atlantic. Cmd. 8071, 716
63. Brazil, exchange of Notes regarding Commercial Transactions. Cmd. 8068, 715
64. France, deletion of Lebanon from list of French Franc Area territories. Cmd. 8075, 716
65. U.S.A., Modification of Leased Bases Agreement. Cmd. 8076, 716
66. Argentina, Trade and Payments Agreement. Cmd. 8079, 716
67. Italy, Sterling Payments Agreement and provisions in respect of Territory of Somaliland under Italian administration. Cmd. 8085, 717
68. Sugar, Protocol for prolongation of International Agreement. Cmd. 8086, 717
69. Belgium, Reciprocal Protection of Trade Marks in Bahama Islands and Belgium. Cmd. 8089, 717
70. Norway, Monetary Agreement. Cmd. 8095, 717
71. France, General Agreement on Social Security, excluding Channel Islands. Cmd. 8096, 718
72. Denmark, Monetary Agreement. Cmd. 8104, 718
73. Sweden, Monetary Agreement. Cmd. 8105, 718
75. International Rice Commission Constitution. Cmd. 8118, 718

Tree :
Fruits, 610
Planting in Urban and Suburban Areas, Memorandum on, 613

Tree (continued) :
Preservation, 621
Roots, Studies on, 194
Trees and Woodlands Preservation, 622
Trench, Col. A. C., Railway Accident Reports, 247, 418, 635
Tretower Castle, guide, 440, 882
Trial of the Major War Criminals, 207, 219, 367, 368, 383, 422, 575, 593
Trichomonas Disease, 517
Trieste, Application of Most-favoured-nation Treatment, Exchange of Notes with U.S.A. Cmd. 7470, 315
Trigonometrical Functions, Five Figure Tables, 176
Trigonometry for Surveyors, Elementary, 222
Trinidad :
and Tobago, Colonial Reports, 343, 532, 749
Trade Union Organisations and Industrial Relations, Report, 186
See also British West Indies.
Tripartite Economic Discussions in Washington. Cmd. 7788, 501
Tristan da Cunha. See Addu Attoll.
Triumph of Caesar, 883
Trolley Vehicles, Memorandum, 420
Tropic Proofing, 607
Trout, Brown, Research Supervisory Committee Report, 832
Truck :
Act, 509, 721
Memorandum, 218
Amendment Act, 506, 720
Trueman, Professor A. E. (Chairman) :
Geological Survey Board, Reports, 226, 392
University Grants Committee, Note on Technology, 877
Trunk Roads Act, 48
Bill, 4, 27
Trust Territories :
What the United Nations is doing for, 870
See also Mandated and Trust Territories.
Trusted, Sir H. : Disturbances in Aden in December 1947, Report, 344
Trustee Savings Banks :
Act, 172
Bill, 12, 30, 122
and Friendly Societies Accounts, 110, 250, 422, 642, 859
Inspection Committee Report, 859

Trusteeship :
Council, United Nations, Public tions, 253, 256, 259, 432, 653, 8
Territories in Africa under U.! Mandate. Cmd. 6840, 37
Trypanosomiasis in Africa, 345
Tsetse :
Fly, 363
Flies in British West Africa, 345
Tubercule Bacillus, Murine Type, 224
Tuberculosis :
and other communicable diseases relation to nurses and other heal workers. Cmd. 8093, 717
Expert Committee Report, 876 in Poultry, 178, 738
in the British Zone of Germany, 3 of Cattle, 178, 738
World War on, 653
Tuberculous Meningitis treated wi Streptomycin, 613
Tubular Scaffolding for Military Pt poses, 438
Tucker, Lord Justice :
(Chairman) : Limitation of Actio Committee, Report. Cmd. 7740, 4
Gilling East Division, Report. Cn 6783, 34
Justices of the Aberayron Distri Inquiry, Proceedings at Hearin Cmd. 7061, 155
Tudor Aircraft :
Committee of Inquiry Report :
Cmd. 7307, 305
Cmd. 7418, 316
Court Investigation Report. Cn 7517, 319
Tunbridge Wells Provisional Order Co firmation Act, 174
Bill, 128, 148
Tunis, Field-Marshal the Viscou Alexander of : Allied Armies Italy, 812
Turkey :
Air Services Agreements :
Cmd. 6755, 32
Cmd. 6928, 43
Cmd. 7254, 312
Drawing Rights Agreements :
Cmd. 7652, 492
Cmd. 7905, 704
Economic and Commercial Con tions, 416
Liquidation of Unexecuted Jud ment of Anglo-Turkish Mix Arbitral Tribunal. Cmd. 6956,

Turkey (continued):
Trade and Payments Agreement. *Cmd.* 6907, 42
Turkish Woven Fabrics, Brief Guide, 878
Turks and Caicos Islands Colonial Reports, 343, 749
Turner, Sir G. W. (Chairman): Motor Manufacturing Industry, National Advisory Council, Report, 238
Turner, H. . Glued and Laminated Wood Bending, 395
Turner, T. (Chairman): Mining Subsidence Committee Report. *Cmd.* 7637, 491
Turnips, Recommended Grades for, 335
Turn-round of Shipping in the United Kingdom Ports, Report, 420
Turntable Ladder, Hand-operated, Instruction Book, 565
Turtle, E. E.: Insect Pests of Food, 193
Turtles. *See* Whales.
Twin Diseases in Ewes (Pregnancy Toxaemia), 738
Two leaf-cast diseases of Douglas Fir, 553
Two-year Part-time Study of Teachers trained in Emergency Colleges, 541,543
Tyndall, Professor A. M. (Chairman): Chemical Engineers Sub-Committee, Technical Register, 811
Tyne:
Improvement Act, 512, 726
to Stainmore Geology, 606
Tunnel Act, 51
Tynemouth Corporation Act, 174
Tyneside. *See* Northumberland.
Type:
Cultures, List of species maintained in the National Collection, 391
Specimens of certain oriental Eucosmidae and Carposinidae (Microlepidoptera), 741
Types of road surfacing and maintenance using tar or asphaltic bitumen, 830
Typewriters, History and Development, 351
Typhus. *See* Chemotherapeutic and other Studies.
Tyre Inflation, 76

U

U-Boat Casualties:
Cmd. 6751, 32
Cmd. 6843, 37
U Boats. *See* Battle of Atlantic.

Uganda:
Civil Service, 344
Colonial Reports, 343, 532, 749
Economic Survey, 416
Water Resources, Report, 533
Ultimus Haeres (Scotland) Accounts and Lists of Estates, 93, 231, 399, 616, 833
Unasylva, 435, 658, 875
Under-developed countries, Relative prices of exports and imports, 870
Unemployment:
and Family Allowances (Northern Ireland Agreement) Act, 171
Bill, 12, 29
Assistance Act, 1934, Old Age and Widows' Pension Act, 1940: Explanatory Memorandum. *Cmd.* 6959, 45
Fund:
Accounts, 15, 138, 287, 471
Financial Condition, 19, 287
Investment Accounts, 20, 140, 288, 465
in Great Britain, Employment and, 369
Insurance:
Acts:
Decisions by the Umpire, 85, 222, 389
Report, 138
Vacant Book, 81
(Eire Volunteers) Act, 50
Bill, 11, 29
Tables. *See* Employment.
UNESCO:
and a World Society, 350
Conference Reports:
Cmd. 7661, 493
Cmd. 7863, 701
Cmd. 8066, 715
Constitution. *Cmd.* 6963, 45
Publications, 113, 259, 433, 653, 870
Uniform, Wearing of, by Officers and Ex-officers released from Military Duty, etc., 117
United:
Kingdom:
Balance of Payments:
Cmd. 7324, 306
Cmd. 7520, 319
Cmd. 7648, 492
Cmd. 7793, 501
Cmd. 7928, 705
Cmd. 8065, 715
Dominion Wool Disposals Ltd., Accounts. *Cmd.* 7714, 496

United (continued):
Kingdom (continued):
Engineering Mission to Canada, 631
Industrial Mission to Pakistan, 846
Maritime:
Authority, Shipping Arrangements. *Cmd.* 6754, 32
Consultative Council, Agreement for establishment of a Provisional Maritime Consultative Council. *Cmd.* 7137, 160
Nations:
Act, 49
Bill, 4, 27
Articles of Agreement, International Monetary Fund. *Cmd.* 6885, 40
Commentary on Report of Preparatory Commission. *Cmd.* 6734, 31
Conference on Road and Motor Transport. *Cmd.* 7997, 710
Dissolution of the International Institute of Agriculture. *Cmd.* 7413, 312
Educational, Scientific and Cultural Organisation. *See* Unesco.
Food and Agriculture:
Conference. *Cmd.* 6731, 31
Organisation. *Cmd.* 6955, 44
Publications, 433, 656, 873
World Food Proposals. *Cmd.* 7031-32, 153
General:
Assembly Proceedings:
relating to non-self-governing and Trust Territories, Memorandum. *Cmd.* 8035, 713
Reports:
Cmd. 7320, 306
Cmd. 7630, 491
Cmd. 7768, 499
Cmd. 7924, 705
Conference on Privileges and Immunities:
Cmd. 6753, 32
Cmd. 7891, 703
International Convention on Privileges and Immunities. *Cmd.* 7673, 494
Maritime Consultative Organisation Conference. *Cmd.* 7412, 312

United (continued):
Nations (continued):
Publications, 110, 250, 422, 642, 859
Relief and Rehabilitation Administration. *See* UNRRA.
World Health Organisation Publications, 658, 875
States of America:
Additional funds for the continued operation of the U.S. Educational Commission in U.K. *Cmd.* 7944, 706
Air:
Bases in Caribbean Area and Bermuda. *Cmd.* 7389, 310
Services Agreement. *Cmd.* 7209, 164
Army:
Air Forces, Third Report of Commanding General, 65
Biennial Report of Chief of Staff, 65
Avoidance of Double Taxation, etc.:
Cmd. 6859, 38
Cmd. 6890, 40
Cmd. 6902, 41
Bizonal Fusion Agreements:
Cmd. 7287, 170
Cmd. 7301, 305
Cmd. 7623, 490
Cmd. 7742, 498
Cmd. 7757, 499
British and American Zones of Occupation in Germany, Agreement:
Cmd. 6984, 46
Cmd. 7001, 47
Civil Aviation Agreement. *Cmd.* 6747, 32
Claims against members and civilian employees of respective Armed Forces. *Cmd.* 7501, 308
Consular Convention. *Cmd.* 7642, 491
Control of Dollar Outpayments. *Cmd.* 7210, 164
Copyright Laws. *Cmd.* 6991, 46
Disposal of surplus lend-lease stores in Middle East. *Cmd.* 7471, 315
Duty Free Treatment of American Relief Goods. *Cmd.* 7583, 323

United (continued):
States of America (continued):
Economic Co-operation:
Cmd. 7446, 314
Cmd. 7469, 315
Cmd. 7570, 322
Cmd. 7654, 492
Cmd. 7961, 708
Establishment of U.S. Educational Commission in the U.K.:
Cmd. 7527, 319
Cmd. 7666, 493
European Jewry and Palestine. *Cmd.* 6822, 36
Ferrous Scrap Exports:
Cmd. 7538, 320
Cmd. 7925, 705
Financial:
Agreement. *Cmd.* 6968, 45
Issues arising out of Bizonal Fusion Agreement Amendment:
Cmd. 7990, 710
Cmd. 8001, 710
Free Importation of Goods into leased bases in Bermuda, the Caribbean, and British Guiana. *Cmd.* 7000, 47
International Authority for the Ruhr Agreement.*Cmd.*7685,494
Interpretation of Para. 6 of Agreement on Settlement of Intergovernmental Claims. *Cmd.* 7132, 159
Leased Bases:
Agreement, Modification of. *Cmd.* 8076, 715
at Argentia, Newfoundland. *Cmd.* 7294, 304
Marine Transport and Litigation:
Cmd. 6847, 38
Cmd. 7218, 165
Most-favoured-nation Treatment:
Western Germany. *Cmd.* 7447, 314
Cmd. 7539, 320
Western Germany and Trieste. *Cmd.* 7470, 315
Motion Picture Industry. *Cmd.* 7421, 312
Mutual Defence Assistance Agreement. *Cmd.* 7894, 703
Non-repatriable Victims of German Action, Allocation of a ReparationShare.*Cmd.*7255,168

United (continued):
States of America (continued):
Overseas Economic Survey, 416
Patent Rights and Information Agreement. *Cmd.* 6795, 34
Prospects for U.K. Exports, 415
Radio Frequencies and Standardisation of Distance Measuring Equipment used as aid to safety of air navigation. *Cmd.* 7622, 490
Settlement:
for Lend-Lease, Joint Memorandum and Agreement. *Cmd.* 6813, 36
of Claims under specific agreements of March 1946. *Cmd.* 7516, 319
of Interests in Joint Installations in the Middle East. *Cmd.* 7514, 319
of Lend-Lease Interest in future sales of surplus stores in the Middle East. *Cmd.* 7513, 318
Synthesis of Penicillin, Principles applying to exchange of information. *Cmd.* 6767, 32
Tariffs and Trade:
Agreement. *Cmd.* 7276, 169
Report on. *Cmd.* 7258, 168
Telecommunications. *Cmd.* 6830, 37
Trinidad, Establishment of U.S. Air Force Base in. *Cmd.* 7864, 701
Unemployment Insurance, Exchange of Notes with U.K. and Canada recording Agreement. *Cmd.* 6900, 41
Use:
and disposal of captured enemy vessels. *Cmd.* 6905, 41
of Gander Airport by U.S. Air Lines. *Cmd.* 7157, 161
Veterans' Pensions Administration Act, 511
Bill, 453, 486
Visas, Exchange of Notes. *Cmd.* 7893, 703
Universal Postal Union:
Agreement. *Cmd.* 7436, 313
Conventions:
Cmd. 7435, 313
Cmd. 7794, 501

Universities:
and University Colleges in receipt of Treasury Grant, 642
of Scotland, Report. *Cmd.* 6853, 38
Report of Preparatory Conference of Representatives, 656
(Scotland) Act, 723
University:
Awards, Working Party Report, 551
Development Report, 422
Education Report, 614
Graduates:
Careers, 75
Possible Openings, 208
Grants Committee Returns, 859
of Glasgow:
Anderson College of Medicine Trust Scheme, 614
Endowments Scheme, 831
of Nottingham Act, 513
of Sheffield (Lands) Act, 330
Reform in Germany, 552
Students, Awards for, 63, 64
Unorthodox use of economisers, 773
UNRRA:
Publications, 113
Resolutions:
Cmd. 6815, 36
Cmd. 6930, 43
Upper Winds over the World, 814
Uranium in Minerals and Ores, Handbook of Chemical Methods for Determination, 830
Urmston Urban District Council Act, 514
Uruguay:
Air Services Agreement. *Cmd.* 7249, 167
British Railway Delegation, Payments Agreement. *Cmd.* 7172, 162
Commercial Conditions, Review of, 416
Payments Agreement. *Cmd.* 7340, 306
Sale of British-owned Railways, Agreement. *Cmd.* 7629, 491
Urwick, Lt. Col. L. (Chairman): Committee on Education for Management, Report, 191
Use:
of Derrick Cranes, 593
of Lime in Agriculture, 334
Using Salty Land, 433
Uthwatt, Rt. Hon. Lord (Chairman): Leasehold Committee on Tenure and Rents of Business Premises, Report. *Cmd.* 7706, 496

Utilisation of Steam, 773
Utility Goods, various publications, see under Board of Trade Publications.

V

Vaagso Island, Raid on Military and Economic Objectives, 385
Vacation Study Supplement, 672
Vaccination:
against Smallpox, Memorandum, 360
Record Card, 398
Valuation:
and Estate Management, Technical Register, 811
See also Rating and Valuation; Railways; Agricultural Valuation.
Valves. *See* Radio Valves.
Vanguard and the Royal Voyage to South Africa, 176
Variable Pitch Propeller Log Book, 525
Vegetable:
Crops, Manuring of, 335
Dehydration, 193
Oils and Oilseeds, Production Trade and Consumption, 186, 345, 753
Vegetables:
and Fruit, Commodity Series, 434
and Salads including Herbs, 352
Diseases of, 738
Domestic Preservation, 517
See also Root Vegetables.
Vehicles:
(Excise) Act, 719
Bill, 446, 455, 487
See also Road Vehicles.
Venereal:
Disease Control in the U.S.A., 877
Diseases, 436
Infections, Expert Committee Report, 877
Venezuela, Oilseed Mission Report, 656
Venn, J. A. (Chairman): Commission of Inquiry into sugar industry of British Guiana, Report, 535
Ventilation:
and Heating, Lighting and Seeing, 603
of Schools, 264
See also Heating and Ventilation.
Vessels. *See* Merchant Vessels.
Veterinary:
Science, Careers, 208, 368

VET—　　　　INDEX 1946-50

Veterinary (continued):
Surgeons Act, 329
Bill, 270, 272, 276, 291, 295, 301, 302
Standing Committee Debates, 463
Vices, Cramps and Clamps, Specifications, 880
Vick, G. Russell (Chairman): Evasions of Petrol Rationing Control, Committee of Inquiry Report. Cmd. 7372, 309
Victoria:
and Albert Museum:
Paintings, etc., Committee Report. Cmd. 6827, 36
Publications, 113, 260, 351, 659, 877
Station, Railway Accident Report, 851
Victory:
Bonds, 219, 385, 594, 812
Celebrations:
Air Navigation Regulations, 57
Official Programme, 70
Vienna, Administration Agreement. Cmd. 6958, 45
Vinegar and Solution of Acetic Acid, 760
Violet:
Commercial Growing, 737
Root Rot, 516
Virgin with the Laughing Child, 660
Virus Diseases in the Potato Crop, Spread of, 390
Visa Agreement with U.S.A. Cmd. 7893, 703
Visas, Abolition of:
Belgium. Cmd. 7038, 153
Denmark:
Cmd. 7101, 157
Cmd. 7577, 323
France. Cmd. 7003, 151
Iceland:
Cmd. 7159, 161
Cmd. 7574, 323
Italy:
Cmd. 7295, 304
Cmd. 7578, 323
Kenya added to list of territories covered. Cmd. 7847, 505
Luxembourg:
Cmd. 7059, 155
Cmd. 7579, 323
Monaco. Cmd. 7589, 324
Netherlands:
Cmd. 7102, 157
Cmd. 7860, 700

Visas, Abolition of (continued):
Newfoundland deleted from list of territories covered. Cmd. 7750, 499
Norway:
Cmd. 7073, 155
Cmd. 7575, 323
Cmd. 7610, 489
San Marino:
Cmd. 7825, 504
Cmd. 7964, 708
Singapore and Federation of Malaya deleted from list of territories covered. Cmd. 8036 to 8043, 713
Sweden:
Cmd. 7103, 157
Cmd. 7576, 323
Switzerland:
Cmd. 7149, 160
Cmd. 7573, 322
Vision, Pupils who are defective in. Cmd. 7855, 832
Visual Training Aids for the Mining Industry, 67
Vitamin A Requirement of Human Adults, 603
Vitreous enamelling of metal or glass, Regulations for, 74
Volunteers, Initial training of, 783
Vose, W. A.: Report of Boiler Explosion at Wimbledon Park, 417
Votes. See Air Votes; Army Votes; Navy Votes.
Voyage Regulations, 263

W

Wadebridge Rural District Council Act, 50
Wages:
Agricultural Wages (Regulation) Bill, 30
Councils:
Act, 510
Bill, 279, 297, 299, 302, 303
Standing Committee Debate, 681
Acts, Reports under, 218, 382, 811
See also Agricultural Wages; Catering Wages; Industrial Court Awards; National Arbitration Tribunal Awards; Cotton Manufacturing Commission.

Waite, Air Commodore R. N. (President): Court of Inquiry into the circumstances of the collision between a Viking Airliner and a Soviet Service Aircraft. Cmd. 7384, 309
Wakefield:
Extension Act, 726
See also Normanton.
Waleran of Uffculme, Lord (Chairman): Petrol Stations Technical Committee, Report, 634
Wales:
and Monmouthshire:
Memorandum by the Council on its Activities, 782
Reports of Government Action:
Cmd. 6938, 43
Cmd. 7267, 168
Cmd. 7532, 320
Cmd. 7820, 504
Cmd. 8062, 715
Secretary of State for, Bill, 483
Education in, 352
Administration, 350
Rural, 543
See also South Wales.
Waley, Sir D. (Chairman): Committee of European Economic Co-operation, Payments Agreement, 194
Walkden, Lord (Chairman): Water Softening Sub-Committee, Report, 561
Walkden, Sir G. T.: Some Correlation Coefficients between certain Upper Air Data, 596
Walker, Sir R. B. (Chairman): Committee on Water Rating in Scotland. Report. Cmd. 6765, 33
Walker, Col. R. J., Railway Accident Reports, 634, 850
Wall:
Maps, 535, 788
Tiler. See Floor.
Wall, J. I. (Chairman): Committee on Celluloid Storage, Report. Cmd. 7929, 705
Wallasey:
Corporation Act, 50
Order Confirmation Act, 51
Bill, 9, 28
Walls and Ceilings, Distemper on, 827
Walmer Castle, guide, 882
Wandsworth and District Gas Act, 512
War:
and Archaeology in Britain, 664
Charities Act, 724

War (continued):
Crimes:
History of Commission, 422
Scientific Results of German Medical, 549
Criminals:
Judgment of the International Military Tribunal. Cmd. 6964, 45
Prosecution and Punishment of, Agreement. Cmd. 6903, 41
Regulations for the Trial of, 116, 263, 663
Trial Reports:
International Military Tribunal, 207, 367, 575
Law Officers' Department, 82, 219, 383, 593, 811
United Nations, 422, 658
Damage:
Account, 286
Act, 719, 724
Agreement with Belgium for Reciprocal Compensation. Cmd. 7495, 317
Amendment Bill, 479, 483, 488, 681
Business and Private Chattels Schemes, Accounts, 25, 470, 678
Commission Report, 250
Compensation:
Equality of Treatment, Agreement with Egypt. Cmd. 7710, 496
Exchange of Notes with France. Cmd. 7012, 152
Land and Buildings Accounts, 287, 471, 878
(Public Utility Undertakings, etc.) Act, 510
Bill, 303, 452, 470, 483, 484
Standing Committee Debate, 681
Statement of Payments and Contributions, 25
Valuations Appeals Act, 48
See also references from War-damaged, separate main entry.
Department Schedules of Prices for Works Services, 881
Despatches. See in each annual section under London Gazette.
Gratuities, 117
Graves:
Mutual Upkeep, Agreement with Czechoslovakia. Cmd. 7691, 495

154

155

WAR—　　　　INDEX 1946-50

War (continued):
Graves (continued):
See also Imperial War Graves Commission.
Great, History of, 362, 568
Medicine, Bulletin of, 86, 225
Memorandum and Supplement, 86
Office Publications (N.P.), 114, 260, 436, 660, 878
Pensions:
Act, 326
(Administrative Provisions) Act, 721
(Extension) Orders, 223, 821
(Special Review) Tribunal, Notes and Digest, 220
Risks (Marine) Insurance Fund Account, 20
Second World, History of, 639, 743
Works. See Requisitioned Land and War Works.
See also references from War-damaged; Wartime; War-handicapped; Warships; Wars; separate main entries.
Ward, F. A. B.: Time Measurement, Handbook of Collections, 192, 826
Ward, W. E. F. (Chairman): Committee on Education in the Colonies, Report, 344
War-damaged:
Areas. See Estate Development.
Sites Act, 719
Bill, 461, 487
Ware:
Case Inquiry. Report. Cmd. 7049, 154
Potatoes, Early and Maincrop, 736
Ware, R. R. (Chairman): Committee on Agricultural Valuation, Report, 738
Ware, W. M.: Mushroom Growing, 54
Warehouses. See Bonded Warehouses.
War-handicapped Children, Report on European Situation, 873
Warkworth:
Castle, guide, 663
Hermitage, guide, 440
Warren Grove Wreck Report, 636
Wars not yet won, 363
Warships on loan to Soviet Union, Protocol on return of. Cmd. 7078, 155
Wartime Tank Production, Reports. Cmd. 6865, 39
Warwick Corporation Act, 330
Water:
Act, 328
Bill, 132, 133, 150, 300

Water (continued):
Acts, Handbook of Local Legislation, 201, 561
Industrial Waste, Re-use, 395
Pollution Research Publications (N.P.), 88, 227, 395, 607, 831
Prevention of Waste, Undue Consumption, Misuse or Contamination of, 200, 560, 778
Rates and Charges, Scotland. Report. Cmd. 6765, 33
Resources of Bechuanaland Protectorate, Northern Rhodesia, Nyasaland, Tanganyika, Kenya and Uganda, 533
(Scotland) Acts:
1946, 49
Bill, 4, 14, 26, 27
1949, 510
Bill, 269, 297, 299, 302, 303, 448, 450, 484
Standing Committee Debates, 681
Softening Sub-Committee Report, 561
Supplies:
Greater London, Report, 359
See also Rural Water Supplies.
Supply:
Handbook of Local Legislation relating to, 782
Pocket Books (Royal Engineers), 438, 439
Systems in Houses, Lagging hot and cold, 881
Treatment, 773
See also Boiler Corrosion.
Watercress, Cultivation of, 177
Waterloo. See Havant.
Waterlow, J. C.: Fatty Liver Disease in Infants in the British West Indies, 391
Watermark Disease of the Cricket Bat Willow, 553
Waters, A. H. S. (Chairman): Advisory Committee on Sand and Gravel, Reports, 409, 841
Waters, Industrial Waste, Treatment and Disposal of, 394
Wath Road Junction Railway Accident Report, 419
Watkins, C. M.: Laying of linoleum upon concrete flooring, 394
Watson, A. (Chairman): Commission of Inquiry into Gold Coast Disturbances, Report, 344

Watson, H.: Woodland Mosses, 194
Watson, R.: East African Rice Mission, Report, 534
Watt, James, Garret Workshop of, 542
Wavell, Field Marshall Viscount, Despatches, 384
Ways and Means:
Chairman of, Select Committee Report, 287
of making the evidence of customary International Law more readily available, 647
We live by words, 246
We, the Peoples, 113
Wealden District, British Regional Geology, 393
Wear Navigation and Sunderland Dock Act, 174, 727
Weather:
Chart, 596
Forecasts, Code for Aviation, 84
in China Seas and North Pacific Ocean, 815
in Home Waters and North East Atlantic, 815
in the Indian Ocean, 816
in the Mediterranean, 816
Maps, 84, 816
Instructions for Preparation, 596, 816
Messages, Codes and Specifications, Handbook of, 387, 596, 817
on the West Coast of Tropical Africa, 596
Reports, 84, 221, 387, 596, 817
Science of, Handbook, 826
See also Ocean Weather Stations.
Weathering Tests on Asbestos-Cement Roofing Materials, 225
Weathering, Preservation and Maintenance of Natural Stone Masonry, 827
Weaver Navigation Act, 50
Webb, S. B.: Soil Survey Procedure and its application to Road Construction, 88
Weed:
Control:
in Cereals by spraying with selective weedkillers, 178, 737
in Linseed and Flax, 516
in Onions and other Horticultural Crops, 55
Killers. See Insecticides.
Weeds, Suppression of, 333

Weeks, Sir R. M. (Chairman): National Advisory Council on Education for Industry and Commerce, Report on Future Development of Higher Technological Education, 757
Weevil, Apple Blossom, 178
Weevils. See Pea and Bean Weevils.
Weights and Measures Act, 506, 723
Notice of Examination of Patterns, 106, 246, 416, 632, 847
See also Sale of Food.
Welch, F. B. A.: Bristol and Gloucester District, British Regional Geology, 393
Welded Ships, Repairs to, 53
Welding:
Memoranda, 100
See also Electric Arc Welding.
Welfare:
of Old People, 780, 782
Pamphlet, 593
Story, 616
Wellington Museum Act, 173
Bill, 125, 130, 149
Select Committee, Special Report, 143
Welsh:
Agricultural Land Sub-Commission, Report on Malltraeth Marsh, 739
Board of Health Publications (N.P.), 201, 782
Borderland, British Regional Geology, 393
Intermediate Education Act, 324
Slate Industry, Report, 264
Welsh, J. (Chairman): Scottish Housing Advisory Committee, Report, 229
Welwyn Garden City Development Corporation Reports, 476, 549
Wessex, Sand and Gravel Advisory Committee Report, 841
West:
African Cocoa, Future Marketing. Cmd. 6950, 44
Bromwich Corporation Act, 514
Indian:
Colonies:
Closer Association. Cmd. 7120, 158
Conference Report. Cmd. 7291, 304
Shipping Services Report, 346
Indies:
Customs Tariffs, 60
Development and Welfare in, 750
See also British West Indies.

156

157

West (continued) :
  Midlands Joint Electricity Authority
    Order Confirmation Act, 51
    Bill, 9, 28
  Riding County Council (General
    Powers) Act, 331
  Sussex County Council Act, 51
  Yorkshire Gas Distribution Act, 52
Western :
  Europe, Coal, Iron and Steel Indus-
    tries, Schuman Plan. Cmd. 7970,
    708
  Germany, Agreement on Most-
    favoured-nation Treatment. Cmd.
    7643, 491
  Highlands and Islands of Scotland,
    Agreements for Maintenance of
    Transport Services, 141, 467
  Pacific Ocean, Monthly Meteorologi-
    cal Charts, 387
  Region, Scottish Hospital Survey
    Report, 90
  Samoa. See Samoa.
  Union :
    Agreement relative to status of
      members of the Armed Forces
      of the Brussels Treaty Powers.
      Cmd. 7868, 701
    Supplementary Protocol.Cmd.
      8057, 715
    Convention concerning Frontier
      Workers. Cmd. 7971, 708
    Convention concerning Student
      Employees. Cmd. 7972, 708
    Treaty of Economic, Social and
      Cultural Collaboration and Col-
      lective Self-Defence. Cmd.
      7599, 488
Westminster Abbey, Pyx Chamber.
  guide, 663
Weston, W. G. (Chairman) : Working
  Party on the turn-round of Shipping
  in the United Kingdom Ports, Report,
  420
Weston-super-Mare Order Confirmation
  Act, 50
Westward, Bt. Hon. Lord (Chairman) :
  Mineral Development Committee, Re-
  port. Cmd. 7732, 497
Weymouth, Geology of the Country
  around, 226
Whalemeat :
  Inspection, Memoranda, 546, 761
  Regulations, 545, 760
Whales and Turtles, Stranded, Guide
  for Identification, 522

Whaling, International Agreements and
  Conventions, etc. :
    Cmd. 6726, 30
    Cmd. 6941, 44
    Cmd. 6990, 46
    Cmd. 7009, 152
    Cmd. 7043, 154
    Cmd. 7354, 307
    Cmd. 7604, 489
    Cmd. 7853, 506
    Cmd. 7918, 705
What :
  goes on in the Colonies, 752
  the United Nations is doing, 433, 653,
    870
Wheare, K. C. (Chairman) : Depart-
  mental Committee on Children and the
  Cinema. Cmd. 7945, 706
Wheat :
  and Barley, Take-all or Whiteheads,
    178
  Bulb Fly, 55
  Commodity Series, 434
  Fund Accounts, 18, 138, 286, 469,
    683
  International Agreement :
    Cmd. 7382, 309
    Cmd. 7680, 494
    Cmd. 7819, 504
  See also Grain Crops.
Wheatley, J. (Chairman) : Scottish
  Nurses' Salaries Committee, Reports.
  Cmd. 7238–9, 304
White :
  Fish and Herring Industries Act,
    329
  Bill, 275, 290, 295, 300, 301
  Standing Committee Debates,
    463
  Rot of Onions and related crops,
    516
  Scour in Calves, 334
White, E. I. : Vertebrate Faunas of
  Lower Red Sandstone of Welsh
  Borders, 741
White, E. W. : British Fishing Boats
  and Coastal Craft, 826
Whitehaven William Colliery Explosion
  Reports :
    Cmd. 7236, 166
    Cmd. 7410, 311
Whitehead, T. H. : Dudley and Bridg-
  north, Geology, 226
Whitehouse West Junction Railway
  Accident Report, 851
Whitley Council. See Civil Service.

Whitley, Rev. H. C. (Chairman) : After-
  care Committee, Report, 832
Whitstable Urban District Council Act,
  331
Whitworth Scolarship Regulations and
  Syllabus, 191, 543, 758
Wholesale Clothing Manufacture, Career,
  793
Widdowson, E. M. :
  Chemical Composition of Foods,
    86
  Experimental Study in Rationing,
    86
  Study of Individual Children's Diets,
    224
Widnes Bridge. See Cheshire and Lan-
  cashire.
Widow's, Orphan's and Old Age Con-
  tributory Pensions Acts, Accounts, 18,
  138, 285, 471
Wigtownshire Educational Trust
  (Amendment) (No. 1) Scheme, 92,
  231
Wilcock, Group Captain C. A. B. (Chair-
  man) : Committee on Recruitment,
  Training and Licensing of Personnel
  for Civil Aviation, Report. Cmd. 7746,
  498
Wild :
  Birds and the Land, 335
  Life Conservation Committee Re-
    port. Cmd. 7122, 159
Wiles, H. H. (afterwards Sir H.) (Chair-
  man) : Standing Committee on Re-
  habilitation and Resettlement of Dis-
  abled Persons, Reports, 81, 592
Will to Co-operate : Discussion Guide on
  United Nations General Assembly,
  869
William Brown Nimmo Charitable Trust
  (Amendment) Order Confirmation
  Act, 330
William Mannell, Wreck Report, 637
Williams, A. E. : Radioactive Tracers in
  Metallurgical Research, 838
Williams, G. C. (Chairman) : University
  Awards Working Party, Report, 351
Williams, John, 363
Williams, O. C. : Historical Develop-
  ment of Private Bill Procedure and
  Standing Orders in the House of
  Commons, 331, 514
Williams, R. E. O. : Infection and
  Sepsis in Industrial Wounds of the
  Hand, 813

Williams, Major-Gen. W. D. A. (Chair-
  man) : Milk Distribution Committee,
  Report. Cmd. 7414, 312
Willink, Rt. Hon. H. U. (Chairman) :
  Royal Commission on Betting, Lot-
  eries and Gaming :
    Evidence, 823
    Report, 608
Willis, Vice-Admiral A. U. :
  Destruction of Enemy Raider by
    H.M.S. Devonshire, 385
  Naval Operations in the Aegean, 386
  Sinking of the German battleship
    Python, 385
Willis, Capt. J. C. T. : Outline of the
  History and Revision of the 25 in.
  Ordnance Survey Plans, 820
Willowdale, Wreck Report, 421
Willow. See Cricket Bat Willow.
Wilson, A. H. : London Airport, Re-
  port, 181
Wilson, D. C. : Thyroid Enlargement,
  391
Wilson, Lt. Col. G. R. S., Railway
  Accident Reports, 247, 418, 634, 851
Wilson, V. : East Yorkshire and Lin-
  colnshire, British Regional Geology,
  393
Windows, Metal, 882
Windward Islands, Arms, 751
Wings of the Phoenix, 520
Winning, Harvesting and Utilisation of
  Peat, 395
Winsford Railway Accident Report, 419
Winter :
  Moths, 333
  Pruning of established Apple and
    Pear Trees, 516
Wire and Wire-rope Industry, Industrial
  Court Report. Cmd. 7097, 157
Wireless :
  Operators' Handbook, 389, 602
  Telegraphy :
    Act, 511
    Bill, 303, 447, 449, 451, 457,
      485
  Handbook, 332, 729
  Specifications, 33
  See also Cable and Wireless.
Wireworms, 178, 737
Wisbech Corporation Act, 727
Witham Junction Railway Accident
  Report, 851
Withdrawal of British Forces from Italy
  and transfer of responsibility to the
  Italian Government. Cmd. 7158, 161

Witnesses' Allowances Order, Depart-
  mental Committee Report, 202
Witney, Geology of country around,
  226
Woking, Railway Accident Report, 108
Wolverhampton Corporation Act, 727
Wolverson Cope : Geology of Southport
  and Formby, 393
Women :
  and Children. See Traffic.
  Officers, Change of Rank Titles, 881
  Status of, 433, 644
  Teachers, Supply of, Working Party
    Report, 543
Women's :
  and Maids' Outerwear, Board of
    Trade Publications (N.P.), 104
  Services, Pay, Retired Pay, etc.
    Cmd. 7607, 489
  See also War Gratuities.
Wood :
  and Plywood, Elasticity of, 391
  Preservation Series, 605
  Requirements and Properties of
    Adhesives for, 828
  Swelling under Stress, 605
Wood, Sir R. S. (Chairman) : Working
  Party on Recruitment and Training of
  Nurses, Report, 199
Woodcutting, Handbook, 828
Woodford Aerodrome Aircraft Accident
  Report, 337
Woodhouse, Lt. Col. E. : Railway
  Accident Reports, 247, 418, 634
Woodland Mosses, 194
Woodlands :
  Dedication of, 354, 769
  Preservation of, 622
Woodman, H. E. : Rations for Live-
  stock, 334
Woodpeckers, 55
Wood pigeon, 737
Woods :
  Shelter or Belts, 610
  See also Forestry (Preservation of
    Woods).
Woods, C. R. (Chairman) :
  Building Research Board, Report,
    117
  Joint Committee of Building Re-
    search Board and Fire Officers
    Committee, Report on precau-
    tions against fire and explosion in
    underground car parks, 683
Woods, Sir W. : Report on Finances of
  the Government of Malta, 61

Woodward, E. L. : Documents on
  British Foreign Policy, 184, 333, 347,
  761
Wool :
  Cloth, etc., Board of Trade Publica-
    tions (N.P.), 102
  Commodity Report, 873
  Disposals. See United Kingdom.
  Export Licence, 632
  Marketing :
    Committee Report, 55
    Draft Scheme for Regulation, 759
    Production and Trade, 536
    Working Party Report, 246
  Textile Industry :
    Proposals for Development Coun-
      cil, 629
    Reports on, 218, 593
Woolley, Lt. Col. Sir L. : Protection of
  Treasures of Art and History in War
  Areas, 440
Woolwich Arsenal Station Railway
  Accident Report, 635
Work :
  of FAO, 658, 875
  of the Organisation, General Assem-
    bly, United Nations, Report, 253
Worker. See Employer and Worker.
Workers. See Dock Workers.
Working :
  Conditions in the Civil Service,
    422
  of the Agricultural Marketing Acts,
    Report, 178
  Party Reports, 106, 201, 246, 416
Workington Pier and Harbour Order
  Confirmation Act, 726
  Bill, 672, 698
Workmen's Compensation :
  Acts, Memorandum, 85
  for Accidents. Cmd. 7626, 490
  Memo on effect of Family Allow-
    ances Act, 1945, 84
  (Pneumoconiosis) Act, 48
  Supplementary Allowances, Claim
    Form, 85
Works :
  Information Conference Report, 373
  Ministry of :
    Publications (N.P.), 117, 263,
      440, 663, 881
    Reports :
      Cmd. 7279, 169
      Cmd. 7541, 320
      Cmd. 7698, 495
      Cmd. 7995, 710

Works (continued) :
  of Art, Losses and Survivals in the
    War, 56
  Services, War Department Schedule
    of Prices for, 881
  See also Public Works.
World :
  Census of Agriculture, Programme
    for, 617
  Communications. See Press, Radio.
  Economic :
    Indices, 121
    Report, 653
  Situation :
    Recent Developments, 870
    Salient Features, 424
  Fiber Survey, 433
  Fibres Review, 656
  Fisheries Abstracts, 875
  Food :
    Appraisal, 658
    Proposals, 435
      Cmd. 7031, 153
    Shortage :
      Cmd. 6785, 34
      Cmd. 6879, 40
  Grain Position, Cmd. 6737, 31
  Health Organisation. See United
    Nations.
  Iron Ore Resources and their Utilisa-
    tion, 870
  Meteorological Organisation, Final
    Act and Convention. Cmd. 7427,
    312
  Outlook and State of Food and
    Agriculture, 875
  Population Trends, 870
  Programme of Unesco, 1947, 260
  Trade, What the United Nations is
    doing, 433
  War on Tuberculosis, 653
  Worms in Poultry, 317
Worthington, E. B. : Middle East
  Science, 107
Woven Fabrics, Persian, 878
Wray, D. A. : Geology of :
  Country around Barnsley, 393
  Southport and Formby, 393
Wreck Reports, 109, 249, 421, 636, 854
Wrestling. See Boxing.
Wrigley, A. : London Clay at Lower
  Swanwick, 521
Wroxeter, Roman City, guide, 663
Wythenshawe Parishes (Transfer)
  Measure, 514

Y

Yalta. See Crimea Conference.
Yangtze Honours, Decorations and
  Medals. Cmd. 7813, 503
Yarn and Cloth, Board of Trade Pub-
  lications (N.P.), 242, 245, 629
Yates, R. : Colliery Explosion Report.
  Cmd. 7041, 307
Yellow :
  Charlock, Destruction of, 55, 737
  Fleea Found, Report, 677
  Yield Tables for Scots Pine and other
    Conifers, 65
Yonge, Professor C. M. (Chairman) :
  Supervisory Committee for Brown
  Trout Research, Report, 832
Yorkshire. See East Yorkshire ; West
  Yorkshire.
You and your Children, 69
Young :
  Citizens at School, 832
  Persons Employment Act, 509
  Abstract of Provisions, 362
Youth :
  Employment Service, Reports, 382,
    593, 811
  Leaders :
    and Community Centre Wardens,
      543
    and Organisers, Recruitment and
      Training of, 92
  Leadership, Careers, 208
Yugoslavia :
  Allocation of a Reparation Share to
    Non-repatriable Victims of Ger-
    man Action. Cmd. 7255, 168
  Compensation for British Property,
    etc., affected by Yugoslav
    Measures of Nationalisation. Cmd.
    7600, 488
  Displaced Persons, Agreement. Cmd.
    7232, 166
  Money and property subjected to
    special measures in consequence of
    Enemy Occupation. Cmd. 7601,
    489
  Terms and Conditions of Payment of
    balance of compensation for
    British property affected by
    Nationalisation, Agreement. Cmd.
    7600.
  Trade Agreements :
    Cmd. 7602, 489
    Cmd. 7880, 702

YUM—   *INDEX 1946–50*

Yumdum Airfield, Gambia, Aircraft
    Accident Report, 181

Z

Zanzibar :
    Civil Service Report, 344

Zanzibar (*continued*) :
    Colonial Reports, 343, 532
    Economic Survey, 416
    Film Strip, 534
Zeila Area, Proposed Cession of Territory to Ethiopia, Exchange of Notes with France. *Cmd. 7758*, 499
Zoology, British Museum (Natural History) Publications, 742

Consolidated Index
to Government
Publications
1951-1955

INDEX

Abbreviations: In addition to the abbreviations in general use, the following are used:
Cmd.=Command Paper; (N.P.)=Non-Parliamentary.

Cross References are to entries consisting of, or beginning with, the word or words indicated.

FOREWORD

With the publication of this quinquennial Index Government publishing of the twenty years from 1936 to 1955 is covered by four indexes. Previous indexes covered the periods 1936 to 1940, 1941 to 1945 (both out of print), and 1946 to 1950 (6s. 0d.). Each includes new titles, revised editions and reprints at revised prices. As in the indexes for the second and third periods Statutory Instruments are omitted and the separately issued Annual Lists of Statutory Instruments should be consulted for information concerning them.

It is suggested that the annual catalogues for 1951 to 1955 should be bound with this consolidated index, discarding the annual index pages and introductions

The page numbering of the annual catalogues indexed in this consolidation is as follows:

1951	1 to 247
1952	249 to 508
1953	1 to 260*
1954	769 to 1023
1955	1025 to 1229

* It is regretted that owing to an error in the pagination of the 1953 catalogue it is necessary to renumber the pages in that issue commencing at No. 509 and finishing at No. 768. The page numbers will then correspond to the references given in this index.

ii

A

Aalsmeer, W. C.: Rice enrichment in the Philippines, 1010
Aaron, J. R.:
  Use of forest produce in sea and river defence in England and Wales, 892
  Use of home-grown timber in wood turning and related trades in Scotland, 892
Aaron, R. I. (Chairman): Central Advisory Council for Education (Wales):
  County colleges in Wales, 99
  Place of Welsh and English in schools in Wales, 614
Abbreviations of place names, 393, 917
A.B.C. of:
  Cookery, 880
  Plain words, 214
  Preserving, 338, 1092
  Vegetables and salads including herbs, 358
Abdul-Hak, S.: Unesco Mission on Syria Museums and Monuments, 1006
Aberdeen:
  and Banff, Sharpe's Trust Scheme memo, 1190
  Census, 635
  Corporation Order Confirmation Act, 1081
    Bill, 1055
  Educational Endowments Scheme memo, 1190
  Extension Order Confirmation Act, 314
    Bill, 284
  Harbour Order Confirmation Act, 573
    Bill, 542
  Widows' Fund, Chartered Accountant's, Order Confirmation Act, 66
    Bill, 3, 32
Aberdeen, Moray and Banff: Education (Scotland) Act memo, 1190
Aberdeenshire:
  Census, 635
  Educational Trust Scheme memo, 957
Abingdon Corporation Act, 66
Abington railway accident report, 974
Abortion Bill, 283, 770
Abrasives, Census of Production, 200, 1199
Abyan Scheme, report, 342
Acarine disease of the honey bee, film strip, 846
Access:
  of women to education, 491
  to books, 1007

Accident reports:
  Aircraft, 85, 338, 594, 973, 1208
  Bus, 468
  Colliery, 301
  Explosive factory, 129
  Garage, 290
  Hydrogen cyanide fumigation, 129
  Railway, 209, 466, 719, 722, 974, 1209
  Tramway, 720
Accidents:
  how they happen and how to prevent them 142, 398, 658, 920, 1157
  Human factor in the causation of, 419
  in paper mills, prevention of, 676
  in the home:
    Circular 140
    Report, 130
  Industrial, Incidence of, upon individuals with special reference to multiple accidents, 679
  Road, 1210
  to Aircraft, survey, 85, 338, 972, 1206
Accommodation Agencies Act, 567
  Bill, 285, 512, 522, 537, 541, 642
Accountancy and cost accountancy, career, 142
Accountant, career, 921
Accuracy of contour charts in forecasting upper winds, 941
Acetylene industry and acetylene chemistry in Germany, 200
Achievement of 21st Army Group, 759
Acorns and beech mast, collection and storage, 117
Acquisition of Land:
  (Assessment of Compensation) Act, 62
  (Authorisation of Procedure) Act, 572
    Bill, 542
Action of the Council, ICAO, 313, 917
Activities:
  of FAO under expanded technical assistance program, 495
  of the United Nations, 476
Acts of Parliament, 59, 307, 567, 828, 1079
  Annotations to 447, 706, 962, 1194
  Distinctions in nature and numbering, 1082, 1147
Actuarial work, career, 658
Acute dehydration in infants, treatment, 420
Acworth, A. W.: Report on buildings of architectural or historic interest, 92
Adam silver, 757
Adamczewski, Stanislaw: Systemics and origin of the generic group Oxyptilus Zeller, 83

1

ADA-AME | 1951-5

Adams, C. D.: List of Gold Coast Pteridophyta, 1101
Adams, F.: Community organisation for irrigation in the United States, 550
Adams, G. H.: Historic astronomical books catalogue, 952
Adams, R: Civil aircraft accident reports, 85, 338, 973
Adelges attacking Japanese and hybrid larches, 368
Aden, Colonial report, 343, 860
Adie, R. J.:
    New evidence of sea level changes in the Falkland Islands, 862
    Petrology of Graham Land, 862, 1110
Administration of:
    Education for handicapped pupils, 286, 443
    Enemy property, legislation in force, 968
    Estates:
        Act, 310, 570
        to National Health Service, Scotland, 191
    Justice:
        and the Urban African, 601
        Bill, 1030, 1031, 1057
        under the Naval Discipline Act, report, 35
Administrative and budgetary questions, Records of, 224, 225
Admiralty publications, 68, 317, 575, 836, 1083
Admission of a State to the United Nations, advisory opinion, 141
Adoption:
    Act, 65
    Mental health aspects, report of experts on, 757
    of Children:
        Departmental Committee report, 819, 900, 903
        Study on practice and procedures, 986
Adult Education:
    England and Wales, 872
    International directory, 1002
    Preliminary survey of bibliographies, 1004
    towards social and political responsibility, 1007
Adult Probation, 986
Advertisement applications, 164
Advertising:
    Career, 659
    Material. *See* Commercial samples.
Advisory:
    Film strips, 77, 586, 846, 1091
    Leaflets:
        Agriculture, 78, 329, 586, 846, 1093
            Scotland, 77, 328, 585, 1030
        Works, 243, 503, 761, 1018
Aedes Scutellaris subgroup review with a study of variation in Aedes Pseudoscutellaris, 853
Aerated concrete, 181
AERE publications, 1098
Aerial triangulation, Stereocomparator technique, 1174
Aerodromes for aircraft, Licensing of, 86
Aerodromes, Air routes, and Ground aids Committee reports, 394, 655
Aeronautical:
    Agreements and arrangements, 138, 394, 655, 917
    Authorities, etc., abbreviations of, 138, 655, 917
    Chart catalogue, 138
    Charts:
        Division, report, 394
        Production progress, 138
        Supplement, 917
    Information services, 394, 917
    Research:
        Committee, technical reports, 69, 318, 577, 838
        Council:
            Current papers, 69, 319, 577, 838, 1084
            Reports and memos, 71, 321, 579, 840, 1087
            Review, 1090
Affiliation Orders Act, 307
    Bill, 253, 266, 277, 281, 283, 383
Afforestation in the Lake District, agreements, 1133
Afghanistan Educational Missions, 491
Africa:
    British West, photo-poster, 389, 651
    Central:
        Closer association, 44, 57, 95
        Economic survey, 345
        Territories, 44, 91
    East:
        High Commission reports, 93, 345
        Introducing, 134, 651, 914
        Land and population, 345
    Economic Conditions, developments, 222, 491, 989
    Fossil mammals of, 84
    General Service Medal, grant of, 1059
        for service in Kenya, 1223
    Map, 864
    Native administration in British African territories, 93
    South:
        Film strip and lecture notes, 134
        Nations of the Commonwealth, 134
        of the Sahara, Investments in overseas territories, 101
    South-West, report of committee on, 993
    Tropical, Enlargement of the exchange economy in, 990
    United Nations Visiting Mission, 229
    West:
        Community development in, film strip, 389
        Economic survey, 345
        Introducing, 651

African:
    Administration, Journal of, 90, 342, 599, 859, 1107
    Consumers in Nyasaland and Tanganyika, 1109
    Development in Southern Rhodesia:
        Film strip, 347
        Picture set, 389
    Land Utilisation Conference report, 91
    Languages and English in education, 237
    Local government in Tanganyika, development of, 93
    Locusts Convention, 551, 621
    Mind in health and disease, 247
    Mothers, infants, and young children, Malnutrition in, 862
    Native market in the Federation of Rhodesia and Nyasaland, 966
    Rickettsioses, report on, 238
    Species of the genus Pardomima Warren, 1102
    Swamp study, 342
    Territories, East, Economic Survey, 862
    Tropical timber, Nomenclature and general information, 100
    University, 651
African-Indian Ocean Region, special meteorological meeting, 140
After-care. *See* Parole.
Aftermath of Munich, 362
Ageing population, 637
Aglen, A. J. (Chairman): Working Party on Valuation for Rating in Scotland, reports, 1193
Agrarian reform and agricultural development, Inter-relationship between, 749
Agricultural:
    Advisory Services in Europe, Development, 876
    Development:
        Land classification for, 550
        Latin America, Prospects for, 552
        Rural reform in Denmark, 549
    Economics:
        and statistics, 549, 1008
        Monthly Bulletin, 495
        Scottish, 329, 586, 1091
    Education:
        British Caribbean Territories, 1107
        Circular, 873, 874
        Working Party report, 847
    Extension services:
        in European countries, 1008
        in the U.S.A., 100
    Holdings Act, 572, 313
        Scotland, 313
    Improvement Council, England and Wales, report, 78
    Land:
        Commission:
            Accounts, 79, 258, 330, 518, 587, 781, 848, 1038, 1091
Agricultural (*continued*):
    Land (*continued*):
        Commission (*continued*):
            Reports, 27, 78, 275, 330, 331, 537, 587, 794, 848, 1048, 1093
        (Removal of Surface Soil) Act, 567
            Bill, 253, 256, 284, 285, 509, 510, 541
            Circular, 648
    Machinery:
        Sub-committee of OEEC, report, 101
        Survey of the trade in, 347
    Marketing Acts, 63, 311, 831, 832
        Draft scheme, 330
        Milk Marketing Scheme, 1091
        Potato Marketing Draft Scheme, 1091
    Produce:
        (Grading and Marking) Amendment Act, 831
        Prices of, 1091
        See also Decontrol of Food.
    Products and fertilizers, prices of, 532, 1010
    Research:
        Bill, 1056
        Council publications, 76, 328, 585, 845, 1090
        in Europe, Organisation of, 751
        in progress, index, 76, 845
        Select Committee on Estimates reports, 791, 1041, 1147
    Statistics:
        England and Wales, 78, 330, 848, 1091, 1094
        Scotland, 328, 585, 845, 1090
        United Kingdom, 77, 330, 331, 585, 587, 848, 1094
    Studies, 234, 549
    Surpluses, disposal of, 1008
    Wages Act, report, 331
Agriculture:
    Account, 16
    Act, 65
    American, 331
    and Fisheries, Ministry of:
        Publications, 77, 329, 585, 846
        Report of the Committee on organisation of, 80
    and Food, Civil Estimates, 783, 1036
    and horticulture, 142, 398
    Annual Review and Determination of Guarantees, 809, 848, 903, 958
    Bulletins, 79, 331, 588, 848, 1091, 1094
    (Calf Subsidies) Act, 307
        Bill, 254, 284
    Development Papers, 750, 1008
    FAO advisory assistance to member countries under the UNRRA-Transfer Fund, 551
    (Fertilisers) Act, 307
        Bill, 250, 282

Agriculture (*continued*):
    for Scotland, Department of, publications, 77, 328, 585, 845, 1090
    Guidance of teachers on setting and marking of examinations, 1191
    (Improvement of Roads) Act, 1080
        Bill, 1030, 1046, 1053, 1054, 1055, 1056, 1147
    in Asia and the Far East, 750
    in Scotland, 40, 77, 290, 328, 550, 585, 810, 845, 1062, 1090
    in the Near East, 750
    Journal, 80, 333, 585, 589, 850, 1092, 1096
        Scottish, 77, 328, 585, 850, 1090
    (Miscellaneous Provisions) Act, 828
        Bill, 544, 771, 773, 784, 797, 800, 802, 906
    (Miscellaneous War Provisions) (No. 2) Act, 312
    of the sand lands, 1091
    (Ploughing Grants) Act, 307
        Bill, 253, 283
    (Poisonous Substances) Act, 307
        Bill, 251, 252, 283
    (Safety, Health and Welfare Provisions) Bill, 1057
    (Scotland) Act, 572
    Technical Bulletins, 81, 850
Agriculture, Animal Health, and Forestry: Colonial Advisory Council publications, 599
Agriculture, Fisheries, and Food, Ministry of, publications, 1091
Agriculture, Forestry and Fishery Products, Survey of, 613
Agriculture, Horticulture, etc., list of books, 848
Agriculture, Production, and Trade: Review of Commonwealth, 347
Aid to South and South-East Asia, film strip, 651
Air:
    Agreement, Portugal and U.K., Exchanges of Notes amending Schedule, 297, 1066
    Almanac, 81, 334, 589, 851, 1097
    and air traffic control, rules 140, 394
    Corporations Acts, 65, 314, 568
        Bill, 519, 544
        Guarantees:
            on loans proposed, 27, 214, 259, 266, 270, 469, 526, 530, 534, 540, 723, 780, 785, 787, 791, 794, 978, 1039, 1044, 1045, 1049, 1051, 1213
            on Stock issued, 280, 469, 786, 978
    Disinfection with ultra-violet irradiation, 940
    Estimates 14, 81, 262, 522, 589, 851, 1035, 1097
        Memos, 39, 81, 289, 548, 589, 807, 851, 1061, 1097
Air (*continued*):
    Force:
        Acts, 314, 1079
            Amendments, 81
            Bill, 803, 1026, 1054
        Career, 921
        Law, 81, 590, 1097
            Amendments, 334, 851
        List, 81, 334, 590, 851, 1097
        Prize Fund, Account, 275, 335
    Masses over British Isles, Characteristics of, 421
    Ministry, publications, 81, 334, 589, 851, 1097
    Navigation:
        Arrangements, Exchange of Notes, U.S.A. and U.K., 37
        Combined meteorological tables, 139
        Conference report, 655
        Meetings reports, 138, 394, 917
        Orders, 338, 595, 973
        Services:
            Conference report, 138
            Procedures for, 138, 394, 655, 917
        Sight reduction tables, 335
    Operations in South-East Asia, despatch, 167
    Photographs, use of oblique, 241
    Pollution Committee reports, 566, 631, 647, 702
    Service, Definition of a scheduled international, 395
    Services:
        Agreements:
            Argentine, 549
            Belgium, 46, 552
            Chile, 295
            Colombia, 303
            Cuba, 557
            Denmark, 298, 552
            Dominican Republic, 53
            Egypt, 50
            France, 38
            Germany, 1073
            India, 287, 556, 823
            Iraq, 56
            Ireland, 556
            Israel, 38
            Italy, 46
            Japan, 549, 560
            Lebanon, 288, 546, 561, 806
            Libya, 550
            Norway, 298, 552, 1075
            Panama, 57
            Philippines, 1074
            Spain, 824, 826
            Sweden, 299, 553
            Switzerland, 48, 300, 550
            Syria, 810
            Thailand, 46, 819
            Turkey, 54
            U.S.A., 1078

Air (*continued*):
    Services (*continued*):
        Appropriation Accounts, 13, 81, 259, 334, 521, 590, 781, 851, 1034, 1097
        Estimates, 12, 81, 261, 262, 334, 782, 851, 1045, 1213
        International Transit Agreement, 917
        Statement of Excess, 524, 590
    Traffic:
        in Western Europe, 394
        Services, supplement, 917
    Transport:
        Advisory Council, reports, 17, 85, 266, 338, 531, 594, 794, 972, 1048, 1207
        Agreements:
            Brazil, 299
            Burma, 548, 561
            France, 560
            Iceland, 36
        in Europe, Conference on co-ordination, report, 917
        Profits exempted from Income Tax, Exchange of Notes with Greece, 36
        Reporting forms, 394
    Votes, Treasury Minutes, 14, 17, 214, 262, 265, 334, 470, 525, 723, 783, 786, 978, 1035, 1039, 1213
Aircraft:
    Accident:
        Investigation, Manual of, 139
        Reports, 85, 338, 594, 859, 1208
        Surveys, 85, 338, 594, 972
    Airworthiness of, 140
    Export Licences, 202, 1203
    Gift to U.S.A., 816
    in agriculture in the U.S.A., Use of, 615
    Landing and taking off in bad weather, report, 37
    Manufacture and repair, Census of Production, 458, 1200
    of the U.K., Accidents to, 1206
    Personnel, Documents of Identity, Exchanges of Notes:
        Belgium, 1059
        Denmark, 1073
        France, 1074
        Netherlands, 1073
        Norway, 1073
        Sweden, 1059
        Switzerland, 1074
    Radio Maintenance Engineers' Licences, 338, 594, 1207
Airdrie Corporation Order Confirmation Act, 66
    Bill, 32
Air-ground communications, Dimensional units to be used, 395
Air/Ops Committee on Performance, report, 139
Airport:
    and air navigation facility tariffs, Manual of, 139, 917
Airport (*continued*):
    Facilities in Bermuda, Exchange of Notes with U.S.A., 48
Airports Licensing Bill, 1094
Airworthiness Division, report, 139
Aitken, Miss J. K. (Chairman): Committee on function, status and training of nurse tutors, report, 901
Albite-Riebeckite-Granites of Nigeria, 375
Alchemical books, Hundred, 436
Alcohol, Expert Committee report, 1013
Aldwyn, Earl St. (Chairman): Advisory Committee on Myxomatosis, report, 1092
Alexander of Tunis, Field Marshal the Viscount, Italian Campaign report, 241
Aliens and British Protected Persons (Naturalisation) Returns, 10, 29, 127, 275, 379, 536, 638, 795, 903, 1050, 1144
Aliens' Employment Act, 1080
    Bill, 1029, 1030, 1054, 1055, 1056
Alkali, etc., Works:
    Regulation Act, 59, 61
        Scotland, 59
            Bill, 1, 13, 14, 26, 31, 130
    Reports, 164, 386, 647, 909, 1150
Allcroft, W. M.: Incubation and hatchery practice, 332, 849
Allen, Sir O.: Selected Arab countries of the Middle East, report, 987
Alliance for peace, 882
Allied High Commission in Germany, agreement, 827, 882
Alloa Junction railway accident report, 209
Allotments Acts, 62, 65, 831
    Bill, 8
    (Scotland) Bill, 8
Allowance Regulations, Army, amendments, 239, 500, 757, 1014, 1221
Alston, A. H. G.:
    Heterophyllous Selaginellae of Continental North America, 1101
    List of Gold Coast Pteridophyta, 1101
    Revision of the West Indian species of Selaginella, 335
Aluminium:
    and aluminium alloys in building, 437
    Dust explosions, prevention of propagation of flame, 142
    Export licences, 202, 561, 719
    Industry in the U.S.A., 357
Amalgamation of the Ministry of Transport and the Ministry of Civil Aviation, 556, 723
Ambatielos Case (Greece/U.K.), 141, 396, 657, 919, 1062
Ambulance:
    Section, Civil Defence, 128
    Services:
        Costing Returns, 378, 638
        Select Committee on Estimates, report, 19
America:
    and West Indies, Calendar of State Papers, 691

America (*continued*):
Central, Population estimates, 996
American:
Aid and European Payments, Accounts, 29, 214, 279, 470, 540, 723, 1037, 1091, 1107, 1198, 1213
Forest:
Operations:
Increase of European Productivity, 357
Tropical Timber Production, 354
Species, Ecology of, 334
Gooseberry mildew, 347
Hesperiidae, catalogue, 83, 335, 591, 1101
Poplar, 100
Public Health Association, 1098
Slipper limpet on Cornish oyster beds, 332
Sylviculture and tropical forest problems, 354
Ammonium nitrate Working Party, 127
Ammonoidea of the Trias, 83
Ampulla and anointing spoon, coloured postcard, 762
Ancient:
and Historical Monuments and Constructions of England, Royal Commission: report on West Dorset, 303, 379
Monuments:
Act, 63
and Historical Buildings guides, 244, 504, 771, 1018, 1225
Boards, reports, 1044
Consolidation and Amendment Act, 569
Lists of, 1018, 1225
Anderson, F. W.: Economic geology of the Fife coalfields: Markinch, Dysart and Leven, 899
Anderson, J. N. D.: Islamic Law in Africa, 1109
Anderson, R. C.: Catalogue of ship models, 430
Anemone growing, Commercial, 1091
Anglesey:
Ancient Monuments, guide, 761
and Caernarvonshire, Census, 1137
Anglo-Egyptian Conversations on the defence of the Suez Canal and on the Sudan, 285, 359
Anglo-Iranian Oil Co. Case (U.K./Iran), 396, 757
Anglo-Norwegian Fisheries Case, 141
Anglo-Soviet Treaty, Correspondence regarding Treaty for Collaboration and Mutual Assistance, 1060, 1122
Angus, County of, Census, 635
Animal:
Health:
Leaflets, 79, 331, 587, 848, 1094
Services, reports, 587, 848, 1094
Animal (*continued*):
Trypanosomiasis in Eastern Africa, 342
Animals:
(Anaesthetics) Act, 310
(Cruel Poisons) Bill, 800, 1053
Ankara Symposium on Arid Zone Hydrology, proceedings, 1002
Annotated bibliography of the fossil mammals of Africa, 854
Annotations to Acts, 191, 447, 706, 962, 1194
Anopheles Gambiae, biology, 497, 1012
Anorthoclase from Nigeria, 336
Anthrax, 587
Anthropology in Kenya, Two Studies in Applied, 92
Antibiotics in:
Livestock feeding, 587
Pig food, 585
Anti-gas instructional diagrams, 127
Antioxidants, Food Standards Committee report, 880
Antiques, export licence, 714
Antiquities of Scotland. *See* National Museum.
Ants, Economic leaflet, 83
Apparatus and materials for teaching Science, Inventory, 230
Apparel and Textiles Order, amendments, 200, 457
Appin murder, Catalogue of documents, 445
Apple:
and Pear:
Scab, 330, 586
Trees, Winter pruning of established, 1093
Aphids, 586, 847
Grading and packing, 1094
Sawfly, 586
Sucker, 847
Apples:
and Pears:
Draft Scheme regulating marketing, 330
Pollination of, 330
Spraying programme, 847
Storage qualities of late dessert varieties, 438
Appleton, Sir E. V. (Chairman):
Committee on Supply of Teachers of Mathematics and Science in Scotland, report, 1062
Scottish Peat Committee, report, 308
Applied:
Research in Europe, the United States, and Canada, Organisation of, 876
Science, Notes on, 177, 687, 943, 1174
Appointment of Sub-Committees and Allocation of Estimates for examination, Select Committee on Estimates, report, 279
Appointments in H.M. Colonial service, 91

Appropriation:
Accounts, Treasury Minute and Abstract, 781
Acts, 59, 307, 567, 828, 1079, 1080
Approved:
School:
Boys, 379
Pupils Reports, Circular, 1190
Schools:
and Remand Homes, report of committee to review punishments, 286
See also Remand Homes; Prisons
Apsley House, guide, 499, 757
Arab:
Countries of the Middle East, Mission report, 987
States of the Middle East, Social Welfare Seminar for, 489, 1002
Arabia, Expedition to South West, 854
Araliaceae, Old World, Contributions to knowledge of, 83
Arbitration:
Acts, 65, 832
Agreement between U.K. (for Ruler of Abu Dhabi and Sultan Said bin Taimur) and Saudi Arabia, 819, 822
Arbroath Abbey, guide, 1018
Archaeopteryx Lithographica, 853
Archdeaconries (Augmentation) Measure, 513, 574, 594
Report, 513, 594
Archer, W. G.:
Bazaar Paintings of Calcutta, 757
Indian Painting in the Punjab Hills, 499
Archibald, E. H. H.: Portraits at the National Maritime Museum, 942
Architect, Career, 142, 1157
Architects Registration Act, 311, 312
Architects' Fees for state-aided housing schemes, circular, 1151
Architecture, Town Planning, and Building Research, Poplar, guide, 103
Ardrossan railway accident report, 974
Argentina:
Air Services Agreement, 549, 621
Trade and Payments Agreements, 44, 46, 105, 546, 621, 809, 882, 1072, 1122
Argyll:
Census, 635
National Forest Park guide, 893
Arid Zone:
Hydrology, Reviews of research, 744
Programmes, 744, 1002
Research, Director of Institutions, 1002
Armadale Pier. *See* Inverness.
Armaments production, Correspondence relating to control under European Defence Community Treaty, 295, 359
Armed Forces (Housing Loans) Act, 568
Bill, 517, 544
Memo, 564, 723
Armer Sir F. (Chairman): Working Party on training of district nurses, report, 1144
Armour made in the Royal Workshops at Greenwich, Exhibition of, 244
Arms and armour of old Japan, 239
Armstrong, F. H.: Strength properties of timber, 696
Army:
Acts, 314, 1079
and Air Force Act, Select Committee, reports, 271, 276, 383, 534, 642
Bill, 803, 1026, 1054
Allowance Regulations, amendments, 239, 500, 757, 1014, 1221
and Air Force:
Acts (Transitional Provisions), 1080
Revision Bill, 1026, 1054
(Annual) Acts, 59, 307, 567, 828
Bills, 2, 31, 251, 282, 283, 514, 542, 773, 801
Appropriation Accounts, 13, 239, 259, 500, 521, 758, 781, 1015, 1035, 1222
Auxiliary Territorial Service Regulations, amendments, 240
Birthday message to H.M. Queen Elizabeth the Queen Mother, 501
Boys' Units, report, 1222
Cadet Force Regulations, amendments, 240, 500, 758, 1015, 1222
Career. *See* H.M. Forces.
Civilian Staff Regulations, 1015
Combined Cadet Force Regulations, 1015
Emergency Reserve Decoration, Regulations, 500, 758, 1222
Engineer Services—Peace 1940 Regulations, amendments, 501
Estimates, 12, 13, 240, 261, 262, 500, 520, 522, 758, 782, 1035, 1045, 1214, 1222
Memos, 39, 240, 289, 500, 548, 758, 807, 1061
Family Pensions and Gratuities, 1015
General Reserve Order, 1015
King's Regulations amendments, 501
List, 240, 500, 758, 1015, 1222
Medical Services, 1143
Administration of (War History), 538
National Service Men, Regulations, 241, 502, 1016
Officers, grant of Honorary Rank, retention of rank, 242
Officers' Service Gratuities, 502
Orders, 240, 500, 758, 1015, 1222
Pay:
Allowances and Bounties for Officers and Other Ranks, 242
Warrant, amendments, 242, 502
Pay, Appointment, etc., amendments, 759, 1016, 1223
Pensions, 501, 1223
Queen's:
Army Schoolmistresses and Acting Queen's Army Schoolmistresses, Special Army Order, 759; pay, 242

Army (*continued*):
Queen' (*scontinued*):
Regulations, Amendments, 502, 759, 1223
Recruiting and Service Regulations, amendments, 758, 1222
Retired Pay, Pensions, and Gratuities, 242, 503
Service Retired Pay, 760
Statement of Excess, 524, 758
Supply, Transport and Barrack Services Regulations, amendments, 243, 503, 1017
Territorial Army Regulations, amendments, 243, 503, 760, 1017, 1224
Votes, Treasury Minutes, 14, 17, 214, 262, 265, 470, 500, 526, 723, 784, 786, 978, 1038, 1039, 1214
Arnold, F. B.: Pakistan, economic survey, 1204
Arnstein, M. G.: National Studies of Nursing Resources, 754
Arran. *See* Island of Arran.
Arsenic, Food Standards Committee, report, 1122
Art:
Examinations, 99, 352, 873, 1119, 1190
Export of works of art, reports, 472, 823, 1074
Films on, 230, 1004
Galleries. *See* Libraries.
in secondary schools, 186
in the House of Commons, Works of, report, 1226
Rules governing Award, 99
Traditional art from the Colonies, catalogue, 94
Arthur, D. W. G.: Stereocomparator technique for aerial triangulation, 1174
Arthur Lee & Sons (Hot Rolling Mills) Ltd., proposal to sell holding of securities, 814
Artificial:
Lighting of building interiors, 1185
Limbs, Standing Advisory Committee, reports, 177
Artist in modern society, 1002
Arts and Letters, 1007
Asbestos, Census of Production reports, 459, 1201
Ash, Sycamore and Maple Seed, collection and storage, 1133
Ashby, Dr. E. (Chairman): Committee on Organisation and Finance of Adult Education in England and Wales, report, 872
Ashby-de-la-Zouch Castle, guide, 761
Ashridge (Bonar Law Memorial) Trust Act, 833
Ashton, L. A.:
Fire endurance of timber beams and floors, 440
Fire tests on structural elements, 598
Ashton, R.:
Selenium, 956
Survey of sulphur and sulphuric acid position, 442
Ashton-under-Lyne, report on areas comprised in Constituencies, 20
Ashworth, W.: Contracts and Finance (War History), 85
Asia:
Air Operations in South East Asia, 167
and the Far East:
Coal and iron resources, 729
Development of mineral resources, 995
Domestic Capital, 485
Economic:
Bulletin, 221, 479, 732, 988
Commission, reports, 480, 481, 491, 732, 733
Developments, 734
Survey of, 223, 734, 990
Flood damage and control, 223, 734
Foreign Investment Law and Regulations, 223
Juvenile delinquency, 994
Progress in, 219
South and South-East, report of Mission, 987
See also Colombo Plan.
South-East:
Commonwealth types, 651
Report on, 243
See also Colombo Plan.
Asia's battle against floods, 229
Asmara, Facilities for U.K. military aircraft, Exchange of Notes with Ethiopia, 557
Asparagus, grading and packing, film strip, 329
Asphalt and coated Macadam, Survey of mixing plants, 699
Assam and Burma, Operations in, despatch, 167
Assessment of:
Psychological qualities by verbal methods, 542
Vibration intensity and its application to the study of building vibrations, 698
Assistance to:
Exporters, 533, 782
Indigent aliens, 489
the needy, Methods of administering, 738
Associated jaws and limb bones of Limnopithecus Macinnesi, 84
Association football, report on difference concerning terms and conditions of players, 400
Assurance Companies:
Acts, 61, 313, 569
Summary of statements, 200, 457, 712, 966, 1199
Returns, 458, 712, 966, 1199
(Winding Up) Acts, 571, 832

Asteroids in British Museum, Notes on, 592
Astronomical results, 376, 899, 1140
Astronomy, Magnetism and Meteorology, Greenwich Observations, 376, 899, 1141
Asylum Case (Colombia/Peru) Judgment, 141
Atlantic, North, Region, 140
Special meteorological meeting, report, 140
Atlantic Duchess explosion and fire, report 129
Atlas of:
End-grain photomicrographs for identification of hardwoods, 696
Framboesia, 237
Atmospheric pollution investigation report, 1187
Atom bomb:
Civil Defence film strip, 640
Research and development. *See* Tube alloys.
Atomic:
Energy:
Act, 833
Agreements:
Belgium, peaceful uses, 1077
U.S.A., civil uses 1068, 1072
Authority:
Act, 828
Bill, 772, 773, 800, 801, 802
See also United Kingdom Atomic Energy Authority.
Civil Estimates, 790, 979
Commission (U.N.):
Check list of documents, 729
Records, 476
for Medical Officers, Notes on, 1083
International bibliography, 220, 729, 986
Production. *See* Britain's Atomic Factories.
Project, Future organisation, 564, 706
Research:
at Harwell, 1221
Establishment, publications, 450, 706, 852, 962, 1098
Information:
Draft agreement on co-operation, 1063, 1122
Mutual defence purposes, agreement, U.S.A., 1068, 1072
Warfare:
Civil Defence Manual of Basic Training, 128
Instructional diagrams, 128
Auctioneering, Estate agency, Land agency, careers, 142, 920
Audio frequency power measurements, 943
Audley End:
Catalogue, 1018
Guide, 1225
Ault, Dr. O. E.: Report on training of Civil Service of Israel, 1000
Aural aids. *See* Visual and aural aids.
Austin Motor Co. Ltd. and National Union of Vehicle Builders, report on dispute, 553
Australia:
Compulsory Education, 233
Country Monograph, 987
Economic Survey, 1204
Industrial, film strip, 389
Social Security Agreement, 556, 604
Australian:
and Tasmanian Gropopterygidae and Nemouridae, Revision of, 336
Industry forges ahead, 389
Austria:
Correspondence with the Soviet Government, 805, 882
Cultural Convention, 548, 551, 621
Documents ancillary to the Austrian State Treaty negotiations, 1077, 1122
Economic Conditions, 877
Exchanges of Notes:
Austrian neutrality, 1078, 1122
Financial aid and Credits, 35, 105
Foreign Currency Bonds, Validation Agreement, 1059, 1122
Sterling Payments Agreement, 810, 882
Foreign Trade Statistical Bulletin, 355, 617, 878
Legal proceedings in civil and commercial matters, 57, 105
Money and Property Agreement, 298, 359
Repayment of Credits granted by European Payments Union, Agreement, 822, 882
State Treaty for the re-establishment of an independent and democratic Austria, 1088, 1123
Sterling Payments Agreement, 40, 105
Austrian State Treaty Act, 1080
Bill, 1028, 1055
Automatic Digital Computation, Symposium proceedings, 943
Automation and Electronics Bill, 1056
Autret, M.:
Kwashiorkor in Africa, 497
Sindrome Policarencial Infantil and its prevention in Central America, 1010
Auxiliary:
Forces Act, 567
Bill, 509, 512, 514, 543
Consolidation Bills report, 509, 514
Territorial Service, regulations. *See* Army.
Availability Question, National Insurance Advisory Committee report, 557
Averages of:
Bright sunshine, 679, 941
Temperature for Great Britain and Northern Ireland, 941
Avery, W. B.: Soils of the Glastonbury district of Somerset, 1092

AVI-BOS | 1951-5

- Aviation:
  - Agreement, Libya, 298
  - Law, Private Pilot's Licence, 85, 338, 594
  - Meteorology of the route Marseilles–Rome–Athens–Cairo, 680
- Awards to inventors, Royal Commission report, 546, 691
- Aycliffe:
  - Development Corporation, reports, 29, 279, 388, 779, 792, 913, 1048
  - School. *See* Approved School.
- Aylwen, Sir George (Chairman): Advisory Committee of the Law Society, reports on Legal Aid and Advice Acts, 168, 678, 939
- Ayr, Census, 635
- Azores. *See* Portugal.
- Azzaroli, A.: Deer of the Weybourne Crag and Forest Bed of Norfolk, 591

B

- Backer, C. A.: Louis Auguste Deschamps, 853
- Bacon:
  - and ham, Insects infesting, 78
  - Curing and sausage, Census of Production, 459, 1201
- Bacteria, National Collection of Industrial, catalogue, 955
- Bacteriological and Chemical Warfare, Correspondence with Soviet Government, 1060, 1123
- Badgers in Woodlands, 1133
- Baechlin, P.: Newsreels across the world, 493
- Bahamas:
  - Colonial Reports, 90, 600, 1108
  - Economic Survey, 602
  - Long Range Proving Ground for Guided Missiles:
    - Exchange of Notes amending Agreement, 1072
    - Extension to Turks and Caicos Islands, 289
- Bahrain Notices, 1123
- Bailey Bridge, normal uses, amendments, 241, 1016
  - *See also* Military Engineering.
- Bailey, Sir D. C. (Chairman): Committee on House Interiors, report, 650
- Baillie Reynolds, P. K.: Thornton Abbey monastic buildings, guide, 1018
- Baker, C. B. (Chairman): Police Council, report on police representative organisations and negotiating machinery, 382
- Baker, Peter Arthur David, indictment, conviction and sentence, 799, 905
- Baker, S. J. (Chairman):
  - Committee of Police Council on Standardisation of Promotion Examinations, 129
- Baker, S. J. (Chairman): (*continued*)
  - Working Party on Sale of Old Metals and Control of Dealers in Old Metals, 1146
- Baking Industry (Hours of Work) Act, 828
  - Bill, 544, 775, 789, 797, 802, 803, 906
- Balance of Payments, 41, 55, 291, 302, 550, 563, 810, 823, 1063, 1074
  - Trends and Policies, 476
  - Yearbook, 658
- Balances, weights, and precise laboratory weighing, 943
- Balfour, Rt. Hon. Earl (Chairman): Royal Commission on Scottish Affairs:
  - Minutes of Evidence, 693, 952
  - Report, 817
- Balfour-Browne, F. L.: Some Himalayan Fungi, 1101
- Balkans:
  - Documents on German Foreign Policy, 625
  - United Nations Special Commission report, 225
- Ballantine, W. M.: Scotland Today, 704
- *Bambo* wreck report, 469
- Bananas, refrigerated gas storage, 696
- Banff, County of, Census, 635
- Banff, Huntly and Turriff, Soils of the country around, 846
- Bangweulu Swamps, Northern Rhodesia, report, 342
- Bank:
  - Holidays (Amendment) Bill, 281
  - of England, reports 50, 214, 299, 470, 558, 723, 818, 978, 1071, 1214
  - of Scotland:
    - Act, 67
    - Order Confirmation Act, 833
      - Bill, 803
- Bankers':
  - Mission to U.S.A., 102
  - Returns, 166, 418, 676, 938, 1170
- Banking, 1157
- Bankruptcy:
  - Act, 309
  - (Amendment) Act, 311
  - Form, 1199
  - (Scotland) Act, 569
- Banks, A.: Freezing and cold storage of herrings, 438
- Banks Shell Collection, catalogue and historical account, 1102
- Bannerman, A.: Ten-stone controlled fish smoking kiln, 438
- Bannon, B. A.: Meteorological aspects of turbulence affecting aircraft at high altitude, 170
- Bannon, J. K.:
  - Classification of upper air temperature according to tropopause pressure, 941
  - Humidity of the upper troposphere and lower stratosphere over Southern England, 421

- Baptist and Congregational Trusts Act, 66
- Barbados:
  - Colonial Reports, 90, 343, 1108
  - Economic Survey, 463, 602
  - *See also* Industrial Development.
- Barcroft, J. C. H., Brunei, Colonial report, 601
- Barker, B. T. P.: Cider apple production, 849
- Barnes, J. M.: Toxic hazards of certain pesticides to man, 755
- Barnes, W. C. (Chairman): Scottish Police Council, reports:
  - Extraneous duties, 642, 702
  - Police Pensions, 704
- Barn-owl, 586
- Barnsley, Geology of the country around, 1140
- Baroque sculpture, 1013
- Barristers and Solicitors. *See* Law.
- Barry. *See* Cardiff.
- Bartram, E. B.: Mosses of Dominica, British West Indies, and Mosses of the Ecuadonian Andes collected by P. R. Bell, 1102
- Basic:
  - and Battle Physical Training, 240, 500
  - Chemical Warfare, 128
  - Facts:
    - about the U.N., 986
    - and Figures (Illiteracy, Education, etc.), 744, 1002
  - Fire fighting, 128
  - Instruments and Selected Documents, G.A.T.T., 373, 634
  - Rescue, 128, 639
  - Statistics of Food and Agriculture, 879
  - Training, Manual of, 128, 380, 639
- Basildon Development Corporation, reports, 29, 279, 388, 779, 792, 913, 1048
- Basiliewsky, P.: Carabidae: Peryphus, 593
- Basra, Port of: Exchange of Notes with Iraq regarding transfer of property, 559
- Basutoland:
  - Colonial reports, 95, 347, 604, 864, 1112
  - Economic survey, 345
  - Land tenure in, 864
  - Medicine murder, report, 42, 95
- Basutoland, the Bechuanaland Protectorate, and Swaziland: history of discussions with the Union of South Africa, 306, 347
- Bath, Boundary Commission report, 38
- Bathgate, Index to Register of Sasines, 704
- Batteries:
  - and accumulators, Census of Production, 459
  - *See also* Defence Lists.
- Battle against erosion, 134
- Bauchard, P.: Child Audience, 1006
- Baxter, G. H. (Chairman): Conference on Closer Association, Central African Territories, 44
- Baynes-Cope, A. D.: Further contributions to the solution of the Piltdown problem, 1102
- Bazaar Paintings of Calcutta, 757, 1221
- B.C. Forms, 1141
- Beans (excluding beans for stock-feeding), 79
- Beattock Summit railway accident report, 209
- Beauly Priory, guide, 1018
- Beaumont, Jacques de: Sphecidae (Hymenoptera) recoltes en Algerie et au Maroc par K. M. Guichard, 83
- Beaver, Sir H. (Chairman):
  - Committee on air pollution, reports, 566, 826
  - Committee of Enquiry into economy in construction of power stations, report, 633
- Bechuanaland Protectorate:
  - Colonial reports, 95, 347, 604, 864, 1112
  - Economic:
    - Development in the Western Kalahari, report, 864
    - Survey, 345
  - Reports on the attitude of the Bamangwato tribe to the return of Tshekedi Khama, 58, 95
- Bedfordshire, Census, 896
- Bedgebury, guide to National Pinetum and forest plots, 117
- Bedwas Colliery explosion report, 894
- Beechwoods, Studies on British, 630
- Beef, breeding and rearing, film strip, 77
- Beehives, 332, 846
- Beekeeping, 79, 1091
  - Migratory, 77
  - Practice making increase, 329
- Beer, Sir Gavin de: Archaeopteryx Lithographica, 853
- Beer, K. E.:
  - Albite-Riebeckite-Granites of Nigeria, 375
  - Petrography of some of the Riebeckite-Granites of Nigeria, 375
- Bees:
  - Acarine disease, 846
  - Diseases of, 79
  - Feeding, 587
- Beet:
  - Eelworm, 78
  - Fodder, 587
- Beetles:
  - Chafer, 329
  - Furniture, 83
- Behar, M.: Sindrome Policarencial Infantil and its prevention in Central America, 1010
- Behrens, C. B. A.: Merchant Shipping and the Demands of War, 1103
- Beit Trust Act, 835
  - Bill. *See* Personal Bills Committee report.
- Belasco, J. E.: Characteristics of air masses over the British Isles, 421
- Belgium:
  - Air Services Agreements, 46, 105, 552, 621

- Belgium (*continued*):
  - and Luxembourg:
    - Economic Survey, 715
    - Foreign Trade Statistical Bulletins, 355, 356, 617, 878
    - Monetary Agreement, 37, 106
  - Avoidance of Double Taxation, 551, 621, 811, 883
  - Construction of a deep-water quay at the port of Dar-es-Salaam, Agreement, 44, 105
  - Co-operation in the peaceful uses of atomic energy, 1077, 1123
  - Discharge by deliveries of defence equipment of a debt, 299, 359, 547, 621, 820, 883
  - Documents of identity for aircraft personnel, 1059, 1123
  - Establishment of a British military base in Belgium, 545, 565, 621
  - Exchange of official publications, 564, 621
  - Graves in Belgian territory of Members of the Armed Forces of the British Commonwealth, 57, 105
  - Loan Agreement, 54, 105
  - Privileges and facilities for British Forces in Belgium, 565, 621
  - Property belonging to persons resident in Belgium, 296, 359
  - Repayment of Credits granted by the European Payments Union, 822, 883
  - Status of Belgian Forces in Germany, 46, 105
- Belgium, Luxembourg, and the Netherlands, Economic conditions, 877
- *Belldock* wreck report, 978
- Bellonte, M.: Civil aviation accident report, 338
- Belper Urban District Council Act, 573
- Belshaw, Professor H.: South and South-East Asia, Mission report, 987
- Ben Lomond, Loch Ard, and Trossachs National Forest Park, guide, 893
- Benefices:
  - (Stabilisation of Incomes) Measure, 2, 67, 84
    - Report by Ecclesiastical Commissioners, 2, 84
  - (Suspension of Presentation) Measure, 515, 574, 594
    - Report, 515, 594
- Benefit for very short spells of unemployment or sickness, report of National Insurance Advisory Committee, 1075
- Benelux, Situations et Problemes de l'Economie, 618
- Beney, F. W. (Chairman): Departmental Committee on Diseases Provisions of the National Insurance (Industrial Injuries) Act, report, 1071
- Bennett, N. H.: Revision of the genus Teriomima Kirby, 591
- Benson, R. B.: Some sawflies of the European Alps and Mediterranean Region, 853
- Benstead, J. G.: Whalemeat bacteriology and hygiene, 696
- Bent, R. A. R.: Ten thousand men of Africa, 348
- Benthall, Sir Edward (Leader, U.K. Trade Mission): Report on markets in the Middle East, 969
- Benzene vapour, Methods for detection in industry, 1189
- Berger, M.: Racial equality and the law, 1007
- Berkeley Hotel Co. Ltd. *See* Savoy Hote Ltd.
- Berkshire:
  - Census, 896
  - County Council Act, 573
    - Bill, 513, 646
- Berlin Conference, Documents relating to the meeting of Foreign Ministers, 808, 883
- Bermuda:
  - and Falkland Islands, Economic survey, 602
  - Colonial reports, 343, 600, 1109
  - Economic survey, 463
- Berwick, Census, 635
- Bespoke tailoring, 1157
- Best, A.C.:
  - Occurrence of high rates of ice accretion on aircraft, 421
  - Temperature and humidity gradients in the first 100 m. over South-East England, 680
- Bethnal Green Station railway accident report, 974
- Betley Road railway accident report, 1209
- Betting and Lotteries Act, 311
- Betting, Lotteries, and Gaming, Royal Commission report, 41, 180
  - Selection of statements submitted, 180
- Beveridge, J.: Register of Privy Seal of Scotland, 446
- Beveridge, Rt. Hon. Lord (Chairman): Broadcasting Committee, reports, 35
- Beverton, R. J. H.: Report on research from the *Ernest Holt* into the fishery near Bear Island, 849
- Bewick, Thomas, Exhibition, 757
- Bibliographical handbooks, 749
- Bibliographies in the social sciences, 230
- Bibliography of recent official demographic statistics, 999
- Bibliotheques du proche et du moyen-orient, Repertoire de 230
- Biesalski, E.: Small farm implements, 751
- Biggs, R.: Diagnosis and treatment of haemophilia and its related conditions, 1171
- Bilateral Trade Negotiations Committee report, 712

- Bilharziasis Expert Committee, report, 756
- Bill of Quantities, notes on preparation, 208
- Bills of Exchange:
  - Act (1882) Amendment:
    - Act (1932), 832
    - Bill (1955), 1053
  - (Time of Noting) Act, 310
- Bills, Reports, Estimates, Accounts, etc. of the House of Commons, 8, 18, 130
- Binder distributors for surface dressing, 185
- Biological standardisation, Expert Committee reports, 238, 499, 756, 1013
- BIOS Surveys Report, 966
- Bird:
  - Life in the Royal Parks, reports, 244, 762, 1225
  - Migration and foot-and-mouth disease, 331
- Birkenhead Corporation Act, 833
- Birley, E:
  - Corbridge Roman Station, guide, 1018
  - Housesteads Roman Fort, guide, 504
- Birmingham Corporation Act, 833
- Births and Deaths Registration Act, 561
  - Bill, 256, 509, 510, 513, 541
  - Memo, 256
- Births, Marriages and Deaths. *See* Registrar-General.
  - Arrangements respecting registration, 373
- Biscuits, Census of Production, 201, 1201
- Bishop, G. R. H.: Breeding for bacon production, 589
- Bishop Auckland, Boundary Commission report, 524
- Bishop's Palace, St. Davids, guide, 761
- Bishops (Retirement) Measure No. 2, 67
- Bituminous:
  - Road materials, Rapid method of analysis, 185, 1188
  - Roads in North America, Research and construction, 185
  - Surfaces, Coloured treatments for, 437
  - Surfacings:
    - for roads carrying tracked vehicles, Recommendations for, 441
    - made by the wet aggregate (hydrated lime) process, 191
- Black:
  - Bean aphid, 846
  - Scurf and stem canker of the potato, 586
- Blacker, R. W.: Report on research from the *Ernest Holt* into tne fishery near Bear Island, 849
- Blackface sheep, Survey of, 586
- Blackhead, 1094
- Blackpool Corporation Act, 314
- Blacksmith, career, 659
- Blast furnaces, Census of Production, 200, 1199
- Blau, G.: Disposal of agricultural surpluses, 1008
- Blaxter, J. H. S.: Storage of herring gametes, 1192
- Blea Moor railway accident report, 719
- Blind persons, Employment of, Working Party reports, 145, 378
- Blindness:
  - and partial sight, Certification of, Circular, 1143
  - in England, Causes of, 631
- Blister blight disease of tea, 599
- Blowing, popping, or pitting of internal plaster, 181
- Blythe, W. L.: Singapore, Colonial reports, 344, 601
- Board:
  - of Control, report, 1143
  - of Trade Departments and their work, Directory of, 714, 967
- Boarding and Hospital Special Schools, Boarding Homes for Handicapped Pupils, etc., List of, 98
- Bohannan, P.: Tiv Farm and Settlement, 1109
- Boiler Explosion Acts, reports, 208, 465, 719, 972, 1207
- Bolen, F.: Films on art, 1004
- Bolivia:
  - Economic survey, 463
  - Technical Assistance Mission, report, 489
- Bologna, Giovanni: Samson and a Philistine, 1014
- Bolster, G. C.: Biology and dispersal of Mytilicota Intestinalis Steuer, 849
- Bomb Reconnaissance Quiz, film strip, 640
- Bombing range near Cuxhaven, Exchange of Notes with Germany, 304
- Bond, M. F.: House of Lords Manuscripts, 511, 647
- Bonded warehouses, Lists, 96, 348, 606, 865, 1113
- Book:
  - Bindings, 239
  - Exhibitions, 694, 952
- Bookbinding and printer's warehouse work, career, 659
- Books:
  - Access to, 1007
  - British, Import into Yugoslavia, 810, 892, 1062
- Boot and shoe, Census of Production, 459
- Booth, C. F.: Quartz vibrators and their applications, 184
- Borax in bacon, 103
- *Borde*, wreck report, 1213
- Border Rivers (Prevention of Pollution) Act, 60
  - Bill, 7, 33, 34
- Boron steels, Production and use, 876
- Borstal. *See* Delinquency, Prisons.
- Borth Bog Investigation Report, 331
- Bosanquet, Capt. H. T. A.: Naval Officer's Sword, 1173

1951-5 | BOT-BUR

BOT— *INDEX 1951-5*

Botanic Gardens. *See* Royal Botanic Gardens.
Botany Bulletin, 83, 335, 591, 853, 1101
Bottling, Census of Production, 967
Bouman, J. C.: Bibliography on filmology as related to the social sciences, 1005
Boundary Commission reports, 20, 22, 29, 38, 39, 127, 188, 269, 305, 379, 443, 524, 639, 825, 903, 958
Bournemouth:
- and District Water Act, 66
- Corporation (Trolley Vehicles) Order Confirmation Act, 1081
  - Bill, 1027, 1054, 1055
- Railway accident report, 1209

Bovine contagious abortion, 1094
Bowden, K. F.: Physical oceanography of the Irish Sea, 1096
Bowie, S. H. U.: Further contributions to the solution of the Piltdown problem, 1102
Bowlby, J.: Maternal care and mental health, 497
Box, H. E.: An undescribed species of Mastichodendron (Sapotaceae) from Barbados and Antigua, 83
Boxboard licence, 204
Boys' Units in the Army, report, 1063, 1222
B.P. Forms, 1141
Brabazon, Lord: Report on the landing and taking off of aircraft in bad weather, 37
Bracken, Control of, 329
Bracknell Development Corporation, reports, 29, 279, 388, 779, 792, 913, 1048
Bradbeer, Alderman A. F. (Chairman): Central Health Services Council, report, 901
Bradford Corporation (Trolley Vehicles):
- Order Confirmation Acts, 573, 833
- Provisional Order Bills, 514, 543, 774, 802

Bradley, K.: Careers in the Oversea Civil Service, 1107
Braille. *See* World Braille usage.
Braithwaite, J. G. (Chairman): Committee on Road Safety reports, 468
Braking performance of motor vehicles and brake testing, 699
Bramley-Harker, R. (Chairman):
- Drop forging industry, report, 661
- Safety in the Use of Power Presses Committee: Report on fencing of press brakes, 401

Brandi, C.: St. Sophia of Ochrida, 747
Brass manufactures, Census of Production, 459, 1200
Brayshaw, J. D.: Movements of salmon off North East Coast of England, 1091
Brazil:
- Air Transport Agreement, 299, 360
- Economic survey, 969
- Military Service Agreement, 1066, 1123
- Settlement of commercial areas, 563, 622, 804, 883, 1075, 1123

Brazil (*continued*):
- Trade and Payments Agreement, 49, 106, 293, 360, 552, 622, 812, 883, 1067, 1072, 1075, 1123

Bread:
- and Flour Confectionery:
  - Census of Production, 459, 1201
  - Distributive trades, Wages Council Commission, Inquiry report, 163
- Order, 112

Brecknockshire and Carmarthenshire, Census, 896
Brecon Gaer, Aberyscir, guide, 1018
Breeding:
- and rearing for beef, 77
- for bacon production, 589

Breslin, J. J. (Chairman): Matchwood Working Party, report, 969
Brewers' wet grains, 78
Brewing and malting, Census of Production, 201, 967
Brick and Fireclay, Census of Production, 458, 1199
Bricklayer, career, 398
Bricks:
- Economy memos, 763
- Firing of common, 244
- Perforated clay, 695
- Selection of clay building, 181
- Using to best advantage, 505

Brickwork, Mortars for, 243
Bridge, P. M.: Suction of moisture held in soil and other porous materials, 441
Bridge-deck systems, Studies on, 1187
Bridges:
- Act, 571
- Wind effects on, 1174

Briggs, A.: Workers' education for international understanding, 1004
Brighton:
- Corporation:
  - Act, 833
  - (Trolley Vehicles):
    - Order Confirmation Act, 314
    - Provisional Order Bill, 253, 283
- Extension Act, 66
- Pier and Harbour Order Confirmation Acts, 315, 834
  - Bills, 253, 283, 774, 802

Bristol:
- Boundary Commission report, 29
- Corporation Acts, 66, 1081
- Explosion and fire report, 290
- Rovers Football Club Ltd., Investigation, reports, 203, 458

Britain:
- and the Colonies, catalogue, 91
- Now, 214
- Official Handbook, 914, 1153

Britain's:
- Atomic factories, 963
- Forests, 116, 630, 638
- Shops, statistical summary, 458

INDEX 1951-5 —BRI

British:
- African:
  - Land Utilisation Conference, report, 91
  - Territories, Native administration in, 862
- Agricultural history, 846
- and Foreign:
  - Medals relating to Naval and Maritime affairs, 177
  - State Papers, 106, 360, 622, 1123
- and Imported Timber Beetles, 591
- Antarctic "Terra Nova" Expedition, report, 1101
- Broadcasting Corporation, reports and accounts, 52, 178, 302, 432, 559, 689, 821, 948, 1070, 1180
- Caribbean:
  - Colonies, Introducing the, 389
  - Federation Plan, 557, 603
- Civil Service, 1854–1954, 978
- Columbia Marine Insurance Rates, report, 605
- Commonwealth:
  - Leaflets, 134, 389, 651
  - Scientific:
    - Conference, Australia, report of proceedings, 590
    - Liaison Offices, publications, 82, 590, 852, 1101
  - Survey Officers Conference, report, 92
- Dependencies in the Caribbean and North Atlantic, 296, 342
- East Africa, economic survey, 715
- Electricity Authority:
  - Guarantees given on:
    - Loans proposed to be raised, 17, 22, 24, 28, 216, 260, 265, 267, 269, 275, 278, 520, 530, 540, 787, 791, 1034
    - Stock issued, 267, 527, 794, 1050
  - Reports and accounts, 272, 273, 370, 532, 792, 1135
- European Airways Corporation:
  - Guarantees given on:
    - Loans proposed to be raised, 27, 214, 259, 270, 534, 540, 785, 787, 791, 794, 978, 1034, 1039, 1045, 1049, 1213
    - Stock issued, 280
  - Reports and accounts, 23, 85, 274, 338, 533, 594, 793, 972, 1048, 1207
- Farming, 79
- Field Products Ltd., Select Committee on Estimates, report, 789, 795
- Fishing-boats and coastal craft, Handbook, 436
- Foreign Policy, Documents on 106, 360, 622, 883, 1123
- Guiana:
  - Colonial reports, 90, 343, 600, 860, 1108, 1109

British (*continued*):
- Guiana (*continued*):
  - Constitution, suspension of 564, 599
  - Constitutional Commission, reports, 91, 822, 859
  - Economic surveys, 563, 602
  - Technical Assistance, Exchange of Notes with U.S.A., 827
  - *See also* Industrial Development.
- Honduras:
  - and Mexico, Telecommunications Agreement, 814
  - Colonial Reports, 91, 344, 860, 1108
  - Economic survey, 602
  - Renewal of Declaration accepting jurisdiction of the International Court of Justice concerning any Treaty relating to its boundaries, 41, 106
  - Report of an Inquiry, 812, 859
- Ichneumoninae, with descriptions of new species, Notes on, 591
- Imperial Calendar and Civil Service List, 190, 446, 705, 961, 1194
- Industries Fair:
  - Board of Trade Journal Supplements 204, 462, 715, 969, 1204
  - (Guarantees and Grants) Acts:
    - Bill, 771, 800
    - Statements of guarantee, 794, 966, 1044, 1214
  - Review of present arrangements, 566, 712
- Intelligence Objectives Sub-Committee Surveys, reports, 200, 437
- Islands in the Southern Hemisphere, 43, 91
- Mammals, List of 335
- Mites of economic importance, 1103
- Museum:
  - Act, 1079
    - Bill, 1027, 1054
  - (Amendment) Bill, 284
  - Bill, 33
  - (Natural History), publications, 83, 335, 591, 853, 1101
  - Publications, 82, 335, 590, 852, 1101
- Nationality Act, 65
- North America Act, 59
  - Bill, 4, 32
- Overseas Airways Corporation:
  - and Cyprus Airways, Exchange of Notes with Israel regarding conversion of earnings into Sterling, 561
  - Guarantees given on:
    - Loans proposed to be raised, 266, 270, 526, 530, 534, 780, 1044, 1049, 1051, 1213
    - Stock issued, 786
  - Reports and accounts, 24, 85, 274, 338, 533, 594, 794, 972, 1048, 1207
- Pacific Islands, Introducing the, 134

BRI— *INDEX 1951-5*

British (*continued*):
- Phosphate Commission, reports and accounts, 47, 93, 298, 347, 554, 604, 814, 864, 1063, 1112
- Poisonous plants, 1095
- Rainfall, 169, 420, 172, 941, 1172
- Regional Geology, 635, 898
- Solomon Islands:
  - Colonial Reports, 90, 600, 1109
  - Economic survey, 602
- Standards Institution, Report of Committee on Organisation and Constitution, 200
- Trade in China, Correspondence between U.K. and China, 300
- Transport Commission:
  - Act, 66, 314, 316, 573, 834
  - and the National Union of Railwaymen Dispute, reports, 1057, 1059, 1162
  - Financial and Statistical Accounts, 295, 465
  - Guarantees given on stock issued, 12, 260, 262, 263, 264, 266, 269, 275, 279, 521, 524, 534, 780, 784, 786, 794, 1040, 1044, 1049
  - Railway Merchandise Charges Scheme, proceedings, 1212
  - Reports and Accounts, 21, 208, 519, 718, 794, 972, 1045, 1207
  - Order Confirmation Acts, 66, 573, 834, 1081
    - Bills, 33, 543, 802, 1055
  - Passenger:
    - Charges Scheme, 212, 469, 721, 977, 1211
    - Fares, Increase in, report, 291
- War Production, 337
- Water-colours, 239
- West Indies:
  - Buildings of architectural or historic interest, 92
  - Eastern Caribbean, economic survey, 463
- West Indies, British Guiana, and British Honduras, Timber Mission, report, 603

Broadcasting:
- Committee, report and appendix, 35, 168, 178
  - Memo, 48, 95, 178, 294, 432
- Copy of:
  - Agreement, 815, 948
  - Licence and Agreement, 296, 432
  - New Charter of Incorporation, 298, 432
- Draft:
  - Licence for Independent Television Authority, 810, 948
  - of Licence and Agreement, 58, 178
  - of Royal Charter, 58, 178, 296, 432
- Estimates, 15, 214, 262, 522, 783, 1036
- Licence granted to Independent Television Authority, 1064, 1180

Broadcasting (*continued*):
- North American Regional Broadcasting Agreement, 30, 108
- Television Policy, Memo on, 565, 689
- to Schools, 230

Broadmoor, report, 297, 377
Brochs of Mousa and Clickhimin, guide, 244
Brock, J. F.: Kwashiorkor in Africa, 497
Bromley Corporation Act, 573
Brooke, H. (Chairman):
- Flats Sub-Committee of the Central Housing Advisory Committee, report on survey in flats, 388
- Housing Management Sub-Committee of the Central Housing Advisory Committee, report on transfers, exchanges and rents, 650

Brooks, C. E. P.: Handbook of statistical methods in meteorology, 680
Brooks, J.: Eggs and egg products, 1186
Brooksby, J. B.: Technique of complement-fixation in foot-and-mouth disease research, 585
Broughton, H. F.:
- Productivity in house building, 699
- Survey of building in sandstone in Scotland, 699
- Thermal insulation of buildings, 1189

Brown:
- Rot diseases of fruit trees, 850
- Trout Research Supervisory Committee reports, 444, 702, 959, 1191

Brown Bayley Steels Ltd., Proposal to sell holdings of securities, 1067
Brown, Clifton. *See* Mr. Speaker.
Brown, D. A.:
- On the Polyzoan genus Crepidacantha Levinsen, 853
- Tertiary Cheilostomatous Polyzoa of New Zealand, 336

Brown, J. M. B.: Studies on British beechwoods, 630
Brown, V.: Aircraft accident reports, 85, 338, 594
Brown, W.: Reports on explosions at:
- Horden Colliery, 1061
- Weetslade Colliery, 1076

Brown, W. B.:
- Fumigation with methyl bromide under gas-proof sheets, 955
- Inspector of Mines report, 895

Browne, J. Nixon (Chairman): Committee on Exchequer Equalisation Grants, report, 1192
Browning, E.:
- Some British mites of economic importance, 1103
- Some inter tidal mites from South West England,592

Brucellosis, Expert reports, 238, 750, 756
Brule, H.: Education of Teachers in England, France, and U.S.A., 1006
Brunei, Colonial reports, 91, 600, 601, 1108

INDEX 1951-5 —BUR

Brushes and Brooms, Census of Production, 460, 967
Brussels:
- Sprouts, 1093
  - *See also* Cabbages.
- Treaty Powers, Conventions (Social and Medical Assistance and Social Security), 43

Bryan, Sir A.: Colliery accident reports:
- Creswell, 296, 370
- Knockshinnock Castle, 40

Bryant, G. E.: Chrysomelidae, Ruwenzori Expedition, 593
Buchan, S.: Geology of country around Chatham, 899
Buchanan, G. (Chairman): National Assistance Board, report on Receipt Centres, 430
Buckingham Palace by floodlight, postcard, 763
Buckinghamshire, Census, 896
Buckley, C.:
- Five Ventures, 1016
- Greece and Crete, 501
- Norway-Commandos-Dieppe, 473

Budget:
- Management Report, 986
- *See also* Financial Statement.

Builders:
- Introduction to:
  - Programming and Progressing for, 243
  - Site Costing for, 243
- Site Records for, 505

Building:
- and Civil Engineering:
  - Contracts, Retention moneys on, report, 1019
  - Works, General Conditions of Government Contracts for, 244
- and Contracting, Gas, Electricity, and Water, Census of Production, 713
- and Housing Research, 993
- Apprenticeship and Training Council report, Training for Management, 504
- Bulletins, 98, 352, 614, 872, 1119
- Byelaws, 387, 140
  - *See also* Model Byelaws.
- Educational, Circular, 872, 874
- Industry:
  - Managerial, executive, and technical posts, careers, 142
  - Restrictive practices, circular, 1150
- Limes, 437
- Mastics: Bonding new concrete to old, 1185
- Materials:
  - and Housing Act, 313
    - Accounts, 9, 244, 258, 504, 523, 648, 762, 784, 1018, 1038, 1225
  - Census of Production, 458, 1199
  - Economy of, 505
- Prosperity, 914

Building (*continued*):
- Research:
  - and Development:
    - Advisory Council report, 762
    - Directory of Organisations in Europe, 220
  - Board, reports, 181, 437, 695, 953, 1185
  - Station Digests, 181, 437, 695, 953, 1185
- Restrictions (Wartime Contravention) Act, 65
- Science Abstracts, [illegible] 1185
- Sites, Welfare arrangements, 163
- Societies:
  - Act, 312, 569
  - Chief Registrar's report, 631, 893
  - Statistical summaries, 118, 370

Buildings:
- Constructions and Engineering Services, Codes of Practice for, 244
- in the Greater London area, report on supply, 793, 969
- Model Byelaws, 388, 650
- of architectural or historic interest in the West Indies, 92
- registered or disused for marriages, 374, 634, 897
- Vibrations in, 1185

Built-up litter system, 330, 1093
Bulgaria, Settlement of financial matters, agreement, 1076, 1123
Bulgaria, Hungary, and Roumania, Interpretation of Peace Treaties with, 141
Bulgarian property, Treasury proposal and directions to Administrator in the U.K., 817, 818, 979, 1064, 1123
Bulk:
- Handling:
  - of grain in U.S.A., 619
  - of home-grown grain, 848
- Storage of potatoes in buildings, 849

Bull pen, 80
Bull, G. A.: Stratus cloud near the east coast of Great Britain, 170
Bullerwell, W.: Geology of the country between Burton-upon-Trent, Rugeley, and Uttoxeter, 1140
Bulletin Statistique, 875
Burcham, J. N.: Dielectric properties of wood, 954
Burgess, G. F. M. *See* Foreign Office Officials.
Burghley, Lord (Leader, United Kingdom Industrial Delegation to Burma), report, 971
Burial and Cremation (Scotland) Bill, draft, 547, 702
Burma:
- Air Transport Agreement, 548, 561, 622

BUR-CHE | 1951-5

Burma (*continued*):
Avoidance of Double Taxation and prevention of fiscal evasion with respect to taxes on income, 47, 106, 292, 360
Campaign, maps, 167
Commercial conditions, review, 712
Educational Mission, report, 491
Industrial Delegation, report, 971
Operations in, despatch, 166, 167
Outstanding financial questions, Exchange of Notes, 814, 883
Burne, R. H.: Cetacean Dissections Handbook, 336
Burnett, P. V. (Chairman): Lighting Committee of Building Research Board, report on lighting of office buildings, 505
Burnham Committee reports, 99, 873
Burrell, J. H. (Chairman): Police Extraneous Duties Committee, report, 642
Burrows, F. J. (Chairman): Agricultural Land Commission, reports, 275, 331, 873
Burrows, R. (Deputy Chairman): Boundary Commission, report on Oldham and Ashton-under-Lyne, 20, 29
Burton, M.: Suberites Domuncula, 592
Burton, W. G.: Storage of ware potatoes in Great Britain, 696
Burton-upon-Trent, Rugeley, and Uttoxeter, Geology of the country between, 1140
Bush fruits, 79
Busia, K. A.: Culture and human fertility, 1006
Business management problems, 876
Bute, County of, Census, 635
Butler, C. G.: Beehives, 332
Butler, Rohan: Documents on British Foreign Policy, 106, 360, 622, 883, 1123
Butter, Use of the word in description of confectionery, 104
Buzzard, Common, 586
Byland Abbey, guide, 504
Bywater, Lt. Col. F. J. (Chairman): Codes of Practice Council, report on Codes of Practice for Buildings Construction and Engineering Services, 244

C

Cabbage:
Aphid, 78, 847
Caterpillars, 329, 586
Root fly, 329
Cabbages, Brussels sprouts, and miscellaneous green crops, 1095
Cabinet Offices publications, 337, 593, 854, 1103
Cable:
and Wireless Ltd., Accounts, 55, 178, 299, 432, 558, 689, 818, 948, 1071, 1181
between Gibraltar and Casablanca, Recovery, Exchange of Notes with Italy, 297
Cacao, Witches' broom disease, 346
Cadastral surveys and records of rights in land, 750
Cadbury, Major E. (Chairman): Central Transport Consultative Committee, report on British Transport Commission (Passenger) Charges Scheme, 291
Caddis-flies. *See* Trichoptera.
Cadet:
Entry into the Royal Navy, report, 553, 575
Force Regulations, 240, 500, 758
Cadman, W. A.: Shelter belts for Welsh hill farms, 631
Caerlaverock Castle, guide, 504
Caerleon Roman ampitheatre, guide, 761
Caernarvon:
Castle and Town Wall, guide, 761
Corporation Act, 834
Caerwent Roman City, guide, 244
Caicos Islands. *See* Turks.
Cain, A. J.: Subdivision of the genus Ptilinopus (Aves, Columbae), 853
Cairnpapple Hill, guide, 244
Cairns, D. A. S.:
(Chairman): Monopolies and Restrictive Practices Commission, reports:
Process of Calico Printing, 787
Supply:
and Export of:
Copper and copper-based alloys, 1047
Pneumatic tyres, 1051
of buildings in Greater London area, 793
Civil Aircraft Accident report, 595
Caithness, Census, 635
Calder, M. G.: Coniferous petrified forest of Patagonia, 591
Calendar:
of Close Rolls, 691, 949
of Inquisitions Post Mortem, etc., 691, 1181
of letters, Despatches, and State Papers relating to negotiations between England and Spain, 949
of State Papers, 180, 445, 691
of Treasury Books, 434, 691, 949
Calf rearing, 588
Calibration of temperature measuring instruments, 1174
Calico printing, Monopolies Commission report, 787
Calver, M. A.: Geology of the country between Burton-upon-Trent, Rugeley, and Uttoxeter, 1140
Calvert, H. R.: Historic astronomical books, catalogue, 952
Calves, lead poisoning, 331
Cambodia, International Commission for supervision and control, 1065, 1070, 1073, 1124

Cambridgeshire and Huntingdonshire, Census, 1137
Cambro-Ordovician limestones and dolomites of the Ord and Torran areas, Skye, and the Kishorn area, 899
Cameo, wreck report, 213
Cameron, (Sir) J. (Chairman): Court of Inquiry into dispute between:
British Transport Commission and National Union of Railwaymen, 1057, 1059
National Federated Electrical Association and Electrical Trades Union, 562
Cameroons:
under French administration, reports, 735, 1001
under United Kingdom administration, 91, 342, 735, 859, 1001, 1107
Campaign:
in Italy, 214
in Norway, 337
Campania Festival Ship, guide-catalogue, 103
Campbell, Sir C. (Chairman): Gatwick Airport Inquiry, report, 817
Camping:
Mobile, 873
Organised, 353
Camps in use for emergency housing purposes, 910
Canada:
and the United States, economic conditions, 877
Exporting to, 202, 968
Economic survey, 204
Film strip, 604
Financial Agreement, 294, 348, 811, 864
Foreign Trade Statistical Bulletin, 355, 617, 878
Relief from Import Duty, articles imported in pursuance of Defence Contracts, Exchange of letters, 1067, 1112
Canada's farm radio forum, 1006
Canal, Dock and Harbour Undertakings, Census of Production, 460, 1202
Cancer registration:
England and Wales, 374
Expert Committee on Health Statistics, report, 498
Cane fruits, 1095
Canned food, production, etc., 1111
Cannock Chase, 116
Canterbury:
and District Water Act, 314
Extension Act, 66
Canvas goods and sacks, Census of Production, 459, 1200
Cape Observatory, Annals, 123, 636, 899, 1140
Capital:
Punishment, Royal Commission, publications, 181, 434, 560, 691
Capital (*continued*):
Works in the Colonial Territories, 345
Caponera, D. A.: Water laws in Moslem countries, 1008
Car parking in the inner area of London, 718
Carbon monoxide, method for detection in industry, 1189
Carboniferous flora of Peru, 853
Carbonatites of the Chilwa Series of Southern Nyasaland, 591
Cardboard box, carton, and fibre-board packing case trades, Census of Production, 460, 1201
Cardiff:
Airport, air navigation order, 973
Corporation Act, 1081
Cardiff, Barry, Monmouth: Boundary Commission report, 22
Cardiganshire and Pembrokeshire, Census, 1137
Cardiolipin antigens, Preparation and chemical and seriological control, 237
Care of:
Builders' machines, 761
Homeless, 380
Senile Persons (Scotland) Bill, 282
Small plant and hand tools, 243
the trawler's fish, 696
Career in the Oversea Civil Service, 1107
Careers guides, 142, 398, 658, 921, 1157
Caribbean:
and North Atlantic, British Dependencies in 296, 342
Area:
Establishment of a Customs Union, 93
Technical Assistance, Exchange of Notes with U.S.A., 812
Colonies:
Food production in, 134
Introducing the, 389
Federation, report on movement of persons within, 1110
Markets in, 715
Region, Air Navigation Meeting, report, 138
Territories, Agricultural education report, 1107
Today, film strips and picture sets, 914
Carlisle Castle, guide, 244
Carnations under glass, 849
Carnegie Park and Scott Trust (Amendment) Scheme:
Memo, 701
Order in Council, 957
Carob-growing areas, report of investigation into rat problem, 92
Carothers, J. C.: African mind in health and disease, 755
Carpenter and joiner, career, 398
Carpet wool, commodity report, 750
Carpets, Census of Production, 201, 967

Carriage:
by Air Act, 311
of Dangerous Goods and Explosives in Ships, 465, 718, 722, 972, 1207
of Goods:
by rail, International Convention, 807, 809, 972
by Sea Act, 310
of Passengers and Luggage by Rail, International Convention, 806, 972
Carrier, N. H.: External migration, 634
Carrier-borne aircraft attack on oil refineries in Palembang area, 167
Carrington, Lord (Chairman):
Advisory Committee on Myxomatosis, report, 850
Agricultural Education Working Party, 847
Carrot fly, 586
Carr-Saunders, Sir A. (Chairman, Inter-University Council): Report on Higher Education Overseas, 1069
Carruthers, N.: Handbook of statistical methods in meteorology, 680, 755
Carter, Sir A. (Chairman, Monopolies and Restrictive Practices Commission):
Electric lamps, 25
Imported timber, 533
Insulated electric lines and cables, 269, 462
Insulin, 274, 462
Matches, 527
Carts, Perambulators, etc., Census of Production, 458, 1200
Cartwright, K. St. G.: Dry rot in wood, 439
Case, R. A. M.: Whalemeat bacteriology and hygiene, 696
Cast iron and rainwater goods, report on supply, 204
Castell Coch, guide, 1018
Castillo, I.: Training of rural school teachers, 1006
Castle Acre Priory, guide, 504
Castle Campbell, guide, 761
Castles of England and Wales, 1019
Catalytic enrichment of industrial gases by the synthesis of methane, 696
Catering:
Establishments, hygiene in, 104
Industry. *See* Hotel.
Wages:
Act, 64
Commission, reports, 19, 142, 268, 398, 528, 659, 789, 920, 1045, 1157
Cathedrals:
(Appointed Commissions) Measure, 2, 67, 84
Report, 2, 84
(Grants) Measure, 770, 835, 855
Report, 770
Cathodic protection of pipelines and storage tanks, 696
Catholic Church and the Race Question 748
Cattle:
Crush, 80
in British Colonial Territories in Africa, Improvement of, 599
of Britain, 1095
Tuberculosis of, 331
Yards, 849
Cattle, Dog and Poultry Foods, Census of Production, 460, 1201
Catto, Rt. Hon. Lord (Chairman): Scottish Financial and Trade Statistics Committee report, 298
Cauliflowers, 332
Causes of blindness in England, 637
Cayman Islands, Colonial reports, 343, 600, 1109
CCC/Works/1 (General Conditions of Contract), 244, 505, 1226
Celluloid and Cinematograph Film Act, 62
Cement:
Census of Production, 200, 966
Economy memo, 505
Engineering and large scale building, 763
High alumina, 181
Housing and small scale building, 763
Census:
Data, application of international standards, 476
explained, 121
Index of place names, 1138
of Distribution and other services, 712, 966, 1199
of Production, 200, 458, 712, 966, 1199
of Woodlands, 117, 630
Reports, 121, 374, 634, 896, 1137
Scotland, 122, 374, 635, 898
Statistics for the calculation of life tables, etc., methods of using, 226
Censuses of Production:
and Distribution, report, 822, 967
Summary tables, 967
Centrimetric aerials for marine navigation, radar, 466
Central:
African Territories, Closer Association, relative reports, 44
After-care Association, reports, 903, 1144
Criminal Court in South Lancashire, Departmental Committee report, 561, 639, 678
Electricity Authority, guarantees on loans proposed to be raised, 1039, 1045, 1049
Government and Finance, Estimates, 15 214, 262, 522, 783, 1036
Health Services Council:
Advisory Committee on Medical Research in Scotland, report on clinical research, 637, 679

Central (*continued*):
Health Services Council (*continued*):
Reports, 125, 266, 377, 530, 637, 679, 790, 901, 1042, 1143
Hospital Pharmaceutical Service report, 1143
Land Board:
Practice Notes, supplementary report, 23, 164
Reports, 271, 386, 529, 647, 791, 909, 958, 1048, 1150
Office of Information, publications, 389, 651
Statistical Office publications, 84, 337, 593, 855, 1103
Transport Consultative Committee, reports, 15, 208, 260, 466, 525, 718, 784, 972, 1036, 1207
Centres Nationaux d'Information Bibliographique, guide, 1005
Century of London Weather, 680
Ceramic industry in the Philippines, 1000
Ceramics and Glass, research reports, 441
Cereal:
Breeding procedures, 751
Foot rots, 329
Root eelworm, 847
Cereals:
and Feeding Stuffs, Decontrol, 546, 620
Deficiency Payments Scheme, 882, 1095
Home grown, Guarantee for, 561, 620
Ceremonials observed at His Late Majesty's funeral, 418
Certification and licensing of aircraft radio personnel, 85
Certificates and Diplomas, Education Rules, 1120
Certified places of worship registered for marriages, 1139
Cestodes of seals from the Antarctic, 336
Cetacea stranded on the British coasts, report, 592
Cetacean dissections, Burne's handbook of, 336
Ceylon:
Economic Survey, 463, 1204
Sterling Assets, etc., Exchange of letters, 39, 95, 302, 347
Chaetognatha and other zooplankton of the Scottish area, 703
Chafer beetles, 78, 329
Chain, Nail, Screw, and Miscellaneous forgings, Census of Production, 459, 1200
Chairs, English, history of, 329
Chaldecott, J. A.: Handbooks of:
Collection relating to heat and cold, 1184
King George III Collection of scientific instruments, 437
Temperature measurement and control, 1185
Chambers, E. G.: Psychological tests for accident proneness and industrial proficiency, summary of reports, 1171
Chambers, S. P. (Chairman): London Transport Committee of Inquiry, report, 1209
Champion, A. J. (Chairman): Committee on Licences, Veterinary Surgeons Act, report, 334
Chandler, M. E. J.:
Schizaeaceae of England in early Tertiary Times, 1102
Some Upper Cretaceous and Eocene fruits from Egypt, 853
Chaplains: Appointment, pay, and conditions of service, 1221
Characteristics:
of air masses over the British Isles, 421
of the ionosphere observed in Great Britain, 698
Charitable Trusts:
Government policy, 1071, 1144
Law and practice, 306, 419
(Validation) Act, 828
Bill, 517, 769, 770, 776, 790, 797, 800, 802, 906
Charity Commission:
Form, 855
Reports of Commissioners, 84, 337, 594, 855, 1104
Charlton, J.:
Lancaster House, guide, 1018
Osborne House, guide, 1225
Charters, H.: Fire in State Forests, 892
Chasen: Handlist of Malaysian Mammals, 1102
Chatfield, C.: Food composition tables, 1010
Chatham:
and District Traction Act, 1081
Geology of the country around, 899
Intra Charity of Richard Watts and Other Charities Scheme Confirmation Act, 1081
Bill, 803, 1025
Chatterton, W. O. (Chairman): Hospitalization Costing Working Party, report, 1143
Chatwin, C. P.: East Anglia and adjoining areas, British Regional Geology, 898
Chauliodini new genus and some new species, 853
Cheadle, Boundary Commission report, 524
Check list of United Nations documents, 729
Chehab, E. M.: Unesco Mission on Lebanon Museum and Monuments, report, 1006
Chemical:
Apparatus in the U.S.A., 354
Caponisation, 78
Control of weeds in forest nursery seedbeds, 368
Engineering research, report, 182
Products:
Committee study, 357
Exportable surpluses, 100

Chemical (*continued*):
Warfare:
Manual of Basic Training, 128
Medical Manual, 1222
Chemical, Gas and Mining Engineering, etc., Career, 920
Chemicals and Allied Trades, Census of Production, 461, 712, 713
Chemistry Research Board, reports, 182, 438, 696, 953, 1186
Chepstow Castle, guide, 1225
Cherries. *See* Plums.
Cherrill, F. R.: Fingerprint system at Scotland Yard, 904
Cheshire:
Brine Pumping (Compensation for Subsidence) Act, 314
Census, 896
County Council Act, 573
Cheshire fatal accident, report, 129
Cheshunt Urban District Council Act, 1081
Chestnut blight, 116
Chettle, G. H.: Hampton Court Palace, guide, 505, 1018
Chick rearing, 330, 847
Child:
and Youth Welfare, 221, 485
Audience, 1006
Care, Select Committee on Estimates report, 270, 276
Feeding, Plant proteins in, 679
Health, report, 636
Labour in relation to compulsory education, 494
Migration to Australia, 639
Child, Youth, and Family Welfare. *See* Legislative and Administrative Series.
Childe, Professor V. G.: Ancient Monuments, Scotland, guide, 504, 1225
Children:
Act, 61, 65, 572
and Young Persons:
Acts, 311, 571, 832
(Amendment) Bill, 1025
Bill (1955), 1031, 1057
(Harmful Publications) Act, 1079
(Scotland) Act, circular, 186
Boarding-out Regulations, memo, 1144
deprived of a normal home life, 477
in the care of Local Authorities, 758, 639, 812, 902, 1067, 1111
United Nations Appeal, Special Committee report, 481
Children's:
Department, work of, 127, 1144
Emergency Fund, 222, 225, 480, 481
See also UNICEF.
Fund, Financial Report and Accounts, 990
Homes, conduct of, 128
Chile:
Air Services Agreement, 295, 360
Chile (*continued*):
Payments Agreement, 55, 106
United Nations Economic Mission, report, 477
Chilton, D.: Navigation today, 694
China:
and Earthenware, Census of Production, 458, 966
British Trade in, 300, 360
Experiment in visual education, 231
Chinese:
Engineering and Mining Co. Ltd. Investigation, report, 1202
Pottery and porcelain, 1184
Chironomidae, Study of African, 1102
Chiropodist, career, 921
Chiswick, wreck report, 213
Chlorine, Methods for detection in industry, 1189
Cholera:
Expert Committee, report, 498
Study Group, report, 237
Chorley, Lord (Chairman): Higher Civil Service Remuneration Committee, report, 217
Christie, J.: Revised yield tables for conifers in Great Britain, 123
Christmas Picture Book, 1013
Chronological Table of the Statutes, 191, 706, 962, 1194
Chrysanthemum:
Eelworm, 1091
Midge, 586
Chrysanthemums, 332, 848
Culture of early flowering, 329
Pests and diseases of, 329
Pot culture of late, 329
Church:
Assembly Measures. *See* Public General Acts.
Revised, 84, 191
of England:
Assembly (Powers) Act, 310
Pensions Board (Powers) Measure, 250, 316, 337
Report by Ecclesiastical Committee, 250, 337
Work, Career, 398
Churches and Universities (Scotland) Widows' and Orphans' Fund Order Confirmation Act, 834
Bill, 803
Churchill, Sir W.:
Exchange of Letters with:
French President, 1062, 1103
Mr. Molotov, 1062, 1103
Message on the occasion of his retirement, 1223
Speech to Congress, U.S.A., 288, 337
Cider apple production, 849
Cinematograph:
Act, 307, 309
Bill, 250, 255, 282, 285
Acts: Safety in cinemas, 1144

Cinematograph (*continued*):
Film:
Printing, Census of Production, 460, 1202
Production (Special Loans) Acts, 307, 828
Accounts, 256, 271, 461, 538, 714, 1037, 1202
Bills, 251, 282, 517, 544, 769
Statement of postponement and remission of payments, 1046, 1202
Films Council, reports, 19, 201, 267, 461, 528, 714, 790, 967, 1044, 1202
Fund Accounts, 23, 179, 271, 533, 690, 791, 1049, 1181
Circular plate ripsaws, Performance of, 696
Citrus:
and dried fruit, 234
Industry. *See* West Indian.
City of London:
(Central Criminal Court) Acts, 66, 573
(Guild Churches) Act, 314
Bill, Select Committee on, report etc., 267, 383
(Various Powers) Acts, 314, 834
Civil:
Aerodromes and ground services, Select Committee on Estimates, report, 1051, 1147
Aircraft accident reports, 85, 338, 594, 973, 1208
Appropriation Accounts, 10, 13, 214, 257, 259, 470, 594, 779, 780, 979, 1032, 1214
Aviation:
Act, 313
Orders, 85, 338
Communications Handbook, amendments, 338, 595, 1208
Convention:
and Agreement, 38, 114
on damage caused by foreign aircraft to third parties on the surface, 48, 114
Ministry of:
Amalgamation with Ministry of Transport, 48
Publications, 85, 338, 594
Protocol relating to amendments to Convention, 819, 823, 883
Contingencies Fund:
Accounts, 30, 214, 280, 470, 784, 979, 1037, 1214
Act, 308
Bill, 255, 285
Defence:
and Allied Services, Publicity and Recruitment, Advisory Committee reports, 306, 811
(Armed Forces) Act, 828
Bill, 773, 777, 803
Civil (*continued*):
Defence (*continued*):
Damage Control pads, 127
(Electricity Undertakings) Act, 828
Bill, 771, 800
Estimates, Select Committee on, report, 782
Film Strips, 380, 639, 903
Home Office publications, 127, 380, 639, 903
Instructional Diagrams, 127
War History, 1103
Report, 52
Welfare Services, 376
Employment, Reinstatement in, Umpire's decisions, 163, 417
Engineering, Career, 658
Estimates, 14, 15, 21, 28, 97, 214, 215, 261, 262, 263, 270, 470, 471, 520, 522, 523, 524, 530, 539, 723, 724, 782, 783, 784, 786, 790, 791, 979, 980, 1035, 1036, 1038, 1045 1214, 1215
Industry and Trade, War History, 337
Judicial Statistics:
England and Wales, 40, 57, 168, 295, 419, 555, 678, 813, 939, 1068, 1170,
Scotland, 35, 54, 188, 300, 443, 555, 702, 815, 959, 1069, 1191
List:
Act, 307
Bill, 254, 284
Select Committee, report, 270, 383
Servants:
Retired pay and pensions, 809
Transfer to other duties, 817, 980
Service:
Appointments Board Bill, 285
Arbitration Tribunal Awards, 142, 398, 659, 921, 1157
Career, 921
Commission, examination papers, 86, 339, 596, 856, 1104
Commissioners' reports, 599, 859, 1107
Digest of Pension Law and Regulations, 471
Executive and Clerical Officers, careers, 398
List. *See* British Imperial Calendar.
Medical staffs, report of Committee on Pay and Organisation, 218
Openings for juniors, 398
Posts for University undergraduates, 850
Professional Accountant Class, report of Committee on Organisation, Structure and Remuneration, 474
Royal Commission on:
Evidence, 950, 1182
Report, 1076, 1182
Selection Board, memo, 86
Staff relations, 1219

Civil (*continued*):
Service (*continued*):
Training and education, 980
Typists' Manual, 1215
Civilian:
Employees at Air Ministry Establishments, regulations, 81, 334, 590, 851, 1098
Health and Medical Services, 638, 1143
Staff Regulations, 240, 501, 758, 1015, 1222
Civilisation of Western Europe and the School, 873
Clackmannan:
and East Stirlingshire and Stirling and Falkirk burghs, Boundary Commission report, 305
Census, 635
Clague, E.: Materials Handling Equipment, 879
Clan Alpine:
Static experiments, 837
Structural trials, 1084
Clapham, Sir A.:
St. Augustine's Abbey, Canterbury, guide, 1225
Whitby Abbey, guide, 504
Clare, K. E.: Use of stablilised soil for road construction in U.S.A., 956
Claringbull, G. F.: Further contributions to the solution of the Piltdown problem, 1101
Clark, A. M.: Notes on asteroids in the British Museum, 592
Clark, W. E. le Gros:
Associated jaws and limb bones of Limnopithecus macinnesi, 84
Miocene Hominoidea of East Africa, 84
Classics in secondary schools, 187
Classification of:
Occupations, 121
Upper air temperature according to tropopause pressure, 941
Classified geological photographs, 375
Clay building bricks, selection, 181
Clay, T.:
Early literature on Mallophaga, 853
Genera and species of Mallophaga, check list, 336
Clean:
Air Bill, 1053, 1056
Catering, 620
Clergy:
Disqualification, Select Committee reports, 271, 383, 529, 642
Pensions Measure, 775, 835, 855
Ecclesiastical Committee report, 775
Clerical Assistant. *See* Junior Clerkships.
Cleugh, E. A.: Panama, economic survey, 1204
Clifton Suspension Bridge Act, 314
Climatological Atlas of the British Isles, 420
Clinical Research. *See* Central Health Services.
Clinton-Pelham, G.: Spain, economic survey, 463
Clipstone West and East Junctions, railway accident, 209
Cloche cultivation, 78, 847
Close:
Rolls, Calendars of, 691, 949
Season for deer in Scotland, 822, 845
Closer association in Central Africa, 57
Clothing Industry Development Council:
Account, 780, 793, 967
Report, 967
Cloud:
Forms, 420
in relation to active warm fronts, 1172
Clowes, G. S. L.: Sailing ships, 437
Clyde Navigation:
Order Confirmation Act, 573
(Superannuation) Order Confirmation Act, 1081
Bill, 1055
Clydebank Station, railway accident, 466
Coal:
Act, 64
and black oils in the West European fuel market, Relationship between, 996
and European economic expansion, 354
and iron ore resources of Asia and the Far East, 729
Gasification, 618
Industry:
Act, 59
Bill, 4, 32
(Improvement of Safety, etc., Regulations) Bill, 33
Nationalisation Act Accounts, 9, 118, 264, 357, 525, 631, 788, 893, 1039, 1134
Mines:
Acts, 61, 311, 569, 570
Regulations, 370, 632, 1134
Census of Production, 712
(Employment of Boys) Act, 63
(Mechanics and Electricians) General Regulations, memo, 893, 895
(Official and Inspections) General Regulations, memo, 118
Regulation Act, 830
Mining:
Careers, 659
(Subsidence) Act, 833
Production, Western Europe, reports, 354, 615
Statistics:
for Europe, 478, 730, 986
Monthly Bulletin, 221, 477
Tar Products, Census of Production, 458, 1199
Trimmers' escape holes in ships loading coal cargoes, circulars, 1208
War History, 217

Coales, H. W. (Chairman): Working Party on Small Diameter Water Pipes, report, 280
Coalfields of Yorkshire and Nottinghamshire, Concealed, memoir, 375
Coast Protection Report, circular, 910
Coastal Flooding:
(Emergency Provisions) Act, 567
Bill, 513, 527, 537, 542, 643
Reports, 559, 588, 640, 649, 704, 814, 849, 904, 912, 959
Cobb, Major M. H.: Measurement of the Ridge Way and Caithness Bases, 687
Cob nuts and filberts, 330
Coca leaf, Report of Commission of Enquiry, 223
Coccidiosis in chickens, 587
Cockfighting Act, 307
Bill, 253, 254, 269, 277, 281, 283, 284, 383
Cockroach, its life history and how to deal with it, 83
Cockroaches, 330
Cocoa:
Commodity report, 234
Situation report, 495
Cocoa, Chocolate, and Sugar Confectionery, Census of Production, 201, 1201
Cocos Islands Act, 1079
Bill, 1025, 1054
Code of Liberalisation, 615
Codes of Practice for Buildings Construction and Engineering Services, report, 244
Codex Sinaiticus and Codex Alexandrinus, 82, 1101
Codling moth, 1093
Coercive Action (Relief) Bill, 1031
Coghill, J. P.: Honduras, economic survey, 970
Cohen, Sir H. (Chairman):
Central Health Services:
Advisory Committee, report on clinical research in relation to the National Health Service, 679
Council, report, 901
Joint Committee on Prescribing, report, 901
Joint Sub-Committee of Standing Medical, Pharmaceutical, and General Practitioners Advisory Committee, report on Definitions of Drugs, 125
Cohen, N. A. J.: Civil aircraft accident report, 595
Cohen, Rt. Hon. Lord Justice (Chairman), Royal Commission on:
Awards to Inventors, report, 546
Taxation of Profits and Income, minutes of evidence, 435
Coil winding wires, 867
Coinage Offences Act, 312
Coke Ovens and By-products, Census of Production, 458, 1199
Cold chain in the U.S.A., 101, 615
Cole, H. A.:
American slipper limpet on Cornish oyster beds, 332
Purification of oysters in simple pits, 849
Coleman, J. D.: Suction of moisture held in soil and other porous materials, 441
Collart, P.: Report of Unesco Mission:
on Lebanon museums and monuments, 1006
on Syria museums and monuments, 1006
Collective:
Defence:
Pacific Charter, 824, 883
South East Asia Treaty, 822, 883
Security:
Correspondence between U.K. and Soviet Government, 822, 826, 884
Progress report, 491
Texts of Notes, 811, 812, 884
Colleges:
of further education, 98
Training, England and Wales, 1121
Colliery:
Explosion reports, 301, 1071, 1076
Management, career, 142
Collins, G. E. P.: Fish farming and inland fishery management in rural economy, 1009
Collision Regulations, 557, 122
Colne Valley Provisional Order Confirmation Act, 1081
Bill, 1028
Colombia:
Agreement for Air Services, 305, 360
Public:
Finance Information Paper, 227
Utilities, 1000
See also Caribbean.
Colombia/Peru Asylum Case, 141, 397
Colombo Plan, 134
Consultative Committee on Economic Development, report, 292, 471
Reports, 566, 724, 827, 980, 1076, 1215
Technical Co-operation Scheme, reports, 604, 864, 1112
See also Progress in Asia.
Colonial:
Advisory Council on Agriculture, Animal Health, and Forestry, publications, 94
Development:
and Welfare Acts, 64, 1079
Bills, 1025, 1054
Despatch to Colonial Governments, 1065, 1108
Report on administration, 1059, 1108
Returns, 19, 91, 269, 342, 529, 599, 789, 859, 1044, 1108
Corporation, reports and accounts, 18, 91, 266, 342, 527, 599, 787, 798, 859, 1040, 1108

COL-CRE | 1951-5

COL— INDEX 1951-5

Colonial (*continued*):
Empire Picture Sets, 134, 389, 914, 1153
Flags, badges, and arms, 860
Geodetic and Topographical Surveys, reports, 599, 860, 1108
Geological Survey publications, 345
Geology and Mineral Resources, 91, 343, 600, 860, 1108
Government Statisticians, conference reports, 92, 860
Loans Act, 308
Bill, 255, 285
Statement of Guarantees, 264, 471, 524, 724, 1039, 1215
Monetary conditions, 93
Office publications, 90, 342, 599, 859, 1107
Plant and Animal Products, 92, 343, 600, 860, 1108
Prisons Bill, 1053
Raw materials, Processing of, Study in location, 94
Regulations, 92, 600, 1108
Reports, 90, 343, 600, 604, 860, 864, 1108, 1112
Research:
Publications (series), 92, 344, 601, 861, 1109
Reports, 49, 92, 302, 344, 563, 601, 824, 861, 1076, 1109
Studies (series), 92, 344, 601, 861, 864, 1109
Road problems, 861
Service:
Appointments in, 91, 342, 599, 859
Reorganisation, 863
Statistics, Digest of, 344, 601, 861, 1110
Territories:
Economic surveys, 345, 862, 1110
General reports, 44, 92, 294, 345, 554, 601, 814, 861, 1067, 1110
Colonies:
in pictures, 861
Introducing the, 390, 1154
Colorado beetle, 847
Colorimetry, Unit and standard of measurement, 430
Colour:
Bar Bill, 30
in School Buildings, 614
Temperatures of stars, 376
Colouring matters, Food Standards Committee, report, 1096, 1122
Colquhoun, M. K.: Wood pigeon in Britain, 76
Colvilles Ltd., proposal to sell holdings, Treasury Minute, 1058
Combined Cadet Force Regulations, 1015, 1222
Combustion, Results achieved in the field of Fuel Advisory Services and technical training, 224
Comet accident. *See* Civil aircraft.
Command Papers, 34, 285, 545, 804, 1057
Commandos. *See* War.
Commerce and Navigation Treaty with Greece, 41
Commercial:
Agreement between U.K. and Egypt, 306
Arrears, Exchange of Notes with Brazil, 1075
Conditions, Reviews (series), 205, 462
Dahlia growing, 1093
Horticulture, Advice to beginners, 329
Pilot's Licence, 338, 1208
Relations, with Cuba, 805
Samples, International Convention to facilitate importation, 806, 884, 1078, 1124
Storage of vegetables, 238
Subjects:
in secondary schools, 187
Setting and marking of examinations, Guidance to teachers, 1191
Commissioners of Prisons, reports, 52, 128, 304, 380, 561, 640, 820, 904, 1071, 1145
Commissioners' Decisions (National Insurance), 422, 681, 688, 943, 1175
Commodity:
Policy studies, 750, 1008
Reports, series, 234, 495, 750, 1008
Series Bulletin, 750, 1008
Trade:
and Economic Development, 986
Statistics, 730, 987
Common:
Informers Act, 59
Bill, 3, 16, 26, 30, 31, 33, 130
Insect pests of stored food products, 1103
Scab of the potato, 78
Services, Civil Estimates, 263, 523, 783, 1036
Commonwealth:
Agricultural Bureaux:
Annual reports, 94, 346, 603, 863, 1111
Review Conference, report, 39, 94
Agriculture, production, prices and trade, 1111
and Foreign Services, Estimates, 15, 214, 262, 522, 783, 1036, 1038
and nuclear development, 1154
and the Sterling Area, Statistical Abstract, 714, 967, 1202
Economic:
Committee, publications, 94, 347, 604, 864, 1111
Conference, final communique, 306, 337
of Nations, map, 864
Parliamentary Association, Select Committee on Estimates report, 271, 276
Relations Office, publications, 95, 347, 604, 864, 1112
Resources and products, wall map, 342

INDEX 1951-5 —CON

Commonwealth (*continued*):
Shipping Committee, publications, 95, 348, 605, 865, 1112
Survey, 651, 914, 1153
Trade, 94, 347, 604, 864, 1111
Statistics, 463
Types, South East Asia, 651
Communal land tenure, 750
Communication Codes and Abbreviations, 395
Communications:
Committee Report, Air Navigation Meeting, 394
Division, reports, 139, 918
Community:
Centre wardens. *See* Youth Leaders.
Development in West Africa, film strip, 389
Factor in modern technology, 748
Organisation and development, series 730, 987
Community, Family and Child Welfare, 750
Compaction of soil and performance of compaction plant, 956
Companies Act, 313
Bill, 281
Reports, 201, 461, 714, 967, 1202
Company secretary, career, 398, 921
Comparability of statistics of causes of death, 497
Comparison of the wind recorded by the anemograph with the geostrophic wind, 941
Compensation:
for war injury suffered by civilians in France, 41
made by the United Nations Administrative Tribunal, 919
Complete Plain Words, 980
Composite:
Action of brick panel walls supported on reinforced concrete beams, 440
Construction, Studies in, 1187
Compressed air illness, investigation during construction of Tyne Tunnel, 940
Compulsory:
Education:
and its prolongation, International Conference, 230
in Pakistan, 1003
Studies on, 230, 233, 494, 748, 1003
Purchase Orders, circular, 909, 911
Registration of title on sale to the County of Surrey, report, 168
Computers, Handbook for, 1174
Comrie, J.: Thermal insulation of buildings, 1189
Concepts and definitions of Capital Formation, 999
Concrete, 437
Aerated, 181
Block making machines, 245
in sulphate-bearing clays and ground waters, 181
Concrete (*continued*):
made with lightweight aggregate, 181
Prestressed, 761, 1019
Roads:
Belgium and West Germany, 1188
Design thickness of, 1188
Thermal expansion of, 184
Concreting methods on housing sites, Study of, 955
Condensation:
in domestic chimneys, 695
of water on refrigerated surfaces, 182
Trails from aircraft, 420, 680, 1172
Congar, Rev. Y. M. J.: Catholic Church and the race question, 748
Coniferous petrified forest in Patagonia, 591
Conifers:
Drought crack of, 892
in Great Britain, Revised yield tables for, 691
Conisbee, L. R.: List of names proposed for genera and sub-genera of recent mammals from the publication of T. S. Palmer's Index Generum Mammalium, 592
Conquest of the air, 694
Conservation and utilisation of resources, International index to films, 221
Consett Iron Co. Ltd., Proposal to sell holding of Ordinary Shares, 1078
Consol: radio aid to navigation, 1208
Consolidated Fund:
Abstract accounts, 13, 215, 260, 471, 521, 780, 980, 1034, 1215
Acts, 59, 60, 307, 567, 568, 724, 828, 1079
Bills, 31, 34, 282, 541, 542, 544, 801, 1054
(Appropriation) Bills, 33, 284, 543, 803, 1055, 1056
(Civil List Provisions) Act, 59
Bill, 6, 33
Consolidation:
Bills, reports, 3, 4, 249, 252, 254, 509 510, 513, 514, 517, 770, 771, 774, 1028, 1029
of Enactments (Procedure) Act, memos, 251, 252, 253, 256, 510, 512, 769, 773, 775
Constabulary, Inspectors' reports:
England and Wales, 19, 129, 269, 382
Scotland, 49, 188, 294, 444, 554, 702, 812, 959, 1067, 1191
Constitutional development in the Commonwealth, 1154
Construction:
and heating of commercial greenhouses, 588
of farm grain silos, 80
of housing estate roads, 699, 1188
Constructional engineering, Census of Production, 459
Consular Conventions:
Belgium, 46, 105

CON— INDEX 1951-5

Consular Conventions (*continued*):
France, 287
Greece, 554
Italy, 815
Mexico, 813
Norway, 45
Sweden, 293, 827
U.S.A., 48
Consultative Assembly of the Council of Europe, publications, 96, 605, 865
Contagious caprine pleuro-pneumonia, 92
Contemporary political science, survey, 230
Continuance of emergency legislation, 564, 640, 825, 904, 1076
Contracts:
and Finance, War History, 593
for building and civil engineering works, general conditions, 505, 1226
Control:
Commission for Germany, report of British High Commissioner, 95
General Board of, for Scotland, report 1071, 1192
of advertisements, 164
of civil building, 910
of communicable diseases in man, 1098
of dividends, 50
of Explosives Order:
Form, 904
Licence, 640
of livestock diseases in European countries, 354
of Raw Materials, War History, 593
of rushes, 1091
of weeds in peas:
with Dinoseb, 587
with DNBP, 78
Controlled grazing, 586
with electric fencing, 78
Convention on Social Security with Luxembourg, 1062
Conviction and sentence of Assize Court at Belfast, case of T. J. Mitchell, 1045, 1146
Cookery, A.B.C., 880
Co-operative:
Farms and smallholdings with centralised services, 332, 588, 849, 1092
Hybrid maize tests in European and Mediterranean countries, Results of, 751
Society, statistical summary, 370
Thrift, credit, and marketing in economically under-developed countries, 751
Co-operatives and fundamental education, 230
Cope, V. Zachary:
(Chairman), Medical Auxiliaries Committees, report, 41
Medical War Histories:
Medicine and Pathology, 378
Surgery, 902, 961
Copper:
and copper-based alloys, supply and export, 1047
and zinc Prohibited Uses Order, Open general licence, 201
Goods, Export Licence, 202, 461, 714, 1203
Smelting and refining in U.S.A., 874
Coppersmith, career, 659
Copyright:
Acts, 61, 569
and Television Exhibiting Right Bill, 1026
Bill (1955), 1030, 1031
Bulletin, 230, 491, 745, 1003
Committee report, 302, 461
Universal, Convention, 558, 622
Corbet, A. S.: Common insect pests of stored food products, 1103
Corbridge Roman Station guide, 1018
Corby Development Corporation, reports, 29, 279, 388, 779, 792, 913, 1048
Corfu Channel Case, judgments, 141, 397
Corlett, J.: Report on research from the *Ernest Holt* into the fishery near Bear Island, 849
Corn Exchange Act, 1081
Corncrake, 586
Corneal Grafting Act, 307
Bill, 252, 283
Cornwall, Census, 1137
Corona, 92, 345, 601, 861, 1110
Coronation:
Celebration, circular, 387
Ceremonial, 677
observed at the Proclamation, 418
Chair, 762
Message:
of thanks from the Queen, 758
to the Army, 758
Proclamation, 418
Rings, coloured postcard, 762
Coroners:
Act, 828
Bill, 772, 800, 801
(Amendment) Act, 570
Bill and the Law Reform (Miscellaneous Provisions) Bill, 785, 797, 906
Coroners' Inquisition Form, 640
"Corps", definition, 240
Corrosion, 876
of steel in steel houses, 440
Corrosion-resistant floors, 1185
Coryza and sinusitis in poultry, 848
Cost:
Accounting and productivity, 354
of house maintenance, 649
of house-building, 387
of Living Advisory Committee, reports, 51, 145, 289, 400
of sickness and price of health, 497
Study (Building Bulletin), 98

INDEX 1951-5 —CRE

Costa Rica, economic survey, 204, 969
Costs:
and efficiency of pig production, 849
in Criminal Cases Act, 307
Bill, 249, 251, 252, 284
Costume illustrations, 17th & 18th centuries, 239
Cotoneasters from the Eastern Himalaya, 853
Cotton:
Act, 828
Bill, 541, 544, 771, 782, 797, 800, 906
(Centralised Buying) Act, accounts, 23, 201, 271, 419, 535, 679, 791, 940, 1046, 1202
Import Committee, reports, 291, 461, 554, 679, 714
Industry Joint Advisory Committee, report on Male Spinners' Cancer, 417
Spinning:
and Doubling, Census of Production, 459
and Weaving machinery, Fencing and safety precautions for, 1169
Career, 659
Textile Industry, Labour productivity of, 484
Weaving:
Census of Production, 459, 1200
Factories, Agreement concerning fencing of machinery, etc., 1159
See also Raw Cotton.
Cotton, Cotton Mixture, and Linen Schedule, 206
Cotton, Rayon, and Linen Schedule, 206
Couch or Twitch, 78
Coulter, Surgeon Commander: Royal Naval Medical Service, war history, 902, 961
Council:
for Wales and Monmouthshire, report on the South Wales ports, 1058
of Europe:
Amendments to the Statute, 48, 106, 561, 622
General Agreement on privileges and immunities, 553, 554, 622, 623
Proceedings of the Consultative Assembly, 40, 106, 563, 623, 1066, 1124
Progress of the United Kingdom proposals, 305, 360
Proposals of H.M. Government, 291, 360
Publications, 96, 605, 865
Reports, 42, 106, 288, 305, 360
Countries' Vaccination Certificate Requirements, 246
Country:
Code for visitors to the countryside, 177
College in Wales, 99
Monographs, 730, 987
County Courts:
Accounts, 11, 171, 257, 280, 422, 457, 785, 942, 1034, 1173
County Courts (*continued*):
Act, 1080
Bill, 1025, 1026, 1029, 1055
Index to parishes, etc., 939
Manual, 168
Court:
of Chancery of Lancaster Act, 307
of International Justice, Declarations concerning optional clause of Statute 1069, 1124
Court Sart Farm occupation level crossing, accident, 209
Court, W. H. B.: Coal, war history, 217
Courts (Emergency Powers) Act, 64
Courts-Martial:
(Appeals) Act, 59
Bill, 3, 4, 5, 17, 26, 32, 33, 130
Procedure:
and administration of justice in the Armed Forces, conclusions, 37, 97
Naval, 1083
Covell, Sir G.: Malaria terminology, 755
Coventry:
Cathedral Act, 573
Corporation Act, 834
Cowes Pier and Harbour:
Order Confirmation Act, 834
Bill, 802
Provisional Order Bill, 774
Cows, Dairy, Feeding of, 1094
Cowshed hygiene, 587
Cox, L. R.: Lower Cretaceous Gastropoda, Lamellibranchia and Annelida from Alexander I Land, 582
Crabs, Some Jurassic and Cretaceous, 83
Craigmillar Castle, guide, 1018
Craster, O. E.:
Anglesey, ancient monuments guide, 761
Brecon Gaer, guide, 1018
Crawford and Balcarres, Earl of (Chairman): Royal Fine Arts Commission, report, 305
Crawford, Major W.: Explosives factory accident, 129
Crawley Development Corporation, reports 29, 279, 388, 779, 792, 913, 1048
Crayshaw, G. (Chairman): Welsh Land Settlement Society Ltd., review and accounts, 332
Cream:
and Use of Milk (Revocation) Order, circular, 620
(Revocation) Order, circular, 103
Standards for, 103
Soups, circular, 881
Credit for the purchase of raw materials, Exchange of Notes with Yugoslavia, 50
Credits for training courses, 554
Creedy, L. A.: Training of rural school teachers, 1006
Cremation Acts, 307, 830
Bill, 252, 265, 278, 282, 383

1951-5 | CRE-DES

CRE— INDEX 1951–5

Cremer, H. W. (Chairman): Committee of Chemical Engineering Research, report, 182
Creswell Colliery, accident report, 296, 370
Cretaceous:
  and Eocene Penduncles of the Cirripede Euscalpellum, 83
  and Tertiary Foraminifera from the Middle East, 336
Crete. *See* Greece.
Crew, F. A. E.: Army Medical Services, administration, 638, 1143
Crew accommodation in merchant ships, handbook, 722
Crewe Corporation Act, 834
Cribbett, Sir G.: Interdepartmental Helicopter Committee, report, 86
Crichel Down, Public Inquiry, 814, 849
Cricket bat willow, Watermark disease of, 1133
Crime:
  Latin-American seminar on prevention, 994
  of Genocide, reservations to Convention on Prevention and Punishment, Order, 141
  Papers relating to large number of, 6, 128
Criminal:
  Justice:
    Acts, 65, 310, 313, 570
    Administration:
      Act, 309
      Bill (1955), 1027, 1028, 1029, 1056
    Amendment Bill, 33
  Law Amendment Act, 59
    Bill, 3, 16, 26, 130
  Policy, International review, 484, 994
  Statistics:
    England and Wales, 49, 128, 299, 380, 560, 640, 816, 904, 1073, 1145
    Scotland, 51, 188, 296, 443, 551, 702, 811, 959, 1063, 1191
Cripples. *See* Deaf.
Critchley, C. E. (Chairman): Commonwealth Economic Committee, report on survey of trade in agricultural machinery, 347
Criteria for correct logging techniques and best methods of work in European countries, 1009
Croft, W. H.: New Trochilliscus from the Downtonian of Podolia, 336
Crofters (Scotland) Act, 1079
  Bill, 883, 1020, 1038, 1043, 1054, 1147
Crofting conditions, Commission of Enquiry, report, 809, 845
Crompton, E.: Soils of the Wem district of Shropshire, 850
Croney, D.: Suction of moisture held in soil and other porous materials, 441
Crook, Lord (Chairman): Interdepartmental Committee, Statutory registration of opticians, 292
Crookall, R.: Fossil plants of the Carboniferous rocks of Great Britain, 1140
Crooke, M.: Adelges attacking Japanese and hybrid larches, 368
Crop yields, estimation of, 1008
Crops for silage, 587, 1093
Crop-year, International Wheat Council, annual report, 141
Crossbill, 1133
Crossland, C.: Madreporaria, Hydrocorallinae, Heliopora and Tubipora, 336
Crouch, G. R.: Dehydration of English fruit, 438
Crown:
  Gall, 1093
  Jewels:
    Guide, 763, 1225
    Postcards, 762
  Lands, abstract accounts, 12, 96, 263, 348, 521, 605, 781, 865, 1035, 1112
    Committee report, 1067, 1215
  Lessees (Protection of Subtenants) Act, 307
    Bill, 252, 266, 278, 281, 283, 383
  Office, publications, 348
  Proceedings Act, 313
    Authorised Government Departments, etc., 471, 980
  See also Most Excellent Majesty.
Crown's Nominee Account, 215, 471, 724, 980, 1215
Cruden, S.:
  Arbroath Abbey, guide, 1018
  Castle Campbell, guide, 761
Cruelty to wild animals, 46, 128, 188
Cruickshank, Professor R. (Chairman): Air Hygiene Committee on Air Disinfection with Ultra-violet Irradiation, report, 940
Crystal Palace. *See* London County Council.
Ctenisicini of the Old World, review and revision, 591
Cuba:
  Abolition of Visas, 41, 106
  Air Services Agreement, 557, 623
  Commercial relations, 805, 884
  Economic Survey, 969
  Trade Agreement, 52, 55, 106
Cucumbers in glasshouses, Cultivation of, 329
Culinary and medicinal herbs, 332
Culling of poultry, 79
  Film strip, 329
Culpin, M.:
  Nervous temperament, 420
  Study of Telegraphist's Cramp, 171
Culter, railway accident, 466
Cultivation:
  of cucumbers in glasshouses, 329
  of ground nuts in West Africa, 615
Cultural:
  Conventions:
    Austria, 548, 551

INDEX 1951–5 —CYR

Cultural (*continued*):
  Conventions (*continued*):
    European, 1061
    Greece, 58, 554, 560, 807
    Italy, 286, 552, 560
    Luxembourg, 564
    Norway, 546
    Portugal, 1057, 1077
  Patterns and technical change, 748
  Relations Agreement, 815, 884
Culture and human fertility, 1006
Cultures by freeze drying, Discussion on maintenance, 852
Cumberbatch, A. N.: Egypt, economic survey, 463
Cumberland and Westmorland, Census, 896
Cumbernauld, Draft New Town Designation Order, memo, 1142
Cummings, W. H.: FAO Advisory Assistance to member countries under the UNRRA Transfer Fund, 751
Cumulus and Cumulonimbus cloud over Malaya, 941
Cunard Insurance Fund accounts, 9, 25, 208, 275, 466, 539, 722, 791, 973
Cunliffe, Geoffrey (Chairman): British Standards Institution Organisation and Constitution, Committee report, 200
Cunningham, A. (Chairman): Committee on Child Health, Scottish Health Services Council, report, 636, 703
Cunningham, Sir C. (Chairman): Committee on Exchequer Equalisation Grants, report, 703
Curia Regis Rolls, 180, 434, 1181
Currant and Gooseberry Aphids, 78
Currants, Black and red, 1090
Currency and Bank Notes Act, 828, 832
  Bill, 282, 544, 724, 770
  Treasury Minutes, 12, 21, 24, 25, 215, 260, 265, 270, 271, 275, 280, 471, 520, 525, 529, 533, 534, 540, 780, 782, 786, 790, 791, 794, 799, 980, 1033, 1040, 1042, 1044, 1046, 1049, 1051, 1052, 1215, 1216
Current Sociology, 491, 745, 1003
Curriculum and community in Wales, 354
Currie, J.: Denmark, economic survey, 1204
Curry, W. T.:
  Laminated beams from two species of timber, 1186
  Strength properties of plywood, 696, 1186
Curves:
  Hydrostatic, 974
  Stability Cross, 974
Cushing, D. H.: Echo sounding experiments on fish, 1092
Customs:
  Agreement for provisional application of Draft International Customs Conventions on Touring, Commercial Road Vehicles, and International Transport of Goods by road, 286, 360
Customs (*continued*):
  and Excise:
    Act, 307
      Bill, 250, 251, 254, 281, 282
    (Amendment) Bill, 802
    Commissioners' Reports, 35, 96, 287, 471, 545, 725, 804, 980, 1058, 1216
    Publications, 96, 348, 606, 865, 1113
    Report of the Committee on the Draft of the Customs and Excise Bill, 287, 471
  Co-operation Council, Conventions, 45, 106, 818, 884
  Formalities, Final Act, Conventions, and Protocol adopted for the Temporary Importation of Private Road Motor Vehicles and Tourism, 1066, 1124
  Forms, 96, 348, 606, 865, 1113
  Tariffs:
    New proposal for the reduction of, 896
    Nomenclature for the classification of goods, Convention, 43, 106
  Valuation of goods, Convention, 45, 107, 818, 884
  Union Study Group, Protocols, 45, 107, 818, 884
Cutlery, Census of Production, 200, 1200
Cuttell, J. R.: Milk Pasteurization, 755
Cutting, C. L.:
  Care of the trawler's fish, 696
  General principles of smoke curing of fish, 438
  Ten stone controlled fish-smoking kiln, 438
Cutworms or surface caterpillars, 586
Cuzco:
  Economic and social development, 482
  Reconstruction report, 747
Cwmbran Development Corporation reports, 29, 279, 388, 779, 792, 913, 1048
Cyclopygid trilobites from Girvan and a note on Bohemilla, 336
Cyprus:
  Colonial reports, 91, 344, 601, 861, 1109
  Economic survey, 602
  Inscription on Agenda of General Assembly, report, 824, 884
  Photo-poster, 1153
  Rat problem, investigation report, 92
  Reciprocal exemption of air transport profits from income tax, 36
  Tripartite Conference. *See* Eastern Mediterranean.
Cyrenaica:
  Air Services Agreement with Thailand, 46
  and Tripolitania:
    Disposal of Italian private property, 50
    Technical Assistance Agreements, 51, 52, 107

CYR— INDEX 1951–5

Cyrenaica (*continued*):
  Disposal and administration of Italian private property, 58
Czechoslovak Refugee Fund accounts, 23, 215, 271, 471, 533, 725, 792, 980, 1046, 1216
Czechoslovakia:
  Payments Agreement, amendment, 292, 360
  Sterling Payments Agreement, extension, 301, 360, 1076, 1124

D

Dahlia growing, commercial, 587, 1093
Daily:
  Press, survey of world situation, 1003
  Telegraph, Complaint of a passage in, Select Committee on Estimates report, 22
Dairy:
  Produce, production trade and consumption, 94, 347, 604, 864, 1111
  Products, Commodity Series bulletin, 750
Dale, Judge E. (Chairman): Committee of Inquiry into Industrial Health Services, report, 39
Dalguise, railway accident, 209
Dalmarnock and Bridgeton Cross, railway accident, 719
Damage control pads, 128
Dampness in buildings, Causes of, 128
Damp-proof courses, 243, 953
Dancing. *See* Dramatic Arts.
Dangerous:
  Drugs:
    Acts, 59, 62, 310
      Bills, 2, 3, 4, 33
    and Poisons (Amendment) Act, 62
  Goods:
    and Explosives in ships, Carriage of, reports, 465, 719, 722
    in Aircraft, Exchanges of Notes with:
      Italy, 58
      Netherlands, 47
Daniel, Admiral Sir Charles (Chairman): Television Advisory Committee, reports 690, 948
Daniels, H. E.: Whalemeat bacteriology and hygiene, 696
Dar-es-Salaam, agreement with Belgium for construction of deep-water quay, 44
Dartmouth Harbour Act, 66
Darwin, Sir Charles (Chairman): Standing Advisory Committee on Artificial Limbs, report, 177
Davey, N.:
  Fire tests on structural elements, 699
  Tests on road bridges, 699
Davidson, C. F.: Further contributions to the solution of the Piltdown problem, 1101
Davies, A. E. M. (Chairman): Working Party on Grants to Training College Students, report, 1120
Davies, A. O. (Chairman): Central Advisory Council for Education; report on drama in the schools of Wales, 872
Davies, C.: Considerations and procedures for the successful introduction of farm mechanisation, 1008
Davison, C. St. C. B.: History of steam road vehicles, 694
Dawihl, W.: Handbook of hard metals, 1187
Day, W. R.: Drought crack of conifers, 892
Day-lighting in buildings, Prediction of levels, 1185
Day-to-day variations in the tropopause, 941
Deacon, E. L.: Vertical profiles of mean wind in the surface layers of the atmosphere, 680
Deaf, cripples, etc., Welfare of, papers relating to preparation of schemes, 123
Deaf-blind persons, special welfare needs, 125
Deal Castle, guide, 761
Dean, R. F. A.: Plant proteins in child feeding, 679
Death:
  Duties, Order in Council, 914
  of Queen Mary, Special Army Order, 758
  of the Speaker, Bill, 541
Deaths:
  by accident at mines and quarries, 120, 370, 893
  See also Registrar-General's Returns.
Debenham, F.: Expedition to Bangweulu Swamps, report, 342
Debiesse, Jean: Compulsory education in France, 494
Debts, Settlement of Pre-War External Bonded, Exchange of Notes with Japan, 547
Decay of wood in boats, Prevention of, 954
Decennial Supplement, Registrar-General's 634, 897
Decimal Currency Bill, 1054
Deck sheathings for cargo and passenger ships, General requirements, 972
Declaration of Human Rights Bill, 281
Decontrol:
  of Cereals and Feeding-stuffs, 546, 588, 620, 702
  of Food and Marketing of Agricultural Produce, 564, 588, 620, 640, 702
Decorations. *See* Honours; Orders.
Dee and Clwyd River Board Act, 66
Deeds:
  of Arrangement Act, 309
  Register of, 961
Deer:
  Abbey of, guide, 504

INDEX 1951–5 —DES

Deer (*continued*):
  of the Weybourne Crag and Forest Bed of Norfolk, 591
  See also Close Season.
Defamation:
  Act, 307
    Bill, 253, 254, 255, 284
  (Amendment) Bill 265, 278, 281, 282, 383
Defence:
  Appropriation Accounts, 13, 97, 260, 350, 520, 607, 779, 867, 1032, 1114
  Discontinuance of, circular, 387
  Equipment:
    Agreement with Belgium, 547, 820
    Gift to Egyptian Government, 1067
  Estimates, 14, 21, 98, 218, 261, 262, 350, 520, 522, 608, 783, 867, 980, 1035, 1036, 1114
  Lists, 867, 1114
  Matters, Exchange of Notes with South Africa, 1069
  Ministry of, publications, 97, 350, 607, 867, 1114
  (Price Control) Regulations. *See* Goods and Services.
  Programme:
    Statement by Prime Minister, 37, 97
    Urgent development by Government Departments, 164
  Regulations, 215, 725, 910, 981, 1216
    Circular, 909
  Services, Storage and Maintenance, Select Committee report, 19
  Specifications, 97, 350, 608, 868, 1114
  Statement, 289, 548, 607, 807, 867, 1060, 1114
  Vote on Account, 263, 523, 784, 1215
  Work, agreement between Postmaster-General and British Broadcasting Corporation, 808, 948
  Works, removal of temporary, 648
Defensive, War at sea, 961
Deficiency diseases in Japanese prison camps, 169
Dehorning of calves, 848
Dehydrated meat, 696
Dehydration of English fruit, 438
Delegated legislation, Select Committee reports, 535, 643, 778, 905
Delegations to the United Nations, 987
Delinquency, Studies in the causes and treatment of offenders, 1145
Democracy in a world of tension, 230
Demographic Year Book, 221, 478, 730, 987
Denbighshire and Flintshire, Census, 1137
Denmark:
  Agricultural development and rural reform, 749
  Air Services Agreements, 298, 361, 552, 623
  Avoidance of double taxation, Convention, 1065, 1124
Denmark (*continued*):
  British Commonwealth war graves in Danish territory, 813, 884
  Documents of identity for aircraft personnel, 1073, 1124
  Economic:
    Conditions, 616
    Survey, 716
  Fisheries outside territorial waters in the ocean surrounding the Faroe Islands, Convention for regulating, 1064, 1124
  Foreign Trade Statistical Bulletin, 355, 356, 617, 878
  Funding of balance of Danish Kroner held for account of Government, 44, 107
  Military Service Agreement, 1065, 1124
  Monetary Agreement, 563, 623
  Money and Property Agreement, 306, 361
  National Accounts Study, 356
  Participation of a Danish contingent in the occupation of Germany, 51, 107
  Payment of compensation for industrial injuries, 805, 813, 884
  Re-imposition of visa requirement for foreign nationals proceeding to North Borneo and Brunei, 56, 107
  Settlement of certain salvage claims, 1064, 1124
Denmark, Iceland, Norway: Economic conditions, 877
Density of residential areas, 387
Dental:
  Care, experiment in, 237
  Caries in children, effect of sugar supplements, 1171
  Radiographers, training notes, 758
  Services, preventive, 377
Dentistry, career, 920
Dentists Bill, 7, 249, 250, 282, 1051, 1053, 1056, 1147
Departmental:
  Records Committee, report, 813, 981
  Replies to reports of Session 1950, Select Committee on Estimates, report, 19
Depressions crossing Labrador and the St. Lawrence basin, 1172
Derby Corporation (Trolley Vehicles):
  Order Confirmation Act, 314
  Provisional Order Bill, 253, 283
Derbyshire:
  Census, 896
  County Council Act, 834
Dermaptera of the world, Systematic monograph of, 1103
Derry, T. K.: Campaign in Norway, 337
Desai, M. J. (Chairman): International Commission for Supervision and Control in Vietnam, report, 1065, 1068
Deschamps, Louis Auguste, 853
Deserted Wives Bill, 30

Design, 134, 389, 650, 914, 1153
and workmanship of non-traditional houses, 123
in the Festival, 134
in town and village, 649
of building, 505
of buildings for grass-drying plants, 333
of farm grain stores, 80
of school kitchens, 1119
Thickness of concrete roads, 1188
Designs. *See* Patents.
Destructive Insects and Pests Act, 830, 831
Detection of insects by their carbon dioxide production, 440
Detergents, synthetic, 913
Development:
and co-ordination of technical annexes to the Convention, 395
and Welfare in the West Indies, 93, 601, 861, 1110
by local authorities and statutory undertakers, 133
Charges, minerals, 43
Commission, publications, 613
Fund, Abstract Accounts, 10, 216, 257, 471, 519, 725, 780, 981, 1035, 1216
of Inventions:
Acts, 828, 833
Bills, 544, 770, 771, 801
Accounts, 256, 272, 461, 538, 714, 1037, 1202
Plans explained, 133
Projects:
Formulation and economic appraisal of, 482
Wokingham School, 352
Devizes, Boundary Commission report, 269, 379
Devon, Census, 1137
Dewsbury Moor Crematorium Act, 1081
Dick Bequest Trust Scheme, memo, 1190
Dickinson, E. J.: Durability of road tar, 956
Die castings, handbook, 709
Dielectric properties of wood, 954
Dieppe. *See* War.
Digest of Statistics, 139, 396
Dillon, Armando, report of Unesco Mission on:
Lebanon museums and monuments, 1006
Syria museums and monuments, 1006
Dines, H. G.: Geology of country around Chatham, 899
Dinsdale, F. E.: Cloud in relation to active warm fronts, 1172
Dining at school, film strip, 615
Diocesan:
Education Committees Measure, 1030, 1104
(Amendment) Measure, 67
Report, 1030, 1103
Stipends Funds Measure, 511, 574, 594
Report, 511, 594
Diphtheria and Pertussis vaccination report, 756
Diplomas leading to admission to Universities, European Convention on Equivalence of, 804, 814, 885
Diplomatic Immunities, 677, 938, 1170
(Commonwealth Countries and Republic of Ireland) Act, 307, 418
Bill, 34, 250
Interdepartmental Committee on State Immunities, report, 288, 361
Restriction Act, 1080
Bill, 1030, 1056
Diptera of Patagonia and South Chile, 83
Direction of International Trade, 730, 987
Direction-finding stations, siting of, 440
Directors, etc., Burden of Proof Bill, 32, 34, 267, 278, 283, 383, 1053
"Diretlo" murders. *See* Basutoland.
Disabled:
Persons:
(Employment) Act, 64
in Government employment, 58, 216, 289, 305, 471, 566, 725, 1057, 1079, 1216
Services for, 1169
Youth in Glasgow, Employment problems of, 420
Disarmament:
Commission (United Nations):
Records, 478, 731, 988
Reports, 367, 816, 885
Sub-committee meetings, reports, 816, 885
Report on, 1077, 1124
Discharged Prisoners' Aid Societies, report, 556, 640
Discipline forms, 640
Diseases:
and insect pests, Forest plantation protection against, 1009
and pests on horticultural planting material, 588
Communicable, Control of, 1098
Notifiable, Cases of and deaths from, 496
of Animals:
Act, 59
Handbook of Orders relating to, 332
of Potatoes, 846
of the chestnut and poplar in Europe, 615
of the oat crop, 328
of Vegetables, 1095
Provisions of the National Insurance (Industrial Injuries) Act, report, 1071, 1175
Disposal:
of agricultural surpluses, 1008
of Internal Restitution Claims in the British Zone of Germany, 107
of Uncollected Goods Act, 307
Bill, 253, 268, 278, 282, 283, 383

Dissolution of Parliament, 167, 1170
Distribution:
and other services, Census of, 712, 966, 1199
of German Enemy Property Act, 307
Bill, 250, 282
Accounts, 787, 968, 1040, 1202
Distinctive school clothing, 98, 100
District heating, 763
Working Party report, 165
Diurnal variation of pressure in the Mediterranean area, 421
Dividends, Control of, 50, 215
Dock strike, report, 55, 145
Docks, London, unofficial stoppages in, report, 44, 163
Dockyards, Select Committee on Estimates, reports, 23, 274, 522
Documentation:
and terminology of science, 1003
in the social sciences, 1003
techniques in the U.S.A., 101
Documents Index, United Nations and Specialised Agencies, 221, 479, 731, 988
Dodecanese, Settlement of claims arising from British Military Administration, Exchange of Notes with Greece, 1066
Dogs:
Act, 830
in food shops, restaurants, etc., 104
(Protection of Livestock) Act, 567
Bill, 514, 528, 537, 541, 543, 643
Doig, A. T.: Health of welders, 145
Dollar exports, 461
Domesday re-bound, 949
Domestic:
Coal Consumers' Council. *See* Industrial Coal Consumers' Council.
Financing of economic development, 221
Food consumption and expenditure, 358, 881, 1096
Preservation of fruit and vegetables, 848, 1094
Science and dietetics, career, 659
Solid fuel appliances, 377, 901
See also Scottish Housing Handbook.
Dominica, Colonial reports, 343, 860, 1109
Dominican Republic:
Air Services Agreement, 53, 107
Long-range proving ground for the testing of guided missiles, 294, 361
See also Caribbean.
Donaldson, G.: Whithorn and Kirkmadrine, guide, 762
Donaldson Trust Scheme:
Memo, 701
Order in Council, 958
Doncaster:
Corporation (Trolley Vehicles) Order Confirmation Act, 1081
Bill, 1027, 1055
Doncaster (*continued*):
Railway accident, 466
Donovanosis, 1012
Dorman Long & Co. Ltd., Proposal to sell holding of Ordinary Shares, 825
Dorothy Lambert, wreck report, 1213
Dorset:
Census, 1137
West, historical monuments:
Inventory, 435
Royal Commission report, 303, 379
Double Taxation Relief Tables, 651, 1154
Doughty, Sir C. (Chairman): Court of Inquiry into causes and circumstances of a dispute between Electrical Trades Union and London Electricity Board, 44
Douglas fir, general volume tables, 368
Douglas, Miss K. G. (Chairman): Standing Nursing Advisory Committee, report, 901
Douglas, Sir W. (Chairman): Civil Service Preparatory Commission, Rhodesia and Nyasaland, report, 303
Douglas, W. S.: Purchase Tax/Utility Committee, report, 287
Dover:
Castle, guide, 761
Harbour:
Act, 65
Consolidation Act, 834
Bill, 770
Dovey, H. O.: Handbook of organisation and methods technique, 657
Dow, Sir Hugh (Chairman): East Africa Royal Commission, report, 1066
Dow-Smith, G. T.: British East Africa, economic survey, 715
Dowson, E.: Land registration, 344
Drainage:
and River Conservancy Authorities, returns, 165, 387, 649, 912
for housing, 695
of the farm homestead, 1092
of trade premises, 810, 900
Drama in the schools of Wales, 872
Dramatic:
and Musical Performers' Protection Act, 310
Art, Dancing, and Music, careers, 398
Dress:
Q.A.R.A.N.C. and W.R.A.C., notification of changes, 240
Regulations for officers, 590, 851, 1098
Dried grass and dried lucerne as stockfeed, 330
Drill (All Arms), 240, 758
Drilling and refining oil equipment in the U.S.A., Production of, 615
Drinks, soft, etc., Census of Production, 460
Drogheda, Earl of (Chairman): Independent Committee of Inquiry into Overseas Information Services, report, 812
Drop forging industry, committee report, 661

Drought crack of conifers, 892
Drug Supervisory Body: Estimated world requirements of narcotic drugs, 221, 479, 988
Drugs:
and Pharmaceutical Preparations, Census of Production, 458
Definition of, report, 125
liable to produce addiction, Expert Committee reports, 499, 1013
See also Narcotic drugs; Potent drugs.
Drums or tanks, repair of, 417
Drumtochty, Britain's Forests, series, 630
Drunkenness, Statistics of offences, 59, 304, 562, 823, 1074, 1146
Dry:
Batteries, 867
Rot in wood, 439
DTD Specifications, 196, 452, 710, 963, 1195
Duckham, A. N.: American agriculture, 331
Duckworth, J.: Substitute feeding stuffs, 333
Dudhope Peerage, proceedings, 509, 646
Dudley Extension Act, 573
Duffus Castle and Church, guide, 244
Duffy, E. A. J.:
British and imported timber beetles, 591
Cerambycidae, Ruwenzori Expedition, 593
Duguid, L. N.: Health of welders, 145
Duke of Edinburgh's birthday, message from the Army, 501
Dumfries, Census, 635
Dunbartonshire:
Boundary Commission report, 38
Census, 898
Dundee:
Census, 635
Corporation (Water, Transport, Finance etc.) Order Confirmation Act, 834
Bill, 801
Harbour and Tay Ferries Order Confirmation Acts, 66, 314
Bill, 284
University Education report, 291
Dunham, K. C.:
Fluorspar, 375
Geology of the country between:
Bradford and Skipton, 635
Burton-upon-Trent, Rugeley and Uttoxeter, 1140
Dunn, Lt. Col. C. L.: Emergency Medical Services, England and Wales, 378
Dunne, Sir L. R.: Report on formal investigation into explosion at Bristol garage, 290
Dunoon Burgh:
Order Confirmation Act, 834
Bill, 802
(Pavilion Expenditure) Order Confirmation Act, 1081
Bill, 803
Dunsfold Airport Customs Order, 85
Dunstable railway accident, 1209
Dunstanburgh Castle, guide, 1225
Durability of road tar, 956
Durham:
Census, 896
Palatine Court, Working Party, report, 299
Durnin, J. V. G. A.: Studies on expenditure of energy and consumption of food by miners and clerks, Fife, 1171
Durst, C. S.: Variation of wind with time and distance, 1172
Dust:
in card rooms, Committee report, 400
in steel foundries, Committee report, 400
Prevention and suppression, instructional pamphlet, 1134
Duststorms of the Anglo-Egyptian Sudan, 421
Duty-free:
Entry of machinery into the United Kingdom, 968
Treatment of American Relief Goods, Exchange of Notes with U.S.A., 46, 48
Dyes and dyestuffs, Census of Production, 458, 1199
Dyestuffs, etc., export licence, 461, 714, 969
Dynamic stresses in cast iron girder bridges, 955
Dynastic Egypt, 1184

E

Earcockles of wheat, 847
Earldom of Dundee, proceedings before the Committee of Privileges and Judgment, 513, 646
Early:
Leaving:
Central Advisory Council for Education report, 873
from senior secondary courses, circular, 1190
Mediaeval art, 1101
Easington Colliery Explosion, 301, 370
East:
Africa:
High Commission, reports, 861, 1110
Royal Commission, report, 1066, 1110
tackles the land problem, 651
today (Picture set), 1153
Anglia and adjoining area, British Regional Geology, 898
Coasts floods, circular, 648
Grinstead, Boundary Commission report, 524
Kilbride and Glenrothes Development Corporation, reports, 11, 22, 189, 199, 273, 531, 791, 960, 1046
Lothian, Census, 898

Easter:
Act (Amendment) Bill, 31
Picture book, 499
Eastern:
Dependencies, Introducing the, 390
Mediterranean and Cyprus, Tripartite Conference, 1074, 1125
Eastwood, C. G.: British African Land Utilisation Conference report, 91
Eastwood, T.: Northern England, British Regional Geology, 635
Ecclesiastical:
Areas, population of, 1138
Committee reports, 2, 67, 250, 255, 511, 513, 515, 770, 775, 778, 855, 1030, 1104
Dilapidations Measure 1923-1929 (Amendment) Measure, 2, 67, 85
Report, 2, 85
Echo sounding experiments on fish, 1092
Economic:
and Employment Commission, check list of documents, 729
and Financial Questions, records, 224, 991
and Social:
Council (United Nations) publications, 222, 480, 732, 989
Development of Libya, 1000
Projects, catalogue, 223, 482, 734, 990
Assistance:
Agreement with Germany, 549
Exchange of Notes with Yugoslavia, 808
Blockade, 337, 473
Bulletins (Asia and the Far East; Europe), 221, 479, 732, 988
Commission for Europe, 744, 989
Conditions, 877
and development in non-self-governing territories, special study on, 732
in Africa, 222
in Denmark, Iceland, Norway, and Sweden, 616
in the Middle East, 222, 732
in the United States, 616
Co-operation with U.S.A., 35, 41, 47, 51, 108, 215, 287, 293, 361, 472, 545, 549, 553, 566, 623, 725, 815, 826, 885, 981
Development, 732, 733
Commission, report, 481
in the U.K. Dependencies, 1154
of under-developed countries, 226, 993
with stability, 920
Developments, summary, 989
Geology of the Fife Coalfields, 899
Growth of twenty republics, 989
Leaflet, Natural History, 83
Measures in favour of the family, 480
Economic (*continued*):
Progress and problems of Western Europe, 101
Series (British Museum, Natural History), 83, 853, 1103
Statistics, Protocol amending International Convention, 54, 108
Survey, 41, 216, 291, 472, 550, 725, 810, 981, 1062, 1216
Asia and the Far East, 223, 734, 990
Colonial Territories, 345, 602, 1110
Europe, 223, 482, 734, 990
Far Eastern Territories, 1110
Latin America, 482, 990
West African Territories, 345
Trends, 593, 855, 1103
Economic, Employment, and Development Commission, United Nations, report, 222
Economic, Social and Cultural Rights, activities of the United Nations, 476
Economical design of rigid steel frames for multi-storey buildings, 184
Economics:
of agriculture in a savannah village, 601
University teaching of social sciences, 1007
Economy:
in house-building, 125, 377
Memoranda, 505, 763
of building materials, 505
of Hausa communities of Zaria, 1109
Ecrehos and Minquiers, agreements with France:
Differences concerning sovereignty, 41, 58, 109
Fishery rights, 39, 287
Ecuador:
Compulsory education, 233
Economic survey, 970
Ecumenical Movement and the Racial Problem, 1007
Eddie, G. C.: Care of the trawler's fish, 696
Eden, D.: Blister blight disease of tea, 599
Eden, J. F.: Study of concreting methods on housing sites, 955
Edgware Road Station, railway accident, 209
Edinburgh:
Botanic Gardens, notes, 849
Census, 375
Chartered Accountants Annuity, etc. Fund Order Confimation Act, 66
Bill, 3, 32
City of, inventory of ancient monuments, 180
Corporation Order Confirmation Act, 834
Bill, 802
Bill (1955), 1056
Educational Endowments Scheme, 958
Memos, 701, 957
Gazette, 98, 352, 613, 872, 1119
Index to Register of Sasines, 704

1951-5 | EDI-EUR

EDI— INDEX 1951-5

Edinburgh (*continued*):
Merchant Company Endowments (Amendment) Order Confirmation Act, 315
Bill, 251, 283
University:
Additional Bursaries:
Educational Endowment Order in Council, 187
Scheme, Memo, 701
(Additional Endowment No. 1) Scheme, memo and Order in Council, 958
Fellowships, Scholarships, and Bursaries Scheme, 690, 701
Scotland Education Act Draft Scheme, 701
Edmunds, F. H.:
Geology of country around Chatham, 899
Wealden District, British Regional Geology, 898
Edmunds, T. H.: Further contributions to the solution of the Piltdown problem, 1102
Education:
Abstracts, 745, 1003
Act, 64, 572
Advisory Council on Secondary Education, report, 186
and Art, 1004
and Broadcasting, Estimates, 262, 522, 783
Memo, 290
Authorities:
and Managers of grant aided educational establishments, accounts and report, 1190
Local expenditure of, 98, 100
Authority Bursaries (Scotland) Regulations, 192
Central Advisory Council report on early leaving, 873
Circulars and administrative memoranda, 98, 186, 352, 614, 615, 873, 1119
Compulsory, Studies on, 230, 233, 748, 1003
during National Service, 501, 1015
Estimates, 15, 214, 522, 979, 1036
Memoranda, 40, 99, 290, 352, 550, 614, 809, 873
Fundamental:
and adult, 238, 1004
Monographs, 230, 747
Higher:
in the Colonies, 93
Overseas, report and review, 1069
in a technological society, 748
in Britain, 1154
in Scotland, annual reports, 41, 187, 287, 291, 443, 551, 701, 812, 957, 1063, 1190
Public, 1190
Education (*continued*):
International:
Bureau of, publications, 1006
Conference on public education, 230, 491, 745, 1003
Yearbook, 492, 1005
Journalism, 1005
Junior Secondary, memo, 1190
Ministry of:
Publications, 98, 352, 614, 872, 1119
Reports, 44, 49, 294, 352, 553, 614, 813, 873, 1069, 1119
Welsh Department, publications, 100, 354, 615, 874, 1121
(Miscellaneous Provisions) Acts, 65, 567
Bills, 285, 513, 514, 523, 537, 542, 543, 643
New Colleges of Further Education, 1119
of handicapped pupils, 614, 615, 1189
of teachers in England, France, and U.S.A., 1006
of women for citizenship, 1006
of youth for international understanding and co-operation, 1004
Organisation and finance, report, 872
Problems in, 234, 748, 1006
Right to, 749
(Scotland) Acts, 65, 313
Publications arising from, 187, 442, 690, 701, 957, 1190
Bill, 1030, 1031
Report, 18, 216
Technical, Select Committee on Estimates report, 533
Unesco Institute for, publications, 1007
Workers', report on Unesco seminar, 745
Educational:
Building, circulars, 872, 873, 874, 1119, 1121, 1189
Commission in U.K., Exchanges of Notes with U.S.A., 545, 630, 818, 1070
Conditions in non-self-governing territories, 990
Developments, 746
Endowments in Scotland, report, 187
Expenditure, 98, 100
Missions, reports, 491, 745, 1004
Organisation and Statistics, world handbook, 491
Studies and documents, 745, 1004
Educational, Scientific, and Cultural Materials, Agreement on Importation, 39
Edwards, H. T. (Chairman), Council for Wales and Monmouthshire:
Memo, 553
South Wales ports, 1058
Edwards, F. L. (Chairman), Committee on Exchequer Equalisation Grants, report, 649
Edwards, L. B.: B.C.G. Vaccination, 755
Edwards, M. V.: Effects of partial soil sterilisation with formalin on the raising of Sitka spruce and other conifer seedlings, 630

INDEX 1951-5 —ELE

Edwards, W.:
Concealed coalfields of Yorkshire and Nottinghamshire, 375
Geology of the country:
around Barnsley, 1140
between Bradford and Skipton, 635
Pennines and adjacent areas, British Regional Geology, 898
Edzell Castle, guide, 504
Eels of Kenya Colony, Observations on the biology of, 1110
Eelworm:
in potatoes, 328
Stem and bulb, 78
Eelworms on strawberries, 587
Effect of sugar supplements on dental caries in children, 1171
Effects:
of National Service, 1159
of partial soil sterilisation with formalin on the raising of Sitka spruce and other conifer seedlings, 630
Efficiency:
Decoration, 501
Medal (Army), Regulations for, 1222
Egerton, Sir A. (Chairman), Heating and Ventilation (Reconstruction) Committee: District Heating report, 763
Egg:
Cookery, 104
Dried (Control of Use) (Revocation) Order, 103
Production:
Faults and their elimination, 330
in poultry yards, 330
Eggs and Egg Products, 1186
Egypt:
Air Services Agreement, 50, 108
British Commonwealth War Cemeteries, graves and memorials in Egyptian territory, agreement, 1064, 1125
Construction of the Owen Falls Dam in Uganda, 811, 885, 1078, 1125
Conversations on defence of Suez Canal and on the Sudan, 58, 108
Economic survey, 463
Financial:
Agreement, 51, 108
Matters, Exchange of Notes, 1076, 1125
Provisional Commercial Agreement, renewal, 306, 361
Public Finance Information Paper, 227
Reserves of petroleum products, 1060, 1125
Revocation of Export Licences, 202
Self-Government and Self-Determination for the Sudan:
Agreement, 558, 623
Documents concerning Constitutional Development in the Sudan, etc., 548, 623
Draft Agreement, 548, 623
Egypt (*continued*):
Self-Government and Self-Determination for the Sudan (*continued*):
International Commission to supervise the process, Agreement establishing, 1079, 1125
Sterling:
Payments Agreement, 52, 108
Releases Agreement, 51, 108
Advance release of £5 million, 551, 623
Suez Canal Base, 824, 890, 1065, 1074, 1075, 1125
Egypt, Sudan, Ethiopia: trade mission report, 1205
Egyptian Government, gift of defence equipment, 1067
Eisenhower, D. D.: North Atlantic Treaty Organisation, report, 431
Election:
Committee Rooms Bill, 282
Expenses returns, 269 380, 443, 1051, 1145
Elections, Select Committee report, 1045, 1046, 1050, 1052, 1147
Electoral:
Registers Act, 568
Bill, 517, 544
Registration Officers and Returning Officers Order, 1139
Electric:
Fencing, 79, 588
Controlled grazing with, 78
Lamps:
Defence list, 607, 867, 1114
Supply of, 25, 204
Lighting:
Accessories and fittings, Census of Production, 200, 1200
Act, 569
Tools for woodworking, 243
Wires and Cables:
Census of Production, 200, 1200
Supply of, 462
Electrical:
Apparatus and circuits, test and certification, 896
Calculations, Examples in, 317
Engineering:
Career, 920
Census of Production, 713
Trades Union and London Electricity Board, inquiry into dispute, 44
Electricite de Beyrouth Company Case, France and Lebanon, 657, 919
Electricity:
Act:
Guarantees given:
on loans proposed to be raised, 17, 22, 24, 28, 216, 260, 265, 267, 269, 275, 278, 471, 520, 526, 530, 534, 540, 725, 787, 791, 981, 1034, 1039, 1045, 1049, 1216

ELE— INDEX 1951-5

Electricity (*continued*):
Act (*continued*):
Guarantess given (*continued*):
on stock issued, 267, 471, 527, 725, 794, 981, 1050, 1216
Report, 533, 632, 702
Boards, Scotland, Guarantee given on loans proposed to be raised, 1040, 1041
for farm and estate, 849
Industry, 614, 877
Price of, 873
Reorganisation (Scotland) Act, 828
Bill, 775, 800, 802
Reports and Accounts, 24, 118, 272, 370, 532, 632, 792, 894, 1047, 1135
Sub-Committee Reports, 145, 400, 761, 923, 1159
Supply:
Industry, Census of Production, 713
(Meters) Acts, 63, 307
Bills, 34, 252, 264, 278, 383
(Supply) Act, 831
Units and standards of measurement, 430
Electronics, Services Textbook of Radio, 1224
Elements:
of forest fire control, 752
of immigration policy, 990
Elephant seal, growth and age, 862
Fleth, wreck report, 469
Elizabeth I, Calendar of State Papers, 180
Elizabeth II, Proclamation on accession, 348, 418
Ellerman, J. R.:
Chasen, 1940, Handlist of Malaysian mammals, 1102
Palaearctic and Indian mammals, check list, 84
Southern African mammals, reclassification, 854
Elliott, T. G.: Survey of production and industrial engineering organisation and practice, 440
Ellis, C. A.: Public utilities in Colombia, 1000
Ellis, Major L. F.: War in France and Flanders, 854, 961
Ellison, M. A.: Photometric survey of solar flares, plages, and prominences in *Ha* light, 436
El Salvador, economic survey, 204, 970
Embarkation cards, Aliens Order, 904
Embroidery:
History of English, 239
Introduction to practical, 1014
Emergency:
Feeding, film strip, 380
Laws:
and Supplies and Services, Statutory Instruments, 191
Emergency (*continued*):
Laws (*continued*):
(Miscellaneous Provisions) Act, 567
Bill, 255, 515, 530, 537, 541, 543, 643
Legislation, Continuance, 56, 128, 304, 380, 1076, 1145
Medical Services, 638
Proclamation, 1170
Emperor Penguin, 602, 862
Empire Settlement Act, 307
Bill, 251, 282
Empire Windrush, wreck report, 977
Employment:
and economic stability, 733
and unemployment in Great Britain, 145
of blind persons, Working Party report, 145
of older men and women, 562, 661, 911, 1077, 1159
of troops in aid of civil power. *See* Military Law Manual.
of Women and Young Persons Act, 832
Problems of disabled youth in Glasgow, 420
See also Civil Employment.
Empress of Canada, wreck report, 977
Emulsion paints, Notes on, 1185
Endersby, H. J.: Performance of circular plate ripsaws, 696
Endowed Schools Acts, scheme, 268, 352
Enemy Property:
Act, 567
Bill, 511, 514, 515, 543
Administration of, 968
Energy in overseas territories, 616
Engineer:
Services, Peace 1940 regulations, 501
Works Services, regulations, 758, 1222
Engineering:
Construction, revised preliminary draft regulations, 145
Dimensional metrology, symposium, 1174
Dispute, inquiry, 808
Draughtsman, career, 1157
Mechanical and electrical, historical events list, 1184
Survey of production and industrial engineering organisation and practice, 440
See also Chemical Engineering.
Engineering, Shipbuilding, and Electrical Goods, Census of Production, 459, 713
England:
Compulsory education, 233
Southern, illustrated guide to ancient monuments, 504
English:
and Scottish Silver, 958
Chintz, 1221
Embroidered pictures, 1221
Furniture, 1221

INDEX 1951-5 —EUR

English (*continued*):
Guidance to teachers on setting and marking examinations, 1191
in secondary schools, 443, 1190
Mediaeval silver, 499
Steel Corporation Ltd., proposal to sell holdings, 815, 1065
Enlargement of exchange economy in tropical Africa, 990
Entertainment:
Film for juvenile audiences, 493
Industry, report on classification of actors for national insurance, 294
of official visitors, 1223
Entomology Bulletins, 83, 336, 591, 853, 1102
Epibionts and parasites of the planktonic copepoda of the Arabian Sea, 84
Epidemiological and vital statistics, 236, 496, 497, 754, 755, 1011, 1012
Epidemiology and control of endemic syphilis, 755
Epileptics. *See* Handicapped persons.
Eppleton Colliery, explosion, 291, 380
Epsom and Walton Downs Regulations (Amendment) Bill, 542
Epstein, A. L.: Administration of justice and the urban African, 601
Equal pay:
Bill, 800
for men and women Civil Servants, Treasury Minute concerning payment from a single Supplementary Estimate 1059, 1216
Equalisation Grant in Scotland, 538, 702, 1049
Equipment:
for the ginning of cotton, 751
of houses, 125
Eritrea:
and Ethiopia, federation of, Exchanges of Notes with Ethiopia, 304, 810, 885
Report of United Nations Commissioner, 736
Shaping a people's destiny, 741
Technical Assistance Agreement, 48, 108, 562
See also Ethiopia.
Eskridge, boiler explosion, 465
Essex:
Census, 896
County Council Act, 315
Establishment of a Customs Union in the Caribbean area, 93
Estate:
Duty and family businesses, 49, 135
Yards, 332
Estimates:
Allocation for examination, 539
Comments on report from Select Committee, 1059, 1125
of the population of England and Wales, 897, 1139
Estimates (*continued*):
Select Committee reports and evidence, 12, 19, 22, 23, 29, 130, 131, 216, 257, 263, 264, 266, 270, 271, 274, 276, 279, 383, 384, 518, 522, 525, 526, 527, 528, 531, 533, 534, 539, 643, 644, 778, 782, 787, 789, 790, 791, 792, 795, 906, 1031, 1036, 1041, 1050, 1051, 1141
Index, 8, 216, 643, 644, 1031, 1147
Supplementary, remuneration of general practitioners, National Health Service, memo, 297, 475
See also Air Estimates; Army Estimates; Civil Estimates; Defence Estimates; Health Estimates; Navy Estimates; Revenue Departments.
Estimation:
of crop yields, 1008
of growth and mortality in commercial fish populations, 1096
Ethiopia:
Demarcation of boundary with Kenya, 40, 108, 808, 885, 1066, 1125
Facilities for military aircraft, 301, 361, 557, 623
Federation with Eritrea, 304, 361, 810 885
Financial arrangements, 304, 361
Termination of lease of Gambella enclave, 1078, 1125
Trade Mission. *See* Egypt, Sudan.
Withdrawal of British Military Administration from Reserved Area, 1057, 1125
Ethiopian region, Simuliidae of the, 593
Etterby Junction, railway accident, 719
Europe:
Council of:
Amendment to Statute, 48
Report, 40, 42
Economic:
Bulletin, 221, 479, 732, 988
Commission for:
Reports, 222, 223, 480, 481, 482, 732, 733, 989, 990
What the United Nations is doing, 229
Survey, 223, 734, 990
OEEC at work on, 879
Steel statistics, 489
Timber statistics, 496, 742, 753
Way ahead, 616
Western, economic progress and problems, 101
European:
Agriculture, 1008
Armour, 239
Bulletin, 234
Coal and Steel Community:
Act, 1080
Bill, 1028, 1055
Joint meeting with Council of Europe, 1066

EUR-FIN | 1951-5

EUR— INDEX 1951-5

European (*continued*):
Coal and Steel Community (*continued*):
Publications, 875, 1121
Relations with U.K.:
Agreement, 828, 885
Correspondence, 812, 885
Conventions, 865
Co-operation in nuclear research, 1007
Cultural Convention, 1071, 1125
Defence Community:
Armaments production, 295
Memorandum, 811, 885
regarding Western support, 295, 361
Relations with U.K., 291, 361
Treaty, 811, 885
Economic Co-operation:
Organisation (OEEC) publications, 100, 354, 615, 876
Survey, 101, 354, 616, 877
Economy, progress and problems, 877
Firearms, 1221
Foundries and productivity, 616
Housing progress and policies, 990
Inland transport:
Protocol to co-ordinate and rationalise, 567, 624, 812, 885
Statistics, 990
Monetary Agreement, 1075, 1126
Payments Union:
Agreement for establishment, 616, 877
Directives for application, 616, 877
Repayment of credits:
Austria, 822
Belgium, 822
Germany, 821
Netherlands, 821
Portugal, 821, 1067
Sweden, 821
Switzerland, 820, 885
Reports, 101, 354, 616, 877
Rules of commercial policy, 616
Supplementary protocol, 54, 108, 301, 361, 559, 624, 820, 885, 1075, 1126
Productivity Agency programme, 877
Rent policies, 734
Seminar on probation, 991
Steel:
Exports and demand in non-European countries, 732
Industry and the wide-strip mill, production and consumption trends, 734
Market, 989
Trends in the setting of the world market, 223
Textile industry in 1953, report, 880
Timber:
Statistics, 750
Trends and prospects, 750

European (*continued*):
Union, Statute of the Council of Europe, 1070, 1126
European-Mediterranean special meetings:
Frequency assignment planning, 655
Meteorological, 140
Evacuation:
in reception areas, 380
in vulnerable areas, 380
Evans, G. O.:
Collection of Mesostigmatid Mites from Alaska, 1102
Revision of the family Epicriidae, 1102
Some British mites of economic importance, 1103
Some inter-tidal mites from South West England, 592
Evans, H.: Nicaragua, economic survey, 970
Evans Murder Case:
Mrs. Beryl Evans and Geraldine, inquiry report, 557, 641
Timothy John Evans, supplementary report, 561, 641
Evans, Brig. W. H.: American Hesperiidae catalogue, 335, 591, 1101
Eve, Sir M. T. (Chairman):
Burnham Committee, report on teachers' salary scales, 99
Crown Lands Committee, report, 1067
Road Haulage Disposal Board, report, 540
Evelyn Rose, wreck report, 1213
Evershed, Rt. Hon. Sir R. (Chairman):
London Docks dispute, court of inquiry report, 824, 825
Supreme Court practice and procedure, Committee reports, 40, 299, 556
Everybody's guide to National Insurance, 1175
Everyman's United Nations, 223, 482, 734
Eves, A. W. D.: El Salvador, economic survey, 970
Evidence Act, 312
Ewe and Togoland unification problem, 1001
Ewenny Priory, guide, 504
Examination:
Papers:
Admiralty, 68, 317, 575, 836
Art, 99, 352, 614, 873, 1119
Civil Aviation, 86, 338, 595, 722, 973, 1208
Civil Service Commission, 86, 339, 596, 856, 1104
Education, Ministry of, 614
Fire Services (Scotland), 959
Fuel and Power, 119, 370, 632, 894, 1135
Scottish Leaving Certificate, 443, 701, 958, 1190
Staff College, War Office entrance examination, 243

INDEX 1951-5 —FAC

Examination (*continued*):
Papers (*continued*):
Transport, 208, 466, 618, 622, 973, 1208
Regulations, 208, 973
Examinations:
Guidance for teachers on setting and marking, 1191
Mining (Certificate of Competency) Rules, 121
Scottish Leaving Certificate, circulars, 443, 1189, 1190
Secondary schools:
Circular, 1119, 1121
Report, 352, 354
Excess Profits Tax, appeals leaflets, 135, 390, 651, 914, 1154
Exchange:
Control Acts, 313, 833
of official publications:
Belgium, 564
France, 554
Exchequer:
Equalisation Grants:
Investigation, 821, 912
Report, 649
See also Local Government.
Grants:
Local authorities, 1153
Local planning authorities, 1142
Exhibition of 1851, Report of Commissioners, 52, 129
Exhibitions, Protocol modifying International Convention, 50, 108
Exna, M.V., 974
Expanded technical assistance program, report, 750
Expedition to South-West Arabia, 83, 854
Expenditure:
of Counterpart Funds from United States Economic Aid Programme, 558 716
of energy and consumption of food by miners and clerks, Fife, 1171
Experiments on living animals, returns, 29, 128, 275, 380, 536, 641, 778, 794, 904, 1048, 1145
Expert Committee on Mental Health, report, 498
Expiring Laws Continuance Acts, 60, 308, 568, 828, 1080
Bills, 7, 33, 256, 285, 517, 544, 776, 803, 1030, 1056
Exploratory Mission of the United Nations, 482
Explosion:
and Fire:
at Bristol, 380
at Queen's Dock, Swansea, 129
at Bedwas Colliery, 804, 894
at Bristol Garage, 290
at Glyncorrwg Colliery, 1071, 1135
at Horden Colliery, 1061, 1135

Explosion (*continued*):
at Weetslade Colliery, 1076, 1135
Explosive Substance, S.R. & O. & S.I. Revised, 192
Explosives:
Act, 310
Guide amendment, 1145
Acts:
Forms, 381, 641
Summaries, 381, 641
and fireworks, Census of Production, 458, 1199
Control of, Order, 904
Factory, accident reports, 129
List of authorised, 129, 381, 641, 904, 1145
Reports of H.M. Inspectors, 12, 129, 260, 381, 518, 534, 641, 795, 904, 1046, 1145
Test of, 896
Export:
Credits, Select Committee on Estimates report, 526, 533
Guarantees Acts, 59, 307, 572
Bills, 1, 31, 251, 282
Licences, 202, 461, 714, 1203
List, key relating to Standard International Trade Classification 968, 1203
of Works of Art, reports, 472, 823, 981, 1074, 1216
Export-Import Bank, Loan Agreement, 36
Exporting:
to Canada, 202, 968, 1203
To U.S.A., 202, 968
External:
Migration, study of available statistics, 634
Parasites of poultry, 79, 1074
Rendered finishes for walls, 184
Extraneous duties, report, 642, 702
Eye, Boundary Commission report, 524
Ezard, C. M.: Costa Rica, economic survey, 969
Ezekiel, M.: Farm and the city, 751

F

Facilitation Division, report, 395
Facilities of Mass Communication, reports on, 1004
Factories:
Act, 63, 65
Chief Inspector's reports, 38, 145, 287, 400, 548, 641, 813, 826, 923, 1075, 1159
Heating and ventilation, 417
S.R.O. & S.I. Revised, 192

FAC— INDEX 1951-5

Factors Act, 309
Factory Forms and Orders, 145, 400, 662, 923, 1159
Falkirk Burgh Extension etc. Order Confirmation Act, 66
Bill, 2, 31
Falkland Islands:
Colonial reports, 90, 343, 860
Dependencies:
Arms, 599
Survey, Scientific reports, 602, 862, 1110
Economic survey, 602
S.R.O. & S.I. Revised, 192
Falmouth:
Docks Act, 834
Pier and Harbour Order Confirmation Act, 315
Bill, 252, 282
Family:
Allowances:
Act, 307, 313
(Amendment) Bill, 1053
and National Insurance Act, 307
Bill, 252, 268, 278, 283, 384
Memo, 291, 422
Report, 292, 422
S.R.O. & S.I. Revised, 192
Census. *See* Population.
Businesses. *See* Estate Duty.
or table service dining, schools, 615
Family, Youth and Child-welfare, International directory of nation-wide organisations, 739
FAO. *See* United Nations Food and Agriculture Organisation.
Far Eastern Territories, economic survey, 1110
Fareham Urban District Council Act, 315
Farm:
and estate hedges, roads, 80
and the city, 751
as a business, 1092, 1096
Book-keeping, 79, 588, 1096
Buildings, maintenance of, 1096
Dairy hygiene, 587, 1093
Gates, 80, 1096
Grain:
Drying and storage, 1095
Silos, construction of, 80
Stores, design of, 80
Implements, small, 751
Incomes in England and Wales, 79, 332, 588, 849, 1092, 1096
Livestock, prevention of disease, 850
Management:
Investigations for agricultural improvement, 750
Principles of, 1097
Mechanisation, considerations and procedures for successful introduction, 1008
Orchard renovation, 77

Farm (*continued*):
Prices, 44, 79, 129, 188, 294, 332, 381, 550, 588, 641, 702
Survey of national measures for control in Western European countries, 750
Tractor, 849
Farmer, E.: Study of telegraphist's cramp, 679
Farmers' Income Tax, 332, 849
Farming in Scotland:
Current economic conditions, 329
Types of, 329
See also Scottish Agricultural Economics.
Farms:
and smallholdings with centralised services in Wales, 588
in European countries, Mechanisation of, 101
Farnborough, Fifty years at, 1195
Faroe Islands, Exchange of Notes with Denmark regulating fishing outside territorial waters, 1064
Farrowing crate, 847
Fatigue and boredom in repetitive work, 420
Fats and oils, commodity reports, 234, 495, 750
Fatstock Guarantee Scheme, 880, 1122
Faulkner, P. (Chairman): Committee on Prevention of Pollution of the Sea by Oil, report, 718
Faversham Navigation Act, 66
Fawcett, Capt. N.: Report on fatal accident at explosives factory, Ardeer, 129
Fecundity of the plaice, 79
Fedorovitch, Sophie, memorial exhibition, 1221
Feeding:
Bees, 587
for winter milk 847
Grass, 585
Mechanisms of a deep sea fish, 592
Nursery children, 124
of chicks and growing stock, 847
of dairy cows, 1094
of separated milk, 1093
Turkeys, 1093
Fellmongery, Census of Production, 201, 1201
Feltwell, R.: Intensive methods of poultry management, 588
Fencing:
and safety precautions for cotton spinning and weaving machinery, 1169
Electric, 79
of hydraulic presses, 401
of press brakes, 401
Ferguson Bequest Fund Order Confirmation Act, 834
Bill, 802
Ferguson, S. M.: Studies in social services 854, 961

INDEX 1951-5 —FIN

Ferguson, T.: Employment problems of disabled youth in Glasgow, 420
Fernhill Farm (Charlton Sidings) occupation level crossing, accident report, 1209
Fertiliser:
Production, distribution, and utilisation in Latin America, 751
Requirements of the Kenya Highlands, 861
Store, 849
Fertiliser, Disinfectant, Insecticide and allied trades, Census of Production, 458, 1199
Fertilisers:
and crop production, 77
and feeding stuffs:
Act, 311
Residual values, 77, 328, 846, 1091
S.R.O. & S.I. Revised, 192
in agricultural recovery programmes, 101
in fishponds, 862
International Rice Commission Working Party, reports, 751, 1008
Methods of analysis, 616
Production, consumption, and trade, 877
Recent trends in consumption in OEEC countries, 355
Trade regulations in OEEC countries, 101
World reports, 495, 1009
See also Manures.
Fertilisers, Fungicides and Insecticides, OEEC Sub-committee report, 101
Fertility, trend and pattern of, 1184
Festival:
Gardens Ltd., Documents relating to, 47, 168
of Britain, 555, 763
(Additional Loans) Act, 59
Bill, 5, 32
Guides, catalogues, souvenir book, 103
(Sunday Opening) Act, 59
Bill, 1, 31
Pleasure Gardens Act, 307
Bill, 34, 250, 384
Select Committee minutes, 259
Fettes Endowment (Amendment) Scheme, 1190
Fiber per caput consumption levels, 1008
Fibers, commodity report, 750
Fibres, industrial, 94
Fibrosis of the liver in West African children, 940
Field:
Archaeology, notes for beginners, 177
Cable construction, Civil Defence handbook, 903
Manual, 655
Surgery pocket book, 240
Tests on wood preservatives used for pressure treatment, 954

Fields of economic development handicapped by lack of training personnel, 734
Fife:
Census, 898
Coalfields, economic geology, 899
Educational Trust Scheme, memos, 701, 957
West, Boundary Commission report, 39
Fifty:
Masterpieces of textiles, 239
Years at Farnborough, 1195
Fight:
at odds, 590, 852
avails, 852
is won, 852
Fiji:
Colonial reports, 90, 343, 600, 601, 1108, 1109
Economic survey, 602
S.R.O. & S.I. Revised, 192
Filho, M. B. L.: Training of rural school teachers, 1006
Filling and sealing materials for joints in concrete roads, 1188
Film:
Industry in six European countries, 230
Non-permitted uses of cellulose, 204
Technicians, professional training of, 232
See also Press.
Filmology as related to the social sciences, bibliography on, 1005
Films:
from Britain, 352
on art, 230, 1004
Training Manual, 918
Finance:
Accounts of the U.K., 20, 216, 268, 472, 725, 790, 981, 1044, 1216
Acts, 62, 63, 64, 65, 307, 309, 310, 312, 313, 567, 570, 571, 572, 828, 830, 831, 1079
Accounts, 18, 216, 267, 472, 521, 529, 725, 788, 981, 1040, 1216
Bills, 5, 32, 33, 59, 253, 282, 283, 515, 542, 543, 776, 801, 802, 1027, 1031, 1055, 1056, 1057, 1216
Draft, 1064
Financial:
Agreements:
Canada, 294, 348, 811
Egypt, 51
India, 289
Libya, 287
Pakistan, 55
Yugoslavia, 57
Aids and credits, Exchange of Notes with Austria, 35
and Military Matters, Exchange of Notes with Libya, 551
Arrangements:
Ethiopia, 304
France, 42
Iraq, 41, 302

1951-5 | FIN-FRA

FIN— INDEX 1951-5

Financial (*continued*):
Arrangements (*continued*):
Yugoslavia, 304, 808, 892
Claims, Exchange of Notes with Iraq, 1078
Limits for unlicensed work, 909
Matters:
and Trade Agreement, Yugoslavia, 306
Bulgaria, 1076
Egypt, 1076
Hungary, 821
Libya, 553
Poland, 827
Turkey, 1059
Obligations, Exchange of Notes with Yugoslavia 1060
Powers (U.S.A. Securities), S.R.O. & S.I. Revised, 192
Questions, Exchange of Notes with Burma, 814
Stability and the fight against inflation, 101
Statements (Budget), 17, 216, 263, 472, 526, 725, 786, 981, 1040, 1049, 1217
Financing improvements to land and buildings, 588
Finch, J. C. W. (Chairman): Welsh Agricultural Land Sub-Commission: report on Mid-Wales Investigation, 1077, 1094
Findlay, W. P. K.: Dry rot in wood, 439
Finger print system at Scotland Yard, 904
Finland:
Avoidance of double taxation, 286, 361, 549, 624
Economic survey, 208
Reciprocal abolition of visas, 826, 885
Sterling Payments Agreement, 300, 303, 361, 552, 558, 624, 812, 816, 885
Fire:
and the atomic bomb, 954
and the design of schools, 352, 1119
Appliances, survey of, 974
Brigade Long Service and Good Conduct Medal, 814
Endurance of timber beams and floors, 440
Grading of buildings, 505
Hazard:
of fuelling aircraft in the open, 182
of internal linings, 955
Prevention and control, 333
Research publications, 182, 438, 696, 954, 1186
Resistance:
of board and joist floors, 695
of reinforced concrete columns, 698
of timber doors, 184
Services:
Annual reports:
England and Wales, 55, 129, 299, 381, 558, 641, 818, 905, 1072, 1145
Fire (*continued*):
Services (*continued*):
Annual reports (*continued*):
Scotland, 43, 188, 292, 443, 551, 702, 812, 959, 1063, 1191
(Scotland) Central Examinations Board, 959
Select Committee on Estimates report, 790, 795
S.R.O. & S.I. Revised, 192
Tests on structural elements, 698
Firearms:
Act, 63
Forms, 381, 1145
Firefighting:
Basic, 128
Survey of science of, 1145
Firemanship, Manual of, 129, 1195
Firemen's Pensions Schemes, 381, 1145
Fires in state forests, 892
Fireworks Act, 59
Bill, 3, 5, 18, 26, 31, 33, 131
Firing of common bricks, 244
First Aid Manual, 127, 639
Firth, Thos., and John Brown Ltd., proposal to sell holdings of securities, 1061
Fischl, C. I.: Fire hazard of internal linings, 955
Fish:
Curing, Census of Production, 460, 1201
Farming and inland fishery management in rural economy, 1009
General principles of smoke-curing, 438
in the Colonial Empire, production of, 863
Marketing in OEEC countries, 355
Notacanthus phasganorus Goode from the Arctic Bear Isle fishing grounds, 83
Some reactions of pelagic fish to light as recorded by echo-sounding, 332
Fisher, Prof. M. G. (Chairman): Scottish Local Government Law Consolidation Committee, report, 545, 547, 564
Fisheries:
Act, 1079
Bill, 1026, 1054
Agreement for the establishment of a General Fisheries Council for the Mediterranean, 291, 362
Bulletins, 235, 495, 751, 862, 1009
Case *v* Norway, Judgment, 397
of Scotland, 49, 188, 294, 444, 551, 702, 811, 959, 1062, 1191
Products Commodity standards for, 752
S.R.O. & S.I. Revised, 192
Statistics Yearbook, 235, 751
Studies, 752, 1009
Technology literature, 752
See also Scottish Sea Fisheries; World Fisheries.
Fishery:
Investigations, 79, 332, 588, 849, 1092, 1096

INDEX 1951-5 —FOO

Fishery (*continued*):
near Bear Island, 849
Publications (Colonial) 93, 345, 602, 862, 1110
Research and educational institutions in North and South America, 235
Rights, Ecrehos and Minquiers, Agreement with France, 39
Fishes of Singapore Straits, Food and feeding relationships of, 93
Fishguard and Goodwick, railway accident, 210
Fish-smoking kiln, ten-stone controlled, 438
Fitness training tables for boys, 240
Fitzgerald, H.: Studies in social services, 854, 961
Five:
European conventions, 865
Ventures, 1016
Fixed equipment of the farm, 80, 333, 588, 849, 1092, 1096
Fixing fibre building board wall linings, 243
Flags, Badges and Arms, Colonial, 599, 860
Flameproof enclosure of electrical apparatus, test and certification, 121, 896
Flats, Living in, 388
Flax processing, Census of Production, 201, 967
Flea from Argentina, 591
Flea-beetles, 78, 586
Fleas:
from the bodies of British birds, 336
Rothschild Collection, 593
Fleck, Dr. A. (Chairman): National Coal Board Advisory Committee on Organisation, report, 1173
Fleet anchorage in Gulf of Paria, Exchange of Notes with U.S.A., 44
Fletcher, Prof. B. A. (Chairman): National Advisory Council on Training and Supply of Teachers, report on recruitment and training of youth leaders and community centre wardens, 100
Fletcher, C. M.: Social consequences of pneumoconiosis among coal-miners in South Wales, 169
Flight:
Navigator's Licence, 339, 595, 722, 974, 1209
Radio Operator's Licence, 339, 1209
Flock and rag, Census of Production, 459, 967
Flood:
Control, series, 729, 991
Damage and control activities in Asia and the Far East, 223
Relief, gift of surplus Government furniture, 550, 725
Warning system:
Circular, 648
Departmental Committee interim report, 559
Floods, East coast, circular, 648
Floor finishes:
based on polyvinyl chloride and polyvinyl acetate, 953
for houses, etc., 440
for industrial buildings, 184
Floud, P.: Castell Coch, guide, 1018
Flour Order, Bread Order, 620
Fluoridation of domestic water supplies in North America, 637
Fluorspar, mineral resources of Great Britain 375
Fodder beet, 587
Fog. *See* Mortality.
Food:
and Agricultural legislation, statistics, 235, 495, 752, 1009
and Agriculture:
basic statistics, 879
Bulletins, 882
Committee of OEEC, report, 101
State of, 235, 496, 533, 1009
and Drugs:
Acts, 312, 1080
Bill, 1028, 1029, 1030
Circular, 1095
Report, 1029
Amendment Act, 828, 881
Bill, 516, 769, 770, 777, 801, 803
Circular, 881
(Milk Dairies, and Artificial Cream) Act, 65
(Scotland) Bill, 516, 769, 770, 772, 801, 1025, 1040, 1043, 1045, 1051, 1053, 1054, 1055, 1057, 1148
S.R.O. & S.I. Revised, 192
(Whalemeat) Regulations, 620
and feeding relationships of the fishes of Singapore Straits, 93
and Nutrition, 104, 359
Appropriation Account, 259
Bulletins, 104, 359, 620
Charts, 359
Circulars (Ministry of Agriculture, Fisheries and Food), 1095
Composition tables, 1010
Consumption levels in OEEC countries, 101
Decontrol and marketing of agricultural produce, 620
Domestic food consumption and expenditure, 358
Estimates, 15, 215, 263, 270, 522, 523, 539, 783, 786, 1036
Growth of policy, 217
Investigation Organisation publications, 182, 438, 696, 954, 1186
Ministry of, publications, 103, 358, 619, 880, 1122
of hailbut from North Atlantic fishing grounds, 703
of the whiting, and comparison with that of the haddock, 960
Poisoning, 1144

FOO— INDEX 1951-5

Food (*continued*):
Preservation:
in the U.K., Research on, 954
See also Scientific and Technological Problems.
Protein, fat and calorie values, 1120
Refrigeration and freezing, some aspects of, 234
Science Abstracts, 183, 438, 696, 954, 1186
Standards:
Committee reports, 882, 1096
(Margarine) Order, 881
Survey, world, 733
Trading Account and Balance Sheet, 23
Values, ready reckoner, 99, 1120
See also National Food.
Food, Drink, and Tobacco, Census of Production, 461, 713
Foot rot in sheep, 1094
Foot-and-mouth disease:
Agricultural Research publications, 328, 585
European Commission for Control, constitution, 565, 624, 823, 885
Report, 817, 850
See also Bird Migration.
Footbridge at Knowsley Street Station, accident, 467
Footpaths and bridleways, circulars, 647, 911
Footwear, Utility rubber, production guide, 206
Forced labour, 734
Forces:
Career, 921
Family Pensions, 546, 607
Women's Services, 1157
Forces' Officers Retired Pay and Pensions, 809
Ford Station railway accident, 466
Foreign:
Compensation:
Act, 65
Commission:
Accounts, 262, 518, 619, 785, 885, 1041, 1126
Reports, 55, 108, 299, 362, 559, 624, 819, 885, 1072, 1126
Currency Bonds, Exchange of Notes with Austria, 1059
Estimates, 15, 214, 522, 262, 1036
Forces in Germany, 1076
Investment Laws and Regulations of countries of Asia and the Far East, 223
Jurisdiction, S.R.O. & S.I. Revised, 192
Office:
Officials, report concerning disappearance, 1073, 1126
Publications, 105, 359, 621, 882, 1122
Ministers of Western Europe, correspondence arising from meeting, 1070
Foreign (*continued*):
Service, Select Committee on Estimates reports, 22, 264, 795, 1036, 1147
Trade:
Statistical Bulletins, 101, 355, 616, 877
Zones in the U.S.A., 878
Foreigners entering and leaving the U.K. statistics, 562, 641, 823, 905, 1074, 1145
Forest:
Fire control, Elements of, 732
Officer, career, 658
Operations series, 117, 1133
Plantation protection against diseases and insect pests, 1009
Policy, Law and Administration, 235
Produce in sea and river defence, use of, 892
Products:
Research publications, 183, 438, 696, 954, 1186
Statistics, yearbook, 235, 495, 752, 1009
Records, 117, 368, 631, 892
Research reports, 117, 369, 631, 893, 1186
Resources, Conservation and utilisation, 478
Forest Gate and Manor Park railway accident, 722
Forestry:
Abstracts coverage list, 752
Acts, 59, 313, 570, 572
Bills, 1, 2, 3, 6, 32, 33
Advisory Committee, reports, 1019, 1225
and fishery products. *See* Agricultural.
and forest products:
Bibliography, 752
Studies, 752, 1009
World directory, 752
as a career, 117, 369
Commission, publications, 116, 368, 630, 892, 1133
Commissioners' reports, 21, 117, 267, 369, 526, 631, 789, 893, 1044, 1133
Criteria and equipment of tractors, 1009
Development paper, 1009
Law of, 1110
Schools, directory, 1009
Workers, vocational training, 1009
See also Unasylva.
Forgery Act, 62
Forlati, F.: St. Sophia of Ochrida, 747
Forsdyke, A. G.: Depressions crossing Labrador and the St. Lawrence basin, 1172
Forster, Sir J. (Chairman): Court of Inquiry reports:
Association football players, Difference regarding terms and conditions, 400
Austin Motor Co. Ltd., Dispute with National Union of Vehicle Builders, 553

INDEX 1951-5 —FRA

Forster, Sir J. (Chairman): Court of Inquiry reports (*continued*):
D. C. Thomson & National Society of Operative Printers and Assistants, 298
Members of N.P.A., A.E.U., and E.T.U. 1063
Forsyth, A. A.: British poisonous plants, 1095
Fortes, M.: Culture and human fertility, 1006
Forth Road Bridge Order Confirmation Act, 034
Bill, 801
Fortifications, Overseas, S.R.O. & S.I. Revised, 192
Fossil:
Amphibians and reptiles, 854
Cephalopoda in the British Museum (Natural History), catalogue, 83
Cirripedia in the Department of Geology, catalogue, 592
Mammals of Africa, 84, 336, 592, 854
Penguins from Mid-Tertiary of Seymour Island, 602
Plants of the Carboniferous rocks of Great Britain, 1140
Foul brood, 587
Foundation, short bored pile, 437
Foundling Hospital Act, 573
Foundry:
Craftsmen, careers, 1157
Ideal, 878
Industry, career, 142
Workers (Health and Safety) Bill, 285
Four Power Talk: correspondence with Soviet Government, 1067, 1126
Fowl:
Cholera, 1094
Nephritis, nature of, 76
Paralysis. *See* Lymphomatosis.
Points of a, 846
Small roasting, 1093
Fowler, R. F. (Chairman): Technical Committee, Cost of Living, report, 289
Fox, Sir C.: South Wales and Monmouthshire, regional guide to monuments, 1225
Fox, L. L.: Heating of panels by flue pipes, 438
Foxell, J. T.: Monarchs of all they surveyed, 433
Framboesia, Atlas of, 237
France:
Air Transport Agreement, 560, 624
Avoidance of double taxation and prevention of fiscal evasion with respect to taxes on income, 47, 52, 109
British Commonwealth war graves in French territory, 55, 624
Cancellation of certain drawing rights, 37, 109
Compensation for British interests in French nationalised gas and electricity undertakings, 43, 53, 109
Compulsory education, 494
France (*continued*):
Consular Convention, 287, 362
Documents of identity for aircraft personnel, 1074, 1126
Economic:
Conditions, 877
Survey, 616
Exchange:
of letters between Prime Minister and French President, 1103
of official publications, 554, 624
Extension of Social Security Agreement to Jersey, 296, 362, 553, 624, 1071, 1126
Financial arrangements, 42, 109
Foreign Trade Statistical Bulletin, 356, 617, 878
Military Service Agreement, 303, 362
Monetary Agreement, 55, 109, 810, 885
Money and property subjected to special measures in consequence of the enemy occupation of France, 555, 624
National Accounts Studies, 356
Non-scheduled commercial air services between U.K. and French territories, 38, 109
Reciprocal:
Abolition of visas, 562, 624
Application of Social Security Schemes, 42, 109, 301, 362
Re-establishment of International Administration of Tangier, 1059, 1126
Regulations for Civil Aviation in the New Hebrides, 54, 109
Rights of fishery in areas of Ecrehos and Minquiers, 39, 109, 287, 362
Social Survey Agreement, 296, 362
Submission to the International Court of Justice of difference concerning sovereignty over Minquiers and Ecrehos Islets, 41, 52, 109
Transit of British and French merchant seamen, 804, 885
War:
Damage compensation, 826, 885, 1071, 1126
Injury suffered by civilians, Compensation for disablement or death, 41, 109
Franklin, H. W. F. (Chairman): Committee to review Punishment, Prisons, Borstal Institutions, Approved Schools, and Remand Homes: reports, 46, 286
Franklin, Sir R. (Chairman): Working Party reports:
Grain drying and storage in Great Britain, 333
Quality milk production, 589
Fraser, F. C.:
Cetacea stranded on British coasts, 592
Hearing in cetaceans, 853
Southern right whale dolphin, 1102
Stranded whales and turtles, 593

Fraser, J. H.:
Chaetogratha and other zooplankton of the Scottish area, 703
Plankton of the waters approaching the British Isles, 1192
Fraser, R. A.: Summarised account of Severn Bridge aerodynamic investigation, 430
Fraudulent Mediums Act, 59
Bill, 3
Fred Borchard wreck report, 469
Free atmosphere in the vicinity of fronts, 1172
Freedom of information and of the Press, 223, 480, 481, 734, 989
Freeman, F. L. (Chairman): National Advisory Committee on Art Examinations, report, 352
Freeman, J. D.: Iban agriculture, 1109
Freeman, M. H.: Dust-storms of Anglo-Egyptian Sudan, 421
Freeman, P.:
Diptera of Patagonia and South Chile, 83
Simuliidae of the Ethiopian region, 593
Study of African Chironomidae, 1102
Freezing and cold storage of herrings, 438
Freight ships, Instructions for masters, 974
Fremantle, Hon. J. (Chairman): Reviewing Committee on Export of Works of Art, report, 1074
Freshwater and Salmon Fisheries Research reports, 188, 444, 702, 959, 1191
Friendly Societies:
Account. *See* Trustee Savings Bank.
Acts, 309, 569
Bill, 1029, 1053, 1055, 1056
in the West Indies, 601
Registry of, publications, 117, 369, 631, 893, 1133
S.R.O. & S.I. Revised, 192
Frit fly, 847
Frith, R.: Humidity of the upper troposphere and lower stratosphere over Southern England, 421
Frog up or frog down, 953
Froidevaux, Y.: St. Sophia of Ochrida, 747
From camps to homes, 482
Frontier workers, Western Union Convention, 293
Frost, R.:
Cumulus and cumulonimbus cloud over Malaya, 941
Upper air circulation in low latitudes in relation to certain climatological discontinuities, 680
Frost, W. E.: Observations on the biology of eels of Kenya Colony, 1110
Frozen pipes, 910
Fruit:
and vegetables:
Domestic preservation, 848
Home freezing, 333, 1093
Fruit (*continued*):
and vegetables (*continued*):
Production, trade, and policies in Europe, 495
Proposals for increased duties, 566
See also Stone fruit.
Dehydration of English fruit, 438
Production and trade, 94, 347, 864, 1111
Fruits, bush, 79
Fruit-tree red spider mite, 586
Fryd, C. F. M.: Further contributions to solution of the Piltdown problem, 1102
Fryer, K. G. H.: Study of concreting methods on housing sites, 955
Fuchs, V. E.: Organisation and methods, Falkland Islands Dependencies Survey, 602
Fuel:
Abstracts, 183, 439, 697, 954, 1186
and energy resources, Conservation and utilisation of, 478
and Power:
Electricity report, 273
Ministry of, publications, 118, 370, 631, 893, 1134
Resources, National policy for use of, 301, 371
Consumption:
in schools, 1119
of thermal power stations, 618, 880
Domestic solid fuel appliances, 377
Efficiency:
Bulletins, 119, 632
News, 119, 371, 632, 894
Estimates, 523, 784, 1036
Manufactured, Census of Production, 458
Market. *See* Coal and black oils.
Research:
Publications, 184, 439, 697, 955, 1187
Specialist conference, 82
Fugitive Criminal, S.R.O. & S.I. Revised, 192
Fumigation:
Precautionary measures, 129
Regulations: buildings, ships, 381
with methyl under gas-proof sheets, 955
Fundamental:
and adult education, 492, 746, 1004
Education, 230, 491, 1006
Processes of electrical contact phenomena, 698
Stars, apparent places of 68, 317, 575, 836, 1083
Funeral of King George VI, Ceremonials observed, 418
Fungi, some Himalayan, 1101
Fungicides. *See* Insecticides.
Fur:
Apparel Order, register of manufacturers, 206, 464
Census of Production, 201, 1201

Furlong, C. R.:
Dehydration of English fruits, 438
Refrigerated gas storage of Gros Michel bananas, 696
Furnished Houses (Rent Control) Act, 313
Furniture:
and Upholstery, Census of Production, 713
How to buy, 134
Manufacture, 659
(Maximum Prices) Order, schedules, 202
Furniture-beetles, 83
Further Education (Scotland) Code, 700
Future takes shape, 914

G

Galvanising techniques in U.S.A., 878
Gambeila, enclave, Termination of lease, 1078
Gambia:
Colonial reports, 90, 600, 1108
Colony, S.R.O. & S.I. Revised, 192
Egg Scheme, Colonial Development Corporation report, 295, 345
Native administration, 93
See also Africa, West.
Game (Duck and Geese) Bill, 285
Game, P. M.:
Oriental Rutile in a High Temperature Andesine from Nigeria, 336
Rock collections in Mineral Department, British Museum (Natural History), 854
Gane, R.: Refrigerated gas storage of Gros Michel bananas, 696
Gardiner, Sir T. (Chairman): reports of Committees on Organisation, etc.:
of Professional Accountant Class in the Civil Service, 474
of Works Group of Professional Civil Servants, 218
Garland, C. E.: Harrison's Digest and Index of Tax Cases, 393, 916
Garner, H. V.: Manures and fertilisers, 331
Garrett, Sir W. (Chairman): Industrial Injuries Advisory Council, reports:
Pneumoconiosis, 555
Raynaud's Phenomenon, 828
Time limits for claiming and obtaining payments of benefits, 291
Garrison and Regimental Institutes, Rules for conduct, 501
Garrod, Sir G.: Despatch on part played by Allied Air Forces in final defeat of enemy in Mediterranean, 167
Garry, R. C.: Studies on expenditure of energy and consumption of food by miners and clerks, Fife, 1171
Gas:
Act, 313
Guarantees given:
on Loans proposed to be raised, 12, 21, 27, 216, 260, 266, 267, 270, 275, 278, 472, 520, 522, 526, 530, 534, 725, 780, 785, 787, 791, 794, 981, 1034, 1039, 1045, 1049, 1217
on Stock issued, 17, 22, 27, 216, 534, 725, 1047, 1217
and Electricity (Borrowing Powers) Act, 828
Bill, 776, 802
Memo., 814, 894
Boards, annual reports and accounts, 10, 27, 119, 274, 371, 532, 632, 793, 894, 1048, 1135
Council, annual report and accounts, 11, 28, 120, 275, 371, 531, 633, 793, 894, 1048, 1135
Examiners' General Directions, 120
Minister of Fuel and Power's reports 11, 28, 119, 275, 371, 533, 632, 793, 894, 1048, 1135
S.R.O. & S.I. Revised, 192
Supply Industry, Census of Production, 460
Undertakings (Scotland) Bill, 30
Volume factors, tables, 120
Gasification of coal, 618
Gasworks, valuation for rating, Working Party report, 1193
Gater, Sir G. (Chairman):
Building Apprenticeship and Training Council: report on training for management, 504
Building Research and Development Advisory Council, report, 762
Gates, farm, 80
Gates Clark, J. F.: Microlepidoptera in the British Museum (Natural History) described by Edward Meyrick, 1102
Gateshead Extension Act, 573
Gatfield, E. N.: Testing concrete by an ultrasonic pulse technique, 1188
GATT in action, 397
Gatwick Airport, 823, 974
Proposed development inquiry, 817, 912
Gauge making and measuring, 943
Gauging and measuring screw threads, 177, 1174
Geddes, W. R.: Land Dyaks of Sarawak, 861
Gedge, M. N. (Chairman): Committee on Shares of No Par Value:
Minutes of evidence, 970
Report, 810, 970
Gee, H. G. (Chairman): Electricity Sub-Committee, report, 661
Gelatine, edible, standards for, 103
Gemstones in the Geological Museum, guide, 123

Genera:
and sub-genera of mammals, List of names proposed, 592
Henricohahnia Breddin, Dicrotelus Erichson, Nyllius Stäl, Orgetorixa China and allied new genera, 853
General:
Agreement on Tariffs and Trade, publications, 373, 634, 896
Assembly. *See* United Nations.
Certificate of Education, 614, 1118, 1120
Conference records, proceedings, 746
Lighthouse Fund, accounts, 16, 209, 265, 466, 523, 718, 789, 974, 1050, 1208
Medical Practitioners' remuneration, memo on, 297, 377, 379
Morbidity, Cancer and Mental Health, supplement, 897
Nursing Councils for England and Wales and Scotland, report, 901
Practice within the National Health Service, 901
Practitioner and the Hospital Service, 376
Practitioners, Distribution of remuneration among, Working Party report, 378
Practitioners' Records, 634
Principles of smoke-curing of fish, 438
Register Office, publications, 121, 373, 634, 896, 1137
Registry Office, Scotland, publications, 122, 374, 635, 897, 1139
Statistics, Bulletin, 101, 618, 878
Geneva:
Conference, documents relating to:
Foreign Ministers' meeting, 1077, 1126
Heads of Governments meeting, 1071, 1126
Indo-China, 819, 887
Korea and Indo-China, 815
Cross, S.R.O. & S.I. Revised, 192
Genocide, Reservations to Convention on prevention and punishment of, 141, 397
Genus:
Epitola Westwood, revisional notes, 1102
Felis, catalogue, 84
Pardomima Warren, 1102
Ptilinopus, subdivisions, 853
Teriomima Kirby, revision, 591
Geodimeter measurement of the Ridgeway and Caithness Bases, 943
Geographical Handbook series, 574
Geography:
Handbook of suggestions for teaching, 494
in secondary schools, 187, 1190
Teaching for international understanding, 234
Geological Survey and Museum, publications, 123, 375, 635, 898, 1140
Geology:
Bulletin, 83, 326, 591, 853, 1102
of the Colony of North Borneo, 345
Geophysical Memoirs, 421, 680, 941, 1172
George VI:
Death of, 418
Special Army Orders, 501
Speech to Parliament, 7, 133
German:
and Japanese:
Industry, Classified list of reports, 190
Experience in extraction of low-grade non-ferrous ores, bibliographical survey, 437
Assets, Settlement of conflicting claims, Agreement with Switzerland, 559, 624
Conventions Act, 1080
Bill, 1028, 1054, 1055
Defence contribution and the European Defence Community, 290, 362
Enemy:
Assets, Settlement of conflicting claims, Agreement with Netherlands, 42
Property:
Report of Advisory Committee on Distribution, 202
Vesting Order, 202
External Debts:
Administrative agreement, 1063, 1126
Report of Conference, 302, 362
Foreign Policy, Documents on, 110, 362, 625, 885
Law, Manual of, 362
Plastics Industry, 966
Potash Syndicate Loan Act, 1081
Property in Switzerland, Agreement, 559, 625
Rayon Industry, 437
German-owned Patents, Agreement for extension of international accord to Italy, 38
Germany:
Acetylene industry and acetylene chemistry, 200
Air Services Agreement, 1073, 1127
and Czechoslovakia, German Foreign Policy, 110
and Italy, Protocol to the Treaty extending Western European Union, 1068
and the Spanish War, German Foreign Policy, 362
Avoidance of double taxation, etc., 820, 885, 1073, 1127
Charter of the Allied High Commission, Instrument of revision, 45, 110
Control Commission, report of British High Commissioner, 95
Conventions between U.K., U.S.A., and France, 295, 296, 363

Germany (*continued*):
Economic conditions, 877
Export of scrap, 293, 363
External Debts, agreement, 54, 110, 549, 625
Foreign Trade Statistical Bulletin, 355, 356, 617, 878
Future of, correspondence, 290, 294, 298, 302, 363, 561, 625
History and administration, 575
Industrial controls in the areas of occupation, agreements, 47, 110, 306, 362, 547, 625
Memo., 817, 885
Monetary Agreement, 554, 625
New practice bombing range near Cuxhaven, Agreement, 304, 363
Non-ferrous metals and alloy steels, Development and use of substitutes, 184
Occupation controls, revision, 45, 110
Participation of a Norwegian Brigade Group in the Occupation, 297
Payments Agreement, 36, 110
Pest control, 200
Post-war economic assistance, settlement of claim, agreement, 549, 625
Presence of foreign forces in the Federal Republic, convention, 1076, 1127
Price, Waterhouse & Co.: report on accounts of Joint Export-Import Agency, 291, 363
Principles governing relationship between Allied Kommandature and Greater Berlin, 295, 363
Protocol to the North Atlantic Treaty on Accession, 1068
Relations with the three Powers, memo, 295, 363
Repayment of credits granted by European Payments Union, agreement, 821 885
Sandbank Bombing Range, use of, 1060, 1127
Statements issued by U.K., U.S.A., and France, 299, 363
Tax treatment of Forces and their members, agreement, 295, 302, 363
Termination:
of occupation regime, 1059, 1127
of war with, 167
Western, Exchange of Notes terminating most-favoured-nation treatment, 303
Germany's place in the New Europe, 364
Gerrard, A. D.: report on matters arising on Rimmer Murder Case, 292
Gibberd, F.: Design in town and village, 649
Gibbs-Smith, C. H.: Apsley House guide, 499, 757
Gibraltar:
Colonial reports, 343, 860
Economic survey, 602
S.R.O. & S.I. Revised, 192
Giffard, General Sir G. J.: Despatches on operations in:
Assam and Burma, 167
Burma and North East India, 166
Gifts:
Aircraft to U.S.A., 816, 982
Defence equipment to Egyptian Government, 1067, 1217
Military equipment to North Atlantic Treaty countries, 816, 982
Synchrotron, to Australia, 813, 982
Vehicles, instruments, etc. to National Industrial Fuel Efficiency Service, 816, 982
Gilbert and Ellice Islands:
Colonial reports, 600, 860
Economic survey, 602
S.R.O. & S.I. Revised, 192
Gilbert, M.: National products, 879
Gillingham bus accident, 468
Gilyard-Beer, R.: Gisborough Priory, guide, 1225
Girdling or banding as a means of increasing cone production in pine plantations, 117
Girdwood, J. G. (Chairman): Committee of Inquiry into cost of:
House building, report, 387
House maintenance, report, 649
Gisborough Priory, guide, 1225
Gittens, John: Approved school boys, 379
Glamorgan:
Census, 896
County Council Act, 315
Gläser, H.: Criteria for correct logging techniques and best methods of work in European countries, 1009
Glasgow:
Census, 375
Corporation:
(Extension of Time) Order Confirmation Act, 1079
Bill, 1055
Order Confirmation Acts, 315, 573, 834
Bills, 282, 542, 801
Sewage Order Confirmation Act, 66
(Water) Order Confirmation Act, 833
Bill, 544
Station, railway accident, 467
Tramway accident, 720
Glass:
Census of Production, 458, 1199
Containers, 458, 966
Window, discoloration, 437
See also Ceramics.
Glass, D. V.: Trend and pattern of fertility in Great Britain, 1184
Glasshouse white fly, 1091
Glasshouses, commercial, construction and heating, 588
Glassware, volumetric, 943

1951-5 | GLA HEA

GLA— INDEX 1951–5

Glastonbury:
Soils of the district, 1092
The Tribunal, guide, 762
Glazier, career, 398
Glen Trool, guide, 893
Glenister, T. W.: Emperor penguin, 862
Glenrothes. *See* East Kilbride.
Glentress, Britain's Forests, 630
Glentworth, R.: Soils of the country around Banff, Huntly, and Turriff, 846
Glossop Water Act, 315
Gloucestershire:
Census, 1138
Regiment in Korea, Citation of U.S. Army, 240
Gloves:
Census of Production, 201, 967
Manufacture and Supply Order Register, 206
Glue, gum, paste, and allied trades, Census of Production, 200, 1199
Glyncorrwg Colliery, explosion, 1071
Goat-keeping, 847
Goddard, Rt. Hon. Lord (Chairman): Committee on Law of Civil Liability for Damage done by Animals, report, 546
Godfrey, W.: Brazil, economic survey, 969
Goitre, endemic, control of, 754
Gold Coast:
Colonial reports, 90, 343, 344, 601, 861
Constitutional reform, Despatches on Government's proposals, 862
Native administration, 93
Pteridophyta, List of, 1101
S.R.O. & S.I. Revised, 192
See also Africa, West.
Golden age of Dutch silver, 757
Gollanfield Junction railway accident, 719
Good farm management, Principles of, 1097
Goodale, Sir E. W. (Chairman): Exhibitions Advisory Committee, report on present arrangements for British Industries Fair, 566
Goodchild, R.: Machine boring of wood, 1186
Goode, C. W.: Poultry on the general farm, 331, 588
Goodey, T.: Laboratory methods for work with plant and soil nematodes, 81
Goods:
and Services (Price Control):
Act, 312
Related Schedules, 202
S.R.O. & S.I. Revised, 192
Vehicles, Licensing Authorities' reports, 976
Gooseberries, 1090, 1093
Gooseberry:
Aphids. *See* Currant.
Red spider mite, 1093
Gordon, D. M.: Peru, economic survey, 463
Gordon, I.:
On Sirpus, a genus of pigmy cancroid crabs, 592
Puerulus stage of some spiny lobsters, 592
Gordon, W. A.: Law of forestry, 1110
Goswick railway accident, 974
Gould, Sir R. (Chairman):
Cost of Living Advisory Committee, reports, 145, 289
Electricity Sub-Committee, reports, 145, 400
Governesses Benevolent Institution Act, 315
Government:
Accounting and Budget execution, 737
Accounts, Budgetary structure and classification of, 225
Annuities, S.R.O. & S.I. Revised, 192
Chemist's Department, annual reports, 375, 636, 899, 1140
Department Electrical Specifications, 196, 711
Departments:
Regional organisations of, Select Committee on Estimates report, 792, 906
Staffs employed in, 39, 45, 52, 57, 219, 289, 294, 300, 304, 475, 548, 553, 559, 566, 727, 809, 814, 819, 826, 1061, 1068, 1072, 1077, 1220
Information Services:
Estimated expenditure, 46, 216, 296, 472, 561, 725, 815, 982, 1074, 1217
Select Committee on Estimates, report, 12
Libraries, guide, 472
of Wales Bill, 1053
Orders, guide, 447, 706, 1194
Publications, catalogues, indexes, 190, 446, 705, 961, 1194
Scientific organisation in the civilian field, 216
Statistical services, 725
Gowers, Sir E.:
A.B.C. of Plain Words, 214
Complete Plain Words, 980
(Chairman):
Departmental Committee on Foot-and-mouth Disease, report, 817
Royal Commission on Capital Punishment:
Minutes of evidence, 181, 434
Report, 560
Gowing, M. M.: Civil industry and trade, 337
Graduate teachers of mathematics and science, 614
Graham Land, Petrology of, 862, 1110
Graham, M.: Research from the *Ernest Holt* into fishery near Bear Island, report 849
Graham, R.: Titchfield Abbey, guide, 1018

INDEX 1951–5 —GRE

Grain:
Bulk handling:
Home grown, 848
in the U.S.A., 619
Commodity reports, 495, 750
Crops, production and trade, 604, 864, 1111
Drying and storage in Great Britain, 333
Exports, 752, 1009
Milling, Census of Production, 459, 1201
Storage, drying and marketing in U.S.A., 333
Grant, C. H. B.: Species and races of yellow wagtails from Western Europe to Western North America, 336
Grant, F. (Chairman): Purchase Tax (Valuation) Committee, report, 552
Grant, Dr. J. B.: report of mission, South and South East Asia, 987
Grant, R. T.: Observations on general effect of injury in Man with special reference to wound shock, 169
Grant-in-aid of Universities and Colleges, Select Committee on Estimates, report, 266, 274
Granton Harbour branch line, railway accident, 975
Grants-in-aid, Select Committee on Estimates, report, 787, 795
Grants to training college students, 1119, 1120
Grass:
Drying, 588
Production, 328
Grassland, 879
Management, 332, 1095
Reclamation, 329
Reseeding, 330
Gratuity for service in Korea, 501
Gray, J. N.: Advisability of extending compulsory registration of title on sale to County of Surrey, report, 168
Gray, W. S.: Preliminary survey of methods of teaching reading and writing, 745
Grazing and forest economy, 752
Great Barrier Reef Expedition, scientific reports, 336, 592
Great Northern London Cemetery (Crematorium) Act, 573
Great Ouse River Board (Revival of Powers, etc.) Act, 573
Great Yarmouth:
Pier and Harbour Order Confirmation Act, 315
Bill, 253, 283
Port and Haven Act, 66
Greaves, I.: Colonial monetary conditions, 601
Greaves, W. M. H.: Spectrophotometric measurements of early type stars, 1184
Grebenik, E.: Trend and pattern of fertility in Great Britain, 1184
Greece:
Ambatielos Case, agreement regarding submission to arbitration, 1062, 1127
and Crete, war history, 501
and Turkey, accession to North Atlantic Treaty, 57, 290
Avoidance of double taxation etc., 557, 625, 807, 887
Commerce and Navigation Treaty, 41, 110
Community Development Programmes, report, 987
Consular Convention, 554, 625
Cultural Convention, 58, 110, 807, 887
Foreign Trade Statistical Bulletin, 355, 356, 617, 878
Money and property subjected to special measures, 820, 887
Nutrition work in, 235
Reciprocal:
Abolition of visas, 555, 625
Exemption of air transport profits from Income Tax, etc., 36, 110
Settlement of claims arising from British Military Administration of the Dodecanese, 1066, 1127
Trading with the Enemy Order, 970
Greek:
Frontier incidents, reports, 486, 740
Loan, account, 1041, 1217
Green:
Belts, 1150
Manuring, 330
Green, Prof. H. N.: Effect of sugar supplements on dental caries in children, 1171
Greene, H.: Using salty land, 749
Greenford, railway accident, 210
Greenland and Faroes Air Navigation Services, report, 138
Greenock Corporation Order Confirmation Act, 573
Bill, 285
Greenwich:
Hospital:
and Travers Foundation:
Accounts, 17, 68, 260, 317, 525, 575, 783, 836, 1038, 1083
Estimated income and expenditure, 20, 68, 268, 317, 529, 575, 786, 836, 1044, 1083
Postcards, 763, 1019
Observatory, publications, 123, 376, 636, 899, 1140
Greenwood, Major:
Incidence of industrial accidents on individuals with special reference to multiple accidents, 625
Labour wastage, 420
Grenada:
Colonial reports, 600, 1108
S.R.O. & S.I. Revised, 1192
Gregory, R. C. L.: County Court Manual, 168

GRE— INDEX 1951–5

Grey squirrel, 640, 1091
Griffith, Wyn: British Civil Service, 1854-1954, 978
Griffiths, Sir William (Chairman): Metallurgists Sub Committee, report on supply and demand for persons with professional qualifications, 163
Grigg, Sir J. (Chairman): Departmental Records Committee, report, 813
Grimes, W. F.: Pentre-Ifan Burial Chambers, guide, 762
Grimsdale, T. F.: Cretaceous and tertiary foraminifera from the Middle East, 336
Grin, E. I.: Epidemiology and control of endemic syphilis, 755
Gritting machines for surface dressing, 185
Ground:
Crop spraying machines, 586
Nuts, cultivation in West Africa, 615
Growing food for a growing world, 1009
Growmore Bulletins, 333
Growth of a Nation, 625
Guam and Trust territories of Pacific Islands, agreement extending territorial scope of South Pacific Commission, 293
Guarantees:
Annual review and determination, 1061, 1092, 1145, 1192
for home-grown cereals, 588, 620, 641, 702
of advances made by societies, 1141, 1150
Guardianship and Maintenance of Infants Act, 60
Bills, 4, 5, 35
Guatemala:
Change of regime, 822, 887
Economic survey, 463
Guava, wreck report, 978
Guest, C. W. G: Civil Aircraft accident report, 1208
Guest Keen Baldwins Iron and Steel Co. Ltd., Proposal to sell shares, 813
Guidance, Manual of, special services, 614, 615
Guided missiles, agreement with U.S.A. for establishment of long-range proving ground in the Bahama Islands, 35
Guides to Official Sources, 121
Guildford, railway accident reports, 719, 975
Guillebaud, C. W. (Chairman): Court of inquiry, reports:
Printing dispute, 560
Railwaymen's wages and salaries, 58
Guiseppi, M. D.: State Papers, Scotland, and Mary Queen of Scots, 445
Gulland, J. A.: Estimation of growth and mortality in commercial fish populations, 1096
Gurney-Dixon, Sir S. (Chairman): Central Advisory Council on Education, England, report on early leaving, 873
Guthe, T.: Treponematoses, 1013
Guthrie, Hon. Lord (Chairman): Scottish Leases Committee, report, 302
Gwydir Uchaf Chapel, guide, 761
Gyro-compass, manual, 575

H

Hadcock, R. H.: Tynemouth Priory and Castle, guide, 504
Haddington, Index to Register of Sasines, 704
Haddock bionomics, 703
Hadfields Ltd., Proposal to sell holdings of securities, 1070
Haemophilia and its related conditions, diagnosis and treatment, 1171
Hague, D. B.: Gwydir Uchaf Chapel, guide, 761
Hague Conference on Private International Law, 819
Hailey, Lord: Native administration in British African Territories, 93, 605, 862
Hair, fibre, and kindred trades, Census of Production, 201, 967
Haiti pilot project, 231
Half-way to Independence. *See* Trust Territory.
Halibut, Statistics of Scottish fishery, 703
Hall, H. D.: North American Supply, 1103
Hall, H. S.: Milk pasteurisation, 755
Ham House, guide, 239
Hamilton Burgh Order Confirmation Act, 315
Bill, 284
Hamilton, J. R. C.: Jarlshof, guide, 762
Hammond, R. J.: Food: Growth of policy, 217
Hampshire, Census, 1138
Hampton Court Palace:
Guide, 505, 1018
Handlist of pictures, 1226
Tapestries, guide, 245
Hanbury, Prof. H. G. (Chairman): Court of Inquiry report into dispute for the omnibus industry, 809
Handel's Messiah, exhibition catalogue, 82
Handford, Sir J. (Chairman): Interdepartmental Committee on Slaughterhouses, Scotland, reports, 806, 1059
Handicapped:
Persons, welfare of, 637
Pupils:
Education of, 1189
Training and supply of teachers, 874
Handley, W. R. C.: Mull and Mor formation in relation to forest soils, 892
Handling concrete on housing sites, 761
Hand-weaving in the Phillippines, 1000
Hankin, G. T.: United Nations at work, 354

INDEX 1951–5 —HAE

Hannan, R. S.: Scientific and technological problems involved in using ionising radiations for the preservation of food, 1186
Hannay, R. K.: Letters of James V, 961
Harbours, Piers and Ferries (Scotland):
Act, 567
Bill, 285, 512, 522, 537, 541, 644
S.R.O. & S.I. Revised, 192
Hard Metals, handbook, 1187
Harding, H.: Patent Office centenary, 687
Harding, J. P.: Ostracod genus Trachyleberis, 592
Hardware, hollow-ware, metal furniture and sheet metal, Census of Production, 713
Hardwood trees, small, volume table, 892
Hardwoods:
Atlas of end-grain photomicrographs, 796
for building and general purposes, 183
Identification of, 439
in building, use of, 693
Lens-key for identification, 438
Hargreaves, E. L.: Civil industry and trade, 337
Harlech, Rt. Hon. Lord:
(Chairman): Standing Commission on Museums and Galleries, report, 983
Illustrated regional guides to ancient monuments, 504, 1018
Harlow Development Corporation, reports, 29, 279, 388, 779, 792, 913, 1048
Harper, F. C.: Floor finishes for houses and other non-industrial buildings, 440
Harrington, J. B.: Cereal breeding procedures, 751
Harris, A. J.: Vehicle headlighting, visibility and glare, 956
Harris, P.: Mechanics of sawing, band and circular saws, 954
Harrison's Digest and Index of Tax Cases, 137, 393, 916
Harrow and Wealdstone Station, railway accident, 719
Hartlepool Port and Harbour Act, 834
Hartlepools, Boundary Commission report, 524
Hartley, W. G.: Movements of salmon off north east coast of England, 1092
Harvey, R. J. P. (Chairman): Mobile Radio Committee, report, 1181
Harwell, 455, 1221
Hassett, wreck report, 978
Hastings, Boundary Commission report, 524
Haswell, M. R.: Economics of agriculture in a savannah village, 601
Hatchery design and disease control, 847
Hatfield Development Corporation, reports, 29, 279, 388, 779, 792, 913, 1048
Hats, Caps, and Millinery, Census of Production, 459, 967
Hausa communities of Zaria, economy of, 1109
Hausberger, F.: Productivity in the distributive trade in Europe, 879
Hawfinch, morphology of head, 1102
Hay, its making and feeding, 330
Haya de la Torre Case (Colombia/Peru), 141, 397
Haymaking, tripod, 587
Hayman, R. W.: Southern African mammals, reclassification, 854
Hayti, economic survey, 716
Hayward, J. T.: European firearms, 1221
Headlighting. *See* Vehicle headlighting.
Health:
Education of the public, expert committee report, 1013
Estimates, 15, 215, 262, 522, 783, 1035, 1036
for Scotland, Department of:
and Scottish Health Services Council, reports, 40, 123, 290, 376, 550, 636, 810, 900, 1062, 1141
Publications, 123, 376, 636, 900, 1141
Hints, simple, 100
Legislation, International digest, 237, 497, 754, 1012
Ministry of:
Publications, 125, 377, 637, 901, 1143
Reports, 52, 126, 296, 302, 378, 549, 560, 566, 637, 638, 824, 825, 902, 1072, 1077, 1143
National Health Service, hospital costing return, 378
of the school child, 352, 873
of welders, 145
Programmes for rural areas, Methodology for planning, 1013
Statistics, expert committee report, 498
Welsh Board of, publications, 126, 379
What local authorities can do to promote health and prevent disease, 125
Healthy village: experiment in visual education in west China, 231
Hearing in Cetaceans, 853
Hearmon, R. F. S.: Dielectric properties of wood, 954
Heat:
and cold, handbook of collection, 1184
Loss from dwellings, 182
Stress, indices of, 1171
Tolerance of domestic animals, 1008
Transfer by radiation, 954
Heathcote-Smith, C. B. B.: Uruguay, economic survey, 970
Heating:
and cooking in local authority houses, list of improved solid fuel appliances, 125
and ventilation in factories, 417
Appliances (Fireguards) Act, 307
Bill, 253, 268, 278, 281, 283, 384
District, 763, 764
of grain, 330
of panels by flue pipes, 438
Stoves, etc., 761

HEA-HOU | 1951-5

Heavy equipment for power stations, 879, 880
Hedgerow and park timber, Census, 730
Helical compression springs, design of, 196
Helicopter Committee, report, 86
Hellenes, King Paul of, appointment to Hon. Admiral in H.M.Fleet, 169
Hemel Hempstead Development Corporation, reports, 29, 279, 388, 779, 792, 913, 1048
Heneage, Sir Arthur (Chairman): Land Drainage Legislation Sub-committee, report, 80
Henderson, I. L.: Paraguay, economic survey, 463
Henderson, J. S.:
(Chairman):
Broadmoor Inquiry Committee, report, 297
Committee on Cruelty to Wild Animals, report, 46
Evans Murder Case, reports, 557, 561
Hepatitis, expert committee report, 756
Hepburn, H. A. (Chairman):
Committee on dust in steel foundries, report, 400
Committee on the safeguarding of milling machines, report, 417
Joint Standing Committee on prevention of accidents in paper mills, report, 676
Joint Standing Committee on safety in use of power presses:
Report on fencing of hydraulic presses, 401
Report on power presses, 168
Herbert, R. (Chairman): Interdepartmental committee on slaughterhouses (England and Wales), reports, 806, 1071
Herbicides. *See* Insecticides.
Herbs, culinary and medicinal, 332
See also Vegetables.
Herefordshire and Shropshire, Census, 1138
Herne Bay:
and Whitstable, Agricultural Land Commission report, 848
Pier and Harbour Order Confirmation Act, 315
Bill, 253, 283
Herring:
Gametes, storage of, 1192
Industry:
Act, 312
Accounts, 9, 25, 188, 280, 444, 780, 1037, 1051, 1192
Draft scheme, 188
Board, reports, 50, 80, 129, 188, 295, 333, 359, 381, 444, 553, 588, 630, 641, 702, 812, 850, 882, 905, 959, 1067, 1096, 1146, 1192
Rearing, 1192
Herrings, freezing and cold storage, 438
Hertfordshire, Census, 896
Herts and Essex Water Act, 573
Hertslet's Commercial Treaties. *See* British and Foreign State Papers.
Heterophyllous Selaginellae of Continental North America, 1101
Hey, M. H.:
Further contributions to solution of Piltdown problem, 1102
Meteorites catalogue, 592
Heywood, V. H.: Notulae criticae ad floram Hispaniae pertinentes, 853
Higgins, B.: Economic and social development in Libya, 1000
High:
Altitude interceptor range, Exchange of Notes with U.S.A., 556
Alumina cement, 181
Commission Territories, economic development and social services, 1073, 1112
Court and Court of Appeal, accounts, 216, 472, 725, 1217
Explosive, instructional diagrams, 128
Higher:
Civil Service, remuneration, 217
Education overseas, 1069, 1110
Technological education, development, statement of Government policy, 53, 99, 168, 188
Highway:
Code, 1209
Road Safety Committee report, 468
England, S.R.O. & S.I. Revised, 192
Hildina, wreck report, 1212
Hilditch, Prof. T. P. (Chairman): Committee on vaporising liquid extinguisning agents, report, 954
Hilf, Prof. H. H.: International performance comparison in the field of logging, 1009
Hill:
Farm research, 77, 585
Farming Act, 313, 829
Bill, 544, 771
Hill, Prof. A. B. (Chairman): Statistics subcommittee, report on medical nomenclature and statistics, 897
Hill, C. P.: Suggestions on teaching history, 748
Hill, E. G.: Selenium, 956
Hill, Lt. Col. F. G. (Chairman): Informal Working Party on treatment and disposal of sewage sludge, report, 913
Hill, J. E.: Land mammals of New Guinea, Celebes, and adjacent islands, 854
Hillingdon Estate Bill, report on petition, 1029, 1149
Hills, I. M.: Introduction to practical embroidery, 1014
Himalayan fungi, 1101
Hinchingbrooke, Viscount (Chairman): Advisory Committee on works of art in the House of Commons, report, 1226

Hincks, W. D.: Systematic monograph of the Dermaptera of the world, 1103
Hinton, H. E.: Common insect pests of stored food products, 1103
Hird, D.: Fire hazard of internal linings, 955
Hire Purchase:
Act, 64, 929
Bill, 544, 773, 775, 787, 797, 803, 906
and Small Debt (Scotland) Act, 571
His Majesty's Declaration of Abdication Act, 63
Historic:
Astronomical Books Catalogue, 952
Buildings:
and Ancient Monuments Act, 567
Bill, 515, 531, 537, 543, 644
Councils, reports, 789, 959, 1019, 1041, 1192, 1226
Historical:
Bulletin series, 591, 853, 1102
Monuments, Royal Commission, 435
Museum of the Register House, Edinburgh, guide, 445
History:
in secondary schools, 187, 1190
of Parliament, Treasury Minute on exhibition, 294, 472
of the Second World War, 217, 337, 378, 473, 501, 593, 638, 759, 854, 902, 961, 1016, 1103, 1143
of the Victoria and Albert Museum, 499
Setting and marking of examinations, guidance of teachers, 1191
Suggestions on teaching, 748
Textbooks:
and international understanding, 748
Bilateral consultations for improvement, 745
History, Geography, and Social Studies, summary of school programmes, 746
Hive:
Smith, 1093
W.B.C., 1091
H.M. Forces, career, 921
Hoary pepperwort, control of, 78
Hodgson, Sir E. H. (Chairman): Committee on Weights and Measures Legislation, report, 43
Holford, W. G.: Design in town and village, 141
Holidays with Pay Act, 64, 571
Holland, E. Milner: Savoy Hotel Ltd. and Berkeley Hotel Co. Ltd., report, 970
Holland House. *See* London County Council.
Holliday, L. G.: Switzerland, economic survey, 463, 1205
Holliday, P.: Witches' broom disease of cacao, 346
Hollingworth, S. E.: Northampton sand ironstone, 123
Hollyfield, J. P.: Annotated bibliography of the fossil mammals of Africa, 854
Holme, R. V.: Fertiliser requirements of Kenya highlands, 861
Holmes, G. D.: Chemical control of weeds in forest nursery seedbeds, 368
Holmes, M.: Crown Jewels in the Wakefield Tower, 763, 1225
Holmes, S. C. A.: Geology of the country around Chatham, 899
Holstein, M. H.: Biology of Anopheles Gambiae, 497, 1012
Home:
Department, Estimates, 15, 214, 262, 522, 783, 1036
Economics and its teaching, material on, 752
Freezing of fruit and vegetables, 333, 1093
Guard Act, 61
Bill, 7, 34
Office publications, 127, 379, 638, 903, 1144
Home-canned Fruit and Vegetables Order, revocation, 619
Homecraft in secondary schools, 443
Home-grown Cereals Deficiency Payments Scheme, 850, 882
Homeless Children. *See* Monograph series.
Homes, new, for old, 1152
Honduras, economic survey, 970
Honey from hive to market, 849
Honeyman, H. L.:
Dunstanburgh Castle, guide, 1225
Warkworth Castle, guide, 1018
Hong Kong:
Colonial reports, 91, 344, 601, 861, 1109
Corona Library, 345
S.R.O. & S.I. Revised, 192
Hong Kong-Japan Open Accounts, procedure for liquidation, Exchange of Notes with Japan, 288
Honours of Scotland, postcard, 763
Honours, Decorations, and Medals:
Committee on Grant of, reports, 47, 217, 1059, 1217
Fire Brigade Medals, institution of, 814, 982
Korea Medal, institution of, 50, 217
Hopfen, H. J.: Small farm implements, 751
Hopkins, G. H. E.:
Early literature on Mallophaga, 853
Genera and species of Mallophaga, check list, 336
Mosquitos of the Ethiopian region, 336
Rothschild Collection of fleas, 593
Hopkins, R. V. M. (Chairman): Cotton Import Committee, reports, 291, 554
Hopkinson, R. C.: Study of interreflection of daylight using model rooms and artificial skies, 955
Hops:
Marketing scheme, 1096
Verticillium wilt of 587

Hopwood, A. T.: Annotated bibliography of fossil mammals of Africa, 854
Hopworthy Farm occupation level crossing, railway accident, 210
Horden Colliery, explosion, 1061
Hormone fattening of cockerels, 78
Hornby, H. E.: Animal trypanosomiasis in Eastern Africa, 342
Horner, F.:
Measurements of atmospheric noise at high frequencies, 698
Siting of direction-finding stations, 440
Horse-breeding Act, 310
Horse-flies of the Ethiopian region, 336, 854
Horsemastership, Equitation, and Animal Transport, Manual of, 241
Horses, Slaughter of, committee report, 559
Horticultural Produce (Sales on Commission) Act, 570
Horticulture. *See* Agriculture.
Horton, C. E. (Chairman): Conference on centrimetric aerials for marine navigational radar, proceedings, 466
Hosiery and other knitted goods, Census of Production, 459
Hospital:
and Specialist Services, England and Wales, Statistics, 378, 638, 902
Boards and Management Committees Estimates, Select Committee report, 264
Costing returns, 378, 636, 638, 902, 1143
Working Party report, 1143
Directory, Scottish, 124, 637, 1142
Endowments:
Fund, accounts, 18, 125, 263, 357, 518, 638, 779, 798, 902
Commission, report, 1069, 1141
(Scotland) Act, 567
Bill, 510, 515, 527, 528, 537, 541, 542, 644
In-patients Statistics, 897, 902, 1139
National Insurance Advisory Committee, report, 298
Morbidity statistics, 122
of St. Mary Magdalen (Colchester) Charity Scheme Confirmation Act, 573
Bill, 512, 542
of the Blessed Trinity (Guildford) Charity Scheme Confirmation Act, 573
Bill, 512, 542
Pharmaceutical Service, report, 1143
Hospital, Local Authority, and General Practitioner Services, report on cooperation, 377
Hospitals:
Analysis of running costs, 901, 1142
Directory, England and Wales, 378
Internal Administration Committee, report, 901
Hospitals (*continued*):
Reception and welfare of in-patients, 637
Hot water:
Service systems, 894
Treatment of plants, 1091
Hotel:
and Catering:
Industry, management, 142
Occupations, careers, 659
Industry in the U.S.A., 101
Proprietors (Liabilities and Rights) Bill, 1054
Houghton-le-Spring, Boundary Commission report, 29
House:
Building:
Cost of, 387
Economy in, 377
Machines for handling materials, 1185
Productivity, 245, 698
Insulation, 761
Interiors, 547, 550
Maintenance, cost of, 549
of Commons:
Accommodation, Select Committee reports, 535, 644, 789, 907
Bills, 30, 281, 541, 799, 1053
Debates, 8, 25, 30, 257, 276, 281, 518, 536, 540, 778, 796, 799, 1031, 1032, 1043, 1052
Disqualification Bill, 1056
Index to Bills, Reports, etc., 8, 18
Journal, 256, 518, 778, 1032, 1043
Kitchen and Refreshment Rooms, 14, 19, 131, 271, 527, 644, 789, 792, 1039, 1148
Library Document, 1082, 1147
Members':
Expenses, Select Committee reports, 535, 644, 782, 907
Fund Accounts, 10, 131, 258, 384, 519, 644, 907, 1036, 1148,
Reports, 14, 131, 1040, 1148
Model Clauses, 574
Papers, 8, 256, 518, 778, 1031
Private Bills, 530, 645
Public:
Accounts, reports, 645, 781, 784, 789, 792
Business, manual of procedure, 30
Publications and Debates, report, 790, 908
Sessional Printed Papers, 8, 518, 645, 1031, 1149
Standing:
Committee:
Debates, 8, 257, 277, 281, 537, 541, 778, 797, 1032, 1043, 1053
Returns, 276, 536, 1042, 1149

House (*continued*):
of Commons (*continued*):
Standing (*continued*):
Orders, 8, 259, 520, 538, 772, 773, 909, 1031, 1149
Works of art in, 1226
of Lords:
Debates, 1, 6, 8, 255, 256, 509, 516, 517, 769, 777, 778, 1025, 1027, 1131
Journal, 17, 509, 769, 1025, 1031
Manuscripts, 511, 647
Model Clauses, 574
Offices, Select Committee reports, 1, 5, 7, 133, 250, 253, 256, 386, 511, 514, 517, 647, 773, 778, 1026, 1028, 1031, 1149
Papers and Bills, 1, 249, 509, 769, 1025
Personal Bills Committee, reports, 513, 772
Procedure of the House, 1, 133
Roll of the Lords Spiritual and Temporal, 255
Select Committee:
Minutes, 772
Reports, 770, 776, 908
Special Orders Committee, reports, 250, 253, 256, 386, 510, 512, 514, 515, 517, 770, 771, 772, 773, 774, 775, 776, 777, 778, 909, 1026, 1027, 1028, 1029, 1030, 1031, 1149
Standing Orders, 5, 772, 773, 909
Report, 515, 647
Select Committee minutes, 515, 647
Painter and decorator, career, 398
Household:
Standards of living in less developed areas, enquiries into, 482
Textiles:
Census of Production, 459
Utility, schedule, 203
Houses, 387, 649
and flats, financing and repair, 910
Design and workmanship of non-traditional, 123
Equipment, 125, 377, 637, 901
for ex-Servicemen, 1150
held on ground lease, 983
Increase in cost of maintaining, 637
Next step, 565, 649
of Parliament by floodlight, postcard, 763
owned by local authorities in Scotland, rents of, 818
saving softwood, 648, 649
Selling price and rental, 648
to be built under licence, 387, 648
Housesteads Roman Fort, guide, 504
House-to-House Collection Act, 312
Housing:
Accommodation:
Grants for improvement or conversion, 912
Housing: (*continued*):
Accommodation (*continued*):
Improvement and conversion of, memo, 910
Act, 63, 308, 312, 387, 571, 833
Bill, 253, 254, 269, 278, 282, 283, 284, 384
Accounts, 217, 473, 625, 982, 1217
Advisory Committee report on transfers, exchanges and rents, 650
and building statistics for Europe, 993
and development, roads and streets, 287
and Local Government, Ministry of, publications, 133, 387, 647, 909, 1150
Report, 1072, 1182
See also Local Government and Planning.
and Town and Country Planning, bulletin, 225, 484, 993
(Emergency Powers) Act, 312
England, S.R.O. & S.I. Revised, 192
Estimates, 15, 215, 262, 522, 649, 783 1036
(Financial and Miscellaneous Provisions) Act, reports, 21, 165, 530, 649, 790, 912
(Financial Provisions) Act, 832
for special purposes, 165
Handbook, Scottish, 125, 377, 1142
in British African territories, 862
Management, career, 1157
Manual, technical appendices, 165, 244
Medals, 911
of calves, 849
of pigs, 588
of small domestic livestock, 333
of special groups, 377
Policy, Scotland, 565, 702
Procedure, 377
Progress, European, 990
Repairs and Rents Act, 829
Bill, 544, 772, 773, 775, 785, 797, 801, 802, 907, 912
Financial resolution, 804
Grants for improvements and conversions, 912
Circulars, 910, 911
Questions and answers, 901, 912
(Repairs and Rents) (Scotland) Act, 829
Bill, 544, 773, 774, 787, 797, 801, 803, 900, 907
Memoranda, 900
Money resolution, 804
Report, 52
Requisitioned properties in use for, 650
Returns:
England and Wales, 37, 43, 50, 56, 133, 165, 287, 292, 299, 305, 387, 547, 552, 558, 564, 649, 806, 811, 817, 823, 900, 1059, 1064, 1071, 1075, 1151
Appendix B, 165, 387, 417, 649, 912, 1151

1951-5 | HOU-INT

HOU— INDEX 1951-5

Housing (*continued*):
Returns (*continued*):
Scotland, 37, 43, 50, 56, 124, 189, 288, 292, 299, 305, 444, 547, 552, 558, 564, 703, 806, 807, 811, 823, 900, 1058, 1064, 1071, 1075, 1141
Revenue Account; Repairs Account, 647
Scotland, S.R.O. & S.I., Revised, 192
(Scotland) Act, 308
Bill, 254, 282, 284
Circulars, 376, 900
Memo, 124
Subsidies:
Bill, 1056
See also Housing (Financial and Miscellaneous Provisions).
Summaries, 35, 40, 41, 46, 48, 53, 54, 58, 124, 125, 133, 165, 189, 286, 289, 290, 295, 297, 301, 302, 305, 388, 444, 545, 548, 550, 554, 556, 560, 566, 634, 649, 703, 804, 808, 810, 814, 815, 819, 822, 827, 900, 912, 1057, 1061, 1062, 1066, 1069, 1072, 1074, 1077, 1141, 1142, 1151
(Temporary Accommodation) Act, accounts, 9, 244, 258, 505, 522, 763, 781, 1019, 1037, 1226
(Temporary Prohibition of Sale of Small Houses) (Scotland) Bill, 34
Housing-estate roads, construction of, 1188
How the United Nations:
Began, 484
Met the challenge of Korea, 737
How to:
Buy furniture, 134
Claim payments under the Town and Country Planning Act, 1152
Howe, R. W.: Detection of insects by their carbon dioxide production, 440
Howell, W. G. R.: Sweden, economic survey, 970
Howitt, Sir H. (Chairman):
Advisory Committee on development of pig production, report, 1074
Pay and Organisation of Civil Service Medical Staffs Committee, report, 218
Huddersfield Corporation Act, 573
Hudson Bay Marine Insurance Rates, reports 95, 348, 605, 865, 1117
Hudson, Rt. Hon. Sir R. J. (Chairman): Judicial Commission, report on Southern and Northern Rhodesia and Nyasaland, 303
Hugh-Jones, P.: Social consequences of pneumoconiosis among coalminers in South Wales, 169
Hull, H. (President): Transport Tribunal, British Transport Passenger Charges Scheme, proceedings, 721
Hulme, A. C.: Dehydration of English fruit, 438
Human:
Relations in industry, 401, 955
Rights:
and fundamental freedoms, Convention for protection of, 36, 110, 293, 364, 562, 625, 817, 887
Commission on:
Checklist of documents, 729
Reports, 480, 481, 482, 733, 990
Draft Covenants, 744
Unesco Exhibition album, 231
Universal declarations of, 748
Impact of, 484, 737
Message of, 484
Yearbook, 225, 484, 993
Humanism and education in east and west, 749, 1008
Humber:
Conservancy Act, 66
Pollution of, 332
Humidity:
Measurement of, 687, 1174
of the upper troposphere and lower stratosphere over Southern England, 421
Hummel, F. C.:
Forest records, general volume tables, Great Britain, 368
Revised yield tables for conifers in Great Britain, 631
Volume-basal area line, 1133
Hundred of Salford, report of Departmental Committee on Court of Record, 54, 164
Hungarian property, Treasury directions, 817, 818, 982, 1063, 1217
Hungary:
Settlement of certain financial matters, 821, 887
Treatment of aircraft and crew of U.S.A., Orders, 919
See also Bulgaria.
Hunt, K. E.: Organisation of recording and estimating statistics for Colonial agriculture, 344
Hunter Blair, C. H.:
Dunstanburgh Castle, guide, 1225
Warkworth Castle, guide, 1018
Huntingdon:
and Offord and Buckden, railway accident, 1210
Railway accident, 467
Huntingdon, G. W. B.: Nandi work and culture, 92
Huntly Castle, guide, 1018
Huq, M. S. : Compulsory education in Pakistan, 1003
Hurcomb, Lord (Chairman): Committee on Bird Sanctuaries in Royal Parks, reports, 244, 762, 1225
Hurst, His Honour Sir G. (Chairman): Departmental Committee on Adoption of Children, report, 819
Hurstfield, J.: Control of raw materials, 593

INDEX 1951-5 —IMP

Husk or hoose in calves, 587, 1094
Hussein, Dr. A.: Mission on rural community organisation and development in the Caribbean area and Mexico, report, 729
Hutson, L. W. (Chairman): Sub-committee of Scottish Building Costs Committee, report on increase in costs of maintaining houses, 637
Hutton, Sir M. (Chairman): Tax Paid Stocks Committee, report, 549
Hybrid maize (corn), 356
Tests in Mediterranean and European countries, progress report, 751
Hydraulics Research Board, reports, 440, 697, 955, 1187
Hydrocarbon oils, S.R.O. & S.I. Revised, 192
Hydro-electric:
Development (Scotland):
Act, 308
Bill, 34, 250, 263, 278, 385
Guarantees given:
on loans proposed to be raised, and accounts, 17, 217, 265, 473, 526, 726, 787, 982, 1041, 1045, 1046, 1049, 1217
on stock issued, 1050, 1051, 1218
North of Scotland Hydro-electric Board Constructional Schemes, explanatory memos, 35, 37, 38, 46, 49, 57, 189, 286, 290, 292, 297, 304, 444, 546, 547, 548, 554, 702, 811, 815, 827, 959, 1062, 1064, 1067, 1072, 1197
S.R.O. & S.I. Revised, 193
Potential in Europe, 732
Hydrogen cyanide fumigation:
Regulations, 381
S.R.O. & S.I. Revised, 193
Hydrometric statistics for British rivers, 389, 1152
Hygiene in catering establishments, 104
Hypnotism Act, 308
Bill, 253, 269, 278, 281, 283, 385

I

Iban agriculture, 1109
ICAO. *See* International Civil Aviation Organisation.
Ice:
Accretion on aircraft, 170, 421
Census of Production, 201, 967
Ice-Cream, 103
Census of Production, 460, 1201
Heat Treatment, etc. Regulations, 125, 126, 378, 379
Iceland:
Air navigation services in, 138
Iceland (*continued*):
Air Transport Services Agreement, 36, 110
Economic conditions, 516
Foreign Trade Statistical Bulletins, 356, 517, 878
Ilchester, Rt. Hon. Earl of (Chairman): Royal Commission on Ancient and Historical Monuments, report on West Dorset, 303
Illingworth, J. R.: Survey of buildings in sandstone in Scotland, 698
Illiteracy, education, libraries, etc., basic facts and figures, 744
Illness among schoolchildren, effect of air disinfection with ultra-violet irradiation, 940
Illumination and visual performance, Relation between, 679
Immigration policy, elements of 990
Immunological procedures for Service personnel, 501, 1016
Impact:
of science on society, 231, 492, 746, 1004
of the Universal Declaration of Human Rights, 484, 737
Imperial:
Calendar. *See* British Imperial Calendar.
Institute, report, 353
State crown, postcard, 762
War:
Graves Commission, reports, 134, 389, 650, 913, 1153
Museum:
Act, 1079
Bill, 803, 1026
Bill and Trustee Savings Banks (Pensions) Bill, 1036, 1043, 1148
Implement shed, 1092
Import:
and export trade, summaries, 349
Duties:
Act, 311
Proposal, 566, 714
Duty, according relief to Canadian Government, 1067
Licences, 968, 1203
Revocation, 205
List, Key relating to Standard International Trade Classification, 968, 1203
of British books into Yugoslavia, 1062
Restrictions, discriminatory application of, 634
Import, Export, and Customs Powers (Defence) Act, 64
Importation of educational scientific and cultural materials, 492
Improvement:
Grants, 1150
of Live Stock (Licensing of Bulls) Act, 63

IMP— INDEX 1951-5

Improvements and conversions, grants for, 912
Incandescent mantles, Census of Production, 201, 967
Incendiary bomb instructional diagrams, 128
Incentives: some experimental studies, 420
Income:
and expenditure, national, statistics, 593
Tax:
Act, 308
Bill, 7, 249, 250, 282
and Finance Acts, with statutory regulations, etc., 390
Acts:
Case commentaries, 651, 1154
Supplements, 135, 641, 915, 1154
and Death Duties on woodlands, 893
Consolidation Bill, drafts, 40, 217
(including Surtax), S.R.O. & S.I. Revised, 193
Tables of, on net income, 135
Wear and tear allowances for machinery or plant, 651
Taxes in the Commonwealth, 135, 390, 651, 915, 1154
Incomes, national and per capita of 70 countries, 488
Increase:
in cost of maintaining houses, 637
of Rent and Mortgage Interest (Restrictions) Act, 62, 571
Increased thermal efficiency of solid fuel through gasification, 879
Incubation and hatchery practice, 332, 849
Incumbents (Discipline) and Church Dignitaries (Retirement) Amendment Measure, 511, 574, 594
Ecclesiastical Committee reports, 511, 594
Independent Television Authority:
Licence granted, 1064
Report and accounts, 1050, 1181
Indeterminate sentence, 993
Index:
Bibliographicus, 492, 746
of place names, 1138
Translationum, 231, 492, 746, 1004
India:
Air Services Agreement, 287, 339, 556, 595, 823, 974
Economic:
Development with stability, 920
Survey, 716
Filmstrip and lecture notes, 134
Financial Agreement, 289, 348, 561, 604
Office Library, guide, 348
Picture set, 134
Public finance survey, 486
S.R.O. & S.I. Revised, 193
Stock, S.R.O. & S.I. Revised, 193
Indian:
Embroidery, 239
Indian (*continued*):
Music, recorded classical and traditional, catalogue, 493
Ocean, weather in, 421
Painting in the Punjab hills, 499
Indian Enterprise, wreck report, 213
Indices of heat stress, 1171
Indictments (Amendments) Bill, 1057
Indo-China, documents of discussion at Geneva conference, 819, 887
Indonesia:
Commercial conditions, 462
Peaceful settlement in, 486
Industrial:
and Agricultural Rates Bill, 1053
and allied research applications, radio isotope techniques, 455
and Provident Societies:
Act, 61, 308, 569
(Amendment) Act, 309, 311, 829
Bill, 773, 787, 797, 800, 801, 907
(No. 1) Bill, 34, 250, 262, 278, 282, 385
and Service medicine, application of scientific methods to, 169
Assurance:
Act, 831
and Friendly Societies Act, 65, 571, 833
Commissioner's reports, 630, 893, 1134
Statistical summaries, 118, 370
Censuses:
and related inquiries, 1000
in Western Europe, 101
Civil Defence Service, 641
Coal Consumer's Council and Domestic Coal Consumers' Council, reports, 21, 120, 270, 371, 530, 633, 790, 895, 1045, 1134
Controls in areas of occupation in Germany, agreement, 306
Court:
Acts, reports, 666, 808, 809, 824, 825, 924
Awards, 146, 401, 662, 924, 1160
Report, 298, 405
Courts:
Act, 62, 570
Reports, 44, 149, 1057, 1059, 1063, 1162
Motor dispute, 553, 666
Printing dispute, 560, 666
Wages and salaries of railwaymen, 38, 149
Delegation to Burma, report, 971
Design, Council of, publications, 134, 389, 650, 914, 1153
Development in Jamaica, Trinidad, Barbados, and British Guiana, 602
Diseases (Benefit) Act, 829
Bill, 544, 771, 782, 797, 907
Disputes Tribunal, awards, 150, 405, 666, 928, 1162

INDEX 1951-5 —INT

Industrial (*continued*):
Fatigue Research Board, reports, 419, 679
Fibres, production trade and consumption, 94, 347, 604, 864, 1111
Health:
Research Board, reports, 420, 679
Services, 39, 217
Injuries:
Advisory Council report on Raynaud's Phenomenon, 828
Fund, account, 20, 171
Payment for Compensation, Convention with Denmark, 803
Organisation and Development:
Act, 833
Accounts, 257, 261, 273, 462, 535, 715, 795, 799, 968, 1033, 1203
Bill, 800
S.R.O. & S.I. Revised, 193
Power, Kelvin Hall, Glasgow, guide-catalogue, 103
Production:
Basic statistics, 618
Index numbers, 228
Relations handbook, 154, 676
Research, Estimates, 523, 784, 1036
Industries, Classification of, Census, 374
Industry:
and employment in Scotland, 43, 189, 292, 444, 550, 703, 809, 959, 1062, 1192
Estimates, 15, 263
Inebriate, S.R.O. & S.I. Revised, 193
Infants' and Girls' Utility Clothing Schedules, 203
Infection in hospitals, cross, control of, 169
Infectious diseases. *See* Registrar-General's returns.
Infective hepatitis, 169
Inferior Court, England, S.R.O. & S.I. Revised, 193
Inflammable textile fabrics, S.R.O. & S.I. Revised, 193
Influenza:
Bulletin, 754
Expert committee report, 756
Review of current research, 755
Information:
Central Office of, publications, 134, 389, 651, 914, 1153
Centres, Civil Defence, 376
Infra-red:
for chicks and piglets, 847
Spectroscopy, bibliography, 1195
Ingram, M.: Whalemeat bacteriology and hygiene, 696
Ingrams, H.: Hong Kong, 345
Inheritance (Family Provision) Act, 312
Injuries in War (Compensation), S.R.O. & S.I. Revised, 193
Injury in Man, with special reference to wound shock, 169
Ink, Census of Production, 200, 966
Inland:
Revenue:
Commissioners' reports, 34, 135, 286, 473, 545, 726, 804, 982, 1057, 1154
Publications, 135, 390, 651, 914, 1154
Transport Committee, draft Customs Convention, 222
Water:
Survey Committee report, 125
Transport in Europe and U.S.A., 993
Innkeepers' liability, Law Reform Committee report, 813, 939
Inoculation and vaccination certificate requirements, 497
Inquisitions post mortem, calendars, 701, 1181
Insect:
Infestation of stored food products in Nigeria, 344
Pests of crops in England and Wales, 850
Insecticides:
Expert committee reports, 238, 498, 756
Manual of specifications, 755
Insecticides, fungicides and herbicides, specifications and methods for analysis, 81
Insects:
and mites in farm-stored grain, 847
infesting bacon and hams, 78
In-Service training:
in social welfare, 484
in the United Nations and the specialised agencies, 737
Insignia of Orders, Decorations, etc., instructions regarding wearing, 1016
Inspection of Churches Measure, 778, 855, 1082
Ecclesiastical Committee report, 778, 855
Instability in export markets of under-developed countries, 737
Installing solid fuel appliances, 761
Institution of Mechanical Engineers Act, 834
Instrument rating, 339, 595
Insulin, supply of, Monopolies Commission report, 269, 274
Insurance:
and re-insurance, agreement with Italy, 817
Careers, 142, 920
Contracts (War Settlement) Act, 308
Bill, 250, 282
S.R.O. & S.I. Revised, 193
Insured letters and boxes, agreement, 565
Intensive methods of poultry management, 588
Interaction of floors and beams in multi-storey buildings, 1187
Inter-Agency agreements, etc., 994
Inter-Allied Reparation Agency, report, 393

INT-JUS | 1951-5

Inter-Commonwealth postgraduate scholarships in science, 82
Inter-Latin-American trade, 994
Interlingual scientific and technical dictionaries, bibliography, 231, 1003
Report, 231
Internal:
Administration of hospitals, committee report, 901
Ballistics, 196
Corrosion of concrete sewer pipes, 1185
Financial situation, 356
Migration, England and Wales, 122
Plastering, avoiding defects in, 953
International:
Airport charges, 918
Arbitral Awards, reports, 484, 737
Bank for reconstruction and development, guarantee on loans proposed, 1039
Bibliography of translations, 492
Bureau of Education, publications, 230, 491, 492, 745, 746, 1006
Children's Emergency Fund, 222, 225, 480, 481, 729, 733, 735, 990
Civil:
Aviation Organisation, publications, 138, 393, 655, 917
Service, Advisory Board reports, 225, 737
Colour Woodcut Exhibition, catalogue, 1014
Commodity problems, review, 225, 486, 737, 994
Conference:
of science abstracting, 231
on pollution of the sea by oil, 816, 974
Conventions on Maritime Law, 561
Court of Justice, publications, 141, 396, 757, 919
What the United Nations is doing, 490
See also Court of International Justice.
Criminal Jurisdiction, committee reports, 484, 993
Digest of Health Legislation, 237, 497, 754, 1012
Directory of Adult Education, 1002
Economic stability, measures for, 485
Exchange of publications, handbook, 492
Finance Corporation Act, 1080
Bill, 1028, 1055
Articles of Agreement and explanatory memo, 1068, 1218
Financial statistics, 658, 920
Institute of Administrative Sciences, 657
Jurisdiction, Tangier zone, reform, 1071
Labour Conference:
Proposed action, 48, 154, 549, 559, 676, 808, 937, 1062 1169
International (*continued*):
Labour Conference (*continued*):
Reports, 40, 154, 289, 416, 552, 566, 676, 1059, 1077, 1169
Law Commission, reports, 225, 735, 737, 993
Meteorological Code, 1172
Migrants, sex and age, 996
Migration statistics, 999
Military Tribunal, proceedings, 417
Monetary Fund, publications, 658, 920
Performance comparison in the field of logging, 1009
Pharmacopoeia, 237
Expert committee report, 498
Political Science Abstracts, 492, 746, 1005
Review of Criminal Policy, 737, 994
Rice Commission Working Party reports:
Fertilisers, 1008
Rice breeding, 751
Road Transport, general agreement, 994
Sanitary Regulations, 238
Special committee proceedings, 498
Scientific Organisations, directory, 231, 1005
Seminar on statistical organisation, 741
Situation, correspondence with Soviet Government, 563, 565, 566, 625, 804, 887
Social Science Bulletin, 231, 492, 746, 1005
Standards:
and recommended practices, 395, 656, 918
in basic industrial statistics, 999
Rules of the air, 918
Status of South West Africa, 141
Tax Agreements, 225, 484
Telecommunication Convention and related documents, 558, 689
Tin Agreement, 817, 887
Trade, 634, 896
Direction of, 730, 987
Organisation, publications, 397
Statistics, Yearbook, 225, 484, 737, 994
Veterinary Congress, report, 333
Wheat:
Council, report, 658
Office, publications, 141
Yearbook of Education, 231, 746, 1005
Interpretation:
Act, 308
of Peace Treaties with Bulgaria, Hungary, and Roumania, 141
Interreflection of daylight using model rooms and artificial skies, 955
Interrelations of cultures, 1008
Intertropical front, 421
Intestates' Estates Act, 308
Bill, 254, 269, 278, 281, 284, 385

Intoxicating Liquor:
(Sales to Persons under Eighteen) Act, 310
S.R.O. & S.I. Revised, 193
Intracranial Gliomata, 940
Intra-European investments, 101
Introducing East Africa, 914
Inventions:
and Designs (Crown Use) Bill, 516
Prolongation of patents, agreement with Italy, 49
Inventories of apparatus and materials for teaching science, 492, 1005
Invercauld, wreck report, 213
Inverness:
Census, 898
County Council (Armadale Pier and Harbour, etc.) Order Confirmation Act, 66
Harbour Order Confirmation Act, 833
Bill, 544
Investigation of atmospheric pollution, 1187
Investigations on building fires, 184, 698
Investment for peace, 1127
Investments in overseas territories in Africa south of the Sahara, 101
Ionian Islands earthquake, Civil Defence aspects, 903
Ionospheric effects on solar flares, 181
Ipswich, Boundary Commission report, 524
Iran:
Export licence revocation order, 204
Payments relations, arrangements to govern, 825, 887, 1057, 1127
Public Finance Information Papers, 227
Settlement of oil dispute, correspondence concerning proposals, 303, 364
Iraq:
Air Services Agreement, 56, 110
British Commonwealth war graves, agreement, 1078, 1127
Compulsory education, 233
Economic survey, 716
Financial:
Arrangements, 41, 110, 302, 364
Claims, settlement of, 1078, 1127
Public Finance Information Papers, 227
Railway system, termination of agreement, 300, 364
Special agreement with U.K. 1071, 1079, 1127
Transfer of certain property in the Port of Basra, 559, 626
Ireland:
Air Services agreement, 556, 595
Economic conditions, 877
Foreign Trade Statistical Bulletins, 355, 617, 878
Trade Agreement, new Annex to, 555, 604
Irish:
Land Purchase Fund, accounts, 8, 171, 256, 422, 519, 681, 779, 795, 942, 1050 1173
Irish (*continued*):
Sailors and Soldiers Land Trust:
Accounts, 217, 473, 726, 982, 1218
Act, 308
Bill, 252, 284
Irk Valley Junction, railway accident, 722
Iron:
and Steel:
Act, 567
Bill, 285, 511, 512, 541, 542
Accounts, 1038, 1218
Guarantees given:
on loans proposed to be raised 14, 217, 260, 266, 270, 473, 520, 526, 726
on stock issued, 14, 16, 27, 120, 217, 262, 275, 473
Arbitration Tribunal Rules, 168
Board, report, 1042, 1195
Consumers' Council, reports, 280, 455, 530, 710
Corporation, report and accounts, 274, 371, 529, 710
Distribution Scheme, 455, 710
Goods, licences, 202, 461, 714, 1203
Holding Realisation Agency:
Proposals to sell:
Holdings, 559, 562, 563, 726, 804, 813, 814, 815, 822, 825, 982, 1058, 1060, 1061, 1065, 1067, 1070, 1078, 1218
Securities, 814, 982
Report and accounts, 1037, 1218
Industry, 299, 455
Development of, 1035, 1195
Melting and rolling, Census of Production, 712
Technology, important developments, 989
Foundries, Census of Production, 458
Ironstone Restoration Fund, explanatory memo, 388, 1151
Irrigation, 849
in the United States, Community organisation for, 750
Need, calculation of, 850
Irvine, Sir J. C. (Chairman): Inter-University Council, report on higher education in the Colonies, 93
Irvine, T. W.: Forest records: General volume tables for Great Britain, 368
Irving, D. J. M.: Hayti, economic survey, 716
Irwin, J.: Shawls, 1221
Isidro, A.: Compulsory education in the Philippines, 748
Islamic law in Africa, 1109
Island of Arran Piers Order Confirmation Act, 66
Bill, 1, 31
Islandmagee, wreck report, 1213
Isle of Man (Customs) Acts, 60, 308, 567 829, 1079

Isle of Man (Customs) Acts (*continued*):
Bills, 6, 33, 254, 284, 515, 543, 776, 802, 1026, 1054
S.R.O. & S.I. Revised, 193
Israel:
Air Services agreement 38, 110
Community settlements, Monograph and report, 987
Conversion into sterling of earnings of BOAC and Cyprus Airways, 551, 626
Reciprocal extension of periods of priority stipulated in Industrial Property Convention, 42, 111
Training of Civil Service, 1000
It pays to co-operate, filmstrips, 914
Italian:
Campaign, 241
Colonies, former, report on disposal, 551, 624
Gothic sculpture, 499
Italy:
Air Services agreement, 46, 111
Allocation of a share in proceeds of sale of certain valuables presumed looted by German Forces, 48, 111
British Commonwealth War Graves, agreement, 1070, 1127
Campaign in, 241
Carriage of dangerous goods in aircraft, 58, 111
Consular Convention, 815, 887
Country Monograph, 987
Cultural Convention, 286, 364, 552, 560, 626
Disposal:
and future administration of Italian private property in Cyrenaica, 58, 111
of Italian private property in:
Cyrenaica and Tripolitania, 50, 111
Eritrea, 290, 364
Early successes against, 854, 961
Economic:
Conditions, 877
Survey, 463, 1204
Extension of the International Accord on German-owned Patents, 38, 111
Foreign Trade Statistical Bulletins, 355, 356, 617, 878
Insurance and re-insurance agreement, 817, 887
Libraries and properties in Italy, agreement, 558, 626
Prolongations of Patents for inventions, 49, 111, 552, 626
Public Finance Information Papers, 227
Reciprocal payment of compensation, war injuries, Southern Rhodesia, 557, 626
Recognition of certain organisations to implement the provisions of the Cultural Convention, 626
Italy (*continued*):
Recovery of submarine cable lying disused between Gibraltar and Casablanca, 297, 364
Revision of certain clauses of the Italian Peace Treaty, 287
Salvage of H.M.S. *Spartan*, 545, 626
Social Insurance Convention, 288, 364, 555, 626
Sterling Payments agreement, 550, 565, 626
Application to Free Territory of Trieste, 36, 111
Transfer of the Provisional Administration of Somalia, 1065, 1128
Ivens, G. W.: Chemical control of weeds in forest nursery seedbeds, 368

J

Jackdaw. *See* Magpie.
Jacks, G. V.: Rice soils and fertilisers, annotated bibliography, 1010
Jamaica:
Colonial reports, 90, 343, 600, 860
Economic survey, 602
S.R.O. & S.I. Revised, 193
Social welfare work, 1006
Jamaica, Trinidad, Barbados, and British Guiana, industrial development, 602
James Hamilton's Trust Scheme:
Memo, 958
Order in Council, 1190
James V, letters of, 961
Jameson, H.: Diurnal variation of pressure in the Mediterranean, 421
Jamieson, K. D.: Peru, economic survey, 1204
Japan:
Air Services agreement, 549, 560, 626
Arms and armour of old Japan, 239
Commercial conditions, 205
Economic survey, 716
Exercise of criminal jurisdiction over United Nations Forces, 807
Liquidation of the Hong-Kong-Japan Open Account, procedure, 288, 364
Pre-war Guarantee Deposits of British Insurance Companies in Japan, 56, 111
Settlement:
of disputes, 303, 364
of the Pre-war External Bonded Debts, 547, 626
Status of United Nations Forces, 818
Sterling Payments Agreement, 55, 111, 298, 302, 364, 547, 626, 805, 807, 825, 887, 1068, 1072, 1073, 1076, 1077, 1078, 1128
Treaty of Peace, 56, 111, 298, 364
Draft, 49, 50, 52, 111

Japanese:
Colour prints, 499
Larch in Great Britain, General Volume Tables, 368
Larches at Dunkeld, 892
Treaty of Peace Act, 61
Bill, 7, 34
Accounts, 787, 969, 1033, 1046, 1204
Jarlshof, guide, 762
Jay. *See* Magpie.
Jay, K. E. B.:
Atomic Energy Research at Harwell, 1221
Britain's Atomic Factories, 963
Jebb, Sir Gladwyn, speeches, United Nations resolution on Chinese intervention in Korea, 39
Jeffers, J. N. R.:
Forest Records, General volume tables for Great Britain, 368
Volume table for small hardwood trees, 892
Jeffery, J. R.:
External migration, 634
Internal migration, 122
Jefferys, J. B.: Productivity in the distributive trade in Europe, 879
Jellies, standard, for table, 1095
Jenkins, Rt. Hon. Lord (Chairman): Law Reform Committee, reports, 551, 813, 824
Jephcott, Sir H. (Chairman): Synthetic Detergents Committee, report, 913
Jersey, application of Social Security Agreement with France, 306, 562
Jewellery and plate, Census of Production, 200, 967
Jewish thought as a factor in civilisation, 1007
John, Hans: Neue Notiophygidae, 853
John Lysaght's Scunthorpe Works Ltd. and Brymbo Steel Works Ltd., proposal to sell holdings, 1078
John Murray Expedition, scientific reports, 84, 592, 854
John Reid's Trust (Amendment) Scheme, 701, 958
John Summers & Sons Ltd., proposal to sell holdings, 822
Johnson, F. C. (Chairman): Police Council Working Party, report, 382
Joint, E. J.: Italy, economic survey, 1204
Jones, C. B. (Chairman, Welsh Agricultural Land Sub-Commission): Borth Bog Investigation, 331
Jones, F. E.:
Reactions between aggregates and cement, 440, 698
Survey of behaviour in use of asbestos-cement pressure pipes, 440
Jones, F. L.: Fundamental processes of electrical contact phenomena, 698
Jones, G. I.: Basutoland Medicine Murders, report, 42
Jones, J. W.:
Salmon on the Cheshire Dee, 79
Salmon Studies, 79, 588
Scales of roach, age and growth of trout, grayling, etc., 849
Jones, R.:
Food of the whiting and a comparison with that of the haddock, 960
State of Haddock stocks in North Sea and at Faroe, 703
Testing concrete by an ultrasonic pulse technique, 1188
Jones, R. F.: Radar echoes from and turbulence within cumulus and cumulonimbus clouds, 941
Jones, T. A.:
Explosion at Bedwas Colliery, 804
Explosion at Glyncorrwg Colliery, 1071
Jones, T. L.: Ashby-de-la-Zouch Castle, guide, 761
Jongmans, W. J.: Carboniferous flora of Peru, 853
Jordan: agreement for settlement of financial matters outstanding as result of termination of mandate of Palestine, 45, 112
Jordan, H. E. K.: Very remarkable flea from Argentina, 591
Joulia, M. P.: Civilisation of Western Europe and the school, 873
Journalism:
and publishing, careers, 920
Education for, 1005
Joyce, J. R. F.: Anorthoclase from Nigeria, 336
Jubilee Book, National Physical Laboratory, 177
Judges' Remuneration Act, 829
Bill, 542, 544, 771
Judgments, S.R.O. & S.I. Revised, 193
Judicial:
Committee, S.R.O. & S.I. Revised, 193
Offices (Salaries, etc.) Act, 308
Bill, 33, 250
Jugenheimer, R. W.: Results of co-operative hybrid maize tests in European and Mediterranean countries, 751, 1008
Jumsai, M. L. M.: Compulsory education in Thailand, 494
Junior:
Clerkships in the Civil Service, 1107
Secondary education, memo, 1190
Juries Act, 829
Bill, 544, 773, 782, 798, 907
Jury, England, S.R.O. & S.I. Revised, 193
Justice of the Peace, S.R.O. & S.I. Revised, 193
Justices of the Peace:
Act, 572
Act, 1361 (Amendment) Bill, 1054
Justices' Licences for sale by retail of intoxicating liquor and registration of clubs, memo, 513

1951-5 | JUS-LEG

JUS— INDEX 1951-5

Justiciary, High Court of England, S.R.O. & S.I. Revised, 193
Jute:
Census of Production, 201, 967
Manufacture, production, prices and trade, 1112
Juvenile delinquency:
Circular, 639
Comparative survey, 737, 994
Psychiatric aspects, 237

K

Kabaka Mutesa II of Buganda, withdrawal of recognition, 567
Kaberry, P. M.: Women of the grassfields, 344
Kalahari, Western, economic development, 864
Kale as a feedingstuff, 330
Kay, H. D.: Milk pasteurisation, 755
Kayser, J.: Comparative study of 17 major dailies, 1006
Kekwick, R. A.: Separation of protein fractions from human plasma with ether, 940
Kennet of The Dene, Lord (Chairman): Committee on the Draft Customs and Excise Bill, report, 287
Kent:
Census, 896
Water Act, 1081
Bill, 1027, 1149
Kenya:
Colonial reports, 90, 91, 344, 601, 861, 1109
Colony, S.R.O. & S.I. Revised, 193
Native administration, 93
Photo-poster, 651
Proposals for a reconstruction of the Government, 809, 862
Report by Parliamentary Delegation, 808, 862
Studies in applied anthropology, 92
Kenya-Ethiopia Boundary:
Appointment of Commission to demarcate, 40
Extension of period for demarcation, 808, 1066
Kenya-Tanganyika Port Facilities, loan for development, 562
Kerrich, G. J.: Cteniscini of the Old World, 331
Kesteven, G. L.: Fish farming and inland fishery management in rural economy, 1009
Kew Bulletin, 180, 434, 691, 949, 1182
Khosla, J. H. (Chairman): International Commission for Supervision and Control in Laos, report, 1064
Kidd, F.: Storage qualities of late dessert varieties of apples, 438
Kidwelly Castle. guide, 504
Kilmarnock Corporation Order Confirmation Act, 315
Bill, 284
Kilmuir, Viscount (Chairman): Malta Round Table Conference, 1078
Kiln Operator's Handbook, 438
Kimmins, D. E.:
New genus and some new species of the Chauliodini, 853
Revision of the Australian and Tasmanian Gripopterygidae and Nemouridae, 336
Trichoptera of Australia and New Zealand, 593
Kincardine, Census, 898
King, J. D.: Effect of sugar supplements on dental caries in children, 1171
King, J. E.: Otariid seals of the Pacific coast of America, 853
King Gustavus of Sweden, appointment as Honorary Admiral in H.M. Fleet, 167
King Sol, wreck report, 1213
King William III's Banqueting House, Hampton Court Palace, guide, 244
King's:
Birthday:
Honours, 167
Message, 241
Recovery from his recent illness, 501
Regulations:
Admiralty Instructions, 68, 317
Air Council Instructions, 82, 334
Army, 241, 501
King's Lynn Pier and Harbour Order Confirmation Act, 315
Bill, 253, 283
Kingston Aquamarine, wreck report, 978
Kingston-upon-Hull Corporation Act, 315
Kinross. *See* Perth.
Kirk, T. H.: Seasonal change of surface temperature of North Atlantic Ocean, 680
Kirkaldy, Prof. H. S. (Chairman): Wages Council Commission of Inquiry, bread and flour confectionery, 163, 417
Kirkbride, railway accident, 210
Kirkcaldy Burgh:
Boundary Commission report, 39
Extension etc. Order Confirmation Act, 66
Kirkcudbright, Census, 898
Kitchen and Refreshment Rooms, House of Commons, 11, 19, 271, 206, 527, 790, 792, 907, 1039, 1148
Kitchens, school, design, 1119
Kitzinger, E.: Early Medieval art, 1101
Knackers' yards, model byelaws, 881, 882
Knight, Mr. Justice: Aircraft accident report, 859
Knighting, E.: Temperature and humidity gradients in the first 100m. over South East England, 680

INDEX 1951-5 —LAN

Knight-Jones, E. W.: Reproduction of oysters in the rivers Crouch and Roach, 332
Knights of the Garter appointments, 167
Knitted Goods (Manufacture and Supply) Order, etc., register of manufacturers, 204, 462
Knockshinnoch Castle Colliery, report on accident, 40, 120
Knowsley Street Station, railway accident, 467
Knox, J.: Economic geology of the Fife coalfields, 899
Kohan, C. M.: Works and buildings, 337
Korea:
and Indo-China, documents relating to discussion at Geneva conference, 815, 887
Chinese intervention, U.N. resolution, 39, 112
Citation of U.S. Army to Gloucester Regiment, 240
Developments in Armistice negotiations and prisoner of war camps, 297, 365
Further summary of events, 54, 112
Gratuity for service in, 501
How the United Nations met the challenge, 737
Indian proposal for solving prisoner of war problem, 306, 365
Medal, 50, 501, 759
Military situation, Armistice negotiations and prisoner of war camps, 550, 626
Our men in, 502
Reconstruction Agency, financial statements, 483
Settlement of advances in Korean currency made to British Commonwealth Forces, 1061, 1128
Treatment of British prisoners of war, 1119
Unification and Rehabilitation, United Nations Commission, reports, 483, 736, 737, 993
Unified Command, report on Armistice Agreement, 560, 626
United Action in, 229
Korean:
Question:
Neutral Nations Repatriation Commission, reports, 992
Report on, 992
Reconstruction:
Agency, financial report and accounts, 735, 737
Agent-General of the United Nations, report, 736
Economic programme, 992, 994
Kow, T. A.: Preliminary study of the physical, chemical, and biological characteristics of Singapore Straits, 602
Kramp, P. L.: Hydromedusae, 592
Kravis, J. B.: National products, 879
Kuwait Notices, 1128
Kwando river, agreement with Portugal regarding certain natives, 1064
Kwashiorkor in Africa, 497

L

Labelling of Food:
(Amendment) Regulations, 1095
Order, Coronation souvenir boxes, 358
Laboratory:
Apparatus for schools, construction of, 1005
Methods for work with plant and soil nematodes, 81
Techniques in rabies, 1012
Labour:
Administration in the Colonial Territories, 93
and National Service, Ministry of:
Publications, 142, 398, 658, 920, 1157
Reports, 52, 154, 300, 417, 557, 676, 1069, 1169
Conference. *See* International Labour Conference.
Estimates, 15, 215, 262, 522, 783, 1036
Force, statistics, 879
Gazette, 154, 417, 676, 937, 1169
Productivity of the cotton textile industry, 484
Wastage. *See* Sickness absence.
Lace:
Census of Production, 201, 1200
Furnishings Industry, accounts, 273, 535
(Export Promotion Levy), 799, 968
Industry:
(Levy) Accounts, 273, 535
Orders, accounts of sums recovered, 462
(Scientific Research Levy) Order, account, 795, 968
Register of Manufacturers, 200, 457
Ladders, Use of, rescue training, 380
Lake District:
Agreements on afforestation, 1133
Film strip, 687
Lakenheath Fen Investigation, 331
Lamb dysentery, 79, 848
Lambert, H. G. (Chairman): Working Group on bulk handling of home-grown grain, report, 898
Lambert, Margaret: Documents on British Foreign Policy, 106
Laminated beams from two species of timber, 1186
Lamp is lit, 237
Lanark, Census, 898
Lancashire:
Census, 896
County Council (General Powers) Act, 66

LAN— INDEX 1951-5

Lancashire (*continued*):
Steel Corporation Ltd., proposal to sell holdings, 804
Lancaster:
(Court of Chancery), S.R.O. & S.I. Revised, 193
House, guide, 1018
Palatine Court (No. 2) Bill, 253, 254, 269, 278, 282, 283, 284, 385
Lancum, F. H.: Wild mammals and the land, 79
Land:
Acquisition of, S.R.O. & S.I. Revised, 193
and population in East Africa, 345
Charges:
Act, 310
England, S.R.O. & S.I. Revised, 193
Dayaks of Sarawak, 861
Drainage:
Act, 311
and Improvement of Land, S.R.O. & S.I. Revised, 193
in England and Wales, 80
(Surrey County Council (Rive Ditch Improvement)) Order Confirmation Act, 573
Bill, 514, 452
Fertility:
(Research) Fund, accounts, 23, 80, 275, 333, 535, 589
S.R.O. & S.I. Revised, 193
for housing, 387
Mammals of New Guinea, Celebes, and adjacent islands, 854
Purchase (Northern Ireland):
Accounts, 23, 272, 880
S.R.O. & S.I. Revised, 193
Reform:
Defects in agrarian structures as obstacles to economic development, 225
Progress in, 996
Registration, 344
Act, 310
England, S.R.O. & S.I. Revised, 193
Registry, publications, 164, 417, 676, 938, 1170
Resources Scientific Conference proceedings, 478
Settlement Association Ltd., report and accounts on small holdings, 334
Tenure, 345
in Basutoland, 864
in the British and British Protected Territories in South East Asia and the Pacific, 344
Transactions, circulars, 910, 1150
Travelling exhibition, guide-catalogue, 103
Values Duties, S.R.O. & S.I. Revised, 193
Landing:
and taking-off of aircraft in bad weather, 37, 88
Cards, Aliens Order, 905
Landlord and Tenant:
Acts, 62, 311, 829, 832
Bills, 544, 774, 775, 776, 788, 798, 801,803, 907
Houses held on ground lease, 983
Security of tenure of business premises, 983
(Rent Control) Acts, 65, 572
(Requisitioned Land) Act, 64
S.R.O. & S.I. Revised, 193
(War Damage):
Act, 832
(Amendment) Act, 572
Landlords, Tenants, etc., rights and obligations, 848
Langdon, J. N.: Fatigue and boredom in repetitive work, 420
Langley, Brig. C. A.: Railway accident reports, 210, 466, 719, 974, 1209
Language, suggestions for teachers, 873
Lanice, wreck report, 469
Laos, International Commission for supervision and control, 1064, 1077, 1128
Larceny Act, 62, 310
Larch, leaf cast of, 117, 1133
Larches, Japanese and hybrid, adelges attacking, 368
Larsen, K.: National bibliographical services, 749
Larval bionomics of mosquitoes and taxonomy of Culicine larvae, 336
Latham, J. P.: Survey of the behaviour in use of asbestos-cement pressure pipes, 440
Latin:
America:
Caracas, Venezuela, nutrition problems, 1010
Documents on German Foreign Policy, 625
Economic:
Commission reports, 480, 481, 482, 733, 989, 990
Surveys, 482, 990
Selected bibiography, 737
American development policy, international co-operation, 994
Laundry, cleaning, job dyeing, and carpet beating: Census of Production, 460, 1201
Laurie, E. M. O.:
Land mammals of New Guinea, Celebes, and adjacent islands, 854
Mammals collected by Shaw Meyer in New Guinea, 336
Lauwerys, J. A.: History textbooks and international understanding, 748
Law:
and Justice, Estimates, 15, 214, 262, 522, 1036

INDEX 1951-5 —LEG

Law (*continued*):
Barristers and solicitors, careers, 142
of civil liability for damage done by animals, 346, 678
of forestry, 1110
of intestate succession, 50, 168
of Property:
Act, 570
(Amendment) Acts, 311, 570
(Entailed Interests) Act, 311
of succession in Scotland, report of committee of inquiry, 37, 189
Officers' Department, publications, 417
Private International, 1074
Reform:
Committee, reports, 551, 678, 813, 824, 939
(Enforcement of Contracts) Act, 829
Bill, 772
(Limitation of Actions, etc.) Act, 829
Bill, 544, 772, 787, 798, 800, 907
(Married Women and Tortfeasors) Act, 832
(Miscellaneous Provisions) Bill, 800, 801
See also Coroners Bill.
(Personal Injuries) (Amendment) Act, 568
(Scotland) Bill, 255, 285
relating to mental illness and mental deficiency:
Evidence taken before Royal Commission, 951, 1182
Scotland, proposals for amendment, 1076, 1142, 1182
Society:
Legal Aid and Advice Act, reports, 168, 678, 939
Scotland, 189
of Scotland, reports etc., 444, 523, 703, 959, 1192
Lawrence, E. N.: Nocturnal winds, 941
Laws:
and regulations on the regime of the High Seas, 484
Register of temporary, 1033, 1044, 1149
Laws, R. M.:
Elephant seal, growth and age, 862
New method of age determination in mammals with special reference to the elephant seal, 602
Lawson, D. I.:
Fire and the atomic bomb, 954
Fire endurance of timber beams and floors, 440
Heating of panels by flue pipes, 438
Laying:
Cages, 330
Drain pipes, 503
Lead:
Export licence, 1203
Limits for lead content of foods, 882
Lead (*continued*):
Paints (Protection against poisoning) Act, 370
Poisoning in calves, 331
Leaf cast of larch, 117, 1133
Leakey, L. S. B.: Miocene hominoidea of East Africa, 84
Leamington Corporation Act, 415
Lear, E.: Nonsense alphabet, 499
Learn and live, 492
Leasehold:
Enfranchisement Bill, 1053
Property:
Act and Long Leases (Scotland) Act Extension Act, 568
Bill, 510, 527, 537, 541, 644
Final report, erratum 34, 199
in England and Wales, Government policy, 545, 641
(Temporary Provisions) Act, 60
Bill, 2, 3, 4, 12, 31, 32, 168
Leases in Scotland, 545, 703
Leather:
Goods, Census of Production, 459, 1201
(Tanning and Dressing), Census of Production, 459, 1201
Leatherjackets, 847
Lebanon:
Air Services Agreement, 288, 365, 546, 561, 627, 806, 888
Museums and monuments, Unesco mission report, 1006
Lee, A. J.: Research from the *Ernest Holt* into the fishery near Bear Island, 849
Lee, A. R.: Durability of road tar, 956
Lee, D. H. K.: Manual of field studies on heat tolerance of domestic animals, 1008
Leeds:
Geology of district north and east 123
Tramway accident, 720
Leese, Lt. Gen. Sir Oliver, despatch on operations in Burma, 167
Leeward Islands:
Bill, 1029, 1056
Colonial report, 90
Economic survey, 463, 602
S.R.O. & S.I. Revised, 193
Legal:
Aid:
and Advice Act:
Accounts, 19, 102, 266, 419, 528, 678, 790, 939, 1041, 1171
Reports on operation etc. 168, 678, 939
(Panel) (Complaints) (Tribunals) Rules, 168
Scheme, Scotland, 189, 444, 703, 959, 1192
(Scotland) Act, reports and accounts 189, 261, 357, 523, 703, 781, 880, 1036, 1192
Committee, ICAO, minutes and documents, 139, 395

LEG-MCC | 1951-5

LEG— INDEX 1951-5

Legal (*continued*):
Documentation in the world, register of, 1003
Preliminaries to marriage in the British Commonwealth and Irish Republic, 121
Proceedings in civil and commercial matters, exchange of notes with Austria, 57
Legg, H. J.: Bolivia, economic survey, 463
Leggett, Sir F. (Chairman): Committee of Inquiry into unofficial stoppages in London Docks, report, 44
Legislation:
Continuance of emergency, 564, 640, 904, 1076
for press, film, and radio, 232
Legislative (and Administrative) series, 738, 994
Legitimacy:
Act, 831
Bill, 1053
Legitimation (Re-registration of Birth) Bill, 1056
Le Gros Clark, W. E.:
History of the primates, 592, 854
Miocene Lemuroids of East Africa, 336
Solution of Piltdown problem, 591, 1102
Legumes in agriculture, 750
Leicestershire, Census, 896
Leigh-Breese, P. L. (Chairman): Housing Management Sub-Committee, reports, 1152, 1153
Leiper, M. A.: Sickness absence, 420
Leith Harbour and Docks Order Confirmation Act, 315
Bill, 284
Lemaitre, H.: Vocabularium bibliothecarii, 749
Lemon sole larvae in the Scottish Plankton Collections, 703
Lend-lease, reciprocal and surplus war property and claims, settlement with U.S.A., 296
Leprosy:
can be cured, 551
Expert Committee report, 757
Survey of recent legislation, 1012
Lerwick Harbour Order Confirmation Act, 315
Bill, 284
Letters of James V, 961
Lettuce:
Aphids, 587
Production, 329
Leubuscher, Charlotte: Processing of Colonial raw materials, 94
Levi-Strauss, C.: Race and history, 493
Lewis, R.: Sierra Leone, 863
Lewis, R. I.: Studies on bridge-deck systems, 1187
Lewis, W. A.: Further studies in the compaction of soil and performance of compaction plant, 956
Lexicon of terms used in connection with international civil aviation, 395
Liabilities (Wartime Adjustment), S.R.O. & S.I. Revised, 193
Liassic ironstones. *See* Mesozoic ironstones.
Liberties of the Subject Bill, 1053
Librarianship, career, 142, 1157
Libraries:
Bulletin for, 232, 493, 747
and properties in Italy, agreement, 558
in adult and fundamental education, 231
Libraries, Museums and Art Galleries, report, 43, 187
Library:
Document, House of Commons, 1082, 1147
in Wales and Welsh studies, 100
United Nations, publications 225, 485, 738, 995
Libya:
Air Services agreement, 550, 627
Civil aviation, temporary agreement, 298, 365
Economic:
Appraisal, general, 738
and social development, 1000
Survey, 463
Financial:
and military matters, agreement, 551 627
temporary agreement, 287, 365
Friendship and alliance, Treaty of 558, 627, 805, 888
Libyan Public Development and Stabilisation Agency, 566, 627
Road to independence through United Nations, 538
Technical assistance, agreement, 49, 112
Transfer of power, agreement relating to financial matters, 553, 627
United Nations:
Commissioner's report 484
Mission, report 745
Lice, 853
Infestation and mange of cattle, 1094
Licensed Premises in New Towns Act, 308
Bill, 254, 255, 274, 278, 282, 284, 285, 385
Licences, 202, 204, 205, 461, 714, 715, 717, 968, 969, 973, 974
Civil Aviation, 1208, 1209, 1211
terminated for non-payment of rent, 1150
Licensing:
Act, 568, 570
Bill, 513, 514, 543
Consolidation Bills, report, 510, 514
(Airports) Bill, 800, 1028, 1056
(Amendment) (Tied Houses) Bill, 281
at Airports Bill, 283

INDEX 1951-5 —LOC

Licensing (*continued*):
Authorities, reports, 209, 468, 718, 722, 1209
(Consolidation) Act, 61
(Seamen's Canteens) Act, 829
Bill, 516, 544, 770
Lichens, moulds, and similar growths on building materials, Control of 437
Liechtenstein and Guatemala Order, 657
Life:
Peers Bill, 256
Tables, supplement, 898
Life-saving appliances, survey of, 1209
Light, unit and standard of measurement, 430
Lighter flints, Standing Committee report, 809
Lighting:
of buildings, some general principles, 953
of office buildings, 505
or road vehicles, 209, 722
Lightweight concrete:
Blocks for housing, 695
in America, 698
Limitation:
Act, 64
(Enemies and War Prisoners) Act, 832
of armaments, draft resolution, 58, 112
Limited Partnerships Act, 569
Lincolnshire and Rutland, Census, 1138
Lindblad, G.: Productivity in the distributive trade in Europe, 879
Lindon, J. B.: Savoy Hotel Ltd. Investigation, report, 716
Lindsay, Sir H. B. (Chairman):
Local Authority Services Standing Advisory Committee: report on what Local Authorities can do to promote health and prevent disease, 125
Medical, Hospital, and Specialist Services and General Practitioner Services Standing Advisory Committee, report on general practitioner and hospital service, 376
Rivers Pollution Prevention Sub-committee, report, 35
Line Communication, handbook of, errata, 501
Linen:
and soft hemp, Census of Production, 459
See also Cotton.
Ling, Lee: Digest of plant quarantine regulations, 751
Lingeman, E. R.: Italy, economic survey, 463
Linklater, E.:
Campaign in Italy, 214
Our men in Korea, 502
Linlithgow:
Index to Register of Sasines, 704
Railway accident, 467
Linoleum, 1185
Linoleum, Leathercloth, and allied trades, Census of Production, 460, 967
Linseed, Home-grown, 847
Linstead, Sir H. (Chairman): Hospital Pharmaceutical Service, report, 1143
Liqueur chocolates, 358
Liquidation of German assets, exchange of notes with Sweden, 826
Litter in the Royal Parks, 1226
Little, K.: Race and society, 748
Liverpool:
Corporation Act, 1081
Court of Passage, S.R.O. & S.I. Revised, 193
Extension Act, 66
Livestock:
Diseases in European countries, Control of 354
Production, report of second Inter-American Meeting, 751
Rearing Act, 60
Bill, 1
Small domestic, housing of, 333
Living:
in flats, 388
traditions of Scotland, 134
Llanelly:
District Traction Act, 315
Pier and Harbour:
Order Confirmation Act, 834
Bill, 802
Provisional Order Bill, 774
Llewellin, Rt. Hon. Lord (Chairman): Ports Efficiency Committee, report on co-ordination of transport and fuel and power, 466
Llewellyn, H. M.: Floor finishes for houses and other non-industrial buildings, 440
Lloyd, Lord (Chairman): Conference on movement of persons within a British Caribbean Federation, report, 1110
Lloyds Act, 66
Loan:
Agreements:
Belgium, 54
Export-Import Bank of Washington, 291, 297, 473
Funds in Uganda Protectorate and Tanganyika, 564
to New Zealand of H.M.S. *Royalist*, 1078, 1218
Lobster fishermen, practical hints for, 444
Lobsters in Scotland, tagged, observations on re-captures, 1192
Local:
Acts, Tables of Short Titles and Index, 573
Ambulance Services costing return, 378
and Personal Acts, Tables of Short Titles and Index, 66, 314, 833, 1080
Authorities:
(Admission of the Press to Meetings) Act, 569

LOC— INDEX 1951-5

Local (*continued*):
Authorities (*continued*):
(Building and Civil Engineering), Census of Production, 460, 1201
Loans Act, 313
Memo on duties, 125
Messages to, 1075
Education Authorities, Excepted Districts, etc., 873
Government:
Act, 65, 571
Equalisation grant in Scotland, reports, 703, 1049, 1192
and Local Government (Financial Provisions) (Scotland) Act, report, 1192
and Planning, Ministry of, publications, 164, 417
See also Housing and Local Government.
Areas, England, statement showing electorates, 1058, 1146
Career, 398, 921
Elections Bill, 1054, 1056
Estimates, 15, 215, 262, 522
(Financial Provisions) (Scotland) Act, 829
Bill, 541, 544, 769, 779
Financial Statistics, England and Wales, 125, 165, 388, 650, 907, 912, 1151
in Britain, 1154
Manpower Committee, report, 58, 217
(Miscellaneous Provisions), Act, 568
Bill, 514, 527, 537, 541, 542, 644
(Public Order) (Scotland) Bill, 545, 703
Report, 52
S.R.O. & S.I. Revised, 193
(Scotland) Act, 60
Bill, 1
Scottish Manpower Committee, report, 302, 445
Statistics, 634
(Street Works) (Scotland) Bill, 1053, 1056
Superannuation:
Acts, 63, 568
Bill, 285, 513, 525, 537, 542, 644
(Administration) Regulations, circular, 911
Allocation of benefits, 1151
(Benefits) Regulations:
Circulars, 910, 911
Memos, 913, 959
Tables, 912, 959
(Benefits) (Scotland) Regulations, memo, 959
Circulars, 648, 910, 911, 1150, 1151
Guide to new benefits, 912, 959
Local (*continued*):
Government (*continued*):
Superannuation (*continued*):
Model form of agreement, 912
Principal, Statutes and Regulations, 1152
Regulations, explanatory memo, 912
Schemes, 648
(Scotland):
Act, 832
Acts, Regulations, explanatory memo, 960
Tables, 912
Land Charges:
Committee report, 286, 419
Register, circular, 1150
Loans:
Fund, accounts, 9, 171, 258, 422, 518, 681, 785, 942, 1038, 1173
S.R.O. & S.I. Revised, 193
Taxation Licences, England, S.R.O. & S.I. Revised, 193
Loch Ard, 116
Locock, Sir G. (Chairman): Standing Committee, report on wood flour, 550
Locust:
Research and control, 92
Wars not yet won, 389
Logan, W. P. D.: General practitioners' records, 634
Loganberry, 329
Logarithms of gas volume factors, tables, 120
Logging techniques and training of forest workers, 1009
Lokur, N. S.: Civil aircraft accident, 595
London:
Airport, 974
Central terminal buildings, 1209
and Home Counties Traffic Advisory Committee, report, 209
Area, supply of buildings, 793
Building:
Act, 316
Acts (Amendment) Act, 316
by floodlight, postcards, 763
Census, 634
County:
Council:
(Crystal Palace) Act, 67
(General Powers) Acts, 67, 315, 573, 834
(Holland House):
Act, 315
Amendment Act, 834
(Loans) Bill, 1046
Joint Committee report, 1029
(Money) Acts, 67, 315, 573, 834, 1081
Courts, directory, 678
S.R.O. & S.I. Revised, 194
Docks, report of court of inquiry into dispute, 824, 825, 924

INDEX 1951-5 —MCC

London (*continued*):
Gazette, 166, 418, 677, 938, 1170
Hydraulic Power Act, 574
Museums and galleries, guide, 190, 705
Passenger Transport Act, 311
Port of, S.R.O. & S.I. Revised, 194
Post Offices and streets, 178, 689, 948
Traffic, 209, 466, 718, 974, 1209
Act, 310
Congestion, report, 209
S.R.O. & S.I. Revised, 194
Transport:
Committee of Inquiry, report, 1209
S.R.O. & S.I. Revised, 194
London's Airports, 557, 595
Long Leases:
(Temporary Provisions):
Bill, 2, 131
(Scotland) Act, 60
Bill, 14, 16, 26, 31
Longhurst, A. R.: Review of the Notostraca, 1102
Longmore, J.: Study of interreflection of daylight using model rooms and artificial skies, 955
Longniddry railway accident, 975
Long-term contract, 750
Looking at the United Nations, 485
Looted gold, agreement for submission of claims to arbitration, 44, 112
Lopez, S. P.: Freedom of information, 734, 989
Loraine, P. (Chairman): Committee on National Stud Policy and Methods of Operation, report, 1096
Lord Chancellor's Department, publications, 168, 419, 678, 939, 1170
Lord President's Office, publications, 1171
Lords:
and Commons: how Parliament began and how it works, 134
Spiritual and Temporal, roll, 7, 133, 255, 386, 516, 647, 777, 909, 1028, 1149
Lorella, wreck report, 1213
Lorimer, F.: Culture and human fertility, 1006
Loss of Employment (Compensation) Bill, 281
Lothian Homes Trust Scheme, memo, 1190
Lotteries Bill, 803, 1053
Louping-ill in sheep, 331
Low-cost radio reception, 232
Lowe, R. H.:
New species of Tilapia from Lake Jipe and the Pangani River, 1102
Tilipia and other fish and fisheries of Lake Nyasa, 345
Lower:
Cretaceous Gastropoda, Lamellibranchia, and Annelida, 602
Tertiary Foraminifera of Qatar Peninsula, 854
Lubricants and Lubrication, research reports, 700
Lucerne, 1091
Ludbrook, N. H.: Scaphopoda, 854
Luddendenfoot, railway accident, 1210
Luke, Sir Stephen: Development and Welfare in the West Indies, 861, 1110
Lunacy:
Act, 569
and Mental Treatment:
Acts, reports of Board of Control, 8, 22, 126, 271, 378, 531, 678, 792, 900, 1046, 1143
England, S.R.O. & S.I. Revised, 194
Scotland, S.R.O. & S.I. Revised, 194
Luton Airport:
Air Navigation Order, 338
Customs Order, 85
Lutte antipaludique par les insecticides a action remanente, 237
Luxembourg:
Compensation for War Damage, 816, 888
Cultural Convention, 564, 627
Extradition Treaty amended, 50, 112
Money and Property Agreement terminated, 306, 365
Social Security Convention, 564, 627, 1062, 1128
See also Belgium.
Lydd (Ferryfield) Airport, Air Navigation Order, 973
Lymington Pier and Harbour:
Order Confirmation Act, 67
Provisional Order Bill, 5, 32
Lympne. *See* Northolt.
Lynton, R. P.: Community factory in modern technology, 748
Lysaght's. *See* John Lysaght's.
Lyttelton, O. (Chairman): Conference on:
Nigerian Constitution, reports, 560, 806
West Indian Federation, report, 45

M

(Note.—The prefixes "Mac", "Mc", etc. are all treated as "Mac" and are listed, subject to that proviso, strictly alphabetically)

Mabane, Rt. Hon. W. (Chairman): Advisory Committee, Publicity and recruitment for Civil Defence and Allied Services, reports, 306, 811
McArthur, D. N. (Chairman): Scottish Standing Committee, report on residual values of fertilisers and feeding stuffs, 77, 328
McCance, R. A.: Studies on the nutritive value of bread and on the effect of variations in the extraction rate of flour on the growth of undernourished children, 940

1951-5 | MCC-MEM

MCC— *INDEX 1951–5*

McClelland, W. (Chairman): Advisory Council on Education in Scotland:
  Administration of education for handicapped pupils, 286
  Further education, 287
  Libraries, museums, and art galleries, 43
  Pupils:
    handicapped by speech disorders, 285
    with mental or educational disabilities, 57
    with physical disabilities, 42
    who are maladjusted because of social handicap, 285
  Visual and aural aids, 34
Macdonald, J. D.: Taxonomy of the Karroo and red-back larks of Western South Africa, 592
Mace, C. A.: Incentives, 420
Macfarlane, R. G.: Diagnosis and treatment of haemophilia and its related conditions, 1171
McGuire, J. H.: Heat transfer by radiation, 954
Machine:
  Boring of wood, 1186
  Milking, 847
  Tools:
    and workshop plant, Defence list, 1114
    Census of Production, 459
    Export licence, 202, 714
Machine-room workers. *See* Printing.
Machinery:
  Accidents, Committee report, 676
  and equipment, export availabilities and delivery periods, 101, 356
  Duty-free entry into U.K., 968
  for consent to the sale, lease, or letting of land, 911
  for silage making, 77
Machines:
  and appliances in Government offices, 983
  builders', care of, 761
  for handling materials in traditional house building, 1155
  Historic books on, exhibition catalogue, 694
MacInnes, D. G.: Miocene and Pleistocene Lagomorpha of East Africa, 592
McIntosh, J. P.: Scottish seed oats, 846
McIntyre, A. D.:
  Food of halibut from North Atlantic fishing grounds, 703
  Statistics of Scottish halibut fishery, 703
Mackay, D.: Hospital morbidity statistics 122
Mackay, M. E.: Separation of protein fractions from human plasma with ether, 940
Mackay, R. A.: Albite-Riebeckite-Granites of Nigeria, 375
Mackenzie, Sir C.: World Braille usage, 1008
Mackenzie, K. E.: Malaya, economic survey, 463
Mackeson, H. R. (Chairman): Bilateral Trade Negotiations Committee, report, 712
Mackie, R. L.: Arbroath Abbey, guide, 1018
Mackie, Prof. T. J. (Chairman): Scottish Hill Farm Research Committee, report, 77
Mackinnon, K. W.: Chinese Engineering and Mining Co. Ltd., report under Companies Act, 1202
Mackintosh, Rt. Hon. Lord (Chairman): Committee of Inquiry into law of succession in Scotland, report, 37
Mackintosh, J.: Feeding of dairy cows, 1094
Mackintosh, Prof. J. M. (Chairman): Committee of Social Workers in the Mental Health Services, report, 46
Mackworth-Praed, C. W.: Species and races of yellow wagtails from Western Europe to Western North America, 336
McLagan, J. (Chairman): Commission on Establishment of Customs Union in the British Caribbean area, 93
Maclean, A. (Chairman): Scottish Housing Advisory Committee:
  Design and workmanship of non-traditional houses, 123
  Housing of special groups, 377
Maclean, F. (Chairman): Committee on administration of Territorial Army, report, 1069
McLintock, W. F. P.: Gemstones, 123
Macmanaway's Indemnity Act, Rev. J. G., 60
  Bill, 2, 31, 32
McMullen, Col. D.: Railway accident reports, 209, 466, 719, 722, 975, 1209
MacNalty, Sir A. S.: Civilian health and medical services, 638, 1143
McNamee, J.: Analysis of symmetrical cylindrical shells, 1189
Maconochie, R. H. (Chairman): Committee on Close Seasons for Deer in Scotland, report, 822
Macphail, A. N.: Employment problems of disabled youth in Glasgow, 420
Macroutilopus problem, 833
McVean, M. I.: Employment problems of disabled youth in Glasgow, 420
McVittie, W. W.: Portugal, economic survey, 1204
Madeira. *See* Portugal.
Made-up household textiles, Census of Production, 1200
Madingley Military Cemetery, terms of use of land, 1058
Madreporaria, Hydrocorallinae, Heliopora, and Tubipora, 336

INDEX 1951–5 —MAR

Magistrates' Courts:
  Act, 308
    Bill, 249, 252, 254, 284
  Memo, 252
  Rules, draft, 295, 382, 419
Magna Carta:
  for refugees, 226
  of King John, translation with facsimile, 180
Magnesian lime and magnesian limestone, 1093
Magnetic and meteorological observations, 376, 899
Magpie, jackdaw, and jay, 78
Maiden Castle, guide, 244
Maidstone Corporation Act, 1081
Main School medical record cards, 1120
Maintenance:
  and safety precautions for powered hand tools, 243
  of dependants, S.R.O. & S.I. Revised, 194
  of standards, Recent developments and techniques, 430
  Orders Act, 314
    Bill, 8
  Rates for students at Universities, 352
Mair, L. P.: Native administration in Central Nyasaland, 344
Maize:
  and maize diets, 752
  for fodder and silage, 847
  Hybrid tests, results, 1008
Making:
  Concrete, 503
  the most of farmyard manure, 1093
Malacca, arms and badges, 599
Maladjusted children, 1120
Malaria:
  British Commonwealth leaflet, 651
  Conference in Equatorial Africa, 238
  Expert Committee reports, 238, 1013
  Terminology, report, 755
Malaya:
  Arms and flag, 599
  Colonial reports, 91, 344, 860. 861, 1109
  Economic survey, 463
  Facts, 345
  New village, 914
  Photoposter, 134
  Service gratuities for locally enlisted personnel, 241
  Today (filmstrip and picture set), 1153
Malaysian mammals, handlist, 1102
Malik, C.: Human rights in the United Nations, 744
Malin Head, wreck report, 213
Mallophaga:
  Checklist of species and genera, 336
  Early literature, 83, 853
Malnutrition in African mothers, infants, and young children, 862
Malta:
  Economic survey, 602
  (Reconstruction) Act, accounts, 9, 25, 93, 279, 345, 534, 602, 790, 862, 1033, 1110
  Round table Conference, 1078, 1110
  S.R.O. & S.I. Revised, 194
Maltese units, retired pay and pensions, 501
Malting industry, power and fuel in, 119
Maltman, W. (Chairman): Scottish Housing Advisory Committee, report on housing of special groups, 377
Mammals:
  Collected by Mr. Shaw Meyer in New Guinea, 336
  New method of age determination, 602
  Southern African, reclassification, 854
Manchester:
  Corporation Act, 834
  (Salford) Dock strike, report, 55
  Ship Canal Act, 315
Manganese in the iron and steel industry, 618
Mangold fly, 586
"Manihine" Expedition to the Gulf of Aqaba, 336
Mann, G. E.: Poultry breeding, 1095
Manners, Miss E. G. (Chairman): Standing Nursing and Midwifery Advisory Committee, reports, 1142
Mannheim, Dr. H.: Studies in the causes of delinquency and the treatment of offenders, 1145
Manning, C. A. W.: University teaching of social sciences, 1007
Manpower. *See* Local Government.
Mansfield, railway accident, 210
Manuels bibliographiques de l'Unesco, 1005
Manufactured:
  Fuel, Census of Production, 1199
  Stationery, paper bag and kindred trades, Census of Production, 1201
Manufacturing industries (including laundries), Census of Production, 461
Manure, farmyard, 1093
Manures and fertilisers, 79, 331, 879
Manuring, green, 330
Mao, Y. T.: Results of co-operative hybrid maize tests in European and Mediterranean countries, 751
Maps, 864
Margarine, Census of Production, 460, 967
Marier, R.: Social welfare work in Jamaica, 1006
Marine:
  Algae, 592
  and Aviation Insurance (Air Risks) Act, 308
    Bill, 254, 271, 278, 282, 284, 385
  Engineering:
    Census of Production, 459, 1200
    Handbook of collections, 694
    See also Naval Architecture.

MAR— *INDEX 1951–5*

Marine (*continued*):
  Insurance Act, 61
  Observer, 109, 421, 600, 940, 1172
  Observer's Handbook, 421
  Research, 703, 960, 1192
  Surveys, etc., list of fees and expenses, 718
Marines, S.R.O. & S.I. Revised, 194
Maritime:
  Conventions Act, 309
  Law, International Conventions, 561
Markets:
  in the Caribbean, 715
  in the Middle East, 969
  Model byelaw, 1152
Markinch, Dysart, and Leven, economic geology of Fife coalfields, 899
Markowski, S.: Cestodes of seals from the Antarctic, 336
Marks, E. N.: Review of the Aedes scutellaris subgroup with a study of variations in Aedes Pseudoscutellaris, 853
Marling and claying, 333
Marples, B. J.: Fossil penguins from the Mid-Tertiary of Seymour Island, 602
Marriage:
  Act, 313
    (1949) Amendment Act, 829
      Bill, 773, 788, 798, 799, 801, 907
  and Divorce, Royal Commission, evidence, 435, 691
  (Certificates of Medical Examinations) Bill, 800
  Legal preliminaries to, 121
  S.R.O. & S.I. Revised, 194
Married women, nationality of, 226
Marsh, B. B.: Whalemeat production and preservation, 696
Marshall:
  Aid:
    Commemoration:
      Act, 568
        Bill, 515, 543
      Commission report, 1061, 1128
    See also Recovery record.
  Scholarship Scheme, proposed arrangements for administration, 552, 627
Marshall, W. A. L.:
  Century of London weather, 680
  Comparison of wind recorded by amenograph with the geostrophic wind, 941
Martin, A.: Collective security, 491
Martin, E. L.: African species of genus Pardomima Warren, 1102
Marwick, H.: Orkney, ancient monuments guide, 504
Mary Queen of Scots, Calendar of State Papers, 445
Mass communication, 232, 747, 1003, 1004, 1005
Massed-start cycle racing, 976
Masterpieces in the Victoria and Albert Museum, 499
Masters, instructions for, 971
Mastic asphalt spreader, career, 659
Match industry, Census of Production, 458, 1199
Matches:
  S.R.O. & S.I. revised, 194
  Supply and export, and supply of match-making machinery, 521
Matchwood Working Party report, 969
Materials:
  Civil Estimates, 523, 783
  Handling equipment:
    and methods in U.S.A., 618
    Cost savings, 879
  Ministry of, 47, 218
    Bill, 5
    Publications, 419
  Strength and testing, 700
Maternal care and mental health, 237, 497
Maternity:
  Benefit, 287
    See also National Insurance Bills.
  Care, expert committee report, 498
Mathematics:
  in secondary schools, 958
  Setting and marking of examinations, guidance to teachers, 1191
Matheson, R. C.: Bird migration and foot-and-mouth disease, 331
Matrimonial Causes Act, 65, 312
  Bill, 18, 26, 30, 131
Matters of life and death, 121
Matthewman, A. G.: Study of warm fronts, 1172
Matthews, J. D.: Japanese larches at Dunkeld, Perthshire, 892
Mattick, A. T. R.: Milk pasteurisation, 755
Mattingly, P. F.: Sub-genus Stegomyia in the Ethiopian Region, 336, 591
Maude, Sir J. (Chairman): Working Party on recruitment, training and qualification of sanitary inspectors, report, 638
Maunder, A. H.: Improvement of agricultural extension services, 1008
Mauritius:
  Colonial reports, 90, 343, 600, 860, 1108
  S.R.O. & S.I. Revised, 194
  Seychelles fisheries survey, 602
Maxwell, Sir A. (Chairman):
  Departmental Committee of the Criminal Court in South Lancashire, report, 561
  Discharged Prisoners' Aid Societies Committee, report, 556
Mayers, N.: Ecuador, economic survey, 970
Mc. *For surnames commencing with this preface, see* Mac.
Measurement:
  of humidity, 1174
  of morbidity, 897

INDEX 1951–5 —MEM

Measurement (*continued*):
  of pressure with the mercury barometer, 1174
  of productivity, 356
  Units and standards, 177, 430, 1174
Measurements:
  of atmospheric noise at high frequencies, 698
  of vessels for Panama Canal, 1211
Measures:
  for economic development of under-developed countries, 226
  passed by the National Assembly of the Church of England, 67, 316, 574, 835, 1082
Meat:
  and livestock, commodity report, 234
  and offal unfit for human consumption, disposal of, 620
  Condemnation of imported canned, 358
  Content and price of sausages, 881
  in small refrigerators, handling of, 182
  Inspection, 105, 358, 359
  Paste, etc., standards, 104
  Pies. *See* Food poisoning.
  Production, trade and consumption, 94, 347, 604, 864, 1112
  Products, 103, 619
    and Canned Meat (Amendment) Order, 103
  Orders 358
Mechanical:
  and electrical engineering, historical events, 1184
  Engineering:
    Careers, 658
    Census of Production, 459, 713, 1200
    Research Board, reports, 184, 440, 697, 955, 1187
  Handling equipment, Census of Production, 459, 1200
  Lighters, S.R.O. & S.I. Revised, 194
Mechanically-propelled road vehicles, returns, 211, 468, 720, 722, 976, 1210
Mechanics of sawing, bank and circular saws, 954
Mechanisation of small farms in European countries, 101
Medals:
  Africa General Service, 1059
  British and foreign, Naval and maritime affairs, 177
  Efficiency, regulations, 1222
  Grant of United Nations Service Medal, 241
Mediaeval tithe barn, Bradford-on-Avon, guide, 762
Medical:
  and auxiliary personnel, professional and technical education, 238, 757
  and biological sciences, 232
  and physiological applications, radio-isotope techniques, 710
Medical (*continued*):
  and population subjects, studies, 122, 374, 634, 897
  Auxiliaries, reports of committees, 41, 126, 189
  Certification of cause of death, instructions for physicians, 497
  Diseases in tropical and subtropical areas, 1016
  Guide, Ship captains, 720, 1211
  History of the Second World War, 638, 902, 1143
  Laboratory technician, career, 921
  Manual of chemical warfare, 1222
  Periodicals, world, 757
  Profession, S.R.O. & S.I. Revised, 194
  Record cards and forms, 187, 1120
  Research:
    Council:
      Publications, 169, 419, 679, 940, 1171
      Reports, 33, 168, 296, 420, 555, 678, 815, 939, 1068, 1171
    Fund, Scottish, proposals, 299
    War History, 638
  Scales, Merchant Shipping, 209, 618
  Schools, world directory, 757
  Services, emergency, 378
  Statistical review of England and Wales, 374, 635
Medical, Pharmaceutical, and General Practitioners Advisory Committee, report on definition of drugs, 125
Medicine:
  and pathology, war history, 378
  Career, 658
Mediterranean:
  and Middle East, early successes against Italy, 854, 961
  and Pacific territories, economic survey 602
  Theatre, part played by Allied Air Forces in final defeat of enemy, 675
Medlicott, W. N.: Economic blockade, 337, 473
Megastigmus flies attacking conifer seed, 1133
Megille, X. B.: Forestry criteria and equipment of tractors, 1009
Megson, N. J. L.: German plastics industry, 966
Meiklereid, E. W.: France, economic survey, 716
Meillon, B. de: Simuliidae of the Ethiopian region, 593
Melanau sago producing community in Sarawak, 601
Mellanby, Lady: Effect of sugar supplements on dental caries in children, 1171
Melville, R. V.: Geology of the country around Chatham, 899
Member-countries of OEEC, combined foreign trade, statistical bulletin, 878

MEM-MOT | 1951-5

MEM— INDEX 1951-5

Member-states of Unesco, reports to Conference, 232, 1007
Memento des statistiques, 875
Men against ignorance, 1006
Mental:
Deficiency:
Act, 569, 570
S.R.O. & S.I. Revised, 194
Health:
Expert committee reports, 238, 498, 757
Services, social workers, committee report, 46, 126
Hygiene in the nursery school, 748
Illness and mental deficiency:
Proposals of amendment to law, 1076
See also Law relating to Mental Illness.
Treatment Act, 63
Mentally subnormal child, expert committee report, 1013
Mercantile Navy List and Maritime Directory, 466, 974
Merchandise Marks:
Act, 62, 308, 309, 568, 569
Bill, 256, 510, 515, 531, 537, 541, 543, 644
Reports, 805, 820, 850, 969, 1070, 1204
(Prosecution) Act, 830
S.R.O. & S.I. Revised, 194
Merchant:
Navy Memorial Act, 315
Seamen, Transit Agreement with France, 804
Shipping:
Act, 61, 308, 309, 829, 830, 832, 833
Bill, 34, 250, 770, 800
Acts (Amendment) Act, 310
and the demands of war, 1103
(Certificates) Act, 309
Circular, 1208
(Equivalent Provisions) Act, 570
(International Labour Conventions) Act, 570
(Liability of Shipowners) Act, 830
Medical Scales, 209
Regulations etc., 1209
S.R.O. & S.I. Revised, 194
(Safety and Load Line Conventions) Act, 311
Survey of life-saving appliances, 1209
Mercury barometer, measurement of pressure, 1174
Mercury-in-glass thermometers, 1174
Merionethshire, Montgomeryshire, and Radnorshire, Census, 1138
Meritorious Service Medal, 241, 759
Mersey:
Docks and Harbour Board Act, 834
Tunnel Act, 1081
Mesostigmatid mites from Alaska, 1102
Mesozoic ironstones of England, 123, 635
Messages:
to local authorities, 1075, 1142, 1152, 1218
Special Army Orders, 501-2
Messer, F. (Chairman): Central Health Services Council:
Annual reports, 266, 530
Co-operation between hospital, local authority, and general practitioner services, 377
Messiah, Handel's, exhibition, 82
Metal:
Goods and precision instruments, Census of Production, 713
Scaffolding, 1018
Metalliferous mines and quarries, Census of Production, 458, 1199
Metals:
Economy Advisory Committee, report, 455
Handbook of hard, 1187
Metallurgy, professional qualifications, 163
Metalwork:
Fifty masterpieces, 239
in secondary schools, 353
Meteorites, catalogue, 592
Meteorological:
Aspects of turbulence affecting aircraft at high altitude, 170
Committee, report, 394
Glossary, amendment, 680
Magazine, 170, 421, 680, 941, 1172
Meeting, final report, 138, 140
Office, publications, 169, 420, 679, 941, 1172
Services, specifications, 139, 918
Meteorology:
Division, report, 918
Handbook of statistical methods in, 680
for aviators, 170
Methods, studies in, 1000
Metric Engineering Tables, comparative British-American, 503
Metropolis:
Commissioner of Police for, reports, 53, 128, 300, 380, 561, 640, 818, 904, 1066
Management (Thames River Prevention of Floods) Amendment Act, 316
Metropolitan:
Common Scheme (Ham):
Amending Scheme Confirmation Act, 772, 834
Provisional Order Bill, 801
Police:
(Borrowing Powers) Act, 308
Bill, 33, 251, 263, 278, 385
Courts, S.R.O. & S.I. Revised, 194
District, S.R.O. & S.I. Revised, 194
Water:
Area, S.R.O. & S.I. Revised, 194
Board Act, 573

INDEX 1951-5 —MIN

Mexico:
Consular Convention, 813, 888
Economic Survey, 716
Telecommunications services with British Honduras, Agreement, 301, 365, 814, 888
See also Caribbean.
Michael Griffith, wreck report, 978.
Microbial growth and its inhibition, 497
Microfilm use, Unesco survey, 494
Microlepidoptera in the British Museum (Natural History), 1103
Micro-organisms, British Commonwealth collections, 82
Middle East:
Communications meeting, report, 918
Economic:
Conditions, 222
Developments, 491, 989
Markets, 969
Middlesex, Census, 896
Mid-Georgian domestic silver, 499
Midlothian, Census, 898
Mid-Wales Investigation Report, maps, 1096
Midwife, S.R.O. & S.I. Revised, 194
Midwives:
Act, 60
Bill, 3, 4, 33
Report, 4
(Scotland) Act, 60
Bill, 3, 4, 33
Report, 4
Survey of recent legislation, 1012
Migrants:
International, sex and age, 996
Protection of, handbook of international measures, 740
Migration, International research, 995
Migratory beekeeping, 77
Mildenhall Treasure handbook, 1101
Mildew, American gooseberry, 847
Miles Davies, A. E. (Chairman): Working Party on grants to training college students, report, 1120
Milford Docks Act, 573, 1081
Milford Viscount, wreck report, 213
Military:
Aircraft:
Provision of facilities, Ethiopia, 301
Supply of, 1060
Engineering, 241, 502, 1016
Equipment, gift to North Atlantic Treaty countries, 816
Law, manual, 502, 759, 1016, 1223
Service, agreements:
Brazil, 1066
Denmark, 1065
France, 303
Milk:
Act, 571
Milk (*continued*):
and Dairies:
(Amendment):
Act, 62
Regulations, circular, 880, 881
Regulations:
Approved oxidising and preserving agents, 103, 104, 358, 619, 620
Circulars, 880, 881, 1095, 1122
Circumstances affecting composition, 78
Feeding for winter, 847
Marketing scheme, 1091, 1096
Pasteurisation, 755
Production, 846
Products, Census of Production, 460, 1201
Quality production, report, 589
Regulations, circulars, 881
Ropy, 847
(Special Designation):
Act, 65
(Pasteurised and Sterilised Milk) Regulations, 103
(Scotland) Order, explanatory memo, 124
(Special Designation, Pasteurised and Sterilised Milk) (Amendment) Regulations, 620
Taints in, 330
Millard, R. S.: Filling and sealing materials for joints in concrete roads, 1188
Miller, A. A.: Food poisoning, 1144
Miller, N. C. E.: Genera Henricohahnia Breddin, Dicrotelus Erichson, Nyllius Stal, Orgetorixa China, and allied new genera, 853
Milling machines, safeguarding, 417
Milne, Sir D. (Chairman): Scottish Local Government Committee, report, 302
Milne, M. K.: Rice soils and fertilisers, annotated bibliography, 1010
Minehead Pier and Harbour Order Confirmation Act, 315
Bill, 253, 283
Mineral:
Deficiencies in plants, diagnosis by visual symptoms, 77
Industry, statistical summaries, 93, 346, 602, 862, 1110
Oil:
in food (Amendment) Order, 358
Regulations, circular, 1095
Refining, Census of Production, 204, 1199
Resources:
Asia and Far East, development, 995
Conservation and utilisation, 478
Great Britain, 375, 899
Working, control of, memo, 199
Workings Act, 60
Bill, 5, 6, 20, 21, 26, 31, 32, 33, 131
Account, 781, 798, 913

MIN— INDEX 1951-5

Mineral (*continued*):
Workings Act (*continued*):
Explanatory memo, 388
Mineralogy Bulletin, 336, 591
Miners' Welfare Act, 308
Bill, 251, 264, 278, 281, 282, 283, 385
Mines:
and Quarries:
Act, 829
Bill, 544, 775, 776, 789, 798, 802, 803, 907
Deaths by accident, provisional statements, 120, 633, 893
Forms, 120, 372, 633, 895, 1136
Reports of Inspectors, 372, 633, 895, 1136
S.R.O. & S.I. Revised, 194
Inspectors' Reports, 120, 372, 633, 895, 1136
List of, 120
Safety research report, 373
(Working Facilities and Support) Act, 62, 831
Mining:
and quarrying, Census of Production, 713
Examinations rules, 373
Surveyors, 633
Industry Act, 62
Qualifications (Mechanics and Electricians) Rules, 1137
Subsidence, effects on small houses, 245
Ministers:
and Heads of Public Departments, 190, 447, 705, 961, 1194
of the Crown:
Acts, 571
(Fisheries) Bill, 800
No. 2, 802
(Parliamentary Under-Secretaries) Act, 61
Bill, 7, 34
(Transfers of Functions, etc.), S.R.O. & S.I. Revised, 194
Ministry:
of Housing and Local Government Provisional Order (Mortlake Crematorium Board) Bill, 1055
of Materials Act, 60
Bill, 5, 33
Report, 47
of National Insurance Act, 572
of Supply Act, 312
of Transport Act, 310
Minor Offences, report of Departmental Committee, 1070, 1146
Minquiers and Ecrehos sovereignty case, 41, 58, 397, 657, 919
Mint, revised Estimate, 1953-4, 530
Miocene:
and Pleistocene Lagomorpha of East Africa, 592
Anthracotheriidae from East Africa, 84
Miocene (*continued*):
Hominoidea of East Africa, 84
Hydracoids of East Africa with observations on Hyracoidea, 854
Lemuroids of East Africa, 336
Miscellaneous:
Financial Provisions Act, 1080
Bill, 1029, 1055
Services:
Appropriation Account, 263
Estimates, 15, 263
Mistakidis, M. N.: Quantitative studies of the bottom fauna of Essex oyster grounds, 332
Mitchell, G. H.: Geology of the country between:
Bradford and Skipton, 635
Burton-on-Trent, Rugeley, and Uttoxeter, 1140
Mitchell, G. R.: Dynamic stresses in cast iron girder bridges, 955
Mitchell, J. P.: Report on materials handling equipment, 879
Mitchell, Sir M. E. (Chairman): Housing Manual Sub-Committee: report on housing for special purposes, 165
Mitchell, Thomas J., Certificate of Conviction and Sentence of the Assize Court at Belfast, 1045, 1146
Mites of economic importance, British, 1103
Mitra, K.: Rice enrichment in the Philippines, 1010
Mixing machines, use and care, 874
M. & M. Mart Garage, Bristol, explosion, 290, 382
Mobile:
Camping, 873
Radio Committee, report, 1181
Mobilisation of domestic capital, 485, 732, 995
Model:
Building byelaws, 900
Byelaws, 165, 388, 648, 882, 913, 1152
Clauses, 574
Modern:
Languages in secondary schools, 187
Site organisation, 243
Mole, 587
Mole, Sir C. (Chairman): Works Directorate of Service Departments, report on economy of building materials, 505
Molesworth, H. D.: Baroque sculpture, 1013
Mollison, P. L.: Rh Blood Groups and their clinical effects, 420, 1171
Molony, Brig. C. J. C.: Early successes against Italy, 854, 961
Molson, H. (Chairman): Road Safety Committee, report on massed-start cycle racing, 976
Monarchs of all they surveyed, 433
Monckton, Sir W.: Civil aircraft accident report, 85

INDEX 1951-5 —MOT

Monetary agreements:
Belgium and Luxembourg, 37
Denmark, 763
France, 55, 810
Germany, 554
Norway, 763
Portugal, 36, 53, 819
Sweden, 806
Switzerland, 36, 41, 49, 57, 292, 297, 301, 548, 558
Monetary gold removed from Rome, 657, 919
Money:
and Property Agreements:
Austria, 298
Denmark, 306
France, 555
Greece, 821
Luxembourg, 306
Payments (Justices Procedure) Act, 571
Money-lender, S.R.O. & S.I. Revised, 194
Moneylenders Act, 831
Monmouth:
Castle and Great Castle House, guide, 244
See also Cardiff.
Monmouthshire:
Census, 896
See also Wales.
Monopolies and Restrictive Practices:
Acts, reports, 15, 16, 25, 204, 263, 462, 523, 715, 783, 969, 1037, 1204
Commission:
Act, 568
Bill, 515, 543
Reports, 204, 269, 274, 462, 527, 533, 715, 787, 793, 969, 1047, 1051, 1068, 1204
Select Committee on Estimates, reports, 528, 533
Montagu, Hon. E. S. (Chairman): Cadet Entry into Royal Navy Committee, report, 553
Monthly Weather Report, 171, 422, 681, 942, 1173
Moore, J. L. M.: Railway accident reports, 210, 619, 975
Moore, R. L.: Rear lights on motor vehicles and pedal cycles, 699
Morant, G. M.: Significance of racial differences, 493
Moray and Nairn Census, 898
Morbidity, measurement of, 897
Morbidity, cancer, and mental health, supplement, 1139
More from every acre, 333
Morocco, rights of nationals of U.S.A., 396, 657
Morphology of the head of the hawfinch, 1102
Morrah, D.: Most excellent Majesty, 651
Morris, Rt. Hon. Lord Justice (Chairman): Court of Inquiry into engineering dispute, report, 808
Morris, H. S.: Melanau sago producing community in Sarawak, 601
Morris, M. O.: Classified geological photographs, 375
Morris, Sir P. (Chairman): National Advisory Council on Training and Supply of Teachers, reports, 100, 614, 874
Morrison, Rt. Hon. W. S. (Chairman): Boundary Commission, reports, 825
Morrison-Scott, T. C. S.:
Chasen 1940, handlist of Malaysian mammals, 1102
List of British mammals, 335
Palaearctic and Indian mammals, check list, 84
Southern African mammals, reclassification, 854
Morrison's Academy Trust (Amendment) Scheme, 442, 701
Mortality:
and morbidity during the London fog, 902
Experience of Government life annuitants, 983
Mortara, G.: Culture and human fertility, 1006
Mortars:
and renderings, addition of gypsum plaster, 437
for brickwork, 243
See also Sands.
Mortimer, C. H.: Fertilisers in Fishponds, 862
Mortlake Crematorium Board, Ministry of Housing and Local Government Provisional Order Bill, 1055
Morton of Henryton, Rt. Hon. Lord (Chairman):
Committee on Law of Intestate Succession, report, 50
Royal Commission on Marriage and Divorce, evidence, 435, 691
Mosley, M. E.:
Protoptila group of the Glossosomatinae, 853
Trichoptera of Australia and New Zealand, 593
Mosquito nuisances in Great Britain, memo on measures for control, 902
Mosquitoes of the Ethiopian region, 336
Moss, J.: Child migration to Australia, 639
Mosses of Dominica and of the Ecuadorian Andes collected by P. R. Bell, 1102
Most Excellent Majesty, 651
Moth:
Codling, 1093
Pine looper, 893
Small ermine, 846
Swift, 847
Vapourer, 329
Motherwell and Wishaw Burgh Order Confirmation Act, 315
Bill, 251, 283

Motherwell, Bothwell, North Lanarkshire, Coatbridge and Airdrie, Boundary Commission report, 305
Moths, Clothes and house, 83
Motion Picture Industry, agreement with U.S.A. industry, 35, 204
Motor:
Transport. *See* Road.
Vehicle industry in U.S.A., 618
Vehicles:
and Cycles, Census of Production, 458, 1200
and tourism, Customs formalities adopted, 1066
(International Circulation) Act, 308,
Bill, 250, 251, 282, 284
Offences, returns, 24, 129, 275, 382, 533, 778, 794, 1050, 1146
Motor-Cycle Accidents, 468
Moulder, foundry craftsmen, 142
Moulinearn, railway accident, 975
Mountbatten, Vice Admiral Earl: South-east Asia, 243
Mourant, A. E.: Rh Blood Groups and their clinical effects, 420, 1171
Mourning, Earl Marshal's order, 418
Movement of population to new and expanded towns, 648
Movements of salmon off the north-east coast of England, 1092
Moving and growing, 353
Mr. Speaker Clifton Brown's Retirement Act, 61
Bill, 7, 34
Muir, Major Kenneth, award of V.C., 166
Muir-Wood, H. M.: Phylum Brachiopoda, 1103
Mule spinners' cancer, 417
Mull and Mor formation in relation to forest soils, 892
Mullen-Strauss, M.: Newsreels across the world, 493
Multilateral conventions, status of, 742, 999
Munich, aftermath of, 110, 362
Murder of Beatrice Alice Rimmer, inquiry report, 292, 382
Murray, J. S.: Rusts of British forest trees, 1133
Murray, R.: On the accuracy of contour charts in forecasting upper winds, 941
Muscat, Treaty of friendship, commerce and navigation, 288, 300, 303
Musee de l'Homme (Paris), Archives of recorded music, 493
Museum:
Monographs, 499, 500, 757, 1014
Quarterly review, 232, 493, 747, 1006
Museums:
and Galleries, Standing Commission, reports, 190, 983
and monuments, 747, 1006
See also Libraries.
Mushroom growing, 77, 1094
Music:
in secondary schools, 443
in the schools of Wales, 614
Recorded, archives of, 493, 747
Setting and marking of examinations, guidance for teachers, 1191
Musical instruments, Census of Production, 459, 1200
Mutual:
Co-operation Pact with Turkey and Iraq, 1063
Security Agency, publications, 422
Myrddin-Evans, Sir G. (Chairman): Human relations in industry conference, report, 401
Mytilicola intestinalis Steuer, biology and dispersal, 849
Myxomatosis:
Advisory Committee reports, 850, 1092
in rabbits and hares, circular, 1092

N

NAAS Quarterly Review, 80, 333, 589, 850, 1092, 1096
Naish, G. P. B.: Ship models picture book, 787
Nall, G. H.: Movements of salmon and sea trout and of brown trout tagged in the Tweed, 1192
Nandi work and culture, 92
Narcissus:
Culture, 79
Flies, 586, 1093
Pests, 331
Narcotic drugs:
Annual reports of Governments, summary, 222
Commission, reports, 222, 223, 480, 481, 733
Commentary on the single convention, 739
Estimated world requirements, 221, 479, 731, 988
Illicit transactions and seizures, 226, 485, 739, 995
Laws and regulations, 222, 480, 732, 989
Narcotics:
Bulletin, 226, 486, 739, 995
Statistics reports, 739, 996
Narrow fabrics, Census of Production, 201, 1200
Nash, G. D.: Thermal insulation of buildings, 1189
Nathan, Rt. Hon. Lord (Chairman): Law and practice relating to Charitable Trusts, 306
National:
Accounts:
Studies, 356, 618
System, simplified, 101
and supporting tables, 742

National (*continued*):
Administration and international organisation, survey of 14 countries, 232
Agricultural Advisory Service:
Journal. *See* NAAS Quarterly Review.
Report, 1096
Arbitration Tribunal awards, 154
Art Collections Bill, 516, 517
Assistance:
Act, 313, 572
Explanatory memo on draft amendment regulation, 47, 171
Amendment Regulations, memos, 291, 423, 1077, 1175
(Amendment) Act, 60
Bill, 5, 32, 33
Board, reports, 47, 171, 300, 423, 557, 681, 816, 943, 1070, 1175
(Determination of Need) Amendment Regulations, 826, 943
Estimates, 522, 1036
S.R.O. & S.I. Revised, 194
Bibliographical services, 749
Brick Advisory Council, paper, 244
Building Studies, 184, 244, 245, 440, 698, 955, 1187
Coal Board, reports and accounts, 19, 121, 268, 373, 527, 633, 788, 896, 1044, 1137
Advisory Committee on Organisation, 1173
Collection of industrial bacteria, catalogue, 955
Commissions, handbook, 232
Debt:
Position of funds, 49, 218, 298, 473, 557, 726, 815, 983, 1070, 1218
Returns, 55, 218, 303, 473, 563, 726, 823, 983, 1070, 1218
S.R.O. & S.I. Revised, 194
Federated Electrical Association and Electrical Trades Union, dispute inquiry, 562
Film Finance Corporation, reports and accounts, 41, 204, 292, 462, 551, 715, 814, 969, 1065, 1204
Food Survey Committee, reports, 105, 881, 1096
Forest:
Parks, guides, 893, 1133
Policies in Europe, 732
Fuel Policy, thermal insulation report, circular, 647
Galleries of Scotland:
Reports, 942, 1173
S.R.O. & S.I. Revised, 194
Gallery, 1173
and Tate Gallery Act, 829
Bill, 517, 769, 771, 772, 776, 801
Health:
Insurance, S.R.O. & S.I. Revised, 194
National (*continued*):
Health (*continued*):
Service:
Accounts, 18, 124, 258, 266, 378, 526, 637, 638, 788, 902, 1041, 1144
Acts, 60, 308, 572
Bills, 3, 32, 251, 282, 283
(Amendment) Act, 65
Central Health Services Council report, 18, 126
Development of consultant services, 126
Distribution of remuneration among general practitioners, Working Party report, 378
Estimates, revised, 21, 215
Hospital:
and specialist services, England and Wales, 638
Analysis of running costs, Scotland, 1142
Costing returns, 636, 638, 902, 1143
S.R.O. & S.I. Revised, 194
Scotland, 901
(Scotland) Act, accounts, 10, 379, 524, 788, 902, 1042, 1142
Superannuation Scheme explained, 379
Supplementary ophthalmic services, 126, 1144
Income:
and Expenditure, 41, 218, 337, 550, 593, 727, 855, 1103
Estimates, 290, 473, 810, 983, 1062, 1219
Statistics, 488, 741, 999
and its distribution in under-developed countries, 488
of Nigeria, 861
Insurance:
Accounts, 258, 423, 523, 682, 785, 944
Acts, 60, 65, 313, 568, 572, 830, 1079
Bills, 4, 32, 514, 528, 537, 542, 543, 644, 778, 803, 1056
(Amendment) Bill, 1054
(No. 2) Bill, 1027, 1055
Advisory Committee reports, 294, 295, 298, 423, 425
Amendment Regulations, 173, 175, 176, 177, 270, 424, 425, 682, 689, 944, 947, 1178, 1180
Reports, 21, 22, 173, 263, 264, 265, 268, 269, 270, 272, 273, 274, 280, 281, 423, 424, 522, 525, 529, 534, 535, 688, 780, 782, 788, 943, 1034, 1039, 1045, 1049, 1051, 1175, 1176
(Amendment) Bill, 31
and Family Allowances, revised Estimate, 530

National (*continued*):
Insurance (*continued*):
and National Assistance, Estimates, 520, 784
Bill:
Memo and report, 827, 944
Proposed changes, memo, 550, 685
Report on financial provisions, 42, 175, 826, 944
Commissioner's decisions:
Index, 422
Claims, 172, 173, 425, 683, 688, 943, 1176
Classification and Insurability, 14, 20, 21, 218, 423, 688, 944
Estimates, 215, 262, 470, 1036
Everybody's guide, 1175
Existing Pensioners' Fund, account, 20, 171
Funds, account, 20, 171, 1040, 1178
Government Actuary's report, 269, 473
(Increase of Benefit and Miscellaneous Provisions) Regulations, 425, 1175
Reports, 280, 1039
Industrial Injuries:
Acts, 313, 568
Bill, 285
Decisions on claims, 174, 175, 176, 428, 429, 430, 685, 686, 689, 945, 946, 947, 1178, 1179
Government Actuary's report, 279, 474
(No. 2) Bill, 513, 530, 537, 543, 644
Raynaud's Phenomenon, 828, 944
Reports, 24, 176, 218, 540, 555, 685, 727, 790, 983, 1033, 1219
Superannuation (Miscellaneous Provisions) Act, accounts, 9, 174
Time limits for claiming benefits, report on, 291, 428
Liability for contributions of persons with small incomes, 1063, 1175
(Maternity Benefit and Miscellaneous Provisions) Regulations, report, 783, 943
Ministry of:
Publications, 171, 422, 681
Reports, 57, 171, 300, 423
See also Pensions and National Insurance.
Regulations, draft report, 528
Reports, 527, 529, 554, 556, 557, 682, 727, 786, 798, 983
Retirement Pensions, report, 947
Scheme, proposed changes, 44, 177
Service, revised estimate, 215
National (*continued*):
Insurance (*continued*):
(Small Incomes) Bill, 890
S.R.O. & S.I. Revised, 194
Unemployment and Sickness Benefit, report, 1075
Land Fund, account, 23, 218, 272, 474, 533, 627, 792, 983, 1046, 1219
Library of Scotland, S.R.O. & S.I. Revised, 194
Maritime Museum, publications, 177, 430, 687, 942, 1173
Museum of Antiquities for Scotland:
Act, 829
Bill, 517, 544
Reports, 298, 444, 1174
Parks:
and Access to the Countryside Act, 314
Reports, 29, 133, 279, 388, 648, 1051, 1152
(Grants) Regulations, explanatory memo, 913
Commission:
Publications, 177, 687
Reports, 279, 388, 539, 650, 799, 913
Film strip, 1174
Physical Laboratory, publications, 177, 430, 687, 943, 1174
Pinetum and forest plots at Bedgebury, guide, 117
Product and expenditure statistics, 879
Products, 879
Registration, S.R.O. & S.I. Revised, 195
Research Development Corporation, reports and accounts, 9, 204, 261, 462, 520, 540, 715, 1033, 1204
Savings Committee:
Report, 1174
Select Committee on Estimates, reports, 1041, 1050, 1147
Service, 1075, 1114, 1169
Act, 572, 676, 314, 1080
Bill, 803, 1026, 1035, 1043, 1148
(Amendment) Act, 313
(Channel Islands) Bill, 1056
(Conscientious Objectors) Bill, 517
Decisions of the Umpire, 163, 676, 937
Education during, 1015
Effects on education and employment of young men, 1059
S.R.O. & S.I. Revised, 195
Servicemen:
Regulations, 241, 502, 1016
Select Committee on Estimates, report, 525, 534
Stereotypes and international understanding, 231
Stud, policy and methods of operation, 1095

National (*continued*):
Studies of nursing resources, guide for, 761
Transport, S.R.O. & S.I. Revised, 195
Trust:
Act, 573
for Scotland Order Confirmation Act, 315
Bill, 283
Union of Railwaymen. *See* British Transport Commission.
Nationalised Industries:
(Membership of Trade Unions) Bill, 282
Select Committee reports, 276, 305, 531, 644, 1050, 1148
Minutes, 1041, 1148
Nationality of married women, 226
Nationals of U.S.A in Morocco, rights of, 141
Nations of the Commonwealth, 134
Native:
Administration:
in the British African territories, 93, 605, 862
in Central Nyasaland, 344
Courts and native customary law in Africa, 599
Natural History Museum, guide, 84, 592
Naturalisation forms, 382
Nature Conservancy, reports, 539, 678, 795, 940, 1050, 1171
Nauru, Trust Territories reports, 490, 1001
Nautical almanac, 68, 317, 576, 836, 1083
Naval:
Architecture and marine engineering, careers, 398
Court-martial procedure, 836, 1083
Discipline Act, report of Committee on Administration of Justice, 35, 68
Electrical:
Manual, 317
Pocket book, 836
Officer's sword, 1173
Navigation:
Admiralty manual of, 836
Today, exhibition, 694
Navy:
and Marines (Wills) Act, 568
Bill, 513, 524, 538, 541, 645
and Naval Reserves, S.R.O. & S.I. Revised, 195
Appropriation accounts, 13, 68, 260, 317, 521, 576, 781, 837, 1034, 1083
Career, 921
Dockyard and Production accounts, 13, 69, 264, 317, 524, 576, 785, 837, 1038, 1084
Estimates, 12, 14, 39, 69, 261, 262, 289, 318, 520, 522, 548, 576, 782, 808, 837, 1035, 1045, 1061, 1084, 1219
Lists, 69, 318, 576, 837, 1084
Statements of excess, 524, 576, 784, 837
Navy (*continued*):
Votes, 14, 17, 218, 261, 265, 318, 474, 526, 727, 786, 983, 1035, 1039, 1219
Navy, Army, and Air Force Reserves Act, 829
Bill, 517, 539, 541, 544, 645
Neden, (Sir) W. (Chairman): Electricity Sub-Committee, reports, 923, 1159
Needles, Pins, Fish hooks, and metal small-wares, Census of Production, 459, 966
Nepal, Treaty, 47, 112
Nervous temperament, 420
Netherlands:
Documents of identity for aircraft personnel, 1073, 1128
Foreign Trade Statistical Bulletin, 355, 356, 617, 878
Graves in Netherlands territories of members of Armed Forces of British Commonwealth, 56, 112
National Accounts Studies, 356
Reciprocal recognition of permits for carriage of dangerous goods in air-craft, 47, 112
Repayment of credits guaranteed by European Payments Union, 821, 888
Settlement:
of conflicting claims to German enemy assets, 41, 112
of wartime debts, 806, 888
Social Security Convention, 822, 888
Netley Abbey, guide, 762
Neue Notiophygidae, 853
Neville-Jones, D.:
Selenium, 956
Survey of sulphur and sulphuric acid position, 442
New:
Colleges of further education, 98, 119
Forest, guide, 117
Gospel fragments, 82, 1101
Guinea, Trust Territories reports, 490, 1001
Hebrides:
Colonial Reports, 90, 860, 1109
Economic survey, 602
Regulation of civil aviation, 54
Himalayan species of Pediculars with special reference to those from eastern Himalaya, 1102
Homes for old, 1152
Horizons at Tzentzenhuaro, 747
Housing Areas (Church Buildings) Measure, 770, 835, 855
Ecclesiastical Commissioners' reports, 770, 855
Primary schools, 1119
School playing fields, 1119
Schools, limits of cost, 872
Secondary schools, 872
Streets Act, 60
Bill, 3, 4, 15, 26, 30, 31, 33, 131
Circular, 140

NEW-PAC | 1951-5

New (*continued*):
Towns:
Accounts, 9, 124, 165, 258, 377, 388, 525, 637, 650, 791, 901, 913, 1042, 1142, 1152
Act, 308, 568, 572, 1080
Bill, 251, 282, 515, 543, 803, 1025
Designation order, 1142
Reports, 11, 22, 29, 133, 189, 199, 277, 279, 388, 444, 531, 704, 779, 791, 792, 913, 960, 1046, 1048, 1152, 1192
Trials in criminal cases, Departmental Committee report, 812, 905
Trochiliscus from the Downtonian of Podolia, 336
Valuation Lists (Postponement) Act, 308
Bill, 255, 285
Village in Malaya, 914
Year's Honours Lists, 166, 418, 677, 938, 1170
Zealand:
Filmstrip, 347
Introducing, 134
S.R.O. & S.I. Revised, 195
Newall, R. S.: Stonehenge, guide, 762, 1225
Newbold, E. M.: Contribution to the study of the human factor in the causation of accidents, 419
Newbury Corporation Act, 573
Newcastle Central Station, railway accident, 467
Newcastle-upon-Tyne Corporation Act, 315, 834
Newfoundland, S.R.O. & S.I. Revised, 195
Newport:
Corporation Act, 574, 834
(Isle of Wight) Pier and Harbour Order Confirmation Act, 834
Bill, 774, 802
News agencies, 1006
Newsham railway accident, 719
Newspaper:
and Periodical Printing and Publishing, Census of Production, 460, 1201
Proprietors' Association, A.E.U. and E.T.U., dispute, 1063, 1162
S.R.O. & S.I. Revised, 195
Newsprint trends, 1005
Newsreels across the world, 493
Newton, L. M.: Marine algae, 592
Newton, M. P.: Internal migration, 122
Niall MacPherson Indemnity Act, 829
Bill, 801
Nicaragua:
Economic surveys, 204, 970
FAO Mission report, 235
Nicol, C. G. M.: Food poisoning report, 1144
Nicol, J.: Canada's Farm Radio Forum, 1006
Nigeria:
Colonial reports, 91, 600, 860, 1108
Nigeria (*continued*):
Colony, S.R.O. & S.I. Revised, 195
Conference report, 806, 862
Fiscal Commissioner's report, 567, 602
Insect infestation of stored food products, 344
National income, 861
Native administration, 93
Today (filmstrip), 1153
See also Africa, West.
Nigerian:
Constitution, report, 560, 603
Livestock Mission report, 93
Night baking, 55, 163
Nilsson-Leissner, G.: Legumes in agriculture, 750
Nine-Power Conference, Final Act, 823, 888
Nitrogenous fertilisers for farm crops, 1093
No room for them? Problem of refugees, 865
Nocturnal winds, 941
Noise measurement techniques, 1174
Non-effective charges (pensions), Estimates, 263, 470
Non-ferrous:
Heavy metal fabrication in U.S.A., 879
Metals:
and alloy steels in Germany, Development and use of substitute materials, 184
(Smelting, rolling, etc.), Census of Production, 458, 1199
Year Book, 102
Ore dressing in U.S.A., 618
Non-industrial Employment Bill, 1041, 1043, 1053, 1148
Non-metalliferous mines and quarries, Census of Production, 712
Non-self-governing territories:
Educational conditions, 990
Reports of Committee on Information, 736, 737, 993
Social conditions, special study, 996
Summaries and analysis of information, 226, 486, 739
Nonsense alphabet, 499
Noppen, J. G.: Chapter House, Westminster Abbey, guide, 761
Norfolk, Census, 1138
North:
America to Europe, meteorological report, 680
Atlantic:
Ocean Stations, conference report, 918
Treaty (Organisation):
Accession of:
Federal republic of Germany, 1068, 1129
Greece and Turkey, 57, 113, 290, 365

North (*continued*):
Atlantic (*continued*):
Treaty (Organisation) (*continued*):
Forces, status of, 47, 112, 1058, 1128
International Military Headquarters, status of, 304, 365
National representatives and international staff, status of, 56, 113, 1060, 1128
Organisation and system of command, 42, 98
Reports, 431, 545, 553, 627
See also Alliance for Peace.
Borneo:
Colonial reports, 91, 344, 601, 861, 1109
Geology, 345
S.R.O. & S.I. Revised, 195
of Scotland:
College of Agriculture Educational Endowment Scheme, memo, 1190
Hydro-electric Board:
Constructional schemes, 290
See also Hydro-electric development.
Explanatory memos, 827, 1062, 1064, 1067, 1072
Guarantees given:
on loans proposed to be raised, 1046, 1049
on stock issued, 1050
Reports and accounts, 19, 189, 267, 444, 523, 704, 783, 960, 1035, 1193
Queensferry Tunnel, railway accident, 975
Wales:
Ancient monuments, 1018
Hydro-electric Power Act, 315, 1082
Bill, 1027
North, J.: Achievement of 21st Army Group, 251
Northampton Sand Ironstone, stratigraphy structure and reserves, 123
Northamptonshire, Census, 896
Northern:
Assurance Act, 834
England:
Ancient monuments, 504
Regional geology, 635
Ireland:
Act, 1080
Bill, 1026, 1054
(Foyle Fisheries) Act, 308
Bill, 7, 34
Geological survey bulletins, 1140
S.R.O. & S.I. Revised, 195
Rhodesia:
and Angola, frontier agreement with Portugal, 1064
Colonial reports, 91, 591, 861
Northolt:
Airport and Lympne Airport, Air Navigation Order, 973
Junction, railway accident, 210
Northumberland, Census, 896
North-West American forests in relation to silviculture in Great Britain, 1133
Norway:
Air Services Agreement, 298, 365, 502, 627, 1075, 1129
Avoidance of double taxation, etc., 45, 54, 113, 1076, 1129
Campaign (war history), 337
Consular Convention, 45, 113
Cultural Convention, 546, 627
Documents of identity for aircraft personnel, 1073, 1129
Economic conditions, 616
Fisheries case, judgment, 397
Foreign Trade Statistical Bulletins, 356, 617, 878
Lobster, distribution, biology and exploitation, 960
Monetary agreement, 563, 627
National Accounts Studies, 618
Participation of a Norwegian Brigade Group in occupation of Germany, 51, 113, 297, 365
Trade agreement, 37, 54, 113
See also War.
Notifiable diseases, Cases of and deaths from, 754, 1011
Notostraca, review of, 1102
Nettebohm case (Liechtenstein v. Guatemala), 657, 919
Nottingham:
City and County Boundaries Act, 67
Corporation Act, 315
Railway accident, 719
South, Boundary Commission report, 269, 379
Nottinghamshire:
and Derbyshire Traction Act, 315
Census, 896
County Council Act, 67
Notulae criticae ad floram Hispaniae pertinentes, 853
Nuclear:
Development. *See* Commonwealth.
Fuels for civil purposes, 826, 888
Power, 1060, 1137, 1171
Research:
Convention for establishment of European Organisation, 565, 627
European co-operation, 1007
Nuneaton Corporation Act, 1081
Nurse tutors, function status and training, 901
Nurseries and plantations, forest, summary methods of establishing, 117
Nurses:
Act, 64, 313
District, training of, 1144

Nurses (*continued*):
Position of enrolled assistant nurse, 901, 1142
Registration Act, 310
(Scotland) Act, 60
Bill, 3, 4, 33
Report, 4
S.R.O. & S.I. Revised, 195
Work of nurses in hospital wards, 1142
Nursing:
Education, Working Conference, 756
Expert Committee reports, 238, 498
Homes, S.R.O. & S.I. Revised, 195
Survey of recent legislation, 755
Nutrition:
Committee for South and East Asia, report, 1010
Expert Committee reports, 495, 498, 1013
Inter-African Conference report, 862
Manual, 620, 1097
Meetings, reports, 1010
Nutritional Studies, 235, 752, 1010
Nutritive value of bread, 940
Nyasaland:
Colonial reports, 91, 600, 860, 1108, 1109
Economic survey, 345
Native administration, 93, 344
See also Rhodesia.
Nyasaland-Mozambique frontier, agreement with Portugal, 1064

O

Oake, G. R. (Chairman): Interdepartmental Committee on Meat Inspection, report, 105
Oakley, K. P.: Solution of Piltdown Problem, 591, 1102
Oat crop, disease of, 328
Oath, S.R.O. & S.I. Revised, 195
Oats. *See* Scottish seed.
Obando, N.: Rice enrichment in the Philippines, 1010
Oberwager, J.: How to print posters, 745
O'Brien, T. H.: Civil Defence (war history), 1103
Obscene publications:
Bill, 1054, 1056
Suppression of circulation agreement, 38, 113, 286, 365
Observer's:
Handbook, 421
Primer, 170
Occupation:
of Germany, participation of:
Danish contingent, 51
Norwegian Brigade Group, 51
Regime in Germany, documents, 1059
Occupational:
Factors in the aetiology of gastric and duodenal ulcers, 169
Occupational (*continued*):
Fertility, decennial supplement, 634
Health, report of joint ILO/WHO committee, 756
Mortality, 897
Therapist, career, 921
Occupations, classification, 121
Occupiers' liability, Law Reform Committee report, 824, 939
Ocean:
Station Vessel Manual, 656, 918
Stations, agreement, 817, 888
Sunfishes, 83
Weather stations, agreement, 556, 628, 1070, 1129
Ocean Vulcan trials, 576, 837, 1084
O'Conor, M. (Chairman): Committee on Welfare of the Deaf, report on special needs of deaf-blind persons
Octopodinae in the collections of the British Museum, revision, 1101
OEEC at work for Europe, 879
Offals in Meat Products Order, circular, 619
Offences:
Drunkenness, 59, 129, 304, 382, 562, 641, 823, 905, 1074
Motor vehicles, 275, 382, 533, 642, 778, 794, 905, 974, 1050
Office worker, career, 1157
Officers, Service gratuities, 502
Official:
List, Registrar-General's, 122, 374, 634, 897, 1139
Secrets:
Acts, 61, 64
S.R.O. & S.I. Revised, 195
Sources, guides to, 634
Statistics, studies in, 337
Ogg, Sir W. (Chairman): Soil Survey Research Board, reports, 77, 328, 585, 845
Ogilvie, L.: Diseases of vegetables, 1095
Ogmore Castle, guide, 762
Oil:
Defence Specification, 98
Dispute, correspondence with Iran, 303
in Navigable Waters:
Act, 62, 1080
Bill, 777, 1025, 1026, 1027, 1040, 1043, 1054, 1055, 1148
S.R.O. & S.I. Revised, 195
Industry, correspondence with Persia, 59
Refinery expansion, reports, 102, 618
Refining and drilling in U.S.A., 356
Swedish shale, 357
Oils:
and greases, Census of Production, 458, 1199
See also Fats.
Old:
Age, Committee report, 826, 983
Metals, sale and control of dealers, 1146

Older men and women, employment, 562
Oldfield-Davies, A. (Chairman): Central Advisory Council for Education (Wales), report on music in schools of Wales, 614
Oldham, areas comprised in East and West constituencies, 20
Oldroyd, H.: House flies of Ethiopian region, 336, 854
Oliver, D. A. (Chairman): Metals Economy Advisory Committee, report, 455
Oman, C.: Wellington Plate, Portuguese service, 1014
Ommanney, F. D.: Mauritius-Seychelles fisheries survey, 602
Omnibus industry, inquiry report, 809, 924
One week's news, 1006
O'Neil, B. H. St. J.:
Audley End, guide, 1225
Caerlaverock Castle, guide, 504
Castles of England and Wales, 1019
Deal Castle, guide, 761
Onion and leek smut, 847
Onions and related crops, 1094
Open fires, 761
Operation Rescue, 650
Operations Division, report, 140
Ophthalmic services, 126, 1144
See also National Health Service.
Opium:
Conference, Protocol and Final Act, 996
Limiting and regulating cultivation of poppy plant, 563, 628
Permanent Central Opium Board, report on narcotics statistics, 226
Opler, M. E.: Social aspects of technical assistance in operation, 1007
Opticians, statutory registration, 292, 379
Orange squash, 103
Orders, Decorations and Medals, etc.:
Instructions regarding wearing, 241, 501, 1016
Order of precedence, 167, 938, 1170
Ordnance:
Factories, Select Committee on Estimates, report, 276
Survey, publications, 177, 687, 943, 1174
Organisation:
and finance of adult education in England and Wales, 872
and methods techniques, handbook, 657
Charts and lists of duties, 983
Organised camping, 353
Oriented rutile of a high-temperature andesine from Nigeria, 336
Origin and destination of passengers, statistical summary, 140
Orkney:
Ancient monuments, 504
Census, 898
Orpington Urban District Council Act, 834
Osborne, E. C.: Manual of travelling exhibitions, 747
Osborne House, guide, 1225
Osmond, D. A.: Soils of the Wem district of Shropshire, 850
Osterley Park, guide, 757, 1014
Ostracod genus Trachyleberis, 592
O'Sullivan, His Honour Judge D. N. (Chairman): Committee on disposal of internal restitution claims in British Zone of Germany, report, 107
Otariid seals of the Pacific coast of America, 853
Our men in Korea, 502
Over and Bare Fens investigation, 331
Overfishing, postponement of operation of Convention, 551, 628
Oversea:
Civil Service, appointments, career, 1107
Education, 93, 346, 603, 863, 1110
Migration Board, report, 820, 864
Overseas:
Broadcasting, Select Committee on Estimates, reports, 274, 522
Economic surveys, 204, 463, 715, 969, 1204
Food Corporation:
Future of, 36, 94, 105, 813, 816, 863
Reports and accounts, 27, 94, 520, 603, 779, 795, 863
Information services, summary of report of independent committee of enquiry 812, 888
Resources Development Acts, 60, 829
Bills, 1, 31, 776, 802
Accounts, 257, 346, 359, 519, 603, 779, 798, 863, 1049, 1111
S.R.O. & S.I. Revised, 195
Trade, 205, 463, 716, 970, 1205
of the United Kingdom, 205
Overseers, England, S.R.O. & S.I. Revised, 195
Owen Falls:
Construction of Dam, exchange of Notes with Egypt, 811, 1078
Picture set, 1153
Owen, R.: India, economic survey, 716
Ox warble fly, 1094
Oxford:
Corporation Act, 574
Motor Services Act, 67
Oxfordshire, Census, 1138
Oxley, T. A.: Detection of insects by their carbon dioxide production, 440
Oysters:
Purification in simple pits, 849
Reproduction in rivers Crouch and Roach, 332

P

Pacific:
Cable, S.R.O. & S.I. Revised, 195
Charter, 824
Islands, trust territories reports, 490, 1001

1951-5 | PAC-POI

PAC— INDEX 1951-5

Packaging and Handling of Food Bill, 31
Packing apples in returnable bushel boxes, 847
Paint and varnish, Census of Production, 458, 1199
Painting:
  Asbestos cement, 457, 503
  Metals in buildings, 953
  Woodwork, 181, 503
Paintings:
  Care of, 230
  Catalogue of colour reproductions, 491, 744
Paints, emulsion, 695
Paisley Technical College Scheme, 958
Pakistan:
  Economic survey, 205, 1204
  Financial agreement, 55, 95
  looks to the future, 914
  Trade agreement, 40, 205
Palaearctic and Indian mammals, checklist, 84
Palaeontology, Great Britain, 1140
Palembang, Sumatra: Carrier-borne aircraft attack on oil refineries, 167
Palestine:
  Refugees in the Near East, United Nations publications, 224, 483, 484, 735, 736, 737, 993
  Settlement of financial matters outstanding as result of termination of mandate agreement with Jordan, 45
  S.R.O. & S.I. Revised, 195
  United Nations Conciliation Commission, reports, 224, 482, 484
Palmer, Sir W. (Chairman): Iron and Steel Consumers Council, report, 530
Palmer, W.: Coronation chair, 762
Panama:
  Air services agreement, 57, 113
  Economic survey, 205, 1204
Pandora, wreck report, 721
Panse, V. G.: Estimation of crop yields, 1008
Paper:
  and Board, Census of Production, 460
  for Printing:
    and writing, tentative forecasts of demands, 1005
    (other than newsprint) and writing, trends, 1005
    Today and tomorrow, 747
  Industry. *See* Pulp.
Paraguay:
  Economic survey, 463
  Trade and payments agreement, 561, 628, 819, 888, 1073, 1129
Paris Conference, documents, 824, 888
Parish Council and Parish Meeting, England, S.R.O. & S.I. Revised, 195
Parishes, townships, etc., Index, 939
Park, Air Chief Marshal Sir K.: Air operations in South East Asia, 167
Parker, H. W.: Stranded whales and turtles, 593
Parliament Act, 831
Parliamentary:
  Agents, etc., rules, 519, 645
  Constituencies, proposed alterations, 825, 905, 960
  Elections:
    England and Wales, 1146
    Scotland, 445
  Returns, S.R.O. & S.I. Revised, 195
Parole and after-care, 996
Parrish, B. B.: State of haddock stocks in North Sea 1946-50 and at Faroe 1914-50, 703
Parry, Mr. Justice Wynn (Chairman): Private International Law Committee, report, 807
Parsnips, 1092
Parthasarathi, G. (Chairman): International Commission for Supervision and Control in Cambodia, report, 1065, 1073
Partnership:
  Act, 61
  S.R.O. & S.I. Revised, 195
Passenger:
  Fares increase, 291, 466
  Ships, survey, 972
Passerini, L.: Advisory assistance to member countries under UNRRA Transfer Fund, 751
Passmore, R.: Studies of expenditure of energy and consumption of food by miners and clerks, Fife, 1171
Pasture and fodder:
  Development in Mediterranean countries, 357
  Production in North West Europe, 879
Patent Office centenary, 687
Patents:
  Act, 65, 314
  and Designs Act, 833
  and technical information for defence purposes, agreement with U.S.A., 547
  European Conventions:
    Formalities required for patent applications, 809, 888, 1070, 1129
    International classification of patents for inventions, 1063, 1129
  for inventions:
    Agreement with Italy, 49, 557
    S.R.O. & S.I. Revised, 195
Patents, Designs, and Trade Marks, reports, 19, 203, 268, 431, 527, 718, 789, 943, 1044, 1175
Patents, Designs, Copyright, and Trade Marks (Emergency) Act, 64
Paterson, T. (Chairman): Non-traditional Sub-Committee of Scottish Housing Advisory Committee, report on design and workmanship of non-traditional houses, 123
Paton, W. D. M.: Compressed air illness, 940

INDEX 1951-5 —PER

Patternmaker, foundry craftsman, career, 142
Pavement design for roads and airfields, 185
Pay:
  and organisation of Civil Service medical staffs, 218
  and pensions, Army, 242
  of Queen's Army Schoolmistresses, 242
  Warrant, amendments, 242, 759, 1016, 1223
Pay, Allowances, and Bounties for officers and other ranks, 242
Pay, Appointment, Promotion, etc. of the Army, 502, 1016, 1223
Payments:
  Agreements:
    Chile, 55
    Czechoslovakia, 292
    Germany, 36
    Peru, 53, 820, 1075
  Balance of (U.K.), 291, 302
  Relations, agreements with Iran, 825, 1057
  to owners of land, guide, 1142
Pea and bean:
  Thrips, 586
  Weevils, 846
Peace:
  Investment for, 1127
  Treaties, S.R.O. & S.I. Revised, 195
  Treaty with Japan, 49, 50, 52, 56, 298, 303
Peace, T. R.: Poplars, 368
Peaceful settlement in Indonesia, 486
Peak District, filmstrip, 1174
Pears and apples, 879
  See also Apples.
Pears, cherries, broccoli, cauliflowers, Brussels sprouts, cabbage, and lettuce, Standing Committee report, 820
Pease, M.: Sex-linkage in poultry breeding, 588, 848
Peat. *See* Scottish Peat Committee.
Pedicularis, new Himalayan species, 1102
Pedlow, R. H.: Temperature and humidity gradients over first 100m. over South East England, 680
Peebles Census, 898
Peebles, T. F.: FAO advisory assistance to member countries under UNRRA Transfer Fund, 751
Peers, Sir C., guides:
  Byland Abbey, 504
  Portchester Castle, 762
  Richmond Castle, 762
Peirse, Air Chief Marshal R. E. C.: Air operations in South East Asia, 167
Pelagic Tunicata, 592
Penang:
  Arms, 599
  Flags and badges, 860
Penicillin (Merchant Ships) Act, 60
Penmaenmawr, railway accident, 210
Penman, J.: Intercranial Gliomata, 940
Pennines and adjacent areas, geology, 898
Penny, F. D.: Handbook on die castings, 709
Pension law and regulations of the Civil Service, digest, 471
Pensioners'
  Guide to the Pensions (Increase) Act, 983
  Milk Bill, 1057
Pensions:
  and National Insurance, Ministry of:
    Publications, 688, 943, 1175
    Reports, 813, 948, 1067, 1180
    Supplementary Estimate, 530
  Appeal Tribunals:
    Act, 312
    (Northern Ireland) (Amendment) Rules, 678
  Board, United Nations, reports, 735, 737, 993
  Estimates, 15, 215, 263, 523, 784, 1036
  House of Commons Members' Fund, report, 1040, 1148
  Increase of, Royal Warrant, 432, 501
  (Increase) Act, 64, 308, 313, 387, 829
    Bills, 254, 270, 278, 283, 284, 385, 771, 800
    Circular, 387
    Forms, etc., 474
  (Mercantile Marine) Act, 832
  Ministry of:
    Proposed transfer of functions, 553, 726
    Publications, 177, 431, 687
    Reports, 257, 274, 431, 533, 687
  (Navy, Army, Air Force, and Mercantile Marine) Act, 312
  Non-effective awards, 1223
  Order, 268, 431
  Retired Pay, 50
    Order, 20, 177, 178
    Royal Warrant amendment, 45, 178
  S.R.O. & S.I. Revised, 195
  Schemes, Order, Firemen, 381, 1145
  See also Police; Retired Pay; Local Government Superannuation; National Insurance.
Pentre-Ifan burial chamber, guide, 762
Per caput fibre consumption levels, 495, 750
Percival, H. V. T.: Apsley House, guide, 499, 757
Percival-Prescott, W.: Coronation chair, 762
Percy of Newcastle, Rt. Hon. Lord (Chairman):
  Burnham Committee reports on teachers' salaries, 873
  Royal Commission on law relating to mental illness and mental deficiency, evidence, 951, 1182
Perforated clay bricks, 695
Performing Animals (Regulation) Act, 831

PER— INDEX 1951-5

Periodicals, handlist of short titles, 694
Peripheral nerve injuries, 940
Perjury Act, 309
Perkins, J. F.: Notes on British Ichneumonidae with descriptions of new species, 591
Perks, J. C.: Chepstow Castle, guide, 1225
Permanent Central Opium Board, reports on statistics of narcotics, 226, 486, 739, 996
Persia, correspondence concerning oil industry, 59, 113
Persian:
  Gulf Gazette, 1129
  Paintings, 499
Personal Bills Committee, reports, 771, 772, 774, 909, 1029, 1149
Personnel:
  Licensing Division, report, 395
  Management, careers, 658
Persons with small incomes, liability for contribution (National Insurance), 1063
Perth and Kinross:
  Census, 898
  Educational Trust Scheme, memo, 701
Peru:
  Economic survey, 463, 1204
  Payments agreements, 53, 113, 820, 888, 1075, 1129
  Public Finance Information Papers, 486
  See also Colombia.
Pest:
  Control in Germany, 200
  Infestation Research, 184, 440, 698, 955, 1187
  of coconut palms in Portuguese East Africa, 591
Pesticides. *See* World Health Organisation.
Pests:
  Act, 829
    Bill, 517, 769, 771, 777, 801, 803
  and diseases of:
    Brassicae, 846
    Chrysanthemums, 329
Pet Animals Act, 60
  Bill, 3, 18, 26, 30, 32, 131
Peterlee New Town, reports, 29, 279, 388, 779, 792, 913, 1048
Peters, Prof. Sir R. (Chairman): Vitamin C Sub-committee, report, 679
Petrography of some of the Riebeckite-granites of Nigeria, 375
Petroleum:
  (Consolidation) Act, 63, 311
  Products, exchange of Notes with Egypt, 1060
  S.R.O. & S.I. Revised, 195
Petrology of Graham Land, 862, 1110
Pevensey Castle, guide, 762
Pharmacopoeias, Expert Committee on unification of, report, 238
Pharmacy:
  Act, 568, 829
    Bill, 512, 526, 538, 541, 645, 773, 774, 777, 801, 803
Pharmacy (*continued*):
  Act (*continued*):
    Consolidation of Enactments (Procedure) Act Memo, 773
    Report, 774, 775
  and Medicines Act, 64
  and Poisons Act, 63, 311
    Form, 642
Philippines:
  Air services agreement, 1074, 1129
  National income and its distribution, 742
  Transfer of Turtle and Mangsee Islands, 50, 113
  Unesco Educational Mission, report, 233
Philip, J. R. (Chairman): Committee on National Museum of Antiquities of Scotland, report, 298, 444
Philipson, W. R.: Contributions to knowledge of Araliaceae; Undescribed species of Mastichodendron (Sapotaceae) from Barbados and Antigua, 83
Phillips, R. W.: FAO Advisory assistance to member countries under UNRRA Transfer Fund, 751
Phillips, Sir T. (Chairman): Economic and financial problems of the provision for old age, committee report, 826
Philosophy, teaching of, 748
Photo-heliographic results, 376, 636, 899, 1141
Photometric survey of solar flares, plages, and prominences in *Ha* light, 436
Photometry, unit and standard of measurement, 430
Phylum Brachiopoda, 1103
Physical:
  Education in the primary school, 614
    Draft syllabus, 958
  Oceanography of the Irish Sea, 1096
  Training:
    and Recreation, Scotland, S.R.O. & S.I. Revised, 195
    Lessons for Cadets, 242
Physically handicapped:
  Children, Expert reports on, 489, 756
  Services for, 998
Physiotherapist, career, 921
Phyto-sanitary Convention for Africa south of the Sahara, 820, 889
Pickford, G. E.: Revision of the Octopodinae in collections of British Museum, 1102
Pictorial, United Nations, 739
Piercy, Rt. Hon. Lord (Chairman):
  Committee on recruitment and training for Youth Employment Service, report, 164
  National Youth Employment Council, report on Youth Employment Service, 937
Piershill Junction, Edinburgh, railway accident, 467

INDEX 1951-5 —POI

Pig:
  Feeding, 586, 1093
  Food, antibiotics in, 585
  Husbandry, 80
    (Breeding and management), 846
  Production:
    Costs and efficiency, 849
    Development of, 1074, 1090, 1097, 1146
Pigeon. *See* Wood pigeon
Pigs, housing of, 588
Pilcher, Mr. Justice (Chairman): Committee on Administration of Justice under the Naval Discipline Act, report, 35
Pillar of Eliseg, guide, 762
Pilotage:
  Act, 309
  Authorities (Limitation of Liability) Act, 312
Pilots and Navigators, Meteorological handbook for, amendments, 421
Pilots' licences, amendment list, 595
Piltdown problem, solution, 591, 1102
Pine:
  Corsican, general volume tables, 117
  Looper moth, 893
  Sawflies, 1133
Pink rot and watery wound rot of potatoes, 1093
Pipelines and storage tanks, cathodic protection of, 696
Pipes, Asbestos-cement pressure, survey of behaviour in use, 440
Pires, E. A.: Training of rural school teachers, 1006
Pit silage, 585
Place of Welsh and English in schools of Wales, 614
Place-names, index, 1138
Plague, 1012
  Expert Committee report, 757
Plaice, fecundity of, 79
Plain Words. *See* Complete Plain Words.
Plankton of the waters approaching the British Isles, 1192
Planning:
  Appeals, circular, 648
  Permissions, drafting of, 164
Plant:
  and animal nutrition in relation to soil and climatic factors, 82
  Breeders, list of, 752
  for pre-stressing concrete, 244
  Pathology, 333, 589, 850, 1092, 1097
  Protection:
    Bulletins, 753, 1010
    International Convention, 297, 365, 808, 889
    See also Phyto-sanitary.
  Proteins in child feeding, 679
  Quarantine regulations, digest, 751
Plantation crops, production trade and consumption, 604, 864, 1111
Plantations, thinning of, 117, 1133
Plaster, internal, blowing, popping or fitting, 181
Plastering, 243
  Internal, avoiding defects in, 953
Plastic:
  Goods and fancy articles, Census of Production, 460, 1202
  White line markings, recommendations for, 185
Plastics:
  in the tropics, 455, 710
  Materials, Census of Production, 1199
  Selected Government Research Reports, 441, 1188
Plate, S.R.O. & S.I. Revised, 195
Platinum, export licence, 202
Play with a purpose, 126
Playfair, E. W. (Chairman): Local Government Manpower Committee, report, 58
Playfair, Maj.-Gen. I. S. O.: Early successes against Italy, 854, 961
Playgrounds for blocks of flats, provision of, 910
Playing-cards, S.R.O. & S.I. Revised, 195
Playing-fields, New school, 1119
Pleadings, oral arguments, etc. *See* International Court of Justice.
Pleistocene fauna of two Blue Nile sites, 84
Plesters, R. J.: Further contributions to solution of Piltdown problem, 1102
Plumage, S.R.O. & S.I. Revised, 195
Plumber, career, 398
Plumbing for housing, 437
Plums and cherries:
  Pollination, 330
  Pruning, 78, 1093
Plymouth, Devonport and Sutton, Boundary Commission, report, 38
Plywood, strength properties of, 1186
Pneumatic and electric tools, 243
Pneumoconiosis:
  among coalminers in South Wales, social consequences, 169
  and Byssinosis:
    Benefit Act, 61
      Bill, 7, 33
    Bill, 33
  Industrial Injuries Advisory Council report, 555
  Statistics:
    Digest, 1137
    in the mining and quarrying industries, 896
Poaching of Deer (Scotland) Bill, 250, 283, 1053
Pocock, R. I.: Catalogue of genus Felis, 84
Podostemaceae, Notes on, for revision of flora of West Tropical Africa, 591
Poisonous plants, British, 1095
Poisons, S.R.O. & S.I. Revised, 195

Poland:
Documents on German Foreign Policy, 625
Financial matters, agreement for settlement, 827, 889
Sterling Payments Agreement, 41, 56, 114, 292, 303, 366, 546, 550, 560, 562, 628, 807, 811, 816, 825, 827, 889
Polesworth, railway accident, 467
Police:
and prison services, careers, 398
Counties and Burghs, reports, 19, 129, 530, 642, 788, 905, 1035, 1146
Extraneous duties, 642
Forces in East and West Germany, 817
Long Service and Good Conduct Medal, Royal Warrant instituting, 47
Pensions, Working Party report, 382, 704
Representative organisations and negotiating machinery, 382, 445
S.R.O. & S.I. Revised, 195
(Scotland) Bill, 1027, 1028, 1030, 1031, 1057
Draft, 563, 704
Explanatory memo, 1063, 1193
Report, 1028
Standardisation of promotion examinations, 129
Stations, design and construction, 1146
See also Metropolis.
Policy for Europe today, 606
Poliomyelitis, Expert committee report, 1013
Polishes, Census of Production, 200, 966
Political:
Activities of Civil Servants, 549, 727
and Security Questions, records, 224, 991
Rights of women, 232
Science, 1007
Bibliography, 986, 1003
International Congress, 746
Pollination, 330
Pollitt, H. W. W.: Colonial road problems, 861
Pollitzer, R.: Plague, 1012
Pollokshields East and Queen's Park, railway accident, 467
Pollution:
of the Humber, 332
of the Sea by oil, international conference, 816
Polychaete fauna of the Gold Coast, 1102
Polythene in the tropics, 710
Polyzoan genus Crepidacantha Levinsen, 853
Pool Betting Act, 829
Bill, 772, 786, 798, 800, 801, 907
Pooling skills for human progress, 739
Pope-Hennessy, J.:
Italian Gothic sculpture, 499
Samson and a Philistine, 1014
Virgin and child, 500
Poplar, American, 100
Poplars, 368
Population:
and Area return. *See* Rates return.
and culture, 1006
and vital statistics, reports, 741, 999
Bulletins, 486, 739, 996
Census methods, handbook, 1000
Commission reports, 222, 480, 481, 732, 733
Ecclesiastical areas, 1138
Estimates of, 121, 374, 634, 897, 1139
Methods of estimating, manual, 739
Movements. *See* Internal migration.
Royal Commission papers, 1182
Studies, 739, 996
Trends, Determinants and consequences of, 996
Welsh-speaking, 1138
See also General Register Office; Census; Decennial supplement: Medical and Population Subjects; Rates in Scotland.
Port of London Act, 315
Portraits at the National Maritime Museum, 942, 1173
Portchester Castle, guide, 762
Ports Efficiency Committee, reports for the co-ordination of transport, fuel and power, 466
Portsmouth Corporation (Trolley Vehicles) Order Confirmation Act, 315
Bill, 253, 283
Portugal:
Air services agreement, 297, 366, 1066, 1130
Cultural Convention, 1057, 1077, 1130
Economic survey, 1204
with annexes on Madeira and the Azores, 205
Foreign Trade Statistical Bulletins, 356, 617, 878
Monetary agreements, 36, 53, 114, 819, 889
Northern-Rhodesia-Angola frontier, etc., agreement, 1064, 1130
Nyasaland-Mozambique frontier agreement, 1064, 1129
Participation in Shire Valley project, 554, 628
Reciprocal abolition of visas, 826, 889
Repayment of credits granted by European Payments Union, 826, 889, 1067, 1130
Portuguese:
East Africa, economic survey, 463, 1205
West Africa, economic survey, 970
Post Office:
Act, 568
Bill, 510, 511, 541
Report, 509
(Amendment) Acts, 308, 569
Bill, 253, 382

Post Office (*continued*):
and Telegraph (Money) Acts, 308, 568, 1080
Bills, 253, 282, 517, 544, 1030, 1056
Commercial accounts, 29, 179, 279, 433, 540, 689, 796, 948, 1052, 1181
Consolidation of Enactments, memo, 510
Departmental Classes Recognition Committee, report, 288, 433
Development and finance reports, 1073, 1181
Estimates, Select Committee reports, 12, 531, 789
Publications, 178, 432, 689, 948, 1180
Savings Bank:
Accounts, 218, 474, 727, 983, 1219
Act, 829
Bill, 773, 774, 803
and Trustee Savings Banks Bill, report, 775
(Site and Railway) Act, 834
Bill, 773, 788, 800, 801, 907
S.R.O. & S.I. Revised, 195
Postage stamps:
of philatelic interest, export licence, 714
Round the world with, 639, 648
Postal:
Addresses, 179, 433, 948, 1181
Agreement concerning insured letters and boxes, 815, 889
Convention, Universal, 815, 889
Postan, M. M.: British war production, 337
Postcards, 762, 1226
Posters, how to print, 745
Posts in the Civil Service for University graduates, 90, 859
Post-war Building Studies, 505, 763
Pot culture of late chrysanthemums, film strip, 329
Potash fertilisers for farm crops, 1093
Potato:
Black scurf and stem canker, 584
Common scab, 178
Crops, certified, register, 77, 328, 584, 846, 1090
Gangrene skin necrosis, and similar diseases, 585
Peeling machines, electrically-operated, use and care, 1120
Root eelworm, 78, 586
Trials and collections at East Craigs, key, 77, 328, 586, 846, 1091
Verticillium wilt and black dot, 847
Potatoes:
Agricultural marketing draft scheme, 1091
Bulk storage, 849
Diseases, 846
Eelworm in, 328
Export licence, 461
Pink rot and watery wound rot, 1093
Seed, 329
Potatoes (*continued*):
Seed (*continued*):
Licence, 202
Ware, export licence, 714
Potent drugs, termination of Brussels agreements for unification of pharmacopoeial formulas, 565, 628
Pottery:
Career, 1157
Domestic and ornamental, licence, 461
English prehistoric, 499
Poultry:
Breeding, 1095
Genetics and systems, 79
Sex-linkage, 848
Culling, 79, 499
External parasites, 79, 1094
for market, preparation, 330
Housing, 1094
Management, intensive methods, 588
Nutrition, 587
on the general farm, 329, 331, 588
Pedigree recording, 587
S.R.O. & S.I. Revised, 195
Trussing, 847
Poupard, H. J. E.: German plastics industry, 966
Powder metallurgy, 205
Power:
and fuel in the malting industry, 119
Estimates, 523, 784, 1037
Loaders, support behind, 1137
Presses, committee report, 676
Stations, economy in construction, 633
Power, Admiral Sir A. J.: Carrier-borne aircraft attack on oil refineries in Palembang area, 167
Powered hand tools, 243
Practice:
Leaflets for solicitors, 676
of O. & M., 983
Pratt, C. H.: Kiln operator's handbook, 438
Precious metals refining, Census of Production, 200, 1200
Precision electrical measurements, symposium, 1174
Preliminary project, 493
Prescribing, Joint Committee report, 901
Preserved:
Foods, Census of Production, 460, 1201
Fruit and vegetables, Census of Production, 201, 1201
Meat, Census of Production, 460, 1201
Preserving, ABC of, 358, 1092
Presiding officers and clerks, instructions, 445
Press Council Bill, 285
Press, Film, and Radio: Unesco publications, 232, 493, 747, 1006
Press, Radio, Film and Television, 232
Prest, A. R.: National income of Nigeria, 861
Preston:
Corporation Act, 315

Preston (*continued*):
South, Boundary Commission report, 524
Prestressed concrete, 761, 1019
Prevention:
and treatment of severe malnutrition in times of disaster, 498
of accidents in paper mills, 676
of Crime Act, 568
Bill, 512, 524, 538, 541, 542, 645
of Damage by Pests Act, 313
of decay of wood in boats, 954
of disease among farm livestock, 850
of Eviction Act, 62
of Fraud (Investment) Act, 64
Particulars, 205, 463, 716, 970, 1205
S.R.O. & S.I. Revised, 195
of nuisance from blowflies, 620
of pollution:
of rivers and other waters, 35, 189
of the sea by oil, 718
of wet-weather damage to surface dressings, 1188
Preventive dental services, report, 377
Price:
Control:
and other Orders (Indemnity) Act, 60
Bill, 6, 33
(No. 1) Bill, 800
Related schedules, 202
of electricity, 879
of peace, 226
Prices for works services, War Department, 503, 760, 1224, 1225
Priestley, Sir R. (Chairman): Royal Commission on Civil Service:
Evidence, 950, 1182
Report, 1076, 1182
Primary:
and secondary schools in England and Wales, 1120
Schools, 958
Plans, 98
Teachers, training, salaries, 745
Primates, history of, 592, 854
Prime Minister:
Exchange of letters with French President, 1062
Statement on Korea, 39
Princess Victoria, wreck report, 721, 977
Printing:
and bookbinding machinery, Census of Production, 459, 1200
and publishing, bookbinding, engraving etc., Census of Production, 713, 1201
Career, 659
Prior, G. T.: Meteorites catalogue, 592
Prison:
Act, 308
Bill, 249, 251, 252, 254, 284
S.R.O. & S.I. Revised:
England, 195
Scotland, 196
Prisoners of War:
in Korea, treatment of, 1119
Indian proposals, 306
Prisons:
and other institutions for offenders, consolidation of enactments, memo, 251, 253
Estimates, Select Committee reports, 270, 522
in Scotland, reports, 46, 189, 294, 445, 551, 704, 812, 960, 1064, 1193
(Scotland) Act, 308
Bill, 249, 253, 254, 284
Prisons, Borstal Institutions, Approved Schools, and Remand Homes, reports of committee to review punishments, 46, 130, 286, 382
Pritula, V. A.: Cathodic protection of pipelines and storage tanks, 696
Private:
Bill Procedure, reports, 777, 909, 1025, 1027, 1149
Bills, rules for practice and procedure, 530, 645
Capital, international flow of, 996
International law:
Air, Conference, 656
Committee, report, 807, 939
Hague Convention, Statute, 819, 889, 1074, 1130
Legislation (Scotland) Procedure, 179, 433, 690, 949, 1181
Street Works Act, 309
Privileges:
and immunities of specialised agencies, convention, 730
Committee on, reports and proceedings, 17, 22, 23, 131, 528, 540, 1040, 1148
Privy:
Council, publications, 433, 690
Seal of Scotland, register of, 446
Prize Courts, S.R.O. & S.I. Revised, 196
Probation:
and related measures, 226
of Offenders, S.R.O. & S.I. Revised, 196
Officers, Directory, 130, 642, 1146
Service, 382
in Scotland, 1193
Problems:
in education, 494, 748, 1006
of business management, 986
Proclamation:
H.M. Queen Elizabeth, 418
Ceremonial observed, 418
Styles and Titles, 677
State of Emergency, 1170
Revocation, 1170
Proctor, P. D. (Chairman):
Local Government Manpower Committee, report, 58
Tate Gallery Trustees, report, 984
Production:
and Distribution, Census of, report, 822

Production (*continued*):
Census of, 200, 458, 712, 966, 1199
Recent changes, 486
Productivity:
in house building, 245, 698
in the distributive trade in Europe, 879
Professional:
Accountant Class in Civil Service, organisation, structure, remuneration, 474
and technical education of medical and auxiliary personnel, 757
Civil Servants, works group, organisation, structure, remuneration, 218
Qualifications. *See* Technical and Scientific Register.
Profits Tax:
Inland Revenue publications, 135, 136, 390, 652, 915, 1154, 1155
S.R.O. & S.I. Revised, 196
Progress:
in Asia, 727
in land reform, 966
of literacy in various countries, 1006
Promotion examinations, Army, 759, 1017
Property in the United Kingdom belonging to persons resident in Belgium, 296
Protecting the refugees, 996
Protection:
against high explosive missiles, basic methods, 380
and electro-deposition of metals, 441
of Animals:
Act, 61, 569
(Amendment) Act, 829
Bill, 285, 515, 773, 784, 800, 907
(Anaesthetics) Act, 829
Bill, 544, 773, 785, 798, 800, 907
(Penalties) Act, 285
of Birds Act, 63, 829
Bill, 516, 517, 541, 544, 772, 773, 781, 798, 800, 802, 907
of buildings and timber against termites, 183
of subgrades and granular bases by surface dressing, 699
Protoptila group of the Glossosomatinae, 853
Protractor, rectangular, 1223
Provisional Order, Scotland, S.R.O. & S.I. Revised, 196
Pruning plums and cherries, 78, 1093
Psychiatric aspects of juvenile delinquency, 237
Psychological tests for accident proneness and industrial efficiency, 1171
Psychotic and neurotic illnesses in twins, 679
Public:
Accounts Committee, reports, 14, 19, 22, 131, 261, 266, 268, 271, 280, 385, 474, 520, 524, 529, 645, 781, 784, 789, 792, 908, 984, 1035, 1037, 1044, 1045, 1051, 1148, 1219
Proceedings, 1042, 1148
Public (*continued*):
Administration:
Short international bibliography, 740
Standards and techniques, 486
Authorities Protection Act, 569
Bills, return, 28, 131, 276, 385, 436, 645, 796, 908, 1042, 1148
Boards, lists of members etc., 286, 306, 567, 727, 827, 984, 1079, 1219
Bodies (Admission of Press) Bill, 30
Business, manual of procedure in, 30
Cleansing, costing returns, 913, 1152
Education:
International Conference, 491, 1003, 1006
Scotland, 443, 1190
Statistics, England and Wales, 44
Finance Information Papers and surveys, 227, 486
General Acts and Church Assembly Measures, short titles, effect, index, 59, 307, 567, 828, 1079
Health:
Act, 63, 310, 571
Administration, expert committee report, 499
and Medical Subjects, series, 902, 1144
(Cleansing of Shellfish) Act, 832
(Condensed Milk) (Amendment) Regulations, circular, 620
(Drainage of Trade Premises) Act, 312
(Imported Food) Regulations, certificates, 103, 358, 619, 881, 1095
(London) Act, 832
(Meat) Regulations, circular, 881
(Amendment) Regulations, 358
(Preservatives etc. in Food) Regulations, circular, 881
S.R.O. & S.I. Revised, 196
(Scotland) Act, 569
(Smoke Abatement) Act, 570
State of, 824
Income and expenditure of the United Kingdom, 18, 218, 267, 474, 527, 727, 788, 984, 1041, 1219
Libraries (Scotland) Act, 1081
Bill, 1027, 1040, 1043, 1054, 1148
Library Manual, 493
Office, Colonies and Dominions, S.R.O. & S.I. Revised, 196
Opinion Research. *See* International Social Science Bulletin.
Order Act, 63
Petitions, committee on, special reports, 16, 131, 273, 385
Record Office, publications, 180, 434, 691, 949, 1181
Rights of Way, survey of, 164
Road Passenger Transport, statistics, 718, 974, 1209

1951-5 | PUB-RET

PUB— INDEX 1951–5

Public (*continued*):
Service Vehicles:
(Contract Carriages and Special Travel Facilities) Bill, 1038, 1043, 1053, 1148
Licensing authorities' reports, 1209
(Travel Concessions) Act, 1081
Bill, 1027, 1054
Trustee Office, reports, 180, 434, 691, 949, 1181
Utilities:
in Colombia, 1000
Street Works Act, notes on, 59, 65, 209
Works Loan:
Acts, 61, 308, 568, 571, 1081
Bills, 7, 33, 255, 285, 517, 1026, 1054
S.R.O. & S.I. Revised, 196
Board, reports, 218, 474, 727, 984, 1219
Publications and Debates, Select Committee reports, 271, 385, 535, 645, 790, 908, 1038, 1041, 1148
Publicity and recruitment for Civil Defence and allied services, advisory committee reports, 379, 382, 445, 811, 902, 905, 960
Puerulus stage of some spiny lobsters, 592
Pullorum disease, 331
Pulp and paper industry:
in Europe, 879
in Latin America, development of, 996
in U.S.A., 102
Pupils:
handicapped by speech disorders, 285, 443
who are maladjusted because of social handicap, 285, 443
with mental or educational disabilities, 57, 187
with physical disabilities, Scotland, 42, 187
Purchase:
of raw materials, exchange of Notes with Yugoslavia, 39
Orders, Compulsory. *See* Housing and Local Government.
Tax:
Report, 552, 727
S.R.O. & S.I. Revised, 196
Tax/Utility Committee, report, 287, 463
Pure chemistry, handbook of Science Museum collections, 181
Purification:
of oysters in simple pits, 849
of the water in swimming baths, 126
Purves, P. C.: Hearing in Cetaceans, 853
Pyefinch, K. A.:
Movements of salmon tagged in the sea, Montrose, 1191
Review of literature on biology of Atlantic salmon, 1191
Pyrope, wreck report, 213

Q

Qatar Notices, 1130
Qualified teachers and temporary teachers, circular, 1119, 1120
Quality milk production, 589
Quantitative:
Inheritance, 585
Studies of the bottom fauna of Essex oyster grounds, 332
Quarantine measures and Vaccination Certificate requirements, 1013
Quartz vibrators and their applications, 184
Queen:
Anne Domestic Silver, 239
Elizabeth II:
Proclamation of, 348
Styles and titles, 677
Speech to both Houses of Parliament, 255, 516, 777, 908, 1028, 1149
Elizabeth the Queen Mother, birthday messages, 759, 1017, 1223
Elizabeth Forest Park Guide, 893
Mary, death of, 677, 758
Mary's art treasures, 1014
Victoria School Scholarship Fund, 701
Queen's:
Army Schoolmistresses, Special Army Order, 759
Birthday:
Honours, 677, 418, 938 1170
Messages, 501, 759, 1016, 1223
Coronation Honours List, 677
Hall, report, 1065, 1219
Regulations:
Admiralty Instructions, 318, 574, 837, 1084
Air Council Instructions, 335, 590, 851, 1098
Army, 502, 759, 1017, 1223
Queensland-British Food Corporation:
Future of, 547, 620
Reports and accounts, 263, 359, 524, 620
Quicker completion of house interiors, 650
Quinquennial review, National Insurance, 798, 1033, 1219

R

Rabbit keeping, modern, 848
Rabbits:
and hares, myxomatosis in, circular, 1122
Mange, worms, ringworm, and miscellaneous disorders, 331
(Prohibition of Spreading) Bill, 1031
Rabies:
Expert committee report, 1013
Laboratory techniques, 1012
Raby, F. J. E.: Castle Acre Priory, guide, 504

INDEX 1951–5 —RAT

Race:
and biology, 233
and class in rural Brazil, 548
and culture, 233
and history, 493
and psychology, 233
and society, 548, 1007
Concept, 548
Mixture, 1007
Question, 234
and modern thought, 548, 1007
in modern science, 233, 493, 548, 1007
Race, R. R.: Rh Blood Groups and their clinical effects, 420, 1171
Racecourse Betting Act, 831
Racial:
Equality and the Law, 1007
Myths, 233
Situation in the Union of South Africa, 992, 993
Radar:
Echoes from and turbulence within cumulus and cumulonimbus clouds, 941
Marine navigational, centrimetric aerials for, 466
Observer Examination Chart, 466
Plotting sheet, 974
Radcliffe, Rt. Hon. Lord. (Chairman): Royal Commission on Taxation of Profits and Income:
Evidence, 436, 810, 952
Reports, 547, 1066
Radford, C. A. R.: Guides to various ancient monuments, 504, 761, 762
Radio:
and Telecommunications, Census of Production, 459
and Television servicing, career, 1157
Direction-finding and navigational aids, 154
Facility charts, 595, 974, 1209
for merchant ships, 179, 433
in fundamental education in undeveloped areas, 232
Purposes, select problems in preparation, properties and application of materials, 598
Research, DSIR publications, 184, 440, 698, 955, 1187
Services textbook, 1224
See also Press.
Radioactive mineral deposits, prospector's guide, 123
Radiographer, career, 659
Radioisotope techniques, 455, 710
Radiological terminology in pulmonary disease, standardisation of, 379
Radiotelephony procedure, 138, 339, 595, 722, 1209
Radmar, wreck report, 721
Radium Commission, short history, 126
Rae, B. B.: Occurrence of lemon sole larvae in Scottish plankton collections, 703
Rag, flock, and other filling materials:
Act, 60
Bill, 1, 2, 3, 6, 32
Circulars, 165, 910
Explanatory memo, 166
Ragge, D. R.: Wing-venation of the Orthoptera Saltatoria with notes of Dictyopteran wing-venation, 1103
Ragwort, 330, 1093
Railroads in the U.S.A., 102, 357
Railway:
Accidents, 209, 466, 719, 974, 1209
Carriages and wagons and trams, Census of Production, 712
Locomotive shops and locomotive manufacturing, Census of Production, 712, 1200
Merchandise Charges Scheme. *See* Transport Tribunal.
Operating and signalling techniques in Europe, Japan, U.S.A., 996
Railwaymen's wages and salaries, inquiry report, 38
Railways:
Act, 310
(Civil Engineering) Census of Production, 460, 1202
Reorganisation Scheme, 815, 975
S.R.O. & S.I. Revised, 448
Rainfall. *See* British Rainfall.
Rainmaking, 996
Raisman, Sir J. (Chairman): Fiscal Commission, Rhodesia-Nyasaland Federation, report, 303
Rajam, R. V., Rangiah, P. N.: Donovanosis, 1012
Ramsden, F.: Food poisoning report, 1144
Raspberry:
Beetle, 329
Cultivation, 847, 1090
Diseases in Scotland, 328
Moth, 1091
Rat problem in Cyprus, 92
Rates and rateable values:
England and Wales, 166, 388, 650, 913, 1152
Scotland, 189, 445, 704, 960, 1193
Ratifications, accessions, withdrawals, 36, 114, 287, 366, 546, 628, 805, 899, 1061, 1130
Rating:
and Valuation:
Act, 63
(Apportionment) Act, 63
Circular, 1151
(Miscellaneous Provisions) Act, 1080
Bill, 1028, 1029, 1054, 1055, 1056
Circular, 1151
S.R.O. & S.I. Revised, 448
(Scotland) Act, 308

RAT— INDEX 1951–5

Rating (*continued*):
and Valuation (*continued*):
(Scotland) (*continued*):
Bill, 250, 253, 265, 267, 278, 282, 385
S.R.O. & S.I. Revised, 448
of site values, committee report, 388
(Scotland) Act, 311
Rations for livestock, 331, 848
Rats and mice on the farm, 588
Raw:
Cotton Commission, reports, accounts 20, 205, 268, 419, 529, 679, 789, 940, 1044, 1205
Materials:
for more paper, 752
See also Colonial.
Raynaud's Phenomenon, 828
Rayon Schedule, 206
See also Cotton.
Rayon, Nylon, etc., Census of Production, 713
Reactions between aggregates and cement, 440, 698
Reading:
Ability, 99
and writing, preliminary survey on methods of teaching, 745
in the primary school, 1191
Ready reckoner of food values, 99, 1120
Ready, A. W. (Chairman): Welsh Language Publishing Committee, report, 302
Rear lights of motor vehicles and pedal cycles, 699
Re-armament, Select Committee on Estimates, reports, 23, 263, 274, 522, 528, 789
Reay, G. A.: Care of the trawler's fish, 696
Rebuilding education in the Republic of Korea, 1004
Reception:
and welfare of patients in hospitals, 124, 637
Centres for persons without a settled way of living, 428
Reclamation of grassland, 329
Record Office, England, S.R.O. & S.I. Revised, 448
Recoveries from Acquiring Authorities Regulations, 1150
Recovery Record (story of Marshall Aid in Britain), 218
Recruitment:
Methods and standards for United Nations and specialised agencies, 225
of scientists and engineers, 1171
Red:
Core of strawberry, 587
Locust, permanent control of outbreak areas, modification of convention, 565, 628
Spider mite on glasshouse crops, 1093
Redundant military equipment, gift to North Atlantic Treaty countries, 546, 727
Reed, Col. W. P.: Railway accident reports, 722, 971, 975, 1010
Rees, Sir F. (Chairman): Committee on night baking, report, 55
Rees, W. J.: Macrotriropus problem, 853
Reeve, E. B.: Observations on the general effect of injury in man with special reference to wound shock, 169
Refrigerated gas-storage of Gros Michel bananas, 696
Refrigeration, agreement replacing International Convention, 1073, 1130
Refugee Emergency Fund, financial report, 993
Refugees:
and stateless persons, status, 228, 288, 366, 814
and surplus elements of population, 606
Protecting, 996
United Nations High Commissioner's reports, 484, 736, 737, 993
See also No room for them?
Refuse:
Collection and disposal. *See* Public Cleansing.
Disposal in flats. *See* Housing and Local Government Circulars.
Regency:
Act, 568
Bill, 516, 544
Domestic silver, 499
Regimental Standing Orders, Royal Army Service Corps, 759
Regional:
Hospital Boards and Hospital Management Committees, Select Committee on Estimates report, 23
Organisation of Government Departments, Select Committee on Estimates report, 792, 795
Supplementary procedures, 140
Register:
of Deeds, 446, 961
House, Edinburgh, guide to historical museum, 445
Registered:
Design Act, 314
Provident Societies, statistical summaries, 118, 369, 631
Trade Unions, statistical summaries, 118, 369
Registers and Records, Scotland, S.R.O. & S.I. Revised, 448
Registrar-General's returns, 122, 374, 634, 897, 1139
Registration:
of Births and Deaths:
Abroad, S.R.O. & S.I. Revised, 448
England and Wales, memo, 256
of Births, Deaths, Marriages, etc., England, Scotland, S.R.O. & S.I. Revised, 448
of Business Names Act, 62

INDEX 1951–5 —RET

Registration (*continued*):
of Title to land, 676
Officers, Lists of 122, 374, 634, 897, 1139
Service:
Act, 568
Bill, 509, 512, 513, 543
in England and Wales, memo, 512
Registry of Friendly Societies, publications, 117, 369, 631, 893, 1133
Rehabilitation of the adult disabled, modern methods, 740
Reiners, W. J.: Productivity in housebuilding, 690
Reinhard, M.: Geology of the Colony of North Borneo, 345
Reining, P.: Culture and human fertility, 1006
Reinstatement in civil employment:
Act, 314
S.R.O. & S.I. Revised, 448
Re-insurance of ships against war risks, agreements, 976
Related schedules, price control, 202
Remand homes, directory, 382
See also Prisons.
Rendering outside walls, 503
Renderings. *See* Sands.
Renfrewshire:
Census, 898
Carnegie Park and Scott Trust Amendment Scheme, memo, 701
East and West, Boundary Commission report, 38
Education (Scotland) Act, memo, Order in Council, 958
Rent:
and Mortgage Interest:
Restrictions:
Act, 572
(Amendment) Act, 311
(Restrictions Continuation) Act, 310
Restriction (Garages) Bill, 31
Restrictions (Notices of Increase) Act, 570
Rents of houses owned by local authorities in Scotland, 302, 445, 818, 901, 1071, 1142
Reorganisation Areas Measure 1944 (Amendment) Measure, 770, 835, 855
Ecclesiastical Committee report, 770, 855
Repair of drums or tanks, 417
Repairs:
and rents:
Handbook, 901
New Act, 912
to mastic asphalt and felt roof coverings, 1185
to welded ships, 1084
Repayment of certain credits relating to armaments, exchange of Notes with Turkey, 810
Representation of the People:
(Amendment) Bill, 30, 281
(St. Albans) Bill, 800
S.R.O. & S.I. Revised, 448
Reptiles, amphibians, and fishes, instructions for collectors, 592
Requisitioned:
Houses and Housing (Amendment) Act, 1080
Bill, 1026, 1039, 1043, 1054, 1149
Circulars, 1130
Land and War Works:
Act, 313, 832
S.R.O. & S.I. Revised, 448
Premises now in use for housing, circular, 648
Properties in use for housing, reports, 388, 650, 913
Resale price maintenance, statement, 47, 205
Rescue:
Manual, 380, 639
Training:
Civil Defence filmstrips, 639, 903
Elements of building construction, 380
Research:
on food preservation in the United Kingdom, 954
Workers and students, notes on grants, 184, 440, 956, 1187
Reserve and Auxiliary Forces:
(Protection of Civil Interests) Act, 60
Bill, 5, 6, 21, 32, 33, 132
Circular, 164
S.R.O. & S.I. Revised, 448
(Training) Act, 60
Bill, 1, 26, 31
Reserves and liabilities, 1931-1945, 53, 219
Reservoirs (Safety Provisions) Act, 571
Residential:
Accommodation for old peoples' homes for the more infirm, 1143
Areas, Density of, 387
Qualifications, 1152
Residual values of fertilisers and feedingstuffs, 328, 846, 1091
Residues in food, 851
Resources, Conservation and utlisation, 478
Rest centres, Civil Defence, 376
Restenneth Priory, guide, 504
Restriction of ribbon development, 387
Restrictive business practices, 226
Retail:
and service trades, general tables, Census of Production, 966
Bread and flour confectionery trade, establishment of wages council, 417
Price lists, 105, 359, 621
Comparisons for international salary determination, 741, 999
Prices, interim index, 417
See also Cost of living.
Trade, short report, 712

RET-SAN | 1951-5

Retention moneys on building and civil engineering contracts, 1019
Retired:
Officers:
Navy, list of, 69
Re-employed, liability for Reserve Service, 1016
Pay, Pensions, etc., 242, 503, 809, 984
Orders, 267, 272, 431, 529, 687, 1033
Orders-in-Council, 178, 431, 1180
Royal Warrants, 293, 299, 432, 554, 555, 1058, 1180
Terminal grants, 1017
Returning Officer, abstract of duties, 445
Revenue:
and expenditure, England and Wales and Scotland, return, 806, 984
Departments:
Appropriation Accounts, 29, 97, 136, 179, 279, 349, 390, 433, 539, 607, 652, 690, 795, 867, 915, 948, 1050, 1112, 1155, 1181
Estimates, 15, 215, 263, 523, 784, 981, 1036
Reverend J. G. Macmanaway's Indemnity Act, 60
Bill, 2, 31, 32
Reviews of research on arid zone hydrology, 236
Revision of the Army and Air Force Acts (Transitional Provisions) Act, 1026, 1054, 1082
Bill, 803
Revue des Nations Unies, 286, 740, 997
Rexford-Welch, Sq. Leader S. C.: R.A.F. Medical Services, administration, 1143
Reynolds, L.:
Manufacture of wood charcoal in Great Britain, 631
Use and manufacture of wood flour, 631
Reynolds, P. K. B.: Castle Acre Priory, guide, 504
Rh Blood Groups and their clinical effects, 420, 1171
Rheology of non-aqueous suspensions, 956
Rheumatic diseases, expert committee report, 1013
Rhoanglo Group Act, 574
Rhodesia:
and Nyasaland:
Economic survey, 205, 1205
Federation:
Act, 568
Bill, 504, 542
Draft Federal Scheme, 296, 346, 348
Reports, 303, 346, 348
Federal Scheme and reports, 547, 603, 605
Order-in-Council (Commencement), 604
Introducing, 134
Rhodesia (*continued*):
Northern:
Colonial report, 344
Economic survey, 345
Mineral rights owned by British South Africa Company, 93
Native administration, 93
Railway agreement, exchange of notes with U.S.A., 56, 1058
Southern:
Filmstrip and lecture notes, 134
Reciprocal payment of compensation for war injuries, agreement with Italy, 557
Rhodesian Selection Trust Ltd. and Associated Companies Act, 834
Rhododendron Bug, 847
Riccall Gates railway accident, 719
Rice:
Breeding, 751
Commission, working party report, 1008
Commodity reports, 234, 750, 1008
Enrichment in the Philippines, 1010
Equipment for processing, 751
Shifting cultivation. *See* Iban agriculture.
Soils and fertilisers, annotated bibliography, 1010
Rice, G. G.: Survey of building in sandstone in Scotland, 698
Richards, A. I.: Culture and human fertility, 1006
Richards, D.: R.A.F. war histories, 590, 852
Richards, O. W.: Ruwenzori Expedition, 84
Richardson, C. A.: Education of teachers in England, France, and U.S.A., 1006
Richardson, I. D.:
Echo-sounding experiments on fish, 1092
Some reactions of pelagic fish to light as recorded by echo-sounding, 332
Richmond Castle, guide, 762
Ridge Way and Caithness Bases, measurement, 687, 943
Riding Establishments (Amendment) Bill, 281
Ridley, Viscount (Chairman): Committee on National Policy for use of fuel and power resources, report, 301
Rigden, P. J.: Rheology of non-aqueous suspensions, 956
Rights:
and obligations of landlords, tenants, and owner-occupiers of agricultural land, 848
of Entry (Gas and Electricity Boards) Act, 829
Bill, 544, 770
of nationals of U.S.A. in Morocco, Order, 396
Rigold, S. E.: Guides to ancient monuments, 504, 761, 1018, 1225
Riot, England, S.R.O. & S.I. Revised, 448

Risks to wild life from toxic chemicals used in agriculture, 1097
Risley, M. K.: Ceramic industry in the Philippines, 1000
River:
Boards Act, 65, 833
Guide to powers and functions, 126
Report, 80, 166
Training and bank protection, 991
Rivers (Prevention of Pollution):
Act, 60
Bill, 4, 5, 16, 26, 31, 33, 132
Circulars, 387, 910
Committee report, 35
(Scotland) Act, 60
Bill, 5, 6, 19, 21, 26, 30, 132
Memo, 124
No. 2 Bill, 31, 33
Roach, scales of, 849
Road:
Abstracts, 185, 441, 699, 956, 1188
Accidents, 719, 976, 1210
Aggregate, sources in Great Britain, 185
and bridge works:
Bill of quantities, 208
Specifications, 211
and motor transport, U.N. Conference, Final Act, 227
and Rail Traffic Act, licensing authorities for goods vehicles, reports, 468, 720, 976, 1210
Bridges, tests on, 698
Construction in U.S.A., use of stabilised soil, 956
Foundation failures, investigation, 185
Fund:
Accounts, 10, 211, 258, 467, 519, 720, 780, 976, 1034, 1210
Reports on administration, 211, 467, 976, 1210
S.R.O. & S.I. Revised, 448
Haulage:
Cases, selected decisions, 212, 469, 720, 977, 1211
Disposal Board, reports, 540, 722, 789, 798, 976, 1044, 1052, 1210
Wages, S.R.O. & S.I. Revised, 448
Motor vehicles and tourism. *See* Customs formalities.
Passenger:
Services, report, 722
Transport, statistics, Great Britain, 466
Research, publications of DSIR, 185, 441, 199, 956, 1188
Safety, 976
Committee reports, 468
to Equality, 740
to the Sixth Form, 99
Traffic:
Acts, 63, 311, 312, 571
Bills, 777, 1025, 1026, 1053, 1054, 1055
Road (*continued*):
Traffic (*continued*):
Acts (*continued*):
Licensing authorities for public service vehicles, 211
and Vehicles, S.R.O. & S.I. Revised, 448
Census, 468
(Driving Licences) Acts, 63, 313, 571
Transport:
International general agreement on economic regulations, 994
Lighting:
Acts, 568, 570
(Amendment) Bill, 514, 525, 538, 541, 542, 645
(Rear Lights) Bill, 512, 513, 514, 523, 538, 541, 543, 645
Vehicles, mechanically-propelled, returns, 211, 468, 720, 722, 976, 1210
Roads:
and Bridges, Scotland, S.R.O. & S.I. Revised, 448
and services, 125, 377
Bituminous, in North America, 185
Concrete, design thickness of, 1188
Improvements Act, 831
Select Committee on Estimates, report, 527, 534
Soil-cement, 333
Robb, W.: Scottish seed oats, 846
Robbie, J. A.: Geology of country around Chatham, 899
Robbins, Prof. L. C. (Chairman):
Export of Works of Art Reviewing Committee, report, 823
Queen's Hall Committee, report, 1065
Roberts, H. C. W.: Easington Colliery explosion, 301
Roberts, N. S.: Japan, economic survey, 716
Roberts-Wray, Sir K. (Chairman): Judicial Advisers' Conference, record of native courts and native customary law in Africa, 599
Robertson, Sir I. (Chairman): British Guiana Constitutional Commission, report, 822
Robinson, B. W.: Persian paintings, 499
Robinson, Prof. G. W. (Chairman): Soil Survey Research Board, report, 77
Robinson, J. E.: Refrigerated gas-storage of Gross-Michel bananas, 696
Robinson, J. F.: Survey of blackface sheep with special reference to their hardiness, 586
Robinson, R. H. M.: Whalemeat bacteriology and hygiene, 696
Robson, W. A.: Political science, 1007
Rochdale Canal Act, 315
Roche Abbey, guide, 1018
Roche, P.: Revisional notes on the genus Epitola Westwood, 1102
Rochester Corporation Act, 316

Rock collections in the Mineral Department, British Museum (Natural History), 854
Rococo art catalogue, 1014
Roderigo, wreck report, 1213
Rodgers, J. (Chairman): Committee on litter in Royal Parks, report 1226
Romania. *See* Bulgaria.
Roofing felts, Census of Production, 200, 966
Root:
Knot eelworm in glasshouses, 587
Vegetables, 332
Roots of prejudice, 233
Rope, twine, and net, Census of Production, 201, 1200
Ropy milk, 847
Rosaura expedition, 853
Rose Theological Bequest Scheme, 187, 443
Roskill, Capt. S. W.: War at sea, 854, 961
Ross and Cromarty:
Census, 898
County Council (Kyle of Lochalsh Fishery Pier) Order Confirmation Act, 67
Ross, W.: Siting of direction-finding stations, 440
Rotations, 1094
Roth, L.: Jewish thought as a factor in civilisation, 1007
Rothesay Castle, guide, 504
Rothschild, Lord (Chairman): Agricultural Research Council, report on foot-and-mouth disease research, 328
Rothschild, M.: Collection of fleas, 336, 593
Roumanian property, Treasury directions, proposals, to Administrator, 816, 818, 984, 1063, 1219
Round Oak Steel Works Ltd., proposal to sell securities, 562, 726
Rowlands, A.: Milk pasteurisation, 755
Roxburgh, Census, 898
Royal:
Air Force (war histories), 590, 852
Medical Services, administration, 1143
Non-flying establishments, Select Committee on Estimates, reports, 795, 1031, 1036, 1147
Prize Fund, accounts, 14, 30, 82, 538, 590, 795, 852, 1046, 1098
Aircraft Establishment. *See* Farnborough.
Albert Hall Act, 67
Army Medical Corps, Standing Orders, 1224
Artillery, Standing Orders and instructions, 1223
Botanic Gardens, publications:
Edinburgh, 180, 434, 691, 949, 1182
Kew 180, 434, 691, 949, 1182
Commissions. *See* title of Commission.
Engineers, supplementary pocket book, amendments, 503
Royal (*continued*):
Fine Art Commission, reports, 305, 382, 556, 642, 814, 905, 1063, 1146
Hospital (Chelsea), accounts 16, 29, 242, 280, 503, 538, 760, 796, 1017, 1052, 1223
Household appointments, 418
Irish Constabulary (Widows' Pensions) Act, 829
Bill, 771, 800
Line, catalogue of documents exhibited, 704
Mint, publications, 181, 694, 952, 1184
Naval:
College, floodlit, postcard, 255
See also Greenwich Hospital.
Medical Service, war history, 902, 961
Prize Fund, accounts, 14, 69, 258, 318, 518, 576, 779, 837, 1033, 1084
Observatory, Edinburgh, publications, 181, 436, 1184
Ordnance Factories, Select Committee on Estimates report, 528
Plate from Buckingham Palace and Windsor Castle, 1014
Scottish Museum publications, 958, 1184
Titles Act, 568
Bill, 511, 541
Warehousemen Clerks and Drapers' Schools Act, 835
Warrant Holders, lists, 166, 418, 677, 938, 1170
Yachts, 687
Royalist, H.M. Cruiser, loan to New Zealand, 1078
Ruanda-Urundi:
Population of, 739
Reports, 229, 743
Rubber:
Census of Production, 460
Investigation. *See* Services.
Ruhr, International authority for, agreement, 305, 366
Runciman, Viscount (Chairman): Committee on Taxicab Service, report, 550
Runcorn-Widnes Bridge Act, 574
Rural:
Community organisation and development in the Caribbean area and Mexico, 730
Electrification, 997
Progress through Co-operatives, 997
Subjects in secondary schools, 443
Transport Improvement Bill, 1046
Wales, 566, 642
Water Supplies and Sewerage Acts, 60, 312, 572, 1080
Bills, 5, 32, 1026, 1030, 1054, 1056
Rushcliffe, Boundary Commission report, 269, 379
Rushes, control of, 1091
Russell, P. F.: Malaria terminology, 755

Rusts of British forest trees, 1133
Rutherglen Burgh Order Confirmation Act, 835
Bill, 801
Ruwenzori Expedition, 84, 593
Ryan, J. (Chairman): Committee appointed to review organisation of Ministry of Agriculture and Fisheries, report, 80

S

Saar:
Agreement between Germany and France, 824, 889
Future position of, 865
Sabrosky, C. W.: Chloropidea, 84
Sacred trust, 997
Safeguarding of Industries:
Act, 310
S.R.O. & S.I. Revised, 448
Safety:
and health, regulations and orders, 370, 632
Circulars, 121, 371, 633, 895, 1137
in cinemas, 1144
in Employment (Inspection and Safety Organisation) Bill, 799
in mines, research, 373, 633, 896, 1137
in use of power presses, fencing of press brakes, 401
Measures in chemical laboratories, 1188
of life at sea, international convention, conference, 545, 628, 805, 889
Pamphlets, 121, 417, 1137, 1169
Precautions, display cards, 187, 443
Sailing ships, history and development, catalogue, 437
Saint Albans Cathedral, guide, 435
Saint Andrews:
Castle, guide, 244
University of, Bill, 509, 510, 511, 515, 526, 528, 538, 542, 543, 646
Saint Augustine's Abbey, Canterbury, guide 1225
Saint Benet Gracechurch Act, 67
Saint Edward's crown, coloured postcard, 762
Saint Helena:
Colonial reports, 343, 860
S.R.O. & S.I. Revised, 448
See also Africa, West.
Saint James's Park by floodlight, postcard, 763
Saint Lucia, Colonial reports, 343, 1108
Saint Oswald Estate Act, 574
Bill, 513
Saint Ronan, wreck report, 721
Saint Sophia of Ochrida, preservation and restoration, 747
Saint Stephen Coleman Street Act, 1081
Saint Vincent, Colonial reports, 90, 600, 1108
Saiyidian, K. G.: Compulsory education in India, 748
Salad crops, outdoor, 331
Salads. *See* Vegetables.
Salaries:
Further education, structure, 1058, 1191
Teachers in primary and secondary schools, 99
Teaching staff of training colleges, England and Wales, 99
See also Teachers' Salaries.
Salcombe Pier and Harbour Order Confirmation Act, 802
Bill, 774, 834
Sale:
of Food (Weights and Measures) Act, 62
of Goods Acts, 61, 309
of Houses, 387
of old metals and the control of dealers in old metals, 1146
Sale, lease, or letting of land, circular, 911
Salford Corporation Act, 1081
Saline water. *See* Arid zone programme.
Salmon:
and Freshwater Fisheries:
Act, 62, 831
(Protection) (Scotland) Act, 60
Bill, 2, 31
and sea trout, movements of, and of brown trout tagged in the Tweed, 1192
Fisheries. *See* Fresh Water.
Movements off North-east coast of England, 1092
of the Cheshire Dee, 79
Review of literature on biology of Atlantic salmon, 1191
Studies, 79, 588
tagged in the sea, Montrose, movements of, 1191
Salmonella. *See* Food poisoning.
Salmonellosis, 1094
Salt:
Mines, brine pits, and salt works, Census of Production, 200, 1199
Treatment of snow and ice on roads, 699
Salvage claims, agreement with Denmark, 1064
Salvaged Goods (Revocation) Order, 620
Sample surveys of current interest, 741
Samson and a Philistine, 1014
Samuels, A. (Chairman):
London and Home Counties Traffic Advisory Committee, report on London traffic congestion, 209
Working Party on car parking in inner London, report, 718
Sand:
and gravel, reports, 388, 650, 913, 1152
Circular, 387
Lands, agriculture of, 1091
Standard, preparation of, 439

Sandbank Bombing Range, exchange of Notes with Germany, 1060
Sanders, H. G.: Rotations, 1094
Sandown-Shanklin Urban District Council Act, 1081
Sands for plasters, mortars and renderings, 243
Sanitary:
  Inspectors:
    (Change of Designation) Bill, 1056
    Working Party report, 638
  International regulations, 56, 114
Sanitation, expert committee reports, 498, 1013
Sao Paulo, wreck report, 1213
Sarawak:
  Colonial reports, 343, 600, 601, 861
  Death duties payable in Northern Ireland, Order-in-Council, 914
  S.R.O. & S.I. Revised, 448
Sasines, index to particular register, 704
Saudi Arabia, arbitration agreement, 819, 822, 890
Saunders, H. St. G.: R.A.F. war histories, 852
Sausages. *See* Meat content.
Savage, W. G. (Chairman): Catering Trade Working Party, report on hygiene in catering establishments, 104
Savings Bank:
  and Friendly Societies, accounts, 219, 474, 727, 984, 1219
  S.R.O. & S.I. Revised, 448
Savory, J. G.: Prevention of decay of wood in boats, 954
Savoy Hotel Ltd., Berkeley Hotel Ltd., investigations, 716, 970
Sawflies of European Alps and Mediterranean region, 853
Sawyer, J. S.:
  Cloud in relation to active warm fronts, 1172
  Day-to-day variations in the tropopause, 941
  Free atmosphere in the vicinity of fronts, 1172
  Intertropical front, memo on, 421
Scaphopoda, 854
Scarborough Castle, guide, 1225
Scheduled airline operations, statistical summary, 139
Scheyven, R.: Economic development of underdeveloped countries, 993
Schizaeaceae of the south of England in early Tertiary times, 1102
School:
  Broadcasts, 353
  Building, 700
    in Scotland, 958
  Child, Health of, 873
  Clothing, 98, 100
  Crossing Patrols Act, 568
    Bill, 513, 515, 543
School (*continued*):
  Dental record card, 1120
  Feeding, 752
  Grammar, suggestions on curriculum, 99
  Health services:
    and Handicapped Pupils Regulations, 614, 615
    Expert committee report, 238
  Kitchens, design of, 1119
  Leaving age, raising, 233
  Library, 353
  Meals:
    and clothing, international conference, 230
    Circular, 614, 615
    Filmstrips, 99, 615, 874, 1120
    Increase of charge, 98, 100
    Memo, 615
    Organisation, 352, 354
  Premises Regulations, standards, circular, 872
  Reading, primary, 1191
Schools:
  Limits of cost, new schools, 1119, 1121
  New:
    Primary, 1119
    Secondary, 98
  Primary and Secondary, England and Wales, 353, 1120
  Recognition of, as efficient, rules, 614
  Registration (Scotland) Rules, 186
  Secondary, subjects of curriculum, 187
  Select Committee on Estimates report, 528
Schools, Boarding Homes, etc.:
  for handicapped pupils, 874
  for training disabled persons, 615
Schuster, W. H.: Fish farming and inland fishing management in rural economy, 1009
Science:
  and technology:
    Directory of current periodical abstracts and bibliographies, 492
    in Western Germany, 1188
  Applied, notes on, 430, 687
  Careers, 398
  Documentation and terminology, 1003
  Exhibition, South Kensington, guide-catalogue, 103
  Guidance to teachers on setting and marking examinations, 1191
  in secondary schools, 187, 1191
  in U.S.A., 590, 852, 1101
  Inter-Commonwealth post-graduate scholarships, 82
  Inventories of apparatus and materials for teaching, 230, 492, 1005
  Museum, publications, 181, 436, 694, 952, 1184
  Scottish Leaving Certificate examination, 442

Scientific:
  and Industrial Research, Department of, publications, 181, 437, 695, 953, 1185
    Reports, 39, 185, 290, 419, 548, 699, 808, 939, 1060, 1171
  and technological problems involved in ionising radiations for preservation of food, 1186
  Aspects, atomic energy, 729
  Conference on conservation and utilisation of land resources, 478
  Instruments, King George III collection, handbook, 437
  Manpower Committee, report on recruitment of scientists and engineers by the engineering industry, 1171
  Policy, annual reports, 49, 168, 295, 419, 555, 678, 820, 940, 1070, 1171
  Reports, Great Barrier Reef expedition, 336
  Research in British Universities, 441, 956, 1188
Scientific, surgical, and photographic instruments, Census of Production, 713, 1200
Scientists' rights, 745
Scotland:
  Ancient monuments, 504, 1225
  Living traditions, 134
  Today, 704
Scott, J. F.: Community factor in modern technology, 748
Scott, M. L.: School feeding, 752
Scott Dow, Dr. R. C. (Chairman): Scottish Dental Advisory Committee: report on preventive dental services, 377
Scott-Moncrieff, G.: Living traditions of Scotland, 134
Scottish:
  Affairs, Royal Commission evidence, 693, 694, 952
    Report, 817, 952
  Agricultural economics, 329, 1091
  Agriculture (journal), 77, 328, 585, 846, 1090
  Amicable Life Assurance Society's Act, 316
  Education Department, publications, 186, 442, 700, 957, 1189
  Estimates, 8, 22, 27, 132, 271, 386, 531, 538, 645, 791, 798, 908
  Farming, studies of current economic conditions, 329
  Financial and trade statistics, report, 208, 445
  Health Services Council, reports, 40, 123, 637, 900, 901, 1142
  Hill Farm Research Committee, survey of blackface sheep, 586
  Home Department, publications, 188, 443, 702, 958, 1191
  Hospitals directory, 124, 637, 1142
  Housing:
    Advisory Committee report, 123
Scottish (*continued*):
  Housing (*continued*):
    Handbook, 125, 377, 637, 901, 1142
  Land Court, reports, proceedings, 35, 189, 287, 445, 545, 564, 704, 819, 960
  Leases, report, 302, 445
  Leaving Certificate Examination, 442, 600, 957, 1189, 1190, 1191
  Local Government Law Consolidation Committee, reports, 545, 547, 564, 704
  Medical Research Fund proposals, memo, 299, 445
  Mutual Assurance Society Act, 316
  Office, publications, 190, 446, 704, 960, 1193
  Peat Committee, report, 960
  Record Office, publications, 445, 704, 961
  Regalia, 190
  Representative Peers, meetings, 7, 133, 251, 1028, 1149
  Sea Fisheries, statistical tables, 190, 960, 1193
  Seed oats, 846
  Statistics, digest, 704, 960, 1193
  Valuation and Rating Committee, report, 819, 960
Scrap:
  Export from Germany, 293
  Metal, metal processing, Census of Production, 458, 1200
Scrivener, R. S.: Venezuela, economic survey, 1205
Scruton, C.: Summarised account of Severn Bridge aerodynamic investigation, 430
Sculpture:
  Baroque, 1013
  from the Colonies, traditional, 94
  Masterpieces, 239
Sea:
  Fish Industry Act, 60, 64
    Bill, 2, 3, 15, 27, 31, 32, 132
  Fisheries Statistical Tables, 80, 334, 589, 704, 850, 1096, 1193
  Transport Service Regulations, 976
Sea-breezes at North Front, Gibraltar, 941
Seafarers and their ships, 1211
Seaham Harbour Pier and Harbour Order Confirmation Act, 315
  Bill, 253, 283
Seal, E. A. (Chairman): Working Party on retention moneys on building and civil engineering contracts, report, 1019
Sea-level changes in the Falkland Islands, new evidence, 862
Seals in the Public Record Office, 949
Seaman's pocketbook, 576
Seamanship, manual, 69, 318, 1084
Search and rescue:
  Committee report, 394
  Division report, 138, 140
  Manual, 148
Searle, W. F. (Chairman): Colonial Government Statisticians Conference, report, 92

Seas, high, laws and regulations on regime, 484
Seasonal:
  Change of surface temperature of North Atlantic, 680
  Workers, committee report, 295
Seats for workers in factories, 163
Second World War, histories, 337, 593, 638, 759, 854, 902, 961, 1193
Secondary:
  School examinations, 352
  Teachers, training, salaries, 1002
Secondment of teachers for overseas service, 98, 873, 874, 957
Securities (Validation), S.R.O. & S.I. Revised, 448
Security:
  Council (United Nations), publications, 227, 232, 486, 997
  of Employment (Service Contracts) Bill, 30
  of tenure of business premises, 983
Sedgefield, Boundary Commission report, 269, 379, 524
Sedgwick, R. J. P.: Guatemala, economic survey, 463
Sediment problem, 991
Seed:
  Crops, threshing and conditioning, 79
  Crushing and oil refining, Census of Production, 458
  Potatoes:
    Export licences, 202, 204, 461, 714
    Maintenance of stocks, 329
    Storage and dressing, 77
  Production etc. in European countries, 879
  Testing for farmers, 78
Seeds:
  Act, 62
  (Amendment) Act, 310
  S.R.O. & S.I. Revised, 448
Seel, Sir G.: Development and welfare in West Indies reports, 345, 601
Selaginella, revision of West Indian species, 335
Selected Government Research Reports, 205, 441, 700, 1188
Selenium, 956
Selkirk, Census, 898
Senior commercial and airline transport pilots' licences, 339, 1211
Separation of protein fractions from human plasma with ether, 940
Septic tanks, design and operation, 755
Service:
  Departments, virement between Votes, 789
  Emoluments, 808, 867
  Estimates, supplementary, 522, 530, 791
  Gratuities, etc., 243
  Retired Pay, etc., 50, 98, 503, 760
Services:
  for the disabled, 1169
  for the physically handicapped, 338
  Rubber investigations, 963
  Textbook of radio, 1224
Servomechanisms, research report, 441
Session, Court of, Scotland, S.R.O. & S.I. Revised, 448
Sessional:
  Index, House of Commons, 778, 908
  Printed papers, 8, 132, 518, 645, 778, 908, 1031, 1149
Settled Land Act, 62
Severn:
  Bridge, aerodynamic investigation, summarised account, 430
  Lower, Sand and Gravel Advisory Committee, report, 388
Sewage:
  Disposal, 648
  Sludge, informal working party report, 913
Sewell, R. B. S.:
  Epibionts and parasites of the planktonic Copepoda of the Arabian Sea, 84
  Pelagic Tunicata, 592
Sewerage and sewage disposal, 911
Sex and age of international migrants, 996
Sex-linkage in poultry breeding, 588, 848
Seychelles:
  Colonial reports, 90, 600, 1109
  S.R.O. & S.I. Revised, 448
Shaping a people's destiny, 741
Shapiro, H. L.: Race mixture, 1007
Shares of no par value:
  Evidence, 970
  Report, 810, 970
Sharing skills, 741
Sharman, T. C.: Portuguese West Africa, economic survey, 970
Sharp, J. G.:
  Dehydrated meat, 696
  Whalemeat production and preservation, 696
Sharp, T.: Design in town and village, 649
Sharpe, Sir R.:
  British Honduras inquiry, report, 812, 859
  (Chairman): Departmental Committee on summary trial of motor offences, report, 1070
Sharpe's Trust Scheme, memo, 1190
Shaw, R. G.:
  Use of chutes for extraction of thinnings, 631
  Use of large diameter wheels and tyres on forest extraction vehicles, 631
Shaw, W. A.: Calendar of Treasury Books, 434, 949
Shawford, railway accident, 467
Shawls, 1221
Shea, A. E.: Canada's farm radio forum, 1006

Sheddick, V.: Land tenure in Basutoland, 864
Sheep, diseases of, shepherd's guide to control, 77
Sheep-dipping baths and handling pens, 80, 847
Sheet metal worker, career, 1157
Sheffield:
  Boundary Commission, report, 524
  Plate, 1221
  Victoria Station, Railway accident, 975
Sheldon, wreck report, 978
Shellard, H. C.: Humidity of the upper troposphere and lower stratosphere over Southern England, 421
Shells. *See* Symmetrical.
Shelterbelts:
  for farmlands, 80
  for Welsh hill farms, 631
Shepherd, H. J.: Refrigerated gas-storage for Gros Michel bananas, 696
Shepherd's guide to prevention and control of diseases of sheep, 77
Sheppard, V. L. O.: Land registration, 344
Shergold, F. A.: Study of single-sized gravel aggregates for road making, 956
Sheriff, Sheriff Court, S.R.O. & S.I. Revised, 448
Sherwood, E. G. P.: Fertiliser requirements of Kenya highlands, 861
Shewan, J. M.: Care of the trawler's fish, 696
Shields, J.: Psychotic and neurotic illnesses in twins, 679
Ship:
  Captain's medical guide, 211, 720, 1211
  Welding Committee reports, 69, 576, 837, 1084
Shipbuilding:
  and engineering dispute, inquiry, 808, 924
  and ship repairing, Census of Production, 459
Ship-models:
  Catalogue, 430
  Picture book, 687
Shipping:
  and War Terminal Services, Select Committee on Estimates, report, 264
  Casualities and deaths, return, 211, 468, 722, 1211
  International Conventions on maritime law, 561, 628
Ships, Registry of, 210, 467, 719, 975, 1210
Shop and office fittings, Census of Production, 460, 1201
Shops:
  Act, 65
    Forms, 130, 1146
  S.R.O. & S.I. Revised, 448
Short, A.: Studies on bridge-deck systems, 1187
Shorthand and typewriting tests, 980
Shrewsbury Estate Act, 835
  Bill, Personal Bills Committee report, 771
Siam, termination of state of war, 37, 114
Sickness:
  Absence and labour wastage, 420
  Benefit. *See* Unemployment.
S.I. Effects, 1195
Siepmann, C. A.: Television and education in U.S.A., 747
Sierra Leone:
  Colonial reports, 343, 344, 860, 1109
  Modern portrait, 863
  Native administration, 93
  S.R.O. & S.I Revised, 448
Sight reduction tables for air navigation, 335, 590
Signal:
  Card, 318
  Letters of British ships, 211, 468, 720, 722, 976, 1211
Signatures, ratifications, acceptances, accessions etc., 488
Significance of racial differences, 493
Silage:
  Crops for, 1093
  from sugar beet tops, 847
  Guide to grading and feeding, 81
  Making, filmstrip, 77
Silk, commodity report, 750
Silk, rayon, nylon, and cotton cloth manufacture, career, 759
Silos, farm grain, construction, 80
Silow, R. A.: Results of co-operative hybrid maize tests in European and Mediterranean countries, 751, 1008
Silver:
  English and Scottish, 958
  Mid-Georgian domestic, 499
Simes, E. (Chairman): Committee of inquiry into rating of site values, report, 388
Simmins, G. J. P.: Canada's farm radio forum, 1006
Simmonds, S.: Economic surveys, Denmark, Iraq, 716
Simplified Spelling Bill, 525, 538, 541, 542, 645
Simpson, A. C.: Fecundity of the plaice, 79
Simpson, I. A.: Rice enrichment in the Philippines, 1010
Simpson, W. D.: Guides to various ancient monuments in Scotland, 504, 1018, 1225
Sims, R. W.: Morphology of the head of the hawfinch with special reference to the myology of the jaw, 1101
Sindrome Policarencial Infantil and its prevention in Central America, 1010
Singapore:
  Aircraft accident, 859
  Colonial reports, 91, 344, 601, 861, 1109
  Filmstrip, 1153
  Photoposter, 1154
  S.R.O. & S.I. Revised, 448

SIN-STA | 1951-5

SIN— INDEX 1951-5

Singapore (*continued*):
Straits, preliminary study of physical, chemical, and biological characteristics, 602
Single-sized gravel aggregates for road-making, 956
Sinking Funds, accounts, 19, 219, 268, 474, 528, 727, 789, 984. 1042, 1219
Rate of accumulation, circular, 1151
Siphonaptera, descriptions of new and little known, 591
Sir William Turner's Hospital at Kirkleatham Charity Scheme Confirmation Act, 67
Bill, 4, 32
Sirpus, a genus of pigmy cancroid crabs, 592
Site:
Costing for builders, 243
Labour studies in school building, 1119
Records for builders, 505
Situation et Problemes economiques, 879
Situation et Problemes de l'economie italienne, 879
Sivaswamy, K. G.: Selected Arab countries of the Middle East, report of mission, 987
Sixth form, road to, 99
Skan, S. W.: Handbook for computers, 1174
Skrubbeltrang, F.: Agricultural development and rural reform in Denmark, 749
Slate quarries and mines, Census of Production, 458, 1199
Slater, E.: Psychotic and neurotic illnesses in twins, 679
Slates, roofing, durability of, 437
Slaughter:
of Animals:
Act, 571
(Amendment) Acts, 60, 829
Bills, 5, 19, 27, 32, 132, 772, 776, 783, 798, 799, 800, 803, 908, 1053
Circulars, 104, 881
(Pigs) Act, 568
Bill, 514, 528, 538, 542, 543, 645
Circular, 881
(Prevention of Cruelty) Regulations, circulars, 881, 1095
of Horses, committee of inquiry, report, 559, 621, 704
Slaughterhouses:
Act, 829
Bill, 771, 772, 774, 789, 798, 801, 802, 908
Circular, 881
Interdepartmental Committee reports:
England and Wales, 806, 882, 1071, 1097
Scotland, 806, 901, 1059, 1142
Licensing and provision of, 881
Slaughtering facilities, circular, 881
Slave Trade, S.R.O. & S.I. Revised, 448
Sloane Shell Collection, catalogue and historical account, 591
Slugs and snails, 78
Slum clearance:
Circulars, 911, 1151
Summary of returns, 1074, 1152
Small:
Arms, Census of Production, 459, 1200
Domestic sewage treatment works, principles of design, 750
Farm implements, 751
Landholders (Scotland) Act, 309
Lotteries and Gaming Bill, 1053, 1056, 1057
Roasting fowl, 1093
Smallholder cheese, 78
Smallholders (Scotland) Acts, Scottish Land Court report of proceedings, 545
Smallholdings:
and Allotments:
Act, 569
S.R.O. & S.I. Revised, 449
Reports and accounts, 81, 334, 589, 850, 1092
Smallpox vaccination, survey of recent legislation, 1013
Smit, F. G. A. M.: Descriptions of new and little known Siphonaptera, 591
Smith hive, 1093
Smith, D. N.: Field tests on wood preservatives used for pressure treatment, 954
Smith, F. E.: Indices of heat stress, 1171
Smith, Sir H. W. (Chairman): Committee on duty-free entry of machinery into Great Britain, report, 968
Smith, M.:
Nervous temperment, 420
Sickness absence and labour wastage, 420
Smith, M. A.: Study of telegraphist's cramp, 679
Smith, M. C.: Intracranial gliomata, 940
Smith, M. G.: Economy of Hausa communities of Zaria, 1109
Smith, Sir S. A. (Chairman):
Hospital Endowments Commission, report, 1069
Standing Medical Advisory Commitee, report on ageing population, 637
Smith, W. C.:
Carbonatites of the Chilwa series of Southern Nigeria, 591
Rock collections in the Mineral Department, British Museum (Natural History), 854
Volcanic rocks of the Ross Archipelago, 1101
Smith, W. H.: Commercial storage of vegetables, 438
Smith, Sir W. R. V. (Chairman): Censuses of Production and Distribution, report, 822
Smoky chimneys, 1185

INDEX 1951-5 —SOU

Smout, A. H.: Lower Tertiary foraminifera of the Qatar Peninsula, 854
Snails. *See* Slugs.
Snowdonia National Forest Park, guide, 1133
Snyder, H. E.: Education of teachers in England, France and U.S.A., 1006
Soap, Candles, and Glycerine, Census of Production, 458, 1199
Social:
and medical assistance, conventions, 43, 114, 814, 890, 1069, 1130
Aspects of technical assistance in operation, 1007
Defence, Legislative and Administrative series, 738, 994
Implications of technical advance in underdeveloped countries, 1003
Insurance conventions:
Italy, 288
Switzerland, 813
Science:
Documentation centres, international repertory, 492
Periodicals, world list, 1003
Sciences:
Documentation in, 1003
Teaching of, 1007
Theses in, 494
University teaching of, 1007
Security:
Agreements etc.:
Australia, 556
European Interim, 809, 890
Old age, invalidity, and survivors, 1069, 1130
Other schemes, 1069, 1131
France, 296, 306, 1071
Italy, 555
Luxembourg, 564, 1062
Netherlands, 822
Switzerland, 549
Convention, Brussels Treaty Powers, 43, 114
Scheme, reciprocal application, France, 42, 301
Services:
in Britain, 1154
Studies in, 854
Stratification and mobility, 1003
Welfare:
Administration, methods of, 227
Evaluation of programme, 734
In-service training, 484
Work in Jamaica, 1006
Work:
Career, 758
Training for, 228
Social, humanitarian, and cultural questions, records, 224, 991
Societies (Miscellaneous Provisions) Act, 572
Sociology, social psychology, and anthropology, 1007
Soft:
Drinks, standards for, 881
Drinks, British wines, and cider, Census of Production, 460, 1201
Furnishings, Census of Production, 460, 1201
Soil:
Mechanics for road engineers, 442
Sterilisation, 330
Survey:
of Great Britain, publications, 77, 328, 585, 845, 846, 850, 1090, 1092
Procedure, 956
Surveys for land development, 749
Soil-cement roads, 333
Solar eclipse, 837
Soldier (magazine), 1017, 1224
Solicitor, S.R.O. & S.I. Revised, 449
Solicitors:
Act, 311
(Amendment) Bill, 1031
Solid fuel, increased thermal efficiency, 879
Solidarity, wreck report, 469
Solomon Islands, economic survey, 602
Somalia, transfer of provisional administration, 291, 1065
Somaliland:
Protectorate:
Arms, Badge, 599
Colonial report, 343, 860
under Italian Administration:
Technical assistance, 742
Trust territory at halfway point, 1004
Trusteeship agreement, 490
United Nations Visiting Mission, report, 743
Some:
Inter-tidal mites in South-West England, 592
Upper Cretaceous and Eocene fruits from Egypt, 853
Somerset:
Census, 1138
North, Boundary Commission report, 38
Somervell, Lord Justice (Chairman): State Immunities Interdepartmental Committee, report on diplomatic immunity, 288
Sooty bark disease of sycamore, 369
Sorghum Mission to certain British African territories, report, 94
Sorn, Hon. Lord (Chairman): Scottish Valuation and Rating Committee, report, 819
Sorsby, A.: Causes of blindness in England, 737
Sound absorbent treatments, 182, 953
South:
Africa:
Defence matters, exchange of letters, 1069, 1114
S.R.O. & S.I. Revised, 449

SOU— INDEX 1951-5

South (*continued*):
Asia and the Pacific, compulsory education, 1003
Bank Exhibition, catalogue, guide, 103
Essex Waterworks Act, 574
Fylde, Boundary Commission report, 524
Georgia, geology, 602
Pacific Commission, agreements, 293, 366, 1058, 1131
Scotland Electricity Board, Guarantees given:
on loans proposed to be raised, 1041, 1045, 1049
on stock issued, 1051
Wales:
and Monmouthshire, guide, 1225
Ports, report, 1058
Southampton Water Airport Air Navigation Order, 595
South-East Asia:
Collective defence treaty, 822
Report on, 243
Southern:
Rhodesia, S.R.O. & S.I. Revised, 449
Right whale dolphin, 1102
Sovereign, references to, 502
Sovereign's orb and head of sovereign's sceptre with cross, postcard, 762
Soviet Government:
Correspondence:
Bacteriological and chemical warfare, 1060
Collective security, 811, 822
Four-Power meeting in Berlin, 804
International situation, 563, 565, 566
Exchange of letters, Prime Minister and Soviet Foreign Minister, 1102
Space-saving designs, 637
Spafford, A. O.: Monarchs of all they surveyed, 433
Spain:
Calendar of letters, despatches, etc., 949
Economic survey, 463
Services agreement, 824, 826, 890
Sterling payments agreement, 288, 366, 804, 890
Trade and payments agreement, 52, 114, 301, 366
Spanish Civil War, 110
Spartan, exchange of Notes with Italy regarding salvage, 545
Spastics. *See* Handicapped persons.
Spath, L. F.:
Ammonoidea of the Trias, 83
Upper Cretaceous cephalopod fauna of Graham Land, 602
Special:
Contribution, S.R.O. & S.I. Revised, 449
Middle East communications meeting, report, 918
Procedure Orders, Scotland, S.R.O. & S.I. Revised, 449
Special (*continued*):
Schools, etc. *See* Schools.
Species maintained in the National Collection of Type Cultures, 169
Specific gravity of spirits, tables, 867
Specifications:
Defence, 97, 350, 608, 868, 1114
D.T.D., 196, 456, 710, 963, 1195
Government Department, 455
Electrical, 196, 455, 711
T.G., 455
Spectrographic abstracts, 1198
Speech therapist, career, 921
Speke Junction and Ditton, railway accident, 975
Spence, Prof. Sir J. (Chairman): Committee on acute infections in infancy:
Treatment of acute dehydration in infants, 420
Spens, Sir W. (Chairman): National Insurance Advisory Committee reports, 287, 289, 294, 295, 298, 534, 535, 555, 557, 780, 782, 783, 788, 1034, 1039, 1045, 1049, 1051, 1063, 1075, 1175
Spes Melior II, wreck report, 1212
Sphecidae and Pompilidae (Hymenoptera) collected by K. M. Guishard:
en Algerie et au Maroc, 83
in West Africa and Ethiopia, 83
Spinach, cultivation of, 847
Spirit:
Distilling, Census of Production, 460, 1201
Rectifying and compounding, Census of Production, 201, 967
Spirits, S.R.O. & S.I. Revised, 449
Sports requisites, Census of Production, 201, 967
Spotted wilt of tomato, 586
Spratt, H. P.: Handbook of collections illustrating marine engineering, 694
Spraying programme for apples and pears, 847
Spring Traps Bill, 5, 7
Spruce, Norway, General volume tables in Great Britain, 117
Squirrel, grey, 631, 1091
S.R.O. & S.I. Numerical table, supplement, 1195
Staff:
College, War Office publications, 242, 243, 503, 760, 1017, 1224
Papers, International Monetary Fund, 658, 920
Relations in the Civil Service, 1219
Staffordshire, Census, 896
Stainton, Sir J. (Chairman): Local Land Charges Committee, report, 286
Stamp:
Act, 569
Duties:
Management Act, 830
S.R.O. & S.I. Revised, 449

INDEX 1951-5 —STA

Stamps, S.R.O. & S.I. Revised, 449
Standard:
Atmosphere and extreme atmospheres, proposals for detailed specifications, 140
International trade classification, statistical papers, 227
Standardisation in U.S.A. and Europe, 879
Standards:
and levels of living, international definition and measurement, 998
and recommended practices, 140, 395
for school premises, 98, 100, 872, 874
for soft drinks, 881
of living. *See* World social situation.
Recent developments and techniques in maintenance, 430
Standing:
Commission on Museums and Galleries, publications, 190, 705, 983
Committee:
Debates, 8, 26, 257, 541, 778, 797, 1032, 1043, 1053
on performance, final report, 656
Reports respecting Merchandise Marks Order, 805
Returns, 28, 132, 276, 386, 536, 646, 796, 908, 1042, 1149
Nursing and Midwifery Advisory Committee, report on State-enrolled assistant nurse in National Health Service, 1142
Orders:
House of Commons, 8, 132, 259, 386, 520, 538, 646, 1031, 1149
House of Lords, 5, 133, 515, 772, 773, 909
R.A.M.C., etc., 503, 759
Stansted Airport Customs, Air Navigation Order, 338
Star:
Almanac for land surveyors, 69, 318, 576, 837, 1084
Atlas for land surveyors, 1224
Starch, Census of Production, 201, 967
Starck, A. R.: British West Indies, Eastern Caribbean, economic survey, 463
Starks, H. J. H.: Braking performance of motor vehicles and brake testing, 699
Stars:
Catalogues, 123, 636
Early type, spectrophotometric measurements, 1184
State:
Crown of Queen Mary, postcard, 762
of the haddock stocks, 703
Management Districts, reports, 29, 190, 520, 535, 642, 796, 905, 1051, 1146
Papers, Calendars, 445, 691, 1123
Stateless person, status of 1069, 1131
Stationers' Goods, Census of Production, 460, 1201
Stationery:
Estimates 15, 215, 263, 523, 783, 1036
Office, publications, 190, 446, 705, 961, 1194
Stationery, Paper Bag, and kindred trades, Census of Production, 460
Statistical:
Abstract for the Commonwealth, 205, 463, 1202
Bulletins, 101, 108, 110, 355, 357, 877, 878, 879
Commission, report, 990
Digest 121, 373, 633, 896, 1137
of the War 217
Methods in meteorology, 680
Office studies, 228
Papers, United Nations, 222, 227, 233, 488, 999
Review, England and Wales, 122, 374, 635, 897, 1139
Summaries:
Friendly Societies, Registry of 118, 369, 631
Mineral industry, 602
Scheduled airline operations, 648
Tables. *See* Sea Fisheries.
Yearbook, United Nations, 228, 488, 742, 999
Statistics:
Annual abstract, 84, 337, 593, 855, 1104
Colonial, 344, 601, 861, 1110
Monthly Bulletin, 228, 489, 742, 999
Monthly Digest, 84, 337, 593, 855, 1104
of Trade Act, 313
S.R.O. & S.I. Revised, 449
Scottish, 704, 960, 1193
Studies in official statistics, 337
Welsh, 905, 1147
The foregoing relate to statistics generally; see also subjects about which statistical information is required.
Status:
of multilateral conventions, 999
of refugees, Convention, 814, 890
of Women, Commission report, 222, 480, 733, 990
Statute Law Revision Act, 568
Bill, 516, 517, 544
Statutes:
Chronological Table, 191, 447, 706, 962, 1194
in force, index, 447, 706, 1195
Statutory:
Instruments:
Effects, 706, 962, 1195
Lists, 191, 447, 705, 961, 1194
Reference Committee, reports, 192

1951-5 | STA-TAX

STA— INDEX 1951-5

Statutory (*continued*):
Instruments (*continued*):
Select Committee proceedings, reports, etc., 13, 14, 15, 16, 17, 18, 19, 20, 21, 22, 28, 29, 132, 261, 262, 263, 264, 265, 266, 267, 268, 269, 270, 271, 272, 275, 280, 386, 521, 522, 523, 524, 525, 527, 528, 529, 530, 531, 533, 535, 538, 539, 646, 779, 799, 908, 1032, 1044, 1149
Volumes, 191, 447, 705, 962, 1083, 1195
Publications Office, publications, 191, 447, 706, 962, 1194
Registration of Opticians, Interdepartmental committee report, 292
Rules and Orders and Statutory Instruments:
Numerical tables, 706, 962
Revised, 192, 448
Steam road vehicles, 694, 1185
Steel:
and aluminium, competition between, 989
Committee, Economic Commission for Europe, 989
Economy Bulletins, 505
European trends, 223
Houses, Corrosion of, 440
Industry. *See* Iron.
Sheets, Census of Production, 458, 1199
Statistics for Europe, 228, 489, 742, 999
Technical improvements in use of, 110
Steel, Capt. J. (Chairman): Sub-Committee of the Standing Advisory Committee on Hospital and Specialist Services, reports on reception and welfare of in-patients in hospitals, 124
Steel, J. L. S. (Leader): Mission of U.K. Industrialists, report on industrial development in Jamaica, Trinidad, Barbados, and British Guiana, 602
Steel, Aluminium, and Tin; agreement with U.S.A. for supply, 288
Steels, boron, 876
Steffens, R. J.: Assessment of vibration intensity and its application to the study of building vibrations, 698
Stem:
and bulb eelworm:
Cereals and other farm crops, 847
Clover, 587
Horticultural crops, 586
Exposure corrections, 1174
Stempffer, H.: Revision of genus Teriomima Kirby, 591
Stephens, J. V.: Geology of country between Bradford and Skipton, 635
Stephens, P. S.: Cuba, economic survey, 969
Stereocomparator technique for aerial triangulation, 1174
Sterilising farm dairy utensils, 847
Sterling:
Area:
American analysis, 422
Statistical summary, 716
Trade summary, 970
See also Commonwealth.
Assets:
and independent gold and dollar reserves, exchange of Notes with Ceylon, 39, 302
of the British Colonies, memo, 603
Payments agreements:
Austria, 40, 810
Czechsolovakia, 301, 1076
Egypt, 51, 52
Finland, 300, 303, 552, 558, 812, 816
Italy, 36, 550, 565
Japan, 55, 298, 302, 547, 805, 807, 825, 1068, 1072, 1073, 1076, 1077, 1078
Poland, 41, 56, 292, 303, 546, 550, 560, 562, 807, 811, 816, 825, 827
Spain, 288, 804
Stevenage New Town, Development Corporation reports, 29, 279, 388, 779, 792, 913, 1048
Stevens, W. C.: Kiln operator's handbook, 438
Stevenson, I. P.: Geology of country between Burton-on-Trent, Rugeley and Uttoxeter, 1140
Stewart, F. O. (Chairman): Scottish Police Council Committee, report on police representative organisations and negotiating machinery, 445
Stewart, I. G.: National income of Nigeria, 861
Stewart, T. G. (Chairman):
Departmental Committee, reports on supply of teachers, 36, 545
Working Party to deal with salaries of teachers in Scotland, report, 1058
Stewarts and Lloyds Ltd., Proposal to sell holdings, 814
Stinging nettles, 586
Stipendiary Magistrate, England, S.R.O. & S.I. Revised, 449
Stirling, Census, 898
Stitt, Cmdr. G. M. S.: Early successes against Italy, 854, 961
Stobcross, railway accident, 210
Stock:
Exchange Clerks' Pension Fund Act, 1082
Feed, town waste for, 1097
Stock, F. G. L.: Fatigue and boredom in repetitive work, 420
Stockport South, Boundary Commission report, 524
Stockton-on-Tees, Boundary Commission report, 269, 379
Stone fruit, structure of intra-European production and markets, 880

INDEX 1951-5 —SUG

Stone, R. G.: Mexico, economic survey, 716
Stonehenge, guide, 762, 1225
Stonehouse, B.: Falkland Islands Dependencies Survey, scientific report, 602
Stones, Prof. H. H.: Effect of sugar supplements on dental caries in children, 1171
Storage:
of herring gametes, 1192
of ware potatoes in Great Britain, 696
Storck, H.: Entertainment film for juvenile audiences, 493
Stormonth, K.: Temperature and humidity gradients in the first 100 M. over south-east England, 680
Straits Settlements, S.R.O. & S.I. Revised, 449
Stranded whales and turtles, guide for identification and reporting, 593
Strasbourg Plan, comments on, 879
Stratford, railway accident, 719
Strathyre Forest, 368
Stratus cloud near the east coast of Great Britain, 170
Straw for fodder, 78
Strawberries, 1094
Diseases and pests, 1090
Preparation for market, 330
Red core of, 587
Street:
Cleansing. *See* Public cleansing.
Widths for carriageways and footways, 166
Strength:
and stability of walls, 1185
of timber struts, 1186
Properties:
of Plywood, 696, 1186
of timber, 696
Stride, H. G.: Royal Mint, 694
Stromness Harbour (Guarantee) Order Confirmation Act, 1082
Bill, 1056
Strong, C. F.: Teaching for international understanding, 353
Stroudwater Navigation Act, 835
Structure of further education salaries, 1058
Stuart, T. A.: Spawning migration, reproduction and young stages of loch trout, 702
Stubblefield, C. J.: Geology of country:
around Barnsley, 1140
between Bradford and Skipton, 635
between Burton-on-Trent, Rugeley, and Uttoxeter, 1140
Student:
Employees, Western Union convention, 289
Pilot's and Private Pilot's licences, 1211
Students at Universities, maintenance rates, 1119
Studies:
in methods, 742
in the social services (war history), 961
Study abroad, international handbook, 233, 494, 748, 1007
Suberites domuncula, synonomy distribution and ecology, 592
Sub-genus Stegomyia in the Ethiopian region, 336, 591
Submarine Telegraph, S.R.O. & S.I. Revised, 449
Substitute feeding stuffs, 333
Succession in Scotland, report on law of, 37
Suction of moisture held in soil and other porous materials, 441
Sudan:
Administration, reports on, 34, 40, 114, 286, 366
Anglo-Egyptian conversation on defence, 58
Commercial conditions, 205, 716
Documents concerning constitutional development and agreement with U.K. and Egypt concerning self-government and self-determination, 548
Electoral Commission, report, 806, 960
International Commission to supervise self-determination, agreement, 1079
Photoposter, 390
Progress in, 651
Self-government and self-determination agreement, 548, 558
(Special Payments) Act, 1081
Bill, 1030, 1056
Trade Mission report. *See* Egypt, Sudan.
See also Growth of a nation.
Sudbury and Woodbridge, Boundary Commission report, 524
Suez Canal:
Anglo-Egyptian conversations on defence, 58
Base, agreements, 818, 824, 890, 1065, 1074, 1075
Shipping and tonnage returns, 890
Suffolk:
Census, 1138
Ministry of Agriculture and Fisheries Provisional Orders Bill, 32
Sugar:
Agreement, proposed international, observations on, 750
and glucose, Census of Production, 460, 1201
Beet:
Cultivation, [illegible]
Eelworm, filmstrip, 329
Sowing to singling, 847
Tops for feeding green, 330, 847
Bill, 1053, 1055
Commodity series bulletin, 495
Conference, 1002
Future arrangements for marketing, 1069, 1097

SUG— INDEX 1951-5

Sugar (*continued*):
Industry (Research and Education) Fund accounts, 25, 81, 279, 334, 539, 589, 1033, 1092
Regulation of production and marketing, international agreement, 286, 366, 548, 565, 629
S.R.O. & S.I. Revised, 449
Sulphur, 357
and sulphuric acid position, survey, 442
Dioxide in imported dehydrated vegetables, 358
Sulphuric acid and the manufacture of phosphatic fertilisers, 618
Summary:
Jurisdiction:
and procedure in Scotland, memo, 769
(Scotland) Act, 829
Bill, 769, 771, 775, 801
Report, 771
Proceedings, S.R.O. & S.I. Revised, 449
Summer Time Act, 570
Sumner, P. L.: Conquest of the air, 694
Sunday:
Entertainments Act, 63
Cinematograph Fund, accounts, 23, 179, 271, 433, 533, 690, 791, 949, 1049, 1181
Observance Bill, 541
Sunderland:
Boundary Commission report, 29
Corporation Act, 67
Sunley, J. G.: Strength of timber struts, 1186
Sunlight, wreck report, 721
Sunshine averages, 679, 941
Sunspot and geomagnetic storm data, 1141
Superannuation:
Acts, 308, 309, 313, 571, 572
and other Trust Funds (Validation): Act, 572
S.R.O. & S.I. Revised, 449
Appeal determinations, 164, 387
Benefits, allocation of part, 1151
Circulars, 910, 1150, 1151
See also Local Government.
(Miscellaneous Provisions) Act, 570
National Health Service scheme, explanation, 379
(President of Industrial Court) Act, 829
Bill, 773, 801
Supervision, records of, forms, 642
Supervisors, training of, 937
Supplies and Services (Defence Purposes) Act, 60
Bill, 2, 31
Supply:
Appropriation accounts, 259, 470
Estimates, 263, 523, 783, 1036
of insulated electric wires and cables, Monopolies Commission report, 269, 462
Supply (*continued*):
of military aircraft, 1060, 1119, 1198
of teachers in Scotland, 36, 187, 545, 702
Services estimates, 15, 21, 215
Ministry of, publications, 196, 450, 706, 962, 1195
Supply, Transport and Barrack Services, regulations, 243, 503, 1017, 1224
Support:
at roadheads, memo, 121
behind power loaders, memo, 1137
Suppression of slavery, 482
Supreme Court:
England, S.R.O. & S.I. Revised, 449
Northern Ireland:
Fees and percentages, 939
Procedure, Order in Council, 939
S.R.O & S.I. Revised, 449
Winter Assize Orders, 168, 419, 678, 939
of Judicature:
Accounts, 12, 199, 257, 457, 518, 529, 619, 712, 786, 966, 1032, 1198
Northern Ireland, Land Purchase Accounts, 23, 102, 272, 357, 531, 619, 792, 880, 1046, 1122
Officers (Pensions) Act, 829
Bill, 773, 801
Practice and procedure, 40, 168, 299, 419, 556, 678
Prize, etc., Deposit Account, 15, 219, 264, 318, 727, 787, 984, 1036, 1220
Rules (Northern Ireland) Orders in Council, 382, 678, 939
Surface Water:
Development in arid regions, 751
Yearbook, Great Britain, 389, 1152
Surgery (war history), 902, 961
Surrey, Census, 896
Surtax Tables, 391
Survey, 475, 728
and Development Plan maps, reproduction of, 165
OEEC, 880
of building in sandstone in Scotland, 698
of some mixing plants for asphalt and coated macadam, 699
Surveyors, instructions to, 1208
Sussex, Census, 896
Sutherland, Census, 898
Sutton and Cheam Corporation Act, 67
Sutton, S. C.: India Office Library, guide, 348
Sutton Coldfield, railway accident, 1210
Sutton Hoo Ship-Burial Guide, 591
Swaffham Prior and Burwell Fens investigation, 331
Swaziland:
Colonial reports, 93, 347, 604, 864, 1112
Economic survey, 345
See also Basutoland.
Sweden:
Air services agreement, 299, 366, 553, 629

INDEX 1951-5 —TAX

Sweden (*continued*):
Avoidance of double taxation, 1065, 1131
Consular Convention, 293, 366, 827, 890, 1037, 1131
Documents of identity for aircraft personnel, 1059, 1131
Double Taxation Convention, extension of, 807, 891, 1060, 1131
Economic conditions, 616, 970
Foreign Trade Statistical Bulletins, 374, 617, 878
Liquidation of German assets in Sweden, 826, 891
Monetary agreement, 806, 891
National accounts study, 618
Repayment of credits granted by the European Payments Union, 821, 890
Trade and Commerce agreement, termination, 566, 629
Swedish shale oil, production methods, 357
Sweetheart Abbey, guide, 244
Swellengrebel, N. H.: Malaria terminology, 755
Swelling of wood under stress, 185
Swift moths, 847
Swimming:
Baths, purification of water, 126
Pool, safety precautions, 443
Swimming, Life saving, Basic and battle physical training, etc., 500
Swindon:
Boundary Commission report, 279, 369
Corporation Act, 67
Swine erysipelas, fever, 331
Swinton:
and Worsley Burial Board Act, 835
Railway accident, 975
Swinton, W. E.: Fossil amphibians and reptiles, 854
Switzerland:
Air services agreements, 48, 114, 300, 367, 550, 629
Avoidance of double taxation, 824, 891 1063, 1131
Documents of identity for aircraft personnel, 1074, 1131
Economic survey, 463, 1205
Foreign Trade Statistical Bulletins, 356, 617, 878
Monetary agreements, 36, 41, 49, 57, 114, 115, 292, 297, 301, 367, 548, 558, 629
National accounts study, 356
Repayment of Credits granted by European Payments Union, 820
Social Insurance Convention, 549, 629, 813, 891
Swords and daggers, 239
Sycamore, sooty bark disease, 369
Sylvester-Bradley, P. C.: Ostracod genus Trachyleberis, 592
Symmetric cylindrical shells, analysis of, 1189
Synchrotron, gift to Australia, 813
Synthetic detergents, Committee report, 913
Syria:
Air services agreement, 810, 891
Commercial conditions, 716
Museums and monuments, Unesco Mission report, 1006
Systematic monograph of Dermaptera of the world, 1103
Systematics and origin of the generic group Oxyptilus Zeller, 83

T

T.A.A. Conference and Seminar series, 489
Tactical training, Civil Defence filmstrip, 903
Taf Fechan Water Supply Act, 1081
Tailoring, Dressmaking, etc., Census of Production, 459, 1201
Tait, M.: Education of women in citizenship, 1006
Take-all or whiteheads of wheat and barley, 847
Tams, W. H. T.: Pest of coconut palms in Portuguese East Africa, 591
Tandy, A. H.: Belgium and Luxembourg, economic survey, 715
Tanganyika:
Administration under U.K. Trusteeship, 94, 346, 603, 863, 1111
Development of African local government, 93
Its present and its future, 744
Native administration, 93
Photoposter, 1154
Population, 739
United Nations reports on, 229, 743
See also Overseas Food Corporation.
Tangier:
Anglo-French agreement amended, 1059
Reform of international jurisdiction, convention, 1071, 1131
Tapestries at Hampton Court Palace, guide, 245
Tar surface dressings, recommendations for, 441
Tariff negotiations, Torquay, report, 43
Tariffs and Trade:
General Agreement, 373, 397, 1062, 1205
Japan's accession, 1064, 1203
Torquay protocol and schedules, 228
Tarleton, R. D.: Reactions between aggregates and cement, 698
Tate Gallery, 966, 984, 1198
See also National Gallery.
Tavistock, Boundary Commission report, 38
Tax:
Cases, Inland Revenue publications, 136, 391, 144, 915, 1155

Tax (*continued*):
  Treatment of Forces and their members, 302
    International agreement, 295
Taxation:
  Agreements:
    Belgium, 551, 811
    Burma, 47, 292
    Denmark, 1065
    Finland, 286, 549
    France, 47, 52
    Germany, 820, 1073
    Greece, 557, 807
    Norway, 45, 54, 1076
    Sweden, 807, 1060, 1065
    Switzerland, 824, 1063
    U.S.A., 817, 1061
  Double Taxation Relief Tables, 651
  of Profits and Income, Royal Commission, evidence, 435, 952, 1184
    Reports, 547, 694, 810, 952, 1066, 1184
  of trading profits, committee report, 41, 219
  Relief from taxation of U.S.A. expenditures in U.K., 290
  Treatment of Provisions for retirement, 806, 985
Taxes. *See* Income Taxes.
Taxes—Subsidies, statistical summary, 140
Taxicab service, committee report, 550, 728
Tax-paid stocks, committee report, 549, 728
Taxonomy of the Karroo and red-back larks of western South Africa, 592
Taylor, A. J.: Caernarvon Castle and Town Wall, guide, 761
Taylor, Dr. C. A.: Rural community organisation and development in the Caribbean area and Mexico, 729
Taylor, D. J.: Eggs and egg products, 1186
Taylor, G.: Notes on Podostermaceae for the revision of the flora of west tropical Africa, 591
Taylor, J. H.: Northampton sand ironstone, 123
Taylor, T. M. (Chairman):
  Commission of inquiry into crofting conditions, report, 809
  Educational endowments in Scotland committee, report, 187
Taylor, Sir W. (Chairman): Advisory Committee on forestry, reports, 1019, 1225
Taylor, W. (Chairman): Working party on employment of blind persons, report, 145
Tchernavin, V. V.: Feeding mechanisms of a deep sea fish, 592
Tea:
  Blending and coffee roasting, Census of Production, 201, 1201
  Blister blight disease, 599
  Commodity report, 750
Teachers:
  in Scotland, supply of, 545
Teachers: (*continued*):
  in Scotland (*continued*):
    Mathematics and science, 1062, 1191
  of handicapped pupils, training and supply, 874
  Qualified and temporary, 1119, 1121
  Secondment for overseas service, 98, 100, 874
  (Superannuation) Acts, 63, 64, 832
    Bills, 800, 1053, 1056
    Reports, 16, 24, 219, 789, 985
  Supply, Departmental committee report, 36, 187
  Training and supply, National Advisory Committee report, 100
  See also Graduate Teachers.
Teachers':
  Salaries, reports, etc., 99, 353, 615, 873, 1121
    (Scotland), regulations, circulars, 186, 957, 1189, 1190
    Structure of further education salaries, 1191
  Superannuation (War Service) Act, 572
Teaching:
  about the United Nations and specialised agencies, 489, 742
  Better nutrition, 235
  for international understanding, 353
  History, 353
  Natural science in secondary schools, 491
  Philosophy, 748
  Social sciences, 1007
Tebble, N.: Polychaete fauna of the Gold Coast, 1102
Technical:
  Advance in underdeveloped countries, social implications, 1003
  and scientific register, supply and demand for persons with professional qualifications, 163
  Assistance:
    Basic agreement for U.K. dependencies, 53, 115
    Commission, reports, 237
    Committee, reports, 734, 990
    Cyrenaica and Tripolitania, 51, 52
    Eritrea, 48
    for economic development etc., 234, 1012
    Libya, 49
    Mission:
      Publications, 615, 618, 619, 879,
      Reports, 489, 734, 876, 878
    Programmes, 495, 742, 1000
    Projects, register of, 618
  Co-operation:
    Africa south of the Sahara, 807, 891
    U.S.A., agreement, 52
  Education:
    Scotland, 702
    Select Committee on Estimates reports, 533, 534

Technical (*continued*):
  Reports (series), 237, 498, 756
  Staff course. *See* Staff College.
  Subjects:
    Guidance to teachers in setting and marking examinations, 1191
    Secondary schools, 187, 1191
Tees:
  Conservancy:
    Act, 835
    (Deposit of Dredged Material) Act, 835
    Superannuation Scheme Act, 574
  Valley Water Act, 574
Teinds, Court of, Scotland, S.R.O. & S.I. Revised, 449
Telecommunication services between British Honduras and Mexico, 301
Telecommunications:
  International convention, 36, 115
  Supplementary agreement, 304, 367
Telegraph Acts, 60, 829
  Bills, 4, 32, 772, 801
Telegraphists' cramp, study of, 679
Telegraphs, S.R.O. & S.I. Revised, 449
Telephone Act, 60
  Bill, 5, 32, 33
Television:
  Act, 829
    Bill, 774, 776, 800, 802, 803
  Advisory Committee reports, 690, 948
  Facilities of mass communication, 1004
  See also Broadcasting.
Temperature:
  and humidity gradients in the first 100M. over south-east England, 680
  Averages, 941
  Measurement and control, collection illustrating, handbook, 1185
  Measuring instruments, calibration of, 1174
Templeborough Rolling Mills Ltd., proposal to sell securities, 559, 726
Temporary Laws, register of, 16, 133, 259, 279, 386, 539, 645, 1033, 1044, 1149
Ten thousand men of Africa, 348
Tenancy of Shops (Scotland) Act, 65
Tenders and specifications, Scottish housing handbook, 1142
Tensions and Technology series, 748, 1007
Te-Phu-Gram, form, 681
Termination of state of war:
  Germany, 167
  Siam (Thailand), 37, 809
Terrington, Lord (Chairman):
  Air Transport Advisory Committee, report, 266
  Post Office Departmental Classes Recognition Committee, report, 288
Territorial:
  and Auxiliary Forces Associations, financial position, 294, 503, 551, 590, 760, 811, 852, 1018, 1069, 1098, 1224
Territorial (*continued*):
  Army:
    Administration, committee report, 1069, 1224
    Manual of military law, 1223
    Regulations, 243, 503, 760, 1017, 1224
    S.R.O. & S.I. Revised, 449
Tertiary Cheilostomatous Polyzoa of New Zealand, 336
Test walls for assessing construction times with new building blocks, 184
Testing:
  Concrete by an ultrasonic pulse technique, 1188
  Memoranda, 121, 896
  of sight and supply or repair of glasses, fees and charges, 1144
Textile:
  Converting, Census of Production, 459, 1200
  Finishing, Census of Production, 459, 1200
  Machinery and accessories, Census of Production, 459, 1200
  Packing, Census of Production, 201, 1200
Textiles:
  Census of Production, 713
  Fifty masterpieces, 239
Textiles, leather, leather goods, fur and clothing, Census of Production, 461, 713
Thailand:
  Air services, 46, 115, 819, 891
  Compulsory education, 494
  Outstanding Commonwealth war claims, 39, 115
  Termination of state of war, 809, 891
Thames, Sand and Gravel Advisory Committee report, 388
Theatre, S.R.O. & S.I. Revised, 449
Theatrical:
  Companies Bill, 801
  Employers Registration:
    Act, 831
    (Amendment) Act, 311
Therapeutic Substances:
  Act, 570
  Bill, 1030, 1057
    Report, 1028, 1030
  (Prevention of Misuse) Act, 568
    Bill, 510, 529, 538, 542, 646
  S.R.O. & S.I. Revised, 449
Thermal:
  Expansion of concrete, 184
  Insulation of houses, 650, 1189
  Power stations:
    Fuel consumption, 880
    Technical development, 102
Thermoplastic flooring tiles, 695
Thesiger, G. A. (Chairman): Licensing of Road Passenger Services Committee, report, 722

Thetford Chase, 368
They can't afford to wait, 748
Thinning of plantations, 1133
Thiourea, Public Health (Preservatives etc. in Food) Regulations, 881
Third Parties (Rights against Insurers) Act, 831
Thirsk, railway accident, 975
Thistles and their control, 585
Thomas, D. P.:
  Associated jaws and limb bones of Limnopithecus Macinnesi, 84
  Miocene Lemuroids of East Africa, 336
Thomas, F. G.: Fire resistance of reinforced concrete columns, 698
Thomas, H. J.:
  Distribution, biology and exploitation of the Norway lobster in Scottish waters, 960
  Recaptures of tagged lobsters in Scotland, 1192
Thomas Bewick Bicentenary Exhibition, catalogue, 757
Thompson, A.: Vocabularium Bibliothecarii, 749
Thompson, A. H.:
  Netley Abbey, guide, 762
  Roche Abbey, guide, 1018
Thomson & Co. Ltd. and members of the National Society of Operative Printers and Assistants, Court of Inquiry report, 298
Thomson, J.: Electronics, 1224
Thornthwaite Forest, 368
Thornton Abbey, guide, 244, 1018
Thorogood, A. L.: Survey of sulphur and sulphuric acid position, 442
Thorogood, C. E.: Ceylon, economic survey, 463, 1204
Threlkeld, T. P. (Chairman): Joint Advisory Committee of the Cotton Industry, reports:
  Dust in card rooms, 400
  Mule spinners' cancer, 417
Threshing and conditioning of herbage, root and vegetable seed crops, 79
Throstle Nest East Junction, railway accident, 210
Tilapia:
  and other fish and fisheries of Lake Nyasa, 345
  New species from Lake Jipe and Pangani river, 1101
Timber:
  African, tropical, nomenclature and general information, 100
  American forest operations and increase of European productivity, 357
  and metal, preservation, 333
  Associations and technical publications, nomenclature, 880
  Building, 763
    Industry, 618
Timber (*continued*):
  Care in use, 761
  Census of Production, 460
  Control, Select Committee on Estimates, report, 19
  from the Colonies, 134
  Furniture industry, 618
  Home-grown, use in wood-turning and related trades in Scotland, 892
  Imported, supply of, 533
  in all building work, use of, 505
  Industries in U.S.A., 618
  Industry in Europe, 880
  Licence, 204, 419, 463
  Mission to British West Indies, British Guiana, and British Honduras, 603
  Statistics, 235, 496, 741, 743, 1010
  Strength properties, 696
  Tropical, 619
Time:
  Limits for claiming benefit:
    Industrial Injuries Advisory Council report, 291, 428
    National Insurance Advisory Committee report, 289, 430
  Measurement, collection illustrating, handbook, 1185
  Rates of wages and hours of labour, 163, 417, 676, 937, 1169
Tin:
  International agreement, 817
  United Nations conference, 1002
  U.S.A., exchange of Notes regarding supply, 300
Tinplate, Census of Production, 458, 1199
Tintern Forest. 116
Titchfield Abbey, guide, 1018
Tithe:
  Act, 60
    Accounts, 9, 171, 219, 258, 422, 475, 519, 728, 783, 942, 1037, 1050, 1173, 1220
  Act 1936 (Amendment) Bill, 1, 6, 31
  (Change of Ownership of Land) Rules, 199
Tithes, England, S.R.O. & S.I. Revised, 449
Title of the Sovereign, 546, 642
Title, Deprivation, S.R.O. & S.I. Revised, 449
Tiv Farm and Settlement, 1109
Tobacco:
  Census of Production, 201, 1201
  Commodity series bulletin, 495
  S.R.O. & S.I. Revised, 449
Tobago. *See* Trinidad.
Togoland:
  under French administration, 1001
  under U.K. administration, 94, 346, 603, 735, 863, 1001, 1111
Toilet preparations and perfumery, Census of Production, 458, 1199
Tollerton, railway accident, 210
Tomato, spotted wilt, 586

Tonga:
  Colonial reports, 343, 860
  Economic survey, 602
Tonnage measurements of ships, instructions, 722, 1211
Tool and implement, Census of Production, 459, 1200
Toomer, Air Vice-Marshal S. E.: Early successes against Italy, 854, 961
Torquay:
  Protocol and schedules, General agreement on tariffs and trade, 228
  Tariff negotiations report, 43, 205
Tortfeasors, S.R.O. & S.I. Revised, 449
Total solar eclipse, 837
Totnes Castle, guide, 504, 1225
Tottenham Corporation Act, 316
Tourism and European recovery, 102
Towards:
  a United Nations world, 739
  World understanding, 494, 748
Towcester Rural District Council (Abthorpe Rating) Act, 835
Tower of London:
  Crown jewels, guide, 763
  Exhibition of armour, 244
  Guide, 764, 1019
  Postcard, 764, 1226
Town:
  and Country Planning:
    Act, 65, 313, 568, 829
      Bill, 281, 285, 511, 512, 520, 542, 646, 776, 777, 790, 798, 801, 802, 803, 908
    Acts, amendment of financial provisions, 305, 389, 445
    (Amendment) Act, 60
      Bill, 1
    Career, 920
    Circulars, 199, 910, 911, 1150, 1151
    (Development Plans) (Amendment) Regulations, circular, 910
    Guide, 1152
      Scotland, 1142
    (Housing Accommodation) Direction, circular, 387
    in Britain, 1154
    Memo, 1153
      Scotland, 1142
    Mineral workings, setting off development charge against payments, 43, 133, 166, 190
    (Minerals) Regulations, circular, 648
    Ministry of, publications, 199
    (National Coal Board) Regulations, explanatory memo, 125, 166
    Planning Payments (War Damage) Schemes, accounts, 519, 593, 779, 799, 855
    Progress report, 42, 166
    (Scotland) Act, 313, 830
      Bill, 777, 790, 798, 801, 802, 903, 908
Town (*continued*):
  and Country Planning (*continued*):
    (Scotland) Act (*continued*):
      Development plans, 377
    Selected appeal decisions, 166, 199, 377, 389
    S.R.O. & S.I. Revised, 449
  and village, Design in, 649
  Development Act, 308
    Bill, 252, 254, 265, 278, 282, 284, 386
    Memo. 389
  Polls Bill, 1054
  Refuse, collection and disposal, 619
  Waste:
    for stock feed, 1097
    in agriculture, use of 956
Toxic:
  Chemicals in agriculture, 81, 851, 1097
  Gases in industry, methods for detection, 1189
  Hazards of certain pesticides to Man, 755
Toxicity of industrial organic solvents, 679
Toy Weapons Bill, 541
Toys and games, Census of Production, 201, 967
Trachoma, expert committee report, 499
Tractor ploughing, 1092
Tractors, wheel and track type, directory, 496
Trade:
  Agreements:
    Cuba, 52, 55
    Ireland, 555
    Norway, 37, 54
    Pakistan, 40
  and Commerce agreement, Sweden, terminated, 566
  and Navigation accounts, 8, 11, 205, 260, 463, 518, 521, 716, 778, 781, 790, 1031, 1034, 1205
  and Payments agreements:
    Argentina, 44, 46, 546, 809, 1065, 1072
    Brazil, 49, 293, 552, 812, 1067, 1072 1075
    Paraguay, 561, 819, 1072
    Spain, 52, 301
  Barriers to knowledge, Manual of regulations, 233
  between Asia and Europe, 1000
  Board of:
    Directory of departments and their work, 462, 1202
    Estimates, 15, 21, 215, 263, 523, 783, 1036
    Journal, 204, 462, 715, 969, 1204
    Publications, 200, 457, 712, 966, 1198
  Boards, S.R.O. & S.I. Revised, 449
  Classification, international, commodity indexes for, 730
  Commonwealth, 1111
  Direction of international, 730, 987

Trade (*continued*):
Disputes:
Act, 569
S.R.O. & S.I. Revised, 449
Facilities Acts, accounts, 18, 219, 267, 527, 728, 788, 985, 1040, 1220
Fairs overseas, 1205
Food and Agricultural Statistics year-book, 752
Foreign, 355
in goods and services between OEEC countries, regulations for liberalisation, 615
Latin America and Europe, 742
Marks:
Act, 312, 832
S.R.O. & S.I. Revised, 449
See also Patent.
Mission report on markets in the Caribbean, 715
of the U.K., annual statement etc., 97, 349, 464, 607, 716, 867, 971, 1114, 1205
Overseas, report, 1205
Statistics:
Commonwealth, 205, 563
International, yearbook, 484
Union:
Act, 61
Bill, 30
S.R.O. & S.I. Revised, 449
Unions, report of Chief Registrar, 893
See also Foreign Trade; Overseas Trade; International Trade; Commodity Trade; Productivity; Sterling Area.
Trading:
Accounts and Balance Sheets, 13, 23, 102, 257, 279, 357, 518, 540, 619, 779, 880, 1122
Profits, taxation of, report, 41
with the Enemy:
Act, 832
Orders, 717, 971
Peace Treaty, etc., 968
S.R.O. & S.I. Revised, 450
Traditional:
Art from the Colonies, catalogue, 94
Sculpture from the Colonies, illustrated handbook, 94
Trafalgar square by floodlight, postcard, 763
Traffic:
Cases, reports, 468, 720, 1211
in women and children, 734
London and Home Counties Advisory Committee reports, 466, 1209
Training:
and supply of teachers, 100
of handicapped pupils, 874
College students grants, 1119, 1120
Colleges in England and Wales, 353, 615, 1121
for management, Building Apprenticeship and Training Council report, 504
Training (*continued*):
for social work, 228
Manual, 140, 918
of Civil Defence general, rescue, and tactical instructors, 639
of District Nurses, 1144
of rural school teachers, 1006
of supervisors, 937
within industry, form, 1169
Training, rehabilitation, and resettlement, Select Committee on Estimates report, 266, 274
Tramway accident, 720
Tramway, trolleybus and omnibus undertakings (civil engineering), Census of Production, 460, 1202
Tramways:
and trolleybus undertakings, return, 212
S.R.O. & S.I. Revised, 450
Transatlantic cable construction and maintenance contract, 539, 728
Transfer of functions (Food and Drugs) Order, 1095
Transhipment, open general licence, 206, 717, 971, 1205
Transmitting world news, 748
Transport:
Act, 313, 568
Bill, 284, 285, 510, 511, 512, 541, 542
Guarantee given on stock issued, 12, 15, 16, 22, 23, 25, 27, 219, 260, 262, 263, 264, 266, 269, 275, 279, 475, 521, 524, 534, 728, 780, 784, 786, 794, 985, 1040, 1044, 1049, 1220
(Amendment) Bill, 17, 27, 133
and Civil Aviation, Ministry of, publications, 722, 972, 1206
and communications:
United Nations Commission, reports, 222, 733, 1000
Checklist of documents, 477
Review, 228, 489, 742, 1000
Arbitration Tribunal, publications, 212, 468, 720, 977, 1211
(Borrowing Powers) Act, 1080
Bill, 803, 1026
Charges, etc., (Miscellaneous Provisions) Act, 830
Bill, 776, 790, 798, 800, 802, 803, 908
(Disposal of Road Haulage Property) Bill, 1057
Estimates, 15, 22, 215, 263, 523, 784, 1036
Select Committee, report, 204
Examinations, 208, 466, 718, 973, 1208
Fund, accounts, 796, 977, 1046, 1211
in U.S.A., Federal regulation of, 619
Inland water, 993
Ministry of:
Amalgamation with Ministry of Civil Aviation, 556
Publications, 208, 464, 718
S.R.O. & S.I. Revised, 450

Transport (*continued*):
Policy, 293, 469
Statistics, 489, 742, 1000
Tribunal, publications, 212, 469, 721, 977, 1211
Users' Consultative Committee, reports, 784, 987, 1041, 1212
Transport, Fuel, and Power, Ports Efficiency Committee on co-ordination, 466
Transport, Shipping, and War Terminal Services, Select Committee on Estimates report, 22
Transports, Instructions for Masters, 974
Transverse contractions and reaction stresses in butt-welded mild steel plates, 69
Travel abroad, 749
Travelling exhibitions, manual, 747
Travers Foundation. *See* Greenwich Hospital.
Treasury:
Bills, S.R.O. & S.I. Revised, 450
Bonds, 1170
Books, Calendars of, 180, 434, 691, 949
Chest Fund, accounts, 12, 219, 259, 475, 512, 728, 783, 795, 985, 1047, 1220
Exchange control, 938
Publications, 214, 469, 723, 978, 1213
Solicitor, S.R.O. & S.I. Revised, 450
Treaties, Laws and Practices concerning their conclusion, 738
Treatment:
and preservation of timber, 618
of British prisoners of war in Korea, 1119
of damp walls, 437
of walls infested with dry rot, 1185
Treaty:
of Peace with Japan, 56
Series, United Nations, 228, 489, 743, 1000
Tree:
Planting on peat, experiment in, 892
Preservation Orders, 165, 376, 648
Root development on upland heaths, 1133
Trees, World festival of, 1009
Trend and pattern of fertility in Great Britain, 1184
Trendall, A. F.: Geology of South Georgia, 602
Trends in economic sectors, 880
Trent River Board Act, 67
Treponematoses, 1013
Trichomonas disease, 331
Trichoptera (caddis-flies) of Australia and New Zealand, 593
Trieste:
Foreign trade statistical bulletin, 356
Memo. of understanding, 294, 367, 823, 891
Trilene, use of, by midwives, 940
Trinidad and Tobago:
Colonial reports, 90, 343, 600, 860, 1109
Economic survey, 463, 602
S.R.O. & S.I. Revised, 450
See also Industrial development.
Tripod haymaking, 587
Tripolitania, air services, 46
Trolley vehicles undertaking. *See* Tramways.
Troops, employment in aid of civil power, 1223
Tropical:
Timber, 102, 619
Woods and agricultural residues as sources of pulp, 752
Trotter, F. M.: Pennines and adjacent areas, geology, 898
Trout:
Research. *See* Freshwater and salmon fisheries.
Spawning migration, reproduction and young stages of loch trout, 602
Trucial States Notice, 1131
Truck Act, 569
Trueman, Sir A. (Chairman): University Grants Committee, report on University development, 289
Trumble, H. C.: Legumes in agriculture, 750
Trunk Roads:
Act, 832, 833
S.R.O. & S.I. Revised, 450
Trussing of poultry, 847
Trust:
Territories, what the United Nations is doing, 490
Territory at the halfway point, 1001
Trustee:
Act, 310, 570
Investment Bill, 1056
Savings Bank:
Accounts, 220, 475, 728, 985, 1220
Act, 830
Bill, 773, 774, 803
Report, 775
Bill. *See* Post Office Savings Bank Bill.
(Pensions):
Act, 1080
Bill, 1026, 1054
Bill. *See* Imperial War Museum Bill.
Reports, 220, 475, 728, 985, 1220
S.R.O. & S.I. Revised, 450
Trusteeship:
Council, United Nations, publications, 229, 490, 743, 992, 1001,
Summary records of meetings, 991
Trusts (Scotland) Act, 310
Tsetse fly, 134
Tse-Tsun Yü: Cotoneasters from the Eastern Himalaya, 853
Tshekedi Khama, report on attitude to his return to Bamangwato Reserve, 58

Tsoong, P. C. : New Himalayan species of Pedicularis with special reference to those from the Eastern Himalaya, 1102
Tube alloys, articles of agreement, 811, 854
Tuberculosis:
Expert committee report, 238
of cattle, 331
Scottish Health Services Committee, report, 125
Vaccination against, 1013
Tucker, Rt. Hon. Lord (Chairman): Departmental Committee on new trials in criminal cases, report, 812
Tucker, J. M. (Chairman):
Committee on taxation of trading profits, 549
Committee on taxation treatment of provisions for retirement, report, 806
Turkey:
Air services agreement, 54, 115
and Iraq, accession of U.K. to pact of mutual co-operation, 1063, 1131
Economic survey, 205
Financial agreement, 1059, 1131
Foreign Trade Statistical Bulletin, 356, 617, 878
Repayment of credits relating to armaments, 810, 891
Visas, abolition of, agreement, 304, 367
See also Greece.
Turkeys:
Feeding, 1093
Rearing, 330
Turkish pottery, 1221
Turks and Caicos Islands, Colonial reports, 343, 600, 1109
Turtle and Mangsee Islands, transfer of administration to Philippine Republic, 50
Tweedie, P. G.: Civil aircraft accident reports, 973, 1208
Tweedsmuir, Lord (Chairman): Imperial Institute Committee of Inquiry, report, 353
Twilli Waters, wreck report, 469
Twins, psychotic and neurotic illnesses, 679
Twitch. *See* Couch.
Two-Power Meeting, Prime Minister's proposal, exchange of letters, 1062, 1103
Tyne:
Improvement Act, 316, 835
Tunnel construction. *See* Compressed air illness.
Tynemouth:
Corporation Act, 574
Priory and Castle, guide, 504
Typists, manual for, 1215
Tyres, pneumatic, Monopolies Commission report on supply and export, 1051

U

Uganda:
Colonial reports, 343, 344, 601, 861, 1109
Uganda (*continued*):
Native administration, 93
Photoposter, 914
Protectorate, Buganda, 825, 863
Withdrawal of recognition from Kabaka Mutesa, 603, 767
U.K.-Dominion Wool Disposals Ltd., accounts, 44, 206, 290, 419, 820, 971
Ultimus Haeres (Scotland) Account and list of estates, 190, 446, 704, 960, 1193
Ultra-violet irradiation, air disinfection with, 940
Umbrellas and walking-sticks, Census of Production, 201, 907
Unasylva, 236, 496, 753, 1010
Underdeveloped countries, Motivations and stimulations in, 1005
Underground Works (London) Bill, 1056
Under-nutrition, studies of, 169
Underwood, Dr. J. E. A. (Chairman): Committee on Maladjusted Children, report, 1120
Unemployment:
and inflation, problems of, 486
Insurance, S.R.O. & S.I. Revised, 450
or sickness, benefit for very short spells, 1075, 1175
Unemployment, Inflation, and Balance of Payments, Government policies, 737
Unesco. *See* United Nations Educational, Scientific and Cultural Organisation.
Unicef:
Agreement for rendering assistance in U.K. dependent territories, 564, 629
Compendium, 747
in Asia, 1002
Pictorial record, 747
Reports, and accounts, 737 739
Union of Benefices (Disused Churches) Measure, 255, 337, 574
Report on, 255, 337
United:
Action in Korea, 229
Kingdom:
Atomic Energy Authority:
Publications, 1221
Report, 1048, 1171
Balance of Payments, 41, 55, 220, 291, 302, 476, 550, 728, 810, 823, 985, 1063, 1074, 1220
Country monograph, 730
Dependent territories, country monograph, 987
Economic conditions, 877
Foreign Trade Statistical Bulletin, 356, 617, 878
Industrial delegation to Burma, 971
Teaching of the social sciences, 1007
Trade Mission to Egypt, Sudan, and Ethiopia, report, 1205
Nations:
Administrative Tribunal, effect of awards of compensation, 919

United (*continued*):
Nations (*continued*):
at work, 334
Basic agreement with World Health Organisation for provision of technical advisory assistance, 301, 367
Disarmament Commission, reports, 297, 367, 816
Educational, Scientific and Cultural:
Materials, agreement on importation, 39, 115
Organisation:
Publications, 230, 491, 744, 1002
Reports, 286, 354, 554, 615, 1074, 1121
Food and Agriculture Organisation, publications, 234, 495, 749, 1008
Forces, Japan:
Agreement regarding status, 818, 891
Exercise of criminal jurisdiction, 807, 891
Publications, 220, 476, 729, 986
Reports on proceedings of General Assembly, etc., 46, 115, 294, 367, 546, 556, 629, 806, 891, 1061, 1131
Ten years' work. *See* Investment for Peace.
Work of the 5th regular session of the General Assembly, 40, 115
World Health Organisation, publications, 236, 496, 754, 1011
States of America:
Additional funds for Educational Commission in U.K., 343, 630, 818, 892
Aluminium industry, 357
Air:
Navigation agreement, 37, 116
Services, agreement, 1078, 1132
Application to Western Germany of most-favoured-nation treatment, 303, 368
Assurances to the Western European Union countries, 1062, 1102
Atomic information for mutual defence purposes, 1068, 1072, 1132
Avoidance of double taxation, etc., 817, 892, 1061, 1132
Bahamas, long-range proving ground for guided missiles, 35, 115, 289, 367, 1072, 1132
Bermuda, civil airport facilities, 48, 116
Consular convention, 48, 116
Continued operation of Educational Commission in the U.K., 1070, 1132
Co-operation on the civil uses of atomic energy, 1068, 1072, 1132
United (*continued*):
States of America (*continued*):
Development:
of port facilities in Kenya and Tanganyika, loan for, 562, 629
of Rhodesia railways, 56, 115, 1058, 1132
Duty-free treatment of American relief goods, 46, 48, 116
Economic:
Aid, 289, 368
Conditions, 616
See also Canada
Co-operation, 47, 116, 287, 293, 549, 630
Survey, 463
Effect of United States Mutual Security Act on agreement for technical assistance to Eritrea, 562, 630
Establishment of a high altitude interceptor range, 556, 630
Exchange of official publications, 53, 116
Expenditure of Counterpart Funds, derived from United States Economic Aid, 548, 629
Foreign Trade Statistical Bulletin, 355, 356, 617, 878
Grain storage, drying, and marketing, 333
Income taxation of private United States investment in Latin America, 744
Interchange of patents and technical information for defence purposes, 547, 629
Lease of a fleet anchorage in the Gulf of Paria, 44, 116
Loan agreement with Import-Export Bank, 36, 116, 297, 368
Mutual assistance in the supply of steel, aluminium and tin, 288, 367
Relief from taxation of U.S. Government expenditures in U.K., 290, 368
Revolving Loan Funds in Uganda Protectorate and Tanganyika, 564, 630
Rights of nationals in Morocco, 396, 657
Settlement for lend-lease, reciprocal aid, surplus war property, and claims, 296, 367
Supply of tin to the U.S., 300, 367
Technical:
Assistance:
British Guiana, 827, 892
Caribbean area, 812, 892
Co-operation, agreement for U.K. dependent territories, 52, 115

UNI-WEL | 1951-5

UNI— INDEX 1951-5

United (*continued*):
States of America (*continued*):
Terms of use of land at Madingley as U.S. military cemetery, 1058, 1132
Steel Companies Ltd., proposal to sell securities, 663, 726
Uniting for peace, 490
Units and standards of measurement, 177, 430
Unity and diversity of cultures, 749, 1008
Universal:
Copyright convention, 558, 749
Declaration of Human Rights, 748
Postal:
Convention, 565, 690, 815
Union, agreement, 565
Universities:
and College Estates Act, 831
in adult education, 494
University:
Development, report, 289, 476, 555, 728
Education in Dundee, Royal Commission report, 291, 445
Graduates, posts in Civil Service, 90, 859
Grants Committee returns, 49, 220, 300, 476, 553, 728, 811, 985, 1066, 1220
of Edinburgh (Royal (Dick) Veterinary College) Order Confirmation Act, 67
Bill, 32
of Hull Act, 1081
of St. Andrews Act, 568
Bill, 255, 509, 510, 511, 515, 526, 528, 538, 542, 543, 646
of Southampton Act, 574
S.R.O. & S.I. Revised, 450
Students Maintenance Rates, 1119
Teaching of social sciences: international relations, 1007
Unsatisfactory tenants, 1153
Upjohn, G. R. (Chairman):
Colonial Development Corporation, report on Gambia Egg Scheme, 295, 345
Departmental Committee on the Court of Record, report, 54
Upper:
Air:
Analysis and tropical forecasting, 170
Circulation in low latitudes, 680
Cretaceous Cephalopod fauna of Graham Land, 602
Urban:
Land problems and policies, 993
Working-class household diet, 105
Uruguay, economic survey, 205, 970
Use:
of chutes for extraction of thinnings, 631
of hardwoods in building, 695
of large diameter wheels and tyres on forest extraction vehicles, 631
Use (*continued*):
of stabilised soil for road construction in U.S.A., 956
Using salty land, 749
Utilisation of saline water, problems of, 1002
Utility goods, Board of Trade publications, 202, 203, 206, 464
Uttoxeter Urban District Council Act, 67
Uvarov, B. P.: Locust research and control, 92

V

Vacations abroad, 1008
Vaccination, 755
against smallpox, 379
against tuberculosis, 1013
Vagrant children, problems in education, 234
Vajda, A. de: Some aspects of surface water development in arid regions, 751
Validation of Elections Acts, 1080
Bills, 1030, 1056
Valle Crucis Abbey, guide, 762
Valuables looted by German forces, 48
Valuation:
for Rating:
Act, 568
Bill, 515, 530, 538, 542, 543, 646
in Scotland, reports on gasworks, waterworks, 1193
and Rating:
in Scotland, 1075, 1193
(Scotland) Bill, 1056
Valve and circuit noise, 184
Vandepeer, D. (Chairman): Agricultural Improvement Council for England and Wales, report, 78
Van Emden, F. I.: Ruwenzori Expedition, 84
Van Steenis, C. G. G. J., and Van Steenis-Kruseman, N. J.: Louis Auguste Deschamps, 853
Vaporising liquid extinguishing agents, 954
Variation:
of rates of interest, 387, 1151
of wind with time and distance, 1172
Varley, E. R.: Vermiculite, 346
Vaughan, G. E.: Portuguese East Africa, economic survey, 463
Vegetable:
Fibres, equipment for processing, 751
Oils and oilseeds, production trade and consumption, 347, 864, 1112
Tanning extracts, 102
Vegetables:
and salads including herbs, 358
Commercial storage, 438
Diseases, 1095
Root, 332
See also Fruit.

INDEX 1951-5 —WAL

Vehicles. *See* Licensing authorities; Motor vehicles; Road vehicles; Mechanically-propelled vehicles.
Vehicles, instruments, etc., gift to National Industrial Fuel Efficiency Service, 816
Venereal:
Disease, international list of treatment centres at ports, 238
Infections and Treponematoses, expert committee reports, 238, 756, 1013
Venezuela:
Economic survey, 205, 1205
Public finance survey, 227
See also Caribbean.
Ventilation of buildings, principles of, 182
Vermiculite, 346
Vernacular languages in education, 747
Vernon, P. E.: Assessment of psychological qualities by verbal method, 420
Vertical profiles of mean wind in the surface layers of the atmosphere, 680
Verticillium wilt:
and black dot of potatoes, 847
of hops, 587
Veterinary:
Science, careers, 398, 1157
Surgeons Act, Committee on licences, report, 334
Vibrations in buildings, 1185
Victoria:
and Albert Museum, publications, 239, 499, 757, 1013, 1221
Cross, award, 166, 167
Victorian and Edwardian decorative arts, 499
Victory Bonds, 167, 418, 677, 938
Vienna, wreck report, 721
Vietnam, International Commission for supervision and control, 1065, 1068, 1078, 1132
Vigoureux, P.: Quartz vibrators and their applications, 184
Vinegar and other condiments, Census of Production, 201, 967
Vintage Port, S.R.O. & S.I. Revised, 450
Virgin and Child, 500
Visa requirements for foreign nationals proceeding to North Borneo and Brunei, 56
Visas:
Abolition of:
Cuba, 41
Finland, 826
France, 562
Greece, 555
Portugal, 826
Turkey, 304
Exemptions for travel to Singapore, etc., for certain countries, 51
Visiting Forces:
Act, 308
Bill, 252, 254, 255, 284
S.R.O. & S.I. Revised, 450
Visser 'T. Hooft, W. A.: Ecumenical movement and racial problem, 1007
Visual:
Aids in fundamental education, 493
and aural aids, 34, 186, 190
Vital:
and health statistics, International conference, 1013
Statistics system, principles for, 741
Vitamin C requirements of human adults, 679
Vocabularium Bibliothecarii, 749
Vocational Training:
of adults including disabled persons, 48
of forestry workers, 1009
Volcanic rocks of the Ross Archipelago, 1101
Volta River Aluminium Scheme, 305, 346, 419
Volume—Basal Area Line, 1133
Volumetric glassware, 943
Voussoir Arch, study of, 184
Vulcanised rubber, specification, 455

W

Waddington, Sir E. J. (Chairman): Constitutional Committee Report on British Guiana, 91
Wage incentive schemes, 154, 1169
Wages:
Council:
Act, 64
Commission of enquiry, bread and flour confectionery distributive trades, 163
Acts, report, 417
Councils:
Act, 313
S.R.O. & S.I. Revised, 450
Protection of, 48
Wagley, C.: Race and class in rural Brazil, 748
Walder, D. N.: Compressed air illness, 940
Wales:
and Monmouthshire:
Council report, 1058, 1146
Memo on Council's activities, 553, 642
Reports on Government action, 55, 126, 303, 383, 562, 642, 823, 905, 1074, 1146
Boundary Commission report, 22
including Monmouthshire, Census, 1138
Library in, 100
North, guide to ancient monuments, 1018
See also Rural Wales.
Walker, Col. R. J.: Railway accident reports, 209, 210, 466, 467, 719
Walker, R. J. B.: Audley End:
Catalogue, 1018
Guide, 1225

WAL— INDEX 1951-5

Wall and ceiling surfaces and condensation, 695
Wallace, L.: Hand-weaving in the Philippines, 1000
Walley, F.: Prestressed concrete, 1019
Wallpaper, Census of Production, 201, 967
Walls:
Damp, treatment of, 437
External rendered finishes for, 184
infested with dry rot, treatment, 1185
Strength and stability, 1185
Walsall Corporation:
Act, 835
(Trolley Vehicles) Order Confirmation Acts, 67, 574
Provisional Order Bills, 4, 32, 514, 543
Walters, J. H.: Fibrosis of the liver in West African Children, 940
Wangle III, wreck report, 213
Wankie Colliery Act, 835
War:
at Sea, 902, 961
Cemeteries etc. in Egyptian territory, agreement, 1064
Charities Act, 572
Claims, settlement of, exchange of Notes with Thailand, 39
Criminals, German, trial proceedings, 417
Damage:
Accounts:
Business and Private Chattels Schemes, 10, 206, 217, 259, 464, 519, 785, 971, 1035, 1206
Land and Buildings, 10, 102, 259, 358, 476, 519, 619, 782, 799, 880, 1014
Public Utility Undertakings, 12, 102, 259, 476
Act, 64
Compensation, exchange of Notes with France, 826, 1071
S.R.O. & S.I. Revised, 450
Department Schedule of Prices, 760, 1018, 1224, 1225
Graves, agreements:
Danish territory, 813
French territory, 555
Iraqi territory, 1078
Italian territory, 1070
History of Second World War, 217, 337, 378, 473, 501, 593, 638, 759, 854, 1103, 1143
in France and Flanders, 854, 961
Office, publications, 239, 500, 757, 1014, 1221
Pensioners, reports, 790, 901, 902, 948, 1044, 1143, 1144, 1180
Pensions:
Committees (Extension) Order, 1180
Estimates, 530
War (*continued*):
Risks Insurance:
Act, 312
S.R.O. & S.I. Revised, 450
Years. *See* German Foreign Policy.
Warcup, G. J. (Chairman): Air Navigation Conference, report, 655
Ward, A.: Sea breezes at North Front, Gibraltar, 941
Ward, A. F.: Report of inspection of Bristol Rovers Football Club, 203
Ward, F. A. B.: Time measurement, handbook of collection, 1185
Warden Section, Civil Defence, 128, 380
Warden's report form, 128
Ward-Jackson, P.: Osterley Park, guide, 1014
Ware potatoes, export licence revocation, 714
Waring, A. B.: Human relations in industry, 955
Warkworth:
Castle, guide, 1018
Harbour, Act, 66
Warm fronts, study of, 1172
Warnock, G. M.: Studies on expenditure of energy and consumption of food by miners and clerks, Fife, 1171
Warrender Estate Bill, report on Petition for, 774
Wars not yet won, series, 134, 389, 651
Wartime debts, settlement with Netherlands, 806
Warrender Estate Bill, report on Petition for, 774
Warwickshire, Census, 896
Washing-up (School Meals series), filmstrip, 99
Washington Talks, documents, 557, 630
Watch:
and Clock, Census of Production, 459, 1200
Wrist, defence specification, 98
Water:
Act, 64, 313
Domestic hot, inquiry into supply in Great Britain, 440
Infusion, means of dust control, 1134
Laws in Moslem countries, 1008
Pipes, report, 389
Pollution, D.S.I.R. publications, 186, 442, 443, 700, 957, 1189
Prevention of waste, etc., 165
Report on, 52
Resources, conservation and utilisation, 478
S.R.O. & S.I. Revised, 450
(Scotland) Act, 65, 833
Supplies:
in North Africa, report on fluoridation, 637
See also Firemanship.

INDEX 1951-5 —WEL

Water (*continued*):
Supply:
and sewage disposal, report, 619
Handbook of local legislation, 166, 389, 650
Transport. *See* Supply, Transport and Barrack Services.
Undertakings, Census of Production, 460
(Waste etc. Prevention), model byelaws, 913
Water-colour paintings by British artists, 500
Waterlow, J. C.: Fibrosis of the liver in West African children, 940
Watermark disease of the cricket-bat willow, 1133
Waters, A. H. S.: Sand and Gravel Advisory Committee reports, 388, 650, 913, 1152
Waters, D. B.: Survey of some mixing plants for asphalt and coated macadam, 700
Waterworks, report of Working Party on rating for valuation, 1195
Watford, railway accident, 975
Watkinson, H. (Chairman): National Advisory Council: report on employment of older men and women, 562
Watson, F. J. B.: Audley End, guide, 1225
Watson, H.: Woodland mosses, 369
Watson, Lord Hill (Chairman): Committee on drainage of trade premises, report, 810
Watt, Dr. J. (Chairman): Joint Tuberculosis Council, report on standardisation of radiological terminology in pulmonary disease, etc., 379
Watts, H. E.:
Accident report, 129
Ammonium Nitrate Working Party report, 129
(Chairman): Departmental Committee, carriage of dangerous goods and explosives in ships, 465
Chief Inspector of Factories report, 129
Explosion and fire at Regent Oil Co., 380
Waverley, Rt. Hon. Lord (Chairman):
Committee on Export of Works of Art, report, 472
Departmental Committee on coastal flooding and flood warning system, reports, 559, 814
W.B.C. Hive, 1091
Wealden District, geology, 898
Wear:
and tear allowances for machinery or plant, 651
Navigation and Sunderland Dock Act, 835
Weather:
and the land, 1095
in the Indian Ocean, 421
London, a century of, 680
Weather (*continued*):
Manual, Admiralty, 574
Maps, 681
Instructions for preparation, 170, 941
Messages etc. Handbook, 170, 421, 681, 941, 1172
Report, monthly, 171, 422, 681, 942, 1173
Service, 171, 1173
Stations:
North Atlantic, agreement, 51, 113
See also Ocean Weather Stations.
Webster, C. T.:
Fire endurance of timber beams and floors, 440
Fire resistance of reinforced concrete columns, 698
Heating of panels by flue pipes, 438
Wedgwood Benn (Renunciation) Bill, 1026
Report from Personal Bills Committee, 1026
Weed control:
by growth-regulating substances, 234
in cereals by selective weedkillers, 1091
in linseed and flax, 587
in peas, 78, 587
Weedon, railway accident, 467
Weeds, England, S.R.O. & S.I. Revised, 450
Weekday Cross, railway accident, 1210
Weetslade Colliery, explosion, 1076
Weevils, large pine, pissodes, 369
Weights and Measures:
Act, notice of examination of patterns, 206, 464, 717, 971, 1206
Legislation, committee report, 43, 208
(Purchase) Act, 830
Sale of Coal (Scotland) Act, 832
S.R.O. & S.I. Revised, 450
Weiner, J. S.: Solution of Piltdown problem, 591, 1102
Welbeck College, formation and aim, 503
Welded:
Ships, repairs to, 1084
Structures, conference structures, 1019
Welder and cutter, career, 659
Welders, health of, 145
Welfare:
Arrangements on building sites, 163
Pamphlets, 163, 380, 417
Report, 52
Section, Civil Defence, 128, 903
Services for handicapped persons, 125, 126
Training, Civil Defence filmstrip, 380, 639
Wellington:
Museum, guide, 499, 757
Plate, Portuguese service, 1041
Wells, A. F. & D.: Friendly Societies in the West Indies, 601
Wells, G. S. (Chairman): District Heating Working Party, report, 165

1951-5 | WEL-ZUC

WEL— INDEX 1951-5

Welsh:
Agricultural Land Sub-Commission reports:
Borth Bog, 331
Mid-Wales, 1077, 1094
and English in the schools of Wales, 614, 615
Board of Health, circulars, 379
Church:
Act, 570
S.R.O. & S.I. Revised, 450
(Temporalities) Act, 570
County details, Census of woodlands, 630
Land Settlement Society, review and accounts, 332
Language publishing, 302, 383
Office, increased function, circular, 1151
Statistics, digest of, 905, 1147
Welsh-speaking population, 1138
Welwyn Garden City Development Corporation, reports, 29, 279, 388, 779, 792, 913, 1048
Wem district of Shropshire, soils, 850
Wenk, E.: Geology of the Colony of North Borneo, 345
Werner, A. E. A.: Further contributions to the solution of the Piltdown Problem, 1102
Wesleyan and General Assurance Society, Act, 835
West:
Africa today, picture set, 914
African Forces, conference report, 863
Bridgford Urban District Council Act, 574
Fife and Kirkcaldy, Boundary Commission report, 305
Hartlepool Extension Act, 316
Indian:
and American territories, economic survey, 602
Citrus industry, 1111
Federation, report, 553, 603
Indies:
British, S.R.O. & S.I. Revised, 450
Development and Welfare reports, 93, 345, 601, 861, 1110
Lothian, Census, 898
Renfrewshire and Greenock, Boundary Commission report, 305
Riding County Council (General Powers) Act, 67
West, C.:
Dehydration of English fruit, 438
Storage qualities of late dessert varieties of apples, 438
Westcott, G. F.: Mechanical and electrical engineering etc., list of events, 1184
Western:
Europe:
Correspondence arising out of meeting of Foreign Ministers, 1070, 1132
Western (*continued*):
Europe (*continued*):
Economic progress and problems, 101
European Union:
Agreement, 1066, 1132
Inclusion of Federal Republic of Germany and Italy, 1068, 1132
Highlands and islands of Scotland, agreement for maintenance of certain transport services, 265, 476
Samoa, reports on, 490, 1001
Union, Conventions:
Frontier workers, 293, 368
Student employees, 289, 368
Westminster Abbey Chapter House, guide, 761
Weston, H. C.: Relation between illumination and visual performance, 679
Weston-super-Mare, Boundary Commission report, 29
Wethered, His Honour E. H. C.: Investigation of Bristol Rovers Football Club, 458
Wetting of slack to assist combustion, 632
Wet-weather damage to surface dressings, prevention of, 441, 1188
Whalemeat:
Bacteriology and hygiene, 696
Production and preservation, 696
Whales and turtles, stranded, guide, 593
Whaling, international convention, amendments to schedule, 305, 368, 805, 892
What:
is race? 494
the United Nations is doing, 229, 490, 744, 1002
Wheat:
Act, 571
Agreement, international, reconsideration of economics, 750
Bulb fly, 1093
Earcockles, 847
International Wheat Council report, 141
Fund, accounts, 16, 81, 262, 334, 518, 589, 785, 851, 1038
Wheatsheaf Junction, railway accident, 719
Wheeler, J. F. G.: Mauritius-Seychelles fisheries survey, 602
Wheeler, Sir M. & Mrs.: Caerleon Roman Amphitheatre, guide, 761
Whitaker, T.: Lightweight concrete in America, 698
Whitby Abbey, guide, 504
White:
Fish:
and Herring Industries Act, 568
Bill, 285, 512, 513, 523, 538, 542, 646
Account, 1037
Authority, reports, accounts, 270, 334, 530, 589, 791, 851, 882, 905, 960, 1047, 1097, 1147, 1193
Line compositions, plastic, analysis, 185

INDEX 1951-5 —WIT

White (*continued*):
Scour in calves, 1094
Slave traffic, international convention for suppression, 805, 892
White, E. W.: British fishing boats and coastal craft, handbook of collections illustrating, 436
White, R. G. (Chairman): Scottish Hill Farm Research Committee, report, 585
Whitehaven Pier and Harbour Order Confirmation Act, 834
Bill, 774, 802
Whitehead Iron & Steel Co., proposal to sell holding of ordinary shares, 1060
Whitehead, T. H.: Mesozoic ironstones of England, 635
Whithorn and Kirkmadrine, guide, 762
Whiting, food of, 960
Whittard, W. F.: Cyclopygid trilobites from Girvan, 336
Whitworth:
Fellowships and prizes, rules and conditions, 1121
Scholarships, regulations and syllabus, 874
Whitworth, T.: Miocene hyracoids of East Africa, 854
Wholesale:
Bottling, Census of Production, 460, 967
Slaughtering, Census of Production, 459, 1201
Trades, Census of Distribution and other services, 1199
Whyte, R. O.: Legumes in agriculture, 750
Wicks Lane, railway accident, 1210
Widdowson, E. M.: Studies on nutritive value of bread, etc. 940
Wigtown, Census, 898
Wild:
Life, risks to, 1097
Mammals and the land, 79
Wildlife and fish resources, conservation and utilisation, 478
Wilkins, G. L.:
Banks shell collection, 1102
Sloane shell collection, catalogue and historical account, 591
Wilkins, L. T.: Studies in the causes of delinquency and the treatment of offenders, 1145
Wilkinson, S. F. (Chairman): Working Party on requisitioned properties in use for housing, reports, 388, 650, 913
Willett, K. C.: Trypanosomiasis, 1017
Williams, F.: Transmitting world news, 748
Willink, Rt. Hon. H. U. (Chairman): Royal Commission on Betting, Lotteries and Gaming, report, 41
Willoughby de Broke Estate Bill, report on petition, 1029, 1149
Wills etc. (Publication) Bill, 1053
Wilnecote and Kingsbury, railway accident, 975
Wilson, Lt. Col. G. R. S., Railway accident reports, 210, 466, 467, 719, 722, 974, 975, 1210
Wilson, H. E.: Cambro-Ordovician Limestones and dolomites of the Ord and Torran areas and Kishorn area, 899
Wilson, P. H. St. J. (Chairman): Training of Supervisors Committee, report, 937
Wilson, R.: Spectrophotometric measurements of early type stars, 1184
Wilson, W. K.: Modern rabbit-keeping, 848
Wilson, W. W.: Bird migration and foot-and-mouth disease, 331
Wiltshire, Census, 1138
Winchester Corporation Act, 316
Winckel, Dr. C.: Selected Arab countries of the Middle East, Mission report, 987
Wind effects on bridges and other flexible structures, 1174
Windmill Bridge Junction, railway accident, 975
Windrow harvesting, 330
Windrum, J. E.: Tonga, report, 860
Windsor, S.R.O. & S.I. Revised, 450
Windward Islands:
Economic surveys, 463, 602
S.R.O. & S.I. Revised, 450
Wingless weevils, 1093
Wing-venation of the Orthoptera Saltatoria with notes on Dictyopteran wing-venation, 1103
Winslow, C. E. A.: Cost of sickness and price of health, 497
Winter:
(Broccoli) and summer cauliflowers, 332
Moths, 586
Pruning established apple and pear trees, 1093
Wire:
and wire manufactures, Census of Production, 459, 1200
for domestic and catering purposes, 1070
Wireless:
Instructions for Civil Defence, 639
Operators:
Electrical and radio notes, 335
Handbook for, 984, 1181
Telegraphy:
Act, 830
Appeal Tribunal Rules, 690
(Blind Persons) Act, 1080
Bill, 1029, 1033
(Validation of Charges) Act, 830
Bill, 779, 802
Wires. *See* Defence List.
Witches' Broom disease of cacao, 346
Withdrawal of British Military Administration from reserved areas, agreement with Ethiopia, 1057
Withers, T. H.:
Cretaceous and Eocene peduncles of the cirripede Euscalpellum, 83
Some Jurassic and Cretaceous crabs, 83

WIT— INDEX 1951-5

Withers, T. H. (*continued*):
Fossil Cirripedia in Department of Geology, Tertiary, catalogue, 592
Witt, L.: Farm and the city, 751
Wokingham School, development projects, 352
Wolfenden, J. F. (Chairman): Secondary Schools Examination Council, report, 352
Wolverhampton Corporation (Trolley Vehicles) Order Confirmation Act, 835
Bill, 802
Provisional Order Bill, 774
Women:
and education, 748
of the grassfields, 344
Women's:
Disabilities, Bill, 281, 541
Services, H.M. Forces, 1157
Wood:
and cork etc. manufactures, Census of Production, 461, 713
Charcoal, manufacture, 631
Dielectric properties, 954
Flour:
Standing Committee report, 550, 717
Use and manufacture, 631
Preservatives. *See* Field tests.
Selected Government Research Reports, 441
Sawyer and woodcutting machinist, careers, 142
Wood, R. F.: Studies of north-west American forests in relation to silviculture in Great Britain, 1133
Wood, R. H.:
Composite action of brick panel walls supported on reinforced concrete beams, 440
Interaction of floors and beams in multi-storey building, 1187
Wood, Sir R. S.: Agricultural education, British Caribbean territories, 1107
Woodcut exhibition catalogue, 1014
Wooden:
Containers and baskets, Census of Production, 460, 1201
Dowels and dowelling, 804, 971
Woodland mosses, 369
Woodlands:
Census, 117, 630
Dedication, 630
Five acres and over, 630
Woodman, H. E.: Rations for livestock, 331, 848
Wood-pigeon in Britain, 76
Woodruff, H. W.: Federation of Rhodesia and Nyasaland, 1205
Woods, C. R. (Chairman): Building Research Board and Fire Officers Committee, report on fire grading of buildings, 505
Woods, H.M.: Incidence of industrial accidents on individuals with special reference to multiple accidents, 679
Woodward, E. L.: Documents on British Foreign Policy, 106, 360, 622, 883, 1123
Woodward, W. B.: Movements of salmon tagged in the sea, Montrose, 1191
Woodware, Technical Assistance Mission report, 618
Woodwork:
Fifty masterpieces, 1221
Painting, 181
Wool:
Production and trade, 94
Reserve prices, plan of, 61, 169
Textile Industry, account, 273, 535, 1033
U.K.—Dominions Wool Disposals Ltd., accounts, 44, 206, 290, 419
World consumption, 95, 864
Woollen and worsted:
Census of Production, 459
Cloth, yarn, manufacture, careers, 398
Woolly aphid, 847
Worcester:
Boundary Commission report, 269, 379
Corporation Act, 67
Worcestershire, Census, 896
Worker in industry, lectures, 417
Workmen's Compensation:
(Pneumoconiosis) Bill, 32
S.R.O. & S.I. Revised, 450
(Supplementation) Act, 60
Bill, 1, 31, 1053
Explanatory memo, 38, 177
Works:
and buildings (war history), 337
Estimates, 15, 215, 263, 523, 783, 1036
Ministry of, publications, 243, 503, 761, 1018, 1225
Report, 49, 244
of art, export licence, 206
Workshop calculations, handbook, 164
World:
against want, 742
Braille usage, 1008
Cartography, 490, 1002
Communications: Press, radio, film, television, 234
Consumption of wool, 95, 864
Directory of medical schools, 757
Economic reports, 229, 491, 744, 1002
Facts and figures, 229, 491, 744, 1002
Festival of trees, 1009
Fisheries Abstracts, 236, 496, 753, 1011
Health Organisation, publications, 236, 496, 754, 1011
List of plant breeders, 753
Medical periodicals, 757
Pulp and paper resources and prospects, 1011
Social situation, 744
War, second, history of. *See* War.
Wormald, H.: Brown rot diseases of fruit trees, 850
Worms in poultry, 848
Wortley West Junction, railway accident, 210

INDEX 1951-5 ZUC

Wreck reports, 213, 469, 721, 977, 1212
Wright, F. C.: African consumers in Nyasaland and Tanganyika, 1108
Wright, J. H.: Finland, economic survey, 716
Wright, N. C. (Chairman):
Food Standards Committee, reports, 880, 882, 1096, 1122
National Food Survey Committee reports:
Domestic food consumption and expenditure, 358
Urban working class household diet, 105
Writers to the Signet Widows' Fund Order Confirmation Act, 1081
Bill, 1055
Wrought iron and steel tubes, Census of Production, 200, 1199
Wyatt, S.: Fatigue and boredom in repetitive work, 420
Wyllie, J.: Principles of good farm management, 1097

Y

Yachts, Royal, 687
Yang, W. Y.: Farm management investigations for agricultural improvement, 750
Yates, R.: Eppleton Colliery explosion report, 291
Yaws control, international symposium, 755
Yearbooks:
Balance of payments, 658
Demographic, 221, 478, 730, 987
Education, international, 492, 746, 1005
Fisheries statistics, 235, 751
Food and agricultural statistics, 235, 495, 752, 1009
Forest products, 235, 752
Human rights, 484
International Court of Justice, 141, 397, 657, 919
International trade statistics, 484
Non-ferrous metals, 102
Surface water, Great Britain, 1152
United Nations, 229, 231, 488, 491, 744, 1002
Statistical, 742, 999
Yeatman, C. W.: Tree root development on upland heaths, 1133
Yellow wagtails, species and races from Western Europe to Western North America, 336
Yemen, relations with, 297, 368
Yeoman Warder, postcard, 764
Yetminster Farm, boundary report, 331
Yewvalley, wreck report, 977
Yorkshire, Census, 896
Young Persons (Employment) Act, 64
Younge, C. M.: (Chairman): Brown Trout Research Supervisory Committee, report, 702
Younger, J. P.:
Scottish Health Services Council's committee report, 125
Standing Advisory Committee report on reception and welfare of in-patients at hospitals, 124
Younger, Hon. K.: Speech at Chatham House, 40
Your:
United Nations, 744
Weather service, 171, 1173
Youth:
Employment Service, 937
Report of Committee on recruitment and training, 164
Leaders and County Centre wardens, 100
Ystrad Caron, railway accident, 719
Yugoslav and Czechoslovak Funds, accounts, 262, 518, 785
Yugoslavia:
Credits for purchases:
Consumer goods, foodstuffs, etc., 38, 116
Raw materials, 50, 57, 116
Financial:
Arrangements, 57, 116, 304, 368
for economic assistance, 808, 892
Matters arising out of Trade Agreement, 306, 368
Obligations, 1060, 1133
Import of British books, 810, 892, 1062, 1133

Z

Zanzibar:
Colonial reports, 343, 600, 1109
Native administration, 93
Zebu cattle of India and Pakistan, 750
Zehetmayr, J. W. L.: Experiments in tree planting on peat, 892
Zetland, Census, 898
Ziegfeld, E.: Education and art, 1004
Zinc: Export licence, 1203
See also Copper.
Zoology Bulletin, 83, 336, 592, 853, 1102
Zoonoses:
Advances in control, 755
Expert group on, 238
Zuckerman, Prof. S. (Chairman):
Natural Resources (Technical Committee) report on use of towns' waste in agriculture, 956
Scientific Manpower Committee, report, 1171
Toxic Chemicals in agriculture, Working Party reports, 81, 851, 1097, 1171

Consolidated Index to Government Publications 1956-1960

INDEX

Abbreviations: In addition to the abbreviations in general use, the following are used:
Cmd. = Command Paper (Jan.-Oct., 1956)
Cmnd. = Command Paper (Oct. 1956 onwards)
A.E.E.W. = Atomic Energy Establishment, Winfrith Heath
A.E.R.E. = Atomic Energy Research Establishment
I.G. = Industrial Group

FOREWORD

With the publication of this quinquennial index Government publishing of the twenty-five years from 1936 to 1960 is covered by five indexes. Previous indexes covered the periods 1936 to 1940, 1941 to 1945, 1946 to 1950, and 1951 to 1955, all of which are now out of print. Each includes new titles, revised editions and reprints at revised prices. As in the indexes for the second, third and fourth periods Statutory Instruments are omitted and the separately issued Annual Lists of Statutory Instruments should be consulted for information concerning them.

International Organisation Publications are now produced in a separate annual catalogue, price 1*s.*, the pages of which are numbered to follow those of the Government publications catalogue of the same year. It is suggested that all catalogues for 1956 to 1960 should be bound with this consolidated index, discarding the annual index pages and introductions.

The page numbering of the annual catalogues indexed in this consolidation is as follows:

Annual and International:

*1956	1 to 247A
*1957	213 to 475
1958	476 to 744
1959	745 to 1002
1960	1003 to 1272

* *Page Nos. 213-247 in the 1956 International Organisation Publications and in the 1957 Annual Catalogue have been duplicated. In order to avoid confusion, the letter* A *has been inserted against the references to the former publication.*

A

Aaron, J. R.:
Use of Home-Grown Softwood in House Construction, 854
Use of Home-Grown Timber in Packaging and Materials Handling, 325
Aaron, Professor R. I. (Chairman: Central Advisory Council for Education) Report, 1116
Abandonment of Animals Act, 1070
Abandonment of Animals Bill, 787, 1007, 1018, 1036, 1041, 1140
Abbeys, 956
Abbot, J. C.:
Marketing Livestock and Meat, 1237
Marketing Problems and Improvement Programs, 967
Abbreviations of Aeronautical Authorities, Services and Aircraft Operating Agencies, 438
Abeele, A. M. V., Method for Analysis and Comparison of Labour Productivity in Cotton Spinning Mills, 449
Abensour, E. S., Principles of Tenancy Legislation, 708
Aberdeen and Banff Counties. Sharpe's Trust Scheme Order-in-Council, 169
Aberdeen and District Milk Marketing Scheme, 553
Aberdeen City Educational Endorsements Scheme, Order-in-Council, 911
Aberdeen Corporation Order Confirmation Act, 273
Aberdeen Corporation Order Confirmation Bill, 248
Aberdeen Harbour Order Confirmation Act, 57, 274, 1071
Aberdeen Harbour Order Confirmation Bill, 35, 249, 786, 1044
Aberdeen Harbour (Superannuation) Order Confirmation Act, 273
Aberdeen Harbour (Superannuation) Order Confirmation Bill, 248
Aberdeenshire Educational Trust Scheme: Memorandum, 169
Order-in-Council, 169
Abingdon County Hall Guide, 208
Abolition of Visas for Refugees. European Agreement, 962
Abrahams, Peter, Jamaica, 302
Abrasive Wheels, Safety in the Use of, 876
Abrasives, Census of Production Report, 394, 1194
Acarine Disease, 555

Accelerated Vocational Training for Unskilled and Semi-skilled Manpower,1245
Access to Current Literature on Education through Periodical Indexes, 466
Accident Reports:
Aircraft, 186–7, 400, 401–2, 670, 826, 928, 1090
Colliery, 263, 377; *Cmnd. 475.* 530, 646
Electrical, 619
Explosives, 334, 371, 604
Railway, 188, 403–4, 672
Tramway, 190
Accidents:
Aircraft:
186–7, 401–2, 670, 826, 928, 1090
Investigation Manual, 1242
Survey, 185, 400, 669, 930, 1093
U.K., 1093
At Windscale No. 1 Pile. *Cmnd. 302.* 269, 412
Childhood. Advisory Group Report, 472
Electrical and their Causes, 875
Factories, Docks, etc. How They Happen and How to Prevent Them, 617, 874, 876, 1152
Fireguards, 340
How They Happen and How to Prevent Them, 135, 347, 429
Railway, 926, 927, 929, 1197, 1198
Road, 168, 656, 673, 930, 1182, 1198
Road, Caused by Dogs, 935
Road, General Summary, 404
Road Traffic, in Europe, 460, 730, 989, 1260
Tramway, 931
When Lifting and Carrying, 621
Accountant, Careers, 876
Accounts:
Of the Masters of Works for Building and Repairing Royal Palaces and Castles, 389
Quantity and Price Indexes in National Accounts, 449
Standardised System of National, 976
Acholi of Uganda, 1103
Ackers, P.:
Charts for the Hydraulic Design of Channels and Pipes, 909
Resistance of Fluids in Channels and Pipes, 909
Acquisition of Land (Assessment of Compensation) Bill, 33
Acrometopae of the Ethiopian Region, 1095

1956-60 | ACT-AIR

ACT— INDEX 1956–60

Actinopterygian and Coelacanth Fishes, Chiefly from the Lower Lias. Revision, 1096
Action of the Council, International Civil Aviation Organisation, 710, 970
Activité de L'Assemblée Parlementaire Européenne, 1232
Activities of GATT, 1239
Activities of the European Coal and Steel Community, General Reports, 704, 963, 964, 965
Activities of the European Economic Community Commission. General Reports, 965
Activities of Unesco. Report, 735, 996
Acton Burnell Castle, Shropshire, Guide, 426
Acts:
55–9, 272–4, 540, 808, 1069
Annotations to, 390, 658, 918, 1190
Privy Council of England, 646
Actualité Européenne et la Presse, 1233
Actuarial Work. Careers, 617
Adams, P. J., Origin and Evolution of Coal, 1132
Addiction-Producing Drugs. *See* Drugs
Addis, Captain C. T.:
India's Most Dangerous Hour, 565, 658
War Against Japan, 296, 389
Adelges Cooleyi, 1129
Adelges Insects of Silver Firs, 112
Aden:
And the Yemen, 1101
Colonial Report, 87, 569
Photo-Poster, 614
Adhesives for Wood:
Efficiency of, 166, 907
Requirements and Properties of, 166
Adie, R. J., Metamorphic Rocks of the Trinity Peninsular Series, 571
Administration of Justice Act, 55, 1070
Administration of Justice Bill, 4, 18, 29, 34, 125, 1005, 1008, 1010, 1029, 1036, 1043, 1044, 1140
Administration of Justice (Amendment) Bill, 520
Administration of Justice (Contempt of Court) Bill, 1004
Administration of Justice (Judges and Pensions) Act, 1071
Administration of Justice (Judges and Pensions) Bill, 1011
Administration of the United Kingdom Dependencies, 344
Administration of War Production, 82, 173
Administrative and Budgetary Questions:
725, 726, 983, 984
Advisory Committee Report, 1255
General Assembly, 229A, 230A
Records, 1254
Administrative Commission Report, International Civil Aviation Organisation, 710, 1242
Administrative Memoranda, 585, 1114
Administrative Procedures involving Inquiries or Hearings. Circular 600, 654
Administrative Tribunals and Enquiries:
Committee Report, 610, 611
Index to the Evidence, 304
Memoranda submitted by Government Departments, 90
Minutes of Evidence, Appendix, 304
Minutes of Evidence taken before the Committee, 90, 304
Report. *Cmnd. 218*. 263, 358
Admiralty:
Headquarters Organisation. Select Committee on Estimates Reports, 1029, 1038, 1143, 1144
Manual of Navigation, Amendment, 276
Publications, 60–1, 276–7, 545, 813, 1074
Adolescent in your Family, 692
Adoption Act, 808, 1070
Adoption Act, 1958 (Amendment) Bill, 1043
Adoption Bill:
486, 488, 521, 1009
Report on Consolidation Bill, 487, 488
Adoption Laws, Comparative Analysis, 224A
Adrian, Lord (Chairman: Committee on Radiological Hazards to Patients). Report, 860, 1136
Adult and Workers' Education Periodicals, 1264
Adult and Youth Education Manual, 1265
Adult Education:
and Leisure Time Activities in Czechoslovakia, 994
Groups and Audio-Visual Techniques, 737
In Community Development, 1264
Advances in Cheese Technology, 706
Advances in Steel Technology, 224A, 720
Advances to Nationalised Industries and Undertakings. Accounts, 496, 587, 765, 766
Advertisements (Hire-Purchase) Act, 272
Advertisements (Hire-Purchase) Bill, 36, 218, 234, 242, 248, 335
Advertising, Career, 136, 347
Advisory Film Strips, 288, 554, 1083
Advisory Leaflets:
Agriculture, 69, 70–1, 287, 553, 819, 820, 1082–3
Works, 207, 426, 697, 956, 1226
Advocates' Widows' Fund Order Confirmation Act, 57
Advocates' Widows' Fund Order Confirmation Bill, 34
A.E.E.W. Publications, 939, 1207
A.E.R.E. Publications, 76–9, 412–18, 681, 939, 1208
Aerial Advertising Bill, 235, 247, 335

INDEX 1956–60 —AGR

Aerial Incidents:
Orders, 219A, 712, 972, 973, 1243
U.S.A. *v.* Czecho-Slovakia, Order, 443
U.S.A. *v.* Union of Soviet Socialist Republics. Order, 443
Aerial Navigation:
844, 845
Agreement on Joint Financing Air Navigation Services in Greenland and the Faroe Islands. *Cmnd. 165*. 260, 314
Agreement on Joint Financing of Air Navigation Services in Iceland. *Cmnd. 166*. 260, 314
Aerodrome Manual, 1240
Aerodromes, Air Routes and Ground Aids Division Report, 438
Aerodynamics, Boundary Layer Effects in, 155
Aeronautical Agreements and Arrangements:
439, 1241
Supplement, 710, 970
Aeronautical History in Pictures, 164
Aeronautical Information Services:
Amendment, 439
And Aeronautical Charts Division Report, 970
Provided by States, 439
Summary, 215A, 710, 972, 1242
Aeronautical Radio Maintenance Mechanic, 219A
Aeronautical Research Council:
Current Papers, 61–6, 277–81, 547, 814, 1075
Reports and Memoranda, 66–9, 281–7, 549, 817, 1078
Technical Reports, 69, 287, 1081
Aeronautical Telecommunications, 439
Aeroplane, 1178
Affiliation Proceedings Act, 272
Affiliation Proceedings Bill, 6, 213, 216, 249
Affiliation Proceedings Report, 217
Afforestation of Upland Heaths, 1129
Afiechydon Defaid, 555
Africa:
Development of, Report, 703
East, High Commission Report, 302
Economic Development, 227A, 722
Economic Survey, 1253
See Europe and Africa
Social Implications of Industrialization and Urbanization in Africa South of the Sahara, 240A
South West:
Admissibility of Hearings by Committee on South West Africa, 219A, 220A
Expedition, Results. *See* Ornithology
Report of Committee, 230A, 456, 726, 984
Africa (*continued*):
Union of South, International Customs Journal, 444
United Nations:
Commission Report on Racial Situation in the Union of South Africa, 229A
Visiting Mission to Trust Territories in East Africa, 235
West, Introducing, 132
African Administration Journal, 86, 299–300, 429, 569, 833, 1103
African Cattle Types and Breeds, 706
African Conference on Bilharziasis, 741
African-Indian Ocean Regional Air Navigation Meeting Report, 1242
African Land Tenure in East and Central Africa Conference Report, 86
African Locusts, Convention regarding Control of the African Migratory Locusts. *Cmnd. 128*. 257, 315
African Species of the Genus Cheumatopsyche, and Ephermeroptera Types of Species, 1095
African Timber Beetles, Monograph of the Immature Stages of, 294
After-care and Supervision of Discharged Prisoners, Report, 603
Ageing of Populations and Its Economic and Social Implications, 459
Aggregates in Great Britain, Sources of White and Coloured, 1182
Aggression, Report of Special Committee on Defining, 456
Aggrey, J. E. Kwegyir, Pioneers Who Served, 344
Agreement on Commercial Debts owed by Residents in Turkey. *Cmnd. 767, 805*. 798, 800, 853; 974, 979
Agricultural Acts. Review and Determination of Guarantees. *Cmnd. 390*. 524, 556, 603, 654
Agricultural Advisory Services in Europe and North America Report, 715
Agricultural Advisory Work, Written Word in, 224A
Agricultural and Food Grants and Subsidies, Revised Supplementary Civil Estimates, 1956–57, 227
Agricultural and Food Statistics, 224A, 598, 977
Agricultural and Horticultural Seeds. Export Licence, 397
Agricultural Commodities and the European Common Market, 707
Agricultural Credit:
In Economically Underdeveloped Countries, 1236
In Latin America. Manual of Supervised, 240A
Agricultural Departments and the Farmers' Unions, Report on Talks. *Cmnd. 1249*. 1069, 1082, 1085, 1137

AGR— INDEX 1956–60

Agricultural Development Papers, 240–1, 435, 706, 966, 1236
Agricultural Economics:
Research in Asia and the Far East, 979
Scottish, 288, 554
Agricultural Economics and Statistics:
241A, 435, 706, 1237
Monthly Bulletins, 967
Agricultural Education Up to University Level, 447
Agricultural Engineering Institutions, International Directory, 435
Agricultural Exhibits in Advisory Work, 716
Agricultural Handbook, 199, 419
Agricultural History, British, 288
Agricultural Holdings (Disturbance Compensation) Bill, 1041
Agricultural Information Bulletin, 199
Agricultural Improvement Council:
289
E. & W. Report, 1084
Agricultural Improvement Grants Act, 808
Agricultural Improvement Grants Bill, 749, 784
Agricultural Land. Rights and Obligations of Landlords and Tenants E. and W., 821
Agricultural Land Commission:
Accounts 17, 71, 228, 289, 498, 556, 786, 821, 1020, 1085
Reports, 26, 71, 239, 289, 513, 555, 779, 821, 1033, 1084
Agricultural Machinery:
Selection, Use and Maintenance, 445
Workshops, 1236
Agricultural Marketing Act, 540
Agricultural Marketing Acts Draft Scheme, 71
Agricultural Marketing Acts Milk Marketing Schemes, 553
Agricultural Marketing Bill, 480, 482, 519
Agricultural Marketing. Report on Consolidation Bill, 477, 482
Agricultural Marketing Schemes Report, 224, 287, 289, 333, 504, 553, 555, 771, 820, 824, 1028, 1082, 1088, 1139
Agricultural Mechanization, 225A, 450, 720, 979, 1250
Agricultural Mortgage Corporation Act, 55, 542
Agricultural Mortgage Corporation Bill, 3, 33, 487, 520
Agricultural or Forestry Buildings, Allowances in respect of Capital Expenditure on, 873
Agricultural Policies in Europe and North America:
445, 974, 1245
Report, 220A
Agricultural Production in Latin America, 450
Agricultural Products and Fertilizers, prices of, 437, 730, 987, 1257
Agricultural Press and Periodicals in OEEC Member Countries, List of, 1246
Agricultural Price Stabilization and Support Policies, Enquiry into the Problems of, 1237
Agricultural Regions in the European Economic Community, 1246
Agricultural Research Act, 55
Agricultural Research Bill, 1
Agricultural Research Council:
Publications, 69, 553, 819, 1081
Report. *Cmnd. 432*. 321, 631, *Cmnd. 750*. 797, 887; *Cmnd. 1069*. 1056, 1160
Agricultural Research Fund, Account, 497, 586, 767, 844, 1021, 1117
Agricultural Research, etc. (Pensions) Bill, 1045
Agricultural Research, Some Aspects of, 819, 1081
Agricultural Sciences, Progress in:
1105
See Commonwealth Agricultural Bureaux Report
Agricultural Sector Accounts and Tables, 435
Agricultural Seeds moving in International Trade, Testing of, 224
Agricultural Situation in Europe, Review, 1258
Agricultural Statistics:
Eastern European Countries, 720
England and Wales, 71, 289, 553, 1084
Scotland, 69, 287, 553, 819, 1081
United Kingdom, 72, 289, 555, 821, 1084
Agricultural Studies, 241A, 435–6, 706, 966, 1236
Agricultural Tractors. Documentation Series, 1245
Agricultural Trade of the USSR and Other Countries of Eastern Europe, 979
Agricultural Value of Phosphate Fertilisers Report, 220A
Agricultural Wages. Report of Proceedings, 289
Agriculture:
Agreements between U.K. and Denmark. *Cmnd. 1071*. 1056, 1119
And Dairy Diploma Courses in Wales, Report, 289
And Horticulture:
Books relating to, 557
Career, 1152
Managerial and Technical Posts, Career, 618
Scottish Certificate of Education, 912
Animal Health and Forestry, Colonial Advisory Council, 300
Bulletins, 72, 290, 556, 821, 1085
Circulars, 72–3, 290–1, 557, 822, 1086

INDEX 1956–60 —AIR

Agriculture (*continued*):
Education Report. *Cmnd. 614*. 539, 558
Estimates:
1956–57, 12
1957–58, 226
1958–59, 494, 676
1959–60, 760
1960–61, 1019, 1201
Higher Education in, 1246
History of Second World War, 82, 174
In European Countries, Output, Expenses and Income, 779
In Scotland. Report. *Cmd. 9745*. 42, 69, 793, 819, *Cmnd. 145*. 259, 287; *Cmnd. 392*. 523, 553; *Cmnd. 1028*. 1053, 1081
In the World Economy, 241A
Journal:
72, 289, 429, 555, 821, 1084
Scottish, 70, 288, 554, 820, 1081, 1082
Leaflets, 199
Long-Term Assurances for. *Cmnd. 23*. 54, 70, 74, 124
Problem Areas in Europe, 447
Review and Determination of Guarantees. *Cmnd. 109*. 256, 289, 333, 386
Technical Bulletins, 293, 560, 824, 1089
World Census:
Program, 706
Report, 436, 706
Agriculture Act:
272, 540
Annual Review and Determination of Guarantees, 1959. *Cmnd. 696*. 793, 821, 860, 913; *Cmnd. 970*. 1049, 1085, 1137, 1186
Agriculture Bill, 217, 218, 219, 233, 242, 247, 248, 249, 336, 484, 485, 504, 512, 517, 519, 520, 605
Agriculture and Fisheries, Department of, for Scotland, Publications, 69–70, 287–8, 553, 819, 1081, 1082
Agriculture, Fisheries and Food, Ministry of:
Publications, 70–5, 288–93, 554, 820, 1083
Report of the Committee on Provincial and Local Organisation and Procedures. *Cmd. 9732*. 41, 72
Agriculture (Safety, Health and Welfare Provisions) Act, 55
Agriculture (Safety, Health and Welfare Provisions) Bill, 4, 16, 29, 33, 125
Agriculture (Silo Subsidies) Act, 56
Agriculture (Silo Subsidies) Bill, 7, 35
Agriculture (Small Farmers) Act, 808
Agriculture (Small Farmers) Bill, 516, 520, 521, 747, 756, 863
Ahrens, M. R., In-Service Teacher Training in the United States of America, 735
A.H.S.B.:
Publications, 1217
A.H.S.B. (*continued*):
Report, 949
Aims and Objectives of ICAO in the Field of Facilitation, 710
Air:
Almanac, 75, 293, 561, 825, 1089
And Water Pollution, 445
High Cost of, 951
Methods for the Detection of Toxic Substances in, 875, 885
Pollution:
Measurement of, 650
Report, 381, 648, 742, 909, 1180
See Air we Live in. High Cost of Air
Air Compressor Plant:
Defence List, 838
For Servicing and Workshop Purposes, 1108
Air Conditions in Horticultural Stores, Control of, 1088
Air Corporations. Nationalised Industries (Reports and Accounts) Select Committee Report, 865
Air Corporations Act:
56, 1070
Guarantee given on:
Loans proposed to be raised, 10, 17, 22, 25, 26, 27, 192, 223, 224, 231, 235, 239, 406, 493, 500, 506, 507, 510, 675, 757, 767, 773, 780, 932, 1018, 1025, 1032, 1034, 1201
Stock issued, 10, 192
Air Corporations Bill:
7, 36, 786, 1003
Select Committee Special Report, 1034
Air Estimates:
1956–57, 12, 75; Memorandum. *Cmd. 9696*. 39, 75
1957–58, 226, 230, 293; Memorandum. *Cmnd. 149*. 259, 293
1958–59, 494, 561; Memorandum. *Cmnd. 373*. 523, 561
Supplementary, 759, 825
1959–60, 759, 825; Memorandum. *Cmnd. 673*. 792, 825
1960–61, 1017, 1089; Memorandum. *Cmnd. 950*. 1048, 1089
Air Flow Over Mountains, 360
Air Force:
Law, Manual of Amendment, 75, 293, 429, 561, 825, 1089
List, 75, 293, 561, 825, 1089
Retired Pay, Pensions, etc., 22, 23, 160
Air Ground Communications:
Dimensional Units. Amendments, 215A
Supplement, 439
Air Law, International Conference on Private Air Law, 215A, 441
Air Mail, Universal Postal Convention. *Cmnd. 576*. 787, 898; *Cmnd. 1218*. 1066, 1128

AIR-ARC | 1956-60

Air Ministry:
  Pamphlet, 293
  Publications, 75–6, 293–4, 561, 825, 1089
Air Navigation Commission, Directives to Panels of, 970
Air Navigation Conferences:
  Report, 215A, 439
  Supplement, 215A, 439, 710
Air Navigation Facilities and Services:
  441
  Charges for International Routes, 216A
  Implementation Panel, 711
Air Navigation Meeting:
  Report, 216A, 439, 710, 971
  Supplement, 216A, 439, 710
Air Navigation Orders, 187, 402, 670, 1090
Air Navigation Plan, 216A, 439, 710, 1241
Air Navigation Problems of World-Wide Concern, 441
Air Navigation Services:
  216A
  Agreement on Joint Financing:
    In Greenland and Faroe Islands, 439; *Cmnd. 678.* 792, 844
    In Iceland, 440; *Cmnd. 677.* 792, 845
  Procedures for, 710, 971, 1242
Air Navigation Sight Reduction Tables, 294
Air Photo Reading. Map Reading, etc., Manual, 954
Air Services:
  Appropriation Account, 11, 75, 224, 293, 492, 561, 758, 825, 1015, 1089
  Estimates:
    1956–57, Revised, 21, 75
    1959–60, 759
  Multilateral Agreement on Commercial Rights, 442
  Supplementary Estimates:
    1956–57, 226, 293
    1957–58, 494, 561
    1958–59, 759, 761, 825
    1959–60, 771, 933, 1019, 1089
    1960–61, 1028, 1202
Air Services Agreements between U.K. and—
  Argentine:
    Cmd. 9720. 40, 103; *Cmnd. 75.* 253
    Exchange of Notes, *Cmnd. 376.* 524, 587; *Cmnd. 1006.* 1051, 1117
  Austria. *Cmnd. 87.* 254
  Australia. *Cmnd. 410.* 526, 670
  Canada, Exchange of Notes amending Schedule of Routes, *Cmnd. 543.* 535, 670; *Cmnd. 1231.* 1068, 1090, 1118
  Ethiopia, *Cmnd. 531.* 534, 589; *Cmnd. 692.* 793, 847
  Cuba. *Cmnd. 258.* 266
  Czechoslovakia. *Cmnd. 1036.* 1053, 1119
Air Services Agreements (*continued*):
  Germany. *Cmnd. 137.* 258
  Ghana. *Cmnd. 567.* 536, 573
  India:
    Amending Air Services Agreement. *Cmnd. 275.* 267; *Cmnd. 837.* 802, 929
  Iran. *Cmnd. 1131.* 1060, 1121
  Ireland:
    Cmnd. 14. 53
    Exchange of Notes amending Agreement. *Cmnd. 535.* 534, 671; *Cmnd. 725.* 795, 930; *Cmnd. 890.* 806, 826; *Cmnd. 1230.* 1068, 1122
  Israel. Exchange of Notes. *Cmnd. 968.* 1049, 1122
  Kuwait. *Cmnd. 1168.* 1063, 1122
  Lebanon. Exchange of Notes amending Schedule of Routes. *Cmnd. 858.* 804, 851
  Malaya. *Cmnd. 356.* 522, 672
  Norway. *Cmnd. 44.* 251
  Pakistan. Amending. *Cmnd. 153.* 259
  Philippines. Exchange of Notes amending Schedule of Routes. *Cmnd. 171.* 260; *Cmnd. 1142.* 1061, 1124
  Poland. Exchange of Notes concerning Introduction of Air Services. *Cmnd. 862.* 804, 852
  South Africa. Exchange of Notes. *Cmnd. 889.* 806, 826
  Spain. Exchange of Notes amending Schedule of Routes. *Cmnd. 853.* 803, 852
  Sweden. *Cmd. 9670.* 37, 110
  Switzerland. Exchange of Notes for Revised Route Schedules. *Cmnd. 217.* 263; *Cmnd. 927.* 1046, 1126
  Thailand. Exchange of Notes amending Schedule of Routes. *Cmnd. 58.* 252; *Cmnd. 1180.* 1064, 1126
  U.S.A. Amending Schedule of Routes. *Cmnd. 82, 85.* 254
  U.S.S.R. *Cmnd. 798.* 800, 852; *Cmnd. 798, 1077.* 1045, 1056, 1127
  Yugoslavia. Exchange of Notes. *Cmnd. 732.* 795, 854; *Cmnd. 972.* 1049, 1128
Air Stations for Single-engined Helicopters, Planning of, 185
Air Terminal in Bermuda. Exchange of Notes between U.K. and U.S.A. extending area. *Cmnd. 1109.* 1058, 1127
Air Traffic:
  Procedures for the Control of, 199
  Services Supplement, 216A, 970
Air Traffic Control, Manual of, 826, 929, 1091
Air Transport Advisory Council Report, 22, 185, 236, 400, 505, 669, 930, 1031, 1091
Air Transport Agreement between U.K. and Burma amending Schedule of Routes. *Cmnd. 83.* 254

Air Votes:
  1954–55, 13, 193
  1955–56, 16, 193, 227, 406
  1956–57, 229, 406, 495, 675
  1957–58, 498, 675, 761, 932
  1958–59, 764, 932, 1019, 1205
  1959–60, 1022, 1206
Air We Live In, 951
Airborne Measurements of the Latitudinal Variation of Frost-Point, Temperature and Wind, 1162
Aircraft:
  Accidents:
    Investigation Manual, 1242
    Reports, 186, 400, 669, 670, 826, 928, 1090
    Survey, 185, 400, 669, 930, 1093
  And Crew of United States of America. Treatment in Hungary, 713
  And Pleasure Boats for Private Use. Customs Convention on Temporary Importation. 226; *Cmnd. 288.* 268; *Cmnd. 650.* 790, 846
  Engine Parts:
    Manufacture and Inspection of Welded Structure, Report, 391
    Report, 659
  Imported. Multilateral Agreement relating to Certificates of Airworthiness. *Cmnd. 1078.* 1056, 1118
  Manufacture and Repair Census of Production Report, 663
  Nationality and Registration Marks Amendment, 440
  Panel on Vertical Separation:
    219A
    Report, 712
  Powerplant Handbook, 199
  Radio Maintenance Engineers' Licences:
    400, 1090
    Amendment, 669
  Supply of Military. *See* Estimates Select Committee Special Report
  See also Personal Aircraft
Aircrew Licences. Exchange of Notes between U.K. and Yugoslavia on Mutual Recognition. *Cmnd. 1061.* 1055, 1128
Airport:
  And Air Navigation Facility Tariffs Manual, 216A, 440, 711, 971, 1242
  Charges Conference Proceedings, 440
Airports Designated in Application of the International Sanitary Regulations, 1267
Air-Seasoning of Converted Green Timber, 907
Airways Operations Training Series. Bulletins, 199
Airworthiness Certificates. Exchange of Notes between U.K. and Netherlands concerning Reciprocal Validation. *Cmnd. 671.* 791, 851
Airworthiness Committee:
  970
  Meeting Report, 1241
Aitken, J. K. (Chairman: Standing Medical, Nursing and Pharmaceutical Advisory Committee Joint Sub-Committee). Report, 602
Aitken, R. S. (Chairman: Hospital Advisory Committee). Report, 303
Akrotiri and Dhekelia. Order-in-Council, 1174, 1175
Akzin, B., New States and International Organisations Report, 239A
Alabaster, J. S., Field and Laboratory Investigation of Fish in Sewage Effluent, 558
Alabasters, English, 203
Alaska:
  Mid-Century, 202
  Pocket Guide, 419
Albemarle, Countess of (Chairman: Youth Service in E. and W. Committee). Report. *Cmnd. 929.* 1046, 1116
Alcohol. Effect of Small Doses on a Skill Resembling Driving, 887
Aldersey-Williams, A. G., Noise in Factories, 1179
Aldhous, J. R., Exotic Forest Trees in Great Britain, 325
Alewell, A., Sea-Fish Marketing in the Federal Republic of Germany, 707
Alexander, C. P., Ruwenzori Expedition, 82
Alexander, R. H., Use of Liquid Manure on Farms, 554
Algae:
  Blue-Green from the Middle Devonian of Rhynie, Aberdeenshire, 827
  Of British Coastal Waters. Introductory Account, 823
Aliabiev, V. I., Ground Winch Skidding in Clear and Selective Felling, 984
Aliens and British Protected Persons (Naturalisation). Return, 221, 233, 333, 504, 603, 776, 860, 1027, 1137
Alignment Charts and Form Height Tables for Determining Stand Volumes of Conifers, Oak, and Beech, 596
Aliment. Procedure in Actions in the Sheriff Courts between Spouses for Payment. *Cmnd. 907,* 807
Alkali, etc., Works:
  Circular, 611
  Report on, 120, 129, 329, 340, 610, 868, 1146
All Hallows The Great Churchyard Act, 543
All Hallows The Less Churchyard Act, 543
All Men are Brothers, 993
All Saints Chelsea Act, 811
Allan, I. R. H., Field and Laboratory Investigation of Fish in a Sewage Effluent, 558

Allan, J. A., Grasses of Barbados, 301
Allanfearn Station Railway Accident, Report, 672
Allen, W. A., Modern Multi-Storey Factories Design, 906
Allied Military Administration of Italy, 1943–45, 565, 658
Allison, M. L., Manual for Evaluators of Films and Filmstrips, 239A
Allium and Milula in the Central and Eastern Himalaya, 1095
Allowance Regulations, Amendments, 204, 423, 693, 952, 1223
Allowances in Respect of Capital Expenditure on Agricultural or Forestry Buildings, 873
Alphabet, Spelling, 218A
"Alpheus", Wreck Report, 406
Alport, C. J. M. (Chairman: Oversea Migration Board). Report. *Cmnd. 336.* 271, 305
Altimeters, 419
Aluminium Goods. Export Licence, 180, 396, 666
Amalgamation and Redesignation of:
  Certain Regiments, 953
  Infantry Regiments, 693
Ambatielos Claim. Award of the Commission of Arbitration, 103
Ambrosia Beetles, Defects caused by, 908
Ambulance and Casualty Collecting Section:
  333
  Amendment, 604
Ambulatory and Domiciliary Medical Care. Role of Hospitals Report, 1000
American Aid and European Payments Accounts, 16, 102, 230, 406, 501, 587, 769, 844, 1026, 1201
American Government. Questions and Answers, 202
American Public Health Association Publication, 1090
American Whelk Tingle on English Oyster Beds. Biology and Control of, 823
Amersham Junior School. Development Projects, 585
Amery, J. (Chairman: Committee on Army Cadet Force). Report. *Cmnd. 268.* 267
Aminoplastic Mouldings, 176
Ammoun, C. D., Study of Discrimination in Education, 721
Amputees, Rehabilitation of, Report, 332
Anaesthetic Explosions Report, 121
Analyses and Projections of Economic Development, 450, 720
Analysis of Running Cost of Hospitals, 121, 330, 600, 1132
Anatomy, Physiology and Body Mechanics for Physical Training Instructors, 696, 1089
Ancient and Historical Monuments and Constructions:
  England. Royal Commission Report. *Cmnd. 743.* 796, 863
  Inventory. Roxburghshire, 162
  Scotland, Royal Commission Publications, 162, 1175
  Selkirkshire. *Cmnd. 276.* 267, 378
  Wales and Monmouthshire. *Cmnd. 1138.* 1060, 1140; 1175
Ancient Monuments:
  And Historic Buildings Guides, 207–8, 426–7, 698, 957, 1226
  Boards:
    For England, Scotland and Wales, 1026, 1226
    Reports, 21, 207, 235, 426, 503, 698, 768, 957
  England and Wales; Supplementary Lists, 207, 426, 957, 1226
  East Caernarvonshire. Royal Commission Report. *Cmd. 9762.* 43, 123
  Illustrated Regional Guide, 207
  Postcards, 697
  Scotland:
    Guide, 956
    Supplementary List, 698
Anderson, Sir C. (Chairman: Committee on Grants to Students). Report. *Cmnd. 1051.* 1054, 1115, 1185
Andrews Diptych. Museum Monograph, 692
Angiosperm Flora of New Guinea, on the Geographical Relationships of, 1095
Angle Ore and Transport Company Act, 811
Anglesey:
  County of, Soils and Agriculture, 553
  Inventory of Ancient Monuments, 1175
Anglo-Hungarian Payments Agreement terminated. *Cmnd. 896.* 806, 850
Anglo-Iraqi Club. Exchange of Notes with U.K. concerning Settlement of Claims. *Cmnd. 187.* 261
Anglo-Soviet Communiqué on the Discussions of the Prime Minister and the Foreign Secretary with Union of Soviet Socialist Republics. *Cmnd. 689.* 792, 845
Angola Birds. Ecology and Taxonomy, 1097
Aniline Vapour, Detection of Toxic Substances in Air, 885
Animal Boarding Establishments Bill, 236, 242, 247, 336
Animal Feedstuffs. Regulations governing their Manufacture and Sale in European Countries, 437
Animal Health:
  Leaflets, 72, 289–90, 556, 821, 1085
  Services in Great Britain, Report, 72, 556, 824, 1088
  Year Book, 966, 1236

Animals:
  Experiments on Living. Return, 26, 124, 239, 334, 509, 604, 776, 862, 1033, 1138
  Management, 204
Annan, R., Historic Books on Mining and Kindred Subjects, 1178
Anniversary Commemorative Session, World Health Assembly, 740
Annotations to Acts:
  390, 658, 918, 1190
  Directions for Noting the Amendments, 175, 390, 1190
Annual Abstract of Statistics, 829
Ansari, M. A. R., Revision of the Brüelia Species Infesting the Corvidae, 80, 295
Antarctic, British ("Terra Nova") Expedition. Natural History Report, 827
Antarctica:
  Cases. Orders, 219A, 713
  Final Act of the Conference together with the Antarctic Treaty. *Cmnd. 913.* 808, 845
Anthrax. Report of the Committee of Inquiry. *Cmnd. 846.* 803, 875
Anthropology, International Bibliography of Social and Cultural, 735, 994, 1264
Anti-Aircraft Equipment loaned to Pakistan. *Cmnd. 367.* 523, 679
Antibiotics in Live-Stock Feeding, 71
Anti-Dumping and Countervailing Duties, 709
Antigua:
  Colonial Report, 569, 1102
  Orders-in-Council, 1173
Antioxidant in Food Regulations, 557
Antiques, Export Licences, 181, 1193
Antiquities of Roman Britain Guide, 562
Antiquities of Scotland National Museum Report, 154, 362, 890
Ants in the House, 1083
Apcar, H. V.:
  Structural Frameworks for Single-Storey Factory Buildings, 1179
  Structural Loading in Factories, 1179
Aphididae of East Africa, 570
Aplysia. Revision of the World Species, 1097
Apples:
  Aphids, 1083
  Blossom Weevil, 820
  Culture, Intensive, 556
  Sawfly, 1083
Apples and Pears:
  557
  Commercial Varieties, 288
  Market:
    221A
    In OEEC Countries, 718
  Pollination of, 555
  Trees, Winter Pruning of Established, 820
Appleton, G. J., Safe Handling of Radioisotopes, 1240
Application de Traite instituant le C.E.C.A. au Cours de la Période Transitoire, 704
Application of Atomic Science in Agriculture and Food, 974
Application of Science to Inland Fisheries, 966
Application of Sprays to Fruit Trees, 288
Applied Mechanics, Examples in, 545
Applied Science, Notes on, 155, 362
Appointments:
  In Overseas Civil Service, etc., 300
  Overseas, 1101
Appraisal of Fellowships Report, 1269
Appropriation Accounts:
  Civil, 9, 193, 222, 407, 491, 676, 757, 932, 1014, 1015, 1201
  Defence, 9, 93, 222, 307, 490, 578, 757, 837, 1015, 1108
  Of Revenue Departments, 514
Appropriation Act, 55, 272, 540, 808, 1070
Approved Probation Hostels and Homes. *See* Probation Officers
Apsley House Guide, 422
Apted, M. R., Claypotts, Angus, Guide, 427
Aquatic Weeds and Algae, Control of, 556
Arab Amirates of the South. Treaty of Friendship and Protection with. *Cmnd. 665.* 791, 833
Arab States, Compulsory Education in, 237A
Arabia, Expedition to South-West, 295
Arabic Printed Books in the British Museum. Supplementary Catalogue, 1095
Arachnids. *See* Insects of Medical Importance
Aradidae, Classification of, 828
Arbitral Award made by the King of Spain:
  Order, 712
  (Honduras *v.* Nicaragua) Order, 1243
Arbitral Procedure, Draft Convention, 225A
Arbuckle, R. H., Land in British Honduras, 1103
Archaeological Report, 427, 698, 1226
Archaeology. Card-Inventory of Important Associated Finds, 1094
Archdeacon Johnson's Almshouse Charity (Oakham and Uppingham) Scheme Confirmation Act, 57
Archdeacon Johnson's Almshouse Charity (Oakham and Uppingham) Scheme Confirmation Bill, 2, 33
Arched Girders. Safety Pamphlet, 645
Archer, M., Tippoo's Tiger, 951
Archer, W. G., Indian Painting in Bundi and Kotah, 1223
Archibald, E. H. H.:
  Sea Fights, 362
  Ship Portraits in National Maritime Museum, 154

1956-60 | ARC-AUS

ARC— INDEX 1956-60

Architect, Careers, 1152
Archives:
  National Register of, List of Accessions to Repositories, 860, 1137
  Of Former German Foreign Office. Exchange of Letters concerning Transfer. *Cmnd. 37.* 251
  Of the Allied High Commission. Protocol Modifying Agreement. *Cmnd. 741.* 796, 845
"Arctic Viking" Wreck Report, 192
Arctiidae, Nolinae, 564
Arctiidae, Thyretidae and Notodontidae, 564
Arden-Clarke, Sir Charles (Chairman: Chaguaramas Joint Commission). Report, 569
Ardsley Station. Railway Accidents Report, 1197
Area Mortality, 597
Areas qualifying for Grant. Town and Country Planning Acts Circular, 611
Argentina:
  Agreement with U.K. on the Consolidation of Debts. *Cmnd. 359.* 523, 587
  Exchange of Notes with U.K. extending the Validity of the Air Services Agreement. *Cmd. 9720.* 40, 103; *Cmnd. 75, 97, 98.* 253, 255, 315; *Cmnd. 376.* 524, 587; *Cmnd. 1006.* 1051, 1117
  Overseas Economic Survey, 182
Argyll, County of:
  Educational Endowments Scheme. Memorandum, 911
  Educational Trust Scheme, 1184
Arid Zone:
  Hydrology. Recent Developments, 994, 1263
  Research, 237A, 465, 735, 994, 1263
Arithmetic:
  In the Primary School Report, 169
  Mathematics and Applied Mathematics. Scottish Certificate of Education, 913
Arkleston Junction Railway Accident. Report, 672
Armaments:
  See Political and Security Questions
  Western European Union Convention concerning Agency for Control *Cmnd. 389.* 524, 596
Armed Forces *see* Forces, H.M.
Armed Forces (Housing Loans) Act, 612
Armed Forces (Housing Loans) Bill: 487, 520
  Memorandum. *Cmnd. 568.* 536, 675
Armer, Sir F. (Chairman: Central Advisory Water Trade Effluents Sub-Committee). Report, 613, 1147
Arms:
  1101
  And Armour in England, 1226
Arms (*continued*):
  And Armour in Tudor and Stuart London, 358
  Colonial, 569
  Hong Kong, 832
  Nigeria, 832, 1101
  Trinidad and Tobago, 832
Armstrong, F. H.:
  Strength Properties of Timber, 166, 1180
  Timbers for Flooring, 382
Army:
  Allowance Regulations, Amendments, 204, 423, 429, 693, 952, 1223
  Appropriation Accounts, 11, 204, 224, 423, 492, 693, 758, 953, 1015, 1223
  Cadet Force:
    Committee Report. *Cmnd. 268.* 267, 423
    Regulations Amendments, 204, 423, 693
  Career, 618
  Catering, Regimental Standing Orders, 206
  Chaplains, Appointment, Pay, etc., 693
  Civilian Staff Regulations, Amendments, 424, 953
  Combined Cadet Force Regulations Amendments, 694
  Conditions of Enlistment Act, 272
  Conditions of Enlistment Bill, 218, 248
  Emergency Reserve of Officers Regulations, 204, 953
  Emergency Reserve Regulations Amendments, 423, 693, 953, 1223
  Engineer Works Services Regulations Amendments, 424
  Enlistment, Regular, and Service Regulations, 424
  Future Organisation. *Cmnd. 230.* 264, 423
  Health, Manual of, 954
  List, 205, 423, 694, 953, 1223
    Supplement, 205
  Magazine, 207, 425, 696
  Medical Services:
    122, 174, 332, 389
    History of Second World War, 859, 916
  Military Law Manual, 206
  Missiles Rockets, 691
  National Service Men Regulations Amendments, 426, 696
  Orders, 205, 423, 429, 694, 953, 1224
    Index, 953, 1224
    Special Issue, 205, 956, 1125
  Pamphlet U.S., 691
  Pay Warrant Amendments, 206, 425, 429, 695, 954, 1224
  Pensions Warrant Amendments, 694, 953
  Physical Training in the, 695, 954

INDEX 1956-60 —ASP

Army (*continued*):
  Prize Money and Legacy Funds Accounts, 222, 246, 425, 955
  Queen's Regulations Amendments, 206, 425, 696, 955, 1224
  Recruiting and Service Regulations Amendments, 205
  Retired Pay, Pensions, etc., 47, 160, 206
  Retirement and Discharge consequent on Reductions, 696
  Supply, Transport and Barrack Services Regulations Amendments, 696
  Territorial Army Regulations Amendments:
    207, 426, 696, 955, 1225
  Votes:
    1954–55, 12, 193
    1955–56, 17, 193, 227, 406
    1956–57, 229, 407, 494, 676
    1957–58, 498, 676, 760, 953
    1958–59, 759, 764, 932, 1019, 1206
    1959–60, 1022, 1206
Army Estimates:
  1956–57, 12, 205
    Memorandum. *Cmd. 9688.* 38, 205
    Revised, 21, 205
  1957–58, 226, 230, 259, 423
    Memorandum. *Cmnd. 150.* 259, 423
    Supplementary, 223, 423
  1958–59, 493, 694
    Memorandum. *Cmnd. 372.* 523, 694
    Supplementary, 505, 694, 761, 953
  1959–60, 759, 953
    Memorandum. *Cmnd. 669.* 791, 953
    Supplementary, 1019, 1223
  1960–61, 1018, 1223
    Memorandum. *Cmnd. 951.* 1048, 1223
    Supplementary, 1028, 1202
Army Reserve:
  Directions for Calling out on Permanent Service, 205
  Proclamation Calling Out, 150
Arnold, D. C., Systematic Revision of the Fishes of the Teleost Family Carapidae, 81
Arnold, F. A., Effect of Fluoridated Public Water Supplies on Dental Caries, Prevalence, 421
Around the World with Unicef, 225A
Arsenic in Food (Amendment) Regulations, Circular, 1086
Arsenic in Food Regulations, Circular, 822
Art:
  Examinations in:
    101, 313, 585, 842, 1115
    Report of the National Advisory Committee, 312
  Export of Works Report. *Cmnd. 856.* 804, 935; *Cmnd. 1175.* 1063, 1204
  Reviewing Committee Report on Export of Works of Art. *Cmnd. 542.* 535, 678
Art (*continued*):
  Rules Governing the Award of Diplomas and Certificates, 101, 586, 1116
  Scottish Certificate of Education, 913
  Secondary Schools Report, 169
  See Export of Works of Art—Royal Fine Art Commission
Art Education:
  National Advisory Committee Report, 585, 586
  National Advisory Council Report, 1116
Artificial Lighting of Laying Hens, 820
Artificial Lights on Fish and Other Marine Organisms at Sea, Effect of, 655
Artificial Limbs in the Rehabilitation of the Disabled, 331
Arts:
  Council of Great Britain Publication, 826, 1090
  Housing the Arts in Britain, 825
  In Britain. *See* Government
  In Education, 100
Arundel Estate Act, 275
Arundel Estate Bill, 215, 219
Asbestos: Census of Production Report, 395, 1194
Asbestos-filled Phenolic Resin, 659
Ascension Island. Agreement between U.K. and U.S.A. for extension of Bahamas Long Range Proving Ground. *Cmd. 9810.* 46, 111
Ash:
  Selecting by Inspection, 908
  Sycamore and Maple Seed. Collection and Storage, 1129
Ashby, A. W., Public Lands, 241A
Ashton, L. A., Sponsored Fire-Resistance Tests on Structural Elements, 1183
Ashton-under-Lyne, Stalybridge and Dukinfield (District) Waterworks Act, 543
Asia and the Far East:
  Economic Bulletin, 227A, 452, 722, 980
  Economic Commission Annual Report, 228A, 723, 981
  Economic Development and Planning, 452, 1252
  Economic Survey, 228A, 453, 723, 982
  Helping Economic Development, 727
  International Action on Housing, Building and Planning, 437
  Mining Development, 231A
  Regional Cartographic Conference Report, 225A
  Regional Conference Report, 436
  Seminar on Population, 450
Asian Flu, What *You* Should Know About, 692
Asian Women in Public Life. Seminar, 720
Asparagus, 1085

ASS— INDEX 1956-60

Assault on John Waters, Allegation of:
  Proceedings of the Tribunal, 915
  Report of the Tribunal. *Cmnd. 718.* 794, 915
Assemblée Commune, Annuaire-Manuel, European Coal and Steel Community, 215A
Assemblée Commune Débates, European Coal and Steel Community, 434, 704, 963
Assemblée Parlementaire dans l'Europe des Six, 704
Assemblée Parlementaire Européenne:
  701
  Annuaire-Manuel, 962
  Bibliographie Méthodique Trimestrielle, 1233
  Cahiers Mensuels de Documentation Européenne, 1233
  Débats, 962, 1233
  Euratom, 1233
  L'Activité de l'Assemblée, 1232
  Publications, 1232
  Rapport Special Concernant la Question Charbonnière, 965
Assembly of Western European Union Proceedings, 738, 997
Assessment of Priority for Road Improvements, 1182
Assistance for Small Farmers. *Cmnd. 553.* 535, 556, 603, 654
Assistance to the Needy, 225A
Assistance to Under-Developed Countries, 468
Assurance Companies:
  Returns, 178, 663, 920, 1191
  Statements of Assurance Business, 178, 393, 663
Assurance Companies Acts:
  Consolidation of Enactments Procedure Act. Memorandum, 481
Aston, G. H., Effects of Variations in the Ambient Air on the Calibration and Use of Ionization Dosemeters, 1163
Astronomical Ephemeris, 813, 1074
Astronomical Results:
  From Observations, 120, 599, 904
  Greenwich, 1178
Astronomy:
  And Magnetism. Greenwich Observations, 1178
  Magnetism and Meteorology Observations, 120, 599, 904
  Text Book of Field, 956
Ataractic and Hallucinogenic Drugs in Psychiatry Report, 999
Aten, A.:
  Copra Processing in Rural Industries, 706
  Processing of Cassava and Cassava Products in Rural Industries, 435
Atherosclerosis and Ischaemic Heart Disease Report, Study Group on, 472
Atheroscleratic Lesions, Classification of. Report, 741
Atkinson, R. J. C., Stonehenge and Avebury and Neighbouring Monuments Guide, 958
Atmosphere and Oceans of the Southern Hemisphere, Exchange of Energy between, 1160
Atmospheric Pollution, Investigation of; Report on Observations, 381, 648, 742, 909, 1180
Atmospheric Water Vapour Pressure World Distribution of, 888
Atom:
  949
  Annual Report, Summary of, 198, 418, 690, 1217
Atomic Achievements in the Commonwealth, 614
Atomic Age, New, 459, 729
Atomic Energy:
  Agreement between U.K. and—
    Germany for Co-operation in Peaceful Uses. *Cmd. 9842.* 48, 106
    Spain for Co-operation in Peaceful Uses. *Cmnd. 936.* 1047, 1125
    Sweden for Co-operation in Peaceful Uses. *Cmnd. 290.* 268
    U.S.A. for Co-operation in Civil Uses. Amendment. *Cmd. 9789, 9847.* 44, 49, 111
  Contribution to Agriculture, 420
  Convention on Establishment of Security Control in Field of Nuclear Energy, *Cmnd. 971.* 1049, 1117
  Decision of the Council of the O.E.E.C. establishing a European Nuclear Energy Agency and Convention on Security Control. *Cmnd. 357.* 522, 587
  Economic Applications of, 450
  Enriched Uranium, Supply of. Exchange of Notes. *Cmnd. 809.* 801, 845
  European Organisation for Nuclear Research. *Cmnd. 928.* 1046, 1117
  Exchange of Notes between U.K. and—
    Belgium amending Agreement for Co-operation in its Peaceful Uses. *Cmd. 9794.* 45, 104
    Denmark regarding Co-operation in Promotion and Development of Peaceful Uses. *Cmnd. 1127.* 1059, 1119
    Norway regarding Peaceful Uses of Atomic Energy. *Cmnd. 245, 277.* 265, 267
    U.S.A. rectifying Agreement for Co-operation on Civil Uses. *Cmd. 9677.* 38, 111
  Glossary of Technical Terms, 720
  In Britain. Guide to Information, 1149

INDEX 1956-60 AUS

Atomic Energy (*continued*):
  Inventions. Agreement between U.K., Canada and U.S.A. as to Disposition of Rights. *Cmnd. 20.* 53, 111
  Medical Officers, Notes on, 545
  Mental Health Aspects of Peaceful Uses, 741
  Mutual Defence Purposes:
    Agreement between U.K. and U.S.A. *Cmnd. 470, 537.* 530, 534, 595; Amendment *Cmnd. 733.* 795, 845
    Co-operation on Uses. *Cmnd. 859.* 804, 833
  Peaceful Uses of:
    199, 231A–2A, 729, 986, 1257
    Agreement between U.K. and—
      Italy. *Cmnd. 349, 458.* 522, 529, 590
      Japan. *Cmnd. 459.* 529, 591; *Cmnd. 625.* 788, 850
      Portugal. *Cmnd. 513.* 532, 592
      Spain. *Cmnd. 936.* 1047, 1125
    Agreement with the European Atomic Energy Community (Euratom). *Cmnd. 649, 702.* 790, 793, 845
    Exchange of Notes between U.K. and Germany. *Cmnd. 375.* 523, 590
    Exchange of Notes between U.K. and Norway. *Cmnd. 245, 277.* 265, 267
    Index to Proceedings of International Conference, 231A–2A, 729, 986, 1257
    Report on the Suspension of Nuclear Tests. *Cmnd. 551.* 535, 588
    Statute of International Atomic Energy Agency. *Cmnd. 92.* 255, 315; *Cmnd. 450.* 528, 588
Atomic Energy Agency Publications, International, 1239
Atomic Energy Authority:
  Balance Sheet, 19, 102, 232, 314, 502, 587, 769, 844, 1024, 1117
  Industrial Group Information Bibliography, 418
  Publications, 198, 412–19, 681, 939, 1207, 1219
  Report:
    21, 198, 235, 419, 505, 691, 771, 1028, 1207
    Of the Committee to Examine the Organisation. *Cmnd. 338.* 271, 418
    Organisation for Control of Health and Safety. *Cmnd. 342.* 521, 690
  Select Committee on Estimates:
    Report, 776, 865
    Special Report, 1143
Atomic Energy Authority Act, 810
Atomic Energy Authority Bill, 754, 786
Atomic Energy of Canada Limited, Catalogue of Nuclear Reactors, 198
Atomic Energy Research Establishment Publications, 76–9, 412–18
Atomic Information. Agreement between the Parties to the North Atlantic Treaty. *Cmd. 9799.* 45, 103
Atomic Laws and Administration, 1248
Atomic Radiation: Statement on the Report of the United Nations Scientific Committee. *Cmnd. 508.* 532, 632; 726
Atomic Science in Agriculture and Food, Applications of. Report, 715, 974
Atomic Terms, Glossary of, 1218
Atomic Weapons, Medical Aspect, 202
Attachment of Earnings Orders, 861
Auchengeich Colliery, Lanarkshire. Report on Underground Fire. *Cmnd. 1022.* 1052, 1173
Auctioneering, Estate Agency and Land Agency. Careers, 617
Audley End, Essex:
  Catalogue of Pictures. Correction Slip, 957
  Guide, 698
Austin, E. C., Upper Air Temperature over the World, 633
Australia, Commonwealth of:
  Agreement with U.K. for Air Services. *Cmnd. 410.* 526, 670
  International Customs Journal, 445, 714, 974, 1244
  On Social Security. *Cmnd. 378.* 524, 573
  Trade Agreement with U.K. *Cmnd. 91.* 254
Australian Chafers, Revision of, 295
Austria:
  Agreement with U.K. for Air Services between and beyond their respective Territories. *Cmnd. 87.* 254, 315
  Convention with U.K. for the Avoidance of Double Taxation and the Prevention of Fiscal Evasion. *Cmd. 9865.* 50, 103; *Cmnd. 135.* 258, 315
  Economic Conditions, 1246
  Exchange of Notes with U.K.:
    Concerning Contracts and Periods of Prescription. *Cmnd. 292.* 269, 315
    Concerning the Repayment of Credit granted by the European Payments Union. *Cmnd. 596.* 538, 588
    Extension of Agreement for the Repayment of Credits granted by the European Payments Union. *Cmd. 9764.* 43, 53; *Cmnd. 21.* 103

AUS-BIG | 1956-60

AUS— INDEX 1956–60

Austria (*continued*)
Exchange of Notes with U.K. (*Contd.*):
For the Re-establishment of an Independent and Democratic Austria. *Cmnd. 784.* 799, 845
Respecting the Repayment of Debts on the Liquidation of the European Payments Union. *Cmnd.755.* 797, 845
Foreign Trade Statistical Bulletin, 222A, 447, 717, 977
International Customs Journal, 974, 1244
Overseas Economic Survey, 398
State Treaty for the Re-establishment of an Independent and Democratic Austria. *Cmnd. 214.* 263, 315
Austria and Switzerland Economic Conditions, 221A, 446, 715
Authorised Officers (Meat Inspection) Regulations. Circular, 1086
Authority Health and Safety Branch. Report, 1217
Automatic Control. Some Non-Linear Problems in the Theory of, 391
Automation:
449
And skill, 1181
In North America. Report, 651
In Perspective Report, 164
Mental Health Problems of, Report, 1000
Report, 164
Social Consequences of, 736
Automobile Seat Belts Report, 691
Average Water-Vapour Content of the Air, 1160
Averages of:
Accumulated Temperature and Standard Deviation of Monthly Mean Temperature over Britain, 889
Earth Temperature for the British Isles, 1160
Aviation:
Law, 400
Law for Applicants for the Private Pilot's Licence, 1090
Meteorology Handbook, 1160
Meteorology of the West Indies, 1161
Private Pilot's Licence, 185, 927
Series, 419
Training Films, 970
Aviation, Ministry of:
Estimates, 1960–61, 1019, 1201
Examination Papers, 826, 1091
Publications, 826, 1090
Revised Estimates, 1960–61, 1027, 1202
Avidor, M., Education in Israel, 736
Avoidance of Cracking in Masonry. Construction of Concrete or Sand-Lime Bricks, 381
Avoidance of Pollution of the Sea by Oil, Manual on, 400, 670
Awards:
For Good Design in Housing Circular, 1146
To Inventors. Royal Commission Report. *Cmd. 9744.* 42, 162
Aycliffe Development Corporation Report, 24, 130, 237, 506, 613, 870, 1147
Aylwen, Sir G. (Chairman: Law Society). Report, 151

B

Babylonian Tablets. Cuneiform Texts from Babylonian Tablets in the British Museum, 827, 1094
Background, 691
Bacon:
Agreed Minute of Discussion between U.K. and Denmark relating to Import of Danish Bacon. *Cmd. 9707, 9823.* 40, 47, 105
Curing and Sausage Census of Production Report, 664
Bacteriological Examination of Water Supplies, 123
Baghdad. Gift of Land. *Cmd. 9814.* 46, 195
Baghdad Pact. Mutual Co-operation between Iraq and Turkey. *Cmd. 9859.* 50, 103
Bahamas:
Arms, 1101
Colonial Reports, 300, 832
Long Range Proving Ground. Establishment of Additional Sites. *Cmd. 9810, 9811.* 46
Orders in Council, 1173
Bahrain:
Notices, 103–4, 315–16, 588, 845, 852, 1117
Treasury Minute concerning Gift of Land. *Cmnd. 110.* 256, 407
Bailey Bridge—Normal Uses, 206
Bailey, S. B., Automation in North America, 651
Baillie Reynolds, P. K.:
Chrysanster, Cornwall, Guide, 1226
Thornton Abbey Guide, 208
Bainbridge, V., Plankton of Inshore Waters off Freetown, Sierra Leone, 1103
Baird Trust Order Confirmation Act, 273
Baird Trust Order Confirmation Bill, 248
Baker, A. Psychiatric Services and Architecture, 1269
Baker, C. G., Report on Proposed British Egg Marketing Scheme. *Cmd. 9805.* 46, 75
Baking, Career, 347
Baking Industry (Small Establishments and Seasonal Resorts) Bill, 767, 778, 784, 865
Bakkensit, Dr. S. C., Investigation into Costs of Distribution in Grocery Retail Trade in Netherlands, 449

INDEX 1956–60 —BAS

Bala to Trawsfynydd Highways (Liverpool Corporation Contribution) Act, 1072
Balaena Expedition, Meteorological Results, 152
Balance of Payments. *Cmd. 9731, 9871.* 41, 51; *Cmnd. 122, 273.* 257, 267; *Cmnd. 399, 540.* 525, 534, 681; *Cmnd. 700, 861.* 793, 804, 939; *Cmnd. 977, 1188.* 1049, 1064
Balfour of Burleigh, Rt. Hon. Lord (Chairman):
Committee on Export of Live Cattle to the Continent for Slaughter. Report. *Cmnd. 154.* 259
Hill Lands (North of Scotland) Commission Report. *Cmd. 9759.* 42
Ball, D. F., Soils and Land Use of the District around Rhyl and Denbigh, 1081
Ball, H. W., Upper Cretaceous Decapoda and Serpulidae from James Ross Island, Graham Land, 1103
Ballantyne, W. M., Scotland Now, 1187
Ballistic Missiles:
Early Warning Station:
Exchange of Notes between U.K. and U.S.A. *Cmnd. 1034.* 1053, 1127
In the United Kingdom. *Cmnd. 946.* 1047, 1089
Exchange of Notes with U.S.A. concerning Supply. *Cmnd. 406.* 526, 595
Supply. *Cmnd. 366.* 523, 578
Balmain, K. H.:
Observations on the Spawning Runs of Brown Trout in the South Queich, Loch Leven, 171
Records of Salmon and Sea Trout Caught at Sea, 171
Balnaguard Halt. Railway Accident Report, 1097
Bank of England Report. *Cmd. 9828.* 47, 193; *Cmnd. 240.* 265, 407; *Cmnd.500.* 532, 676; *Cmnd. 801.* 800, 932; 1093
Bank Rate. Tribunal appointed to Inquire into Allegations that Information about the Raising of Bank Rate was Improperly Disclosed:
Proceedings, 603
Report. *Cmnd. 350.* 522, 603
Bankers Returns, 150, 357, 631, 917, 1190
Banking and the Stock Exchange, Careers, 618, 1152
Bankruptcy:
And Companies (Winding-Up) Proceedings Account, 228, 393, 489, 663, 756, 764, 920, 1023, 1191
General Annual Report, 178, 393, 920, 1191
Law and Deeds of Arrangement Law Amendment:
Minutes of Evidence, 663
Report. *Cmnd. 221.* 264, 393
Report, 663
Bannon, J. K., Average Water Vapour Content of the Air, 1160
Baptist Chapel and Other Charities (Totnes and Tuckenhay) Scheme Confirmation Act, 57
Baptist Chapel and Other Charities (Totnes and Tuckenhay) Scheme Confirmation Bill, 2, 33
Barbados Colonial Report, 300, 832
Barby Sidings Railway Accident Report, 188
Barcelona Traction Light and Power Co. Ltd. (Belgium *v.* Spain). Order, 713, 1243
Barclays Bank D.C.O. Act, 273
Barker, D., Commonwealth we Live In, 1106
Barker, R. E., Books for All, 237A
Barking Machines, Provisional Protocol for the Testing, 987
Barley:
821
World Catalogue of Genetic Stocks, 1238
Barn Hay Drying, 558
Barnard, G. P.:
Effects of Variations in the Ambient Air on the Calibration and Use of Ionization Dosemeters, 1163
Mass Spectrometer Researches, 155
Barnard Castle, Co. Durham, Guide, 957
Barnburgh Main Colliery Explosion Report. *Cmnd. 279.* 268
Barnes Railway Accident Report, 188
Barnett, L. D., Hindi Printed Books Supplementary Catalogue, 562
Barnett, R. D., Nimrod Ivories Catalogue, 294
Barnsley Boundary Commission for England. Report, 1137
Barnsley Corporation Act, 57
Barometric Changes and the Efflux of Gas in Mines, 153
Barrack Services Regulations Amendments, 207, 955
Barrott, J. P., Films recommended for Children and Adolescents up to 16 years, 468
Barry, Hon. Mr. Justice (Chairman: Advisory Council on Treatment of Offenders). Report, 863; *Cmnd. 1213.* 1066
Barry Corporation (Barry Harbour) Act, 57, 274
Bartlett, Sir F. (Chairman: Individual Efficiency in Industry Committee). Report, 650
Bary, Lt.-Cdr. B. McK., Effect of Electric Fields on Marine Fishes, 172
Basement System, Structural Analysis of, at Turoka, Kenya, 834
Basic Chemistry in Nuclear Energy, 986

BAS— INDEX 1956–60

Basic Design Temperatures for Space-Heating, 208
Basic Documents, World Health Organisation, 243A, 739, 1267
Basic Facts:
About the United Nations, 1251
And Figures, 1263
Basic Instruments and Selected Documents, General Agreement on Tariffs and Trade, 220A, 438
Basic Metallurgy and Fabrication of Fuels, 986
Basic Stitches of Embroidery, 1222
Basildon Development Corporation Report, 24, 130, 237, 506, 613, 870, 1147
Bastardy. Consolidation of Enactments relating to. Memorandum, 6
Basutoland:
Agreement for the Avoidance of Double Taxation, etc. *Cmnd. 898.* 807, 835
Annual Report, 835
Bechuanaland and Protectorate and Swaziland Economic Survey Mission Report, 1106
Colonial Report, 91, 573, 1106
Constitutional Arrangements. *Cmnd. 897.* 807, 835
Order-in-Council, 1174
Report on Constitutional Discussions held in London. *Cmnd. 637.* 789, 835
Bathing Beaches, E. and W., Sewage Contamination, 887
Batteries:
And Accumulators. Census of Production Report, 394
Secondary, 94
Battle Honours. Special Army Orders, 205
Battle Physical Training, 695
Battles, Actions and Engagements:
Official Names, 694
2nd World War, 205
Bazley, E. N., Sound Absorbing Materials, 1163
B.C. Form Lunacy, 857
Bean Weevils. *See* Pea, Bean and Clover Leaf Weevils
Bear Island Cod. Migrations and Movements, 559
Beardmore, Wm., and Co. Ltd., Proposal to sell Holdings of Securities. *Cmnd. 59.* 252
Beaumaris Castle, Anglesey, Coloured Postcard, 697
Beaumont, Jacques de:
Sphecidae (Hym) Récoltés en Libye et au Tibesti par M. Kenneth M. Guichard, 80
Sphecidae Récoltés en Tripolitaine et en Cyrénaique par M. Kenneth M. Guichard, 1095
Bechuanaland Protectorate:
Agreement for the Avoidance of Double Taxation, etc. *Cmnd. 899.* 807, 835
Colonial Report, 91, 573, 835
Constitutional Proposals. *Cmnd. 1159.* 1062, 1106
Economic Survey Mission Report, 1106
Beckwith, J.:
Andrews Diptych, 692
Caskets from Cordoba, 1222
Bedford Corporation Act, 57
Bedgebury National Pinetum and Forest Plots Guide, 113
Beebe, C. W., Leather Bookbindings. How to Preserve Them, 199
Beech, Steaming of Home Grown, 907
Beef:
Production, 822
Quality, Studies on 382, 649, 1180
Beekeepers, Advice to Intending, 288
Beekeeping:
290
Migratory, 288
Beer, Sir Gavin de:
Darwin's Journal, 1096
Darwin's Notebooks on Transmutation of Species, 1096
Evolution of Ratites, 81
Identity of Isopyrum Aquiligioides, 1095
Bees, Diseases of, 821
Beesley, M. E., London-Birmingham Motorway Traffic and Economies. Economic Assessment, 1182
Beeswax from the Apiary, 1083
Beet Eelworm, 1083
Beetles:
Common Furniture, 907, 1180
Death Watch, 1180
From the London Clay of Bognor Regis, Sussex, 1096
House Longhorn, 907
Lyctus Powder-Post, 1180
Monograph of the Immature Stages of Neotropical Timber Beetles, 1097
Saw-Toothed Grain, 1084
See African Timber Beetles
Beever, C., Financial Assistance Schemes for Acquisition or Improvement of Fishing Craft, 1237
Begley, C. D., Growth and Yield of Sweet Chestnut Coppice, 112
Behavioural Research, Some Applications of, 468
Beitrag mur Kenntnis der Erotyliden, 562
Belgian Congo:
And Ruanda-Urundi. Overseas Economic Survey, 398
International Customs Journal, 444, 713, 973, 1244

INDEX 1956–60 —BIG

Belgium:
Agreement with U.K.:
Relating to Compensation for Disablement and Death due to War Injury. *Cmnd. 311.* 270, 315
Respecting the Repayment of the Debt on the Liquidation of the European Payments Union. *Cmnd. 756.* 797, 845
Convention with U.K. on Social Security and Protocol concerning Benefits in Kind. *Cmnd. 199.* 262, 315; *Cmnd. 460.* 529, 588
Exchange of Letters with U.K. concerning Repayment of Credits granted by the European Payments Union. *Cmd. 9836.* 48, 104; *Cmnd. 248.* 265, 316
Exchange of Notes with U.K.:
Amending Agreement for Co-operation in the Peaceful Uses of Atomic Energy. *Cmd. 9794.* 45, 104
Concerning arrangements to Facilitate Travel. *Cmnd. 1091.* 1057, 1118
Extending the Provisions of the Visa Abolition Agreement. *Cmd. 9711.* 40, 104
Belgium—Luxembourg:
Economic Union. Economic Conditions, 1246
Foreign Trade Statistical Bulletin, 222A, 447, 448, 717, 977
Belgium, Luxembourg—Netherlands:
Economic Conditions, 221A, 446
International Customs Journal, 444, 713, 973, 1244
Beloe, R. (Chairman: Secondary School Examinations Council). Report, 1116
Belshaw, D. H., Agricultural Credit in Economically Underdeveloped Countries, 1236
Belt Conveyers at Quarries. Safety Circular, 900
"Ben Meidie" Wreck Report, 931
Bending of Solid Timber, 907
Beneficial Insects, 556
Benelux Economic Conditions, 715
Benge, R. C., Technical and Vocational Education in United Kingdom, 736
Benjamin, B.:
Emmetropia and Its Aberrations, 359
Tuberculosis Statistics for E. and W., 327
Benson, H., Report on Methods adopted by the London Electricity Board on Disposal of Scrap Cable. *Cmnd. 605.* 539, 641
Benson, R. B., Studies in Pontania, 1095
Benthic Animals as Indicators of Hydrographic Conditions and Climatic Change in Svalbard Waters, 291
Bentley, E. W.:
Biological Methods for the Evaluation of Rodenticides, 560
Control of Rats in Sewers, 1089
Bentwick, J. S., Education in Israel, 736
Benzene Vapour. Methods for the Detection of Toxic Substances in Air, 630
Berks County (Consent to Letting) Ministry of Housing and Local Government Provisional Order Act, 274
Berks County (Consent to Letting) Ministry of Housing and Local Government Provisional Order Bill, 248
Berlin. *See* Germany. Documents
Bermuda:
Colonial Report, 569, 1102
Conference. Final Communiqué. *Cmnd. 126.* 257, 316
International Customs Journal, 444, 974
Berney Arms Mill, Reedham, Norfolk Guide, 426
Berwickshire Educational Trust Scheme, Memorandum, 1184
Betio Island. Weather Station. Exchange of Notes between U.K. and U.S.A. *Cmd. 9693.* 39
Bettenson, A. S. (Chairman: Joint Advisory Committee of the Cotton Industry). Report, 348, 1154
Betting and Gaming Act, 1070
Betting and Gaming Bill, 783, 786, 1007, 1008, 1009, 1023, 1036, 1042, 1044, 1140
Betting Bill, 250
Betting Levy Bill, 1012, 1044, 1045
Betting Reform Bill, 784
Beutick, Dr. D. E., Investigation into Costs of Distribution in Grocery Retail Trade in Netherlands, 449
Beveridge, J., Register of Privy Seal of Scotland, 389
Beverton, R. J. H.:
Echo-Sounding Experiments in the Barents Sea, 1087
On the Dynamics of Exploited Fish Populations, 559
Beware Firedamp, 640
Bhattacharyya, R. N., Food and Feeding Habits of Larval and Post-Larval Herring in the Northern North Sea, 388
Bibliographical Handbooks, 237A, 465, 735
Bibliographical Series, 225A, 1239
Bibliographie Analytique du Plan Schuman et de la C.E.C.A., 214A
Bibliographie Méthodique Trimestrielle, 214A, 434, 704, 962, 1233
Bickershaw Colliery Explosion Report. *Cmnd. 1000.* 1051, 1171
Bickley, F., Report on the Manuscripts of the late Allan George Finch, 380
Bindweeds, 289
Big Ben, Story of, 958

Bilharziasis:
African Conference on, 741
Bibliography on, 1267
International Work in, 1268
2nd African Conference, 1270
Billard, G., Films recommended Children and Adolescents up to 16 years, 468
Binders, 823
Binney, G. (Leader U.K. Trade and Industrial Mission to Ghana). Report, 923
Biological Effects of Radiation, 232A, 986
Biological Methods for the Evaluation of Rodenticides, 560
Biological Standardization, Export Committee Report, 245A, 473, 741, 1000, 1269
Biological Substances, Requirements for, 1269
Biological Warfare, 123
Biology:
And Control of the American Whelk Tingle Urosalpinx cinerca (Say) on English Oyster Beds, 823
And Distribution of the Slipper Limpet Crepidula fornicata in Essex Rivers, 74
Of the Treponematoses, 471
Biostatistics, Inter-American Centre Report, 731
Bird Life in the Royal Parks, Report, 427, 957
Bird Paintings, Some Eighteenth Century, in the Library of Sir Joseph Banks, 828
Birds Collected by Mr. F. Shaw-Mayer in the Central Highlands of New Guinea, 81
Birkett, Sir Norman (Chairman: Committee of Privy Councillors). Report. *Cmnd. 283.* 268
Birley, E., Chesters Roman Fort, Northumberland, 1226
Birmingham Corporation Act, 543, 811
Birsay Early Christian and Norse Settlements Guide, 957
Birth of a Prince, 1190
Births. *See* Registrar General's Returns
Biscuits. Census of Production Report, 395, 1193
Bituminous Materials, Testing Mixers for, 384
Black, W. P. M., Field Studies of the Movement of Soil Mixture, 652
Blacker, R. W.:
Benthic Animals as Indicators of Hydrographic Conditions and Climatic Change in Svalbard Waters, 291
Echo-Sounding Experiments in the Barents Sea, 1087
Blackfriars Bridgehead Improvement Act, 1072
Blackhead, 556
Blackpool Building Society. Report on Affairs, 597
Blackpool Corporation Act, 543
Blackshaw, M. B., Utilisation of Space in Dwellings Report, 1262
Blacksmith. Career, 1152
Blackwood, A. C., British Micro-biology in British Commonwealth Countries, 826
Blaenhirwaun Colliery, Carmarthenshire, Explosion Report. *Cmnd. 287.* 268
Blagden, His Honour Judge J. B. (Chairman: Bankruptcy Law and Deeds of Arrangement Law Amendment Committee):
Cmnd. 221. 263
Minutes of Evidence, 663
Blast Furnaces. Census of Production Report, 394
Blaxter, J. H. S.:
Effect of Artificial Lights on Fish and Other Marine Organisms at Sea, 655
Herring in Aquaria, 656
Herring Rearing:
II. Effect of Temperature and Other Factors on Development, 388
III. Effect of Temperature and Other Factors on Myotome Counts, 388
Blew, J. O., Preservative Treatment of Fence Posts and Farm Timber, 420
Blinded Veterans of World War II and Korea, Occupations of, 421
Blindness in England Report, 121
Bloch, H. S.:
Programme for Technical Assistance in the Fiscal and Financial Field, 732
Revenue Administration and Policy in Israel, 732
Blokhine, P., Utilisation of Space in Dwellings Report, 1262
Blood, Sir H. (Chairman: Civil Service Commission). Report on Plan for British Caribbean Federation. *Cmd. 9619.* 36, 89
Blood Groups for Transfusion, Determination of ABO and Rh(D), 633
"Blue Crusader" Wreck Report, 931
Blue-Green Algae from the Middle Devonian of Rhynie, Aberdeenshire, 827
Blumhardt, J. F., Hindi Printed Books, Supplementary Catalogue, 562
Blunting of Wood-Cutting Edges, 166
Blyth Generating Station (Ancillary Powers) Act, 57
Blyth Harbour Act, 274
Board Mill Survey, Economic Study, U.K., 854
Boarding Education. Assistance with Cost. Report, 1116
Boarding-Out of Children. Memorandum on, 915
Boats:
And Harbour Craft, Operation of Small, 203

Boats (*continued*):
Pleasure, and Aircraft, Temporary Importation for Private Use of. *Cmnd. 650.* 790, 846
"Bobara" Wreck Report, 192
Body Building Foods, 1083
Boiler Explosions Acts:
Report on Working of the Acts, 927
Reports 185–6, 400–1, 670, 926, 927, 1196
Boilers for Nursery Use, 559
Boldt, G.:
Représentation des Travailleurs sur le Plan de l'Entreprise dans le Droit des Pays Membres de la C.E.C.A., 965
Stabilité de l'Emploi dans le Droit des Pays Membres de la C.E.C.A., 965
Bolivia:
Exchange of Notes with U.K. regarding the Reciprocal Abolition of Visas. *Cmnd. 1081.* 1056, 1118
International Customs Journal, 444
Overseas Economic Survey:
182
Addendum, 398
Bolton, W., Poultry Nutrition, 1085
Bombach, G., Comparison of National Output and Productivity of U.K. and U.S., 975
Bond, M., Historic Parliamentary Documents in the Palace of Westminster, 1145
Bonded Warehouses:
1108
Amending Supplements, 92, 305–6, 429, 574, 837
Bonner, W. Nigel, Introduced Reindeer to South Georgia, 571
Books:
And Other Material of Educational Nature. Agreement between U.K. and Israel for Importation. *Cmnd. 1185.* 1064, 1122
Exchange of Notes between U.K. and Yugoslavia regarding Import of British Books. *Cmd. 9726.* 41
Exhibitions, 1178
For All, 237A
Printed in Italy, etc. Short-Title Catalogue, 826
Production and Translations, 468
Relating to Agriculture, Horticulture, etc. Selected and Classified List of, 337
Boom Defence Equipment. Treasury Minute relative to Gift to N.A.T.O. *Cmnd. 910.* 807, 934
Boot and Shoe Census of Production Report, 179, 664
Bootle Corporation Act, 811
Borasio, L., Illustrated Glossary of Rice Processing Machines, 708
Border National Forest Park Guide, 596
Borneo, British Territories in. Photo-Poster, 131
Borough Market Junction, Railway Accident Report, 929, 1197
Borrie, W. D., Cultural Integration of Immigrants, 996
Borstals. *See* Prisons
Bosanquet, Dr. C. J. C. (Chairman: Reorganisation Committee on Pigs and Bacon). Report. *Cmd. 9795.* 45
Boswell, V. R., Growing Vegetables in Town and City, 951
"Bosworth" Wreck Report, 932
Botanic Gardens:
Edinburgh, 901
Kew Guide, 824
Botany Bulletins, 80, 562, 1095
Bothwell Castle, Lanarkshire Guide, 698
Bottle Tickets, 692
Boucher, C. A., Survey of Services Available to the Chronic Sick and Elderly, 332
Boundaries, Areas, Geographic Centres, and Attitudes of the United States and the Several States, 201
Boundary Commission Reports:
England, 15, 123, 772, 861, 1015, 1137
Scotland, 1016, 1186
Boundary Layer Effects in Aerodynamics, Proceedings of a Symposium, 155
Bournemouth Corporation Act, 1072
Bournemouth—Swanage Motor Road and Ferry Act, 57
Bouton, P. E., Studies on Beef Quality, 649
Bouvarel, Pierre, Sur le Reboisement et l'Amélioration des Forêts en Macédoine Yougoslave, 240A
Bovingdon Aerodrome Air Navigation Order, 402
Bow Porcelain, 1744 to 1776. Special Exhibition, 827
Bowen, G., Canada Overseas Economic Survey, 398
Bowes, H. L. (Chairman: Inland Waterways) Committee Report. *Cmnd. 486.* 531
Boys' Physical Training, 695
BP Trading Act, 274
Brachiopoda of the John Murray Expedition, Report on, 1097
Brachyopid Labryinthodonts, 80
Bracknell Development Corporation Report, 24, 130, 237, 506, 613, 870, 1147
Bradford Corporation Act, 810
Bradford Corporation (Trolley Vehicles) Order Confirmation Act, 543
Bradford Corporation (Trolley Vehicles) Order Confirmation Bill, 483
Bradford Corporation (Trolley Vehicles) Provisional Order Bill, 483, 518
Bradley, J. D., Records and Descriptions of Microlepidoptera from Lord Howe Island and Norfolk Island collected by Rennel Island Expedition, 80

Bradley, K., Britain's Purpose in Africa, 872
Brain, Sir R. (Chairman: Interdepartmental Committee on Drug Addiction) Report, 1133
Brambell, Professor F. W. R., Voles and Field Mice, 596
Bramley-Harker, P. (Chairman: Joint Standing Committee on Safety in Use of Power Presses) Report, [illegible]
Brand, W., Requirements and Resources of Scientific and Technical Personnel in 10 Asian Countries, 1266
Brass Manufacturers. Census of Production Report, 394
Brazier, J. D., Meranti Seraya and Allied Timbers, 166
Brazil:
And U.K. Protocol relating to General Agreement on Tariffs and Trade, 969
Economic Development, 430
Exchange of Notes with U.K. prolonging Articles of the Trade and Payments Agreement. *Cmnd. 323.* 270, 316
International Customs Journal, 713
Brazilian Traction Subsidiaries Act, 543
Bread and Flour:
Confectionery. Census of Production Report, 664
Food Standards Committee Report, 1087
Breeding:
Behaviour and Reproductive Cycle of the Weddell Seal, 571
Methods for Cattle, Pigs and Poultry in U.S., 445
Breuning, S., Révision du Genre Exocentrus Mulsant, 563
Brewing and Malting. Census of Production Report, 395
Brick-built Silo Construction, 74
Bricklayer, Career, 876
Bricks:
And Fireclay Census of Production Report, 663
Fireclay and Refractory. Census of Production Report, 1194
Packed, 905
Brickwork, Sulphate Attack on, 905
Bridge-deck Systems, Studies on, 1181
Bridgeman, Viscount. Chairman:
Advisory Committee of the Legal Aid and Advice Act. Report. *Cmnd. 962.* 1048, 1159
Advisory Committee on Financial Provisions of Legal Aid and Advice Act Report. *Cmnd. 918.* 808, 887
Advisory Committee on Operation and Finance of Legal Aid and Advice Act Report, 632
Law Society Advisory Committee Report, 359, 1159
Bridgeman, Viscount (*continued*):
Law Society on Operation and Finance of Legal Aid and Advice Act Report, 886
Bridges, Rt. Hon. Lord (Chairman: Royal Fine Art Commission) Report. *Cmnd. 909.* 807, 863
Bridport and Yeovil, Geology of the Country Around, 857
Briggs Motor Bodies Ltd., Report of a Court of Inquiry into Dispute. *Cmnd. 131.* 257
Brighton Corporation Act, 1072
Brinck, P., Ruwenzori Expedition, 828
Brindley, T. A., Pea Weevil and Methods for its Control, 420
Bristol Airport Orders, 402
Bristol Corporation Act, 57, 1072
Britain:
614
And the Gold Coast, 344
In Brief, 344, 872, 1149
Looks at the Commonwealth. Photo-Poster, 1149
Official Handbook, 131, 872, 1149
Britain's Economy, 50 facts, 344, 614, 1149
Britain's Forests, 112
Britain's Overseas Territories, 1149
Britain's Purpose in Africa, 872
British Agricultural History Film Strip, 288
British and Foreign State Papers, 104, 316, 588, 845
British Antarctic ("Terra Nova") Expedition. Natural History Report, 827
British Broadcasting Corporation:
Privileges Committee Report on Complaint, 225
Reports and Accounts. *Cmd. 9803.* 45, 161; *Cmnd. 267.* 267, 369; *Cmnd. 533.* 534, 640; *Cmnd. 834.* 802, 897; *Cmnd. 1174.* 1063, 1169
British Caribbean. A Fiscal Survey, 302
British Caribbean Bill, 3, 35
British Caribbean Federal Capital, Commission Report, 300
British Caribbean Federation Act, 55
British Caribbean Federation Plan:
Civil Service Commission Report. *Cmd. 9619.* 36, 89
Fiscal Commission Report. *Cmd. 9618.* 36, 89
Judicial Commission Report. *Cmd. 9620.* 36, 89
Report by the Conference. *Cmnd. 9733.* 41, 86
British Commonwealth:
Collections of Micro-Organisms. Directory of Collections and List of Species Maintained, 1094
Leaflets, 131, 344, 872, 1149
Scientific Office Publications, 79, 561, 826, 1094
Statisticians Conference Report, 296

British Council, Annual Report, 1094
British Cretaceous Pleurotomariidae, 1096
British European Airways Corporation:
Guarantee given on Loans proposed to be raised, 10, 17, 22, 25, 26, 27, 192, 224, 239, 406, 493, 500, 506, 510, 675, 767, 773, 780, 932, 1032, 1034, 1201
Report and Accounts, 24, 186, 237, 401, 505, 561, 670, 772, 826, 927, 1030, 1090
British Film Fund Agency. Report and Accounts, 773, 920, 1031, 1191
British Foreign Policy:
Documents on, 104, 316, 588, 847, 1120
Reference Pamphlet, 132
British Fortunes Reach Their Lowest Ebb, 1098, 1189
British Fracture Research in the United Kingdom Report, 277
British Guiana:
300
Arms, 87
Badges, 87
Colonial Reports, 88, 301, 570, 833
Constitutional Conference Report. *Cmnd. 998.* 1051, 1104
Photo-Poster, 131
British Guiana Today:
Film Strip, 132
Picture Set, 131
British Honduras:
Colonial Report, 87, 301, 569, 833, 1102
Conference Report. *Cmnd. 994.* 1050, 1104
Land Use Survey Team Report, 1103
Orders-in-Council, 1175
Picture Set, 1149
British Imperial Calendar and Civil Service List, 174, 390, 658, 917, 1189
British Industries Fair (Guarantees and Grants) Act Account, 771, 932
British Military Administration in the Far East, 82, 174
British Mites of the Subfamily Macrochelinae Trägårdh, 81
British Museum:
Natural History Publications, 80–2, 294–6, 562, 827, 1095
Publications, 79–80, 294, 561, 826, 1094
Quarterly, 79, 294, 561, 1094
British Nationality Act, 540
British Nationality Bill, 220, 250
British North America Act, 1071
British North America Bill, 1011, 1044
British Overseas Airways Corporation:
And the Merchant Navy and Airline Officers' Association. Report into a Dispute. *Cmnd. 105.* 256
Guarantee given on Loans proposed to be raised, 10, 17, 22, 27, 192, 223,
B.O.A.C. (*continued*):
239, 406, 493, 500, 507, 510, 675, 767, 773, 780, 932, 1032, 1034, 1201
Guarantee given on Stock Issued, 10, 192
Reports and Accounts, 24, 186, 237, 401, 505, 772, 927, 1030, 1090
British Parliament, 873
British Phosphate Commission. Reports and Accounts. *Cmd. 9743.* 42, 91; *Cmnd. 133.* 258, 304; *Cmnd. 511.* 532, 573; *Cmnd. 715.* 794, 835; *Cmnd. 1155.* 1062, 1106
British Railway Locomotive, 1803 to 1853, 648
British Railways:
British Transport Commission. Report. Reappraisal of the Plan for the Modernisation and Re-equipment. *Cmnd. 813.* 801, 927
Nationalised Industries Select Committee Report, 1029, 1141
British Rainfall. Report on Distribution, 152, 359, 887, 1160
British Regional Geology, 1131
British School, National Gallery Catalogue, 890
British School of Painting, Illustrations and Catalogue, 154
British Seaweeds, Handbook of, 828
British Solomon Islands:
And Rennell Island, Natural History of, 828
Colonial Report, 569, 1102
British Solomon Islands Protectorate:
Colonial Arms, 569
Order-in-Council, 1174
British South Atlantic Islands, Picture Set, 872
British Species of Sappaphis Matsumura, 293
British System of Taxation, 132, 615, 1150
British Transport Commission:
Exchange of Correspondence with Ministry of Transport and Civil Aviation. *Cmnd. 585.* 538, 672
Guarantee given on Loans proposed to be raised, 22, 26, 27, 224, 231, 236, 240, 493, 501, 507, 510, 681, 758, 768, 774, 780, 938, 1018, 1026, 1032, 1034, 1206
Guarantee given on Stock Issued, 17, 27, 232
Passengers Charges Scheme:
Interim Decision, 931
Transport Tribunal Order, 190
Transport Tribunal Proceedings, 191, 405, 931
Railway Merchandise Charges Scheme:
405
Confirmation, 401
Decision, 190
Proceedings, 191

BRI-CAN | 1956-60

BRI— INDEX 1956-60

British Transport Commission (*continued*):
  Railways Proposals. *Cmd. 9880.* 51, 186
  Report and Accounts, 20, 186, 233, 401, 504, 670, 770, 927, 1027, 1196
  Report on the Purchasing Procedure. *Cmnd. 262.* 266, 401
  Select Committee on Statutory Instruments Report, 244, 339
  Standing Orders Committee, Special Report—Petition for Additional Provision, 763, 866
British Transport Commission Act, 57, 274, 543, 810, 1072
British Transport Commission Charges Schemes:
  Harbours, 1199
  Harbours Order Confirmation, 674
  Harbours Transport Tribunal Proceedings, 674
  Inland Waterways:
    Order Confirmation, 674
    Transport Tribunal Proceedings, 674
  Passengers Transport Tribunal Proceedings, 674
  Railway Merchandise Alterations, 670
British Transport Commission Order Confirmation Act, 542, 543, 810
British Transport Commission Order Confirmation Bill:
  250, 786
  No. 2, 519
British Trials in Underground Gasification, 114
British Universities, Scientific Research in, 652, 1182
British Vascular Plants, List of, 562
British Virgin Islands. Colonial Report, 569, 1102
British West Indies. Film Strip, 344
British West Indies Today. Picture Set, 131
Briton Ferry Steel Company Ltd. Proposal to sell its Holding of Securities. *Cmd. 9740.* 41
Britton, E. B.:
  Beetles from the London Clay of Bognor Regis, Sussex, 1096
  Revision of Australian Chafers, 294
Broadcasting:
  Agreement between the Postmaster-General and the British Broadcasting Corporation. *Cmnd. 1066.* 1055, 1169
  Agreement Supplemental to Licence and Agreement. *Cmnd. 80.* 254, 369
  (Anticipation of Debates) Select Committee Report, 19, 125
Broadcasting Estimates:
  1956–57, 12
  1957–58, 226
  1958–59, 494, 676
  1959–60, 760, 933
  1960–61, 1019, 1201
Broadcasting Without Barriers, 994
Brock, G. R., Strength of Nailed Joints, 382
Brockwood and Farnborough Railway Accident Report, 403
Broderick, G. G., Television in Education, 691
Broiler House, 292
Bromley College and other Charities Confirmation Act, 1072
Bromley College and other Charities Confirmation Bill, 1007, 1042
Bromley Railway Accident Report, 188
Brook, A. J., Fertilization Experiments in Scottish Freshwater Lochs. Loch Kinardochy, 387
Brook, Sir N., Report on Misuse of Official Facilities. *Cmnd. 583.* 537
Brooke, E. M., Survey of Sickness, 1943 to 1952, 598
Brooks, C. E. P., Glazed Frost of January 1940, 152
Broughton, H. F., Mobile Tower Cranes for Town and Three Storey Building, 1181
Brown, A. F. C., Experimental Stress Analysis in U.S.A. and Canada, 167
Brown, A. W. A., Insecticide Resistance in Arthropods, 740
Brown Coal in Europe, Mining and Upgrading, 458
Brown Scale, 1083
Brown Skua of South Georgia, 89
Brown, T. J., Old Royal Library, 394
Brown Trout Research Supervisory Committee Report, 171, 387, 655, 914
Brown, W.:
  Burns. Fumigation with Methyl Bromide under Gas-Proof Sheets, 909
  Mines:
    And Quarries Report, 645
    Report, 116, 642
Brown, W. B.:
  Mines:
    And Quarries Report, 645
    Report, 642
Browning, E., British Mites of the Subfamily Macrochelinae Trägårdh, 81
Brucellosis, Expert Committee Report, 741
Brue Valley and Northmoor, Somerset, Report, 71
Brüelia:
  (Mallophaga) Species Infesting the Corvidae, Revision of the, 80
  Revision of, 295
Brummel, L., Union Catalogues, their Problems and Organisation, 237A
Brunei:
  Colonial Report, 86, 301, 570, 833, 1102
  Flat Badge, 1103
Brunt, Sir David (Chairman: Study Committee) Report on Basic Design Temperatures for Space-Heating, 208

INDEX 1956-60 —BUR

Brunton, J. S. (Chairman: Working Party on Curriculum of Senior Secondary School) Report, 911
Brushes and Brooms. Census of Production Report, 396
Brussels Convention, Activities of the Council and the Implementation of, 213
Brussels Nomenclature:
  214A
  Alphabetical Index, 962
  Classification of Chemicals, 574
  Omnibus Corrigenda, 704
Brussels Treaty. Western European Union Agreement. *Cmnd. 388.* 524, 595
Bryan, D. A., New Zealand, Overseas Economic Survey, 182
Bryant, G. E., Ruwenzori Expedition, 828
Buchanan, C. D., Report on Nuclear Power Station at Trawsfynydd, 645
Buckinghamshire County Council Act, 274
Buckle, D., Child Guidance Centres, 1268
Buckrakes and Green-crop Loaders, 823
Bucks Water Board Act, 811
Buddhism and the Race Question, 737
Bude-Stratton Urban District Council Act, 1072
Budget. *See* Financial Statement
Budget Estimates:
  And Information Annex, General Assembly, 229A
  General Assembly, 726, 983, 984
  United Nations, 1254, 1255
Budget Management. Report of the Workshop, 225A
Budgetary Control, 974
Budgetary Structure and Classification of Government Accounts, 1251
Budgets Familaux des Ouvriers de la C.E.C.A., 1234
Buedeler, W., International Geophysical Year, 469
Bufton, A. W. J., Industrial and Economic Microbiology in North America, 651
Building. *See* Post-War Building Studies
Building:
  And Civil Engineering Industries. Report on Safety and Health. *Cmnd. 953.* 1048, 1158
  And Contracting Census of Production Report, 180, 665
  And Repairing Royal Palaces and Castles. Accounts of Masters of Works, 389
  Apprenticeship and Training Council Report, 427
  Bulletins:
    100, 313, 585, 842, 1115
  Byelaws, 869
  Economics, Cost Planning, 648
  For the Future:
    Film Strip, 132
    Picture Set, 131
  Industry, Incentives in, 909
Building (*continued*):
  Legislation in Scotland Report. *Cmnd. 269.* 267, 329
  Materials and Structures Reports, 419
  Materials Census of Production Report, 663
  Modular Co-ordination in, 223A
  Principles of Modern, 909
  Research Report, 164, 381, 648, 905, 1178
  Research Station Digests Index, 164, 381, 429, 648, 905, 1178
  Science Abstracts, 165, 381–2, 429, 649, 906, 1179
  Standardization and Modular Co-ordination, 1257
Building (Scotland) Act, 809
Building (Scotland) Bill, 514, 516, 520, 521, 605, 747, 748, 749, 756, 785, 863
Building Sites, Organisation of, 909
Building Societies Act, 1070
Building Societies Bill, 1006, 1007, 1010, 1029, 1036, 1043, 1044, 1140
Building Societies. Chief Registrar's Report, 114, 326, 597, 855, 1130
Buildings:
  Dampness in, 956
  For Grain Drying and Storage, 1087
  For the Storage of Crops in Warm Climates, 1183
  Model Byelaws, 130
  Registered or disused for Marriages, 118, 328
  See also Official List
Bulbs:
  Scale Mite, 71
  Spring Flowering, 951
Bulganin. Correspondence with Sir Anthony Eden. *Cmnd. 182.* 261
Bulgaria. Exchange of Notes with U.K. concerning Settlement of Financial Matters. *Cmnd. 752.* 797, 845
Bulgarian Property:
  Accounts of the Administrator. *Cmnd. 464.* 529, 676
  In the U.K. Accounts of the Administrator. *Cmnd. 772.* 799, 932; *Cmnd. 979.* 1049, 1200
Bulinus Jousseaumei. Studies on the Structure and Taxonomy of, 295
Bulk Storage of Potatoes in Buildings, 1085
Bulletin for Libraries, 994
Bulletin Statistique, European Coal and Steel Community, 214, 434, 704, 963, 1233
Bullfinch, 1083
Bulmer, B. F., Rainfall on Malta, 1162
Buoys and Shore Marks for Inland Waterways in Asia and the Far East, Uniform System of, 733
Burd, A. C., On the Herring of the Southern North Sea, 291

BUR— INDEX 1956-60

Burdette, R. J., Marketing Livestock and Meat, 1237
Burgess, A. H., Hop Growing and Drying, 290
Burgess, G. H. O., Temperature of British Fish During Distribution in Summer, 910
Burgess, W. R., Remodelled Economic Organisation Report, 1248
Burma:
  Agreement with Hong Kong for Supply of Cotton Textiles. *Cmnd. 738.* 796, 846
  Exchange of Notes with U.K.:
    Amending the Burmese Schedule of Routes annexed to the Air Transport Agreement. *Cmnd. 83.* 254, 316
    Concerning Export of Cotton Textiles. *Cmnd. 724.* 795, 846
    Concerning the Export of Cotton Textiles and/or Yarn and the Acceptance of Raw Cotton from the United States. *Cmd. 9860.* 50, 104
  Overseas Economic Survey, 398
Burma-Yunnan Boundary. Exchange of Notes concerning Boundary. *Cmnd. 40.* 54, 104.
Burnham Committee Report. *See* Teachers' Salaries
Burrow, F. J. (Chairman: Agricultural Land Commission), Report on Land in Brue Valley and Northmoor, Somerset, 71
Burt, C. S. S., Report on Allegations relating to Carlisle and District State Management Scheme. *Cmnd. 168.* 260, 333
Burton Agnes Old Manor House, Yorkshire, Guide, 207
Burton, M., Sponges, 1097
Bury, J. P. T.:
  Chinese Question, 1929–1931, 1120
  Documents on British Foreign Policy, 588, 847, 1120
  German Affairs:
    1120
    And Plebiscite Problems, 1120
Bush Fruits, 821
Bushe-Fox, J. P., Richborough Castle Guide, 208
Business Education Series. *See* Vocational Division Bulletin
Business Leadership, Education for, 221A
Business Management, European Guide to General Courses, 1247
Bute Educational Trust Scheme, Memorandum, 1184
Butcher, R. W., Introductory Account of the Smaller Algae of British Coastal Waters, 823
Butler, C. G., Beekeeping, 290
Butler, H. E., Spectrophotometric Measurements of Early Type Stars, 648, 1178
Butler, Professor J. R. M., Grand Strategy, 296
Butler, P. M.:
  Contributions to the Odontology of Oreopithecus, 828
  Erinaceidae from the Miocene of East Africa, 81
  Insectivora and Chiroptera from the Miocene Rocks of Kenya Colony, 295
Butler, R.:
  Chinese Question, 1929–1931, 1120
  Documents on British Foreign Policy, 316, 588, 847, 1120
  German Affairs:
    1120
    And Plebiscite Problems, 1120
Butler, R. A., Documents on British Foreign Policy, 104
Butterflies from Malaya. New or Little Known, 827
Butter-Making. Farmhouse, 289
Byelaws, Model, 72, 74, 130, 342, 612
Bykov, D. V., Working Metals by Electro-Sparking, 168
Bynea Steel Works Limited. Proposal to Sell Holdings of Securities. *Cmnd. 188.* 261
Byssinosis:
  Report of the Industrial Injuries Advisory Council. *Cmd. 9673.* 37, 158
  Within the Cotton Industry. Industrial Injuries Advisory Council Review. *Cmnd. 1095.* 1057, 1167

C

C.A.A. Technical Manual, 199
Cabbage and Savoy:
  Commercial Production of, Film Strip, 288
  Winter, 555
Cabbage Aphid, 1083
Cabbage Root Fly, 70, 288
Cabbage, Spring, 288
Cabinet Office Publications, 82, 296, 565, 828, 1098
Cable and Wireless Limited, Accounts and Report. *Cmd. 9830.* 47, 161; *Cmnd. 239.* 265, 369; *Cmnd. 502.* 532, 640; *Cmnd. 839.* 802, 897; *Cmnd. 1116.* 1059, 1169
Cable System. *See* Submarine Telecommunications Cable System
Caborn, J. M., Shelterbelts and Microclimate, 325
Cacao, Production, Price and Consumption, 241A

INDEX 1956-60 —CAN

Cadbury, P. S. (Chairman: Royal Commission on Local Government in Greater London), Minutes of Evidence, 1176
Cade, R. C., Handbook of British Colonial Stamps, 305
Cadmium Poisoning. Industrial Injuries Advisory Council Report. *Cmd. 9674.* 38, 158
Caernarvon Castle Postcards, 697
Caernarvonshire:
  Inventory of Ancient Monuments, 1175
  Royal Commission Report on Ancient Monuments. *Cmnd. 1138.* 1060, 1140
Caernarvonshire, East:
  Cantref of Arllechwedd and the Commote of Creuddyn. Survey and Inventory, 162
  Royal Commission on Ancient Monuments Report. *Cmd. 9762.* 43
Caerphilly Castle, Glamorgan, Guide, 698
Cahiers Mensuels de Documentation Européenne, 1233
Caine, Sir Sydney. Chairman:
  Fiscal Commission. Report on Plan for a British Caribbean Federation. *Cmd. 9618.* 36, 89
  Grassland Utilisation Committee. Report. *Cmnd. 547.* 535
Cairns, Sir David (Chairman: Monopolies and Restrictive Practices Commission), Reports, 15, 20, 22, 24, 221, 223
Calculation in the Median Sky Wave Field Strength in Tropical Regions, 910
Calculations of Deformations of Welded Metal Structures, 649
Calder Hall, 949
Calder, N., What They Read and Why, 909
Calderbank, P. H., Chemical Engineering in the U.S.A., 167
Calendar of:
  Close Rolls, 161
  Inquisitions, Miscellaneous, 378
  Inquisitions Post Mortem, 161
  Liberate Rolls, 1175
  State Papers. Domestic Series, 1175
  Treasury Books, 161, 646, 901
Calf Rearing, 1085
Calf Slaughter. Circular, 1086
Calibration of Temperature Measuring Instruments, 636
Call up of Men to the Forces. *Cmnd. 175.* 261, 347
Calorie Requirements Committee Report, 437
Calver, M. A.:
  Economic Geology of the Stirling and Clackmannan Coalfield, Scotland, Area North of the River Forth, 119
  Geology of Midlothian Coalfield, 599
Calvinistic Methodist or Presbyterian Church of Wales (Amendment) Act, 811
Cambodia. International Commission for Supervision and Control. Report. *Cmd. 9671.* 37, 104; *Cmnd. 253.* 266. 316; *Cmnd. 526.* 534, 589; *Cmnd. 887.* 806, 846
Cambrian Forests, 854
Cambridge, City of:
  Ancient Monuments of the City. Royal Commission Report. *Cmnd. 743.* 796, 863
  Inventory of the Historical Monuments, 902
Cameron, Lord (Chairman: Court of Inquiry into Dispute of the Port Transport Industry), Report. *Cmnd. 510.* 532
Cameron, State of. International Customs Journal, 974
Cameron, Hon. Lord. Report of Court of Inquiry into Dispute at Briggs Motor Bodies Ltd. *Cmnd. 131.* 257
Cameron, J. M., Methods of Testing Small Fire Extinguishers, 419
Cameron, R.:
  Mix Design for Vibrated Concrete, 428
  Vibrated Concrete in Building, 427
Cameroons, Reports Under:
  French Administration, 236A
  United Kingdom Administration, 86, 236A, 300, 569, 832
Cammell Laird and Company Act, 57, 543
Camp Stoves and Fireplaces, 199
Campaign in Italy, 1098, 1189
Campaigns, Royal Air Force Medical Services, 602, 657
Campbell, Dr. Bruce, Crested Tit, 596
Campbell, R. N., Effect of Flooding on the Growth Rate of Brown Trout in Loch Tummel, 387
Canada:
  And United States Economic Conditions, 221A, 446, 714, 715, 975, 1246
  Exchange of Letters with U.K. on Social Security. *Cmnd. 925.* 1046, 1106
  Exchange of Notes with U.K. amending the Air Services Agreement. *Cmnd. 543.* 535, 670; *Cmnd. 1231.* 1068, 1090, 1118
  Financial Agreement to amend the Financial Agreement with U.K. *Cmnd. 121.* 257, 407
  Foreign Trade Statistical Bulletin, 222A, 447, 717, 977
  International Customs Journal, 444, 714, 973
  Overseas Economic Survey, 398
  Submarine Telecommunication Cable System. Agreement with U.K. and Others, 897

1956-60 | CAN-CHI

CAN— *INDEX 1956–60*

Canal, Dock and Harbour Undertakings. Census of Production Report, 396
Canberra Symposium Proceedings, Climatology and Microclimatology, 735
Cancellation of All Outstanding Claims. Exchange of Notes between U.K. and Cyrenaica. *Cmnd. 691.* 793, 847
Cancer:
  Statistical Review Supplement, 328, 598
  Statistics for England and Wales, 598
  Statistics. *See* Health Statistics
Cancer of the Lung:
  Epidemiology of, 1269
  Quest into the Environmental Causes of, 203
  See Tobacco Smoking
Cancer of the Mouth and Respiratory Tract, 419
Cannibalism and Feather Picking in Poultry, 1084
Canteens and Messrooms for Small Factories, 630
Canterbury and District Water Act, 1072
Canvas Goods and Sacks Census of Production Report, 664
Cape Observatory Annals, 904
"Cape St. Mary." Gift of Fishery Research Vessel, to Government of Hong Kong. *Cmnd. 817.* 801, 934
Capel Garmon, Chambered Long Cairn, Denbighshire Guide, 698
Capercailzie, 113
Capital Expenditure:
  Continuance of Restriction. Circular, 129
  On Agricultural or Forestry Buildings, Allowances, 873
Capital Funds for Industrial Development in Europe, Supply of, 449
Capital, International Flow of Private, 984
Capital Investment:
  Circular, 611
  In the Coal, Gas and Electricity Industries. *Cmnd. 132.* 258, 370, 386; *Cmnd. 415.* 526, 641, 654; *Cmnd. 713.* 794, 898, 913; *Cmnd. 993.* 1050, 1170
Capital Movements. Code of Liberalisation, 1245
Capitate Hydroids and Medusae, Evolutionary Trends in the Classification, 295
Caravan Sites and Control of Development:
  Circular, 1146
  Model Standards, 1146
Caravan Sites and Control of Development Act, 1070
Caravan Sites and Control of Development Bill, 1008, 1009, 1010, 1026, 1037, 1042, 1043, 1044, 1140
Caravans as Homes. Report. *Cmnd. 872.* 805, 868
Carbon Bisulphide Vapour, 875
Cardboard Boxes, Cartons and Fibreboard Packing Cases. Census of Production Report, 395, 1194
Cardigan Police Force. *See* Carmarthen
Cardiganshire Constabulary. Report. *Cmnd. 251.* 266, 333
Cardiovascular Diseases and Hypertension, Expert Committee Report, 1000
Care of the Eyes, 420
Careers:
  Choice of, 136, 347, 617, 875, 876, 1152
  For Men and Women, 136, 347, 617
  Guide, 136, 876
"Carency" Wreck Report, 675
Caribbean:
  See British Caribbean
  Organisation. Agreement for Establishment. *Cmnd. 1144.* 1061, 1118
  Region. Air Navigation Plan, 1241
Carisbrooke Castle Guide, 208
Carlisle and District State Management. Inquiry into Allegations. Report. *Cmnd. 168.* 260, 333
Carlton Approved School. Report of Inquiry into Disturbances. *Cmnd. 937.* 1047, 1138
Carmarthen and Cardigan, Proposed Compulsory Amalgamation of Police Forces. *Cmnd. 374.* 523, 605
Carnegie Park and Scott Trust Scheme:
  385
  Memorandum, 385, 911
  Order-in-Council, 1184
Carnovsky, Leon, Report on a Programme of Library Education in Israel, 240A
Caroli Linnaei Systema Naturae, 81
Carpenter, G. A., Preservation of Fish and Fish Offal for Oil and Meal Manufacture, 907, 1183
Carpets. Census of Production Report, 395, 1194
Carr, R. (Chairman: National Joint Advisory Council Sub-Committee), Report on Training for Skill, 630
Carreg Cennan Castle, Carmarthenshire, Guide, 1226
Carriage of Dangerous Goods and Explosives in Ships Report. Amendments, 186, 401, 670, 927, 1196
Carriage of Dangerous Goods. European Agreement. *Cmnd. 734.* 796, 850
Carriage of Goods by Rail, International Convention. *Cmd. 9889.* 52, 186; 403, 536, 593, 671; *Cmnd. 1124.* 1059, 1197
Carriage of Passengers and Luggage by Rail. International Convention. *Cmd. 9852.* 49, 186; *Cmnd. 1125.* 1059, 1197
Carrington, Sir W. S.:
  Hide & Co. Ltd., Investigation into Affairs, 921
  Investigation into Affairs of Wright Hamer Textiles Ltd. Report, 1192

INDEX 1956–60 —CEN

Carroll, O. J., Korea, 1951–53, 421
Carrots, Parsnips, Parsley. Chemical Weed Control, 1084
Carruthers, J. F. S., Heat Penetration in the Pressure of Plywood, 907
Carter, Professor C. F. (Chairman: Economics Committee of the Council for Scientific and Industrial Research), Report, 1180
Cartographic Conference for Asia and Far East, Proceedings, 451, 992
Carts, Perambulators, etc., Census of Production Report, 394
Cartwright, A., Noise in Three Groups of Flats with Different Floor Insulations, 909
Cartwright, K. St. G., Decay in Timber and Its Prevention, 906
Case Commentary on the Income Tax Acts. Supplement, 132, 873
Case Notes, 857
Case, R. A. M., Cancer Statistics, E. & W. 598
Casey, R., London and Thames Valley, British Regional Geology, 1131
Caskets from Cordoba, 1222
Cassava and Cassava Products in Rural Industries, Processing of, 435
Cast Acrylic Sheet, 918
Castle Gate Congregational Church Burial Ground (Nottingham) Act, 57
Catalogue of Printed Books, Maps and Music, Rules for Compiling, 1094
Catering:
  Hotel Keeping and Arrangements and Conditions for the Award of National Diplomas, 843
  Wages Commission Report, 26, 136, 239, 347, 773, 876
Catherine McCaig's Trust Scheme, Memorandum, 1184
Cathodic, Galvanic Anode and Drainage Protection of Main Gas Pipe Lines against Underground Corrosion, 382
Cattedown Wharves Act, 274
Cattle:
  Crush, 292
  Diseases of, 821
  Dog and Poultry Foods. Census of Production Report, 395
  For Slaughter. *See* Export of Live Cattle
  Yards, 1087
Caunter, C. F.:
  Cycles, Handbook of Collection, 648
  History and Development. Light Cars, 648
  History and Development of Cycles, 164
  Motor Cars, Handbook of Collection, 1178
  Motor Cycles, 164, 648
Cavitation in Hydrodynamics. Proceedings of a Symposium, 155
Cayman Islands:
  Arms, 569
  Colonial Report, 301, 1102
  Flag Badge, 833
Cayman Islands and Turks and Caicos Islands Act, 540
Cayman Islands and Turks and Caicos Islands Bill, 250, 479
Celluloid and Cellulose Nitrate Compositions Report, 659
Cement. Census of Production Report, 394, 1194
Cement Industry:
  In Europe Statistics, 445, 978, 1250
  Recent Developments in O.E.E.C. Countries, 224A
Cement or Lime Content of Cement—or Lime-stablized Soil, Determination of, 1182
Cements other than Ordinary Portland Cement, 426
Cemeteries Model Bye-Law, 342
Census:
  1951, 118
  England and Wales, 118, 327
  Isle of Man, 327
  Jersey, Guernsey, etc., 327
  Report, England and Wales, 856
  Reports, 327, 597
  Scotland, 119
Census of Distribution and other Services Report, 923
Census of Production:
  Index of Products, 920
  Introductory Notes, 923
  Reports, 179–80, 180, 394–6, 663, 1193
  Summary Tables, 179, 394, 663, 921
Census of Traffic on Main International Traffic Arteries, 720
Central Advisory Water Committee:
  Report, 868
  Sub-Committee Report, 1146
Central After-Care Association Council, Report, 123, 333, 603, 861, 1137
Central and Scottish Health Services Councils Standing Medical Advisory Committees Report, 331
Central Electricity Authority Guarantee given on Loans proposed to be raised, 13, 17, 22, 26, 27, 224, 231, 235, 239
Central Electricity Generating Board. Report and Accounts, 775, 898, 1033, 1170
Central Government and Finance Estimates:
  1956–57, 12
  1957–58, 226
  1958–59, 494
  1959–60, 759, 933
  1960–61, 1019, 1201

CEN— *INDEX 1956–60*

Central Health Services Council:
  Report, 22, 121, 122, 331, 332, 303, 602, 770, 859, 891, 1133
  Standing Nursing Advisory Committee. Report on the Design of Nurses' Uniforms, 859
Central Land Board:
  1098
  Publications, 296
  Report, 20, 129, 237, 340, 386, 506, 600, 610; *Cmnd. 908.* 807, 858, 871
Central Office of Information:
  Publications 131–2, 872
  Select Committee on Estimates. Report, 1029, 1143
Central Organisation for Defence. *Cmnd. 476.* 530, 676
Central Statistical Office Publications, 83, 296–7, 565, 829, 1098
Central Transport Consultative Committee:
  Great Britain Report, 20, 186, 497, 670, 768, 928, 1023, 1196
  Lewes–East Grinstead Branch Railway Report. *Cmnd. 360.* 523, 671
  Report, 229, 401
Centrocneminae, A new Sub-family of the Reduviidae, 80
Cephalo chordata, 296
Cephalopoda of Madeira, Records and Distribution, 80
Cereals:
  Choosing Selective Weed-Killers for, 820
  Contracts for sale of, 721
  Deficiency Payments Scheme, 822
  Harvesting and Storage of, 450
Cerebral Vascular Disease and Strokes, 421
Ceremonial (Provisional) Amendments, 423, 694
Certificates:
  And Diplomas, Arrangements and Conditions for the Award of, 586
  Of Airworthiness. Multilateral Agreement. *Cmnd. 1078.* 1056, 1118
Ceylon:
  Exchange of Letters with U.K. Service Establishments in Ceylon. *Cmnd. 197.* 262, 307
  International Customs Journals, 973, 1244
Chafers. *See* Australian Chafers
Chagas' Disease. Study Group Report, 1270
Chaguaramas Joint Commission Report, 569
Chain, Nail, Screw and Miscellaneous Forgings Census of Production Report, 664
Chaldaen Kings Chronicles, 79
Chalmers, R. A., Chromiferous Ultrabasic Rocks of Eastern Sierra Leone, 572
Chamberlain, R. N., Report on Confidential Enquiries into Maternal Deaths in England and Wales, 1130
Chamberlin, J. C., Pea Weevil and Its Control, 420
Champion, F. J., Preservative Treatment of Fence Posts and Farm Timber, 420
Chance, Sir Hugh (Chairman: Technical Education Advisory Panel), Report, 586
Chancellor, A. P., Control of Aquatic Weeds and Algae, 556
Chancellor, R. J., Seedlings of Common Weeds, 1085
Chancery Chambers and the Chancery Registrar's Office. Report of the Committee. *Cmnd. 967.* 1049, 1159
Chandler, K. N., Reflex Reflectors, 652
Chandler, M. E. J.:
  Oligocene Flora of Bovey Tracey Lake Basin, Devonshire, 563
  Plant Remains of the Hengistbury and Barton Beds, 1096
Chandos, J., London Airport, Text, 187
Changes in Composition of Military Forces, 694
Channel Islands (Church Legislation) Measure, 1931 (Amendment):
  Measure, 217, 275, 297
  Report, 217, 297
Chapel-en-le-Frith (South) Railway Accident Report, 403
Chaplains, Appointment, Pay and Conditions of Service of, 693
Chaplais, Pierre, Treaty Rolls, 162
Charities Act, 1070
Charities and Kindred Bodies, Rating of. *Cmnd. 831.* 802, 871
Charities Bill, 1004, 1006, 1010, 1029, 1037, 1042, 1043, 1140
Charity Commission:
  Form 829, 1099
  Report, 83, 297, 565, 929, 1099
Charity of Francis Barker and Certain other Charities (City of York) Bill, 4, 34
Charles Beattie Indemnity Act, 55
Charles Beattie Indemnity Bill, 1, 33
Charlesworth, D., Roman Site at Wall Museum Guide, 698
Charlesworth, G., Road Junctions in Rural Areas, 1182
Charlton, J.:
  Chiswick House and Gardens Guide, 698
  Kew Palace Guide, 208
  Lancaster House Guide, 427
  Osborne House Guide, 1227
Charollais Cattle. Report of the Committee on the Proposed Experimental Importation. *Cmnd. 1140.* 1060, 1082, 1088
Chart of all the Oceans, 225A
Charter and Rules, Western Europe Union, 470

INDEX 1956–60 —CHI

Charter of the United Nations, Guide to, 720
Charts for the Hydraulic Design of Channels and Pipes, 909
Cheese:
  Processed, and Cheese Spread Report, 74
  Soft, 289
  Technology, Advances in, 706
Cheesemaking, Starters for, 71, 555, 821
Chemical Analyses of Igneous Rocks, Metamorphic Rocks and Minerals, 119
Chemical Composition of Fish Tissues, 907
Chemical Compounds used in Agriculture and Food Storage. Circular, 357
Chemical Effects of Radiation, 986
Chemical Engineer, Function and Training of. International Conference, 223A
Chemical Engineering in the U.S.A., 167
Chemical Fertilisers. Monopolies Commission. Report on the Supply, 1013, 1193
Chemical Industry in Europe, 450, 719, 978, 1250
Chemical Research Board Report, 382
Chemical Warfare:
  Casualties, Treatment of, 422
  Defence Series, 420
Chemical Weed Control:
  In Carrots, Parsnip and Parsley, 1084
  In Flower Crops, 1084
  In Horticultural Crops, 1084
  In Onions and Leeks, 1084
Chemical Weed-Killers for Bindweed, 1088
Chemicals:
  Census of Production Report, 179
  Classification of, in Brussels Nomenclature, 574, 836
  (General) Census of Production Report, 663
Chemistry Research Board Report, 165, 649
Chemotherapy and Chemoprophylaxis in Tuberculosis Control. Report, 741
Chepstow Castle Postcard, 697
Cheque Endorsement. Report. *Cmnd. 3.* 52, 193
Cheques Act, 272
Cheques Bill, 217
Cheques Bill No. 2, 247, 248
Chequers Estate Act, 540
Chequers Estate Bill, 485, 519
Chertsey Urban District Council Act, 57
Chest Clinics, 859
Chesters Roman Fort, Northumberland Guide, 1226
Chestnut. *See* Growth and Yield
Chests of Drawers and Commodes, 1222
Chettle, G. H.:
  Hampton Court Palace Guide, 208
  Palais de Hampton Court, 1227
  Triangular Lodge, Rushton, Guide, 208
Chevening Estate Act, 809
Chevening Estate Bill, 751, 795
Chick Rearing, Infra-Red Heat for, 200, 1083
Chickens:
  Hybrid, 822
  Rearing of, 72
  Table, 821
Chicory as a Root Crop, 820
Chief Land Registrar's Report, 886
Chief Medical Officer's Report. *Cmnd. 871.* 805, 860
Child Cyclists:
  Committee on Road Safety Report, 186
  Working Party Report, 670
Child Declaration of Rights. *Cmnd. 1073.* 1056, 1127
Child Guidance Centres, 1268
Child Migration to Australia. Report. *Cmd. 9832.* 47, 91
Childbirth, Emergency. Welfare Section Training Bulletin, 861
Childe, Professor V. Gordon, Ancient Monuments, Scotland, Guide, 956
Children:
  And Young Persons. Report. *Cmnd. 1191.* 1065, 1139
  Care of Memorandum, 123
  Employment of, in the Potato Harvest. Report. *Cmd. 9738.* 41
  From the National Gallery Paintings, 154
  In Britain, 873
  In Hospital. Report on Their Welfare, 859
  Institutional Care of, 457
  In The Care of Local Authorities:
    Cmd. 9881. 51, 123
    E. and W. *Cmnd. 411.* 526, 603; *Cmnd. 632, 914.* 788, 808, 861; *Cmnd. 1237.* 1068, 1137
    Scotland. *Cmnd. 461.* 529, 654; *Cmnd. 779.* 799, 913
  Jurisdiction affecting. Report of Committee on Conflicts. *Cmnd. 842.* 803, 887
  Memorandum on Boarding-out of, 915
  Research relating to, 419
  Work of UNICEF, 724
Children Act, 540
Children and Young Persons Act, 55
Children and Young Persons (Registered Clubs) Bill, 247, 250
Children Bill, 479, 480, 481, 485, 505, 512, 519, 605
Children's Bureau:
  Folder, 692
  Publications, 419–20, 692
Children's Fund Report:
  453
  Of the Executive Board, 1253
  United Nations, 227A

CHI-COA | 1956-60

CHI— INDEX 1956–60

Children's Homes. Memorandum, 915
Chile:
Exchange of Notes with U.K. concerning a Loan. *Cmnd. 1195.* 1065, 1118
International Customs Journal, 445, 714, 1244
Military Service Agreement with U.K. *Cmd. 9668.* 37, 104
Overseas Economic Survey, 667
Chimneys:
For Domestic Boilers and Other Slow Burning Appliances, 1226
Smoky, 697
China:
Exchanges of Notes with U.K. and Burma concerning the Burma–Yunnan Boundary. *Cmnd. 40.* 54, 104
Republic of. International Customs Journal, 1244
China and Earthenware. Census of Production Report, 394
China, W. E., Check-List and Keys to the Families and Sub-families of Hemiptera-Heteroptera, 827
Chinese Family and Marriage in Singapore, 301
Chinese Manuscripts from Tunhuang Descriptive Catalogue, 562
Chinese Porcelain of the Ch'ing Dynasty, 692
Chinese Question, 1929–1931, 1120
Chinley Railway Accident Report, 672
Chinn, G. M., Machine Gun, 202
Chintz, English, Exhibition, 1223
Chipping Sodbury Town Trust Scheme Confirmation Act, 1072
Chipping Sodbury Town Trust Scheme Confirmation Bill, 1007, 1042
Chironomidae of Africa South of the Sahara, Study of, 80, 562, 563
Chironomidae, Study of the New Zealand, 827
Chiropodist. Careers, 1152
Chiswick House and Gardens Guide, 698
Chiva, L., Rural Communities, Problems, Methods and Types of Research, 996
Chlorophora Report, 300
Choice of Careers, 136, 347, 617, 875, 876 1152
Cholera, 998
Choosing Selective Weed-Killers for Cereals, 820
Choosing Your Career, 1152
Christchurch Castle, Hampshire, Guide, 208
Christie, J. M.:
Alignment Charts and Form Height Tables for Determining Stand Volumes of Conifers, Oak and Beech, 596
Code of Sample Plot Procedure, 854
Christie J. M. (*continued*):
Preliminary Yield Table for Poplar, 854
Provisional Yield Tables for:
Oakand Beech in Great Britain, 596
Western Hemlock in Great Britain, 325
Christmas Island Act, 540
Christmas Island Bill, 480, 518
Chromiferous Ultrabasic Rocks of Eastern Sierra Leone, 572
Chronic Sick and Elderly. Survey of Services available, 332
Chronological Table of Statutes, 175, 390, 658, 918, 1190
Chrysanthemums, 290
Church Assembly:
Measures, 59, 812, 829
Publications, 83
Church Funds Investment:
Ecclesiastical Committee Report, 478 566
Measure, 478, 544, 566
Church of England. Measures passed by National Assembly, 1073
Church of Scotland (General Trustees) Order Confirmation Act, 542
Church of Scotland (General Trustees) Order Confirmation Bill, 249
Church of Scotland Home for Children (Hawthornbrae) Trust:
Order-in-Council, 385
Scheme, 285
Church of Scotland (Property and Endowments) Act, 272
Church of Scotland (Property and Endowments) Bill, 214, 247
Church of Scotland Trust Order Confirmation Act, 811
Church of Scotland Trust Order Confirmation Bill, 520
Church Property (Miscellaneous Provisions) Measure:
1006, 1073, 1099
Ecclesiastical Committee Report, 1006, 1099
Church, R., Royal Parks of London, 208
Church Schools (Assistance by Church Commissioners):
Ecclesiastical Committee Report, 478, 566
Measure, 478, 544, 566
Churchill Endowment Fund for Exchange Students between U.K. and Denmark. Accounts and Statements. *Cmnd. 885.* 806, 847
Chysauster, Cornwall, Guide, 1226
Cichlid Fishes in Lake Victoria, Monotypic Genera of, 81
Cilgerran Castle, Pembrokeshire, Guide, 426
Cinemas. Recommendations on Safety in, 123

INDEX 1956–60 —CIV

Cinematograph Acts, Circular. Corrigenda, 123
Cinematograph Film Printing. Census of Production Report, 396
Cinematograph Film Production Census of Production Report, 180, 665
Cinematograph Film Production (Special Loans) Acts:
Accounts, 15, 180, 232, 396, 496, 665, 769, 772, 921, 1016, 1191
Statement, 921, 1029, 1191
Cinematograph Films Act, 272, 1070
Cinematograph Films Bill, 7, 214, 215, 229, 242, 247, 336, 783, 786, 787, 1003, 1014, 1140
Cinematograph Films Council Report, 23, 180, 236, 396, 505, 665, 771, 923, 1032, 1194
Cinematograph Fund Account, 23, 244, 514, 646, 780, 901
Circular Saws, 907
Circulars and Administrative Memoranda, 1115
Citizen Participation in Political Life, 1265
Citizenship Education for Girls, 995
"Citrine" Wreck Report, 192
Citrus Fruit, General Conditions for International Sale, 720
City of Aberdeen Educational Endowments Scheme:
Memorandum, 653
1958, Order-in-Council, 911
City of London (Guild Churches) Act, 1072
City of London (Various Powers) Act 57, 274, 543, 811, 1072
"City of Sydney" Wreck Report, 192, 406
Civil Aerodromes and Ground Services. Select Committee on Estimates Report, 222, 336
Civil Aeronautics:
Board Report, 692
Manual, 199
Civil Air Regulations, 199–200, 420
Civil Air Transport. Agreement between U.K. and Poland. *Cmnd. 1226.* 1067, 1124
Civil Aircraft Accidents Reports, 186–7, 401–2, 670, 826, 928, 1090
Civil and Commercial Matters. Convention between U.K. and Germany for Reciprocal Recognition and Enforcement of Judgments. *Cmnd. 1118.* 1059, 1118
Civil Appropriation Accounts, 9, 193, 222, 407, 491, 676, 757, 932, 1014, 1015, 1201
Civil Aviation:
Agreement between U.K. and Hungary. *Cmnd. 1236.* 1068, 1121
Commercial Rights. *Cmnd.879.* 805, 846
Communications Handbook Amendment, 187, 402, 928, 1090
Civil Aviation (*continued*):
Facilities and Long-Range Proving Grounds for Guided Missiles in West Indies. Exchange of Notes between U.K. and U.S.A. *Cmnd. 142.* 258
Gatwick Airport Order, 187
Lympne Airport Order, 187
Multilateral Agreement. *Cmnd. 1099.* 1058, 1118
Protocol relating to:
An Amendment to the Convention. *Cmnd. 482.* 530, 589
Certain Amendments. *Cmnd. 107.* 256, 316
Unification of Certain Rules relating to International Carriage by Air. *Cmd. 9824.* 47, 104
Civil Aviation Act:
Air Navigation Order, 670
Orders, 402, 1090
Civil Aviation (Licensing) Act, 1070
Civil Aviation (Licensing) Bill, 1006, 1007, 1022, 1037, 1041, 1042, 1043, 1070, 1141
Civil Contingencies Fund Accounts, 12, 31, 193, 499, 676, 765, 933, 1023, 1201
Civil Defence:
Circulars Index, 333
Film Strips, 123
Form, 333
General Training Bulletin, 603, 861, 1137
Handbook, 333, 604, 694, 861, 1137
Industrial Bulletin, 333, 861
Instructional Diagrams, 333
Instructors' Notes, 33, 604, 861, 1138
Manual of, 123
Manual of Basic Training, 123
Manual, Pamphlets, 862
National Plan, 421
Operations, Control of, 861
Pocket Book, 334, 1138
Section Training Bulletins, 603
See Ministry of Health Report
Technical Bulletin, 200, 420
Training Memoranda, 861, 1137
Civil Defence Corps, Welfare Section, 861, 869
Civil Defence Department Bulletins, 861
Civil Engineering. Arrangements and Conditions for the Award of Higher National Certificates, 1116
Civil Estimates:
1954–55. Statement of Excesses, 14, 193
1955–56. Statement of Excesses, 227, 407
1956–57:
193–4
Revised, 21, 194
Revised Supplementary, 227, 407
Statement of Excesses, 495, 676
Supplementary, 225

CIV— INDEX 1956–60

Civil Estimates (*continued*):
1957–58:
Revised, 235, 407
Statement of Excesses, 761, 933
Supplementary, 491, 493, 676
1958–59:
494, 676
Supplementary, 505, 677, 758, 761, 933
1959–60:
759, 933
Revised, 771, 933
Supplementary, 771, 781, 933, 1020, 1201
1960–61:
1019
Revised, 1024, 1027
Supplementary, 1028, 1038
Civil Estimates and Estimates for Revenue Departments:
1955–56. Supplementary, 12, 194
1956–57:
12, 21, 194, 195
Index, 12, 194
Memorandum, 12, 194
Supplementary, 21, 194
Vote on Account, 12, 194
1957–58:
226
Index, 226, 407
Memorandum, 226, 408
Supplementary, 235, 408, 493, 677
Vote on Account, 226, 407
1958–59:
494, 677
Index, 494, 677
Memorandum, 494, 677
Supplementary, 758, 933
Vote on Account, 494, 677
1959–60:
759, 933
Index, 759, 933
Memorandum, 759, 933
Supplementary, 1017, 1202
Vote on Account, 760
1960–61:
1019, 1202
Index, 1019, 1202
Memorandum, 1019, 1202
Revised Estimate, 1202
Supplementary, 1202
Vote on Account, 1019
Civil Judicial Statistics:
England and Wales. *Cmd. 9775.* 43, 150; *Cmnd. 224.* 264, 358; *Cmnd. 434.* 527, 632
Scotland. *Cmd. 9808.* 46, 171; *Cmnd. 215.* 263, 387; *Cmnd. 478.* 530
Civil Jury Trial in Scotland. Report. *Cmnd. 851.* 803, 913
Civil Registration, Final Report of Seminar, 233
Civil Service:
And Foreign Service, Recruitment to. *Cmnd. 232.* 264
Arbitration Tribunal Awards, 136–7, 348, 618, 875, 876, 1152
Careers, 136
Estimates Revised, 1956–57, 21
List. *See* British Imperial Calendar
Oversea. *See* Overseas
Pay Research Unit Report, 568, 832, 1101
Posts for Graduates, 83
Remuneration:
Payment. *Cmnd. 963.* 1048, 1203
Sums required for Payment of Arrears. *Cmnd. 682.* 792, 934
Royal Commission Index, 163
Training and Education:
677, 934, 1202
Shorthand and Typewriting Proficiency Tests, 194
Civil Service Commission:
Examination Papers, 83–6, 297–9, 566, 830, 1099
Publications, 83–6, 297–9, 830, 1099
Civil Service Commissioner's Report, 86, 299, 566, 832, 1101
Civil Services. Civil Estimate, 1955–56 Excesses, 227
Civil Tables. Statistical Review, 599
Civilian Employees at Air Ministry Establishments. Regulations Amendment, 76, 561, 825, 1090
Civilian Service, Organisation maintained by British Forces in Germany, Disbandment of. *Cmnd. 226.* 264
Civilian Staff Regulations Amendment, 205, 424, 694, 953, 1224
Clackmannan, County of, Education (Scotland) Act:
Draft Scheme, 385
Memorandum, 385
Order-in-Council, 385
Clackmannan, County of, Educational Trust Scheme, 170
Clackmannan Dollar Academy Trust Scheme Memorandum, 513, 653
Claims:
Arrangements between U.K. and Japan regarding Settlement. *Cmnd. 1229.* 1067, 1122
Under Treaty of Peace. Memorandum of Understanding between U.K. and Italy. *Cmnd. 241.* 265
Clapham, Sir. A., Thornton Abbey Guide, 208
Clappier, B., Remodelled Economic Organisation Report, 1248
Clark, Sir K. (Chairman: Arts Council of Great Britain), Report, 826
Clark, Sir W. E. Le Gros:
History of the Primates, 1097
Introduction to Study of Fossil Man, 564

INDEX 1956–60 —COA

Clarke, S. H. (Chairman: Warren Spring Laboratory), Report, 1183
Classics, Suggestions for the Teaching of, 842
Classification of Chemicals in the Brussels Nomenclature, 574, 836
Classification of Goods in Customs Tariffs. *Cmnd. 305.* 269, 396
Classification of Mental Disorders, 1267
Classification of Occupations, 118, 1130
Classification of Pharmaceutical Preparations, 1267
Classification of Proprietary Preparations, Report, 859
Clausen, H., Pig Breeding Recording and Progeny Testing in European Countries, 966
Clausentum, Southampton, Excavations at, 698
Clay, H. M., Older Worker and His Job, 1181
Clay, T.:
Early Literature on Mallophaga, 1095
Revisions of Mallophaga Genera. Degeeriella from the Falconiformes, 563
Claypotts, Angus, Guide, 427
Clean Air Act:
55
Circular, 129, 340, 610, 868, 869, 1146
Industrial Provisions, 857
Memoranda, 129, 329, 611
Clean Air Bill:
3, 4, 16, 29, 33, 35, 125
Clean Catering, 601
Clean Food:
Code, 857
Notice, 857
Pack, 857
Clean Rivers (Estuaries and Tidal Waters) Act, 1070
Clean Rivers (Estuaries and Tidal Waters) Bill:
787, 1006, 1008, 1016, 1037, 1041, 1043, 1141
Circular, 1146
Cleaning and Chemical Sterilization of Farm Dairy Utensils, 820
Clearance of Z Zones by Road, 1137
Clearances on Transport Roads in Coal Mines Report, 370
Cleeve Abbey, Somerset. Guide, 1226
Clements, F. W., Report of an International Seminar on Education in Health and Nutrition, 437
Clergy Orphan Corporation Act, 543
Clerical and Secretarial Works. Careers, 875
Climatological Charts of the North Atlantic, 360, 633
Climatology:
735
And Microclimatology, 735
Cloakroom Accommodation and Washing Facilities in Factories, 885
Closure of Schools, Memorandum on, 100, 121
Clothing Industry Development Council Account, 15, 180, 501, 665
Clothing Industry Development Council (Dissolution) Account, 237, 396, 766, 921, 1015, 1039, 1191
Clotted Cream, 289
Cloud Forms:
According to the International Classification, 888
Amendment, 152
And Codes for States of the Sky, Manual, 200
Clough, R. H.:
Explosion at Colliery Report. *Cmnd. 1000.* 1051
Inspectors of Mines and Quarries. Report, 900, 1172
Clover Leaf Weevils. *See* Pea, Bean and Clover Leaf Weevils
Clyde Lighthouses Order Confirmation Act, 542
Clyde Lighthouses Order Confirmation Bill, 250
Clyde Navigation Order Confirmation Act, 59, 274, 1071
Clyde Navigation Order Confirmation Bill, 35, 786, 1044
Clyde Navigation Order Confirmation No. 2 Bill, 249
Coal:
And Other Mines. Regulations Circular, 900
Derivatives Committee Report. *Cmnd. 1120.* 1059, 1173
Distribution Costs in Great Britain Report. *Cmnd. 446.* 528, 641
Domestic Consumers' Council Reports, 772, 899
Electricity and Gas Industries, Capital Investment in, 153; *Cmnd. 132.* 258; *Cmnd. 415.* 526, 641; *Cmnd. 713.* 794, 898, 913; *Cmnd. 993.* 1050, 1170, 1186
International Classification of Hard Coals, 456
Origin and Evolution, 1132
Production Methods, 720
Revised Plan, 890
Statistics for Europe, 225A, 451, 720, 979, 1258
Coal-fired Automatic Stoker Warm Air System Tests, 1115
Coal Industry Act, 55, 1070
Coal Industry Bill:
5, 34, 787, 1005, 1041
Memorandum. *Cmd. 9747.* 42, 114; *Cmnd. 895.* 806, 900
Coal Industry in Europe, 224A, 450, 1250

1956-60 | COA-CON

COA— INDEX 1956–60

Coal Industry Nationalisation Act Account, 19, 114, 230, 370, 503, 641, 766, 898, 1022, 1170
Coal Industry Nationalisation (Superannuation) Regulations. Statutory Instruments, Select Committee Report, 221, 339
Coal Mines:
  Census of Production Report, 179, 394, 1193
  Draft Clearances in Transport Roads Regulations—Circular, 900
  Regulations Circulars, 1172
Coal Mines (Ventilation) General Regulations, 114
Coal Mining. Census of Production Report, 1193
Coal Mining (Subsidence) Act, 272
Coal Mining (Subsidence) Bill, 218, 219, 233, 242, 247, 248, 249, 336
Coal Tar Products. Census of Production Report, 394, 1194
Coalfield Papers of the Geological Survey of Great Britain, 119, 906
Coburn, T. M., London–Birmingham Motorway Traffic and Economies Traffic Investigation, 1182
Coccidiosis in Chickens, 290
Cockburn, R. M., Temperature of British Fish during Distribution in Summer, 910
Cocoa:
  Chocolate and Sugar Confectionery. Census of Production Report, 395
  Main Products of the Overseas Territories, 223A
  Statistics, 706, 966, 1236
Coconut Situation, 966, 1236
Cod. *See* Bear Island Cod
Codding, G. A. Junior, Broadcasting Without Barriers, 994
Code of Liberalisation:
  221A
  Of Capital Movements, 1245
Code of Practice for Protection of Persons exposed to Ionizing Radiations, 331
Code of Sample Plot Procedure, 854
Codex Alexandrinus. Old Testament, 562
Codling Moth, 555
Coed Y Brenin, Merioneth, 112
Coffee:
  In Latin America, 979
  International Agreement, *Cmnd. 803.* 806, 846
Cohen, Baron (Chairman: Royal Commission on Awards to Inventors), Report. *Cmd. 9744.* 42
Cohen, Lord, Chairman:
  Council on Prices, Productivity and Incomes, Report, 646, 901
  Royal Commission on Awards to Inventors, Compendium of Principles and Procedure adopted, 378
Cohen, Lord, Chairman (*continued*):
  Standing Joint Committee, Central Health Services Council. Report, 859
  Standing Medical Advisory Committee. Sub-Committee Report, 859
Cohen, Professor Sir Henry, Chairman:
  Central Health Services Council. Report on Medical Care of Epileptics, 121
  Panel on Composition and Nutritive Value of Flour. Report. *Cmd. 9757.* 42
Cohen of Birkenhead, Lord, Chairman:
  Standing Joint Committee on Classification of Proprietary Preparations. Report, 1133
  Standing Medical Advisory Committee. Report on Welfare Foods, 331
Coins:
  Arab-Byzantine and Post Reform Umaiyod, Catalogue, 80
  English Copper, Tin and Bronze, 1094
  Guide to the Principal Coins of the Greeks, 827
Coke Ovens:
  And By-products. Census of Production Report, 394
  And Manufactured Fuel. Census of Production Report, 1194
Cold Storage Undertakings—Report, 877
Coldstream, Sir William (Chairman: National Advisory Council on Art Education), Report, 1116
Cole, H. A.:
  Notes on the Biology of the Common Prawn, 823
  Oyster Cultivation in Britain, 74
Cole, H. G., Corrosion of Metals by Vapours from Organic Materials, 659
Cole, Sonia, Neolithic Revolution, 828
Coleraine, Rt. Hon. Lord, Chairman:
  Central Transport Consultative Committee. Report. *Cmnd. 360.* 523
  National Youth Employment Council. Report. 149, 876
Collection of Cones from Standing Trees, 1129
Collective Defence. *Cmnd. 265.* 267, 316
Collectors, Instructions for, 295, 1097
Collenette, C. L., Lymantziidae, 564
Collier, B., Defence of the United Kingdom, 296
Colliery Accident Report. *Cmnd. 205.* 263
Colliery Explosion Report. *Cmnd. 310, 327.* 270, 271; *Cmnd. 331, 396, 414, 467, 485.* 521, 525, 526, 529, 531, 642, 1047, 1051, 1171
Colliery Spoil Heaps, 868
Collins, A. C., Great Barrier Reef Expedition Scientific Report. Foraminifera, 564
Collins, A. J., Jewels and Plate of Queen Elizabeth I, 79

INDEX 1956–60 —COM

Colman, J. S., Rosawra Expedition, 828
Colne Valley Sewerage Board, Ministry of Housing and Local Government Provisional Order Confirmation Act, 2, 58
Colne Valley Sewerage Board, Ministry of Housing and Local Government Provisional Order Bill, 784
Colne Valley Sewerage Board (No. 2), Ministry of Housing and Local Government Provisional Order Confirmation Bill, 33
Colombia:
  Economic Development, 720
  International Customs Journal, 714, 974, 1244
Colombo Plan:
  See Technical Co-operation
  For Co-operative Economic Development in South and South-East Asia. Consultative Committee Report. *Cmnd. 920.* 1046, 1202
  Picture Set, 614
  Report, 573. *Cmnd. 610.* 539, 677
  5th Annual Report. *Cmnd. 50.* 251, 408
  6th Annual Report. *Cmnd. 315.* 270, 408
  Technical Co-operation Scheme:
    91
    Report, 304, 835
Colonial Advisory Council of Agriculture, Animal Health and Forestry Publications, 300, 569
Colonial Agriculture Statistics, 301
Colonial Arms, 569
Colonial Development and Welfare, 87
Colonial Development and Welfare Acts:
  809
  Report. *Cmnd. 672.* 792, 832
  Return of Schemes, 21, 87, 234, 300, 504, 569, 771, 832, 1028, 1101
Colonial Development and Welfare (Amendment) Act, 809
Colonial Development and Welfare (Amendment) Bill, 749
Colonial Development and Welfare Bill:
  751, 784, 786
  Consolidation Bills Report, 746, 752, 867
Colonial Development Corporation:
  Report and Accounts, 18, 87, 231, 300, 500, 770, 832, 1026, 1101
  Report of the Committee of Enquiry into the Financial Structure. *Cmnd. 780.* 799, 834
Colonial Empire Picture Sets, 131, 344
Colonial Flags, Badges and Arms, 87
Colonial (Geodetic and Topographical) Surveys, Directorate of, Report, 88, 302
Colonial Geological Surveys, 1947–56 Ten Years' Progress, 300
Colonial Geology and Mineral Resources:
  87, 300, 429
  Bulletins Supplement, 87, 300
Colonial Loans Acts. Guarantee given on Loans to:
  22, 194
  Kenya, 1027, 1202
  Nigeria, 503, 677
  Rhodesia and Nyasaland, 506, 677, 1025, 1202
Colonial Office:
  Digest of Statistics, 1101
  List 87, 300, 569, 832, 1101
  Picture Sets, 614, 872, 1149
  Publications, 86–90, 299–303, 569, 832, 1101
  Reports, 1102, 1106
  Select Committee on Estimates:
    Report, 1029, 1143
    Special Report, 1039, 1144
Colonial Plant and Animal Products:
  87, 300, 429, 569
  See also Tropical Science
Colonial Regulations, 88
Colonial Reports, 87, 91, 300–1, 305, 569, 573, 832, 835
Colonial Research:
  Publications, 88, 301, 570, 1103
  Reports:
    1955–56. *Cmnd. 52.* 251, 301
    1956–57. *Cmnd. 321.* 270, 301
    Cmnd. 591. 538, 570; *Cmnd. 938,* 1215, 1047, 1066, 1102
  Studies 88, 301–2, 570, 833, 1103
Colonial Statistics Digest, 88, 302, 429, 570, 834, 1101
Colonial Territories. *Cmd. 9769.* 43, 88; *Cmnd. 195.* 262, 302; *Cmnd. 451.* 528, 570; *Cmnd. 780.* 799, 833; *Cmnd. 1065.* 1055, 1103
Colonies in Pictures, 88
Colour:
  In School Buildings, 100
  Reproductions of Paintings Catalogue, 994
  Visual Problems of, 636
Colouring Matter in Food Regulations. Circular, 291
Colourless Waterproofing Treatment for Damp Walls, 164
Colours, B. S. 2660 Range of, 381
Colquhoun, W. P., Effect of Small Doses of Alchohol on a Skill Resembling Driving, 887
"Colwyn Bay" Wreck Report, 675
Comben, A. J., Effect of Depth on the Strength Properties of Timber Beams with an Analysis of the Stresses and Strains Developed, 382
Combine Harvesters, 558
Combined Cadet Force Regulations. Amendments, 205, 424, 694, 954, 1224
Combustible Contents in Buildings, 419
Comenius, John Amos. Selection from his Works, 465
Comintern and the CPUSA, 200

COM— INDEX 1956–60

Command Papers, 36–55, 250–71, 521, 787, 1045
Commerce:
  And Navigation between U.K. and Shereefian Empire. Exchange of Notes between U.K. and Morocco. *Cmnd. 144.* 259
  Establishment and Navigation. Treaty between U.K. and Iran. *Cmnd. 698.* 703, 850
Commercial Debts Owed by Residents in Turkey. Agreement between U.K. and Turkey. *Cmnd. 767, 805.* 798, 800, 853, 974, 979
Commercial Matters. Exchange of Notes between U.K. and Turkey. *Cmnd. 136.* 258
Commercial Pilot Examination Guide, 200
Commercial Pilot's Licence:
  402
  (Flying Machines), 928
Commercial Policy, 709
Commercial Production of Cabbage and Savoy. Film Strip, 288
Commercial Relations:
  Agreement between U.K. and European Coal and Steel Community. *Cmnd. 693.* 793, 847
  European Coal and Steel Community Agreement. *Cmnd. 326.* 271
  Exchange of Notes between U.K. and Cuba. *Cmd. 9758.* 42, 105; *Cmnd. 96.* 255; *Cmnd. 358.* 528, 589; *Cmnd. 688.* 792, 846
Commercial Rights of Non-Scheduled Air Services:
  In Europe Multilateral Agreement on. *Cmnd. 879.* 803, 846
  Multilateral Agreement. *Cmnd. 1099.* 1058, 1118
Commercial Road Vehicles. Customs Convention on Temporary Importation. *Cmnd. 255.* 266; *Cmnd. 919.* 1045, 1118
Commercial Samples. Customs Convention regarding E.C.S. Carnets. *Cmd. 9863.* 50, 105; *Cmnd. 711.* 794, 846
Commercial Subjects. Scottish Certificate of Education, 913
Commercial Varieties of Apples and Pears, 288
Commercial Violet Growing, 71
Commissioner of Police of the Metropolis Report. *Cmnd. 487.* 531, 604
Commissioner's Decisions:
  Claims for Benefit, etc., 363–9
  Index Amendments, 156, 362, 636, 891, 1164
Commissioners of Prisons Report. *See* Prisons
Committee on Administrative Tribunals and Enquiries. *See* Administrative Tribunals and Enquiries
Committees of the Consultative Assembly. Council of Europe, Supplement, 961
Commodity Policy Studies, 241A, 707, 1236
Commodity Reports:
  241A, 707, 900
  Rice, 436
Commodity Series Bulletins, 241A, 436, 707, 1236
Commodity Survey, 720, 979, 1251
Commodity Trade Statistics, 225, 451, 720, 979, 1251
Common Furniture Beetle, 997, 1190
Common Land Royal Commission:
  Index, 647
  Minutes of Evidence:
    163, 370
    Appendix, 647
  Report. *Cmnd. 462.* 529, 647
Common Names of British Insect and Other Pests, 559
Common Prawn, Notes on the Biology of, 823
Common Services Estimates:
  1956–57, 12
  1957–58, 226
  1958–59, 494, 676
  1959–60, 760, 933
  1960–61, 1019, 1201
Common Worms of the Pig, 556
Commonwealth:
  And Nuclear Development, 132
  And the Sterling Area. Statistical Abstract, 180, 396, 665, 921, 1192
  Association in Brief, 872, 1149
  Britain Looks at. Photoposter, 1149
  Cameos, 1149
  Constitutional Developments in, 1150
  Development. United Kingdom's Role. *Cmnd. 237.* 264, 305
  Economic Committee:
    Annual Report, 835
    Publications, 91, 304, 572, 835, 1105
    Report, 304, 572, 835, 1105
  Economic Development, 132, 615
  Education:
    872
    Conference Report. *Cmnd. 841.* 803, 836
  Educational Co-operation. *Cmnd. 1032.* 1053, 1103, 1106
  Estimates:
    1956–57, 12
    1957–58, 226
    1958–59, 494
    1959–60, 759, 933
    1960–61, 1019, 1201
  In Brief, 344, 872, 1149
  Of Nations, 344
  Of Nations Wall Map, 573
  Partnership, 614, 1149
  Picture of the, 344
  Raw Materials Review, Report, 572, 1105
  Reference Pamphlets, 344

INDEX 1956 60 —CON

Commonwealth (*continued*):
  Scholarship and Fellowship Plan. *Cmnd. 894.* 808, 833, 835
  Survey:
    132, 344, 429, 614, 872, 1149
    Officers' Conference Proceedings Report, 302, 1103
  This is The, 873
  Today, 429
  Trade:
    91, 572, 835, 1105
    And Economic Conference Report. *Cmnd. 539.* 534, 572, 677
    With the U.S., 833
  War Graves Commission Report, 1107
  We Live in, 1106
  What is the? 132, 615, 872
Commonwealth Agricultural Bureaux:
  Review Conference. Report. *Cmd. 9664.* 37, 91
  Report, 91, 304, 572, 834, 1105
Commonwealth Institute Act, 540
Commonwealth Institute Bill, 479, 517
Commonwealth Relations Office:
  List 91, 305, 573, 835, 1106
  Publications, 91, 304–5, 573, 835, 1105
  Select Committee on Estimates, Special Report, 772, 865, 1029, 1143
Commonwealth Scholarships Act, 810
Commonwealth Scholarships Bill, 755, 787
Commonwealth Settlement Act, 272
Commonwealth Settlement Bill, 214
Commonwealth Shipping Committee, Publications, 91, 305, 574, 836, 1107
Commonwealth Teachers Act, 1070
Commonwealth Teachers Bill, 1008, 1042
Communicable Diseases:
  In Man, Control of, 1090
  In Schools, 998
  Notification of, 999
Communication Codes and Abbreviations, 217A, 440
Communications Division:
  International Civil Aviation Organisation, 217A
  Report, 711
  Supplement, 441
Communications, Interceptions of, Report. *Cmnd. 283.* 268
Communications Meeting, Special Middle East Supplement, 218A
Communist Activities Around the World, 200
Communist Conspiracy, 200
Community Coal Mining and Iron and Steel Industries, Investment in, 1234
Community Development:
  Handbook, 570
  Photoposter, 1149
  Study Kit on Training for, 462
"Compagnie du Port, des Quais et des Entrepôts de Beyrouth" and the "Société Radio-Orient" (France *v.* Lebanon) Order, 972, 1243
Companies Act. Investigations, 921, 1192
Companies Act, 1948 (Amendment) Bill, 1041
Companies General Annual Report, 180, 396, 665, 921, 1192
Company Assets and Income, 1192
Company Law Committee. Minutes of Evidence, 1192
Company Planning and Production Control, 71f
Comparative Cross National Research, 738A
Comparative Education, 736
Comparative Fishing Trials with Shrimp Nets, 559
Comparative National Products and Price Levels, 715
Comparative Studies of Customs Procedures Study, 1232
Comparison of Capital Costs of Heating Systems in Houses, 165
Comparison of National Output and Productivity of the United Kingdom and the United States, 975
Compensation (Acquisition and Planning) Bill, 516
Compensation for:
  British Property affected by Czechoslovak Measures of Nationalisation. Exchange of Notes with U.K. *Cmnd. 56.* 252
  Compulsory Acquisition of Land. Circular, 611
  Disablement and Death due to War Injury. Agreement between U.K. and Belgium. *Cmnd. 311.* 270
  Premature Retirement from the Armed Forces. *Cmnd. 231.* 264, 307
Composite Construction, Studies in, 1181
Composition in the Primary School, 385
Composition of Foods, 1160
Composting:
  Film Strip, 554
  Sanitary Disposal and Reclamation of Organic Wastes, 244A
Composts, Seed and Potting, 555
Compressed Air for Ventilation Purposes, Use of, 900
Compulsory Acquisition of Land (Assessment of Compensation) and Repurchase of Rights Bill, 34
Compulsory Education Studies, 237A
Compulsory Insurance against Civil Liability in Respect of Motor Vehicles. European Convention, 962
Computer Techniques for Clerical Work, Report, 155
Concrete:
  Amendment, 424
  Lightweight, 207
  Lintels, Simple, 1226
  Manual of Military Engineering. Amendment, 954

CON-CRE | 1956-60

Concrete (*continued*):
Materials for, 1179
Ready-Mixed, 649
Roads, 165, 292
See National Building Studies Special Reports
Condensation:
And the Design of Factory Roofs, 649
In Dwellings, 1179
In Sheeted Roofs, 651
Condensed Milk Regulations. Circular, 822
Conduct of ICAO Meetings, Directives of the Council concerning, 970
Conference of Foreign Ministers at Geneva. *Cmnd. 797, 829, 868*. 800, 802, 805, 846, 848
Congressional Directory for the Use of the United States Congress, 200
Conifers:
New Ways of Using the General Tariff Tables, 325
Tariff Tables for Great Britain, 112
Conisbrough Castle, Yorkshire, Guide, 957
Conklin, H. C., Hanunóo Agriculture, 437
Conlon, M., Education in Belgium, 466
Conservation of the Living Resources of the Sea, 225A
Conservation of Vorticity at 100 Millibars, 1162
Consolidated Fund Abstract Account, 11, 194, 225, 408, 492, 677, 758, 934, 1015, 1203
Consolidated Fund Act, 55, 272, 540, 809, 1070
Consolidated Fund (Appropriation) Bill, 249, 520, 786, 1044
Consolidated Fund (Appropriation) (No. 2) Bill, 35
Consolidated Fund Bill, 33, 247, 517, 784, 1042, 1045
Consolidated Fund (No. 2) Act, 272, 540
Consolidated Fund (No. 2) Bill, 247, 517
Consolidated Municipal Charity and Certain Other Charities (Ludlow) Act, 57
Consolidated Municipal Charity and Certain Other Charities (Ludlow) Bill, 4, 34
Consolidation Bills Report, 1, 2, 6, 7, 8, 213–14, 215, 216, 217, 218, 220, 477, 478, 479, 481, 482, 484, 487, 488, 745, 866, 1003, 1004, 1005, 1007, 1009, 1144
Consolidation of Debts. Agreement between U.K. and Argentine. *Cmnd. 359*. 523, 587
Consolidation of Enactments (Procedure) Act, Memorandum, 1, 4, 6, 8, 214, 217, 748, 755, 867
Constable, Application for Appointment as, 861
Constable Collection, Catalogue, 1222
Constabulary; Report of Her Majesty's Inspector for Scotland. *Cmd. 9771*. 43, 171; *Cmnd. 172*. 260, 387; *Cmnd. 437*. 528, 654; *Cmnd. 770*. 799, 914; *Cmnd. 1046*. 1054, 1186
Constitution:
FAO. Rules adopted by the Conference, 707
Of Security over Moveable Property; and Floating Charges. *Cmnd. 1017*. 1052, 1159
U.S.A., 422
Constitutional Development in the Commonwealth, 615, 1150
Construction and:
Heating of Commercial Glasshouses, 1085
Operation of Charcoal Kilns, 908
Constructional Engineering. Census of Production Report, 179, 663
Consular Convention between U.K. and:
France. *Cmnd. 617*. 788, 844
Germany. *Cmnd. 5*. 52, 106; *Cmnd. 607*. 788, 849
Greece. *Cmnd. 525*. 533, 590
Italy. *Cmnd. 1135*. 1060, 1122
Mexico. *Cmnd. 633*. 789, 851
U.S.A. *Cmnd. 524*. 533, 595
Consultant Engineering in the United States, Aspects of, 715
Consultation and Co-operation in the Commonwealth, 345
Consultation with Executive Councils. Circular, 868
Consultative Assembly and Common Assembly of European Coal and Steel Community Report, 703
Consultative Assembly. *See* Council of Europe
Consumer Protection. Report of the Committee. *Cmnd. 1011*. 1052, 1193
Consumers' Food Buying Habits Report, 715
Consumption of Food in the United States, 199
Containers. Customs Convention: *Cmnd. 235*. 264; *Cmnd. 905*. 807, 846
And Protocol of Signature, 226A
Continental Schools Painting Illustrations, 154
Continental Shelf, Law of the Sea, 728
Continuance of Emergency Legislation. *Cmnd. 7*. 52, 123
Contracts:
And Periods of Prescription. Exchange of Notes between U.K. and Austria. *Cmnd. 292*. 269
Building and Civil Engineering Works, 1226
Model Standing Order, 342
Of Sale of Cereals, 721

Contribution Conditions and Credits Provision. National Insurance Advisory Committee. Report. *Cmd. 9854*. 49
Contribution of Home Economies Towards Rural Development Projects, 1246
Contributions:
Report of the Committee, 725, 726, 984
To Voluntary Bodies, 868
Toward a Classification of Modern Isospondylous Fishes, 1097
Control, Board of:
Annual Report, 21
Scotland, Report of the General Board. *Cmd. 9807*. 46; *Cmnd. 546*. 535, 600; *Cmnd. 892*. 806, 857; *Cmnd. 1160*. 1062, 1132
Control of:
Advertisements, Code of Standards. Circular, 1146
Borrowing Order:
General Consent, 934
Rules of the Supreme Court. Statutory Instruments Select Committee Report, 513, 609
Civil Defence Operations in E. and W., 603, 861
Development Alongside Special Roads. Circular, 611
Insect Vectors in International Air Traffic, 243A
Losses in Young Farm Animals, 446
Mineral Working, 1146
Radioactive Wastes. *Cmnd. 884*. 806, 869, 913
Rats in Sewers, 1089
Control Systems and Armaments, Precision Gearing for, 1075
Controlled Fusion Devices, 987
Convalescent Treatment:
Report of a Working Party. Corrigendum, 1136
Working Party Report, 859
Convention on:
International Civil Aviation. Amendments, 441
Taxation of Road Vehicles for Private Use in International Traffic. *Cmnd. 220*. 263
The Nationality of Married Women. *Cmnd. 200*. 262
Conventions and Protocols of Signature, 225A
Conversion of Ionospheric Virtual Height-Frequency Curves to Electron Density-Height Profiles, 910
Conversion Tables for Forest Research Workers, 1128
Conway Castle:
And Town Walls. Caernarvonshire, Guide, 427
Postcard, 697
Cook, B. C. A., Burma. Overseas Economic Survey, 398
Cook, J. W. (Chairman: Inter-Departmental Committee on Milk Composition in the U.K. *Cmnd. 1147*. 1061
Cooke, F. C., Copra Processing in Rural Industries, 706
Cooke, Dr. G. W., Agricultural Value of Phosphate Fertilisers which Economise in the Use of Sulphuric Acid. Report, 220A
Cooking Equipment Standard Specifications, 370
Cooling of the Uneviscerated Poultry Carcase by Various Methods in Common Use, 165
Cooper, J. P., Grasses in Agriculture, 1236
Co-operation:
Between the European Atomic Energy Community (EURATOM) and the Government of the United States of America, 963
For Economic Progress, 1251
Select Bibliography on, 436
Co-operative Farms and Smallholdings:
Reports and Accounts, 73, 291, 822
Wales. Report and Accounts, 558, 1086
Co-operative Marketing for Agricultural Producers, 241A
Co-operatives and Land Use, 706
Copper:
Food Standards Committee Report, 73
Goods Export Licence, 181, 397, 666
In Food Circular, 557
Copra Processing in Rural Industries, 706
Copyright:
Bulletin, 237A, 466, 735, 994, 1263
International Convention. *Cmnd. 361*. 523, 589
Laws and Treaties of the World, 735, 1263
Universal Copyright Convention. *Cmnd. 289*. 268, 316
Copyright Act, 55
Copyright Bill, 1, 2, 6, 23, 29, 34, 35, 125
Corby, G. A., Air Flow Over Mountains, 360
Corby Development Corporation Report, 24, 130, 237, 506, 613, 870, 1147
"Corchester" Wreck Report, 192, 406
Corfield, J. D., Historical Survey of the Origins and Growth of Man. *Cmnd. 1030*. 1053, 1103
Corn Drills, 558
Cornwall County Council Act, 1072
Cornwall. Saxton's Map, 1094
"Cornwood" Wreck Report, 675
Corona:
88, 302, 429, 570, 833, 1103
Library Series, 89, 300, 302, 1103
Corporal Punishment. Report on the Treatment of Offenders. *Cmnd. 1213*. 1066, 1138

Corporate Bodies' Contracts Act, 1070
Corporate Bodies' Contracts Bill, 787, 1007, 1024, 1037, 1042, 1141
Corporate Bodies' Contracts Circular, 1146
Corporation Houses in Glasgow. Report on Review of Rents, 601
Corporation of the Sons of the Clergy Charities Bill, 518
Corporation of the Sons of the Clergy Charities Scheme Confirmation Act, 543
Corporation of the Sons of the Clergy Charities Scheme Bill, 481
"Corps", Definition for the Purposes of the Army Act, 424, 694
Corps Warrant. Amendments, 424
Correspondence between:
Mr. Bulganin and Sir Anthony Eden. *Cmnd. 182*. 261, 408
The Prime Minister and Mr. Bulganin. *Cmnd. 380, 381*. 524, 589
Corrosion:
And its Prevention at Bimetallic Contacts, 175, 659
Of Metals by Vapours from Organic Materials, 659
Of Non-Ferrous Metals, 648
Corsets and Miscellaneous Dress Industries. Census of Production Report, 1194
Corsica International Customs Journal, 444
Cosciani, C., Effects of Differential Tax Treatment of Corporate and Non-Corporate Enterprises, 975
Cosmetic, Food and Drug Act, Requirements of. Guide, 951
Cost of:
Boarding Education, Assistance with. Report, 1116
Living Advisory Committee Report on New Index of Retail Prices. *Cmd. 9710*. 138
Prescribing:
Committee Report, 602
Final Report of the Committee, 859
The National Health Service Report. *Cmd. 9663*. 37, 122
Cost Study Building Bulletin, 313
Costa Rica International Customs Journal, 714
Costing of Powered Vehicles and Machines, 242A
Costs:
And Efficiency in Milk Production. Report, 1086
Of Mechanical Plant, 648
Costs of Leases Act, 540
Costs of Leases Bill, 484, 504, 512, 518, 605
Cottam, P. A., Pelecaniform Characters of the Skeleton of the Shoe-Bill Stork, Balaeniceps Rex, 295
Cottesloe, Lord (Chairman: Reviewing Committee on Export of Works of Art), Report. *Cmd. 9882*. 52; *Cmnd. 270*. 267; *Cmnd. 542*. 535; *Cmnd. 856*. 804, 935; *Cmnd. 1175*. 1063
Cotton (Centralised Buying) Act, Accounts, 23, 180, 495, 665, 766, 773, 921, 1030, 1192
Cotton Finishing—Reorganisation Scheme (Confirmation) Order—Select Committee Statutory Instruments Report, 1143
Cotton Industry:
Future of European, 448
Joint Advisory Committee Report: 1057, 1167
On Dust in Card Rooms, 348
Reorganisation. *Cmnd. 744*. 796, 923
Cotton Industry Act, 809
Cotton Industry Bill, 751, 785, 787
Cotton Industry (Compensation for Redundancy) Bill, 786
Cotton, J. R., Belgian Congo and Ruanda-Urundi Overseas Economic Survey, 398
Cotton, M. A., Excavations at Clausentum, Southampton, 698
Cotton Spinning:
And Doubling Census of Production Report, 179, 664
Career, 617
Cotton Textiles:
Agreement between Hong Kong, with consent of the U.K. and Burma *Cmnd. 738*. 796, 846
And/or Yarn. Exchange of Notes between U.K. and Burma concerning Export and Acceptance of Raw Cotton from U.S. *Cmd. 9860*. 50, 104
Exchange of Notes between U.K. and Burma concerning Export. *Cmnd. 724*. 795, 846
Cotton Weaving Census of Production Report, 664
Cotton Yarn: Exchange of Notes between U.K. and Indonesia:
Amending Memorandum of Understanding for Export from Hong Kong. *Cmnd. 250*. 265
Relating to Arrangements for Export. *Cmnd. 45*. 251
Couch or Twitch, 288
Coulter, Surgeon Captain J. L. S., Royal Naval Medical Services, 122, 174
Council for Wales and Monmouthshire Memorandum. *Cmnd. 53*. 252, 334; *Cmnd. 631*. 788, 869
Council of Association between the U.K. and the High Authority of the European Coal and Steel Community. Report. *Cmnd. 794*. 800, 848
Council of Europe:
1949–59, 1232

Council of Europe (*continued*):
Consultative Assembly:
433
Documents, Working Papers, 433, 703, 961, 1231
Meeting with Common Assembly of the European Coal and Steel Community Official Report, 213A;
Official Report of Debates, 703, 961, 1231
Orders and Minutes, 213A 703, 961, 1231
Proceedings Report. *Cmnd. 400*. 525, 589; 703, 961; *Cmnd. 1072*. 1056, 1119
Publications, 213A, 433, 703–4, 961, 1231
Records. Index, 1231
Texts Adopted, 433, 703, 961, 1231
Convention between Member Countries. *Cmnd. 41*. 251, 316
Directorate of Information, 433
European Coal and Steel Community Joint Meeting Report, 433
Medical, Surgical and Laboratory Equipment on Free Loan in Hospitals. *Cmnd. 1136*. 1060, 1119
Protection of Television Broadcast Agreement. *Cmnd. 1163*. 1063, 1119
Protocol to the General Agreement of Privileges and Immunities. *Cmnd. 84*. 254, 317
Report on Proceedings. *Cmnd. 26* 54, 104; *Cmnd. 274*. 267, 317
2nd Protocol to the General Agreement on Privileges and Immunities. *Cmnd. 139*. 258, 317; *Cmnd. 579*. 537, 589
Texts of a Statutory Character for Ultimate Inclusion in a Revised Statute. *Cmnd. 118*. 257, 317
Council of Industrial Design:
Publications, 1148
Report, 613
Council on Prices, Productivity and Incomes Reports, 646, 901
Council to the Assembly, International Civil Aviation Organisation, 217
Councils and their Houses:
Circular, 868
Report, 869
Counterfeit Currency. International Convention for the Suppression. *Cmnd. 666*. 791, 846; *Cmnd. 932*. 1046, 1119
County Court Parishes, etc. Index, 886
County Courts Accounts, 14, 154, 228, 361, 500, 635, 762, 889, 1020, 1162
County Courts Act, 809
County Courts Bill, 487, 747, 784
County Courts Consolidation Bills Report, 745, 746, 747, 866
County Courts Consolidation of Enactments Memorandum, 487
County Courts Manual, 358
County Hall, Abingdon, Berkshire, Guide, 208
County of Argyll Educational Endowments Scheme. Memorandum, 911
County of Berks (Consent to Letting) Ministry of Housing and Local Government Provisional Order Confirmation Act, 274
County of Berks (Consent to Letting) Ministry of Housing and Local Government Provisional Order Confirmation Bill, 217
Court-Brown, W. M., Leukaemia and Aplastic Anaemia in Patients Irradiated for Ankylosing Spondylitis, 359
Courts of Summary Jurisdiction in the Metropolitan Area. Report of the Departmental Committee, 862
Covent Garden Bill, 1044
Coventry Corporation Act, 543
Cowhouses in Modern Practice, 823
Cows, Feeding Diary, 1085
Cox, L. R.:
British Cretaceous Pleurotomariidae, 1096
Two new Radioitids (Rudistid Lamellibranchia) from the Upper Cretaceous Tukey, 1096
Coypu, 1084
Cracherode Shell Collection, 295
Cracking in Brickwork, etc., Question and Answers, 648
Cracking of Asbestos—Cement Sheets, 1178
Craddock, J. M., Synoptic Study of Anomalies of Surface Air Temperature over the Atlantic Half of the Northern Hemisphere, 889
Craig, R. E., Hydrography of Scottish Coastal Waters, 914
Cranbrook, Earl of (Chairman: Maternity Services Committee), Report, 859
Cranes for Building, 906
Craster, O. E.:
Cilgerran Castle, Pembrokeshire, Guide, 426
Tintern Abbey, Monmouthshire, Guide, 208
Crawford and Balcarres, Rt. Hon. the Earl of, Chairman:
Preservation of Downing Street Committee Report. *Cmnd. 457*. 529
Royal Fine Art Commission Report. *Cmnd. 70*. 253
Crawford, Major W., Explosives Factory Accident Report, 604
Crawley Development Corporation Report, 24, 130, 237, 506, 613, 870, 1147
Cream Cheese, 288
Cream Coloured Earthenware, 1222

Credit:
For Purchase of Goods in U.K. Exchange of Notes between U.K. and Yugoslavia. *Cmnd. 722*. 795, 854
Problems of Small Farmers in Asia and Far East, 451
Credits granted by European Payments Union Repayment. Exchange of Notes between U.K. and Austria. *Cmd. 9764*. 43, 53, 103
Creed, Sir Thomas, Chairman:
Committee on Scales of Salaries for Teachers. Reports, 842
Forest of Dean Committee. Report. *Cmnd. 686*. 792, 855
Creep and Fracture of Metals at High Temperatures, 155
Cremer, H. W. (Chairman: Synthetic Detergents Standing Technical Committee), Report, 613, 870, 1147
Cren, E. D. le, Application of Science to Inland Fisheries, 966
Creosoting Plant at Thetford Chase, 1129
Crested Tit, 596
Cretaceous Pleurotomariidae, British, 1096
Crew, F. A. E., Army Medical Services, 122, 174, 332, 859, 916
Crichton Castle, Midlothian, Guide, 427
Cricket Bat Willow, Cultivation of, 596
Crime:
And Treatment of Offenders, Prevention of, Report, 459
Disease and Social Affliction, Half-a-Century of Successful Struggle against, 1262
Of Genocide:
979
United Nations Convention, 226A
Problems, European Committee, 1232
Criminal Injuries (Compensation) Bill, 787, 1044
Criminal Justice Administration Act, 55
Criminal Justice Administration Bill, 2, 14, 29, 33, 125
Criminal Justice Administration (Amendment) Act, 809
Criminal Justice Administration (Amendment) Bill, 749, 784, 785
Criminal Justice Bill, 1040, 1044
Criminal Justice (Scotland) Act, Forms, 171
Criminal Justice Supervision Record Cover, 287
Criminal Law Revision Committee. *Cmnd. 835*, 802, 861; *Cmnd. 1187*. 1064, 1138
Criminal Matters, European Convention on Mutual Assistance, 962
Criminal Policy, International Review of, 230A, 457, 728, 985, 1255
Criminal Statistics:
England and Wales. *Cmd. 9884*. 52, 123; *Cmnd. 286*. 268, 334; *Cmnd. 529*. 534, 604; *Cmnd. 803*. 800, 862; *Cmnd. 1100*. 1058, 1138
Criminal Statistics (*continued*):
Scotland. *Cmd. 9750*. 42, 171; *Cmnd. 157*. 259, 387; *Cmnd. 426*. 527, 654; *Cmnd. 746*. 796, 913; *Cmnd. 1024*. 1053, 1186
Criminology, Teaching in the Social Sciences, 469
Croft, W. N., Blue-Green Algae from the Middle Devonian of Rhynie, Aberdeenshire, 827
Crofters Commission Report, 287, 554, 819, 1029, 1081, 1141
Crofting, 1037
Croney, D., Field Studies of the Movement of Soil Mixture, 652
Crook, A. E., Winding Accident, Brookhouse Colliery, Report. *Cmnd. 475*. 530
Crookall, R., Fossil Plants of the Carboniferous Rocks of Great Britain, 857
Crooke, M., Adelges Cooleyi, 1129
Croome, H., Human Problems of Innovation, 1181
Crop and Livestock Insurance. Report, 436
Crosby Corporation Act, 57
Crossfill, J. W. L., Hazards to Men in Ships Lost at Sea, 151
Cross-Cultural Education and Educational Travel, 467
Crosskey, R. W., Taxonomic Study of the Larvae of West African Simuliidae with Comments on the Morphology of the Larval Black-Fly Head, 1096
Crossley, A. F., Temperature—Compensated Equivalent Head-winds for Jet Aircraft, 360
Crossman, E. R. F. W., Automation and Skill, 1181
Cross-Shaft Overhead Fan Kiln, 907
Crow, D., Commonwealth Education, 872
Crown Agents for Oversea Governments and Administrations Publications, 305
Crown Estate Act, 55
Crown Estate Bill, 6, 35
Crown Estate Commissioner's:
Abstract Accounts, 492, 574, 758, 836, 1015, 1107
Historical Essay, 1107
Publications, 836, 1107
Report, 305, 574, 836, 1107
Statement on Future of Regent's Park Terraces, 305
Crown Lands. Abstract Accounts, 11, 91, 225, 305
Crown Proceedings Act. Authorised Government Departments, etc., 408, 934
Crown's Nominee Account, 194, 408, 677, 934, 1203
Crowther, Sir G. (Chairman: Central Advisory Council for Education):
(England), Correspondence re Future Demand for Teachers, 585
Report, 842

Croydon Airport. Air Navigation Order, 1090
Croydon Corporation Act, 57, 274, 1072
Crude Oil and Natural Gas, Search and Exploitation, 715
Cruden, S.:
Early Christian and Pictish Monuments of Scotland, 427
Scottish Abbeys, 1227
"Crush Hour" Travel in Central London, Report, 671
Crushing and Grinding, 649
Crustacea, Penaeidae. Series Benthesicymae, 1097
Cruz, H. S., F.A.O.'s Role in Rural Welfare, 966
Crystallographic Data for the Calcium Silicates, 165
Cuba:
Exchange of Notes with U.K.:
Cmnd. 688, 792, 846
Amending the Schedules to the Air Services Agreement. *Cmnd. 258*. 266, 317
Modifying the Agreement concerning Commercial Relations. *Cmnd. 96*. 255, 317
On Commercial Relations. *Cmd. 9758*. 42, 105; *Cmnd. 358*. 522, 589
International Customs Journal, 444
Cucumber Growing, 1084
Culicine Mosquitoes of the Indo-Malayan Area, 295, 564
Cullen, G., Chiswick House and Gardens Guide Illustrations, 698
Cullen, London Airport, Architectural Drawings, 187
Culpin, C., Methods of Green Fodder Conservation, 225A
Cultivation of the Cricket Bat Willow, 596
Cultural Agreement Between U.K. and:
Iraq. *Cmnd. 969*, *1129*. 1049, 1060
Turkey. *Cmd. 9767*. 43, 111; *Cmnd. 401*. 525, 594
Cultural Assimilation and Tensions in Israel, 238A
Cultural Convention between U.K. and:
Germany. *Cmnd. 441*. 528, 590; *Cmnd. 742*. 796, 849
Iran. *Cmnd. 865*. 804, 850
Netherlands. *Cmnd. 382*. 524, 592
Spain. *Cmnd. 1134*. 1060, 1175
Cultural Convention. Exchange of Notes between U.K. and Luxembourg. *Cmd. 9782*. 44, 107
Cultural Division Partial Agreement Section, 1232
Cultural Fund, Council of Europe Report, 1232
Cultural Integration of Immigrants, 996
Cultural Property Final Act, Convention and Protocol on Protection in the Event of Armed Conflict. *Cmd. 9837*. 48, 105
Cultural Radio Broadcasts, 468
Culture and Human Fertility, 737
Cumbernauld Development Corporation Report, 236, 613, 656, 776, 779, 870, 915, 1187
Cuneiform Texts from:
Babylonian Tablets in the British Museum, 827, 1094
Cappadocian Tablets in the British Museum, 294
Cunliffe, Lord. (Chairman: Central Health Services Council Committee). Report, 1133
Curia Regis Rolls:
378
Reign of Henry III, 1175
Curing, Trilingual Dictionary, 1238
Curnow, P. E., King William III Banqueting House, Hampton Court, Guide, 698
Currant and Gooseberry Aphids, 288
Currency and Bank Notes Act, Treasury Minute, 10, 17, 20, 21, 23, 26, 31, 194, 224, 225, 230, 234, 236, 239, 245, 408, 491, 499, 504, 506, 510, 515, 677, 757, 758, 764, 771, 772, 776, 777, 781, 935, 1015, 1016, 1018, 1020, 1022, 1024, 1029, 1032, 1034, 1039, 1040, 1203
Currency Exchange Rates. Exchange of Notes between U.K. and Argentine. *Cmnd. 97*. 255
Current Bibliography of National Official Publications, 735
Current Food Additives Legislation, 436, 707, 966, 1236
Current Mass Communication Research, 468
Current Medical Research, 633, 887, 1160
Current School Enrolment Statistics, 237A, 466, 735, 994
Current Sociology, 237A, 466, 735
Curricula, Preparation of, General Secondary School, 1265
Curriculum:
Of the Senior Secondary School:
Circular, 911
Report, 911
Revision and Development, Planning for, 736
Revision and Research, 736
Curry, W. T., Strength Properties of Plywood: Working Stresses, 302, 630
Curtiss, L. F., Geiger-Muller Counter, 202
Cushing, D. H.:
Echo-Sounding Experiments in the Barents Sea, 1087
Interpretation of Echo Traces, 292
Number of Pilchards in the Channel, 292
On the Herring of the Southern North Sea, 291

Cushing, D. H. (*continued*):
On the Nature of Production in the Sea, 823
Phytoplankton and the Herring, 73
Production and a Pelagic Fishery, 73
Triple Frequency Echo Sounder, 73
Cushion, A. A., Morbidity Statistics from General Practice, 598
Custodial Sentences for Young Offenders Report, 1186
Customs and Excise:
Areas of the World, 989
Convention and Protocol of Signature, 226A
Convention on:
Containers. *Cmnd. 235*. 264, 317; *Cmnd. 905*. 807, 846
International Transport of Goods. *Cmnd. 790*. 800, 846
Temporary Importation for Private Use of Aircraft and Pleasure Boats. *Cmnd. 288*, 268, 317; *Cmnd. 650*. 790, 846
Temporary Importation of Commercial Road Vehicles. *Cmnd. 255*. 266, 317
The International Transport of Goods, 980
Convention Regarding E.C.S. Carnets for Commercial Samples. *Cmd. 9863*. 50, 105
Co-operation Council:
Activities, 434, 704, 1232
Bulletin, 434
Publications, 213A–14A, 704, 962, 1232
Estimates:
1956–57, 12
1957–58, 226
1958–59, 494
1959–60, 760, 933
1960–61, 1202
Forms, 92–3, 306, 574, 836, 1107
Procedures, Comparative Study, 434, 704, 1232
Publications, 92–3, 305–7, 574, 836, 1107
Regulations and Procedure, U.K., 577
Report of the Commissioners. *Cmd. 9675*. 38, 194; *Cmnd. 69*. 253, 408; *Cmnd. 344*. 521, 678; *Cmnd. 613*. 539, 678
Reports. *Cmnd. 912*, *1234*. 1045, 1068, 1203
Select Committee on Estimates Special Report, 233, 240, 336, 1031, 1144
Tariffs:
And Supplement, 430
Classification of Goods, Convention on Nomenclature. *Cmnd. 305*. 269
Customs and Excise (*continued*):
Tariffs (*continued*):
Nomenclature for Classification of Goods, 214A; *Cmnd. 1070*. 1056, 1119
Of the U.K., 1107
Protocol of Amendment to the Convention for the Classification of Goods. *Cmnd. 127*. 257, 317
Valuation. Explanatory Notes, 1232
Customs Duties (Dumping and Subsidies) Act:
272
Report, 505, 665, 777, 921, 1032, 1192
Customs Duties (Dumping and Subsidies) Bill:
36, 215, 247
Memorandum. *Cmnd. 6*. 52, 180
Cutler, F., U.S. Investments in the Latin American Economy, 692
Cutlery:
Census of Production Report, 664, 1194
English, 422
Cutting, C. L.:
Dehydration of Fish, 165
Temperature of British Fish during Distribution in Summer, 910
Cutting, Theory of, 1180
Cutworms, 288, 820
Cwmbran Development Corporation Report, 24, 130, 237, 506, 613, 870, 1147
Cycles:
Handbook of the Collection, 648
History and Development, 164
Some Safety Aspects of Pedal and Motor-assisted Cycles, 384
Cycling. *See* Safe Cycling
Cyclists. *See* Child Cyclists
Cyprus:
Cmnd. 1093. 1057, 1103, 1108, 1119
Colonial Report, 88, 301, 570, 833
Conference:
Documents. *Cmnd. 679*. 792, 846
Final Statements. *Cmnd. 680*. 792, 846
Constitutional Proposals Report. *Cmnd. 42*. 55, 88
Correspondence Exchanged between the Governor and Archbishop Makarios. *Cmd. 9708*. 40, 88
Discussion in the North Atlantic Treaty Organisation. *Cmnd. 566*. 536, 589
International Customs Journal, 973
Order-in-Council, 1174
Statement of Policy. *Cmnd. 455*. 529, 571
Terrorism in, 90
Text of Notes from U.K. reimposing the Visa Requirement for Travel to Cyprus. *Cmnd. 73*. 253
Today, Picture Set, 131
Cyprus Act, 1070

Cyprus Bill, 1010, 1041
Cyrenaica. Exchange of Notes with U.K. on Mutual Cancellation of All Outstanding Claims. *Cmnd. 691*. 793, 847
Czecho-Slovak Refugee Fund Accounts, 23, 195, 237, 408, 765, 781, 935
Czechoslovakia:
Adult Education and Leisure Time Activities, 994
Agreement with U.K. for Air Services. *Cmnd. 1036*. 1053, 1119
Exchange of Letters with U.K. concerning Offers made in Settlement of certain Sterling Bonded Debts. *Cmnd. 1009*. 1051, 1119
Exchange of Notes with U.K.:
Concerning Agreement on certain Inter-Governmental Debts. *Cmnd. 55*. 317; *Cmnd. 720*. 794, 847, 1045, 1119
Concerning the Agreement on Compensation for British Property affected by Nationalisation. *Cmnd. 56*. 252, 317
Prolonging the Sterling Payments Agreement. *Cmd. 9687*, *9819*, *9875*. 38, 47, 51, 105: *Cmnd. 129*. 257, 317
International Customs Journal, 1244
Poland and U.S.S.R., Education in, 466

D

Dagenham East Station Railway Accident Report, 672
Dairy Economics, Some Aspects of, 560
Dairy Farms, Mechanization of, 450
Dairy Herd, Disease, Wastage and Husbandry, 1087
Dairy Policy, Agricultural Policies in Europe and N. America Report, 1245
Dairy Produce, Production, Trade, Consumption, etc., 91, 572, 1105
"Dalhanna" Wreck Report, 1200
Damages Assessment. *See* Law Reform, Scotland
Dampness in Buildings, 956
Damp-proof Course Insertion, 648
Damp-proof Treatments for Solid Floors, 164
Dancing, Choice of Careers, 1152
Dandy, J. D., Sloane Herbarium, 564
Dandy, J. E., British Vascular Plants List, 562
Dangerous Drugs Act, and Regulations, Duties of Doctors and Dentists, 123
Dangerous Goods. *See* Carriage of
Daniel, Admiral Sir C. (Chairman: Television Advisory Committee), Report, 1170
Danish Bacon. Arrangements relating to Import. Agreed Minute of Discussions between U.K. and Denmark. *Cmd. 9823*. 40, 47, 105
Danish Ships, Re-Insurance against War Risks Agreement, 404
Dartford Tunnel Act, 274
Dartmoor National Park:
362
Film Strip, 155
Darwen and Mostyn Iron Co. Ltd., Proposal to sell Holdings of Securities. *Cmnd. 703*. 793, 937
Darwin, Sir Charles (Chairman: Radioactive Substances Standing Advisory Committee), Code of Practice, 331
Darwin's Journal, 1096
Darwin's Notebooks on Transmutation of Species, 1096
Data Processing Methods, Handbook on, 1237
Data Sheets, 1091
Davey, J. B., Emmetropia and Its Aberrations, 359
David, P. M., Sagitta Planctonis and Related Forms, 295
Davies, Professor D. S. (Chairman: Committee on Agriculture and Dairy Diploma Courses in Wales), Report, 289
Davies, Mr. Justice A. (Chairman: Departmental Committee on Matrimonial Proceedings in Magistrate's Courts). *Cmnd. 638*. 789, 862
Davies, Martin:
British School Catalogue, 154, 890
Earlier Italian Schools Catalogue, 154
Early Netherlandish School Catalogue, 154
French School Text Catalogue, 361
Paintings and Drawings on the Backs of National Gallery Pictures, 154
Davies, R. L., Psychiatric Services and Architecture, 1269
Davis, F. M., Account of the Fishing Gear of E. and W., 823
Davis, M. E., Disease, Wastage and Husbandry in British Dairy Herd, 1087
Davis P. R., Fore-Limb Skeleton and Associated Remains of Proconsul Africanus, 828
Daw, S. E. H., Austria Overseas Economic Survey, 398
Daws, L. F., Heat Transfer in Deep Underground Tunnels, 651
Day E.I.S.N. Schools, 100
Day, W. R., Sitka Spruce in British Columbia, 325
Daylight Tables Simplified, 651
Dean Forest and Wye Valley, 325
Dean, H. T., Effect of Fluoridated Public Water Supplies on Dental Caries Prevalence, 421

DEA-DIV | 1956-60

DEA— INDEX 1956–60

Dean Orphanage and Cauvin's Trust (Amendment No. 3) Scheme:
Memorandum, 912
Order-in-Council, 1185
Dean, W. J., Ordovician Tribolite Faunas of South Shropshire, 1096
Dean, W. T., Faunal Succession in the Caradoc Series of South Shropshire, 563
Death Duties Bill, 1041
Death Duties in Canton de Vaud. Exchange of Notes between U.K. and Switzerland abrogating Declaration. *Cmnd. 514.* 533, 594
Death Grant Question. National Insurance Advisory Committee Report. *Cmnd. 33.* 54
Death Penalty (Abolition) Bill, 5, 32, 34, 36
Death Warrant of King Charles I. Document Reproduction, 1145
Death-Watch Beetle, 1180
Deaths of Eleven Mau Mau Detainees at Hola Camp in Kenya, Documents. *Cmnd. 778, 795, 816.* 799, 800, 801, 833
Deaths. *See* Registrar General's Returns
Débats de l'Assemblée Commune, European Coal and Steel Community, 214A, 434, 704, 962
Debenham, F. Nyasaland, 89
Debts:
Owed by Residents of Turkey, Agreement on Commercial, 974, 979
U.K. and Denmark. Exchange of Notes. *Cmnd. 754.* 797, 847
Decade of Co-operation, Achievements and Perspectives, 718
Decay of Timber and its Prevention, 906
Decennial Supplement, E. and W., 327, 597
Declaration of the Rights of the Child. *Cmnd. 1073.* 1056, 1127
Dedication of Woodlands, 112
Deeds, Register of, Index, 173, 389, 657, 916, 1188
Deepfrozen Foods, Experts Report, 1245
Deep Litter Hen House, 823
Deer (Scotland) Act, 809
Deer (Scotland) Bill, 486, 488, 746, 750, 765, 778, 784, 785, 863
Defects Caused by Ambrosia (Pinhole Borer) Beetles, 908
Defence:
See also Civil Defence
Agreement between U.K. and Nigeria. *Cmnd. 1212.* 1066
Appropriation Account, 9, 93, 222, 307, 490, 578, 757, 837, 1015, 1108
Central Organisation. *Cmnd. 476.* 530, 676
Collective. *Cmnd. 265.* 267
Contracts. Report of the Committee of Enquiry. *Cmd. 9788.* 44, 180
Defence (*continued*):
Cost of U.K. Forces:
Exchange of Notes between U.K. and Germany. *Cmnd. 588.* 538, 590
Stationed in Germany and related Measures of Mutual Aid. *Cmnd. 256.* 266
Estimates:
93
1956–57, 12, 13
1957–58, 226, 307
1958–59, 494, 578
1959–60, 759, 837, 933
1960–61, 1019, 1108
Future Policy. *Cmnd. 124.* 257, 307
Guides, 837
Lists, 93, 307, 578, 837, 1108
Ministry of, publications, 93–100, 307–12, 578, 837, 1108, 1114
Of the United Kingdom, 296, 380
Plan. *Cmnd. 662.* 791, 838
Programme Equipment:
Disposal of Surplus. *Cmnd. 1233.* 1057, 1068
Exchange of Notes between U.K. and U.S.A. concerning Disposal. *Cmnd. 714.* 794, 853
Regulations, 408
Report. *Cmnd. 363.* 523, 578; *Cmnd. 952.* 1048, 1114
Requirements in Caribbean, etc. Exchange of Notes between U.K. and U.S.A. *Cmd. 9812.* 46, 111
Specifications:
94–100, 307–12, 578, 838, 1109
Index, 585, 841
Statement. *Cmd. 9691.* 39, 93
Statistics:
1957–58, *Cmnd.* 130. 257, 307
1958–59, *Cmnd. 364.* 523, 578
1959–60, *Cmnd. 661.* 791, 842
Supplementary Estimates:
1956–57, 223, 307
1957–58, 493, 578
1959–60, 1017, 1108
Vote on Account, 494, 677, 1019, 1202
Defence Contracts Act, 540
Defence Contracts Bill, 250, 481, 500, 512, 518, 606
Defense Against Radioactive Fall-out on the Farm, 692
Deformation of Metals, Effect of a Surface-Active Medium on, 906
DEG:
Information Series, 1217
Reports, 1217
Dehydrated Vegetables for the Caterer, 558, 1086
Dehydration of Fish, 165
Delhi Public Library, 468
Delegations to the United Nations General Assembly, 451

INDEX 1956–60 —DES

Delinquency, Causes of, and Treatment of Offenders, Studies in, 1140
Delkeskamp, K., Neue Erotyliden aus dem Britischen Museum. Beitrag zur Kenntris der Erotyliden, 562
Delphacidae from the Lesser Antilles, 1095
Demange, J. M., Les Types D'Harpagophoridae de R.I. Pocock Conservé's au British Museum, Natural History, 1097
Demographic and Social Characteristics of the Population, 1260
Demographic Trends in Western Europe, 221A
Demographic Yearbook, 221A, 451, 721, 980, 1251
Demography, University Teaching of Social Sciences, 469
Demolitions. Royal Engineers Supplementary Pocket Book Amendments, 207, 425
Demotic Papyri, Catalogue of, 79
Denmark:
Agreed Minute of Discussions with U.K. on Arrangements relating to Import of Danish Bacon. *Cmd. 9787, 9823.* 40, 47, 105
Agreement on Agriculture with U.K. *Cmnd. 1071.* 1056, 1119
Agreement with U.K. relating to Trade and Commerce. *Cmnd. 337.* 521, 589
And U.K. Churchill Endowment Fund for the Exchange of Students Account and Statements. *Cmnd. 885.* 806, 847
Convention on Social Security with U.K. *Cmnd. 860.* 804, 847; *Cmnd. 990*; 1050, 1119
Convention with U.K.:
On Payment in respect of Industrial Injuries as relating to Denmark and Northern Ireland. *Cmd. 9839.* 48, 105
Payment of Compensation or Benefit in respect of Industrial Injuries. *Cmnd. 76.* 253, 317
Exchange of Notes with U.K.:
Concerning the Convention on Rights of Foreign Forces in Germany and the Finance Convention. *Cmnd. 22.* 54, 105
Concerning the Regulation of Fishing around the Faroe Islands. *Cmnd. 776.* 799, 847
Extending the Convention for the Avoidance of Double Taxation and the Prevention of Fiscal Evasion. *Cmnd. 705.* 794, 847
Extending the Provision of the Military Service Agreement. *Cmd. 9669.* 37, 105
Denmark (*continued*):
Exchange of Notes with U.K. (*continued*)
Extending to Rhodesia and Nyasaland, etc., the Convention for the Avoidance of Double Taxation, etc. *Cmnd. 903.* 807, 847
Regarding Co-operation in the Promotion and Development of the Peaceful Uses of Atomic Energy. *Cmnd. 1127.* 1059, 1119
Foreign Trade Statistical Bulletin, 222A, 447, 717, 977
Iceland, Norway and Sweden Economic Conditions, 221A, 446, 715, 1246
International Customs Journal, 444, 1244
Respecting the Reciprocal Repayment of Debts on the Liquidation of the European Payments Union. *Cmnd. 754.* 797, 847
Densities in Housing Areas, 1183
Dental Health Education Scottish Standing Committee Report, 1132
Dental Personnel, Auxiliary, Expert Committee Report, 999
Dental Profession. Report of the Committee on Recruitment. *Cmd. 9861.* 50, 120, 121
Dental Surgery Assistants, Royal Navy, Handbook, 547
Dentistry. Careers, 876
Dentists Act, 55, 272
Dentists Bill, 1, 2, 33, 214, 215, 248
Dentists Consolidation Bills Report, 213, 215
Department of Scientific and Industrial Research. *See* Scientific and Industrial Research
Department of Scientific and Industrial Research Act, 55
Department of Scientific and Industrial Research Bill, 2, 3, 5, 21, 29, 34, 35, 125
Departmental Road Safety Committee Report, 1021, 1196
Dependency Provisions. National Insurance Advisory Committee Report on the Question of Dependency Provisions. *Cmd. 9855.* 50
Dependent Peoples. *See* Sacred Trust
Depth of the Wind-Produced Homogeneous Layer in the Oceans, 73
Deratting Certificates, Ports approved and designated for Issue, 471
Derby Corporation Act, 1072
Derbyshire County Council Act, 1072
Dermaptera of the World based on Material in the British Museum (Natural History). Systematic Monograph, 828
Derwent Valley Water Order Amendments, 215
Derwent Water Order, 1957 Bill, 480
Design:
131, 343, 430, 613, 871, 1148

DES— INDEX 1956–60

Design (*continued*):
And Cropping of Mobile Glasshouses, 555
For Livability, 202
Of Horticultural Packing Sheds, 1087
Of Houses and Housing Estates Circular, 341
Of Poplar Experiments, 854
Of School Kitchens, 313
Designing for Safety in the Home, 857
Desoer, Air Vice-Marshal N. L.:
India's Most Dangerous Hour, 565, 658
War Against Japan, 296, 389
Detection of Toxic Substances in Air, Methods for, 885
Detergents. *See* Synthetic Detergents
Determination of Guarantee, Annual Review. *Cmd. 9721.* 41, 73, 171
Determination of the ABO and Rh(D) Blood Groups for Transfusion, 633
Deuterium and Tritium Compounds, Bibliography of Research on, 202
Deutschman, Z., Disease Control and International Travel, 243A
Developing Mass Media in Asia, 1265
Development and Application of Scientific Knowledge in Scotland, 772, 778, 863
Development and Engineering Group:
Information Series, 1217
Publications, 1217
Reports, 1217
Development and Welfare in West Indies Report, 571
Development Areas. Select Committee on Estimates Report, 9, 125, 230, 337
Development Fund Abstract Account, 11, 195, 225, 408, 492, 678, 758, 935, 1016, 1203
Development of Inventions Acts:
542
Accounts, 14, 180, 232, 396, 496, 665, 763, 921, 1016, 1192
Development of Inventions Bill, 487, 520
Development Plans Review Circular, 1146
Development Projects, Secondary School, Arnold, 1115
Developmental Progress of Infants and Young Children, 1136
Devlin, Hon. Mr. Justice, Chairman:
Committee appointed to Inquire into Operation of Dock Workers (Regulation of Employment) Scheme. *Cmd. 9813.* 46
Nyasaland Commission of Inquiry. Report. *Cmnd. 814.* 801, 834
Devonshire. Saxton's Maps, 79, 1094
D.H.S. Housing Techs. 329
Diabetes, Taking Care of, 692
Diagnosis of Occupational Diseases, Notes on, 636
Diakonoff, A., Additions to Descriptions of New Olethreutinae and Carposiniclae in the British Museum (Natural History), 827
Diaspidini (Coccoidea: Homoptera) from Africa, Some New, 1096
Dicercomyzon Demoulin. New Species of Genus, 562
Dick Bequest Trust Scheme:
Memorandum, 169
Order-in-Council, 169
Dick, J. B., Temperatures and Humidities in Pig Houses, 1181
Dickens, Admiral Sir Gerald, Dress of the British Sailor, 362
Dickens. Excerpt from the General Catalogue of Printed Books, 1094
Dickson, B. T., Guide Book to Research Data for Arid Zone Development, 465
Die Castings, Handbook:
Addendum, 659
Amendment, 175
Diets. Studies in Urban Household Diets, Report, 73
Dieuzeide, H., Teaching Through Television, 1249
Differences, Rules for the Settlement of, 971
Differential Diagnosis of Yaws, 1268
Differential Rent Schemes, Circular, 129
Diffusion and Equilibrium Properties of Water in Starch, 382
Digby, M.:
Co-operative Marketing for Agricultural Producers, 241A
Co-operatives and Land Use, 706
Diligence. Report of the Committee. *Cmnd. 456.* 529, 654
Dillon, L. S., Revision of the Neotropical Acanthocinini Genus Lagocheirus, 562
Din, U. Aung, Tropical Silviculture, 1237
Dines, H. G., Metalliferous Mining Region of South-West England, 119
Dinsdale, D. H. (Chairman: National Investigation into Economics of Milk Production), Report, 1086
Diocesan Education Committees Measure, 59
Diphtheria Immunization, 471
Diplock, K. (Deputy Chairman: Boundary Commission for England), Report, 861, 1059, 1137
Diplomatic and Consular Privileges and Immunities Laws and Regulations, 728
Diplomatic Immunities, 150, 357, 631, 1189, 1190
Diplomatic Immunities (Conferences with Commonwealth Countries and Republic of Ireland) Bill, 1045
Direction de la Documentation Parlementaire et de l'Information, 963
Direction of International Trade, 226A, 451, 721, 980, 1251

INDEX 1956–60 —DIV

Directorate of:
Colonial (Geodetic and Topographical) Surveys Report, 88
Overseas (Geodetic and Topographical) Surveys Report, 571
Directory of:
International Standards for Statistics, 1259
Nuclear Reactors, 1239
Probation Officers, etc. Amendments, 1138
Disabled Persons:
In Government Employment. *Cmnd. 90.* 255, 408; *Cmnd. 370.* 523, 678; *Cmnd. 664.* 791, 935; *Cmnd. 957.* 1048, 1204
Report of the Committee of Inquiry on the Rehabilitation, Training and Resettlement. *Cmd. 9883.* 52, 137
Report of the Standing Committee on Rehabilitation and Resettlement, 619
Disabled Persons (Employment) Act, 541
Disabled Persons (Employment) Bill, 482, 502, 512, 517, 606
Disablement, Rules governing Assessment of, Industrial Injuries Advisory Council Report. *Cmd. 9827.* 47, 159
Disappearing Culture. *See* International Social Science Bulletin
Disarmament:
And the United Nations, 721
Commission, United Nations, Records, 226, 451, 721, 980, 1252
Committee Meeting:
Records. *Cmd. 9648, 9649, 9650, 9651, 9652.* 36, 37, 105, 106; *Cmnd. 1152.* 1062, 1119
Text of the Plan. *Cmnd. 981.* 1049, 1119
Question, 344
Report on the Proceedings of the:
Sub-Committee. *Cmnd. 333.* 271, 318
United Nations Disarmament Commission. *Cmd. 9770.* 43, 105
Search for, 1150
Talks, Report on. *Cmnd. 228.* 264, 318
United Nations Effort, 226A
Disciplinary Tribunals Departmental Committee on Powers of Subpoena Report. *Cmnd. 1033.* 1053, 1140, 1187
Discrimination in Education, Study of, 721
Diseases:
And Pests on Horticultural Planting Material, 558
Control and International Travel, 243A
In Cattle and Sheep at Pasture, Control of, 715
Injuries and Causes of Death, International Statistical Classification, 327, 598
Of Animals, Handbook of Orders relating to, 558
Of Bees, 821
Diseases (*continued*):
Of Cattle, 821
Of Onions, Leeks and Shallots, 287
Of Pigs, 290
Of Sheep:
See also Afiechydon Defaid
557
Shepherd's Guide to Prevention and Control, 70
Of Turkeys, 290
Of Vegetables, 72
Wastage and Husbandry in the British Dairy Herd. Report, 1087
Diseases of Animals Act. Return of Proceedings, 824, 1088
Disposal of:
Radioactive Wastes Proceedings of the Scientific Conference, 1239
Scrap Cable. Report on Inquiry into the Methods adopted by the London Electricity Board. *Cmnd. 605.* 539, 641
Special Fund. Exchange of Notes between U.K. and Jordan. *Cmnd. 1007.* 1051, 1122
Surplus United States Mutual Defence Programme Equipment. *Cmnd. 198.* 262; *Cmnd. 1084, 1233.* 1114, 1127
Disputes. European Convention for Peaceful Settlement. *Cmnd. 1060.* 1055, 1119
Dissolution of Parliament:
918
Honours, 918
Distress for Rates Act, 1070
Distress for Rates Bill, 755, 1041
Distress for Rates Consolidation Bills Report, 1003, 1004, 1144
Distress for Rates Consolidation of Enactments, 755
Distribution and other Services, Report on Census, 923
Distribution, International Recommendations in Statistics, 989
Distribution of German Enemy Property Acts Accounts, 15, 180, 230, 396, 502, 665, 769, 781, 921
Distribution of Industry Act, Circular, 868
Distribution of Industry (Industrial Finance) Act, 541
Distribution of Industry (Industrial Finance) Bill, 484, 503, 513, 518, 606
Distribution of Wet-Bulb Temperature at Aberdeen and Eskdalemuir, 153
District Nurses, Training of, Report, 859
Disturbances at the Carlton Approved School Report. *Cmnd. 937.* 1047, 1138
Ditton Laboratory, Reports of the Low Temperature Research Station and, 907
Diverted Cargoes Claims. Exchange of Notes between U.K. and Greece on Final Settlement. *Cmnd. 996.* 1050, 1121
Divorce (Insanity and Desertion) Act, 541
Divorce (Insanity and Desertion) Bill, 250, 480, 483, 491, 512, 517, 519, 606

Dixey, F.:
Colonial Geological Surveys, 1947–56, 300
East African Rift System, 87
Overseas Geological Survey Report, 832
Dock Workers (Pensions) Act, 1070
Dock Workers (Pensions) Bill, 1007, 1042
Dock Workers (Regulation of Employment) Enquiry. *See* Cold Store Undertakings Report
Docks and Sorrels, 71
Doctors. *See* General *and* Medical Practitioners
Doctors' and Dentists' Remuneration, Royal Commission:
Minutes of Evidence, 647, 901, 1175
Report. *Cmnd. 939.* 1047, 1175
Supplement. *Cmnd. 1064.* 1055, 1175
Written Evidence, 380, 1176
Doctors' and Midwives' Certificates for National Insurance Purposes. Report of the National Insurance Advisory Committee. *Cmnd. 1021.* 1052, 1167
Document de Travail sur la situation de l'Agriculture dans la Communauté, 963
Documentation:
And Terminology of Sciences, 466, 994
In the Social Sciences, 237A, 466, 735, 994, 1263
Resolution and Index, ICAO, 711
Series, 1245
Documents:
Index, United Nations and Specialised Agencies, 226A, 452, 721, 992, 1261
On British Foreign Policy, 316, 1120
On German Foreign Policy, 106
Dodson, R. H. T., Education for Business Leadership Report, 221A
Dog Licences Act, 809
Dog Licences Bill, 750, 786
Dog Licences Consolidation Bills Report, 745, 751, 867
Dogs. Road Accidents in which they are the Cause, 755, 935
Doll, R., Leukaemia and Aplastic Anaemia in Patients Irradiated for Ankylosing Spondylitis, 359
Dollar:
Sterling Exchange Rate applicable to Outgoings diverted from Greek Ports during Late War. Exchange of Notes between U.K. and Greece. *Cmd. 9754.* 42, 107
Trade, Liberalisation of Europe's, Report, 223A, 448
Dollar Academy Trust Scheme:
513, 653
County of Clackmannon Order-in-Council, 912
Draft Scheme and Memorandum, 385
Dolls, 1222
Domestic Coal Consumers' Council. *See* Industrial Coal Consumers' Council
Domestic Commerce Series, 420
Domestic Food Consumption and Expenditure Report, 73, 291, 558, 822, 1087
Domestic Heating:
And Thermal Insulation, 1179
Estimation of Seasonal Heat Requirements and Fuel Consumption in Houses, 165
Domestic Preservation:
Fruit and Vegetables, 556
Meat and Poultry, 558
Domestic Science and Dietetics:
136
Careers, 617
Domestic Work in Hospitals, Organisation and Management of, 1134
Domicile Bill, 482, 485, 746, 784
Dominica:
Colonial Report, 569, 1102
Order-in-Council, 1173
Dominican Republic. Overseas Economic Survey, 398
Donaldson, G., Register of Privy Seal of Scotland, 389
Donaldson Trust (Amendment No. 1) Scheme:
Memoranda, 912
Order-in-Council, 912
Doncaster Corporation (Trolley Vehicles) Order Confirmation Act, 274
Doncaster Corporation (Trolley Vehicles) Provisional Order Bill, 217, 248
Donnelly, H. H., Chairman:
Committee on Qualifications of Teachers in School Holding the Teacher's Technical Certificate, Report, 170
Working Party on Remuneration of Part-time Further Education Teachers, Report, 911
Donnison, F. S. V., British Military Administration in the Far East, 82, 174
Dosemeters. Effects of Variations in the Ambient Air on the Calibration and Use of Ionization Dosemeters, 1163
Dosser, D. G. M., National Income of Tanganyika, 370
Double Death Duties Bill, 250
Double Taxation Relief. Tables, 873
Douglas, E. M., Boundaries, Areas, Geographic Centers and Altitudes of the United States and the Several States, 201
Douglas Fir, Two Leaf-Cast Diseases, 112
Douglas, C. K. M., Glazed Frost of Jan., 1940, 152
Douglas, Sir J. B. (Chairman: Scottish Committee on Prescribing Costs), Report, 858

Douglas, K. G. (Chairman: Central Health Services Standing Nursing Advisory Committee). Report on Design of Nurses' Uniforms, 859
Dover Castle:
Guide, 957
Postcard, 697
Dover Corporation Act, 57
Downing Street, Preservation of, Report. *Cmnd. 457.* 529, 680
Dowson, Sir Ernest, Land Registration, 88
Draft Coal and Other Mines Regulations, M.P. Safety Circular, 645
Dragon High Temperature Reactor Project Report, 1246
Drainage:
And River Conservancy Authorities. Return of Income and Expenditure, 129, 869
And Use of Methane from Coal Fields (Fire-damp), 221A
Pipework in Dwellings, 649
Drainage Rates Act, 541
Drainage Rates Bill, 482, 516
Drains and Sewers, Small Underground, 906
Dramatic and Musical Performers' Protection Act, 541
Dramatic and Musical Performers' Protection Bill, 480, 518
Dramatic and Musical Performers' Protection, Report on Consolidation Bill, 477, 481
Dramatic Art. Careers, 875
Dredge and other Mixed Corn, 289
Dress of the British Sailor, 362
Dress Regulations for Officers Amendment, 294, 561
Dressmaking and Millinery. Career, 347
Drew, G. C., Effect of Small Doses of Alcohol on a Skill Resembling Driving, 887
Drill (All Arms) Amendment, 424, 694, 1224
Drinking Water, International Standards, 740
Drinnan, R. E., Winter Feeding of the Oystercatcher on the Edible Mussel in the Conway Estuary North Wales, 559
Driving, Effect of Small Doses of Alcohol on a Skill Resembling, 887
Driving Instruction:
Manual of, 124
See Roadcraft
Drogheda, Rt. Hon. Earl of (Chairman: Advisory Council on Treatment of Offenders), Report, 334
Droit du Travail, 965
Drought, Circular, Short Term Measures, 869
Droylsden Station Railway Accident Report, 403
Drugs:
See also Narcotic Drugs
Addiction. Interdepartmental Committee Interim Report, 1133
Addiction Producing. Expert Committee Report, 472, 741, 999, 1269
Addicts. Treatment and Care. Report, 473
And Pharmaceutical Preparations Census of Production Report, 179, 663
And Poisons in Hospitals, Report on the Control of Dangerous, 602
Comparative Pharmacology of Some Psychotropic Drugs, 1267
Definition of, Report, 1133
Food and Cosmetic Act, Requirements of. Guide, 951
Liable to Produce Addiction, Expert Committee Report, 245A
Public Health and Social Problems in the Use of Tranquilizing Drugs, 421
Supervisory Body Supplement, 452, 722, 980, 1252
Drunkenness, Offences of, England and Wales Statistics. *Cmd. 9888.* 52, 124; *Cmnd. 280.* 268, 335; *Cmnd. 573.* 537, 605; *Cmnd. 807.* 801, 862; *Cmnd. 1094.* 1057, 1139
Dry Rot:
1226
In Buildings, 907
In Wood, 1180
Drying of Moulds by Portable Dryers Report, 138
D.T.D. Specifications, 176–8, 391–3, 659, 826, 918, 1091
Duck Stamps and Wildlife Refuges, 201
Duffy, E. A. J.:
Monograph of the Immature Stages of African Timber Beetles, 294
Monograph of the Immature Stages of Neo-Tropical Timber Beetles, 1097
Duke-Elder, Sir Stewart (Chairman: Committee on Trial Case Lenses), Report, 123
Dumazedier, Joffre:
Kinescope and Adult Education, 996
Tele-Clubs in France, 239A
Dumbarton Castle, Dunbartonshire Guide, 698
Dumfries:
Academy Endowments Trust Scheme Memorandum, 1184
And Galloway Girls' Home Trust Scheme:
Memoranda, 912
Order-in-Council, 1185
Boys' Home Trust Scheme:
Memoranda, 912
Order-in-Council, 1185
Kirkcudbright and Wigtown Hannahfield Trust Scheme. Memorandum, 653

Duncan MacLeod of Skeabost Scholarship Fund (Amendment No. 2) Scheme:
Memoranda, 912, 1184
Order-in-Council, 1184
Dundee Corporation Act, 57
Dundee Corporation (Consolidated Powers) Order Confirmation Act, 542
Dundee Corporation (Consolidated Powers) Order Confirmation Bill, 221, 249
Dunham, F.:
Television in Education, 691
Television in Our Schools, 419
Dunham, F. C., Chromiferous Ultrabasic Rocks of Eastern Sierra Leone, 572
Dunham, J. W., Combustible Contents in Buildings, 419
Dunlop, J. (Chairman: Scottish Health Services Council Committee), Reports, 601, 858
Dunning, G. C.:
Maison Dieu Guide, 698
Richborough Castle Guide, 208
Durability of Reinforced Concrete:
In Buildings. Report, 383
In Sea Water. Report, 1181
Durand, P.:
Représentation des Travailleurs sur le Plan de l'Entreprise dans le Droit des Pay Membres de la CECA, 965
Stabilité de l'Emploi dans le Droit des Pay Membres de la CECA, 965
Durand, Victor, Report of Inquiry into Disturbances at the Carlton Approved School. *Cmnd. 937.* 1047, 1138
Durham County Council (Darmston-Coxgreen Footbridge) Act, 274
Durst, C. S.:
Barometric Changes and the Efflux of Gas in Mines, 153
Preparation of Statistical Wind Forecasts and Assessment of their Accuracy in Comparison with Forecasts made by Synoptic Techniques, 1162
Statistical Study of the Variation of Wind with Height, 360
Dust:
In Card Rooms Report, 348, 1154
Prevention and Suppression Instructional Pamphlet, 114
Dutch School. National Gallery Catalogues, 635, 1163
Duties, etc., of the Medical Branch of the Factory Inspectorate. *Cmnd. 736.* 796, 877
Dyes and Dystuffs. Census of Production Report, 394, 1194

E

Eales, N. B., Revision of the World Species of Aplysia, 1097
Eames, J. E., Eocene **Mollusca from** Nigeria, 785
Ear Plug Laminations in relation to the Age Composition of a Population of Fin Whales, 828
Earlier Italian Schools of Painting, Catalogues, 154
Early Christian and Norse Settlements, Birsay, Guide Book, 957
Early Christian and Pictish Monuments of Scotland, 427
Early Keyboard Instruments, 1222
Early Literature on Mallophaga, 1095
Early Netherlandish School of Painting Catalogues, 154
Early Pleistocene Mammalian Fauna from Bethlehem, 563
Earnings Limits for Benefits. National Insurance Advisory Committee Report. *Cmd. 9752.* 42
Earthenware, Cream Coloured, 1222
East Africa:
High Commission Report, 88, 570, 833, 1102
Royal Commission Report:
Commentary on the Despatches from the Governors. *Cmd. 9804.* 45, 88
Despatches from the Governors. *Cmd. 9801.* 45, 88
United Nations Visiting Mission to Trust Territories, 991
East African:
Epheroptera, with Descriptions of New Species, Notes on, 1095
Forces. Correspondence with the Governor of Kenya, Uganda and Tanganyika, concerning Financial Arrangements applicable on Transfer of Local East African Forces. *Cmnd. 281.* 268, 302
Rift System, 87
East Anglia and the Midlands Illustrated Regional Guide, 207
East Ham Corporation Act, 274
East Ham. Railway Accident Report, 1197
East Kilbride Development Corporations Report, 21, 172, 236, 613, 656, 776, 779, 870, 915, 1187
East Lothian Educational Trust Scheme:
Draft, 386
Memorandum, 386
Order-in-Council, 653
Eastbourne Station Railway Accident Report, 929
Eastern Mediterranean Despatch, 357
Eastop, V. F., Study of Aphididae of East Africa, 570
Eaton, O. N., Hamster Raising, 199
ECAFE, Work of, 1255
Ecclesiastical Commission **Reports,** 3, 217, 478, 747, 829, 1099

Echo-Sounder Surveys in the Autumn of 1956, 559
Echo Sounding Experiments in the Barents Sea, 1087
Echo Traces. Interpretation of, 292
Ecological of the West African Marine Benthos, 571
Ecology of Intermediate Snail Hosts of Bilharziasis, Report, 472
Ecology of Scottish Inshore Fishing Grounds, 655
Economic and Financial Policy Formation, 238A
Economic and Financial Questions. General Assembly, United Nations, 983, 1254
Economic and Social Council, United Nations:
Commission on Narcotic Drugs Report, 722, 981
Governing Council of the Special Fund Report, 1253
Index to Proceedings, 227A, 453, 722, 981, 1252
Narcotic Drugs. National Laws and Regulations Index, 981
Publications, 722–3, 981
Records, 227A–8A, 453, 723, 981, 1252
Report, 726, 984, 1255
Rules of Procedure, 723
Summary, 227A
Economic and Social Development, Statistical Series for the Use of Less Developed Countries, 989
Economic Applications of Atomic Energy, 450
Economic Assistance Agreement between U.K. and Germany for Settlement of Claim. *Cmnd. 627.* 788, 849
Economic Blockade, 828, 916
Economic Bulletins:
Asia and Far East, 227A, 452, 722, 980, 1252
Europe, 227A, 452, 722, 981, 1252
Latin America, 227A, 452, 722, 981, 1252
Economic Characteristics of the Population, 732
Economic Commission Reports:
303
Africa, 982, 1253
Asia and the Far East, 723, 981, 1253
Europe, 228A, 453, 723, 981, 982, 1253
ICAO, 1242
Latin America, 453, 723, 981, 1253
See also "In the Service of Europe"
Economic Conditions:
221A, 446
Member and Associated Countries of OEEC, 715, 975, 1246
Non-Self-Governing Territories, 721
Economic Co-operation and Development. Convention on the Organisation. *Cmnd. 1257.* 1069
Economic Developments:
227A
Africa, 452, 722
Analyses and Projections, 1251
And Planning in Asia and Far East, 227A, 452, 722
Brazil, 450
Colombia, 720
In the Commonwealth, 132, 615
In the Middle East, 452, 722, 981, 1252
In the United Kingdom Dependencies, 344, 1150
Overseas Countries and Territories associated with OEEC Member Countries, 715
Projects Manual, 1256
Economic Forces in the U.S.A. in Facts and Figures, 201
Economic Geology of the Stirling and Clackmannan Coalfield, 906
Economic Growth:
Of Twenty Republics, 227A
Policies for Sound, 976
Economic Implications of:
Automation in Europe, 981
Full Employment. *Cmd. 9725.* 41, 195
Economic Leaflet, 295
Economic Role of Middleman and Co-operatives in Indo-Pacific Fisheries, 1237
Economic Series. British Museum, Natural History, 564, 1097
Economic Statistics, New Contributions to, 829
Economic Survey:
Cmd. 113. 256, 409; *Cmnd. 394.* 525, 678; *Cmnd. 708.* 794, 935; *Cmnd. 976.* 1049, 1204
Africa since 1950, 1253
Asia and Far East, 228A, 453, 723, 982, 1253
Europe, 228A, 454, 723, 982, 1253
Latin America, 228A, 723, 982, 1253
Overseas, 182, 398, 667, 923
1956. *Cmd. 9728.* 41, 195
Economic Trends, 83, 297, 430, 565, 829, 1098
Economics:
Committee of Council for Scientific and Industrial Research Report, 1180
International Bibliography, 237A, 466, 735, 994, 1263
United States of America, 237A
Economy in Expenditure, 610
Ecuador International Customs Journal, 444
Edelman, C. H., Bibliography of Land and Water Utilization and Conservation in Europe, 242A
Eden, Sir Anthony. Correspondence with Mr. Bulganin. *Cmnd. 182.* 261
Eden, J. F., **Mobile Tower Cranes for Two and Three-Storey Buildings,** 1181

EDE-EPA | 1956-60

Eden, R. A., Geology of the Country around Sheffield, 329
Edinburgh Castle Guide, 698, 1226
Edinburgh, City of. Fettes Endowment Amendment Scheme Order-in-Council, 169
Edinburgh College of Art Order Confirmation Act, 811
Edinburgh College of Art Order Confirmation Bill, 786
Edinburgh Corporation Order Confirmation Act, 57, 811
Edinburgh Corporation Order Confirmation Bill, 520
Edinburgh Gazette, 100, 312, 430, 585, 901, 1175
Edinburgh, H.R.H. the Duke of Edinburgh's Birthday. Message from Army Council, 205, 695, 956
Edinburgh Merchant Company Educational Endowments Scheme, Memorandum, 911, 1184
Edinburgh Merchant Company Order Confirmation Act, 1072
Edinburgh Merchant Company Order Confirmation Bill, 1043
Edinburgh, Register House, Official Guide to the Documents Exhibited in Historical Museum, 916
Education:
  Abstracts, 238A, 466, 735, 994, 1264
  Administrative Memorandum, 100, 312
  And Nuclear Energy Report, 1239
  And Training for Distribution, 975
  Belgian Congo, 736
  Belgium, 466
  Brazil, 994
  Britain, 615
  British Caribbean, Higher Technical. Report, 302
  Bulletin, 100, 201
  Business Leadership Report, 221A
  Central Advisory Council:
    (England) Survey, 1115
    Report, 842
  Circulars:
    102, 313, 585, 842, 843, 1115, 1116
    And Administrative Memoranda, 100, 313, 585; Index 313, 585, 1115
  Clearing Houses and Documentation Centre, 467
  Compulsory Studies, 237A
  Culture and Mass Communication:
    International Statistics, 1263
    Statistics, 237A
  Czechoslovakia, Poland and USSR, 466
  Draft Schemes, 170
  Egypt, 735
  For Agriculture, Report. *Cmnd. 614.* 539, 558, 585
  For Industry and Commerce, National Advisory Council, 842

Education (*continued*):
  For the Age of Science, 951
  Fundamental, Monograph on, 468
  Further. Circular, 911
  Immigrants for Citizenship, 238A
  In Exile, 101
  In the U.K. Dependencies, 872
  International Conference on Public Education, 237A, 468, 737, 995, 1264
  International Understanding, 995
  International Year Book, 238A, 467, 736, 995, 1265
  Israel, 736
  Italy, 995
  Memorandum, 169
  Ministry of:
    Publications, 100–2, 312–14, 585, 842, 1114, 1116
    Reports, *Cmnd. 223.* 313; *Cmnd. 777.* 799, 842; *Cmnd. 1088.* 1057, 1115
  Order-in-Council, 169
  Pamphlets, 101, 201, 313, 585, 842, 1116
  Percentage of 13 year olds receiving Secondary Education in Different Types of School, 1116
  Post Fourth Year Examination Structure in Scotland. *Cmnd. 1068.* 1055, 1185
  Primary, 842
  Publications, Unesco Institute for, 469
  Report and Statistics of Public Education. *Cmd. 9785.* 44, 101; *Cmnd. 454.* 529, 585
  Research in, 466
  Rules, 101, 313, 586, 843, 1116
  Rural Wales. Report, 1115
  Scotland:
    1039, 1040, 1141
    Report. *Cmd. 9722.* 41, 170; *Cmnd. 162.* 260, 385; *Cmnd. 407.* 526, 653; *Cmnd. 740.* 796, 911; *Cmnd. 1018.* 1052, 1184
    Superannuation Scheme, 169, 170
    The Next Step. *Cmnd. 603.* 539, 653
    See also Scottish Education Department
  Secondary, E. and W., 843
  Special Statistics, 1266
  Wales:
    1037
    Central Advisory Council Report, 100
  Welsh Department:
    586, 843
    Circulars, 102, 314
  West Indies, Fundamental, Adult, Literacy and Community, 238A
  See also Sandwich Courses—Secondary—Primary—Technical and Vocational

Education Act:
  809
  Registration of Independent Schools. Memorandum, 101
Education (Amendment) Bill, 1007
Education and Broadcasting Estimates, 1959–60, 760, 933
Education Association, International Directory, 995
Education Authorities and Managers of Grant-Aided Educational Establishments:
  Abstract of Accounts, Report, 169, 911
  Accounts, 385, 653
Education Authority Bursaries (Scotland) Regulations, 385
Education Bill, 1, 6, 33, 35, 752, 785
Education. Estimates:
  1956–57:
    12, 101
    Memorandum on. *Cmd. 9709.* 40
  1957–58:
    226
    Memorandum. *Cmnd. 99.* 255, 313
  1958–59:
    494, 676
    Memorandum. *Cmnd. 377.* 524, 585
  1960–61:
    1019, 1201
Education (Scotland) Acts:
  55
  Educational Scheme, Draft, 385–6
  Memorandum, 385–6, 653, 911, 912, 1184
  Orders-in-Council, 385–6, 653, 911, 912, 1184
Educational Building:
  102, 1115, 1116
  Capital Investment Circular, 313, 314
  Limits of Cost. Circular, 842, 843, 1115, 1116
Educational Conditions in Non-Self-Governing Territories, 1259
Educational Courses, 1232
Educational Endowments:
  Accounts, 386
  Scheme, City of Aberdeen, 911
Educational Information Services in USSR, 735
Educational Maintenance Allowances Report, 313
Educational Periodicals, International List, 467
Educational Research:
  1264
  International Conference, Report, 466
Educational, Scientific and Cultural Materials, Agreement on Importation. Guide, 736
Educational Studies and Documents, 238A, 466–7, 736, 995, 1264
Edwards, Alderman H. T. (Chairman:

Edwards (*continued*):
  Council for Wales and Monmouthshire), Memorandum. *Cmnd. 53.* 252
Edwards, I. E. S., Hieratic Papyri in the British Museum, 1094
Edwards, Professor J. G. (Chairman: Royal Commission. Ancient and Historical Monuments, Wales and Monmouthshire), Report. *Cmnd. 1138.* 1060, 1140
Edwards, M. V., Exotic Forest Trees in Great Britain, 325
Edwards, R.:
  Georgian Furniture, 693
  Ham House Guide, 422, 951
Edwards, W., Geology of the Country Around Sheffield, 329
Eelworms:
  In Potatoes, 1082
  In Strawberries, 1083
Eeuwens, B. E. P. Bibliography on Land and Water Utilization and Conservation in Europe, 242A
Effect of Draughts on the Burning of Portable Oil Heaters, 1179
Effect of Flooding on the Growth Rate of Brown Trout in Loch Tummel, 387
Effect of Tax Liability on Damages. Law Reform Committee Report. *Cmnd. 501.* 532
Effects of Differential Tax Treatment of Corporate and Non-Corporate Enterprises, 975
Effects of Small Doses of Alcohol on a Skill Resembling Driving, 887
Effects of Taxation on Foreign Trade and Investment, 1253
Efficiency of Adhesives for Wood, 166, 907
Efficient Uses of Fertilizers, 966
Efficient Uses of Fuel, 641
Egg Marketing Scheme, Proposed British. Report. *Cmd. 9805.* 46, 75
Egglestone Abbey, Yorkshire, Guide, 698
Eggs:
  And Larvae of Haddock at Faroe, 172
  Draft Scheme for Regulating Marketing, 71
  Export Licence, 397
Egypt:
  Agreement between U.K. and United Arab Republic concerning Financial and Commercial Relations. *Cmnd. 723.* 795, 847
  Agreement between U.K. and United Arab Republic concerning Financial and Commercial Relations and British Property in Egypt. *Cmnd. 639.* 789, 935
  Exchange of Notes with U.K. extending the Provisions of the Suez Canal Base Agreement. *Cmd. 9858.* 50, 106
  Operation in, 357

Egyptian Region. United Kingdom Trade Mission Report, 1194
Ehrman, J., Grand Strategy, 82, 174
Eibl-Eibesfeldt, Dr. Irenäus, Survey on Galapagos Islands, 995
Eisteddfod Act, 809
Eisteddfod Bill, 521, 748
Elder Yard Chapel, Chesterfield Act, 57
Election Expenses:
  Amendment, 32, 124
  Return, 1023, 1138, 1186
Elections Select Committee Report, 9, 125
Electric Energy Statistics for Europe, 454, 724, 982, 1251, 1258
Electric Fencing, 290
Electric Fields on Marine Fishes, Effect of, 172
Electric Gravity Feed Slicing Machines, Film Strip, 313
Electric House Heating, 692
Electric Lamps. Defence List, 307
Electric Lighting Accessories and Fittings. Census of Production Report, 394
Electric Power:
  Asia and Far East, 724
  Committee on. Supplement, 724
  Consumption Forecasts, Methods employed for Determination, 228A
  Equipment Survey of, 446, 715, 978, 1249
  Possibilities of Exchanges, 730
  Services in Europe, Organisation of, 228A
  Situation in Europe:
    454, 724, 1253
    And Its Future Prospects, 1253
Electric Stunning, Circular, 557
Electric Wires and Cables, Census of Production Report, 664
Electrical Accidents and Their Causes, Report, 619, 875, 1154
Electrical and Allied Machinery and Plant, Report on the Supply and Exports, 223
Electrical and Electronics Industries, Use of Technical Literature, 909
Electrical Apparatus, Test and Certification of Flameproof Enclosure, 901
Electrical Applications, Printed Wiring for, Defence Guide, 837
Electrical Engineering:
  Award of National Certificates and Diplomas, 1116
  Census of Production Report, 179
  (General) Census of Production Report, 664
  See Radio, Services Textbook of
Electrical Fishing, 707
Electrical Pocket Book, Naval, 545
Electrician. Career, 347
"Electricité de Beyrouth" Company Case, 443

Electricity:
  And Gas Boards Report. *Cmnd. 695.* 793, 899
  Council Reports and Accounts, 24–5, 114–15, 237–8, 370–1, 775, 898, 1033, 1170
  For Farm and Estate, 1087
  In Europe, 446
  Rates Report, 446
  Report of the Minister of Power, 25, 114, 239, 371, 508, 641, 775, 898, 1033, 1170
  South of Scotland Board Report and Accounts, 227, 389
  Trend of Selling Price, 719
Electricity Act:
  272
  Guarantee given on Loans proposed to be raised, 11, 13, 17, 22, 26, 195, 224, 231, 235, 239, 409, 493, 500, 507, 510, 678, 757, 764, 767, 780, 935, 1018, 1025, 1032, 1034, 1204
  New Generating Stations and Overhead Lines. Circulars, 611
Electricity (Amendment) Bill, 1011, 1044
Electricity Bill, 36, 216, 217, 218, 229, 242, 247, 249, 336
Electricity Board Reports and Accounts, 507, 641, 775, 899, 1032, 1033, 1171
Electricity (Borrowing Powers) Act, 809
Electricity (Borrowing Powers) Bill:
  521, 747
  Memorandum. *Cmnd. 618.* 540, 641, 655
Electricity (Publications and Applications) (Scotland) Regulations, Statutory Instruments. Select Committee Report, 490, 609
Electricity Supply Industry:
  Census of Production Report, 180, 396, 1194
  In Europe, 224A, 450, 719, 978, 1251
  Reorganisation. *Cmnd. 27.* 54, 115
  Report. *Cmd. 9672.* 37, 115
Electrification in Europe, State of Rural, 1259
Electrification. *See* Rural Electrification
Electro-Sparking, Working Metals by, 168
Electronic and Allied Equipment, Production of, Defence Guide, 837
Electronic Computer, Wage Accounting by, Report, 155
Electronic Valves and Cathode Ray Tubes Monopolies and Restrictive Practices Commission, Report on Supply of, 221, 223
Eledone, Notes on European Species, 80
Elementary Meteorology for Air-Crew, 633
Elements of First Aid, 334
Elephant Seal:
  88
  Physiology of Reproduction, 302

Elimination of Double Taxation Report, 715, 975, 1247
Eliot, Lt. Col. J. H., New or Little Known Butterflies from Malaya, 827
Ellis, R. W., Whiting in the North Sea, 172
Ellison, M. A., Spectrum of Quiescent Prominences, 380
Elm Diseases:
  596
  In Britain, Status and Development of, 1129
Eltham Palace, Kent, Guide, 698
Elvin, H. L., Social Development Through Family and Home, 1104
Embroidery, Basic Stitches, 1222
Emergency Childbirth, Welfare Section Training Bulletin, 861
Emergency Feeding. Civil Defence Handbook, 1138
Emergency Force, United Nations. Budget Estimates, 726, 983
Emergency Laws (Repeal) Act, 809
Emergency Laws (Repeal) Bill, 489, 516, 520, 756, 863
Emergency Legislation:
  Cmnd. 563. 536, 678
  Continuance of, *Cmnd. 7.* 52, 123; *Cmnd. 297.* 269, 334
Emerson, J. P., Establishing and Operating a Flower Shop, 201
Emesinae in the British Museum (Natural History), New and Little Known, 563
Emmetropia and its Aberrations, 359
Empire Settlement Bill, 36
Employers' Association, Trade Unions, etc., Directory, 619, 1154
Employment:
  And Industry in Wales, 1037
  Economic Implications of Full, *Cmd. 9725.* 41, 195
  In Scotland, 1027, 1037, 1141
  Must Full Employment Mean Ever-Rising Prices, 196
  Of Children in the Potato Harvest Report. *Cmd. 9738.* 41, 170
  Positive Employment Policies, 630
Emsweller, S. L., Roses for the Home, 201
Emulsifying and Stabilising Agents in Foods Report, 73
Emulsion Paint, 207
Enactments Relating to the Profits Tax, 873
Encyclopaedias and Dictionaries of Education, 735
Endemic Goitre, 1267, 1268
Endersby, H. J., Blunting of Wood-Cutting Edges, 166
Energy Advisory Commission Report, 1250
Energy and Economic Development, New Sources of, 459
Energy Development in Latin America, 724

Energy Foods, 1083
Energy for OEEC Countries. Basic Statistics, 977
Engholm, B. C. (Chairman: Committee on Transactions in Seeds), Report. *Cmnd. 300.* 269; *Cmnd. 1092.* 1057
Engineer. *See* Chemical Engineer—Professional Engineer
Engineer Works Services, Regulations, Amendments, 205, 424, 695, 955
Engineering:
  And Allied Employers' National Federation of Shipbuilding and Engineering Unions. Report of Court of Inquiry into Dispute. *Cmnd. 159.* 259
  And Scientific Manpower in the United States, Western Europe and Soviet Russia, 201
  And Traffic Aspects of Highway Safety. Report of the Seminar, 987
  Books on, 381
  Industries in Europe, 224A, 719, 1250
  Institutions, International Directory of Agricultural, 435
  Production, Arrangements for Awards of Certificates, 313
  Reports, Selected Piezoelectricity, 370
  Shipbuilding and Vehicles. Census of Production Report, 180, 923
  Work, Careers, 618
Engineers, Royal, Supplementary Pocket Book, 1225
Engledow, Sir F. (Chairman: Agricultural Improvement Council, E. and W.), Report, 560
English Alabasters from the Hildburgh Collection, 203
English Chintz, 1223
English Copper, Tin and Bronze Coins in the British Museum, 1094
English Cutlery, 422
English Furniture Designs of the Eighteenth Century, 951
English in Secondary Schools. Report on the Teaching, 170
English Printed Textiles, 1222
English. Scottish Certificate of Education, 913
English Watches, 203
Entertainments Duty Act, 541
Entertainments Duty Bill, 220, 250
Entertainments Duty Consolidation Bill Report, 220, 477
Entomology, Bulletins, 80, 294, 562, 827, 1095
Entreprises Sidérurgiques. European Coal and Steel Community, 1233
Entwistle, A., Incentives in the Building Industry, 909
Eocene Mollusca from Nigeria, 295
EPA European Technical Digests, 221A, 446, 716, 975

Ephemeroptera from Uganda, New Species of, 80
Epidemiological and Vital Statistics:
  Annual, 243A, 470, 739
  Report, 244A, 471, 739, 998, 1267
Epidemiological Methods in the Study of Mental Disorders, 1269
Epidemiological Record, Weekly, 243A, 470
Epileptics, Report on Medical Care, 121
Equal Pay:
  For Equal Work, 1253
  For Women, 203
  Primer, 203
Equivalent Headwinds at Heights of 30,000 feet and 40,000 feet along Air Routes, 634
Ergonomics of Automation, 1181
Erinaceidae from the Miocene of East Africa, 81
Essex County Council Act, 543
Essex County Council (Fullbridge, Maldon) Act, 1072
Esso Petroleum Company Act, 274
Esso Petroleum Company Bill. Select Committee:
  Report, 1031, 1142
  Special Report, 1031, 1143
Establishments for the Training of Teachers, E. and W. recognised by the Minister, 842, 1115
Estimated Damage from Nuclear Attack, 604
Estimates:
  Allocation to Sub-Committees, 1038
  Select Committee:
    Minutes of Proceedings, 27, 125, 240, 336, 509, 606, 776, 863
    Reports, 9, 13, 14, 16, 21, 23, 125, 222, 224, 233, 234, 235, 236, 240, 336, 490, 503, 505, 506, 606, 770, 772, 776, 781, 864, 1017, 1029, 1030, 1042
    Special Reports, 222, 227, 230, 234, 240, 245, 336–7, 491, 493, 497, 506, 514, 515, 606, 757, 763, 770, 865, 1023, 1029, 1031, 1038, 1039, 1040, 1043
  See Air — Army — Civil — Defence — Navy — Revenue Departments — Royal Ordnance Factories — Scottish —War Office Purchasing Services
Ethiopia:
  Agreement with U.K. for Air Services. *Cmnd. 531.* 534, 589; *Cmnd. 692.* 793, 847
  International Customs Journal, 444, 714
Ethiopian, Mascarene and Australian Reduviidae in the British Museum. New Genera and Species of, 294
Études et Documents, European Coal and Steel Community, 434
Euratom Bibliographie, 704, 963
Europe:
  And Africa, 1232
  And the World Economy. Economic Review, 1247
  Economic Bulletin, 227A, 452, 722, 981, 1252
  Economic Commission Report, 228A, 723, 981, 982
  Economic Survey, 228A, 454, 723, 982, 1253
  Today and in 1960, 446
European Agreement:
  Concerning International Carriage of Dangerous Goods by Road. *Cmnd. 734.* 796, 850
  On the Protection of Television Broadcasts. *Cmnd. 1163.* 1063, 1119
European and British Commonwealth Series, 201
European Atomic Energy Community:
  Agreement with U.K. for Co-operation in Peaceful Uses of Atomic Energy. *Cmnd. 702.* 793, 845
  General Report on Activities, 963, 1233
  Publications, 963
  Report on Nuclear Industries in the Community, 963
  Treaty establishing, 438
European Civil Aviation Conference Report, 217A, 441, 711, 970
European Coal and Steel Community:
  Cmnd. 424. 527, 589
  Activities of the Community Report, 214A, 963, 1233
  And U.K. Report of the Council of Association. *Cmnd. 1104.* 1058, 1120
  Agreement concerning the Relations with U.K. *Cmnd. 13.* 53, 106; *Cmnd. 326.* 271, 318; *Cmnd. 693.* 793, 847
  Annual Report. *Cmnd. 116.* 256, 318
  Assemblée Commune Manuel, 435, 704, 962
  Assemblée Parlementaire Européenne Débats, 962, 1233
  Bulletin Statistique, 214A, 434, 704, 963, 1233
  Consultative Assembly Joint Meeting with Members of the Council of Europe, 214A
  Débats de L'Assemblée Commune, 704
  Études et Documents, 705
  Official Gazette, 102, 430
  Publications, 102, 214A–15A, 434, 704–6, 962, 1232
  Rapport Général sur L'activité de la Communanté. 963, 1235
  Report. *Cmnd. 794.* 800, 848
European Coal, Rational Utilization of, 724
European Commission of Human Rights, 703

European Committee on Crime Problems, 1232
European Common Market. *See* Agricultural Commodities
European Conference of Local Authorities, 433
European Convention:
  For the Peaceful Settlement of Disputes, 434; *Cmnd. 1060.* 1055, 1119
  On Establishment, 213A
European Co-operation Report, 961, 1232
European Culture and the Council of Europe, 434
European Economic Community Commission:
  Bulletin, 965, 1235
  General Reports, 965, 1236
  Publications, 965, 1235
  Treaty Establishing, 438
European Economic Co-operation Survey, 221A
European Economy, Structure of, 978
European Free Trade Area:
  Negotiations:
    Documents. *Cmnd. 641.* 789, 937
    Report. *Cmnd. 648.* 790, 937
  United Kingdom Memorandum. *Cmnd. 72.* 253, 396, 409
European Free Trade Association:
  966
  Booklet, 935
  Compendium, 1192
  Convention and Documents. *Cmnd. 906.* 807, 921, 935; *Cmnd. 1026.* 1053, 1120
  Forms, 1192
  Protocol on the Legal Capacity, Privileges and Immunities. *Cmnd. 1194.* 1065, 1120
  Publications, 966
  Schedules to Convention approved at Stockholm. *Cmnd. 906–7.* 807, 921, 935
  Stockholm Draft Plan. *Cmnd. 823.* 801, 938
European Free Trade Association Act, 1070
European Free Trade Association Bill, 1005, 1041
European Gas Economy Trends, 228A
European Housing:
  Progress and Policies, 228A
  Situation, 228A
  Trends and Policies, 454, 724, 982
European Interim Agreement. Social Security Schemes Amendment. *Cmnd. 1161, 1162, 1182, 1183.* 1062, 1064, 1125
European–Mediterranean Communications Meeting Supplement, 218A
European–Mediterranean Regional Air Navigation:
  Meeting Report, 1242
  Plan, 1241
European Monetary Agreement:
  Amendments. *Cmnd. 959.* 1048, 1120
  As Amended, 1247
  Directives for Application of, 975, 1245
  Report, 1247
  Supplementary Protocol. *Cmnd. 554.* 535, 589
European Monetary Agreement Act, 809
European Monetary Agreement Bill, 747, 784
European Nuclear Energy and the Eurochemic Company Report, 716
European Organisations Handbook, 213A
European Parliament, Towards a, 704
European Payments Union:
  Agreement for Establishment, 221A
  Exchange of Letters between U.K. and:
    Belgium concerning Repayment of Credits. *Cmnd. 248.* 265
    Germany for Repayment of Credits. *Cmnd. 291.* 268
    Sweden on Repayment of Balance of U.K. Debts. *Cmnd. 81.* 254
    Sweden on Repayment of Part of Debt. *Cmd. 9712.* 40, 110
  Exchange of Notes between U.K. and:
    Austria concerning Repayment of Credit. *Cmnd. 596.* 538, 588
    Sweden on Repayment of Debt on Liquidation. *Cmnd. 991.* 1050, 1126
  Report, 221A, 446, 716, 975
  Reports of Debts on Liquidation. *Cmnd. 754, 755, 756, 757, 758, 759, 760, 761, 762, 763, 764, 768, 769.* 797, 798, 845, 850, 852
  Supplementary Protocol:
    Cmd. 9867. 50, 106; *Cmnd. 555.* 535, 589
    Amending the Agreement. *Cmnd. 259.* 266, 318
European Refrigeration Research and its Practical Applications, 975
European Steel Market, 228A, 454, 724, 982
European Technical Conference on Food-Borne Infections and Intoxications Report, 1269
European Technical Digests, 221A, 446, 716, 975, 1247
European Treaty Series, 213A, 434, 703, 962, 1232
European University Rectors and Vice-Chancellors Report of Conference, 245A
Europe's Growing Needs of Energy. How Can They Be Met? Report, 221A
Europe's Need for Oil, 716
Evans, E. J., Sound Absorbing Materials, 1163
Evans, G. Owen:
  British Mites of the Subfamily Macrochelidae Trägårdh, 81

Evans, G. Owen (*continued*):
  Revision of the Platyseiinae based on Material in the Collections of the British Museum (Natural History), 1097
  Ruwenzori Expedition, Introduction with List of Localities, 564
Evans, Sir Ifor (Chairman: National Insurance Advisory Committee), Reports, 230, 234, 236, 237, 239, 243, 244, 245, 246; *Cmnd. 206.* 263; 502, 504, 506, 513, 892; *Cmnd. 984, 1021.* 1048, 1052
Evans, R. E., Rations for Livestock, 1085
Evans, W. E. Revision of the Arhopala Group of Oriental Lycaenidae, 295
Evans, W. R., Provisional Yield Table for Western Hemlock in Great Britain, 325
Eve, Sir M. T., Chairman:
  Crown Estate Commissioners: Statement on Future of Regent's Park Terraces, 305, 836
  Road Haulage Disposal Board, 26
Evening Institutes, 101
"Evening News" Drawing and Text Complaint. Committee of Privileges Report, 223, 338
Everett Interpolation Coefficients, 636
Everybody's Guide to National Insurance, 636, 891
Everyman's United Nations, 228A, 1254
Evolution, Handbook on, 564, 1097
Evolution of Ratites, 81
Evolution Récente de la Situation Économique, 963
Examination. Extra-Masters in the Mercantile Marine, 929
Examination (Introduction of Ordinary Grade) Circular, 911
Examination Papers:
  Aviation, Ministry of, 826, 1091
  Civil Service Commission, 83–6, 297–9, 566, 830, 1099
  Fuel and Power, Ministry of, 115, 326
  Power, Ministry of, 641, 645, 899, 900, 1171, 1172
  Scottish Leaving Certificate:
    171, 654, 1185
    Circular, 169, 386
  Secondary Schools, Circular, 313, 314
  Transport and Civil Aviation, 187, 402, 671, 830, 928
  Transport, Ministry of, 926, 1117
Examination Regulations:
  Ministry of Transport, 1198
  Transport and Civil Aviation, 671
Examinations:
  Art, 101, 313, 585, 842, 1115
  Mining Qualifications Board, 900
  Secondary Schools:
    General Certificate of Education and Sixth Form Studies Report, 1115
    Other than G.E.C. Report, 1116
Examples in Applied Mechanics, 545
Excavations:
  At Clausentum, Southampton, 698
  At Jarlshof, Shetland, 427
  On Defence Sites. Mainly Neolithic-Bronze Age, 1226
Excess Profits Levy. Appeal Leaflet, 873
Exchange of Dwellings Bill, 520
Exchange of Energy between the Atmosphere and the Oceans of the Southern Hemisphere, 1160
Exchequer and Audit Departments Act, 777
Exchequer and Audit Departments Bill, 218, 249
Exchequer and Audit Department Publications, 586, 844, 1117
Excreta Disposal for Rural Areas and Small Communities, 740
Execution of Sentences and Military Penal Establishments, Rules, etc., 695
Executive Board, World Health Organisation. Resolutions, 999
Executive Committee Report. International Civil Aviation Organisation, 1242
Exell, A. W., Vascular Plants of S. Tomé, 82
Exhibition Galleries Guide, 81
Exocentrus Mulsant, Révision du Genre, 563
Exodus from Hungary, 454
Exotic Forest Trees in Great Britain, 325
Expansion of School Building, 468
Expedition to South-West Arabia, 295
Expenditure:
  Economy in, 610
  On Furniture and Equipment Circular, 100, 102
  Treasury Control of, 770, 866
Experience in Radiological Protection, 986
Experimental Horticulture, 558, 822, 1087
Experimental Husbandry:
  73, 291, 558, 822
  Farms and Experimental Horticulture Stations Report, 1087
Experimental Rearing of the Larvae of Ostrea edulis L. in the Laboratory, 74
Experimental Stress Analysis in the U.S.A. and Canada, 167
Experiments in Rectilinear Cutting, 1180
Experiments on Living Animals, Return, 26, 124, 239, 334, 509, 604, 776, 862, 1033, 1138
Experiments on the Chemical Control of Rhododendron Ponticum, 325
Experiments on the Treatment of Redwood Sapwood by Dipping, 650
Expiring Laws Continuance Act, 56, 273, 542, 810, 1071
Expiring Laws Continuance Bill, 7, 35, 220, 249, 487, 520, 754, 786, 1011, 1044

Exploitation of Sea Birds in Seychelles, 570
Explosion Reports:
  Bickershaw Colliery. *Cmnd. 1000.* 1051, 1171
  Colliery. *Cmnd. 279, 287, 327.* 268, 270, 271, 371; *Cmnd. 331, 396, 414, 467, 485.* 521, 525, 526, 529, 531, 642
  St. John's Colliery. *Cmnd. 935.* 1047, 1171
  Walton Colliery. *Cmnd. 843.* 803, 899
Explosives:
  And Fireworks. Census of Production Report, 394, 1194
  Carriage by Sea. Rules for Packing, Stowage and Labelling Report, 402, 671, 928
  Factory Accident Report, 334, 604
  Inspectors Report, 27, 124, 235, 334, 504, 604, 1038, 1140
  List of Authorised, 124, 334, 604, 862
Explosives Acts:
  Authorised Explosives, 1139
  Memorandum for the Guidance of Applicants, 604
  Report, 777, 862
  Summary, 1139
Export Guarantees Act, 272, 809
Export Guarantees Bill, 216, 247, 753, 786
Export/Import Bank of Washington Agreement with U.K. providing for a Line of Credit. *Cmnd. 104.* 256, 409
Exporters, Compendium Amendment, 1192
Exporting to the United States, 951
Exports:
  Food Products to Canada. Certificate, 559
  Licences:
    180–1, 396–7, 666, 921
    Antiques, 1193
    Open General Revocation, 666
  List, 1108
  List, Relating to the Standard International Trade Classification. Amendment, 181
  Live Cattle. Committee of Enquiry Report. *Cmnd. 154.* 259, 291, 387
  Surplus War Material. *Cmd. 9676.* 38, 94, 106
  Works of Art. Report of the Reviewing Committee. *Cmd. 9882.* 52, 195; *Cmnd. 270.* 267, 409; *Cmnd. 542.* 535, 678; *Cmnd. 856.* 804, 935; *Cmnd. 1175.* 1063, 1204
Exports from Overseas Territories of OEEC Countries, Statistics of, 719
External Defence and Mutual Assistance. Proposed Agreement between U.K. and Malaya. *Cmnd. 263.* 266
External Rendered Finishes, 1178
Extradition, Agreement between U.K. and Israel. *Cmnd. 1013, 1223.* 1052, 1067, 1122
Eyes, Care of, 420
Eyespot of Wheat and Barley, 820

F

Facilitation Division, International Civil Aviation Organisation:
  Report, 217A, 1241
  Supplement, 217A
Facilities for Education in Rural Areas, 737
Factories:
  And Plant, History of Second World War, 565, 657
  Building Studies, 906, 1179
  Buildings, Structural Frameworks for Single-Storey, 1179
  Chief Inspector's Report. *Cmnd. 8.* 53, 138; *Cmnd. 329.* 521, 619; *Cmnd. 521.* 533, 619; *Cmnd. 810.* 801, 876; *Cmnd. 1107.* 1058, 1152
  Docks, etc. Accidents. How They Happen and How to Prevent Them, 874, 876
  Forms, 138, 348, 620, 875, 1154
  Inspectorate:
    Guide to Statistics, 1155
    Medical Branch, Duties, etc. *Cmnd. 736.* 796, 877
    Staffing and Organisation. *Cmd. 9879.* 51, 138
  Ionising Radiations, Special Regulations Draft, 348, 1154
  Modern Multi-Storey, 906
  Orders, 138, 621, 878
  Work, Study of Attitudes to, 151
Factories Acts:
  809
  Memorandum, 138
  Regulations. Revision, 619
Factories Bill, 516, 520, 749, 751, 752, 762, 778, 784, 786
Facts and Figures, Basic, 994
Facts of Flight, 201
Fair Labour Standards Act (Federal Wage-Hour Law) Handy Reference Guide, 201
Falkland Islands Dependencies:
  Colonial Reports, 87, 88, 832
  Gazetteer, 848, 1120
  Survey Scientific Reports, 302, 571, 833, 1103
Fallout and the Winds, 420
Falmouth Docks Act, 543, 811
Falmouth Harbour Act, 543
False Indications of Origin of Goods. International Agreement. *Cmnd. 876.* 805, 848
Family Allowances Act, Decisions, 1164
Family Allowances and National Insurance Act, 55, 809

FAM-FLE | 1956-60

FAM— INDEX 1956-60

Family Allowances and National Insurance Bill, 5, 20, 29, 34, 126, 516, 520, 747, 756, 863
Family and Child Welfare. *See* International Social Service Review
Family Fare. Food Management and Receipes, 201
Family Levels of Living. Report, 724
FAO Group Report, 968
FAO's Role in Rural Welfare, 966
Farley, J. L., Duck Stamps and Wildlife Refuges, 201
Farmers:
 Assistance for Small. *Cmnd. 553.* 535, 556, 603, 654
 Book-keeping and Income Tax, 823
 Bulletins, 201, 420, 692
 In Asia and Far East, Credit Problems of Small, 451
 Income Tax, 73, 291
Farmhouse Butter-Making, 289
Farmhouses and Cottages, 559
Farming:
 Current Economic Conditions in Scottish, 70
 In the United States, Generalized Types of, 199
 Some Studies of Current Economic Conditions in Scottish Farming, 1081
Farms:
 And Estates, Procedure for Building and other Work, 74
 And Horticultural Workers, Choice of Career, 618
 And Smallholdings. *See* Co-operative Farms
 Animals, Control of Losses, 446
 As a Business. Handbook of Standards and Statistics, 291
 Book-keeping, 554
 Buildings:
  Construction, 823
  Pocketbook, 1087
  Remodelling and Adaptation, 716
  Report of Survey, 1247
  Roof Coverings, 1087
  Wall Construction, 823
 Dairies:
  1087
  Utensils, Cleaning and Chemical Sterilization, 820
 Grain Drying and Storage, 72, 1085
 Income Series, 558
 Incomes in England and Wales Report:
  291, 558, 1087
  1956–57, 822
  1957–58, 822
 Machinery:
  558
  Leaflets, 558, 823, 1087
Farms (*continued*):
 Management:
  716
  Handbook, 819
  In the United States. Report, 716
  Investigations, 966
  Records and Accounts, 557
 Produce, Output and Utilization, 559
 Roads, 290
 Workshop, 292
Farmyard Manure Handling, 823
Farnham Castle Measure:
 1011, 1099
 Report, 1011, 1099
Faroe-Shetland Channel, Hydrography of, 388
Farr, C. A., Ring Circuit Electrical Installations for Housing, 427
Fashionable Lady in the 19th Century, 1222
Fatal Accidents Act, 809
Fatal Accidents Bill, 520, 750, 751, 752, 760, 778, 784, 786, 863
Fatis Review, 221A, 446–7, 716, 975, 976, 1247
Fats and Oils Commodity Report, 241A, 707, 966
Fatstock Guarantee Scheme, 73, 291, 823, 1087
Faunal Succession in the Caradoc Series of South Shropshire, 563
Faulkner, P. (Chairman: Committee on Safety of Nuclear-Powered Merchant Ships), Report. *Cmnd. 958.* 1048
Fay, E. S., Report on Investigation into Affairs of General, London and Urban Properties Ltd., 1192
Federation of Malaya Independence Act, 272
Federation of Malaya Independence Bill, 219, 249
Feeding Dairy Cows, 1085
Feeding for Winter Milk, 555
Feeding Grass, 69
Feeding Layers on the General Farm, 71
Feeding of Children from One to Five Years, 1133
Feeding of Separated Milk, 555
Fees and Charges for the Testing of Sight and the Supply or Repair of Glasses. Amendments, 1137
Fees for Certificates of Outcome of Civil Trial (Army) Regulations, 424
Felixstowe Dock and Railway Act, 57
Fellmongery, Census of Production Report, 395
Fellowships, Scholarships, Educational Exchange International Handbook, 996
Felted Beech Coccus, 112
Feltwell, R:
 Methods of Intensive Poultry Management, 821
 Turkeys, 821

INDEX 1956-60 —FIN

Fencing:
 And Safety Precautions for Cotton Spinning and Weaving Machinery, 149, 1158
 Of Machinery Circular, 900
Fennah, R. G., Delphacidae from the Lesser Antilles, 1095
Fernando Po and Rio Muni. International Customs Journal, 1244
Fertilisation Experiments in Scottish Freshwater Lochs, 387, 914
Fertilisers:
 Agricultural Value of Phosphate Fertilisers. Report, 220
 And Crop Production, 1082
 And Feeding Stuffs, Residual Value, 70, 554, 820, 1082
 Disinfectant, Insecticide and Allied Industries, Census of Production Report, 394
 Distributors, 823
 Efficient Use of, 966
 In the Commonwealth, 1105
 Legislation, Latin America, 241A
 Placement for Arable Crops, 69
 Production and Consumption, 221A, 241A, 447, 707, 716, 966, 976, 1247
 World Production and Consumption, 436, 1236
Fertility:
 And Hatchability, Aids to, 71
 In Industrialized Countries, Recent Trends in, 730
 Of Marriage, 119
 Report, 856
Fettes Endowment (Amendment No. 3) Scheme, Order-in-Council, 169
Feversham, Earl of (Chairman: Departmental Committee on Human Artificial Insemination), Report. *Cmnd. 1105.* 1058
Fiber Consumption Levels, 1236
Fibre Building Board Industry in Europe, 221A
Fibreboard and Particle Board Report, 707
Field and Laboratory Investigation of Fish in a Sewage Effluent, 558
Field Astronomy, Text Book, 956
Field Beans, 558
Field Cable:
 Construction, 861
 Laying and Despatch Riders, 1138
Field Crop Sprayers, 558
Field, H. I., Diseases of Pigs, 290
Field Manual:
 Amendment, 441, 970
 Communication Procedures, 217A
Field Studies of the Movement of Soil Moisture, 652
Fife Educational Trust Scheme, 1185; Memorandum, 386, 653
Fifteen to Eighteen Report, 842, 1115
Fifteen-Year Exposure Test of Porcelain Enamels, 419
Fifty Facts about Britain's Economy, 1149
Figulla, H. H., Cuneiform Tests from Babylonian Tablets in the British Museum, 827
Fiji:
 Colonial Report, 301, 570, 833, 1102
 Order-in-Council, 1174
 Photo-Poster, 614
Filey Holiday Camp Station Railway Accident, 403
Filho, M. B. L., Primary School Curricula in Latin America, 736
Films:
 And Cinema Statistics. Report on Methodology, 240A
 Catalogue of French Ethnological, 239A
 Filmstrips:
  132, 155, 288, 313, 344, 362, 554, 614, 1083
  International Rules for Cataloguing, 467
  Manual for Evaluators, 239A
  Use. Evaluation and Production, 1265
 Making on a Low Budget, 1265
 Programmes for the Young Report, 996
 Popular Science Catalogue, 468
 Recommended for Children and Adolescents, 468
 Vocabulary, 738
Films Act, 1070
Films Act Consolidation Bills Report, 1004, 1144
Films Bill, 1006, 1007, 1043
Finance:
 Accounts:
  765, 936
  Of the United Kingdom, 20, 195, 234, 409, 489, 504, 678, 770, 936, 1027, 1204
 Advances to Nationalised Industries and Undertakings, 496, 587, 766, 844, 1017, 1020, 1027, 1117, 1171
 Convention between U.K., France, U.S.A. and Germany. *Cmnd. 655.* 790, 849
 Statistics of Sources and Uses, 1249
Finance Act, 55, 272, 541, 809, 1070
Finance Act Accounts, 18, 195, 231, 409, 501, 678, 1024, 1204
Finance No. 2 Act, 5, 34, 35
Finance Bill, 5, 34, 35, 219, 248, 249, 485, 518, 519, 753, 785, 786, 1009, 1042, 1043
Finance Estimates:
 1956–57, 12
 1957–58, 226
 1958–59, 494
 1959–60, 759, 933
 1960–61, 1019, 1201

FIN— INDEX 1956-60

Financial and Commercial Relations:
 Agreement between U.K. and United Arab Republic. *Cmnd. 723.* 795, 847.
 And British Property in Egypt. Agreement with U.K. *Cmnd. 639.* 789, 935
Financial Arrangements. Exchange of Notes between U.K. and Turkey. *Cmnd. 1256.* 1069, 1126
Financial Assistance Schemes for the Acquisition or Improvement of Fishing Craft, 1237
Financial Matters:
 Agreement between U.K. and:
  Canada amended. *Cmnd. 121.* 257
  Hungary. *Cmd. 9820.* 47, 107
  U.S.A. *Cmnd. 120.* 257; *Cmnd. 178.* 261
 Exchange of Notes between U.K. and Bulgaria concerning Settlement. *Cmnd. 752.* 797, 845
 Protocol modifying Agreement between U.K. and Turkey. *Cmnd. 117.* 257
 Settlement. Agreement between U.K. and Roumania. *Cmnd. 1232.* 1068, 1125
Financial Obligations. Exchange of Notes between U.K. and Yugoslavia. *Cmd. 9730.* 41, 112
Financial Policy, 1939–45, 82, 174
Financial Questions. Exchange of Notes between U.K. and Poland for Settlement. *Cmnd. 1057.* 1055, 1124
Financial Regulations, ICAO, 711
Financial Reports:
 General Assembly, 726
 World Health Organisation, 740, 1268
Financial Statement:
 1956–57, 17, 195
 1957–58, 230, 409
 1958–59, 500, 678
 1959–60, 764, 936
 1960–61, 1022, 1204
Financing Improvements to Land and Buildings, 74
Financing of Housing:
 And Community Improvement Programes, 454
 In Europe, 724
Finch, H. D. S., New Ways of Using the General Tariff Tables for Conifers, 325
Finch, J. C. W. (Chairman: Welsh Agricultural Land Sub-Commission), Report on Monmouthshire Moors Investigation, 75
Finch, The Late Allan George, Report on the Manuscripts of, 380
Findlay, W. P. K.:
 Decay of Timber and Its Prevention, 906
 Dry Rot in Wood, 1180
Fines Bill, 1004
Finger and Palm Prints, Instructions in the Method of Taking, 1139
Finland:
 Convention with U.K. on Social Security. *Cmnd. 878.* 805, 848; *Cmnd. 1240.* 1068, 1120
 Education in, 1264
 Exchange of Notes with U.K. regarding the Reciprocal Abolition of Visas. *Cmnd. 523.* 533, 589
 International Customs Journal, 444, 714
 Pulp and Paper Statistics, 1250
Finsbury Square Act, 274, 811
Fire Appliances:
 And Equipment, Emergency Drill Book, 1138
 For Mobile Fire Columns, Manual of, 124
Fire Extinguishers, Methods of Testing Small, 419
Fire Fighting:
 Elementary, 333
 For Householders, 201
 Ship, 422
Fire, Materials and Structures, 648
Fire Precautions for Houses, Memorandum on Structural, 329
Fire Research Board Report:
 165, 382, 649, 907, 1179
 Special Report, 1180
Fire Resistance:
 Of Pre-stressed Concrete, Chlorinated Rubber Paints, etc., 164
 Tests on Structural Elements, Sponsored, 1183
Fire Service Drill Book, 1139
Fire Services Act, 809
Fire Services Bill, 750, 752, 786
Fire Services, Counties and County Boroughs, Chief Inspector's Reports:
 England and Wales. *Cmd. 9845.* 49, 124; *Cmnd. 246.* 265, 334; *Cmnd. 499.* 531, 604; *Cmnd. 844.* 803, 862; *Cmnd. 1122.* 1059, 1140
 Scotland. *Cmd. 9756.* 42, 171; *Cmnd. 152.* 259, 387; *Cmnd. 425.* 527, 655. *Cmnd. 747.* 796, 914; *Cmnd. 1031.* 1053, 1186
Firedamp, 640
Fireguards, 340
Firemen's Pension Scheme:
 Commutation, 862
 Order, 334
Firs, Adelges Insect of Silver, 112
First Aid:
 And Early Treatment of Burns in the R.A.F., 293
 Civil Defence Handbooks, 604
 Elements of, 334
 In the Laboratory. Display Card, 170
First Conference of London. Documents on British Foreign Policy, 588

INDEX 1956-60 —FLE

First Offenders Act, 541
First Offenders Bill, 481, 482, 517, 519
First Offenders (Scotland) Act, 1070
First Offenders (Scotland) Bill, 1005, 1041
First Ten Years of the World Health Organisation, 740
Fiscal and Financial Field, Programme for Technical Assistance in, 732
Fish:
 And Fish Offal for Oil and Meal Manufacture, Preservation of, 1183
 And Meat Curing Brines, Microbiology, 649
 And Wildlife Service. Circular, 201
 Curing. Census of Production Report, 395
 Dehydration of, 165
 Frozen, 223A
 Hygienic Transport and Handling, 1133
 Marketing and Consumption of Frozen, 1245
 Marketing in Western Europe, 447
 On the Dynamics of Exploited Fish Populations, 559
 Tissues, Chemical Composition, 907
 Trade, Hygiene in, 1133
Fish, B. P., Diffusion and Equilibrium Properties of Water in Starch, 382
Fish, G. R., Seiche Movement and Its Effect on Hydrology of Lake Victoria, 302
Fisheries:
 Abstracts, World, 969
 Agreement between U.K. and:
  Norway. *Cmnd. 1324.* 1067, 1123
  U.S.S.R. *Cmd. 9778.* 44, 111; *Cmnd. 148.* 259
 Agreement relating to the International Convention for regulating the Police of the North Sea Fisheries. *Cmnd. 517.* 533, 590
 Bulletin, 241A, 436, 707
 Investigations, 73–4, 291, 558, 823, 1087
 North-East Atlantic Fisheries Convention. *Cmnd. 659.* 791, 848
 On the Fishing Effort in English Demersal Fisheries, 73
 Police of North Sea. Agreement relating to International Convention. *Cmnd. 4.* 52, 109
 Policies in Western Europe and North America, 1247
 Protocol to the International Convention for the North-West Atlantic Fisheries. *Cmnd. 687.* 792, 848
 Publications, 89, 302, 571, 833, 1103
 Scotland. Report. *Cmd. 9739.* 41, 171; *Cmnd. 146.* 259, 387; *Cmnd. 395.* 525, 655; *Cmnd. 704.* 794, 914; *Cmnd. 1097.* 1057, 1082
Fisheries (*continued*):
 Scottish Sea Fisheries Statistical Tables, 172, 388, 656, 915, 1082
 Statistics Yearbook, 241A, 436, 707, 969, 1239
 Study, 436, 707, 966, 1237
Fishermen's Organisation and the Regulation of Fish Prices in Sweden, 436
Fishing:
 Around Faroe Islands. Exchange of Notes between U.K. and Denmark. *Cmnd. 776.* 799, 847
 Boat Tank Tests, 241A, 966
 Careers, 875
 Gear of E. and W. Account, 823
Fitters, Turners, Machinists. Careers, 136
Fitting the Job to the Worker, 716, 1247
Fitzgerald, J. (Chairman: Committee for Staggering of Working Hours in Central London), Report, 671
Fitzmaurice, R., Manual on Stabilized Soil Construction for Housing, 732
Five-Year Perspective. Consolidated Report, 1254
Five-Year Trade Agreement between U.K. and U.S.S.R. *Cmnd. 771.* 799, 922
Fixed Equipment of Farm Leaflets, 74, 292, 559, 823, 1087
Fixed Price Tendering Circular, 340
Fixed Services Meeting, North Atlantic, 972
Flags:
 And Map Kit, United Nations, 1262
 Badges:
  1103
  And Arms, 571
  Cayman Islands, 833
  Hong Kong, 833
 Of All Nations, 60, 545, 813
Flameproof Enclosure of Electrical Apparatus, Test and Certification of, 646, 901
Flame-Retardant Building Materials, 907
Flatlets For Old People:
 611, 1147
 Circular, 611, 1146
Flats and Houses:
 611
 Circular, 611
Flats, Plumbing for Multi-Storey, 906
Flax Processing. Census of Production Report, 395
Flea Beetles, 1083
Fleas:
 Illustrated Catalogue of the Rothschild Collection, 81
 See also Insects of Medical Importance Their Medical and Veterinary Importance, 564
Fleck, Sir A., Chairman:
 Committee appointed to obtain Information relating to Windscale Piles, Report. *Cmnd. 471.* 530

1956-60 | FLE-FRU

FLE— INDEX 1956-60

Fleck, Sir A., Chairman (*continued*):
Committee to Examine Organisation for Control of Health and Safety in U.K. Atomic Energy Authority Report. *Cmnd. 342.* 521
United Kingdom Atomic Energy Authority Report. *Cmnd. 338.* 271
Fleetwood Harbour. British Transport Commission Charges Scheme, 1199
Fletcher, D. S.:
Arctiidae Nolinae, 564
Geometridae, 564
Ruwenzori Expedition Introduction, 564
Flight Engineering, 202
Flight Engineer's Licence, 402
Flight, Facts of, 201
Flight, Information Manual, 201
Flight Instructors':
Handbook, 199
Oral Examination Guidebook, 201
Flight Navigator's Licence, 187, 671, 926, 928, 1091
Flight, Path of, 202
Flight Radio Operator's Licences, 402, 671; Amendment, 926
Flint Implements, 79
Flock and Rag. Census of Production Report, 395
Flood Control Series, 228A, 454, 724, 982, 1254
Flood Prevention (Scotland) Bill, 1039, 1040, 1044, 1045, 1141
Floor Coverings, Laying Screeds as an Underlay, 1226
Floor Finishes for Factories, 909
Flour:
Composition Regulations, etc. Circular, 73
Report on Composition and Nutritive Value. *Cmd. 9757.* 42, 74, 120, 121
Flower Shop, Establishing and Operating, 201
Fluke or Liver Rot in Sheep, 1085
Fluoridated Public Water Supplies on Dental Caries Prevalence, Effect of, 421
Fluorine Food Standards Committee Report, 292
Fluorine in Food Regulations, Circulars, 822
Fly, as a Danger to Health, Its Life History and How to Deal With It, 1097
Flying Fish, Recent Developments in the Barbadian Flying-Fish Fishery and Contributions to the Biology of the Flying-Fish Hirundichthys Affinis, 89
Flynn, Captain, F. C.:
British Fortunes Reach Their Lowest Ebb, 1098, 1189
"The Germans Come to the Help of Their Ally", 82, 174
Focus on East-West Relations, 213A
Fomes Annosus in Great Britain, 1129
Fontes et Aciers, 705, 963, 1233
Food:
Circulars of, 72–3
Composition of, 1160
Estimates:
1956–57, 12
1957–58, 226
1958–59, 494, 676
1959–60, 760
1960–61, 1019, 1201
From Gardens and Allotments, 74
Hygiene:
Codes of Practice, 859, 1133
Docks, Carriers, etc., Regulations, Circular, 1133
Expert Committee on Environmental Sanitation Report, 245A
Regulations, Circular, 121, 331, 1133
Scotland Regulations Statutory Instruments. Select Committee Report, 756
Investigation:
Board Report, 166, 382, 649, 907
Index to Literature, 165
Leaflet, 649
Special Reports, 165, 382, 649, 907, 1180
Technical Paper, 165, 382, 907
Mixers, 558
National Food Reserve Policies, 707
National Food Survey Committee, 73, 291, 558, 822, 1087
Poisoning:
Investigation of Circular, 602
Memorandum, 602
Science Abstracts, 166, 382, 650, 1180
See also Advisory Filmstrips
Standards Committee Report, 74, 292, 823, 1087
Standards (Ice-Cream) Regulations, Labelling of Food (Amendment) Regulations, Circular, 822
Studies in Administration and Control, 82, 174
Supplies in Armed Forces Estimates, Select Committee Special Report, 491, 606
Supplies of the Armed Services. Select Committee on Estimates Report, 21, 125
Supply, Time Series, 1237
Food Additives:
Control in the United Kingdom, 1237
Control Series, 966
General Principles governing Use of, 437, 473
Joint FAO/WHO Conference Report, 245A
Legislation, Current, 707, 966
Food and Agriculture:
Documentation Series, 1245

INDEX 1956-60 —FOR

Food and Agriculture (*continued*):
Expansion in Far East, Problems of, 242A
Legislation, 241A–2A, 436, 707, 967, 1237
Price Policies, 967
State of, 242A, 436, 708, 968, 1238
Statistics Yearbook, 242A, 436
Technical Services, 446–7, 716, 975
See Fatis Review
Food and Agriculture Organisation:
Agreement for Latin American Forest Research and Training Institute. *Cmnd. 1171.* 1063, 1120
Conference Report, 707, 1238
Exchange of Notes with U.K. establishing International Desert Locust Information Service. *Cmnd. 600.* 539, 590
Group Report, 968
Publications, 435–7, 706–9, 966, 1236
Role in Rural Welfare, 966
Statistics Yearbook, 708
Food and Drugs Act. Circular, 73
Food and Drugs (Scotland) Act, 55
Food and Drugs (Scotland) Bill, 1
Food and Drugs. *See* Ministry of Health Report
Food and Feeding Habits:
Of Larval and Post-Larval Herring in the Northern North Sea, 388
Of the Lemon Sole, 172
Food-borne Infections and Intoxications, European Technical Conference Report, 1269
Food, Drug and Cosmetic Act, Requirements of. Guide, 951
Foods Your Children Need, 692
Food-and-Mouth Disease Viruses, Methods of Typing and Cultivation of, 447
Foot Rot in Sheep, 821
Footwear:
Report on the Supply of Certain Rubber, 22, 182
Trade. Distribution in Europe, 716
For Human Welfare, 982
For The Children, Work of UNICEF in the Americas, 724
Forage Harvesters, 1087
Foraminifera. Great Barrier Reef Expedition Scientific Reports, 564
Forbes, Sir A. (Chairman: Iron and Steel Board), Special Report, 235, 370
Forces, H. M.:
Career, 136
In Germany. Exchanges of Letters with Netherlands prolonging agreement concerning Responsibility for Rights and Obligations. *Cmnd. 413.* 526, 592
Medical and Dental Services Committee Report, 94
Royal Navy. Career, 347
Forces, H. M. (*continued*):
Stationed in Territory of Federal Republic of Germany, Documents relating to. *Cmd. 9802.* 45, 106
See also Service Pay
Forecasting Cirrus Cloud over the British Isles, 360
Forecasting Manpower Needs for the Age of Science, 1247
Foreign Compensation Commission:
Accounts, 17, 106, 228, 318, 502, 590, 769, 848, 1027, 1120
Reports. *Cmd. 9849.* 49, 106; *Cmnd. 299.* 269, 318; *Cmnd. 611.* 539, 590; *Cmnd. 901.* 807, 845; *Cmnd. 1204.* 1066, 1120
Foreign Estimates:
1956–57, 12
1957–58, 226
1958–59, 494, 676
1959–60, 759, 933
1960–61, 1019, 1201
Foreign Forces in Germany. Exchange of Notes between U.K. and Denmark concerning Convention on Rights, and Finance Convention. *Cmnd. 22.* 54, 105
Foreign Law in Turkey, Reception of, 467
Foreign Ministers Conference at Geneva. Principal Documents. *Cmnd. 797, 829, 868.* 800. 802, 805, 846, 848
Foreign Office:
Publications, 103–12, 314–25, 587, 844, 1117
Foreign Service Act, 1070
Foreign Service Bill, 783, 786, 1003, 1014, 1141
Foreign Student and Post Graduate Public Health Courses Report, 999
Foreign Trade Statistical Bulletin, 221A–2A, 447–8, 717–18, 977, 1248
Foreigners Entering and Leaving the United Kingdom. Statistics. *Cmnd. 34.* 54, 124; *Cmnd. 163.* 260, 334; *Cmnd. 405.* 526, 604; *Cmnd. 701.* 793, 863; *Cmnd. 994.* 1050, 1140
Fore-Limb Skeleton and Associated Remains of Proconsul Africanus, 828
Foremen in Europe, Selection and Training of, 223A
Forest Products Research:
Board Report, 166, 382, 650
Bulletins, 112, 166, 382, 650, 907, 1180
Laboratory Leaflets, 907, 1180
Records, 112, 325, 596, 650, 854, 908, 1129
Reports, 112, 325, 596, 854, 907, 1129, 1180
Research Workers, Conversion Tables for, 1128
Special Report, 166, 382, 650, 1180
Forestry:
Advisory Committee Report, 427

FOR— INDEX 1956-60

Forestry (*continued*):
Agriculture and Marginal Land Report, 382
And Forest Products Study, 708, 1237
Buildings, Allowances in respect of Capital Expenditure on Agricultural, 873
Career, 347, 1152
Criteria and Equipment of Tractors Report, 242A
Development Papers, 242A, 437, 967, 1237
Practice. Forest Nurseries and Plantations, 596
Forestry Commission:
Booklet, 112, 1128
Bulletins, 325, 596, 854, 1129
Guide, 854, 1129
Leaflets, 112–13, 325, 596, 855, 1129
Publications, 112–13, 325, 596, 854, 1128
Reports, 23, 112, 233, 325, 504, 596, 773, 855, 1023, 1128
Forests:
Accident Statistics, Collection, Compilation and Analysis, 724
Inventory, World, 1238
Of Dean Committee Report. *Cmnd. 686.* 792, 855
Products:
Statistics Yearbook, 242A, 436, 708, 967, 1239
World Statistics, 709
Seed Directory, 242A
Tractors:
228A
Protocol for the Testing of, 1257
Working Techniques and Training of Forest Workers Joint Committee Reports, 242A, 437, 708, 724, 967
Form F. Sigs. Message Form, 1139
Form of Claim in Answer to Notice to Treat, 857, 936
Formal Validity of Wills. Private International Law Committee Report. *Cmnd. 491.* 531, 632
Formation Professionnelle dans les Houillères des Pays de la Communauté, 215
Formation Professionelle dans les Mines de Fer des Pays de la Communauté, 963
"Forresbank" Wreck Reports, 1200
Forster, Sir J. (Chairman: Court of Inquiry into Dispute between London Master Printers Association and London Typographical Society and Association of Correctors of the Press), Report. *Cmd. 9717.* 40
Forsyth, R. J., Use of Liquid Manure on Farms, 554
Forth and Forth Road Bridge. Report on the Proposed Underwater Crossing. *Cmd. 9741.* 41, 171
Forth Road Bridge Order Confirmation Act, 543
Forth Road Bridge Order Confirmation Bill, 517, 1044
Fossils:
Amphibians and Reptiles, 564
Birds, 564
British Caenozoic Fossils (Tertiary and Quaternary), 1095
Denticipitid Fishes from East Africa, 1096
Mammals of Africa, 81, [illegible], [illegible], [illegible], 1097
Man:
Introduction to Study, 564
See Primates, History of
Metacarpals from Swartkrans, 1097
Minerals and Rocks, Instructions for Collectors, 82, 1097
Plants of the Carboniferous Rocks of Great Britain, 857
Tubulidentata from East Africa, 81
Foster-Sutton, Sir S. W. P. (Chairman: Tribunal inquiring into Allegations reflecting on Official Conduct of Premier, etc.), Report. *Cmnd. 51.* 251
Foundations with Social Science Activities, 468
Foundry Industry. Career, 347
Fourastié, J., Productivity, Prices and Wages, 449
Fowey Pier and Harbour Order Confirmation Act, 1072
Fowey Pier and Harbour Order Confirmation Bill, 1008, 1043
Fowl Typhoid, 556
Fox, L.:
Tables of Everett Interpolation Coefficients, 636
Tables of Weber Parabolic Cylinder Functions and other Functions for Large Arguments, 1163
Use and Construction of Mathematical Tables, 362
Framlingham Castle, Suffolk, Guide, 957
France:
Agreement with U.K. on the Liquidation of the European Payments Union. *Cmnd. 757.* 797, 848
And U.K. Protocol to the Convention on Social Security. *Cmnd. 999.* 1049, 1120
Consular Convention with U.K. *Cmnd. 617.* 788, 848
Convention on Relations between the Three Powers, U.K., France and U.S.A. with Germany. *Cmnd. 653.* 790, 849
Convention on Social Security with U.K. *Cmnd. 9877.* 51, 106; *Cmnd. 560.* 536, 590
Doing Business with France, 692

INDEX 1956-60 —FRU

France (*continued*):
Economic Conditions, 221, 446, 715 1246
Exchange of Notes with U.K.:
Concerning Exemption from Turnover Tax on Royalties. *Cmnd. 808.* 801, 848
Concerning Mining Regulations to be applied in the New Hebrides. *Cmnd. 667.* 791, 848
Concerning the Revision of the Penal System in the New Hebrides. *Cmnd. 668.* 791, 848
Extending to the Island of Jersey the Anglo-French Social Security Convention. *Cmnd. 840.* 803, 848
Foreign Trade Statistical Bulletin, 222A, 447, 448, 717, 977
History and Administration, 545
International Customs Journal, 444 713, 973, 1244
Military Service Agreement with U.K. *Cmnd. 57.* 252, 318
Frances Barker and certain other Charities (City of York) Scheme Confirmation Act, 57
Francis, E. H., Economic Geology of the Stirling and Clackmannan Coalfield, Scotland, Area North of the River Forth, 119
Francis, F. C., Catalogues of Oriental Printed Books and Manuscripts, 827
Francis, G. H., Petrological Studies of Glen Urquhart, Inverness-shire, 563
Franciscolo, M., Ruwenzori Expedition, 828
Franklyn, General Sir Harold (Chairman: Battle Nomenclature Committee), Report, 205, 694
Franks, Rt. Hon. Sir Oliver (Chairman: Committee on Administrative Tribunals and Enquiries):
Minutes of Evidence, 90, 304
Report. *Cmnd. 218.* 263
Fraser, D. K. (Chairman: Scottish Advisory Council on Welfare of Handicapped Persons), Report, 331
Fraser, F. C., Hearing in Cetaceans, 1097
Fraud, Prevention of. Particulars, 182
Free Trade Report, 448
Free World Ally—Japan, 692
Freedman, M., Chinese Family and Marriage in Singapore, 301
Freedom from Arbitrary Arrest, Detention and Exile, 1254
Freedom of Entry into Industry and Trade, 718
Freeman, F. L. (Chairman: National Advisory Commission on Art Examinations), Report, 312
Freeman, Paul:
Ruwenzori Expedition, 828
Freeman, Paul (*continued*):
Study of Chironomidae of Africa, South of the Sahara, 80, [illegible], [illegible]
Study of the New Zealand Chironomidae, 827
Freer Trade in Europe, 409
French:
Domestic Silver, 1223
Equatorial Africa, International Customs Journal, 714, 973
Ethnographical Films, Catalogue, 239A
Guiana International Customs Journal, 444
Polynesia International Customs Journal, 714
School of Painting, Catalogue, 154
School Text Catalogue, 361
West Africa International Customs Journal, 445, 714
Freshwater and Salmon Fisheries Research Reports, 171, 387, 655, 914
Friendly Societies Act, 55
Friendly Societies, Registry of:
Annual Return Forms, 113–14, 325–6, 596, 855, 1129
Membership of Trade Unions Bill, 247
Publications, 113–14, 325–6, 596, 855, 1129
Report of Chief Registrar, 114, 326, 597, 855, 1130
Friendship and Protection Treaty between U.K. and:
Arab Amirates of the South. *Cmnd. 665.* 791, 833
Tonga. *Cmnd. 606.* 539, 594; *Cmnd. 848.* 803, 852
Frit Fly, 820
Frontier Workers:
And Student Employees. Accession of Germany and Italy to Convention. *Cmnd. 1209.* 1066, 1128
Protocol concerning Accession of Germany and Italy to Convention. *Cmnd. 138.* 258
Frost Precautions in Household Water Supply, 207
Frost, R., Pressure Variation over Malaya and the Resonance Theory, 1162
Frozen Fish, 223A
Frozen Food Industry, New Developments in the, 951
Frozen Pipes. Circular, 129
Fruit:
Citrus. General Conditions for International Sale, 720
Exchange of Notes between U.K. and U.S.A. concerning Sale for Sterling. *Cmnd. 402.* 525, 595
Production and Trade, 91, 304, 572, 1105
Fruit and Fruit Products. Exchange of Notes between U.K. and U.S.A. concerning Sale. *Cmnd. 1010.* 1052, 1127

FRU-GIF | 1956-60

Fruit and Vegetables:
  Census of Production Report, 1193
  Domestic Preservation, 556
  In Europe, Marketing of, 223A
  In OEEC Countries, Consumption of, 1246
  Standardisation of Wooden Packaging, 1246
Fruit Trees:
  Application of Sprays, 288, 1083
  Capsid Bugs, 288
  Raising, 290
  Red Spider Mite, 288, 1083
  Spraying, 290
Frye, Thomas. *See* Bow Porcelain
FSH Circulars, 72–3
Fuel:
  Abstracts, 166–7, 383, 430, 650, 908
  And Firing Equipment for Nurseries, 1088
  Appliances, List of Recommended Domestic Solid, 331
  Consumption for Household and Domestic Uses in Europe, Trends in, 229A
  Consumption in Schools, 585, 1115
  Efficient Use of, 641
  Estimates, 1956–57, 12
  Research Board Report, 167, 383, 561, 650, 1180
Fuel and Power, Ministry of:
  Examinations, 115
  Publications, 114–18, 326–7
  See also Power, Ministry of
Fugitive Criminals. Agreement between U.K. and Germany for Extradition. *Cmnd. 1002, 1200.* 1051, 1065, 1121
Fulton, A. S., Supplementary Catalogue of Arabic Printed Books in the British Museum, 1095
Fumigation with Methyl Bromide under Gas-Proof Sheets, 909
Function and Training of Chemical Engineers, 223A
Fundamental and Adult Education: 238A, 467, 736, 995, 1264
  Literary and Community Education in West Indies, 238A
  Monographs, 737, 996
  Recent Publications, 238
Fundamental Physics, 986
Fundamental Stars, Apparent Place of, 60, 545
Funds in Court, Committee Report. *Cmnd. 818.* 801, 887
Fungi Pathogenic to Man and Animals, Nomenclature of, 633
Funtham's Lane Occupation Level Crossing Railway Accident Report, 672
Fur. Census of Production Report, 395
Furnished Houses (Rent Control) Bill, 784
Furniture:
  And Upholstery Census of Production Report, 179, 664
  Designs, English, of the Eighteenth Century, 951
  Manufacture, Careers, 876
Furskins and Manufactures of Furskins and Sheepskin Goods. Export Licence, 666
Further Education Circular, 911
Future Demand for Teachers, 585
Future of the European Cotton Industry Report, 448
Future Population Estimates by Sex and Age Report, 987, 1257
Fyfe, G. M. (Chairman: Mental Health Sub-Committee), Report, 330
Fylde Water Board Act, 57

G

Gabbard, H. F., Preparing Your Child for School, 201
Gaelic. Scottish Certificate of Education, 913
Galapagos Islands Survey, 995
Galbraith, I. C. J., Variation Relationships and Evolution in the Pachycephala Pectoralis Superspecies, 81
Galvin, H. R., Small Public Library Building, 996
Gambia:
  Colonial Report, 300, 570
  Colony Letters Patent. Order-in-Council, 1174
  Order-in-Council, 1174
Game Laws (Amendment) Act, 1070
Game Laws (Amendment) Bill, 1005, 1007, 1041, 1043
Gaming Bill, 786
Gammelgaard, Søren, Resale Price Maintenance, 719
Garde, P. K., Directory of Reference Works published in Asia, 465
Gardiner, B. G., Revision of certain Actinspterygian and Coelacanth Fishes, Chiefly from Lower Lias, 1096
Gardner, E., Recreation Leaders Handbook, 421
Gardner, F. M., Delhi Public Library, 468
Garforth and Micklefield, Railway Accident Report, 1197
Gariboldi, F., Illustrated Glossary of Rice Processing Machines, 708
Garland, C. E.:
  Case Commentary on Income Tax Acts, Supplement, 132, 615, 873
  Harrison's Index to Tax Cases: 617, 873
    Supplement, 617

Garments made from Woven Cloth Standing Committee Report. *Cmnd. 440.* 528, 667
Garner, H. V., Manures and Fertilizers, 556
Garston and Hunts Cross West Railway Accident Report, 188
Gas:
  Boards and Gas Council, 239, 371
  Boards Annual Reports and Accounts, 25, 115, 238–9, 371, 508, 642, 774, 899, 1033, 1171
  Census of Production Report, 1194
  Council Annual Reports and Accounts, 115, 239, 509, 642, 774, 899, 1033, 1171
  Economy, Trend of European, 228A
  Examiners' General (Amendment) Directions, 371
  Examiners' General Directions, 327
  In Europe:
    719
    Production, etc., 1250
  Industry, 982
  Memorandum on Bill. *Cmnd. 947.* 1047, 1172
  Methods of Forecasting Demand, 724
  Report of the Minister of Fuel and Power, 25, 115
  Report of the Minister of Power, 239, 371, 509, 642, 774, 899, 1033, 1171
  See Natural Gas
  Statistics for Europe, 454, 724, 979, 1251
  Town, 648
  Transport in the United States, Long-Distance, 223A
Gas Act:
  1070
  Guarantee given on Loans proposed to be raised, 10, 16, 17, 22, 26, 27, 195, 224, 231, 235, 240, 409, 493, 501, 507, 510, 698, 757, 767, 774, 936, 1018, 1025, 1032, 1034, 1204
Gas Bill, 1006, 1041
Gas Supply Industry, Census of Production Report, 180, 396
Gases. Report on Supply of Certain Industrial and Medical, 221, 397
Gasification, British Trials in Underground, 114
Gas-Turbine Collaboration Committee Welding Panel Report, 391
Gater, Sir G., (Chairman: University Grants Committee Sub-Committee), Report on Methods used of Contracting and Recording and Controlling Expenditure. *Cmnd. 9.* 53
Gates Clarke, J. F., Catalogue of Type Specimens described by Edward Meyrick, 564
Gateshead. Gift of Land at East Gateshead. *Cmnd. 822.* 801, 934
Gathercole, P. W., Excavations at Clausentum, Southampton, 698
Gatwick Airport Air Navigation Order, 187, 671
Gauging and Measuring Screw Threads, 890
Gear, H. S., Disease Control and International Travel, 243A
Geiger-Miller Counter, 202
Gelatine, Adhesives, etc. Census of Production Report, 1194
Genera Nidalia and Bellonella, with an Emendation of Nomenclature and Taxonomic Definitions for the Family Nidaliidae, Revision of, 563
General Agreement on Tariffs and Trade:
  Activities of GATT, 1239
  Basic Instruments and Selected Documents, 709, 969, 1239
  Negotiations for Establishment of New Schedules, 969
  Protocol of Rectifications, etc., 438
  Publications, 438, 709–10, 969, 1239
  Rectifications and Modifications, 709, 969
  Supplementary Concessions, 220A
General Aspects of a Population Census, 732
General Board of Control, Scotland. Report. *Cmd. 9807.* 46, 120; *Cmnd. 212.* 263, 387
General Certificate of Education Requirements, 585, 586
General Conference Records, UNESCO, Resolutions, 736, 995, 1265
General Drafting Technical Manual, 203
General Lighthouse Fund Accounts, 30, 187, 234, 402, 510, 671, 765, 929, 1030, 1197
General London and Urban Properties Limited. Investigation into the Affairs. Report, 1192
General Practitioners:
  Conference on Public Health Training. Report, 741
  Records. Analysis of the Clinical Records, 118
General Register Office:
  Publications, 118–19, 327–8, 597, 855, 1130
  Scotland Publications, 856
General Service Medal for Service in Cyprus, Grant of, 424
General Statistics Statistical Bulletin, 223A, 448, 718, 978, 1249
Generating Stations and Overhead Lines, Circular, 611
Genetic Stocks, World Catalogue, 243A, 709, 968, 1238
Geneva Conference:
  Cmnd. 797, 829, 868. 800, 802, 805, 846, 848
  See Ten-Power Disarmament Committee

Geneva Conventions Act, 272
Geneva Conventions Bill, 217, 218, 249
Geneva Tariff Negotiations Report. *Cmd. 9779.* 44, 181
Genocide, Crime of. U.N. Convention, 226A, 979
Genus Neozephyrus Sibatani and Its (Lepidoptera: Lycaenidae) Revision of, 295
Genus Tridrepana Swinhoe, Revision of, 294
Geographical Handbook Series, 545
Geography:
  Guiding of Teachers on Setting and Marking of Examinations, 171
  In Secondary Schools, Teaching of, 654
  Scottish Certificate of Education, 913
Geological Column exhibited in the Museum of Practical Geology Guide, 328
Geological Survey and Museum:
  Guide, 599
  Memoirs, 119, 329, 599, 857
  Progress and Report, 119, 599, 857, 1132
  Publications, 328–9, 599, 857, 1131
  Summary of Progress, 329
Geological Survey Bulletin, 119, 201, 328, 599, 1131
Geological Time, Succession of Life Through, 828
"Geologist" Wreck Report, 192
Geology:
  Bulletins, 80, 295, 563, 827, 1096
  Of the Country around Sheffield, 329
Geometridae, 564
Geophysical Memoirs, 152, 360, 633, 888, 1160
Geophysics Handbook, 381
George, E. A., Blue-Green Algae from the Middle Devonian of Rhynnie, Aberdeenshire, 827
George, H., Hastie. Wreck Report, 927
Georgian Furniture, 693
German Affairs:
  1120
  And Plebiscite Problems, 1120
German Assets in:
  Italy. Memorandum of Understanding. *Cmnd. 236.* 264
  Portugal Agreement. *Cmnd. 863.* 804, 848
  Spain. Protocol terminating Obligations. *Cmnd. 833.* 802, 848
German Enemy Property, Distribution of, Acts. Account, 769, 921
German External Debts:
  Agreement Amended. *Cmnd. 177.* 261, 318; *Cmnd. 626.* 788, 848
  Agreement concerning the Arbitral Tribunal and the Mixed Commission. *Cmnd. 1239.* 1068, 1120
German Foreign Policy, Documents on, 106, 318, 590, 847
German School. National Gallery Catalogue, 1163
"Germans Come to the Help of Their Ally". *See* Mediterranean and Middle East
Germany:
  Agreement regarding:
    Foreign Forces stationed in the Federal Republic of Germany. *Cmnd. 852.* 803, 849
    The War Graves, Cemeteries and Memorials of the British Commonwealth. *Cmd. 9833, 9838.* 48, 106, 112
  Agreement with U.K.:
    And Canada concerning the Conduct of Manoeuvres and other Training Exercises in the Soltau-Luneburg Area. *Cmnd. 1025.* 1053, 1120
    Concerning Contracts of Insurance and Contracts and Treaties of Reinsurance. *Cmnd. 1041.* 1054, 1121
    For Air Services. *Cmnd. 137.* 258, 319
    For Co-operation in the Peaceful Uses of Atomic Energy. *Cmd. 9842.* 48, 106
    For Extradition of Fugitive Criminals. *Cmnd. 1002, 1200.* 1051, 1065, 1121
    France and U.S.A. on the Tax Treatment of the Forces and their Members. *Cmnd. 657.* 790, 849
    Regarding German War Graves in the U.K. *Cmnd. 930.* 1046, 1121
    Regarding the Settlement of the Claim in respect of Post-War Economic Assistance. *Cmnd. 627.* 788, 849
  Consular Convention with U.K. *Cmnd. 5.* 52, 106; *Cmnd. 607.* 788, 849
  Convention between U.K., France and U.S.A. on the Settlement of Matters arising out of the War and the Occupation. *Cmnd. 656.* 790, 849
  Convention on Relations between the Three Powers, U.K., France and the U.S.A. *Cmnd. 653.* 790, 849
  Convention on the Rights and Obligations of Foreign Forces and their Members. *Cmnd. 654.* 790, 849
  Convention with U.K.:
    For the Reciprocal Recognition and Enforcement of Judgments in Civil and Commercial Matters. *Cmnd. 1118.* 1059, 1118
    On Social Security. *Cmnd. 78.* 254, 318; *Cmnd. 1055.* 1055, 1121

Germany (*continued*):
  Convention with U.K. (*continued*):
    On Unemployment Insurance. *Cmnd. 77.* 253, 318; *Cmnd. 1054.* 1054, 1121
  Correspondence about the Future of. *Cmnd. 29.* 54, 106
  Cultural Convention with U.K. *Cmnd. 441.* 528, 590; *Cmnd. 742.* 796, 849
  Documents:
    About the Future. *Cmnd. 634, 670, 719.* 789, 791, 794, 849
    Relating to the Further Support of the United Kingdom Forces stationed in the Territory of the Federal Republic. *Cmd. 9802.* 45, 106
  Exchange of Letters with U.K. concerning the:
    Agreement for Repayment of Credits granted by the European Payments Union. *Cmnd. 291.* 268, 318
    Transfer of Archives of the Former German Foreign Office. *Cmnd. 37.* 251, 318
  Exchange of Notes with U.K.:
    Amending the Agreement regarding German War Graves in the U.K. *Cmnd. 1170.* 1063, 1121
    Applying the Agreement for Co-operation in the Peaceful Uses of Atomic Energy. *Cmnd. 375.* 523, 590
    Concerning Arrangements to Facilitate Travel between them. *Cmnd. 1157.* 1062, 1121
    Concerning Disbandment of the Civilian Service Organisations maintained by British Forces in Germany. *Cmnd. 226.* 264, 318
    Concerning Local Defence Costs of U.K. Forces and related Measures of Mutual Aid. *Cmnd. 256.* 266, 319
    Concerning Local Defence Costs of United Kingdom Forces stationed in the Federal Republic. *Cmnd. 588.* 538, 590
    Constituting a Supplementary Agreement regarding the Use of the Sandbank Bombing Range. *Cmnd. 244.* 265, 319
    On the Liquidation of the European Payments Union. *Cmnd. 760.* 798, 849
    Regarding Extension concerning Legal Proceedings in Civil and Commercial Matters. *Cmnd. 1202.* 1065, 1121
  Federal Republic:
    Economic Conditions, 221A, 466, 715, 1246
Germany (*continued*):
  Federal Republic (*continued*):
    Foreign Trade Statistical Bulletin, 222A, 448, 717, 977
    International Customs Journal, 444, 713, 973, 1244
    Overseas Economic Survey, 182
  Finance Convention. U.K., France and U.S.A. *Cmnd. 655.* 790, 849
  Occupation Regime. Protocol on Termination. *Cmnd. 658.* 791, 850
  Pocket Guide, 202
  Protocol on the Termination of the Occupation Regime. *Cmnd. 658.* 791, 850
Gerwig, C., Pig Breeding, Recording and Progeny Testing in European Countries, 966
Ghana:
  Agreement with U.K. for Air Services. *Cmnd. 567.* 536, 573
  Gold Coast Becomes, 344
  Hearing by Judicial Committee of Privy Council of Appeals. Exchange of Letter with U.K. *Cmnd. 1190.* 1065, 1106
  International Customs Journal, 714, 974
  International Rights and Obligations. Exchange of Letters with U.K. *Cmnd. 345.* 522, 573
  Making of, 344, 1150
  Proposed Constitution. *Cmnd. 71.* 253, 302
  Public Officers Agreement with U.K., *Cmnd. 158.* 259, 305
  U.K. Trade and Industrial Mission Report, 923
Ghana Act, 272
Ghana Bill, 214
Ghana (Consequential Provisions) Act, 1070
Ghana (Consequential Provisions) Bill, 1008, 1043
Ghana Independence Bill, 8, 36
Ghandi. *See* All Men Are Brothers
Giant in the Sun, 890
Gibbs-Smith, C. H.:
  Aeroplane, 1178
  Apsley House, 422
  Fashionable Lady of the 19th Century, 1222
Gibraltar:
  Colonial Report, 87, 301, 570, 1102
  Order-in-Council, 1174
  Picture Set, 614
Gibson, E., Time Spent Awaiting Trial, 1140
Gifts:
  Boom Defence Equipment to the North Atlantic Treaty Organisation. *Cmnd. 910.* 807, 934
  Fishery Research Vessel to Government of Hong Kong. *Cmnd. 817.* 801, 934

1956-60 | GIF-HAB

GIF— INDEX 1956–60

Gifts (*continued*):
  Inshore Minesweeper, to the Governments of East Africa. *Cmnd. 418.* 527, 678
  Land in Baghdad. Treasury Minute. *Cmd. 9814.* 46, 195
  Land to Bahrain. *Cmnd. 110.* 256
  Land to the County Borough of Gateshead. *Cmnd. 822.* 801, 934
  Line Barracks, Mauritius. Treasury Minute. *Cmd. 9746.* 42, 195
  Pig Progeny Testing Stations to the Pig Industry Development Authority. *Cmnd. 821.* 801, 934
  School Building to Milan. *Cmnd. 987.* 1050, 1203
  Slipway Repair Base to Sierra Leone. *Cmnd. 1110.* 1058, 1203
  Stores and Equipment to the Federation of Rhodesia and Nyasaland. *Cmnd. 409, 492.* 526, 531, 678
  Tower Hill Barracks to Sierra Leone. *Cmnd. 1111.* 1058, 1203
  Treasury Minute relative to the Gifts of Ocean Escort H.M.S. Hare. Motor Launch S.D.M.L. 3515 and certain Training Equipment to the Federal Government of Nigeria. *Cmnd. 636.* 789, 934
Gilbert and Ellice Islands Colony. Colonial Report, 300, 832
Gilbert, M., Comparative National Products and Price Levels, 715
Gilchrist, A., Winds between 300 and 100 MB in the Tropics and Subtropics, 152
Giles, L., Descriptive Catalogue of Chinese Manuscripts from Tunhuang in the British Museum, 562
Gillett, J. B., Indiofera in Tropical Africa, 647
Gillie, Blaise (Chairman: Wales and Monmouthshire Development and Government Action), Report. *Cmnd. 684.* 792
Gilson, J. C., Lung Function in Coal Workers' Pneumoconiosis, 151
Gilyard-Beer, R.:
  Abbeys, 956
  Cleeve Abbey, Somerset, Guide, 1226
  County Hall, Abingdon, Guide, 208
Giordana, G., Logging Cableways, 983
"Girdleness" Wreck Report, 675
Girling, F. K., Acholi of Uganda, 1103
Gladman, R. J., Fomes Annosus in Great Britain, 1129
Glamorgan County Council Act, 811
Glanville, S. R. K., Catalogue of Demotic Papyri. Instructions of Onchoheshonqy, 79
Glasgow Corporation Consolidation (General Powers) Order Confirmation Act, 1072
Glasgow Corporation Consolidation (General Powers) Order Confirmation Bill, 1042
Glasgow Corporation Order Confirmation Act, 57, 274, 811, 1072
Glasgow Corporation Order Confirmation Bill, 35, 248, 520, 1044
Glasgow Corporation Order Confirmation (No. 2) Bill, 785
Glasgow Tramway Accident Report, 190, 931
Glass:
  Containers Census of Production Report, 663
  Other than Containers. Census of Production Report, 663
Glasses:
  Fees and Charges for (Testing Sight, etc.) Amendments, 1137
  See Ophthalmic Services
Glassey, S. D., Notes on Weather Analysis in Falkland Islands Dependencies, 571
Glasshouse Heating Systems, 559, 1088
Glasshouses:
  Construction and Heating of Commercial, 1085
  Design and Cropping of Mobile Glasshouses, 555
Glazed Frost of Jan., 1940, 152
Glazier, Career, 876
Glazier, E. V. D., Transmission and Propagation, 955
"Gleaner" Wreck Report, 1200
Gleave, Group Captain T. P., British Fortunes Reach Their Lowest Ebb, 1098, 1189
Glen More, Cairngorms, Guide, 325, 1129
Glenrothes Development Corporation Report, 21, 172, 236, 613, 656, 776, 779, 870, 915, 1187
Gloag, H. L., Lighting of Factories, 906
Gloucester and Sharpness Canal (Water) Act, 1072
Gloucester Candlestick, 951
Gloucester Corporation Act, 543
Gloucester County Council Act, 811
Gloucester, H.R.H., The Duke of, Promotion to Marshal of the Royal Air Force, 631
Gloucester Pier and Harbour Order Confirmation Act, 812
Gloucester Pier and Harbour Order Confirmation Bill, 752, 785
Gloucester Road Junction Railway Accident, 672
Gloucestershire County Council Act, 57
Glove. Census of Production Report, 395
Glue, Gum, Paste and Allied Industries. Census of Production Report, 394
Goats, Milk, 201
Goddard, H. A., Principles of Administration applied to Nursing Service, 740
Goitre, Endemic, 1267, 1268

INDEX 1956–60 —GRA

Gold Coast Becomes Ghana:
  Film Strip, 344
  Photo-Poster, 344
  Picture Set. 12 plates, 344
Gold Coast Colonial Report, 87
Goldie, N., Upper Air Temperature over the World, 633
Goldsmith, P., High Cloud over Southern England, 153
Good, R., On the Geographical Relationships of the Angiosperm Flora of New Guinea, 1095
Goodchild, R., Experiments on Rectilinear Cutting, 1180
Goode, C. W., Poultry on the General Farm, 290
Goodey, J. B., Laboratory Methods for Work with Plant and Soil Nematodes, 293
Goodman, N. M. (Chairman: Working Party on Convalescent Treatment), Report, 859
Goodrich Castle, Herefordshire, Guide, 698
Goods:
  Customs Convention on the International Transport of, 980
  Transport, Convention on Taxes of Road Vehicles, 462
Goodwin, D., Taxonomy of the Genus Columbia, 828
Goody, J. R., Social Organisation of the Lowiili, 88
Gooseberry:
  And Blackcurrant Sawflies, 1083
  Red Spider Mite, 820
Gorbatchensky, V. A., Timber Transport on Snow and Ice Roads, 1260
Gordon Hotels Ltd. Investigation, 397
Gordon, I.:
  On a Stygiomysis from the West Indies with a Note on Spelaeogriphus, 1097
  On Spelaeogriphus, New Cavernicolous Crustacean from South Africa, 295
  Sergestidae of the Great Barrier Reef Expedition, 81
Gore-Booth, Sir Paul, Remodelled Economic Organisation Report, 1248
Gorell-Barnes, W. L. (Chairman: Conference on African Land Tenure in East and Central Africa), Report, 88
Gosline, W. A., Contributions towards a Classification of Modern Isospondylous Fishes, 1097
Gotaas, H. B., Composting, 244A
Gough, C. M., Sampling and Analysis of Rolled Asphalt and Coated Macadam, 168
Gould, C., 16th Century Venetian School, 890
Government:
  Accounts, Budgetary Structure and Classification of, 1251
  Administration in Wales. *See* Council for Wales
  Administration of the U.K., 872, 1150
  And the Arts in Britain, 678
  Departments, Staffs Employed in. *Cmd. 9701, 9784, 9840.* 39, 44, 48, 54; *Cmnd. 25.* 197; *Cmnd. 89, 184.* 255, 261, 411; *Cmnd. 442.* 528, 680
  Information Services Estimated Expenditure. *Cmd. 9868.* 51, 195
  Libraries, Guide to, 678
  Offices, Whitehall Gardens, Tests on, 1181
  Orders, Guide to, 390, 918
  Personnel System, 421
  Policies and the Cost of Building, 1255
  Publications:
    Catalogue, 174, 390, 658, 917, 1189
    Consolidated Index, 658
  Transactions, 727
Government Chemist Department Report, 119, 329, 599, 1181
Governors' Pensions Act, 56, 272
Governors' Pensions Act Report, 214
Governors' Pensions Bill, 5, 34, 217, 218, 249
Grabe, S., Selection and Training of Foremen in Europe, 222A
Grading of Sawn British Softwoods, 908
Graduate Students and Research Workers. Notes on Grants, 383, 650, 908
Graduates, Civil Service Posts for, 83
Graham, A. (Chairman: Safety, Health and Welfare Conditions in Non-Ferrous Foundries Technical Sub-Committee), Report, 875
Graham, A. M., Simplified Daylight Tables, 651
Graham, R., Egglestone Abbey Guide, 698
Graham, V., Story of W.V.S., 863
Graham Guest, C. W.:
  Deputy-Chairman. Boundary Commission for Scotland Report, 1016
  Chairman, Committee on Building Legislation in Scotland Report. *Cmnd. 269.* 267
Grain:
  Cleaning and Sorting Report, 979
  Crops, Production, Trade and Consumption, 304, 833
  Driers, 558
  Drying and Storage, Buildings for, 1087
  Exports by Source and Destination, 242A
  Legumes, Tropical and Subtropical, Tabulated Information on, 968
  Milling. Census of Production Report, 395

GRA— INDEX 1956–60

Grain (*continued*):
  Policies, National, 1237
  See National Grain
  Storage Problems in Nyasaland, Investigations into, 570
  Trade:
    See World Grain
    Statistics, World, 709, 969, 1239
  Underground Storage of, 88
  Weevils, 71, 820
Grainger, L., Behaviour of Reactor Components under Irradiation, 1240
Grains, Report of the F.A.O. Group on, 707, 960
Grand Strategy, 82, 174, 296, 389
Grants:
  Improvement and Conversions. Housing Repairs and Rent Act, 341
  New Grants for Better Homes, 858, 870
  Research, 1179
  Students Report. *Cmnd. 1051.* 1054, 1115, 1185
  To Recognised Training College Students, 585
Grass:
  Clover and Lucerne Trials in OEEC Countries, 1246
  Production, 69
  Tetany in Cattle. *See* Hypomagnesaemia
  Winter, 289
Grasses:
  In Agriculture, 1236
  Of Barbados, 301
Grassland Utilisation Committee Report. *Cmnd. 547.* 535, 554, 559, 604
Gratuities in respect of Service in the Women's Royal Army Corps. Special Army Order, 424
Gravels. *See* Matter of Lime
Gray, Sir J. (Chairman: Salmon Research Committee Pass Investigation Sub-Committee), Report, 388
Gray, P. G.:
  Noise in Three Groups of Flats with Different Floor Insulations, 909
  Report of Inquiry into Rent Act. *Cmnd. 1246.* 1069, 1148
Gray, W. S., International Survey on Teaching of Reading and Writing, 239A
Grayson Rolls and Clover Docks Act, 58
Graystone, P., Equivalent Headwinds at Heights of 30,000 feet and 40,000 feet along Air Routes, 634
Great Barrier Reef Expedition Scientific Reports, 81, 564
Great Britain and Northern Ireland International Customs Journal, 443, 713, 973, 1244
Great Exuma Island included in Bahamas Long Range Proving Ground. Exchange of Notes between U.K. and U.S.A. *Cmnd. 266.* 267
Great Yarmouth Pier and Harbour Order Confirmation Act, 543
Great Yarmouth Pier and Harbour Order Confirmation Bill, 483
Great Yarmouth Pier and Harbour Provisional Order Bill, 518
Great Yarmouth Port and Haven Pier and Harbour Order Confirmation Act, 58
Great Yarmouth Port and Haven Pier and Harbour Order Bill, 5, 34
Greece:
  Agreement with U.K. respecting the Repayment of the Debt on the Liquidation of the European Payments Union. *Cmnd. 769.* 798, 850
  Consular Convention with U.K. *Cmnd. 525.* 533, 590
  Economic Conditions, 221A, 446, 715, 975, 1246
  Exchange of Notes with U.K.:
    And on the Final Settlement of the Diverted Cargoes Claims. *Cmnd. 996.* 1050, 1121
    Concerning Dollar/Sterling Exchange Rate applicable to Cargoes diverted from Great Ports during the late War. *Cmd. 9754.* 42, 107
  Foreign Trade Statistical Bulletins, 222A, 447, 448, 717, 977
  International Customs Journal, 444
  Norway and Sweden Protocol concerning the Accession to the Convention concerning Student Employees. *Cmnd. 942.* 1047, 1128
  Overseas Economic Survey, 182
Greek Loan Account, 18, 195, 231, 409, 501, 678, 766, 936, 1024, 1204
Green Belts Circular, 341
Green Fodder Conservation, Methods of, 225A
Green, G. W., Geology of the Country Around Bridport and Yeovil, 857
Greenland and Barent Seas Charts, 888
Greenland and Faroe Islands. Agreement on Joint Financing of Air Navigation Services. *Cmnd. 165.* 260, 314, 439; *Cmnd. 678.* 792, 844
Greenock Burgh Extension etc. Order Confirmation Act, 58
Greenock Burgh Extension etc. Order Confirmation Bill, 33
Greenock Port and Harbours Order Confirmation Act, 274
Greenock Port and Harbours Order Confirmation Bill, 249
Greenwich Hospital and Travers Foundation:
  Accounts, 16, 60, 232, 276, 499, 545, 763, 813, 1022, 1074
  Estimated Income and Expenditure, 20, 60, 234, 276, 504, 545, 771, 813, 1026, 1074

INDEX 1956–60 —HAB

Greenwich Magnetic and Meteorological Observations. Results, 329, 904
Greenwich Observations in Astronomy, Magnetism and Meteorology, 120, 904
Greenwich Observatory:
  Bulletins, 904, 1178
  Publications, 120, 329, 599
Greenwich Photo-Heliographic Results, 905
Greenwood, P. H.:
  Fossil Denticipitid Fishes from East Africa, 1006
  Monotypic Genera of Cichlid Fishes in Lake Victoria:
    81
    And Revision of the Lake Victoria Haplochromis Species, 828
  Revision of the Lake Victoria Haplochromis Species, 81, 295, 1097
Grégoire, R., National Administrative and International Organisations Report, 239A
Gregory, R. C. L., County Court Manual, 358
Greig, J. R.:
  Sheep Dog Management and Feeding, 70
  Shepherd's Guide to Prevention and Control of Diseases of Sheep, 70, 554
Grenada:
  Colonial Report, 300, 569
  Order-in-Council, 1173
Gresty, C., Drying of Moulds by Portable Dryers, 138
Gretton, R. H., Co-operative Marketing for Agricultural Producers, 241A
Grigg, Rt. Hon. Sir James (Chairman: Advisory Committee on Recruiting), Report. *Cmnd. 545.* 535
Grigor'ev, I. A., Measurement of Small Holes, 167
Grimes, Professor W. F.:
  Capel Garmon, Chambered Long Cairn, Guide, 698
  Excavations on Defence Sites Mainly Neolithic-Bronze Age 1226 Pentre-ifan Burial Chamber, Nevern, Guide, 1226
Grimmit, H. W., Report on Nuclear Power Station at Trawsfynydd, 645
Grimsby Harbour British Transport Commission Charges Scheme, 1199
Grinsell, L. V., Stanton Drew Stone Circles Guide, 208
Grocery Retail Trade in the Netherlands, Investigation into Costs of Distribution, 449
Gronovious Fish Collection. Catalogue and Historical Account, 563
Ground Winch Skidding in Clear and Selective Felling, 984
Group Teaching in Primary Schools, 654
Groves, A. E., Gypsum and Anhydrite, 571
Groves, R. (Chairman: Food Standards Committee), Report, 1087
Growing Demand for Water Sub-Committee Report, 868, 1146
Growing Field Peas for Stock Feeding, 71
Growing Vegetables in Town and City, 951
Growth and Structure of Wood, 650
Growth and Yield of Sweet Chestnut Coppice, 112
Grundy, F., Teaching of Hygiene and Public Health in Europe, 471
Gruneburg, Professor H., Annotated Catalogue of the Mutant Genes of the House Mouse, 151
Guadalcanal Campaign, 202
Guadeloupe International Customs Journal, 444
Guarantees:
  Determination of, Review. *Cmd. 9721.* 124
  To Building Societies. Circular, 611
Guardianship of an Infant:
  Case concerning Order, 443, 713
  Judgment, 972, 973
Guardianship of Infants Bill, 479
Guatemala Overseas Economic Survey, 182
Guest, Rt. Hon. Lord (Chairman: Scottish Licensing Law), Report. *Cmnd. 1217.* 1066
Guide to Government Orders, 918
Guide to Official Sources, 598
Guide to the Trade Union Acts, 1130
Guildford Cathedral Measure:
  812, 829
  Reports, 748, 829
Guillebaud, C. W. (Chairman: Committee of Enquiry into cost of National Health Service), Report. *Cmd. 9663.* 37
Gulland, J. A., On the Fishing Effort in English Demersal Fisheries, 73
Gun Barrel Proof (Alteration of Maximum Prices) Order, 176
Guppy, E. M., Chemical Analysis of Igneous Rocks, Metamorphic Rocks and Minerals, 119
Gurkha Rifles, Changes in Designations, 956
Guthrie, Hon. Lord (Chairman: Committee on Legal Aid in Criminal Proceedings), Report. *Cmnd. 1015.* 1052
Gymru, Darluno, 123
Gypsum and Anhydrite, 571

H

Habershon & Sons Ltd. Proposal to sell holdings of Securities. *Cmnd. 1053.* 1054, 1205

HAC-HOL | 1956-60

HAC— *INDEX 1956–60*

Hackett, C. Y., Differential Diagnosis of Yaws, 1268
Hackett, G. J., International Nomenclature of Yaws Lesions, 740
Haig, I. T., Tropical Silviculture, 1237
Hair, Fibre and Kindred Industries. Census of Production Report, 395
Halcrow, Sir William, Volta River Project Engineering Report, 183
Hale, Sir E. (Chairman: Committee on Superannuation of University Teachers), Report, 1207
Half a Century of Successful Struggle against Crime, Disease and Social Affliction, 1262
Halibut—Observations on its Size at First Maturity, Sex Ratio and Length/Weight Relationship, 914
Halifax Corporation Act, 811
Halifax, Survey of Industrial Health, 629
Hall, B. P., Ecology and Taxonomy of Some Angola Birds, 1097
Hall, D. N. F., Recent Developments in the Barbadian Flying-Fish Fishery and Contributions to the Biology of the Flying-Fish Hirundichthys Affinis, 89
Hall, D. W., Underground Storage of Grain, 88
Hall, H. D., Studies of Overseas Supply, 82, 174
Hall, Sir N., Hospital Service Report, 331
Hallmarking. Report of the Departmental Committee. *Cmnd. 663.* 791, 923
Halls of Residence Report, 409
Ham House. Guide, 422, 951
Hamilton, J. R. C., Excavations of Jarlshof, Shetland, 427
Hamilton, S. B.:
  Note on History of Reinforced Concrete in Buildings, 383
  Short History of the Structural Fire Protection of Buildings, 651
Hammond, R. J., Food, Studies in Administration and Control, 82, 174
Hampshire Saxton's Maps, 1094
Hampson, M. A., Laverbread Industry in South Wales and the Laverweed, 559
Hampton Court, Le Palais de, 1227
Hampton Court Palace:
  Guide, 208
  Hand-List of Pictures, 699
  Postcards, 697, 957
Hamster Raising, 199
Hancock, D. A., Biology and Control of American Whelk Tingle on English Oyster Beds, 823
Handel, George Frideric, Commemorative Exhibition Catalogue, 827
Handicapped Pupils:
  Education of the, 101
  England and Wales List of Special Schools, 1115
  Special Schools, 101
Handling and Transport of Timber in Mountainous Regions, 724
Hanes Coed Y Brenin, Meirionydd, 112
Hannahfield Trust Scheme. Order-in-Council, 912
Hannan, R. S., Cooling of the Uneviscerated Poultry Carcase by Various Methods in Common Use, 165
Hanunóo Agriculture, 437
Harbour Charges Schemes. Transport Tribunal Proceedings, 674, 1199
Hard Coals by Type, International Classification, 456
Hard Fibre Cordage, Report on Supply 20, 182
Harden Jones, F. R., Echo Sounding Experiments in the Barents Sea, 1087
Hardie, H. G. M., Limestones of Scotland, 119
Hardware, Hollow-ware, Metal Furniture and Sheet Metal Census of Production, Report, 179, 664
Hardwoods:
  And Softwoods Longitudinal Permeability, 650
  For Industrial Flooring, 908
  Grading of Sawn British, 908
  Handbook of, 167
  Identification of, 1180
Hardy, D. E., Walker Type of Fruit Flies in British Museum Collection, 1095
Harker, R. B. (Chairman: Joint Standing Committee Non-Ferrous Foundries), Report, 356
Harlech, Rt. Hon. Lord, East Anglia and the Midlands Illustrated Regional Guide, 207
Harlow Development Corporation Report, 24, 130, 237, 506, 613, 870, 1147
Harman, Rt. Hon. Lord Justice, Chairman:
  Committee on Chancery Chambers and the Chancery Registrars' Office. Report. *Cmnd. 967.* 1049
  Rights of Light Committee. Report. *Cmnd. 473.* 530
D'Harpagophoridae de R. I. Pocock Conservés au British Museum (Natural History), 1097
Harper, F. C., Floor Finishes for Factories, 907
Harris, C. R. S., Allied Military Administration of Italy, 565, 658
Harrison, W. N., Fifteen-Year Exposure Test of Porcelain Enamels, 419
Harrison's Index to Tax Cases. Cumulative Supplement, 617, 873
Hartwell, B. J. (Chairman: Sub-Committee Advisory Council on Treatment of Offenders), Report, 603
Harvesting:
  And Conservation of:
    Green Fodder in Dry Regions, 720
    Maize Stalks for Forage, 225A

INDEX 1956 60 —HEA

Harvesting (*continued*):
  And Storage of:
    Grain Maize, 979
    More Common Cereals, 450
  Transport and Storage of Green Fodder in Mountainous Regions, 720
Haselgrove, D. C., Chairman:
  Management Group Slough Experiment. Report, 404
  Working Party on Child Cyclists. Report, 670
Hashimite Kingdom of Jordan, International Customs Journal, 444
"Haslemere" Wreck Report, 192
Hastings Pier Act, 1072
Hastings Tramways Act, 274
Haswell, G. A., Underground Storage of Grain, 88
Hatchery Design and Disease Control, 71
Hatfield Development Corporation Report, 24, 130, 237, 506, 613, 870, 1147
Hatfield New Town, Report into the Causes of Damage to Houses, 611
Hats, Caps and Millinery, Census of Production Report, 395
Hawaii Pocket Guide, 202
Hawkstone Wreck Report, 931
Hawthornbrae. *See* Church of Scotland Home for Children
Hay:
  And Haymaking, 71
  Quality and Feeding, 71
Hay, J. (Chairman: Departmental Road Safety Committee), Report, 1021
Hayes, J., Thomas Rowlandson Catalogue of Watercolour Drawings, 1159
Hayes, S. P., Measuring the Results of Development Projects, 996
Haymaking Tripods and Racks for, 558
Hayti Overseas Economic Survey, 182
Hayward, J. F.:
  Chest of Drawers and Commodes, 1222
  English Cutlery, 422
  English Watches, 203
Hazards to Man of Nuclear and Allied Radiations Report. *Cmd. 9780.* 44, 151; *Cmnd. 1225.* 1067, 1160
Hazards to Men in Ships Lost at Sea, 151
Hazel Coppice, Utilization of, 325
Headquarters Section. Civil Defence, 603, 604
Heady, J. A., Social and Biological Factors in Infant Mortality, 856
Health:
  And Nutrition, Report of an International Seminar on Education, 437
  And Safety: Dosimetry and Standards, 986
  Department of, for Scotland:
    Circulars, 120, 600, 857
    Forms, 120
    Publications, 120–1, 329–31, 600, 857, 1132
Health (*continued*):
  Department of, for Scotland (*contd.*):
    Report. *Cmnd. 140.* 258, 329; *Cmnd. 385.* 524, 600; *Cmnd. 697.* 793, 858; *Cmnd. 983.* 1050, 1153
    Scottish Health Services Council Report. *Cmd. 9742.* 42, 120; 331, 858
  Education:
    313
    Bibliography, 238A
    In Schools, 1185
    Teacher Preparation of, 1269
  Estimates:
    1956–57, 12
    1957–58, 226
    1958–59, 494, 676
    1959–60, 760
    1960–61, 1019, 1201
  In the United Kingdom Dependencies, 132 ,1150
  Information Series, 420
  Laboratory Methods Report, 999
  Legislation, International Digest, 244A, 471, 740, 998, 1268
  Of the School Child. Report, 100, 842
  Personnel, Training of, in Health Education of Public. Report, 999
  Physics in Nuclear Installations, 1248
  Services:
    Britain, 344, 872, 1150
    U.S.S.R. Report, 1269
  Statistics:
    Expert Committee Report, 741
    Report, 999
    Scottish, 1133
  Visiting Report, 101, 120, 122
Health, Ministry of:
  Circulars:
    121, 331, 602, 859, 1088, 1133
    Index, 331
  Memorandum, 121, 122, 602
  Publications, 121–3, 331–2, 601, 859, 1133
  Report:
    Cmd. 9857. 50, 53; *Cmnd. 16.* 121; *Cmnd. 293.* 269, 331; *Cmnd. 806, 871.* 801, 805, 860; *Cmnd. 1086, 1206.* 1057, 1066, 1136
    Part II, 1956. *Cmnd. 325.* 521, 602
    Part I, 1957. *Cmnd. 495.* 531, 602
    Part II, 1957. *Cmnd. 559.* 536, 602
Hearing in Cetaceans, 1097
Heasman, M. A., Social and Biological Factors in Infant Mortality, 856
Heastie, H., Upper Winds over the World, 1160
Heat Bibliography, 1180
Heat Penetration in the Pressing of Plywood, 907
Heat Transfer in Deep Underground Tunnels, 651

HEA— *INDEX 1956–60*

Heating Systems in Houses, Comparison of Capital Costs, 165
Heavy Equipment for Power Stations, Survey, 223A
Heavy Water Lattices, 1239
Hedgerow and Farm Timber Committee Report, 112
Helgeson, E. A., Methods of Weed Control, 706
Heller, F., Crystallographic Data for the Calcium Silicates, 165
Hellifield Railway Accident Report, 188
Helliwell, H. C., Airborne Measurements of the Latitudinal Variation of Front-Point, Temperature and Wind, 1162
Helping Economic Development in Asia and the Far East, 727, 1255
Helping South East Asia to Help Itself, 727
Hemel Hempstead Development Corporation Report, 24, 130, 237, 506, 613, 870, 1147
Hemiptera—Heteroptera—Check list and Keys to the Families and Sub-Families, 827
Hen House, Deep Litter, 823
Henderson, Sir G. (Chairman: Standing Advisory Committee on Hospital and Specialist Services) Report, 330
Henderson, Dr. P. (Chairman: Standards of Normal Weight in Infancy Committee) Report, 860
Hengistbury and Barton Beds, Plant Remains of, 1096
Henksmeier, Dr. K. H., Economic Performance of Self Service in Europe, Report, 1246
Henry VII:
  Calendar of Close Rolls, 161
  Calender of Inquisitions Post Mortem, 161
Henshaw, J. E.:
  Inspector of Mines Report, 116, 642, 645
Hepper, B. T., Environmental Factors Governing the Infection of Mussels, 73
Her Majesty's Most Gracious Speech to Both Houses of Parliament, 754, 867
Heraldy in the Victoria and Albert Museum, 1223
Herbage Seeds Mixtures, 71
Herbert, D. W. M., Field and Laboratory Investigation of Fish in Sewage Effluent, 558
Herbert, Sir E., Chairman:
  Damage and Casualties in Port Said Report. *Cmnd. 47.* 55, 94
  Electricity Supply Industry Committee. Report. *Cmd. 9672.* 37
  Royal Commission on Local Government in Greater London:
    Minutes of Evidence, 902, 1176
    Report. *Cmnd. 1164.* 1063, 1177
Herbs, Savory, 201
Hercik, Dr. F., Safe Handling of Radioisotopes, 1240
Herefordshire Water Board Order Bill, 752
Heritable Property. Power of Trustees to sell, purchase or otherwise deal with. *Cmnd. 1102.* 1058, 1159
Hermitage Castle, Roxburghshire. Guide, 427
Herne Hill Railway Accident Report, 673, 1198
Herring:
  Clyde Estuary, 1187
  In Aquaria, 656
  Industry Board Report, *Cmd. 9765.* 43, 172; *Cmnd. 183.* 261, 292, 334, 387; *Cmnd. 435.* 528, 559, 604, 655; *Cmnd. 787.* 799, 823, 862, 914; *Cmnd. 1050.* 1054, 1088, 1139, 1186
  Rearing:
    Effect of Temperature and other Factors on Development, 388
    Effect of Temperature and Other Factors on Myotome Counts, 388
  Southern North Sea, 291
Herring Industry Acts Accounts, 31, 124, 171, 492, 655, 763, 782, 913
Hertfordshire County Council Act, 1072
Hertfordshire, 1577. Saxton's Map, 827
Hessle, C., Fishermen's Organisations and the Regulation of Fish Prices in Sweden, 436
Hetherington, Sir H. (Chairman: Royal Fine Art Commission for Scotland) Report. *Cmnd. 982.* 1050
Hey, M. H., Mineral Species and Varieties arranged Chemically, Index, 82
Heywood and Middleton Water Act, 58
Hide and Co. Ltd. Investigation into Affairs, 921
Hides and Skins:
  Industry in Europe, 224A, 450, 976, 1248, 1250
  Sector, Statistics of, 450
Hieratic Papyri in the British Museum, 1094
Higgins, R. A., Catalogue of Terracottas in Department of Greek and Roman Antiquities, British Museum, 1094
High Cloud Over Southern England, 153
High Cost of Air, 951
High Court and Court of Appeal, Account, 195, 358, 409, 632, 886, 1159
High Seas:
  Fishing, Conservation of Living Resources, Law of the Sea, 728
  General Régime. Law of the Sea, 728
High-Temperature Reactions of Uranium Dioxide with various Metal Oxides, 202
High Voltage Impulse Testing, 155
Higher Education in Agriculture, 1246
Higher Technical Education in the British Carribean Report, 302

INDEX 1956–60 —HOL

Highland Orphanage Trust Scheme:
  Memorandum, 912
  Order-in-Council, 912
Highland Policy, Review of, *Cmnd. 785.* 799, 915
Highlands and Islands Shipping Services Act, 1070
Highlands and Islands Shipping Services Bill, 783, 787, 1005, 1014, 1037, 1041, 1141
High-Voltage Bridge Measurements at Power Frequencies, 362
Highway Code:
  187, 402, 926
  Welsh, 189
Highway Law. Report on Consolidation. *Cmnd. 630.* 788, 871, 929
Highway Practice in the United States of America, 201
Highways Act, 809
Highways Act Report, 748
Highways Bill, 746, 748, 749, 785
Highways (Public Authorities' Liability) Bill, 1043
"Hildebrand" Wreck Report, 675
Hill Farming Act, 56
Hill Farming Bill, 6, 34
Hill, H. O., Instruments of Navigation, 635
Hill, J. E., North Bornean Pygmy Squirrel Glyphotes Simus Thomas and its Relationships, 828
Hill Lands (North of Scotland) Commission Report. *Cmd. 9759.* 42, 70
Hillingdon Estate Act, 59
Himsworth, Sir H., Chairman:
  Hazards to Man of Nuclear and Allied Radiations. Report. *Cmnd. 1225.* 1067, 1160
  Medical Research Committee. Report on Hazards to Man of Nuclear and Allied Radiations. *Cmd. 9780.* 44
Hinchliffe, Sir Henry, (Chairman: Cost of Prescribing Committee) Report, 602, 859
Hincks, W. D., Systematic Monograph of Dermaptera of the World based on Material in British Museum (Natural History), 828
Hindi Printed Books, Supplementary Catalogue, 562
Hinton, C. L., Food Additive Control in the U.K., 1237
Hirsch Library, Books in, 827
Hirst, K. M., Maternal Deaths in England and Wales Report, 332
Hispano Moresque Pottery, 693
Historic Buildings:
  And Ancient Monuments. Select Committee on Estimates Report, 1143
  Council Reports:
    England, 19, 208, 233, 427, 502, 699, 767, 957, 1024, 1227
Historic Buildings (*continued*):
  Council Reports (*continued*):
    Scotland, 20, 208, 233, 387, 503, 699, 768, 957, 1024, 1227
    Wales, 19, 208, 233, 427, 502, 699, 767, 957, 1024, 1227
Historic Parliamentary Documents:
  In the Palace of Westminster, 1145
  Reproductions Postcards, 1145
Historical Bulletin Series, 295, 563, 828, 1096
Historical Manuscripts Commission Publications, 380, 860, 1137
Historical Monuments:
  Archaeological Survey, 1176
  England, 902
Historical Museum, Register House, Official Guide to Documents exhibited, 916
History:
  In Secondary Schools, Teaching of, 654
  Of the Second World War, 82, 122, 173, 296, 389, 565, 602, 657, 828, 859, 916, 1098
  Scottish Certificates of Education, 913
Hitchin Railway Accident Report, 929
Hitchman, Sir A. (Chairman: Agricultural Improvement Council for England and Wales) Report, 289
Hive, Modified Commercial, 555, 1083
Hive, Smith, 1083
Hodson, Rt. Hon. Lord Justice (Chairman: Committee on Conflicts of Jurisdiction affecting Children) Report. *Cmnd. 842.* 803, 887
Hola Camp Documents. *Cmnd. 778, 795, 816.* 799, 800, 801, 833
Holden, A. V., Fertilization Experiments in Scottish Fresh-Water Lochs:
  914
  Loch Kinardochy, 387
Holden, H. S., Morphology and Relationship of Rachioptuis Cylindrica, 1096
Holes, Measurement of Small, 167
Hollander, D. H., Biology of Treponematoses, 471
Holleman, L. W. J., Processing of Cassava and Cassava Products in Rural Industries, 435
Holliday, F. G. T., Herring in Aquaria, 656
Holmes Chapel and Sandbach. Railway Accident Report, 1198
Holmes, G. D., Experiments on Chemical Control of Rhododendron Ponticum, 325
Holmes, Sir M. G. (Chairman: Public Trustee Office Committee) Report. *Cmd. 9755.* 42
Holmes, M. R., Arms and Armour in Tudor and Stuart London, 358
Holmes, S. C. A., London and Thames Valley, British Regional Geology, 1131

1956-60 | HOL-HUN

HOL— INDEX 1956–60

Holt, S. J., On the Dynamics of Exploited Fish Populations, 559
Holyroodhouse Palace Guide, 698, 1227
Holy Trinity, Hounslow Act, 543
Home and Garden Bulletins, 201, 692, 951
Home Defence and the Farmer, 559
Home Department Estimates:
1956–57, 12
1957–58, 226
1958–59, 494, 676
1959–60, 759, 933
1960–61, 1019, 1201
Home Designing for Safety in the Home, 857
Home Economics for South and East Asia, Report of Technical Meeting, 708
Home Freezers, 202
Home Grown Sugar Beet (Research and Education) Fund. Account, 763, 780
Home, Sir J. M., Shelter Woods or Belts, 69, 819
Home Office Publications 123–5, 333–5, 603, 860, 1137
Home, Rt. Hon. the Earl of (Chairman: Constitutional Discussions on Basutoland). *Cmnd. 637.* 789, 835
Home Safety Bill, 1045
Homecraft:
In Secondary Schools, Teaching of, 1185
Rooms, Safety Precautions in, Display Cards, 170
Scottish Certificate of Education, 913
Homeless:
Conduct and Care of. Exercises and Local Competitions, 869
Families. Circular, 868
Homes, New Grants for Better, 858, 870
Homicide Act, 272
Homicide Bill, 35, 214
Homosexual Offences and Prostitution Report. *Cmnd. 247.* 265, 334, 387
Honey Fungus, 596
Honeyman, G. G. (Chairman: Advisory Committee on Examination of Steam Boilers in Industry) Report. *Cmnd. 1173.* 1063
Hong Kong:
Agreement with Burma for Supply of Cotton Textiles. *Cmnd. 738.* 796, 846
Arms, 832
Badges, 87
Colonial Office Picture Set, 614
Colonial Report, 88, 301, 570, 833, 1102
Flag Badge, 833
International Customs Journal, 1244
Orders-in-Council, 1174
Treasury Minute relative to Loan of two Minesweepers. *Cmnd. 651.* 790, 934
Honours, Decorations and Medals, Committee on the Grant of. *Cmnd. 190.* 261, 409
Hooijer, D. A., Early Pleistocene Mamalian Fauna from Bethlehem, 563
Hooper, Sir Frederick (Chairman: Resettlement Advisory Board) Progress Report. *Cmnd. 789.* 800, 885
Hooton South Junction Railway Accident Report, 673
Hop Growing and Drying, 290
Hopkins, G. H. E.:
Early Literature on Mallophaga, 1095
Fleas, 81
Notes on Some Mallophaga from Mammals, 1096
Hopkinson, R. G., Simplified Daylight Tables, 651
Hop-Pickers and Pickers, etc., of Fruit, Flowers, etc. Model Byelaw, 342
Hopwood, A. T., Insectivora and Chiroptera from the Miocene Rocks of Kenya Colony, 295
Horion, P.:
Représentation des Travailleurs sur le Plan de l'Entreprise dans le Droit des Pays Membres de la CECA, 965
Stabilité de l'Emploi dans le Droit des Pays Membres de la CECA, 965
Hornby, W., Factories and Plant, 565, 657
Horse Breeding Act, 541
Horse Breeding Bill, 480, 518
Horse Breeding, Report on Consolidation Bill, 477, 480
Horse-Flies of the Ethiopian Region, 295
Horse Numbers in European Countries, Effects of Farm Mechanization, 720
Horse Races. Report of the Departmental Committee on a Levy on Betting. *Cmnd. 1003.* 1051, 1139
Horses, Live, Exports Licence, 181
Horticultural Crops. Chemical Weed Control, 1084
Horticultural Machinery Leaflets, 559, 824, 1088
Horticultural Marketing. Report of the Committee. *Cmnd. 61.* 252, 292, 334, 387
Horticultural Packing Sheds, Design in, 1087
Horticulture:
Experimental, 558, 822, 1087
Improvement of Production and Marketing of Produce. *Cmnd. 880.* 805, 820, 824, 862
See also Experimental Husbandry
Horticulture Act, 1070
Horticulture Bill, 783, 786, 1005, 1006, 1019, 1037, 1041, 1042, 1141
Hosiery:
And Other Knitted Goods Census of Production Report, 179, 664
Knitwear and Lace. Career, 1152
Hospital of Robert Earl of Leicester Charity (Warwick) Scheme Confirmation Act, 58

INDEX 1956–60 —HOU

Hospital of Robert Earl of Leicester Charity (Warwick) Scheme Confirmation Bill, 4, 34
Hospital of St. Mary Magdalene and Other Charities (Newcastle upon Tyne) Charity Scheme Confirmation Act, 811
Hospital of St. Mary Magdalene and Other Charities (Newcastle upon Tyne) Charity Scheme Confirmation Bill, 750, 785
Hospital of St. Nicholas (Salisbury) Charity Scheme Confirmation Act, 811
Hospital of St. Nicholas (Salisbury) Charity Scheme Confirmation Bill, 750, 785
Hospitals:
Analysis of Running Costs of, 121, 330, 1132
And Specialist Services:
England and Wales, Statistics, 122
Standing Advisory Committee Report, 330
Building Bulletin, 602
Costing Returns, 122, 333, 602, 859, 1135
Directory:
England and Wales, 122, 332
Scottish, 601, 1132
Endowments Fund Account, 10, 122, 227, 331, 497, 601, 602, 769, 857, 1027, 1134
Endowment Research Trust Report and Accounts, Scottish, 1038
In-patients:
Enquiry Report, 1130
Statistics, 856
In Programmes of Community Health Protection, Role of, 472
Laundry Arrangements Report, 1133
O. and M. Service Reports, 602, 859, 1134
Running Costs of, Select Committee on Estimates Report, 235
Service Report, 331
Supplies. Central Health Services Council Committee Report, 332, 602
Hot and Cold Open-Tank Method of Impregnating Timber, 907
Hotel and Catering:
Management. Career, 347
Occupations. Career, 136
Hotel Keeping and Catering. Arrangements and Conditions for the Award of National Diplomas, 843
Hotel Proprietors Act, 56
Hotel Proprietors Act Notice, 150
Hotel Proprietors Bill, 4, 5, 6, 18, 29, 33, 35, 126
Hotel Proprietors (Liabilities and Rights) Bill. *See* Hotel Proprietors Bill
House, D. V., Report on Investigation into the Affairs of Gordon Hotels Ltd., 397
House of Commons:
Accommodation Select Committee Minutes, 27, 126
Bills, 32–6, 247–50, 516, 784, 1041
Committee of Public Accounts Report, 866
Debates, 28–9, 30, 32, 221, 241–2, 243, 246, 429, 490, 510, 513, 516, 756, 777, 783, 1013, 1035, 1036, 1040
Disqualification Act, 272
Disqualification Bill, 23, 35, 36, 126, 215, 247, 248
Journals, 490, 756, 1013
Kitchen and Refreshment Rooms. Select Committee Report, 18, 233, 337, 503, 607, 766
Library Documents, 59, 275
Members' Fund:
Accounts, 14, 126, 229, 337, 499, 607, 762, 863, 1140
Report 10, 126
Model Clauses, 1073
Papers, 8–32, 221–46, 489, 605, 755, 863, 1012
Privileges Committee Report, 32, 223, 225, 240, 338
Procedure Report from Select Committee, 235, 761, 865
Public Accounts:
221, 225, 227, 233, 236, 238
Index, 221, 243
Reports, 761, 769, 771, 865, 1014, 1026, 1029, 1039, 1142, 1143
Publications, 1140
Sessional Index, 8
Sessional Printed Papers, Titles and Contents, 8, 489, 1012, 1013, 1144
Standing Committee:
Debates, 8, 29, 242, 246, 489, 490, 512, 516, 783, 1012, 1013, 1036, 1037, 1038, 1040
Returns, 28, 866, 1035
Standing Orders:
27, 126, 491, 506, 609, 772, 780, 1018, 1027, 1034, 1038, 1144
Committee, Special Reports, 866
House of Commons Disqualification Act, 272, 808, 1069
House of Commons Disqualification Bill, 215, 247, 248
House of Commons Members Fund Act, 272, 1070
House of Commons Members' Fund Bill, 216, 248, 1000, 1018, 1042, 1145
House of Commons (Redistribution of Seats) Act, 541
House of Commons (Redistribution of Seats) Bill, 480, 517
House of Lords:
Debates, 6–7, 8, 213, 219–20, 429, 477, 485, 489, 745, 753, 755, 1003, 1010, 1012
Journals, 477, 1003

HOU— INDEX 1956 60

House of Lords (*continued*):
Model Clauses, 275, 1073
Offices, Select Committee Reports, 2, 3, 6, 7, 214, 219, 220, 340, 479, 484, 488, 609, 610, 748, 753, 755, 867
Papers and Bills, 1–8, 213–21, 477, 745, 866, 1003
Publications, 1144
Select Committee:
On Procedure Report, 8, 128, 217, 340
Reports, 485, 488, 609, 753, 867, 1006, 1007, 1008, 1012, 1143
Special Orders; Committee Reports, 2–8, 128, 214, 215, 216, 217, 218, 219, 220, 339–40, 479, 480, 481, 482, 483, 484, 485, 487, 488, 609, 610, 747, 748, 749, 750, 751, 752, 753, 754, 755, 867, 1004, 1005, 1006, 1007, 1008, 1009, 1010, 1011, 1012, 1145
Standing Orders:
2, 6, 129, 216, 219, 340, 485, 487, 610, 1005, 1007, 1010, 1011, 1144
Amendments, 747, 755
House Purchase and Housing Act, 809
House Purchase and Housing Act Circular, 69
House Purchase and Housing Bill, 520, 748, 750, 784, 785
Household Expenditure Report, 348
Houses:
Building, Programming of, 164
Construction, Study of Alternative Methods, 909
Design, 121
Held on Ground Lease, 358
Longhorn Beetle, 907
Purchase. Proposed Government Scheme. *Cmnd. 571.* 536, 600, 612
Refuse. Duties in Connection with Removal, 342
Temporary, 340
Housing:
Accommodation, Improvement and Conversion, 858
And Building Materials in Asia and Far East, 456
And Building Statistics for Europe, 230, 457, 727, 984, 1251, 1257
And Community Improvement Programme, Financing of, 454
And Town and Country Planning in the U.K. Dependencies, 1150
Building and Planning, 456, 457, 727, 1255
Census, General Principles for, 731
Europe, Financing of, 724
Ghana, 732
Handbook, Scottish, 331
Layout, 601
Management:
Careers, 617
Housing (*continued*):
Management (*continued*):
Sub-Committee of the Central Housing Advisory Committee Report, 130
Procedure for Local Authorities, 601
Progress, European, 228A
Report, 118
Research Reprint Series, 202
Returns:
England and Wales. *Cmd. 9681, 9749, 9817, 9885.* 38, 42, 46, 52, 130; *Cmnd. 65, 155, 233, 248.* 253, 259, 264, 268, 341; *Cmnd. 354, 420, 489, 548.* 522, 527, 531, 535, 612; *Cmnd. 646, 729, 819, 873.* 789, 795, 801, 805, 870; *Cmnd. 941, 1016, 1119, 1208.* 1047, 1052, 1059, 1066, 1147, Appendix, 130, 341, 612, 1147
Scotland, *Cmd. 9680, 9748, 9818, 9886.* 38, 42, 46, 52, 120; *Cmnd. 66, 156, 234, 285.* 253, 259, 264, 268, 330; *Cmnd. 355, 421, 490, 552.* 522, 527, 531, 535, 600; *Cmnd. 647, 728, 820, 869.* 789, 795, 801, 805, 858; *Cmnd. 934, 1014, 1112, 1205.* 1047, 1052, 1058, 1066, 1132
Situation, European, 228A
Statistics. Circulars, 611
Subsidies:
610; Circular, 1146
In Scotland Working Party Report, 120
Summaries. *Cmd. 9665, 9702, 9727, 9774, 9796, 9846, 9869.* 37, 39, 41, 43, 45, 49, 51, 54, 120. *Cmnd. 28.* 130; *Cmnd. 49, 95, 115, 179, 204, 254, 271, 324.* 251, 255, 256, 261, 263, 266, 267, 271, 330, 341; *Cmnd. 340, 379, 397, 438, 463, 519, 536, 598.* 521, 524, 525, 528, 529, 533, 534, 539, 600, 612; *Cmnd. 624, 683, 709, 766, 793, 838, 845, 904.* 788, 792, 794, 798, 800, 802, 803, 807, 858, 870; *Cmnd. 921, 955, 986, 1056, 1087, 1045, 1172, 1228.* 1046, 1048, 1050, 1055, 1057, 1061, 1063, 1067, 1132, 1147
Techs. *See* D.H.S. Housing
The Arts in Great Britain Report, 826
Through Non-profit Organisations, 457, 732
Trends and Policies, European, 724, 982
Housing Act, 272
Housing Act Account, 196, 272, 409, 679
Housing Act, Tables of Comparison, 341
Housing Bill, 214, 218, 249
Housing Bill Report, 218
Housing and Local Government, Ministry of:
Circular, 129–31, 340–1, 610 868, 1146

INDEX 1956 60 HUN

Housing and Local Government, Ministry of (*continued*):
Estimates:
1956–57, 12
1957–58, 226
1958–59, 494, 676
1959–60, 760
1960–61, 1091, 1201
Forms, 129, 869
Index, 341
Publications, 129–31, 340–3, 610, 868, 1146
Report. *Cmd. 9876.* 51, 130; *Cmnd. 193.* 262, 342; *Cmnd. 419.* 521, 612; *Cmnd. 737.* 796, 871; *Cmnd. 1027.* 1053, 1148
Housing and Town Development (Scotland) Act, 272
Housing and Town Development (Scotland) Bill, 217, 233, 242, 247, 248, 337
Housing (Financial Provisions) Act, 541
Housing (Financial Provisions) Bill, 478, 479, 517
Housing (Financial Provisions) Report on Consolidation Bill, 477, 479
Housing Repairs and Rent Act. Grants for Improvement, 341
Housing Subsidies Act, 56
Housing Subsidies Act Circular, 129
Housing Subsidies Bill, 1, 33
Housing (Temporary Accommodation) Act Account, 10, 208, 225, 427
Housing (Underground Rooms) Act, 809
Housing (Underground Rooms) Act Circular, 869
Housing (Underground Rooms) Bill, 521, 748, 761, 778, 784, 863
How Accidents Happen When Lifting and Carrying, 621
How to Find Out about the United Nations, 230A
How to make Grass Silage, 1084
Howard, A., Studies on Beef Quality, 382, 649, 1180
Howarth, I. G., Revision of the Genus Neozephyrus Sibatani and Its (Lepidoptera Lycaenidae), 295
Howarth, M. K., Upper Jurassic and Cretaceous Ammonite Faunas of Alexander Land and Graham Land, 571
Howes, Dr. H. W., Fundamental, Adult, Literacy and Community Education in the West Indies, 238
Howitt, Sir H.:
Chairman: Committee of Inquiry on the Powers of the Crown to Authorise the Use of Unpatented Inventions and Unregistered Designs in Connection with Defence Contracts. *Cmd. 9788.* 44
Report on Purchasing Procedure, British Transport Commission. *Cmnd. 262.* 266
Hoyle, G.:
Explosion Report. *Cmnd. 331, 414.* 321, 320
Mines and Quarries Report, 642, 645
North Western Mines Report, 116
Hoyle, H. D., Subtropical Jet Stream of the Eastern North Pacific Ocean, 360
Huberman, M. A., Tropical Silviculture 1237
Huddersfield Corporation Act, 58
Hudson Bay Marine Insurance Rates Report, 91, 305, 574, 836, 1107
Hueper, W. C., Quest into the Environmental Causes of Cancer of the Lung, 203
Hugh-Jones, P., Lung Function in Coal-Workers Pneumoconiosis, 151
Hughes, R., Administration of War Production, 82, 173
Hull, R., Sugar Beet Diseases, 1085
Hull Harbour British Transport Commission Charges Scheme Order, 1199
Human and Animal Ecology, 465
Human Artificial Insemination Departmental Committee Report. *Cmnd. 1105.* 1058, 1139, 1187
Human Heredity, Effect of Radiation on, 1269
Human Problems of Innovation, 1181
Human Protein Requirements and Their Fulfilment in Practice. Conference Proceedings, 437
Human Relations in Industry Report, 223, 650
Human Rights:
Commission Report, 228A, 723, 982, 1253
European Commission of, 703
United Nations Work, 457, 727, 734
Universal Declaration, 727, 993
Yearbook, 230A, 457, 727, 1262
Human Rights Bill, 250
Human Tissue Bill, 1045
Human Welfare, 724, 982
Humanism and Education in East and West, 469
Humber Bridge Act, 811
Humber Bridge Bill. Special Report from the Standing Orders Committee, 767, 866
Hume, A. B. (Chairman: Scottish Advisory Council Committee on Treatment of Offenders) Report, 1188
Humid Tropics Research, 736
Humidity, Measurement of, 636
Hummel, F. C.:
Code of Sample Plot Procedure, 854
Tariff Tables for Conifers in Great Britain, 112
Hungarian Property in the U.K. Accounts of the Administrator. *Cmnd. 465.* 529, 679; *Cmnd. 774.* 799, 936; *Cmnd. 978.* 1049, 1200

Hungarian Uprising, 319
Hungary:
Agreement with U.K.:
Concerning Civil Aviation. *Cmnd. 1236*. 1068, 1121
Relating to the Settlement of Financial Matters. *Cmd. 9820*. 47, 107
Exchange of Notes with U.K. terminating the Anglo-Hungarian Payments Agreement. *Cmnd. 896*. 806, 850
Exodus from, 454
Problems. Summary of Report, 457
Special Committee Report, 455
Hunt, K. E., Colonial Agriculture Statistics, 301
Hunterston, Ayrshire, Nuclear Generating Station Report, 388
Huntly Castle, Aberdeenshire. Guide Book, 1227
Hurcomb, Lord (Chairman: Committee on Bird Life in the Royal Parks) Report, 427, 957
Hurricane Research Station. Exchange of Notes between U.K. and U.S.A. *Cmnd. 1035*. 1053, 1127
Husk or Hoose in Calves, 1083
Hyatt, K. H., Revision of the Platysseiinae based on Material in the Collections of the British Museum (Natural History), 1097
Hybrid Chickens, 822
Hyde, H.:
Explosion Report. *Cmnd. 396*. 525
Inspectors of Mines and Quarries Reports, 642, 645, 900, 1172
Northumberland and Cumberland Mines Report, 116
Hydractinia, Three Northern Species, 81
Hydraulics Research Board:
Papers, 909, 1183
Report, 167, 383, 650, 908, 1180
Hydrocarbon Oil Duties (Temporary Increase) Act, 56
Hydrocarbon Oil Duties (Temporary Increase) Bill, 8, 36
Hydrodynamics, Caviation in, 155
Hydro-Electric Development (Scotland) Act:
Guarantee given on Loans proposed to be raised, 10, 17, 18, 19, 22, 26, 27, 31, 172, 196, 224, 231, 235, 236, 240, 409–10, 493, 501, 507, 510, 515, 679, 757, 760, 767, 768, 774, 780, 936, 1018, 1025, 1031, 1034, 1204
North of Scotland Hydro-Electric Development Scheme. *Cmnd. 32*. 54, 172; *Cmnd. 408*, *494*. 526, 531, 655; *Cmnd. 681*. 792, 914
Hydro-Electric Plant Construction, Bibliographical Index, 727, 1251
Hydro-Electric Power Plants, Mechanization in Construction, 458
Hydrogen Bomb, 334
Hydrogen Sulphide. Methods for Detection of Toxic Substances in Air, 630
Hydrographical Observations in the Irish Sea, 1087
Hydrographical Survey of the River Usk, 291
Hydrography:
Of the British East African Coastal Waters, 302, 833
Of Faroe-Shetland Channel, 388
Of Scottish Coastal Waters, 914
Of the North-Western Approaches to the British Isles, 914
Hydroid Genus Perigonimus M. Sars, 1846. Revision of the, 81
Hydrologic Terms used in Asia and Far East Glossary, 454
Hydrological Survey, River Great Ouse Basin, 1148
Hydrology, Arid Zone. Recent Developments, 994
Hydrometric Statistics for British Rivers, 131, 343, 613, 871
Hygiene:
And Public Health in Europe, Teaching of, 471
And Sanitation in Aviation:
Expert Committee Report, 1000
Guide, 1268
Catering Establishments. *See* Clean Catering
Retail Fish Trade, 1133
Retail Meat Trade, 859
Transport and Handling of:
Fish, 1133
Meat, 859
Hypomagnesaemia, 821
Hystrichopsyllid Siphonaptera, New, 562

I

Ice. Census of Production Report, 395
Ice Cream:
Census of Production Report, 664
Heat Treatment, etc. Regulations Circulars, 859
Standard. Food Standards Committee Report, 292
Iceland:
Aerial Navigation Agreement. *Cmnd. 166*. 260, 314
Agreement on Joint Financing of Air Navigation Services, 440. *Cmnd. 677*. 792, 845
Agreement with U.K. respecting the Repayment of the Debt on the Liquidation of the European Payments Union. *Cmnd. 763*. 798, 850
Economic Conditions, 1246
Foreign Trade Statistical Bulletin, 222A, 447, 448, 717, 977

Iceland (*continued*):
Submarine Telecommunication Cable System. Agreement with U.K. and others, 783, 897
Idea in Action, 421
Identification of Hardwoods, 1180
Identification of Timbers, 908
Ignatieff, V., Efficient Use of Fertilizers, 966
IGRL:
Publications, 691
Ill-treatment of Prisoners in H.M. Prison, Liverpool. Report of Inquiry. *Cmnd. 503*. 532, 603
Illustrated Booklet, Victoria and Albert Museum, 693, 1222
Immigration and Passports Bill, 517
Immunological and Haematological Surveys Report, 1000
Immunological Procedures, Memorandum, 206, 424
Impact of Science on Society, 238, 467, 737, 995, 1264
Imperial Standards. Report on the comparisons of the Parliamentary Copies, 666
Imperial War Graves Commission Reports, 343, 871
Imperial War Museum Short Guide, 343
Implementation Panel:
441
Air Navigation Facilities and Services, 711
Report, 971
Import Duties:
European Free Trade Association. Order. *See* Statutory Instruments Select Committee Report
Ways and Means Resolution. *Cmnd. 304*. 269, 397
Import Duties Act:
541
Report, 1034, 1193
Import Duties Bill, 250, 479, 517
Import Licence Amendments, 181, 397, 666, 922, 1193
Import List. Key relating to the Standard International Trade Classification. Amendment, 181
Import of British Books and Films. Exchange of Notes between U.K. and Yugoslavia. *Cmnd. 404*. 525, 596. *Cmnd. 1023*. 1052, 1128
Importance of Thermal Insulation in Building, 427
Importation by air, Formalities on Arrival of Aircraft, 1232
Importation by Inland Frontiers; Formalities on Arrival, Up to Presentation of Goods Declarations, 1232
Importation by Sea:
434
Unloading, 704
Importation, Temporary:
Private Road Vehicles. *Cmnd. 602*. 787, 846
Private Use of Aircraft and Pleasure Boats. *Cmnd. 650*. 790, 846
Imported Goods and Re-exported Goods, Statistical Classification, 577, 837, 1108
Imported Timber. Monopolies Commission Report, 507, 666
Imprisonment:
Alternatives to Short Terms of. Report, 334
Use of Short Sentences Report, 1188
Improvement and Conversion of Housing Accommodation, 858
Improvement Grants. Circular, 341
Improvement of Family Levels of Living through Social Security and Related Social Services, 1256
Improvements in National Assistance. *Cmnd. 782*. 799, 891
Improving Agricultural Tenancy, 436
Improving Marginal Land, 69
In the Service of Europe, 727
Incandescent Mantles. Census of Production Report, 396
Ince Moss Junction Railway Accident Report, 673
Ince, Sir Godfrey (Chairman: Committee of Inquiry into Welsh Broadcasting) Report. *Cmnd. 39*. 54
Incentives in the Building Industry, 909
Income and Expenditure. *See* National
Income Tax:
And Estate Duty on Woodlands, 1129
Double Taxation Relief Tables, 873
Form, 873
In the Commonwealth, 132, 615, 1150
Outside the Commonwealth, 132, 345, 615, 873, 1150
Income Tax Acts:
Case Commentary, 132, 615, 873
Supplement, 132, 615, 873, 1150
Income Tax (Repayment of Post War Credits) Act, 809
Income Tax (Repayment of Post-War Credits) Bill, 749, 785
Increase of certain Pensions. Royal Warrant, 956
Indecency with Children Act, 1070
Indecency with Children Bill, 755, 1003, 1024, 1037, 1042, 1141
See Criminal Law Revision Committee Report
Independence of Somaliland. Agreement and Exchange of Letters with U.K. *Cmnd. 1101*. 1058
Independent Primary and Secondary Schools E. and W. recognised as efficient 586
Independent Television Authority. Report and Accounts, 24, 161, 243, 369, 513, 640, 779, 897, 1038, 1169

Index of Retail Prices:
Cost of Living Advisory Committee Report. *Cmd. 9710*. 40, 138
Method of Construction and Calculation, 138, 886
Index Translationum, 238A, 467, 736, 995, 1264
India:
Exchange of Notes with U.K.:
Amending Air Services Agreement. *Cmnd. 275*. 267, 402
Constituting an Agreement to amend the Air Services Agreement. *Cmnd. 837*. 802, 929
International Customs Journal, 713
Teaching of the Social Sciences, 240A
Indian Painting in Bundi and Kotah, 1223
Indian Territory, Right of Passage Over. Order, 220A, 443, 713, 972
India's Most Dangerous Hour, 565, 658
Indigenous Cattle of the British Dependent Territories in Africa, 569
Indigofera in Tropical Africa, 647
Individual Differences in Night-Vision Efficiency, 359
Individual Efficiency in Industry. *See* Human Relations in Industry
Indo-Australian Geometridae. New Species, 563
Indonesia:
Exchange of Notes with U.K.:
Amending the Memorandum of Understanding for the Export of Cotton Yarn from Hong Kong. *Cmnd. 250*. 265, 319
Relating to Arrangements for the Export of Cotton Yarn. *Cmnd. 45*. 251, 319
Indo-Pacific Fisheries, Economic Role of Middlemen and Co-operatives, 1237
Indus Basin Development Fund Act, 1071
Indus Basin Development Fund Agreement. *Cmnd. 1199*. 1065, 1106
Indus Basin Development Fund Bill, 1011, 1044
Industrial Accident Prevention. Industrial Safety Sub-Committee Report, 138
Industrial and Economic Microbiology in North America, 651
Industrial and Provident Societies Bill, 1044
Industrial and Provident Societies. Chief Registrar's Report, 326
Industrial Assurance Commissioner's Report, 114, 326, 596, 855, 1130
Industrial Assurance and Friendly Societies Act, 1948 (Amendment) Act, 541
Industrial Assurance and Friendly Societies Act, 1948 (Amendment) Bill, 481, 517
Industrial Challenge of Nuclear Energy, Conference Papers, 448, 718, 976, 1248
Industrial Classification of All Economic Activities, Index to International Standard, 233A
Industrial Coal Consumers' Council. Domestic Coal Consumers' Council Reports, 20, 115, 235, 371, 505, 642, 772, 899, 1031, 1171
Industrial Court Awards, 138–41, 349–50, 621, 875, 1155
Industrial Court. Report on London Airport Dispute. *Cmnd. 608*. 539, 623
Industrial Courts Act:
Court of Inquiry Report. *Cmnd. 510*. 532, 623
Reports. *Cmd. 9717*, *9843*. 40, 49, 138; *Cmnd. 105*, *131*, *159*, *160*. 256, 257, 259, 260, 349
Industrial Design, Council of:
Publications, 131, 343, 613, 871, 1148
Report, 131, 343, 613, 872, 1148
Industrial Design in the United States, 976
Industrial Development:
In the United Kingdom Dependencies, 345
Of Peru, 1251
Industrial Diseases (Benefit) Acts, Pneumoconiosis and Byssinosis Benefit Scheme. Decision of the Commissioner, 1164
Industrial Disputes Tribunal Awards, 141–9, 351–6, 623, 880
Industrial Enterprises in Under-developed Countries, Management of, 729
Industrial Fibres, Production, Trade, etc., 304, 572, 835, 1105
Industrial Fire Precautions in War, 861
Industrial Flooring, Hardwood for, 908
Industrial Group:
Information Bibliography, 418, 949
Publications, 418, 690, 949, 950, 1218
Report, 949, 1218
United Kingdom Atomic Energy Authority Publications, 690
Industrial Growth, Patterns of, 1257
Industrial Health:
And Safety Centre Guide, 629
Chief Inspector of Factories' Report. *Cmnd. 558*. 536, 629; *Cmnd. 811*. 801, 876; *Cmnd. 1137*. 1060, 1152
Survey:
In Halifax Report, 629
In the Pottery Industry, 885
Industrial Injuries. Convention between U.K. and Denmark on Payment of Compensation or Benefit. *Cmd. 9839*. 48, 105; *Cmnd. 76*. 253
Industrial Microbiology in British Commonwealth. Review, 826
Industrial Organisation and Development Act:
Account, 14, 15, 181, 231, 232, 397, 762, 781, 922, 1040, 1193

Industrial Organisation and Development Act (*continued*):
Lace Furnishings Industry (Export Promotion Levy) Account, 500, 515, 666
Lace Industry (Levy) Account, 500, 515, 666
Wool Textile Industry:
(Export Promotion Levy) Account, 500, 667
(Scientific Research Levy) Account, 500, 667
Industrial Production, Indices of, 719, 1099
Industrial Property. International Convention for Protection:
Cmnd. 875. 805, 850
Explanatory Notes, 922
Industrial Rating Bill, 18, 29, 31, 126
Industrial Research:
And Development Expenditure Report, 1180
Associations. Summary of Work, 651
Estimates:
1956–57, 12
1957–58, 226
1958–59, 494
1959–60, 760, 933
1960–61, 1019, 1201
Industrial (Small Business) Series, 202
Industrial Statistics:
224A
1900 to 1957, 718
Industrial Use of Woodwaste, 224A
Industrialization and Productivity Bulletin, 727, 984, 1255
Industrialization in Under-Developed Countries, Bibliography on, 225A
Industries:
Scotland and Wales Census of Production Report, 923
Standard Industrial Classification, 829
Industry:
And Commerce, Education for, 842
And Employment in Scotland:
Cmd. 9737. 41, 172
And Scottish Roads Report. *Cmnd. 125*. 257, 387; *Cmnd. 384*. 524, 655; *Cmnd. 706*. 794, 914; *Cmnd. 1045*. 1054, 1187
Human Relations in, Reports, 650
Problems of Progress in, 383, 651, 909, 1181
Research for, Report, 1181
Tables, Census E. and W., 327
Infancy, Standards of Normal Weight. Committee Report, 860
Infant Care, 419
Infant Mortality, Social and Biological Factors, 856
Infantry Regiments, Amalgamation and Re-designation of, 693
Infectious Diseases:
European Technical Conference on the Control through Vaccination Programmes, 1269
See Registrar General's Returns
Infestation Control, 824
Influence of Sales Taxes on Productivity, 718
Influenza Epidemic, E. and W., 1136
Information, Central Office of:
Publications, 131–2, 344–5, 614, 872, 1149
Select Committee on Estimates Report, 1029, 1143
Information on Water Resources Report, 868
Informations Mensuelles, 214–15, 434, 705, 964
Informations Statistiques, 1234
Infra-Red and Roman Spectroscopy Abstracts of Literature on, 393
Infra-Red Heat for Chick Rearing, 288, 1083
Ingall, D. H. (Chairman: Training of District Nurses Advisory Committee) Report, 859
Ingeberg, S. H., Combustible Contents in Buildings, 419
Ingleby, Rt. Hon. Viscount (Chairman: Committee on Children and Young Persons) Report. *Cmnd. 1191*. 1065
Ingrams, H., Uganda. Crisis of Nationhood, 1103
Ink, Census of Production Reports, 394
Inland Fisheries, Application of Science to, 966
Inland Navigation. Convention regarding Measurement and Registration of Vessels Employed, 734
Inland Revenue:
Estimates:
1956–57, 12
1957–58, 226
1958–59, 494, 676
1959–60, 760, 933
1960–61, 1019, 1202
Publications, 132–5, 345–7, 615, 873, 1150
Report. *Cmd. 9667*. 37, 196; *Cmnd. 54*. 252, 410; *Cmnd. 341*. 521, 679; *Cmnd. 628*. 788, 936; *Cmnd. 922*. 1046, 1204
Inland Telegraph Service. Report of the Advisory Committee, 640
Inland Transport, 296, 389
Inland Waterways:
Charges Scheme. Transport Tribunal Proceedings, 674
Government Proposals. *Cmnd. 676*. 792, 929
Report of the Committee of Inquiry. *Cmnd. 486*. 531, 671

Inman, P., Labour in the Munitions Industries, 296
Inquisitions, Calendar of Miscellaneous, 378
In-Sack Grain Drying, 823
Insecticides:
Expert Committee Report, 245, 472
Resistance and Vector Control. Expert Committee Report, 1269
Resistance in Arthropods, 740
Spray Accumulations in Soil on Crop Plants, Some Effects on, 422
Insectivora and Chiroptera from the Miscene Rocks of Kenya Colony, 295
Insects:
And Mites:
In Sacks, Destruction of, 1083
In Farm-Stored Grain, 555
Medical Importance, Handbook for the Identification of, 81
Other Pests, Common Names of British, 559
Pest of Douglas Tin and Sitka Spruce. *See* Adelges Cooleyi
Pests of Graminaceous Crops in East Africa, Report, 1103
Resistance and Vector Control Report, 741
Their World, 1097
In-Service Teaching Training in the United States of America, 735
Installing Solid Fuel Appliances, 1226
Instalments due under Treaty Termination Settlement. Exchange of Notes concerning Payment. *Cmnd. 515*. 533, 591
Institutional Care of Children, 457
Instruments:
For Surface Observations, 152
Of Navigation, 635
Pilot Examination Guide, 692
Insurance:
Agreement between U.K. and Germany concerning Contracts of Insurance and Contracts and Treaties of Re-Insurance. *Cmnd. 1041*. 1054, 1121
And Re-Insurance Agreement between U.K. and Italy concerning contracts. *Cmnd. 504*. 532, 590
Careers, 1152
Policies. *See* Law Reform Committee for Scotland
Insurance Companies Act:
541
Life Assurance and Bond Investment Business, 1191
Report on Consolidation Bill, 478, 484
Statements of Insurance Business, 1193
Insurance Companies Bill, 481, 483, 519
Insured Letters and Boxes. Postal Parcels, Agreements concerning. *Cmnd. 1219*. 1067, 1128
Integrated Data Processing and Computers. European Experts Report, 1248
Integrated River Basin Development Report, 727
Intense Radio-Frequency Radiation Safety Precautions, 1170
Intensive Apple Culture, 556
Intentional Food Additives to Establish their Safety in Use, Procedures for Testing. Report, 741
Interception of Communications. Committee of Privy Councillors Report. *Cmnd. 283*. 268, 334
Inter-Governmental Copyright Committee, 735
Inter-Firm Comparison, 718
Inter-Governmental Debts. Exchange of Notes Between U.K. and Czechoslovakia. *Cmnd. 720*. 794, 847
Inter-Governmental Maritime Consultative Organisation Publication, 1152
Interest on Damages (Scotland) Act, 541
Interest on Damages (Scotland) Bill, 483, 503, 512, 517, 519, 607
Interferometry, 1163
Interhandel Case (Switzerland *v.* United States of America) Judgment, 713, 973, 1243
Inter Latin American Trade:
Report, 457
Study, 457
Interim Committee for the Common Market and Euratom Publications, 438
Intermediate Hosts of Schistosoma, 740
Internal Migration, 327
International Agreement regarding False Indications of Origin on Goods. *Cmnd. 876*. 805, 848
International Air Traffic, Control of Insect Vectors, 243A
International Airport Charges, 441
International Arbitral Awards Report, 230, 727, 1258
International Atomic Energy Agency:
Agreement on the Privileges and Immunities. *Cmnd. 1176*. 1063, 1124
Exchange of Notes with U.K. relating to the Supply of Enriched Uranium. *Cmnd. 809*. 801, 845
Publications, 969, 1239
Review Series, 1240
International Bank and Monetary Fund Act, 809
International Bank and Monetary Fund Bill, 748, 784
International Bank for Reconstruction and Development:
Guarantee given on a loan proposed to be made to the Federal Power Board of the Federation of Rhodesia and Nyasaland, 194
Loan to Nigeria, 503, 677
Proposals. *Cmnd. 652*. 790, 936

International Bibliography:
Economics, 237, 466, 735, 994
Political Science, 237, 466, 735, 994
Public Administration, 732
Social and Cultural Anthropology, 994
Sociology, 237, 466, 735, 994
Translations, 238, 467
International Book Trade. *See* Books for All
International Bureau of Education Publications, 238, 1264
International Carriage by Air. Protocol to amend the Convention for Unification of Rules. *Cmd. 9824*. 47, 217
International Carriage of Goods by Road, Contract, 225
International Civil Aviation Convention, 970
International Civil Aviation Organisation:
Action of the Council, 215A, 438, 710, 970, 1240
Assembly Reports, 440, 1242
Circulars, 216A–17A, 441, 711, 970, 1241
Council to the Assembly Annual Report, 217A, 441, 711, 970, 1241
Directives of the Council Concerning the Conduct of ICAO Meetings, 970
Executive Committee Report, 711
Financial Regulations, 217A, 711, 1241
Joint Financing Conference for Revision of the Danish and Icelandic Arrangements Report, 442
Publications, 215A–19A, 438–43, 710–12, 970, 1240
Publications Regulations, 217, 441, 711, 1241
Resolutions, 1242
Rules of Procedure for the Council, 971
Technical Meetings and Rules of Procedure, 217A
International Coffee Agreement. Declaration. *Cmnd. 883*. 806, 846
International Commercial Arbitration, Conference on, 979
International Commodity Trade Commission Report, 227A, 453, 982
International Conferences:
On Private Air Law, 215A
On Public Education, 237, 737, 995, 1264
On Safety of Life at Sea, 1152
On High Policy, 817
International Convention:
Concerning the Carriage of Goods by rail, 403
For the Protection of Industrial Property:
Cmnd. 875. 805, 850
Explanatory Notes, 922
International Court of Justice:
Booklet, 457
International Court of Justice (*continued*):
Declarations concerning the Optional Clause of the Statute. *Cmd. 9719*. 40, 107; *Cmnd. 249*. 265, 319; *Cmnd. 599*. 539, 590
Publications, 219A–20A, 443, 712–13, 972, 1243
Yearbook, 220A, 443, 713, 973, 1243
International Customs:
Journals, 443–5, 713–14, 973, 1243
Tariffs Bureau, Publications, 443–5, 713 14, 973, 1243
International Development Association Act, 1070
International Development Association Articles of Agreements. *Cmnd. 965*. 1049, 1204
International Development Association Bill, 1006, 1042
International Digests of Health Legislation, 244A, 471, 740, 998, 1268
International Directory of Education Associations, 995
International Directory of Radioisotopes, 969, 1239
International Effects of National Grain Policies, 241A
International Exchange of Publications:
Convention. *Cmnd. 1242*. 1069, 1127
Handbook, 238A
International Financial Statistics, 220A, 445, 714, 974, 1245
International Flight Information Manual, 202, 692
International Flow of Private Capital, 984
International Geophysical Year, 381, 469
International Guide to European Sources of Technical Information, 448
International Labour Conference:
Proposed Action by H.M. Government. *Cmnd. 1*. 52, 149; *Cmnd. 111, 313*. 256, 270, 356; *Cmnd. 522*. 533, 630; *Cmnd. 783, 886*. 799, 806, 875, 885
Reports. *Cmnd. 36*. 54, 149; *Cmnd. 328*. 271, 356; *Cmnd. 592, 593*. 538, 630; *Cmnd. 923, 1189*. 1046, 1065, 1158
International Labour Organisation. Judgments of the Administrative Tribunal upon Complaints made against Unesco, 220A, 443
International Law Commission:
Report, 225A, 230A, 456, 726, 984, 1055
Yearbook, 457, 727, 1263
International Map of World on Millionth Scale. Report, 457, 465, 728, 985
International Meteorological Code Amendment, 152, 360, 633
International Monetary Fund:
And the International Bank for Reconstruction and Development. Proposals. *Cmnd. 652*. 790, 936

International Monetary Fund (*continued*):
Publications, 220, 445, 714, 974, 1245
Staff Papers, 1245
International Nomenclature of Yaws Lesion, 740
International Organisations:
In the Social Sciences, 239A
Legal Status, etc., 1239
Publications Catalogue, 174, 390, 917 1189
International Pharmacopoeia, 998
International Quarantine, Proceedings and Reports, 244A
International Recommendations in Basic Industrial Statistics, 1259
International Repertory of Institutions conducting Population Studies, 996
International Review of Criminal Policy, 230A, 457, 728, 985, 1255
International Rice Commission Constitution. *Cmnd. 997*. 1050, 1121
International Rights and Obligations. Exchange of Letters between U.K. and:
Ghana. *Cmnd. 345*. 522, 573
Malaya. *Cmnd. 346*. 522, 573
Nigeria. *Cmnd. 1214*. 1066, 1106
International Sanitary Regulations:
Cmnd. 30. 250, 319; 471
Airports Designated, 471
Amendment. *Cmnd. 1165*. 1063, 1128
Certificate of Vaccination against Smallpox. *Cmnd. 312*. 270, 319
Review, 243A
International Social Science:
Bibliographies, 735, 995
Bulletin, 238A, 467, 736, 995
Journal, 1263
Review, 230A, 457, 728, 985, 1256
International Sociological Association. Nature of Conflict, 469
International Standards:
And Recommended Practices, 217–18, 441–2, 711, 971, 1241
For Drinking Water, 740
Industrial Classification, 989
International Statistical Classification of Diseases, Injuries and Causes of Death, Manual of, 327, 598
International Sugar Agreement. *Cmnd. 1146*. 1061, 1126
International Survey of Programmes of Social Development, 985
International Tax Agreements, 230, 728, 1256
International Telecommunication Convention:
Cmnd. 520. 533, 590
And Related Documents. *Cmnd. 1075*. 1056, 1169
International Tin Agreement. *Cmnd. 12*. 53, 107
International Tin Council Resolution. *Cmnd. 38*. 54
International Tracing Service Agreement. *Cmd. 9713*. 40, 107
International Trade:
220A, 223A, 438, 710, 969
And Payments and National Accounts, Terms used in, 719
Direction of, 226, 451, 721, 980, 1251
Organisation Publications, 220A
Statistics, Yearbook, 230A, 457, 728, 985, 1263
International Transport of Goods. Customs Convention on. 980; *Cmnd. 1012*. 1052, 1121
International Travel:
Survey of, 421
United States Participation in, 692
International Understanding, Education for, 995
International Whaling Convention Revised Schedule. *Cmnd. 694*. 793, 854
International Wheat Agreement. *Cmnd. 730*. 790, 854; *Cmnd. 1074*. 1056, 1128
International Work in:
Bilharziasis, 1268
Leprosy, 1268
International Yearbook of Education, 238A, 467, 736, 995, 1265
Interpolation and Allied Tables, 60
Interpretation of Echo Traces, 292
Intestate Husband's Estate (Scotland) Act, 809
Intestate Husband's Estate (Scotland) Bill, 520, 747, 758, 778, 863
Introduced Reindeer of South Georgia, 571
Inventaria Archaeologica:
1094
Illustrated Card-Inventory, 562
Inventions and Designs by Government Department, Use of, 378
Inventors Royal Commission Report on Awards. *Cmd. 9744*. 162
Inverness Royal Academy Endowments Trust Scheme:
Memorandum, 912, 1184
Order-in-Council, 1184
Inverness-shire Educational Trust Scheme:
Memorandum, 912, 1184
Order-in-Council, 1184
Investigations:
Atmospherics Pollution Report, 648, 909, 1180
Food Poisoning Circulars, 602
Grain Storage Problems in Nyasaland, 570
Of the Performance of Pneumatic-tyred Rollers in the Compaction of Soil, 910
Record Forms, 171
Investing in Coal, 153
Investissements dans les Industries du Charbon et de l'Acier de la Communauté, 215, 705, 964

Investments:
Australia, 471
Central America, 421
Community Coalmining and Iron and Steel Industries Report, 1234
European Coal Steel Community, 964
Iodine Prophylaxies, Legislation on, 1267
Ionising Radiations:
Code of Practice for the Protection of Persons exposed to, 331
See Factories
Ionospheric Virtual Height Frequency Curves, Conversion to Electron Density-Height Profiles, 910
Ipswich Dock Act, 58
Iran:
Agreement with U.K. for Air Services between and beyond their respective Territories. *Cmnd. 1131*. 1060, 1121
Cultural Convention with U.K. *Cmnd. 865*. 804, 850
Exchange of Notes with U.K. concerning the Avoidance of Double Taxation on Income derived from Air Transport Services. *Cmnd. 1143*. 1061, 1121
International Customs Journal, 1244
Overseas Economic Surveys, 667, 923
Treaty of Commerce, Establishment and Navigation with U.K. *Cmnd. 698*. 793, 850
Iraq:
Cultural Agreement with U.K. *Cmnd. 969, 1129*. 1049, 1060, 1121
Exchange of Notes with U.K.:
Concerning the Settlement of Financial Claims by the Establishment of an Anglo-Iraqi Club. *Cmnd. 187*. 261, 319
Referring to Special Agreement. *Cmd. 9695, 9772*. 39, 43, 107
International Customs Journal, 444
Ireland:
Agreement with U.K.:
On Social Security. *Cmnd. 1020*. 1052, 1121
With respect to Certain Exemptions from Tax. *Cmnd. 717*. 794, 938; *Cmnd. 1089*. 1057, 1204
And Portugal Economic Conditions, 221, 446, 448, 975
Economic Conditions, 1246
Exchange of Notes with U.K.:
Amending the Air Services Agreement. *Cmnd. 535*. 534, 671; *Cmnd. 725, 890*. 795, 806, 826, 930; *Cmnd. 1230*. 1068, 1090, 1122
Concerning an Agreement with respect to Exemptions from Tax. *Cmnd. 874*. 805, 938; *Cmnd. 1192*. 1065, 1205
Ireland (*continued*):
Exchange of Notes with U.K. (*continued*):
Introducing a New Annex to the Air Services Agreement. *Cmnd. 14*. 53, 189
Foreign Trade Statistical Bulletins, 222, 447, 717, 977
Trade Agreement with U.K. *Cmnd. 1019*. 1052, 1194
Irish Land Purchase Fund Accounts, 226, 361, 494, 515, 635, 1162
Irish Republic International Customs Journal, 714
Irish Sailors and Soldiers Land Trust Accounts, 196, 410, 679
Irish Silver, 952
Iron and Steel Act:
Accounts, 19, 232, 410, 499, 679, 764, 936, 1017, 1023, 1203
Statement in regard to Remuneration, Allowances, etc. to Sir Cyril Musgrave, 762, 900
Iron and Steel Board:
Remuneration and Allowances payable to the Deputy Chairman, 1020, 1171
Reports, 23, 181, 235, 372, 505, 642, 770, 898, 1026, 1170
Salaries Determined by the Minister, 245, 372
Iron and Steel (Financial Provisions) Act, 1070
Iron and Steel (Financial Provisions) Bill, 1006, 1041
Iron and Steel Goods Export Licence, 181, 397, 666
Iron and Steel Holding and Realisation Agency:
Proposal to sell Holding of Securities. *Cmd. 9679, 9699, 9740*. 38, 39, 41, 196; *Cmnd. 59, 106, 188*. 252, 256, 261, 410; *Cmnd. 532*. 534, 679; *Cmnd. 703*. 793, 937; *Cmnd. 1053, 1115, 1121, 1156, 1227*. 1054, 1059, 1062, 1067, 1203, 1205
Reports and Accounts, 9, 196, 223, 410, 494, 515, 679, 1015, 1039, 1205
Iron and Steel Industry:
Development, 235, 371
In Europe, 224A, 450, 719, 978, 1250
Iron and Steel (Melting and Rolling) Census of Production Report, 179, 663
Iron and Steel Products Market Sampling Study, 718
Iron and Steel Scrap. Export Licence, 666
Iron and Steel Trades Employers' Association and the National Joint Trade Unions' Craftsmen's Iron and Steel Committee. Report of a Court of Inquiry on Disputes. *Cmd. 9843*. 49
Iron and Steel Works, Water Economy in, 720
Iron Deficiency Anaemia Report, 1000

IRO-KIN | 1956-60

Iron Foundries:
Census of Production Report, 179, 663
Report of the Joint Standing Committee on Conditions in, 138, 149
Ironstone Restoration Fund:
Account, 226, 766, 870
See Mineral Workings Account
Irrigation:
By Sprinkling, 1236
System for Use under Glass, Low-Level Sprinkler, 824
I Saw Technical Assistance Change Lives, 457
Isle of Man:
Agreements regarding Customs and Other Matters. *Cmnd. 317.* 270, 334
Census Report, 327
Isle of Man Act, 541
Isle of Man Bill, 249, 479
Isopyrum Aquilegioides L, Identity, 1095
Isopondylous Fishes. Contributions toward a Classification of Modern, 1097
Isotopes:
Agriculture, 986
Biochemistry and Physiology, 986
Industrial Use, 986
Medicine, 986
Research, 986
Utilisation, Social and Economic Aspects, 736
Israel:
Agreement with U.K. on Extradition. *Cmnd. 1013, 1223.* 1052, 1067, 1122
Convention with U.K. on Social Security. *Cmnd. 174.* 260, 319; *Cmnd. 347.* 522, 590
Exchange of Notes with U.K.:
Amending the Air Services Agreement. *Cmnd. 968.* 1049, 1122
Concerning the Import of British Books of an Educational Nature. *Cmnd. 1185.* 1064, 1122
International Customs Journal, 444, 973, 1244
Programme of Library Education. Report, 240A
Revenue Administration and Policy, 732
Italian Books in British Museum. Short Title Catalogue, 826
Italian Schools:
National Gallery Catalogue, 361
Of Painting. 18th Century:
Catalogues, 154
Illustrations, 154
Italy:
Agreement with U.K.:
Concerning Contracts of Insurance and Reinsurance. *Cmnd. 504.* 532, 590
For Co-operation in the Peaceful Uses of Atomic Energy. *Cmnd. 349, 458.* 522, 529, 590
Italy (*continued*):
Consular Convention with U.K. *Cmnd. 1135.* 1060, 1122
Convention with U.K.:
For the Avoidance of Double Taxation and the Prevention of Fiscal Evasion. *Cmnd. 1210.* 1066, 1122
On Social Insurance. *Cmnd. 112.* 256, 319; *Cmnd. 572.* 536, 590
Economic Conditions, 221, 446, 975, 1246
Exchange of Notes with U.K.:
Concerning the Practice of the Medical Profession by Italian and British Doctors. *Cmnd. 238.* 264, 319
Extending to Island of Jersey the Anglo-Italian Social Insurance Convention. *Cmnd. 716.* 794, 850
Respecting the Repayment of the Debt on the Liquidation of the European Payments Union. *Cmnd. 759.* 797, 850
Foreign Trade Statistical Bulletin, 222 448, 717, 977, 978, 1244
Memorandum of Understanding:
With France regarding German Trade Marks in Italy. *Cmnd. 19.* 53, 107
With U.K. regarding Claims under the Treaty of Peace. *Cmnd. 241.* 265, 320
With U.K., France and the U.S.A. regarding German Assets in Italy. *Cmnd. 236.* 264, 320
Pocket Guide, 202
Ito, Ryoji, Education in Japan, 238A
ITU Radio Conference, Special Communications Meeting Report, 712

J

Jack, Professor D. T. (Chairman: Court of Inquiry) Report into Disputes. *Cmnd. 105, 159, 160.* 256, 259, 260; *Cmnd. 608.* 539
Jackson, R. G. A., Volta River Project Report, 183
Jackson, W. (Chairman: Special Committee) Report on Supply and Training of Teachers for Technical Colleges, 314
Jacobs, J. C., Field Studies of the Movement of Soil Mixture, 652
Jacobsen, E., Comparative Pharmacology of Some Psychotropic Drugs, 1267
Jacoby, E. G., Methods of School Enrolment Protection, 995
Jacoby, E. H., Principles of Tenancy Legislation, 708
Jahoda, M., Race Relations and Mental Health, 1265

Jamaica:
302
Colonial Arms, 569
Colonial Report, 87, 88, 301, 1102
James, D. G., Forecasting Cirrus Cloud over the British Isles, 360
Jameson, Sir W. (Chairman: On Field of Work, Training and Recruitment of Health Visitors) Report, 122
Jamides Euchylas Complex and Two New Species of the Genus Jamides, 1095
Jammet, Dr. H., Safe Handling of Radioisotopes, 1240
Janson, H. W., Common Names of British Insect and Other Pests, 560
Japan:
Agreement Regarding British Commonwealth War Graves in Japanese Territory. *Cmnd. 134.* 258, 320
Agreement with U.K.:
For Co-operation in the Peaceful Uses of Atomic Energy. *Cmnd. 459.* 529, 591; *Cmnd. 625.* 788, 850
Regarding Settlement of Claims. *Cmnd. 1229.* 1067, 1122
Education in, 238A
Exchange of Notes with U.K.:
Concerning the Grant of Continuous Visas. *Cmnd. 412.* 526, 591
Prolonging the Sterling Payments Agreement. *Cmnd. 86.* 254, 320
Free World Ally, 692
International Customs Journal, 444, 714
Status of United Nations' Forces. *Cmnd. 67.* 253
War Against, 296, 389
Japanese Beetle, 71
Japanese Treaty of Peace Act Accounts, 24, 181, 499, 667, 767, 773, 922
Jarlshof, Shetland, Excavations of, 427
Jarvis, R. A., Soils of the Country Round Kilmarnock, 288
Jay, P., Effect of Fluoridated Public Water Supplies on Dental Caries Prevalence, 421
Jayatilleke, K. N., Buddhism and the Race Question, 737
Jayne, Sears, Lumley Library Catalogue, 80
"Jean Stephen" Wreck Report, 675
Jeannel, R.:
Ruwenzori Expedition, 828
Sur les Pselaphides de l'Inde Septentrionale, 1096
Jedburgh and Morebattle. Soils of the Country round, 70
Jeffers, J. N. R.:
Code of Sample Plot Procedure, 854
Design of Poplar Experiments, 854
Jeffrey, A. G., Records and Accounts for Farm Management, 557
Jehu, V. J., Vehicle Headlamp Testing, 652
Jenkins, Rt. Hon. Lord (Chairman):
Company Law Committee. Minutes of Evidence, 1192
Law Reform Committee. Reports. *Cmnd. 18.* 53; *Cmnd. 62, 310.* 252, 269; *Cmnd. 501, 622.* 532, 540
Jennings, Sir Ivor (Chairman):
Royal Commission on Common Lands: Minutes of Evidence, 163, 378
Report. *Cmnd. 462.* 529, 647
Jephcott, Sir H. (Chairman):
Committee of Inquiry. Report on Department of Scientific and Industrial Research. *Cmd. 9734.* 41
Committee on Synthetic Detergents. Report, 131
Warren Spring Laboratory Steering Committee. Report, 1183
Jersey. Exchange of Notes between U.K. and Italy extending the Anglo-Italian Social Insurance Convention. *Cmnd. 716.* 794, 850
Jersey, Guernsey and Adjacent Islands Census Report, 327
Jesus Hospital (Rothwell) Charity Act, 811
Jesus Hospital (Rothwell) Charity Bill, 750, 785
Jet Aircraft:
Economic Implications of Introduction into Service, 711
Flight Planning Data for use in Examinations, 1091
Jet Operations Requirements Panel:
Meeting, 1242
Report, 712
Jet Streams as shown by Aircraft Observations, Some Features of, 152
Jewel Tower, Westminster, Guide, 208
Jewellery and Plate:
Census of Production Report, 394
Of Queen Elizabeth I, Inventory, 79
Jewish People, Biological History, 1265
Jindra, J., Use of Power Saws in Forest Operations Report, 993
Job Analysis, 223A
Jobling, J., Establishment Methods for Poplars, 1129
John Murray Expedition, Scientific Reports, 296, 1097
John Reid's Trust Scheme:
Memorandum, 912
Order in Council, 1185
John Watson's Trust (Amendment No. 1) Scheme, Memorandum, 912
Johne's Disease in Cattle, Sheep and Goats, Control of, 223A
Johnson, D. H.:
Preparation of Statistical Wind Forecasts and an Assessment of their Accuracy in Comparison with Forecasts made by Synoptic Techniques, 1162

Johnson, D. H. (*continued*):
Variations of the Measured Heights of Pressure Surfaces, 152
Johnson, F. R., Lumley Library Catalogue, 80
Johnston, Miss A. C. (Acting Chairman Royal Commission on Local Government) Minutes of Evidence, 903
Joint Consultation in Practice, 976
Jones, D. A., Chromiferous Ultra-basic Rocks of Eastern Sierra Leone, 572
Jones, E. S., Manual for Evaluators of Films and Filmstrips, 239A
Jones, Dr. E. W., Report on Chloraphora, 300
Jones, F. E., Reactions between Aggregates and Cement, 651
Jones, F. G. W., Sugar Beet Pests, 557
Jones, J. M., (Chairman: Working Party on a Welsh Agricultural College) Report, 1088
Jones, N. R., Chemical Composition of Fish Tissues, 907
Jones, R., Whiting in the North Sea, 172
Jones, T. A.:
Colliery Explosion Reports. *Cmnd.* 287, *316.* 268, 270
Inspectors of Mines and Quarries Reports, 642, 645, 900
South Western Division Mines Report, 116
Jones, T. L., Lauceston Castle, Cornwall, Guide, 957
Jordan:
Exchange of Notes with U.K.:
Concerning a Loan. *Cmnd. 483.* 531, 591; *Cmnd. 484.* 531, 591; *Cmnd. 847.* 803, 850; *Cmnd. 1090.* 1057, 1122
Concerning the Disposal of the Special Fund. *Cmnd. 1007.* 1051, 1122
Concerning the Payment of Instalments due under the Treaty Termination Settlement. *Cmnd. 515.* 533, 591
Modifying the Annex, terminating the Treaty of Alliance. *Cmnd. 1158.* 1062, 1122
Postponing Payment of Second Instalment of Debt. *Cmnd. 943.* 1047, 1122
Terminating the Treaty of Alliance. *Cmnd. 186.* 261, 320
Hashimite Kingdom of, International Customs Journal, 444
Jordan, Colin, Committee of Privileges Report on Complaint of a Letter to a Member, 1031, 1142
Jordan, K., Contribution to the Taxonomy of Stenoponia J. & R. (1911) Genus of Palaearctic and Nearctic Fleas, 562
Joseph and John Morrison Bursaries Fund Draft Scheme:
170
Memorandum, 386
Order-in-Council, 386
Joseph Rowntree Memorial Trust Act, 811
Joshi, N. R., Types and Breeds of African Cattle, 706
Joslen, Lt. Colonel H. F., Orders of Battle. U.K. and Colonial Formations and Units in the Second World War, 1098
Journal Officiel des Communantés Européennes, 705, 964, 965, 1234
Journalism and Press Photography. Career, 618, 1152
Journalists, Training of, 737
Judgments, Advisory Opinions and Orders:
Index, 713, 973
Reports, 219–20, 443, 712, 972, 973, 1243
Judicial Offices (Salaries and Pensions) Act, 272
Judicial Offices (Salaries and Pensions) Bill, 218, 249
Judicial Pensions Act, 810
Judicial Pensions Bill, 755, 786
Judicial Statistics:
E. and W. *Cmnd. 802.* 800, 886; *Cmnd. 1126.* 1059, 1159
Scotland. *Cmnd. 850.* 803, 914; *Cmnd. 1047.* 1054, 1187
Jugenheimer, R. W., Hybrid Maize Breeding and Seed Production, 1236
Jurisdiction Affecting Children. Report of the Committee on Conflicts. *Cmnd. 842.* 803, 887
Justice Estimates 1956–57, 12
Justices of the Peace Act 1361 (Amendment) Bill, 2, 15, 29, 32, 126
See also Magistrates' Courts (Appeals from Binding Over Orders) Bill
Jute:
Census of Production Report, 395, 1194
Markets, Manufacturing and Production, 436
Juvenile Delinquency:
Comparative Survey of, 728
In Post-War Europe, 1232
New Perspectives for Research Report, 420
Prevention of, 230A
Juvenile Epilepsy Report, 473

K

Kabata, Z., Lernaeocera obtusa n. sp. Biology and Effects on Haddock, 655
Kale as a Feedingstuff, 555
Kantola, M., Mechanical Loading of Timbers on Trucks, 967

Kariba. Photo-Poster, 1149
Karpenko, G. V., Effect of a Surface-Active Medium on Deformation of Metals, 906
Kayser, A.:
Représentation des Travailleurs sur le Plan de l'Entreprise dans le Droit des Pays Membres de la CECA, 965
Stabilité de L'Emploi dans le Droit des Pays Membres de la CECA, 965
Keightley, General Sir C. F., Operations in Egypt Despatch, 357
Keithia Disease of Thuja Plicata, 596
Kelham, Dr. R. L.:
Artificial Limbs in the Rehabilitation of the Disabled, 331
Chairman: Sub-Committee of Brussels Treaty Organisation Report on Rehabilitation of Amputees, 332
Kelso and Lauder, Soils of the Country Round, 1082
Kelsterton Technical College. Provision of Advanced Technical Education Report, 586
Kenilworth Castle Guide, 698
Kensington Palace Guide, 150, 886
Kent County Council Act, 811
Kent, Sussex, Surrey and Middlesex. Saxton's Map, 1094
Kenya:
Colonial Report, 88, 301, 570, 1102
Colony and Protectorate International Customs Journal, 445
Constitutional Conference Report. *Cmnd. 960.* 1048, 1104
Guarantee given on Loan by International Bank for Re-construction and Development, 1202
International Customs Journal, 1244
New Constitutional Arrangements. *Cmnd. 369.* 523, 571
Proposals for New Constitutional Arrangements. *Cmnd. 309.* 269, 302
Set of 12 Plates, 872
Uganda and Tanganyika. Correspondence with U.K. concerning Financial Arrangements applicable on Transfer of East African Forces. *Cmnd. 281.* 268
See also Mau Mau
Kew:
Bulletin:
162, 378, 646, 901, 1175
Index, 901
Gardens Guide, 378, 824
Palace Guide, 208
Key, A., (Chairman: Committee on Methods of Chemical Analysis as applied to Sewage and Sewage Effluents) Report, 131
Key, To Have a, 462
Keyboard Instruments, Early, 1222
Keyte, M. J., Lighting of Factories, 906
Kildrummy and Glenbuchat Castles, Aberdeenshire. Guidebook, 427
Kilmarnock Corporation Order Confirmation Act, 274
Kilmarnock Corporation Order Confirmation Bill, 248
Kilmarnock, Soils of Country round, 288
Kiln Drying Schedules, 907
Kiln Sterilization of Lyctys-infested Timber, 907
Kimmins, D. E.:
African Species of the Genus Chevmatopsyche and Ephemeroptera Types of Species, 1095
Identity of Stenopsyche Griseipennis McLachlan, 563
Lectotypes of Trichoptera from the McLachlan Collection in the British Museum (Natural History), 562
Miss L. E. Cheesman's Expedition to New Hebrides, 563
Neuroptera and Trichoptera collected by Mr. J. D. Bradley on Guadalcanal Island, 295
New and Little-Known Species of African Trichoptera, 562
New Species and Subspecies of Odonata and on some Trichoptera from S. Rhodesia and Portuguese East Africa, 563
New Species of Ephemeroptera from Uganda, 80
New Species of the Germs Dicercomyzon Demoulin (Ephemeroptera, Fam. Tricorythidae), 562
Notes on East African Ephemeroptera with Descriptions on New Species, 1095
Odonata collected by Mr. J. D. Bradley on Guadalcanal Island, 295
Ruwenzori Expedition, 828
Kinescope and Adult Education, 996
King, D., Samplers, 1223
King, F. H. H., Money in British East Asia, 301
King, J. E., Monk Seals, 80
King Olav V, of Norway, Appointment as Honorary Admiral, 631
King Penguin Aptenodytes Patagonica of South Georgia, Breeding Behaviour and Development, 1103
King William III Banqueting House, Hampton Court Palace Guide, 698
King Wilson, W., Modern Rabbit-Keeping, 821
King's Lynn Conservancy Pier and Harbour Order Confirmation Act, 543
King's Lynn Conservancy Pier and Harbour Order Confirmation Bill, 483
King's Lynn Conservancy Pier and Harbour Provisional Order Bill, 518
Kingsley, E., Oats, 824
Kingsley, Mary, "Pioneer Who Served", 344

Kintyre Club Bursaries Trust Draft Scheme, 170
Kintyre Club Bursaries Trust Scheme:
Memorandum, 386
Order-in-Council, 386
Kirby Muxloe Castle, Leicestershire. Guide, 427
Kirkcudbright Educational Trust Scheme Memorandum, 912
Kiriakoff, S. G., Arctiidae Thyretidae and Notodontidae, 564
Kirkaldy, Professor H. S. (Chairman: Wages Council Commission) Report, 149
Kitchen and Refreshment Rooms, House of Commons, Select Committee Report, 18, 126, 233, 337, 503, 607, 866, 1029, 1144
Kitchens, Planning School, 386
Klineberg, O., Race and Psychology, 737
Knight, K. L., Mosquitoes of Arabia, 80
Knight, R. A. G.:
Efficiency of Adhesives for Wood, 166, 907
Requirements and Properties of Adhesives for Wood, 166
Knotgrass and Allied Weeds, 71
Know Your Capital City, 201
Knox, George, Catalogue of Tiepolo Drawings in the Victoria and Albert Museum, 1222
Knox, T. M. Chairman:
Advisory Council on Education in Scotland Special Committee. Report. *Cmnd. 202.* 262; *Cmnd. 644.* 789, 913; *Cmnd. 1068.* 1055
Knutson, J. W., Effect of Fluoridated Public Water Supplies on Dental Caries Prevalence, 421
Kon, S. K., Milk and Milk Products in Human Nutrition, 968
Korea:
1951–53, 421
Reconstruction Agency:
Report and Accounts, 455, 456, 725, 726, 983
See Unkra in Action
Unification and Rehabilitation of Korea. Commission Report, 230A, 725, 726, 984, 1255
Utilities Claims Settlement Agreement with U.S.A. *Cmnd. 796.* 800, 850
Korolev, V. F., Milking Methods and Milking Machines, 979
Kosikowski, F. V., Advances in Cheese Technology, 706
Kott, P., Sessile Tunicata, 296
Kramer, M., Public Health and Social Problems in the Use of Tranquilizing Drugs, 421
Krishnamoorthy, P. N., Safe Handling of Radioisotopes, 1240
Krohn, Klaus-Hinrich, Sea-Fish Marketing in the Federal Republic of Germany, 707
Kuhne, W. G., Liassic Therapsid Oligokyphus, 82
Kuwait:
Agreement with U.K. for Air Services. *Cmnd. 1168.* 1063, 1122
Notices, 107, 320, 591, 851, 1122
Kuzin, A. M., Application of Radioisotopes in Biology, 1240
Kuznetsov, V. D., Surface Energy of Solids, 652

L

Labelling of Food (Amendment) Regulations, 557
Labelling of Food. *See* Food Standards
Laboratories:
Methods for Work with Plant and Soil Nematodes, 293
Precautions Display Card, 170
Services Organisation. Report by a Committee, 601
Technicians and Assistants. Career, 1152
Labour and National Service, Ministry of:
Publications, 135–49, 347–56, 617, 874, 876, 1152
Report. *Cmd. 9791.* 45, 149; *Cmnd. 242.* 265, 356; *Cmnd. 468.* 529, 630; *Cmnd. 745.* 796, 876; *Cmnd. 1059.* 1055, 1152
Labour Estimates:
1956–57, 12
1957–58, 226
1958–59, 494, 676
1959–60, 760, 933
1960–61, 1019, 1201
Labour Gazette, 150, 356, 430, 630, 875, 885, 1158
Labour in the Munitions Industries, 296
Labour in the United Kingdom Dependencies, 344
Labour Management on the Farm, 448
Labour Productivity in Cotton Spinning Mills, Method for Analysis and Comparison of, 449
Labour Relations and Working Conditions in Britain, 615
Labour Statistics, 598
Lace. Census of Production Report, 395
Lace Furnishings Industry (Export Promotion Levy) Account, 14, 232, 500, 666, 922, 1040
Lace Industry (Levy) Account, 500, 666
Lace Industry (Scientific Research Levy) Order Account, 14, 232
Lackey Moth, 1083

Laing, J. A.:
Trichomonas Foetus Infection of Cattle, 435
Vibrio Fetus Infection of Cattle, 241A
Lake Victoria Haplochromis Species (Pisces, Cichlidae), Revision of, 81, 295, 1097
Lamb, H. H.:
Meteorological Results of the Balaena Expedition, 152
Tornadoes in England, 360
Lambert, E. B., Mushroom Growing in the United States, 201
Lambert, M. E.:
Chinese Questions, 1929–31, 1120
German Affairs:
1120
And Plebiscite Problems, 1120
Laminated Timber, 223A
Lamont, H. R. L., Transmission and Propagation, 955
Lancashire County Council (Industrial Development, etc.) Act, 1072
Lancaster House Guide, 427
Land and Water Utilization and Conservation in Europe, Bibliography on, 242A
Land Branches of the Service Departments. Select Committee on Estimates Special Report, 505, 606, 763, 865
Land Charges. Report. *Cmd. 9825.* 47, 151
Land Consolidation, 448
Land Drainage Bill, 1040, 1044
Land Drainage in England and Wales Bill. *Cmnd. 916.* 808, 824
Land Drainage (Scotland) Act, 541
Land Drainage (Scotland) Bill, 246, 249, 480, 490, 495, 512, 517, 607
Land in British Honduras. Report, 1103
Land-Locked Countries, Free Access to Sea, 728
Land Powers (Defence) Act, 541
Land Powers (Defence) Act Replacement of Emergency Legislation. *Cmnd. 352.* 522, 695
Land Powers (Defence) Bill, 481, 498, 512, 517, 518, 607
Land Reform, Progress Report, 458
Land Registrar's Report, 150
Land Registration, 88
Land Registration Acts. Forms, 357
Land Registry:
Publications, 357, 1158
Report, 357, 630, 886, 1158
Land Tenure:
And Land Administration in Nigeria and the Cameroons, 302
Supplement to Bibliography, 968
Landlord and Tenant Act, Security of Tenure, 358
Landlord and Tenant (Furniture and Fittings) Act, 809
Landlord and Tenant (Furniture and Fittings) Act Circular, 869
Landlord and Tenant (Furniture and Fittings) Bill, 520, 749, 751, 760, 778, 786, 863
Landlord and Tenant (Temporary Provisions) Act, 541
Landlord and Tenant (Temporary Provisions) Act Circular, 611
Landlord and Tenant (Temporary Provisions) Bill, 483, 485, 503, 512, 518, 519, 520, 607
Landlord's and Tenant's Rights explained, 358
Lane, A., Guide to Collection of Tiles, 1223
Lang, D. M., Soils of Malta and Gozo, 1103
Langdon, D., Story of W.V.S. Decorations, 863
Langley, Brigadier C. A.:
Railway Accident Report, 188, 403, 404, 672, 673, 926, 927, 929, 1197, 1198
Tramway Accident Report, 190
Language Problem, Scientific and Technical Translating and Other Aspects of, 466
Languages, Modern, 101
Lanoix, J. N.:
Excreta Disposal for Rural Areas and Small Communities, 740
Water Supply for Rural Areas and Small Communities, 998
Laos, Report of the International Commission for Supervision and Control. *Cmnd. 314.* 270, 320; *Cmnd. 541.* 535, 591
Large Radiation Sources in Industry. Proceedings of a Conference, 1239
Larson, F. E., Guidebook for Manufacturers Developing and Selling New Products, 200
Larson, G. E., Selling the United States Market, 420
Larvin Africa. *See* Native Courts
L'Assemblée Commune, Débats de, 214A
Last Days of Peace, 318
Last Months of Peace. *See* German Foreign Policy
Latin America:
Common Market, 1256
Economic Bulletin, 227A, 452, 981
Economic Commission, 227A, 228A, 453, 981, 1253
Economic Survey, 228A, 982, 1253
Forest Research and Training Institute. Agreement. *Cmnd. 1171.* 1063, 1120
Pulp and Paper Prospects. Report, 242
Regional Census Training Centre Report, 989
Regional Conference Report, 437
Latin and Greek:
Guidance of Teachers on the Setting and Marking of Examinations, 171
Scottish Certificate of Education, 913

Launceston Castle, Cornwall. Guide, 957
Laundry and Dry Cleaning. Career, 136
Laverbread Industry in South Wales and the Laverweed, 559
Law and Justice Estimates:
1956–57, 12
1957–58, 226
1958–59, 494
1959–60, 759, 933
1960–61, 1019, 1201
Law, Barristers and Solicitors. Careers, 617
Law Commission, International Yearbook, 727, 993
Law of the Sea. United Nations Conference Report. *Cmnd. 584.* 537, 591, 728, 992, 1261
Law of War on Land. Manual of Military Law, 954
Law Reform Committee Reports:
Cmnd. 18. 53, 151; *Cmnd. 62, 310.* 252, 269, 358; *Cmnd. 501, 622.* 532, 540, 632
Scotland. *Cmnd. 88, 114, 141, 330.* 254, 256, 258, 271, 358; *Cmnd. 449.* 528, 632; *Cmnd. 635, 907.* 789, 886, 907; *Cmnd. 1017, 1102, 1103.* 1052, 1058, 1159
Law Relating to Mental Illness and Mental Deficiency:
Index, 380
Minutes of Evidence taken before the Royal Commission, 380
Report. *Cmnd. 169.* 260, 380
Law Relating to Safety and Health. Mines and Quarries, 643
Law Society:
Account, 230
Report, 151, 359, 632, 886, 1048, 1159
Scotland, 226, 1187
Lawrie, R. A., Study on Beef Quality, 382, 649, 1180
Laws, R. M., Elephant Seal, 88, 302
Laws, Register of Temporary, 245, 339, 1014
Laying Screeds as an Underlay for Floor Coverings, 1226
Lea, F. M., Durability of Reinforced Concrete in Sea Water, 1181
Lead. Export Licence, 397
Leadburning, 956
Leadership and Group Discussion, 466
Leakey, L. S. B., Some East African Pleistocene Suidae, 564
Lease. Houses held on Ground Lease, 358
Leasehold. Enfranchisement Bill, 33
Leasehold Enfranchisement and Restrictive Covenants Bill, 752
Leasehold Tenure (Wales) Bill, 1041
Leather:
Bookbindings. How to Preserve them, 199
Goods. Census of Production Report, 395
Leather (*continued*):
(Tanning and Dressing) Census of Production Report, 205
Leatherjackets, 555
Leave of Absence. House of Lords Select Committee Report, 480, 485, 609, 754, 867
Lebanon:
Exchange of Notes with U.K.:
Amending the Schedule of Routes annexed to the Air Services Agreement. *Cmnd. 838.* 804, 831
Concerning the Loans of Arms. *Cmnd. 518.* 533, 591
Lebegge, M., Utilization of Space in Dwellings Report, 1262
Lebovici, S., Child Guidance Centres, 1268
Lectotypes of Trichoptera from the McLachlan Collection now in the British Museum (Natural History), 562
Ledingham, G. A., Industrial Microbiology in British Commonwealth Countries, 826
Lee, A., Hydrographical Observations in the Irish Sea, 1087
Lee, A. R., Types of Road Surfacing and Maintenance Using Tar or Asphaltic Bitumen, 652
Lee, C. A., Study on Beef Quality, 1180
Lee, E., Longitudinal Permeability on Some Hardwoods and Softwoods, 650
Lee, T. G., Methods of Testing Small Fire Extinguishers, 419
Lee Valley Water Act, 811
Leech, F. R., Disease Wastage and Husbandry in the British Dairy Herd, 1087
Leeds Corporation Act, 58
Leeward Islands Act, 56
Leeward Islands Colonial Reports, 87
Leeward and Windward Islands Constitutional Conference Report. *Cmnd. 804.* 800, 834
Legal, Administrative Health and Safety Aspects of Large Scale Use of Nuclear Energy, 232A
Legal Aid:
Handbook, 359
In Criminal Proceedings. Report. *Cmnd. 1015.* 1052, 1187
Scheme. Law Society of Scotland Report, 172, 387, 655, 1187
Select Committee on Estimates Report, 14, 125
Legal Aid and Advice Act:
1070
Accounts, 17, 151, 230, 358, 502, 632, 768, 886, 1025, 1159
And Legal Aid (Assessment of Resources) Regulations. Report of the Advisory Committee on Financial Provisions. *Cmnd. 918.* 808, 887
Report of the Law Society, 151, 359, 632, 886, 1048, 1159

Legal Aid Bill, 787, 1006, 1021, 1037, 1042, 1141
Legal Aid (Scotland) Act Accounts, 13, 102, 226, 387, 500, 587, 768, 844, 1023, 1117
Legal Commission Report ICAO, 971, 1242
Legal Documentation in the World, Register of, 466
Legal Proceedings in Civil and Commercial Matters. Exchange of Notes between U.K. and Germany. *Cmnd. 1202.* 1065, 1121
Legal Questions. General Assembly Records, 229A, 455, 725, 983, 1234
Legal Status of Married Women. Reports, 728
Leggett, Sir F., Building Apprenticeship and Training Council Report, 427
Legislative Series, 230, 437, 708, 985, 1239, 1256
Legitimacy Act, 809
Legitimacy Bill, 750, 752, 753, 764, 778, 784, 785, 786, 864
Legitimation (Re-Registration of Birth) Act, 272
Legitimation (Re-Registration of Birth) Bill, 36, 218, 233, 242, 337
Legitimation (Re-Registration of Birth) (No. 2) Bill, 35
Le Gros Clark, Sir W.:
History of Primates, 82
Miocene Lemuroid Skull from East Africa, 81
Leicester Central Station Railway Accident Report, 404
Leicester Corporation Act, 58
Leicestershire Map. *See* Warwickshire
Leigh Almshouse, Stoneleigh, and other Charities Scheme Confirmation Act, 58
Leigh Almshouse, Stoneleigh, and other Charities Scheme Confirmation Bill, 2, 33
Leigh, C., Inspector of Mines and Quarries Report, 1172
Leiris, Michel, Race and Culture, 737
Leith Harbour and Docks Order Confirmation Act, 811
Leith Harbour and Docks Order Confirmation Bill, 786
Lending Library Unit Translations Bulletins, 909, 1180
Lend-Lease, Reciprocal Aid, Supplies War Property and Claims. Exchange of Notes between U.K. and U.S.A. *Cmnd. 201.* 262
Length of Working Life of Males in Great Britain, 885
Lennox-Boyd, Rt. Hon. Alan. (Chairman).
Nigeria Constitutional Conference. Report. *Cmnd. 207.* 263; *Cmnd. 569.* 536
Singapore Constitutional Conference. Report. *Cmnd. 147.* 259
Lenses, Trial Case, Report, 123
Lepentzov, P. A., Timber Skidding by Tractors in the U.S.S.R., 990
Leprosy:
Demystified, 1270
Expert Committee Report, 1269
International Work in, 1268
War Not Yet Won, 344
Leptospirosis, Diagnosis and Typing in. Report, 172
Lernaeocera obtusa n. sp. Its Biology and its Effects on the Haddock, 655
Leslie, H. R.:
Nuclear Generating Station Report, 388
Chairman: Scottish Advisory Council on Treatment of Offenders. Report, 1186
Lethem, W. A., Principles of Milk Legislation. and Control, 241A
Lettuce Aphids, 820
Leukaemia and Aplastic Anaemia in Patients Irradiated for Ankylosing Spondylitis, 359
Level Crossing Protection Report, 403
Levey, M., 18th Century Italian School of Painting, Catalogue, 154
Levin, B., Weight Gains, Serum Protein Levels, and Health of Breast Fed and Artificially Fed Infants, Full Term and Premature, 887
Levy, M., German School, National Gallery Catalogue, 1163
Levy, R. F., Chairman:
Committee of Inquiry on Anthrax. Report. *Cmnd. 846.* 803, 875
Monopolies Commission:
On Imported Timber. Report, 507
Report on Supply of Chemical Fertilizers, 1013
Levi-Strauss, C., Race and History, 737
Lewes–East Grinstead Branch Railway. Proposed withdrawal of Train Services Report. *Cmnd. 360.* 523, 671
Lewis, J. M. Carreg Cennan Castle Guide, 1226
Lewis Merthyr Colliery, Glamorganshire Explosion Report. *Cmnd. 316.* 270
Lewis, Ray, Colonial Development and Welfare, 87
Lewis, W. A., Investigation of the Performance of Pneumatic Tyred Rollers in the Compaction of the Soil, 910
Liability of Owners of Sea-going Ships, International Convention relating to Limitation. *Cmnd. 353.* 522, 591
Liassic Therapsid Oligokyphus, 82
Liberal Education in Technical Colleges. Circular, 313, 314
Liberalisation, Code of, 221, 715, 975, 1245
Liberalisation of Europe's Dollar Trade, 223A, 448
Liberate Rolls, Calendar of, 1175

LIB-McC | 1956-60

Liberties of the Subject Bill, 218
Librarianship. Career, 1152
Libraries:
- Bulletin for, 239, 467, 737, 994, 1263
- For Asia, Public, 239A
- Documents, House of Commons, 59
- Education in Israel Report, 240A
- Geneva:
  - Monthly List of Books, Catalogued, 230–1, 458, 729, 985, 1256
  - Monthly list of Selected Articles, 231, 458, 729, 985, 1256
- Guide to Government, 678
- Manuals for, 239A, 468, 996, 1265
- National:
  - Scotland, Report, 154, 635, 1163
  - Their Problems and Prospects, 1265
- Service, Public, E. and W. Report on Structure. *Cmnd. 660.* 791, 843
- Services for Children, 468
- Statistics on, 996

Libraries (Public Lending Right) Bill, 1044, 1045
Libya:
- Overseas Economic Survey, 182
- United Kingdom of, International Customs Journal, 444

Licences:
- 396–7, 402, 921, 922
- Export, 180–1
- Import:
  - 181
  - Amendments, 666
- Pilots, 927

Licensing Act. State Management Districts Report, 513, 605
Licensing (Airports) Act, 56
Licensing (Airports) Bill, 3, 18, 29, 34, 126
Licensing (Amendment) Bill, 8
Licensing Authorities:
- Annual Reports, 930
- For Goods Vehicles Reports, 404
- For Public Service Vehicles Reports, 187, 672

Licensing Bill, 1044
Licensing in Scotland. Consolidation of Enactments (Procedure) Act Memorandum, 748
Licensing Law Report, Scottish. *Cmnd. 1217.* 1066
Licensing of Bulls and Boars Bill, 483, 519
Licensing (Scotland) Act, 809
Licensing (Scotland) Bill, 748, 750, 785
Licensing (Scotland) Consolidation Bills Reports, 745, 750, 867
Lidgettonia, New Type of Fertile Glossopteris, 563
Life and Death, Matters of, 118
Life Peerages, 631, 917
Life Peerages Act, 541
Life Peerages Bill, 220, 478, 517
Life Saving Appliances, Merchant Shipping Survey of, 929
Lifesaving Challenge in America Today, 951
Life Tables, Decennial Supplement, 327
Lifting and Carrying:
- Accidents, 621
- Safety, Health and Welfare New Series, 630

Light Cars, History and Development of, 648
Light Cladding, 381
Light Rescue. Civil Defence Handbooks, 604
Lighting in Factories, 906
Lighting, Short History, 905
Lights and Sounds Signals, Survey of. Instructions to Surveyors, 187
Lightweight Concrete, 207
Lignite Resources of Asia and Far East, 458
Likhtman, V. I., Effect of a Surface-Active Medium on the Deformation of Metals, 906
Lime-Blowing in Brickwork, 381
Lime In Agriculture, Use of, 72
Limestones of Scotland, 119
Lincolnshire and Nottinghamshire, 1957, Saxton's Map, 827
Lindsey, K., Towards a European Parliament, 704
Line and Wireless Instruction, 1137
Line Barracks, Mauritius. Gift to Government. *Cmd. 9746.* 42, 195
Line Communications, Royal Signals Handbooks, 695
Linen and Soft Hemp. Census of Production Report, 179, 664
Lings, M., Supplementary Catalogue of Arabic Printed Books in the British Museum, 1095
Linklater, E., Campaign in Italy, 1098, 1189
Linoleum:
- Leathercloth and Allied Industries. Census of Production Report, 396, 1194
- Monopolies and Restrictive Practices Commission Report on Supply, 24, 182

Liquid Manure on Farms, Use of, 554
Liquidation of German Assets. Exchange of Notes between U.K. and Sweden. *Cmnd. 219.* 263
Lister, R. D., Some Safety Aspects of Pedal and Motor-Assisted Cycles, 384
Lister v. The Romford Ice and Cold Storage Co. Ltd., Report, 885
Literacy Teaching, 238A
Literature. Access to Current Literature on Education, 466
Litter Act, 541
Litter Act Circular, 611, 868, 1146
Litter Bill, 33, 247, 481, 495, 512, 517, 607
Little, K. Z., Race and Society, 737

Little London Railway Accident Report, 673
Liverpool Corporation Act, 274
Liverpool Hydraulic Power Act, 274
Liverpool Overhead Railway Act, 58
Livestock and Meat in OEEC Countries, Marketing and Distribution Margins for, 1245
Livestock Production in the Americas, Recent Developments affecting, 435
Living Resources of the Sea, Conservation of, 225A
Livingstone, David, 131
Lizard Genus Aprasia; Its Taxonomy and Temperature—Correlated Variation, 81
Llanelly Steel Company (1907) Limited. Proposal to sell Holding of Securities. *Cmnd. 1121.* 1059, 1203
Lloyd-Williams, Hugh (Chairman):
- Cold Store Undertakings Report, 877
- Dock Workers (Regulation of Employment) Inquiry Report, 1158
- Ocean Shipowners' Tally Clerks Committee Report, 1158

Loader, P. T., Temperatures and Humidities in Pig Houses, 1181
Loading of Steam and Sailing Ships Notes, 929
Loan Exhibition of English Chintz, 1223
Loans:
- Exchange of Notes between U.K. and:
  - Chile. *Cmnd. 1195.* 1065, 1118
  - Jordan. *Cmnd. 483, 484.* 531, 591; *Cmnd. 1090.* 1057, 1122
  - Lebanon. Arms. *Cmnd. 518.* 533, 591
  - Kenya. Map Printing Equipment. *Cmnd. 616.* 540, 679
  - Pakistan. Anti-Aircraft Equipment. *Cmnd. 367.* 523, 679
  - Police and Fire Authorities, E. and W. and Scotland, Respirators. *Cmnd. 577.* 537, 679
  - Treasury Minute relative to Loan to the Government of Hong Kong of the Inshore Minesweepers. *Cmnd. 651.* 790, 934
  - Turkey. Agreement with U.K. *Cmnd. 615.* 539, 594

Lobster:
- And Crab Fisheries in Scotland, 656
- Fishery of Wales, 559
- Storage, 655

Local and Personal Acts, 57, 273, 542, 810, 1071
Local Authorities (Building and Civil Engineering) Census of Production Report, 665
Local Authorities (Expenditure on Special Purposes) (Scotland) Bill, 1039, 1040, 1044, 1141
Local Authorities (Expenses) Act, 56
Local Authorities (Expenses) Bill, 2, 13, 29, 32, 126
Local Contributions to the Scottish Universities Report. *Cmnd. 640.* 789, 912
Local Education Authorities:
- E. and W. Statistics, 586, 1116
- Excepted Districts List, 313, 1115
- On Scales of Salaries for Teachers Report 842

Local Employment Act, 1070
Local Employment Act Circular, 1146
Local Employment Bill, 786, 787, 1004
Local Government:
- And Central Departments in Scotland. *Cmnd. 445.* 528, 655
- Areas and Status of Local Authorities. *Cmd. 9831.* 47, 130
- Estimates, 1959–60, 760
- Functions E. and W. *Cmnd. 161.* 260, 342
- In Britain, 132, 614, 872
- In Greater London. Royal Commission:
  - Index, 1176
  - Memoranda of Evidence, 902
  - Minutes of Evidence, 902, 1176
  - Report. *Cmnd. 1164.* 1063, 1177
- In Scotland, 655
- Superannuation:
  - Circular, 1146
  - Scotland, Principal Statutes and Regulations, 172

Local Government Act:
- 541
- Circular, 868
- Financial Provision Circular, 611

Local Government and Miscellaneous Financial Provisions (Scotland) Act:
- 541
- Circular, 911

Local Government and Miscellaneous Financial Provisions (Scotland) Bill; 250, 482, 484, 485, 502, 512, 518, 519, 607
Local Government Bill, 250, 482, 483, 484, 501, 512, 518, 519, 607
Local Government Elections Act, 56
Local Government Elections Bill, 4, 17, 30, 34, 126
Local Government Finance:
- E. and W.:
  - *Cmnd. 209.* 263, 342
  - General Grant Order:
    - Report, 514, 612, 782, 870
    - Supplement, 514, 612
  - In Africa, Principles of, 86
  - Report, 1039, 1147
  - Statistics, 130, 342, 612, 870, 1147
- Scotland:
  - *Cmnd. 208.* 263, 388
  - General Grant (Scotland) Order Report, 514, 655
  - Report. 1017, 1039, 1147

Local Government (Omnibus Shelters and Queue Barriers) Scotland Act, 541

Local Government (Omnibus Shelters and Queue Barriers) Scotland Bill, 250, 483, 503, 512, 518, 607
Local Government (Promotion of Bills) Bill, 236, 242, 247, 337
Local Government Service. Career, 1152
Local Government Services: Restriction of Capital Expenditure. Circular, 129
Local Government (Street Works) (Scotland) Act, 56
Local Government (Street Works) (Scotland) Bill, 3, 11, 30, 33, 126
Local Government Superannuation Act Circular, 611
Local Government Superannuation (Investment of Funds) Bill, 787
Local Health Service Report, 1269
Local Loans Fund Accounts, 10, 154, 228, 361, 498, 635, 760, 889, 1020, 1162
Location Indicators, 971
Locock, Sir G. (Chairman: Standing Committee on Oil Burning Apparatus) Report. *Cmd. 9686.* 38
Locke, G. M. L., Code of Sample Plot Procedure, 854
Lockwood, Dr. J. F. (Chairman: Secondary School Examinations Council) Report, 1115
Locomotives:
- And Railway Track Equipment. Census of Production Report, 1194
- Boiler Water Treatment Report, 458

Locusts:
- 344, 1149
- African Locusts, Convention regarding Control of the African migratory Locusts. *Cmnd. 128.* 257, 315
- International Desert Locust Information Service. Exchange of Notes between U.K. and F.A.O. *Cmnd. 600.* 539, 590

Lodigiani, L., Rice Harvesting, 225
Log Saw Catalogue, 437
Logan, W. P. D.:
- Morbidity Statistics from General Practice, 598, 1131
- Rubella and Other Virus Infections during Pregnancy, 1136
- Survey of Sickness, 1943 to 1953, 598
- Tuberculosis Statistics for E. and W., 327

Loganberry, 1083
Logging Cableways, 985
London and Home Counties Traffic Advisory Committee Report, 929
London and Surrey (River Wandle and River Graveney) (Jurisdiction) Act, 1072
London and Thames Valley, 1131
London Airport:
- 187, 1091
- Aircraft Accident Report, 400
- Development Committee Report, 403
- Dispute. Court of Inquiry Report. *Cmnd. 608.* 539, 623

London–Birmingham Motorway Traffic and Economics, 1182
London Bridge Station Railway Accident Report, 404
London County Council (General Powers) Act, 57, 58, 274, 543, 811, 1072
London County Council (Loans) Act, 57
London County Council (Money) Act, 58, 274, 543, 811, 1072
London County Courts Directory, 886
London Electricity Board:
- Committee of Privileges Report. Complaint of Certain Actions, 240, 338
- Report and Accounts, 774

London Gazette, 150, 357–8, 430, 631, 917, 1189
London, Greater, Census Report, 118
London Master Printers' Association and the London Typographical Society and the Association of the Correctors of the Press. Report of a Court of Inquiry. *Cmd. 9717.* 40
London Museum:
- Catalogue, 1159
- Guide, 1158
- Publications, 150, 358, 886

London Museums and Galleries Guide, 174, 916
London Necropolis Act, 58
London Parking Survey, 188
London Post Offices and Streets, 161, 640, 1169
London Roads Committee Report. *Cmnd. 812.* 801, 930
London Traffic Report, 187, 403, 672, 929, 1197
London Travel Committee Report, 927
London–Yorkshire Motorway, 1197
Long, H. A., Effect of Small Doses of Alcohol on a Skill Resembling Driving, 887
Long Range Aid to Navigation Station. Agreement between U.K. and U.S.A. concerning Establishment in Bahama Islands. *Cmnd. 1179.* 1064, 1127
Long Range Educational Planning, 466
Long Range Proving Ground Sites in Ascension Island. Exchange of Notes between U.K. and U.S.A. *Cmnd. 867.* 805, 853
Long-Term Assurances for Agriculture. *Cmnd. 23.* 54, 70
Long-Term Hospital Patients. Report of the National Insurance Advisory Committee. *Cmnd. 964.* 1048, 1165
Long Term Trends and Problems of the European Steel Industry, 1256
Longhurst, A. R., Ecological Survey of the West African Marine Benthos, 571
Longitudinal Permeability of Some Hardwoods and Softwoods, 650
Longmore, J., Simplified Daylight Tables 651

Look and Live, 202
Look at London Airport, 1091
"Loradore" Wreck Report, 192
Lord Chancellor's Department Publications, 150–1, 358–9, 632, 886, 1159
Lord High Commissioner (Church of Scotland) Act, 810
Lord High Commissioner (Church of Scotland) Bill, 755, 783, 786, 1014, 1141
Lord President's Office Publications, 151
Lords Spiritual and Temporal, Roll of, 7, 129, 220, 340, 486, 610, 754, 867, 1011, 1145
Lorimer, F., Culture and Human Fertility, 737
Loss of or damage to Guests' Property. Notice, 150
Lot, F., Radioisotopes in the Service of Man, 997
Lothian Homes Trust Scheme Order-in-Council, 169
Lotto, G. De, Pseudo-coccidae described by:
- C. K. Brain from South Africa, 563
- H. C. James from East Africa, 295

Love, R. M., Chemical Composition of Fish Tissues, 907
Lovern, J. A., Chemical Composition of Fish Tissues, 907
Low Countries Pocket Guide, 421
Low Grade Ores, 718
Low, J. D., Fomes Annosus in Great Britain, 1129
Low-Level Sprinkler Irrigation System for Use under Glass, 824
Low Temperature Research Station and the Ditton Laboratory. Reports of the Superintendents, 907
Lowdermilk, R. R.:
- Television in Education, 691
- Television in our Schools, 419

Lowenthal, L. J. A., Differential Diagnoses of Yaws, 1268
Lowestoft Harbour. British Transport Commission Charges Scheme, 1199
Lowiili, Social Organisation of, 88
Lowman, M. S., Savoury Herbs: Culture and Use, 201
Lowndes, C. A. S., Synoptic Study of Anomalies of Surface Air Temperatures over the Atlantic Half of the Northern Hemisphere, 889
Loy, R. M., Rubella and other Virus Infections during Pregnancy, 1136
Lubbock, A., (Chairman) Royal Commission on Common Land, Minutes of Evidence, 163, 378–9
Lubricating Oils and Greases. Census of Production Report, 1194
Lucerne, 288
Lucke, E. R., Social Welfare Project, 234A
Ludlow Consolidated Municipal Charity and Certain other Charities Scheme Confirmation Act, 57
Ludlow Consolidated Municipal Charity and Certain other Charities Scheme Confirmation Bill, 4, 34
Ludlow Railway Accident Report, 404
Lugard, F. D., Pioneers who Served, 872
Luke, Sir Stephen, Report on Development and Welfare in the West Indies, 302, 571
Lullingstone Roman Villa, Kent, Guide, 698
Lumby, B. R., Depth of the Wind-Produced Homogeneous Layer in the Oceans, 73
Lumley Library. Catalogue, 80
Lunacy and Mental Treatment Acts Report, 21, 122, 236, 332, 506, 602, 772, 886, 1030, 1159
Lunacy, B. C. Form, 857
Lunacy (Scotland) Acts. Forms, 329
Lunan Bay, Railway Accident Report, 929
Lung Function in Coal Workers' Pneumoconiosis, 151
Lupins as a Farm Crop, 289
Lur'e, A. I. Some Non-Linear Problems in the Theory of Automatic Control, 391
Lusby, R. M., Training Restaurant Sales Personnel, 203
Luton Station Railway Accident Report, 188
Luxembourg:
- Exchange of Notes with U.K.:
  - Amending Cultural Convention. *Cmd. 9782.* 44, 107
  - Concerning Arrangements to Facilitate Travel. *Cmnd. 1079.* 1056, 1123

Lyctus:
- Attack in Sawn Hardwoods, Prevention of, 1180
- Attack on Sawn Logs, Spray Treatment for, 908
- Powder Pest Beetles, 1180

Lymantriidae, 564
Lymm. Report on Proposed Development of Land for Manchester Overspill, 612
Lymphomatosis and Avian Leucosis Complex, 556
Lympne Airport. Civil Aviation Order, 187
Lysaght, Averil, Some 18th Century Bird Paintings in the Library of Sir Joseph Banks, 828

M

McArthur, D. N. (Chairman: Scottish Standing Committee on Residual Values of Fertilisers and Feeding Stuffs) Report, 70, 288, 554, 820
McCance, R. A.:
- Composition of Foods, 1160
- Hazards to Men in Ships Lost at Sea, 151

1956-60 | McC-MAU

McC— INDEX 1956–60

McClellen, W. D., Roses for the Home, 201
McColvin, L. R., Public Library Services for Children, 468
McCullough, T. W. (Chairman):
  Joint Standing Committee on:
    Conditions in Iron Foundries Report, 149
    Power Presses Report, 356
Macdonald, J., Exotic Forest Trees in Great Britain, 325
MacDonald, J. D., Contribution to Ornithology of Western South Africa, 362
Mace in the House of Commons, 275, 337
Machacek, D., Mechanization of the application of Chemical Fertilisers in Form of Liquid, 1250
Machine Gun, 202
Machine Milking, 821
Machine Tool Industry Report, 1193
Machine Tools:
  And Workshop Plant Amendment, 1108
  Census of Production Report, 179, 663
Machinery:
  Agricultural, 445
  Fencing of. Circular, 900
  Leaflet Horticultural, 824
MacInnes, D. G.:
  Fossil Tubulidentata from East Africa, 81
  New Miocene Rodent from East Africa, 295
McIntosh, T. P., Key to Oat Varieties described in Scottish Seed Oats, 70
McIntyre, A. D., Ecology of Scottish Inshore Fishing Grounds, 655
Macivor, I., Dumbarton Castle Guide, 698
Mackay, H. M. M., Weight Gains, Serum Protein Levels and Health of Breast Fed and Artificially Fed Infants, Full Term and Premature, 887
McKechnie, Sheriff H., (Chairman): Committee on Diligence Report. *Cmnd. 456.* 529
McKenzie, A., Cancer Statistics E. and W., 598
Mackinlay, W. M., (Chairman: Scottish Standing Committee on Dental Health Education), 1132
McKinney, R., (Chairman: Joint Committee on Atomic Energy) Report on Impact of Peaceful Uses of Atomic Energy, 199
Mackinnon-MacNeill Trust Scheme:
  Memorandum, 912, 1185
  Order-in-Council, 1185
Mackintosh, J. M.:
  Chairman: Housing Management Sub-Committee of the Central Housing Advisory Committee. Report, 130
  Teaching of Hygiene and Public Health in Europe, 471
MacLaren, Neil:
  Dutch School, National Gallery Catalogues, 1163
  Spanish School Catalogue, 154
McLaughlin, E. A., Types and Breeds of African Cattle, 706
MacLean, D. J., Polishing of Roadstone in relation to the Resistance to Skidding of Bituminous Road Surfacings, 652
MacLeod, Rt. Hon. Iain: (Chairman):
  Industrial Health Advisory Committee. Report, 629
  Kenya Constitutional Conference Report. *Cmnd. 960.* 1048
  Nyasaland Constitutional Conference Report. *Cmnd. 1132.* 1060
McMeeking, J. G. (Chairman: National Advisory Council on Education for Industry and Commerce) Report, 842
McMullen, Colonel D.:
  Railway Accident Report, 188, 189, 403, 404, 672, 673, 929, 1197, 1198
  Tramway Accident Report, 931
McNair, Rt. Hon. Lord: (Chairman):
  Burnham Committee, Report on Teachers' Salaries, 101, 102
  Committee on Recruitment to Dental Profession. Report. *Cmd. 9861.* 50
Macrae, W. D., Disease, Wastage and Husbandry in British Dairy Herd, 1087
MacRobert, I. M., Printed Books, 422
Made-up Household Textiles. Census of Production Report, 395
Magistrates' Courts Act, 272
Magistrates' Courts Bill, 214, 215, 216, 232, 242, 248, 337
Magistrates' Courts (Appeals from Binding Over Orders) Act, 56
Magistrates' Courts (Appeals from Binding Over Orders) Bill. *See* Justices of the Peace Act, 1361. (Amendment) Bill
Magnesian Lime and Magnesian Limestone, 1083
Magnesium Fabricating and Casting, 223A
Magnetic and Meteorological Observations, Results of, 600, 904
Magnetic Observations Results, 904
Magnus Hannaford, R. G., Education and Training for Distribution, 975
Magpie Moth, 288
Magslip Elements. Handbook, 1074
Maidstone Corporation (Trolley Vehicles) Order Confirmation Act, 543
Maidstone Corporation (Trolley Vehicles) Order Confirmation Bill, 483
Maidstone Corporation (Trolley Vehicles) Provisional Order Bill, 518
Main products of Overseas Territories, 223, 448
Maincrop Potatoes, 555
Mainstone, R. J., Tests on New Government Offices, Whitehall Gardens, 1181
Maintenance Agreements Act, 272

INDEX 1956–60 —MAN

Maintenance Agreements Bill, 216, 217, 230, 242, 247, 249, 337
Maintenance Grants for Students at Universities, 585
Maintenance Obligations, United Nations Conference, 458
Maintenance Orders Act, 541
Maintenance Orders (Attachment of Income) Bill, 242, 244, 247, 337
Maintenance Orders Bill, 250, 480, 481, 483, 495, 512, 517, 519, 607
Maintenance Orders, Scotland, Need for Provision Allowing Enforcement. Report. *Cmnd. 449.* 528, 632
Maison Dieu, Ospringe, Kent, Guide, 698
Maize:
  For Fodder and Silage, 820
  Hybrid Maize Breeding and Seed Production, 1236
  Stalks for Forage, Harvesting and Conservation, 225
Makarios, Archbishop. Correspondence with Governor of Cyprus. *Cmd. 9708.* 40, 88
Making of Ghana, 344, 1150
Making the Most of Farmyard Manure, 1083
Malalasekera, G. P., Buddhism and the Race Question, 737
Malaria:
  1149
  Conference for Eastern Mediterranean and European Regions, 741
  Conference for the Western Pacific and South-East Asia Regions Report, 245A
  Eradication. Programme and Estimates, 740
  Existing Legislation, 471
  Expert Committee Report, 472, 999
  See World Health
Malaya:
  Agreement with U.K. for:
    Air Services. *Cmnd. 356.* 522, 672
    Establishment of the Tropical Fish Culture Research Institute at Batu Berendam. *Cmnd. 1067.* 1055, 1106
    Reference of Appeals from the Supreme Court to the Judicial Committee of the Privy Council. *Cmnd. 383.* 524, 573
  Arrangements for Employment of Overseas Commonwealth Forces in Emergency Operations. *Cmnd. 264.* 267, 307
  Becomes a Sovereign Nation:
    Film Strip, 614
    Photo Poster, 344
    Picture Set, 344
  Colonial Report, 88, 573
  Constitutional Proposals for the Federation of Malaya. *Cmnd. 210.* 263, 303
Malaya (*continued*):
  Exchange of Letters with U.K. about Representation on the Internal Security Council. *Cmnd. 620.* 540, 573
  Federation of Malaya Constitutional Conference Report. *Cmd. 9714.* 40, 89
  International Customs Journal, 444, 713, 973, 1244
  International Rights and Obligations. Exchange of Letters with U.K. *Cmnd. 346.* 522, 573
  Making of a Nation, 345
  Proposed Agreement on External Defence and Mutual Assistance with U.K. *Cmnd. 263.* 266, 307
  Public Officers Agreement with U.K. *Cmnd. 854.* 804, 835
  Report of the Constitutional Commission, 303
Malaya, Federation of, Independence Act, 272
Malaya, Federation of, Independence Bill, 219, 249
Maldive Islands. Agreement with U.K. *Cmnd. 948.* 1048, 1106
Male, P. J. E., Guatemala, Overseas Economic Survey, 182
Mallophaga:
  Early Literature on, 1095
  From Mammals, Notes on Some, 1096
  Genera, Revisions, Degeeriella from the Falconiformes, 563
Malnutrition:
  Chez la Mère, Le Nourrisson et le Jeune Enfant en Afrique. Rapport, 89
  In African Mothers, Infants and Young Children. Report, 89
  See Protein Malnutrition
Malta:
  Economic Commission Report, 303
  Order-in-Council, 1175
Malta (Letters Patent) Act, 809
Malta (Letters Patent) Bill, 747, 784
Malta (Reconstruction) Act Account, 21, 89, 229, 303, 513, 579, 779, 833
Man and Hunger, 709
Man the Tool-maker, 82, 564
Management and Manuring of Orchard Soils, 288
Management and Technology, 651
Management of Ware Potato Stores, 1084
Managers for To-morrow, 383
Manchester Corporation Act, 58, 811
Manchester Ship Canal Act, 58, 1072
Mandahl-Barth, G., Intermediate Hosts of Schistosoma, 740
Mangold Fly, 1083
Mangoldt, H. K. Von. (Chairman: European Payments Union Managing Board) Report, 975

MAN INDEX 1956–60

Mann, G. E., Poultry Breeding, 1085
Mann, Sir J., Arms and Armour in England, 1226
Mann, M., Copra Processing in Rural Industries, 706
Manoeuvres Act, 808
Manoeuvres Bill, 486, 520
Manoeuvres Bill Report on Consolidation Bill, 487
Manpower:
  206
  Accelerated Vocational Training for Unskilled and Semi-Skilled, 1245
  In Great Britian, Scientific and Engineering, 149
  Population, 1900–1958, 978
  Report on Practices Impeding the Full and Efficient Use of, 885
Mansfield, A. W.:
  Breeding Behaviour and Reproductive Cycle of the Weddell Seal, 571
  Notes on Weather-Analysis in Falkland Islands Dependencies, Antarctica, 571
Manson, M. M., Rubella and Other Virus Infections during Pregnancy, 1136
Mantegna, Andrea. Series of Nine Paintings, 1227
Manufacture and Inspection of Welded Structures for Aircraft Engine Parts. Report, 391
Manufactured Fuel, Census of Production Report, 394
Manufactured Stationery, Paper Bag and Kindred Industries. Census of Production Report, 395
Manufacturing Industry in Egypt, Israel and Turkey, Development of, 980
Manures:
  And Fertilizers, 556
  Liquid Manure on Farms, Use of, 554
  Making Most of Farmyard, 1083
Maps:
  79
  Commonwealth of Nations, 573
  International, of the World. Report, 457, 728
  Reading, Air Photo Reading and Field Sketching, Manual of 206, 424, 695, 954
  Saxton's, 1094
Marche Commun, 704, 963
Margarine. Census of Production Report, 395, 1193
Margate Pier and Harbour Confirmation Act, 543
Margate Pier and Harbour Confirmation Bill, 483
Margate Pier and Harbour Provisional Order Bill, 518
Marginal Cost and Electricity Rates, Theory of, 719
Marine and Aviation Insurance (War Risks) Act. Agreements, 672
Marine and Aviation Insurance (War Risks). Reinsurance of British Ships against War Risks, 927
Marine Borers and Methods of Preserving Timber against Their Attack, 908
Marine Corps Monograph, 202
Marine Engineering. Census of Production Report, 663
Marine Observer:
  152, 360, 430, 633, 888, 1161
  Handbook Amendment, 152
Marine Radar, Performance Standards, 403
Marine Research, 172, 388, 655, 914, 1082, 1187
Marine Society Act, 274
Marine Surveyors and Other Mercantile Marine Services, Fees and Expenses, 929
Marine Surveys Fees and Expenses payable, 187
Mariners, Meteorology for, 360
Maritime Law. International Convention. *Cmnd. 1128.* 1059, 1125
Maritime Safety Committee:
  Constitution (Request for Advisory Opinion) Order, 973
  Of the Inter-Governmental Maritime Consultative Organisation. Constitution Advisory Opinion, 1243
Maritime Transport, 224A, 450, 719, 978, 1250
Market for Apples and Pears in OEEC Countries, 718
Market for Nuclear Equipment and Instrumentation, 1248
Market, Latin American Common, 1256
Market Research:
  Methods in Europe, 223
  On a European Scale, 1248
Marketing:
  Agreement between U.K. and New Zealand. *Cmnd. 194.* 262
  Agricultural Products. Consolidation of Enactments (Procedure) Act. Memorandum, 480
  And Woodland Produce Report, 113
  By Manufacturers. Report of the International Conference, 448
  Costs and Margins for Fresh Milk, 421
  Fruit and Vegetables:
    967
    Spain and Turkey, 1246
  Guides, 967, 1237
  Livestock and Meat, 1237
  Major Edible Oils (Liquid) and Oil-Seeds in the Ecafe Region, 231A
  Problems and Improvement Programs, 967
  Research Report, 951
Marking and Regeneration of Fins, 655
Marriage Acts Amendment Act, 541
Marriage Acts Amendment Bill, 480, 497, 512, 516, 517, 607

INDEX 1956–60 —MAU

Marriage and Divorce, Royal Commission on Appendix to Minutes of Evidence Report. *Cmd. 9678.* 38
Marriage (Enabling) Act, 1070
Marriage (Enabling) Bill, 754, 1003, 1005, 1041
Marriage (Scotland) Act, 56
Marriage (Scotland) Bill, 4, 5, 20, 30, 33, 34, 35, 126
Marriage (Secretaries of Synagogues) Act, 809
Marriage (Secretaries of Synagogues) Bill, 488, 520
Marriott, F. H. C., Individual Differences in Night-Vision Efficiency, 359
Marriott, R., Study of Attitudes to Factory Work, 151
Marsden, S. J., Turkey Raising, 201
Marsh, A. R. S., Effects of Variations in the Ambient Air on the Calibration and Use of Ionization Dosemeters, 1163
Marshall Aid Commemoration Commission:
  Account, 19, 107, 234, 320, 495, 591, 766, 851, 937, 1020, 1123
  Report. *Cmd. 9736.* 41, 107; *Cmnd. 167.* 260, 320; *Cmnd. 433.* 527, 591; *Cmnd. 753.* 797, 851; *Cmnd. 1042.* 1054, 1127
Marshall, Sir G. A. K., Otiorrhychine Curculionidae of the Tribe Celeuthetini, 82
Marshall Scholarships Act, 810
Marshall Scholarships Bill, 754, 786
Marston, A. D., Maternal Deaths in England and Wales Report, 332
Martin, L. C. J., (Chairman: Working Party on Assistance with Cost of Boarding Education) Report, 1116
Martin, W. J.:
  Maternal Deaths in England and Wales Report, 332
  Report on Confidential Enquiries into Maternal Deaths in England and Wales, 1136
Marxist Classics, 200
Mason, F. C.:
  Greece Overseas Economic Survey, 182
  Iran Overseas Economic Survey, 667, 923
Mason, J., Occurrence of Nicothoe Astaci Andouin and Milne Edwards on Scottish Lobsters, 656
Mass Communication Reports and Papers, 239A, 467–8, 737, 996, 1265
Mass Spectrometer Researches, 155
Mass Spectrometry for Uranium Isotopic Measurements, 1240
Masterpieces from the National Gallery, Book of, 1163
Masters of Transports, Instructions for. Amendment, 403
Masters of Works for Building and Repairing Royal Palaces and Castles, Accounts of, 389
Mastitis in Cattle, 72
Match. Census of Production Report, 394
Materials for Concrete, 1179
Maternal and Child Health Services, Administration of, 472
Maternal Deaths in England and Wales. Report on Confidential Enquiries, 332, 1136
Maternity Services:
  Committee Report, 859
  Scotland Report, 858
Mathematical Tables:
  636, 1163
  Use and Construction of, 362
Mathematics:
  In Secondary Schools, Teaching of, 1185
  Teaching of, 1264
Matrimonial Causes Bill, 516
Matrimonial Causes (Decree Absolute) General Order, 359
Matrimonial Causes Jurisdiction Bill, 217
Matrimonial Causes (Property and Maintenance) Act, 541
Matrimonial Causes (Property and Maintenance) Bill, 482, 501, 512, 516, 607
Matrimonial Proceedings (Children) Act, 541
Matrimonial Proceedings (Children) Bill, 481, 483, 497, 512, 516, 517, 519, 607
Matrimonial Proceedings in Magistrates' Courts. Report of the Departmental Committee. *Cmnd. 638.* 789, 862
Matrimonial Proceedings (Magistrates' Courts) Act, 1070
Matrimonial Proceedings (Magistrates' Courts) Bill, 218, 220, 754, 1003, 1004, 1005, 1009, 1025, 1037, 1041, 1042, 1141
Matrimonial Proceedings (Magistrates' Courts) Memorandum, 217
Matsuda, R., Classification of the Aradidae, 828
Matter of Lime. Archaeological Survey of the River Gravels, 1176
Matters of Life and Death, 118, 856
Matthews, R. D., Use of Liquid Manure on Farms, 554
Mattingly, P. F.:
  Culicine Mosquitoes of the Indo-Malayan Area, 295, 564
  Mosquitoes of Arabia, 80
Mau Mau:
  Detainees in Hola Camp:
    Documents. *Cmnd. 778.* 799, 833
    Further Documents. *Cmnd. 816.* 801, 833
    Proceedings and Evidence in the Inquiry into Deaths. *Cmnd. 795.* 800, 834
  Historical Survey of the Origins and Growth. *Cmnd. 1030.* 1053, 1103

MAU-MIN | 1956-60

Maul, G. E., Cephalopoda of Madeira and Distribution, 80
Mauritius:
  Colonial Report, 87, 301, 833, 1102
  Constitution, Orders-in-Council, 1173
  International Customs Journal, 444
Maxwell, Sir A. (Chairman: Departmental Committee, Courts of Summary Jurisdiction in the Metropolitan Area) Report, 862
Mayer, Speech by Monsieur René, 215A
Maze Hill Railway Accident Report, 929
Mealy-Bugs from the Ethiopian Region, 563
Means of Escape in Case of Fire. Memorandum, 138
Measurement of Air Pollution, 650
Measurement of Humidity, 636
Measurement of Levels of Health. Report, 741
Measurement of Levels of Living with Special Reference to Jamaica, 302
Measurement of Ships in Port. Exchange of Notes between U.K. and Venezuela concerning Reciprocal Exemption. *Cmnd. 857*. 804, 854
Measurement of Small Holes, 167
Measurement, Units and Standards of, 155
Measures for the Economic Development of Under-Developed Countries, 1256
Measures Passed by the National Assembly of the Church of England, 59, 275, 544, 812, 1073
Measures to Improve the Supply of Teachers in Scotland Report. *Cmnd. 202*. 262
Measuring the Results of Development Projects, 996
Meat:
  And Dairy Products. Marketing and Distribution in the United States. Report, 718
  And Poultry, Domestic Preservation of, 588
  Circular, 290
  Contents and Price of Sausages. Circular, 557
  Hygiene:
    436, 471
    Expert Committee Report, 241A, 245A
    In the Retail Meat Trade, 859
  Hygienic Transport and Handling of Meat, 859
  Inspection. Grants Circular, 290
  Production, Trade, etc., 304, 835, 1105
  Regulations, Circular, 1086
  Staining and Sterilisation Regulations:
    Circular, 822
    Revocation, Circular, 822
Meates, Lt. Col. G. W., Lullingstone Roman Villa Guide, 698
Mecca Pilgrimage of the Hegira Report, 470
Mechanical and Electrical Engineering, 1178
Mechanical Barking of Timber, 437
Mechanical Engineering:
  Census of Production Report, 179, 664
  Research Board Report, 167, 383, 651, 909, 1181
Mechanical Handling Equipment. Census of Production Report, 664
Mechanically Propelled Road Vehicles:
  Census, 405, 673, 990, 1199
  Returns, 189, 405
Mechanical Thinning and Gapping of Row Crops, 823
Mechanization:
  In the Construction of Hydro-Electric Power Plants, 458
  Of Dairy Farms, 450
  Of the Application of Chemical Fertilizers in the Form of Liquid, 1250
  Of the Cultivation and Harvesting of Sugar Beet, 1250
  Of Thought Processes. Proceedings of Symposium, 890
Medals for Service in Cyprus, Grant of, 424
Medical Act, 56
Medical Bill, 4, 6, 35
Medical Act, 1956 (Amendment) Act, 541
Medical Act, 1956 (Amendment) Bill, 483, 519
Medical and Population Subjects Studies, 327, 598, 856, 1131
Medical Aspects of Atomic Weapons, 202
Medical Aspects of Nuclear Radiation, 420
Medical Care of Epileptics. Central Health Services Council Report, 121
Medical Care Organisation Expert Committee Report, 472
Medical Education, 998
Medical History of the Second World War, 122, 174, 332
Medical Laboratory Technician. Career, 347, 876, 1152
Medical Practitioners:
  Consolidation of Enactments relating to, 4
  Report of the Committee to consider the Future Numbers and the Appropriate Intake of Medical Students, 332
Medical Profession. Exchange of Notes between U.K. and Italy. *Cmnd. 238*. 264
Medical Radioisotope Scanning. Proceedings of a Seminar, 1240
Medical Records and Secretarial Services, 859
Medical Rehabilitation. Expert Committee Report, 742
Medical Research Council:
  Memoranda, 151, 633, 887

Medical Research Council (*continued*):
  Publications, 151, 359, 633, 887, 1160
  Report. *Cmd. 9787*. 44, 151; *Cmnd. 180*. 261, 359; *Cmnd. 453*. 529, 632; *Cmnd. 792*. 800, 887; *Cmnd. 1082*. 1057, 1160
  Special Report Series, 151, 359, 887, 1160
Medical Research, Current, 359
Medical Schools, World Directory, 473
Medical Services of the Armed Forces. Select Committee on Estimates Report, 772, 865, 1031, 1144
Medical Specialization, 740
Medical, Surgical and Laboratory Equipment. Temporary Importation, *Cmnd. 1136*. 1060, 1119; 1232
Medical Superintendents and Medical Staff Committees Sub-Committee Report, 330
Medical Tables, Statistical Review, 599
Medicinal Plants of the Arid Zones, 1263
Medicine:
  Careers, 347
  Isotopes in, 986
Medieval Catalogue, London Museum, 150
Medieval Near Eastern Pottery, 693
Mediterranean:
  And Middle East History of the Second World War, 82, 174, 1098, 1189
  Development Project, 967
Medlicott, W. N., Economic Blockade, 916
Medway Lower Navigation Pier and Harbour Order Confirmation Act, 812
Medway Lower Navigation Pier and Harbour Order Confirmation Bill, 752, 875
Meek, C. K., Land Tenure and Land Administration in Nigeria and the Cameroons, 302
Meetings between France, U.S.A., U.S.S.R. and U.K., Documents relating to, *Cmnd. 1052*. 1054, 1123
Mégille, X. B. de:
  Forestry Criteria and Equipment of Tractors, 242A
  Tractors for Logging, 242A
Meigle Collection. *See* Early Christian
Meigle Museum, Perthshire. Catalogue, 427
Meiklejohn, Colonel J. F.:
  India's Most Dangerous Hour, 565, 658
  War Against Japan, 296, 389
  Member Countries Combined Foreign Trade Statistical Bulletin, 222A, 448, 718, 978
Member States Reports, 737
Men, Steel and Technical Change, 383
Mengoni, L.:
  Représentation des Travailleurs sur le Plan de L'Entreprise dans le Droit des Pays Membres de la CECA, 965
  Stabilité de l'Emploi dans le Droit des Pays Membres de la CECA, 965
Mental Deficiency and Lunacy (Scotland) Act Forms, 600
Mental Deficiency in Scotland Report, 330
Mental Disorders:
  Classification of, 1267
  Epidemiological Methods in Study, 1269
  Epidemiology of, Report, 1269
Mental Health:
  Aspects of the Peaceful Uses of Atomic Energy Report, 741
  Legislation Report, 601, 858
  Problems of the Aging and Aged, Report, 1000
  Problems of Automation Report, 1000
  Review, Tribunal Forms, 1135
  Social Aspects, 995
  Statistical Review, Supplement, 598, 1131
Mental Health Act, 809
Mental Health Act, Forms, 1134
Mental Health Bill, 750, 752, 753, 765, 779, 784, 785, 786, 864
Mental Health Scotland Act, 1071
Mental Health (Scotland) Bill, 1008, 1009, 1025, 1037, 1041, 1042, 1044, 1141
Mental Health (Scotland) Memorandum on Bill. *Cmnd. 931*. 1046, 1132
Mental Hospital Patients. Area of Residence, 1131
Mental Illness and Mental Deficiency. Royal Commission on Law relating to Report. *Cmnd. 169*. 260, 380
Mentally Deficient Children, Organisation of Special Education for, 1265
Mentally Handicapped Persons, Welfare Needs of. Report, 331
Mentally Retarded Children, Teachers of. Report, 419
Meranti, Seraya, and Allied Timbers, 166
Mercantile Marine, Examination for Extra Masters in the, 926
Mercantile Navy List and Maritime Directory, 188, 672, 929, 1197
Merchandise Marks Act Standing Committee Report. *Cmnd. 282*. 268, 397; *Cmnd. 439*, *440*, *575*. 528, 537, 667; *Cmnd. 1001*, *1039*. 1051, 1054, 1193
Merchant Navy:
  Officers. Career, 618
  Ratings. Career, 136
Merchant Shipping:
  Instructions to Surveyors, 401
  Survey of Life-Saving Appliances, 929
  Survey of Passenger Ships, 188, 672
Merchant Shipping (Liability of Shipowners and Others) Act, 541

Merchant Shipping (Liability of Shipowners and Others Bill, 250, 482, 484, 497, 512, 518, 519, 607
Merchant Shipping (Minicoy Lighthouse) Act, 1071
Merchant Shipping (Minicoy Lighthouse) Bill, 1008, 1042
Mercury and Compounds. Methods for the Detection of Toxic Substances in Air, 630
Meritorious Service Medal. Royal Warrant, 424
Mersey Docks and Harbour Board Act, 58, 543
Merthyr, The Lord (Chairman: Hedgerow and Farm Timber Committee) Report, 112
Message Form F. Sigs. Home Office, 1139
Messer, Sir F. (Chairman: Central Health Services Council Committee) Report, 332, 602
Metalliferous Mines and Quarries. Census of Production Report, 394, 1193
Metalliferous Mining Region of South-West England, 119
Metallurgy. Arrangements and Conditions for the Award of National Certificates and Diplomas, 1116
Metals:
  Deformation of. Effect of a Surface-Active Medium on, 906
  Statistics of Non-Ferrous, 450
  Testing in the United States, 1248
Metamorphic Rocks of the Trinity Peninsular Series, 571
Meteorological Charts, Monthly, 888
Meteorological Glossary, 360, 633
Meteorological Instruments, Handbook of, 152
Meteorological Magazine, 152, 360, 430, 633, 888, 1161
Meteorological Office:
  Forms, 360
  Publications, 151–3, 359–61, 633, 887, 1160
  Report, 151, 359, 360, 633, 889, 1162
Meteorological Reports, 152, 634, 1161
Meteorological Results of the Balaena Expedition, 152
Meteorological Services and the Royal Greenwich Observatory. Select Committee on Estimates Report, 234, 336, 506, 607
Meteorological Telecommunications Meeting Report, 712
Meteorology Division Report, 1242
Methane, 976
Methodist Church Funds Act, 1072
Methods of Estimating Population, Manuals on, 232A, 459
Methods of Intensive Poultry Management, 821
Methods, Studies in 1260
Metropolis, Commissioner of Police. Report. *Cmd. 9786*. 44, 123
Metropolitan Magistrates' Courts Act, 809
Metropolitan Magistrates' Courts Bill, 749, 751, 752, 785
Metropolitan Police Act, 1839 (Amendment) Act, 541
Metropolitan Police Act, 1839 (Amendment) Bill, 482, 499, 512, 516, 518, 607
Metropolitan Police Driving School, Manual of Driving Instructions, 124
Metz, Professor B., Fitting the Job to the Worker, 1247
Mexborough and Swinton Traction Act, 1072
Mexico:
  Consular Convention with U.K. *Cmnd. 633*. 789, 851
  Exchange of Notes with U.K. concerning the Reciprocal Abolition of Visas. *Cmnd. 985*. 1050, 1123
  International Customs Journal, 714, 973, 1244
  Overseas Economic Survey, 182
Meyer-Waarden, P. F., Electrical Fishing, 707
M.F. Circular, 73
M.F.P. Safety Circular, 115
M.H.S. (Transport) Forms, 334–5
Mialaret, G., Teaching of Mathematics, 1264
Microbiology of Fish and Meat Curing Brines. Proceedings, 649
Microlepidoptera:
  Catalogue of the Type Specimens described by Edward Meyrick, 564
  From Lord Howe Island and Norfolk Island collected by the Rennel Island Expedition. Records and Descriptions, 80
Micro-Organisms:
  British Commonwealth Collections of, 1094
  Directory, 79
Middle East:
  Communications Meeting, 218A
  Economic Development, 227A, 722, 981, 1252
  Region Air Navigation Plan, 1241
Middlesbrough. Boundary Commission for England Report, 1137
Middlesex County Council Act, 58, 811
Midlothian and Edinburgh Boundary Commission Report, 1116, 1186
Midlothian Coalfield Geology, 599
Mid-Wales Investigation Report. *Cmd. 9809*. 46, 74
Mid-Wessex Water Act, 812
Migration:
  Analytical Bibliography of International Statistics, 232A
  Internal, 327

Migration (*continued*):
  See Child Migration — Oversea Migration
Migrations and Homing Behaviour of Brown Trout, 655
Migratory Beekeeping, 288
Milford Docks Act, 274
Milford Haven Conservancy Act, 541
Milford Haven Conservancy Bill, 220, 249, 478, 479, 480, 518
Military Aircraft, Supply of. Select Committee on Estimates Report, 222, 240, 336
Military Engineering, 206, 424, 954
Military Equipment Sale Abroad. Select Committee on Estimates Special Report, 770, 865, 1143
Military Forces, Changes in Composition of, 694
Military Law, Manual of. Amendments, 206, 424, 430, 695, 954, 1224
Military Service Agreements between U.K. and:
  Chile. *Cmd. 9668*. 37, 104
  Denmark. *Cmd. 9669*. 37, 105
  France. *Cmnd. 57*. 252
Milk:
  And Dairies (General) Regulations. Approved Chemical Agents. Circulars, 72, 73, 291, 557, 558, 822, 1086
  And Milk Products in:
    Human Nutrition, 968
    OEEC Countries, Marketing and Distribution Margins for, 1246
  Chemical Composition and Quality, 70
  Composition in the U.K. Report. *Cmnd. 1147*. 1061, 1082, 1088, 1135, 1139
  Feeding for Winter, 555
  Getting Enough, 692
  Goats, 201
  Hygiene, Joint FAO/WHO Expert Committee Report, 472, 1269
  Legislation and Control, Principles of, 241A
  Marketing Scheme. *See* Scottish
  Production, Costs and Efficiency in Report, 1086
  Products. Census of Production Report, 664
  Regulations, Circular, 1086
  Survey, *See* Small Pulp
Milking Methods and Milking Machines, 979
Milking Parlour, 823
Millar, O., Triumph of Caesar. Series of Nine Paintings, 1227
Millbourn, Sir E. (Chairman: London Airport Development Committee) Report, 403
Miller, G. F., Tables of Generalised Exponential Integrals, 1163
Miller, J., Korea, 1951–53, 421
Miller, J. C. P., Tables of Weber Parabolic Cylinder Functions, 155
Miller, N. C. E.:
  Centrocneminae. New Sub-Family of Reduriidae, 80
  Check List and Keys to the Families and Sub-Families of the Hemiptera-Heteroptra, 827
  New Genera and Species of Ethiopian Mascarene and Australian Reduviidae in the British Museum, 294
  New Sub-Family, New Genera and New Species of Reduviidae (Hemiptera-Heteroptera), 827
Millions Still Go Hungry, 437
Millipedes and Centipedes, 555
Millom and Askam Hematite Iron Co. Ltd. and Hodbarrow Mining Co. Ltd. Proposal to sell holding of Securities. *Cmnd. 532*. 534, 679
Millport Piers (Amendment) Order Confirmation Act, 58
Millport Piers (Amendment) Order Confirmation Bill, 35
Mills, J. R. E., Contribution to the Odontology of Oreopithecus, 828
Milngavie Junction Railway Accident Report, 673
Milton Railway Accident Report, 188
Mine Air, Notes on Sampling of, 114
Mineral Industry. Statistical Summary Production, etc., 89, 303, 572, 834, 1104
Mineral Oil Refining. Census of Production Report, 394, 1194
Mineral Resources:
  Development Series, 231A, 458, 729, 985, 1256
  Of Great Britain, Special Reports, 119
Mineral Species and Varieties arranged Chemically. Index, 82
Mineral Working, Control of, 1146
Mineral Workings Act:
  Account, 10, 130, 496, 612, 766, 870, 1018, 1147
  Ironstone Restoration Fund Account, 226, 342
Mineralogy Bulletin, 563
Minerals Yearbook, 202
Mines and Quarries:
  Books Prepared and Designated by the Minister, 643
  Chief Inspector's Reports, 116, 372, 642, 645, 900, 901, 1172, 1173
  Clearance on Transport Roads in Coal Mines, 370
  Forms, 116–17, 327, 372–7, 643, 900, 1172
  Principal Electrical Inspector's Report, 116
  Regulations, 643
  Safety Circulars, 645, 900
Mines and Quarries Act. Law relating to Safety and Health, 372

Mines (Notification of Dangerous Occurrences) Order Circular, 900
Minesweepers:
Gift of Inshore Minesweeper to Government of East Africa. *Cmnd. 418.* 527, 678
Loan to Hong Kong. *Cmnd. 651.* 790, 934
Mingledale Railway Accident Report, 188
Mining:
And Kindred Subjects, Historic Books on, 1178
And Upgrading of Brown Coal in Europe, 458
Development in Asia and Far East, 231A, 729, 1257
Engineering, 467
Examinations (Surveyors) (Amendment) Rules, 645
Legislation, Survey of, 729
Products, Non-Metalliferous other than Coal, Treatment of. Chemicals and Allied Trades; Metal Manufacture. Report on the Censuses of Production, 923
Qualifications:
Board Examinations for Certificates of Competency, 900, 1172
Mechanics and Electricians (Amendment) Rules, 377, 645
Regulations in New Hebrides. Exchange of Notes between U.K. and France. *Cmnd. 667.* 791, 848
Ministerial Salaries Act, 272
Ministerial Salaries Bill, 218, 249
Ministers and Heads of Public Departments, 175, 390, 430, 658, 917, 1189
Ministers of the Crown (Parliamentary Secretaries) Act, 1071
Ministers of the Crown (Parliamentary Secretaries) Bill, 1011, 1044
Ministry of Housing and Local Government Provisional Order Confirmation (West Hertfordshire Main Drainage) Act, 812
Ministry of Housing and Local Government Provisional Order Confirmation (West Hertfordshire Main Drainage) Bill, 749
Minster Lovell Hall, Oxfordshire, Guide, 698
Miocene Lemuroid Skull from East Africa, 81
Miocene Ruminants of East Africa, 564
Miscellaneous 1956.
1. Washington Declaration, U.S.A. and U.K. *Cmd. 9700.* 39
2. War Cripples, Agreement on Exchange. *Cmd. 9705.* 39
3. International Court of Justice Declaration concerning Optional Clause of the Statute. *Cmd. 9719.* 40
Miscellaneous 1956 (*continued*):
4. Plant Protection Agreement for South East Asia and Pacific Region. *Cmd. 9783.* 44
5. Civil Aviation, Convention for Unification of Rules relating to International Carriage by Air. *Cmd. 9824.* 47
6. Cultural Property. Final Act, Convention and Protocol on Protection in the Event of Armed Conflict. *Cmd. 9837.* 48
7. Customs Convention regarding E.C.S. Carnets for Commercial Samples. *Cmd. 9863.* 50
8. Agreement regarding War Graves, etc., of the British Commonwealth. *Cmd. 9833.* 48
9. Foreign Compensation Commission Report. *Cmd. 9849.* 49
10. European Payments Union Supplementary Protocol. *Cmd. 9867.* 50
11. Northwest Atlantic Fisheries. Protocol to International Convention. *Cmd. 9874.* 51
12. Convention on Abolition of Slavery. *Cmd. 9870.* 51
13. Agreement relating to International Convention for regulating the Police of the North Sea Fisheries. *Cmnd. 4.* 52
14. Council of Europe. Report on Proceedings. *Cmnd. 26.* 54
15. International Tin Council Resolution. *Cmnd. 38.* 54
Miscellaneous 1957:
1. Council of Europe Convention between Member Countries on Establishment. *Cmnd. 41.* 251
2. Protocol to the International Convention for Regulation of Whaling. *Cmnd. 100.* 255
3. International Sanitary Regulations. *Cmnd. 30.* 250
4. Statute of the International Atomic Energy Agency. *Cmnd. 92.* 255
5. European Convention on Equivalence of Periods of University Study. *Cmnd. 93.* 255
6. Protocol amending International Sugar Agreement. *Cmnd. 101.* 256
7. Council of Europe Texts of Statutory Character for Inclusion in Revised Statute. *Cmnd. 118.* 257
8. European Coal and Steel Community Annual Report. *Cmnd. 116.* 256
9. Customs Tariffs. Protocol of Amendment to Convention for Classification of Goods. *Cmnd. 127.* 257
10. Bermuda Conference. *Cmnd. 126.* 257

Miscellaneous 1957 (*continued*):
11. Western European Union. Protocol Concerning Accession of Germany and Italy to Conventions on Frontier Workers. *Cmnd. 138.* 258
12. Council of Europe. Protocol to General Agreement on Privileges and Immunities. *Cmnd. 139.* 258
13. Aerial Navigation Agreement on Financing Air Navigation Services in Greenland and Faroe Islands. *Cmnd. 165.* 260
14. Aerial Navigation Agreement on Financing Air Navigation Services in Iceland. *Cmnd. 166.* 260
15. Convention on Nationality of Married Women. *Cmnd. 200.* 262
16. Convention on Taxation of Road Vehicles. *Cmnd. 220.* 263
17. Report on Disarmament Talks. *Cmnd. 228.* 264
18. Customs Conventions on Containers. *Cmnd. 235.* 264
19. International Court of Justice. Declaration concerning the Optional Clause of the Statute. *Cmnd. 249.* 265
20. Customs Convention on Temporary Importation of Commercial Road Vehicles. *Cmnd. 255.* 266
21. European Payments Union. Supplementary Protocol amending Agreement. *Cmnd. 259.* 266
22. Council of Europe. Report on Proceedings of Consultative Assembly. *Cmnd. 274.* 267
23. Customs Convention on Temporary Importation of Aircraft and Pleasure Boats. *Cmnd. 288.* 268
24. Foreign Compensation Commission Report. *Cmnd. 299.* 269
25. International Sanitary Regulations. Certificate of Vaccination against Smallpox. *Cmnd. 312.* 270
26. Convention on Taxation of Road Vehicles. *Cmnd. 320.* 270
27. European Coal and Steel Community Agreement Concerning Commercial Relations. *Cmnd. 326.* 271
28. North Atlantic Council Ministerial Meeting. *Cmnd. 339.* 271
Miscellaneous 1958:
1. Trade Marks. Arrangement concerning International Classification of Goods and Services. *Cmnd. 348.* 522
2. Decision of Council of O.E.E.C. establishing European Nuclear Energy Agency and Convention on Security Control. *Cmnd. 357.* 522
3. International Convention relating to Limitation of Liability of Owners of Sea-Going Ships. *Cmnd. 353.* 522
Miscellaneous 1958 (*continued*):
4. Western European Union Agreement. *Cmnd. 388.* 524
5. Western European Union Convention. *Cmnd. 389.* 524
6. Council of Europe Consultative Assembly Proceedings Report. *Cmnd. 400.* 525
7. European Coal and Steel Community Report. *Cmnd. 424.* 527
8. Refugee Seamen Agreement. *Cmnd. 427.* 527
9. Road Markings. European Agreement. *Cmnd. 480.* 530
10. International Agreement on Olive Oil. *Cmnd. 549.* 535
11. Atomic Energy. Reports of Conference of Experts to Study Methods of Detecting Violations of a Possible Agreement on Suspension of Nuclear Tests. *Cmnd. 551.* 535
12. European Monetary Agreement. Supplementary Protocol. *Cmnd. 554.* 535
13. European Payments Union. Supplementary Protocol. *Cmnd. 555.* 535
14. Cyprus. Discussion in North Atlantic Treaty Organisation. *Cmnd. 566.* 535
15. Law of the Sea. United Nations Conference Report. *Cmnd. 584.* 537
16. Sugar. Draft International Agreement. *Cmnd. 587.* 538
17. International Court of Justice. Declarations concerning Optional Clause of Statute, *Cmnd. 599.* 539
18. Foreign Compensation Report. *Cmnd. 611.* 539
Miscellaneous 1959:
1. Agreement between U.K. and European Atomic Energy Community for Co-operation in Peaceful Uses of Atomic Energy. *Cmnd. 649.* 790
2. International Convention for Suppression of Counterfeit Currency. *Cmnd. 666.* 791
3. North East Atlantic Fisheries Convention. *Cmnd. 659.* 791
4. Cyprus Conference Documents. *Cmnd. 679.* 792
5. Cyprus Conference Final Statements. *Cmnd. 680.* 792
6. European Agreement concerning International Carriage of Dangerous Goods by Road. *Cmnd. 734.* 796
7. International Wheat Agreement. *Cmnd. 730.* 795
8. Agreement on Commercial Debts owed by Residents of Turkey. *Cmnd. 767.* 798
9. Customs Convention on International Transport of Goods. *Cmnd. 790.* 800

Miscellaneous 1959 (*continued*):
10. Council of Association between U.K. and High Authority of European Coal and Steel Community Report. *Cmnd. 794.* 800
11. Conference of Foreign Ministers at Geneva. *Cmnd. 797.* 800
12. Foreign Forces stationed in Germany Agreement. *Cmnd. 852.* 803
13. Conference of Foreign Ministers at Geneva. Principal Documents. *Cmnd. 829.* 802
14. Conference of Foreign Ministers at Geneva. *Cmnd. 868.* 805
15. International Convention for Protection of Industrial Property. *Cmnd. 875.* 805
16. International Agreement regarding False Indications of Origin on Goods. *Cmnd. 876.* 805
17. World Health Organisation. Constitution Amendment. *Cmnd. 877.* 805.
18. Multilateral Agreement on Commercial Rights of Non-Scheduled Air Services in Europe. *Cmnd. 879.* 805
19. International Coffee Agreement Declaration. *Cmnd. 883.* 806
20. Foreign Compensation Commission Report. *Cmnd. 901.* 807
21. Conference on Antarctica with Antarctic Treaty. *Cmnd. 913.* 808
Miscellaneous 1960:
1. Greece, Norway, Sweden. Protocol concerning Accession to Convention concerning Student Employees. *Cmnd. 942.* 1047
2. European Monetary Agreement Amendments. *Cmnd. 959.* 1048
3. Plan for Comprehensive Disarmament tabled at Conference of Ten Nation Committee. *Cmnd. 981.* 1049
4. European Convention on Academic Recognition of University Qualifications. *Cmnd. 1037.* 1053
5. Paris Meetings between France, U.S.A., U.S.S.R. and U.K. *Cmnd. 1052.* 1054.
6. European Convention for Peaceful Settlement of Disputes. *Cmnd. 1060.* 1055
7. Report on the Proceedings of the Consultative Assembly of the Council of Europe. *Cmnd. 1072.* 1056
8. Airworthiness for Imported Aircraft. Multilateral Agreement. *Cmnd. 1078.* 1056
9. U.K. and European Coal and Steel Community, Council of Association Report. *Cmnd. 1104.* 1058
Miscellaneous 1960 (*continued*):
10. Verbatim Records of Meetings of Ten-Power Disarmament Committee Geneva. *Cmnd. 1152.* 1062
11. Caribbean Organisation Agreement for Establishment. *Cmnd. 1144.* 1061
12. European Agreement on Protection of Television Broadcasts. *Cmnd. 1163.* 1063
13. International Sanitary Regulations Amendment. *Cmnd. 1165.* 1063.
14. International Atomic Energy Agency. Agreement on Privileges and Immunities. *Cmnd. 1176.* 1063
15. Foreign Compensation Committee Report. *Cmnd. 1204.* 1066
16. European Free Trade Association. Legal Capacity Privileges and Immunities. *Cmnd. 1194.* 1065
17. Convention of Third Party Liability in the Field of Nuclear Energy. *Cmnd. 1211.* 1066
18. North Atlantic Treaty Organisation Agreement for Mutual Safeguarding of Secrecy of Inventions. *Cmnd. 1220.* 1067
Miscellaneous Financial Provisions Act Account, 230, 244, 292, 314, 514, 559, 773, 824, 1038, 1088
Miscellaneous Mines (Explosives) Regulations, Safety Circular, 900
Miscellaneous Preserved Foods. Census of Production Reports, 664
Miscellaneous Stationers' Goods. Census of Production Report, 396
Miss L. E. Cheeseman's Expedition to New Hebrides, 563
Mission Report, 995
Mistakidis, M. N.:
Biology of Pandalus Montagui Leach, 292
Comparative Fishing Trials with Shrimp Nets, 559
Misuse of Official Facilities Report. *Cmnd. 583.* 537, 679
Mitchell, B. D., Soils of the Country round Kilmarnock, 288
Mitchell, R. L., Limestones of Scotland, 119
Mitchell, Sir Steuart (Chairman: Machine Tool Advisory Council Sub-Committee) Report, 1193
Mix Design for Vibrated Concrete, 428
Mixed Claims Commission Decisions, 727
Mixing Feeding Stuffs on the Farm, 71
Moat Hostel (Amendment No. 1) Scheme:
Memorandum, 1184
Order-in-Council, 1184
Mobile Radio Committee Report, 161, 897, 1170
Mobile Tower Cranes for Two and Three Storey Building, 1181

Mocatta, A. A. (Chairman: Cheque Endorsement) Report. *Cmnd. 3.* 52
Mock Auctions Bill, 747, 750, 785, 787, 1044
Mocquot, G., Advances in Cheese Technology, 706
Model Byelaws, 72, 74, 130, 342, 612
Model Clauses, House of Lords, House of Commons, 275, 1073
Model Standing Orders Contracts, 342
Modern Building, Principles of, 909
Modern Computing Methods, 362
Modern Languages:
101
Guidance of Teachers on the Setting and Marking of Examinations, 171
Scottish Certificate of Education, 913
Modern Multi-Storey Factories, 906
Modern Studies. Scottish Certificate of Education, 913
Modified Commercial Hive, 555, 1083
Modular Co-ordination in Building, 223A
Moir, T. R. G., Grasses in Agriculture, 1236
Moisture Content:
Determination by the Oven-Drying Method, 907
Of Timber in Use, 907
Mole, 555, 1083
Molenaar, A.:
Irrigation by Sprinkling, 1236
Représentation des Travailleurs sur la Plan de l'Entreprise dans le Droit des Pays Membres de la CECA, 965
Stabilité de L'Emploi dans le Droit des Pays Membres de la CECA, 965
Water Lifting Devices for Irrigation, 241A
Molitar, A., University Teaching of Social Sciences Public Administration, 996
Molluscan Anatomy for Parasitologists in Africa, Guide, 296
Molony, Brigadier C. J. C.:
British Fortunes Reach Their Lowest Ebb, 1098, 1189
"The Germans Come to the Help of their Ally", 82, 174
Molony, J. T. (Chairman: Committee on Consumer Protection) Report. *Cmnd. 1011.* 1052
Molson, H. (Chairman: Committee on Road Safety) Report, 186
Monckton, Rt. Hon. Viscount, of Brenchley (Chairman: Advisory Commission on Review of Constitution of Rhodesia and Nyasaland) Report. *Cmnd. 1148.* 1061
Monetary Gold Removed from Rome in 1943. Judgment, 220A
Monetary System, Committee on the Working of:
Cmnd. 827. 802, 934
Minutes of Evidence, 1202
Money in British East Asia, 301
Monitoring Report Series, 1160
Monk Seals, 80
Monmouthshire County Council Act, 58
Monmouthshire Moors Investigation Report, 75
Monograph on Fundamental Education, 239A, 737
Monographs in Applied Social Sciences, 996
Monopolies and Restrictive Practices Acts; Report, 13, 20, 182, 227, 495, 667, 761, 923, 1020, 1193
Monopolies and Restrictive Practices Commission Reports, 15, 22, 24, 182, 221, 223, 397–8, 1013, 1193
Monopolies and Restrictive Practices (Imported Hardwood and Softwood Timber) Orders. Statutory Instruments Select Committee Report, 1143
Monoszon, E. I., Educational Information Services in U.S.S.R., 735
Monotypic Genera of Cichlid Fishes in Lake Victoria Haplochromis Species, 828
Montgomery, Professor G. L. (Chairman: Scottish Health Services Council Sub-Committee) Report, 858
Monthly Digest of Statistics, 83, 297, 430, 565, 829, 1098
Monthly Weather Report, 153, 361, 634, 888, 1161
Montreal Conference. *See* Commonwealth Trade and Economic Conference
Montserrat:
Colonial Report, 569, 1102
Orders-in-Council, 1173
Moore, D. G., Fifteen-Year Exposure Test of Porcelain Enamels, 419
Moore, J. G., Upper Air Temperature over the World, 633
Moral-Lopez, P., Principles of Tenancy Legislation, 708
Morbidity Statistics from General Practice, 598, 1131
More Flatlets for Old People:
1147
Circular, 1146
Moreau, R., Variation in the Western Zosteropidae, 295
Moreton, B. D., Beneficial Insects, 556
Morocco:
Exchange of Notes:
For the Mutual Abolition of Visas on Passports. *Cmnd. 623.* 788, 851
With U.K. concerning the Convention of Commerce and Navigation between U.K. and the Shereefian Empire. *Cmnd. 144.* 259, 320
International Conference Final Declaration. *Cmnd. 60.* 252, 320
International Customs Journal, 714, 974, 1244

MOR-NAT | 1956-60

Morrah, D., Queen and People, 872
Morris, Sir Charles. (Acting Chairman: Royal Commission on Local Government in Greater London) Minutes of Evidence, 903, 1176
Morris, Sir Philip. (Chairman):
  Commonwealth Education Conference. Report. *Cmnd. 841.* 803, 836
  National Advisory Council. Report on Training and Supply of Teachers, 102, 314
Morrison, Joseph and John, Bursaries Fund Draft Scheme, 170
Morse, C. (Chairman: Economic Survey Mission, Basutoland, Bechuanaland Protectorate, Swaziland) Report, 1106
Mortality:
  Age and Sex Patterns, 232A
  Statistics. *See* Demographic Yearbook
Mortars for Jointing, 906
Morton of Henryton, Rt. Hon. Lord (Chairman: Royal Commission on Marriage and Divorce):
  Minutes of Evidence, 163
  Report. *Cmd. 9678.* 38, 163
Mortuaries and Post-Mortem Accommodation Planning, 130
Moscow's European Satellites. Handbook, 201
Moser, C. A., Measurement of Levels of Living with Special Reference to Jamaica, 302
Mosquitoes:
  Arabia, 80
  British. Their Control, 564
  Culicine, of Indo-Malayan Area, 295, 564
  Their Relation to Disease, 564
Moss, Louis, Consumer's Food Buying Habits. Report, 715
Motor Cars. Handbook of the Collection, 1178
Motor Cycles:
  Handbook of the Collection, 648
  History and Development, 164
Motor Cyclists. Committee on Road Safety Report on the Minimum Age, 403
Motor Mechanic. Career, 136
Motor Rules. *See* Highway Code
Motor Vehicles:
  And Cycles Census of Production Reports, 405, 663, 673, 990, 1199
  Offences relating to, Return, 31, 124, 189, 245, 335, 405, 515, 605, 771, 862, 1028, 1139
  See Road Vehicles
Motor Vessels Mercantile Navy List, 1197
Motorway:
  London to Yorkshire, 1197
  Ross, 1199
Mountbatten—Windsor. Declaration concerning Descendants who shall bear the Surname, 1190
Mount Grace Priory, Yorkshire. Guide, 957
Mountford, W. D., Ear Plug Laminations in relation to the Age Composition of a Population of Fin Whales, 828
Mouse, Annotated Catalogue of the Mutant Genes of the House Mouse, 151
Movement of Timbers, 908
Movements of Salmon Tagged in the Sea, 655
Moving from the Slums Report, 130
Morsovic, M. I., Technical and Vocational Education in the U.S.S.R., 995
Mowers, 823
Mozart in the British Museum, 80
M.P. Safety Circular, 377
Mr. Speaker Morrison's Retirement Act, 810
Mr. Speaker Morrison's Retirement Bill, 754, 787
Mudie, Sir Francis (Chairman: British Caribbean Federal Capital Commission) Report, 300
Muhammadan Coins in the British Museum, 80
Muir, A., Limestones of Scotland, 119
Muir, J. W., Soils of the Country round Jedburgh and Morebattle, 70
Muir-Wood, H. M.:
  Report on the Brachiopoda of the John Murray Expedition, 1097
  Succession of Life through Geological Time, 296, 828
Multilateral Agreements, 1239
Multilateral Conventions, Status of, 234, 462, 731, 989, 1260
Multilingual Demographic Dictionary, 987
Multilingual Vocabulary of Soil Science, 1237
Multi-Purpose River Basin Development, 228A, 454, 1254
Mungo Park, 344
Munro, H. K., Trypetidae, 296
Munro, W. R.:
  Observations on the Spawning Runs of Brown Trout in the South Queich, Loch Leven, 171
  Pike of Loch Choin, 387
Munthe, P., Freedom of Entry into Industry and Trade, 718
Murchison of Taradale Memorial Trust Scheme:
  Memoranda, 912
  Order-in-Council, 912
Murgatroyd, R. J.:
  High Cloud over Southern England, 153
  Wind and Temperature to 50° KM over England, 152
Murrant, Sir E. (Chairman: Ports Efficiency Committee) Report, 188
Murray, Sir K. (Chairman: University Grants Committee) Report *Cmnd. 79.* 254; *Cmnd. 534.* 534

Murray, Sir K. A. H., Agriculture, 82, 174
Murray, R., Some Features of Jet Streams as shown by Aircraft Observations, 152
Muscat:
  And Oman. Exchange of Letters with U.K. concerning the Sultan's Armed Forces, Civil Aviation, etc. *Cmnd. 507.* 532, 592
  Notices, 108, 320–1, 591, 851, 1123
Museums:
  239, 468, 737, 996, 1265
  And Galleries. Standing Commission Report, 916
  And Monuments, 737, 1265
  In Education, 238A
  Monographs, 692, 951, 1223
  Organisation of, 1265
  Seminar on the Educational Role Report, 1264
  Techniques in Fundamental Education, 466
  See Name of Museum
Musgrave, Sir C., Statement in regard to Remuneration, etc., 762, 900
Mushroom Growing:
  1085
  In the United States, 201
Music:
  Careers, 1152
  In Schools, 101, 1116
  Scottish Certificate of Education, 913
Musical Instruments. Census of Production Report, 395
Mussel Purification Simplified System, 74
Mussels:
  Environmental Factors Governing the Infection of, 73
  Great Spatfall of Mussels in the River Conway Estuary in Spring, 1940, 74
Must Full Employment Mean Ever-Rising Prices, 196
Mutual Co-operation between Iraq and Turkey. *Cmd. 9859.* 50
Mykura, W., Geology of Midlothian Coalfield, 599
Mylne Bursary Scheme:
  Memoranda, 912
  Order-in-Council, 912

N

N.A.A.S. Quarterly Review, 74, 292, 559, 824, 1088
Naish, G. P. B., Nelson and Bronte, 635
Napier, J. R.:
  Fore Limb Skeleton and Associated Remains of Proconsul Africanus, 828
  Fossil Metacarpals from Swartkrans, 1097
Narcissus Pests, 556
Narcotic Drugs:
  Bulletin on, 231A, 458-9, 729, 979, 1251
  Commission on, Report, 227A, 453, 723, 982
  Estimated World Requirements, 226A–7A, 452, 722, 980, 1252
  Multilingual List, 729
  National Laws and Regulations:
    Index, 722, 981
    Relating to control, 1252
  Reports relating to Opium, etc., 453, 722, 981
  Summary of Laws and Regulations, 227A, 453
  See also United Nations
Narrow Fabrics. Census of Production Report, 395
Narva Wreck Report, 931
Nasutitermitinae, A Revision of the East African, 294
Natality Statistics Demographic Yearbook, 1251
National Accounts:
  And Supporting Tables, System of, 1260
  Statistics Yearbook, 729, 993, 1263
National Administration and International Organisations. Administrative Problems, 239A
National Advisory Council, on Training and Supply of Teachers:
  Correspondence with Minister of Education, 585
  Report, 314
National Agricultural Advisory Service Journal, 74, 292, 430, 559, 824, 1088
National Assistance:
  Amendment Regulations. *Cmnd. 296.* 269, 363; *Cmnd. 1198.* 1065, 1164
  Estimates:
    1956–57, 12, 495, 676
    1957–58, 226
    1958–59, 494, 676
    1959–60, 760, 933
    1960–61, 1019, 1201
  Improvements in. *Cmnd. 782.* 799, 891
  Report. *Cmd. 9781.* 44, 156; *Cmnd. 181.* 261, 363; *Cmnd. 444.* 528, 636; *Cmnd. 781.* 799, 896; *Cmnd. 1085.* 1057, 1169
National Assistance Act, 809
National Assistance Act (Amendment) Bill, 235, 242, 247, 249, 250, 337, 1045
National Assistance (Amendment) Act, 809
National Assistance (Amendment) Bill, 520, 748, 786
National Assistance Bill, 752
National Building Studies:
  Research Papers, 651, 909, 1181
  Special Reports, 383, 651, 909, 1181
National Bureau of Standards:
  Circular, 202
  Handbook, 202, 692

National Chemical Laboratory Report, 910, 1181
National Coal Board:
  Publications, 153, 890
  Report and Accounts, 18, 118, 233, 377, 501, 645, 766, 900, 1024, 1025, 1172
National Dairy Policies in Advanced Countries, 1236
National Debt:
  Cmnd. 498. 531, 680; *Cmnd. 791.* 800, 937
  Papers Relative to the Position. *Cmd. 9816.* 46, 196; *Cmnd. 203.* 262, 410; *Cmnd. 1139.* 1060, 1205
  Returns. *Cmnd. 48.* 251, 410; *Cmnd. 351, 574.* 522, 537, 680; *Cmd. 924, 1221.* 1046, 1067
National Debt Act, 542
National Debt Act, Report on Consolidation Bill, 487, 488
National Debt Bill, 486, 488, 521
National Engineering Laboratory Steering Committee Report, 1181
National Film Finance Corporation Report and Accounts. *Cmd. 9751.* 42, 182; *Cmnd. 176.* 261, 398; *Cmnd. 448.* 528, 667; *Cmnd. 799.* 800, 923; *Cmnd. 1096.* 1057, 1193
National Food Reserve Policies, 707
National Food Survey Committee. Report on Domestic Food Consumption and Expenditure, 73, 291, 558, 822, 1087
National Forest:
  Park Guides, 325, 596, 1129
  Vacations, 202
National Galleries of Scotland Act, 809
National Galleries of Scotland Bill, 752, 770, 779, 785, 864
National Galleries of Scotland Report, 154, 361, 635, 890, 1162
National Gallery:
  Catalogues:
    154, 361, 635, 890, 1163
    Dutch School, 635
  Masterpieces, 635, 1163
  Publications, 154, 361
  Report, 635, 1162
National Grain Policies, 967, 1237
National Health Service:
  Accounts:
    18, 122, 229, 332, 498, 602, 761, 770
    Scotland, 499, 600
  Central Health Services Council Report, 232, 332, 503, 602, 1027, 1136
  Hospitals:
    And Specialists Services, England and Wales Statistics Report. *Cmd. 9663.* 37
    Costings Returns, 332, 602, 859, 860, 1135
  Revised Estimate, 1957–58, 235, 407
  Report, 22, 770, 859, 891
National Health Service (*continued*):
  Scotland:
    1132
    Publications, 121, 330, 600
  Superannuation Scheme:
    122
    Allocation of Pensions. Explanatory Memorandum, 330
    Report, 859
    Scotland, 330, 858
  Supplementary Ophthalmic Services. Fees and Charges for Testing Sight and Supply or Repair of Glasses, 332
  Summarised Accounts, 1021, 1136
National Health Service (Amendment) Act, 272
National Health Service (Amendment) Bill, 218, 243, 247, 248
National Health Service (Amendment) Bill and the Parish Councils (Miscellaneous Provisions) Bill, 234
National Health Service (Amendment) (No. 2) Bill, 249
National Health Service Contributions Act, 272, 541
National Health Service Contributions Bill, 217, 248, 480, 517
National Health Service (Scotland) Acts. Accounts, 18, 121, 229, 230, 761, 858, 1021, 1132
National Health Services Acts:
  Circular, 341
National Income and Expenditure:
  Cmd. 9729. 41, 83, 197; 297, 410, 829, 1098
  Preliminary Estimates. *Cmnd. 123.* 257; *Cmnd. 398.* 525, 565, 680; *Cmnd. 712.* 794, 937; *Cmnd. 988.* 1050, 1205
  Statistics, 83, 233A, 461
National Income of Tanganyika, 570
National Insurance:
  Accounts:
    16, 197, 228
    Of the National Insurance Fund, etc., 498, 636, 891
  Amendment Regulations:
    Draft, 158, 160, 234, 366, 368, 1164
    Reports, 13, 32, 227, 230, 236, 237, 239, 243, 244, 245, 246, 363, 364, 365, 366, 501, 504, 506, 515, 638, 763, 764, 768, 772, 779, 893, 895, 896, 1165
  Benefit. Quinquennial Review of the Rates and Amounts. Report, 1027, 1167
  Circular, 1146
  Contribution Rates, 638
  Decisions of the Commissioner, 1165
  Decisions on Claims:
    156, 363–4, 366–8, 369, 637
    Index, 362

National Insurance (*continued*):
  Decisions on Questions of Classification and Insurability, 156, 636
  Draft Regulations, 366, 368, 638, 639, 892, 894, 895, 896
  Estimates:
    1956–57, 12
    1957–58, 226
    1958–59, 494, 676
    1959–60, 760, 933
    1960–61, 1019
  Everybody's Guide, 636, 891
  Government Actuary Report, 1205
  Regulations Reports, 19, 239, 501, 680, 761, 781, 783, 896, 937
  Report on the Financial Provisions of the Bill. *Cmnd. 294.* 269, 410; *Cmnd. 629.* 788, 893; *Cmnd. 1197.* 1065, 1167
  Report on the Question of Widow's Benefits. *Cmd. 9684.* 38, 156
  Schemes:
    For Provision for Old Age. *Cmnd. 538.* 534, 639
    Proposed Changes. *Cmnd. 295.* 269, 368; *Cmnd. 1196.* 1065, 1168
National Insurance Act, 56, 272, 809, 1071
National Insurance Act Report, 232, 410
National Insurance Advisory Committee Reports. *Cmd. 9684, 9752, 9854, 9855.* 38, 42, 49, 50, 54; *Cmnd. 33.* 156; 227, 239, 243, 244, 245, 246; *Cmnd. 206.* 263, 363; 1024, 1025, 1026, 1028, 1029, 1030, 1031, 1039, 1048, 1052, 1165, 1167
National Insurance and Industrial Injuries Preliminary Draft, 638
National Insurance (Annulled Marriages) Regulations. Draft, 366
National Insurance (Assessment of Graduated Contributions) Regulations:
  Draft, 1164
  Report, 1026, 1165
National Insurance Bill, 3, 19, 30, 34, 126, 216, 220, 230, 243, 247, 248, 249, 337, 751, 766, 785, 864, 893, 1011, 1044
National Insurance (Child's Special Allowance) Regulations Draft, 366
National Insurance (Collection of Graduated Contributions) Regulations:
  Draft, 1164
  Report, 1026, 1165
  Select Committee Report, 1143
  See also Statutory Instruments
National Insurance (Death Grant) Regulations. Draft, 366
National Insurance (Earnings) Regulations:
  Draft, 1015
  Report, 1015, 1166
National Insurance (Extension of Unemployment Benefit) Bill, 520
National Insurance Fund, etc. Accounts, 1022, 1165
National Insurance (Graduated Contributions and Non-Participating Employments—Miscellaneous Provisions) Regulations, Report, 1029, 1166
National Insurance (Industrial Injuries) Acts:
  Decision on Claims, 156, 159, 366–8, 638, 892, 894, 1167
  Report. 20, 156, 197; *Cmd. 9673, 9674, 9827.* 37, 38, 47, 158, 159; 234, 363, 410, 504, 680, 759, 767, 770, 892, 896, 937, 1032, 1205
  Review of Prescribed Diseases Schedule. *Cmnd. 416.* 526, 639
National Insurance (Industrial Injuries) Bill, 32
National Insurance (Industrial Injuries) Byssinosis Review. *Cmnd. 1095.* 1057, 1167
National Insurance (Industrial Injuries) Regulations, Preliminary Draft, 1167
National Insurance (No. 2) Act, 273
National Insurance (Non-Participation—Assurance of Equivalent Pension Benefits) Regulations:
  Draft, 1164
  Report, 1028, 1166
National Insurance (Non-Participation—Continuity of Employment) Regulations, Draft, 1164
National Insurance (Widowed Mothers) Bill, 1041
National Land Fund Account, 23, 197, 502, 680, 769, 937, 1021, 1205
National Libraries:
  Scotland, Report, 154, 635, 1163
  Their Problems and Prospects, 1265
National Maritime Museum:
  Greenwich Guide, 1163
  Publications, 154, 362, 635
National Museum of Antiquities of Scotland:
  Publications, 154
  Report, 362, 635, 890, 1163
National Park Guides, 362, 1163
National Parks (Amendment) Bill, 784
National Parks and Access to the Countryside Act Report, 490, 612, 782, 870, 1014, 1147
National Parks Commission:
  Publications, 155, 362
  Report, 31, 130, 515, 612
National Parks Film Strips, 155, 1163
National Physical Laboratory:
  Publications, 155, 362, 636, 890, 1163
  Report, 155, 362, 636, 890, 1163
  Symposium, 1163
National Pinetum and Forest Plots Guide, 113
National Plan for Civil Defence Administration, 421

National Population Censuses, Principles and Recommendations for, 731
National Portrait Gallery, Report, 362, 636, 890, 1163
National Products:
  And Expenditure. Statistics, 449
  Of 55 Countries, 461
National Register of Archives:
  860
  List of Accessions to Repositories, 1137
National Research Development Corporation. Report and Accounts, 16, 182, 228, 398, 495, 515, 667, 782, 923
National Retail Distribution:
  Certificates, Award of, 101
  Retail Management, Arrangements and Conditions for the Award of Certificates, 843
National Savings Committee Report, 155, 362, 636, 1163
National Service Acts:
  Decisions in respect of Liability to be called up for Service, 630
  Decisions on Applications for Postponement of Liability to be called up, 356, 885
  Reinstatement in Civil Employment, 1158
National Service. Decisions by Umpire in respect of Postponement for Call Up. Pamphlet, 149
National Service Men:
  Committee Report on their Employment in the U.K. *Cmnd. 35*. 54, 206
  Regulations Amendments, 425, 695, 955
National Social Service Programmes, Development of, 1251
National Youth Employment Council Report, 876
Nationalised Industries and Undertakings:
  Accounts, 496, 587, 765, 766, 1020, 1171
  Select Committee Reports, 240, 337, 502, 509, 607, 770, 773, 865, 866, 1029, 1143
  Special Report, 1034, 1144
Nationalised Industries Loans Act, 541
Nationalised Industries Loans Bill, 480, 517
Nationalised Transport Undertakings Reorganisation. *Cmnd. 1248*. 1069
Nationality of Married Women, Convention on. *Cmnd. 200*. 181, 311, *Cmnd. 601*. 539, 592
Native Courts and Native Customary Law in Africa. Judicial Advisers' Conference, 300, 1104
Natural Durability of Timber, 908
Natural Gas. Report on Position in European Economy, 459
Natural Hatching, 71
Natural History Museum Guide, 296, 564
Natural History of Rennell Islands, British Solomon Islands, 564, 828, 1098
Natural Resources Technical Committee Report, 382, 652
Naturalization Return, 221
Nature Conservancy:
  Report, 30, 151, 244, 359, 514, 632, 781, 887, 1039, 1178
  Select Committee on Estimates Report, 506, 606, 1023, 1143
  The First Ten Years, 890
Nature of Conflict, 469
Nature of Production in the Sea, 823
Nauru. United Nations Visiting Mission to Trust Territories in the Pacific. Report, 464, 1261
Nautical Almanac:
  60, 276, 545, 813, 1075
  And Astronomical Ephemeris, 60, 276, 545
Nautical Subjects. Teaching in Secondary Schools, 386
Naval and Marine Reserves Pay Act, 272
Naval and Marine Reserves Pay Bill, 216 248
Naval and Military Forces (Attachment) Regulations, 956
Naval Architecture. Arrangements and Conditions for the Award of National Certificates, 843
Naval Court-Martial Procedure:
  Amendment, 60, 276
  Memorandum, 545
Naval Discipline Act, 272
Naval Discipline Act, Select Committee Report, 27, 126
Naval Discipline Bill, 216, 218, 247, 248, 249
Naval Electrical Pocket-Book, Amendments, 276, 545
Naval Marine Engineering Practice, 60, 1074
Naval Research and Development:
  Select Committee on Estimates Report, 23 125
Navigation:
  Admiralty Manual of, 60, 276, 546, 813, 1074
  Instruments of, 635
  Scottish Certificate of Education, 913
Navy:
  Appropriation Account, 11, 60, 225, 276, 492, 546, 759, 813, 1016, 1074
  Career, 347
  Dockyard and Production Accounts, 15, 61, 228, 276, 497, 546, 762, 813, 1021, 1074
  Estimates:
    1955–56 Supplementary, 13, 61
    1956–57:
      12, 21, 61
      Revised, 21, 61
      Statement. *Cmd. 9697*. 39, 61

Navy (*continued*):
  Estimates (*continued*):
    1956–57 (*continued*)
      Supplementary, 226, 277
    1957–58:
      226, 230, 277
      Explanatory Statement. *Cmnd. 151*. 259, 277
      Supplementary, 493, 546
    1958–59:
      493, 546
      Explanatory Statement. *Cmnd. 371*. 523, 546
      Supplementary, 759, 813
    1959–60:
      759, 813
      Explanatory Statement. *Cmnd. 674*. 792, 813
      Supplementary, 1017, 1074
    1960–61:
      1017, 1074
      Explanatory Statement. *Cmnd. 949*. 1048, 1074
      Supplementary, 1028, 1202
  List:
    61, 277, 546, 813, 1074
    Appendix, 277
  Retired Pay, Pensions, 160
  Statement of Excess, 1956–57, 496, 546
  Training Courses, 202, 421
  Votes:
    1954–55, 12, 197
    1955–56, 17, 197, 226, 410
    1956–57, 229, 410
    1957–58, 498, 680, 761, 814
    1958–59, 770, 937, 1020, 1206
    1959–60, 1022, 1206
Navy, Army and Air Force Reserves Act, 809
Navy, Army and Air Force Reserves Bill, 488, 520
Neden, Sir W. (Chairman: Cost of Living Advisory Committee) Report on Proposals for New Index of Retail Prices. *Cmd. 9710*. 40
Needles, Pins, Fish Hooks and Metal Smallwares. Census of Production Report, 664
Negotiations for a European Free Trade Area:
  Documents. *Cmnd. 641*. 789, 937
  Report. *Cmnd. 648*. 790, 937
Negro in the United States of America, 736
Neighbouring Rights, 237A
Neill, C. A., Weight Gains, Serum Protein Levels and Health of Breast Fed and Artificially Fed Infants, Full Term and Premature, 887
Nelson and Bronte, 635
Nelson, H. I., Report on Inquiry into Proposed Compulsory Amalgamation of Police Forces in Counties of Carmarthen and Cardigan. *Cmnd. 374*. 523, 605
Nematodirus Disease in Lambs, 1084
Neolithic Revolution, 828
Neotropical Acanthocinini (Coleoptera: Cerambycidae). 11. Genus Lagocheirus, Revision of, 562
Netherlands:
  Convention with U.K. on Social Security. *Cmd. 9792*. 44, 108
  Economic Conditions, 1246
  Exchange of Letters with U.K.:
    Concerning the Agreement for Repayment of Credits granted by the European Payments Union. *Cmd. 9848*. 49, 108
    Concerning the Convention on the Rights and Obligations of Foreign Forces in Germany. *Cmd. 9872*. 51, 108
    Prolonging the Agreement concerning the Division of Responsibility for Rights and Obligations of Forces in Germany. *Cmnd. 413*. 526, 592
  Exchange of Notes with U.K.:
    Amending the Cultural Convention. *Cmnd. 382*. 524, 592
    Concerning the Arrangements to Facilitate Travel. *Cmnd. 1080*. 1056, 1123
    Concerning the Reciprocal Validation of Airworthiness Certificates. *Cmnd. 671*. 791, 851
    Extending to the Netherlands Antilles Convention for the Avoidance of Double Taxation, etc. *Cmd. 9766*. 43, 108; *Cmnd. 452*. 528, 592
    Respecting the Repayment of the Debt on the Liquidation of the European Payments Union. *Cmnd. 764*. 798, 851
  Foreign Trade Statistical Bulletin, 222A, 447, 448, 717, 977, 978
Network of Intra-European Trade, 447, 718, 978
Neue Erotyliden Aus Dem Britischen Museum, 562
Neuroptera and Trichoptera Collected by Mr. J. D. Bradley on Guadalcanal Island, 295
New Atomic Achievements in the Commonwealth. Poster, 614
New Atomic Age, 459
New Caledonia and Dependencies. International Customs Journal, 714, 1244
New College of Further Education, 842
New Contributions to Economic Statistics, 829
New Grants for Better Homes, 858, 870
New Guinea:
  International Customs Journal, 444
  Special Questionnaire for the Trust Territory, 992

New Guinea (*continued*):
  United Nations Visiting Mission to the Trust Territories. Report, 464, 1261
New Hebrides:
  Colonial Report, 569
  Condominium. International Customs Journal, 1244
  Exchange of Notes between U.K. and France concerning:
    Mining Regulations. *Cmnd. 667*. 791, 848
    Revision of Penal System in the New Hebrides. *Cmnd. 668*. 791, 848
  Report, 1102
New Houses in the Country. Circular, 1146
New Industrial Revolutions, 231A
New Labyrinthodont (Paracyclotosaurus) from the Upper Trias of New South Wales, 563
New Products. Guidebook for Manufacturers Developing and Selling, 200
New Siphonaptera from Eastern Mediterranean Countries, 1095
New States and International Organisations Report, 239A
New Streets Act, 1951 (Amendment) Act, 273
New Streets Act, 1951 (Amendment) Act, Circular, 341
New Streets Act, 1951 (Amendment) Bill, 36, 225, 243, 247, 337
New Towns, 1266
New Towns Act:
  541, 809
  Accounts, 19, 121, 130, 232, 330, 342, 495, 613, 760, 870, 1021, 1132, 1147
  Development Corporations Reports, 21, 24, 130, 172, 236, 237, 342, 505, 506, 613, 656, 776, 779, 870, 915, 1030, 1031, 1147, 1187
  Reports, 236, 237, 388
New Towns Bill, 249, 479, 520, 752, 769, 779, 864
New Trends in Youth Organisations, 1264
New Year's Honours Lists, 150, 357, 631, 917, 1189, 1190
New Zealand:
  Agreement with U.K. on Social Security. *Cmd. 9682*. 38, 91
  International Customs Journal, 444, 973
  Marketing Agreement with U.K. *Cmnd. 194*. 262, 398
  Overseas Economic Survey, 182
  School Publications Branch, 736
  Trade Agreement. *Cmnd. 830*. 802, 923
Newall, R. S., Stonehenge, Wiltshire, Guide, 957
Newcastle and Gateshead Water (No. 2) Order Bill, 1005
Newcastle Central Station. Railway Accident Report, 1198
Newcastle-upon-Tyne Corporation Act, 58, 1072
Newcomer to World Trade Guide, 421
Newcraighall Colliery. Midlothian, Haulage Accident Report. *Cmnd. 205*. 263, 377
Newell, B. S.:
  Hydrography of the British East African Coastal Waters, 833
  Preliminary Survey of the Hydrography of the British East African Coastal Waters, 302
Newlay and Horsforth Railway Accident Report, 404
Newman, O. F., Hydrographical Survey of the River Usk, 291
Newspapers and Periodicals:
  Printing and Publishing. Census of Production Report, 665
  Statistics of, 996, 1266
Newton, L. British Seaweeds Handbook, 828
Niblett, Professor W. R. (Chairman: University Grants Committee Sub-Committee) Report, 409
Nicaragua:
  Exchange of Notes with U.K. extending Treaty for Regulation of Turtle Fishing by the Cayman Islanders in Nicaraguan Territorial Waters. *Cmnd. 1201*. 1065, 1123
  International Customs Journal, 444, 974
Nicothoe astaci Auduin and Milne Edwards on Scottish Lobsters, Occurrence of, 656
Nigeria:
  And Cameroons Land Tenure and Land Administration, 302
  And Southern Cameroons. Order-in-Council, 1174
  Arms, 1101
  Becomes a Sovereign Nation:
    Photoposter, 1150
    Picture Set, 1149
  Colonial Report, 569
  Constitutional Conference Report. *Cmnd. 207*. 263, 303; *Cmnd. 596*. 536, 571
  Constitutional Discussions. *Cmnd. 1063*. 1055, 1104
  Eastern Region of Arms, 1101
  Fears of Minorities and the Means of Allaying Them. Report. *Cmnd. 505*. 532, 571
  Fiscal Commission Report, *Cmnd. 481*. 530, 571
  Flag Badge, 1103
  International Bank Loan, 503, 677
  International Customs Journal, 444, 1244
  International Rights and Obligations. Exchange of Letters with U.K. *Cmnd. 1214*. 1066, 1106

Nigeria (*continued*):
  Northern Region, Arms, 832
  Overseas Economic Survey, 398
  Proposed Defence Agreement with U.K. *Cmnd. 1212*. 1066, 1106, 1114
  Statement of Policy regarding Overseas Officers. *Cmnd. 497*. 531, 571
  The Making of a Nation, 1150
  Traffic and Transport in, 1103
  Treasury Minute relative to Gifts. *Cmnd. 636*. 789, 934
  Tribunal of Inquiry Report on Allegations reflecting on the Official Conduct of the Premier. *Cmnd. 51*. 251, 303
  Western Region, Colonial Arms, 569
Nigerian Independence Act, 1071
Nigerian Independence Bill, 1010, 1043
Nimrud Ivories. Catalogue, 294
Nitrogen. Industrial Uses, 449
Nitrogeneous Fertilisers for Farm Crops, 1083
Nixon, H. M., Royal English Bookbindings in the British Museum, 294
Noakes, G. R., Electrical Fundamental, 425
Noble, Commander Allan (Chairman: Oversea Migration Board) Report. *Cmd. 9835*. 48
Noblecourt, A., Protection of Cultural Property in the Event of Armed Conflict, 737
Noise Abatement Act, 1071
Noise Abatement Act Circular, 1146
Noise Abatement Bill, 1008, 1009, 1010, 1025, 1037, 1041, 1043, 1044, 1141
Noise in Factories, 1179
Noise in Three Groups of Flats with Different Floor Insulations, 909
Nomads and Migrants, Education of, 238A
Nomads and Nomadism in the Arid Zone, 1265
Nomenclature of Fungi Pathogenic to Man and Animals, 633
Non-Ferrous Foundries. Joint Standing Committee Report on Safety, Health and Welfare Conditions, 356
Non-Ferrous Metals:
  Census of Production Report, 663
  Corrosion of, 648
  Industry in Europe, 224A
  In Under-Developed Countries, 231A
  Statistics of, 450, 718, 978
Non-Metalliferous Mines and Quarries Census of Production Report, 179, 663
Non-Metalliferous Mining Products except Coal, Treatment of Censuses of Production Report, 180
Non-Self-Governing Territories:
  Committee of Information Report, 230A, 456, 726, 984, 1255
Non-Self-Governing Territories (*continued*):
  Economic Conditions, 722
  Special Study on Social Conditions, 233A
  Summaries and Analyses of Information, 231A, 459
"Nordicstar" Wreck Report, 675
North Atlantic:
  Climatological Charts, 360
  Council Ministerial Meeting. *Cmnd. 339*. 271, 321
  Fixed Services Meeting:
    972
    Report, 442
    Supplement, 442
  Ice Patrol. Agreement regarding the Financial Support. *Cmd. 9864*. 50, 108
  Region Air Navigation Plans, 1241
North Atlantic Treaty Organisation:
  220A, 445
  Agreement for the Mutual Safeguarding of Secrecy of Inventions. *Cmnd. 1220*. 1067, 1123
North Borneo:
  1103
  Colonial Report, 88, 301, 570, 833
  Order-in-Council, 1174
North Devon Water Act, 812
North-East Surrey Crematorium Board Act, 58
North Almham Saxon Cathedral, Norfolk. Guide, 1226
North, Sir George (Chairman: Inter-Departmental Committee on Social and Economic Research) Report, 151
North of Scotland College of Agriculture Educational Endowments Scheme:
  Memorandum, 169
  Order-in-Council, 169
North of Scotland Development Corporation Bill, 247
North of Scotland Electricity Order Confirmation Act, 811
North of Scotland Electricity Order Confirmation Bill, 520
North of Scotland Hydro-Electric Board:
  Constructional Scheme:
    Cmnd. 408. 526
    Explanatory Memorandum. *Cmnd. 32*. 172; *Cmnd. 494*. 531; *Cmnd. 681*. 792, 914
  Guarantee given on Loans proposed to be raised, 10, 18, 19, 22, 26, 27, 172, 196, 224, 231, 235, 240, 493, 501, 507, 510, 515, 679, 767, 774, 780, 936, 1018, 1025, 1031, 1034, 1204
  Report and Accounts, 13, 172, 225, 388, 495, 656, 760, 915, 1017, 1187
North of Scotland Milk Marketing Scheme, 553

NOR-OUT | 1956-60

NOR— INDEX 1956-60

North York Moors National Park, 362
Northampton County Council Act, 1072
"Northern Crown" Wreck Report, 406
Northern Highlands, British Regional Geology, 1131
Northern Ireland (Compensation for Compulsory Purchase) Act, 273
Northern Ireland (Compensation for Compulsory Purchase) Bill, 32, 36, 214, 222, 338
Northern Ireland, Disqualification of Certain Members. *Cmd. 9698*. 39, 124
Northern Rhodesia:
  Colonial Report, 87, 301, 570, 833, 1102
  Order-in-Council, 1174
  Proposals for Constitutional Change. *Cmnd. 530*. 534, 571
Northwest Atlantic Fisheries. Protocol to the International Convention. *Cmd. 9874*. 51, 108
Norway:
  Agreement with U.K. respecting the Repayment of the Debt on the Liquidation of the European Payments Union. *Cmnd. 758*. 797, 851
  Consular Convention with U.K. *Cmnd. 590*. 538, 592
  Convention on Social Security with U.K. *Cmnd. 252*. 266, 321; *Cmnd. 422*. 527, 592
  Economic Conditions, 1246
  Exchange of Notes with U.K.:
    Amending the Air Services Agreement. *Cmnd. 44*. 251, 321
    Extending to Rhodesia and Nyasaland the Convention for the Avoidance of Double Taxation, etc. *Cmnd. 1062*. 1055, 1123
    Regarding Co-operation in the Promotion and Development of the Peaceful Uses of Atomic Energy. *Cmnd. 245, 277*. 265, 267, 321
  Fishery Agreement with U.K. *Cmnd. 1224*. 1067, 1123
  Foreign Trade Statistical Bulletin, 222A, 448, 717, 977, 978
  International Customs Journal, 444, 714, 1244
Norwegian Loans (France *v*. Norway) Order, 219A, 443, 713, 973
Nosema Disease, 820
Nosov, A. V., Working Metals by Electro-Sparking, 168
Notice to Treat, Form of Claim in Answer to, 857, 936
Notifiable Diseases. *See* Epidemiological and Vital Statistics
Notification of Communicable Diseases, 999
Nottebohm Case (Liechtenstein *v*. Guatemala) Judgment, 220A
Nottinghamshire Map, *See* Lincolnshire
Novitates Himalaicae—I, 80
Now Wash Your Hands Notice, 857
Nuclear and Allied Radiations. Report on Hazards to Man. *Cmd. 9780*. 44, 151; *Cmnd. 1225*. 1067, 1160
Nuclear Attack, Estimated Damage from, Diagrams, 604
Nuclear Chemistry and Effects of Irradiation, 231A
Nuclear Data and Reactor Theory, 986
Nuclear Electronics. Proceedings of the International Symposium, 1240
Nuclear Energy:
  As a New Source, Outlook for, 1257
  Convention on the Establishment of a Security Control. *Cmnd. 971*. 1049, 1117
  Convention on Third Party Liability. *Cmnd. 1211*. 1066, 1124
  Developments in Peaceful Applications, 1240
  In Britain, 345
  Industrial Challenge, 448, 718, 976, 1248
  Industry of the United Kingdom, 951
  Joint Action by OEEC Countries, 223
  Legal, Administrative, Health and Safety Aspects, 232
  Physics in, 986
  Possibilities of Action. Report, 223A
  Post-Graduate Training in Public Health Aspects Report, 742
  Production Technology of Materials Used, 231A
  See also Atomic Energy
Nuclear Equipment and Instrumentation, Market for, 1248
Nuclear Explosions, Effects of High-Yield, 421
Nuclear Generating Station Report, 388
Nuclear Industries in the Community. European Atomic Energy Community, Report on the Position, 963
Nuclear Installations, Health Physics in, 1248
Nuclear Installations (Licensing and Insurance) Act, 809
Nuclear Installations (Licensing and Insurance) Bill, 486, 488, 489, 521, 752, 768, 779, 783, 864
Nuclear Materials and Isotopes Production of, 986
Nuclear Physics and Instrumentation, 986
Nuclear Power:
  Plants, 986
  Programme. *Cmnd. 1083*. 1057, 1173
  Role of, 231A
  Station at Trawsfynydd Report, 645
Nuclear-Powered Merchant Ships. Report of the Committee on Safety. *Cmnd. 958*. 1048, 1198

INDEX 1956-60 —OCC

Nuclear Reactors:
  1239
  Catalogue of, 198
  Directory of, 969, 1239
Nuclear Research. Convention for the Establishment of a European Organisation. *Cmnd. 928*. 1046, 1117
Nuclear Tests, Suspension of. *Cmnd. 551*. 535
Nuclear Weapons:
  123, 862
  Effects of, 421
Nugent, G. R. H. (Chairman):
  Committee on London Roads. Report. *Cmnd. 812*. 801
  Road Safety Committee Report, 403
Numerical Tables, S.R. and O. and S.I. Supplement, 918, 1191
Nunney Castle, Somerset, Guide, 427
Nurses Act, 273
Nurses Agencies Act, 273
Nurses Agencies Act, Report, 7, 8
Nurses Agencies Bill, 6, 36
Nurses (Amendment) Bill, 1045
Nurses Bill, 6, 36
Nurses Bill, Report, 7, 8
Nurses Uniforms. Report of Sub-Committee on Design, 859
Nursing:
  And Midwifery. Career, 618
  Education Programmes for Foreign Students. Report of a Conference, 1269
  Expert Committee Report, 999
  For Men. Career, 618
  Service. Principles of Administration applied to, 740
Nutrition:
  And Society, 243A
  Committee for South and East Asia Report, 437
  Committee for the Middle East Report, 1237
  Expert Committee Report, 741
  Manual of, 824
  Meetings Reports, 437, 708, 967, 1237
  Principles of Good, 692
  Problems in Latin America, 967
Nutritional Study, 242A, 437, 708, 968
Nyasaland:
  Colonial Report, 88, 301, 570, 833, 1102
  Commission of Inquiry Report. *Cmnd. 814*. 801, 834
  Constitutional Conference Report. *Cmnd. 1132*. 1060, 1104
  Despatch by the Governor. *Cmnd. 815*. 801, 834
  Land of the Lake, 89
  State of Emergency. *Cmnd. 707*. 794, 834
Nyasaland-Mozambique Frontier Agreement between U.K. and Portugal. *Cmnd. 528*. 534
Nye, J. W. B., Insect Pests of Graminaceous Crops in East Africa, 1103
Nylon Monofilaments, 391

O

Oak and Beech, Provisional Yield Tables, 596
Oak Leaf Roller Moth, 112
Oak Mildew, 113
Oakley, K. P.:
  Man the Tool-Maker, 82, 564
  Succession of Life through Geological Time, 296, 828
Oaths Act 1888 (Amendment) Bill, 1045
Oats:
  824
  Varieties, Key to, 70
Oban Burgh Order Confirmation Act, 59
Oban Burgh Order Confirmation Bill, 36
Oberholzer, V. G., Weight Gains, Serum Protein Levels and Health of Breast Fed and Artificially Fed Infants, Full Term and Premature, 887
Obscene and Profane Words Bill, 1045
Obscene Publications Act, 809
Obscene Publications Bill:
  237, 247, 338, 497, 520, 608, 749, 751, 764, 779, 784, 786, 864
  Select Committee Report, 497, 608
  Special Report, 237
Observations in Astronomy, Magnetism and Meteorology, 120, 599
Observatories' Year Book, 152, 360, 634, 889, 1161
Observer's Handbook:
  360
  Amendment, 889
Occasional Licences and Young Persons Act, 56
Occasional Licences and Young Persons Bill, 3, 18, 30, 33, 126
Occupation Regime, Germany. Protocol on Termination. *Cmnd. 658*. 791, 850
Occupation Tables, Census, E. and W., 327
Occupational Accidents in the United States, Prevention of, 449
Occupational Diseases, Notes on Diagnosis of, 636
Occupational Health:
  Committee Report, 741
  Public Health Service in, 421
Occupational Mortality, 597
Occupational Pension Schemes, 680
Occupational Therapist, Career, 876
Occupations and Industries, 119
Occupations, Classification of, 118, 1130
Occupations of Totally Blinded Veterans of World War II and Korea, 421
Occupiers' Liability Act, 273

OCC— INDEX 1956-60

Occupiers' Liability Bill, 4, 36, 216, 229, 243, 338
Occupiers' Liability (Scotland) Act, 1071
Occupiers' Liability (Scotland) Bill, 749, 752, 783, 786, 1005, 1014, 1017, 1037, 1141
Occurrence of Nicothoe astaci Andouin and Milne Edwards on Scottish Lobsters, 656
"Ocean Harvest" Wreck Report, 1200
"Ocean Layer" Wreck Report, 1200
Ocean Shipowners' Tally Clerks. Report, 1158
Ocean Station Vessel Manual Amendment, 218A
Oceanographic Research Stations:
  Agreement between U.K. and U.S.A.:
    Barbados. *Cmnd. 68*. 253
    Bahama Islands. *Cmnd. 343*. 521, 595
    Turks and Caicos Islands. *Cmnd. 94*. 255
Oceanography. *See* Mariners, Meteorology for
O'Dea, W. T., Short History of Lighting, 905
O'Doherty, E. F., Individual Differences in Light. Vision Efficiency, 359
Odonata and some Trichoptera from S. Rhodesia and Portuguese East Africa, New Species and Subspecies, 563
Odonata collected by Mr. J. D. Bradley on Guadalcanal Island, 295
Odontology of Oreopithecus, Contribution to, 828
OEEC:
  And the Common Market, 718
  Bibliography, 223A, 449
  Countries. Statistical Bulletins Foreign Trade, 1248
  General Catalogue of Books, 719
  Publications, 220–4, 445, 715–20, 974, 1245
  Report, 223A, 718, 979
Off the Beaten Track, 985
Offences of Drunkenness; E. and W. Statistics. *Cmd. 9888*. 52, 124; *Cmnd. 280*. 268, 335; *Cmnd. 573*. 537, 605; *Cmnd. 807*. 801, 862; *Cmnd. 1094*. 1057, 1139
Offences Relating to Motor Vehicles. Return, 31, 124, 189, 245, 335, 405, 515, 605, 771, 862, 1028, 1139
Offenders for Probation, Selection of, 989
Offenders in Britain, Treatment of, 1150
Offenders, Young, Custodial Sentences for. Report, 1186
Offensive, The, 1098, 1189
Offices Act, 1071
Offices Bill, 787, 1006, 1008, 1021, 1037, 1042, 1043, 1141
Offices Regulation Bill, 250, 784
Official Gazette, European Coal and Steel Community, 102, 435
Official Guide to the Documents exhibited in Historical Museum, Register House, Edinburgh, 916
Official Lists:
  118, 328, 1130
  Buildings for Marriages, 855
  Registration Officers, 598, 856
Official Publications:
  680
  And Government Documents, Convention concerning Exchange between States. *Cmnd. 1241*. 1069, 1127
  Brief Guide, 1190
Official Sources, Guide to, 598
Official Statistics, Studies in, 83, 885, 886, 1099
Oil:
  And New World, 240A
  Europe's Need for, 716
  Heaters. *See* Effects of Draught
  Outlook for Europe, 224A
Oil Burners (Standards) Act, 1071
Oil Burners (Standards) Bill, 1008, 1042, 1043
Oil Burning Apparatus. Standing Committee Report. *Cmd. 9686*. 38, 182
Oil-Fired Warm Air System Test, 585
Oils:
  and Greases, Census of Production Report, 394
  Marketing of Major Edible, 231A
Oilseeds, 448
Okerblom, N.O., Calculations of Deformations of Welded Metal Structures, 649
Okinawa. Victory in the Pacific, 202
Old Age. Provision for. National Insurance Scheme. *Cmnd. 538*. 534, 639
Old Royal Library, 294
Old Trafford Junction Railway Accident Report, 189
Older Worker and his Job, 1181
Oldfield-Davies, A., (Chairman: Central Advisory Council for Education in Wales) Report, 100, 1115
Oldham Corporation Act, 1072
Oldroyd, H.:
  Horse Flies of the Ethiopian Region, 295
  Insects and Their World, 1097
Olethreutinae and Carposinidae in the British Museum (Natural History) Additions to Descriptions of New, 827
Oligocene Flora of the Bovey Tracey Lake Basin, Devonshire, 563
Olive Oil:
  International Agreement and Protocol of Amendment. *Cmnd. 549*. 535, 592; *Cmnd. 954*. 1048, 1124
  Market, Stabilisation of, 241A
  Processing in Rural Mills, 435

INDEX 1956-60 —OUT

Olive Oil (*continued*):
  United Nations Conference Proceedings, 231A
Oliver, E. I., Nigeria. Overseas Economic Survey, 398
Olley, J., Preservation of Fish and Fish Offal for Oil and Meal Manufacture, 907, 1183
Olson, W. C., Psychological Foundations of the Curriculum, 736
Oman, C., Gloucester Candlestick, 951
On the Nature of Production in the Sea, 823
Onchsheshorqy, Instructions of, 79
One Hundred Masterpieces from the National Gallery, 154
One-Man Work in Mixed Stands of Beech, Spruce and Fir, 437
Onion Fly, 555
Onions:
  820
  And Leeks:
    Chemical Weed Control, 1084
    Shallots, Diseases of, 287
Opencast Coal Act, 541
Opencast Coal Bill, 250, 483, 484, 485, 502, 512, 518, 519, 608
Operating Costs of Machinery in Tropical Agriculture, Symposium on, 300
Operating Theatre Suites, 602
Operation and Finance of the Legal Aid and Advice Act. Law Society Report, 632
Operations in Egypt. Despatch, 357
Ophthalmic Optician and the Dispensing Optician. Career, 136
Ophthalmic Services:
  Fees and Charges, 1137
  Supplementary, 860
  Supply and Repair of Glasses, 332
Opium:
  And Other Narcotic Drugs Report, 227A, 1252
  See Poppy Plant
Optical Grade of Polystyrene, 391
Opticians Act, 541A
Opticians Bill, 250, 480, 494, 512, 517, 608
Oracular Amuletic Decrees of the Late New Kingdom, 1094
Oram, P. A., Pastures and Fodder Crops in Rotations in Mediterranean Agriculture, 241A
Orchards:
  Renovation and Improvement, 288
  Soils, Management and Manuring, 288
Orders, Decorations and Medals. Order of Precedence, 631
Orders-in-Council, 1168, 1173
Orders of Battle. U.K. Colonial Formations and Units in the Second World War, 1098
Ordnance Survey Report, 155, 362, 636, 1163
Ordovician Trilobite Faunas of South Shropshire, 1096
Ores, Low Grade, 718
Organe, G. S. W., Report on Confidential Enquiries into Maternal Deaths in England and Wales, 1136
Organisation and Management of Domestic Work in Hospitals, 1134
Organisation and Methods Division. Procedure Records, 937
Organisation for Control of Health and Safety in United Kingdom Atomic Energy Authority. *Cmnd. 342*. 521, 690
Organisation of Building Sites, 909
Organisation of Museums. Practical Advice, 1265
Oriental Books and Manuscripts. Catalogues, 827
Oriental Lycaenidae, Revision of the Arhopala Group, 295
Origin and Evolution of Coal, 1132
Origin of Goods. False Indications of. International Agreement. *Cmnd. 876*. 805, 848
Ornithology of Western South Africa, Contribution to. Results of British Museum (Natural History) South West Africa Expedition, 1949–50, 562
Orthoptist. Career, 136
Osborne House, Isle of Wight. Guide, 1227
Ostracod Hinge Structure, Evolution and Nomenclature, 80
O'Sullivan, R., (Chairman: Committee of Investigation on Complaints made against Operation of British Wool Marketing Scheme) Report, 556
Otiorrhynchine Curculionidae of the Tribe Celeuthetini, 82
Ouin, Marc, OEEC and the Common Market, 718
Our Children's Teeth. Report, 1132
Our Rights as Human Beings, 231A
Our Unknown Planet, 459
Ouse. *See* River Great Ouse
Outdoor Rhubarb. Film Strip, 554
Outdoor Salad Crops, 72
Outdoor Tomatoes, 288
Outer Seven Plan. *See* Stockholm Draft Plan
Outlook for Energy Sources. Resources for Freedom Report, 203
Outlook for Key Commodities. Resources for Freedom Report, 203
Outlook for Nuclear Energy as a New Source of Power, 1257
Out-Patient Waiting Time. Report, 602
Output and Utilization of Farm Produce in the U.K., 559
Output, Expenses and Income of Agriculture in Some European Countries. Report, 729

1956-60 | OVE-PHA

OVE— INDEX 1956-60

Overfishing:
Amendments to the Convention. *Cmnd. 1181.* 1064, 1124
Convention for Regulations. *Cmd. 9704.* 39, 106; *Cmnd. 731.* 795, 851
Overseas:
Civil Service:
Appointments, 300
Organisation. *Cmd. 9768.* 43, 89
Statement of Policy regarding Overseas Officers serving in Nigeria. *Cmnd. 497.* 531, 571
Commonwealth Forces. Arrangements for Employment in Emergency Operations in Malaya. *Cmnd. 264.* 267
Development Assistance from the U.K. *Cmnd. 974.* 1049, 1201
Economic Surveys, 182, 398, 667, 923
Education, 89, 303, 430, 572, 834, 1104
Food Corporation Report and Accounts, 13, 89
Geodetic and Topographical Surveys, Directorate of, Report, 833
Geological Surveys:
572
Mineral Resources Division, 1104
Report, 832, 1104
Geology and Mineral Resources:
430, 572, 834, 1104
Bulletin Supplement, 572
Governments, Service with. *Cmnd. 1193.* 1065, 1104
Information Services. *Cmnd. 225.* 264, 303, 305, 321, 357, 398, 410; *Cmnd. 685.* 792, 834, 836, 851, 886, 923, 937
Migration Board:
Report. *Cmd. 9835.* 48, 91; *Cmnd. 336.* 271, 305; *Cmnd. 619.* 540, 572; *Cmnd. 975, 1243.* 1049, 1069, 1107
Statistics, 91
Supply, Studies of, 82, 174
Technical Reports, 167, 651
Territories, Main Products, 223A
Trade Reports, 182, 398, 430, 667, 923, 1194
Overseas Resources Development Act:
56, 542, 810
Account, 225, 303, 492, 572, 756, 834, 1018, 1104
Overseas Resources Development Bill, 6, 95, 250, 479, 480, 701
Overseas Resources Development, Consolidation Bills Report, 745, 747, 866
Overseas Service Act, 542
Overseas Service Bill, 250, 479, 1045
"Overton" Wreck Report, 192
Owner Cultivator in a Progressive Agriculture, 706
Oxley, T. A., Underground Storage of Grain, 88
Oyster:
Cultivation in Britain, 74
Production in the Rivers Crouch and Roach, 292
Stock in the Rivers Crouch and Roach, 292
Oystercatcher, Winter Feeding of, on Edible Mussel in Conway Estuary, North Wales, 559

P

Pachycephala Pectoralis. Super-Species, Variation, Relationships and Evolution in the, 81
Pacific Islands:
Trust Territory Report, 464
Trusteeship Agreement for Trust Territory, 464
United Nations Visiting Mission to the Trust Territories Report, 1261
Pacific Region Air Navigation:
Meeting Report, 216A
Plan, 1241
Packed Bricks, 905
Packaging for Fruit and Vegetables, Wooden, 720
Paediatric Education Report, Study Group on, 472
Page, H. J., Efficient Use of Fertilisers, 966
Paget-Tomlinson, E. W., Instruments of Navigation, 635
Paige, D., Comparison of National Output and Productivity of U.K. and U.S., 975
Paint:
And Printing Ink, Report on the Census of Production, 1194
And Varnish. Census of Production Report, 394
Emulsion, 207
Painter and Decorator. Career, 1152
Painting and Decorating Contracting Business, Establishing and Operating, 202
Painting Catalogues:
British School, 154
Children from the National Gallery, 154
Colour Reproductions, 237A, 468, 994
Earlier Italian Schools, 154
Early Netherlandish School, 154
One Hundred Masterpieces from the National Gallery, 154
Paintings and Drawings on the Backs of National Gallery Pictures, 154
Spanish School, 154
Paintings:
Illustrations:
British School, 154
Continental Schools, 154
Italian Schools, 154

INDEX 1956-60 —PAR

Paintings (*continued*):
National Maritime Museum, Greenwich, Concise Catalogue, 635
Prior to 1860, Catalogue of Colour Reproductions, 1263
Some Eighteenth Century Bird, in the Library of Sir Joseph Banks, 828
Pakistan:
Exchange of Notes with U.K. constituting an Agreement to amend the Air Services Agreement. *Cmnd. 153.* 259, 403
Loan of Anti-Aircraft Equipment. *Cmnd. 367.* 523, 679
Pakistan (Consequential Provision) Act, 56
Pakistan (Consequential Provision) Bill, 2, 33
Palace of Holyrood House. Guide, 1227
Palaeontology. Geological Survey Memoir, 857
Palestine Refugees in the Near East. United Nations Relief and Works Agency:
Accounts, 455, 726, 1255
Announcements:
984
Of Pledges of Contributions, Report, 983
Report, 455, 725, 983, 984
Special Report of the Director, 455
Palmar, C. E., Woodpeckers in Woodlands, 596
Panama International Customs Journal, 974
Pandalus Montagui Leach, Biology of, 292
Panel on Vertical Separation of Aircraft. Report, 712
Pant, D. D., Structure of Some Leaves and Fructifications of the Glossopteris Flora of Tanganyika, 563
Papal Letters, 1471, and 1484, 162
Papal Registers. Calendar of Entries relating to Great Britain and Ireland, 162
Paper:
And Board. Census of Production Report, 179, 395
World Demand to 1975, 1238
Papua International Customs Journal, 445
Parade and Rifle Drill. Royal Naval Handbook Amendment, 277, 814, 1075
Paraguay: Agreement with U.K. on Trade and Payments. *Cmd. 9683, 9850.* 38, 49, 108
Parish Councils Act, 273
Parish Councils Act Circular, 341
Parish Councils (Miscellaneous Provisions) Bill, 218, 247
See also National Health Service (Amendment) Bill
Parishes, etc., Index to, 359, 886, 1159
Park Gate Iron and Steel Co. Ltd., Proposal to Sell Holdings of Securities. *Cmd. 9699.* 39
Park Lane Improvement Act, 542
Park Lane Improvement Act, Select Committee Special Report, 497, 608
Park Lane Improvement Bill, 249, 481, 484, 497, 513, 518, 519, 608
Parker, Rt. Hon. Sir H. L. (Chairman: Tribunal to Inquire into Allegations that Information about the Raising of Bank Rate was Improperly Disclosed):
Proceedings, 603
Report. *Cmnd. 350.* 522, 603
Parker, H. M. D., Manpower, 296
Parker, H. W., Lizard Genus Apraisia, Its Taxonomy and Temperature—Correlated Variation, 81
Parking, P. H., Noise in Three Groups of Flats with Different Floor Insulations, 909
Parking Places in:
St. Marylebone Plan, 929
Westminster Plan, 672
Parking Survey Inner London Report, 188, 672
Parliament Bill, 517
Parliament, Dissolution of:
918
Honours, 918
Parliamentary Agents, Attornies, Solicitors and Others, List of Charges, 7, 29, 126, 128
Parliamentary Debates of Great Britain, 59, 126
Parliamentary Elections (Scotland). Instructions, 915
Parliamentary Institutions in the Commonwealth, 345
Parliamentary Papers, House of Commons and Command Sessional Index, 8, 126, 338, 755, 864, 1012, 1142
Parliamentary Privilege Act Order-in-Council. *Cmnd. 431.* 527, 605
Parochial Church Councils (Powers) Measure:
3, 59, 83
Ecclesiastical Committee Report, 3, 83
Parr, E., Report of Inquiry into Rent Act. *Cmnd. 1246.* 1069, 1148
Parrish, B. B.:
Effect of Artificial Lights on Fish and Other Marine Organisms at Sea, 633
Herring in Aquaria, 656
Parry, Hon. Mr. Justice Wynn, (Chairman: Private International Law Committee) Report. *Cmnd. 491.* 531
Parsons, K. H., Owner Cultivator in a Progressive Agriculture, 706
Part-Time Employment Report. *Cmnd. 206.* 263, 363

PAR INDEX 1956-60

Parthasarathi, G. (Chairman: International Commission for Supervision and Control in Cambodia) Report. *Cmd. 9671.* 37
Passage of Smolts and Kelts through Fish Passes. Report, 388
Passenger Charges Scheme. Transport Tribunal Proceedings, 405
Passenger Ships, Survey of:
Circular, 186
Instructions to Surveyors, 188, 672
Passenger Transport, Convention on, Taxation of Road Vehicles, 462
Pastures and Fodder Crops in Rotations in Mediterranean Agriculture, 241A
Patent Office:
Library. Periodical Publications, 362, 636, 1164
Publications, 362, 636, 1164
Patents:
Designs and Trade Marks Report, 20, 155, 233, 362, 503, 636, 768, 890, 1026, 1164
European Convention on the International Classification of Patents for Invention. *Cmd. 9862.* 50, 108
Patents Act, 273
Patents and Designs (Renewals, Extensions and Fees) Bill, 1011, 1045
Patents Bill, 7, 36
Patents Bill (Lords), 215, 225, 243, 338
Path of Flight, 202
Pathology, Preventative Aspects in the Teaching of. Report, 1000
Paton Educational Trust Scheme:
Draft, 170
Memorandum, 385
Order-in-Council, 385
Paton, H. M., Accounts of Masters of Works for Building and Repairing Royal Palaces and Castles, 389
Patterns of Industrial Growth, 1257
Pavements. Guide to Structural Design, 1182
Pavlova, Anna, Catalogue of the Commemorative Exhibition, 150
Pawnbrokers Act, 1071
Pawnbrokers Bill, 787, 1005, 1037, 1041, 1141
Pay and Pensions, Service. *Cmd. 9692.* 39, 94
Pay Warrants:
954
Amendments, 206, 425, 695, 954, 1224
Payment of Debt Incurred on Termination of Treaty of Alliance. Exchange of Notes between U.K. and Jordan. *Cmnd. 943.* 1047, 1122
Payment of Wages Act, 1071
Payments of Wages Bill, 787, 1006, 1007, 1019, 1020, 1037, 1041, 1043, 1141
Pea and Bean Beetles, 820
Pea, Bean and Clover Leaf Weevils, 819
Pea Root Eelworm, 289
Pea Weevil and Methods for Its Control, 420
Peace, Last Months of, 106
Peace, T. R., Status and Development of Elm Disease in Britain, 1129
Peaceful Applications of Nuclear Energy, Developments in, 1240
Peaceful Settlement of Disputes, European Convention for. *Cmnd. 1060.* 1055, 1119
Peaceful Uses of Atomic Energy.
See Atomic Energy, Peaceful Uses of
Peacock, A. T., National Income of Tanganyika, 370
Peak District. National Park Guide, 1163
Pear and Apple Trees, Winter Pruning of Established, 820
Pearson, Hon. Mr. Justice (Chairman: Committee on Funds in Court) Report. *Cmnd. 818.* 801, 887
Pearson, J. T., Cancer Statistics, E. and W., 598
Peas, 290
Peck, C. Wilson, English Copper, Tin and Bronze Coins in British Museum, 1094
Pedgley, D. E., Summer Sea-Breeze at Ismailia, 634
Peebleshire Educational Trust Scheme, Memorandum, 1184
Peech, N. M. (Chairman: Committee on Solid Smokeless Fuels) Report. *Cmnd. 999.* 1051, 1173
Peers, Sir C., Kirby Muxloe Castle Guide, 427
Pelagic Fishery Production, 73
Pelagic Fishes of East Africa, Preliminary Survey, 89
Pelayo, Wreck Report, 927
Pelecaniform Characters of the Skeleton of the Shoe-Bill Stork, Balaeniceps Rex, 295
Pembrokeshire Coast National Park Film Strip, 155
Penal Practice in a Changing Society. *Cmnd. 645.* 789, 862
Penal System in New Hebrides. Exchange of Notes between U.K. and France. *Cmnd. 668.* 791, 848
Penguins, Pygoscelid, 571
Penman, A. D. M., Sites and Foundations, 1179
Penny, F. D., Handbook on Die Casting, 659
Pensions:
Allocation of, Memorandum, 314, 386
Appeal Tribunals (Scotland) (Amendment) Rules. Select Committee on Statutory Instruments Report, 1143
Estimates:
1956–57, 12
1957–58, 226
1958–59, 494, 676
1959–60, 760, 933

INDEX 1956–60 —PHA

Pensions (*continued*):
Estimates (*continued*):
1960–61, 1013, 1201
For the Widows, Children and Dependants of Teachers in Scotland Report. *Cmnd. 527.* 534, 654
Increase:
Circular, 869
Guide, 937
Ready Reckoner Tables, 937
Schemes, Occupational, 680
Warrant, Army, 206, 423, 956
See also under Army—Firemen—National Health Service—Police—Retired Pay—War
Pensions and National Insurance, Ministry of:
Publications, 156–60, 362–9, 636, 891, 1164
Report. *Cmd. 9826.* 47, 156; *Cmnd. 229.* 264, 368; *Cmnd. 493.* 531, 639; *Cmnd. 826.* 802, 896; *Cmnd. 1133.* 1060, 1168
Pensions (Increase) Act:
56, 810
Circular, 129
Guide, 197
Pensions (Increase) Act (Extension) Order. Circular, 340
Pensions (Increase) Bill, 3, 16, 30, 33, 34, 126, 751, 770, 779, 785, 864
Pentre-Ifan Burial Chamber, Nevern, Pembrokeshire, Guide, 1226
Penybont Main Sewerage Act, 543
People and Timber, 421
People's Dispensary for Sick Animals Act, 58
Peppiatt, L. E. (Chairman: Departmental Committee on Levy on Betting on Horse Races) Report. *Cmnd. 1003.* 1051
Perambulators, Hand-Trucks, etc. Census of Production Report, 1194
Percival, H. V. T., Apsley House, 422
Percy, Lord Richard, Exploitation of Sea Birds in Seychelles, 570
Percy of Newcastle, Rt. Hon. Lord (Chairman: Royal Commission on Law relating to Mental Illness and Mental Deficiency) Report. *Cmnd. 169.* 380
Perfilov, M. A.:
Ground Winch Skidding in Clear and Selective Felling, 984
Timber Skidding by Tractor in the U.S.S.R., 990
Periodic Vehicle Tests. *Cmnd. 430.* 527, 674
Periodical Publications in the Patent Office Library, 362, 636, 1164
Periodicals:
Adult and Workers' Education, 1264
For New Literates, 468, 737
Primary Education, 1264
Science Library. Hand List of Short Titles, 381
Periodicals (*continued*):
Selected Educational, 994
Permanent Central Opium Board Report, 232A, 459, 729, 987, 1257
Permanent Supplementary Artificial Lighting of Interiors, 1179
Perrins, H. J.:
Explosion at Colliery Report. *Cmnd. 935.* 1047, 1171
Mines and Quarries Report, 900, 1172
Persian Gulf Gazette, 108–9, 321, 392, 831, 1124
Personal Aircraft:
Inspection Manual, 199
Owner's Guide, 202
Personal Record Card, 335
Personnel Card, 335
Personnel Management:
Career, 136
Series, 421
Peru:
International Customs Journal, 444
Industrial Development, 1251
Pest Infestation Research Board:
Bulletin, 909
Report, 167, 383, 651, 909, 1081
Pesticides:
Insecticides, etc. Specifications, 245A
Specifications and Methods of Analysis, 560
Toxic Hazards of, to Man, 245A
Pests. Control of Pests in Stored Agricultural Products. Report, 715
Pests Act, 1954 (Amendment) Bill, 219, 220
Peterlee Development Corporation Report, 24, 130, 237, 506, 613, 870, 1147
Petrik, Milivoj, Training of Sanitary Engineers, 244A
Petrini, E., Education in Italy, 995
Petrol Filling Stations:
Circular, 600
Planning Applications. Circular, 611
Petroleum:
Oils and Lubricants and Allied Products, Defence List, 837, 1108
Resources of Asia and the Far East:
Proceedings of the Symposium, 985
Symposium on the Development, 1256
Petroleum Spirit (Conveyance by Road) Regulations. Certificate, 335
Petrological Studies in Glen Urquhart, Inverness-shire, 563
Petrology of Graham Land, 571
Petter, G. S. V. (Chairman: Mission on Higher Technical Education in the British Caribbean) Report, 302
P.G. Reports, 1219
Pharmaceutical Preparations:
Classification of, 1267
Use of Specifications for Report, 741
Pharmacist, Career, 876
Pharmacy and Poisons Act. Form of Application to Sell Poisons, 1139

PHE-POT | 1956-60

PHE— INDEX 1956–60

Phemister, J.:
Limestones of Scotland, 119
Northern Highlands. British Regional Geology, 1131
Petrographical Notes to Metalliferous Mining Region of South-West England, 119
Phenolic Mouldings, 176
Phenolic Resin Bonded Paper Tube, 659
Phillippines:
Exchange of Notes with U.K. amending the Schedule of Routes to the Air Services Agreement. *Cmnd. 1142.* 1061, 1124
Exchange of Notes with U.K. concerning the Air Services Agreement. *Cmnd. 171.* 260, 321
International Customs Journal, 714
Phillips, A., Story of Big Ben, 958
Phillips, R., Chromiferous Ultrabasic Rocks of Eastern Sierra Leone, 572
Phillips, R. W.:
Recent Developments affecting Livestock Production in the Americas, 435
Types and Breeds of African Cattle, 706
Phosphate Fertilizers for Farm Crops, 71
Photo-Heliographic Results, 120, 329, 905
Photo Posters, 614, 1149
Photographic Zenith Tube, 1178
Photography, 202
Photometry of Telescopes and Binoculars, 155
Physical Chemistry of Metallic Solutions and Intermetallic Compounds, 890
Physical Education:
Official Primary and Secondary Programmes, 994
Primary Schools. Syllabus, 1185
Safety Precautions Display Card, 170
Secondary Schools, 386, 1186
Physical Training:
Army Pamphlets, 695, 954, 1224
Instructors, Principles of Anatomy and Physiology, 1089
Physical Training and Recreation Act, 542
Physical Training and Recreation Bill, 482, 502, 513, 517, 518, 608
Physically Handicapped, Rehabilitation of, 457
Physics:
In Nuclear Energy, 986
Research Reactors, 231A
Physio-Therapist and Remedial Gymnast. Career, 136
Phytoplankton and the Herring, 73
Phyto-Sanitary Convention for Africa South of the Sahara. *Cmd. 9834.* 109
Piaget, J., Introduction to Selection of Works from John Amos Comenius, 465
Pickering Castle, Yorkshire, Guide, 698
Pick-up Balers, 558
Picture Books, 886, 1222, 1223
Piercy, Rt. Hon. Lord (Chairman: Committee on Rehabilitation Training and Resettlement of Disabled Persons) Report. *Cmd. 9883.* 52
Piezoelectricity, Selected Engineering Report, 370
Pig Houses, Temperatures and Humidities, 1181
Pig Industry:
Cmnd. 24. 54, 70, 74, 124
Development Authority Report and Accounts, 640
Piggot, W. R., Calculation of the Median Sky Wave Field Strength in Tropical Regions, 909
Piglet Anaemia, 289
Pigs:
And Bacon. Reorganisation Commission Report. *Cmd. 9795.* 45, 70, 74
Breeding, Recording and Progeny Testing in European Countries, 966
Diseases of, 290
Feeding, 820
Progeny Testing Stations. Transferred to the Pig Industry Development Authority. *Cmnd. 821.* 801, 934
Pike of Loch Choin, 387
Pilchards in the Channel, Number, 292
Pilkington, Sir H. (Chairman):
Royal Commission on Doctors' and Dentists' Remuneration:
Minutes of Evidence, 647, 901
Report. *Cmnd. 939.* 1047; *Cmnd. 1063.* 1055
Pilot—Area in Sardinia, 1248
Pilot Instruction Manual, 951
Pilot's Licence, Private, Aviation Law for Applicants, 927
Pilot's Radio Handbook, 199
Pine Looper Moth, 855
Pine Shoot Moth and Related Species, 325
Pine Weevil, Large, 1129
Pioneers Who Served, 131, 344, 872
Pipes. Actual Internal Diameters of Various Classes of Pipe, etc. Supplement, 1183
Pirenne, M. H., Individual Differences in Light-Vision Efficiency, 359
Pit, Trench, Clamp and Tower Silos, 559
Pizer, S., U.S. Investments in the Latin American Economy, 692
Plague, Expert Committee Report, 999
Plaice in the North Sea, Spawning of, 823
Plan for a British Caribbean Federation. *Cmd. 9618, 9619, 9620, 9621.* 36
Plan, Schuman, Catalogue Analytique du Fonds, 215A
Plancke, R., Education in Belgium, 466
Planet, Our Unknown, 459
Planetary Co-ordinates, 1960–1980, 546

INDEX 1956–60 —POL

Plankton of Inshore Waters off Freetown, Sierra Leone, 1103
Planktonic Stages of the Haddock in Scottish Waters, 914
Planning Appeals:
Circular, 869
Selected, 871, 1148
Planning Grants under the Town and Country Planning Act, Explanatory Memorandum, 869
Planning School Kitchens, 386
Planning, Study and Practice of, 995
Plant, Professor Sir A. (Chairman: Industrial Injuries Advisory Council) Reports. *Cmnd. 416.* 526; *Cmd. 9673, 9674, 9827.* 37, 38, 47
Plant and Machinery:
For Export, General Conditions for Supply, 232A
Rating of, Report, 871
Supply and Erection, 459
Plant Breeders' Rights Report. *Cmnd. 1092.* 1057, 1082, 1088, 1139
Plant Exploration, Collection and Introduction, 1236
Plant Level Measurements, Methods and Results, 223A
Plant Nematology, 825
Plant Pathology, 75, 292, 430, 559, 824, 1088
Plant Production in the Northern North Sea, 656
Plant Protection:
Cmd. 9834. 48, 109
Agreement for the South-East Asia and Pacific Region. *Cmd. 9783.* 44, 109; *Cmnd. 170.* 260, 321
Bulletins, 242A, 437, 708, 968, 1238
Convention for Establishment of Organisation. *Cmd. 9878.* 51, 109
Plant Remains of the Hengistbury and Barton Beds, 1096
Plantation Crops. Production, Trade and Consumption, 91, 573, 1105
Plants, Instructions for Collectors, 295
Plastering on Dense Concrete, etc., 381
Plastics:
For Building, 381
Goods and Fancy Articles Census of Production Report, 665
In the Tropics Report, 176, 391, 659, 918, 1091
Materials. Census of Production Report, 394
Platt, Sir H. (Chairman: Committee on Welfare of Children in Hospital) Report, 859
Platyseiinae. Based on Material in the Collections of the British Museum. (Natural History) Revision of, 1097
Playfair, Major-General, I.S.O.:
British Fortunes Reach Their Lowest Ebb, 1098, 1189
Playfair, Major-General, I.S.O., (*continued*):
"The Germans Come to the Help of their Ally", 82, 174
Playing Fields Safety Precautions, Display Cards, 170
Pleadings, Oral Arguments, Documents, International Court of Justice:
220A, 443, 713, 973, 1243
Judgments of Administrative Tribunals, 443
Pleistocene Suidae, Some East African, 564
Plenary Meetings. ICAO Minutes, 1242
Plerocercoid Larvae of Grillotia erinaceus in Halibut, Occurrence of, 655
Plotting Chart (Fishing), 926
Ploughs:
Overhaul, 558
Setting, 823
Plum Aphids, 555, 1083
Plumber. Career, 876
Plumbing:
For Multi-Storey Flats, 906
Repairs in the Home, Simple, 201
Simplified, 427
Plums, Pollination of, 1084
Plywood:
Heat Penetration in the Pressing of, 907
Strength Properties of, 382, 650
Pneumatic-tyred Rollers in the Compaction of Soil, Investigation of the Performance of, 910
Pneumoconiosis:
In the Mining and Quarrying Industries Statistics, 118, 645
Lung Function in Coal Workers, 151
Statistics, Digest of, 898, 901, 1170
Pocket Guides, 202
Poisons. *See* Pharmacy and Poisons
Poland:
Agreement with U.K. concerning Civil Air Transport. *Cmnd. 1226.* 1067, 1124
Exchange of Notes with U.K.:
Concerning the Introduction of Air Services. *Cmnd. 862.* 804, 852
Further prolonging the Sterling Payments Agreements. *Cmnd. 74.* 258, 321
Modifying the Agreement for the Settlement of Outstanding Financial Questions. *Cmnd. 1057.* 1055, 1124
Poles, History of Committee for Education of, 101
Police:
Career, 347
Counties and Boroughs, England and Wales. Report, 13, 124, 234, 335, 504, 605, 769, 862, 1029, 1139

POL— INDEX 1956–60

Police (*continued*):
Drivers' Manual. *See* Road-craft
England and Wales. Select Committee on Estimates:
Report, 491, 606
Special Report, 506, 515, 606, 607
Forces of the County of Carmarthen and the County of Cardigan Report, Amalgamation. *Cmnd. 374.* 523, 605
Metropolis. Report of the Commissioner. *Cmnd. 222.* 264, 334; *Cmnd. 800.* 800, 862; *Cmnd. 1106.* 1058, 1139
Of the North Sea Fisheries. Agreement relating to the International Convention. *Cmnd. 4.* 52, 109
Pensions:
Forms, 172, 1187
Regulations. Commutation and Allocation, 605, 656
Promotion. Examinations, 299
Royal Commission:
Minutes of Evidence, 1177
Report. *Cmnd. 1222.* 1067, 1140
Scotland Examination Board. Question Papers and Syllabus, 173, 1187
Uniform. Committee of the Police Council for E. and W. Report, 605
Widow's Pension Form, 1187
See also Commissioner of Police—Metropolis
Police Federation Act, 810
Police Federation Bill, 749, 784
Police, Fire and Probation Officers Remuneration Act, 56
Police, Fire and Probation Officers Remuneration Bill, 7, 35
Police (Scotland) Act, 56
Poliomyelitis:
Expert Committee Report, 741, 1270
Infantile Paralysis, 420
Vaccination, 245A
Polishes. Census of Production Report, 394, 1194
Polishing of Roadstone in Relation to the Resistance to Skidding of Bituminous Road Surfacings, 652
Political Advance in the United Kingdom Dependencies, 615, 1150
Political and Security Questions, General Assembly Records, 229A, 725, 983, 1254
Political Rights of Women, Convention on, 232A
Political Science:
In the U.S.A. Report, 237A
International Bibliography of, 237A, 466, 735, 994, 1264
Political Sociology, Essay and Bibliography, 735
Pollard, F. S., Inspector of Mines and Quarries Report, 900, 1172
Pollination:
Apples and Pears, 555
Plums:
1084
And Cherries, 555
Pollitzer, R., Cholera, 998
Pollution of the Sea by Oil:
232A
International Convention for Prevention. *Cmnd. 595.* 538, 593
Manual of Avoidance of, 400, 670
Polypodiaceae and Grammitidaceae of Ceylon, 1095
Polystyrene:
Mouldings, 1091
Optical Grade of, 391
Polythene Tubes for Cold Water Services, 427
Polyvinyl Chloride, 1091
Pontania, Studies in, 1095
Pontypool Water Act, 58
Pooling Skills for Human Progress, 232A
Poor's Coal Charity (Wavendon) Charity Scheme Confirmation Act, 812
Poor's Coal Charity (Wavendon) Charity Scheme Confirmation Bill, 750, 785
Pope, R. D., Revision of the Species of Schizonycha Dejean from Southern Africa, 1095
Poplars:
Establishment Methods for, 1129
Experiments, Design of, 854
In Forestry and Land Use, 708
Planting, 113
Plants, Quality of, 325
Preliminary Yield Table, 855
Poppy Plant. Limiting and Regulating the Cultivation, 232A
Popular Science Films Catalogue, 468
Population:
And Culture:
737, 996
Positive Contribution by Immigrants, 239A
And Vital Statistics Reports, 232A, 233A, 459, 730, 987, 1257
Asia and the Far East Seminar, 450, 1257
Bulletin, 459
Census Methods, Handbook of, 732, 1260
Censuses. *See* Demographic Yearbook
Commission Report, 453, 981
Employment, etc., Statistical Data, Member Countries, Council of Europe, 1232
Estimates:
England and Wales and Local Authority Areas, 118, 327, 598, 856, 1130
Scotland, 599, 856, 1131
Future Growth of World, 730
Studies, 232A, 459, 730, 987, 1257

INDEX 1956–60 —POT

Population (*continued*):
See also National Population Censuses—Rates and Rateable Values—Rates Returns—Registrar General's Returns—Scotland, Return—Statistical Review—World Population
Population (Statistics) Act, 1071
Population (Statistics) Bill, 754, 787, 1006, 1021, 1037, 1042, 1141
Porcelain Enamels. Fifteen Years' Exposure Test, 419
Port of London Act, 274, 812
Port of London (Superannuation) Act, 543
Port Said. Damage and Casualties. *Cmnd. 47.* 55, 94
Port Transport Industry:
Report of a Committee appointed to inquire into the Operation of the Dock Workers (Regulation of Employment) Scheme. *Cmd. 9813.* 46, 149
Report of a Court of Inquiry. *Cmnd. 510.* 532, 623
Portrait Miniatures, 952
Ports:
Efficiency Committee Report, 188
List of. Timber and Pitwood. Report of Inquiry, 1158
Portslade and Southwick Outfall Sewerage Board Act, 274
Portsmouth and Southsea Station Railway Accident Report, 404
Portsmouth Corporation Act, 812
Portugal:
Agreement on German Assets in Portugal and on Claims regarding Monetary Gold. *Cmnd. 863.* 804, 848
Agreement with U.K.:
for Co-operation in the Peaceful Uses of Atomic Energy. *Cmnd. 513.* 532, 592, 787, 852
Regarding Nyasaland-Mozambique Frontier. *Cmnd. 528.* 534, 592
Economic Conditions, 1246
Exchange of Notes with U.K. on the Repayment of the Debt on the Liquidation of the European Payments Union. *Cmnd. 762.* 798, 852
Foreign Trade Statistical Bulletin, 222A, 447, 448, 717, 977, 978
International Customs Journal, 973
Portugal *v.* India. Right of Passage over Indian Territory, 443
Positive Employment Policies, 630
Possible Impact of the European Economic Community, in particular the Common Market, upon World Trade, 710
Post-Fourth Year Examination Structure in Scotland Report. *Cmnd. 1068.* 1055, 1185
Post-Graduate Training in the Public Health Aspects of Nuclear Energy Report, 742
Post Office:
And Streets, London, 161, 640, 1169
Capital Expenditure. *Cmnd. 690.* 793, 897; *Cmnd. 973.* 1049, 1169
Commercial Accounts, 222, 244, 369–70
Estimates:
1956–57, 12
1957–58:
226
Revised Supplementary, 494, 676
1958–59, 494, 676
1959–60, 760, 933
1960–61, 1019, 1202
Guide, 161, 370, 640, 897, 1169
In the U.K., 370, 640, 1169
Publications, 161, 202, 369–70, 640, 897, 1169
Report and Commercial Accounts. *Cmnd. 621.* 540, 640; *Cmnd. 870.* 805, 897; *Cmnd. 1206.* 1066, 1169
Savings Bank Account, 197, 410, 680, 937, 1205
Status of. *Cmnd. 989.* 1050, 1170
Post Office and Telegraph (Money) Act, 542, 810
Post Office and Telegraph (Money) Bill, 250, 479, 754, 786
Post Office and Telegraph (Money). Proposed Resolution. *Cmnd. 318.* 270, 370; Memorandum. *Cmnd. 882.* 806, 897
Post Office Bill:
1045
Memorandum. *Cmnd. 1247.* 1069, 1169
Post Office Works Act, 810
Post Office Works Bill, 487, 746, 748, 770, 779, 784, 785, 864
Post War Building Studies, 208
Postage Stamps of the United States, 202, 692, 1222
Postal Addresses, 370, 640, 1169
Postcards:
208, 697, 1226
Victoria and Albert Museum, 952
Works, Ministry of, 957
Pot Plants, 821
Potatoes:
290
And Tomato Blight, 1083
Bulk Storage, in Buildings, 1085
Crops Certified, Register of, 70, 287, 554, 820, 1082
Diggers, 558
Harvesting, 1251
Maincrop, 555
Marketing Board. *See* Miscellaneous Financial Provisions Act
Root Eelworm, 71
Seed, 70
Skin Spot and Silver Scurf, 288
Stock-Feeding, 555
Storage and Dressing of Seed, 553

1956-60 | POT-PUB

POT— INDEX 1956–60

Potatoes (*continued*):
- Trials and Collections, Key to, 70, 287, 554, 820, 1082
- Ware, 69
- Wart Disease of, 820

Poteat, M. N., Selling the United States Market, 420

Potent Drugs. Protocol for the Termination of the Brussels Agreements and the Unification of Pharmacopoeial Formulas. *Cmnd. 2.* 52, 109

Pottery:
- Hispano Moresque, 693
- Industry in Stoke-on-Trent. Industrial Health Survey Report, 885
- Medieval Near Eastern, 693
- Report respecting Certain Articles. *Cmnd. 282.* 268

Potts, C. G., Milk Goats, 201

Poultry:
- Breeding:
  - 1085
  - Stock, Feeding of, 71
- Management, Methods of Intensive, 821
- Nutrition, 1085
- On the General Farm, 290
- Quality Control in Marketing Fresh, 907

Pound and Our Future, 411

Power, 381

Power Getting and Loading Machines, Dust Suppression with, 114

Power of Investment of Trustees in Great Britain. *Cmnd. 915.* 808, 937

Power, Ministry of:
- Estimates:
  - 1956–57, 12
  - 1957–58, 226
  - 1958–59, 494, 676
  - 1959–60, 760, 933
  - 1960–61, 1019, 1201
  - Select Committee Report, 503, 606
- Examination Papers, 371, 641, 899, 900, 1171, 1172
- Nationalised Industries and Undertakings Account, 496, 587
- Publications, 370–7, 640, 898, 1170
- Safety Circulars, 900
- Special Report, 515, 606

Power Presses:
- Joint Standing Committee Report on Safety in the Use of, 356
- Safety in the Use of, 885

Power Reactors, 231A, 969

Power Saws in Forest Operations, Use of, 993

Power Stations, Heavy Equipment for Survey, 223A

Powers of the House, Select Committee Report, 1, 129

Powers of Trustees to Sell, Purchase or otherwise Deal with Heritable Property, etc. Law Reform Committee for Scotland. Report. *Cmnd. 1102.* 1058, 1159

Poynton, Sir Hilton (Chairman: Public Services Conference) Report, 1104

Practice, Code of:
- 307
- Publication, 578

Practice Leaflet for Solicitors, 357

Pratt, A. W.:
- Condensation in Sheeted Roofs, 651
- Heat Transfer in Deep Underground Tunnels, 651

Precepts Rules, Circular, 868

Precious Metals Refining. Census of Production Report, 394

Precision Gearing for Control Systems and Armaments, 1075

Precision Measuring Instruments (Mechanical), Defence List, 93

Prefabricated Building, 976

Premium Savings Bonds, 357, 631, 917, 918, 1189, 1190

Pre-natal Care, 421

Preparation of General Secondary School Curricula, 1265

Preparation of Statistical Wind Forecasts and an Assessment of their Accuracy in Comparison with Forecasts made by Synoptic Techniques, 1162

Preparation of Wood for Microscopic Examination, 908

Preparing Your Child for School, 201

Presbyterian Church of England Act, 1072

Pre-School Education, 1264

Prescribed Diseases Schedule Review. Report of the Industrial Injuries Advisory Council. *Cmnd. 416.* 526, 639

Prescribing Costs:
- Committee's Report, 602
- Scottish Committee Report, 858

Preservation of Downing Street Report. *Cmnd. 457.* 529, 680

Preservation of Fish and Fish Offal for Oil and Meal Manufacture, 907

Preservation of Timber and Metal, 292

Preservative Treatment of Fence Posts and Farm Timbers, 420

Preservatives in Food Report, 823

Preserved Fruit and Vegetables. Census of Production Report, 395

Preserved Meat. Census of Production Report, 395

Press Authority Bill, 5, 7

Press, Film and Radio:
- In the World Today, 239A, 737, 1265
- Television:
  - Organisations Handbook, 996
  - World Communications, 240A

Press Messages. Problems of Transmitting, 239A

INDEX 1956–60 —PRI

Pressure Gauges:
- Bourdon Tube Type, 1108
- Defence List, 307

Pressure Surfaces, Variations of the Measured Heights of, 152

Pressure Variation over Malaya and the Resonance Theory, 1162

Prest, A. R., Fiscal Survey of British Caribbean, 302

Preston Railway Accident Report, 673

Preston, T. R., Calf Rearing, 1085

Pre-Stressed Concrete, 428

Preventing the Keeping of Animals so as to be prejudicial to Health, 612

Prevention of Fraud (Investments) Act, 542

Prevention of Fraud (Investments) Act, Report on Consolidation Bill, 478, 482

Prevention of Fraud (Investments) Bill, 480, 519

Prevention of Fraud (Investments) Particulars, 182, 398, 667, 923

Prevention of Lyctus Attacks in Sawn Hardwoods, 1180

Preventive Medicine, Handbook, 825

Prevett, P. F., Investigation into Storage Problems of Rice in Sierra Leone, 833

Price Indexes, Methods used in compiling, 989

Prices:
- For Works Services War Department Schedule, 426
- Of Agricultural Products and Fertilizers, 437

Primary Batteries. Defence List, 307

Primary Education:
- 842
- In Asia, 1264
- Periodicals, 1264

Primary Schools:
- Composition in, 385
- Curricula in Latin America, 736
- Preparation and Issuing of Curriculum, 737
- Textbooks, 995

Primates, History of, 82, 564, 1097

Prime Minister and Mr. Bulganin, Correspondence between. *Cmnd. 380, 381.* 524, 589

Prince Henry the Navigator and Portuguese Maritime Enterprise. Catalogue, 1094

Principles of Administration applied to Nursing Service, 740

Principles of Modern Building, 909

Printed Books:
- 422
- In British Museum. Accessions Catalogue, 827
- Maps and Music in the British Museum. Rules for compiling the Catalogues, 1094

Printed Wiring for Electrical Applications. Defence Guide, 837

Printer's Imprint Bill, 1044

Printing:
- And Bookbinding Machinery. Census of Production Report, 664
- And Publishing, Bookbinding, Engraving, etc. Census of Production Report, 665
- Career, 618, 876
- Machine Room Workers. Career, 347

Priorities of Patronage, 1090

Prison Commission Publication, 1173

Prison Service:
- Career, 136
- Journal, 1173
- Report. *Cmnd. 544.* 535, 605, 656

Prisons:
- And Borstals, England and Wales:
  - 335
  - Policy and Practice in Administration, 1139
- Commissioners Report. *Cmnd. 10.* 53, 124; *Cmnd. 322.* 270; *Cmnd. 496.* 531, 604; *Cmnd. 825.* 802, 862; *Cmnd. 1117.* 1059, 1139
- Liverpool. Report of Inquiry into Allegations of Illtreatment of Prisoners. *Cmnd. 503.* 532, 603
- Scotland, Report. *Cmd. 9760.* 42, 172; *Cmnd. 164.* 260, 335, 388; *Cmnd. 429.* 527, 656; *Cmnd. 765.* 798, 915; *Cmnd. 1048.* 1054, 1187

Prisoners. After-Care and Supervision of Discharged Prisoners Report, 603

Pritchard, F. E. (Chairman: Committee on the Rating of Charities and Kindred Bodies) Report. *Cmnd. 831.* 802, 871

Private Business. House of Commons, 1034, 1144

Private International Law Committee Report. *Cmnd. 491.* 531, 632

Private Legislation (Scotland) Procedure Journal, 161, 388, 657, 916, 1188

Private Mobile Radio Services:
- 898
- Performance Specifications, 1170

Private Pilots, Questions and Answers for, 203

Privett, D. W., Exchange of Energy between the Atmosphere and the Oceans of the Southern Hemisphere, 1160

Privileges and Immunities:
- Council of Europe:
  - 434
  - Protocol to General Agreement, *Cmnd. 84.* 254; 962
- Specialized Agencies of the United Nations, Convention on. *Cmnd. 855.* 804, 853

PRI— INDEX 1956 60

Privileges Committee:
- Report, 125, 223, 225, 240, 338, 504, 603
- Report on Complaint of a Letter to a Member, 1031, 1142

Privy Council:
- Orders-in-Council, 1173
- Publications, 1173

Privy Council of England Acts, 646

Privy Seal of Scotland, Register of, 389

Probation Officers and Approved Probations Hostels and Homes Directory, 605, 1138

Probert-Jones, J. R., Conservation of Vorticity at 100 Millibars, 1162

Problems and Perspectives. Report on the International Meeting on Social Research, 1248

Problems of Humid Tropical Regions, 736

Problems of Progress in Industry, 383, 651, 909, 1181

Problems of Rural Wales, 1037

Procedure for the Council, Rules of. ICAO, 971

Procedure in the Public Business, Manual. House of Commons, 778, 863

Procedure Records. Organisation and Methods Division, 937

Procedure. Select Committee:
- House of Commons Report, 761, 865
- House of Lords Report, 753, 867, 1145
- Reports, 217, 228, 338
- Special Report, 488, 506, 608, 609

Proceedings before Examining Justices Report. *Cmnd. 479.* 530, 605

Processing Irradiated Fuels and Radioactive Materials, 986

Processing of Raw Materials, 986

Proclamation for Calling Out the Army Reserves, 150

Production and Trade in the Near East, 242A

Production, Census of:
- 179–80, 394–6, 663, 932, 1193
- Tables, 179, 394, 921

Production Group:
- Publications, 1219
- Reports, 1219

Production Technology of the Materials used for Nuclear Energy, 231A

Production Yearbook, 968, 1238

Productivity, Bibliography on, 223A

Productivity in the Wholesale Trade, 224A

Productivity Measurement:
- 223A, 1248
- Review, 223A, 449, 718, 976

Productivity, Prices and Wages, 449

Professional and Technical Education of Medical and Auxiliary Personnel, Expert Committee Report, 245A

Professional Association in the Mass Media, 996

Professional Engineers, Career, 876

Professional Notes, 152, 360, 889, 1162

Professions Supplementary to Medicine Act, 1071

Professions Supplementary to Medicine Bill, 787, 1007, 1009, 1017, 1037, 1041, 1043, 1141

Profits Tax:
- Appeal Leaflets, 133, 345, 615, 873, 1150
- Enactments relating to, 873
- Provisions of the Finance Acts Supplement, 345, 615, 1150

Programme Exchanges by means of Television Films, European Agreement, 962

Programming of House Building, 164

Progress in Atomic Energy, 986

Progress in Industry, Problems of, 1181

Promise of Technology. Resources for Freedom Report, 203

Promotion of Private Bills. Joint Committee Report, 753, 863, 867

Proofing of Farm Buildings Against Rats and Mice, 559

Properties of Reactor Materials, 986

Proposed Experimental Importation of Charollais Cattle Report. *Cmnd. 1140.* 1060, 1082, 1088

Proprietary Preparations, Standing Joint Committee on Classification Report, 859, 1133

Prostitution. *See* Traffic in Persons

Protection Against Neutron Radiation up to 30 Million Electron Volts, 692

Protection of Cultural Property in the Event of Armed Conflict, 737

Protection of Deer Bill, 516, 786, 1043

Protection of Tenants (Local Authorities) Bill, 784, 1042

Protective Clothing against Flames and Heat, 1180

Protective Foods, 1083

Protein Malnutrition in Brazil, 242A

Protein Requirements Report, 708

Proudman, Professor J. (Chairman Sub-Committee):
- Central Advisory Watch Committee. Report, 868
- On Growing Demand for Water. Report, 1146

Prout, L. B., New Species of Indo-Australian Geometridae, 563

Provision of Popular Reading Materials, 996

Provisions for Old Age. *Cmnd. 538.* 534, 639

Provisional Yield Tables for Oak and Beech in Great Britain, 596

Pselaphides (Coleoptera) De L'Inde Septentrionale, 1096

Pseudococcidae:
- Described by C. K. Brain from South Africa, 563

INDEX 1956–60 —PUB

Pseudococcidae (*continued*):
- Described by H. C. James from East Africa, 295
- Of the Solomon Islands, 1095

Psychiatric Hospital as a Centre for Preventive Work in Mental Health. Report, 741

Psychiatric Nursing, Expert Committee Report, 245A

Psychiatric Services and Architecture, 1269

Psychological Foundations of the Curriculum, 736

Psychological Services for Schools, 469

P.T. Instructors. *See* Physical Training in the Army

Public Accounts:
- Committee Report, 8, 9, 13, 16, 19, 23, 126, 127, 221, 225, 227, 233, 236, 338, 495, 503, 506, 608, 761, 769, 771, 865, 1014, 1026, 1029, 1142
- Index, 338
- Navy Votes, 770, 937
- Special Reports, 493, 608, 759, 866, 1014, 1039, 1143
- Treasury Minutes, 1022, 1205

Public Administration:
- Aspects of Community Development Programmes, 1260
- International Bibliography, 732
- Training in, 732
- *See* University Teaching of Social Sciences

Public Analysts Regulations Circular, 290

Public Bills Return, 27, 127, 240, 338, 509, 608, 776, 864, 1034, 1142

Public Boards:
- List of Members. *Cmd. 9660,* 37, 55; *Cmnd. 43.* 197; *Cmnd. 332.* 271, 411; *Cmnd. 609.* 539, 680
- Of a Commercial Character, Members, with Salaries and Allowances. *Cmnd. 911.* 808, 937; *Cmnd. 1250.* 1069, 1206

Public Bodies (Admission of the Press to Meetings) Bill, 35, 1023, 1037, 1041, 1042, 1141

Public Bodies (Admission to Meetings) Act, 1071

Public Bodies (Admission to Meetings) Bill, 1007, 1009, 1023, 1042, 1044, 1141

Public Business:
- House of Commons Standing Orders, 753, 866, 868, 1018, 1027, 1038, 1144
- House of Lords, 1007, 1144
- Manual of Procedure, 778, 863

Public Cleansing Costing Returns, 130, 342, 613, 871, 1147

Public Education:
- International Conference, 237A, 468, 737, 995, 1264
- Report and Statistics, *Cmd. 9785.* 44, 101; *Cmnd. 454.* 529, 585
- Scotland, 654

Public General Acts and Church Assembly Measures:
- 55, 271, 540, 808, 1069
- Short Titles, 55, 272

Public Health:
- And Medical Subjects. Reports, 123, 332, 860, 1136
- And Social Problems in the Use of Tranquilizing Drugs, 421
- Imported Food. Regulations. Circulars, 72, 73, 291, 822, 1086, 1088, 1133
- Laboratory Service Report, 473
- Monograph, 203, 421
- Papers, 1269
- Regulations Circulars, 557
- Report on the State of. *Cmnd. 18.* 122; 421
- Service Publications, 421, 692

Public Health Bill, 1011

Public Health Laboratory Service Act, 1071

Public Health Laboratory Service Bill, 755, 1003, 1005, 1009, 1026, 1037, 1042, 1043, 1141

Public Health Officers (Deputies) Act, 273

Public Health Officers (Deputies) Bill, 36, 215, 226, 243, 338

Public Income and Expenditure of the United Kingdom, Accounts, 18, 197, 231, 411, 502, 680, 766, 937, 1024, 1206

Public Investment in Great Britain. *Cmnd. 1203.* 1066, 1206

Public Lands, 241A

Public Library. *See* Libraries

Public Officers Agreement between U.K. and Malaya. *Cmnd. 854.* 804, 835

Public Petitions. Special Report from the Committee, 1027, 1143

Public Records Act, 542

Public Records Bill, 220, 478, 479, 484, 504, 513, 517, 519, 608

Public Records Office:
- Deputy Keeper's Report, 378
- Publications, 161–2, 378, 646, 901, 1175
- Report, 162, 646, 901, 1159

Public Road Passenger Transport Statistics, 188, 403, 929, 1197, 1199

Public Sanitary Conveniences, 342

Public Service Vehicles. Licensing Authorities Reports, 672

Public Service Vehicles (School Children) Bill, 517

Public Service Vehicles (Travel Concessions) Act, 1955

Public Service Vehicles (Travel Concessions) (Amendment) Bill, 1041

Public Services Conference Report, 1104

Public Trustee (Fees) Act, 273

Public Trustee (Fees) Bill, 8, 247

Public Trustee Office:
- Committee of Enquiry Report. *Cmd. 9755.* 42, 151
- Report, 162, 378, 646, 901, 1175

PUB-REG | 1956-60

PUB— INDEX 1956–60

Public Works Loan Bill, 5, 35, 220, 249
Public Works Loan Board Report, 197, 411, 680, 932, 1201
Public Works Loans Act, 56, 273
Publications:
 And Debates, Reports, 27, 127
 General Catalogue of OEEC Books, 719
 Handbook on the International Exchange, 238A
 Study of Current Bibliographies of National Official Publications, 735
Published by H.M.S.O., 1190
Pugh, R. B., Crown Estate, 1107
Pugsley, L. J., Food Additive Control in Canada, 966
Pullorum Disease, 290
Pulp and Paper:
 Industry in Europe Report, 449, 976
 Production, etc., 1250
 Prospects in Latin America, Report, 242A
 Statistics, 224A, 449, 719, 976, 1250
Pulp Mills, Small Economic Enquiry, 1248
Pulpy Kidney Disease or Enterotoxaemia of Sheep, 72
Pulverised Fuel Ash in Building Materials, 164
Pumps and Pipework for Heating Systems, 1088
Pupil's Progress Record, 170
Purcell, Henry. Commemorative Exhibition Catalogue, 827
Purchase of certain Ships of British Reserve Fleet. Agreement between U.K. and Turkey. *Cmnd. 751.* 797, 853
Purchase Notices Circular, 869
Purslow, D. F., Experiments on the Treatment of Redwood Sapwood by Dipping, 650
Purves, P. E.:
 Ear Plug Laminations in relation to the Age Composition of a Population of Fin Whales, 828
 Hearing in Cetecean, 1097
Pyefinch, K. A.:
 Movements of Salmon Tagged in the Sea, Altens, Kincardineshire, 655
 Trout in Scotland, 1188
Pygmy Squirrel, North Bornean, Glyphotes Simus Thomas, and its Relationships, 828

Q

Qatar Notices, 109, 321–2, 592, 852, 1124
Qualifications of Teachers in Schools Holding the Teacher's Technical Certificate Report, 170
Qualified Teachers and Temporary Teachers, 585, 586, 843
Quality control in Marketing Fresh Poultry, 907
Quality of Poplar Plants, 325
Quantity and Price Indexes in National Accounts, 449
Quarantine:
 Measures and Vaccination Certificate Requirements, 245A, 472, 741
 Proceedings and Reports relating to International Quarantine, 244A
Quarries:
 Explosives Regulations, Draft Circular, 900
 Notification of Dangerous Occurrences. Order, Circular, 900
Queen and People, 872
Queen Elizabeth I Inventory of Jewels and Plate, 79
Queen Elizabeth II Speech to Both Houses of Parliament, 7, 220, 486, 609, 754, 867, 1011, 1145
Queen Elizabeth the Queen Mother. Birthday Message, 206, 425, 696, 956
Queen, H.M. and H.R.H. Prince Philip. Birth of a Son, 1225
Queen's and Lord Treasurer's Remembrancer Publications, 901, 1175
Queen's Birthday:
 Honours Lists, 150, 357, 631, 917, 918, 1190
 Message from the Army, 205, 424, 695, 956
Queen's Regulations:
 And Admiralty Instructions Amendments, 61, 277, 546, 814, 1075
 Air Council Instruction's Amendments, 76, 294, 430, 561, 825, 1089
 Appendices, 61
 Army Amendments, 206, 425, 430, 696, 955, 1224
 Persian Gulf, 852
Questions and Answers Building Research Station Digest, 164, 165, 1179
Question Papers:
 Civil Service Commission, 830, 1099
 Scottish Certificate of Education, 912
Quick, H. E., British Slugs, 1097
Quinquennial Review:
 Government Actuary Report, 1027, 1205
 Of Rates and Amounts of National Insurance Benefit Report, 1027, 1165

R

R. & D.B.R. Publications, 691
R. & D.B. (W) Publications, 691
Rabbit-Keeping Modern, 821
Rabbits Bill, 2, 3, 34
Rabbits (Prohibition of Spreading) Bill, 1
Rabies, Expert Committee Report, 472, 1270

INDEX 1956–60 —RAE

Raby, F. J. E., Framlingham Castle Guide, 957
Race and Culture, 737
Race and History, 737
Race and Psychology, 737
Race and Society, 737
Race Discrimination Bill, 34, 36, 518, 520, 1042, 1045
Race Question:
 In Modern Science, 468, 737, 1265
 In Modern Thought, 737
Race Relations:
 And Mental Health, 1265
 Recent Research on, 736
 Selected Documentation for Study, 738
Rachiopteris Cylindrica, Morphology and Relationships of, 1096
Racial and Religious Insults Bill, 1041
Racial Situation in Union of South Africa, United Nations Commission Report, 229A
Radar Station on Island of Grand Turk. Exchange of Notes between U.K. and U.S.A. concerning. Establishment and Operation. *Cmnd. 836.* 802, 853
Radarman 3 and 2. Navy Training Courses, 421
Radcliffe, Rt. Hon. Lord:
 Chairman Committee on the Working of the Monetary System:
  Minutes of Evidence, 1202
  Report. *Cmnd. 827.* 802, 934
 Report on Constitutional Proposals for Cyprus. *Cmnd. 42.* 55, 88
Radford, C.A.R.:
 Acton Burnell Castle Guide, 426
 Dover Castle Guide, 957
 Early Christian and Norse Settlements Guide, 957
 Goodrich Castle Guide, 698
 Sandbach Crosses, Cheshire, Guide, 208
 Tretower Court Guide, 957
Radiation:
 Biological Effects of, 986
 Chemical Effects of, 986
 Effect of, on Human Heredity, 472, 1269
 Medicine into the Undergraduate Medical Curriculum, Introduction of. Report, 742
 Sources in Industry Conference, 1239
 See Atomic Energy
 See Large Radiation
Radio:
 And Radar for Merchant Ships. Performance Specification, 640, 898, 1170
 And Telecommunications. Census of Production Report, 179, 664
 And Television Servicing. Career, 875
 Conference, ITV, 712
Radio (*continued*):
 Facility Charts, United Kingdom, 188, 403, 672, 926, 929, 1091
 Frequency Cables, 578, 1108
 Research Board Report, 167, 384, 651, 910, 1181
 Services:
  Private Mobile, 898, 1170
  Textbook of, 425, 955
Radioactive Deposits, Surveying and Evaluating, 1240
Radioactive Fall-out, 862
Radioactive Isotopes:
 And Supervoltage, Use of, 1240
 Fission Products in Research and Industry, Applications of, 232A
 General Aspects of the Use of, 232A
 In Biology, Application of, 1240
 In the Service of Man, 997
 International Directory of, 969, 1239
 Ionizing Radiations in Agriculture, Physiology and Bio-Chemistry, 232A
 Nuclear Radiations in Medicine, 232A
 Safe Handling of, 202, 969, 1240
 Teletherapy Equipment International Directory, 1240
Radioactive Markers in Go-Devils. Safety Precautions, 885
Radioactive Substances Act, 1071
Radioactive Substances Bill, 754, 1003, 1004, 1005, 1007, 1023, 1037, 1041, 1042, 1141
Radioactive Wastes:
 Control of. *Cmnd. 884.* 806, 869, 913
 Disposal of. Conference, 1239
Radioactivity Circular, 869
Radiobiological Laboratory Report, 819, 1081
Radiochemical Analysis, Methods of. Expert Committee Report 1000
Radiochemical Centre, Amersham, 1222
Radiographer. Career, 136
Radiolitids (Rudistid Lamellibrachia) from the Upper Cretaceous of Turkey, 1096
Radiological Defense Series, 420
Radiological Hazards to Patients. Committee Report, 860, 1136
Radiological Health and Safety Report, 1207
Radiological Protection, Experience in, 986
Radionuclides, Metrology of. Proceedings of a Symposium, 1240
Radiotelephony Procedure Amendment, 188, 403, 672, 926
Radiotelephony Training and Reference Manual, 971
Rae, B. B.:
 Food and Feeding Habits of the Lemon Sole, 172
 Halibut. Observations on its Size at First Maturity, Sex Ratio and Length/Weight Relationship, 914

RAE— INDEX 1956–60

Rae, B. B. (*continued*):
 Occurrence of Plerocercoid Larvae of Grillotia erinaceus in Halibut, 655
 Seals and Scottish Fisheries, 1082
Raffles, T. S., Pioneer Who Served, 344
Ragg, R. M., Soils of the Country around Kelso and Lauder, 1082
Ragge, D. R., Acrometopae of the Ethiopian Region, 1095
Ragwort, 288
Rail Traffic. International Convention concerning Carriage of:
 Goods by Rail. *Cmnd. 564.* 536, 593, 671
 Passengers and Luggage by Rail. *Cmnd. 565.* 536, 593
Railway Clearing System Superannuation Fund Act, 812
Railway Passengers Assurance Act, 812
Railways:
 Accident Reports, 188, 403–4, 672, 926, 927, 929, 1197, 1198
 And Steel, 459
 Career, 1152
 Carriages and Wagons and Trams. Census of Production Report, 179, 663
 Civil Engineering. Census of Production Report, 396
 Locomotive Shops and Locomotive Manufacturing. Census of Production Report, 394
 Merchandise:
  British Transport Commission Charges Scheme, 405, 670
  Charges Scheme Transport Tribunal Proceedings, 191
 Proposals. *Cmd. 9880.* 51, 186
Rainfall:
 Averages, 887
 British, 152, 359, 887
 Of Depressions which pass Eastward over or near the British Isles, 153
 Of Malta, 1162
 Register of, 152, 360
Raisman, J., Fiscal Commission, Nigeria, Report. *Cmnd. 481.* 530
Rance, V. E., Corrosion of Metals by Vapours from Organic Materials, 659
Ransom, W. H., Buildings for Storage of Crops in Warm Climates, 1183
Raspberries, Cultivation of, 819, 820
Rate-Demands Rules Circular, 868
Rateable Values in England and Wales Distribution of. *Cmnd. 718.* 40, 129
Rates:
 And Rateable Values:
  England and Wales, 131, 342, 613, 871, 1147
  Scotland, 915, 1187
 Consolidation of Certain Enactments relating to Distress, 755
 Scotland Return, 172, 388, 656
Ratifications, etc., Supplementary List. *Cmd. 9723.* 41, 109; *Cmnd. 102.* 256, 322; *Cmnd. 386.* 524, 593; *Cmnd. 642,* 322; *Cmnd. 386.* 524, 593; *Cmnd. 642, 727, 828, 866.* 789, 795, 802, 805, 852; *Cmnd. 933, 1008, 1114, 1186.* 1047, 1051, 1059, 1064, 1124
Rating and Valuation Act, 273, 810
Rating and Valuation Act Circular, 340
Rating and Valuation Bill, 36, 215, 247, 749, 784, 1040, 1044
Rating of Charities and Kindred Bodies:
 Committee. Circular, 610, 611
 Report of the Committee, *Cmnd. 831.* 802, 871
Rating of Machinery. Circular, 340
Rating of Plant and Machinery. Report, 871
Rations for Livestock, 290, 1085
Ratites, Evolution of, 81
Rats in Sewers, Control of, 1089
Rauscher, M., Harvesting and Storage of Grain Maize, 979
Ravensdale, T. C., Dominican Republic. Overseas Economic Survey, 398
Raw Hides and Skins, Production, Utilisation, etc., 1105
Raw Materials:
 Commonwealth, 572, 1105
 Processing of, 986
 Resources Survey, 729
Raynes, F., Barley, 821
Rayon, Nylon, etc. and Silk, Production. Census of Production Report, 179, 395, 664
Razso, Professor T., General Problem of Transport on the Farm, 979
REA Bulletin, 692
Reaction Wood (Tension Wood and Compression Wood), 908
Reactions between Aggregates and Cement, 651
Reactor Components under Irradiation, Behaviour of, 1240
Reactor Design:
 Cross Sections, Important to, 231A
 Physics of, 231A
Reactor Physics:
 986
 And Economics, 986
Reactor Safety and Control, 986
Reactor Technology:
 986
 And Chemical Processing, 232A
 See also Nuclear Reactors
Read, W. A., Economic Geology of the Stirling and Clackmannan Coalfield, Scotland, Area South of the River Forth, 906
Reading Almshouse and Municipal Charities Bill, 518
Reading Almshouse and Municipal Charities Scheme Confirmation Act, 543

INDEX 1956–60 —REG

Reading Almshouse and Municipal Charities Scheme Confirmation Bill, 481
Reading and Berkshire Water, etc. Act, 812
Reading Corporation (Trolley Vehicles) Order Confirmation Act, 274
Reading Corporation (Trolley Vehicles) Provisional Order Bill, 217, 248
Reading, Dowager Marchioness, (Chairman: Housing Management Sub-Committee) Report, 869
Reading Most. Hon. the Marquess (Chairman):
 Committee on Consolidation of Highway Law) Report. *Cmnd. 630.* 788, 871, 929
 Council on Tribunals. Report, 1159
Reading Materials, Provision of Popular, 996
Reading, Standards of, 313
Ready-Mixed Concrete, 649
Ready Reckoner Tables, Pensions Increase, 937
Rearing of Chickens, 72
Rearing Turkeys, 71
Reay, G. A., Dehydration of Fish, 165
Rebinder, P. A., Effect of a Surface-Active Medium on the Deformation of Metals, 906
Reclassification of Government Expenditure and Receipts in Selected Countries, 730
Recreation Leaders, Handbook for, 421
Recreational Charities Act, 542
Recreational Charities Bill, 220, 478, 517
Recruiting:
 Advisory Committee Report. *Cmnd. 545.* 535, 578
 Government's Comments. *Cmnd. 570.* 536, 578
Recruitment to the Home Civil Service and the Foreign Service. Government Policy and Report. *Cmnd. 232.* 264, 411
Recruits' Physical Training Pamphlets, 695
Rectifications and Modifications to Texts of Schedules. GATT, 969
Rector and Vice-Chancellors, European Universities. Conference Report, 245A
Red Spider Mite:
 On Glasshouse Crops, 820, 1083
 On Hops and Others Crops in the Open, 555
Reducing Laboratory Vibrations, 905
Reduviidae, (Hemiptera-Heteroptera) New Sub-Family of, New Genera and New Species of, 80, 827
Reed, Colonel W. P., Railway Accident Reports, 188, 189, 403, 404, 672, 673, 929, 930, 1198
Rees, W. J.:
 Cephalopoda of Madeira Records and Distribution, 80
Rees, W. J. (*continued*):
 Evolutionary Trends in the Classification of Capitate Hydroids and Medusae, 295
 Notes on the European Species of Eledone, 80
 Revision of the Hydroid Genus Perigonimus M. Sars, 81
 Three Northern Species of Hydractinia, 81
Reference Pamphlets, 132, 344-5, 614, 872, 1150
Reference Works published in Asia, Directory of, 465
Reflex Reflectors, 652
Refractory Bricks, Blocks and Tiles Standing Committee Report. *Cmnd. 439.* 528, 667
Refrigerated Stores for Fruit, 72
Refrigeration Research, European, and its Practical Application, 975
Refrigerator. How to Choose and Use, 692
Refugee Fund. United Nations Accounts and Reports, 984
Refugee Seamen Agreement. *Cmnd. 427.* 527, 592
Refugees:
 Report of the United Nations High Commissioner, 455, 456, 726, 983, 984, 1254, 1255
 Voluntary Funds Administered by the United Nations. High Commissioner Accounts, 1255
 See also Palestine Refugees
Refuse Collection, etc. Costing Return, 613
Regents Park Terraces, Future of. Crown Estate Commissioners' Statement, 305, 836
"Reggio" Wreck Report, 192
Regimental Standing Orders:
 Army Catering Corps, 206
 Royal Army Service Corps, 206
Regiments, Amalgamation and Re-designation of certain, 953
Regional Census Training Centres:
 Asia and the Far East Report, 1259
 Latin America Report, 989
Regional Planning, 1255
Register of Deeds:
 389
 Index, 657
Registered Designs Act, 1949
Registered Designs (Amendment) Bill, 516
Registrar General:
 Returns, 118, 119, 328, 430, 598, 856, 1131
 Scotland:
  Report, 119, 328, 599, 1131
  Returns, 599
Registration and Licensing Authorities. Index Marks and Addresses, 189

1956-60 | REG-ROB

REG— INDEX 1956–60

Registration of Births, Deaths and Marriages (Navy, Marines and Service Civilians) (Overseas) Bill, 218, 219, 234, 243, 247, 249, 338
Registration of Births, Deaths and Marriages (Special Provisions) Act, 273
Registration of Births, Deaths and Marriages (Special Provisions) Bill, 219, 249
Registration of Independent Schools:
  169
  Circular, 385
  Memorandum, 401
Registration Officers:
  List of, 118, 328, 856, 1130
  Official List. Re-Grouping of Water Undertakings. Circular, 611
Registry of Friendly Societies Forms, 855
Rehabilitation and Resettlement of Disabled Persons Standing Committee Report, 619
Rehabilitation of Amputees. General Principles, 332
Rehabilitation of Derelict, etc. Land Circular, 1146
Rehabilitation of the Physically Handicapped, 457
Reid, D. D. Epidemiological Methods in the Study of Mental Disorders, 1269
Reid, J. A. Reflex Reflectors, 652
Reid, J. H., Spectrum of Quiescent Prominences, 380
Reid, Rt. Hon. Lord (Chairman: Malaya Constitutional Commission) Report, 303
Reilly, Sir Bernard, Aden and the Yemen, 1101
Reindeer, Introduced Reindeer to South Georgia, 571
Reiners, W. J., Incentives in the Building Industry, 909
Reinforced Concrete in Buildings, Note on the History of, 383
Re-Insurance of British Ships against War Risks. Amending Agreements, 927
Re-Insurance of Danish Ships against War Risks. Agreement, 404
Reiss, H., On the Synonymy of Some Zygaena Species, 1096
Reitz, Stonehenge and Avebury and Neighbouring Monuments Guide Map, 958
Relations between U.K. France and U.S.A. Convention with Germany. *Cmnd. 653*. 790, 849
Religions, Sociology of, 237A
Religious Houses. *See* Abbeys
Remodelled Economic Organisation Report, 1248
Remodelling of Old Schools, Circular, 842
Removal of House Refuse and the Cleansing of Earth Closets, etc., 612
Removal through Streets of Offensive Matter, 612
Removing and Erecting. Procedural Law relating to. *Cmnd. 114*. 256
Rendle, B. J., Growth and Structure of Wood, 650
Renfrewshire Educational Trust Scheme, Memorandum, 1184
Rennel Island, British Solomon Islands, Natural History of, 564, 828, 1098
Rent Act:
  273
  Circular, 340, 1146
  Forms, 342
  Report of Enquiry. *Cmnd. 1246*. 1069, 1148
Rent Act and You:
  343
  Scottish Edition, 330
  Welsh Edition, 343
Rent Bill, 32, 35, 215, 216, 217, 228, 243, 247, 248, 339, 1044
Rent Control, Statistical Information. *Cmnd. 17*. 53, 121, 131
Rent Policy, Voting by Councillor Tenants on, Circular, 129
Rents of Corporation Houses in Glasgow Report, 601
Rents of Houses Owned by Local Authorities:
  Circular, 120
  Scotland. *Cmd. 9773*. 43, 121; *Cmnd. 185*. 261, 330; *Cmnd. 393*. 525, 601, 656; *Cmnd. 710*. 794, 856; *Cmnd. 944*. 1047, 1133
Reorganisation of the Cotton Industry. *Cmnd. 744*. 796, 923
Repairing Brickwork, 1179
Repayment of Credits granted:
  By European Payments Union, Exchange of Letters between U.K. and:
    Austria. *Cmd. 9764*. 43, 48, 53; *Cmnd. 21*. 103
    Netherlands. *Cmd. 9848*. 49
    Switzerland. *Cmd. 9844*. 49
  to U.K. by European Payments Union and by Belgium-Luxembourg Economic Union to the European Payments Union. *Cmd. 9836*. 48, 104
Repayment of the Debt on the Liquidation of the European Payments Union. Exchange of Notes with U.K.:
  Netherlands. *Cmnd. 671*. 791, 851
  Norway. *Cmnd. 758*. 797, 851
Répertoire des Organisations Agricoles non Gouvernementales Groupées dans le Cadre de la Communanté Economique Européenne, 1235
Répertoire des Prodits Siderurgiques, 215A
Repertory of Practice of United Nations Organs:
  232A
  Supplement, 730

INDEX 1956–60 —REV

Replacement of Certain Emergency Legislation by the Land Powers (Defence) Bill. *Cmnd. 532*. 322
Repositories. *See* Archives
Représentation des Travailleurs sur le Plan de l'Entreprise dans le Droit des Pays Membres de la CECA, 965
Representation of the Laity Measure:
  3, 59, 83
  Ecclesiastical Committee Report, 3, 83
Representation of the People Act. 1949 (Amendment) Bill, 1041
Representation of the People (Amendment) Act, 273, 542
Representation of the People (Amendment) Bill, 36, 218, 234, 243, 339, 487, 520
Requirements and Properties of Adhesives for Wood, 166
Requirements for Biological Substances Report, 1269
Requisitioned Houses Act:
  1071
  Circulars, 1146
Requisitioned Houses and Housing (Amendment) Act. Circular, 340, 341, 868
Requisitioned Houses Bill, 1005, 1020, 1038, 1041, 1141
Resale Price Maintenance, 719
Rescue, 1137
Rescue Section, Civil Defence Instructors' Notes, 333, 603, 604, 1138
Rescue Training:
  Bulletin, 1137
  Instructional Diagrams, 333
Research:
  And Development Publications, 418-19
  And Its Users, 1179
  Councils in the Social Sciences, 468
  Data for Arid Zone Development Guide Book, 465
  Establishments, Direction of, 362
  For Industry Report, 651, 910, 1181
  Grants, 1179
  In Education, 466
  In Scotland, 504, 513, 608
  On Injuries Sustained in Road Accidents, 168
  Projects in Progress and in Plan, Register of Mass Communication, 468
  Reactors, 986
  Relating to Children: Studies in Progress, 419
  Workers and Students. Notes on Grants, 167
  Workers. *See* Scientific Manpower
Réseau Mondial. Pressure, Temperature and Precipitation Summaries, 360
Reserve Fleet Estimates. Select Committee Report, 606, 770, 866
Reserve Service of Short Service Officers, Liability from, etc., 956
Resettlement Advisory Board Progress Report. *Cmnd. 789*. 800, 885
Residual Values of Fertilizers and Feeding Stuffs. Report, 70, 288, 554, 820, 1082
Resistance of Fluids Flowing in Channels and Pipes, 909
Resources for Freedom Reports, 203
Respirators. Treasury Minute on Loan to Police and Fire Authorities. *Cmnd. 577*. 537, 679
Respiratory Virus Diseases. Expert Committee Report, 1000
Restriction of Capital Expenditure. Circular, 129
Restriction of Capital Investment. Circular, 341
Restriction of Imprisonment of Children Bill, 1042
Restriction of Offensive Weapons Act, 810
Restriction of Offensive Weapons Bill, 749, 764, 779, 784, 785, 864
Restrictive Business Practices:
  969
  Guide to Legislation on, 1248
Restrictive Trade Practices Act:
  56
  Export Agreements, 183
  Registration of Agreements Guide, 162
Restrictive Trade Practices Bill, 4, 5, 6, 33, 34, 35
Restrictive Trading Agreements Registry Publications, 162
Retail Price Comparisons for International Salary Determination, 989
Retail Prices Index of:
  Cost of Living Advisory Committee Report. *Cmd. 9710*. 40, 138
  Method of Construction and Calculation, 138, 886
Retail Selling. Career, 347
Retired Officers, Navy List, 813
Retired Pay, Pensions, etc.:
  Order Amending, 22, 23, 160, 223, 244, 368–9
  Order-in-Council, 160, 368, 639, 678, 769, 896, 1023, 1168
  Royal Warrant Amending. *Cmd. 9821, 9822*. 47, 160; *Cmnd. 63, 64, 306, 307*. 252, 253, 269, 369; *Cmnd. 748, 749*. 796, 797, 897; *Cmnd. 1004, 1005*. 1031, 1169
  Special Army Orders, 206, 425
Retirement and Discharge, Army, 696
Reunion Island International Customs Journal, 714
Revenue Departments:
  Appropriation Accounts, 31, 93, 133, 161, 244, 306, 345, 370, 578, 615, 640, 781, 837, 873, 898, 1038, 1108 1150, 1170

REV— INDEX 1956–60

Revenue Departments (*continued*):
  Estimates:
    1957–58, 226, 493, 494, 677
    1958–59, 494, 677
    1959–60, 760
    1960–61, 1019
Review Series, 1240
Revised Plan for Coal, 890
Revue des Nations Unies, 232A–3A, 459–60, 730, 987, 1258
Revue Internationale de Service Social, 987
Rexford-Welch, Squadron Leader S. G., Royal Air Force Medical Services:
  Commands, 122, 174
  Campaigns, 602, 657
Reynolds, D. J.:
  Assessment of Priority for Road Improvement, 1182
  London-Birmingham Motorway Traffic and Economics, Economic Assessment, 1182
Reynolds, G., Catalogue of Constable Collection, 1222
Reynolds, N., Simplified System of Mussel Purification, 74
Reynolds, P. K. B.:
  Egglestone Abbey Guide, 698
  Framlingham Castle Guide, 957
Rheolau'r Ffordd Fawr, 189
Rheumatic Fever, Prevention of, Expert Committee Report, 473
Rhodesia and Nyasaland:
  Constitution Amendment Bill:
    Cmnd. 298. 269, 305
    Order-in-Council, 305
  Electoral Bill. *Cmnd. 362*. 523, 573
  Gift of Stores and Equipment. *Cmnd. 492*. 531, 678
  Guarantee given on Loans to be made by International Bank for Reconstruction and Development, 506, 677, 1025, 1202
  International Customs Journal, 444, 714, 974
  Investment in Federation, 22, 203
  Report of the Advisory Commission on the Review of the Constitution. *Cmnd. 1148, 1149, 1150, 1151, 1151 I to IV*. 1061, 1062, 1105–6
Rhododendron Ponticum. Experiments on Chemical Control, 325
Rhubarb, Outdoor, 554
Rhuddlan Castle, Flintshire, Guide, 208
Rhyl and Denbigh, Soils and Land use of the District Around, 1081
Rhyl Urban District Council Act, 58
Ricard, R., Animal Feedstuffs, Regulations governing Manufacture and Sale, 437
Rice:
  709
Rice (*continued*):
  Commodity Report, 241A, 436, 707, 966
  Harvesting, 225A
  Industry, Economic Aspects Report, 242A
  In Sierra Leone. Investigation into Storage Problems, 833
  International Rice Commission Constitution. *Cmnd. 997*. 1050, 1121
  Processing Machines, 708
  Trade Glossary, 427
Richard II. Calendar of Inquisitions, 378
Richards, C. G., Provision of Popular Reading Materials, 996
Richards, R. (Chairman: Royal Commission on Ancient and Historical Monuments and Constructions of Wales and Monmouthshire) Report. *Cmd. 9762*. 43
Richardson, I. D.:
  Echo-Sounding Experiments in the Barents Sea, 1087
  Triple Frequency Echo Sounder, 73
Richborough Castle, Kent, Guide, 208
Ridley, Hon. M. W., Exploitation of Sea Birds in Seychelles, 570
Right of Passage over Indian Territory:
  Order, 713, 973
  Portugal *v.* India. Judgment, 1243
Rights and Obligations of Foreign Forces and their Members. Convention with Germany. *Cmnd. 654*. 790, 849
Rights of Light Act:
  810
  Committee Report. *Cmnd. 473*. 530, 632
Rights of Light Bill, 488, 746, 747, 748, 752, 784
Rigold, S. E.:
  Maison Dieu Guide, 611, 698
  North Elmham Saxon Cathedral, Norfolk, Guide, 1226
  Nunney Castle Guide, 427
  Yarmouth Castle Guide, 957
Riman, P. H. (Chairman: Gas Turbine Collaboration Committee Welding Panel) Report, 391
Ring Circuit Electrical Installations for Housing, 427
Ritchie, A., Scottish Seine Net Fishery, 1082
Ritchie, C. C., Studies on Bridge-Deck Systems. Bending Moments in a Plate-and-Girder System, 1181
Ritson, Sir E. H. (Chairman: Committee on Rating of Plant and Machinery) Report, 871
River Great Ouse Basin Hydrological Survey, 1148
River Severn Basin Hydrological Survey, 1148
Rivers (Prevention of Pollution) Act Circular, 611

INDEX 1956–60 —ROB

Road and Rail Traffic Act, Reports of the Licensing Authorities for Goods Vehicles, 404, 674, 930
Road Haulage:
  Cases, England and Wales. Decisions by Transport Arbitration Tribunal, 190
  Disposal Board Report, 20, 26, 189
Road Safety Bill, 1041
Road Safety (Protective Headgear) Bill, 1045
Road Traffic Act:
  56, 1071
  Periodic Vehicle Tests. *Cmnd. 430*. 527, 674
  Traffic Commissioner's Reports, 674, 927, 1199
Road Traffic (Amendment) Act, 1071
Road Traffic (Amendment) Bill, 1008, 1041, 1043
Road Traffic (Amendment) Bill and Road Traffic (Driving of Motor Cycles and Mopeds) Bill, 1026, 1038, 1142
Road Traffic and Roads Improvement Act, 1071
Road Traffic and Roads Improvement Bill, 1008, 1009, 1026, 1038, 1042, 1044, 1142
Road Traffic Bill, 4, 5, 6, 12, 30, 33, 35, 127, 755, 1003, 1005, 1042
Road Traffic Consolidation Bills Report, 1004, 1005, 1144
Road Traffic (Driving of Motor Cycles) Act, 1071
Road Traffic (Driving of Motor Cycles and Mopeds) Bill, 1041, 1043
Road Traffic (Driving of Motor Cycles) Bill, 1009, 1010, 1026, 1038, 1043, 1044, 1142
Road Transport Lighting Act:
  273, 540
  Report, 216
Road Transport Lighting (Amendment) Act, 542
Road Transport Lighting (Amendment) Bill, 248, 250, 479, 495, 513, 608
Road Transport Lighting Bill, 213, 215
Road Vehicles:
  Mechanically Propelled:
    Annual Census, 405, 673, 990, 1199
    Return, 189, 405
  Private, Temporary Importation for Use of. *Cmnd. 602*. 787, 846
Roadcraft:
  863
  Manual of Driving Instructions for Students, 124
  Police Drivers' Manual, 1140
Roadmaking Aggregates. A Study of the Granulators Used in the Production of, 1182
Roads:
  Abstracts, 167–8, 384, 430, 651, 910, 1182
  Accidents:
    404, 656, 673, 930, 1182, 1198
    Caused by Dogs, 935
    Christmas, 1959, 1182
    Research on Injuries sustained, 168
    Summary and Tables, 189
  And Airfields, Military Engineering, 954
  And Bridge Works Specification, 404, 673
  And Motor Transport. United Nations Conference, 1261
  And Road Problems in South-East Asia and the Caribbean, Report on, 301
  Concrete, 165, 292
  Construction Over Peat, Review of Existing Methods, 652
  England and Wales Report, 515, 673, 674, 782, 927
  Fund:
    Account, 11, 189, 225, 404
    Administration Report, 189, 404
  Junctions in Rural Areas, 1182
  Local Material, 559
  Markings, European Agreement. *Cmnd. 480*. 530, 593
  Notes, 1182
  Report, Scottish. *See* Industry and Employment in Scotland
  Research:
    Board Report, 168, 384, 652, 910, 1182
    Index of Publications, Addendum, 384
    Road Notes, 168, 384, 652, 910, 1182
    Technical Papers, 168, 384, 652, 910, 1182
  Safety Committee Report on Minimum Age for Motor-Cyclists, 403
  Safety Report *see* Sense and Safety
  Safety. Slough Experiment Report, 404
  Safety. *See* Departmental Road Safety
  Surfacing and Maintenance. Using Tar or Asphaltic Bitumen, Types of, 652
  Traffic:
    Accidents in Europe. Statistics, 233A, 460, 730, 989, 1260
    Consolidation of Certain Enactments relating to, 755, 867
    Convention on, *Cmnd. 578*. 537, 593
Roadstone Test Data, 910, 1182
Robb, W., Key to Oat Varieties described in Scottish Seed Oats, 70
Robb, W. B. Temperature of British Fish during Distribution in Summer, 910
Robbie, J. A., Geology of the Country Around Bridport and Yeovil, 857

ROB-SAY | 1956-60

ROB— INDEX 1956–60

Roberts, E., County of Anglesey Soils and Agriculture, 553
Roberts, Sir H., Colliery Explosion Reports. *Cmnd. 467, 485.* 529, 531
Roberts, Brigadier M. R., India's Most Dangerous Hour, 565, 658
Roberts, Sir S., (Chairman: Committee on Structure of Public Library Service In England and Wales) Report. *Cmnd. 660.* 791, 843
Robertson, General Sir Brian, (Chairman: British Transport Commission) Report. *Cmnd. 813.* 801, 927
Robertson, Colonel J. R. H., Railway Accident Report, 1197
Roberts-Wray, Sir Kenneth (Chairman: Judicial Advisers' Conference), 1104
Robinson, Professor Austin. (Chairman: Energy Advisory Commission) Report, 1250
Robinson, D. H., Wheat, 560
Robson, Sir T. B. (Chairman: Coal Distribution Costs) Report. *Cmnd. 446.* 528
Rochdale Corporation Act, 543
Rodent from East Africa, New Miocene, 295
Rodenticides, Biological Methods for the Evaluation of, 560
Roe Deer, 1129
Rogers, J. S., Leather Book-bindings. How to Preserve them, 199
Rogers, T. A.:
Explosion Report. *Cmnd. 843.* 803, 898
Underground Fire. Auchengeich Colliery. Report. *Cmnd. 1022.* 1052
Rogers, T. E., Spain. Overseas Economic Survey, 398
Role of the Executive in the Modern State, 736
Rolled Asphalt and Coated Macadam, Sampling and Analysis of, 168
Roman Britain. Guide to Antiquities, 562
Roman Lettering. Alphabets and Inscriptions, 693
Roman Site at Wall, Staffordshire, Guide, 698
Romanesque Art, 422
Romford Ice and Cold Storage Co. Ltd. *See* Lister v.
"Romford Recorder" Newspaper. Privileges Committee Report on Complaint, 225, 338
Romney, D. H., Land in British Honduras, 1103
Roof Drainage, 649
Roofing. Safety, Health and Welfare Pamphlet, 630
Roofs. Condensation and Design of Factory Roofs, 649
Rook, 71
Rootstocks for Apples and Pears, 288
Rope, Twine and Net. Census of Production Report, 395, 1194
Rosaura Expedition, 828
Rose, Sir. H. (Chairman: Committee on Employment of Children in the Potato Harvest) Report. *Cmd. 9738.* 41
Roses for the Home, 201
Roskill, Captain S. W., War at Sea, 296, 1098, 1189
Ross, J., (Chairman: Fact Finding Mission on Child Migration to Australia) Report. *Cmd. 9832.* 47
Ross and Cromarty Educational Trust Scheme. Memorandum, 912, 1185
Ross Motorway, 1199
Rosse, The Earl of (Chairman: Standing Commission on Museums and Galleries) Report, 916
Rothschild, M., Fleas, 81
Roumania. Agreement with U.K. relating to the Settlement of Financial Matters. *Cmnd. 1232.* 1068, 1125
Roumanian Property. Accounts of the Administrator. *Cmnd. 466.* 529, 680; *Cmnd. 773.* 799, 938; *Cmnd. 980.* 1049, 1200
Round Oak Steel Works (Level Crossings) Act, 811
Round Timber from the Farm, 1087
Route Facilities Charges:
Conference Proceedings, 712
Statement, 971
Rowe, M. E., Hatfield New Town Report, 611
Rowlands, W. T.:
Aiechydon Defaid, 555
Diseases of Sheep, 557
Rowlandson, Thomas. Catalogue of Water-colour Drawings, 1159
Rowntree, J. A., Internal Migration, 327
Roxburgh County Council (Ale Water) Order Confirmation Act, 58
Roxburgh County Council (Ale Water) Order Confirmation Bill, 3, 34
Roxburgh Educational Trust Scheme. Draft and Memorandum, 386, 653
Roxburgh, Hon. Mr. Justice (Chairman: Land Charges Committee) Report. *Cmd. 9825.* 47
Roxburghshire:
Ancient Monuments Royal Commission Report. *Cmd. 9735.* 41, 172
Inventory of Ancient and Historical Monuments, 162
Royal Air Force:
Manual. *See* Elementary Meteorology for Aircrew
Medical Services, Campaigns, 122, 174, 602, 657
Prize Fund Account, 23, 76, 240, 294, 762, 781, 826
Royal Army Medical Corps, etc. Standing Orders, 426, 956, 1125

INDEX 1956–60 —RUR

Royal Army Service Corps Regimental Standing Orders, 206
Royal Badge for Wales on Flags, Use of, 610
Royal Botanic Gardens:
Edinburgh:
Descriptive and Illustrated Account, 378
Notes, 162, 378, 646, 901, 1175
Kew:
Guide, 378, 824
Publications, 162, 378, 646, 901, 1175
Royal College of Physicians of London Act, 1073
Royal Commissions:
Ancient and Historical Monuments and Constructions:
England. Report. *Cmnd. 743.* 796, 863, 902, 1176
Scotland. *Cmd. 9735.* 41, 162, 172, 378, 1175
Selkirkshire. *Cmnd. 276.* 267, 378
Wales and Monmouthshire, 123, 162, 1060, 1140, 1175
Awards to Inventors, 378
Civil Service, 163
Common Land, 163, 378–80, 647; *Cmnd. 462.* 529, 647
Doctors' and Dentists' Remuneration, 380, 647, 901; *Cmnd. 939, 1064.* 1047, 1055, 1175, 1176
Historical Manuscripts, 380
Law Relating to Mental Illness and Mental Deficiency. Minutes of Evidence, 380
Local Government in Greater London, 902; *Cmnd. 1164.* 1063, 1176
Marriage and Divorce, 163
Police. *Cmnd. 1222.* 1067, 1140, 1177
Royal Engineers. Supplementary Pocket Book Amendments, 207, 425, 696, 1225
Royal English Bookbindings in the British Museum, 294
Royal Exchange Assurance Act, 1073
Royal Fine Art Commission:
Report. *Cmnd. 70.* 253, 335; *Cmnd. 447.* 528, 605; *Cmnd. 909.* 807, 863
Scotland Report, *Cmnd. 982.* 1050, 1187
Royal Greenwich Observatory:
Bulletins, 904, 1178
Publications, 904, 1178
Royal Hospital, Chelsea, Army Prize Money and Legacy Funds, Account. 222, 246, 425, 757, 955, 1015, 1225
Royal Institution of Great Britain Charity Bill, 518
Royal Institution of Great Britain Charity Scheme Confirmation Act, 543
Royal Institution of Great Britain Charity Scheme Confirmation Bill, 481
Royal Marines Enlistment and Service Orders and Regulations, 1075
Royal Marines Enlistment and Service (Amending) Orders and Regulations, 1075
Royal Mint:
Outline History, 1178
Publications, 164, 1178
Report, 164, 380, 648, 905, 1178
Royal Naval Dental Surgery Assistants Handbook, 547
Royal Naval Medical Services, 122, 174
Royal Naval Sick Berth Staff Handbook, 813
Royal Navy Prize Fund Account, 10, 61, 228, 277
Royal Observatory, Edinburgh. Publications, 164, 380, 648, 1178
Royal Ordnance Factories:
Estimate, 1960–61, 1019, 1225
Supplementary Estimate, 1959–60, 1019, 1225
Royal Parks of London, 208
Royal School for Deaf Children Margate Act, 543
Royal Scottish Museum, Publications, 164, 381
Royal Society for the Prevention of Cruelty to Animals Act, 544
Royal Wanstead School Act, 812
Royal Warrant Holders List, 150, 357, 631, 917, 1189
Royal Warrant to Amend Retired Pay, Pensions, etc. *Cmnd. 1004, 1005.* 1051 1169
Ruanda-Urundi. United Nations Visiting Mission to Trust Territories Report, 733
Rubber:
Census of Production Report, 179, 665
Proofed Garment Making. Industry Report on Application for Establishment of a Wages Council, 149
Rubella and Other Virus Infections during Pregnancy. Report. 1136
Rucker, Sir Arthur. Review of University Grants Committee Methods. *Cmnd. 1235.* 1068
Rugby Corporation Act, 58
Rule Against Perpetuities. *See* Law Reform Committee Report
Runciman of Doxford, Rt. Hon. Viscount (Chairman: Horticultural Marketing) Report. *Cmnd. 61.* 252
Runcorn–Widnes Bridge Act, 57
Running Costs of Hospitals:
Analysis of, 121, 600, 1132
Select Committee on Estimates:
Report, 336, 763, 866
Special Report, 497, 606
Rural Communities. Problems, Methods and Types of Research, 996
Rural Education, 238A, 736

RUR— INDEX 1956–60

Rural Electrification:
233A, 460, 987, 1259
In Europe, 730
Rural Home Economics:
Advisers, Training of, 1247
In Europe, Advisory Work on, 719
Rural Sociology. 466
Rural Subjects. Teaching in Secondary Schools, 386
Rural Television in Japan Report, 1265
Rural Wales, Problems of, 1037
Rural Welfare, F.A.O.'s role in, 966
Rural Youth, Education of, 238A
Rushes, Control of, 1083
Russell, R., Early Keyboard Instruments, 1222
Russell, W. L.:
Testing Mixers for Bituminous Materials, 384
Tests on the Efficiency of a Twin-Shaft Paddle Mixer with Various Settings of the Paddle Tips, 168
Russell Greig, J., Shepherd's Guide to the Prevention and Control of Diseases of the Sheep, 70
Ruud, K., Financial Assistance Schemes for the Acquisition or Improvement of Fishing Craft, 1237
Ruwenzori Expedition, 82, 296, 564, 828
Ruzicic, Professor N., Cleaning and Storing of Grain Survey, 979

S

Sabine, P. A., Chemical Analysis of Igneous Rocks, Metamorphic Rocks and Minerals, 119
Sacred Trust, 233A, 460, 1259
Safe Cycling, 405
Safe Handling of Radioisotopes, 1240
Safeguarding of Agricultural Land. *See* Town and Country Planning Circular
Safety:
And Health:
In the Building and Civil Engineering Industries, Report. *Cmnd. 953.* 1048, 1158
Law relating to, 643
Under Mines and Quarries Act, Law relating to, 372
Aspects of Pedal and Motor Assisted Cycles, 384
Building Operations, 630
Circulars, 115, 645, 900, 1172
Devices for Hand and Foot Operated Presses, 630
Health and Welfare Conditions in Non-Ferrous Foundries. Joint Standing Committee Report, 875
Safety (*continued*):
Health and Welfare:
New Series, 1158
Pamphlets, 26, 149, 630, 645, 876, 885, 1158
In Mines Research. Report, 327, 645, 901, 1173
In the Home, Designing for, 857
In the Use of Power Presses, Joint Standing Committee Report, 885
Lamps for Use in Mines, Test and Approval of, 646
Of Life at Sea, International Conference, 1152
Precautions in Schools Display Cards, 170
Precautions, intense Radio-Frequency Radiation, 1170
Series, 969, 1240
Sagitta Planctonis and Related Forms, 295
Sailor, Dress of the British, 362
"St. Celestin" Wreck Report, 192
Saint Christopher, Nevis and Anguilla:
Colonial Arms, 569
Orders-in-Council, 1173
St. Helena Colonial Report, 87, 832
St. James's Dwellings Charity Scheme Confirmation Act, 544
St. James's Dwellings Charity Scheme Confirmation Bill, 481
St. Johns Colliery, Yorkshire. Explosion Report. *Cmnd. 935.* 1047, 1171
St. John's Station, Lewisham, Railway Accident Report, 673
St. Kitts-Nevis-Anguilla Colonial Report, 569
Saint Lucia:
Administrator of the Colony. Orders-in-Council, 1173
Agreement between U.K. and U.S.A. for extension of Bahamas Long Range Proving Grounds. *Cmd. 9811.* 46, 111
Colonial Report, 87, 569
Constitution. Order-in-Council, 1174
Saint Martin's Parish Church Birmingham Act, 1073
St. Marylebone, Parking Places, 929
St. Paul's Cathedral Order, 357
Saint Peter Upper Thames Street Churchyard Act, 1073
Saint Peter's Church Nottingham (Broad Marsh Burial Ground) Act, 1073
St. Stephen Bristol (Burial Grounds etc.) Act, 1073
Saint Stephen Walbrook (Saint Antholin's Churchyard) Act, 58
St. Vincent:
Colonial Report, 301
Orders-in-Council, 1173
Salad and Other Food Crops in Glasshouses, 72
Salad Crops, Outdoor, 72

INDEX 1956–60 —SAY

Salaires et les Charges Sociales dans les Industries de la Communauté, 215A
Sale and Leasing of Houses Circular, 1146
Sale of Military Equipment abroad. Select Committee on Estimates Report, 770, 865
Sale of Milk Bill, 513, 518, 608
Sale of Tobacco and Construction of Housing Facilities. Exchange of Notes between U.K. and U.S.A. *Cmd. 9793.* 45, 111; *Cmnd. 143, 272.* 258, 267
Sales Taxes on Productivity, Influence of, 718
Salford Corporation Act, 1073
Saline Water, Utilisation of, 465
Salisbury, Most Hon. The Marquess (Chairman: Royal Commission on Ancient and Historical Monuments and Constructions of England) Report. *Cmnd. 743.* 796, 863
Salmon:
And Sea Trout caught at Sea, Records of, 171
Fishing. Weekly Close Time, 915
Research Committee Pass Investigation. Sub-Committee Report, 388
Tagged in the Sea, Altens, Kincardineshire, Movements of, 655
Salmond, Dr. K. F., Investigation into Grain Storage Problems in Nyasaland 570
Salt Mines, Brine Pits and Salt Works. Census of Production Report, 394
Sample Surveys of Current Interest. Reports, 461, 1259
Samplers, 1223
Samuels, A. (Chairman):
Committee on Parking Survey of Inner London. Report, 188, 672
London and Home Counties Traffic Advisory Committee Report on 30 m.p.h. Speed Limit, 188
London Travel Committee. Report, 927
Sanbach Crosses, Cheshire, Guide, 208
Sand and Gravel:
In Central Scotland, Report on the Supply, 182
Production, 699, 958, 1227
Sand for Concrete, 648
Sandbank Bombing Range. Exchange of Notes between U.K. and Germany constituting a Supplementary Agreement. *Cmnd. 244.* 265
Sands, for Plasters, Mortars and Renderings, 1226
Sands, W. A.:
Revision of the East-African Nasutitermitanae, 294
Revision of the Termites of the Genus Amitermes from the Ethiopian Region (Isoptera, Termintidae, Amitermitirae), 827
Sandwell and Company Limited:
Board Mill Survey, Economic Survey, 854
Small Pulp Survey, Economic Study, 855
Sandwich Courses:
And Block Release Courses E. and W., 1115
Approved, 842
List of, 313, 586
Sanitary Conditions and Management of Slaughterhouses Model Byelaws, 74
Sanitary Engineers, Training of, 244A
Sanitary Inspectors (Change of Designation Act), 56
Sanitary Inspectors (Change of Designation) Bill, 5, 21, 30, 127
Sanitary Regulations, International. *Cmnd. 30, 312.* 250, 270; 471
Sansom, R. C., Organisation of Building Sites, 909
Sappaphis Matsumura, British Species of, 293
Sap-Stain in Timber, 907
Sarawak:
Colonial Report, 87, 88, 301, 570, 1102
Constitution, Order-in-Council, 1174
Sardinia, Pilot Area in, 1248
Sasines, Index to Particular Register for Sheriffdoms, 173, 389, 657, 916, 1188
Saunders, A. D.:
Barnard Castle Guide, 957
Tilbury Fort, Essex, Guide, 1226
Sausages. Food Standards Committee Report, 74
Savage, C. I., Inland Transport, 296
Savage, R. E., Great Spatfall of Mussels in the River Conway Estuary in Spring, 1940, 74
Saville, Alan:
Eggs and Larvae of Haddock at Faroe, 172
Planktonic Stages of the Haddock in Scottish Waters, 914
Savings Banks Funds Account, 197, 411, 680, 938, 1206
Savory Herbs. Culture and Use, 201
Savory, J. G., Dry Rot in Wood, 1180
Sawflies, Gooseberry and Blackcurrant, 1083
Saw-Toothed Grain Beetle, 1084
Sawn Softwood, 460
Sawnwood. *See* Timber Statistics
Saws, Circular, 907
Sawyer, J. S., Rainfall of Depressions which pass Eastward over or near the British Isles, 153
Saxifraga of the Himalaya, 562
Saxtead Green Mill, Framlingham, Suffolk, Guide, 1226
Saxton's Maps, 79, 827, 1094
Sayers, R. S., Financial Policy, 1939–45, 82, 174

1956-60 | SCA-SHI

SCA— INDEX 1956-60

Scales of Salaries for Teachers. Report of the Committee, 842
Scandinavian Silver, 952
Scarborough Castle:
Guide, 1227
Postcard, 697
Schistosoma, Intermediate Hosts of, 740
Schizonycha Dejean from Southern Africa, Revision of the Species, 1095
Schoeller, H., Arid Zone Hydrology:
994
Recent Developments, 1263
Schofield, E. T., Manual for Evaluators of Films and Filmstrips, 239A
Schofield, H. H., Report on Total Accident at Bramble Island Explosives Factory, 334
Scholarships awarded under Churchill Endowment Fund for Exchange of Students. *Cmnd. 885.* 806, 847
Schools:
And the Countryside, 585
Buildings:
466
Colour in, 100
Expansion of, 468
Gift to Milan. *Cmnd. 987.* 1050, 1203
Scotland, 170, 386
Story of Post-War, 313
Children, Report on Health of, 101, 842
Closure of, Memorandum, 100
Co-operatives, 238A
Curricula, Preparation of General Secondary, 1265
Enrolment:
Projection Methods, 995
Statistics, Current, 237A, 466, 994
Examinations in Secondary. Report, 1115
Feeding in Asia and the Far East. Report of the Regional Seminar, 967
Furniture and Equipment, 994
Handicapped Pupils England and Wales, 101
Inspection and Supervision, 237A, 238A
Kitchens, Design of, 313
Limits of Cost for New Schools, Circular, 100
Lunchrooms, Planning and Equipping, 422
Meals:
Film Strips, 313
Service and the Schools Circular, 1184
Service and the Teacher. Circular, 842, 843
Services Report, 100, 101
Premises. Standards for, Regulations. Circular, 842, 843
Recognised as Efficient, E. and W., 101, 586
Schools (*continued*):
Registers and Records, 100
Registration of Independent:
169
Circular, 385
Memorandum, 101
Remodelling of Old. Circular, 842, 843
Scotland Code, 109
Syllabus of Physical Education, 1185
See also Secondary School
Schöpp, R., Pea Weevil and Methods of Its Control, 420
Schuman, Bibliographie Analytique du Plan Schuman et de la CECA, 214A
Science:
And Society, 468
Career, 347
Chemistry, Physics, Botany, Zoology, Biology. Scottish Certificate of Education, 913
Education for the Age of, 951
Inventories of Apparatus and Materials for Teaching, 467
Notes on Applied, 155, 362, 636, 890
Office of the Minister for, 905
Report on Teaching Science by Use of Television in Schools, 1249
Teaching in Secondary Schools, 386, 1116
Teaching, Unesco Source Book for, 469
Science Museum:
First Hundred Years, 381
Publications, 164, 381, 648, 905, 1178
Scientific and Engineering Manpower:
Great Britain Report, 149; *Cmnd. 902.* 807, 887, 905
Shortage of. Report, 422
Scientific and Engineering Research. Estimates of Resources devoted to, 910
Scientific and Industrial Research, Department of:
Grants for Graduate Students and Research Workers, 908
Publications, 164–8, 381–5, 648, 905, 1178
Report. *Cmd. 9690, 9734.* 39, 41, 151; *Cmnd. 213.* 263; *Cmnd. 428.* 527, 632; *Cmnd. 739.* 796, 887; *Cmnd. 1049.* 1054, 1160
Select Committee on Estimates:
Report, 505, 606, 770, 866
Special Report, 1023, 1143
Scientific and Industrial Research, Department of, Act, 55
Scientific and Industrial Research, Department of, Bill, 2, 3, 5, 21, 29, 34, 35, 125
Scientific and Technical Personnel in 10 Asian Countries, Requirements and Resources of, 1266

INDEX 1956-6 —SCO

Scientific and Technical Translating and other Aspects of the Language Problem, 466
Scientific Cleaning for the Fish Industry, Principles of, 649
Scientific Knowledge in Scotland, Development and Application of 772, 778, 863
Scientific Manpower for Applied Research, 449
Scientific Papers, 1162
Scientific Policy Report of the Advisory Council. *Cmnd. 11.* 53, 151; *Cmnd. 278.* 268, 359; *Cmnd. 597.* 539, 632; *Cmnd. 893.* 806, 887, 905; *Cmnd. 1167.* 1063, 1159, 1178
Scientific Research:
British Universities, 168, 384, 652, 910, 1182
Natural History Museum, 82
Scientific Results of the Danish Rennell Expedition, and British Museum (Natural History) Expedition, 564, 828
Scientific, Surgical and Photographic Instruments, etc. Census of Production Report, 664
Scientific Technological Educational and Cultural Fields. Agreement between U.K. and U.S.S.R. *Cmnd. 917.* 808, 853
Scientist. Careers, 1152
Scotland Now, 1187
Scott, C. W.:
Colliery Explosion Report. *Cmnd. 279.* 268
Mines and Quarries Report, 116, 642, 645
Scott, J. D.:
Administration of War Production, 82, 173
Studies of Overseas Supply, 82, 174
Scott, P. H., Bolivia Overseas Economic Survey, 182
Scottish Abbeys, 1227
Scottish Administration. Handbook, 172
Scottish Agricultural Economics:
70, 288, 430, 554, 1081, 1082
Studies, 288
Scottish American Investment Company Limited Order Confirmation Act, 1073
Scottish American Investment Company Limited Order Confirmation Bill, 1042
Scottish Castles, 958
Scottish Certificate of Education. Syllabuses and Specimen Question Papers, 912
Scottish Education Department:
Circulars, 169, 385, 653, 911, 1184
Publications, 169–71, 385–6, 653, 911, 1184
Report and Accounts, 170
Rules, 654
Scottish Estimates, 22, 30, 127, 236, 243, 339, 505, 513, 608, 779, 864, 1029, 1038, 1142
Scottish Health Services Council:
331, 601, 858, 1133
Standing Joint Committee Report, 1133
Scottish Health Statistics, 1133
Scottish Home Department:
Circular, 654, 1186
Publications, 171–3, 386–9, 654, 913, 1186
Scottish Hospitals:
Directory, 601, 1132
Endowments Research Trust. Report and Accounts, 222, 330, 494, 601, 767, 857, 1024, 1133
Scottish Housing Handbook, 121, 331, 601
Scottish Land Court:
Proceedings Report. *Cmd. 9689.* 38, 53; *Cmnd. 15.* 172, 173; *Cmnd. 506.* 532, 656, 657
Publications, 389, 915, 1188
Report: *Cmnd. 216.* 263, 388; *Cmnd. 788.* 800, 915; *Cmnd. 1038.* 1053, 1188
Appendices, 657, 915
Scottish Leaving Certificate:
Circular, 653, 1184
Examination Circular, 169, 385, 654, 911, 1185
Memorandum, 170
Papers, 171
Scottish Licensing Law Report. *Cmnd. 1217.* 1066, 1188
Scottish Milk Marketing Scheme, 70
Scottish Office Publications, 173, 389, 657, 916, 1188
Scottish Record Office Publications, 173, 389, 657, 916, 1188
Scottish Regalia, Postcard, 427
Scottish Representative Peers:
Election of a Representative, 486, 610
Minutes of Meeting of Election, 754, 867
Scottish Roads Report. *See* Industry and Employment in Scotland
Scottish Sea Fisheries Statistical Tables, 172, 388, 656, 915, 1082
Scottish Seine Net Fishery, 1082
Scottish Services, Civil Estimate, Revised, 1960–61, 1202
Scottish Standing Committee Debates:
489, 490
Volume, 1013
Scottish Statistics, Digest, 173, 389, 656, 913, 1186
Scottish Union and National Insurance Company's Act, 58
Scottish Universities. Local Contributions to Report. *Cmnd. 640.* 789, 912
Scottish Valuation Advisory Council Report, 656, 1186
Scottish Woollen Technical College Educational Endowments Scheme:
Memoranda, 654
Order-in-Council, 654

SCR— INDEX 1956-60

Scrap Metal Processing Census of Production Report, 663
Screw Threads, Gauging and Measuring, 890
Sea Action Committee of the Institute of Civil Engineers Report, 1181
Sea Fights. Oil Paintings, 362
Sea Fish Industry Act, 810
Sea Fish Industry Bill, 755, 783, 786, 1014, 1142
Sea Fish Industry of Great Britain, Governmental Services to, 707
Sea Fish Marketing in the Federal Republic of Germany, 707
Sea Fisheries (Compensation) (Scotland) Act, 810
Sea Fisheries (Compensation) (Scotland) Bill, 748
Sea Fisheries (Scotland) Bill, 520, 758, 778, 863
Sea Fisheries Statistical Tables:
75, 293, 560, 824, 1082, 1088
Scottish, 656
Sea Transport Service Regulations. Amendment, 405, 930
Sea. United Nations Conference on the Law, 982
Seaham Harbour Dock Act, 544
Seal, D. T., Collection of Cones from Standing Trees, 1129
Seals:
And Scottish Fisheries, 1082
Monk, 80
Seamanship. Manual of Amendment, 277, 547, 1074
Search and Rescue Division Report, 218A
Search for Disarmament, 1150
Seats. Southeast Asia Treaty Organisation Report, 203
Second World War:
Battles, Actions and Engagements, 205
History Publications, 82, 173, 389, 565, 602, 657, 1189
Secondary Batteries (Lead Acid and Alkaline Type), 94
Secondary Education. A Look Ahead, 419
Secondary Education For All. *Cmnd. 604.* 539, 586
Secondary Education in England and Wales, 313, 586, 843
Secondary School Plant, 422
Secondary Schools. Physical Education, 386
Secondary Technical and Vocational Education in Underdeveloped Countries, 995
Secretary of State for Scotland. Nationalised Industries and Undertakings Account, 496, 587
Securities and Unit Trusts. Particulars of Dealers in, 1193
Security. Conference of Privy Councillors, Statement. *Cmd. 9715.* 40, 161
Security Council, United Nations:
Records, 233A, 460–1, 730–1, 988, 989, 1239
Repertoire of the Practice, 461, 1258
Report, 983
Security of Tenure of Business Premises, 358
Seddon, H., Spectrophotometric Measurements of Early Type Stars, 648, 1178
Seed and Potting Composts, 555
Seed Crushing and Oil Refining. Census of Production Report, 179, 394
Seed Potatoes Stock Maintenance, 70
Seedlings of Common Weeds, 1083
Seeds:
For Leys, 1083
Testing for Farmers, 288
Testing of Agricultural Seeds moving in International Trade, 224A
Transactions in. Report *Cmnd. 300.* 269, 293, 335
Seeds of Progress, 233A
Seiche Movement and its Effect on the Hydrology of Lake Victoria, 302
Seismology, 381
"Seistan". Wreck Reports, 1200
Selecting Ash by Inspection, 908
Selective Weed Control in Cereals, 820
Self-Service in Europe. Report on Economic Performance, 1246
Selkirkshire:
Ancient and Historical Monuments Royal Commission. Report. *Cmnd. 276.* 267, 378
Educational Trust Draft Scheme:
170
Memorandum, 386
Order-in-Council, 386
Inventory of Ancient and Historical Monuments, 378
Sellers, Rt. Hon. Lord Justice (Chairman: Criminal Law Revision Committee) Report. *Cmnd. 835.* 802, 861; *Cmnd. 1187.* 1064
Selling the United States Market, 420
Senate and House of Commons Northern Ireland. Disqualification of Certain Members. *Cmd. 9698.* 39, 124
Senior Commercial and Airline Transport Pilots' Licences:
190, 405, 930
Examination Papers, 1091
Sense and Safety, 190
Sergestidae of the Great Barrier Reef Expedition, 81
Service Departments Public Accounts. Report, 233
Services Estimates (Major Variations) Select Committee on Estimates Reports, 1031, 1038, 1144
Service Lubricants and Temporary Protectives Handbook, 918

INDEX 1956-60 —SHI

Service Pay:
Allowances. *Cmnd. 365.* 523, 572
Pensions. *Cmd. 9692.* 20, 91; *Cmnd. 945.* 1047, 1114
Service with Overseas Governments. *Cmnd. 1193.* 1065, 1104
Services Available to the Chronic Sick and Elderly, Survey of, 332
Services' Textbook of Radio, 955
Sessile Tunicata, 296
Sessional Index, House of Commons, 8, 127
Sessional Printed Papers:
House of Commons Papers, 8, 127, 755
Titles and Contents, House of Commons, 8, 127, 489, 608, 1012, 1013, 1144
Setting out on Site, 956
Settle Railway Accident Report, 1198
Settlement of Debts. Exchange of Notes between U.K. and Czechoslovakia concerning Agreement. *Cmnd. 55.* 252
Settlement of Differences, Rules for, 971
Seven-Figure Trigonometrical Tables for Every Second of Time, 814
Severn. *See* River Severn
Sewage, and Sewage Effluents, Methods of Chemical Analysis, as applied to, Committee Report, 131
Sewage Contamination of Bathing Beaches in England and Wales, 887
Sexual Offences Act, 56
Sexual Offences Bill, 2, 34
Sexual Offences Bill Joint Committee Report, 1
Seychelles:
Colonial Report, 569, 1102
Orders-in-Council, 1174
Shapiro, H. L., Jewish People, Bibliographical History, 1265
Sharpe's Trust Scheme. Order-in-Council, 169
Shaw, C. J. D. Rents of Corporation Houses in Glasgow Report, 601
Shaw, W. A., Calendar of Treasury Books, 161, 646
"Sheaf Royal" Wreck Report, 406
Shearer, I. A. (Chairman: Tenancy of Shops Committee) Report. *Cmnd. 472.* 530
Shearer, W. M.:
Movement of Salmon Tagged in Sea, 655
Records of Salmon and Sea Trout caught at Sea, 171
Sheep:
Breeding and Management, 290, 1085
Diseases of, 557
Foot Rot in, 821
Industry in Britain Report, 652
Maggot Fly, 556
Prevention and Control of the Diseases, 554
Sheepdog. Management and Feeding, 70
Sheerness Pier and Harbour Order Confirmation Act, 542
Sheerness Pier and Harbour Order Confirmation Bill, 483, 485
Sheerness Pier and Harbour Provisional Order Bill, 518
Sheet Metal Worker and Coppersmith. Career, 1152
Sheffield. Geology of Country Around, 329
Shell, Hon. Mr. Justice (Chairman: Supreme Court of Northern Ireland Committee) Report. *Cmnd. 227.* 264
Shelbourne, J. E., Oyster Stock in Rivers Crouch and Roach, 292
Shell (Stanlow to Partington Pipeline) Act, 544
Shellard, H. C., Averages of Accumulated Temperature and Standard Deviation of Monthly Mean Temperature over Britain, 889
Shell-Mex and B.P. (London Airport Pipeline) Act, 812
Shelter Belts:
And Microclimate, 325
For Farmland, 292
Shelter from Radioactive Fallout, 200
Shelter Woods or Belts, 69, 819
Shepheard, Sir V. G. (Chairman: Admiralty Advisory Committee) Report, 277
Shepherd, H. J., Cooling of the Uneviscerated Poultry Carcase by Various Methods in Common Use, 165
Shepherds Bush and Holland Park. Railway Accident Report, 929
Shepherd's Guide:
554
To the Prevention and Control of Diseases of the Sheep, 70
Sheppard, V. L. O., Land Registration, 88
Shereefian Empire. Exchange of Notes between U. K. and Morocco concerning Convention of Commerce and Navigation. *Cmnd. 144.* 259
Shergold, F. A.:
Polishing of Roadstone in Relation to the Resistance to Skidding of Bituminous Road Surfacings, 652
Study in the Granulators Used in Production of Roadmaking Aggregates, 1182
Sheridan, M., Emmetropia and Its Aberrations, 359
Sheridan, M. D., Developmental Progress of Infants and Young Children, 1136
Sherlock, R. L.:
Geological Column, 328
London and Thames Valley. British Regional Geology, 1131
Shewan, J. M., Dehydration of Fish, 165
Shifting Cultivation in Philippines. Report on an Integral System, 437

SHI-SOL | 1956-60

Shimmin, A. N., (Chairman: Catering Wages Commission) Report, 773, 876
Ship Models, 164
Ship Portraits in the National Maritime Museum, 154
Shipbuilding:
And Marine Engineering Industries, Research and Development Requirements, 1181
And Ship Repairing:
Census of Production Report, 179, 663
Revision of Regulations, 619
Shipbuilding Employers' Federation and Confederation of Shipbuilding and Engineering Unions. Report of a Court of Inquiry into Dispute. *Cmnd. 160*. 260
Shipping:
Casualties and Deaths Return, U.K., 190, 405, 674, 1198, 1199
Convention for the Establishment of the Intergovernmental Maritime Consultative Organisation. *Cmnd. 589*. 538, 593
International Convention for the Prevention of Pollution of the Sea by Oil. *Cmnd. 595*. 538, 593
International Conventions on Maritime Law. *Cmnd. 1128*. 1059, 1125
Ships:
British Reserve Fleet:
Exchange of Notes between U.K. and Turkey concerning Purchase. *Cmnd. 260*. 266
Purchase of certain. Agreement between U.K. and Turkey. *Cmnd. 751*. 797, 853
Laws concerning the Nationality, 230A
Manual, Bureau of, 422
Registry of, 189, 404, 430, 673, 926, 930, 1198
Shop and Office Fitting Census of Production Report, 665
Shops Act Forms, 1140
Shops Bill, 7, 213, 215, 216, 248
Shortage of Scientific and Engineering Manpower Report, 422
Shorthand and Typewriting Proficiency Tests, 194
Shoub, H., Methods of Testing Small Fire Extinguishers, 419
Shrew-Flea Doratopsylla Dasycnema and Palaeopsylla, Notes on, 1096
Shrimpton, D. H., Quality Control in Marketing Fresh Poultry, 907
S.I. Effects, 390, 658, 918, 1190
Siberer, P., Selection and Training of Foremen in Europe, 222A
Sickness:
Experience of Insured Persons. *See* National Insurance Report
Survey of 1943 to 1952, 598
Sierra Leone:
And the Gambia Colonial Office Picture Set, 614
Colonial Report, 87, 301, 570, 1102
Constitutional Conference Report. *Cmnd. 1029*. 1053, 1104
International Customs Journal, 974, 1244
Investigation into Storage Problems of Rice in, 833
Orders-in-Council, 1174, 1175
Report, 833
Slipway Repair Base. Gift. *Cmnd. 1110*. 1058, 1203
Tower Hill Barracks. Gift. *Cmnd. 1111*. 1058, 1203
Sight Reduction Tables for Air Navigation, 294
Sight Testing: *See* Ophthalmic Services
Signal Generators, Attenuators, Voltmeters and Ammeters at Radio Frequencies, 636
Signal Letters of British Ships, 190, 405, 430, 674, 927, 930, 1199
Signal Office Practice, 1138
Signals. Civil Defence Instructors' Notes, 1138
Signing of United Nations Charter, 10th Anniversary, 234A
Silage:
72
How to Make Grass, 1084
Making and Feeding of, 449
Silo Construction, Brick Built, 74
Silver Fish and Firebrat, 295
Silviculture, Tropical, 1237
Simes, E. (Deputy Chairman: Boundary Commission) Report, 15
Simmonds, S., Hayti Overseas Economic Survey, 182
Simmons, D.:
Explosives Factory Accident Report, 334, 604
Simonds, Rt. Hon. Viscount (Chairman: Departmental Committee on Powers of Subpoena of Disciplinary Tribunals) Report. *Cmnd. 1033*. 1053
Simple Farm Book-keeping, 554
Simplification, Standardization, Specialisation, 719, 976
Simplified Plumbing:
427
For Multi-Storey Flats, 906
Simpson, A. C.:
Lobster Fishery of Wales, 559
Spawning of Plaice:
Irish Sea, 1087
North Sea, 823, 958
Simpson, W. D.:
Ancient Monuments, Scotland Guide, 956
Bothwell Castle Guide, 698
Crichton Castle Guide, 427

Simpson, W. D. (*continued*):
Hermitage Castle Guide, 427
Huntley Castle, Aberdeenshire, Guide, 1227
Kildrummy and Glenbuchat Castle Guide, 427
Scottish Castles, 958
Sims, R. W., Birds Collected by F. Shaw-Mayer in Central Highlands of New Guinea, 81
Sinclair, Sir Leonard (Chairman: Advisory Committee on Inland Telegraph Service) Report, 640
Sinclair of Cleeve, Lord (Chairman: Committee of Enquiry into Financial Structure of Colonial Development Corporation) Report. *Cmnd. 786*. 799, 834
Singapore:
Colonial Report, 301, 570, 1102
Commonwealth Leaflet. Cameo Series, 1149
Constitutional Conference Report *Cmd. 9777*. 44, 89; *Cmnd. 147*. 259, 303
Loss of, 296, 389
Picture Set, 1149
State of Arms, 1101
State of, Flag Badge, 1103
Singapore, State of, Act, 542
Singapore, State of, Bill, 485, 519
Singh Ghanshyam, (Chairman: International Commission for Supervision and Control in Cambodia) Report. *Cmnd. 887*. 806, 846
Sion College Act, 58
Sites:
And Foundations, 1179
Setting out on, 956
Sitka Spruce in British Columbia, 325
Situation Economique dans les Pays de la Communauté Rapport, 965
Sivadon, P., Psychiatric Services and Architecture, 1269
Skelhorn, N. J.:
Hide & Co. Ltd., Investigation into Affairs, 921
Investigation into the Affairs of Wright Textiles Ltd. Report, 1192
Skid-Resistance Tester, Instructions for Using the Portable, 1182
Skimmed Milk Regulations. Circular, 1086
Skin Spot and Silver Scurf of Potatoes, 288
Skippers and Second Hands of Fishing Boats, Regulations for Examination, 187
Sky Factor Diagram, Scottish Housing Handbook, 601
Slade Green and Dartford. Railway Accident Report, 1198
Slade Lane Junction, Levenshulme. Railway Accident Report, 1198
Sladen, W. J. L., Pygoscelid Penguins, 571
Slate Quarries and Mines. Census of Production Report, 394
Slaughter of Animals Act:
808
Calf Slaughter. Circular, 1086
Circular, 822
Slaughter of Animals Bill:
486, 517
Report on Consolidation Bill, 487, 488
Slaughter of Animals. Electric Stunning. Circular, 557
Slaughter of Pigs (Anaesthesia) Regulations. Circular, 557
Slaughterhouses:
Circular, 72
Construction, etc., 291
England and Wales. *Cmd. 9761*. 43, 75
Hygiene Regulations. Etc. Circular, 557
Licences Regulations Circular, 822
Meat Inspection Grant Regulations. Circular, 557, 822, 1086
Model Byelaws, 74
Recommended Minimum Standards for the Construction, Lay-out and Equipment in E. and W. *Cmnd. 243*. 265, 293
Reports (Appointed Day) Order. Circular, 822, 1086
Slaughterhouses Act:
542
Circular, 557
Slaughterhouses Bill, 246, 249, 481, 483, 485, 497, 513, 519, 520, 608
Slavery:
Convention on Abolition, the Slave Trade and Institutions and Practices similar to Slavery. *Cmd. 9797, 9870*. 45, 51, 109; *Cmnd. 257*. 266, 322
United Nations Conference of Plenipotentiaries, 461
Sledge, W. A., Polypodiaceae and Grammitidaceae of Ceylon, 1095
Sloane Herbarium, 564
Slough:
Experiment, 404
Station Railway Accidents Report, 926
Slugs:
And Snails, 555, 820
British, 1097
Slum Clearance:
Circular, 129, 869, 1146
Subsidy—Indirect Re-Housing. Circular, 340
Summary of Proposals. *Cmd. 9685*. 38, 121
Slum Clearance (Compensation) Act:
56
Circular, 129
Slum Clearance (Compensation) Bill, 4, 5, 18, 30, 33, 35, 127, 129
Slums, Moving from, 130
Small Arms. Census of Production Report, 663

Small Business Dwelling-Houses Bill, 784, 787
Small, D., Creosoting Plant at Thetford Chase, 1129
Small Estates (Representation) Bill, 1045
Small Family Farm, European Problem, 976
Small Landholders (Scotland) Act. Appendices to Report as to Proceedings, 389, 915, 1188
Small Lotteries and Gaming Act, 56
Small Lotteries and Gaming (Amendment) Act, 1956, 810
Small Lotteries and Gaming Bill, 3, 9, 34, 127
Small Lotteries and Gaming Act, 1956 (Amendment) Bill, 749, 784
Small Picture Books, 952, 1222, 1223
Small Public Library Building, 996
Small Pulp Mill Survey, Economic Study, United Kingdom, 855
Small Underground Drains and Sewers, 906
Smallholdings Organised on the Basis of Centralised Services. Report and Accounts, 75, 293, 560, 822, 824, 1088
Smart, J., Handbook for Identification of Insects of Medical Importance, 81
Smart, P. M. T., Sponsored Fire-Resistance Tests on Structural Elements, 1183
Smedley Viaduct Signal Box Railway Accident Report, 1198
Smieton, Dame Mary. (Chairman):
Industrial Safety Sub-Committee National Joint Advisory Council Report, 138
Standing Committee on Rehabilitation and Resettlement of Disabled Persons Report, 619
Smit, F.G.A.M.:
African Species of Stivalius, Genus of Siphonaptera, 563
New Hystrichochopsyllid Siphonaptera, 562
New Siphonaptera from Eastern Mediterranean Countries, 1095
Notes on the Shrew-Flea Doratopsylla Darycnema and Notes on Paleopsylla, 1096
Smith, Sir A. C., (Chairman: Judicial Commission) Report on Plan for British Caribbean Federation. *Cmd. 9620*. 38, 89
Smith, C. V., Synoptic Evolution of 500 Millibar Flow Patterns, 1161
Smith, D. M., Natural Durability of Timber, 908
Smith, D. N., Longitudinal Permeability of Some Hardwoods and Softwoods, 650
Smith, F. F., Roses for the Home, 201
Smith, H., Saxifraga of Himalaya, 562
Smith Hive, 1083
Smith, M. A., Inventaria Archaeologica, 562
Smith, S., Cuneiform Texts from Cappadocian Tablets in the British Museum, 294
Smith, W. Campbell, Volcanic Rocks of Cape Adare, South Victoria, 827
Smithburn, K. C., Yellow Fever Vaccination, 244
Smithfield Market Report, 630
Smoke Control Areas:
129, 329
E. and W. Programmes for the Establishment of Smoke Control Areas. *Cmnd. 1113*. 1058, 1148
See also Clean Air Act
Smoky Chimneys, 697
Smolts and Kelts, Passage of, through Fish Passes, 388
Snow, Filth, Dust, etc. Preventing the Occurrence of Nuisances, 612
Snowdonia, 635
Snowdonia National Park. Film Strip, 1163
Soap, Candles and Glycerine. Census of Production Report, 394
Soap Detergents, Paint, Varnishes. Marketing Techniques, 449
Social and Biological Factors in Infant Mortality, 856
Social and Cultural Anthropology, International Bibliography of, 994, 1264
Social and Economic Research, Interdepartmental Committee Report, 151
Social and Medical Assistance. Amendment to the European Convention. *Cmnd. 1169, 1184*. 1063, 1064, 1125
Social Aspects of Mental Health, 995
Social Commission:
Report, 453
United Nations Report, 1253
Social Conditions in Non-Self-Governing Territories, 233A, 989
Social Consequences of Automation, 736
Social Development:
International Survey of Programmes, 985
Through Family and Home. Report, 1104
Social Factors in Economic Growths, 735
Social Humanitarian and Cultural Questions. Records of Meetings, 455, 725, 983, 1254
Social Implications of Industrialisation and Urbanisation in Africa South of the Sahara, 240A
Social Insurance:
Convention between U.K. and:
Italy. *Cmnd. 112*. 256; *Cmnd. 572*. 536, 590
Switzerland. *Cmnd. 926, 1108*. 1046, 1058, 1126
Turkey. *Cmnd. 864*. 804, 853
Exchange of Notes between U.K. and Italy. *Cmnd. 716*. 794, 850

Social Progress through Community Development, 233A
Social Psychiatry and Community Attitudes Report, 1000
Social Research and Industry in Europe, 1248
Social Science Department. London School of Economics, Woman, Wife, Worker, 1181
Social Sciences:
And Peaceful Co-operation, 1265
Documentation in, 237A, 466, 735, 994
In Secondary Schools. Report, 239A
Periodicals, World List, 466
Reports and Papers, 239A, 468, 735, 996, 1266
Research Council in, 468
Teaching in, 240A, 469
Social Security:
Agreement between U.K. and:
Australia. *Cmnd. 378*. 524
Ireland. *Cmnd. 1020*. 1052, 1121
New Zealand. *Cmd. 9682*. 38, 91
And Protocol concerning Benefits in Kind between U.K. and Belgium. *Cmnd. 199*. 262
Convention between U.K. and:
Belgium. *Cmnd. 460*. 529, 588
Denmark. *Cmnd. 860*. 804, 847; *Cmnd. 990*. 1050, 1119
Finland. *Cmnd. 878*. 805, 848; *Cmnd. 1240*. 1068, 1120
France. *Cmd. 9877*. 45, 51, 106; *Cmnd. 560*. 536, 590
Germany. *Cmnd. 78*. 254; *Cmnd. 1055*. 1055, 1121
Israel. *Cmnd. 174*. 260; *Cmnd. 347*. 522, 590
Norway. *Cmnd. 252*. 266; *Cmnd. 422*. 527, 592
Sweden. *Cmnd. 46, 192*. 251, 262
Yugoslavia. *Cmnd. 443, 561*. 528, 536, 596
Exchange of Notes between U.K. and:
Canada. *Cmnd. 925*. 1046, 1106
France on Extension to Island of Jersey. *Cmnd. 840*. 803, 848
Protocol to Convention between U.K. and France. *Cmnd. 966*. 1049, 1120
Schemes European Interim Agreement Amendment. *Cmnd. 1161, 1162, 1182, 1183*. 1062, 1064, 1125
Social Services:
Britain, 132, 614, 1150
Community Development, 1256
Organisation and Administration, 728
Social Welfare:
In the United Kingdom Dependencies, 1150
Project, 234A
Training, 985
Social Workers in the Local Authority Health and Welfare Services. Working Party Report, 860
Society in Scotland for Propagating Christian Knowledge Order Confirmation Act, 811
Society in Scotland for Propagating Christian Knowledge Order Confirmation Bill, 520
Sociology:
In the U.S.A., 237A
International Bibliography of, 466, 735, 994, 1264
Of Science, 466
Sodium Fluoracetate as a Rodenticide, Use of, 560
Soft Cheese, 289
Soft Drinks:
British Wines and Cider Census of Production Report, 664
Food Standards, Committee Report, 824
Soft Furnishings Census of Production Report, 665
Softwoods:
Grading of Sawn British, 908
Handbook of, 384
In House Construction, Use of Home-Grown, 854
Key. Forest Products Research Bulletin, 1180
Working Stresses for Structural, 166
Soil Analysis:
For Advisory Purposes, 71
Organisation and Rationalisation, 449
Soil Moisture. Field Studies of Movement, 652
Soil Science, Multilingual Vocabulary, 1237
Soil Sterilization, 71, 1083, 1085
Soil Survey:
Great Britain:
69, 70, 1081
Memoir, 553, 1081, 1082
Report, 819
Research Board Report, 553
Scotland Memoir, 70, 288
Soils and Land use of the District around Rhyl and Denbigh, 1081
Soils and Manures for:
Fruit, 72
Vegetables, 1085
Soils of Malta and Gozo, 1103
Soils of the Country around Kilmarnock, 288
Soldier, 207, 425, 696, 956, 1225
Sole, Food and Feeding Habits of the Lemon Sole, 172
Solicitors Act:
273
Consolidation Bills Report, 213
Solicitors (Amendment) Act, 56, 810
Solicitors (Amendment) Bill, 1, 2, 3, 8, 34, 749, 785

Solicitors Bill:
8, 214, 215, 247
Memorandum, 8
Solicitors (Scotland) Act, 542
Solicitors (Scotland) Bill, 220, 478, 479, 482, 517
Solid Smokeless Fuels Committee Report. *Cmnd. 999.* 1051, 1173
Soltau-Luneberg Area. Agreement concerning Conduct of Manoeuvres and other Training Exercises. *Cmnd. 1025.* 1053, 1120
Somaliland:
Agreements and Exchanges of Letters with U.K. in Connexion with the Attainment of Independence. *Cmnd. 1101.* 1058, 1125
Colonial Report, 301, 832, 1102
Commonwealth Cameos, 1149
Constitutional Conference Report. *Cmnd. 1044.* 1054, 1104
Protectorate:
Colonial Office Picture Set, 614
Governor and Commander-in Chief, Orders-in-Council, 1174
Grants-in-Aid of the Administration. *Cmd. 9666.* 37, 89
Under Italian Administration Report, 235A
Some Aspects of Agricultural Research, 819
Some Eighteenth Century Bird Paintings in the Library of Sir Joseph Banks, 828
Some Typical Weather Maps, 361
Somerset County Council Act, 1073
Soper, M. H. R., Field Beans, 558
Sorn, Hon. Lord (Chairman):
Local Contributions to Scottish Universities Report. *Cmnd. 640.* 789, 912
Tribunal of Inquiry into Allegations of Assault of John Waters. *Cmnd. 718.* 794, 914
Sorrell, A., Stonehenge and Avebury and Neighbouring Monuments Guide, Illustrations, 958
Sorsby, Professor A.:
Blindness in England. Report, 121
Emmetropia and Its Aberrations, 359
Sound Absorbing Materials, 1163
Sound Insulation:
Of Dwellings, 164
In Houses, 331
Sources du Troit du Travail, Etude Comparative des, 705
Sources of Educational Publications of an Official Nature, 466
Sources of Road Aggregate, 1182
Sources of White and Coloured Aggregate in Great Britain, 1182
South Africa:
Exchange of Notes with U.K. supplementary to the Air Services Agreement. *Cmnd. 889.* 806, 826
South Africa (*continued*):
International Customs Journals, 714, 973, 1244
South Durham Steel and Iron Co., Ltd., Proposal to sell Holdings of Securities. *Cmd. 9679.* 38
South-East Asia:
Collective Defence Treaty. *Cmnd. 265.* 267
Region Air Navigation Plan, 1241
South Georgia-11, Geology of, 833
South Lancashire Transport Act, 544
South of Scotland Electricity Board:
Guarantee given to Loans proposed to be raised, 10, 17, 22, 26, 27, 31, 196, 224, 231, 236, 240, 493, 501, 507, 510, 679, 768, 774, 780, 936, 1018, 1025, 1031, 1034, 1204
Reports and Accounts, 15, 173, 227, 389, 495, 656, 761, 915, 1018, 1187
South of Scotland Electricity Order Confirmation Act, 58
South of Scotland Electricity Order Confirmation Bill, 35
South Wales Transport Act, 812
South West Africa, Committee's Report, 984
Southampton Corporation Act, 1073
Southampton Water Airport Civil Aviation Order, 671
Southend-on-Sea Corporation Act, 1073
Southey, J. F., Plant Nematology, 825
Sovereignty over certain Frontier Land (Belgium/Netherlands):
Judgment, 972
Order, 713
Soviet Patent and Trade Mark Law. Report, 1164
Space-Heating, Basic Design Temperatures for, 208
Spacing of Machinery. Wool Textile Industry, 1158
Spain:
Agreement with U.K. for Co-operation in the Peaceful Uses of Atomic Energy. *Cmnd. 936.* 1047, 1125
Cultural Convention with U.K. *Cmnd. 1134.* 1060, 1125
Economic Conditions, 975, 1246
Exchange of Notes with U.K.:
Amending the Schedule of Routes annexed to the Air Services Agreement. *Cmnd. 852.* 801, 852
Regarding the Reciprocal Abolition of Visas. *Cmnd. 1130.* 1060, 1125
Overseas Economic Survey, 398
Pocket Guide, 1222
Spanish Royal Armour in the Tower of London, Exhibition, 1226
Spanish School Paintings Catalogues, 154
Spanish Territories in the Gulf of Guinea International Customs Journal, 714

Spawning of Plaice in the:
Irish Sea, 1087
North Sea, 823
Speaker Morrison's Retirement Bill, *See* under Mr. Speaker
Special Army Orders, 956
Special COM/OPS/RAC Meeting Report, 972
Special Fund, Governing Council Report, 1253
Special Political Committee Records, 1254
Special Report Series. Medical Research Council, 1160
Special Schools for Handicapped Pupils, 101
Specifications:
Cooking Equipment, Standard, 370
Defence, 94–100, 307–12, 578, 838, 1109
D.T.D., 176 8, 391–3, 659, 826, 918, 1091
Road and Bridge Works, 404
Transmitters and Receivers Performance, 898
Spectrographic Abstracts, 178, 393, 662
Spectrophotometric Measurements of Early Type Stars, 164, 648, 1178
Spectrum of Quiescent Prominences, 380
Speech Therapist, Career, 618
Speed Limit, London:
and Home Counties Traffic Advisory Committee Report, 188
Traffic Area Report, 1197
Spelaeogriphus, A New Cavernicolous Crustacean from South Africa, 295
Spelling Alphabet, 218A
Spencer, R., Principles of Scientific Cleaning for the Fish Industry, 649
Spens, Sir W., (Chairman: National Insurance Advisory Committee) Reports. *Cmd. 9684, 9752, 9854, 9855*; *Cmnd. 33.* 13, 32, 38, 42, 49, 50, 54; 227
Sphecidae (Hym) Récoltés en Libye et au Tibesti par M. Kenneth M. Guichard, 80
Sphecidae (Hym) Récoltés en Tripolitaine et en Cyrénaique par M. Kenneth M. Guichard, 1095
Spirit Distilling. Census of Production Report, 395
Spirit Rectifying and Compounding. Census of Production Report, 395
Sponges. John Murray Expedition, Scientific Reports, 1097
Sponsored Fire Resistance Tests on Structural Elements, 1183
Sport in Education, Place of, 467
Sports Requisites. Census of Production Report, 396
Spratt, H. P., Mechanical and Electrical Engineering, 1178
Spray Taps, 905
Spray Treatment for Prevention of Lyctus Attack in Sawn Logs, 908
Spring Cabbage, 288
Spring-Flowering Bulbs, 951
Spring Strips, Application of to Instrument Design, 155
Spurr, N. F., Film-making on a low Budget, 1265
Squab Raising, 201
Squirrel, Grey, 1129
S.R. & O. and S.I. Numerical Table. Supplement, 390, 658, 918
Stabilisation of the Olive Oil Market, 241A
Stabilité de l'Emploi dans le Droit de Pays Membres de la CECA, 965
Stabilized Soil Construction for Housing. Manual on, 732
Staffordshire. Saxton's Maps, 1094
Staff:
Employed in Government Departments. *Cmnd. 442.* 528, 680; *Cmnd. 775.* 799, 938; *Cmnd. 1058.* 1055, 1206
Papers, International Monetary Fund, 220A, 445, 714, 974, 1245
Pension Board Report, Joint, 983
Relations in the Civil Service, 680
Staff College, War Office List, 207, 426
Staggering of Working Hours in Central London Committee Report, 671
Staines Central Station Railway Accident Report, 673
Stamp, Professor L. D. (In the Chair: Royal Commission on Common Land) Minutes of Evidence, 379
Stamps:
Handbook of British Colonial Stamps in Current Use, 305
Of the United States, 692
United Nations Postage, 464
Standard Capacitors and Their Accuracy in Practice, 155
Standard Industrial Classification:
565
Alphabetical List of Industries, 829
Standard International Trade Classification, 1259
Standard Specifications for Cooking Equipment, 370
Standard Sunlight Indicators:
Diagrams, 601
Scottish Housing Handbook, 601
Standards for School Premises Regulations Circular, 842, 843
Standards of Normal Weight in Infancy, Committee Report, 860
Standards, *See* Imperial
Standing Commission on Museums and Galleries:
Publications, 174, 916
Report, 916
Standing Committees:
Debates, 8, 29, 32, 242–3, 489, 490, 778, 783, 1012, 1013, 1040
Returns, 28, 127, 241, 339, 509, 609, 776, 866, 1144

Standing Orders:
House of Commons:
27, 126, 491, 500, 669, 866, 1010, 1027, 1034, 1038, 1144
Committee Special Report, 866
House of Lords:
2, 6, 129, 214, 340, 485, 487, 610, 747, 753, 755, 868, 1005, 1007, 1010, 1011, 1144
Public Business. 485, 610, 753, 866, 868
Royal Army Medical Corps, etc., 426, 696, 956, 1225
Stanton, G. S., Path of Flight, 202
Stanton Drew Stone Circles, Somerset, Guide, 208
"Stanvac Japan" Wreck Report, 1200
Staphylococcal Infections in Hospitals, 859
Star Almanac for Land Surveyors, 61, 277, 547, 814, 1075
Starch. Census of Production Report, 395
Starks, H. J. H.:
Research on Injuries sustained in Road Accidents, 168
Some Safety Aspects of Pedal and Motor Assisted Cycles, 384
Stars:
Apparent Places of Fundamental, 276
Spectrophotometric Measurements of Early Type, 164, 648, 1178
Starters for Cheese-making, 71, 555
State Management Districts (Licensing Act, 1949 and 1953) Report, 124, 244, 335, 513, 605, 780, 863, 1039, 1140
State of Food and Agriculture, 968
State of Singapore Act, 542
State of Singapore Bill, 485, 519
State Papers, Calendar of, 1175
Stateless Persons:
Convention relating to their Status. *Cmnd. 1098.* 1057, 1125
Status of, 234A
Stationery Estimates:
1956–57, 12, 30
1957–58, 226
1958–59, 494, 676
1959–60, 760, 933
1960–61, 1019, 1201
Stationery Office:
Publications, 174–5, 390, 658, 917, 1189
Select Committee on Estimates Report, 222, 234, 337
Statistical Bulletins:
Agriculture and Food, 977
Definitions and Methods, 719, 1248
Energy for OEEC Countries, 977
Foreign Trade, 221A–2A, 447–8, 717–18, 977, 1248
General Statistics, 978, 1249
Industrial Statistics, 224A
Manpower, Population, 1900–1958, 978
Statistical Bulletins (*continued*):
Network of Intra-European Trade, 978
Statistical Classification of Imported Goods and Re-Exported Goods, 577, 837, 1108
Statistical Commission Report, 228A, 1253
Statistical Data:
For the Use of the Council of Europe, 704
Population, Employment, etc., 962, 1232
Statistical Digest:
118, 218A–19A, 377, 442–3, 646, 712, 901, 970, 1173, 1241
Scottish, 173, 389, 656, 913, 1186
Statistical Office of European Communities Publications, 1250
Statistical Papers:
731, 989, 1259
International Trade, 226A
United Nations, 233A, 461
Statistical Quality Control, 224A
Statistical Reports and Studies, 240A, 468, 996, 1266
Statistical Review England and Wales, 118, 328, 598, 856, 1131
Statistical Study of the Variation of Wind with Height, 360
Statistical Summary, Mineral Industry, 303
Statistical Tables:
Scottish Sea Fisheries, 656, 824
Sea Fisheries, 75, 560
Statistical Yearbook, United Nations, 233A, 462, 731, 989, 1260
Statistics:
Agricultural:
And Food, 224A, 598, 977
Eastern European Countries, 720
Economies, 241A, 435, 706, 967, 1237
England and Wales, 71, 289, 555, 1084
Scotland, 69, 287, 553, 819, 1081
United Kingdom, 72, 289, 555, 821, 1084
Annual Abstract, 83, 297, 565, 829, 1098
Basic Industrial, International Recommendations, 1259
Cancer, 598
Cement Industry in Europe, 445, 978, 1250
Civil Judicial:
England and Wales. *Cmd. 9775.* 43, 150; *Cmnd. 224.* 264; *Cmnd. 434.* 527, 632
Scotland, 46, 171; *Cmnd. 215.* 263; *Cmnd. 478.* 530
Coal for Europe, 225A, 451, 720, 979, 1258
Cocoa, 706, 966, 1236
Colonial:
302, 834, 1101
Agriculture, 301
Digest of, 88, 302, 570, 834

Statistics (*Continued*):
Commodity Trade, 225A, 451, 720, 979, 1251
Criminal:
England and Wales. *Cmd. 9884.* 52, 123; *Cmnd. 286.* 334; *Cmnd. 529.* 534, 604; *Cmnd. 803.* 800, 862; *Cmnd. 1100.* 1058, 1138
Scotland. *Cmd. 9750.* 42, 171; *Cmnd. 157.* 259; *Cmnd. 426.* 527, 654; *Cmnd. 746.* 796, 913; *Cmnd. 1024.* 1053, 1186
Current School Enrolment, 237A, 466, 733, 994
Defence. *Cmnd. 130.* 307; *Cmnd. 661.* 791, 842
Directory of International Standards, 1245
Drunkenness. *Cmd. 9888.* 32, 124, *Cmnd. 280.* 335; *Cmnd. 573.* 537, 605; *Cmnd. 807.* 801, 862, *Cmnd. 1094.* 1057, 1139
Economic, New Contributions, 829
Education:
Cmnd. 777. 799, 842
Culture and Mass Communication, 237
England and Wales. *Cmnd. 1088.* 1057, 1115
Electric Energy, Europe, 454, 724, 982, 1251, 1257
Energy for OEEC Countries, 977
Epidemiological and Vital, 243A, 244A, 470, 471, 739, 998, 1267
Exports from Overseas Territories of OEEC Countries, 719
Factory Inspectorate, 1155
Film and Cinema, 240A
Fishery, Yearbook, 241A, 436, 707, 969, 1239
Food and Agricultural Yearbook, 242A, 436, 708
Foreign Trade, 448
Foreigners Entering and Leaving the U.K. *Cmnd. 34.* 54, 124; *Cmnd. 163.* 334; 526, 604; *Cmnd. 701.* 793, 863; *Cmnd. 994.* 1050, 1140
Forest Accidents, 724
Forest Products, Yearbook, 242A, 436, 708, 967, 1239
Gas, Europe, 454, 724, 979, 1251
General, 223A, 448, 718, 978, 1249
Health:
Expert Committee Report, 741, 999
Scottish, 1133
Hides and Skins:
450
Industry in Europe, 450, 1248
Hospitals:
And Specialist Services. England and Wales, 122
In-patient, 856
Statistics (*continued*):
Housing:
612
And Building, for Europe, 230A, 457, 727, 984, 1251, 1258
Hydrometric, British Rivers, 131, 343, 613, 871, 1148
Industrial, 224A, 718
International, Financial, 220A, 445, 714, 974, 1245
International, Education, Culture and Mass Communication, 1263
International Migration, 232A
International Trade Yearbook, 230A, 457, 728, 985, 1263
Judicial, England and Wales, *Cmnd. 802.* 800 886; *Cmnd. 1126.* 1059, 1159
Judicial, Scotland. *Cmnd. 850.* 803, 914; *Cmnd. 1047.* 1054, 1187
Labour, 598
Libraries, 996
Local Education Authorities England and Wales, 1116
Local Government:
Authorities, E. and W., 586, 612
Financial, 130, 342, 870, 1147
Monthly Bulletin, 234A, 462, 731, 986, 1257
Monthly Digest of:
83, 297, 430, 565, 829, 1098
Supplement, 565, 829
Morbidity, 598, 1131
Natality, 1251
National Accounts Yearbook, 729, 993, 1263
National Income and Expenditure, 83, 233A, 461
National Product and Expenditure, 449
Newspapers and Periodicals, 996, 1266
Non-Ferrous Metals, 450, 718, 978
Official Study, 83
Oversea Migration, 91
Pneumoconiosis in Mining and Quarrying Industries, 118, 645, 898, 901, 1170
Population and Vital, 232A, 233A, 459, 730, 987, 1257
Population Bill, 754, 787, 1006, 1021, 1037, 1042, 1141
Public Education. E. and W. *Cmd. 9785.* 44; *Cmnd. 223.* 313; *Cmnd. 454.* 529, 585
Public Road Passenger Transport, 188, 403, 929, 1197, 1199
Pulp and Paper, 224A, 449, 719, 976, 1250
Road Accidents:
404
In Europe, 233A, 460, 730, 989, 1260
Scottish, Digest of, 173, 389, 656, 913, 1186

STA-SUT | 1956-60

STA— INDEX 1956-60

Statistics (*continued*):
Scottish, Health, 1133
Sea Fisheries:
293
Scottish, 172
Sources and Uses of Finance, 1249
Special Education, 1266
Steel for Europe, 234A, 462, 731, 989, 1258
Studies in Official, 829, 885, 886, 1099
Textiles Production and Consumption, 449, 719
Timber:
450, 719, 978, 1250
Bulletin, 708, 990
Industry in Europe, 224A, 437
Price, 462
Tropical, 719, 978, 1249
Transport, for Europe, 234A, 462, 732, 990, 1251
Tuberculosis, E. and W., 327
University Teaching in Social Sciences, 469
Vital, Handbook, 234A
Welsh, Digest of, 124, 343, 869, 1147
World Facts and Figures, 734
World Forest Products, 709
World Grain Trade, 438, 709, 969, 1239
Statistics Division. ICAO Report, 972
Statistique Bulletin, 214A
Statistiques, Memento de, 215A, 435
Statistiques Sociales, 1250
Status of Multilateral Conventions, 234A, 462, 731, 989
Status of Stateless Persons. Final Act and Convention, 234A
Status of Women. Commission Report, 228A, 453, 723, 982, 1253
Statute Law Revision Act, 542, 810, 1071
Statute Law Revision Act. Report on Consolidation Bill, 478, 483, 746, 751, 867, 1004, 1145
Statute Law Revision Bill, 480, 519, 751, 786, 1008, 1044
Statutes:
Chronological Tables of, 175, 390, 658, 918, 1190
In Force, Index, 175, 390, 658, 918, 1190
Statutory Inquiries, Procedure, 601
Statutory Instruments:
1955, 175
1956, 390
1957, 659
Effects, 175
List of, 175, 390, 430, 658, 917, 1189, 1191
Select Committee:
Minutes of Proceedings, 9, 30, 127, 221, 244, 339, 490, 513, 609, 756, 780, 781, 864, 1013, 1014, 1038, 1142

Statutory Instruments (*continued*):
Select Committee (*continued*):
Report, 9, 30, 127, 244, 339, 513, 609, 756, 780, 865, 1013, 1014, 1143
Statutory Publications Office Publications, 175, 390, 658, 918, 1190
Statutory Rules and Orders and Statutory Numerical Table, 175
Staveley Iron and Chemical Company Limited. Proposal to Sell Holding of Securities. *Cmnd. 1156*. 1062, 1205
"Staxton Wyke" Wreck Report, 1200
Stead, Professor G. (Chairman: Working Party on Anaesthetic Explosions) Report, 121
Steam Bending Properties of Various Timbers, 908
Steam Boilers in Industry. Report of the Advisory Committee on Examination. *Cmnd. 1173*. 1063, 1158
Steaming and Sailing Vessels. Mercantile Navy List, 929, 1197
Steaming of Home-Grown Beech, 907
Stearn, W. T.:
Allium and Milula in the Central and Eastern Himalaya, 1095
Identity of Isopyrum Aquilegroides L., 1095
Steel:
And Its Alternatives, 234A
Industry, European. Long-Term Trends and Problems, 1256
Making and Transforming Industries in Latin America, Problems of, 731
Market, European, 228A, 454, 724, 982
Sheets. Census of Production Report, 394
Statistics for Europe, 234A, 462, 731, 989, 1258
Technology, Advances in, 224A, 720
Workers and Technical Progress, 978
Steel Company of Wales Ltd. Proposal to sell Holdings. *Cmnd. 106*. 256
Steele, J. H., Plant Production in the Northern North Sea, 656
Steele, L. P., Average Water Vapour Content of the Air, 1160
Steering Committee for Nuclear Energy Report, 716
Steinlin, H. J., One-Man Work in Mixed Stands of Beech, Spruce and Fir, 437
"Stella Orion" Wreck Report, 192
Stem and Bulb Eelworm on:
Narcissi, etc., 289
Tulips, 289
Vegetables, 71, 1083
Stengel, E., Classification of Mental Disorders, 1267
Stenopsyche Griseipennis McLachlan, Identity of, 563
Step-Saving U Kitchen, 201
Stepanov, M. A., Harvesting and Conservation of Green Fodder in Dry Regions, 720

INDEX 1956-60 —STR

Stepanov, M. J., Mechanisation of the Cultivation and Harvesting of Sugar Beet, 1250
"Stephens" Wreck Report, 406
Stephenson, H. S., Inspector of Mines and Quarries Report, 900, 1172
Stephenson, P. M., Upper Winds Over the World, 1160
Sterling Area. Statistical Abstract, 180, 396 665, 921, 1192
Sterling Bonded Debts. Exchange of Letters between U.K. and Czechoslovakia concerning Offers made in Settlement. *Cmnd. 1009*. 1051, 1119
Sterling Payments Agreement. Exchange of Notes between U.K. and:
Czechoslovakia. *Cmd. 9687, 9819, 9875*. 38, 47, 51, 105; *Cmnd. 129*. 257
Japan. *Cmnd. 86*. 254
Poland for Prolongation. *Cmnd. 74*. 253
Stevenage Development Corporation Report, 24, 130, 237, 506, 613, 870, 1147
Stevens, P. H. M., Densities in Housing Area, 1183
Stevenson, I. P., Geology of the Country Around Sheffield, 329
Stevenson, S. M., Report on Investigation into the Affairs of Gordon Hotels Ltd. 397
Stewart, E. G., Town Gas, 648
Stewart, Sir John (Chairman: Industrial Court of Inquiry) Report on Dispute between Iron and Steel Trades Employers' Association and National Joint Trade Unions' Craftsmen's Iron and Steel Committee. *Cmd. 9843*. 49
Stewart, R., Managers for To-morrow, 383
Stewart, T. G. (Chairman):
Departmental Committee on Supply of Teachers in Scotland. Report. *Cmnd. 196*. 262
Working Party on Pensions for Widows, Children, and Dependants of Teachers in Scotland. Report. *Cmnd. 527*. 534
Stewarty of Kirkcudbright. Educational Trust Scheme:
Memorandum, 912, 1185
Order-in-Council, 1185
Stinging Nettles, 71
Stirling and Clackmannan Coalfield, Economic Geology, 119, 906
Stirling Heads, 1175
Stirlingshire Educational Trust Draft Scheme:
170
Memorandum, 386
Order-in-Council, 654
Stivalius African Species, Genus of Siphonatera, 563

Stobswood Occupational Level Crossing. Railway Accident Report, 1198
Stockholm:
Convention and Freer World Trade, 966
Draft Plan for a European Free Trade Association. *Cmnd. 823*. 801, 938
Stone, Sir Leonard, (Chairman: Departmental Committee on Hallmarking). Report. *Cmnd. 663*. 791, 923
Stone, P. A., Floor Finishes for Factories, 907
Stone Preservatives. Jointing Plasterboard, 906
Stone, R., Quantity and Price Indexes in National Accounts, 449
Stone, R. G., Mexico Overseas Economic Survey, 182
Stonehenge:
And Avebury and Neighbouring Monuments. Guide, 958
Postcard, 697
Wiltshire. Guide, 957
Stonehouse, B.:
Brown Skua of South Georgia, 89
King Penguin Aptenodytes Patagonica of South Georgia. Breeding and Development, 1103
Stoneley, H. M. M., Upper Permian Flora of England, 563
Stonemasonry, Career, 876
Storage:
And Dressing of Seed Potatoes, 553
Of Crops in Warm Climates, Building for, 1183
Stores:
And Equipment. Gift to Rhodesia and Nyasaland. *Cmnd. 409, 492*. 526, 531, 678
And Ordnance Depots of the Service Departments. Select Committee on Estimates Report, 224, 241,336
Stormonth, K., Rainfall on Malta, 1162
Story of Big Ben, 958
Story of W.V.S. 863
Strachan, Hon. Lord (Chairman: Civil Jury Trial in Scotland Committee) Report. *Cmnd. 851*. 803, 913
"Strathcoe" Wreck Reports, 1200
Strawberries, 821
Street Offences Act, 810
Street Offences Bill, 520, 749, 764, 779, 785, 864
Streets. Guide to Engineers on the Making Up of Private Streets. 1182
Strength of Nailed Joints, 382
Strength Properties of Plywood, Working Stresses, 382, 650
Strength Properties of Timber, 166, 1180
Stresa Conference. Industrial Challenge of Nuclear Energy, 976
Stride, H. G., Royal Mint, 1178
Strong, D. E., Eltham Palace Guide, 698

STR— INDEX 1956-60

Strontium 90:
In Human Bone in the U.K., Assay of, 1160
In Human Diet in the United Kingdom, 819, 1081
In Milk and Agricultural Materials in the United Kingdom, 1081
Stroyan, H. L. G., British Species of Sappaphis Matsumura, 293
Structural Analysis of the Basement System at Turoka, Kenya, 834
Structural Design of Flexible and Rigid Pavements for New Roads. Guide, 1182
Structural Fire Protection of Buildings, particularly in England, Short History, 651
Structural Frameworks for Single Storey Factory Buildings, 1179
Structural Loading in Factories, 1179
Structural Steel. Admiralty Advisory Committee Report, 277
Structure and Growth of Selected African Economics, 731
Structure of Some Leaves and Fructifications of the Glossopteris Flora of Tanganyika, 563
Structure of the Public Library Service in England and Wales. Report. *Cmnd. 660*. 791, 843
Stuart, T. A.:
Marking and Regeneration of Fins, 655
Migrations and Homing Behaviour of Brown Trout, 655
Student Employees. Protocol concerning Accession to Convention. *Cmnd. 942*. 1047, 1128
Student Pilot's and Private Pilot's Licences, 405, 930
Students and Research Workers. Notes on Grants, 908
Studentships and Fellowships, 1179
Studies in Methods, 234A, 732
Studies in Official Statistics, 829, 885, 886
Study Abroad. International Handbook, 240A, 468, 738, 996, 1266
Study and Practice of Planning, 995
Study of Attitudes to Factory Work, 151
Study on Traffic in Persons and Prostitution, 990
"Sturdee" Wreck Report, 192
Stygiomysis from the West Indies with a Note on Spelaeogriphus, 1097
Sub-Committees, Appointment of, and Allocation of Estimates, 514
Submarine Telecommunications Cable System:
Agreement between the U.K. and U.S.A., 1028, 1169
Agreement with Canada, the Eastern Telegraph Company Limited and the Canadian Overseas Telecommunication Corporation, 783, 897

Submarine Telecommunications Cable System (*continued*):
Agreement with Iceland, Denmark and the Great Northern Telegraph Co. Ltd., 783, 897
Subtabulation, 547
Sub-Tropical Jet Stream of the Eastern North Pacific Ocean, 360
Succession of Life through Geological Time, 296, 828
Sudan:
Middle East Bridge to Africa, 691
Report on Administration. *Cmd. 9798, 9841*. 45, 48, 110
Self-Determination. *Cmd. 9829*. 47, 110
Sudanese Republic. International Customs Journal, 444, 973, 1244
Suez Canal:
Base Agreement. Exchange of Notes between U.K. and Egypt extending Provisions. *Cmd. 9858*. 50, 106
Conference Selected Documents. *Cmd. 9853*. 49, 110
Exchange of Correspondence regarding the Future Operation. *Cmd. 9856*. 50, 110
Problem, 422
Returns of Shipping and Tonnage, 110
Sugar:
Agreement, International. *Cmnd. 1146*. 1061, 1126
And Glucose. Census of Production Report, 395
Beet:
Cultivation, 1085
Diseases, 1085
Mechanisation of the Cultivation and Harvesting, 1250
Pests, 557
Pulp for Feeding, 555
Yellows, 555
Board Report and Accounts, 509, 560, 773, 825, 844, 1031, 1089
Census of Production Report, 1193
Conference, United Nations, Summary, 734
Draft International Sugar Agreement. *Cmnd. 587*. 538, 593
Industry (Research and Education) Fund Account, 11, 75, 229, 293, 492, 605
International Agreement for the Regulation of Production and Marketing *Cmd. 9815*. 46, 110
Protocol amending the International Sugar Agreement. *Cmnd. 101*. 256, 322: *Cmnd. 557*. 536, 593
Sugar Act:
56, 128
Account, 499, 560, 765, 766, 773, 824, 844, 1021, 1034, 1089
Home Grown Sugar Beet (Research and Education) Fund Account, 763, 780

INDEX 1956-60 —SUT

Sugar Bill, 2, 14, 30, 33
Suggestions for the Teaching of Classics, 842
Suicide. *See* Criminal Law Revision Committee Report
Sulphate Attack on Brickwork, 905
Sultan's Armed Forces, Civil Aviation, etc., Exchange of Notes between U.K. and Muscat and Oman. *Cmnd. 507*. 532, 592
Summer Sea-Breeze at Ismailia, 634
Summit Meetings. *See* Meetings—U.S.S.R.
Sun Diagram. Scottish Housing Handbook, 601
Sunday Entertainment Act. Cinematograph Fund Account, 23, 161, 244, 378, 514, 646, 780, 901
"Sunday Express" Newspaper, Complaint of a Passage in. Committee of Privileges Report, 223, 338
Sundberg, U., Mechanical Barking of Timber, 437
Sunderland Corporation Act, 274
Sundial. True to Scale Print. Scottish Housing Handbook, 601
Sunley, J. G., Working Stresses for Structural Softwoods, 166
Sunlight Indicators, Standard. Diagrams, 601, 613
Sunlighting and Daylighting Working Diagrams for Testing, 601
"Sunprincess" Wreck Report. *See* "Geologist"
Superannuation Act, 273
Superannuation Bill, 218, 248
Superannuation Interchange Rules. Circulars, 610, 611
Superannuation (Miscellaneous Provisions) Act, etc. Circulars, 340, 341, 868, 869
Superannuation of University Teachers Report, 1207
Superannuation Scheme:
England and Wales National Health Service, 122
National Health Service, Scotland, 330
Teachers (Scotland), 169, 170
Superannuation (Transfer between Metropolitan Police Staff and Local Government) Rules Circular, 868
Superannuation. *See* National Health Service
Supersonic Aircraft, Introduction into Commercial Service, 1243
Supersulphate Cement, 1178
Supervision Record Forms, 171
Supply:
And Training of Teachers for Technical Colleges. Report, 314

Supply (*continued*):
Estimates:
1956–57, 12
1957–58, 226
1958–59, 494, 676
1959–60, 760, 933
Of Hard Fibre Cordage Report, 20, 182
Teachers:
In Scotland. Departmental Committee Report. *Cmnd. 196*. 262, 386
In the 1960's, 586
Transport and Barrack Services Regulations. Amendment, 207, 426, 696, 955
Supply, Ministry of: Publications, 175–8, 391–3, 659, 918
Support of Roadheads in Advance of Rippings, 645
Supreme Court:
Northern Ireland. Report of the Committee. *Cmnd. 227*. 264, 359
Prize, etc., Deposit Account, 21, 197
Rules. Select Committee on Statutory Instruments Special Report, 513, 609
Supreme Court of Judicature:
Account, 16, 178, 228, 393, 499, 662, 765, 920, 1021, 1191
Land Purchase Account. Northern Ireland, 24, 103, 237, 393, 756, 773, 920, 1030, 1191
Order, 359
Supreme Court of Judicature (Amendment) Act, 810
Supreme Court of Judicature (Amendment) Bill, 749, 784
Sur le Reboisement et l'Amélioration des Forêts en Macédoine Yougoslave, 240A
Surface Current Charts of the Eastern North Pacific Ocean, 1162
Surface Energy of Solids, 652
Surface Observations, Manual of, 203
Surface Texture, Guide to the Assessment, 578
Surface Water Yearbook of Great Britain, 131, 343, 613, 871, 1148
Surgical Operations, Code of, 118
Surinam International Customs Journal, 444, 973, 1244
Surrey County Council Act, 544
Surveys:
Accidents to Aircraft, U.K., 930
Of Mining Legislation, 729
Of Sickness, 1943 to 1952, 598
Surveying. Career, 618
Suspension of Payments, Repayments and Consolidation. Exchange of Letters between U.K. and Switzerland. *Cmnd. 512*. 532, 593
Suter, H. H., General and Economic Geology of Trinidad, B.W.I., 1104

1956-60 | SUT-TEM

SUT— INDEX 1956–60

Sutherland Educational Trust Scheme. Memorandum, 1185
Sutton, A. G., Importance of Thermal Insulation in Building, 427
Sutton Colliery. Nottinghamshire Explosion Report. *Cmnd. 327.* 271
Sutton's Hospital (Charterhouse) Charity Bill, 4, 34
Sutton's Hospital (Charterhouse) Charity Scheme Confirmation Act, 58
Swain, A., Hydrographical Survey of the River Usk, 291
Swan, M., British Guiana, 300
Swansea Corporation (Fairwood Common) Act, 58
Swaziland:
  Agreement for the Avoidance of Double Taxation, etc. *Cmnd. 900.* 807, 836
  Colonial Report, 305, 573, 835, 1106
  Economic Survey Mission Report, 1106
  Picture Set, 1149
Sweden:
  Agreement with U.K. for Co-operation in the Peaceful Uses of Atomic Energy. *Cmnd. 290.* 268, 322
  Convention on Social Security with U.K. *Cmnd. 46, 192.* 251, 262, 322
  Convention with U.K. for the:
    Avoidance of Double Taxation and the Prevention of Fiscal Evasion. *Cmnd. 1153.* 1062, 1126
    Relief from Double Taxation with Respect to Duties on the Estates of Deceased Persons. *Cmnd. 1154.* 1063, 1126
  Economic Conditions, 1246
  Exchange of Letters with U.K. on Repayment:
    Of Part of the Debt owed in Connection with the European Payments Union. *Cmd. 9712.* 40, 110
    Of the Balance of the U.K. Debt owed in Connection with the European Payments Union. *Cmnd. 81.* 254, 322
  Exchange of Notes with U.K.:
    Amending the Air Services Agreement. *Cmd. 9670.* 37, 110
    Extending to Rhodesia and Nyasaland and to Kenya, Uganda, Tanganyika and Zanzibar the Convention for the Avoidance of Double Taxation, etc. *Cmnd. 891.* 806, 852
    Regarding the Liquidation of German Assets. *Cmnd. 219.* 263, 322
    Repayment of the Debt on the Liquidation of the European Payments Union. *Cmnd. 761.* 798, 852; *Cmnd. 991.* 1050, 1126
Sweden (*continued*):
  Foreign Trade Statistical Bulletin, 222A, 447, 448, 717, 977, 978
  International Customs Journal, 444, 714, 1244
Swimming Pools, Safety Precautions Display Card, 170
Swinton, W. E.:
  Fossil Amphibians and Reptiles, 564
  Fossil Birds, 564
Swiss Confederation. Declaration on Provisional Accession to GATT, 709, 969
Switzerland:
  Convention with U.K. for Relief from Double Taxation with Respect to Taxes on the Estates of Deceased Persons. *Cmd. 9806.* 46, 110; *Cmnd. 119.* 257, 322
  Exchange of Letters with U.K.:
    Concerning suspension of Payments and for Repayments and Consolidation, *Cmnd. 512.* 532, 593
  For the Repayment of Credits granted by the European Payments Union. *Cmd. 9844.* 49, 110
  Exchange of Notes with U.K.:
    Abrogating the Declaration concerning Death Duties in the Canton de Vaud. *Cmnd. 514.* 533, 594
    Concerning Revised Route Schedules Annexed to Air Services Agreement. *Cmnd. 927.* 1046, 1126
    Respecting the Repayment of the Debt on the Liquidation of the European Payments Union. *Cmnd. 768.* 798, 852
    Revising the Route Annexed to the Air Services Agreement. *Cmnd. 217.* 263, 322
  Foreign Trade Statistical Bulletin, 222A, 448, 717, 977, 978, 1246
  International Customs Journal, 713, 1243
  Supplementary Convention on Social Insurance with U.K. *Cmnd. 926, 1108.* 1046, 1058, 1126
Sylvester-Bradley, P. C., Structure, Evolution and Nomenclature of the Ostracod Hinge, 80
Sylwan, Barbro, Kinescope and Adult Education, 996
Symposium on the Operating Costs of Machinery in Tropical Agriculture, 300
Synoptic Evolution of 500-Millibar Flow Patterns, 1161
Synoptic Study of Anomalies of Surface Air Temperature over the Atlantic Half of the Northern Hemisphere, 889
Synthetic Detergents, Standing Technical Committee Progress Report, 131, 613, 870, 1147

INDEX 1956–60 —TAX

Synthetic Food Colours Series, 707
Synthetic Resin Bonded Laminated Sheet, 918

T

Table Chickens, 821
Tables, 7-figure Trigonometrical, 814
Tables of Generalised Exponential Integrals, 1163
Tabor, C. D., Mass Spectrometry for Uranium Isotopic Measurements, 1240
Tabular Presentation, Bureau of Census Manual, 203
Tackley, M. E., Korea, 1953–54, 421
Tailoring, Dressmaking, etc. Census of Production Report, 664
Tait, J. B.:
  Hydrography of Faroe-Shetland Channel, 388
  Hydrography of the North-Western Approaches to the British Isles, 914
Taking Stock. Building Research Station Digest, 381
Tally Clerks. Committee Report, 1158
Tamar Bridge Act, 274
Tandy, A. H., Argentina Overseas Economic Survey, 182
Tanganyika:
  International Customs Journal, 444, 1244
  National Income, 570
  Orders-in-Council, 1174
  Picture Set, 1149
  Under U.K. Administration Report, 89, 303, 572, 834, 1105
  United Nations Visiting Mission to Trust Territories in East Africa Report, 235A
Tanganyika Agricultural Corporation Act, 273
Tanganyika Agricultural Corporation Bill, 219, 248
Tanner, J. C., Road Junctions in Rural Areas, 1182
Tanner, J. M. Emmetropia and its Aberrations, 359
Tar Surface Dressings. Recommendations, 652
Tariff:
  Amendments, 836, 1107
  Customs and Excise, 1107
Tariffs and Trade:
  Declaration on Provisional Accession of Swiss Confederation to the General Agreement, 709, 969
  General Agreement. Supplementary Concessions, 220A
Tarleton, R. D., Reactions between Aggregates and Cement, 651
Tarlo, L. B., Review of Upper Jurassic Pliosaurs, 1096
Tate Gallery Report, 178, 393, 920, 1191
Tax Cases:
  Appeals to the High Court, etc. Leaflets, 133–5, 345–6, 430, 615, 873, 1151
  Harrison's Index to:
    135
    Cumulative Supplement, 617
  Reports, 135, 347, 431, 617, 874, 1151
Taxation:
  Agreement between U.K. and Ireland with Respect to certain Exemptions. *Cmnd. 717, 874.* 794, 805, 938; *Cmnd. 1089.* 1057, 1204
  Agreement for Avoidance of Double Taxation, U.K. and:
    Basutoland. *Cmnd. 898.* 807, 835
    Bechuanaland. *Cmnd. 899.* 807, 835
    Swaziland. *Cmnd. 900.* 807, 836
  Agreement of the Forces and their Members. Agreement between U.K., France, U.S.A. and Germany. *Cmnd. 657.* 790, 849
  Agreements. *See* International
  British System of, 132, 1150
  Convention between U.K. and:
    Austria for the Avoidance of Double Taxation and the Prevention of Fiscal Evasion. *Cmd. 9865.* 50, 103; *Cmnd. 135.* 258
    Italy for Avoidance of Double Taxation, etc. *Cmnd. 1210.* 1066, 1122
    Sweden:
      For Avoidance of Double Taxation and Prevention of Fiscal Evasion. *Cmnd. 1153.* 1062, 1126
      For Relief from Double Taxation with Respect to Duties on Estates of Deceased Persons. *Cmnd. 1154.* 1062, 1126
    Switzerland for Relief from Double Taxation with Respect to Taxes on Estates of Deceased Persons. *Cmnd. 119.* 257
    U.S.A. for Relief from Double Taxation etc. *Cmd. 9806.* 46, 110
  Effects of, on Foreign Trade and Investment, 1253
  Elimination of Double, Report, 715, 975, 1247
  Exchange of Notes between U.K. and:
    Denmark for Avoidance of Double Taxation, etc. Extension to Rhodesia, Nyasaland, etc. *Cmnd. 705.* 794, 847; *Cmnd. 903.* 807, 847
    Iran concerning Avoidance of Double Taxation derived from Air Transport Services. *Cmnd. 1143.* 1061, 1121

TAX— INDEX 1956–60

Taxation (*continued*):
  Exchange of Notes between U.K. and (*continued*):
    Ireland concerning certain exemptions. *Cmnd. 874.* 805, 938; *Cmnd. 1192.* 1065, 1205
    Netherlands for Avoidance of Double Taxation, etc. *Cmd. 9766.* 43, 108; *Cmnd. 452.* 528, 592
    Norway extending Convention for Avoidance of Double Taxation, etc. to Rhodesia and Nyasaland. *Cmnd. 1062.* 1055, 1123
    Sweden extending Convention for Avoidance of Double Taxation, etc. to Rhodesia, Nyasaland, Kenya, Uganda, Tanganyika and Zanzibar. *Cmnd. 891.* 806, 852
    U.S.A.:
      Extending Provisions of Double Taxation Convention to certain U.K. Overseas Territories. *Cmnd. 824.* 802, 853
      For Prevention of Fiscal Evasion, etc. *Cmnd. 721.* 794, 854
  Farmer's Income, 73
  International Agreements, 230, 728, 1256
  Protocol between U.K. and U.S.A. for Avoidance of Double Taxation and Prevention of Fiscal Evasion. *Cmnd. 191.* 262
  Road Vehicles Convention. *Cmnd. 220, 320.* 263, 270, 322, 323; 462
  Road Vehicles for Private Use in International Traffic, 225A
Taxonomic Study of the Larvae of West African Simuliidae with Comments on the Morphology of the Larval-Black-Fly Head, 1096
Taxonomy of the Genus Columbia, 828
Taxonomy of Stenoponia J. & R. (1911), Genus of Palearctic and Nearctic Fleas, Contribution to the, 562
Taylor, A. D., Camp Stoves and Fireplaces, 199
Taylor, A. J.:
  Conway Castle and Town Walls, Caernarvonshire, Guide, 427
  Jewel Tower, Westminster, Guide, 208
  Minster Lovell Hall Guide, 698
  Rhuddlan Castle Guide, 208
Taylor, F. W., Crystallographic Data for the Calcium Silicates, 165
Taylor, J. L., Secondary School Plant, 422
Taylor, Sir W. (Chairman: Advisory Committee on Forestry) Report, 427, 1227
Tea:
  Monopolies and Restrictive Practices Commission. Report on Supply, 221
  Sampling on Importation, 557
  Trends and Prospects, 1236
Teachers:
  Basis of Remuneration of Part-Time Further Education Teachers, 911
  Children:
    Deaf, 419
    Mentally Retarded. Report, 419
  Future Demand for, 585
  Handbook for, 1264
  Measures to Improve the Supply of Teachers in Scotland. Report. *Cmnd. 202.* 262, 386
  Preparation for Health Education Report, 1269
  Qualified and Temporary Circular, 102, 585, 586, 842, 843
  Salaries:
    842
    Committee Reports:
      842
      Establishments for Further Education, England and Wales, 101
      Primary and Secondary Schools, England and Wales, 101
      Teaching Staff of Farm Institutes and Teachers of Agricultural Subjects, 102
      Training Colleges, England and Wales, 101
    Scotland:
      Regulations. Circular, 169, 385, 653, 911, 1143
      Report on Pensions. *Cmnd. 527.* 534, 654
      Report on Supply. *Cmnd. 196.* 262; *Cmnd. 644.* 789, 913
  Superannuation Scheme Scotland, Draft, 169
  Superannuation (Scotland) Regulations:
    Allocation of Pension Memorandum, 386
    Rules. Circular, 385
    Supply of, in 1960, 586
  Technical Certificate Qualification Report, 100, 170
  Three Years Training Report, 102
  Training:
    313, 1114
    Authorities (Scotland) Regulations. Circular, 653
    Establishments for England and Wales, 842, 1115
    Scope and Content of 3 year Course, 314
Teachers (Superannuation) Act, 56
Teachers (Superannuation) Acts. Allocation of Pension Memorandum, 314
Teachers (Superannuation) Bill, 2, 4, 13, 30, 33, 35, 128
Teaching:
  Abroad, 738
  Classics, Suggestions for, 842

INDEX 1956–60 —TEM

Teaching (*continued*):
  Human Rights, 989
  Hygiene and Public Health in Europe, 471
  Mathematics:
    1264
    Secondary Schools, 237A
  Reading and Writing, 239A
  Secondary Schools:
    Geography, 654
    History, 654
    Report, 386
  Service in the Commonwealth and Other Countries Overseas. Circular, 1115, 1116, 1184
  Social Sciences:
    240A, 469, 996
    U.S.S.R., 995
  Through Television Report, 1249
Technical and Vocational Education:
  Cmd. 9703. 39, 102, 171, 995
  Underdeveloped Countries, 995
  U.K., 736
  U.S.A., 1264
  U.S.S.R., 995
Technical Assistance:
  Board Reports, 228A, 723, 982
  British Guiana. Exchange of Notes between U.K. and U.S.A. extending Agreement. *Cmnd. 1238.* 1068, 1128
  Committee Report, 228A, 453, 1253
  Economic Development of Under-Developed Countries Programme and Budget Estimates, 244A, 472, 740
  Fiscal and Financial Field, 732
  International Co-operation, 234A
  Mission Publications, 223A
  Programme, 234A, 732, 1260
  Special Report, 240A
  Trust, and Other Territories. Agreement between U.K. and the United Nations, etc. *Cmnd. 1178.* 1064, 1126
  Your Questions Answered, 732
  See also Seeds of Progress
Technical Bulletins, 293, 422, 560, 1089
Technical Change and Political Decision, 1265
Technical Colleges:
  467
  Liberal Education in, 313
  Organisation of, 100, 102
Technical Commission Report. International Civil Aviation Organisation, 1242
Technical Co-operation:
  Agreement for the Establishment of the Commission for Technical Co-operation in Africa South of the Sahara. *Cmnd. 612.* 788, 852
  Scheme of the Colombo Plan. Reciprocal Waiver of Import Duties on Goods Supplied. *Cmnd. 474.* 530, 594
  Under the Colombo Plan Report, 1107
Technical Education. Advisory Panel Report. *Cmd. 9703.* 39, 102, 171; 586
Technical Information:
  And the Smaller Firm, 978
  International Guide to European Sources, 448
  Services in Europe. Report, 224A, 719
Technical Manuals, 203
Technical Memorandum. Department of Health for Scotland, 331
Technical Notes, 427 8
Technical Possibilities of a Thames Flood Barrier. *Cmnd. 930.* 1046, 1148
Technical Problems of Welsh Agriculture Report, 560
Technical Reports:
  Series, 472, 741, 999
  Special Volumes, 287
Technical Services to the Smaller Firm by Basic Suppliers, 1250
Technical Subjects:
  Scottish Certificate of Education, 913
  Teaching in Secondary Schools, 386
Techniques for Tomorrow, 234A
Technological Centres, 234A
Technological Education in Britain, 344, 1150
Tees Conservancy Act, 58, 811
Tees Valley and Cleveland Water Act, 544, 811
Teeth, Our Children's, 1132
Tele-Clubs in France. *See* Press, Film, Radio
Teleost Family Carapidae (Percomorphi, Blennioidea) Systematic Revision of the Fishes of the, 81
Telephone Policy. *Cmnd. 436.* 528, 640
Telephone System, Full Automation. *Cmnd. 303.* 269, 370
Telescopes and Binoculars, Photometry of, 155
Teletypewriter Operating Practices, Manual of, 971
Television:
  Advisory Committee Report, 1170
  Agricultural Advisory Work, 1247
  And Rural Adult Education, 239A
  Broadcasts, European Agreement on Protection of. *Cmnd. 1163.* 1063, 1119; 1232
  Education, 691
  Japan, Rural, 1265
  Our Schools, 419
Television Act Account, 13, 31, 161, 495, 640, 760, 782, 898
Television (Commercial Advertisements) (No. 2) Bill, 784
Television (Limitation of Advertising) Bill, 785
Témoignage sur le Communanté des Six, 435
Temperance (Scotland) Act. Return of Voting Areas, 173

TEM-TRA | 1956-60

- Temperature:
  - And Humidities in Pig Houses, 1181
  - Calibration of Measuring Instruments, 636
  - Compensated Equivalent Headwinds for Jet Aircraft, 360
  - Of British Fish during Distribution in Summer, 910
  - Relative Humidity and Precipitation Tables, 634, 889, 1162
  - Standard Deviation of Monthly Mean Temperatures over Britain, Averages of Accumulated, 889
  - Synoptic Study of Anomalies of Surface Air, over the Atlantic Half of the Northern Hemisphere, 889
- Temple of Preah Vihear (Cambodia *v.* Thailand) Order, 1243
- Temporary Houses, 340
- Temporary Laws, Register of, 31, 127, 245, 339, 514, 609, 1142
- Temporary Teachers, Circular, 1115, 1116
- Ten-Nation Disarmament Committee Held at Geneva:
  - Text of Plan. *Cmnd. 981.* 1049, 1119
  - Verbatim Records of the Meetings. *Cmnd. 1152.* 1062, 1119
- Ten Steps Forward, 742
- Ten Years of the Council of Europe, 1232
- Tenancy Legislation, Principles of, 708
- Tenancy of Shops (Scotland) Committee Report. *Cmnd. 472.* 530, 656
- Tenants' Protection Bill, 517
- Tensions and Technology Series, 240, 469, 738
- Tents, Vans, Sheds, etc., Model Byelaws, 130
- Tephigram, 153
- Termites:
  - Of the Genus Amitermes from the Ethiopian Region (Isoptera, Termitidae, Amitermitinae) Revision of, 827
  - Proofing of Timber for Use in the Tropics, 908
- Terms and Conditions of Employment Act, 810
- Terms and Condit ons of Employment Bill:
  - 749, 764, 779, 785, 864
  - *See also* Wages Council Bill and Wages Council (Amendment) Bill
- "Terra Nova"—British Antarctic Expedition—Natural History Report, 827
- Terracottas in the Department of Greek and Roman Antiquities, British Museum Catalogue, 1094
- Terrington, Lord (Chairman: Committee on Proposed Experimental Importation of Charollais Cattle) Report. *Cmnd. 1140.* 1060
- Territorial and Auxiliary Forces Associations Financial Position. *Cmd. 9866.* 50, 76, 207; *Cmnd. 261.* 266, 294, 426; *Cmnd. 488.* 531, 561, 697; *Cmnd. 881.* 805, 826, 956; *Cmnd. 1141.* 1061, 1090, 1225
- Territorial Army:
  - Regulations Amendments, 207, 426, 696, 955, 1225
  - Reorganisation. *Cmnd. 1216.* 1066, 1225
  - Special Army Orders, 956
  - Territorial Army Reserve and County Associations, Regulations:
    - 955
    - Amendments, 955
  - *See* Military Law, Manual of
- Territorial Sea:
  - Contiguous Zone, Law of the Sea, 728
  - Laws and Regulations on the Regime, 728
- Terrorism in Cyprus, 90
- Tester's Manual. Explanatory Notes, 1200
- Testing Concrete, 697
- Testing Memoranda, 646, 901
- Testing Mixers for Bituminous Materials, 384
- Testing of Sight:
  - Fees and Charges, 1137
  - Supply and Repair of Glasses. Statement Specifying Fees and Charges, 332
- Textbooks and International Understanding, 994
- Textiles:
  - Converting. Census of Production Report, 395
  - English Printed, 1222
  - Fabrics and Threads. Defence List, 578, 837
  - Finishing. Census of Production Report, 664
  - Foreign Trade Statistical Bulletin, 448, 718, 978
  - Industry in Europe, 224A, 450, 719, 978
  - Leather and Clothing. Food, Drink and Tobacco Censuses of Production Report, 180, 923
  - Machinery and Accessories. Census of Production Report, 663
  - Packing. Census of Production Report, 395
  - Production and Consumption Statistics, 449, 719
- Thailand:
  - Agreement with U.K. etc., regarding British Commonwealth War Graves. *Cmd. 9776.* 44, 110
  - Exchange of Notes with U.K.:
    - Amending the Schedule to the Air Services Agreement, *Cmnd. 58.* 252, 323; *Cmnd. 1180.* 1064, 1126

- Thailand (*continued*):
  - Exchange of Notes with U.K. (*contd*):
    - Concerning the Reciprocal Waiver of Import Duties on Goods supplied under the Technical Cooperation Scheme of the Colombo Plan. *Cmnd. 474.* 530, 594
  - International Customs Journal, 444
  - Memorandum on the Disposal of Former German Assets. *Cmnd. 108.* 256, 323
- Thames Conservancy Act, 812
- Thames Flood Barrier, Technical Possibilities. *Cmnd. 956.* 1048, 1148
- Thapar, R., Visual Aids in Fundamental Education and Community Development, 996
- Theoretical and Experimental Aspects of Controlled Nuclear Fusion, 987
- Therapeutic Substances Act, 56
- Therapeutic Substances of Human Origin, European Agreement on the Exchange, 962
- Therapy, Application of High Energy Radiations in, 1239
- Thermal Insulation (Dwellings) Bill, 517
- Thermal Insulation in Building, Importance of, 427
- Thermal Insulation (Industrial Buildings) Act:
  - 273
  - And Regulations, Memorandum, 1173
  - Explanatory Memorandum, 646
- Thermal Insulation (Industrial Buildings) Bill, 218, 233, 243, 247, 248, 339
- Thermonuclear Fusion, Recent Research on Controlled, 1240
- Thinning and Gapping of Row Crops, Mechanical, 823
- Third Reich. First Phase. Documents on German Foreign Policy, 590, 847
- This is Civil Defence, 422
- This is the Commonwealth, 873
- Thomas, H. H.:
  - Libya Overseas Economic Survey, 182
  - Lidgettonia. New Type of Fertile Glossopteris, 563
- Thomas, H. J.:
  - Lobster and Crab Fisheries in Scotland, 656
  - Lobster Storage, 655
- Thomas, I., Common Names of British Insect and Other Pests, 560
- Thomas, J. O., Convention of Ionospheric Virtual Height-Frequency Curves to Electron Density-Height Profiles, 910
- "Thomas L. Devlin" Wreck Report, 1200
- Thompson, A., Vocabularium Bibliothecarii, 735
- Thompson, J. P., Combustible Contents in Buildings, 419
- Thompson, M. W.:
  - Conisbrough Castle Guide, 957
  - Pickering Castle Guide, 698
- Thomson, A. B., Distribution of Wet-Bulb Temperature at Aberdeen and Eskdalemuir, 153
- Thornton Abbey, Lincolnshire, Guide, 208
- Thought Processes, Mechanisation of Proceedings of Symposium, 890
- Three Year Training for Teachers. Report of the National Advisory Council, 102
- Threlkeld, T., Animal Feedstuffs. Regulations governing Manufacture and Sale, 437
- Threshers, 558
- Tiepolo Drawings in the Victoria and Albert Museum, Catalogue of, 1222
- Tilbury Fort, Essex. Guide, 1226
- Tiles. Guide to Collection, 1223
- Timber:
  - Air Seasoning of Converted Green, 907
  - And Metal, Preservation of, 292
  - And Pitwood, Report of Inquiry, 1158
  - Beams, Effect of Depth on the Strength Properties of, 382
  - Bulletin for Europe, 242A, 437, 708, 990, 1238, 1260
  - Census of Production Report, 179, 664
  - Decay and Its Control, 908
  - Decay of, and Its Prevention, 906
  - For Flooring, 382
  - Handling and Transport in Mountainous Regions, 708
  - Hot and Cold Open-Tank Method of Impregnating Timber, 907
  - Identification of, 908
  - Imported, Monopolies Commission Report, 507, 666
  - Industry in Europe, Statistics, 224A
  - Laminated, 223A
  - Mechanical Barking of, 437
  - Mechanical Loading on Trucks, 967
  - Meranti, Seraya and Allied, 166
  - Modern Techniques for the Drying and Conditioning of, 449
  - Natural Durability of, 908
  - Paper:
    - And Other Manufacturing Industries. Censuses of Production Report, 396
    - Censuses of Production Report, 923
  - Price Statistics, 462
  - Sap-Stain in, 907
  - Skidding by Tractor in the USSR, 990
  - Statistics, 450, 719, 978, 1250
  - Strength Properties of, 166
  - Transport on Snow and Ice Roads, 1260
  - Tropical Statistics, 719, 978
  - Use of Home Grown Timber in Packaging and Materials Handling, 325
    - *See* Forest Products Research Leaflets
    - *See* Tropical Timber

- Timber (*continued*):
  - Time Measurement, Handbook of the Collection Illustrating, 648
  - Time Rates of Wages and Hours of Labour, 149, 356, 630, 886, 1158
  - Time Service, 1178
  - Time Spent Awaiting Trial Report, 1140
  - Timmons, J. F., Improving Agricultural Tenancy, 436
- Tin:
  - Agreement, International, 107
  - Amendment to International Tin Agreement. *Cmnd. 556.* 535, 594
- Tinplate. Census of Production Report, 394
- Tintern Abbey, Monmouthshire, Guide, 208, 1227
- Tipulidae, 82
- Tirmizi, N. M., Crustacea Penaeidae Series Benthesicymae, 1097
- Titanium, Zirconium and Some Other Elements of Growing Industrial Importance, 224A
- Tite, G. E., Jamides Euchylas Complex and Two New Species of the Genu Gamides, 1095
- Tithe Act Account, 227, 361, 411, 498, 681, 763, 938, 1016, 1162, 1206
- Title to Land, Registration of, 1158
- Titles and Contents, Sessional Printed Papers, 755
- To Have a Key, 462
- Tobacco:
  - Census of Production Report, 395, 1194
  - Exchange of Notes between U.K. and U.S.A. concerning Sale of Tobacco and Construction of Housing and/or Community Facilities. *Cmnd. 403.* 525, 595
  - Pipe Bowls. Report of the Standing Committee Respecting Certain Wooden Tobacco Pipe Bowls. *Cmnd. 1001.* 1051, 1193
  - Smoking and Cancer of the Lung Statement, 312, 359
- Togoland:
  - Report under United Kingdom Administration, 90
  - Under British Administration. United Nations Visiting Mission Report, 463, 464
  - Under French Administration. United Nations Commission Report, 236A, 733
- Toilet Preparations and Perfumery. Census of Production Report, 394
- Tomatoes:
  - 1085
  - Cultivation, Diseases and Pests, 290
  - Foot Rot, 69
  - Outdoor, 288
  - Spotted Wilt, 1083
- Tonga:
  - Biennial Report, 90
  - Colonial Report, 832
  - Friendly Islands International Customs Journal, 445
  - Treaty of Friendship with U.K. *Cmnd. 606.* 539, 594; *Cmnd. 848.* 803, 852
- Tonnage Measurement of Ships, Surveyors' Instruction, 190
- Tools:
  - And Implements. Census of Production Report, 394
  - Common User Hand, 93
  - Hand and Machine Screw Cutting Tools, 307
  - Standing Committee Report Respecting Certain Hand Tools. *Cmnd. 1039.* 1054, 1193
- Toomer, Air Vice-Marshal S. E., "The Germans Come to the Help of their Ally", 82, 174
- Topolski, F., London Airport, Drawings, 187
- Toppoo's Tiger, 951
- Tornadoes:
  - England, 360
  - What They are and What To Do About Them, 203
- Torry Research Station:
  - Handling and Preservation of Fish. Report, 910, 1183
  - Technical Paper, 910, 1183
- Touch, Dr. A. G., Aircraft Accident Report, 400
- Tour De Londres. Guide Book, 1227
- Touring. Convention concerning Customs Facilities for Touring. *Cmnd. 308.* 269, 323
- Tourism in Europe, 224A, 1250
- Tourist Industry in Scotland, 768, 779, 864
- Toward the Economic Development of the Republic of Viet Nam, 990
- Towards a European Parliament, 704
- Towards a New Energy Pattern in Europe, Report, 1250
- Tower Hill Barracks. Sierra Leone, Gift. *Cmnd. 1111.* 1058, 1203
- Tower of London:
  - Guide Book, 428
  - Postcards, 208, 697, 957, 1226
- Town and Country Planning:
  - Britain, 872
  - Control of Advertisements. Amendment Regulations, Circular, 1146
  - Development Plans. Amendment Regulations. Circular, 869
  - General Development (Amendment) Order, Circular, 1146
  - Minerals. Regulations. Circular, 341
  - Planning Payments (War Damage) Schemes, 1949, Account, 10, 83, 224, 296, 492, 565, 759, 829, 1016, 1098

- Town and Country Planning Act:
  - 810
  - Circulars:
    - 610, 869, 1146
    - Scotland, 600
  - Report of the Compensation and Contributions, 1033, 1148
  - Selected Appeal Decisions:
    - Bulletin, 343
    - E. and W., 613
    - Scotland, 601
- Town and Country Planning Bill:
  - 516, 520, 749, 750, 751, 753, 762, 779, 784, 864
  - Explanatory Memorandum. *Cmnd. 562.* 536, 613, 657
- Town and Country Planning (Scotland) Act:
  - 810
  - Accounts, 20, 83, 121, 131, 227, 296, 331, 343, 496, 565, 601, 613, 769, 829, 858, 871, 1022, 1133, 1148
  - Appeals Decisions, 858
  - Circular, 857
  - Consolidation Bills Report, 746, 753, 867
  - Purchase Notices Circular, 857
- Town and Country Planning (Scotland) Bill, 753, 786
- Town Gas. Its Manufacture and Distribution, 648
- Toxic Hazards of Pesticides to Man. Report, 245A
- Toxic Substances:
  - In Air, Methods for the Detection of, 630, 875, 885
  - In Factory Atmospheres, 1158
- Toys and Games:
  - Census of Production Report, 396
  - Picture Book, 886
- Trachoma. Expert Committee Report, 245A
- Tractors:
  - Engine Overhaul, 558
  - Equipment, 242A
  - For Logging, 242A
  - Forest, 228A
  - Fuel Store, 292
  - Provisional Protocol for Testing Forest Tractors, 724
- Trade:
  - Agreement between U.K. and:
    - Australia. *Cmnd. 91.* 255, 398
    - Denmark. *Cmnd. 337.* 521, 589
    - Ireland. *Cmnd. 1019.* 1052, 1194
    - New Zealand. *Cmnd. 830.* 802, 923
    - U.S.S.R. *Cmnd. 771.* 799, 922; *Cmnd. 1076.* 1056, 1127
  - And Industrial Mission to Ghana Report, 923
  - And Navigation Accounts, 8, 11–12, 183, 221, 223, 398–9, 429, 489, 491, 667, 755, 758, 924, 1013, 1017, 1194
- Trade (*continued*):
  - And Payments Agreements:
    - Between U.K. and Paraguay. *Cmd. 9683, 9850.* 38, 49, 108
    - Exchange of Notes between U.K. and:
      - Argentina. *Cmnd. 98.* 255
      - Brazil prolonging. *Cmnd. 323.* 270
  - Barriers to Knowledge, 240A
  - Classification, Standard International, 1259
  - Direction of International, 226A, 451, 721, 980, 1251
  - Directory of Board of Trade Departments and Their Work, 665
  - Effluents Sub-Committee of the Central Advisory Water Committee Report, 613, 1147
  - Estimates:
    - 1956–57, 12
    - 1957–58, 226
    - 1958–59, 494, 676
    - 1959–60, 760, 933
    - 1960–61, 1019, 1201
  - Guides for the Newcomer to World, 421
  - International, 220A, 223A, 230A, 438, 453, 457
  - Marks:
    - Arrangement concerning the International Classification of Goods and Services. *Cmnd. 348.* 522, 594
    - Protection. Exchange of Notes between U.K. and Vietnam. *Cmd. 9694.* 39, 111
    - Understanding between U.K. French Republic, U.S.A. and Italy. *Cmnd. 19.* 53, 107
  - Mission to the Egyptian Region of the United Arabs Republic. Report, 1194
  - Of the U.K.:
    - 578
    - Annual Statement, 836
    - With the Commonwealth and Foreign Countries Statement, 93, 306–7, 1107
    - With Selected Countries, 183
  - Yearbook, 968, 1238
  - *See* Commodity Trade—International Commodity Trade
- Trade, Board of:
  - Departments and Their Work. Directory, 180, 1192
  - Journal, 181–2, 397, 431, 667, 922, 1193
  - Publications, 178–85, 393–400, 663, 920, 1191
  - Report, 1143
  - Select Committee on Estimates, 1029
  - Special Report, 1040, 1144
- Trade Facilities Acts. Account, 18, 198, 231, 398, 501, 681, 765, 938, 1024, 1206

Trade Unions:
  Acts, Guide to, 1130
  Chief Registrar's Report, 114, 326, 597, 855, 1130
  Directory. *See* Employers' Association Training in Europe, 1250
Trades Selected in Scotland and Wales. Censuses of Production Report, 396
Trading Accounts and Balance Sheets, 9, 31, 103, 245, 314, 514, 587, 1014, 1117
Trading Representations (Disabled Persons) Act, 542
Trading Representations (Disabled Persons) Bill, 483, 503, 513, 517, 519, 609
Traditional Cultures in South-East Asia, 997
Trafalgar Square Draft Regulations. Select Committee on Statutory Instruments Report, 780
Traffic:
  And Transport in Nigeria, 1103
  Cases Reports, 405, 431, 674, 930, 1199
  Commissioners Reports, 674, 927, 1199
  In Persons and Prostitution, Study, 989
  London, 929
  On Main International Traffic Arteries Census, 720
  Safety Code for Road Works, 403
  Signal Settings, 652
Traffic Control (Temporary Provisions) Bill, 787
Training:
  And Administration of Personnel in the Public Service, 732
  College Hostels, 313
  Colleges, England and Wales, 102, 314, 586
  District Nurses Report, 859
  For Skill. Recruitment and Training of Young Workers in Industry Report, 630
  For Social Welfare, 985
  For Social Work, 990
  For Town and Country Planning, 727
  In Radiological Health and Safety. Report, 1207
  Journalists, 737
  Made Easier, 1181
  Manual:
    712, 1243
    International Civil Aviation, 219A, 443, 972
  Primary Teacher Training Staffs, 468
  Public Administration, 732
  Teachers:
    313
    Grants to Recognised Training College Students, 1114
  Technical and Scientific Staff, 995
  Workers within the Factory, 450
Traité CECA Devant les Parlements Nationaux, 704
Traité instituant le Communauté Européenne du Charbon et de l'Acier, Révision du, 706
Tramway Accident Report, 190, 931
Tramway, Trolley Bus and Omnibus Undertakings. Census of Production Report, 396
Transactions in Seeds. Report. *Cmnd. 300.* 269, 293, 335, 389
Transhipment Licence:
  924
  Amendments, 183, 399
Translations:
  Bulletin, Lending Library Unit, 909
  International Bibliography, 238A, 467, 1264
Transmission and Propagation, 955
Transmitters-Receivers and Performance Specifications, 898
Transport:
  And Communications Commission Report, 453, 982
  Arbitration Tribunal. Road Haulage Cases Decisions, 190
  Consultative Committee. *See* Central Transport
  Estimates:
    1956–57, 12
    1957–58, 226
    1958–59, 494, 676
    1960–61, 1019, 1201
  Fund Account, 24, 190, 496, 674
  Instructions for Masters of, 929
  Of Dangerous Goods. Classification, Listing and Labelling, 462
  Of Goods by Road:
    International. *Cmnd. 1012.* 1052, 1121
    Sample Survey Report, 931
  Of Goods under TIR Carnets, Customs Convention. *Cmnd. 790.* 800, 846
  Of Perishable Foodstuffs, 732
  On the Farm, General Problem of, 979
  Power, and Industrial Research Estimates, 1959–60, 760, 933
  Standing Committee Debates, 1040
  Statistics:
    For Europe, 234A, 462, 732, 990, 1251
    Public Road Passenger Transport, Great Britain, 188, 929, 1197, 1199
  See Nationalised Transport
Transport Act:
  Guarantee given on Loans proposed to be raised, 22, 26, 27, 198, 224, 231, 236, 240, 411, 493, 501, 507, 510, 681, 758, 768, 774, 780, 938, 1018, 1026, 1032, 1034, 1206
  Guarantee Given on Stock issued, 17, 27, 198, 232, 411

Transport and Civil Aviation, Minister of, Exchange of Correspondence with the Chairman of the British Transport Commission. *Cmnd. 585.* 538, 672
Transport and Civil Aviation, Ministry of:
  Circulars, 186, 401
  Examination Papers, 187, 402, 671, 928
  Memorandum, 403
  Publications, 185–92, 400–6, 669, 927
Transport (Borrowing Powers) Act, 810
Transport (Borrowing Powers) Bill, 520, 746
Transport (Disposal of Road Haulage Property) Act, 56
Transport (Disposal of Road Haulage Property) Bill, 3, 4, 16, 30, 33, 35, 128
Transport, Ministry of:
  Examination Papers, 926, 1197
  Publications, 926, 1196
Transport (Railway Finances) Act:
  273
  Account, 765, 1027
  Advances to Nationalised Industries and Undertakings Account, 496, 587
Transport (Railway Finances) Bill, 32, 35, 36, 214, 222, 339
Transport Tribunal, British Transport Commission Charges Schemes:
  Harbour:
    Order, 674, 1199
    Proceedings, 674, 1199
  Inland Waterways:
    Order, 674
    Proceedings, 674
  Passenger:
    Interim Decision, 931
    Order, 190, 405, 931
    Proceedings, 191, 405, 674, 931
  Railway Merchandise:
    Interim Decision, 190
    Proceedings, 191, 405
Transport Users' Consultative Committee Reports:
  Scotland, 20, 191, 229, 406, 497, 675, 768, 931, 1024, 1200
  Wales and Monmouthshire, 20, 191, 229, 406, 498, 675, 768, 931, 1024, 1200
"Traquair", Wreck Report, 406
Traung, Jan Olaf, Fishing Boat Tank Tests, 241A, 966
Travel:
  Exchanges of Notes concerning Arrangements to facilitate Travel. U.K. and:
    Belgium. *Cmnd. 1091.* 1057, 1118
    Germany. *Cmnd. 1157.* 1062, 1121
    Luxembourg. *Cmnd. 1079.* 1056, 1123
    Netherlands. *Cmnd. 1080.* 1056, 1122
  United States Participation in International, 692
Travelling Journeyman takes the Road again, 469
Trawsfynydd, Proposed Nuclear Power Station, Report, 645
Treasury:
  Books, Calendar of, 161, 646, 901
  Chest Fund, Account, 23, 198, 497, 681, 763, 938
  Control of Expenditure. Estimates. Select Committee Report, 506, 606, 866
  Publications, 192–8, 406–12, 675, 932, 1200
Treat, Form of Claim in Answer to a Notice, 1204
Treat, Notice to, Form of Claim (Scotland), 857
Treatment and Care of Drug Addicts Report, 473
Treatment of Non-Metalliferous Mining Products other than Coal; Chemicals and Allied Trades; Metal Manufacture. Report on the Censuses of Production, 923
Treatment of Offenders:
  Britain, 1150
  Scottish Advisory Council Report, 1186
  Selection of for Probation, 989
  Young Offenders. Report, 863, 1186
  See Imprisonment
Treatment of Timber in a Drying-Kiln, 907
Treatment of Wound Shock, 359
Treaty Collections, List of, 234A
Treaty of Alliance. Exchange of Notes between U.K. and Jordan Modifying the Termination. *Cmnd. 1158.* 1062, 1122
Treaty Rolls, 162
Treaty Series:
  European, 434
  General Index, 1952–54. *Cmnd. 368.* 523, 594
  United Nations, 234A–5A, 462–3, 732–3, 990, 1260
  1955:
    91 Ratifications, etc., Supplementary List. *Cmd. 9723.* 41
    92 Index. *Cmd. 9724.* 41, 110
  1956:
    1. U.K. and Denmark. Exchange of Notes extending the Provisions of the Military Service Agreement. *Cmd. 9669.* 37
    2. U.K. and Sweden. Exchange of Notes amending Air Service Agreement. *Cmd. 9670.* 37
    3. U.K. and U.S.A. Exchange of Notes rectifying Agreement for Co-operation on Civil Uses of Atomic Energy. *Cmd. 9677.* 38
    4. U.K. and Czechoslovakia. Exchange of Notes prolonging

Treaty Series (*continued*):
  1956 (*continued*):
    Sterling Payments Agreement. *Cmd. 9687.* 38
    5. U.K. and U.S.A. Exchange of Notes on Construction and Operation of a Weather Station on Betio Islands. *Cmd. 9693.* 39
    6. U.K. and Vietnam. Exchange of Notes for Protection of Trade Marks. *Cmd. 9694.* 39
    7. U.K. and Iraq. Exchange of Notes referring to Special Agreement. *Cmd. 9695.* 39; *Cmd. 9772.* 43
    8. Overfishing. Conventions. *Cmd. 9704.* 39
    9. U.K. and Belgium. Exchange of Notes extending Visa Abolition Agreement. *Cmd. 9711.* 40
    10. U.K. and Sweden. Exchange of Letters on Repayment of Debt owed in connection with European Payments Union. *Cmd. 9712.* 40
    11. International Tracing Service. Agreement. *Cmd. 9713.* 40
    12. U.K. and Argentine. Exchange of Notes prolonging Air Services Agreement. *Cmd. 9720.* 40
    13. U.K. and Yugoslavia. Exchange of Notes regarding Import of British Books. *Cmd. 9726.* 41
    14. U.K. and Yugoslavia. Exchange of Notes regarding certain Financial Obligations. *Cmd. 9730.* 41
    15. U.K. and Greece. Dollar-Sterling Exchange Rate Applicable to Cargoes Diverted from Greek Ports. *Cmd. 9754.* 42
    16. U.K. and Cuba. Exchange of Notes regarding Commercial Relations. *Cmd. 9758.* 42
    17. U.K. and Austria. Repayment of Credits granted by European Payments Union. *Cmd. 9764.* 43
    18. U.K. etc., and Thailand, Agreement regarding War Graves. *Cmd. 9776.* 44
    19. U.K. and Luxembourg. Exchange of Notes amending Cultural Convention. *Cmd. 9782.* 44
    20. U.K. and Netherlands. Convention on Social Security. *Cmd. 9792.* 45
    21. Atomic Information. Agreement between the Parties to the North Atlantic Treaty. *Cmd. 9799.* 45
    22. U.K. and U.S.A. Exchange of Notes relating to Sale of Tobacco by U.S. and Construction of Housing Facilities by U.K. *Cmd. 9793.* 45
    23. U.K. and Belgium. Exchange of Notes amending Agreement for Co-operation in Peaceful Uses of Atomic Energy. *Cmd. 9794.* 45
    24. Slavery Convention. *Cmd. 9797.* 45
    25. U.K. and U.S.A. Agreement concerning Extension of Bahamas Long Range Proving Ground by Establishment of Additional Sites in St. Lucia. *Cmd. 9811.* 46
    26. U.K. and U.S.A. Exchange of Notes concerning Defence Requirements in Caribbean and Adjacent Areas and in South Atlantic. *Cmd. 9812.* 46
    27. U.K. and Czechoslovakia. Exchange of Notes prolonging Sterling Payments Agreement. *Cmd. 9819.* 47
    28. Sugar. International Agreement. *Cmd. 9815.* 46
    29. U.K. and Denmark Arrangements relating to Import of Danish Bacon. *Cmd. 9823.* 47
    30. U.K. and Hungary. Agreement relating to Settlement of Financial Matters. *Cmd. 9820.* 47
    31. Plant Protection. *Cmd. 9834.* 48
    32. U.K. and Belgium. Exchange of Letters regarding Repayment of Credit. *Cmd. 9836.* 48
    33. U.K. and Federal Republic of Germany. Agreement for Co-operation in Peaceful Uses of Atomic Energy. *Cmd. 9842.* 48
    34. U.K. and Switzerland. Exchange of Letters for Repayment of Credits granted by European Payments Union. *Cmd. 9844.* 49
    35. U.K. and U.S.A. Amendment to Agreement for Co-operation in Civil Uses of Atomic Energy. *Cmd. 9847.* 49
    36. U.K. and Netherlands. Exchange of Letters concerning Agreement for Repayment of Credits granted by European Payments Unions. *Cmd. 9848.* 49
    37. U.K. and Paraguay. Agreement on Trade and Payments. *Cmd. 9850.* 49
    38. War Cripples. Agreement on Exchange with a View to Medical Treatment. *Cmd. 9851.* 49
    39. Bagdad Pact of Mutual Co-operation between Iraq and Turkey. *Cmd. 9859.* 50
    40. U.K. and Egypt. Exchange of Notes extending provisions of

Treaty Series (*continued*):
  1956 (*continued*):
    Suez Canal Base Agreement. *Cmd. 9858.* 50
    41. U.K. and Burma, Exchange of Notes concerning the Export of Cotton Textiles and/or yarn and the Acceptance of Raw Cotton from U.S. *Cmd. 9860.* 50
    42. European Convention on the International Classification of Patents for Invention. *Cmd. 9862.* 50
    43. Agreement regarding Financial Support of the North Atlantic Ice Patrol. *Cmd. 9864.* 50
    44. Plant Protection. Convention for Organisation. *Cmd. 9878.* 51
    45. U.K. and Netherlands. Exchange of Letters concerning Conventions on Rights and Obligations of Foreign Forces in Germany. *Cmd. 9872.* 51
    46. U.K. Dependent Territories. Basic Agreement with Unesco regarding Aid. *Cmd. 9873.* 51
    47. U.K. and Czechoslovakia. Exchange of Notes prolonging Sterling Payments Agreement. *Cmd. 9875.* 51
    48. U.K., Burma and China. Exchange of Notes concerning Burma-Yunnan Boundary. *Cmnd. 40.* 34
    49. Potent Drugs. Protocol for Termination of Brussels Agreements and for Unification of Pharmacopocial Formulas. *Cmnd. 2.* 52
    50. International Tin Agreement. *Cmnd. 12.* 53
    51. Agreement concerning Relations between U.K. and European Coal and Steel Community. *Cmnd. 13.* 53
    52. Understanding between U.K., French Republic, U.S.A. and Italy regarding German Trade-Marks in Italy. *Cmnd. 19.* 53
    53. Atomic Energy Inventions. Agreement between U.K., Canada and U.S.A. as to Disposition of Rights. *Cmnd. 20.* 53
    54. U.K. and Austria. Exchange of Notes concerning Extension of Agreement for Repayments of Credits granted by European Payments Union. *Cmnd. 21.* 53
    55. U.K. and Denmark. Exchange of Notes concerning Rights of Foreign Forces in Germany and Finance Convention. *Cmnd. 22.* 54
    56. Ratifications, etc. *Cmnd. 102.* 256, 322
    57. Treaty Series, Index. *Cmnd. 103.* 256, 323
  1957:
    1. U.K. and Indonesia. Exchange of Notes relating to Arrangements for Export of Cotton Yarn. *Cmnd. 45.* 251
    2. Agreement between U.K. and U.S.A. for an Oceanographic Research Station in Barbados. *Cmnd. 68.* 253
    3. U.K. and Norway. Exchange of Notes amending Air Services Agreement. *Cmnd. 44.* 251
    4. U.K. and Czechoslovakia. Exchange of Notes concerning Agreement on Settlements of Debts. *Cmnd. 55.* 252
    5. U.K. and Czechoslovakia. Exchange of Notes concerning Agreement on Compensation for British Property. *Cmnd. 56.* 252
    6. U.K. and France. Military Service Agreement. *Cmnd. 57.* 252
    7. U.K. and Thailand. Exchange of Notes amending Schedule to Air Services Agreement. *Cmnd. 58.* 252
    8. Visas. Text of Notes from U.K. re-imposing Visa Requirements for Travellers to Cyprus. *Cmnd. 73.* 253
    9. Morocco. International Conference Final Declaration. *Cmnd. 60.* 252
    10. United Nations Forces, Japan. Agreement regarding Status. *Cmnd. 67.* 253
    11. U.K. and Poland. Exchange of Notes prolonging the Sterling Payments Agreement. *Cmnd. 74.* 253
    12. U.K. and Argentine. Exchange of Notes prolonging Air Services Agreement. *Cmnd. 75.* 253
    13. U.K. and Denmark. Convention on Payment of Compensation or Benefit in respect of Industrial Injuries. *Cmnd. 76.* 253
    14. U.K. and U.S.A. Exchange of Notes amending the Schedule of Routes annexed to Air Services Agreement. *Cmnd. 82.* 254
    15. U.K. and Sweden. Exchange of Letters on Repayment of Balance of U.K. Debt owed in connection with European Payments Union. *Cmnd. 81.* 254

Treaty Series (*continued*):
1957 (*continued*):
16. U.K. and Burma. Exchange of Notes amending Burmese Schedule of Routes annexed to Air Transport Agreement. *Cmnd. 83.* 254
17. Council of Europe. Protocol to General Agreement on Privileges and Immunities. *Cmnd. 84.* 254
18. U.K. and Japan. Exchange of Notes prolonging Sterling Payments Agreements. *Cmnd. 86.* 254
19. U.K. and U.S.A. Exchange of Notes amending the Schedule of Routes annexed to Air Services Agreement. *Cmnd. 85.* 254
20. U.K. and Turkey. Protocol regarding Financial Matters. *Cmnd. 117.* 257
21. U.K. and Austria. Agreement for Air Services. *Cmnd. 87.* 254
22. U.K. and U.S.A. Agreement for Establishment of Oceanographic Research Station in Turks and Caicos Islands. *Cmnd. 94.* 255
23. U.K. and Cuba. Exchange of Notes modifying Agreement concerning Commercial Relations. *Cmnd. 96.* 255
24. U.K. and Argentine Republic. Exchange of Notes about Currency Exchange Rates. *Cmnd. 97.* 255
25. U.K. and Argentine Republic. Exchange of Notes on Trade and Payments Agreement. *Cmnd. 98.* 255
26. Civil Aviation. Protocol relating to certain Amendments. *Cmnd. 107.* 256
27. Thailand. Memorandum on Disposal of former German Assets. *Cmnd. 108.* 256
28. U.K. and Switzerland. Convention for Relief from Double Taxation with respect to taxes on Estates of Deceased Persons. *Cmnd. 119.* 257
29. Convention regarding Control of African Migratory Locusts. *Cmnd. 128.* 257
30. U.K. and Czechoslovakia. Exchange of Notes prolonging Sterling Payments Agreement. *Cmnd. 129.* 257
31. U.K. and U.S.A. Exchange of Notes concerning Civil Aviation Facilities and Long Range Proving Grounds for Guided Missiles in West Indies. *Cmnd. 142.* 258

Treaty Series (*continued*):
1957 (*continued*):
32. Japan. Agreement regarding British Commonwealth War Graves in Japanese Territory. *Cmnd. 134.* 258
33. U.K. and Austria. Convention for Avoidance of Double Taxation and Prevention of Fiscal Evasion. *Cmnd. 135.* 258
34. U.K. and Turkey. Exchange of Notes relating to Commercial Matters. *Cmnd. 136.* 258
35. U.K. and Germany. Agreement for Air Services. *Cmnd. 137.* 258
36. U.K. and U.S.S.R. Fisheries Agreement. *Cmnd. 148.* 259
37. U.K. and U.S.A. Exchange of Notes referring to Sales of Tobacco and Construction of Housing and/or Community Facilities. *Cmnd. 143.* 258
38. U.K. and Morocco. Exchange of Notes concerning Convention of Commerce and Navigation between U.K. and Shereefian Empire. *Cmnd. 144.* 259
39. U.K. and Jordan. Exchange of Notes terminating Treaty of Alliance. *Cmnd. 186.* 261
40. Plant Protection Agreements for the South-East Asia and Pacific Region. *Cmnd. 170.* 260
41. U.K. and Philippine Republic. Exchange of Notes concerning the Air Services Agreement. *Cmnd. 171.* 260
42. Western European Union. Agreement on Status. *Cmnd. 173.* 260
43. German External Debts. Agreement amended. *Cmnd. 177.* 261
44. U.K. and U.S.A. Financial Agreement. *Cmnd. 178.* 261
45. U.K. and Iraq. Exchange of Notes concerning Settlement of Financial Claims by Establishment of Anglo-Iraqi Club. *Cmnd. 187.* 261
46. Convention on Social Security between U.K. and Sweden. *Cmnd. 192.* 262
47. U.K. and U.S.A. Exchange of Notes on Disposal of Surplus Mutual Defence Assistance Programme Equipment. *Cmnd. 198.* 262
48. U.K. and U.S.A. Exchange of Notes concerning Settlement for Lend-Lease, Reciprocal Aid, Surplus War Property Claims. *Cmnd. 201.* 262

Treaty Series (*continued*):
1957 (*continued*):
49. U.K. and Switzerland. Exchange of Notes revising the Route Schedule annexed to Air Services Agreement. *Cmnd. 217.* 263
50. U.K. and Sweden. Liquidation of German Assets. *Cmnd. 219.* 263
51. U.K. and Italy. Memorandum of Understanding regarding Claims under Treaty of Peace. *Cmnd. 241.* 265
52. U.K., France, U.S.A. and Italy. Memorandum of Understanding regarding German Assets in Italy. *Cmnd. 236.* 264
53. U.K. and Germany. Exchange of Notes concerning Disbandment of Civilian Service Organisation. *Cmnd. 226.* 264
54. U.K. and Italy. Exchange of Notes concerning Practice of Medical Profession. *Cmnd. 238.* 265
55. U.K. and Germany. Exchange of Notes constituting Supplementary Agreement regarding Use of the Sandbank Bombing Range. *Cmnd. 244.* 265
56. U.K. and Belgium. Exchange of Letters concerning Repayment of Credits granted by European Payments Union. *Cmnd. 248.* 265
57. U.K. and Indonesia. Exchange of Notes amending Memorandum of Understanding for Export of Cotton Yarn from Hong Kong. *Cmnd. 250.* 265
58. Austria. State Treaty for Re-establishment of Independent and Democratic Austria. *Cmnd. 214.* 263
59. Convention on Abolition of Slavery. *Cmnd. 257.* 266
60. U.K. and Cuba. Exchange of Notes amending the Schedules to the Air Services Agreement. *Cmnd. 258.* 266
61. U.K. and Turkey. Exchange of Notes concerning Purchase of Ships of British Reserve Fleet. *Cmnd. 260.* 266
62. U.K. and U.S.A. Exchange of Notes concerning Extension of Bahamas Long Range Proving Ground to include Island of Great Exuma. *Cmnd. 266.* 267
63. South-East Asia Collective Defence. *Cmnd. 265.* 267

Treaty Series (*continued*):
1957 (*continued*):
64. U.K. and U.S.A. Exchange of Notes concerning Sale of Tobacco and Construction of Housing and Community Facilities. *Cmnd. 272.* 267
65. U.K. and Norway. Exchange of Notes regarding Peaceful Uses of Atomic Energy. *Cmnd. 277.* 267
66. Universal Copyright Convention. *Cmnd. 289.* 268
67. U.K. and Sweden. Agreement for Co-operation in Peaceful Uses of Atomic Energy. *Cmnd. 290.* 268
68. U.K. and Germany. Exchange of Letters concerning Repayment of Credits to European Payments Union. *Cmnd. 291.* 268
69. U.K. and Austria. Exchange of Notes concerning Contracts and Periods of Prescription. *Cmnd. 292.* 269
70. Convention concerning Customs Facilities for Touring. *Cmnd. 308.* 269
71. University Study European Convention on Equivalence of Periods. *Cmnd. 301.* 269
72. U.K. and Brazil. Exchange of Notes prolonging Articles of Trade and Payments Agreement. *Cmnd. 323.* 270
73. Ratifications, Accessions, Withdrawals, etc. *Cmnd. 386.* 524
74. Treaty Series Index. *Cmnd. 387.* 524

1958:
Index. *Cmnd. 643.* 789, 853
1. U.K. and U.S.A. Agreement for Establishment of Oceanograph Research Stations in Bahama Islands. *Cmnd. 343.* 521
2. U.K. and Israel. Convention on Social Security. *Cmnd. 347.* 522
3. U.K. and Cuba. Exchange of Notes regarding Commercial Relations. *Cmnd. 358.* 522
4. International Convention revising Berne Convention for Protection of Literary and Artistic Works. *Cmnd. 361.* 523
5. U.K. and Argentine. Agreement on Consolidation of Debts. *Cmnd. 359.* 523
6. Treaty Series General Index. *Cmnd. 368.* 523
7. U.K. and Germany. Exchange of Notes for Co-operation in Peaceful Uses of Atomic Energy. *Cmnd. 375.* 523

Treaty Series (*continued*):
1958 (*continued*):
8. U.K. and Argentina. Exchange of Notes further prolonging Air Services Agreement. *Cmnd. 376.* 524
9. U.K. and Netherlands. Exchange of Notes amending Cultural Convention. *Cmnd. 382.* 524
10. U.K. and U.S.A. Exchange of Notes about the Weather Station on Betio Island. *Cmnd. 391.* 525
11. U.K. and Turkey. Cultural Agreement. *Cmnd. 401.* 525
12. U.K. and U.S.A. Exchange of Notes concerning Sale for Sterling of Fruit and Fruit Products. *Cmnd. 402.* 525
13. U.K. and U.S.A. Exchange of Notes concerning Sale of Tocacco and Construction of Housing and/or Community Facilities. *Cmnd. 403.* 525
14. U.K. and U.S.A. Exchange of Notes concerning Supply of Intermediate Range Ballistic Missiles. *Cmnd. 406.* 526
15. U.K. and Yugoslavia. Exchange of Notes terminating Agreement regarding Import of British Books. *Cmnd. 404.* 525
16. U.K. and Japan. Exchange of Notes concerning Grant of Continuous Visas. *Cmnd. 412.* 526
17. U.K. and Netherlands. Exchange of Letters prolonging Agreement concerning Division of Responsibility for Rights and Obligations of Forces in Germany. *Cmnd. 413.* 526
18. U.K. and Norway. Convention on Social Security. *Cmnd. 422.* 527
19. Statute of International Atomic Energy. *Cmnd. 450.* 528
20. U.K. and Netherlands. Exchange of Notes for Avoidance of Double Taxation, etc. *Cmnd. 542.* 528
21. U.K. and Italy. Agreement for Co-operation in the Peaceful Uses of Atomic Energy. *Cmnd. 458.* 529
22. U.K. and Belgium. Convention on Social Security, etc. *Cmnd. 460.* 529
23. U.K. and Thailand. Exchange of Notes concerning Reciprocal Waiver of Import Duties on Goods supplied under Technical Co-operation Scheme of Colombo Plan. *Cmnd. 474.* 530

Treaty Series (*continued*):
1958 (*continued*):
24. Protocol relating to Amendment to Convention on International Civil Aviation. *Cmnd.* 482. 530
25. U.K. and Jordan. Exchange of Notes concerning a Loan. *Cmnd. 483.* 531
26. U.K. and Jordan. Exchange of Notes concerning a Loan. *Cmnd. 484.* 531
27. U.K. and Italy. Agreement concerning Contracts of Insurance and Re-Insurance. *Cmnd. 504.* 532
28. U.K. and Muscat and Oman. Exchange of Letters concerning Sultan's Armed Forces, Civil Aviation, etc. *Cmnd. 507.* 532
29. U.K. and Switzerland. Exchange of Letters concerning Suspension of Payments and for Repayment and Consolidation. *Cmnd. 512.* 532
30. Agreement with U.K. and Portugal for Co-operation in the Peaceful Uses of Atomic Energy. *Cmnd. 513.* 532, 787
31. U.K. and Switzerland. Exchange of Notes abrogating Declaration concerning Death Duties in Canton de Vaud. *Cmnd. 514.* 533
32. U.K. and Jordan. Exchange of Notes concerning Payment of Instalments due under Treaty Termination Settlement. *Cmnd. 515.* 533
33. International Convention for regulating the Police of the North Sea Fisheries Agreement. *Cmnd. 517.* 533
34. U.K. and Lebanon. Exchange of Notes concerning Loans of Arms. *Cmnd. 518.* 533
35. U.K. and Finland. Exchange of Notes regarding Reciprocal Abolition of Visas. *Cmnd. 523.* 533
36. International Telecommunication Convention. *Cmnd. 520.* 533
37. U.K. and U.S.A. Consular Convention. *Cmnd. 524.* 533
38. U.K. and Greece. Consular Convention. *Cmnd. 525.* 533
39. Convention for the Protection of War Victims. *Cmnd. 550.* 535
40. U.K. and Portugal. Agreement regarding Nyasaland–Mozambique Frontier. *Cmnd. 528.* 534
41. U.K. and U.S.A. Agreement for Co-operation on Uses of

Treaty Series (*continued*):
1958 (*continued*):
Atomic Energy for Mutual Defence Purposes. *Cmnd. 537.* 534
42. International Tin Agreement Amendment. *Cmnd. 556.* 535
43. Sugar. Protocol Amending International Sugar Agreement. *Cmnd. 557.* 536
44. France and U.K. Convention on Social Security. *Cmnd. 560.* 536
45. U.K. and Yugoslavia. Convention on Social Security. *Cmnd. 561.* 536
46. Rail Traffic. International Convention concerning Carriage of Goods by Rail. *Cmnd. 564.* 536
47. International Convention concerning Carriage of Passengers and Luggage by Rail. *Cmnd. 565.* 536
48. U.K. and Italy. Convention on Social Insurance. *Cmnd. 572.* 536
49. Road Traffic Convention. *Cmnd. 578.* 537
50. Council of Europe. 2nd Protocol to General Agreement on Privileges and Immunities. *Cmnd. 579.* 537
51. U.K. and U.S.A. Exchange of Notes concerning continued Operation of U.S. Educational Commission in U.K. *Cmnd. 580.* 537
52. War Graves Agreement. *Cmnd. 581.* 537
53. War Graves in Federal Republic of Germany Territory. *Cmnd. 582.* 537
54. Shipping Convention for Establishment of Intergovernmental Maritime Consultative Organisation. *Cmnd. 589.* 538
55. U.K. and Norway. Consular Convention. *Cmnd. 590.* 538
56. International Convention for Prevention of Pollution of Sea by Oil. *Cmnd. 595.* 538
57. U.K. and Austria. Exchange of Notes concerning Repayment of Credit granted by European Payments Union. *Cmnd. 596.* 538
58. U.K. and F.A.O. Exchange of Notes establishing International Desert Locust Information Service. *Cmnd. 600.* 539
59. Convention of Nationality of Married Women. *Cmnd. 601.* 539
60. U.K. and Turkey. Agreement concerning a Loan. *Cmnd. 615.* 539
61. Ratifications, etc. Supplementary List. *Cmnd. 642.* 789
62. Treaty Series Index. *Cmnd. 643.* 789

Treaty Series (*continued*):
1959:
1. Customs Convention on Temporary Importation of Private Road Vehicles. *Cmnd. 602.* 787
2. U.K. and Germany. Consular Convention. *Cmnd. 607.* 788
3. Technical Co-operation Agreement for Establishment of Commission in Africa South of the Sahara. *Cmnd. 612.* 788
4. U.K. and France. Consular Convention. *Cmnd. 617.* 788
5. Morocco. Exchange of Notes for the Mutual Abolition of Visas on Passports. *Cmnd. 623.* 788
6. U.K. and Japan. Agreement for Co-operation in Peaceful Uses of Atomic Energy. *Cmnd. 625.* 788
7. U.K. and Germany. External Debts Agreement. *Cmnd. 626.* 788
8. U.K. and Germany. Agreement regarding Settlement of Claim in Respect of Post-War Economic Assistance. *Cmnd. 627.* 788
9. U.K. and Mexico. Consular Convention. *Cmnd. 633.* 789
10. U.K., France, U.S.A. and Germany. Convention on Relations. *Cmnd. 653.* 790
11. U.K. and Germany. Convention on Rights and Obligations of Foreign Forces and Their Members. *Cmnd. 654.* 790
12. U.K., France, U.S.A. and Germany. Finance Convention. *Cmnd. 655.* 790
13. U.K., France, U.S.A. and Germany. Convention and Settlement arising out of the War and the Occupation. *Cmnd. 656.* 790
14. U.K., France, U.S.A. and Germany. Agreement on Tax Treatment of the Forces and Their Members. *Cmnd. 657.* 790
15. Protocol on the Termination of the Occupation Régime. *Cmnd. 658.* 791
16. Customs Convention on Temporary Importation for Private Use of Aircraft and Pleasure Boats. *Cmnd. 650.* 790
17. U.K. and France. Exchange of Notes concerning Mining Regulations to be applied to New Hebrides. *Cmnd. 667.* 791
18. U.K. and France. Exchange of Notes concerning Revision of Penal System in the New Hebrides. *Cmnd. 668.* 791

1956-60 | TRE

TRE— INDEX 1956–60

Treaty Series (*continued*):
1959 (*continued*):
19. U.K. and Netherlands. Exchange of Notes concerning Reciprocal Validation of Airworthiness Certificates. *Cmnd. 671*. 791
20. Air Navigation Services, Iceland. Agreement on Joint Financing. *Cmnd. 677*. 792
21. Air Navigation Services, Greenland and Faroe Islands. Agreement on Joint Financing. *Cmnd. 678*. 792
22. Protocol to International Convention for Northwest Atlantic Fisheries. *Cmnd. 687*. 792
23. U.K. and Cuba. Exchange of Notes on Commercial Relations. *Cmnd. 688*. 792
24. U.K. and Cyrenaica. Exchange of Notes on the Mutual Cancellation of all Outstanding Claims. *Cmnd. 691*, 793
25. U.K. and Ethiopia. Agreement for Air Services. *Cmnd. 692*. 793
26. U.K. and European Coal and Steel Community Agreement concerning Commercial Relations. *Cmnd. 693*. 793
27. Schedule to the International Whaling Convention Revised. *Cmnd. 694*. 793
28. U.K. and European Atomic Energy Community. Agreement for Co-operation in the Peaceful Uses of Atomic Energy. *Cmnd. 702*. 793
29. Customs Convention regarding Carnets for Commercial Samples. *Cmnd. 711*. 794
30. U.K. and U.S.A. Exchange of Notes concerning the Disposal of Surplus United States Mutual Defence Programme Equipment. *Cmnd. 714*. 794
31. U.K. and Italy. Exchange of Notes extending to the Island of Jersey the Anglo-Italian Social Insurance Convention. *Cmnd. 716*. 794
32. U.K. and Czechoslovakia. Exchange of Notes concerning the Agreement on Certain Inter-Governmental Debts. *Cmnd. 720*. 794, 1045
33. U.K. and U.S.A. Supplementary Protocol amending the Convention for Avoidance of Double Taxation, etc. *Cmnd. 721*. 794
34. U.K. and Yugoslavia. Exchange of Notes regarding a Credit for Purchase of Goods in the United Kingdom. *Cmnd. 722*. 795
35. U.K. and United Arab Republic. Agreement concerning Financial and Commercial Relations and British Property in Egypt. *Cmnd. 723*. 795
36. U.K. and Burma. Exchange of Notes concerning Export of Cotton Textiles and/or Yarn. *Cmnd. 724*. 795
37. Agreement between Hong Kong acting with consent of U.K. and Burma for Supply of Cotton Textiles and/or Yarns. *Cmnd. 738*. 796
38. Convention for Regulation of Meshes of Fishing Nets and Size Limits of Fish. *Cmnd. 731*. 795
39. Ratifications, Accessions, Withdrawals, etc. Supplementary List. *Cmnd. 727*. 795
40. Protocol modifying Agreement concerning Archives of Allied High Commission. *Cmnd. 741*. 796
41. U.K. and Germany Cultural Convention. *Cmnd. 742*. 796
42. U.K. and Turkey. Exchange of Notes modifying Agreement for Purchase of Certain Ships of British Reserve Fleet. *Cmnd. 751*. 797
43. U.K. and Bulgaria. Exchange of Notes concerning Settlement of Financial Matters. *Cmnd. 752*. 797
44. U.K. and Denmark. Exchange of Notes respecting Repayment of Debts on Liquidation of European Payments Union. *Cmnd. 754*. 797
45. U.K. and Austria. Exchange of Notes respecting Repayment of Debts on Liquidation of European Payments Union. *Cmnd. 735*. 797
46. U.K. and Belgium. Agreement respecting Repayment of Debt on Liquidation of European Payments Union. *Cmnd. 756*. 797
47. U.K. and France. Agreement respecting Repayment of Debt on Liquidation of European Payments Union. *Cmnd. 757*. 797
48. U.K. and Norway. Agreement respecting Repayment of Debt on Liquidation of European Payments Union. *Cmnd. 758*. 797

INDEX 1956–60 —TRE

Treaty Series (*continued*):
1959 (*continued*):
49. U.K. and Italy. Exchange of Notes respecting Repayment of Debt on Liquidation of European Payments Union. *Cmnd. 759*. 797
50. U.K. and Germany. Exchange of Notes respecting Repayment of Debt on Liquidation of European Payments Union. *Cmnd. 760*. 798
51. U.K. and Iceland. Agreement respecting Repayment of Debt on Liquidation of European Payments Union. *Cmnd. 763*. 798
52. U.K. and Netherlands. Exchange of Notes respecting Repayment of Debt on Liquidation of European Payments Union. *Cmnd. 764*. 798
53. U.K. and Switzerland. Exchange of Notes respecting Repayment of Debt on Liquidation of European Payments Union. *Cmnd. 768*. 798
54. U.K. and Greece. Agreement respecting Repayment of Debt on Liquidation of European Payments Union. *Cmnd. 769*. 798
55. U.K. and Denmark. Exchange of Notes concerning Regulation of Fishing Around Faroe Islands. *Cmnd. 776*. 799
56. U.K. and Austria. Claims for Re-Establishment of an Independent and Democratic Austria. *Cmnd. 784*. 799
57. U.S.A. and Korea. Utilities Claims Settlement Agreement. *Cmnd. 796*. 800
58. U.K. and U.S.S.R. Agreement concerning Air Services. *Cmnd. 798*. 800, 1045
59. U.K. and Turkey. Agreement on Commercial Debts owed by Residents in Turkey. *Cmnd. 805*. 800
60. U.K. and France. Exchange of Notes concerning Exemption from Turnover Tax on Royalties. *Cmnd. 808*. 801
61. U.K. and International Atomic Energy Agency. Exchange of Notes relating to supply of enriched Uranium. *Cmnd. 809*. 801
62. U.K. and U.S.A. Exchange of Notes extending Provisions of Double Taxation Convention to U.K. Overseas Territories. *Cmnd. 824*. 802
63. Ratifications, Accessions, etc. Supplementary List. *Cmnd. 828*. 802
64. Protocol terminating Obligations regarding German Assets in Spain. *Cmnd. 833*. 802
65. U.K. and U.S.A. Exchange of Notes concerning Establishment and Operation of Radar Station on Island of Grand Turk in Turks and Caicos Islands. *Cmnd. 836*. 802
66. U.K. and Jordan. Exchange of Notes concerning Loan during 1959–60. *Cmnd. 847*. 803
67. U.K. and Tonga. Treaty of Friendship. *Cmnd. 848*. 803
68. Protocol to International Convention for Regulation of Whaling. *Cmnd. 849*. 803
69. Convention on Privilege and Immunities of Specialised Agencies of the United Nations. *Cmnd. 855*. 804
70. U.K. and Venezuela. Exchange of Notes concerning Reciprocal Exemption from Measurement of Ships in Port. *Cmnd. 857*. 804
71. U.K. and Lebanon. Exchange of Notes amending Schedule of Routes annexed to Air Services Agreement. *Cmnd. 858*. 804
72. U.K. and U.S.A. Amendment to Agreement for Co-operation on Uses of Atomic Energy for Mutual Defence Purposes. *Cmnd. 859*. 804
73. U.K. and Poland. Exchange of Notes concerning Introduction of Air Services. *Cmnd. 862*. 804
74. Agreement on German Assets in Portugal and on Claims regarding Monetary Gold. *Cmnd. 863*. 804
75. U.K. and Sweden. Exchange of Notes extending Convention for Avoidance of Double Taxation to Rhodesia, Nyasaland, etc. *Cmnd. 891*. 806.
76. Ratifications, Accessions, Withdrawals, etc. *Cmnd. 866*. 806
77. U.K. and U.S.A. Exchange of Notes concerning Agreement for Additional Long Range Proving Ground Sites in Ascension Island. *Cmnd. 867*. 805
78. U.K. and U.N. International Children's Emergency Fund. Protocol to Agreement for rendering Assistance. *Cmnd. 888*. 806

TRE— INDEX 1956–60

Treaty Series (*continued*):
1959 (*continued*):
79. U.K. and Hungary. Exchange of Notes terminating Anglo-Hungarian Payments Agreement. *Cmnd. 896*. 806
80. Customs Convention on Containers. *Cmnd. 905*. 807
81. U.K. and Rhodesia and Nyasaland. Exchange of Notes with Denmark for Avoidance of Double Taxation, etc. *Cmnd. 903*. 807
82. U.K. and U.S.S.R. Agreement on Relations in Scientific, Technological. Educational and Cultural Fields. *Cmnd. 917*. 808
83. Ratifications, Accessions. Withdrawals, etc. *Cmnd. 932*. 1047
84. Index. *Cmnd. 940*. 1047, 1126
1960:
1. Customs Convention on Temporary Importation of Commercial Road Vehicles. *Cmnd. 919*. 1045
2. U.K. and Switzerland Exchange of Notes concerning Revised Route Schedules annexed to Air Services Agreement. *Cmnd. 927*. 1046
3. Convention for Establishment of European Organisation for Nuclear Research. *Cmnd. 928*. 1046
4. U.K. and Germany Agreement regarding German War Graves in U.K. *Cmnd. 930*. 1046
5. International Convention for Suppression of Counterfeiting Currency. *Cmnd. 932*. 1046
6. U.K. and Jordan. Exchange of Notes postponing Payment of Debt. *Cmnd. 943*. 1047
7. International Agreement on Olive Oil and Protocol of Amendment. *Cmnd. 954*. 1048
8. Nuclear Energy. Convention on Establishment of Security Control. *Cmnd. 971*. 1049
9. U.K. and France. Protocol to Convention on Social Security. *Cmnd. 966*. 1049
10. U.K. and Yugoslavia. Agreement concerning Air Services. *Cmnd. 972*. 1049
11. U.K. and Israel. Exchange of Notes amending Air Services Agreement. *Cmnd. 986*. 1050
12. U.K. and Mexico. Exchange of Notes concerning Reciprocal Abolition of Visas. *Cmnd. 985*. 1050
13. U.K. and Denmark. Convention on Social Security. *Cmnd. 990*. 1050
14. U.K. and Sweden. Exchange of Notes for Repayment of Debt on Liquidation of European Payments Union. *Cmnd. 991*. 1050
15. U.K. and United Nations Special Fund. Agreement concerning Assistance. *Cmnd. 995*. 1050
16. U.K. and Greece. Exchange of Notes on Final Settlement of Diverted Cargoes Claims. *Cmnd. 996*. 1050
17. International Rice Commission Constitution. *Cmnd. 997*. 1050
18. Customs Convention on International Transport of Goods by Road. *Cmnd. 1012*. 1052
19. U.K. and Argentina. Exchange of Notes extending Validity of Air Services Agreement. *Cmnd. 1006*. 1051
20. U.K. and Jordan. Exchange of Notes concerning Disposal of Special Fund. *Cmnd. 1007*. 1051
21. Ratifications, etc. Supplementary List. *Cmnd. 1008*. 1051
22. U.K. and U.S.A. Exchange of Notes concerning Sale of Fruit and Fruit Products. *Cmnd. 1010*. 1052
23. U.K. and Yugoslavia. Exchange of Notes regarding Import of British Books and Films. *Cmnd. 1023*. 1052
24. U.K. and U.S.A. Exchange of Notes on Setting up Ballistic Missile Early Warning Station in U.K. *Cmnd. 1034*. 1053
25. U.K. and U.S.A. Exchange of Notes relating to Establishment of Hurricane Research Stations on Jamaica and Grand Cayman Islands. *Cmnd. 1035*. 1053
26. U.K. and Czechoslovakia. Agreement for Air Services. *Cmnd. 1036*. 1053
27. U.K. and Turkey. Exchange of Notes constituting an Agreement for Abolition of Visas. *Cmnd. 1043*. 1054
28. International Wheat Agreement. *Cmnd. 1074*. 1056
29. Convention on Nomenclature for Classification of Goods in Customs Tariff. *Cmnd. 1070*. 1056
30. Convention Establishing European Free Trade Association. *Cmnd. 1026*. 1053

INDEX 1956 60 —TRE

Treaty Series (*continued*):
1960 (*continued*):
31. Agreement between U.K. and Denmark on Agriculture. *Cmnd. 1071*. 1056
32. U.K. and Poland. Exchange of Notes modifying Agreement for Settlement of Outstanding Financial Questions. *Cmnd. 1057*. 1055
33. U.K. and Yugoslavia. Exchange of Notes on Mutual Recognition of Aircrew Licences. *Cmnd. 1061*. 1055
34. U.K. and U.S.S.R. Five Year Trade Agreement. *Cmnd. 1076*. 1056
35. U.K. and U.S.S.R. Exchange of Notes amending Air Services Agreement. *Cmnd. 1077*. 1056
36. U.K. and Luxembourg. Exchange of Notes concerning Arrangement to Facilitate Travel. *Cmnd. 1079*. 1056
37. U.K. and Netherlands. Exchange of Notes concerning Arrangements to Facilitate Travel. *Cmnd. 1080*. 1056
38. U.K. and Bolivia. Exchange of Notes regarding Reciprocal Abolition of Visas. *Cmnd. 1081*. 1056
39. U.K. and Jordan. Exchange of Notes concerning Loan. *Cmnd. 1090*. 1056
40. U.K. and Belgium Exchange of Notes concerning Arrangements to Facilitate Travel. *Cmnd. 1091*. 1057
41. Convention relating to Status of Stateless Persons. *Cmnd. 1098*. 1057
42. Multilateral Agreement on Commercial Rights on Non-Scheduled Air Services in Europe. *Cmnd. 1099*. 1058
43. U.K. and Switzerland. Supplementary Convention on Social Insurance. *Cmnd. 1108*. 1058
44. U.K. and Somaliland. Agreement and Exchange of Letters in Connexion with Independence. *Cmnd. 1101*. 1058
45. U.K. and U.S.A. Exchange of Notes extending Area of Civil Air Terminal in Bermuda. *Cmnd. 1109*. 1058
46. U.K. and Denmark. Exchange of Notes regarding Co-operation in Promotion and Development of Peaceful Uses of Atomic Energy. *Cmnd. 1127*. 1059
47. International Convention on Maritime Law. *Cmnd. 1128*. 1059
48. Ratifications, Accessions, etc. *Cmnd. 1114*. 1059
49. U.K. and Spain. Exchange of Notes regarding Reciprocal Abolition of Visas. *Cmnd. 1130*. 1060
50. U.K. and Iraq. Cultural Agreement. *Cmnd. [illegible]*. 1060
51. U.K. and Italy. Cultural Convention. *Cmnd. 1135*. 1060
52. Council of Europe. Agreement on Temporary Importation of Medical, Surgical and Laboratory Equipment. *Cmnd. 1136*. 1060
53. U.K. and Philippines. Exchange of Notes amending Air Services Agreement Schedule of Routes. *Cmnd. 1142*. 1061
54. U.K. and Iran. Exchange of Notes concerning Avoidance of Double Taxation on Income Derived from Air Transport Services. *Cmnd. 1143*. 1061
55. International Sugar Agreement. *Cmnd. 1146*. 1061
56. U.K. and Germany. Exchange of Notes concerning Arrangements to Facilitate Travel. *Cmnd. 1157*. 1062
57. U.K. and Jordan. Exchange of Notes modifying the Annex terminating Treaty of Alliance. *Cmnd. 1158*. 1062
58. European Interim Agreement on Social Security Schemes. Amendment. *Cmnd. 1161*. 1062
59. European Interim Agreement on Social Security Schemes Amendment. *Cmnd. 1162*. 1062
60. U.K. and Kuwait. Agreement for Air Services. *Cmnd. 1168*. 1063
61. Social and Medical Assistance. European Convention Amendment. *Cmnd. 1169*. 1063
62. U.K. and Germany. Exchange of Notes amending Agreement regarding German War Graves in U.K. *Cmnd. 1170*. 1063
63. U.K. and United Nations, etc., Agreement for Technical and Other Territories. *Cmnd. 1178*. 1064
64. U.K. and U.S.A. Agreement concerning Long Range Aid to Navigation Station in Bahama Islands. *Cmnd. 1179*. 1064
65. U.K. and Thailand. Exchange of Notes amending Air Services Agreement Schedule of Routes. *Cmnd. 1180*. 1064

TRE-UNI | 1956-60

Treaty Series (*continued*):
1960 (*continued*):
66. Overfishing. Amendments to Convention. *Cmnd. 1181.* 1064
67. Social Security Schemes. European Interim Agreement Amendments. *Cmnd. 1182.* 1064
68. Social Security Schemes. European Interim Agreement Amendment. *Cmnd. 1183.* 1064
69. Social and Medical Assistance European Convention Amendment. *Cmnd. 1184.* 1064
70. U.K. and Germany. Agreement for Extradition of Fugitive Criminals. *Cmnd. 1200.* 1065
71. U.K. and Nicaragua. Exchange of Notes for Regulation of Turtle Fishing by Cayman Islanders in Nicaraguan Territorial Waters. *Cmnd. 1201.* 1065
72. U.K. and Israel. Exchange of Notes concerning Import of British Books of Educational Nature. *Cmnd. 1185.* 1064
73. U.K. and Germany. Exchange of Notes regarding Extension of Legal Proceedings in Civil and Commercial Matters. *Cmnd. 1202.* 1065
74. Ratifications, Accessions, etc. *Cmnd. 1186.* 1064
75. U.K. and Chile. Exchange of Notes concerning Loan. *Cmnd. 1195.* 1065
76. Accession of Germany and Italy to the Conventions on Frontier Workers and Student Employees. *Cmnd. 1209.* 1066
81. U.K. and Japan. Arrangement regarding Settlement of Claims. *Cmnd. 1229.* 1067

Trees:
Bush and Stump Clearance, 823
Circular, 129
In Kensington Gardens. Report, 1227
In Town and City, 613
Planting Practices:
In Temperate Asia, 242A, 967
In Tropical Africa, 437
In Tropical Asia, 437
Species, Choice of, 1237

Tregonning, K. G., North Borneo, 1103
Tremewan, W. G., On the Synonymy of Some Zygaena Species, 1096
Tresidder, J. O., Review of Existing Methods of Road Construction Over Peat, 652
"Tresillian" Wreck Report, 192
Trend of the Selling Price of Electricity, 719
Trendall, A. F., Geology of South Georgia, 833
Trends in Economic Sectors, 224A, 450, 719, 978, 1250
Trends in International Trade Report, 710
Trends in Utilisation of Wood and Its Products in Housing, 463
Treponematoses, Biology of, 471
Tretower Court, Breconshire Guide, 957
Trial Case Lenses Report, 123
Triangular Lodge, Rushton, Northamptonshire, Guide, 208

Tribunals:
Inquiring into Allegation of Assault on John Waters Report. *Cmnd. 718.* 794
Report of the Council, 1159

Tribunals and Inquiries Act, 542
Tribunals and Inquiries Bill, 479, 482, 485, 505, 513, 519, 609
Trichiuroid Fishes, Studies on the, 81
Trichomonas Foetus Infection of Cattle, 435
Trichoptera. New and Little Known Species of African, 562
Trifonov, L. K., Harvesting and Conservation of Maize Stalks for Forage, 225A
Trigonometrical Tables, Seven Figure, for Every Second of Time, 814
Trilingual Dictionary of Fisheries Technological Terms, 1238

Trinidad:
And Tobago:
Annual Report, 832
Arms, 832
Colonial Report, 87, 569
Constitutional Discussions Report. *Cmnd. 1123.* 1059, 1104
General and Economic Geology of, 1104
Oil Company. Proposed Purchase. *Cmd. 9790.* 44, 198

Triple Frequency Echo Sounder, 73
Tripods and Racks for Haymaking, 558
Triumph of Caesar. Series of Nine Paintings, 1227
Tropical and Subtropical Grain Legumes, Tabulated Information, 968
Tropical Building Studies, 1183
Tropical Fish Culture Research Institute. Agreement between U.K. and Malaya of Establishment at Batu Barendam. *Cmnd. 1067.* 1055, 1106
Tropical Products Institute, Report, 1183
Tropical Science, 431, 834, 1183
Tropical Silviculture, 1237
Tropical Timber, Statistics on, 719, 978, 1249
Tropical Vegetation, Study of, 736

Trout:
In Loch Tummel, Effect of Flooding on the Growth Rate of, 387
Migrations and Homing Behaviour of Brown, 655

Trout (*continued*):
Observations on the Spawning Runs of Brown Trout in the South Queich, Loch Leven, 171
Scotland, 1188

Trout, G. C., Bear Island Cod. Migrations and Movements, 559
Trucial State Notices, 110–11, 323, 594, 1126
Trunk Roads. Select Committee on Estimates Report, 770, 864, 1143

Truro Cathedral Measure:
812, 829
Report, 747, 829

Trustee Investments Bill, 1011, 1012, 1045
Trustee, Power of Investment. *Cmnd. 915.* 808, 937

Trustee Savings Banks:
Increase of Pensions Order. Select Committee on Statutory Instruments Report, 780
Report, 198, 411, 681, 938, 1207

Trustee Savings Banks Act:
542
Account, 198, 411, 681, 938, 1207

Trustee Savings Banks Bill, 220, 245, 246, 249, 250, 339

Trusteeship Council:
General Assembly Records, 229A, 1254
Index to Proceedings, 235A, 463, 733, 991, 1261
Records, 235A–6A, 463–4, 733, 983, 991, 1261
Report, 726, 984, 1255
Rules of Procedure, 236A, 733
Summary Records of Meetings, 455
Trust Territory Agreement, 464

Trusts (Scotland) Bill, 1039, 1040, 1044, 1142
Trypetidae, 296
Tsetse-Fly, 344

Tuberculosis:
Control Programme for General Hospitals Guide, 422
Control Report, 245A
Expert Committee Report, 1269
Of Cattle, 290
Statistics for England and Wales, 327

Tucker, D. W., Preliminary Studies on the Trichiuroid Fishes, 81
Tucker, Rt. Hon. Lord (Chairman: Departmental Committee on Proceedings before Examining Justices) Report. *Cmnd. 479.* 530
Tulloch, D. S., Hydrography of North-Western Approaches to British Isles, 914
Tulloch, W., Geology of Midlothian Coalfield, 599
Tungate, D. S., Echo-Sounder Survey in the Autumn of 1956, 559
Tunisia International Customs Journal, 444
Tunnell, G. A., World Distribution of Atmospheric Water Vapour Pressure, 888

Turkey:
Agreement on Commercial Debts owed by Residents. *Cmnd. 767.* 798, 853; *Cmnd. 805.* 800, 853; 974, 979
Agreement with U.K. concerning a Loan. *Cmnd. 615.* 539, 594
Convention on Social Insurance with U.K. *Cmnd. 864.* 804, 853
Cultural Agreement with U.K. *Cmd. 9767.* 43, 111; *Cmnd. 401.* 525, 594
Economic Conditions, 221A, 446, 715, 975
Exchange of Notes with U.K.:
Concerning Financial Arrangements. *Cmnd. 1256.* 1069, 1126
Concerning the Purchase of Ships of the British Reserve Fleet. *Cmnd. 260.* 266, 323
Constituting an Agreement for the Abolition of Visas. *Cmnd. 1043.* 1054, 1126
Modifying the Agreement for the Purchase of Certain Ships of the British Reserve Fleet. *Cmnd. 751.* 797, 853
Relating to Commercial Matters. *Cmnd. 136.* 258, 323
Foreign Trade Statistical Bulletin, 222A, 448, 717, 718, 977, 978
Protocol with U.K. modifying the Agreement regarding certain Financial matters. *Cmnd. 117.* 257, 323
Work of the Conference on Financial Assistance to Turkey and on Turkish Debts. Memorandum, 979

Turkeys:
821
Disease of, 290
Raising, 201
Rearing, 71

Turks and Caicos Islands:
Colonial Report, 301, 1102
International Customs Journal, 974

Turner, R., Use of Liquid Manures on Farms, 554
Turner, T. B., Biology of Treponematoses, 471
Turnip Gall Weevil, 555
Turnover Tax on Royalties. Exchange of Notes between U.K. and France concerning Exemption. *Cmnd. 808.* 801, 848
Turoka, Kenya, Structural Analysis of the Basement System, 834
Turtle Fishing in Nicaraguan Territorial Waters. Exchange of Notes extending Treaty for Regulating. *Cmnd. 1201.* 1065, 1123
Tweedie, P. G., Civil Aircraft Accident Report, 186–7

Twemlow, J. A., Papal Letters, 162
Twin Disease in Ewes, 290
Twin-Shaft Paddle Mixer with Various Settings of the Paddle Tips, Tests on the Efficiency, 168
Two Leaf-Cast Diseases of Douglas Fir, 112
Tyne Improvement Act, 274, 544
Tyne Tunnel Act, 59, 1073
Type Cultures, National Collection of, 633
Typewriting Proficiency Tests. Keys and Papers, 677, 934, 1202
Typography. *See* Printed Books

U

Uddington, Near Glasgow, Railway Accident Report, 673

Uganda:
A Crisis of Nationhood, 1103
Acholi of, 1103
Colonial Report, 88, 301, 570, 833, 1102
Colonial Office Picture Set, 614
International Customs Journal, 445, 1244

U.K.A.E.A. Documents, Guide to, 1218
Ultimus Haeres (Scotland) Account and List of Estates, 173, 389, 657, 916, 1188
Umbrella and Walking Stick. Census of Production Report, 395
Unasylva, 243A, 438, 709, 968, 1238
Underground Drainage. Questions and Answers, 1179
Underground Fire. Auchengeich, Report. *Cmnd. 1022.* 1052, 1173
Underground Plants for Industry, 203
Underground Storage of Grain, 88

Underground Works (London) Act:
56
Select Committee Special Report, 128

Underground Works (London) Bill, 5, 20, 34
Unemployment Insurance. Convention between U.K. and Germany. *Cmnd. 77.* 253; *Cmnd. 1054.* 1054, 1121

UNESCO:
Activities of, Report, 237
And Its Programme, 469, 996
Basic Facts and Figures, 994
Chronicle, 240A, 469, 738, 997, 1266
Courier, 240A, 469, 738, 997, 1266
General Conference Records, 238A, 467, 736, 995
Institute for Education Publications, 469
Member States Reports, 239A, 737, 1265
Publications, 237A–40A, 465–9, 735–8, 993, 1263
Report on Activities, 237A, 996, 1265

Ungley, C. C., Hazards to Men in Ships Lost at Sea, 151

UNICEF:
Around the World with, 225A
Compendium, 236A
Financial Report and Accounts, 229A, 453, 456, 726, 984, 1253, 1255
Protocol to the Agreement with U.K. for the Rendering of Assistance. *Cmnd. 888.* 806, 853
Report, 227, 228, 723, 981

Uniform and Personal Equipment Record Card, 335
Uniform Traffic Control Devices for Streets and Highways, Manual on, 203
Union Catalogues, Their Problems and Organisation, 237A

United Arab Republic:
Agreement with U.K. on Financial and Commercial Relations. *Cmnd. 723.* 795, 847
Province of Egypt. International Customs Journal, 973

United Charities of Nathaniel Waterhouse, and Other Charities (Halifax) Scheme Confirmation Act, 1073
United Charities of Nathaniel Waterhouse, and Other Charities (Halifax) Scheme Confirmation Bill, 1007, 1042

United Kingdom:
And Soviet Union, Statement on the Discussions. *Cmd. 9753.* 42
Balance of Payments. *Cmd. 9731, 9871.* 41, 51, 198; *Cmnd. 122, 273.* 257, 267, 411; *Cmnd. 399, 540.* 525, 534, 681; *Cmnd. 700, 861.* 793, 804, 939; *Cmnd. 977, 1188.* 1049, 1064, 1207
Economic Conditions, 221A, 446, 715, 1246
Foreign Trade Statistical Bulletins, 222A, 447, 448, 717, 718, 977, 978
Financial Institutions, 345
Role in Commonwealth Development. *Cmnd. 237.* 264, 305

United Kingdom Atomic Energy Authority. *See* Atomic Energy Authority

United Kingdom Dependencies:
Basic Agreement with United Nations Educational Scientific and Cultural Organisation regarding Aid. *Cmd. 9873.* 51, 111
Economic Development in, 1150
Health in, 1150
In Brief, 345, 873, 1150
Political Advance in, 1150
Social Welfare in, 1150

United Nations:
76 Countries, 422
Administrative Tribunal, Statute and Rules, 236A, 992
Agreement with U.K. concerning Assistance from Special Fund. *Cmnd. 995.* 1050, 1127

United Nations (*continued*):
Annual Report, 229A
Basic Facts, 225A, 451, 734, 1251
Charter, 234A, 720
Children's Fund:
Financial Report and Accounts, 229A, 453, 456, 726, 984, 1253, 1255
Report, 227A, 228A, 723, 981
Conference on the Law of the Sea, 992
Convention concerning the Exchange of Official Publications and Government Documents between States. *Cmnd. 1241.* 1069, 1127
Convention concerning the International Exchange of Publications. *Cmnd. 1242.* 1069, 1127
Convention on Privileges and Immunities of the Specialized Agencies. *Cmnd. 855.* 804, 853
Declaration of the Rights of the Child. *Cmnd. 1073.* 1056, 1127
Delegations, 451
Disarmament Commission Report. *Cmd. 9770.* 105; *Cmnd. 333.* 1045, 1125
Documents:
Index, 992, 1261
Series Symbols, 225A
Emergency Force Budget, 983, 1254
Facts about United Nations and Material Available, 734
Five Year Perspective, 1254
Food and Agriculture Organisation:
Conference Report, 241A
Publications, 240A–3A
Forces. Japan. Agreement regarding the Status. *Cmnd. 67.* 253, 323
General Assembly:
Administrative and Budgetary Questions. Report, 455
Budget Estimates and Information Annex, 456, 983, 984
Index to Proceedings, 454, 725, 982, 1254
Records, 229A–30A, 454–6, 725, 982, 1254
Report. *Cmnd. 189.* 261
Report on the Work of the Organisation, 726, 983
Resolutions, 983, 1254
Rules of Procedure, 229A, 726
Work of the Organisation, 455
How to Find Out About, 230A
In the Mainstream of History, 422
Joint Staff Pension Board Report, 230A, 456, 983, 984, 1254, 1255
Legislative Series, 985
Narcotic Drugs, 1262
Organs. Repertory of Practice, 464, 730, 734

United Nations (*continued*):
Publications, 224–36, 450–65, 720–34, 979, 1250
Postage Stamps, 464
Refugee Fund Accounts, 229A, 456, 726, 984
Relief and Works Agency for Palestine Refugees in Near East. Report and Accounts, 983, 984
Report on Proceedings of the General Assembly. *Cmd. 9716.* 40, 111; *Cmnd. 189.* 261, 323; *Cmnd. 417.* 527, 594; *Cmnd. 735.* 796, 853; *Cmnd. 992.* 1050, 1127
Review, 236A, 464–5, 734, 993, 1262
Signing of Charter, 10th Anniversary, 234A
Special Fund, 1253
Specialized Agencies:
Convention on the Privileges and Immunities. *Cmnd. 1177.* 1064, 1127
Documents:
and Publications, 452
Index, 992, 1261
Teaching About, 995
Statistical Yearbook, 233
Trust Funds and Special Accounts, etc. 984, 1255
U.K. Agreement for Provision of Technical Assistance for Trust and Other Territories. *Cmnd. 1178.* 1064, 1126
Visiting Mission to Trust Territories Reports, 463, 464, 991, 992, 1261
What You Should Know About It, 992
Wheat Conference Proceedings, 465
Work for Human Rights, 727, 734
Work of the Organisation Report, 983, 1255
World Health Organisation Publications, 243A–5A
Yearbook, 236, 734, 993, 1263
See also World Health Organisation

United States:
Agreement relating to Provision and Maintenance of Submarine Telecommunication Cable System, 1028, 1169
Agreement to Amend Financial Agreement with U.K. *Cmnd. 120.* 257, 411
Agreement with U.K.:
And Canada as to Disposition of Rights in Atomic Energy Inventions. *Cmnd. 20.* 53, 111
Concerning the Establishment in the Bahama Islands of a Long Range Aid to Navigation Station. *Cmnd. 1179.* 1064, 1127
Concerning the Extension of the Bahamas Long Range Proving Ground by the Establishment of

1956-60 | UNI-WAG

UNI— INDEX 1956–60

United States (*continued*):
Additional Sites. *Cmd. 9810, 9811.* 46, 111
For Co-operation on the Uses of Atomic Energy for Mutual Defence Purposes. *Cmnd. 470, 537.* 530, 534, 595
For the Establishment of Oceanographic Research Stations in the Bahama Islands. *Cmnd. 343.* 521, 595
For the Establishment in Barbados of an Oceanographic Research Station. *Cmnd. 68.* 253, 324
For the Establishment of an Oceanographic Research Station in the Turks and Caicos Islands. *Cmnd. 94.* 255, 324
Amendment to Agreement with U.K. for Co-operation:
On the Civil Uses of Atomic Energy. *Cmd. 9789, 9847.* 44, 49, 111
On the Uses of Atomic Energy for Mutual Defence Purposes. *Cmnd. 733, 859.* 795, 804, 853
Civil Defense, 422
Consular Convention with U.K. *Cmnd. 524.* 533, 595
Economic Conditions, 975
Exchange of Notes with U.K.:
About the Weather Station on Betio Island. *Cmnd. 391.* 525, 595
Amending the Schedule of Routes annexed to the Air Services Agreement. *Cmnd. 82, 85.* 254, 324
Concerning Civil Aviation Facilities and Long Range Proving Grounds for Guided Missiles in the West Indies. *Cmnd. 142.* 258, 324
Concerning Defence Requirements in the Caribbean and Adjacent Areas and in the South Atlantic. *Cmd. 9812.* 46, 111
Concerning Disposal of Surplus United States Mutual Defence Programme Equipment. *Cmnd. 714.* 794, 853
Concerning the Agreement for the Addition to the Bahamas Long Range Proving Ground of Sites in Ascension Island. *Cmnd. 867.* 805, 853
Concerning the Continued Operation of the U.S. Educational Commission in the U.K. *Cmnd. 580.* 537, 595
Concerning the Establishment and Operation of a Radar Station on the Island of Grand Turk in the Turks and Caicos Islands. *Cmnd. 836.* 802, 853
Concerning the Extension of the Bahamas Long Range Proving Ground to include the Island of Great Exuma. *Cmnd. 266.* 267, 324
Concerning the Sale of Fruit and Fruit Products. *Cmnd. 402.* 525, 595; *Cmnd. 1010.* 1052, 1127
Concerning the Sale of Tobacco and the Construction of Housing and/or Community Facilities. *Cmnd. 272.* 267, 324; *Cmnd. 403.* 525, 595
Concerning Settlement for Lend-Lease, Reciprocal Aid, Surplus War Property and Claims. *Cmnd. 201.* 262, 324
Concerning the Supply of Intermediate Range Ballistic Missiles. *Cmnd. 406.* 526, 595
Extending the Agreement regarding Technical Assistance for British Guiana. *Cmnd. 1238.* 1068, 1128
Extending Area of the Civil Air Terminal in Bermuda. *Cmnd. 1109.* 1058, 1127
Extending the Provisions of the Double Taxation Convention to certain U.K. Overseas Territories. *Cmnd. 824.* 802, 853
For the Construction and Operation of a Weather Station on Betio Island. *Cmd. 9693.* 39, 111
On Disposal of Surplus United States Mutual Defence Assistance Programme Equipment. *Cmnd. 198.* 262, 324
On the Setting up of a Ballistic Missile Early Warning Station. *Cmnd. 1034.* 1053, 1127
Rectifying the Agreement for Co-operation on the Civil Uses of Atomic Energy. *Cmd. 9677.* 38, 111
Referring to the Sale of Tobacco and the Construction of Housing and/or Community Facilities. *Cmd. 9703.* 45, 111; *Cmnd. 143.* 258, 324
Relating to Hurricane Research Stations. *Cmnd. 1035.* 1053, 1127
Financial Agreement with U.K. *Cmnd. 178.* 261, 324
Foreign Trade Statistical Bulletin, 222A, 447, 448, 717, 718, 977, 978, 1244
Government Printing Office Publications, 199–203, 419–22, 691, 951, 1222
Government Purchasing Directory, 203
International Customs Journal, 444, 973, 1244

INDEX 1956–60 —USS

United States (*continued*):
Investments in the Latin American Economy, 692
M.D.A.P. Equipment Disposal Deposit Account. *Cmnd. 1084, 1233.* 1057, 1068, 1114, 1127
Overseas Economic Survey, 182
Report of the Marshall Aid Commemoration Commission. *Cmnd. 1042.* 1054, 1127
Supplementary Protocol with U.K.:
Amending Convention for Avoidance of Double Taxation, etc. *Cmnd. 721.* 794, 854
For the Avoidance of Double Taxation and the Prevention of Fiscal Evasion. *Cmnd. 191.* 262, 324
Units and Standards of Measurement employed at the National Physical Laboratory, 155
Unity and Diversity of Cultures, 240A, 469
Universal Copyright Convention. *Cmnd. 289.* 268
Universal Postal Union. *Cmnd. 576, 586.* 787, 898; *Cmnd. 1218, 1219.* 1066, 1128
Universities:
And Adult Education Report, 314
College of the West Indies Teaching Hospital. Report, 303
Development. Interim Report. *Cmnd. 79.* 254, 411; *Cmnd. 534.* 534, 681
European, Council of Europe Consultative Assembly, 433
Grants Committee:
Methods for Contracting and Recording and Controlling Expenditure Review. *Cmnd. 1235.* 1068, 1207
Report, 1207
Returns. *Cmd. 9800.* 45, 198; *Cmnd. 211.* 263, 412; *Cmnd. 477.* 530, 681; *Cmnd. 832.* 802, 939; *Cmnd. 1166.* 1063, 1207
Sub-Committee Report on Methods used for Contracting and Recording and Controlling Expenditure. *Cmnd. 9.* 53, 198
Institutions. Formal Programmes of International Co-operation, 1264
Local Contributions to Scottish. Report. *Cmnd. 640.* 789, 912
Professors and Lecturers Willing to Teach Abroad, List of, 738
Qualifications. European Convention on Academic Recognition of. *Cmnd. 1037.* 1053, 1128; 1232
Scientific Research in British, 384
Study:
434
European Convention. *Cmnd. 93, 301.* 255, 269, 324
Teaching of Social Sciences, 469, 996
University of Bristol Act, 1073
University of Exeter Act, 274
University of Leicester Act, 544
University of St. Andrew's (Scholarships and Bursaries) Scheme. Memorandum, 1185
Unkra in Action, 236A
Unprocessed and Processed Radioisotope Preparations and Special Radiation Sources, 969
Upper Air Temperature over the World, 633
Upper Cretaceous Decapoda and Serpulidae from James Ross Island, Graham Land, 1103
Upper Jurassic and Cretaceous Ammonite Faunas of Alexander Land and Graham Land, 571
Upper Jurassic Pliosaurs, Review of, 1096
Upper Permian Flora of England, 563
Upper Wind Code Manual, 203
Upper Winds Over the World, 1160
Ur Excavations, 80
Uranium:
And Thorium, Geology of, 231A
Exchange of Notes between U.K. and International Atomic Energy Agency relating to supply of Enriched Uranium. *Cmnd. 809.* 801, 845
Urban Sociology. Research in Great Britain and Scandinavian Countries, 237
Urbanization in Asia and Far East. Proceedings of Seminar, 738
Urmston and Trafford Park Railway Accident Report, 930
Urquhart, Sir Robert (Chairman: Crofters Commission) Report, 287
Use of Power Saws in Forest Operations Report, 993
Use of Vernacular Languages in Education, 737
Usinger, R. L., Classification of Aradidae, 828
Usk River, Hydrographical Survey, 291
U.S.S.R.:
200
Agreement with U.K.:
Concerning Air Services. *Cmnd. 798.* 800, 852; *Cmnd. 798.* 1045, 1127
On Relations in the Scientific, Technological, Educational and Cultural Fields. *Cmnd. 917.* 808, 853
Anglo-Soviet Communiqué on Discussions with the Prime Minister and Foreign Secretary. *Cmnd. 689.* 792, 845
Correspondence on Summit Talks. *Cmnd. 423, 469.* 527, 530, 593
Exchange of Notes with U.K. amending the Air Services Agreement. *Cmnd. 1077.* 1056, 1127

USS— INDEX 1956–60

U.S.S.R. (*continued*):
Fisheries Agreement with U.K. *Cmd. 9778.* 43, 111
Fisheries Agreement with U.K. *Cmnd. 148.* 259, 322
Five Year Trade Agreement with U.K. *Cmnd. 1076.* 1056, 1127
Further Correspondence. *Cmnd. 516, 594.* 533, 538, 593
Health Services Report, 1269
Statement on Discussions with United Kingdom. *Cmd. 9753.* 42
Teaching of Social Science, 995
Technical and Vocational Education, 995
Trade Agreement with U.K. *Cmnd. 771.* 799, 922
Utilisation of Hazel Coppice, 325
Utilisation of Saline Water, 465
Utilisation of Space in Dwellings Report, 1262
Utilities Claims Settlement Agreement between U.S.A. and Korea. *Cmnd. 796.* 800, 850
Utinomi, Huzio, Revision of the Genera Nidalia and Bellonella with an emendation of Nomenclature and Taxonomic Definitions for the Family Nidaliidae, 564
"U" Values, Memorandum on Calculation of, 1173

V

Vacancies in Sees Measure, 748, 812, 829, 830
Vacations Abroad, 240, 469, 738, 997, 1266
Vaccination Against Smallpox:
Additional International Sanitary Regulations. *Cmnd. 312.* 270
Memorandum on, 122
Vaccinations. *See* Poliomyelitis—Quarantine Measures
Validation of Elections (Northern Ireland) Act, 56
Validation of Elections (Northern Ireland) Bill, 2, 33
Vallings, H. G., Mobile Tower Cranes for Two and Three Storey Buildings, 1181
Valuation and Rating (Scotland) Act:
56
Report, 656, 915
Valuation and Rating (Scotland) Bill, 5, 19, 30, 34, 128
Valuation Offices Inland Revenue Services available to Local Authorities, 601, 656
Van Buren, M., Small Public Library Building, 996
Vapourer Moth, 1083
Variations of Trusts Act:
542
See Law Reform Committee's Report
Variation of Trusts Bill, 246, 250, 480, 484 491, 519, 609
Variation of Wind with Time and Distance, 152
Variety Reduction, Case Studies on, 719
Varty, I. W., Adelges Insects of Silver Firs, 112
Vascular Plants of S. Tomé, Catalogue Supplement, 82
Veale, Sir D. (Chairman: Committee to consider Training in Radiological Health and Safety) Report, 1207
Vegetable Oils and Oilseeds, Production, Trade, etc., 91, 304, 573, 835, 1105
Vegetables:
Dehydrated for Caterers, 558
Diseases of, 72
Growing in Town and City, 951
Vehicles:
Customs Convention on Temporary Importation of Private Road Vehicles. *Cmnd. 602.* 787, 846
Headlamps Testing, 652
Return. *See* Road Motor Vehicles
Temporary Importation of Commercial Road, 226A
Testing. Tester's Manual, 1200
Venereal Disease:
Agreement for facilities to be given to Merchant Seamen for Treatment, 741
Existing Legislation, 245A
Infections and Treponematoses. Expert Committee Report, 1269
Treatment Centres at Ports. World Directory, 1000, 1270
Venetian School. Sixteenth Century, 890
Venezuela:
Exchange of Notes with U.K. concerning Reciprocal Exemption from the Measurement of Ships in Port. *Cmnd. 857.* 804, 854
International Customs Journal, 973
Ventilation:
And Insulation, 559
Of Rippings, 327
Vergara, Dr. A., Protein Malnutrition in Brazil, 242A
Vernacular Languages in Education, 737
Verstandig, S., Fishermen's Organisations and the Regulation of Fish Prices in Sweden, 436
Vessels employed in Inland Navigation. Convention regarding Measurement and Registration, 734
Veterinary Public Health. Advisory Group Report, 245A
Veterinary Science. Career, 617
V.H.F. Transmitters and Receivers. Performance Specifications, 1170
Vial, V. E., Land in British Honduras, 1103
Vibrated Concrete in Buildings, 427

INDEX 1956 60 —WAG

Vibrio Fetus Infection of Cattle, 241A
Vick, Sir G. R., Report of Inquiry into Allegations of Ill-Treatment of Prisoners at H.M. Prison, Liverpool. *Cmnd. 503.* 532, 603
Vickers, M. D., Conversion of Ionospheric Virtual Height-Frequency Curves to Electron Density-Height Profiles, 910
Victoria and Albert Museum:
Guide, 422
Publications, 203, 422, 692, 951, 1222
Postcards, 952
Victoria Line. Report, 927
Victory Bonds, 150, 357, 631, 918, 1190
Viet, J.:
New Towns, 1266
Selected Documentation for the Study on Race Relations, 738
Vietnam:
And the Geneva Agreements. Documents concerning the Discussions with Government of the Union of Soviet Socialist Republics. *Cmd. 9763.* 43, 111
Exchange of Notes with U.K. for the Protection of Trade Marks. *Cmd. 9694.* 39, 111
International Commission for Supervision and Control Report. *Cmd. 9706.* 39, 112; *Cmnd. 31.* 251, 324; *Cmnd. 335, 509.* 521, 532, 595; *Cmnd. 726.* 795, 854; *Cmnd. 1040.* 1054, 1128
Toward the Economic Development of the Republic, 990
Village Bus, 191
Villiers, A., Ruwenzori Expedition, 828
Vinegar and other Condiments. Census of Production Report, 395
Vining, Rutledge, Economics in the U.S.A. 237A
Virgin Islands. Orders-in-Council, 1173, 1174
Visas:
Abolition:
Exchange of Notes between U.K. and Belgium extending Agreement. *Cmnd. 9711.* 40, 104
For Refugees. European Agreement, 962
Exchange of Notes between U.K. and:
Bolivia regarding Reciprocal Abolition. *Cmnd. 1081.* 1056, 1118
Finland regarding Reciprocal Abolition. *Cmnd. 523.* 533, 589
Japan for Grant of Continuous Visas. *Cmnd. 412.* 526, 591
Mexico concerning Reciprocal Abolition. *Cmnd. 985.* 1050, 1123
Morocco for Abolition of Visas on Passports. *Cmnd. 623.* 788, 851
Visas (*continued*):
Exchange of Notes between U.K. and (*continued*):
Spain regarding Reciprocal Abolition of Visas. *Cmnd. 1130.* 1060, 1125
Turkey constituting an Agreement for Abolition of Visas. *Cmnd. 1043.* 1054, 1126
Text of Notes reimposing the Visa Requirement for Nationals travelling to Cyprus. *Cmnd. 73.* 253, 324
Visual Aids in Fundamental Education and Community Development Report, 996
Visual Problems of Colour. Proceedings of Symposium, 636
Vital Statistics Methods Handbook, 234A
Vocabularium Bibliothecarii, 735
Vocational Division Bulletin, 203
Volcanic Rocks of Cape Adare, South Victoria Land, 827
Voles and Field Mice, 596
Vollmar, A., Blackpool Building Society Report, 597
Voronitsin, K. I.:
Ground Winch Skidding in Clear and Selective Felling, 984
Timber:
Skidding by tractor in the U.S.S.R., 990
Transport on Snow and Ice Roads, 1260
Volta River Project. Reports and Appendices, 183
Voting Areas Return. *See* Temperance (Scotland) Act

W

Wade, N. V., Basic Stitches of Embroidery, 1222
Wage Accounting by Electronic Computer. Report, 155
Wages Arrestment Limitation (Amendment) (Scotland) Act, 1071
Wages Arrestment Limitation (Amendment) (Scotland) Bill, 783, 787, 1004, 1014, 1142
Wages Bill, 517, 520
Wages Councils Act:
810
Commission of Inquiry Report, 149
Consolidation Bills Report, 746, 752, 867
Wages Councils (Amendment) Bill:
486, 520
See Terms and Conditions of Employment Bill
Wages Councils Bill, 786
Wagner, B., Design for Livability, 202
Wagner, E. G.:
Excreta Disposal for Rural Areas and Small Communities, 740

WAG-WHI | 1956-60

Wagner, E. G. (*continued*):
- Water Supply for Rural Areas and Small Communities, 998

Wailes, R.:
- Berney Arms Mill Guide, 426
- Saxtead Green Mill Guide, 1226

Wakefield, Boundary Commission for England Report, 1137
Wakefield Corporation Act, 274
Waldo, D., Political Science in the U.S.A. Report, 237A
Wales:
- 124
- And Monmouthshire:
  - Council Memorandum. *Cmnd. 53.* 334; *Cmnd. 631.* 788, 869
  - Report on Development and Government Action. *Cmd. 9887.* 52, 124, 250, 335; *Cmnd. 319.* 270, 343; *Cmnd. 684.* 792, 871; *Cmnd. 961.* 1048, 1148
  - Welsh Grand Committee Report on Development and Government Action, 1028, 1141
- Government Administration. *Cmnd. 334.* 271, 343
- Report. *See* Mid-Wales

Walker, A. L.:
- Maternal Deaths in England and Wales Report, 332
- Report on Confidential Inquiries into Maternal Deaths in England and Wales, 1136

Walker, G., Traffic and Transport in Nigeria, 1103
Walker, Hon. Lord (Chairman: Law Reform Committee for Scotland) Report. *Cmnd. 88, 114, 141, 330.* 254, 256, 258, 271; *Cmnd. 449.* 528; *Cmnd. 635, 907.* 789, 807; *Cmnd. 1017, 1102, 1103.* 1052, 1058
Walker, J., Muhammadan Coins in British Museum, 80
Walker, K. J. S., Experiments in Rectilinear Cutting, 1180
Walker Types of Fruit Flies in the British Museum Collection, 1095
Wall and Floor Tiler. Career, 876
Wall, Staffordshire, Roman Site, Guide, 698
Wallace, T., Soils and Manures for Fruit, 72
Wallasey Corporation Act, 544
Walley, F., Pre-Stressed Concrete, 428
Wallis and Futuna Islands. International Customs Journal, 1244
Wallpaper. Census of Production Report, 395
Walne, P. R.:
- Biology and Distribution of the Slipper Limpet Crepidula Fornicata in Essex Rivers, with Notes on the Distribution of the Larger Epi-Benthic Invertebrates, 74

Walne, P. R. (*continued*):
- Experimental Rearing of the Larvae of Ostrea edulis L. in the Laboratory, 74

Walsall. Boundary Commission for England Report, 1137
Waltham Holy Cross Urban District Council Act, 544
Walthamstow Corporation Act, 59
Walton Colliery, Yorkshire, Explosion Report. *Cmnd. 843.* 803, 899
Walton, H. S., Midlothian Coalfield, Geology of, 599
Walton, J., Glen More. Cairngorms Guide, 1129
War:
- Against Japan, 296, 565, 658
- And Occupation of Germany. Convention with U.K., France and U.S.A. on matters arising therefrom. *Cmnd. 656.* 790, 849
- At Sea, 1939–45, 296, 339, 1098, 1189
- Cripples. Agreement between Member Countries of the Council of Europe on their Exchange with a View to Medical Treatment. *Cmd. 9705, 9851.* 39, 49, 112; 213A
- Histories. Select Committee on Estimates Report, 240, 336, 757, 865
- History of Second World War, 173–4, 296, 389, 564, 602, 657, 828, 859, 916, 1098, 1189
- Material, Export of Surplus. *Cmd. 9676.* 94, 106
- Pensioners Report, 22, 121, 123, 160, 236, 331, 332, 369, 505, 601, 603, 639, 774, 858, 860, 896, 1031, 1133, 1136, 1169
- Pensions Committees (Extension) Order:
  - 1169
  - No. 2, 1169
- Production:
  - Administration of, 82, 173
  - History of Second World War, 564, 657
- Victims. Convention for their Protection. *Cmnd. 550.* 535, 595
- Years:
  - 106
  - Documents on German Foreign Policy, 318

War Damage Accounts:
- Business and Private Chattels Schemes, 11, 183, 223, 399, 495, 668, 762, 781, 924
- Land and Buildings, 9, 31, 203, 492, 693, 764, 780, 952

War Damage (Clearance Payments) Act, 1071
War Damage (Clearance Payments) Bill, 1006, 1021, 1038, 1041, 1142

War Department, Schedule of Prices for Works Services, 426
War Graves:
- Agreement. *Cmnd. 581, 582.* 537, 595
- Agreement regarding War Cemeteries of the British Commonwealth. *Cmd. 9833.* 48, 112
- Agreement with Federal Republic of Germany. *Cmd. 9838.* 48, 106
- Commission Report, 1107
- German, in U.K.:
  - Agreement between U.K. and Germany. *Cmnd. 930.* 1046, 1121
  - Exchange of Notes amending Agreement. *Cmnd. 1170.* 1063, 1121
- In Japanese Territory. Agreement with Japan. *Cmnd. 134.* 258
- Thai Territory. Agreement with U.K. etc. *Cmd. 9776.* 44, 110

War Office:
- Publications, 204–7, 423–6, 693, 952, 1223
- Purchasing (Repayment) Services Estimate, 1960–61, 1019, 1225
- Supplementary Estimates, 1959–60, 781, 956

Warble Fly Infestation in Cattle, Organisation of Control of, 450
Ward, F. A. B., Time Measurement, 648
Ward-Jackson, P.:
- English Furniture Designs in the 18th Century, 951
- Ham House Guide, 422, 951

Warden Section:
- Civil Defence Instructors' Notes, 333, 603, 604, 1138
- Training Bulletin, 861

Ware Potatoes:
- Early and Main Crop, 69
- Stores. Management of, 1084

Wards, Colonel G. T.:
- India's Most Dangerous Hour, 565, 658
- War Against Japan, 296, 389

Waring, A. B., (Chairman: Human Relations in Industry Committee) Report, 650
Warmth without Waste, 697
Warning Station. *See* Ballistic Missile
Warr, Rt. Hon. Earl de la (Chairman: Committee on Further Education for Agriculture) Report. *Cmnd. 614.* 539
Warren, G. M., Simple Plumbing Repairs in the Home, 201
Warren Spring Laboratory, Report, 1183
"Wars Not Yet Won", 344, 1149
Wart Disease of Potatoes, 820
Wartnaby, J.:
- International Geophysical Year, 381
- Seismology, 381

Warwickshire and Leicestershire, 1576, Saxton's Map, 827
Wash Your Hands, Now. Notice, 857
Washington Declaration by the President of the U.S.A. and the Prime Minister of the U.K. *Cmd. 9700.* 39, 112
Wasps, 71
Waste Treatment and Environmental Aspects of Atomic Energy, 986
Wastes. *See* Composting
Watches:
- And Clocks. Census of Production Report, 664, 1194
- English, 203

Water:
- And the World Today, 465
- Central Advisory Committee Sub-Committee Reports, 868
- Charges. Circular, 129
- Economy in Iron and Steel Works, 720
- Facilities in Civil Defense Emergencies Operation and Repair, 422
- Fluoridation. Expert Committee Report, 741
- For Industrial Use, 734
- Growing Demand for. Sub-Committee Report, 1146
- Lifting Devices for Irrigation, 241A
- Pollution:
  - Abstracts, 168, 384–5, 431, 652, 910, 1183
  - Research Board Report, 168, 385, 653, 911, 1184
- Resources:
  - Development:
    - 228A
    - Asia and Far East, 454, 982
    - Burma, India and Pakistan, 454
    - Centre Report, 1253
    - In British Borneo, Federation of Malaya, Indonesia and Thailand, 1254
    - In the Lower Mekong Basin, Development of, 724
- Supplies:
  - Bacteriological Examination of, 123
  - For Rural Areas and Small Communities, 998
  - Royal Engineers Supplementary Pocket Book. Amendments, 425
- Undertakings:
  - Census of Production Report, 180, 665
  - Re-grouping of, Circular, 129, 611
- Vapour Content of the Air, Average, 1160

Water Act:
- 542
- Circular, 611

Water Bill, 479, 480, 481, 485, 505, 513, 518, 519, 609
Water Officers Compensation Act, 1071
Water Officers Compensation Bill, 754, 787, 1020, 1038, 1142
Water-Colours, Twentieth Century British, 693

Watercress Cultivation, 72
Waterlow, Dr. J., Protein Malnutrition in Brazil, 242A
Waters, John:
- Proceedings of Tribunal Inquiring into allegation of Assault, 915
- Report of Tribunal inquiring into allegation of Assault. *Cmnd. 718.* 794, 915

Waters, W. T., Provisional Yield Tables for Oak and Beech in Great Britain, 596
Watkins, C. M., Durability of Reinforced Concrete in Sea Water, 1181
Watson, A., Revision of the Genus Tridrepana Swinhoe, 294
Watson, D. M. S.:
- Brachyopid Labyrinthodonts, 80
- New Labyrinthodont from the Upper Trias of New South Wales, 563

Watson, H., (Chairman: Committee on Marketing of Woodland Produce) Report, 113
Watts, Sir H. E. (Chairman: Advisory Committee on Carriage of Dangerous Goods and Explosives in Ships) Report, 401
Waugh, G. D., Oyster Production in Rivers Crouch and Roach, 292
Waverley, Rt. Hon. Viscount (Chairman: Forces Medical and Dental Services Committee) Report, 94
Weather:
- Analysis in Falkland Islands Dependencies, Antarctica, 571
- And the Builder, 207
- Maps:
  - 361
  - Instruction for Preparation, 634, 889, 1161
  - Some Typical, 361
- Messages, Handbook of, 153, 361, 634, 888, 1160
- Report, Monthly, 153, 361, 431, 634, 888, 1161
- Service, Your, 889
- Station on Betio Island. Exchange of Notes between U.K. and U.S.A. *Cmd. 9693.* 39, 111; *Cmnd. 391.* 525, 595

Weatherproof Outerwear. Census of Production Report, 1194
Weaver, T. R. (Chairman: Educational Working Paper) Report, 313
Webb, J. E., Cephalo Chordata, 296
Weber Parabolic Cylinder Functions and Other Functions for Large Arguments, Tables of, 155, 1163
Webster, F. V., Traffic Signal Settings, 652
Webster, G., Roman Site at Wall, Guide, 698
Wedgwood, 693
Weeds:
- Choosing Selective Weed Killers for Cereals, 820
- Control, Methods of, 706
- Seedlings of Common, 1085
- Selective Weed Control in Cereals, 820

Weeds Act:
- 810
- Consolidation Bills Report, 745, 750 866

Weeds Bill, 747, 785
Weekly Close Time for Salmon Fishing Report, 915
Weevils, Pea, Bean, and Clover Leaf, 819
Weight Gains, Serum Protein Levels, and Health of Breast Fed and Artificially Fed Infants, Full Term and Premature, 887
Weights and Measures Act, Notices of Examinations of Patterns, 183–5, 399–400, 668, 924, 1195
Weights and Measures Bill, 1011, 1012
Weir, Sir C. (Chairman: Committee on Co-operation between Area and Scottish Electricity and Gas Boards) Report. *Cmnd. 695.* 793, 899
Weiss, L. E., Structural Analysis of the Basement System at Turoka, Kenya, 834
Welch, F.B.A., Geology of the Country around Bridport and Yeovil, 857
Welded Metal Structures, Calculations of Deformations of, 649
Welder and Cutter. Career, 347
Welfare:
- Foods, Report on, 331
- Needs of Mentally Handicapped Persons, Report, 331
- Of Children in Hospital Report, 859
- Section, Training Bulletin, 861
- Training. Emergency Feeding, Film Strip, 123
- *See* Ministry of Health Report

Welford, A. T., Ergonomics of Automation, 1181
Wellington Museum. *See* Apsley House
Welsh Agricultural College Working Party Report, 1088
Welsh Agricultural Land Sub-Commission Report, 75
Welsh Agriculture Technical Problems Report, 560
Welsh and English in the Schools of Wales. Report of the Central Advisory Council for Education, 1116
Welsh Broadcasting Report. *Cmnd. 39.* 54, 161
Welsh Statistics Digest, 124, 343, 869, 1147
Welwyn Garden City:
- Development Corporation Report, 24, 130, 237, 506, 613, 870, 1147
- Station Railway Accident Report, 404

Wemyss, Earl of, (Chairman):
- Ancient and Historical Monuments Royal Commission. Report. *Cmnd. 276.* 267, 378
- Royal Commission on Ancient and Historical Monuments and Constructions, Scotland. Report. *Cmd. 9735.* 41

W. Wesson & Co. Ltd. Proposal to sell its Holdings of Securities. *Cmnd. 1115.* 1059, 1205
West Africa, United Nations Visiting Mission to the Trust Territory, 992
West Cumberland Water Board Order, 1012
West Fife and Dunfermline Burghs. Boundary Commission for Scotland Report, 1016, 1186
West Hertfordshire Main Drainage Act, Ministry of Housing and Local Government Provisional Order Confirmation, 749
- *See also* Ministry of Housing and Local Government

West Indies:
- British, Photo-Poster, 131
- Colonial Arms, 569
- Constitution (Amendment) Order-in-Council, 1174
- Development and Welfare Report, 302, 571
- Flag Badge Plate, 571
- Nation in the Making, 615
- Teaching Hospital Report, 303

West Lothian Educational Trust Scheme:
- Draft, 170
- Memorandum, 386
- Order-in-Council, 386

West Renfrewshire and Greenock Boundary Commission Report, 1016, 1186
West Sleekburn. Railway Accident Report, 1198
West, W. J.:
- Potato Harvesting, 1251
- "Yard and Parlour" System in Milk Production in the U.K., 225A

Westcott, G. F.:
- British Railway Locomotive, 1803 to 1853, 648
- Mechanical and Electrical Engineering, 1178

Wester, R. E., Growing Vegetables in Town and City, 951
Western Co-operation:
- 132
- In Brief, 615, 1150

Western European Union:
- Accession of Germany and Italy to Convention on Frontier Workers and Student Employees. *Cmnd. 1209.* 1066, 1128
- Accession of Greece, Norway and Sweden to Convention concerning Student Employees. *Cmnd. 942.* 1047, 1128

Western European Union (*continued*):
- Agreement of the Brussels Treaty. *Cmnd. 388.* 524, 595
- Agreement on Status. *Cmnd. 173.* 260, 325
- Assembly Proceedings, 245A, 470, 738, 997, 1266
- Charter and Rules of Procedure, 470
- Convention concerning the Agency for the Control of Armaments. *Cmnd. 389.* 524, 596
- Protocol concerning the Accession of Germany and Italy to the Conventions on Frontier Workers. *Cmnd. 138.* 258, 325
- Publications, 245A, 470, 738, 997

Western Hemlock. Yield Tables, 325
Western Samoa. United Nations Visiting Mission to Trust Territories in Pacific. Report, 464, 992
Western Zosteropidae, Variation in the, 295
Westonbirt Arboretum Guide, 1129
Westwood Junction Railway Accident Report, 189
Whaling:
- International Whaling Convention Schedule. *Cmnd. 694.* 793, 854
- Protocol to the International Convention for the Regulation of Whaling. *Cmnd. 100.* 255, 325; *Cmnd. 849.* 803, 854

What is the Commonwealth?, 132, 615, 872
What They Read and Why, Use of Technical Literature in the Electrical and Electronics Industries, 909
Wheat:
- 71, 560
- Agreement:
  - *Cmnd. 1074.* 1056, 1128
  - International. *Cmnd. 730.* 795, 854
- And Barley, Eyespot of, 820
- Conference, United Nations, 465, 1262
- Fund Account, 14, 75, 227, 244, 293, 491, 560
- World Catalogue of Genetic Stocks, 243, 438, 968

Wheeler, A. C., Gronevious Fish Collection, 563
White Fish and Herring Industries Act:
- 273
- Accounts, 499, 560, 1016, 1089

White Fish and Herring Industries Bill, 35
White Fish and Herring Industries (No. 2) Bill, 215, 247
White Fish Authority:
- Account, 14, 75, 224, 314
- Report and Accounts, 23, 75, 125, 173, 237, 293, 335, 389, 505, 560, 605.

1956-60 | WHI-YEA

WHI— INDEX 1956–60

White Fish Authority (*continued*):
656, 766, 770, 825, 863, 915, 1028, 1082, 1089, 1140
Whitehead Iron and Steel Company Limited. Proposal to Sell its Holding of Debenture Stock. *Cmnd. 1227.* 1067, 1205
Whitehead, T. P., Weight Gains, Serum Protein Levels and Health of Breast Fed and Artificially Fed Infants, Full Term and Premature, 887
Whiting (Gadus Merlangus L) in the North Sea, 172
Whitstable Harbour Act, 274
Whitworth Fellowships and Exhibitions. Rules and Conditions for Award, 843
Whitworth, T., Miocene Ruminants of East Africa, 564
Wholesale Bottling. Census of Production Report, 664
Wholesale Clothing Manufacture, Career, 136
Wholesale Trade, Productivity in, 224A
Whyte, R.O.:
Grasses in Agriculture, 1236
Plant Exploration Collection and Introduction, 1236
Widdas, W.:
Inspector of Mines and Quarries Report, 642, 645, 900, 1172
Newcraighall Colliery Haulage Accident Report. *Cmnd. 205.* 263
Scottish Division Mines Report, 116
Widdowson, E. M.:
Composition of Foods, 1160
Hazards to Men in Ships Lost at Sea, 151
Widow's Benefits. Report of the National Insurance Advisory Committee. *Cmd. 9684.* 38
Wigtownshire Educational Trust Scheme. Memorandum, 1185
Wilcox, F. O., United Nations in the Mainstream of History, 422
Wild Oats, 71, 555
Wild Onion and Ramsoms, 1083
Wilkins, G. L., Cracherode Shell Collection, 295
Wilkinson, J. V. S., Hindi Printed Books, Supplementary Catalogue, 562
Willcocksen, M., Know Your Capital City, 201
William Morris, 693
Williams, D. J.:
Mealy-Bugs from the Ethiopian Region, 563
Pseudococcidae of the Solomon Islands, 1095
Some New Diaspidini from Africa, 1096
Williams, F., Preliminary Survey of the Pelagic Fishes of East Africa, 89
Williams, F. H. P.:
Report on Roads and Road Problems, 301
Testing Mixers for Bituminous Materials, 384
Williams, John, Pioneers who Served, 872
Willink, H., (Chairman: Commission appointed to Inquire into Fears of Minorities and Means of Allaying them in Nigeria) Report. *Cmnd. 505.* 532
Willink, Sir H. (Chairman):
Committee to Consider the Future Numbers of Medical Practitioners, etc. Report, 332
Royal Commission on Police:
Minutes of Evidence, 1177
Report. *Cmnd. 1222.* 1067
Willoughby de Broke Estate Act, 59
Willis, W. J. A., (Chairman: Committee of the Police Council for England and Wales) Report, 605
Wills, etc. (Publication) Bill, 32, 516, 520, 758, 779, 784, 864
Wills, J. R., Report on Proposed Development of Land at Lymm for Manchester Overspill, 612
Willson, F. M. G., Governmental Services to the Sea-Fish Industry of Great Britain, 707
Wilson, Sir A. (Chairman):
Ministry of Agriculture, Fisheries and Food Local Organisation and Procedure Report. *Cmd. 9732.* 41
Report on Caravans as Homes. *Cmnd. 872.* 805, 868
Wilson, A. H. (Chairman: Coal Derivatives Committee) Report. *Cmnd. 1120.* 1059
Wilson, Lt. Col. G. R. S., Railway Accident Report, 188, 189, 404
Wilson, H. E., Geology of Midlothian Coalfield, 599
Wilson, H. F., Inspector of Mines and Quarries Report, 900, 1172
Wilson, J. C., (Chairman: Housing Subsidies in Scotland Working Party) Reports, 120
Wilson, P. H. St. J., (Chairman: Inter-Departmental Committee) Report, 885
Wilson, R., Spectrophotometric Measurements of Early Type Stars, 164, 648
Wilson, R. B.:
Economic Geology of the Stirling and Clackmannan Coalfield, Scotland:
Area North of the River Forth, 119
Area South of the River Forth, 906
Geology of Midlothian Coalfield, 599
Wilson, R. M., (Chairman: Committee of Inquiry as to whether there are any Causes of Industrial Unrest arising from Present Arrangements in Smithfield Market) Report, 630

INDEX 1956–60 —WOO

Wilson, V.:
Geology of Country around Bridport and Yeovil, 857
London and Thames Valley, British Regional Geology, 1131
"Wimbledon" Wreck Report, 406
Wimpenny, R. S., Young Plaice Hauls off the English East Coast, 1087
Winches:
Protocol for the Testing of, 968
Provisional Protocol for Testing, 708
"Winchester" and "Haslemere" Wreck Reports, 192
Wind and Solar Energy, 237A
Wind and Temperatures to 50 KM. Over England, 152
Wind Effects on Roofs, 905
Winding Accident, Brookhouse Colliery, Yorkshire, Report. *Cmnd. 475.* 530, 646
Windows and Doors, Standard Metal, Monopolies and Restrictive Practices Commission Report, 398
Windrow Harvesting, 288
Winds between 300 and 100 MB. in the Tropics and Subtropics, 152
Windscale:
Accident at No. 1 Pile. *Cmnd. 302.* 269, 412
Piles. Report of the Committee appointed to make a Technical Evaluation of Information relating to the Design and Operation, etc. *Cmnd. 471.* 530, 691
Winfrith Heath Act, 273
Winfrith Heath Bill, 218, 248
Winnifrith, A. J. D., (Chairman: Agricultural Improvement Council E. and W.) Report, 1084
Winstanley, A., Explosion Report. *Cmnd. 327.* 271
Winter Cabbage and Savoys, 555
Winter Feeding of the Oyster-catcher on the Edible Mussel in the Conway Estuary, North Wales, 559
Winter Grass, 289
Winter, M., Film-making on a Low Budget, 1265
Winter Pruning Established Apple and Pear Trees, 820
Wire:
and Wire Manufacturers. Census of Production Report, 394
Goods for Domestic and Catering Purposes. Standing Committee Report. *Cmnd. 575.* 537, 667
Wireless Operators Handbook, 370
Wireworms, 555
Wisbech Port and Harbour Pier and Harbour Order Confirmation Act, 34, 58
Wisbech Port and Harbour Pier and Harbour Provisional Order Bill, 5
Wise, A. F. E., Drainage Pipework in Dwellings, 649
Wiseman, D. J.:
Chronicles of Chaldaean Kings, 79
Cuneiform Texts from Cappadocian Tablets in the British Museum, 294
Withers, F. W., Disease, Wastage and Husbandry in the British Dairy Herd, 1087
Wittmer, W., Ruwenzori Expedition, 828
Woking Railway Accident Report, 189
Wolfenden, Sir J. (Chairman):
Committee Report on Employment of National Service Men in United Kingdom. *Cmnd. 35.* 54
Homosexual Offences and Prostitution Committee. Report. *Cmnd. 247.* 265, 334
Wolff, Torben, Natural History of Rennel Island, 564, 1098
Wolstencroft, A. (Chairman: Mobile Radio Committee) Report, 1170
Wolverhampton Water Order, 747
Wolverson, W. A. (Chairman: Mobile Radio Committee) Report, 161, 897
Woman, Wife and Worker, 1181
Women and Technical Assistance, 734
Women's:
Bureau Leaflets, 203
Fashions. 19th Century, 1223
Measurements and Sizes, 400
Services. Career, 347
Wood:
And Its Products. Utilisation in Housing, 463
Colours and Kinds, 419
Efficiency of Adhesives for, 907
Growth and Structure of, 650
Preparation of for Microscopic Examination, 908
Sawyer and Woodcutting Machinist. Career, 347
Waste as a Fuel, 908
Wood, Henry. Herring of the Clyde Estuary, 1187
Wood, M.:
Burton Agnes Old Manor House Guide, 207
Christchurch Castle, Hampshire, Guide, 208
Wood, R. F., Exotic Forest Trees in Great Britain, 325
Woodburn Kirby, Major General S.:
India's Most Dangerous Hour, 565, 658
War Against Japan, 296, 389
Wooden Containers and Baskets. Census of Production Report, 665
Wooden Packaging for Fruit and Vegetables:
720
Standardisation of, 1246

WOO— INDEX 1956–60

Woodlands:
Dedication of, 112
Income Tax and Estate Duty on, 1109
Produce, Marketing of, Report, 113
Woodman, H. E., Rations for Livestock, 290
Woodpeckers in Woodlands, 596
Wood-Pigeon, 1083
"Woods" Wreck Report, 1200
Woodward, E. L., Documents on British Foreign Policy, 104, 316, 588
Woodward, J., Management and Technology, 651
Woodwaste, Industrial Use of, 221A
Woodworking Craftsmen. Career, 876
Woodworm, 426
Wool:
Marketing Scheme, British Report, 556
Production and Trade, 91
Textiles Industry:
Accounts:
922, 1040, 1193
Export Promotion Levy, 14, 231, 500, 667, 762, 922
Scientific Research Levy, 15, 231, 500, 667, 762, 922
Spacing of Machinery, 1158
Woollen and Worsted. Census of Production Report, 179, 664
Woolley, Sir L., Ur Excavations, 80
Worcestershire. Saxton's Maps, 1094
Work of OEEC Report, 979
Work of W.H.O. Annual Report, 244, 472, 740, 999, 1268
Work of Youth Employment Service Report, 149, 876
Work Study Terms, Glossary of, 720
Workers Abroad, 469
Workers. Readaptation and Re-employment Report, 215A
Working Conditions in Industry. *See* Fitting the Job to the Worker
Working in Winter or Bad Weather, 1179
Working Life of Males in Great Britain, Length of, 885
Working Metals by Electro-Sparking, 168
Working of the Monetary System. Committee Report. *Cmnd. 827.* 802, 934
Working Stresses for Structural Softwoods, 166
Workington Harbour and Dock (Transfer) Act, 274
Workmen's Compensation and Benefit (Supplementation) Act:
56
Decisions on Claims, 369, 640
Workmen's Compensation and Benefit (Supplementation) Bill, 5, 20, 30, 32, 34, 35, 128, 516, 520
Works:
And Buildings of Service Departments (Army). Estimates Select Committee Report, 13, 125
Works (*continued*):
Estimates:
1956–57, 12
1957–58, 226
1958–59, 494, 676
1959–60, 760, 933
1960–61, 1019, 1201
Works, Ministry of:
Directorate-General of Works, Select Committee on Estimates Report, 16, 125
Publications, 207–8, 426–9, 697, 956, 1226
Works of Art Export Licences, 181
Workshops, Safety Precautions in, Display Card, 170
World Cartography, 236A, 465, 734
World Catalogue of Genetic Stocks, 243A, 438, 709, 968
World Communications. Press, Radio, Film, Television, 240A
World Congresses of the Communist International, 200
World Crop Harvest Calendar, 968
World Demand for Paper to 1975, 1238
World Directory:
Of Medical Schools, 473
Of Venereal Disease Treatment Centres at Ports, 1000
World Distribution of Atmospheric Water Vapour Pressure, 888
World Economic Survey, 236A, 465, 734, 993, 1262
World Energy Supplies:
1259
Statistical Papers, 461
World Facts and Figures, 734
World Fisheries Abstracts, 243A, 438, 709, 969, 1238
World Food:
Problems, 243A, 709
Reserve, Functions, Scope and Limitations, 241A
World Forest:
Inventory, 1238
Products Statistics, 709
World Grain Trade Statistics, 438, 709, 969, 1239
World Health, 1948–1958, 742, 1270
World Health Assembly:
Records, 244A, 740, 999
Resolutions and Decisions Handbook, 245A, 472, 742, 1268
World Health Organisation:
Basic Documents, 243A, 739, 1267
Bulletin, 243A, 470, 739, 997, 998, 1267
Chronicle, 243A, 470, 739, 998, 1270
Constitution Amendments. *Cmnd. 877.* 805, 854
Executive Board:
Proposed Programme and Budget Estimates Report, 244A, 472, 1268
Resolutions, etc., 244A, 472–3

INDEX 1956–60 —YEA

World Health Organisation (*continued*):
Financial Report, 244A, 740, 999
International Sanitary Regulations Amendments. *Cmnd. 1165.* 1063, 1128
Monograph Series, 244A, 471, 740, 998, 1268
Official Records, 244A, 471–2, 740, 999, 1268
Publications, 470–3, 739–42, 997, 1267
Records, 244A, 1268
Situation Report, 999
Technical Report Series, 245A, 472, 741, 999, 1269
World Illiteracy at Mid-Century, 468
World Population:
Conference Proceedings Report, 236A, 465
Future Growth of, 730
World Production, Consumption and Trade of Fertilizers, 1236
World Social Situation Report, 465
World Survey of Education, 997
World Trade. *See* Possible Impact
World's Requirements for Energy, 231A
Wormit Railway Accident Report, 189
Worms in Poultry, 290
Wound Shock, Treatment of, 359
Wreck Reports, 192, 406, 675, 927, 931, 1200
Wrexham Technical College. Provision of Advanced Technical Education Report, 586
Wright, A. C. S., Land in British Honduras, 1103
Wright, C. A.:
Molluscan Anatomy for Parasitologists in Africa, 296
Studies on the Structure and Taxonomy of Bulinus Jousseaumei, 295
Wright Hamer Textiles Limited, Investigation into the Affairs. Report, 1192
Wright, J. H., Chile Overseas Economic Survey, 667
Wright, N. C. (Chairman):
Food Standards Committee. Report, 73, 74, 292, 824
National Food Survey Committee Report, 73
Wrigley, A. J.:
Maternal Deaths in England and Wales Report, 332
Report on Confidential Enquiries into Maternal Deaths in England and Wales, 1136
Wrigley, C. G., Studies of Overseas Supply, 82, 174
Wrigley, Sir John (Acting Chairman: Royal Commission on Local Government in Greater London) Minutes of Evidence, 902, 903, 904, 1176
Wrought and Cast Aluminium and Magnesium Alloys at Room and Elevated Temperatures, Properties of, 391
Wrought Iron and Steel Tubes. Census of Production Report, 394
Wüster, E., Documentation and Terminology of Science, 994
W.V.S., Story of, 863
Wyatt, S., Study of Attitudes to Factory Work, 151
Wye Valley. *See* Dean Forest
Wygodzinsky, P., New and Little Known Emesinae in the British Museum (Natural History), 563
Wynn-Parry, Hon. Mr. Justice, (Chairman: Committee on Remuneration and Conditions of Service of Certain Grades in the Prison Services) Report. *Cmnd. 544.* 535
"Wyre Majestic" Wreck Report, 675, 1200

Y

Yang, W. Y., Methods of Farm Management Investigations for Improving Farm Productivity, 966
"Yard and Parlour" System in Milk Production in U.K., 225A
Yarmouth Castle, Isle of Wight. Guide, 937
Yarmouth (Isle of Wight) Pier and Harbour Order Confirmation Act, 1072
Yarmouth (Isle of Wight) Pier and Harbour Order Confirmation Bill, 1008, 1043
Yarmouth Naval Hospital Transfer Act, 273
Yarmouth Naval Hospital Transfer Bill, 220, 249
Yarmouth Vauxhall Station Railway Accident Report, 404
Yates, R. (Chairman: Clearances on Transport Road in Coal Mines Committee) Report, 370
Yates, Alderman R. C. (Chairman: Central Water Advisory Committee Sub-Committee) Report, 868
Yaws:
Differential Diagnosis of, 1268
Lesions, International Nomenclature, 740
Y Ddeddf Yn Gryno. Y Ddeddf Rent, 343
Yearbooks:
Animal Health, 966, 1236
Commonwealth Relations Office, 305
Demographic, 226A, 451, 721, 980
Education, International, 238A, 736, 995
Fishery Statistics, 241A, 436, 707, 969, 1239
Food and Agriculture Statistics, 242A, 436, 708
Forest Products Statistics, 242A, 436, 708, 967, 1239
Human Rights, 230A, 457, 727, 1262

YEA—   INDEX 1956–60

Yearbooks (continued):
International Court of Justice, 220A,
    443, 713, 973, 1243
International Education, 467, 1265
International Law Commission, 457,
    727, 993, 1263
International Trade Statistics, 230A, 457,
    728, 985, 1263
National Accounts Statistics, 729, 993,
    1263
Observatories, 360, 889, 1161
Production, 968, 1238
Statistical, 989
Surface Water, 131, 343, 613, 871, 1148
Trade, 1238
United Nations:
    236A, 734, 993, 1263
    Statistical, 233A, 462, 731
Yellow Fever:
    Arrangements for Vaccination against,
        243A
    Vaccination:
        244A
        Expert Committee Report, 741
Yield Table for Western Hemlock in
    Great Britain, Provisional, 325
You and Your U.S.A., The Constitution,
    422
Youard, G. B., Farm Roads, 290
Young Farmers and Farm Workers,
    Training of, 1245
Young Offenders, Treatment of, Report,
    863
Young Plaice Hauls Off the English East
    Coast, 1087
Young Workers in Industry, Report on
    Recruitment and Training, 630
Younghusband, Miss E. L., (Chairman:
    Working Party on Social Workers in
    Local Authority Health and Welfare
    Services) Report, 860
Your Child:
    From One to Six, 419]
    From Six to Twelve, 419
Your United Nations, Guide Book, 236A,
    465, 993
Your Weather Service, 889
Youth:
    Courses, 1232
    Education of Rural, 238A
    Employment Service:
        And Youth Service Grants. Select
        Committee on Estimates Report,
        236, 336
    Council Report, 876
    Work of, Report, 149, 876
    Organisations, New Trends in, 1264

Youth Service:
    1115, 1116, 1184
    Grants. Select Committee Esti-
        mates. Special Report, 493, 606
    In England and Wales Committee
        Report. Cmnd. 929. 1046, 1116
Yugoslav and Czecho-Slovak Fund
    Accounts, 106
Yugoslavia:
    Agreement with U.K. concerning Air
        Services. Cmnd. 732. 795, 854;
        Cmnd. 972. 1049, 1128
    Convention on Social Security with
        U.K. Cmnd. 443, 561. 528, 536, 596
    Education. Documentation of, 1264
    Exchange of Notes with U.K.:
        On the Mutual Recognition of
            Aircrew Licences. Cmnd. 1061.
            1055, 1128
        Regarding Certain Financial Obli-
            gations. Cmnd. 9730. 41, 112
        Regarding Credit for Purchase of
            Goods in U.K. Cmnd.722. 795, 854
        Regarding the Import of British
            Books. Cmnd. 9726. 41, 112
        Regarding the Import of British
            Books and Films. Cmnd. 1023.
            1052, 1128
        Terminating the Agreement for
            Import of British Books. Cmnd.
            404. 525, 596

                        Z

Zanzibar:
    Colonial Report, 569, 833
Zarembo, K. S., Cathodic, Galvanic
    Anode and Drainage Protection of Main
    Gas Pipe Lines against Underground
    Corrosion, 382
Zehetmayr, J. W. T., Afforestation of
    Upland Heaths, 1129
Zinc. Export Licence, 397
Zolotas, X., Remodelled Economic Organi-
    sation Report, 1248
Zone de Libre-Echange, 706
Zoology Bulletins, 80, 295 563, 828, 1097
Zoonoses. Expert Committee Report, 1000
Zuckerman, Professor Sir S. (Chairman:
    Committee On Scientific Manpower.
    Report. Cmnd. 902. 807, 887, 905
    Natural Resources Technical Com-
        mittee. Report, 382, 652
Zygaena Species. On the Synonymy of
    Some, 1096
Z Zones, Clearance of, by Road, 1137

Consolidated Index to Government Publications 1961-1965

FOREWORD

Scope

This index, covering the period January 1961 to December 1965, includes all titles as listed in the five annual volumes of Government Publications i.e. it does not include Statutory Instruments or publications of international organisations for which there are separate lists and indexes.† Reprints at revised prices are not generally included.

Previous quinquennial indexes have been compiled from 1936 to 1960 but with the exception of 1955–60 they are out of print.

Notes on Compilation

The first significant word as well as the most important word of the title has been indexed and cross-references have been made where helpful, except for Acts and Bills which are indexed under first word of the title only. 'Word-by-word' order has been followed. Personal names are in small capitals. Where there are joint-authors, only the first-named is indexed, but names of all chairmen are indexed. Titles listed in the catalogues in two or more places, mainly under "Parliamentary Publications" and "Classified List" Headings, are only indexed once under the latter page reference.

Pagination

The five annual volumes were paginated consecutively as follows:

1961	pp 1–224
1962	pp 225–445
1963	pp 447–696
1964	pp 697–962
1965	pp 963–1226

This information is repeated for convenience at the foot of each page of the index and the particular year of publication can thereby be identified.

Omissions

Individual titles within the following series are not indexed separately:

Boiler Explosion Inquiries
Business Monitor. Production
Civil Aircraft Accidents
Civil Estimates
Civil Service Arbitration Tribunal
  Awards
Civil Service Commission.
  Question Papers
Current Papers (Aeronautical
  Research Council)
Customs Forms
D.E.F. Specifications (Defence)
Defence Guides and Lists
D.T.D. Specifications (Aviation)
European Atomic Energy
  (EURATOM) Regulations
European Economic Community
  (EEC) Regulations
Factory Forms
Friendly Societies
  (Annual Return Forms)
F.S.H. Circulars

†*The 1965 annual volume of Government Publications also omitted overseas agency titles which are to be found in "International Organisations and Overseas Agencies Publications 1965."*

Omissions (continued)

Honours Lists
Industrial Court Awards
Land Registry Forms
Meteorological Office Forms
Mines and Quarries. Forms
National Institute for Research
  into Nuclear Science
New Towns and Development
  Corporation Reports
Profit Tax Leaflets
Public Health (Imported Foods)
  etc. Regulations
Queens Regulations and
  Admiralty Instructions

Railway Accident Reports
Reports and Memoranda
  (Aeronautical Research Council)
Royal Commissions. Evidence
Tax Case Leaflets
Trucial States Notices
United Kingdom Atomic Energy
  Authority Reports (A.E.E.W.
  etc.)
War Pensions Committee
Weights and Measures.
  Examination of Patterns
Wreck Reports.

Abbreviations

* = Exchange of Notes, Letters. Agreements etc.

B.M.	=	British Museum
E. and W.	=	England and Wales
H.C.	=	House of Commons
H.L.	=	House of Lords
N.I.	=	Northern Ireland
OIC	=	Order in Council
PRO	=	Public Record Office
S.I.	=	Statutory Instrument
UKAEA	=	United Kingdom Atomic Energy Authority.

INDEX

A

AANENSEN, C. J. M., Gales in Yorkshire, 1154
AARON, J. R., Mineral nutrient status of heather, 1121
AARON, R. I. (Chairman):
Rural transport in Wales, 281
Welsh holiday industry, 495
Welsh language, 513
AARVOLD, JUDGE, C. D. (Chairman), Magistrates' Courts in London, 357

Abatement of electrical interference, Hospitals, 1126
Abberley, Geology of country around, 396
ABC:
of cookery, 300
of preserving, 81
Aberdare Markets & Town Hall Act, 1041
Aberdeen:
Census:
Leaflet. Population, etc., 590
Report 590
Harbour Order Confirmation Act, 69
Royal Aberdeen Workshops for Blind Scheme, 400, 645
Soils of country around, 528
Aberdour Castle, Guide, 221
Abies Grandis & Abies Nobilis. Yield tables, 127
Abnormalities of sex chromosome complement, 883
Abolition of Resale Price Maintenance Bill, 741
Abortion:
Bill, 975, 1012
Report, 1127
Abrasive wheels:
Form, 1153
Safety in use, 1152
Absolute magnitudes of RR Lyrae Variable stars, 1169
Abstracts. See specific subjects
Abu Simbel temples*, 844

Academic staff in universities etc. Remuneration, 887
Acari, Terrestial, 313
Acarus L, 1758, 797
Accelerated freeze—drying methods of food preservation, 81
Access to:
public buildings for disabled, 1222
sub-ordinate legislation, 596
Accession:
of Aden to South Arabia*, 316
to repositories, 134, 354, 594, 1127

Accident(s):
and Emergency:
Department. Hospital, 852, 1126
services, 352
at factories etc. (Periodical) 151, 368, 611, 874, 1146
Notice of, O.S.R. Form, 880
See also Aircraft, Railways, etc.
Accommodation:
for:
nursing staff, 133, 592
psychiatric patients, 592
needs of Scottish Record Office etc., 646
Residential, for:
elderly people, 353
hospital staff, 852
Accountant (Careers), 612
Accuracy of industrial measurement, 641
ACKERS, P.:
Charts for hydraulic design of channels etc., 640
Critical-depth flumes, 640
Table for hydraulic design of storm-drains etc., 640
Acorns & beech mast. Collection & storage, 586
Acridoidea, 94, 311, 541
Actornithophilus Ferris, 310
Acts:
Annotations to, 187, 409, 649, 915, 1177
Local 68–70, 289–90, 517–9, 774–5, 1041–2
of Parliament (Numbering & Citation) Act, 287
Bill, 9, 261
of Privy Council, 174, 901
Personal, 519
Public General, 67–8, 287–9, 516–7, 771–3, 1039–41
See also Statutes

Adair Lodge Convalescent Home, 427
ADAMS, P. J., Geology & ceramics, 129
Aden:
Accession to South Arabia*, 316
Archaeology in Protectorates, 888
Flag, 803
Instructions OIC, 174
Report, 100
Royal Instructions OIC, 632, 1166
Stratigraphy Eastern Protectorate, 1159
Adhesives for wood, 639, 905
Administration of:
Estates (Small Payments) Act, 1039
Bill, 972, 1006, 1009, 1010, 1131
Justice Acts, 771, 1039
Bills, 456, 457, 697, 703, 709, 710, 734, 741, 742, 746, 857, 966, 1006, 1009, 1131

Administration of Justice Acts (continued): Circular, 1138
Administrative:
and clerical staff. Electricity Supply industry, 1156
arrangements. Hospital, 352, 850, 851, 1125
Department. Hospital, 592, 852
Services. Hospital, 132
Admiralty:
Advisory Committee on Structural Steel 71, 291, 819, 1087
Headquarters Organisation. Estimates Committee, 519
Manual of:
navigation, 71, 818, 1086
seamanship, 71, 519, 818
memo on court-martial procedure, 71, 291, 1086
Publications, 71–2, 291–2, 519–20
See also Defence, Ministry of, Navy Dept.
Adoption Act, 771
Bill, 705, 735, 741, 744, 857
Adult:
offender, 1128
training centres, 853
Advertisements, Control of, Circular, 361
Advertising. (Careers), 612
Advisory:
Bulletins, Agriculture, 1050
Leaflets:
Agriculture 81–2, 300–1, 529–30, 783–4, 1051–3
Works (and Public Building), 221, 389, 633, 899, 1166

AEEW reports, 206–7, 428–9, 676–8, 942–5, 1207–9
Aerated concrete, 178
AERE reports, 207–13, 429–34, 678–82, 945–52, 1209–16
Aerial:
installations for sound & T.V., 865
navigation, 115, 507
Aerodromes:
Civil, and navigational services, 89
Licensing, 89
Aeronautical Research Council:
Current papers, 72–5, 294–4, 520–4, 775–9, 1043–7
Publications, 72–9, 292–8, 520–7, 775–81, 1043–9
Reports & memoranda, 75–9, 294–8, 524–7, 779–81, 1047–9
Technical reports, 79, 298, 527, 781
Aeronautics, Sir George Cayley's, 393
Aeroplane flights, World's first, 1170

Affiliation Proceedings:
(Amendment) Bill, 1011
Blood Tests Bill, 2, 4, 41

African:
administration. Journal, 102
Assistance Plan, 550, 804, 1075
charaxes, 541, 796
mealy bugs, 796
After-care:
Inmates & prisoners, 184
organisation, 595, 647

Age by marital condition, Census:
England & Wales, 849
Scotland, 850
Ageing & semi-skilled. Survey, 160
AGHMATI, Z. B. J., Commentaries on Talmud, 95
Agricultural:
Advisory Service, National, See National Agriculture Advisory Service.
and food grants etc.: Estimates Committee, 359
and Forestry Associations (Trading Agreements) Act, 287
Bill, 228, 255, 260, 261, 358
Censuses & Production, 82, 301, 784, 785, 1053
graduates. Demand for, 855
Improvement Council, 530
Land Commission:
Accounts, 83, 301, 530, 784–5
Annual reports, 82, 301, 530, 784
Marketing:
Acts. North of Scotland Milk Scheme, 784
Schemes. Reports, 86, 305, 533, 789, 1060
Nuisances Bill, 742
Research:
Aspects of, 79
Council:
Publications, 79, 298, 439, 527, 781–2, 1049–50
Report, 160, 394, 505, 527, 781, 1050
Fund. Accounts, 115, 329, 566, 822, 1091
Index, 1049
Pensions Act, 67
Bill, 2
Service, 527
Scotland, 730, 858
Scottish Grand Committee, 735
Soviet Union*, 1117
Sciences Review, 103, 319, 550, 803
Statistics:
England & Wales, 82, 301, 784, 1053
Scotland, 299, 782, 1050
U.K., 82, 301, 785, 1053
Agriculture:
Acts 1947 & 1957. Annual review, 83, 302, 530, 785, 1052
Agreement. Denmark, 569

Agriculture (continued):
and Fisheries for Scotland, Department of, Publications, 79–81, 299–300, 527–9, 782–3, 1050–1
and food storage. Chemicals, 87
and Horticulture Act, 771
Bill, 491, 700, 735, 742, 858
Animal Health etc. Technical assistance, 889
Bill, 1008, 1013
Commonwealth, 804
Development of, 1058
Fisheries & Food, Ministry of:
Advisory Leaflets, 81–2, 300–1, 529–30, 783–4, 1051–3
Bulletins, 83–4, 303, 531, 785–6, 1054
Circulars, 84–5, 86, 302–3, 531–2, 786–7, 1054–8
Economic Series, 85
Estimates Committee, 140, 141, 360
Publications, 81–7, 300–5, 529–34, 783–90, 1051–61
Soviet Union. Co-operation*, 1117
Technical Bulletin, 87, 534, 790, 1061
in:
Britain, 148, 366, 871, 1144
Dependencies, 148
Scotland, 79, 299, 527, 782, 1050
Wales & Monmouthshire. Welsh Grand Committee, 255, 1006, 1131
Journal, 83, 301, 530, 784, 1053
Miscellaneous Provisions Act, 516
Bill, 260, 263, 449, 450, 465, 482, 488, 489, 597
Poisonous substances used in, 789
Safety, health, welfare, & wages, 305, 533, 789, 1060
Scottish. See Scottish
Technical assistance from Britain, 889
Yearbook of (USA), 957
Agromyzidae, 1067

AHMAD, I., Leptocorisinae, 1067
AHMED, F.:
Pleiades, 1169
Southern galactic clusters, 636
A.H.S.B. reports, 213, 434–5, 683, 952–3
Aid:
from Britain, Financial & technical, 871
to developing:
countries, 671
nations, 870
Aids to:
management (Farms), 532, 787, 1058
working conifer thinnings, 403
Air:
Almanac, 87, 305, 534, 808, 1078
Clean, Tall buildings & emissions, 1139, 1222

Air (continued):
Corporations Acts, 516, 771
Advances, 790, 1061
Bills, 232, 257, 260, 263, 456, 491, 1008, 1013, 1014
Loans, 200, 422, 671, 936, 1201
Estimates & memoranda, 88, 305, 534
Force:
Careers, 368
Department. Publications, 808–9, 1078–9
law. Manual, 88, 306, 534, 808, 1079
List, 88, 306, 534, 808, 1079
Operational research, 534
Queen's Regulations, 88, 306, 534–5, 808, 1079
freight. Working party, 537
Guns & Shot Guns etc. Act, 287
Bill, 42, 228, 255, 261, 358
Ministry:
establishments, Civilian employees, 88, 535, 809, 1079
Publications, 87–8, 305–6, 534–5
See also Defence, Ministry, Air Force Department
navigation:
safety. Convention, 115, 507
services & civil aerodromes, 89
Sight reduction tables, 88
Photo reading Manual, 440
pollution. Measurement & research, 143
routes. West Indies/USA*, 347
seasoning of timber, 906
services:
Agreements. See respective countries
Appropriation Accounts, 88, 306, 534, 808, 1079
Supplementary Estimates, 88, 248, 306, 534, 808, 1079
stations for helicopters, 308
temperatures:
Measurement & control, 304
over Northern Hemisphere, 885
traffic:
Argentine/Netherlands*, 1092
control Manual, 89, 307, 535, 792, 1064
Transport:
Advisory Council. Final report, 89
Burma, 1093
Licensing Board, 90, 308, 537, 792, 1064
route schedules. France*, 118
Votes, 205, 426, 674, 940, 1205
Aircraft:
accidents U.K., survey, 92, 309, 539, 795, 1061
British military, Transit facilities. Azores*, 123
Civil supersonic transport. France*, 577
engine parts. Welded structures, 307

Aircraft (continued):
Fuelling of landplanes, 89
Ice accretion, 1155
industry report, 1038
log book, 88
materials & process specifications
D.T.D. See D.T.D.
noise. Guide, 823
offences committed on board. Convention, 825
passenger manifesto. Yugoslavia*, 846
Private navigation & piloting, 567
Radio maintenance engineers' licences, 306, 535, 1062
structure. Fatigue structures, 524
See also Civil aircraft
Airfields:
Birds on, 536
Soils, 398
Vegetation, 181, 642
Airflow around a model of Gibraltar, 622
Airports Authority Act, 1039
Bill, 740, 745, 746, 963, 966, 967, 980, 1011
Loans, 1201
Airthrey Castle Maternity Hospital. Gift, 1207
AITKENHEAD, P., Diseases & pests on horticultural planting material, 303

ALBERMARLE, COUNTESS OF (Chairman), Youth employment service, 1146
Alcohol & traffic safety, 958
Alcoholics. Health services, 1174
ALDERSEY-WILLIAMS, A. G., Electricity supply & distribution, 178
ALDHOUS, J. R., Chemical control of weeds, 1122
Aldridge. Proposed county district, 145
ALEXANDER, C. P., Tipulidae, 796
ALEXANDER, J. B., Magellanic clouds, 393
ALEXANDER, W. B., River Tees, 181
ALEXANDRA, PRINCESS. Wedding Programme, 611
Aleyrodidae of western Africa, 1068
Algae, 304, 788, 1067
Algol. Programming in, 792
Aliens & British protected persons (Naturalisation), 135, 355
Alkali etc. Works reports, 142, 360, 601, 864, 1138
ALLAN, J. K., Geology of Fife coalfields, 130
ALLAN, J. M. (Chairman). Mental health services, 131
ALLCROFT, W. M., Incubation & hatchery practice, 83, 785
ALLEN, R. G. D. (Chairman), Impact of rates on households, 1139
Allhallows Staining Churchyard Act, 69
Allowance regulations. Army, 218–9, 220, 439, 690, 809, 1079

Alosinae. Indo-pacific, 1069
Altimeter Committee report, 1064
Aluminium:
houses, 865
in building, 395, 637
in building materials, 638
Overseas Geological Survey, 381

Amblecote. Proposed new borough, 145
Ambulance:
and first aid (civil defence), 135, 355, 356, 594
service. Hospital, 852
stations. Building, 1126
Ameniinae, 1067
America(n):
and West Indies. State papers, 634
Military Insurance Association, 1181
road construction plant, 931
Amphibians & reptiles. Fossil, 1069

Anaesthetising areas. Flooring in, 1126
Anchors & Chain Cables:
Bill, 1006, 1010, 1012, 1131
for unclassed ships, 665
Ancient monuments:
and historic buildings in care of Ministry, open to public, 221, 633, 900
Boards for England, Scotland & Wales.
Annual reports, 221, 247, 633, 899, 1167
Guides, 221, 389, 633, 899–900, 1166–7
in:
England & Wales. List, 390, 633, 1167
Scotland, 221, 222, 390, 634
See also Monuments and Royal Commission
Ancient trial plates, 636
Andaspis, 796
ANDERSON, SIR C. (Chairman) Traffic signs, 421
ANDREWS, R. W., Cobalt, 381
Anemones, 300, 1052
Aneroid barometer, 884
Angiosperms of Cambridge Annobon Island Expedition, 1069
Anglesey:
Census report, 588
Saxton map, 560
Anglo-:
Egyptian financial agreement, 329
French Condominium, 802
Japanese:
commercial treaty, 413
Property Commission, 115
Saxon:
ornamental metalwork, 794
pennies, 794
Soviet Trade* Prolongation, 760

Angus. Census:
Leaflet. Population etc., 590
Report, 590
Animal(s):
Boarding Establishments Act, 516
Bill, 264, 451, 453, 482, 489, 490, 597
Breeding Research Organisation, 527, 782, 1049
Control of Intensified Methods of Food Production Bill, 39
Cruel Poisons Act, 287
Bill, 8, 225, 228, 262
Diseases:
Handbook of orders, 1059
Return of proceedings, 87, 305, 533, 789, 1060
Surveys report, 785, 1054
Experiments on:
Departmental Committee, 1130
living animals, 136, 356, 594, 855, 1129
Feeding anti-biotics, 298
Health:
A Centenary, 1054
services, 87, 305, 789, 1060
Physiology Institute, 298, 782
Restriction of Importation Act, 771
Bill, 706, 743
Welfare of, 1037
ANNAN, N. G. (Chairman), Teaching of Russian, 328
Annotations to Acts, 187, 409, 649, 915, 1177
Annual:
Abstract of Statistics, 96, 314, 544, 1070
nettle, 783
statement of trade, 105, 321, 552, 807, 1077
ANSON, SIR W. (Chairman):
Employment of prisoners, 137, 596
Organisation of work for prisoners, 856
Antarctic:
Fauna & flora conservation, 1036
lichens, 794
pelagic whaling*, 281, 585, 838
Treaty, 115, 1036
Anti-:
biotics in:
animal feeding, 298
milk, 531
cyclones over Scandinavia, 162
locust Research Centre, 1159
oxidants in food, 333
static precautions. Hospitals, 353, 1126
swine fever vaccine to Phillipines, 1203
Antigua:
Report, 547, 1074
St. Kitts etc. Constitutional proposals, 1074
Visas. Uruguay*, 585

Antiques. Export licences, 1191
Antiquities:
Early Chinese. Handbook, 795
Later Saxon period. Catalogue, 794
Roman Britain. Guide, 795
Ants indoors, 784
Anvers Islands. Petrology, 318

Ao Stars. Distribution, 393

Aphididae of West Africa, 95
Aphids:
Apple, 783
Cabbage, 1052
Currant & gooseberry, 81
Lettuce, 1052
Plum, 1051
Walker, Francis, 95
Woolly, 81
Appearance of bridges, 931
Apple(s):
aphids, 783
blossom weevil, 300, 1051
brown rot & blossom wilt, 1051
cider. See Cider
powdery mildew, 81, 1052
Apples & pears:
commercial varieties, 82
Pollination of, 82
rootstock, 300
scab, 300
APPLETON SIR E. V. (Chairman), Scottish peat, 299
Appliances. Repair vouchers*, 569, 751
Applied:
biology. Certificates, 565
science. Notes, 164, 397, 641, 907
Application of:
sprays to fruit trees, 82
water to machine undercutting etc., 171
Apprenticeship training in engineering, 877
Appropriations:
Account Abstract, 140
Acts, 67, 287, 516, 771, 1039
of Land. Circular, 142
Approved schools etc.:
Directory, 136, 1128
Statistics, 596, 857, 1130
Appuldurcombe House. Guide, 899
Apsley House:
Guide. 959
Paintings, 1222
APTED, M. R., Aberdour Castle, 221

Arable crops & grass, 1058
Arbitration. Controversy. Chile*, 1092
Arbour Low. Guide, 633
Archaeology:
Field, 884
in Aden Protectorates, 888
reports, 389

ARCHANGELSKY, S.:
Eocene ginkgoales, 1068
Mesozoic flora, 541
ARCHER, M., Natural history drawings in India Office Library, 320
ARCHIBALD, E. H. H., Travellers by sea, 380
Architect (Careers), 611
Architectural physics. Lighting, 637
Archives, National Register of, 134, 354, 394, 1127
Are you good at cycling? 393
Areas of:
great landscape value (Eastland). Circular, 399
Special Scientific Interest Bill, 744
Argentina(line):
Air service*, 116, 1092
Cereals*, 824
Consolidation of debts*, 115
Cultural Convention, 115, 567
Islands. Petrology, 794
Loan*, 567
Military service*, 823
Argyll:
Census:
Leaflet. Population etc., 590
Report, 590
County Council:
Arinagour & Craignure Piers etc.
Act, 69
Bill, 41
Soulnaig Pier etc. Act, 289
Bill, 43
Educational Trust Scheme, 400
Armed Forces:
Bill, 1014
Housing Loan Act, 1039
Bill, 967, 1009
Memorandum, 1201
Armed Trespass Bill, 1009
Armillaria root rot, 82
ARMITAGE, A. (Chairman), Pay of postmen, 937
Armour:
European, 1222
Japanese, 1168
Arms (Colonial Office), 100, 316, 547, 802, 1073
Army:
Allowance Regulations, 218–9, 220, 439, 690, 809, 1079
and Air Force Act, 67
Bill, 6, 39, 40
Select Committee. Special Report, 140
Appropriation Account, 219, 439, 690, 809, 1079
Cadet Force regulations, 220, 691, 1079
Careers. Opening for boys, 368, 612
Catering Corps, 220
Department. Publications, 809–12, 1079–81

Army (continued):
See also War Office
Emergency Reserve regulations, 219, 439, 690, 809, 1079
Estimates, 26, 201, 219, 426, 439, 442, 464, 690, 809
Handbook. Practical radiography, 690
health. Manual, 1080
List, 219, 439, 690, 809, 1079
medical services, 353
Orders, 219, 439–40, 690, 809–10, 1080
Special, 220, 441, 692, 811–2, 1081
Pay Warrant, 219, 440, 691, 810, 1080, 1081
Pensions. Warrant, 219, 440, 692, 810, 1080
Queens Regulations, 219–20, 440–1, 691, 810–1, 1080
Reserve(s):
Act, 287
Bill, 42, 226, 261
Estimates Committee. Special report 141, 359
Regulations, 220, 441, 691, 811
Re-organisation, 1081
Territorial. Regulations, 220, 441, 691–2, 811, 1080–1
Votes, 205, 426, 675, 940, 1205
Art(s):
Ancient near-eastern, 93
and:
amenities in Scotland, 33, 138, 1006, 1131
design:
Careers, 152, 875
Post diploma studies, 822
Antique & Byzantine, 689
Christian & Byzantine, 439
Council, 88, 306, 535, 1061
Diplomas & Certificates, 114, 824
Examinations. Question papers, 113, 327, 564, 821
Export of works of, 203, 282, 673, 939, 1203
Government & the, 939
Housing the, 88
Indian. Guide, 689
Medieval. Early, 795
Museum. Teaching in, 218
Noveau & Alphonse Mucha, 689
Policy for the, 1089
Secondary Schools, 911
Sale of Works of, 941
Arthritis & Rheumatism, 688
Articles. Imported & exported, 105, 321, 552, 807, 1077
Artificial insemination of poultry, 530, 1053
Ascension Island, U.S.A.*, 1120
Ascertainment of maladjusted children, 911

ASHLEY, J., Magnetic survey of N.E. Trinity Peninsular, 318
Asilidae, 796
ASLAN, N. A., Cleoninae etc., 541
Aspirated psychrometer readings, 377, 884
Asplenium. Ceylon species, 1067
Assay:
of stronsium 90 in bone, 160, 376–7, 619, 893, 1154
Office Act, 289
Assessment of:
disablement, 1162
new building products, 1167
Associated Society of Locomotive Engineers. Inquiry, 1149
Assur-Nasir-Apil II Sculptures, 310
Astronomical:
discussions on interstellar structure, 903
Ephemeris, 71, 291, 319, 888, 1169
results, 176
Astronomy & magnetism. Greenwich Observations, 176, 392

Athaliini, 301
Athyrioid ferns of Ceylon, 310
ATKINS, H. J. B. (Chairman), Treatment of acute poisoning, 352
ATKINSON, R. D'E., Mirror transit circle axis, 176
ATKINSON-WILLES, G. L., Wildfowl in Great Birtain, 625
Atlantic:
salmon. Ross-shire, 528, 782
Undersea Test Centre*, 585
Atlantide, 808
Atmosphere:
diffusion equations, 1156
turbulence. Aircraft, 535
Atom, 213, 434, 682, 953, 1218
Atomic:
Energy:
of. See United Kingdom
Atomic Energy Authority
Co-operation*, 124, 568, 584, 841, 843, 845, 1092, 1118, 1119, 1120
NATO Co-operation*, 839, 1113
physics. Handbook of conduction, 637
terms. Glossary, 214, 433, 1219

Auctioneer & estate agent (Careers), 875
Audio-visual aids in higher scientific education, 1091
Audley End. Pictures, 900
Auroral Observatories. Halley Bay, 539, 794
Australasian timber beetles, 543
Australia(n):
Agricultural Company Act, 289
Air tankers*, 504
Cereals*, 824
Commonwealth Development & its financing, 550

Australia(n) (continued):
Customs arrangements Aircraft*, 306
Nauru*, 1113
Space Vehicle Launchers*, 843, 1117
Austria:
Consular Convention, 116, 823
Extradition Treaty, 568
Judgments. Convention, 116, 329
Authority Code (UKAEA), 213
Automatic:
data processing, 178, 394
keying device. Ships Radio, 895
Auxiliary Fire Service, 814
Aveling & Porter traction engine. Print, 1080
AVERY, B. W., Soil around Aylesbury., 782
Avian leucosis complex, 1052
Aviation:
Flight Guide, 89
kerosene & gasoline, 308
law. Private pilots' licence, 88, 535, 790
Ministry of:
Contracts:
Guided weapons, 861
Pricing, 792, 1064
Examination papers, 90, 307–8, 536, 792, 1064
Notification to, of tall buildings etc., 602
Publications 88–92, 306–9, 535–9, 790–3, 1061–5
Specifications. See D.T.D.
safety, 306
See also Civil Aviation
Avoiding losses in calf rearing, 784, 1053

Award(s):
for first degree etc. courses, 326, 328, 564, 566, 820
for good design in housing, 361, 601, 864, 1138
of costs at statutory inquiries, 882, 1139, 1223
AWRE Reports, 1216–8

Aylesbury & Hemel Hempstead. Soils, 782
Ayr. Census:
Leaflet. Population etc., 590
Report, 850

Azores. Transit facilities. Portugal*, 123

B

B-type stars, 177, 636, 1170
Baby's first year, 689
Babylonian:
legend of Flood, 309
tablets, 93, 310, 540, 795, 1066
Talmud, 95

BAC— *INDEX 1961-5*

Bacillariophyceae, 788
Backing of Warrants (Republic of Ireland)
Act, 1039
Bill, 710, 963, 964, 1006, 1009, 1131
Bacon:
cut into slices, 86
to U.K. market, 788
Bacteria. Industrial, National collection,
1181
Bahama Islands (Constitution) Act, 516
Bill, 456, 490
Bahamas:
Atlantic Undersea Test Centre, U.S.A.*,
585
Constitutional Conference, 549
flag, 803
meetings. Communique, 568
Public Officers*, 889
reports, 100, 548, 1074
Royal Instructions OIC, 899
Bahrain Notices, 116, 329, 568, 824, 1092–3
BAILEY, D. M., Greek & Roman pottery
lamps, 540
BAILEY, E. B., Geology of Ben Nevis etc.,
130
Bailey (Malta) Ltd. report, 547
BAIN, N. W., Steam tables, 906
Bairds & Scottish Steel Ltd. etc. Security
holdings, 672
BAKER, HON. MR. JUSTICE (Chairman)
Mechanical recording of court proceed-
ings, 1154
BAKER, E. B. H. (Chairman), Inter-library
co-operation, 327
Bakeries. Safety in use of machinery, 375
Baking:
Careers, 875
Wages Council. Scotland, 618
Balance of payments, 206, 427, 545, 799,
1071
Balarus amphitrite, 542
Balers. Pick-up, 303
BALL, D. F., Soils around Bangor etc., 527
BALL, H. W., Sandstone of Brown Clee
Hill, 94
BALL, P. W., Petrorhagia, 796
Ball (or Roller) Bearings. Merchandise
Marks, 191, 515, 663
Balmer Line intensities of stars, 636
Banbury & Edge Hill. Geology, 1124
Banff. Census:
Leaflet. Population etc., 590
Report, 590
Bangor & Beaumaris. Soils etc. around, 527
Bank of England. Report, 200, 422, 671,
936, 1201
Bankers' Returns. London Gazette 186,
408, 915
Banking:
and Stock Exchange (Careers), 612
system. British, 871

Bankruptcy:
and Companies (Winding-up) Proceed-
ings. Account, 188, 652, 1181
General Annual report, 188, 410, 652,
916, 1182
BANKS, SIR J., Supplementary letters, 312,
1066
Banqueting House, Whitehall. Guides, 900
BANWELL, SIR H. (Chairman), Contracts for
building & civil engineering work, 901
Baptismal Registers Measure, 70, 97
Barbados:
Flora, 1159
High Altitude Research Project*, 547
Instructions OIC, 174
Letters Patent OIC, 174
Public Officers*, 549
Reports, 100, 548, 1074
Barbizon School, 1221
Barbus (Pisces, Cyprindae), 312, 1069
Barclays Bank D.C.O. Act, 1041
Barclodiad y Gawres chambered cairn, 902
Bark form etc. in birch, 639
BARKER, D.:
British aid to developing nations, 870
Commonwealth we live in, 104, 806
Swaziland, 1074
Barley:
Eyespot, 1052
High-moisture Silos, 1049
BARLOW, N., Darwin's ornithological notes,
543
Barn:
feed record, 785
hay drying, 303
BARNES, D. C. (Chairman), Selection &
training of supervisors, 374
BARNETT, R. D.:
Masterpieces of ancient near eastern art,
93
Panjabi printed books, 93
Saurashtra books, 93
Sculptures of Assur-Nasir etc., 310
Baroteseland agreement, 805
Barristers (Qualification for Office) Act, 67
Bill, 6, 41
Barrow:
Ironworks Ltd. Stock, 672
Steel Works Ltd. Securities, 202
BARRY, HON. MR. JUSTICE (Chairman),
Treatment of offenders, 357
Barry Corporation Act, 774
Basement complex of Neny Fjord, 539
Basic electricity, 535
Basilewsky situla, 689
Basutoland:
Constitution OIC, 632, 899, 1166
Constitutional:
Commission report, 793
Conference, 802
Council Publication, 793

Basutoland (*continued*):
Electoral provisions OIC, 899
National Council (Extension) OIC, 899
Order OIC, 1166
Photoposter, 365
Picture sets, 147
Public Service Commission OIC, 389,
899
Reports, 320, 548, 803, 1074
Resident Commissioner, OIC, 632
Royal Instructions, OIC, 632, 899
BATE, R. H., Middle Jurassic ostracoda,
542, 797
BATE, S. C. C., Impact loading on concrete
beams, 395
Bath:
Alteration of area, 604
Corporation Act, 518
BATHE, B. W.:
British small craft, 1170
Ship models, 903, 904
Bats of West Africa, 1067
Battle:
of Normandy, 313
Physical training, 810
Bauxite etc., 381
BAWDEN, F. C. (Chairman), Technical
assistance from Britain in agriculture, etc.,
889
BAWN, C. E. H. (Chairman), National
Chemical Laboratory. Report, 1180

B.B.C. *See* British Broadcasting Corporation

B.E.A. *See* British European Airways
BEACHAM, A. (Chairman), Depopulation in
mid-Wales, 865
Bean(s):
Agricultural Bulletin, 302
Dwarf & climbing, 82
thrips, 81
Bearings, Ball or roller. Merchandise Marks,
191, 515, 663
Beaumaris Castle. Souvenir, 221
Beauty culture (Careers), 369
Bechuanaland:
Additional Instructions OIC, 899
Constitutional proposals, 802
Double taxation. Sweden*, 345
Instructions to High Commissioner OIC,
173
Photoposter, 147
Reports, 320, 551, 805, 1074
Royal Instructions OIC, 632, 1166
BECKETT, R. B., John Constable's corres-
pondence, 354
BECKWITH, J.:
Basilewsky situla, 689
Veroli casket, 439
Bed cleaning service. Hospital, 1125

—BEN

Bedding plants, 784
Bedford:
Corporation Act, 774
Northampton & North Bucks. Study,
1141
Bedfordshire:
and Luton. Police area amalgamation,
1130
Census:
Leaflet. Population, 589
Occupation Groups, 1123
Report, 588
Saxton map, 93
Bedgebury pinetum. Guides, 348, 349
BEECHING report. Railways, 665
Beef:
Aids to management, 532
cattle & carcasses. Measurement, 1050
production, 1054
Beehives, 785
BEER, SIR G. DE, Darwin's notebooks, 94
Bees. Feeding, 530
Beeston Castle. Guide, 389
Beet:
Eelworm, 81, 1052
Mangels & Fodder, 300, 1052
See also Sugar Beet
Beetle:
Common furniture, 905
Death watch, 639
Domestic wood-boring, 95
Flea, 81, 783
House Longhorn, 640, 1180
Japanese, 1052
Lyctus Powder-Post, 639
Pine shoot, 348
Raspberry, 1052
Saw-toothed grain, 530, 1053
Timber. Australasian, 543
BELBIN, E., Training the adult worker, 907
Belgium:
British visitors' passports*, 116
Cereals*, 1093
Compensation for war injury*, 116
Consular Convention, 116, 1093
BELL, A. C., Blockade of Central Empires,
1914–18, 186
Bembridge Pier & Harbour Act, 518
Bill, 453, 454, 489
Ben Nevis & Glen Coe. Geology, 130
BENEDICT, B., Indians in a plural society,
409
Benefices (Suspension of Presentation)
Measure, 1042, 1071
BENNETT, N., Spectroscopic binaries,
393, 636
BENSON, R. B.:
Athaliini, 311
Holarctic sawflies, 311

BEN— *INDEX 1961-5*

Bentley Car print, 1170
Benue Valley. Geology, 1159
BENZIAN, B., Nurtition problems, 1121
Berkshire:
and Bucks. County Council Act, 69
Census:
Leaflet. Population etc., 589
Occupation groups, 1123
Report, 848
Berlin:
Documents, 119
Meaning of, 365
Bermuda:
Canadian forces*, 806
Letters Patent OIC, 388
Reports, 317, 803
Space Vehicle Tracking Station*, 126,
515
Berwick Census:
Leaflet. Population etc., 590
Report, 850
Berwickshire Educational Trust Scheme,
182
Beryllium, Determination, 640
Bespoke tailoring (Careers), 368
Bessel functions. Tables, 397
BESSEY, G. S. (Chairman), Training of youth
leaders, 328
Betio Island. Weather station*, 347
BETTENSON, A. S. (Chairman), Cotton
industry, 153
Better opportunities in technical education,
112
Betting:
and Gaming Act. Permits & licenses,
135, 355, 460
Duties Act, 516
Bill, 232, 233, 264, 600
Gaming & Lotteries Acts, 516, 771
Bills, 232, 233, 264, 600, 706, 707,
735, 741, 743, 745, 858
Permits & licenses, 854, 982
Levy Act, 67
Bill, 1, 2, 40
Beupre, Old. Castle. Guide, 1167
BEVAN, D., Pine shoot beetles, 348
Beware firedamp, 170
BEYDOUN, Z. R., Stratigraphy of eastern
Aden, 1159

BHATTACHARYYA, S. K., British mites, 543

Biblionidae, 1067
Bibliography of:
cuneiform tablets, 794
farm building research, 1049
Bideford Harbour Provisional Order Act,
774
Bill, 706, 744
BIGG, P. H., Metric values in scientific
papers, 906

BILHAM, E. G., Heavy falls of rain, 377
Bilingualism in education, 1088
Binders. (Farm machinery), 788
Bindweeds. Perennial, 784
Biology:
and medicine. Mathematics etc. in, 1154
Applied. Certificate, 565
Bionomics of:
fisheries resources. Atlantic, 549
lobster, 303
Birch, Bark form etc., 639
Bird(s):
and woodlands, 846
land, of Gaadacanal, 312
life in Royal parks, 389, 900
on airfields, 536
Rare, African, 312
Birkenhead Corporation (Mersey Tunnel
Approaches) Act, 1041
BIRLEY, A. R., Hadrian's wall, 633
Birmingham:
Alteration of area, 144
Corporation Acts, 69, 1041
Dipped headlights campaign, 642
See also West Midlands
Birthday Honours Lists, 187, 408, 649, 915,
1177
Birthplace & Nationality Tables. Census,
849
Births etc. Registrar General's Returns.
See Registrar General
Bishop's Palace, Kirkwall. Guide, 1166
Bituminous materials in road construction,
642
Bivalvia jurassic, 1068

BLACK, H. K., Authorised explosives, 136,
594
Black:
country. County boroughs, 364
currant. Varieties, 534
grass, 530
leg of potatoes, 81, 1051
Sea, Weather in, 622
Blackhead. Advisory leaflet, 783
BLACKIE, J. R., Auroral observations, 794
BLAXTER, J. H. S., Herring rearing, 299
BLEDISOE, VISCOUNT (Chairman), Salmon
& freshwater fisheries Committee, 87
Blind, Workshops for, 374
Blockade of Central Empires 1914–18, 96
BLOOD, SIR G. (Chairman), Malta Consti-
tutional Conference, 103
Blood-grouping of reagents*, 824, 1093
Blood transfusion services. Hospital, 132,
352
Blossom end of apples, 1051
Blow flies, 796
BLUMHARDT, J. F., Pashto Mss, 1066
BLUNDELL, D. J., Palaeomagnetic investiga-
tions, 539

B.O.A.C. *See* British Overseas Airways
Corporation
Board of:
Inquiry. Prime Minister. Security, 1206
Trade. *See* Trade, Board of
Boarding school for maladjusted children,
1088
BOGLE, D. B. (Chairman): Award of costs
at statutory inquiries, 882
Bognor Regis inquiry, 1142
Bohemian glass, 1221
Boiler(s):
Domestic. Chimney design, 1178
Explosions Acts:
Inquiries, 196, 418, 665, 931, 1182
Working of, 420, 669, 934, 1196
house & steam plants. Hospitals, 353,
852, 1126
BOLTON, W., Poultry nutrition, 531
Bolton. Provisional Order Act, 518
Bill, 450, 488
Bombyliidae, 1068
BOND, M. F., Manuscripts H.L., 447
Bonded warehouses, 106, 321, 552, 808,
1078
Book(s):
and titles to Yugoslavia*, 127, 348, 585,
845, 1121
English. Illustration, 1066
Exhibition:
Science Museum, 636
Shakespeare, 796
Fifteenth century, 309, 540
Georgian etc. 309
Hebrew, 795
in Science Museum, 177
Modern. Subject Index, 310
on chemical & allied industries, 177
Panjabi, 93
Saurashtra, 93
Shakespeare, 796
Short title catalogue, 540, 1066
Syriac, 309
Use of, 822
Bookbindings:
Grolier, 1065
Illustrated book, 439
BOON, G. C., Segontium Roman Fort, 390,
1167
Boot & shoe manufacture. Careers, 368
BORCHSENIUS, N. S., Disaspididae, 541
Border Forest Park. Guide, 127, 349
Borneo, North. *See* North Borneo
Borrowing (Control & Guarantees) Act.
Advances, 1201
Borstal:
training. Prediction methods, 1130
Work & vocational training, 996
BOSANQUET, C. I. C. (Chairman), Agricul-
tural graduates, 855
Boscobel House. Guide, 1166

—BRI

BOSSARD & ALLEN cases. Prime Minister's
inquiry, 1206
Botany bulletins, 93, 310, 541, 796, 1067
Botryopteris antiqua, 311
Bottom fishing. North Kenya, 1074
Boundary Commission for England. Report,
486
BOURDILLON, H. T. (Chairman), Standards
in public library service, 328
Bovine contagious abortion. (Brucellosis),
300
BOWDEN, J., Bombyliidae, 1068
BOWERS, A. B., Histological changes in
gonad, 80
Boxing Bill, 228
BOYNTON, L. O. J., Appuldurcombe House,
899
Boys:
and girls, Good posture, 958
Physical training, 691, 810

BP Refinery (Kwinana) Act, 518

BRACEWELL, S., Bauxite etc., 381
Brachiopod:
genus cyctothyris, 311
suborder chonetoidea, 313
BRADFIELD, G., Elasticity measurements in
metals, 907
Bradford:
Alteration of area. Map, 866
Corporation (Conditioning House) Act,
518
BRADLEY, J. D., Microlepidoptera, 94, 311,
1070
BRADSHAW, P., Turbulence measurements,
641
BRAILSFORD, J. W., Hod Hill, 310
BRAIN, LORD (Chairman), Drug addiction,
132, 1125
BRAMBELL, F. W. R. (Chairman), Welfare of
animals, 1037
BRAND, M. (Chairman), Pottery industry,
613
BRAZIER, J. D., Identification of hardwoods,
278
Brazil:
Loan*, 116, 1093
Military service*, 116
Bread & Flour:
Prices, 1156
Regulations, 531
Brecknockshire. Saxton map, 1066
Breconshire. Census. Report, 588
Brent Cross Crane accident, 1031
Brewers' grains, 300
Bricklaying in cold weather, 1166
Bricks:
Heat insulating etc. Merchandise Marks,
191

Bricks (*continued*):
Selection of clay building, 1179
Brickwork etc., Strength of, 1178
Bridge(s):
Appearance, 931
Deck systems tests, 638
Highway:
Rubber bearings, 667
Working stresses, 197, 667
BRIDGER, J. P., Downs herring, 85
BRIDGES, RT. HON. LORD (Chairman):
Royal Fine Art Commission, 137, 566
Security at National Gallery, 275
Training in public administration, 651
BRIGGS, J., Airflow around model of Gibraltar, 622
Brighouse:
Proposed county district. Map, 867
Provisional Order Act, 289
Bill, 229, 262
Brighter Prospect. Arts Council Report, 306
Brighton Skydeck Act, 1041
Bristol:
Corporation Act, 69
County borough. Alteration of area, 604
Britain(s):
and:
education in Commonwealth, 871
European Communities, 422, 871
Colonial achievement, 318
Economy. Fifty facts, 365
in brief, 147, 608, 870
Official Handbook, 147, 365, 608, 869, 1143
See also British *and Specific Subjects*
British:
aid to developing Nations, 870
Airports Authority loan, 1201
and Foreign State Papers, 116, 329, 568, 1093
Antarctic:
Survey, 539, 794
Territory:
Arms, 802
Gazetteer, 340, 836
Instructions OIC, 388
See also Falkland Islands
banking system, 871
books & films into Yugoslavia*, 127, 348, 585, 845, 1121
Broadcasting Corporation:
Licence, 170, 515, 895
Reports & accounts, 170, 384, 615, 895, 1162
Royal Charter, 170, 384, 515, 895
caenozoic fossils, 541
claimants under Anglo-Egyptian financial agreement, 329
Commonwealth. *See* Commonwealth
Council. Reports, 92, 309, 539, 794, 1065
British (*continued*):
dairy herd:
Brucellosis, 785
disease, wastage & husbandry, 785
drawings. Catalogue, 93
European Airways Corporation:
Advances, 89, 307, 536, 790, 1061
Loans, 200, 422, 671, 936, 1201
Reports & accounts, 88, 306, 535, 790, 1062
Report (Private edition), 92, 309, 539, 794, 1065
Film:
Fund Agency. Annual report, 188, 410, 597, 916, 1182
Institute Report, 1065
Foreign Policy:
Documents, 117, 570, 1095
Fact & quotation, 148
in second world war, 313
Guiana:
Conference, 551
Disturbances. Commission, 318
Election report, 1074
Financial position, 802
Independence Conference, 284, 1038
Instructions OIC, 174
Loans, 202
Reports, 100, 317, 548
Technical assistance USA*, 845
Honduras:
Constitutional Conference, 549
Photoposter, 147
Reports, 548, 1074
Royal Instructions OIC, 899
Visas*, 580
Imperial Calendar, 186, 407, 671, 936, 1201
Indian Ocean Territory, Royal Instructions OIC, 1166
inventions, 608
livestock breeding, 531
mammals. Identification, 797
marine cretaceous ostracoda, 1068
mesozoic fossils, 310
Museum:
Acts, 287, 516
Bills, 227, 261, 263, 449, 451, 452, 468, 482, 488, 490
Calendars, 95, 539, 794, 1067
General information, 310
Guide, 93, 309
Publications, 93, 309–10, 539–40, 794–6, 1065–7
Quarterly, 93, 309, 539, 794, 1065
Museum (Natural History):
Bulletins, 93–5, 310–2, 541–3, 796–7, 1067–9
Exhibition Galleries, 95, 313
Expedition to Nepal, 1068
Historical Series, 94, 312, 543

British (*continued*):
Museum (Natural History) (*continued*):
Publications, 93–5, 310–3, 541–3, 796–8, 1067–70
Scientific research at, 313
national hive, 82
Nationality:
Acts, 771, 1039
Bills, 490, 700, 741, 972, 1006, 1010, 1131
Forms, 355
No. 2 Act, 771
Bill, 704, 743
North America Act, 771
Bill, 707, 744
Overseas Airways Corporation:
Advances, 89, 307, 536, 790, 1061
Annual report, 89, 306, 535, 790, 1062
Financial problems, 536
Loans, 200, 422, 671, 936, 1201
Select committee, 792, 1135
overseas territories. Double taxation*, 117
palaeozoic fossils, 796
parliament. Reference pamphlet, 148, 366, 1144
pewter, 218
Phosphate Commissioners, 104, 320, 551, 805, 1076
pseudococcidae, 311
Railways:
Acts, 518, 774, 1041
Board:
Court of inquiry, 1031
Loans, 670, 675, 676, 941, 942, 1206, 1207
Reports, 726, 1198
Experience with diesel & electric traction, 196
Fares. London, 666, 935, 936, 1200
Re-shaping, 665
Select committee, 141
See also Railways
rainfall, 620, 883
Regional Geology, 129, 1124
seaweeds, 95
small craft, 1170
Solomon Islands:
Report, 317, 548, 1074
Royal Instructions OIC, 899
system of taxation, 365, 1144
Transport:
Commission:
Acts, 69, 289
Accounts, 115, 418, 666, 932
Loans, 205–6, 427
Order Confirmation:
Act, 69
Bill, 41
No. 2 Act, 69
Bill, 41
British (*continued*):
Transport Commission (*continued*):
Passenger charges scheme, 199, 421
Report, 24, 247, 665
Docks:
Act, 774
Board:
Loans, 675, 942, 1207
Report, 931, 1198
Virgin Islands:
Arms, 100
Reports, 317, 1074
Waterways:
Acts, 518, 1041
Board:
Annual Reports, 931, 1198
Loans, 675, 942, 1207
Publications, 798, 1070
Order Confirmation Act, 1041
Bill, 1012
Wool Marketing Scheme. Complaints, 299
Brittle fracture. Steel, 291, 819
BRITTON, E. B., Wood-boring beetles, 95
Broadcasting:
(Advertising Contracts) Bill, 744
Committee on, 281, 384, 385
House of Commons proceedings, 1135–6
in Wales, 358
organisations. Protection of performers. Convention, 329
services in Great Britain, 871
Standing Committee Debate, 38
stations. European*, 1093
BROCKMAN, J. ST. L., Family allowances etc. Law, 165
Broilers. Production, 82, 1052
Bronchitis. Scottish Health Services Council Report, 646
BROOKE, E. M., Patients in mental hospitals, 589
BROOKS, A. C., Thomson's gazelle, 101
BROTHERSTON, J. H. F. (Chairman), Experimental nurses training, 646
BROTHWELL, D. R., Digging up bones, 543
BROWN, D. S., Gastropod mollusca, 1068
BROWN, H. P. (Chairman), Pay etc. London Transport drivers, 617, 881
BROWN, R. A.:
History of King's Works, 633
Orford Castle, 900
BROWN, W. M. C., Sex chromosome complement, 883
Brown:
rot etc. of apples, 1051
trout, 528, 782
Brownhills. Proposed county district, 145
BRS. *See* Building Research Station
Brucellosis, 300, 785, 1051

BRUNDRETT, SIR F. (Chairman), Technical assistance for overseas geology & mining, 889
Brunei, State of:
Medals, 672
Report, 317
BRUNTON, J. S. (Chairman), Linkage of secondary & further education, 646
Brunton report, 735, 858
Brussels nomenclature, Classification:
Chemicals, 105, 321, 807, 1077
Opinions, 807, 1078
Brussels sprouts, 83, 300, 1052
Brussels treaty*, 329
BRYAN, J., Applying wood preservatives, 179
BRYDEN, W. J. (Chairman), Treatment of offenders, 402
Bryocorinae, 311
BUCHANAN, C.:
Traffic in towns, 670
Circular, 864
Whitehall plan (Traffic), 1168
Buchenavia etc., 541
Buckinghamshire:
Census:
Leaflet. Population etc., 589
Occupation groups etc., 1123
Report, 848
North. Northampton, Bedford, Study, 1141
Budget:
Financial statement, 203, 424, 673, 939, 1204
Supplementary, 941
Buganda & Bunyoro dispute, 319
Bugs. African mealey, 796
Building(s):
and civil engineering:
Careers, 612
maintenance. Hospitals, 1125
organisation & practice, 901
works. Contracts, 390, 901
Bulletins. Education, 112, 326, 564, 820, 1088
Components in shipyards, 634
Control:
Bill, 1008, 1014
Circular, 864, 1167
Educational. *See* Education
Engineering & allied industries. Craft courses, 645
Farm. *See* Farm
for:
hospital service, 133
pigs, 1049
potatoes, 85
poultry, 1049
Historic. *See* Historic buildings
in London area. Qualitative study, 905
Building(s) (*continued*):
Industrial. *See* Industrial Building
Industrialised (Education), 820
management Handbooks, 1167
materials. Thermal effects, 399
National Certificates etc., 114
over 300 ft. Notification to Ministry of Aviation, 602
plant & equipment. Maintenance. Hospital, 853
Principles of Modern, 180, 1180
products. New, 1167
Proofing of, against Rats and Mice, 1061
Public. Access for disabled, 1222
Regulations:
Advisory committee, 900
Guide, 1168
Research:
and information services, 900
Report, 178, 394, 637, 904, 1178
Station:
Digests, 178, 394–5, 637, 904, 1178–9
Index, 394, 904, 1178
Publications, 178, 394–5, 637–8
Technical statement, 486
Schools. *See* Schools. Building
Science Abstracts, 178, 395, 638, 904–5, 1179
Scotland Act 1959, Buildings standards regulation, 131, 644, 861, 909, 910, 1171
Societies:
Act, 287
Bill, 227, 228, 262, 360
Lloyds' Permanent Building Society affairs, 128, 350
Advances, 143, 604, 866, 1139
Chief Registrar's report, 128, 350, 588, 848, 1122
Consolidation of certain enactments, 376
Forms, 127
standards. Regulations. Scotland, 131, 644, 861, 909, 910, 1171
studies. National, 179–80, 395, 638, 905, 1179
Tall & industrial emissions, 1139, 1222
Temporary, of pole construction, 86
Wind effects, 1180
Winter, 634, 1139, 1222
Built-up felt roofs, 178
Bulb:
and corm production, 83, 785
scale mite, 301
Bulgarian Property accounts, 200, 422, 671, 939, 1201
Bulk storage of petroleum gas, 1152
Bull pen, 1058
Bullfinch, 81
BULLOCK, A. L. C. (Chairman), Demand for teachers, 1089

BUNNETT, R. J. A., Spofforth Castle, 1167
BURD, A. C., Herring of North Sea, 303
Bureau of:
the Census, U.S.A., 688
Intelligence, U.S.A., 688
International Commerce, U.S.A., 688
Standards, U.S.A., 688
BURGESS, G. H. O., Fish smoking, 643
Burgh Police Amendment (Scotland) Act, 771
Bill, 701, 742
Code of modified provisions, 1171
Burial:
and Cremation Bill, 233
of Offenders Bill, 42
Burma:
Air transport*, 1093
Reconquest of, 1070
Supply of cotton yarns*, 568
Burnham Committee reports, 113, 114, 565–6
BURNS, SIR A., Fiji, 548
BURNS, K. N., Fluorosis in cattle, 785
BURNS, T., Child care service, 645
Burry Inlet Cockle Fishery Order. Select committee, 979
BURTON, M. A., Calcareous sponges, 543
Burton-on-Trent Order. Select committee, 861
Bus services:
in Highlands, 196
Rural, 199, 1200
Bush fruits, 1054
Bushy Park. Trees, 634
Business:
Monitor. Production Series, 191–4, 410–1, 652–9, 916–24, 1182–90
Studies:
Award of certificates, 114
Higher award, 821
BUTCHER, R. W., Smaller algae, 304
Bute:
Census:
Leaflet. Population etc., 590
Report, 850
Educational Trust Scheme, 182
BUTLER, H. E., Measurements of stars, 177
BUTLER, J. R. M., Grand strategy, 798
BUTLER, P. M., Mammals, 1068
BUTLER, R., British Foreign Policy, 117
BUTLER, RT. HON. R. A. (Chairman):
Central Africa Conference, 543
Nyasaland Constitutional Conference, 313
Butt rots of conifers, 349, 1121
Buzzard, Common, 82

Byelaws, Model. *See* Model Bylaws
Byssinosis. Flax & hemp workers (National Insurance), 1161

C

Cabbage(s):
aphid, 1052
brussels, sprouts etc., 83
Caterpillars, 300
root fly, 300
Spring, 530
Summer & autumn, 82
Cabinet:
Office Publications, 95–6, 313, 798, 1070
Papers. List, 901
Cabinets. English, 959
Cable and:
cords. Colour code. Hospitals, 353
Wireless Ltd. Report & accounts, 170, 384, 629, 895, 1163
Caddis-flies. New African, 311
Cadet Force regulations:
Army, 220, 691, 1079
Combined, 219, 440, 691, 1080
CADMAN, W. A., Shelterbelts for farms, 586
Caenozoic fossils, 541
Caernarvon Castle. Guide, 221
Caernarvonshire:
Census. Report, 588
Saxton map, 540
West. Ancient Monuments, 902
CAIRNS, HON. MR. JUSTICE (Chairman), Civil aircraft accidents, 90
Caithness. Census. Report & leaflet, 590
Calcereous sponges, 543
Calder Hall, 213
Calendars. *See specific subjects*
Calf (Calves):
Housing, 1059
Rearing. Avoiding losses, 784, 1053
tetany, 301
Calibration of temperature measuring instruments, 907
Calliptamus serville, 541
Calluna heathland afforestation, 586
Cambodia. Diplomatic exchanges, 1093
Cambrian Colliery explosion, 1164
Cambridge, University of, & Agricultural Research Council Publication, 439
Cambridgeshire:
Census:
Leaflet. Population etc., 589
Report, 848
Saxton map, 93
CAMERON, HON. LORD (Chairman):
Bus services in Highlands, 196
Highland transport, 670
Land use in Highlands, 782
National Union of Bank Employees. Complaint, 618
Cameroon (Cameroun):
Commercial co-operation*, 508
Cultural co-operation*, 568, 824

CAM-CIV | 1961-5

Cameroon (Cameroun) (*continued*):
  Gift of camps, 202
  under U.K. administration, 100
  See also Northern Cameroons
CAMPBELL B.:
  Birds & woodlands, 846
  Crested tit, 1121
CAMPBELL, R. H., Linen manufacture, 914
CAMPBELL, R. N., Brown trout, 528
Camping & education, 113
Camps. Gift to Cameroun Republic, 202
Canada(ian):
  army in first World War, 623
  cereals*, 824
  Commonwealth development & Financing, 103
  Department of:
    Northern Affairs, 112
    Transport (Meteorology), 112, 417
  Dominion Bureau of Statistics, 112, 564, 820
  forces in Bermuda*, 806
  Official Handbook, 112, 564, 820
  Social security*, 320
  U.K. Housing Mission, 634
  wildlife, 112
  Yearbook, 112, 564, 820
Candalides, 796
Cane fruits, 302
Canned meat. Food standards, 304
Canton Island. Space vehicle tracking station*, 126
Cantref of Lleyn, 902
C.A.P. Civil aircraft accidents, 89, 306–7, 535–6, 791, 1062–3
Capacitors etc. at radio frequencies, 164
Capercalzie, 1121
Capillary watering of plants, 1059
Capital gains. Taxation, 1206
Capparidacae, 1077
Car parking facilities. Hospital, 850
Caradocian brachiopod faunas, 542
Caravan:
  Fire hazards, 905
  parks, 360, 361
  Sites:
    Circular, 1138
    No. 2 Bill, 1009
Carbon:
  monoxide poisoning, 1152
  tetrachloride etc. Precautions, 533
Card rooms, Dust in, 153
Cardiff:
  Corporation Act, 69
  County Borough. Alteration of boundary. Map, 605
Cardiganshire:
  Census. Report, 588
  Saxton map, 1066
Cardowan Colliery. Explosion, 171
Care of elderly in Scotland, 482, 597
Careers:
  Choice of, Series, 151–2, 368–9, 611–2, 874–5, 1146–7
  Guidance in schools, 1088
  Guide, 368, 611, 874, 1146
  Leaflets, 151
  Wallsheets, 151
Caribbean Organisation. Establishment*, 330
  See also East Caribbean
Carlton House Terrace, Future of, 105
Carmarthenshire:
  Census Report, 588
  Saxton map, 1066
Carnations under glass, 83
Carnets, 116, 569, 825
Carpets (Careers), 369
Carriage by Air:
  Act, 67
    Bill, 3, 33, 39, 137
  International Convention, 120, 757
  Supplementary Provisions Act, 287
    Bill, 229, 246, 255, 260
Carriage of:
  dangerous goods etc. in ships, 199, 418, 931, 1190
  goods by:
    rail, 278, 330, 666, 667, 841–2, 1115
      Convention, 196
    Road:
      Act, 1039
        Bill, 973, 1006, 1009, 1131
      Convention, 838
  passengers by rail. Convention, 278, 666, 841–2, 1115
Carriers' licensing. Report, 1198
Carrot(s):
  fly, 81
  parsnips & parsley. Weed control, 301, 1052
CARRUTHERS, J. F. S., Glues in joints, 395
Cars. *See* Motor vehicles
CARSON, R. A. G., Coins of Roman Empire, 540
CARTER, H., Tonal system of Northern Rhodesian plateau Tonga, 317
CARTER, W. (Chairman), Criminal Injuries Compensation Board, 1128
Cartulary of:
  Missenden Abbey, 354
  Tutbury Priory, 354
Case commentary on Income Tax Acts, 148, 366, 609, 871
CASEMENT, SIR R., Bill, 40
Castleford. Proposed county district. Map, 867
Casualty(ies):
  and accident departments. Hospital, 130
  Evacuation of, 356
Catalogues. *See specific subjects*

Catering:
  Clean. Handbook, 591
  department. Hospital, 352, 591, 1125
  Hospital, 353, 403
  industry. Management (Careers), 151, 874
Caterpillars. Cabbage, 300
Cathedrals Measure, 519, 545
Catherine McCaig's Trust Scheme, 401, 645
Cattle:
  diseases, 786
  Fluorosis, 785, 1054
  Grass tetany, 301
  grids for roads, 304
  Mastitis, 783, 1052
  of Britain, 83, 531
Cauliflower(s):
  and related crops, 1054
  mosaic, 1052
Causes of delinquency etc. Studies, 137, 596
Caustic soda immersion cleaning, 82
CAYLEY, SIR G., Aeronautics, 393
Cayman Islands:
  Instructions OIC, 389
  Report, 101

Celery:
  fly, 1051
  Leaf spot, 529
Cellular plastics for building, 637
Celyphidae, 1068
Cement in commonwealth, 551
Census 1961:
  England & Wales:
    Age, Marital condition. Tables, 849
    Birthplace & nationality tables, 849
    Commonwealth immigrants in conurbations, 1122
    County reports, 588, 848–9
    Housing:
      National summary tables, 849
      tables, 1122
    Migration. National summary tables, 1123
    Occupation:
      and industry. National summary tables, 1123
      Industry etc. Groups, 1123
    Place names. Index, 1122
    Population, dwellings households, 351, 588–9
    Preliminary report, 128
    Usual residence, 849
    Welsh speaking population, 351
  Scientific & technical qualifications, 351
  Scotland:
    County Reports, 590, 850
    Housing. National summary tables, 850
    Local housing indices, 1123
    Occupation & industry, 1124
Census 1961 (*continued*):
  Scotland (*continued*):
    Population:
      age by marital condition, 850
      dwellings, households, 352, 590
    Preliminary report, 129
    Usual residence, 1123
  Why? 129
Census of:
  distribution, 663, 928
  production, 191–4, 415, 663, 928
    Guide to official sources, 151
Cento. Status*, 330, 569
Central:
  Advisory Water Committee, 361, 601
  After-care Association, 135, 357, 595, 1130
  Africa(n):
    Conference, 543
    Office, 313, 543
    Power Corporation loan, 937
    Public officers*, 805
  Electricity Generating Board, 171, 385, 629, 895, 1163
  government of:
    Britain, 366, 871, 1144
    U.K., 148
  Health Services Council:
    Advisory Committees, 352, 591, 1125
    Reports, 132, 133, 248, 352, 591, 593, 851, 853, 1127
    Scottish, 131, 132, 406, 591, 647, 851, 913, 1125, 1175
  Office of Information. *See* Information
  organisation for defence, 553
  Scotland. Programme, 659
  sterile supply. Hospitals, 133, 403, 1125
  Statistical Office, 96, 313–4, 544–5, 798–9, 1070–1
  Training Council Report, 1146
  Transport Consultative Committee, 196, 418, 665, 931, 1198
  Treaty Organisation*, 330, 569
  Youth Employment Executive. Working party, 1146
Cephalopod "Beaks", 542
Cereal(s):
  Deficiency Payments Scheme, 84, 1054
  diseases, 302
  Exchanges of notes etc. *See respective countries*
  Marketing Act, 1039
    Bill, 746, 967, 1006, 1010, 1131
  pests, 1054
  root eelworm, 82
  Stem eelworm on, 529, 783
  take-all, 1052
Cerebral infarction, 161
Ceremonial:
  House of Commons, 137
  War Office, 440

Certificate(s):
  courses in Scottish schools, 1172
  National. *See* National *& specific subjects*
  of:
    air worthiness*, 330
    competency examinations, 171, 387, 631, 897, 1165
    Secondary Education, 113, 327, 566, 822, 1089
Ceylon species of asplenium, 1067

Chaetotaxy of legs in gamasina, 542
Chairs. English, 1222
Chaldaean Kings. Chronicle, 310
CHALFONT, LORD, Disarmament. Text of speeches, 1095
Chalicotheres. East African, 1068
Chalk downland afforestation, 348
CHALLENOR, DET.-SGT., Report, 1130
CHAMBERLAIN, Y. M., Marine algae, 1067
CHAMBERS, J. D., Laxton guide, 788
CHANCELLOR, R. J., Water weeds, 302
Chancellor of Exchequer. Complaint concerning speech, 1134
Chancery Masters practice form, 1153
Chancery of Lancaster Rules. S.I. report, 140
CHANDLER, M. E. J.:
  Flora of Hampshire etc., 94, 797
  Lower tertiary floras, 95
  Osmundites Doukevi Carruthers, 1068
  Post-ypresian plant remains, 94
Change & response. Schools Council, 1090
Changing pattern of economic activity in Gambian village, 651
Channel Islands. Passports*:
  Belgium, 116
  Denmark, 117
  Finland, 118
  France, 118
  Germany, 119
  Greece, 119
  Iceland, 120
  Luxembourg, 121
  Monaco, 122
  Norway, 122
  Spain, 124
  Sweden, 345
  Switzerland, 125
  Turkey, 346
Channel Tunnel:
  Geological survey*, 836
  Proposals for fixed link, 667
Channels:
  and pipes. Hydraulic design, 640
  open. Flow measurement, 640
Chapel Street Congregational Church (Southport), Burial Ground Act, 774
Charaxes. African, 541, 796
Charcoal wood, 348
CHARD, J. R. S., Roe deer, 846
CHARIG, A. J., Gastropod genus Thatcheria, 541
Charity Commissioners. Reports, 97, 259, 485, 856, 1130
CHARLTON, J., Marlborough House, 390
CHARTERS, H., Fires in state forests, 127
Charts for:
  contracts, 1167
  hydraulic design of channels, 640
Chateau de Douvres (Dover Castle) Guide, 389
Chattel Mortgages Bill, 1013
CHATWIN, C. P.:
  East Anglia etc. Geology, 129
  Hampshire basin etc. Geology, 129
Chebyshev series for mathematical functions, 397
Cheese. Food standards, 304
Cheesemaking. Starters, 1052
CHEESMAN'S, MISS L. E., Expedition to New Guinea, 310
Cheilostomatous Polyzoa Neoeuthyris Woosteri, 797
Chelsea Hospital Accounts, 220, 692, 811, 1081
Cheltenham. Proposed new county borough, 604
Chemical(s):
  and allied industries. Books, 177
  classification, 105, 321, 807, 1077
  control of weeds in forest, 1122
  engineering. Certificate, 328
  for the gardener, 531, 1054
  laboratories. Safety measures, 906
  Toxic, 87, 1050
  weed control in:
    carrots etc., 301, 1053
    forest, 1122
    horticultural crops, 301, 1053
    onions & leeks, 301
Chemistry of complex cyanides, 906
Cherries:
  and:
    pear slugworm, 300
    plums. Agriculture Bulletin ,83
  Polination, 82 530
  Pruning 81
Chert specimens. Fractured, 94
CHESHAM, LORD (Chairman), Control of motor rallies, 931
Cheshire:
  Brine Pumping Act, 774
  Census:
    Leaflet. Population etc., 589
    Report, 848
  Saxton map, 795
CHETTLE, G. H., Hampton Court guide:
  English edition, 1167
  German edition, 390
Chichester Rural District Council Act, 774

Chick(ens):
  Broilers Production, 82, 1052
  cocidiosis, 529, 1051
  embryo development chart, 84
  rearing:
    Agricultural Bulletin, 785
    for egg production, 530, 1052
  table, 1054
Chickweed. Common, 784
Chief Registrar of Friendly Societies. Report, 128, 350, 587–8, 848, 1122
Child(s):
  care:
    Scottish, 401, 645, 911, 1172
    service at work, 645
  the family & the young offender, 1128
  guidance medical services, 406
  Special Allowance. Decisions, 166
  welfare services, 958
CHILDE, V. G., Ancient monuments. Scotland, 221
Children(s):
  and Young Persons:
    Act, 516
      Bill, 232, 233, 448, 454, 482, 488, 489, 597
    Scotland:
      Minutes, 858
      Report, 912
  Bureau U.S.A. Publication, 688
  Deaf. Survey, 565
  Department, 137, 857
    Staffing. Scotland, 647
  Gallery guide, 903
  Illness among. U.S. survey, 958
  in:
    Britain, 366, 1144
    Care, 355, 854, 856
  Maladjusted. *See* Maladjusted children
  Prevention of neglect, 646
  ward. Hospital, 852, 1126
Chile:
  Abolition of visas*, 116
  Arbitration*, 1092
Chilean species of eupsophus, 312
Chimney(s):
  design for domestic boilers, 1178
  heights, 601, 602, 865
  flues etc. Installation of appliances. Regulations, 910
Chinese:
  antiquities, 795
  periodicals in libraries, 1066
Chiropodist (Careers), 368
Choice of Careers, 151–2, 368–9, 611–2, 874–5, 1146–7
Choosing specifications for plastering, 904
CHOWN, S. M., Ageing & semi-skilled, 160
Christian & Byzantine art, 439
CHRISTIE, J. M., Provisional yield tables, 127
Chronic:
  respiratory infections of poultry, 1052
  sick, 913
Chronicles of Chaldean Kings, 310
Chronological Table of Statutes, 187, 409, 649, 915, 1177
Chrysanthemum(s):
  Bulletin, 83
  eelworm, 300
CHURCH, R., Royal parks of London, 1168
Church:
  Assembly:
    Measures, 70, 97, 290, 314, 519, 545, 775, 799–800, 1042, 1071
    Publications, 97, 314, 545, 799–800, 1071
  Commissioners Measures, 698, 775, 799, 800
  of England Convocation Bill, 975, 1014
Churchill Endowment Fund. Exchange of students. Denmark, 117, 1093
Churchwardens (Appointment & Resignation) Measure, 698, 775, 799
CHURMS, J., Proper Motions in declination for stars, 636

Cicadelline types, 1068
Cichlid fishes, 1069
Cider apple:
  orchard, 784
  Production, 302, 531
Cigarette(s):
  and tobacco etc. Monopolies Commission, 191
  cigar & pipe lighters. Merchandise Marks, 191
  Health Hazards Bill, 742
Cinema. Pre-history of, 903
Cinematograph(y):
  Careers, 875
  Film(s):
    Council, 194, 249, 476, 928, 1191
    Production (Special Loans) Acts, 188, 249, 257, 485, 823
  Fund. Account, 174, 389, 465, 632, 823, 1091
  See also Films
Circular saws. Merchandise Marks, 928
Citizen's guide to aircraft noise, 823
Citizenship of U.K. & colonies. Statistics, 596, 857, 1130
City of London:
  Courts Act, 774
  Various Powers Acts, 69, 289, 518, 1041
Civil:
  aerodromes & air navigational services, 89
  affairs & military government. N.W. Europe, 95
  aircraft accident(s):
    Investigation etc., 90

CIV—   INDEX 1961-5

Civil (continued):
aircraft accident(s) (continued):
Reports, 89, 306–7, 535–6, 791, 1062–3
See also Aircraft
Appropriation Accounts, 201, 422–3, 671, 936, 1202
aviation:
Act 1949 Orders, 89, 307, 536, 791, 1063
Careers, 875
Communications Handbook, 89, 536, 792
Customs Airport Orders, 89, 307, 536, 791, 1063
Euro control Act, 287
Bill, 9, 42
Hungary*, 119
International Convention, 116, 120, 330, 578
Offences etc. on aircraft. Convention, 825
See also Aviation
Contingencies Fund accounts, 201, 423, 671, 936, 1202,
Defence:
Ambulance & first aid, 135, 355, 356, 594
Care of homeless, 864
Corps deployment, 1128
Dispersal Circular, 361, 362
Films for training, 355, 854
General Training Bulletin, 355, 854
Handbooks, 135, 355, 594, 854, 1128
Headquarters Section:
Bulletin, 135, 136, 355
Notes, 135, 855
Syllabus, 355, 356, 594
Instructors' Notes, 135, 355, 594, 854–5
Medals, 202, 672
Message Forms. Cover, 595
Pocket Book, 135, 356, 1128
Rescue, 135, 355, 356, 855, 1128
Signals, 135, 355, 855
Syllabuses for local training, 356, 594
Training memorandum, 135, 356, 1128
W.V.S., 1938–63, 596
Warden Section, 356, 594, 855
Welfare, 594
Engineering contracting etc. (Careers), 613
See also Building & civil engineering
Estimates: 201–2, 247, 248, 423, 426, 485, 671–2, 937, 1202
Form of, 464, 598
Statement of Excesses, 675, 941, 1206
Vote on Account, 206, 428, 466, 942, 1207

Civil (continued):
liability for loss etc. Law, 619, 882
Proceedings (Registration of Change of Address) Bill, 744
science, Organisation, 637
Service:
Arbitration awards, 152–3, 369, 612–3, 875, 1147–8
Commission(ers):
Annual report, 316, 547, 802, 1073
Publications, 97–9, 314–6, 545–7, 801–2, 1071–3
Question papers, 97–9, 314–6, 545–7, 801–2, 1071–3
General, scientific & technical posts (Careers), 151, 874
Junior Posts (Careers), 151, 1147
List. See British Imperial Calendar
Pay Research Unit, 99, 547, 1073
Recruitment. Estimates Committee, 1133
remuneration, 202, 942
Scientific, Organisation of, 1205
shorthand tests, 423
Staff relations, 1206
Superannuation law, 1203
Typists:
Manual, 425
Tests, 202, 423, 672, 676, 925
War. Siegeworks, Newark-on-Trent, 902
Civilian industrial employees (Air Force) Regulations, 88, 535, 809, 1079

Clackmannan. Census:
Leaflet. Population etc. 590
Report, 850
CLARE, K. E.:
Road-making materials in Nigeria, 398
Vegetation on roads etc., 181, 642
CLARK, A. M.:
Ophiuroids, 1069
Starfishes, 341, 1118
CLARK, J. D., Fractured chert specimens, 94
CLARK, SIR W. L. G., Primates, 543, 1069
CLARKE, J. F. G., Microlepidoptera, 1069
CLARKE, M. R., Cephalopod "Beaks", 542
CLARKE, N. W. B.:
External loads in buried pipelines, 395
Pipe-laying principles, 905
CLARKE, R., Grime's Graves, 633
CLARK, SIR H., Identification of hard woods, 179
Clasp, Story of, 112
Classics. Teaching. Schools, 183
Classification.:
Brussels Nomenclature:
chemicals, 105, 321, 807, 1077
goods, 1095
opinions, 807, 1078
proprietary preparations, 132, 1125

Classification (continued):
of heavy falls of rain, 377
Statistical, for goods, 106, 322, 553, 808, 10/8
Classified:
geological photographs, 640
roads, 248, 464
Classifying individuals, 1131
CLAY, H. M., How research can help training, 907
CLAY, T.:
Actornithophilus ferris, 310
Mallophaga, 94
Clay building bricks. Selection, 1179
CLAYE, SIR A. (Chairman), Prematurity, 132
CLAYTON, G. A., Turkey breeding, 302
Clean:
Air Act:
Chimney heights, 601, 602, 865
Circulars, 142, 143, 361, 362, 601, 865, 1138, 1139
Grant arrangements, 1139, 1222
Tall buildings, 1139, 1222
See also specific subjects. Smoke control areas etc.
air policy & domestic fuel supplies, 603
catering. Handbook, 591
Clearance of Z Zones by road. Civil Defence, 135, 1128
CLENSHAW, C. W., Chebyshev series, 397
Cleonemae, 541
Clergy:
Ministration to non-resident Electors Measure, 775, 799
Ordination & Miscellaneous Provisions Measure, 775, 799, 800
Pensions Measure, 70, 97
Clerical, Medical & General Life Assurance Act, 69
Clients' Money Accounts Bill, 1009
Clinical dosimetry, 688
Clinics. Local Health Authority, 353
Clitheroe & Nelson. Geology, 129
CLM reports, 213–4, 435, 683, 953, 1218
Cloche cultivation, 300, 1052
Close Rolls. Calendar, 634
Clothing:
Industry Development Council (Dissolution) Account, 189, 257, 480, 925
manufacture (Careers), 152
Cloud types for observers, 377
Cloud, Benn Network on, 300
CLUBE, S. V. M., Photometry of cluster, 1169
Clube. General mixed (Education Build-ing), 112
Clusters, 176, 393, 1169
and stellar evolution, 903
Clyde:
Navigation:
Orders Confirmation Acts, 69, 518, 1041

Clyde (continued):
Navigation (continued):
Bills, 488, 746
Superannuation Order Confirmation Bill, 1014
Port Authority Order Confirmation Bill, 1013
Clytha Estate. Transfer to National Trust, 518
Clywedog Reservoir Joint Authority Act,

Coal:
and other Mines. Regulations:
First aid, 387
Managers & officials, 173, 387, 631
Mechanics & electricians, 173, 1165
and Steel Community. See European Coal & Steel Community
Board. See National Coal Board
Consumers' Council.
Northern Irish Interests Act, 287
Bill, 42, 228, 255, 261, 358
See also Domestic & Industrial Coal Consumers' Councils
Industry:
Acts, 68, 516, 1039
Bills, 9, 42, 232, 258, 260, 264, 976, 1013
Finances, 1164
Nationalisation Act:
Accounts. 171, 385, 629, 896, 1202
Loans, 630, 937, 1203
Mines:
Law, 897
Safety. Regulations, 173, 387, 631, 897, 1165
Mining:
Areas. Surface development, 143
Industry:
Careers, 152
Difference. National Union of Mineworkers etc., 881
Coast erosion & defence, 179
Coastal preservation & development, 602
Coatbridge Burgh Extension Order Confirmation Act, 1041
Bill, 1011
Cobalt, 381
COBBOLD, RT. HON. LORD (Chairman), Commission of Inquiry. North Borneo & Sarawak, 319
Coccidea, 1068
Coccidosis in chickens, 529, 1051
Coccinellidae, 541
COCKRAM, J. (Chairman), Water charges, 601
Cockroaches, 300, 1052
COCKROFT, SIR J. (Chairman), Protection against ionizing radiations, 883

COD—   INDEX 1961-5

Cod. Larvae, 528
Code of practice for:
protection of persons against radiations, 177, 851, 875
safe use etc. for electronic equipment, 683
Codex Siniaticus & Codex Alexandrinus, 540
Codling moth, 300, 783
COE, R. L. Syrphidae, 796
Coffee:
in Britain (World's coffee), 657
International agreement, 330, 341, 1093
COHEN, LORD, OF BIRKENHEAD (Chairman).
Classification of proprietary preparations, 132
Communications between doctors, nurses & patients, 591
Health education, 851
Safety of drugs, 591
Coins:
English, 795
Roman, 540, 1066
Viking, 1067
COLBY, R., Waterloo despatch, 1222
Cold water services. Design bulletin, 1139
COLDSTREAM, SIR W. (Chairman):
Post-diploma studies. Art & design, 822
Vocational courses in college etc., 328
COLE, S.:
Neolithic revolution, 95, 543
Races of man, 543, 1070
COLERAINE, RT. HON. LORD (Chairman):
Employment & training of young people, 158
COLES, R., Small poultry flock, 786
Collection of:
acorns, 586
cones, 586
Collective:
Contracts of Employment Bill, 1009
passports. European*, 825
Collectors. Instructions for, 312, 543, 1069
Colleges:
of Education:
Falkirk & Ayr, 911
Teaching staff salaries, 1090
Rating Relief (Oxford & Cambridge) Bill, 742
Colliery explosions, 171, 385, 1164
Collisions at sea. Regulations, 669
Colombia. Abolition of visas*, 116
Colombo Plan:
Consultative Committee. Annual report, 202, 423, 551, 704, 1075
Reference Pamphlet, 871
Technical co-operation under, 188, 410, 652, 889, 1159
Thailand*, 583
Colonial:
and Dominions Offices. Records, 901

Colonial (continued):
Development:
and Welfare Acts.
Accounts. Loans, 100, 316, 547, 802, 1076
Return of schemes, 100, 317, 547, 803, 1074
Corporation report & accounts, 100, 102, 317, 318, 547, 552, 806
Loans Act, 287
Bill, 229, 245, 255, 261
Statements of guarantee, 202, 423, 672, 937
Office.:
Confidential print to 1916, 1168
Digest of statistics, 318, 548, 803
List, 100, 317, 547, 803, 1074
Picture sets, 147
Publications, 100–3, 316–9, 547–9, 802–3, 1073–5
Quarterly digest of statistics, 100, 318
Records, 901
Reports, 100–1, 317, 320, 547–8, 551, 803, 1074
Research:
Review, 1940–60, 889
Reports, 317
Studies, 101, 317, 409, 651
Territories, 101, 317
Colour:
code of cables & cords. Hospitals, 353
in school buildings, 326
printing in Japan, 795
Colouring:
in factories, 178
matters (Food), 788
COLVIN, H.M.: Star Abbey, 634
Combine harvesters, 303
Command Papers, 43–66, 264–87, 491–515, 746–71, 1014–38
Commerce:
Higher education for, 912
rooms. Secondary schools, 1172
Commercial:
Court users' Conference, 376
glasshouses, 83, 785
horticulture. Advice to beginners, 300
pilots' Licences, 89
production of pot plants, 302
strawberry growing, 1050
subjects. Teaching, 402
varieties. Apples & pears, 82
Commissioned service. H.M. Forces (Careers), 368
Commissioners' decisions. See respective Acts
Committees. See specific subjects
Common:
buzzard, 82
chickweed, 784
European Language Bill, 261

Common (continued):
furniture beetle, 905
Insect pests, 543
Market in action, 423
scab of potatoes, 1051
water weeds, 302
Commons Registration Act, 1039
Bill, 710, 963, 966, 967, 974, 1006, 1010, 1012, 1131
Circular, 1153
Commonwealth:
Agricultural Bureaux:
Annual reports, 103, 319, 550, 803
Conference, 103
agriculture, 804
and sterling area. Statistics, 189, 411, 660, 925, 1191
Britain & education in, 871
cameo West Indies, 147
Centre. Photopacket, 365
Conference. Photopacket, 870
constitutional development, 147, 871
consultation & co-operation, 365, 871
consultations on European Economic Community, 104
Development:
Act, 516
Bill, 453, 490
Despatch, 548
and its financing, 103, 550, 804
Corporation Accounts & reports, 806, 993, 1076–7
Finance Company Act, 518
Economic Committee:
Annual report, 103, 319, 550, 803, 1075
Publications, 103–4, 319, 550–1, 803–4, 1075–6
economic development, 148
education:
Britain's contribution, 365
Conference, 327, 822
Liaison Committee, 104, 320, 551, 804, 1076
Foundation. Memo. Prime Minister's meeting, 1076
future of. Conference, 551
Immigrants:
Act, 288
Bill, 42, 227, 261, 262
Advisory Council, 596, 856, 1128
Control. Statistics, 554, 855, 1128
Instructions to immigration officers, 317, 356
in consultations. Census, 1122
See also Immigrants.
Immigration from, 1129
Income Taxes, 148, 366, 609, 877, 1144
Institute:
Photopacket, 609
Picture set, 147

Commonwealth (continued):
Language & communication, 1076
Leaflets, 147
links in education, 1143
Member nations. Wallsheet, 871
Merchant shipping*, 806
Modern, 365
parliamentarians. Photopacket, 365
Parliamentary goverment in, 148
Picture of, 147
Prime Ministers' meeting, 330, 806, 1076
Relations Office:
List, 104, 320, 551, 806, 1076
Publications, 104–5, 320, 551–2, 805–7, 1076–7
Scholarship:
Amendment Act, 516
Bill, 263, 448
and Fellowship Plan. 104, 320, 551, 804, 1076
Commission, 104, 320, 551, 805
Sciences in, Promotion of, 609
Scientific Committee, 320
Secretariat:
Bill, 976
Memo. Prime Ministers' meeting, 1076
Settlement Act, 288
Bill, 227, 243, 255, 261
Shipping Committee, 105, 320
stamp design, 1066
Survey, 147, 365, 608–9, 870, 1143–4
Survey Officers' Conference, 888
Telegraphs*, 629
today, 870, 1144
trade, 103, 319, 550, 804, 1075
Wallsheet. Member nations, 871
War Graves Commission:
Annual reports, 105, 320, 552, 807, 1077
Italian dues. Exemption*, 121, 578
we live in, 104, 806
What is the ?, 365
Communication(s):
between doctors, nurses & patients, 591
in industry, 618
Problem of, Conference, 394
Community:
care. Development of, 591, 851
development. British contribution, 366
facilities in new towns, 1139
Compaction:
of concrete road slabs, 398
plant, 181
Company(ies):
Act 1948. Investigations, 189, 660, 925, 1191
assets income & finance, 412, 660, 1191
Bill, 261
Floating Charges (Scotland) Act, 67
Bill, 6, 33, 39, 41, 138

COM— *INDEX 1961–5*

Company(ies) (continued):
General Annual report, 189, 411, 660, 925, 1191
investigations, 189, 660, 925, 1191
Law Committee, 189, 412
Profits. Income Tax, 872
Share Transfers Bill, 42
secretary. (Careers), 612
Compendium for exporters (EFTA), 190, 413, 660, 926, 1191
Compensation:
Appeals tribunals, 1139
for:
victims of:
crimes, 135, 855
National-Socialists*, 836
Nazis*, 825
war injury. Belgium*, 116
Complex cyanides. Chemistry, 906
Complex-stress creep etc. of metallic alloys, 396
Compositional quality of milk, 783
Composts. Seed & potting, 301
Compound fertilizers, 530
Comprehensive education. Circular, 1088, 1172
Compressive strength of pit-props, 1180
Compulsory
acquisitions of interest in land. Compensation, 141, 601
Purchase:
Act, 1039
Bill, 969, 971, 1013, 1136
by local authorities. Circular, 361
Computer(s):
in offices, 1152
Introducing, 1204
programming, International language, 792
Computing methods. Modern, 164
Concentrates. Feeding to cows, 1053
Conciliation Act 1896. Inquiry, 875
Concrete:
Aerated, 178
beams, 395
Flexural strength, 908
Granolithic etc., 904
Lightweight aggregate, 394, 637
Military engineering, 810
mix. Proportioning & control, 178
Natural aggregates. Shrinkage, 637
on farm & estate, 85
road, 1059
staved silos for barley, 1049
Steel corrosion, 1178
CONDE, B., Ruwenzori expedition, 95
Condensate systems. Hospitals, 592
Condensation of super heated steam. Conference, 640
Conditions:
favourable to faster growth, 623

Conditions (continued):
in steel foundries, 153
of work. Reference pamphlet, 148, 366, 1144
Conduct of mental nursing homes. Select Committee S.I., 257
Cones. Collection, 586
Conflict of law, 330, 844
Congo. Loan*, 1094
Coniferae etc., 391
Conifers:
Butt rots, 349, 1121
Decay, 1121
Group dying, 127
Pruning, 586
Thinnings, 348, 846
Consol. A radio aid to navigation, 1063
Consolidated Fund:
Abstract Accounts, 202, 423, 460, 713, 980
Act, 67, 287, 516, 771, 1039
Bill, 2, 261, 488, 741, 1009
Appropriation Bill, 42, 263, 490, 745, 1013
Loans from, 1205
No. 2 Act, 67, 288, 516, 771, 1039
Bill, 40, 261, 488, 742, 1010
Consolidation:
Bills reports, 141, 226, 228, 230, 233, 360, 600–1, 863, 965, 1136–7
of Enactments (Procedure) Act Memo., 141, 601
Consortium of Local Authorities Special Programme (CLASP), 112
CONSTABLE'S conduct, 354
Constabulary:
Report. Chief inspector, 136, 247, 595, 596, 857, 1130
Report. Inspector. Scotland, 184, 402, 646, 913, 1027
See also Police
Constitution (al):
development in Commonwealth, 147, 871
U.K. Selected quotations, 148
See also specific countries
Construction:
and handling of glasshouses, 83
industry:
Manpower study, 1152
N.E.D.C., 887
Training Board. Report, 1148
lifting operations etc. Regulations inquiry, 153
work. Safety, 375, 618
Consular:
conventions See respective countries
relations. Vienna Convention, 569
Consultation:
and co-operation in Commonwealth, 365
on educational matters, 400

Consumer:
Council:
Annual report, 807, 1077
Publications, 807, 1077
education. Information for, 1077
Protection:
Act, 67
Bill, 5, 33, 38, 40, 138
Committee. Final report, 413
Test Registration Bill, 260
Contact:
binaries, 176
insecticides, 906
Continental Shelf:
Act, 771
Bill, 456, 491, 702, 735, 742, 858
Convention, 839
Netherlands & Norway*, 1094
Report, 1163
Contracts:
for building & civil engineering work, 390, 901
Model Standing Orders, 865, 868
of:
Employment Act, 516
Bill, 264, 451, 454, 482, 489, 490, 597
insurance etc. Germany*, 119
Contribution to voluntary bodies. Circular, 865
Control of:
borrowing Order. General consent, 204, 939
hiring (Television sets) Licence, 661, 926
Immigration. Statistics, 594, 855, 1128
mites, 82
motor rallies, 931
noise, 397
Office de Industrial Development Act, 1039
Bill, 746, 969, 970, 971, 1006, 1010, 1012, 1131
Circular, 1139
public expenditure, 202
rats etc., 84, 530
Venereal Diseases Bill, 263
Control for Scotland. General Board of, 130, 402
Controlling dimensions for educational building, 820
Conveniences. Public, Hand-washing facilities, 1138
Convocation Bill, 975, 1014
Conway:
Castle. Guide, 222
Corporation Act, 1041
Co-operative(s):
farms etc. in Wales, 85, 303
overseas. Advisory Committee, 888
COOK, SIR J. (Chairman):
Pesticides, 789

Cook, Sir J. (Chairman) (continued):
Poisonous substances in agriculture etc., 789
COOK, P. L., Polyzoa, 797, 1069
Cookery. ABC of, 300
Cool stars, 903
COOPER, ASTRONAUT. Triumph of, 622
Copyright Convention, 825
Coral caryophyllia Smithii, 312
CORBET, G. B., Identification of British mammals, 797
Corm production, 83, 785
Cormorant. Distribution & food, 1050
Corn:
drills, 532
marigold, 784
Rents Act, 516
Bill, 450, 482, 487, 597
Sweet, 82, 1052
Cornwall & Isles of Scilly. Census:
Leaflet. Population etc, 589
Report, 848
Corona:
Library Series, 548, 1074
Periodical, 101, 317, 548
Corporal punishment. Correction, 136
Corporation:
of Trinity House of Leith Order Confirmation Bill, 1013
Tax, 1203
Correspondence:
Courses (Registration) Bill, 260
of Rev. J. Greene, 1127
Corrosion and its prevention at bimetallic contacts, 536
Cost(s):
and efficiency in milk production, 787
guidance for housing, 602
of:
hospital buildings, 133
Living Advisory Committee, 369
COSTA, M., Mites, 312
Costing:
and building procedures. Local authority, 353
of management etc. Local authority housing, 864, 869
COTTESLOE, LORD (Chairman), Works of art:
Export of, 203, 282, 939
Sale by Public bodies, 941
Cotton:
Centralised Buying Act. Accounts, 190, 660, 925
industry:
Assistance, 246
Committee, 153
spinning (Careers), 874
yarns:
Burma*, 568
Israel*, 1111

1961 pp 1–224, 1962 pp 225–445, 1963 pp 447–696, 1964 pp 697–962, 1965 pp 963–1226

24

INDEX 1961–5 **—COT**

1961 pp 1–224, 1962 pp 225–445, 1963 pp 447–696, 1964 pp 697–962, 1965 pp 963–1226

25

COU— *INDEX 1961–5*

Couch or twitch, 81, 300, 783
Council:
for Wales, 281, 495, 513
of:
After-care Association, 135, 357, 595, 1130
Europe:
Consultative Assembly, 117
Repair of appliances*, 569
Statute Amendment, 330, 569, 1030
Industrial Design. See Industrial Design
on:
Prices, production & incomes, 173
Tribunals 160, 278, 376, 619, 882, 1153
Countryside:
and Tourist Amenities (Scotland) Bill, 487, 491, 597
in 1970. Conference, 888
County:
Court(s):
Accounts, 163, 379, 622, 886, 1156
Jurisdiction Act, 516
Bill, 264, 448
Manual, 619
Reviews. Circular, 361
See also respective counties.
Course in elementary meteorology, 377
Court:
of:
Chancery of Lancaster (Amendment) Act, 67
Bill, 4, 34, 39, 138
Criminal Appeal. Interdepartmental Committee, 1130
Justice. European Communities. Rules, 330, 1094
Session. Scotland. Rules, 1077
Proceedings, Mechanical recording, 1154
COUSINS, A. W. J.:
E-Region zero-point programmes, 636
Northern & Southern photometric systems, 636
Photoelectric magnitudes & colours of Southern stars, 635
Standard magnitudes in E. Regions, 393
Three-colour photoelectric photometry, 176
Covent Garden Market:
Act, 67
Bill, 4, 5, 6, 40, 42, 138, 142
Authority:
Accounts, 460, 532, 787, 1058
Report, 532, 787, 1058
Coventry. Alteration of area. Map, 145
Cow(s):
cubicles, 782
Dairy feeding, 530, 785, 1053
Slatted floors, 1049

Cowdenbeath & Central Fife. Economic geology, 130
COX, E. S., British Railway's experience with diesel etc., 196
COX, L. R., Jurassic bivalvia, 1068
COX, P. J., Report of inquiry, 857
Coypu, 82, 784

C.P.M. explained, 904

CRADDOCK, J. M.:
Air temperatures over Northern Hemisphere, 885
Temperature anomalies, 378
Craft courses for building etc. industries, 645
CRAIG, C. N., Multi-storey flats design etc., 638
CRAIG, R. E., Undersea photography, 528
CRAIGIE, J. (Chairman), Consultation on educational matters, 400
Cranes. Lifting equipment, 178
CRANSTONE, B. A. L., Melanasia, 93
CRASTER, SIR J., Dunstanburgh Castle Point, 633
CRASTER, O. E.:
Llanthony Priory, 633
Tintern Abbey, 633
CRATHORNE, RT. HON. LORD (Chairman), Sunday Observance Law, 857
CRAWFORD, B. H., Photographic emulsions, 164
Cream, (Advisory Leaflet), 82
Credit-Sale Agreements (Scotland) Act, 67
Bill, 6, 34, 41, 138
Creditors of goods. Diligence (Law Reform), 882
CREED, SIR T. (Chairman), Salaries. Teachers, 113, 114, 327, 565
CREMER, H. W.:
Discharges on Thames estuary, 1181
Synthetic detergents, 146, 363, 607, 869
Crestaceous cribrimorph polyzoa, 311
Crested tit, 1121
CREW, F. A. E., N–W Europe. Medical services, 353
CRICK, W. F., (Chairman) Award in business studies, 821
Crime(s):
of violence. Compensation, 855
War against 1959–64, 857
Criminal:
Appeal:
Act, 771
Bill, 457, 697, 703, 735, 742, 858
Court of, 1130
Courts. Business of, 137
Evidence Act, 1039
Bill, 969, 1006, 1009, 1131
Injuries Compensation:
Bill, 488
Board Report, 1128

Criminal (continued):
Justice:
Acts, 67, 1039
Bills, 3, 4, 5, 34, 39, 41, 138, 746, 969, 1006, 1131
Notices, 356
Administration Act, 288
Bill, 8, 9, 43, 227, 255, 261, 358
Scotland Act, 516
Bill, 232, 264, 455, 482, 490, 597
Explanatory note, 646
Notices, 911
Supervision record cover, 402
Law:
Bill, 1014
Revision. Committee reports, 594, 855, 856, 1128
matters. Assistance between U.K. & German police*, 119
Procedure:
Attendance of Witnesses Act, 1039
Bill, 970, 972, 1006, 1009, 1011, 1012, 1131
Insanity:
Act, 771
Bill, 704, 744
Law Revision Committee, 594
Jurors, 855
Right of Reply Act, 771
Bill, 702, 735, 741, 858
Scotland Act, 1039
Bill, 973, 1010, 1132
proceedings Legal aid, 356, 595
Statistics:
England & Wales, 136, 356, 594, 855, 1128
Scotland, 184, 402, 646, 912, 1174
Criminals. Persistent, 596
Critical-depth flumes for flow measurement, 640
CROFT-MURRAY, E., British drawings. Catalogue, 93
Crofters:
Commission report, 79, 299, 532, 782, 1050
Scotland Act, 67
Bill, 6, 18, 34, 39, 41, 138,
Crofting counties. Census. Leaflet, 590
Cromarty. Census. Leaflet & Report, 590
CROMPTON, A. W., Skull of oligokyphus, 797
CROMWELL, OLIVER., Facsimile, 635
CROOKALL, R., Fossil plants, 906
Cropping. Protective, 83
Crops. See Farm, Field, Grain & Horticultural Crops
CROSS, HON. MR. JUSTICE (Chairman), Private International Law Committee, 619
Crossbills, 586
Crossings. Push button control. Directions, 420
CROSSKEY, R. W., Ameniianae, 1067

CROSSLEY, A. F., Extremes of wind shear, 622
Crown(s):
Agents. Publication, 1077
Estate:
Act, 67
Bill, 6, 39
Commissioners:
Abstract Accounts, 105, 320, 552, 807, 1077
Publications, 105, 320, 552, 807, 1077
Report, 105, 320, 552, 807, 1077
gall & leafy galls, 589
Jewels, 389
Nominate Account, 203, 424, 672, 938, 1203
Office buildings, 900
Proceedings Act. Solicitors, 424, 938
CROWTHER, SIR G. (Chairman), Traffic in towns, 670
CROWTHER, R. E.:
Double drum winch technique, 846
Extraction of conifer thinnings, 846
Felling & converting thinnings, 586
Crude Oil Terminals (Humber) Act, 1041
CRUDEN, S., Early Christian & Pictish monuments of Scotland, 900
Cruelty to Animals Act. Experiments on living animals return, 136, 356, 594, 855, 1129
Crustacea. John Murray expedition, 1069
Cryptostigmatid mites, 1069
Ctenophthalmus, 541
Ctenozamites cycadea, 94

Cucumbers. Imported raw, Merchandise Marks, 533
Culicine mosquitoes, 95, 1069
Culinary & medicinal herbs, 83
Culling laying hens, 530
Cultural agreements etc. See respective countries
Cumberland:
Census:
Leaflet. Population etc., 589
Report, 588
County Council Act, 774
Bill, 703
Saxton map, 540
Cuneiform:
tablets, 794
texts, 93, 310, 540, 795, 1066
CUNNINGHAM, SIR C. (Chairman), Vassall case, 284
Cupuladriidae, 1069
Curia Regis Rolls, 391
Currant:
and gooseberry aphids, 81
Red, 530

1961 pp 1–224, 1962 pp 225–445, 1963 pp 447–696, 1964 pp 697–962, 1965 pp 963–1226

26

INDEX 1961–5 **—CUR**

1961 pp 1–224, 1962 pp 225–445, 1963 pp 447–696, 1964 pp 697–962, 1965 pp 963–1226

27

CUR—   *INDEX 1961-5*

Currency:
and Bank Notes Act. Treasury Minutes, 203, 250, 424, 427, 485, 672–3, 712, 713, 938, 1003, 1203
difficulties. Forces in Europe*, 340
Current:
measuring by electrodes, 1058
medical research, 160, 376, 619, 883
Papers A.R.C., 72–5, 292–4, 520–4, 775–9, 1043–7
serials received by N.L.L., 1089
Curriculum Bulletin. Schools Council, 1090
CURRY, W. T.:
Home-grown softwoods, 1180
Working stresses for timber, 179
CURTIS, A. A., Mathematical tables, 906
CUSACK, R. V., Investigation into affairs of F.M.S. Rubber Planters Estates Ltd. etc., 925
CUSHING, D. H.:
Echo sounding for fisherman, 534
Herring in North Sea, 303
Custodial training for young offenders, 402
Customs:
Airports Orders, 89, 307, 536, 791, 1063
and Excise:
Commissioners' Reports 205, 553, 675, 808, 1078
Publications 105–6, 321–2, 552–3, 807–8, 1077–8
Tariff amendments 105, 321, 552, 807, 1078
Warehousing Manual 106, 552, 553, 807, 1078
Annuity & Benevolent Fund Act, 774
Civil aircraft. Australia*, 306
Conventions:
Carnets 116, 569, 825
Importation of:
goods for display 273, 569
professional equipment 272, 569
International transport of goods 825
Seafarers' welfare 1094
treatment of pallets 584
Co-operation Council:
Bulletin 320
Classification opinions 807, 1078
Duties:
Dumping & Subsidies Act 190, 412, 660, 925, 1191
Italy*, 1008
Forms 106, 321
Regulations & procedures 106
Tariff:
of European Communities 190, 412–3
Nomenclature, 1095
Treatment of pallets. Convention, 584
Cut flowers & foliage under glass, 786
Cuticular studies, 1067
Cutlery & silverware trades in Sheffield & district, 881

Cyanide:
in salmon & trout, 782
poisoning. Notice, 1153
Cycling:
Are you good at ?, 393
Skilful. Manual, 1170
Cygnus II association. Photometries, 1169
Cylinder seals, 310
Cyngor cymru a mynwy, 603
Cyprus:
Cereals*, 805
Establishment of Republic*, 117
New grain bins, 102
Report, 101
Treaty of guarantee, 117
Cysticercosis. Analysis, 160
Cytology etc. of leukaemias, 883

Czecho-Slovak(ia):
Inter-governmental debts*, 330, 569, 82;
Refugee Fund Account, 203, 424, 47e
823

D

Dahlias, 82
Dairy:
byelaws. Model, 131
cows. Feeding, 530, 875, 1053
economics, 531
goat-keeping, 300
herd, British. See British
Dairying:
aids to management, 787
Low cost, 1054
DALTON, O. M., Treasure of the Oxus, 795
Damp-proof course. Insertion, 1166
Damp-proofing solid floors, 1178
Damping off. Tomato, 1053
Dangerous:
Drugs Acts, 772, 1039
Bills, 701, 735, 741, 858, 964, 967, 1010, 1136
machines. Precautions needed, 881
Danials:
expedition to West Africa, 808
language guide 957
Science Press Ltd., 808
Danjon astrolabe, 1169
Darlington & Simpson Rolling Mills Ltd.
Stocks, 202
Darlington. Alteration of area Map, 605
Dartford Tunnel Acts, 69, 289
Dartmoor, New forests of 1121
Dartmouth Castle. Guide, 1167

INDEX 1961-5   **—DEF**

DARWIN'S:
notebooks. Transmutation of species, 94
ornithological notes, 543
type specimens of Balarus amphitrite, 542
Data sheets (Aviation), 792
DAVIES, HON. MR. JUSTICE (Chairman). Limitation of actions, 376
DAVIES, K. G., State papers, 634
DAVIS, G. R. C., Magna Carta, 540
DAVIS, I. T. M. (Chairman), Winter building, 634
DAVIS, R. A., Control of rats & mice, 84
DAVISON, C. ST.C. B., Historic books on machines, 636
DAY, F. E. F.:
Passenger-mileage by road, 398
Road improvement schemes, 180
DAWSON, W. R., Letters of Sir J Banks, 312
DAY, J. H., Polychaete fauna, 543
DAY, L. R., Books on chemical & allied industries, 177
DAY, W. R., Douglas fir plantations, 586
Day release report, 821
Daylight:
and sunlight. Planning for, 868
in buildings. Estimating, 637, 904
indicators, 865
Daylighting & space about houses. Regulations, 910

DE BEER, SIR G.:
Darwin's notebooks, 94
Evolution, 1069
DE FERRANTI, S. Z., Pioneer of electric power, 904
DE L'ISLE, RT. HON. VISCOUNT. Manuscripts, 354
DE LOTTO, G.:
African mealy bugs, 796
coccidae, 1066
pseudococcidae, 94
Dead Sea Scrolls. Exhibition guide, 1066
Deaf children. Survey, 565
Deal & Walmer Castles. Guide, 633
Dealers in securities, 191, 415, 663, 928, 1195
Dealfishes, 95
DEAN, W. T.:
Geology of Ordovician strata, 797
Lingle Ammonite zones, 94
Ordovician tribolite faunas, 311, 541, 542
Stile etc. in Lake District, 541
Tribolites of Caradoc series, 311
Dean & Wye Valley Forest Park. Guide, 586, 846
DEANS, E., Elementary school mathematics, 958
Death(s):
benefit. Decisions, 1160

Death(s) *(continued):*
grant. Decisions, 626
in fires, 1179
of pedunculate oak, 1121
Sudden, in infancy, 1127
Registrar General's Returns. *See* Registrar General
Death-watch beetle, 639
Debates. *See* House of Commons & House of Lords
Debts. Consolidation. Argentine*, 115
Decay in standing conifers, 1121
Deception Island. Geology, 101
Dechenellid trilobites, 1068
Decimal:
Coinage Bill, 43
Currency:
Bill, 1011
Inquiry, 675
Decisions of the Commissioner etc. *See* respective subjects
Deck sheathings for ships, 665
Decorations. *See* Honours
Deeds. Register of, (Scotland) Indexes, 185, 407, 648, 914, 1176
Deep:
litter system, 784
plan (race-track) ward units, 592
Deer Act: 516,
Bill, 452, 454, 473, 482, 487, 489
Deer. Roe, 846
D.E.F. specifications, 106–11, 322–6, 554–63, 812–8
Defence:
areas in West Indies*, 100
Central Organisation for, 553
Departments. Form of estimates, 860, 862
Estimates, 106, 326, 553, 812, 1081
Form of, 246, 251, 861
Statement, 326, 563, 820, 1088
Supplementary, 553, 820
Vote on Account, 206, 428, 466, 942, 1207
See also Air, Army, etc.
Guides, 106, 322, 553, 812, 1081–2
Lists, 106–7, 322, 554–63, 812, 1082
Ministry of:
Air Force Dept. Publications, 808–9, 1078–9
See also Air Force & Air Ministry
Appropriation Account, 106, 322, 486, 563, 1086
Army Dept. Publications, 809–12, 1079–81
See also Army
Estimates. *See* Defence Estimates
Navy Dept. Publications, 818–20, 1086–8
See also Admiralty

DEF—   *INDEX 1961-5*

Defence *(continued):*
Ministry of *(continued):*
Publications, 106–11, 322–6, 553–63, 808–20, 1078–88
Vote on Account, 206, 428, 466, 942, 1207
Publications. Index, 111, 326, 818, 1086
Report on, 111
Royal Ordnance Factories. *See* Royal Ordnance Factories
Specifications, 106–11, 322–6, 554, 812–8, 1082–6
Statement, 326, 563, 820, 1088
Transfer of Functions Act, 772
Bill, 487, 490, 491, 690, 742, 858
Deformities caused by thalidomide, 854
D.E.G. reports, (UKAEA), 214, 435, 683
Degrees of mental handicap, 182
Delinquency & treatment of offenders. Studies, 137, 596, 1130–1
Delinquent generation, 137
Delphacidae, 1068
Demand for:
agricultural graduates, 855
places in higher education, 564
Denbighshire (and Flintshire):
Census. Report, 588
Saxton Map, 795
Denmark:
Agriculture*, 569
Bacon. Supply*, 788
British visitors' passport*, 117
Cereals*, 1095
Churchill Endowment Fund. Student exchange, 117, 1093
Consular Convention, 330, 569
Double taxation*, 117, 331
"Red Crusader" incidents*, 117
Structural fire protection of ships*, 843
Student employees, 331
Trade & commerce*, 117
DENNING, RT. HON. LORD (Chairman):
Legal education for students, 159
Report, 674
Dental:
caries. Controlling, 851
Department. Hospital, 591
services. Estimates Committee, 359, 600
technicians. Manual of training, 691
Work. Hospital, 131
Dentistry (Careers), 875
Dentists' & Doctors' remuneration:
Review body, 1127
Royal Commission. Index, 175
De-population. mid-Wales, *See* Mid-Wales
Departmental records in P.R.O. Guide, 634
Dependencies. *See* United Kingdom Dependencies
Deputies & shot firers in coal mines, Books, 387
Derby. Alteration of area Map, 867

Derbyshire:
Census:
Leaflet. Population etc., 589
Report, 848
Prehistoric sites, 633
Saxton map, 540
D.E.R.E. booklet, 214
Deretrichia weise, 541
Dermatitis. Industrial, 375
Desert Locust Information Service*, 118
Design:
and:
appearance (Building), 904
development of weapons, 798
Bulletins (M.H.L.G.), 362, 601, 602, 603, 865, 1139
Centre Book, 147, 364
Magazine, 146, 364, 608, 869, 1143
National Diploma, 113, 327, 564, 821
of:
forms in goverment depts., 424
gutters, 637
roads, 197
roof-venting systems, 905
surface water sewerage Systems, 602
timber floors, 394
urban sewer systems, 398
See also Art & Design
Designing for old people, 362
Detection of underground explosions, 1218
Detergents. Synthetic, 146, 363, 607, 869
Determination of:
beryllium. Handbook, 640
uranium & thorium. Handbook, 641
Developing:
countries:
Aid, 671
Research assistance, 889
nations. Aid, 870
Development(s):
and:
Engineering Group. Reports (UKAEA), 214, 435, 683,
government action. Wales, 34, 138, 146, 358, 364, 607, 869
growth in Scotland, 910
Commissioners' report, 205, 675
Corporation reports, 145, 251, 363, 606, 868, 1141
Fund Accounts, 203, 424, 673, 938, 1203
in roofing, 904
near:
buildings of architectural interest, 602
railways, 602
of:
agriculture, 1058
community care, 591, 851
Inventions:
Act 1948–58 Accounts, 190, 413, 660, 925, 1191

INDEX 1961-5   **—DIS**

Development(s) *(continued):*
of *(continued):*
Act 1965, 1039
Bill, 969, 976, 1006, 1009, 1011, 1131
natural resources overseas. Assistance, 889
plans:
Circulars, 399, 1139, 1222
Future of, 1139
Maps, 865, 868
Projects. Education. Building, 564
DEVLIN, RT. HON. LORD, (Chairman) Port transport industry, 881, 1149
Devon:
Census:
Leaflet. Population etc., 589
Report, 848
County Council Acts, 69, 1041
Dewsbury. Proposed county borough. Map, 867
Diadem, H.M.S., Loan to Pakistan, 427
Diagnosis of:
mineral deficiencies in plants, 298
occupational diseases, 628, 1162
Dialkyld 311, 541
Diatom genus Capartogramma, 543
DICK, J. B., Space & water heating in local authority flats, 180
DICKENS, R J., year variables, 1169
DICKINSON, J. C., Furness Abbey, 1167
DICKSON, W., Trawl performance, 80
Die castings. Handbook, 440
Diesel:
and eletric traction. British Railways experience, 196
Fumes Bill, 260
Diet. Radioactivity in, 79
Dietetics etc., 1151, 1146
Dietitians etc. in National Health Service, 354
Differential curve growth analyses of stars, 903
DIGBY, A., Maya jades, 795
Digest of:
commentaries. Talmud, 95
statistics:
Monthly, 162, 378, 621–2, 885, 1156
See also specific subject
Digging up bones, 543
DILLON, L. S., Monochamini, 94
Dimensional co-ordination:
and industrialised building. Hospital, 832
in house building. Circular, 602
for:
Crown Office building, 900
industrialised building, 633, 900
Dimensions & components for housing, 603

Dining room. Hospitals, 133, 852
Dinosaurs 10'w, 95
Dinoicoterus blur., 93
DINWOODIE, J. M., Picea sitchensis Carr, 639
Diplomas. Protocol. Equivalence of, 1095
See also specific subjects
Diplomatic:
documents PRO, 901
Immunities:
Conferences with Commonwealth, Act, 67
Bill, 2
London Gazette, 187, 408
List. London, 839, 1112–3
Privileges, Act, 772
Bill, 703, 704, 735, 744, 858
relations Conventions, 126, 1095
Dipped headlights campaigns, 908
Birmingham, 642
Diptera from Nepal, 796, 1068
Dipterus Valenciennesi, 1068
Direct:
acting electric space-heaters, designation. Circular, 865
grant grammar schools. List, 821
Direction finding equipment, 1163
Directorate. *See specific subject*
Directory. *See specific subject*
DIRSH, V. M.:
Acridoidea, 94, 311, 541
Pneumoridae, 1067
Disabled:
Access to public buildings, 1222
persons in government employment, 203
Services for, 375
Disablement. Assesment of, 1162
Disarmament:
18-Nation Committee Conference:
Documents, 272, 329, 331, 570, 580, 825, 1095
Speech. Lord Chalfont, 1095
Discipline form. Police regulations, 1128
Discretionary payments to occupiers displaced, 602
Discrimination in education:
Protocol, 570
UNESCO Convention, 331, 347
Disease(s):
and pests. Horticulture, 303
in general practice, 351
Wastage & husbandry in British dairy herd, 785
See also respective subjects
Disinfection of poultry houses, 530, 1053
Disposal of:
old motor vechicles, 1138
surplus:
government land, 602
U.S. defence equipment, 326, 563, 818, 1021

DIS-EGG | 1961-5

Disputes. Settlement:
European Convention, 118, 331
Germany*, 837
Switzerland*, 1116
Distinguished Conduct Medal, 220
Distributing & generating electricity. Scotland, 138
Distribution of:
Ao stars, 393
coral Caryophyllia Smithii, 312
cormorant, 1050
German enemy property, 190, 413, 660, 926, 1191
moisture. Airfields, 398
rateable values, 603
District general hospital (Building notes), 133
Ditton & Covent Garden Laboratories reports, 298, 527, 782, 1049
Diving manual. U.S. Navy, 957
Divorce (Scotland) Act, 772
Bill, 697, 701, 707, 735, 743, 745, 858,
Dixon, H. B. F., Cysticercosis, 160

Dock:
foremen at Southampton, 875
workers' regulations, 159
Docks & sorrels, 300, 1051
Dockyards, H.M.:
Accounts, 71, 291, 520, 819, 1087
Estimates Committee, 250, 464
Doctor(s):
and dentists' remuneration:
Review body, 1127
Royal Commission. Index, 175
Family. Work of, 591
nurses & patients. Communication, 591
Documents on:
British foreign policy, 117, 570, 1095
German foreign policy, 117, 331, 826
Dog Racing (Betting Days) Act, 516
Bill, 450, 453, 488, 490
Dogs Bill, 709
Doig, A. T., Health of welders, 371
Dolley, M.:
Anglo-saxon pennies, 794
Viking coins, 1067
Dolls' houses, 218
Domestic:
Coal Consumers' Council reports, 172, 386, 630, 897, 1165
food consumption & expenditure, 85, 303, 532, 787, 1058
fuel supplies & clean air policy, 603
preservation of fruit & vegetables, 302
science & dietetics (Careers), 151, 1146
services. Hospital, 352, 591, 851, 1125
wood-boring beetles, 95
Domicile. Law of, 619
Dominica:
Arms, 316
Report, 317
Dominion Bureau of Statistics, Ottawa, Publications, 112, 564, 820
Dominions Office. Records, 901
Donaldson, G., Register of Privy Seal of Scotland, 648
Doncaster, J. P., Francis Walker's aphids, 95
Doncaster:
Alteration of area. Map, 867
Provisional Order Confirmation Act, 290
Bill, 229, 262
Done, J. T., Rhinitis of swine, 785
Donelly, H.H. (Chairman):
Appointment of teachers. Scotland, 400
Pensions for teachers' widows, 401
Donnington Castle. Guide, 900
Donnison, F. S. V., History of second World War. Civil affairs etc., 95
Donovan, Lord (Chairman), Court of Criminal Appeal, 1130
Dorset. Census. Leaflet & report, 588
Dorsetshire. Saxton map, 93
Double drum winch technique, 846
Double-lined spectroscopic binary, 176
Double-star observations, 176, 903
Double taxation:
agreements etc. *See respective countries*
relief tables, 872
Douglas fir:
home grown timbers, 905
plantations, 586
Dounreay experimental reactor establishment. Information booklet, 214
Dove Prion, 318
Dover:
Castle Guide. French edn., 389
Harbour Act, 518
Downing Street & Old Treasury Buildings Estimates Committee, 599, 862
Downs Herring. Fecundity & larval abundance, 85

Draft undertakings Secretary of State for Scotland, 79–80, 527, 782
See also Undertakings
Dragon flies of eastern Africa, 95
Drainage:
and:
river conservancy authorities. Return form 143, 603, 1139
sanitary appliances. Regulations, 910
for housing, 178
of the farm homestead, 788
Rates Acts, 288, 516
Bills, 229, 262, 449, 488
Dramatic art (Careers), 875
Draughtsmen's & Allied Technicians Association. Inquiry, 1149
Drawing offices. Layout & lighting, 394

Drawings:
Italian, 310
Natural history, 806
of Rembrandt, 310
Drepanidae, 94, 1067
Dress regulations for R.A.F. officers, 88
Dressmaking, etc. (Careers), 1146
Dried milk food standards Committee, 304
Drill book for emergency fire appliances & equipment, 594
Drilling machines. Fencing 618
Drills. Unit, for seeds, 1059
Drivers & conductors, London Transport, Pay & conditions, 617, 881
Droitwich, Geology of country around, 396
Drop forging hammers etc., 375
Dropmore Pinetum, 586
Drug(s):
addiction. Inter-Departmental Committee, 132, 1125
Advisory Board Bill, 487
Narcotic. Convention, 342, 1096
Prevention of Misuse Act, 772
Bill, 705, 735, 743, 744, 858
Saftey of, Report, 591, 1125
Drunkenness. Offences, 136, 357, 595, 856, 1129
Dry:
cleaning:
Careers, 874
plant. Precautions, 375
-lined interiors. Dwellings, 178
Rot:
Design of floors, 394
in buildings, 905
Drymadusa Stein, 94

D.S.I.R. *See* Scientific & Industrial Research

D.T.D.:
Lists, 92, 306, 309, 535, 790, 1062
Specifications, 90–2, 308–9, 537–9, 792–3, 1064–5

Dubai Notice, 117
Ducetia Stal, 94
Ducks:
and geese, 83
at a distance, 958
Dudley. Proposed county borough, 144
Duffy, E. A. J., Timber beetles, 543
Duffy, P., Committee of Privileges, 1134
Dumbarton. *See* Dunbartonshire
Dumfries:
Academy Endowments Trust Scheme, 182
Census:
Leaflet. Population etc., 590
Report, 850
Moat Hostel Scheme, 645, 912
Dumfriesshire. Educational Trust Scheme, 182, 400
Dunbartonshire (Dumbarton):
Census:
Leaflet. Population etc., 590
Report, 850
Council House Rents, 130
Educational Trust Scheme, 182, 400
Dundee:
Census. Leaflet & report, 590
Children's Home Trust Scheme, 400
Educational Trust Scheme, 911, 1172
High School Scheme, 401, 1173
Home for deaf children. Scheme, 1172
Hostel for deaf children. Scheme, 645
Orphanage Trust Scheme, 645
Rents of corporation houses, 644
Dunlop, J. (Chairman), Visiting patients in hospital, 406
Dunnett, Sir J.:
Nuclear power for ship propulsion, 933
Shipbuilding Advisory Committee, 199
Dunstanburgh Castle Point. Natural history 633
Durham:
Census:
Leaflet. Population, 589
Report, 588
County Council Act, 518
Markets Company Act, 1041
Prison. Ill treatment, 596
Saxton map, 795
University. Act, 519
Dust:
and fumes in factory atmospheres, 1152
control in potteries, 613
explosions in factories, 618
in card rooms, 153
prevention & suppression, 171
Duties of Local Authorities. Factories Act, 876

Dwarf & climbing beans, 82
Dwellings. Compulsory improvement of, 865
See also Houses

Dyrham Park, Transfer, 202
Dysaphis Borner. Revision, 533, 1059

E

Early:
Chinese antiquities, 795
Christian and:
Byzantine art, 439
Pictish Monuments, 900
Gothic illuminated Mss., 1066

Early (*continued*):
medieval art, 795
printers' marks, 439
type stars, 177
warning system, 1034
Earp, J. R., Geology of country around Clitheroe, 129
Earth temperatures, 378
East, O. G., Wright Brothers Memorial U.S.A., 958
East:
Africa(n):
Common Services Organisation, 101, 102, 316, 889
Economic & Fiscal Commission, 101
flora, 1077
oyster, 318
and Central Africa. Wild resources, 103
Anglia(n):
and Lincolnshire. Local Government Commission, 1140
British Regional Geology, 129
Rivers. Hydrological survey, 603
Carribean Territories. Federation:
Civil Service Commission, 498
Conference, 317
Fiscal Commissioner, 498
Proposals, 1075
Devon water (Re-grouping) Order, 701
Lothian. Census. Leaflet & report, 590
Midlands. General review area, 144, 145, 603
Nepal. Expedition, 1068
Suffolk. Census. *See* Suffolk
Sussex. Census. *See* Sussex
Eastern:
Aden Protectorate. Stratigraphy, 1159
entropôt, 889
Nigeria. Public officers*, 651
Easton, P. H.:
Herringbone parlour literature, 1049
Slatted floor systems for pigs. Literature, 1049
Eastop, V. F., Aphididae (Homoptera), 95

Ecclesiastical:
Committee Reports, 97, 314, 545, 800, 975, 1071
Fees Measure, 290, 314
Jurisdiction Measure, 519, 545
Echo sounding for fishermen, 534
Ecology of young stages of salmon, 782
Economic:
activity in a Gambia village, 651
Affairs. Department of, 1088
aspects of farming. Tanganyika, 548
co-operation & development. Convention, 331
development in Commonwealth, 148
Leaflet. B.M. (Nat. History), 312
plant diseases. Scotland, 81
Economic (*continued*):
potential of Leeward Islands, 651
report, 544, 798, 1070
Series:
Agriculture, 85
B.M. (Nat. History), 95, 543
situation:
Circular. Housing & Local Govt., 143
Prime Minister's Office, 898
statistics:
New contributions, 314, 799
Principal series, 1070
survey, 203, 424
trends, 96, 313–4, 544, 798, 1070
Economics of factory buildings, 395
Economy of Northern Ireland. Working party, 357
Ecuador. Abolition of visas*, 826

Edgell, Sir J., Sea surveys, 1158
Edinburgh, Duke Of (Chairman), Queen's award to industry, 1166
Edinburgh:
Borderers' Association Educational Trust Scheme, 1172
Census:
Leaflet. Population etc., 352, 590
Report, 590
Corporation Order Confirmation Acts, 289, 518, 1041
Bills, 42, 264, 746
Fettes College Scheme, 645, 911, 1172
Gazette, 175, 391, 635, 902, 1168
Geology, 396
John Watson's Trust Scheme, 182, 400
Merchant Company Educational Endowments Scheme, 182
Royal Botanic Gardens. *See* Royal Botanic Gardens.
Edlin, H. L.:
Dean Forest & Wye Valley. Guide, 846
Forestry practice, 846
Edmonds, E. A., Geology of country around Banbury etc., 1124
Education(al):
Acts, 288, 772
Bills, 38, 42, 227, 255, 261, 358, 702, 703, 735, 743, 744, 858
and Science, Department of (formerly Ministry):
Diplomas & Certificates. *See specific subjects*
Publications, 112–4, 326–8, 564–6, 820–2, 1088–91
Authorities, Scotland:
Accounts, 182, 400, 645, 911, 1173
Bursaries, 645
Teachers. Relations, 401
See also Education, Scotland
Bilingualism in, 1088

Education(al) (*continued*):
building:
Bulletins, 112, 326, 564, 820, 1088
Consortia, 820
Controlling dimensions, 820
Notes. (Scotland), 911, 1172
Commonwealth:
Britain's contribution, 365
links in 1143
Comprehensive, 1088, 1172
Discrimination in, Convention, 331, 347, 570
General Certificate of. *See* General Certificate
health, 327, 851
Higher:
for commerce, 912
in:
Britain, 148
Commonwealth & Britain, 871
France, 958
Robbins report, 564, 821
Legal. African students, 159
matters. Consultation on, 400
Ministry of. *See* Education & Science, Dept. of
of maladjusted children, 1089
Scotland:
Acts, 288, 516, 1039
Bills, 226, 229, 230, 260, 263, 264, 451, 482, 489, 597, 746, 964, 1006, 1131
Circular, 400
Education Authorities accounts, 182, 400, 645, 911, 1173
Teachers' Superannuation Scheme, 400
Trust Schemes etc., 182–3, 400–1, 645–6, 911–2, 1172–3
Building notes, 911, 1172
Comprehensive, 1172
Further. Teachers, 1172
Primary, 1173
Transfer to secondary education, 183, 400
Public, 183, 912
Secretary of State's report, 182, 401, 645, 911, 912, 1020
Technical, 183
See also Education Authorities. Scotland
Sea in, 822
Secondary:
and further education. Linkage, 646
Certificate of, 113, 327, 566, 822, 1089
in each local education authority, 327, 565, 821, 1090
New ways in junior (Scotland), 646
re-organisation of, 1088, 1172
Statistics of, 328, 566, 822, 1090
Education(al) (*continued*):
Technical:
Better opportunities, 112
in:
Britain, 609
Scotland, 183
Wales, 114
Transfer from primary to secondary (Scotland), 183, 400
Wales (Welsh Dept.):
Circulars, 114, 328, 566
Minutes of Proceedings H.C., 358
Publications, 114, 328, 566
Science, 1090
Technical, 114
Edwards, F. L. (Chairman), Rate-deficiency grants, 364
Edwards, J. G. (Chairman), Ancient monuments of W. Caernarvonshire, 902
Edwards, M. V., Wind-loosening of trees, 586
Edwards, R., Ham House, 689

Eelworm(s):
Beet, 81, 1052
Cereal root, 82
Chrysanthemum, 300
Potato:
root, 529, 1052
tuber, 784
Root-knot, 82, 529
Stem on:
cereals, 529, 783
clover, 300
narcissi etc., 301
Strawberries, 1052

Effect of:
impact loading on beams, 395
nuclear explosions of experiments, 637
rotation on stars, 636
soil organic matter on soil-cement mixtures, 398
Efficiency:
of adhesives for wood, 639
studies. Hospital, 131, 352, 591, 850–1, 1124–5
Efficient milking, 1053

E.G. report (UKAEA), 1218
Egg production:
Intensive poultry management for, 1054
Rearing chickens for, 530, 1052
Eggen, O. J.:
Cluster Melotte, 393
Clusters & stellar evolution, 903
High-velocity stars. Catalogue, 903
Period-colour relation for contact binaries, 176
Photometry of cluster, 176

EGG—   *INDEX 1961-5*

EGGEN, O. J. (*continued*):
Space motions & distribution of B-type stars, 177
Space velocity vectors, 393
Three-colour photometry, 176
Eglinton Hotels (Scotland) Ltd. Investigation into affairs, 189
Egypt. *See* United Arab Republic
Egyptian:
collections in B.M., 795
stelae. Hieroglyphic texts, 310
El Salvador. Abolition of visas*, 331
Elasmobranchs. Vitamin A etc. in livers, 783
Elasticity. Measurements in metals, 907
Elderly:
Care of, Scotland, 482, 597
people. Accommodation, 353
See also Old people
E.L.D.O. *See* European Launcher Development & European Organisation
Election(s):
expenses, 1128
Welsh Forms Act, 772
Bill, 491, 701, 735, 858
Parliamentary. Scotland. Forms, 405
Select Committee, 599
Electoral registration officers, 1129
Electric(al):
accidents, 369
and electronic:
engineering certificates, 1090
equipment for services, 1133
apparatus & circuits. Test, 173
calculations. Examples, 71, 1086
contracting in engineering agreements, 623
current abroad, 688
equipment for vehicles. Monopolies Commission, 485
heating for glues, 395
incandescent lamps. Merchandise Marks, 515, 928, 1194
interference. Hospitals, 1126
lighting on the farm, 788
limit switches, 1152
Pocket Book. Navy, 71, 520
services. Hospital, 592, 852
testing. Safety in, 1152
Electricity:
Act (1957) Loans, 203, 424, 673, 938, 1203
Amendment Act, 67
Bill, 1
and Gas:
Act, 516
Bill, 456, 491
Memorandum, 630
Tariffs, 1156
Basic, 535

Electricity (*continued*):
Boards. Reports, & accounts, 171, 385, 630, 896, 1164
Borrowing Powers (Scotland) Act, 516
Bill, 233, 260, 263, 358
Order. Memo, 172
Consultative Councils, 171, 385, 630, 896, 1164
Council:
Advances, 171, 386, 896, 1164
Loans, 203, 424, 673, 938, 1203
Report & accounts, 171, 385, 630, 896, 1163
current etc. Standards of measurements, 397
for farm & estate, 1058
Minister of Power report, 171, 385, 630, 896, 1163
Scotland:
Minutes of Proceedings, 138, 597
Report, 399
Standing Committee Debate, 34, 482
supply:
and distribution (Factory), 178
industry:
Dispute. Court of enquiry, 877
Remuneration of staff, 1156
Standing Committee, 631, 862
Electro-medical apparatus. Hospitals, 592
Electronic equipment manual, 683
Electronics. Services textbook, 692
Elementary:
firefighting (Civil Defence), 135
meteorology:
course, 377
for aircrew. Amdt., 161
radar, 1079
school mathematics, U.S.A., 958
Elgin calendar, 95
Elim Church Moor Lane Bolton Burial Ground Act, 774
Elland. Proposed county district. Map, 867
ELLFERS, J., Flora of East Africa, 1077
ELLIOT OF HARWOOD, BARONESS (Chairman), Child care, 647
ELLIOT, D. H., Petrology of Argentine Islands, 794
ELLIOTT, R. A. (Chairman), Storm overflows etc., 607
ELLIS, L. F., Battle of Normandy, 313
ELLIS, R W R (Chairman). Remand homes, 401
Elm disease, 586
Elopود & clupéoid fishes, 1069
Fly, Isle of, *See* Isle of

Embroidery:
Flowers in English, 689
Gospel stories in, 959
Emergency:
electrical services. Hospital, 852

Emergency (*continued*):
feeding. Civil Defence, 135
Laws (Re-enactments & Repeals) Act, 772
Bill, 706, 735, 743, 744, 858
Powers Act, 772
Bill, 702, 735, 742, 858
treatment. Poisoning, 352
EMERY, D. (Chairman), Special hospitals, 134
EMMERSON, SIR H. Construction industries, 390
Emoluments of Top Management Bill, 1008
Empididae, 1068
Employer(s):
associations etc. Directory, 153, 369, 613, 875, 1148
Insurance Bill, 1012
Recovering damages, 619
sick pay schemes, 893
Employment:
Agencies (Regulation) Bill, 1012
and training of young people, 158
of Women Bill, 246, 467, 482
EMPSON, D. W., Cereal pests, 1054
EMSLIE, G. C., Rents of council houses in Dunbarton, 130
—
Endotricha Zeller, 541
Endowed Schools Acts Scheme, 113
Ends & means. Arts Council report, 535
Energy balance. Terms, 378
Engineer construction plant, 440, 810
Engineering:
and shipbuilding industries. Agreements, 887, 1157
apprenticeship training, 877
design. Committee report, 638
Electrical & Electronic. Awards to students, 1090
Industry Training Board, 1148
Measurement of angle in, 164
Ordinary National Certificates etc., 328, 822
plant & services. Hospitals, 1126
practice. Naval Marine, 520, 1087
Engineers:
and technologists. Post-graduate courses, 1089
department. Hospitals, 352
in Merchant Navy & Mercantile Marine. Examinations, 196, 665–6
Professional (Careers), 152
England & Wales. Saxon map, 540
English:
and Scottish Law Commission, 1154
for immigrants, 565
language. Examining, 821
Low Price Book Society:
Electrical calculations, 1086
Principles of modern building, 1180
See also specific subjects.

INDEX 1961-5   **—ETH**

Engraved work of Eric Gill, 689
Entertainment Clubs Bill, 1012, 1014
Entomology. Bulletins, 94, 310–1, 541, 796–7, 1067–8
Environment of a herring fishery, 80
—
Eocene:
Primate Genus Cantius, 311
tarsioids, 94
Episcopal Church (Scotland) Act, 772
Bill, 457, 742
Epitolinae, 311, 796
—
Equalisation grant. Scotland, 256
Equipping a hospital building, 353
—
E-Region zero-point programmes, 636
Ergonomics in industry. Conference, 178
Ermine moths, 1011
Ernobius mollis, 639
—
Escape from fire & assistance to fire service. Means of, 910
ESSEN, L., Measurement of frequency, 397
Essex:
Census:
Leaflet (Population etc.) & report, 588
Occupation groups, 1123
rivers & Stour. Hydrological survey, 143
Esso Petroleum Company Act, 69
Establishments. Treasury control, 862
Estate:
Agents Bill, 487, 1012
Duty (Deferment of Payment) Bill, 1008
Estimates:
Committees:
Minutes of Proceedings, 139, 457, 597, 858, 1001
Reports, 139–40, 246, 247, 248, 249, 250, 359, 598–9, 860, 1133–4
Special Reports, 140–1, 246, 250, 251, 359–60, 464, 468, 600, 861–2, 1133
Sub-committees. *See* Sub-committees
Form of, 140
Memo. by Financial Secretary, 201, 424, 672, 939, 1203
Supplementary: 139, 140, 598
Winter, 599, 860, 861, 1134, 1135
Spring, 250, 359, 598, 860, 1133, 1135
Variations in, 140, 247, 490, 600, 860, 862, 1133, 1135.
See also Civil Estimates, Defence Estimates etc.
Estimating daylight in buildings, 637, 904
Estuary of River Mersey. Sewage, 181
—
Ethiopian drepanidae, 1067

ETR—   *INDEX 1961-5*

Etruscan bronze utensils, 1066
—
Euchromadora de Man, 1069
Euglenophyceae, 304
Eupsilophus, 312
Euratom. *See* European Atomic Energy Community
Eurocontrol. Convention, 115, 507
European:
and Mediterranean Plant Protection Organisation, 343
armour, 1222
Atomic Energy Community:
Regulations, 331–2, 570, 826–7, 1096–7
Statement. Lord Privy Seal, 331
Treaty*, 346
Coal & Steel Community:
Annual reports, 117, 322, 570, 827, 1097
General regulations on organisation, 1097
Regulations, officials etc., 570
Statement. Lord Privy Seal, 332
Treaty, 346, 1118
Communities:
Britain and, 423, 871
Court of Justice. Rules, 330, 1094
Glossary of legal terms, 332, 1097
Court of Human Rights, 340
Economic Co-operation Convention, 331
Economic Community:
Commonwealth Consultations, 104
Conventions, 1097
Regulations, 333 9, 570 6, 827 35, 1097–1109
Report by Lord Privy Seal, 332, 333
Statement by Lord Privy Seal, 160
Treaty, 346
U.K. and, Statement, 118
Fisheries Conference, 835
Free Trade Association:
Amendments to Convention, 339, 576, 835, 1109
Compendium, 190, 413, 660, 926, 1191
Finland*, 118, 835, 1109
Legal capacity, 118
Launcher Development Organisation, Privileges & immunities, Protocol, 1115
Select Committee, 1134
See also below European, Organisation
migration, 339, 576
monetary*, 339
Organisation for Development of Space Vehicle Launchers*, 345, 843, 1117
Parliament rules, 570
Patent law. Draft Convention, 416

European (*continued*):
Pharmacopoeia Convention, 1109
Political Union. Statement, 339
Social Charter, 339, 1109
Space Research Organisation, 339, 841, 843, 1134
Eurotrust Ltd., 1191
—
Evacuation:
and care of homeless. Civil Defence, 135
casualties, 356
EVANS, SIR D. L. (Chairman), Record depositories, 854
EVANS, D. S.:
Double-lined spectroscopic binary, 176
Fundamental data for southern stars, 393, 903
Observations of single-lined variables, 392
Radial velocity, 636
EVANS, G. O.:
Chaetotaxy in gamasina, 541
Mites of macrocheles, 542
Terrestial acari, 313
EVANS, SIR I. (Chairman), National Insurance Advisory Committee reports 36, 167, 383, 384, 626, 892
EVANS, J. C.:
Inspection of gauging dimensions, 397
Measurement of angle in engineering, 164, 907
Pneumatic gauging, 907
EVANS, TIMOTHY JOHN, Bill, 39
EVE, SIR M. T.:
Carlton House Terrace, 105
Regent's Park Terraces, 320
EVERSHED, RT. HON. LORD (Chairman) Royal Commission Historical Mss., 134
Everybody's guide to National Insurance, 164, 890, 1160
Eviction from Rented Dwellings Bill, 741
Evidence (Road Traffic) (Scotland) Bill, 1009
Evolution. Handbook, 312, 1069
—
Ewes. Breeding loss, 785
—
Ex-servicemen housing, 1139, 1222
Examination(s):
Art, 113, 327, 564, 821
Aviation. Ministry of, 90, 307–8, 536, 792, 1064
Bulletins, 566, 822, 1089
Certificates of competency, 171, 387, 631, 897, 1165
Civil Service, 97–9, 314–6, 545–7, 801–2, 1071–3
Experimental, 822, 1089
Fire Services. Scotland, 184, 1174
Flight Navigators, 90, 308, 536, 792, 1064

INDEX 1961-5   **—EXP**

Examination(s) (*continued*):
Masters & Mates. *See* Masters & Mates
Mercantile Marine, 196, 413, 665–6, 931, 1191
Merchant Navy, 196, 665
Mining, 171, 387, 631, 897, 1165
National Diploma in Design, 113, 327, 564, 821
Objective-type, 822
Pilot's, 90, 308, 536, 792, 1064
School-based, 1089
Secondary Education Certificate. *See* Certificate
Examining:
of English language, 821
Some techniques of, 822
Examples in electrical calculations, 71, 1086
Excavations. Annual report, 389, 633, 901, 1167
Excess profits:
Levy. Appeals, 609, 872, 1144
Tax. Appeals, 148
Excess Votes. Public Accounts Committee, 139, 359, 599, 861, 1134
Exchange of:
Notes etc. *See specific subject or country*
Official publications:
Convention, 340
Germany*, 577
Thailand*, 583
Vietnam*, 585
Exchequer:
Accounts. Reform of, 675
and Audit Dept. Publications, 115, 329, 566–7, 822–3, 1091–2
Execution of sentences. Rules etc., 441, 692, 811
EXELL, A. W.:
Angiosperms, 541
Buchenavia, 541
Exercises & studies. Civil Defence, 854
EXETER, BISHOP OF, (Chairman), Treatment of offenders, 595
Exeter. Alteration of area, 604
Exhibition:
Galleries of National History Museum, 95, 313
of:
1851, 136
1862, 439
forgeries, 93
printing, 540
Roman coins, 540
Shakespeare, 796
Exmouth Pier & Harbour Order Confirmation Act, 69
Bill, 5, 41
Expedition:
to East Nepal, 1068
John Murray, 1069

Experiment(s):
in:
numerical forecasting, 162
operational weather prediction, 378
verification of forecast charts, 163
on animals:
Departmental Committee, 1130
Return to H.C., 136, 356, 594, 855, 1129
Experimental:
communications satellites. Testing*, 126
examinations (Mathematics), 822
farm buildings, 782, 1049
horticulture, 85, 303, 332, 787, 1058
husbandry:
farms. Progress reports, 85, 303, 532, 789, 1059
(Periodical), 85, 303, 532, 787
nurses training. Glasgow, 646
Expiring Laws Continuance Acts, 68, 289, 517, 772, 1039
Bills, 8, 42, 232, 263, 456, 491, 709, 745, 975, 1013
Exploitation of sea. Convention, 1109
Explosion reports, 171, 385, 1164
Explosives:
Application Form, 1129
at quarries, 173
Authorised, 136, 356, 594, 855, 1129
for carriage by sea, 199, 420, 934–5, 1196
H.M. Inspector Report, 137, 596, 855, 1129
Underground, 1208
Export(s):
Guarantees Acts, 68, 772
Bills, 8, 42, 491, 698
Import Bank of Washington*, 1092
Licences:
Antiques, 1191
Iron & steel scrap, 190, 413, 660, 926, 1191
Open general, 190, 413, 660–1, 926, 1191–2, 1195
Scrap & metallic residues, 413, 660–1, 660, 926, 1191, 1195
Southern Rhodesia, 1196
List, 106, 321, 552, 807, 1077
of:
produce & manufactures U.K., 105, 321, 552, 807
works of art, 203, 282, 673, 939, 1203
to U.S.A., 689, 1075
trends, 623
Exporters Compendium (EFTA), 190, 413, 660, 926, 1191
Exporting to U.S.A., 689
Exposure:
of population to radiation from fallout, 883
to driving rain. Index, 394

EXT-FLI | 1961-5

Extended aeration sewage treatment plants. Circular, 1139
Extension of:
compulsory after-care to inmates etc., 184
Leases Bill, 260
Extra Masters. *See* Masters
Extraction of conifer thinnings, 846
Extradition treaty:
Austria*, 568
Sweden*, 583
Extremes of Wind Shear, 622

Eyemouth Harbour Order Confirmation Act, 69
Bill, 41
Eyespot of wheat & barley, 1052
Eynsford Castle. Guide, 900

F

Facsimile:
Great Fire of London, 1176
Magna Carta, 1168
Summons from Cromwell, 635
Factory(ies):
Act(s), 67
Bill, 3, 4, 41, 141
Duties of local authorities, 876
Regulations, 153
Short guide, 375
Structural requirements, 375
atmospheres, 1152
Building Studies, 178, 394, 395
Chief Inspector. Annual reports, 151, 368, 611, 874, 1146
Colouring in, 178
Dust explosions, 618
Economics of buildings, 395
Fire protection, 178
Firefighting, 159
Forms, 153–5, 369–71, 613–4, 876–7, 1148–9
Lane, Warrington (Level Crossing) Act, 518
Orders, 614
Thermal insulation, 395
Facts about the waterways, 1070
Faculty Jurisdiction Measure, 700, 775, 800
Faint stars, 1169
Fair:
Trade Practices Bill, 260
Wages Clause Bill, 744
Fairfield Shipbuilding & Engineering Co. Ltd., Advances, 1201
Falkland Islands (and Dependencies):
Forecasting in, 162
Gazeteer, 119
Falkland Islands (and Dependencies) (*continued*):
Instructions OIC, 899
Letters Patent OIC, 388
Palaeomagnetic investigations, 539
Reports, 100, 318
Scientific reports, 101, 318, 1074
See also British Antarctic Survey
False or misleading indications of origin on goods. Prevention*, 576
Family:
allowances:
Act(s): 1039
Bill, 965, 968, 971, 1013, 1136
Decisions of:
Commissioners, 164–5, 381, 625, 890, 1160
Reported, 384
Tribunal, 381
and National Insurance:
Acts, 68, 772
Bills, 9, 38, 42, 43, 358, 699, 741
Law, 165, 381, 625, 890, 1160
doctor. Field of work, 591
expenditure survey, 155, 371 614, 1149
or table service dining (School), 1090
pension benefits for teachers, 1089
Preservation Bill, 746
Far Eastern crisis. Documents. 1095
Farm(s):
and:
estate. Electricity for, 1058
Garden Chemicals Bill, 743, 1009
horticultural workers (Careers), 152
as a business. Management, 532, 787 1058
buildings:
Experimental. Reports, 782, 1049
Repair & maintenance, 1059
Research. Bibliography, 1049
Unit, 782, 1049
classification, 1058
Co-operative, in Wales, 85, 303
crops:
Arable & grass, 1058
Irrigation, 82
Fertilisers, 300, 1052
Potash for, 82, 530
Row, Mechanical thinning, 303
Electric lighting, 788
fences. Permanent, 304
fertilisers. *See* Fertilisers
gates, 788
grinding, 532
homestead. Drainage, 788
Hospital, 132
incomes, 85, 303, 788, 1058
Institutes. Salaries, 566, 1090
Land & building improvements, 304
livestock, 527

Farm(s) (*continued*):
machinery leaflets, 85, 303, 532, 788
management records & accounts, 786
produce, 86, 1060
rats. Control of, 530
seed cleaning machinery, 85
sprayers, 302
Upland, Making it pay, 80
work. Planning, 83
Farmers:
and growers. Mechanisation leaflets, 1059
book-keeping & income tax, 788
lung. National Insurance, 892
weather, 1054
Farming:
Mechanised, in Tanganyika, 548
restored opencast land, 301
Scale of enterprise in, 177
Scottish, Current economic conditions, 81, 299, 529, 783, 1051
Farmyard manure. Handling, 1059
Farnham Castle:
Guide, 221
Measure, 70
Faroe Islands. Double taxation. Denmark*, 117
Fatigue fractures in aircraft, 524
Fatstock:
and carcase meat, 787
guarantee Scheme 85, 303, 532, 788, 1058
Faulks, N., Investigation into affairs of:
H. Jasper & Co. Ltd., 189
Pilot Assurance Co. Ltd., 190
Fauna:
and flora. Antarctic. Conservation, 1036
Carodocian Brachiopod & Ordovician Tribolite, 542
of Portrane limestone, 542, 797

Featherstone. Proposed county district. Map, 867
Fecundity:
and larval abundance of herring, 85
of Atlantic salmon, 80
Federal Aviation Agency, U.S.A., 567, 823
Federation of. *See respective countries*
Feeding:
bees 530
dairy cows, 530, 785, 1053
layers on farm, 784
pigs, 1051
poultry, 530
separated milk, 784
silage, 82
tomatoes, 530
turkeys, 784
value of grass silage, 82, 1053
Fees and:
charges. Opthalmic services, 134, 354, 593, 853, 1126, 1127
Fees and (*continued*):
expenses. Marine surveys etc., 196, 415, 418, 932
Feilden, G. B. R. (Chairman), Engineering design, 638
Felixstowe Dock & Railway Act, 518
Fellgett, P. B., Register encoder & serializer, 393
Felling & converting thinnings, 586
Felonies & misdemeanors, 1128
Fences. Permanent farm, 304
Fennah, R. G.:
Delphacidea, 1068
Fulgoroidea, 1068
Ugyops, 796
Ferguson, Sir J., Security at National Gallery, 275
Ferns of Ceylon, 310
Ferranti, S. Z. de, 904
Ferranti Ltd., Guided weapons contract, 861
Fertility etc. in fowls, 1052
Fertilizers:
and feeding stuffs, 81, 299, 528, 783, 1050
Compound, 530
for the farm, 786
handling & distribution, 532
Nitrogenous, 300, 1052
Fettes College Scheme, 645, 911, 1172

Fibre(s):
Industrial, Production, 104, 319, 550, 804, 1075
reinforcement of metals, 1063
Fiduciary note issue, 203, 250, 424, 427, 485, 672–3, 712, 713, 938, 1003, 1203
Field, Hon. Mr. Justice F. E. (Chairman), Public expenditure in Grenada, 318
Field, H. I., Pig diseases, 786
Field:
archaeology, 888
cable & despatch riders (Civil Defence), 355, 855
crop sprayers, 303, 1059
measurements of sound insulation, 180
of work of family doctor, 591
studies. Scotland, 912
surgery pocket book, 691
Fife:
Census:
Leaflet. Population etc., 590
Report, 850
coalfields. Geology, 130
Fifty:
facts about Britain's economy, 365
masterpieces of:
near Eastern art, 93
pottery etc., 959
sculpture, 959

Fifty (*continued*):
miles per hour (Temporary speed limit), 667, 933, 1199, 1223
point traffic census, 398
things to see (Science Museum), 1170
Figulla, H. H., Babylonian tablets, 93, 540
Fiji:
Constitution OIC, 632, 899
Constitutional Conference, 1074
Corona Library Series, 548
Electoral Provisions OIC, 388, 1166
Land use & population, 1159
Letters Patent OIC, 174, 389
Public Service Amendment OIC, 1166
Reports 101, 317, 548, 803, 1074
Royal Instructions OIC, 632
Filing of management papers. Hospitals, 133
Film(s):
Act, 772
Bill, 702, 703, 743
Civil Defence training, 355, 854
Finance Corporation. *See* National Film Finance Corporation.
France*, 1109
Fund Agency. *See* British Film Fund Agency
industry. Structure & trading practices, 929
See also Cinematographic films
Finance:
Accounts of U.K. 203, 247, 673, 939, 1203
Acts, 67, 288, 517, 772, 1039
Advances. *See respective* Nationalised Industries
Bills, 6, 40, 41, 230, 262, 263, 453, 488, 490, 706, 709, 743, 744, 745, 746
Expediting, 599
Gaming inquiry, 857
Guaranteed Land Stock Account, 939
No 2 Act, 772
Bill, 974, 1011, 1012
of coal industry, 1164
Financial:
and:
economic obligations. Nationalised industries, 203
technical aid from Britain, 871
arrangements. Hospitals, 132, 352
institutions U.K., 148
loss allowance (Local Government), 361
statement, 203, 424, 673, 939, 1204
Supplementary, 941
statistics:
England & Wales (Local Government), 144, 362, 606, 1140
Periodical, 314, 544, 798, 1070–1
Series available, 1070
Financing improvements to land & buildings, 304
Fine Rolls. Calendar, 174, 634
Finland:
Abolition of visas*, 118
Air services*, 1109
Association with EFTA*, 118, 835, 1109
British visitors' passport*, 118
Cereals*, 1109
Tonnage certificates. Merchant ships*, 340
Finnegan, R. H., Limba people, 1159
Fire(s):
and:
design of schools, 112
roofs, 639
appliances:
Drill book, 594
Manual, 1129
associated with:
blankets, 639
cooking appliances, 639
kerosine-burning appliances, 395
columns. Mobile, Standing Orders, 137
Deaths in, 1179
Escape from, (Building Standards) 910
extinction. Shock hazard, 1179
fighting. *See* Firefighting
hazards of:
caravans, 905
electricity, 395
Heat radiation from, 639
in State forests, 127
involving:
electrical equipment, 1179
liquified petroleum gas, 639
Means of escape from. (Building Regulations Scotland), 910
Notes, 179, 639, 1179
Open, for coke burning, 143
precautions:
Fish fryers. Hospitals, 353
in home (Filmstrip), 856
protection:
against, Hospitals, 1126
in factories, 178
research:
Report, 179, 395, 639, 905, 1179
Station, 395, 639, 905, 1179
Technical Papers, 395, 639, 905, 1179
resistance of floors & ceilings, 179
Service(s):
Careers, 875
Department, 594, 856, 1129
Drill Book, 594
England & Wales, 137, 276, 596, 857, 1130
Exam. papers. Scotland, 184, 1174
Scotland, 184, 402, 646, 913, 1175
spread. Risk. Circular, 602
statistics, 181, 639, 905, 1179
venting in buildings, 1179

Firearms Act, 1039
Bill, 970, 972, 973, 1006, 1010, 1012, 1131
Fireboats, 856
Firedamp, 170
Firefighting:
Elementary (Civil Defence), 135
in factories, 159
theory, 595
Firemanship. Manual, 356, 595, 856, 1129
Firemen & firewomen. Training record, 854
Fireworks Act, 772
Bills, 262, 491, 700, 735, 858
First:
aid:
and home nursing (Civil Defence), 594
Order O.S.R. Form, 1152
Treatment. Advice on, S.H.W., 881
degree & comparable courses. Awards, 820
employment of graduates, 676, 1091
hundred families, 1139
negatives, 1170
year apprenticeship training in engineering, 877
Fish(es):
and:
meat paste. Food standards, 1059
wildlife service U.S.A., 958
Cichlid, 1069
Elopoid & Clupeoid, 1069
Food supply, and insect emergence, 80
fryers. Fire precautions, Hospital, 353
frying & offensive trades. Byelaws, 145
Instructions for collectors, 1069
Jurassic, 541
Macristium & ctenothrissid, 95
Palaeoniscoid, 542
populations, 548
Size limits. Convention, 342, 577, 581
Smoking, 643
Fisher, L. R.:
Vitamin A etc. in:
herring, 528
livers of elasmobranchs, 783
Fisher, N. (Chairman): Bahamas Constitutional Conference, 549
Fisheries & Fishing:
Bottom, in Kenya, 1074
Convention*, 835, 836, 1109
European Conference, 835
Freshwater & salmon research, 80, 299, 528, 782, 1050
General Council for Mediterranean, 835
Iceland:
Dispute*, 120
Stocks, 85
industry, 87, 136
investigations, 85, 303–4, 788, 1058
Fisheries & Fishing (*continued*):
Limits:
Act, 772
Bill, 706, 735, 744, 858
Norway*, 835
Poland*, 841
nets, Meshes, 342, 577, 581
North-east Atlantic Convention, 576
North-west Atlantic Convention, 576
Norway* 122, 835
Norwegian vessels*, 835
Publications (Colonial), 101, 318, 548–9, 1074
regime. Soviet Union*, 842
resources. Atlantic, 549
Salmon, *See* Salmon
Scotland, 80, 299, 528, 782, 1050
Sea, Statistical tables, 87, 305, 534, 789, 1060
Whiting, Scottish, 528
Fixed:
Channel Link, 667
equipment of the farm, 85, 304, 788, 1058–9
Fixings. Making, to hard materials, 389

Flag(s):
and ensigns, 1086
Colonial Office etc., 104, 549, 803, 1074
of all nations, 71, 291, 818, 1086
Use of, Trial plantations, 586
Flame arresters & explosion reliefs, 1152
Flammable Materials Bill, 742
Flanders, A. D., Dock foreman at Southampton, 875
Flats:
for disabled, 865
Heating in, 178, 180, 904
Landscaping for, 601, 603
Multi-storey, 638, 904
Service cores, 362, 603, 865, 1139
Flavouring agents. Report, 1059
Flax & hemp workers. Byssinosis, 1161
Flea(s):
beetles, 81, 783
Rothschild Collection, 312
Fleck, Lord, (formerly Sir A.):
Fishing industry, 44, 87
Radio astronomy, 1171
Fletcher, D. S., Ruwenzori Expedition. Noctuidea, 95
Flies:
and other insects in poultry houses, 1053
Blow, 796
Cabbage root, 300
Celery, 1051
Fruit, 783, 796
House etc., 300, 1052
Narcissus, 81
Onion, 81, 1052

Flies (*continued*):
  Warble, 784
  Wheat bulb, 81
Flight:
  navigator's licence, 89, 307, 1063
    Exam. papers, 90, 308, 536, 792, 1064
  Path of, 567
  radio operators' licences, 89, 307, 1063
  Realm of, 567
Flintshire:
  Census report, 588
  County Council (Higher Ferry Saltney Footbridge) Act, 1042
  Saxton map, 795
Flood. Babylonian legend, 309
Flood Prevention (Scotland) Act, 67
  Bill, 2, 40, 138
Floodlight. Guide to evening classes, 882, 1124
Floor(s) & flooring:
  and:
    ceilings. Fire-resistance, 179
    roofs. (Principles of modern building), 180
  coverings. Laying screeds, 1166
  Damp-proofing solid, 1178
  design to prevent dry rot, 394
  Forces applied to, 179
  Granolithic concrete etc., 904
  in anaesthetising areas, 353, 1126
  Sheet & tile, 637
  Slatted, for cows, etc., 1049
  strips, 663
Flora(s):
  Barbados, 1159
  Bournemouth beds, 797
  Fossil, 311
  Lower Headon beds, 94
  Mesozoic, 542
  Palaeocene, London Clay, 95
  Tropical, East Africa, 1077
  Vascular, 794
Flow:
  measurement in closed conduits, 396
  of hot gases, 639
Flowers:
  Cut, under glass, 786
  in English embroidery, 689
  Outdoor, for cutting, 302
Fluoridation:
  of domestic water supplies, 851
  studies. Conduct, 354
Fluoroacetamide as rodenticide. Precautionary measures, 1081
Fluorosis in cattle, 785, 1054
Fly. *See* Flies.
Flying in Royal Navy 1914–64, 887

F.M.S. Rubber Planters Estates Limited, Investigation into affairs, 925

Fodder:
  beet, 1052
  Maize for, 81
Foerster's genera, 311
FOISTER, C. E., Economic plant diseases of Scotland, 81
Fomes Annosus. Fungus, 349
Food:
  additives and methods of toxity testing, 1059
  and Agriculture Organisation:
    Constitution, 116, 1110
    Desert Locust Information Service*, 118
    Latin-American forest research, 118
  Antioxidants in, 533
  Colouring matters, 788
  consumption. Domestic, Annual reports, 85, 303, 532, 787, 1058
  hygiene. Code of practice. Poultry, 132
  Irradiation of, 851
  Labelling:
    Bill, 1009, 1014
    Food Standards Committee, 788
    Regulations, 84
  mites, 87
  mixers, 85
  of:
    megrim, 328
    Norway lobster, 299
  policy. Medical & nutritional aspects. Committee, 851
  preservation. Freeze-drying methods, 81
  regulations. *See* Public Health. Imported food.
  Standards Committee reports, 304, 533, 788, 1059
  store. Insect pests in, 82
  U.K. Civil Series, 313
  values:
    Ready reckoner, 822
    Table, 377
  waste. Hospitals, 591
  you eat & heart disease, 688
Footwear Materials Marketing Bill, 743
For those in peril. Lifesaving, 624
Forces applied to floor by the foot, 179
Ford Model 'N' Print, 1170
Ford Motor Co. Dispute, 614
FORD-SMITH, M. A., Complex cyanides, 906
Forecast charts. Verification, 163
Forecasting in Falkland Islands, 162
Foreign:
  arbitral awards, 159
  Compensation:
    Act, 516
      Bill, 233, 257, 260, 264
    Commission:
      Egyptian claims rules. Select Committee, 359

Foreign (*continued*):
  Compensation (*continued*):
    Commission (*continued*):
      Report & accounts, 118, 340, 577, 836, 1110
  Exchange:
    costs Germany*, 836
    expenditure. Germany*, 837, 1110
  Office. Publications, 115–27, 329–48, 567–86, 823–46, 1092–1121
  Policy. British. *See* British Foreign Policy
  Public documents. Legislation for, Convention, 119, 1112
Foreigners entering & leaving U.K., 137, 358, 596, 857, 1130
Forest(s):
  fires in State, 127
  North-east Scotland, 586
  nurseries:
    Establishing, 846
    Grey mould in, 846
    Nutrition problems, 1121
  Park Guides, 127, 349, 586, 846, 1121
  Products Research. Bulletins etc., 179, 395, 639–40, 905–6, 1179–80
  records, 127, 348, 586, 846, 1121
  Research report, 127, 349, 586, 846, 1122
  Statistician's report, 1121
  Weed control, 1122
Forestry:
  Advisory Committee, 390, 634, 899
  Careers, 1147
  Commission(ers):
    Annual report, 127, 348, 586, 846, 1121
    Estimates Committee, 860, 1135
    Publications, 127, 348–9, 586, 846, 1121–2
  in Scotland. Minutes of proceedings, 858
  practice, 846
  Sale of Land (Scotland) Act, 517
    Bill, 264, 452, 483, 597
  Scottish Grand Committee, 735
Forgeries & deceptive copies. Exhibition, 93
Form design:
  Guide Sheet 939, 1204
  in government departments, 424
FORRESTER, S., Aids to working conifer thinnings, 348
FORSTER OF HARRABY, RT. HON. LORD, Fort Transport Industry, 159
Fort William Pulp & Paper Mills Act, 517
  Bill, 451, 483, 488, 597
Forth & Clyde (Extinguishment of Rights of Navigation) Act, 288
  Bill, 42, 226
Forth Road Bridge Order Confirmation Act, 69
  No. 2 Bill, 41
Forward from school, 327

Fossil(s):
  amphibians & reptiles, 312, 1069
  British Caenozoic, 541
  flora in Forest of Dean, 311
  ginkgoales, 1068
  insects from Charmouth, 312
  Instructions for collectors, 312
  mammals of Africa, 1068
  man, 1069
  Palaeozoic, 796
  plants of rocks, 906
FOSTER-SUTTON, SIR S.:
  Kenya:
    Constituencies de-limitation, 549
    Regional boundaries, 318
  Zanzibar. Disturbances, 103
Foundations & soils, 1178
Foundry(ies):
  craftsmen. Patternmaker (Careers), 612
  environment. Improving, 375
  goggles, 881
  industry (Careers), 612, 1146
  Steel conditions in, 153
  technology. Certificates etc., 327
Four hundred years of music printing, 795
Fowl(s):
  Fertility & hatchability, 1052
  pest policy, 304
  pox, 1051
  typhoid, 1051
FOWLER, W. A., Star formation, 636
FOX, B. H., Alcohol & traffic safety, 958

Fractured chert specimens, 94
France:
  Air transport. Routes*, 118
  British visitors' passports*, 118
  Catalogue of books in B.M., 540
  Cereals*, 836
  Channel Tunnel, 836
  Civil supersonic transport aircraft*, 577
  Double taxation*, 577, 750, 836, 1110
  Education in, 958
  Family allowances. Jersey*, 1110
  Film Company production*, 1109
  Fisheries*, 836
  New Hebrides*, 577
  Postal communications*, 577
  Travel arrangements*, 118
FRANCIS, E. H., Cowdenbeath & Central Fife economic geology, 130
FRANCIS, G. H., Petrological studies in Glen Urquhart, 797
FRANCIS WALKER'S aphids, 95
FRASER, HON. H. (Chairman):
  Trinidad and Tobago Independence Conference, 319
  Leeward Islands & Windward Islands Constitution Conference, 56, 103
FRASER, J. H., Oceanic & bathypelagic plankton, 80

Freehold Land Finance Co. Ltd. Investigation into affairs, [illegible]
Freezing of fruit & vegetables, 300
French Language guides, 957
Frequency. Measurement, 397
Freshwater:
  and salmon fisheries research 80, 299, 528, 782, 1050
  gastropod molluscs, 312, 542, 543, 1068, 1069
FRIEND, P. D., Large-span glasshouse, 1049
Friendly Societies:
  Acts, etc. Guide, 350
  Annual Return forms, 127–8, 349–50, 586–7, 846–8, 1122
  Membership of Trade Unions Bill, 744
  Publications, 127–8, 349–51, 586–8, 846–8, 1122
  Report of Chief Registrar, 128, 350, 587–8, 848, 1122
Frit fly, 783
From school to further education, 646
FROST, R., Mean streamlines & isotachs, 1155
Frost:
  damage to pipes, 602
  precautions, 602
Fruit(s):
  and vegetables:
    domestic preservation, 302
    home freezing, 300
  Bush, 1054
  Cane, 302
  flies, 796
  plants. Inspection & certification, 1053
  production. Commonwealth, 103, 319, 550, 804, 1075
  Refrigerated stores for, 1054
  Scale insects, 783
  Soft, in garden, 301
  Soils & manures for, 1054
  Top, in garden, 301
  tree(s):
    grafting, 530
    Raising, 785
    Red spider mite, 300, 1051
    sprays, 82
    Tortrix moths, 784
FRY, J. F., Fire(s):
  associated with:
    electric blankets etc., 639
    kerosene-burning appliances, 395
  hazards of electricity, 395
FRY, W. G., Pycnogonida, 1069

F.S.H. Circulars, 84, 302–3, 531–2, 786–7, 1054–8

Fuel:
  policy, 1164

Fuel (*continued*):
  research:
    Conference, 539
    organisation D.S.I.R., 179
  Smokeless supplies, 1138
  storage in housing, 361
Fuelling of aircraft, 89
Fulgoridea, 1068
FULTON, J. S. (Chairman), Teachers:
  Demand & supply, 326
  Future pattern of education & training, 327
Fumigation:
  research conductivity meters, 79
  with:
    liquid fumigants, 533
    methyl bromide, 136
Functions of Secretary of State. Wales, 740, 1131
Fungi, Larger British, 95
Furnaces. Industrial Clean Air Act, 143
Furness Abbey, Guide, 1167
Furniture:
  Gift to Sierra Leone, 427
  trade & consumer, 1077
  Victorian, 688
Further education. Welsh Grand Committee, 34
Furunculosis in kelts, 299
Future:
  development of Youth Employment Service, 1146
  of:
    Carlton House Terrace, 105
    Commonwealth, 551
    development plans, 1139
    East Africa High Commission Services, 102
    Germany. Documents, 119
    Regent's Park Terraces, 320
    sound radio & T.V., 384
    waterways, 798
  pattern of education & training of teachers, 327

G

GADD, C. J., Ur Excavations. Text, 795, 1067
Gaelic in secondary schools. Teaching, 402
GALBRAITH, I. C. J., Land birds of Guadalcanal etc., 312
Gales in Yorkshire, 1154
Gall. Crown & leafy, 529
GALLOIS, R. W., Geology. Wealden district, 1124
Gamasina. Chaetotaxy of legs, 542
GAMBELL, R., Scottish whiting fishery, 528

Gambia:
  Arms, 1070
  Constitutional Conference, 107
  Flags, 1074
  Gift of furniture etc., 424
  Independence:
    Act, 772
      Bill, 709, 745
    Booklet, 1144
    Conference, 803
  Instructions OIC, 388
  Photoposter, 1144
  Picture set, 365
  Public officers'*, 1076, 1159
  Reference Pamphlet, 114
  Reports, 100, 548, 803
  Royal Instructions OIC, 632
  Village:
    Economic activity, 651
    Trachoma in, 1154
Game Licences & Gun Licences (Miscellaneous Provisions), etc., Bill, 38
Gaming under Section 2 of Finance Act, Enquiry, 857
Garden companion, 901
Gardener. Chemicals for, 1054
Gardens. Manuring & liming, 301
GARDINER, B. G., Palaeoniscoid fishes etc., 542
Garforth. Proposed county district. Map, 867
GARLAND, C. E.:
  Case commentary on Income Tax Acts, 148, 366, 609, 871
  Harrison's index to Tax cases, 148, 366, 609
GARNER, E. H. (Chairman), Irrigation, 394
Garton Collection of English table glass, 1153
Gas:
  Act 1948 Loans, 203–4, 424, 673, 939, 1204
  Act 1965, 1039
    Bill, 969, 972, 973, 1006, 1009, 1010, 1012, 1131
  and Electricity (Resale) Bill, 743
  Boards Reports & Accounts, 171–2, 386, 630, 711, 896–7, 1164
  Borrowing Powers Act, 1040
    Bill, 974, 1012
    Memorandum, 1165
  Consultative Councils, 171–2, 386, 630, 896–7, 1164
  Council:
    Advances, 171, 386, 896, 1164
    Annual report, 171, 386, 630, 896, 1165
    Loans, 203–4, 424, 673, 939, 1204
  Fitter (Careers), 368, 1146
  Industry. Select Committee, 140, 247, 898

Gas (*continued*):
  Minister of Power report, 172, 386, 630, 896, 1165
  Turbine Collaboration Committee, 307
Gascon Rolls P.R.O., 901
Gastropods, 94, 541, 1169
Gates. Farm, 788
Gateshead. Proposed borough. Map, 605
Gauging:
  dimensions, 397
  Pneumatic, 907
GAUNT, J. F., Fire hazards. Caravans, 905
Gazetteer. British Antarctic Territories (Falkland Islands), 119, 340, 836

Gear selectivity & fishing effort, 80
GEDDES, LORD (Chairman), Carriers' licensing, 1198
Geese & ducks, 83
General:
  Agreement on Tariffs & Trade, 346, 1021
  Aviation Flight guide, 89
  Board of Control. Scotland, 130, 402
  Certificate of Education, 112, 114, 326, 328, 821
  conditions. Government building etc. Contracts, 390
  consent under Control of Borrowing Order, 204, 939
  Fisheries Council, 835
  Grant:
    Increase Order:
      England & Wales, 362–3, 606, 867–8, 1140
      Scotland, 258, 401, 646, 910, 1171
    Order. Scotland, 258, 402, 901
    Relevant expenditure regs., 361
  Licence control of hiring (T.V. sets), 661, 926
  Lighthouse Fund, 196, 418, 666, 932, 1198
  Post Office. *See* Post Office
  Register Office, 128–9, 351, 558–9, 848–9, 1122–3
  Registry Office Scotland, 129, 352, 590, 849, 1123–4
  Service Medal, 202, 220, 672, 692, 812, 937, 1203
  studies in technical colleges, 327
Geneva Tariff negotiations, 346
Genieri village. Gambia. Survey, 651
Geography & education, 113
Geology(ical)
  and ceramics, 129
  Bulletins:
    British Museum, Natural History, 94, 311–2, 541–2, 797, 1068
    Geological Survey, 129, 396, 640, 906, 1124
  Column. Guide, 640
  of . . . *See respective towns, etc.*

Geology(ical) (continued):
photographs, 640
Survey:
and Museum. Publications 129–30, 396, 640, 906, 1124
Bulletin, 129, 396, 640, 906, 1124
Channel Tunnel Project*, 836
England & Wales:
Memoirs, 129, 396, 640, 906, 1124
Summary of Progress, 130 396, 640, 906, 1124
Memoirs (Palaeontology), 906
Scotland. Memoirs, 130, 396
time, 313
Geomagnetic:
field, 635
secular variation, 393
Geophysical:
investigations of Scotia Arc, 794
memoirs, 161, 377, 620, 1154–5
paper, 1159
GEORGE, T. N. British Regional Geology. N. Wales, 129
George:
Heriot's Trust Scheme, 1172
Medal. London Gazette, 915
Georgian etc. Books in B.M., 309
German(y):
Air:
offensive against, 96
Services*, 340
Books. Catalogues, 540
British:
forces, 340, 836, 837, 1110
visitors' passport*, 119
Compensation for:
U.K. nationals*, 836
victims of Nazi persecution*, 825
Contracts of insurance etc.*, 119
Criminal matters*, 119
Documents on, 119
Domestic silver, 218, 1222
Double taxation*, 826
Economic assistance*, 119
Enemy property. Account, 190, 413, 660, 926, 1191
Exchange of official publications*, 577
Forces in U.K.*, 119
Foreign:
exchange:
costs*, 836
expenditure*, 837
forces in*, 837, 839–40
policy. Documents, 117, 331, 826
Future of, Documents, 119
Judgment in civil matters, 119
Local defence costs*, 119
Manoeuvres*, 113
N.A.T.O. forces, 839–40
Official publications. Exchange*, 577
School. National Gallery, 163

German(y) (continued):
Science in, 624
Settlement of:
disputes*, 837
U.K. claims. Economic assistance*, 119
Social security, 119, 1117
Unemployment insurance, 340
West German forces in U.K. facilities*, 340

GHAURI, M. S. K., Morphology & taxonomy of insects, 313

GIBBS-SMITH, C. H.:
Sir George Cayley's Aeronautics, 393
Wellington Museum, 959
World's first aeroplane flights, 1170
Wright Brothers, 637
Gibraltar:
Airflow around model, 622
Aliens OIC, 389
Constitution OIC, 899
Instructions OIC, 632, 899
Legislative Council OIC, 632
Photoposter, 1144
Reports, 101, 317, 548, 803, 1074
Royal Instructions OIC, 899
Spain. Difference with, 1110
GIBSON, SIR, D. (Chairman), New building products, 1167
GIBSON, E., Murder, 137
GILBERT, K. R., Portsmouth blockmaking machinery, 1170
Gilbert & Ellice Islands:
OIC, 632
Reports, 100, 548
Royal Instructions OIC, 632
GILES, C. G., Portable skid-resistance tester, 908
GILL, E., Engraved work, 689
GILLHAM, E. J., Radiometric standards & measurements, 164
GILLIE, A. (Chairman), Field of work of family doctor, 591
GILMORE, R. S., Geometry calculations in scattering experiments, 623
GILYARD-BEER, R., Shap Abbey, 634
Ginkgoales. Fossil, 1068
GIRGIS, S., Heart in trionychidae, 312
GIUSEPPI, M. S., Public Record Office guide, 634

Glaciological observations in Trinity Peninsular etc., 794
GLADMAN, R. J. Principal butt rotts of conifers, 1121
Glamorgan (shire) (and Monmouthshire):
Census:
Leaflet. Population etc., 351
Report, 588

Glamorgan (shire) (and Monmouthshire) (continued):
Forests. Guide, 127
Saxton. Map, 1066
Glasgow:
Census. Leaflet & report, 590
Corporation:
Consolidation (Water etc.) Order Confirmation Act, 1041
Bill, 746
Order Confirmation Acts, 69, 289, 518, 1042
Bills, 41, 263, 490, 1010
No. 2 Order Confirmation Bill, 1014
Parking Meters Order Confirmation Act, 289
Bill, 42
Education Trust Scheme, 1172–3
Royal:
College of Science & Technology. Scheme, 182, 400
Infirmary. Nurses training, 646
Glass:
Bohemian, 1221
English, 903
English table, 1153
manufacture (Careers), 369
Glasses. Fees & charges, 134, 354, 593, 853, 1126, 1127
GLASSEY, S. D., Forecasting in Falkland Islands, 162
Glasshouse(s):
Construction etc. of commercial, 83, 785
Light & heat in, 1049
Mobile, 1052
Salads etc. in, 785
symphylids, 82, 1053
ventilation, 1059
whitefly, 300, 1051
Glen Trool. Forest Park Guide, 1121
Glenbuchat Castle. Guide, 1167
Glenlivet report, 80
GLENTWORTH, R., Soils of country around Aberdeen etc., 528
GLOAG, H. L., Colouring in factories, 178
Global clusters, 1169
Globular clusters, 177, 393, 1169
Glossary of:
atomic terms, 214, 435, 1219
legal terms, 332, 1097
Gloucester(shire):
Census:
Leaflet. Population etc., 589
Report, 848
Harbour Provisional Order Act, 518
Bill, 453, 489
Proposed alteration of area. Map, 604
Saxton. map, 93
Glues. Synthetic. Heating, 395

Goat-keeping. Dairy, 300

Gold & coin. Imports & exports, 105, 321, 552, 807
GOLDRING, D. C. Geology of Loubet Coast, 539
Gonad. Histological changes, 80
Good:
design in housing awards, 361, 601, 864, 1138
posture for boys & girls, 958
GOODEY, J. B., Laboratory methods for work with nematodes, 790
GOODING, E. G., B. Flora of Barbados, 1159
GOODISON, R. R. (Chairman), Aviation kerosene etc., 308
GOODMAN, A. (Chairman), London orchestras, 1061
Goods:
Carriage. See Carriage
Classification. See Classification
False or misleading indications of origin*, 576
Imported. See Imported goods
Goosander & redbreasted merganser, 528
Goose production, 300
Gooseberry(ies):
Advisory leaflet, 529
aphids, 81
powdery mildews, 529, 1052
Gordiodrilus beddard, 542
Gospel stories in English embroidery, 959
Gothic illuminated mss., 1066
GOULD, C., 16th century Italian Schools, 623
Government:
Actuary report, 204, 425, 626, 892, 1161
and the arts, 939
Central. See Central
Chemist report, 180, 396, 640, 906, 1180
contracts for building etc. Works, 390
expenditure. Below the line, 204, 271, 673, 939
organisation booklet, 425
orders in force. Index (Guide), 187, 650, 1177
Publications:
Catalogues, 186, 407, 648, 914, 1176
Consolidated index, 408
Statistical services, 425

G.P.O. See Post Office

Graduates. First employment, 676, 1091
Grafting fruit trees, 530
GRAHAM, R., Wenlock Priory, 1167
GRAHAM-HARRISON, F. L. T. (Chairman), Police cadets, 1130
Grain:
beetle saw-toothed, 530, 1053
bins, in Cyprus, 102
crops. Production (Commonwealth), 104, 319, 550, 1075

Grain (continued):
driers, 85
Drying, 788
Insects & mites in, 1052
weevils, 529
Grand strategy (Second World War), 798
GRANDISON, A. G. C., Genus eupsophus, 312
Grangemouth Burgh Bill, 230
Granolithic concrete etc. Flooring, 904
Grants:
for better homes, 399, 866
Non-recurrent. Notes on procedure, 676, 1091
of honours etc. Committee, 202, 672, 937, 1203
Research, D.S.I.R., 178, 394, 638
to universities & colleges, 1133, 1135
Granular base material, 181
Granulators. Rock, 1200
Graphite. Natural Production & uses, 909
Grass:
Arable crops, &, 1058
Black, 530
Intensive, for grazing, 1050
seeds. Saving, 82
silage:
Advisory leaflet, 1050
Feeding value, 82, 1053
Self-feeding, 1050
staggers in sheep, 301
tetany in cattle, 301
Winter, 784
Grassland management, 83
Gravel see Sand & Gravel
Graves. Servicemen. Netherlands*, 580, 839
GRAY, CAPTAIN J., Undertaking with Secretary of State. Scotland, 527, 529
Grazing. Spring rye, 82
Great:
fire of London. Facsimile, 1176
Northern London Cemetery Act, 69
Ouse Water Act, 69
Yarmouth & Pier Harbour Provisional Order Acts, 290, 518
Bills, 230, 262
Greater London:
Council:
Appointment of officers, 864
General Powers Act, 1042
Money Bill, 1042
Publications, 1124
See also London County Council
Housing, 1142
Greece:
Abolition of visas*, 1110
and Turkey*, 1133
British visitors' passports*, 119
Greek:
and Roman pottery lamps, 540
terracotta figures, 540

GREEN, B., Grimes Grave. Young people's guide, 901
GREEN, G. W., Geology of country around Wells, 1124
GREEN, SIR S. L., Hospital staff recruitment, 593
Green:
belts, 362
manuring, 82
GREENE, REV. J., Correspondence, 1127
GREENE. S. W., Vascular flora, 794
Greenwich:
Hospital:
Accounts, 71, 291, 519, 818, 1086
Income & expenditure, 71, 247, 519, 818, 1087
observations in astronomy etc., 176, 392
Observatory. See Royal Observatory
Park trees, 899
GREENWOOD, P. H.:
Barbus (Cyprinidae), 312
Cichlid fishes, 1069
Dinotopterus blgr., 95
Lake Victoria Haplochromis species, 542
Swimbladder in notopteridae, 797
GREGORY, R. C. L., County Court Manual, 619
GREIRSON, DR., Museum Trust Scheme, 912, 1172
Grenada:
Instructions OIC, 389
Public expenditure, 274
Reports, 100, 803
Grey:
mould in nurseries, 846
seals & fisheries, 624
squirrels, 349
GRIFFITH, J., Jurassic fish, 541
GRIFFITHS, D. A. A., Acarus, 797
GRIFFITHS, D. H., Scotia arc, 794
GRIFFITHS, W. E. B. (Chairman), Altimeter Commitee, 1064
Grime's Grave guide, 633, 901
Grimsby:
Alteration of area, Map, 1140
Corporation Act, 289
GRINNELL, L. V., Stoney Littleton Long Barrow, 633
GROLIER, J., Bookbindings, 1065
Group:
dying of conifers, 127
of Ten. Statement, 941
Grouped flatlets for old people, 362
GROVES, R. (Chairman), Food Standards, 304, 533
Growth:
and recruitment in herring, 303
of economy, 623, 887

Guaranteed Land Stock account, 939

Guarantees. Annual review, (Agriculture), 83, 302, 530, 785, 1021
Guardian's allowance decisions, 382
Guardianship of Infants Bills, 261, 487, 1006, 1011, 1012, 1132
Guarding of platen machines, 375
GUEST, HON. LORD (Chairman), Scottish licensing law, 647
Guided weapons contracts, 861
Gulf Oil Refining Act, 1042
GULLAND, J. A., Fishing in Iceland, 85
GUMLEY, C. S. (Chairman), Hospital catering. Scotland, 403
Guns (3rd Party Insurance) Bill, 742
Gurkhas & Nepal, 1080
GUTENBURG, J., 540
GUTHRIE, B. N. G.:
Rapidly rotating pole on B-type stars, 1170
Rotation of Balmer line intensities, 636
Silicon manganese stars, 1170
Gutters & rainwater pipes. Design, 637

GWYER, J. M. A., Grand strategy, 798
GWYNN, E. H. (Chairman), Prison medical service, 856

Gypsum plasters, 899
Gypsy(ies):
Camps Compensation Bill, 488
Circular, 361

H

Haddock bionomics, 299
Hadleigh Castle. Guide, 633
Hadrian's Wall. Guide, 390, 633
HAIGH, J. H., Radiolocation techniques, 220
Hairdressers (Registration) Act, 772
Bill, 706, 707, 735, 742, 744, 745, 858
Hairdressing & beauty culture (Careers), 369
HALE, SIR E. (Chairman), University teaching methods, 676, 822
Halesowen. Alteration of area, 145
Half:
our future, 594
velocity of radio waves, 812
Halifax. Alteration of area. Map, 866
HALL, B.P.:
Rare birds of Africa, 312
Taxonomy & identification of pipits, 95
HALL, D. N. F., Penaeidae, 548
HALL, J. A., Calibration of temperature measuring instruments, 897
HALL, SIR R. (Chairman):
Economy of Northern Ireland, 357
Transport needs in next 20 years, 670

HALL, W. J., New diaspididae, 311
Hallen Bay. Auroral observations, 539, 794
HALLORAN, T., Report of inquiry into case of, 857
HALSBURY, RT. HON. EARL (Chairman), Decimal currency, 675
Ham House. Guide, 689
HAMILTON, DUKE OF (Chairman), Pilot training, 537
HAMILTON, S. B., Buildings in London (Careers), 369
HAMMOND, R. J., Food. Studies in administration & control, 313
HAMMOND, W. H., Persistent criminals, 596
Hampshire:
Basin. Geology, 129
Census. Leaflet & report, 588
Hampton Court:
Guide, 1167
German edn., 390
Postcards, 221
tapestries, 390
trees, 634
HANCOCK, H. D. (Chairman), Local Government Commission for England, 144, 604, 605, 866
Hand-list of:
coniferae, 391
music in periodicals, 540, 1066
orchids, 391
Hand-washing facilities in public conveniences, 1138
Handbooks. See respective subjects
Handicapped pupils. Special schools, 565
HANDLEY, W. R. C., Mycorrhizal associations etc., 586
Handling of:
purchased seed potatoes, 1053
unit loads, 533
HANDOVER, P. M., History of London Gazette, 1176
Hansard. See House of Commons & House of Lords Debates
Hapton Valley Colliery explosion, 385
Harbours Act, 712
Bill, 487, 491, 701, 703, 735, 742, 743, 858
Hard, soft & cream cheeses (Food standards), 304
HARDING, G. A., Radial velocities, 1169
HARDING, G. L., Archaeology in Aden, 858
HARDING, J. P., Darwin's type specimens, 542
Hardship allowance. National Insurance, 383
Hardwoods:
Identification, 179
Lyctus attack, 906
HARDY, D. E.:
Bibionidae, 1067
Fruit flies, 796

Harlech Castle:
  Guide, 900
  Souvenir, 221
HARPER, F. C., Forces applied to the floor by the foot in walking, 179
HARRIS, R., Political organisation of Mbembe, 1159
HARRIS, T. M.:
  Ctenozamites cycadea, 94
  Yorkshire jurassic flora, 95, 798
HARRISON, D. N., Errors of Meteorological Office Radiosonde, Mark 2B, 378
HARRISON-HALL, M. K., Investigation into affairs of Madingley Investments Ltd., 925
Harrison's Index to tax cases. Supplement, 148, 366, 609, 872
HARROLD, T. W., Estimation of rainfall, 1155
HARRY GOVIER SEELEY & Karoo reptiles, 312
HARTHAN, J. P., Bookbindings, 439
Hartlepool. Proposed county borough. Map, 605
HARTLEY, F. ST. A., Children's Gallery, 903
HARTWELL, B. J. (Chairman), Treatment of offenders, 595
Harunobu and his age, 795
Harvesters. Combine, Potatoes, 788
Harwich Harbour Act, 774
HASTINGS, A. B., Cheilostomatous polyzoa etc., 797
HASWELL, M. R., Economic activity in a Gambia village, 651
Hatchery practice, 83, 785
HAWKES, D. D., Geology of South Shetland Islands, 101
HAWKINS, E. K., Roads etc. in an under-developed country, 409
HAWKINS, J. C., Tractor ploughing, 305
HAWTON, SIR J. (Chairman), British Water-ways Board report, 798
Hay(making):
  Barn drying, 303
  Growing the crop, 82
  Quality & feeding, 82
  Quick, 786
  Swath treatment, 303
HAYES, J.:
  Garton Collection of table glass, 1153
  London since 1912, 376
HAYHOE, F. G. J., Acute leukaemias, 883
HAYNES, D. E. L., Portland vase, 795
HAYNES, S. Etruscan bronze utensils, 1066
HAYTER, SIR W. (Chairman), University Grants Committee, 206
HAYWARD, J. F.:
  English cabinets, 959
  European armour, 1222
  Swords & daggers, 689
  Tables in Victoria & Albert Museum, 218

Hazards to man of nuclear & allied radiations, 160

Headquarters Section. Civil Defence, 135, 136, 355, 356, 394, 855
Health:
  and welfare:
    Development of Community care, 591, 851
    services:
      Ministry of Health, 134, 354, 593, 853
      Scotland, 131, 405, 646, 912, 1174
  Army manual, 1080
  circulars:
    Agriculture, 86
    Health, 132, 133, 853
  Department of Scotland. Publications, 130-1, 402-6, 646-7, 912-3, 1174-5
  Report, 131, 405, 646, 912, 1174
  education, 327, 851
  information for travellers to U.S.A., 688
  Ministry of:
    Annual report, 134, 354, 593, 853, 1127
    Circulars. Index, 132, 133, 853
    Memoranda, 353
    Publications, 131-4, 352-4, 591-3, 850-4, 1124-7
    Report of Chief Medical Officer, 134, 354, 593, 853, 1127
    Statistical Report Series, 1127
  of school child, 113, 327, 821
  of welders, 371
  Service(s):
    in Britain, 365, 871
    in Wales & Monmouthshire, 858
    Superannuation Scheme. Scotland, 912
    Welsh Grand Committee, 735
    Statistics. Scottish, 131, 406, 913, 1175
    Visitors & Social Workers (Training) Act, 288
    Bill, 38, 42, 229, 255, 261, 358
    Accounts & report, 1091
Heart:
  disease & the food you eat, 688
  in trionychidae, 312
HEASMAN, M. A., Mass miniature radiography, 129
Heat:
  bibliography, 179, 394, 396, 641, 906, 1180
  insulating bricks etc., 191
  radiation from fires, 633
  transmission. Building Standards Regulation (Scotland), 644
Heaters, Room, etc. installing, 1166
Heather mineral nutrient status, 1121
Heating:
  in local-authority flats, 178, 180, 904
  systems. Farm, 1059

Hebrew:
  and Samaritan mss., 1066
  Printed books. B. M., 795
Helicopter stations in London area, Planning, 90, 308
HENDEY, N. I., Smaller algae, 788
HENMAN, D. W., Pruning conifers, 586
HENNIKER-HEATON, C. (Chairman), Day release, 821
HENRY IV. Letters, 1168
Hens. Culling laying, 530
HEPBURN, H. A. (Chairman), Accidents in paper mills, 374
Her Majesty's:
  Dockyards. See Dockyards
    Forces (Careers), 368, 612, 1147
    Inspectors. See specific subject. Constabulary etc.
    Ministers etc. 186, 408, 673, 939, 1204
    speech to Parliament, 141, 232, 456, 709, 975
HERBERT, J. A., Romances. Catalogue, 540
Herbs. Culinary & medicinal, 83
Herefordshire:
  Census:
    Leaflet. Population etc., 589
    Report, 848
    Saxton map, 795
HERIOT, GEORGE. Trust Scheme, 1172
Heriot-Watt College Order Confirmation Bill, 1014
HERON, A., Ageing & the semi-skilled, 160
Herring:
  downs. Fecundity, 85
  fishery. Environment of, 80
  Growth & recruitment, 303
  Histological change in gonad, 80
  Industry:
    Acts. Accounts, 86, 402, 533, 788, 1059
    Board, 86, 304, 533, 788, 1059
    rearing, 299
    Recent round, 543
    Vitamin A & fat, 528
  Herringbone parlour. Recent literature, 1049
Hertfordshire. Census:
  Leaflet. Population, 589
  Occupation Groups, 1123
  Reports, 588
HESELTINE, H. K., Thermal conductivity meters, 79
Hetaerina Takasei Nakas, f 12
Heterosporous plants, 1068
HETHERINGTON, SIR H. (Chairman), Royal Fine Arts Commission. Scotland, 406
HEWETT, P. C., Investigation. Eurotrust Ltd., 1191
HEY, M. H., Mineral species & varieties, 312

HEYWORTH, RT. HON. LORD (Chairman):
  Council on prices productivity & incomes, 173
  Social studies, 1090
  University Appointments Board, 822
Hieroglyphic texts from Egyptian stelae, 310
HIGGINS, R., Jewellery, 1066
HIGGINS, R. A., Greek terracotta figures, 540
High:
  altitude:
    nuclear explosions, 637
    research project*, 547
  Court & Court of Appeal. Receipts & expenditure, 159, 376, 619, 882
  seas. Convention, 577
  Velocity stars, 903
Higher:
  Award in business studies, 821
  Education. See Education, Higher
  National Certificates. See specific subjects
  Police Training, 357, 595
Highland(s):
  and Islands:
    Advisory Panel. Land use, 782
    Development (Scotland) Act, 1040
    Bill, 972, 974, 1006, 1009, 1011, 1013, 1132
    Shipping Services Act. Undertaking, 79
  Transport services in, 670
  transport enquiry, 196, 670
Highway(s):
  Act 1959. Circular, 361
  Amendment Act, 1040
  Bill, 746, 970, 1006, 1132
  Bridges. See Bridges.
  Code. Welsh edition, 420
  Loadings. Standard, 197
  Liability for animals Bill, 39
  Miscellaneous Provisions Act, 67
  Bill, 6, 7, 34, 38, 41, 42, 138
  Statistics, 933, 1198
  Straying Animals Bill, 741, 1010
HILL, F. G. (Chairman), Home refuse disposal, 146
HILL, J. E., Hipposideros, 543
HILL-BURTON, S., Inquiry, 857
HILLIER, R. (Chairman), Cutlery & silverware trades. Sheffield, 881
HINES, B., DUCKS, 938
HINTON, H. E., Pests in food, 543
Hipparrinus etc., 797
Hipposideros, 543
Hire Purchase:
  Acts, 772, 1040
  Bills, 42, 232, 456, 697, 699, 705, 735, 742, 743, 858, 969, 1013, 1136-7
  Consolidation of enactments, 969
  Index to government orders, 1177

Hire Purchase (continued):
  Limitation of Payments Bill, 489
  of Motor Vehicles Bill, 39
  Scotland Act, 1040
    Bill, 969, 1013, 1136-7
Histological changes in gonad, 80
Historic(al):
  books on machines, 616
  Buildings:
    and Ancient Monuments. Estimates committee, 140
    See also Ancient monuments.
    Bill, 487
    Council. Annual reports, 221-2, 390, 633, 901, 1167
    Repair & preservation, 1167
  guide to sculptures of Parthenon, 310
  Manuscripts Commission, 134, 354, 593-4, 854, 1127
  Monuments. York, 392
    See also Royal Commission & Ancient Monuments.
    Series. B. M., 94, 312, 543, 1066
  Hive. British National, 82
H.M. Customs. See Customs
H.O. (Transport) Forms, 358
HOBMAN, D., Voluntary service, 939
Hod Hill antiquities, 310
HOGARTH, WILLIAM. Calendar, 1067
HOGG, J. M.:
  Fires associated with electric cooking appliances, 639
  Fires involving liquified petroleum gas, 639
HOGG, RT. HON. Q., Complaint concerning speech, 860
Holarctic sawflies, 311
HOLDEN, A. V., Cyanide in salmon & trout, 782
HOLDEN, H. S., Botryopteris antiqua, 311
HOLDEN, M. J. Fish populations, 548
HOLDER, D. W. Schlieren methods, 641
HOLE, G. V. (Chairman):
  Air freight, 137
  Third London airport, 792
Holidays. Staggered, 663
HOLLAND, C. H., Silurian rocks of Ludlow district, 542
HOLLAND, SIR M. (Chairman), Housing in Greater London, 1142
HOLLIS, D. Diptera of Nepal, 796
HOLLOWAY, A. (Chairman), Gas turbine collaboration, 307
HOLMES, M. Crown Jewels in Tower of London, 389
HOLMES, M. B. Moorfields in 1559, 618
HOLTAM, H. W., Roundwood, 846
Holy:
  Table Measure, 700, 775, 800
  Trinity Brompton Act, 69

Holyrood House. Guide, 633
Home(s):
  for today & tomorrow:
    Circular, 361
    Report, 143
    freezing of fruit & vegetables, 300
    grown:
      roundwood, 846
      timbers, 905, 1180
    Office:
      Children's Dept. Work, 137, 857
      Circular, 854
      Estimates Committee, 599, 600
      Publications, 134-7, 355-8, 594-6, 854-7, 1128-31
      Safety Act, 67
        Bill, 3, 34, 138
      Honduras. Abolition of visas*, 340
      Honey from hive to market, 551
      Honeybees use in orchards, 300
      HONEYBONE, R. M., Milletts Holdings. Investigation, 660
      HONEYMAN, G. (Chairman):
        Salaries of teachers, 1089
        Sugar confectionery etc. Wages Council, 159
  Hong Kong:
    History, 899
    Instructions OIC, 899
    Photoposter, 609
  HONOURABLE LADY HYLTON-FOSTER. See Hylton-Foster
  Honours:
    decorations & medals. committee on grants, 202, 672, 937, 1203
    lists, 186, 187, 408, 649, 914, 915, 1176-7
  HOOPER, P. R., Petrology of Anvers Island, 318
  HOPKINS, G. H. E., Fleas. Catalogue, 312
  HOPKINSON, R. G., Architectural physics. Lighting, 637
  HOPSON, A. J., Barbus, 1069
  Horticulture(al):
    Co-operative marketing, 85
    Commercial, 300
    crops:
      Chemical weed control, 301, 1053
      Watering equipment, 1059
      machinery. Leaflets, 304, 533, 1059
      planting material, 303
  Hospital(s):
    abstracts, 133, 353, 591-2, 851-2, 1125-6
    boards. Regional. Accounts, 133, 354, 593, 853, 1127
    Scotland, 131, 405, 647, 913, 1174
    building:
      bulletin, 133, 852, 1126
      Cost, 133

Hospital(s) (continued):
  building (continued):
    Maintenance, 853
    notes, 133, 353, 592, 852, 1126
    Progress report, 353, 592, 852, 853, 1126
    Scotland, 403, 647
    catering: 353
    Scotland, 403
    caring. grants, 134, 354, 593, 853, 1126
    Children's Dept. Work, 137, 857
    design:
      in use. Scotland, 647, 1174
      notes, 852, 1126
      District General. Building, 133
      Endowments Fund. Account, 133, 592, 852, 1126
      engineers, 354
      equipment notes, 353, 592, 852, 1126
      Equipping, 353
      grounds etc., 132
      medical records. Standardisation, 1125
      Mental patients, 589
      O & M. reports, 133, 593, 852
      patients. See Patients
      Plan:
        England & Wales, 353, 593, 853
        Scotland, 403, 913
        planning notes Scotland, 130, 403, 647, 1174
      redevelopment, 852
      Regional Boards. See Hospital Boards
      Scottish. See Scottish Hospitals
      service. Abstracts of efficiency studies, 131, 352, 591, 850-1, 1124-5
      Special, 134
      staff:
        Accommodation, 852
        Recruitment etc., 593
        Technical Memorandum, 353, 592, 852, 1126
        transport, 132, 591, 592, 851
        Working Party Report, 134
      See also respective departments & services etc. & National Health Service, Hospitals.
  Hot & cold open-tank process of impregnating timber, 906
  Hotel:
    and catering industry. (Careers), 151, 874
    keeping & catering. Diplomas, 565
    keepers. Liability for property, 577
  Hours of employment, 618
  HOUSE, D. V. (Chairman), Shipping services to N.I., 670
  House(s):
    Aluminium, 865
    building:
      Dimensional co-ordination. Circular, 602

House(s) (continued):
  building (continued):
    Industrialised. Circular, 1139
    Protection of Purchasers Bill, 1008
    Buyers Protection Bill, 742, 1010
    Daylighting & space, 910
    flies etc., 300, 1052
    improvement. Circulars, 361, 1139
    in multiple occupation 361, 865
    Longhorn beetle, 640, 1180
    Purchase & Housing Act:
      Accounts, 143, 604, 866, 1139
      Circular, 361
      refuse disposal, 146
      socket outlet wiring, 394
      sparrow, 529
      See also Housing, & Dwellings
  House of Commons: 137-41, 358-60, 596-600, 857-63, 1131-6
    Bills, 38-41, 260-4, 487-91, 741-6, 1008-14
    Broadcasting of proceedings, 1135-6
    Ceremonial, 137
    Debates, 32-3, 38, 254-5, 259-60, 481-2, 486, 733-4, 740, 1001, 1007
    Bound volumes, 10, 33, 234, 255, 457, 482, 711, 734, 1004, 1005 6
    Disqualification Acts, 287, 516, 771, 1039
    Dress, Official, 139
    History, 1754-90, 854
    Journals, 10
    Kitchen (and Refreshment Rooms), 141, 250, 600, 862, 1135
    Letter to members. Privileges report, 1134
    Library:
      Documents, 70, 519
      Estimates Committee report, 139, 140
    Members:
      Fund:
        Accounts, 137, 258, 597, 857, 1131
        Act, 288
        Bill, 230, 263
        Sick. Arrangements, 1134
    Minutes of Proceedings, 137-9, 358-9, 597-8, 857-60, 1131-3
      See also specific subjects
    Official Dress, 139
    Papers, 9-38, 233-60, 457-81, 710-40, 978-1003
    Index, 137, 139, 359, 360, 598, 860, 1133
    Special report. Select Committee, 1136
    Privileges Committee, 139, 860, 1134
    Procedure. Select Committee, 248, 599, 861, 1134

HOU— INDEX 1961-5

House of Commons (continued):
Public:
Accounts Committee, 139, 140, 235, 249, 359, 458, 485, 599, 861, 862, 1134, 1135
Bills. Returns, 139, 359, 598, 860, 1001
Publications & Deb tes. Select Committee, 599, 1135
Reports, 139-40, 359, 598-600, 860-1, 1133
Select Committee. See specific subjects
Services. Select Committee, 1135
Special reports, 140-1, 359-60, 600, 861-2, 1135
See also specific subjects
Standing:
Committee Debates. See Standing Committee
Orders. See Standing Orders
House of Lords: 141-2, 360, 600-1, 863-4, 1136-8
Consolidation Bills, 141, 226, 228, 230, 233, 360, 600-1, 863, 1136-7
Debates, 7-8, 9, 231-2, 233, 455, 457, 708-9, 710, 976-8
Bound volumes, 1, 8, 225, 447, 697, 976, 978
Manuscripts, 447
Offices. Select Committee, 141, 231, 232, 450, 455, 456, 703, 863, 968, 1137
Papers & Bills, 1-9, 225-33, 447-57, 697-710, 963-76
Privileges Committee, 600, 863
Procedure, 142, 454, 456, 863, 1137
Reform, 231, 233
Roll of Lords, 141, 232, 456, 863, 1137
Select Committee, 5, 6, 8, 141, 142, 230, 231, 232, 701
Special Orders Committee, 142, 227, 228, 229, 230, 232, 233, 360, 448, 449, 452, 453, 455, 701, 710, 863, 1137
Standing Orders, 142, 231, 701, 864, 1137, 1138
Household & Wardrobe documents, 902
Housing:
Acts, 67, 772
Accounts, 673, 866, 1204
Bills, 6, 7, 34, 39, 41, 42, 138, 487, 490, 702, 704, 706, 735, 742, 744, 858
Circulars, 142, 361, 865
Forms, 361
and Local Government. Ministry of, Circulars, 142-3, 361-2, 601-2, 864-5, 1138-9
Forms, 143, 603
Provisional Orders. See respective towns
Publications, 142-6, 360-4, 601-7, 864-9, 1138-43
Report, 146, 363, 607, 868, 1142

1961 pp 1-224, 1962 pp 225-445, 1963 pp 447-696, 1964 pp 697-962, 1965 pp 963-1226

56

INDEX 1961-5 —IMP

Housing (continued):
the Arts, 88
Association. Circular, 361
calves, 1059
Circular, 1138
Command Paper, 604
Corporation report, 1140
Cost:
guidance, 602
yardstick, 603
Design:
Awards, 361, 601, 864, 1138
Bulletin, 362
dimensions & components, 603
Exchange of accommodation. London, 1138
Financial Provisions Act. Circular, 361
for ex-servicemen. Circular, 1139, 1222
Good design. Awards, 361, 601, 864, 1138
in:
Britain, 148
England & Wales, 143
Greater London, 1142
Scotland, 130
indices. Local, 1123
management. Circular, 1139
mission to Canada, 634
National summary tables, 849, 850
pigs, 302
Planning & environment (Scottish Health Dept.), 131, 405
Programme:
1965-70, 1140
1965-70 Scottish, 1175
provisions. Greater London Council, 1138
return:
England & Wales, 143-4, 362, 604, 866, 1019, 1140
Scotland, 130, 399, 403, 644, 910, 1018, 1171
Scotland(tish): 130
Accounts, 910, 1171, 1204
Act, 288
Bill, 42, 228, 244, 255, 262
Amendment Act, 1040
Bill, 973, 1006, 1011, 1132
Command Paper, 130
Financial Provisions Bill, 1014
Handbook, 644
Programme, 1175
Return, 130, 399, 403, 644, 910, 1018, 1171
Slum Clearance Compensation Act, 1040
Bill, 975, 976, 1013, 1014
standards. Regulations (Scotland), 910
Subsidies Bill, 1014
summary, 144, 281, 282, 286, 362, 604, 866, 1020, 1025, 1140

Housing (continued):
tables. Census, 1123
tenders. Procedure, 602
Welsh Grand Committee, 256
How research can help training, 907

Huddersfield:
Alteration of area. Map, 866
Corporation Act, 1042
Hudson Bay Marine Insurance Rates report, 105, 320
HUGHES, A. M., Mites in stored food, 87
HUGHES, L. E., Post-mortem examinations of sheep, 785
HUGHES-HUGHES, A., Manuscript music. Catalogue, 795
Hull. Alteration of area. Map, 867
Human:
bone. Strontium 90 in, 160, 376-7, 619, 883, 1154
relations in obstetrics, 132
rights & fundamental freedoms. Convention, 344, 577-8, 837
sciences:
Aid to industry, 180
Register of research, 399, 643, 1181
skeletal remains, 543
Tissue Act, 67
Bill, 6
HUMMEL, F. C., Tariff tables, 348
Hungary(ian):
Civil aviation*, 119
Property accounts, 200, 422, 671, 936, 1201
HUNTER, LORD (Chairman), Scottish fisheries, 529, 1051
HUNTER, J. (Chairman), Central Training Council, 1146
HUNTER, J. O. M., Investigation into Eglinton Hotels (Scotland) Ltd., 189
Huntingdon & Biggleswade. Geology, 1124
Huntingdonshire:
and Soke of Peterborough. Amalgamation, 603
Census:
Leaflet. Population etc., 589
Report, 848
Saxton map, 93
HURCOMBE, LORD (Chairman), Bird life in Royal Parks, 389
HUTCHINSON, J. C., Modern foreign languages, 688
Hyades stars, 1169
HYATT, K. H., Mesostigmata, 797
Hyde Park (Underground Parking) Act, 67
Bill, 3, 34, 39, 138
Map, 197
Hydraulic Research:
Papers, 179, 181, 640, 1180
Station. Publications & report, 179, 396, 640, 906, 1180

Hydro-electric:
Boards. See North of Scotland & South of Scotland
Development (Scotland) Act Loans, 204, 425, 673, 939, 1204
Hydrogen:
Cyanide vapour detection, 159
Sulphide detection, 168
Hydrographical surveys. River Tyne, 303
Hydrography. Britain's contribution, 1158
Hydroids of cytaeidae, 312
Hydrological surveys, 144, 362, 603, 866, 868
Hydrometers & hydrometry, 397
Hydrometric statistics for British rivers, 146, 364, 869, 1142
Hygiene in milk production, 82
Hygrometric tables, 377, 884, 1155
HYLTON-FOSTER, HON. LADY, Act, 1040
Bill, 975, 1013
Hypomagnesaemia, 301

I

Ice accretion on aircraft, 1155
Iceland:
British visitors' passports*, 120
Fisheries dispute*, 120

Identification of:
British mammals, 797
cephalopod "Beaks" 542
common water weeds, 302
hardwoods, 179
I.G. reports, 215, 435, 953
Igneous rocks of Midlands, 542

Ill-treatment of Durham prisoners, 596
Illness among children. U.S. survey, 958
Illuminated manuscripts & printed books, 1066

Immature stages of Australasian timber beetles, 543
Immigrant(tion):
Control of, Statistics 594, 855, 1128
English for, 565
from Commonwealth, 1129
Officers. Instructions, 317, 356
See also Commonwealth Immigrants
Immunological procedures. Memo., 219, 810
Impact:
loading on concrete beams, 395
of rates on households, 1139
Imperial:
Calendar & Civil Service List, 186, 407, 671, 936, 1201

1961 pp 1-224, 1962 pp 225-445, 1963 pp 447-696, 1964 pp 697-962, 1965 pp 963-1226

57

IMP— INDEX 1961-5

Imperial (continued):
Defence Committee. Papers, 902
Ottoman Loans, 425, 674
War Museum. Handbook, 607
Import:
Duties Act. Annual report, 190, 251, 661, 926, 1192
Licences, 190, 413, 661, 926, 1191
Importation of Rare Animals Bill, 741
Imported:
goods:
entered for home use, 106, 553, 808, 1078
Statistical classification, 106, 322, 553, 808, 1078
manufactures. Competitiveness, 1157
raw cucumbers. Merchandise marks, 533
Improvement(ing):
and conversion grants. Circular, 361
of foundry environment, 375
houses. Circular, 361, 1139
to land and buildings. Farm, 304

In-patients. See Patients
In-sack grain drying, 788
Incapacity for work. Incidence of, 893
Inclusion of equivalent metric values in scientific papers, 906
Income(s):
policy, 425
prices, employment & production. Statistics, 375, 618, 881, 1153
Tax:
Acts. Supplements, 148, 366, 609, 871, 872, 1144
and estate duty on woodlands, 846
in and outside Commonwealth, 148, 366, 609, 872, 1144
Management Act, 772
Bill, 702, 735, 741, 742, 858
on company profits, 872
Incubation & hatchery practice, 83, 785
Incumbents & Churchwardens (Trusts) Measure, 698, 775, 800
Independent:
Chapel, Bolton Act, 289
Schools:
England & Wales, 113, 565
Protection Bill, 745
Television Authority:
Advances, 170
Annual report, 256, 384, 629, 895, 1163
Payments by contractors, 1163
Index:
and Digest. Commissioners. National Insurance, 890, 1160
of:
defence publications, 111, 326, 818, 1086
exposure to driving rain, 394

Index (continued):
of (continued):
mineral species, 312, 541
place names (Census), 1122
published infra-red spectra, 89
retail prices, 369, 880
to:
Army Orders, 219, 440, 690, 810, 1080
BRS digests, 394, 904, 1178
Commissioners' decisions, 165, 381, 625, 890
Education circulars, 113, 327, 565, 821, 1089
Government:
Orders, 187, 650, 1177
Publications, 408
Health Circulars, 133, 853
Parliamentary papers. See Parliamentary papers
registers. Scottish Record Office, 185, 407, 648, 914, 1176
Statutes in force, 187, 409, 650, 915, 1177
Treaty Series, 125, 268, 344, 584, 844, 1110
India(ns):
and Pakistan. Royal tour. Photoposter, 147
art. Guide, 689
British, Ocean territory OIC, 1166
Cereals*, 805
Commonwealth development & its financing, 550
in a plural society, 409
Mazagon Dockyard etc. Credit*, 806
Office Library. Drawings, 320
Indo-China. British involvement, 1111
Indo-Pacific alosinae, 1069
Indo-Pakistan cleoninae, 541
Indo-West Pacific plankton, 101
Indonesia:
Air services*, 120
War cemeteries etc.*, 578
Indus Basin Development Fund. Agreement, 120, 1159
Industrial(ised):
accident declaration. National Insurance, 383, 892
and Provident Societies:
Acts, 67, 1040
Bills, 3, 4, 34, 39, 41, 138, 710, 963, 964, 967, 1010, 1136
Report of Chief Registrar, 128, 350, 587, 848, 1122
Assurance Commissioner. Reports, 128, 351, 587, 848, 1122
bacteria, 1181
building:
and educational building. Consortia, 820
Dimensional co-ordination, 900

Industrial(ised) (continued):
building (continued):
Dimensions & components, 603
classification. Standard, 544
Coal Consumers Council, 172, 386, 630, 897, 1165
Court(s):
Act. Reports of inquiries, 614, 877, 1149
Awards, 155-8, 371-4, 614-7, 877-80, 1149-51
death benefit. Decisions, 168, 169, 383, 892, 1161
dermatitis. Precautionary measures, 375
Design(s):
Council of:
Publications, 146-7, 364, 608, 869, 1143
Report, 146, 364, 608, 869, 1143
Departmental Committee, 415
Papers. H.L., 926
development:
Certificate, 361
in U.K. Dependencies, 148
disablement benefit. Decisions, 168, 383, 627, 892, 893, 1161
diseases (Byssinosis) Bills, 264, 1007, 1009, 1132
Estate Management Corporations, 415, 662, 715, 1193
fibres. Production (Commonwealth), 104, 319, 550, 804, 1075
furnaces. Clean Air Act, 143
Group. Reports (UKAEA), 215
health:
Annual report. Chief Inspector Factories, 151, 368, 611, 874, 1146
Services. Organisation, 375
housebuilding, 1139
injury benefits. Decisions, 168, 169, 383, 627, 893, 1161
See also National Insurance (Industrial Injuries)
inspection. Subjective standards, 907
Insurance Acts Guide, 350
Organisation & Development Act Accounts, 414, 466, 929, 1192
property. Convention, 340
relations. Handbook, 1158
safety & education service, 400
Training:
Act, 772
Bills, 487, 491, 698, 700, 701, 742, 858
Government Proposals, 374
Industry(ies):
Alphabetical list, 544
and employment:
in Scotland, 184, 246, 256, 403, 406, 644
in Wales, 467, 483

Industry(ies) (continued):
Ergonomics in, 178
Problems of progress in, 180, 641, 907
Queen's award to, 1166
Research for, 180, 394, 642, 907, 1180
Infancy. Sudden death in, 1127
Infanticide Bill, 1012
Infarction. Cerebral, 161
Infestation control 1959-61, 304
Influence of metal abundance of spectra in late-type dwarfs, 393
Information:
Central Office of:
Estimates Committee, 140
Publications, 147-8, 365-6, 608-9, 869-71, 1143-4
for consumer education, 1077
Informatory signs. Roads, 932, 1198
Infra-red spectra. Index, 89
INGLIS, W. G.:
Enoplida, 797
Nematodes, 95, 312, 543
Strongyles, 1069
Inland Revenue:
Commissioners' reports, 205, 426, 610, 872, 1145
Estimates Committee, 140, 141, 600
Publications, 148-51, 366-8, 609-11, 871-4, 1144-6
Tax Cases. See Tax Cases
Inland telephone service, 629
Innocent misrepresentation. Law Reform Committee, 376
Input-output tables, U.K., 96
Inquisitions Miscellanea. Calendar, 634
Insect(s):
and mice in grain, 1052
emergence from Loch, 80
fossil. Charmouth, 312
Instructions for collectors, 543
Male scale, 313
pests in food stores, 82, 543
scale on fruit, 783
Inserting damp-proof course, 1166
Inspection:
and certification of fruit plants, 1053
of gauging dimensions involving linear & angular measurements, 397
Inspector of Weights & Measures. Examination, 1191
Installing solid-fuel appliances, 1166
Institute of Animal Physiology, 298, 782
Instructions:
for collectors:
Fishes & plants, 1069
Fossils etc., 312
Insects, 543
to:
Immigration Officers, 317, 356
Presiding Officers, 405

Insurance:
  business. Statements, 191, 414, 661, 1192
  Careers, 875
  Companies:
    Act:
      Insurance business, 191, 414, 661, 1192
    Investigation, 190
    Life assurance, 190, 414, 661
  Share Capital. Bill, 260
Insured letters etc.*, 126
Intensive:
  grass for grazing, 1050
  livestock husbandry system, 1037
  poultry management, 1054
  stocking of sheep, 301
Inter-allied Reparation Agency. Final Report, 611
Inter-continental testing U.S.A.*, 126
Inter-departmental Committee on social & economic research, 151
Inter-governmental:
  debts, Czechoslovakia*, 330, 569, 825
  Maritime Consultative Organisation, 151, 842
Inter-library co-operation, 327
Inter-stellar:
  medium & galactic structure, 903
  reddening, 1169, 1170
International:
  Atomic Energy Agency, 270, 578
  Bank for Reconstruction, 672, 939, 1111
  carriage by air. Convention, 120, 757
  civil aviation. Convention, 116, 120, 330, 578
  code of signals. Supp., 196
  coffee*, 330, 341, 1093
  Commission. Vietnam, 126, 348, 1120
  conventions. See specific subject
  Court of Justice. Declaration, 837
  Development Association:
    Act, 772
    Bill, 700, 741
    Articles of agreement, 120
    Executive directors. Report, 674
  exchange of publications, 341
  Exhibition of 1862, 439
  Finance Corporation, 120, 425, 576
  Headquarters & Defence Organisation Act, 772
  Bill, 456, 491
  Institute of Refrigeration, 582
  Labour:
    Conference, 120, 158, 374, 617, 837
    Convention, 341, 374, 579, 617, 837
    Organisation, 120, 837, 1111
  law. Private. See Private International Law
  military H.Q. Protocol NATO, 1114

International (continued):
  Monetary Fund:
    Acts, 288, 1040
    Bills, 227, 261, 974, 1011
    Arrangements for borrowing, 422
    Resources, 1025
    monetary system (Group of Ten), 941
  organisation(s):
    of legal metrology, 342
    publications. Catalogue, 187, 408, 648, 914, 1176
  Patents Bureau*, 1114
  Poplar Commission, 120, 343
  Printing Machinery & Allied Trades Exhibition, 540
  Rice Commission, 582
  rights & obligations. Sierra Leone*, 123
  sale of goods. Law, 837
  sanitary regulations, 341, 582, 842
  science reports, 624
  scientific organisations. Guide, 689
  sugar agreement, 843
  telecommunications Convention, 120
  tin agreement, 125, 346
  tracing service, 120
  transport:
    Goods by road, 838
    Pallets, 120
  Whaling. Convention, 126, 1120
  wheat agreement, 348, 585, 1120
Intestacy (Scotland) Bill, 40
Introducing computers, 1204
Inventions:
  British, 608
  Development of. See Development
  Secrecy of*, 342, 582, 839
  Inveraray. Transfer of Old Town, 202
  Inverness. Census:
    Leaflet. Population etc., 590
    Report, 590
Investment:
  appraisal, 1157
  disputes report, 1111
  Machine tools, 1157

Ionising radiations:
  at exhibitions, 177
  Industrial users, 159
  Protection of:
    persons. Code of practice, 851, 875
    workers. Convention, 579
I.P.E.X., 540
Ipswich. Alteration of area. Map, 1110
Iran:
  Commerce & navigation, 838
  Cultural Convention, 121
Iraq. Trade with, 194
Ireland:
  Air services*, 123, 842, 1077

Ireland (continued):
  Bacon supply*, 788
  Cereals*, 803
  Free trade area*, 1038
Irish:
  Land Purchase Fund. Accounts, 163, 379, 622, 886, 1156
  Peers. Petition, 976
Iron:
  and Steel:
    Act. Accounts, 204, 425, 674, 1204
    Statement on pension, 386
    and Alloying Metals. Production (Commonwealth), 319, 1075
  Board:
    Annual reports, 170, 247, 630, 897, 1165
    Chairman's remuneration, 172
    Members' pension, 386
    Special report, 172, 630, 897
  Careers, 152
  Financial Provisions Act Loans, 386, 897, 1204
  Holdings & Realisation Agency:
    Reports, 204, 674, 939, 1204
    Selling securities etc., 202, 204, 427, 672
  Industry:
    Development in, 172, 897
    Research in, 630
    Training Board, 1151
  Realisation account, 204, 425, 674, 1204
  scrap. Export licenses, 190, 413, 660, 926, 1191
  Ore:
    imports into South Wales, 1223
    ports & industrial development. Wales, 1007, 1131
  Ironstone Restoration Fund Account, 145, 363, 606, 868, 1140
  Irradiation of Food. Working party, 851
  Irrigation:
    Agricultural Bulletin, 302
    in Great Britain, 394
    of farm crops, 82
    Outdoor, 82, 1053

Isle(s) of:
  Ely. Census:
    Leaflet. Population etc., 589
    Report, 849
  Man. Financial agreement, 136
  Bull).:
    Ancient monuments, 221
    Census:
      Leaflet. Population etc., 589
      Report, 848
  Wight:
    Census. Leaflet. Population etc., 588
    River & Water Authority Act, 774

Isobella F. McDonald, Bequest Fund Scheme, 912, 1173
Israel:
  Double taxation*, 341, 578
  Financial matters*, 1111
  Trade in cotton yarn*, 1111

Italy(ian):
  Air services. Route schedules, 578, 838
  books. 15th century, 540
  British visitors' passport*, 121
  Customs, dollar*, 1095
  Double Taxation*, 578
  drawings. Raphael, 310
  Fuels & lubricants. War Graves Commission, 121, 578
  Judgment in civil & commercial matters, 838
  language guide, 957
  Local taxation*, 1112
  school. Catalogue, 623, 1157
  sculpture in Victoria & Albert Museum, 959
  secular silver, 439
  Vehicle rear lights etc.*, 341

Ivory Coast. Visas*, 1111

J

Jack, D. T. (Chairman):
  Dispute at Spitalfields etc., Markets, 881
  Ford Motor Co. Dispute, 614
  Rural bus services, 199
  Salaries of teachers, 1090
Jackson, C. J. (Chairman), Water Pollution Research Board, 1181
Jackson, T. H. E., Epitolinae, 311, 796
Jacobian elliptic functions. Tables, 906
Jacobs, K. C., British Guiana. Financial position, 862
Jades. Maya, 795
Jago, N. D., Caliptamus Serville, 541
Jakubski, A. W., Margarodidae, 1069
Jamaica:
  Arms, 542
  becomes a sovereign nation, 365
  Commonwealth development & financing, 804
  Double taxation*, 1111
  Flag, 519
  Independence:
    Act, 288
    Bill, 230, 263
    Conference, 318
  International rights & obligations*, 551
  Making of a nation. Reference Pamphlet, 366

Jamaica (continued):
  Photoposter, 365
  Public officers*, 103
  Reports, 100, 317, 548, 1074
James, A. E., Inquiry. Det. Sgt. Challenor, 1130
James, M. T., Blow flies, 796
Jameson, C., Stamp trading, 807
Jamieson, B. G. M., Gordiodrilus Beddard, 542
Japan(ese):
  Abolition of visas*, 578
  and other nephrids, 1069
  Antarctic pelagic whaling*, 838
  armour, 1168
  beetle, 1012
  Consular Convention, 838
  Cultural agreement, 121
  Double taxation*, 341, 578
  Money orders*, 1111, 1113
  Treaty of:
    commerce etc., 341, 579
    Peace Act. Accounts, 191, 661, 926, 1112
  War against, 96, 313, 1070
Jasper & Co. Ltd., Investigation into affairs, 189

Jeannel, R., Pselaphides de Ceylon, 94
Jeffers, J. N. R., Forest statisticians, 1121
Jeffrey, A. G., Records & accounts for farm management, 786
Jeffries, Sir C., Review of Colonial research, 1940-1960, 889
Jellicoe, Earl, (Chairman), Water resources in North West, 602
Jenkins, Rt. Hon. Lord (Chairman):
  Company law, 189, 412
  Law reform committee, 159, 376, 619
Jenkins, E., Index & digest of decisions given by Commissioner, 890
Jennings, Sir I. Magna Carta, 1144
Jenour, Sir M. (Chairman), Conference on science & industry, 394
Jenson, A. G.:
  Proofing of buildings against rats, 1061
Jersey:
  Double taxation*, 1110
  Family allowance*, 1110
Jewel Tower, Westminster. Guide, 1167
Jewellery from classical lands, 1066

Jobbing, J., Poplar cultivation, 586
John Constable's correspondence, 354
John F. Kennedy. See Kennedy
John Murray expedition, 542
John Watson, Trust Scheme, 182, 400
Johnson, A. E., Complex-stress creep etc. of metallic alloys, 396
Johnson, G. A. L., Geology of Moor House, 624

Johnston, K. (Chairman), Industrial designs, 415
Johore Para Rubber Co. Ltd. Investigation into affairs, 925
Joint Services:
  handbook of lubricants, 691
  non-metallic materials Advisory Board, 1064
Jointing with mastics & gaskets, 637
Jones, A. (Chairman), National Board for prices & incomes, 1156
Jones, B. (Chairman), Audio visual aids, 1091
Jones, D. H. P.:
  Ao stars, 393
  Radial velocities, 176
Jones, F. E., Aluminium etc. in building materials, 638
Jones, J. D. (Chairman), Piccadilly Circus, 1141
Jones, R.:
  Changes in gear selectivity & fishing effort, 80
  Haddock bionomics, 299
Jones, S. L., London Government, 363
Jones, T. I.:
  Capacitors etc, 164
  Signal generators etc, 397
Jordan, K., Tunga Caecigena, 311
Jordan:
  Loans*, 121, 341, 579, 838, 1028, 1111-2
  Money orders*, 579
  Treaty of alliance*, 121, 579
Journal of:
  African administration, 102
  local administration overseas, 410, 651, 889, 1159
Journalism (Careers), 875
Judges:
  Remuneration Act, 1040
    Bill, 974, 1012
  Rules etc, to police, 854
Judgment in civil & commercial matters. See respective countries
Judicial:
  business (Legal Aid) Standing orders, 142
  Proceedings (Regulation of Reports) Bill, 40
  statistics:
    England & Wales, 159, 376, 619, 882, 1154
    Scotland, 184, 275, 504, 913, 1174
Junior:
  secondary education. New ways, 646
  training centres. Building note, 592
Jurassic:
  bivalvia, 1068
  fish, 541
  flora, 95, 798
  ostracoda, 542, 797

Jurors. Criminal procedure, 855
Justices of the Peace:
  Act, 1040
    Bill, 967, 1007, 1011, 1132
  Subsistence Allowances Bill, 1011
  Training of, 1154

K

Kaines-Thomas, E. G., Donnington Castle, 900
Kale as feedingstuff, 300, 1052
Kamaran Royal Instructions OIC, 632
Kapur, A. P., Coccinellidae, 541
Karabag, T., Drymadusa Stein, 94
Karmeli, D. (Chairman):
  British wool marketing scheme, 299
  Truck Acts, 159
Kautmann, C. M.:
  Barbizon School, 1221
  Legend of St. Ursula, 959
  Paintings at Apsley House, 1222
Kay, A. E., Marine molluscs, 1069
Kay, H., Teaching machines, 641
Kaye, P., Marine Cretaceous ostracoda, 1068
Keele University Act, 290
Keen, A. M., Gastropod family Vermetidae, 94
Keith Of Avonholm Rt. Hon. Lord (Chairman), Scottish Record Office, 646
Keitha disease, 586
Kelly, A., Fibre re-inforcement of metals, 1063
Kelsall, R. K., Women & teaching, 566
Kelts. Furunculosis, 299
Kennedy, J. F.:
  Assassination. President's Commission, 958
  Eulogies, 957
  Memorial Act, 772
    Bill, 707, 745
Kent:
  Census:
    Leaflet population etc, 589
    Occupation groups, 1123
    Report, 588
  Quarter Sessions Act, 289
  rivers. Hydrological survey, 866
Kenya:
  Arms, 802
  becomes a sovereign nation. Photoposter, 609
  Cereals*, 805
  Coastal strip:
    Agreement, 102, 549
    Conference, 318
    Joint Statement, 549

Kenya (continued):
  Constituencies Delimitation Conference, 549
  Constitution. Proposed, 549
  Constitutional Conference, 319
  Flags, 803
  Independence:
    Act, 517
    Conference, 549
  Instructions OIC, 174
  Loan, 423
  Northern Frontier District Commission, 319
  Photoposter, 609
  Preparations for independence, 549
  Public officers*, 889
  Reference Pamphlet, 871
  Regional Boundaries Commission, 318, 549
  Reports, 101, 548, 803
  Republic Act, 1040
    Bills, 746, 964
Kenyatta, Jomo. Release, 101
Kerosene & gasoline. Working party, 308
Kettering etc. Geology of country around, 640
Kew:
  Bulletin, 175, 391, 635, 902, 1168
  Gardens:
    Guide, 87
    Publications, 175, 391, 635, 902, 1168
Key, A. (Chairman), Experimental disposal of house refuse, 146
Key to:
  disarmament, 870
  potato trials, 80, 299, 528, 782, 1050

Kidd, J. (Chairman), Maladjusted children, 911
Kidderminster. Geology of country around, 396
Kilbrandon, Lord (Chairman):
  Bus services in Highlands, 196
  Children & young persons. Scotland, 912
  Highland transport, 670
  Scottish:
    Grand Committee, 735
Kildrumny Castle. Guide, 1167
Killingholme Jetty Act, 518
Kilmuir, Rt. Hon. Earl (Chairman), Future of Commonwealth, 551
Kiln sterilization of timber, 395
Kimmins, D. E.:
  Leptocerinae, 796
  New African caddis-flies, 311
  Trichoptera, 310, 796

Kincardine(shire):
Census. Leaflet, Population etc. & report, 590
Educational trust scheme, 182, 400, 401
KINDERSLEY, LORD (Chairman), Doctors' & dentists' remuneration, 1127
KING, A. H., Four hundred year's of music printing, 795
KING, D. J. C., Llanstephan Castle. Guide, 633
KING, J. E., Seals, 797
King George:
Island. Petrology 101
Jubilee Trust publication, 611
King's:
Lynn Conservancy Provisional Order Act, 774
Bill, 706, 744
Works. History, 633
KINGSTON, T. A., Report of inquiry, 857
Kingston-upon-Hull. Alteration of area. Map, 867
KINMAN, T. D., Southern RR lyrae stars, 176
Kinross. Census. Leaflet, population etc, 590
KIRBY, S. W.:
Reconquest of Burma, 1070
War against Japan, 313
KIRK, J. H. (Chairman), Domestic food consumption, 532
KIRK, T. H., Tornado at Malta, 620
KIRKALDY, H. S. (Chairman), Baking Wages Council, 618
Kirkaldy, Victoria Hospital, 1174
Kirkcudbright. Census:
Leaflet. Population etc, 590
Report, 850
KIRKHAM, R. H. H., Concrete road:
Riding quality, 642
slabs, 398
Kirkham House, Paignton. Guide, 633
KISSEN, M., Rents of corporation houses in Dundee, 644
Kitchen(s). Hospital:
Building Notes, 133
Equipment Notes, 852
KITZINGER, E., Early medieval art, 795

KLEIN, L., Multiproducts etc, 909

KNIGHT, R. A. G., Adhesives for wood, 639, 905
KNIGHTING, E.:
Numerical forecasting, 162
Operational numerical weather prediction, 378
Knotgrass & allied weeds, 82, 300
Knottingley. Proposed county district. Map, 867

KNOX, SIR M. (Chairman), Transfer from primary to secondary education, 183
KNUDSEN, J., Danish expedition to West Africa, 808

KOERNER, R. M., Glaciological observations, 794

Kuniyoshi, 218
Kuria Muria Islands Royal Instructions OIC, 632
Kuwait:
Notices, 121
Operation, 440
Relations with U.K.*, 121
Route schedules*, 579
Kuyunjik Collection B.M., 93, 794

L

Labelling of food. See Food
Laboratory methods for work with nematodes, 790
Labour:
and machinery (Farms), 787
Gazette, 158, 374, 617–8, 880, 1151–2
Ministry of:
Annual report, 151
publications 151–9, 368–75, 611–8, 874–81, 1146–53
relations & conditions of work, 148, 366, 1144
Lace Industry etc. (Levy) Accounts, 414, 661, 926, 1192
LACEY, J., Dust from barley grain, 1049
Ladybirds, 312
Laemophloeinae, 311
Lake Victoria Haplochromis, 542
LAMB, I. M., Antarctic lichens, 794
Lamb(s):
Disease, 1053
wintering sheds, 86
LAMBERT, W. G., Babylonian literary texts, 1066
LAMONT, J. M., Plaice investigations in Scottish waters, 783
Lamps:
Electric incandescent. Merchandise Marks, 515, 928, 1194
Greek & Roman pottery, 540
Lanark. Census:
Leaflet. Population etc, 590
Report, 850
Lancashire:
Census:
Leaflet. Population etc, 589
Report, 849
North, Rivers, 868
Quarter Sessions Act, 69
Saxton map, 93

Land:
agent (Careers), 875
and natural resources. Circulars, 1153
Appropriation of (acquired under Housing Act), 142
birds of Guadalcanal, 312
Commission:
Bill, 1014
Command Paper, 1032
Compensation Act, 67
Amendment Bill, 746
Bill, 2, 4, 41, 141
Circular, 143
Tables of comparison, 144
Compensation. Scotland Act, 517
Bill, 452, 454, 490, 601
Tables of comparison, 454, 644
Derelict, Treatment of, 602
Drainage Act, 67
Bill, 5, 6, 34, 39, 41, 138
Form, 603
Guide, 304
Government. Disposal of surplus, 602
Interests in, Compulsory acquisition, 141, 601
Mergers affecting, 1153
Minister's Order, 1153
Opencast, Farming restored, 301
Positive covenants affecting, 1154
purchase accounts. N.I., 997
Registered. Mergers affecting, 1153
Registration Acts:
Forms, 375, 882, 1153
Practice leaflets, 1153
Title to land, 1153
Registry:
Publications, 159, 375, 618, 882, 1153
Report to Lord Chancellor, 159, 375, 618, 882, 1153
Settlement Association. Smallholdings, 87, 305, 534, 789, 1060
tenure in Zanzibar, 101
use:
and population in Fiji, 1159
in highlands & islands, 782
Landlord and Tenant Act, 288
Bill, 229, 256, 260, 263, 358
Circular, 362
Lands, Dead, New life for, 606
Landscaping for flats:
Circular, 601
Design Bulletin, 603
LANDSDOWNE, MARQUESS (Chairman), Malaysia, 495
LANG, D. M.:
Georgian etc. books, 309
Soils of Malta & Gozo. 101
LANG, SIR J. (Chairman), Ministry of Aviation contracts, 792, 1064
LANGDON-THOMAS, G. J., Fire protection in factory building, 178

LANGLEY, C. A., Rail accidents, 198
Langstone Harbour, Pier & Harbour Provisional Order Act, 290
Bill, 230, 262
Language(s):
and communications in Commonwealth, 1076
guides, 957
laboratory, 688
Machine translation, 641
Modern:
in high school U.S.A., 688
in secondary schools, 402
Laos:
Economic aid*, 580, 838, 1112
Foreign exchange operations fund*, 839, 1112
Laotian Question Conference, 341
Neutrality, 580
Larch:
canker & dieback, 349
Comparative study of properties, 1180
Leaf cast, 586
Larger British fungi, 95
Largs Burgh Order Confirmation Act, 289
Bill, 261
Larvae in cod, 528
LARWOOD, G. P.:
Cretaceous cribimorph polyzoa, 311
Last English open field village. Laxton, 788
Late antique & Byzantine art, 689
Latin American:
Forest Research Establishment*, 118
Studies, 1091
Laundry(ies):
and dry cleaning (Careers), 874
Hospital:
Building Notes, 852
Efficiency Study, 131, 352, 591, 850
Equipment Notes, 1126
Safety, 618
LAVER, F. J. M., Introducing computers, 1040
LAW, M., Heat radiation from fires etc, 639
LAW, R. J., Steam engine, 1170
Law:
Careers, 612
Commissioners. Proposals, 1154
Commissions:
Act, 1040
Bill, 968, 969, 1007, 1009, 1010, 1011, 1132
First Programme, 1154
Scottish, 1174
Reform:
Committee, 159, 376, 619
Scotland, 619, 882
Damages & Solatium (Scotland) Act, 288
Bill, 42, 228, 245, 256, 262

Law (continued):
Reform (continued):
Husband & Wife Act, 288
Bill, 42, 229, 245, 256, 262
Miscellaneous Provisions (Scotland) Bill, 975, 976
Succession etc (Scotland) Bill, 483, 489, 597
Society. See Legal Aid
See also specific subjects
LAWRENCE, SIR G. (Chairman):
National Incomes Commission reports, 623, 887, 1157
Remuneration Ministers & M.P's., 941
LAWRENCE, L. C., Cygnus II association, 1169
Laxton. Guide, 788
Laying:
cages, 300, 784
screeds as underlay, 1166
Layout & equipment of drawing offices, 394
Lead & compounds. Detection, 374
Leaf:
cast of larch, 586
spot of celery, 529
Leafy gall, 529
Leaping behaviour of salmon & trout, 299
Leasehold:
Bill, 264
Enfranchisement (Wales) Bill, 39
property, 364
Tenure (Wales) Bill, 39
LEATON, B. R.:
Geomagnetic secular variation, 393
Mechanisation of spherical harmonic analysis, 176
Solar. Daily variation, 635
Lebanon:
Air services*, 580
Disarmament*, 580
Double taxation*, 839, 1112
Lebetus, 542
Lee, River. Basin, hydrometric area, 362
LEECH, F. B.:
Brucellosis in dairy herd, 785
Disease etc. in dairy herd, 785
Losses of breeding ewes, 785
Leeds:
Alteration of area. Map, 867
Confirmation Act, 518
Bill, 452, 489
University Act, 1042
Leek(s):
Advisory Leaflet, 82
and onions chemical weed control, 301
smut, 1052
LEEVEN, J., Talmud, 95
Leeward Island:
Constitutional Conference, 103
Economic potential, 651

LEFKOVITCH, L. P., Laemophloeinae, 311
Legal:
Aid:
Act, 772
Bill, 449, 491, 698, 700, 743
and Advice:
Acts. Account, 159, 376, 619, 882, 1154
Law Society report, 159, 376, 619, 882, 1154
in criminal proceedings, 356, 595
scheme. Law Society Scotland, 185, 405, 647, 1175
Scotland fund. Account, 115, 329, 567, 823, 1091
education. African students, 159
metrology. Convention, 342
proceedings. Expenses, 137
profession (Qualifications for Office) Bill, 34, 40, 138
See also Barristers (Qualifications for Office)
records in P.R.O. Guide, 634
status of Welsh language, 1008, 1223
system. English, 366, 871
terms. Glossary, 332, 1097
Legend of St. Ursula, 959
Legislation for foreign public documents, 1112
Leicester. County borough. Alteration of area, 144
Leicestershire:
and Rutland. Amalgamation, 603
Census:
Leaflet. Population etc, 589
Report, 849
LEICHTY, E., Cuneiform tablets. Bibliography, 794
LEIGH, C., Tower Colliery explosion, 385
Leith Harbour & Docks Confirmation Act, 289
Bill, 263
LELE, K. M., Fossil flora, 311
Length, mass etc. Standards of measurement, 397
Leopoldville. Loan*, 1094
Leprosy. "Wars not yet won", 147
Leptocorisinae, 796, 1067
LESLIE, H. R. (Chairman), Treatment of offenders, 184, 647
Letchworth Garden City Corporation Act, 289
Bill, 247
Lethrinus in West Indian Ocean, 101
Letter(s):
Banks, Sir Joseph, 312, 1066
Henry IV, 1168
Luke, Sir Samuel, 693
Letterpress printing. Productivity, 180
Lettuce aphids, 1052
Leucotomy in England & Wales, 134

LEVY, R. F. (Chairman), Monopolies Commission:
Petrol, 1194
Wallpaper, 928
LEWIS, D. J., Simuliidae, 796
LEWIS, W. A., Compaction plans, 181
Leys, seeds for, 300

Liability:
for deportation form, 356
in tort between husband & wife, 159
Liaison between Planning Authorities & River Boards, 361
Liassic ammonite zones etc., 94
Liberate Rolls. Calendar, 390, 901
Librarianship (Careers), 874
Library(ies):
co-operation E. & W., 327
Public, See Public Libraries
School & college. Scotland, 646
Libya. Treaty of friendship*, 580
Licensed:
Betting Offices (Restriction) Bill, 1009
residential establishment etc. inquiry, 881
Licences:
Aircraft radio maintenance engineer, 306, 535, 1062
Commercial, senior commercial & airline transport pilots, 89, 792
Examination Papers. See Examinations
Flight navigators, 89, 307, 1063
Flight radio operators, 89, 307, 1063
Private pilots. Law for applicants, 88, 535, 790
Student pilots & private pilots, 92, 539
Licensing:
Acts, 68, 772
Bills, 5, 7, 34, 40, 41, 42, 138, 456, 697, 699, 701, 742, 863
aerodromes, 89
Authorities. Annual report, 198, 199, 420, 669, 934, 1200
Consolidation of certain enactments, 456
planning. Departmental Committee, 1130
Scotland. Act, 288
Bills, 8, 9, 225, 230, 256, 261, 263, 358, 966, 968, 1011
Lichens. Antarctic, 794
Liechtenstein. Travel U.K. & Switzerland*, 125
Life:
and other long term insurance business, 1193
Association of Scotland Ltd., Act, 774
assurance. Statements, 190, 414, 661
peerages, 186, 408, 914
saving:
appliances, 667
then & now, 624
Lifeboats. Plastic, 667

Lifting equipment for cranes, 178
Light:
and heat. Glasshouse, 1049
Photometry etc. Standards of measurement, 907
rescue. Civil Defence, 355
sources for clinical purposes, 1154
Lighting:
Architectural physics, 637
of drawing offices, 394
Lightweight aggregate concretes, 394, 637
Limba people of Sierra Leone, 1159
Lime:
for soil stabilization, 398
in:
agriculture, 1053
horticulture, 530
Liming gardens, 301
Limitation(s):
Act, 517
Bill, 451, 454, 483, 487, 488, 490, 597
of actions. Personal injury, 376
Lincoln. Alteration of area. Map, 1140
Lincolnshire:
and East Anglia. Local Government Commission, 1140
Census:
Leaflet. Population etc, 389
Report, 849
Lindingapais, 796
Line & wireless instruction. (Civil Defence), 135
Linen:
manufacture in Scotland, 914
services. Hospital, 131, 132, 352, 591, 850, 851
LINES, R., Use of flags, 586
Linkage of secondary & further education, 646
Liptninae, 541
Liquid feeding of tomatoes, 530
Liquified petroleum gas storage, 1152
Listening eye. Teaching in an art museum, 218
LITTLEWOOD, S. W. G. (Chairman), Experiments on animals, 1130
Liverpool:
Corporation Act, 289
Exchange Act, 1042
Livestock:
breeding, 531
Marketing, 1059
Nutrient requirements (Poultry), 527
LIVINGSTON, H. R.:
Cow cubicles, 782
Slatted floors, 1049
Livingston. New Town Order, 405

Llanelly:
and District Water Board Order, 229
Provisional Order. See Welsh Office

LLA— INDEX 1961-5

Llanstephan Castle. Guide, 633
Llanthony Priory. Guide, 633
LLEWELLYN-JONES, F., Science & education in Wales, 1090
Lloyds Permanent Building Society. Affairs, 128, 350

Loan(s):
agreements. See respective countries
for Theological colleges. Measures, 698, 775, 799
Lobster:
Bionomics, 303
Norway. Food, 299
Local:
Acts (and Personal), 68–70, 289–90, 517–9, 774–5, 1041–2
Administration Overseas. Journal, 410, 651, 889, 1159
authority(ies):
Amenities Bill, 260
bonds. Regulations, 865
borrowing, 674
Building Notes, 353, 592, 853, 1126
Children's Department. Scotland. Staffing, 647
contracts, 865
duties, Factories Act, 876
Expenditure on special purposes Act, 68
Bill, 4, 34, 39, 138
Historic Buildings Act, 288
Bill, 229, 244, 256, 260, 261
Circular, 362
housing. Costing, 864, 869
Land Act, 517
Bill, 452, 483, 487, 489, 597
Circular, 602
Members. Travelling allowances, 361
Proceedings & business. Model Standing Orders, 602, 868
education authority(ies):
and National Agriculture Advisory Service, 112, 114, 820
England & Wales. Statistics, 114, 327, 565, 821
Excepted Districts, 565
Secondary education in each, 327, 565, 821, 1090
Elections (Greater London) Bill, 1011
Employment Acts, 517
Accounts, 415, 662, 715, 1193
Administration, 599, 600
Annual Reports, 191, 251, 662, 928, 1194
Bill, 452, 483, 489, 597
Circular, 361
financial returns (Scotland), 184, 403, 644, 910, 1171

Local (continued):
government:
Acts,
Bill, 261, 487
Circulars, 361, 602, 1138, 1139, 1222
Commission:
England & Wales, 144–5, 603, 604–5, 866–7, 1140
Wales, 605–6
Compensation Regulations, 602, 606, 1138
Conferences Regulations, 1139, 1222
Finance (ial):
General Grant Increase Order, 362–3, 606, 867–8, 1140
Provisions Act, 517
Bill, 452, 453, 454, 473, 483, 487, 489
Circular, 490, 865
Scotland. See Local Government. Scotland
statistics, 144, 362, 606, 1140
in:
Britain, 147, 609, 871, 1144
Greater London. Royal Commission, 391
Pecuniary Interests Act, 772
Bill, 705, 707, 735, 741, 745, 859
Records Act, 288
Bill, 229, 230, 246, 256, 260, 262, 263
Circular, 361
Scotland:
Acts, 1040
Bills, 746, 973, 1007, 1009, 1012, 1132
Financial Returns, 184, 403, 644, 910, 1171
Development & Finance Act, 772
Bill, 706, 735, 741, 744, 858
Expenditure on Special Purposes Act, 68
Bill, 4, 34, 39, 138
Finance(ial):
General Grant Order, 258, 401, 402, 646, 910, 1171
Provisions Acts, 288, 517
Bills, 38, 42, 138, 226, 259, 260, 264, 358, 450, 483, 488, 597
Circular, 602
Modernisation, 483, 597, 644
Pecuniary Interests. Bill, 1008, 1013, 1132
Re-organisation, 910
Superannuation:
Circulars, 184
Modification. Select Committee, 140
service (Careers), 368

INDEX 1961-5 —LOR

Local (continued):
government (continued):
superannuation:
benefits. New Towns staffs, 362
Circulars, 142, 143, 362, 602, 864, 1138
schemes. Modification. Select Committee, 140
Health Authority clinics, 353
housing indices. Census. Scotland, 1123
land charges register, 603
loans fund. Accounts, 163, 379, 622, 886, 1157
taxation. Italy*, 1112
Loch Turret Water Board (Hydro-electric development) Order Confirmation Act, 518
Bill, 490
LOCKWOOD, SIR J. (Chairman):
Certificate of secondary education, 113, 327, 566
Examining of English language, 821
Schools' curricula & exams., 822
Sixth form studies, 328
Logistic & training facilities. W. German forces in U.K.*, 340
London:
Airport(s):
Estimates Committee, 140, 141
Third, 792
and Home Counties. Traffic Advisory Committee, 428, 667
Authorities (Staff) Order, 1138
borough(s):
Councils. Appointments of officers, 864
Maps:
Possible grouping, 145
Proposed grouping, 363
Recording new titles, 868
Report, 363
Bridge Improvements Act, 289
Building Acts, Constructional bye-laws, 1124
Census:
Leaflet. Population, 351
Occupation groups, 1123
Report, 588
City of. See City of London
County Council:
General Powers Acts, 69, 289, 518, 774
Improvements Acts, 289, 518
Money Acts, 69, 289, 518, 774
Publications, 882
See also Greater London Council
Courts Directory, 159, 376
Diplomatic List, 839, 1112–3
Employment. Housing. Land, 606
fares, 666, 935–6, 1200–1
Gazette, 186–7, 408, 649, 914, 1176–7
Facsimile, 1176
History, 1176

London (continued):
Government:
Act, 517
Amendments to 1933 Act Circular, 602
Bill, 264, 450, 452, 453, 483, 488, 490, 597
Circulars, 602, 865
Circulars, 143, 361, 601, 1138
Compensation Regulations, 865
Government proposals, 145
Maps, 145, 363, 868
Staff Commission. Officers, 864
Great Fire. Facsimile, 1176
Hackney Carriage Bill, 263
Magistrates courts, 357
Museum Publications, 376, 618
See also Museum of London
Museums & galleries. Guide, 914
Opera Centre. Criticisms, 882
orchestras, 1061
parks, Royal, 1168
post offices & streets, 384, 895
Roman, 376
since, 1912, 376
traffic, 418, 667
Transport:
Acts, 518, 774, 1042
Board:
Annual reports, 932, 1199
Drivers & conductors. Pay etc., 617, 881
Fares, 666, 935, 936, 1200, 1201
Loans, 695, 942, 1207
Select Committee, 1134, 1135
Long:
range area. Communications scheme, 1163
term demand for scientific manpower, 160
Longer-term postgraduate courses for engineers, 1089
LONGHURST, A. R., Bionomics of fisheries resources, 549
LONGSON, J., Photographic study. Fatigue fractures in aircraft, 524
Longthorpe Tower. Guide, 900
Look around monasteries of N.E. Yorkshire, 390
LORD, CYRIL., Excess Profit Levy Appeal 609, 872, 1144
LORD, R. E., Mechanised farming at Nacherton, 940
Lord:
Advocate's Department, 619, 882
Chamberlain. Plays submitted, 795
Chancellor's Department, 159–60, 376, 619, 882, 1153–4
President's Office, 160, 376
Privy Seal's Office, 160

LOR— INDEX 1961-5

...ords. Spiritual & temporal. Roll of, 141, 377, 456, 863, 1137
...oss of services etc. (Law reform), 619
...ost Property (Scotland) Act, 1040
Bill, 905, 1007, 1009, 1132
...otteries & Gaming Act, 288
Bill, 42, 229, 230, 247, 256, 263
...OTTO, G. De., Pseudococcidae, 544
...oubet coast. Geology, 539
...OVATT, B. A., Strawberry growing, 1030
...ow:
cost dairying, 1054
pressure glass-fibre laminates, 517
Priced Book Society publications, 1086, 1180
temperature research Station, 79, 298, 439, 527
...ower:
cretaceous terebratelloidea, 1068
tertiary floras, 95, 797
Usutu basin, 1159
...OWSON, PATRICK ALEXANDER., Memorial scholarship scheme, 645

...ubricants. Joint Services handbook, 691
...ucas Estate Act, 519
Bill. Personal Bills Committee, 449
...ucerne, 529
...UKE, SIR SAMUEL, Letter books, 593
...ullingstone Roman villa. Guide, 633
...UMB, F. E., Variation of temperature in coastal waters, 162
...UPTON, T., Money for effort, 180
...uton:
Police area. Amalgamation, 1130
Proposed county borough, 144
...uxembourg:
British visitors' passports*, 121
Cereals*, 1093

...yctus:
attack in hardwoods, 906
powder-post beetles, 639
...ydford Castle. Guide, 900
...ymphomatosis, 1052

M

ICARTHUR, D. N. (Chairman), Residual value of fertilizers, 299, 528, 783
IcBOYLE, J. (Chairman), Child care, 646
IACBRAYNE, D. LTD., Undertaking, 79, 300
IcCAIG, CATHERINE, Trust Scheme, 401, 645
IcCORQUODALE, LORD (Chairman), Disablement, 1162
IcCOWAN, P. K. (Chairman), Child guidance, 406

McDONALD, RT. HON. LORD (Chairman), Young chronic sick, 913
McDONALD, ISABELLA, Bequest Fund Scheme, 912, 1173
Madduff Harbour Order Confirmation Act, 774
Bill, 697, 743
McGREGOR, A. G., Tertiary volcanic districts. Scotland, 129
McGREGOR, I., Mass radiography. campaign, Scotland, 131
Machine:
milking (Correction), 84
tools. Investment, 1157
translation of languages, 641
undercutting. Application of water, 171
Machinery:
for swath treatment of hay, 303
of:
Government Bill. See Ministers of Crown Bill
prices & incomes policy, 1008
Machines, Historic books, 636
MCINTOSH, D. H., Meteorological glossary, 884
MACKAY, J. A.:
Collection of postage etc stamps, 795
Commonwealth stamp design, 1066
MACKENZIE, C. H. (Chairman), Electricity in Scotland, 399
MACKENZIE, P. K. (Chairman), Milk powder, 86
MACKENZIE, Bequest Scheme, 183, 401
MCLAREN Trust scheme, 1173
MACLEOD, RT. HON. I. (Chairman), West Indies Constitution Conference, 103
MACPHERSON, R. K., Physiological responses to hot environments, 160
MACRAE, A. K. M. (Chairman), Alcoholics, 1174
Macristium, 95
Macrocheles Latr, 542
MCVEAN, D. N., Plant communities, 394
Madingley Investments Ltd. Investigation, 925
Magellanic clouds, 393, 635, 636, 1169
Magistrates' Courts. London, 357
Magna Carta: 540
and its influence, 1144
Translation & facsimile, 1168
Magnetic:
results, 176, 635
survey. Graham Land, 318
Magpie moth, 529
Maidstone:
Corporation (Trolley Vehicles):
Order Confirmation Act, 289
Provisional Order Bill, 230, 262
Geology of country around, 640
Maintenance of buildings etc. Hospital, 853
Maize for fodder & silage, 81

INDEX 1961-5 —MAN

Majestic Insurance Co. Ltd. Investigation, 923
Major ports of Britain, 420
Making:
an upland farm pay, 80
fire. Wood friction etc., 903
fixings to hard materials, 389
Maladjusted children:
Ascertainment of, 911
Boarding schools for, 1088
Education of, 1089
Malaria:
Arms, 802
Cereals*, 805
Flag, 803
Independence Act, 772
Bill, 704, 743
Reference Pamphlet, 871
Malayan offshore trawling grounds, 318
Malaysia:
Act, 517
Bill, 455, 490
Agreements, 549
Air services*, 806
Federal Court. Appeals, 806
Inter-government Committee, 495
Joint statement, 104
Overseas officers in Sabah & Sarawak*, 1113
Public officers,*, 889
Reference Pamphlet, 609
Release of crown lands to services, 549
Maldive Islands*, 1113
MALE, G. M., Education in France, 958
Male scale insects, 313
Malicious Damage Act, 772
Bill, 706, 744, 745,
Mallophaga (Insecta), 94
Malta:
Arms, 1073
Constitution OIC, 174, 389, 632, 899
Constitutional Commission, 103
Electoral Provisions OIC, 174
Financial assistance*, 803
Flag, 1074
Gift of colors, 1203
Independence:
Act, 772
Bill, 707, 745
booklet, 870
Conference, 549
Constitution, 803
Inheritance of international rights*, 1022
Loan, 480
Mutual defence & assistance*, 803
Photoposter, 870
Reconstruction Act accounts, 102, 252, 479, 726, 1074
Reference Pamphlet, 871
Soils of, 101
Tornado, 620

Mammals:
British identification, 797
Fossil, 1068
in Scotland, 903
Man(e):
antiquity, 797
Races of, 1070
requirements for protein, 854
Sex chromosome complement in, 883
the tool-maker, 95
Management(s):
and control of research & development, 177
consultants' association survey, 1157
farm aid, 532, 787, 1058
in hotel & catering (Careers), 151, 874
of:
vegetation on airfields, 642
young pigs, 301
papers. Hospital. Filing, 133
recruitment & development, 1157
studies:
Diploma in, 328, 565, 1089
in technical colleges, 327
Manchester:
Corporation Acts, 69, 289, 1042
Ship Canal Act, 289
Mangolds & fodder beet, 300, 1052
MANKTELOW, SIR R.:
Civil Service Commission. East Caribbean, 498
Skelmersdale New Town Order, 146
Manned spacecraft centre, 622, 886
MANNHEIM, D. H., Borstal training, 1130
Manoeuvres, in Soltau-Luneburg*, 1113
Manpower:
Presidents' report, U.S.A., 958
resources for science & technology, 1179
slides, 880, 1152
Manuals. See specific subjects
Manufacture(rs)*:
and inspection of welded structures, 1180
Aircraft, 307
Imported. Competitiveness, 1157
Manure(s):
Handling, Farmyard, 1059
Poultry, 82, 1052
Soils and, for fruit, 1054
Seaweed as, 300
Manuring:
and liming gardens, 301
of grassland, 785
Manuscript(s):
Additions to, B. M., 794, 1066
collections B.M., 310
De L'Isle & Dudley, 354
Early Gothic, 1066
Hebrew & Samaritan, 1066
Illuminated, 1066
Maps, etc, 309, 540

MAN-MIN | 1961-5

Manuscript(s) (*continued*):
Music, 795
Pashto, 1066
Persian illuminated, 1066
Polwarth, Lord, 134
Romances, 309, 540
Map(s):
Manuscripts, 309, 540
reading. Manual, 440
Saxton, 93, 540, 795, 1066
MARCOUSE, R., Listening eye, 218
Margarodidae & termitococcidae, 1069
MARGOLIOUTH, G., Hebrew & Samaritan Mss., 1066
Marigold. Corn, 784
MARILLIER, H. C., Hampton Court Palace. Tapestries, 390
Marine:
algae, 1067
corps. U.S. Shape up, 957
cretaceous ostracoda, 1068
engineering practice, 520, 1087
enoplida, 797
molluscs, 1069
nematode, 312, 797, 1069
Observer, 161, 377, 621, 884, 1155
observers' handbook, 621, 884
radio equipment, 1163
reactor research group, 933
research, 80, 299, 528, 783, 1050
research. Undersea photography, 528
Society Act, 518
surveys. Fees payable, 196, 415, 418, 932
Marines, Royal. Orders & regulations, 292, 820
Maritime travel conference, 1117
Marketing:
in United States, 1075
of:
meat & livestock, 1059
minor crops, Uganda, 651
Marlborough House. Guide, 390
MARLOWE, C., Exhibition, 796
MARRE, A. S. (Chairman):
Occupational sick pay schemes, 881
Selection & training of supervisors, 881
Marriage (Wales & Monmouthshire) Act, 288
Bill, 43, 228, 256, 262, 358
Marriages. Official list of places for, 128, 351, 588, 848, 1123
Married women's:
Property Act, 772
Bill, 456, 491
Savings Bill, 452
MARS-JONES, W. L., Inquiry into case of Thomas Hollaron, etc. 857
Mars training ship fund scheme, 183, 401
MARSHALL, N. B.:
Heteromi, 542
Macristium etc., 95
Marshall Aid Commemoration Commission:
Account, 204, 342, 674, 940, 1205
Report, 126, 347, 584, 845, 1119
MARTIN, A., Marketing of crops in Uganda, 651
MARTIN, MRS. ISOBELLA BLYTH, Bursary Trust scheme, 401, 645
MARTIN, L., Whitehall plan, 1168
Masarid wasps, 313
MASNER, L., Proctotrupoida, 1067
MASON, SIR F. (Chairman), National Engineering Laboratory Steering Committee, 396
Mass:
miniature radiography, 129
Radiography campaign. Scotland, 131
Masterpieces of Print Room B.M., 1066
Masters:
and mates:
Regulations for examinations, 420, 934
Specimen sets of examination papers, 931
Extra, in Mercantile Marine examinations, 196, 418, 666, 931, 1191
Mastics & gaskets, jointing, 637
Mastitis in cattle, 783, 1052
Maternal deaths. Confidential enquiries, 593
Maternity:
and midwifery. Advisory Committee, 132
benefit, 166, 382, 1160
department. Hospitals, 352, 592, 852, 1125
Mathematical tables, 397, 906
Mathematicians. (Careers), 369, 1147
Mathematics:
and computer science in biology & medicine, 1154
Elementary school (U.S.A.), 958
Experimental examination, 822
in primary schools, 1090
Modern, & your Child, 958
MATLEY, W., Punched tape units, 903, 1170
Matrimonial Causes:
Acts, 517, 1040
Bills, 451, 483, 487, 488, 490, 597, 971, 974, 1013, 1137
Consolidation of enactments, 971
MATTINGLY, H., Coins of Roman Empire, 1066
MATTINGLY, P. F., Culcine mosquitoes, 95, 1069
MAUDLING, RT. HON. R. (Chairman):
East Caribbean Federation Conference, 317
Kenya:
Coastal Strip Conference, 318
Constitutional Conference, 319

MAUDLING, RT. HON. R. (Chairman) (*continued*)
Trinidad & Tobago Independence Conference, 319
Uganda Independence Conference, 319
Zanzibar Constitutional Conference, 319
Mauritius:
Constitution OIC, 174, 389, 899
Constitutional Conference, 1075
Electoral Provisions OIC, 1166
Indians in a plural society, 409
Language of laws OIC, 388
Letters Patent OIC, 174
Loan, 480
Reports, 101, 317, 803, 1074
MAY, W. E., Naval swords & firearms, 380
Maya jades, 795
Mazagon dockyard credit*, 806

Mbembe, Nigeria. Political organisation, 1159

Mealey bugs. African, 796
Meals:
School, Service. Memorandum, 1090
service to hospital wards, 1125
Mean streamlines & isotachs, 1155
Meaning of Berlin, 365
Measurement:
and control of air temperature, 304
of:
angle in engineering, 164, 907
beef cattle, 1050
frequency, 397
length & diameter, 641
load by elastic devices, 164
upper winds, 377
units & standards, 397, 907
Measures. Church of England, 70, 97, 290, 314, 519, 545, 775, 799–800, 1039, 1071
Measuring tapes etc. Merchandise Marks, 415, 928
Meat:
and livestock marketing, 1059
Canned. (Food Standards), 304
Imported (Merchandise Marks), 1194
Industry (Scientific Research Levy) Account, 1192
Inspection etc. Regulations, 84, 302, 303, 531, 786, 1056, 1057
marketing & distribution, 787
pies (Food Standards), 533
Pre-packed cuts of imported. Merchandise Marks, 1194
Production (Commonwealth), 104, 319, 550, 804, 1075
MEATES, G. W., Lullingstone Roman villa, 633
Mechanical(ised):
farming. Tanganyika, 548
recording. Court proceedings, 1154
Mechanical(ised) (*continued*):
thinning. Crops, 303
ventilation of rooms, 603
Mechanics & electricians at mines of coal etc. Books, 387
Mechanisation:
leaflets. Farmers, 1059
of spherical harmonic analysis, 176
Medals:
Civil Defence, 202, 672
Distinguished Conduct, 220
General Service, 202, 220, 672, 692, 812, 937, 1203
Naval General Service, 202, 672
Royal Naval Auxiliary Service, 1203
Royal Red Cross, 220
United Nations, 812
Victoria Cross, 220
Medical:
aid to developing countries, 410, 651
and:
nutritional aspects of food policy, 851
population studies, 129, 351, 589
Appeal Tribunal, 168–9, 383, 627, 892, 1161
appliances. Vouchers*, 569, 751
guide. Ship Captain's, 199, 669
laboratory technician. (Careers), 1147
photography & medical illustration. Hospital, 133, 592
record card, 356
records. Hospital, 132, 591
Research:
Council:
Memorandum, 160, 376, 883, 1154
Monitoring Report Series, 160, 376–7, 883, 1154
Publications, 160–1, 376–7, 619, 883, 1154
Reports, 160, 278, 619, 759, 1154
Special reports, 160–1, 377, 883, 1154
in Britain, 871
scales. Merchant shipping, 197
secretarial services. Hospital, 132
services for child guidance, 406
staffing structure:
Hospital service, 133
Scottish hospitals, 913
tables, 129, 351, 589, 849, 1123
termination of pregnancy Bill, 38
treatments. European*, 281
Medicine & surgery (Careers), 369, 875
Medieval:
Early, Art, 795
silver nefs, 689
Medway Conservancy Act, 518
Megrim. Food of, 528
Melanesia. Ethnography, 93

Melton Mowbray Provisional Order Act, 1042
Bill, 970, 1011
Melville Trust Order Confirmation Act, 289
Bill, 263
Member nations of Commonwealth. Wall-sheet, 871
Members of Parliament. Remuneration, 941
Mental:
handicap. Degrees of, 182
Health:
Scotland Act:
Forms, 403–5
Notes, 131, 404, 405, 647
Visiting book, 405
Statistical review. G.R.O., 129, 351, 849
hospitals. Patients. 589
nursing homes. Select Committee S.I., 257
Mentally sub-normal. Training centres. Staff, 352
Mercantile:
Marine examinations, 196, 418, 665, 666, 931, 1191
Navy lists, 197, 419, 667, 932, 1194
Merchandise Marks Act. Reports, 86, 191, 415, 515, 533, 663, 928, 1194
Merchant:
Navy:
Examinations, 196, 665–6, 931, 934
Officers (Careers), 142, 874
shipping:
Act, 1894. Wreck reports, 200, 421–2, 670, 932–3, 1194
Acts, 772, 1040
Bills, 491, 702, 735, 743, 859, 973, 1007, 1011, 1012, 1132
Acts, of Parliament. List of principal, 667
Life saving appliances, 667
medical scales, 197
Survey of passenger ships, 197
ships:
Radio for, 1163
Tonnage certificates. Finland, 340
Mercury project summary, 886
MEREDITH-OWENS, G. M.:
Turkish:
manuscripts, 1066
miniatures, 540
Merioneth. Saxton map, 1066
Merionethshire. Census. Report, 588
Mersey:
Discharge of sewage, 181
Docks & Harbour Board Act, 518
River Board Act, 774
Tunnel Act, 69
Tunnel (Liverpool/Wallasey) etc. Act, 1042
Merseyside, Problems of, 1088
Meshes of fishing nets etc., 342, 577, 581
Meso-synoptic analysis of thunderstorms, 377
Mesostigmata (Acari), 797
Mesozoic flora, 542
MESSER, H. J. M., Silos for barley, 1049
Metal(s):
Elasticity measurements in, 907
Fibre reinforcement, 1063
Industries. Occupational trends, 1152
Structure & mechanical properties, 907
Metallic alloys. Creep etc., 396
Metalwork:
Anglo-saxon, 794
Early Oriental, 795
Meteorology(ical):
Elementary:
Course in, 377
for aircrew, 161
General, 379
glossary, 884
instruments, 161, 377, 622
Magazine, 161–2, 377–8, 621, 884–5, 1155
Office:
Annual report, 162, 378, 620, 883, 1154
Forms, 620, 883, 1155–6
Publications, 161–3, 377–9, 620–2, 883–6, 1154–6
Radiosonde errors, 378
R.A.F. forms, 620, 885
Reports, 1155
Scientific papers, 162–3, 378, 622, 885, 1155, 1156
World Organisation:
Convention, 121, 839
personnel, 1113
Methods:
for detection of toxic substances, 159, 374, 618, 1152
of:
assessing life of road surfacings, 398
construction etc. of Retail Price Index, 880
instruction. Civil Defence, 355
Methyl bromide fumigation, 136
Metric values in scientific papers, 906
Metrology. Legal, International Organisation, 342
Metropolitan Police. Mr. Herman Woolf Case, 857
See also Police
Mexico. Abolition of visas*, 580
MEYRICK, E., Microlepidoptera, 543, 1069

M. F. Circulars, 84–5, 787

Mice. *See* Rats & mice
Microgasterini, 1067
Microlepidoptera, 94, 311, 543, 1069, 1070

Micropentila Aurivillius, 1067
Mid-Wales:
Development & de-population, 1007, 1131
Depopulation. Report, 865
Middle jurassic ostracoda, 542, 797
Middlesex:
Census:
Leaflet & report, 588
Occupation groups, 1123
County Council Act, 69
MIDDLETON, J., Land tenure in Zanzibar, 101
MIDGLEY, M. M., Intensive poultry management, 1054
Midland Bank staff. Salaries, 1156
Midlothian:
Census. Leaflet & report, 590
Educational Trust Scheme, 182, 401
Midwifery:
Careers, 368, 1147
services in Scotland. Staffing, 1175
Migration:
European, 339, 576
National Summary tables. Census, 1123
Oversea. Board, 105, 320, 552, 1076
Mildew:
Apple powdery, 81, 1052
Gooseberry Powder, 529, 1052
MILES, M. K., Anticyclones over Scandinavia, 162
Military:
engineering, 440, 810
expenditure overseas. Estimates Committee, 599, 860, 861
law. Manual, 219, 440, 691, 810, 1080
penal establishments. Execution of sentences, 811
Service*:
Argentina, 823
Brazil, 116
Milk:
and dairies regulations, 84, 302, 303, 531, 532, 786, 787, 1054–7
Anti-biotics in, 531
Compositional quality, 783
cooling on farm, 530
distributors. Remuneration, 305
Dried, Food standards, 304
Marketing Scheme:
Complaint, 533
North of Scotland, 784
powder, 86
production:
Economics, 531, 787
Hygiene, 82
Radioactivity in, 298, 527, 782, 1050
Ropy, 300
Separated. Feeding, 784
Taints in, 300
Milking:
Efficient, 1053
Machine (correction), 84
MILLAR, R. H., Scottish oyster investigations, 80
MILLER, C. (Chairman), Commercial Court Users' Conference, 376
MILLER, P. J., Lebetus, 542
Milletts Holdings (St. Pauls) Ltd. Investigation into affairs, 660
MILLS, D. H.:
Atlantic salmon, 782
Cormorant, 1050
Goosander & merganser, 528
MILNE, SIR D. (Chairman), Aberdeen typhoid outbreak, 912
Mineral(s):
deficiencies in plants, 298
dust in industry, 642
industry. Statistical summary, 102, 318, 625, 889, 1159
Instructions. for collectors, 312
nutrient status of heather, 1121
oil in food, 304
species & varieties, 312, 541
Systematic collection in B.M. (Natural History), 1070
Workings Act. Account, 145, 363, 606, 868, 1140
Mineralogy Bulletin, 542, 797
Mines:
and quarries:
Books, 172, 386–7
Chief Inspectors' report, 173, 388, 631, 898, 1165
Divisional reports, 172, 388, 631, 898, 1165
Forms, 172–3, 387, 897–8
Law, safety & health, 895, 1165
Medical examinations. Regulations, 897
Miscellaneous, Law, 1165
of coal. Law, 897
Research. Safety in, Annual report, 173, 388, 631, 898, 1166
Working Facilities & Support Bill, 975, 1137
Miniatures. Turkish, 540
Mining:
Examination Rules, 387
National Certificates, 822
Qualifications:
Board examinations, 171, 387, 631, 897, 1165
Rules, 388
Minister of Space Research & Development Bill, 40
Ministerial Salaries:
and Members' Pensions Act, 1040
Bill, 746, 964, 967, 1009, 1010
Consolidation Act, 1040
Bill, 969, 972–3, 1013, 1136

MIN— *INDEX 1961-5*

Ministers:
and heads of public Depts., 186, 408, 673, 939, 1204
of Crown Act, 772
Bills, 40, 710, 743, 746
of Group of Ten, 941
Ministry of Housing & Local Government.
Provisional Orders Acts & Bills.
See respective towns
Mint. *See Royal Mint*
Mirror transit circle axis, 176
Misrepresentation Bill, 1014
Missenden Abbey. Cartulary, 354
Missile defence alarm system U.S.A.*, 126
MITCHELL, A. F., Dropmore pinetum, 586
MITCHELL, C. (Chairman), Scottish Water Advisory Committee, 644
MITCHELL, G. H., Geology. Droitwich etc. & Edinburgh, 396
Mite(s):
associated with rodents in Israel, 312
British, 543
Bulb scale, 301
Control of, in stored commodities, 82
in farm-stored grain, 1052
Macrochates Latr, 542
of stored food, 87
Primitive cryptostigmated, 1069
Red spider, 300, 1051

Moat Hostel Scheme, 645, 912
Mobile glasshouse, 1052
Mock Auctions Act, 68
Bill, 6, 34, 41, 138
Model:
Byelaws, 131, 145, 602, 606
Dairy Byelaws, 131
Standing Orders, 602, 606, 865, 868
Water Byelaws, 606
Modern:
building. Principles of, 180, 1180
Commonwealth, 365
computing methods, 164
languages. *See* Languages, modern
mathematics & your child, 958
rabbit-keeping, 785
Modernisation of local government in Scotland, 483, 597, 644
Moisture content of timber, 905
Mole. Advisory leaflets, 300. 529
Molluscs, 312, 342, 343, 1068, 1069
MOLONY, J. T. (Chairman), Consumer protection, 112
MOLSON, LORD (Chairman), Buganda & Bunyoto dispute, 319
Monaco:
Arrangements to facilitate travel*, 122
British visitors' passports*, 122
Monasteries of N. E Yorkshire, 390
Monetary Law Draft Convention, 376

Money:
for effort, 180
orders:
Japan*, 1111, 1113
Jordan*, 579
Monitoring Report series (MRC) 160, 376–7, 619, 883, 1154
Monmouth & Chepstow, Geology of country, 129–30
Monmouthshire:
Census:
Leaflet population etc., 351
Report, 588
Saxton map, 795
Monochamini (Cerambycidae), 94
Monopolies:
and Mergers Act, 1040
Bill, 973, 1007, 1010, 1011, 1013, 1132
and Restrictive Practices Acts. Annual reports, 191, 415, 663, 928, 1194
Commission reports, 191, 485, 928, 1194
Divestment Bill, 261
mergers & restrictive practices, 928
Montgomeryshire & (Merioneth):
Census. Report, 588
Saxton map, 1066
Monthly:
Digest of Statistics, 96, 314, 544–5, 799, 1071
Weather report, 162, 378, 621–2, 885, 1156
Montrose Burgh & Harbour (Amendment) Order Confirmation Act, 69
Bill, 41
Montserrat. Reports, 547, 803
Monuments:
Christian & Pictish. Scotland, 900
Roman. York, 391
threatened or destroyed, 635
See also Ancient monuments
Moor House. Geology, 624
MOORE, J. G., Temperatures & humidities, 885
MOORE, W. C., Cereal diseases, 302
Moorfields in 1559, 618
Moray (& Nairn) Census. Leaflet & report, 590
Morbidity statistics from general practice, 331
MORE, SIR T., Play, 796
Morgan, M. C., Insect emergence, 90
Morgan Trust scheme, 645
MORGANS, J. F. C., Bottom fishing, 1074
MORISON, SIR R. (Chairman), Probation service, 357
MORLEY, D. W., Automatic data processing, 178
Morley. Alteration of area. Map, 867

1961 pp 1–224, 1962 pp 225–445, 1963 pp 447–696, 1964 pp 697–962, 1965 pp 963–1226

76

INDEX 1961-5 **—NAN**

Morphology:
and:
systematics of polyzoa, 311
taxonomy of insects, 313
of Botryoteris Antigua, 311
MORRIS, OF NORTH-Y-GEST, LORD (Chairman), Jury service, 1130
MORRIS, G. I. (Chairman), Helicopter stations, 90
MORRIS, I. R., Sheep recording, 85
MORRIS, M. O., Geological photographs, 640
MORRIS, SIR P. (Chairman), Homes for today & tomorrow, 143
Morrisons' Academy Trust Scheme, 401, 912, 1173
Mortars for jointing, 1178
Morthology & classification of brachiopod, 313
MORTIMER, RT. REV. R. C. (Chairman), Treatment of offenders, 595
MORTON, J. E., Vermetidae, 1068
Mortuary & post-mortem room, 592
Mosquito(es):
Culicine, 95, 1069
nuisances in Great Britain, 353
MOSS, C., Syriac printed books. Catalogue, 309
Moth(s):
Codling, 300, 783
Magpie, 529
Pea, 300, 1052
Raspberry, 529
Small ermine, 1051
Swift, 529
Tortrix, 784
Winter, 81
Motherwell & Wishaw Burgh Extension etc. Order Confirmation Act, 774
Bill, 742
Motion picture, Origins, 903
Motor:
cycle roadcraft, 1129
rallies. Control, 931
Vehicle(s):
Disposal of old, 1138
Driving Establishments Bill, 743, 1010
equipment,* 342, 1118
Noise from, 394
offences, 136, 357, 595, 856, 1129
Passenger insurance Bill, 34, 38, 40, 138
sundry mechanics. Certificate, 111
Mouldboard plough setting, 788
MOUND, L. A., Aleyrodidae, 1068
Movement of timbers, 1180
Mowers, 303

M.P. Safety circulars, 173, 387, 631, 897, 1165

1961 pp 1–224, 1962 pp 225–445, 1963 pp 447–696, 1964 pp 697–962, 1965 pp 963–1226

F   77

MUCHA, ALPHONSE & Art Noveau, 689
MUIR-WOOD, H. M., Brachiopod, 313
MURIE, J. R., Bailey (Malta) Ltd., 547
MULHALL, J. A., Public Service Commission, 410
Multi-storey flats, 904
Multiple nationality & military obligations. Convention, 580
Multiproducts Ltd., 909
Murder:
(Abolition of Death Penalty) Act, 1040
Bill, 746, 973, 974, 975, 1007, 1011, 1013, 1132
Home Office Research Unit, 137
MURDOCH, G., Soil & irrigability. Lower Usutu Basin, 1159
MURRAY, C. A., Clusters, 1169
MURRAY, J. S., Group dying of conifers, 127
MURRAY, JOHN, Expedition, 1069
MURRAY, SIR K. (Chairman):
University:
development, 942
graduates. First employment, 676
Murres. Distribution etc, 112
Muscat notice, 122
Museum(s):
and galleries. Standing Commission, 186
648, 914, 1176
London, Guide, 914
of London Act, 1040
Bill, 709, 710, 746, 969, 1132
See also London Museum
of practical geology, 396
Provincial, 648
Music:
manuscripts, 795
printing. 400 years, 795
published in periodicals, 540, 1066
rooms. Secondary schools, 1172
Sacred vocal. Catalogue, 795
Teaching. Schools, 183
Mussel scale & brown scale, 1051

Mycorrhizal associations etc., 586
MYRDDIN-EVANS, SIR G. (Chairman), Local Government Commission for Wales, 605

N

N.A.A.S. *See* National Agricultural Advisory Service
Nachingwea. Mechanised farming, 548
Nairn. Census, Leaflet & report, 590
NASH, C. P. B., Royal yachts, 887
NAMIER, SIR L., History of Parliament, 854
NANDY, K., Interstellar reddening, 1169
1170

1961 pp 1–224, 1962 pp 225–445, 1963 pp 447–696, 1964 pp 697–962, 1965 pp 963–1226

NAR— *INDEX 1961-5*

Narcissus:
Eelworm, 301
flies, 01
Narcotic drugs. Convention, 342, 1096
NASH, G. D., Thermal insulation of factories, 395
National:
Advisory Council on education for industry, 821
Aeronautics & Space Administration U.S.A., 622, 886
Agricultural Advisory Service:
Local education authority, 112, 114, 820
Progress report, 85, 303, 532, 789, 1059
Quarterly review, 86, 304, 533, 789, 1060
Assistance:
Act, 288
Bills, 42, 228, 256, 260, 359, 710, 963, 967, 1010
Board reports, 169, 384, 628, 893, 1162
Statement of Excess, 941
Conduct of homes. Select Committee S.I., 257
Determination of need. Regulations, 381, 625, 890
Board for prices & incomes, 1156
Building:
Agency, 633
Studies:
Research papers, 179–80, 395, 638, 1179
Special reports, 395, 638, 905, 1179
Bureau of Standards, U.S.A., 688
Certificates & diplomas, 182, 183, 911, 912
See also specific subjects
Chemical Laboratory publications, 180, 396, 640–1, 906, 1180
Coal Board:
Advances, 171, 385, 629, 896, 1202
Loans, 630, 937, 1203
Report & accounts, 173, 246, 631, 898, 1165
Collection of industrial bacteria, 1181
debt:
Commissioners. Account, 163, 379, 622, 886, 1156
Office, 163, 379, 622, 886–7, 1156–7
Reduction of capital, 204, 425, 674, 886, 1028
Returns, 204, 494, 886, 1205
Defence, Dept. of, Canada, 623
diplomas. *See specific subjects*
Economic Development Council.
Publications, 623, 887, 1157

National (*continued*):
Engineering Laboratory, 180, 396, 641, 906, 1180
Film Finance Corporation:
Advances, 188, 257, 485, 823
Annual report, 191, 278, 663, 928, 1032
flags & ensigns, 1086
Forest Parks, 127
Galleries of Scotland, 163, 379, 623, 887, 1157
Gallery. London:
Catalogue, 163, 623, 1157
Report, 379, 1157
Security, 279
Health Service:
Acts, 68
Bills, 3, 34, 39, 40, 138, 1009
Central Health Services Council.
See Central Health
Hospitals Accounts. *See* Hospital Boards
Contributions Acts, 68, 1040
Bills, 2, 39, 965, 968, 1013, 1136
Dieticians etc., in, 354
Hospitals:
Boards Act, 772
Bill, 491, 701, 735, 859
Costings returns, 134, 354, 593, 853, 1126
See also Hospitals
Prescribing, 854, 1127
Scotland. Acts Hospital Boards etc.
Accounts, 131, 405, 647, 913, 1174
Hospital. Running costs, 402, 647, 912, 1174
Superannuation scheme:
England & Wales, 134, 354, 853, 1127
Scotland, 647
Supplementary opthalmic services.
Fees & charges, 134, 354, 593, 853, 1136
Income(s).
and:
balance of payments. Preliminary estimates, 204, 425, 674, 940, 1205
expenditure, 96, 314, 544, 798, 1070
Commission, 283, 623, 887, 1157
Institute for research into nuclear science, 163–4, 379–80, 623–4, 887, 1157–8
Insurance:
Acts, 517, 773, 1040
Accounts, 165–6, 382, 626, 891, 1160
Amendment Bills, 487, 1009
Bills, 448, 487, 488, 627, 709, 745, 968, 970, 1013, 1136

1961 pp 1–224, 1962 pp 225–445, 1963 pp 447–696, 1964 pp 697–962, 1965 pp 963–1226

78

INDEX 1961 5 **—NAT**

National (*continued*):
Insurance (*continued*):
Decisions of Commissioner, 165–7, 382–3, 625–6, 891–2, 1160–1
Index:
Amendments, 165, 381, 625, 890
and digest, 890, 1160
Reported, 384
Decisions of Tribunal, 166, 167, 383, 626
Financial provisions, 627, 892
Government Actuary report, 204, 425, 626, 892, 1161
Local government superannuation. Circulars, 142, 864
Memo, 890
Advisory Committee reports, 36, 167–8, 383–4, 626–7, 892, 1161
Amendment Regulations:
Draft, 165, 166
Reports, 12, 24, 27, 36, 37
Assessment of graduated contributions Regulations, 382, 384
Claims & payments Amendment Regulations, 890, 892
Classification Amendment Regulations, 165, 167
Collection of graduated contributions:
Draft, 165, 382
Reports, 167, 256
Continental Shelf Regulations:
Draft, 893
Report, 892
Contributions. Amendment Regulations:
Draft, 165, 381
Reports, 167, 383–4, 626
Earnings. Regulations, 382, 892
Everybody's guide, 164, 890, 1160
Fund etc., Accounts, 165–6, 382, 626, 891, 1161
Further Provisions Bill, 968, 1008
General benefits Amendment Regulations:
Draft, 165, 1162
Reports, 167, 1161
Graduated retirement benefit:
Draft, 165
Report, 167
Industrial injuries:
Acts, 1040
Bill, 965, 968, 971, 1013, 1136
Government Actuary, 204, 425, 627, 893, 1161
Byssinosis, 1161

National (*continued*):
Insurance (*continued*):
Industrial injuries (*continued*):
Decisions of:
Commissioner, 168, 169, 383, 384, 627, 892–3, 1161
Decisions of:
Reported, 384
Tribunal, 168, 169, 383, 627, 893
Farmers' lung, 892
Law, 165, 381, 625, 890, 1160
Occupational diseases, 628, 1162
Law, 165, 381, 625, 890, 1160
Local Government superannuation
Circulars, 142, 184, 864
Married women. Amendment Regulations, 36, 165
Medical Certification Regulations, 890, 1161, 1162
Members of H.M. Forces, 165, 167
Modification of local government superannuation schemes. Select Committee, 140
New entrants. Transitional Regulations, 382
Non-participation Regulations, 165, 167, 625, 626, 627
Preliminary drafts, 165, 381–2, 625, 890, 1162
Schemes. Proposed changes, 628
Scotland. Local government superannuation:
Circulars, 184
Select Committee S.I., 140
Unemployment & sickness Regulations, 890, 892
Widowed Mothers' Bill, 42
Land Fund, 204, 425, 674, 940, 1205
Lending Library:
Current Serials, 1089
Translations Bulletin, 179, 396, 641, 907, 1089
Livestock breeding Conference, 531
Maritime Museum, 380, 624, 887, 1158
Museum of Antiquities. Scotland, 164, 380, 624, 888, 1158
Park(s):
Commission report, 145, 363, 486, 868, 1141
Service. Historical handbook, 958
Physical Laboratory:
Conference, 397, 641
Mathematical tables, 397, 906
Notes on applied science, 164, 397, 641, 907
Publications, 164, 397, 641, 906–7, 1180
Report, 164, 397, 641, 906, 1180
Symposium, 397, 641, 907, 1180
Units & standards of measurement, 397, 907

1961 pp 1–224, 1962 pp 225–445, 1963 pp 447–696, 1964 pp 697–962, 1965 pp 963–1226

79

National (continued):
  Plan, 1088
  Plan in brief, 1088
  Portrait Gallery, 164, 380, 624, 888
  Ports Council:
    Annual report, 1199
    Port developments, 1158
  Provident Institution Act, 774
  Register of archives, 134, 354, 594, 1127
  Research Development Corporation:
    Advances, 190, 413, 660, 925, 1191
    Report & accounts, 191, 486, 663, 928, 1180
  Savings Committee. Annual reports, 380, 624, 888, 1158
  Science Foundation. U.S.A., 624
  Servicemen in army. Regulations, 441, 811
  Trust for Scotland Order Confirmation Act, 69
    Bill, 41
  Union of:
    Bank Employees. Complaint, 618
    Mineworkers. Difference, 881
  Water Safety Campaign Circular, 1139
  Youth Employment Council. Interim report, 158
Nationalised:
  industries:
    and undertakings. Advances. See respective industries
    Financial & economic obligations, 203
    Select Committee reports, 140, 141, 247, 250, 359, 631, 792, 862, 898, 1134, 1135
  transport undertakings. Accounts, 932, 1091
NATO. See North Atlantic Treaty Organisation
Natural:
  graphite, 909
  history:
    drawings, 320
    Dunstanburgh Castle Point, 633
    Museum. See British Museum. N.H. of snakes, 1070
    Rennell Island, 313
  Resources Technical Committee (Agriculture), 177
Naturalisation:
  forms, 356
  return, 135, 355
Nature Conservancy reports & publications, 164, 380, 394, 624–5, 888
Nauru*, 1113
Nautical:
  Almanac, 71, 291, 520, 818, 1087
  Office publications, 888, 1169
  subjects in secondary schools, 183

Naval:
  and marine pensions (London Gazette), 916
  Court Martial procedure, 71, 291, 519, 1086
  craft. Gifts, 938
  Electrical pocket book, 71, 520
  General Service Medal, 202, 672
  Marine engineering practice, 520, 1087
  swords & firearms, 380
  See also Royal Naval
Navigation:
  Admiralty manual, 71, 818, 1086
  Radio aid, 1063
Navy:
  Appropriation accounts, 71, 291, 520, 818, 1087
  Army & Air Force Reserves Act, 773
    Bill, 491, 699, 735, 859
  Careers, 368
  Department publications, 818–20, 1086–8
    See also Admiralty
  Dockyard & Production accounts, 71, 291, 520, 819, 1087
  estimates, 72, 291, 520
  Flying in, 887
  List, 71, 72, 292, 520, 819, 1087
  Queen's Regulations & Admiralty Instructions, 72, 292, 520, 819, 1087
  Votes, 205, 426, 675, 819, 940, 1206

Near & Middle East. Documents on British foreign policy, 570
Near-eastern art, 93
Needle-cast of pine, 846
Needs of young children in care, 856
Nefs. Medieval silver, 689
Negatives. First, 1170
Nematodes, 95, 312, 543, 790, 1069
Nematodirus disease in lambs, 1053
Nene rivers. Hydrological survey, 869
Neny Fiord. Basement complex, 539
Neolithic revolution, 95, 543
Neotunga euloidea, 311
Nepal:
  and Gurkhas, 1080
  Diptera from, 1068
  Expedition to, 1068
Netherlands:
  Air services*, 1092
  British visitors' passport*, 122
  Cereals, etc* 824
  Continental Shelf*, 1094
  Double taxation*, 342, 840
  Graves of servicemen*, 580, 839
  Inventions & secrecy*, 839
NETHERTHORPE, LORD (Chairman), Antibiotics in animal feeding, 298
Nettle. Annual, 783

New:
  colleges of education. Falkirk & Ayr, 911
  Commonwealth Institute. Photoposter 609
  contributions to economic statistics, 314, 799
  Forest(s):
    Act, 773
    Bill, 456, 697, 701, 702, 707, 743, 745, 861
    guide, 349
    of Dartmoor, 1121
    grain bins in Cyprus, 102
    grants for better homes. Scotland, 399
  Hebrides:
    Land snails, 542
    Protocol. France*, 577
    Reports, 317, 802
    Visas. Turkey*, 584
  horizons, 551
  life for dead lands, 606
  streets. Greater London Order, 1138
  Towns:
    Acts, 773, 1040
    Bills, 491, 699, 709, 963, 972, 1013, 1136
    Development Corporations, 445, 184, 251, 363, 606, 868, 1141
    Lord Chancellor's Memo. Consolidation of enactments, 709
    No. 2 Act, 773
      Bill, 705, 735, 743, 744, 859
    of Britain, 148, 871
    Livingston Order, 405
  traffic signs, 1199
  types of paint, 394, 899
  valuation lists, 362
  ways in junior secondary education, Scotland, 646
  Years Honours list, 408, 649, 914–5, 1176
Zealand:
  Air services*, 89
  Commonwealth development & financing, 550
  Nauru*, 1113
NEWALL, R. J., Bark form etc., in birch, 639
Newark on Trent. Siegeworks, 902
NEWBY, R. F., Dipped headlights campaign, 642
Newcastle-under-Lyme Corporation Act, 774
Newcastle upon Tyne:
  Corporation Act, 774
  Proposed borough. Map, 605
  R. H. E., World in space, 622
  Newer types of paint, 394, 899
Newport:
  Boundary alteration. Map, 605
  Corporation Act, 69

NEWSOM, J. H., Half our future, 564
NEWTON, L., Seaweeds, 95
Newton-le-Willows Provisional Order Act, 1042
  Bill, 970, 1011

N.H.S. See National Health Service

NICHOLSON, G. W. L., Canadian expeditionary force, 1914–1919, 623
Nigeria:
  Commonwealth development & its financing, 550
  Northern Cameroons. Incorporation, 104, 320
  Public officers*, 651
  Report, 100
  Republic Act, 517
    Bill, 456, 491,
  Soils & other road-making materials, 398
  Western Region flag badge, 104
NIRL. See National Institute for Research into Nuclear Science
Nitrate salt baths. Notice, 881, 1153
Nitrogenous fertilizers for farm crops, 300, 1052
NIXON, G. E. J., Tribe microgasterini, 1067

N.L.L. See National Lending Library

Noctuidae, 95
Nodini & eumolpidae, 1068
Noise:
  Aircraft, Citizens' guide, 823
  and:
    buildings, 637
    the worker, 618
  Control of, 397
  from motor vehicles, 394
  in the home, 178
  Problem of, 637
Nomenclature of disease, 134
Non-
  ferrous metal production (Commonwealth), 550
  metallic:
    materials Board, 1064
    minerals. Review, 804
    recurrent grants. Procedure, 676, 1091
    residential treatment of offenders, 357
    war-like stores. Services, 1133–4
Norfolk:
  Census:
    Leaflet population etc., 589
    Report, 849
  Estuary Act, 774
  Saxton map, 540
Normandy. Battle of, 313
Normanton. Proposed county district, 867

North:
  Atlantic:
    Shipping Act, 68
      Bill, 6, 40
    Treaty Organisation:
      Accession of Greece & Turkey*, 1113
      Co-operation on atomic energy, 839, 1113
      Foreign forces in Germany*, 839–40
      German forces in U.K.*, 119
      International Military H.Q., 1113
      Inventions. Secrecy*, 342
      U.K. Forces. Germany*, 119
  Borneo (and Sarawak):
    Commission of enquiry, 319
    Instructions OIC, 388
    Peace corps U.S.A.*, 385
    Reports, 101, 548
    Roadmaking materials, 1200
  East(ern):
    Atlantic fisheries. Convention, 576
    general review area, 605, 1141
    regional development, 663
    Scotland forests, 586
  Lancashire rivers, 868
  of Scotland. Hydro-electric Board:
    Advances, 115, 567, 912, 1164
    Annual report, 184, 405, 647, 910
    Constructional scheme, 1171
    Loans, 204, 425, 673, 674, 939, 1204
    Milk marketing scheme, 784
    Orkney & Shetland Shipping Co. Undertaking, 782, 1051
  Wales geology, 129
  West:
    Atlantic fisheries. Convention, 576
    regional study, 663
    Yorkshire forests guide, 846
  Northampton:
    Alteration of area, 144
    Bedford & N. Bucks study, 1141
    Corporation Act, 290
    Police area. Amalgamation, 1129
  Northamptonshire (etc.):
    Census:
      Leaflet population etc., 589
      Report, 849
    Police area. Amalgamation, 1129
    Saxton map, 93
  Northern:
    Affairs & National Resources. Canada. Publication, 112
    and southern photometric systems, 636
    Cameroons. Incorporation, 104, 320
    Ireland:
      Act, 288
      Bill, 225, 227, 229, 246, 256, 261, 262
      Economy of, 357
      Shipping services to, 669

Northern (continued):
  Nigeria. Public officers*, 651
  Rhodesia:
    Anglea frontier*, 1115
    becomes Zambia. Photoposter, 870
    Cereals,* 805
    Independence:
      booklet, 870
      Conference, 806
      Instructions OIC, 389
      Photoposter, 870
      Proposals for constitutional change, 102,
      Provision of personnel. United Nations*, 845
      Reports, 101, 548, 803
      Royal Instructions OIC, 899
      See also Zambia
NORTHUMBERLAND, DUKE OF (Chairman), Recruitment for veterinary profession, 789, 856
Northumberland:
  Census:
    Leaflet population, 589
    Report, 588
  Saxton map, 795
Norway:
  Air services*, 1114
  British visitors' passports*, 122
  Continental Shelf*, 1094
  Double taxation*, 342, 840
  Fisheries(ing)*, 122, 835, 1114
  Judgments in civil matters*, 122, 342
  Lobster food of, 299
Norwich. Alteration of area. Map, 1140
Not yet five, 327
Notch tough steel, 1087
Notes on applied science, 164, 397, 641, 907
Notices of recall & release. Criminal Justice (Scotland) Act, 911
Notopteridae. Swimbladder, 797
Nottingham:
  Alteration of area. Map, 867
  Local Government Commission, 1142–3
Nottinghamshire. Census:
  Leaflet. Population etc., 589
  Report, 849
Nuclear:
  and allied radiation hazards to man, 160
  attack. Advising householder, 594
  Energy:
    Civil liability*, 840
    on Britain, 148, 365
    industry of U.K., 215
    Third Party liability, 581, 840
  explosions. Effect on scientific experiments, 637
  Installations:
    Act, 1040
    Bill, 969, 1013, 1136

Nuclear (continued):
  Installations (continued):
    Amendment Act, 1040
    Bills, 740, 745, 746, 964, 1132
  power:
    for ship propulsion, 933
    programme. 2nd, 898
    weapon tests, 122, 581, 840
NUGENT, SIR R. (Chairman), British Overseas Airways Corporation, 792
Numerical forecasting, 162
Nurses & nursing:
  Act, 773
    Bill, 702, 736, 741, 859
  Amendment Act, 68
    Bill, 2, 34, 138
  and midwifery (Careers), 368, 1147
  for men (Careers), 368
  Health records, 851
  Homes:
    Act, 517
      Bill, 264, 450, 483, 487, 597
    Domestic services, 352
    services. Hospital, 352, 591
  staff:
    Accommodation, 133, 592
    Recording sickness, 352
  training:
    Experimental, at Glasgow, 646
    School for, 133, 592
  Nutrient requirements of farm livestock, 527
  Nutrition:
    Manual, 86
    problems in forest nurseries, 1121

Nyasaland:
  Constitutional Conference, 313
  Independence booklet, 870
  Instructions OIC, 174, 632
  Mozambique:
    Boundary Commission*, 1115
    Frontier*, 343
    Photoposter, 870
    Public officers*, 889
    Reports, 101, 317, 806
    Royal Instructions, OIC, 632
    See also Rhodesia & Nyasaland

O

O. & M. Practice of, 1205
Oak, Death of pedunculate, 1121
OAKLEY, K. P.:
  Man the tool-maker, 95
  Problem of man's antiquity, 797
  Succession of life, 313, 797
OASTLER, E. G. (Chairman), Scottish Health Services Council, 646

Oaths:
  Act, 68
    Bill, 3, 34, 40, 138
  and Evidence (Overseas Authorities & Countries) Act, 517
    Bill, 452, 483, 487, 489, 597
Oats. Wild, 82, 784

Objective-type examinations (Certificate of Secondary Education), 822
Obscene Publications Act, 773
  Bill, 706, 736, 743, 744, 859
Observations of:
  southern RR Lyrae stars, 176
  twenty-four single-lined variables, 392
Observatories' Year book, 162, 378, 622, 885
Observers' handbook, 162
Obstetrics. Human relations in, 132

Occultation of Regulus, 636
Occupation(al):
  and industry. National summary tables. Census, 1123, 1124
  diseases. Diagnosis, 628, 1162
  Industry, socio-economic groups. Census, 1123
  Therapist:
    Careers, 874
    in National Health Service, 354
    Therapy Dept., 353, 592
  Occupiers displaced by land acquisition, etc., 602
Occurrence & pathology of Dee disease, 782
  378
Ocean weather stations in North Atlantic, 378
Oceanic & bathypelagic plankton, 80
Oceanographic & meteorological research, 304

Odda's Chapel. Guide, 1167
O'DEA, W. T., Making fire, 903
ODHIAMBO, T. R., Bryocorinae, 311

Offences:
  Drunkenness. Statistics, 136, 357, 595, 856, 1129
  Motor vehicles, 136, 357, 595, 856, 1129
Offenders:
  Custodial training for young, 402
  Treatment of. See Treatment:
Office(s):
  and industrial development. See Control of offices
  Computers in, 1152
  of:
    education U.S.A., 688, 958
    Industrial Assurance Commissioner. See Industrial Assurance
    International Science Activities U.S.A., 624

OFF—   *INDEX 1961-5*

Office(s) (continued):
Shops & Railway Premises Act, 517
Bill, 260, 264, 449, 450, 455, 483, 488, 489, 597
Explanatory book, employees, 1152
Forms, 880–1, 1152
General guide, 880, 1152
Report, 1152
Statement, 898
work (Careers), 874
Official:
dress in House of Commons, 139
List:
Buildings for marriages, 128, 351, 588, 848, 1123
Registration Officers, etc., 128, 351, 589, 849, 1123
publications, Exchange:
Convention, 340
Germany*, 577
Thailand*, 583
Vietnam*, 585
sources. Guide, 128, 151
statistics. Studies in, 96, 314, 799, 880, 1070

OGDEN, W. M. (Chairman), De-population in Mid-Wales, 865
OGILVIE, L., Diseases of vegetables, 83

Oil:
in Navigable Waters Act, 517
Bill, 452, 467, 483, 487
Mineral, in food, 304

Old:
Beaupre Castle. Guide, 1167
people:
Designing for, 362
Grouped flatlets, 362
Services for, 142
See also Elderly People
red sandstone of Brown Clee Hill, 94
Sarum. Guide, 1167
OLDFIELD-DAVIES, A. B. (Chairman), Technical education. Wales, 114
OLDROYD, H., Asilidae, 796
Oligokyphus. Skull of, 797
Olive oil*, 581, 841
OLIVER, F. W. J., Mathematical tables, 397
O'LOUGHLIN, C., Leeward Islands. Survey, 651

OMAN, C. Medieval silver nefs 689
Ombudsman. Parliamentary Commissioner, 1031
OMMANNEY, F. D., Malayan offshore trawling grounds, 318

One hundred things to see. V. & A. Museum 439

O'NEIL, B. H. ST. J., Ancient monuments, Isles of Scilly, 221
Onion(s):
Advisory leaflet, 530
and lock(s):
smut, 1052
Weed control, 301
and related crops, 1054
fly, 81, 1052

Open:
fires for coke burning, 143
General licences:
Export, 190, 413, 660–1, 666, 926, 1191–2, 1195
Import, 190, 413, 661, 926, 1191
Operating theatres, Hospitals. 850
Operation & management. Small sewage works, 1141
Operational research in R.A.F., 534
Opex. Turkey*, 584
Ophiuroids, 1069
Opthalmic optician & dispensing optician (Careers), 152, 1147

Orbital elements of binaries, 393
Orchestras. London, 1061
Orchids. Hand-list, 391
Orders:
by Her Majesty. Pensions etc., 169, 277, 628, 893, 1162
decorations, medals. Order of precedence, 187
Diseases of animals, 1059
in Council:
Home Office, 856
Pensions & National Insurance, 169, 384, 628, 893, 1162
Privy Council, 173–4, 388–9, 632, 899, 1166
Ordinary National Certificates. See specific subjects
Ordnance:
Factories. See Royal Ordnance Factories
Survey:
Annual reports, 380, 625, 988, 1158
Estimates Committee, 599, 861
Professional paper, 888
Ordovician:
and adjacent strata. Geology, 797
trilobite faunas, 311
Orford Castle. Guide, 900
Organic halogen compounds 159
Organisation:
and practices. Building & civil engineering, 901
of:
after-care, 595, 647
Civil Service, 637
Industrial Health Services, 375

1961 pp 1–224, 1962 pp 225–445, 1963 pp 447–696, 1964 pp 697–962, 1965 pp 963–1226

84

INDEX 1961-5   **—PAK**

Organisation (continued):
of (continued):
prison medical service, 856
science in Germany, 624
Scientific Civil Service, 1205
secondary education, 1088, 1172
work for prisoners, 856
Oriental, Slavonic, East European & African studies, 206
Origins of:
motion picture, 903
operational research, 534
Orkney:
Census. Leaflet & report, 590
Educational Trust Scheme, 182, 401
Islands. Shipping Co. Undertaking, 79, 300
Steam Navigation Co. Undertaking, 80
Orpington Urban District Council Act, 290
Orthoptist (Careers), 152, 1147

Osborne House. Catalogue, 1167
Osmudites Doukevi Carruthers, 1068
OSR forms, 880, 1152
Ostracoda:
Cretaceous, 1068
Middle jurassic, 542, 797

Outdoor:
flowers for cutting, 302
irrigation, 82, 1053
salad crops, 302
tomatoes, 300, 1052
Outpatients. See Patients
Output & utilisation of farm produce, 86, 1060

Overfishing. Meshes of nets etc., 581
Oversea(s):
Development:
and Service Act, 1040
Ministry of:
Publications, 888–9, 1159–60
Work of, 1029
Technical assistance, 103
Education, 102, 188, 410, 651
geodetic & topographical surveys, 101, 318, 409, 651, 888, 1159
Geological survey:
Annual reports, 100, 410, 651, 889, 1159
Publications 102 318 381 625 889 1159
geology and:
mineral resources, 102, 188, 410, 651, 889, 1159
mining. Technical assistance, 889
Migration Board, 105, 320, 552, 1076
Research publications, 651, 889, 1159

Oversea(s) (continued):
Resources Development Acts. Accounts, 102, 318, 552, 806, 1076–7
Service(s):
Act, 68
Bill, 2
Pensions. Supplement Regulation, 651
trade:
Accounts, 1195
Report on, 194, 415–6, 663, 929, 1195
OWEN, D. E., Silurian polyzoa, 1068
OWEN, E. F., Brachiopod genus Cyclothyris, 311
OWEN, L. O. (Chairman), Welsh Advisory Water Committee, 146
OWEN-EVANS, G.:
chaetotaxy of legs in free-living Gamasina, 542
Mites of Genus Macrocheles Latr, 542

Oxfordshire. Census:
Leaflet, population etc., 589
Report, 849

Oyster(s):
Biology & culture, 318
Scottish, Investigations, 80
Water sterilization, 85

P

Pacific Islands:
Fiji (Constitution) OIC, 632
Gilbert & Ellice Islands OIC, 632
PADMORE, SIR T. (Chairman), Nuclear power for ship propulsion, 933
PAGEL, B. E. J.:
Influence of metal abundance of spectra etc., 393
Radial velocity & spectrum, 392
Some cool stars, 903
Paint. New types, 394, 899
Painting(s):
Apsley House, 1222
in tropical climates, 399
Persian, 1222
Portrait. Egypt, 310
Victorian, 609
walls, 1178
Paisley Corporation Order Confirmation Act, 518
Bill, 264
Pakistan:
Commonwealth development & its financing, 103
Double taxation*, 204
Loan of H.M.S. Diadem, 427

1961 pp 1–224, 1962 pp 225–445, 1963 pp 447–696, 1964 pp 697–962, 1965 pp 963–1226

85

PAL—   *INDEX 1961-5*

Palace of Westminster. Select Committee, 1134
Palaeomagnetic investigations in Falkland Islands, 539
Palaeoniscoid fishes, 542
Palaeontology:
Geological Survey. Memoirs, 905
Old red sandstone, 94
Pallets. Customs treatment, 584
PALMAR, C. E.:
Capercaillie, 1121
Titmice in woodlands, 349
Woodpeckers in woodlands, 1122
PALMER, G., Deadlishes, 95
Panama. Air services*, 1114
Panjabi. Printed books. Catalogue, 93
Papal registers. Calendar, 174
Paper mills:
Prevention of accidents, 374
Safety in, 881
Parade & rifle drill. R. N. Handbook, 72, 292, 520
Paraguay. Trade & payments*, 122, 342
PARISH, D. E. W. (Chairman), Building research etc., 900
PARKER, H. W., Snakes, 1070
PARKER, K. A. L. (Chairman), Higher police training, 356, 595
PARKER, W. E., American Military International Insurance Association, 1181
PARKIN, P. H., Sound insulation between dwellings, 180
Parking:
in town centres, 1138, 1141
Next stage. London's problems, 667
Places (Plymouth) Order. Select Committee, 599–600
Parks. Royal, of London, 1168
Parliamentary:
Act, 1911. Anniversary exhibition, 93
Bill, 1011
British, Reference pamphlet, 148, 366, 1144
Commissioner for Administration, 1031
Debates. See House of Commons and House of Lords
Dissolution. Queen's proclamation, 915
elections. See Elections
government:
in Britain, 609
in Commonwealth, 148
History, 854
Papers:
General Index, 137, 598
Sessional Index, 139, 359, 598, 860, 1133
Title & Contents, 234, 360, 598, 863, 1136
Photocopier (1215–1965), 1144
State opening, 366
See also Palace of Westminster

PARRY, SIR D. H. (Chairman), Legal status of Welsh language, 1223
PARRY, HELI, EIR H. W. (Chairman), Disturbances in British Guiana, 318
PARRY, J. H. (Chairman), Latin American studies, 1091
Parsley. Chemical weed control, 301, 1052
Parsnips:
Advisory Leaflet, 1051
Chemical weed control, 301, 1052
Parthenon. Sculptures, 310
Partners in patronage. Arts Council report, 88
Pashto mss. catalogue, 1066
Passenger:
mileage by road in Greater London, 398
ships. Merchant shipping, 197
transport in Great Britain, 670, 933, 1199
Passports:
agreements etc. See respective countries
Collective*, 823
Pastes. Fish & meat, 1059
Patent(s):
and Design (Renewals etc.) Act, 68
Bureau. International*, 1114
Designs & trade marks reports, 164, 381, 663, 928, 1195
Employees' Inventions Bill, 968, 971, 1012
for invention:
International classification, 1119
Unification of substantive law, 841, 1119
International Bureau, 1114
law:
European. Convention, 416
U.K., 1119
Office Library. Periodical publications, 1160
Rolls. Calendar, 174, 901
Path of flight, 567
Pathology:
department, Hospital, 132, 352, 353, 852
Measurement of work, 1162
Patients:
admitted to mental hospital, 589
concerned in criminal proceedings, 405
In:
day. Pattern, 1162
enquiry, 128, 351, 589, 849
statistics, 313, 1175
in hospital:
Mental Health Scotland Act, 405
Visiting, 406
Out:
Arrangements. Hospital, 132, 850, 1125
departments. Hospital. 353, 592, 852, 1126
Psychiatric. Accomodation, 592

1961 pp 1–224, 1962 pp 225–445, 1963 pp 447–696, 1964 pp 697–962, 1965 pp 963–1226

86

INDEX 1961-5   **—PER**

PATON, T. R., Soil survey of Semporna Peninsula, 651
PATRICK ALEXANDER Lecture, Memorial Scholarship Scheme, 645
Pattern of:
in-patients day, 1162
the future (Manpower), 880
Patternmaker (Careers), 1162
Pavements. Structural design, 394
PAWSEY, R. G.:
Grey mould, 846
Needle-cast of pine, 846
Resin-top disease of Pine, 846
Pay Warrants. Army, 210, 440, 691, 810, 1080, 1081
Pea(s):
and bean thrips, 81
for drying, 81
moth, 300, 1052
Weed control, 82, 1052
Peace corps in:
North Borneo, 585
Sarawak, 584–5
Peaceful settlement of disputes, 118
Pear(s):
and cherry slugworm, 300
midge, 81
See also Apples & pears
PEASE, W. H., Marine molluscs, 1069
Peat Marwick Mitchell & Co. Shipbuilding orders, 199
Peat:
Scottish Committee, 299
surveys. S.W. Scotland, 1051
PECK, C. W., English copper etc. coins, 795
PEDDIE, Lord (Chairman), Co-operatives, 888
PEDGLEY, D. E.:
Elementary meteorology, 377
Thunderstorms, 377
Pedunculate oak. Death, 1121
Peebles. Census:
Leaflet. Population etc., 590
Report, 850
Peebleshire. Educational Trust Scheme, 182
Peerage:
Act, 517
Bill, 453, 454, 490
Renunciation Bill, 40
PEERS, SIR C., ST. Botolph's Priory, 900
Pelagic:
polychaetes, 312
whaling*, 281, 585, 838
Pembrokeshire:
Census. Report, 588
County Council Act, 1042
Saxton map, 795
Penaeidea, 548
Penalties for Drunkenness Act, 288
Bill, 229, 262

Pencils etc. Merchandise Marks, 663
Pendennis & St. Mawes Castles. Guide, 634
Pennine Anglo-saxon, 794
Penney, F. D., Die castings, 440
Pension(s):
Air Forces. Order, 169, 277, 628, 893, 1162
Allocation of. Explanatory memo. 1201
and National Insurance, Ministry of:
Annual report, 169, 384, 628, 893, 1162
Estimates Committee, 1133, 1135
Publications, 164–70, 381–4, 623–9, 890–4, 1162
Army. See Army, Pensions:
Bill, 261
Home Guard. Order & Warrant, 1162
Increase:
Acts, 516, 1040
Bills, 232, 263, 264, 975, 1013
Circulars, 601, 864, 865
Pensioners' guides, 674, 940
Military Forces. Warrant, 170, 277, 629, 894, 1162
Naval Forces. Order, 169, 384, 628, 893, 1162
Officers etc., OIC etc., 1914–18 War, 169, 170, 277, 384, 628–9, 893, 894
Teachers' widows, 401
Wives & widows. Increments, 168
Pensioners' guide to Pensions Increase Acts, 674, 940
People at work, 618
Percussion musical instruments. Merchandise Marks, 663
PERCY, T. R. (Chairman), Ill-treatment of prisoners, 596
Perennial bindweeds, 784
Performers' Protection Act, 517
Bill, 448, 483, 489, 597
Performing Animals Bill, 963
Perim Royal Instructions OIC, 632
Period-colour relation for contact binaries, 176
Periodicals:
Chinese, in British libraries, 1066
in Patent Office Library, 1160
Perjury & attendance of witnesses, 856
PERKINS, J. F., Foerster's genera, 311
Permanent farm fences, 364
Permissible working stresses in bridges etc., 197, 667
Permits & Licences, Betting & Gaming Acts, 135, 355, 460, 854, 982
Perpetuities & Accumulations Act, 773
Bill, 700, 701, 706, 736, 743, 744, 859
PERRIN, M. W. (Chairman), Food Standards Committee, 788, 1059
Persian:
art. Calendar, 539
Gulf Gazette, 122, 343, 581, 841, 1114

1961 pp 1–224, 1962 pp 225–445, 1963 pp 447–696, 1964 pp 697–962, 1965 pp 963–1226

87

PER-POU | 1961-5

Persian (*continued*):
illustrated mss., 1066
paintings, 1222
Persistent:
criminals, 596
organochlorine pesticides review, 789
Personal:
Acts, 519
Bills Committee, 449
Persons acquiring U.K. citizenship, 596, 857, 1130
Pert guide for management use, 894
Perth (and Kinross):
Census:
Leaflet. Population etc., 590
Report, 850
Educational Trust Scheme, 645, 911
Morrison's Academy Trust Scheme, 401, 912, 1173
Peru. Air services*, 122
Pest(s):
Cereal, 1054
Infestation Research:
Board report, 298
Bulletin, 79
Laboratory reports, 298, 527, 782, 1049
Insect, in food stores, 82, 543
Pesticides. Persistent organochloride, 789
Peterborough. Soke of:
Amalgamation with Huntingdonshire, 603
Census:
Leaflet. Population etc., 589
Report, 849
Petrol(eum):
filling stations. Circular. Scotland, 1171
Production Act 1934. Account, 1165
supply. Monopolies Commission, 1194
Petrology(ical):
of:
Anvers Island etc., 318
Argentine Islands, 794
Deception Island, 101
King George Island, 101
studies. Glen Urquhart, 797
Petrorhagia, 796
PETTIT, J. M., Heterosporous plants, 1068
Pewter. British, 218

P.G. Information series & reports (UKAEA), 215–8, 435–8, 683–5, 953–5, 1219

Pharmacy:
and Poisons:
Act 1933 Form, 1129
Amendment Act, 773
Bill, 701, 736, 741, 859
Bill, 704, 706, 736, 742, 859
Pharmacy (*continued*):
Careers, 1147
department. Hospital, 132, 591, 851
Philippines. Anti-swine fever vaccine, 1203
PHILLIPS, A.:
Castle Guides, 221, 222
Monasteries of N.E. Yorkshire, 390
PHILLIPS, D. H., Leaf cast of larch, 586
PHILLIPS, L., Modern mathematics & your child, 958
Phlaurocentrum Karsch, 311
Phosgene detection, 374
Photoelectric magnitudes of stars, 393, 635
Photographic:
emulsions, 164
photometry of globular cluster, 177
study of fatigue structures. Aircraft, 524
zenith tube instrument, 903
Photography:
and cinematography (Careers), 875
Undersea, Marine research, 528
Photoheliographic results, 176, 635
Photometric standards & unit of light, 164
Photometry:
of:
cluster NGG, 176, 1169
RR Lyrae variables, 1169
Physical, 397
Photoposters, 147, 365, 609, 870, 1144
Physical:
education in primary schools. Scotland, 912
photometry, 397
training in Army, 440, 691, 810
PHYSICK, J.:
Duke of Wellington in Caricature, 1221
Eric Gill. Engraved work, 689
Physiological responses to hot environments, 160
Physiotherapy(ist):
and remedial gymnast (Careers), 152, 612
department. Hospital, 133, 352, 592, 1124, 1125
in National Health service, 354
Phyto-sanitary Convention, 343

Piccadilly Circus. Working party, 1141
Picea sitchensis Carr, 639
Pick-up balers, 303
PICKERING, SIR G. (Chairman), University Grants Committee, 354
PICTON, J. G. (Chairman):
Licensed residential establishment, 881
South Wales coalfield, 1152
Picture(s):
of Commonwealth, 147
sets, 365
Pier & Harbour Confirmation Acts & Bills. *See respective towns*
Pies. Meat, Food standards, 533

Pig(s):
Aids to management, 532
Buildings for, Bibliography, 1049
Diseases of, 786
fattening houses, 1059
feeding, 531, 1051
Housing, 302
Industry Development Authority, 170
Slatted floor systems for, Research literature, 1049
Young, Management, 301
PIGOTT, S., West Kennett. Long barrow, 389, 633
PILE, W. D. (Chairman), Family pensions benefits for teachers, 1089
PILKINGTON, SIR H. (Chairman), Broadcasting, 384, 385
Pilot Assurance Co. Ltd., Investigation into affairs, 190
Pilot(s):
licenses:
Exam, 536
Law, 535
Training Committee, 537
PINCHES, T. G., Cuneiform texts from Babylonian tablets, 540, 795
Pine(s):
Needle-cast, 846
Scots, 846, 1180
shoot beetles, 348
Termite infestation, 1159
PINHEY, E. C. G., Dragon-flies, 95
Pink rot etc. of potatoes, 529
Pioneers who served, 147
Pipe(s):
and fittings for domestic water supply, 178
laying principles. Construction methods, 905
Lines:
Act, 288
Bill, 227, 228, 231, 256, 262, 263, 358
Circular, 362
Buried, External loads, 395
Pipits. Taxonomy, 95
PIPPARD, A. J. S. (Chairman), Pollution of Thames, 145
Pitcairn etc., Islands Instructions, OIC. 632
Pitprops. Strength, 1180
PITTAM, R. R., Legal aid in criminal proceedings, 356, 595

Place:
names Index, 1122
to live. Yearbook of Agriculture U.S.A., 957
Placing & management of contracts for engineering work, 901
Plaice investigations in Scottish waters, 783
Plan of operations for woodlands, 348
Plankton:
Indo-West-Pacific, 101
Oceanic & bathypelagic, 80
Planned preventive maintenance. Hospitals, 1126
Planning
and control of hospital external transport, 592
appeals:
Inquiries, 278
Selected, 146, 364, 869
Written representations, 1139
applications, 143, 607, 869, 1142
Authorities & River Boards liaison, 361
Bulletins, 361, 363, 606–7, 865, 868, 1138, 1141
Conditions for Private Development Bill, 260
farm work, 84
for daylight & sunlight, 868
of:
central sterile supply depts. 403
helicopter stations, 90
PLANT, SIR A. (Chairman):
Byssinosis etc., Workers, 1161
Farmers' lung, 892
Fowl pest policy, 304
Plant(s):
and machinery maintenance, 881
Capillary, Watering, 1059
communities of Highlands, 394
diseases. Scotland, 81
Diagnosis of mineral deficiencies, 298
Instructions for collectors, 1069
nematology, 1061
New varieties. Protection. Convention, 495
pathology, 86, 304, 533, 789, 1060
protection. Conventions, 343
remains from Isle of Wight, 94
taxonomy, 1067
Varieties & Seeds:
Act, 773
Bill, 456, 457, 491, 700, 736, 742, 859
Gazette, 1060
Plantation crops production (Commonwealth), 550, 804,
Plastering. Specifications, 904
Plastics in tropics, 537
Platen machines. Guarding, 375
PLATT, B. S., Foods in tropical countries, 377
PLATT, SIR H. (Chairman), Standing Medical Advisory Committee, 352
PLATT, J. W. (Chairman), Studies in technical colleges, 327
PLATT, SIR R. (Chairman), Medical staffing structure. Hospital service, 133
Plays submitted to Lord Chamberlain, 795
Pleiades, 1169
Ploughing. Tractor, 305

PLOWDEN, LORD (Chairman):
Aircraft industry, 1038
Control of public expenditure, 202
Representational services overseas, 842
Plum(s):
Advisory Leaflet, 783
and cherries:
Agricultural Bulletin, 83
Pruning, 81
aphids, 1051
Plumber(s):
and gas fitter (Careers), 368, 1146
Registration Bill, 1009
Plumbing. Simplified, for housing, 637
Plywood. Strength properties, 905

Pneumatic:
gauging, 907
tube communication system. Hospital, 592
Pneumonoconiosis. Statistics, 171, 385, 896, 1163
Pneumoridae, 1067

POCHIN, E. E. (Chairman), Protection against ionizing radiations, 160
Poisoning:
Acute, Hospital treatment, 352
Carbon monoxide, 1152
Poisonous substances in agriculture etc., 789
Poisons. Form for selling, 1129
Polack Travelling Scholarship Fund Scheme, 1173
Poland. Vessels within fishery limits*, 841
Polaris sales U.S.A.*, 581, 584
Pole construction. Buildings of, 86
Police:
Act, 773
Bill, 487, 491, 702, 704, 736, 742, 744, 859
Circular, 1138
and public relations, 392
apprehensions & criminal proceedings. Scotland, 184, 402, 646, 912, 1174
areas:
Bedfordshire & Luton, 1130
Northamptonshire & Northampton, 1129
cadets. Working party, 1130
Careers, 612
College. Special course, 595
Council. Higher police training, 356, 595
Counties & boroughs. E. & W., 136, 247, 595, 596, 857, 1130
Discipline regulations. Forms, 1128
dogs, 595
Federation Acts, 68, 288
Bills, 5, 6, 34, 38, 42, 138, 228, 244, 256, 260
Judges' Rules & Administrative Directions to, 854
Police (*continued*):
of Metropolis, 136, 357, 596, 856, 1027
Pensions Act, 68
Bill, 3, 41
Royal Commission, 175–6, 392, 635
Scotland:
Apprehensions, 1174
Exam. papers, 647
service in Britain, 1144
Sheffield Appeal Inquiry, 596
training, 136, 357, 595
See also Constabulary
Policy:
for the arts, 1089
into practice. Arts Council report, 1061
Poliomyelitis in Hull & East Riding, 593
Political:
advance in U.K. Dependencies, 147
organisation of Mbembe, 1159
scene, 1901–14, 93
Pollination of:
apples & pears, 82
cherries, 82, 530
Polluting discharges on Thames Estuary, 1181
Pollution of:
sea by oil, 343
tidal Thames, 145
water by tipped refuse, 146
POLWARTH, RT. HON. LORD, Manuscripts of, 134
Polychaete fauna of South Africa, 543
Polymer assessment, 1064
Polyvinyl chloride sheeting, 194
Polyzoa:
cretaceous cribrimorph, 311
from West Africa, 797, 1069
Silurian, 1068
Pontefract etc. Proposed country district. Map, 867
Pontypridd & Maesteg. Country around, Geology, 906
Poole Corporation Acts, 69, 1042
POPE, J. A., Fecundity of salmon, 80
POPE-HENNESSY, J. Italian sculpture. Catalogue, 959
Poplar:
cultivation, 586
International Convention, 120, 343
Population:
estimates:
England & Wales, 128, 351, 589, 849, 1123
Scotland, 129, 590, 849, 1123
of fish, 548
tables, 129, 351, 589, 849, 1123
See also Census
PORRITT, SIR A. (Chairman), Medical aid to developing countries, 410, 651
Port(s):
Council. *See* National Ports Council

Port(s) (*continued*):
development. Interim plan, 1158
Major, of Great Britain, 420
of London:
Acts, 69, 290, 518, 774, 1042
Extension of Seaward Limit Act, 774
transport industry, 159, 881, 1149
Portable skid-resistance tester, 908
Portchester Castle. Guide, 1167
Portering services. Hospital, 132, 352, 591, 851, 1125
Portland:
Castle. Guide, 1167
vase, 795
Portrait painting from Roman Egypt, 310
Portsmouth blockmaking machinery, 1170
Portugal:
British visitors' passport*, 123
Double taxation*, 123, 343
Northern Rhodesia-Angola frontier*, 1115
Nyasaland-Mozambique:
Boundary Commission*, 1115
frontier*, 343
Railway between Swaziland & Mozambique*, 841
Transit facilities in Azores*, 123
Positive covenants affecting land, 1154
Post:
diploma studies. Art & design, 822
graduate courses. engineers etc., 1089
medical education, 354
Office:
Act, 68
Bill, 2, 34, 39, 138
Loans, 204, 425, 674, 940, 1205
Borrowing Powers Act, 773
Bill, 491, 697
Giro, 1163
Guide, 170, 384, 629, 895, 1163
How it works, 365
prospects, 170, 384, 629, 895, 1163
Publications, 170, 384–5, 629, 894–5, 1162–3
Report & accounts, 170, 385, 629, 895, 1163
Savings Bank(s):
Account, 204, 425, 674, 940, 1163
Bill, 1013
Fund, 205, 426, 675, 941, 1206
Subway Bill, 1014
telephone installations, 865
Offices:
in U.K., 170, 629, 895
London, 384, 895
radiac log form, 1130
war economic assistance. Germany*, 119
ypresian plant remains, 94
Postage stamps etc., Tapling Collection, 795
Postal:
addresses, 170, 629, 895
and Proxy Voting Bill, 1014
parcels*, 126
POSTAN, M. M., Design & development of weapons, 798
Postcards:
Hampton Court, 221
Stonehenge, 1167
Tower of London, 390
Postmen. Pay, 937
Posture for boys & girls, 958
Pot plants. Commercial production, 302
Potash for farm crops, 82, 530
Potato(es):
Agriculture Bulletin, 1054
as a stock feed, 530
Black leg of, 81, 1051
Bulk storage. Buildings, 85
chitting houses, 86
Common scab, 1051
crops. Register, 80, 299, 528, 783, 1050
harvesting with:
complete harvesters, 788
diggers, 532
Marketing Scheme, 301, 303
Pink rot etc., 529
Powdery scab, 783
root eelworm, 529, 1052
Seed:
Handling of purchased, 1053
Maintenance of stocks, 81
Sprouting, 301, 1053
Skin spot & silver scurf, 529, 1052
trails, 80, 299, 528, 782, 1050
tuber:
Eelworm, 784
Spraing etc., 1052
Virus diseases, 1051
Potteries. Dust control, 613
Pottery:
Careers, 151
Fifty masterpieces, 959
Potting composts, 301
Poultry:
Aids to management, 532
Artificial insemination, 530, 1053
breeding stock. Feeding, 530
buildings. Bibliography, 1049
Chronic respiratory infections, 1052
dressing & packing, 132
flock. Small, 786
houses:
Disinfection, 530, 1053
Flies etc., in, 1053
management for egg production, 1054
manure, 82, 1052
Nutrient requirements, 527
nutrition, 531
Preparation & trussing for market, 530
Progency Testing Stations. Transfer, 938

Poultry (continued):
  Research Centre. Report, 1050
  Salmonella infection, 82
POUNCEY, P., Italian drawings, 310
Powdery scab of potatoes, 783
POWELL, M. B. (Chairman), Central Health Services Council, 132
POWELL, T. G. E., Barclodiady Y Gawres chambered cairn, 900
Power:
  Ministry of:
    Publications, 170–3, 385–8, 629–31, 895–8, 1163–6
    Statistical Digest, 173, 388, 631, 898, 1166
  press safety, 375, 1152
Pox. Fowl, 1051

Practical:
  firemanship, 356
  radiography (Army), 690
Practice:
  leaflet for solicitors, 1153
  of O. & M., 1205
PRATT, N. M., Interstellar medium & galactic structure, 903
Prayer Book Measures, 800, 975, 1042, 1071
Pre-cast concrete building. Collapse, Ministry of Public Building & Works, 486
Pre-employment courses. Scotland, 183
Pre-packed cuts of meat. Merchandise Marks, 1194
Pre-stressed concrete design, 810
Precautions needed on dangerous machines, 1066
Prediction methods. Borstal training, 1130
Prefabrication. History, 1179
Preferred dimensions for:
  educational etc. Buildings, 900
  housing, 633
Prematurity report, 132
Premium Bonds, 186–7, 408, 649, 914–5, 1176, 1177
Preparation:
  and trussing poultry, 530
  of strawberries, 82
Preparing to build, 1167
Prescribing:
  Cost of (Correction slip), 1125
  National Health Service, 854, 1127
Preservation of:
  fruit & vegetables, 302
  Superannuation Benefits Bill, 1009
Preservative treatment of timber, 395
Preserving. ABC of, 81
President's Commission on assassination of President Kennedy, 958
Presiding officers & clerks. Instructions. Scotland, 405
Press. Royal Commission, 392

Pressure steam sterilisers. Hospitals, 592
PRESTON, J. S., Photometric standards, 164
Preston:
  Corporation Act, 774
  Geology of country around, 640
Prevention of:
  accidents in paper mills, 374
  collisions at sea, 669
  Fraud (Investments) Act:
    Dealers, 191, 415, 663, 928, 1195
    General permission, 191
  lycus attack in hardwoods, 906
  neglect in children, 646
  wet-weather damage. Roads, 908
Preventive:
  detention, 595
  medicine. Handbook, 88, 534, 1079
PRICE, D., Geology of country around Preston, 640
PRICE, P. S. (Chairman), Police areas of Northamptonshire & Northampton, 1129
Prices:
  and incomes:
    National Board. Reports, 1156
    Policy, 1088
    Early Warning System, 1034
    Machinery of, 1088
  of bread, soaps etc. Reports, 1156
  Productivity & Incomes Council's report, 173
Pricing of Ministry of Aviation contracts, 792, 1064
Primary:
  education in Scotland, 1173
  schools:
    Mathematics in, 1090
    plans, 820
    Science, 113
    Social training in, 401
    Transfer to secondary education. Scotland, 183, 400
Primates. History of, 543, 1069
Prime Minister(s):
  Board of Inquiry. Bossard & Allen cases, 1206
  Office. Publications, 898, 1166
Principles of modern building, 180, 1180
Print(s):
  Room B.M. Masterpieces, 1066
  Science Museum, 1170
Printer's:
  Imprint Act, 68
  marks, 3, 34, 39, 138
  marks, 439
Printing:
  and the mind of man, 540
  Colour, in Japan, 795
  exhibition, 540
  Graphic reproduction processes (Careers), 368
  industry. Wages etc., 1156

Printing (continued):
  Inventor, 540
  Letterpress, Productivity, 180
Prison(s):
  and:
    after-care. Annual report, 135, 357, 595, 1130
    Borstals, 856
    Statistical tables, 1130
Commission Publications, 173, 388
Commissioners reports, 137, 279, 596, 836
Department:
  Publications, 631, 898, 1166
  Report on work, 856, 1130
Medical Service organisation, 856
Scotland, 185, 405, 647, 913, 1175
Service:
  Careers, 152
  Journal, 173, 388, 631, 898, 1166
Prisoners:
  after-care, 184
  Employment. Borstal, 596
  Ill-treatment. Durham, 596
  Organisation of work for, 856
  Work for, 137
Private:
  air law, 757
  House Owners Protection Bill, 262, 263, 488
  International Law:
    Committee, 159, 376, 619
    Conference, 1115
  land mobile radio services, 895
  law unification, 1112
  legislation (Scotland) procedure, 185, 406–7, 648, 913–4, 1175
  mobile radio services, 385, 629
  pilots licence. Law, 790
  point-to-point system, 629
Street Works:
  Act, 68
  Bill, 3, 39, 233
  Circular, 143
Privileges Committee reports, 139, 860, 863, 1134
Privy:
  Council:
    Acts of, 174, 901
    Publications & Orders in Council, 173–4, 388–9, 631, 899, 1166
    Seal of Scotland. Register, 648
Probation:
  officers:
    and approved hostels & homes, 136, 356, 594, 855, 1128
    superannuation Regulations, 1138
  service:
    Departmental Committee, 357
    England & Wales, 856
    Scotland, 185

Problem(s) of:
  communication, 394
  man's antiquity, 797
  Merseyside, 1088
  progress in industry, 180, 641, 907
Procedure:
  House of Commons, 248, 599, 861, 991, 1134
  Disclosure of matters, 861
House of Lords, 863, 1137
Proceedings & business of local authorities. Model Standing Orders, 868
Prototropoidea, 1067
Production:
  Census of, 191–4, 415, 663, 928
  See also Business Monitor
  Group Reports (UKAEA). See P. G. Reports
  of building components. Shipyards, 634
Productivity in letterpress printing, 180
Professional:
  bodies requirements. General Certificate of education, 326, 328
  engineers (Careers), 152
  equipment. Temporary importation, 569
Profits Tax:
  Appeal leaflets, 149, 366, 609, 872
  Provisions of Finance Acts, 366, 609, 872, 1144
  See also Excess profits
Programme & progress. Charts for contracts, 1167
Programming in Algol, 792
Project Mercury orbital flight, 886
Promotion of the sciences in Commonwealth, 609
Proofing of buildings against rats & mice, 1061
Proper motions stars, 636, 1169
Properties of spruce timber, 395
Property (Joint Tenants) Act, 772
  Bill, 705, 735, 742, 858
Proprietary preparations. Classifications, 132, 1125
Protected:
  cropping, 83
  polythene, 537
Protection:
  against corrosion of steel in concrete, 1178
  from Lushton Act, 773
    Bill, 709, 745, 746
of:
  Amenity Bill, 260
  Animals (Anaesthetics) Act, 773
    Bill, 698, 743
  Birds Act, 773
    Bills, 491, 705, 736, 744, 859, 969, 972, 973, 1014
  condensate systems. Filming amines, 592

Protection (continued):
  of (continued):
    Deer Bill, 1009
    Depositors Act, 517
      Bill, 260, 264, 450, 483, 488, 489, 597
    structural steel against fire, 179
    Tenants (Local Authorities) Bill, 40
Protective duties, 106, 553, 808, 1078
Protein:
  fat & calorie values of foods. Ready Reckoner, 822
  requirements of man, 854
Protura, 95
Proud record. Britain's colonial achievement, 338
PROUDMAN, J. (Chairman):
  Growing demand for water, 361
  Oceanographic & meteorological research, 304
PROVAN, A. L. (Chairman), Milk hygiene sub-committee, 531
Provincial museums & galleries, 640
Provision of:
  facilities for sport, 865
  handwashing facilities. Public conveniences, 1138
Pruning:
  conifers, 586
  plums & cherries, 81
  softwoods, 1180

Pselaplides of Ceylan, 94
Pseudococcidae, 94, 311
Psychiatric:
  patients. Accommodation, 592
  unit. Short-stay, 133
  ward. Hospitals, 852, 1126
Psychodidae, 1068

Pteruchus, 311

Public:
  Accounts. Committee of:
    Reports, 139, 235, 249, 359, 458, 599, 861, 862, 1037, 1134, 1135
    Special reports, 140, 235, 359, 458, 485, 862, 1135
  See also Air, Army & Navy Votes administration. Training, 651
  Authorities (Allowances) Act, 68
    Bill, 6, 40
    Circular, 143
  Bills. Returns, 31, 359, 598, 860, 1001
  Boards. List of members, 205, 426, 940, 1206
  Bodies (Admission to Meetings) Act. Circular, 143
  Building(s):
    Access to, for disabled, 1222
    and Works. Ministry of,

Public (continued):
  Building(s) (continued):
    Advisory leaflets, 389, 633, 899, 1166
    Circular, 1167
    Publications, 389–90, 633–4, 899–901, 1166–8
    Re-organisation, 634
    See also Works, Ministry of
  cleansing. Costing returns, 146, 363, 607, 1141
  conveniences. Handwashing facilities, 1138
  documents. Foreign, Convention, 119
  education. Scotland, 183, 912
  expenditure:
    Circulars, M.H.L.G., 1139, 1222
    Control of, 202
    in Granada, 274
    in 1963–4 & 1967–8, 515
  General Acts (& Church Assembly Measures), 67–8, 287–9, 516–7, 771–3, 1039–41
  Health:
    Act, 68
      Bill, 1, 2, 7, 34, 39, 42, 138, 489
      Circular, 143, 1167
      Guide to building regulations, 1168
      and medical subjects reports, 134, 354, 593, 854, 1127
    Chief Medical Officer. Report, 134, 354, 593, 853, 1127
    imported food regulations, 84–5, 86, 302, 531, 532, 786–7, 1054–8
    Laboratory Service Act. Accounts, 593, 853, 1206
    Notification of Births Act, 1040
      Bill, 972, 1007, 1009, 1132
    Service (U.S.A.) Publications, 688, 958
    Washing Facilities Bill, 40
  income & expenditure. Account, 205, 426, 675, 941, 1206
  investment in Great Britain, 205, 426, 675
  Lavatories (Abolition of Turnstiles) Bill, 42, 488
  Lavatories (Turnstiles) Act, 517
    Bill, 453, 483, 488, 490, 598
    Circular, 602
  Libraries (and Museums):
    Act, 773
      Bill, 704, 736, 741, 743, 745, 859
      Circular, 1088, 1138
    Standards of service, 328
  Officers' agreements. See respective countries
  Order Act, 517
    Bills, 263, 264, 452, 490

Public (continued):
  Record Office:
    Annual report, 159, 376, 619, 882, 1153
    Guide to contents, 634
    Handbooks, 901–2, 1168
    Publications. 174–5, 390–1, 634–5, 901–2, 1168
  road passenger transport statistics, 197, 667
  sanitary conveniences. Model bye-laws, 1138
  Service:
    Commission in overseas territories. Notes, 410
    Vehicles (Travel Concessions) Act (Amendment) Bill, 488, 743
    Trustee Office. Annual report, 175, 391, 635, 902, 1168
    Works Loans:
      Acts, 773, 1040
        Bills, 491, 699, 736, 859, 974, 1012
      Board. Annual report, 200, 426, 675, 941, 1206
  Publications:
    and debates. Report. Special Select Committee, 599, 1135–6
    List of, available to public (UKAEA), 215, 435, 688, 957, 1219
  Pudsey. Proposed alteration of area. Map, 867
  PUGH, I. V., Future of development plans, 1139
  PUGH, R. B., Records of Colonial & Dominions Offices, 901
  Pullorum disease, 529
  Pumps & pipework for heating systems, (Farm), 1059
  Punched tape:
    code conversion unit, 903
    editing unit, 1170
  Purchase Tax Act, 517
    Bill, 448, 488, 600

Pycnogonida. Feeding mechanisms, 1069
PYEFINCH, K. A., Atlantic salmon, 528
Pyraustinae revision, 94

Q

Qatar notices, 123, 343–4, 581, 842, 1115

Qualified & temporary teachers. Circular, 112, 114, 564, 566, 1088
Qualitative study of buildings in London, 905
Quality:
  Milk Producers Ltd., 533
  in seeds, 300

Quarries. Law, 1165
  See also Mines & quarries
Quarter Sessions Officers (Superannuation) regulations, 1138
Quarterly returns of Registrar General. See Registrar General
Qu'est-ce que Stonehenge?, 634
Queen:
  Elizabeth Forest Park. Guide, 846
  Mary. Plenipotentiary, 198
Queen's:
  and Lord Treasurer's Remembrancer:
    Edinburgh Gazette, 175, 391, 635, 902, 1168
  Ultimus Haeres, 185, 407, 648, 914, 1173
  award to industry, 1166
  Bench Masters' Practice forms, 882
  Birthday Honours lists, 187, 408, 649, 915, 1177
  Regulations:
    and Admiralty Instructions, 72, 292, 520, 819, 1087
    for Army, 219–20, 440–1, 691, 810–2, 1080
    for Royal Air Force, 88, 306, 534–5, 808, 1079
    speech to Parliament, 141, 232, 456, 709, 975
Question papers. See Examination papers
Quick haymaking, 786

R

Rabbit control in woodlands, 1121
Rabbit-keeping. Modern, 785
Race(s):
  of man, 543, 1070
  Relations Act, 1040
    Bill, 974, 975, 1007, 1011, 1012, 1013, 1132
Racial Discrimination:
  and Incitement Bill, 43, 487, 741
  Bill, 227
Radar. Elementary, 1079
RADCLIFFE, RT. HON. VISCOUNT (Chairman), Security procedures in Public Service, 271
Vassall case, 596
RADFORD, E.:
  St. Dogmael Abbey, 390
  Segontium Roman Fort, 390
  White Castle, 390
Radial velocity(ies), 176, 392, 636, 1169
Radiation(s):
  from fallout. Exposure of population, 883
  hazards to man, 160
  Ionising. See Ionising radiations

RAD-ROA | 1961-5

Radio:
aid to navigation, 1063
and television:
Future of (Pilkington), 384
servicing (Careers), 874
astronomy, 1171
engineering trade group, 535, 1079
equipment for ships. Specifications, 895, 1163
facility charts, 90
for merchant ships. Specifications, 895, 1163
operators' handbook, 170, 1163
receiver for ships. Specification, 895
research, 180, 397, 641, 907, 1171
Services textbook, 220, 692
telegraph. Specifications:
Alarm equipment, 895
Receiver, 895
Transmitter, 1163
telephone. Specifications:
Alarm signal, 895
Distress equipment, 895, 1163
waves. Half velocity, 812
Radioactive:
chemicals, 686
materials. Control of health hazards, 160
Substances Act:
Circular, 601
Explanatory memorandum, 607
Radioactivity in:
drinking water, 607, 868, 1141
human diet, 79, 298
milk, 298, 527, 782, 1050
Radiobiological Laboratory, 79, 298, 527, 782, 1050
Radiochemical Manual, 391, 686
Radiographers:
Careers, 151, 874
in National Health Service, 354
Radiography:
campaign. Scotland, 131
Mass miniature, 129
Practical, Army handbook, 690
Radiolocation techniques, 220
Radiometric standards & measurements, 164
Radiostrontium etc. in drinking water, 363
Radiotelephony procedure, 90, 537, 1064
Radiotherapy dept. Hospital, 352
Radnorshire etc.:
Census, 588
Saxton map, 1066
RAE, B. B.:
Food of megrim, 528
Larvae in Cod, 528
Seal damage to salmon fisheries, 1050
R.A.F. forms (Meteorological Office), 620, 885
See also Air Force
Rag, flock etc. Act. Circular, 143
RAGGE, D. R.:
Ducetia Stal., 94
Geneta Phlaurocentrum Karsch, 311
Tylopsis Fieber, 797
Ragwort, 529
Railway(s):
Accidents:
Minister of Transport. Report, 198, 419, 668, 933, 1199
Reports, 197–8, 419–20, 667–8, 933–4, 1199
Closures Bill. 969, 1009
Development near, 602
Science Museum booklet, 1170
See also British Railways.
Rain:
Classification, 377
Exposure to driving, Index, 394
Rainfall:
British, 620, 883
Estimation of, 1155
Raising the school-leaving age, 1090
RAISMAN, SIR J. (Chairman), Economic & Fiscal Commission. East Africa, 101
RAITT, D. F. S., Trispterus Esmarkii, 1050
RAMSBOTTOM, J., Larger British fungi, 95
RANDS, J. B., Hydrometers & hydrometry, 397
RANSOM, W. H.:
Soil stabilization, 638
Solar radiation, 399
Raphael & his circle. Drawings in B.M., 310
Rare birds of Africa, 312
Raspberry(ies):
Advisory leaflet, 783
beetle, 1052
moth, 529
RATCLIFFE, J. A. (Chairman), High altitude nuclear explosions, 637
Rate(s):
and rateable values:
England & Wales, 146, 363, 607, 868, 1141
Scotland, 185, 399, 644, 910, 1171
books order. Circular, 361
deficiency grants, 364
Impact of, on households, 1139
Revaluation, 364
Rateable values between properties. Distribution, 603
Ratifications etc. Treaty Series. Lists, 123, 344, 581–2, 836, 842, 1116
Rating:
and Valuation Act, 68
Bill, 4, 5, 6, 34, 40, 41, 138
Circular, 143
Bill, 1008, 1014
Interim Relief Act, 773
Bill, 491, 700, 736, 859
Circulars, 864

Rating (*continued*):
of owners. Circular, 362
Unoccupied Hereditaments Bill, 1010
Rationalised production. Social effects, 909
Rats & mice:
Control of, 84, 530
Proofing of buildings, 1061

R.C.C. reports, 686, 955, 1219

READE, B., Art Nouveau & Alphonse Mucha, 689
READING, S. (Chairman), Commonwealth Immigrants Advisory Council, 1128
Ready reckoner of food values, 822
Realm of flight, 567
Rearing:
chickens, 530, 785, 1052
turkeys, 784
Reciprocating engine. History, 1170
Recognition of rapidly rotating pole, 1170
Reconnaissance soil survey of Semporna Peninsula, 651
Reconquest of Burma, 1070
Record(s):
and accounts for farm management, 786
of Colonial & Dominions Offices, 901
repositories in Great Britain, 854
Recorded Delivery Service Act, 288
Bill, 43, 228, 256, 261, 358
Recruitment:
for service overseas, 410
for veterinary profession, 789
to Civil Service. Estimates Committee, 1133
Recruits' physical training, 691
Red:
core of strawberry, 82, 1052
Crusader. Inquiry*, 117
currants, 530
Deer Commission, 80, 299, 533, 783, 1050
Sea lights*, 344
spider mite, 300, 529
Redundancy Payments Act, 1040
Bill, 974, 1007, 1010, 1012, 1132
Redundancy. Progress in provision for, 159
Redundant workers (Severance Pay) Bill, 262, 488, 741
REES, W. J.:
Coral Caryophillia Smithii, 312
Hydroids of cytaeidae, 312
Reference Pamphlets (C.O.I.), 147–8, 365–6, 609, 871, 1144
Reform of Exchequer accounts, 675
Refraction & its components:
during growth of the eye, 161
in twins, 377
Refreshment Houses Act, 773
Bill, 706, 707, 744, 745
Refrigerated stores for fruit, 1054
Refrigeration. International Institute*, 582
Refrigerators. Merchandise Marks, 191
Refugee seamen*, 344
Refuse:
and swill. Hospital Services study, 1125
collection. Costing returns, 146, 363, 607, 1141
disposal in blocks of flats, 637
Pollution of water, 146
Regent Refining Company Act, 290
Regents Park Terraces. Future, 320
Regimental Standing Orders, Army Catering Corps, 220
Regional:
development:
in Wales, 858
Welsh Grand Committee, 487, 736
statistics:
Abstracts, 1070
series available, 1070
Register encoder & serialiser, 393
Register of. *See respective subjects*
Registrar General(s):
Annual Estimates. Population. *See* Population
Quarterly & Weekly Returns:
England & Wales, 128, 351, 589, 849, 1123
Scotland, 129, 352, 590, 850, 1124
Scotland. Annual report, 129, 590, 849
Statistical Review E. & W., 129, 351, 589, 849, 1123
Registrar of Restrictive Trading Agreements:
Guide, 902
Reports, 191, 415, 928
Registration:
and Licensing authorities, 198, 668, 1199
of births, deaths & marriages (Scotland):
Act, 1040
Bill, 710, 963, 966, 967, 975, 994, 1007, 1010, 1012, 1132
Select Committee S.I., 1134
of goods under Resale Prices Act. Guide, 902
of title to land, 1153
Scotland, 647
Officers. Official List, 128, 351, 589, 849, 1123
Registry of:
Friendly Societies, *See* Friendly Societies
Ships, 198, 420, 668, 934, 1195
Regular Reserve. Regulations, 220, 441, 691, 811
Regulations: *See respective subject*
REID, RT. HON. LORD (Chairman), Registration of title to land. Scotland, 647
REID, A., Road tunnels, 1200
Reinforced:
concrete design, 810
plastic lifeboats, 667

Reinforcing steel in concrete protection, 1178
Relations between Education Authorities & teachers, 401
Remand Homes. Report, 401
Rembrandt. Drawings of, 310
Remedial gymnast (Careers), 152, 612
Remodelling old schools, 564
Remuneration of:
academic staff in universities etc., 887
administrative staff etc. in electricity supply industry, 1156
Ministers & M.P's., 941
Teachers Acts, 517, 1040
Bills, 452, 483, 489, 598, 710, 740, 745, 746, 859, 963, 964, 1010
Renfrew. Census:
Leaflet. Population etc., 590
Report, 850
Renfrewshire Educational Trust scheme, 183, 912, 1173
Rennell Island, British Solomon Islands, natural history, 313
RENOUARD, Y., Gascon Rolls, 901
Rent(s):
Act, 1040
Act & you:
156 questions answered, 1142
Guide for Scotland, 1171
and security of tenure. Rent Bill, 1142
Bill, 973, 974, 975, 1007, 1010, 1012, 1013, 1132
of council houses in:
Dunbarton, 130
Dundee, 644
of houses owned by local authorities. Scotland, 131, 405, 644, 910, 1171
Re-organisation of. *See specific subject*
Repair:
and maintenence of farm buildings, 1059
and preservation of historic buildings, 1167
Report on Overseas Trade, 194, 415–6, 663, 929, 1195
Reports & memoranda. Aeronautical Research Council, 75–9, 294–8, 542–7, 779–81, 1047–9
Repositories. List of accessions, 134, 354, 594, 1127
Representation of People:
Act 1949:
Amendment Bill, 736, 741, 746, 859
Amendment Bill No. 2, 491
Extension of Voting Facilities Bill, 1008
Representational services overseas, 842
Reproductions from illuminated mss., 1066
Republic of South Africa (Temporary Provisions) Act, 68
Bill, 4, 40
Requirements:
and properties of adhesives for wood, 905
of man for protein, 854
Resale Prices Act, 773
Bill, 704, 705, 706, 742, 743, 745
Guide to registration of goods, 902
Rescue:
Civil Defence, 135, 355, 356, 855, 1128
signal table, 1196
Research:
and development. Management & control, 177
assistance for developing countries, 889
Council, 160, 394, 638, 905, 1179
for industry, 180, 394, 642, 907, 1180
Grants. (D.S.I.R.), 178, 394, 638
See also specific subjects
Reshaping of British Railways, 665
Residential:
accommodation for:
elderly people, 353
staff. Hospital, 852
areas, higher densities:
Bulletin, 363
Circular, 361
leasehold property, 364
Residual values for fertilizers & feeding stuffs, 81, 299, 528, 783, 1050
Resin-top disease of Scots pine, 846
Resistance to transmission of heat & sound, 644
Restriction of Offensive Weapons Act, 68
Bill, 3, 34, 39, 40, 138
Restrictive practice — *See* Monopolies
Restrictive trading agreements:
Registrar. Publication, 902
Reports, 191, 415, 928
Resuscitation manual, 811
Retail:
distribution certificates, 328
prices. Index, 369, 880
selling (Careers), 368
trading hours, 1130
Retired pay etc.:
Orders by Her Majesty & in Council, 169, 277, 384, 628, 893, 1162
Royal Warrant, 169–70, 277, 628–9, 894, 1162
Retirement pension. Decisions, 166, 382, 891, 1160
Returning Officer. Elections. Scotland. Duties, 405
Revaluation for rates, 364
Revenue departments:
Appropriation accounts, 106, 321
Estimates, 201, 202, 426
REYNOLDS, L., Wood charcoal, 348

Rheolau'r Ffordd Fawr, 420
Rhine navigation. Convention, 842

Rhinitis of swine, 785
Rhodesia & Nyasaland:
Act, 517
Bill, 454, 490
Commonwealth development & financing, 103
Double taxation:
Norway*, 342
Switzerland*, 125, 580
Federation. Establishment, 543
Nyasaland-Mozambique frontier*, 343
See also Northern & Southern Rhodesia

Rice. Constitution of International Commission, 582
RICHARDS, G. T., Typewriters, 903
RICHARDS, O. W., Masarid wasps, 313
RICHARDSON, G. (Chairman), Turnover taxation, 872
RICHEY, J. E., Tertiary volcanic districts, Scotland, 129
Richmond Park. Trees in, 390
RIDDING, A., S. Z. de Ferranti, 904
Riding Establishments Act, 773
Bill, 704, 706, 707, 736, 741, 743, 745, 859
Riding quality of concrete roads, 642
Right of Privacy Bill, 2
Rights of way. Effect of development. Circular, 602
RIGOLD, S. E., Guides:
Eynsford Castle, 900
Portchester Castle, 1167
Temple Manor, 389
Rio Tinto Rhodesian Mining Limited Act, 69
Rising damp in walls, 394
Risk of fire spread from storage areas, Circular, 602
RITSON, SIR E. H., East Midlands general review area, 603
River(s):
Authorities (Compensation Regulations), 1138
Dart. Navigation Act, 290
Prevention of pollution:
Act, 68
Bill, 5, 6, 34, 38, 40, 42, 138
Circular, 143, 601
Scotland Act, 1040
Bill, 740, 741, 745, 746, 859, 964, 967, 968, 1010, 1132
Ravensbourne etc. Act, 70
Wear Watch Act, 70
See also under name of river

Road(s):
Abstracts, 180, 397–8, 642, 908, 1199–1200
Accidents: 198, 420, 669, 934, 1200
Fatal, at Christmas 1963, 908
Roads(s) (*continued*):
and:
bridge works. Specifications, 667, 669
Rail Traffic Act. Licensing Authorities, 198
See also Road Traffic Act, 1960
road transport in an under-developed country, 409
services (Housing handbook), 644
traffic. Survey, 398
Bituminous-surfaced. Design, 398
Classified, 248, 464
Concrete:
Farm, 1059
Riding quality, 642
construction:
American, 931
Bituminous materials, 642
Design of, 197
experiments using rubberised surfacing materials, 908
Goods transport, Survey, 935
haulage rates, 1156
High-speed. Traffic signals, 1200
improvement schemes. Cost, 181
in England & Wales, 198, 420, 669, 934
materials. Rubberised bituminous, 908
motor vehicles. Census, 198, 420, 669
movement (Civil Defence), 356
notes, 394, 642, 908, 1200
Passenger-mileage by London, 398
pricing, 934
progress, 198
research. Notes, Technical papers etc., 180–1, 397–8, 642, 908, 1199–1200
Royal Engineers' pocket book, 220
safety:
Bills, 741, 1009
Legislation, 1200
Research, 642
Scottish, 184, 403, 406, 644,
signs:
and signals*, 1116
Informatory, 932, 1198
See also Traffic signs
slabs. Concrete, 398
Soil-cement (Farms), 304
Surface dressings, 908
surfacings. Assessing life, 398
Traffic:
Act 1930–62. Traffic Commissioners, 198, 199, 420, 669, 934, 1200
Act 1956 Amendment Bill, 744
Act 1960:
Amendment Bill, 262
Licensing Authorities, 199, 420, 669, 934, 1200
Vehicle testing, 669
Act 1962, 288
Bill, 3, 4, 5, 8, 9, 41, 231, 248, 256, 261, 263

1961-5 | ROA-SCH

ROA— INDEX 1961-5

Road(s) (*continued*):
Traffic (*continued*):
Act 1964, 773
Bill, 703, 743
European agreement, 1116
Main international arteries, 123
Research on, 1199
See also Traffic
transport. Crews*, 344
tunnels, 1200
Vegetation on, 181
vehicles. Taxation Convention, 582
See also Vehicles
Roadheads. Support, 631
Roadmaking materials:
Borneo, 1200
Nigeria, 398
Roadstone tests data (Addendum), 1200
Robbins, Lord (Chairman), Higher education, 564, 821
Robertson, J. W., Kenya coastal strip, 102
Robinson, B. W.:
Kuniyoshi, 218
Persian paintings, 1222
Robinson, H. R., Japanese armour, 1168
Rochdale, Viscount (Chairman), Major ports, 420
Rochdale Canal Act, 1042
Rochester:
Bridge Act, 1042
Castle. Guide, 901
Rock granulators. Testing, 1200
Rocks:
Igneous, 542
Instructions for collectors, 312
Silurian, 542
Rodenticides. Precautionary measures, 1061
Rodger, A. G. (Chairman), Teachers in Scotland:
Further education service conditions, 1172
Supply, 401
Roe deer, 846
Rogers, E. V., Rabbit control, 1121
Rogers, T. A., Explosion. Six Bells Colliery, 171
Roll of Lords Spiritual & Temporal, 141, 232, 456, 863, 1137
Roman:
Britain. Antiquities, 795
coins: Exhibition guide, 540
Empire. Coins of, 1066
forts of the Saxon shore, 901
London, 376
York: 392
Monuments, 391
Romances in B.M. Catalogue, 309, 540
Roof(s):
and fire, 639
Built-up felt, 178
constructions. Fires, 639
Roof(s) (*continued*):
venting:
Flow of hot gases, 639
systems. Designs, 905
Roofing:
Developments in, 904
Safety in construction work, 618
Rook, 1052
Room heaters etc. Installing, 1166
Root-knot eelworm in glasshouses, 82, 529
Rootstock for apples & pears, 300
Rope milk, 300
Rosevear, D. R., Bats of West Africa, 1067
Roskill, S. W., War ar sea, 96
Ross, R., Diatom genus Capartogramma, 541
Ross & Cromarty:
Census. Leaflet & report, 590
Educational Trust Scheme, 183
Mackenzie Bequest Scheme, 183, 401
Rosse, Earl of (Chairman), Museums & galleries, 648, 1176
Rotation of silicon & manganese stars, 1170
Rotherham:
Alteration of area. Map, 867
Proposed Order Confirmation Act, 1042
Bill, 971, 1011
Rothesay Burgh Order Confirmation Act, 289
Bill, 42
Rothwell, Garforth & Stanley. Proposed county district. Map, 867
Roumanian property. Accounts, 200, 422, 671, 936, 1201
Round timber from the farm, 304
Rounding errors in algebraic processes, 641
Roundwood. Home-grown, 846
Rouse, E. C., Longthorpe Tower, 900
Rouse, G. D., New forests of Dartmoor, 1121
Rowe, H. W. F., World's coffee, 652
Roxburgh. Census:
Leaflet population etc., 590
Report, 850
Royal:
Aberdeen workshop for blind. Scheme, 400, 645
Air Force. *See* Air Force, Royal
and historical letters. Henry IV, 1168
Army Medical Corps etc. Standing Orders, 220, 441, 692, 812, 1081
Birth. London Gazette, 913
Botanic Garden(s):
Edinburgh:
Garden companion, 901
Notes, 175, 391, 635, 902, 1168
Kew. *See* Kew
College of:
Physicians & Surgeons. Glasgow. Act, 518
Bill, 264

1961 pp 1–224, 1962 pp 225–445, 1963 pp 447–696, 1964 pp 697–962, 1965 pp 963–1226

100

INDEX 1961-5 —SAB

Royal (*continued*):
College of (*continued*):
Science & Technology. Glasgow scheme, 182, 400
Commission(s):
Ancient & historical monuments:
England, 391, 635, 902
Scotland, 635
Wales & Monmouthshire, 902
Doctors & dentists remuneration, 175
Historical mss., 134, 354
Local Government. Greater London, 391
Police, 175, 392, 635
Press, 392
Trade unions, 1168
Engineers. Pocket book, 220
Fine Art Commission, 137, 596
Scotland, 406, 913
Four Towns Fishing Order Confirmation Act, 1042
Bill, 1011
Greenwich Observatory. *See* Royal Observatory
Holloway College Act, 290
Hospital Chelsea. *See* Chelsea
Marines. Orders & Regulations, 292, 820
Mint:
Annual report, 177, 393, 636, 1169
Publication, 636
Naval:
Auxiliary Service Medal, 1203
Handbook. Drill, 72, 292, 520
See also Naval
Navy (Careers), 368
See also Navy
Observatory:
Annals, 392
Bulletin & publications, 176–7, 392–3 635–6, 902–3, 1169
Edinburgh, 177, 393, 636, 903, 1169–70
Observations, 176, 392
Ordnance factories:
Appropriation Accounts, 220, 440, 691, 810, 1080, 1081
Estimates, 220, 441
Vote. Grants for service, 220
parks of London, 1168
Red Cross, 220
Russell School Act, 290
Scottish Museum, 903
Society for Prevention of Accidents, 393, 1170
tour to India & Pakistan, 147
visit. West Africa. Photoposter, 365
Warrant:
Army, 218, 219, 440, 441, 691, 692, 809, 810, 1080, 1081
Holders, 186, 408, 649, 915, 1176
Royal (*continued*):
Warrant (*continued*):
Retired Pay etc., 169–70, 277, 628–9, 894, 1162
See also Pay Warrant, Army Pensions Warrant
yachts, 887
R.R. Lyrae stars, 176, 1169
RSPP (UKAEA), 686
R/T procedures. (Air traffic), 1064
Rubber:
bearings in highway bridges, 667
plastics & fabrics. Anti-static precautions. Hospitals, 353
Rubberized:
bituminous road materials & binders. Specification, 908
surfacing materials. Full-scale road experiments, 908
Rules:
Court of Session. Scotland, 1077
Execution of sentences, 441, 692, 811
Runcorn District Water Board, Act 290
Rural:
bus services, 199, 1200
development:
in Wales & Monmouthshire, 858
Welsh Grand Committee, 736
transport:
Local Authorities Bill, 262
problems in Wales, 281
surveys, 669
Water Supply & Sewerage Acts, 68, 1040
Bills, 4, 39, 976, 1013
Rushton Hall. Transfer to R.N.I.B. 202
Russam, K., Moisture in soils at overseas airfields, 398
Russell, E. L. (Chairman), Teachers for further education, 113
Russell, R. C. H., Coast erosion & defence, 179
Russia. *See* Soviet Union
Russian. Teaching of, 328
Rutland:
and Leicestershire. Amalgamation, 603
Census:
Leaflet. Population etc., 589
Report, 849
Saxton map, 93
Ruwenzori expedition, 95, 1070
Rye. Winter, 82

S

Sabah:
Overseas officers. Malaysia*, 1113
Public officers. Malaysia*, 889

1961 pp 1–224, 1962 pp 225–445, 1963 pp 447–696, 1964 pp 697–962, 1965 pp 963–1226

101

SAB— INDEX 1961-5

Sabah (*continued*):
Report, 1074
Sabrosky, C. W., Stenomicra, 1060
Sacred vocal music. Catalogue, 795
Safety:
afloat, 393
and health (Mines & quarries) Law, 897, 1165
circular. Mines regulations, 173, 387, 631, 897, 1165
code for electro-medical apparatus, 592
health & welfare:
Booklets, 159, 375, 618, 881, 1152
Forms, 1152
health, welfare & wages in agriculture, 305, 533, 789, 1060
in:
construction work, 375, 618
domestic building, 904
electrical testing, 1152
laundries, 618
mines. Research, 173, 388, 631, 898, 1166
paper mills, 881
use of:
abrasive wheels, 1152
machinery in bakeries, 375
mechanical power presses, 375
power presses, 1152
measures in chemical laboratories, 906
of:
air navigation (Eurocontrol), 115, 507
drugs, 591, 1125
life at sea, 151, 1116
Pamphlet. Ministry of Power, 631
precautions in schools, 113, 565
Sailing ships from 1700 A.D., 904
Saint:
Andrews University scheme, 183
Anne Soho Act, 1042
Benet Sherelog Churchyard Act, 70
Botolph's Priory. Guide, 900
Dionis Backchurch Churchyard:
Act, 518
Bill, 450
Amendment Act, 774
Dogmael's Abbey. Guide, 390
George Hanover Square Burial Ground Act, 774
Helena:
Instruction OIC, 389
Reports, 100, 548, 1074
John's Church, Smith Square Act, 775
Kitts – Nevis – Anguilla report, 100
Laurence Catford Act, 1042
Lucia:
Beane field *, 845
Reports, 317, 548, 1074
Validation of election OIC, 174
Mark, Camberwell Act, 1042
Saint (*continued*):
Mary, Alverstoke, Burial Ground Act, 1042
Nicholas Acons Churchyard Act, 519
Bill, 450
Olave's & St. Saviour's Grammar School Foundation Scheme, 113
Pancras Lane, Churchyard Act, 70
Paul, Covent Garden Act, 290
Paul, Portman Square, Saint Marylebone Act, 775
Peter's Church Nottingham Churchyard Act, 290
Thomas Apostle (Queen Street) Churchyard Act, 290
Ursula, Legend, 959
Vincent reports, 100, 317, 548
Salad:
and other food crops in glasshouses, 785
crops. Outdoor, 302
Salaries:
Midland Bank staff, 1156
Teachers. *See* Teachers
Sale(s) of:
Dead Wild Geese (Prohibition) Bill, 449, 453
Houses & Land (Legal Costs) Bill, 743
works of art by public bodies, 941
Salisbury, Marquess Of (Chairman), Royal Commission on Ancient & Historial Monuments, 391, 635
Salisbury Isolation Hospital. Treasury minute, 203
Salk poliomyelitis vaccine, Treasury minute, 676, 942
Salmon:
and:
Freshwater Fisheries
Acts, 773, 1041
Bills, 491, 700, 717, 736, 742, 968, 969, 970, 1009, 1012
Committee report, 87
research, 80, 299, 528, 782, 1050
trout:
Cyanide, 782
fisheries. Scotland, 529, 1051
Leaping behaviour, 299
Atlantic:
Ecology, 782
Fecundity, 80
Movements, 528
Fisheries. Seal damage to, 1050
Predators, 528
Salmonella infection in poultry, 82
Salvage & special services (Navy Department), 820
Salvation Army Act, 519
San Marino:
British visitors' passports*, 123, 344
War damage*, 123

1961 pp 1–224, 1962 pp 225–445, 1963 pp 447–696, 1964 pp 697–962, 1965 pp 963–1226

102

INDEX 1961-5 —SCH

Sand & gravel:
Production, 222, 390, 634, 901, 1168
working. Circular, 143
Sanders, H. G. (Chairman), Toxic chemicals in agriculture & food storage. 87
Sands, W. A., Termite subfamily Nasutitermitinae, 1067
Sandstone. Old red, 94
Sandwich courses & block release courses in further education establishments, 113
Sandys, Rt. Hon. D. (Chairman & Author):
British Guiana:
Conference, 551
Independence Conference, 284
Gambia Independence Conference, 803
Kenya Independence Conference, 549
Malta Independence Conference, 549
Modern Commonwealth, 365
Northern Rhodesia Independence Conference, 806
Southern Rhodesia Constitutional Conference, 105
Zanzibar Independence Conference, 549
Sanitary regulations, 341, 582, 842
Sappaphis Matsumura, 1059
Sarawak:
Compensation & retiring benefits. OIC, 632
Constitution, OIC. 389, 632
Peace Corps*, 584
Public:
officers*, 889
service Commission. OIC, 174
Reports, 101, 317, 548
See also North Borneo & Sarawak
Sarson, P. B., Variation of earth temperatures, 378
Sarum, Old. Guide, 1167
Sasines for Sheriffdoms, 185, 407, 648, 1176
Satelite communications, 126, 895
Saturation flow at traffic signals. Measuring, 908
Saunders, A. D., Deal & Walmer Castles, 633
Saurashtra books. Catalogue, 93
"Savannah" visits*, 845
Savings Banks Funds account, 205, 426, 675, 941, 1206
Savory, H. N., Tinkinswood & St. Lythans long cairns, 900
Saw-toothed grain beetle, 530, 1053
Sawmill study. Work cycle times, 639
Saxifraga of Himalaya, 93
Saxton maps, 93, 540, 795, 1066
S.C.A.A.P., Reports, 550, 804, 1075
Scaffolding. Safety in construction work, 618
Scale(s):
insects on fruit, 783
mussel & brown, 1051
of enterprise in farming, 177
Scamp, A. J. (Chairman), Court of inquiry between British Railways & Unions, 1149
Scarborough, Earl Of (Chairman), Commonwealth Scholarship Commission, 104
Scarman, Hon. Mr. Justice (Chairman), Law Commission, 1154
Schiffer, C. G., Illness among children, 958
Schlieren methods, 641
Schloss Hampton Court, 390
Scholderer, V., Johann Gutenberg, 540
Scholefield, C. E. (Chairman), Police area. Bedfordshire & Luton 1130
School(s)
and:
college libraries, 646
Commonwealth, 113
Approved etc. *See* Approved Schools
Boarding, for maladjusted children, 1088
building:
Estimates Committee, 140, 141
Survey, 1090
Careers. guidance in, 1088
Child. Health of, 113, 327, 821
Council:
Curriculum Bulletins, 1090
Examination Bulletins, 1089
Publications, 1090
Working paper, 1090
See also Schools. Secondary Examination Council
curricula & examinations, 822
Fire & design, 112
Forward from, 327
From, to further education, 646
Grammar, Direct-grant. List, 821
in U.S.A., 112
Independent, List, 113, 565
leaving age. Raising, 1090
meals service. Memo., 1090
Old, Remodelling, 564
Premises. Scotland. Regulations. Select Committee, 1134
Primary. *See* Primary
Safety precautions, 113, 565
Science teaching, 805
Scottish Secondary. Certificate Courses, 1172
Secondary:
design. Sixth form and staff, 1088
Examinations Council:
Bulletins, 566, 822
Reports, 113, 328, 566, 821
See also Schools, Council
rooms. Building Notes, 911, 1172
Slow learners at, 822
Special, for handicapped pupils, 565
to further education, 646
Village, (Building), 112

1961 pp 1–224, 1962 pp 225–445, 1963 pp 447–696, 1964 pp 697–962, 1965 pp 963–1226

103

Science:
and:
education. Exchanges. United Arab Republic*, 347
industry:
Conference, 394
in Scotland, 34, 138, 256, 358
technology, Act 1041
Bill, 745, 963, 967, 1010
Applied, Notes on, 164, 397, 641, 907
Civil, Organisation, 637
Education in, Conference U.S.A., 688
Experimental Examination, 1089
in:
education in Wales, 1090
Germany, 624
primary schools, 113
Minister for, Office, 177, 394, 637
Museum:
Book exhibition, 636
Booklets, 903–4, 1170
Children's Gallery, 903
Current periodicals in library, 1090
Fifty things to see, 1170
Guide, 177, 637, 1170
Monograph, 1170
Publications, 177, 393, 636–7, 903–4, 1170
of firefighting, 356
Research Council Publications, 1171
rooms. Secondary schools, 1172
teaching. School, 805
Sciences. Promotion of, in Commonwealth, 609
Scientific:
and:
Industrial Research. Dept. of:
Publications, 178–81, 394–9, 637–44, 904–9
See also Technology, Ministry of, 1178–81
Research:
Council, 160, 394, 638, 905, 1179
Grants, 178, 399, 638
Studentships & fellowships, 178, 394, 638
Universities & colleges. Support, 394
technological:
manpower, 637, 1179
qualifications. Census, 351
Civil Service. Organisation of, 1205
education. Higher, Audio-visual aids, 1091
equipment to universities, 672
experiments. Effect of nuclear explosions, 637
manpower, 160, 637, 1179
Papers (Meteorological Office), 162–3, 378, 622, 885, 1156
Scientific (*continued*):
policy. Advisory Council, 376, 637, 904
Reports (British Antarctic Survey), 101, 318, 539, 794
research:
at Natural History Museum, 313
in British Universities, 181, 394, 642, 908, 1090
technological educational & cultural fields. Soviet Union*, 124, 1094
Scilly Isles. *See* Isles of Scilly
Scope & standards of Certificate of Secondary Education, 566
Scotia Arc. Geophysical investigation, 794
Scotland:
Ancient Monuments Guide, 221
Central. Programme, 659
Development & growth in, 910
Fisheries of, 80, 299, 528, 782, 1050
North-east forests, 586
Prisons in, 1175
Secretary of State Undertakings, 79–80, 300, 527, 529, 782, 1051
Tertiary volcanic districts, 129
See also Scottish
Scots pine, 846, 1180
Scotswood Bridge Act, 290
Scott, J. A. (Chairman), Training staff for mentally subnormal, 352
Scott, P., Wildfowl in Great Britain, 625
Scott-Moncrieff, G., Scottish Border Abbeys, 901
Scottish:
Agricultural Economics, 81, 299, 529, 783, 1051
Agriculture (Journal), 81, 299, 529, 783, 1051
Border Abbeys, 901
Certificate of Education arrangement. Papers etc. ,182, 183, 400, 401, 645, 646, 911, 912, 1174
College of Commerce. Endowment Scheme, 1173
Development Department:
Circulars, 399, 1171
Publications, 399, 644, 909–11, 1171–2
Report, 644, 911, 1171
Technical broadsheet, 399
Education Department:
Circulars, 182, 400, 645, 911, 1172
Publications, 182–3, 400–2, 645–6, 911–2, 1172–4
Rules, 183, 912
Estimates:
Minutes of proceedings, 139, 358, 598, 859, 1132
Standing Committee Debates, 34, 256, 483, 736, 1007
farming. Current economic conditions, 81, 299, 529, 783, 1051

Scottish (*continued*):
Grand & Standing Committee, 9, 35
Health:
Services Council Reports, 131, 132, 406, 591, 647, 913, 1175
statistics, 131, 406, 913, 1175
See also Health Department for Scotland
Home (and Health) Department publications, 183–5, 402–6, 646–7, 912–3, 1174–5
hospital(s):
directory, 406
Endowments Research Trust, 131, 406, 647, 913, 1175
in patients statistics, 913, 1175
Medical staffing structure, 913
running costs, 402, 647, 912, 1174
See also Hospitals:
housing. *See* Housing, Scotland
Land Court, 185, 406, 647–8, 913, 1175
Law Commission. First programme, 1174
licensing law, 647
Office, 185, 406–7, 648, 913–4, 1175
oyster investigation, 80
peat, 299, 1051
plumbers' & scottish builders' Agreement, 498, 623
Pulp Mill (Water Supply) Order Confirmation Act, 519
Bill, 488
Record Office:
Accommodation, 646
Publications, 185, 407, 648, 914, 1176
roads, 184, 403, 406, 644
salmon & trout fisheries, 529, 1051
sea fisheries. Statistical tables, 81, 300, 529, 783, 1051
Statistical Office, 648, 914, 1176
statistics, Digest. 184, 399, 402, 644, 648, 914, 1171, 1176
Valuation Advisory Council Report, 183, 402, 644, 909, 1171
whiting fishery, 528
Wool Trades Consultative Committee, 299
Scrap & metallic residues. Licence, 413, 660–1, 666, 926, 1191, 1195
Scrap Metal Dealers Act, 773
Bill, 491, 703, 705, 736, 744, 859
Screeds as underlay for floor coverings, 1166
Scrolls from Dead Sea. Exhibition guide, 1066
Sculpture(s):
Fifty masterpieces, 959
Italian, Catalogue, 959
of:
Assur-Nasir-Apli, 310
the Parthenon, 310
Sea:
cards, State of, 163
defence. Research, 304
Exploration of, Convention, 1109
Fish Industry Act, 288
Bill, 38, 42, 228, 230, 256, 261, 358
fisheries, Statistical tables, 87, 305, 534, 789, 1060
in education, 822
Law of:
Continental Shelf Convention, 839
disputes protocol, 580
Pollution by oil, 343
Safety of life at, 151, 1116
surface temperatures, 162
surveys. Britain's contribution to hydrography, 1158
Sea-going qualities of ships. Seminar, 907
Seaborne, A. E. M., Industrial inspection, 907
Seafarers:
national identity documents, 1111
welfare, 1094
Seal(s):
damage to salmon fisheries, 1050
of the World, 797
Seals:
Cylinder, 310
Western Asiatic, 310
Seamanship. Admiralty manual, 71, 519, 818
Seamen. Refugee*, 344
Seasonable variation of sea temperature, 162
Seasonal Workers Bill, 40
SEATO. Privileges and immunities*, 1116
Seaweed(s):
as manure, 300
Handbook, 95
Second:
nuclear power programme, 898
world war. History, 95–6, 313, 353, 798, 1070
Secondary:
education. *See* Education, Secondary
schools. *See* Schools, Secondary
Secrecy of inventions. Safeguarding, 342, 582, 839
Secretary. Company, (Careers), 612
Secretary of State for:
Scotland. Undertakings, 79–80, 300, 527, 529, 782, 1051
Wales:
Circular, 1222
Function of ,740, 1131
Security(ies)
and:
Change, 159
unit trusts. Dealers, 191, 415, 663, 928, 1195
at National Gallery, 275

Security(ies) (*continued*):
Commission:
Board of inquiry, 1206
Standing. Report, 1070
procedures in public service, 271
Standing Commission, 1070
Sediment transport by currents, 1180
Seed(s):
and potting composts, 301
for leys, 300
Potato. *See* Potato
Quality in, 300
Unit drills, 1059
Seeley, H. G., & Karroo Reptiles, 312
Segontium Roman Fort. Guide, 390, 633
Select Committees. *See respective subjects*
Selected planning appeals, 146, 364, 869
Selection:
and training of supervisors, 374, 881
of clay building bricks, 1179
Selective tendering for local authorities, 1167
Self-feeding of grass silage, 1050
Selkirk. Census:
Leaflet. Population etc., 590
Report, 850
Sellers, Rt. Hon. Lord Justice, (Chairman), Criminal Law Revision Committee:
Closing speeches, 594
Criminal procedure:
Insanity, 594
Jurors, 855
Perjury & attendance of witnesses, 856
Selman, B. J.:
Deretrichia Weise, 541
Nodini & Eumolpidae, 1068
Selwood, E. B., Dechenelid tribolites, 1068
Semporna Peninsular soil survey, 651
Senate document (U.S. Congress), 957
Senior commercial & airline transport pilots' licenses Exam. Papers, 92, 307, 536, 792, 1064
Sentence of the Court. Handbook, 857
Service(s):
colleges. Estimates Committee, 860, 1135
cores in high flats, 362, 603, 865, 1139
departments. Virement, 139, 359, 599, 861, 1134
Disability Pensions Bill, 264, 1009
for:
disabled, 375
old people Circular, 142
overseas. Recruitment, 410
pay & pensions, 326, 820
textbook of radio, 220, 692
Settled Land Act 1925 (Amendment) Bill, 263
Settlement of disputes. *See* Disputes
Seventy m.p.h. Temporary speed limit Order, 1199, 1223
Severn Bridge Tolls Act, 1041
Bill, 746, 974, 1010, 1132
Re-committed Bill, 1007, 1133
Sewage:
plants. Circular, 1139
works:
Operation & management of, 1141
Operator's Handbook, 1142
Sewer(age) systems. Design of:
storm, 642
surface water, 602
urban, 398
Sex chromosomes complement in man, 883
Sexual Offences Bill, 260, 970, 972, 974, 975
Seychelles:
Capital offences OIC, 174
Court of Appeal OIC, 899
Flag badge, 102
Instructions OIC, 632
Judicature OIC, 899
Legislative Council (Amendment) OIC, 632
Report, 101, 548

Shakespeare:
Birthplace etc. Trust Act, 70
Exhibition of books etc., 796
Fascimile of deed & leaf of play, 796
General catalogue of books. Excerpt, 796
in Public Records Office, 901
Shanks, J. (Chairman), Primary education in Scotland, 1173
Shanwick oceanic control area (Air traffic), 1064
Shap Abbey. Guide, 634
Shape up. Fitness exercises, 957
Shaw, C. J. D. *See* Kilbrandon, Lord
Shawcross, Rt. Hon. Lord (Chairman), Royal Commission on press, 392
Sheals, J. G.:
Cryptostigmatid mites, 1069
Expedition to East Nepal, 1068
Sheathings. Deck, for ships, 665
Sheep:
Aids to management, 532
Breeding & management, 786
Calf tetany etc., 301
Handling pens & baths, 788
Post-mortem examination, 785
Recording & progeny testing, 85
Stocking. Intensive, 301
Sheet & tile flooring from thermoplastic binders, 637
Sheffield:
Alteration of area. Map, 867
Police appeal inquiry, 596
Shell:
Brazil Act, 70

Shell (*continued*):
Chemicals Distributing Company of Egypt Act, 519
Company of Australia Act, 775
Shellard, H. C.:
Calculation of terms. Weather station, 378
Forecasting temperature inversions, 163
Shelter belts for:
farmland, 85
Western hill farms, 586
Sheret, M. A., Auroral observations, 539
Sheriff Courts (Civil Jurisdiction & Procedure) (Scotland) Act, 517
Bill, 452, 473, 483, 487
Sheriffs (Pensions) (Scotland) Act, 68
Bill, 3, 5, 34, 39, 41, 139
Sherlock, R. L., Geological column, 640
Sherwood, P. T., Soil-cement mixtures, 398
Ship(s):
captain's medical guide, 199, 669
code & decode book, 163, 885
fires, 856
models, 903, 1170
Mortgage Finance Company Act, 290
Passenger, Instructions to surveyors, 197
Registry of, 198, 420, 668, 934, 1195
Sailing (from 1700), 904
Sea-going qualities, 907
Signal letters, 199, 421, 669, 935, 1196
Structural fire protection. Denmark*, 843
Tonnage measurement. Sweden*, 345
Shipbuilding:
Advisory Committee, 199
and ship repairing (Careers), 152
Credit Act, 773
Bill, 491, 698
Employers' Federation inquiry, 1149
Industry Training Board, 1152
orders placed overseas, 199
services to N. Ireland, 669
Shipping:
casualties & deaths, 199, 421, 669, 1196
Contracts & Commercial Documents Act, 773
Bill, 707, 745
Intergovernmental Maritime Consultation Organisation, 151, 842
Maritime Travel Conference, 1117,
Shipyards, Production of building components, 634
Shock hazard, Extinction of fires, 1179
Shops:
Act 1950:
Forms, 857
Provisions for amending (Trading hours), 1130
Airports Act, 288
Bill, 229, 246, 256, 260, 262
Shops (*continued*):
Early Closing Days Act, 1041
Bill, 970, 1007, 1010, 1133
Scotland Bill, 859
Shore, A. F., Portrait painting, 310
Shoreham:
and Lancing. Provisional Order Act, 774
Bill, 706, 743
Harbour Act, 290
Short, A., Bridge-deck systems, 638
Short stay psychiatric unit, 133
Short-term gains taxation, 426
Short-title catalogue of books, 540, 1066
Shorten, M., Squirrels, 302
Shorthand & typing proficiency tests, 423, 937
Shrinkage of natural aggregates in concrete, 637
Shropshire:
Census:
Leaflet. Population etc., 589
Report, 849
Saxton map, 540
S.H.W. forms, 881, 1153

Sick:
members of House of Commons. Voting, 1134
pay schemes, 881, 893
Sickness benefit:
decisions, 166, 167, 382, 625, 626, 627, 891, 1161
Time limits for claiming, 892
Sidmouth. Provisional Order Act, 290
Bill, 262
Sidney papers. Mss., 354
Sierra Leone:
achieves independence. Photoposter, 147
Air services*, 344
Arms, 100
Flag badge, 102
Independence Act, 68
Bill, 3, 40
International rights & obligations, 123
Library Board. Gift, 427
Limba people of Northern, 1159
Making of a nation, 148
Photoposter, 147
Picture set, 147
Public officers*, 105
Reference pamphlet, 148
Structure & petrology, 410
Sight:
reduction tables, Air navigation, 88, 535
testing & supply of glasses. Fees, 134, 354, 593, 853, 1126, 1127
Signal(s):
Civil Defence instructors' notes, 135, 355, 855
generators etc., 397
letters of ships, 199, 421, 669, 935, 1196

Signal(s) (continued):
office:
and wireless operation procedure (Civil Defence), 355, 855
practice (Civil Defence), 135, 854
Signs of the Zodiac, 959
Silage:
Agricultural Bulletin, 83
Grass:
Advisory leaflet, 79, 82
Feeding value of, 82, 1053
Self-feeding, 1050
Maize for, 81
Methods of feeding, 82
stores, 1059
Wilting for, 301, 530
Silicon & manganese stars, 1170
Sillimanite, 1159
Silos:
Concrete staved, 1049
Grain, 85
Silurian:
polyzoa, 1068
rocks of Ludlow district, 542
Silver:
German & Swiss domestic, 218
German domestic, 1222
Italian secular, 439
scurf of potatoes, 529, 1052
Silverware trades in Sheffield, 881
SIMMONS, T. M., Railways, 1170
SIMONS, E. L.:
Eocene tarsioids, 94
New eocene primate genus Cantius, 311
SIMPSON, A. C., Bionomics of lobster, 303
SIMPSON, W. D.:
Bishop's & Earl's Palaces Kirkwall, 1166
Kildrummy & Glenbuchat Castles, 1167
Urquhart Castle, 900
SIMS, SIR A. (Chairman), Structural Steel Committee, 71, 291, 819, 1087
Simuliidae, 796
Singapore:
Armed forces. Crown land, 549
Badges. Marine ensign, 104
Loan, 474
Public officers*, 889
Reports, 317, 540
SIR GEORGE CAYLEY'S, Aeronautics, 393
SIR ROGER CAYLEY'S Bill 40
Sitka spruce timber, 395
Six Bells Colliery explosion, 171
Sixth form studies & university entrance requirements, 328

SKEAT, T. C., Manuscript collections. Catalogues, 310

SKELHORN, N. J., Inquiry Mr. Herman Woolf & police, 857
Skelmersdale New Town (Designation) Order inquiry, 146
Skid-resistance tester, 908
Skilful cycling. Manual, 1170
Skin spot & silver scurf of potatoes, 529, 1052
Skull of the oligokyphus, 797
SKYRME, W. T. C. (Chairman), Expenses of legal proceedings, 137

Slatted floors for dairy cows & pigs, 1049
Slaughterhouses. Regulations, 84, 302, 303, 531, 786
SLEDGE, W. A.:
Asplenium, 1067
Athyrioid ferns, 310
Slender wall construction for houses, 131
Slow learners in school, 822
Slugs & snails, 529
Slugworm. Pear & cherry, 300

Small:
ermine moths, 1051
Estates (Representation) Act, 68
Bill, 5, 35, 40, 139
poultry flock, 786
Small-scale preparation of photographic emulsions, 164
Smallholdings:
in Wales, 85, 303
Reports & accounts, 87, 305, 534, 789, 1060
Smallpox:
Control of outbreak, 853
Report 1961-2, 593
Vaccination against, 353
SMART, J., Instructions for collectors, 543
SMEED, R. J. (Chairman), Road pricing, 934
Smethwick. Proposed county borough, 144
SMIT, F.G.A.M. :
Ctenophtalmus, 541
Neotunga euloidae, 311
SMITH, B., North Wales geology, 129
SMITH, H., Saxifraga, 93
SMITH I. W.:
Dee disease, 782
Furunculosis in kelts, 299
SMITH, J. A. B. (Chairman), Model dairy byelaws, 131
SMITH, K. G. V., Diptera from Nepal, 1068
Smoke control areas:
Circulars, 142, 361, 362, 602, 1138
Programmes, 362, 364
Smokeless fuel supplies, 1138
Smoking & health report (U.S.A.), 958
SMYTH, M. J., Photometry of southern galactic clusters, 636

Snails:
and slugs, 529
New Hebridean land, 542
Snakes. Natural history, 1070
Snow & slush measurement (Air traffic), 1064
Snowdonia National Forest Park. Guide, 349, 586

Soaps etc. Prices, 1156
Social:
and:
Economic Research Committee, 151
medical assistance. Convention, 123, 344
Insurance. Convention. Turkey, 346
security:
agreements. Amendments, 123, 124, 344, 582, 842, 1117
Canada*, 320
France*, 1117
Germany Convention, 119, 1117
programmes throughout world, 958
services in Britain, 365, 871
statistics, 128
studies report, 1090
training in primary school, 401
workers (Careers), 152, 612, 1147
Socket outlet wiring, 394
Soft:
drinks Regulations, 531, 786
fruit in garden, 301
Softwoods:
Bark borer, 639
Home-grown, Effect of pruning on, 1180
Soil(s):
and:
foundations, 1178
irrigability. Usutu Basin, 1159
land use around. See respective towns
manures for fruit, 1054
other roadmaking material. Nigeria, 398
at overseas airfields, 398
cement:
mixtures, 398
roads, 304
of Malta & Gozo, 101
organic matter, 398
stabilization, 398, 638
Survey of Great Britain:
Memoirs, 327, 328, 782
Reports, 79, 298, 527, 782, 1050
Survey of Sampang Peninsula, 651
Solar:
and luni-solar daily variation, 635
radiation, 399
Soldier:
humour, 220
Periodical, 220, 441, 692, 811, 1081
SOLEM, A., New Hebridean land snails, 542

Solicitors:
Act, 1041
Bill, 710, 963, 967, 973, 1007, 1010, 1011, 1133
Practice leaflets, 1153
Scotland Act, 1041
Bill, 968, 1012, 1132
Solid fuel appliances. Installing, 1166
Solihull. Proposed county borough, 145
SOLLBERGER, E., Babylonian legend of the Flood, 909
Solomon Islands. See British Solomon Islands
Soltau-Lüneburg manoeuvres*, 1113
Somerset:
Census:
Leaflet. Population etc., 589
Report, 849
man, 93
Saxton map, 93
SOPER, J. P., Future of Commonwealth, 551
Sorrels. Docks &, 300, 1051
SORSBY, A. A., Refraction, 161, 377
Sound:
and television broadcasting services in Britain, 871
insulation. Measurements, 180
transmission. Building standards Regulations (Scotland), 644
South:
Africa:
Act, 288
Bill, 227, 228, 256, 261, 262, 359
Cereals*, 824
Double taxation*, 344–5, 826
Arabia:
Accession of Aden, 803
Army financial arrangements, 285
Conference, 803
Royal Instructions OIC, 632
East:
Asia Treaty Organisation*, 1116
England, 869
Study, 869
Essex Waterworks Act, 290
Georgia, Flora, 794
of Scotland Electricity Boards:
Advances, 115, 567, 912, 1164
Loans, 204, 425, 673, 674, 939, 1204
Reports, 185, 406, 644, 911, 1172
Pacific Commission*, 1017, 1117
Shetland Islands. Geology, 101
Shields. Proposed Tyneside borough.
Staffordshire Water Act, 238
Wales:
Coalfield:
Geology, 906
Inquiry, 1152
Iron ore imports into, 1223
Western General Review Area (Local Government), 604, 1142

Southampton docks. Foreman inquiry, 785
Southern
Rhodesia:
Act, 1041
Bill, 1013
Cereals*, 824
Constitution:
Act, 68
Bill, 8, 42
Order. Select Committee, 1134
Proposed changes & provisions, 105
Constitutional Conference report, 105
Correspondence with H.M. Government, 543
Instructions OIC, 388
Joint statement on Independence, 807
Negotiations between governments. Documents, 1077
Revocation of export licenses, 1196
Visas. Re-imposition, 1120
spectroscopic binaries, 636
stars:
Fundamental data, 176, 393, 903
Photoelectric magnitudes, 393, 635
Soviet Union:
Agricultural research co-operation*, 1117
Air services U.K.*, 124
Cultural relations*, 124, 582, 1094
English magazine distribution*, 124
Fishery regime*, 842
Scientific etc. fields. Relations*, 495
trade agreement*, 1117
Visas. Abolition of fees*, 842
SOWA, S., Trachoma & allied infections, 1154
Sowing grass seeds, 82

Space:
and water heating in flats, 180, 904
heaters. Designation of electric. Circular, 865
in the home, 602, 603
motions & distribution of stars, 177
research:
and Development, Ministry of, 40
co-operation U.S.A.*, 124
European:
Collaboration*, 124, 345, 583, 843
Organisation, 339, 841, 843, 1134
vehicle:
launchers European organisation*, 345, 843, 1117
See also European Organisation for Development

Space (continued):
vehicle (continued):
tracking stations:
Bermuda*, 126, 515
Canton Island*, 126, 515
U.K.*, 126
Zanzibar*, 126
velocity vectors, 393
Spain:
Air services*, 124
Atomic energy*, 124
British visitors' passports*, 124
Consular Convention*, 124, 583
Cultural Convention*, 124
Sparrow. House, 529
Special:
Commonwealth African Assistance Plan, 550, 804, 1075
hospitals. Working party, 134
schools for handicapped pupils, 565
Specification:
for road and bridge work, 667, 669
See also DEF & DTD
Spectacles. Merchandise Marks, 415
Spectral requirements of light sources, 1154
Spectrographic abstracts, 92
Spectrophotometric measurements of stars, 177
Speech therapist (Careers), 1147
Speed limits:
Temporary orders, 667, 933, 1199, 1223
Traffic signs, 420
Spence Bursary Trust Scheme, 401, 646
SPENCER, K. A., Agromyzidae, 1067
Spinach, 300
Spitalfields etc. markets. Dispute, 881
Spofforth Castle. Guide, 1167
Sponges. Calcareous, 543
Sport(s):
Facilities Bill, 1080
Provision of facilities. Circulars, 865
Spraing. Potato tuber, 1052
Spray Irrigation (Scotland) Act, 773
Bill, 703, 704, 705, 707, 744
Sprayers:
Farm, 307
Field crop, 303, 1059
Sprays. Application. Fruit trees, 82
Spring cabbage, 530
Sprouts. Brussels, 83, 300, 1052
Spruce. Properties of, 395
Spurrey, 83
Squirrels:
Biology & control, 302
Grey, 249

Staffing of:
local authority children's depts. Scotland, 647
midwifery service. Scotland, 1175
Stafford Corporation Act, 775
Staffordshire. Census:
Leaflet. Population etc., 589
Report, 588
Staggered holidays, 663
Stamp:
design. Commonwealth, 1066
Enterprising Bill, 191
trading, 807
Stanchions. Strength of encased, 1179
Standard:
highway loadings, 197
industrial classification, 544
magnitudes in E regions, 393
stars. Measures, 636
technical training notes, 535, 1079
Standards of:
ascertainment. Scottish schoolchildren, 182
public library service, 328
Standing:
Commission on Museums etc., 186, 648, 914, 1176
Committee(s):
Debates, 9, 33–5, 38, 233–4, 255–6, 260, 482–3, 487, 710–1, 734–6, 740–1, 1006–7, 1008
Returns, 31, 141, 253, 360, 480, 862, 1001
Orders:
for road movement, 137
House of Commons, 141, 599, 600, 862, 1136
House of Lords, 142, 231, 701, 864, 1137, 1138
R.A.M.C. etc., 220, 441, 692, 812, 1081
revision H.C. Select Committee, 599
Security Commission, 1070
STANFORD, W. P. (Chairman), Basutoland Constitutional Commission, 793
Stanley, Garforth & Rothwell. Proposed county district. Map, 867
Star(s):
almanac, 72, 252, 520, 888, 1169
Declination, 636
formation, 636
Fundamental data, 176
See also Cool, Hyades etc.
Starfishes & their relations, 313
Starling, 300
Starters for cheese-making, 1052
State:
Building Society. Affairs of, 128
House, Holborn. Estimates Committee, 599, 862

State (continued):
Management Districts, 137, 437, 484, 857, 1000
of sea cards, 163
opening of Parliament, 366
Papers:
British & Foreign, 116, 329, 568, 1093
Calendar, 634, 900, 901
Guide, 634
Statelessness:
Convention, 281
U.N. Conference, 303
Statement:
of:
excesses, 426, 675, 941, 1206
Ministers, of Group of Ten, 941
trade, 105, 321, 552, 807, 1077
on defence, 326, 563, 820, 1088
States of annual progress of linen manufacture in Scotland, 914
STATHAM, P. M., Geological photographs, 640
Stationers:
and Newspaper Makers' Company Act, 70
sundries & school rules. Merchandise Marks, 663
Stationery Office Publications, 186–7, 407–8, 648–9, 914–5, 1176–7
Statistical:
Abstract U.S.A., 688
Classification for goods, 106, 322, 555, 1066
digest (Power), 173, 388, 631, 898, 1166
papers (Transport), 670, 935
relationships. Temperature, 378
report series, N.H.S. Prescribing, 1127
review. E. & W., 129, 351, 589, 849, 1123
series available. List, 1070
services. Government, 425
summary. Mineral industry, 102, 318, 625, 889, 1159
techniques for classifying individuals, 1131
Statistics:
Annual Abstracts, 96, 314, 544, 1070
Digest (Colonial Office), 318, 548, 803
Monthly Digest of, 96, 314, 544–5, 799, 1071
Official. Studies in, 96, 314, 799, 1070
Quarterly digest (Colonial Office), 100, 318
See also subject Agricultural etc.
Status of world's nations, 688
Statute(s):
Chronological table, 187, 409, 649, 915, 1177
in force. Index, 187, 409, 650, 915, 1177
Law Revision:
Acts, 517, 773

STA— INDEX 1961-5

Statute(s) (continued):
Law Revision (continued):
Bills, 450, 490, 600, 704, 705, 745, 863, 976
Consequential Repeals Act, 1041
Bill, 965, 968, 971, 1013, 1136, 1137
Scotland Act, 773
Bill, 452, 601, 705, 745, 863
See also Acts
Statutory:
inquiries. Award of costs, 882, 1139, 1223
Instruments (and S.R. & O.):
Bound annual volumes, 187–8, 409, 650, 916, 1178
effects, 187, 409, 650, 916, 1178
lists. Monthly & annual, 186, 409, 650, 916, 1177–8
numerical table. Supp., 188, 409, 650, 916, 1178
Select Committee, 10, 139, 140, 141, 234, 235, 257, 359, 598, 599, 600, 859, 861, 1132–3, 1134
Orders (Special Procedure) Act, 1041
Bill, 969, 972, 1007, 1009, 1011, 1012, 1133
Draft Order, 284, 362, 421
Publication Office, 187–8, 409, 649–50, 915–6, 1177–8
Statws Cyfreithiol Yr Iaith Gymraeg, 1223
Steam:
engine. History, 1170
Superheated, Condensation, 641
tables, 906
Steatonyssus Kolenati, 797
Steel(s):
Brittle fracture in, 291, 819
foundries. Conditions, 153
in concrete. Protection against corrosion, 1178
nationalisation, 1166
Notch tough, 1087
specifications. Working party, 1087
Structural:
Navy (Admiralty) Dept., 71, 291, 819, 1087
Protection against fire, 179
Tests on, 71, 219, 1087
Transition temperatures, 1087
STEELE, J. H., Herring fishery, 80
Stem:
and bulb eelworm on:
narcissi, 301
tulip, 301
eelworm on:
cereals etc., 529, 783
clover, 360
STEMPFFER, H.:
Lipterinae, 541
Micropentila Aurivillino, 1067

Stenomicra, 1068
STEPHENSON, H. S., Colliery explosions:
Cambrian, 1164
Hampton Valley, 385
Sterilisation of syringes, 376
Sterilisers. Pressure steam, Hospitals, 592
Sterilising arrangements. Hospitals, 1125
Stevenson screen readings, 377, 884, 1155
STEWART, J. F. (Chairman). Relations between education authorities and teachers, 401
STEWART, J. G. (Chairman), Workshops for blind, 374
Stile End beds etc., 542
Stirling. Census:
Leaflet. Population etc., 590
Report, 850
Stirlingshire. Ancient Monuments, 635
Stock:
Exchange (Careers), 612
Transfer Act, 517
Bill, 449, 483, 489, 598
Stockport & Knutsford. Geology, 640
Stocks of Trisopterus Esmarkii, 1050
Stoke-on-Trent. Alteration of areas. Map, 145
STONE, P.A., Economics of factory buildings, 395
Stonehenge:
Postcard, 1167
What is:
English Edn., 390
French Edn., 634
Stoney Littleton Long Barrow. Guide, 633
Stores. Gift, to Malta, 1203
Storm:
overflows & disposal of sewage:
Circular, 602
Interim report, 607
sewage systems. Guide, 642
Storm-drains, sewage etc. Tables for design, 640
Stourbridge. Proposed new borough, 145
Strategic:
air offensive against Germany, 96
reconnaissance in damaged areas, 135
Stratigraphy of Eastern Aden Protectorate, 1159
Strawberry(ies):
Agricultural Bulletin, 531
Eelworms on, 1052
Growing commercial, 1050
Preparation for market, 822
Red core of, 82, 1052
Virus diseases, 1053
Streamlines & isotachs, 1155
STREATFIELD, HON. M. JUSTICE (Chairman),
Business of criminal Courts, 137
Street(s):
New, Town & country planning, 1138
widths. Byelaws, 361

INDEX 1961-5 —SUP

Strength:
of:
brickwork etc. walls, 1178
encased stanchions, 1179
properties of:
plywood, 905
timber, 179
Strengthening of Marriage Bill, 745, 1011
Strongyles (Nematoda), 1069
Strontium 90 in:
human bone, 160, 376–7, 619, 883, 1154
milk, 79
STROYAN, H. L. G.:
Dysaphis Börner, 533
Sappaphis Matsumura, 1059
Structural:
design:
in architecture, 178
of roads, 398
fire:
precautions. Building Standards Regulations (Scotland), 910
protection of ships*, 843
requirements of Factories Act, 375
steel. See Steel
strength & stability. Building Standard Regulations (Scotland), 910
timbers. Working stresses, 179, 1179
Structure and:
petrology of Sierra Leone, 410
relationships of Jurassic fish, 541
trading practices of films industry, 929
STUART, M. C. (Chairman), Red Deer Commission, 80, 299
STUART, T. A., Leaping behaviour of salmon & trout, 299
STUBBEFIELD, C. J., Geological column, 640
Student pilot's & private pilot's licences, 539
Students:
and their education (Robbin's report), 821
use of vacations, 676
Studentships & fellowships D.S.I.R., 178, 394, 638
Studies in. See respective subjects
STURROCK, F. G., Planning farm work, 83

Sub judice matters in H.C., 599
Sub-committees (Estimates Committee):
Allocation of matters, 141, 360
Appointment of, etc., 141, 359, 468, 600, 861, 1135
Sitting of, Overseas, 1135
Subject Index of modern books B.M., 310
Subjective standards in industrial inspection, 907
Subordinate legislation. Access to, 596
Succession of life through geological time, 313, 797
Succession (Scotland) Act, 773
Bill, 487, 491, 598, 700, 701, 702, 736, 741, 743, 859

Sudan. Air services*, 124, 345
Sudden death in infancy, 1127
Suffolk. Census:
East:
Leaflet. Population etc., 589
Report, 848
West:
Leaflet. Population etc., 589
Report, 849
Sugar:
agreement Protocol, 843
beet:
Fund, 87, 305, 466, 790, 1061
Harvesting, 303
pulp for feeding, 82
virus. Yellow, 1052
Board. Accounts etc., 87, 115, 250, 305, 476, 534, 790, 1061
Confectionery & Food Preserving Wages Council, 159
Suicide Act, 68
Bill, 2, 35, 40, 139
Sulphur dioxide. Detection, 374
Summary Jurisdiction Bill, 490
Summer & autumn cabbage, 82
Summons from Oliver Cromwell. Facsimile, 635
Sunday:
Entertainments Act. Cinematograph Fund Account, 174, 389, 465, 632, 823, 1091
Observance:
Bill, 743
Law on, 857
Sunderland:
Alteration of area, 605
Corporation Act, 519
SUNLEY, J. G.:
Home-grown pit-props, 1180
Testing of structural timbers etc., 639
Working stresses for structural timbers, 179, 1179
Sunshine for Great Britain & N.I., 1931–60, 620
Superannuation:
Act, 1041
Bill, 741, 745, 859, 971, 974, 975, 1013, 1137
Amendment Act, 1041
Bill, 746, 964, 967, 1010
Civil service etc. Digest of law, 1203
Interchange rules, 142, 143, 865, 1139
Miscellaneous Provisions Act. Circulars, 142, 143, 1139
Scheme (E. & W.) National Health Service, 1127
Supervision for quality education in science. Conference, 688
Supervisor(s):
and his job, 641
Selection & training, 374, 881

SUP— INDEX 1961-5

Supplementary, See respective subjects
Supreme Court of Judicature:
Accounts, 188, 409, 650, 886, 1178
Northern Ireland, Land Purchase Accounts, 188, 409, 650, 916, 997,
Queens Bench Master's Practice forms, 882
Sur les Pselaphides, 94
Surface:
development in coal mining areas, 143
dressings. Wet-weather damage (Roads), 908
water Year book, 146, 364, 869, 1142
workmen at coalmines etc. Books, 387
Surgery (Careers), 369, 875
Surrey. Census:
Leaflet. Population etc., 589
Occupation groups, 1123
Report, 588
Surveyor(s):
Instructions, 665
Land agent etc. (Careers), 875
Sussex. Census:
Leaflet. Population etc., 589
Occupation groups, 1123
Reports, 848, 849
Sussex University Act, 290
Sutherland (and Zetland):
Census. Leaflet & report, 590
Educational Trust Scheme, 183
Sutton Coldfield:
Alteration of area, 145
Corporation Act, 70
Sutton Hoo ship burial, 795

SWAIN, A., Fishery investigations, 303
Swansea. Alteration of boundary. Map, 605
SWANWICK, G. R. (Chairman), Police appeal inquiry, 596
Swaziland:
and Mozambique. Connecting railway*, 841
Constitution, 549
Corona Library, 1074
Double taxation. Sweden*, 345
Instructions OIC, 173, 899
Loan, 672
Lowveld. Soil etc., 1159
Photoposter, 147
Reports, 104, 320, 551, 807, 1174
Royal Instructions OIC, 632, 899
Sweden:
Atomic energy. Peaceful uses*, 843
British visitors' passports*, 124, 345
Cereals*, 843
Double taxation, 124, 345, 1117
Extraction Treaty, 583
Tonnage measurement of ships*, 345
Swedes & turnips, 301
Sweepstakes on Horse Races (Authorisation) Bill, 963, 968

Sweet corn, 82, 1052
Swift moths, 529
Swimbladder in notopteridae, 797
Swimming:
bath colds, 1139
pools, 362
SWINDELLS, B., Measurement of load, 164
Swine:
fever, 529
Rhinitis, 785
SWINTON. W, E:
Dinosaurs, 312, 797
Fossil amphibians & reptiles, 312, 1069
Harry Govier Seely etc., 312
Switzerland:
Arrangements to facilitate travel*, 125, 583
Atomic energy. Peaceful uses*, 841, 1118
British visitors' passports*, 125
Double taxation*, 125, 844
Loans*, 124, 345
Settlement of disputes*, 1116
Swords and:
daggers, 689
firearms. Naval, 380
Symbister Harbour. See Zetland
Symphylids. Glasshouse, 82, 1053
Synthetic detergents. Standing Technical Committee, 146, 363, 607, 869
Syria:
Air services*, 281
Cereals*, 1118
Syriac printed books etc. Catalogue, 309
Syringes sterilization etc., 376
Syrphidae, 796
SYX-RRL Vehicle counter. Using, 642

T

Table(s):
chickens, 1054
for:
Bessel functions, 397
hydraulic design of storm-drains, etc., 640
glass. English, 1153
in Victoria & Albert Museum, 218
of:
half velocity of radio waves, 812
Jacobean elliptic functions, 906
values of foods, 377
Taf Fechan Water Board Order, 973
Tailoring. Bespoke, (Careers), 368
Taints in milk, 300
Tall buildings & industrial emissions, 1139, 1222
Talmud. Babylonian, 95

INDEX 1961-5 —TEA

Tanganyika:
and Zanzibar. Cereals*, 805
Appeals from Court of Appeal*, 552
Arms, 316
Constitutional Conference, 103
Flag, 104
Independence Act, 68
Bill, 8, 42
Instructions to Governor OIC, 173, 174
Making of a nation, 148
Mechanised farming in, 548
Photoposter, 147
Public Officers*, 410
Reference pamphlet, 148
Republic Act, 289
Bill, 232, 263
Story of progress, 148
under U.K. Administration, 103
TANNER, J. C.:
Factors affecting amount of travel, 181
Fifty-point traffic census, 398
Sample survey of roads & traffic, 398
Tapestries at Hampton Court Palace, 399
Tapling collection of postage stamps etc., 795
Tar surface dressings, 1200
Taraxicum, 93
Tariff(s):
Amendments, 105, 321, 552, 807, 1078, 1095
tables. Forestry, 348
Tate (Gallery):
Reports, 188, 651, 916
Review, 651
Taw River, Mussel Fishery Order. Select Committee S.I., 257
Tax. Cases:
Appeals leaflets, 149–50, 366–7, 610–1, 872–3, 1145–6
Harrison's Index, 148, 366, 609, 872
Selection etc., 367, 611, 873–4, 1146
Taxation:
British system, 365, 1144
Capital gains, 1206
Double*. See respective countries
Short-term gains, 426
Taxonomic study of drepanidae, 94
Taxonomy:
and biology of:
lebetus, 542
penaeidae, 548
of pipits, 95
Tay Road Bridge Order Confirmation Act, 290
Bill, 263
TAYLOR, A. J., Jewel Tower, Westminster, 1167
TAYLOR, B. J., Geology of country around Stockport & Knutsford, 630
TAYLOR, G. E., Occultation of regulus, 636

TAYLOR, J. H., Geology of country around Kettering etc., 630
TAYLOR, Sir W. (Chairman):
Forestry, 634
Trees in:
Greenwich Park, 899
Richmond Park, 390
Teachers:
Demand for & supply of, 326, 1089
Education & training. Future pattern, 327
Family pension benefits, 1089
for further education, 113
in higher education (Robbins), 564
Pensions for widows etc., 1089
Qualified & temporary, 112, 114, 564, 566, 1088
Remuneration. See Remuneration
Salaries, 113–4, 565–6, 1089, 1090
Scotland:
and Education Authorities, 401
Appointment to Education Committees, 400
Education, training & certification, 182, 400, 911
Entry requirements, 1174
Further education, 1172
Salaries Regulations, 645
Superannuation scheme. Actuary report, 400
Supply, 401
Widows etc. pensions, 401
Superannuation Act(s): 1041
Bill, 975, 1013
Government Actuary:
Reports, 205, 427
Tables (Allocation of pension), 1091
Training:
and supply. National Advisory Council reports, 113, 326, 327, 1089
courses (Establishments), 113, 327, 565, 821, 1089
Grants, 112, 114, 326, 328, 1088
Teaching:
Careers booklet, 1147
classics, 183.
commercial subjects, 402
Council (Scotland) Act, 1041
Bill, 969, 1007, 1010, 1133
gaelic, 402
in an art museum, 218
machines & use in industry, 641.
methods. University, 676, 822
modern languages, 402
music, 183
profession. Scotland, 646
Russian, 328
service in Commonwealth etc., 820

Teaching (*continued*):
staff. Training colleges, Salaries, 565
Women &, 566
TEBBLE, N., Pelagic polychaetes, 312
Technical:
assistance:
for:
British Guiana/U.S.A.*, 845
development of natural resources, 889
overseas:
geology & mining, 889
development, 103
Sub-committees. Estimates Committee, 1135
from Britain in agriculture etc., 889
United Nations*, 844
Broadsheet. Scotland, 399
Bulletin. Agriculture, 81, 87, 534, 790, 1061
colleges:
General studies, 327
management studies, 327
Co-operation:
Department of:
Act, 67
Bill, 4, 40
Estimates Committee, 860, 1135
Progress Report, 410
Publications, 188, 409–10, 651–2
See also Overseas Development. Ministry of,
under Colombo Plan, 188, 410, 652, 889, 1159
drawing. Examination Bulletin, 1089
education. *See* Education
Memorandum Health Dept. Scotland, 131
Techniques of examining. (Certificate of Secondary Education), 822.
Technology. Ministry of, Publications, 1178–81
Tees:
Conservancy Act, 775
Hydrological Survey, 144
Water Pollution, 181
Teeside:
County borough:
Local Government Commission, 1141
Proposed new map, 605
Railless Traction Board (Additional Route) Order Confirmation Act, 70
Bill, 5, 41
Telegraph Act, 288
Bill, 225, 261, 360
Telephone:
installations. Flats, 865
service:
Hospitals, 1125
in an expanding economy, 629
Inland, 629
Television:
Acts: 517, 773
Bills, 264, 453, 455, 483, 489, 490, 598, 697, 742, 863
I.T.A. Payments by contractors, 1163
broadcasting services in Britain, 871
broadcasts. Protection*, 125, 346, 1030, 1118
future of, (Pilkington), 384
Higher Education Service Bill, 40
or broadcasting service. (Prohibition of Control by Newspaper Proprietor) Bill, 39
Programme exchanges*, 125
servicing (Careers), 874
sets. Hiring. Licence, 661, 926
Temperance polls. Return of voting areas. Scotland, 406
Temperature(s):
and humidities near cloud, 885
anomalies. Europe & Siberia, 378
averages, 1931–60, 620
Earth, Variation, 378
inversions over Atlantic, 163
measuring instruments. Calibration, 907
over Northern Hemisphere, 885
Sea surface, Variations, 162
Standards of measurement, 397
Temple Manor, Strood. Guide, 389
Temporary:
buildings of pole construction, 86
speed limits. Orders, 667, 933, 1199, 1223
Tenancy of Shops (Scotland) Act, 773
Bill, 702, 721, 736, 742, 860
TENBY, RT. HON. VISCOUNT (Chairman):
Award of costs at Statutory Inquiries, 882
Third parties at Appeal Inquiries, 278
Tendering. Selective, for local authorities, 1167
TENNANT, SIR M. (Chairman), Scientific civil service, 1205
Terebratelloida. Cretaceous, 1068
Termite(s):
and protection of timber, 1180
infestation of pines, 1159
subfamily nasutitermitinae, 1067
Terracotta figures, 540
Terrestrial acari, 313
Territorial:
and Auxiliary Forces Association, 442, 515, 1091
Army. Regulations, 220, 441, 691–2, 811, 1080–1
Sea Convention, 1118
Waters. OIC, 856
Tertiary volcanic districts. Scotland, 129
Testamentary dispositions. Convention, 330, 844

Testing memorandum (Ministry of Power), 173
Testing of:
sight & supply or repair of glasses. Fees & charges, 134, 354, 593, 853, 1126, 1127
structural timbers, poles etc., 639

Thailand:
Air services*, 125
Exports. Colombo Plan*, 583
Official publications*, 583
Thalidomide. Deformities, 854
Thallophyta. Pteridophyta, 95
Thames:
Effects of polluting discharges, 1181
Pollution of tidal, 145
Thatcheria, 541
Theological Colleges etc. Loans. Measure, 775, 799
Therapeutic substances of human origin*, 844, 1118
Thermal:
conductivity meters, 79
insulation of factory buildings, 395
Thermoplastic binders. Flooring, 637
Thinnings. Felling by hand, 586
Third:
Reich. First phase, 331
London Airport. Inter-departmental Committee, 792
Thistles & their control, 81, 300, 1051
THOMAS, D. B.:
First negatives, 1170
origins of the motion picture, 903
THOMAS, D. V.:
Danjon astrolabe, 1169
Photographic Zenith Tube instrument, 903
THOMAS, H. J., Food of Norway lobster, 299
THOMAS, P. H.:
Flow of hot gases in roof venting, 639
Roof venting systems 905
THOMPSON D., Arbor Low, 633
THOMPSON, M. W., Farnham Castle, 221
THOMPSON, P. D., Full-scale road experiments, 908
THOMSON, J., Electronics, 692
Thomson's gazelle, 101
THOROLD, SIR G. (Chairman), Remuneration of milk distributors, 305
Three:
colour photometry, 176, 636
parameter numerical forecasts, 378
Thunderstorms of 1958. Analysis, 377
THURLEY, K. E., The supervisor & his job, 641

TICKELL, W. L. N., Dove Prion, 318
Ticket Touting Bill, 39
TILL, W. M., Steatonyssus Kolenati, 797
Timber(s):
beetles. Australasian, 543
floors. Design, 394
Home-grown:
Douglas fir, 905
Scots pine, 1180
Impregnating, 906
Lyctus-infested, 395
Moisture content, 905
Movement of, 1180
Preservative treatment, 395
Protection of, & termites, 1180
Quality. Production. Pruning Conifers, 586
Round, from farm, 304
Sawn, Air-seasoning, 906
Sitka spruce. Properties, 395
sizes for small buildings, 389
Strength properties, 179
Structural:
Testing, 639
Working stresses, 179, 1179
Termites & protection of, 1180
Timberwork. Repair & preservation of historic buildings, 1167
Time:
and latitude service, 636, 902, 903, 1169
rates of wages & hours of work, 159, 375, 618, 881, 1153
service, 176, 177, 393
Timekeepers. Clocks etc., 904
TIMOTHY, J. E., Bill, 39
Tin. International agreements, 125, 346
Tinkinswood & St. Lythans Long Cairns. Guide, 900
Tintern Abbey. Guide, 900
Tipulidae from Tibet etc., 796
TISDALL, P. A. Inquiry into case of, 857
Tit. Crested, 1121
TITE, G. E., Candalides, 796
Tithe:
Act Accounts, 163, 379, 622, 886, 1157
Changes of ownership of land Rules. Notice, 410
Redemption Committee, 410
Titles (Abolition) Bill, 741
Titmice in woodlands, 349

Tobago. *See* Trinidad
TODD, LORD (formerly SIR A.) (Chairman), Advisory Council on scientific policy, 376, 904
TODD, J. C., Black currant varieties, 534
Tomatoes:
Agricultural Bulletin, 302
Damping-off & foot rot, 1053
Liquid feeding, 530
Outdoor, 300, 1052
Tonal system of Northern Rhodesia Plateau Tonga, 317

Tonga:
Instructions OIC, 174
Report, 100, 548, 1074
Royal Instructions OIC, 1166
Treaty of Friendship. Amendment*, 844
Tonnage:
certificates of merchant ships*, 340
measurement of sea fishing boats, 665
TOOTH, G. C., Leucotomy, 134
Top fruit in garden, 301
Topographical surveying. Textbook, 1081
Torbay. Proposed new county borough, 604
Tornado at Malta, 620
Torre de Londres, La, 390
Torre di Londra. La, 634
Torry kiln operator's handbook, 643
Torry Research Station, 181, 398, 643, 908, 1181
Tourism in:
Scotland, 399, 1007, 1131
Wales & Monmouthshire, 483, 597
Tourist development proposals. Circular, 399
Tower Colliery. Explosion report, 385
Tower of London:
guides:
English edn., 222
French edn., 390
German edn., 222
Italian edn., 634
postcard, 390
Tower zu London, 222
Town & Country Planning:
Acts (incl. Scotland): 288, 517
Accounts, 146, 364, 607, 869, 1142
Bills, 227, 229, 263, 360, 450, 483, 488, 598
Circulars, 143, 361, 601 602 1138
Development plan maps, 868
Explanatory memo, 607
No. 2 Bill, 489
Tables of comparison, 607
Amendment Bill, 1009
Control of advertisements, 361
Development plans. Direction, 1139, 1223
Grants. Regulations, 864
Greater London Development Order, 1138
in Britain, 365
Inquiries procedure. Rules, 361, 1138
Land Values Bill, 742
Minerals Regulations, 602
National Coal Board Regulations, 601, 607
Planning Payments (War Damage) Schemes Account, 146, 1142
Use Classes Order, 1138
Town Centres:
Approach to renewal, 361, 363
Current practice, 607
Town Centres (*continued*):
Parking in. Circular, 1138, 1141
Redevelopment, 607
TOWNROW, J. A., Pteruchus, 311
Towyn Trewan Common Act, 517
Bill, 233, 263
Toxic:
chemicals, 87, 782, 1050
substances in air. Methods for detection, 159, 374, 610, 1152
Toxicity testing methods, 1059

Trachoma & allied infections, 1154
Tractor ploughing, 305
Trade:
and:
commerce. Denmark*, 117
development. U.N. Conference, 929
industries. Mission to Iraq, 194
navigation. Accounts, 194, 416, 463, 663–4, 716, 929, 1196
payments. Paraguay*, 122, 342
Annual Statement of, 105, 321, 552, 807, 1077
Board of:
Business Monitor. Production series, 191–4, 410–1, 652–9, 916–24, 1182–90
Journal, 191, 414–5, 661–2, 927–8, 1192–3
Publications, 188–96, 410–7, 652–65, 916–30, 1181–98
Disputes Act, 1041
Bill, 970, 972, 973, 974, 1007, 1009, 1012, 1133
Facilities Acts. Accounts, 205, 427
Import & export, 105, 321, 552, 807, 1077
marks*, 583
Union(s):
Amalgamation etc. Act, 773
Bill, 701, 741
and Employers' Association. Royal Commission, 1168
Chief Registrar of Friendly Societies. Report, 128, 350, 588, 848, 1122
Commission No. 2 Bill, 745
with:
Commonwealth & foreign countries. Annual Statement, 105, 321, 552, 807, 1077
Iraq Mission, 194
Trading:
accounts & balance sheets, 115, 458, 567, 823, 1091
Retail Hours, 1130
Stamps Act, 773
Bill, 703, 706, 707, 736, 741, 743, 745, 860
with the enemy (Yugoslavia) Order, 416

Traffic:
cases, 199, 421, 670, 935, 1196
census. First five years, 598
Commissioners. Annual report, 199, 420, 669, 934, 1200
in towns, 670
Circular, 864
safety code for road works, 419, 421, 667
signals:
for high-speed roads, 1200
Saturation flow. Measurement, 908
signs:
Directions, 406, 420
for:
all-purpose roads, 670
motorways, 421
Manual, 1200
New, 1199
Push button control, 420
Speed limits, 406, 420
See also Road signs
See also Road traffic
Training:
the adult worker, 906
colleges. Salaries of staff, 565
health visitors. Council report, 1091
How research can help, 907
in public administration. Overseas, 651
Justices of Peace, 1154
part-time youth leaders, 328
Physical, Army, 440, 691, 810
school for nurses, 133, 592
staff of centres for mentally sub-normal, 352
teachers. *See* Teachers, Training
Transfer from primary to secondary education:
Circular, 400
Report, 183
Transhipment. Open General Licence, 664, 1196
Transmutation of species, 94
Transport:
Act(s): 288
Bill, 38, 42, 228, 230, 244, 256, 262, 263
Loans, 205–6, 427, 670, 675–6, 932, 941 2, 1091, 1206–7
Aircraft. Estimates Committee, 860, 862
Dept. of, Canada, Meteorology Branch, 112, 417
Holding Company:
Annual report 726, 1200
Loans, 675, 942, 1091–2, 1207
Hospital, 132, 591, 592, 851
in Wales & Monmouthshire, 598
Ministry of:
Circulars, 665
Examinations, 196, 418, 665–6, 931–2
Memoranda, 197, 419, 421, 667
Transport (*continued*):
Ministry of (*continued*):
Publications, 196–200, 418–22, 665–70, 931–6, 1198–201
Statistical papers, 670, 935
needs in next 20 years, 670
services in highlands & islands, 670
Tribunal:
British Transport Commission (Passenger) Charges, 199, 421
London fares, 666, 935, 1200–1
Users Consultative Committee. Annual reports, 200, 421, 670, 936, 1201
Welsh Grand Committee, 236, 483, 598
Travel:
Agencies (Registration) Bills, 488, 741
Agents Bill, 1008
arrangements:
France*, 118
Monaco*, 122
Switzerland*, 125, 583
by young persons*, 346
Concessions Act, 773
Bill, 709, 745
Factors affecting amount, 181
performance, 80
Travellers by sea, 380
Travelling allowances to members of local authorities, etc., 363
Travers' Foundation. *See* Greenwich hospital
Treasure of the Oxus, 795
Treasury:
Books. Calendar, 175, 390
Control of Establishments, 862
Minutes, 202–3, 427, 672, 676, 938, 942, 1207
Fiduciary Note Issue, 203, 250, 424, 427, 485, 672–3, 712, 713, 938, 1203
publications, 200–6, 422–8, 671–6, 936–42, 1201–7
Treatment of:
derelict land, 602
offenders:
Advisory Council reports, 595
Court Handbook, 857
Non-residential under 21, 357
Reference Pamphlet, 871
Scottish Advisory Council, 184
Treaty Series:
Index, 125, 268, 344, 584, 844, 1110
ratifications, 123, 344, 581–2, 836, 842, 1116
See also under specific country, organisation or subject
Trees:
in:
Greenwich Park, 899
Hampton Court & Bushy Parks, 634
Richmond Park, 390
Wind-loosening of young, 596

TREMEWAN, W. G., Zygena Fabrics Sepidoptera, 94
TREMLOW, J. A., Papal letters, 174
TREND, SIR B. (Chairman), Civil science, 637
TRG Information Series & Reports (UKAEA.), 218, 438, 686-8, 955-7, 1220-1
Trial:
 plantations. Use of flags, 586
 plates, 636
Tribe Microgasterini, 1067
Tribunals:
 Council on, 160, 278, 376, 619, 882, 1153
 of Inquiry:
 Evidence Act. Vassall Case, 596
 Repeal Bill, 1010
Trichloroethylene. Detection, 1152
Trichoptera, 310, 796
Trilobites:
 Dechenellid, 1068
 of Caradoc series, 311
Trinidad (and Tobago):
 Arms, 547
 becomes a sovereign nation, 365
 Flag, 549
 Independence:
 Act, 288
 Bill, 230, 263
 Conference, 319
 Instructions OIC, 174
 International rights & obligations*, 552
 Loans, 202
 Making of a nation. Reference Pamphlet, 366
 Photoposter, 365
 Public officers*, 103
 Report, 100
Trinity Peninsula:
 Glaciology, 794
 Magnetic survey, 318
Trionychidae, 312
Trisopterus esmarkii, 1050
Trolley vehicles. Memorandum, 200
TRON, A. R., Natural graphite, 909
Trooping. Estimates Committee report, 246, 359
Tropical:
 Building Studies, 399, 638
 Health Hints, 410
 Products Institute, 180, 398, 643, 909, 1160
 Science, 181, 398, 643, 909, 1160
Trout:
 Brown, 528, 782
 Leaping behaviour, 299
 loch, 80
 See also Salmon & Trout
Trucial States notices, 125, 346, 584, 844, 1118
Trucks Acts. Committee, 159

Trustee Investments Act, 68
 Bill, 6, 7, 35, 40, 139
 Circular, 143
Trustee Savings Bank:
 Accounts & reports, 206, 427, 676, 942, 1207
 Act, 773
 Bill, 456, 741
Trusts (Scotland) Act, 68
 Bill, 6, 35, 39, 139
Tuberculosis case finding. Scotland, 131
TUCK, L. M., Murres, 112
TUCKER, G. B., Upper winds over the world, 161
Tulip(s):
 Eelworm, 301
 fire, 1053
TUNBRIDGE, R. E. (Chairman), Hospital medical records, 1125
Tunga Caecigena, 311
Tunisia. Abolition of vias*, 584
Tunnels. Road, 1200
Turbulence measurements with hot wire anemometers, 641
Turkey:
 British visitors' passport*, 125, 346
 Commercial debts*, 1119
 Financial arrangements*, 125, 346, 508, 584, 844, 1118-9
 Loan*, 844
 Social Insurance Convention, 346
 Visa Abolition*, 346, 584
Turkey(s):
 breeding, 302
 Diseases, 530
 Feeding, 784
 Rearing, 784
Turkish miniatures, 540
Turks & Caicos Islands:
 Instructions OIC, 389, 1166
 Reports, 317, 548
TURNER, D. H., Early Gothic illuminated Mss., 1066
Turnip(s):
 and swedes, 301
 Gall weevil, 1052
Turnover taxation. Report of Committee, 872
Tutbury Priory. Cartulary, 354
Twitch or couch, 81, 300, 783
TYLDESLEY, J. B., Atmospheric diffusion equations, 1156
TYLER, SIR L. (Chairman), Hospital engineers, 354
Tylopsis fieber, 797
Tyne. River, Hydrographical survey, 303
Tynemouth. Proposed Tyneside borough including Map, 605

Tyneside:
 Proposed borough. Maps, 605
 Special review area, 604, 1142
Typewriters. History & development, 903
Typewriting proficiency tests, 202, 423, 672, 676
Typhoid. Fowl, 1051
Typists. Civil Service. Manual, 425
Tyres & wheels. Warning poster, 1153

U

Uganda:
 Act, 773
 Bill, 700, 742
 Arms, 547
 becomes a sovereign nation. Photoposter, 365
 Commission report Dispute, 319
 Constitutional Conference, 103
 Flag, 549
 Independence:
 Act, 288
 Bill, 231, 263
 Conference, 319
 Instructions OIC, 174, 388
 Loan, 202
 Making of a nation, 366
 Marketing of minor crops, 651
 Photoposter, 365
 Picture set, 365
 Public officers*, 651
 Reports, 101, 548
 Roads & transport, 409
Ugyops from S. America, 796

U.K. See United Kingdom
U.K.A.E.A. See United Kingdom Atomic Energy Authority

Ultimus Haeres Scotland account etc., 185, 407, 648, 914, 1175

Umbrella(s):
 and umbrella parts. Merchandise Marks, 928
 handles. Standing Committee, 416

Underground:
 explosions. Detection, 1218
 workmen. Coal mines. Books, 387
Undersea photography in marine research, 528
Undertakings of Secretary for Scotland, 300, 529, 1051
 See also Draft Undertakings

Unemployability Supplement. National Insurance, 168
Unemployment:
 benefit. Decisions, 166-7, 382-3, 625-6, 891-2, 1161
 insurance. Germany, 340
UNESCO. See United Nations Educational, Scientific & Cultural Organisation
Union of Soviet Socialist Republics. See Soviet Union
Unit drills for seeds, 1059
United:
 Arab Republic:
 Exchanges of professors etc.*, 347, 1119
 Financial & commercial relations etc.*, 281, 347
 Kingdom:
 Altimeter Committee report, 1064
 Atomic Energy Authority:
 Annual report, 206, 247, 688, 957, 1221
 Illustrated summary, 213, 434, 682, 953, 1218
 Balance sheet & accounts, 115, 245, 567, 823, 1218
 Documents guide, 683
 Publications, 206-18, 428-38, 676-88, 942-57, 1207-21
 Cumulations, 215, 435, 688, 957, 1219
 See also A.E.R.E. etc.
 Balance of payments, 206, 427, 545, 799, 1071
 Civil Series. History of War, 313, 798
 Constitution, 148
 Dependencies:
 Agriculture, 148
 in brief, 148
 Industrial development, 148
 Political advance, 147
 Economy. Growth of, 623
 Fire Statistics, 181, 639, 905, 1179
 Information Agency. Yugoslavia*, 348
 Medical Series, 353
 Military Series, 95-6, 313, 798, 1070
 See also specific subjects
 Nations:
 Charter. Resolutions to amend, 1119
 General Assembly. Proceedings, 126, 347, 585, 845, 1119
 Medal, 812
 Provision of personnel:
 Northern Rhodesia & Nyasaland*, 845
 Overseas territories of U.K.*, 585
 Technical Assistance Board, 844
 Trade & development Conference, 929

United (continued):
 Nations Educational, Scientific & Cultural Organisation:
 Constitution, 117, 1119
 Discrimination in education. Convention, 331, 347
 Exchange of official publications. Convention, 340
 General Conference, 114
 States of America:
 Air routes. West Indies*, 347
 Ascension Island*, 347, 1120
 Atomic energy*, 568, 584, 845, 1119, 1120
 Bahama Islands. Test Centre*, 585
 Bermuda. Tracking Station*, 126, 515
 Betio Island. Weather Station*, 347
 British Guiana, Technical assistance*, 845
 Bureau of:
 Customs, 689
 Naval personnel, 957
 Canton Island. Tracking Station*, 126, 515
 Cereals*, 824
 Congress. Publications, 957
 Defence Areas. West Indies, 100
 Department of:
 Agriculture, 957
 Commerce, 688
 Defence, 957
 Health, Education & Welfare, 688, 958
 Interior, 958
 Labour, 958
 Navy, 957
 State, 688
 Treasury, 689
 Educational & cultural exchange programmes*, 1120
 Exporting to, 689
 Exports, Committee, 1075
 Federal Aviation Agency, 567, 823
 Government Printing Office, 688, 958
 Library of Congress, 689
 Marketing in, 1075
 Marshall Aid Commission. See Marshall Aid
 Mutual Defence Programme equipment, 236, 347(*), 563, 585(*), 818, 1021
 National Aeronautics & Space Administration*, 1120
 Navy. Diving manual, 957
 North Borneo. Peace Corps*, 585
 Polaris sales. U.K.*, 581, 584
 St. Lucia. Beane Field*, 845
 Sarawak Peace Corps*, 584
 Satellite testing*, 126

United (continued):
 States of America (continued):
 "Savanah" visits*, 845
 Space research co-operation*, 126
 Statistical abstract, 688
 travellers to, Health information, 688
 Treasury Department, 689
 United Kingdom:
 Missile defence alarm system*, 126
 Tracking Station*, 126
 Weapons production programme*, 347
 West Indies:
 Air routes*, 347
 Defence area*, 100
 Zanzibar. Tracking Station*, 126
Units:
 and standards of measurements. N.P.L., 397, 907
 of measurement. Air/ground communications, 792
Universal:
 Postal Union, 126
 resistance diagram, 181
University(ies):
 admission. Diplomas. Convention, 1095
 and Colleges:
 Estates Act, 773
 Bill, 704, 736, 741, 860
 Grants, 1133, 1135
 Remuneration of staff, 887
 Returns 206, 428, 676, 822, 1091
 Appointment Boards, 822
 awards, 112, 114, 326, 328, 564, 566, 820
 Cambridge, & Agricultural Research Council. Publication, 439
 Development, 328, 942
 Durham & Newcastle. Act, 519
 Graduates. First employment, 676, 1091
 Grants:
 Committee:
 Annual survey, 1018, 1091
 Publications, 206, 328, 354, 428, 676, 822, 942, 1091
 Estimates Committee, 1133, 1135
 Keele Act, 290
 Leeds Act, 290
 Non-recurrent grants, 1091
 qualifications. European Convention, 347
 St. Andrews Scheme, 183
 Scotland Bill, 1002, 1008, 1013
 Sussex Act, 290
 Teaching methods, 676, 822
Unsealed radioactive substances. Regulations, 153

Upper:
 Silesia etc. Documents on British Foreign Policy, 117
 winds over world, 161
Ur excavations, 310, 795, 1067
Uruguay. Visas*, 126, 348, 585
Uranium & thorium. Determination, 641
Urban:
 sewer systems. Design, 398
 traffic engineering, 1201
Urquhart Castle. Guide, 900

U.S.A. See United States of America
Use of, See specific subjects
U.S.S.R. See Soviet Union
Usual residence tables. Census:
 England & Wales, 849
 Scotland, 1123
Usutu Basin. Soil etc., 1159

Utensils. Etruscan, 1066

V

Vacations by students. Use of, 676
Vaccination against smallpox, 353
Vaccine:
 Anti-swine fever, Phillipines, 1203
 Salk poliomyelitis, 676, 942
VAILLANT, F., Psychodidae, 1068
Vale of Leven Hospital, 647
Valuation:
 for rating, 602
 lists:
 New, 362
 Rules, 362
VAN SOEST, J. L., Taraxacum, 93
VAN SOMEREN, V.:
 African chamaes, 541, 796
 East African oyster, 318
VANSCHUYTBROECK, P. Celyphidae, 1068
Variable pitch propeller. Log book, 92
Variables. Observations on twenty-four single-lined, 392
Variation(s):
 in trachlid length, 639
 of difference. Earth temperatures, 378
Vascular flora, 794
Vassall Case:
 Committee of inquiry, 284
 Minutes of evidence at public hearings, 596
 Tribunal report, 596

Vegetable(s):
 diseases, 83
 oils & oilseeds production (Commonwealth), 104, 319, 551, 804, 1075
 See also Fruit & vegetables
Vegetation on roads & airfields, 181, 642
Vehicle(s):
 counter. Using, 642
 Excise Act, 288
 Bill, 225, 226, 261, 360
 or appliance long sheets & record book, 358
 rear lights. U.K. & Italy*, 341
 taxation. Convention, 582
 testing. Testers' manual, 664, 669
Ventilated silo grain driers, 85
Ventilation. Building Standards Regulations (Scotland), 910
VERDON-SMITH, SIR W. R. (Chairman), Fattstock etc. Marketing & distribution, 787
Vermetidae, 1068
VERNON, P. E., Certificate of Secondary Education, 822
Veroli casket, 439
Vestures of Ministers Measure, 800
Veterinary:
 profession. Recruitment for, 789, 856
 science (Careers), 369, 875
 Surgeons Bill, 975

Victoria:
 and Albert Museum:
 Bulletin, 1221
 One hundred things to see, 439
 Publications, 218, 439, 689, 959, 1221-2
 Hospital. Kirkcaldy, 1174
Victorian:
 furniture, 689
 paintings, 689
Victory:
 Bonds, 187, 408, 915
 in the West, 313
Vietnam:
 Attempts at settlement, 1120
 Exchange of official publications*, 347
 Supervision & control, 126, 348, 1120
Village schools (Building), 112
Violets, 300
Virement between Service depts. Votes, 139, 359, 599, 861, 1134
Virgin Islands. British. See British Virgin Islands
Virus:
 diseases:
 Potatoes, 1051
 Strawberry, 1053
 yellows of sugar beet, 1052
Visas*. See respective countries

Visiting patients in hospital, 406
Vitamin A etc. in:
  elasmobranchs, 783
  herring, 528

Vocational courses in colleges & schools of art, 328
Vole. Water, 82
Voluntary:
  bodies. Contributions, 865
  service. Guide, 939
Vote on Account, 206, 428, 466, 942, 1207
Voting arrangements for sick members, 1134

W

Wages:
  cost & prices in printing industry, 1156
  Councils Act. Commission of inquiry, 159, 618, 881
Wakefield. Proposed borough. Map, 867
Waldegrave, Earl (Chairman):
  Forest research, 1122
  Horticultural co-operative marketing, 85
Wales (and Monmouthshire):
  1964, 1223
  Agriculture in, 255, 1006, 1131
  Ancient & Historical Monuments, 902
  Broadcasting, 358
  Census:
    Population etc. 588
    Welsh-speaking population, 351
  Command Paper, 1223
  Constitutional changes, 740, 1131
  Council for, 281, 495, 513
  De-population in Mid-, 865
  Development & de-population in Mid-, 1007, 1131
  Development & government action, 34, 138, 146, 358, 364, 607, 869
  Difference in coalfield, 1152
  Education. *See* Education
  Geology. North, 129
  Iron ore:
    imports into South, 1223
    ports, 1007, 1131
  Local Government Commission, 605–6
  Regional development, 736, 858
  Rural:
    development, 736, 858
    transport, 281
  Tourism, 597
  Transport, 598
Walker, Hon. Lord (Chairman), Law Reform Committee, 619, 882
Walker, A. L., Maternal deaths, 593
Walker, F., Aphids, 95
Walker, K. J. S., Sawmill study, 639
Walker, N. D. (Chairman), Degrees of mental handicap, 182
Walker, R. J. B., Audley End. Pictures. Catalogue, 900
Wallace, T., Mineral deficiencies in plants, 298
Wallasey Corporation Act, 290
Wallington, C. E.:
  Numerical forecasts at Dunstable, 378
  Verification of forecast charts, 163
Wallpaper. Monopolies Commission, 928
Walls:
  Painting, 1178
  Strength of, 1178
Wallsheet. Commonwealth, 871
Walsall. Proposed county borough, 144
Walmer Castle. Guide, 633
Walton & Weybridge Urban District Council Act, 1042
War(s):
  against:
    crime, 857
    Japan, 96, 313, 1070
  at sea, 96
  cemeteries etc. Indonesia*, 578
  Damage:
    Acts, 773, 1041
      Bills, 700, 741, 746, 966, 968, 970, 1007, 1011, 1133
    Business & Private Chattels Schemes. Accounts, 194, 676, 689, 1222
    Commission publications, 218, 689–90, 1222
    Land & Buildings. Accounts, 218, 689, 690, 1222
    Payments. Final settlement, 66
    San Marino. Payments*, 123
  Department. Schedule of prices for Works services, 221, 634, 901, 1168
  graves. Netherlands*, 580, 839
  histories, 95–6, 313, 353, 798, 1070
  not yet won, 147
  Office:
    Estimates Committee, 249, 360
    Publications, 218–21, 439–42, 690–2
    Purchasing (Repayment) Services. Account, 221, 442, 692, 812, 1081
    Supply. Appropriation account, 221
    See also Army Dept.
  Pensioners. Report, 134, 248, 593, 894, 1162
  Pensions Committees. Orders, 894, 1162
  Years 1940–1. Documents. German Foreign Policy, 117, 331, 826
Warble fly, 784
Ward, A. G. (Chairman), Fish & meat pastes, 1059
Ward, F. A. B.:
  Atom physics. Handbook, 637
  Timekeepers, 904

Ward, F. J. (Chairman), Local authority housing, 869
Ward, H. C. D., Romances. B.M. Catalogue, 309
Ward, R. G., Land use & population in Fiji, 1159
Ward:
  design. Hospitals, 647, 1174
  units. Hospitals, 133, 592
Warden Section. Civil Defence, 356, 594, 855
Warehouses. Bonded, 106, 321, 552, 808, 1078
Warehousing Manual, 106, 552, 553, 807, 1078
Warren, Chief Justice (Chairman), Assassination of President Kennedy, 958
Warren Spring Laboratory, 180, 399, 643, 909, 1181
Warwickshire. Census:
  Leaflet. Population etc., 589
  Report, 588
Wasps, 82, 313
Watch straps. Merchandise Marks, 663
Water:
  and steam. Physical properties, 906
  Application, to machine undercutting, 171
  Byelaws, Model 606
  charges, 362, 601
  Cold, Services, 1139
  conservation, 364
  Drinking, Radioactivity, 607, 868, 1141
  Growing demand for, 361
  officers compensation Regulations, 864, 1174
  pollution:
    abstracts, 181, 399, 643–4, 909, 1181
    by tipped refuse, 146
    Research Laboratory publications, 181, 399, 644, 909, 1181
  Resources:
    Act, 517
      Bill, 232, 233, 448, 449, 454, 483, 488, 490, 598
      River Authorities Compensation Regulations, 1138
    Board. Annual report, 869, 1001
    in North-West, 602
    Licences Regulations, 1139, 1222
    of Wales, 35, 146
  safety:
    campaign. National, 1139
    code, 393
  service. Central Scotland, 644
  sterilization (Fisheries), 85
  supplies, Domestic, in N. America, 851
  vole, 82
  waste etc. Model Byelaws, 602
  weeds, 302
Waterfowl identification guide, 958
Waterhouse, D. B., Harunobu & his age, 795
Watering:
  Capillary, of plants, 1059
  equipment for crops under glass, 1059
Waterloo despatch, 1222
Watertight basement, 221
Waterways:
  Facts about, 1070
  Future of, 798
Watford Corporation Act, 519
Watkins, L. H., Design of urban sewer systems, 398
Watson, A., Drepamidae, 94, 1067
Watson, J. H., Ancient trial plates, 636
Watson, John, Trust Scheme, 182, 400
Watson, W., Early Chinese antiquities, 795
Watts, Sir H. E. (Chairman), Carriage of dangerous goods, 418
Wayman, P. A.:
  Hyades stars, 1169
  Southern stars, 176, 393

Wealden district. Geology, 1124
Weapons:
  Design & development of, 798
  Production Programme U.S.A.*, 347
Wear & Tees Hydrological survey, 144
Weather:
  and the builder, 221
  Farmers, 1054
  in:
    Black Sea, 622
    Home Fleet Waters, 886, 1156
    Mediterranean, 379, 886
  maps. Preparation, 161, 1155
  messages. Handbook, 161, 377, 621, 884, 1155
  prediction, 378
  Report. Monthly, 162, 378, 621–2, 885, 1156
  Station on Betio Island*, 347
  ways, 417
  work, 112
Weaver, O. J., Boscobel House & White Ladies Priory, 1166
Webster, Sir C., Strategic air offensive, 96
Webster, F. V., Traffic signals, 1200
Webster & Davidson Mortification for Blind Scheme, 401, 646
Wedding of Princess Alexandra. Souvenir programme, 611
Wedgwood Benn, A. N., Committee of Privileges, 139
Weed(s):
  Control:
    Chemical:
      carrots, parsnips & parsley, 301, 1053
      forests, 1122
      horticultural crops, 301, 1053
    in peas, 82, 1052

Weed(s) (*continued*):
  Knotgrass & allied, 82, 300
  Research Organisation, 1050
  Water, 302
Weevil(s):
  Apple blossom, 300, 1051
  Grain, 529
  Turnip gall, 1052
  Wingless, 529
Weights & measures:
  Act, 517
    Bill, 1, 2, 39, 260, 263, 449, 451, 453, 483, 488, 490, 598
    No. 2 Bill, 41
  Examination of pattern, 194–6, 416–7, 664–5, 929–30, 1196–8
  Inspector of, Examination, 1191
Welch, F. B. A., Geology of country around Monmouth, 130
Welder & cutter (Careers), 368
Welders. Health of, 371
Welfare:
  administration. Children's Bureau U.S.A., 958
  foods. S.I. Select Committee, 140
  Section. Home Office, 135, 137, 594
Welland & Nene rivers. Hydrological survey, 869
Wellington:
  Duke of:
    in caricature, 1221
    Official despatch. Waterloo, 1222
  Museum, 959, 1222
Wells, M. K., Freetown layered basic complex of Sierra Leone, 410
Wells & Cheddar. Geology, 1124
Welsh:
  Advisory Water Committee, 146
  holiday industry, 495
  language,:
    Legal status, 1008, 1223
    today:
      English edition, 513
      Welsh edition, 603
  Office:
    Circulars, 1222–3
    Provisional Order Confirmation (Llanelly) Act, 1042
      Bill, 970, 1011
    Publications, 1222
  Shipping Agency Act, 1042
  speaking population. Census, 351
  statistics. Digest of, 143, 362, 603, 866, 1223
Wemyss & March, Rt. Hon. Earl (Chairman), Royal Commission. Ancient & Historical Monuments. Scotland, 635
Wenlock Priory. Guide, 1167
Wentworth Estate Act, 775
Wernham, R. B., State papers in P.R.O., 901
West:
  Africa. Royal visit. Photoposter, 365
  Bromwich. Proposed county borough, 144
  Hartlepool C.B. & Hartlepool. M.B. Proposed county borough. Map, 605
  Indies:
    Act, 288
      Bill, 227, 261
    Air route U.S.A.*, 347
    Commonwealth cameo, 147
    Consitution:
      Conference, 103
      OIC, 173, 388
    Defence area U.S.A.*, 100
    Picture set, 365
  Kennett. Long Barrow:
    Excavations, 389
    Guide, 633
  Lothian. Census. Leaflet & report, 590
  Midlands:
    Regional study, 1088
    Review area, 144–5
    Special review area. Local Government Commission, 364
  Riding County Council (General Powers) Act, 775
  Suffolk. Census:
    Leaflet. Population etc., 589
    Report, 849
  Yorkshire. Special review area. Local Government Commission, 866
Western:
  and Central Europe. Documents, 570
  Asiatic seals. Catalogue, 310
  co-operation in brief, 366
  European Union, 585, 845
  hill farms. Shelterbelt, 586
  Nigeria. Public officers*, 651
  Samoa. Air services*, 89
Westmorland (and Cumberland):
  Census:
    Leaflet. Population etc., 589
    Report, 588
  Saxton map, 540

Whaling:
  Antarctic pelagic whaling, 281, 585, 838
  International Convention, 126, 1120
Whalley, P. E. S.:
  Endotricha Zeller, 541
  Pyraustinae, 94
What is:
  the Commonwealth?, 365
  Stonehenge?, 390, 634
Wheat:
  and barley eyespot, 1052
  bulb fly, 81
  International agreement, 348, 585, 1120
  Yellow rust, 784

Wheatley, Rt. Hon. Lord (Chairman), Teaching profession in Scotland, 646
Wheeler, J. F. G., Lethrinus, 101
Wheeler, M. M., Investigation into affairs of Freehold Land Finance Co., 925
White, C.:
  Drawings of Rembrandt, 310
  Foreign artists, drawings, 93
White, E.:
  Dipterus valenciennesi, 1068
  Sandstone of Brown Clee Hill area, 94
White:
  Castle. Guide, 390
  Fish:
    and Herring Industry Act, 68
      Bill, 3, 39
    Authority:
      Annual report & accounts, 87, 248, 534, 790, 1061
      Receipts & grants, 87, 305, 790, 1061
Whitefly. Glasshouse, 300, 1051
Whitehall plan, 1168
Whitehaven Harbour Act, 290
Whitehead, P. J. P.:
  Alosinae, 1069
  Elopoid & clupeoid fishes, 1069
  Herrings, 543
Whiteley, P., Painting in tropical climates, 399
Whiting fishery. Scottish, 528
Whittenbury, R., Changes in grain, 1049
Whitworth Fellowships & Exhibitions, 565
Why a Census?, 129

Wickstead, J. H., Indo-West Pacific plankton, 101
Wideawake Airfield U.S.A.*, 347
Widowed mother's allowance. Decisions, 166
Widows':
  Benefit. Decisions, 167, 382, 383, 626, 891, 892, 1161
  Pensions Bill, 264, 741
Wigtown, Census:
  Leaflet. Population etc., 590
  Report, 850
Wigtownshire Education Trust Scheme, 183
Wilberforce, Lord (Chairman), Positive covenants affecting land, 1154
Wilberforce. "Pioneer who served", 147
Wild:
  oats, 82, 784
  resources of Africa, 103
Wildfowl in Great Britain, 625
Wilkins, L. T., Delinquent generations, 137
Wilkinson, J. H., Rounding errors, 641
Williams, A., Caradecion brachiopod faunas, 542
Williams, D. J.:
  Lindingaspis & anaspis, 796
  Pseudococcidae, 311
Williams, R. M. C., Termite infestation of pines, 1159
Willink, Sir H. (Chairman), Royal Commission. Police, 175, 392
Willis, J. R.:
  Bognor Regis inquiry, 1142
  Licensing planning, 1130
Wills Act, 517
  Bill, 452, 454, 483, 487, 490, 598
Wilson, Sir A. (Chairman):
  Noise from motor vehicles, 394
  Problem of noise, 637
Wilson, D. M., Antiquities of later Saxon period. Catalogue, 794
Wilson, I. M. (Chairman), Ascertainment of maladjusted children, 911
Wilson, P. H. St. J. (Chairman), Cost of living, 369
Wilson, Sir R. (Chairman):
  Coal mining industry. Difference, 881
  Omnibus industry. Difference, 1152
Wilson, W. K., Modern rabbit-keeping, 785
Wilting for silage, 301, 530
Wiltshire:
  Census:
    Leaflet. Population etc., 589
    Report, 849
  Saxton map, 93
Winchester Cathedral Close. Act, 70
Wind:
  effect on buildings, 1180
  loosening of young trees, 586
  shear, 622
Winding enginemen etc. Books, 387
Windward Islands. *See* Leeward Islands
Wing, J. K., Rehabilitation of schizophrenic patients, 883
Wingless weevils, 529
Winn, Lord Justice (Chairman), Standing Security Commission, 1070
Winter:
  building:
    Circular, 1139, 1222
    Report, 634
  grass, 784
  moths, 81
  rye, 82
Wireworms, 783
Wiring. Socket outlet, 394
Wiseman, D. J.:
  Chronicles of Chaldaean kings, 310
  Western Asiastic seals, 310
Witnesses. Criminal Law Pension Committee, 856

Wolrige-Gordon, J. (Chairman), Midwifery services, 1175
Wolverhampton. Proposed county borough, 145
Women(s):
  and teaching. Nuffield survey, 566

Women(s) (continued):
  in Britain, 871
  migration, 551
  services (Careers), 368, 1147
Wood, M., Donnington Castle, 900
Wood, P. C., Water sterilisation, 85
Wood, R. F., Chalk downland afforestation,
  348
Wood:
  adhesives, 639, 905
  charcoal, 348
  preservatives, 179
Woodlands:
  Birds and, 846
  Dedicated & approved, 348
  Income tax etc. on, 846
  Rabbit control in, 1121
  Woodpeckers in, 1122
Woods, H. (Chairman):
  Foundry goggles, 881
  Paper mills. Safety, 881
  Steel foundries. Conditions in, 153
Woodsawyer & woodcutting machinist
  (Careers), 368
Woodward, Sir L., British foreign policy,
  313
Woodworking machinery for builders, 633
Wool:
  and wool textiles. World trade, 1076
  Industry Training Board, 1153
  textiles & carpets (Careers), 369
Woolf, H., Action of Metropolitan Police,
  857
Woolley, Sir L., Ur excavations, 310, 1067
Woolley, Sir R.:
  Double-star observations, 176, 903
  Globular clusters, 177, 393, 1169
  Magellanic clouds, 393, 635, 1169
  Radial velocity from Coude plates, 176,
  1169
  RR Lyrae variable stars, 1169
Woolly aphid, 81
Worboys, Sir W. (Chairman), Traffic
  signs, 670
Worcester Corporation Act, 775
Worcestershire. Census:
  Leaflet. Population etc., 589
  Report, 588
Work:
  and vocational training. Borstals, 596
  for prisoners, 137, 856
  grading etc. Hospital engineers, 354
  of Youth Employment Service, 375, 1153
Working:
  for prosperity, 1088
  of rate deficiency grants, 364
  paper. Schools Council, 1090
  stresses for:
    bridges, 197, 667
    timbers, 179, 1179

Workmen at mines & quarries. Books, 172,
  386-7
Workmen's Compensation:
  Acts. Memo, 381
  and Benefit (Amendment) Act, 1041
  Bill, 976, 1013
Works:
  department. Hospitals, 1125
  Ministry of:
    Advisory Leaflets, 221
    Guides, 221, 222
    Publications, 221-2
    See also Public Buildings & Works
  services. War Dept. Prices, 221, 634, 901,
  1168
Workshops for blind, 374
World(s):
  coffee, 652
  first aeroplane flights, 1170
  Health Organisation, 126, 1121(*)
  in space, 622
  Meteorological Organisation, 121, 839,
  1113(*)
  Security Agency Bill, 488
  trade in wool etc., 1076
Worssam, B. C., Geology of country around
  Maidstone, 640
Worthington, E. B.:
  Grey seals & fisheries, 624
  Wild resources of Africa, 103

Wreck reports, 200, 421-2, 670, 932-3, 1194
Wright, A. D., Fauna of Portrane lime-
  stone, 542, 797
Wright Brothers:
  Account of work, 637
  Memorial U.S.A., 958
Wright, C. A., Gastropod molluscs, 312,
  542, 543, 1069
Wright, J. H. (Chairman), Medical staffing
  structure. Scottish hospitals, 913
Wright, P. J. F., Strength of concrete, 908
Writers to Signet Widow's Fund Order
  Confirmation Act, 1042
  Bill, 1011

W.V.S. Civil Defence, 1938-63, 596

Wye:
  Basin. Hydrological survey, 1142
  Valley. Forest Park. Guide, 586, 846
Wynne-Edwards, R. M., (Chairman),
  Building Regulations, 900

X

X-ray departments. Hospitals, 133, 352, 353,
  591, 1125

Y

Yachts. Royal, 887
Yalin, M. S., Sediment transport, 1180
Yang Di-Pertuan Negera. Standard flag
  badge, 104
Yarmouth (Isle of Wight) Pier & Harbour
  Provisional Order Act, 518
  Bill, 453, 489
Yates, P. O., Cerebral Infarction, 161

Yellow rust of wheat, 784

Yield tables for Abies-Grandis, 127

York:
  and North Midlands. General Review
  area, 867, 1142
  City. Roman monuments, 391, 392
  County borough. Alteration of area.
  Map, 867
Yorkshire:
  East Riding. Census:
    Leaflet. Population etc., 589
    Report, 849
  North Riding. Census:
    Leaflet. Population etc., 589
    Report, 849
  Saxton map, 540
  West Riding. Census:
    Leaflet. Population etc., 589
    Report, 588
  West. Special Review Area. Local Gov-
  ernment Commission, 866
  Winding Engineers Association. Differ-
  ence, 881
Young, D. A., Cicadelline types, 1068
Young, F. G. (Chairman), Irradiation of
  food, 851
Young, H. W., Roman London, 376
Young:
  children in care. Needs of, 856
  chronic sick. Report, 913
  people. Employment & training, 158
  Persons (Employment) Act, 773
Younger, W. McE. (Chairman), Building &
  civil engineering procedure. Scotland, 901
Youth:
  club. Education. building, 564
  Employment Service:
    Future development, 1146
    Work of, 375, 1153
  leaders. Training, 328
  service buildings. Mixed clubs, 112

Yugoslavia:
  Aircraft passenger manifests*, 846
  British books & films*, 127, 348, 585,
  845, 1121

Yugoslavia (continued):
  Consular Convention, 1094
  Credit facilities*, 127
  Information Agency*, 348
  Money & property*, 348
  Visas*, 1121

Z

Z zones. Clearance of, 1128
Zambia:
  Cereals*, 1076
  Independence Act, 773
  Bill, 707, 744
  Photoposter, 870
  Public officers*, 889
  Reference Pamphlet, 871
  See also Northern Rhodesia
Zanzibar:
  Act, 517
  Bill, 456
  Agreement 1890 terminated,* 549
  becomes a sovereign nation. Photo-
  poster, 609
  Constitutional Conference, 319
  Disturbances, 103
  Independence Conference, 549
  Isle of Cloves, 871
  Kenya. Coastal strip, 549
  Land tenure in, 101
  Photoposter, 609
  Reference Pamphlet, 871
  Report, 548
  Space vehicle tracking station*, 126

Zedner, J., Hebrew printed books. Cata-
  logue, 795
Zetland:
  Census. Leaflet & report, 590
  County Council (Symbister Harbour)
  Confirmation Act, 70
  Bill, 39
  Educational Trust Scheme, 183, 1173
Zeuner, F. E., Fossil insects, 312

Zinc Corporation Act, 290

Zoology Bulletins, 94-5, 312, 542-3, 797,
  1068-9
Zuckerman, Sir S. (Chairman):
  Management & control of research &
  development, 177
  Natural resources. Agriculture, 177
  Scientific manpower, 160, 637

Zygaena Fabricius, Lepidoptera. Catalogue, 94

Consolidated Index to Government Publications 1966-1970

FOREWORD

Scope

This index, covering the period January 1966 to December 1970, includes all titles as listed in the five annual volumes of Government Publications, i.e. it does not include Statutory Instruments or publications of international organisations for which there are separate lists and indexes. Reprints at revised prices are not generally included.

Previous quinquennial indexes have been compiled from 1936 to 1965 but they are out of print.

Notes on Compilation

The first significant word as well as the most important word of the title has been indexed and cross-references have been made where helpful, except for Acts and Bills which are generally indexed under first word of the title only. 'Word-by-word' order has been followed. Personal names are in small capitals. Where there are joint-authors, only the first-named is indexed, but names of all chairmen are indexed. Titles listed in the catalogues in two or more places, mainly under "Parliamentary Publications" and "Classified List" Headings, are only indexed once under the latter page reference.

Pagination

The five annual volumes were paginated consecutively as follows:

1966	pp	1–272
1967	pp	273–604
1968	pp	605–990
1969	pp	991–1402
1970	pp	1403–1740

This information is repeated for convenience at the foot of each page of the index and the particular year of publication can thereby be identified.

Omissions

Individual titles within the following series are not indexed separately:

Boiler Explosion Inquiries
Business Monitor Series
Civil Aircraft Accidents
Civil Estimates
Civil Service Arbitration Tribunal
  Awards
Civil Service Commission
  Question Papers
Current Papers (Aeronautical
  Research Council)
Customs Forms
DEF Specifications (Defence)
Defence Guides and Lists
DTD Specifications (Aviation)

Electricity Boards Regional
  Reports
European Atomic Energy
  (EURATOM) Regulations
European Economic Community
  (EEC) Regulations
Factory Forms
Friendly Societies
  (Annual Return Forms)
FSH Circulars
Gas Boards Regional Reports
Honours Lists
IFR (Imported Food Regulations)
  Circulars

Omissions (continued)

Industrial Court Awards
Land Registry Forms
Meteorological Office Forms
Mines and Quarries Forms
National Insurance (Unemployed
  Benefit and Industrial Injuries)
  Commissioners' Decision
New Town and Development
  Corporation Reports
Profit Tax Leaflets
Public Health (Imported Foods)
  etc. Regulations
Queens Regulations and
  Admiralty Instructions

Railway Accident Reports
Reports and Memoranda
  (Aeronautical Research Council)
Royal Commissions. Evidence
Tax Case Leaflets
Trucial States Notices
United Kingdom Atomic Energy
  Authority Reports (AEEW etc)
Weights and Measures
  Examination of Patterns
Wreck Reports

Abbreviations

*	=	Exchange of Notes, Letters, Agreements etc.
B.M.	=	British Museum
CSE	=	Certificate of Secondary Education
E. and W.	=	England and Wales
GRO	=	General Register Office
H.C.	=	House of Commons
H.L.	=	House of Lords
LEA	=	Local Education Authority
N.I.	=	Northern Ireland
OIC	=	Order in Council
PRO	=	Public Record Office
S.I.	=	Statutory Instrument
UKAEA	=	United Kingdom Atomic Energy Authority

INDEX

A

AARON, L. R.: Drying and scaling pine billets, 1612

ABEL, A.: Nursing attachment to general practice, 1268
Aberdeen:
City, Aberdeen County, Banff, Kincardine, Moray, and Nairn:
census, 155
sample census, 469, 1261
Corporation Order Confirmation Bill, 1484
Extension Order Confirmation Act, 1517
(Fish Market) Order Confirmation Act, 1113
Marine Laboratory, 1520
see also City of Aberdeen
Aberdeenshire Educational Trust Scheme, 210
Aberfan:
technical reports, 1397
Tribunal's reports, 286
Aberlour:
Orphanage Trust (Amendment) Scheme, 533
Trust:
(Amendment) Scheme, 1679
Scheme, 926
Abortion:
Act, 367
Bill, 1, 2, 3, 4, 339
Law (Reform) Bill, 1479
(No. 2) Bill, 287
Supplement, Reg. Gen. 1665
see also Medical Termination of Pregnancy
Abrasive(s):
census of production, 567
Wheels Regulations, Inquiry, 1566
Abstracts see specific subjects

Acanthodrilidae, 723
Acari Cryptostigmata, 1127
Acaridae, 1539
Accessions to repositories, lists, 159, 473, 871, 1269, 1674
Accident(s):
and fire, at Esso Petroleum Co., 874
at:
factories etc., 179, 498, 746, 1148, 1564, 1627
Hixon Level Crossing, 963
Scunthorpe blast furnace, 874
drowning, and water safety, 1293
in construction industry, 498
to young motor cyclists, 863
see also Aircraft, Railway, etc.

Accommodation designed for old people, 1293
Account of the British Aid Programme, 1666
Accountant, (careers), 180
Accuracy in building, 523
ACKERS, P.: Hydraulic design of storm drains etc., 1692
ACKLAND, D. M.: Anthomyiidae, 385
ACLAND, A. S.: Safety in the home, 490
Acoustics, 523
Acquisition of Easements and Profits by Prescription, Law Reform, 189
Acridoidea, 722, 1125
Acrylonitrile, 186
Activated-sludge sewerage treatment, 1293, 1297
Activity Data method of recording user requirements, 203
Acts:
Annotations to, 218, 542, 931, 1342, 1689
Local: 78–9, 543, 705–7, 113–4, 1516–18 and personal, supplementary index, 543
of:
Parliaments of Scotland, 218
Sederunt, S. I. select committee, 1640
Public General, 76–8, 367, 703–5, 1110–12, 1514–16

ADAM, W.: Cephalopod Family Sepiidae, 104
ADAMS, C. G.: East Indian letter classification of the tertiary, 1538
Foraminiferal genus *Austrotillina* Parr, 722
ADAMS, F. S.: Surface Spread of Flame, 221
ADAMS, I. H.: Descriptive list of plans in Scottish Record Office, 1683
ADAMS, Chief Master P. (Chairman): Civil Judicial statistics, 899
ADAMS, P. J.: The Moon, its Geology and Geography, 907
Additional Accommodation for Members, H. C. (Services) select committee, 1636
Additions to Manuscripts, B. M., catalogues, 99, 383, 719, 1134, 1683
Ad-Drefnu Llywodraeth Leol Im Morganng a Sir Fynwy, 1736
Adelaide Island, geology, 1662
Adelgids, attacking spruce and other conifers, 860
Aden:
income tax, 1300
Perim, and Kuria Muria Islands Act, 367
Bill, 284, 337, 338
suspected terrorists, 130
Adhesives:
census of production, 957
for wood, 939

Adhesives (continued):
used in building, 1320
addendum, 1669
Adjustment of Agricultural guaranteed prices, 1521
Administration:
Bonds, etc., Law Commission, 1654
of:
Estates (Small Payments) Act, circular, 170
Justice Act, 703, 1111, 1515
Bill, 290, 334, 339, 606, 619, 620, 671, 874, 1003, 1060, 1073, 1273, 1403, 1410, 1465, 1479, 1481, 1628
Overseas, Journal, 196, 515, 907, 1314, 1667
Administrative:
arrangements, hospital, 155, 469, 470, 864, 1262, 1615
law, submission to Lord Chancellor, 1303
structure of medical and related services, E. and W., 867
Admiralty:
Hydrographic Service, 411
instructions, 123
manual of navigation, 123, 411, 735, 1140
oar maces of, 1174
see also Defence, Navy department
Adolescents. See Adults and Adolescents
Adoption:
Act, 703
Bill, 612, 661, 665, 669, 874
of children:
European Convention, 418, 756
Working paper, 1624
practice, guide, 1624
Adoration of the Magi, 266
ADRIAN, Lord (Chairman): Radiological hazards to patients, 158
Adult(s):
and adolescents' smoking habits and attitudes, 864
trainee, challenge of change, 1147
Advertisements (Hire Purchase) Act, 367
Bill 4, 274, 280, 337, 485
Advertising, (careers), 180, 1564
Advocates' Widows' and Orphans' Fund Order Confirmation:
Act, 1113
Bill, 670

A.E.E.W. Reports 252–3, 387–8, 972–3, 1185–6, 1727–8
Aelothripidae, 385
AERE:
reports, 245–7, 588–92, 973–7, 1386–90, 1728–30
translations, 257–9, 592–4, 977–8, 1390–2, 1730–1

Aerodromes, pay of ground staff, 1308
Aerological cross-sections, daily, 191, 508, 900
Aeronautical:
Booklet, 207
Information publication, 1716
Research Council:
current papers, 81–4, 543–8, 932–4, 1343–6, 1527–31
publications, 81–5, 543–54, 932–8, 1343–51, 1527–35
reports and memoranda, 84–5, 548–52, 934–7, 1346–9, 1531–3
technical report, 552, 937
Aeronautics:
Leonardo da Vinci's, 530
Science Museum, 207
Aeroplanes:
and helicopters, pilots' licences, 1370
first, directory and nomenclature, 207
Aerospace material specifications, DTD series 96–8, 552–4, 937–8, 1349–51, 1534–5

Afghanistan, cultural relations, 132, 759–60
AFIFI, S. A., Pseudococcidae and Eriococcidae, 1125
Africa:
Information Office pamphlet, 1649
South Atlantic, and Indian Oceans, relative humidity and precipitation, 510
After-care:
Place of voluntary service, 474
see also Probation and after-care
Aftermath of Locarno, British foreign policy, 132

Agamidae, 723
Agarics, 1326, 1674
Age:
Level of Employment Bill, 666, 1073, 1480
of Majority:
report, 508
(Scotland) Act, 1111
Bill, 999, 1060, 1072, 1074, 1273
Aggregate, survey of, 244, 1663
Agribusiness Ltd., investigation, 951
Agricultural:
Advisory Service See National Agricultural Advisory Service
and:
food statistics, 1130
horticultural subjects, teachers' salaries, 1147
censuses and production:
E. and W., 1521
U.K., 95, 1521

Agricultural (continued):
economics:
progress report, 728
Scottish. See Scottish
guaranteed prices, adjustment, 1521
Holdings:
Bill, 665
(Scotland) Act, 348
Horticultural, and Forestry Industry Training Board, 448, 746, 1148, 1564
Industry, Economic Development Committee, 904
land:
improvement, estimates committee, 479, 878
landlords and tenants, 1116
machinery, census of production, 957
Marketing:
Act(s):
British Wool Marketing Scheme, 89
Draft amendment to a scheme, 1120
Scottish Milk Marketing Scheme, 86
Schemes, report, 95, 381, 717, 1116, 1526
Mechanic, and Blacksmith (careers), 1149
Research:
Council:
annual report, 86, 373, 709, 1115, 1519
occasional papers, 1519
publications, 85–6, 373, 709, 1115, 1519
Index, 1519
Service 1115
Workers. see Forestry and Agricultural Research Workers
Sciences, 392, 728, 1133
statistics:
Century of, 711
E. and W. 89, 375, 710, 1521
Scotland, 86, 373, 1115, 1519
U.K., 711, 1521
Training Board (Abolition) Bill, 671
Valuation, 1116
workers' pay, E. and W., 1307
see also Farm(s) and Farmer(s)
Agriculture, 89, 375, 711, 1117, 1521
Agriculture('s):
Acts, 367, 1515
annual review, 89, 375, 711, 1117, 1521
Bill, 42, 45, 52, 63, 276, 278, 280, 334, 336, 476, 1069, 1076, 1408, 1410, 1466, 1480, 1483

Agriculture('s) (continued):
and:
Fisheries, Department of, for Scotland:
advisory bulletins, 1115
publications 86–7, 373–4, 709–10, 1115–16, 1519–21
technical bulletin, 710
Horticulture (careers), 180, 1564
Fisheries and Food, Ministry of:
advisory leaflets, 374–5
bulletins, 89–90, 376, 711, 1117, 1521–2
circulars, 90–2, 376, 711
fixed equipment, leaflets, 1120
publications, 87–96, 374–82, 710–18, 1116–23, 1521–7
technical bulletins, 95, 382, 718, 1123
Hand Tools to Mechanization, 530
import saving role, 904
in:
Britain, 495, 1649
Scotland, 86, 373, 709, 1116, 1519
(Miscellaneous Provisions) Act, 703
Bill, 334, 339, 607, 609, 611, 614, 661, 665, 875
pay of workers, E. and W., 1516
safety:
arrangements for toxic chemicals, 414
health, welfare, and wages, 95, 381, 717, 1122, 1526
(Scotland) Act, Proceedings, 536, 1335
select committee, 379, 481, 880–1, 1281
(Spring Traps) (Scotland) Act, 1111
Bill, 664, 670, 671, 875, 991, 1073, 1273
structure, 95, 1522
supply estimates, 1725
Wales and Monmouthshire, 875
see also farm(s) and farmer(s)

A.H.S.B. reports, 259, 594, 979, 1392, 1731

A.I. Levy (Holdings) Ltd., 234
Aids to management:
beef, 1120
dairying, 1524
farm labour and machinery, 1524
poultry, 1120
sheep, 1120
Ail Adroddiad Cyfnodol, Comisiwn Ffinian i Cymru, 1272
Aiolopus Fieber, 722
Air Almanac, 114, 397–8, 731, 1136, 1548

Air:
conditioning and ventilation, hospitals, 1616
conditions in horticultural stores, 94
Corporations Acts, 76, 367, 703, 1111
accounts, 232, 557, 941, 1354
Bill, 1, 11, 163, 275, 279, 336, 611, 666, 1000, 1060, 1073, 1074, 1415, 1484
loans, 246, 579–80, 965–6, 1377, 1720
detection of toxic substances in, booklets, 186, 750
Force:
civilian industrial employees, regulations, 398
Department see Defence, Ministry of
Law, manual, 114, 398, 731, 1136
List, 114, 398, 731, 1136, 1548
Queen's Regulations, 114, 398, 731, 1137, 1548
motion in frontal precipitation, 901
Navigation:
Order and Regulations, 232, 557, 941, 1354, 1720
safety, 1574
sight reduction tables, 398, 732
Pollution:
Bill, 1334
effect on plants and soil, 373
Publication (826), 398
Services:
agreements see respective countries
tariffs*, 418, 756
Surveys, photogrammetry, 1314
Traffic:
Control:
Manual, 234, 572, 954, 1369, 1712
Training manual, 955–6, 1354, 1696
international carriage rules, 418
route schedule*, 1160
Transport:
and Travel Industry Training Board, 1564
Licensing Board, 232, 557, 941, 1354, 1696
votes, 250, 584–5, 970, 1382, 1724
Airborne:
Radio apparatus, 1696
Sound insulation of partitions, 222
Aircraft:
accidents:
civil, 231–4, 567, 950–1, 1364–5, 1706–8
survey, 232, 557, 1695
design, noise measurement, 1713
disinfecting, 146
fires, 554
manufacturing and repairing, census of production, 957

Aircraft (continued):
material and process specifications, 96, 552
Noise:
Bill, 50, 339
report, 557
offences committed on board, 1163
propulsion, 208
radio maintenance engineers' licences, 557, 941
radioactive contamination, 84
Aircrew(s):
avoidance of excessive fatigue, 952
elementary meteorology, 1137
Airdrie Court House Commissioners (Dissolution) Order Confirmation Act, 705
Bill, 665
Airline operators, U.K., safety performance, 959
Airports Authority Act:
accounts, 941, 1354
loans, 246, 580, 966, 1377, 1720

ALABASTER, J. S., Effect of heated effluents on fish, 92
ALBEMARLE, COUNTESS OF (Chairman), National Youth Employment Council, 754
Aldborough Roman Town, Yorkshire, guide, 912, 1670
ALDHOUS, J. R., Chemical control of forest weeds, 1255
Aldrin and dieldrin residues in food, 380
Alepocephaloid fishes, 1128
ALEXANDER, J. B.:
B–V of the sun, 206
G–R and R–I colours of late-type dwarfs, 920
Alexandra Park and Palace Order, S.I., 167
Aleyrodidae, 101
Algae:
calcareous, 723
food value of 1524
red, 102
smaller, British coastal waters, 379
Algeria, Air Services*, 1574
Algorithms and logical trees, tables, 1543
Aliens, 1624
Alkali, annual report, 169, 486, 888, 1290, 1643
All Saints, Streatham Act, 705
ALLAN, J.: Cults of ancient India, 383
ALLEN, A.:
Magnetic survey, Graham Land, 98
Seismic refraction investigations in Scotia Sea, 99
ALLEN BROWN, R.: Rochester Castle, 1321
ALLEN, J. B.: Nepheline-Syenite and phonolite, 906
ALLEN, W. D.: Electrostatic generator group, 209

Allied Brewers, Ltd. Monopolies Commission, 1370
Allied Produce Co. Ltd., 234
ALLISON, SIR C. (Chairman): Teeside, 1297
Allotments inquiry, 1294
Allowance(s):
Regulations, army, 114, 398, 732, 1137, 1548
amendments, 732, 734
to members of local authorities, 171, 490, 1643
Alloys, corrosion at high temperatures, 938
Almanac. See Nautical Almanac, and Star Almanac
Aloeides Thyra Complex, 721
Alphabetical list of industries, 105, 1129
Altar-piece of the Apocalypse, 984
Aluminium:
primary, production, 953
semi-manufactures:
costs and prices, 510
Monopolies Commission, 510

Amalgamated:
Dental Co. Ltd., Monopolies Commission, 34
Union of Building Trade Workers, dispute, 499
Amateur radio operators licences*, 844
Amber, carved, catalogue, 98
Amblycera, 1125, 1538
Ambrosia beetles, 222
Ambulance training and equipment, 158, 472
Amendment of Statutory Instruments Bill, 1479
America(n):
and West Indies, State papers, 1324
Questions, British foreign policy, 1164
studio pottery, 985
Amines, filming, 1618
Ammody tidae, 93
Ammonites and Nautiloids, 102
Ampelaceae, 1127
Amphetamines:
and lysergic acid diethylamide, (LSD), 1624
barbiturates, LSD and cannabis, 1622
Amphipoda, 1127
Amphiuridae, 1539
Amusement:
Arcades (Regulation) Bill, 1075, 1480
centres, development control, 1646

Amoyrine Essyridae, 29f
Anchors and Chain Cables Act, 367
Ancient:
and historical monuments:
and constructions of England, 874
Royal Commission, 1628
of Peeblesshire, 521

Ancient (continued):
Chinese weapons and belt hooks, 1123
Monument(s):
and historic buildings:
guides, 201–2, 521–2, 912, 1321, 1670
lists, 522, 912
open to the public, 201
Boards:
England, 1669
Scotland and Wales, 202, 522, 912, 1320
Scotland, 1676
Wales, 1736
in England and Wales, list, 202, 522, 912, 1320, 1670
Scotland:
illustrated guide, 522
list, 522, 912, 1321, 1677
Royal Commission, 525
Southern England, 202
West Cambridgeshire, 874
Musical instruments of West Asia, 1123
ANDERSON, PROF. D. S. (Chairman): Commercial rating, 1678
ANDERSON, F. W.:
Northern Skye, geological survey, 195
Ostracoda, 102
ANDERSON, M. M.: Brachiopods, 1126
Anderson and Woodman Library Trust Scheme, 1332
ANDERTON, P.: Changing to the metric system, 222, 555, 1352
ANDREW, E. M.: Lesser Antilles, 1662
ANDREWS, R. W.: Wollastonite, 1663
Aneline vapour, detection, 750
Angle Ore and Transport Company Act 1959 (Amendment) Order, 126
Anglesey:
census, 152
sample census, 467, 1459
Anglo-Saxon pennies, 1535
Anguilla:
conference report, 392
problem, report of inquiry, 1602
Angus, Kinross, and Perth, census, 155
Animal(s):
and poultry foods, census of production, 957
Bill, 1002, 1004, 1077, 1411, 1413, 1414, 1483
Breeding:
Establishments Bill, 1074
Research Organisation, 85, 373, 709, 1115, 1519
review, 1133
Civil liability, Royal Commission, 507
(Control of Intensified Methods of Food Production) Bill, 334
Cruelty to, Bill, 665

Animal(s) (continued):
Diseases:
handbook of orders, 93, 715
Institute for Research, 1115, 1519
return of proceedings under Act, 95, 382, 717
survey, 711
Export of, for Research, Bill, 334, 619, 666
Health Services, 95, 381, 717, 1122, 1526
husbandry, antibiotics, 1264
Importation, Bill 337
living, experiments on, 161, 474, 872, 1270, 1625
Physiology, Institute of, 86, 709, 1519
Protection of:
Bill, 10/4
International transport, 1249
(Restriction of Experiments) Act:
Advisory Committee report, 474
summary of statistics, 612, 1145
Annotations to Acts, 218, 542, 931, 1342, 1689

Antarctic:
lichens, 1311
moss flora, 1662
Treaty:
Act, 367
Bill, 49, 279, 306, 331, 476
consultative meeting, 418, 1160
Anthoza, 1127
Antibiotics in animal husbandry and veterinary medicine, 1264
Anti-Discrimination Bill, 667, 1072, 1077
Antigua:
Arms, 392
Colonial report, 109
Constitutional Conference report, 109
Flag, 394
race relations and immigration, select committee, 1618
space vehicle tracking*, 464
Anti-static precautions, hospitals, 866
Antiques, licence, 236
Ants indoors, 375

Aoridae, 1127

Apanteles Förster, 386
Aphids, woolly, 88
Apidae, 722
Appeal(s):
Court. See Court of Appeal
from decisions of Medical Appeals Tribunal, 216, 539, 869, 1266, 1621
to the High Court, tax cases, 178–9, 496–7, 896–7, 1300–2, 1650–2
Appearance of bridges, 1716
Apple and pear:
scab, 88
suckers, 375

APPLEBY, R. (Chairman): Clothing E.D.C., 1309
APPLETON, J. H.: Disused railways, 1343
Application:
for official search of Land Register, 1653
of computers in the construction industry, 1672
Applied:
mechanics, 1551
science, notes, 555, 1352, 1713
Appropriation:
accounts:
abstract, 251, 586, 972, 1384, 1726
civil, 246, 580, 966, 1377, 1720
Act, 76, 367, 703, 1111, 1513
(No. 2) Act, 76, 1515
Approved school(s):
punishment at Court Lees, 473
remand homes, and attendance centres, statistics, 32, 476, 874, 1273, 1628
Appuldurcombe House, I.O.W., guide, 521
APTED, M. R.: Painted Ceilings of Scotland, 202

Aquatic weeds, control, 711
Aquifers, ground-water statistics, 1736
Aquifoliaceae, 729
Arabia, South, Treaty of Friendship, 61
Araliaceae, 729
Arbitration:
compulsory, in Britain
grievance, in U.S.A., 919
International:
disputes, 1160
Investment Disputes Act: 76
(No. 9, 51
taxation liability of Euratom employees, 419
Archaeocyatha, 1126
Archaeological:
excavations. See Excavations
reports, 913, 1321
ARCHANGELSKY, S.: New Gymnosperms, 103
ARCHER, A. A.: Gwendraeth Valley and adjoining areas 1312
ARCHER, M.: British Drawings, India Office Library, 1576
ARCHER, W. G.: Paintings of the Sikhs, 266
Architects:
costs and fees, 902
Registration (Amendment) Act: 1111
Bill, 999, 1060, 1071, 1073, 1274
Architecture, (careers), 747
Archives:
and education, 744
National register, 159, 473, 871
Area(s):
improvement, 1292
mortality tables, 861
of Special Scientific Interest Bill, 337

Argentine(a):
Air Services*, 130, 419, 756
arbitration of boundary controversy, 131
cereals*, 1162
loan*, 419
military service*, 419, 756
visas*, 419 1160
Argyll:
Caithness, Inverness, Orkney, Ross and Cromarty, Sutherland, and Zetland, sample census, 466, 1361
Forest Park Guide, 465
Argyllshire, mineral resources, 1312
Armed Forces:
Act: 76
Bill, 9, 10, 48, 51, 52, 167, 1412, 1414, 1485
pay. 192,
standing reference: 902, 1307, 1657
Armour, European, in the Tower of London, 914
Arms:
and Armour:
in England, 1321
in Tudor and Stuart London, 1653
granted by Royal Warrant, 108, 392
ARMSTRONG, M.: Lower old red sandstone, 1562
Armstrong Patents Co. Ltd, Industrial Relations Commission, 1545
Army:
Allowance regulations, 114, 398, 732, 733, 734, 1137, 1548
Cadet Force regulations, 732, 1548
Department publications, see Defence, Ministry of
drill, 115
Emergency Reserve regulations, 115
estimates: 401, 1141
Act, 76, 1560
list, 115, 399, 732, 1137, 1548
Long Term Reserve, regulations and administrative instructions, 733
Officers:
dress regulations, 1138, 1549
in receipt of retired pay, list, 1137
Orders, 115, 399, 732, 1137–8, 1549
special, 1140
Pensions Warrants, 115, 116, 400, 540, 734, 870, 1139, 1268, 1549, 1622
physical training, 115, 399, 733, 1138
Queen's regulations, 116, 399, 733, 1138
Regular Reserve, regulations and administrative instructions, 733
Reserve Act, 1111
Bill, 995, 1060, 1072, 1274
Special orders, 117, 400, 734, 1140, 1551

Army (continued):
Territorial regulations, 116, 399, 731
trumpet and bugle calls, 117
votes, 250, 401, 585, 970, 1383, 1724
see also Military
Aromatic Isocyanates, 1568
Arsine, 186
Art(s):
ancient Near Eastern, 1123
and:
amenities, Scotland, 1066, 1274
centre:
in the primary schools, 925
rooms, safety in, 1680
Design Education, 1563
classical, fifty masterpieces, 1536
Council:
of Great Britain:
Annual report, 97
and accounts, 382, 718, 1527
estimates committee, 879
publications, 97, 382, 718, 1123, 1527
Theatre inquiry, 1527
early medieval, 1123
education, 126
examinations in, 126, 413
export of works of, 249, 582, 968, 1380, 1562
grants, estimates committee, 878, 1277
Japanese, 1123
Nouveau and Alphonse Mucha, large picture book, 985
Sumerian, 1537
ARTHURE, H.: Maternal deaths, E. and W., report, 1267
Artificial Limb Service in Scotland, future, 1681
Asbestos:
cement, painting, 521, 523
health precautions in industry, 1567
problems arising from use of, 750
Ascophora imperfecta, 387
Ash, quality of wood, 222
Ashford Study, consultants' proposals, 487
Asian:
Development Bank:
conference, 131
contribution to special funds*, 1574
establishment*, 756
musical instruments, ancient, 1123
Scripts, handbook, 100
Asilidae, 101, 1537
Asparagus, 1117
Aspects of administration in a large Local Authority, 916
Assay of Strontium 90 on human bone, see Strontium
Assessing the fishing industry, estimates committee, 479, 483

ASS-BEV | 1966-70

ASS— INDEX 1966–70

Assizes and Quarter Sessions, Royal Commission, 1326
Associated Industrial Consultants Ltd., 1661
Associated Octel Company Ltd., Industrial Relations Commission, 1544
Association of:
  Education Committees, select committee 1635
  Municipal Corporations, select committee, 1634
Astata Latreille, 385
Asterids, 387
Astronomical ephemeries, 205, 529, 920, 1328, 1675
Astronomy:
  field, textbook, 1551
  globes, orreries, and other models, 922

Atkinson, R. D'E.: Cooke transit circle, 206
Atlantic, crossing under sail, 1310
Atlas:
  Computer Laboratory, 208
  of speciation, African passerine birds, 1537
Atmospheric:
  diffusion:
    equation, 901
    slide rule, 192
  pollution, investigation, 556
Atom–66, 259
  –67, 594
Atomic:
  energy:
    agreements etc., *see respective countries*
    application of safeguards*, 340, 1160
    Article VI amendment, 1574
    Authority:
      Bill, 1406, 1409, 1482, 1485
      see also United Kingdom
    European organisation for Nuclear Research, 1160
  terms, glossary, 262
Attachment of Earnings:
  Bill, 1411, 1412, 1642
  Orders, 871

Auction (Bidding Agreements) Act, 1111
  Bill, 996, 1000, 1060, 1071, 1072, 1073, 1075, 1274
Audio, shorthand, and typewriting tests, 1379
Auroral observations, analysis, 383
Australia(n):
  and New Zealand Banking Group Act 1517
  air services*, 108
  cereals*, 1162
  double taxation*, 393, [illegible]7
  Edinburgh airfield, 968
Australia(n) (*continued*):
  micro-organism collection, 413
  War graves*, 1254, 1610
  see also South Australia
Austria:
  air services*, 1160
  double taxation*, 366, 1164
  extradition*, 1238, 1575
  judgments, 1575
  visas*, 757, 1161, 1575
  war cemetery*, 419
Austrotillina Parr, 722
Authorised:
  explosives, list, 161, 474, 872, 1270, 1625
  Sweepstakes Bill 665
Automatic bubble chamber film measurement, 1330
Automation in photogrammetry, 1314

Aviation:
  historical survey, 1675
  law for applicants for private pilots' licence, 232, 557, 941, 1354, 1696
  Ministry of, 96–8
    see also Technology, Ministry of Supply, Ministry of, publications, 1527–35
    see also Technology, *and* Aviation, Ministries of
Avoidance of:
  excessive fatigue in aircrews, 952
  pollution of the sea by oil, 955

Awards:
  and finance, E. and W., statistics of education, 746
  Civil Service Arbitration Tribunal, 180–1, 499
  for good design in housing, 170, 488, 889, 1291, 1644
    Wales, 266, 600, 985, 1396, 1736
  Industrial Court, 183–5, 502–4, 750–2, 1153–4, 1568–9
  of:
    General Service Medals, 66, 581
    National certificates and diplomas in Scotland, 533
  to students, circular, 125
A.W.R.E.:
  Library bibliographies, 258, 594–5, 979, 1392–3, 1733
  reports, 260–1, 594–5, 979–80, 1392–3, 1731–3

Ayr and Bute:
  census, 155
  sample census, 469

Azodicarbonamide, 715

1966 pp 1–272, 1967 pp 273–604, 1968 pp 605–990, 1969 pp 991–1402, 1970 pp 1403–1740
8

INDEX 1966–70 —BAN

B

Babylonian tablets, 100, 384, 720, 1124
Bacillery White Diarrhoea (BWD), 88
Bacon, Sir E. (Chairman):
  Agriculture's import saving role, 904
Bacon:
  Curing:
    Industry Stabilising Scheme, S.I. select committee, 1287, 1640
    meat, and fish products, census of production, 957
  supply*, 1245
Baconsthorpe Castle, guide, 201
Bacteriological:
  examination of water supplies, 1267
  techniques for dairy purposes, 718
Bagus Umbara, Prince of Koripan, 719
Bahamas:
  colonial report, 393
  constitutional conference, 757
  long-range proving ground*, 464
Bahrain:
  Alcoholic Drinks (Amendment) Regulations, 757
  Aliens (Immigration and residence) Regulation, 131
  Contract Law (Amendment) Regulation, 758
  criminal procedure (Amendment) Rules 758
  Currency:
    Amendment) Regulation, 758
    (Specifications) Regulation, 758
  Explosives (Amendment) Regulation, 757
  Import of Currency (Repeal) Regulation, 131
  Income Tax (Amendment) Regulation, 419
  International Organisations (Immunities and Privileges) Regulations, 758
  Notices, 131, 419–20, 757–8
  Penal Code (Amendment) Regulations, 420
  Persian Gulf Gazette, 459
  Possession of and Traffic in Arms (Amendment) Regulation, 757
  Post Regulation, 419
  Prison Rules (Amendment) Regulation, 420
  Traffic (Amendment):
    (No. 2) Regulation, 758
    Regulation, 757
  Transfer of Jurisdiction:
    (Assaults and Stealing) Regulation, 758
    (Control of Dangerous Drugs) Regulation, 757
    (Immigration and Residence of Aliens) Regulation, 757
Bahrain (*continued*):
  Transfer of Jurisdiction (*continued*):
    (Labour and Kindred Matters) Regulation, 419
    (Leases of Land or Buidlings) Regulation, 420
    (Miscellaneous Matters) Regulation, 758
    (Municipal Rules and Bye-Laws) Regulation, 757
    (Patents, Designs, and Trade Marks) Regulation, 419
    (Traffic) Regulation, 757
  United Nations Children's Fund*, 857
Baillie, E. D.: Protective clothing, report, 914
Baines, A.: Non-keyboard Instruments, 985
Baird, R. H.: Growth and condition of mussels, 93
Baird and Hamilton Ltd, Monopoly Commission, 1713
Bairstow, R.: Magnostrictive readout of wire spark chambers, 923
Baker, Hon. Mr. Justice (Chairman): Mechanical recording of Court proceedings, 189
Bakeries, safety in use of machinery, 753
Baking:
  Industry:
    bread prices, and pay, 1657, 1658
    wages, 192
  Powder and Golden Raising Powder, Food Standards Committee, 1525
Balance of Payments, U.K., 106, 389, 725, 1130, 1542:
  preliminary estimates, 250, 584, 970, 1382, 1724
Bale handling equipment and systems, 381
Balfour-Browne, F. L.: Fungi of Nepal, 721
Ballet, designs and illustrations, 599
Ballistic Missile Early Warning Station, 1253
Balloons. *See* Pilot Balloons
Bane, W. T.: Operational research, models and government, 966
Banister, F. E.: *Indostromus paradoxus*, 1539
Bank, M. A. L. (Chairman): British Patent, System, 1697
Bank:
  charges, 510
  holidays, proclamation, 1341
  of England:
    annual report, 246, 580, 966, 1377, 1720
    Nationalised Industries select committee, 1636
  of Nova Scotia, loans, 1377

1966 pp 1–272, 1967 pp 273–604, 1968 pp 605–990, 1969 pp 991–1402, 1970 pp 1403–1740
9

BAN— INDEX 1966–70

Bank (*continued*):
  of Scotland Order Confirmation Order Act, 1517
    Bill, 1483
Bankers returns, 218, 541, 930, 1337
Banking:
  and:
    accounting table, Decimal Currency Board, 1547
    the Stock Exchange, (Careers), 747
  decimal currency booklet, 1136
  system, British, 895
Bankruptcy:
  and Companies (Winding Up) Proceedings:
  account, 223–4, 557, 941, 1354, 1696
  annual report, 223, 557, 941, 1354, 1696
Banwell Report, action on, 511
Barbados:
  Arms, 108
  constitutional conference, 109
  double taxation*, 1575
  Flag: 394
    Governor-General, 394
  Independence Act: 77
    Bill, 9, 51
  Information Office pamphlet, 177
  Race relations, Immigration select committee, 1638
Barbican and Horseferry Road construction sites, Court of inquiry, 501
Barbiturates, use and misuse, 1622
Barclays:
  Bank:
    Act, 1113
    D.C.O. Act, 1517
    Trust Company Act, 1517
  Lloyds, and Martins Banks, merger, 955
Barker, E. S.: Spectroscopic binaries, 920
Barlow, A. R.: Resin pressure and Scolyted beetle activity, 151
Barn hay drying, 716
Barnett, R. D.:
  Ancient Near Eastern Art, 1123
  Illustrations of Old Testament History, 100
Barnsley Corporation Act, 1113
Barque running before a gale, Print, 512
Barr, H.: Probation, 162
Barraclough, J. W.: Timber extraction by tractor, 465
Barrington, C. A.: Forestry in the Weald, 859
Barry Corporation Act, 78
Barton C. M.: Stratigraphy of King George Island, 98
Basellaceae, 729
Basements, watertight, 1669
Basildon Development Corporation, Public Accounts committee, 1280
Basingstoke Corporation Act, 1517
Basingwerk Abbey, guide, 201
Baskets, census of production, 1371
Baskett, Sir R. (Chairman): Nutrient requirements of pigs, 373
Basle Facility and the Sterling Area, 966
Basutoland:
  (Benefits under Retirement Scheme) Order OIC, 201
  Corona Library Series, 110
  Independence:
    booklet, 177
    conference, 110
  (Public Service) Order OIC, 201
Batchelor, Prof. I. R. C. (Chairman): Staffing mental deficiency hospitals, 1681
Batchelor, K.: calibration measurement of PLA, 922
Bate, R. H.:
  Oolites and limestone, 386
  Ostracoda, 102, 386, 1126
Bates, D. E. B.: brachiopods and trilobites, 722, 1126
Bath, Marquess of: manuscripts at Longleat, 871
Bath:
  conservation study, 1290
  University of Technology Act, 370
Bathe, B. W.:
  British Warships, 1675
  Ship Models, 208
Batholomew, D. J.: Manpower planning, 1543
Bathonian Ostracoda, 1126
Batiks, large picture book, 1396
Batty, C. J. (Editor): PLA progress report, 530, 923, 1676
Bawden, Sir F. (Chairman): Forestry Research, 465, 860
Bayliss, B. T.: Transport for Industry, 1376

Beaches, oil pollution, 890
Beam:
  bending magnets, 530
  ion, from mercury pool arc source, 209
  lines, 922
  loading, 923
  measurements, 530
  Proton Nimrod extracted, 209
  sensing radial and phase control systems for Nimrod, 194
  vertical blow-up, 1330
Bean weevil, 88
Beardsley, Aubrey, picture book, 266
Beaton portraits, 905
Beaumont, J. de: *Sphecidae des Iles Vanaries*, 721
Bechuanaland:
  colonial report, 109
  Corona Library Series, 110

1966 pp 1–272, 1967 pp 273–604, 1968 pp 605–990, 1969 pp 991–1402, 1970 pp 1403–1740
10

INDEX 1966–70 —BEV

Bechuanaland (*continued*):
  Independence:
    booklet, 177
    conference, 110
Beckwith, J.: Adoration of the Magi, 266
Bedding and soft furnishings, census of production, 1371
Bedford Corporation Act, 1113
Bedfordshire:
  sample census, 467, 862
  Sessions of the Peace, 1624
Bedgebury pinetum and forest plots, 1255
Bedingfeld, A. L.: Creake Abbey, 1670
Beeby, G. H. (Chairman): Manpower in the chemical industry, 512
Beechey, Sir W.: Nelson, colour poster, 1662
Beeching, Lord (Chairman): Assizes and Quarter Sessions, Royal Commission, 1326
Beef:
  aids to management, 1120
  breeding herds, slatted floors for, 512
  cattle, housing, 1525
Beehives, 711
Beekeepers, advice, 375
Beekeeping, 89
Beer, monopoly commission, 1369
Bees:
  diseases, 1117
  male humble, 723
  swarming, 1522
Beeston, G. R. (Chairman): Arts in Wales, 267
Beethoven, 1535, 1536
Beetles:
  ambrosia, 222
  carpet, 384
  colorado, 88
  common furniture, 1351
  death watch, 939
  great spruce bark, 151
  lyctus powder-post, 1351
  oriental timber, 724
  pinhole borer, 222
  scolytid, 151
Begone Dull Care, residential care of children, 871
Belas Gap, long barrow, guide, 201
Belgium:
  double taxation*, 421, 1575
  driving licences*, 1161
  goods transport by road*, 1607
  taxation of road vehicles*, 1607
Bell, S. B. M.: computer graphics patching of failed cyclops events, 1676
Bell, T. T. W.: Spruce seedlings, 860
Bellamy, R. G. (Chairman): Training training officers, 180, 498
Bellis, B. T. (Chairman): Computers and schools, 1332
Bellshill Maternity Hospital, 927, 1681
Belt:
  conveyors at quarries, 1352
  hooks. Ancient Chinese, 1123
Bembo's Library, 100
Benedict, B.: People of the Seychelles, 196, 1667
Bennett, J. R. J.: Beam measurements, 530
Bennettitales: 1128
  fossil, 102
Benson, R. B.: Symphyta, 722
Benson, Sir H. (Chairman): National Trust, 1311
Benzine toluene and xylene styrene, 186
Berberidaceae, 112
Berkshire, sample census, 467, 862
Berlin and the problem of German reunification, 1649
Bermuda:
  civil airport facilities*, 858
  colonial report, 109
  Constitution Bill, 285, 337, 367
  constitutional conference, 393
  report, 758, 1161, 1571
  space vehicle tracking and communication station*, 858
Berridge, N. G.: Mineral resources of the crofter counties of Scotland, 1312
Berrill, K. (Chairman): Teaching computing, 1735
Berwick, Peebles, Roxburgh, and Selkirk, sample census, 469, 1261
Berwick-upon-Tweed fortifications, guide, 522
Berycoid fishes, 386
Bessey, G. S. (Chairman): Youth service, 128
Betterment Levy:
  (Exemption in Case C) Order, S.I. select committee, 1641
  explanatory memorandum, 487
  modifications, 1296
  (Scotland), 531
  (Waiver of Interest) (No. 2) Regulations S.I. select committee, 483
Betting:
  and Gaming Appeals:
    and Fees of Clerks to Licensing Authorities, Act of Sederunt, S.I. select committee, 1640
    (No. 2) Act of Sederunt, S.I. select committee, 1640
  Bill, 48, 50, 275
  Gaming, and Lotteries:
    Act, Permits and licences, 159, 473, 871, 1625
    (Amendment) Act, 1111
      Bill, 992, 995, 996, 1073
  Premises (Licence Duty) Regulations S.I. select committee, 1288
Bevan, D.: Pine looper moth, 151

1966 pp 1–272, 1967 pp 273–604, 1968 pp 605–990, 1969 pp 991–1402, 1970 pp 1403–1740
11

Bewcastle, geology of the country around, 1663
BEYNON, V. H.: Dairy economics, 376
BIBBY, J. S.: Stratigraphy, Graham Land and James Ross Island Group, 719
Bibliography of farm building research, 85, 373, 709, 1115, 1519
Bill of Rights, 1411 (No. 2) Bill, 1075
Binary(ies): Peculiar A Star HR-4072, 529 Spectroscopic, 920
Dingo Duty Regulations S.I. select committee, 1288
Biochemical research in psychiatry, 1655
Biological: sciences, 415, 746, 1147, 1563 warfare, prohibition, 1245
Bird(s): African passerine, 1536 and bird sanctuaries in the Royal Parks, 202, 913, 1670 fossil, 104 instructions for collectors, 1540 life in Royal Parks, 202, 913, 1670 Protection Bill, 52, 283, 332, 336 type specimens in the Natural History Museum, 388
Birmingham: Aluminium Castings Ltd, inquiry, 501, 1545 Corporation Act, 705, 1517
BIRSAY, LORD, (Chairman), General Medical Services, Highlands and Islands, 534
Births, deaths, and marriages: (Local Registration Authorities' Officers) Compensation (Scotland) Regulations, 212 see also Registrar General's returns
Birthday Honours, see Queen's Birthday Honours
Biscuits, census of production, 957
BISHOP, D., Coding and data co-ordination for the construction industry, 1322
Bitumen, cut-back, for surface dressing roads, 963
Bituminous: and other roads in Africa, vehicle operating costs, 578 materials in road construction, 576, 963 road materials, rapid methods of analysis, 578
Bivalvia, 1128

BLACK, H. K.: List of authorised explosives, 474
Black: currants, 89 grass, 375 Papers, contributors to, Educ. and Sci. select committee, 1635

Blackburn Corporation Act, 1517
Blackfriars Bridgehead Improvements Act, 78
Blackgame, 860
BLACKIE, J.: Inside the Primary School, 413
BLACKMORE, H. L.: Royal sporting guns at Windsor, 915
Blackpool: and Stourbridge Provisional Orders Act: 706 Bill, 668
Corporation Act, 1113
Pier and Great Yarmouth New Britannia Pier, Confirmation Order Act, 79 Bill, 6, 7, 49
Blacksmith (careers), 1149
Blackwater estuary, Hydrography, 715
BLACKWELL, K. C.: Semi-regular and RV Tauri Variables, 1327
Blackwood Papers, 1805-1900, 905
BLAIR, C. H.: Norham Castle, Northumberland, 202
BLESZNSKI, S.: Chilo zincken, 1538
BLETCHLEY, J. D., Insect and Marine borer damage
Blight: Potato, 88 Tomato, 88
Blind: and partially sighted children, 744 mobility and reading habits, 864
Blindness in E. and W., 158
Blood: tests, proof of paternity, 899 transfusion service, hospital, 470
Blood-grouping reagents*, 758
BLOUNT, B. K. (Chairman): Government Steering committee, 222
Blowflies, 375
Blue stain, 151
BLUNDELL, G.: Halley Bay, 383

BOALER, S. B.: Pterocarpus angolensis, 196
Board(s) of: Governors of teaching hospitals, 158, 471, 867, 1265, 1619 Trade: Aircraft Radio Maintenance Engineers' Licences, 557 see also Trade, Board of
Board of Trade Journal, 237-8, 570-1, 933-4, 1368-9, 1111 see also Trade and Industry
Bonzio's map of Ireland, 100
Boiler(s): corrosion and water treatment, 1551 Explosion Acts, inquiries, 224, 557-8, 941, 1355, 1696 for nursery use, 716 independent, installing, 1669 plant, hospital, 1616

Boletaceae, 1674
Boleti, 1326, 1674
Bolton Corporation Act, 1517
Bolts, Nuts, Screws, rivets, etc., census of production, 958
Bombus Latreille, 722
Bombycidae, 724
Bombyliidae, 1125
Bonded Warehouses, See Warehouses, bonded
BONHAM-CARTER, SIR D.: Functions of district general hospitals, 1262
BONHAM-CARTER, RT. HON. M.(Chairman): Race Relations Board, 475, 1628
BONNER, W. N.: The Fur Seal of South Georgia, 719
BONNER, R. S. P.: Vehicle operating costs, 578
Books: large picture, 266, 599, 985, 1396, 1735 printed before 1701, Foreign Office Library, catalogue, 146 small picture, 1396
Bookbindings, leather, preservation, 385
BOOTH, T. C.: Plantations of mediaeval Rigg and Furr cultivation strips, 465
Border(s): Counties, census, Scotland, 155 Development (Scotland) Bill, 1071
Boreham Wood Research Station, 939
Borrowing (Control and Guarantees) Act, advances, 246, 580, 966
Borstal: after-care, 161 see also Prisons, Borstals etc.
BOSWORTH, DR. G. S. (Chairman): Education and training requirements for electrical and mechanical industries, 127
Engineering training, 1692
Botany bulletins, 385, 721, 1124, 1537 see also genus(era)
Botrytis cinera, 1255
Botswana: armed forces*, 410 double taxation*, 1575 Independence Act, 77 Bill, 5, 6, 50 Information Office pamphlet, 177 public officers*, 392, 420, 515, 758 reserves in sterling*, 1161 training or police forces*, 1161 wireless and ancillary equipment, 968
BOULTON, W.: Poultry nutrition, 376
Boundary Commission: for Wales, 1272 reports, 1269
Bournemouth Corporation Act, 1113
BOWDEN, SIR F. (Chairman): Forest Research, 1612
BOWEN, R.: Aden report, 130

BOWERS, B.: R.E.B. Crompton, Pioneer Electrical Engineer, 1329 X-Rays, 1675
Boy entrants and Young servicemen, 1560
BOYNTON, L. O. J.: Appuldurcombe House, 521

BP Trading Act 1957 (Amendment) Order, 126

BRABIN, MR. JUSTICE, inquiry into Timothy John Evans case, 159
Brachiopods: early arenig, 1126 eifelian, 1126 Kinninae Elliot, 1538 lower palaeozoic, 722 neocomian, rhynconelloid, 722 rhyncholelid, 1126 silicified, 722 silurian, 1538 strophomenacean, 722
Braconidae, 386, 721, 1537
Bradford: cathedral and churchyard, 78 Corporation Act, 1113
BRADLEY, J. C.: types of Scoliidae described by Frederick Smith, 385
BRADLEY, R. T.: Forest management tables, 151 Thinning control in British woodlands, 465
Bradwell Nuclear Power Station, 419
Brain drain, 413
Bransford, W. de, calendar of register, 159
Brass rubbings, catalogue, 1396
BRAZELL, J. H.: London weather, 900
Brazil: double taxation*, 758 technical co-operation*, 758, 1576
Breach of promise of marriage, Law Commission, 1304
Bread: and flour confectionery, census of production, 1371 and rye, pay, baking industry, 1657, 1658
Breath Test Device (Approval): (No. 1) Order, 874 (No. 2) Order, 734
Brecon Beacons, National Parks guide, 313
Breconshire: census, 152 sample census, 467, 1259
BRENNAN, J. P. M.: Caesalpininioideae, 396
Brewing: and malting, census of production, 957 industry, costs, prices, and profits, 192

Brexiaceae 729
Brick(s): calcium silicate, 521, 1669 clay building, 220 fireclay, and refractory goods, census of production, 958 fletton and non-fletton, 511 flintlime, 1669 sandlime, 1669
Bricklaying in cold weather, 1320
Brickwork: and blockwork, mortars for, 912 efflorescence and stains, 1320 sulphate attack, 323
Bridge: and structures, permissible working stresses, 576 appearance, 1716
Bridgewater Canal water for cooling purposes, chemical problems, 530
Bright Northern A stars, radial velocities etc., 920
Brighton: Corporation Act, 1113 Marina Act, 705 Bill, 608
Brinkburn Priory, abridged guide, 522
Bristol: and Avonmouth Docks dispute, 187 Clifton and West of England Zoological Society Act, 1113
Bristol Siddely Engines Ltd.: inquiry, 940 Public Accounts, 880 report, 940 special reports, 483, 880
Britain('s): and (the): developing countries, 177, 495, 895, 1299, 1649 European Economic Community, economic background, 412 International: co-operation, 895 Labour Organisation, 1149 Latin America, 895 process of decolonisation, 1649 United Nations, 1649 as market for the developing countries, 895 associated states and dependencies, 1299 by car, 1540 caravan and camping sites, 1540 Central Government, Information Office pamphlet, 495 children in, Information Office pamphlet, 495 economy, fifty facts, 495, 895 forest resources, 1611 holidays on inland waterways, 1540 in brief, 176, 494, 894, 1299, 1648

Britain('s) (continued): Information Office handbook, 176 invisible exports, 1649 new coins, 731, 1136 Official Handbook, 176, 495, 894, 1298, 1648 regional development, Information Office pamphlet, 895 share in Commonwealth education, 894 See also United Kingdom
British: Agriculture, Fisheries and Food and the European Economic Community, 481 aid: programme, 1313, 1666 to developing countries, statistics, 195, 514, 907, 1313, 1616 Air: Line Pilots Association, Industrial Court inquiry, 502, 750 Transport in the Seventies, 1355
Airports Authority: advances, 1354 Annual report and accounts, 558, 941, 1355, 1696 loans, 966, 1377, 1720
Aleyrodidae, 101
and: Commonwealth affairs, survey, 495-6, 895-6, 1299-1300, 1649 see also Commonwealth Survey Foreign state papers, 131, 420, 1161
Antarctic: Survey, 98-9, 383, 717-19, 1311, 1662 Territory, 758
Armed Forces, programmed instruction, 124
Avonian (carboniferous) conodont faunas, 1126
banking system, Information Office pamphlet, 895
Broadcasting Corporation: annual report and accounts, 196, 515, 909, 1315 Bill, 1072 Court of Inquiry, 1153 Estimates Committee, 1277, 1279, 1668 licence and agreement, 1315 Royal Charter, 1315 see also Broadcasting
Dependencies, Information Office pamphlet, 176
Drawings, India Office Library, 1576
European Airways: Corporation: Annual report and accounts, 232, 515, 909, 1315 loans, 246, 579, 966, 1377, 1720 select committee on Nationalised industries, 481

British (continued): Film: Fluid Agency, annual report and accounts, 224, 558, 941, 1355, 1696 Institute, 99, 383, 719 estimates committee, 879
Financial Institutions, Information Office pamphlet, 177, 1299
Foreign Policy documents, 132, 421, 760, 1164, 1577
fossils, 721
Guiana flora, 1326, 1674
Guiana-Venezuela frontier,* 131
Honduras: Corona Library Series, 759 Letters Patent OIC, 911 report, 758 OIC, 911 report, 758
Imperial Calendar and Civil Service List, 246, 580, 966, 1377, 1543
Indian Ocean Territory, 464
Institute of Recorded Sound, estimates committee, 879
Insulated: Callender's Cable Ltd.: Monopolies commission, 572 pay of staff, 1307
involvement in Indo-China conflict, 132
Machine Tool Industry, marketing practice, 16
mammals, identification, 1128
Motor Corporation Ltd and Pressed Steel Company Ltd, merger, 239
Museum: bicentenary publications, 99 booklets, 1123 Calendar, 99, 383, 719, 1123, 1536 catalogue of printed maps, charts and plans, 386 guide and maps, 384, 720, 1536 Mozart in, 721 (Natural History) See Natural History Museum Old, 384 public services, guide, 1536 publications, 99-101, 383-5, 719-21, 1535 report of Trustees, 383, 1124 Neocomian Rhynchonelloid Brachiopods, 722 official statistics, development, 725, 1542
Overseas Airways: Corporation: Annual report and accounts, 233, 558, 941, 1355, 1696 debt, 966 loans, 246, 579, 966, 1377, 1720 pay of pilots, 903, 1308 Industrial Court inquiry, 750

British (continued): Parliament, Information Office pamphlet, 495, 895
Patent system, 1697
Pharmacopoeia Commission, medicines commission approved names, 1616
Phosphate Commissioners, report and accounts, 108, 393, 758, 1161, 1576
poisonous plants, 711
property in Egypt, 463
Railways: Board: Act, 78, 370, 705, 1113 and National Union of Railwaymen, Court of Inquiry, 502 annual report and accounts, 241, 576, 961, 1374, 1716 countrywide fares and charges increase Prices and Incomes, 902 loans, 251, 578, 971, 1384, 1726 London area fare increases, Prices and Incomes, 902 organisation, 1374 (Mersey Railway Extensions) Act, 705 staff, pay and conditions of service, 192 rainfall, 900 regional geology: Central England, 1311 Grampian Highlands, 514 South Wales, 1662 South West England, 1311 Relief Advisory Mission, Nigeria, 850 rivers: hydrometric statistics, 985 rainfalls and river water temperature, 985 Road Services, pay of vehicle maintenance workers, 903 ships, re-insurance against war risks, 1317 Sidac Ltd, Monopolies Commission, 1713 Solomon Islands: Colonial report, 393 report, 758, 1161, 1576 Royal Instructions OIC, 520, 1668 Standard Time: (Abolition) Bill, 1479 Act, 703 Bill, 288, 340, 616, 661, 669, 875 Act (Repeal) Bill, 671 review, 1628 Steel Corporation: accounts of publicly-owned Companies, 1316, 1690 advances, 1318 annual report and accounts, 1316, 1690

British (continued):
Steel Corporation (continued):
Industrial Court of Inquiry, 750
loan, 583, 1381
organisation, 515, 1316
Port Talbot inquiry, 1153
Select committee on Nationalised
Industries, 882
System of Taxation, Information Office
pamphlet, 177, 1299
Transport Docks:
Act, 78, 370, 1113
Board:
annual report and accounts,
242, 576, 961, 1384, 1716
loan, 251, 579, 971, 1384, 1726
Order Confirmation Act: 1517
Bill, 1482
Travel Association:
publications, 1540
report, 1134
turtles, identification, 383
Universities and Colleges, scientific:
equipment, 1721
research, 128, 414, 745, 1147, 1593
Virgin Islands, reports, 109
warships, illustrated booklet, 1675
watercolours, 1396
Waterways:
Act 78
Board:
annual report and accounts, 242,
576, 961, 1374, 1716
Leisure and Waterways, 388
loan, 251, 579, 971, 1384, 1726
recreation and amenity, 576
Wines. Census of production, 957
woodlands, thinning control, 465
British Museum Quarterly, 99, 383, 719,
1124, 1536
BRITTON, E. L. (Chairman): Raising the
school leaving age, 415
BRITTON, J. N.: Multiple Marking of
English Compositions, 128
Broad Sanctuary Site, Westminster, 493
Broadcasting: 196
charters and licences, 1315
in Britain, Information Office pamphlet,
177
proceedings:
H.C., 166, 167, 289, 882
H.L., 888
Stations*, 1576
see also British Broadcasting
Brochs of Mousa and Clickhimin, guide,
1670
Brocks Fireworks Ltd., Industrial Relations
Commission, 1545
Broiler houses, 93
BRON GERSMA, L. D.: British turtles, 383
Bronze Age finds in Co. Durham, 720

BROOKE, E. M.: Patients in psychiatric beds,
census, 472
BROWN, PROF. A. J. (Chairman): Student
maintenance grants, 743
BROWN, C. J.: Changing structure of
agriculture, 1522
BROWN, J. M. B.: Great spruce bark beetle,
151
BROWN, R. A.: Dover Castle, 201, 912
BROWN, W. H.: Royal Botanic Garden,
Edinburgh, 1520
BROWNE, H. H. (Chairman): Refuse storage
and collection, 493
BROWNING, PROF. F. (Chairman): Hospital
endowments, 1334
BROWNLIE, C. C. (Chairman): Scottish
Housing Advisory Committee, 1678
BRS, *see* Building Research Station
BRUCE, A. H. (Chairman): Paper and Paper
Products Training Board, 1570
BRUCE, R. H. W. (Chairman): Highland
Transport Services, 374
BRUCE-MITFORD, R. L. S.: Sutton Hoo
Ship Burial, 721
BRÜCK, M. T.: Three Colour Photometry of
Southern Galactic Clusters, 207, 921
Brunchorstia die-back of corsican pine, 465
Brunel University Act, 370
BRUNTON, C. H. C.:
silicified:
brachiopods, 722
productoids, 103
Brush(es) and broom(s):
census of production, 1372
Wages Council (Great Britain), 505
Brussels Nomenclature, classification:
of chemicals, 397, 730
opinions, 113, 397, 1547
Bryobia Mites, 88
Bryozoa, 723, 1128

B.S.R. Ltd., Industrial Relations Commission, 1545

Bubble Chamber Events, 208
Buckinghamshire, sample census, 467, 862
Budget, financial statement, 249, 583, 969,
1380, 1722
BUGLER, A. J.: *HMS Victory*, 123
Builder(s)*:
and weather, 521
machines, care of, 1320
Materials and Builders' Merchants
(careers), 747
Building(s):
accuracy, 523
adhesives, 1320, 1669
and:
Civil Engineering:
Contracting, (careers), 1565
Labour, inquiry, 753

Building(s) (continued):
and (continued):
Natural resources:
assistance to the fishing industry,
295
estimates committee, 316
boards:
fibre, 1669
plastering on, 1320
bulletins, Educ. and Sci., 125, 412, 743,
1145, 1560
by direct labour organisations, 1292
cellular plastics, 913
changing appearance, 523
cleaning external surface, 1671
Control:
Act, 77:
Bill 6, 7, 43, 45, 48, 49, 50, 163
Minister's report, 1321
report, 913
circular, 170
cracking, 220
Crafts, (careers), 1564
dampness, 521, 1320
design, cost control, 914
dimensional co-ordination, 524, 914
domestic, safety, 1671
educational, co-ordination of components, 743
estimating daylight, 1671
external electrical distribution systems,
914
farm, pocket book, 379
(First Amendment) Regulations S. I.
select committee, 167
for General Medical Practice, 865
heating, water, etc. installations, 914
hospital, 471
in bad weather, 489
industrial, corrosion-resisting floors,
1671
Industry:
operatives, 864
pay and conditions, 903, 1306
integrated day– and artificial light, 220
limes, 220, 1320
maintenance:
interim report, 1323
manual, 1672
management:
handbook, 1672
studies, 1570
materials:
miscellaneous, census of production,
958
pulverised fuel ash in, 523
stainless steel, 1671
operations, accidents, 179
operative work, 219
overseas in warm climates, 913
planning a major programme, 203

Building(s) (continued):
process, case study, 1672
programming and progressing in design,
1323
reducing noise, 521
regulations:
Agreement Board, circulars, 889,
1643
circulars, 170, 171, 487, 489, 889,
1291, 1292, 1643, 1645
commercial glasshouses, 202
Fire, Stairs, Space, 202
metric:
equivalents of dimensions, 889,
893
values, 1297
metrication, 1292
multi-storey car parks, 889
prefabricated chimneys, 170
public health, 489
PVC sheeting, 487
selected decisions, 489
sound insulation, 171
Research:
Station: 219
annual report, 1671
daylight protractors, 913
digests, 220, 523, 913, 1321–2,
1671
publications, 220, 522–3, 913–14,
1321–2, 1671–2
reports, 220, 522, 913, 1321,
1671
sky component protractors, 913
technical paper, 220
science abstracts, 220, 523, 913–14,
1322, 1671–2
(Scotland) Act: 1515
Bill, 1077, 1407, 1409, 1466, 1470,
1482, 1628, 1629
selective tendering, standard forms of
contract, 1644
single storey, PVC rooflights, 221
sites:
co-ordination of underground
services: 914, 1323
electricity on, 201
fire risks, 521, 1669
noise control, 912, 1320
(6th Amendment) Regulations S. I.
select committee, 1644
small, timber sizes, 1669
Society(ies):
Chief Registrar of Friendly Societies'
report, 152, 466, 861, 1257, 1613
mortgages, rate of interest, 193
Standards (Scotland):
Amendment Regulations, memorandum, 532, 1677
metric equivalents of dimensions, 923
system for higher education, 1560

Building(s) (continued):
vibrations, 1671
wind loading, 913
without accidents, 521
work(s):
Local Authority tender and contract
procedures, 490
schedule of rates: 203, 524, 915, 1323
metric edition, 1673
Bulbs and corms, flowers from, 376
Bulgaria:
air services*, 1576
Consular convention*, 759, 1161
medical services*, 849, 1161
property accounts, 969, 765, 1377, 1719
trade*, 1576
Bulk grain dryers, 94, 380
BULLEN, F. R. (Chairman): Disused tips,
1316
BULLERWELL, W.: Seismic reflection survey,
Southern Irish Sea, 1312
Bullfinch, the, 68
BULLOCK, R. H. W. (Chairman): Problems
of cyclical pattern of machine T., 223
Bunker silos, force on walls by silage, 1519
BURGESS, T.: Inside comprehensive schools,
1562
Burgh Castle, abridged guide, 522
BURGHARD, REAR ADM. G. F. (Chairman):
Common standards for electronic parts,
554
Burma(ese):
income tax, 1300
printed books, catalogue, 1162
BURNS, W.: Hearing and noise in industry,
1617
BURRELLS, W.: Low background counting
room and ancillary apparatus, 923
BURREN, J. W.: Modifications to RHEL
geometrical reconstruction programme,
922
BURROWS, G. S.: Chichester, 1290
BURT, M. D. B.: Cyclophyllidean cestodes
from birds in Borneo, 1127
BURTON, A. L. (Chairman): Local Authority purchasing, 1297
BURTON OF COVENTRY, BARONESS (Chairman): Council of Tribunals, 1654
BURTT, B. L.: Notes for Botanic Garden,
Edinburgh, 1674
Bury, *see* Manchester Corporation
Bus:
Fuel Grants Act, 77
Bill, 11, 52
productivity agreements, 511
Business:
efficiency, ABC of advisory services, 904
Monitor:
civil aviation series, 942, 1355–6,
1697
miscellaneous series, 1356, 1698

Business (continued):
Monitor (continued):
production series 224–32, 558–67,
942–50, 1356–64, 1698–1706
service and distributive series, 1706
premises, security of tenure, 899, 1654
Busmen, pay and conditions, 192, 902, 903
BUSTARD, H. E.: Cedura Tryoni Complex,
103
BUTCHER, E. G.:
Fire and car-park buildings, 393
temperature attained by steel in building
fires, 221
BUTCHER, R. W. Smaller algae of British
coastal waters, 379
Bute Education Trust (Amendment)
Scheme, 1332
BUTLER, J. R.: Occupational choice, 745
Butt rot, 1611
Butterflies:
generic names and type species, 386
in woodlands, 860
Butyl rubber, price, 902
Buxton, Stockport, and York, Provisional
Order, 284, 370
Buying and selling, (careers), 1149
Buzzard, common, 375

B–V of the sun, 206

BWD, 88

BYATT, I. C. R.: Science policy study, 1147
BYNNER, J. M.: The Young Smoker, 1271
Byssinosis, 866

C

Cab Bill, 1484
Cabinet:
Office:
publications, 104, 338, 724, 1128–9,
1540
records, P.R.O., 203
Papers, list, P.R.O., 203
Cable and Wireless Ltd, 197, 515, 908, 1315,
1644
Cactaceae, 729
Cadco Developments Ltd., 232
Caerleon Roman amphitheatres, guide, 1670
Caernarvon Castle:
pictorial guide, 1321
watercolour reproduction, 914
Caernarvonshire:
census, 133
sample census, 467, 1259
Caesalpinioideae, 396

Cairngorm area, Technical Group report,
531, 1330
Caithness, mineral resources, 1312
Calcareous algae, 723
Calcichordata, 722
Calcium silicate bricks, 1669
Calculations in S.I. units, 1672
CALDECOTE, VISCOUNT (Chairman): Movement of freight, 193
Calderdale Water Bill, 1001
Calendars. *see specific subject*
Calf:
housing, 1121
rearing, 376
tetany, 375
wastage and husbandry in Britain, 711
Caligidae, 723
Caligus longicaudatus Brady, 723
Cambodia, power and irrigation*, 1162
Cambrian Coast Line, retention of railway
services, 1717
Cambridge:
geology of the country around, 1663
Low Temperature Research Station, 86
Reading, and Walsall Provisional Order
Confirmation Act, 79
Bill, 5, 49
Cambridgeshire:
census, 133
historical monuments, inventory, 916
sample census, 467, 1259
Cameras, aeronautics, 207
CAMERON, I. B.:
Rocks at Sandy Bay, Co. Antrim, 1312
Sources of aggregate in N. I., 1663
CAMERON, LORD (Chairman):
Printing Industry inquiry, 501
Scottish Inshore Fisheries, 1520
Cameroon:
loan, 420
telecommunication system*, 360
Cameroons, income tax, 1300
CAMPBELL PROF. A. D.: Electricity Supply
Industry Inquiry, 1568
CAMPBELL, A. D. (Chairman): Teachers'
salaries, Scotland, 1680
CAMPBELL-SMITH, W.: History of the
mineral collection in the B.M., 1128
Canada(ian):
cereals*, 1162
double taxation*, 108, 393
Federal Civil Service, 1133
forces in Bermuda*, 1759
micro-organism collections, 413
pension plan*, 759
war graves*, 1254, 1610
Cancer, 467, 861, 1664
Candles, census of production, 957
Cane fruits, 1171
Canker, larch, 1255
Cannabis, 1269, 1622

Cans, and metal boxes, census of production, 598
Canteens, Messrooms and Refreshment
Services, booklet, 187
Canvas goods, and sacks, census of production, 958
Cape Lyot heliograph results, 1328
Cape:
Observatory annals, 205
photographic catalogue, 205
Capital:
Allowances Act, 703
Bill, 275, 288, 340, 484, 485
programmes, circular, 1572
projects code, hospital building procedure, 1616
Capricode, 1616
Caprifoliaceae, 729
Captain James Cook, poster, 1661
Car Delivery Industry, pay and productivity, 1307
Caravan:
and camping sites, 1540
sites:
Act: 703
Bill, 613, 616, 661, 665, 668, 669,
875
circular, 890
gypsy encampments, 1644
development control, 1294
Carbon:
disulphate vapour, 1152
fibres, memoranda, 1639
tetrachloride, precautionary measures,
380
Carboniferous rocks of Great Britain,
fossil plants, 1663
Carchemish, excavations, 1536
Carcinogenic substances, use in educational
establishments, 1678
Cardboard boxes, cartons, and fibre board
packing cases, census of production,
1372
Cardiff Corporation Act, 1113
Cardiganshire:
census, 133
sample census, 467, 1259
Cardio-vascular Department, hospital, 1615
Cardium eduli, 913
Care:
and health of hospital staff, 856
in use of timber, 1320
of builders' machines, 1320
Careers:
choice of, 180, 498, 747, 1149, 1564
guide, 180, 498, 747, 1149
Cargo ship safety, fees and expenses, 238
Caribbean Development Bank*, 1567
CARLILE, T. (Chairman): Shipbuilding
Industry Training Board, 1571

CAR— INDEX 1966-70

Carmarthenshire:
census, 153
sample census, 467, 1259
Carn Euny, Cornwall, guide, 912
Carnation production, manual, 376
Car-park(s):
buildings, fire note, 939
multi-storey, 889
Car-parking facilities, developers' contributions, 489
Carpet(s):
beetles, 384
census of production, 958
Industry Training Board, 180, 498, 746, 1149, 1564
knotting and weaving, notes ,1396
Carriage of:
dangerous goods in ships, 950
goods by rail, international convention, 962, 1162, 1249
goods by Sea (Amendment) Bill,1410,1480
passengers and luggage by rail, 1162
Cartiages, illustrated booklet, 1675
CARROLL, A. S., Kinematical analysis of two neutral Pi-Meson Final States, 208
Cars:
in housing, 490
light, Technical history 1675
CARTER, S.:
Juncaceae, 112
Tecophilaeaceae, 112
CARTER, SIR W. (Chairman): Criminal Injuries Compensation Board, 1625
Cartographers Training and qualifications, 1314
Cartography, Commonwealth conference, 1314
Cartoons, Raphael, 266
CAS Occasional Papers, 586, 966, 1131, 1377, 1543
Cash transactions during change over, decimal currency booklet, 1136
Catasaurus Schönherr, 1125
Catering, hospital, 156, 469, 864, 1262, 1613
Catherine McCaig's Trust (Amendment) Scheme, 926
CATION, P. G. F.: Study of vertical air motion and particle size, 309
Catoptopteryx Karsch, 1537
Cattle:
beef, housing, 1525
buildings, 83
crushes and equipment, 715
direct feeding, 512
grids for private roads, 1121
Caudal skeleton:
ancanthopterygian fishes, 723
pholidophorid fishes, 722
CAUNTER, C. F.: The light Car, 1675
CAWDOR, EARL (Chairman): Historic Buildings Council for Scotland, 1677

Cayley, Sir George, Biography, 922
Cayman Islands:
colonial report, 393
hurricane research stations*, 963-4

Cedar, western red, 465
Cedura Tryoni Complex, 103
Ceiling tiles, polystyrene, fire risks, 1669
Ceilings Painted, of Scotland, 202
Celery leaf spot, 88
CELORIA, F., Dated post-medieval pottery, 188
Cement(s):
painting, 201
census of production, 567
special, 912
Censorship of the theatre, 485
Census:
constituency tables, 1257
distribution and other services, 1714
England and Wales, 152-4
general report, 861
Isle of Man, 153
Jersey, Guernsey, and adjacent Islands, 159
Northern Ireland, 906
of:
children and adolescents in non-psychiatric wards, 472
patients in psychiatric beds, 472
production:
index of products, 1715
introductory notes, 957
reports, 567, 957-8, 1371-2, 1715
summary tables, 1372, 1715
woodlands, 1611
sample:
England and Wales, 467-8
Scotland, 469
Scotland, 155
Central:
Advisory Council for Education (Wales), 743
After-Care Association, 161
and:
Scottish Health Services Councils, 470, 865
Southern Line Islands, annual report 109, 845, 1240, 1598
Borders, plan for expansion, 923
Castings Ltd, investigation, 499
Committee on English, 925
Danish, ancient monuments, 1628
Electricity:
Board, bulk supply tariff, 902
Generating Board:
annual report and accounts, 198, 516, 909, 1317, 1691
Power Stations, inquiry, 1319
Select Committee, 883

1966 pp 1–272, 1967 p ρ 273–604, 1968 pp 605–990, 1969 pp 991–1402, 1970 pp 1403–1740

20

INDEX 1966-70 **—CHE**

Central (continued):
England, geology, 1311
Government:
of Britain, Information Office pamphlet, 177, 495
re-organisation, 1540
Health Services Council:
District General Hospital, functions of, 1262
publications, 156, 470, 865
report, 158, 471, 867, 1264, 1616
heating etc. installations for dwellings, 1672
Housing Advisory Committee, needs of new communities, 492
Lancashire, New Town proposals, 487, 888
Office of Information See Information Office
Statistical Office publications, 105-6, 388-9, 724-5, 1129-30, 1541-2
Sterile Supply, hospital, 1615
Training Council, reports 180, 313, 498, 746, 1149, 1571
Transport Consultative Committee for G.B. annual report and accounts, 242, 576, 961, 1374, 1717
Unit for environmental planning, 1145
Youth Employment Executive (careers), 717, 1149, 1564-5
Centralised Services, smallholdings, 95, 382, 717
Centre for Administration Studies. See CAS occasional papers
Century of agricultural statistics, 711
Cephalopod family Sepudae, 104
Cepheids, photometry, 529
Cerambycidae, 724
Ceramics, glass, and mineral Products Industry Training Board, 180, 498, 747, 1150, 1565
Cereals:
deficiency payments scheme, 376, 1522
home grown, annual report, 94, 380, 716, 1121, 1525
international*, 759, 1162
root eel worm, 88
Ceramoporidae, 1611
Cerebral Palsy, children, 1561
Certificate(s) of:
comprising in the Merchant Navy, examination 569, 952, 1366, 1709
Secondary education:
experimental and trial examinations, 128, 415
geography, 128
history, 921
home economics, 128
monitoring experiment, 128, 1329
working papers, 128
Cesar Mange de Hauke Bequest, 720

Cestodes, 1127
Ceylon:
air services*, 1162
public officers*, 1162
CHADWICK, REV. PROF. O.: Church and State, 1543
Chairs, English, 1735
Chalcidoidea, 385, 1126
Chalk, clay, sand, and gravel extraction, census of production, 1371
Chamosite in Weald clay, 1663
CHANDLER, M. E.:
A new Tempskya from Kent, 722
Fruiting organs from Morrison Formation, 103
CHANDLER, S. E.:
Fires in Hotels, 1351
Multiple death fires, 1351
Change for a pound, 921, 1675
Changing:
to the Metric System, 222, 555, 1352
wage payment systems, 920
Channels and pipes, charts for hydraulic design, 1352
CHANTLER, P. (Chairman), Dee Crossing Study, 490
Charaxes, 101, 385, 1125, 1538
Charge exchange reactions, 530
Charges Schemes, Water Resources Act, 492
Charitable Causes (Medical research and Disabled Persons) Bill, 1485
Charity Commissioners for England and Wales, 162, 473, 644, 1272, 1627
CHARLICK, R. H.: Housing Pigs, 905
Chateau de Douvres, 1670
Chattel(s):
Mortgages Bill, 17
Transfer of Title, Law Reform, 189
Chebyshev series for Bessel Functions of Fractional Order, 222
Check-off agreements in Britain, 919
CHEETHAM, A. H.: Cheilostomatous polyzoa, 103
Chelsea:
College, University of London Act, 1113
Hospital accounts, 116, 490, 1319, 1560
Chemical(s):
and Allied Products Industry Training Board, 740, 1150, 1565
balance, development, 1329
control of weeds in the forest 1255
for:
the gardener, 376
pest control, census of production, 957
in:
Brussels Nomenclature, 397
hand cleansing of farm dairy equipment, 89

1966 pp 1–272, 1967 pp 273–604, 1968 pp 605–990, 1969 pp 991–1402, 1970 pp 1403–1740

21

CHE INDEX 1966-70

Chemical(s) (continued):
industry, manpower, 512
making, 922
toxic, safety arrangements, 414
Chemistry:
atoms, elements and molecules, 922
chemical laboratories and apparatus, 207
making chemicals, 922
Chepstow Castle, guide, 522
Cheshire:
census, 153
County Council Act, 705
sample census, 467, 867
Chest Services, future, 865
CHESTER, D. N. (Chairman): Football, 745
Chester, conservation study, 1290
CHETTLE, G. H.· Hampton Court Palace, 522
CHEW, V. K.:
Early history of the gramophone, 530
Physics for Princes, 1329
Chichester, conservation study, 1290
Chick-s(-ens):
and growing stock, feeding, 89
coccidiosis, 374
Chief:
Land Registrar, report to the Lord Chancellor, 506
Registrar of Friendly Societies, report of 152, 466, 861, 1257, 1613
Child('s) (and Children's) and:
adolescents in non-psychiatric wards, report on census, 472
their primary schools, 412
Young Persons Act, 1111
Bill, 997, 1000, 1001, 1002, 1060, 1072, 1074, 1075, 1274
guide for Courts and practitioners, 1625
1963 (Amendment) Bill, 1073, 1480
blind, and partially sighted, 744
Care:
Home Office Advisory Council, 871
in Scotland, 928, 1333
(including Approved Schools)
Secretary of State for Scotland's report, 533
Service, Dorset County Council, 160
Clothing, distributors' margin, 903
Deaf, education of, 413
Department, Home Office:
report on the work of, 475, 1628
workloads, 1270
handicapped, in care, 1679

Child('s) (and Children('s)) (continued):
in:
Britain, Information Office pamphlet, 495
Care, E. and W., 159, 473, 871, 1269, 1625
trouble, 871
Nutrition, 1622
Partially hearing, 413
Performances, regulations, 072
Play on housing estates, 221
With:
cerebral palsy, 1561
hearing defects, 532
visual handicaps, ascertainment, 1331
CHILDE, PROF. V. G.: Illustrated guide to ancient monuments, Scotland, 522
CHILDS, A.: Brachiopods, 1126
Chile:
Arbitration on boundary with Argentine, 131
atomic energy*, 1160, 1162
cultural relations*, 345, 420
irrigation scheme,* 1164
loan*, 131, 1577
military service*, 420
Nuclear Research Reactor*, 1577
Visas*, 759
Chilo zincken, 1538
Chimney(s):
boiler and furnace, grit and dust emission, 490
domestic boiler, 221
height, 487, 489
mild steel, 1323
smoking, 912
China. Sail and Sweep in, 208
Chinese:
fish drawings, Reeves collection, 1538
fishes, 387
periodicals in British libraries, handlist, 1124
Chintz, origins, 1736
Chiropodist, (careers) 499
Chiroptera, 103
Chitting houses, 512
CHITTY, T. B.: Fire note, 1691
Chlorine:
detection, 186
liquid, precautions in handling etc., 505
Chocolate:
and Sugar Confectionery Industry, costs and prices, 902
Confectionery, Census of Production, 957
Choice of Careers, booklets. See Careers, choice
Chondrostei, 386

Choosing:
a bicycle, 579
a type of pile, 913
your house, 888
Christ Church with Saint Andrew and Saint Michael, East Greenwich Act, 705
CHRISTIE, P. M.: Carn Euny, Cornwall, 912
Chromic Acid Mist, 501
Chronically Sick and Disabled Persons Bill, 1609, 1407, 1410, 1460, 1480, 1483, 1619
Chronological tables of Statutes, 718, 374, 931, 1342, 1689
Chrysanthemum eelworm, 375
Church(es):
and:
State, 1543
Universities (Scotland) Widows' and Orphans' Fund (Amendment) Order Confirmation Bill, 337, 370
Assembly Measures, 389–90, 725–6, 1130–1, 1542–3
Commissioners Measure, 1518, 1542, 1543
Information Office, 1543
of England Convocation Act, 77
Church function area, geology, 905, 906
Churchill:
Endowment Fund, 1163
statue, H. C., 1628
Cicadellidae, 721
Cicadelloidea, 102
Cichlidae, 387, 1127
Cider, Census of production, 957
Cigarette(s):
filter rods, Monopolies Commission, 1369
(Health Hazards) Bill, 669, 1479
Cinematograph:
Film(s):
Council:
annual report, 232, 567, 950, 1364, 1706
legislation, 958
Production (Special Loans) Acts, accounts, 129, 754
Fund account, 130, 418, 755, 1157, 1572
Cinque Ports, calendar of White and Black Books, 473
Circular saws, 515
Circumpolar stars, Cape catalogue, 206
Circumstances of Families, 1537
Cirripid fauna, 387
City:
and County of Bristol Dock undertaking, pay awards to staff, 903
of:
Aberdeen Education Endowments (Amendment) Scheme, 1679

INDEX 1966-70 **—CIV**

City (continued):
of (continued):
Dundee Educational Trust Scheme, 210
Edinburgh Corporation, Tron Kirk, 1721
London (Various Powers) Act, 705, 1113
Oxford Provisional Order Confirmation Act, 79
University Act, 371
Civic Amenities Act, 367, 489
Bill, 49, 280, 203, 302, 331, 335, 338, 416
Civil:
Aeronautical fixed service, telecommunication procedures, 1715
Affairs and Military Government, 104
Air Transport:
Industry Training Board, 499, 568, 748, 1150
Inquiry, 1355
Aircraft accidents, reports, 233-4, 567-8 950-1, 1364-5, 1706-8
and Political Rights, International covenant, 454
Appropriation Accounts, 246, 580, 966, 1378, 1720
Aviation:
Acts:
1949, Orders, 234, 568, 951, 1365, 1708
1968, 703
Bill, 288, 289, 290, 340, 617, 661, 669, 875
Air base on Grand Turk Island*, 420
convention, 1163
(Declaratory Provisions) Bill, 1415, 1477, 1484
Department publications, 232-4
Orders, directions, grants, and agreements, 1304
policy, 1365
Contingencies Fund accounts, 247, 580, 966, 1378, 1720
Defence:
Corps Training Syllabuses, 473
handbook, 871
Instructors' Notes, 473, 1625
Engineering:
contracting since Banwell, 904
economic development, 512, 904
Industry, pay and conditions, 903, 1306
tender and contract procedure, 1291
Engineers, surveying for, Commonwealth conference, 1314
Estimates:
Miscellaneous, 247, 581, 967, 1378
Statement of Excesses, 247, 971, 1383, 1725

1966 pp 1–272, 1967 pp 273–604, 1968 pp 605–990, 1969 pp 991–1402, 1970 pp 1403–1740

22 23

CIV—   *INDEX 1966–70*

Civil (*continued*):
Estimates (*continued*):
Supplementary, 247, 580–1, 967, 1378, 1720
Revised, 247, 580, 967, 1720
Vote on Account, 252, 586, 972, 1384, 1726
Evidence Act, 703
Bill, 290, 606, 608, 617, 661, 666, 669, 875
Judicial statistics, *see* Judicial statistics.
Liability:
for:
animals, 507
dangerous things and activities, 1654
vendors and lessors of defective premises, 1655
proceedings:
hearsay evidence, 189
privilege, 507
Servants, 192
Service:
Arbitration Tribunal awards, 180–1, 499, 748, 1150, 1565
(careers), 1149
Commission:
annual report, 107, 390, 726
publications, 106–7, 390–1, 726–7
Question papers, 106–7, 390, 726–7, 1131–2, 1543–4
Department:
publications, 1131–3, 1543–4
report, 1544
Factual, statistical, and explanatory papers, 967
Fulton Report, 967
List, 246, 580, 966, 1377, 1543
Management:
by objectives, 1131
Consultancy Group report, 967
Non-industrial, London weighting, 511
of North America, 1133
Pay Research Unit, 391
proposals and opinions, 967
recruitment, estimates committee, 167
surveys and investigations, 967, 1379
Training, 1133
and education, 247, 581, 967, 1133, 1379
report, 967
Use of logical trees, 1543
Civilian Industrial employees at Defence Ministry, regulations, 398

Clackmannan, Fife, and Kinross, sample census, 469, 1261
Claims and misleading descriptions, Food Standards, 93

CLARK, A. McG.:
Amphiuridae, 1539
Nardoa and other Ophidiasterids, 387
CLARK, D. H. (Chairman): Psychiatric nursing, 865
CLARK, E. (Chairman): Housing management in Scotland, 531
CLARKE, A. W. (Chairman): Carriage of dangerous goods in ships, 950
CLARKE, J. F. G.: Microlepidoptera, catalogue, 1128
Classics teaching in schools, 534
Classification:
Brussels Nomenclature:
chemicals, 397, 730
opinions, 113, 397, 1547
of:
diseases, 466
farms, E. and W., 379, 1524
overseas trade statistics, guide, 1547
proprietary preparations, 470, 867
snakes, 387
the tertiary, 1538
trade marks, 462
statistical, of imported and re-exported goods, 397
to alphabetical list of industries, 105
Classified index of Local Authorities and New Towns E. and W., 891
CLAY, T.:
Amblycera, 1538
Menoponidae, 721, 1125
Myrsidea Waterston, 101
Clay tile flooring, 523
CLAYTON, M., Rubbings of brasses and incised slabs, 1396
CLAYTON, W. D.:
Gramineae, 1546
Clean:
air:
Act: 703
Bill, 611, 615, 616, 665, 669
chimney heights, 488
circulars, 170, 483, 489, 890, 1290, 1291, 1292, 1293, 1330
direct acting electric space heaters, 890
exempted fireplaces, 1572, 1644
grant arrangements, 266
grit and dust, 489
memorandum, 487
question and answer book, 266
smoke control areas:
Authorised Fuels: 170, 1644
(No. 2) Regulations, 1645
estimates and final costs, 170
supplies of solid smokeless fuels, 488

Clean (*continued*):
air (*continued*):
(Height of Chimneys) Regulations, 1291
(Measurement of Grit and Dust) Regulations, 889
rivers, 1644
CLEGG, H. A.: Fork lift trucks inquiry, 182
Clement Ader's flight claims and place in history, 922
CLENSHAW, C. W.: Chebyshev Series, 222
Clergy Pensions (Amendment) Measure, 277, 371, 389, 390, 995, 1114, 1130, 1131
Clerical work measurement, 966
CLERK, A. M.: Ophiuroidea, 723
Clickhimin, Shetlands, excavations, 913
Clients' Money (Accounts) Bill, 49, 666
Clinical and post mortem diagnoses, agreement between, 154
CLM. *see* Culham Laboratory
Cloak room accommodation, and washing facilities, 753
Clocks:
Census of production, 957
in the B.M., 720
Closed circuit television annunciator system, H.C. (Services) select committee, 481
Cloth manufacture, silk, man-made fibres and cotton, (careers) 180
Clothes moths and carpet beetles, 384
Clothing:
and Allied Products Industry Training Board, 1565
Children's, distributors margin, 903
Industry:
Development Council (Dissolution) account, 234, 558, 951, 1365
Economic Development Committee, 904, 1309
future market, 1661
manufacturing industries, pay and conditions, 1307
CLOUGH, C. H.: Pietro Bembo's library, B.M., 100
Clover:
weevils, 88
see also grass and clover
Club root, 375
CLUBE, S. V. M.:
Proper motions:
in the field of NGC, 206
of RR Lyrae Variables, 920
Clubs, Unlicensed, Registration and Control of Bill, 4
Clupeoid fishes, 387, 1127, 1139
Clupeomorph fishes, 723

Cluster(s):
flies, 375
globular, 529
M67 II and III, proper motions, 1327
OB, 921
Southern galactic, 207, 921
Clutch mechanising for road vehicles, Monopolies Commission, 955
Clyde:
Navigation (Superannuation) Order Confirmation Act, 78
Port Authority Order Confirmation Act, 78, 1113
Bill, 1075

COAD, J. G.: Hailes Abbey
Coal:
and Other Mines (Shafts, Outlets and Roads) (Amendment) Regulations, 520
distribution costs, 193
Industry:
Acts, 367
accounts, 581, 909, 1316
loan, 247, 248, 581, 967, 1379, 1720
Nationalisation Act:
account, 198
loan, 247, 248, 581, 967, 1379, 1720
loading dispute, 1571
mining, census of production 957
prices, 192, 1307, 1657, 1658
trimmers, employment in ports, 505
Coast(s):
and ship stations, VHF transmitter and receiver, 908, 1668
circular, 170
Nature conservation, 1545
of:
England and Wales, 728
High quality scenery, 1545
Coastal:
heritage, 1545
pollution, Science and Technology, select committee, 482, 883, 884, 1270
preservation and development, 513, 728, 1134, 1545
recreation and holidays, 1134
Coastline planning and studies, 728, 1545
Coatbridge Burgh Order Confirmation Act, 1518
Bill, 1482
COATES, A.: Basutoland, 110
Cob-nuts and filberts, 88
Coccidae, 386
Coccidiosis in chickens, 374
Coccoidea, 386, 1125
COCKBURN, C.: Construction Statistics, report, 914

1966 pp 1–272, 1967 pp 273–604, 1968 pp 605–990, 1969 pp 991–1402, 1970 pp 1403–1740
24

COC—   *INDEX 1966–70*

Cockermouth and Caldbeck, geology, 1311
Cockles, 93
COCKS, L. R. M.: Brachiopods, 722, 1538
Cocoa, chocolate, and sugar confectionery, census of production, 957
Coconut germ plasm, 196
Cod:
and cod fishery at Faroe, 93
food of 374, 709, 710
Coding and data co-ordination, 1322
Coding moth, 87
Coffee*, 759, 1163, 1248
COGAN, B. H.: *Ephydridae*, 721
COHEN, A. V.: Sophistication factor in science expenditure, 415
Coil winding irregularities in super conducting magnets, 1676
Coinage Bill, 1414, 1415, 1654
Coins in:
British Museum:
Arab-Sassanian, 384
Carolingian, 99
English, 1536
Greek Sicily, 100
Hiberno-Norse, 101
in the British Isles, Sylloge, 101
India, 383
Muhammadan, 384
Roman, 100, 384, 720, 1536
circulation, U.K., numbers, 1542
Coke ovens, and manufactured fuel, census of production, 957
Cold blast cupolas, 1291, 1294
COLDSTREAM, SIR W. (Chairman): Art and design education, 1563
COLE, S.: Neolithic Revolution, 388
COLEMAN-COOKE, J.: Exmoor National Park, 1546
Coleoptera, 385, 1125
Coleraine, Portrush, and Portstewart Area Plan, 906
Collecting in Turkey, 385
Collective bargaining, studies, 919
Collectors:
in Edinburgh Herbarium, index, 1674
instructions for 724, 1540
College(s):
of:
Arms, 392
Education:
entrants, 744
government of, 127
teachers' salaries, 414, 1147
technical, management studies, 126
Year, pattern and organisation, 1562
Collegiate Churches (Capital Endowments) Measure, 1046, 1518, 1542
Colombo Plan:
Annual report, 514, 907, 1313, 1667
technical co-operation, 196, 907

Colonial:
Development and Welfare Acts:
accounts, 108, 195, 393, 907, 1313
schemes and loans, 108, 393, 759, 1163, 1666
Loans Acts, 581, 967, 1379, 1720
Office List, 109
Phillipsastraeidae, 722
Reports, 109, 393
Colorado beetle, 88
Colour(ed):
film, supply and processing, Mono polies Commission, 239
in school buildings, 1143
school leavers, problems of, 1284, 128
Columnea, Jamaican species, 1125
COLYERS, B.: Helium, 530, 1676
Combine harvesters, 716
Command Papers, 52–76, 340–67, 671–703 1077–1110, 1485–1514
Commerce, teachers, and industry, close links, 128
Commercial:
and Clerical Training Council, report 746
data processing, 556
rating, inquiry, 1678
studies in schools, 1561
Commissary Court of London, testa mentary records, index, 1269
Commission for Industry and Manpowe Bill, 1480
Commissioners' decisions. *See* respective Acts
Commodity:
coding, 1659
information systems, 1659
Common:
Market:
patents, 1714
see also European Economic Community
names of British Insects and other pests, 718
Commons Registration Act, 188, 889, 1643, 1644
Commonwealth:
Agricultural Bureaux:
annual report, 107, 392, 728, 1133
review conference, 107
and:
Foreign supply estimates, 1725
Sterling area, statistical abstract, 234, 558, 951
Citizens, 1625
collections of micro-organism, 413, 743
Conference on Anguilla, 392
Development Corporation, annual report and accounts, 109, 393, 907, 1313, 1667
Community:
of interests, Schools, Youth Service, Community Service, etc., 925

Commonwealth (*continued*):
Economic Committee:
Annual report, 107
publications, 107–8
report, 108
Education:
Britain's share, 894
Conference, 907
Liaison Committee publications, 108
392
Immigrants Act, 703
Bill, 608, 666, 871
control of immigration, 159, 473, 871, 1270, 1625
instructions of Immigration Officers, 159, 473, 871, 1270, 1625
(No. 2) Bill, 608
Immigration control, Race Relations etc. select committee, 1285
in:
brief, 495, 1299
education, 127
Income taxes, 177
Medical Conference, 196
Office:
publications, 108–12, 392–5
Year book, 109, 393, 759
see also Foreign and Commonwealth Office
Prime Ministers' meetings, 109, 1163
Relations Office, *see* Commonwealth Office
Scholarship:
and Fellowship Plan, 108, 392
Commission, annual report, 195, 392, 907, 1313, 1667
Secretariat Act, 77
Bill, 48
Settlement Act, 367
Bill, 48
Survey, 176, 495
Officers, conference, 1313–14
see also British and Commonwealth Affairs Survey
Telecommunications:
Act, 703
Bill, 607, 661, 666, 875
Organisation, 759, 1252
Telegraphs*, 1252
Today, 176, 495
trade, 392
War Graves Commission, annual report, 112, 395, 728, 1133, 1545
Year book, 1254, 1610
Communication(s):
satellites*, 131, 420
services, hospital, 1616
supply estimates, 1725
Community:

Community (*continued*):
Relations Commission, 1272, 1627
Service:
and the curriculum, 921
Youth and 1680
Company(ies):
Acts, 367
Bill, 9, 11, 47, 275, 286, 331, 335, 337, 467, 1061, 1074, 1075, 1274
investigation, 234, 568, 951
reports, 951, 952
(Floating Charges) (Scotland) Act, 1715
General annual, and annual reports, 235, 568, 952, 1365, 1709
manpower planning, 753
(Political Contributions) Bill, 1001, 1003
Secretary, (careers), 1564
Compendium of Teacher Training courses, E. and W., 413
Compensation for:
compulsory purchase, 1644
dispossessed tenant farmers, 488
loss etc. following statutory re-organisation, 889
Competition, monopoly, and restrictive practices, 1709
Components in wide double and multiple systems, three colour photometry, 206
Compound fertilisers, prices, 510
Comprehensive:
development, grants to Local Authorities, 1293
schools, 743, 1562
Compulsory:
Acquisition, right to claim professional fees, 498
Purchase:
date of assessment of compensation, 1644
Orders, 1304
Computer(s):
aided production control, 1659
and:
Managers Series, 1659
People Series, 1659
schools, 1332
application:
in the:
construction industry, 1322
distributive trade, 1659
packages, 1659
assisted control, using ion source, 1330
Board for universities and research councils, 1561
control, real-time interpreter, 1676
education:
facilities, 1659
report, 413
Evidence in:
Court of Session, Act of Sederunt, S.I. select committee, 1640

1966 pp 1–272, 1967 pp 273–604, 1968 pp 605–990, 1969 pp 991–1402, 1970 pp 1403–1740
26

1966-70 | COM-CUM

COM— INDEX 1966–70

Computer(s) (*continued*):
Evidence in (*continued*):
Sheriff Court, Act of Sederunt, S.I. select committee, 1640
file creation for manufacturing control, 1659
for research, 127
Fortran programming manual, 1659
graphics patching of failed cyclops events, 1676
in:
distribution, 1659
textiles, 1659
vehicle scheduling, 1659
industry, U.K., Science and Technology select committee, 1639
installations, accommodation and fire precaution, 938
laboratory, 208
magneto-static programme TRIM, 1330
merger project, 940
new courses, 1660
packages, Local Government, 1660
peripherals and typesetting, 929, 1683
Standards Series, 1659
techniques, impact on road transport planning, 1659
use, petrological-mineralogical code for, 1663
user's guide to decimalisation, 1659
Computer-based data processing, 1659
Computing:
modern methods, 1713
teaching in Universities, 1735
Conciliation Act, reports, 499
Concrete:
aerated, 1671
breakers, noise, 890
floors, 1322
granolithic, 1671
handling on housing sites, 521, 1669
in sulphate-bearing soils and ground-waters, 913
insulated magnet for accelerator, 1330
lightweight, 1320
aggregate, 1322, 1671
making, 521
mix proportioning and control, 1671
pre-stressed, 521
ready mixed, 201
re-inforced, for highway structures, 1374
roads, 242
testing, 1669
tiles and terrazzo flooring, 1671
wall panels, joints, 323
zinc-coated reinforcement, 1322
Concreting in cold weather, 912
Condensate systems, protection, 1618
Condensation:
advisory leaflets, 201, 1669
building digest, 1322
Condensation (*continued*):
in dwellings, 1645, 1672
prevention, 913
Condensed milk, Food Standards Committee, 1121
Cones from standing trees, 151
Congo (Kinshasa) commercial and economic co-operation*, 1578
Conifers, 151, 465, 1611
Conopidae, 101
Consent to marriage, convention, 848, 1603
Conservation of Seals Act, 1515
Bill, 610, 996, 999, 1076, 1408, 1467, 1480, 1629
Consol, radio aid to navigation, 96
Consolidated Fund:
abstract account, 129, 416, 755, 1157
Act: 77, 367, 703, 111, 1515
Bill, 10, 47, 335, 665, 666, 1071, 1479
and National Loans Fund accounts, 1379, 1572, 1573
(Appropriation):
Bill, 48, 50, 669, 1075, 1482, 1483
(No. 2) Bill, 338
loan, 249, 584
(No. 2) Act: 368, 703, 111, 1515
Bill, 335, 1072, 1481
Consolidation Bills, 168, 484–5, 886–7, 1289, 1642
Constabulary, report:
Chief Inspector, 162, 475, 874, 1272, 1627
Scotland, 213, 535, 927, 1334, 1681
Constitution Commission, 1133, 1544
Constitutional Conference Reports, 109, 393
Construction:
census of production, 1372
design, network analysis, 1323
Industry:
accidents in, 498
application of computers, 1322, 1672
Contracts Bill, 1467, 1481, 1482, 1629
going metric, 524, 1323, 1672
pay and conditions, 903
Research and Information Association, 1672
Survey of research and development, 914, 1673
Training Board, 181, 500, 748, 1150, 1565
Research Advisory Council, 1672
Sites:
electrical supplies, 523
large industrial, 1661
protective clothing for workers, 914
sound insulation, and new forms of, 913
statistics, directory, 914
Surveys and certificates, fees and expenses, 238

1966 pp 1–272, 1967 pp 273–604, 1968 pp 605–990, 1969 pp 991–1402, 1970 pp 1403–1740

28

INDEX 1966–70 —COS

Construction (*continued*):
works:
scaffolding, safety, 753
system building, safety, 753
Consular:
conventions. *See* respective countries
Relations Act, 703
Bill, 287, 340, 610, 661, 875
Consultant grade, responsibilities, 1268
Consumer:
consultative machinery in nationalised industries, 728
Council:
annual report, 112, 395, 728, 1134, 1545
publications, 112, 395, 728, 1134, 1545
Protection:
(Amendment) Bill, 1410, 1411
Bill, 287–8, 289, 606, 607, 1411, 1484
Continental Shelf:
Denmark*, 131, 421
Netherlands*, 457–8
reports, 516, 1216, 1690
Contingencies Fund Act, 1515
Bill, 1414, 1477, 1484, 1629
Contractors' plant, and quarrying machinery, census of production, 957
Contracts:
Exemption Clauses, Law Commission, 1304
of Employment Bill, 1071
Contributors to Black Papers, select committee, 1635
Control of:
Borrowing Order, 585
Commonwealth immigration, select committee, 1638
Hiring (Television Sets) Licence, 1709
Ice-cream etc. Vans Bill, 47
immigration, statistics, 1625
Liquid Fuel Act, 368
Bill, 285, 338
Office and Industrial Development Act, 235, 568, 952, 1365, 1646
Venereal Diseases Bill, 671
Conversion:
of accounting records, Decimal Currency booklet, 1136
tables for forestry agricultural workers, 151
Conveyancing:
and Feudal Reform (Scotland) Act, 1313
Bill, 1410, 1467, 1480, 1481, 1629
legislation and practice, 212
Conway Fishery. Young mussels, 1120
Cook, P. L.: Polyzoa, 387, 1127
Cook, Captain James, 1124
Cook Transit Circle, 206
Cooke, Sir L. (Chairman): Hotel Loans, 1712
Cookers, installing, 1669
Cooking fats. Prices and Incomes Board, 1658
Cool Halo Subdwarf HD 25329, analysis, 529
Cope, J. C. W.: Dorset Clay, 386
Copestake, Crampton and Co. Ltd. investigation, 568
Coppard, G.: With a Machine Gun to Cambrai, 1298
Copper water pipes, 170
Copyright:
Bill, 1076, 1411, 1479, 1485
International Convention, 1577
literary and artistic works, 421
revising Berne Convention, 358
(Royalties on Records) Bill, 1004
Coral, official definition, 1714
Corbet, G. B.:
Elephant shrews, 723
Identification of British mammals, 1128
Corby Tube works, dispute, 501
Cordullidae, 722
Corn drills, 716
Corn Exchange Act, 1113
Cornwall:
and the Isles of Scilly, sample census, 467, 1259
census, 153
(Lostwithiel) Order, S.I. select committee, 885
(Padstow) Order, S.I. select committee, 885
(St. Austell with Fowey) Order, S.I. select committee, 885
see also Devon and Cornwall
Corona Library series, 110, 759
Coroners' Inquisition Form, 160
Corporation of the Trinity House of Leith Order Confirmation Act, 78
Correspondence Courses in the Training of Teachers, 108
Corsets, and miscellaneous dress industries, census of production, 958
Corsican pine, 465
Cossidae, 724
Cost(s):
and:
efficiency, gas industry, 1658
revenue, National Newspapers, 1657
control in building design, 911
of:
Living Advisory Committee report, 753
personal services in hotels, 904
private building in Scotland, 1677
prices and profitability in the ice-cream manufacturing industry, 1658

1966 pp 1–272, 1967 pp 273–604, 1968 pp 605–990, 1969 pp 991–1402, 1970 pp 1403–1740

29

COS— INDEX 1966–70

Costa Rica, visas*, 1163
Cost-benefit:
analysis, current issues, 1131
aspects, manpower retraining, 1570
Costing:
and building procedures, 1619
of handling and storage in warehouses, 1709
Cotton:
and Allied:
Fibres Spinning Industry, 1156
Textiles Industry Training Board, 500, 748, 1150, 1165
(Centralised Buying) Act, accounts, 235, 1365
spinning and doubling, census of production, 1371
weaving, census of production, 1371
Cotton-paintings, indo-European, 1736
Coude spectrograph, 1327
Counselling in schools, 415
Council:
for:
scientific policy, 125, 413, 743
technical co-operation in South and South East Asia, 907
Training:
Health visitors, accounts, 1159
in Social Work, accounts, 1159, 1617
Wales and Monmouthshire, 267
Western European Union, 354
House Communities, policy for progress, 1677
Housing, purposes, procedures, and priorities, 1293, 1294
of:
Association with European Coal and Steel Community, 134
Europe, Human rights, 132, 1577
Industrial Design, 175
on Tribunals, annual report, 189, 507, 899, 1654
Tenants:
Charter Bill, 667, 1074, 1482
Scotland, rate rebates, 1678
Countryside:
Act: 703
Bill, 334, 339, 610, 612, 615, 661, 666, 668, 875
circulars, 890, 1644
reports, 728, 1134
Commission:
for Scotland, 1134, 1546
publications, 728, 1134, 1545
disused railways, 1545
farm buildings, 1292, 1294
(Scotland) Act, 368
Bill, 284, 286, 331, 336, 338, 339, 476
settlement, 489, 493
County:
Councils Association, select committee, 1634
Courts:
accounts, 193
index to parishes, 189
London directory, 507
of Argyll Educational Trust (Amendment) Scheme, 1332
population forecasts, South East Study, 170
tables, census, Scotland, 155
Coupland, J. H.: magnets with air cored windings of saddle coil type, 1676
Court Lees Approved School, inquiry, 473
Courts:
Bill, 1412, 1414, 1485
of:
Appeal:
accounts, 188, 507, 898
powers to sit in private, 189
Session, (Scotland) Rules of Court, 112, 395–6
Proceedings, mechanical recording, 189
Courts-Martial:
(Appeals) Act, 703
Bill, 606, 607, 666
Navy:
manual, 1551
memorandum, 411
Cousins, A. W. J.: Southern stars, 206
Cousins, Rt Hon. F. (Chairman):
Central Training Board, 1571
Community relations, 1627
Covent Garden Market:
Acts, 78, 1113
accounts, 92, 378–9, 1120
Authority report, 92, 379, 714
Coventry Corporation Act, 1113
Cowan, C. F.: *Lycaenidae*, 101, 385
Cowan, T. J. (Chairman): Northern Pennines Rural Development Board, 1525
Cowhouses, 1524
Cowley shopping centre, 904
Cox, C. B.:
dicynodonts from Ntawere Formation in Zambia, 1126
Eunotosaurus, 1126
Coypu, 89

Craftsman's pocketbook, metrication, 1672
Craigfoodie Endowment Scheme, 211, 533
Cranbrook, Earl of (Chairman): Animals (Restriction of Importation) Act, 412
Cranch, John: Zoologist, 1538
Crane, Sir H. W. (Chairman): Industrial injuries, 1621
Crassostrea, food value of algae, 1524
Craster, O. E.: Skenfrith Castle, 1670
Craven Arms area, geology, 1311
Creake Abbey, guide, 1670

1966 pp 1–272, 1967 pp 273–604, 1968 pp 605–990, 1969 pp 991–1402, 1970 pp 1403–1740

30

INDEX 1966–70 —CUM

Cream:
cheese, 88
Food Standards Committee report, 380
Cremer, H. W. (Chairman): Synthetic detergents, 174, 1297, 1648
Crewe, F. A. E.: Medical History of the Second World War, 157
Criccieth Castle, guide, 1670
Cricket bat willow, 859
Crime Recording, Scottish criminal statistics, 927
Crimes of Absolute Prohibition (Defence) Bill, 668
Criminal:
Appeal:
Act, 77, 703
Bill, 3, 4, 5, 8, 49, 606, 607, 666, 886
(Northern Ireland) Act, 703
Bill, 606, 697, 666, 886
Injuries Compensation Board, 160, 473, 872, 1625
intent, imputed, 507
Justice:
Act, 368
(Amendment) Bill, 1479
Bill, 52, 281, 282, 284, 286, 331, 336, 338, 476
Law:
Act, 368
Bill, 7, 10, 43, 163, 275, 276, 286, 331, 336, 338, 476,
Report, 1654
Revision Committee, 160, 872
offences, ancient, proposals to abolish, 189
proceedings, legal aid, 190
Responsibility Bill, 334
statistics:
Departmental Committee report, 475
England and Wales, 160, 473, 872, 1270, 1625
Scotland, 212, 534, 927, 1334, 1681
Crippled Persons (Miscellaneous Provisions) Bill, 47
Cripps, J. (Chairman): Coastal preservation, 1545
Cripps Mission to India, 1599
Crofters:
Commission, annual report, 86, 373, 709, 1116, 1519
(Scotland) Acts, 348
Crofting Counties, census, 155
Cromer, Rt. Hon. Earl of: Export business from Capital Overseas, 953
Crompton, pioneer electrical engineer, 1329
Cronan, D. S.: Recent sedimentation in Irish sea, 1312, 1664
Crookall, R.: Fossil plants, 1663
Crosby Corporation Act, 705
Crosskey, R. W.:
Simuliidae, 1125
Tachinidae, 385, 386
Crossraguel Abbey, guide, 1670
Crowd behaviour at football matches, 1297
Crowe, S.: Forestry in the landscape, 151
Crown('s):
Agents for Overseas Governments and Administrations, 112, 396, 728, 1134, 1546
Estate:
abstract accounts, 112, 396, 729–30, 1135, 1546
Commissioners report, 112, 396, 730, 1135, 1546
gall, 88
jewels:
coloured post-card, 522
guide, 522, 912
souvenir guide, French and German editions, 1321
Nominee account, 248, 582
Office, Constitution Commission, 1133
Proceedings Act, 248, 582, 968, 1379, 1721
Crowther, Lord (Chairman), Constitution Commission, 1133
Cruelty to Animals:
Act 1876 (Amendment) Bill, 665, 1484
Bill, 1072
Cruickshank, Prof. R. (Chairman): Rheumatic fever in Scotland, 536
Crum Rubber Plant project, loan, 1599
Crustacea, 1127
Cryptochaetidae, 102
Crytophyceae, 379

CS gas, medical and toxilogical aspects, 1272

Cublington Wing, local hearings, 1365
Cucumber:
mosaic, 88
production, manual, 1522
cucurbitaceae, 396
Cufodontis, G., Pittosporaceae, 112
Culham Laboratory:
physics conference, 1394
reports, 261–2, 595–6, 980–1, 1393–4, 1733
select committee, 883, 884
Cullingworth, J. B. (Chairman):
Needs of new communities, 492
Ownership and management of housing in new towns, 893
Cultural agreements etc, *see respective countries*
Cumberland:
census, 153
County Council Act, 1517
sample census, 467, 1259

1966 pp 1–272, 1967 pp 273–604, 1968 pp 605–990, 1969 pp 991–1402, 1970 pp 1403–1740

31

CUM-DIP | 1966-70

CUM— INDEX 1966–70

Cumbrian rivers, hydrological survey, 171
Cuneiform:
  tablets, Kouyunjik collection, catalogue, 719
  texts from Babylonian tablets, 100, 384, 720, 1124
CUNNINGHAM, W. (Chairman): Modern Languages, 1679
Cupolas, cold blast, 1291, 1294
Curculionidae, 1125
CURDS, C. R.: British Freshwater ciliated protozoa, 1354
Currants, black, 88
Currency:
  and Bank Notes Act, treasury minutes, 248, 582, 968, 1379, 1721
  decimal, 248
Current:
  Acts of Parliament, Scotland, index of short titles, 542
  Medical Research, 190, 508, 899
  Papers, aeronautical Research Council, 81–4, 543–8, 932–4, 1343–6, 1527–31
Curriculum:
  bulletin, Schools Council, 128, 414
  Consultative Committee, 925, 1332, 1678
  development, 415
  Innovation in practice, 921
  papers, Scotland, 925, 1332, 1678
CURRY, D.: Geological and geophysical investigations, English Channel, 1663
CURRY, W. T.:
  European redwood and whitewood, 1351
  Plywoods, 554, 1351
  Timber, 1692
    laminated, 555
Curry powder, Food Standards Committee, 1525
CURTIS, R.: Petrology, Graham Land, 383
CUSHING D. H.:
  Abundance of hake off South Africa, 715
  Stock of herring in the North Sea, 93
Customary Holidays Bill, 667, 1071
Customs:
  and Excise:
    annual statement of trade, 113, 396, 730, 1135, 1546
    Commissioners' report, 113, 396, 1136, 1547
    examination papers, 106
    export list, 113
    publications, 113, 396–7, 730–1, 1135–6, 1546–7
  Convention:
    importation of scientific equipment, 1164
    International transport of goods, 132
    Touring formalities, 421
Customs (*continued*):
  Duties (Dumping and Subsidies):
    Act, 111
      annual report, 1366, 1709
      Bill, 614, 661, 666, 992, 1073, 1289
    Amendment Act, 703
      Bill, 875
  formalities for touring, 421
  (Import Deposits) Act, 703, 1111
    Bill, 619, 670, 1076
CUTHBERTSON, SIR D. (Joint Chairman): Nutrient requirements of pigs, 373
Cutlery:
  and:
    silverware trades, problems, 505
    stainless steel flatware Industry (Scientific Research Levy) accounts, 570, 953, 1367, 1373, 1710
  census of production, 958
  Wages Council (Great Britain) order to abolish, 1156

Cyclamates, 93, 380
Cyclopoid copepods, 1128
Cyclotrons as booster injector, 209
Cygnus II Association, 207
Cymru, 987, 1397, 1736
Cyngor Adeiladau Hanesyddol Cymru, 524, 914, 1323, 1672
Cyprus:
  British army training team*, 760
  double taxation*, 760
  excavations, 1536
  social insurance*, 1577
Cystoids, 386

Czecho-slovak(ia):
  Refugee Fund Account, 130, 416, 755, 1157, 1573
  Science and technology*, 760

D

D'ABREU, PROF. A. L. (Chairman): Surgery for the newborn, 865
DAINTON, DR F. S. (Chairman):
  Flow of candidates in science and technology into higher education, 125, 743
  National Libraries Committee, 1146
Dairy(ies):
  economics, aspects, 376
  effluents, 1120
  farm, 1121
  floors, 379
  produce, production, trade, consumption, and prices, 107
  science and technology, progress review, 728

1966 pp 1–272, 1967 pp 273–604, 1968 pp 605–990, 1969 pp 991–1402, 1970 pp 1403–1740

32

INDEX 1966–70 —DEF

Dairying:
  aids to management, 379, 1524
  cow cost, 1522
Dale Abbey, cartulary, 473
DALL, M. B.: German wood statuettes, 599
Damage to property, offences of, 1654
Damages, liquidated, 129
Dampness in buildings, 521, 1320
Damp-proof courses, 220, 1669
Dancing and drama (careers), 1564
Dangerous:
  Drugs Act, 368
    Bill, 281, 285, 331, 336, 338, 476
  goods and explosives, carriage in ships, 232
  things and activities, civil liability, 1654
DARE, P. J.: oystercatchers, 93, 1524
Daresbury Nuclear Physics Laboratory, 530
Dartford Tunnel Act, 370
Dartmoor rivers, hydrological survey, 171
Dartmouth Auto Castings Ltd, Industrial Relations Committee, 1545
Darwin('s):
  Notebooks, 387
  on the routes of male humble bees, 723
Dasycladaceae, 723
Data Surveillance Bill, 1074
DAVEY, R. J.:
  cysts, 387, 1538
  microplankton, 1538
DAVID, D.: computer assisted control using an ion source, 1330
DAVIDSON, P. E.: oystercatchers and cockles fishery, 379
DAVIES, SIR H. E. (Chairman): Aberfan Tribunal, 286
DAVIES, J. G. W. (Chairman): Selection Committee, Civil Service, 1133
DAVIES, J. M.: Adelgids, 860
DAVIES, M. (Editor): Brecon Beacons, 513
DAVIES, M.: Jesness Inventory, 476
DAVIS, J. (Chairman): Health, safety, and welfare, drop forging industry, 181
DAVIS, M. G.: New Forest, 1612
Dawley: Wellington: Oakengates, development proposals, 171
DAWSON, W. R.: Mummies and human remains, 719
DAY, VICE-ADM. SIR A.: Admiralty Hydrographic Service, 1795–1919, 411
DAY, J. B. W.: geology of the country around Bewcastle, 1663
Day hospitals, patients attending, 1269
Daylight:
  and artificial light integrated in buildings, 220
  factors, protractors for computation, 220
Deaf:
  children, education, 744
  peripatetic teachers of, 1146
Deal Castle, guide, 201
Dealers in securities, and Unit Trusts, particulars of, 573, 956, 1714
DEAN, W. T.: Ordovician trilobites, 103, 386
DEARING, G. E. (Chairman): East Midlands Economic Planning Council, 124
Death(s):
  accuracy in certificate of cause, 154
  in fires attended by fire brigades, 1709
  maternal, E. and W., 158
  postneonatal, 1622
Death watch beetle, 939
DE BEAUMONT, J.: Sphecidae, 385
DEBRENNE, F.: Lower Cambrian Archaeocyatha, 1126
Decimal Currency:
  Act, 368, 1111
    Bill, 284, 331, 335, 476, 995, 996, 1061, 1071, 1072, 1274
    circular, 1293, 1645
  and metric measures, teaching guide, 921
  Board:
    annual report, 731, 1136, 1547
    publications, 731, 1136, 1547–8
  booklets, 731, 1136, 1547
  change-over, 1380
  in the U.K., 248, 533
  stage 2, 925
Decimalisation, computer users' guide, 1659
Decisions:
  of the Commissioner, *see respective subjects*
  on planning applications, E. and W., statistics, 175, 494, 894
Declaration of Arbroath 1320, facsimile and translation, 1682
Declaratory and compulsory Purchase Orders, 1304
Dee Crossing Study, 490
Deeds, index to register of, 929
DEEMING, J. C.: Diptera from Nepal, *sphaeroceridae*, 1125
Deeplish, improvement possibilities, 171
Deer:
  (Amendment) (Scotland) Act, 368
    Bill, 9, 274, 278, 331, 336, 476
  fallow, 151
  Hunting, and Hare Coursing Abolition Bill, 1076
  red. *See* Red Deer Commission
  roe, 1611
D.E.F. specifications, 118–23, 401–10, 747–42, 1142–4, 1553–60
Defeat of Germany, 1129
Defective premises, civil liability, 1655
Defence:
  accounts, 117, 416, 735, 1158, 1552
  and Overseas Affairs, 479

1966 pp 1–272, 1967 pp 273–604, 1968 pp 605–990, 1969 pp 991–1402, 1970 pp 1403–1740

C 33

DEF— INDEX 1966–70

Defence (*continued*):
  appropriation accounts, 117, 416, 1158
  (Army) Purchasing (Repayment) Services, statement of excess, 736
  estimates, 400, 736
    and related matters, 880
    form of, 880
    statement, 124, 400, 736, 1141, 1560
    supplementary:
      Air, 736, 1141
      Army, 401, 736, 1141, 1560
      Central, 117, 401, 736, 1141, 1560
      Navy, 117, 401, 736, 1141
      Purchasing (Repayment) Services, 1560
      Royal Ordnance Factories, 117, 401, 736, 1560
      Vote on Account, 252, 586, 972, 1384, 1726
  Guides, 117–8, 401, 736–7, 1141, 1552–3
  Lists, 118, 401, 737, 1141, 1552
  Ministry of:
    Air Force Department, 113–14, 397–8, 731–2, 1136–7, 1548
      see also Air Force
    Army Department, 114–17, 398–400, 732–5, 1137–40, 1548–51
      see also Army
    Civilian industrial employees, regulations, 398
    Navy Department, 123–4, 411, 735, 1140–1, 1551–2
      See also Navy
    publications, 113–24, 397–411, 731–42, 1136–44, 1548–60
      index, 410, 1553
  policy, supplementary statement, 411, 736
  Research:
    and Development, 1142
    select committee, 88304, 1286
  Secretary of State's Order, 1550
  Specifications, 118–23, 401–10, 737–42, 1142–4, 1553–60
  Supply estimates, 1725
  Votes, 250, 584–5, 970–1, 1382–3, 1724
    see also Defence estimates, supplementary
Definition of drugs, 470
DE GLANVILLE, R. G.: Numbers of coins in circulation in the U.K., 1542
Dehydrated vegetables for the caterer, 714
De la Rue company merger, 1370
DELAFONS, J. (Chairman): Housing Revenue accounts, 1295
Delinquency:
  causes, and treatment of offenders, 162, 476, 1273
  types of, and home background, 476
De L'isle and Dudley Manuscripts, Sidney papers, 473
Denbighshire:
  area, geochemical reconnaissance, 1663
  census, 153
  sample census, 467, 1259
DENINGTON, E. (Chairman): standards of housing fitness, 173
Denmark:
  atomic energy*, 1577
  bacon*, 1245
  Churchill Endowment Fund, 1163
  Continental shelf*, 131, 421
  double taxation*, 133, 422, 761, 1164, 1165
DENNING, RT HON. LORD (Chairman):
  Historical Manuscripts Commission, 1674
  Legal Records, 190
DENNIS, R. W. G.: Fungus flora of Venezuela, 1674
DENNY, Mrs. M. B. A. (Chairman): Artificial Limb Service, 1681
Dental:
  anaesthesia, 470
  department, hospital, 1618
  Estimates Board, accounts:
    E. and W. 158, 471, 867, 1265, 1619
    Scotland, 212, 535, 928, 1334, 1681
  health in E. and W., adult, 1664
  Manufacturing Co. Ltd, Monopolies Commission, 239
  services in health centres, 1334
Denticipitidae, 723
Dentists' Supply Co. of New York, Monopolies Commission, 239
Dentistry (careers), 1149
Dentroctonus micans, 151
Departmental Papers, classes of, P.R.O., 203
Derby:
  Churches (Saint Christopher's, Saint Peter's and Saint Paul's) Act, 78
  Corporation Act, 1113
Derbyshire:
  area, geochemical reconnaissance, 1663
  census, 153
  County Council Act, 1113
  sample census, 467, 862
Dermanyssidae, 103
Dermatitis from flour, dough, or sugar, 187
Desalinisation, E. and W., 1396
Desert Locust Information Service, 457
Design(s):
  and construction, underground pipe sewers, 489, 494, 1644
  bulletin(s):
    circular, 889
    Housing and Local Government, 171 490, 891, 1294, 1646
  Copyright Act, 703
    Bill, 617, 661, 666, 669, 875
  for English sculpture, 1396

1966 pp 1–272, 1967 pp 273–604, 1968 pp 605–990, 1969 pp 991–1402, 1970 pp 1403–1740

34

INDEX 1966–70 —DIP

Design(s) (*continued*):
  hospital, 471
  maintenance and operation, 202
  of:
    Beam Lines with high resolving power, 922
    buildings, programming and progressing, 1323
    horticultural:
      buildings, 716
      packing sheds, 715
    information-processing systems for government, 586
    public conveniences, 889
Design Magazine, 175, 494, 894, 1298, 1648
Designing:
  buildings, professional collaboration, 914
  for:
    old people, metric edition, 1294
    science, 743
  low-rise housing system, Sheffield, 1646
Desks and bureaux, English, 985
Detention centre(s):
  detention of girls, 872
  report, 1625
  see also Prisons, Borstals and detention centres
Detergents:
  census of production, 957
  synthetic, 493, 1297, 1648
De Tweede Engelse Oorlog, 1665–1667, 513
Deuterium, vapour pressure and molar volume for, 194
Developing countries:
  education in, 1667
  Information Office pamphlets:
    Africa, 1649
    agriculture, 495
    Britain as a market, 895
    economic aid, 895
    engineering, 1299
    South and South East Asia, 177, 895
Development:
  and application of very strong steels, 96
  areas, 412
  Commissioners' report, 246
  Control:
    general principles, 1294
    management study, 490, 492
    policy notes, 1294, 1646
      circular, 1291
  Corporation report, 173
  cost estimating, 1351
  for agricultural purposes, 890
  Fund Accounts, 248, 582, 968, 1280, 1722
  in:
    British Official Statistics, 1130
    residential areas, 1294
    rural areas, 1294
    town centres, 1294
Development (*continued*):
  of:
    Inventions Acts:
      accounts, 235, 368
      Bill, 274, 279, 336, 484
    Play-Groups:
      Bill, 667
      (No. 2) Bill, 338
    Tourism Act, 1111
      Bill 998, 1001, 1007, 1061, 1071, 1074, 1075, 1274
  plans, 1646
  progress of infants and young children, 870
  projects, handbook, 1351
DEVLIN, LORD: Level of pay for dock workers, inquiry, 187
Devon:
  and Cornwall, holiday industry, 1646
  census, 153
  sample census, 467, 862
DEWAR, G. J.: Geology of Adelaide Island, 1662
DEWDNEY, D. A. C. (Chairman): Production planning control, conference, 194, 904
D'ewes, Sir Simond, Library, bi-centenary publication, 99
Dew-point temperatures over the Indian Ocean, monthly charts, 1656

Diagnostic X-ray department, 866
Diastatidae, 102
Dichaetomyiini Emden, 1125
DICKENS, R. J.: Globular Cluster W Centauri, 529
DICKSON, J. A. (Joint Chairman): Pulpwood supply and the paper industry, 1255
Dieback, Larch, 1255
Dieldrin residues in food, 380
Diesel engines, maintenance, 1672
Digests. *See* specific subject
Dilleniaceae, 729
Dimensional co-ordination, building, 914
DINES, H. G.: Geology of the country around Sevenoaks and Tonbridge, 1663
Dinoflagellate cysts, 387
  and acritarchs, 1538
Dinosaurs, 387, 1539
Diploma in management studies, memorandum, 744
Diplomatic:
  buildings overseas, estimates committee, 480, 879
  List, London, 144, 457, 847, 1145, 1602
  Privileges:
    and International Organisations Bill, 1481, 1629
    Bill, 47

1966 pp 1–272, 1967 pp 273–604, 1968 pp 605–990, 1969 pp 991–1402, 1970 pp 1403–1740

35

DIP— INDEX 1966-70

Diplomatic (continued):
Service:
Administration Office, 124, 411, 742, 1145
List, 124, 411, 742, 1145, 1577
Dipsacaceae, 729
Diptera:
Asilidae, 101, 1537
Bombyliidae, 1125
Conopidae, 101
Cryptochaetidae, 102
Diastatidae, 102
Dolichopodidae, 101
Diosophilidae, 102
Ephydridae, 721
from Nepal, 101, 385, 1125
Heleomyzidae, 101
Muscidae, 1125
Nemestrinidae, 1125
Pipunculidae, 101
Platypezidae, 101
Psychodidae, 385
Rhinophoridae, 101
Sarcophagidae, 101
Simuliidae, 1125
Tachinidae, 385, 386, 1125
Direct:
acting executive space-heaters, 890
Grant Grammar Schools, 1562
labour:
on new constructions, 1296
organisations, building, 1292
Directorate, see specific subject
Directory, see specific subject
Disabled:
facilities for, in public conveniences, 889
Persons' Pensions and Miscellaneous
Provisions Bill, 1070
Disablement:
Commission Bill, 1076
Income Commission, 669
Disarmament:
documents, 132, 421, 760
further documents, 1164, 1598
nuclear weapons, 760, 1577
path to peace, 760
Disease(s):
and mosquitoes, 723
infectious, Registrar General's returns, 154
injuries, and causes of death 466
international classification, 466, 1257
keitha, of cedar 465
occupational, 1622
of:
Animals:
Act, return of proceedings, 95, 382, 717, 1112, 1526
handbook of Orders, 93, 715
bees, 1117

Disease(s) (continued):
of (continued):
raspberry, 1115
sheep, 90
vegetables, 1117
Plant, 380, 717, 1525
Pullorum, 88
Reversion of blackcurrants, 88
Silver leaf of fruit trees 88
Wart, of potato, 88
Disinfecting ships and aircraft, 146
Dismissal:
Appeals Board Bill, 336, 669
procedures, 500
Disposal of:
liquid manure, 1525
solid toxic wastes, 1646
surplus U.S. defence equipment, 123, 411, 742, 1144, 1560
Disputes:
check-off, in Britain, 919
compulsory settlement, convention, 1608
procedures in Britain, 919
Dissolution of Parliament, proclamation, 1686
Distribution of:
Drepaninae, 722
German Enemy Property Acts, accounts, 23, 568, 952, 1366, 1709
Norway pout, 710
Stars and interstellar matter, 207
Distributive:
Industry Training Board, 1151, 1565
Trade(s):
computer applications, 1659
Economic Development Committee, 904
management training, 1309
Selective Employment Tax, 1722
statistics, 1660
District general hospitals, functions, 1262
Disused:
Railways:
and agriculture, 1545
in the countryside, 1545
Tips, guidance for initial inspection, 1316
Ditton Laboratory, 86, 373, 709
Divorce(s):
and legal separation, Hague Convention, 1654
Reform:
Act, 1111
Bill, 661, 665, 668, 670, 875, 998, 1000, 1002, 1061, 1073, 1075, 1274
of grounds, 189
(Scotland) Bill, 1479
"D" Notice:
matters, inquiry, 388
system, 388
Dixon, P. J. (Joint Chairman): Pulpwood
supply and the paper industry, 1255

Dixon, R.: Orthogonal plynomials, 1657

Dobson Spectrophotometer, 509
Dock(s):
accidents, 179
and Harbours Act, 77
account, 1158
Bill, 6, 7, 45, 48, 49, 50, 51, 163
workers:
in Liverpool, payment and earnings
system, inquiry, 505
retirement age, 753
wages and level of pay, 187
Doctors' and dentists' remuneration, 158, 870, 1268, 1540
Documents:
application form for office copies, 898
abolition of legislation, 1244, 1602
export control of, 1561
memoranda, and questionaire, select
committee, 1635
on British foreign policy, 132, 421, 760, 1164, 1577
Dog fish, food of, 374
Dogs in food shops etc., 865
Do-it-yourself with safety, film strip, 872
Dolley, R. H. M.: Carolingian coins in the
B.M., 99
Dolls, small picture book, 1396
Dolphins, stranded, identification guide, 104, 1124
Domestic:
and:
Appellate Proceedings (Restriction
of publicity) Act, 703
Bill, 339, 609, 661, 666, 670, 875
boiler chimneys, 221
Coal Consumers' Council, annual report, 199, 518, 910, 1318, 1710
electrical appliances, census of production, 1371
food consumption and expenditure, 92
See also Household Food Consumption
preservation of fruit and vegetables, 89
refuse, 1671
services, hospital, 156, 1615
Domiciliary midwifery and maternity bed
needs, 1616
Dominica:
colonial report, 109, 393
Flag, 110
Dominican Republic, 412, 760
Donald, Prof. K. W. (Chairman): Oxygen
therapy, 1335
Donaldson, G. (Editor): Register of the
Privy Seal of Scotland, 537
Donaldson, Lord (Chairman): Boy En-
trants and Young Servicemen, 1560
Herbage seed supplies, 717
Doncaster:
area study, 1145

Doncaster (continued):
Corporation Act, 1517
Donnison, Prof. D. (Chairman): Public
Schools, 1562
Donnison, F. S. V.: Central organisation
and planning, 104
Donovan, Rt Hon. Lord (Chairman):
Trade Unions and Employers' Associa-
tions, 919
Doorstep Selling Bill, 47
Doppler radar, 509
Dorset:
census, 153
Central, and South East, ancient
monuments, 1628
clay, 386
County Council Child Care Service, 160
inventory of historical monuments, 1674
sample census, 467, 1259
Water Order, 613
Jersey fabric, materials control, 1660
taxation:
agreements:
of the U.K., 1300
see also respective countries
relief, tables, 177
Dover Castle:
guide, 201
German edition, 912
souvenir guide: 912
French edition, 1670
Doves, 724
Downey, W. G. (Chairman): development
cost estimating, 1351
Draft:
Police Pensions (Amendment) (No. 3)
Regulations S.I. select committee, 1288
Strategy for the South West, 412
Synopsis of the Orders, Families, and
Genera of recent fishes and fishlike
vertebrates, 412
Wales Rural Development Board Order,
S.I. select committee, 1288
Drain and sewer pipes, flexible, 521
Drained joints in precast concrete cladding, 1308
Drama:
and music, Secondary School Design, 123
survey, 744
Drapery, see Retail Drapery
Draughtsman(men's):
and Allied Technician's Association, 902
Engineering, (careers), 180
Drawings, British, in the India Office
Library, 1576
Drepanidae, 385, 722, 724

1966 pp 1–272, 1967 pp 273–604, 1968 pp 605–990, 1969 pp 991–1402, 1970 pp 1403–1740

DRE— INDEX 1966-70

Dress(es):
lingerie, infants' wear, etc., census of
production, 1371
regulations for army officers, 1138, 1549
Drill (all arms), 115
Drilling:
machines, guarding spindles and attachments, 1567
rig accidents, 359
Drills, corn, 716
Driver('s'):
record book, 1717
Training for young people, 1374
understanding of road traffic signs, 864
Driving manual, 1374
Drop forging:
hammers, safety, 505
industry, conditions, 181
Drosophilidae, 102
Drowning accidents and water safety, 1293
Drug(s):
addicts, rehabilitation, 1272
and medicines, forthcoming legislation, 470
Committee on safety of, 156, 470, 865
definition of, 470
Dependence Committee, 1269, 1272
Narcotic:
Commission on, 422
convention, 133
translation errors, 422
offences, powers of arrest and search, 1626
prescribing and administration, 864
safety of, 1263
Drunkenness, offences of, statistics, 161, 474, 872, 1271, 1626
Dry rot, 521
Drying:
and scaling pine billets, 1612
hops, 711
out, building advisory leaflet, 1320

D.T.D. specifications 96-8, 552-4, 937-8, 1349-51, 1534-5

Dudgeons Wharf fire, 1627
Dudley Corporation Act, 1516
Duffy, E. A. J.: Oriental timber beetles, 724
Dufton, A. F., Protractors for the com-
putation of daylight factors, 220
Duffy, A. R.:
European Armour in the Tower of
London, 914
Mann's Arms and Armour Revision, 1321
Dumfries, Kirkcudbright, and Wigton:
census, 153
sample census, 469, 1261

Dunbarton:
and Renfrew, sample census, 469, 1261
census, 155
Duncan, Sir V. (Chairman): Overseas
representation, 1245
Dundee:
Angus, and Perth, sample census, 469, 1261
City of, Educational Trust Scheme, 210
Clackmannan, and Fife, census, 155
Corporation:
Busmen, pay and conditions, 903
Order Confirmation Act, 1113
Bill, 1494
Dunkeld, old red sandstone iginimbrites, 1312
Dunlop, Sir D. (Chairman): Safety of
Drugs, 263
Dunn, J. E.:
Brigade attendance times at fires in
buildings, 939
Fires fought with five or more jets, 1292
Dunnet, Sir G. (Chairman): Sugar Board, 1526
Dunning, F. W.: Geophysical exploration, 1662
Durability of metals in natural waters, 913
Durban Navigation Colleries Act, 705
Durham:
and West Hartlepool, geology of the
country between, 906
census, 153
County Council Act, 705
Local Education Authority, dispute, 1156
sample census, 467, 862
Dust:
and fumes in factory atmosphere, 187, 1156
explosions in factories, 754, 1567
Duthie, Dr. J. H.: Primary School Survey, 1679
Dwarfs, late type, G-R and R-I colours, 920
D.W.B.A. calculation of charge-exchange
reactions, and inelastic scattering, 530
Dwelling(s):
central heating etc. installations, 1670
houses, 1145, 1672
houses, existing, selected decisions, 1678
in good repair, etc, rent, 1293
Dyestuffs:
census of production, 957
synthetic, prices, 1306
Dyfnallt, G. (Editor): Salisbury (Cecil)
Manuscripts, 1624

Economic (continued):
activity (continued):
sub-regional tables, sample census, 1666
tables, sample census, 862, 1261
Affairs, Department of, publications, 124, 412, 742, 1145
Aid to developing countries, statistics, 195, 514, 907
benefits of scientific research, 1147
Development Committees. See specific
industry
Planning:
Councils, 124
in Scotland, select committee, 1640
prospects, revised assessment, 1722
reports, 388, 968
Series, Natural History Museum, 1539
Social and Cultural Rights, International Covenant, 454
statistics, new contributions, 1542
trends, 105, 388, 724, 1129, 1543
Economies of scale in Local Government
research studies, 916
Ecuador:
loan*, 1578
visas*, 1405

Eden, R. A.: Marine geological and geo-
physical work, East coast of Scotland, 1663
Edible gelatine, Food Standards Com-
mittee, 1525
Edinburgh:
and the Lothians:
census, 155
sample census, 469, 1261
Corporation Order Confirmation Act, 370, 1516,
Bill, 279, 335, 1076, 1485
Gazette, 201, 525, 915, 1374-5, 1673
Herbarium, index of collectors, 674
Trades Maiden Fund Order Con-
firmation Act, 1113
see also City of Edinburgh
Edlin, H. L.:
Check list of Forestry Commission
publications, 151
Forests of Central and Southern
Scotland, 1255
Know your:
Broadleaves, 859
Conifers, 151, 1611
Snowdonia (editor), 1255
Timber:
Your growing Investment, 1255
Edmonds, E. A.:
Geology of the Country around Oke-
hampton, 1312
South West England, 1311

Dixon, R.: Orthogonal plynomials, 1657

Eames, E. S.: Medieval tiles, 721
Early:
flying, 207
Gothic illuminated manuscripts, 1536
medieval Art in the B.M., 1123
warning system, Prices and Incomes
policy, 170
Earnings, new survey, 1571
Earnings-related short term benefits, 214, 1268
Earth temperature averages for U.K., 900
Earthworms, 723
Eason, E. H.: Eupolybothrus Verhoeff, 1539
East:
Africa, Overseas Aid select committee, 1637
Anglia:
and the Midlands, guide, 912
coasts, 728
Planning Council, 742
sample census, 862
study, 742
Caribbean, tripartite economic survey, 515
Craigs key to potato trials and collec-
tions, 87, 374, 709
Green, Aberdeen Order Confirmation
Act, 1113
Bill, 1075
Kilbride Burgh Act, 370
Midland(s):
Economic Planning Council, 124, 1145
opportunity, 1145
region, sample census, 862
Suffolk, sample census, 467
Sussex, sample census, 467
Eastern Pacific Ocean, monthly meteor-
ological charts, 1306
Easton, P. H.: Bunker silos, 1519
East-West Highway*, 1245
Eastwood, T.: Geology of the country
around Cockermouth and Caldbeck, 1312

Ebdon, R. A.:
Temperature, contour heights, and
winds over the northern hemisphere, 1656
Upper air observations at the Seychelles, 900

Eccles, Rt Hon. Viscount (Chairman):
British Museum Trustees, 1124
Ecclesiastical Commission reports, 390, 725-6, 995, 1130-1, 1542
Economic:
activity:
County:
leaflets, 862-3, 1259
Tables, Scotland, 1261

Education:
Act, 368, 703
Bill, 11, 45, 50, 163, 287, 289, 339, 340, 614, 661, 665, 667, 875, 1468, 1480, 1631
1870, centenary document reproductions, 1561
and:
Science, Department of:
building bulletins, 125, 412, 743, 1145, 1560
circulars and administrative memoranda, 125, 412, 743, 1145, 1561
index, 126, 744, 1562
H. M. Inspectorate:
E. and W., 745, 882
Scotland, 882
leaflets, 126
lists, 126, 413, 744, 1146, 1561
output budgeting, 1561
publications, 125-9 412-16, 743-6, 1145-8, 1560-3
regulations and administration memoranda, index, 1146
reports, 125, 413, 744, 1145, 1561
Schools Council, see Schools Council
select committee reports, 745, 881, 927, 1281-2, 1634-5
Supply estimates, 1725
training of teachers, 412
Research, lubrication, 126
Training:
for scientific and technological library and information work, 744
of technicians, 392
Authority Bursaries (Scotland) Regulations, 1332
census tables, 153
Commonwealth in, 127
computer, 413
Department, Scottish. See Scottish Education Department
Discrimination convention, 1165
for industry and commerce:
agricultural education, 126
use of buildings and equipment, 744
(Handicapped Children) Act, 5;5
Bill, 1411, 1483
Higher, inquiry, 125
in:
Britain, Information Office pamphlet, 495
developing countries, 1667
health, 127
Scotland, Secretary of State for Scotland's report, 210, 533, 925, 1322, 1678
Wales and Monmouthshire, 45, 163

Education (continued):
(Miscellaneous Provisions) Bill, 1407, 1408, 1483
(No. 2) Act, 703
Bill 608
nursing, 850
of deaf children, 744
pamphlets, 127, 413, 414, 744, 1145, 1561
physical, primary schools, 927
planning papers, 1561
(re-committed) Bill, 1468, 1629
(School Milk) Bill, 1405, 1479
(Scotland) Act, 1111
Bill, 670, 997, 999, 1000, 1001, 1062, 1072, 1075, 1274, 1477, 1484
circular, 1332
Government Actuary's report, 211
reports, 533, 925, 1332
Trust Schemes, 210-11, 533-4, 926-7, 1332-3, 1679
Services, psychologists, 745
statistics, 129, 415, 746, 1148, 1563
survey, 413, 744, 1146, 1563
trends, 129, 416, 746, 1148, 1563
Educational:
and cultural exchange programme*, 464
building:
co-ordination of components, 743
notes, Scotland, 211, 533, 1333, 1679
establishments, use of carcinogenic substances in, 1678
Research, in Wales, 921
National Foundation report, 128
statistics, Scottish, 534, 927, 1333, 1680
Edward Gordon Craig, large picture book, 599
Edward Johnston's Book of Sample Scripts, V. and A. Museum, 266
EDWARDS, PROF. SIR R. (Chairman): Civil Air Transport, 1355
EDWARDS, V. W.: Fast shutter magnets for separated particle beams, 922
EDWARDS, W. N.:
Geology of the country around Ollerton, 906
Palaeontology, 387
Eelworm:
cereal root, 88
chrysanthemem, 375
potato tuber, 88
stem, on tulips, 89
Efficiency:
in industry, attitudes to, 180
studies, in the hospital service, abstracts, 469
Efflorescence and stains on brickwork, 1320
Effluents:
dairy, 1120
fish toxicity test, 1643

Effluents (continued):
from nerve agent production, disposal, 1550
industrial, 891, 894
standard tests, 1643
to rivers, standards, 894
Egg(s):
production:
intensive poultry management, 1521
lighting for, 89, 375
(Protection of Guarantees) Order, S.I. select committee, 1287
Re-organisation Commission, 717
EGGEN, O. J.:
Giants of types K and M, 529
Three-colour photometry, 206, 1327
EGGLISHAW, H. J.: Freshwater and Salmon Fisheries Research, 373
Egyptian:
antiquities in the B.M., catalogue, 719
collections in the B.M., 1536
Funds, accounts, 844, 1558
stelae, hieroglyphic texts, 1536
tomb painting, 720
Eifelian brachiopods, 1126
Eire. See Ireland, Republic of
El Salvador:
technical co-operation*, 461, 671
visas*, 761
Elatinaceae, 724
Elderly:
nutrition of, 1622
patients, care of in certain hospitals, inquiry, 867
social welfare for, 864
with mental disorder, 1681
ELDO, see European Launcher Development Organisation
Election(s):
expenses, 160
Parliamentary:
E. and W., 161, 474, 873, 1271, 1626
Law, 871
Electoral:
law, conference, 160, 473, 872
Registration:
Mauritius, 393
Officers and Returning Officers Order, 161, 474, 873, 1271, 1626
Electric(al):
and:
electronic:
engineering, higher national certificates and diplomas, 126
equipment for the Services, 167
mechanical manufacturing industries, education and training requirements, 127

Electric(al) (continued):
appliances:
census of production, 1371
domestic, distributors' costs and margins, 903
arc welding, 754
Contracting Industry:
Scotland, pay and conditions, 1307
wages and conditions, Prices and Incomes Board, 193
distribution systems external to buildings, 914
engineers. See mechanical and electrical engineers
fencing, 89
goods, miscellaneous, census of production, 1371
installations:
hospital, 1616
in buildings, 1323
traditional, 1323
lamps:
Monopolies Commission, 955
screw cap, 754
machinery, census of production, 957
prices, Prices and Incomes Board, 1657
Services, see Mechanical and Electrical Services
supplies for construction sites, 523
units and standards, 1713
see also Units and standards of measurement
welding apparatus, dangers in use, 1319
wiring:
harnesses for motor vehicles, Monopolies Commission, 239
installations and power consuming apparatus, inspection and testing, 914
Electricians, see Mechanics and electricians
Electricity:
Act:
annual report and accounts, 909
Bearer Bonds, 1380
Bill, 288, 1468, 1480, 1629
loans, 248, 582, 968, 1380, 1722
and:
Gas Act, accounts, 198, 517, 909, 1317
magnetism, S.I. units, 1713
Boards:
report and accounts, 198, 517, 909, 1317, 1691
South of Scotland:
advances, 198, 517, 909, 1317
annual report and accounts, 200, 532, 925, 1331, 1678
loans, 249, 583, 969, 1381, 1722
census of production, 958

Electricity (continued):
Consultative Council(s), 198, 517, 909, 1317, 169
North of Scotland, 210, 213, 532, 924, 1331, 1677
Council:
advances, 198, 517, 1317
loans, 248, 582, 968, 1380, 1722
report and accounts, 198, 517, 909, 1317, 1691
select committee, 883
Minister's report, 198, 517, 909, 1317, 1690
on building sites, 201
(Scotland) Act, 1111
Bill, 620, 664, 670, 875, 924
Supply:
Industry:
Court of inquiry, 1568
productivity payments, 903
Training Board, 181, 500, 749, 1151, 1566
workers, pay, 511
see also Central Electricity Generating Board
Electromagnetic distance measurement, Commonwealth Conference, 1314
Electro-medical apparatus, safety code, 1618
Electronic(s):
contracting industry, pay and conditions, 1307
EDC, data communications, guide, 1309
manpower study, 505
parts, common standards, 554
Research Council, 96
Electro-sensitive safety devices, 1566
Electrostatic:
generator(s):
beam bending magnets for use with, 530
group, 209
inflector, 209
Elementary:
ideas of game theory, 586
meteorology for aircrews, 1137
scattering theory, 208
Elephant-shrews, 723
Elevational control, Housing circular, 170, 266
Elgin district, geology, 906
ELLERMAN, J. R.: Checklist of Palaearctic and Indian mammals, 104
Ellice Islands:
income tax, 1300
see also Gilbert and Ellice Islands
ELLIOT OF HARWOOD, BARONESS (Chairman): Consumer Council, 112
ELLIOT, J. N.: Nymphalidae, 1126
ELLIOTT, G. F.: Calcareous algae, 723

ELLIOTT, R. A. (Chairman): Underground pipe sewers, 175, 494
ELLIOTT, R. T.: Pulsed magnet command systems, 1330
ELLIOTT-BINNS, E. U. E. (Chairman): Suggestions and complaints in hospitals, 1335
Elliotts of Newbury, Industrial Relations Commission, 1545
ELLIS, MAJ. L. F.: The Defeat of Germany, 1129
ELLIS, S. E.: Petrology and provenance of honestones, 1127
EL-NAGGAR, Z. R.: Stratigraphy and planktonic Foraminifera, 102
ELSTUB, SIR J. (Chairman): National Aircraft Effort, productivity report, 1352
Ely:
Hospital, Cardiff, inquiry, 1267
Ouse-Essex Water Act, 705
Embioptera, 101
Embroidery:
basic stitches, 266
English, 1735
Emergency(ies):
natural, 1396
powers, revoking of, proclamation, 1687
printing arrangements, H.C. (Services) select committee, 1283
EMMERSON, SIR H. (Chairman): London Government Staff Commission, 173
EMMET OF AMBERLEY, BARONESS (Chairman): Legal advice and assistance, 1655
Employed Persons:
(Health and Safety) Bill, 1468, 1480, 1629
securing safety, 1156
Employee(s):
Protection Bill, 49
re-instatement, inquiry, 1571
Security Bill, 1071
Employer(s):
Associations:
functions and organisation, 919
survey of official, 1571
Trade Unions, Joint Organisations etc., directory, 181, 500, 748, 1151, 1565
Liability:
(Compulsory Insurance) Act, 1111
Bill, 1000, 1074, 1075
see also Insurance (Employers' Liability) Bill
(Defective Equipment) Act, 1111
Bill, 661, 664, 665, 670, 875, 994, 1062, 1071, 1074, 1274
Employment:
Agencies:
Bill, 49, 334, 476

Employment (continued):
Agencies (continued):
charges and salaries, office staff, 903
(Regulation) Bill, 45, 47, 331
and Productivity, Department of, publications, 746-54, 1148-57
See also Labour, Ministry of
Department of, publications, 1564-72
of:
troops in aid of Civil Power, 733
University graduates, 206
Employment and Productivity Gazette, 749, 1151, 1566
see also Labour Gazette
Emulsifiers and stabilisers, food regulations, 1525
Emulsion paints, 201
Energy:
and momentum in the troposphere and stratosphere, 1656
statistics, digest, 1316, 1690
Engineering:
Bench and Machine Work, (careers), 1564
construction works, accidents, 179
directorate, 1643
draughtsman, 180
Industry Training Board, 181, 500, 749, 1151,
modern, census of production, 957
specifications, 914, 1323, 1672
trades, pay and conditions of service, 511, 1307
Engineers('):
Merchant Navy examinations, 569
professional, 180, 556
small tools and gauges, census of production, 957
technologists etc, manpower survey, 125
England:
Ancient Monument Board, 1320
and Wales, agricultural census, 1521
Boundary Commission, 1269
reform of Local Government, 1648
English:
Channel, 1663
compositions, multiple marking, 128
for:
children of immigrants, 415
young school leavers, 1678
legal system, Information Office pamphlet, 1299
oral, C.S.E. trial examination, 128
teaching, research and development, 128
Wealden flora, 1126
see also specific subjects
Engravings by S. W. Hayter, large picture book, 599
Ensiling grass, 89

Entertainment:
Employment Agencies Bill, 1074
Licensing of Private Places Bill, 11, 275, 277, 335
Enticement Actions (Abolition) Bill, 1074
Entomology:
applied, 1133
bulletins, 101-2, 385-6, 721-2, 1125-6, 1527-8
see also genus(era)
Entry Certificates, Race Relations select committee, 1285
Environment('):
and poultry houses, 1521
Department of:
circulars, 1572
publications, 1572
protection of, 1647
Ephemeris, astronomical, 205, 529, 920, 1328, 1675
Ephydridae, 721
Epilepsy:
in Scotland, medical care, 928
people with, 1622
Epoxy resin(s):
gas evolution from, 1676
glass composites, 1676
systems, 922
Epping Forest (Waterworks Corner) Act, 705
Equal Pay Act, 1515
Bill, 669, 1073, 1077
(No. 2) Bill, 1409, 1469, 1481, 1483, 1629
Eric George Millar bequest of manuscripts and drawings, B. M., 720
Eriococcidae, 1125
Ermine moth, small, 87
Erskine Bridge Tolls Act, 703
Bill, 290, 334, 339, 875
Esdaile Trust:
(Amendment) Scheme, 533
Scheme, 926
ESHER, VISCOUNT: York, 1298
Eskdalemuir Observatory, 1306
ESRANGE see European Space Research Organisation Launching Range
ESRO, see European Space Research Organisation
Essex:
County Council (Canvey Island Approaches etc.) Act, 1113
River and South Essex Water Act, 1113
University, privileges committee, 1280
Esso Petroleum:
Company Act 1957 (Amendment) Order, 126
fatal accident at West London Terminal, 874

1966-70 | EST-FIE

EST— INDEX 1966–70

Estate(s):
Agents:
Bill, 23, 43, 47, 163
Monopolies Commission, 1370
Duty:
on settled property, 1380
(Surviving Spouse) Bill, 1071
Proceedings against, Law Commission, 1303
Estimates:
Chief Secretary's Memorandum, 1722
Committees:
Minutes of Proceedings, 163, 476, 479, 875, 1274, 1629
reports, 165, 479, 480, 870, 878–9, 1277–80, 1632–4, 1650
special reports, 167, 483, 878–9, 1634
sub-committees. *See* sub-committees
Financial Secretary's Memorandum, 248, 582, 968, 1380
National Income and balance of payments, 250, 584, 970
Scottish:
Minutes of Proceedings, 164, 478, 877, 1275
Standing Committee Debates, 46, 332, 662, 1066
Supplementary, 1725
Spring, 165, 479, 878, 879
Winter, 165, 480, 483, 878, 1277, 1634, 1726
revised, 878, 1725
Supply, 1725
see also Civil estimates, Defence Estimates
Estimating daylight in buildings, 1671

ETHERIDGE, R.: Iguanid lizard genera, 723, 1128, 1539
Ethiopia(n):
Art, B.M. Calendar, 719
British Council*, 1166
manuscript painting, 1123
Notiphilini, species 721
War graves*, 858
Ethylene oxide, fumigation, 1525

Eudulidae, 723
Euphthiracaroid mites, 1127
Eupolybothrus Verhoeff, 1539
Eupterotidae, 724
Eurasian and Australian *Neptini*, 1126
Euratom, *see* European Atomic Energy Community
Europe(an):
and:
Mediterranean Plant Protection Organisation, 1247
North Atlantic Ocean, relative humidity and precipitation, 510
armour in the Tower of London, 914
Europe(an) (*continued*):
Atomic Energy Community:
arbitration*, 419
regulations, 133–4, 422–4, 761–2
setting up, 424
Broadcasting Stations*, 759
Coal and Steel Community:
rate of levies, 1164
report, 134, 424, 1166
Code of Social Security, 460, 1250
Commission of Human Rights, 455
Communities:
membership of, 388
regulations, *see* European Economic Community
setting up single Council and single Commission, 462
Council of, Human Rights*, 132, 1577
Court of Human Rights, 455, 1599
Economic Community:
association with:
Greece*, 424
Turkey*, 134
common agricultural policy, 348
regulations, 134–41, 424–53, 762–843, 1166–1238, 1579–95
setting up, 453
Firearms, 1396
Free Trade Association:
amendments to Convention, 141, 843, 1596
compendium for exporters, 235
amendment, 569
Declaration forms, 235
Finland*, 142, 844, 1596
Launcher Development Organisation, 422, 1165
redwood and whitewood, 555, 1351
Space Research Organisation:
Esrange*, 1165, 1579
Esro launching range*, 1165
privileges and immunities, 852
Special TD project*, 1579
Telemetry Station*, 761
300 GeV Accelerator, 1330

EVANS, D.: Epoxy resin glass composites, 1676
EVANS, D. S.: Fundamental Data for Southern Stars, 206
EVANS, F. J. (Chairman): Cairngorm Area Technical Group, 531, 1330
EVANS, G. O.: British Dermanyssidae, 103
EVANS, SIR IFOR (Chairman): National Insurance Advisory Committee, 538
EVANS, OF HUNGERSHALL, LORD (Chairman): National Insurance Advisory Committee, 1621
Evans, Timothy John, case of, 159
EVANS, W. B.: geology of the country around Macclesfield, 906

1966 pp 1–272, 1967 pp 273–604, 1968 pp 605–990, 1969 pp 991–1402, 1970 pp 1403–1740
44

INDEX 1966–70 —EXP

Eveline Lowe Primary School, 412
Evening Classes, guide, 469, 1262, 1615
Ever Ready Company, prices of batteries, 1658
Everybody's guide to Social Security, 537
Evidence:
Criminal Law Revision Committee, 160
Expert, Law Reform Committee, 1655
hearsay. Law Reform Committee, 189
of opinion, Law Reform Committee, 1655

EWING, J. L.: Correspondence Courses in teacher training, 108

Examination(s):
Board, Scottish Certificate of Education, 211, 534, 927
bulletins, Schools Council, 128, 415, 921
for certificates of:
competency:
Merchant Navy, 569, 952, 1366, 1709
Mining Qualifications Board, 199
qualification, Inspector of Weights and Measures, 952
papers:
Art, 126, 413
for licences:
Flight Navigator, 234, 573, 956, 1370, 1714
Senior Commercial Airline Transport Pilot, 234, 573, 956, 1370, 1714
Examining:
at 16 plus, 126
methods, sixth form, 921
Excavations:
annual report, 202, 524, 914, 1321, 1670
at:
Clickhimin, Shetland, 913
Hod Hill, 720
Jerablus, 1536
Ur, 101
in Cyprus, 1536
Excess Votes:
and Atomic Energy Authority, Public Accounts, 165
Public Accounts, 440, 1280, 1634
Exchange:
Control, Act and Instruments, 1380
of Young Persons Bill, 667
Exchequer and Audit, Department of, publications, 129–30, 416–18, 754–6, 1157–60, 1572–4
Execution of Sentences, Army, 734, 1550
Exemption Clauses in Contracts, Law Commission, 1304
Exeter Corporation Act, 78
Exhibition(s):
Contracting industry, pay and conditions, 1307
International, 843
Exmoor National Park, 1546
Expansion of:
Ipswich, 171, 891, 1295
Northampton, 171
Peterborough, 171
Warrington, 171
Expenditure, public, planning and control, 124
Experiment(s):
in Radio Broadcasting, H.C., 882
on living animals, 161, 474, 872, 1270, 1625
Experimental:
farm building, 512, 905
farms, 1524
horticultural stations and husbandry farms, 92, 379, 1120, 1524
horticulture, 92, 379, 714, 1120, 1524
husbandry, 92, 379, 714, 1120, 1524
Expert evidence, Law Reform Committee, 1655
Expiring Laws:
Act, 1111
Bill, 1003, 1076
Continuance Act, 77, 368, 704, 1515
Bill, 9, 51, 288, 339, 619, 670, 1413, 1414, 1484, 1485
Exploitation of North Sea Gas, Nationalised Industries select committee, 883
Exploration of the sea, convention, 843
Explosibility tests for industrial dusts, 939
Explosions:
dust, in factories, 754
venting a building, 923
see also Boiler Explosion Acts
Explosives:
Acts:
forms, 1625
H.M. Inspector's annual report, 474, 872, 1270, 1625
list of authorised explosives, 161, 474, 872, 1270, 1625
(Age of Purchaser) Bill, 1408, 1409
and fireworks, census of production, 957
carriage:
by sea, 240
in ships, 232
licence to import, application form, 1625
mixed, stores for, 1273
Export(s):
and the industrial training of people from overseas, 1366
business from capital projects overseas, 952
by air, 512
control of documents, 1561

1966 pp 1–272, 1967 pp 273–604, 1968 pp 605–990, 1969 pp 991–1402, 1970 pp 1403–1740
45

EXP— INDEX 1966–70

Export(s) (*continued*):
Encouragement Bill, 335
Guarantees:
Act, 368, 704
Bill, 52, 277, 606, 667, 887
and Payments Act, 1515
Bill, 1407, 1469, 1479, 1629
invisible, Britain's, 1649
licences:
open general:
antiques, 236, 1709
copper scrap, 1709
iron and steel scrap, 236, 952, 1366
metallic residues, 952, 1366
printed matter and film for Southern Rhodesia, 236, 952
revocation:
iron and steel scrap, 1715
pork and live cattle etc., 1715
Southern Rhodesia, 236
List, 113, 397, 730
of:
Animals for Research Bill, 334, 619, 666
Manuscripts Bill, 1071
works of art, 249, 582, 968, 1380, 1562
promotion, 878, 956
staff, training of, 754
through movement to Europe, 193
trade statistics, 1135
Export-Import Bank of Washington, U.S.A.*, 246, 579, 965, 1377
Exposure to driving rain, index, 1671
Expression of amounts in printing etc., decimal currency booklet, 731
External loads on buried pipelines, simplified tables, 1672
Extradition:
Austria*, 1238
Sweden, 141
Extra-parochial Ministry Measure, 390

F

Fabric quality, control of, 1660
Fabry photometry, 206
Facsimile telegraphy, 471
Factory(ies):
Act:
Abrasive wheels inquiry, 1566
Commissioner's report, 181
Draft Construction (Working Places) Regulation, inquiry, 181
Appointed Doctor Service, 179
atmospheres, dust and fumes, 1151
Chief Inspector's report, 179, 498, 746, 1148, 1564
Factory(ies) (*continued*):
docks, etc., accidents, how to prevent, 179, 190, 746, 1140, 1564
dust explosions, 754, 1567
fire fighting in, 187
Forms, 181–2, 500–1, 749–50, 1151–2, 1567
hours of employment, women and young persons, 1153
Inspectorate, H.M., 501, 749, 1151, 1567
Facts:
and forecasts, decimal currency booklet, 1136
to Fortunes, guide to bigger profits, 1661
Fairfield:
Rowan Ltd., financial assistance, 246, 580, 966
Shipbuilding and Engineering Ltd., financial assistance, 246, 580, 966
Fairey Surveys Report, Aberfan, 1397
FAIRLIE, H. (Chairman), Pupils' Progress, 1333
Fairweather Recording Calorimeter, 518
Falkirk Ward, hospital design, 1334
Falkland Islands:
and Dependencies:
colonial report, 393
report, 1238
Dependencies Survey. *See* British Antarctic Survey
income tax, 1300
Telemetry Station*, 761
vascular flora, 719
Fallow deer, 151
False indication of origin of goods, 453
Family(ies):
Allowances:
Acts:
decisions, 214, 540, 865, 1263, 1617
index, 214–15, 537–8, 866, 1264, 1618
school leavers, 1617
and National Insurance:
Act: 77, 368, 704
Bill, 289, 339
(No. 2) Bill, 613, 666
Law relating, 215, 538, 866, 1264, 1618
at home, Sheffield, 1646
circumstances of, 537
expenditure survey, 182, 501, 749, 1151, 1261, 1566
houses at West Ham, 1294
Income Supplements Act, 1515
Bill, 1414, 1484
Law:
Commission, 1304, 1654
Reform Act: 1111
Bill, 619, 620, 991, 1000, 1062, 1071, 1073, 1274

1966 pp 1–272, 1967 pp 273–604, 1968 pp 605–990, 1969 pp 991–1402, 1970 pp 1403–1740
46

INDEX 1966–70 —FIE

Family(ies) (*continued*)
living at high density, Leeds, Liverpool, and London, 1646
Planning Bill, 311
Provision Act, 77
Bill, 4, 5, 6, 48, 50
Far Eastern Affairs, British Foreign Policy, 132, 1164
Farm(s):
and:
estate hedges, 1525
Garden Chemicals Act, 368
Bill, 47, 50, 331, 477
animals, feeding, 86
as a business, 379, 715, 1120, 1524
buildings:
and the countryside, 1292, 1294
Department, reports, 512
experimental, 86, 905
pocket book, 379
Research, bibliography, 85, 373, 709, 1115, 1519
business, planning, 374
classification, E. and W., 379, 715, 1524
crops, potash for, 375
dairies, 1121
equipment:
dairy, use of chemicals in hand cleaning, 89
fixed, leaflets, 93, 380, 713, 1120–1, 1524
experimental, 1524
fences, permanent, 1121
grain drying and storage, 89
grinding, 716
husbandry, experimental, 1524
incomes, E. and W., 92, 379, 715, 1120, 1524
Institutes, salaries of teaching staff, 1147
inventories for Oxfordshire, 159
livestock, nutrient requirements, 86, 373
management survey, report on farm incomes, 1524
produce in U.K., output and utilisation, 381
seed cleaning and grading machinery, 94
FARMER ALD. P.: complaint about statement, Privileges Committee, 1280
Farmer and Company Ltd (Transfer of Registration) Act, 1113
Farmers: and growers, mechanisation leaflets, 94, 380, 716, 1525
(Farms (and Farmers)), *see also* Agricultural and Agriculture
Farmland shelter belts, 1121
FARQUHARSON, W. M (Chairman): Hospital Boards in Scotland, 212
FARRER, M. I. (Chairman): Relieving nurses of non-nursing duties, 865
FARRER-BROWN, L. (Chairman): Research and development in modern languages, 743
Fast shutter magnets for separated particle beams, 922
Fatstock Guarantee Scheme, 92, 379, 715, 1120, 1524
FAULKNER, R.: Progeny testing in British forest nurseries, 465
Fauna(s):
British Avonian (carboniferous) conodont, 1126
highest ordovician graptolite, 1538
of the Portrane limestone, 102
Ordovician trilobite
Favia valenciennesii, 1127
Faviidae, 1127

Federal Republic of Germany, *see* germany
Fees:
and charges:
supply and repair of glasses, 1268, 1623
testing sight etc., 158, 472, 870, 1268, 1623
Marine Surveys etc., 1366
Felixstowe Dock and Railways Act, 706
Fellmongery, census of production, 1371
Fencing, electric, 89
Fenitization, 1127
FERGUSON, PROF. T. (Chairman): Carcinogenic action of mineral oils, 900
FERGUSON, W. K. (Chairman): Modern studies for school leavers, 925
Fertilization experiments in Scottish freshwater lochs, 87
Fertility, census tables, 153
Scotland, 155
Fertilizer(s):
and:
chemicals for pest control, census of production, 957
feeding stuffs, residual values, 87, 374, 717, 1116, 1520
handling and broadcasting, 380
Feudal Reform (Scotland) Bill, 1072
Feudities, Multures, and Long Leases (Scotland) Bill, 337, 665

Fibre(s):
building boards, fixing, 521
industrial, production, trade, and consumption, 107
FIELD, E.: Validation Study of Hewitt and Jenkins' Hypothesis, 476
Field:
astronomy, textbook, 1551
monuments, protection, 1323
surgery, pocket book, 115

1966 pp 1–272, 1967 pp 273–604, 1968 pp 605–990, 1969 pp 991–1402, 1970 pp 1403–1740
47

FIF-FOR | 1966-70

FIF— INDEX 1966–70

Fife County Council Order Confirmation Act, 1517
Bill, 1483
Fifteen to Seventy Me V separated orbit cyclotron as booster injector, 209
Fifty:
masterpieces of:
Ancient Near East Art, 1123
Classical Art, 1536
Pence Coin Withdrawal Bill, 1077
Fight against pollution, 1647
Figulla, H. H.: Cuneiform texts from Babylonian tablets, 384
Figures help, 904
Fiji:
annual report, 1239, 1596
colonial report, 109
(Compensation and Retiring Benefits) Order, OIC, 1668
(Constitution):
(Amendment) Order OIC, 911, 1669
Order, OIC, 201
Constitutional Conference, 1607
Flag, 1596
Independence:
Act, 1515
Bill, 1411, 1483
Order OIC, 1669
Information Office pamphlet, 1649
(Retiring Benefits) Order OIC, 1668
Royal Instructions, OIC, 201
Film(s):
Act, 77, 1515
Bill, 10, 45, 51, 163, 1077, 1406, 1408, 1410, 1469, 1482, 1629
Artistes' Association and Film Production Association, difference, 499
legislation, review, 958
Monopoly Commission report, 239
Processing industry, pay of certain employees, 1308
(Statutory Deposit) Bill, 1071
see also Cinematographic films
Filming Amines, 1618
Fimmonds, G. E.: A method of explosion venting a building, 923
Finance:
Acts, 77, 368, 704, 1111, 1515
Bill, 7, 48, 50, 615, 661, 666, 668, 876, 1001, 1062, 1073, 1074, 1274, 1481
(No. 2) Bill, 284, 336, 338
provisions, 1650
Accounts, U.K., 249, 583, 969
and awards, statistics of education, 1563
Financial:
circumstances of pensioners, 214
institutions, British, Information Office pamphlet, 1299
position, Territorial and Auxiliary Forces Associations, 742
Financial (*continued*):
Statement, 249, 583, 969
and Budget Report, 1380, 1722
statistics, 105–6, 389, 725, 1129–30, 1541
Finch Manuscripts, 159
Findlater, J.: Surveys and 900 mb wind relationships, 192
Fine, Dr S.: Blind and partially-sighted children, 744
Finger:
rings in B.M., catalogue, 719
spelling and signing, 744
Finland:
association with EFTA*, 142, 844
atomic energy*, 756, 1239
double taxation*, 133, 453, 1165, 1596
visas*, 1239
Fire(s):
and:
car park buildings, 939
external walls, 221
rescue services, heliports, 1367
at Dudgeons Wharf, inquiry, 1627
attended by fire brigades, deaths, 1709
Brigade medal, 1273
Department:
film strips, 161, 872
manual on firemanship, 872, 1270
Service drill book, 1270
engines and other fire fighting appliances, 208
extinction by foam, 1691
fighting:
appliances, catalogue, 1329
in factories, booklet, 187
science, 872
fought with five or more jets, 221
in:
buildings, brigade attendance times, 939
a compartment, radiation from, 939
hotels, 1351
offices, etc., 1156
multiple death, 1351
Notes, 221, 939, 1351, 1691
precautions:
Bill, 1477, 1484, 1485
for campers, film strip, 872
in pleasure craft, 161
film strip, 872
memorandum, 1263
propagation test, 1691
Research:
report, 221, 554, 939, 1351, 1691
Station:
publications, 221, 554, 939, 1691
symposiums, 939
technical papers, 221, 554, 939, 1351, 1691, 1709

1966 pp 1–272, 1967 pp 273–604, 1968 pp 605–990, 1969 pp 991–1402, 1970 pp 1403–1740

48

INDEX 1966–70 —FLE

Fire(s) (*continued*):
risks:
on building sites, 521, 1669
with polystyrene ceiling tiles, 1669
safety, film strips, 161
Service(s):
(careers), 1149
Departmental Committee report: 1627
Scotland, 927
Drill book, 1270
H. M. Chief Inspector's report, 162, 475, 874, 1272, 1628
H. M. Inspector for Scotland's report, 213, 535, 927, 1334
pay, 510
personnel, 1262
(Scotland) Central Examinations, 927, 1334
systems, hospital, 1616
statistics, U.K., 221, 554, 939, 1692
Firearms:
Act, 704
Bill, 608, 609, 667, 887, 1073
1968 (Amendment) Bill, 1073
Certificates, 1270
Dealers registration, 1270
European, V. and A. Museum, 1396
Forms, 1270
sale, hire, gift, or loan, 1270
Firemen's Pension Scheme:
Amendment Order S.I. select committee, 885
part time firemen, 161
S.I. select committee, 872, 885
Firemanship, manual, 872, 1270
Fireplaces, exempted, Clean Air Act circular, 1291
Fire-resistance of brick and block walls, 221
Fire-retardent plastics rooflights, weathering properties, 1351
Fireworks:
census of production, 957
Safety Bill, 1406
Firm price tendering, 1572
First:
Aid and Home Nursing, Civil Defence, 473
Class Engineer, Merchant Navy examination, 569
colour motion pictures, 1329
National City Bank, loan, 580, 1377
Three Years, Schools Council, 921
Fish(es):
alepocephaloid, 1128
and:
fish products, handling and preservation, 223, 1353, 1695
fishlike vertebrates, 387
berycoid, 386
cakes, Food Standards Committee, 1525
Fish(es) (*continued*):
Caudal skeletons, 722, 723
Chinese, 387
clupeoid, 103, 387, 1127, 1539
clupeomorph, 723
Commonwealth Economic Committee report, 108
drawings, Chinese, 1538
effect of heated effluents, 92
elopoid, 103
farming, net enclosures, 1520
handling and processing, 223
palaeniscoid, 386
products, census of production, 957
teleost, 1539
toxicity tests, 1643, 1646
Fishery(ies):
Convention*, 142
France*, 844
investigations, 92–3, 379, 715, 1120, 1524
North West Atlantic, 142, 1596, 1597
of Scotland, 86, 373, 709, 1116, 1524
operations in North Atlantic, 844
policing, conference, 844
Research:
directorate, 1116, 1520
Freshwater and Salmon, 86
see also various categories, Cockle, Inshore etc.
Fishing:
boat(s):
medical scales, 1366
Skippers and Second Hands, examination papers, 1366
(careers), 1149
industry, assistance, estimates committee, 479, 483
Vessel(s):
Grants Act, 368
accounts, 1121, 1123, 1520, 1526
Bill, 282, 336
(Safety Provisions) Act, 1515
Bill, 1410, 1469, 1480, 1482, 1629
Fitz-Gerald, D.: Georgian Furniture, 1396
Fixed farm equipment leaflets, 93, 380, 715, 1120, 1524

FK4, proper motions on the system of, 1327

Flags of all Nations, 1551
see also specific country
Flame, surface spread of, 221
Flanders, A.: Investigation into Bristol and Avonmouth Docks dispute, 187
Flat glass, Monopolies Commission, 955
Flatlets, Grouped, for old people, 1294
Flax, census of production, 1371
Fleas, Catalogue, 388
Fleet, M.: Geology of the Oscar Coast, Graham Land, 1311

1966 pp 1–272, 1967 pp 273–604, 1968 pp 605–990, 1969 pp 991–1402, 1970 pp 1403–1740

D 49

FLE— INDEX 1966–70

Fletcher, Prof. B. A. (Chairman): English for children of immigrants, 415
Fletcher, D. S.:
Ethiopian species of *Cleora*, 386
Ruwenzori expedition, 724
Fletcher, H. R.: Royal Botanic Garden, Edinburgh, 1674
Fletton Brickworks Industry, pay and conditions, 1658
Flexible sealing materials, 912
Flight:
Engineers' licence, 569
Navigators':
examination papers for licence, 234, 573, 956, 1370, 1714
licence, 234, 569, 952, 1366, 1709
time limits, 952
Flint implements, 720
Flintlime bricks, 1669
Flintshire:
census, 153
County Council Act, 1517
sample census, 467, 1259
Flood, Babylonian legend, 99
Floodlight, guide to evening classes, 469, 864, 1262, 1615
Floor(s) and flooring:
clay tile, 523
concrete, 1322
corrosion-resistant, 1671
force of foot pressure, 523
screeds:
B.R.S. digest, 1322
laying, 521, 1320
space, industrial, shopping, and office use, 1297
terrazzo, 1671
Flora:
English Wealden, 1126
of:
Antarctic moss, 1662
British fungi, 1326, 1674
tropical East Africa, 112, 396, 729, 1134, 1546
Venezuelan fungus, 1674
West tropical Africa, 728
vascular, of the Falkland Islands, 719
Yorkshire jurassic, 1128
Zambesiaca, 112, 1546
Flour, iron in, 870
Flow charts, logical trees, and algorithms for rules and regulations, 586
Flowers, Prof. B. H. (Chairman): Computers for research, 127
Flowers from bulbs and corms, 376
Fluke or liver rot in sheep, 88
Fluoridation:
of water supplies, 1292
studies, 1268
Fluoroacetamide, use as rodenticide, 1526
Fly(ies):
blow, 375
cluster, 375
gout, 88
house, 375
mangel, 88
sand, 85
warble, 89
wheat bulb, 375
Flying:
from Myth to Space Travel, 922
since 1913, 207

Fodder, buildings for processing and storing, 86
Folkard, S.: Delinquency, causes and treatment research, 162
Fomes annosus, 465, 1611
Food:
additives and contaminants, 93, 380, 715, 1525
and Drugs (Milk) Act, 1515
Bill, 1077
domestic, consumption and expenditure, 92
Drink, and Tobacco Industry Training Board, 1151, 1566
growth, and population structure of salmon, 373
hygiene:
codes of practice, 156, 470, 1263
coin operated vending machines, 470
Labelling Bill, 50
leaching of substances from packaging materials, 1525
mixers, 716
of:
cod, 374, 709, 710
seals, 710
the witch, 1161
regulations, emulsifiers and stabilisers, 1515
Research Institute, 709, 1115
retailing, 1154
restaurants, etc., dogs in, 865
Standards Committee reports, 93, 380, 715, 1121, 1525
storage:
and direct feeding of cattle, 512
safety arrangements for use of toxic chemicals, 141
Foot, M. R. D.: History of the Second World War, 143
Foot-and-Mouth disease:
Committee report, 1122
epidemic, origin, 717
Football:
Committee report, 745
matches, crowd behaviour, 1297
Footpaths Committee report, 893

1966 pp 1–272, 1967 pp 273–604, 1968 pp 605–990, 1969 pp 991–1402, 1970 pp 1403–1740

50

INDEX 1966–70 —FOR

Footwear:
and the consumer, 728
census of production, 958
Leather, and Fur Skin Industry Training Board, 1151, 1566
Prices and Income Board, 510, 903
Forage harvesters, 380
Foraminifera, 102
Ford Motor Company Ltd., Industrial Court inquiry, 750
Foreign:
and Commonwealth Office publications, 756–859, 1160–1254, 1574–1611
see also Commonwealth Office, and Foreign Office
Compensation:
Act, 1111
accounts, 142, 454, 844, 1158
Bill, 664, 670, 876, 991, 992, 996, 1073
Commission:
accounts, 142, 454, 844, 1158, 1597
report, 142, 454, 844, 1597
Exchange Operations Fund for Laos*, 144, 456, 847, 1243, 1602
Law, European convention, 1243
Office:
and Commonwealth Office, merger, 849
Correspondence, index, 1302
Library, catalogue of books, 146
publications, 130–51, 418–65
See also Foreign and Commonwealth Office
Records, P.R.O. handbook, 1324
small craft, 208
travel, select committees H.C., 882
Foreigners entering and leaving U.K., statistics, 162, 475, 874, 1273, 1628
Foremen and Staff Mutual Benefit Society (Application of Rules) etc., Act, 1113
Forensic psychiatry, 1334
Forest(s):
management:
in Sweden, 465
mathematical models, 151
tables, 151, 465
nurseries:
grey mould, 1255
progeny testing, 465
of:
Central and Southern Scotland, 1255
North and Mid-Wales, guide to site types, 1612
Park(s):
booklet, 1255
Guide, 151
Products Research Laboratory:
bulletins, 554, 939, 1351, 1692
leaflets, 222, 555, 939, 1351–2
Forest(s) (*continued*):
Products Research Laboratory (*continued*):
reports, 221, 939
special reports, 555
Records, 151, 465–60, 1255, 1611–12
Research, 151, 465, 860, 1612
Station publications, 1691
resources, Britain, 1611
weeds, chemical control, 1255
Forestry:
Act, 368
Bill, 5, 10, 52, 168, 277, 485
and agricultural research workers, conversion tables for, 151
Commission:
annual report, 151, 465
and accounts, 859, 1611
booklets, 151, 465, 859, 1255, 1611
bulletins, 465, 859, 1255
guide, 860, 1255
leaflets, 151, 465, 860, 1255, 1611
ploughing practice, 1612
publications, 151, 465, 859–60, 1255, 1611–12
consolidation of Acts, Lord Chancellor's memorandum, 168
in the:
British scene, 859
landscape, 151
Weald, 859
metric guide, 1255
pastures, and field crops, progress review, 728
quarantine, biological background, 465
research, 860
use of land within the proprietory land unit, 1255
Form(s):
A.44, application for office copies of documents, 898
E.30 A. and B, designs guide sheet, 969
H.20, return of income and expenditure, 490, 891, 1294
S.H.W. 395, dangers from gassing and chemical burns, 505, 754
207 Pen, teachers' pensions, 413
Forming a new organisation, network analysis, 1377
Forsyth, A. A.: british poisonous plants, 711
Fort:
George, guide, 1670
William and surroundings, sample census, 863
Forth:
Harbour Reorganisation Scheme Confirmation (Special Procedure) Act: 370
Bill, 339

1966 pp 1–272, 1967 pp 273–604, 1968 pp 605–990, 1969 pp 991–1402, 1970 pp 1403–1740

51

FOR— INDEX 1966-70

Forth (continued):
 Ports Authority:
  account, 1158
  Order Confirmation Act, 1114, 1517
  Bill, 1483
Fossil(s):
 Bennettitales, 102
 birds, 104
 British:
  Caenozoic, 721
  Mesozoic, 721
  Palaeozoic, 101, 1537
 chordates, 722
 hominids, catalogues, 387
 mammals, 102, 103, 386
 plants of the carboniferous rocks of G.B., 195, 1312, 1663
 spores and pollen, 386
Foster, J. R. M.: Prawns, 1524
Foul brood, 375
Foulness (off-shore) local hearings, 1365
Fountains Abbey, guide, 912, 1670
Four hundred years of music printing, 720
Fowler, R. F.: Duration of unemployment of wholly unemployed, 725
Fox, A., Industrial sociology and industrial relations, 205
Foyers Project, 1331

France:
 air transport*, 143, 1597
 amateur radio operators*, 844
 Customs privileges*, 1598
 double taxation*, 760, 1597
 Film co-production*, 142, 454, 1597
 Fisheries*, 844
 International Road Transport*, 1242
 New Hebrides*, 454, 1239, 1598
 social:
  insurance*, 1598
  security, Channel Islands*, 142
  taxation of Road vehicles*, 1597
Francis, E. H.: Geology of the Stirling district, 1663
Fraser, A. G.: Petrology of Stonington and Trepassey Islands, 98
Fraser, A. I.: Sitka Spruce, 464
Fraser, F. C.: Stranded whales etc., identification, 104, 1124
Frederick Parker Ltd, Industrial Relations Commission, 1549
Free postage facilities for MPs, 166
Freedom of Publication (Protection) Bill, 49, 665, 1065, 1070, 1073, 1274, 1478
Freeman, R. B.: Charles Darwin on the routes of male humble bees, 723
Freight:
 forwarders, 1660
 Integration Council, 1717
 transport of, 368

French in Primary Schools, 128, 1333
Fresh fruit and vegetables, distribution costs, 510
Freshwater:
 and Salmon Fisheries Research, 86, 373, 1116
 Fisheries Laboratory, Pitlochry, 1520
Freyssinet-concrete hinges, 242
Friedman, E.: Charge-exchange reactions and inelastic scattering, 530
Friendly:
 and Industrial and Provident Societies Act: 704
  Bill, 613, 615, 661, 668, 669, 876,
 Societies:
  Bill, 1406, 1407, 1408, 1414, 1481, 1629
  Chief Registrar's report, 152, 466, 861, 1257, 1613
  Registry of:
   annual return forms, 152, 466, 860-1, 1255-6, 1612
   Industrial Assurance Commissioner's report, 152, 466, 861, 1257, 1613
   publications, 152, 466, 860-1, 1255-7, 1612-13
Frogs, parasites in, 723
Frontal calcification in some bryozoa, 1128
Frost, R.: Beaufort Force Wind Speed and Wave Height, relationship, 192
Frost precautions, 1669
Fruit:
 and vegetable(s):
  domestic preservation, 89
  home preservation, 1117
  products, census of production, 957
  spraying machines, 376
 tree(s):
  raising, rootstocks, and propagation, 1117
  Silver leaf disease, 88
Fruiting organs from Morrison Formation, 103
Frye, J. (Chairman): Iron and Steel Consumers' Council, 1693

FSH circulars, 90-2, 376-8, 711-13, 1117, 1522

Fuel:
 pulverised, in building materials, 323
 for the future, 517

Fuelling landplanes and helicopters, 569, 1366
Fugitive Offenders:
 Act, 368
 Bill, 279, 283, 331, 335, 477
 within the Commonwealth, rendition, 162
Future of the sixpence, 1548

INDEX 1966-70 **—GAS**

Fullwood, N. (Chairman): Curricula in Latin and Greek, 534
Fulton, Lord (Chairman): The Civil Service, 967, 1379
Fumes from welding and flame cutting, 1566
Fumigation with:
 ethylene oxide, 1525
 liquid fumigants, precautionary measures, 380
Functions and effects of grievance arbitration, U.S.A., 919
Funds in Court, E. and W., accounts, 416-17, 755, 1158, 1573
Fungus(i):
 cause of rot and death in conifers, 465
 flora:
  British, 1326, 1674
  Venezuela and adjacent countries, 1764
 fomes annosus, 1611
 honey, 465
 larger British, handbook, 104
 Nepal, 721
 pathogenic to man and animals, 508
Fur:
 census of production, 1371
 seals, 719
Furniture:
 and:
  equipment dimensions, further and higher education, 1560
  Timber Industry Training Board, 182, 501, 749, 1151, 1566
  upholstery, census of production, 1371
 beetle, 1351
 domestic electrical appliances, and footwear, distributors' costs and margins, 903
 English, short history, 266
 Georgian, 1396
 manufacture (careers), 499
Further:
 and higher education, furniture and equipment, 1560
 education:
  centres, salaries of teachers, 745, 1147, 1333, 1680
  general student, 413
  (Scotland) (Amendment) Regulations, 925
  statistics, 746, 1662
  structure of Art and Design education, 1563
 supply and training of teachers, 129

G

Gadd, C. J.: Literary and religious texts, Ur excavations, 101
Gaelic, census, Scotland, 155
Galactic clusters, three-colour photometry, 207, 921
Galatheidae, 104
Gale Damage:
 Bill, 662
 Scotland, 875
Gall:
 crown, 88
 leafy, 88
 mite of black currants, 88
Gall-bladder parasites in whiting, 374
Galleries of H.C., guide for visitors, 1628
Gambia, Republic of:
 Act, 1516
 Bill, 1409, 1482
 double taxation*, 1239
 International rights and obligations*, 110
Game, P. M.: The younger volcanics, 1539
Game(s):
 Act, 1515
 Bill, 1403, 1405, 1407, 1480
 census of production, 958
 theory, elementary ideas, 1377
Gaming:
 Act, 704
 (Amendment Bill), 620, 992
 Bill, 340, 614, 616, 622, 662, 667, 670, 876, 991, 1004
 Board for G.B., 1627
 Extablishments Bill, 339
 Machine (Licence Duty) Regulations, and S.I. select committee, 1288
Gammaridea, 1217
Garden Companion, 1674
Gardener, chemicals for, 376
Gardiner, B. G.: Chondrostei, 386
Gardner, I. S. K.: Beam sensing radial and phase control systems for Nimrod, 194
Garland, C. E.: Case commentary on Income Tax Acts, 496
Garrett, J.: Management by objectives, 1131
Garrod, D. J.: Whiting, 93
Gas:
 and:
  Bearer Bonds, 1381
  Bill, 1070, 1080, 1463, 1819
  loans, 249, 583, 969, 1381, 1722
 and:
  Electricity Act, 704
  Bill, 614, 667, 910
  Water Supply, manual workers' pay and conditions, 510
 Boards, annual report and accounts, 199, 517-18, 910, 1318, 1692

GAS— INDEX 1966-70

Gas (continued):
 census of production, 958
 centrifuge process, 1605
 Consultative Council report and accounts 199, 517-18, 910, 1318, 1692
 Council:
  advances, 1317
  Annual report and accounts, 199, 518, 910, 1318, 1692
  loan, 249, 583, 969, 1722
  select committee on Nationalised Industries, 882, 883
  Electricity, and Coal Industries, select committee on Nationalised Industries, 166
  evolution from epoxy resins, 1676
  examiner's working notebook, 518
  Industry:
   costs and efficiency, 1608
   staff workers pay, 903
   Training Board, 182, 501, 749, 1151, 1566
  Minister of Power's report, 199, 518, 910, 1318, 1692
  North sea, 883, 1317
  prices, 902, 1307
  supplies, shortage in West Midlands, 200
 Gaseous spheres, self gravitating dynamics, 206
 Gassing and chemical burns, cautionary notice, 505
Gatherer, W. A. (Chairman):
 English for the young school leaver, 1678
 Teaching of literature, 925
Gauge making and measuring, 555
gauging stations, descriptions, 985

Geckos, 103
Geddes, R. M. (Chairman): Shipbuilding Inquiry, 240
Gekkonidae, 103
Gelechiidae, 1128
Gelatine, adhesives, etc., census of production, 957
General:
 Accident, Fire, and Life Assurance Corporation Ltd:
  Industrial Relations Commission, 1545
  Prices and Incomes Board, 510
 and Parliamentary Constituency tables, U.K., G.R.O., 1257
 Chemicals, census of productions, 1371
 G.C.E., C.S.E., and School Leavers, statistics, 746
 Grant (Increase):
  Order, 173
  (Scotland) Order, 209
 Index, Treaty Series, 1599

General (continued):
 Lighthouse Fund accounts, 236, 576, 331, 1374, 1710
 mechanical engineering, census of production, 1371
 Medical:
  Practice, buildings, 865
  Services, Highlands and Islands, 534
  for sight testing etc., 1764
 Optical Council (Disciplinary Committee) (Procedure) Order of Council, S.I. select committee, 1640
 Practice:
  Finance Corporation:
   financial assistance, 584, 969, 970, 1382, 1723
   report, 471, 867, 1265, 1619
  nursing attachments, 1268
 Printing, publishing, bookbinding, engraving, etc. census of production, 1372
 Rate Act, 1515
  (Amendment) Bill, 666, 1479
  Bill, 11, 275, 335, 358, 484, 488, 1069, 1076, 1403, 1407, 1481, 1629
  circulars, 488, 889
  rate product rules, 889
  tables of comparison, 489
 Register:
  and Record Office of Shipping and Seamen, 1366, 1710
  Office, 152-4, 466-9, 861-3, 1257-9, Scotland, 154-5, 468-9, 863, 1259-61, 1613-15
 Teaching Council, 1333
 Transport Consultative Committee for G.B., 297
Generating Plant breakdowns, Science and Technology select committee, 1639
Genocide:
 Act, 1111
 Bill, 619, 670, 1063, 1274
 prevention and punishment, 143, 1598
Gentianaceae, 1537
Gentry, A. W.:
 Fossil mammals of Africa, 102
 Pelorovis Oldwayensis Reck, 386
Genus(era):
 Acarus, 1539
 Agama, 723
 Alloplectus, 1128
 Ancistrotermes, 101
 Andreaea
 Antanartia, 101
 Anthene, 102
 Boleti, 1326, 1674
 Buellia, 1311
 Callomyia, 101
 Cheritrini, 385

INDEX 1966-70 **—GIB**

Genus(era) (continued):
 Cleora, 386
 Columnea, 1125
 Crassostrea, 1524
 Cribrimorpha, 387
 Dikraneura, 721
 Echiura, 1539
 Elaphoglossum, 385
 Enyalus, 1128
 Eurotessarana, 1126
 Haplochromis, 387
 Hyparrhenia, 1674
 Kellaria, 1128
 Lycoptera, 1539
 Macrotermes, 1537
 Mercenaria, 1524
 Mytilus, 1524
 Neptini, 1126
 Notiphilus, 721
 Oretinae, 385
 Orosius, 102
 Ostrea, 1524
 Palorus, 385
 Phileitor, 103
 Platypeza, 101
 Plica, 1539
 Pohlia, 1662
 Polytrichum, 1662
 Pseudoste ga, 387
 Psilopilum, 1662
 Rhipidocephala, 101
 Rinodina, 1311
 Sarconeurus, 1662
 Sipuncula, 1539
 Strobilurus, 723
 Swertia, 1537
 Uracentron, 723
 Veratrilla, 1537
 See also binomial entries
Geochemical reconnaissance of the:
 Denbighshire area, 1663
 Derbyshire area, 1663
Geochemistry of:
 recent sediments, Irish Sea, 1664
 sedimentary rocks, 1312
Geodetic observations and field surveys, Commonwealth Conference, 1314
Geography, C.S.E. trial examination, 128
Geological:
 Museum, 195, 514, 1662
 Sciences:
  annual report, 195, 514, 906, 1311, 1662
  publications, 195, 514, 905-6, 1311-12, 1662-4
Survey:
 and Museum, Scotland, 906
 of Great Britain:
  bulletins, 195, 514, 1311, 1662

Geological (continued):
 Survey (continued):
  memoirs:
   E. and W., 195, 514, 906, 1311-12, 1663
   Scotland, 195, 906, 1663
   summary of progress, 195
   overseas, 195
Geology:
 bulletins, 102-3, 386-7, 721-3, 1126, 1538, see also genus (era)
 of:
  South Orkney Islands, 711, 719
  South Shetland Islands, 719
Geomagnetic elements, annual values, 920
Geometridae, 386
Geophysical:
 exploration, 1662
 memoirs, 191, 900, 1656
 papers, 906, 1311, 1662
 surveys, Shetland, Islands, 906
George, T. N.: South Wales, 1662
George Heriot's Trust:
 (Amendment) Scheme, 926
 Scheme, 211
George Outram and Co. Ltd, Monopolies Commission, 1713
George III Collection, physics, 1329
Georgian furniture, large picture book, 1396
German(y):
 British:
  Forces*, 453, 1238, 1596
  Foreign policy, 760
  defeat, 1129
  domestic silver, small picture book, 599
  double taxation*, 453, 1578
  external debts*, 1239
  foreign exchange expenditure*, 843
  foreign policy, 132
  gas centrifuge process*, 1605
  return of 6 brigade, 1596
  reunification problem, 1669
  social security*, 454, 843
  termination of military control, 1164
  training exercises*, 1598
  wood statuettes, 599
Ghana, debts*, 246, 1239
Ghauri, M. S. K., Orosius Distant, 102
Giants of types K and M, Royal Greenwich Observatory, 524
Gibbons, E. B.: Court Lees Approved School, inquiry, 473
Gibbs, J. (Chairman): Smallholdings, 382
Gibbs-Smith, C. H.:
 Aviation, 1675
 Clement Ader, 922
 Early Flying, 207
 First Aeroplanes, directory and nomenclature, 207
 Flying from Myth to Space Travel, 922

GIB-HAR | 1966-70

Gibbs-Smith, C. H. (*continued*):
Leonardo da Vinci's Aeronautics, 530
Sir George Cayley, 922
Gibraltar:
colonial report, 109, 393
Constitutional Order OIC, 1320
further documents, 454, 844
(Referendum) Order OIC, 520
report, 844, 1598
talks with Spain, 143
Gilbert, K. R.:
Fire engines and other fire fighting appliances, 208
Fire fighting appliances, catalogue, 1329
Machine tool exhibits in Science Museum, catalogue, 208
Gilbert and Ellice Islands:
(Amendment) Order OIC, 1320
colonial report, 109
(Electoral Provisions):
(Amendment) Order OIC, 521
Order OIC, 520,
Order OIC, 521
report, 845, 1240, 1598
Royal Instructions, OIC 521, 1669
Gilbert Island, teleost fishes, 1539
Giliomee, J. H.: Coccidae, 386
Gilmore, R. S.: Correlated dead time effects in high rate coincidence measurements, 209
Gilyard-Beer, R.: Fountains Abbey, 1670
Girard, P. M.: Rough digitising merger programme, 1676
Girling Ltd, Industrial Court Inquiry, 750
Girt, J. L.: social and economic assessment, 1267
Giuseppi, M. S.: Salisbury (Cecil) Manuscripts, 1269

Glamorgan:
and Monmouthshire, Local Government re-organisation, 1631, 1736
census, 153
sample census, 467, 1259
Glasgow:
and Lanark:
census, 155
sample census, 469, 1261
Cathedral, guide, 1670
Corporation:
(Carnoustie Street) (Bridge) Order Confirmation Act, 78
Bill, 48
Order Confirmation Act, 370, 1516, 1517
Bill, 335, 1076
(No. 2) Order Confirmation Act, 78
Bill, 1480
(Superannuation etc.) Order Confirmation Act, 1114
Bill, 1073
Glasgow (*continued*):
Corporation (*continued*):
(Works etc.) Order Confirmation Bill, 1484
Glass(es):
census of production, 1371
masterpieces, 721
supply or repair, fees and charges, 1268, 1623
technology, catalogue, 1329
Glasshouse:
crops, red spider mite on, 88
heating systems, 1525
Glen More Cairngorms, guide, 151
Glennie, J. F. (Joint Chairman): Water resources of the North, 599
Gliese, W.: Cape catalogue of circumpolar stars for the equinox, 206
Globular cluster W. Centauri, 529
Glossary of:
atomic terms, 262
management techniques, 583
mental disorders, 863
training terms, 501
Gloucestershire:
census, 153
County Council Act, 1517
sample census, 467, 862
Gloves, census of production, 958
Glycerine, census of production, 957
Glyn Mills and Company, advances, 584, 969–70, 1382, 1723
Glyphipterigidae, 1128

Godber, Sir G. (Chairman): Organisation of medical work in hospitals, 470
Going metric:
first five years, 1657
implication for primary and secondary schools, 925
in construction industry, 524
metric units, 1657
Gold in your hands, 194
Gomphidiaceae, 1674
Good design in housing, awards, 170, 488 889, 1291, 1644
Wales, 266, 600, 985, 1396, 1736
Goode, Sir W. (Chairman): Water Resources Board, 1736
Goodlet, G. A.: sands and gravels, Scotland, 1663
Goods:
imported and re-exported, 113
transport by road:
geographical analysis, 244
international, 456, 1242
Customs Convention, 113
see also agreements with specific Countries
methodological report, 244

Goods (*continued*):
vehicles:
plating and testing. 961–2, 1717
testers' manual, 567, 962
Goodwin, D.:
pigeons and doves of the world, 724
woodpeckers, 723
Goody, P.C.: teleosts and myclophoids, 1126
Gooseberries, 88
Gosline, W. A.: alepocephaloid fishes, 1128
Gosling, Sir A. (Chairman): footpaths, 983
Gosport Corporation Act, 1517
Gout fly, 88
Government:
accounting, 1381
and Finance, Supply Estimates, 1725
Central, *see* Central Government
Chemist('s):
report, 222, 556, 940, 1353, 1694
Steering Committee's laboratory, 222
Contracts Review Board, 1673
Laboratories, industrial research and development, 1693
of Wales Bill, 288, 335
Orders:
in force, index, 542, 1689
tables, 219, 543, 932, 1342, 1690
publications, catalogue, 217, 541, 929, 1336, 1683
Research Establishments, liaison with Universities, 413
Social Survey publications, 86–4, 1261–2
Statistical Services, Estimates Committee 165, 479, 483, 1542
Statutes in force, index, 218, 542, 931, 1690

Grade stress:
European redwood and whitewood, 1351
laminated timber, 555, 1692
plywood, 1351
Graduate training, manufacturing technology, 1692
Graham, M. W. R. de V.: Pteromalidae, 1126
Graham, R.: Titchfield Abbey, 1321
Graham Hall, J. (Chairman): Statutory maintenance limits, 874
Graham Land:
geology, 1311
magnetic survey, 98
petrology, 383
stratigraphy, 719
Grain:
crops, production, trade, consumption, and prices, 107
dryers, 94, 716
drying and storage, 89
buildings, 86
farm-stored, insects and mites in, 88
heating in store, 375
Grain (*continued*):
milling, census of production, 957
Gramineae, 1546
Grampian Highlands, geology, 514
G–R and R–I colours of late-type dwarfs, 920
Grand Baham Island, Apollo Unified S-Band Facility*, 858
Grand Turk Island, air base*, 420
Grandison, A. G. C.: Nigerian lizards, 723
Grangemouth—Falkirk regional survey and plan, 923
Gransby, D.: The House of Stuart, 1310
Grant, Rt Hon. Lord (Chairman): Sheriff Court, 536
Grant(s):
for:
Arts, Estimates Committee, 878, 1277
Comprehensive Development, 1293
investment, 953
non-recurrent, 1735
of honours, decorations and medals, 66, 581
to students on teacher training courses, 743, 1561
under Rural Waterways and Sewerage Acts, 490
Graptolites, 1126
Grass:
and:
clover crops for seed, 711
grassland, 89
Black, 375
ensiling, 89
Staggers, 375
Tetany, 375
Grassland leafhopper, 721
Gray, D. E.: Nimrod operation and development, 53, 923, 1676
Gray, E.: Workloads in Children's Departments, 1270
Gray, J. E.: Type specimens of Sipuncula and Echiura, 1539
Gray, P. G.:
Adult dental health, E. and W., 1664
Drivers' understanding of road traffic signs, 864
Mobility and reading habits of the blind, 864
Private motoring in E. and W., 1261
Grayson, A. J.: Imports and consumption of wood products, 1612
Great:
auk eggs, 104
Barrier Reef Expedition, 724
Britain:
agricultural census, 1521
geological survey, 1662
history of retriangulation, 906
labour costs, 753
Summary Tables, 468
see also Britain

Great (*continued*):
Migration, the, 1310
Northern London Cemetery Corporation Act, 706
poets, illustrated booklet, 1310
Yarmouth:
Corporation busmen, pay, 903
New Britannia Pier, *see* Blackpool Pier
Greater London:
census, 153
Council:
(General Powers) Act, 78, 370, 706, 1114
Housing Role within London, 491
Inner London Education Authority, 469, 864, 1262
(Money) Act, 78, 370, 706, 1114,1517
pay of Chief and Senior Officers, 511
publications, 469, 864, 1262, 1615
(Vauxhall Cross Improvement) Act, 706
Parks and Open Spaces Provisional Order Act, 370
Bill, 284, 337
Rate Equalisation Scheme, 892
sample census, 862
Greathead, D. J.: *Bombydiidae* and *Nemestrinidae*, 1125
Greece:
and Turkey, British Foreign policy, 1577
Anglo-French Crimean War cemetery*, 143
association with EEC*, 424
atomic safeguards*, 1240
Commonwealth War graves*, 1254, 1610
driving licences*, 1598
loan of 1898, account, 583
visas*, 1240
Green, S. W.: Antarctic moss flora, 1662
Greenaway, F.:
Atoms, elements, and molecules, 922
Chemical laboratories and apparatus, 207
Greenhill, B.: The Great Migration, 1310
Greenock Corporation Order Confirmation Act, 370
Bill, 335
Greenough, A. P.: Interfacial cohesion, 940
Greenwich Hospital:
Act, 368
Bill, 286, 338
and Travers Foundation:
accounts, 123, 417, 735, 1158, 1551
estimated income and expenditure, 123, 411
Greenwood, P. H.:
Cichlidae, 387
clupeomorph fishes, 723
Haplochromis species, 1127
Lycoptera and *Hiodontidae*, 1539
Megalopidae, 1539
Gregg, A. R.: British Honduras, 759
Greig, J.: John Hopkinson, Electrical Engineer, 1675
Grenada:
Colonial report, 109
report, 1240
Grenville Library, B.M., illuminated manuscripts, 384
Gresham, A. T.:
concrete insulated magnet for 300 GeV accelerator, 1330
magnets for particle accelerator physics, 1330
Grey mould in forest nurseries, 1255
Griffiths, D. A.: *Acaridae*, 1539
Griffiths, H. (Chairman): Ronan Point Flats, inquiry, 893
Grinsell, L. V.: Belas Knap Long Barrow, Gloucestershire, 201
Grinstead, E. D.: Chinese periodicals in British libraries, 1124
Grint, E. T. C., BBC dispute, inquiry, 1153
Grit and dust:
Clean Air Act, 489
emmission from chimneys, 490
report, 493
Gromia oviformis, 1127
Grosset, J. B. (Chairman): Standard Pharmaceutical Advisory Committee, 213
Ground(s):
and gardens maintenance, hospital, 1262
space treatment on high density housing estates, 490
staff at aerodromes, pay, 1308
Water Year Book, 1736
Grouped flatlets for old people, 1294
Grow your own sales staff, 904
Grueber, H. A.: Coins of the Roman Republic, B.M., 1536

Guarantees, agricultural, annual review and determination, 1521
Guardian's Allowance, 215, 868
Guardianship of Minors Bill, 1411, 1412, 1485, 1642
Guernsey, Alderney, Herm, and Jethou, social insurance, 360
Guest, Keen and Nettlefold Ltd and Birfield Ltd, Monopolies Commission, 572
Guichard, K. M.: Collecting in Turkey, 385
Guide:
and map to the British Museum, 720
to:
London museums and galleries, 901
Seals in the PRO, 915
See also specific places
Guildford Corporation Act, 370

Gun(s):
Barrel Proof:
Act, maximum prices, 1550
(Alteration of Maximum Prices) Order, 1550
sporting, 915
Gutenburg, Johann, 1536
Guthrie, B. N. G.:
binary peculiar A Star HR 4072, 529
chemical composition of manganese Star 53 Tauri, 207
Guyana:
armed forces personnel*, 845
Arms, 108
Flag:
Governor General, 101, 394
National, 110
Independence:
Act, 77
Bill, 3, 48
booklet, 177
public officers*, 110, 196
Republic Act, 1515
Bill, 1407, 1481
status of H.M. Forces*, 110
Venezuela Frontier*, 1598

Gwasanaeth iechyd Gwladol, 1736
Gwendraeth Valley and adjoining areas, geology, 1312

Gymnosperms, 103
Gypsy(s):
and other Travellers, 489, 491
circular, 170
Wales, 266
encampments, circular, 1644

H

Hackett, M. (Chairman): Strategy for the South-East, 412
Haddington, Earl of (Chairman): National Museum of Antiquities of Scotland, 194
Hadley, H. (Editor): Magnet technology, international conference, 922
Haematopus ostralegus, 93, 379, 1524
Hagenbuch, Prof. (Chairman): Reinstatement of former employees, 1571
Hague Convention, divorces and Legal separation, 1654
Hailes Abbey, guide, 1670
Hains, B. A.:
Central England, 1311
Geology of the Craven Arms Area, 1311
Hair, Bass, and Fibre Wages Council (Great Britain), inquiry, 505
Haircutting Services. Monopolies Commission, 955
Hairdressing and:
Allied Services Industry Board, 1566
Beauty Culture (careers), 1149
Hake off South Africa, 715
Halifax and Calder Valley, area study, 742
Hall, B. P.: African passerine birds, 1537
Hall, D. H.: regional magnetic anomolies, 1664
Hall, J. S.: Milk quality, 1115
Hall, Sir N. (Chairman): Pharmaceutical Services, 1622
Halls, Z.:
Men's Costume, 1653
Women's Costume, 1303
Halley Bay, scientific reports, 383
Halliday, Prof. J. M. (Chairman): Conveyancing, legislation and practice, 212
Hallmarking Bill, 1481
Halo Red-giant, 206
Halosaur leptocephalus, 103
Halstead, D. G. H.: Tenebrionidae, 385
Hambros Bank Act, 1517
Hamilton, J.: Brochs of Mousa and Clickhimin, 1670
Hamilton, J. R. C.: Excavations at Clickhimin, Shetland, 913
Hamilton, R. A.: Extraterrestrial constant of a Dobson spectrometer, 509
Hamilton Advertisers Ltd., Monopolies Commission, 1713
Hampshire:
census, 153
County Council Act, 1517
sample census, 467, 862
Hampton Court Palaces:
Gardens and park, plan, 522
guide, 522
Hancock, D. A.: Cockles, 93
Hancock, P.: Corrosion of alloys at high temperatures, 938
Hand tools, powered, 1320, 1669
Handbook of statistics, 171, 491, 891
Handel and his autographs, 384
Handicapped:
children in care, 1679
pupils, special schools, E. and W., 413
Handicraft, CSE trial examination, 128
Handkerchiefs, census of production, 1371
Handlist of Persian Manuscripts, 720
Handwriting, English, 1735
Hand trucks, census of production, 958
Hanger, J. E. and Co., 510
Hanley, F. (Chairman): soil potassium and magnesium, 382
Hansard. *See* H.L. and H.C. debates
Haplochromis species, 387, 1127
Harbours:
Act, loans, 417, 962, 1158, 1558
(Amendment) Act, 1515
Bill, 1411, 1483
Harden, D. B.: Masterpieces of Glass, 721

HAR—   INDEX 1966-70   INDEX 1966-70   **—HIE**

Hardie, C. E. M. (Chairman): British Overseas Airways Corporation, 1355
Harding, G. A.:
Photometric observations of RR Lyrae variables, 206
Radial velocity observations of standard stars, 1327
Hardman, Sir H. (Chairman), Home grown cereals, 1121
Hardwoods, machine planing, 555
Hardy Brothers Ltd. (Transfer of Registration) Act, 1114
Hare Coursing:
(Abolition) Bill, 1076, 1485
Bill, 1482
See also Deer hunting and hare coursing
Harisson, C. M. H., Radiicephalus Elongatus Osorio, necoytype, 723
Harlech, Lord:
East Anglia and the Midlands, 912
Southern England, 202
Harmer, L. C., Clerical work measurement, 966
Harold, M. R., A resonant extraction system for Nimrod, 1330
Harper, F. C., Forces applied to floors by walking, 523
Harper, J. (Chairman), Forensic psychiatry, 1334
Harris, A. L., Social welfare for the elderly, 864
Harris, G. L., Sand and gravel, 1663
Harris, M., The housewife and the Garchey system of refuse disposal, 863
Harris, T. M., Yorkshire jurassic flora, 1128
Harris, W. G. (Chairman), Contracting in civil engineering since Banwell, 904
Harris, W. V., Genus Ancistrotermes, 101
Harris College, Preston, building bulletin, 125
Harrison, C. J. O., Birds, instructions for collectors, 1540
Harrison, M., Local Government administration in E. and W., 490
Harrison, R. K. (Editor), Petrological and mineralogical code for computer use, 1663
Harrison's index for class names, 177, 469, 1300, 1650
Harrisson, C. M. H., First Halosaur leptocephalus, 103
Harrold, T. W., Air motion in frontal precipitation, 901
Harvesting:
combine, 716
forage, 380
Harwell variable energy cyclotron, beam measurements, 530
Haslegrave, Dr. H. L. (Chairman), Technician courses and examinations, 1146

Haslemere, geology, 1312
Hastings, A. B.:
Stylopoma Levinson, 723
type material of some genera and species of polyzoa, 103
Hastings Hours, B.M. Calendar, 1123
Hats, caps, and millinery, census of production, 958
Haustoriidae, 1127
Havering Corporation Act, 1517
Hay, barn drying, 716
Hayes, J., Oil paintings, 1653
Hayter, W., large picture book of his engravings, 599
Hayward, J. F.:
English:
desks and bureau, 895
watches, 1396
European firearms, 1396
Hayward, R. (Chairman), Administration of the wage shop, 537

Headlamps, use of, 579
Health:
and:
safety at work, 1566
Social Security, Department of:
annual report, 1262, 1617
circular, 865
Family Allowance, Decision of the Commissioner, 865, 1617
publications, 864-70, 1262-9, 1615-24
statistical report series, 1268
See also Health and Social Security, Ministries of
Welfare:
community care, 156
Services:
Scotland, 212, 535, 927, 1334
Wales, 1274
Welsh Grand Committee, 1063
Centres, 1617
Education, handbook, 744
in:
agriculture, 95
education, 127
Industrial, Chief Inspector of Factories' report, 178
Ministry of:
annual report, 156, 470, 867
Chief Medical Officer's report on state of public health, 472
hospital in-patients, report, 467
index to circulars, 157
publications, 155-8, 469-72
See also Health and Social Security, Department of the school child, 126, 1562

Health (continued):
Service(s):
and Public Health Act, 704
Bill, 339, 610, 612, 613, 616, 662, 666, 668, 876
Convention, Poland, 454
design note, 1263
in:
Britain, Information Office pamphlet, 895
Scotland, 1681
superannuation scheme, 927
statistics:
E. and W., digest, 1263
Scottish, 928
Visiting and Social Work (Training) Act, accounts, 156, 417, 865, 1159, 1617
Hearing:
Aid(s):
Bill, 334, 665
Council Act, 704
Bill, 611, 614, 615, 669
and noise in industry, 1617
Hearsay evidence in Civil Proceedings, Law Reform Committee, 189
Heasman, M. A.: Accuracy of certification of cause of death, 154
Heat:
bibliography, 222, 555, 940, 1352, 1694
transfer:
and pressure drop for forced flow of helium, 1676
through low pressure helium gas, 531
Heathery Burn Cave, Bronze Age finds, 720
Heathrow (London) Airport, disruption, 1571
Heating:
and drying out, 1320
hospitals, 1616
hot and cold water, etc. installations for buildings, 914
Heavy particles:
energy loss(es):
multiple scattering correction to, 922
straggling distributions of, 923
Hedgehogs, 1612
Hedges, farm and estate, 1525
Hedley, R. H.: Gromia oviformis, 1127
Heleomyzidae, 101
Helicopters:
fuelling, 569, 1366
Professional pilots' licenses, 1370
Heliport Fire and Rescue Services, 1367
Helium-3 and Helium-4, cryogenic properties, 530
Helmsley Castle, Yorkshire, guide, 201

Hemiptera:
Ciccadellidae, 721
Coccoidea, 1125
Homoptera, 101
Lygaeidae, 385
Hemming, P. J.: Rhopalocera, 386
Hemsley, J. H.: Sapotaceae, 729
Henderson, D. M.: British fungus flora, 1326
Hendry, A. W.: Introduction to the higher symmetries, 208
Henig, Sir M. (Chairman): East Midlands Economic Planning Council, 1145
Henry, Prof. G. L. F. (Chairman): Title to land in Scotland, 1335
Henry Lawes Manuscript, 1124
Henry Millar Trust Scheme, 1332
Her Majesty('s):
Forces, (careers), 1149
Inspectors, see specific subject, Constabulary, etc.
Ministers and Heads of Public Departments, 249, 583, 969, 1381, 1544
Most Gracious Speech to Both Houses of Parliament, 2, 287, 618, 1002, 1411
Queen Elizabeth II, Argentine-Chile arbitration, 131
Heralds of England, 392
Herbage seed supplies, 717
Herbst, L. J.: Transistor circuit techniques, 530
Herefordshire:
census, 153
sample census, 468, 1259
Heriot-Watt College:
Edinburgh Scheme, 1333
Order Confirmation Act, 78
Herring:
changes of stock in the North Sea, 93
Industry:
Acts, accounts, 93, 380, 715, 1121, 1520
Board, annual report, 94, 380, 716, 1121, 1520
Herstmonceux Reflector, cassegrain spectrograph, 206
Hertfordshire, sample census, 468, 862
Heterakoidea, 387
Heterocera, 721
Hewitt and Jenkins' hypothesis, delinquency, 176
Hewsham, D. B.: Challenge of change to the adult trainee, 1156
Hey, M. H.: Catalogue of meteorites, 104
Hickman, M. J.: Measurement of humidity, 1713
Hicks, D. (Chairman): Grit and dust emissions, 493
Hieroglyphic texts from Egyptian stelae etc., 1536

HIG—   INDEX 1966-70   INDEX 1966-70   **—HOP**

Higgins, R. A.: Terracottas in the B.M., 1537
High:
blocks, appraisal and strengthening, 1644
Court and Court of Appeal, accounts, 188, 507, 898, 1303, 1654
rate coincidence measurements, correlated dead time effects, 209
voltage apparatus in vacuum support insulators, 209
Higher:
Civil Service pay, 192
education:
building system, 1560
flow of candidates from Science and technology, 125, 743
in the further education system, 127
mission to the South Pacific, 196
student numbers:
E. and W., 1561
Scotland, 1680
National Certificates in mining Surveying, 126
police training in Scotland, 927
High-frequency single-sideband radiotelephone transmitter, 909
receiver, 909
Highland(s):
and Islands:
Development:
Board, report, 472, 871, 1269, 1624
(Scotland) Act, 704
accounts, 417, 755, 1159, 1573
Bill, 613, 616, 667, 669
see also Highlands and Islands Development (Scotland) bill
Livestock Producers Ltd., investigation, 951
Transport:
Bill, 331
Board, 374, 476
Services, 374, 476
see also Scottish Highlands
Highly specialised graduates, employment, 745
Highway(s):
Act:
Bill, 1484
1959 (Amendment) Bill, 1077
Street width byelaws, 988
bridges and structures, 576
code, English and Welsh editions, 1374
maintenance, 1717
statistics, 242, 576, 962, 1374, 1717

Highway(s) (continued):
(Straying Animals):
Bill, 48, 51
(No. 2) Bill, 1072
Hill, Prof. Sir S. (Chairman): Hospital treatment of acute poisoning, 865
Hill, J. E.: Review of the genus philetor, 103
Himsworth, Sir H. (Chairman): CS gas, 1272
Hinksey, P. I.: Rooflights for venting fires in single-storey buildings, 1268
Hiodontidae and Lycoptera relationship, 1539
Hispanic silver, 1396
Historic(al):
buildings:
and: areas, preservation, 1294
circulars, 170, 890
Council for:
England, 202, 524, 914, 1323
Scotland, 202, 524, 1323, 1677
Wales, 202, 524, 914, 1323, 1672
Manuscripts:
Commission, publications, 159, 473, 871, 1269, 1624
Royal Commission on:
centenary exhibition, 1269
guides to reports, 159
reports, 871, 1624, 1674
Monuments:
in:
Dorset, 1674
England, Royal Commission, 916
Series, Natural History Museum, 104, 1536
Towns, preservation and change, 491
History:
CSE, examination bulletin, 921
Second World War, 1128, 1540
Hixon Level Crossing accident, public inquiry, 963

HMS Fearless, discussions with Rhodesia, 853
HMS Victory, building restoration and repair, 123

Hoare, Sir F. A. (Chairman): General Practice Finance Corporation, 1265, 1619
Hobbs, G. J.: The geology of Livingstone Island, 719
Hobman, D.: Guide to Voluntary Service, 1320
Hod Hill excavations, 720
Hodgson, E. W. (Chairman):
Power Presses, 753, 1156
Sheffield cutlery and silverware problems, 505

Holden, A. V.: Chemical study of Rain and stream water in the Scottish Highlands, 87
Holden, M. J.: Spurdogs, 93, 715
Hole, W. V.: Houses and people, 221
Holiday(s):
Industry, Devon and Cornwall, 1646
motives in timing, 863
on inland waterways, 1540
Holland, See Netherlands
Holland-Martin, Adm. Sir D. (Chairman): Trawler safety, 959, 1373
Holler, R. H.: Work flow in batch production, 222
Hollington and Hewthorn, rule in, Law Reform Commission, 507
Hollis, D.: Acridoidea, 722
Holmes, M.:
Crown Jewels at the Tower of London, guide, 522, 912
Les Joyaux de la Couronne, 1321
Holmes, M. R.: Stage costumes and accessories in the London Museum, 898
Holothurioidea, 1128
Holtam, B. W.:
Blue Stain effect on wood of home grown conifers, 151
Forestry in Sweden, 465
Home grown roundwood, 465
Holy Trinity, West Hampstead Act, 706
Home(s):
Civil Service, Method II system of selection for the administrative class, 1133
economics:
CSE trial examination, 178
departments in secondary schools, 1679
rooms, safety, 1680
Grown:
Cereals Authority, annual report and accounts, 94, 380, 1121, 1525
conifers, effect and control of Blue Stain, 151
roundwood, 465
softwoods for building, 220
Sugar Beet Research and Education Fund, account, 95, 382, 718, 1122, 1526
timbers, 555, 918
Help Service, E. and W., 1664
Office:
Advisory Council, child care, 871
Amendment lists, 475
and Scottish Home and Health Department Prison Service examination papers, 620
Children's Department, 475
Constitution Commission, 1133
Fire Department, see Fire Department

Home(s) (continued):
Office (continued):
Prison Department, see Prison Department
publications, 159-62, 473-6, 871-4, 1269-73, 1624-8
studies, 1270
Unit reports, 162, 476
Statistical Department, report on murder, 1273
older, standards of fitness, 173
ownership, help towards, 171
preservation of fruit and vegetables, 1117
Homeless discharged offenders, residential provision, 162
Homoptera:
Aleyrodidae, 101
Cicadellidae, 721
Cicadelloidea, 102
Coccidae, 386
Coccoidea, 386, 1125
Eriococcidae, 1125
Pseudococcidae, 1125
Honduras, visas*, 1240
Honestones, 1127
Honey:
from hive to market, 711
fungus, 465
Honeyman, Sir G. (Chairman):
Dockworkers (Regulation of Employment) Act, inquiry, 186
Teachers' salaries, arbitral report, 414, 745, 1333
Tube works, inquiry, 501
Hong Kong:
Additional Instructions OIC, 201, 521, 1320, 1669
annual report, 394, 845, 1240, 1599
colonial report, 109
income tax, 1300
Letters Patent OIC, 521, 1669
(Non-domiciled Parties) Divorce Rules, S.I. select committee, 1640
Honours, decorations, and medals, Committee on grants of, 248, 581
Hooijer, D. A., Miocene rhinoceroses of Africa, 103
Hooker Estates Ltd. (Transfer of Registration) Act, 1517
Hoover (Ltd):
domestic appliances, price, 902
Industrial Relations Commission, 1545
Hooykaas, Dr C.: Bagus Umbara, Prince of Koripan, 719
Hop(s):
growing and drying, 711
marketing scheme, 94
Verticillium Wilt, 88
Hopkins, G. H. E.: Hystrichopsyllidae, 388

HOP-HUM | 1966-70

HOP— *INDEX 1966-70*

HOPKINSON, JOHN: Electrical engineer, 1675
Horagini, 101
Horserace Betting Levy Act, 1111
Bill, 671, 993, 994, 1063, 1072, 1073, 1274
Horticultural:
buildings, pocket book, 716
Industry, examination of, 92, 714
packing sheds, 715
stores, air conditions in, 94
Horticulture:
and plantation crops, 1133
experimental, 92, 379, 1120, 1524
in Britain, 380
stations, experimental, 92, 379, 1120, 1524
sub-committee, 881
HORTON, A.: Drift sequence and topography, Ouse and Nene basin, 1664
Hosiery:
and:
Knitwear:
Economic Development Committee, 1660
in the 1970s, 1661
Industry (Scientific Research Levy) account, 1710
making up, 1660
other knitted goods, census of production, 958
knitwear and lace (careers), 1564
HOSKINS, R. F. (Editor): Handbook of Asian Scripts, 100
Hospital(s):
Abstracts, 156–7, 470–1, 866, 1263, 1617–81
Accident and Emergency Department, 469
administrative arrangements. *See* Administrative arrangements, hospital
Boards:
in Scotland, administrative practice, 212
of Management and Executive Councils for Scotland, accounts, 1681
building(s):
cost, 1618
in G.B. estimates committee, 1632
maintenance, 1618
notes, 157, 471, 866, 1263, 1618
procedure notes, 1616
communication services, 1616
costing returns, 472, 867, 1619
day, *see* day hospitals
design:
in use:
Falkirk Ward, 1334
Bellshill Maternity Hospital, 927, 1681
note, 157, 471, 927
Hospital(s) (*continued*):
Endowment(s):
Allocation, 1334
Fund account, 157, 471, 866, 1618
Research Trust, Scottish, 213, 536, 928
(Scotland) Bill, 1477, 1482, 1484, 1629
Engineering Services, commissioning of, 471
equipment note, staff accommodation, 1263
hot and cold water services, 1616
in-patient inquiry, GRO tables, 154, 467, 861, 1257, 1665
laundries, 1263
Management Committees and Executive Councils, 158, 471, 867, 1265, 1619
medical records in Scotland, 536
mental deficiency, *see* Mental deficiency hospitals
O and M:
and work study reports, 1263
Service reports, 157, 866
pharmaceutical service, 1622
in Scotland, 213
plan for Scotland, review, 213
planning note, Scotland, 535
portering services, 1263
psychiatric, *see* psychiatric hospitals
running costs, Scotland, 212, 535, 928
sanitary services, 523
scientific and technical services, 866
Service:
abstract of efficiency studies, 155, 469–70, 864, 262, 1615
index, 865
Scotland, organisation of medical work, 535
special and state, estimates committee, 870, 878
staff, care and health, 865
suggestions and complaints, 1335
sweepstakes, 1479
technical memorandum, 157, 471, 866 1263, 1616
treatment of acute poisoning, 865
Hot and cold water:
services, hospital, 1616
Systems:
Installation of, 914
lagging, 912
Hotel(s):
accounting, 1309
and:
business travellers, 1661
Catering:
(careers), 1149
Economic Development Committee, 512, 904, 1309

INDEX 1966-70 **—HOU**

Hotel(s) (*continued*):
and (*continued*):
Catering (*continued*):
Industry Training Board, 501, 750, 1153, 1568
investment in, 904
occupations, Ministry of Labour booklet, 180
staff turnover, 1309
restaurants:
in Britain, 1540
London, 1540
development:
incentives, 952
loans, 1712
fires in, 1351
keepers, liability for guests' property, 456
keeping and Catering, national diplomas, 129
Service, 904
HOUGHTON, SIR W. (Chairman):
Adoption of children, 1624
Training:
for office supervision, 746
of export staff, 754
Hounslow Corporation Act, 706
Hours:
and overtime, London Clearing Banks, 1657
of:
employment, women and young persons, 1153
work, overtime, and shift working, 1658
House(s):
and people, 221
building, programming by line of balance, 1308
Buyers Protection Bill, 49
conditions survey, Welsh Office, 1397
held on a Ground Lease, rights under Landlord and Tenant Act, 491
improvement and repair, circular, 1292
in multiple occupation, circular, 1293
Local Authority owned, Scotland, rents, 1335
of:
Commons, 163–8, 476–84, 874–86, 1273–88, 1628–41
Bills, 47–52, 334–40, 665–71, 1070–7, 1478–85
broadcasting proceedings, 166, 167, 882
Churchill statue, 1628
closed circuit television annunciator system, 481
debates, 41–7, 328–34, 658–64, 1054–70, 1460–78
House(s) (*continued*):
of (*continued*):
Commons (*continued*):
debates (*continued*):
bound volumes, 41, 42, 45, 330, 658, 660, 1054, 1055, 1059, 1460, 1465, 1477
general index, 42, 658, 1460
Disqualification Act, 76, 367, 704, 1110, 1515
foreign travel by select committees, 166, 882
free postage facilities for Members, 166
Guide for visitors to galleries, 1628
Inner court and cloisters, 166
library, new accommodation, 166
Member(s):
additional accommodation, 1636
Contributary Pension Fund, accounts, 130, 417, 705, 1573, 1628
detained in prison, rights of, Privileges Committee, 1634
Fund, accounts, 163, 476, 874, 1159, 1573
serving legal documents, Privileges Committee, 1634
Minutes of Proceedings, 163–4, 476–9, 874–7, 1273–6, 1628–31
new parliamentary buildings, 166, 481, 882
Notices of Motions, time limit for handing in, 166
Papers, 13–41, 292–328, 623–58, 1009–54, 1419–60
index, 164, 1276, 1631
photo-statting papers for Members, 882
Privileges Committee, 480, 880, 1280, 1634
Procedure select committee, 166, 481, 883, 1284, 1637
radio broadcasting experiment, 882
(Redistribution of Seats):
(Amendment) Bill, 1070
Bill, 1001, 1074, 1075, 1479
(No. 2) Bill, 1000, 1002, 1074
Refreshment department, accounts, 166, 882
security, 1636
Select committees, 165–8, 479–84, 878–85, 1277–88, 1631–41
see also specific subjects
Services select committee, 164, 166, 167, 478, 481, 877, 882, 1282, 1631, 1636

HOU— *INDEX 1966-70*

House(s) (*continued*):
of (*continued*):
Commons (*continued*):
Special reports of committees, 167, 483, 1631
Standing committees, *see* Standing committees
Standing Orders, *see* Standing Orders
stationery, 481, 882
tape-recording of standing committees, 166
telephone services, 481, 882
Hanover, 905
Lords, 168–9, 284–6, 886–8, 1289–90, 1642–3
(Abolition of Delaying Powers) Bill, 50
broadcasting proceedings, select committee, 888
(Composition Functions) Bill, 288
Consolidation Bills, 168, 484–5, 886–7, 1289, 1642
debates, 11–13, 290–2, 630–3, 1004–9, 1415–19
bound volumes, 11, 12, 13, 291, 620, 622, 1004, 1008, 1415, 1417
cumulative indexes, 12, 13, 1005, 1008, 1418, 1419
Offices, committee reports, 168–9, 485, 887, 888, 1289, 1642
papers and bills, 1–11, 273–90, 605–20, 991–1004, 1403–15
Privileges Committee reports, 169
Procedure, 169, 486, 887, 1289
Reform, 887
Select committee reports, 486, 888, 1289, 1642
Sessional Papers, titles and tables of contents, 1290, 1643
Special orders, 169, 486, 888, 1290, 1642–3
Standing Committee, *see* Standing Committee
Standing orders, 169, 486, 611, 1290, 1643
televising proceedings, 486
Stuart, 1310
Tudor, 513
Windsor, 513
owned by Local Authorities in Scotland, rents, 532, 1678
planning, circular, 889
Purchase and Housing Act, 171, 491, 891, 1294
purchasers, protection, 1293
sale of, 488
House(s) (*continued*):
shells, metric:
circular, 1293
two storey, 1308
two or three storey, generic plans, 1308
Housebuilding:
in U.S.A., 172
industrialised, 266
metrication, 888, 890
(Protection of Purchasers) Bill, 47
progress in metrification, 1644
value for money, 1293
Houseflies, 374
Household:
and farm inventories for Oxfordshire, 159
composition:
census tables, 153
national summary, 154
Scotland, 155
tables, sample census, Scotland, 863
detergents, Monopolies Commission, 239
food consumption and expenditure, 716, 1121
see also Domestic food consumption
textiles:
and handkerchiefs, census of production, 1371
distributors' margins, 903
House-sparrow, 375
Housewife and the Garchey system of refuse disposal, 863
Housing:
Act(s):
circulars, 489, 890, 1292, 1293, 1645
1961, accounts, 172, 531, 891, 1295
1964:
accounts, 172, 209, 491, 532, 892, 924, 1295, 1331
Corporation report, 491, 1646
1969, 1112
sale of houses, 488
(Amendment) Scotland Act, 1515
Bill, 1069, 1076, 1274, 1404
and:
households, census, Scotland, 155
Local Government, Ministry of:
circulars, 170–1, 487–90, 888–91, 1290–3, 1643–5
design bulletins, 171, 490, 891, 1294, 1646
handbook of statistics, 1646
model standing orders, circulars, 889
Provisional Orders, *see respective Towns*
publications, 169–75, 486–94, 888–94, 1290–8, 1643–8
report, 349, 1297

INDEX 1966-70 **—HUM**

Housing (*continued*):
and (*continued*):
Local Government, Ministry of (*continued*):
Sociological Research Section, 491
redeployment of labour, circular, 487
Associations, subsidies, 489–90
Authorities, continuity in contracting, 1308
awards for good design, *see* Awards
beef cattle, 1525
Bill, 999, 1001, 1002, 1063, 1071, 1074, 1075, 1274
co-ordination of components, 1646
cost yardstick, 1291, 1645
metric, 1292
development, land costs, 1308
estates:
cars in, 171
children's play, 221
high density treatment of ground space, 490
telephone facilities, 488
(Financial Provisions etc.) (Scotland) Bill, 21, 45, 51, 52, 368, 477, 611
(Financial Provisions) (Scotland) Act:
Bill, 43, 163, 277, 607, 611, 668, 704, 887
tables of comparison, 924
improvement and repair, circular, 1645
in:
Britain, Information Office pamphlet, 1649
New Towns, ownership and management, 893
Wales and Monmouth, 1629
land availability, 1572
Local Authority:
Contributions Bill, 1071
owned, rent increases, 490
management in Scotland, report, 531
of calves, 1121
returns:
E. and W., 172
Scotland, 209, 531, 924, 1331, 1677
race relations, circular, 891
Revenue accounts:
circular, 1292
report, 1295
Role of Greater London Council within London, 491
(Scotland) Acts, 367, 1112
accounts, 172, 209, 531, 532, 891, 924, 1295, 1331
Bill, 6, 8, 51, 168, 999, 1000, 1064, 1071, 1074, 1075, 1274
Tables of Comparison, 532
sites, handling concrete on, 1669
(Slum Clearance Compensation) Act, circular, 170
Housing (*continued*):
soil and waste pipe systems, 523, 1671
sow and litter, 380
standards:
and costs, circular, 1293
costs and subsidies, circulars, 488, 600
statistics, 172, 491, 892, 1295, 1647
Subsidies:
Act, 368
Bill, 52, 278, 279, 281, 331, 335, 337, 477
circulars, 488, 489, 889, 1292
representative borrowing rate, circulars, 890, 1645
supplementary subsidies, circulars, 890, 1292, 1645
Estimates committee, 1277, 1278
manual, 488, 491, 1645
Summaries, 172, 491–2
survey in E. and W., 864, 1295, 1647
tables, Scotland, 863
two-storey, industrialised, 1658
vertical dimensional standards, 488
(Wales and Monmouthshire) Bill, 1470
Hove Corporation Act, 370
Hovercraft Act, 704
Bill, 616, 662, 667, 669, 876
How fast? Paper for discussion, 962
HOWARTH, T. G.: Revisional notes on Genus Antanartia, 101
HOWE, G. (Chairman): Ely Hospital, Cardiff, inquiry, 1267
HOWLETT, R. (Chairman): Nutritional standard of the school dinner, 127

HPD failed events, computer graphics patching, 1676

Huddersfield:
and Colne Valley area study, 1145
Corporation Act, 1517
HUDSON, W. M.: Strength properties of European redwood and whitewood, 555
HUGHES, H. M.: Experimental horticulture, 1524
HUGHES, J.: Membership participation and Trade Union Government, 1919
HUGHES-HUGHES, A.: Manuscript music in the B.M., catalogue, 99
HULL, F. (Editor): Calendar of White and Black Books of the Cinque Ports, 473
HULTON, P. H.: Cesar Mange de Hauke bequest, 720
Human:
Rights:
and fundamental freedoms, protection, 132, 1599
civil and political, 454
competence of European Commission, 143, 455, 1240

Human (continued):
  Rights (continued):
    conventions, 1599
    European Court of, 143, 455, 1240, 1599
  International Year, 495
  political rights of women, 455
  skeletal material from Ceylon, 102
  Tissue Act, 1264
Humanities for the young school leaver, 415, 921
Humber investigations, cruise report, 1312
Humberside, 1145
Humes, A. G.:
  Lichomolgidae, 1128
  Stellicola, 387
Humidity, measurement of, 1713
Hungary(ian):
  cereals*, 1240
  co-operation in applied science and technology*, 1240
  Funds account, Foreign Compensation Commission, 844, 1158
  property accounts, 579, 965, 1377, 1719
  road transport of goods*, 1607
Hunt, A.:
  Home Help Service, 1664
  Survey of:
    Scottish tourism, 864
    Women's employment, 864
Hunt, D. R.:
  Cactaceae, 729
  Tamaricaceae, 112
Hunt, Sir J.:
  (Chairman):
    Intermediate areas, 1145
    management training and development, 1149
    pattern and organisation of the college year, 1562
    training:
      and development of managers, 498
      for commerce and the office, 187
  (Joint Chairman):
    Education for industry and commerce, 744
    technical college resources, 1146
Hunt, Lord (Chairman):
  Immigrants and the Youth Service, 413
  Parole Board, 1628
  Police in Northern Ireland, 1313
Hunt, T. (Chairman): West Midlands, patterns of growth, 113
Hunter, J. (Chairman): training and development of managers, 2nd report, 498
Huntingdon and Peterborough:
  County Council Act, 1517
  sample census, 468, 1259
Huntingdonshire, census, 153

Hurcomb, Lord (Chairman): Bird life in Royal Parks, 1670
Hurrell, H. G.: Pine martens, 859
Husbandry:
  experimental, 92, 379, 1120
  farms, experimental, 92, 379, 1120
Hutchinson, Prof. J. H. (Chairman): Epilepsy in Scotland, 928
Hutchinson, W.: Higher police training in Scotland, 927
Huxley, J.: Tettigoniidae, 1537
Huyton-with-Roby Urban District Council Act, 78
Hyades, the, proper motions in the region of, 206
Hyatt King, A.: Handel and his autographs, 384
Hydraulic(s):
  and water supplies, survey of the science of firefighting, manual, 872
  design(s):
    channels and pipes, 1352
    stormdrains, sewers, and pipelines, tables, 1692
  Research:
    paper, 1352, 1692
    Station report, 222, 555, 1352, 1692
Hydrocarbon Oil (Customs and Excise) Act, 1413
Hydrocephalus, pathology, 508
Hydro-electric:
  Boards, North of Scotland, 210, 213
  Development (Scotland) Act:
    explanatory memorandum, 1331
    loans, 249, 583, 969, 1381, 1722
Hydrogen:
  fluoride and inorganic fluorides, 1568
  liquid, vapour pressure and molar volume for, 194
  sulphide, 1568
Hydrographic:
  and magnetic surveys, Commonwealth conference, 1313
  Service, Admiralty, 411
Hydrography:
  Convention, 845
  of Blackwater Estuary, 715
Hydrological survey, Wessex rivers, 494
Hydrometric statistics for British rivers, 985
Hygiene:
  food, codes of practice, 156, 470
  in:
    commerce and offices, 843
    meat trades, 1263
Hygenic milk production, 88
Hymenoptera:
  Apidae, 722
  Braconidae, 386, 1537
  Chalcidoidea, 385
  Encyrtidae, 385

Hymenoptera (continued):
  from Turkey, 385, 722
  Pteromalidae, 1126
  Scoliidae, 385
  Sphecidae, 385, 721
  Symphyta, 722
Hypomagnesaemia in cattle and sheep, 375
Hystrichopsyllidae, 388

I

IBM United Kingdom Ltd., increase in rental charges for equipment, 902
Icacinaceae, 729
Ice cream industry, costs, prices, and profitability, 1658
Identification parades, 1270
IFR circulars, 713-13, 1117-20, 1522
IG report, 262
Iguanid lizards, 1539
Iliff, N. (Chairman): Printing in a competitive world, 1661
Illuminated manuscripts, 100, 1536
Illustrated:
  booklets, Science Museum, 1329
  catalogue of the Rothschild collection of fleas, 388
ILO, see International Labour Organisation
Immigrant(s):
  and the Youth Service, 413
  children, English for, 415
  Commonwealth, see Commonwealth Immigrants Act
Immigration:
  Appeals:
    Act, 1112
    Bill, 670, 872, 994, 996, 1064, 1072, 1271, 1274
    Committee report, 475
  control, Commonwealth select committee, 1183
Immunities and privileges, 845, 1240
Immunological procedures, Service personnel and their families, 733
Imperial:
  Chemical Industries Ltd., pay of:
    general workers and craftsmen, 1307
    salaried staff, 1307

Imperial (continued):
  War Museum:
    handbook, 894
    publication, 1298
Implement shed and farm workshop, 1121
Import(s):
  and consumption of wood products, 1612
  Duties:
    Act, annual report, 236, 318, 952, 1367, 1710
    (General) (No. 8) Order S.I. select committee, 885, 1287
    (Temporary Exemptions) (No. 6) Order S.I. select committee, 1287
  Licences:
    Open general, 236, 569, 953, 1367, 1710
    Revocation, Southern Rhodesia, 236
Importation of Animals Bill, 337
Imported:
  and re-exported goods, statistical classification, 731
  Food Standards, see FSH- and IFR circulars
Improvement(s):
  of agricultural land, 479, 878
  to land and buildings, financing, 1120
Imputed criminal intent, 507
In Place of Strife, 1155
Incapacity for work, incidence of, 217
Incentive Bonus Schemes, circular, 487
Income(s):
  and:
    Corporation Taxes:
      Act, 1515
      Bill, 1403, 1413, 1480, 1484, 1642
      tables of comparison, 1650
    (No. 2) Act, 1515
  expenditure:
    National, 106, 389, 774, 1129, 1541
    return, 389, 490, 891, 1294
  policy, circular, 889
  prices, employment, and production statistics, 187, 506, 754, 1156
  tax(es):
    case commentary, 1650
    supplementary, 177, 496, 896, 1300, 1650
    in the Commonwealth, 177
    outside:
      the Commonwealth, 178
      the U.K., 896, 1300, 1650
Indecent Advertisements (Amendment) Act, 1515
  Bill, 1409, 1483

Independence:
  booklets, Information Office, 177
  Conferences reports, 110
Independent:
  Day Schools, 1562
  Schools in E. and W., lists, 126, 744, 1562
  Television:
    Authority:
      additional payment by programme contractors, 197, 316, 909, 1315, 1668
      annual reports and accounts, 197, 816, 908, 1315, 1668
      licence, 1315
    Companies, costs and revenues, 1658
Index:
  and:
    digest of decisions, National insurance Acts, 214, 537, 866, 1264, 1618
    Title page, London Gazette, 218, 541, 931, 1341, 1689
  classified, of Local Authorities and New Towns, E. and W., 891
  general, to Treaty Series, 1599
  Harrison's, to Tax Cases, 177, 496, 1300, 1650
  locorum, 384
  number construction, problems, 1542
  of:
    agricultural research, 1519
    collectors in the Edinburgh Herbarium, 1674
    Defence publications, 410
    industrial production, 1542
    products, census of production, 1715
    Religious Houses etc., 384
    retail prices, method of construction and calculation, 506
  sessional, H.C. Papers, 164, 885, 1276, 1631
  subject, Public General Acts and Church Assembly Measures, 76, 367, 703, 1111, 1514
  supplementary, to Local and Personal Acts, 543
  to:
    additional manuscripts in B.M. (1783-1835), 384
    Army Allowances Regulations, 733
    catalogue of additions to manuscripts in B.M. (1854-1875), 720
    Charters and Rolls, B.M. Manuscript Department, 384
    Civil Estimates, 247, 581, 967, 1318
    Education and Science circulars, regulations and administrative memoranda, 126, 413, 744, 1146, 1562
    experimental husbandry, 714

Index (continued):
  to (continued):
    Foreign Office correspondence, 1302
    Government Orders in Force, 542, 1689
    hospital abstracts, 156, 866, 1617
    H.C. debates. See House of Commons debates
    H.L. debates, see House of Lords debates
    Industrial Tribunal's decisions, 504, 752, 1155, 1570
    lists of accessions to repositories, Historical Manuscripts, 473
    Parishes, County Courts, 189
    Particular Registers of Sasines for Sheriffdoms, 214, 537, 929
    Public General Acts, 76, 367, 703, 1111, 1514
    Register of Deeds in Scottish Record Office, 214, 537, 929
    Statutes in force, 218, 542, 931, 1690
    Testamentary Records, Commissary Court of London, 1269
    Treaty series, 143, 455, 845, 1241, 1599
Index-catalogue:
  African phaneropterinae, 722
  Genus-group names of Tachinidae, 385
India(n):
  Air Services*, 394
  and Pakistan, Overseas Aid select committee, 1637
  Art, large picture book, 1396
  coins in B.M., 383
  income tax, 1300
  Office:
    Library:
      British drawings, 1576
      Burmese books, 1162
      Guide, 394, 1240
    records, note, 394
  transfer of power, 1599
  War graves*, 1254, 1610
Indian Ocean currents, 191
Indo-China, British involvement in, 132
Indo-European cotton-paintings, 1736
Indonesia:
  Air Services*, 1241
  British losses*, 455
  commercial debts*, 845, 1241
  Crum Rubber Plant Project loan*, 1600
  loan*, 845, 1241, 1599, 1600
Indo-Oriental horagini, 101
Indostromus paradoxus, 1539
Indus Basin, development, 145
Industrial:
  and Provident Societies:
    Act, 368
    Bill, 49, 283, 331, 336, 477
    forms, 152, 466, 860, 1256, 1613

Industrial (continued):
  and Provident Societies (continued):
    Chief Registrar's report, 152, 466, 861, 1257, 1613
  archaeology, Wales, 1310
  Assurance Commissioner's report, 152, 466, 861, 1257, 1613
  bacteria, national collection, 556, 1694
  buildings, corrosion-resistant floors, 1671
  Civil Servants, pay and conditions, 1657
  classification, standard, 723
  Coal Consumers' Council, annual report, 199, 518, 910, 1318, 1710
  construction sites, large, 1661
  Court(s):
    Act, report of inquiries, 182, 501, 750, 1153, 1568
    Awards, 183-5, 502-4, 750-2, 1153-4, 1568-9
  death benefit claims, 869
  demand for transport, 1717
  Design, Council of:
    Annual report, 175, 494, 894, 1298
    publications, 175, 494, 894, 1298, 1648
  Development:
    Act, 77
    accounts, 715, 718, 1121, 1520, 1526
    annual report, 570
    Bill, 6, 8, 48, 50, 51, 163
    certificates, circular, 170
    circular, 890
    (Ships) Act, 1515
  Disablement Benefit, Decisions of the Commissioner, 539, 869, 1266, 1621
  Diseases (Benefits) Acts, accounts, 539
  Disputes Tribunal, work of, 919
  dusts, explosibility tests, 939
  effluents, circular, 891
  engines, census of production, 957
  Expansion, 940
    Act, 704
    Bill, 610, 612, 662, 665, 666, 668, 876
    report, 1352
  fibres, production, trade, and consumption, 722
  fires, extinction by foam, 1691
  health, Chief Inspector of Factories' report, 179, 498
  Information Bill, 610
  Injury(ies):
    Act:
      decisions of the Commissioner, 540
      see also National Insurance (Industrial Injuries)

Industrial (continued):
  Injury(ies) (continued):
    and Diseases (Old Cases) Act, 368
      accounts, 1265, 1621
    Bill, O, 274, 279, 336, 484, 485
      decisions of the Commissioner, 866
    Benefit, decisions of the Commissioner, 539, 540, 869
    Fund accounts, 213, 539, 868, 1265, 1621
    (Independent Contractors) Bill, 1072
    Medical Boards, handbook, 1671
  investment:
    computers merger project, 940
    primary aluminium production, 953
  noise, 488, 1266, 1292
  Organisation and Development Act, accounts, 94, 236, 380, 570, 716, 953, 1367, 1710
  plant and steel work, census of production, 1371
  production and other output measures, index, 1542
  property:
    conventions, 1600
    protection, 455
  Relations:
    Bill, 1482, 1484
    Commission, 1544-5
    (Improvements) Bill, 1479
    policy, In Place of Strife, 1155
    studies, 920
    workplace, 864
  Reorganisation Corporation, 124
    Bill, 10, 11, 145, 49, 50, 51, 52, 471
    loan, 1381
    report and accounts, 742, 1145, 1693
  research and development in Government Laboratories, 1693
  sociology and industrial relations, 205
  Training:
    Bill, 1470, 1479, 1481, 1630
    of people from overseas, exports, 1366
  Research Register, 504
  Tribunals, decisions, 185-6, 504, 752, 1154-5, 1570
Industrialised:
  building bulletin, 203
  two-storey housing, 1658
Industry(ies):
  alphabetical list, 105, 1129
  and commerce, education for, 744
    related to efficiency, 180
  Bill, 1485
  census tables:
    E. and W., 154
    Scotland, 155
    Summary, 468

IND-JO | 1966-70

Industry(ies) (*continued*):
commerce, and teachers, closer links, 128
different, relative frequency, 221
disputes procedures, 205
hearing and noise, 1617
in Wales and Monmouthshire, 45, 163
manpower training, estimates committee 483
position of women, 920
problems of progress, 222
Queen's Award, 541, 930, 1338, 1685
Inelastic scattering, calculation programme, 530
Inertia Selling Bill, 1410, 1470, 1478, 1481, 1630
INESON, E.: Development and application of very strong steel, 96
Infant(s):
and young children, development progress, 870
milk foods, Monopolies Commission, 573
Wear, census of production, 1371
Infanticide Bill, 1479
Infectious diseases, GRO returns, 154, 155
Infestation Control Laboratory report, 94, 1121
Inflector electrostatic, 209
Information:
Central Office of:
publications, 176, 494–6, 894–6, 1298–1300, 1648–9
reference pamphlets, 177, 495, 895, 1299, 1649
public interest, 1133
systems, theoretical analysis, 1660
INGLIS, W. C.: Nematodes, 103, 387, 723, 1127
INGRAM, PROF. J. T. (Chairman): Nomenclature of fungi pathogenic to man and animals, 508
Injury playing football in lunch hour, decision of the Commissioner, 1266
Inland:
parcel post and remittance services, charges, 1307
Revenue:
Association of H.M. Inspectors of Taxes, estimates committee, 1279
estimates committee, 1277, 1278
First Division Association, estimates committee, 1279
H.M. Commissioners' report, 178, 496, 896, 1300, 1650
publications, 177–9, 496–8, 896–8, 1300–2, 1650–3
statistics, 1650
Waterways, holidays on, 1540
Inner London Education Authority:
publications, 469, 864, 1262, 1615
research study, 916
Inns:
noted for good food, round London, 1540
of Britain, 1540
In-patient:
inquiry, hospital, 1665
statistics, psychiatric hospitals, 1623
Input-output tables, U.K., 1542
Inquiries, *see* specific subject
Inquisitions:
miscellaneous, calendar, 1324
post mortem etc. documents, calendar, 1673
INSALL, D. W.: Chester, 1290
Insect(s):
and:
marine borer damage to timber and woodwork, 555
mites:
beneficial, 1521
in farm-stored grain, 88
of medical importance, identification, handbook, 104
their world, 104
In-service training for teachers, survey, 1563
Inshore fisheries, Scottish, regulation, 1520
Insolvency Services (Accounting and Investment) Bill, 1004, 1069, 1076, 1274, 1403 1405, 1480
Installing (ations):
electrical: 1323
wiring, inspection and testing, 914
licensed by PMG, 908
of heating, hot and cold water, etc, 914
open fires and convectors, 1320
rebuilding programme, army, 203
room heaters, independent boilers, and cookers, 1669
solid fuel appliances, 1320, 1669
Institute:
Food Research, 1115
for Research on Animal Diseases, 1115, 1519
of:
Animal Physiology, 709
Geological Sciences:
annual report, 195, 1311, 1662
publications, 195, 514, 905–6, 1310,1662–3
Local Government Studies, 1327
Tropical Products, 196, 515, 907
Instructions:
and application of physical training in the army, 733
for collectors, 724, 1540
to immigration officers, 159, 473, 871, 1270, 1625

Instructors('s):
Notes, Civil Defence, 473
training and use of operators as, 1157
Instrumental music, treatises, etc. B.M., 99
Insulated wires and cables, census of production, 957
Insulation:
sound, 913, 1322
thermal, *see* Thermal insulation
Insulators, support, for high voltage apparatus, 209
Insurance:
Business:
accounts, 570
annual report, 1367, 1710
statistics, 1367
(careers), 1149
(Employers' Liability) Bill, 1064, 1071, 1275
Insured letters and boxes*, 197
Intellectual property, convention, 1601
Intensive:
poultry management for egg production, 1521
therapy unit, hospital building note, 1618
Inter-American Development Bank*, 143, 1600
Inter-facial cohesion, 940
Inter-Governmental Maritime Consultative Organisation:
amendments to convention*, 143, 460
headquarters*, 845, 1241
oil pollution, 1605
safety at sea, 1250
specialised agencies*, 1248
Intermediate areas, 1145
Internal migrations, census, Scotland, 155
International:
Atomic Energy Agency:
Bradwell Nuclear Power Station*, 419
general conference, 1574
safeguards*, 410, 757
Bank for Reconstruction and Development loan, 141, 142, 581
carriage of:
dangerous goods by road*, 474
goods by:
rail, convention*, 962
road*, 1242
see also International Transport of goods
certificates of vaccination, 146
Civil Aviation, trilingual text*, 1163
classification of:
diseases:
alphabetical list, 1257
Statistical, 466
International (*continued*):
classification of (*continued*):
goods and services for registration of Trade Marks*, 364, 1609
code of signals, 1367
Coffee:
agreement, 759
Organisation*, 1248
computer bibliography, 1659
Conferences and Conversations, British Foreign policy, 421
Conventions, *see* specific subject
Council for the Exploration of the Sea*, 843
Court of Justice, 1241
Curriculum Conference, 921
Development Association, replenishment of resources, 907, 1600
Eisteddfod Bill, 314, 332, 335, 477
see also Llangollen International Musical Eisteddfod Bill
exhibitions*, 843
goods transport, taxation of vehicles, 1252
Grains arrangement*, 759
Harvester Company of Great Britain Ltd., Industrial Relations Commission, 1545
Health Regulations, 1599
Hydrographic Organisation, 845
Investment Disputes Bill, 9
Labour:
Conference, 143, 504, 752, 1242, 1600
Convention:
Fitness for employment in mines, 455
Hygiene in commerce and office, 845
Organisation, 455, 845
maritime traffic, facilitations*, 457
Monetary Fund:
Act, 704, 1515
Bill, 615, 668, 1411, 1482, 1483
resources, 1724
special drawing rights, 971
Motor Insurance Cards, Monopolies Commission, 573
obligations and Local Authority purchasing, 487
Organisation(s):
Act, 704
Bill, 610, 612, 662, 668, 876
and Overseas Agencies, publications 541, 929, 1336, 1683
of legal metrology, 847
practical temperature scale, 1352
Road Transport:
carriage of goods*, 1242
France*, 1242
Netherlands*, 1242
taxation of vehicles*, 1242

International (*continued*):
Sales, Uniform Laws, Act, 369
Bill, 282, 299, 302, 304, 333, 335, 338, 478
Sugar:
agreement, 1251
Organisation*, 1248
system of Units, 1713
Telecommunication Convention and related documents, 144
transport:
of goods, 132, 456, 1242
see also International carriage of goods
Wheat:
Agreement, 464, 845
Council, immunities and privileges*, 1240
Year for Human Rights, 495
Interpretation of Statutes, Law Commission, 1303
Inter-Service Metallurgical Research Council, 940
Interstellar reddening, observations, 207, 529, 921
Introduction:
of:
decimal currency, water charges, 1645
shift working, 752
to the projection for Ordnance Survey Maps, 907
Inventaria Archaeologica, 720
Inventory of historical monuments in Cambridgeshire, 916
Inverness-shire, mineral resources, 1312
Investment:
appraisal, 512, 1309
disputes, international, settlement, 460
Grants, annual report, 953, 1367, 1710
in hotels and catering, 904
incentives, 124, 1723

Ion beams for mercury pool arc source, 209
Ionising radiations:
in:
research and teaching, 748
schools etc., 925
precautions for industrial users, 754, 1156
protection of persons exposed in research and teaching, 499

Ipswich expansion proposals, 171, 891, 1295

Iran, Air Traffic*, 144
Iraq, cereals*, 1242
IRELAND, J. G.: Effect of rotation by stellar luminosity, 207
Ireland:
Map, 100
Republic of:
air services*, 394, 459
bacon*, 1245
free trade*, 111, 852, 1249
social security*, 111, 853, 854
Irish:
Land Purchase Fund, accounts, 193, 511, 903, 1309, 1660
Peers, petition, 5
Sailors and Soldiers Land Trust Act, 368
Bill, 282, 338
Iron:
and Steel:
Act, 368, 1112
accounts, 249, 583, 910, 1318
Bill, 45, 52, 276, 277, 278, 335, 476, 1000, 1064, 1073, 1275, 1318
loans, 583, 969, 1381
Board, 199, 518
Consumers' Council, 1318, 1693
(Financial Provisions) Act, loans, 199, 249, 583, 1318, 1693
(General), census of production, 1371
Holding and Realisation Agency, accounts, 249, 584
Industry Training Board, 186, 504, 753, 1155, 1570
scrap, export licence, 236, 1366
revocation, 1715
Castings:
etc., census of production, 957
Industry (Scientific Research Levy) Accounts, 910, 1693, 1710
foundries, cold blast cupolas, 1291, 1294
in:
buildings, painting, 220
flour, 870
Ironfounding capacity survey, 518
Ironstone Restoration Fund accounts, 173, 492, 893, 1296, 1647
Irrigation:
and hydrology, potential transpiration, 710
water for, 376
Irvine New Town, planning proposals, 532
IRWIN, J.: Origins of chintz, 1736

Isle of Ely, census, 153
Isle of Man:
constitutional relationship, 1272
migration, economic activity etc, 153
Isle of Wight:
census, 153
geology, 906
sample census, 468, 862
(Yarmouth I.W. Bridge) Scheme 1964 Confirmation Instrument, 286

Isocyanates, aromatic, 1586
Isoptera, 101, 1537
Isotope:
separation*, 1605
services, radioactive, organisation, 1622
Israel:
cultural relations*, 1164, 1601
double taxation*, 1578
judgements, 1579
legal proceedings*, 144, 846
visas*, 456, 1242

Italian drawings in B.M., 384
Italy:
air services*, 351
double taxation*, 133, 846
film co-production*, 361, 846
judgments, 1602
social insurance*, 360, 1250
tax exemption*, 846

J

Jack Holmes Planning Group, 871
JACKSON, T. H. E.: Lycaenidae, 1125
JACKSON, SIR W. (Chairman): Manpower resources of Science and technology, 125
Jamaica:
air services*, 1601
income tax, 1300
double taxation*, 1242
James Cook, The opening of the Pacific, 1661
James G. H. Glass Trust Scheme, 926
James Ross Island group, stratigraphy, 719
James Watt and the separate condenser, 1329
JAMISON, C.: Shrewsbury manuscripts, 159
Jams and other preserves, 1121
JANSON, S. E.:
Glass technology, 1329
Making chemicals, 922
Japan(ese):
air services*, 456, 1601
Art, 1123
atomic energy*, 144, 757, 1160, 1242
consular convention, 131
double taxation*, 1165
income tax, 1300
surrender, 1128
Treaty of Peace Act, accounts 237, 570, 953, 1367, 1710

JEANES, R. E.: Building operatives work, 219
JEFFERIES, R. P. S.: *Subphylum calcichordata*, 722
JEFFREY, C.: Cucurbitaceae, 396
JEGER, L. (Chairman): Sewage disposal, 1648
J. E. Hanger and Company, pay and conditions of employees, 510
JENKINS, K.: Coins of Greek Sicily, 100
Jerablus, excavations, 1536
Jersey, Guernsey, and adjacent Islands, census, 159
Jesness inventory:
application to Approved School boys, 1273
on a sample of British probationers, 476
JESSUP, F. W. (Chairman): Supply and training of Librarians, 745
JESTER, general statistics programme, 531
Jewellery, plate, and refining of precious metals, census of production, 958

Job evaluation, 903
Johann Gutenberg, inventor of printing, 1536
John Cranch, zoologist, 1538
John VIII Palaeogus, medallion, 100
John Hopkinson, electrical engineer, 1675
John Murray Expedition (1933–1934), 104, 388
JOHNS C. N.: Criccieth Castle, 1670
JOHNSON, J. H.: Tertiary red algai, 102
JOHNSON, P. O.: Wash Sprat Fishery, 1524
JOHNSTON, E.: Book of Sample Scripts, 266
JOHNSTON, HON. LORD (Chairman): Royal Fine Art Commission for Scotland, 1674
JOHNSTONE, C.: Fatal accident in Scunthorpe blast furnace, report, 874
JOHNSTONE, G. S.: The Grampian Highlands 514
Joints:
between concrete wall panels, 523
open drained, 523
JOKING system, analysis of bubble chamber events, 208
JONES, RT HON. A. (Chairman): Prices and Incomes Board, 192, 193, 510–11, 901–3, 1306–8, 1657–8
JONES, B. W.: Cod and Cod Fishery at Faroe, 93
JONES, D. H. P.:
Late-type stars of differing metal deficiency, 529
Photoelectric photometry of RR Lyrae stars, 206
JONES, D. P.: Elementary scattering theory, 208
JONES, David Lloyd, decision of the Commissioner, 1266
JONES, DR F. E. (Chairman): The Brain Drain, 413
JONES, F. G. W.: Sugar beet pests, 1117
JONES, O. C.: Photometric standards and the unit of light, 1352
JONES, DR S.: Design of instruction, 754

1966-70 | JON-LEI

JON— INDEX 1966–70

Jon-Landor Ltd., investigation, 236
Jordan:
air services*, 1160, 1601
financial arrangement*, 456
loan*, 456, 1243, 1601
repayment of loans*, 144
Journal of Administration Overseas, 196, 515, 907, 1314, 1667
Journalists' pay, 1307
Joyaux de la Couronne, souvenir guide, 1321

Judgment debts, enforcement, 1304
Judicial:
and extra-judicial documents, service abroad, 1577
Committee (Dissenting Opinions) Order OIC, 201
statistics, Civil, 189, 507, 899, 1303, 1654
Scotland, 212, 534, 899, 1334, 1681
Juncaceae, 112
Jurassic cheilostomatous Polyzoa, 723
Jury room, secrecy, 872
Justice(s):
administration of, 290
of the Peace:
Act, 704
Bill, 610, 612, 662, 665, 667, 668, 876
(Subsistence Allowances) Bill, 47, 51
Out of Reach, 1545
Jute, census of production, 1371

K

Kabata, Z.: Gall-bladder parasites of whiting, 374
Kaljo, D.: Corals, 102
Kauffmann, C. M.: An altar-piece of the Apocalypse, from Master Bertram's workship, 984
Kay, J. B. (Chairman): Allocating Council houses to Scotland, 532

Keeper of Public Records, annual report, 189, 507, 915, 1324, 1673
Keith, K. A. (Chairman): East Anglia, 742
Keithia disease of western red cedar, 465
189, 507, 915, 1324, 1673
Kemsley, W. F. F.: Family expenditure, handbook, 1261
Kendrew, J. C. (Chairman): Council for Scientific Policy, 743
Kenilworth Castle, guide, 1321
Kennedy, A. (Chairman): National Museum of Antiquities of Scotland, 1662
Kennedy, D. A.: Late-Babylonian economic texts, 1124
Kennedy, K. A. R.: Human skeletal material from Ceylon, 102
Kennedy, W. J.: Lower Chalk of Southern England, 387
Kennedy Round of Trade Negotiations, 571
Kent:
County Council Act, 1518
Quarter Sessions Act, 78
sample census, 468, 862
see also West Kent.
Kenya:
British training team*, 846
U.K. forces*, 846
Kerrich, G. J.: Anagyrine Encyntidae, 385
Kerslake, J.: House of Hanover, 905
Kew:
Gardens, 203, 525, 916, 1326
Observatory, 1306
Kew Bulletin, 203, 525, 916, 1326, 1674
Key, Dr A. (Chairman):
Fish toxicity, 1646
Solid toxic wastes, 1646
Keyboard instruments, 985

Kidd, Sheriff M. H. (Chairman): Sheriff Court Records, 536
Kidderminster Corporation Act, 1114
Kidney transplant, *see* Renal Transplantation Bill
Kilbrandon, Hon. Lord:
(Chairman):
Companies (Floating Charges) (Scotland) Act, 1715
Marriage Law of Scotland, 1334
Scottish Law Commission, 536, 1335, 1654, 1682
(Joint Chairman): Law Commission, 1304
Kilmun arboretum and forest plots, 1255
Kimmins, D. E.:
Type specimens of:
Libellulidae and *Cordullidae*, 722
Odonata, 101, 1125, 1537
Plecoptera and Megaloptera, 1537
Kindersley, Lord (Chairman): Doctors' and dentists' remuneration, 158, 870, 1268, 1540
King, A. H.: Four Hundred Years of Music Printing, 720
King, J. E.: The Ross Seal, 1662
Kingeninae Elliott, 1538
Kings and Queens:
of Britain, poster, 513
series, House of:
Hanover, 905
Stuart, 1310
Tudor, 513
Windsor, 513

INDEX 1966–70 —LAN

King's Lynn Provisional Order Act, 1114
Bill, 999, 1074
Kings Norton, Lord (Chairman): Cars for cities, 576
Kingston-upon-Hull Corporation Act, 370
Kirby, Sir A. (Chairman): Movement of exports, 1660
Kirby, J. E.: Kilmun arboretum and forest plots, 1255
Kirkhill Primary School Broxburn, development project, 1679
Kitchens, hospital, 1616
Kitzinger, E.: Early medieval Art in the B.M., 1123

Klagenfurt Commonwealth War cemetery, 419

Knight, R. A. G.: Efficiency of adhesives for wood, 939
Knight, W. J.: *Cicadellidae*, 721
Knitted goods, census of production, 958
Knitting, Lace, and Net Industry Training Board, 186, 504, 753, 1155, 1570
Know Your:
Broadleaves, 859
Conifers, 151, 1611
Knudsen, J.: Deep-sea bivalvia, 388

Kokoschka, Word and Vision, 384
Kokwaro, J. O.: *Valarianaceae*, 729, 1134
Korea, visas*, 1602
Koripan, Prince Bagus Umbara of, 719
Kouyunjik collection of cuneiform tablets, B.M., 719

Kraus-Thomson Organisation Ltd, Index to British Foreign Office Correspondence, 1302

Kuria Muria Islands, treaty of Cession, 849
Kuwait:
air services*, 1243
cultural relations*, 421, 846
money orders*, 456
relations with U. K.*, 847

L

La Sainte Union College of Education, Southampton, Education and Science select committee, 1635
Labelling of:
Cigarette Packets Bill, 1074
Food:
and Toilet Preparations Bill, 1073, 1077
Bill, 50
Laboratory:
culture of the prawn, 1120
of the Government Chemist Steering Committee, 222
precautions, display card, 1333
technicians and assistants (careers), 1149
Labour:
costs in G.B., 753
Ministry of, publications, 179–87, 498–506
see also Employment and Productivity, Department of, and Employment, Department of
relations and conditions of work in Britain, Information Office pamphlet, 495
turnover, following training of middle aged for new skills, 1156
Labour Gazette, 186, 504–5
see also Employment and Productivity Gazette
Lace:
census of production, 958
Furnishings Industry (Export Promotion Levy) accounts, 570
Lacey, G. W. B.: Flying since 1913, 207
Lackey moth, 87
Lagging hot and cold water systems, 912
Lagos, Commonwealth Prime Ministers' meeting, 109
Lake:
District:
guide, 1134
weekend motorists, 1134
of Menteith Fisheries Order Confirmation Act, 1518
Bill, 1483
Lamb, H. H.: Variations of atmospheric circulation, 191
Lamb, I. M.: Antarctic lichens, 1311
Lambert, W. G.: Catalogue of the cuneiform tablets in the Kouyunjik collection, 719
Lambeth Palace Library, Shrewsbury and Talbot papers, 159
Lamont, J. M.: Plaice in Scottish waters, 374
Lanarkshire Educational Trust Amendment Scheme, 211, 334
Lancashire:
census, 152
County Council (General Powers) Act, 796
sample census, 468, 862
Land(s):
acquisition and disposal, 1291
agricultural, improvement of, estimates committee, 479, 878

LAN— INDEX 1966–70

Lands (*continued*):
and:
buildings, financing improvements, 1120
Natural Resources, Ministry of:
circulars, 188
see also National Parks Commission
availability for housing, 1572
Charges:
Act, form, 898, 1303
local, register, 174
Commission:
Act, 368, 1302
Bill, 9, 11, 43, 45, 48, 51, 163, 275, 276, 334
report and accounts, 892, 1295, 1647
Betterment Levy Case notes, 1302
circular, 487
(Dissolution) Bill, 1485
Costs and housing development, 1308
Court, Scottish, 213, 536
derelict, neglected, or unsightly, rehabilitation, 600
Improvement Company's Amendment Act, 1114
Purchase account, N.I., 219, 543, 932, 1343, 1690
Register, application for search, 1653
Registration:
Act, 77
Bill, 3, 4, 46, 50, 163, 477
forms, 188, 506, 898, 1653
Practice leaflets for solicitors, 506
registration of title to land, 898
cadastral surveys, Commonwealth Conference, 1314
Fee Order S.I. select committee, 1641
(Official Searches) Rules, 1303, 1653
Registry:
Chief Registrar's report, 188, 506, 898, 1304, 1653
publications, 188, 506, 898, 1303, 1653
Settlement Association Ltd, Smallholdings, 717
Surveyors, Star Almanac, 205, 529, 920, 1328, 1675
Tenure in Scotland, 1334
transfer, *see* Transfer of Land
use:
forestry, agriculture, and multiple use of rural land, 127
wooded private estates, E. and W., 1255
Landlocked States, transit trade, 1252
Landlord(s) and Tenant(s):
Act:
circular, 170
Law Commission, 1303
Security of tenure of business premises, 1654
some rights under, 491
Interim report on distress for rent, 189
rights and obligations, 1116
Landplanes, 569, 1366
Landscape:
forestry in, 151
roads in, 378
Landscaping for flats, 490
Lang, J. (Chairman): Crowd behaviour at football matches, 1297
Langdon, F. J.: Modern offices, a user survey, 221
Langdon-Thomas, G. J.: Fire and the external wall, 221
Langholm, geology of the neighbourhood, 906
Langkon North Borneo Rubber Ltd., investigation, 236
Langstone Harbour Order Confirmation Act, 1962 (Amendment) Order, 126
Language(s):
Laboratories, 744
modern:
and the less able pupil, 1679
in:
Comprehensive Schools, 1679
Further Education, 1679
research and development, 743
Laos, Foreign Exchange Operations Fund* 144, 456, 847, 1243, 1602
Larch:
canker and dieback, 1255
home grown timber, 555
Large picture books, V. and A. Museum, 266, 599, 985, 1396, 1735
Larvae of *Ostrea edulis*, 93
Larwood, G. P.: bryozoa, 1128
Lasers, use of in schools etc., 1678
Lasiocampidae, 724
Late Night Refreshment Houses:
Act, 1112
Bill, 995, 1002, 1075, 1289
Lord Chancellor's memorandum, 995
Late-type stars:
abundance determination, 1328
of differing metal deficiency, 529
Latey, Hon. Mr Justice (Chairman): Age of majority, 508
Latin America, nuclear weapons, 850, 1605
Launceston, Restormel, Totnes, guide, 1670
Launching Middle Schools, 1561
Laundry(ies):
and dry cleaning:
charges, 193
(careers), 747

INDEX 1966–70 —LEI

Laundry(ies) (*continued*)
hospital, 1616
work, hospital, 804
Launert, E.: *Malpighiaceae*, 729
Lavers, G. M.: Strength properties of timber, 554
Law, M.: Radiation from fires in a compartment, 939
Law, R. J.: James Watt and the separate condenser, 1220
Law:
(careers), 1564
Commission:
annual report, 189, 507, 899, 1304, 1654
First programme, 189
reports, 189, 507, 899, 1303–4, 1654–5
Sea Fisheries (Shellfish) Bill, 348
see also Scottish Law Commission
European convention, 1243
of:
Contempt, Tribunals of Inquiry, 1304
Property Act, 1112
Bill, 994, 995, 997, 1002, 1064, 1074, 1075, 1275
Succession, illegitimate persons, 190
the sea, fishing and conservation, convention, 144
Treaties, Vienna convention, 1244
Reform:
Committee reports, 189, 507, 1655
(Miscellaneous Provisions):
Act, 1515
Bill, 1076, 1408, 1470, 1480, 1630
(Scotland) Act, 77, 704
Bill, 1, 5, 6, 43, 45, 47, 48, 49, 50, 163, 611, 614, 616, 618, 662, 666, 667, 669, 876
Second Programme, 899
Society:
of Scotland, Legal Aid Scheme, 212, 213, 928, 1334, 1681
see also Legal Aid
Lawson, Sir W. (Chairman). Review Board for Government Contracts, 1673
Laying cages, 88
Laying floor screed, 1320
Layout, roads in rural areas, 1374

Leach, E. B. (Chairman): Mechanical engineering, Economic Development Committee, 1310
Leaching of substances into food, 1525
Leadburning, 1320
Leaf Spot of celery, 88
Leafhopper, grassland, 721
Leafy gall, 88
Learning about space, 1561
Leasehold Reform:
Act, 368
Bill, 283, 285, 286, 287, 332, 335, 337, 338, 477
E. and W., 188
Leather:
bookbindings, preservation, 385
goods, census of production, 1371
(tanning and dressing) and fellmongery, census of production, 1371
Leathercloth, census of production, 958
Leatherjackets, 88
Lebanon, air services*, 1244
Lee, Dr E. (Chairman):
Fire research, 1351
Government Chemist's report, 1353
Hydraulics Research, 1352
Water Pollution Research, 1695
Lee Valley Regional Park Act, 370
Leeds:
Approach, planning and transport, 1375
Corporation Act, 78
Liverpool, and London, design bulletin, 1646
Legal:
Advice and Assistance, better provision, 1655
Aid:
Acts, accounts, 189, 507, 899, 1304, 1655
and advice, Law Society's report, 190, 507, 899, 1304, 1655
booklet, 597
handbook, 190, 508, 1655
in criminal proceedings, 190
Scheme, Law Society of Scotland's report, 212, 928, 1334, 1681
(Scotland) Acts, 368
accounts, 130, 417, 755, 1159, 1579
Bill, 10, 275, 338, 485
documents served on M.P.s, Privileges committee, 1634
metrology, international organisation, 847
proceedings, civil and commercial matter, Israel, 144
Records, 190
System, English, Information Office pamphlet, 1299
Legislation:
Decimal currency booklet, 1136
forthcoming, safety, quality, and description of drugs and medicine, 358
of documents, European Convention, 1244, 1602
Legitimation (Scotland) Act, 704
Bill, 288, 340, 610, 662, 666, 876
Leicester Corporation Act, 706

LEI— INDEX 1966–70

Leicestershire:
census, 153
County Council Act, 1518
sample census, 468, 862
Leisure:
and the waterways, 388
in the countryside, 188
planning, 1262
Lemon and orange peeling, cautionary
notice, 187
Leonardo da Vinci's Aeronautics, 530
Lepidoptera:
Drepanidae, 385, 722
Geometridae, 386
Heterocera, 721
Lycaenidae, 101, 102, 385, 386, 721, 1125
Nymphalidae, 101, 1125, 1126, 1538
Pyralidae, 1538
Rhopalocera, 386
Lerwick Observatory, 1306
Lesotho:
(Compensation and Retiring Benefits)
Order OIC, 201
double taxation*, 1244
Independence Act, 77
Bill, 6, 50
Information Office pamphlet, 177
public officers*, 394, 515
reserves of sterling*, 1602
Lesser Antilles, gravity anomolies, 1662
Lessons of the London Government
reforms, 916
Letcombe Laboratory:
annual report, 1519
see also Radiological Laboratory
Lever Park Act, 1114
Levy, R. F. (Chairman): Monopolies
Commission, 239
Lewin J. D.: Radiation dose rates for
super-conducting magnets, 209
Lewis, Sir A.: A glossary of mental dis-
orders, 863
Lewis, B. N.:
Algorithms and logical trees, 1543
Flow charts, logical trees and algo-
rithms, 586
Lewis, D. J.: Phlebotomine sandflies, 385
Lewis, Prof. M. M. (Chairman): Education
of deaf children, 744
Lewis and Harris, Livingston New Town,
and surroundings, sample census, 863
Leys School, Cambridge, conference of
Commonwealth officers, 1313

Libellulidae, 722
Librarians, supply and training of, 745
Library(ies):
Bibliography, UKAEA, 1733
Grenville, illuminated manuscripts, 384
Information and Archive work, (careers),
747

Library(ies) (continued)
National:
for Scotland, *see* National Library
for Scotland
lending, for Science and Technology, 414, 1146
Maritime Museum, catalogue, 1661
of Sir Simond D'Elwes, 99
Pietro Bembo's, B.M., 512
School, 414
Scotland, standards of public service,
1333
University Grants Committtee report,
599
Lice, 1539
Licence(s):
(Aeroplanes and Helicopters) professional pilots', 1370
Aircraft radio maintenance engineers',
912
Amateur radio operators*, 844
examination papers for:
Flight Navigator, 234, 573, 956,
1370, 1714
Senior Commercial Airline Trans-
port Pilot, 234, 573, 956, 1370,
1714
export, *See* Export licences
Flight Engineers', 569
Flight Navigators', 234, 569, 952, 1366,
1709
Flight radio operators', 234, 569
general, hiring television sets, 1709
import. *See* Import Licences
Private Pilots', 569, 959
aviation law for application, 941,
1354, 1696
Senior Commercial Airline Transport
Pilots'. *See above,* examination papers
for
Student Pilots', 569, 959
to import explosives, 1625
Licensing:
(Amendment) Act, 368
Bill, 51, 283, 332, 336, 477
Authorities report to Ministry of
Transport, 1719
(Certificates in Suspense) (Scotland)
Act, 368
Bill, 7, 46, 50, 163
of Marriages on Unlicensed Premises
Bill, 1470, 1478, 1630
Private Places of Entertainment Act, 369
Bill, 11, 275, 277
(Scotland) Act, 1112
Bill, 992, 1071
Lichens, 1311
Lichomolgidae, 1128
Life:
Peerages, 1686
sciences, 128

1966 pp 1–272, 1967 pp 273–604, 1968 pp 605–990, 1969 pp 991–1402, 1970 pp 1403–1740

80

INDEX 1966–70 **—LOB**

Life (continued):
tables, GRO, 861
Scotland, 1260
Lifting and carrying, do's and dont's, wall
sheet, 506
Lifts and escalators, hospital, 1616
Light:
cars, technical history, 1675
Unit of photometric standards, 1352
Lighting:
early oil lamps and candles, 208
for egg production, 89, 175
gas, mineral oil, electricity, 530
in schools, 412
of motor vehicles, 579
offices, shops, and railway premises,
1156
other than in the home, illustrated
booklet, 1675
site, 912
Light-keepers, pay and duties, 1307
Lightweight concrete, 1320
Lilleshall Abbey, guide, 1321
Limacodidae, 724
Limbfitters, pay and conditions, 510
Lime(s):
and liming, 1117
building, 220, 1320
Limitation Act, Law Commission, 1654
Linaceae, 112
Lincolnshire:
census, 153
Parts of:
Holland, sample census, 468
Kesteven and Lincoln CB, sample
census, 468
Lindsay excluding Lincoln CB,
sample census, 468
sample census, 1259
Linen:
Census of production, 1371
services, hospital, 156, 469, 864, 1262,
1615
Lingerie, census of production, 1371
Linoleum, leathercloth, etc., census of
production, 958
Liquid(s):
and gases, physical properties, 1694
chlorine, precautions, 1156
Fuel, Control Bill, 285
hydrogen, vapour pressure and molar
volume for, 194
manure disposal, tanker equipment,
1525
Liquidated damages, 1291
List 70, Independent Schools in E. and W.,
1562
Live Hare Coursing (Abolition) Bill, 335,
339, 671
Liver rot in sheep, 88

Liverpool:
Corporation:
Act, 370, 1114
(General Powers) Act, 370
design bulletin, 1646
Livestock:
Export Control Bill, 51
Marketing Co. Ltd., investigation, 951
Living:
animals, experiments, 161, 474, 872,
1270, 1625
in a:
caravan, 395
slum, 1646
Livingston, H. R.:
Partially slatted floors in pig fattening
houses, 512
slatted floors for beef breeding herds,
512
Livingston Island, South Shetlands, geology,
719
Lizards:
iguanid, 723, 1128, 1539
Nigerian, 723

Llangollen International Musical Eisteded-
fod Act, 368
Bill, 283, 337, 477
see also International Eisteddfod Bill
Llewellyn, L. C.: Pontobdellinae, 103
Lloyd, D. H.: Business control in poultry
keeping, 176
Lloyd, Dr J. D. (Chairman): Ancient
Monument Board for Wales, 1736
Lloyd, Lord (Chairman): Need for Nation-
al Film School, 1414
Lloyd Davies, T. A. (Chairman): Problems
of use of asbestos, 750
Llywodraeth Leol Yng Nghymru, 600

Load Line(s):
fees, 238
International:
conference, 144, 145, 847
convention, correction of errors,
1244
Merchant Shipping Bill, 279
Loading charts for design of buried rigid
pipes, 524
Loan(s):
agreements, *see* respective countries
consents to small amounts, 1291, 1396
from the:
Consolidated Fund, 249, 584
National Loans Fund, 969, 1381,
1723
period for all loans, 1291
Societies, 152
Lobster storage, 1116

1966 pp 1–272, 1967 pp 273–604, 1968 pp 605–990, 1969 pp 991–1402, 1970 pp 1403–1740

F 81

LOC— INDEX 1966–70

Local:
Acts, 78–9, 370–1, 705–6, 1113–4,
1516–18
and Personal Acts:
supplementary index, 543
tables and index, 78, 370, 705, 1113,
1516
Authority(ies):
and:
Allied Personal Social Services,
893
New Towns, E. and W. classified
index, 891
building notes, 471, 1619
(Expenditure on Special Purposes)
(Scotland) Bill, 97
general contract to certain transactions, 969
(Goods and Services) Act, 1516
Bill, 339, 1069, 1076, 1077, 1404,
1410, 1481, 1630
Housing:
Increases in rent:
circulars, 490, 889, 890
Prices and Incomes Board, 902
Rent (Control of Increases) Act,
circular, 1643
large, aspects of administration, 916
manual workers' pay and conditions,
510
Members:
allowances, 170, 490, 1643
pecuniary interests, 487
Mutual Investment Trust Act, 704
Bill, 339, 609, 662, 666, 876
owned houses, Scotland, rents, 1335
purchasing:
international obligations, circulars 487, 1645
report, 1297
(Qualification of Members) Bill,
1415, 1485
records (Scottish), 535
Scotland:
rents of houses, 200
reorganisation proposals, 213
Services, 916
Social Services Act, 1516
Bill, 1410, 1470, 1480, 1482, 1483,
1630
Tender and contract procedures:
civil engineering, 1292
for building work, 490
Education Authorities:
awards to students, 744
entrants to colleges of Education,
126, 744
excepted executives in E. and W., 126
lists, 126, 1146
performance and size, research
study, 916

Local (continued):
Education Authorities (continued):
secondary education, 126, 744
Employment Act, 1516
accounts, 238, 571, 954, 1369, 1712
annual report, 238, 571, 954, 1369,
1693
Bill, 1070, 1076, 1404, 1630
expenditure, circular, 889
financial returns (Scotland), 208, 532,
924
Government:
Act, 17
Bill, 8, 10, 11, 46, 47, 49, 50, 51,
52, 163, 607, 662, 667, 876
circulars, 487, 490, 889, 1291,
1293, 1643, 1645
derelict, neglected, or unsightly
land, 487
financial:
provision, 487
statistics, E. and W., 172,
492, 892
grants to Local Authorities, 889
Greater London Rate Equalisation Scheme, 892
Rate Support Grant Regulations,
488
administration:
abroad, 490
E. and W., 490
Committee on management, 171, 490
computer packages, 1660
Councillor, 490
Elector, 490
England, Royal Commission
see Royal Commission
Finance(ial):
General Grant (Increase) Order:
E. and W., 173
Scotland, 209
Rate Support Grant:
(Increase) Order:
E. and W., 1572
Scotland, 537, 924, 1678
Order:
E. and W., 173, 492, 892,
1296, 1572
Scotland, 537, 1331
Scotland, 209
statistics, E. and W., 172, 492,
892, 1296
(Footpaths and Open Spaces) (Scot-
land) Act, 1516
Bill, 1076, 1407, 1471, 1630
Grants (Social Needs) Act, 1112
Bill, 620, 664, 670, 876
Housing, and Social Services, supply
estimates, 1725

1966 pp 1–272, 1967 pp 273–604, 1968 pp 605–990, 1969 pp 991–1402, 1970 pp 1403–1740

82

INDEX 1966–70 **—LON**

Local (continued):
Government (continued):
in:
England:
reform, 1648
Royal Commission, 525–6,
916
Scotland:
Bill, 1471
Royal Commission, 526,
917–9, 1629
Wales, reorganisation, 600, 664,
875
New Areas, map, 1647
(Pecuniary Interests):
Bill, 43
(Scotland) Act, 77
Bill, 2, 43, 46, 163
(Promotion of Bills) Bill, 49
(Qualification of Councillors) Bill,
1478, 1483, 1630
Reorganisation in Glamorgan and
Monmouthshire, 1471, 1631, 1736
Reform:
England, 1648
E. and W., areas and boundaries,
1644
(Rights of the Public) Bill, 5
(Scotland):
Acts, 367
Bill, 10,11, 49, 51, 52, 163
Local financial returns, 532
Royal Commission, 1327
Service(s):
booklet, 180
economics of scale, research
study, 916
pay of Chief and Senior Officers,
511
staffing, 490
statistics, circular, 1644
Superannuation:
Act, tables, 492, 535, 1292, 1645
(Benefits):
Regulations, 489
tables, 492
(Scotland) Regulations,
tables, 535
Interchange Rules, circular, 1291
(Termination of Reviews) Act, 368
Bill, 46, 51, 277, 477
housing statistics, E. and W., 492, 892,
1296, 1647
Land charge(s):
register, 174, 1304, 1655
rules, 1655
Loans Fund, accounts, 193, 511, 904,
1309
Locarno aftermath, documents, 132
Locke, G. M. L.: Britain's forest resources,
1611

Locomotives, and railway track equipment,
census of production, 1371
Locusts, 457
Lodgepole pine, 939
Lofthouse, J. A. (Chairman): Civil Engin-
eering, 193
Logical trees, 586, 1543
Lok Kawi Rubber, Ltd., 234
London:
Brick Company, prices charged, 1658
Bridge Act, 368
Building Acts, constructional by-laws,
1615
Cab Act, 704
Bill, 290, 334, 339, 876
Clearing Banks:
Hours and Overtime, 1657
pay, 1307
Commonwealth Prime Ministers' meet-
ing, 109
County Courts Directory, 507
design bulletins, 1646
Diplomatic List, 144, 457, 847, 1244,
1602
Fares:
(British Rail) Order, 965
(London Transport) Order, 962,
965
from:
Bankside, print, 1536
the River, 1540
Gazette, 217–8, 541–2, 929–31, 1336–41,
1683–9
Title page and index, 218, 541, 931,
1341, 1689
good food inns, 1540
Government:
Act, 368
Bill, 275, 276, 335
Greater London Rate Equal-
isation Scheme, 892
reforms, research study, 916
(Scotland) Act, Local Financial
Returns, Scotland, 924
Staff Commission, 173
Hotels and restaurants, 1540
Maps, Information, excursions, 1540
Museum(s):
and galleries, guide, 901
oil paintings, 1653
publications, 188, 506, 898, 1303,
1653
stage costumes and accessories, 898
Noise survey, 914
Post offices and streets, 197, 908
taxicab:
fares, proposed increase, 903
trade, Departmental Committee
report, 1627

1966 pp 1–272, 1967 pp 273–604, 1968 pp 605–990, 1969 pp 991–1402, 1970 pp 1403–1740

83

London (continued):
Transport:
Act, 78, 370, 706, 1114
(Alteration, of Wages Grades Pension Schemes) Order, S.I. select committee, 482
Board:
annual report and accounts, 242, 576, 962, 1374, 1717
loan, 251, 579, 971, 1384
Fare increases in the London area, 902, 1307
Fares, Prices and Incomes Board, 1658
Tribunal, 962
Weather, 900
Long:
Distance Footpath guide, 1134
Term trade, Soviet Union*, 1369
View of London from Bankside, print, 1536
Longleat, manuscripts of the Marquess of Bath, 871
LONGMORE, J.: B.R.S. Daylight protractors, 913
LORD, D. H.: Rutherford Laboratory DDP-224 system handbook, 530
Lord:
Advocate's Department, Constitution Commission, 1133
Chancellor's:
Advisory Committee, 507
Office:
County Courts Branch, Index to Parishes, 188-9, 507-8, 898, 1303-5, 1654-5
publications, 188-9, 507-8, 898, 1303-5, 1654-5
Lord Howe Island, Petrology, 1593
Lords' Attendances, Return to an Order re..., 289, 721
Lords Spiritual and Temporal, Roll of, 169, 486, 888, 1289, 1642
Lothians Regional Survey Plan:
economic and social aspects, 209
physical planning aspects, 210
Lotteries (Greater London Council) Bill, 620
Loughborough University of Technology Act, 78
LOUTIT, J. F. (Chairman): Assay of Strontium-90 in human bones, 308, 899
Low:
background counting room and ancillary apparatus
cost dairying, 1522
Lower:
Cambrian Archaeocyatha, 1126
Carboniferous trilobites, 386
Chalk of Southern England, 387
Llandovery (Silurian) trilobites, 1538

Lower (continued):
Old Red Sandstone:
Ignimbrites, 1312
Strathmore region, 1664
Palaeozoic Brachiopods, 722

LSD:
report, 1622, 1624
use and misuse, 1622

Lubricating oils and greases, census of production, 1371
Lubrication (tribology):
Committee report, 938
present position and industry's needs, 126
LUCAS, G. Ll.: Flora of Tropical East Africa, 729
Lullingstone Roman Villa, guide, 202, 1321
LUMSDEN, G. I.: Geology of the neighbourhood of Langholm, 906
Lunar occultations, discussions, 206
Luton Corporation Act, 1114
Luxembourg, double taxation*, 421, 847

Lycaenidae, 101, 385, 721, 1125
Lyctus powder-post beetles, 1351
Lysianassidae, 1127

M

M. and Q. Form No. 215, 721
MABILLE, P.: Types of Lepidoptera heterocera, 721
MCBOYLE, J. (Chairman): Local Authority records (Scotland), 535
MCCALL, A. H. (Chairman): Scottish Health Services Council, 1335
MCCARTHY, M. C.: employment of highly specialised graduates, 745
MCCARTHY, DR W. E. J. (Chairman): Durham L.E.A. and N.A.S. dispute, 1156
MCCARTHY, W. E. J.:
Shop Stewards:
and workshop relations, 920
role in British industrial relations, 205
MACCHESNEY, Congleton, Crewe, and Middlewich, geology of country around, 906
MACDERMOTT, RT HON. LORD (Chairman): Supreme Court of Judicature, N.I., 1655
MCDONALD, R. H. (Chairman): Community care of mentally handicapped, 1681
MACER, C. T.: Sand eels, 93

1966 pp 1-272, 1967 pp 273-604, 1968 pp 605-990, 1969 pp 991-1402, 1970 pp 1403-1740

MACGREGOR, PROF. A. G. (Chairman): Classification of proprietary preparations, 863
Machine:
planing, hardwoods, 555
tool:
collection, catalogue, 208
orders, problems of cyclical pattern, 223
Machinery:
biscuit making, safety in use, 187
handbook on marketing, 1660
in bakeries, safety in use, 753
Machines, temporary adaptations, decimal currency, 1547
Machynlleth-Pwllheli Line, analysis of retention, 1717
MACIVOR, I.:
Fort George, 1670
Fortifications of Berwick-upon-Tweed, 522
MCKENNELL, A. C.:
Adults' and Adolescents' smoking habits and attitudes, 864
Motives in the timing of holidays, 863
Noise annoyance in Central London, 863
MACKENZIE, K.: Parasites of O-group plaice, 710
MCKERSIE, R. B.: Changing wage payment systems, 920
Mackinnon-Macneill Trust (Amendment) Scheme, 211
MCLELLAN, A. G. (Chairman): Water resources of the North, 599
MACLENNAN, SIR H. (Chairman): Human Tissue Act, 1264
MACLURE, J. S.: Curriculum innovation in practice, report, 921
MCMILLAN, COL. D. (Chairman): Cable and Wireless, 1315, 1667
MACNALTY, SIR A. S. (Editor): Medical Services in war, 1264
MCNEILL, F. A.: Great Barrier Reef Expedition, scientific report, 724
MCQUILLIN, R.:
Geophysical Surveys in the:
Shetland Islands, 906
Orkney Islands, 1311
Humber investigations, cruise report, 1312
MACROBERT, T. M.: Fine Illustrations in European Printed Books, 1396
Macroscelididae, 723
MACWALTER DR R. J. (Chairman): Dairy effluents, 1120
MCWILLIAM, J. (Chairman): Countryside Commission for Scotland, 1134
MADDES, SIR G. (Chairman): University Teachers' Superannuation, 746

MADDOCK, I. (Chairman): Maintenance engineering, 1694
Madras College (St. Andrews) Trust Scheme, 534, 926
Magnet(s):
beam bending for use with electrostatic generators, 530
Command systems pulsed, 1330
concrete insulated, for European 300 GeV accelerator, 1330
fast shutter, for separated particle beams, 922
for particle accelerator physics, 1330
plunging, system for Nimrod extracted proton beam, 209
superconducting:
coil winding irregularities, 1676
estimate of radiation dose rate, 209
technology, international conference, 922
with air-cored windings of saddle coil type, 1676
Magnetic:
results, 528, 1328
spectrometers, 1329
Magneto-resistor temperature stabilised, 1676
Magnetostatic computer programme TRIM, 1330
Magnetostrictive readout of wire spark chambers, 923
Maintenance:
and champerty, proposals for reforms of law, 189
engineering, 1694
manuals for buildings, 1672
obligations to children, 1602
of Diesel engines, 1672
Orders Act, 704
Bill, 339, 609, 612, 662, 665, 668, 876
recovery abroad, 1602
workers, bus companies, pay, 1306
Maize for fodder and silage, 88
MAJOR, J. H.: Plunging magnetic system for Nimrod extracted proton beam, 209
Major aircraft fires, symposium, 554
Malacostega, 1127
Malawi:
air service*, 1244
double taxation*, 848
public service:
British added conditions', 848
extra contribution*, 847
Republic Act, 77
Bill, 4, 50
Malay Peninsula/Singapore, General Service Medals, 581
Malaysia:
air services*, 848
armed forces*, 848

1966 pp 1-272, 1967 pp 273-604, 1968 pp 605-990, 1969 pp 991-1402, 1970 pp 1403-1740

Malaysia (continued):
double taxation*, 848
gift of assets, 1519, 1121
mutual defence and assistance*, 110
transfer of land and assets, 968
MALHOTRA, H. L.: Fire resistance of brick and block walls, 221
MALLABY, G. (Chairman): Staffing of Local Government, 490
Mallaig Harbour:
Order Confirmation Act, 1518
Bill, 1483
Revision Order, S.I. select Committee, 885
Mallophaga, 1125
Mallory Batteries Ltd, price increase of hearing aid batteries, 902
Malpighiaceae, 729
Malta:
air services*, 394, 1244
Commonwealth Development, 107
Joint Mission's report, 394
(Reconstruction) Act, accounts, 110-11, 394, 848, 1245
Mammals:
British, identification, 1128
fossil, 102, 386
non-marine, instructions for collectors, 724
palaearctic and Indian, 104
see also specific animal
Man:
is not lost, record of astronomical navigation, 905
the tool-maker, 388
Management:
consultants, code of practice, 1544
eductaoin in the 1970s, 1661
of computer-based data processing, 1659
studies, diploma, 744
techniques, glossary, 583
Training:
and Development Committee, report, 498
in distributive trades, 1309
Manchester:
Corporation:
Act, 370, 1518
(Walshaw, Bury) Housing Compulsory Purchase Confirmation Order, 278
Ship Canal Act, 78
(Ullswater and Windermere) Water Order, 277
Manganese Star 53 Tauri, chemical composition, 207
Mangel flies, 88
Man-made:
cellulosic fibres, Monopolies Commission, 955

Man-made (continued):
Fibre(s):
and cotton yarn prices, 1307, 1308
census of production, 958, 1371
Producing Industry Training Board, 186, 505, 753, 1155
MANN, SIR J.: Arms and Armour in England, 1321
MANNING, CAPT. G. E.: Weather radar for pilots, 1716
Manpower:
efficient use of, 500
in the chemical industry, 512
papers, 753, 1570
planning, statistical techniques, 1543
Resources for Science and Technology, 125, 413, 743
retraining, cost-benefit aspects, 1570
studies:
electronics, 505
food retailing, 1155
growth of office employment, 753
occupational changes, 753
technological, 1659
training for industry, estimates committee, 479, 483
MANSERGH, N. (Editor): India, the transfer of power, 1599
Manuals, see specific subject
Manufactures, miscellaneous, of paper and board, census of production, 1372
Manufacturing:
control, computer file creation, 1659
industry(ies):
miscellaneous, census of production, 1372
movement of, 955
Manure Disposal of liquid, 1525
Manuscript(s):
acquired since 1925, National Library of Scotland, catalogue, 194, 905
and:
drawings, first George Millar Bequest, 720
Men, centenary exhibition, 1269
at Longleat, 871
catalogue of additions to the B.M., 99, 383, 719, 1124, 1536
index, 384, 720
Department, B.M., index to Charters and Rolls, 100
Export of, Bill, 1071
Henry Lawes, 1124
illuminated:
early Gothic, 1536
in the Grenville Library, 384
Romanesque, 100
in the National Library for Scotland, 194, 905

1966 pp 1-272, 1967 pp 273-604, 1968 pp 605-990, 1969 pp 991-1402, 1970 pp 1403-1740

Manuscript(s) (continued):
made in the B.M., catalogue, 99
handlist, 1536
of Lord Sackville of Knole, catalogue, 159
Persian, 100, 720
Salisbury (Cecil), at Hatfield House, 159, 1624
Map(s):
and plans, PRO 525
Proposed new Local Government areas, 1647
Margarine:
and compound cooking fats, Prices and census of production, 957
Incomes Board, 1658
Marguerite Bay, petrology of Islands, 98
MARIEN, E. (Founder): Inventaria Archaeologica, 720
Marine:
engineering practice, 411, 1140
etc:
and Sea Broadcasting (Offences) Bill, 50
Broadcasting (Offences) Act, 368
Bill, 279, 281, 332, 336, 337, 477
fish, reaction to moving nets etc. in tanks, 87
geological and geophysical work, east coast of Scotland, 1663
Laboratory, Aberdeen, 1520
observer's handbook, 1305
pollution damage, 1603
radar performance specification, 955
Research, 87, 374, 709-10, 1116, 1520
science and technology, 1353
search and rescue operations, U.K., 1715
surveys and other Marine services fees and expenses, 238, 569, 1366
Marine Observer, 191, 508, 900, 1305, 1656
Maritime:
conventions, 457
Law:
Bills of lading, 848
liability of owners of sea-going ships, 848
liens and mortgages, 853
meteorology, 900
traffic facilitation, 457
Market Harborough, geology, 1312
Marketing Schemes, agricultural, 1116
Marks and Spencer Ltd., case study, 1672
MARQUAND, H. A. (Deputy Chairman): Prices Incomes Board, 193
MARRE, A. S. (Chairman): Cost of Living, 753
Marriage:
breach of promise, Law Commission, 1304
convention, 848, 1603

Marriage (continued):
law of Scotland, 1334
nullity, 1654
(Registrar General's Licence) Act, 1516
Bill, 1409, 1481
Strengthening Bill, 7, 48
MARRIS, R. L.: multiple shiftwork, 1661
MARSH, A. I.: Disputes procedures in British Industry, 205, 919
MARSHALL, DR A. H. (Chairman): Highway Maintenance, 1717
MARSHALL, T. H.: Catalogue of Finger rings in the B.M., 719
Marshall:
Aid Commemoration Act:
Account, 249, 584, 969, 1381, 1723
annual report, 148, 463, 858, 1245, 1603
Scholarships, 1245, 1603
Mary, Queen of Scots, Calendar of State Papers, 1336
Masonry, Natural stone, weathering, preservation and maintenance, 523
Mass spectrometry bulletin, 262, 596, 981, 1394, 1733
MASSEY, SIR H. (Chairman): Council for Scientific policy, 125
Master Bertram's workshop in Hamburg, Altarpiece of the Apocolypse, 984
Masters and Mates, Merchant Navy:
examinations, 569
regulations, 569
Masterpieces of:
European painting in the National Gallery, 194
glass, 721
MASTON, C. J. (Chairman): Hours of employment, 1153
Materials:
brittle, designing in, 96
test rig, low temperature, some typical data, 1676
Maternal deaths in E. and W., 158, 1267
Maternity:
bed needs, 1616
benefit claims decision of the Commissioner, 868
Mathematical:
models in forest management, 151
tables, 222
Mathematics:
for majority, 415
in the Primary Schools, 128, 1328
Matrimonial:
Causes Act, 368
Bill, 276, 278, 285, 332, 334, 336, 338, 477, 1074
Homes Act, 368
Bill, 2, 3, 5, 51, 286, 332, 338, 477
Forms, 848

1966 pp 1-272, 1967 pp 273-604, 1968 pp 605-990, 1969 pp 991-1402, 1970 pp 1403-1740

Matrimonial (continued):
Proceedings:
and Property Act, 1516
Bill, 1102, 1103, 1104, 1077, 1410, 1471, 1630
Financial Provision, Law Commission, 1304
Property Bill, 1070
Remedy of Restitution, proposal for abolition, Law Commission, 1303
MATTHEWS, D. H.: Signy Island, geology, 718
MATTINGLY, H.: Coins of the Roman Empire, 384
MAUD, SIR J. (Chairman): management of Local Government, 171, 490
Mauritius:
Banwell Commission report on electoral system, 109
Colonial report, 109, 393
Compensation and Retiring Benefits Order OIC, 520
Constitution (Amendment) Orders OIC, 520, 521
(Constitution) Order OIC, 520
Detection station*, 849
(Electoral Provisions) Order OIC, 201
(Electoral Registers) OIC, 520
Electoral registration, 393
(Former Legislative Council) Order OIC, 520
General election, 393
Independence:
Act, 704
Bill, 339, 607
Order OIC, 911
Information Office pamphlet, 895
Mutual defence and assistance*, 849
police forces*, 849
public officers*, 849, 907
report, 849, 1603
Royal Instructions OIC, 520
transfer of land and fixed assets, 968
Maximum security regime for long term prisoners, 873
MAY, W. E.: Dress of Naval Officers, 194
MAYHEW, E. DE N.: Sketches by Thornhill, 599

Measurement:
of humidity, 1713
units and standards, National Physical Laboratory, 222
Measures passed by the National Assembly of the C. of E., 389, 726, 1131, 1542-3
Meat:
and Livestock Commission, 1379
Industry (Scientific Research Levy) account, 94, 380, 570, 716
products, census of production, 957

Meat (continued):
Research Institute, annual report, 1519
trades, hygiene, 1263
MEATES, LT COL. G. W.: Lullingstone Roman Villa, 1321
Mechanical:
and electrical:
engineers, examination, 199
medical plant, 1616
services, planned maintenance and operation, 914
Engineering:
Economic Development:
conference, 904
Committee, better delivery, 1310
Industry, report, 1310
handling:
equipment, census of production, 957
safety, 1567
power presses, safety in use, 1566
Mechanics and electricians, examination, 199
Mechanisation leaflet for farmers and growers, 94, 380, 716, 1525
Medal, general service, in:
Malay Peninsula/Singapore, 581
South Arabia, 66
Medical:
Act, 1112
Bill, 996, 1064, 1073, 1075
and:
population subjects, studies, 154, 468, 863
related services, E. and W., 867
Appeals Tribunal, 216, 539, 869, 1266, 1621
education, Royal Commission, 919
gas and suction systems, 1617
guide, Ship Captain, 574, 1372
history of second World War, 157, 1264
Inspection (Evidence of Drug-Taking) (School Pupils) Bill, 1485
Mycology Committee, 508
Records Department, hospitals, 1615
Research:
Council:
annual report, 190, 508, 899, 1305, 1655
Industrial Relations Commission, 1545
memorandum, 508
monitoring report, 190, 508, 899
publications, 190, 508, 899, 900, 1305, 1655
special report series, 190, 508, 900, 1655
current, 190, 509, 899
scales, fishing boats, 1366
Services:
Bulgaria, 849
in War, 1264

Medical (continued):
tables, GRO, 154, 467, 861, 1257, 1665
Termination of Pregnancy Bill, 47, 49, 285, 287, 332, 336, 339, 477
see also Abortion Bill and Abortion (No. 2) Bill
work, organisation of, in hospital(s): 470
service, Scotland, 535
Medicine(s):
Act, 704
Bill, 615, 617, 618, 662, 665, 669, 876
and Surgery (careers), 747
Commission, approved names, 1616
preventative, handbook, 114
proprietary, distributors' margins, 903
therapeutic substances*, 1603
Medieval:
Art in B.M., 1123
catalogue in London Museum, 898
Rigg and Furr cultivation strips, 465
Sites, see Prehistoric, Roman and Medieval sites
tiles, 721
Mediterranean and the Middle East, U.K. military series, 104
Medway Water (Bewl Bridge Resevoir) Act, 1112
MEE, A. J. (Chairman): Science for General Education, 1332
Megalopidae, 1539
Megaloptera, type specimens, 1537
Megaloptera, Water Order, 286
MELLICK, J. (Chairman): Legal Aid Scheme, Scotland, 1334
Melton Mowbray and Sheffield Provisional Orders Bill, 1415, 1482, 1484
Members:
Interests (Declaration) H. C. select committee, 1283
of the House of Commons (Conditions of Service) Bill, 1484
travel, H. C. (Services) select committee, 1282
Membership of European Communities, 388
Memoirs of the geological survey of:
E. and W., 195, 514, 906, 1311, 1663
Scotland, 906
Memoranda Rolls (Exchequer), calendar, 1324
MENENDEZ, C. A.: Fossil Bennettitales, 102
Menoponidae, 101, 721
Men('s):
Costume, illustrated booklet, 1653
haircutting services, Monopolies Commission, 955
on site, building management studies, 1570
Mental:
Deficiency hospitals, staffing, 1681
disorders, glossary, 863

—MER

Mental (continued):
Health Act, 1959 (Amendment) Bill, 1072
Welfare Commission for Scotland, 1681
Mentally:
disordered:
residential hospitals for, 471
training centres, 868
handicapped, community care, 1681
Mercantile:
Marine, Extra Masters examinations, 235
see also Merchant Navy examination papers
Navy List:
motor vessels, 572, 955, 1369, 1712
steam and sailing vessels, 238, 572, 955, 1369
Merchandise Marks Act, 238
Merchant:
Navigation, Soviet Union, 849
Navy:
Examination(s):
for certificates of competency, 1366, 1709
papers:
Extra:
First Class Engineer, 569
Master, 235, 569, 952, 1366, 1709
Masters and Mates, 569
Second Class Engineers, 569
Skippers and Second Hands of Fishing boats, 1366
Officers, pay and conditions, 510
Ratings (careers), 499
seamen, code of safe working practices, 1708
ships:
radio for, 516, 908, 1668
to 1880, 1329
Shipping:
Act, 368, 1516
Bill, 50, 278, 332, 477, 1070, 1075
1076, 1406, 1408, 1409, 1410
1471, 1480, 1482, 1630
Reports of Court, 238, 572, 1369, 1712-13
(Load Lines) Act, 368
Bill, 279, 336
medical scales, 955
Mercator Projection, Transverse, 1666
Mercurial poisoning, 187
Mercury:
and mercury compounds, 1153
hearing aid batteries, increase in prices, 902
MEREDITH-OWENS, G. M.: Handlist of Persian Manuscripts, 720

Mergers:
guide to practice, 1369
survey, 1713
Merionethshire:
census, 153
sample census, 468, 1259
Mersey Docks and Harbour Board:
Act, 78, 370, 706
(Seaforth Works) Act, 79
Merseyside:
conurbation, house condition survey, 1647
Passenger Transport Area (Designation) Order S.I. select committee, 1287
Mesozoic:
and cainozoic dinoflagellate cysts, 1538
anthopterygian fishes, caudal skeletons, 723
MESSER, H. J. M.:
Building for food storage and direct feeding of cattle, 512
chitting houses, 512
Metal(s):
containers, supply, Monopolies Commission, 1713
durability in natural waters, 913
in buildings, painting, 220
manufactures, miscellaneous, census of production, 1371
non-ferrous:
Commonwealth Economic Committee, 392
in buildings, painting, 220
precious, refining, census of production, 958
scaffolding, 912, 1320
surfaces, preparing for painting, 201
work, painting, 512
working:
machine tools, census of production, 957
welding, and cutting, (careers), 1564
Metalliferous mining and quarrying, census of production, 957
Metarbelidae, 724
Meteorites:
Concise account, 388
in the B.M., catalogue, 104
Meteorological Magazine, 191, 508, 900, 1305, 1656
Meteorological:
Office:
annual report, 191, 508, 900, 1305, 1656
forms, 191, 509, 1305
monthly weather reports, 191-2, 509, 901, 1306, 1657
publications, 191-2, 508-9, 900, 1305-6, 1656-7
scientific papers, 192, 509, 901, 1657
services, estimates committee, 165, 483

Meteorology:
convention, 1245
for:
Air Traffic Controllers, 1696
Aircrew, 1137
Mariners, 509
Metric:
equivalents of dimensions, 923
guide for forestry, 1255
house shells:
circular, 1293
two storey, 1308, 1658
cost guide, 1658
housing:
cost yardstick, circular, 1292
dimensional framework, 1659
dimensions and areas, 1659
transitional period, 1308
what it means, 1308
in practice, 1672
space standards, 924
system:
change to, 222, 555, 938
conversion factors, 1352
tariff tables, forestry, 1611
top diameter sawlog tables, 1611
volume ready reckoner, round timber, 6111
units, water, sewage, and related subjects:
circular, 888
report, 892
wall charts, 1659
Metrication:
and building regulations, circular, 1292
Board:
publications, 1657
report, 1657
in the construction industry, 1673
of housebuilding:
circular, 888, 890
progress, 1644
Metrology, Legal, International Organisation of, 847
Metropolitan:
Police, Commissioner's report, 162, 475, 1627
Water Board Act, 370
Meyrick types of microlepidoptera, catalogue, 1128

Microdeutopus costa, 1127
Microgaster Latreille, 721
Microlepidoptera, Meyrick types, catalogue, 1128
Micro-organisms, Commonwealth collections, 413, 743
Microphotometer, automatic, 207
Microplankton, 1126, 1538
Microplitus Förster, 1537

Microscopy spores and pollens, 386
Middle:
East, Overseas Aid select committee,1637
Eastern and American questions, British Foreign policy, 1164
Schools:
launching, 1561
new problems in school design, 125
towards, 1561
MIDDLETON, A. J.:
Fatigue tests on pressurised polyethylene terephthalate, 530
Low temperature materials test rig, 1676
Mid-Glamorgan Water Act, 706
Midland Motor Cylinder Company Ltd, Industrial Relations Commission, 1545
Midlothian County Council Order, Confirmation Act, 1518
Bill, 1483
Mid-Wales, New Town, 267
Midwifery, domiciliary needs, 1616
Migration tables:
census, 154
sample census:
E. and W., 1666
Scotland, 863
Mild steel chimneys, 1323
Military:
Aircraft (Loans):
Act, 77
Bill, 4, 48
memorandum, 249
establishments, rules, regulations etc. relating to, 734, 1550
law, manual, 115, 399, 732, 1138, 1149
see also Army and Defence
Milk:
and Milk Products Technical Advisory Committee, 1120
condensed, 1121
distribution in E. and W., inquiry into methods, 92
distributors, remuneration, 510, 511
industry workers, pay and conditions, 1657
production:
costs and efficiency, 378
hygiene, 863
products, census of productions, 957
quality, 1153
radioactivity in, 86
Milking parlour, leaflet, 715
Milky Way, OB stars in, 921
Mill Lane, Kirk Ella, Burying Ground Act, 706
MILLAR, E. L. M. (Chairman): Ambulance training and equipment, 158, 472
MILLAR, R. H.: Oyster population in Loch Ryan, 710
MILLAR, PROF. M. M. (Chairman): Elderly with mental disorder, 1681

—MIN

Milling machines, horizontal guarding of cutters, 1567
MILLS, D. H.: Survival of hatchery-reared salmon fry, 1116
MILNE, P. H.: Net enclosures for fish farming, 1520
Mineral(s):
collection in B.M., history of, 1128
industry:
statistical summary, 195, 514, 906, 1312, 1663
world production, exports, and imports, 514, 1663
oil(s):
carcinogenic action, 900
gas, and water, methods of search, 1662
refining, census of production, 957
Resources:
Division, Natural Environment Research Council, 906
of the crofter Counties of Scotland, 1312
overseas geology, 1663
Workings Act, accounts, 173, 492, 893, 1296, 1647
Mine workings, support of, 200
Mineralogy bulletins, 1539
Mines:
and quarries:
Act:
Book 4, 199
forms, 518-19
Divisional Inspector's report, 200, 519
grants to Local Authorities, 1644
H.M. Chief Inspector's report, 200, 519, 911, 1353, 1663
law relating to safety and health, 1693, 1712
(Notification of Tipping Operations) Regulations, 1319
Safety circulars, 1352
(Tips) Act, 1112
Bill, 664, 670, 671, 876, 991, 992, 1072
circular, 1292, 1644
workmen at quarries, 1693
Management Bill, 1408, 1411, 1413, 1482, 1485
Mills, and Furnaces, National Museum of Wales, 1310
(Notification of Dangerous Occurrences) (Amendment) Order, 520, 1319
Research, safety in, annual report, 200, 520, 911, 1319, 1694
(Working Facilities and Support) Act, 77
Bill, 48, 168
Minimum age for marriage, convention, 848, 1603

1966-70 | MIN-NAT

MIN— INDEX 1966–70

Mining:
Examinations (Surveyors) (Amendment) Rules, 519, 1693
National certificates and diplomas, 126
Qualification Examination:
Mechanical and electrical engineers, 199
Mechanics and electricians, 199
surveying, higher national certificates, 126
Ministerial control, nationalised industries, 483, 882 3
Minister's awards for good design in housing, *see* Awards
Ministry of Social Security Act, 77
Bill, 5, 6, 48, 50, 62, 77
circular, 487
Ministry of Housing and Local Government Provisional Order, *see respective towns*
Miocene:
carnivora, 102
rhinoceroses, 103
Miscellaneous:
civil estimates, *see* Civil estimates
components, hospital, 1616
Financial Provisions Act, 704
Bill, 619, 670
supply estimates, 1725
see also specific subject
Misrepresentation Act, 369
Bill, 3, 8, 43, 46, 51, 164, 332, 477
Misuse of Drugs Bill, 1415, 1471, 1478, 1480, 1484, 1630
MITCHELL, A. F.: Westonbirt in colour, 860
MITCHELL, K. W.: Criteria for designing in brittle materials, 96
MITCHELL, PROF. R. G. (Chairman): Scottish Advisory Committee on Child Care, 1679
Mites:
beneficial, 1521
bryobia, 88
bulb scale, 88
euphthiracaroid, 1127
gall, 88
in farm-stored grain, 88
red spider, 88, 375
Mixed Hereditaments (Certificates) Regulations, 488

Mobile Radio Committee report, 516
Model:
clauses, 707
Water Byelaws, 173
(Scotland), 532
Modern:
building principles, floors and roofs, 524
computing methods, 1713
engineering, census of production, 957
language teaching, 1329
see also Languages, modern
Modern (*continued*):
offices, user survey, 221
Modular electronic data acquisition system, 923
Moisture content determination by oven-drying, 222
Molecular biology*, 743, 1603
Monimiaceae, 729
Monitoring report, strontium 90 in human bone, 190, 508, 899, 1305, 1655
Monk Bretton Priory, Yorkshire, guide, 202
Monmouthshire:
census, 153
sample census, 468, 1259
Sewerage Board Bill, 5, 7, 48
MONOD, T.: John Cranch, *Zoologiste de l'Expédition du Congo* (1816), 1538
Monopolies:
and Mergers Acts, annual report, 238, 572, 955, 1370, 1570
Commission reports, 239, 572, 955, 1369–70, 1713
Monoponidae, 1125
Montague Burton Chair of International Relations (Amendment) Scheme, 926
Montague Burton, Monopolies Commission, 573
Montgomeryshire:
census, 153
sample census, 468, 1259
Monthly:
charts of dew-point temperatures, Indian Ocean, 1656
digest of statistics, 105–6, 389, 725, 1130, 1541
meteorological charts, Eastern Pacific Ocean, 1306
weather reports, *see* Weather reports
Montserrat:
Colonial report, 109
Report, 849
Moon, the, geology and geography, 906
MOORE, D. M.: Vascular flora of the Falkland Islands, 719
MOORE, D. R.: Tests on circular diaphragms of polyethylene terephthalate film, 208
MOORE, J. R.: Recent sedimentation in Northern Cardigan Bay, 1127
Moray Firth, plan for growth, 871
Morecambe Bay:
and Solway Barrages, report on desk studies, 599
Barrage, desk study, 599
More Points for Businessmen, decimal currency booklet, 1547
MORETON, B. D.: Beneficial insects and mites, 1521
MORGAN, A. M. (Chairman): Pension Rights, 186
MORGAN J. T.: Gas evolution from epoxy resins, 1676

1966 pp 1–272, 1967 pp 273–604, 1968 pp 605–990, 1969 pp 991–1402, 1970 pp 1403–1740

92

INDEX 1966–70 —MUS

MORGAN, N. C.: Fertiliser experiments in Scottish freshwater lochs, 87
MORGAN REES, D.: Mines, Mills, and Furnaces, 1310
Morgan Guaranty Trust Company of New York, loan, 966, 1377, 1720
Morocco, air services*, 130, 1245, 1603
MORRIS, A.: Chemical problems in use of Canal water for cooling at Daresbury Nuclear Physics Laboratory, 530
MORRIS, SIR C. (Chairman): Higher Education mission to South Pacific
MORRIS, J. (Chairman): Railway policy, 577
MORRIS, P.: Hedgehogs, 1612
MORRIS, W. R.: Beam bending magnets, 530
Mortality, area tables, GRO, 861
Mortars for brickwork, 912
MORTON, PROF. F.: Safety of natural gas, 1694
MORTON, PROF. R. A. (Chairman):
Azodicarbonamide, 715
Food additives:
and contaminants, 93, 380, 715, 1525
further classes, 715
MORTON-WILLIAMS, R.:
Undergraduates attitude to school teaching as a career, 864
Young school leavers, 921
Mosaic:
and streak of tomato, 375
of cucumber, 88
MOSLEY ISLE, W. H. (Chairman): Wool textile industry, 1310
Mosquitoes, relation to disease, 723
Moss, A. A.: Meteorites, 388
Motels, 1294
Moth(s):
codling, 87
clothes, 384
lackey, 87
pine looper, 511
small ermine, 87
Motor:
cars up to 1930, illustrated booklet, 1329
cycle, three-wheel vehicle, and pedal cycle manufacturing, census of production 1371
cyclists, young, accidents, 863
Industry:
Joint Labour Council, activities, 186, 753
statistics, 1310
Insurers' Bureau, 1375
lifeboat radio equipment, 908
repairing and servicing industry, costs and charges, 510
Vehicles:
(Driving Licences) Regulations, S.I. select committee, 1641
lighting, 579
Motor (*continued*):
Vehicles (*continued*):
manufacturing, census of production, 1371
offences relating to, 161, 474, 873, 1271, 1626
vessels, *see* Mercantile Navy List
Motoring, private, E. and W., 1261
Motorways:
and trunk roads, estimates committee, 1277
Corporation Bill, 666
MOTT, PROF. SIR N. (Chairman): Electronics Research Council, 96
MOUND, L. A.:
Australian *Aeolothripidae*, 385
British *Aleyrodidae*, 101
Thysanoptera,
from the Solomon Islands, 1537
R. S. Bagnall's collections, 722
Mountain rescue, 731
MOUNTBATTEN OF BURMA, EARL: Prison escapes and security, 162
Mousa and Clicklimin brochs, guide, 1670
Movement of:
exports, Economic Development Committee, 193, 1660
manufacturing industry in the U.K., 955
oystercatchers, 1524
Service personnel and stores, 479
Moving out of a slum, 1646
Mowers, 1525
Mozart in the B.M., 721

Multiple:
death fires, 1351
Health Screening Clinic, Rotherham, 1267
Scattering correction, 922
shiftwork, monograph, 1661
Multi-storey car parks, circular, 889
Mummies and human remains, B.M., 719
MUNDY, E. J.: Experimental husbandry farms and horticulture stations, 1524
Municipal:
busmen, pay, 902
Docks Bill, 334
Murder 1957–1968, Home Office Statistical Department, 1273
Muridae, 103
MURRAY, A. S.: Excavations in Cyprus, 1536
MURRAY, C. A.:
Proper motions in the:
field of Cluster M 67. II and III, 1327
region of the hyades, 206
Muscat and Oman, Kuria Muria Islands, 849
Muscidae, 1125

1966 pp 1–272, 1967 pp 273–604, 1968 pp 605–990, 1969 pp 991–1402, 1970 pp 1403–1740

93

MUS— INDEX 1966–70

Museum(s):
and Galleries, standing committee, 510, 901, 1083
Galleries, and the Arts, supply estimate, 1725
of Practical Geology, 195
see also specific museum
Music:
(careers), 1564
CSE experimental examination, 178
in:
the British Museum:
catalogue, 99
handlist, 1536
schools, 1145
instrumental, 99
printing, four hundred years of, 720
secular vocal, 99
Musical instruments:
Ancient West Asian, 1123
as works of art, 985
catalogue, 985
Mussels, 93, 1120
Mustard, Food Standards Committee, 1525
MUTCH, W. E. S.: Public recreation in National Forests, 859

Myclophoids, relationship with teleosts, 1126
Mycology, biological control, 728
MYERS, A. A.: Aoridae, 1127
MYKURA, W.: Sodic scapolite in the Shetland Islands, 1312
Myrsidea Waterston, 101, 721
Myrsinaceae, Jamaican, 1124
Mytilus:
edulis, 93
juvenile, food value of algae, 1524

N

NAAS Quarterly Review, 94, 381, 716, 1121, 1526
NAISBY, J. (Chairman): Sight tests for seafarers, 1715
NAISH, G. P. B.: The Wasa, her place in history, 905
NANDY, K.: Interstellar reddening, 207, 921
NAPOLITAN, L.: Costs and efficiency in Milk production, 378
NAPPER, D. M.: *Dipsacaceae*, 729
Narcissus pests, 1521
Nardoa and other ophidiasterids, 387
Narrow fabrics, census of production, 958
NASH, G.: Edward Gordon Craig, 599
National:
accounts statistics, 725
Advisory Council on Education for Industry and Commerce, 126, 744, 1146
Agricultural Advisory Service, soil chemists conference, 382
Air Traffic Control Service training manual, 955
Aircraft Effort, productivity report, 1332
Assembly of the Church of England Measures, *see* Measures
Assistance Board;
annual report, 217
homeless single persons, 215
Association of:
Head Teachers, Education and Science select committee, 1634
Schoolmasters:
dispute, 1147
Education and Science select committee, 1635
Board for Prices and Incomes, *see* Prices and Incomes Board
Building:
Agency, publications, 1308–9, 1658
Studies, research papers, 221, 523
Bus Company:
annual report and accounts, 1718
loans, 1384, 1726
Certificates and Diplomas:
electrical and electronic engineering, 126
mining, and higher National certificates in mining surveying, 126
revision of rules, Scottish Education Department circular, 533
Coal Board:
accounts and statistical tables, 199, 519, 911, 1319, 1694
(Additional Powers) Act, 77
Bill, 10, 46, 50, 164
loans, 581, 967, 1720
report, 199, 519, 911, 1319, 1694
select committee on Nationalised industries, 882, 1283, 1694
collection of industrial bacteria, 556, 1694
Computing Centre, publications, 1659–60
Daily Newspapers, costs and revenue, 511
Debt:
Funds in Trust, 193, 511, 904, 1309, 1660
Office publications, 193, 511, 903–4, 1309, 1660
return, 249, 584, 969, 1382
Economic Development:
Council, publications, 193–4

1966 pp 1–272, 1967 pp 273–604, 1968 pp 605–990, 1969 pp 991–1402, 1970 pp 1403–1740

94

INDEX 1966–70 NAT

National (*continued*):
Economic Development (*continued*):
Office:
data book, 1310
publications, 511–12, 904, 1309–10, 1660–1
Talking Shop series, 1661
Engineering Laboratory:
annual report, 222, 555
publications, 222, 555, 1352, 1694
Film:
Finance Corporation, annual report and accounts, 239, 573, 956, 1370, 1713
School, need for, 414
Food Survey Committee, annual report, 92, 716, 1121
Forests, public recreation, 859
Foundation for Educational Research, Education and Science select committee, 1635
Freight Corporation:
annual report and accounts, 1718
loans, 1383
organisation, 1718
Gallery(ies):
London, 194, 512, 1310
of Scotland, Trustees' report, 194, 512, 904, 1310, 1661
Health Service:
Act(s), 77
accounts, 158, 471, 867, 1265, 1619
Bill, 2, 47, 281, 334, 477
Central Health Services Council report, 158, 471, 867, 1264
General Practice Finance Corporation, *see* General Practice
Anniversary Conference, 867
Contributions Bill, 1409, 1481
(Family Planning) Act, 369
Bill, 2, 47, 281, 334, 477
Future structure, 1619
Hospital:
Building, 157
costing returns, 157–8, 472, 867
Manual workers, pay and conditions, 510
pay of nurses and midwives, 902
(Regional Hospital Areas) Order, S.I. select committee, 1287
Relationship with pharmaceutical industry, 472
reorganisation in Wales, 1736
(Scotland):
Acts:
accounts, 212, 535, 928, 1334, 1681
Government Actuary's report, 535
running costs of Scottish hospitals, 212, 535, 928
National (*continued*):
Health Service (*continued*):
Superannuation Scheme:
allocation of pension, 1619
E. and W., an explanation, 472
Government Actuary's report, 158, 1619
Supplementary Ophthalmic Services, 472, 867
Transplantation problems, 1264
Income and:
balance of payments, preliminary estimates, 250, 584, 970, 1387, 1724
expenditure, 105, 389, 724, 1129, 1541
Institute:
for Research in Nuclear Science, publications, 194
of Agricultural Engineering, publications, 512, 905
Insurance:
Act(s), 1112
accounts, 215, 539, 868, 1265, 1619
(Amendment) Bill, 49, 335, 477, 666
Bill, 49, 216, 332, 671, 1071
circular, 1292
decisions of the;
Commissioner, 215–6, 538–9, 868–9, 1265, 1620–1
index and digest, 214–5, 537–8, 866, 1264, 1618
Tribunal, 1265
Government Actuary's report, 215, 539
memorandum, 538
(No. 2) Bill, 285, 338, 353, 1000, 1065, 1074, 1075, 1275
Government Actuary's report, 540, 1266
memorandum, 538, 1266
Advisory Committee, 215, 538, 867, 1265, 1621
and Industrial Injuries (Stamps) Regulations, S.I. select committee, 1288, 1621
(Claims and Payments) Amendment:
Regulations, 538, 540, 1267
(No. 2) Regulations, 1265
(Classification) Amendment:
Regulations, 867, 870, 1268, 1619
(No. 2) Regulations, 1619, 1623
(Collection of Graduated Contributions) Regulations, 1619, 1622
(Computation of Earnings) Regulations, 540
(Contributions) Amendment Regulations, 361, 538, 540

1966 pp 1–272, 1967 pp 273–604, 1968 pp 605–990, 1969 pp 991–1402, 1970 pp 1403–1740

95

NAT—   INDEX 1966-70

National (continued):
Insurance (continued):
(Determination of Claims and Questions) Amendment:
Regulations, 216, 538
(No. 2) Regulations, 538, 540
(Earnings):
limit for Retirement Pensions, 558
Regulations, 539
Earnings-related short term benefit, 214
Etc. Act, 1112
Bill, 992
Existing pensioners Fund, accounts, 215, 539, 868, 1265, 1621
Family Allowance Act, 540
Fund accounts, 215, 539, 868, 1265, 1621
(Further Provision) Bill, 47, 665, 1070, 1076
(General Benefit) Amendment Regulations, 216
(Industrial Injuries):
Acts:
accounts, 215, 539, 868, 1265, 1621
Decisions of the:
Commissioner, 216, 539, 540, 869, 1266, 1620
index, 214–15, 537–8, 866, 1264, 1618
Tribunal, 540, 869, 1621
Government Actuary's report, 216, 540
(Amendment) Act, 369
Bill, 278, 1070
erosion of teeth, 216
industrial noise, 1266
(Insurable and Excepted Employments) Amendment Regulations, 870
Law relating, 215, 538, 867, 1264, 1618
vibration syndrome, 1621
(Mariners) Amendment:
Regulations, 309
(No. 2) Regulations, 217
Maternity Benefit, 539
(Medical Certification) Amendment Regulations, 216
(Members of the Forces) Regulations, 867
(Members of the Police Forces), Regulations, 867, 870
(Occupational Pensioners) (Unemployment Benefit):
and Contribution credits, 867
Regulations, 870, 1619
S.I. select committee, 1641

National (continued):
Insurance (continued):
(Old Persons' and Widows' Pensions and Attendance Allowance) Act, 1516
Bill, 1411, 1483
(Overlapping Benefits) Amendment Regulations, 539, 540
Regulations, Preliminary Drafts, 216–7, 540, 870, 1267, 1622
Reserve Fund, accounts, 215, 539, 868, 1265, 1621
(Residence and Persons Abroad) Amendment Regulations, 539, 540
Schemes, proposed changes, 214
Sickness Benefit, 539
Supplements, law relating, 215
Time limit for obtaining payment of benefits, 868
(Unemployment:
and Sickness Benefit) Amendment Regulations, 1622
Benefit, 538
Joint:
Advisory Council:
dismissal procedures, 500
pension rights, 186
Council for Air Transport, Industrial Court of Inquiry, 502
Land Fund, accounts, 250, 584, 1382, 1723
Lending Library for Science and Technology:
current serials, 414
translations bulletins, 126, 414, 744, 1146, 1562
Library(ies):
Committee, documentary evidence and report, 1146
for Scotland, catalogue of Manuscripts, 194, 905
Loans:
Act, 704
Bill, 339, 607, 662, 665, 876
Fund:
accounts, 1157, 1723
loans from, 969, 1381, 1723
Lottery Bill, 662, 665, 879
Maritime Museum:
catalogue of library:
biography, 1661
voyages and travel, 905
gift, 1379
publications, 194, 512–13, 905, 1310, 1661
minimum wage, 1155
Mod (Scotland) Act, 1112
Bill, 998, 1065, 1073, 1275

National (continued):
Museum of:
Antiquities, Scotland, Trustees' report 194, 513, 905, 1310, 1662
Wales, publications, 1310
Newspapers, cost and revenue, 1657
Parks:
and Access to the Countryside Act, 188, 728, 893, 1134, 1644
Commission:
publications, 188, 513
report, 893
Guide, 188, 513, 1334, 1546
Physical Laboratory:
annual report, 222, 555, 940, 1352
Electric units and standards, 1713
Notes on Applied Science, 555, 1352, 1713
publications, 222, 555–6, 1352, 1713
report, 222, 555, 940, 1352
SI:
International system of units, 1713
units in electricity and magnetism, 1713
Units and standards of measurement employed, 222, 555
Portrait Gallery:
annual report of the Trustees, 194, 513, 905
illustrated booklets, 513
publications, 1310, 1662
Ports Council:
annual report and accounts, 242, 308, 576, 962, 1375, 1718
digest of port statistics, 194, 513, 905, 1311, 1662
loan, 417, 962, 1158
Reference Library of Science and Invention:
list of non-Slavonic titles, 1124
periodical publications, 1537
Register of Archives, accession to repositories:
list, 159, 473, 871
index to lists, 473
Research:
Development Corporation:
annual report and accounts, 556, 940, 1352, 1694
report, 222
Station:
publications, 523–4
special reports, 524
Savings Committee, annual report, 195, 513, 905, 1311, 1662
Service men, Army, regulations for, 1139
Society of Metal Mechanics, Court of Inquiry, 501
Steel Corporation, loan, 583

National (continued):
Superannuation:
and Social Insurance:
Bill, 1077, 1472, 1482, 1630
explanatory memorandum, 1266
Government Actuary's report, 1266
Earnings-related Social Security proposals, 1266
terms for partial contracting out, 1266
Theatre Act, 1112
Bill, 671, 993, 1065, 1275
Trust, Benson Report, 1311
Union of:
Students, Education and Science select committee, 1635
Teachers, Young Teacher Advisory Committee, 1634
Water Safety:
Campaign, 488
Committee, 921
Westminster Bank Act, 1114
Nationalised:
Industries:
consumer consultative machinery, 728
economic and financial objectives, 584
Ministerial control, 1381
Private sector, top salaries, 1307
select committee on, 1283, 1636, 1694
Transport Undertakings, loans, 245, 964, 1376
Natural:
emergencies, circulars, 1293, 1396
Environment Research Council:
Mineral Resources Division, 906, 1663
Ordnance Survey, annual report, 514
publications, 195, 514, 905–6, 1311–12, 1662–4
reports, 195, 514, 906, 1312, 1663–4
gas, safety as a fuel, 1694
History Museum:
bulletins, 101–3, 385–7, 721–3, 1124–8, 1537–9
economic series, 723
guide to exhibition galleries, 104
historical series, 104, 387, 723, 1128
library, list of serial publications, 724, 1128
publications, 101–4, 385–8, 721–4, 1124–8, 1537–40
stone masonry, weathering, preservation, and maintenance, 523

1966 pp 1–272, 1967 pp 273–604, 1968 pp 605–990, 1969 pp 991–1402, 1970 pp 1403–1740

96   97

NAT—   INDEX 1966-70   —NOR

Nature:
Conservancy:
handbook, 906
progress, 906
conservation at the coast, 1545
Nautical Almanac, 205, 529, 920, 1328, 1675
astronomical navigation with, 905
Office, publications, 205, 529, 920, 1328, 1675
Naval:
Court Martial:
Admiralty memorandum, 411, 1140
manual, 1551
Marine Engineering practice, 411, 1140
Medical Branch, ratings' handbook, 735
Officers' dress, 94
Navigation:
Admiralty manual, 123, 411, 735
air, 557
astronomical, 905
Rhine, 459
Navy:
Court Martial, see Naval Court Martial
Department:
production accounts, 117, 416, 735, 1158, 1552
publications, 123–4, 411, 735, 1140–1, 1551–2
estimates, 124, 401, 736, 1141
List, 123, 411, 735, 1140, 1551
appendix, 123, 1140
Retired Officers, 735, 1551
Queen's Regulations, 123, 411, 735, 1140, 1551
Votes, 250, 585, 971, 1383, 1724
see also Admiralty, Defence and Royal Navy

NEALE, J. W., Ostracod fauna, 383
Nedo:
and Talking Shop series, 1661
see also National Economic Development Office
Nelson, coloured poster, 1662
Nematodes:
classification, 387
Euchromadora species, 1127
marine, 103, 1539
parasitic in frogs, 723
Nemestrinidae, 1125
Neolithic Revolution, 388
Nepal:
Diptera, 101, 385, 1125
East-West Highway*, 1245
financial assistance*, 1245
Secondary School for boys*, 1245
Nepheline-syenite and phonolite, 906

Nerve agents:
disposal of effluent, 1551
report on transport, 1551
Net, census of production, 958
Netherlands:
airworthiness certificates*, 458
bacon*, 1245
Continental shelf*, 457–8
customs privileges*, 1604
double taxation*, 457, 850, 1578
gas centrifuge process*, 1605
judgments in civil matters*, 850, 1245–6, 1604
legal proceedings convention, 849, 1604
road transport of goods*, 1250, 1604
taxation of road vehicles*, 1604
uranium*, 1605
Nettle, annual, 87
Network analysis in forming a new organisation, 586
Neutron spectronomy, 922
New:
City, study in urban development, 173
communities, needs, 492
computer course, 1604
curriculum, Schools Council, 414
earnings survey, 1570
Forest:
Act, 1516
Bill, 1003, 1473, 1480, 1482, 1630
guide, 151, 1612
Guinea, Sepik Head-waters, 100
Hebrides:
District agents etc.*, 1598
economic survey, 515
registration of births etc.*, 454
report, 109, 850, 1579
money:
conversions, 1548
in your shop, 1548
Parliamentary buildings, H.C. (Services) select committee, 481, 882, 1282, 1636
Scottish housing handbooks, 924, 1331, 1677
Town(s):
Act(s), 1112
accounts, 173, 493, 893, 1296
Bill, 10, 51, 670, 992
Commission report, 173, 493, 893, 1296, 1647
Development Corporation reports, 173, 493, 893, 1296, 1647
Draft New Town (Irvine) Designation Order, 210
report, 492
tables of comparison, 173
Mid-Wales, 267
of Britain, 1299

New (continued):
Town(s) (continued):
(Scotland):
Act, 704
accounts, 1296
Bill, 288, 605, 607, 666, 886
reports, 924, 1331, 1677
Secretary of State's memorandum, 532
Year's Honours List, 217–18, 541, 930, 1336, 1683
Zealand:
butter imports*, 394
collection of micro-organisms, 743
Commonwealth War Cemetery at Klagenfurt*, 419
double taxation*, 111
income tax, 1300
social security*, 1250, 1604
trade*, 395
War graves*, 1254, 1610
Newcastle-upon-Tyne Corporation Act, 706
Newlyn Pier and Harbour Commissioners, inquiry, 1571
Newport:
Corporation Act, 1518
(Mon.) geology, 1312
Newquay Urban District Council Act, 370
NEWSOM, SIR J. (Chairman): Public Schools Commission, 745

NGC 6522, proper motions in the field of, 206

Nicaragua, visas*, 1246
NICHOL, T.: Geochemical reconnaissance, Derbyshire area, 1663
NICHOLLS, D. C.: wooded private land for forestry, 1255
NICHOLS, R. W. (Chairman): pressure vessels, 1352
Nicobar Islands, income tax, 1300
NICOL, A. J. (Chairman): efficient use of manpower, 500
Nigeria:
British Relief Advisory Mission, 850
Lord Hunt's Mission, 1604
Observer Team report, 1246
Nimrod:
A 7 GeV proton sychrotron, 194
beam sensing radial and phase control systems for, 194
calculation of perturbed orbits for resonant extraction from, 923
electrostatic inflector, 209
extracted proton beam, plunging magnet system for, 209
injection of beam from 50 MeV PLA, 531

Nimrod (continued):
operation and development quarterly report, 531, 923, 1330, 1676
resonant extraction system, 1330
symposium on use for nuclear structure physics, 923
Nitrogen and soil organic matter, conference, 1123
Nitrous fumes, 1152, 1153
NIXON, G. E. J.: Braconidae, 386, 721, 1537

No Folks of their Own, community care of mentally handicapped, 1681
NOBLE, T. A. F. (Chairman): Work of Probation and After-care Department, 162
Noise:
aircraft, 557
and the worker, 754
annoyance in central London, 863
control on building sites, 912, 1320
from concrete breakers, circular, 890
in:
buildings, reducing, 521
industry, hearing, 1617
industrial:
circulars, 488, 1292
decisions of the Commissioner, Industrial Injuries, 1266
London, survey, 914
measurement for aircraft design, 1713
Nomenclature:
(and directory) of the first aeroplanes, 207
Brussels, 113, 397, 730
fungi, 508
Non–:
alloy bright steel bars, prices, 1307
calcareous microplankton, 1126, 1538
custodial and semicustodial penalties, 1626
electrical machinery, miscellaneous, census of production, 1371
ferrous metals:
census of production, 1371
Commonwealth Economic Committee, 392
Industrial Civil Service, London weighting, 511
marine mammals, instructions for collectors, 724
nursing duties, relieving nurses of, 865
proliferation of nuclear weapons, 760
recurrent grants, 984, 1735
warlike stores of the Services, estimates committee, 167
Norfolk:
census, 153
sample census, 468, 862

1966 pp 1–272, 1967 pp 273–604, 1968 pp 605–990, 1969 pp 991–1402, 1970 pp 1403–1740

98   99

NOR— INDEX 1966-70

Norham Castle, Northumberland, guide, 202
NORMAN, J. R.: Recent fishes and fishlike vertebrates, 387
NORRIS, W. H. (Chairman): metric units, 892
North:
Atlantic:
Ocean Stations*, 1246
Treaty:
accommodation in Germany*, 1246
Organisation, International Military Headquarters*, 1604, 1605
status of personnel*, 1246
changing, challenge of, 124
Devon (Meldon Reservoir) Water Order, 286
of Scotland:
Hydro-electric Board:
advances, 909, 1317
Bonds, 1722
Constructional Scheme No. 40, 1331
loan, 583, 969, 1722
report and accounts, 213, 517, 924, 1331, 1677
Orkney, and Shetland Shipping Company Ltd., passenger fares and freight charges, 902
Riding County Council Act, 1518
Sea:
Gas, exploitation, select committee on Nationalised industries, 883, 1317
oil pollution*, 1246
Wales, coasts, 728
York Moors, guide, 188
Yorkshire forests, guide, 151
Northampton:
County Council Act, 1114
expansion proposals, 171
Northamptonshire:
census, 153
sample census, 168, 862
North-east:
England, coasts, 728
Lincolnshire Water Act, 1114
Scotland, survey, 1331
North-eastern Irish Sea, recent sedimentation, 1312
Northern:
Economic Planning Council, 124
hemisphere, average temperature, contour heights, and winds, 1656
Ireland:
agricultural census, 1521
Boundary Commission, 1269
census of population, 906
economic report, 906

Northern (continued):
Ireland (continued):
Government:
Departments, Constitution Commission, 1133
of, publications, 906, 1313
Land purchase accounts, 219, 543, 932, 1343, 1690
police, 1313
sources of aggregate, 1663
status in U.K., 1133
Supreme Court of Judicature, 219, 543, 932, 1343, 1655
texts of communiques, Home Secretary's visit, 1271
Livestock Producers Ltd, 951
Milky Way, distribution of OB stars, 921
Pennines Rural Development Board, annual report, 1525
Region, sample census, migration, 863
stars:
radial velocity, 920
three-colour photometry, 1327
Northerners, challenge to, 124
North-west:
Atlantic Fisheries, International convention, 1596
Economic Planning Council, 742
England, coasts, 728
North-western Region, sample census, migration, 862
NORTHUMBERLAND, DUKE OF (Chairman): Foot-and-Mouth, 1122
Northumberland:
census, 153
County Council Act, 1518
National Park, guide, 1134
sample census, 468, 862
Norway:
atomic energy*, 850
double taxation*, 145, 458, 1165, 1605
pout, distribution, 710
road transport of goods*, 1607
spruce, 931
Norwich Corporation Act, 1518
Nottinghamshire:
census, 153
sample census, 468, 862

Nuclear:
energy:
gas centrifuge process*, 169f
information Office pamphlet, 177, 1299
isotope separation*, 1605
third party liability, 850
uranium*, 1605
Installations Act, 1112
Bill, 995, 1065, 1071, 1073, 1275

Nuclear (continued):
reactor programme, review, 482
Research reactor, Chile*, 1577
structure physics, symposium on the use of Nimrod, 923
weapons:
Latin America, 850, 1605
non-proliferation, 760
Nuculacene, 1128
Nullity of Marriage:
Bill, 1484
Law Commission, 1654
Numbers of coins in circulation, U.K., 1542
Nursery Schools (Parental Contributions) Bill, 1070
Nurses:
Act: 1112
Bill, 994, 996, 1001, 1065, 1071, 1075, 1275
and midwives, National Health Service, 902
Nursing:
education*, 850, 1605
(careers), 499
out-patient departments, 1262
relief, hospital services, 1615
services, ward books, 1262
staff, senior, structure, 158
student progress, hospital service, 1615
ward etc., staffing, hospital service, 1615
work, hospital, 156
Nuthampstead, Local hearings, 1365
Nutrient(s):
recommended intakes, U.K., 1267
requirements:
farm livestock, 373
pigs, 373
ruminants, 86
Nutrition:
child, 1622
manual, 1525
of:
the elderly, 1622
young children, 870
report, 1133
Nuts and bolts etc, census of production, 958
NYBELIN, O.: Pholidophoridae, 102
Nymphalidae, 101, 385, 1125, 1126, 1538

—OFF INDEX 1966-70

Oar Maces of Admiralty, 194

OB:
clusters and associations, 921
stars in the Northern Milky Way, 921
Obscene Publications (Amendments) Bill, 1073
Observatories Year Book, Meteorological Office, 901, 1306
Observer's handbook, Meteorological Office, 1306
Observer Newspaper, Privilege committee, 1306
Obsidian, perlite, 1664

Occupation(s):
and industry, County tables, Census, Scotland, 155
census tables, 154
Scotland, 155
classification, 154
industry, socio-economic groups, 152-3
Occupational:
choice, 745
diseases, 1622
pension schemes, 250, 1267
therapist (careers), 180
Ocean:
Stations, North Atlantic*, 1246
wave statistics, 555
O'CONNOR, J.: painting of St. Pancras Hotel and Station, 506

O'DEA, W. T.:
Aeronautics, 207
Early oil lamps and candles, 208
gas, mineral oil, electricity, 208
lighting other than in the home, 1675
Odonata:
Corduliidae, 722
Libellulidae, 722
type specimens, 101, 1125, 1537

Offences:
and other acts on board aircraft, 1163
of:
damage to property, 1654
drunkenness, statistics, 161, 474, 872, 1271, 1626
relating to motor vehicles, 161, 474, 873, 1271, 1626
Offender(s):
delinquent, treatment of, 176
female, study of, 476
Fugitive:
Act, 368
Bill, 331, 477
within the Commonwealth, 162
homeless discharged, residential provision, 162

1966 pp 1-272, 1967 pp 273-604, 1968 pp 605-990, 1969 pp 991-1402, 1970 pp 1403-1740
100
101

OFF— INDEX 1966-70

Offender(s) (continued):
in Britain, treatment, Information Office pamphlet, 895
probation, 161
reparation by, 1627
treatment, handbook, 1273
Office(s):
buildings, soil and waste pipe systems, 1671
machinery, census of production, 957
shops, and railway premises:
Act, Minister's report, 186, 505, 751, 1155, 1570
certificate of approval, 505, 1155
firefighting equipment, 186
First Aid Order, 505, 1155
Lighting, 1156
means of escape from fire, 1156
training organisations, 505, 1155
staff employment agencies, charges and salaries, 903
supervision, training for, 746
Work, (careers), 1149
Officers(s):
and soldiers, relation to civil life, 733
dress, navy, 194
in receipt of retired pay, list, 1137, 1548
Official:
list of registration officers etc., 154, 466, 861, 1257, 1664
Paid envelopes, H.C. (Services) select committee, 1636
statistics:
British, development, 1130, 1542
studies, 506, 725, 1130, 1542

OGILVIE, L.: Diseases of vegetables, 1117

Oil(s):
and fats, census of production, 957
in Navigable Waters Bill, 1478, 1482, 1483, 1485, 1630
mineral, carcinogenic action, 900
paintings in London Museum, catalogue 1653
pollution:
at sea:
casualties, 1603
convention on prevention, 1605
North Sea*, 1246
of beaches, circular, 890
of the sea, manual on avoidance, 955

OKADA, T.: Diptera from Nepal, 102
Okehampton:
Castle, guide, 1321
geology, 1312

Olaeaceae, 721

Old:
British Museum, 384
houses into new homes, 893
people:
designing for, 1293, 1294
grouped flatlets, 1294
Testament History, illustrations, 100
Wardour Castle, Wiltshire, guide, 912
Old-Babylonian Legal documents, 720
Older houses, Scotland, 934
Oldham Corporation Act, 79
OLDROYD, H.:
African Asilidae, 1537
Genus Rhipidocephala, 101
Insects and their world, 104
Olive Oil*, 850, 1606
Ollerton, geology of the country around, 906

OMAN, C.:
English Silversmith's Work, 266
The Golden Age of Hispanic Silver, 1396
Ombudsman, see Parliamentary Commissioner
Ommatophoca rossi, 1662

On the Water. In the Water, 921
O'NEILL, B. H. St. J.. Deal Castle, 201
Onions, advisory leaflet, 88

Oolites:
and limestone, 386
Yorkshire, stratigraphy and palaeogeography, 386

Open:
drained joints, 523
fires and convectors, installing, 1320
general:
export licences, see Export licences
import licence, 569
University:
Education and Science select committee, 1635
gifts, 1721
Planning Committee report, 1146
Opera and Ballet in the U.K., 1123
Operational research, models and government, 966
Operations and industrial relations at Heathrow, disruption, 1571
Operatives in the building industry, 864
Operators as instructors, training and use, 1157
Ophidiasterids, 387
Ophiodermatids, 723
Ophiotrichids, 723
Ophiuroidea, 723, 1339
Ophthalmic services, supplementary, 472, 867
Opiliaceae, 729

Opportunity(ies) in the:
East Midlands, 1145
professions, industry, and commerce, 747

Orbits, perturbed, calculation of, for resonant extraction from Nimrod, 923
Orchard sprayers, 1525
Orchestral resources of G.B., 1527
Orchidaceae, 729
Orders:
by Her Majesty, pensions etc., 717, 540, 869, 1267, 1622
in Council:
Health and Social Security, 1267, 1622
Pensions, 217, 540, 870
Privy Council, 200-1, 911, 1668
prerogative, 520, 911, 1320, 1668
Ordnance:
and small arms, census of production, 1371
Survey:
annual report, 514, 907, 1313
maps and the National reference system, 907
retriangulation of G.B., 906
transverse mercator projection, 1666
Ordovician trilobite faunas, 386, 1126
Organ(s):
Transplants Bill, 1072
fruiting, Morrison formation, 103
Organic heating, census of production, 186
Organisation of Secondary Education, 1561
Organochlorine pesticides, 1146
Origins of:
chintz, 1736
goods, false indications*, 1596
Orkney:
and Shetland, mineral resources, 1312
Educational Trust (Amendment) Scheme, 1313
Islands, geophysical surveys, 1311
ORMOND, D. R.: House of Wonder, 1310
ORMOND, R. and M.: Great poets, 1310
Orthochlorobenzylidene Malononitrile, 1622
Orthogonal Polynomials, 1657
Orthoptera, 722, 1125, 1537

OSBORNE WHITE, H. J.: Geology of the Isle of Wight, 204
Oscar II Coast, Graham Land, geology, 1312, 1663
O.S.R. 19, 505
see also Offices, Shops, and Railway premises
Osteoglossomorpha, 1539
Ostracod fauna, 383

Ostracoda:
Bathonian, 386, 1126
Cretaceous, 100
Middle jurassic, 102
New British Albion, 102
Ostrea:
edulis, 93, 1524
juvenile, 1524

Otters, Protection Bill, 1074

Oune and Nene basin, drift sequence and sub-glacial topography, 1664
Outer space:
exploration and use, 158, 851
rescue of astronauts and return of objects*, 850, 1246
Outfitting trade, pay of workers, 510
Outlawries, (No. 2) Bill, 668
Outlook, report and review of the British Film Institute, 99, 383, 719
Out-patient(s):
arrangements, hospital, 470
department:
dental department, 1618
hospital service, 1615
organisation and design, 535
Output budgeting:
and macro-economics, 1561
for Department of Education and Science, 1561
Overalls, and mens' shirts, underwear, etc., census of production, 958
Overhead electric lines, danger from, 520
Overseas:
Aid:
Act, 77, 704
accounts, 515, 1314
Bill, 5, 29, 46, 48, 50, 164, 668
estimates committee, 878
select committee on, 1636
and Other Clergy (Ministry and Ordination) Measure, 390
Development:
Indus Basin Development Fund*, 145
Ministry of, publications, 195-6, 514-15, 907-8, 1313-15, 1666-7
Tarbela Development Fund*, 851
work in hand, 515
Geological survey, 195
Geology and Mineral resources, 514, 1312, 1663
Representation, Review Committee, 1245
Research publications, 196, 515, 907, 1268
Resources Development Act(s), 1112
accounts, 196, 515, 1314
Bill, 997, 1065, 1073, 1275

1966 pp 1-272, 1967 pp 273-604, 1968 pp 605-990, 1969 pp 991-1402, 1970 pp 1403-1740
102
103

OVE-PIC | 1966-70

Overseas (*continued*):
Service:
guide, 1314
Malawi*, 851
(Pensions Supplement):
Regulations and the Pensions Increase Act, 514
(Special Provisions) Regulations, S.I. select committee, 167
Zambia*, 851
Surveys, directorate, annual report, 514, 907, 1314, 1667
Trade:
Accounts of U.K., 239, 573, 956, 1370, 1714
report, 240, 574, 958, 1372, 1715
statistics:
guide to classification, 1547
U.K., 1714
Overtime working in Britain, 919

OWEN, E. F.: Brachiopods, 722, 1538
Ownership and management, housing in new towns, 893

Oxford:
City of, Provisional Order Act, 79
Bill, 50
School Development Project, designing for science, 743
Oxfordshire:
census, 153
household and farm inventories (1550–1590), 159
sample census, 468, 1259
Oxygen therapy, uses and dangers, 1335

Oystercatchers, 93, 379, 1524
Oysters, 710, 1524

Ozone, in presence of nitrous fumes, 1153

P

PAGEL, B. E. J.:
analysis of:
Cool Halo Subdwarf HD 25329, 529
Halo Red-Giant, 206
Paint(s):
and printing ink, census of production, 1371
Childrens' clothing, household textiles, and proprietary medicines, distributors' margins, 903
emulsion, how to use, 201
new types, 220
Painted Ceilings of Scotland, 202
Painting(s):
asbestos cement, 521, 523
Egyptian tomb, 720
Ethiopian manuscript, 1123
metal(s):
in buildings:
coatings, 220
iron and steel, 220
non-ferrous, 220
surfaces, preparation, 201
metalwork, 521
new plaster and cement, 201
of the Sikhs, 266
oil, in the London Museum, 1653
South Italian vase, 100
walls, 1671
woodwork, 201, 912, 1322
Paisley College of Technology (Amendment) Scheme, 1679
Pakistan:
select committee on Overseas Aid, 1637
War Graves*, 1254, 1610
Palace of Westminster:
additional accommodation, H.C. (Services) select committee, 1283
telephone services, H.C. (Services) select committee, 882
Palaemon serratus, 1120, 1524
Paleogeography. Yorkshire oolites, 386
Palaeoniscoid fishes, 386
Palaeoniscoidea-Schuppen, 722
Palaeontology:
and stratigraphy, Dorset clay, 386
early history, 387
fossil plants of British carboniferous rocks, 195, 1312, 1663
Palexorista Townsend, 386
PALMER, A. (Chairman): Culham Laboratory, 884
PALMER, C. E.: Blackgame, 860
PALMER, D. R.: radial velocities etc. of, 663
Bright Northern A Stars, 920
PALMER, G.: teleost fishes, 1539
Panama, visas*, 145, 1246
Paper:
and:
board, census of production, 1371
Paper Products Industry Training Board, 1155, 1570
Industry, pulpwood supply, 1255
Paraguay:
trade and payments*, 458, 1246, 1247, 1606
visas*, 458, 1247
Parasites:
in frogs, 723
of:
O-group plaice, 710
poultry, 88
whiting gall bladder, 374

Parent/teacher relations in Primary Schools, 744
Parish Councils and Burial Authorities (Miscellaneous Provisions) Act, 1516, 1645
Bill, 1409, 1473, 1479, 1481, 1630
PARKER, A. E.: Geophysical memoir, 1656
PARKER, R. R.: *Caligus longicaudatus*, 723
PARKIN, P. H.: London noise survey, 914
Parking garages, multi-storey, 490
Parks, Royal, bird life in, 202, 913, 1670
Parliament:
and control of university expeditions, Public Accounts special report, 483
Bill, 607, 169, 1003
British, Information Office pamphlet, 495, 895
dissolution, proclamation, 1686
(No. 2) Bill, 671
(No. 4) Bill, 1072
(No. 5) Bill, 1072
(No. 6) Bill, 995
of Scotland, index of short titles to current Acts, 542
publication of proceedings, Joint Committee on, 1004, 1642
Parliamentary:
Commissioner:
Act, 369
(Amendment Bill), 666
Bill, 46, 48, 50, 52, 275, 277, 278, 325, 328, 335, 477
for Local Government (Scotland) Bill, 1071
reports, 479, 877, 1276, 1280, 1631
select committee reports, 478, 1284, 1637
debates, *see* H.C. and H.L.
elections, *see* Elections
Papers:
delivery to Members etc., H.C. (Services) select committee, 1282
sessional index, 164, 1276, 1631
titles and contents, 164, 886, 1276, 1641
Parole Board report, 1272, 1628
Scotland, 1681
Privileges Committee, H.C., 883
PARRY, DR T. (Chairman): Libraries, 599
Partially hearing children, 413
Particle:
accelerator, construction:
effect of radiation, 922
of magnets for, 1330
beams, separated, 922
heavy, *see* Heavy particles
production by the thermodynamic model, 923
Particulars of dealers in securities and of Unit Trusts, 239, 753, 956, 1370, 1714
Partitions, airborne sound insulation, 222
PASLEY-TYLER, CMDR H.: Defence research, 884
Passenger(s):
at London's Airports, origin and destination survey, 1714
fares and freight charges, North of Scotland, Orkney, and Shetland Shipping Company Ltd., 902
transport in G.B., 576, 962, 1375, 1718
PASSMORE, DR. R. (Chairman): Nutrient allowance, 1267
Pastoral Measure, 726
Patent(s):
designs and trade marks, 239, 573, 956, 1370, 1714
in the Common Market, 1714
Rolls, Elizabeth I, 203
system and patent law, 1697
PATERSON, I. B.: Old red sandstone ignimbrites, 1312
Pathology:
department, hospital, 156, 470
organisation, management, and methods 866
Patients:
attending day hospitals, 1269
Ely Hospital, Cardiff, ill-treatment inquiry, 1267
in psychiatric beds, 472
PATON, T. A. L. (Chairman): Large industrial sites, 1661
PATTERSON, C.:
British Wealden Sharks, 102
Caudal skeleton of pholidopherid fishes, 722
Cretaceous berycoid fishes, 386
PAU reports, 1734
PAUL, C. R. C.: Silurian cystoids, 383
Pawnbrokers Bill, 1479
PAWSEY, R. G., Grey mould in forest nurseries, 1255
Paxillaceae, 1674
Pay:
and:
condition etc. of workers, *see* specific industry or employment
Pensions Service, 124, 1144
maintenance workers of bus companies, 1306
of:
Armed Forces, standing references: 1657
Senior Officers, 1658
Separation Allowances, 1658
University Teachers, standing reference, 1657
Warrants, Army, 116, 400, 734, 1139, 1549
Payment by results system, 902

Payrolling, decimal currency booklet, 1547
PAYNE, HON. MR JUSTICE (Chairman): Enforcement of Judgment debts, 1304

Pea(s), 1117
Bean, and Clover weevils, 88
PEACOCK, PROF. A. (Chairman): Orchestral resources, 1527
PEACOCK, J. D.: Geology of the Elgin district, 906
Pearl Assurance Company Ltd., terms and conditions of employment, 902
PEARSALL, W. H. (Editor): Lake District, 1134
PEARSON, LORD (Chairman):
Industrial Courts Act, disputes, 183, 501, 750, 1568
Law Reform Committee, 189, 1655
Peat:
Congress, Second International, 710
surveys, Scottish, 87, 710
Peculiar A Stars, origin, 921
Pecuniary Interests of Local Authority Members, circular, 487
PEDDIE, LORD (Chairman): Prices and Incomes Board, 1658
Peebleshire, ancient and historical monuments, 521
PEERS, SIR C.: Rievaulx Abbey, guide, 522
Pelorovis oldowayensis, 386
Pembrokeshire:
census, 153
sample census, 468, 1259
Penal system in E. and W., Royal Commission, 527
Penalties, non-custodial and semi-custodial, 1626
Pennies, Anglo-Saxon, 1535
Pennine Way, 1134
Pension(s):
Air Force Order, 217, 540
allocation, National Health Service Superannuation, 1619
and National Insurance, annual report, 217
Army:
Order, 540
Warrant, 115
(Increase) Act, 1112
Bill, 992, 1065, 1071, 1275
Circulars, 170, 890, 1291, 1293
overseas service, 1314
pensioner's guide, 250, 1133
Naval Forces Order, 217, 540
Occupational schemes, 250
police, 202
widows, 212
retirement, 540
Pension(s) (*continued*):
scheme:
firemen:
allocation, 161
Order, 161
new, 1266
occupational, 1267
Supplement Regulations and Pensions Increase Act, guide to Overseas Service, 514, 1314
Under Teachers' Superannuation Regulations, 413
War, 1268
Warrants, Army, *see* Army Pensions Warrant
The Way Forward, 1267
see also Pay and pensions
Pensioners('s):
guide to Pensions (Increase) Act, 250, 1133
occupational, benefit and contribution credits, 867
retirement, financial circumstances, 214
War, 217, 540, 870, 1622
PENSTON, M. V.: Collapse of an isothermal gas sphere, 206
People:
and planning, 1297
in prison, E. and W., 1271
with epilepsy, 1622
Perambulators, hand-trucks, etc., census of production, 958
PERCIVAL, V.: The Duke of Wellington, 1396
Performances by children, law, 872
Periodical Publications (Protection of Subscribers) Bill, 1072, 1479
PERKS, J. C.: Chepstow Castle, guide, 522
PERKS, W. (Chairman): criminal statistics, 475
Perlitic obsidian, devitrification and volumetric relationships, 1664
Perry, census of production, 957
Persian Gulf Gazette, 145, 459, 851, 1247, 1606
Persian:
manuscripts, B.M.:
catalogue, 100
handlist, 720
miniature painting, large picture book, 599
Personal:
injuries litigation, committee report, 899
Records (Computers) Bill, 998
Persons acquiring citizenship of the U.K. and Colonies, statistics, 162, 476, 874, 1273, 1628
PERTH, LORD (Chairman): Crown Estate Commissioners, 1135

Peru:
air services*, 145, 1247
loan*, 459, 851
technical co-operation*, 147
Pest(s):
and diseases:
plant, 381, 717, 1525
raspberry, Scotland, 1115
Control, chemicals for, census of production, 957
Infestation:
Laboratory report, 86, 373, 709, 1115, 1519
Research, 86, 373, 709, 1115, 1519
narcissus, 1521
sugarbeet, 1117
Pesticides:
and other toxic chemicals, 1145
persistent organochlorine, 1146
PESTON, M:
elementary ideas of Game Theory, 856, 1377
statistical decision theory, 966
Pet Animals Act 1951 (Amendment) Bill, 1073, 1479
Peterborough:
expansion proposals, 171
new town, Royal Commission, 1326
PETHERBRIDGE, P.: Solar heat gain calculations, 1672
Petition of Irish Peers, 5
Petrography and chemistry, arenaceous rocks, 1312
Petrol(eum):
(Consolidation) Act 1928, construction and licensing conditions, 873
distribution depots and major installations, 873
filling stations:
and motels, 1294
storage of cans, drums, etc., 873
Industry Training Board, 753, 1155, 1570
(Production) Act, accounts, 519, 1319, 1694
Petrological-mineralogical code for computer use, 1663
Petrology of:
Graham Coast, Graham Land, 383
Lord Howe Island, 1539
PETTITT, J. M.: Spores and pollen, exine structure, 386
Pevensey Castle, souvenir guide, 1670

PG:
information series, 262
reports, 263–4, 596–7, 981–3, 1394, 1734

Phaneropterinae, index catalogue, 722
Pharmaceutical:
industry, relations with National Health Service, 472
Pharmaceutical (*continued*):
preparations, census of production, 957
service, hospital, 1622
Pharmacy:
and Poisons Act, 1933, application to sell, 1271
arrangements, hospital, 864
(careers), 499, 1564
department, hospital, 1615
PHELPS BROWN PROF. E. H.: Labour in building and civil engineering, inquiry, 753
PHILLIPS, A.: Fountains Abbey, 912
PHILLIPS, A. H.: Computer peripherals and typesetting, 929, 1683
PHILLIPS ROSS, J. R. P.: Polyzoa, 102
Phocidae, 1662
Phoenix Assurance Company Act, 1114
Pholidophoridae, triassic and liassic, 102
Phosgene in the air, detection, 750
Photogrammetrists Training and qualifications, 1314
Photogrammetry:
air surveys, 1314
automation, Commonwealth conference, 1314
Photographic:
instruments, census of production, 1371
Measures of polarization of Starlight in h and x persei, 921
Photography and Cinematography (careers), 747
Photoheliographic results, 206, 920, 1327
Photometer, iris, semi-automatic, 207
Photometric standards and the unit of light, 1352
Photometry:
Fabry, 206
of cepheids, 529
Three-colour, 206, 207, 921, 1327
Phthiraptera, 1538
Phycitinae, 1538
Physical:
education:
in the Primary School, 927
Secondary School design, 125
sciences, 128, 415, 745, 1147, 1563
training in the army, 399, 733, 1138
PHYSICK, J.: Designs for English Sculpture (1680–1860), 1396
Physics for Princes, 1329
Physiotherapist and Remedial Gymnast, (careers), 747

Picidae, 723
PICKEN, C.: Chebyshev series for Bessel functions of fractional order, 222
PICKLES, D. C.: Heat transfer through low pressure helium gas, 531
Pick-up balers, 94

1966-70 | PIC-PRE

PIC— INDEX 1966–70

Picnic sites, 1134
Picture books:
large, 266, 599, 985, 1396, 1735
small, 599, 1396
Pier and Harbour Orders Confirmation Acts and Bills, *see respective towns*
Pietro Bembo's Library, B.M., 100
Pig(s):
fattening houses, partially slatted floors, 512
housing in one pen from birth to slaughter, 905
management, 715
nutrient requirements, 373
Pigeons and doves of the world, 724
Pile, choosing a type, building digest, 913
PILKINGTON, SIR H. (Chairman):
Agricultural education, 126
Education for industry and commerce, 744
PILKINGTON, LORD (Joint Chairman), Technical College resources, 1146
Pilkington Bros. Ltd, dispute, 1571
Pilot balloons, upper wind measurement, 900
Pilots':
licence:
examination for, 234, 573, 956
private, 569, 959
professional, aeroplanes and helicopters, 1370
student, 569, 959
pay, BOAC, 903
weather radar, 1716
Pi-Meson final states, kinematical analysis, 208
Pine:
billets, close piled, drying and scaling, 1612
lodgepole, 939
looper moth, 151
martens, 859
PING, J. W., investigations into the affairs of:
Jon-Landor Ltd, 236
Langkon North Borneo Rubber Ltd, 236
Selama (Malaya) Rubber Estates Ltd, 236
Pipe(s):
buried, rigid, loading charts for design, 524
Pitch fibre, drain and sewer, 521
plastic, cold water supply, 1320
PVC, 521
sewers, underground, design and construction, 175
system, soil and waste:
housing, 1671
office buildings, 1671
Pipe(s) (*continued*):
unreinforced concrete and clayware, high strength bedding for, 624
Pipelines, buried, external loads, 1672
PIPER, J.: Watercolour of Caernarvon Castle, reproduction, 914
Pipunculidae, 101
Pisanello's medallion of Emperor John VIII Palaeogus, 100
Pitcairn:
Arms, 1574
Henderson, Ducie, and Oeno Islands, Instructions OIC, 201
Royal Instructions OIC, 1669
Pitch fibre drain and sewer pipes, 521
Pitlochry Freshwater Fisheries Laboratory, 1520
PITT, L. J.: Polyzoa of some British jurassic clays, 1126
Pittenweem Harbour:
Bill, 337
Order Confirmation Act, 370
Pittosporaceae, 112

PLA:
calibration measurements, 922
final progress report, 1676
progress report, 208, 530, 923, 1329, 1676
Place:
names and population, Scotland, 468–9
of Marriage Bill, 47
Plaice:
investigations in Scottish waters, 374
O-group, parasites, 710
Planktonic foraminifera, 102
PLANNER, C. W.: Transporting Beam from 50 MeV PLA for injection into Nimrod, 531
Planning:
and transport, Leeds approach, 1375
appeals, transfer for determination by inspectors, 1645
applications, statistics of decisions, 175, 494, 894
Blight:
and Worsenment Bill, 1478
circular, 1644
bulletins, 493
control:
enforcement, 1291
of radio masts, circular, 889
decisions, E. and W. statistics, 1297
farm business, 374
for leisure, outdoor physical recreation, 1262
investment and town centre redevelopment, circular, 170
payments (War Damage) Schemes, accounts, 1298

INDEX 1966–70 —POL

Planning (*continued*):
permissions:
time-limit, circular, 1291
use of conditions, circular, 888
public participation, 1297
Plans in Scottish Record Office, descriptive list, 537
Plant(s):
and soil, effect of air pollution, 373
breeding and genetics, progress review, 728
diseases and pests, 380, 717, 1525
fossil, 1663
Health Act, 369
Bill, 10, 52, 168
material, hot-water treatment, 376
pathology, 94, 381, 717, 1121, 1525
poisonous, British, 711
Pot, bulletin, 1521
Protection:
European and Mediterranean Organisation, 1247
of new varieties, 1247
South-east Asia and Pacific*, 851, 1247
Plant Varieties and Seeds Gazette, 94, 381, 717, 1112, 1526
Plantations on medieval rigg and furr strips, York East Forest, 465
Plaster(s):
and cement, new, painting, 201
gypsum, used in building, 201
mixes for inside work, 201
Plasterboard:
dry linings, 521
prices, 1308
Plastering on building boards, 1320
Plastics:
application and durability, 220
cellular, for building, 913
materials, census of production, 1371
moulding and fabrication, census of production, 1372
pipes for cold water supply, 1320
Plate, census of production, 958
Plating and testing goods vehicles, 961–2, 1717
Platypezidae, 101
PLAYFAIR, MAJ. GEN. I. S. O.: Destruction of the Axis Forces in Africa, 104
Play-groups:
Bill, 667
(No. 2) Bill, 338
Playing fields and hard surface areas, 125
Plecoptera, type specimens, 1537
Plectambonitaceae, 1538
PLEDGE, H. T.: Science since 1500, 208
PLENDERLEITH, H. J.: Preservation of leather bookbinding, 385
Pleuronectes platessa, 710
Ploughing practice, Forestry Commission, 1612
PLOWDEN, LADY (Chairman): Children and their Primary schools, 412
Plumbing:
single stack, 912
with stainless steel, 523
Plunging magnet system for the Nimrod extracted proton beam, 209
Plywood, strength properties, 554, 1351

Pneumoconiosis:
and allied occupational chest diseases, diagnosis and benefit claims, 540, 1267
byssinosis, and miscellaneous diseases benefit scheme, 866
decision of the Commissioners, 866
digest of statistics, 198, 516, 909, 1690
Poisoning, acute, hospital treatment, 865
Poisonous plants, British, 711
Points for businessmen, decimal currency booklet, 1136
Poland:
Consular convention, 421
Health Services*, 454, 1606
science and technology*, 853, 1247
Polarization of starlight in h and x Persei, photographic measures, 921
Polecats, 1612
POLHILL, R. M.:
Berberidaceae, 112
Ulmaceae, 112
Police:
Act, 1112
Bill, 1003, 1076
objections to proposed amalgamation, 161, 474, 873, 1271
(Amendments) (No. 3) Regulations, S.I. select committee, 482
(careers), 747
(Discipline) (Scotland) Regulations:
discipline form, 535
investigation form, 535
drivers' manual, 1273
estimates committee, 165, 483, 1271, 1277
in N.I., 1313
manpower equipment, and efficiency reports, 474
of the Metropolis, *see* Metropolitan Police
pension form, 212
(Scotland):
Act, 77, 260
Bill, 9, 11, 34, 46, 50, 52, 164, 292, 477
(No. 2) Bill, 281, 338, 485
Objections to amalgamation, inquiries, 928
Examination Board, question papers, 535

POL— INDEX 1966–70

Police (*continued*):
Service:
in Britain, Information Office pamphlet, 1299
recruitment of people with Higher Education qualifications, 475
Training Centres E. and W., 1626
widows pension form, 212
Polishes, census of production, 957
Political rights of women, convention, 455, 461
Pollution:
air, effects on plants and soil, 373
atmospheric, 556
coastal, 320, 482, 883
fight against, 1647
water, abstracts and research, 556, 940
see also oil pollution
Polyethylene terephthalate:
film(s):
mechanical properties, effect of radiation, 530
tests on circular diaphragms, 208
pressurised membrane fatigue tests, 530
Polystyrene ceiling tiles, fire risks, 1669
Polytechnics and other colleges, plan for, 127
Polyzoa:
British:
jurassic clays, 1126
Marine, nomenclatural index, 1127
cheilostomatous, 103
genera and species, 102
jurassic cheilostomatous, 723
pearl-bearing, 103
Portrane limestone, 102
stylopoma Levinson, 723
West African, 387, 1127
Ponies Act, 1112
Bill, 49, 290, 606, 611, 614, 670, 996, 1065, 1275
PONT, A. C.: *Dichaetomyiini* Emden, 1125
Pontederiaceae, 729
Pontobdellinae, 103
POOLE, E. G.:
geology of the country around:
Market Harborough, 1312
Nantwich and Whitchurch, 514
POOLE, J. B.: Solid-liquid separation, 223
POPE, J. D.: Cassegrain spectrograph of Yapp reflector at Herstmonceux, 206
Population:
annual estimates GRO, 154, 467, 861, 1257, 1664
Scotland, 154, 468, 863, 1259, 1613
Censuses and Surveys, Office of:
list of registration officers, 1664
official list, 1664
publications, 1663–5
see also General Register Office
forecast, South-east study, circular, 170
Population (*continued*):
projections for the South-east, studies on, 168
radiation risk to, from environmental contamination, 190
Science and Technology select committee, 1639
tables, GRO, 154, 467, 861, 1257, 1665
Porcelain Figures, small picture book, 1396
Pork, and live cattle, sheep and swine, revocation of export licences, 1715
Porpoises, Stranded, identification guide, 104, 1124
Port(s):
Bill, 1077, 1473, 1481, 1630
of London:
Act, 371, 706
Authority Revision Order, 286
reorganisation, 1375
statistics, digest, 194, 513, 905, 1311, 1662
Transport Industry:
Court of Inquiry, 1568
Dock Workers (Regulation of Employment) Act, inquiry, 186
Portable skid-resistance tester, instructions for using, 1376
Portbury new dock not authorised, 242
Portering services, hospital, index, 156
Portland cement, prices, 510, 1308
Portrait(s):
Beaton, 905
Gallery, *see* National Portrait Gallery
Tudor and Jacobean, 1310
Portsmouth Corporation Act, 371, 1114
Portugal:
atomic energy*, 852, 1248, 1606, 1607
double taxation*, 760, 1248
local air service*, 145
Post Office(s):
Act, 1112
Bill, 664, 667, 996, 998, 1000, 1001, 1065, 1072, 1075, 1275
1292
loans, 250, 584, 970, 1382, 1724
and streets, London, 197
(Borrowing Powers) Act, 369
Bill, 52, 277
charges, 1307
(Data Processing Service) Act, 369
Bill, 285, 332, 336, 338, 477
examination papers, 107
Guide, 197, 516, 908, 1315
in the U.K., 197, 908, 1668
London Gazette, 1340
prospects, 197, 516, 908, 1315
publications, 196–7, 515–16, 908–9, 1315–16
reorganisation, 516
report and accounts, 197, 516, 649, 1315, 1668

INDEX 1966–70 —PRE

Post Office(s) (*continued*):
Savings Bank:
Act, 77
accounts, 250, 584, 970, 1382
Bill, 2, 43, 164
Fund accounts, 585, 970, 1315, 1382
Investment accounts, 516, 908, 1316
Scheme, 1685
select committee on Nationalised Industries, 481, 483
(Subway) Act, 77
Bill, 4, 46, 48, 49, 164
Users' National Council, 1668
see also Posts and Telecommunications
Post Surrender Tasks, Earl Mountbatten's report, 1138
Postal:
addresses, 197, 516, 1316
and Proxy Voting Bill, 49
parcels, Universal Postal Union*, 197
Postneonatal deaths, 1622
Posts and Telecommunications, Ministry of, publications, 1667–8
Pot plants, bulletin, 1521
Potash for farm crops, 375
Potato(s):
and Tomato blight, 88
crisping, building for storing in stillages, 86
crops, register, 87, 374, 710, 1116, 1520
gangrene, 89
harvesting with:
complete harvesters, 716
diggers, 381
storage buildings, 85, 86
Trials and Collections at East Craigs, key to, 87, 374, 709, 1116
tuber eelworm, 88
wart disease, 88
Pottery:
American studio, 985
census of production, 1371
dated post medieval, 188
industry, pay and conditions of employment of workers, 1658
manufacture, (careers), 1149
POTTS, P. G. (Chairman): Action on the Banwell Committee's recommendations on building contracts, 511
Poultry:
aids to management, 1120
breeding, sex linkage, 89
external parasites, 88
housing and the environment, 1521
keeping, business control, 376
nutrition, 376
Research Centre report, 1115
Slaughter Act, 369
Bill, 48, 49, 278, 332, 335, 478
worms in, 88
Pout, Norway
POWELL, A. L. T.: van de Held curves of growth, 1328
Power(ed):
consuming apparatus, *see* Electrical wiring installations, etc.
hand-tools:
electric, 1320
pneumatic, 1320
safety and maintenance, 1669
Ministry of:
publications, 198–200, 516–20, 909–11, 1316–19
safety circulars, 200, 520
statistical digest, 200, 520, 911
see also Technology, Ministry of
of Attorney, Law Commission, 1654
press(es), 186
toolsetting and tool design, 753
stations, inquiry, 1319
to fly, 208

Practice Leaflets for Solicitors, 898
PRATT, N. M.: Photographic measures of the polarization of starlight in h and x Persei, 921
Prawns, 1120, 1524
Prayer Book (Further Provisions):
Measure, 726
(No. 2) Measure, 618
Precious metals, refining, census of production, 958
Precision approach radar, 1714
Pregnancy, Medical Termination:
(Abortion (No. 2)), Bill, 287
Bill, 47, 49, 285, 332, 336, 339, 477
Prehistoric, Roman, and Medieval sites, 202, 524, 914, 1321, 1670
Prek Thnot (Cambodia) Power and Irrigation Development Project*, 1162
Premium:
Bonds, 218, 541, 930, 1336, 1683
supplements, 1337
Savings Bonds, 217, 218
PRENTICE, J. E.: Lower carboniferous trilobites, 386
Prerogative Orders in Council, 520–1, 911, 1320, 1668
Prescription and limitation of Actions, reform of law, 1682
Preservation of:
fruit and vegetables, domestic, 89
historic buildings and areas, 1294
timber and metal, 1121
Press brakes:
friction clutch, safety devices, 1566
safety in use, 1156
Pressed Steel Fisher Ltd., Industrial Court inquiry, 750
Pressure:
steam sterilizers, precautions, 866
vessels, inquiry, 1352

Preston, Harris College, 125
Prevention of:
  Crime (Scotland) Bill, 339
  Fraud (Investments) Act, dealers in securities, and Unit Trusts, 239
Preventive medicine, handbook, 114
Prices and Incomes:
  Act, 77, 369, 704
    Bill, 8, 46, 48, 50, 51, 164, 615, 662, 667, 668, 876
    1966 (Amendment) Bill, 336
    (No. 2) Bill, 284, 285, 332, 337, 338, 477, 615
    Rent increases of Local Authority housing, 890
  National Board for:
    general report, 193, 510, 902
    reports 192-3, 510-11, 901-3, 1306-8, 1657-8
  Policy:
    after June 30th 1967, 412, 488
    Early Warning system, 170
    Return to an Order, H.L., 7, 124, 168
    standstill, period of severe restraint, 124, 487
Primary:
  aluminium production, 953
  and Secondary Schools, salaries of teachers:
    E. and W., 414, 1147
    registered, Scotland, 1333
  Education:
    Bill, 662
    Wales and Monmouth, 875
  School(s):
    French in, 1333
    inside, 413
    mathematics in, 128, 1328
    parent/teacher relations, 744
    safety in, 1680
    (Scotland):
      arts and crafts, 925
      implications of going metric, 925
      physical education, 927
    survey, 1679
Prime Ministers' Papers (1801-1902), 871
Principles of control, new construction by direct labour, 1296
Printed:
  maps, charts, and plans, B.M., excerpt from catalogues, 384
  matter and film for export to Southern Rhodesia, export licence, 236
Printing:
  and publishing:
    Economic Development Committee's report, 1661
    Industry Training Board, 1155, 1571
    manpower Papers, 1570
    of newspapers and periodicals, census of production, 1372

Printing (continued):
  crafts (careers), 1564
  graphic reproduction processes, booklet, 180
  in a competitive world, 1661
  Industry, Web-Offset machines, Court of Inquiry, 501
Prison(s):
  and Borstal After-care, annual report, 161
  Borstals, and Detention Centres, estimates committee, 480, 878
  Department:
    Home Office report, 872
    publications, 200, 520, 911, 1319, 1668
    report on the work of, statistical tables, 162, 475, 874, 1273, 1626, 1628
  escapes and security, inquiry, 162
  in Scotland, 213, 535, 818, 1681
Prison Service Journal, 200, 520, 911, 1319-20, 1668
Prisoners, long term, in maximum security, 875
Private:
  building in Scotland, cost, 1677
  International Law, Hague Conference, 1248
  investigators Bill, 1073
  land mobile radio services, 908
  Legislation (Scotland) Procedure, 213-14, 537, 929, 1335-6, 1682
  mobile radio services, 197, 908
  motoring, E. and W., 1261
  Places of Entertainment (Licencing) Act, 369
    Bill, 11, 275, 277, 335
Privilege(s):
  and Immunities*, 852, 1248
  Committee reports, 169, 480, 880, 1280, 1634
  in civil proceedings, Law Reform report, 507
Privy:
  Council:
    of Scotland, register, 929
    Orders and Prerogative Orders in Council 200-1, 520-1, 911, 1320, 1668
    Registers preserved in PRO, 525, 915
    Seal of Scotland, Register, 537
Probation:
  and After-Care:
    Department, report on work, 162, 1273
    Directory, 475, 873, 1626, 1627
    amended lists, 873, 1271-2
  areas, directory of, 160
  Grant (Deduction) Regulations, 161

Probation (continued):
  Hostels:
    and Homes, Approved, 160
    in Scotland, 213
  National study, 162
  of offenders, England, 161
  Officers, 160
  Service, Scotland, forms, 536
Probationers in their social environment, 1273
Problems:
  arising from use of asbestos, 750
  of young school leavers, 1627
Procedure:
  H.C. select committee, 166, 482, 883, 1284, 1637-8
  H.L., 169, 486, 887, 1289
Proceedings Against Estates Act, 1516
  Bill, 1404, 1481
Process plant, expert committee report, 1353
Proclamations, 1341, 1686, 1687, 1688
Proctor, F. (Chairman): Dairy floors, 379
Production:
  Census of, report, 567, 957-8, 1371-2 and summary tables, 1715
  planning and control, 194, 904
Productivity:
  agreements, 510, 1307
  and pay, period of severe restraint, 193
  handbook of advisory services, 512
  prices and incomes:
    N.E.D.O., 512, 904
    policy, 742, 1155,
    water rates and charges, 890
Productoids, silicified, 103
Professional:
  collaboration in designing buildings, 914
  engineers, survey, 1695
  pilots' licences, aeroplanes and helicopters, 1370
  scientists, survey, 1695
  Sport, (careers), 1149
  Surveyors, training and qualifications, 1314
Professions, Industry, and Commerce, opportunities in, 747, 1149
Profits Tax:
  appeals to the High court, 1300
  provisions of the Finance Acts, 178, 306, 1300
  supplement, 1650
Programme(s):
  Analysis Unit, UKAEA, 1394
  for DWBA, 530
  Jester, general statistics, 530
  Rough digitising "Merge", 1676
Project(s):
  co-ordination, 1308
  in practice, central committee on English, 1678

Project Magazine, 127, 414, 745, 1147, 1562
Promotion of exports, estimates committee, 878
Proper motions:
  in the:
    field of:
      Clusters, M67 II and III, 1327
      NGC 6522, 206
    region of the Hyades, 206
  of RR Lyrae variables, 920
Property:
  maintenance management, 1672
  settled, estate duty, 1381
Proposed 300 GeV accelerator, 745
Proprietary:
  medicines, Prices and Incomes Board, 903
  preparations, revision of system of classification, 865
Protection:
  from Dogs Bill, 1072
  of:
    Animals Bill, 1074
    Birds Act, 369
      Bill, 6, 8, 52, 283, 309, 332, 336, 477
    Consumers (Trade Descriptions) Bill 1
    the Environment, fight against pollution, 1647
    house purchasers, 1293
    Otters Bill, 1074
    Pension Rights Bill, 1478, 1481
    persons exposed to ionising radiations in research and teaching, 748
Protective:
  clothing for workers on construction sites
  Duties, imported goods, 397
  screens and enclosures, building leaflet, 1320
Protestant Telegraph, Privileges committee, 480
Proton:
  beam, Nimrod extracted, plunging magnet for, 209
  -proton scattering at high energies, 1330
  synchrotron:
    Nimrod A 7 GeV, 194 with beam loading control of the RF, 923
Protozoa:
  British freshwater ciliated, 1354
  Gromia oviformis, 1127
Provident Societies Bill, 49
Provincial Agricultural Economics Service, 376
Provision of Milk and Meals amending Regulations, S.I. select committee, 885
Provisional Collection of Taxes Act, 704
  Bill, 287, 340, 485
Proxy Voting Bill, 49

Prudential Assurance Company Ltd, terms and conditions of employment, 902
Prysig Field Barrack Building, guide, 1670

Pseudococcidae, 1125
Pseudorhynchus Serville, 1125
Psychiatric:
  hospitals:
    activities, 870
    and units, E. and W., in-patients statistics, 1268, 1623
    E. and W., facilities and services, 1269, 1623
  nursing today and tomorrow, 865
  report series, 1623
Psychiatry:
  biochemical research, 1655
  forensic, 1334
Psychidae, 385, 724
Psychologists in education services, 745

Pteridophyta, 1546
Pterocarpus angiolensis, 196
Pteromalidae, 1126

Public:
  Accounts:
    Committee, return, 1724
  Defence:
    (Air) Votes, 250, 584, 970, 1382, 1724
    (Army) Votes, 250, 585, 970, 1383, 1724
    (Navy) Votes, 250, 585, 971, 1383, 1724
    Excess Votes, 480, 1280, 1634
      and Atomic Energy Authority, 165
    reports from committee, 165, 166, 480, 1280, 1726
    special reports, 483, 880
    Treasury Minutes, 251, 586, 972
    Virement, 165, 480, 880, 1280, 1634
    Bills, 165, 479, 877, 1276
    return, 1631
  Boards, list of members, 250, 585, 971, 1383, 1724
  Building:
    and:
      common governmental services, Supply estimates, 1725
      Works, Ministry of:
        advisory leaflets, 201, 521, 912, 1320, 1669
        circulars, 202
        publications, 201-3, 521-4, 912-15, 1320-3, 1669-73
      programme:
        estimates committee, 878, 1323

Public (continued):
  Business, Standing Orders:
    H.C., 168, 484, 886, 1288
    H.L., 169, 486, 611, 1290, 1643
  cleansing, costing returns, 174, 493, 893
  conveniences, design, circular, 889
  education in Scotland, 534
  Expenditure:
    and Receipts Act, 704
      Bill, 608, 665, 971
    miscellaneous schemes, circular, 170
    new presentation, 1383
    1968-9 and 1969-70, 971
    1968-74, 1383
    planning and control, 124
    selection of unit costs, 971
  General Acts (and Church Assembly Measures), 76-8, 367-9, 703-5, 1110-12, 1514-16
  Health:
    Act:
      (Amendment) Bill, 1065, 1070, 1275
      see also Public Health (Recurring nuisances) Bill
      (Amendment) (No. 2) Bill, 1075
    Building Regulations:
      Circulars, 170, 487, 889, 1643, 1645
      Metric:
        equivalents on dimensions, 893
        values, 1297
      selected decisions, 493
    Circulars, 170, 489, 889, 1291, 1292, 1643
    and medical subjects, 158, 472, 870, 1267, 1622
    (Imported Food) Regulations, circulars, 90-2
    Laboratory Service Act, accounts, 158, 472, 870, 1267, 1622
    (Recurring Nuisances) Act, 1112
      Bill, 996, 1072
      see also Public Health Act (Amendment) Bill
    state of, Chief Medical Officer's report, 158, 472, 869, 1267, 1622
  Income and Expenditure, accounts, 251, 585, 971
  Library Service, Scotland, standards, 1333
    officers agreements, see respective countries
  participation in planning, 1297
  Path Orders, circular, 1281
  petitions, special report, 1281
  purchasing and industrial efficiency, 585

Public (continued):
  Record(s):
    Act, 369
      Bill, 280, 337
    Office:
      Advisory Council's report, 1324
      Calendar of the Patent Rolls, Elizabeth I, 203
      guide to contents, 1324
      handbooks, 203, 915, 1324
      Keeper's annual report, 189, 507, 915, 1324, 1673
      maps and plans, 525
      publications, 203, 525, 915, 1324, 1673
  recreation in National Forests, 859
  Right(s):
    Bill, 5
    of Way Orders Regulation, extinguishment, 1291
  Schools Commission:
    report, 745, 1562
    Scotland, 1562
  Service(s):
    and Armed Forces Pensions: Commission Bill, 334
    Review Bill, 339
    guide, 1536
    overseas, future, 1314
    spending, new policies, 1742
    transport and traffic, 377
    Trustee Office, annual report of the Public Trustee, 203, 525, 915, 1324, 1673
    Utilities Street Work Act, 242
    Works Loans Act, 77, 369
      Bill, 4, 48
      Board, annual report, 251, 585, 971, 1383, 1725
      (No. 2) Bill, 284, 337
  Publication(s):
    available to the public, UKAEA, list, 262
    of Proceedings in Parliament, report, 1004, 1634, 1642
  Published, Bill, 49
PUGH, R. B.: Old Wardour Castle, Wiltshire, guide, 912
PULASKI, W. J.: Sphecidae, 385
Pullorum disease (BWD), 88
Pulpwood supply and the paper industry, 1255
Pulsed magnet command systems, 1330
Pump design, testing and operation, 555
Pupil(s'):
  less able, and modern languages, 1679
  progress records, 1333, 1679
Purchase notices, circular, 1291
PVC:
  drain and sewer pipes

PVC (continued):
  rooflights, 221
  sheeting, self-extinguishing grades, circular, 487

Pyralidae, 1538
Pyrotenax Ltd., Monopolies Commission, 313, 572
Pyzer, H.: Report on Copestoke, Crampton and Co. Ltd., 568

Q

Qatar:
  Contract Law (Amendment) Regulation, 852
  Criminal Procedure (Amendment) Rules, 852
  Dangerous Drugs (Amendment) Regulation, 852
  International Organisations (Immunities and Privileges) Regulations, 852
  Notices, 459, 852
  Penal Code (Amendment) Regulation, 459
  Prison Rules (Amendment) Regulation, 459
  Queen's Regulations, 459
  technical assistance*, 858
  United Nations Children's Fund*, 857
Qualified teachers and other persons in schools, 743
Qualitative studies of buildings, 221
Quantity surveyors, working in metric, 1659
Quarry(ies):
  belt conveyors, 1352
  (Notification of Dangerous Occurrences) (Amendment) Order, 520, 1319
  Vehicle(s):
    Regulations, 1319, 1694
    Requirements, 1352
  See also Mines and quarries
Queen Elizabeth II, poster, 905
Queen's:
  and Lord Treasurer's Remembrancer, 203, 525, 915, 1324, 1673
  Award to Industry:
    London Gazette, 541, 930, 1338, 1685
    Report, 1714
  Birthday Honours Lists, 218, 541, 930, 1339, 1687
  Cottage, Kew, guide, 202

Queen's (*continued*):
Regulations:
and Admiralty Instructions, 123
Army, 116, 399, 733, 1139, 1549
Bahrain Orders, 420, 757
Qatar Orders, 459, 852
Royal Air Force, 114, 398, 731, 1137, 1548
Royal Navy, 123, 411, 735, 1140, 1551
Trucial States Orders, 462
Question:
papers:
Civil Service Commission, 106–7, 390, 726, 1131, 1543
examinations in Art, 413
See also Examination
Time, Procedure select committee, 1637

R

Rabbit(s), 375
meat production, 89
Rabies, inquiry, 1524
Race Relations:
Act(s), 704
(Amendment) Bill, 49, 1074, 1478
Bill, 615, 617, 618, 662, 667, 669, 670, 876, 1479
booklet, 873
Repeal Bill, 1479
and immigration, select committee, 1284–5, 1638
Board, 475, 874, 1272, 1628
in housing, circular, 891
Racial:
and Religious Discrimination Bill, 10
Discrimination, convention, 1249
Radar:
precision approach, 1714
wind data and reduction sheet, 1305, 1657
RADCLIFFE, LORD (Chairman):
British Museum Trustees, 383
D Notice inquiry, 388
RADFORD, C. A. R.:
Crossraguel Abbey, 1670
Glasgow Cathedral, 1670
St. Dogmael's Abbey, 1321
Tretower Court and Castle, 1321
Radial Velocities, 920, 1327
Radiation:
dose rates for superconducting magnets, 209
effects on mechanical properties of polyethylene terephthalate films, 530
from fires in a compartment, 939
Radiation (*continued*):
high energy, effect on mechanical properties of epoxy resin system, 922
risk from environmental contamination, 190
Radicephalus elongatus osorio, 723
Radio:
and:
other electronic apparatus, census of production, 957
Space Research:
report, 922
Station, 922
Television:
Rental and Relay Industry, Prices and Incomes Board, 901
Servicing, (careers), 1149
broadcasting experiment, H.C., 882
equipment for medical and biological telemetry devices, 909
for merchant ships, 516, 908, 1168
masts, planning and control, 889
operators:
handbook, 908
amendment, 197
Rentals Ltd, Monopolies Commission, 955
telephone equipment for distress, urgency, and safety purposes, 908
Radioactive:
contamination of aircraft, 84
isotope services, organisation, 1622
risk to the population from environmental contamination, 190
Radioactivity:
genetic effects in South India, 190
in:
drinking water, 174, 493
milk, 86
Radiobiological Laboratory:
annual report, 86, 373, 709
see also Letcombe Laboratory
Radiochemical Centre, Amersham, 203
Radiographer, (careers), 747
Radiological:
hazards to patients, 158
Protection Act:
Bill, 1002, 1003, 1077
Radiomechanical manual, 203
Radiotelephony procedure, 1370
Radnorshire:
census, 153
sample census, 468, 1259
RAE, D. B.:
Food of:
cod, 374, 709, 710
dogfish, 374
seals, 710
the witch, 1116
RAFTERY, M. F.: Explosibility tests for industrial dusts, 939

RAGG, J. M.: Soils round Haddington and Eyemouth, 374
RAGGE, D. R.: *Tettigoniidae*, 722, 1125
Rail:
links with Heathrow Airport, 1719
convention, 1249
Railway(s):
accident reports 242–3, 577, 962–3, 1375, 1572, 1718–19
carriages, wagons, and trams, census of production, 1371
in G.B., safety record, 577, 962, 1572
policy, 577
track equipment, census of production, 1371
Twentieth century, illustrated booklet, 1675
Rain and stream waters in the Scottish Highlands, chemical study, 87
Rainfall, British, 900
Raising the school leaving age, 1680
RAITT, D. F. S.:
Norway pout in the North sea, 710
Scottish cod fishery in the North Sea, 374
RAMSAY, W. J. (Editor): Heat bibliography, 1352
RAMSBOTTOM, J.: Handbook of the larger British fungi, 104
RAMSEY, G. W.: *Acari cryptostigmata*, 1127
R and D, *see* Research and Development
RANDLE, T. C., Coil winding irregularities in superconducting magnets, 1676
RANFT, J.:
Calculation of perturbed orbits for resonant extraction from Nimrod, 923
particle production by the thermodynamic model, 923
Vertical beam blow-up during resonant ejection from Nimrod, 1330
Rank Organisation Ltd, merger, 1370
Raphael Cartoons in the V. and A. Museum, 266
RAPSON, E. J.: Indian coins, 383
Raspberry pests and diseases in Scotland, 1115
Rate(s):
and rateable values:
E. and W., 174, 493, 893
Tables, 1297
Scotland, 210, 532, 924, 1331, 1677
demands:
and rebates, circular, 889
reductions in poundage, 487
of:
pay etc., Navy, 1551
surtax, 896
wages and hours of work, changes, 1150, 1565
Rate(s) (*continued*):
Product (Amendment of Enactments) Regulations, 488
rebates:
circular, 890
E. and W., 893, 1647
tables, 1297
Scotland, 928, 1677
Support Grant:
(Amendment) Regulations, circulars, 1291, 1645
central forecasting, 1644
(Increase):
Order, 492, 1296, 1572
(Scotland) Order, 537, 924, 1678
Order:
report, 173, 492, 892
S.I. select committee, 482
Regulations, 488
(Scotland) Order, 537, 1331
Ratifications, Treaty series, lists, 145, 459, 852, 1249, 1607
Rating Act, 77
Bill, 2, 43, 48, 164
and valuation, Secretary of State for Scotland's report, 311
RAY, H. A. (Chairman): Service in Hotels, 904
RAYMOND, SIR S. (Chairman): Gaming Board, 1627
RAYNER, G. H.: SI Units, 1713
RCC-R179, UKAEA, 264
READ D. J.: Brunchorstia die-back of Corsican pine, 465
READE, B.:
Art Nouveau and Alphonse Mucha, large picture book, 985
Aubrey Beardsley, 266
Ballet designs and illustrations, 599
READING, DOWAGER MARCHIONESS (Chairman), Place of voluntary service in after-care, 162, 474
Reading:
Provisional Order Act, 79
Bill, 5, 49
University, scientific equipment, 1721
Reading:
progress, 127
teaching of, Education and Science select committee, 1635
Re-allocation of School-Children (Scotland) Bill, 338
Real-time interpreter for computer control, 1676
Recommended resale prices, Monopolies Commission, 1370
Record repositories in G.B., list, *see Repositories*
Recreation and holidays, coastal, 1134

Recruitment to the Civil Service, estimates committee, 167
Red:
Crescent Society, gift, 586
Deer Commission, annual report, 87, 374, 710, 1116, 1520
Sea Lights, maintenance*, 459
spider mite:
crops in the open, 375
glasshouse crops, 88
REDCLIFFE-MAUD, RT. HON. LORD (Chairman): Local Government in England, 916, 1326
REDDAWAY, W. B. (Chairman): Selective Employment Tax, 1722
REDDISH, V. C.:
Distribution of stars and interstellar matter, 207
Wolf-Rayet stars, 329
Redeployment, study, 1571
REDFERN, P.: Input-output analysis, 586
Redundancy:
Fund account, 417, 755, 1159, 1574
Payments Act 1965 (Amendment) Bill, 1071
Rebates Act, 1112
Bill, 992, 1071
Redundant Churches and Other Religious Buildings Act, 1112
Bill, 995, 1066, 1071, 1275
Redwood and whitewood, European, strength properties, 555
REED, S.: *Outlook*, 383, 719
REES, G. H.: Control of the RF in a proton synchrotron with beam loading, 923
REEVE, M. R.: Laboratory culture of the prawn, 1120
REEVE, P. A.: Design of beam lines with high resolving power, 922
Reeves collection of Chinese fish drawings, 1538
Reform of Local Government:
England, 1648
E. and W., areas and boundaries, 1644
Refraction during growth, 1655
Refreshment:
Department, H.C. (Services) select committee, 166, 481, 882, 1283, 1636
Houses Act, 369
Bill, 48, 276, 283, 332, 336, 337, 477
Refrigerators, disused, safe disposal, 1645
Refugees:
status, 459, 1249
visas*, 1254
Refusal to supply goods, Monopolies Commission, 1713
Refuse:
collection:
and disposal, costing returns, 174, 493
working party report, 488
Refuse (*continued*):
disposal, Garchey system, 863
domestic, 1671
storage and collection, 493
Regalia, Scottish, 1673
Regent, Royal, and Carlton Terrace Gardens, Edinburgh Order Confirmation Act, 1518
Bill, 1482
Regime for long term prisoners in maximum security, 873
Region with a future, strategy for the South-west, 412
Regional:
coastal conferences, 513
development in Britain, Information Office pamphlet, 895
employment premium, development areas, 412
Hospital Boards, accounts: 158, 471, 867, 1265, 1619
Scotland, 212, 535, 928, 1334, 1681
magnetic anomolies, 1664
statistics, abstract, 105, 388, 724, 1129, 1541
Register of, *see respective subject*
Registrar General:
annual estimates, population, *see* Population
decennial supplement E. and W., 861, 1664
for Scotland:
annual report, 155, 468, 863, 1260, 1613
life tables, 1260
mortality statistics, 1260
occupational mortality, 1613
place names and population, alphabetical list, 468
population and vital statistics, 1260
quarterly and weekly returns, 155, 469, 863, 1260-1, 1613-14
quarterly and weekly returns E. and W., 154, 467, 862, 1257-9, 1665-6
statistical review, E. and W., 154, 467, 861, 1257, 1664
Registration:
and Licencing Authorities in G.B., N.I., and Republic of Ireland, index marks and addresses, 936
of:
Marriage, convention, 848, 1603
Title to land, 898
Scotland, 1335
Officers, list, 154, 466, 861, 1257, 1664
Registry of:
Friendly Societies, *see* Friendly Societies
Ships, 239–40, 573, 956, 1366, 1710
Regulations, *see respective subject*
Rehabilitation of derelict, neglected, or unsightly land, 487

REID, J. H.: Cape Lyot Heliograph results, 1328
REINERS, W. J. (Chairman): Coding and data co-ordination, 1322
Reinsurance of British Ships against war risks, 575–6
Remand Homes, *see* Approved Schools
Rembrandt drawings, B.M., 100
Remedial Gymnast, (careers), 747
Removal and Disposal of Vehicles (Alteration of Enactments) Order, S.I. select committee, 885
Remuneration of Teachers (Scotland):
Act, 369
Bill, 280, 332, 334, 477, 478
Order:
circular, 925
S.I. select committee, 885
teachers' salaries memorandum, 1678
Renal Transplantation Bill, 662, 666, 669, 671, 876
Rendering outside walls, 201
Renfrew, census tables, 155
RENN, D. F.:
Pevensey Castle, 1670
Three Shell Keeps, 1670
RENNIE, E. M. (Chairman): Consultative Committee on the Curriculum, 925
Rent(s):
Act, 704
(Amendment) Bill, 334
Bill, 605, 608, 611, 667, 887
circulars, 170, 889
1968 (Amendment) Bill, 1071
tables of comparison, 893
Book (Forms of Notice) (Scotland) Regulations, S.I. select committee, 885
(Control of Increases) Act, 1112
Bill, 1003, 1071
dwellings in good repair etc., 1293
houses owned by:
Local Authorities Scotland, 210, 532, 924, 1335
Public Authorities Scotland, 1678
rebates, 488
for council tenants Scotland, 1678
(Scotland) Bill, 1412
tenants in receipt of supplementary benefit, 1572
Reorganisation:
Commission for eggs, 717
of Central Government, 1540
Reparation by the offender, 1627
Repositories:
Record, 159, 871
Lists of accessions to, 159, 473, 871, 1269, 1674
index, 473
Representation of the People Act, 1112
(Amendment) Bill, 337
Bill, 620, 670, 671, 991, 992, 1072, 1479
1949 (Amendment) (No. 2) Bill, 665
Representative borrowing rate circular, 1292
Republic of Gambia Act, 1516
see also Gambia, Republic of
Republic of Ireland, *see* Ireland, Republic of
Research:
and:
Development:
Building management handbooks, 524, 914, 1323, 1672
bulletins, 524, 914, 1322, 1672
Information, directorate, 1322
computers, 127
Papers, Royal Commission, 528, 919
series, official statistics, 1542
Services Ltd., community survey, Scotland, 1327
studies, 1273
Reserve Forces Act, 77
Bill, 6, 7, 46, 48, 50, 51, 164
Reservoirs (Safety Provisions) Act, circular, 1293
Residential:
areas, development, 1294
hostels for mentally disordered, 471
Residual values, fertilisers and feeding stuffs, 87, 374, 1116, 1520
Residue data, collection of, 1145
Resin(s):
pressure and scolytid beetle activity, 151
synthetic, census of production, 1371
see also epoxy resins
Restenneth and Aberlemno, guide, 1321
Restraint, severe:
Prices and Incomes standstill, 124, 487
Productivity and pay during, 193
Restrictive:
practices, Monopolies Commission, 1713
Trade Practices Act, 705
Bill, 615, 617, 662, 667, 668, 669, 876
Trading agreements, report:
of the Registrar General, 1571
to the Registrar General, 574
Retail Drapery:
Outfitting, and Footwear trades:
pay of workers, 510
statistical supplement, 510
Retailing, (careers), 1149
Retired Officers, Navy, list, 735, 1551
Retirement:
age, compulsory, of Dock workers, 753
Pension(s):
decision of the Commissioner, 215, 540, 868, 1265
deferred retirement, increase, 868

RET-RUS | 1966-70

RET— *INDEX 1966–70*

Retirement (*continued*):
  Pensioners, financial and other circumstances, 214
Retriangulation of G.B., history, Ordnance Survey, 906
Revenue Act, 705
  Bill, 340
  (No. 2) Bill, 607, 665
Reversion Disease and gall mite of Black currant, 88
Review of British Standard Time, 1628
Revocation of import and export licences, Southern Rhodesia, 236
Revoking:
  of emergency powers, proclamation, 1687
  state of emergency, proclamation, 1688
REYNOLDS, G.:
  British water-colours, 1396
  The engravings of S. W. Hayter, 599
REYNOLDS, N.: Settlement and survival of young mussels in the Conway fishery, 1120

RHEL:
  geometrical reconstruction programme modifications, 922
  see also Rutherford Laboratory
Rheumatic fever in Scotland, 536
Rhine navigation, amendment, 459
Rhinoceroses, miocene, 103
Rhinophoridae, 101
Rhizopodea, 1127
RHODES, F. H. T.: British Avonian (Carboniferous) conodont faunas, 1126
Rhodesia:
  exchanges with the regime, 1249
  H.M.S. *Fearless* discussions, 853
  Independence Bill, 336, 1479
  Settlement proposals, 111
  see also Southern Rhodesia
Rhopalocera, 386
Rhymney Valley Sewerage Board Act, 371
Rhyparochrominae types, 385

RICHARDS, O. W.: *Apidae*, 722
RICHMOND, SIR I.: Hod Hill Excavations, 720
Riding Establishments Act, 1516
  Bill, 1003, 1403, 1405, 1406, 1410, 1474, 1481, 1630
Rievaulx Abbey:
  guide, 522
  picture book, 522
RIGBY, N. L. (Chairman): Associated Industrial Consultants Ltd., 1661
Right(s):
  of:
    Light Act, 1959, forms, 190
    M.P.s detained in prison, Privileges committee, 1634
    Privacy Bill, 335, 1478
Right(s) (*continued*):
  to claim professional fees on compulsory acquisition, 489
RIGOLD, S. E.:
  Baconsthorpe Castle, Norfolk, 201
  Lilleshall Abbey, Shropshire, 1321
RITCHIE CALDER, LORD (Chairman): Metrication Board, 1657
River(s):
  Authorities and Sewage Disposal Authorites, technical problems, 175
  Cumbrian, hydrological survey, 171
  Dartmoor, hydrological survey, 171
  Wessex, hydrological survey, 494
Rivets, census of production, 958

Road(s):
  abstracts, 243–4, 578
  accidents, 243, 577, 963
    tables and graphs, 1376
  aggregate in G.B., sources, 964
  and:
    Bridge works, specifications, 1376
    communications, Wales and Monmouthshire, 332, 476
  bituminous-surfaced in tropics and sub-tropics, 244
  circular, traffic and transport plans, 963
  concrete, 242
  construction:
    bituminous materials, 576
    efficiency, 193, 512
  for the future, inter-urban plan, 1376, 1719
  goods transport, survey, 244
  Haulage:
    Industry:
      Charges: 192
        Costs and wages, 511
      Productivity agreements, 903
    Wages Council, field of operations, inquiry, 1571
  in:
    England, 244, 578, 964, 1376, 1711
    the landscape, 578
    rural areas, layout, 1374
    urban areas, 244
  markings, manual, 244
  new, flexible, and rigid pavements, 244
  Notes, 244, 578, 963, 1376
  Public Utilities Street Works Act, circular, 242
  Research:
    Board, report, 243
    Director's report, 243
    estimate committee, 480, 878
    Laboratory, annual report, 963, 1376, 1719
      publications, 243–4, 578, 963, 1376, 1719
      special report, speed limit trial, 244, 578

1966 pp 1–272, 1967 pp 273–604, 1968 pp 605–990, 1969 pp 991–1402, 1970 pp 1403–1740

120

INDEX 1966–70 —ROG

Road(s) (*continued*):
  Research (*continued*):
    Laboratory, annual report (*continued*):
      technical papers, 578, 963
    1965–1966, 578
  rubberised bituminous materials and binders, 963
  rural, traffic prediction, 1374
  Safety:
    Act, 369
      Bill, 43, 46, 47, 51, 52, 164, 277, 280, 337, 478
      goods vehicles examination and plating, 964
    1967 (Amendment) Bill, 665
    and traffic requirements, 1294
    fresh approach, 578
  Salt treatment for snow and ice, 963
  (Scotland) Act, 1516
    Bill, 1070, 1076, 1405, 1407, 1408, 1474, 1479, 1482, 1630
  signs and signals, convention, 1163
  Sources of white and coloured aggregates in G.B., 244
  sub-grades, and granular sub-bases and bases, protection, 963
  surface dressing with cut-back bitumen, recommendations, 963
  town, better use of, 576
  track costs, ministry report, 964
  Traffic:
    Act(s):
      Bill, 46
      fees, collection procedure, hospital, 864
      Licensing Authorities, 244, 578, 964, 1376, 1719
      Traffic Commissioners' report, 578, 1376
    (Amendment) Act, 369
      Bill, 49, 50, 52, 277, 279, 283, 284, 332, 336, 338, 478, 667, 1474, 1479, 1630
    (Burden of Responsibilities) Bill, 665
    convention, 1249
    (Disqualification) Act, 1516
      Bill, 1408, 1481
    (Driving Instruction) Act, 369
      Bill, 283, 332, 334, 337, 338, 478
    European road signs and signals*, 146
    (Insurance) Bill, 1072
    International traffic arteries, 460, 853, 1249
    (Miscellaneous Provisions) Bill, 335
    Regulation Act, 369
      Bill, 279, 280, 283, 286, 338, 485
      proposed text with amendments, 964
    road signs and signals, protocol, 460
Road(s) (*continued*):
  Transport:
    Industry Training Board, 505, 1156, 1571
    international carriage of goods*, 1607
    Lighting Act, 369
      Bill, 282, 337
    Netherlands*, 1250
    planning, impact of computer techniques, 1659
    Sweden*, 853
  urban, restraint of traffic, 575
Roadcraft, police drivers' manual, 1273
ROBENS, LORD (Chairman): Joint mission for Malta, 394
ROBERTS, DAME J. (Chairman): Distribution of teachers in Scotland, 211
ROBERTSON, C. L. (Compiler): Short title catalogue of books printed before 1701, in Foreign Office Library, 146
ROBERTSON, PROF. D. J.:
  (Chairman): Disruption at Heathrow, 1571
  Girling Ltd, Bromsborough, dispute, 750
  Railway guards and shunters, dispute, 502
  Steel Corporation, Port Talbot, dispute, 1153
ROBERTSON, I. M. (Chairman): Public Library Service, Scotland, 1333
ROBERTSON, J. H.: Information-processing systems, 586
ROBERTSON, LORD (Chairman): Scottish teachers' salaries, 927, 1680
ROBINSON, B. W.: Persian miniature painting, 599
ROBINSON, T. C.: Butterflies in woodlands, 860
ROBSON, T. O.: Control of aquatic weeds, 711
ROCHDALE, RT. HON. VISCOUNT (Chairman): Shipping, 1709
Rochdale Road Passenger Transport Department, terms and conditions of employment, 903
Rochester Castle, guide, 1321
Rocks:
  arenaceous, 1312
  sedimentary, 1312
  tertiary welded-tuff vent agglomerate, 1312
Rodentia, 103
Rodenticides, precautionary measures, 1526
Rodents of West Africa, 1128
RODGERS, A. G. (Chairman): Children with hearing defects, 533
Roe deer, 1611
ROGOWSKI, B. F. W.: Fire propagation test, 1691

1966 pp 1–272, 1967 pp 273–604, 1968 pp 605–990, 1969 pp 991–1402, 1970 pp 1403–1740

121

ROL— *INDEX 1966–70*

Roll of the Lords Spiritual and Temporal, 169, 486, 888, 1289, 1642
Roman:
  coins in the B.M., 100, 384, 720, 1536
  sites, *see* Prehistoric, Roman, and medieval sites
Romano-British cemetery, York, 1321
Ronan Point, collapse of flats, inquiry, 893
Roof(s):
  constructions subjected to fire tests, 1691
  drainage, 1322
  felt, built up, 1671
Room heaters, installing, 1669
Root rot of conifers, 1611
Rootes Motors Ltd, Industrial Court inquiry, 750
Rope, twine, and net, census of production, 958
ROSE, PROF. H.: Management education, 1661
Rosebery County School for Girls, sixth-form centre, 743
ROSEN, B. G.: Faviidae, 1127
ROSEVEARE, D. R.: Rodents of East Africa, 1128
ROSKILL, SIR A., (Chairman): Monopolies Commission, 239, 572–3, 955, 1369–70, 1714
ROSKILL, HON MR JUSTICE (Chairman): Third London Airport, 1365, 1708
ROSPA, *see* Royal Society for Prevention of Accidents
ROSS, E. S.: Embioptera, 101
ROSS, H. H.: Grassland leafhopper, 721
Ross and Cromarty:
  mineral resources, 1312
  (Strathcarron-South Strome Road):
    Bill, 51
    Order Confirmation Act, 370
Ross Group Ltd and Associated Fisheries Ltd, Monopolies Commission, 239
Ross seal, anatomy, 1662
ROSSE, EARL OF (Chairman):
  Area Museum services, 510
  Museums and Galleries, 1683
  Universities and Museums, 901
Rotary Cultivation, 716
Rotation by stellar luminosity, effect, 207
Rothampstead Experimental Station, annual report, 1115
Rotherham Multiple Health Screening Clinic, 1267
Rothschild collection of fleas, catalogue, 388
Rough digitisings "Merge" programme, 1676
Roumania. *See* Rumania
Round Timber, ready reckoner, metric, 1611
Roundwood, home grown, 465
ROWE, F. W. E.: Holothuriidae, 1128
Roxburgh, Sutherland, and Zetland Counties, special study area, sample census, 863
Royal:
  Air Force:
    manual, 1137
    Mountain Rescue Teams, 731
    Museum:
      gift of:
        land and buildings, 1379
        stores and equipment, 586
    Queen's Regulations, 114, 398, 731, 1137, 1548
    see also Air Force
  Albert Hall Act, 79
  Assent Act, 369
    Bill, 277, 336
  Bank of Scotland:
    Act, 1518
    Order Confirmation Act, 371, 1113
      Bill, 337, 670, 1482
  Botanic Garden(s):
    Edinburgh:
      (1670–1970), 1520
      publications, 203, 525, 915, 1325, 1674
    Kew, 203, 525, 916, 1326, 1674
  Charter, British Broadcasting Corporation, 1315
  College of:
    Art Act, 706
    Science and Technology, Glasgow Scheme, 926
  Commission on:
    Ancient:
      and historical monuments and constructions of England, 1628
      monuments, Scotland, 525
    Assizes and Quarter Sessions, 1326
    historical:
      manuscripts:
        centenary exhibition, 1269
        reports, 871, 1624, 1674
          guide to, 159
      monuments, England, 1326
    Local Government:
      England, 525–6, 916, 1326–7
      Scotland, 526–7, 917–19, 1327
    medical education, 919
    penal system in E. and W., 527
    Trade Unions and Employers Associations, 204–5, 527–8, 919–20
    Tribunals of inquiry, 205
  Engineers supplementary pocket book, 116
  Fine Art Commission, 205, 1272
    for Scotland, 528, 1674
  Greenwich Observatory publications, 205–6, 528–9, 920, 1327–8, 1675
  Hospital, Chelsea, 115, 400, 1139, 1560

1966 pp 1–272, 1967 pp 273–604, 1968 pp 605–990, 1969 pp 991–1402, 1970 pp 1403–1740

122

INDEX 1966–70 —RUS

Royal (*continued*):
  Lineage, poster, 513
  Marines:
    Enlistment and Service Orders and Regulations, 735
    Uniform regulations, 124, 375, 1552
  Mint:
    Deputy Master and Comptroller's annual report, 207, 529, 920, 1328, 1675
    estimate committee, 878, 1277
    outline history, 529, 1675
  Navy:
    and Royal Marines Uniform Regulations, 124, 735, 1552
    Queen's Regulations, 411, 735, 1140, 1551–2
      and Admiralty Instructions, 123
    see also Navy, and Admiralty
  Observatory:
    annals, 206
    bulletins, 206, 528–9, 1327
      see also Royal Greenwich Observatory
    Edinburgh, 207, 529, 921, 1328
  Ordnance Factories:
    Appropriation accounts, 117, 401, 735, 1158, 1552
    Defence, Supplementary estimates, 117, 401, 736, 1560
    manufacturing accounts, 117, 416, 735
    operating accounts, 1158, 1552
  Parks, bird life, 202, 913, 1670
  Society for the Prevention of Accidents, 529, 921
  sporting guns at Windsor, 915
  Ulster Constabulary Reserve, 1313
  Warrant(s):
    Arms, 108, 392, 1574
    Army, 114, 115, 116, 398, 400, 732, 734, 1137, 1139, 1548, 1549
    Fire Brigade Medal, 1273
    holders, 218, 541, 930, 1336, 1683
    see also Pay Warrants and Army Pensions Warrant

RR Lyrae:
  stars, photoelectric photometry, 206
  variables, photometric observations, 206, 920

R. S. Bagnall's Thysanoptera collections, review, 722

Rubber:
  and Plastic Processing Industry Training Board, 753, 1156, 1571
  census of production, 598
Rubberised bituminous road materials and binders, 963
RUELLE, J. E.: Termites, 1537
Rule(s):
  in Hollington and Hewthorn, Law Reform report, 507
  of:
    the Air and Air Traffic Control (sixth Amendment) Regulations, S.I. select committee, 885
    Court:
      Amendment (No. 3) Act of Sederunt S.I. select committee, 1640
      of Session, 112, 395
    the Supreme Court, 190, 508, 899, 1305, 1655
Rumania(n):
  cereals*, 146
  Consular convention, 1163
  driving licences*, 1607
  funds, accounts, 844, 1158
  International road transport*, 1608
  nuclear research material and equipment*, 1250
  property accounts, 579, 965, 1377, 1719
  road transport*, 1250
  scientific and technical co-operation*, 460
Ruminants, nutrient requirements, 86
Rural:
  areas:
    development, 1294
    mains water, 1293
  development:
    aspects, 246
    in Wales and Monmouthshire, 478
  roads, traffic prediction, 1374
  Water Supplies and Sewerage:
    Acts, grants, 490
    (Scotland) Act, 1516
      Bill, 1070, 1076, 1275, 1404, 1630
Rushes, control, 375
Rushton Triangular Lodge, guide, 1670
RUSSELL, D. S.: Pathology of hydrocephalus, 508
RUSSELL, F. M.:
  (Editor), 15 to 70 MeV separated orbit cyclotron as a booster injector, 209
  New target material for the Rutherford frozen target, 1676
RUSSELL, J. D.: St. Martin Preserving Co. Ltd., investigation, 236
RUSSELL, RT. HON. LORD JUSTICE (Chairman): Law of Succession, 190
RUSSELL, R.: Keyboard instruments, V. and A. museum, catalogue, 985
Russia:
  China, and the West, Information Office pamphlet, 895
  see also Soviet Union

1966 pp 1–272, 1967 pp 273–604, 1968 pp 605–990, 1969 pp 991–1402, 1970 pp 1403–1740

123

1966-70 | RUT-SCO

RUT— INDEX 1966–70

Rutherford:
frozen target, new material, 1676
Laboratory:
DDP-224 system handbook, 530
reports, 208–9, 530–1, 922–3, 1329–30, 1676
work of, 530, 531, 923, 1331, 1676
RUTHVEN, B. (Chairman): Courses leading to Scottish Certificate of Education, 533
Rutland:
census, 153
sample census, 468, 862
Ruwenzori Expedition, 724

RYAN, W. S.:
Forming a new organisation, 586, 1377
Use of logical trees in the Civil Service, 1543
Rycote Chapel, Oxfordshire, guide, 522
Ryde Corporation Act, 1114
RYDZ, B. (Joint Chairman): Water resources of the North, 599
Ryhope, a pit closes, 1571
RYLAND, J. S.: British marine polyzoa, nomenclatural index, 1127

S

SABINE, P. A.:
perlitic obsidian, 1664
petography and chemistry of arenaceous rocks, 1312
SABROSKY, C. W.: *Tachinidae* described by Baranov, 1125
SACHARIDIS, E. J.: Wide angle elastic proton-proton scattering at high energies, 1330
Sachsenhausen, Parliamentary Commissioner's report, 880
Sacks, census of production, 958
SACKVILLE OF KNOLE, RT. HON. LORD: Calendar of manuscripts, 159
SADLER, F. MCB.: Lunar occultations, 206
Safe disposal of disused refrigerators, circular, 1645
Safeguards in Waterworks:
circular, 489
operation and management, 494
Safety:
and:
health:
at work, basic rules, 754
in mines and quarries, law, 1693, 1712
maintenance, powered hand-tools, 1669

Safety (*continued*):
at:
drop forging hammers, 505
school, 744
circulars (M. and Q.), 1319
code, electro-medical apparatus, 1618
Health:
and Welfare:
booklets, 187, 505, 753–4, 1156
forms, 187, 505, 754
Welfare, and Wages in Agriculture, 95, 381, 717, 1122, 1572
in:
art and craft rooms, 1680
construction work:
general site safety practice, 187
roofing, 1156
system building, 753
domestic buildings, 1671
(the) home, 490
economics rooms, 1680
mechanical handling, 1567
mines research, annual report, 200, 520, 911, 1319, 1694
physical education in Secondary Schools, 1680
Primary Schools, 1680
science laboratories, 1680
sewers and at sewerage works, circular, 1293
technical workshops, 1680
use of:
biscuit-making machinery, 187
machinery in baking, 753
power presses:
committee report, 1566
mechanical, 1566
press brakes, 1156
woodworking machines, 1567
of:
cargo ships, 238
drugs, 865, 1263
life at sea, 146, 460, 1250, 1608
merchant seamen, code of practice, 1708
natural gas as fuel, inquiry, 1694
seamen, 1715
performance of U.K. airline operators, 959
precautions in schools, 1680
quality, and description of drugs and medicines, 470
record of railways, see Railways
road, 280
trawler, 959
Sail and sweep in China, 208
Sailing ships and small craft, 208
SAINSBURY, LORD (Chairman): Relationship between pharmaceutical industry and NHS, 472

INDEX 1966–70 —SAN

Saint:
Andrew's Links Order Confirmation Act, 371
Bill, 337
Barnabas, Lewisham Act, 371
Christopher–Nevis–Anguilla, *see* Saint Kitts–Nevis–Anguilla
Dogmael's Abbey, guide, 1321
Edward's Crown, coloured post card, 522
George, Botolph Lane Churchyard Act, 706
Helena:
Colonial report, 393
double taxation*, 1250
income tax, 1300
Royal Instructions OIC, 201
James and Saint Paul, Plumstead Act, 706
John's College, York, Education and Science select committee, 1635
Kitts–Nevis–Anguilla:
Arms, 392
Colonial report, 109
Constitutional conference report, 109
Flag, 394
Inquiry, 1603
Lucia:
Colonial report, 393
Flag, 394
income tax, 1300
race relations and immigration select committee, 1638
Martin Preserving Co. Ltd., investigation, 236
Mary(s):
Ealing Act, 79
Hornsey Act, 1114
Bill, 620
Oldham, design bulletins, 1646
Summertown Act, 706
Mary-le-Park, Battersea Act, 371
Mildred, Bread Street Act, 1114
Pancras Hotel and Station, painting in London Museum, 506
Saviour, Paddington Act, 1114
Bill, 995
Stephen:
Clapham Park Act, 1114
South Lambeth Act, 371
Vincent:
Colonial report, 109
Constitutional conference report, 393, 1245
public officers*, 1667
report, 853
Salaries of teachers in Further Education Centres, Scotland, 1680

Salary:
scales for teachers, 1147
in:
Farm Institutes, E. and W., 745
Further Education Establishments, E. and W., 745
of Agricultural and Horticultural subjects, E. and W., 745
structures, 1308
Sale(s):
of:
Goods Bill, 3
Tickets:
(Offences):
Bill, 1072, 1481
(No. 2) Bill, 1481
(Street Offences) Bill, 668
Venison (Scotland) Act, 705
(No. 2) Bill, 613, 662, 666, 668, 876
Salisbury (Cecil) Manuscripts, 159, 1269, 1624
Salisbury Railway and Market House Act, 1114
SALMON, B. (Chairman): Senior Nursing staff structure, 158
SALMON, J. (Chairman): Hotel and Catering Industry Training Board, 1153
SALMON, J.: Rycote Chapel, guide, 522
SALMON, RT. HON. LORD JUSTICE (Chairman):
Law of Contempt, 1304
Royal Commission on Tribunals of Inquiry, 205
Salmon:
and trout fisheries, 332, 476
fisheries research, 373
fry, hatchery research, 1116
Salop County Council Act, 1518
Salt:
and miscellaneous non-metaliferous mining and quarrying, census of production, 957
treatment of snow and ice on roads, 963
SALTMAN, A. (Editor): Cartulary of Dale Abbey, 473
Salvadoraceae, 729
Salvation Army Act, 706
Sample census:
E. and W.: 467–8, 862–3, 1259, 1666
Scotland, 469, 863, 1261
SAMSON, W. B.: Abundance determination of late-type stars, 1328
Sand(s):
and gravel(s):
Production, 203, 524, 915, 1323, 1673
resources, inner Moray Firth, 1663
Southern Counties of Scotland, 1663
eels, 93
flies, 385
Sandlime bricks, 1669

SAN— INDEX 1966–70

Sandstone, lower old red, 1664
Sandy Braes, Co. Antrim, rocks, 1312
SANGAI, G. R. W.: *Sonneratiaceae*, 729
Sanitary regulations, international, 146
Sapotaceae, 729
Sap-stain in timber, 1352
Sarcophagidae, 101
Sasines, Particular Register, index, 214, 537, 929
Saturniidae, 724
SAUNDERS, A. D., Upnor Castle, Kent, guide, 522
Savings Banks Fund accounts, 251, 585–6
Sawflies, currant and gooseberry, 87
Sawlog tables, metric top diameter, 1611
Sawyers and woodcutting machinists, agreement on pay, 903

SCAAP, *see* Special Commonwealth African Assistance Plan
Scab, apple and pear, 88
SCADDING, PROF. J. G. (Chairman): Chest Services, future, 865
Scaffolding:
metal, 912, 1320
safety, 753
Scale insects, 1125
SCAMP, SIR (A). J.:
Coal:
loading dispute, 1571
trimmers in ports, inquiry, 505
Industrial Court Inquiries, 183, 501, 502, 750
Liverpool dockworkers payment and earnings system, inquiry, 505
Motor Industry Joint Labour Council, report, 186, 753
Vickers Ltd, dispute, 1153
SCARMAN, HON. MR. JUSTICE (Chairman): Law Commission, 189, 507, 899, 1303–4, 1654–5
Scattering:
Inelastic, calculation problem for DWBA, 530
Multiple, correction, 992
Wide-angle elastic proton-proton at high levels, 1330
Scawsby College, Doncaster, Education and Science select committee, 1635
SCHELPE, E. A. C. L. E.: Pteridophyta, 1546
Schmidt Camera objective prism spectra, 1328
Scholarships, Commonwealth Commission, 392
School(s):
based examining, teachers' experience, 415
buildings, colour in, 1145
child, health, 126, 1562
Colleges of Education, etc., use of lasers, 1678

School(s) (*continued*):
commercial studies, 1561
Comprehensive, 1562
Council:
curriculum:
bulletins, 1328
innovation in practice, 921
gifts, 1721
Project Technology, 921
publications, 128, 414–15, 921, 1328–9, 1675
Welsh Committee report, 921
working papers, 128, 415, 921, 1329
design, new problems, 743
dinner, nutritional standard, 127
Direct Grant Grammar, 1562
furniture dimensions, 412
Independent Day, 1562
list, 1562
leavers:
coloured, problems, Race Relations and Immigration select committee, 1284, 1285
G.C.E. and C.S.E., 746
modern studies for, 925
on sandwich type training course, 1617
statistics, 1563
leaving age, raising, 211, 1680
library, Education and Science pamphlet, 414
lighting in, 412
management and government, research study, 916
meal series, film strips, 127
Middle:
launching, 1561
new problems, 125
Primary, *see* Primary Schools
Public:
Commission report, 745, 1562
Scotland, 1562
safety precautions, 1680
(Scotland) code, draft, 925
Secondary, *see* Secondary Schools
Teaching as a career, undergraduates' attitudes, 864
Schooling, middle years, 1329
SCHULTZE, H. P.: *Palaeoniscoidea* Schuppen, 722
SCHUR, H.: Education and Training for Scientific and Technological Library and Information work, 744
Science(s):
and Technology:
co-operation*, *see specific countries*
flow of candidates into higher education, 125, 743
manpower resources, 125, 413
National Lending Library, 414, 744, 1146, 1562

INDEX 1966–70 SCO—

Science(s) (*continued*):
and Technology (*continued*):
select committee reports, 482, 484, 883–4, 1284–5, 1638–9
on coastal pollution, 1270
statistics, 415, 1148, 1563
triennial manpower survey of engineers etc., 125
applied, notes, 1713
for general education, 1332
laboratories, safety in, 1680
Museum:
booklets, 1675
Four in One Books, 208
Illustrated:
booklets, 207, 530, 922, 1329, 1675
guide, 922
photography collection, 1329
publications, 207–8, 530, 922, 1329, 1675
of firefighting, hydraulics and water supply, 872
policy studies, 415, 745, 1147
Research Council:
Mathematics group, Atlas Computer Laboratory, 208
reports, 128, 415, 745, 1147, 1562
Rutherford High Energy Laboratory reports, 208–9, 530–1, 922–3, 1329–40, 1676
since 1500, 208
sixth form, 128
teaching, Education and Science select committee, 1635
Scientific:
and Technological Library and Information work, education and training for, 744
equipment, Customs convention, 1164
growth, manpower parameters, 125
papers, Meteorological Office, 901
Policy, Council for, 125, 411, 743
reports, British Antarctic Survey, 98, 383, 718
research in British universities and colleges, 128, 415, 745–6, 1147, 1563
surgical, and photographic instruments, etc., census of production, 1371
Scientist(s):
(careers), 1565
engineers, and technologists, flow in employment, 743
etc., manpower survey, 125
Scoliidae, 385
Scolytid beetle, 151
Scotia Sea seismic refraction investigations, 99
Scotland:
Acts of Parliament, 218
Agricultural statistics, 1519

Scotland (*continued*):
Agriculture:
and Fisheries, Department of. *See* Agriculture and Fisheries
in, 86, 373, 709, 1116, 1519
Ancient Monuments:
Board, 202, 522, 912, 1320, 1676
illustrated guide, 522
list, 912, 1322, 1677
and Wales (Referenda) Bill, 1070
arts and amenities, 1066, 1274
Boundary Commission report, 1109
census, 155
Central and Southern forests, 1255
child care, 210, 533, 928, 1333
Constitution Commission, 1544
Countryside Commission, 1134
Court of Sessions, 112, 395–6
criminal statistics, 212, 534, 927, 1334, 1681
East coast, marine geological and geophysical work, 1663
economic affairs, 1640
education, 210, 533, 925, 1332, 1678
epilepsy, 928
finance, 209
fire services, 535
fisheries, 86, 373, 709, 1116, 1520
gale damage, 875
Geological Survey and Museum, 906
Health:
and Welfare services, 212, 535, 927, 1334
Service Superannuation Scheme, 927
Hospital:
medical records, 536
Pharmaceutical Service, 213
housing:
management, 531
return, 209, 531, 925, 1331, 1677
judicial statistics, 212, 534, 928, 1334, 1681
Local Government, consideration, 1629
Memoirs of Geological Survey, 195, 906
National:
Galleries, *see* National Galleries
Library, 194, 905
Museum of Antiquities, 194, 513, 905, 1310, 1662
North-east, survey, 1331
older houses, 532, 924
Parole Board, 1334
prisons, 213, 535, 928, 1681
probation hostels, 213
Public:
Library service, 1333
Schools Commission, 1562
rates and rateable values, 210, 532, 924, 1331, 1677
rents of Local Authority owned houses, 210, 532, 924, 1335, 1678

SCO   INDEX 1966–70

Scotland (continued):
Royal Fine Art Commission, 528, 1674
sample census, 863
State Papers, calendar, 1336
Transport Users Consultative Committee, annual report, 245, 579, 965, 1276, 1719
Ultimus Haeres, 214, 537
Water Service, 210
see also Scottish
SCOTT, C.: Accidents to young motorcyclists, 863
SCOTT, D. B.: Computer graphics patching of HPD failed events, 1676
Scott, Sir Walter, Scholarships, 211
Scottish:
Administration, handbook, 535
Affairs, select committee, 1275, 1266, 1639–40
Agricultural economics, 87, 374, 710, 1116, 1520
Certificate of Education:
alternative chemistry syllabus, 533
Examination:
Board, 211, 534, 927
papers, 211
syllabus and specimen question papers, 212
cod fishery, North Sea, 374
Development Department:
annual report, 209, 532, 923, 1331, 1678
circulars, 1330
publications, 209–10, 531, 923–5, 1330–1, 1676–8
economy, 214
Education Department:
bulletin, 533
Central Committee on English, bulletin, 1678
circulars, 210, 533, 925, 1332, 1678
Community of Interests, 925
Curriculum:
Consultative Committee, 533
papers, 1332
publications, 210–12, 533–4, 925–7, 1331–3, 1678–80
educational statistics, 534, 927, 1333, 1680
Estimates:
Bill, 662
minutes of proceedings, 164, 478, 877, 1275
Standing Committee, 46, 332, 662, 1066
Health:
Services:
administrative reorganisation, 927
Council, 213, 536, 928, 1335, 1681
statistics, 213, 536, 928, 1335, 1682

Scottish (continued):
Highlands:
chemical study of rain and stream water, 87
salmon and trout research, 373
see also Highlands and Islands
Home and Health Department:
H.M. Chief Inspector of Constabulary for Scotland's report, 213, 535, 927, 1334, 1681
Prison Service examination papers, 107
publications, 212–13, 534–6, 927–9, 1333–5, 1681–2
Registration of Births, Deaths and Marriages (Local Registration Authorities' Officers) Compensation (Scotland) Regulations, 212
Hospital(s):
analysis of running costs, 212, 535, 928
Endowments Research Trust, 213, 536, 928, 1335, 1682
Housing Advisory Committee:
allocating council houses, 532
rent rebates for council tenants, 1678
Infantry, uniform, 1673
inshore fisheries, regulation, 1520
Land Court reports: 213, 536, 929, 1335, 1682
appendices, 1335
Law:
Commission:
annual report, 212, 536, 928, 1335, 1682
exemption clauses in contracts, 1304
First Programme, 212
grounds for divorce, 536
interpretation of statutes, 1303
law of evidence relating to corroboration, 536
legitimation per subsequens matrimonium, 536
prescription and limitation of actions, 1682
reports, 1654, 1655
Sale of Goods Act, amendments, 1304
Second Programme, 928
Shellfish fisheries and shellfish, 507
Society, 212, 213
Life Assurance Company 1968 Act, 706
Milk Marketing Scheme, 86
Office:
Constitution Commission, 1133
publications, 213–14, 537, 929, 1335–6, 1682
peat surveys, 87, 710
Record Office:
descriptive list of plans, 537, 1683

INDEX 1966–70   —SEC

Scottish (continued):
Record Office (continued):
publications, 214, 537, 929, 1336, 1682–3
regalia, 1673
roads in the 1970s, 1331
salmon and trout fisheries, 332, 476
sea fisheries, statistical tables, 87, 374, 710, 1116, 1521
Secondary Schools, guidance, 1333
Self-Government bid, 334
statistics, digest, 214, 532, 924, 1330, 1677
teachers' salaries:
memorandum, 925, 927, 1678, 1680
Prices and Incomes Board, 192
Tourism survey, 864
Transport Group:
annual report and accounts, 1682
Union and National Insurance Company's Act, 79
United Services Museum, uniform of Scottish Infantry, 1673
Valuation Advisory Council, annual report, 209, 531, 923, 1330, 1677
see also Scotland
Scottish Agriculture, 87, 374, 710, 1116, 1520
Screeds, floor, laying, 521
Screens and enclosures, protective, 1320
Screw(s):
cap electric lamps, precautions, 754
census of production, 958
Scripts:
Asian, 100
sample, Edward Johnston's Book, 266
SCRUTTON, C. T.: Colonial Phillipsastraeidae, 722
SCUDDER, G. G. E.: Rhyparochrominae types
Sculpture, English, designs for, 1396
Scytopetalaceae, 729, 1134

Sea:
Broadcasting (Offences) Bill, 50
Fish:
(Conservation) Act, 369
Bill, 281, 285, 338, 485
Lord Chancellor's memorandum, 281
Industries Acts, accounts, 93, 95, 380, 382, 715, 718, 1121, 1123, 1520, 1526
Fisheries:
Act, 705, 1516
accounts, 1520
Bill, 619, 620, 670, 671, 998, 1004, 1403, 1404, 1480, 1642
1968 (Commencement No. 1) Order S.I. select committee, 1288

Sea (continued):
Fisheries (continued):
Regulation:
Act, 77
Bill, 3, 8, 51, 168
consolidation of Acts, Lord Chancellor's memorandum, 169
Scottish, statistical tables, 87, 374, 710, 1521
(Shellfish) Act, 369
Bill, 281, 285, 338, 485, 507
Statistical tables, 382, 717, 1122, 1526
Law:
assistance and salvage, 853
convention, 144
level, problems, Commonwealth conference, 1314
safety of life at, 146, 1608
Sea Gem, drilling rig, accident, 519
Seafarers, sight tests, 1715
Sea-going ships, owners liability, 848
SEAL, D. T.: Collections of cones from standing trees, 151
Sealing materials, flexible, 912
Seals:
Conservation Act, 1515
Bill, 610, 996, 999, 1076, 1408, 1467, 1480, 1629
food of, 710
fur, 710
Ross, 1602
Seals in the PRO, guide, 915
Seamanship, Admiralty Manual, 1551
Seamen:
safety of, 1715
see also Shipping and seamen
Seashells, bivalve, 101
Second:
Class Engineer, Merchant Navy examination, 569
Dutch War, 513
World War:
British foreign policy, 1540
History:
British special operations, 143
medical, 157
Secondary:
batteries, prices, 902
Education:
awards to students, 126
Certificate, of trial examinations, 415
entries to Colleges of Education, 126
organisation, 1561
School(s):
design:
arts and crafts, 412
drama and music, 125
Middle Schools, new problems, 125

SEC—   INDEX 1966–70

Secondary (continued):
School(s) (continued):
design (continued):
modern languages, 743
Physical education, 125
workshop crafts, 125
home economics departments, 1679
modern language teaching, 1329
safety in physical education, 1680
Scotland:
implication of going metric, 925
staffing, 1333
circular, 1332
(Scottish) guidance, 1333
see also Primary and Secondary Schools
Secrecy of the jury room, 872
Securities, particulars of dealers in, 239, 753, 956, 1370, 1714
Security:
and tenure, business premises, 899
building digest, 1671
Commission report, 251, 585, 724, 1129
in H.C., (Services) select committee, 1636
SEDDON, H.:
Automatic Micrometer, 207
Semi-automatic iris photometer, 297
Sedimentation in Northern Cardigan Bay, 1127
SEDMAN, E. C.: The JOKING system, 208
SEEAR, N.: Position of Women in industry, 920
SEEBOHM, F. (Chairman): Local Authority and allied personal social services, 893
Seeds, quality, 88
Selama (Malaya) Rubber Estates Ltd., investigation, 236
Select Committees:
return, 1634
see also respective subject
Selective:
Employment:
Payments Act, 77
Bill, 8, 49, 50, 1481
Tax, 251, 1722
tendering, building, standard forms of contract, 1644
SELLERS, RT. HON. LORD JUSTICE (SIR F.) (Chairman): Criminal Law Revision, 160, 872
SELWOOD, E. B.: Thysanoepeltidae from Irish Devonian, 103
Senior:
Commercial Airline Transport Pilot, examination papers for licence, 234, 573, 956, 1370, 1714
nursing staff structure, 158
Sentence of the Court, handbook, 1273
Sepulae, 104
Serial tendering, case studies, 524, 1673

SERVICE, M. J. (Chairman): Safety of Seamen, 1715
Service(s):
by youth, 128
cores in high flats, protection against lightning, 490
for elderly with mental disorder, 1681
hospital, see hospital
in hotels, 904
pay and pensions, 124, 742, 1144
personnel and stores, movement, estimates committee, 479, 483
virement, see virement
Sessional:
index, Parliamentary papers, 164, 885, 1276, 1631
Papers, H.L., tables of titles and contents, 1290, 1643
Sessions of the Peace for Bedfordshire (1355–59 and 1363–64), 1624
Setting Out:
accuracy, building digest, 1671
on site, 1320
Settlement in the Countryside, planning, 489, 4493
Sevenoaks and Tonbridge, geology of the country around, 1663
Severn Bridge Tolls Act, accounts, 964, 1159, 1719
Sewage:
Disposal:
Authorities, technical problems, 175
Taken for granted, 1648
effluents:
and trade, 489
circular, 170
Sewerage:
and drainage, hospital, 1617
(Scotland) Act, 705
Bill, 340, 610, 612, 614, 663, 666, 668, 877
treatment plants, activated sludge type, 1293
Sewers:
and sewerage works, safety, circular, 1293
underground pipe, design and construction, 1644
Sewing:
machines, illustrated booklet, 1675
machinists, Industrial Court inquiry, 750
Sex linkage in poultry breeding, 89
Sexual Offences Act, 369
Bill, 3, 47, 50
(No. 2) Bill, 284, 332, 336, 478
Seychelles:
(Amendment) Order, OIC, 1320
and British Indian Ocean Territory (Commissions) Order OIC, 520

Seychelles (continued):
Civil Appeals:
(Amendment) Order OIC, 911
Order OIC, 521
Colonial report, 109
Constitutional:
advance proposals, 395
conference report, 1607
(Electoral Provisions):
(No. 2) Order OIC, 521
Order OIC, 520
Judicature Order OIC, 521
Legislative Council (Extension of Duration) Order OIC, 521
Order OIC, 521, 1669
people of, 196
reports, 853, 1608
Royal Instructions, OIC, 521, 1669
tracking and telemetry facilities*, 464
upper air observations, geophysical memoirs, 900
Seymour Papers at Longleat, 871

SHACKLETON, RT. HON. LORD: Report on Civil Service Department, 1544
Sharing of Church Buildings Measure, 1112, 1406, 1518, 1643
Bill, 620, 991, 992, 998, 1066, 1072, 1074, 1276
Sharks, British Wealden, 102
SHARP, LADY: Tranport planning—The Men for the Job, 1719
SHAW, H. K. A.: Sphenoecleaceae, 720
SHAW, R. M. (Chairman): Fluoridation, 1268
SHAW, W. A.: Calendar of Treasury Books, 1324
Sheep:
aids to management, 1120
and miscellaneous items, buildings for, 86
diseases of, 90
fluke or liver rot, 88
handling pens, and baths, 1121
Sheffield, design bulletins, 1646
SHELDEN, SIR W. (Chairman): Child Welfare Centres, 470
SHELDON, R.: Effect of high energy radiation on epoxy resin systems used for particle accelerator construction, 922
Shelter belts for farm land, 1121
SHEPHARD-THORN, E. R.: Around Tenterden, 195
SHERIDAN, M.: Developmental progress of infants and young children, 870
Sheriff Court Records, Scotland, 536
Shetland Islands:
Geological surveys, 906
sodic scapolite (dipyre), 1312
Shift:
work, multiple, 1661
working, introduction, 752

Ship(s):
Captain's medical guide, 574, 1372
carriage of dangerous goods, 950
and explosives, 232
code and decode book, 509
disinfecting, 146
establishments, and Officers of the Fleet, list, 1551
models, 208
provisions, inspection fees, 238
registry of, see Registry of ships
Stations, VHF transmitter and receiver, 1668
see also Mercantile Navy List
Shipbuilding:
and:
modern engineering, census of production, 957
Ship Repairing:
(careers), 747
Industry, report, 1566
Credit Act, loans and accounts, 240, 574, 959, 1372
Industry:
Act, 369, 1112
account, 1353
Bill, 281–2, 332, 335, 336, 478, 671, 992, 1066, 1276, 1481
Board, report and accounts, 506, 1353, 1694
Training Board, 187, 754, 1156, 1571
Inquiry Committee, 240
Shipowners, loans, 574, 959, 1372
Shipping:
and seamen, General Register and Record Office, 1366, 1710
assistance and salvage at sea, 853
carriage of passenger luggage, 853
casualties and deaths, 240, 574, 959, 1372, 1715
industry, Court of Inquiry report, 501
Inter-Governmental Maritime Consultative Organisation, Convention, 460, 853–4
maritime liens and mortgages, 853
report, inquiry, 1709
tonnage measurement, 1608
Shirts:
census of production, 958
in the Seventies, 1661
Shop(s):
and office fittings, census of production, 958
Bill, 665
Stewards:
and workshop relations, research, paper, 920
role in British industrial relations, 205

1966-70 | SHO-SQU

SHO— INDEX 1966–70

Shop(s) (*continued*):
  (Sunday Trading):
    Bill, 290, 1412
    (No. 2) Bill, 609, 611, 668
  (Weekday Trading) Bill, 1484
Shopkeepers, independent, guide to bigger profits, 1661
Shoppers' Table, decimal currency poster, 1548
Short Title(s):
  and index, Public General Acts, tables, 76, 367, 703, 1111, 1514
  catalogue of:
    books printed:
      before 1701 in the Foreign Office Library, 146
      in France, 100
    Spanish, Spanish American, and Portugese Books, 100
Shrewsbury and Talbot Papers, calendar, 159
Shropshire:
  census, 153
  sample census, 468, 862

SI:
  International system of Units, 1713
  Units in electricity and magnetism, 1713
Sickness benefit, decision of the Commissioner, 868, 1265, 1620
Sidney Papers, Historical Manuscripts, 473
Sierra Leone, double taxation*, 1250
Sight:
  fees and charges for testing, 158, 472, 870, 1268, 1623
  reduction tables for air navigation, 732
  tests for seafarers, 1715
Signal(s):
  International code, 1367
  letters of U.K. and Commonwealth ships, 240, 574, 959, 1372
Signs and posters, planning control, 174
Signy Island, South Orkneys:
  geology, 718
  petrology, 719
Sikh(s):
  marriage and customary divorce in India, decision of the Commissioner, 1620
  paintings, 266
Silage:
  bulletin
  forces exerted on bunker silo walls, 1519
Silicified productoids, 103
SILLITOE, K. K.: Planning for leisure, 1262
Silver:
  German domestic, small picture book, 599
  Hispanic, the Golden Age, 1396
  Leaf disease of fruit trees, 88
  Tudor domestic, 1736
Silversmith's work, English, 266
SIM, M. E.:
  Distribution of OB Stars in the Northern Milky Way, 921
  Search for globules in OB clusters, 921
SIMMONS, D.: Report on accident at Stevenston explosives factory, 475
SIMMONS, T. M.: Railways, 1675
SIMS, R. W.: Earthworms, 723
Simuliidae, 1125
Singapore:
  Act, 77
    Bill, 6, 50
  air services*, 395
  double taxation*, 395
  gift, 1721
  transfer of land and assets, 968
Single stack plumbing, 912
Single-sideband radio equipment, 909
SINGLETON, N. (Chairman):
  Appointed Factory Doctor Service, 179
  Dismissal procedures, 500
Siphonophora, synopsis, 104
Sir George Cayley (1773–1857) biography, 922
Sir John Leng's Trust Scheme, 211, 534
Sir Walter Scott Scholarship and Bursaries Fund (Amendment) Scheme, 211, 534
Site(s):
  costing for builders, 201
  excavated in advance of destruction, 202, 524, 914, 1321, 1670
  lighting, 912
  picnic, 1134
  prehistoric, Roman, and medieval, 202, 524, 914, 1321, 1670
  safety practice in construction work, 187
  types, forests of North- and Mid-Wales, 1612
Sitka:
  and Norway Spruce, 939
  spruce, 465
Sitpro report, 1661
Sixpence, future, 548
Sixteen plus, examinations, 126
Sixth Form:
  curriculum and examinations, 128
  examining methods, 921
  science, 128
  work, further proposals, 921

SKEFFINGTON, A. M. (Chairman): Public participation in planning, 1297
SKELTON, R. A.: Captain James Cook after Two Hundred Years, 1124
Skenfrith Castle, Monmouthshire, guide, 1670
Sketches by Thornhill, monograph, 599
Skid-resistance tester, 1376

INDEX 1966–70 —SOC

Skills in working with people, improving, 1157
SKINNER, F. G.: Origin and development of weights and measures, 530
Skippers of fishing boats, examinations, 1366
SKURNIK, L. S.: CSE Monitory experiment, 1329
Sky component protractors, 913
Skye, Northern, geology, 195

Slatted floors for beef breeding herds, 512
Slaughter of poultry Act, 369
  Bill, 48, 49, 278, 332, 335, 478
SLEDGE, W. A.: Genus *Elaphoglossum*, 385
Slum(s):
  clearance, 489, 1293
  studies, 1646

Small:
  Claims Courts, 1545
  picture books, 599, 1396
  plant, and hand tools, care of, 521
Smallholdings:
  organised on the basis of Centralised Services, 718
  report and accounts, 95, 382
  statutory, inquiry, 92
Smallpox vaccination:
  certificates, 146
  memorandum, 471
SMART, J.: Identification of insects of medical importance, 104
SMART, J. G. O.: Geology of the country around Canterbury and Folkstone, 514
SMITH, D. B.: Geology of the country between Durham and West Hartlepool, 906
SMITH, D. L.: *Linaceae*, 112
SMITH, E. G.: Geology of the Country around Chesterfield, Matlock, and Mansfield, 514
SMITH, H.: *Gentianaceae*, 1537
SMITH, J. B.: Talley Abbey, Carmarthenshire, guide, 522
SMITH, T. D., (Chairman):
  Development Corporations for new towns, 1647
  Northern Economic Planning Council, 124
Smithfield Market, 1208
SMM in metric, 1309
Smoke Control Areas:
  (Authorised Fuels):
    (No. 2) Regulations, circular, 1645
    Regulations, circulars, 1293, 1644
  estimates and final costs, 170, 266
Smoker, young, study, 1261
Smoking:
  among schoolboys, 1261
  habits and attitudes, adults and adolescents, 864
Smoky Chimneys, 912

Snakes, classification, 387
Snow and slush, measurement and reporting action, 572
Snowdonia, Forest Park guide, 1255

Soap, detergents, candles, and glycerine, census of production, 957
Social:
  Affairs, estimate committee, 480
  and:
    economic change, education implications, 415
    medical assistance, European convention, 146
  Insurance, earnings related benefits, 126
  Science(s), 415, 746, 1147, 1653
    Research:
      Council, annual report, 127, 746, 1147, 1563
      Unit:
        report, 1267
        study, 1268
  Security:
    European:
      code, 460
      interim agreements, 460, 1250
    Everybody's guide, 537
    in Britain, 1649
    Italy, convention, 1250,
    Ministry of:
      annual report, 538, 867
      Order by Her Majesty, pensions etc., 540
      publications, 214–17, 537–40
      Royal Warrant, Army pensions, 540
      see also Health and Social Security
    New Zealand*, 1250
    Preliminary Draft of the National Insurance (Classification) Amendment Regulations, 1268
    Republic of Ireland*, 111, 854
    Switzerland*, 854
  Services in Britain, Information Office pamphlet, 177, 1299
  Survey reports, 863–4, 1261–2
  trends, 1542
  welfare for the elderly, 864
  Work:
    and the community, 213
    Council for Training in, 156
    in Scotland, 1680

SOC— INDEX 1966–70

Social (*continued*):
  Work (*continued*):
    (Scotland) Act, 703
      Bill, 608, 610, 616, 663, 667, 669, 877
      notes, 1680
    Services Group:
      child care in Scotland, 928
      children's hearings, 1680
Society and the young school leaver, 415
Socio-economic group, census tables, 154
Sodic scapolite (dipyre), Shetland Islands, 1312
Soft drinks, British wines, cider, and perry, census of production, 957
Softwoods, home-grown, for building, 220
Soil(s):
  agricultural science progress, 1133
  analysis for advisory purposes, 88
  and:
    foundations, 220
    manures for vegetables, 711
    waste pipe systems:
      housing, 523, 1671
      office building, 1671
      potassium and magnesium, 382
      around Haddington and Eyemouth, 374
  sulphate bearing, concrete in, 913
  Survey:
    of G.B., 709, 1115
    Research Board, 86, 709
  technical bulletin, 95
Soke of Peterborough, census, 153
Solar heat gain calculations, 1672
Soldier Magazine, 116 17, 400, 734, 1140, 1550–1
Solicitors:
  practice leaflets, 898
  remuneration, Prices and Incomes Board, 902
  standing reference, 1308
Solid:
  fuel appliances, installing, 1320, 1669
  smokeless fuels, supplies, 488
  toxic wastes, disposal, 1646
Solid-liquid separation, 223
SOLLBERGER, E:
  Babylonian legend of the flood, 99
  Royal inscriptions, Ur excavations, 101
Solomon Islands, Thysanoptera, 1537
Solus Petrol Order, 8, 10
Solvents, food additives, 93
Solway Barrage, 599
SOMERSCALES, T. J.: Large print in National Maritime Museum, 512
Somerset:
  census, 153
  County Council Act, 371, 1518
  sample census, 468, 862
Sonneratiaceae, 729
SORSBY, A.:
  Incidence and causes of blindness E. and W., 158
  Refraction and its components during growth, 1655
Sound:
  and television Broadcasting in Britain, Information Office pamphlet, 1299
  insulation:
    and new forms of construction, 913
    of traditional dwellings, concrete floors, 1322
Soups, Food Standards Committee report, 715
Sources of energy, review, 108
South:
  Africa:
    customs privileges*, 854
    double taxation*, 422, 460, 854, 1165, 1251
    War graves*, 1254, 1610
  and South-East Asia:
    Colombo Plan, 1313
    Information Office pamphlet, 895
  Arabia(n):
    Authorities, gifts, 586
    Federation, friendship and protection*, 112
    Service awards, 246
    See also Southern Yemen
  Atcham Scheme, 1297
  Australia, ownership of property, 968
  East:
    Dorset, ancient monuments, 1628
    Economic Planning Council, 412
    Lancashire:
      and North Cheshire Passenger Transport Area (Designation) Order, S.I. select committee, 1287
      conurbation housing condition, survey, 1295
    Strategic plan, 1648
    Strategy, 412
  Georgia, fur seal, 719
  Hampshire study, 174
  of Scotland:
    Electricity Board:
      advances, 198, 517, 909, 1317
      annual report and accounts, 200, 532, 925, 1331, 1678
      loan, 969, 1381, 1722
    Hydro-Electric Board, loan, 249, 583
  Orkney Islands:
    geology, 718
    petrology, 719
  Pacific:
    Higher education mission, 196
    quarterly surface current charts, 509

INDEX 1966–70 —SQU

South (*continued*):
  Shetland Islands, geology, 98, 719
  Wales:
    and the Severn Estuary coasts, 728
    coalfield, geology, 1312
    geology, 1662
  West(ern):
    Economic Planning Council, 412
    England, geology, 1311
    Region, sample census, 863
    Scotland, strategy for, 1678
Southampton Corporation Act, 1518
Southern:
  Counties of Scotland, sands and gravels, 1663
  England, guide to ancient monuments, 202
  galactic clusters, three-colour photometry, 207, 921
  Irish Sea, seismic reflection survey, 1312
  Livestock Producers Ltd, investigation, 951
  Rhodesia, import and export licences, 236
  stars, fundamental data, 206
  Yemen, independence, 854
Southport, Lancashire, fatal accident, 1627
Soviet Union:
  air services*, 1608
  Consular convention*, 146, 854
  co-operation in applied science and technology*, 854
  direct communication link*, 461
  financial and property claims*, 854
  long term trade*, 1251, 1369
  merchant navigation*, 849
  scientific, educational and cultural relations*, 461, 1251
  visas*, 855
Sow and litter, housing, 380

Space:
  in the home, metric edition, 888
  introduction to, 731
  learning about, 1561
  Research and Development, estimates committee, 480, 878
Spain, double taxation*, 1251
Sparrow, *see* House-sparrow
Speaker of the House of Commons (Chairman), Boundary Commission, 1269
Special:
  Army Orders, 117, 400, 734–5, 1140, 1551
  cements, 912
  Commonwealth African Assistance Plan, report, 108
  drawing rights, International Monetary Fund, 971
  education, 534
Special (*continued*):
  hardship allowance, decision of the Commissioner, 1266
  Hospitals and State Hospitals, estimates committee, 878
  Inter-governmental conference on the status of teachers, 743
  missions, convention, 1608
  Orders, H.C., *see* House of Commons
  Report series, Medical Research Council, 190, 508, 900, 1655
  Schools for handicapped pupils, E. and W., 413
    lists, 1146
  study areas, Scotland, 863
Specification, road and bridge works, 1376
Spectometers, magnetic, 1329
Spectrometry, neutron, 922
Spectrophotometry, automated, 529
Spectroscopic binaries, orbital elements, 920
Speech Therapist (careers), 747
Spence Bursary Trust Scheme, 211
Sphaeroceridae, 1125
Sphecidae, 385, 721
Sphenocleaceae, 729
Sphingidae, 724
SPICER, C. C.: Regional and social factors in infant mortality, 154
Spinning:
  and doubling of cotton, flax, and man-made fibres, census of production, 1371
  cotton and man-made fibres (careers), 497, 1564
Spirit distilling and compounding, census of production, 957
Spores and pollen revealed by light and electron microscopy, 386
Sporting Events (Betting) Bill, 48, 50, 275
Sports:
  Council report, 1134
  equipment, census of production, 958
  Facilities and Planning Acts, circular, 1644
Sprat fishery, Wash, 1524
Sprayers, orchard, 1525
Spring Traps Bill, *see* Agriculture (Spring Traps), Scotland Bill
Spruce:
  and other conifers, adelgid attack, 860
  great bark beetle, 151
  Norway, 939
  seedling survival and growth, 860
  sitka:
    rooting and stability, 465
    timber, 939
Spurdogs, 93, 715

Squalus acanthius, 93, 374, 715
SQUIRREL, H. C., the country around Newport, (Mon.), 1312

SRI-SYM | 1966-70

Srivastava, K. D.:
Nimrod electrostatic inflector
Support insulator for high voltage apparatus in vacuum, 209

Staff(ing):
location systems, precautions, 866
of:
Mental Deficiency Hospitals, 1681
Secondary Schools, circular, 1332
titles and job description in commercial data processing, 556
turnover, hotels and catering, 1309
Staffordshire:
census, 153
County Council Act, 1518
sample census, 468, 862
Stage costume and accessories, London Museum, 898
Stag-Hunting with Hounds (Abolition) Bill, 667
Stainless steel:
as a building material, 1671
plumbing, 523
Stains:
chart, 1152, 1153
on brickwork, 1320
Stamp, Hon. M. (Chairman): London taxicabs, 1627
Stamps Bill, 1479
Standard(s):
capacitors, accuracy in practice, 1352
in CSE and GCE, 415
industrial classification, 725, 1129
newsprint, prices, 510
Public Library service in Scotland, 1333
specification (M and E), 1673
stars, radial velocity observations, 1327
systems of hotel accounting, 1309
Standard-Triumph (Liverpool) Ltd., Court of Inquiry, 1153
Standing:
committees:
debates, 41, 45, 331, 334, 661, 664, 1054–5, 1060–7, 1460, 1465–74
returns, 167–8, 885, 1288, 1641
Dental Advisory Committee, 865
Medical Advisory Committee:
child welfare, 470
dental anaesthesia, 470
Orders:
H.C., 168, 484, 885–6, 1288, 1641
H.L., 169, 486, 1290, 1643
(Revision), select committee on, 1640
Stansted:
Airport, Council on Tribunals special report, 899
objections to development as third London airport, 493
Star Explorations Ltd. investigation, 952
Star(s):
Almanac for land surveyors, 205, 529, 920, 1328, 1675
and interstellar matter, distribution, 207
binary peculiar A, 529, 921
bright, Fabry photometry, 206
circumpolar, catalogue, 206
late-type, 529, 1328
manganese, 53 Tauri, 207
Northern:
A, 920
three-colour photometry, 1327
OB, distribution, Milky Way, 921
photoelectric magnitudes and colours, 206
RR Lyrae, 206
Southern, fundamental data, 206
standard, 1327
Wolf-Rayet, 529
Starch and miscellaneous foods, census of production, 957
Starfishes, 387
Starlight in h and x Persei, 921
State:
Management Districts Licensing Acts, annual reports, 162, 475, 874, 1628
of:
Emergency, proclamation, 1688
revoking, 1688
public health, *see* Public health
Papers:
calendar, 1324
list and analysis, 1324
Statement of:
excesses, 971, 1383, 1725
trade, 113, 369, 730, 1135, 1546
Stationers' goods, miscellaneous, census of production, 1372
Stationery Office:
question papers, Civil Service Commission, 106
publications, 217–8, 541–2, 929–31, 1336–42, 1683–9
Statistical:
abstract, Commonwealth and Sterling area, 234, 568, 951
classification:
goods, 397
imported and re-exported goods, 731
decision theory, 966
digest, Ministry of Power, 200
News, 725, 1130, 1542
Papers, Ministry of Transport, 244
report series, 472, 870, 1268, 1623
review, E. and W. GRO, 861
Services, Government, 479
summary of the mineral industry, 195, 514, 906, 1312, 1663

1966 pp 1–272, 1967 pp 273–604, 1968 pp 605–990, 1969 pp 991–1402, 1970 pp 1403–1740

136

Statistical (*continued*):
tables:
National Coal Board, 1319, 1694
Prison Department, 162, 872, 874, 1626, 1628
Sea Fisheries, 382, 717, 1122, 1526
Scottish, 374, 710, 1116, 1521
Statistics:
annual abstract, 105, 369, 1129, 1541
handbook, 171, 491, 891, 1294, 1646
monthly digest, 105–6, 389, 725, 1130, 1541
official, studies in 389, 506, 725, 1130, 1542
regional abstracts, 105, 388, 724, 1129, 1541
see also subject, agricultural etc.
Status of:
teachers, English and Welsh editions, 743
women, political rights, 461
Statute(s):
chronological table, 128, 542, 931, 1342, 1689
in force, 218, 546, 931, 1690
interpretation, Law Commission, 1303
Law:
(Repeals) Act, 1112
Bill, 997, 1001, 1066, 1075, 1289, 1303, 1415, 1654
Revision:
Act, 77
Bill, 48
Law Commission, 1303, 1654
Statutory:
Harbour Authorities (Minister of Transport) loans, 417, 962, 1158
Instruments:
Bound annual volumes, 219, 542–3, 931, 1342, 1690
lists, annual and monthly, 219, 542–3 931, 1342, 1689
select committee, 164, 167, 478, 482–3, 877, 885, 1276, 1287, 1631, 1640
maintenance limits, committee report, 874
Orders, tables and index, 705
Publications Office, publications, 218–9, 542–3, 931–2, 1342, 1689–90
Smallholdings, inquiry, 92, 379
Steam and Sailing vessels, *see* Mercantile Navy List
Steamship(s):
Merchant ships to 1880, 1329
Mutual Underwriting Association Ltd., 576
Stearn, W. T.:
Jamaican species of *Columnea* and *Alloplectus*, 1125
Synopsis of Jamaican *Myrsinaceae*, 1124
Steel(s):
Company of Wales, dispute, 499–500
prices, 1307
temperature attained in Building fires, 221
tubes, census of production, 457
very strong, 96
Steers, J. A. (Chairman): Regional Coastal conference, 728
Stegocephalidae, 1127
Stellar luminosity, effect of rotation by, 207
Stellicola:
caerulus, 387
new species, 387
Stem eelworm on tulips, 89
Stempfer, H.: Lycaenidae, 386
Stephens, Sir E. (Chairman): Centenary exhibition, Historical Manuscripts Commission, 1269
Stephenson, T.: The Pennine Way, 1134
Sterilizers and disinfectors, hospital, 1616
Sterling, overseas, minimum proportion*, 855
Stevenson, G. R.: Neutron spectrometry, 922
Stevenston Explosives Factory, fatal accident, 475
Stewart, M.: Britain and the ILO, 1149
Stewarts and Lloyds Ltd, Court of Inquiry, 501
Stirling:
census tables, 155
County Council Order Confirmation Bill, 1484
District, geology, 1663
Stock, J. T.: Development of the Chemical Balance, 1329
Stoke-on-Trent Corporation Act, 1518
Stone:
Age, techniques and cultures, 720
and slate quarrying and mining, census of production, 957
Stonham, Lord (Chairman): Constitutional relationship, I.O.M. and U.K., 1272
Stonehenge, What is? German edition, 912
Stonemasonry (careers), 499
Stores for mixed expolsives, 1273
Storm:
Overflows:
circular, 1643
technical committee, 1648
sewage disposal:
circular, 1643
report, 1648
Storm-drains, sewers, and pipelines, hydraulic design, 1692
Strachan, I.: W. Carruthers' type graptlites, 1126
Strategic plan for the South-East, 1648

1966 pp 1–272, 1967 pp 273–604, 1968 pp 605–990, 1969 pp 991–1402, 1970 pp 1403–1740

137

Strategy for the:
South-East, 412
South-West, 412
Stratigraphy:
and:
palaeogeography of Yorkshire oolites, 386
planktonic foraminifera, 102
Graham Land and James Ross Island group, 386
Lower ordovician, 103
Strauss, G. R. (Chairman), Censorship of the theatre, 485
Strawberries, bulletin, 1521
Street:
cleansing, costing returns, 174, 493, 893
Offences Bill, 289, 991, 1004
widths for new streets, 488
Strength properties of:
plywood, 554, 1351
timber, 554, 1351
Strengthening of Marriage Bill, 7, 48
Strong, D. E.: Carved amber, catalogue, 99
Strong, R.:
House of Tudor, 513
Tudor and Jacobean Portraits, 1310
Strontium–90 in human bone in the U.K., 190, 508, 899, 1305, 1655
Strophomenacean brachiopods, 722
Structural:
fire precautions, circular, 1291
steel, behaviour in fire, 939
Structure of Art and Design Education, 1563
Stuart, House of, 1310
Stubbings, H. G.: Cirriped fauna, 387
Student(s):
at Teacher Training establishments, grants, 125
awards:
circulars, English and Welsh editions, 125
entries to Colleges of Education, 126
National Diplomas in hotel keeping and catering, 127
maintenance grants, Advisory Panel, 743
numbers in Higher Education, 1561
Scotland, 1680
on Teacher Training courses, grants, 743, 1561
Pilots' and Private Pilots' licence, 959
progress, inquiry, 984
relations, select committee on Education and Science, 1281, 1282

Sub-committees (Estimates Committee):
Allocation of matters, 167, 483, 879, 1277
Appointments of, 167, 483, 879, 1277
Subphyum calcichordata, 722
Subsidies:
for Housing Associations, 489–90
Housing, manual, 491
Suckers, apple and pear, 375
Sudan:
Interest free loan*, 1608, 1251
technical assistance*, 1609
Suet, Food Standards Committee, 1525
Suffolk, census, 153
Sugar:
Act, accounts, 95, 382, 718, 1122, 1526
Beet:
cultivation, 1521
harvesting, 94
home grown. *See* Home grown sugar beet
pests, 1117
Board, report and accounts, 95, 382, 718, 1122, 1526
census of production, 957
confectionery industry:
census of production, 957
costs and prices, 902
International agreement, 147, 355, 1251
Sulphate, attack on brickwork, 523
Sumerian Art, 1537
Summerfield report on psychologists in education services, 745
Summerhayes, V. S.: *Orchidaceae*, 729
Sumner, P:
Carriages, 1675
Motor Cars up to 1930, 1392
Sunday Entertainments Act:
Bill, 9, 274, 337, 339, 663, 666, 877, 1066, 1070, 1077, 1276, 1411
Cinematograph Fund account, 130, 418, 755
Sunday Times, Privileges Committee, 1280, 1634
Sunley, J. G.: Grade stresses for structural timbers, 939
Sunpath diagrams and overlays for solar heat gain calculations, 1672
Superannuation:
(Civil Service and Local Government) Interchange Rules, circular, 888
(Local Government and:
Approved Employment) Interchange Rules, circular, 1292
Other Employments) Interchange Rules, circular, 1292
Overseas Employment) Interchange Rules, circular, 1292
(Miscellaneous Provisions) Act, 369, 539
Bill, 280, 333, 336, 478
(Scottish Teaching and English Local Government) Interchange Rules, circular, 1292
(Teaching and Local Government) Interchange Rules
Supervisory Training, 187

1966 pp 1–272, 1967 pp 273–604, 1968 pp 605–990, 1969 pp 991–1402, 1970 pp 1403–1740

138

Supplementary:
Benefits Commission:
handbook, 1623
report, 537
Estimates, Defence (Central), *see* Defence Estimates, Supplementary, Central
Supply Estimates, 1725, 1726
index, 1725
Supreme Court:
of Judicature:
Account, 193
Masters' Practice, Directions, Tables and Forms, 190
Northern Ireland, Land Purchase, 219, 543, 932, 1343, 1690
of Northern Ireland, report on, 1655
Rules, 190, 508, 899, 1305, 1655
Surface:
Water:
run off from development, circular, 1293
Year book of G.B., 175, 985
Supplement, 985
wind speed and direction, U.K., tables, 901, 1306
Surgery for the newborn, 865
Surgical instruments, census of production, 1371
Surplus:
Land, circular, 171
United States Defence equipment, disposal, 123, 410, 742, 1144, 1560
Surrender of Japan, 1128
Surrey, sample census, 468, 862
Surtax:
rates, 896
tables, 896
Survey(s):
and 900 mb wind relationships, 192
geological, *see* Geological Surveys
geophysical, *see* Geophysical surveys
of:
British and Commonwealth Affairs, 495, 895, 1299, 1649
mergers, Monopolies Commission, 1713
professional engineers, 556
Surveying:
for civil engineers, Commonwealth conference, 1314
instruments and methods, 922
Surveyor, Land Agent, Auctioneer, and Estate Agent, (careers), 747
Sussex, sample census, 1259
Sutherland:
mineral resources, 1312
see also County of Sutherland
Sutton, Sir Graham (Chairman): Natural Environment Research Council, 514
Sutton, S. C.: Guide to India Office Library, 394, 1240
Sutton Hoo Ship Burial, 721

Swallow, Sir W. (Chairman):
Investment in hotels and catering, 904
Manpower statistics of the hotel and catering industry, 512
Staff turnover, hotels and catering, 1309
visitors to Britain, 512
Swann, Prof. M. M. (Chairman):
Antibiotics in animal husbandry, 1264
Manpower for scientific growth, 125, 743
Swansea Corporation Act, 1518
Swarming of bees, 1522
Swaziland:
Arms, 1251
Colonial report, 109, 393
Constitutional proposals, 111
double taxation*, 1251
Independence:
Act, 705
Bill, 615, 668
Booklet, 896
Conference, 855
Information Office pamphlet, 895
loan, 581
public officers*, 855
report, 1251
Sweden:
atomic energy*, 461
double taxation, 133, 761, 855, 1252
extradition*, 147
interchange of information for defence*, 461
international carriage of goods by road*, 853, 855
taxation of road vehicles*, 855
transfer of nuclear material to Switzerland*, 1252
Swine erysipelas, 87
Swinton, W. E.:
Dinosaurs, 387, 1539
Fossil birds, 104
Swiss, R. G. (Chairman):
Dental:
anaesthesia, 470
technicians, 865
Switzerland:
double taxation*, 133, 461
income tax, 1300
judicial settlement arbitration*, 461
licences for amateur radio operators*, 461
loans, 1377
nuclear material transfer*, 1252
social security*, 854, 1252

Sylloge of coins in the British Isles, 101
Symmetries, higher, introduction to, 208

1966 pp 1–272, 1967 pp 273–604, 1968 pp 605–990, 1969 pp 991–1402, 1970 pp 1403–1740

139

Symphyta, 722
Synchrotrons, proton, 194, 923
Synodical Government:
  Measure, 997, 1131, 1415, 1543
  No. 2, 1131
  (Special Majorities) Measure, 1542, 1543
Synthetic:
  detergents, 174, 493, 1297, 1648
  resins, and plastics materials, census of production, 1371
System(s):
  analysis report, 1660
  analysts:
    (commercial), training, 1157
    selection, 1660
  building, safety, 753

T

Tables, see specific subject
Tachinidae, 385, 386, 1125
Tachysphex kohl, 385
TAIT, H.: Clocks in the B.M., 720
Taken for granted, sewage disposal, 1648
TALBOT, J. W.: Hydrography of the estuary of the River Blackwater, 715
Talking machines (1877–1914), 530
Talley Abbey, Carmarthenshire, guide, 522
Tamaricaceae, 112
Tanah Estates Ltd, investigation, 234
Tanker equipment, liquid manure disposal, 1525
Tanzania:
  Act, 1112
  Bill, 996, 1074
  income tax, 1300
TAPPER R. J.: Vapour pressure and molar volume for liquid hydrogen and deuterium, 194
Tarbela Development Fund*, 851
Tariff:
  amendments, Customs and Excise, 113, 397, 730, 1135, 1547
  and overseas trade, classification, 1135
  tables, metric, forestry, 1611
Task ahead, economic assessment, 1145
Tate Gallery reports, 219, 543
Tattooing of Minors Act, 1118
  Bill, 995, 1066, 1071, 1072, 1276
TAVERNE, D. (Chairman):
  Police manpower, equipment, and efficiency, 474
  Recruitment into the police service, 475
Tax(es):
  Association of H.M. Inspectors, 1279

Tax(es) (continued):
  Cases:
    appeals to the High Court, 178–9, 496–7, 896, 1300–2, 1650–2
    Board of Inland Revenue, 179, 498, 897–8, 1302, 1652–3
    Harrison's Index, 177, 496, 1300, 1650
  Management Act, 1516
    Bill, 1403, 1480, 1642
    Tables of comparison, 1650
Taxation:
  British system, Information Office pamphlet, 177, 1299
  Double:
    relief, 177
    agreements, see respective countries of:
      goods vehicles, Turkey*, 856, 857
      Road vehicles:
        convention, 1252
        Sweden*, 855
      woodland, 465
Taxicab fares, proposed increase, London, 903
TAYLOR, A. J.: Basinwerk Abbey, Flintshire, 201
TAYLOR, J. D.: Bivalvia, 1128
Tayside, potential for development, 1678

Tea prices, Prices and Incomes Board, 1658
Teacher(s):
  British, in France, social insurance, 1598
  Education, Training, and:
    Certification, entry requirements and courses, 212, 534
    Registration, 483, 927, 1680
    (Scotland) Regulations S.I. select committee, 483
  experience of school based examining, 415
  future recruitment and training, 211
  in:
    E. and W., statistics, 1563
    Further Education, salaries, 745, 1333, 1680
    Primary and Secondary Schools:
      arbitral report on payment, 745
      salary scales, 414, 1333
    Scotland, more equitable distribution, 211
    Secondary Schools, curriculum and deployment, 746
  industry, and summers, shown links, 128
  of Nursing Act, 369
    Bill, 34, 46, 49, 164, 278
    qualified, in schools, 743
  salary(ies):
    memorandum, Scottish, 927, 1680
    scales, 1147

Teacher(s) (continued):
  salary(ies) (continued):
    Scottish, Prices and Incomes Board, 192
  Scotland, Remuneration Act, see Remuneration of Teachers (Scotland) Act
  statistics of education, 746
  status of, 743
  Unesco recommendation concerning, 925
Superannuation:
  Acts, 129, 369
    Bill 8, 335, 484
    Government Actuary's report, 1133
  (Family Benefits) (Scotland) Regulations:
    circular, 1332
    S.I. select committee, 482, 1287
  Scheme:
    E. and W., 1133
    Scotland, Government Actuary's report, 211
  (Scotland):
    Act, 705
      Bill, 478
      Government Actuary's report, 1680
    Regulations, circular, 1332
  Supply and training for Further Education, 129
  survey of in-service training, 1563
Training:
  Correspondence Courses in the Commonwealth, 108
  Grants to recognised students, 125, 1561
  revision of regulations, circular, 533
  select committee on Education and Science, 1282, 1634, 1635
University:
  standing reference on pay, 1657
  superannuation, 746
Teaching:
  (careers), 747
  computing in Universities, 1735
  Council:
    for E. and W., 1563
    (Scotland) Bill, 1414, 1474, 1479, 1482, 1483, 1631
  of:
    classics in schools, 534, 1329
    literature, Central Committee on English, 925
    reading, select committee on Education and Science, 1635
    sciences, select committee on Education and Science, 1635

Teaching (continued):
  staff:
    Colleges of Education:
      report on salaries, 414
      salary scales, E. and W., 1147
    Farm Institutes, salary scales, 1147
    Training Courses in E. and W., compendium, 125, 413
TEBBLE, N.: British bivalve seashells, 101
Technical:
  College(s):
    management studies, 126
    resources:
      effective use, 1562
      more effective use, 1146
    use of costing etc., 1146
  co-operation:
    Peru*, 147
    under the Colombo Plan, 907
    workshops, 1680
  Technician(s):
    courses and examinations, 1146
    education and training of, 392
    surveyors, cartographers, and photogrammetrists, training and qualifications, 1314
Technological:
  and scientific affairs, estimates committee, 480
  innovation in Britain, 724
  manpower, studies in, 1695
Technologists etc., manpower survey, 125
Technology:
  and the schools, 921
  Ministry of, publications, 219–23, 543–56, 930, 1343–54, 1690–5
    see also Ministries of Aviation, Aviation Supply, and Power
Tecophilaeaceae, 112
Tees:
  and Hartlepools Port Authority Act, 79, 1114
    accounts, 1159
  Valley and Cleveland Water Act, 371
    Bill, 276, 486
Teesside:
  Corporation Act, 1114
  Survey and plan, 1297
Teeth, erosion, 216
Telecommunications:
  Commonwealth Telegraphs*, 1282
  International convention*, 462
Telegraph and telephone apparatus, census of production, 957
Teleos(s):
  and mylophoids, 1126
  fishes, Gilbert Islands, 1539
Telephone:
  facilities on new housing estates, 488
  Regulations, S.I. select committee, 885

Telephone (continued):
  services:
    H.Q., 481
    Palace of Westminster, 882
Televising proceedings of H.L., 278, 384, 486
Television:
  Act, accounts, 197, 516, 909
  (Advertisements) Bill, 1409
  Advisory Committee report, 909
  and:
    Race Relations Select Committee, 1285
    Sound Radio Communal Aerial Systems, U.K., 1673
Telipna aurivillius, 1125
Temperance polls, 928
Temperature tables, relative humidity and precipitation, 192, 510
TEMPLE, J. T.: Trilobites, 1538
Temporary adaption of machines, decimal currency booklet, 1547
Tempskya from Kent, 722
Tenant(s):
  farmers, displaced on acquisition of land, compensation, 488
  in receipt of supplementary benefit, rent, 1572
  Tendering documents with a production bias, 911
Tenebrionidae, 385
Ten-minute rule motions, Procedure select committee, 1637
TENNANT, J. R.: Araliaceae, 729
Termination of military control, Germany, British Foreign policy, 1164
Termites, 1137
Termitidae, 1537
Terracottas in the B.M., 1537
Territorial:
  and:
    Army Volunteer Reserve Regulations, 734, 1139, 1550
    Auxiliary Forces Associations, financial position, 124, 411, 742
  Army:
    Regulations, 116
    Volunteer Reserve Regulations, 399
Tertiary, East Indian Letter Classification, 1538
Testing:
  concrete, 1669
  of sight:
    and supply of glasses, fees and charges, 1268
    fees and charges, 158, 472
Tettigoniidae, 722, 1125, 1537
Textile:
  finishing, census of production, 958

Textile (continued):
  industries, miscellaneous, census of production, 958
  machinery and accessories, census of production, 957

Thailand, air services*, 856
Thames:
  Conservancy Act, 79
  Valley Water Act, 706
Theatre(s):
  Act, 705
    Bill, 611, 615, 663, 665, 667, 669, 877
  censorship, 485
  today in E. and W., 1527
Theft:
  Act, 705
    Bill, 290, 606, 609, 610, 617, 663, 667, 669, 877
  and related offences, Criminal Law Revision Committee, 160
Therapeutic substances of human origin*, 462, 856, 1603
Thermal Insulation:
  advisory leaflets, 1320, 1669
  Contracting Industry, pay of certain workers, 903
  (Industrial Buildings) Act, explanatory memorandum, 520
  Think metric, 1323
Third:
  Lanark Athletic Club Ltd., investigation, 951
  London Airport, 575
    Commission on, 1365, 1708
    objections to Stansted, inquiry, 493
  Reich, German Foreign policy, 132
THOMAS, A. H. (Chairman): Cutlery wages, 1156
THOMAS, D. B.:
  Cameras photographs and accessories, 207
  First Colour Motion Pictures, 1329
  Science Museum photography collection, 1329
THOMAS, D. V.: Observing programme, optimization, 529
THOMAS, G.: Operatives in the building industry, 864
THOMAS, H.: Catalogues of Spanish, Spanish-American, and Portugese Books, 100
THOMAS, H. J.: Lobster storage, 1116
THOMAS, I.: Common names of British insects and other pests, 718
THOMAS, M.: The fire service and its personnel, 1262
THOMAS, P. M. (Chairman): Scottish Transport Group, 1682

THOMPSON, E. J.: Population projections for the South-East, 468
THOMPSON, G. L.: Automated spectrophotometry, 529
THOMPSON, PROF. R. H. S. (Chairman): Transport of nerve agents, 1550
THOMPSON, R. T.: Curculionidae, 1125
THOMSON, A. (Chairman): Scottish criminal statistics, 927
THOMSON, I. W.: Petrology of Signy Island, 719
Thomson Newspapers Ltd. and Crusha and Son Ltd., Monopolies Commission, 933
THORBURN, W. A.: Uniform of the Scottish Infantry 1740–1900, 1673
Thorn Electrical Industries Ltd. and Radio Rentals Ltd., proposed merger, 955
Thornhill, sketches by, monograph, 599
THORPE, PROF. H. (Chairman): Allotments, 1294
Three:
  Shell Keeps (Launceston, Restormel, Totnes) guide, 1670
  years to go, facts and forecasts, decimal currency booklet, 731
Three-colour photometry, 200, 921, 1327
Thuja plicata, 465
Thurleigh (Bedford) local hearings, Third London Airport, 1365
THURRELL, R. G.:
  Chamosite in weald clay, 1663
  Geology of the country around Haslemere, 112
THURSTON, M. H.: Amphipoda, 1127
Thysanoepeltidae, 103
Thysanoptera, 385, 722, 1537

Tile(s):
  clay, flooring, 523
  concrete, 1671
  medieval, 721
  polystyrene ceiling, 1669
Timber(s):
  and:
    metal, preservation, 1121
    woodwork, insect and marine borer damage, 555
  care in use, 1320
  census of production, 1371
  connectors, 521
  extraction by tractor, 465
  movement of, 555
  round, ready reckoner, 1611
  sap-stain, 1352
  steam bending properties, 555
  sizes for small buildings, 1669
  strength, 222, 554, 1351
  structural laminated, grade stresses, 555, 939, 1692
  Your growing investment, 1255

Time:
  and latitude service, Royal Greenwich Observatory, 509, 920, 1328
  British Standard, 288
  measurement, 530
  rates of wages and hours of work, 187, 506, 754, 1156, 1571
Time-limited planning permissions, 1291
Times and Sunday Times Newspapers, new proprietor, Monopolies Commission, 230
Tin*, 147, 462, 1609
TIMMIS, A.: Inner London Education Authority, study of divisional administration, 916
Tip(s):
  disused, 1316
  safety, 1316
TIRNIZE, N. M.: Galatheidae, 104
Titchfield Abbey, Hampshire, guide, 1321
TITE, G. E.: Lycaenidae, 102, 721
Tithe:
  Act, accounts, 251, 511, 971, 1383, 1725
  redemption, 514, 971
Title(s):
  Abolition Bill, 51
  and contents, parliamentary papers, H.C. and Command, 886, 1276, 1641
  page and index, London Gazette, 218, 541, 931, 1341, 1689
  Tables of contents, and index, H.L. Sessional Papers, 1290, 1643

Tobacco:
  and snuff (Health Hazards), 1485
  census of production, 957
TODD, RT. HON. LORD (Chairman): Medical Education, 919
Toilet preparations:
  census of production, 957
  manufacturers' prices, 1307
Tokyo Convention Act, 369
  Bill, 49, 283, 333, 337, 478
Tomato:
  blight, 88
  ketchup, Food Standards Committee, 1525
  mosaic and streak, 375
TOMLINSON, P. M. L.: Eggs of the Great Auk, 104
Tonga:
  Act, 1516
    Bill, 1408, 1482
    external relations*, 1609
    extradition*, 149
  Tools and Implements, census of production, 958
TOPHILL, P.: Graptolite faunas, 1538

Tor Bay Harbour Act, 1518
Torrey Canyon disaster, 476, 724
Torry Research Station, annual report, 223, 556, 940, 1353, 1695
Totton, A. K.: Synopsis of the siphonophora, 104
Tourism, Scottish, 864
Tourist Trade Facility Bill, 334
Towards the Middle School, 1561
Tower of London:
Crown Jewels, guide, 912
European Armour, 914
guide, 522
souvenir guide, 522
Town:
and Country Planning, 494
Act, 704
accounts, 175, 494, 894, 1297
(Amendment) Bill, 663, 665, 669, 877
Bill, 340, 612, 615, 617, 618, 663, 667, 670, 877, 998
circulars, 170, 488, 890, 891, 1290, 1291, 1644, 1645
(Aerodromes) Direction, 170
(Control of Advertisements) Regulations, 1293
Determination of planning appeals, rules for local inquiries in relation, 891
General:
Development:
(Amendment) Order, 890
Order, 488
Requirements, 1291
Historic buildings and conservation, 890
in Britain, Information Office pamphlet, 895
(Inquiries Procedure) rules, 1292
amendment, 891
New development plan system, manual, 1645
(Public Path Orders) Regulation, 1291
Regulations (London) (Indemnity) Act, 1516
Bill, 1414, 1484
(Scotland) Act(s), 1112
accounts, 175, 494, 894, 1297–8
Bill, 619, 620, 671, 1066, 1074, 1276
statistics, 1297, 1648
transfer of planning appeals, 1645
(Tree Preservation Order) Regulations, 1290
Centre(s):
and Shopping precincts, building regulations, 1291
development, 1294
Town (*continued*):
Centre(s) (*continued*):
Properties Ltd, investigation, 952
redevelopment, 170
Historic, preservation and change, 491
roads, better use of, 576
Town Magazine, Privileges Committee, 880
Toxic:
chemicals, 414, 1145, 1146, 1519
substances in the air, methods of detection, booklets, 186, 501, 750, 1152, 1568
wastes, solid, disposal, 1646
Toxicity tests, fish, 1646
Toys:
games, and sports equipment, census of production, 958
in the London Museum, 1653
small picture book, 599

Tractor:
fuel storage, 1525
timber extraction, 465
Trade and Industry, 1715–16
see also Board of Trade Journal
Trade:
and:
Industry:
Department of, publications 1695–1716
Supply Estimates, 1725
sewage effluents, 489
Board of:
Business Monitor, 224–32, 558–67, 942–50, 1355–64, 1697–1706
Journal, see Board of Trade Journal
publications, 223–41, 557–75, 941–60, 1354–74
Description Act, 705
Bill, 665
(No. 2) Bill, 607, 611, 663, 665, 667, 877
Disputes Bill, 1479
Marks:
classification of goods and services*, 462
International registration*, 1609
Negotiations, Kennedy Round, 571
New Zealand*, 395
Overseas:
report, 574
U.K. accounts, 573
transit, land-locked states, 1252
Union(s):
Acts, 152
and Employers' Associations, Royal Commission, 204–5, 527, 919–20
index to published evidence, 919
research papers, 205, 528, 919–20
selected written evidence, 920

Trade (*continued*):
Union(s) (*continued*):
Chief Registrar of Friendly Societies' report, 152, 466, 861, 1257, 1613
Commission Bill, 335
Structure and Government, 919
U.K. and Commonwealth, and foreign countries, 113, 396, 730, 1135, 1546
Trading accounts and balance sheets, Government Departments, 130, 418, 756, 1159, 1574
Traditional dwellings:
electrical installation, 1323
sound insulation, 1322
Traffic:
Air, *see* Air traffic
and:
public transport, 577
transport plans, 963
Cases, Transport Tribunal decisions, 244, 578, 1376, 1719
prediction, rural roads, 1374
restraint on urban roads, 575
signs:
construction and mounting, 578
illumination, 578
manual, 244, 578, 964
signals, 578
see also Road Traffic
Training:
and:
development of managers, 498, 1149
qualifications:
professional surveyors, 1314
technician surveyors, cartographers, and photogrammetrists, 1314
use of operators as instructors, 1157
Boards, *see specific* Board
Central Council, 180
Centre for Mentally Disordered, 868
Course:
sandwich type, 1617
teaching, 125
for commerce and the office, 187
Information Papers, 754, 1156
of:
Export staff, 754
Probationary constables, 1626
Systems Analysts (Commercial), 1157
Training officers, 498
Research Register, 754, 1157
terms, glossary, 501
Transfer of:
land, Law Commission, 507, 1303
title to chattels, Law Reform Committee, 189
Transistor circuit techniques, 530
Transit trade of land-locked States, 1252
Transparent Paper Ltd., Monopolies Commission, 1713
Transplantation problems, human tissue, 1264
Transport:
Act, 705
Bill, 339, 613, 617, 618, 663, 667, 670, 964, 1276
loans, 245, 251, 418, 578, 964, 971, 1376, 1383–4, 1726
1968 (Amendment) Bill, 1071
and General Workers Union, inquiry, 501, 1571
Central Consultative Committee for G.B., 576
Finances Act, 77
Bill, 4, 48
for industry (Summary report), 1376
freight, 579
Highland, *see* Highland transport
Holding Company Act, 705
annual report and accounts, 245, 579, 964, 1376, 1719
Bill, 339, 607
loans, 251, 418, 579, 971, 1384, 1726
hospital, 156, 1262
in London, 965
industrial demand, 1717
International carriage of goods by road*, 456, 856, 1252
(London):
Act, 1112
Bill, 670, 997, 1000, 1002, 1074, 1075, 1288
Amendment Act, 1112
Bill, 1003, 1076
(Re-committed) Bill, 1067, 1276
Ministry of:
advisory manuals, 1374
and British Railways Board, 579
circular, 242
memorandum, 242, 576, 1374
publications, 241–6, 575–9, 961–5, 1374–6, 1716–19
re-insurance of British ships against War risks, 575–6
statistical papers, 244
Motor vehicle equipment and parts*, 856
passenger in G.B., 962
planning, men for the job, 1719
policy, 245
Road Lighting Bill, 282
Tribunal:
London fares, 245, 965
Traffic cases, 244, 578, 1376, 1719
Users Consultative Committee:
annual reports, 245, 579, 965, 1376, 1719
Bill, 4
for Scotland, annual report to Secretary of State, 1682

Transverse Mercator projection, 1666
Travel:
Agents, and Tour and Charter Operators Registration Bill, 1484
Concessions Bill, 47, 335, 339
Trade Registration Bill, 335
Trawler(s):
deep sea, casualties and accidents, 1709
safety, inquiry, 959, 1373
Treasury:
Books, calendar, 1324
Centre for Administration Studies, 586, 966, 1131, 1377, 1543
Minutes, 251, 586, 972, 1379, 1384, 1726
fiduciary note issue, 248, 582, 968, 1379–80, 1721
publications, 246–52, 578–86, 965–72, 1377–84, 1719–26
Treaties, Law of, Vienna Convention, 1244
Treaty series:
general index (1961–1964), 53
index, 143, 455, 845, 1241, 1599
ratifications, 145–6, 459, 852, 1249, 1607
see also under specific country, organisation, or subject
Trees:
Act, 1516
Bill, 1408, 1480, 1483
Circular, 1644
and woodland, memorandum on preservation, 188
bush, and stump clearance, 715
Preservation Orders, circular, 188
Trendall, A. D.: South Italian Vase painting, 100
Trends in education, 129, 416, 746, 1148, 1563
Tress, Prof. T. C. (Chairman): South-West Economic Planning Council, 412
Tretower Court:
and Castle, guide, 1321
Breconshire, guide, 912
TRG:
information series, 264, 597, 983, 1734
reports, 264–6, 597–8, 983–4, 1395, 1734–5
Triassic Ntawere Formation, Zambia, dicynodonts, 1126
Tribology, 126, 938, 1351, 1690
Tribunals:
and Inquiries Act, 77
annual report of Council, 189, 507, 899, 1654
Bill, 2, 4, 5, 11, 47, 49, 51, 164
of Inquiry:
and the law of contempt, 1304
Royal Commission, 205
Trigonacea, 1128
Trilobite faunas of Anglesey, 722
Trilobites, 102, 103, 386, 1126, 1538
Trim, further developments, 1330
Trinidad and Tobago:
air services*, 395
double taxation*, 395, 1578, 1609
public officers*, 395
Trinity House of Leith, Corporation of, Order Confirmation Act, 78
Tripartite economic survey of the East Caribbean, 515
Tron Kirk, Edinburgh, 1721
Troops, employment in aid of civil power, 733
Tropical:
plant pathology, progress review, 728
Products Institute:
report, 196, 515, 907
Tropical Science, 196, 515, 907, 1314, 1667
Trowbridge, C. W.: Analysis of ion beams from a mercury pool arc source, 209
Trucial States:
Notices, 147, 462, 856
United Nations Children's Fund*, 1253
Trumpet and Bugle Calls, 117
Trustee:
Investments (National Debt Commissioners) Amendment Bill, 999, 1003
Savings Bank(s):
Act, 705, 1112
accounts, 252, 586, 972, 1384, 1726
Bill, 290, 334, 339, 877, 995, 998, 1001, 1075, 1289, 1304
annual report of Inspection Committee, 252, 586, 972, 1384, 1726

Tschalär, C.: Energy losses of heavy particles, 922, 923

Tuck, W. J.: Aircraft propulsion, 208
Tucker, T. F. (Chairman): Child care, 1624
Tudor:
and:
Jacobean Portraits, 1310
Stuart London, Arms and Armour, 1653
domestic silver, illustrated booklet, 1736
House of, 513
Tulips, stem eelworm, 89
Tunbridge, Prof. Sir S. (Chairman): Care and health of hospital staff, 865
Turkey:
Bosphorus Bridge Loan*, 1609
British Foreign policy, 1577
Commercial credit*, 856
financial arrangments*, 463, 857
gift to Red Cresent Society, 586
loans*, 147, 463, 856, 857, 1252, 1253, 1609
purchase of ships*, 1609
road taxes of goods vehicles*, 857
steel pipe plant loan*, 1609
Turkeys, feeding, 89

Turks and Caicos Islands:
additional instructions OIC, 911
arms, 108
Colonial report, 109
(Constitution) (Amendments) Order OIC, 885
Flag, 1239
reports, 857
Turner, D. H.:
Early Gothic Illuminated Manuscripts, 1536
Romanesque Illuminated Manuscripts, 100
Turner, D. H.: Raspberry pests and diseases in Scotland, 1115
Turner, J. M.: Third Lanark Athletic Club, investigation, 951
Turnips and swedes, 1115
Turtles, British, guide to identification, 383

Tweed Fisheries Act, 1114
Twine, census of production, 958

Tyneside:
Conurbation, house condition survey, 1647
Passenger Transport Area (Designation) Order, S.I. select committee, 1287
Types of, *see specific subjects*

U

Uganda, Commonwealth Development, 107

U.K., *see* United Kingdom
U.K.A.E.A., *see* United Kingdom Atomic Energy Authority
UKRAS, *see* United Kingdom Railway Advisory Service

Ulmaceae, 112
Ulster Defence Regiment:
Act, 1112
Bill, 1003, 1076, 1077
formation, 1144
regulations for use, 1550
Ultimus Haeres (Scotland), account and list of Estates, 214, 537

Unauthorised Telephone Monitoring Bill, 335
Undergraduates' attitude to School teaching as a career, 864
Underground:
pipe sewers, design and construction, 489, 494, 1644
services, co-ordination, 1658
Underwear, men's, census of production, 958
Underwood, G.: Contribution to the classification of snakes, 387
Unemployment:
and Sickness Benefit regulations, decisions of the Commissioner, 1265
Benefit, decisions of the Commissioner, 215, 868, 869, 1265, 1620
Unesco, *see* United Nations Educational, Scientific, and Cultural Organisation
Unicef, *see* United Nations Children's Fund
Uniform:
Laws on International Sales Act, 369
Bill, 279, 282, 333, 335, 338, 478
of the Scottish Infantry, 1673
Royal Navy and Royal Marines, 1552
Unilever Ltd and Allied Breweries Ltd proposed merger, 1370
Union Bank of Switzerland, loan, 1377
Unit(s):
and standards of measurement, National Physics Laboratory, 222, 556
see also Electric Units and standards of light, National Physics Laboratory, 1352
Trusts, particulars, 239, 573, 956, 1370, 1714
United:
Arab Republic:
British property in Egypt*, 463
cultural convention*, 132, 857
financial and commercial arrangements*, 463
Drapery Stores Ltd and Montague Burton Ltd, proposed merger, 573
Kingdom:
Advisory Council on Education for Management, 126
Agricultural censuses and production, 375
Air Pilot, Aeronautical Information Publication, 1716
Airline operators, safety performance, 959
and:
Colonies, persons acquiring citizenship, 162, 874, 1273, 1628
European Communities, Statements, 477, 1540
U.S.A., employment of highly specialised graduates, 745
Assay of Strontium–90, 190, 508, 899, 1305, 1655
Atomic Energy Authority:
Act, report and accounts, 259, 594, 972, 1384, 1727
Excess votes and, 165
guide to documents, 196
publications, 252–66, 587–98, 972–84, 1384–95, 1727–35
available to the public, 262, 598, 981, 1385, 1727

United (continued):
  Kingdom (continued):
    Atomic Energy Authority: (contd.):
      Specification and Guide 2000, 264
      Averages of earth temperature, 900
    balance of payments, 106, 389, 725, 1130, 1542
    Committee for the simplication of international trade procedures, 1661
    Computer Industry, 1639
    finance accounts, 249, 583, 969
    fire statistics, 221, 554, 939, 1692
    General and Parliamentary Constituency Tables, 1257
    marine search and rescue operations, 1715
    membership of European Communities, 351, 388
    military series, 104, 1128
    Nuclear Reactor Programme, Science and Technology select committee, 482
    Oil Pipelines Act, 79
    Overseas Trade:
      accounts, 239, 573, 956, 1370, 1714
      statistics, 1714
    Railway Advisory Service, technical bulletin, 246, 579
    relationship with the Isle of Man, 1272
    statistics of foreigners entering and leaving, 162, 475, 874, 1273, 1628
    trade with Commonwealth and foreign countries, 113, 396, 730, 1135, 1546
    War graves*, 1254, 1610
  Nations:
    Charter, amendments to Articles, 60, 148, 1253
    Children's Fund:
      Bahrain*, 857
      Qatar*, 857
      Trucial States*, 1253
    Economic and Social Council, drugs, 422
    Educational, Scientific, and Cultural Organisation:
      amendments to Article V, 1610
      status of teachers, 925
    Food and Agriculture Organisation: locusts*, 457
      plant protection*, 1347
    freedom of association*, 858
    General Assembly, reports on proceedings, 147, 463, 857, 1253, 1610
    peace-keeping force in Cyprus*, 148
    privileges and immunities of specialised agencies, 852

United (continued):
  Nations (continued):
    technical assistance:
      Bahrain*, 858
      Qatar*, 858
  States of America:
    air services*, 131, 148
    amateur radio operators, licences*, 148
    Apollo unified S-Band facility, Grand Baham Island*, 858
    Atomic Energy*, 148, 149, 757, 1253, 1610
    Bahamas long-range proving ground, 464
    Ballistic missile Early Warning Station*, 1253
    British Indian Ocean Territory*, 464
    carriage of conventional type ammunition*, 463
    cereals*, 1162
    civil:
      aircraft use of base at Grand Turk Island*, 420
      airport facilities at Kindley Air Force Base, Bermuda*, 858
    defence programme equipment disposal, 123, 410, 742, 1144, 1560
    double taxation*, 147, 148, 149
    extradition, Tonga*, 149
    Federal Civil Service, 1133
    financing educational and cultural exchange programmes*, 464
    grievance arbitration, functions and effects, 919
    Hurricane Research Station, Cayman Islands*, 463
    Marshall Aid:
      see Marshall Aid
      see also Marshall scholarships
    NS Savannah visits to U.K. territory*, 464
    radio licences*, 1610
    Social Security Pensions*, 1253
    space vehicle tracking station(s):
      Antigua*, 464
      Bermuda*, 858
      U.K.*, 148, 149, 464
    tracking and telemetry facilities, Seychelles*, 464
  Universal Postal:
    Convention, 149, 197
    Union:
      constitution, 149
      giro transfers*, 1253, 1316
      insured letters and boxes*, 149, 197
      postal parcels*, 149, 197
  University(ies):
    and:
      Colleges, scientific research, 128, 415, 745, 1147, 1563

University(ies) (continued):
  and (continued):
    museums, 901
    Research Councils, Computer Board, 1561
    University Colleges, returns, 127, 746
  Building Notes, 266, 599
  Council for the education of teachers, Education and Science select committee, 1635
  development, review, 416, 746
  expenditure, control, 483
  graduates, first employment, 266, 589, 984, 1735
  Grants Committee:
    annual survey, 416, 984, 1148, 1735
    publications, 266, 598-9, 984, 1148, 1735
    returns, 746
  of:
    Aberdeen, 1282
    the air, 129
    Aston in Birmingham Act, 371
    Bradford Act, 371
    Essex, Privileges committee, 1280
    Lancaster School of Education, Education and Science select committee, 1635
    London Institute of Education, Education and Science select committee, 1635
    Reading, Scientific equipment, 1721
    Salford Act, 706
    St. Andrews (Scholarships and Bursaries) (Amendment) Scheme, 926
    Southampton School of Education, Education and Science select committee, 1635
    Surrey Act, 79
    Wales Institute of Science and Technology Act, 706
  of:
    Open. See Open University (Scotland)
      Act, 78
      Bill, 2, 43, 47, 48, 164
  Teachers':
    standing reference on pay, 903, 1657
    superannuation, 746
  Unlicensed Clubs, registration and control Bill, 4
  Unsolicited Goods and Services Bill, 1484

Upton Castle, Rent, guide, 588
Upper:
  cretaceous teleosts and myclophids, 1126
  jurassic Rhyncholellid brachiopods, 1126
  estuarine ostracoda, 386
  Silesia, British Foreign policy, 760
  wind measurement by pilot balloons, 900

Ur excavations, 101
Uraniidae, 724
Urban:
  growth, major, feasibility
  restraint of traffic, 575
  see also Town
Use of:
  Bridgewater Canal water at Daresbury Physics Laboratory, 530
  chemicals:
    in hand cleansing farm dairy equipment, 89
    toxic, in agriculture and food storage, 414
  headlamps, 579
  Jesness inventory on British probationers, 476
  management consultants by Government Departments, code of practice, 1544
  Nimrod for Nuclear Structure Physics, symposium on, 923
Usual residence tables, GRO, 1259
U.S.S.R., see Soviet Union

U-values, standardised, 1322

V

Vaccination:
  against smallpox, memorandum, 471
  yellow fever, certificates, 146
Vachell collection of Chinese fishes, 387
Valarianaceae, 729, 1134
Valuation:
  British Aluminium Company Ltd and Lochaber Power Company) (Scotland Order, 311
  for Rating (Scotland) Act, 1516
Value Added Tax, 1310
Van der Held curves of growth, 1328
VAN RIEMSDIJK, J.: In the Science Museum, 922
VAN SOMEREN, V. G. L.: African Charaxes, 101, 385, 1125, 1538
Vapour:
  barriers, 1669
  pressure and molar volume for liquid hydrogen and deuterium, 194
Variables:
  RR Lyrae, 206, 920
  semi-regular and RV Tauri, 1327
Vascular Flora of the Falkland Islands, 719
Vase painting, South Italian, 100

Vegetable(s): 380
  and animal oils and fats, census of production, 951
  dehydrated, for the caterer, 714
  diseases, 1117
  oil and oilseeds, 392
  soils and manures for, 711
Vehicle(s):
  and:
    Driving Licences Act, 1117
      Bill, 664, 670, 992, 994, 995, 1067, 1071, 1073, 1276
    other refuse disposal, 489
    designed for use in towns, 378
    maintenance workers, British Road Service, pay, 903
    mechanically propelled:
      excise duties, 1654
      licensing and registration, 1655
    operating costs on different road surfaces, 378
    testing, manual, 246
VENABLES, SIR P. (Chairman), Open University, 1146
Venereal Diseases Bill, 671
Venezuela:
  frontier with British Guiana*, 131, 1598
  fungus flora, 1674
Ventilation, internal bathrooms and W.C.s, 523
VERDCOURT, B.:
  Flora of Tropical East Africa, 729, 1134
  Kew Bulletin, 1674
Verticillium wilt of hops, 88
Vespertilionidae, 103
Vessels:
  motor. See Mercantile Navy list
  pressure, inquiry, 1352
  Protection Act, 369
    Bill, 47, 333, 334, 338, 478
  steam and sailing. See Mercantile Navy list
  See also Ships
Veterinary:
  Science:
    and Surgery, (careers), 1149
    progress review, 728
  Surgeons Act, 77
    Bill, 1, 2, 3, 4, 10, 43, 50, 51, 164

VHF transmitters and receivers, 908

Vibration:
  in buildings, 1671
  syndrome, report, 1621
Vickers Ltd, dispute, 1153
Victims of untraced drivers, compensation, 1374

Victoria and Albert Museum:
  bulletin, 266, 599, 905
  monographs, 266
  publications, 266, 399, 984-5, 1396, 1735-6
Victory:
  Bonds, 930, 1339, 1686
  H.M.S. building, restoration, and repair, 123
  in the West 1129
Vienna Convention, Law of Treaties, 1244
Vienna, Information Office pamphlet, 1649
VIGOUREUX, P., Electric Units and Standards, 1713
Virement between Service departments, votes, 165, 480, 880, 1280, 1634
Visas:
  for refugees, abolition*, 1254
  See also respective countries
Visiting Forces Bill, 1417
Visitors to Britain, 512
Vitamin D, report, 1622

VOIGT, G., Cretaceous age of jurassic cheilostomatous polyzoa, 723
Voluntary:
  Colleges of Education, Education and Science select committee, 1635
  service:
    guide, 1320
    in After Care, 474
Votes:
  excess. See Excess votes
    on Account, Civil Estimates and Defence (Central) Estimates, 252, 586, 972, 1384, 1726
  See also Defence votes
Voyages and Travel, 905

W

Wage(s):
  and hours of work:
    changes in rates, 180, 499, 747, 1150, 1565
    time rates, 187, 506, 754, 1156, 1571
    in agriculture, 95
    Stop, administration, 537
WAGNER, SIR A., Heralds of England, 392
WAGON, D. J., General statistics programme
JESTER, 531

Wales (and Monmouthshire):
  agriculture, 873
  Ancient Monuments Board, 202, 522, 912, 1320, 1736
  Arts, 267
  Boundary Commission, 1269, 1272
  Central Advisory Council for Education, 743
  Constitution Commission, 1544
  Council for, 267
  Education:
    consideration, 163
    Primary, 743, 875
  Educational Research, 921
  Forests, 1612
  Government of Bill, 788
  Health and welfare services, 1274
  Historic Buildings Council, 202, 524, 914, 1323
  Housing Bill, 1629
  industrial archaeology, 1310
  industry, 45, 163
  Local Government, 600, 664, 875
  National:
    Health Service reorganisation, 1736
    Museum, 1310
  New Town, 267
  roads and communications, 332, 476
  Rural Development, 478
    Board Order, see Draft Wales Rural etc.
  sample census, 863
  Transport Users Consultative Committee, annual report, 245, 579, 965, 1376, 1719
  The Way Ahead, 600
  see also Welsh
WALKER, J.: Arab-Sassanian coins, 384
WALKER, PROF. J. (Chairman): Hospital medical records in Scotland, 536
Wallasey Corporation Act, 371, 1518
WALLINGTON, C. E.: Numerical solution of atmospheric diffusion equation, 901
WALLIS, D.: Programmed instruction in British armed forces, 124
Wall(s):
  Brick, and Block, fire resistance, 221
  external, and fire, 221
  outside, rendering, 201
  panels, concrete, cracks, 1536
WALNE, P. R.: Ostrea edulis, 93, 1524
Walsall:
  Corporation Act, 516
  Provisional Orders Bill, 49, 79
WALSH, DR D. (Chairman): Protection of Field Monuments, 1323
WALSH, H. V.: Current issues in cost-benefit analysis, 1131
Walshaw, see Manchester Corporation
WALTON, J.: Glen More Cairngorms, 151

War:
  against Japan, 1128
  damage accounts, 252, 418, 386, 730, 1139
  graves of Commonwealth forces, in Greece*, 858, 1254, 1610
Pensions Committee(s):
  (Amendment and Extension) Order, 1624
  Orders, 1623-4
  (Revocation) Order, 1624
  pensioners, report, 217, 540, 870, 1268, 1623
Warble fly, 89
WARD, REV. A. G. (Chairman): Food standards, 93, 380, 715, 1121, 1525
WARR, F. A. B.: Time measurement, descriptive catalogue of collection, 530
WARD:
  units, hospital building note, 1263
  waitress service, hospital, 864
Wardour Castle, Wiltshire, guide, 912
Warehouses:
  bonded, list, 113, 397, 731, 1136, 1547
  costing handling and storage in, 1709
Warehousing manual, 113, 397, 730, 1136, 1547
WARFORD, D. J.: South Atcham Scheme, 1297
Warley Corporation Act, 1516
Warmth without waste, 912
WARR, P. B.: Identifying supervisory training needs, 754
WARREN, R. L. M.: Type specimens of non-passerine birds in the B.M., 388
Warren Spring Laboratory, 223, 556, 940, 1695
Warrington expansion proposals, 171
Warships, British, 1845-1945, 1675
Wart disease of potatoes, 88
WARTNABY, J.: Surveying, instruments and methods, 922
WARWICK, R. M.: Nematodes, 1539
Warwickshire:
  census, 153
  County Council Act, 1518
  sample census, 468, 862
Wash:
  estuary storage, 1736
  sprat fishery, 1524
Washing up, film strips, 127
Washington Export-Import Bank, loans, 130, 246, 579, 965
Wasps, 89
Watches:
  and clocks, census of production, 1371
  English, 1396
Water(s):
  and sewerage schemes, 487, 600
  byelaws, circular, 171, 600
  charges, decimal currency, 1645

WAT-WST | 1966-70

WAT— INDEX 1966–70

Water(s) (*continued*):
  drinking, radioactivity in, 174, 493
  for irrigation, 376
  hot and cold, *see* Hot and cold
  natural, durability of metals in, 913
  on, and in, 921
  pipes, copper, circular, 170
  pollution:
    abstracts, 223, 556, 940, 1553, 1695
    control engineering, 1695
    Research:
      Laboratory publications, 223, 556, 940, 1695
      report, 223, 556, 940, 1353, 1695
      technical paper, 1354
  Rates and charges, circular, 487, 890
  Resources:
    Act, 705
      annual report, 1736
      Bill, 612, 663, 666, 667, 877, 1411, 1413, 1414, 1485
      charging schemes, 489
      circular, 489, 890
      report, 188, 494, 894
    Board:
      Annual report, 188, 494, 894, 1736
      desalinisation, E. and W., 1396
      publications, 599, 985, 1396, 1736
    in the North, 599, 1736
  safety campaign, 188
  (Scotland) Act, 369
    Bill, 280, 283, 333, 334, 336, 338, 479
  Service(s):
    Scotland, 210
    hot and cold, hospital, 1616
  supply(ies):
    bacteriological examination, 1267
    fluoridation, 1292
    in South-East England, 188
    Industry:
      Training Board, 187, 506, 754, 1157, 1571
      Pay and productivity, 1658
  Surface, year-book, 175
Water-colours, British, 1396
Watercress growing, 376
WATERHOUSE, R. (Chairman): Rabies, 1524
Watertight basements, 1669
Waterways, inland, holidays, 1540
Waterworks, safeguards, 489, 494
WATSON, A.: *Drepanidae*, 385, 722
WATSON, J.: English Wealden flora, 1126
WATSON, SIR S. L. (Chairman): Residual values of fertilizers and feeding stuffs, 87, 1116, 1520
WAY, R. (Chairman): London Transport Board, 1717
WAYNE, (SIR) E. (Chairman): Drug dependence, 1296, 1272, 1624, 1626
Weald clay, chamosite in, 1663

Weapons and belt hooks, ancient Chinese, 1123
Weather:
  and the builder, 521, 912, 1669
  London, 900
  messages, handbook, 191, 508, 900, 1305, 1656
  monthly reports, 191, 509, 901, 1306, 1657
  radar for Pilots, 1716
Weatherproof outerwear, census of production, 958
WEAVER, T. R. (Chairman):
  Government of Colleges of Education, 127
  Teaching Council for E. and W., 1563
Weaving:
  of cotton, linen, and man-made fibres, census of production, 1371
  silk, man-made fibres, and cotton, (careers), 1564
Web-Offset printing machines, 501
WEBSTER, F. V.: Traffic signals, 578
WEBSTER, G.: Wroxeter Roman City, 202
Weeds:
  aquatic, control, 711
  forest, chemical control, 1255
  Research Organisation, 373, 1115
WEEDON, PROF. B. C. L. (Chairman): Food regulations, 1525
Weevils, pea, bean, and clover, 88
Weights and Measures:
  examination:
    for Inspector's Certificate, 952
    of patterns, 241, 575, 959, 1373, 1716
  origins and development, 530
  report, 1373
WEISS, R., Pisanello's medallion of Emperor John VIII Palaeogus, 100
Welding and flame cutting, fumes, 1566
Welfare:
  in agriculture, 95
  material for seafarers, 132
  services, Scotland, *see* Health and Welfare, etc.
Welland and Nene (Empingham Reservoir) and Mid-Northamptonshire Water Act, 1518
  Bill, 1642
Wellington, development proposals, 171
Wellington, the Duke of, pictorial survey, 1396
WELLS, SIR H. (Chairman), Commission for New Towns, 1647
Welsh:
  Committee:
    Educational research, 921
    raising the school leaving age, 415
    research and development of Welsh, 415
  economy, public expenditure, 1477

INDEX 1966–70 —WHI

Welsh (*continued*):
  house conditions survey, 1397
  Language:
    Act, 369
      Bill, 282, 338
    consideration, 1629
    legal status, 14
    Welsh Grand Committee, 1474
  Office:
    circulars, 170–1, 266–7, 488–90, 600, 888–91, 985, 1290–3, 1396, 1572, 1643–5, 1736
    Constitution Commission, 1133
    Provisional Order Confirmation (Western Valleys) (Mon) Sewerage Board Act, 79
      Bill, 5, 7, 48
    publications, 266–7, 600, 985, 1396–7, 1736
  statistics, digest, 267, 600, 985, 1397, 1736
  See also Wales
WENHAM, L. P.: Romano-British Cemetery, York, 1321
Wessex Rivers, 494
WEST, L. A.: Hand Tools to Mechanization, 530
West:
  Bromwich Corporation Act, 1517
  Cambridgeshire, ancient monuments, 874
  Ham, family houses, 1294
  Hertfordshire Main Drainage:
    Act, 1518
    District Provisional Order Act, 370
      Bill, 284, 337
  Indies Act, 369
    Bill, 52, 276
  Kent Main Sewerage District Provision Order Act, 79, 669, 706
    Bill, 5, 49
  Lothian County Council Order Confirmation Act, 1518
    Bill, 1483
  Midlands:
    Conurbation housing condition survey, 1295
    Economic Planning Council, 412
    Passenger Transport Area (Designation) Order, S.I. select committee, 1287
  patterns for growth, 412
  region, sample census, 863
  Suffolk, sample census, 468
  Sussex:
    County Council Order Confirmation Act, 1518
    sample census, 468
  Yorkshire Conurbation house condition survey, 1647

Western:
  Approaches, geological and geophysical investigations, 1663
  European:
    printed books, fine illustrations, 1396
    Union, meeting at the Hague, 457
  Livestock Producers Ltd, investigation, 951
  Red Cedar, 465
  Samoa, sterling proportions*, 1254
  Valleys (Mon) Sewerage Board Provisional Order Act, 79
    Bill, 5, 7, 48
Westmorland:
  census, 153
  sample census, 468, 862
Westonbirt:
  arboretum, guide, 1155
  in colour, 860

Whales, dolphins, and porpoises, stranded, identification guide, 104, 1124
Whaling, international conventions, 150, 1254
WHALLEY, J. I.: English Handwriting, 1735
WHALLEY, P. E. S.: *Phycitinae*, 1538
What is Stonehenge? guide, German edition, 912
Wheat:
  bulb fly, 375
  international agreement, 150, 464
WHEELER, M. M.: Town Centre Properties Ltd, and Star Explorations Ltd, investigation, 952
WHITE, C.: Drawings of Rembrandt, 100
White, R. B.:
  Changing appearance of buildings, 523
  Qualitative studies of buildings, 221
White:
  and Black Books of the Cinque Ports, calendar, 473
  Fish:
    and Herring Industries Acts, accounts, 95–6, 380, 382, 718, 1123, 1526
    Authority, annual report and accounts, 95, 382, 718, 1038, 1527
    (Deep Sea Vessels) (United Kingdom) Scheme, S.I. select committee, 1287
Whitehaven Harbour Act, 1518
WHITEHEAD, P. J. P.:
  Clupeoid fishes, 387, 1127, 1539
  Elopoid and clupeoid fishes, 103
  Reeves collection of Chinese fish drawings, 1538
  Vachell collection of Chinese fishes, 387
WHITEHEAD, R. A.: Sample survey and collection of coconut germ plasm in the Pacific, 196
Whitgift Charities Act, 1114

WHI— INDEX 1966–70

Whiting:
  Irish Sea and Clyde, 93
  stocks and gall-bladder parasites, 374
Whitley Bay Pier Act, 79
WHITTINGTON, H. B.: Trilobites of the Henllan Ash, Merioneth, 102
WHYBREW, E. G.: Overtime working in Britain, 919

WIDGERY, RT. HON. LORD (HON. MR JUSTICE) (Chairman):
  Legal Aid in Criminal Proceedings, 190
  Penal system, 1627
Widows benefit, decisions of the Commissioner, 1265, 1620
Wigan Corporation Busmen, pay, 903
Wild:
  Creatures and Forest Laws Bill, 1414, 1654
  Plant Protection Bill, 665
WILLETTS, P.: Beethoven and England, 1536
WILLETTS, P. J.: Henry Lawes Manuscript, 1124
WILLIAMS, A.: Output budgeting and contribution of micro-economics to Government efficiency, 586
WILLIAMS, C. E.: Costing of handling and storage in warehouses, 1709
WILLIAMS, D. J.: Scale insects, 1125
Williams Glyn's Bank Act, 1518
Willow, Cricket bat, 859
Wills Act, 705
  Bill, 690, 666
WILSON, PROF. A. (Chairman): Collection of residue data, 1145
WILSON, SIR A. (Chairman): Power stations, 1319
WILSON, PROF. J. S. G.: Economic survey of the New Hebrides, 515
WILSON, DR. M.: Children with cerebral palsy, 1561
WILSON, R. (Chairman): Immigration appeals, 475
WILSON, SIR R. (Chairman):
  National Freight Corporation, organisation, 1718
  Strike of Stevedores and Dockers, 183
WILSON PECK, C.: English Copper, tin, and bronze coins, 1536
Wilt of hops, 88
Wiltshire:
  census, 153
  sample census 468, 862
Wind:
  load(ing):
    assessment, 1671
    on buildings, 913, 1321, 1322
  speed and:
    direction, tables, 1306
    wave height, relation, 192

WINDEYER, PROF. SIR B. W. (Chairman): Ionising radiation in research and teaching, 748
Window:
  design and solar heat gain, 220
  joinery, prevention of decay, 220
Windsor, House of, 513
Windward Islands, Constitutional Conference report, 109
Wine, British, census of production, 947
WINN, RT. HON. LORD JUSTICE (Chairman): Personal injuries litigation, 899
WINTERBOTTOM, LORD (Chairman): Building maintenance, 1323
Wire, and wire manufactures, census of production, 958
Wireless Telegraphy Act, 369
  Bill, 283, 285, 333, 335, 337, 338, 479
Wireworms, 88
WISE, PROF. M. J. (Chairman): Statutory smallholdings, 379
Witch, the, food of, 1116
With a Machine Gun to Cambrai, 1298
Witham Navigation Company Act, 1114

WOLFENDEN, SIR J. (Chairman): University development, 746
Wolf-Rayet stars, 529
Wollastonite, monograph, 1663
Wolstan de Bransford, calendar of the Register of, 159
Wolverhampton Corporation Act, 151
Women('s):
  and:
    girls' tailored outerwear, census of production, 1371
    young persons, hours of employment in factories, 1153
  Costumes, 1600–1750, booklet, 1303
  employment survey, tables, 864
  political rights, convention, 455, 461
  position in industry, research paper, 920
WOOD, PROF. J. C.:
  Pilkington Bros, Ltd., inquiry, 1571
  Road Haulage, 1571
  Standard-Triumph (Liverpool) Ltd., Court of Inquiry, 1153
WOOD, R. F.: Forestry in the British Scene, 859
Wood:
  and cork manufactures, census of production, 1371
  bending, handbook, 1716
  efficiency of adhesives for, 939
  preparation for microscopic examination, 939
  products, imports and consumption, U.K., 1612
WOODBINE PARISH, D. (Chairman): Hospital building maintenance, 1618

INDEX 1966–70 —WST

WOODBURN KIRBY MAJ. GEN. S.: The Surrender of Japan, 1128
WOODCOCK, G. (Chairman): Industrial relations, 1544–5
Woodcutting Machinist, (careers), 1564
Wooden containers, and baskets, census of production, 1371
WOODING, RT. HON. SIR H. (Chairman): Anguilla, 1603
Woodlands:
  butterflies in, 860
  census, 1611
  plan of operations, 151
  taxation, 465
Woodpeckers, 723
Woodsawyer, (careers), 1564
WOODWARD, SIR LL., British Foreign Policy in the Second World War, 1540
Woodwork(ing):
  crafts, (careers), 1564
  exposed, maintaining, 521
  machines, safety in use, 1567
  painting, 201, 912, 1322
Woodworm, 521, 1669
Wool(len):
  and worsted, census of production, 1371
  Industry Training Board, 187
  Jute, and Flax Industry Training Board, 506, 754, 1157, 1571
  Textile:
    Economic Development Committee, 1310
    Industry:
      (Export Promotion Levy):
        accounts, 256, 570, 953, 1367, 1373, 1710
        Order, S.I. select committee, 1640
      Safety, Health, and Welfare, 1572
      (Scientific Research Levy):
        accounts, 236, 570, 953, 1367, 1373, 1710
        Order, S.I. select committee, 1640
    strategic future, 1310
WOOLF, M.: The Housing Survey in E. and W., 864
WOOLLEY, A. R.: Fenitization, 1127
WOOLLEY, SIR R.: Radial-velocity observations of RR Lyrae variables at Kottamia, 206
Woolly aphid, 88
WOOSTER, C. E. D. (Chairman): Network analysis in construction design, 524
WOOTTON OF ABINGER, BARONESS (Chairman): Countryside Commission, 1134
WORCESTER, G. R. G.: Sail and Sweep in China, 208
Worcestershire:
  census, 153
  County Council Act, 1517

Worcestershire (*continued*):
  sample census, 468, 862
WORDIE, J. S. (Chairman): Teachers' salaries scales, 414, 745
Work(s):
  department, hospital, 1615
  of:
    Art, export of, 582, 1380, 1562
    the Rutherford Laboratory, 530, 531, 923, 1330, 1676
    the Youth Employment Service, 754
  Safety Committees in practice, case studies, 754
Working:
  in metric, quantity surveyors, 1659
  installations licenced by PMG, 908
  papers, Schools Council, 415
  with computers, guide to jobs and careers, 1659
Workloads in Children's Departments, 1270
Workmen's Compensation:
  and Benefit:
    (Amendment) Act:
      accounts, 539
      Bill, 671
    (Supplementation) Act, accounts, 539
  (Supplementary Allowances) Act, 217
Workplace:
  and transport tables, Scotland 863
  Industrial Relations, 864
Workshop(s):
  crafts, Secondary School design, 125
  hospital, 1616
World:
  Health:
    Assembly, 464
    Organisation:
      amendment of Articles, 464
      nomenclature regulations, 1240
  Intellectual Property Organisation, convention, 360, 455
  Meteorological Organisation*, 1245
  production, exports, and imports, mineral industry, 906
Worms in poultry, 88
WORSSAM, B. C.: Geology of the country around Cambridge, 1663
Worsted, census of production, 1371

Wreck reports, 238, 572, 955, 1369, 1712–13
WRIGHT, J. E.: Geology of the Church Stretton area, 905
WRIGHT, R. (Chairman): Reorganisation Commission for eggs, 717
WRIGHT, R. W. (Chairman): Process plant, 1353
Wroxeter Roman City, guide, 202

W. Stevenson and Sons, Sutton, Cornwall Ltd., Industrial Relations Commission 1545

WYN—   INDEX 1966-70

WYNN, A. H. A. (Chairman): Metrication Committee, 938
WYNN-EDWARDS, SIR R.: Shortages of gas supplies in West Midlands, report, 200

X

X-ray(s):
  departments, hospital, 469, 470, 1262, 1615
  discovery and application, 1675
Xylene Styrene, 186

Y

YAPP, W. B.: The weekend motorist in the Lake District, 1134
Yarn:
  issue, and control of losses, 1660
  purchasing and storage, 1660
  testing, 1660

Yearbook of the Commonwealth, 1254, 1610
Yellow fever, vaccination certificates, 146

York:
  and North Midlands General Review Area, 175
  conservation study, 1298
  Corporation Act, 1114
Yorkshire:
  and:
    Humberside:
      Economic Planning Council:
        and Board, Halifax and Calder Valley, 742
        review, 124
      Region, sample census, 863
    Lincolnshire coasts, 728
  Castles, picture book, 912
  East Riding:
    census, 153
    sample census, 468, 1259
  Jurassic flora, 1128
  North:
    forests, guide, 151

Yorkshire (continued):
  North (continued):
    Riding:
      census, 153
      sample census, 468, 1259
    Oolites, 386
    Registries Amendment Act, 79
  West Riding:
    census, 153
    County Council, case study, 1673
    sample census, 468, 1259
YOUNG, D. A.: Bechuanaland, 110
YOUNG, C. W. T.: Larch canker and dieback, 1255
YOUNG, O. C.:
  External loads on buried pipelines, 1672
  High-strength beddings for unreinforced concrete and clayware pipes, 524
Young:
  children:
    nutrition, 870
    Our, 1267
  mussels in Conway fishery, 1120
  people, driver training, 1374
  school leavers:
    English, 1678
    Humanities, 415, 921
    problems, 1627
    report, 921
    Society and, 415
    smoker, 1261
YOUNGER, RT. HON. K. (Chairman): Penal system, 872, 873-4, 1625, 1626
Your:
  manpower, guide to manpower statistics, hotel and catering, 512
  future in clothing, 1661
Youth:
  and community:
    service, 1680
    work in the 1970s, 1148
  Employment Service, the work of, 754
  leaders and assistants, part time, training, 129
  Service:
    immigrants and, 413
    proposals, 1148
    report, 128

Yugoslavia:
  air services*, 150, 859, 1611
  consular convention*, 150
  cultural convention*, 132, 150
  exchange of money orders*, 858
  import of British books and films*, 150, 465
  international carriage of goods by road*, 1252
  science and technology*, 853, 1254
  visas*, 1254, 1611

INDEX 1966-70   —ZUC

Z

Zambia:
  air services*, 392, 1254
  armed forces*, 859
  double taxation*, 1611
  public service*, 851, 859
Zanzibar, income tax, 1300

Zinc-coated reinforcement of concrete, 1322

Zoology bulletins, 103, 387-8, 723, 1127-8, 1539
  see also genus(era)

ZUCKERMAN, SIR S. (Chairman):
  Hospital scientific and technical services, 866
  Technological innovation in Britain, 724
  Torrey Canyon disaster, 724

1966 pp 1-272, 1967 pp 273-604, 1968 pp 605-990, 1969 pp 991-1402, 1970 pp 1403-1740

1966 pp 1-272, 1967 pp 273-604, 1968 pp 605-990, 1969 pp 991-1402, 1970 pp 1403-1740